Frommer's

✓ P9-DFY-935

Europe
from $85 a Day

46th Edition

Here's what the critics say about Frommer's:

"Amazingly easy to use. Very portable, very complete."

—*Booklist*

"Detailed, accurate, and easy-to-read information for all price ranges."
—*Glamour Magazine*

"Hotel information is close to encyclopedic."

—*Des Moines Sunday Register*

"Frommer's Guides have a way of giving you a real feel for a place."
—*Knight Ridder Newspapers*

WILEY

Wiley Publishing, Inc.

Wiley Publishing, Inc.

111 River St.
Hoboken, NJ 07030-5774

ISBN 0-7645-6890-6

Editor: Lorraine Festa
Additional editing by Elizabeth Albertson, Stephen Bassman, Kendra Falkenstein, and Naomi P. Kraus.
Production Editor: Heather Wilcox
Cartographer: Elizabeth Puhl
Photo Editor: Richard Fox
Production by Wiley Indianapolis Composition Services

Front cover photo: Detail of Michelangelo's *David,* at the Galleria dell'Accademia, Florence.

For information on our other products and services or to obtain technical support, please contact our Customer Care Department within the U.S. at 800/762-2974, outside the U.S. at 317/572-3993 or fax 317/572-4002.

Wiley also publishes its books in a variety of electronic formats. Some content that appears in print may not be available in electronic formats.

Manufactured in the United States of America

5   4   3   2   1

Contents

4 Athens & Delphi   101

by Sherry Marker

5 Barcelona & Environs   145

by Sascha Segan & Herbert Bailey Livesey

6 Berlin & Potsdam   188

by Beth Reiber

20 Prague & Environs   752

by Hana Mastrini

21 Rome & Environs   784

by Reid Bramblett

22 Salzburg & Innsbruck   847

by Beth Reiber

23   Seville & the Best of Andalusia   882

by Sascha Segan & Herbert Bailey Livesey

24   Stockholm & Environs   920

by Darwin Porter & Danforth Prince

25   Venice & Environs   950

by Reid Bramblett

(26) Vienna & Krems   998

by Beth Reiber

Index   1042

List of Maps

About the Authors

Reid Bramblett is the author of *Frommer's Tuscany & Umbria, Frommer's Northern Italy*, and *Europe For Dummies*, as well as coauthor of *Frommer's Italy from $70 a Day*. He also helped found guidebookwriters.com. When not on the road, he splits his time between his native Philadelphia and Columbia, Missouri.

Londoner **Richard Jones**, author of *Frommer's Memorable Walks in London*, has been devising tours of Britain since 1982. He is the author of *Walking Haunted London, Haunted Britain and Ireland, Myths and Legends of Britain and Ireland*, and *Walking Dickensian London*. A regular contributor to programs on the Discovery, History, Mystery, and Travel channels, he was recently featured in the documentary *The Making of From Hell*, providing analysis of the infamous Jack the Ripper murders. He also wrote and presented the drama-documentaries *Shakespeare in London* (1999).

Suzanne Rowan Kelleher is a travel writer and the former Europe editor of *Travel Holiday* magazine. She has traveled extensively in Ireland, is married to an Irishman, and currently lives in County Dublin. She is the author of *Frommer's Ireland*.

All four of **Joseph S. Lieber**'s grandparents emigrated from Eastern Europe at the turn of the 20th century, settling in New York City, where he was born and raised. Mr. Lieber lived in Hungary for several years in the early 1990s. He presently practices law in Boston and is the coauthor of *Frommer's Budapest & the Best of Hungary* and *Frommer's Europe*.

Herbert Bailey Livesey is a native New Yorker. After an early career as a university administrator, he decided to devote himself to writing full time. He's the author or coauthor of 10 travel guides (including *Frommer's New England, Frommer's Canada*, and *Frommer's Montréal & Québec City*), a novel about deep-sea sportfishing, and several books on education and sociology. His articles have appeared in *Travel & Leisure, Food & Wine*, and *Playboy*.

Sherry Marker's love of Greece began when she majored in classical Greek at Harvard. She has attended the American School of Classical Studies in Athens and studied ancient history at the University of California at Berkeley. Author or coauthor of a number of guides to Greece (such as *Frommer's Greece* and *Frommer's Greek Islands*), she has published articles in the *New York Times, Travel & Leisure*, and *Hampshire Life*. She's also the coauthor of *Frommer's Europe* and has written books on a variety of subjects, including a history of London for young adults.

Hana Mastrini, a native of the western Czech spa town of Karlovy Vary, became a veteran of the "Velvet Revolution" as a student in Prague in 1989. She began contributing to *Frommer's* guides while helping her husband, John, better understand his new home in the Czech Republic.

George McDonald has lived and worked in both Amsterdam and Brussels, as deputy editor of the KLM in-flight magazine and as editor-in-chief of the Sabena in-flight magazine. Now a freelance journalist and travel writer, he has written extensively on both the Netherlands and Belgium for magazines and guidebooks. He's the author of *Frommer's Amsterdam, Frommer's Brussels, Bruges, Ghent & Antwerp*, and *Frommer's Belgium, Holland & Luxembourg*.

Haas Mroue is a freelance travel writer who grew up spending summers in the South of France. He lived in Paris while studying at the American University, then returned to the States to graduate from the UCLA Film School. His articles, poems, and short stories have been widely published, and he's coauthor of *Frommer's Gay & Lesbian Europe* and author of *Frommer's Memorable Walks in Paris*. When not on the road, he lives on the beach in Port Townsend, Washington.

Cheryl A. Pientka is a freelance journalist. She is the author of *Paris For Dummies* and coauthor of *Frommer's Paris from $80 a Day* and *France For Dummies*. A graduate of Columbia University Graduate School of Journalism and the University of Delaware, she splits her time between New York and Paris.

As a team of veteran travel writers, **Darwin Porter** and **Danforth Prince** have produced numerous titles for Frommer's, including bestselling guides to Italy, France, the Caribbean, England, and Germany. Porter, a former bureau chief of *The Miami Herald*, is also a Hollywood biographer—his most recent releases include *The Secret Life of Humphrey Bogart* and *Katharine the Great*, the latter a close-up of the private life of the late Katharine Hepburn. Prince was formerly employed by the Paris bureau of the *New York Times*, and is today the president of Blood Moon Productions and other media-related firms.

Beth Reiber lived for 4 years in Germany and 3 years in Japan, selling travel articles to the *Los Angeles Times, Chicago Tribune, Washington Post,* and many other publications. Now residing in Lawrence, Kansas, she's the author of *Frommer's Japan, Frommer's Tokyo,* and *Frommer's Hong Kong,* and is a contributor to *Frommer's USA*.

Sascha Segan, a freelance writer, is a columnist on air travel and destinations for Frommers.com. He also wrote *Frommer's Fly Safe, Fly Smart* and the Spain chapter for *Frommer's Europe 2005,* and contributed to many of the 2004 *Frommer's* guides. In his spare time, he writes about gadgets for technology magazines. He lives in New York City.

Christina Shea, a native of Hartford, Connecticut, served as a Peace Corps volunteer in Hungary and subsequently directed Peace Corps language-training programs in Lithuania and Kyrghyzstan. She is the author of the novel *Moira's Crossing* (St. Martin's Press) and a coauthor of *Frommer's Budapest & the Best of Hungary* and *Frommer's Europe*.

An Invitation to the Reader

In researching this book, we discovered many wonderful places—hotels, restaurants, shops, and more. We're sure you'll find others. Please tell us about them, so we can share the information with your fellow travelers in upcoming editions. If you were disappointed with a recommendation, we'd love to know that, too. Please write to:

Frommer's Europe from $85 a Day, 46th Edition
Wiley Publishing, Inc. • 111 River St. • Hoboken, NJ 07030-5774

An Additional Note

Please be advised that travel information is subject to change at any time—and this is especially true of prices. We therefore suggest that you write or call ahead for confirmation when making your travel plans. The authors, editors, and publisher cannot be held responsible for the experiences of readers while traveling. Your safety is important to us, however, so we encourage you to stay alert and be aware of your surroundings. Keep a close eye on cameras, purses, and wallets, all favorite targets of thieves and pickpockets.

Other Great Guides for Your Trip:

Frommer's England from $70 a Day

Frommer's London from $85 a Day

Frommer's Paris from $80 a Day

Frommer's Italy from $70 a Day

Frommer's Ireland from $60 a Day

Frommer's Greece from $50 a Day

Frommer's Europe

Europe For Dummies

Frommer's Gay & Lesbian Europe

Frommer's Europe by Rail

Frommer's Road Atlas Europe

For even more guides, see the beginning of each city chapter.

Frommer's Star Ratings, Icons & Abbreviations

Every hotel, restaurant, and attraction listing in this guide has been ranked for quality, value, service, amenities, and special features using a **star-rating system.** In country, state, and regional guides, we also rate towns and regions to help you narrow down your choices and budget your time accordingly. Hotels and restaurants are rated on a scale of zero (recommended) to three stars (exceptional). Attractions, shopping, nightlife, towns, and regions are rated according to the following scale: zero stars (recommended), one star (highly recommended), two stars (very highly recommended), and three stars (must-see).

In addition to the star-rating system, we also use **seven feature icons** that point you to the great deals, in-the-know advice, and unique experiences that separate travelers from tourists. Throughout the book, look for:

Finds	Special finds—those places only insiders know about
Fun Fact	Fun facts—details that make travelers more informed and their trips more fun
Kids	Best bets for kids, and advice for the whole family
Moments	Special moments—those experiences that memories are made of
Overrated	Places or experiences not worth your time or money
Tips	Insider tips—great ways to save time and money
Value	Great values—where to get the best deals

The following **abbreviations** are used for credit cards:

AE	American Express	DISC	Discover	V	Visa
DC	Diners Club	MC	MasterCard		

Frommers.com

Now that you have the guidebook to a great trip, visit our website at **www.frommers.com** for travel information on more than 3,000 destinations. With features updated regularly, we give you instant access to the most current trip-planning information available. At Frommers.com, you'll also find the best prices on airfares, accommodations, and car rentals—and you can even book travel online through our travel booking partners. At Frommers.com, you'll also find the following:

- Online updates to our most popular guidebooks
- Vacation sweepstakes and contest giveaways
- Newsletter highlighting the hottest travel trends
- Online travel message boards with featured travel discussions

What's New in Europe

What's new in Europe? Read on to find out what recently opened, what's changed, and what's hot for your trip.

AMSTERDAM

Museum fans face a double whammy in Amsterdam. The Rijksmuseum, Holland's top museum, continues its years-long partial closure for renovation, with "only" the finest paintings by the Dutch Masters and some other elements of the collection on display in the sole wing that remains open. In 2004, the modern art Stedelijk Museum also closed for a period of years, for rebuilding. The Stedelijk's collection should be back on display in 2005, somewhere, once appropriate temporary accommodations have been secured.

In at least partial compensation, a glittering new piece in the mosaic of Amsterdam's old-harbor redevelopment should be in place, with the opening of the **Muziekgebouw** concert hall on the waterfront just east of Centraal Station. This ultramodern facility will be the new home to the BIMhuis jazz and De IJsbreker contemporary and experimental music operations.

ATHENS

The **Greek National Tourist Office (GNTO),** also known as the Hellenic Tourism Organization (EOT), closed its main office just off Syntagma Square, and reopened at 7 Tsochas St., Ambelokopi (© 210/870-0000; www.gnto.gr), well out of central Athens. At press time, the GNTO announced plans to open several smaller information centers in and around Syntagma Square.

Take advantage of the newly **pedestrianized streets** that link Athens's main monuments: You can stroll from Hadrian's Gate, past the Acropolis and Ancient Agora, to the Kerameikos. There are often exhibits and sometimes concerts along the way.

Both the **Grande Bretagne** and the **Hilton** have reopened after extensive renovations; it's well worth taking a glance at the ornate gold gilt lobby of the Grande Bretagne and the sleek lines of the Hilton's vast lobby.

Aigli (© 2210/336-9363), the very chic, very pricey bistro in Athens's Zappeion Gardens, just off Syntagma Square, has reopened. Aigli has both cafe and restaurant sections, so you can have a coffee at a table in the cafe and enjoy watching stylish Athenians at nearby restaurant tables toying with their fois gras and oysters.

A number of museums, including the **National Archaeological Museum** in Athens and the archaeological museums in Olympia and Delphi, underwent renovations in honor of the 2004 Olympics. All should be open when you visit, but be sure to double-check before you head to Delphi: There are persistent rumors that Delphi's important archaeological museum (© 22650/82-312) may open for the Olympics (Aug 2004) and then close again for further renovations.

If you are **driving** from Athens Eleftherios Venizelos International

Airport to the Peloponnese, be sure that you have an up-to-date map showing the new Athens's ring road, which saves you plowing through Athens's perpetual gridlock.

BARCELONA

Barcelona has been buzzing about the arrival of Forum 2004, a summer-long event of performances, speeches, and exhibitions, concluding soon after this book goes to press. If you arrive after Forum departs, don't fret—it'll leave behind a new convention center; new parks; two entirely new neighborhoods, Diagonal Mar and 22@, east of the city center; and loads of new hotels. Most of the hotels are higher-end properties, but good budget options include the new **Banys Orientales** hotel, located in the center of town at Argenteria 37 (© 93/268-8460); it may be one of the city's best buys. It's 3 blocks from the cathedral, sparkling clean, and reasonably priced. It even sits above a classy yet inexpensive restaurant. The **Nouvel,** Santa Ana 18–20 (© 93/301-8274), and **Ciudad Condal,** Mallorca 255 (© 93/215-1040), have also gotten attractive face-lifts.

Recent moves by Barcelona's public transit company have made it easier to get around town. The same ticket now works on all subways, buses, and commuter trains within the Barcelona metro area. Reflecting the new regime, several train lines have been renumbered. Outside of town, the newly restored Montserrat Rack Railway (www.cremallerademontserrat.com) provides a tremendously picturesque way to get to the popular mountaintop monastery complex.

BERLIN & POTSDAM

The final soccer game of the **2006 World Cup** is expected to take place at the Berlin Olympiastadion on July 9. Since Berlin is expecting a sell-out crowd, book early for hotels.

EurAide, geared toward English-speaking travelers and answering questions on train travel and local sightseeing, has moved from its obscure location inside Bahnhof Zoologischer Garten to the station's more visible Reisezentrum (Travel Center). Incidentally, in 2006, Bahnhof Zoologischer Garten's status as the main train station will end with the opening of the **Hauptbahnhof** farther east (presently Lehrter Bahnhof).

Berlin Tourismus has changed its website to **www.berlin-tourist-information.de**.

The price of a **single journey** on Berlin's public transportation network has decreased from 2.10€ ($2.40) to 2€ ($2.30), but this is no great savings. Before, you could travel as much as you wanted within a 2-hour period, including round-trip excursions; the new ticket is good for only one journey in one direction.

The **Deutsches Historisches Museum,** Unter den Linden 2 (© 030/20 30 40), has partly reopened following many years of expansion and renovation. An addition by I. M. Pei, housing special exhibits, is now open for business.

The Story of Berlin, Kurfürstendamm 207–208 (© 030/88 72 01 00), which portrays 8 centuries of the city's history, has added a nearby 1970s underground bunker to its exhibits. Luckily, the bunker, built to house 3,500 people in the event of an atomic bomb, was never called into action during the decades of the Cold War, since it was equipped with only enough food and water to last 2 weeks.

BERN & THE BEST OF THE BERNER OBERLAND

The ridiculously low ceiling that the Swiss government used to place on bets in its gambling casinos has been removed. Switzerland will never be Las Vegas, but its casinos are now gambling parlors that have become, well, at least more serious. Typical of the reorganized casinos in the country is the newly reopened **Grand Casino Kursaal,** Kornhausstrasse 3 (© 031/ 339-5555), which attracts an international crowd, often in the diplomatic corps.

BRUSSELS

The city has introduced the **Brussels Card,** a chip-equipped plastic card, to smooth access for visitors. The card, which costs 30€ ($35), is enabled for 3 days, and affords free or reduced admission to around 30 city museums and attractions, along with free use of public transportation, and discounts on a range of other services.

BUDAPEST & LAKE BALATON

As of 2004, Hungary will be a member of the European Union, and the current plan calls for adoption of the euro as currency in 2007.

Groundbreaking for the long-planned new metro line (from Keleti Station in Pest across the river to Southern Buda) remains on hold, due to funding problems. Construction may start in 2004 with E.U. infrastructure money.

Nagymező utca between Andrássy and Bajcsi-zsilinszky utca, the **"Broadway of Budapest,"** has been at long last turned into a pedestrian-only area. The floodlights in the pavement and the fountain have turned the once ugly area into a most attractive hub of the city's theater life, providing a pleasant atmosphere for an evening stroll.

The biggest reconstruction project in the downtown area of Pest in recent years is **St. Stephen's Basilica** and the spacious square in front of it, which has been turned into a Mediterranean "plaza" with lots of plants and terraces in the summer.

COPENHAGEN & HELSINGØR

Once again, *The Little Mermaid (Den Lille Havfrue),* one of Copenhagen's most enduring monuments, had to suffer yet another attack by vandals in 2003. By now the city has become adept at restoring limbs or lost body parts to this bronze statue, created in 1913 and inspired by Hans Christian Andersen's famous fairy tale. The good news is that it's been restored and will be posed on an offshore rock waiting to greet you at the Copenhagen harbor at the time of your visit.

DUBLIN

The newest addition to Dublin's public transportation network—the sleek light-rail tram known as **LUAS**—is due for completion in mid-2004. Traveling at a maximum speed of 70kmph (45 mph) and departing every 5 minutes in peak hours, LUAS aims to appease Dublin's congestion problems and bring the city's transportation into the 21st century. Three lines will link the city center at **Connolly Station** and **St. Stephen's Green** with the suburbs of Tallaght in the southwest and Dundrum and Sandyford to the south. For further information, contact **LUAS** (© 01/703-2029; www.luas.ie).

Though eating out has gotten more expensive in recent years, some restaurants still offer exceptional bang for your buck. Our favorite affordable eateries include **Mimo Cafe,** the superlative vegetarian restaurant **Juice,** and **Aya @ Brown Thomas**'s conveyor-belt sushi bar. They all prove that you don't have to sacrifice taste and trendiness when you want to save money.

Hoping to bring home some chic **souvenirs?** The hippest new shopping destination is the up-and-coming **Old City** neighborhood, just west of Temple Bar. The area is centered on the pedestrianized Cow's Lane and is particularly good for fashion and smart, craft-based housewares. On weekends, a clothing and crafts market is set up in the district, accentuating the bohemian feel.

EDINBURGH & ENVIRONS

As prices in the heart of Edinburgh soar higher and higher, more frugal visitors head to the outskirts of town for cheaper living costs. Because of the good public transportation network, this is no hardship. In 2003, more readers than ever wrote in praising **A-Haven,** 180 Ferry Rd. (✆ **0131/ 554-6559**), only a 5-minute bus ride north of the main rail station. Guest rooms overlook the Firth of Forth.

As the cuisine of Auld Reekie continues to improve, more and more British food magazines have discovered such recently uncovered delights as **Duck's at Le Marché Noir,** 2/4 Eyre Place (✆ **0131/558-1608**), with its sophisticated blend of Scottish and French cuisine and one of the best fixed-price lunch deals in town. Another recent discovery is **Dubh Prais,** 123B High St., Royal Mile (✆ **0131/557-5 732**). "The Black Pot" (its English name) is one of the best places to introduce yourself to moderately priced and old-fashioned Scottish cuisine, such as suprême of freshly caught salmon or saddle of venison in juniper sauce.

FLORENCE

Santa Croce, the last of Florence's three major churches, has capitulated and begun charging admission ($4.60), a disturbing trend that began with Santa Maria Novella and then San Lorenzo.

In late 2003, **Michelangelo's** *David* started getting a thorough, 7-month scrubbing that should leave the artistic icon sparkling clean by May 2004— just in time to celebrate his 500th birthday.

Another development making us a bit wary of rising prices is that several of the famously cheap hotels lining Via Faenza are renovating and going mid-scale on us. Luckily, rates have barely budged at the **Albergo Azzi,** even though they've added TVs, air-conditioning, and other amenities to the rooms and jumped up a price category. The similar work on its neighbor, **Albergo Mia Cara,** was just getting started when this edition went to press; it will be transformed into a three-star, moderate hotel—at nearly double the present rates.

In other Tuscan news, although we already announced in the last edition that the **Leaning Tower of Pisa** finally reopened to the public after more than a decade, that happy event had only just occurred when we went to press. Turns out that someone decided the already lofty price they were charging to climb the tower when it first opened, $13, wasn't enough, and the cost has skyrocketed to $20—the priciest single admission to a major sight or museum in all of Italy. Ah, well. It's still worth it.

LISBON & ENVIRONS

The clean, efficient **Metro system** has been upgraded and is being extended even further. The 52-hectare (130-acre) **Expo '98 site,** which has been converted to permanent uses, including a grand aquarium and shopping center, now boasts a sweeping waterfront plaza that is the largest of Lisbon's burgeoning list of wireless Internet hotspots. The initial designs for a new casino, slated for construction in Lisbon's port area, are finally getting underway after much discussion.

LONDON

Brick Lane (over in the city's East End), with its numerous Indian restaurants, is booming and blooming. It has seen the emergence of several classy, cafe-style restaurants where it is still possible for two people to enjoy quality Indian food inexpensively.

As far as accommodations go, the budget end of the market is being badly neglected as hoteliers expand upmarket. It's nice to see that the previous urban jungles that once surrounded the Tower of London have been replaced by an altogether more pleasing landscape that includes several hotels, which, although not budget hotels, are at least situated in the heart of the old city.

Speaking of the old city—those of you who have visited in the last couple of years may have noticed an eye-catching, conical building that has come to dominate the very center of the city (in truth, it's impossible to miss). This is the new **Swiss Re building,** designed by Norman Foster (also responsible for the Millennium Bridge); Londoners have affectionately nicknamed it the "erotic gherkin."

In 2003, the old © 192 **directory assistance** was replaced by a plethora of new directory services, all with the prefix © 118. *Warning:* If you phone any of them, the operator will ask if you want to be put through to the number. If you do, you will be charged a premium rate for the call. It's better to track down the number and make the call yourself.

MADRID

Art lovers rejoice! Three major Madrid museums will fly with new wings by late 2004. Both the **Prado** and the **Museum Thyssen-Bournemiza** will use their new spaces to display more of their impressive permanent collections, which at the Prado stretches to 20,000 works. At the **Centro de Arte Reina Sofía,** the new wing is devoted to temporary exhibits. The Thyssen extension opens in March, the Reina Sofía extension in June, and the Prado should be ready by October. Another museum, the **Museo Lázaro Galdiano,** should be done with its multi-year renovation by the end of 2004, but call ahead.

Madrid's museum renovators aren't out of work, though. They're busy refitting the **Museo Municipal** and **Museo Romántico,** so if you intend to visit either of those, check to see if they're open.

The owners of high-quality *hostal* T.I.J.C.A.L. got tired of turning people away, so they opened **T.I.J.C.A.L. 2,** Cruz 26 (© **91/360-4628**), near the Puerta del Sol, in 2003. So far, it seems to be held to the same high standards as the original. The **Europa,** Carmen 4 (© **91/521-2900**), also opened 35 attractive rooms in a new wing in 2003, improving its rank among Madrid's budget hotels.

Madrid's **subway Line 8** from the airport has also been extended to Nuevos Ministerios nearer the center of town, and you can check in for many airlines at the Nuevos Ministerios station. It's only a 12-minute trip from Nuevos Ministerios to the airport. That makes taking a cab to Nuevos Ministerios a cheaper alternative to riding all the way to the airport.

MUNICH & NEUSCHWANSTEIN

The opening soccer game of the **2006 World Cup** is expected to take place in Munich on June 9. Since Munich is expecting a sell-out crowd, book early for hotels.

Planet Hollywood has closed its doors, but another world-renowned institution, the **Hard Rock Cafe,** has taken up residence at this great location just across from the Hofbräuhaus at Platzl 1 (© **089/242 949 0**).

The **Deutsches Museum,** Museuminsel 1 (© **089/217 9 1**), the world's oldest and largest technological museum, has added a children's section, called the **Kinderreich,** with interactive displays geared for kids 8 and younger.

The **Pinakothek der Moderne,** Barer Strasse 40 (© **089/238 05-360**), which opened in 2003 and houses four major collections under one roof—art, graphics, architecture, and design—is now Munich's second-most visited museum after the Deutsches Museum.

After many years of renovation, the **Antikensammlungen,** Königsplatz 1 (© **089/59 98 88 30**), with its Greek, Roman, and Etruscan antiquities, is again open to the public.

Munich nightlife suffered a blow when the massive Kunstpark Ost closed in 2003. It has been resurrected, however, as **Kultfabrik,** Grafingerstrasse 6 (© 089/49 00 90 70), offering more than two dozen concert venues, themed bars, and dance clubs.

To avoid long lines at **Neuschwanstein,** Bavaria's most popular castle, reserve admission tickets in advance online at www.hohenschwangau.de.

NICE

The new **Terminal 2** at Nice Airport has opened and construction is finally complete at all roads leading to both terminals. The new space is airy and bright and has a few excellent cafes, bars, and one fine-dining restaurant. The shopping area (past security) is excellent and includes several specialty stores selling Provençal goods.

Check out the website for budget airline **easyJet** (www.easyjet.com), which has been increasing service to Nice and offering incredibly low fares.

The highly recommended **Hotel Le Lido** (© 04/93-88-43-15), a block from the sea, has been renovating its very affordable rooms. The most talked-about hotel in Nice is the **Hi Hotel** (© 04/97-07-26-26), opened in 2003. The ultra-modern decor is attracting a steady stream of European yuppies. Its basement Happy Bar pulls in local young professionals who come to see and be seen.

On the popular Cours Saleya, **Eclat du Cours** (© 04/93-85-68-76) is our latest bargain discovery. It offers a delicious three-course meal for only 15€ ($17). You can opt to sit on the sun-splashed terrace or in the cozy dining room. Also in Vieux Nice, near the beautiful place Rosetti, the new **Samsara** (© 04/93-80-70-63) offers an elegant and intimate dining experience at an affordable price; the three-course prix fixe menu is 17€ ($19).

If you're heading to **Cannes,** the newly renovated **Hotel America**

(© 04/93-06-75-75) is one of the best splurge choices on the Cote d'Azur. A block from the sea and close to the Film Festival building, it boasts luxurious rooms with spacious marble bathrooms at reasonable prices. In high season, doubles are 145€ ($167).

PARIS

Due to a decline in visitors, many hotels have decided not to raise their rates in 2004, and some restaurants have kept their prices untouched from 2002.

In May 2004, the roof of Charles-de-Gaulle's new Terminal 2E collapsed, killing four people. At press time, details of the reorganization of flights was not determined.

Many hotels seem to have taken the dip in occupancy rates in 2003 as an opportunity to begin renovations. On a charming narrow street a few minutes from the Eiffel Tower, **Hôtel de L'Alma,** 32 rue de l'Exposition, 7e (© 01-47-05-45-70), is renovating all of its rooms and has added minibars, safes, and marble bathrooms.

New dining venues just keep opening up. One of our favorites, and celebrity chef Alain Ducasse's latest creation, is the exquisite **Aux Lyonnais,** 32 rue St-Marc, 2e (© 01-42-96-65-04), which serves surprisingly affordable and delicious authentic dishes from Lyon.

PRAGUE & ENVIRONS

The latest addition to Prague's hotel address book is the **Hotel Neruda,** Nerudova 44 (© 257-535-557; www.hotelneruda-praha.cz), a renovated and refurbished place with a perfect location for exploring the Prague Castle just a few steps up the hill.

For a fine-dining experience, visit the **Hergetova Cihelná,** Cihelná 2b (© 257-535-534; www.cihelna.com), which offers an international menu in a great location on the bank of the Vltava River next to Charles Bridge. This expansive former brick factory has been divided into a restaurant, cocktail bar, cafe, music lounge, and large summer terrace

Another place with a close connection to the Vltava was recently rebuilt and opened to the public. An old mill on Kampa Island, called Sovovy Mlýny, has been transformed into **Museum Kampa** (© **257-286-147;** www.museumkampa.cz) and now presents an exhibition of Czech and eastern European modern art.

ROME

There's now a **shuttle bus direct from Ciampino Airport downtown** (though it costs 8€/$9 compared to the old public transport's 2€/$2.30).

The no. 64 bus no longer carries you all the way to St. Peter's! In fact, no cross-town bus does anymore. Now they all stop at Piazza Pia next to Castel Sant'Angelo (the most convenient bus there is the no. 40 Express from Termini), where you can either walk the 4 long blocks or grab the no. 62, which circles continuously to St. Peter's and back.

Those convenient **J-line buses** (put in place for the papal Jubilee crowds of 2000) have been retired as planned.

Nearly all **Roman hotels** have been bit by the renovation and inflation bug. A slew of the wonderfully cheap old standbys (including the Abruzzi and Smeraldo) have been renovated into three-star blandness, and are now charging the inflated prices to prove it. Several others (including the Coronet) have similar plans in the works. It's getting hard to find a double room in Rome for less than $100. On the plus side, one hotel, the Marcus, actually got cheaper.

Many of Rome's galleries, museums, and sights now offer **advance reservations** through a single reservations service called Pierreci (www.pierreci.it) for 1.50€ ($1.75) per ticket. The sights covered are some biggies: the Colosseum, Roman Forum, Palatine and Palatine Museum, Capitoline Museums, Baths of Caracalla, Castel Sant' Angelo, Palazzo Massimo, Palazzo Altemps, Crypta Balbi, Baths of Diocletian, Centrale Montemartini, Domus Aurea, Mausoleo di Cecilia Metella, Villa dei Quintili, Hadrian's Villa at Tivoli, and Museo Arceologico at Palestrina.

Admission to the Vatican Museums went up yet again, to 12€ ($14). Still worth it, though.

The **restoration of Michelangelo's** *Moses* in San Pietro in Vincoli church has been finished.

In November 2003, Renzo Piano's gorgeous new **Parco della Musica** complex of performance halls opened on the north side of town, near the Stadio Falminio. The premier Accademia Nazionale di Santa Cecilia musical association was the first outfit to take up residence in one of its auditoriums.

SALZBURG & INNSBRUCK

It costs more to get around in Salzburg nowadays, as both buses and taxis have raised their rates. A single bus trip now costs 1.70€ ($1.95), while taxi fares start at 3€ ($3.45). The **Salzburg Card,** which allows unlimited transportation and includes admission to virtually all the city's attractions, now costs 19€ ($22) for 24 hours, except from mid-June to mid-September when it costs 2€ ($2.30) more.

A new museum is taking shape atop Mönchsberg. The **Museum der Moderne Salzburg** (© **0662/80 42-2541**), slated to open its doors at the end of 2004, will feature changing exhibitions of art and photography from the 20th and 21st centuries.

The hottest attraction in Innsbruck is currently the redesigned **Bergisel** (© **0512/58 92 59**), a ski jump first built in 1925. The sleek and futuristic-looking tower houses an observatory and a cafe.

SEVILLE & ANDALUSIA

One of Seville's oldest buildings is now one of its newest hotels. The **Hotel Convento La Gloria,** Argote de Molina 26–28 (© **95/429-3670**), dates from 1363. It's not the only new historic hotel in Andalusia, though; Granada seems to be crawling with them. The most affordable of Granada's new/old bunch is the **Casa del Capitel Nazari,** Cuesta Aceituneros 6 (© **95/821-5260**), in a building dating from 1503.

Also in Granada, **Iberos y Patagonicos,** Escudo de Carmen 36 (© **95/822-0772**), has recently opened to serve exciting "new Spanish" cuisine, a long shot from typical stick-to-your-ribs Andalusian food.

Back in Seville, **Sol Café Cantante,** Sol 5 (© **95/422-5165**), says it's a new kind of flamenco studio for a new generation. They specialize in young local performers and offer dance lessons; the two, obviously, are linked. They're a good alternative to the beaten path of *tablas.*

The place to be for youthful nightlife in Seville nowadays is the **Alameda de Hercules,** a long plaza just north of most of the tourist attractions. A slew of bars around the plaza attracts a crowd of patrons from 18 to 35, both straight and gay.

Depending on when you read this, you may see work for Seville's first **Metro line** around town. The line, scheduled to open in 2006, won't be of much use to tourists.

STOCKHOLM & ENVIRONS

It's a rare day when a moderately priced hotel opens in central Stockholm, but **Hotel Rival,** Mariatorget 3 (© **08/545-789-00**), made its debut in 2003 on Södermalm in the center of the much-frequented restaurant district. Much of the hotel honors old movies, including the Gösta Berling saga that starred Greta Garbo. Scandinavian modern design is showcased here.

Stockholm's much-attended **Moderna Museet,** Skeppsholmen (© **08/519-552-00**), underwent a massive rejuvenation in 2004 and is now much more user friendly. Combined with the Museum of Architecture, the showcase of modern paintings has a permanent collection of 20th-century masters but keeps abreast of post-millennium developments by its roster of changing exhibitions that feature new themes.

VENICE

The Phoenix has risen from the ashes! **La Fenice opera house,** devastated by a fire in 1996, has been painstakingly reconstructed and held an inaugural concert in December 2003. However, until the theater begins hosting a regular schedule in November 2004, performances will continue to take place at the Palafenice (a giant tent near the city parking lot).

As **St. Mark's Basilica** no longer allows you to bring in bags, they've set up an experimental "left luggage" service outside.

A number of museums now allow you to **reserve tickets and entry times** before you arrive, including the Accademia (where it can be worth it during the ling lines of summer) and the Ca d'Oro (where it's really unnecessary).

Admission prices have risen (by a whopping 25%–35%) at some top sights, including the Accademia, which now costs 9€ ($10), and the Peggy Guggenheim, which now charges 10€ ($12).

The Church Association which regulates entry to most of Venice's top churches now offers cheap (.50€/60¢) **audioguides** at most of its member churches.

In nearby Padova, **restoration of the Scrovegni Chapel,** completely frescoed by Giotto, has been finished—and the admission has more than doubled to 11€ ($13). And that doesn't count the absolutely necessary 1€ ($1.15) booking fee that you need in order to snag one of the limited, timed entries available each day.

VIENNA & KREMS

Vienna Tourist Information has changed its website; you'll now find it at **www.info.wien**.

Two museums that were closed many years for renovations have now reopened. The **Albertina Museum,** Albertinaplatz 1 (© 01/534 83-540), houses one of the world's largest collections of graphic art, only a portion of which is shown in exhibitions that change every 3 months. The **Liechtenstein Museum,** Fürstengasse 1 (© 01/ 319 57 67-252), is housed in a palace filled with a private collection of Renaissance and baroque portraits, Dutch still lifes and landscapes, and Biedermeier art. The Historisches Museum der Stadt Wien, in an attempt to create a new image, is now called the **Wien Museum,** Karlsplatz 4 (© 01/ 505 87 47-0), with a new addition of temporary exhibitions complementing the museum's displays of Vienna's 7,000 years of history.

1

Enjoying Europe
on a Budget

by Reid Bramblett

Americans have such a love affair with Europe that more than eight million cross the Atlantic every year to explore its cities, discover its countryside, delight in its food and wine, meet its people, trace their roots, and soak up the incomparable culture, history, art, and architecture.

This book can serve as your trusty guide so you can get the most out of Europe on a budget; it provides all the hints, advice, practical information, and historical background you'll need—whether your goal is to see all the Renaissance museums of Florence, ponder life from a sidewalk table of a Parisian cafe, bask in the baroque beauty of Prague, explore the hill towns of Andalusia, or hit the theaters of London's West End.

1 About the $85-a-Day Premise

Times—and most definitely prices—have changed since Arthur Frommer himself published the first edition of this book, *Europe on $5 a Day*, in 1957. This 46th edition of ***Frommer's Europe from $85 a Day*** has been completely revised, yet it retains the ever-dependable Frommer's emphasis: *finding great value for your money.*

This guide is not about just barely scraping by, but about traveling comfortably on a reasonable budget. Spend too little and you suck all the fun out of travel; you shortchange yourself, your vacation, and your experiences. Spend too much and you insulate yourself from the local side of Europe.

Frommer's Europe from $85 a Day takes you down the middle road, where the joys and experiences of Europe open wide to let you in. Doing Europe "from $85 a day" means $85 is the average starting amount per person you'll need to spend on *accommodations and meals*

only; transportation, sightseeing, shopping, souvenirs, entertainment, and other expenses are not included. Expect to use a little over half your $85 each day on accommodations. Obviously, two people can travel within this budget more easily than one—$90 for a double room and $40 each for meals.

Of course, since our budget is *from* $85 a day, we don't limit our hotel and restaurant recommendations to only the rock-bottom places. You'll also find moderately priced choices as well as more expensive options for those who'd like to splurge here and there—say on a romantic dinner in Paris or a room overlooking the Grand Canal in Venice.

This chapter and chapter 2, "Planning an Affordable Trip to Europe," will show you how to squeeze the most out of your budget. Refer to the individual city chapters for specifics, such as when to go, where to stay, what to do, and how to save money once you arrive.

2 Frommer's Money-Saving Strategies

GETTING THE BEST DEAL ON ACCOMMODATIONS

Most tourist offices, some travel agents, and often hotel reservation booths at airports or train stations provide listings of B&Bs, inns, rooms for rent in homes, farmhouses, and small hotels where a couple might spend only $30 to $80 for a double. Besides the more traditional options below, creative travel alternatives in which lodging costs nothing or next to nothing include home exchanges and educational vacations (see "Educational Travel," in chapter 2).

BRINGING THE RATES DOWN

Keep prices low by traveling off season and off the beaten track. In cities, seek out local, not touristy, neighborhoods or those frequented largely by students (often around the train station). Small family-run B&Bs, inns, and pensions tend to be cheaper—not to mention friendlier—than larger hotels. Although you'll find more and more properties in Europe sporting the familiar names of American chains, they're almost always standardized business hotels with rates two to four times higher than what the same chain charges in the States.

Getting a good rate at any hotel is an exercise in trade-offs. You can get lower prices by looking for hotels away from the town center or opting for a smaller room, one without a private bathroom, or one without a TV

or other amenities. Ask to see several rooms—desk clerks will often try to move the most expensive or least appealing rooms first, so let them know you're a smart shopper who will stay only in a room you approve of and that's a fair price. Politely negotiate the rates—especially off season or if you sense the hotel has plenty of empty rooms—and you might pay around 25% less. Always ask about discounts for stays of 3 or more days, for stays over the weekend, or for students or seniors.

If you haven't reserved a room before leaving home, call around to a few hotels before you begin visiting them to gauge how full the city's inns seem to be. If there are plenty of extra rooms, you've got more bargaining leverage. If one proprietor isn't easily persuaded to give you a worthwhile deal, try elsewhere. If, however, hotels in town seem booked, bed down in the first reasonable place and hope for better bargaining luck next time. Pick your top few choices from the reviews in this book before you hit town (perhaps on the train ride in); when you arrive at the train station of a new town, buy a phone card from a newspaper stand (that's always where they're sold) and head over to the pay phones to start calling those hotel choices for an available room (or head to the station's room reservations desk if there is one). This way you get a

---

Tips A Note on Special Rates

In a couple of chapters you'll see that some hotels offer special rates "for Frommer's readers." We don't solicit these rates or offer anything (like a guaranteed rosy write-up) in return, but hoteliers sometimes offer them, and we're only too happy to accept on your behalf! The hotel owners request that you please *make it clear on booking or arrival* (or both) that you're a Frommer's reader, in order to avoid confusion about those special rates. Note that the actual rates might have changed by the time you plan your trip, but the hotels will still offer our readers a discount.

Europe

jump on those who head out to search on foot.

OVERNIGHT TRAINS   One of the great European deals is the **sleeping couchette,** where for only about $20 (2nd class) you get a reserved bunk for the night in a shared sleeping compartment (sometimes sleeping two, but usually four to six people). When you wake up, you've gotten where you're going without wasting your daylight hours on a train, plus you've saved yourself a night's hotel charges—along with hotel comfort.

PACKAGE TOURS   Airlines and tour operators offer package tours that, unlike fully escorted guided tours, book only air transportation and hotels and leave the sightseeing up to you. It's a good mix of the joys and freedom of independent travel at the (sometimes) cut rates of a tour. See "Escorted General-Interest Tours," in chapter 2, for more details.

RENTING   Imagine living for a week in a studio apartment in London for $500 to $600, or in a cottage in France for $450 to $600. If you rent a room, an apartment, a cottage, or a farmhouse, you can live like a European, if only for a few days or weeks. In cities, you can often broker rental rooms and apartments through the tourist office or a private lodging service in the train station. Rooms for rent usually offer great rates (much cheaper than hotel rates) even for the single traveler staying just 1 night, although some might require a minimum stay of a few nights. Apartments start making economic sense when you have three or more people and are staying in town for a week or longer.

Renting villas, cottages, farmhouses, and the like is a much trickier business, with a wide range of rates— and quality. It can be a downright budget option (usually, again, for groups of three or four renting for a few weeks), or it can be a hedonistic splurge on an overpriced historic castle. Shop around. Contact local tourist offices before leaving home; they might have lists or catalogs of available properties. Or read through travel magazines and newspaper supplements for ads.

Or you can try **Barclay International** (© 800/845-6636; www.barclayweb.com), which since 1963 has represented properties across Europe, including some 3,000 apartments and 5,000 villas, many off the beaten path. Book as early as possible. Or take the guesswork out of the process by booking with 30-year-old **Untours** (© 888/868-6871; www.untours.com), which sets you up with plane tickets, a rental car, an apartment in any of a dozen European countries for 1 to 2 weeks, plus a local contact who will help you settle in and is available by phone to dispense advice during your stay. A wee bit pricier than going it alone, perhaps, but many readers report that it's worth it.

HOSTELS   One of the least expensive ways to keep a roof over your head and meet other travelers is a stay in a hostel. Although more and more families and intrepid seniors are appearing in the common rooms lately (only those in Bavaria still enforce an under-26 age limit), hostels are still primarily student stomping grounds. In fact, in summer especially, they fill up early each morning, often with high school and college students partying their way through Europe. If that's not your scene, you might want to look elsewhere.

Hostels charge around $10 to $35 per night for what's usually a bunk in a dormlike room (often sex-segregated) that sleeps anywhere from 4 to 50 people or more and a single big bathroom down the hall, college dorm–style. Happily, the recent trend at hostels has been away from gymnasium-sized dorms and toward smaller shared units of four to six, often with a bathroom attached to each.

There are usually lockers for your bags, and you often must bring your

> **Tips City-Specific Savings**
>
> For city-specific savings on all these topics, see the "Getting the Best Deal" boxes throughout this guide.

own sleep-sack (basically a sheet folded in half and sewn up the side to make a very thin sleeping bag) or buy one on-site. For many, you need an **HI membership card** (see below)—at some, the card is required for you to stay there; at others, it gets you a discount; and at some private hostels, the card doesn't matter at all.

There's usually a lockout from morning to mid-afternoon and a curfew of around 10pm to 1am—which can seriously cramp your evening plans, especially since many hostels are at the edge of town, meaning you have to finish dinner rather early to catch that long bus or metro ride back out.

Membership in **Hostelling International,** 8401 Colesville Rd., Suite 600, Silver Spring, MD 20910 (© **301/495-1240;** www.hiusa.org), an affiliate of the International Youth Hostel Federation (IYH), is free for those under 18, $28 per year for people 18 to 54, $18 for those 55 and older, or $250 for a lifetime membership. HI sells the annual *International Guide—Europe* for $13.95. But in the days of the Internet, the official website of **Hostelling International** (www.hihostels.com) and that of independent **www.hostels.com** are free, more up to date, and far more useful than any book in print.

GETTING THE BEST DEAL ON DINING

Some hotels include dinner or breakfast in their rates or offer them as extras. For dinner, this is sometimes a fine meal at a good price, but you can almost always eat just as cheaply—and find considerably more variety—by dining at local restaurants. **Hotel breakfasts**—with the exception of the cholesterol-laden minifeasts of the

British Isles—are invariably overpriced. A "continental breakfast" means a roll with jam and coffee or tea, occasionally with some sliced ham, cheese, or fruit to justify the $4 to $20 price. Many hotels include breakfast in the rates, but if there's any way you can get out of paying for it, do so. You can pick up the same food at the corner cafe or bar for $2 to $4.

When it comes to **choosing your restaurant,** a local bistro, trattoria, taverna, or pub is not only cheaper than a fancier restaurant, but also offers you the opportunity to rub elbows with Europeans. Ask locals you meet for recommendations of places *they* like, not places they think you as a visitor would like. Pick restaurants that are packed with locals, not those abandoned or filled only with tourists. At any restaurant, the **house table wine** will usually be just fine, if not excellent, and cheap. Similarly, **beer** is plentiful, cheap, and excellent on the British Isles and in central and eastern countries (Belgium, Germany, the Czech Republic, and so on).

The **fixed-price menu** (or tourist menu) is a budget option that gets you a semi- to full meal at a cheaper price—but a much more limited selection—than if you ordered each dish from the full menu. The best deals include wine (a glass or quarter carafe) or beer, coffee, and dessert along with choices for first and second courses.

If you love fine food but not huge bills, consider patronizing **top restaurants at lunch.** Outstanding places often serve the same or similar dishes at both meals, but with lunch prices two-thirds to one-half of dinner prices. Plus, lunch reservations are easier to come by.

In Britain and Ireland, indulge in afternoon tea, in Spain do a tapas bar crawl, and in Italy nibble during the evening *passeggiata* (stroll)—all inexpensive popular customs that'll cut your appetite for a huge meal later. Wherever you eat, be sure to check the menu and ask your waiter to see if a **service charge** is automatically included; don't tip twice by accident.

In the **bars and cafes** of many European countries, the price on any item consumed while you stand at the bar is lower (sometimes by as much as half) than the price you'd pay sitting at a table, and three times lower than the price charged at the outdoor tables.

If your day is filled with sightseeing, lunch can be as quick as local cheeses and salamis, ripe fruit, a loaf of freshly baked bread, and a bottle of wine or mineral water eaten on the steps of the cathedral, on a park bench, or in your hotel room. **Picnic** ingredients in Europe, purchased from outdoor markets and tiny neighborhood shops, are ultrafresh and so cheap you usually won't spend more than $5 to $10 per person.

GETTING THE BEST DEAL ON SIGHTSEEING

You've heard that the best things in life are **free.** Well, some of the best things in sightseeing are, too. You can't get much better than strolling through Paris's Luxembourg Gardens or spending an afternoon in London's British Museum. And how about peeking into Rome's many churches or lounging on the Spanish Steps, exploring Barcelona's medieval quarter, hiking the Alps around Salzburg, or relaxing on a St-Tropez beach? The website **www. europeforfree.com** lists hundreds of free things to see and do across Europe. Or just stroll around town, drinking in the European ambience—city tourist offices often offer free booklets of walking tours for exploring the city on foot. Also note that Frommer's publishes

Memorable Walks in Paris and *Memorable Walks in London* (both $12.99).

Visit the tourist offices and pump them for free maps, information, brochures, and museum lists—everything you need to plan your sightseeing. Find out if some museums offer free entry on a particular day or reduced admission after a certain hour, and go then (but be prepared for crowds—you're not the only one looking to save some money). Keep in mind that many European museums are closed on Monday (in Paris, it's Tues) and open just a half-day on Sunday, so check the schedule before you go.

Always inquire about **special passes** or **combination tickets** that include reduced admission to several or even all of a city's museums. Sometimes these passes even include reduced public transportation fares.

GETTING THE BEST DEAL ON SHOPPING

GETTING YOUR VAT REFUND

First the bad news: All European countries charge a **value-added tax (VAT)** of 15% to 33% on goods and services—it's like a sales tax that's already included in the price. Rates vary from country to country, although the goal in E.U. countries is to arrive at a uniform rate of about 18%.

Now the good news: Non-E.U. citizens are entitled to have some or all of the VAT refunded on purchases if they spend more than a certain amount *at any one store* (how much ranges from as low as $80 in England—but some stores, like Harrods, require as much as £50/$90—up to nearly $200 in France and Italy). The actual amounts in each country—as well as lots of VAT-free shopping advice—are listed at the website of **Global Refund** (© 800/566-9828; www.globalrefund.com).

Ask the store for an official VAT receipt, and carry it with you. Many shops are now part of the "Tax-Free for Tourists" network. (Look for the sticker in the window.) Stores participating in this network issue a check along with your invoice at the time of purchase.

You actually don't "redeem" the receipts you're carrying around until you are getting ready to leave the last E.U. country (which includes all of western Europe except Switzerland, Norway, and Iceland; and all of eastern Europe minus Bulgaria, Romania, and Turkey—the latter three are up for membership) you visit on your trip. That means you should bring all your receipts for every E.U. country to the airport from which you depart; so if you're flying home from Paris, you can take your Italian, German, and French receipts to the Customs agent at Charles de Gaulle Airport.

Before you even check in for your flight, you must visit the local Customs office at the airport with the receipts and the items you purchased, in case the officer wishes to inspect your purchases (which rarely happens). The Customs agent will stamp your receipt and give you further directions—usually, after going through check-in and security, you head to another VAT refund desk inside the airport and deal with more paperwork there. In some cases, they give you a refund on the spot. More often, the stamped receipt is sent back to the store and your reimbursement is credited against your credit card or sent to you by check. Either way, it can take months.

CUSTOMS For U.S. Citizens
Longtime travelers rejoice! In 2003, the personal exemption rule—how much you can bring back into the States without paying a duty on it—was doubled to $800 worth of goods per person. This applies to returning U.S. citizens who have been away for at least 48 hours, and can be used once every 30 days. On the first $1,000 worth of goods over $800, you pay a flat 3% duty. Beyond that, it works on

an item-by-item basis. There are a few restrictions on amount: 1 liter of alcohol (you must be over 21), 200 cigarettes, and 100 cigars. Antiques more than 100 years old and works of fine art are exempt from the $800 limit, as is anything you mail home. Once per day, you can mail yourself $200 worth of goods duty-free; mark the package "For Personal Use." You can also mail gifts to other people without paying duty as long as the recipient doesn't receive more than $100 worth of gifts in a single day. Label each gift package "Unsolicited Gift." Any package must state on the exterior a description of the contents and their values. You can't mail alcohol, perfume (it contains alcohol), or tobacco products worth more than $5.

For more information on regulations, check out the **U.S. Customs and Border Protection website** (www.cbp. gov) or write to them at 1300 Pennsylvania Ave. NW, Washington, DC 20229, to request the free *Know Before You Go* pamphlet.

To prevent the spread of diseases, **you cannot bring into the States** any plants, fruits, vegetables, meats, or most other foodstuffs. This includes even cured meats like salami (no matter what the shopkeeper in Europe says). You may bring in the following: bakery goods, all but the softest cheeses (the rule is vague, but if the cheese is at all spreadable, don't risk confiscation), candies, roasted coffee beans and dried tea, fish, seeds for veggies and flowers (but not for trees), and mushrooms. Check out the **USDA's website** (www.aphis. usda.gov/oa/travel) for more info.

For British Citizens You can bring home almost as many goods as you like from any E.U. country as long as the goods are for your own use. You're likely to be questioned by Customs if you bring back more than 90 liters of wine, 3,200 cigarettes, or 200 cigars. If you're returning home from a non-E.U. country or if you buy your goods in a duty-free shop, you're allowed to bring home 200 cigarettes or 50 cigars, 2 liters of table wine, plus 1 liter of spirits or 2 liters of fortified wine. Get in touch with **Her Majesty's Customs and Excise Office,** New King's Beam House, 22 Upper Ground, London SE1 9PJ (© **020/7620-1313;** www. hmce.gov.uk), or call their Advice Service (© 0845/010-9000) for more information.

For Canadian Citizens For a clear summary of Canadian rules, write for the booklet *I Declare,* issued by **Revenue Canada,** 2265 St. Laurent Blvd., Ottawa K1G 4KE (© **800/959-2221** or 613/993-0534; www.ccra-adrc. gc.ca). Canada allows citizens a C$750 exemption if you've been out of the country for at least 7 days. You're allowed to bring back duty-free 200 cigarettes, 2.2 pounds of tobacco, 40 imperial ounces of liquor, 50 cigars, and 1.5 liters of wine. In addition, you're allowed to mail gifts to Canada from abroad at the rate of C$60 a day, provided they're unsolicited and aren't alcohol or tobacco (write on the package "Unsolicited Gift, Under C$60 Value"). All valuables should be declared on the Y-38 form before departure from Canada, including serial numbers of, for example, expensive foreign cameras that you already own. *Note:* The C$500 exemption can be used only once a year and only after an absence of 7 days. For more information, call the **Automated Customs Service** (© **800/ 461-9999** toll-free within Canada, or 204/983-3500 outside Canada).

For Australian Citizens The duty-free allowance in Australia is A$400 or, for those under 18, A$200. Personal property mailed back from Europe should be marked "Australian Goods Returned" to avoid payment of duty. On returning to Australia, citizens can bring in 250 cigarettes or 250 grams of loose tobacco, and 1,125ml of alcohol. If you're returning with valuable goods you already own, such as foreign-made cameras, you should file form B263. A helpful brochure, available from Australian consulates or Customs offices, is *Know Before You Go.* For more information, contact **Australian Customs Services,** GPO Box 8, Sydney, NSW 2001 (© **1300-363-263** within Australia; 02-6275-6666 from overseas; www. customs.gov.au).

For New Zealand Citizens The duty-free allowance for New Zealand is NZ$700. Citizens over 17 years can bring in 200 cigarettes, or 50 cigars, or 250 grams of tobacco (or a mixture of all three if their combined weight doesn't exceed 250 grams); plus 4.5 liters of wine or beer, or 1.125 liters of liquor. New Zealand currency doesn't carry import or export restrictions. Fill out a certificate of export, listing the valuables you are taking out of the country; that way, you can bring them back without paying duty. Most questions are answered in a free pamphlet available at New Zealand consulates and Customs offices: *New Zealand Customs Guide for Travellers, Notice no. 4.* For more information, contact **New Zealand Customshouse,** 50 Anzac Ave., Box 29,

---

Tips **But I Bought That Before I Left Home!**

If you plan to travel with expensive items (especially foreign-made) you already own, like cameras, video or computer equipment, or valuable jewelry (particularly inadvisable), check with your home country's Customs office about filing a form of ownership. If it's undeclared beforehand, officials might assume you bought the item abroad and try to make you pay duty on it.

Auckland, NZ (© **0800-428-786** within New Zealand, 09-359-6655 from overseas; www.customs.govt.nz).

BARGAINING   Bargaining may be more prevalent in parts of the world other than Europe, but it's still done in Spain, Portugal, Greece, and, to some degree, Italy. In other countries, store prices are pretty firm, but you'll have the opportunity to haggle in street markets anywhere.

These tips will help ease the process: Never appear too interested or too anxious; offer only half or even a third of the original asking price and slowly work your way up from there (the price should never jump up—it should inch up, so take the time to inch it properly); tantalize with cash and have the exact amount you want to pay ready in your pocket. Finally, don't take bargaining, the vendor, or yourself too seriously. The seller will act shocked, hurt, or angry, but isn't really; it's all just part of the ritual. And don't worry about taking advantage of the vendor; he'll only sell the item to you for the price he's willing to accept. Ideally, bargaining should be fun for both parties.

GETTING THE BEST DEAL ON EVENING ENTERTAINMENT

If you're interested in the **theater, ballet,** or **opera,** ask at the tourist office if discount or last-minute tickets are available and where to get them (at the theater itself or a special outlet or booth, like the famous "tkts" half-price ticket booth on London's Leicester Sq.). Some theaters sell standing room or discount seats on the day of the performance, and students and seniors may qualify for special admission.

Nightclubs tend to be expensive, but you might be able to avoid a cover charge by sitting or standing at the bar rather than taking a table, or by arriving before a certain hour. If you decide to splurge, keep a lid on your alcohol intake; that's where the costs mount

astronomically. If you've arrived during a **public holiday** or **festival,** there might be abundant free entertainment, much of it in the streets. For more leads on stretching your entertainment dollar, check "Deals & Discounts" and "After Dark" in each city chapter.

GETTING THE BEST DEAL ON PHONE CALLS & E-MAIL

LOCAL CALLS   In most European countries these days, public phones work with **prepaid phone cards**— many don't even take coins anymore— sold at newsstands, tobacconists, and post offices. These cards are put out by the phone company itself and are legit, not like the scams prevalent in the United States. Calls cost the same whether made with coins or cards. If you'll be in town a while, phone cards pay off in convenience. If you're in a country for just a few days, you probably won't use up an entire card (but good luck finding a coin-op phone in Paris or Athens anymore).

OVERSEAS CALLS   If you can avoid it, never pay European rates for a transcontinental call; American rates are cheaper, so have friends and family call *you* at your hotel. AT&T, MCI, and Sprint all have local (usually) free numbers in each country that link you directly to an American operator, who can place a **collect call** or take your calling-card number. You'll find these local numbers under the "Telephone" entry in "Fast Facts" in every destination chapter of this book, or you can get a wallet card from the phone company.

Calling cards, not to be confused with phone cards, are like credit cards for phone calls and usually offer the easiest and cheapest way for you to call home. They're issued by major long-distance carriers such as AT&T, MCI, and Sprint. Since the rates and calling plans change regularly, shop around to find out which one is currently offering the best deal on Europe-to-the-U.S. rates.

Tips **Number, Please: Calling Europe**

To make a phone call from the United States to Europe, dial the **international access code, 011;** then the **country code** for the country you're calling; then (sometimes) the **city code** for the city you're calling (usually dropping the initial zero, which has conveniently been left off numbers in the list below); followed by the regular telephone number. For an operator-assisted call, dial **01,** then the country code, the city code, and the regular telephone number; an operator will then come on the line.

Following are codes for the countries and major cities in this guide. These are the codes you use to call from overseas or from another European country; if you're calling from within the country, see the "Country & City Codes" boxes within each destination chapter.

European phone systems are currently undergoing a prolonged confusing change. *Italy, France, Spain, Monaco, Copenhagen, and Portugal no longer use separate city codes:* The old codes are now built into all phone numbers, and (except for France) you must *always* dial that initial zero or nine (which was previously—and still is in most other countries—included before a city code only when dialing from another city within the country itself).

Austria	43		**Hungary**	36
Salzburg	662		Budapest	1
Vienna	1		**Ireland**	353
Belgium	32		Dublin	1
Brussels	2		**Italy**	39
Czech Republic	420		**Monaco**	377
Prague	2		**The Netherlands**	31
Denmark	45		Amsterdam	20
England	44		**Portugal**	351
London	20		**Scotland**	44
France	33		Edinburgh	131
Germany	49		**Spain**	34
Berlin	30		**Sweden**	46
Munich	89		Stockholm	8
Greece	30		**Switzerland**	41
Athens	1		Bern	31

Avoid making any calls from European hotels. They often charge exorbitant rates—especially for transatlantic calls, but even for a local call like ringing up a nearby restaurant for reservations—and they often add a "surcharge" on top of that, sometimes bringing the total anywhere from 200% to 400% above what the same call would cost from a pay phone. Strangely enough,

the small, inexpensive hotels are least likely to charge obscenely high rates, while the plusher, pricier inns are the ones that tend to hit you with those ridiculous charges.

Calling cards are the cheapest way to call home, but if you choose to travel without one, you have two choices. Since phone cards (above) come in a variety of increments, you can buy a few of the more expensive versions and call abroad by feeding them into a pay phone, one after the other, as they get used up. Or go to a big-city post office where you can call home from a little booth on a toll phone, then pay when you're done.

E-MAIL Cybercafes have popped up all over Europe faster than you can say *"le e-mail."* You can find one in most cities, check your e-mail, and send virtual postcards to your friends back home for around 10¢ to 30¢ per minute. Most also offer temporary mailboxes you can rent for the day, week, or month if you'll be sticking around town for a while. Some countries (Spain, the Netherlands) also provide public Internet kiosks scattered about town (often in post offices), but the speed is usually excruciatingly slow.

The best guides to cybercafes on the Web are **www.cybercaptive.com** and **www.cybercafe.com**. For much more on this subject, see "The 21st-Century Traveler" in chapter 2, and for specifics, check the "Internet Access" entry in the "Fast Facts" section for each city chapter.

3 Getting Around Without Going Broke

BY TRAIN

The train is the primary way to go in Europe. European trains are less expensive than those in the United States and far more advanced in many ways, and the system is much more extensive, with over 100,000 miles of rails. Modern high-speed trains make the rails faster than planes for short journeys, and overnight trains get you where you're going without wasting valuable daylight hours—and you save money on lodging to boot.

If you plan on doing a lot of train travel, *Frommer's Europe by Rail* is the official guidebook of Rail Europe. The user-friendly guide will help you plan your train trip through Europe, detailing the reservation process and highlighting the scenic lines, the high-speed routes, and lodging, dining, and charming stops along the way. Detailed itineraries help you make the most of your time.

For specific routes and schedules, the 500-page *Thomas Cook European Timetable* is the definitive book listing all official European train routes and schedules. It's available in the United States for $27.95 (plus $4.50 shipping and handling) from Forsyth Travel Library, P.O. Box 2975, Shawnee Mission, KS 66201 (© **800/367-7984**); at travel specialty stores; or online at **www.thomascooktimetables.com**.

You can get even more information about train travel in Europe, plus research schedules and fares (largely for major routes) online at **Rail Europe** (© **877/272-RAIL;** www.raileurope.com). For more on using Europe's trains, including resources for finding each country's national railway website—which will include much more detailed schedule and fare info than Rail Europe, sometimes even in English!—check out **www.europetrains.org**.

SUPPLEMENTS & RESERVATIONS Europe has a rainbow of train classifications ranging from **local milk runs** that stop at every tiny station to **high-speed bullet trains** that cruise at 209kmph (130 mph) between major cities. Many high-speed trains throughout Europe, including the popular ES (Eurostar), EC (EuroCity), IC (Inter-City), and EN (EuroNight), require you to pay a **supplement** of around $5 to $15 in addition to the regular ticket fare. It's included when you buy regular tickets and (on most trains) is covered by rail passes.

The few trains that charge rail pass holders additional supplements (includes seat reservations) are

---

Tips **Class Consciousness**

The difference between seats in **first class** and **second class** on European trains is minor—a matter of 1 or 2 inches of extra padding and maybe a bit more elbow room (and only four bunks per sleeping couchette rather than 2nd class's six). For up to 50% less, a second-class ticket still gets you there at the same time.

Artesia (between France and Italy), Cisalpino (between Switzerland and Italy), Thalys (between Amsterdam or Brussels and Paris), Eurostar Italia (between major Italian cities), and AVE (between Madrid and Seville). If you didn't buy the supplement at the ticket counter (usually a special window at one end of the ticket banks) before boarding, the conductor will sell you the supplement on the train—along with a fine.

Seat reservations are also required on some of the speediest of the high-speed runs—Eurostar (between London and Paris or Brussels through the Chunnel), France's TGV, Germany's ICE, Spain's AVE and EUROMED, Italy's ETR/Pendolino and Eurostar, Sweden's X2000, and any other train marked with an "R" on a printed train schedule. Reservations range from $10 to $50 or more (when a meal is included). You can almost always reserve a seat within a few hours of the train's departure, but to be on the safe side, you'll probably want to book a few days in advance.

You'll also need to **reserve a sleeping couchette**—compartments with bunk beds to sleep four (1st class) or six (2nd class); a bunk costs around $20 and isn't terribly comfortable, but it does get you where you're going without wasting your vacation time. Lock the couchette door, keep your money belt on under your clothes, and don't flash valuables (you're sharing the couchettes with strangers).

With two exceptions, there's no need to buy individual train tickets or make seat reservations before you leave the States. However, on the high-speed Artesia run (Paris to Turin in 5½ hr.), you must buy a supplement beforehand—on which you can get a substantial discount if you have a rail pass, but only if you buy the supplement in the States along with the pass. It's also wise to reserve a seat on the Chunnel's Eurostar, as England's frequent "bank holidays" (long weekends) book the train solid with Londoners taking a short vacation to Paris.

TRAIN STATIONS Most European stations are brilliantly efficient and clean, if a bit chaotic at times. In stations, you'll find posters showing the track number and timetables for regularly scheduled runs that pass through (departures are often on a yellow poster, arrivals on white). In many stations you'll find automated ticket machines that can save you much standing-in-line time. Many stations also have tourist office outposts and hotel reservations desks, banks with ATMs, and newsstands where you can buy phone cards, bus and metro tickets, city maps, English-language newspapers, and local events magazines. The bathrooms often leave much to be desired; bring a packet of tissues with you as well as some spare change, as many require a nominal fee to get in.

RAIL PASSES One of the greatest values in European travel is the **rail pass,** a single ticket allowing you unlimited travel—or travel on a select number of days—within a set time period. If you plan on getting all over Europe by train, purchasing a rail pass will be much less expensive than buying individual tickets. Plus, a rail pass gives you the freedom to hop on a train whenever you feel like it, and unless you need to reserve a couchette, there's no waiting in ticket lines. For more focused trips, you might want to look into national or regional passes, or just buy individual tickets as you go. Use Rail Europe (www.raileurope.com) and Europetrains.org (www.europetrains.org) as resources to help you work out a rough trip plan and do some quick math to see whether a pass will save you money.

Passes Available in the United States
The granddaddy of passes is the **Eurailpass,** covering 17 countries (most of western Europe except the U.K.; see the "Eurail Countries" sidebar). The more modest but flexible **Selectpass** covers three to five contiguous countries for more focused trips. The passes include bonuses such as free or reduced prices on some ferries and river cruise boats, scenic buses, and certain private rail lines (for example, 25% off the Jungfrau train in Switzerland).

Rail passes are available in either **consecutive-day** or **flexipass** versions (in which you have 2 months to use, say, 10 or 15 days of train travel of your choosing as you go along). Consecutive-day passes are best for those taking the train very frequently (every few days), covering a lot of ground, and making many short train hops. Flexipasses are for folks who want to travel far and wide but plan on taking their time over a long trip and intend to stay in each city for a while. There are also **saverpasses** for families and small groups, and **rail/drive** passes that mix train days with car-rental days.

If you're **under age 26,** you can opt to buy a regular first-class pass or a second-class youth pass; if you're 26 or over, you're stuck with the first-class pass. Passes for **kids 4 to 11** are half price, and kids under 4 travel free.

The rates quoted below are for 2004:

- **Eurailpass:** Consecutive-day Eurailpass $588 for 15 days, $762 for 21 days, $946 for 1 month, $1,338 for 2 months, or $1,654 for 3 months.
- **Eurailpass Flexi:** Good for 2 months of travel, within which you can travel by train for 10 days (consecutive or not) for $694; or 15 days for $914.
- **Eurailpass Saver:** Good for two to five people traveling together, costing $498 per person for 15 days, $648 for 21 days, $804 for 1 month, $1,138 for 2 months, or $1,408 for 3 months.
- **Eurailpass Saver Flexi:** Good for two to five people traveling together, costing $592 per person for 10 days within 2 months, or $778 per person for 15 days within 2 months.
- **Eurailpass Youth:** The second-class rail pass for travelers under 26, costing $414 for 15 days, $534 for 21 days, $664 for 1 month, $938 for 2 months, or $1,160 for 3 months.
- **Eurailpass Youth Flexi:** Only for travelers under 26, allowing for 10 days of travel within 2 months for $488; or 15 days within 2 months for $642.
- **Eurail Selectpass:** For the most tightly focused of trips, covering

---

Eurail Countries

Austria, Belgium, Denmark, Finland, France, Germany, Greece, Hungary, Ireland, Italy, Luxembourg, the Netherlands, Norway, Portugal, Spain, Sweden, and Switzerland all participate in the Eurail system.

Note: The United Kingdom (England, Scotland, Wales, and Northern Ireland) isn't included.

three to five contiguous Eurail countries connected by rail or ship. It's valid for 2 months, and its cost varies according to the number of countries you plan to visit. A pass for three countries is $356 for 5 days, $394 for 6 days, $470 for 8 days, and $542 for 10 days. A four-country pass costs $398 for 5 days, $436 for 6 days, $512 for 8 days, and $584 for 10 days. A pass for five countries costs $438 for 5 days, $476 for 6 days, $552 for 8 days, $624 for 10 days, and $794 for 15 days.

- **Eurail Selectpass Saver:** Same as the Eurail Selectpass (and slightly less expensive) but for two to five people traveling together. Per person, the three-country pass is $304 for 5 days, $336 for 6 days, $400 for 8 days, and $460 for 10 days. A pass for four countries is $340 for 5 days, $372 for 6 days, $436 for 8 days, and $496 for 10 days. A five-country pass is $3,744 for 5 days, $406 for 6 days, $470 for 8 days, $530 for 10 days, and $674 for 15 days.

- **Eurail Selectpass Youth:** Good in second class only for travelers under 26. Cost varies according to the number of countries you plan to visit, but all passes are valid for 2 months. For three countries, it's $249 for 5 days, $276 for 6 days, $329 for 8 days, and $379 for 10 days. A four-country pass costs $279 for 5 days, $306 for 6 days, $359 for 8 days, and $409 for 10 days. A five-country pass is $307 for 5 days, $334 for 6 days, $387 for 8 days, $437 for 10 days, and $556 for 15 days.

- **EurailDrive Pass:** This pass offers the best of both worlds, mixing train travel and rental cars (through Hertz or Avis) for less money than it would cost to do them separately (and one of the only ways to get around the high daily car-rental rates in Europe when you rent for less than a week). You get 4 first-class rail days and 2 car days within a 2-month period. Prices (per person for one adult/two adults) vary with the class of the car: $452/$409 economy, $481/$423 compact, $496/$431 midsize, and $531/$447 small automatic (Hertz only). You can add up to 6 extra car days ($49 each economy, $64 compact, $75 midsize, $95 small automatic [Hertz only]). You have to reserve the first "car day" a week before leaving the States but can make the other reservations as you go (subject to availability). If there are more than two adults, the extra passengers get the car portion free but must buy the 4-day rail pass for about $365.

- **Eurail SelectPass Drive:** This pass, like the EurailDrive Pass, offers combined train and rental car travel, but only for very focused trips: within any three to five adjoining Eurail countries. A flexipass, it includes 3 days of unlimited, first-class rail travel and 2 days of unlimited-mileage car rental (through Avis or Hertz) within a 2-month period. Prices (per person for one adult/two adults) are $335/$291 economy, $365/$305 compact, $392/$315 midsize, and $429/$331 small automatic. You can add up to 7 additional rail days for $39 each and unlimited extra car days for $49 to $95 each, depending on the class of car.

There are also **national rail passes** of various kinds (flexi, consecutive, rail/drive, and so on) for each country, **dual country passes** ("France 'n Italy," or "Switzerland 'n Austria"), and **regional passes** like ScanRail (Scandinavia), BritRail (covering Great Britain—which Eurail and Europass don't), and the European East Pass (good in Austria, the Czech Republic, Slovakia, Hungary, and Poland). Some types of

> **Tips A Train Discount**
>
> Remember that seniors, students, and youths can usually get discounts on
> European trains—in some countries just by asking, in others by buying a
> discount card good for a year (or whatever). Rail Europe or your travel
> agent can fill you in on all the details.

national passes you have to buy in the States, some you can get on either side of the Atlantic, and still others you must purchase in Europe itself.

For the Eurailpass and Eurorail Selectpass, you must scribble the date on the pass as you hop on the train; you don't have to wait in line at the ticket window. However, you will need to go to the ticket window if the train you want to take requires you to reserve a seat (such as the Pendolino, which, as a 1st-class train, doesn't accept the 2nd-class youth passes) or if you want a spot in a sleeper couchette. The Eurailpass gets you only a 33% discount on the TGV train through the Chunnel from London to Paris.

The passes above are available in the United States through **Rail Europe** (© **877/272-RAIL** in the U.S., 800/ 361-RAIL in Canada; www.raileurope. com). No matter what everyone tells you, they *can* be bought in Europe as well (at the major train stations), but they are more expensive. Rail Europe can also give you information on the rail-and-drive versions of the passes.

Passes Available in the United Kingdom Many rail passes are available in the United Kingdom for travel in Britain and Europe.

The **InterRail Pass** is the most popular ticket for anyone who has lived in Europe at least 6 months. Its price depends on the trip duration and how many of the eight "zones" you pick (covering 28 countries—but, as with Eurail, none in the U.K.). The zones are: Zone A (Republic of Ireland), Zone B (Finland, Norway, Sweden), Zone C (Austria, Denmark,

Germany, Switzerland), Zone D (Czech and Slovak republics, Croatia, Hungary, Poland), Zone E (Belgium, France, Luxembourg, Netherlands), Zone F (Morocco, Portugal, Spain), Zone G (Greece, Italy, Turkey, Slovenia), or Zone H (Bulgaria, Macedonia, Romania, Yugoslavia).

You can choose one zone (£182 for 12 days, £219 for 22 days), two zones (£275 for a month), three zones £320 for a month), or all eight zones (£379 for a month). Folks under 26 pay a bit less. As with the Eurail, you'll likely have to pony up a supplement for high-speed trains across Europe. You can purchase the pass at the U.K.'s version of **Rail Europe** (www.raileurope.co.uk/ inter rail).

Another good option for travelers 26 and under, **BIJ** tickets (Billet International de Jeunesse, French for "youth ticket") cost 30% to 50% less than the standard one-way, second-class fare; are valid for a full month; and allow you to choose your own route to a final destination, stopping as many times as you like along the way. **Explorer** tickets are slightly more expensive but allow you to travel from London to your final destination along one route and back on another; you choose from a selection of predetermined circular routes (covering northern Europe, central and eastern Europe, or western Europe).

BIJ tickets are sold only in Europe, under the names of Wasteels and Eurotrain, but you can get further information on them at **Wasteels Travel** (www.wasteels.com). In London, you can get the tickets at the

Wasteels office at Victoria Station (© 020/7834-7066).

BY CAR

Getting around Europe by car might not be the pricey endeavor you imagine. True, rental and parking rates can be quite high, and gasoline costs as much as three times more than in the States. But once the math is done, three or more people traveling together can actually go cheaper by car than by train (even with rail passes).

In addition, driving is the best way to explore the rural and small-town sides of Europe, like France's Riviera, Italy's Tuscany, and southern Spain's Andalusia. You might want to mix-and-match train travel to get between cities and the occasional rental car to explore a region or two; if so, look into the rail/drive versions of rail passes (see "By Train," earlier in this chapter).

Never rent a car just to tool around a European city—the motorists and traffic patterns can drive anyone crazy, parking is difficult and expensive, and the public transportation is usually excellent anyway. Never leave anything of value in the car overnight and nothing visible any time you leave the car. (This applies doubly in Italy, triply in Seville.)

TAXES & INSURANCE When you reserve a car, be sure to ask if the price includes the E.U. **value-added tax (VAT), personal accident insurance (PAI), collision-damage waiver (CDW),** and any other insurance options. If not, ask what these extras will cost, because at the end of your rental they can make a big difference in your bottom line. The CDW—which

at around $10 to $15 a day can buy you great peace of mind—and other insurance may be covered by your credit card if you use the card to pay for the rental; check with the card issuer to be sure and don't double-pay if you can avoid it! Remember that most CDWs come with an often-hefty deductible ($500 or so), so while they can be a wallet-saver if the car is totaled, most bumps or scratches will still be paid for from your pocket.

If your credit card doesn't cover CDW, **Travel Guard International** (© 800/826-4919; www.travelguard. com) offers it for $7 per day (plus a small plan fee). Many rental companies *require* you to buy or have CDW and theft-protection insurance to rent in Italy and Spain.

RENTAL AGENCIES The main car-rental companies include **Avis** (© 800/230-4898; www.avis.com); **Budget** (© 800/527-0700; www. budget.com); **Dollar,** known as **Europcar** in Europe (© 800/800-3665; www.dollarcar.com); **Hertz** (© 800/ 654-3131; www.hertz.com); and **National** (© 800/227-7368; www. nationalcar.com).

However, the best prices on rentals in Europe are usually found at **Auto Europe** (© 888/223-5555; www.auto europe.com), which acts as a sort of consolidator for rentals—you actually pick up your car at, say, the Avis or Hertz office in the destination, but you pay a rate below what those rental agencies charge the public. This company will also work out long-term leases for periods longer than 17 days; it saves you lots over a rental, plus you get a brand-new car and *full* insurance coverage, as

---

⎛Tips Rent Before You Go

Many car-rental companies grant discounts if you reserve in advance (usually 48 hr.), and it's *always* cheaper to reserve from your home country. Weekly rentals are less expensive than day rates.

⌜Tips⌟ The Rules of the Road

- Drive on the right, except in England, Scotland, and Ireland, where you drive on the left.
- Don't cruise in the left lane on a four-lane highway; in Europe it truly *is* only for passing . . . and sports cars opened up.
- If someone comes up behind your car and flashes their lights at you, it's a signal for you to slow and drive closer to the shoulder so they can pass you.
- Except for portions of the German Autobahn, most highways do indeed have speed limits of around 100kmph to 135kmph (60 mph–80 mph).
- Remember, everything's measured in kilometers (mileage and speed limits). For a rough conversion: 1km = 0.62 miles.
- Gas might *look* reasonably priced, but remember that the price is per liter (3.8 liters = 1 gal.), so multiply by four to estimate the per-gallon price.
- European drivers tend to be more aggressive than their American counterparts, so drive defensively and carefully—assume that the other drivers have a better idea of the local traffic laws and norms, and take your cues from them.

with **Europe By Car** (© **800/223-1516,** in New York 212/581-3040; www.europebycar.com).

PERMITS & HIGHWAY STICKERS   Although a valid U.S. state driver's license usually suffices, it's wise to carry an **International Driving Permit** (required in Poland, Hungary, and Spain), which costs $10 from any AAA branch (www.aaa.com). (You don't have to be a member; bring a passport-size photo.)

Some countries, like Austria and Switzerland, require that cars on the national highways have special stickers. If you rent within the country, the car will already have one, but if you're crossing a border, check at the crossing station to see whether you need to purchase a sticker on the spot for a nominal fee.

BY BUS

Bus transportation is readily available throughout Europe; it occasionally is less expensive than train travel, but not usually, and covers a more extensive area but can be slower and much less comfortable. European buses, like the trains, outshine their American counterparts, but they're perhaps best used only to pick up where the extensive train network leaves off in some rural areas.

BY PLANE

Over the past few years, air travel in Europe has gone from laughably expensive excess only enjoyed by businesspeople with huge expense accounts to the fastest, and often cheapest, way to bop around Europe. It's called the **no-frills airline** revolution, and not only has it caused more than a dozen new little airlines to crop up, each selling one-way tickets that crisscross Europe for well under $100, but it has also forced the major European airlines to drastically lower their own inflated prices.

Europe's **no-frills airlines,** such as easyJet and Ryanair, were modeled on American upstarts like Southwest, but have proven even more successful at the concept. By keeping their overheads down—using electronic ticketing, foregoing meal service, and servicing either major cities' secondary airports or smaller cities—these airlines are able to offer amazingly low fares. Now you can save time *and* money over long train hauls. Ryanair even frequently runs promotions during which it gives away tickets *for free,* and many other sales on one-way tickets where they cost £1.99 (a little more than $3). Seriously, this happens all the time. Even when not on sale, their tickets cost only around $10 to $50, tops. And flights rarely take more than 2 hours—whereas the same train trip might take 2 days.

The system is still evolving, with new players appearing every year and a few failing or, more commonly, being gobbled up by the growing competition. The phenomenon started in London, and many companies are still based there (although they now also have smaller hubs across Europe). Plus, there are now no-frills outfits setting up shop in Brussels, across Germany, and even in Italy and Spain. So far, only France has had bad luck, with its few start-ups failing and disappearing.

The two Big Boys in the business are **easyJet** (© **44-870/600-0000;** www.easyjet.com), which has hubs in London, Liverpool, Bristol, Barcelona, Amsterdam, and Paris; and **Ryanair** (© **353-1/249-7851;** www.ryanair.ie), which flies out of London, Glasgow, Dublin, Shannon, Frankfurt, Stockholm, Brussels, and Milan.

The current shortlist of the most dependable among the other choices includes: **Virgin Express** in Brussels (www.virgin-express.com), **Germanwings** (www.germanwings.com) and **Hapag-Lloyd Express** (www.hlx.com) in Germany, **Volare Web** (www.volareweb.com) and **Air One** (www.air-one.it) in Italy, **Sterling** (www.sterlingticket.com) and SAS's offshoot **Snowflake** (www.flysnowflake) in Scandinavia, and **Air Europa** (www.air-europa.com) and **Spanair** (www.spanair.es) in Spain.

Of less use to casual travelers, but a growing force among budget-savvy Brits, is **bmibaby** (www.bmibaby.com), which flies from several central English cities (East Midlands, Manchester, Teeside), plus from Cardiff in Wales.

Be aware, though, that the names might change because these small airlines are often economically vulnerable and can fail or merge with a big airline. Still, as quickly as one disappears, another takes off. Independent websites **www.lowcostairlines.org** and **www.nofrillsair.com** keep track of the industry. Another site, **Applefares.com,** will do a pricing metasearch of some two dozen low-cost European airlines, including some, but not all, of those listed above, plus other, smaller ones. That way, you can see the going rate for, say, a London-to-Rome ticket—though it's not a booking engine, but a search engine.

Lower airfares are also available throughout Europe on **charter flights** rather than on regularly scheduled ones. Look in local newspapers to find out about them. **Consolidators** cluster in cities like London and Athens.

2

Planning an Affordable Trip to Europe

by Reid Bramblett

The secret to enjoying a great hassle-free trip to Europe is advance planning. This chapter provides the lowdown on what you need to do before you leave, all the tips you need to make the wisest decisions, and all the choices on how to get to Europe cheaply but still comfortably.

1 Visitor Information

TOURIST OFFICES

Start with the national **European tourist offices** in your own country—for a complete list of offices and their websites, see below. If you aren't sure which countries you want to visit, check out the website **www.visiteurope.com** to sign up for the virtual *VisitEurope Newsletter,* published online monthly by the 33-nation European Travel Commission. For more information, call © **212/218-1200** or e-mail info@visit europe.com. Or pick up a copy of *Europe For Dummies* (Wiley Publishing, Inc.).

AUSTRIAN NATIONAL TOURIST OFFICE

IN THE U.S. & CANADA   P.O. Box 1142, Times Square Station, New York, NY 10108-1142 (© **212/944-6880;** fax 212/730-4568).

IN THE U.K.   P.O. Box 2363, London, W1A 2QB (© **020/7629-0461;** fax 020/7499-6038).

IN AUSTRALIA   36 Carrington St., 1st Floor, Sydney, NSW 2000 (© **02/9299-3621;** fax 02/9299-3808).

WEBSITE   www.austria-tourism.at

BELGIAN TOURIST OFFICE

IN THE U.S.   780 Third Ave., New York, NY 10017 (© **212/758-8130;** fax 212/355-7675).

IN CANADA   P.O. Box 760, Succursale NDG, Montréal, PQ H4A 3S2 (© **514/457-2888;** fax 514/457-9447).

IN THE U.K.   31 Pepper St., London E14 9RW (© **0891/887-799;** fax 020/7458-0045).

WEBSITE   www.visitbelgium.com

BRITISH TOURIST AUTHORITY

IN THE U.S.   551 Fifth Ave., Suite 701, New York, NY 10176-0799 (© **800/462-2748** or 212/986-2266; fax 212/986-1188); 625 N. Michigan Ave., Chicago, IL 60611 (© **800/ 462-2748**).

IN CANADA   5915 Airport Rd., Suite 120, Mississauga, ON L4V 1T1 (© **888/8676885** in Canada or 905/405-1720 in Mississauga; fax 905/405-1835).

IN AUSTRALIA   Level 16, Gateway, 1 Macquarie Place, Sydney, NSW 2000 (© **02/9377-4400;** fax 02/9377 4499).

WEBSITES www.travelbritain.org or www.visitbritain.com

CZECH TOURIST AUTHORITY

IN THE U.S. 1109 Madison Ave., New York, NY 10028 (© **212/288-0830,** ext. 101 or 105; fax 212/288-0971).

IN CANADA Simpson Tower, 401 Bay St., Suite 1510, Toronto, ON M5H 2Y4 (© **416/363-9928;** fax 416/363-0239).

IN THE U.K. Morley House, 320 Regent St., London W1B 3BG (© **020/7631-0427;** fax 020/7631-0419).

WEBSITES www.czechtourism.com or www.czechcenter.cz

DENMARK TOURIST BOARD

IN THE U.S. & CANADA 655 Third Ave., 18th Floor, New York, NY 10017 (© **212/885-9700;** fax 212/885-9710).

IN THE U.K. 55 Sloane St., London SW1X 9SY (© **020/7259-5959;** fax 020/7259-5955).

WEBSITE www.visitdenmark.com

FINLAND TOURIST BOARD

IN THE U.S. & CANADA P.O. Box 4649, Grand Central Station, New York, NY 10163-4649 (© **800/FIN-INFO** or 212/885-9700; fax 212/885-9710).

IN THE U.K. P.O. Box 33213, London W6 8JX (© **020/7365-2512;** fax 020/8600-5681).

WEBSITE www.finland-tourism.com

FRENCH GOVERNMENT TOURIST OFFICE

IN THE U.S. 444 Madison Ave., 16th Floor, New York, NY 10022 (© **212/838-7800**); 875 N. Michigan Ave., Suite 3214, Chicago, IL 60611 (© **312/751-7800;** fax 312/337-6339); 9454 Wilshire Blvd., Suite 715,

Beverly Hills, CA 90212 (© **310/271-6665;** fax 310/276-2835). To request information at any of these offices, call the **France on Call hot line** at © **410/286-8310** (50¢ per minute).

IN CANADA Maison de la France/French Government Tourist Office, 1981 av. McGill College, Suite 490, Montréal, PQ H3A 2W9 (© **514/876-9881;** fax 514/845-4868 or 514/288-4264).

IN THE U.K. Maison de la France/French Government Tourist Office, 178 Piccadilly, London, W1J 9AL (© **09068/244-123** [60p per min.]; fax 020/7493-6594).

IN AUSTRALIA French Tourist Bureau, level 22, 25 Bligh St., Sydney, NSW 2000 (© **02/9231-5244;** fax 02/9221-8682).

WEBSITES www.francetourism.com or www.franceguide.com

GERMAN NATIONAL TOURIST OFFICE

IN THE U.S. 122 E. 42nd St., 52nd Floor, New York, NY 10168-0072 (© **800/637-1171** or 212/661-7200; fax 212/661-7174); 8484 Wilshire Blvd., Suite 440, Beverly Hills, CA 90211 (© **323/655-6085;** fax 323/655-6086); P.O. Box 59594, Chicago, IL 60659 (© **773/539-6303;** fax 773/539-6378).

IN CANADA German National Tourist Office, North Tower, Suite 604, 175 Bloor St. E., Toronto, ON M4W 3R8 (© **416/968-1570;** fax 416/968-1986).

IN THE U.K. P.O. Box 2695, London W1A 3TN (© **020/7317-0908** or 9001/600-100; fax 020/495-6129).

IN AUSTRALIA G.P.O. Box A 980, Sydney South, NSW 1235 (© **02/9267-8148;** fax 02/9267-9035).

WEBSITES www.germanytourism.de or www.visits-to-germany.com

GREEK NATIONAL TOURIST ORGANIZATION

IN THE U.S. Olympic Tower, 645 Fifth Ave., Suite 903, New York, NY 10022 (℃ 212/421-5777; fax 212/826-6940).

IN CANADA 91 Scollard St., 2nd Floor, Toronto, ON M5R 1G4 (℃ 416/968-2220; fax 416/968-6533); 1170 place du Frere Andre, 3rd Floor, Montréal, PQ H3B 3C6 (℃ 514/871-1535; fax 514/871-1498).

IN THE U.K. 4 Conduit St., London W1S 2DJ (℃ 020/7495-9300; fax 020/7287-1369).

IN AUSTRALIA 51–57 Pitt St., Sydney, NSW 2000 (℃ 02/9241-1663 or 02/9252-1441; fax 02/9241-2499).

WEBSITE www.gnto.gr

HUNGARIAN NATIONAL TOURIST OFFICE

IN THE U.S. & CANADA 150 E. 58th St., 33rd Floor, New York, NY 10155-3398 (℃ 212/355-0240; fax 212/207-4103).

IN THE U.K. 46 Eaton Place, London, SW1X 8AL (℃ 020/7823-1055; fax 020/7823-1459).

WEBSITES www.gotohungary.com or www.hungarytourism.hu

IRISH TOURIST BOARD

IN THE U.S. 345 Park Ave., New York, NY 10154 (℃ 800/223-6470 or 212/418-0800; fax 212/371-9052).

IN THE U.K. 150 New Bond St., London W1Y 0AQ (℃ 0800/039-7000 or 171/493 3201; fax 020/7493-9065).

IN AUSTRALIA 36 Carrington St., 5th Level, Sydney, NSW 2000 (℃ 02/9299-6177; fax 02/2999-6323).

WEBSITES www.ireland.travel.ie or www.irelandvacations.com

ITALIAN GOVERNMENT TOURIST BOARD

IN THE U.S. 630 Fifth Ave., Suite 1565, New York, NY 10111

(℃ 212/245-4822 or 212/245-5618; fax 212/586-9249); 500 N. Michigan Ave, Suite 2240, Chicago, IL 60611 (℃ 312/644-0996 or 312/644-0990; fax 312/644-3019); 12400 Wilshire Blvd., Suite 550, Los Angeles, CA 90025 (℃ 310/820-1898; fax 310/820-6357).

IN CANADA 175 Bloor St. E., Suite 907, South Tower, Toronto, ON M4W 3R8 (℃ 02/416-925-4882; fax 02/416-925-4799).

IN THE U.K. 1 Princes St., London W1B 2AY (℃ 020/7408-1254; fax 020/7493-6695).

IN AUSTRALIA Level 26, 44 Market St., Sydney, NSW 2000 (℃ 02/9262-1666; fax 02/9262-1677).

WEBSITES www.italiantourism.com or www.enit.it

MONACO GOVERNMENT TOURIST OFFICE

IN THE U.S. & CANADA 565 Fifth Ave., New York, NY 10017 (℃ 800/753-9696 or 212/286-3330; fax 212/286-9890).

IN THE U.K. The Chambers, Chelsea Harbour, London, SW10 0XF (℃ 0500/006-114 or 020/7352-9962; fax 020/7352-2103).

WEBSITES www.monaco tourism.com or www.monaco.mc

NETHERLANDS BOARD OF TOURISM

IN THE U.S. 355 Lexington Ave., 19th Floor, New York, NY 10017 (℃ 888/464-6552 or 212/557-3500; fax 212/370-9507).

IN CANADA 25 Adelaide St. E., Suite 710, Toronto, ON M5C 1Y2 (℃ 888/GOHOLLAND [800/PAYS-BAS en français] or 416/363-1577; fax 416/363-1470).

IN THE U.K. P.O. Box 30783, London, WC2B 6DH (℃ 020/7539-7950 or 906/871-7777; fax 020/7539-7953).

WEBSITE www.holland.com

NORWEGIAN TOURIST BOARD

IN THE U.S. & CANADA 655 Third Ave., Suite 1810, New York, NY 10017 (© **212/885-9700;** fax 212/885-9710).

IN THE U.K. Charles House, 5th Floor, 5 Regent St., London SW1Y 4LR (© **020/7839-2650;** fax 020/7839-6014).

WEBSITE www.visitnorway.com

PORTUGUESE NATIONAL TOURIST OFFICE

IN THE U.S. 590 Fifth Ave., 3rd Floor, New York, NY 10036 (© **212/354-4610;** fax 212/575-4737); 88 Kearny St., Suite 1770, San Francisco, CA 94108 (© **415/391-7080;** fax 415/391-7147).

IN CANADA 60 Bloor St. W., Suite 1005, Toronto, ON M4W 3B8 (© **416/921-7376;** fax 416/921-1353).

IN THE U.K. 22 Sackville St., 2nd Floor, London W1S 3LY (© **020/7494-1517;** fax 020/7494-1508).

WEBSITE www.portugal.org

SWEDEN TOURIST BOARD

IN THE U.S. & CANADA P.O. Box 4649, Grand Central Station, New York, NY 10163-4649 (© **800/FININFO** or 212/885-9700; fax 212/885-9710).

IN THE U.K. Swedish Travel and Tourism Council, 11 Montague Place, London W1H 2AL

(© **800/3080-3080** or 020/7870-5600; fax 020/7724-5872).

WEBSITE www.visit-sweden.com

SWITZERLAND TOURISM

IN THE U.S. & CANADA 608 Fifth Ave., New York, NY 10020 (© **877/794-8037** in the U.S, or 800/100-200-30 elsewhere; fax 212/262-6116 in the U.S. or 416/695-2774 in Canada).

IN THE U.K. Swiss Centre, 10 Wardour St., London, W1D 6QF (© **00-0800/100-200-30** or 020/7292-1550; fax 00-800/100-200-31).

WEBSITE www.switzerland tourism.com

TOURIST OFFICE OF SPAIN

IN THE U.S. 666 Fifth Ave., 35th Floor, New York, NY 10103 (© **212/265-8822;** fax 212/265-8864); 845 N. Michigan Ave., Suite 915-E, Chicago, IL 60611 (© **312/642-1992;** fax 312/642-9817); 8383 Wilshire Blvd., Suite 956, Beverly Hills, CA 90211 (© **323/658-7188;** fax 323/658-1061); 1221 Brickell Ave., Suite 1850, Miami, FL 33131 (© **305/358-1992;** fax 305/358-8223).

IN CANADA 2 Bloor St. W., 34th Floor, Toronto, ON M4W 3E2 (© **416/961-3131;** fax 416/961-1992).

IN THE U.K. 22–23 Manchester Sq., London W1M 5AP (© **0891/669-920** [50p per min.] or 020/7486-8077; fax 020/7486-8034).

WEBSITE www.okspain.org

2 Entry Requirements & Customs

ENTRY REQUIREMENTS

U.S., U.K., Irish, Canadian, Australian, and New Zealand citizens with a **valid passport** don't need a visa to enter any European country if you don't expect to stay more than 90 days and don't expect to work there. If after entering Europe you find you want to stay more than 90 days, you can apply for a permit for an extra 90 days, which, as a rule, is granted immediately. Go to your home country's consulate.

In these halcyon days of the European Union, there are no more border controls between countries within the E.U. (except for the island nations of the U.K. and the Republic of Ireland), or when crossing into Norway or Iceland (neither of which are E.U.). That said, in these security-obsessed times,

Allow plenty of time before your trip to apply for a passport; processing usually takes 3 weeks but can take longer during busy periods (especially spring). And keep in mind that if you need a passport in a hurry, you'll pay a higher processing fee. When traveling, safeguard your passport in an inconspicuous, inaccessible place like a money belt and keep a copy of the critical pages with your passport number in a separate place.

airport arrivals are often scrutinized regardless.

Switzerland, however—which is not a member of the E.U., nor even of the U.N.—does keep border guards, making it one of the few places where you still must undergo a passport check even when driving into the country. The same holds for those three Eastern European nations—Bulgaria, Romania, and Turkey—that are still waiting in the wings for E.U. membership.

No matter where you are, if your passport is lost or stolen, head to your consulate as soon as possible for a replacement.

Passport specifics and downloadable applications can be found on the Internet at the following sites: **www.travel.state.gov** (U.S.), **www.dfait-maeci.gc.ca/passport** (Canada), **www.passports.gov.uk** (U.K.), **www.irlgov.ie/iveagh/services/passports/passportforms.htm** (Ireland), **www.dfat.gov.au/passports** (Australia), and **www.passports.govt.nz** (New Zealand).

CUSTOMS: WHAT YOU CAN BRING INTO EUROPE

Foreign visitors can bring along most items for personal use duty-free, including fishing tackle; a sporting gun and 200 cartridges; a pair of skis; two tennis racquets; a baby carriage; two hand cameras with 10 rolls of film; and 200 cigarettes or 50 cigars or pipe tobacco not exceeding 250 grams. There are strict limits on importing alcoholic beverages. However, limits are much more liberal for alcohol bought tax-paid in other countries of the European Union.

3 Money

Luckily, ATMs (automated teller machines) can now be found just about everywhere, even in the smallest towns, so cash is readily available. As luck would have it, banks in Europe do not (yet) charge a fee for using their bank—though your home bank probably will for your use of an out-of-network ATM, and these days the bank will often also charge a premium for withdrawal of foreign currency (see "ATMs," below).

It's a good idea to exchange at least some money—just enough to cover airport incidentals and transportation to your hotel—before you leave home, so you can avoid lines at airport ATMs.

You can exchange money at your local American Express or Thomas Cook office or at your bank (often, though, only at the major branches). If you're far away from a bank with currency-exchange services, American Express offers traveler's checks and foreign currency, though with a $15 order fee and additional shipping costs, at www.americanexpress.com or © **800/807-6233.**

CURRENCY

In January 2002, most of western Europe (except the U.K., Switzerland, Denmark, Norway, and Sweden) retired their francs, lire, guilders, and marks and switched over to the single

European currency called the **euro.** Euro coins are issued in denominations of .01€, .02€, .05€, .10€, .20€, and .50€ as well as 1€ and 2€; bills come in denominations of 5€, 10€, 20€, 50€, 100€, 200€, and 500€.

Exchange rates (see box below) are established daily and listed in most international newspapers. To get a transaction as close to this rate as possible, pay for as much as possible with credit cards and withdraw cash from ATMs.

Traveler's checks, while still the safest way to carry money, are something of an anachronism from the days before the ATM made cash accessible at any time. The aggressive evolution of international computerized banking and consolidated ATM networks has led to the triumph of plastic throughout Europe—even if cold cash is still the most trusted currency, especially in smaller towns or cheaper mom-and-pop joints, where credit cards may not be accepted.

You'll get the best rate if you **exchange money** at a bank or at one of its ATMs. The rates at "Cambio/ change/wechsel" exchange booths are invariably less favorable but still a good deal better than what you'd get if you exchange money at a hotel or shop (a last-resort tactic only). The bill-to-bill changers you see in some touristy places exist solely to rip you off.

ATMS

The ability to access your personal checking account through the **Cirrus** (© 800/424-7787; www.mastercard. com) or **PLUS** (© 800/843-7587; www.visa.com) network of ATMs—or get a cash advance on an enabled Visa or MasterCard—has been growing by leaps and bounds in Europe over the last decade. It works just like at home. All you need do is search out a machine that displays your network's symbol (which these days is practically all of them), pop in your card, and punch in your PIN, or personal identification number (see "A PIN Alert," below). The machine will spit out local currency drawn directly from your home checking account (and at a more favorable rate than you'd get converting traveler's checks or cash).

Keep in mind that many banks impose a fee every time a card is used at a different bank's ATM, and that fee can be higher for international transactions (up to $5 or more) than for domestic ones (where they're rarely more than $1.50). However, as I mentioned above, banks in Europe do not (at least yet) charge you a second fee to use their ATMs. To compare banks' ATM fees within the U.S., use **www.bankrate. com**. For international withdrawal fees, ask your bank.

An ATM in most of Europe is called *Bankomat.* Increased internationalism has been slowly doing away

---

Tips Dear Visa: I'm Off to Europe!

Some credit card companies recommend that you notify them of any impending trip abroad. This way, they won't become suspicious when the card is used numerous times in a foreign destination and they won't block your charges. Even if you don't call your credit card company in advance, you can call always the card's toll-free emergency number (see "Credit Cards," later in this chapter) if a charge is refused—a good reason to carry the phone number with you. But perhaps the most important lesson is to carry more than one card on your trip; if a card doesn't work for any number of reasons, you'll have a backup.

A PIN Alert

Make sure the PINs on your bank cards and credit cards will work in Europe. You'll need a **four-digit code** (six digits often won't work), so if you have a six-digit code, play it safe by getting a new four-digit PIN for your trip. If you're unsure about this, contact Cirrus or PLUS (see "ATMs," above). Be sure to check the daily withdrawal limit at the same time.

with the old worry that your card's PIN, be it on a bank card or credit card, must be specially enabled to work abroad, but it always pays to check with the issuing bank to be sure (see "A PIN Alert," above). If at the ATM you get a message saying your card isn't valid for international transactions, it's likely the bank just can't make the phone connection to check it (occasionally this can be a citywide epidemic); try another ATM or another town.

When you withdraw money with your **bank card,** you technically get the interbank exchange rate—about 4% better than the "street rate" you'd get exchanging cash or traveler's checks. Note, however, that some U.S. banks are now charging a 1% to 3% "exchange fee" to convert the currency. (Ask your bank before you leave.)

Similarly, **Visa** has begun charging a standard 1% conversion fee for cash advances, and many credit card–issuing banks have begun tacking on an additional 1% to 3%. Basically, they've gotten into the "commission" game, too. And, unlike with purchases, interest on a credit card cash advance starts accruing *immediately,* not when your statement cycles. Both methods are still a slightly better deal than converting traveler's checks or cash and considerably more convenient (no waiting in bank lines and pulling out your passport as ID). Savvy travelers use credit card advances only as an emergency option and get most of their euros with their bank cards.

ATM withdrawals are often limited to 200€ ($230) or sometimes 300€ ($345) per transaction, regardless of your cash advance allowance. **American Express** card cash advances are usually available only from American Express offices (see the "Fast Facts" section of each city chapter throughout the book).

CREDIT CARDS

Visa and **MasterCard** are now almost universally accepted at most hotels, restaurants, and shops; the majority also accepts **American Express. Diners Club** is gaining some ground, especially in big cities and in more expensive establishments. If you arrange with your card issuer to enable the card's cash advance option (and get a PIN as well), you can also use it at ATMs.

Prepare for the worst: Go to the websites for each of your credit cards and figure out what local number to call in each country should you **lose your card.** The bank that issues each Visa or MasterCard should also have a regular U.S. number with a local area code (*not* an 800 or other toll-free number) that you can call collect from abroad should you lose the card. For **American Express,** that number is ⓒ **336/393-1111.**

TRAVELER'S CHECKS

Traveler's checks used to be the only sound alternative to traveling with dangerously large amounts of cash. They were as reliable as currency but, unlike cash, they could be replaced if lost or stolen.

The Euro, the U.S. Dollar & the U.K. Pound

At press time, US$1 = approximately .87€ (or 1€ = $1.15). The rate fluctuates from day to day, depending on a complicated series of economic and political factors, and might not be the same when you travel.

Likewise, the ratio of the U.S. dollar to the British pound fluctuates constantly. At press time, $1 = approximately 60p (or £1 = $1.85).

These are the rates reflected in the table below, and the ones used to translate euro amounts in ballpark dollar figures throughout this book, rounded to the nearest nickel for amounts under $10, to the nearest dollar for amounts $10 and above (though this table will be precise to the penny).

Euro	U.S.$	U.K.£	Euro	U.S.$	U.K.£
.50	.57	.31	30.00	34.50	18.65
1.00	1.15	.62	40.00	46.00	24.86
2.00	2.30	1.24	50.00	57.50	31.08
3.00	3.45	1.86	60.00	69.00	37.30
4.00	4.60	2.49	70.00	80.45	43.49
5.00	5.75	3.11	80.00	92.00	49.73
6.00	6.90	3.73	90.00	103.00	55.68
7.00	8.05	4.35	100.00	115.00	62.16
8.00	9.20	4.97	125.00	144.00	77.83
9.00	10.35	5.59	150.00	172.00	92.97
10.00	11.50	6.21	200.00	230.00	124.32
15.00	17.24	9.32	300.00	345.00	186.48
20.00	23.00	12.43	400.00	460.00	248.64
25.00	28.75	15.54	500.00	575.00	310.81

These days, traveler's checks are less necessary because most cities have 24-hour ATMs that allow you to withdraw small amounts of cash as needed. However, keep in mind that you will likely be charged an ATM withdrawal fee if the bank is not your own, so if you're withdrawing money every day, you might be better off with traveler's checks—provided that you don't mind showing identification every time you want to cash one.

Most banks issue checks under the names of **American Express** (© **800/721-9768** in the United States and Canada, or 801/945-9450 collect from anywhere else in the world; www.americanexpress.com); **Thomas Cook** (© **800/223-7373** in the U.S. and Canada, or 44-1733-318-950 collect from anywhere in the world; www.thomascook.com); **Visa** (© **800/227-6811** in the U.S. and Canada, or 44-171-937-8091 collect from anywhere in the world; www.visa.com); or **Citicorp** (© **800/645-6556** in the U.S. and Canada, or 1-813-623-1709 collect from anywhere in the world). American Express and Thomas Cook offer versions that can be countersigned by you or your companion. **AAA** will sell Amex checks to their members without a commission. *Note:* You'll get the worst possible exchange rate if you pay for a purchase or hotel room directly with a traveler's check; it's better to trade in the traveler's checks for euros at a bank or the American Express office. Call the numbers listed above to report **lost or stolen traveler's checks.**

WIRE SERVICES

If you find yourself out of money, a wire service can help you tap willing friends and family for funds. Through **TravelersExpress/MoneyGram**, 3940 S. Teller St., Lakewood, CO 80235 (© 800/666-3947; www.moneygram. com), you can get money sent around the world in less than 10 minutes. Cash is the only acceptable form of payment. MoneyGram's fees vary based on the cities the money is wired from and to, but a good estimate is $20 for the first $200, and $30 for up to $400, with a sliding scale for larger sums.

A similar service is offered by **Western Union** (© 800/CALL-CASH), which accepts Visa and MasterCard credit or debit cards, or Discover. You can arrange for the service over the phone, at a Western Union office, or online at www.westernunion.com. A sliding scale begins at $15 for the first $100. A currency exchange rate will also apply. Additionally, your credit card company may charge a fee for the cash advance as well as a higher interest rate.

4 Travel Insurance

Check your existing insurance policies and credit card coverage before you buy travel insurance. You may already be covered for lost luggage, cancelled tickets, or medical expenses. The cost of travel insurance varies widely, depending on the cost and length of your trip, your age, your health, and the type of trip you're taking.

TRIP-CANCELLATION INSURANCE Trip-cancellation insurance helps you get your money back if you have to back out of a trip, if you have to go home early, or if your travel supplier goes bankrupt. Allowed reasons for cancellation can range from sickness to natural disaster to the State Department's declaration that your destination is unsafe for travel. (Insurers usually won't cover vague fears, though, as many travelers discovered who tried to cancel their trips in Oct 2001 because they were wary of flying.) In this unstable world, trip-cancellation insurance is a good buy if you're getting tickets well in advance—who knows what the state of the world, or of your airline, will be in 9 months? Insurance policy details vary, so read the fine print—and make sure that your airline or cruise line is on the list of carriers covered in case of bankruptcy. A good resource is **"Travel Guard Alerts,"** a list of companies considered high-risk by Travel Guard International (see website below). Protect yourself further by paying for the insurance with a credit card—by law, consumers can get their money back on goods and services not received if you report the loss within 60 days after the charge is listed on your credit card statement.

Note: Many tour operators, particularly those offering trips to remote or high-risk areas, include insurance in the cost of the trip or can arrange insurance policies through a partnering provider, a convenient and often cost-effective way for the traveler to obtain insurance. Make sure the tour company is a reputable one, however: Some experts suggest you avoid buying insurance from the tour or cruise company you're traveling with, saying it's better to buy from a "third party" insurer than to put all your money in one place.

For more information, contact one of the following recommended insurers: **Access America** (© 866/807-3982; www.accessamerica.com); **Travel Guard International** (© 800/826-4919; www.travelguard.com); **Travel Insured International** (© 800/243-3174; www.travelinsured.com); and **Travelex Insurance Services** (© 888/457-4602; www.travelex-insurance.com).

MEDICAL INSURANCE For travel overseas, most health plans (including Medicare and Medicaid) do not provide coverage, and the ones that do often require you to pay for services upfront and will reimburse you only after you return home. Even if your plan does cover overseas treatment, most out-of-country hospitals make you pay your bills upfront, and they send you a refund only after you've returned home and filed the necessary paperwork with your insurance company. As a safety net, you may want to buy travel medical insurance, particularly if you're traveling to a remote or high-risk area where emergency evacuation is a possible scenario. If you require additional medical insurance, try **MEDEX Assistance** (© 410/453-6300; www.medexassist. com) or **Travel Assistance International** (© 800/821-2828; www.travel assistance.com; for general information on services, call the company's Worldwide Assistance Services, Inc., at © 800/777-8710).

Note: **Blue Cross/Blue Shield members** (© 800/810-BLUE or www. bluecares.com for a list of participating hospitals) can now use their plans and cards at select hospitals abroad as they would at home, which means much lower out-of-pocket costs. There are member hospitals in most cities across Europe.

LOST-LUGGAGE   INSURANCE On international flights (including U.S. portions of international trips), checked baggage coverage is limited to approximately $9.05 per pound, up to approximately $635 per checked bag. If you plan to check items more valuable than the standard liability, see if your valuables are covered by your homeowner's policy, get baggage insurance as part of your comprehensive travel-insurance package, or buy Travel Guard's "Bag-Trak" product. Don't buy insurance at the airport, as it's usually overpriced. Be sure to take any valuables or irreplaceable items with you in your carry-on luggage, as many valuables (including books, money, and electronics) aren't covered by airline policies.

If your luggage is lost, immediately file a lost-luggage claim at the airport, detailing the luggage contents. For most airlines, you must report delayed, damaged, or lost baggage within 4 hours of arrival. The airlines are required to deliver luggage, once it's found, directly to your house or destination free of charge.

5 Health & Safety

STAYING HEALTHY

There are no special health risks you'll encounter in most of Europe. The tap water is safe, and medical resources are of a high quality. In fact, with most of Europe enjoying at least partially socialized medicine, you can usually stop by any hospital emergency room with an ailment, get swift and courteous service, be given a diagnosis and a prescription, and be sent on your way with a wave and a smile—and not even a sheet of paperwork to fill out. (Though note that a Dec 2003 decision in Britain to force non–U.K. residents to pay upfront for hospital visits—an attempt to crack down on foreign freeloaders who travel to London just to have expensive medical procedures and care regimens performed—may spell the beginning of the end to free health care in Europe.)

Contact the **International Association for Medical Assistance to Travelers (IAMAT;** © 716/754-4883 or 416/ 652-0137; www.iamat.org) for tips on travel and health concerns in the countries you're visiting, and for lists of local, English-speaking doctors. In **Canada,** contact them at 40 Regal Rd., Guelph, ON, N1K 1B5 (© **519/836-0102;** fax 519/836-3412); and in **New Zealand** at P.O. Box 5049, Christchurch 5 (fax 643/352-4630).

The United States **Centers for Disease Control and Prevention** (© 800/311-3435; www.cdc.gov) provides up-to-date information on necessary vaccines and health hazards by region or country. Any foreign consulate can provide a list of area doctors who speak English. If you get sick, consider asking your hotel concierge to recommend a local doctor—even his or her own. You can also try the emergency room at a local hospital; many have walk-in clinics for emergency cases that are not life threatening. You may not get immediate attention, but you won't pay the high price of an emergency room visit.

WHAT TO DO IF YOU GET SICK AWAY FROM HOME

Any foreign consulate can provide a list of area doctors who speak English. If you get sick, consider asking your hotel concierge to recommend a local doctor—even his or her own. You can also try the emergency room at a local hospital. Many hospitals have walk-in clinics for emergency cases that are not life threatening; you may not get immediate attention, but you won't pay the high price of an emergency-room visit. We list hospitals and emergency numbers under the "Fast Facts" section in each city chapter.

If you suffer from a chronic illness, consult your doctor before your departure. For conditions like epilepsy, diabetes, or heart problems, wear a **MedicAlert identification tag** (© 888/633-4298; www.medicalert.org), which will immediately alert doctors to your condition and give them access to your records through MedicAlert's 24-hour hot line.

Pack **prescription medications** in your carry-on luggage, and carry prescription medications in their original containers, with pharmacy labels—otherwise they won't make it through airport security. Also bring along copies of your prescriptions in case you lose your pills or run out. Don't forget an extra pair of contact lenses or prescription glasses. Carry the generic name of prescription medicines, in case a local pharmacist is unfamiliar with the brand name.

STAYING SAFE

Europe is, by and large, a remarkably safe place. The worst threats you'll likely face are the pickpockets that sometimes frequent touristy areas and public buses; just keep your valuables in an under-the-clothes money belt and you should be fine. There are, of course, thieves in Europe as there are everywhere, so be smart; don't leave anything in your rental car overnight, and leave nothing visible in it at any time that might tempt a would-be thief.

6 Specialized Travel Resources

TRAVELERS WITH DISABILITIES

While Europe won't win any medals for handicapped accessibility, in the past few years its big cities have made an effort to accommodate travelers with disabilities.

Many nations have recently passed laws compelling rail stations, airports, hotels, and most restaurants to follow a stricter set of regulations concerning **wheelchair** accessibility to restrooms,

ticket counters, and so on. A few of the top museums and churches are beginning at least to install ramps at the entrances, and a few hotels are converting first-floor rooms into accessible units by widening the doors and bathrooms.

Other than that, don't expect to find much of the landscape easy to tackle. Builders in the Middle Ages and Renaissance didn't have wheelchairs or mobility impairments in mind when they built narrow door-ways and spiral staircases, and preservation laws keep modern Europeans from being able to do much about this. Buses and trains can cause problems as well, with high, narrow doors and steep steps at entrances. There are, however, usually seats reserved on public transportation for travelers with disabilities.

A disability shouldn't stop anyone from traveling. Here are some organizations that can offer you specific advice.

Many **travel agencies** offer customized tours and itineraries for travelers with disabilities. **Flying Wheels Travel** (© 507/451-5005; www.flyingwheelstravel.com) offers escorted tours and cruises that emphasize sports and private tours in minivans with lifts. **Access-Able Travel Source** (© 303/232-2979; www.access-able.com) offers extensive access information and advice for traveling around the world with disabilities. **Rumpleduck Travel** (© 877/401-7736 or 310/850-5340; www.rumpleduck.com) brings a personal touch to designing itineraries and specializes in trips to the U.K., Hawaii, and Las Vegas. **Accessible Journeys** (© 800/846-4537 or 610/521-0339; www.disabilitytravel.com) caters specifically to slow walkers and wheelchair travelers and their families and friends.

Organizations that offer assistance to disabled travelers include the **MossRehab Hospital** www.mossresourcenet.org), which provides a library of accessible-travel resources online; **SATH (Society for Accessible Travel and Hospitality;** © 212/447-7284; www.sath.org; annual membership fees: $45 adults, $30 seniors and students), which offers a wealth of travel resources for all types of disabilities and informed recommendations on destinations, access guides, travel agents, tour operators,

vehicle rentals, and companion services; and the **American Foundation for the Blind** (© 800/232-5463; www.afb.org), a referral resource for the blind or visually impaired that includes information on traveling with Seeing Eye dogs.

For more information specifically targeted at travelers with disabilities, the community website **iCan** (www.icanonline.net/channels/travel/index.cfm) has destination guides and several regular columns on accessible travel. Also, check out the quarterly magazine *Emerging Horizons* ($14.95 per year, $19.95 outside the U.S.; www.emerginghorizons.com) and *Open World Magazine,* published by the Society for Accessible Travel and Hospitality (see above; subscription: $18 per year, $35 outside the U.S.).

GAY & LESBIAN TRAVELERS

Much of Europe has grown to accept same-sex couples over the past few decades, and in most countries homosexual sex acts are legal. To be on the safe side, do a bit of research and test the waters for acceptability in any one city or area. As you might expect, smaller towns tend to be less accepting than cities. Gay centers include London, Paris, Amsterdam, Berlin, Milan, and the Greek islands.

The **International Gay and Lesbian Travel Association (IGLTA;** © 800/448-8550 or 954/776-2626; www.iglta.org) is the trade association for the gay and lesbian travel industry, and offers an online directory of gay and lesbian-friendly travel businesses; go to their website and click on "Members."

Many agencies offer tours and travel itineraries specifically for gay and lesbian travelers. **Above and Beyond Tours** (© 800/397-2681; www.abovebeyondtours.com) is the exclusive gay and lesbian tour operator

> **Value Savings for Seniors & Families**
>
> At many museums, children under 18 and seniors get in free but only if they hail from one of the countries that has signed a reciprocal international cultural agreement to allow children and seniors this privilege. These countries include England, Canada, Ireland, Australia, New Zealand, and indeed much of the world—but *not* the United States. (However, many museum guards either don't ask for citizenship ID or wave kids and seniors on through anyway.) Children and seniors, no matter what their nationality, also get discounts on trains.

for United Airlines. **Now, Voyager** (© **800/255-6951;** www.nowvoyager.com) is a well-known San Francisco–based gay-owned and operated travel service.

The following travel guides are available at most travel bookstores and at gay and lesbian bookstores, or you can order them from **Giovanni's Room** bookstore, 1145 Pine St., Philadelphia, PA 19107 (© **215/923-2960;** www.giovannisroom.com): *Frommer's Gay & Lesbian Europe* (www.frommers.com), an excellent travel resource; *Out and About* (© **800/929-2268;** www.outandabout.com), which offers guidebooks and a newsletter ($20 per year; 10 issues) packed with solid information on the global gay and lesbian scene; *Spartacus International Gay Guide* (Bruno Gmünder Verlag; www.spartacusworld.com/gayguide) and *Odysseus: The International Gay Travel Planner* (Odysseus Enterprises Ltd.), both good, annual English-language guidebooks focused on gay men; the *Damron* guides (www.damron.com), with separate, annual books for gay men and lesbians; and *Gay Travel A to Z: The World of Gay & Lesbian Travel Options at Your Fingertips* by Marianne Ferrari (Ferrari International; Box 35575, Phoenix, AZ 85069), a very good gay and lesbian guidebook series.

SENIORS

Europe is a multigenerational culture that doesn't tend to marginalize its seniors, and older people are treated with a great deal of respect and deference throughout the Continent. But there are few specific programs, associations, or concessions made for them. The one exception is on admission prices for museums and sights, where those over 60 or 65 will often get in at a reduced rate or even free (see "Savings for Seniors & Families," above). There are also special train passes and reductions on bus tickets and the like in various towns.

Members of **AARP** (formerly known as the American Association of Retired Persons), 601 E St. NW, Washington, DC 20049 (© **800/424-3410** or 202/434-2277; www.aarp.org), get discounts on hotels, airfares, and car rentals. AARP offers members a wide range of benefits, including *Modern Maturity* magazine and a monthly newsletter. Anyone over 50 can join.

Sadly, most major **airlines** have in recent years cancelled their discount programs for seniors, but you can always ask when booking. Of the big **car-rental** agencies, only National currently gives an AARP discount, but the many rental dealers that specialize in Europe—Auto Europe, Kemwel, Europe-by-Car—offer seniors 5% off their already low rates. In most European cities, people over 60 or 65 get reduced admission at theaters, museums, and other attractions, and they can often get discount fares or cards on public transportation and national rail systems. Carrying an ID with proof of age can pay off in all these situations.

Grand Circle Travel, 347 Congress St., Boston, MA 02210 (✆ **800/959-0405** or 800/321-2835; www.gct.com), is one of the literally hundreds of travel agencies specializing in vacations for seniors. But beware: Many packages are of the tour-bus variety. Seniors seeking more independent travel should probably consult a regular travel agent. **SAGA Holidays,** 1161 Boylston St., Boston, MA 02115 (✆ **800/343-0273;** www.sagaholidays.com), has 40 years of experience running all-inclusive tours and cruises for those 50 and older. They also sponsor the more substantial "Road Scholar Tours" (✆ **800/621-2151**), fun-loving tours with an educational bent.

Many reliable agencies and organizations target the 50-plus market. **Elderhostel** (✆ **877/426-8056;** www.elderhostel.org) arranges study programs for those ages 55 and over (and a spouse or companion of any age) in the U.S. and in more than 80 countries around the world. Most courses last 5 to 7 days in the U.S. (2–4 weeks abroad), and many include airfare, accommodations in university dormitories or modest inns, meals, and tuition. **ElderTreks** (✆ **800/741-7956;** www.eldertreks.com) offers small-group tours to off-the-beaten-path or adventure-travel locations, restricted to travelers 50 and older. **INTRAV** (✆ **800/456-8100;** www.intrav.com) is a high-end tour operator that caters to the mature, discerning traveler, not specifically seniors, with trips around the world that include guided safaris, polar expeditions, private-jet adventures, and small-boat cruises down jungle rivers.

Recommended publications offering travel resources and discounts for seniors include: the quarterly magazine *Travel 50 & Beyond* (www.travel50andbeyond.com);   *Travel Unlimited: Uncommon Adventures for the Mature Traveler* (Avalon); *101 Tips for Mature Travelers,* available from Grand Circle Travel (✆ **800/221-2610** or 617/350-7500; www.gct.com); and *Unbelievably Good Deals and Great Adventures That You Absolutely Can't Get Unless You're Over 50* (McGraw-Hill), by Joann Rattner Heilman.

FAMILY TRAVEL

Europeans expect to see families traveling together and tend to love kids. You'll often find that a child guarantees you an even warmer reception at hotels and restaurants.

At **restaurants,** ask waiters for a half portion to fit junior's appetite. If you're traveling with small children, government-rated three- and four-star hotels may be your best bet—**babysitters** are on call, and such hotels have a better general ability to help you access the city and its services. But even cheaper hotels can usually find you a sitter. Traveling with a pint-size person usually entails pint-size rates. An **extra cot** in the room won't cost more than 30% extra—if anything—and most museums and sights offer **reduced-price** or free admission for children under a certain age (6–18). Kids almost always get discounts on plane and train tickets.

Familyhostel (✆ **800/733-9753;** www.learn.unh.edu/familyhostel) takes the whole family, including kids ages 8 to 15, on moderately priced domestic and international learning vacations. Lectures, field trips, and sightseeing are guided by a team of academics.

Recommended family travel Internet sites include **Family Travel Forum** (www.familytravelforum.com), a comprehensive site that offers customized trip planning; **Family Travel Network** (www.familytravelnetwork.com), an award-winning site that offers travel features, deals, and tips; **Traveling Internationally with Your Kids** (www.travelwithyourkids.com), a comprehensive site offering sound advice for long-distance and international travel with children; and **Family Travel Files** (www.thefamilytravelfiles.com), which offers an online magazine and a directory of off-the-beaten-path tours and tour operators for families.

WOMEN TRAVELERS

Women travelers will receive a warm welcome throughout most of Europe—sometimes a bit too warm, actually, when it comes to the Mediterranean cultures of Italy, Spain, Greece, and southern France. Flirting back at these would-be Romeos, even mildly, convinces them that you're interested. Heck, mere eye contact encourages them to redouble their efforts. Unless you want all this attention, take your cue from the local women, who usually ignore the men around them entirely unless it's someone they're already walking with.

    Women Welcome Women World Wide (5W; © 203/259-7832 in the U.S.; www.womenwelcomewomen. org.uk) works to foster international friendships by enabling women of different countries to visit one another (men can come along on the trips; they just can't join the club). It's a big, active organization, with more than 3,500 members from all walks of life in some 70 countries.

    Check out the award-winning website **Journeywoman** (www.journey woman.com), a "real life" women's travel information network where you can sign up for a free e-mail newsletter and get advice on everything from etiquette and dress to safety; or the travel guide *Safety and Security for Women Who Travel* by Sheila Swan and Peter Laufer (Travelers' Tales, Inc.), offering common-sense tips on safe travel.

STUDENTS & YOUTHS

If you plan to travel outside the U.S., you'd be wise to arm yourself with an **International Student Identity Card (ISIC),** which offers substantial savings on rail passes, plane tickets, and entrance fees—note that your own school's ID will often *usually* suffice to snag you those discount admissions at sights and museums across Europe; you need the ISIC. It also provides you with basic health and life insurance and a 24-hour help line. The card is available for $22 from **STA Travel** (© 800/781-4040, and if you're not in North America there's probably a local number in your country; www.sta.com or www.statravel.com), the biggest student travel agency in the world. If you're no longer a student but are still under 26, you can get an **International Youth Travel Card (IYTC)** for the same price from the same people, which entitles you to some discounts (but not on museum admissions). (*Note:* In 2002, STA Travel bought competitors **Council Travel** and **USIT Campus** after they went bankrupt. Some offices still operate under the Council name, but it's owned by STA.) **Travel CUTS** (© 800/667-2887 or 416/614-2887; www.travelcuts.com) offers similar services for both Canadians and U.S. residents. They also have a London office, 295A Regent St., London W1B 2H9 (© 0207-255-2082); or try **Campus Travel,** 52 Grosvenor Gardens, London SW1W 0AG (© 020/ 7730-3402; www.campustravel.co.uk), Britain's leading specialist in student and youth travel. Irish students should turn to **USIT** (© 01/602-1600; www.usitnow.ie).

Tips **Book 'em Early**

Most youth hostels fill up in the summer, so be sure to book ahead.

If you enjoy meeting other young travelers on the road—and want to save money—consider staying in **hostels.** Some are quite nice and charge only $10 to $25 per night for what's generally a bunk in a dormlike room (often sex-segregated) sleeping anywhere from 4 to 50 or more. However, they're usually on the outskirts of town, there's usually a lockout from morning to midafternoon, and there's a curfew of around 10pm to 1am. For more, see chapter 1.

7 Planning Your Trip Online

SURFING FOR AIRFARES

The "big three" online travel agencies, **Expedia.com, Travelocity.com,** and **Orbitz.com,** sell most of the air tickets bought on the Internet. (Canadian travelers should try Expedia.ca and Travelocity.ca; U.K. residents can go to Expedia.co.uk and Opodo.co.uk.) Each has different business deals with the airlines and may offer different fares on the same flights, so it's wise to shop around. Expedia and Travelocity will also send you **e-mail notification** when a cheap fare to your favorite destination becomes available. Of the smaller travel agency websites, **Side-Step** (www.sidestep.com) has gotten the best reviews from Frommer's authors. It's a browser add-on (you have to download it) that "searches 140 sites at once," saving you the trouble of doing so independently, but it only works on PCs.

Also remember to check **airline websites,** especially those for low-fare carriers in Europe (see the very last section of chapter 1) such as easyJet (www.easyjet.com) and Ryanair (www.ryanair.com), whose fares are often misreported or simply missing from travel agency websites. Even with major airlines, you can often shave a few bucks from a fare by booking directly through the airline and avoiding a travel agency's transaction fee.

But you'll get these discounts only by **booking online:** Most airlines now offer online-only fares that even their phone agents know nothing about.

Great **last-minute deals** are available through free weekly e-mail services provided directly by the airlines. Most of these are announced on Tuesday or Wednesday and must be purchased online. Most are only valid for travel that weekend, but some (such as Southwest's) can be booked weeks or months in advance. Sign up for weekly e-mail alerts at airline websites or check mega-sites that compile comprehensive lists of last-minute specials, such as **Smarter Living** (smarterliving.com). For last-minute trips, **site59.com** and **lastminute.com** in Europe often have better air-and-hotel package deals than the major-label sites.

If you're willing to give up some control over your flight details, use what is called an **"opaque" fare service** like **Priceline** (www.priceline.com; www.priceline.co.uk for Europeans) or its smaller competitor **Hotwire** (www.hotwire.com). Both offer rock-bottom prices in exchange for travel on a "mystery airline" at a mysterious time of day, often with a mysterious change of planes en route. The mystery airlines are all major, well-known carriers—and the possibility of being sent from Philadelphia to Chicago via

Tampa is remote; the airlines' routing computers have gotten a lot better than they used to be. But your chances of getting a 6am or 11pm flight are pretty high. Hotwire tells you flight prices before you buy; Priceline usually has better deals than Hotwire, but you have to play their "name our price" game. If you're new at this, the helpful folks at **BiddingForTravel** (www.biddingfortravel.com) do a good job of demystifying Priceline's prices and strategies. Priceline and Hotwire are great for flights within North America and between the U.S. and Europe. But for flights to other parts of the world, consolidators will almost always beat their fares. *Note:* In 2004, Priceline added non-opaque service to its roster. You now have the option to pick exact flights, times, and airlines from a list of offers—or you can opt to bid on opaque fares as before.

For much more about airfares and savvy air-travel tips and advice, pick up a copy of *Frommer's Fly Safe, Fly Smart* (Wiley Publishing, Inc.).

SURFING FOR HOTELS

Shopping online for hotels is generally done one of two ways: by booking through the hotel's own website or through an independent booking agency (or a fare-service agency like Priceline; see above). These Internet hotel agencies have multiplied in mind-boggling numbers of late, competing for the business of millions of consumers surfing for accommodations around the world. This competitiveness can be a boon to consumers who have the patience and time to shop and compare the online sites for good deals—but shop you must, for prices can vary considerably from site to site. And keep in mind that hotels at the top of a site's listing may be there for no other reason than that they paid money to get the placement. However, note that most smaller hotels and B&Bs (especially outside the U.S.) don't show up on these booking engine websites at all—a shame since, by and large, those smaller places tend to be the most charming and least expensive.

Frommers.com: The Complete Travel Resource

For an excellent travel-planning resource, we highly recommend **Frommers.com** (www.frommers.com), voted Best Travel Site by *PC Magazine*. We're a little biased, of course, but we guarantee that you'll find the travel tips, reviews, monthly vacation giveaways, bookstore, and online-booking capabilities thoroughly indispensable. Among the special features are our popular **Destinations** section, where you'll get expert travel tips, hotel and dining recommendations, and advice on the sights to see for more than 3,500 destinations around the globe; the **Frommers.com Newsletter,** with the latest deals, travel trends, and money-saving secrets; our **Community** area featuring **Message Boards,** where Frommer's readers post queries and share advice (sometimes even our authors show up to answer questions); and our **Photo Center,** where you can post queries and share money-saving tips. When your research is done, the **Online Reservations System** (www.frommers.com/book_a_trip) takes you to Frommer's preferred online partners to book your vacation at affordable prices.

Of the "big three" sites, **Expedia** may be the top hotel booking choice, thanks to its long list of special deals and "virtual tours" or photos of available rooms so you can see what you're paying for (a feature that helps counter the claims that the best rooms are often held back from bargain booking websites). Running a close second is **Travelocity,** which posts unvarnished customer reviews and ranks its properties according to the AAA rating system. Also reliable are **Hotels.com** and **Quikbook.com**. An excellent free program, **TravelAxe** (www.travelaxe.net), can help you search multiple hotel sites at once, even ones you may never have heard of. The newest booking site, **Travelweb** (www.travelweb.com), is partly owned by the hotels it represents (including the Hilton, Hyatt, and Starwood chains) and is therefore plugged directly into the hotels' reservations systems—unlike independent online agencies, which have to fax or e-mail reservation requests to the hotel, a good portion of which get misplaced in the shuffle. More than once, travelers have arrived at the hotel, only to be told that they have no reservation. To be fair, many of the major sites are undergoing improvements in service and ease of use, and Expedia will soon be able to plug directly into the reservations systems of many hotel chains—none of which can be bad news for consumers. In the meantime, it's a good idea to **get a confirmation number** and **make a printout** of any online booking transaction.

8 The 21st-Century Traveler

INTERNET ACCESS AWAY FROM HOME

Travelers have any number of ways to check e-mail and access the Internet on the road. Of course, using your own laptop—or even PDA or electronic organizer with modem—gives you the most flexibility. And if you don't have a computer, you can still access your e-mail and your office computer from cybercafes.

It's hard nowadays to find a city that *doesn't* have a few cybercafes. Although there's no definitive directory for cybercafes—these are independent businesses, after all—three places to start looking are at **www.cybercaptive.com** and **www.cybercafe.com**.

Aside from formal cybercafes, most **public libraries** across the world offer Internet access free or for a small charge. **Hotels** that cater to business travelers often have **in-room dataports** and **business centers,** but the charges can be exorbitant. Also, most **youth hostels** nowadays have at least one computer where you can access the Internet.

Most major airports now have **Internet kiosks** scattered throughout their gates. These kiosks, which you'll also see in shopping malls, hotel lobbies, and tourist information offices around the world, give you basic Web access for a per-minute fee that's usually higher than cybercafe prices. The kiosks' clunkiness and high price means they should be avoided whenever possible.

To retrieve your e-mail, ask your **Internet Service Provider (ISP)** if it has a Web-based interface tied to your existing e-mail account. If your ISP doesn't have such an interface, you can use the free **mail2web** service (www.mail2web.com) to view (but not reply to) your home e-mail. For more flexibility, you may want to open a free, Web-based e-mail account with **Yahoo! Mail** (mail.yahoo.com). (Microsoft's Hotmail is another popular option, but Hotmail has severe spam problems.) Your home ISP may be able to forward your e-mail to the Web-based account automatically.

USING A CELLPHONE

The three letters that define much of the world's wireless capabilities are GSM (Global System for Mobiles), a big, seamless network that makes for easy cross-border cellphone use throughout Europe and dozens of other countries worldwide. In the U.S., T-Mobile, AT&T Wireless, and Cingular use this quasi-universal system; in Canada, Microcell and some Rogers customers use GSM, and all Europeans and most Australians use GSM.

If your cellphone is on a GSM system, and you have a world-capable multiband phone such as many Sony Ericsson, Motorola, or Samsung models, you can make and receive calls across civilized areas on much of the globe, from Andorra to Uganda. Just call your wireless operator and ask for "international roaming" to be activated on your account. Unfortunately, per-minute charges can be high—usually $1 to $1.50 in western Europe and up to $5 in places like Russia and Indonesia.

That's why it's important to buy an "unlocked" world phone from the get-go. Many cellphone operators sell "locked" phones that restrict you from using any removable computer memory phone chip (called a **SIM card**) card other than the ones they supply. Having an unlocked phone allows you to install a cheap, prepaid SIM card (found at a local retailer) in your destination country. (Show your phone to the salesperson; not all phones work on all networks.) You'll get a local phone number—and much, much lower calling rates. Getting an already locked phone unlocked can be a complicated process, but it can be done; just call your cellular operator and say you'll be going abroad for several months and want to use the phone with a local provider.

For many, **renting** a phone is a good idea. (Even worldphone owners will have to rent new phones if they're traveling to non-GSM regions, such as Japan or Korea.) While you can rent a phone from any number of overseas sites, including kiosks at airports and car-rental agencies, we suggest renting the phone before you leave home. That way you can give loved ones and business associates your new number, make sure the phone works, and take the phone wherever you go—especially helpful for overseas trips through several countries, where local phone-rental agencies often bill in local currency and may not let you take the phone to another country.

Phone rental isn't cheap. You'll usually pay $40 to $50 per week, plus airtime fees of at least a dollar a minute. If you're traveling to Europe, though, local rental companies often offer free incoming calls within their home country, which can save you big bucks. The bottom line: Shop around. Two good wireless rental companies are **InTouch USA** (© 800/872-7626; www.intouchglobal.com) and **Road-Post** (www.roadpost.com; © 888/290-1606 or 905/272-5665). Give them your itinerary, and they'll tell you what wireless products you need. InTouch will also, for free, advise you on whether your existing phone will work overseas; simply call © 703/222-7161 between 9am and 4pm ET, or go to http://intouchglobal.com/travel.htm. You can also usually lease a cellphone from major car-rental firms; as with the best rates on the cars themselves, the prices at consolidator Auto Europe (www.autoeurope.com) tend to be better than those at the major firms like Hertz or Avis.

Online Traveler's Toolbox

Veteran travelers usually carry some essential items to make their trips easier. Following is a selection of online tools to bookmark and use.

- **Visa ATM Locator** (www.visa.com), for locations of PLUS ATMs worldwide, or **MasterCard ATM Locator** (www.mastercard.com), for locations of Cirrus ATMs worldwide.
- **Foreign Languages for Travelers** (www.travlang.com). Learn basic terms in more than 70 languages and click on any underlined phrase to hear what it sounds like.
- **Intellicast** (www.intellicast.com) and **Weather.com** (www.weather.com). Both give weather forecasts for all 50 states and for cities around the world.
- **Mapquest** (www.mapquest.com). This best of the mapping sites lets you choose a specific address or destination and, in seconds, returns a map and detailed directions.
- **Subway Navigator** (www.subwaynavigator.com). Download subway maps and get savvy advice on using subway systems in dozens of major cities around the world.
- **Universal Currency Converter** (www.xe.com/ucc). See what your dollar or pound is worth in more than 100 other countries.
- **Travel Warnings** (http://travel.state.gov/travel_warnings.html, www.fco.gov.uk/travel, www.voyage.gc.ca, www.dfat.gov.au/consular/advice). These sites report on places where health concerns or unrest might threaten American, British, Canadian, and Australian travelers. Generally, U.S. warnings are the most paranoid; Australian warnings are the most relaxed.

9 Getting There Without Going Broke

A round-trip plane ticket from the States can run to thousands of dollars or be as cheap as $179. Although $179 is the sort of deal you run across only rarely (and usually on New York–London routes), there's no need to pay more than $500 to $800 even on a regularly scheduled flight. You just have to plan ahead and know how to find such fares. Here are some tips.

BY PLANE FROM NORTH AMERICA

Most major airlines charge competitive fares to European cities, but price wars break out regularly and fares can change overnight. For a list of the **major North American and European national airlines** and their toll-free numbers and

websites, see "The Major Airlines," below.

Tickets tend to be cheaper if you fly midweek or off season. **High season** on most airline routes is usually June to mid-September, the most expensive and most crowded time to travel. **Shoulder season** is April to May, mid-September to October, and December 15 to 24. **Low season**—with the cheapest fares—is November to December 14 and December 25 to March.

GETTING THROUGH THE AIRPORT

With the federalization of airport security, security procedures at U.S. airports are more stable and consistent than ever. Generally, you'll be fine if you arrive at the airport **2 hours** before an international flight; if you show up late, tell an airline employee and she'll probably whisk you to the front of the line.

Bring your **passport** as photo ID (you need that to get into Europe anyway!) and if you've got an E-ticket, print out the **official confirmation page;** you might need to show it at the security checkpoint. Keep your ID at the ready to show at check-in, the security checkpoint, and sometimes even the gate. (Children under 18 do not need government-issued photo IDs for domestic flights, but they do for international flights to most countries.)

In 2003, the TSA phased out **gate check-in** at all U.S. airports. And **E-tickets** have made paper tickets nearly obsolete. Passengers with E-tickets can beat the ticket-counter lines by using airport **electronic kiosks** or even **online check-in** from you're a home computer. Online check-in involves logging onto your airlines' website, accessing your reservation, and printing out your boarding pass—and the airline may even offer you bonus miles to do so! If you're using a kiosk at the airport, bring the credit card you used to book the ticket or your frequent-flier card. Print out your boarding pass from the kiosk and proceed to the security checkpoint with your pass and a photo ID. If you're checking bags or looking to snag an exit-row seat, you will be able to do so using most airline kiosks. Even the smaller airlines are employing the kiosk system, but always call your airline to make sure these alternatives are available. **Curbside check-in** is also a good way to avoid lines, although a few airlines still ban curbside check-in; call before you go.

Security lines are getting shorter than they were during 2001 and 2002, but some doozies remain. If you have trouble standing for long periods of time, tell an airline employee; the airline will provide a wheelchair. Speed up security by **not wearing metal objects** such as big belt buckles or clanky earrings. If you've got metallic body parts, a note from your doctor can prevent a long chat with the security screeners. Keep in mind that only **ticketed passengers** are allowed past security, except for folks escorting disabled passengers or children.

Federalization has stabilized **what you can carry on** and **what you can't.** The general rule is that sharp things are out, nail clippers are okay, and food and beverages must be passed through the X-ray machine—but that security screeners can't make you drink from your coffee cup. Bring food in your carry-on rather than checking it, as explosive-detection machines used on checked luggage have been known to mistake food (especially chocolate, for some reason) for bombs. Travelers in the U.S. are allowed one carry-on bag, plus a "personal item" such as a purse, briefcase, or laptop bag. Carry-on hoarders can stuff all sorts of things into a laptop bag; as long as it has a laptop in it, it's still considered a personal item. The Transportation Security Administration (TSA) has issued a list of restricted items; check its website (www.tsa.gov/public/index.jsp) for details.

Airport screeners may decide that your checked luggage needs to be searched by hand. You can now purchase luggage locks that allow screeners to open and re-lock a checked bag if hand-searching is necessary. Look for Travel Sentry certified locks at luggage or travel shops and Brookstone stores (you can buy them online at www.brookstone.com). These locks, approved by the TSA, can be opened by luggage inspectors with a special code or key. For more information on the locks, visit www.travelsentry.org. If you use something other than

TSA-approved locks, your lock will be cut off your suitcase if a TSA agent needs to hand-search your luggage.

FLYING FOR LESS: TIPS FOR GETTING THE BEST AIRFARE

Passengers sharing the same airplane cabin rarely pay the same fare. Travelers who need to purchase tickets at the last minute, change their itinerary at a moment's notice, or fly one-way often get stuck paying the premium rate. Here are some ways to keep your airfare costs down.

- Passengers who can book their ticket **long in advance,** who can **stay over Saturday night,** or who can **fly midweek or at less-trafficked hours** may pay a fraction of the full fare. If your schedule is flexible, say so, and ask if you can secure a cheaper fare by changing your flight plans.
- You can also save on airfares by watching local newspapers for **promotional specials** or **fare wars,** when airlines lower prices on their most popular routes. You rarely see fare wars offered during peak travel times, but if you can travel in the off months, you may snag a bargain.
- Search **the Internet** for cheap fares (see "Planning Your Trip Online").
- **Consolidators,** also known as bucket shops, are great sources for international tickets. Start by looking in Sunday newspaper travel sections; U.S. travelers should focus on the *New York Times, Los Angeles Times,* and *Miami Herald.* For less-developed destinations, small travel agents who cater to immigrant communities in large cities often have the best deals. *Beware:* Bucket shop tickets are usually nonrefundable or rigged with stiff cancellation penalties, often as high as 50% to 75% of the ticket price, and some put you on charter airlines, which may leave at inconvenient times and experience delays. Several reliable consolidators are worldwide and available on the Net. **STA Travel** is now the world's leader in student travel, thanks to its purchase of Council Travel. It also offers good fares for travelers of all ages. **ELTExpress** (© 800/ **TRAV-800;** www.eltexpress.com or www.flights.com) started in Europe and has excellent fares worldwide, but particularly to that continent. It also has "local" websites in 12 countries. **FlyCheap** (© 800/FLY-CHEAP; www.flycheap.com) is owned by package-holiday megalith My Travel and so has especially good access to fares for sunny destinations. **Air Tickets Direct** (© 800/ **778-3447;** www.airticketsdirect. com) is based in Montréal and leverages the currently weak Canadian dollar for low fares; it'll also book trips to places that U.S. travel agents won't touch, such as Cuba.
- Join **frequent-flier clubs.** Accrue enough miles, and you'll be rewarded with free flights and elite status. It's free, and you'll get the best choice of seats, faster response to phone inquiries, and prompter service if your luggage is stolen, if your flight is canceled or delayed, or if you want to change your seat. You don't need to fly to build frequent-flier miles—**frequent-flier credit cards** can provide thousands of miles for doing your everyday shopping.
- For many more tips about air travel, including a rundown of the major frequent-flier credit cards, pick up a copy of *Frommer's Fly Safe, Fly Smart* (Wiley Publishing, Inc.).

LONG-HAUL FLIGHTS: HOW TO STAY COMFORTABLE

Long flights can be trying; stuffy air and cramped seats can make you feel as if you're being sent parcel post in a small box. But with a little advance planning, you can make an otherwise unpleasant experience almost bearable.

- Your choice of airline and airplane will definitely affect your legroom. Among U.S. airlines, American Airlines has the best average seat pitch (the distance between a seat and the row in front of it), though they recently announced they'll be refitting the planes to do away with the extra legroom, so this may not last long. Find out more at www.seatguru.com, which has extensive details about almost every seat on six major U.S. airlines. For international airlines, research firm Skytrax has posted a list of average seat pitches at www.airlinequality.com.

- Emergency exit seats and bulkhead seats typically have the most legroom. Emergency exit seats are usually held back to be assigned the day of a flight (to ensure that the seat is filled by someone able-bodied); it's worth getting to the ticket counter early to snag one of these spots for a long flight. Many passengers find that bulkhead seating (the row facing the wall at the front of the cabin) offers more legroom, but keep in mind that bulkheads are where airlines often put baby bassinets, so you may be sitting next to an infant.

- To have two seats for yourself in a three-seat row, try for an aisle seat in a center section toward the back of coach. If you're traveling with a companion, book an aisle and a window seat. Middle seats are usually booked last, so chances are good you'll end up with three seats

to yourselves. And in the event that a third passenger is assigned the middle seat, he or she will probably be more than happy to trade for a window or an aisle seat.

- Ask about entertainment options. Many airlines offer seatback video systems where you get to choose your movies or play video games—but only on some of their planes. (Boeing 777s are your best bet.)

- To sleep, avoid the last row of any section or a row in front of an emergency exit, as these seats are the least likely to recline. Avoid seats near highly trafficked toilet areas. Avoid seats in the back of many jets—these are often considerably more narrow than those in the rest of coach class. You also may want to reserve a window seat so that you can rest your head and avoid being bumped in the aisle.

- Get up, walk around, and stretch every 60 to 90 minutes to keep your blood flowing. This helps avoid **deep vein thrombosis,** or "economy-class syndrome," a rare and deadly condition that can be caused by sitting in cramped conditions for too long. Other preventative measures include drinking lots of water and avoiding alcohol (see next bullet).

- Drink water before, during, and after your flight to combat the lack of humidity in airplane cabins—which can be drier than the Sahara. Bring a bottle of water on board. Avoid alcohol, which will dehydrate you.

- If you're flying with kids, don't forget to carry on toys, books, pacifiers, and chewing gum to help them relieve ear pressure buildup during ascent and descent. Let each child pack his or her own backpack with favorite toys.

Tips Coping with Jet Lag

Jetlag is a pitfall of traveling across time zones. If you're flying north-south and you feel sluggish when you touch down, your symptoms will be caused by dehydration and the general stress of air travel. When you travel east to west or vice-versa, however, your body becomes thoroughly confused about what time it is, and everything from your digestion to your brain gets knocked for a loop. Traveling east, say, from Chicago to Paris, is more difficult on your internal clock than traveling west, say from Atlanta to Hawaii, as most peoples' bodies find it more acceptable to stay up late than to fall asleep early.

Here are some tips for combating jet lag:

- **Reset your watch** to your destination time before you board the plane.
- **Drink lots of water** before, during, and after your flight. Avoid alcohol.
- **Exercise and sleep well** for a few days before your trip.
- If you have trouble sleeping on planes, **fly eastward on morning flights.**
- **Daylight** is the key to resetting your body clock. At the website for **Outside In** (www.bodyclock.com), you can get a customized plan of when to seek and avoid light.
- If you need help getting to sleep earlier than you usually would, some doctors recommend taking either the hormone **melatonin** or the sleeping pill **Ambien**—but not together. Some recommend that you take 2 to 5 milligrams of melatonin about 2 hours before your planned bedtime—but again, always check with your doctor on the best course of action for you.

THE MAJOR AIRLINES

NORTH AMERICAN AIRLINES North American carriers with frequent service and flights to Europe are **Air Canada** (© 888/247-2262; www.aircanada.ca), **American Airlines** (© 800/433-7300; www.aa.com), **Continental Airlines** (© 800/231-0856; www.continental.com), **Delta Airlines** (© 800/241-4141; www.delta.com), **Northwest Airlines** (© 800/447-4747; www.nwa.com), **United** (© 800/538-2929; www.united.com), and **US Airways** (© 800/622-1015; www.usairways.com).

EUROPEAN NATIONAL AIRLINES Not only do the national carriers of European countries offer the greatest number of direct flights from the States (and can easily book you through to cities beyond the major hubs), but since their entire U.S. market is to fly you to their home country, they often run more competitive deals than most North American carriers. In fact, the competition between British Airways and Virgin Atlantic leads them to offer incredible deals to London—already the cheapest European gateway. And most national airlines—particularly Iceland Air, Lufthansa, and Air France—offer great deals on flights from the States to many European cities besides those of their own country (although usually with a transfer via their home hub).

Major national and country-affiliated European airlines include the following:

- **Austria:** Austrian Airlines. *In the U.S.:* 800/843-0002. *In Canada:* 888/817-4444. *In the U.K.:* 0845/601-0948. www.aua.com.

- **Czech Republic:** CSA Czech Airlines. *In the U.S. & Canada:* 800/223-2365, *In the U.K.:* 020/7255-1898. www.czechairlines.com.
- **France:** Air France. *In the U.S.:* 800/237-2747. *In Canada:* 800/667-2747. *In the U.K.:* 0845/359-1000. *In Australia:* 1300-361-400 or 02/9244-2100. www.airfrance.com.
- **Germany:** Lufthansa. *In the U.S.:* 800/645-3880. *In Canada:* 800/563-5954. *In the U.K.:* 0845/773-7747. *In Australia:* 300/655-727. www.lufthansa.com.
- **Greece:** Olympic Airlines. *In the U.S.:* 800/223-1226. *In Canada:* 514/878-3891 (Montréal) or 416/964-7137 (Toronto). *In the U.K.:* 0870/606-0460. *In Australia:* 612/9251-2044. www.olympicairlines.com.
- **Iceland:** IcelandAir. *In the U.S. & Canada:* 800/223-5500. *In the U.K.:* 020/7874-1000. www.icelandair.com.
- **Ireland:** Aer Lingus. *In the U.S. and Canada:* 800/IRISH-AIR. *In the U.K.:* 0845/084-4444. www.aerlingus.com.
- **Italy:** Alitalia. *In the U.S.:* 800/223-5730. *In Canada:* 800/361-8336. *In the U.K.:* 0870/544-8259. www.alitalia.com.
- **The Netherlands:** KLM Royal Dutch Airlines. *In the U.S. and Canada:* 800/447-4747. *In the U.K.:* 08705/074-074. *In Australia:* 300/303-747. *In New Zealand:* 09/309-1782. www.klm.com.
- **Portugal:** TAP Air Portugal. *In the U.S.:* 800/221-7370. *In the U.K.:* 0870/607-2024. *In Australia:* 02/9244-2344. www.tap-airportugal.com.
- **Scandinavia (Denmark, Norway, Sweden):** Scandinavian Airlines. *In the U.S. and Canada:* 800/221-2350. *In the U.K.:* 0870/6072-7727. *In Australia:* 300/727 707. www.scandinavian.net.
- **Spain:** Iberia. *In the U.S.:* 800/772-4642. *In the U.K.:* 0845/601-2845. www.iberia.com.
- **Switzerland:** Swiss International. *In the U.S. and Canada:* 877/359-7947. *In the U.K.:* 0845/601-0956. *In Australia:* 800/883-199. www.swiss.com.
- **United Kingdom:** (1) Virgin Atlantic. *In the U.S. and Canada:* 800/862-8621. *In the U.K.:* 0870/380-2007. *In Australia:* 02/9244-2747. www.virgin-atlantic.com. (2) British Airways. *In the U.S. and Canada:* 800/247-9297. *In the U.K.:* 0870/850-9850. *In Australia:* 300/767-177. *In New Zealand:* 800/247-847. www.britishairways.com.

FROM THE UNITED KINGDOM BY TRAIN

For **European rail passes** and other special tickets available in Britain to U.K. citizens, see "Getting Around Without Going Broke" in chapter 1.

BY CHUNNEL TRAIN The **Eurostar train** screams between London and Paris or Brussels at 300kmph (186 mph) in less than 3 hours (compared to 10 or more hours on the train-ferry-train route). As of 2004, one-way fares from London to either Paris or Brussels in **standard/second class** range from $45 to $90 for an adult "Leisure" ticket, depending on how far in advance you book your ticket and how exchangeable/refundable it is. Holders of certain rail passes (Eurail, Eurorail, BritRail, France, or Benelux) pay $75 each way; youths under 26 pay $45 ($75 during peak times), and children ages 4 to 11 pay $38. First-class tickets get quite ridiculous (up as high as $798 round-trip).

You can phone for Eurostar reservations at ℂ **0990/186-186** or 020/7928-5163 in London, 338/36-35-35-39 in France or 01-53-44-60-03 in Paris, or **800/EUROSTAR** in the U.S. (www.eurostar.com). Eurostar trains arrive at and depart from Waterloo Station in London, Gare du Nord in Paris, and Brussels Zuid/Midi in Brussels.

BY HOVERCRAFT

The quicker and slightly cheaper hovercrafts operated by **Hoverspeed** (ℂ **0870/240-8070;** www.hoverspeed.co.uk) make the 35-minute crossing between Dover and Calais up to 12 times daily; Dover to Oostende, Belgium, three to five times daily; Folkstone to Boulogne four times a day; New Haven to Dieppe one to three times daily (those last two not in winter). Rates for foot passengers are £24 to £28 (35€–40€/$40–$46); rates with a car are £99 to £146 (142€–210€/$163–$241).

BY FERRY

P&O Ferries (ℂ **44-1304/864-003;** www.poferries.com) is a consolidation of what used to be three separate ferry lines crisscrossing the English Channel and the North Sea. It now operates the popular car ferries between Dover, England, and Calais, France, 24 hours a day (every half-hour at peak times, hourly at night; 1¼ hr.), as well as the connections between Hull, England, and either Zeebrugge, Belgium (one daily; departs at 6:15pm to arrive at 8:30am the next day), or Rotterdam, Netherlands (one daily; departs at 6:30pm to arrive at 8am the next day). It also handles the old "P&O European" car and passenger service between Portsmouth and Cherbourg, France (three to six departures a day, but only one daily in Jan; 5–9 hr.); between Portsmouth and Le Havre, France (three a day; 4½–6½ hr.); and between Portsmouth and Bilbao, Spain (two a week; 36 hr.).

For an idea of prices: Return fare in standard class on the classic Dover-to-Calais ferry, for a car with driver and one to two passengers, costs around £128 (183€/$211), varying widely with the season and time of day. There's a hefty surcharge of anywhere from $20 to $100 if you buy your tickets at the port on the day of departure rather than order ahead of time online or by phone.

In the U.S., book P&O Ferries through the helpful **Scots-American Travel** (ℂ **800/247-7268;** www.scotsamerican.com).

A major competitor is **Brittany Ferries** (ℂ **08703/665-333** in the U.K.; www.brittany-ferries.co.uk), sailing from the southern coast of England to five destinations in Spain and France. From Portsmouth, sailings reach St-Malo, Caen, and Cherbourg; from Poole, they reach Cherbourg. From Plymouth, sailings go to Santander, Spain, and Roscoff, France.

DFDS (Scandinavia) Seaways (ℂ **800/533-3755** in the U.S., 08705/333-000 in the U.K. or 44-1255-240-240 from outside the U.K.; www.scansea.com) offers sea links from England to ports in the Netherlands, Germany, and all the Scandinavian countries.

BY CAR

Many car-rental companies won't let you rent a car in Britain and take it to the Continent, so always check ahead. There are many "drive-on/drive-off" car-ferry services across the Channel (see "By Ferry" above). There is also **Eurotunnel** (ℂ **08705/353-535** in the U.K., 03/21-00-61-00 in France, or 0990/353-535 from elsewhere in the world; www.eurotunnel.co.uk), with trains through the Channel Tunnel that run a drive-on/drive-off service every 15 minutes (once an hour at night) for the 35-minute ride between Folkstone, England, and Calais,

France. It can cost anywhere from £19 to £313 (27€–449€/$31–$516) round-trip, depending on the date, time of day, the length of time before you return, and more. One-way tickets are a flat £111.50 (160€/$184).

BY COACH

Although travel by coach is considerably slower and less comfortable than train travel, if you're on a budget you might opt for one of **Eurolines's** regular departures from London's Victoria Coach Station to destinations throughout Europe. Contact Eurolines's British branch, the National Express at Ensign Court, 4 Vicarage Rd., Edgbaston, Birmingham, B15 3ES (© **08705/808-080;** www. eurolines.com).

10 Packages for the Independent Traveler

Before you start your search for the lowest airfare, you may want to consider booking your flight as part of a travel package. Package tours are not the same thing as escorted tours. Package tours are simply a way to buy the airfare, accommodations, and other elements of your trip (such as car rentals, airport transfers, and sometimes even activities) at the same time and often at discounted prices—kind of like one-stop shopping. Packages are sold in bulk to tour operators—who resell them to the public at a cost that usually undercuts standard rates.

One good source of package deals is the airlines themselves. Most major airlines offer air/land packages, including **American Airlines Vacations** (© 800/321-2121; www.aavacations. com), **Delta Vacations** (© 800/221-6666; www.deltavacations.com), **Continental Airlines Vacations** (© 800/301-3800; www.covacations.com), and **United Vacations** (© 888/854-3899; www.unitedvacations.com).

The single best-priced packager to Europe, though, is Internet-only travel agent **Go-Today.com** (www.go-today.com), offering excellent 4- and 6-night air/hotel packages throughout the Continent, as well as airfare/car-rental deals. Its up-and-coming rival **Octopus Travel** (© 877/330-7765; www.octopuspackages.com) sometimes undercuts Go-Today.com's rates, but look carefully at the hotels you get. Often with Octopus, the lodgings

are located way on the outskirts of town. By the time you "upgrade" to a property near the historic center and take a look at the new rate, Go-Today.com turns out to be the real price champ.

Among the more traditional travel agencies, **Liberty Travel** (© 888/271-1584; www.libertytravel.com) is one of the biggest packagers in the Northeast and usually boasts a full-page ad in Sunday papers. **American Express Vacations** (© 800/241-1700; www.americanexpress.com) is one of the most reputable national operators. Several big **online travel agencies**—Expedia, Travelocity, Orbitz, Site59, and Lastminute.com—also do a brisk business in packages. If you're unsure about the pedigree of a smaller packager, check with the Better Business Bureau in the city where the company is based, or go online at www.bbb.org. If a packager won't tell you where it's based, don't fly with it.

Travel packages are also listed in the travel section of your local Sunday newspaper. Or check ads in the national travel magazines such as *Arthur Frommer's Budget Travel, Travel + Leisure, National Geographic Traveler,* and *Condé Nast Traveler.*

Package tours can vary by leaps and bounds. Some offer a better class of hotel than others. Some offer the same hotels for lower prices. Some offer flights on scheduled airlines, while others book charters. Some limit your choices of accommodations and travel days. You are often required to make a large payment upfront. On the plus side, packages can save you money, offering group prices but allowing for independent travel. Some even let you add on a few guided excursions or escorted day trips (also at prices lower than if you booked them yourself) without booking an entirely escorted tour.

Before you invest in a package tour, get some answers. Ask about the **accommodations choices** and prices for each. Then look up the hotels' reviews in a Frommer's guide (note, however, that most hotels offered with package tours are cookie-cutter chain places very short on atmosphere,

hence they might not appear within this book; use the Internet to suss them out and see some pictures) and check their rates for your specific dates of travel online. You'll also want to find out what **type of room** you get. If you need a certain type of room, ask for it; don't take whatever is thrown your way. Request a nonsmoking room, a quiet room, a room with a view, or whatever you fancy.

Finally, look for **hidden expenses.** Ask whether airport departure fees and taxes, for example, are included in the total cost.

Finally, if you plan to travel alone, you'll need to know if a **single supplement** will be charged and if the company can match you with a roommate.

11 Escorted General-Interest Tours

Escorted tours are structured group tours, with a group leader. The price usually includes everything from airfare to hotels, meals, tours, admission costs, and local transportation.

Again, **American Express Vacations** (see "Packages for the Independent Traveler," above) offers the most comprehensive escorted tours to Europe, but there are hundreds of other operators, some specializing in Europe-wide tours, others in specific countries. Ask your travel agent. If you want a tour balancing independent-style travel and plenty of free time with all the pluses of a guided tour, you have two choices.

The more mainstream are the popular itineraries offered by **Europe Through the Back Door,** 120 Fourth Ave. N., P.O. Box 2009, Edmonds, WA 98020-2009 (© **425/771-8303;** www.ricksteves.com), designed by Rick Steves, of public TV's *Travels in Europe* fame. For more funk and fun, check out the new (as of 2004) European itineraries being offered by that most excellent Australia-based tour

operator **Intrepid Travel,** with U.S. offices at 5222 Lee St., Torrance, CA 90503 (© **877/448-1616;** www. intrepidtravel.com). The company has long been admired in Asia for its small group size (no more than 12 participants), fun travel philosophy (they travel like solo tourists do: using public transport, staying in family-run B&Bs, eating in local bistros and such), and commitment to social causes.

Many people derive a certain ease and security from escorted trips. Escorted tours—whether by bus, motor coach, train, or boat—let travelers sit back and enjoy their trip without having to spend lots of time behind the wheel. All the little details are taken care of; you know your costs upfront; and there are few surprises. Escorted tours can take you to the maximum number of sights in the minimum amount of time with the least amount of hassle—you don't have to sweat over the plotting and planning of a vacation schedule. Escorted tours are particularly convenient for people with limited mobility.

> **Tips   A Tour Warning**
>
> Before you sign up with any tour, check on its quality and business practices. Ask the operator if you can see surveys and observations filled out by past participants. Check any tour company with the local **Better Business Bureau** and/or with the **U.S. Tour Operators Association (USTOA)**, 342 Madison Ave., Suite 1522, New York, NY 10173 (© **212/599-6599**; www.ustoa.com), which keeps tabs on its members.

On the downside, an escorted tour often requires a big deposit upfront, and lodging and dining choices are predetermined. As part of a cloud of tourists, you'll get little opportunity for serendipitous interactions with locals. The tours can be jam-packed with activities, leaving little room for individual sightseeing, whim, or adventure—plus they also often focus only on the heavily touristed sites, so you miss out on the lesser-known gems.

Before you invest in an escorted tour, ask about the **cancellation policy:** Is a deposit required? Can they cancel the trip if they don't get enough people? Do you get a refund if they cancel? If *you* cancel? How late can you cancel if you are unable to go? When do you pay in full? *Note:* If you choose an escorted tour, think strongly about purchasing trip-cancellation insurance, especially if the tour operator asks you to pay upfront. See the section on "Travel Insurance," earlier in this chapter.

You'll also want to get a complete **schedule** of the trip to find out how much sightseeing is planned each day and whether enough time has been allotted for relaxing or wandering solo.

The **size** of the group is also important to know upfront. Generally, the smaller the group, the more flexible the itinerary, and the less time you'll spend waiting for people to get on and off the bus. Find out the **demographics** of the group as well. What is the age range? What is the gender breakdown? Is this mostly a trip for couples or singles?

Discuss what is included in the **price.** You may have to pay for transportation to and from the airport. A box lunch may be included on an excursion, but drinks might cost extra. Tips may not be included. Find out if you will be charged if you decide to opt out of certain activities or meals. The sections on accommodations choices, hidden expenses, and single supplements discussed above under "Packages for the Independent Traveler" apply here as well.

12 Special-Interest Vacations

If a plain-Jane tour is just not for you, consider one of these themed vacations, whether it's getting into the great outdoors on a hiking or biking trip across the Alps, exchanging your home with a Parisian, taking cooking lessons in Florence, or going on an archeological dig in the south of France.

ARCHAEOLOGICAL DIGS

Earthwatch, 3 Clock Tower Place, Suite 100, Box 75, Maynard, MA 01754 (© **800/776-0188** or 978/461-0081; www.earthwatch.org), and **Earthwatch Europe,** 267 Banbury Rd., Oxford, England OX2 7HT (© **01865/318-838**), offer education-packed participation in worldwide archaeological digs, animal behavioral patterns studies, and more.

BIKE TOURS

Cycling is the best way to see Europe at your own pace. You can rent bicycles at train stations or private agencies in just about any city or town, and, in some countries, you can pick up a bike at one train station and drop it off at another. In parts of Germany, Scandinavia, and especially the pancake-flat Netherlands, biking is a way of life, and the opportunities and resources for pedalers are extensive. In fact, in Copenhagen, thousands of rickety old free bikes are scattered at racks throughout town; just grab one, pop in a few coins to unlock it (they're refunded when you reattach the bike to another rack), and pedal away.

Avid cyclists who plan to tour a whole region by bike will probably want to bring their own. Neophytes might want to try a short trip at home first to learn the basics and figure out the essential gear. Some airlines charge extra to bring a bike; many count it as one of your pieces of checked luggage. Either way, your bicycle must be properly boxed—remove the pedals and front wheel; buy the box at a bike shop or the airport for around $10. You can take a bike onto just about any train, but on many you have to pay a fee ranging from nominal to ridiculously high (up to 75% of the cost of your own ticket).

The best tour resource is the annual **Tourfinder** issue of *Bicycle USA*. A copy costs $15 from the League of American Bicyclists, 1612 K St. NW, Suite 401, Washington, DC 20006 (© **202/822-1333;** www.bikeleague. org). Membership is $30 per year and includes the Tourfinder and the annual almanac with information on European bicycling organizations. **Holland Bicycling Tours,** P.O. Box 6086, Huntington Beach, CA 92615-6086 (© **800/852-3258;** www.hollandbicyclingtours.com), leads 8- to 12-day tours throughout Europe (not just in the Netherlands). **Experience Plus,** 415 Mason Ct., Suite 1, Fort Collins, CO 80524 (© **800/685-4565;** www.xplus.com), runs bike tours across Europe; **Ciclismo Classico,** 30 Marathon St., Arlington, MA 02174 (© **800/866-7314;** www.ciclismoclassico.com), is an excellent outfit specializing in tours through Italy but also through France, Austria, and Switzerland.

WALKING TOURS

Wilderness Travel, 1102 Ninth St., Berkeley, CA 94710 (© **800/368-2794;** www.wildernesstravel.com), specializes in walking tours, treks, and inn-to-inn hiking tours of Europe. **Sherpa Expeditions,** 131A Heston Rd., Hounslow, Middlesex, England TW5 ORF (© **44-(0)20/8577-2717;** www.sherpaexpeditions.com), offers both self-guided and group treks through off-the-beaten-track regions. Two long-established, somewhat upscale walking tour companies are **Butterfield & Robinson,** 70 Bond St.,

---

Tips **Specialty Travel Websites**

At **InfoHub Specialty Travel Guide** (www.infohub.com), you can find tours centered around just about anything and everything: antiques, archaeology, art history, churches, cooking, gay life, nudism, religion, wineries, and much more. If this sounds expensive to you, don't worry—while searching the site, you can even set your own price limit. Two other good resource sites for specialty tours and travels are the **Specialty Travel Index** (www.specialtytravel.com) and **Shaw Guides** (www.shawguides.com).

Suite 300, Toronto, ON M5B 1X3 (© **800/678-1147** in North America, 416/864-1354 elsewhere; www. butterfield.com), and **Country Walkers,** P.O. Box 180, Waterbury, VT 05676 (© **800/464-9255** in North America, 802/244-1387 elsewhere; www.countrywalkers.com). The bike tour companies **Experience Plus** and **Ciclismo Classico,** listed above under "Bike Tours," also do walking tours.

Most European countries have associations geared toward aiding hikers and walkers, where membership usually gets you discounts at the countries' networks of mountain huts. In the U.S., try the **American Alpine Club,** 710 Tenth St., Suite 100, Golden, CO 80401 (© **303/384-0110;** www.americanalpineclub.org). In Britain, it's the **Ramblers' Association,** 2nd Floor, Camelford House, 87–90 Albert Embankment, London SE1 7TW (© **020/7339-8500** in the U.K.; www.ramblers.org.uk). In France, call the **Club Alpin Français,** 24 av. de Laumière, 75019 Paris (© **01-53-72-87-00** in France; www.clubalpin. com). In Italy, contact the **Club Alpino Italiano,** 7 Via E. Petrella 19, 20124 Milano (© **02-205-7231** in Italy; www.cai.it). Germany's club is the **Deutscher Alpenverein,** Von-Karh Strasse 2–4, Postfach 500 220, 80972 München (© **089/140-030** in Germany; www.alpenverein.de). Switzerland's is called the **Schweizer Alpenclub,** Monbijoustrasse 61, 3000 Bern 23 (© **031/370-1818** in Switzerland; www.sac-cas.ch). For Austria, try the **Österreichischer Alpenverein,** Wilhelm-Greil-Strasse 15, Innsbruck, A-6010 (© **0512/59-547** in Austria; www.alpenverein.at).

HORSEBACK RIDING

One of the best companies out there is **Equitour,** P.O. Box 807, 10 Stalnaker St., Dubois, WY 82513 (© **800/545-0019;** www.ridingtours.com).

WILDERNESS & ADVENTURE TRAVEL

Adventure Center, 1311 63rd St., Suite 200, Emeryville, CA 94608 (© **800/228-8747** or 510/654-1879; www.adventure-center.com), offers slow-paced, flexible trips ranging from hiking in Tuscany to canoeing the Danube to sailing along the Turkish coast. **Above the Clouds,** P.O. Box 388, Hinesburg, VT 05461 (© **802/482-4848;** www.aboveclouds.com), and **Mountain Travel–Sobek,** 1266 66th St., Emeryville, CA 94608 (© **888/687-6235** or 510/527-8100; www.mtsobek.com), also offer European trips. In the United Kingdom, especially for skiing, walking, and trekking, try **HF Holidays,** Imperial House, Edgware Road, London NW9 5AL (© **020/8905-9556;** www.hf holidays.co.uk), and **Sherpa Expeditions** (see "Walking Tours," above). For skiing and walking holidays, try **Waymark Holidays,** 44 Windsor Rd., Slough SL1 2EJ (© **01753/516-477;** www.waymarkholidays.co.uk).

HOME EXCHANGES

Intervac U.S., 30 Corte San Fernando, Tiburon, CA 94920 (© **800/756-4663;** www.intervac.com), is part of the largest worldwide home-exchange network, with a special emphasis on Europe. It publishes five catalogs a year, listing over 11,000 homes in some 50 countries. Call for details.

Intervac also has program representatives in **Canada,** 606 Alexander Crescent NW, Calgary, Alberta T2M 4T3 (© **403/284-3747**); the **U.K.,** 24 The Causeway, Chippenham, Wiltshire SN15 3DB (© **01249/461-101**); **Ireland,** Philipstown, Ballymakenny Road, Drogheda, Co. Louth (© **041/983-0930**); **Australia,** 2/55 Kareela Rd., 2090 Cremorne Point NSW 2090 (© **02/8969-6236**); and **New Zealand,** 54 McKinley Crescent, Wellington 6002 (© **049/344-258**).

EDUCATIONAL TRAVEL

The best—and one of the most expensive—of the escorted cultural tour operators is brainy **Smithsonian Journeys,** P.O. Box 23293, Washington, DC 20026-3293 (© 877/ 338-8687 or 202/357-4700; www. smithsonianjourneys.org). Also contact **your alma mater or local university** to see if they offer summer tours open to the public and guided by a professor specialist.

The **National Registration Center for Studies Abroad,** P.O. Box 1393, Milwaukee, WI 53201 (© 414/ 278-7410; www.nrcsa.com), and the **American Institute for Foreign Study,** River Plaza, 9 W. Broad St., Stamford, CT 06902-3788 (© 800/ 727-2437; www.aifs.com), can help you arrange study programs and summer programs abroad. The biggest organization dealing with higher education around the world— and administrator of the Fulbright program—is the **Institute of International Education,** 809 United Nations Plaza, New York, NY 10017-3580 (© 212/883-8200, or 800/445-0443 to order publications; www.iie.org). A clearinghouse for information on European-based language schools is **Lingua Service Worldwide,** 75 Prospect St., Suite 4, Huntington, NY 11743 (© 800/ 394-LEARN or 631/424-0777; www. itctravel.com).

CULINARY SCHOOLS

Cuisine International, P.O. Box 25228, Dallas, TX 75225 (© 214/ 373-1161; www.cuisineinternational. com), brings together some of the top independent cooking schools and teachers based in Italy, France, Portugal, Greece, and England. Following are other cooking schools worth checking out.

IN ITALY

- **Divina Cucina,** Via Taddea 31, 50123 Florence, Italy (© 925/ 939-6346 in the U.S., 055-292-578 in Italy; www.divina cucina.com).
- **Lorenza de' Medici's Cooking School,** contact Louise Owens, 3128 Purdue, Dallas, TX 75225 (© 214/739-2846 in the U.S., 0577/744-832 in Italy; www. colitbuono.com).
- **Giuliano Bugialli,** 252 Seventh Ave., no. 7R, New York, NY 10001 (© 646/638-1099; www. bugialli.com).

IN FRANCE

- **Le Cordon Bleu,** rue Léon-Delhomme 8, 75015 Paris; or 40 Enterprise Ave., Secaucus, NJ 07094 (© 800/457-2433 in the U.S. or Canada, 33/01-53-68-22-50 elsewhere; www.cordon bleu.net).
- **Les Saveurs de Provence,** La Lumière, 26170 Merindol-les-Oliviers, Drôme Provençal, France (© 04/75-28-78-12 in France; www.ifrance.com/saveurs).

3

Amsterdam & Environs

by George McDonald

Amsterdam has never entirely shed its twofold reputation as a hippie haven and a tulips-and-windmills landmark, even with an economy that has moved far beyond these clichés. Powered more by business than by the combustion of semi-legal exotic plants, prosperity has settled like a North Sea mist around the graceful cityscape of canals and 17th-century town houses. The historic center recalls Amsterdam's Golden Age as the command post of a vast trading network and colonial empire, when wealthy merchants constructed gabled residences along neatly laid-out canals.

A delicious irony is that the placid old structures also host brothels, smoke shops, and some extravagant nightlife. The city's inhabitants, proud of their live-and-let-live attitude, which is based on pragmatism as much as a long history of tolerance, have decided to control what they cannot effectively outlaw. They permit licensed prostitution in the Red Light District and the sale of hashish and marijuana in designated "coffee shops."

But don't think Amsterdammers drift around town in a drug-induced haze. They are too busy whizzing around on bikes, jogging through Vondelpark, feasting on arrays of ethnic dishes, or simply watching the parade of street life from sidewalk cafes. A new generation of entrepreneurs has revitalized old neighborhoods like the Jordaan, turning some of the distinctive houses into offbeat stores and bustling cafes, hotels, and restaurants.

Between dips into Amsterdam's artistic and historical treasures as well as all its other pleasures, be sure to take time out to absorb the freewheeling spirit of Europe's most vibrant city.

For more on Amsterdam and its environs, see *Frommer's Amsterdam; Frommer's Portable Amsterdam; Frommer's Irreverent Guide to Amsterdam;* or *Frommer's Belgium, Holland & Luxembourg.*

1 Essentials

ARRIVING

BY PLANE If you fly into Amsterdam, you arrive at the efficient, single-terminal **Amsterdam Airport Schiphol** (© **0900/0141** for flight information; www.schiphol.nl), 13km (8 miles) southwest of the center city. You exit from Customs into Schiphol Plaza, a combined arrivals hall and mall, with currency exchange offices, ATMs, bars, restaurants, and shops. You can get questions answered and make hotel reservations at the **Holland Tourist Information** desk, open daily 7am to 10pm.

A **train** from Schiphol Station, a floor below Schiphol Plaza, connects the airport with Amsterdam's Centraal Station. The fare is 2.95€ ($3.40) one-way

Value Budget Bests

Amsterdam's best deal by far is a simple stroll along the shady canals, where you can admire their bridges and 17th-century houses. Few cities have so many buildings of this vintage still standing. While strolling, you're likely to see many street performers, from marionettes to five-piece rock bands. Their entertainment costs as much as you wish to toss into the hat. Here are some other things to do or see for free:

- View 15 paintings from the 17th century of the Amsterdam Civic Guards in the **Schuttersgalerij,** a covered passage between the Begijn-hof (free admission) and the Amsterdams Historisch Museum.
- Judge horseflesh at the **Hollandsche Manège (Dutch Stables),** Von-delstraat 140, built in 1882 and inspired by the Spanish Riding School in Vienna.
- Breathe scented air in the **Rijksmuseum Garden** and view interesting sculptural elements and other fragments of old buildings "stored" there.
- Cross the bridge over Reguliersgracht at Herengracht and take in a photogenic view of no fewer than 15 bridges, saving yourself the cost of a canal-boat tour, on which this is one of the primary sights.
- Visit the "floating" **Flower Market** on Singel, which doesn't really float, exactly, but has been there since 1862.
- Check the level of the sea at the **Normaal Amsterdams Peil (Normal Amsterdam Level),** a bronze plaque set in the passage between the Muziektheater and the Stadhuis on Waterlooplein. This sets the standard for Europe's altitude measurements. Beside it are three glass columns filled with water—the first two show the current sea level at Vlissingen and IJmuiden, and the third, 5m (16 ft.) above your head, the high-water mark during the disastrous 1953 floods in Zeeland.
- Hear the **lunchtime rehearsal concerts** (12:30–1pm) at the Muziektheater (Tues) and the Concertgebouw (Wed) every week October to June.
- Listen to the tinkling chimes of four **17th-century carillons** in concert: Westertoren (Tues noon–1pm), Zuidertoren (Thurs noon–1pm), Munttoren (Fri noon–1pm), and Oude Kerkstoren (Sat 4–5pm).

and the trip takes 20 minutes. The train's frequency ranges from six trains an hour at peak times to one an hour at night.

The **Connexxion Hotel Bus** (☎ **0900/9292**) shuttles between the airport and the city center on a circular route directly connecting 16 top hotels that are close to many others. A bus leaves from in front of Schiphol Plaza every 20 minutes from 7am to 5pm, every 30 minutes from 5 to 7pm, and every hour from 7 to 9pm. The fare is 8.50€ to 11€ ($10–$12) one-way. **Bus** no. 197 connects the airport and the city center every half-hour and costs 3.40€ ($3.90) one-way. A **taxi** from the airport to the city center is around 45€ ($52).

Amsterdam Deals & Discounts

SPECIAL DISCOUNTS   One of the best discounts in town is the **Amsterdam Pass**, available at VVV tourist offices for 31€ ($36) for 1 day, 41€ ($47) for 2 days, and 51€ ($59) for 3 days. It provides up to 150€ ($125) in savings, offering free or discounted admission to 38 museums and attractions (including the Rijksmuseum, Rembrandthuis, and Oude Kerk), a free canal cruise, and discounts on selected restaurants and stores. A free 1-, 2-, or 3-day transport ticket is included.

If you're under 26 and not necessarily a student, you can buy a **Cultureel Jongeren Pas (CJP; Cultural Youth Passport)** entitling you to free admission to many of the city's museums and to discounts on theater performances, concerts, and other events. It costs only 13€ ($14) and is good for a year. You can get a CJP at the VVV tourist offices. Bring your passport and a passport-size photo of yourself.

WORTH A SPLURGE   You don't need to dress like a toff to go to the opera, ballet, or a classical music concert in Amsterdam (though you can if you want to). Some tickets for the **Muziektheater** and the **Concertgebouw** are eminently affordable, even for visitors whose financial assets consist of little more than a discount coupon for McDonald's. And the resident Netherlands Opera, Netherlands Ballet, and Royal Concertgebouw Orchestra are well worth a bit of trimming and squeezing in other departments.

BY TRAIN   Whether you arrive by Thalys high-speed train from Brussels or Paris, an ordinary international train, or a train from elsewhere in the Netherlands, you'll likely find yourself deposited in the city center at **Centraal Station.** For information on trains (and other public transportation) in the Netherlands, call © **0900/9292** or visit www.9292ov.nl. For international trains, call © **0900/9296.** Right in front of the station is an array of tram and bus stops, and a Metro station (downstairs).

BY BUS   Buses from London, Paris, Brussels, and other cities, operated by **Eurolines** (© **020/560-8788;** www.eurolines.com), arrive at the bus station adjoining Amstel railway station (Metro: Amstel) in the south of the city.

BY CAR   European expressways E19, E35, E231, and E22 converge on Amsterdam from France and Belgium to the south, and from Germany to the north and east.

VISITOR INFORMATION
TOURIST OFFICES   VVV Amsterdam, Stationsplein 10 (© **0900/400-4040;** fax 020/625-2869; www.visitamsterdam.nl; tram: 1, 2, 4, 5, 6, 9, 13, 16, 17, 24, or 25), is in front of Centraal Station. The office is open daily 9am to 5pm (to 4:30pm Nov–Mar). Another office, on Platform 2 in the railway station, is open Monday to Saturday 8am to 8pm, and Sunday 8:30am to 4:30pm. Both offices provide maps, brochures, and details about the city; reserve hotels and tours; and sell theater and concert tickets. A VVV information center at Leidsplein 1 (Tram: 1, 2, 5, 6, 7, or 10) is open Monday to Saturday 9am to 8pm and Sunday 9am to 5pm.

Be sure to pick up a copy of *Amsterdam Day by Day* for 1.50€ ($1.75). This monthly magazine is full of details about art exhibits, concerts, and theater performances, and also lists bars, dance clubs, and restaurants.

For more details on cultural events and to reserve and purchase tickets for almost every venue in the city, stop by the **Amsterdam Uit Buro (AUB),** on the corner of Leidseplein and Marnixstraat (𝒞 **020/621-1211;** tram: 1, 2, 5, 6, 7, or 10), open Monday to Saturday 10am to 6pm.

WEBSITES The official website of the Netherlands Board of Tourism (**www.visitholland.com**) has useful advice for upcoming events, bicycling, and culture—and it even lets you know when the tulips bloom. Amsterdam's most comprehensive site, **www.visitamsterdam.nl**, lays out the details on sightseeing, walking routes, wining and dining, shopping for antiques, and current events. For information on many of Amsterdam's more than 40 museums, go to **www.hollandmuseums.nl**. To book a hotel online, visit **www.go-amsterdam. org**. One of the best virtual tours on the Net is **www.channels.nl**—the images are clear, you can direct your own tour, and you can chat with others about Amsterdam. Here, visitors give their impressions of restaurants, hotels, museums, and hash houses. At **www.amsterdamhotspots.nl**, they mean "hot." Here are *the* places to fill your nights, from eating and drinking to where to toke, what the top gay bars are, and where to see those famous working girls on display behind picture windows. Good restaurant info is available at **www.dinner-in-amsterdam.nl**.

CITY LAYOUT

Although Amsterdam center is small enough that residents think of it as a village, it can be confusing until you get the hang of it. A map like the handy *VVV Amsterdam Map,* available from VVV tourist offices for 3.50€ ($4.05), is essential.

When you step out of Centraal Station's main entrance, you're facing south toward the center. From here the **Old City** is laid out along five concentric semicircles of canals: **Singel, Herengracht, Keizersgracht, Prinsengracht,** and **Singelgracht** (*gracht* means "canal"). Along this necklace of man-made waterways, wealthy 17th-century merchants built their elegant homes, most of which are still standing. Within these canals are many smaller canals and connecting streets, radiating from the center.

Damrak, a busy tourist street, leads from Centraal Station to the **Dam,** once the location of the original dam on the Amstel River that gave the city its name and now a large open square on which stands the Royal Palace. To the left is the famous **Red Light District,** where government-licensed prostitutes sit in their windows, waiting for customers. A block to the right of Damrak is **Nieuwendijk** (which becomes **Kalverstraat** when it crosses the Dam), a pedestrian-only shopping street. If you follow Kalverstraat to the end, you'll be at **Muntplein** (*plein* means "square"), identified by the old Mint Tower. Cross Singel and continue in the same direction to reach **Rembrandtplein,** one of the main nightlife areas. Beyond Rembrandtplein is **Waterlooplein,** which hosts the Muziektheater and a great flea market.

At the heart of another important nightlife zone is **Leidseplein,** on Singelgracht. Leidseplein is at the end of Leidsestraat, a pedestrianized shopping street. **Museumplein,** where you find Amsterdam's three most famous museums—the Rijksmuseum, Van Gogh Museum, and Stedelijk Museum (though the Stedelijk has been temporarily rehoused near Centraal Station so its premises can be renovated and expanded)——is a short walk along Singelgracht from Leidseplein.

The **Jordaan,** a fast-developing old neighborhood now filled with inexpensive restaurants, unusual stores, and small galleries, lies between Prinsengracht, Brouwersgracht, Singelgracht, and Rozengracht. Turn right off Damrak at any point between Centraal Station and the Dam, and when you cross Prinsengracht, you're in the Jordaan.

GETTING AROUND

When looking at a map of Amsterdam, you might think the city is too large to explore on foot. This isn't true: It's possible to see almost every important sight in the Old City on a 4-hour walk.

BY TRAM, BUS & METRO Public transportation begins at around 6am and the regular service ends around midnight. After that, there are infrequent night buses. The distinctive yellow **trams** (streetcars) are the most convenient means of getting around; they're fast, cheap, and fun, and provide a great view of the sights. Of 16 tram routes in the city, 11 begin and end at Centraal Station.

An extensive **bus** net complements the trams and reaches many points the trams don't cover.

The city's four **Metro** (subway) lines don't serve most areas you'll want to visit, being used mainly to get people to and from the suburbs, but from Centraal Station you can use Metro trains to reach Nieuwmarkt and Waterlooplein, both stops in the central zone.

Maps showing the transportation net and fare zones are posted at most tram/bus shelters and all Metro stations. A detailed map is available from VVV tourist offices and the **GVB Amsterdam Tickets & Info** office (© **0900/9292**) on Stationsplein in front of Centraal Station.

Tickets & Passes You can buy tickets from drivers, conductors, ticket dispensers, the GVB Amsterdam Tickets & Info office, VVV tourist offices, and many news vendors. An *enkeltje* (single-journey ticket) is 1.60€ ($1.85) for one zone and 2.40€ ($2.75) for two zones. Tourists rarely travel outside the central zone.

A *dagkaart* (day ticket) is good for unlimited travel in all city zones for up to 9 days. A 1-day card is 6.30€ ($7.25) from the GVB Amsterdam Tickets & Info office. Also available are tickets valid for 2 and 3 days, for 10€ ($12) and 13€ ($15).

A flexible option is to buy a *strippenkaart* (strip card) that you can use throughout your stay. You can buy an 8-strip card for 6.40€ ($7) from drivers and conductors, or the more cost-effective 15-strip card for 6.40€ ($7) and 45-strip card for 19€ ($22) from the locations referred to above. Before boarding a tram or bus, determine how many zones you'll be traversing. Fold your strip card so that one more box than the number of zones is facing up, and stick this end into the yellow box near the door as you enter. The machine stamps your card. (Some trams have a conductor who stamps the card.) On buses, have the driver stamp your card. The ticket includes transfers to other tram, bus, and Metro lines within 1 hour of the time stamped.

Keep in mind that inspectors, sometimes undercover, may demand to see your ticket at any time. If you haven't paid the proper fare, you'll be fined 30€ ($35) plus the fare for the ride.

BY BIKE Follow the Dutch example and pedal. A bike is one of the best ways of getting around in this flat city where too many cars clog the narrow streets.

You'll see children barely old enough to walk, their great-grandparents, and even businesswomen in high heels pedaling through the city in any weather. Sunday, when the city is quiet, is a good day to pedal through the parks and to practice riding on cobblestones and dealing with trams before venturing into a rush-hour fray.

Warning: Watch out for unpredictable car drivers and always lock your bike and its front wheel to something fixed and solid—theft is common.

Bike-rental rates average 7€ ($8) a day or 30€ ($35) a week, with a deposit required. The following outfits are located in the center and have good rates and service: **Take a Bike,** in the basement of Centraal Station, to the right of the main entrance as you face the station (© 020/624-8391; tram: 1, 2, 4, 5, 6, 9, 13, 16, 17, 24, or 25); **Damstraat Rent-a-Bike,** Damstraat 22–24 (© 020/ 625-5029; tram: 4, 9, 14, 16, 24, or 25); **MacBike,** Mr. Visserplein 2 (© 020/ 620-0985; tram: 4, 9, or 14); **MacBike Too,** Marnixstraat 220 (© 020/626-6964; tram: 10 or 17); and **Bike City,** Bloemgracht 70 (© 020/626-3721; tram: 6, 13, 14, or 17).

BY TAXI Officially, you can't simply hail a cab, but often they'll stop if you do. You can get a taxi in front of any major hotel and at Centraal Station, the Dam, Leidseplein, Rembrandtplein, and other locations. To phone for a cab, call **Taxi Centrale** (© 020/677-7777). Fares start at 2.90€ ($3.35) and increase by 1.80€ ($2.05) per kilometer, or about 2.90€ ($3.35) per mile; waiting time is 32€ ($36) per hour.

BY BOAT The **Museumboot** (© 020/622-2181) stops near virtually all of Amsterdam's museums and attractions. The boats leave from in front of Centraal Station every 30 minutes daily from 10am to 5pm. Tickets are available at the Lovers Canal Cruises counter near the dock. A day ticket is 14€ ($16) adults, 9.50€ ($11) children ages 4 to 12, children under 4 free; after 1pm, tickets are, respectively, 13€ ($14) and 7.25€ ($8). The ticket also allows reduced admission to most of the city's museums and attractions.

For pretty much the same experience and the same price, you can also try the **Canal Bus** (© 020/623-9886), whose boats operate daily 10am to 5pm on three fixed routes—Green, Red, and Blue—that connect important museums and shopping and entertainment districts, with two buses an hour at peak times. A day pass, valid until noon the next day and including a museum admissions discount, costs 13€ ($17) for adults and 7.95€ ($9) for children under 14.

And since you're in the city of canals, you might like to splurge on a **water taxi,** which takes up to eight passengers, at 60€ ($69) for the first half-hour and

---

Native Behavior

The bicycle might have been invented with Amsterdam in mind, and it is believed that there are at least 600,000 bikes in the city. To get close to the Amsterdam experience, you positively have to get into the saddle and ride. It takes a while to get used to moving smoothly and safely through the whirl of trams, cars, buses, trucks, fellow bikers, and pedestrians, particularly if you're on a typically ancient, one-speed, much-battered *stadfiets* (city bike), also known as an *omafiets* (grandmother bike)—the only kind that makes economic sense here, since anything fancier will attract a crowd of people wanting to steal it.

Country & City Codes

The country code for the Netherlands is **31**. The **city code** for Amsterdam is **20**; use this code when you're calling from outside the Netherlands. If you're within the Netherlands but not in Amsterdam, use **020**. If you're calling within Amsterdam, simply leave off the code and dial the regular seven-digit phone number.

25€ ($29) for every subsequent half-hour. You can move faster in the boat than on land, and you'll get your very own canal cruise. Taxis are docked outside Centraal Station. Call **Watertaxi** (© 020/535-6363) for more information.

BY RENTAL CAR   Don't drive in Amsterdam. The city is a jumble of one-way streets, narrow bridges, and trams and cyclists darting every which way, along with tough measures in place to make driving as difficult as possible. No-parking zones are rigorously enforced and the limited parking spaces are expensive. Plus, car break-ins are common.

Outside the city, driving is a different story, and you may want to rent a car to see the nearby countryside. All the top international firms rent here: **Avis,** Nassaukade 380 (© 020/683-6061; tram: 1 or 6); **Budget,** Overtoom 121 (© 020/612-6066; tram: 1 or 6); **Europcar,** Overtoom 197 (© 020/683-2123; tram: 1 or 6); and **Hertz,** Overtoom 333 (© 020/201-5312; tram: 1 or 6). All of these firms also have desks at the airport. Rates begin at around 45€ ($52) per day for a small car with unlimited mileage.

Remember: You get the best deal if you arrange for the rental before leaving home. For more options, see the "Getting Around Without Going Broke" section of chapter 1, beginning on p. 21.

FAST FACTS: Amsterdam

American Express   The office at Damrak 66, 1012 LM Amsterdam (© 020/504-8780; tram: 4, 9, 16, 24, or 25), close to Centraal Station, is open Monday to Friday 9am to 5pm; Saturday 9am to noon.

Business Hours   **Banks** are open Monday to Friday 9am to 4 or 5pm, and some until 7pm on Thursday. Open hours for **offices** are Monday to Friday 9 or 10am to 4 or 5pm. Regular **shopping** hours are Monday 10 or 11am to 6pm; Tuesday, Wednesday, and Friday 9am to 6pm; Thursday 9am to 9pm; Saturday 9am to 5pm; some stores are open Sunday noon to 5pm.

Currency   In 2002, The Netherlands adopted the **euro** (€) for its currency. At press time, $1 = .87€, or 1€ = $1.15.

Currency Exchange   Change your money at **banks** or **VVV tourist offices.** Hotels and *bureaux de change* (currency-exchange offices), open regular hours plus evenings and weekends, charge a low commission (or none at all) but give a low rate. If you carry American Express traveler's checks, you may exchange them at an **American Express** office (see above), where there's no commission charge. Other fair-dealing options are the **GWK exchange** at Centraal Station, and **Thomas Cook,** Damrak 125 (© 020/620-3236; tram: 4, 9, 16, 24, or 25).

Two conveniently located branches of **ABN-AMRO Bank,** both with ATMs, are Rokin 82 ((© **020/624-2590;** tram: 4, 9, 14, 16, 24, or 25) and Rokin 16 ((© **020/520-6666;** tram: 4, 9, 14, 16, 24, or 25), though if you're just looking for an ATM, you shouldn't have a problem finding one: They're everywhere.

Dentists & Doctors For 24-hour doctor and dentist referrals, contact the **Central Medical Service** ((© **020/592-3434**).

Drugstores & Pharmacies For both prescription and non-prescription medicines, go to an *apotheek* (pharmacy). Regular pharmacy hours are Monday to Saturday 9am to 5:30pm. Try **Dam Apotheek,** Damstraat 2 ((© **020/624-4331;** tram: 4, 9, 14, 16, 24, or 25). All pharmacies post locations of nearby all-night and Sunday pharmacies on their doors.

Embassies & Consulates **U.S. Consulate:** Museumplein 19 ((© **020/575-5309;** tram: 3, 5, 12, or 16), open Monday to Friday 8:30am to noon and 1:30 to 3:30pm; **U.K. Consulate-General:** Koningslaan 44 ((© **020/676-4343;** tram: 2), open Monday to Friday 9am to noon and 2 to 4pm. Australia, Canada, Ireland, and New Zealand do not have consulates in Amsterdam.

Embassies are in The Hague (Den Haag): **U.S.:** Lange Voorhout 102 ((© **070/310-9209**); **Canada:** Sophialaan 7 ((© **070/311-1600**); **U.K.:** Lange Voorhout 10 ((© **070/427-0427**); **Ireland:** Dr. Kuyperstraat 9 ((© **070/363-0993**); **Australia:** Carnegielaan 4 ((© **070/310-8200**); **New Zealand:** Carnegielaan 10 ((© **070/346-9324**).

Emergencies For police assistance, an ambulance, or the fire department, call (© **112.** This is a free call.

Holidays January 1 (New Year's Day); Good Friday; Easter Monday; April 30 (Queen's Day/Koninginnedag); Ascension Day; Pentecost Monday; December 25 (Christmas) and 26. Easter, Ascension, and Pentecost change each year. In 2005, the dates are Good Friday, March 25; Easter Monday, March 28; Ascension, May 5; Pentecost Monday, May 16.

Hospitals Two hospitals with a first-aid department (emergency room) are **Onze-Lieve-Vrouwe Gasthuis,** Eerste Oosterparkstraat 179 ((© **020/599-9111;** tram: 3, 6, or 10), and the **Academisch Medisch Centrum (AMC),** Meibergdreef 9 ((© **020/566-3333;** Metro: Holendrecht).

Internet Access In the center, the two Internet cafes of **easyEverything** are at Damrak 33 ((© **020/320-8082;** tram: 4, 9, 16, 17, 24, or 25), open daily 7:30am to 11pm, and Reguliersbreestraat 22 ((© **020/320-6291;** tram: 4, 9, or 14), open 24 hours a day. Access begins at 1.50€ ($1.75) an hour.

A less crowded choice is **The Internet Café,** Martelaarsgracht 11 ((© **020/627-1052;** info@internetcafe.nl; tram: 1, 2, 5, 6, 13, or 17), open Sunday to Thursday 9am to 1am, Friday to Saturday 9am to 3am; access is 2.75€ ($3.15) an hour.

Laundry & Dry Cleaning Most *wasserettes* (self-serve laundries) are open daily 7 or 8am to 9 or 10pm. Central locations include Oudebrugsgracht 22 (tram: 4, 9, 14, 16, 24, or 25), between Damrak and Nieuwendijk; Ferdinand Bolstraat 9 (tram: 16, 24, or 25), near the Heineken brewery; and Rozengracht 59 (tram: 6, 13, 14, or 17), on the edge of the Jordaan. A wash usually costs about 5€ ($5.75) and a dry about .50€ (60¢) for 10 minutes. You can get dry cleaning done at **Palthé**, Vijzelstraat 59 (*②* **020/ 623-0337**; tram: 16, 24, or 25), just south of Muntplein, with the cost depending on the garment and how soon it's needed.

Mail Most **post offices** are open Monday to Friday 9am to 5pm. The office at Singel 256, at the corner of Raadhuisstraat (tram: 6, 13, 14, or 17), is open Monday to Friday 9am to 6pm (to 8pm Thurs); Saturday 9am to 3pm.

Postage for a postcard or letter to the United States, Canada, Australia, or New Zealand is .75€ (85¢); to Britain and Ireland it's .45€ (50¢).

Police In an emergency, call *②* **112**. This is a free call. In non-urgent situations, contact **Police Headquarters,** Elandsgracht 117 (*②* **020/559-9111**).

Safety Random violent crime is not common in Amsterdam, though it does happen. Nonviolent crimes like pickpocketing and theft from cars are common and tourists in particular are targets. Muggings are more rare, but you need to watch out in some places and circumstances, such as a stroll through the Red Light District or along a deserted canalside at night.

Taxes There's a value-added tax (BTW) of 6% on hotel and restaurant bills (19% on beer, wine, and liquor), and 6% or 19% (the amount depends on the product) on purchases. For information on how to recover some of the 19% tax rate on purchases, see "Shopping," later in this chapter.

Telephone Both local and long-distance calls from a pay phone are .30€ (35¢) a minute. International calls, per minute, cost: **U.S.** and **Canada** .30€ (35¢); **U.K.** and **Ireland** .33€ (40¢); **Australia** and **New Zealand** .40€ (45¢). You can use pay phones in booths all around town with a KPN *telekaart* (phone card), selling for 5€ ($6), 13€ ($15), and 25€ ($29) from post offices, train ticket counters, and newsstands. Some pay phones take coins of .10€, .20€, .50€, and 1€. For information inside the Netherlands, call *②* **0900/8008;** for international information, call *②* **0900/8418.**

To charge a call to your calling card, dial **AT&T** (*②* 0800/022-9111); **MCI** (*②* 0800/022-9122); **Sprint** (*②* 0800/022-9119); **Canada Direct** (*②* 0800/ 022-9116); or **British Telecom** (*②* 0800/022-9944).

Tipping A 15% service charge is included in the price of meals at almost all restaurants (if it isn't, it will generally say so on the menu), so it's not necessary to leave a tip. But waitstaff do appreciate tips and if the service was good, you might want to leave a small tip by rounding up in cash, not on a credit card slip, to the nearest euro or the nearest 5€, depending on the price of the meal. (In an expensive restaurant you might feel obliged to go to the nearest 10€.) Taxi fares are high and include a service charge, and though drivers appreciate a tip, it's not really necessary to give one unless you have a reason for doing so.

2 Affordable Places to Stay

There was a time when canal-house hotels were quite cheap, but most of them have now raised their rates beyond the budget range. They make a great splurge choice, but even if you don't stay in a canal house, you'll most likely stay in a building built 250 to 350 years ago during Amsterdam's Golden Age.

In most cases, a Dutch breakfast is included in the room rate. It usually includes ham, cheese, a boiled egg, several types of bread, butter, milk, and sometimes chocolate sprinkles, which are very popular.

Booking ahead is always advised. The Dutch hotel industry runs a free hotel-booking service, the **Netherlands Reservation Center,** P.O. Box 404, 2260 AK Leidschendam (© **070/419-5500;** fax 070/419-5519; www.hotelres.nl). If you arrive in Amsterdam without a reservation, consult the **VVV tourist offices** (see "Visitor Information" on p. 63) or contact the VVV's **Amsterdam Reservation Center** (© **0777/000-888;** reservations@amsterdamtourist.nl). If you plan to stay in a hostel or student hotel in summer, look for a room early in the day—by late afternoon, hostels are usually full.

Note: You'll find the lodging choices below plotted on the map on p. 82.

AROUND CENTRAAL STATION & THE DAM

Amstel Botel ⚓   Amsterdam's only floating hotel has become quite popular, largely because of its location, seemingly adventurous nature, and rates. The rooms, on four decks of a moored boat, are connected by an elevator, are furnished in no-nonsense but comfortable modern style, and come with small showers. To get here, turn left from Centraal Station, passing the bike rental—the "botel" is painted white and is directly in front of you. Be sure to ask for a room with a view on the water side, not on the uninspiring quay side.

Oosterdokskade 2–4 (beside Centraal Station), 1011 AE Amsterdam. © 020/626-4247. Fax 020/639-1952. www.amstelbotel.com. 176 units. 87€–92€ ($100–$106) single or double; 117€–122€ ($135–$140) triple. Buffet breakfast 10€ ($12). AE, DC, MC, V. Limited parking on quay. Tram: 1, 2, 4, 5, 6, 9, 13, 16, 17, 24, or 25 to Centraal Station. **Amenities:** Lounge; concierge; dry cleaning. *In room:* TV w/pay movies, safe.

De Westertoren   This is the best of the hotels on this block near the Anne Frankhuis. The two rooms with balconies in the front are attractive but tend to be a bit noisy; the quieter rooms in back are large and bright. Full breakfast is served in the rooms, and proprietors Tony and Chris van der Veen are happy to share a wealth of information about the city.

Raadhuisstraat 35B (near Westermarkt), 1016 DC Amsterdam. ©/fax 020/624-4639. www.hotelwestertoren.nl. 8 units, 4 with bathroom. 55€ ($63) single with shower only; 70€–80€ ($81–$92) double with shower only, 90€ ($104) double with bathroom; 110€ ($127) triple with shower only, 125€ ($144) triple with bathroom; 140€ ($161) quad; 140€–205€ ($161–$236) family room for up to 6 people. Rates include continental breakfast. AE, DC, MC, V. Limited street parking. Tram: 6, 13, 14, or 17 to Westermarkt. *In room:* TV, coffeemaker.

Pax   Most rooms at the Pax, near the Anne Frankhuis, are large, and all are simply furnished and clean; two have small balconies overlooking the street. Room no. 19, with four beds and plenty of space, is particularly well suited to students or young people traveling together. There's no elevator.

Raadhuisstraat 37B (near Westermarkt), 1016 DC Amsterdam. ©/fax 020/624-9735. 8 units, none with bathroom. 29€–45€ ($33–$52) single; 36€–70€ ($41–$81) double. AE, MC, V. Limited street parking. Tram: 6, 13, 14, or 17 to Westermarkt. *In room:* TV.

 ⁀*Tips* **Booking a Room in a B&B**

B&B accommodations are available by contacting **Bed & Breakfast Holland,** Theophile de Bockstraat 3, 1058 TV Amsterdam (© **020/615-7527;** fax 020/669-1573). Rates per person range from 18€ to 35€ ($21–$40), depending on amenities and location. There's a 2-night minimum stay.

> **Value Getting the Best Deal on Accommodations**
>
> - Stick to hotels recommended by the VVV Amsterdam tourist office. Politely decline the offers of young men and women in the railway stations who want to take you to a hotel.
> - Be aware that hotels near the Jordaan and Leidseplein make good deals.
> - Take advantage of discounts often offered in winter. Even if the rates haven't been lowered, it's often possible to get a few euros off the quoted price.
> - Note that advance reservations are extremely important in summer, when Amsterdam is the youth vacation capital of Europe.
> - Consider taking a room without a private bathroom. Hallway showers and toilets are usually well maintained, and the price reduction is substantial.

ALONG THE CANAL BELT

Adolesce   Quilts and parrots are the themes here. You find live parrots in the lobby, parrot prints decorating the rooms and halls, and old quilts displayed throughout. Rooms are outfitted with new furnishings. The breakfast room includes a small bar, a patio garden, and a TV lounge. This six-story building has steep stairs and no elevator, but a few rooms are on the ground floor, including two off the back patio.

Nieuwe Keizersgracht 26 (at the Amstel River), 1018 DS Amsterdam. ✆ 020/626-3959. Fax 020/627-4249. www.adolesce.nl. 10 units. 65€ ($75) single; 85€–100€ ($98–$115) double; 115€ ($132) triple. MC, V. Limited street parking. Tram: 9 or 14 to Waterlooplein. **Amenities:** Bar/lounge.

Agora ⭐   Two 1735 houses have been fully restored to create this fine hotel, steps from the floating flower market. Rooms are attractively furnished with new beds and a few antiques. The large family room has three windows overlooking the Singel Canal. Although this communal room and guest rooms at the front are exposed by day to the hustle and bustle of a busy street, the canal view makes it worth it. The hotel is efficiently run and well maintained by friendly Yvo Muthert and Els Bruijnse. There is no elevator.

Singel 462 (at the Flower Market), 1017 AW Amsterdam. ✆ 020/627-2200. Fax 020/627-2202. www. hotelagora.nl. 16 units, 13 with bathroom. 65€ ($75) single without bathroom, 100€ ($115) single with bathroom; 115€ ($132) double without bathroom, 140€ ($161) double with bathroom. Rates include continental breakfast. AE, DC, MC, V. Limited street parking. Tram: 1, 2, or 5 to Koningsplein. *In room:* TV, hair dryer.

Keizershof ⭐   This hotel, in a large old canal house, is run by the genial Mrs. de Vries, and her son Ernest and daughter Hanneke. Rooms are named after movie stars, the ceilings of most rooms have exposed beams, and several other special touches make a stay here memorable. To reach the upper floors, you must climb a wooden spiral staircase built from a ship's mast. A Dutch breakfast is served.

Keizersgracht 618 (at Nieuwe Spiegelstraat), 1017 ER Amsterdam. ✆ 020/622-2855. Fax 020/624-8412. www.hotelkeizershof.nl. 6 units, 2 with shower only, 2 with bathroom. 50€ ($58) single without bathroom; 65€ ($75) double without bathroom, 75€ ($86) double with shower only, 90€–92€ ($104–$106) double with bathroom. Rates include Dutch breakfast. MC, V. Limited street parking. Tram: 16, 24, or 25 to Keizersgracht.

Tips **A Canal-House Warning**

Be prepared to climb hard-to-navigate stairways if you want to save money on lodging in Amsterdam. Narrow and steep as ladders, these stairways were designed to conserve space in the narrow houses along the canals. If you have difficulty climbing stairs, ask for a room on a lower floor.

Prinsenhof ☆ *Value*   One of the best deals in Amsterdam, the Prinsenhof isn't far from the Amstel River in a renovated canal house. Most of the rooms are large, with beamed ceilings and basic yet reasonably comfortable beds. The hotel has recently been redecorated, with new showers and carpets installed. Front rooms look onto Prinsengracht. A large breakfast is served. The proprietor takes pride in the hotel's quality and makes you feel at home. There's no elevator, but a pulley will haul your bags up and down the stairs.

Prinsengracht 810 (at Utrechtsestraat), 1017 JL Amsterdam. ℂ 020/623-1772. Fax 020/638-3368. www.hotelprinsenhof.com. 10 units, 4 with bathroom. 40€ ($46) single without bathroom, 75€ ($86) single with bathroom; 60€ ($69) double without bathroom, 80€ ($92) double with bathroom; 85€ ($98) triple without bathroom, 100€ ($115) triple with bathroom; 100€ ($115) quad without bathroom, 135€ ($155) quad with bathroom. Rates include continental breakfast. AE, MC, V. Limited street parking. Tram: 4 to Prinsengracht. *In room:* TV.

AROUND LEIDSEPLEIN

Impala   Around the corner from Leidseplein, the Impala is at the junction of two canals. The singles and doubles are small but the triples and quads large, and one is particularly popular for its bay window overlooking the canals. Breakfast is served in a large room with an unusual modern wall tapestry. The hotel has always been under the same family management.

Leidsekade 77 (off Leidseplein), 1017 PM Amsterdam. ℂ 020/623-4706. Fax 020/638-9274. 16 units, 7 with bathroom. 35€ ($40) single without bathroom, 45€ ($52) single with bathroom; 55€ ($63) double without bathroom, 65€ ($75) double with bathroom; 75€ ($86) triple without bathroom, 80€ ($92) triple with bathroom; 90€ ($104) quad without bathroom, 95€ ($109) quad with bathroom; 105€ ($121) quint without bathroom, 110€ ($127) quint with bathroom. Rates include continental breakfast. MC, V. Tram: 1, 2, 5, 6, 7, or 10 to Leidseplein. **Amenities:** Lounge.

Stayokay Amsterdam Vondelpark ☆   "The new generation of city hostel" is how the Dutch youth hostel organization describes their flagship establishment on the edge of Vondelpark facing Leidseplein. The core is a former Girl's Housekeeping School. Rooms are simply but modernly furnished, and the four- and six-bed rooms are ideal for families or groups of friends. Some rooms are adapted for travelers with disabilities. The hostel is open 24 hours, and all guests have key cards. The Backpacker's Lounge is a great place to meet fellow travelers.

Zandpad 5 (in Vondelpark), 1054 GA Amsterdam. ℂ 020/589-8999. Fax 020/589-8955. www. stayokay.com/vondelpark. 105 units. 65€–77€ ($75–$89) double; 104€–112€ ($97–$129) quad; 138€–150€ ($159–$173) 6-bed room; 184€–200€ ($212–$230) 8-bed room; 21€ ($24) bed in 10- to 20-bed dormitory. 2.50€ ($2.90) discount for IYHF members. Rates include Dutch breakfast. AE, MC, V. No parking. Tram: 1, 2, 5, 6, 7, or 10 to Leidseplein. **Amenities:** Bar/lounge; Internet access.

AROUND MUSEUMPLEIN

Euphemia   A 5-minute walk from the Rijksmuseum and Museumplein, the Euphemia, without elevator, is popular with students, young travelers, and gays. It's clean and inexpensive, with ground-floor rooms that are wheelchair accessible. There's a TV and VCR in the breakfast room; you can even rent videos. Inexpensive snacks are sold later in the day.

Fokke Simonszstraat 1–9 (off Vijzelgracht), 1017 TD Amsterdam. © 020/622-9045. Fax 020/638-9673. www.euphemiahotel.com. 30 units, 25 with bathroom. 35€ ($40) single without bathroom; 50€–90€ ($58–$104) double without bathroom, 70€–120€ ($81–$138) double with bathroom; 25€–46€ ($29–$53) per person triple or quad with bathroom. Continental breakfast 5€ ($6). AE, DC, MC, V. Limited street parking. Tram: 16, 24, or 25 to Weteringcircuit. *In room:* TV (some units).

Museumzicht This hotel is ideal for museumgoers. Located behind the Rijksmuseum, it occupies the top floors of a Victorian house (no elevator). The breakfast room commands an excellent view of the museum with its numerous stained-glass windows. Robin de Jong, the proprietor, has filled the rooms with an eclectic furniture collection, from 1930s English wicker to 1950s pieces.

Jan Luykenstraat 22 (near the Rijksmuseum), 1071 CN Amsterdam. © 020/671-2954. Fax 020/671-3597. hotelmuseumzicht@planet.nl. 14 units, 3 with bathroom. 45€ ($52) single without bathroom; 70€ ($81) double without bathroom, 95€ ($109) double with bathroom. Rates include continental breakfast. AE, DC, MC, V. Limited street parking. Tram: 2 or 5 to Hobbemastraat.

P.C. Hooft ★ Imagine staying on Amsterdam's most upscale shopping street, amid chic boutiques and classy restaurants, for no more than you'd pay in any other budget hotel in town. That's what you get at the P.C. Hooft, even though you have to climb quite a few stairs to enjoy your stay. Most rooms have been updated, and some have full bathrooms. The breakfast room, guaranteed to wake you up, is painted wild shades of orange and blue.

Pieter Cornelisz Hooftstraat 63 (near the Van Gogh Museum), 1071 BN Amsterdam. © 020/662-7107. Fax 020/675-8961. www.pchoofthotel.nl. 16 units, 3 with bathroom. 30€–35€ ($35–$40) single without bathroom, 45€ ($52) single with bathroom; 50€–55€ ($58–$63) double without bathroom, 65€ ($75) double with bathroom; 85€ ($98) triple; 105€ ($121) quad. Rates include continental breakfast. MC, V. Limited street parking. Tram: 2 or 5 to Hobbemastraat. **Amenities:** Lounge. *In room:* TV.

Wynnobel Around the corner from the chic boutiques of Pieter Cornelisz Hooftstraat, the Wynnobel is a few minutes' walk from the Rijksmuseum. It overlooks part of Vondelpark and is run by friendly Pierre Wynnobel and his wife, who sees to it the hotel is kept clean. If you can convince Mr. Wynnobel to play the piano in the lobby, you have an added treat. The large rooms, some of which are equipped as triples and quads, are furnished with vintage or antique furniture, and a large breakfast is served in your room.

Vossiusstraat 9 (off Eerste Constantijn Huygensstraat), 1071 AB Amsterdam. © 020/662-2298. 12 units, none with bathroom. 25€–35€ ($29–$40) single; 50€–70€ ($58–$81) double; 90€–110€ ($104–$127) triple; 100€–120€ ($115–$138) quad. Rates include continental breakfast. No credit cards. Limited street parking. Tram: 2 or 5 to Hobbemastraat. **Amenities:** Lounge.

IN THE JORDAAN

Acacia ★ The young owners, Hans and Marlene van Vliet, are justifiably proud of their hotel in an unusual triangular corner building, without elevator, facing a picturesque canal in the Jordaan. Rooms are furnished with modern beds, new carpets, and desks. The large front-corner rooms sleep as many as five and have windows on three sides. There are also a couple of studios with tiny kitchenettes, plus two houseboats (moored in the canal across the street) that add an authentic local touch. On the ground floor is a cozy Old Dutch breakfast room.

Lindengracht 251 (off Prinsengracht and Brouwersgracht), 1015 KH Amsterdam. © 020/622-1460. Fax 020/638-0748. www.hotelacacia.nl. 18 units, including houseboats. 65€ ($75) single; 80€–90€ ($92–$104) double; 99€ ($114) triple; 95€–110€ ($109–$127) houseboat double. Rates include continental breakfast. MC, V. Limited street parking. Tram: 3 or 10 to Marnixplein. *In room:* TV.

Van Onna Consisting of three canal houses, this hotel has grown over the years, but genial owner Loek van Onna continues to keep his prices reasonable. Mr. van Onna has lived here since he was a boy and will gladly tell you about the building's history. Accommodations vary considerably, with the best rooms in the newest building. However, the oldest and simplest rooms have a great deal of charm. Whichever building you stay in, ask for a room in front overlooking the canal.

Bloemgracht 102–104 and 108 (off Prinsengracht), 1015 TN Amsterdam. ℂ 020/626-5801. 41 units. 40€ ($46) single; 80€ ($92) double; 120€ ($138) triple; 160€ ($184) quad. Rates include continental breakfast. No credit cards. Limited street parking. Tram: 6, 13, 14, or 17 to Westermarkt.

IN DE PIJP

Van Ostade Bicycle Hotel ⭐ The young owners cater to visitors who want to explore Amsterdam on bikes, and they are helpful in planning biking routes through and around the city. You can rent bikes here for only 5€ ($5.75) daily, no deposit. Rooms have been recently renovated and have plain but comfortable modern furnishings; some have kitchenettes and small balconies, and there are large rooms for families. The hotel, which has no elevator, is a few blocks from the popular Albert Cuyp street market, in the somewhat raggedy De Pijp neighborhood.

Van Ostadestraat 123 (off Ferdinand Bolstraat), 1072 SV Amsterdam. ℂ 020/679-3452. Fax 020/671-5213. www.bicyclehotel.com. 16 units, 8 with bathroom. 60€–65€ ($69–$75) double without bathroom, 70€–99€ ($81–$114) double with bathroom; 95€ ($109) triple without bathroom, 115€ ($132) triple with bathroom. Rates include continental breakfast. AE, MC, V. Parking 17€ ($20). Tram: 3, 12, or 25 to Ceintuurbaan-Ferdinand Bolstraat. **Amenities:** Bike rental. *In room:* TV.

WORTH A SPLURGE

De Filosoof ⭐⭐ On a quiet street of brick houses near Vondelpark, this extraordinary, elegant hotel should at least make you think. One of the owners, a philosophy professor, has decorated rooms with posters, framed quotes, and unusual objects chosen to represent philosophical and cultural themes. Ponder the meaning of life in rooms dedicated to thinkers such as Goethe, Nietzsche, or Marx, or to motifs like Eros, the Renaissance, or astrology. You can even consult your private bookshelf of philosophical works or join in a weekly philosophical debate. The rooms in an annex across the street are larger; some open onto a private terrace.

Anna van den Vondelstraat 4–6 (at Vondelpark), 1054 GZ Amsterdam. ℂ 020/683-3013. Fax 020/685-3750. www.hotelfilosoof.nl. 38 units. 100€–115€ ($115–$132) single; 115€–138€ ($132–$159) double; 160€–170€ ($184–$196) triple; 185€–195€ ($213–$224) quad. Rates include buffet breakfast. AE, MC, V. Limited street parking. Tram: 1 or 6 to Jan Pieter Heijestraat. **Amenities:** Lounge. *In room:* TV.

Seven Bridges ⭐⭐ If you're going to splurge, this is a fine place to do so. Each huge room is unique, with antique furnishings, plush carpets, and reproductions of modern art; one room even has a bathroom with a skylight and wooden walls similar to those in a sauna. Decor includes handmade Italian drapes, hand-painted tiles, and wood-tiled floors. Some attic rooms have sloped ceilings and exposed beams. There's no elevator. The front rooms overlook a small canal, and the rear rooms overlook a garden. Proprietors Pierre Keulers and Gunter Glaner are extremely helpful.

Reguliersgracht 31 (2 blocks from Rembrandtplein), 1017 LK Amsterdam. ℂ 020/623-1329. 8 units. 100€–170€ ($115–$196) single; 120€–200€ ($138–$230) double. Rates include continental breakfast. AE, MC, V. Limited street parking. Tram: 4 to Keizersgracht. *In room:* TV, hair dryer.

3 Great Deals on Dining

As a trading and gateway city that positively revels in its status as a melting pot, Amsterdam has absorbed culinary influences from far and wide, making it easy to find dozens of ethnic eateries serving everything from Argentine to Yugoslavian food. Indonesian food is extremely popular, notably the *rijsttafel* (see the "Spice of Life" box below). Many of these ethnic places serve hearty and delicious meals at very reasonable prices. And there are plenty of traditional Dutch restaurants as well.

Amsterdam's favorite lunch is the *broodje,* a small sandwich made with a soft roll or French bread and filled with meat or fish. You find these inexpensive tasty sandwiches at sandwich counters and street stands all over. An especially popular street food is *broodje haring,* raw herring and chopped onions in a soft bun for around 2.75€ ($3.15). The traditional method for eating herring is to tip your head back and lower the fish headfirst (well, where the head would be if it hadn't already been cut off) into your mouth. Another traditional Dutch lunch is an *uitsmijter* (pronounced *out*-smayter; the name means "bouncer"): two pieces of toast topped with ham or cheese and two fried eggs, often served with a small salad.

In general, with the exception of late-night restaurants, kitchens in Amsterdam take their last dinner orders at 10 or 11pm. Restaurants with outside terraces are always in big demand on pleasant summer evenings, and few take reservations. One way to combat escalating dinner tabs is to take advantage of the low-cost *dagschotel* (plate of the day) many restaurants serve. Two great areas for discovering new restaurants are around **Leidseplein** and in the **Jordaan.**

AROUND CENTRAAL STATION

Kam Yin *(Value* SURINAMESE/CHINESE   The neon-and-tile interior might remind you of the waiting room in a bus station, but this restaurant is extremely popular with budget-conscious Amsterdammers. The constant turnover keeps the cooks busy all day, ensuring your meal is freshly prepared. Heaping mounds of rice and noodles are topped with fish, meat, or vegetables blending Chinese, Indonesian, and South American flavors. Try the *moksi meti,* a hearty plate of mixed meats with noodles or rice as a main meal, or inexpensive *broodjes* (sandwiches) as a snack.

Warmoesstraat 6 (off Damrak). ℭ **020/625-3115.** Main courses 3.95€–6.95€ ($4.55–$8); fixed-price menus 5.95€–8.95€ ($7–$10). No credit cards. Daily noon–midnight. Tram: 1, 2, 4, 5, 6, 9, 13, 16, 17, 24, or 25 to Centraal Station.

Moments Spice of Life

Even if you're on a tight budget, try to have at least one **Indonesian** *rijsttafel.* This traditional "rice table" banquet of as many as 20 succulent and spicy foods served in tiny bowls usually costs between 18€ and 30€ ($21–$35). Pick and choose from among the bowls and add your choices to the pile of rice on your plate. It's almost impossible to eat all the food set on your table, but give it a shot—it's delicious and a true taste of multicultural Amsterdam. For an abbreviated version served on one plate, try *nasi rames.* At lunch, the standard Indonesian fare is *nasi goreng* (fried rice with meat and vegetables) or *bami goreng* (fried noodles prepared the same way).

> ### ⌒Value Getting the Best Deal on Dining
>
> • Take advantage of the *dagschotel* (plate of the day) and the *dag-menu* (menu of the day) for good food at bargain rates.
> • Look for fixed-price or tourist menus—the selection of dishes is limited, but you can eat at restaurants normally out of your price range.
> • For lunch, try those Dutch favorites, *broodjes* and *uitsmijters,* both tasty and inexpensive.
> • Sample Dutch cheese—it's wonderful and makes an ideal picnic food.
> • For a filling, hot, vegetarian snack, try a falafel from one of the Israeli and Lebanese snack bars around Leidseplein and Rembrandtplein.
> • Note that a Dutch-style cone of hot fries with mayo can be a filling and inexpensive snack—not to mention delicious.

Moeder's Pot DUTCH   This restaurant is small, but the meals it serves are huge. The steak dinner is a justifiable favorite and is typical of the unambitious but tasty food served here. The daily specials are a particularly good deal. Moeder's Pot, managed since 1970 by the friendly Mr. Cor, is a popular neighborhood hangout, though smoke will get in your eyes and up your nose in the small dining room. Nevertheless, you'll find it especially convenient if you're staying at the Hotel Acacia (p. 73).

Vinkenstraat 119 (near Haarlemmerplein). ⓒ 020/623-7643. Main courses 4.75€–11€ ($5–$12). No credit cards. Mon–Fri 5–10pm; Sat 5–9:30pm. Tram: 3 to Haarlemmerplein.

ALONG THE CANAL BELT
Pancake Bakery 𝕱 (Kids) PANCAKES   Located in a 17th-century canal warehouse, this two-story restaurant with winding staircases and exposed beams serves some of the most delicious and unusual pancakes you'll ever taste. There are several dozen varieties, almost all of which are a full meal. Choices include salami and cheese, cheese and ginger, honey nuts and whipped cream, and ice cream and *advokaat* (a Dutch eggnoglike cocktail). One of the best sellers is the "American" pancake: with fried chicken, sweet corn, peppers, carrots, Cajun sauce, and salad. You'll have a fine view of the canal from the upper-floor windows. In summer, a few tables are placed in front overlooking the canal.

Prinsengracht 191 (near the Anne Frankhuis). ⓒ 020/625-1333. www.pancake.nl. Pancakes 4€–10€ ($4.60–$12). AE, MC, V. Daily noon–9:30pm. Tram: 6, 13, 14, or 17 to Westermarkt.

AROUND SPUI
De Visscher SEAFOOD   If you're walking down crowded Kalverstraat, it's the colorful sandwich display that will draw you in. This fast-foodery has a fresh-fish counter for takeout shrimp, tuna, and crab sandwiches in front, plus a restaurant in back. The raw herring, baked mackerel, and fried mussels are delicious.

Kalverstraat 122 (at Spui). ⓒ 020/623-7337. Main courses 3.75€–7.75€ ($4.30–$9). No credit cards. Mon–Sat 9:30am–6:30pm; Sun noon–4:30pm. Tram: 4, 9, 14, 16, 24, or 25 to Spui.

AROUND REMBRANDTPLEIN

Atrium DUTCH   This spectacular facility is the self-service student restaurant on the grounds of Amsterdam's old university. A courtyard between four restored buildings has been covered with a glass roof that lets in plenty of light all year. To reach the food lines, walk up the stairs just inside the door and cross the pedestrian bridge. The menu mixes standard Dutch fare with exotic influences.

Oudezijds Achterburgwal 237 (at the University of Amsterdam). © 020/525-3999. Main courses 3.75€–4.75€ ($4.30–$5). No credit cards. Mon–Fri noon–2pm and 5–7pm. Tram: 4, 9, 14, 16, 24, or 25 to Spui.

Cantharel DUTCH   Small and dark, this restaurant is a classic eatery that's been serving up hearty meals for years. Meat and potatoes are the order of the day, but the choices can be surprising—from liver and onions to *schnitzel paprikasaus,* marinated spareribs to chicken Cordon Bleu. You'll find Cantharel across from the old wooden church.

Kerkstraat 377 (off Utrechtsestraat). © 020/626-6400. Main courses 6.50€–8.75€ ($7–$10); daily specials 6.95€–8.95€ ($8–$10). AE, DC, MC, V. Daily 5–10pm. Tram: 4 to Utrechtsestraat.

De Jaren ⭐ CONTINENTAL   If you admire picturesque surroundings, you'll love this large cafe/restaurant. Originally a bank, the renovated building has high ceilings, a tiled mosaic floor, and two terraces overlooking the Amstel. Many students eat lunch here since it's near the university. Supposedly Rembrandt lived and worked in part of this house. You can enjoy ham and eggs for breakfast, help yourself to the extensive salad bar for lunch, and have dinner with a main course like pasta, steak, or couscous.

Nieuwe Doelenstraat 20–22 (off Muntplein). © 020/625-5771. www.cafe-de-jaren.nl. Main courses 8.50€–14€ ($10–$16); fixed price menus 18€–20€ ($20–$23). No credit cards. Daily 10am–1am (Fri–Sat until 2am). Tram: 4, 9, 14, 16, 24, or 25 to Muntplein.

Golden Temple ⭐ VEGETARIAN   In its 4th decade of tickling meat-shunning palates, this temple of taste is still one of the best vegetarian (and vegan) options in town. The first thing you notice when you enter is that you can actually *see* the place—the veil of cigarette smoke that obscures most Amsterdam restaurants has been lifted here by a nonsmoking policy that adds a heavenly touch all its own. If anything, the limpid atmosphere is a tad too hallowed, an effect enhanced by a Zenlike absence of decorative flourishes. The menu livens things up, with an unlikely roster of Indian, Middle Eastern, and Mexican dishes; the multiple-choice platters are a good way to go.

Utrechtsestraat 126 (close to Frederiksplein). © 020/626-8560. www.restaurantgoldentemple.nl. Main courses 6.50€–9.50€ ($7–$11); mixed platter 12€ ($14). MC, V. Daily 5–10pm. Tram: 4 to Prinsengracht.

La Place DUTCH/CONTINENTAL   This vast multilevel food depot has something for everyone. On the ground floor you'll find quiche, pizzas, and delicious fresh breads. (The cheese-onion loaf is a meal in itself.) An airy glass-topped cafeteria covers the three upstairs floors. Main dishes include a meat or fish of the day, often with a vaguely Indonesian touch, with vegetables and potatoes. Vegetarians love the soup and salad selection, and there's an assortment of freshly squeezed fruit juices.

Rokin 160 (at Muntplein). © 020/622-0171. Main courses 3.50€–7.95€ ($4–$9). AE, MC, V. Mon–Sat 9:30am–8pm; Sun 11am–8pm. Tram 4, 9, 14, 16, 24, or 25 to Muntplein.

Piet de Leeuw Steakhouse ✿ DUTCH (STEAKS)   Think of it as "Piet's Place," the kind of joint you feel right at home in. There's a cigarette machine on one wall, and the dark, cozy interior that smells slightly of beer was probably last decorated circa 1955. The famous, cholesterol-rich, artery-clogging killer beefsteaks, pan-fried in margarine with onions, come with a slice of white bread and are fantastic. Waiters check you out before bringing you toothpicks with tiny national flags with which to spear your raw herring, sweet pickles, and triangles of toast. On weekends, you can get a pan-fried steak or a plate of herring until midnight.

Noorderstraat 11 (at Vijzelgracht). ✆ 020/623-7181. Main courses 14€–18€ ($16–$21). AE, MC, V. Mon–Fri noon–11pm; Sat–Sun 5–11pm. AE, MC, V. Tram 16, 24, or 25 to Prinsengracht.

AROUND NIEUWMARKT

Nam Kee ✿ CHINESE   Stylish it isn't, but this modest place attracts throngs of locals in search of cheap, authentic Chinese dishes. Its popularity occasionally means lines out to the street. Whether your taste is for sweet-and-sour prawns, sliced pork, or stir-fried vegetables, your choice is guaranteed to be fresh and filling. The noodle soups are a one-dish meal at 4.55€ ($5.25). My favorite is the *bami soep* goulash, a peppery soup with huge chunks of beef.

Zeedijk 111–113 (at Nieuwmarkt). ✆ 020/624-3470. www.namkee.nl. Main courses 5.25€–15€ ($6–$17). AE, MC, V. Daily 11:30am–12:30am. Metro: Nieuwmarkt.

AROUND LEIDSEPLEIN

Bojo 🔲Value INDONESIAN   This excellent, inexpensive restaurant, conveniently close to Leidseplein, is open late on weekends. So if hunger strikes you after a late night on the town, drop in for a flavorful special boiled rice *(longtong rames)*, which is served with chewy rice cakes. If the place looks too crowded, be sure to check the adjoining dining room with a separate entrance.

Lange Leidsedwarsstraat 51 (off Leidseplein). ✆ 020/622-7434. Main courses 6.75€–13€ ($8–$15). No credit cards. Mon–Thurs 5pm–2am; Fri–Sat noon–3am. Tram: 1, 2, 5, 6, 7, or 10 to Leidseplein.

Van Altena ✿ SEAFOOD   Raw herring is a Dutch specialty, and there are dozens of *herringhuis* fish stands in town. The best of all is this class operation across from the Rijksmuseum. Owner Pieter van Altena has spent a lot of time and money perfecting the raw herring preservation process; connoisseurs stock up on his fresh herring from May through summer, and on the frozen and pickled variety year-round. You can also feast on delicious salmon or crab salad, and a dozen other fishy delights, on warm whole-grain buns. You use proper stainless-steel flatware and drink chilled white wine in a stemmed glass. Though it is basically a stand, a few lucky diners can even sit down to eat at a couple of tiny tables.

Stadhouderskade (no number, at Jan Luijkenstraat). ✆ 020/676-9139. Snacks 3€–7.70€ ($3.45–$9). No credit cards. Tues–Sun 11am–7pm. Tram: 6, 7, or 10 to Weteringschans.

IN THE JORDAAN

De Prins ✿✿ 🔲Value MODERN DUTCH/CONTINENTAL   In a 17th-century canal house, this companionable brown cafe (traditional Dutch bar) and restaurant opposite the Anne Frankhuis serves the kind of food you'd expect from a much more expensive place. The clientele is loyal, so the relatively few tables fill up quickly. It's a quiet neighborhood restaurant—nothing fancy or trendy, but quite appealing, with the bar on a slightly lower level than the restaurant and a sidewalk terrace for drinks in summer.

Prinsengracht 124 (at Egelantiersgracht). ✆ 020/624-9382. Main courses 7.50€–15€ ($9–$17); dish of the day 9.90€ ($12); specials 11€–15€ ($13–$17). AE, DC, MC, V. Daily 10am–1 or 2am (kitchen to 10pm). Tram: 6, 13, 14, or 17 to Westermarkt.

> ## *Value* Quick Bites
>
> As in most European cities, you'll find the best meal bargains are
> the offerings of the most recent immigrants. In Amsterdam's case, the
> **Middle-Eastern snack bars** and **Surinamese fast-food restaurants** have
> the cheapest meals. The former specialize in *showarma* and falafel,
> and can be found in high concentrations around Leidseplein and Rem-
> brandtplein; the latter are known for their chicken *roti,* mildly curried
> pieces of chicken served with a pancakelike bread, and can be found
> in the vicinity of Albert Cuypstraat, the site of a popular daily market.
> About 2.75€ to 7€ ($3.15–$8) gets you a filling meal in either type of
> place.
>
> A good Dutch alternative is **Broodje Van Kootje,** Leidseplein 20
> (© 020/623-2036; tram: 1, 2, 5, 6, 7, or 10), which, as the name implies,
> sells *broodjes* (sandwiches) plus snacks at 2.50€ to 5.50€ ($2.90–$6).
> Brightly lit, and with only a few tables, it's popular with Amster-
> dammers on the go. If you can't stomach the idea of eating raw her-
> ring from a street vendor, maybe it'll seem more palatable here. A
> specialty is the creamy *kroket broodje.* There's an equally popular
> branch at Spui 28 (© 020/623-7451; tram: 1, 2, or 5).
>
> If you're fed up with burgers and fries, try **The Hot Potato,** Leidses-
> traat 44 (© 020/623-2301; tram: 1, 2, 5, 6, 7, or 10), near Leidseplein.
> This tiny diner with only stools (no chairs) serves up 30 varieties of
> baked potato platters, ranging from one with butter or cream to a
> deluxe spud prepared with crabmeat, at 2€ to 3.90€ ($2.30–$4.50).
> Equally renowned are its super-filled American sub and torpedo sand-
> wiches, for 2.95€ to 4.75€ ($3.90–$5.45). It's open daily 10am to 10pm.
>
> Another quick-bite alternative, particularly for seriously cash-
> strapped budget travelers, are the branches of **Febo Automatiek** that
> you'll find all around town. They open directly on the sidewalk and
> look like giant street-side vending machines. Drop a few euro coins in
> the appropriate slots and—voilà!—you have a lunch of Indonesian *nasi*
> or *bami goreng,* hamburger, fries, and milkshake. I wouldn't say the
> portions are small, but they do have a compact form factor.

Hostaria ✦ ITALIAN   Owners Marjolein and Massimo Pasquinoli have
transformed this tiny space in the Jordaan into a showcase for the kind of cuisine Italian mothers only wish they could equal. When you sit down, Marjolein brings a dish of garlicky *tapenade* and warm bread. As an appetizer, you
might select a perfectly balanced fish soup with a slice of salmon or lightly
grilled eggplant slices with fresh herbs. The *zuppa di gamberone con l'acquetta,*
a plate of prawns and shellfish from the market, is terrific, and you also have
a choice of wonderful pastas—the tagliatelle with arugula and truffles is a particular treat.

Tweede Egelantiersdwarsstraat 9 (off Egelantiersstraat). © 020/626-0028. Reservations recommended on
weekends. Main courses 6.75€–14€ ($8–$16); fixed-price menu 16€ ($18). No credit cards. Tues–Sun
6:30–10pm. Tram: 6, 13, 14, or 17 to Westermarkt.

Sweet Stuff

If you have a sweet tooth, be sure to try some traditional Dutch desserts, like *poffertjes* (miniature pancakes), *oliebollen* (similar to powdered sugar–covered doughnut holes), or pancakes. All these come with various fillings or toppings, many of which contain a liqueur of some sort. Traditional *poffertje* restaurants are garish affairs that look as though they're part of a circus. There's one on Weteringcircuit, west of Leidseplein.

PICNICKING

You can pick up almost anything you might want for a picnic, from cold cuts to a bottle of wine, at the **Albert Heijn supermarket,** at the corner of Leidsestraat and Koningsplein, near Spui (tram: 1, 2, or 5), open Monday to Friday 9am to 8pm and Saturday 9am to 6pm. Then head over to Vondelpark, only a 15-minute walk. If it's summer, you might even catch a free concert at the outdoor theater.

WORTH A SPLURGE

De Belhamel 𝕽𝕽 *Finds* CONTINENTAL   At this restaurant, classical music complements Art Nouveau in a graceful setting overlooking the Herengracht and Brouwersgracht canals. The menu changes seasonally, and game is a specialty. You can expect such menu dishes as puffed pastries layered with salmon, shellfish, crayfish tails, and *chervil beurre-blanc* to start; and beef tenderloin in Madeira sauce with zucchini *rösti* and puffed garlic for a main course. They serve vegetarian dishes, too.

Brouwersgracht 60 (at Herengracht). 𝄐 020/622-1095. Main courses 19€–20€ ($21–$23); fixed-price menu 32€ ($37). AE, MC, V. Sun–Thurs 6–10pm; Fri–Sat 6–10:30pm. Tram: 1, 2, 5, 6, 13, or 17 to Martelaarsgracht.

D'Vijff Vlieghen 𝕽 MODERN DUTCH   Touristy? Yes. This is a kind of Dutch theme park, with seven dining rooms in five canal houses decorated with artifacts from Holland's Golden Age—among them four original Rembrandt etchings. But the chef is passionate about an updated form of Dutch cuisine he calls "the new Dutch kitchen." The menu has a selection of seasonal fish and game, often marinated with fresh herbs and served with unusual vegetables like chard, wild spinach, and Brussels sprouts.

Spuistraat 294–302 (at Spui). 𝄐 020/530-4060. www.thefiveflies.com. Reservations recommended on weekends. Main courses 21€–30€ ($24–$35); seasonal menu 32€–53€ ($36–$60). AE, DC, MC, V. Daily 5:30–10pm. Tram 1, 2, or 5 to Spui.

4 Seeing the Sights

Amsterdam has an almost bewildering embarrassment of riches. There are 160 canals to cruise (with a combined length of 76km/47 miles spanned by 1,281 bridges), hundreds of narrow streets to wander, almost 8,000 historic buildings to see in the city center, more than 40 museums of all types to visit, diamond cutters and craftspeople to watch as they practice generations-old skills . . . the list is as long as every visitor's individual interests—and then some.

THREE KEY MUSEUMS

Anne Frankhuis 𝕽𝕽   On July 6, 1942, the family of Anne Frank and another Jewish family went into hiding to avoid being deported to Nazi concentration camps. With the eyes of a child and the writing skills of a girl who hoped one day to be a writer, young Anne chronicled the almost-silent life in hiding of the *onderduikers* (divers or hiders), the continued persecution of Jews by Hitler, the progress of the war, and her personal growth as a young woman. The cramped, gloomy hiding place, where the families were forced to maintain nearly total silence, kept them safe for more than 2 years until they were betrayed and pro-Germany Dutch police raided their refuge on August 4, 1944. Anne died of typhus in March 1945 at Bergen-Belsen, tragically close to the war's end; six of the others also died in concentration camps.

The rooms here contain no furniture and are as bare as they were when Anne's father—Otto, the only survivor—returned, but the exhibits, including a year-by-year chronology of Anne's life, fill in the missing details. This lack of distraction allows you to project yourself into Anne's claustrophobic, fear-filled world. A new wing next door mounts temporary exhibits on themes like intolerance and racism.

The museum is operated by the Anne Frank Foundation, an organization founded to eliminate anti-Semitism, fascism, and neo-Nazism, and continues Anne's struggle for a better world. Anne achieved her dream of being a famous writer: Today more than 13 million copies of *The Diary of Anne Frank* have been sold, in 50 languages.

Note: Lines here can be very long, especially in summer. Try going on a weekday morning—this advice isn't as useful as it once was, because everybody is both giving it and heeding it, but it should still save you some waiting time. An alternative strategy if you're in town from April to August, when the museum is open until 9pm, is to go in the evening, as it is invariably quiet then—now at any rate. Once you're inside, an hour should do it, though many people do linger.

Prinsengracht 263 (at Westermarkt). © 020/556-7100. www.annefrank.nl. Admission 7.50€ ($9) adults, 3.50€ ($4.05) children 10–17, free for children under 10. Apr–Aug daily 9am–9pm; Sept–Mar daily 9am–7pm; Jan 1 and Dec 25 noon–7pm. Closed Yom Kippur. Tram: 6, 13, 14, or 17 to Westermarkt.

Rijksmuseum ✿✿✿

Most of Holland's premier museum, at Museumplein, is closed for renovation until mid-2008. During this period, key paintings from the magnificent 17th-century Dutch Golden Age collection can be viewed in the museum's own Philips Wing. Other elements of the collection likely will be on view at other venues in the city. The three-star rating given here is an indicator of the Rijksmuseum's importance when it is fully open. This rating is justified even for the highlights of Golden Age art alone, but remember that most of the museum's complete collection will be "invisible" to visitors for some time to come. During the renovation period, you can find a complete review of the Rijksmuseum at www.frommers.com.

Stadhouderskade 42 (at Museumplein). © 020/647-7000. www.rijksmuseum.com. Admission 8.50€ ($10) adults, free for those under 18. Daily 10am–5pm. Closed Jan 1. Tram: 2 or 5 to Hobbemastraat; 6, 7, or 10 to Weteringschans.

Van Gogh Museum ✿✿✿

Step through the portals here and you enter the imagination of Vincent van Gogh (pronounce it *fan khokh;* 1853–90), the 19th century's most important Dutch artist and arguably the world's best-known and best-loved painter—though he was neither of these during his short life. Designed by Gerrit Rietveld, an architect associated with the de Stijl movement, and opened in 1973, this museum houses the world's largest collection of the works of van Gogh—200 paintings and 600 drawings. It gives a chronological

Central Amsterdam

ⓘ Information
✉ Post office
--- Railway

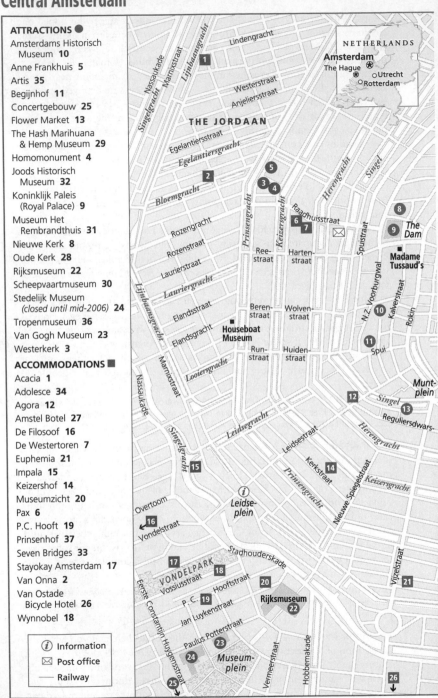

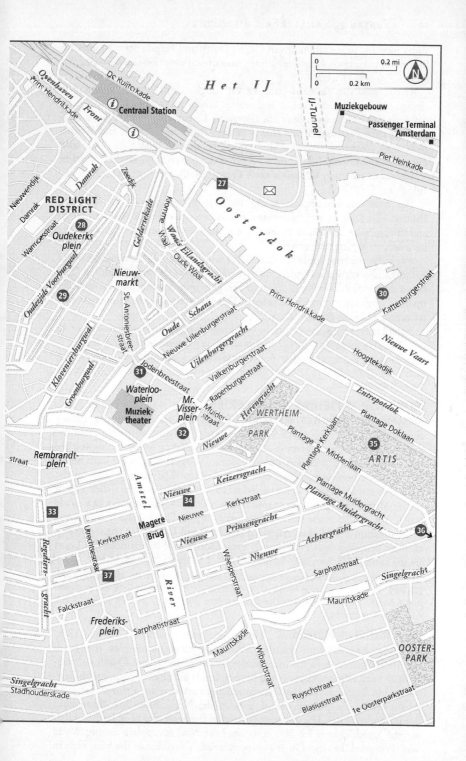

and a thematic presentation of van Gogh's Dutch and French periods; includes his private collection of Japanese prints, magazine illustrations, and books; and houses 750 of his letters.

As you view the paintings, you see van Gogh's early, gloomy style slowly change to one of vibrant colors and see his brushstrokes getting bolder as he developed his unique style. Seek out *Gauguin's Chair, The Yellow House, Self-portrait with Pipe and Straw Hat, Vincent's Bedroom at Arles,* and *Wheatfield with Reaper.* Of course, the star of the show is *Still Life Vase with Fourteen Sunflowers,* best known simply as *Sunflowers.* The somber mood in Vincent's last painting, *Cornfield with Crows* (1890), seems to presage his suicide at age 37.

The museum also displays works by contemporaries such as Toulouse-Lautrec, Gauguin, Monet, Sisley, and others, who both influenced van Gogh and in turn were influenced by him; the periods before he was born and after his death are represented as well.

You reach the new annex, built in 1999 and designed by Japanese architect Kisho Kurokawa, via an underground walkway from the main building. The facade of the oval building is titanium and gray-brown stone, and its roof lifts up like a frog's eye to provide extra light. This space contains the museum's print collection and temporary exhibits.

Note: Lines at the museum can be very long, especially in summer—try going on a weekday morning. Allow 2 to 4 hours to get around once you're inside.

Paulus Potterstraat 7 (at Museumplein). 𝄃 020/570-5200. www.vangoghmuseum.nl. Admission 9€ ($10) adults, 2.50€ ($2.90) children 13–17, free for children under 13. Daily 10am–6pm. Closed Jan 1. Tram: 2, 3, 5, or 12 to Van Baerlestraat.

MORE TOP MUSEUMS & GALLERIES

Amsterdams Historisch Museum ✹✹
In a huge 17th-century former orphanage, now housing exhibits covering nearly 700 years of the city's history, this fascinating museum gives you a better understanding of everything you see as you explore the city. Gallery by gallery, century by century, you'll learn how a fishing village became a major world-trading center. The main focus is on the city's 17th-century golden age, a period when Amsterdam was the richest city in the world, and some of the most interesting exhibits are of the trades that made it rich. You can also view many famous paintings by Dutch masters here. Next to the museum is the **Schuttersgalerij (Civic Guard Gallery),** a narrow, sky-lit chamber bedecked with 17th-century group portraits of militiamen. The hours are the same as for the museum, and admission is free.

Kalverstraat 92, Nieuwezijds Voorburgwal 357, and Sint-Luciënsteeg 27 (next to the Begijnhof). 𝄃 020/ 523-1822. www.ahm.nl. Admission 6€ ($7) adults, 4.50€ ($5) seniors and children 6–16, free for children under 6. Mon–Fri 10am–5pm; Sat–Sun and holidays 11am–5pm. Closed Jan 1, Apr 30, Dec 25. Tram: 1, 2, 4, 5, 9, 14, 16, 24, or 25 to Spui.

Joods Historisch Museum ✹
Housed in the four restored 17th- and 18th-century synagogues of the beautiful Ashkenazi Synagogue complex, the Jewish Historical Museum tells the intertwining stories of the Jewish Dutch community's identity, religion, culture, and history. Inside are objects, photographs, artworks, and interactive displays. Jewish religious artifacts are a major focus. An exhibit covers the persecution of Jews in the Netherlands and throughout Europe under Hitler. The synagogues stand at the heart of a neighborhood that was the Jewish quarter for 300 years until the Nazi occupation during World War II emptied the city of its Jewish population. The oldest of the four, built in

---

Value Good Deals on Sightseeing

- Check out the Amsterdam Pass (see the "Amsterdam Deals & Discounts" box on p. 63).
- Remember that the best (and cheapest) way to see Amsterdam is by wandering its streets and along its canals. You really can't get lost—if you're unsure where you are, just ask a passerby for directions (in English), or board any tram marked CENTRAAL STATION to return to the city center.
- Take advantage of the free admission to Vondelpark, 48 hectares (120 acres) of trees, ponds, flower beds, and picnic grounds where, in summer, concerts and all kinds of open-air activities are held. Call © 020/644-4216 to find out what's going on.
- Get the best panoramic views of Amsterdam by climbing the stairway or taking the elevator to the top of the Westerkerk Tower, for 3€ ($3.45). For a free view, take the elevator to the top of the Okura Hotel, Ferdinand Bolstraat 333, a few blocks south of the Rijksmuseum; or walk up to the rooftop terrace of the Nemo Science and Technology Center, just west of Centraal Station, along Prins Hendrikkade.

1670, is the oldest public synagogue in western Europe; the newest dates from 1752.

Jonas Daniël Meijerplein 2–4 (at Waterlooplein). © 020/625-4229. www.jhm.nl. Admission 6.50€ ($7) adults, 4€ ($4.60) seniors and students, 3€ ($3.45) children 13–17, 2€ ($2.30) children 6–12, free for children under 6. Daily 11am–5pm. Closed Yom Kippur. Tram: 9 or 14 to Waterlooplein.

Museum Het Rembrandthuis 🎨 When Rembrandt van Rijn moved into this three-story house in 1639, he was already a well-established wealthy artist. However, the cost of buying and furnishing the house led to his financial downfall in 1656. When Rembrandt was declared insolvent, an inventory of the house's contents listed more than 300 paintings by Rembrandt and some by his teacher, Pieter Lasteman, and his friends Peter Paul Rubens and Jan Lievens. In 1658, Rembrandt was forced to sell the house and most of his possessions to meet his debts. He remained there until 1660, and then moved to much less grandiose accommodations on Rozengracht, in the Jordaan.

The museum houses a nearly complete collection of Rembrandt's etchings, and the artist's printing press. Of the 300 prints he made, 250 are here, with about half hanging on the walls at any one time. Rembrandt's prints show amazing detail, and you can see his use of shadow and light for dramatic effect. Wizened patriarchs, emaciated beggars, children at play, Rembrandt himself in numerous self-portraits, and Dutch landscapes are the subjects you'll long remember after a visit here. Temporary exhibits are mounted in an adjacent house that belonged to Rembrandt's wife, Saskia.

Jodenbreestraat 4 (at Waterlooplein). © 020/520-0400. www.rembrandthuis.nl. Admission 7€ ($8) adults, 5€ ($6) students, 1.50€ ($1.75) children 6–15, free for children under 6. Mon–Sat 10am–5pm; Sun and holidays 1–5pm. Closed Jan 1. Tram: 9 or 14 to Waterlooplein.

Scheepvaartmuseum 🎨🎨 A bonanza for anyone who loves the sea, the Maritime Museum is housed in a former arsenal of the Amsterdam Admiralty dating from 1656 and appropriately overlooks the busy harbor. Around the inner courtyard are 25 rooms with exhibits: ship models, charts, instruments, maps, prints, and paintings—a chronicle of Holland's abiding ties to the sea through commerce, fishing, yachting, navigational development, and war. Old maps include a 15th-century Ptolemaic atlas and a sumptuously bound edition of the *Great Atlas* by Jan Blaeu, master cartographer of Holland's golden age. Among the historic papers on display are several pertaining to Nieuwe Amsterdam (New York City) and Nieuwe Nederland (New York State).

A full-size replica of the Dutch East India Company's *Amsterdam,* which in 1749 foundered off Hastings on her maiden voyage to the fabled Spice Islands (Indonesia), is moored at the museum's wharf, as is a recently completed replica of the *Stad Amsterdam,* a three-masted iron clipper from 1854. Other ships include a steam icebreaker, a motor lifeboat, and a herring lugger. Environmentalists will be interested in going aboard Greenpeace's *Rainbow Warrior,* a Trojan of environmental protection on the high seas. You can reach this museum by taking a 20-minute walk along the historical waterfront, the Nautisch Kwartier (Nautical Quarter).

Kattenburgerplein 1 (in the Eastern Dock). ℂ 020/523-2222. www.scheepvaartmuseum.nl. Admission 7.50€ ($9) adults, 6€ ($7) seniors, 4€ ($4.60) children 6–17, free for children under 6. Tues–Sat 10am–5pm (also Mon during school vacations); Sun noon–5pm. Bus: 22 or 32 to Kattenburgerplein.

Stedelijk Museum 𝆑   *Note:* At this writing, the Stedelijk Museum's premises on Paulus Potterstraat at Museumplein are closed until mid-2006 for renovation and expansion. The collection was due to move during 2004 to temporary quarters, probably but not certainly to the TPG building beside Centraal Station. Admirers of modern art should check the current situation with the Stedelijk's website or the VVV Amsterdam tourist office. The following review serves as a guide to the collection, and the practical details reflect probabilities at press time.

Focusing on modern art from 1850 to 2000, the Stedelijk is Amsterdam's most innovative major museum. The extensive permanent collection centers around the de Stijl movement, Cobra (an expressive, abstract 1950s style that originated with artists from Copenhagen, Brussels, and Amsterdam) and post-Cobra painting, nouveau réalisme, pop art, color-field painting, zero and minimalist art, and conceptual art. On display are selections from its permanent collection—including works by **Chagall, Picasso, Monet, Manet, Cézanne, Mondrian, Matisse, Dubuffet, de Kooning, Appel,** and **Rauschenberg.** The museum has the largest collection outside Russia of the abstract painter Kasimir Malevich. In addition to the paintings, sculptures, drawings, and engravings, there are exhibits of applied arts, videos, industrial design, and photography.

Temporary address: Oosterdokskade 3–5. ℂ 020/573-2737. www.stedelijk.nl. Admission 7€ ($8.05) adults, 3.50€ ($4.05) seniors and children 7–17, free for children under 7. Daily 11am–5pm. Closed Jan 1. Tram: 1, 2, 4, 5, 6, 9, 13, 16, 17, 24, or 25 to Centraal Station.

Tropenmuseum 𝆑 *(Kids)*   One of Amsterdam's most interesting museums, the Tropical Museum focuses on contemporary culture and problems in tropical areas. On the three floors surrounding the spacious main hall are numerous life-size tableaux depicting life in tropical countries. There are displays of beautiful handicrafts and antiquities from these regions, but the main focus is the life of the people today. There are hovels from the ghettoes of Calcutta and Bombay, and mud-walled houses from the villages of rural India. Bamboo huts from Indonesia and crowded little stores no bigger than closets show you how people live in areas like Southeast Asia, Latin America, and Africa. Sound effects play over hidden speakers: Dogs bark, children scream, car horns blare, and vendors call out their wares.

In the **Kindermuseum (Children's Museum) TM Junior,** youngsters 6 to 12 can explore and participate in all sorts of activities. (One adult is allowed to accompany each child.)

Linnaeusstraat 2 (at Mauritskade). (C) 020/568-8215. www.tropenmuseum.nl. Admission 7.50€ ($9) adults, 5€ ($6) seniors and students, 3.75€ ($4.30) children 6–17, free for children under 6. Daily 10am–5pm (until 3pm Dec 5, 24, 31). Closed Jan 1, Apr 30, May 5, Dec 25. Tram: 7, 9, 10, or 14 to Mauritskade.

AN ALTERNATIVE MUSEUM

The Hash Marihuana & Hemp Museum   Well, it wouldn't really be Amsterdam, would it, without its fascination with intoxicating weeds. This museum will teach you everything you ever wanted to know, and much you maybe didn't, about hash, marijuana, and related products. The museum does not promote drug use but aims to make you better informed before you decide whether to light up and, of course, whether to inhale. One way it does this is by having a cannabis garden in the joint (sorry) . . . on the premises. Plants at various stages of development fill the air with an unmistakable, heady, resinous fragrance. And hemp, not plastic, could be the future if the exhibit on the multifarious uses of the fiber through the ages is anything to go by. Some exhibits shed light on the medicinal uses of cannabis and on hemp's past and present-day uses as a natural fiber. Among several notable artworks in the museum's collection is David Teniers the Younger's painting, *Hemp-Smoking Peasants in a Smoke House* (1660).

Oudezijds Achterburgwal 130 (Red Light District). (C) 020/623-5961. www.hashmuseum.com. Admission 5.70€ ($7), free for children under 13 (must be accompanied by an adult). Daily 11am–11pm. Tram: 4, 9, 14, 16, 24, or 25 to the Dam.

HISTORIC BUILDINGS

Only steps from busy shopping streets, the **Begijnhof** ⭑, at Spui (tram: 1, 2, or 5), is the city's most tranquil spot. Hidden behind a nondescript facade is a 14th-century courtyard with a central garden ringed with restored almshouses formerly occupied by *begijns,* pious laywomen of the order of the Beguines. Most of the tiny 17th- and 18th-century buildings house elderly widows, and you should respect their privacy, especially after sunset. In the southwest corner of the cloister, at no. 34, stands Het Houten Huys, one of Amsterdam's pair of surviving timber houses, built around 1425. (The authorities prohibited construction of timber houses in 1452 after a series of disastrous fires.) The complex includes a clandestine Roman Catholic church and the former Beguine church from 1419, donated by the city's Protestant rulers to Scottish Presbyterian exiles in 1607, and now misnamed slightly as the Engelse Kerk (English Church). Allow an hour to wander and see it all.

Narrow-Minded Housing?

You can see the **narrowest house** in Amsterdam at **Singel 7.** It's just 1m (3⅓ ft.) wide—barely wider than the front door! However, it's a cheat. Only the front facade is really this narrow; behind it, the house broadens out to more usual proportions. The *genuine* narrowest house is **Oude Hoogstraat 22,** near Nieuwmarkt. With a typical Amsterdam bell gable, it's 2.02m (6½ ft.) wide and 6m (20 ft.) deep. A close rival is nearby at **Kloveniersburgwal 26,** the cornice-gabled **Kleine Trippenhuis,** at 2.44m (8 ft.) wide.

Finds **Gay Remembrance**

The *Homomonument,* Westermarkt (tram: 13, 14, or 17), a sculpture group of three pink granite triangles near the Anne Frankhuis, memorializes gays and lesbians killed during World War II, or as a result of oppression and persecution because of their sexuality. People also visit to remember those who have died of AIDS.

Koninklijk Paleis   The 17th-century neoclassical Royal Palace, built on top of 13,659 wooden pilings to prevent it from sinking into the soft Amsterdam soil, was Amsterdam's town hall for 153 years. It was first used as a palace during Napoléon's rule in the early 19th century when, from 1806 to 1810, the French emperor's brother Louis Bonaparte was king of the Netherlands. You can visit its high-ceilinged Citizens' Hall, Burgomasters' Chambers, and Council Room, as well as the Vierschaar—a marble tribunal where, in the 17th century, death sentences were pronounced. Although this is the monarch's official palace, Queen Beatrix rarely uses it for more than occasional receptions or official ceremonies.

Dam. ✆ 020/620-4060. www.koninklijkhuis.nl. Admission 4.50€ ($5) adults, 3.60€ ($4.15) seniors, students, and children 6–16, free for children under 6. Easter holidays and June–Aug daily 11am–5pm; Sept to mid-Dec and mid-Feb to May (except Easter holidays) generally Tues–Thurs 12:30–5pm (open days and hours vary; check before going). Guided tours usually Wed 2pm. Closed during periods of royal residence and state receptions. Tram: 1, 2, 4, 5, 6, 9, 13, 14, 16, 17, 24, or 25 to the Dam.

HISTORIC CHURCHES

Nieuwe Kerk   This church, across from the Royal Palace, is new in name only. Construction on this late-Gothic structure began about 1400, but much of the interior, including the organ, dates from the 17th century. Since 1815, all Dutch kings and queens have been crowned here. Today the church is used primarily as a cultural center where special art exhibits are held. Regular performances on the church's huge organ are held in summer.

Dam (next to the Royal Palace). ✆ 020/638-6909. www.nieuwekerk.nl. Daily 10am–6pm (Thurs to 10pm during exhibits). Admission varies with different events; free when there's no exhibit. Tram: 1, 2, 4, 5, 6, 9, 13, 14, 16, 17, 24, or 25 to the Dam.

Oude Kerk ⋆   This Gothic church from the 13th century is the city's oldest, and its many stained-glass windows are particularly beautiful. It now stands smack dab in the middle of the Red Light District, surrounded by old almshouses turned into prostitutes' rooms. Inside are monumental tombs, including that of Rembrandt's wife, Saskia van Uylenburg. The organ, built in 1724, is played regularly in summer; many connoisseurs believe it has the best tone of any organ in the world.

Oudekerksplein (at Oudezijds Voorburgwal). ✆ 020/625-8284. www.oudekerk.nl. Admission 4€ ($4.60) adults, 3.20€ ($3.70) seniors and students, free for children under 12; rates may vary for special exhibits. Church Mon–Sat 11am–5pm; Sun 1–5pm. Tower June–Sept Wed–Sun 2–4pm; Sept–Apr Sun–Fri 1–5pm, Sat 11–5pm. Tram: 1, 2, 4, 5, 6, 9, 13, 14, 16, 17, 24, or 25 to the Dam.

Westerkerk ⋆   Built between 1620 and 1630, this church is a masterpiece of Dutch Renaissance style. At the top of the 84m (276-ft.) tower, the highest, most beautiful tower in Amsterdam, is a giant replica of the imperial crown of Maximillian of Austria. Somewhere in this church (no one knows where) is Rembrandt's grave. During summer, regular organ concerts are played on a

300-year-old instrument, and you can climb the tower or go by elevator to the top for a great view.

Westermarkt. © 020/624 7766. Free admission to church; admission to tower 3€ ($3.45). Church Apr–June and Sept Mon–Fri 11am–3pm; July–Aug Mon–Sat 11am–3pm. Tower June–Sept Mon–Sat 10am–5pm. Tram: 6, 13, 14, or 17 to Westermarkt.

A GREAT ZOO

Artis 🎭🎭 *(Kids)* If you're at a loss for what to do with the kids, Artis is a safe bet— 1.2 million visitors a year agree. Established in 1838, the oldest zoo in the Netherlands houses 6,000 animals from 1,400 species. Of course, you find the usual tigers, lions, giraffes, wolves, leopards, elephants, camels, monkeys, penguins, and peacocks no self-respecting zoo can do without. The African residents even stroll around on a miniature savannah. Yet there's also much more, for no extra charge, such as an excellent Planetarium (closed Mon mornings) and a Geological and Zoological Museum. The Aquarium, built in 1882 and refurbished since, is superbly presented, particularly the sections on the Amazon River, coral reefs, and Amsterdam's own canals with their fish populations and burden of wrecked cars, rusted bikes, and other urban detritus. Finally, there's a children's farm, where kids can stroke and help tend to the needs of resident Dutch species, including moorland sheep, long-haired Veluwe goats, and tufted ducks. You can rest for a while and have a snack or lunch at Artis Restaurant.

Plantage Kerklaan 38–40 (at Plantage Middenlaan). © 020/523-3400. www.artis.nl. Admission 15€ ($17) adults, 11€ ($13) children 3–9, free for children under 3. Daily 9am–5pm. Tram: 9 or 14 to Plantage Kerklaan, 6 to Plantage Doklaan.

PARKS

When the sun shines in Amsterdam, people head for the parks. The most popular and conveniently located of Amsterdam's 20 parks is the 49-hectare (122-acre) **Vondelpark** 🎭🎭 (tram: 1, 2, 3, 5, 6, 7, 10, or 12), home to skateboarding, Frisbee-flipping, in-line skating, model-boat sailing, soccer, softball, basketball, open-air concerts and theater, smooching in the undergrowth, parties, picnics, craft stalls, topless sunbathing—you name it. Its lakes, ponds, and streams are surrounded by meadows, trees, and colorful flowers. Vondelpark lies generally southwest of Leidseplein and has entrances all around; the most popular is adjacent to Leidseplein, on Stadhouderskade. Watch out for the tasty-looking

---

Checking Out the Red Light District

The warren of streets east of the Dam, around Oudezijds Achterburgwal and Oudezijds Voorburgwal, is the *Rosse Buurt* **(Red Light District)**, one of the most famous features of Amsterdam sightseeing (Metro: Nieuwmarkt). Here, you'll see women of all nationalities dressed in exotic underwear and perched in windows waiting for customers.

The Red Light District is a major attraction, not only for customers of storefront sex but also for sightseers. If you do choose to look around, you need to exercise some caution. Watch out for pickpockets. Also, in a neighborhood where anything seems permissible, the one no-no is taking pictures. Violate this rule and your camera could be taken from you and broken.

Special & Free Events

In keeping with Amsterdammers' enthusiasm about life, every day in the city is filled with special events. Some of Amsterdam's best freebies are its **street performers**. You find them primarily in front of Centraal Station during the day and on Leidseplein and Rembrandtplein in the evening.

April 30 is **Koninginnedag (Queen's Day)**, and both Amsterdammers and out-of-towners crowd the streets to enjoy performances, parades, markets, and general merrymaking. The area around the *Homomonument* becomes a huge outdoor dance club.

The single most important event in the Netherlands is the **flowering of the bulb fields** each spring from March to mid-May. Two-thirds of all the cut flowers sold in the world come from the Netherlands. The best flower-viewing areas are between Haarlem and Leiden and between Haarlem and Den Helder. Most people take a guided bus tour given by any of the tour companies referred to under the "Organized Tours" section on p. 91. You can also drive between these towns. The highlight of the season is the annual **flower parade** from Haarlem to Noordwijk in late April. There's another flower parade from Aalsmeer (home of the world's largest flower auction) to Amsterdam on the first Saturday in September.

In June, July, and August, **open-air concerts** are held in Vondelpark. Check at the VVV Amsterdam tourist office for times and dates. In June, there's also the **Holland Festival,** an extravaganza of music, dance, and other cultural activities that take place all over the city and highlights a different theme each year. In September, the **Jordaan Festival** showcases this old neighborhood where small inexpensive restaurants, secondhand stores, and unusual boutiques and galleries are found.

The **August Gay Pride Festival** in Europe's gay-friendliest city is a big event. A crowd of 150,000 turns out to watch its highlight: the Boat Parade's display of a hundred or so outrageously decorated boats cruising the canals. In addition, there are street discos and open-air theater performances, a sports program, and a film festival. For more information, contact Gay Business Amsterdam at ℂ/fax **020/620-8807.**

"gateau" they sell here, or you might find yourself floating above the trees: Drug-laced "space cake" is an acquired taste. This park, open daily 8am to sunset, is extremely popular in summer with young people from all over the world; admission is free.

To enjoy scenery and fresh air, head out to the giant **Amsterdamse Bos** (tram: 16 or 24 to Stadionplein, and then any bus, except the no. 23, south on Amstelveenseweg to the main entrance) in the Amstelveen southern suburb. Nature on the city's doorstep, the park was laid out during the Depression years as a public works project. By now the trees, birds, insects, and small animals are firmly established. From the entrance, follow a path to the **Roeibaan,** a rowing course 2km (1¼ miles) long. Beyond its western end, at the **Bosmuseum**

(© 020/676-2152), you can trace the park's history and learn about its wildlife. The museum is open daily 10am to 5pm; admission is free. Nearby is a big pond called the **Grote Vijver,** where you can rent boats (© 020/644-5119), and the **Openluchttheater (Open-Air Theater),** which often has performances on summer evenings. In 2000, the **Kersenbloesempark (Cherry Blossom Park)** opened in the Amsterdamse Bos. Its 400 cherry trees, donated by the Japan Women's Club, mark 400 years of cultural ties between the Netherlands and Japan. The Bos is open 24 hours; admission is free.

ORGANIZED TOURS

Although you could see most of Amsterdam's important sights in one long walking tour, it's best to break the city into shorter walks. Luckily, the **VVV Amsterdam** tourist office has done that. For 1.80€ ($2.05), you can buy a brochure outlining one of four walking tours: *Voyage of Discovery Through Amsterdam, A Walk Through Jewish Amsterdam, A Walk Through the Jordaan,* and *A Walk Through Maritime Amsterdam.*

BOAT TOURS   A **canal-boat cruise** ✿✿ is the best way to view the old houses and warehouses. If you have to choose among a walking tour, a bus tour, and a boat tour, definitely take a boat. This is a city built on the shipping trade, so it's only fitting you should see it from the water, just as the Golden Age merchants saw their city. There are several canal-boat jetties, all of which have signs stating the time of their next tour. The greatest concentration of canal-boat operators is along Damrak and Rokin from Centraal Station; another cluster is on Singelgracht, near Leidseplein. Most tours last 1 hour and are around 8.50€ ($9.80) for adults, 5.75€ ($6.60) for children 4 to 12, and free for children under 4 (prices may vary a little from company to company). Since the tours are all basically the same, simply pick the one that's most convenient for you. Some cruises include snacks and drinks; floating candlelit dinners are extra.

You can take a self-guided, self-powered tour on a **canal bike.** These small pedal boats for two to four are available from **Canal Bike** (© 020/626-5574) at Leidseplein near the Rijksmuseum (tram: 1, 2, 5, 6, 7, or 10), at Westerkerk (tram: 6, 13, 14, or 17), and on Keizersgracht near Leidsestraat (tram: 1, 2, or 5). Canal bikes are available daily 10am to 4pm in spring and autumn (to 10pm in summer). The hourly rate is 8€ ($9.20) a head for one or two people and 7€ ($8.05) a head for three or four. There's a 50€ ($58) refundable deposit. You can pick one up at one jetty and drop it off at another.

BUS TOURS   A 2½ hour bus tour of the city is around 18€ ($21). Children 4 to 13 are usually charged half-price, and children under 4 are free. Tour companies include **The Best of Holland,** Damrak 34 (© 020/623-1539); **Holland International Excursions,** Dam 6 (© 020/551-2800); **Holland Keytours,** Dam 19 (© 020/624-7304); and **Lindbergh Excursions,** Damrak 26 (© 020/622-2766).

Value A Ferry Tale

Free ferries connect the city center with Amsterdam Noord (North). The short crossings for foot passengers and bikes make ideal mini-cruises for the cash-strapped and provide a good view of the harbor. Ferries depart from piers along De Ruyterkade behind Centraal Station every 10 to 15 minutes from 6:30am to 6pm.

5 Shopping

Strolling Amsterdam's streets, you could get the impression the city is one giant outdoor mall. Everywhere you look are stores ranging in price and variety from the Jordaan's used-clothing stores and bookstores to Pieter Cornelisz Hooft-straat's designer boutiques. Alas, most stores have little in the way of bargains. However, many typically Dutch souvenirs and gift items might appeal to you and can be real bargains if you shop around.

Amsterdam's best buys are Dutch-made, such as Delftware, pewter, crystal, and old-fashioned clocks, or commodities in which they have significantly cornered a market, such as diamonds. If cost is an important consideration, remember that the Dutch also have inexpensive specialties like cheese, flower bulbs, and chocolate.

For jewelry, trendy clothing, and athletic gear, try the department stores and specialized stores around the **Dam.** On the long, pedestrianized **Nieuwendijk–Kalverstraat** shopping street and on **Leidsestraat,** you'll find inexpensive clothing stores and souvenir stores. For designer boutiques and upscale fashion and accessories, shop on **Pieter Cornelisz Hooftstraat** and **Van Baerlestraat.** Pricey antiques and art dealers congregate on **Nieuwe Spiegelstraat.** For fashion boutiques and funky little specialty stores, or a good browse through a flea market or secondhand store, roam through the streets of the **Jordaan.** The **Red Light District** specializes in stores selling erotic clothing, sex aids and accessories, and pornographic books and magazines.

Should you see the words SOLDEN or TOTAAL UITVERKOOP on a store window, go immediately into bargain-hunting mode. The former means "Sale" and the latter "Everything Must Go." Both are pointers to reductions of anything from 10% to 75%.

STORES WORTH A VISIT

The city's top department store, with the best selection of goods and a great cafe, is **De Bijenkorf,** Dam 1 (© **020/621-8080;** tram: 4, 9, 14, 16, 24, or 25). **Magna Plaza** (tram: 1, 2, 5, 6, 13, 14, or 17) is a splendid three-story mall in the old main post office building, behind the Dam at the corner of Nieuwezijds Voorburgwal and Raadhuisstraat.

Focke & Meltzer, Gelderlandplein 149, Buitenveldert (© **020/644-4429;** tram: 5 or 51), is the best one-stop store for authentic Delft Blue and Makkumware porcelain, Hummel figurines, Leerdam crystal, and a world of other fine china, porcelain, silver, glass, and crystal. Unless you simply must have brand-name articles, you can save considerably on hand-painted pottery at

---

Tips **Tax Saver**

Watch for the TAX-FREE SHOPPING sign in some store windows. These stores provide visitors who are not residents of the European Union the check they need for recovering the **value-added tax** (BTW in the Netherlands) when they leave the E.U. This refund amounts to 13.5% of the total cost of purchases of more than 137€ ($158) in a participating store. When you're leaving by air, present the check to Customs, along with your purchases and receipts; they will stamp it and you can get an immediate refund from the ABN-AMRO bank at Schiphol Airport.

Heinen, Prinsengracht 440, off Leidsestraat (℗ **020/627-8299;** tram: 1, 2, or 5), and even watch the product being made. Also recommendable is **Delftware,** Nieuwendijk 24 (℗ **020/627-3974;** tram: 1, 2, 4, 5, 6, 9, 13, 16, 17, 24, or 25).

Diamond showrooms offering free individual and small-group tours of their diamond-cutting and -polishing facility include: **Amsterdam Diamond Center,** Rokin 1 (℗ **020/624-5787;** tram: 4, 9, 14, 16, 24, or 25), just off the Dam; **Coster Diamonds,** Paulus Potterstraat 2–6 (℗ **020/676-2222;** tram: 2 or 5), near the Rijksmuseum; and **Van Moppes Diamonds,** Albert Cuypstraat 2–6 (℗ **020/676-1242;** tram: 4), at the street market.

MARKETS

Buying flowers at the **Bloemenmarkt (Flower Market),** on a row of barges permanently moored along Singel between Muntplein and Leidsestraat (tram: 1, 2, 4, 5, 9, 14, 16, 24, or 25), is an Amsterdam ritual. The market is open Monday to Saturday from 9am to 5pm.

You can still find a few antiques and near-antiques at the **Waterlooplein flea market** (tram: 9 or 14), on the square around the Muziektheater, but most of what's for sale there these days is used and cheap clothing. The open-air **Albert Cuyp market,** Albert Cuypstraat (tram: 4, 16, 24, or 25), has more cheap clothing, plus fresh fish and flowers, Asian vegetables, textiles, electronics, cosmetics, and more. Both markets are open Monday to Saturday from 9am to 5pm. There's also a **flea market** on Noordermarkt in the Jordaan (tram: 1, 2, 5, 6, 13, or 17) on Monday morning from 8am until midday; and a market for **organic food** on Noordermarkt Saturday from 10am to 4pm.

Spread through several old warehouses along the Jordaan canals, **Kunst & Antiekcentrum de Looier,** Elandsgracht 109 (℗ **020/624-9038;** tram: 6, 7, 10, 17), is a big art and antiques market. Individual dealers rent booths and corners here to show their best wares in antique jewelry, prints, and engravings.

Other great markets are the **antiques market** on Nieuwmarkt (Metro: Nieuwmarkt), on Sunday from May to October 10am to 4pm; the **secondhand book market** in Oudemanhuispoort (tram: 4, 9, 14, 16, 24, or 25), a covered passageway between Oudezijds Voorburgwal and Kloveniersburgwal, held Monday to Saturday 10am to 4pm; another **secondhand book market,** on Spui (tram: 1, 2, or 5), held on Friday 10am to 6pm; the **art market** at the same location on Sunday 10am to 5pm; and the **modern art market** on Thorbeckeplein (tram: 4, 9, or 14), held on Sunday from March to December, with sculptures, paintings, jewelry, and mixed-media pieces.

6 Amsterdam After Dark

Nightlife in Amsterdam centers on **Leidseplein** and **Rembrandtplein,** and you find dozens of bars, nightclubs, cafes, dance clubs, and movie theaters around these two squares. More cultured evening entertainments can be found in other parts of the city.

For listings of performances, consult the monthly magazine *Amsterdam Day by Day* available for 1.50€ ($1.75) from VVV Amsterdam tourist offices. *De Uitkrant,* a free monthly magazine in Dutch, has an even more thorough listing of events (which is not hard for English-speakers to follow) and is available at performance venues, clubs, and VVV offices.

For tickets to theatrical and musical events (including rock concerts), contact **Amsterdam Uit Buro (AUB) Ticketshop,** Leidseplein 26 (℗ **0900/0191;**

http://amsterdam.aub.nl; tram: 1, 2, 5, 6, 7, or 10), which can book tickets for almost every venue in town, for 2€ ($2.30) per ticket. VVV offices also reserve tickets, for a 2.50€ ($2.90) fee.

THE PERFORMING ARTS

CLASSICAL MUSIC   The renowned **Royal Concertgebouw Orchestra** is based at the **Concertgebouw,** Concertgebouwplein 2–6 (© **020/671-8345;** www.concertgebouw.nl; tram: 3, 5, 12, or 16), which has an ornate Greek Revival facade and some of the best acoustics of any hall in the world. Performances, by this and other orchestras, are held almost every night in the building's two halls. There are free half-hour rehearsal concerts on Wednesday at 12:30pm. The box office is open daily 10am to 7pm, with tickets at 12€ to 90€ ($14–$104).

The **Netherlands Philharmonic Orchestra** (the "NedPho") and the **Netherlands Chamber Orchestra** both perform at the impressive **Beurs van Berlage,** Damrak 243 (© **020/627-0466;** www.beursvanberlage.nl; tram: 4, 9, 14, 16, 24, or 25), which was once the Amsterdam stock exchange, and now houses two concert halls for symphonies and chamber music. The box office is open Tuesday to Friday 12:30 to 6pm and Saturday noon to 5pm, with tickets at 7.50€ to 25€ ($8.65–$29).

OPERA & DANCE   The **Netherlands Opera** and the **National Ballet** both perform regularly at the modern **Muziektheater,** Waterlooplein (© **020/ 625-5455;** www.muziektheater.nl; tram: 9 or 14); and the innovative **Netherlands Dance Theater** company from The Hague is a frequent visitor. The box office is open Monday to Saturday 10am to 8pm and Sunday 11:30am to 6pm, with tickets at 15€ to 60€ ($17–$58). Music and dance performances are occasionally held at the **Stadsschouwburg** (see "Theater," below).

THEATER   The **Koninklijk Theater Carré,** Amstel 115–125 (© **020/ 622-5225;** Metro: Weesperplein), a huge old domed former circus-theater on the Amstel River near the Magere Brug (Skinny Bridge), occasionally presents touring shows from New York's Broadway or London's West End. The box office is open Monday to Saturday 10am to 7pm and Sunday 1 to 7pm, and tickets go for 12€ to 53€ ($13–$60). At the Dutch Renaissance **Stadsschouwburg,** Leidseplein 26 (© **020/624-2311;** tram: 1, 2, 5, 6, 7, or 10), built in 1894, performances include plays in Dutch and occasionally English, plus music and dance performances by international companies. The box office is open daily 10am to 6pm, with tickets at 7€ to 35€ ($8.05–$40).

Compared by *Time* to Chicago's famous Second City troupe, **Boom Chicago Theater,** Leidsepleintheater, Leidseplein 12 (© **020/423-0101;** www.boom chicago.nl; tram: 1, 2, 5, 6, 7, or 10), puts on great improvisational comedy, and Dutch audiences have no problem with the English sketches. You can have dinner and a drink while enjoying the show at a candlelit table. It's open daily in summer, closed Sunday in winter. The cover is 11€ to 32€ ($13–$36), but that doesn't include dinner.

LIVE-MUSIC CLUBS & BARS

Amsterdam's biggest and most popular clubs book up-and-coming acts and always charge admission. But there are also plenty of smaller clubs in cafes that showcase local bands and charge no admission.

Housed in an old canalside warehouse, **Bimhuis,** Oude Schans 73–77 (© **020/623-3373;** Metro: Nieuwmarkt), is Amsterdam's premier jazz club. It's open Wednesday to Sunday from 8pm to 1am, with a 10€ to 15€ ($12–$17) cover. You can impress your ears with a never-routine mix of electronic music, avant-garde jazz, and anything else that goes out on a musical limb, in the small concert hall at **De IJsbreker,** Weesperzijde 23 ((C) **020/668-1805;** Metro: Weesperplein), a pleasant cafe with an outdoor terrace on the banks of the Amstel. The cover is 7€ to 12€ ($8.05–$14).

Note: Sometime early in 2005, both BIMhuis and De IJsbreker are due to pack up their music and instruments and decamp to the new, state-of-the-art **Muzickgcbouw** (www.muziekgebouw.nl) on the waterfront. At this writing, the concert hall is under construction in the old harbor, between Centraal Station and the cruise-liner Passenger Terminal Amsterdam.

A regular crowd frequents the small, intimate **Alto Jazz Café,** Korte Leidsedwarsstraat 115 ((C) **020/626-3249**), for nightly performances by both regular and guest combos. Also check out the **Bamboo Bar,** Lange Leidsedwarsstraat 64 ((C) **020/624-3993**), and funky **Bourbon Street,** Leidsekruisstraat 6–8 ((C) **020/623-3440**), for late night blues and rock. All three bars are near Leidseplein, reached by tram 1, 2, 5, 6, 7, or 10.

THE BAR SCENE

There are countless bars—or cafes, as they're called here—in the city, many around **Leidseplein** and **Rembrandtplein.** Many of them don't start to get busy until at least 8pm, but they usually open at noon and stay open all day. The most popular drink is draft pilsner served in small glasses with two fingers of head on top. Also popular is *jenever* (Dutch gin) available in *jonge* (young) and *oude* (old) varieties—*oude* is stronger and more refined in taste and higher in alcoholic content.

BROWN CAFES Particularly old and traditional bars often earn the appellation of *bruine kroeg* **(brown cafe),** a name said to have been derived as much from the preponderance of wood furnishings as from the browning of the walls from years of dense tobacco smoke. Some have been around since Rembrandt's time. At these warm and friendly (and smoky) cafes, you can sit and sip a glass of beer or a mixed drink; at some you can even get a cheap meal.

Papeneiland, Prinsengracht 2, at the corner of Brouwersgracht ((C) **020/624-1989;** tram: 1, 2, 5, 6, 13, or 17), is Amsterdam's oldest cafe: Since 1600 or thereabouts, folks have been dropping by for shots of *jenever* and glasses of beer. Originally a tasting house where people could try liqueurs distilled and aged on the premises, **De Drie Fleschjes,** Gravenstraat 18, between the Nieuwe Kerk and Nieuwendijk ((C) **020/624-8443;** tram: 1, 2, 4, 5, 6, 9, 13, 14, 16, 17, 24, or 25), has been in business for more than 300 years. It's popular with businesspeople and journalists, who stop by to sample the wide variety of *jenevers*.

The dark walls, low ceilings, and old wooden furniture at **Hoppe,** Spui 18–20 ((C) **020/420-4420;** tram: 1, 2, or 5), one of Amsterdam's oldest and most popular brown cafes, have literally remained unchanged since the cafe opened in 1670. It has become a tourist attraction, but locals love it too, often stopping for a drink on their way home. There's usually standing room only and the crowds overflow onto the sidewalk.

Said to be where the builders of the Westerkerk were paid, **Café Chris,** Bloemstraat 42 ((C) **020/624-5942;** tram: 6, 13, 14, or 17), opened in 1624 and has some curious old features, including a toilet that flushes from outside the bathroom door. In a medieval alley, wood-paneled **In de Wildeman,** Kolksteeg 3 ((C) **020/638-2348;** tram: 1, 2, 5, 6, 13, or 17), serves more than 200 kinds of beer. The tile floor and rows of bottles and jars behind the counters are remnants from its early days as a distillery's retail store.

In the Jordaan, **De Twee Zwaantjes,** Prinsengracht 114 (© **020/625-2729;** tram: 6, 13, 14, or 17), is a small brown cafe popular with locals and visitors alike for its weekend singalongs. Late in the evening the musical instruments begin to show up, and once everyone has had enough Heineken and *jenever,* the old music begins.

MODERN CAFES Flea-market tables, armchairs left over from the 1970s, and rotating exhibits of puzzling artwork have made **Café Schuim,** Spuistraat 189 (© **020/638-9357;** tram: 1, 2, or 5), the cafe of the moment in the Dam area. The rumpled surroundings attract an assortment of creative types who debate and discuss during the week and try to avoid being crushed by mobs on weekends.

Other notable hangouts are **Café Dante,** Spuistraat 320 (© **020/638-8839;** tram 1, 2, or 5), where a different modern art exhibit is mounted every month; and **Café Schiller,** Rembrandtplein 26 (© **020/624-9846;** tram: 4, 9, or 14), which has a bright, glassed-in terrace on the square, and a finely carved Art Deco interior; it's popular with artists and writers.

The concept of the Grand Cafe—combining drinks and food in elegant surroundings—has taken Amsterdam by storm. One of the best is **Café Luxembourg,** Spuistraat 24 (© **020/620-6264;** tram 1, 2, or 5), a chic rendezvous that takes some of its menu dishes from top eateries around town. Whether you're in jeans or theater attire, you'll feel comfortable at **Royal Café De Kroon,** Rembrandtplein 15 (© **020/625-2011;** tram: 4, 9, or 14), with fine views on the square through the big picture windows upstairs, amid a decor that's rigorously modern.

On summer evenings, trendies head to the terrace of **Café Vertigo,** Vondelpark 3 (© **020/612-3021;** tram: 2 or 5), in Vondelpark, for one of the liveliest scenes in town. The low arched ceilings, subtle lighting, and unobtrusive music set a mood of casual sophistication.

GAY & LESBIAN CLUBS & BARS

Amsterdam bills itself as the gay capital of Europe, proud of its open and tolerant attitude toward homosexuality. To find out more about the gay and lesbian scenes, stop by **COC,** Rozenstraat 14 (© **020/623-4079;** tram: 6, 13, 14, or 17), 2 blocks off Westerkerk. It houses a cafe (open Mon–Sat 11pm–4am) and a dance club. The dance club is primarily for men on Fridays and primarily for women on Saturdays. Sundays attract a mixed crowd. You can also call the **Gay and Lesbian Switchboard** at © **020/623-6565,** open daily 10am to 10pm.

Gay News Amsterdam, a new monthly newspaper in English, is available free in gay establishments throughout Amsterdam. Of course, you find great coverage of the Gay Capital of Europe in *Frommer's Gay & Lesbian Europe.*

There are lots of bars and dance clubs for gay men all over the city, but far fewer lesbian spots. Generally you find the trendier spots around **Rembrandtplein** and on **Reguliersdwarsstraat** (immediately off Leidsestraat, a block south of Singel), a more casual atmosphere on **Kerkstraat** near Leidseplein, and leather bars on **Warmoesstraat.**

Popular men's bars include **April,** Reguliersdwarsstraat 37 (© **020/ 625-9572;** tram: 1, 2, or 5), a sleek modern bar; **Exit,** Reguliersdwarsstraat 42 (© **020/624-7778;** tram: 1, 2, or 5), a dance club that attracts a younger crowd; **iT,** Amstelstraat 24 (© **020/625-0111;** tram: 4, 9, or 14), Amsterdam's most famous and flamboyant dance club with a mixed gay and straight crowd;

Cockring, Warmoesstraat 96 ((C) **020/623-9604;** tram: 4, 9, 14, 16, 24, or 25), a popular dance club; **Argos,** Warmoesstraat 95 ((C) **020/622-6572;** tram: 4, 9, 14, 16, 24, or 25), Europe's oldest leather bar; and **Cosmo,** Kerkstraat 42 ((C) **020/624-7778;** tram: 1, 2, or 5), a late-night bar.

Vive la Vie, Amstelstraat 7 ((C) **020/624-0114;** tram: 4, 9, or 14), on the edge of Rembrandtplein, is the city's only lesbian bar; this convivial little corner spot on Rembrandtplein hosts periodic parties. **Saarein,** Elandsstraat 119 ((C) **020/623-4901;** tram: 6, 7, 10, or 17), near Leidseplein, is a women-only bar/cafe that's not exclusively lesbian but has a large following.

DANCE CLUBS

You'll find dozens of large and small clubs around **Leidseplein** and **Rembrandtplein.** They tend to rise and fall in popularity, so ask someone in a cafe what the current favorites are. Drinks can be expensive—a beer or Coke averages 5€ ($5.75), and a whiskey or cocktail 7.50€ ($8.65). Most dance clubs are open Thursday to Sunday 9 or 10pm to 2 or 3am.

Popular clubs include **Arena,** Gravesandestraat 51 ((C) **020/625-8788;** tram 7 or 10); **Escape,** Rembrandtplein 11 ((C) **020/625-2011;** tram: 4, 9, or 14); **West Pacific,** Haarlemmerweg 8–10 ((C) **020/488-7778;** tram: 10); **Odeon,** Singel 460 ((C) **020/624-9711;** tram: 1, 2, or 5); **Paradiso,** Weteringschans 6–8 ((C) **020/626-4521;** tram: 1, 2, 5, 6, 7, or 10); **Akhnaton,** Nieuwezijds Kolk 25 ((C) **020/624-3396;** tram: 1, 2, 5, 6, 13, or 17); and **Melkweg** 🎭, Lijnbaansgracht 234A ((C) **020/624-1777;** tram: 1, 2, 5, 6, 7, or 10). Cover and music vary.

"COFFEE SHOPS"

Amsterdam is a mecca for the marijuana smoker and seems likely to remain that way. Visitors often get confused about "smoking" coffee shops and how they differ from "nonsmoking" ones. Well, to begin with, "smoking" and "nonsmoking" don't refer to cigarettes—they refer to cannabis. "Smoking" coffee shops not only sell cannabis, most commonly in the form of hashish, but also provide somewhere patrons can sit and smoke it all day if they so choose. Generally, these smoking coffee shops are the only places in Amsterdam called "coffee shops"—regular cafes are called *cafes* or *eetcafes.*

You are allowed to buy only 5 grams (.2 oz.) of soft drugs at a time for personal use, but you're allowed to be in possession of 30 grams (1.2 oz) for personal use.

Coffee shops are not allowed to sell alcohol, so they sell coffee, tea, and fruit juices. You won't be able to get any food (except maybe drug-laced "space cake"), so don't expect to grab a quick bite while you're at one. You're even allowed to smoke your own stuff in the coffee shop, as long as you buy a drink.

Some of the most popular smoking coffee shops are **The Rookies,** Korte Leidsedwarsstraat 145–147 ((C) **020/694-2353;** tram: 1, 2, 5, 6, 7, or 10); **Borderline,** Amstelstraat 37 ((C) **020/622-0540;** tram: 9 or 14); and, with tourists, the shops of the **Bulldog** chain, which has branches around the city. The **Bulldog Palace** is at Leidseplein 15 ((C) **020/627-1908;** tram: 1, 2, 5, 6, 7, or 10).

Tips **Toker Talk**

Don't buy on the street. You stand a fair chance of being ripped off, the quality is doubtful, and there may be unpleasant additives. Stick with the "smoking" coffee shops.

---

7 Side Trips: Haarlem ★★ & Delft ★★

If Amsterdam is your only stop in the Netherlands, try to make at least one excursion into the countryside. Dikes, windmills, and some of Holland's quaintest villages await you just beyond the city limits. And you don't need to travel much farther to reach one of the Netherlands' many historic art towns.

HISTORIC HAARLEM

Just 20km (12 miles) west of Amsterdam, **Haarlem** is a graceful town of winding canals and medieval neighborhoods that also holds several fine museums. The best time to visit is Saturday, for the market on the **Grote Markt,** or in tulip season (Mar to mid-May), when the city explodes with flowers. Haarlem is 15 minutes from Amsterdam by **train,** and two or three depart every hour from Centraal Station. A round-trip ticket is 5.25€ ($6). There are frequent **buses** from outside Centraal Station. If you go by **car,** take N5 and then A5 west.

VISITOR INFORMATION   **VVV Haarlem,** Stationsplein 1, 2011 Haarlem (✆ **0900/61-61-600;** fax 023/534-0537; www.vvvzk.nl), is just outside the railway station. The office is open Monday to Friday from 9:30am to 5:30pm, Saturday 10am to 2pm.

SEEING THE SIGHTS   Haarlem is where Frans Hals, Jacob van Ruysdael, and Pieter Saenredam were living and painting their famous portraits, landscapes, and church interiors, while Rembrandt was living and working in Amsterdam.

Handel and Mozart made special visits here just to play the magnificent organ of **Sint-Bavokerk (St. Bavo's Church),** also known as the **Grote Kerk** ★, Oude Groenmarkt 23 (✆ **023/532-4399**). Look for the tombstone of painter Frans Hals and for a cannonball that has been embedded in the church's wall ever since it came flying through a window during the 1572–73 siege of Haarlem. And, of course, don't miss the famous Christian Müller Organ, built in 1738. You can hear it at one of the free concerts given on Tuesday and Thursday, April to October. It has 5,068 pipes and is nearly 30m (98 ft.) tall. The woodwork was done by Jan van Logteren. Mozart played the organ in 1766 when he was just 10 years old. St. Bavo's is open Monday to Saturday from 10am to 4pm. Admission is 1.50€ ($1.75), and 1€ ($1.15) for children under 15.

From St. Bavo's, it's an easy walk to the **Frans Halsmuseum** ★★, Groot Heiligland 62 (✆ **023/516-4200;** www.franshalsmuseum.nl), where the galleries are the halls and furnished chambers of a former pensioners' home, and famous paintings by the masters of the Haarlem school hang in settings that look like the 17th-century homes they were intended to adorn. It's open Tuesday to Saturday 11am to 5pm, Sunday and holidays noon to 5pm; closed January 1 and December 25. Admission is 5.40€ ($6.20) adults, 4€ ($4.60) seniors, free for visitors under 19.

The oldest and perhaps the most unusual museum in the Netherlands, the **Teylers Museum,** Spaarne 16 (✆ **023/531-9010;** www.teylersmuseum.nl), contains a curious collection. There are drawings by Michelangelo, Raphael, and Rembrandt; fossils, minerals, and skeletons; instruments of physics; and an odd assortment of inventions, including the world's largest electrostatic generator, dating from 1784, and a 19th-century radarscope. It's open Tuesday to Saturday 10am to 5pm and Sunday and holidays noon to 5pm; closed January 1 and December 25. Admission is 5.50€ ($6.35) adults, 1€ ($1.15) children 5 to 18, and free for children under 5.

An ideal way to tour the city is by **canal boat cruise,** operated by **Woltheus Cruises** (© **023/535-7723**) from their Spaarne River jetty, Gravensteenbrug. Cruises run from April to October at 10:30am, noon, 1:30, 3, and 4:30pm (during some months the 1st and last tours are on request only), and are 6.50€ ($7.50) adults, 4€ ($4.60) children 3 to 11, free for children under 3.

WHERE TO DINE   You can get reasonably priced meals at **Café Mephisto,** Grote Markt 29 (© **023/532-9742**). At this comfortable brown cafe, the decor is Art Nouveau and the music leans toward classic jazz. *Broodjes* are 2.75€ to 4.50€ ($3.15–$5.20), and the kitchen turns out a respectable chicken satay for 8.75€ ($10). It opens daily at 9am (meals begin at noon) and closes at 2am on weekdays, 3am on weekends. No credit cards are accepted.

DELFT: BEYOND THE BLUE & WHITE

Yes, **Delft,** 54km (33 miles) south of Amsterdam, is the home of the famous blue-and-white porcelain. And, yes, you can visit the factory of Koninklijke Porceleyne Fles. But don't let Delftware be your only reason to visit. This is one of the prettiest small cities in the Netherlands, and is also important as a cradle of the Dutch Republic and the traditional burial place of the royal family. Plus, it was the birthplace, and inspiration, of the 17th-century master of light and subtle emotion painter Jan Vermeer. To this day, Delft remains a quiet little town, with flowers in its flower boxes and linden trees bending over its gracious canals.

There are several **trains** an hour from Amsterdam's Centraal Station to Delft. The trip takes about 1 hour and is 15€ ($17) round-trip. If you go by **car,** take A4/E19 then A13/E19 past Den Haag (The Hague), and watch for the Delft exit.

VISITOR INFORMATION   **Tourist Information Delft,** Hippolytusbuurt 4, 2611 HN Delft (© **015/215-4051;** www.delft.nl), is in the center of town and open daily.

SEEING THE SIGHTS   Vermeer's house is long gone from Delft, as are his paintings. But you can visit the **Oude Kerk,** Roland Holstlaan 753 (© **015/212-3015**), where he's buried. You might also want to visit the **Nieuwe Kerk** , Markt (© **015/212-3025**), where Prince William of Orange and other members of the House of Oranje-Nassau are buried, and to climb its tower, which is 109m (357 ft.) high. Both churches are open April to October, Monday to Saturday 9am to 6pm; November to March, Monday to Friday 11am to 4pm, Saturday 11am to 5pm. Separate admission to each is 3€ ($3.45) adults, 1.50€ ($1.75) children 5 to 14, and free for children under 5; separate admission to the Nieuwe Kerk tower is 2€ ($2.30) adults, 1€ ($1.15) children 5 to 14, and free for children under 5.

The **Prinsenhof Museum** , Sint-Agathaplein 1 (© **015/260-2358**), on the nearby Oude Delft Canal, is where William I of Orange (William the Silent) lived and had his headquarters during the years he helped found the Dutch Republic. It's also where he was assassinated in 1584. (You can still see the musket-ball holes in the stairwell.) Today, the Prinsenhof is a museum of paintings, tapestries, silverware, and pottery. It's open Tuesday to Saturday 10am to 5pm, Sunday 1 to 5pm; closed January 1 and December 25. Admission is 5€ ($5.75) adults, 4€ ($4.60) children 12 to 16, and free for children under 12.

In the same neighborhood, you can see a fine collection of old Delft tiles displayed in the wood-paneled setting of a 19th-century mansion museum called **Lambert van Meerten,** Oude Delft 199 (© **015/260-2358**). It's open Tuesday to Saturday 10am to 5pm, Sunday 1 to 5pm; closed January 1 and December 25. Admission is 3.50€ ($4) adults, 3€ ($3.45) children 12 to 16, and free for children under 12.

To see a demonstration of the traditional art of making and hand-painting Delftware, visit the factory and showroom of **Koninklijke Porceleyne Fles,** Rotterdamseweg 196 (℧ **015/251-2030;** bus: 63, 121, or 129 to Jaffalaan), founded in 1653. It's open year-round, Monday to Saturday 9am to 5pm and Sunday (Apr–Oct only) from 9:30am to 4pm; closed December 25 to January 1. Admission is 2.50€ ($2.90), free for children under 13.

WHERE TO STAY   In a pinch, you could try the pensions near the railway station, but they fill up fast in summer. Another possibility is **'t Raedthuys,** Markt 38–40, 2611 GV Delft (℧ **015/212-5115;** fax 015/213-6069), with nine units (some with bathroom). Singles are 40€ to 55€ ($46–$63), doubles are 45€ to 65€ ($52–$75). American Express, Diners Club, MasterCard, and Visa are accepted. Also in the town center is the slightly pricier **De Koophandel,** Beestenmarkt 30, 2611 GC Delft (℧ **015/214-2302;** fax 015/214-0674), which has 21 units for 70€ ($81) single, 85€ ($98) double, breakfast included. American Express, Diners Club, MasterCard, and Visa are accepted.

WHERE TO DINE   The best Dutch restaurant is **Spijshuis de Dis** ⟨, Beestenmarkt 36 (℧ **015/213-1782**), where a meal is around 20€ ($23) and the specialty is steak. It's open Thursday to Tuesday from 5 to 10:30pm and accepts American Express, Diners Club, MasterCard, and Visa. The large **Stadsherberg De Mol,** Molslaan 104 (℧ **015/212-1343**), serving Dutch food, has live music and dancing, and serves a fixed-price menu for 65€ ($75). The food is served medieval style in wooden bowls, and you eat with your hands. It's open Tuesday to Sunday from 6 to 11pm and accepts MasterCard and Visa.

4

Athens & Delphi

by Sherry Marker

Athens is the city Greeks love to hate. They complain that it's too expensive, crowded, and polluted. It seems about to burst at the seams, with at least five million people and streets so congested you'll suspect each Athenian has a car. The Athens Metro now makes it much easier to get around central Athens and has significantly reduced pollution as well as traffic. Construction of Athens's "archaeological park"—a network of pedestrian walkways linking the major archaeological sites—makes walking in much of central Athens a real pleasure.

Even though you've probably come to see the glory that was Greece—perhaps best symbolized by the Parthenon and the superb statues and vases in the National Archaeological Museum—allow some time to make haste slowly in Athens. Your best moments may come at a small cafe, sipping a tiny cup of the sweet sludge Greeks call coffee, or getting lost in the Plaka, only to find yourself in the shady courtyard of an old church or being guided to your destination by a stranger who takes the time to see you on your way. With some advance planning, you should find a pleasant and inexpensive hotel, eat well in convivial restaurants, and leave Athens planning to return, as the Greeks say, *tou chronou* (next year).

For more on Athens and its environs, see *Frommer's Greece* or *Frommer's Greek Islands*.

1 Essentials

GETTING THERE

BY PLANE   The **Athens International Airport Eleftherios Venizelos** (_(C)_ **210/ 353-0000;** www.aia.gr), 27km (17 miles) northeast of Athens at Spata, opened in 2001. The good news is that this is a large, modern facility, with ample restrooms, interesting shops, and acceptable restaurants. The bad news is that unlike Hellinikon Airport, which was virtually in Athens, the new airport is a serious slog from Athens. Although the direct six-lane link road to Athens and the ring road that links up with the National Highway into the Peloponnese at Eleusis are officially complete, not all exits, entrances, and feeder roads are in place, nor are they accurately signposted. At present, allow at least an hour for the journey from the airport to Athens (and vice-versa) by bus or taxi; you may be pleasantly surprised that you need less time, or you may find yourself glad you allowed the full hour. Bus service to Syntagma Square or to Piraeus costs about 4€ ($4.60). Officially, there's one bus to Syntagma and one to Piraeus every 20 minutes. A taxi into central Athens usually costs around 20€ to 30€ ($23–$35), depending on the time of day and traffic. Bus and taxi stations are signposted at the airport.

> ### ⌒Tips Airport Diversion
>
> The very impressive, privately operated **Attica Zoological Park** ⋆⋆ (© **210/663-4724**; atticapark@internet.gr) in Spata, not far from the new airport at Spata, is home to more than 2,000 birds from some 320 species, a butterfly garden, and a small farm. The zoo, which plans to add more exhibits, is open daily from 10am to 7pm and charges 8€ ($9.20) admission (4€/$4.60 for children). Given the state of most airports in the summer, the zoo might seem an oasis of tranquillity.

Keep in mind that the airport's website and official publications cannot always be relied on for accurate, up-to-date information. The airport has shops (including a good bookstore, and stores carrying attractively priced perfumes and colognes) and restaurants (including the inevitable McDonald's).

When planning your carry-on luggage for the Athens airport, keep in mind that you may have quite a trek from your arrival point to the baggage-claim area. Also keep in mind that the luggage allowance for most flights within Europe is 20 kilos (44 lb.). This is almost certainly less than you were allowed if you flew to Greece from the U.S. or Canada.

Tourist information, currency exchange, a post office, baggage storage (left luggage), and car rentals are available at the arrivals level of the main terminal. ATMs, telephones, toilets, and luggage carts (1€/$1.15) are available at the baggage-claim area. There are also several free phones from which you can call for a porter. *Note:* Porters' fees are highly negotiable.

Travelers complain frequently that adequate information on arrivals, departures, cancellations, delays, and gate changes is not always posted on the flight information screens. Nonetheless, it is important to check these screens and at the information desks, as there are currently no flight announcements. Arrive at your gate as early as possible; gates are sometimes changed at the last minute, necessitating a considerable scramble to reach the new gate in time.

Note: Rumors continue to circulate that Olympic Airways will announce bankruptcy. Thus far, Olympic has managed to pull itself back from the brink but it has cut back significantly on scheduled flights. Virgin Atlantic Airline has closed its Athens office, increasing the fares of other carriers that fly the London–Athens route.

BY TRAIN   Central Athens claims two train stations, both located just off Dilyianni, northwest of Omonia Square. Trains from the west, including Eurail connections via Patra, arrive at the **Stathmos Peloponnissou (Peloponnese Station),** about 1.5km (1 mile) northwest of Omonia Square. Trains from the north arrive 3 blocks further north at the **Stathmos Larissis (Larissa Station),** on the opposite side of the tracks from the Peloponnese Station. If you are making connections from one station to the other, allow 10 to 15 minutes for the walk. Both stations have currency-exchange offices usually open daily from 8am to 9:15pm; they also have luggage-storage offices charging 4€ ($4.60) per bag per day, open daily from 6:30am to 9:30pm. The cafe and waiting room are sometimes closed. A **taxi** into the center of town should cost about 6€ ($6.90). For information on schedules and fares, contact the **Greek Railroad Company (OSE;** © **210/512-4913** or 210/529-7777; www.ose.gr).

BY BOAT   Piraeus, the main harbor of Athens's main seaport, 11km (7 miles) southwest of central Athens, is a 15-minute subway (Metro) ride from Monastiraki and Omonia squares. The subway runs from about 5am to midnight and costs 1€ ($1.15). The far-slower bus no. 040 runs from Piraeus to central Athens (with a stop at Filellinon off Syntagma Sq.) every 15 minutes between 5am and 1am and hourly from 1am to 5am, for .50€ (60¢).

You might prefer to take a **taxi** to avoid what can be a long hike from your boat to the bus stop or subway terminal. Be prepared for some serious bargaining. The normal fare on the meter from Piraeus to Syntagma should be about 7€ to 12€ ($8.05–$14), but many drivers simply offer a flat fare, which can be as much as 20€ ($23). Pay it if you're desperate, or walk to a nearby street, hail another taxi, and insist that the meter be turned on.

If you travel to Piraeus by hydrofoil *(Flying Dolphin),* you'll probably arrive at the **Zea Marina** harbor, about a dozen blocks south across the peninsula from the main harbor. Even our Greek friends admit that getting a taxi from Zea Marina into Athens can involve a wait of an hour or more—and that drivers usually drive a hard (and exorbitant) bargain. To avoid both the wait and the big fare, walk up the hill from the hydrofoil station and catch bus no. 905 for .50€ (60¢); it connects Zea to the Piraeus subway station, where you can complete your journey into Athens. You must buy a ticket at the small ticket stand near the bus stop or at a newsstand before boarding the bus. *Warning:* If you arrive late at night, you might not be able to do this, as both the newsstand and the ticket stand may be closed.

VISITOR INFORMATION

TOURIST OFFICE   In 2003, the **Greek National Tourism Organization** (GNTO or EOT, also known as the Hellenic Tourism Organization) closed its main office just off Syntagma Square. The new main office is at 7 Tsochas St., Ambelokipi (© **210/870-0000;** www.gnto.gr), well out of central Athens, but the GNTO promised to open mini-information centers in and around Syntagma Square by summer 2004 (after this book went to press). The Tsochas office is open Monday through Friday from 8am to 3pm and is closed weekends. Information about Athens, free city maps, transportation schedules, hotel lists, and booklets on other regions of Greece are available in Greek, English, French, and German, although many publications on popular sights seem to be perpetually out of print.

WEBSITES   Sites include **www.greece.gr, www.culture.gr, www.phantis. com,** and **www.ellada.com** for Athens and Greece in general; **http://city.net** (Athens information); **www.athensnews.gr** (*The Athens News,* Greece's English-language newspaper); **www.eKathimerini.com** (an insert of translations from

---

Tips Taxi Savvy

If you decide to splurge on a taxi, ask an airline official or a policeman what the fare should be, and let the taxi driver know you've been told the official rate before you begin your journey. If you're taking a taxi to the airport, try to have the desk clerk at your hotel order it for you well in advance of your departure. Many taxis refuse to go to the airport, fearing that they'll have a long wait before they get a return fare.

> ⌒*Value* **Budget Bests**
>
> From hotels and restaurants to transportation and sights (many museums and monuments are free on Sun), Athens has long been one of the least expensive European capitals. Inflation since Greece joined the Common Market has made Athens significantly less of a bargain, but it remains very cheap compared to virtually every other Common Market country capital.
>
> If you're here in winter, you may be able to take advantage of the low prices usually offered at Athens's hotels, including many luxury hotels; do not hesitate to ask about special seasonal offers when you make reservations. This can even be true of two of Athens's finest hotels, the **Hilton** and the **Grande Bretagne,** which underwent extensive renovations in anticipation of the 2004 Athens Summer Olympics.
>
> And remember that at most Greek cafes, including the chic spots in Kolonaki Square and the very pleasant Aigli in the National Gardens, you're perfectly welcome to sit as long as you like and enjoy the passing scene for the price of a coffee. When you feel like stretching your legs, explore the former royal gardens for free!
>
> Art lovers should keep an eye out for notices in the English-language newspapers the *Athens News* and "Kathimerini" (an insert in the Athens edition of the *Herald Tribune*), which announce gallery openings. Openings are usually free and open to the public—and sometimes even include free nibbles!

the Greek press sold with the *International Herald Tribune*); **www.all-hotels.gr/intro.asp** (information on hotels); **www.dilos.com** (travel information, including discounted hotel prices); **www.gtp.gr** (information on ferry service); **www.greekislands.gr** (information on the islands); **www.greektravel.com** (a helpful site on all aspects of Greece run by American Matt Barrett); **www.ancientgreece.com** and **www.perseus.tufts.edu** (an excellent source about ancient Greece); and **www.greekbooks.com**, **www.book.culture.gr**, **www.nbc.gr**, and **www.greekbooks.gr** (useful sites for information on books on many aspects of Greece). For information on the Olympics, check out **www.athens2004.com** and **www.cultural-olympiad.gr**.

CITY LAYOUT

If you, like the Greek mathematician Euclid, find it easy to imagine geometric forms, it will help you to think of central Athens as an almost perfect equilateral triangle, with its points at **Syntagma (Constitution) Square, Omonia (Harmony) Square,** and **Monastiraki (Little Monastery) Square,** near the **Acropolis.** In government jargon, the area bounded by Syntagma, Omonia, and Monastiraki squares is defined as the commercial center, from which cars are banned (in theory, if not in practice) except for several cross streets. Most Greeks consider Omonia the city center, but visitors usually get their bearings from Syntagma, where the House of Parliament is. Few Athenians were enchanted with Omonia's "face-lift" in honor of the Olympics; 27 months and two million euros later, it is now possible to walk somewhat safely across Omonia Square—on lots of cement. The promised trees, at least at press time, had not appeared. Syntagma Square was also redesigned, losing several lanes of traffic—and gaining congestion, as well as several fountains and some greenery. Omonia and Syntagma squares are connected by the parallel **Stadiou Street** and **Panepistimiou Street,** also called **Eleftheriou Venizelou.** West from Syntagma Square, ancient **Ermou Street** and broader **Mitropoleos Street** lead slightly downhill to **Monastiraki Square.** Here you'll find the **flea market,** the **Ancient Agora (Market)** below the Acropolis, and the **Plaka,** the oldest neighborhood, with many street names and a scattering of monuments from antiquity. A special bonus: **Adrianou,** the main drag in Plaka, which once teemed with traffic, is now pedestrian-only, as is **Odos Dionissiou Areopayitou,** at the foot of the Acropolis. From Monastiraki Square, **Athinas Street** leads north past the modern market (the Central Market) to Omonia Square. Bustling with shoppers in the daytime, Athinas Street is less savory and to be avoided at night, when prostitutes and drug dealers tend to hang out. Newly fashionable **Psirri** (until recently a run-down warehouse district), with galleries, cafes, and restaurants, runs between Ermou and Athinas.

Athens Deals & Discounts

SPECIAL DISCOUNTS With an **International Student Identification Card (ISIC),** students get a substantial discount—usually 50%—on admission to archaeological sites and museums, and to most artistic events, theater performances, and festivals. If you have documents proving you're a student, you can get a student card (8€/$9.20) at the **International Student and Youth Travel Service,** on the second floor of 11 Nikis St., 2 blocks southeast of Syntagma Square (© 210/323-3767). It's open Monday to Friday 9am to 5pm, Saturday 9am to 1pm. (Discounts are sometimes available merely with a student ID from a college or university.) Those under 26, student or not, can buy international rail tickets for up to 40% below official prices here.

Most museums also grant 30% to 50% ticket discounts to **seniors**—women over 60 and men over 65 who have proof they're citizens of a European Union country. Some museums also offer a senior discount to U.S. citizens—you have to ask and hope for the best, as only inconsistency is reliably consistent in Greece.

WORTH A SPLURGE Why not get tickets to a concert or an opera at Athens's handsome new **Megaron Mousikis Concert Hall** (© 210/728-2333)? For 20€ ($23) you can often get wonderful seats, hear terrific music, and see elegant Athenians in silks and furs mingling with counter-culture students in jeans and T-shirts. After the performance, treat yourself to a glass of wine or a very serious martini at one of Kolonaki's fashionable watering holes. **To Ouzadiko,** 25–29 Karneadou St. (© 210/729-5484), in the Lemnos International Shopping Center, has at least 40 kinds of ouzo and at least that many kinds of *mezédes,* including superb zesty *horta* (greens). **To Prytaneion,** 7 Millioni (© 210/364-3353), is the place to go for smoked salmon and beef carpaccio. It's easy to spend another 20€ ($23) and more at either place, but the people-watching alone is worth the price of admission.

In general, finding your way around Athens is easy, except in the Plaka, at the foot of the Acropolis. This labyrinth of narrow, winding streets can challenge even the best navigators. Don't panic: The area is small enough that you can't go far astray, and its side streets, with small houses and neighborhood churches, are so charming that you won't mind being lost. One excellent map may help: the Greek Archaeological Service's **Historical Map of Athens,** which includes the Plaka and the city center and shows the major archaeological sites. The map costs about 4€ ($4.60) and is sold at many bookstores, museums, ancient sites, and newspaper kiosks.

GETTING AROUND

BY BUS, TROLLEY BUS & METRO (SUBWAY) The **blue-and-white buses** run regular routes in Athens and its suburbs every 15 minutes daily from 5am to midnight. The **orange electric trolley buses** serve areas in the city center daily from 5am to midnight. The **green buses** run between the city center and Piraeus every 20 minutes daily from 6am to midnight, then hourly to 6am. At press time, tickets cost .50€ (60¢) and must be bought in advance, usually in groups of 10, from any news kiosk or special bus ticket kiosks at the main stations. When you board, validate your ticket in the automatic machine. Hold onto it: Uniformed and plainclothes inspectors periodically check tickets and can levy a basic fine of 5€ ($5.75) or a more punitive fine of 20€, on the spot.

The major bus stations in Athens are: Suburban bus terminal at Areos Park; Long Distance Bus Terminal A, 100 Kiffissou (reached by bus no. 051 from Zinonos and Menandrou sts., off Omonia Sq.); and Long Distance Bus Terminal B, 260 Liossion (reached by bus no. 024 from Amalias Ave., Syntagma Sq.). *Important:* Keep in mind that the numbers of buses serving these routes may have changed by the time you visit Athens—and fares are certain to increase.

The original **Metro** line links Piraeus, Athens's seaport; central Athens itself; and Kifissia, an upscale northern suburb. A second line, with its main station in Syntagma Square, links the Defense Ministry on Mesogheion Avenue with central Athens and the northwest suburb of Sepolia. Original plans for the entire 21-station Metro to be running by the end of 2002 were changed to target the August 2004 Summer Olympics. (Now, if someone would just build adequate parking lots near the new Metro stops so that commuters can leave their cars there rather than park them on every available inch of the sidewalks. . . .) In the city center, the main stops are **Syntagma, Acropolis, Monastiraki, Omonia,** and **Viktorias (Victoria).** Trains run about every 5 to 15 minutes daily from 5am to midnight. At present, tickets on the old line cost .60€ (70¢); tickets on the new line cost .75€ (85¢); and a day pass costs 3€ ($3.45)—but don't be surprised if these prices have gone up by the time you arrive. Validate your ticket in the machine as you enter the waiting platform, or risk a fine. Metro and bus tickets are not interchangeable.

BY TAXI Supposedly there are 17,000 taxis in Athens, but finding one empty is almost never easy. Especially if you have travel connections to make, it's a good

---

Metro Museums

Allow a little extra time when you catch the Metro in central Athens. Two stations—**Syntagma Square** and **Acropolis**—handsomely display finds from the subway excavations in what amounts to Athens's newest small museums. For more on the Athens Metro, go to **www.ametro.gr**.

> **Tips A Taxi Warning**
>
> There are increasing numbers of unlicensed cab drivers In Athens and Piraeus. Usually, these pirate cabbies (many from eastern Europe) drive a gray car you might mistake for the standard gray Athens taxi. It's always a good idea to make sure your cab driver has a meter and a photo ID. Many of the unlicensed cab drivers are uninsured and unfamiliar with the metropolitan area; some are outright crooks and have robbed passengers.

idea to pay the 2€ ($2.30) surcharge and reserve a radio taxi. The minimum fare in a taxi is 2€ ($2.30). Some radio taxi companies and phone numbers are: **Athina** © 210/921-7942; **Express** © 210/993-4812; **Parthenon** © 210/532-3300; and **Piraeus** © 210/418-2333. Most hotels and restaurants will call a radio taxi for you without charge.

When you get into a taxi, check to see that the meter is turned on and set on "1" rather than "2"; it should be set on "2" (double fare) only from midnight to 5am or if you take a taxi outside the city limits. (If you plan to take a cab out of town, it is best to negotiate a flat rate in advance.) Unless your cab is caught in very heavy traffic, a trip to the center of town from the airport between 5am and midnight shouldn't cost more than 15€ to 25€ ($17–$29). Don't be surprised if your driver picks up other passengers en route; he'll work out everyone's share, and probably the worst that will happen is you'll get less of a break on the shared fare than you would if you spoke Greek. Most Greek passengers at least round out the fare—for example, from 2.90€ to 3€—and some give a bit more of a tip.

If you suspect you've been overcharged, ask for help at your hotel or other destination before you pay the fare. Keep in mind that your driver may have difficulty understanding your pronunciation of your destination. If you are taking a taxi from your hotel, a staff member can tell the driver your destination or write down the address for you to show to the driver. If you carry a business card from your hotel, you can show it to the driver when you return. Most restaurants will call for a taxi at no charge. The Greek National Tourist Organization's pamphlet *Helpful Hints for Taxi Users* has information on taxi fares as well as a complaint form, which you can send to the Ministry of Transport and Communication, 13 Xenophondos, 101 91 Athens. (Replies to complaints should be forwarded to the *Guinness Book of Records*.)

BY CAR & MOPED   In Athens a car is more trouble than convenience. Use a car only for trips outside the city—and keep in mind that on any day trip (to Sounion or Eleusis, for example), you'll spend at least several hours leaving and reentering central Athens. And remember this: Greece has the second highest traffic fatality rate in Europe. (Only Portugal has a worse record.) Be careful.

Car-rental agencies in the Syntagma Square area include **Avis,** 48 Amalias Ave. (© **800/331-1084** or 210/322-4951); **AutoEurope,** 29 Hatzihristou St., right off Syngrou (© **800/223-5555** or 210/924-2206); and **Budget,** 8 Syngrou Ave. (© **800/527-0700** or 210/921-4711).

Remember: You get the best deal if you arrange the rental before leaving home. You will usually get the worst possible deal if you arrive in Athens and want a car for only 1 day.

In season, prices for rentals from well-known international companies range from about 40€ to 100€ ($46–$115). *Warning:* Be sure to take full insurance and ask if the price you are quoted includes everything. Often the price quoted

Country & City Codes

Greek telephone codes have changed several times in the past few years. Currently, to dial a number in Athens from outside Greece, dial 011 30 (Greece) + 210 (Athens) + the seven-digit Athens number. To dial Athens from within Greece, dial 210 + the seven-digit Athens number. To dial a number outside of Athens from outside Greece, dial 011 30 (Greece) + the local area code + the local number. To dial a number outside of Athens from within Greece, dial the local area code + the local number. Remember: When you are in Greece, you must use the area code even if you are phoning within the same area—even if you are just phoning across the street!

doesn't include all taxes, drop-off fee, gasoline charges, and so on. Be particularly vigilant if you intend to collect or return your car at an airport: Many companies charge a hefty fee for this—but they do not mention it to you when you reserve your car.

You can rent mopeds from **Meintanis,** 4 Dionyssiou Areopagitou St., near the intersection with Amalias Avenue, Plaka (© **210/323-2346**), for about 25€ ($29), tax included. Ask for the 20% discount if you rent for a week. *Note:* Riding a moped in Athens is *not* for the faint of heart.

ON FOOT   Most of what you probably want to see and do in Athens is in the city center, allowing you to sightsee mostly on foot. The pedestrian zones in sections of the Plaka, the commercial center, and Kolonaki make strolling, window-shopping, and sightseeing infinitely more pleasant than on other, traffic-clogged streets. Nonetheless, visitors should keep in mind that here, as in many busy cities, a red traffic light or stop sign is no guarantee that cars (or motorcycles) will stop for pedestrians.

FAST FACTS: Athens

American Express   The office at 2 Ermou St., near the southwest corner of Syntagma Square, 102 25 Athens, Greece (© **210/324-4975**), offers currency exchange and other services Monday to Friday 8:30am to 4pm and Saturday 8:30am to 1:30pm.

ATMs   ATMs are increasingly common in Athens, and the National Bank of Greece operates a 24-hour ATM on Syntagma Square. However, it's not a good idea to rely on using ATMs exclusively in Athens: The machines are sometimes out of service when you need them most, on holidays, or during bank strikes.

Banks   Banks are generally open Monday to Thursday 8am to 2pm and Friday 8am to 1:30pm. Most have currency-exchange counters that use the rates set daily by the government; these rates are usually more favorable than those offered at unofficial exchange bureaus. It's worthwhile to do a little comparison-shopping: For example, some hotels offer rates (usually only for cash) better than the official bank rate. If you need money after bank hours and your hotel can't help, try **Acropole,** 21 Kidathineon, Plaka (© **210/331-2764**), usually open daily 8am to midnight.

Business Hours In winter, **shops** are generally open Monday and Wednesday 9am to 5pm; Tuesday, Thursday, and Friday 10am to 7pm; and Saturday 8:30am to 3:30pm. In summer, shops are generally open Monday, Wednesday, and Saturday 8am to 3pm; and Tuesday, Thursday, and Friday 8am to 1:30pm and 5:30 to 10pm. Many shops geared to visitors keep especially long hours, but some close daily 2 to 5pm. Most **food stores** and the **Central Market** are open Monday and Wednesday 9am to 4:30pm, Tuesday 9am to 6pm, Thursday 9:30am to 6.30pm, Friday 9:30am to 7pm, and Saturday 8:30am to at least 4:30pm.

Currency In 2002, Greece adopted the **euro** (€) for its currency. At press time, 1€ = $1.15 or $1 = 87€.

Dentists & Doctors If you need an English-speaking doctor or dentist, call your embassy for advice; or try **SOS Doctor** (© 210/331-0310 or 210/331-0311). The English-language *Athens News* lists some American- and British-trained doctors and hospitals offering emergency services. Most of the larger hotels have doctors whom they can call for you in an emergency.

Embassies & Consulates **Australia,** Leoforos Dimitriou Soutsou 37 (© 210/645-0404-5); **Canada,** Odos Ioannou Yenadiou 4 (© 210/727-3400 or 210/725-4011); **Ireland,** Vasilissis Konstantinou 7 (© 210/723-2771); **New Zealand,** Xenias 24, Ambelokipi (© 210/771-0112); **South Africa,** Kifissias 60, Maroussi (© 210/680-6645); **United Kingdom,** Odos Ploutarchou 1 (© 210/723-6211); and **United States,** Leoforos Vasilissis Sofias 91 (© 210/721-2951; emergency number 210/729-4301). Be sure to phone ahead before you go to any embassy; most are open for business 9am to noon only and are usually closed on their own as well as Greek holidays.

Emergencies In an emergency, dial © **100** for fast police assistance and © **171** for the Tourist Police (see "Police," below). Dial © **199** to report a fire and © **166** for an ambulance or a hospital.

Holidays Major public holidays in Athens include New Year's Day (Jan 1), Epiphany (Jan 6), Ash Wednesday, Independence Day (Mar 25), Good Friday, Easter Sunday and Monday (Orthodox Easter can coincide with or vary by 2 weeks from Catholic and Protestant Easter), Labor Day (May 1), Assumption Day (Aug 15), National Day (better known as Oxi Day; Oct 28), and Christmas (Dec 25–26). It's not unusual for some shops and offices to close for at least a week at Christmas and Easter.

Internet Access As a general rule, most cybercafes charge about 5€ ($5.75) an hour. The very efficient and helpful **Sofokleous.com Internet C@fe** 🔍, Stadiou 5, a block off Syntagma Square (©/fax 210/324-8105; www.sofokleous.com), is open daily 10am to 10pm. The **Astor Internet Café,** Odos Patission 27, a block off Omonia Square (© 210/523-8546), is open Monday to Saturday 10am to 10pm and Sunday 10am to 4pm. Across from the National Archaeological Museum is the **Museum Internet Cafe,** Odos Octobriou 28, also called Odos Patission (© 210/883-3418; www.museumcafe.gr), open daily 9am to 11pm. To find out about more cybercafes in Greece, check out **www.netcafeguide.com/countries/greece.htm**.

Mail The main **post offices** in central Athens are at 100 Eolou St., just south of Omonia Square, and in Syntagma Square on the corner of

Mitropoleos Street. They're open Monday to Friday 7:30am to 8pm, Saturday 7:30am to 2pm, and Sunday 9am to 1pm.

All the post offices can accept small parcels. The (usually very crowded) **parcel post office**, 4 Stadiou St., inside the arcade (© **210/322-8940**), is open Monday to Friday 7:30am to 8pm. Parcels must be open for inspection before you seal them at the post office. Bring your own sealing tape and string.

Pharmacies Pharmakia, identified by green crosses, are scattered throughout Athens. Hours are usually Monday to Friday 8am to 2pm. In the evening and on weekends most are closed, but they usually post a notice listing the names and addresses of pharmacies that are open or will open in an emergency. Newspapers, including the *Athens News,* list the pharmacies open outside regular hours.

Police In an emergency, dial © **100.** For help dealing with a troublesome taxi driver or hotel, restaurant, or shop owner, call the Tourist Police at © **171;** they're on call 24 hours and usually speak English, as well as other foreign languages.

Taxes A **value-added tax (VAT)** is included in the price of all goods and services in Athens, ranging from 4% on books to 36% on certain luxury items. Although in theory you should be able to get a refund on VAT at the airport, the red tape involved makes it virtually impossible in practice. If you want to try for a refund, keep all your receipts and look for the VAT booth (often closed) at the airport.

Telephone Many of the city's public phones now accept only phone cards, available at newsstands and OTE offices in several denominations starting at 5€ ($5.75). The card works for 100 short local calls (or briefer long distance or international calls). Some kiosks still have metered phones; you pay what the meter records. North Americans can phone home directly by contacting **AT&T** (© **00-800-1311**), **MCI** (© **00-800-1211**), or **Sprint** (© **00-800-1411**). You can send a telegram or fax from offices of the **Telecommunications Organization of Greece (OTE).** There are OTE offices in central Athens at 15 Stadiou, near Syntagma, in Omonia Square, and in Victoria Square Office at 85 Patission St.

Outside Athens, most OTEs are closed on weekends, although in major ports and tourist centers this is not always the case.

Tipping Restaurants include a service charge in the bill, but many Greeks and visitors add a 10% or more tip. Most Greeks don't give a percentage tip to taxi drivers, but they sometimes add a small tip for especially good service or a long ride.

2 Affordable Places to Stay

To avoid settling for a bad or expensive room, book in advance or arrive with a considerable reserve of time and energy. Staff at the **Greek National Tourist Organization** booth (see "Visitor Information," earlier in this chapter) at the Spata airport will sometimes help travelers find a hotel, but remember: Rooms

---

Credit Card Alert

Some small hotels require a credit card number to guarantee your reservation, but demand actual payment in cash.

---

are scarce every July and August—and virtually every hotel room for the 2004 Olympics was booked months in advance of the Games. If you decide to head into town and look yourself, you can drop off your baggage (about 2€/$2.30 per bag) at **Pacific Ltd.**, 26 Nikis St. (℃ **210/324-1007**), 2 blocks southwest of Syntagma Square. Its official hours are Monday to Saturday 7am to 8pm and Sunday 7am to 2pm. **Bellair Travel and Tourism Inc.**, 15 Nikis St. (℃ **210/ 323-9261** or 210/321-6136), is open Monday to Friday 9am to 5pm and has similar fees. Although both Pacific and Bellair keep regular hours, it's always a good idea to phone ahead to make sure they are open—and not full.

Almost every Greek hotel is very clean, although few are cozy, charming, or elegant. Don't expect frills (or even eye-appeal) at most budget hotels: Most rooms are rather spartan, furnished with simple beds and bureaus. If shower and tub facilities are important to you, be sure to have a look at the bathroom before you accept a unit; many Greek tubs are tiny and the showers hand-held. Most budget hotels (and some grand ones) don't offer hair dryers in the rooms, but sometimes one is available at the front desk or from housekeeping. It's a good idea to make sure the air-conditioning or central heat work before you check into your room.

The Plaka is the first choice for most budget travelers, but because of its popularity, an affordable room could be hard to find. Try hotels adjacent to the Plaka between Monastiraki and Syntagma squares, on the south side of the Acropolis in Makriyanni, or farther south in Koukaki—but keep in mind that if you stay in Koukaki, you'll spend extra time getting to and from most places you want to go.

Note: You'll find the lodging choices below plotted on the map on p. 132.

IN THE PLAKA

Acropolis House Hotel   Location is practically everything in this venerable small hotel in a renovated 150-year-old villa with minimalist furnishings in the guest rooms. Try to get room no. 401 or 402 for an Acropolis view. The relatively quiet pedestrianized Plaka side street is a real plus, although motorcycles can be a problem. The newer wing (only 65 years old) isn't architecturally special, and the toilets (one for each room) are across the hall. There's a washing machine (for a small fee; free after a 4-day stay). If the Acropolis House is full, try the less appealing Adonis or (still less appealing) Kouros on the same street (see below).

6–8 Kodrou, 105 58 Athens. ℃ **210/322-2344**. Fax 210/324-4143. 25 units, 15 with bathroom. 70€ ($80) double without bathroom, 85€ ($98) double with bathroom. 10€ ($12) surcharge for A/C. Rates include continental breakfast. V. Walk 2 blocks out of Syntagma Sq. on Mitropoleos and turn left on Voulis, which becomes pedestrianized Kodrou. *In room:* A/C.

Adams Hotel   Some of my friends always stay at this small hotel on a delightful square across from St. Catherine's, one of the loveliest churches in Athens. They report that the hotel is quiet, the staff very accommodating, and the rooms clean. On the other hand, when I've been here, other guests have been noisy, my room less than spotless, and the staff unhelpful. If you do stay here, let me know what you think—and try to get one of the rooms on the top floor with Acropolis views.

Herefondos 6 and Thalou, 105 58 Athens. ℭ 210/322-5381. Fax 210/323-8553. 15 units, 11 with bathroom. 60€ ($69) double without bathroom, 72€ ($83) double with bathroom. Take Amalias out of Syntagma about 8 blocks to Thalou; turn left on Thalou, which intersects Herefondos.

Byron Hotel   Every year I come close to eliminating the Byron, where the indifferent-at-best service is a real drawback. Still, it offers two real pluses: the relatively quiet central Plaka location just off recently pedestrianized Dionyssiou Areopagitou Street, and a few rooms with Acropolis views. The price is fair (and often highly negotiable). That said, if you don't remember the dingy Byron before its remodeling 4 years ago, the new decor, which lacks charm, might not impress you. I've also had reports that the air-conditioning is temperamental at best. Alas, the same can be said for the service, which is usually haphazard and often curt.

19 Vyronos, 105 58 Athens. ℭ 210/325-3554. Fax 210/323-0327. 20 units. 85€–95€ ($98–$109) double. Rates include breakfast. No credit cards. From Syntagma Sq., walk south on Amalias Ave. past Hadrian's Arch, stay right, and turn right on Dionyssiou Areopagitou; Vyronos ("Byron" in Greek) is the 2nd street on the right, and the hotel (with a portrait of Lord Byron by the door) is on the right. **Amenities:** Bar. *In room:* A/C, TV.

Hotel Adonis 𝕽   The architecturally undistinguished Adonis redecorated its rooms in 2001, but if you hadn't seen the rooms before then, you might not know it. Units are small (all with bathrooms with shower only), but the location, just off Kidathineon Street, is appealing. The view from the rooftop garden overlooking the Acropolis and Lykavitos Hill is a plus, as are the individual balconies with table and chairs. The hotel is popular with students and seldom quiet.

3 Kodrou St., 105 58 Athens. ℭ 210/324-9737. Fax 210/323-1602. 25 units. 80€ ($92) double. Rates include breakfast. AE, V. Walk 2 blocks out of Syntagma Sq. on Mitropoleos St., turn left on Voulis, and continue along the pedestrian-only extension, which is Kodrou. *In room:* A/C, TV.

Hotel Nefeli 𝕽   Rooms at the little Nefeli, just steps from the main Plaka shopping and restaurant streets, are small but comfortable, the quietest overlooking pedestrianized Angelikis Hatzimihali Street (although illegal motorcycle

---

(*Tips* **Olympics Alert**

If you plan to visit Greece around the time of the Athens Summer Olympics (just as this book is being published in Aug 2004), be forewarned: Hotel rooms in and around Athens for the Olympics were booked months before the games. Many hotel rooms have been booked for several weeks before and after the games as well. In addition, *all* prices, including those of transportation, hotels, restaurants, and even museum and archaeological sites, are likely to be in considerable flux during the Olympics season. Price increases of more than 100% are common—and may be in place for some time to come. Nonetheless, some hotels and restaurants are braced to lower their prices if the Olympics do not bring the expected tourism boon to Greece. Still, 2004 is not shaping up to be a good year for a budget trip to Greece—and it remains to be seen if hotel, restaurant, and transportation prices will return to pre-Olympics inflation levels in 2005.

Tips **Get It in Writing**

To say that prices in Greece are in flux is a considerable understatement. Formerly, most hotels pegged their prices to the drachma/dollar exchange rate, and raised their rates whenever the drachma fell. Similar fluctuation now occurs with the euro/dollar exchange rate. What will happen to hotel rates as a result of the 2004 Olympics is anyone's guess. Double-check any price you are quoted on a hotel and get the price you are offered in writing (i.e., print out and bring with you a copy of any e-mail confirmation).

---

traffic can be a real problem at night). I've found the staff courteous and helpful, and friends who've stayed here say the same. I was, therefore, surprised by one reader's report of curt service, sleep interrupted by a noisy tour group, and a grubby bathroom.

16 Iperidou, 105 58 Athens. © **210/322-8044.** Fax 210/322-5800. 18 units (5 with shower only). 85€–95€ ($98–$109) double. Rates often considerably less off season. Rates include continental breakfast. AE, V. Walk 2 blocks west from Syntagma Sq. on Mitropoleos, turn left on Voulis, cross Nikodimou, and turn right on Iperidou. **Amenities:** Breakfast room. *In room:* A/C, TV.

Kouros Hotel   Like the Adonis and Acropolis House, the Kouros has a great location on pedestrianized Kodrou Street in the heart of the Plaka. From the street, the Kouros is charming: a 200-year-old house with nice architectural details and three attractive balconies. The rooms with balconies get more light but also more street noise. Alas, the small rooms are gloomy—and so is the staff. Many guests tend to stay out late and come back at hours when those less fond of nightlife might be trying to sleep.

11 Kodrou St., 105 58 Athens. © **210/322-7431.** 10 units, none with bathroom. From 65€ ($72) double. No credit cards. Walk 2 blocks west from Syntagma Sq. on Mitropoleos St., turn left on Voulis, and continue along pedestrian-only extension.

Student Inn 🏛   This is as cheap a deal as you'll get in the Plaka. Student friends who've stayed here found the staff very helpful, enjoyed the small garden, and didn't mind the cramped rooms, the Plaka noise, or the lack of air-conditioning and ceiling fans. Ah, to be young again!

16 Kidathineon, 105 58 Athens. © **210/324-4808.** Fax 210/321-0065. 12 units, none with bathroom. From 30€ ($35) double. No credit cards. Breakfast 4€ ($4.60). From Syntagma Sq., walk south on Amalias Ave. until Queen Sophia Ave. and Hadrian's Arch are on your left; turn right onto Thalou, which runs into Pittakou.

NEAR SYNTAGMA SQUARE

Athens Cypria 🏛🏛   After extensive renovations, the former Diomia Hotel was reborn in 2000 as the Athens Cypria. Gone are the Diomia's gloomy lobby and rooms, but the very convenient central location on a street with (usually) no traffic and the splendid Acropolis views from room nos. 603 to 607 remain (as do the less-than-enchanting views of walls and rooftops from other rooms). The breakfast buffet offers hot and cold dishes from 7 to 10am in a mirrored dining room. *One criticism:* Responses to requests for information and reservations are often sluggish.

5 Diomias, 105 62 Athens. © **210/323-8034.** Fax 210/324-8792. 71 units. 130€–150€ ($150–$173) double. Reductions possible off season. Rates include buffet breakfast. AE, MC, V. Take Karayiori Servias out of Syntagma Sq.; Diomias is on the left, after Lekka. **Amenities:** Bar and snack bar; luggage storage. *In room:* A/C, TV, minibar, hair dryer.

> ### _Tips_ More Hotels near Plaka & Syntagma
>
> Although I've never been tempted to stay here because all three hotels seem to focus on tour groups, it's worth knowing that there are three hotels on Odos Apollonos, between Syntagma Square and the Plaka: the **Aphrodite,** Odos Apollonos 21 (© **210/323-4357;** fax 210/322-5244); the **Hermes,** Odos Apollonos 19 (© **210/323-5514;** fax 210/323-2073); and the less expensive **Kimon,** Odos Apollonos 27 (© **210/331-4658;** fax 210/ 502-0134). All three have doubles for less than 100€ ($115)—sometimes for less than 70€ ($80). The lobbies at all three have been noisy and crowded with groups checking in and out when I've visited; the Hermes less so than the other two. I'd appreciate hearing from readers who have stayed at any of these conveniently located hotels.

Hotel Achilleas   The Achilleas (Achilles) has a great location on a relatively quiet side street steps from Syntagma Square and was completely renovated in 2001. Guest rooms here are sometimes heavily discounted off season. Rooms are a good size. Some rear ones have small balconies. Several rooms on the fifth floor can be used as interconnecting family suites. The very central location and fair prices make this hotel a good choice, and the breakfast room is pleasant.

21 Lekka, 105 62 Athens. © 210/323-3197. Fax 210/322-2412. www.achilleashotel.gr. 34 units. 155€ ($178) double. Rates include breakfast. AE, DC, MC, V. With Hotel Grande Bretagne on your right, walk 2 blocks out of Syntagma Sq. on Karayioryi Servias and turn right onto Lekka. **Amenities:** Snack bar. _In room:_ A/C, TV, minibar; hair dryer and safe in most units.

Hotel Astor   A widely traveled journalist tells me he always stays here when in Athens because of the central location, bright rooms (some with Acropolis views), rooftop bar, and efficient (if not pleasant) front desk staff. The journalist also says he usually succeeds in bargaining down the room price. Those in the know report that the Astor sometimes unofficially rents rooms by the hour.

16 Karayioryi Servias St., 105 62 Athens. © 210/335-1000. Fax 210/325-5115. 131 units. From 120€ ($138) double. Rates include buffet breakfast. AE, V. With Hotel Grande Bretagne on your right, walk 3 blocks out of Syntagma Sq. on Karayioryi Servias to the Astor. **Amenities:** Restaurant; bar; snack bar. _In room:_ A/C, TV, minibar.

Hotel Carolina ☆☆   The family-owned and -operated Carolina, on the outskirts of the Plaka, a brisk 5-minute walk from Syntagma, has always been popular with students. Recently, the hotel underwent extensive remodeling and now attracts a wide range of frugal travelers who enjoy its casual atmosphere. Guest rooms have double-glazed windows and air-conditioning; many, like room nos. 407 and 308, have large balconies. Several rooms, such as no. 308, have four or five beds, which make them popular with families and students.

55 Kolokotroni, 105 60 Athens. © 210/324-3551. Fax 210/324-3350. hotelcarolina@galaxtnet.gr. 31 units. 75€–110€ ($86–$127) double; breakfast 5€ ($5.75). MC, V. Take Stadiou out of Syntagma Sq. to Kolokotroni St. (on left). **Amenities:** Breakfast room. _In room:_ A/C, TV.

NEAR MONASTIRAKI SQUARE

Attalos Hotel ☆   The six-story Attalos, recently totally renovated, is well situated for those wanting to take in the exuberant daytime street life of the nearby Central Market and the exuberant nighttime scene at the cafes and restaurants of the Psirri district. The rooms here are plain, but not gloomy; 40 have balconies and 12 have Acropolis views. Unusual for Greece, nonsmoking rooms are available. The roof garden offers fine views of the city and the Acropolis. The hotel often gives a 10% discount to Frommer's readers. As well, good discounts may be given in the off season. *One caution:* Drug dealing and prostitution are not unknown on Athinas Street.

29 Athinas, 105 54 Athens. © **210/391-2801.** Fax 210/324-3124. www.attalos.gr. 80 units. 150€–170€ ($173–$196) double. Rates include buffet breakfast. AE, MC, V. From Monastiraki Sq., walk about 1½ blocks north on Athinas. **Amenities:** Luggage storage. *In room:* A/C, TV, hair dryer (most rooms).

Hotel Cecil *(R)(R) (Value)*   For years, the Cecil was rather grim, but now, recently refurnished, it is positively gracious. The good-sized rooms (with high ceilings) are in a 150-year-old town house. The management tries hard to make guests comfortable—and there's a very appealing roof garden.

39 Athinas, 105 54 Athens. © **210/321-2810.** Fax 210/321-8005. 20 units. 75€ ($86) double. Rates include buffet breakfast. MC, V. From Monastiraki Sq., walk about 1½ blocks north on Athinas. **Amenities:** Breakfast room; roof garden. *In room:* A/C.

Hotel Tempi *(Value)*   For those who need no frills and require minimal comforts, the Tempi is a good choice in a charming location on a pedestrianized square with a small church and a flower market. Rooms are very simply furnished (bed, table, chair), but the beds are decent, and the showers (usually) hot. Ten rooms have balconies from which, if you lean, you can see the Acropolis. There's a rooftop lounge and a book exchange. Two problems: The plumbing leaves a good deal to be desired, and the shared bathrooms can be smelly and in need of cleaning.

29 Eolou, 105 51 Athens. © **210/321-3175.** Fax 210/325-4179. tempihotel@travelling.gr. 24 units, 8 with bathroom. From 65€ ($72) double without bathroom, from 80€ ($92) double with bathroom. AE, MC, V. From Monastiraki Sq., walk 1 block toward Syntagma Sq. on Hermou St. and turn left up Eolou. **Amenities:** Lounge; laundry; luggage storage.

(Value) Getting the Best Deal on Accommodations

- Try to avoid Athens in July and August, when the city is hot and crowded. You can get a better deal in other months (especially Jan–Mar), when rates are reduced about 30% and it's more of a buyer's market.
- If you ask to see a room before you take it, you're more likely to be shown a better room. You might also check out several rooms and ask for a lower price for a smaller, less attractive, or less convenient room.
- Take a room without a private bathroom. Most rooms have a washbasin, and common bathrooms are usually clean and shared by only two or three rooms. If the kind of tub or shower you want is important, ask to see the room. Many Greek tubs are cramped and many showers flimsy.
- Ask for the reduced rate for a stay over 3 nights.
- If you reserve ahead, be sure to ask for information on special packages and reductions. Hotels seldom volunteer this information unless asked.

Jason Inn Hotel 🇷🇷 (value)   If you don't mind walking a few extra blocks to Syntagma, this is one of the best values in Athens, with a staff that's usually very helpful. You're just out of the Plaka, around the corner from the newly fashionable Psirri district and steps from bustling Athinas Street. The hotel is redecorated on a regular basis and has bright, attractive, decent-sized rooms with modern amenities and double-paned windows to keep out traffic noise. If the Jason is full, the staff may be able to find you a room in one of its other hotels: the similarly priced Adrian, in the Plaka; or the slightly less expensive **King Jason** or **Jason,** both a few blocks from Omonia Square.

12 Ayion Assomaton, 105 53 Athens. © 210/325-1106. Fax 210/324-3123 or 210/523-4786. Douros@ hotelnet.gr. 57 units. 95€–155€ ($109–$178) double. Rates include American buffet breakfast. AE, MC, V. From Monastiraki Sq., head west on Ermou, turn right at Thisio Metro station, pass the small below-ground-level church, and bear left. *In room:* A/C, TV, minibar.

IN MAKRIYANNI & KOUKAKI

Acropolis View Hotel 🇷🇷   This nicely maintained hotel is on a residential side street off Rovertou Galli Street, not far from the Herodes Atticus Theater. The usually quiet neighborhood, at the base of Philopappos Hill, is a 10- to 15-minute walk from the heart of the Plaka. Rooms (most freshly painted each year) are small but clean and pleasant, with good bathrooms; 16 have balconies. Some, like no. 405, overlook Philopappos Hill, and others, like no. 407, face the Acropolis.

Rovertou Galli St. and 10 Webster St., 117 42 Athens. © 210/921-7303. Fax 210/923-0705. www. acropolisview.gr. 32 units. 130€ ($150) double. Rates include generous buffet breakfast. Substantial reductions Nov–Apr 1. MC, V. From Syntagma Sq. take Amalias Ave. to Dionyssiou Areopagitou; head west past Herodes Atticus Theater to Rovertou Galli St. Webster (*Gouemster* on some maps) is the little street intersecting Rovertou Galli St. between Propilion and Garabaldi. **Amenities:** Bar. *In room:* A/C, TV, minibar.

Art Gallery Hotel 🇷🇷   As you might expect, this small hotel—in a half-century-old house that has been home to several artists—has an artistic flair (and a nice old-fashioned cage elevator). Customers tend to be loyal, many of them on repeat visits, greeting old friends and cordial to newcomers. Rooms are small and plain but comfortable, some with ceiling fans, although all now have air-conditioning. There's a nice Victorian-style breakfast room on the fourth floor.

5 Erechthiou, Koukaki, 117 42 Athens. © 210/923-8376. Fax 210/923-3025. ecotec@otenet.gr. 22 units. 60€–90€ ($69–$104) double. Rates include generous breakfast. Hotel sometimes closed Nov–Mar; when open then, prices reduced. AE, MC, V. *In room:* A/C, TV.

Austria Hotel 🇷🇷   This very well-maintained hotel at the base of wooded Philopappos Hill is operated by a Greek-Austrian family, who can point you to local sights (including a convenient neighborhood laundry!). The Austria's guest rooms and bathrooms are rather spartan, but more than acceptable—and the very efficient staff is a real plus here. There's a great view over Athens and out to sea from the rooftop (I could see the island of Aegina), where you can sun or sit under an awning.

7 Mousson, Filopappou, 117 42 Athens. © 210/923-5151. Fax 210/924-7350. www.austriahotel.com. 36 units (11 with shower only). 135€ ($155) double. Rates include breakfast. AE, DC, MC, V. Follow Dionyssiou Areopagitou around south side of Acropolis to where it meets Robertou Galli; take Garibaldi around base of Filopappou Hill until you reach Mousson. **Amenities:** Breakfast room; rooftop terrace. *In room:* A/C, fax.

Marble House Pension 🇷🇷 (value)   Named for its marble facade, usually covered by bougainvillea, this small hotel, whose front rooms offer balconies overlooking quiet Zinni Street, is popular with budget travelers (including many teachers). Over the last several years, the pension has been remodeled and redecorated, gaining new bathrooms and guest room furniture. There are two easy-access ground-floor guest rooms, two guest rooms with kitchenettes, and nine guest rooms with air-conditioning. If you're spending more than a few days in Athens and don't mind being out of the center, this is a homey base. We have had one worrying report recently of a decline in the service—let us know what you think.

35 A. Zinni, Koukaki, 117 41 Athens. ℂ 210/923-4058. Fax 210/922-6461. 16 units, 12 with bathroom. From 60€ ($69) double without bathroom, 75€ ($86) double with bathroom. 10€ ($12) supplement for A/C. Monthly rates available off season. No credit cards. From Syntagma Sq. take Amalias Ave. to Syngrou Ave; turn right onto Zinni; the hotel is in the cul-de-sac beside the small church. **Amenities:** Luggage storage. *In room:* TV, minibar.

Parthenon Hotel 𝒜   This recently redecorated hotel has an excellent location just steps from the Plaka and the Acropolis. The Parthenon is one of the AirOtel group of four Athenian hotels; if it's full, the management will try to get you a room at the **Christina,** a few blocks away, or at the **Riva** or **Alexandros,** near the Megaron (Athens Concert Hall). *Warning:* On occasion I've found the desk staff less than helpful and infuriatingly vague about room prices.

6 Makri, 115 27 Athens. ℂ 210/923-4594. Fax 210/644-1084. 79 units. 115€–125€ ($132–$144) double. MC, V. From Syntagma, take Amalias into Dionyssiou Areopagitou; Makri is the 2nd street on the left. **Amenities:** Restaurant; bar; garden. *In room:* A/C, TV.

Tony's Hotel 𝒜 *Value*   Many students, singles, and thrifty couples dominate the scene at Tony's (also known as Tony's Pension), where there's a communal kitchen and TV lounge. If Tony's is full, Tony or his multilingual wife, Charo, will contact their pension peers and try to find you alternate lodgings. If you're planning a stay of a week or more, Tony's also has 11 studios (some with balconies) with kitchenettes in a small building nearby.

26 Zacharitsa St., 117 41 Athens. ℂ 210/523-4170. 50€–80€ ($58–$92) double; substantial off-season discounts. From Syntagma Sq., take Amalias Ave. into Dionyssiou Areopagitou St. until you reach Propileon St.; turn left on Propileon and walk downhill 5 blocks to its end; zig right, then zag left to Zaharitsa. *In room:* A/C, TV (some units), kitchen, minibar (studios).

NEAR OMONIA SQUARE & THE NATIONAL ARCHAEOLOGICAL MUSEUM

Athens International Youth Hostel 𝒜𝒜   This is easily the best hostel in Athens (in an uninteresting, but basically trouble-free, neighborhood, a brisk 10-min. walk from Omonia Sq.). The rooms sleep two to four in decent beds and have private showers and lockers. You must join the IYHF—14€ ($16)—or pay an additional 2.50€ ($2.90) daily. There's no curfew. The neighborhood is dull, but you probably won't spend much time there.

16 Victor Hugo, 104 38 Athens. ℂ 210/523-4170. Fax 210/523-4115. 138 beds. From 20€ ($23) per person. Rates include breakfast. No credit cards. Walk west from Omonia Sq. 3 blocks on Ayiou Konstantinou and turn right on Koumoundourou St.; Victor Hugo is 2 blocks up. **Amenities:** Shared kitchen; self-service laundry.

Hotel Exarchion 𝒜   The no-frills Hotel Exarchion has decent-size rooms, most of which have balconies. You can drink and snack at the rooftop bar while you watch (and listen to) University of Athens students debating and sometimes demonstrating in the square below.

55 Odos Themistokleous, 106 83 Athens. ℂ 210/360-1256. Fax 210/360-3296. 49 units. From 65€ ($72) double. No credit cards. From Syntagma Sq., take Panepistimiou Ave. to Omonia Sq.; Themistokleos intersects Panepistimiou on your right. **Amenities:** Bar. *In room:* A/C, TV (some units).

Tips **A Hotel Warning**

I tend not to recommend hotels near Omonia Square, which has become a hangout for petty criminals. Some hotels are home to many eastern European prostitutes. There are, however, still some acceptable hotels north of Omonia near Exarchia Square and the National Archaeological Museum; they aren't terribly central and are most useful for those planning to spend a good deal of time exploring the National Archaeology Museum and University district. I also do not suggest hotels on traffic-plagued Syngrou Avenue. These hotels—usually very expensive and comfortable—are precisely where you do not want to be in Athens, unless you are at a convention and will hardly leave the hotel.

Museum Hotel *☆☆*   This venerable hotel, now managed by the Best Western Chain, is so close to the Archaeological Museum that its balconies overlook the museum's relatively quiet tree-filled park. Rooms are bland but have recently been spruced up. This is a you-get-what-you-pay-for good-value businesspeople's hotel, although the traffic here is, as almost everywhere in Athens, steady and noisy.

16 Odos Bouboulinas, 106 82 Athens. ☎ **800/428-2627** or 210/360-5611. Fax 210/380-0057. 58 units. From 110€ ($127) double. Rates include breakfast. AE, DC, V. From Syntagma Sq., take Panepistimiou Ave. to Omonia Sq.; take 28 Oktobriou (also signposted as Patission) out of Omonia Sq. to Solomos; turn right on Solomos and left onto Odos Bouboulinas.

WORTH A SPLURGE

Athenian Inn *☆*   Kolonaki is a fashionable residential-and-shopping neighborhood northeast of Syntagma Square at the foot of Mount Likavitos. If you stay here, you are likely to be tempted by its pricey restaurants and boutiques (but see our Kolonaki budget dining suggestions, below). The Athenian Inn is on a relatively quiet side street 3 blocks from Kolonaki Square and has a loyal following, including many teachers, despite its small rooms (many of which have small balconies). A quote from the guest book: "At last the ideal Athens hotel, good and modest in scale but perfect in service and goodwill." Keep in mind that if you stay here, you will do a good deal of walking (some of it fairly steeply uphill) to get to and from the central attractions. Neighborhood doves coo vigorously at night, a sound you will probably find either soothing or infuriating.

22 Haritos St., Kolonaki, 106 75 Athens. ☎ 210/723-8097. Fax 210/724-2268. 28 units. 135€ ($155) double. Rates include breakfast. AE, DC, V. From Syntagma Sq., go east on Vasilissis Sofias Ave. to Loukianou; turn left on Loukianou and take it 6 blocks uphill to Haritos. *In room:* A/C.

Hotel Plaka *☆☆*   This hotel—popular with Greeks, who prefer its modern conveniences to the old-fashioned charms of most other hotels in the Plaka area—has a terrific location and fair prices. Many rooms have balconies. Fifth- and sixth-floor rooms in the rear (where it's usually quieter) have views of the Plaka and the Acropolis, also splendidly visible from the roof garden bar (open in summer). Friends who stayed here recently weren't charmed by the service but loved the Hotel Plaka's central and relatively quiet location. Rates here are usually considerably cheaper off season.

Mitropoleos and 7 Kapnikareas St., 105 56 Athens. ☎ 210/322-2096. Fax 210/322-2412. plaka@tourhotel.gr. 67 units, 38 with shower only. 100€–125€ ($115–$144) double. Rates include breakfast. AE, MC, V. Follow Mitropoleos St. out of Syntagma Sq. past cathedral; turn left onto Kapnikareas. **Amenities:** Bar; roof garden. *In room:* A/C, TV, minibar, hair dryer.

3 Great Deals on Dining

Athens has an astonishing number of restaurants and tavernas (and a growing number of fast-food and takeout joints) serving everything from good, cheap Greek food in plain surroundings to fine Greek, French, Asian, and other international cuisines in luxurious settings. Cost-conscious travelers might not experience the top of the line but can eat very well here.

Most restaurants have menus printed in both Greek and English, but many don't keep their printed (or handwritten) menus up to date. If a menu isn't in English, there's almost always someone working at the restaurant who can translate or give suggestions in English. You might be offered some fairly repetitive suggestions because restaurant staff members tend to suggest what most tourists request. That means *moussaka* (baked eggplant casserole, usually with ground meat), *souvlakia* (chunks of beef, chicken, pork, or lamb grilled on a skewer), *pastitsio* (baked pasta, usually with ground meat and béchamel sauce), or *dolmadakia* (grape leaves, usually stuffed with rice and ground meat). Although all these dishes can be delicious—you've likely eaten them at home and looked forward to enjoying the real thing here—the truth is that you might be disappointed. All too often, restaurants catering heavily to tourists serve profoundly dull *moussaka* and unpleasantly chewy *souvlakia*. I hope the places I suggest do better.

To avoid the ubiquitous favorites-for-foreigners, you might indicate to your waiter that you'd like to look at the food display case, often just outside the kitchen, and then point to what you'd like to order. Many restaurants are perfectly happy to have you take a look in the kitchen itself, but be sure to check first: Many restaurateurs are understandably fed up with tourists barging into their kitchens without asking permission.

Mezédes (appetizers served with bread) are one of the great delights of Greek cuisine and often can be enjoyed in lieu of a main course. Perennial favorites are *tzatzíki* (garlic, cucumber, dill, and yogurt dip), *melitzanosalata* (eggplant dip), *skordalia* (garlic dip), *taramosalata* (fish roe dip), *keftedes* (crispy meatballs), *kalamaria* (squid), *yigantes* (white beans in tomato sauce), *loukanika* (little sausages), and octopus. *Beware:* Virtually all the squid served in Greece is frozen, and many restaurants serve dreadful *keftedes, taramosalata,* and *melitzanosalata* made with more bread than any other ingredient.

When it's not being used as filler, fresh Greek bread is generally tasty, substantial, nutritious, and inexpensive. If you're buying bread at a bakery, ask for *mavro somi* (black bread)—it's almost always better than the blander white. An exception is the white bread in the *koulouria* (pretzel-like rolls covered with sesame seeds) you'll see Greeks buying on their way to work in the morning from street vendors carrying wooden trays of the bracelet-shaped snacks.

If you're wondering what to wash all this food down with, the most popular Greek wine is *retsina,* usually white, but often rosé or red, flavored with pine resin. In theory, the European Union now controls the amount of resin added, so you're less likely to come across the harsh *retsina* some compare to turpentine. If you don't like the taste, try *aretsinato* (wine without resin). The best-known Greek beer is Amstel, and you'll also find many European brands. (Henniger is especially popular.)

When it comes time for dessert or a midafternoon infusion of sugar, Greeks usually head to a *zaharoplastion* (sweet shop), so restaurants tend not to offer a wide variety of desserts. Almost all restaurants do serve fruit (stewed in winter, fresh in season). If you're in Athens when cherries, apricots, peaches, or melon are in season, you might try an assortment for dessert or even a light meal. Increasingly, many restaurants serve sweets like *baklava* (pastry and ground nuts with honey), *halva* (sesame, chopped nuts, and honey), and *kataifi* (shredded wheat with chopped nuts and lots of honey).

If you want coffee with your dessert, keep in mind that for Greeks, regular coffee usually includes a mere heaping teaspoon of sugar. Sweet coffee seems to be about a 50/50 mixture of coffee and sugar. If you've never had Greek coffee before, you may find it tastes a bit like espresso. Watch out for the grounds in the bottom of the cup.

Greek brandy is a popular after-dinner drink (but a bit sweet for non-Greek tastes), but the most popular Greek hard drink is *ouzo,* an anise-flavored liqueur. In fact, there are many cafes *(ouzeri)* where ouzo, wine, and a selection of *mezédes* are served from breakfast to bedtime. Ouzo is taken either straight or with water, which turns it cloudy white. You might see Greeks—usually men, or women with men—drinking quarter- and even half-bottles of ouzo with their lunch; if you do the same, you'll find out why the after-lunch siesta is so popular.

IN THE PLAKA

Some of the most charming old restaurants in Athens are in the Plaka—and so are some of the worst tourist traps. Here are a few things to keep in mind when you head out for a meal.

Waiters from some Plaka restaurants hustle business outside their restaurants; they don't merely urge you to come in and sit down, but virtually pursue you down the street. The hard sell is almost always a giveaway that the place caters to tourists.

If you're lucky enough to be in Athens in winter, you'll see the Plaka as it once was: thronged with Greek families. In summer, Greeks tend to abandon the Plaka to tourists. In general, avoid Plaka places with floor shows; many are clip joints charging outrageous amounts (and levying surcharges not always stated on menus) for drinks and food. If you do get burned, stand your ground, phone the Tourist Police at ✆ **171,** and pay nothing before they arrive. Often just the threat that you'll call the Tourist Police has the miraculous effect of lowering a bill.

Damigos (The Bakaliarakia) ☆☆ GREEK/CODFISH   Since 1865, Damigos has been serving delicious deep-fried codfish and eggplant, as well as chops and stews for inveterate meat-eaters. This basement taverna with enormous wine barrels in the back room and an ancient column supporting the roof in the front serves wine from family vineyards. (If you like it, you can usually buy a bottle to take away.) There are few pleasures greater than sipping the white or rosé *retsina* while watching the cook turn out unending meals in his absurdly small kitchen. Don't miss the delicious *skordalia* (garlic sauce), equally good with cod, eggplant, bread—well, you get the idea.

41 Kidathineon St. ✆ 210/322-5084. Main courses 5€–10€ ($5.75–$12). No credit cards. Daily 7pm to anytime between 11pm and 1am. Usually closed July–Sept. From Syntagma Sq., head south on Filellinon or Nikis St. to Kidathineon; Damigos is downstairs on the left just before Adrianou St.

Credit Card Alert

Most Athenian restaurants—even very well-known ones—don't accept credit cards. Check first!

> ## *Value* Getting the Best Deal on Dining
>
> - Snack on a *koulouria* (round pretzel-like roll covered with sesame seeds), which costs about .30€ (25¢).
> - For a cheap and tasty meal, buy a *gyro* (sliced lamb served in pita bread); *souvlakia* (usually grilled bits of pork, lamb, or chicken) with pita; *tyropita* (cheese pie); *spanokopita* (spinach-and cheese pie); or a sandwich at a *souvlakatzidiko* (souvlakia stand), *zaharoplastlon* (confectioner), or other sandwich shop. If you're not exhausted from sightseeing, get it to go: Table service costs more.
> - Buy water and other drinks at a grocery store or kiosk, where they can cost a fourth of what you'll be charged at a restaurant.
> - Be aware that seafood isn't a good choice in Athens; it's always expensive and its freshness is often questionable.
> - Try a few *mezédes* (appetizers), usually about 2€ to 10€ ($2.30–$12) a portion. If you're eating with friends, all the better: You can order a variety to share with others, and find out what you like best.
> - Note that *krasí* (wine, whether *retsina* or non-resinated) and ouzo are generally less expensive than beer and soft drinks. Check whether a restaurant has its own wine from the barrel. Many restaurants have both a resinated and a non-resinated house wine, but they customarily suggest the more expensive bottled wines to foreigners.
> - Be aware that domestic beer, such as Amstel, is usually less expensive than imported beer.

Eden Vegetarian Restaurant *☆* VEGETARIAN   You can find vegetarian dishes at almost every Greek restaurant, but if you want to experience organically grown products, soy (rather than eggplant) *moussaka*, mushroom pie with a whole-wheat crust, freshly squeezed juices, and salads with bean sprouts, join the young Athenians and Europeans who patronize the Eden. The prices are reasonable if not cheap, and the decor is engaging, with 1920s-style prints and mirrors and wrought-iron lamps.

12 Lissiou St. *⟨℃⟩*/fax 210/324-8858. Main courses 8€–15€ ($9.20–$17). AE, MC, V. Wed–Mon noon–midnight. Usually closed Aug. From Syntagma Sq., head south on Filellinon or Nikis St. to Kidathineon, which intersects Adrianou St.; turn right on Adrianou and take Mnissikleos up 2 blocks toward Acropolis to Lissiou.

Kouklis Ouzeri (To Yerani) *☆* GREEK/MEZEDES   Sit down at one of the small tables and a waiter will present you with a large tray of about a dozen plates of *mezédes*—appetizer portions of fried fish, beans, grilled eggplant, *taramosalata*, cucumber-and-tomato salad, olives, fried cheese, sausages, and other seasonal specialties. Accept the ones that appeal. If you don't order all 12, you can enjoy a tasty and inexpensive meal, washed down with the house *krasí* (wine). No prices are posted, but the waiter will tell you what everything costs if you ask. Now, if only the staff could be just a bit more patient when foreign visitors are deciding what to order. . . .

14 Tripodon St. *℃* 210/324-7605. Appetizers 3€–12€ ($3.45–$14). No credit cards. Daily 11am–2am. From Syntagma Sq., head south on Filellinon or Nikis St. to Kidathineon; take Kidathineon across Adrianou to Thespidos and climb toward Acropolis; Tripodon is the 1st street on the right after Adrianou.

Quick Bites

The **Apollonion Bakery,** 10 Nikis St., and the **Elleniki Gonia,** 10 Karayior-yis Servias St., are among a number of places around Syntagma Square that make sandwiches to order and sell croissants, both stuffed and plain. **Ariston** is a small chain of *zaharoplastia* (confectioners), with a branch at the corner of Karayioryis Servias and Voulis streets (just off Syntagma Sq.) selling snacks as well as pastries. The seductive little **Vasilopoulos Delicatessen,** 19 Stadiou St., has wonderful *halva* and other delicacies to go.

For the quintessential Greek sweet, *loukoumades* (round doughnut-center-like pastries deep-fried, drenched with honey, and topped with powdered sugar and cinnamon), nothing beats **Doris,** 30 Praxiteles St., a continuation of Lekka Street, a few blocks from Syntagma Square. If you're still hungry, Doris serves hearty stews and pasta dishes for absurdly low prices Monday to Saturday 8am to 3:30pm. **Aigaion,** 46 Panepistimiou St., is a good place to stop on the way to or from the National Archaeological Museum for some *loukoumades* or creamy rice pudding.

Everest is another chain worth trying; there's one a block north of Kolonaki Square at Tsakalof and Iraklitou. On Kolonaki Square, **To Kotopolo** serves succulent grilled chicken to take out or eat in. In the Plaka, the **Center of Hellenic Tradition,** opening onto both 36 Pandrossou St. and 59 Mitropoleos St., has a small cafe with a spectacular view of the Acropolis where you can revive yourself with a cappuccino, snack on pastries, and buy excellent reproductions of traditional folk crafts in the shop.

Platanos Taverna 🎇🎇 TRADITIONAL GREEK   This taverna on a quiet pedestrian square has tables outdoors in good weather beneath a spreading *platanos* (plane tree). Inside, where locals usually congregate to escape the summer sun at midday and the tourists in the evening, you can enjoy looking at the old paintings and photos on the walls. The Platanos has been serving good *spitiko fageto* (home cooking) since 1932, and has managed to keep steady customers happy while enchanting visitors. If artichokes or spinach with lamb are on the menu, you're in luck: They're delicious. The house wine is tasty, and there's a wide choice of bottled wines from many regions of Greece.

4 Dioyenous St. © **210/322-0666.** Fax 210/322-8624. Main courses 7€–15€ ($8.05–$17). No credit cards. Mon–Sat noon–4:30pm and 8pm–midnight; Sun in Mar–May and Sept–Oct noon–4:30pm. From Syntagma Sq., head south on Filellinon or Nikis St. to Kidathineon; turn right on Adrianou St., take Mnissikleos up 1 block toward the Acropolis, and turn right on Dioyenous.

Taverna Xinos 🎇🎇 TRADITIONAL GREEK   Despite the forgivable spelling lapse, Xinos's business card says it best: "In the heart of old Athens there is still a flace [sic] where the traditional Greek way of cooking is upheld." In summer, there are tables in the courtyard; in winter, you can warm yourself by the coal-burning stove. While the strolling musicians may not be as good as the Three Tenors, they do sing wonderful Greek golden oldies, accompanying themselves on the guitar and *bouzouki*. (If you're serenaded, you might want to give the musicians a tip. If you want to hear the theme from *Never on Sunday*, ask for "Ena Zorbas.") Most evenings, tourists predominate until after 10pm, when locals begin to arrive.

4 Geronta St. ℂ 210/322-1065. Main courses 7€–15€ ($8.05–$17). No credit cards. Daily 8pm to anywhere from 11pm to 1am; sometimes closed Sun, usually closed part of July and Aug. From Syntaqma Sq., head south on Filellinon or Nikis St. to Kidathineon; turn right on Geronta and look for the sign for Xlnos in the cul-de-sac.

Tristrato SNACKS/PASTRY   Tristrato calls itself a "traditional milk bar" but has delicious cakes, yogurts with fresh fruits, fresh fruit juices, and herbal teas as well as the more traditional rice and milk puddings. This is a congenial spot at which to take a break from sightseeing in the Plaka, with tables outside overlooking little Filomousou Eterias Square in fair weather. If the weather is not fair, the interior, with its small tables and often soft music, is cozy.

34 Dedalou and 12 Geronta sts. ℂ 210/324-4472. Ice cream, pastries, beverages 3€–8€ ($3.45–$9.20). No credit cards. Daily 11am–midnight. Closed Aug. From Syntagma Sq., head south on Filellinon or Nikis St. to Kidathineon and turn right on Geronta.

NEAR SYNTAGMA SQUARE

Restaurant Kentrikon GREEK   The Kentrikon has been here for decades, setting up tables out in the arcade in summer and serving indoors (air-conditioned in summer) year-round. This restaurant's central location, reasonable prices, and coffee bar make it popular with locals as well as tourists. I can't remember ever having a dreadful meal here—neither can I remember a really good one, although the lamb stew with spinach is usually trustworthy. The large interior can be terribly noisy, and the service seems to alternate between rushed and desultory.

3 Kolokotroni St. (several blocks north of Syntagma Sq.) ℂ 210/323-2482. 8€–17€ ($9.20–$20). AE, DC, MC, V. Mon–Fri noon–5 or 6pm.

NEAR MONASTIRAKI SQUARE

Abyssinia Cafe ⍟ *(Finds* GREEK/MEZEDES   You'll know you're not in Kansas any more when you sit in this small cafe in a ramshackle building overlooking a lopsided square where furniture restorers ply their trade. You can sit indoors (wonderful dark wood, copper, and old prints) or outside and have just a coffee, but it's tempting to snack on cheese Abyssinia (feta cheese scrambled with spices and garlic), mussels and rice pilaf, or *keftedes* (meatballs). This is a great place to take a break from "doing" the nearby monuments of the Acropolis and Agora.

Plateia Abyssinia. ℂ 210/321-7047. Appetizers and main courses 5€–15€ ($5.75–$17). No credit cards. Tues–Sun 10:30am–2pm (often open evenings as well). Usually closed for a week at Christmas and Easter, sometimes closed part of Jan and Feb. Abyssinia Sq. is just off Ifaistou (Hephaistos) St. across from entrance to Ancient Agora on Adrianou.

Diporto *(Finds* GREEK   This little place, sandwiched between olive shops, serves up salads, stews, and delicious *revithia* (chickpeas), a Greek winter dish popular among stall owners, shoppers, and Athenians who make their way to the market for cheap and delicious food. If you like Diporto, try Papandreou, also in the Central Market and famous for its restorative tripe soup, a Greek remedy for hangovers.

Athens Central Market. No phone. 4€–9€ ($4.60–$10). No credit cards. Mon–Sat 6am–6pm. From Syntagma Sq., follow Hermou to Athinas St.; the Central Market is on the right side of the street.

Taverna Sigalas *Finds* TRADITIONAL GREEK This longtime Plaka taverna, housed in a vintage 1879 commercial building, boasts that it is open 365 days a year. Its lively interior has huge old *retsina* kegs in the back and dozens of black-and-white photos of Greek movie stars on the walls. After 8pm nightly, there's Greek Muzak. At all hours, Greeks and tourists wolf down large portions of stew, *moussaka,* grilled meatballs, baked tomatoes, gyros, and other hearty dishes, washing it all down with the house red and white *retsinas.*

Plateia Monastiraki 2. © 210/321-3036. Fax: 210/325-2488. Main courses 5€–16€ ($5.75–$18). AE, DC, MC, V. Daily 7pm–2am. Across Monastiraki Sq. from the Metro station.

Thanasis *Finds* *Value* GREEK/SOUVLAKIA Thanasis serves *souvlakia* and pita and exceptionally good fries, both to go and at its outdoor and indoor tables; as always, the prices are higher if you sit down. On weekends, it often takes the strength and determination of an Olympic athlete to get through the door and place an order. It's worth the effort: This is both a great budget choice and a great place to take in the local scene, which often includes a fair sprinkling of Gypsies, including some cute and very determined child beggars.

69 Mitropoleos St. © 210/324-4705. Main courses 3€–10€ ($3.45–$12). No credit cards. Daily 9am–2am. On northeast corner of Monastiraki Sq. Hermou St. leads directly from Syntagma Sq. to Monastiraki Sq.

IN MAKRIYANNI & KOUKAKI

Socrates' Prison *Finds* GREEK/CONTINENTAL In 2001, this long-standing favorite (also known as the **Samaria**) moved around the corner to a new location with a roof garden (a real plus for summer evenings). Socrates' Prison remains an excellent place to head when you want good food but want to avoid the frenzy of the central Plaka. This is a favorite with Greeks and with American and European expats living in Athens, who lounge at tables outdoors in good weather and in the pleasant indoor rooms year-round. The food is somewhat more imaginative than average Greek fare (try the veggie croquettes) and includes Continental dishes like salade niçoise and vegetable-stuffed pork roll. The *retsina* is excellent, and there's a wide choice of bottled wines and beers.

17 Robertou Galli St. © 210/922-3434. Main courses 10€–17€ ($12–$20). AE, DC, MC, V. Mon–Sat 11am–4pm and 7pm–1am. Closed Aug. From Syntagma Sq., take Amalias Ave. to pedestrianized Dionyssiou Areopagitou St., walk away from Temple of Zeus on the side of Dionyssiou Areopagitou across from Acropolis, and turn left onto Mitseon and right onto Robertou Galli.

NEAR THE NATIONAL ARCHAEOLOGICAL MUSEUM & OMONIA SQUARE

Athinaikon *Finds* GREEK/OUZERIE Not many tourists come to this favorite haunt of lawyers and businesspeople working in the Omonia Square area. You can have just appetizers (technically, this is an *ouzerie*) or a full meal. For a reasonably priced snack, stick to the appetizers, including delicious *loukanika* (sausages) and *keftedes* (meatballs), and pass on the more pricey grilled shrimp or seafood casserole. Whatever you eat, you'll enjoy taking in the old photos on the walls, the handsome tiled floor, and the regular customers, who combine serious eating with animated conversation.

2 Themistokleous St. © 210/383-8485. Main courses 4€–16€ ($4.60–$18). No credit cards. Mon–Sat 11am–midnight. Closed Aug. From Omonia Sq., take Panepistimou St. a block to Themistokleous St.; the Athinaikon is almost immediately on your right.

Taygetos *Value* GREEK/SOUVLAKIA This is a great place to stop for a quick meal on your way to or from the National Archaeological Museum. The service is usually swift, and the *souvlakia* and fried potatoes are excellent, as are the grilled lamb and chicken (priced by the kilo). The menu sometimes includes delicious *kokoretsi* (grilled entrails). The Ellinikon Restaurant next door is also a good value.

4 Satovriandou St. ℂ 210/523-5352. Main courses 6€–12€ ($6.90–$14). No credit cards, Mon–Sat 9am–1am. From Omonia Sq., take Patission (28 Oktovriou) toward the National Museum; Satovriandou is 3rd major turning on your left.

IN KOLONAKI

Neon 👨 *(Value)* GREEK/INTERNATIONAL The Kolonaki Neon serves the same food and is open the same hours as the Syntagma and Omonia branches (see below), but the fair prices are especially welcome in this expensive neighborhood. Tsakalof is a shady pedestrian arcade, and you can usually sit indoors or outdoors; on weekends, this is a great place to watch chic young Athenians resting from their Kolonaki shopping expeditions. The other branches are at 1 Dorou, Omonia Square (ℂ 210/522-9939); and at 3 Mitropoleos St., on the southwest corner of Syntagma Square (ℂ 210/322-8155). Fair prices, consistently good food, and the chance to see what you are ordering are the reasons to head to any of the Neons.

Odos Tsakalof 6, Kolonaki Sq. ℂ 210/364-6873. Snacks 2€–6€ ($2.30–$6.90); sandwiches 4€–8€ ($4.60–$9.20); main courses 5€–20€ ($5.75–$23). No credit cards. Daily 9am–midnight.

Rhodia 👨 TRADITIONAL GREEK This taverna in a handsome old house has tables in its small garden in good weather—although the interior, with its tile floor and old prints, is so charming you might be tempted to eat indoors. The Rhodia is a favorite of visiting archaeologists from the nearby British and American Schools of Classical Studies, as well as of locals. It might not sound like just what you'd always craved, but the octopus in mustard sauce is terrific, as are the perhaps less intimidating veal or *dolmades* (stuffed grape leaves) in egg-lemon sauce. The house wine is excellent, as is the *halva*, which manages to be both creamy and crunchy.

44 Aristipou St. ℂ 210/722-9883. 7.50€–16€ ($8.65–$18). No credit cards. Mon–Sat 8pm–2am. From Kolonaki Sq., take Patriarkou Ioakim uphill to Loukianou; turn left on Loukianou, climb steeply uphill to Aristipou, and turn right.

WORTH A SPLURGE

To Kafeneio 👨👨 GREEK/INTERNATIONAL This is hardly a typical *kafeneio* (coffee shop/cafe), with its pictures on the walls, crowd of ladies who lunch, and staff members from the many embassies in Kolonaki. If you relax, you can easily run up a substantial tab ($60 for lunch or dinner for two is easy), but you can also eat more modestly and equally elegantly. If you have something light, like the artichokes a la *polita*, leeks in crème fraîche, or onion pie, washed down with draft beer or the house wine, you can finish with profiteroles and not put too big a dent in your budget. This is an especially congenial spot if you're eating alone.

26 Loukianou St. ℂ 210/722-9056. 6€–25€ ($6.90–$29). No credit cards. Mon–Sat 11am–midnight or later. Closed Sun and most of Aug. From Kolonaki Sq., follow Patriarkou Ioakim St. several blocks uphill to Loukianou and turn right on Loukianou.

Vlassis 👨👨 TRADITIONAL GREEK Greeks call this kind of food *paradisiako*—traditional, but paradisiacal is just as good a description. This very reasonably priced food is fit for the gods: delicious fluffy vegetable croquettes, eggplant salad that tastes like no other, and hauntingly tender lamb in egg-lemon sauce. It's a sign of Vlassis's popularity with Athenians that there's not even a discreet sign announcing its presence in a small apartment building on hard-to-find Paster. If you arrive at 8pm, you'll probably wonder why I recommend reservations; from 10pm, Vlassis is usually packed. What makes Vlassis a splurge is not its prices, which are very reasonable, but the fact that you will probably want to take a taxi (10€/$12 round-trip from Syntagma) there. On the other hand, you might feel so giddy with delight after eating that you won't mind the half-hour walk back to Syntagma.

8 Paster St. (off Plateia Mavili). ℂ 210/646-3060. 8€–20€ ($9.20–$23). No credit cards. Mon–Sat 8pm–1am. Closed much of June–Sept. From Syntagma Sq., take Vasilissis Sophias Ave. to Plateia Mavili, and follow D. Tsoustou out of Plateia Mavili to Chatzikosta; Paster is the cul-de-sac on the left after you turn right onto Chatzikosta.

Zeidoron ☆ GREEK/MEZEDES   This *mezedopolio* (hors d'oeuvres place) is one of a number of restaurants springing up in the old warehouse district of Psirri, now busily being transformed into a chic art gallery and cafe district. There are lots of delicious *mezédes* to choose from, including vegetable croquettes, several eggplant dishes, and some heartier meat dishes, like pork in mustard. You can have a varied and delicious meal—and keep the price tab reasonable—by avoiding the more expensive *mezédes* like shrimp. There's a wide variety of wines, beers, and ouzos. And you can take in the passing scene, which gets more and more lively as the night wears on and stylish young Athenians arrive.

10 Taki and Ayios Anaryiron. ℂ 210/321-5368. www.psirri.gr/zeidoron. Reservations recommended. Most appetizers and main courses 6€–15€ ($6.90–$17). No credit cards. Mon–Sat 11am till at least midnight. Closed Aug. From Syntagma Sq., take Ermou to Navarchou Apostoli, which runs into Taki, which intersects Ayios Anayiron.

4 Seeing the Sights

At press time, the Ministry of Culture had not reached a final decision on scheduled price hikes for admission to most monuments and museums. Our prices are based on the few prices determined at press time and "guesstimates" offered by some museums. As there is—surprise!—no fixed policy on cheaper tickets for students and seniors, be sure to ask about a discounted ticket if you are a senior or a student.

Note: Strikes that close museums and archaeological sites can occur without warning. Decide what you most want to see and go there as soon as possible after your arrival. If you're here off season, check with the **Greek National Tourist Organization** at ℂ 210/331-0437 or 210/331-0562 for abbreviated winter hours. Bear in mind that the hours posted at many sites are inaccurate.

THE ACROPOLIS & ANCIENT AGORA

The Acropolis ☆☆☆   *Note:* The monuments of the Acropolis underwent extensive renovation in honor of the 2004 Summer Olympics. At press time, these renovations had not been completed. The Temple of Nike, which had been entirely dismantled for restoration, was partially re-erected. The Propylaia and Parthenon were encased in scaffolding. What follows is an attempt to describe what you should see when the renovations are completed.

The Acropolis is one of a handful of places in the world that is so well known it's hard not to be nervous when you finally get here. Will it be as beautiful as its photographs? Will it be, ever so slightly, a disappointment? Rest assured: The Acropolis does not disappoint—but it usually *is* infuriatingly crowded. What

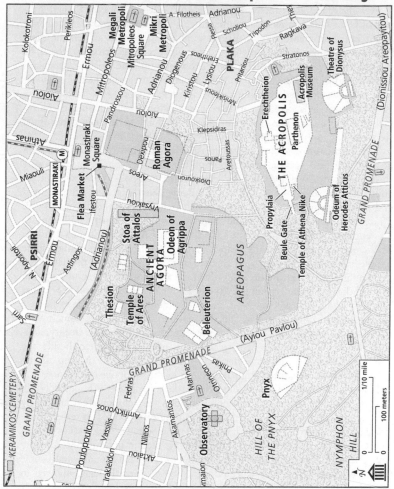

you want here is time—time to watch as the columns of the Parthenon appear first beige, then golden, then rose, then stark white in changing light; time to stand on the Belvedere and take in the view over Athens; and time to realize that you really are here, and to think of all those who have been here before you.

When you climb up the Acropolis—the heights above the city—you'll realize why people seem to have lived here as long ago as 5000 B.C. The sheer sides of the Acropolis make it a superb natural defense. And, of course, it helped that in antiquity there was a spring here, ensuring a steady water supply.

In classical times, when Athens's population had grown to around 250,000, people lived on the slopes below the Acropolis. Athens's civic and business center, the Agora, and its cultural center, with several theaters and concert halls, bracketed the Acropolis; when you peer over the sides at the houses in the Plaka and the remains of the ancient Agora and the Theater of Dionysos, you'll see the layout of the ancient city. Syntagma and Omonia squares, the heart of today's Athens, were well out of the ancient city center.

Even the Acropolis's superb heights couldn't protect it from the Persian invasion of 480 B.C., when most of its monuments were burned and destroyed. You might notice immense column drums built into the walls. When the great Athenian statesman Pericles ordered the monuments of the Acropolis rebuilt, he had the drums from the destroyed Parthenon built into the walls lest Athenians forget what had happened—and so they would remember they had rebuilt what they had lost. Pericles' rebuilding program began about 448 B.C.; the new Parthenon was dedicated 10 years later, but work on other monuments continued for a century. It seems that restoration and rebuilding here never end: You'll see scaffolding on the Acropolis monuments.

The **Parthenon** 𝕜𝕜𝕜, dedicated to Athena Parthenos (the Virgin), patron goddess of Athens, was the most important religious shrine here, but there were shrines to many other gods and goddesses on the Acropolis's broad summit. As you climb up, you'll first go through the **Beule Gate** 𝕜, built by the Romans and today known by the name of the French archaeologist who discovered it in 1852. As you continue through the **Propylaia** 𝕜, the monumental 5th-century B.C. entranceway, you'll notice the little **Temple of Athena Nike** 𝕜𝕜 (Athena of Victory) perched above the Propylaia. This beautifully proportioned Ionic temple was built in 424 B.C. and restored in the 1930s. Off to the left of the Parthenon is the **Erechtheion** 𝕜𝕜, which the Athenians honored as the tomb of Erechtheus, a legendary king of Athens. A hole in the ceiling and floor of the northern porch indicates the spot where Poseidon's trident struck to make a spring (symbolizing control of the sea) gush forth during his contest with Athena to be the city's chief deity. Athena countered with an olive tree (symbolizing control of the rich Attic plain); the olive tree planted beside the Erechtheion reminds visitors of her victory. Be sure to see the delicate carving on the Erechtheion and the original caryatids in the Acropolis Museum.

However charmed you are by these elegant little temples, you're probably still heading resolutely toward the Parthenon, eight of whose columns are painstakingly being taken apart and reassembled. You might be disappointed to realize you're not allowed inside the temple, both to protect the monument and to allow restoration to proceed safely. If you find this frustrating, keep in mind that in antiquity only priests and honored visitors were allowed in to see the monumental—some 11m (36 ft.) tall—statue of Athena designed by the great Phidias, who was in charge of Pericles' building program. Nothing of this huge gold-and-ivory statue remains, but there's a small Roman copy in the National Archaeological Museum—and horrific renditions on souvenirs ranging from T-shirts to ouzo bottles. Admittedly, the original statue wasn't understated: The 2nd century A.D. traveler Pausanias, one of the first guidebook writers, recorded that the statue stood upright in an ankle-length tunic with a head of Medusa carved in ivory on her breast. She held a spear and a figure representing Victory that was about 2.5m (8¼ ft.) high. A shield lay at her feet, with a snake beside the shield, possibly representing Erechtheus. The floor of the room in which the statue stood was covered in olive oil so the gold and ivory were reflected through the dimness.

If you look over the edge of the Acropolis toward the Temple of Hephaistos in the ancient Agora and then back up at the Parthenon, you can't help but be struck by how much lighter and more graceful the Parthenon is than the Theseion, as the Temple of Hephaistos is known today. Scholars tell us this is because Iktinos, the Parthenon's architect, was something of a magician of optical illusions: The columns and stairs—the very floor—of the Parthenon all

Value **Getting the Best Deal on Sightseeing**

- Take advantage of the free admission to many sites and museums every Sunday—but beware of the crowds doing the same thing. Admission is always free at the Center for Acropolis Studies (see below); the Center of Folk Art and Tradition (aka the Cultural Center of the Municipality of Athens), 6 Angelikis Hatzimihali St.; the Children's Museum, 14 Kidathineon St.; the Museum of Greek Costume, 7 Dimokritou St.; the Museum of Greek Popular Musical Instruments, 1–3 Diogenous St.; and several other small museums.

- Note that if you're a student, your current ID could net you a discount; if you run into trouble, take documentation to the International Student and Youth Travel Service (see the box "Athens Deals & Discounts," earlier in this chapter). It can issue a student card entitling you to half-price admission to most archaeological sites and museums, as well as discounts on many performances and events.

- Be aware that if you're studying archaeology, art history, or the classics, you can get a free pass to museums and sites by writing to the Museum Section, Ministry of Science and Culture, 14 Aristidou St., 105 59 Athens, where you should be able to collect your pass when you produce a copy of your letter and documentation. Apply at least a month in advance and include verification from your college or university.

- Be aware that if you arrive an hour or so before closing, some sites and museums will, if you ask nicely, stamp your entrance ticket so you can make a free return visit the next day.

appear straight because they're minutely curved. The exterior columns, for example, are slightly thicker in the middle, which makes the entire column appear straight. That's why the Parthenon, with 17 columns on each side and 8 at each end (creating a peristyle of 46 relatively slender columns), looks so graceful, while the Theseion, with only 6 columns at each end and 13 along each side, seems so stolid.

Of course, another reason the Parthenon looks so airy is that it's literally open to the air. The entire roof and much of the interior were blown to smithereens in 1687, when a party of Venetians attempted to take the Acropolis from the Turks. A shell fired from nearby Mouseion Hill struck the Parthenon—where the Turks were storing gunpowder and munitions—and caused appalling damage. Most of the remaining sculptures were carted off to London by Lord Elgin in the first decade of the 19th century. Those surviving sculptures—long known as the Elgin Marbles—are on display in the British Museum, causing ongoing pain to generations of Greeks, who continue to press for their return (and make a point of calling them the Parthenon Marbles).

The Parthenon originally had sculpture in both its pediments, as well as a frieze running around the entire temple. The frieze was made up of alternating triglyphs (panels with three incised grooves) and metopes (sculptured panels). The east pediment showed scenes from the birth of Athena, and the west pediment, Athena and Poseidon's contest for possession of Athens. The long frieze showed the battle of the Athenians, led by the hero Theseus, against the Amazons; scenes from the Trojan War; and the struggles of the Olympian gods against giants and centaurs. The message of most of this sculpture was the triumph of knowledge and civilization (read: Athens) over the forces of darkness and barbarians. An interior frieze showed scenes from the Panathenaic Festival each August, when citizens proceeded through the streets, bringing a new *peplos* (tunic) for the statue of Athena. Only a few fragments of any of the sculptures remain in place, and you'll have to decide whether it's a good or a bad thing that Lord Elgin removed so much before the *nefos* (smog) spread over Athens and ate away at the remaining sculpture.

If you're lucky enough to visit the Acropolis on a smog-free sunny day, you'll see the golden and cream tones of the Parthenon's handsome Pentelic marble at their most subtle. It might come as something of a shock to realize that the Parthenon, like most other monuments here, was painted in antiquity, with gay colors that have since faded, revealing the tones of the natural marble.

The **Acropolis Archaeological Museum** ☆☆ hugs the ground to detract as little as possible from the ancient monuments. Inside, you'll see the four original caryatids from the Erechtheion that are still in Athens (one disappeared during the Ottoman occupation, and one is in the British Museum). Other delights are sculpture from the Parthenon burned by the Persians, statues of *korai* (maidens) dedicated to Athena, figures of *kouroi* (young men), and a wide range of finds from the Acropolis. Allow at least an hour for your visit, and remember that the museum is often very crowded.

Those interested in learning more about the Acropolis should check to see if the **Center for Acropolis Studies,** on Makriyanni Street just southeast of the Acropolis (© **210/923-9381**), has reopened. Its hours are daily 9am to 2:30pm; admission is free. On display are artifacts, reconstructions, photographs, drawings, and plaster casts of the Elgin/Parthenon Marbles. Construction of a museum to house the marbles when—if—they are returned to Athens has been slowed by the discovery of important Byzantine remains beneath the museum site. In February of 2002, London's British Museum refused to lend the marbles to Athens for the August 2004 Olympics, citing fears that the marbles would never be returned to London.

You'll probably want to spend at least half a day on the Acropolis.

Dionyssiou Areopagitou. © **210/321-0219**. Admission 12€ ($14) adults. Free Sun. This ticket, which is valid for 1 week, includes admission to the Acropolis, Acropolis Museum, Ancient Agora, Theater of Dionysos, Karameikos Cemetery, Roman Forum, Tower of the Winds, and Temple of Olympian Zeus. It is still possible to buy individual tickets at the other sites. The Acropolis is usually open summer daily 8am–7pm; winter daily 8:30am–2:30pm. The Acropolis Museum usually closes at least half an hour earlier than the Acropolis. From Syntagma Sq., take Amalias Ave. into pedestrianized Dionyssiou Areopagitou, and follow the marble path up to the Acropolis. The ticket booth, along with a small post office and a snack bar, are slightly below the Acropolis entrance.

Ancient Agora ☆☆   The Agora was Athens's commercial/civic center, with buildings used for a wide range of political, educational, philosophical, theatrical, and athletic purposes—which may be why what remains seems such a jumble. This is a nice place to wander and enjoy the views up toward the Acropolis, and take in the herb garden and flowers planted around the 5th-century B.C. Temple of Hephaistos and Athena (the Theseion), peek into the heavily restored 11th-century church of Ayii Apostoli (Holy Apostles), and admire the 2nd-century B.C. Stoa of Attalos, reconstructed by American archaeologists in the

1950s. The museum in the Stoa's ground floor has finds from 5,000 years of Athenian history, including sculpture and pottery, as well as a voting machine and a child's potty seat, all with labels in English. The museum (which has excellent restrooms) closes 15 minutes before the site does. Allow several hours to visit the Ancient Agora and its museum.

Below the Acropolis on the edge of Monastiraki (entrance on Adrianou, near Ayiou Philippou Sq., east of Monastiraki Sq. and on Ay. Apostoli, the road leading down into Plaka from the Acropolis). © 210/ 321-0185. Admission (includes museum) 4€ ($4.60).

THE TOP MUSEUMS

The National Archaeological Museum ★★★ *Note:* The museum closed
for renovations in 2002 and was scheduled to reopen in time for the August 2004 Summer Olympics. The second floor of the museum, where most of the extensive collection of Greek vases was housed, had already been closed since 1999, when an earthquake shook Athens. It was not known at press time where objects would be displayed; therefore, for now, we can only detail the museum's main attractions, not where they will be displayed. Be sure to check ahead for updated opening times and prices.

This is an enormous and enormously popular museum; try to arrive as soon as it opens (or the hour before it closes) so that you can see the exhibits and not just the backs of other visitors. The collection includes objects from the Neolithic to the Roman eras. Don't miss the stunning gold masks, cups, dishes, and jewelry unearthed from the site of Mycenae by Heinrich Schliemann in 1876; the elegant marble Cycladic figurines (ca. 2000 B.C.); and the famous marble and bronze statues. The museum's extensive collection of black-and-red figure vases is, not surprisingly, the finest in the world. The museum shop has reproductions and books on aspects of the collection. You'll probably want to spend a minimum of 3 hours here—and wish you'd spent more.

44 Patission. © 210/821-7717. protocol@eam.culture.gr. Admission 6€ ($6.90). Mon 12:30–6pm; Tues–Fri 8am–6pm; Sat–Sun and holidays 8:30am–3pm. From Omonia Sq., walk about a half km (⅓ mile or 10 min.) north on the road officially named 28 Oktovriou (Oct 28) Ave. but usually called Patission.

N. P. Goulandris Foundation Museum of Cycladic Art ★★★ This handsome museum houses the largest collection of Cycladic art outside the National Archaeological Museum. See if you agree with those who have compared the faces of the Cycladic figurines to the works of the Italian painter Modigliani. Be sure to go through the courtyard into the museum's newest acquisition: an elegant 19th-century house with some of its original furnishings and visiting exhibits. The museum shop has a wide variety of books and reproductions—and a resolutely unhelpful staff. You'll want to spend at least 3 hours here; be sure to take a break in the garden cafe.

4 Neophytou Douka. © 210/722-8321. www.cycladic-m.gr. Admission 4€ ($4.60). Mon and Wed–Fri 10am–4pm; Sat 10am–3pm. From Syntagma Sq., walk 7 blocks east along Vasilissis Sofias Ave., then a half block north on Neophytou Douka.

Tips Online Museum Updates

Information on most Greek museums and archaeological sites—and an update on any price hikes—should be available at **www.culture.gr**.

Athens

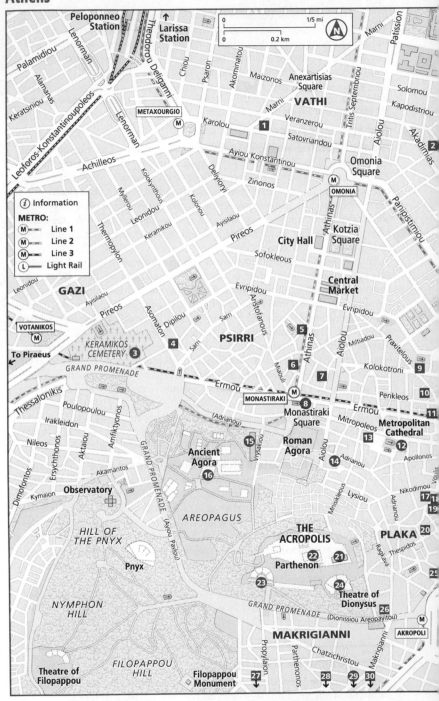

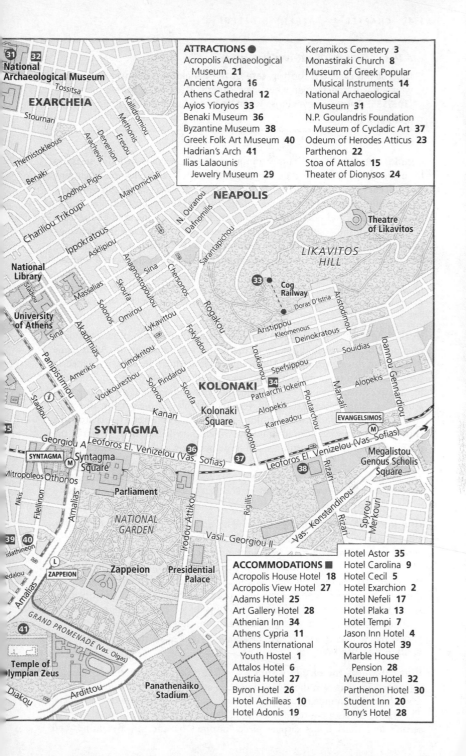

ATTRACTIONS ●
Acropolis Archaeological
  Museum **21**
Ancient Agora **16**
Athens Cathedral **12**
Ayios Yioryios **33**
Benaki Museum **36**
Byzantine Museum **38**
Greek Folk Art Museum **40**
Hadrian's Arch **41**
Ilias Lalaounis
  Jewelry Museum **29**

Keramikos Cemetery **3**
Monastiraki Church **8**
Museum of Greek Popular
  Musical Instruments **14**
National Archaeological
  Museum **31**
N.P. Goulandris Foundation
  Museum of Cycladic Art **37**
Odeum of Herodes Atticus **23**
Parthenon **22**
Stoa of Attalos **15**
Theater of Dionysos **24**

ACCOMMODATIONS ■
Acropolis House Hotel **18**
Acropolis View Hotel **27**
Adams Hotel **25**
Art Gallery Hotel **28**
Athenian Inn **34**
Athens Cypria **11**
Athens International
  Youth Hostel **1**
Attalos Hotel **6**
Austria Hotel **27**
Byron Hotel **26**
Hotel Achilleas **10**
Hotel Adonis **19**

Hotel Astor **35**
Hotel Carolina **9**
Hotel Cecil **5**
Hotel Exarchion **2**
Hotel Nefeli **17**
Hotel Plaka **13**
Hotel Tempi **7**
Jason Inn Hotel **4**
Kouros Hotel **39**
Marble House
  Pension **28**
Museum Hotel **32**
Parthenon Hotel **30**
Student Inn **20**
Tony's Hotel **28**

Tips **Museum Cafe with a View**

Dine at the excellent rooftop cafe of the **Benaki Museum** (see below), which has a spectacular view over Athens. It offers a buffet supper (30€/$35) Thursday evenings, when the museum remains open until midnight.

Benaki Museum *★★* This stunning private collection includes treasures from the Neolithic era to the 20th century. The folk art collection (including magnificent costumes and icons) is superb, as are the two complete rooms from 18th-century northern Greek mansions, ancient Greek bronzes, gold cups, Fayum portraits, and rare early Christian textiles. A new wing doubles the exhibition space of the original 20th-century neoclassical town house that belonged to the wealthy Benaki family. The museum shop is excellent, and new galleries have special exhibitions. This is a very pleasant place to spend several hours—or days.

Koumbari 1 (at Leoforos Vasilissis Sofias, Kolonaki, 5 blocks east of Syntagma Sq.). © **210/367-1000.** www.benaki.gr. Admission 6€ ($6.90); free on Thurs. Mon, Wed, Fri, Sat 9am–5pm; Thurs 9am–midnight; Sun 9am–3pm.

Byzantine Museum *★* If you love icons (paintings, usually of saints, usually on wood) or want to find out about them, this is the place to go. As its name makes clear, this museum, in a 19th-century Florentine-style villa, is devoted to the art and history of the Byzantine era (roughly the 4th–15th c.). Selections from Greece's most important collection of icons and religious art—along with sculptures, altars, mosaics, religious vestments, bibles, and a small-scale reconstruction of an early Christian basilica—are exhibited on several floors around a courtyard. If you visit, keep in mind that when the villa was built, it was in the countryside—Athens was still a small, provincial town. Allow at least an hour for your visit.

22 Vasilissis Sofias Ave. © **210/723-1570** or 210/721-1027. Admission 4€ ($4.60). Tues–Sun 8:30am–3pm. From Syntagma Sq., walk along Queen Sophias Ave. (aka Venizelou Ave.) for about 15 min. The museum is on your right.

Greek Folk Art Museum *★★* *Kids* This endearing small museum has dazzling embroideries and costumes, carved wood furniture, tools, and ceramic and copper utensils from all over the country, plus a small room with zany frescoes of gods and heroes done by eccentric artist Theofilos Hadjimichael, who painted in the early part of the 20th century. Lots of Greek schoolchildren visit here, and there are sometimes puppet shows and special exhibits. This is a great place to spend several hours—and it's easy to nip outside for a cool drink or snack on Kidathineon Street when you want a break from sightseeing.

17 Kidathineon St., Plaka. © **210/322-9031.** Admission 2€ ($2.30). Tues–Sun 10am–2pm. From Syntagma Sq., take Filellinon St. to Kidathineon.

Ilias Lalaounis Jewelry Museum *★★* The 3,000 pieces on display here are so spectacular that even those who don't care about jewelry will enjoy this glitzy small museum, founded by one of Greece's most successful jewelry designers. The first floor has a boutique stocking 2,000 items and a small workshop. The second and third floors display pieces inspired by ancient, Byzantine, and

Special Events

Early June to early October brings the annual **Athens Festival** ⟨★★★⟩, the city's main celebration of the arts. The Odeum (Odion) of Herodes Atticus, built in A.D. 174 and known as the *Irodio*, is the setting for performances by well-known Greek and foreign orchestras, ballet companies, singers, and dancers; offerings include classical Greek tragedies and comedies (usually done in modern Greek) and operas. The only drawbacks are that the stone seats are hard, with thin foam cushions, and there are no backrests. Tickets usually cost about 17€ to 56€ ($19–$64). Find out what's playing in the English-language press or at the Hellenic/Athens Festival Office, 39 Panepistimiou St. (© 210/322-1459), usually open Monday to Saturday 8:30am to 2pm and 5 to 7pm, and Sunday 10:30am to 1pm. If they're available, tickets can also be purchased at the Odeum (© 210/323-2771) for several hours before performances, which usually begin at 9pm.

The **Lykavitos Festival** ⟨★⟩, an outdoor event held atop Mount Lykavitos each summer, features more contemporary entertainers (the Pet Shop Boys appeared recently), at prices usually a bit lower than those at the Athens Festival. For schedule and ticket information, contact the Hellenic/Athens Festival Office (as above) or the Lykavitos Theater at © 210/722-0209. You can buy tickets at the Athens Festival box office or at the gate. Sometimes a free shuttle bus takes ticket holders from central Athens to the theater. Otherwise, you'll need to take a taxi or the funicular from the top of Ploutarchou Street.

Beyond Athens, the annual **Epidauros Festival** ⟨★★★⟩ presents performances of ancient Greek drama at the world's most perfect amphitheater, usually late June to early September. Special buses, and sometimes excursion boats, usually run from Athens and Piraeus during the festival. Check with the Hellenic/Athens Festival box office (as above) for schedules and tickets. Tickets are also usually available at the box office at the theater in Epidauros (© 27530/22-026).

Additional information on these festivals is available online at **www.hellenicfestival.gr**, **www.cultureguide.gr**, and **www.greektourism.com**.

Cycladic designs, as well as by plants and animals. The museum has frequent special exhibits and a cafe. Many of the exhibits are small and detailed, so you'll probably want to spend several hours here.

12 Kalisperi (at Karyatidon). © 210/922-1044. Fax 210/923-7358. www.lalaounis-jewelrymuseum.gr. Admission 4€ ($4.60) Mon and Thurs–Sat 9am–4pm; Wed 9am–9pm (free after 3pm); Sun 10am–4pm. Walk 1 block south of the Acropolis between Theater of Dionysos and Odeum of Herodes Atticus.

Museum of Greek Popular Musical Instruments ⟨★★⟩ ⟨Value⟩   Photos show the musicians, and recordings let you listen to the tambourines, Cretan lyres, lutes, pottery drums, and clarinets on display in this enchanting museum. The shop has a wide selection of CDs and cassettes, and the excellent Platanos Taverna (p. 122) is across the street. It's easy to spend the morning here, have lunch

---

⟨Tips⟩ Take the Plaka Tram

Keep an eye out for the Plaka tram. For 4€ ($4.60), the half-hour ride begins in Palia Agora Square, loops through the Plaka, and then runs along the Acropolis before heading back into the Plaka. It runs daily 10am to 10pm in summer (weekends only in the off season).

---

at the Platanos, and find yourself wandering back to the museum to hear another tambourine or two after lunch.

1–3 Diogenous St. ⓒ 210/325-0198. Free admission. Tues and Thurs–Sun 10am–2pm; Wed noon–8pm.

GALLERIES

One of the great (usually free) pleasures of visiting Athens is browsing in its small art galleries. Very occasionally a gallery has an admission fee for a special exhibit, but usually there is no charge. This is a wonderful way to get a sense of the contemporary Greek art scene—and possibly buy something to take home. Openings are usually not by invitation only, so if you see a notice of an opening, feel free to stop by. Here are some galleries to keep an eye out for in central Athens: The **Epistrofi Gallery,** 6 Taki (ⓒ 210/321-8640), in trendy Psirri, has occasional concerts as well as shows; the **Epikentro Gallery,** 10 Armodiou (ⓒ 210/331-2187), stages frequent exhibits in its improbable location in the Athens Central Market; the **Rebecca Kamhi Gallery,** 23 Sophokleous (ⓒ 210/321-0448), not far from the Central Market, and one of Athens's best-known galleries, is open by appointment only in August; **Bernier/Eliades Gallery,** 11 Eptachalkou, Theseion (ⓒ 210/341-3935), stages group exhibitions, as does **Kappatos,** Agias Irenes 6 (ⓒ 210/321-7931).

There are also frequent shows at the **Melina Mercouri Cultural Center,** Iraklidon and Thessalonikis 66 (ⓒ 210/345-2150), not far from the Theseion and at the **Melina Mercouri Foundation,** 9–11 Polygnotou (ⓒ 210/331-5601), in Plaka. The fashionable Kolonaki district is chock-a-block with galleries: The **Athens Art Center,** 4 Glyconos, Dexameni, Kolonaki (ⓒ 210/721-3938); **Photohoros,** 44 Tsakalof (ⓒ 210/321-0448); and **Medussa,** Xenokratous 7 (ⓒ 210/724-4552), are three to look for. The **Athens Arts and Technology School** (ⓒ 210/381-3700) usually stages shows around Athens in July and August when many galleries close or move out of town. One just-out-of-town suburban gallery that's open year-round and well worth a visit (in part for its great cafe and shop) is **The Deste Foundation for Contemporary Art,** 8 Omirou, Nea Psychico (ⓒ 210/672-9460; www.deste.gr), a 20-minute cab ride from Syntagma Square.

A GARDEN, A HILL & A MONASTERY

The **National Garden,** between Amalias Avenue and Irodou Attikou, south of Vasilissis Sofias Avenue, was originally the garden of the Royal Palace. Today, the former palace houses the Parliament; the tomb of the Unknown Soldier in front of the Parliament building is guarded by Greek soldiers (Evzones) wearing bright red slippers and short, pleated kilts. There's usually an especially impressive changing of the guard on Sunday at 11am. The garden contains more than 500 varieties of plants and trees, as well as duck ponds and a small, sad zoo with some peacocks. There are several cafes and one excellent expensive restaurant (Aigli Bistrot, near the Zappeion); you can also picnic here—or just escape the summer heat on one of the benches under shade trees. Keep an eye out for the bust of Melina Mercouri, the Greek actress and political figure, across from the garden on Vasilissis Amalias Avenue. The garden is officially open daily 7am to 10pm, with free admission. This isn't a good place to wander alone at night, unless you enjoy encounters with strangers.

Mount Lykavitos (Lycabettus), dominating the northeast of the city, is a favorite retreat for Athenians and a great place to get a bird's-eye view of Athens and its environs—if the *nefos* (smog) isn't too bad. Even when the *nefos* is bad, sunsets can be spectacular here. On top is a small chapel of Ayios Yioryios (St. George), whose name day is celebrated on April 23. Nearby are the Lykavitos Theater, an important venue for summer music performances, as well as a couple of overpriced cafes. You can take the funicular from the top of Ploutarchou Street (3€/$3.45 10am–10pm, about every 20 min. in summer) or walk up from Dexameni Square, the route preferred by young lovers and the energetic.

The **Kaisariani Monastery,** just 7km (4½ miles) east on the cool forested slope of Mount Imittos (Hymettus), is another lovely place to escape Athens's noise and *nefos,* although a number of recent summer forest fires severely damaged the pine groves. The monastery is open Tuesday to Sunday 8:30am to 3pm. The small church was built in the 5th century, probably over an ancient temple; its pretty frescoes date from the 16th century. Bus 224 leaves from Kaningos Square on Acadamias Street and from Panepistimiou Street and Vasilissis Sofias Avenue, northeast of Syntagma Square, about every 20 minutes. A taxi to take you here, wait an hour while you visit, and then return, should cost about 20€ ($23). Better yet, take the bus here, spend as long as you like, and take a taxi back into central Athens.

ORGANIZED TOURS

You can book tours of Athens through most hotels or any travel agency. A half-day tour of city highlights should cost about 50€ ($58). Night tours can include a sound-and-light show, Greek folk dancing at the Dora Stratou Dance Theater, or dinner and Greek dancing; they range from about 50€ to 150€ ($58–$173). Since many Athenian nightclubs are clip joints, the safety-in-numbers aspect of a visit with a tour group may appeal to you. **CHAT Tours,** 9 Xenofondos (Syntagma, 4th floor; *©* **210/322-3137;** fax 210/323-1200; chat@chatours.gr); **GO Tours,** 20 A. Diakou St., Makriyanni (*©* **210/921-5650**); and **Key Tours,** 4 Kalirois St. (*©* **210/923-3166**), are reliable companies offering tours of Athens and various day trips. Tours are often no more expensive—and considerably less stressful—than renting a car for the day and driving yourself. Also keep in mind that finding many sites if you don't speak Greek (Daphni, Eleusis, Kessaraini, Marathon) isn't easy.

5 Shopping

If you want to pick up retro clothes or old copper, try the flea market, a daily spectacle between the Plaka and Monastiraki Square. It's most lively on Sunday, but you can find the usual trinkets, copies of ancient artifacts, jewelry, sandals, and various handmade goods, including embroideries, any day. *Warning:* Not everything sold as an antique is genuine, and it's illegal to take antiquities and icons more than 100 years old out of the country without an export license.

In the Plaka–Monastiraki area, several shops with nicer-than-usual arts and crafts and fair prices are **Stavros Melissinos,** the Poet-Sandalmaker of Athens,

89 Pandrossou St. (© 210/321-9247); **Emanuel Masmanidis' Gold Rose Jewelry,** 85 Pandroussou St. (© 210/321-5662); the **Center of Hellenic Tradition,** 59 Metropoleos St. and 36 Pandrossou St. (© 210/321-3023), which has a lovely cafe; and the **Hellenic Folk-Art Gallery,** 6 Ipatias and Apollonos streets, Plaka (© 210/324-0017).

Clothes in Greece are expensive, and it isn't a good place to add to your wardrobe unless you hit the January or August sales. If you need to get something, try the moderately priced shops in the Omonia/Syntagma/Monastiraki squares triangle—and resist the tempting boutiques around Kolonaki Square.

6 Athens After Dark

Greeks enjoy their nightlife so much they take an afternoon nap to rest up for it. The evening often begins with a leisurely *volta* (stroll); you'll see it happening in many neighborhoods, including the Plaka and Kolonaki Square. Most Greeks don't even begin to think about eating dinner until at least 9pm—and even then there's no hurry. Around midnight, diners often move on to a club for music and dancing. Feel free to try places on your own, although you might feel like the odd man out because Greeks seldom go anywhere alone. If you're a woman on your own and want to be left alone, you'll probably find hitting the bars and dance clubs uncongenial.

Check the *Athens News* or the daily "Kathimerini" insert in the *International Herald Tribune,* sold at most major newsstands, for current cultural and entertainment events, including films, lectures, theater, music, and dance. The weekly *Hellenic Times* and *Athenscope* and the monthly *Now in Athens* have good lists of nightspots, restaurants, movies, theater, and much else. *Athinorama* (published weekly in Greek) has restaurant, theater, music, and special events listings, as does the excellent *Odyssey* magazine (published about six times a year in English).

Best of all, if you have a Greek friend, ask for pointers on what's currently on. If you ask a taxi driver, he's likely to take you to either his cousin George's joint or the place that gives him a kickback for bringing you. Be especially wary of heading out of the city to the places that spring up each summer on the airport road; these spots are usually overpriced and often unsavory. That said, the **Asteria Club** (© 210/894-4558) and the **Bio-Bio Club** (© 210/894-1300) in Glyfada were both popular during the summer of 2001, as was **Riba's** (© 210/965-5555) in Varkiza. Admission can cost as much as 50€ ($58) at live-music joints; expect to pay an additional 20€ ($23) for one or two drinks.

THE PERFORMING ARTS

The acoustically marvelous new **Megaron Mousikis Concert Hall,** 89 Vasilissis Sofias Ave. (© 210/728-2333), hosts a wide range of classical music programs that include quartets, operas in concert, symphonies, and recitals. The box office is open Monday to Friday 10am to 6pm, Saturday 10am to 2pm, and Sunday 6 to 10:30pm on performance nights. Tickets, usually costing from as little as 5€ to 100€ ($5.75–$115), are also sold weekdays 10am to 5pm in the Megaron's convenient downtown kiosk in the Spiromillios Arcade, 4 Stadiou St. (the arcade is in the courtyard off Stadiou). The Megaron has a limited summer season but is in full swing the rest of the year.

Most major jazz and rock concerts, as well as some classical performances, are held at the **Pallas Theater,** 1 Voukourestiou St. (© 210/322-8275).

English-language theater and American-style music are performed at the **Hellenic American Union Auditorium,** 22 Massalias St., between Kolonaki and Omonia squares ((C) **210/362-9886**); you can usually get a ticket from 10€ ($12). Arrive early and check out the art show or photo exhibit at the adjacent gallery. The **Greek National Opera** performs at the **Olympia Theater,** 59 Akadimias St., at Mavromihali ((C) **210/361-2461**).

The **Dora Stratou Folk Dance Theater,** which performs May to October on Philopappos Hill, is the best known of the traditional dance troupes. Performances are Tuesday through Sunday at 10:15pm, with additional shows at 8:15pm on Wednesday and Sunday. You can buy tickets for about 12€ to 25€ ($14–$29) 8am to 2pm at the box office, 8 Scholio St., Plaka ((C) **210/924-4395** or 210/921-4650 after 5:30pm).

Sound-and-light shows, seen from the Pnyx, the hill across Dionyssiou Areopagitou Street from the Acropolis, illuminate (sorry) Athens's history by focusing on the history of the Acropolis. Try to sit away from the too-loud speakers and concentrate instead on the play of lights on the monuments of the Acropolis. Shows are held April to October. Performances in English begin at 9pm and last 45 minutes. Tickets can be purchased at the **Athens Festival Office,** 4 Stadiou St. ((C) **210/322-7944**), or at the entrance to the sound-and-light show ((C) **210/922-6210**), which is signposted on the Pnyx. Tickets cost from 10€ ($12).

LIVE-MUSIC CLUBS

Walk the streets of the Plaka on any night and you'll find lots of tavernas offering pseudo-traditional live music (usually at clip-joint prices) and a few offering the real thing. **Taverna Mostrou,** 22 Mnissikleos St. ((C) **210/324-2441**), is one of the largest, oldest, and best known for traditional Greek music and dancing. Shows begin about 11pm and usually last to 2am. The 30€ ($35) cover includes a fixed-price supper; a la carte fare is available but expensive. Nearby, **Palia Taverna Kritikou,** 24 Odos Mnissikleos ((C) **210/322-2809**), is another lively open-air taverna with music and dancing. Other reliable tavernas with live traditional music are **Nefeli,** 24 Panos St. ((C) **210/321-2475**); **Dioyenis,** 3 Sellei St. ((C) **210/324-7933**); **Stamatopoulou,** 26 Lissiou St. ((C) **210/322-8722**); and **Xinos,** 4 Geronta St. ((C) **210/322-1065**).

For Greek pop music, try **Zoom,** 37 Kidathineon St., in the heart of the Plaka ((C) **210/322-5920**). If you want to check out the local rock and blues scene along with small doses of metal, Athenian popsters play at **Memphis,** 5 Ventiri St., near the Hilton Hotel east of Syntagma ((C) **210/722-4104**), Tuesday to Friday. Cover varies.

Nightlife in August

Many popular after-dark spots close in August, when Athenians flee the summer heat and head to the country. You'll find that a number of bars, cafes, *ouzeries,* and tavernas on the pedestrianized **Irakleidon** walkway off Apostolos Pauvlos Street across from the Theseion stay open in August: **Stavlos,** the restaurant/bar/disco popular with all ages, remains open on August weekends. A few doors away, the **Berlin Club,** which caters to a young crowd and specializes in rock, is open most nights, and **Ambibagio** has quite genuine Greek music. The sweet shop **Aistisis** offers great views of the Acropolis and stays open as late as the nearby bars.

Those interested in authentic *rebetika* (music of the urban poor and dispossessed) should consult their hotel receptionist or the current issue of *Athenscope* or *Athinorama* (in Greek) to see which clubs are featuring the best performers. Shows usually don't start until nearly midnight, and although there's usually no cover, a 20€ ($23) charge per drink isn't uncommon. Most clubs are closed in summer, and many that are open are far from the town center, so budget at least another 30€ ($35) for round-trip taxi fare.

The downscale, smoke-filled **Rebetiki Istoria,** 181 Ippokratous St. (© 210/ 642-4937), features old-style *rebetika* music, played to a mixed crowd of older regulars and younger students and intellectuals. The music usually starts at 11pm, but arrive earlier to get a seat. The legendary Maryo I Thessaloniki (Maryo from Thessaloniki), sometimes described as the Bessie Smith of Greece, sometimes sings *rebetika* at **Perivoli t'Ouranou,** 19 Lysikratous St. in the Plaka (© 210/323-5517 or 210/322-2048). A number of clubs and cafes specialize in jazz but also offer everything from Indian sitar music to rock to punk. A few to try: **Café Asante,** 78 Damareos in Pangrati (© 210/756-0102); **Half Note Jazz Club,** 17 Trivonianou St., Mets (© 210/921-3310); and **The Rodon Club,** 24 Marni St., west of Omonia Square (© 210/523-6293). **The House of Art,** 4 Sahtouri and Sari, Psirri (© 210/321-7678); and **Pinakothiki,** 5 Agias Theklas (© 210/324-7741), are both in newly fashionable Psirri (so fashionable that it has its own website: **www.psirri.gr**). Admission varies at these clubs depending on who's performing, but expect to pay between 15€ and 30€ ($17–$35) for admission; drinks are often 10€ ($12). Sometimes admission includes the price of one drink. Ask.

GAY & LESBIAN BARS

The gay scene is fairly low-key; get-togethers are sometimes advertised in the English-language press. Information is also available from the Greek national gay and lesbian organization **AKOE-AMPHI,** P.O. Box 26002, 100 22 Athens. Its office is at 6 Zalongou (© 210/771-9221).

The friendliest bar is **Aleko's Island,** 42 Tsakalof St., Kolonaki (no phone). **Granazi,** 20 Lebesi St. (© 210/325-3979), attracts a loud and lively young crowd. The disco **Lambda,** 15 Lembessi St. and 9 Syngrou Ave. (© 210/ 922-4202), is hip and trendy with the young locals. In Kolonaki, **Alexander's,** 44 Anagnostopoulou, Kolonaki (© 210/364-6660), is more sedate, with more variety. **Porta,** 10 Phalirou St. (© 210/924-3858), and **Fairytale,** 25 Kolleti (© 210/330-1763), are well-established lesbian bars. There's usually a lively nighttime transvestite cruising scene along Syngrou Avenue in Makriyanni. **Koukles** (the name means "dolls"), at Zan Moreas and Syngrou Avenue, Koukaki (no phone), has drag shows most evenings.

DANCE CLUBS

Hidden on the outskirts of the Plaka, **Booze,** 57 Kolokotroni St., second floor (© 210/324-0944), blasts danceable rock to a hip student crowd. For disco, head to **Absolut,** 23 Filellinon St. (no phone); **Q Base,** 49 Evripidou, Omonia (© 210/321-8256); or **R-Load,** 161 Ermou (© 210/345-6187). If you feel a bit too old there, head north to Panepistimiou Street, where the **Wild Rose,** in the arcade at 10 Panepistimiou (© 210/364-2160), and **Mercedes Rex,** at 48 Panepistimiou (© 210/361-4591), usually have varied programs. Admission at all these clubs is at least 10€ ($12).

7 A Side Trip to Delphi & Its Archaeological Site ⟨★

Many tour groups offer day trips to **Delphi,** stopping at the Byzantine Monastery of Osios Loukas. In summer, tour groups clog Delphi's few streets by day, but many head elsewhere for the night, which means hotel rooms are usually available—although often all the cheap rooms are gone by midmorning. In winter, thousands of Greeks head here each weekend, not for the archaeological site but for the excellent skiing on Mount Parnassus. The influx of skiers has made getting a room in the formerly sleepy nearby hamlet of Arachova virtually impossible without a reservation on winter weekends, and Delphi itself is often full. The tourist office on the main street (© **22650/82-900**) is usually open daily 7:30am to 2:30pm (sometimes later in summer)—but is sometimes mysteriously closed.

Public **buses** leave Athens for Delphi five times daily from Bus Terminal B (© **210/831-7096**), some distance north of Omonia Square; the trip takes about 3 hours, and buses are often very crowded. The address is given as 260 Liossion St., which is actually where you get off the local bus; turn right onto Gousiou Street and you'll see the terminal at the end of the road.

SEEING THE SITES   Throughout antiquity, pilgrims came to Delphi from all over the Greek—and much of the non-Greek—world to ask Apollo's advice on affairs of state as well as personal matters. Alas, the god's words were famously hard to interpret. "Invade and you will destroy a great empire," the oracle told Lydian King Croesus when he asked whether he should go to war with his Persian neighbors. Croesus invaded and destroyed a great empire: his own. Since Delphi was also the site of the Pythian Games, the most famous athletic festival in Greece after the Olympics, there's a lot to see here.

If you begin at the **Archaeology Museum** (© 22650/82-1313), just outside the site entrance, the displays help you visualize many of the works of art that decorated the site. Each of the museum's original 13 rooms had a specific focus, although the museum's expansion has caused some exhibits to be moved around. Keep an eye out for the sculpture from the Siphnian Treasury, finds from the Temple of Apollo, sculpture from the Roman era, and the famous 5th-century B.C. bronze known as the *Charioteer of Delphi.* Don't miss the handsome youth's delicate eyelashes shading his wide enamel-and-stone eyes. Admission (which includes the site) is 9€ ($10). Summer hours: Monday noon to 5:30pm; Tuesday to Friday 7:30am to 6:30pm; Saturday and Sunday 8:30am to 3pm. In the winter, it's usually open daily 8:30am to 3pm. *Note:* The museum is closed for renovation until the 2004 Olympics; it will reopen for the Olympics (Aug 13–29, 2004) but may close indefinitely for renovations thereafter.

The Festival of Delphi

Every summer (usually in June), the European Cultural Center of Delphi sponsors a festival featuring ancient Greek drama and works inspired by ancient drama. Tickets and schedules are usually available at the Center's Athens office at 9 Frynihou, Plaka (© 210/331-2798), and at the Center's Delphi office (© 22650/82-733). *Budget travelers take note:* Tickets are sometimes substantially discounted or even free close to performance time.

The **Sanctuary of Apollo** is just beyond the museum, and the famous Castalian Spring is on the road leading to the Sanctuary of Athena Pronaia on the lower slopes of Mount Parnassus. As you enter the Sanctuary of Apollo, you'll walk along the marble **Sacred Way** that pilgrims used in antiquity. Climbing toward the **Temple of Apollo,** you'll pass the remains of the small treasuries Greek cities built to house works of art dedicated to Apollo, as well as a number of Roman stoae. Many of the works of art in the museum were found along the Sacred Way; some ornamented the Temple of Apollo itself. Several of the columns of this massive 4th-century B.C. temple have been re-erected; the others lie where they fell when the earthquakes that had destroyed earlier temples struck again and toppled this one. Somewhere deep inside this temple sat the Pythian priestess who gave voice to Apollo's utterances. From the temple, the path continues uphill through pine trees to the well-preserved 4th-century B.C. **theater** that seated 5,000; it's still used for performances during the Festival of Delphi (although the Archaeological Service has announced that it is considering putting an end to this to protect the theater). Above the theater, the path becomes even steeper, continuing to the **Greek stadium,** which was enlarged by the Romans. You might want to curl your toes into the parallel grooves carved into stone at the starting line and attempt a lap or two.

When you leave the Sanctuary, continue along the main road to the sacred **Spring of Castalia** (no admission charge), tucked away in a cleft in the rocks behind a bend in the road. This is where Apollo planted a laurel he brought from the beautiful Vale of Tempe and where poets drank from the spring in search of inspiration. Alas, the sacred spring is now off-limits because of the threat of falling rocks, and it shows signs of becoming an unattractive cesspool. Across from the spring, farther along the road, you'll see the entrance to the **Sanctuary of Athena Pronaia** (Athena the Guardian of the Temple). This area is also known as the Marmaria because of all the marble found here, much of which was hacked up and carted off for building after the Sanctuary lost its power during the early Christian era. The antiquities here, including sections of two temples and a gymnasium, are poorly preserved, and you might prefer just to peer down at the elegant 4th-century **Tholos** (a round building of unknown function), whose slender Doric columns are easy to spot.

You can easily spend a full day visiting Delphi; at a bare minimum, allow 4 hours to visit the museum and site. Admission (which includes the museum) is 9€ ($10). Summer hours are Monday noon to 5:30pm; Tuesday to Friday 7:30am to 6:30pm; Saturday and Sunday 8:30am to 3pm. In the winter, it's usually open daily 8:30am to 3pm.

WHERE TO STAY   The small family-owned **Hotel Varonos,** 27 Pavlou and Frederikis (Delphi's main street), 330 54 Delphi (℃/fax **22650/82-345**), renovates each year and has 11 rooms with spectacular views over the plain. The room rate is 75€ to 90€ ($86–$104). American Express, MasterCard, and Visa are accepted, and discounts are sometimes available. In addition to the Varonos, we've had good reports about the similarly priced **Pan Hotel,** 53 Vasileos Pavlou and Frederikis (℃ **22650/82-294**); the adjacent **Olympic Hotel,** 53a Vasileos Pavlou and Frederikis (℃ **22650/82-793;** fax 22650/82-780); and the **Hermes Hotel,** 29 Vasileos Pavlou and Frederikis (℃ **22650/82-318;** fax 22650/ 82-639). The last two are both owned by the Droseros family.

Delphi Site Plan

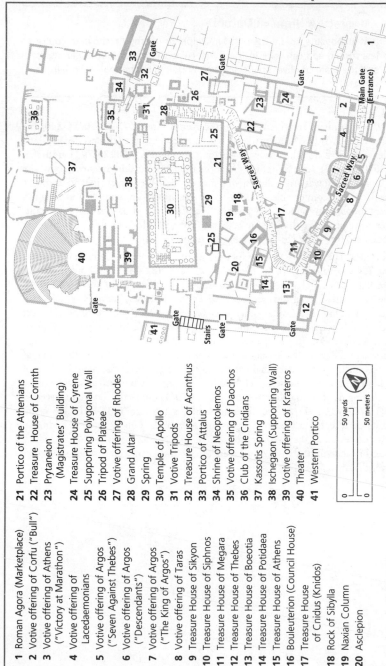

1 Roman Agora (Marketplace)
2 Votive offering of Corfu ("Bull")
3 Votive offering of Athens
   ("Victory at Marathon")
4 Votive offering of
   Lacedaemonians
5 Votive offering of Argos
   ("Seven Against Thebes")
6 Votive offering of Argos
   ("Descendants")
7 Votive offering of Argos
   ("The King of Argos")
8 Votive offering of Taras
9 Treasure House of Sikyon
10 Treasure House of Siphnos
11 Treasure House of Megara
12 Treasure House of Thebes
13 Treasure House of Boeotia
14 Treasure House of Potidaea
15 Treasure House of Athens
16 Bouleuterion (Council House)
17 Treasure House
   of Cnidus (Knidos)
18 Rock of Sibylla
19 Naxian Column
20 Asclepion

21 Portico of the Athenians
22 Treasure House of Corinth
23 Prytaneion
   (Magistrates' Building)
24 Treasure House of Cyrene
25 Supporting Polygonal Wall
26 Tripod of Plataea
27 Votive offering of Rhodes
28 Grand Altar
29 Spring
30 Temple of Apollo
31 Votive Tripods
32 Treasure House of Acanthus
33 Portico of Attalus
34 Shrine of Neoptolemos
35 Votive offering of Daochos
36 Club of the Cnidians
37 Kassotis Spring
38 Ischegaon (Supporting Wall)
39 Votive offering of Krateros
40 Theater
41 Western Portico

0 ___ 50 yards
0 ___ 50 meters

143

Moments A Night in Delphi

If at all possible, spend the night in Delphi or nearby Arachova so you're less rushed and can take in the spectacular scenery of Mount Parnassus and the plain of olives stretching below Delphi to the sea—especially at sunset.

If you want to stay in Arachova, the **Xenia Hotel** (℗ **22670/31-230;** fax 22670/32-175) has 44 rooms, each with a balcony (but charmless decor); doubles cost 80€ ($92). The very pleasant **Anemolia** (℗ **22670/31-640;** fax 22670/31-642), with 52 rooms, is set on a hill just outside Arachova above the Delphi road; it was originally a member of the Best Western chain, and its rooms are large and comfortable. The 44-room **Arachova Inn,** with 42 rooms and a cozy fireplace in the lobby, is just outside of town and has its own restaurant. Tentative prices for all three for 2004 are 85€ ($98) for a double (sometimes as much as 20€–50€/$23–$58 higher on the weekend).

WHERE TO DINE   Most Delphi restaurants serve bland tourist fare; prices at the **Taverna Vakchos,** 31 Apollonos St. (℗ **22650/82-448**), are about as good as you'll get. The family-run **Taverna Lekaria,** 33 Apollonos St. (℗ **22650/82-864**), has nice toasted bread and excellent *saganaki* (fried cheese), but the service is often desultory. Dinner for two at either place begins at 30€ ($35). You'll probably eat better and escape the summer tourists if you take a bus or cab to the village of **Arachova,** 9.7km (6 miles) north. You can sit in the little town square, drink glasses of the water that gushes from freshwater springs, and browse the string of shops on the main street that offer local weavings and crafts, reproductions of antiques, and local cheeses. Then, you can eat modestly but well at local tavernas, including the **Taverna Karathanassi** (℗ **22670/31-360**), the **Taverna Dasargyri** (℗ **22670/31-391**), or the **Taverna Kaplanis** (℗ **22670/31-891**). No credit cards are accepted at these restaurants; all are open daily about noon to midnight. Two can eat at all these restaurants for 25€ to 40€ ($29–$46), which includes a beer or carafe of house wine; prices are usually higher in winter, when skiers take over the town.

5

Barcelona & Environs

by Sascha Segan & Herbert Bailey Livesey

Barcelona is a miracle. With an unforgettable visual style, a passion for living, and a continuous churn of old and new, the capital of the autonomous region of Catalonia (don't call it Spanish!) is easily Spain's most enjoyable city. Barcelona is a laughing jewel that winks at businesslike Madrid and goes on partying. It says something that Catalonia's favorite sons have been four artists known for their brilliant eccentricity: Gaudí, Miró, Picasso, and Dalí.

A walk through Barcelona captures the best of Western civilization. First a major Roman outpost, the city was by the 13th century the capital of the Kingdom of Catalonia and Aragón, whose colonial influence extended into southern France, down to Valencia, and over to Sicily and Greece. Catalonians consider themselves a distinct nationality, speaking a language that owes as much to French as it does to Spanish.

Since the 19th century, the Catalan metropolis has always been at the forefront of modernity. Barcelona was the nation's first industrial center, expanding from its ancient settlement into the surrounding hills by the 1920s. The end of the 20th century brought another burst of expansion: first for the 1992 Olympics, and now for Expo 2004, a 6-month festival demanding the construction of an entire new neighborhood on the waterfront.

Barcelona is perfectly harmonious with its surroundings. The city sits in a bowl valley bracketed by the hill of Montjuïc and the river Besós, backed by a wall of mountains dominated by the Tibidabo peak. The low-slung city rises gently up the slope; a lack of skyscrapers means Gaudí's masterpiece, the towering Sagrada Família church, is visible from all over town.

Barcelona's quirky personality and willingness to take risks has netted the city with some of Europe's most amazing architecture, from the Gothic cathedral to the parade of Modernist masterpieces along the Passeig de Grácia. The region has given birth to some of history's most visionary artists. Now, the city is also becoming known for brilliant, almost surrealist cuisine. Joyously joining the Europe of the 21st century, Barcelona has everything going for it—good looks, a sharp business sense, an appreciation for all forms of culture, and an unerring eye for style.

For more on Barcelona and its environs, see *Frommer's Madrid, Barcelona & Seville; Frommer's Spain;* or *Spain For Dummies.*

1 Essentials

ARRIVING

BY PLANE Barcelona's modern **El Prat Airport** is about 13km (8 miles) from the city center. A **train** runs between the airport and the Estació Sants rail station every 30 minutes from 6:13am to 11:40pm, taking about 20 minutes to

Barcelona Deals & Discounts

SPECIAL DISCOUNTS   Most four- and five-star hotels have adopted the North American practice of sharply **reduced weekend rates,** often including extras not provided during the week, like breakfast and a morning newspaper. These lowered rates aren't always volunteered, so ask if less expensive rooms are available Friday to Sunday nights. Booklets of **discount coupons** on tours, meals, shopping, nightclubs, casinos, car rentals, concerts, and museum admissions are frequently offered. For more details and even reservations, contact the **Centre d'Informació,** Plaça de Catalunya, 08015 Barcelona (© **93/304-3135;** fax 93/ 423-2649; Metro: Catalunya).

Also available at the Centre d'Informació is the **Barcelona Card,** giving you free travel on the bus and Metro, discounts of 15% to 50% off admission to almost 40 museums and other attractions, and smaller discounts at a selection of shops and restaurants. The card is good for 1 through 5 days and costs 16€ ($19), 19€ ($22), 22€ ($26), 24€ ($28), and 26€ ($30), respectively; 3€ ($3.45) less for children 4 to 12 in each level.

The architectural achievements of *modernisme* set Barcelona apart. While Antoni Gaudí and Lluís Domènech were the leaders, they and their contemporary adherents produced well over 150 remarkable structures, concentrated in the Eixample. The **Ruta del Modernisme** multi-ticket (www.rutamodernisme.com) provides 50% discounts on admissions to several of the most prominent **buildings;** it's good for 30 days, and you can buy it at Casa Amatller, Passeig de Gràcia 41, for 3.60€ ($3.20) adults and 2.40€ ($2.15) students and seniors. It pays for itself if you visit at least two of its sites: La Pedrera (regular admission 7€/$8.05); Palau de la Música Catalana (7€/$8.05), Temple de la Sagrada Família (8€/$9.20), Fundació Tàpies (4.20€/$4.85), Palau Güell

---

Estació Sants and continuing to the more central Plaça de Catalunya; it costs 2.25€ ($2.60). **Aerobuses** (© **93/415-6020**) run among the three terminals at the airport and to Plaça de Catalunya (with intermediate stops) Monday to Friday every 12 minutes from 6:30am to midnight. The trip takes 25 to 40 minutes and costs 3.45€ ($4). Tickets are sold on the bus, which is air-conditioned and has a low entry without steps. A **taxi** into town is about 20€ to 25€ ($23–$29), plus tip and supplements for luggage (about .85€/$1 per piece).

Note: When departing Barcelona, make sure to determine which of the three terminals you need. The shuttle to Madrid called the **Pont Aeri/Puente Aéreo (Air Bridge)** has its own location, separate from the **Terminal Nacional,** where you can get flights to other parts of Spain.

BY TRAIN   National and international trains arrive at the **Estació Sants** or the **Estació de França,** both slightly outside the city center but linked to the municipal Metro network. Many trains also stop at the Metro station at **Plaça de Catalunya.** For schedules and prices, call **RENFE** (© **90/224-0202;** www.renfe.es) or **Rail Europe** (© **888/382-7245;** www.raileurope.com).

BY BUS   Not all bus lines use it, but the principal terminal is the **Estació del Nord,** Ali-bei 80 (© **93/265-6508;** Metro: Arc de Triomf), not far from the

(4€/$4.60), and Museu d'Art Modern (3€/$3.45). In addition, there are guided tours in English of the "Block of Discord," which includes buildings by Gaudí and Domènech, daily at 10am, noon, 1, 3, 4, and 6pm.

When it comes time to visit neighboring provinces to the north and south, the **Spain Rail & Drive Pass** sold by **Rail Europe** (© **888/382-7245;** www.raileurope.com) provides 3 days of rail travel and 2 days' use of a rental car within a 2-month period, making it a good way to reach the resorts of the Costa Brava and Sitges, the cities of Girona and Tarragona, and the small villages of the Pyrenees and the wine country.

Students with appropriate ID can enjoy reduced or free admission to most of the city's museums and monuments. The pamphlet with the **Carnet Joven (Youth Card)** issued by the Generalitat de Catalunya lists almost 8,000 places offering discounts. It isn't so easy to obtain one, however. When you go to the **Punt d'Informació Juvenil,** Secretaria General de Joventut, Calabria 147, 08001 Barcelona (© **93/483-8384;** Metro: Tarragona), you're likely to be shunted from office to office, and English probably won't be spoken by any of the clerks. The center is open Monday to Friday 9am to 2pm and 3 to 5:30pm. Better yet, see if the mobile booth at the corner of Portal de l'Angel and Plaça de Catalunya is open.

WORTH A SPLURGE   If you want to splurge on a special night, tickets for performances at the **Palau de la Música Catalana** give top value, if only because you get to view its remarkable interior. Sampling Catalunya's *cavas* (wines made by the champagne method) in a sophisticated *xampanyeria* or nursing a pricey beer in one of the city's celebrated **designer bars** also makes for a memorable splurge evening.

Old Town and Plaça de Catalunya. Some companies stop near the Estació Sants, which has a Metro station.

BY CAR   Despite all the new roads and beltways, traffic is heavy and often chaotic, especially in the Eixample and on the Old Town's narrow streets. Find a detailed street map before your arrival, if possible, and once you're at your destination, consider garaging the car until departure. Leave no possessions inside, even in the trunk. If your hotel has no garage, there are usually nearby lots or facilities. One of the easiest to find is the garage beneath the plaza in front of the cathedral.

VISITOR INFORMATION

TOURIST OFFICES   The most central and helpful of the several information offices is the subterranean **Centre d'Informació,** at the southeast corner of Plaça Catalunya (© **93/368-9730;** Metro: Catalunya), open daily, 9am to 9pm. The multilingual attendants can provide street maps, answer questions, change money, and make hotel reservations. The office has a shop selling books and souvenirs.

In addition, the following **tourist offices** offer maps, brochures, and schedules of current exhibits, concerts, and other cultural events: **Estació Sants,** open

---

Value Budget Bests

At lunch—and at dinner in some restaurants—the three-course *menú del día* is nearly always a bargain. Make that your main meal and supplement it with snacks, sandwiches, pizza, or tapas (assorted bar snacks) at other times.

January, February, and July are **sale months,** when signs on almost every type of store shriek ¡REBAIXES! (Catalan) or ¡REBAJAS! (Spanish). Toward the end of these months, prices hit rock bottom.

Monday to Friday 8am to 8pm, and Saturday, Sunday, and holidays 8am to 2pm; **Plaça Sant Jaume,** open Monday to Friday 9am to 8pm, Saturday 10am to 8pm, and Sunday and holidays 10am to 2pm; and the **airport information office,** open daily 9am to 9pm.

For information on Barcelona and the entire region of Catalunya, try the **Oficina de Informació Turística,** Gran Vía del Corts Catalanes 658 (© 93/ 301-7443; Metro: Catalunya), open Monday to Friday 9am to 7pm and Saturday 9am to 2pm.

During summer, over 100 young people known as **Red Jackets** (for their crimson-and-white uniforms) roam the principal tourist areas offering assistance in various languages between 10am and 8pm.

For **information on what's happening** in Barcelona, dial © 010 Monday to Friday 7am to 11pm and Saturday 9am to 2pm. English-speaking attendants are available. Also see the brochure *Facil parlar,* available at tourist offices.

WEBSITES The official site of the Tourist Office of Spain is **www. okspain.org.** With far greater depth of coverage, **www.bcn.es** details restaurants, hotels, shops, markets, and even current traffic conditions, and includes a calendar of events updated daily. Another source of general information is provided by the municipal authorities at **www.barcelonaturisme.com.** Short on dining and shopping but fairly useful for essential addresses, phone numbers, and sightseeing is **www.bcn-guide.com.** At **www.tmb.net,** site of the Barcelona Transport Authority (Transports Metropolitans de Barcelona, or TMB), you'll find as much as you want to know about the Metro and bus systems, with detailed maps, hours, and prices.

CITY LAYOUT

Barcelona took shape under the Romans and later expanded from a walled medieval core at the water's edge. Between the harbor and the ordered grid of the 19th-century Eixample district lies the **Ciutat Vella (Old Town),** bordered by the Parc de la Ciutadella to the northeast and the fortress-topped hill of Montjuïc to the southwest. Its focal point is the **Barri Gòtic (Gothic Quarter),** which once contained the Call, a medieval Jewish neighborhood.

To the east is the **Barri de la Ribera,** developed during Barcelona's 13th- and 14th-century colonial and commercial expansion. Below the Parc de la Ciutadella and enclosing the east end of the harbor is **Barceloneta,** originally home to the city's mariners and fishermen and now known primarily for its seafood restaurants. It connects to the southwestern edge of the **Port Olímpic** in **Poble Nou,** an urbanized satellite of the central city containing what was the Olympic Village. A long **beach** reopened to the public runs from the tip of Barceloneta to the Port Olímpic and beyond. Way out to the east of the Olympic region is the brand-new **Diagonal Mar** neighborhood, created for the summer-long Forum 2004 festival.

At the Barri Gòtic's western edge, bisecting the Old Town, is **La Rambla,** a boulevard (comprising five individually named sections) curving a little over a mile from the port to Plaça de Catalunya. On the other side, down by the port, is the notorious **Barri Xinés (Chinese Quarter),** best avoided at night. Above the Barri Xinés, roughly north of the street called Nou de la Rambla, is the residential **El Raval** district, currently balancing on the knife-edge between marginally unsafe and breathtakingly hip.

To the north of Plaça de Catalunya is the **Eixample,** a grid of wide streets and Modernist buildings that's the product of Barcelona's growing prosperity in the late 19th century. North of the Eixample are **Gràcia,** an area of small squares and lively bars and restaurants that's known as "Barcelona's Greenwich Village"; **Sarría,** a quiet residential area; and **Tibidabo,** Barcelona's tallest mountain.

GETTING AROUND

The several important districts of the city are accessible on foot as well as by Metro (subway), bus, funicular, cable car, taxi, and train. Given persistent traffic congestion, the Metro and walking are quickest. For **public transport information,** call ✆ **010** Monday to Saturday 8am to 10pm. Note that fares are slightly higher on weekends and holidays.

BY METRO (SUBWAY)   The Metro and integrated commuter train lines (called FGC) operate Monday to Thursday 5am to midnight; Friday and Saturday 5am to 2am; and Sunday and holidays 6am to midnight. The lines you'll want to use within the city are numbered L1 through L8; other lines, starting with L, R, and S, serve various suburbs.

The one-way fare is 1.05€ ($1.20), but several types of **discount passes** may be used on the Metro, buses, and FGC trains. The best deal is the T10 10-ride pass, which costs 5.80€ ($6.65) and can be shared by multiple people. If you're really going to be zipping around, a 1-day pass costs 4.40€ ($5.05), a 2-day pass costs 8€ ($9.20), and there are 3-, 4-, and 5-day versions, too. Remember, you must use your ticket to exit the system as well as to enter.

All Metro stations have automated machines that sell tickets and passes; instructions are available in English, and the machines accept coins, bills, and credit cards. Many Metro ticket windows, *estancos* (tobacco shops), lottery booths, and even some bakeries also sell passes. A free Metro map is available at most Metro stations and tourist offices.

BY BUS   TMB also runs Barcelona's bus system. For schedules and route information, visit one of the service offices mentioned above, call ✆ **93/ 318-7074,** or visit TMB's website at www.tmb.net. The single fare is 1.05€ ($1.20), same as the Metro fare.

⌒*Tips*   A Note on Addresses

In Spain, street numbers follow street names and the ° sign indicates the floor. The Spanish first floor (1°) is the American second and is the convention used in this chapter. The Catalan words for "street," "avenue," "boulevard," and "plaza" are *carrer, avinguda, passeig,* and *plaça,* respectively.

A private, luxury bus, the **Tombbus Shopping Line,** runs from Plaça de Catalunya up the Passeig de Grácia and then northwest up Avenida Diagonal, every 5 minutes from 7:30am to 9:30pm Monday through Friday and 9:30am to 9:20pm Saturday. This bus doesn't accept Metro tickets. Tickets bought on the bus cost 1.25€ ($1.45) per ride, 8€ ($9.20) for a seven-ride card, or 5€ ($5.75) for a 1-day pass.

BY TELEFERIC, TRAMVIA BLAU & FUNICULAR   The **Transbordador Aeri del Puerto** is an aerial cable car running hundreds of feet above the port between Barceloneta and Montjuïc hill. An intermediate stop is made at the Moll de Barcelona, a jetty thrusting into the harbor from the plaza near the south end (harbor end) of La Rambla (with the Columbus Monument). Although the city views are spectacular, this isn't a ride for the even mildly acrophobic. June to September, the cable car operates daily 10:30am to 8pm; hours vary the rest of the year but it always runs between noon and 6pm. It runs about every 15 minutes, with the one-way fare at 7.50€ ($8.60) and round-trip fare at 9€ ($10) adults.

The **Funicular Montjuïc** runs between the Paral-lel Metro stop (Lines L2 and L3) and its terminus near the Fundació Joan Miró, halfway up Montjuïc. It runs daily late March to mid-September 9am to 10pm and late September to early March 9am to 8pm. It's part of the Metro system, so fares are the same as the subway fares.

The **Teleféric de Montjuïc** (aerial cable car) links the funicular with the castle at the top of Montjuïc, with a single stop near the Parc d'Atraccions, an amusement park. From mid-March to mid-June and mid-September to early November, it runs daily from 11am to 7:15pm; during high summer it runs from 11:15am to 9pm; and the rest of the year, the schedule is subject to change but the cable car usually runs Saturday, Sunday, and holidays from 11am to 7:15pm. The fare is 3.40€ ($3.90) one-way and 4.80€ ($5.50) round-trip.

The **Tramvía Blau,** a replica of an antique wooden tram running from Passeig de Sant Gervasi (Metro: L7/Avinguda del Tibidabo) to the bottom of the Tibidabo funicular, operates weekends in summer from 10am to 9pm, in winter from 10am to 6pm. Buses provide the service during the week, and schedules are subject to unpredictable change. The fare is 2€ ($2.30) one-way and 2.90€ ($3.35) round-trip. From the end of the line, about halfway up Tibidabo, you can take the **Tibidabo funicular** to the amusement park and basilica at the top. Late March to late October, it runs at least once every half-hour 10:30am to 10pm (to 6pm weekends in winter). The amusement park at the top is open noon to 8pm. The one-way fare is 2€ ($2.30); round-trip is 3€ ($3.45).

Note: All fares and schedules for cable cars, trams, and funiculars are subject to frequent changes. When in doubt, as during fiestas and seasonal changes, call ⓒ **010.**

BY TAXI   Most Barcelona taxis are black and yellow. When available, they display a sign reading LIBRE (Spanish) or LLIURE (Catalan) and/or an illuminated green roof light. On weekdays between 6am and 10pm, the fare starts at 1.15€ ($1.30) and increases by .69€ (80¢) per kilometer; at other times, the fare starts at 1.30€ ($1.50) and increases by .88€ ($1) per kilometer. Additional charges apply if you're going to the airport or the cruise port, riding on major holidays, or carrying luggage. Rates are listed on a sticker on the inside of the window. Taxi stands are abundant, and you can hail a cab on the street or call for one at ⓒ **93/433-1020,** 93/357-7755, 93/391-2222, or 93/490-2222.

Barcelona Metro

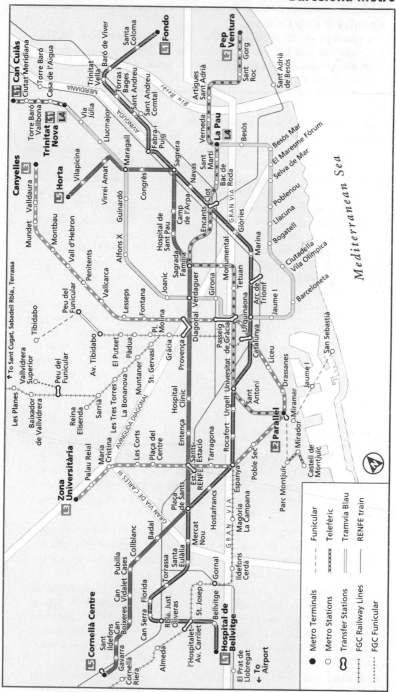

Country & City Codes

The **country code** for Spain is **34**. The **city code** for Barcelona is **93**. The city code has now been incorporated into all phone numbers, so you must always dial it, whether you're outside Spain, within Spain, or even within Barcelona.

BY CAR   Spain has one of the worst traffic fatality rates in Europe—almost five times that of Holland, the safest country in that regard. Use a car only for out-of-town excursions. Renting a car is expensive, but if one is a necessity, an airline fly/drive package may be the most economical solution.

Remember: You get the best deal if you arrange the rental before leaving home.

Otherwise, shop for the best deal among the following agencies with town and airport offices: **Atesa,** Sants railway station (© **93/491-0189,** or 93/298-3433 at the airport; www.atesa.es; Metro: Estacio Sants); **Avis,** Pallars 457 (© **93/303-1066,** or 93/298-3600 at the airport; www.avis.com; Metro: El Maresme/Forum); **Europcar,** Sants railway station (© **93/491-4822,** or 93/298-3300 at the airport; www.europcar.com; Metro: Estacio Sants); and **Hertz,** Viriat 45 (© **93/419-6156,** or 93/298-3638 at the airport; www.hertz.com; Metro: Estacio Sants).

Note: You'll need only your state or provincial driver's license to rent a car, but if you're in an accident or stopped on the road by police, a new regulation stipulates you must produce an **International Driver's License,** available at AAA offices in the United States for $10. Take along two passport-size photos, or they can take your picture for another $10. Also, be aware that Spain has toughened its rules of the road, including driving while holding a cellphone and driving under the influence, with the possibility of fines well over $500.

FAST FACTS: Barcelona

American Express The office at Ramblas 74, 08002 Barcelona (© **93/301-3531;** Metro: Liceu), is open daily 9am to 9pm. They'll hold mail for holders of their cards or traveler's checks for up to 1 month free. They'll also exchange currency and let you take out advances on your American Express card.

Babysitters Concierges in the larger hotels have lists of people and agencies available to provide child care. In the smaller hotels and pensions, this service is less certain, but in family-run places you can sometimes hire the teenage children of the managers.

Business Hours Hours at **banks** vary but usually are Monday to Friday 8:30am to 2pm and Saturday 9am to 1pm (closed Sat June–Sept). Typical **office** hours are Monday to Friday 9am to 1:30pm and 4 to 7pm, but some offices have special summer hours 8am to 3pm. **Shop** hours vary widely, but the norm is Monday to Friday 10am to 2pm and 4 to 8pm, and Saturday 10am to 2pm.

Consulates The consulate of the **United States** is at Passeig Reina Elisenda 23 (© **93/280-2227;** Metro: Reina Elisenda), open Monday to Friday 9am to noon and 3 to 5pm; the consulate of **Canada** is at Passeig de Gràcia 77

(© **93/215-0704;** Metro: Passeig de Gràcia), open Monday to Friday 10am to noon; the consulate of the **United Kingdom** is at Av. Diagonal 477 (© **93/366-6200;** Metro: Hospital Clínic), open Monday to Friday 9:30am to 1:30pm and 4 to 5pm, closed afternoons in summer; the consulate of **Ireland** is at Gran Vía 94 (© **93/491-5021;** Metro: María Cristina), open Monday to Friday 10am to 1pm; the consulate of **Australia** is at Gran Vía Carles III 98 (© **93/330-9494;** Metro: María Cristina), open Monday to Friday 10am to noon; and the consulate of **New Zealand** is at Travessera de Gràcia 64 (© **93/209-0399;** Metro: Gràcia), open Monday to Friday 9:30am to 1:30pm and 4:30 to 7:30pm.

Crime The street crime for which Barcelona once drew unwanted attention has diminished, due in part to an increased police presence and new lighting on dark streets in the Old Town. Some wariness is still required, however. A favorite maneuver of criminals is to spit or spill a messy substance on you—while one member of the team offers to "help," another relieves you of valuables. Men are more likely to suffer this; women are more often the victims of purse snatchings. Be especially alert in the older parts of town and around major sights. Take the usual urban precautions, and use hotel safes for jewelry, traveler's checks, extra credit cards, and any cash not required for each excursion.

An office that can help is **Turisme Atenció (Tourist Attention),** La Rambla 43 (© **93/301-9060;** Metro: Liceu). Operated by the municipal police Sunday to Thursday 7am to midnight and Friday to Saturday 7am to 2am, it has English-speaking attendants who can aid crime victims in reporting losses and obtaining new documents.

Currency In 2002, Spain adopted the **euro (€)** for its currency. At press time, 1€ = $1.15, or $1 = 0.87€.

Currency Exchange Change money and traveler's checks at any bank advertising a *cambio.* A set commission is nearly always charged, which makes cashing small amounts expensive. When banks are closed, you can change money at the Estació Sants daily 8am to 10pm or at the airport daily 7am to 11pm.

Only in a pinch, there are **Chequepoint** offices on La Rambla and near the cathedral, as well as at other locations, where you can change money or traveler's checks daily 9am to midnight. They don't charge a commission, but their exchange rate is significantly lower than the bank rates.

ATMs are located throughout the city, especially in tourist and commercial areas. Some stateside banks charge excessive fees for this service and others charge little or nothing, so check that out before you leave. Be sure you have a four-digit PIN.

Dentist For local referral service, call © **93/415-9922.**

Doctor Call © **061.** Consulates keep lists of English-speaking physicians, as do most hotel concierges.

Drugstores Pharmacies stay open late in rotation—*farmàcias de guardia.* They're listed in the daily newspapers and have signs on their front doors giving the location of the nearest *farmàcia* that's open late.

Emergencies In a medical emergency, call © **061** for an ambulance. For the police, call © **092.** In the event of fire, call © **080.**

Holidays See the "Special & Free Events" sidebar later in this chapter. Other holidays are New Year's Day (Jan 1), Epiphany (Jan 6), Good Friday, Easter Monday, Labor Day (May 1), Whitsun (a local holiday, June 1), Sant Joan Day (June 24), Feast of the Assumption (Aug 15), Catalunya Day (Sept 11), Hispanitat/Columbus Day (Oct 12), Tots Sants/All Saints Day (Nov 1), Constitution Day (Dec 6), Feast of the Immaculate Conception (Dec 8), and Christmas (Dec 25–26).

Hospitals Three have emergency departments *(urgencias):* **Hospital Clínic,** Villarroel 170 (© **93/227-5400;** Metro: Hospital Clínic); **Hospital Creu Roja de Barcelona,** Dos de Maig 301 (© **93/433-1551;** Metro: Hospital de Sant Pau); and **Hospital de la Santa Creu I Sant Pau,** Sant Antoni Maria Claret 167 (© **93/291-9000;** Metro: Hospital de Sant Pau).

Internet Access It's difficult to walk more than a few blocks in central Barcelona without tripping over a cybercafe. Just off the Plaça de Catalunya, two branches of the **CyberMundo Internet Centre,** Bergara 3 and Balmes 8 (© **93/317-7142;** Metro: Plaça de Catalunya), are open from 9am Monday through Friday (10am on Sat, 11am on Sun) to 1am. With more than 80 computers, an hour at a terminal costs as little as 1.20€ ($1.40), 1.80€ ($1.60) for students. Coffee and soft drinks are served. Several branches of the global **EasyEverything** chain also dot the city; there's one at La Rambla 31 (Metro: Drassanes), open daily from 8am to 2:30am, and another at Ronda Universitat 35 (Metro: Plaça de Catalunya), open daily 8am to 2am. Rates vary, but can be as low as 1€ ($1.15) per hour. Incidentally, on most newer Spanish keyboards, the "@" is brought up by pressing the 'Alt Gr' and '2' keys together.

Language Catalan *(Català),* the indigenous language of Catalunya, is the official language of the region, and most signs appear either solely in Catalan or in both Catalan and Spanish. It is a distinct, separate language, not a dialect, and is related to *langue d'oc* and *provençal,* spoken across the Pyrenees in southern France. To the casual ear, spoken Catalan sounds like a mix of French and Spanish.

Laundry Even in moderately priced hotels, the cost of sending out laundry will be three to four times that charged by independent shops. One of the latter in the Gothic Quarter is **Lavandería C. Roca,** Roca 3 (© **93/302-2487;** Metro: Liceu), on a side street between Plaça del Pi and La Rambla.

Mail The **central post office** on Plaça Antoni López, 08002 Barcelona (© **93/318-3831**), is open Monday to Friday 8am to 9pm and Saturday 8am to 2pm. Other offices *(correos)* are generally open Monday to Friday 9am to 2pm. Most will hold mail addressed to you and labeled *Lista de Correos.* Take your passport when collecting mail. Letters and postcards to the United States cost .76€ (85¢). You can also buy stamps *(sellos* or *estampillas)* at tobacco stores *(estanco* or *estanc).* Mailboxes are yellow and identified by the word *correos* or *correu.* When mailing or receiving packages, it's best to use one of the familiar international shippers—Federal Express, DHL, or UPS. Parcel delivery through the Spanish postal service is painfully slow.

Restrooms Lavatories in train and Metro stations are unappealing and potentially unsafe, and an experiment with coin-operated electronic booths installed on streets appears to have ended. Rely on the restrooms in bars, restaurants, museums, or hotel lobbies. Ask for *los aseos* or *los servicios*.

Telephone If you're calling long distance from a hotel, expect a hefty surcharge. Most **public phone** *cabinas* provide clear instructions In English. A local call is .25€ (30¢).

To make an **international call,** dial ✆ **00,** wait for the tone, and dial the country code, the area code, and the number. Since an international call from a phone booth requires stacks of coins, it's easier to use a major credit card, accepted by most public phones.

Or purchase a **phone card** worth 12€ ($14), good for 150 minutes. Use it to make international calls from properly equipped booths, which are clearly identified. Phone cards are available at tobacco shops *(estancos)* and post offices. Or you can make calls and pay for them after completion at the currency-exchange booth at La Rambla 88, open Monday to Saturday 10am to 11pm and Sunday 10am to 1:30pm. Contact **MCI** at ✆ **900/99-0014** or **AT&T** at ✆ **900/99-0011** directly from any phone.

Tipping While tipping for certain services is customary, large amounts aren't expected. A bellhop should get about 1€ ($1.15) per bag. Taxi drivers usually get 10%. Virtually all restaurants include a service charge in the bill, so a 5% to 10% additional tip usually suffices. Ushers in cinemas and theaters and at the bullring get about .50€ (60¢).

2 Affordable Places to Stay

Barcelona hasn't been a cheap place to stay for years. At press time, the coming of the summer-long Forum 2004 led to a frenzy of high-end hotel building. Add that to the crashing dollar-euro exchange rate, and you'll find that it's increasingly harder to find a cheap room in this tremendously popular city. (Even the *hostales,* the old reliable limited-service properties, are less affordable.) Most hotels have increased their rates relatively little in euro terms over the past few years, but their prices have jumped by 30% or more in dollars. Barcelona is now almost as expensive to stay in as New York City.

Most of the desirable inexpensive digs are in the Old Town, a block or 2 to either side of La Rambla, with a few scattered throughout the Eixample. Rooms without showers or tubs usually have at least wash basins. Unless otherwise indicated, the rates below don't include breakfast or taxes (IVA in Spain).

Note: You'll find the lodging choices below plotted on the map on p. 170.

⒯ᵢₚₛ Discounts on the Web

If you're thinking of spending 70€ ($80) or more on a room, check out the websites for the major chains **Sol Melia** (www.solmelia.com) and **Husa** (www.husa.com). Both sites deeply discount their three- and four-star properties, often to 70€ ($80) or 80€ ($92) per night. *(Note:* Few Sol Melia and Husa hotels are listed below because their regular rack rates are much higher than the Web discounted rates.)

IN THE BARRI GOTIC & EL BORN

Banys Orientales 🖢🖢 Possibly Barcelona's best buy, this new budget hotel is two notches above its price mates. Rooms are spare, yet romantic, with modern four-poster beds and prints of Egyptian obelisks or Turkish harem scenes. All rooms have free, high-speed Internet access, and everything, from bathtub to bedside table, is new and sparkling clean. The hotel is 3 blocks from the Cathedral and on top of Senyor Pareyllada, a classy yet inexpensive seafood restaurant.

Argenteria 37 (east of Via Laietana), 08003 Barcelona. © 93/268-8460. Fax 93/268-8461. www.hotelbanys orientales.com. 43 units. 74€ ($85) single; 89€ ($102) double. AE, DC, MC, V. Metro: Jaume 1. *In room:* A/C, TV, minibar.

Call This renovated hostel, in what used to be the Jewish Quarter (the Call) of medieval Barcelona, combines basic functionality with a location ideal for exploring the Old City. The cathedral and La Rambla are only minutes away. Some English is spoken.

Arc de Sant Ramón del Call 4 (2 blocks west of Plaça Sant Jaume off Carrer del Call), 08002 Barcelona. © 93/302-1123. Fax 93/301-3486. 25 units. 42€ ($48) single; 60€ ($69) double. MC, V. Metro: Liceu. *In room:* TV (most units).

Cortés This long-popular hotel became more desirable after it undertook renovations that included new bathrooms. Its prices didn't jump too high for what you get, with rooms (including 16 singles) that are simply furnished but decently maintained. Next to the streetside lobby is the cafe where the included breakfast is served. Guests get a 10% discount on other meals in the restaurant. A sister hotel, the **Cataluña** (Santa Anna 24; © 93/301-9150), directly across the narrow street, has re-opened after its own extensive rehab; rates are slightly lower.

Santa Anna 25 (about a block east of the upper Rambla), 08013 Barcelona. © 93/317-9112. Fax 93/302-7870. 45 units. 70€ ($81) single; 103€ ($118) double. Rates include breakfast. AE, DC, MC, V. Metro: Plaça de Catalunya. *In room:* A/C, TV, safe.

Condal 🖢 A spiffy little lobby leads to spic-and-span little rooms in this hotel managed by the same crew as the Call (above). It isn't that the snug rooms are different in dimension or furnishings from those at competitors in its class—but everything is fresh, with firm mattresses, nick-free walls and desks, and electrically operated shutters to block out noise and light. The rooms meant for single

---

Forum 2004

At press time, the summer-long Forum 2004 (www.barcelona2004.org), a festival devoted to the themes of "cultural diversity, sustainable development, and conditions for peace," was expected to bring many thousands into the city. Scheduled were some 423 concerts by 170 different musical groups, in addition to performances, speeches, and exhibitions. Check the website for details, and expect sky-high hotel rates during the festival. If you're coming after the fact, you can enjoy the new convention center, parks, even entire new neighborhoods—Diagonal Mar and 22@, mostly populated by expensive business hotels—left behind by the Forum. We don't advise staying in the new areas after the Forum is over, though; they're far from the center of town and not particularly interesting. If you'd still like to check out the area, take the L4 Metro line to the Forum station.

> ### (*Value* Getting the Best Deal on Accommodations
>
> - Note that some lodgings offer reductions if you pay in cash rather than with a credit card.
> - Be aware that discounts are often available for stays of a week or more.
> - Don't accept the first rate quoted. Ask for a cheaper room—especially off season.
> - Ask if there's a surcharge for local or long-distance phone calls. Usually there is and it can be as high as 40%. Make calls at the nearest telephone office instead.
> - Inquire if service and taxes (IVA) are included in the quoted price or will be added to the final bill.

guests are somewhat smaller but have full-size beds (most of the others have twins). Some English is reluctantly spoken by the grumps at the front desk.

Boquería 23 (a block east of La Rambla), 08002 Barcelona. © 93/318-1882. Fax 93/318-1978. 31 units. 54€ ($67) single; 68€ ($79) double. MC, V. Metro: Liceu. *In room:* A/C, TV.

Inglés   On a busy narrow street off La Rambla, this four-story hotel offers surprisingly quiet rooms, especially those in back. The furnishings are utilitarian, the floors vinyl tile, and the bathrooms marble, with hand-held shower heads. English is spoken. This is no longer the bargain it was a few years ago but is still within budget parameters, especially for single rooms. Next to the lobby is a bar/restaurant serving several special fixed-price meals, starting at 8€ ($9.20).

Boquería 17, 08002 Barcelona. © 93/317-3770. Fax 93/302-7870. 28 units. 47€ ($53) single; 74€ ($86) double. Rates include breakfast. AE, DC, MC, V. Metro: Liceu. *In room:* TV, safe.

Jardi   The Jardi (without elevator) overlooks the enchanting plazas embracing the 14th-century Santa Maria del Pi church. Down below is a bar favored by the district's artists and students. The routinely furnished rooms vary significantly in size and layout. The lowest rates listed are for small rooms facing an inner courtyard; the higher rates are for rooms facing the street, or doubles with balconies.

Plaça Sant Josep Oriol 1 (a block from the middle of La Rambla), 08002 Barcelona. © 93/301-5900 or 93/301-5958. Fax 93/318-3664. 42 units. 65€–80€ ($75–$92) single; 75€–90€ ($86–$104) double. AE, DC, MC, V. Metro: Liceu. **Amenities:** Bar. *In room:* TV (4 units).

Nouvel   A recent renovation buffed the 1917 Nouvel to a glamorous shine; unfortunately, it's buffed up the prices as well. Past the front desk is a refurbished dining room presided over by a talented Basque chef who changes his menu seasonally. Try to get a room on the fifth floor, where the furnishings are new and the double-glazed windows provide blissful silence. The four suites have Jacuzzis.

Santa Ana 18–20 (a block from La Rambla), 08002 Barcelona. © 93/301-8274. Fax 93/301-8370. 78 units. 106€ ($121) single; 166€ ($191) double. Rates include breakfast. MC, V. Metro: Catalunya. **Amenities:** Restaurant; bar; in-room massage. *In room:* A/C, TV, fridge (some units), hair dryer, safe.

Rey Don Jaime I   East of Plaça Sant Jaume, the main plaza of the Barri Gòtic, this unassuming hotel offers three floors of renovated rooms and bathrooms.

Most rooms have writing desks; some have small balconies. Since the hotel is on a busy street, the rooms in back are quieter. There's also a TV salon.

Jaume I 11, 08002 Barcelona. ☎/fax **93/310-6208**. r.d.jaime@atriumhotels.com. 30 units. 42€ ($48) single; 65€ ($75) double. AE, DC, MC, V. Metro: Jaume I.

IN THE EIXAMPLE

Ciudad Condal   At press time, hotel renovations promised to bring up the standard, but not the prices, of this hotel. The Ciudad Condal is in a late-19th-century *modernista* building on one of Barcelona's tonier blocks. The 2004 renovation adds air-conditioning and modernist touches to the place; call to make sure you're getting a renovated room. The rooms facing the street have balconies, while the interior rooms overlook a garden rather than the usual airshaft. The hostel is three flights up (no elevator).

Mallorca 255 (between Passeig de Gràcia and Rambla de Catalunya), 08008 Barcelona. ☎ **93/215-1040**. 11 units. 69€ ($79) single; 100€ ($115) double. AE, DC, DISC, MC, V. Metro: Passeig de Gràcia or Diagonal. **Amenities:** Limited room service. *In room:* A/C, TV, safe.

Granvía ✿   A leaded-glass portico leads into as grandly proportioned a lobby and staircase as you'll find this side of the Ritz, down the street. This impression is reinforced by the amusingly overblown first-floor salon, surely once the ballroom of a grandee, now home to a big-screen TV. Doors from the salon open onto a large terrace. Elsewhere, you'll find lots of wood and marble in the halls and rooms, most of the latter large enough for desks and sitting areas. The beds are mostly of swaybacked vintage, but some newer ones are sprinkled throughout. English is spoken.

Gran Vía de les Corts Catalanes 642 (east of Passeig de Gràcia), 08007 Barcelona. ☎ **93/318-1900** or 93/302-5046. Fax 93/318-9997. www.nnhotels.es. 53 units. 70€ ($81) single; 110€ ($127) double. AE, DC, MC, V. Metro: Passeig de Gràcia. *In room:* A/C, TV, minibar.

Neutral   An economy choice in a luxury area, the spic-and-span Neutral has an entrance one flight up, on the mezzanine. Antique floor tiles and a fresh paint job help brighten the small but high-ceilinged rooms, which are furnished with odds and ends, the better ones with easy chairs. Most have balconies. The breakfast room boasts an impressive coffered ceiling. English is spoken.

Rambla de Catalunya 42 (at the corner of Carrer de Consell de Cent), 08007 Barcelona. ☎ **93/487-6390** or 93/487-6848. 28 units, 10 with shower only, 18 with bathroom. 28€ ($32) single with shower, 42€ ($48) single with bathroom; 45€ ($52) double with shower, 48€ ($55) double with bathroom. MC, V. Metro: Passeig de Gràcia. *In room:* TV, safe.

Oliva ✿   Rates at this pension have risen slowly, but it's still a relative bargain in increasingly pricey Barcelona. Above a tony clothing store, it has a fine vintage elevator that ascends in stately manner to the fourth floor's high-ceilinged rooms with tile floors, lace curtains, and sinks. Several offer views of the Passeig de Gràcia but are nevertheless quiet. A few are cramped, though, so ask to see the room first.

Passeig de Gràcia 32 (at the corner of Carrer Diputació), 08007 Barcelona. ☎ **93/488-0162**. www. lasguias.com/hostaloliva. 16 units, 9 with bathroom. 26€ ($30) single without bathroom; 48€ ($55) double without bathroom, 55€ ($63) double with bathroom. No credit cards. Metro: Passeig de Gràcia. **Amenities:** Laundry service. *In room:* TV, no phone.

Universal   Once you're buzzed into the well-lit entry, an elevator carries you up to the narrow first-floor lobby. Beer and soft drinks are served in the adjacent sitting room. The rooms are spare and clean, usually with built-in desks and twin beds. This is a good bet for those who want to be near the center of the pricey Eixample. It's a step up from the Neutral (p. 158), which is under the same ownership. Some staff speaks English.

Aragó 281 (near Carrer de Pau Claris), 08009 Barcelona. ℂ 93/487-9762. Fax 93/487-4028. 18 units. 47€ ($54) single; 62€ ($71) double. MC, V. Metro; Passeig de Gràcia. In room: TV, safe.

Urquinaona   Tucked into a narrow building off the plaza of the same name, this little hostel-turned-hotel was recently renovated, but seems to have backslid a bit in the past year or 2. Rooms are as equipped as those of a three-star property, but on our last visit the furniture looked cheap, the walls were dirty, and the rooms were beginning to look a bit tired. Outside the heaviest tourist trails, it's nonetheless handy to La Ribera and the Eixample districts. Breakfast can be served in your room. English is spoken.

Ronda de Sant Pere 24, 08010 Barcelona. ℂ 93/268-1336. Fax 93/295-4137. www.barcelonahotel.com/ urquinaona. 16 units. 70€ ($81) single; 90€ ($103) double. MC, V. Metro: Urquinaona. **Amenities:** Laundry service. In room: A/C, TV, minibar, hair dryer, safe.

Windsor   As befits this upscale neighborhood, this hostel's lobby, halls, and TV room are elegantly outfitted, and they just got out the paintbrush again. The carpeted rooms, though small, are quiet; some have balconies. The four without bathrooms share the facilities with just one other room, but that's grounds for bargaining. The hostel is two long flights up, but there's an elevator. The owner speaks English.

Rambla de Catalunya 84, 08008 Barcelona. ℂ 93/215-1198. 15 units, 11 with bathroom. 38€ ($44) single without bathroom, 45€ ($52) single with bathroom; 55€ ($63) double without bathroom, 64€ ($74) double with bathroom. No credit cards. Metro: Passeig de Gràcia or Provença. In room: No phone.

IN GRACIA

Hotel Silver 🎇   Your sense of adventure is rewarded here: Two subway stops from the Eixample, in an attractive neighborhood of hip bars and pubs, this charming, affordable, family-run hotel offers 49 pleasant rooms with kitchenettes in each one. The rooms vary widely, from cozy little nooks with older furnishings to shiny renovated units with blond wood furnishings, convection ovens, and spacious terraces. The back garden is a perfect place to sip your morning coffee. The staff bends over backwards to help and reservations manager Dafne Benedito speaks perfect English, so ask her and she'll tell you all about the rooms.

Bretón de los Herreros 26, 08012 Barcelona. ℂ 93/218-9100. Fax 93/416-1447. www.hotelsilver.com. 49 units. 69€–98€ ($79–$113) single; 72€–120€ ($83–$138) double. Breakfast 6.50€ ($7.50). AE, DC, MC, V. Parking 11€ ($12). Metro: Fontana. **Amenities:** Bar; limited room service; laundry service; free Internet access in lobby. In room: A/C, TV, kitchen, safe.

ON LA RAMBLA

Internacional   This member of the all-embracing HUSA chain is across from the Liceu opera house. The functional rooms are of good size, with ample bathrooms; a dozen of them have tiny balconies. Some sleep three or four, providing a substantial savings over renting two separate rooms. The bright breakfast room overlooks La Rambla, where the hotel also runs an alfresco balcony cafe in summer. There's no elevator, and you could probably get a discounted rate at a three-star hotel for these prices, but you're paying for location here.

La Rambla 78–80, 08002 Barcelona. ℂ 93/302-2566. Fax 93/317-6190. www.husa.es. 60 units. 68€ ($78) single; 86€ ($99) double. AE, DC, MC, V. Metro: Liceu. **Amenities:** Bar. In room: Safe.

Mare Nostrum _Value_   In 1992, this old building was stripped down and spruced up with comforts not often found at this price level (though there's no elevator). The attractive breakfast salon's wide window displays the pageant of La Rambla, looking down on the sidewalk mural by Joan Miró. Many rooms have balconies, and five have double beds. Apart from a slightly haphazard quality to the architecture and the administration, the Mare Nostrum represents good value. Discounts are usually given to guests who say they read about the hotel in Frommer's (depending on who's working at the reception desk, one flight up).

Sant Pau 2 (directly on La Rambla), 08001 Barcelona. Ⓒ✆ 93/318-5340. Fax 93/412-3069. 30 units, 21 with bathroom. 52€ ($60) single without bathroom, 63€ ($72) single with bathroom; 56€ ($64) double without bathroom, 67€ ($77) double with bathroom. Rates include breakfast in high season only. AE, DC, MC, V. Metro: Liceu. *In room:* A/C, TV.

IN EL RAVAL

España Seeing the inside of a *modernista* building (most of which are in private hands) is rare, so it's almost an honor to enjoy a meal in one of the dining rooms here. This 1904 hotel was designed by Domènech i Montaner, a contemporary of Antoni Gaudí. A mural in one dining room was painted by Ramón Casas, one of the most prominent artists of his time; the fantastical limestone fireplace in another was carved by Eusebi Arnau, who did the proscenium sculptures in Domènech's Palau de la Música. It's difficult to maintain a landmark, though, and the facilities are worn, largely due to the parade of student groups. The rooms are of widely varying sizes, with ceiling fans and clean tile bathrooms.

Sant Pau 9–11 (a block west of La Rambla), 08026 Barcelona. Ⓒ✆ 93/318-1758. Fax 93/317-1134. 90 units. 50€ ($58) single; 98€ ($113) double. AE, MC, V. Metro: Liceu. **Amenities:** Restaurant. *In room:* Safe.

Gaudí Across the narrow street is the 1888 Palau Güell, designed by Antoni Gaudí. Get a top-floor room at this hotel for a good look at the legendary architect's forest of individually shaped and decorated chimneys. The Gaudí boasts a number of *modernista* decorative elements, too, including a colorful free-form fountain in the lobby. The rooms are unfailingly clean, albeit sometimes absent reading chairs. The place is only a few steps west of the lower end of La Rambla, but you probably won't want to go too far in the opposite direction into the seedy heart of the Barri Xinés.

Nou de la Rambla 12, 08001 Barcelona. Ⓒ✆ 93/317-9032. Fax 93/412-2636. www.hotelgaudi.es. 73 units. 90€–115€ ($104–$132) single; 120€–150€ ($138–$173) double. AE, DC, DISC, MC, V. Metro: Drassanes. **Amenities:** Cafeteria; bar; exercise room; concierge; limited room service; in-room massage; same-day laundry/dry cleaning. *In room:* A/C, TV, hair dryer, safe.

San Agustí Ⓐ *Kids* The San Agustí is no longer the remarkable value it once was, but at least breakfast is still included. On a square shaded by plane trees and recently repaved and cleaned (comparatively), it was converted from a convent to a hotel in 1840, making it one of the city's oldest. The attractive lobby makes effective use of ancient stone-and-brick arches and windows overlooking the plaza. While most rooms are ordinary, some ceilings soar and hand-hewn wood beams in other sections are head-knockers. Particularly good for families are the two-room suites with two bathrooms. The new attic rooms (nos. 401–408) are desirable, and the restaurant offers three-course fixed-price lunches and dinners. The manager and some staffers speak English.

Plaça Sant Agustín 3 (a block west of La Rambla, off Carrer Hospital), 08001 Barcelona. Ⓒ✆ 93/318-1658. Fax 93/317-2928. www.hotelsa.com. 77 units. 95€–105€ ($109–$121) single; 126€–142€ ($145–$163) double; 140€–158€ ($161–$182) attic room. Rates include breakfast. AE, MC, V. Metro: Liceu. **Amenities:** Restaurant; bar; concierge; laundry/dry-cleaning service. *In room:* A/C, TV, hair dryer (some units), safe.

WORTH A SPLURGE

The steep prices listed below are about average in this high three- and low four-star category, but remember that they're rack rates and you should be able to get a discount of 20% or more unless there are three conventions in town.

Albinoni *★★*   Until recently, this was called the Allegro, and some confusion still persists. (Tell your cab driver its former name, too.) It's worth the trouble of finding it. First, there is the building, a stately 1886 neoclassical mansion. Imagine the horse-drawn carriages wheeling into what is now the lobby, depositing their guests at the grand staircase, and continuing on to the stables beyond. (There's a tented breakfast room back there now.) Rooms are of decent dimension, with 18 facing the courtyard and another 18 in front, over the street. These all have balconies and are the ones to request. Unusual for a city-center hotel, they rent bicycles.

Av. Portal de l'Angel 17 (south of Plaça de Catalunya), 08002 Barcelona. ⓒ **93/318-4141**. Fax 93/301-2631. www.hoteles-catalonia.es. 74 units. 118€ ($136) single; 167€ ($192) double. AE, DC, MC, V. Metro: Catalunya. **Amenities:** Bar; bike rental; limited room service; same-day laundry/dry cleaning. *In room:* A/C, TV w/pay movies, minibar, hair dryer, safe.

Lleó *★*   Although the rooms don't quite deliver on the promise of the gleaming lobby, they contain comforts and conveniences not seen in many hotels costing only a few euros less. Not least among these are firm mattresses, balconies (with 32 rooms), and a substantial buffet breakfast. The 19th-century building was renovated for the Olympics and has held up pretty well. It's handy to the Plaça de Catalunya and La Rambla.

Pelai 22 (about midway between the University and Plaça de Catalunya), 08001 Barcelona. ⓒ **93/318-1312**. Fax 93/412-2657. www.hotel-lleo.es. 89 units. 116€ ($133) single; 144€ ($166) double. AE, DC, MC, V. Metro: Universitat. **Amenities:** Restaurant; bar; concierge; limited room service; same-day dry cleaning/laundry. *In room:* A/C, TV, minibar, hair dryer, safe.

Gallery Hotel *★★*   Perched at the start of the Passeig de Grácia, this super-stylish, ultramodern hotel is a perfect base for attacking the shops of both the Eixample and Grácia. The spare but spacious rooms have an almost Asian feel to them, with furnishings in red and black, firm beds, and big bathtubs. Service is impeccable.

Roselló 249, 08008 Barcelona. ⓒ **93/415-9911**. Fax 93/415-9184. www.galleryhotel.com. 110 units. 93€–187€ ($107–$215) single; 118€–254€ ($136–$292) double. AE, DC, MC, V. Metro: Diagonal. **Amenities:** Restaurant; bar; exercise room; sauna; concierge; business center; room service; same-day laundry/dry cleaning. *In room:* A/C, TV, minibar, hair dryer, safe.

3 Great Deals on Dining

Eating well in Barcelona is easy. Eating inexpensively is only a bit more challenging. The city's restaurants offer a wealth of dishes, primarily Mediterranean in their ingredients—olive oil, almonds, garlic, aromatic herbs, and tomatoes. Sausages (like the traditional *butifarra*), robust game, delicate seafood, savory rice dishes and stews, and myriad treatments of mushrooms are mainstays of the Catalan repertoire, often in such unusual combinations as fruit with poultry or shellfish with game. Look for **fideos** (*fideus* in Catalan), a form of paella made with fine noodles instead of rice. The highest concentration of low-priced eateries is in the Ciutat Vella.

A heightened local enthusiasm for **tapas** (*tapes* in Catalan), the bar snacks for which other parts of Spain have long been noted, has resulted in the opening of

> **Value Getting the Best Deal on Dining**
>
> • Take advantage of the three-course *menú del día* offered at lunch in most restaurants and at dinner in some.
> • Note that appetizer *(entrant)* portions are nearly as large as main courses but usually less expensive, so you might want to settle for two of them instead of the usual combination.
> • Order the *plat combinat* offered at many taverns and restaurants— it's a one-dish meal consisting usually of meat, fish, or chicken with fried potatoes and a salad or vegetable. Bread and a beverage are often included, at a price that rarely exceeds 8€ ($9.20) and that can be much less.
> • Try eating or drinking standing up inside. Many places have three prices for the same items, cheapest at the *barra* (bar), more at an inside *taula* (table), and most expensive at outside tables.
> • Enjoy a meal in a tapas bar. Two or three tapas (in Catalan, *tapes*) or larger *ración (racció)* portions can constitute a great inexpensive meal.

big gleaming places whose long bars are laden with food platters. Dished up in small *tape* servings or in larger **ración** (*racció* in Catalan) portions, two or three can constitute a meal. Just be sure to check the prices, for many kinds of shellfish and the delicacy *angulas* (baby eels boiled in oil) can do severe damage to a food budget.

Also often found in tapas bars are meal-size treats called **tostadas** (*torrades* in Catalan). Similar to Italian *crostini,* they're slabs of toasted or grilled bread rubbed with garlic and tomato pulp, drizzled with olive oil, then topped with any of dozens of diverse ingredients, including *xorico* (chorizo) sausage, beef tartare, mushrooms, slices of pork loin, cheese, anchovies, and sardines. One or two can make a lunch. Smaller versions of *torrades* are **montaditos.**

Spaniards drink red or white wine as they wish, without regard for the parroted fish-or-meat shibboleths, and some even unabashedly choose Coke as their beverage throughout meals. Brewed decaf coffee is now widely available in bars and restaurants. Ask *"¿Descafinado en máquina?"*

If you arrive at the restaurants recommended below before 2pm for lunch or 10pm for dinner, you'll almost certainly be seated quickly without a reservation. After those times, lines form at the more popular places. A tax (IVA) of 7% is added to every bill. And not even the busiest high-turnover restaurant will drop a check on your table before you request it.

IN THE BARRI GOTIC & EL BORN

El Gran Café SPANISH   The tobacco-brown ceiling is high enough to accommodate 5m (15-ft.) windows and a dining balcony over the service bar. The building is 19th century, and the restaurant has been given a Belle Epoque appearance. A piano player adds to the mood in the evening, when the crowd has a polished look. Fish and game dominate the menu, but specific ingredients are changed frequently, a sign the chef follows the market. The fast-moving staff wastes not a step bringing his creations to the table.

Avinyo 9 (a block south of Carrer Ferrán). ℂ **93/318-7986.** Main courses 5.75€–19€ ($7–$22); *menú del día* 11€ ($13). AE, DC, MC, V. Daily 1–3pm and 8pm–12:30am. Metro: Liceu or Jaume I.

La Dolça Hermína ✹ MEDITERRANEAN   This stylish space doesn't *look* as if it qualifies as a budget choice, and the fashionable people lined up for tables might not seem likely to be patrons. But it's easy to walk away from lunch here with your wallet only $10 lighter. La Dolça Hermína offers simply sauced, handsome interpretations of Catalan classics like cannelloni and sausage with white beans; the food isn't too rich, and lights up with little bursts of flavors like the cherry tomatoes in the ham-and-green-bean salad. The menu lists several vegetarian dishes too. Given the high volume, the service is swift and understandably impersonal.

Magdalenes 27 (near the intersection of Vía Laietana and Carrer Comtal). ℭ 93/317-0676. Main courses 4.45€–9.90€ ($5.10–$11). AE, DC, MC, V. Daily 1–3:45pm and 8:30–11:30pm. Metro: Urquinaona.

La Fonda ✹ MEDITERRANEAN   Knowledgeable locals leave the nearby ancient Los Caracoles *taberna* to the tourists and line up at this spiffy two tiered place framed behind high arched windows. (There's another floor downstairs.) Casually stylish and mostly under 35, especially in the evening, the locals come to check one another out and enjoy seafood paella, other rice dishes, and meat-and-fruit combos. Several vegetarian dishes are offered. Prices here have recently shot up sharply, moving it from a bargain find into the realm of mid-priced respectable restaurants, but the reliable quality of the food means it's a place still worth coming back to. Arrive early, as it fills up quickly.

Escudellers 10 (east of La Rambla). ℭ 93/301-7515. Main courses 8€–15€ ($9–$17); *menú del día* 14€ ($16). AE, MC, V. Daily 1–5:30pm and 8:30–11:30pm. Metro: Liceu.

La Pineda SPANISH   The windows of this *xarcutería* (charcuterie) are draped with loops of sausages and whole hams, and its interior is enclosed by dark beams, cracked tiles, and shelves and cabinets lined with bottles. This kind of atmosphere isn't planned; it just happens. Take a small marble-topped table at the back. A usual order (there's no menu) is *jamón, queso, pan,* and *tinto*—air-cured ham, Manchego cheese, bread, and a tumbler of red wine. Don't put too much faith in the listed hours, which are flexible.

Pi 16 (near Plaça del Pi). ℭ 93/302-4393. Meals under 11€ ($13). MC, V. Mon–Sat 9am–8pm. Metro: Liceu.

Les Quinze Nits ✹ MEDITERRANEAN   As Barcelona restaurant prices have increased over the past few years, Les Quinze Nits has kept theirs down, making meals here much better buys than in the past. The large front room overlooks the enclosed plaza, with tables out under the loggia most of the year. A smaller, quieter room in back suits couples who don't need to be seen. The earnest, if not always precise, young staff swiftly brings on fare like spinach-filled cannelloni under a blanket of melted cheese, and traditional Catalan *butifarra* sausage with white beans. Vegetarian dishes include a plate of grilled vegetables and a mushroom salad with cheese and grilled asparagus.

Plaça Reial 6 (east of La Rambla). ℭ 93/317-3075. Main courses 4.45€–9.95€ ($5.10–$11); *menú del día* 7€ ($8). AE, MC, V. Daily 1–3:30pm and 8:30–11:30pm. Metro: Liceu.

Pitarra ✹ SPANISH   Pitarra occupies the former home/watch shop of the prolific and much honored Catalan playwright/poet Federic Soler Hubert (pseudonym Pitarra). The atmosphere is friendly, the service swift, and the food hearty. Look for game dishes in winter, like partridges in vinaigrette and jugged wild boar in a sauce perfumed by bitter chocolate. The *menú* price includes a beverage and taxes. While Pitarra offers excellent value, its location deep in the Barri Gòtic means you might prefer to come for lunch rather than dinner.

Avinyó 56 (south of Carrer Ferrán). ℭ 93/301-1647. Main courses 7€–22€ ($8.05–$25); *menú del día* (lunch only) 9€ ($10). MC, V. Mon–Sat 1–4pm and 8:30–11pm. Closed Aug. Metro: Liceu or Jaume I.

Senyor Parellada ✪ SPANISH   Masonry arches in the dining room give this seafood-focused bistro next door to the Banys Orientals hotel a Middle Eastern feel, but the menu is Spanish through and through. Expect a wide range of seafood, such as baked monkfish with mustard and garlic sauce; and the occasional meat dish, such as roasted rack of lamb or stuffed cannelloni. The menu labels each dish with the region of Spain where it's most popular, and the chefs turn out admirably precise flavors.

Argenteria 37 (east of Via Leitana). ✆ **93/310-5094.** Main courses 4.45€–14€ ($5–$16). AE, MC, V. Mon–Sat 1–4pm and 8:30pm–midnight. Reservations recommended. Metro: Jaume I.

Taxidermista ✪ CATALAN/INTERNATIONAL   If you're stuck waiting in line at nearby Les Quinze Nits (p. 163), you might want to give this place a try for similar quality food at only slightly higher prices. Though it's named for the business of a previous tenant, you'll be the one stuffed. The creative kitchen provides worthy antidotes to usually vegetable-free Spanish meals. Ringing the couscous and lamb at the center of its plate, for example, are discreet portions of chickpeas, zucchini, carrots, and potatoes, served with a small pitcher of broth and a spoonful of hot sauce on the side. A tasty little *aperitivo* (say, a pig's foot stuffed with duck confit) arrives with your drink order. The setting is an effective blend of 19th-century space and hand-hewn beams with post-industrial lighting.

Plaça Reial 8. ✆ **93/412-4536.** Main courses 8.30€–17€ ($9.55–$19). DC, MC, V. Dining room Tues–Sun 1:30–4pm and 8:30pm–12:30am; tapas bar Tues–Sun noon–1am. Metro: Liceu.

IN THE EIXAMPLE

Citrus ✪ CATALAN   Inexpensive yet elegant, with a mixed crowd of locals and tourists, Citrus is a gentle introduction to Catalan cuisine. The second-floor dining room (located above Tapa Tapa) has wraparound windows looking out on the Passeig de Gràcia. Citrus offers a pre-appetizer for around 1€ ($1.15)—take it, even if you haven't a clue what it might be (say, a mound of cod tartare sprinkled with lumpfish caviar). Subsequent saucings are light, often only the juices of the central ingredients, and portions are about half the humongous Spanish norm. One possibility is the *mar y montaña,* a skewer of four baby shrimp joined with rabbit parts garnished with mushrooms and rosemary; another is *fideos con sepia,* tangy black noodles with chunks of cuttlefish. Daily specials are in the 5€ to 9€ ($5.75–$10) range, so it's easy enough to walk out of here spending under $20 per person including wine. The service is proper, although the staff rushes endlessly about. Citrus is run by the AN Group, which also owns several other excellent Barcelona restaurants, each one different.

Passeig de Gràcia 44. ✆ **93/487-2345.** Main courses 4.90€–13€ ($5.65–$14). AE, DC, DISC, MC, V. Mon–Sat 1–4:30pm and 7:30pm–12:30am; Sun 1–4:30pm. Metro: Passeig de Gràcia.

L'Hostal de Rita ✪ MEDITERRANEAN   Be standing at the door at 1pm or 8:30pm, or be prepared to wait. The prices here are unbeatable, the regional specialties impeccable, and the setting immaculate; expect hungry hordes at this cheerful little joint. Diners range from college kids to their prosperous elders who routinely pay a lot more for pretentious food of no greater quality. The *menú* always offers three choices of appetizer, main course, and dessert, and comes with a carafe of house wine. To keep things moving, the preparations are quite simple. Typical is the quickly grilled fish drizzled with a parsley-flecked olive oil.

Aragó 279 (at Pau Claris). ✆ **93/487-2376.** Main courses 2.35€–8€ ($2.70–$9.20); *menú del día* 7€ ($8.05). AE, DC, MC, V. Daily 1–3:45pm and 8:30–11:30pm. Metro: Passeig de Gràcia.

Madrid-Barcelona CATALAN   Despite the name, a reference to the train from Madrid that once ran along this street, this place is Catalan through and through—from the menu language and the waitperson's rushed recitation of the daily specials to the food itself. You'll find *arròs negre*, paella made with squid ink; *entrecot al roquefort*, steak with cheese; and *paperina de verdures*, thinly sliced zucchini, onions, and other vegetables lightly fried and served in a paper cone. The garlic mayo, pungent *ali-oli*, is perfect with the grilled seafood and rice dishes. The triangular menu makes no distinction among appetizers, soups, and main courses, so you might want to order a salad since few mains come with vegetables. They push the *pa amb tomàquet*—slabs of bread rubbed with tomato pulp and garlic—but there are better versions elsewhere.

Aragó 282 (east of Passeig de Gràcia). ⓒ 93/215-7026. Main courses 4.30€–14€ ($4.95–$16). AE, DC, MC, V. Mon–Sat 1–4pm and 8:30–11:30pm. Metro: Passeig de Gràcia.

Qu Qu (Quasi Queviures) SPANISH   Yet another AN Group joint, this one is a laid-back tapas bar. On the left is a takeout counter for meats, salads, and pastas, and on the right a bar for the consumption of the delectable *tapes;* in back is a sit-down section for light meals. Funky jazz and alternative rock on the stereo proclaim this isn't your grandpa's tapas bar.

Passeig de Gràcia 24. ⓒ 93/317-4512. Meals under 12€ ($11); *plats combinats* 4.40€–6.65€ ($3.95–$5.95). AE, DC, DISC, MC, V. Daily 8:30am–1am. Metro: Passeig de Gràcia.

Tapa Tapa SPANISH   Slick and contemporary, this wildly popular tapas emporium was the vanguard of the AN Group conquest of the Eixample. With its sidewalk tables under big umbrellas, twin long bars open to the street, and large elevated dining room, it's perfect for drop-in meals and snacks, although there might be a wait at peak hours. It offers over 50 tapas, with an additional four or five daily specials, usually under 3€ ($3.45) apiece. The paper place mats picture and describe most of the menu, making ordering easy. Do specify the *tapa* size of each dish, or they'll automatically give you the larger and more expensive *racciós* (rations).

Passeig de Gràcia 44. ⓒ 93/488-3369. Tapas 1.75€–4.95€ ($2–$5.70); *racciós* 3.55€–7.80€ ($4.10–$8.95). AE, DC, DISC, MC, V. Mon–Thurs 7:30am–1:30am; Fri–Sat 7:30am–2am; Sun 8am–1am. Metro: Passeig de Gràcia.

WEST OF LA RAMBLA

El Turia SPANISH   This is a family affair: Dad tends the zinc-topped bar, Mom works the stove, and the daughter runs the dining room. It's frequented by actors and writers, many of whom are gay and live and work nearby. They come for the simple food, such as the daily *plats combinats,* so even with an appetizer and wine, lunch needn't be more than 13€ ($15). Find El Turia down the lightly used pedestrian lane just below La Boquería. The restaurant now opens and closes early, so this is a place for breakfast and lunch, perhaps after a tour of the market next door.

Petxina 7 (off La Rambla). ⓒ 93/317-9509. Main courses 9€–17€ ($10–$20); *menú del día* 11€ ($13). MC, V. Mon–Fri 8am–8pm; Sat–Sun 8am–6pm. Closed Aug. Metro: Liceu.

Pollo Rico 🎇 SPANISH   Every budgeter seeks out this place sooner or later, yet local workers still chow down at the long front counter for lunch. The ground-floor windows are covered with gaudy colors and cartoons, nearly masking the golden birds turning slowly on their spits. This "rich chicken" refers to the taste, not the cost, and how they keep the prices this low remains a mystery. A half bird comes with various trimmings, but a typical deal includes fries, bread, and a glass of wine for 6.30€ ($7.25). A mild splurge can be paella for two—only 17€ ($20). The service and surroundings are strictly rough-and-ready, with wooden booths in the tile-dadoed upstairs room.

Sant Pau 31 (2 blocks west of La Rambla). (☎ 93/441-3184. Main courses 2.90€–12€ ($3.35–$13); *menú del día* 6.30€ ($7). No credit cards. Thurs–Tues 1pm–midnight. Metro: Liceu.

NEAR THE MUSEU PICASSO

Cal Pep SPANISH   This fine little tapas bar just south of the Picasso Museum is popular with both locals and tourists. There are 20 seats at the long marble bar and a tiny sit-down back room. While you'll probably get a seat if you arrive at 1:30pm during the week, expect a wait after 2pm and on weekends. (If it *is* full, there are two other cafes on the same square.) There's no menu—the manager will tell you what's available and use his lapel mike to relay your order to the kitchen when it gets busy. It isn't that what comes forth strays far from the traditional repertoire, only that it's so much better prepared. This is the way *pescados fritos* (fried fish), *almejas con jamón* (steamed clams with ham), and *pan con tomate* (Catalan tomato bread) rarely taste in less skilled hands. The bunch behind the bar joke and laugh with patrons and each other all the while.

Plaça de les Olles 8. (☎ 93-310-7961. Reservations required for dining room. Main courses and tapas 3.60€–13€ ($4.15–$14); *menú del día* 15€ ($17). AE, DC, MC, V. Tues–Sat 1:15–4pm and 8–11:30pm; Mon 8–11:30pm. Closed Aug. Metro: Jaume I.

El Xampanyet SPANISH   As long as anyone can remember, a sign stating HAY SIDRA FRESCA ("We have fresh cider") has hung on the door frame of this 1929 *bodega*. They do have fresh cider, of the alcoholic Asturian variety, but the primary tipple is a sweetish wine with a *cava*-like spritz called Ca l'Esteve. A relentlessly cheerful family greets every new patron as a great friend, and while the tapas are mostly limited to anchovies, tortillas, and a selection of canned fish, people stay on just to bask in the friendly glow. Antique tile dadoes, large dark casks, and bottles black with decades of tobacco smoke provide the setting.

Montcada 22. (☎ 93/319-7003. Tapas 1.10€–2.90€ ($1.30–$3.35). No credit cards. Tues–Sun noon–4pm and 6:30pm–midnight. Metro: Jaume I.

Euskal Etxea BASQUE/SPANISH   A short walk down Carrer Montçada from the Picasso Museum, this is billed as a Basque "Cultural Center," but people pile through the door for the trays of *pintxos* set out on the bar at opening time. These are mostly slices of bread piled with a variety of toppings. The drill is to take a plate and grab as many tapas as you want. Individually, they cost 1.20€ ($1.65). This is on the honor system, so you report your consumption after the fact. Go early: When the initial supply at each session is gobbled up, they don't make any more. There are tables in back for sit-down meals, including a three-course *menú* with bread, dessert, and a half-liter of wine. All this has proven so popular, they've opened an annex, **Nou Euskal Etxea Berri,** next door at no. 5 ((☎ 93/315-1447), a fancier place with a sit-down bar, a few tables, and a complete menu where entrees cost around 12€ to 20€ ($14–$23).

Placeta Montcada 1–3. (☎ 93/310-2185. No credit cards. Tues–Sat 12:30–4pm and 7:30pm–midnight; Sun 7:30pm–midnight. Metro: Jaume I.

La Pizza Nostra *(Kids)* ITALIAN   Within the walls of a medieval mansion on the same block as the Picasso Museum, throngs of mostly young locals (few tourists) enjoy some of the best pizza in town. These pizzas are of the knife-and-fork variety, partly because that's the way Spaniards eat almost everything but more because the pizzas are heaped with all manner of toppings. Some are conventional (sausage or shrimp) but others quite surprising (spinach with béchamel sauce, squid, or bits of cod)—27 versions in all. A plate of pasta or an 8-inch pizza should satisfy most appetites, especially when accompanied by *sangría* or a respectable René Barbier wine. Salads are also available. The service is rushed but pleasant enough.

Mont|,.ula 29. ℂ **93/319-9058.** Pizzas, pastas, and main courses 6€–10€ ($6.90–$12); *menú del día* 8€ ($9.20). AE, DC, MC, V. Tues–Sun 1:30–4pm and 8:45–11:30pm (to midnight Fri–Sat). Metro: Jaume I.

Little Italy MEDITERRANEAN   New street lamps have made this a more approachable after-dark destination in the resurgent Born area. Once trendy, it has settled into middle age in restaurant years, making it more comfortable for people who aren't necessarily pale, thin, and artistic. The waitstaff is still dressed in black and the crowd mostly on the giddy side of 35. Pastas are the best deal, so a good way to keep the tab within reason is to have one of them preceded by soup or salad. The two levels are framed by stone walls and 19th-century iron beams and pillars. Sinatra is a near-constant presence on the stereo, abetted by live jazz Wednesday and Thursday nights.

Rec 30 (near Passeig Born). ℂ **93/319-7973.** Main courses 10€–16€ ($12–$19); *menú del día* 11€ ($13). AE, V. Daily 1.30–4pm and 9pm–midnight; Sat until 2am. Metro: Jaume I.

THE CHAINS

A native Catalan chain of sandwich shops with roughly the same ambience and prices as McDonald's, **Pans & Company** has branches throughout the city, three on La Rambla alone, including a two-floor location at no. 84 and another at Passeig de Gràcia 39. Most are open Monday to Saturday 9am to midnight and Sunday 10am to midnight. **Bocatta** claims, in four languages, to make the "Best Sandwiches in Town." Among its branches are one on Plaça Sant Jaume, another at Rambla de Catalunya 80, and a two-story version at La Rambla 85. An outpost of a Dutch chain, **Maoz,** at Carrer de Ferran 13, dishes up far fresher falafel than other joints on or near the Rambla. **Pastafiore** specializes in pizzas and pastas, evident at its main branch at La Rambla 125.

PICNICKING

Found in almost every neighborhood, *xarcuterias* (*charcuterías* in Spanish) specialize in sausages, meats, and cheeses and usually have bottles of wine and stocks of canned goods that can compose a memorable picnic. One of the most appetizing is **La Pineda,** near Plaça del Pi (p. 163). A more complete selection is found in the *supermercado* that occupies much of the cellar of the giant **El Cortes Inglés** department store on Plaça de Catalunya. Everything from bread to cold cuts to wine and a deli is on offer. Or stock up on everything at the incomparable **La Boquería** market on La Rambla.

Wherever you load up on supplies, head for the **Parc de la Ciutadella,** the **Barceloneta** beach, or the park at the Montjuïc end of the **Transbordador del Puerto** to enjoy your picnic.

WORTH A SPLURGE

Agut ✰✰ SPANISH   If it weren't for Agut's location in a dark corner of the Gothic Quarter, you might not be able to get in at all. As it is, be there when the doors open to have even a chance for a table without a reservation. The chefs give all their attention to the delicate balancing of ingredients, allowing every flavor to take its bow. That shows up even in salads, such as young basil and arugula leaves with toasted pine nuts and croutons on a bed of diced tomatoes, draped with slivers of smoked fish. The beef is superb—look for *filetitos de buey con salsa trufa* and *trompetas de la muerte* (beef filets with truffle sauce and black mushrooms). Open since 1924, the restaurant occupies several rooms on two floors with wooden wainscoting, marble floors, and early-1900s paintings. The ingratiating waitstaff inquires often about your satisfaction. Don't confuse this Agut with the far more expensive Agut d'Avignon on Calle Trinitat.

Gignàs 16 (a block south of the main post office). © **93/315-1709.** Reservations strongly advised. Main courses 17€–19€ ($20–$22). DC, MC, V. Tues–Sat 1:30–4pm and 9pm–midnight; Sun 1:30–4pm. Metro: Barceloneta.

Botafumeiro *&&* SEAFOOD   Widely regarded as Barcelona's best seafood restaurant, this is where the king of Spain comes for his fish. The menu is stacked with dozens of preparations of fish, mussels, clams, lobster, scallops, and other sea life. Whether grilled, fried, or served in *paella,* they're always fresh and often heartbreakingly simple, showcasing the beauty of Galician seafood. The Mariscos Botafumeiro specialty is a grand parade of everything fresh available that day. A few meat dishes lurk at the edges of the menu, but that's not why you're here. White-jacketed waiters, always snapping to attention, make you feel like royalty. If the prices here are too high, Neira owns several other restaurants in town, including **Moncho's Barcelona,** Traverssera de Grácia 44–46 (© 93/ 414-6622; www.monchos.com), where grilled seafood is the specialty.

Gran de Grácia 81. © **93/218-4230.** Reservations recommended. Main courses 21€–60€ ($24–$69). AE, DC, MC, V. Daily 1pm–1am. Metro: Fontana.

7 Portes *&&* CATALAN/SPANISH   Said to be Barcelona's oldest restaurant, with over 160 years behind it, this is still one of the most popular. These "seven doors" open onto as many rooms, with smaller salons on the second floor. Cloth-covered hanging lamps provide a peachy glow for the businesspeople, trendies, families, and tourists, all served by an efficient staff. House specialties are rice dishes, including paella, and Catalan combinations of fruit with seafood or meats. Careful selection (avoiding costly shellfish and crustaceans) can keep your meal near budget level. Traditional specialties such as Catalan sausage, for instance, can be as little as 9€ ($10). Most nights, a piano player enhances the jovial mood.

Passeig Isabel II 14. © **93/319-3033.** www.setportes.com. Reservations required weekends. Main courses 9€–48€ ($10–$55). AE, DC, MC, V. Daily 1pm–1am. Metro: Barceloneta.

4 Seeing the Sights

Nurtured by the Catalan veneration of the creative impulse, innovative artists and architects have been at least tolerated and more often encouraged to allow their talents and instincts to run free. In Barcelona, the results lie open to view in museums dedicated to individual artists—Picasso and Miró among them— and in scores of buildings brought into being by architects of the native form of Art Nouveau called *modernisme,* led by Antoni Gaudí and Lluís Domènech.

Tips **A Museum Note**

All Barcelona's municipal museums are free for those under 18 and for students with international ID cards. Municipal museums are closed January 1 and 6, April 12 and 19, May 1 and 31, June 24, September 11 and 24, October 12, November 1, and December 6, 8, and 25. Nearly all museums are closed on Monday, but many now stay open through the afternoon siesta on other days, when most stores are closed.

> ## (Value) Getting the Best Deal on Sightseeing
>
> - Remember that admission is free to most major museums on the first Sunday of every month and discounted every Wednesday that isn't a holiday. But be prepared to deal with heavy crowds.
> - Some of Barcelona's greatest attractions are free for you to admire from the street: the Gaudí houses, the Sagrada Família, and the Modernist fantasia of Parc Guêll. And a drink at the bar of the Grand Hotel La Florida gives you an unparalleled view for a tiny fraction of the price of staying at that super-luxe Tibidabo aerie.
> - Enjoy the savings offered by the Barcelona Card and La Ruta del Modernisme multi-ticket (see "Barcelona Deals & Discounts" at the beginning of this chapter).
> - Be aware that the special Bus Turístic makes 24 stops on its two circular routes, north and south, of the major sights and neighborhoods—you can get on and off as often as you like for the price of a 1- or 2-day pass. With free guidebooks and attendants, this is a far less expensive option than those offered by commercial tour companies.
> - Note that seniors are eligible for discounted or even free museum admission, and those under 18 or 16 get into many museums free.
> - Take advantage of the best sightseeing bargain of all: people-watching along La Rambla; its northerly extension, the Rambla de Catalunya; and the Moll de la Fusta, bordering the port. All have benches scattered around to relax on, or you can nurse a soft drink or coffee at one of the scores of sidewalk cafes.

THE TOP MUSEUMS

Museu Picasso 🏛🏛🏛 Barcelona's most popular single attraction, this museum focuses on the early years of Picasso's long and varied career. The paintings, drawings, engravings, and ceramics here go all the way back to juvenilia, but the museum is light on his most famous later paintings—except for the series based on Velázquez's *Las Meninas,* which are on display here. The observation that the museum itself is at least as interesting as the artworks within is even more true now that galleries in the original three Renaissance mansions have been expanded into two more adjoining palaces.

Montcada 15–23. ℂ 93/319-6310. www.museupicasso.bcn.es. Admission to permanent collection 5€ ($5.75) adults, 2.50€ ($2.90) seniors and students under 25, free for visitors under 16, free for everyone 1st Sun of every month; temporary exhibits up to 5€ ($5.75) extra. Tues–Sat and holidays 10am–8pm; Sun 10am–3pm. Metro: Jaume I.

Fundació Antoni Tàpies 🏛 Housed in a *modernista* building designed by Lluís Domènech i Muntaner and refurbished by his great-grandson in 1989, this museum continues the Barcelona tradition of honoring prominent native artists. Tàpies is thought by many to be the living heir to Miró and Picasso, and this exhibit space rotates examples of his work and that of younger Catalan artists. The tangle of tubing atop the building is a Tàpies sculpture that makes more sense when you realize it's called *Chair and Cloud.*

Aragó 255. ℂ 93/487-0315. www.fundaciotapies.org. Admission 4.20€ ($4.85) adults, 2.10€ ($2.40) seniors and students. Tues–Sun 10am–8pm. Metro: Passeig de Gràcia.

Barcelona

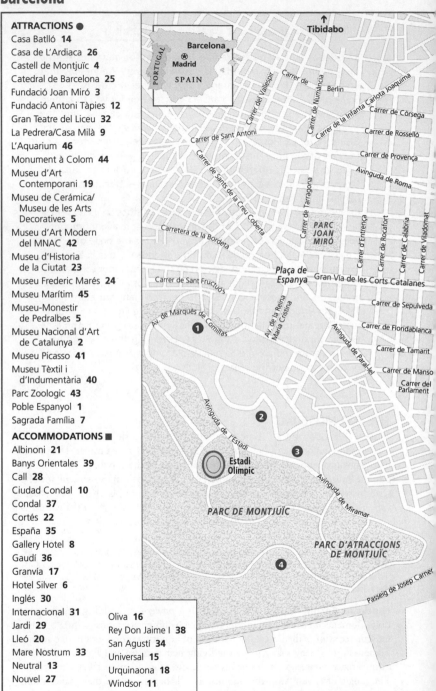

⑤ Plaça de Francesc Macià

⑥

ⓘ Information

0   1/4 mi
0   0.25 km

Travessera de Gràcia

Gran de Gràcia

Carrer de Buenos Aires

Carrer de Londres

Carrer de Paris

Avinguda Diagonal

Carrer de Còrsega

Travessera de Gràcia

Av. de Sant Antoni Maria Claret

Carrer de la Indústria

EIXAMPLE ⑧ⓘ

⑨

Carrer de Rosselló

Avinguda Diagonal

Carrer de Roger de Flor

Plaça de la Sagrada Família ⑦

Carrer de Provença

Carrer d'Enric Granados

Carrer de Balmes

Rambla de Catalunya

Passeig de Gràcia

Carrer de Pau Claris

⑩

Carrer de Mallorca

Carrer de València

⑪

⑫

⑮

Carrer d'Aragó

Passeig de Sant Joan

⑬⑭

Carrer de Nàpols

Carrer de Sicília

Carrer de Comte Borrell

Carrer del Comte d'Urgell

Carrer de Villarroel

Carrer de Casanova

Carrer de Muntaner

Carrer d'Aribau

Carrer del Consell de Cent

Carrer de la Diputació

⑯

Carrer de R. de Llúria

Carrer del Bruc

Carrer de Girona

Carrer de Bailèn

Plaça de la Universitat

Gran Via de les Corts Catalanes

⑰

Plaça de Tetuan

Carrer de Sardenya

Ronda Universitat

Carrer   de Casp

Ronda de Sant Antoni

Carrer de Pelai

Plaça Catalunya ⓘ

Plaça ⑱ **Urquinaona**

Ronda de Sant Pere

Carrer   d'Ausias Marc

Carrer   d'Ali Bei

Carrer de Ribes

⑳

RAVAL

⑲

Av. Portal de l'Àngel

㉑

㉒

Carrer de Sant Antoni

Carrer de Hospital

La Rambla

BARRI GÒTIC

㉗

㉙ ㉖

㉘

Via Laietana

Passeig de Lluís Companys

㉞

㉝

㉚

㉕

㉔㉓

Carrer de Sant Pau

㉟

㉜㉛

C. de ㉞ Ferran

C. de la Princesa

Carrer del Comerç

Passeig de Pujades

Carrer de la Marina

Carrer Nou de la Rambla

㊱

㊲

㊳㊴㊵

LA RIBERA

Avda. de les Drassanes

La Rambla

Carrer Ample

Passeig de Picasso

PARC DE LA CIUTADELLA

Carrer de Wellington

㊺

㊹

Plaça Portal de la Pau

Passeig de Colom

Pg. Isabell II

Moll de la Fusta

Avinguda d'Icària

㊷

PARC ZOOLÒGIC

㊸

Villa Olímpica →

Moll d'Espanya

Port Vell

BARCELONETA

㊻

Passeig   Marítim

Tips **Art at a Discount**

The "Articket" allows visits to six major art centers in Barcelona—Museu Nacional d'Art de Catalunya, Museu d'Art Contemporàni de Barcelona, Fundació Antoni Tàpies, Fundació Joan Miró, Centre de Cultura Contemporània de Barcelona, and Centro Cultural Caixa Catalunya—for 15€ ($17). Even if you go to only the four most important spots, that's a savings of over 6€ ($6.90), which buys a beer and a couple of tapas to round out the cultural experience. Buy the ticket at any of the six museums or at the tourist office at Plaça de Catalunya.

Fundació Joan Miró ★★ A tribute to Catalan lyrical surrealist Joan Miró, this contemporary museum follows his work from 1914 to 1978 and includes many of his sculptures, paintings, and multimedia tapestries. Even the roof boasts his whimsical sculptures as well as impressive city vistas. Temporary exhibits of other contemporary artists, often two or three at a time, are held on a regular basis. The restaurant adheres to high standards but isn't too expensive. From the top of the Montjuïc funicular, turn left, and walk down to the museum.

Parc de Montjuïc. ✆ **93/443-9470.** www.bcn.fjmiro.es. Admission 7.20€ ($8.30) adults, 3.90€ ($4.50) students, free for children under 15; temporary exhibitions 3.60€ ($4.15) adults, 1.80€ ($2.10) students. July–Sept Tues–Wed and Fri–Sat 10am–8pm, Thurs 10am–9:30pm, Sun and holidays 10am–2:30pm; Oct–June Tues–Sat 10am–7pm, Sun and holidays 10am–2:30pm. Funicular: Montjuïc. Bus: 50 from Plaça de Espanya.

Museu d'Art Contemporàni (MACBA) ★ Much excitement attended the 1995 opening of this stunning, light-filled building by American architect Richard Meier. Standing in stark contrast to the 16th-century convent opposite and the surrounding tenements with laundry drying on their balconies, it has generated a renewal of the El Raval neighborhood. The permanent collection comprises only about 1,300 paintings and sculptures from the late 1940s, including works by many Catalan and Spanish artists and a few by non-Spaniards like Calder and Dubuffet. Critical assessments of the museum will depend on future acquisitions and the success of temporary exhibits, which have so far proved to be cutting edge. In the meantime, at least see it for the architecture. Walk 5 blocks west from the upper Rambla along Carrer Bonsucces, which changes to Elisabets. After a visit, you might want to check out the **Centre de Cultura Contemporània (Contemporary Cultural Center)** next door at Montalegre 5 (✆ **93/306-4100;** www.cccb.org), which combines a modern glass wing with a former monastery and mounts provocative exhibits and installations. Admission is 5.50€ ($6.35), 4€ ($4.60) for students. It's open Tuesday, Thursday, and Friday from 11am to 2pm and 4 to 8pm, Wednesday and Saturday from 11am to 8pm, and Sunday and holidays from 11am to 7pm.

Plaça de les Angels 1. ✆ **93/412-0810.** www.macba.es. General admission 7€ ($8.05) adults, 5.50€ ($6.35) students, 3€ ($3.45) non-holiday Wed. Mon–Fri 11am–7:30pm; Sat 10am–8pm; Sun and holidays 10am–3pm. Metro: Catalunya or Universitat.

Museu Nacional d'Art de Catalunya (National Museum of Catalan Art) ★ In this building—meant to last only for the year of the 1929 World's Fair and redesigned inside by controversial Italian architect Gae Aulenti in the 1990s—is a collection of Catalan art from the Romanesque and Gothic periods as well as from the 16th to the 18th centuries, along with works by high-caliber non-Catalan artists like El Greco, Velázquez, Zurbarán, and Tintoretto. Pride of place goes to the sculptures and frescoes removed from the Romanesque churches strung across Catalunya's northern tier. The view of the city from the front steps is a bonus.

In the Palau Nacional, Parc de Montjuïc. ② 93/622-0375. www.mnac.es. Admission to permanent collection 4.80€ ($5.50) adults, 2.40€ ($2.75) seniors and students, free for everyone 1st Thurs of the month; extra fee for special exhibits. Tues–Sat 10am–7pm; Sun and holidays 10am–2:30pm. Metro: Espanya.

THE IMPORTANT CHURCHES

Catedral de Barcelona (La Seu) ✦✦✦
Begun in the late 13th century and completed in the mid–15th century (except for the main facade, which is from the late 19th c.), this Gothic cathedral attests to the splendor of medieval Barcelona. Its main points of interest are the **central choir;** the **crypt of Santa Eulàlia,** whose alabaster sepulcher is of 14th-century Italian craftsmanship; and the *Cristo de Lepanto,* whose twisted torso allegedly dodged a bullet during the naval battle of the same name. Racks in front of the side chapels are typically ablaze with scarlet votive candles. A popular feature is the adjoining **cloister** ✦, with access down on the right from the front entrance. It encloses palm trees, magnolias, flowering medlars, a fountain erupting from a moss-covered rock, and a gaggle of live geese, said to be reminders of the Roman occupation (or of the Apostles or the virtuous St. Eulàlia, depending on the various convictions of writers and guides). Try not to miss the cathedral exterior in the evenings when it's illuminated, usually Friday, Saturday, and Sunday. (The schedule isn't consistent.) On the steps at Sunday noon, a band with ancient instruments plays the eerily haunting *sardana,* the music of the hallowed Catalan folk dance.

Plaça de la Seu. ② 93/315-3555. www.catedralbcn.org. Fre admission to cathedral and cloister; admission to choir 1.50€ ($1.75); admission to Museu de la Catedral 1€ ($1.15). Cathedral daily 9am–1:30pm and 4–7pm; museum daily 10am–1pm and 5–7pm. Metro: Jaume I. Bus: 17, 19, 40, or 45.

Temple de la Sagrada Família ✦✦✦ (Kids)
If you see one monument in Barcelona, this should be it. Looking like something halfway between a feverish dream and a giant sandcastle, this *modernista* cathedral will be Europe's largest, with a 158m (525-ft.) high central dome—that is, if it's ever finished. In 1884, architect Antoni Gaudí i Cornet took over the then 2-year-old project and turned it into the ultimate statement of his flamboyant, surrealist vision. At the pinnacles of the completed towers, for example, are vivid mosaic sunbursts of gold and crimson, and much of the east facade appears to have melted under the blast of a giant blowtorch. Unfortunately, Gaudí died in 1926 after being run over by a tram, and left no detailed plans. Construction has continued off and on, with different additions reflecting different eras, sometimes quite dissonantly (such as the aggressively Cubist sculptures on the west facade). As Robert Hughes has written,

---

Moments **Amble Along La Rambla**

Even if you don't have time to visit a single museum or monument, be sure to take a stroll along La Rambla. The flamboyant spectacle is ever-changing, unending, street theater, coursing at all hours with families, sailors, transvestites, mimes, lovers, lowlifes, pickpockets, sketch artists, punks, puppeteers, models, "living statues," beggars, buskers, shell game sharpies, and political activists. Keep a firm hand on your wallet, though.

Tips **Other Gaudí Greats**

Barcelona abounds in examples of the master's work, and UNESCO lists all his creations as World Trust Properties. In 1997, his masterpiece apartment building at Provença 261–265 (at the corner of Passeig de Gràcia), **La Pedrera** (aka **Casa Milà**), was lovingly restored (see "More Attractions," later in this chapter). The **Parc Güell** (whose hallmark is its fanciful animal sculptures) and the **Casa Batlló**, Passeig de Gràcia 43, are other remarkable examples.

Gaudí "is not someone with whom one can collaborate posthumously." One of the towers has an elevator that takes you up to a magnificent view. The crypt's **Museu del Temple** chronicles the cathedral's structural evolution.

Mallorca 401. © **93/455-0247.** www.sagradafamilia.org. Admission 8€ ($9.20) adults; 5€ ($5.75) students. Guided tour 3€ ($3.45) extra. Elevator 2€ ($2.30). Apr–Sept daily 9am–8pm; Oct–Mar daily 9am–6pm. Metro: Sagrada Família. Bus: 19, 33, 34, 43, 44, 50, or 51.

OTHER MUSEUMS

Museu d'Art Modern del MNAC   Despite its name, this museum focuses somewhat narrowly on the work of Catalan painters and sculptors who worked during the *modernista* period (1880–1930), along with examples of furniture and decorative arts by like-minded craftspeople and designers of the time. Its importance has been markedly diminished by the Museu Nacional d'Art de Catalunya (p. 172), which has appropriated much of this museum's collection, so inquire ahead to be certain it's still open.

Plaça de les Armes, Parc de la Ciutadella. © **93/319-5728.** www.mnac.es. Admission 3€ ($3.45) adults, 2.10€ ($2.40) seniors and students, free to all 1st Thurs of the month. Tues–Sat 10am–7pm; Sun and holidays 10am–2:30pm. Metro: Arc de Triomf.

Museu de Ceràmicà/Museu de les Arts Decoratives   In a 1920s palace, the **Ceramics Museum** collection traces the history of Spanish ceramics from the 13th century to the present. It's one of the most important museums of its kind in Europe, and included are a few rare Moorish pieces as well as plates executed by Picasso and Miró. Also contained in the palace is the less interesting **Decorative Art Museum,** open the same hours. The building sits on attractive parklike grounds that are worth a visit by themselves, if you're in the neighborhood.

Diagonal 686. © **93/280-5024.** www.museuceramica.bcn.es. Admission to each museum 3.50€ ($4.05) adults, 2€ ($2.30) students and seniors, free to all 1st Sun of each month. Tues–Sat 10am–6pm; Sun and holidays 10am–3pm. Metro: Palau Reial.

Museu d'Historia de la Ciutat (Museum of the History of the City) *R*   Housed in a 15th-century mansion that was moved here stone by stone from Carrer Mercaders, several blocks away, this museum features **excavations** *R* of Roman and Visigothic remains underground, for which further excavations are again underway. On the upper floors are jumbled assortments of sculptures, weapons, ceramics, household implements, and more—a sort of municipal attic.

Plaça del Rei. © **93/315-1111.** www.museuhistoria.bcn.es. Admission 4€ ($4.60) adults, 2.50€ ($2.90) students and seniors, 2.75€ ($2.45) non-holiday Wed, free for children under 16, free to all 1st Sat afternoon of the month. June–Sept Tues–Sat 10am–8pm, Sun and holidays 10am–3pm (the rest of the year closes 2–4pm). Metro: Jaume I.

Museu Marítim (Maritime Museum) Installed in the Drassanes, the 14th-century Gothic royal shipyards, this museum's superb collection of maritime vessels and artifacts is distinguished by a full-size replica of Don Juan of Austria's **galleon** . The baroque flagship of the Spanish and Italian fleet defeated a naval force of the Ottoman Empire in the 1571 Battle of Lepanto. There are also humbler fishing boats, many intricate ship models, and a map owned by Amerigo Vespucci.

Av. de les Drassanes 1. © 93/3301-1831. www.diba.es/mmaritim. Admission 5.40€ ($6.20) adults; 2.75€ ($3.10) seniors, students, and children 7–16, free for children under 7, free for all 1st Sat each month 3–6pm. Daily 10am–7pm. Metro: Drassanes.

Museu-Monestir de Pedralbes (Pedralbes Museum-Monastery) This 14th-century monastery, with impressive stained-glass windows, was founded by Queen Elisenda de Montcada, whose sepulcher is inside the **early Gothic church.** The **cloisters** provide glimpses of several monks' cells, an apothecary, a kitchen that was used until recently, a 16th-century infirmary, and **St. Michael's Chapel,** which features 14th-century murals. A renovated wing, the **Sala Thyssen** , has over 80 medieval paintings and sculptures from the Thyssen-Bornemisza collection, the bulk of which is now housed in its own museum in Madrid (see chapter 16, "Madrid & Environs").

Baixada del Monestir 9. © 93/203-9282 for monastery, or 93/280-1434 for Sala Thyssen. www.museu historia.bcn.es. Admission to monastery and Sala Thyssen 5.50€ ($6.35) adults, 3.50€ ($4.05) seniors and students, free for children under 16. Tues–Sun 10am–2pm. Closed holidays. Metro: L6 to Reina Elisenda. Bus: 22 or 64.

Museu Tèxtil i d'Indumentària (Museum of Textiles and Industry) Occupying two 13th-century Gothic palaces opposite the Museu Picasso (p. 169), this museum contains a collection of textiles spanning ancient times to the 21st century. Temporary exhibitions can get very avant-garde, such as the works of 1980s art/fashion bad boy Leigh Bowery. The pleasant courtyard cafe invites lingering. Occupying a restored portion of the same structure is the **Museu Barbier-Mueller** (same phone), housing a 6,000-piece collection of pre-Columbian art recently acquired by the municipal government. Descriptions of the objects are in English. A separate admission of 3€ ($3.45) is charged; it's open the same hours as the textile museum.

Montcada 12–14. © 93/319-7603. www.museutextil.bcn.es. Admission 3.50€ ($2.70) adults, 2€ ($2.30) seniors and students, free for children under 16, free to all 1st Sat of the month 3–6pm. Tues–Sat 10am–6pm; Sun and holidays 10am–3pm. Metro: Jaume I.

MORE ATTRACTIONS

La Pedrera It's formally called Casa Milà, but the popular name of this apartment/office block means the "Stone Quarry." It was so dubbed because of the widely held public view that Gaudí had finally gone off the deep end. Its undulating exterior of carved stone gives the building the aspect of the lair of a mythical dragon, its balconies enclosed by free-form wrought iron. Following extensive restoration, the top floor and roof and a separate apartment now

---

Moments Dancing with Gaudí

You can drink and dance to live music on summer Friday and Saturday nights on the otherworldly rooftop of Gaudí's La Pedrera. All that and stunning vistas of the city, too.

Special & Free Events

Locals gather regularly to dance the *sardana,* a sedate, precisely chor-eographed Catalan folk dance. They're accompanied by a *cobla,* a band composed of 10 to 20 brass and reed instruments, several of them with origins in the distant past. Citizens of all ages and aptitudes form circles to perform its complex steps. Watch them in front of the cathedral on Saturday at 6:30pm and Sunday at noon; at Plaça Sant Jaume on Sunday and holidays at 7pm in summer and 6:30pm in win-ter; at Plaça Sant Felip Neri the first Saturday of the month at 6pm; and at Plaça de la Sagrada Família on Sunday at noon.

On the night of June 23, Barcelona celebrates the **Verbena de Sant Joan** with bonfires in the streets and plazas. It's customary to eat *coca,* a special sweet made from fruit and pine nuts, and festivities held on Montjuïc culminate in an impressive fireworks display.

During the week of September 24 are the celebrations of the **fiestas de la Mercé,** Barcelona's most important popular festival. Concerts and theatrical performances animate Plaças Sant Jaume, de la Seu, del Rei, Sot del Migdia, Escorxador, and Reial; and giants, devils, dragons, and other fantastic creatures parade through the Old Town. At the end of it all are a music pageant and fireworks.

The days-long, pre-Lenten **Carnaval** has grown in importance in recent years, with a parade and elaborately costumed citizens partying all night in the streets and nightspots.

During November, the **Festival Internacional de Jazz de Barcelona** takes place in the Palau de la Música Catalana.

explore the architect's career through slide shows, models, drawings, and photo-graphs. A fourth-floor apartment is dressed up as the home of a typical Barcelona bourgeois family. Don't miss the roof terrace, populated with highly sculptural chimneys and vents that might have been imagined by H. G. Wells.

Provença 261–265 (at the corner of Passeig de Gràcia). (℃) **90/240-0973.** Admission to attic, terrace, and apt 7€ ($8.05). Daily 10am–8pm; guided tours daily at 4pm. Metro: Diagonal.

L'Aquàrium 🐾 *(Kids* This carefully conceived aquarium is said to be the largest in Europe. It exhibits more than 8,000 marine creatures of 450 species in 21 tanks. The rainbow-hued fishes and spectacular invertebrates are each identified by their Catalan, Spanish, Latin, and English (that is, British) names. A high-light is the clear plastic tunnel allowing you to glide on a moving walkway through a tank stocked with prowling sharks and gliding rays. The admission fee was recently boosted to truly fearsome levels.

On the Moll d'Espanya, in the harbor. (℃) **93/221-7474.** www.aquariumbcn.com. Admission 14€ ($16) adults, 9.25€ ($11) seniors and children 4–12, free for children under 4. July–Aug daily 9:30am–11pm; June and Sept daily 9:30am–9:30pm; Oct–May daily 9:30am–9pm. Metro: Drassanes or Barceloneta. Bus: 14, 17, 19, 36, 38, 39, 40, 45, 57, 59, 64, 91, or 100.

Moll d'Espanya, Port Vell (Old Port) *(Kids* The final phase of a long-term rehabilitation effort, this comma-shaped wharf with palm trees and lawns thrusts diagonally from the northeast corner into the center of the harbor. It carves out packed marinas of working and pleasure boats while providing for **Maremagnum,** a complex of shops, nightclubs, an IMAX theater, and an eight-screen cineplex. A footbridge connects the tip of the wharf with the traffic circle ringing the Columbus Monument at the foot of La Rambla.

At the harbor. Metro: Drassanes or Barceloneta. Bus: 14, 17, 19, 36, 38, 39, 40, 45, 57, 59, 64, 91, or 157.

Monument à Colom (Columbus Monument)
This waterfront landmark was erected for the 1888 Universal Exhibition to commemorate Columbus's triumphant return after his first expedition to the New World. After sailing into Barcelona, he delivered news of his discoveries to Queen Isabella and King Ferdinand. A 7.5m (25-ft.) bronze statue of the explorer surmounts the Victorian-era monument. Oddly, it has been positioned so he's pointing vaguely off to Africa, rather than toward the New World. Inside the iron column on which he stands is a creaking elevator that ascends to a panoramic view.

Plaça Portal de la Pau. © 93/302-5224. Admission 2€ ($2.30) adults, 1.30€ ($1.50) seniors and students 4–12, free for children under 4. June–Sept daily 9am–8:30pm; Oct–May daily 10am–6:30pm. Metro: Drassanes. Bus: 14, 36, 38, 57, 59, 64, or 91.

Poble Espanyol ★ *Kids*
This consolidated village showing examples of the architectural styles found throughout Spain was conceived and executed for the 1929 World's Fair. After substantial renovations and alterations in operational philosophy, the once-stuffy open-air museum has become almost a village in its own right, with working artisans, dozens of crafts shops, restaurants, and assorted nightclubs and bars, a few of which are much in vogue. Some visitors judge it a slightly kitschy theme park but, in fact, the buildings are accurate full-size replicas of specific structures in various regional styles throughout the country.

Marqués de Comillas, Montjuïc. © 93/508-6330. www.poble-espanyol.com. Admission 5.95€ ($5.30) adults, 4.75€ ($4.25) students, 3.55€ ($3.15) seniors and children 7–14, free for children under 7. Mon 9am–8pm; Tues–Thurs 9am–2am; Fri–Sat 9am–4am; Sun 9am–midnight. Metro: Plaça de Espanya, then bus 61 or the free double-decker Poble Espanyol shuttle bus (on the half-hour).

STROLLING AROUND THE BARRI GOTIC
This walk passes the Gothic Quarter's most important structures and should take under 2 hours, not counting closer looks and lingering. Begin at **Plaça Nova,** to the right of **La Seu** (cathedral) as you face it, where there are remnants of the Roman wall. Walk up the ramp between the cylindrical towers that were once a gateway to the medieval city. Emerge into Carrer del Bisbe Irurita, where the first building on your left is the **Casa de l'Ardiaca (Archbishop's House).** Its 18th-century portal opens onto an attractive courtyard with Romanesque details below and Gothic above. At the top of the stairway is a patio with a 13th-century mural and a splendid coffered ceiling. The courtyard is open daily 10am to 1:30pm.

Opposite the Casa de l'Ardiaca on Carrer Santa Llúcia is the Romanesque doorway to the **Capilla de Santa Llúcia** (open daily 8am–1:30pm and 4–7:30pm), a vestige of the 11th-century cathedral that preceded the current one. Walk through the chapel and exit at the far side, entering the cathedral cloisters. After a circuit of the cloisters, enter the cathedral proper and walk through it and out the main entrance.

Turn right, then right again, and proceed up Carrer dels Comtes (look up to see some classic Gothic gargoyles); make yet another right along Carrer de la Pietat behind the cathedral. Leading off to the left is Carrer del Paradís, where inside the **Centre Excursionista de Catalunya** (no. 10) are surviving columns of the city's largest Roman temple, which honored Augustus. Return to Carrer de la Pietat and continue to the left behind the cathedral.

The Barri Gòtic

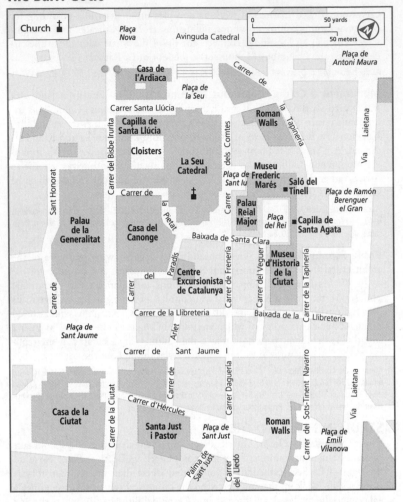

Church ✝

Plaça Nova

Avinguda Catedral

50 yards
50 meters

Plaça de Antoni Maura

Casa de l'Ardiaca

Plaça de la Seu

Carrer de

la Tapineria

Via Laietana

Carrer Santa Llúcia

Roman Walls

Capilla de Santa Llúcia

dels Comtes

Carrer del Bisbe Irurita

Cloisters

La Seu Catedral

Plaça de Sant Iu

Museu Frederic Marés

Saló del Tinell

Plaça de Ramón Berenguer el Gran

Sant Honorat

Carrer de

la pietat

Carrer

Palau Reial Major

Plaça del Rei

Capilla de Santa Agata

Palau de la Generalitat

Casa del Canonge

Baixada de Santa Clara

Paradís

Carrer de Freneria

Carrer del Veguer

Museu d'Historia de la Ciutat

Carrer de la Tapineria

Carrer de

Carrer

del

Centre Excursionista de Catalunya

Carrer de la Llibreria

Baixada de la Llibreria

Plaça de Sant Jaume

Arlet

Carrer de Sant Jaume I

Carrer de

Carrer de la Ciutat

Carrer d'Hércules

Carrer Dagueria

Via Laietana

Casa de la Ciutat

Santa Just i Pastor

Plaça de Sant Just

Roman Walls

Carrer dels Sots-Tinent Navarro

Plaça de Emili Vilanova

Palma de Sant Just

Carrer del Lledó

Turn left on Carrer del Bisbe Irurita and walk to **Plaça de Sant Jaume.** On the right is the **Palau de la Generalitat,** seat of the regional Catalan government; its main 16th-century Renaissance facade faces the plaza and the **Casa de la Ciutat (City Hall),** whose 19th-century neoclassical facade supersedes a Gothic one. To the left off Carrer de la Ciutat runs the narrow Carrer d'Hércules, leading into **Plaça de Sant Just.** Notice the 18th-century mansions with sgraffito decoration and the **Sants Just i Pastor** church.

Now turn left onto Carrer Daguería, cross Carrer Jaume I and Carrer de la Llibretería, and continue along Carrer Frenería. Turn right onto the Baixada de Santa Clara and in a few yards enter the enclosed **Plaça del Rei.** At the corner on the left is the **Palau Reial Major,** the former residence of the counts of Barcelona and the kings of Aragón. At the farthest corner, to the right, the staircase with semicircular risers leads up to (on the left) the **Saló del Tinell,** where Isabella and Ferdinand are said to have received Columbus on his return from the New World, and (on the right) the **Capilla de Santa Agata**, built atop the Roman wall and featuring a handsome 15th-century retablo.

Turn right on Carrer del Veguer to the entrance of the **Museu d'Historia de la Ciutat** (p. 174). Housed in a 15th-century mansion that was moved here stone by stone from Carrer Mercaders, several blocks away, the museum features excavations of Roman and Visigothic remains below ground and up above a gallimaufry of sculptures, weapons, ceramics, household implements, and more.

Returning to the Baixada de Santa Clara, turn right on Carrer dels Comtes. Alongside the cathedral in **Plaça de Sant Iu** is the **Museu Frederic Marès** (© **93-310-5800**; www.museumares.bcn.es), open Tuesday to Saturday 10am to 7pm and Sunday and holidays 10am to 3pm; admission is 3€ ($3.45) adults and 1.50€ ($1.75) seniors and students 16 to 25, free for children under 16 and for everyone the first Sunday of the month. It houses the eclectic antiquities and curios of benefactor Marès, a Catalan sculptor, and recently added more gallery space for its bewildering numbers of crucifixion sculptures. At the far end of the peaceful exterior courtyard is a section of the Roman wall.

PARKS & GARDENS

The **Parc de la Ciutadella** ✿ occupies the former site of a detested 18th-century citadel, some remnants of which remain. Here, too, are found the **Museu d'Art Modern**, the **Museu de Zoología**, the **Museu de Geología**, the regional **Parliament**, the **zoo**, and an **ornate fountain** that's in small part the work of the young Gaudí.

The **Parc Güell** ✿, on the northern rim of the Gràcia section, was to be an upper-crust development of 60 homes with a full complement of roads, markets, and schools. Financed by Eusebi Güell and designed by Gaudí, the project was aborted after only two houses and a few public areas were built. One of the two houses is now the **Casa-Museu Gaudí**, Carretera del Carmel (© **93/219-3811**). Don't miss the ceramic mosaic lizard at the park's entrance stairway, the Hall of a Hundred Columns, and the view from the plaza above. The park is open daily 10am to 8pm (to 9pm in summer); admission is free. The museum is open daily 10am to 6pm (to 8pm Apr–Sept); admission is 4€ ($4.60).

TOURS

Take advantage of the bargain **Bus Turístic** ✿. A single ticket permits unlimited travel on these buses, many of them open-topped double-deckers. Originating at Plaça de Catalunya, the red bus makes two circular sweeps. Highlights of the northern route are the Parc Güell, La Sagrada Família, the base of Tibidabo, and the Monestir de Pedralbes. The southern circuit makes stops on Montjuïc, at the Port Olímpic, and in the Barri Gòtic. Together, they make 26 stops, and you can get off and reboard as often as you please. The buses run daily, about every 15 minutes in summer and every 30 minutes the rest of the year, 9am to 9:30pm. If you stay on the bus, without debarking, each tour takes about 2 hours. An all-day ticket is 15€ ($17), and a ticket good for 2 consecutive days is 19€ ($22); tickets for children 4 to 12 years cost 9€ ($11) for 1 day and 12€ ($14) for 2. Admission is free for children under 4. You can buy tickets on the bus, and they come with a guidebook in six languages and vouchers providing discounts on entrance to attractions like the zoo and the Poble Espanyol. Multilingual guide/conductors announce stops and answer questions.

Children and adults enjoy **Las Golondrinas** (© **93/442-3106**; www. lasgolondrinas.com; Metro: Drassanes), the 30-minute round-trip boat ride from the Portal de la Pau, near the Monument à Colom, to the lighthouse on the harbor breakwater and back. The mini-voyage bestows close-up views of the maritime traffic and the skyline. While room has been made for pleasure craft, this is a working harbor, with tugs, cranes off-loading freighters, dry docks, and shipyards. The company also offers 2-hour cruises to the Forum 2004 area and back for 8.50€ ($10) adults, 6.10€ ($7) seniors and students, 3.70€ ($4.25) children 4 to 10, and free for children under 4. Departures are year-round at 11:30am and 1:30pm, with trips at 4:30, 6:30, and 8:30pm during warmer months.

5 Shopping

Barcelona's **value-added tax** (known as **IVA** in Spain) is now 7% for most items and services, but 16% for those defined as luxury goods. IVA recovery is possible for residents of countries outside the European Union, but only on purchases of more than 90€ ($104) bought at individual stores with the TAX-FREE sticker displayed. Get a certificate at the store and cash it in at airport Customs. See chapter 1, "Enjoying Europe on a Budget," for details.

The **main shopping streets** in the Old Town are Avinguda Portal de l'Angel, Carrer Portaferrissa, Carrer del Pi, Carrer de la Palla, and Carrer Pelai. In the Eixample, they're Passeig de Gràcia and Rambla de Catalunya; in the northern reaches of town, Avinguda de la Diagonal, Gran de Gràcia, Travessera de Gràcia, Carrer de Balmes, and Carrer Verdi.

El Corte Inglés is Spain's most prominent department store. Its main Barcelona emporium is at Plaça de Catalunya 14 (© **93/302-1212;** www.elcorteingles.es; Metro: Catalunya), with a large new branch a block away on Portal de l'Angel, in a building once occupied by its departed rival, Galería Preciados, and another at the top of La Rambla, in what was recently a Marks & Spencer outlet. It stays open all day and has a full-size supermarket in the basement and a pleasant cafeteria/restaurant with views on the ninth floor. El Corte Inglés's major competitor in the areas of electronics and entertainment is **FNAC,** at the corner of Bergara and Plaça Catalunya (© **93/318-0108;** www.fnac.es; Metro: Catalunya). In the same building, stretching along the Carrer de Pelai side, are many boutiques of international clothing brands. Up in the Eixample, the **Bulevard Rosa** (51–53 Passeig de Gràcia; no phone; www.bulevardrosa.com) is a mall of 110 shops, mostly mid-range clothing boutiques.

Barcelona's strengths are fashion and design, examples of which are nearly always costly. **Vinçon,** Passeig de Gràcia 96 (© **93/215-6050;** Metro: Diagonal), carries the latest gadgets and home furnishings. A number of shops offer authentic ceramics from prominent regions of the country. Two worthwhile stops are **La Caixa de Frang,** Carrer Freneria (no phone; Metro: Jaume I), behind the cathedral; and **Itaca,** Carrer Ferrán 26 (© **93/301-3044;** Metro: Jaume I), near Plaça Sant Jaume. Cutting-edge boutiques catering to locals line **Carrer Verdi** in the Gràcia neighborhood, from the Plaça Revolució stretching about 6 blocks north and onto side streets. Pick up a shopping map from any of the Verdi boutiques.

ART Escudellers, Escudellers 5 (© **93/342-4164;** Metro: Drassanes), is a large space with individual stalls selling pottery and handicrafts of varying levels of aptitude. A potter demonstrates his work technique. **La Manual Alpargatera,** Avinyo 7 (© **93/301-0172;** Metro: Jaume I), is the best shop for the handmade espadrilles seen on dancers of the *sardana*. It has many styles and also sells hats and some folk art.

Several stores carry English-language volumes, but the **Come In Bookshop,** Provença 203 (© **93/453-1204;** Metro: Diagonal or Hospital Clínic), specializes in British and American travel guides, novels, and nonfiction. A larger, more central store is **Casa del Llibre,** Passeig de Gràcia 62 (© 93/272-3480), with a large selection of English-language books in a discreet section as well as scattered throughout, especially in the part devoted to travel.

Angel Jobal, Princesa 38 (no phone; Metro: Jaume I), offers a variety of teas and spices, along with especially good prices on thread saffron, the world's costliest spice. Find it a block past the turn for the Picasso Museum. **La Boquería,** officially the Mercat de Sant Josep, is Spain's most extensive, most fascinating market, purveying glistening-fresh produce, meats, cheeses, fish, and every imaginable edible. In Plaça del Pi (Metro: Liceu) on Friday, Saturday, and Sunday, an **open market** of artisan food items, including cheeses, honey, vinegars, pâtés, fruit preserves, and quince pastes, is held. Antiques lovers will enjoy the open-air **Mercat Gòtic de Antigüedades** by the cathedral (Metro: Jaume I), held every Thursday from 9am to 8pm (except Aug). Other days, stroll down nearby **Carrer de la Palla,** which has at least 18 shops and galleries. The indoor antiques mall at **55 Passeig de Gràcia** is open Monday through Saturday from 10:30am to 8:30pm; it's home to 73 independent retailers selling everything from French neoclassical furniture to African idols.

6 Barcelona After Dark

Barcelona's nightlife runs from the campy burlesque of El Molino to the bizarre opulence of the Palau de la Música Catalana. For the latest information on concerts and other musical events, call the **Amics de la Música de Barcelona** at © **93/302-6870,** Monday to Friday from 10am to 1pm and 3 to 8pm. For information on the **Ballet Contemporáneo de Barcelona,** call © **93/322-1037.**

For a comprehensive list of evening activities, pick up a copy of the weekly *Guía del Ocio* or the entertainment guide offered with the Thursday edition of *El País.* For a guide to the gay and lesbian scene, pick up a **map of gay Barcelona** at Sex Tienda, Carrer Rauric 11 (© **93/318-8676;** Metro: Liceu).

THE PERFORMING ARTS

The **Gran Teatre del Liceu,** La Rambla 51–59 (© **93/485-9913;** www. liceubarcelona.com; Metro: Liceu), is the traditional home to opera and ballet. It suffered a devastating fire in 1994 but has reopened after extensive renovations. The result is glorious. The theater presents 8 to 12 operas every season and strives to make them more accessible to a wider audience: Prices can be as low as 5.75€ ($6.60) for operas, concerts, ballets, and recitals. You can book tickets with credit cards from outside the country daily 10am to 10pm Barcelona time at © **93/274-6411.** In Barcelona, call © **90/253-3353** any time up to 3 hours before the performance desired.

A magnificent *modernista* concert hall, the **Palau de la Música Catalana,** Amadeu Vives 1 (© **93/295-7200;** www.palaumusica.org; Metro: Urquinaona), is the work of Catalan architect Lluís Domènech i Montaner, a rival of Antoni Gaudí. The Palau is home to the Orquestra Simfònica de Barcelona, one of whose directors is American Lawrence Foster, and hosts a variety of classical and jazz concerts and recitals. Tickets can cost anywhere from 5€ ($5.75) to over 70€ ($80), depending on who's playing and how good your seat is. The box office is open Monday to Saturday 10am to 9pm.

Symphonic and chamber music have a new home at **L'Auditori,** Lepant 150 (© **93/247-9300;** www.auditori.org; Metro: Glòries), with both large and small performance spaces. Appearances by the Barcelona Symphony Orchestra are augmented by traveling groups, the Joven Orquestra de España (Young Orchestra of Spain), and string quartets. Tickets are 14€ to 43€ ($16–$49), half-price for students. You can buy them outside the country with a credit card 24 hours a day at © **34/93-326-2946;** or inside Spain at © **90/210-1212.** The performance space of the FNAC mall, **El Triangle,** Pelai 39 (© **93/318-0108;** Metro: Catalunya), is on Plaça Catalunya, at the top of La Rambla. The programs, usually free and starting at 7pm Monday to Saturday, hit every cultural note—from folk singers and jazz combos to new-wave electronic music to lecturers on books and films. Pick up an agenda at the store.

LIVE-MUSIC CLUBS

At nightfall, the **Poble Espanyol,** on Montjuïc hill (© **93/508-6330;** Metro: Plaça de Espanya, then bus 61), switches from museum village to entertainment complex, offering everything from jazz and flamenco to dance clubs and designer bars, including the **Torres de Avila,** Marquès de Comillas 25 (© **93/425-4788**). On warm nights, head for the open-air roof for a spangled city view. It's open Thursday through Saturday from 11pm to 5am, with no cover. Also in the village is **El Tablao de Carmen,** Arcs 9 (© **93/325-6895;** www.tablaodecarmen. com), the best place in Barcelona to see flamenco. That isn't much of a compliment, however, for the passionate dance of Andalusia is generally performed better in Madrid or Seville. Admission is 55€ ($63) for dinner and the first show, or 29€ ($33) for the first show and a drink. Dinner begins at 9pm; the first show is at 9:30pm, the second at 11:55pm. Closed Monday.

Big-time rockers who can fill arenas usually book into the **Palau d'Esports,** Passeig Minici Natai 5, Montjuïc (© **93/426-2089;** Metro: Avenida de l'Estadi). Top-drawer jazz performers can be found Wednesday through Saturday at **La Cova del Drac,** Vallmajor 33 (© **93/200-7032;** www.masimas.com; Metro: Muntaner or La Bonanova).

Run by the same crew as La Cova Del Drac, the popular **Jamboree,** Plaça Reial 17 (© **93/301-7564;** www.masimas.com; Metro: Liceu), is located on a raucously diverse plaza off the lower Rambla. Jazz, blues, and/or Latin bands appear most nights; the website has a full schedule. Across the square from the Jamboree is **Sidecar,** Heures 4–6 (© **93/302-1586;** Metro: Liceu). The music is live rock—pop or alternative or in between—and there's a terrace in warm weather. A popular old-timer is the **Harlem Jazz Club,** Comtessa de Sobradiel 8 (© **93/310-0755**), with live jazz in all its permutations—flamenco fusion, Brazilian salsa, Afro-Caribbean, and blues, nightly.

There are two reasons to make the trip to the **London Bar,** Nou de la Rambla 34 (© **93/318-5261;** www.londonbarbcn.com; Metro: Paral-lel): Live music—swing, rock, or whatever is presented in the back room most nights. And it's the only place in town to pour a half-strength version of the madness-inducing liqueur absinthe. Dating from 1910, with a few surviving *modernista* motifs, this long, high-ceilinged establishment is in the notorious Barri Xinés (take a cab).

DESIGNER BARS & DANCE CLUBS

In summer, the lower end of **Rambla de Catalunya** blossoms with outdoor cafe/bars. The bars of **Carrer Santaló,** near Plaça de Francesc Macià on the Diagonal, are popular with the younger crowd. And **Passeig del Born,** near the Museu Picasso, has several low-key "bars of the night."

Over in **Poble Nou,** near the Parc de la Ciutadella, are two skyscrapers marking the location of the former Olympic Port. The artificial harbor is now lined on three sides with over 200 bars and cafes that pound on toward dawn. The area is also one of the safest nightlife districts.

Standouts among the "designer" bars and the larger disco/bar/restaurants sometimes known as *multispacios* are **Otto Zutz,** Lincoln 15 (© **93/238-0722;** www.ottozutz.com; Metro: Plaça Molina); and **Velvet,** Balmes 161 (© **93/217-6714;** Metro: Diagonal). Shops and bars around town give away little cards that let you get into Otto Zutz without paying a cover charge. Don't even try to go clubbing before 1am.

PUBS & OTHER BARS

Increasingly popular are more or less accurate replications of Irish and British pubs. Featuring pints of Guinness Stout and Irish folk music, here are three that have opened over the past few years: **The Quiet Man,** Marquès de Barberà 11 (in Barri Xinés; © **93/412-1219;** Metro: Liccu); **Kitty O'Shea's,** Nau Santa María 5, just east of Numancia (© **93/280-3675;** Metro: María Cristina); and **Flann O'Brien's,** Casanova 264 (© **93/201-1606;** Metro: Urgell).

GAY & LESBIAN BARS

Gays have a number of beguiling bars and dance clubs to choose from, but lesbians very few. For the latest on the scene, log on to **www.gaybarcelona.net.** It's in Spanish, but not too difficult to decipher. Ads and listings in such weekly guides as *Guía del Ocio* referring to *el ambiente* nearly always mean places with a mostly or totally gay clientele. The gay sex shops **Sex Tienda,** Rauric 11 (© **93/318-8676**), and **Zeus,** Riera Alta 20 (© **93/442-9795**), have friendly, chatty staffs that can suggest the latest, hottest, coolest possibilities.

Women should check in at **Cafe-Bar Aire,** Valencia 236 (© **93/451-8462;** Metro: Passeig de Gràcia), the hub of the city's lesbian scene. Patrons and staff offer advice on what else is happening in town. **Café de la Calle,** Vic 11 (© **93/218-3863;** Metro: Diagonal), caters to both gays and lesbians and is often used as a place to meet before embarking on a night out; it's open daily from 6pm to 3am. A popular longtime standby, the **Dietrich Gay Teatro Cafe,** Consell de Cent 255 (© **93/451-7707;** Metro: Universitat or Urgüell), has frequent drag shows, with music for dancing and a long black bar leading into a lounge area. The crowd at Dietrich is a bit older than the guys at other clubs.

Arena Sala Madre, Balmes 32 (© **93/487-8342;** Metro: Universitat), is probably Barcelona's most popular mainstream gay club. Depending on the DJ, the music switches from techno to house to classic disco. Admission changes by day and event. It's one corner of a triangle that includes **Arena Classic,** Diputació 233 (© **93/487-8342**), which plays more retro tunes and has a ladies' night on Thursday, and **Arena VIP,** Gran Vía 593 (© **93/487-8342**), which plays disco and house. Remember, never go clubbing before 1am.

COCTELERIAS

More than any other Spanish city, Barcelona enjoys its cocktail lounges *(coctelerías)*. Typically open from early evening to the small hours, they're meeting places before dinner or for postprandial nightcaps; little or no food is served. Many are named for their specialties, like **El Dry Martini,** Aribau 166 (© **93/217-5072;** Metro: Provença). With over 90 gins and vodkas in stock, they cover a lot of bibulous ground. It's open daily 6:30pm to 2:30am (to 3:30am Fri and Sat). Popular enough to duplicate itself, the two versions of **Gimlet,** Rec 24 (© **93/310-1027;** Metro: Jaume I), and Santaló 46 (© **93/201-5306;** Metro: Hospital Clínic), are open daily 7pm to 2:30am (to 3am Fri and Sat). Some have

English names, such as **Blue Moon,** La Rambla 128 (© **93/302-6643;** Metro: Liceu), a lounge in the Hotel Rivoli with a piano player (7–10pm) and an expert mixologist. It's open daily 4pm to 1am.

An exceptional retreat that eclipses all the rest for elegance and panache is the **Palau Dalmases,** Montcada 20 (© **93/310-0673;** Metro: Jaume I), a 16th-century mansion a few doors down from the Picasso Museum. You enter at the end of an enclosed courtyard. The multiple archways and ancient stone walls are hung with large copies of florid baroque paintings, and candles are lit on the marble-topped tables. Vivaldi and Bach provide the stereo underscore for murmured confidences and romantic intimacies. It's open Tuesday to Friday 8pm to 2am and Saturday 6 to 10pm; opera singers perform Thursdays at 11pm. On those nights, the cover (including a drink) is 18€ ($21). No food is served.

CAFES

The Spanish tradition of the *tertulia,* a semi-formalized debate/conversation, is carried on at a handful of smoke-filled early-1900s cafes. Most are open from breakfast until after midnight.

On the scene for over 100 years, the **Café de l'Opera,** La Rambla 74 (© **93/ 317-7585;** Metro: Liceu), remains a good lookout on the often eyebrow-raising doings on La Rambla, best for breakfast or an afternoon caffeine reinforcement. For a brief burst of time in the first decade of the 20th century, **Els Quatre Gats,** Montsió 3 (© **93/302-4140;** Metro: Catalunya), was *the* gathering place for the artists, designers, and poets (including Picasso) who were making Barcelona a creative hot spot. You can eat there, but skip the indifferent food and go for a drink to take in the atmosphere. A dark Disney doppelgänger looks to have been at work at **Bosc de les Fades,** Pasaje de la Banca 7 (© **93/317-2649;** Metro: Drassanes). It attempts to evoke a woodland dell, fairy-tale style, with fake twisted tree trunks forming scary faces amid dangling faux branches. Twenty-somethings constitute most of the crowd dawdling over sandwiches, drinks, and smokes daily 6pm to 2:30am. Find it down the alley to the right of the entrance to the wax museum, at the harbor end of La Rambla. It looks older, but while it opened only a few years ago, **Schilling,** Ferran 23 (© **93/317-6787**), carries on in true cafe tradition. Given its Austro-Hungarian look, easily viewed through its wide glass front, and a stylish crowd of yuppies, polished execs, artistes, and gays, it has no difficulty keeping the tables filled. There's a limited menu of tapas and *bocadillos* (sandwiches), but this is a venue for meeting, seeing, and being seen. Open daily 10am to 2:30am.

7 Side Trips: Beaches, Dalí & More

MONTSERRAT MONASTERY

The vast **Montserrat Monastery** complex (www.abadiamontserrat.net), 52km (32 miles) northwest of Barcelona, contains a basilica with a venerated Black Virgin, a museum, hotels, restaurants, and an abundance of souvenir shops and food stalls.

The monastery—a 19th-century structure that replaced one leveled by Napoleon's army in 1812—is 1,680m (2,400 ft.) up Montserrat. Its name refers to the serrated peaks of the massif: bulbous elongated formations that provided shelter for 11th-century Benedictine monks. One of the noted institutions of the monastery is the 50-voice **Boys' Choir** ✿, begun in the 13th century; the boys sing at 1 and 6:45pm. Their performances are thrilling to the faithful and curious alike, and are the best reason for a visit. Second on that list is the newly constituted subterranean **Museu de Montserrat** (© 93/877-7777), near the entrance to the basilica. It brings together artworks once scattered around the complex, including gold and silver liturgical objects, archaeological artifacts from the Holy Land, and paintings from both the Renaissance and the 21st century. Admission is 3.60€ ($4.15), and it's open Monday to Friday from 10am to 6pm; Saturday, Sunday, and holidays from 9:30am to 6pm. Numerous funiculars and paths lead to **hermitages** and **shrines** higher up the mountain.

The least expensive transport from Barcelona is the R5 train from Plaça de Espanya. It leaves hourly for the Aeri de Montserrat station, where a funicular carries you to the complex. If you're not in a screaming hurry, though, stay on to Monistrol de Montserrat (another 4 min.) and ride to the monastery on the restored rack railway (www.cremalleradmontserrat.com), which offers the most spectacular views. "Trans Montserrat" tickets, available at any city FGC station, offer round-trip train, Metro, and rack railway use, and unlimited funicular and cable-car rides for 21€ ($24). "Tot Montserrat" tickets add in admission to the museum and lunch at the cafeteria for a total of 35€ ($40). Call © 93/205-1515 or try www.fgc.es.

Several tour companies offer daily **bus tours,** but they cost upward of 45€ ($52). Families, in particular, can find better ways to spend their money.

WHERE TO STAY & DINE   One strategy to avoid the worst of the crowds, especially in summer, is to check into the central **Hotel Abat Cisneros,** Plaça Monestir, Montserrat, 08691 Barcelona (© **93/877-7701;** fax 93/877-7724), in late afternoon in time to hear the choir. The units are comfortable enough, with doubles at 68€ to 74€ ($78–$85). The kitchen and dining room staffs are capable, serving regional Catalonian food; dining hours are daily from 1 to 4:30pm and 8:30 to 11:30pm. American Express, MasterCard, and Visa are accepted.

SITGES & ITS BEACHES

A popular beach destination 40km (25 miles) south of Barcelona, **Sitges** (*seet-jes*) really swings in summer, especially with young Barcelonans and gays from everywhere. By mid-October it goes into hibernation, but its scenic charms and museums may be motive enough for a winter visit. Things pick up with Carnaval in late February, a riotously turbulent event with costumed revelers partying for days.

The beaches here have showers, bathing cabins, and stalls. Kiosks rent items like air cushions and motorboats. Those beaches on the eastern end and those inside the town center are the most peaceful, such as **Aiguadoiç** and **Els Balomins.** The **Playa San Sebastián, Playa Fregata,** and **Playa de los Barcos** (**Beach of the Boats,** under the church, next to the yacht club) are the family beaches. Most young people go to the **Playa de la Ribera,** in the west. The main gay beach is the **Playa del Mort (Beach of the Dead).**

The **Museu Cau Ferrat,** Fonollars (© 93/894-0364), is the legacy of wealthy Catalan painter Santiago Rusinyol, and home to a collection of his works but also several pieces by Picasso and El Greco, much ornate wrought iron (a Catalan specialty), and more. Next door is the **Museu Maricel de Mar** (© 93/894-0364), the legacy of Dr. Pérez Rosales, whose impressive accumulation of furniture, porcelain, and tapestries draws largely from the medieval, Renaissance, and baroque periods. Both museums are open June 15 to September 30, Tuesday to Sunday from 10am to 2pm and 5 to 9pm. During the rest of the year, they're open Tuesday to Friday from 10am to 1:30pm and 3 to 6:30pm, Saturday from 10am to 7pm, and Sunday from 10am to 3pm. Admission to each is 3€ ($3.45), 1.50€ ($1.75) for seniors and students.

Trains (line C2) run daily to Sitges (a 40-min. trip) from Barcelona's Estació Sants. The round-trip fare is 5.50€ ($6.35).

WHERE TO STAY 🌾 The 58-unit **Hotel Romàntic y la Renaixença,** Sant Isidre 33, 08870 Sitges (© **93/894-8375;** fax 93/894-8167; www.hotelromantic. com), is composed of a series of former villas along one of Sitges's quietest streets. The rooms are medium-size and tastefully appointed, with doubles at 68€ to 101€ ($78–$116). American Express, Diners Club, MasterCard, and Visa are accepted.

WHERE TO DINE **Mare Nostrum** at Passeig de la Ribera 60 (© **93/ 894-3393**) has been serving local seafood dishes since 1950. The dining room, in a former private home dating back to 1890, has a waterfront view. Grilled fish take pride of place on the menu; the fish soup is also excellent. Main courses run 9€ to 15€ ($10–$17). Next door, an even cheaper cafe dishes out sandwiches, ice cream, and tapas. American Express, Diners Club, MasterCard, and Visa are accepted. The restaurant is open Thursday to Tuesday from 1 to 4pm and 8 to 11pm; make reservations during the summer.

HELLO, DALI

Irrepressibly eccentric and enormously skilled at self-promotion, surrealist Salvador Dalí traveled widely, especially to the United States, but always returned to his home territory of northeastern Catalunya. With the opening of two of Dalí's former residences, not far from his museum in Figueres, near the French border, a more fully rounded picture of his complex life and enthusiasms has emerged. The only difficulty is that although you can reach Figueres and Girona, the region's main city, by bus and train from Barcelona, the much smaller towns of Púbol and Port Lligat require a car. You won't need the car for more than a day, but more extended touring of this lovely region easily justifies a 2- or 3-day rental.

A logical scheme is to travel first to Girona by **train** (trains leave hourly from Barcelona's Sants station, take 70–90 min., and cost 5€–5.75€/$5.75–$6.60 each way) or by the **A-7** *autopista* (toll highway) from Barcelona, a distance of 97km (60 miles). From the train station, it's a 10-minute walk or a cheap cab ride to the **tourist information office** (© **972/226-575**) at Rambla de la Llibertat 1. Girona deserves at least a 2- or 3-hour exploration. The old town is on the other side of the Onyar River from the tourist office and can be taken in easily on foot. Several car-rental agencies are around the train station. From there, drive north about 4km (2½ miles) to pick up Route 255 heading east toward La Bisbal. In 24km (15 miles), watch for signs directing you to the small village of Púbol.

SEEING THE SIGHTS Dalí's favorite model and lifelong love was Gala, another man's wife when he met her in 1929. They ran away to Paris and led a tempestuous life together and apart, through their mutual experimentations in art and sexuality. He bought her a mansion in Púbol and vowed he wouldn't come there unless she specifically invited him, in writing. This was fortunate, since she had a steady stream of young lovers from the village, although she didn't move in until she was in her 70s. In 1996, the **Casa-Museu Castell Gala Dalí** (© **972/511-800;** www.salvador-dali.org) opened. It houses a fascinating collection of antiques, tapestries, and Dalí's inimitable contributions, including a stuffed horse and a painting of two radiators on a panel covering two real ones. March 15 to November 1, it's open Tuesday to Sunday 10:30am to 6pm (to 8pm June 15 Sept 15). Admission is 5.50€ ($6.35), 4€ ($4.60) for seniors and students.

From Púbol, pick up Route 252 north, which arrives in central Figueres in about 44km (27 miles). You can also take frequent, inexpensive trains from Barcelona or Girona to Figueres; the ride takes, on average, half an hour from Girona and costs no more than 3€ ($3.45). Signs point the way to the **Teatre-Museu Dalí** (© **972/511-976;** www.salvador-dali.org). Billed as the "world's largest surrealist object," the museum was designed by the artist himself, who is now entombed in one of the exhibits. The four floors are a riotous, relentless assault of Dalí: surrealism on the walls, floors, and ceilings of every corridor. The famous couch designed from Mae West's lips is here (as part of an entire room designed to look like her head, from a distance). In the central patio is a car surmounted by a giant sculpture that reveals different details depending on the height and angle from which you look at it. The museum also has a unique set of jewelry designed by Dalí, including a rendition of his famous melted watch. The museum is open daily October to June 10:30am to 5:45pm, and July to September 9am to 7:45pm. Admission is 9€ ($10) adults and 6.50€ ($7) seniors and students. Children under 9 enter free.

If the experience leaves you in the mood for a modest splurge, one of the best restaurants in the region is about 3.2km (2 miles) from Figueres: the **Hotel Empordà** on the Antiga Carretera de França (© **972/500-562;** www.hotel emporda.com). Inventive Catalan cuisine is efficiently brought to the table, with fixed-price menus starting at 30€ ($34). Simple double rooms upstairs go for 115€ to 135€ ($132–$155). The restaurant is open daily from 1 to 3:30pm and 8:30 to 11:30pm and accepts American Express, Diners Club, MasterCard, and Visa.

The last corner of this Dalí triangle, a cluster of cottages on the shore of the fishing village of Port Lligat, opened in 1997. You'll need a car to reach this landmark, or you can take a bus from Figueres to Cadaqués and call a taxi from there. From the Dalí museum in Figueres, drive east on Route 260 about 32km (20 miles) toward Cadaqués. On a protected cove a couple of miles north of that town, the connected white-stucco structures that became Dalí's home nudge a beach banked with heaps of seaweed and crowded with working boats and Zodiacs. Called the **Casa-Museu Dalí Port Lligat** (© **972/258-063;** www.salvador-dali.org), the rambling house contains his studio with a motorized easel, a rearing stuffed bear, and an extensive library (albeit with fake books replacing the originals). English-speaking docents are on duty in most rooms, nudging you along to the next room after your brief inspection. The tour ends on the patio, where parents might not want to point out that the long pool with bulges at each end outline the shape of a phallus. March 15 to June 14, the museum is open daily 10:30am to 6pm. From June 15 to September 15, it's open 10:30am to 9pm, and September 16 to January 6, it's open 10:30am to 6pm. Visits must be reserved in advance, a task best accomplished by a hotel *conserje*. Admission is 8€ ($9.20) adults and 5€ ($5.75) seniors and students. Children under 9 enter free.

6

Berlin & Potsdam

by Beth Reiber

The history of **Berlin** in the 20th century—particularly since the late 1980s—is one of Europe's most compelling stories. Even in the mid-1980s, who'd have imagined the Wall would come tumbling down, communism would be defeated throughout eastern Europe, and the two Germanys would reunite, with Berlin as the new capital?

Ironically, Berlin began as a divided city in the 13th century, when two settlements were founded on opposite banks of the Spree River, later growing and merging. Berlin served as capital of Prussia under the Hohenzollerns and in 1871 became capital of the German nation. After the turn of the 20th century, Berlin began to challenge Munich as the cultural capital as well, attracting artists like Max Liebermann, Lovis Corinth, and Max Slevogt. Max Reinhardt took over as director of the Deutsches Theater, Richard Strauss became conductor at the Royal Opera, and Albert Einstein was named director of physics at what became the Max Planck Institute.

After the German defeat in World War II, Germany and its former capital were carved into four sections: Soviet, American, French, and British. Berlin, deep in the Soviet sector, was divided into East and West, with East Berlin serving as the capital of East Germany. In 1961, after a series of disputes and standoffs, a 4.4m (13-ft.) wall was erected around West Berlin, in part to stop a mass exodus of East Germans to the West. Three million had already fled, most of them young, draining East Germany of many of its brightest and most educated. How ironic that in 1989 it was another exodus from the East to the West that triggered the Wall's sudden demise.

Again the nation's capital, Berlin is changing so rapidly it's impossible to keep abreast of everything, particularly in eastern Berlin, where you'll find dazzling shopping centers, office high-rises, and new government buildings. Although, along with the rest of the nation, Berlin has suffered economic recession and ideological differences between eastern and western Germans, Germany's largest city (pop. 3.5 million) is one of Europe's hottest destinations, with some of the best museums, a thriving nightlife, and a rich cultural legacy. Almost half of Berlin's visitors are younger than 35. Only London, Paris, and Rome boast more overnight stays.

For more on Berlin and its environs, see *Frommer's Portable Berlin, Frommer's Germany,* and *Frommer's Germany's Best-Loved Driving Tours.*

1 Essentials

ARRIVING

BY PLANE If you're flying on Lufthansa or any of the other airlines serving the city from Frankfurt, Munich, or western Europe, most likely you'll arrive at **Tegel Airport,** 8km (5 miles) from the center and the city's largest airport. Stop

(*Value* Budget Bests

If you're on a tight budget but love museums, note that Berlin's state-owned museums offer **free admission** the first Sunday of every month, including the most famous: the Pergamon, Altes Museum, Gemäldegalerie, Alte Nationalgalerie, Neue Nationalgalerie, Egyptian Museum, Berggruen Sammlung, and Museum für Gegenwart at the Hamburger Bahnhof. (Note, however, that admission may be charged during special exhibitions.) There are also a couple other ways to save on museum admissions; see "Berlin Deals & Discounts," below.

More bargains may be found in Berlin's **theaters**, **operas**, and **concerts**, particularly those offering 25% to 50% off unsold tickets for that evening's performance. Insiders make **Hekticket**, a half-price ticket office for that evening's performances, one of their first stops in Berlin. As for dining, your ticket to cheap meals is the *Imbiss*, a streetside food stall or tiny locale serving food for takeout or dining while you stand at chest-high counters. Sausages, Berliner *Boulette*, hamburgers, trench fries, pizza by the slice, Turkish pizza, *döner kabob*, and other finger foods are common fare, as well as beer and soft drinks. You can easily dine for less than 6€ ($6.90). You'll find *Imbisse* along side streets off the Ku'damm, on Friedrichstrasse near the S-Bahn station, Wittenbergplatz, and many other thoroughfares and squares throughout Berlin and at major train and S-Bahn stations.

---

by the Airport Service Center in the Haupthalle (Main Hall, across from Gate 0) to get a city map and directions to your hotel. The best and easiest way to get into town, particularly if your destination is one of the hotels on or around Kurfürstendamm, is by **bus,** which costs 2€ ($2.30) one-way. **City bus no. 109,** departing every 10 to 15 minutes from outside the arrivals hall, travels to Stuttgarter Platz and along Kurfürstendamm to Bahnhof Zoologischer Garten (the main train station, usually called Bahnhof Zoo) in about 30 minutes. **Bus no. X9** travels a more direct route with fewer stops (it does *not* travel along Kurfürstendamm), between Tegel Airport and Bahnhof Zoo, in less than 20 minutes for the same fare. If you're staying in Berlin-Mitte, take one of the buses above to Bahnhof Zoo and transfer to the S-Bahn, or take the **JetExpressBus TXL** directly to Berlin-Mitte for 2€ ($2.30). If you think you'll be using public transportation more than one more time during the rest of the day, consider purchasing a Tageskarte (day ticket) for 6€ ($7); see "Getting Around," below. The trip by **taxi** to Bahnhof Zoo is about 16€ ($18).

Schönefeld Airport, which once served as East Berlin's major airport, is the destination for most flights from Russia and the Middle East. The easiest way to get from Schönefeld to Bahnhof Zoo and the center of Berlin is via **S-Bahn S-9** from Schönefeld Station (a 5-min. walk from the airport), which also stops at Alexanderplatz and Savignyplatz. Another option is the **ExpressBus SXF,** which makes runs to Potsdamer Platz and Wittenbergplatz. The fare for both buses is 2€ ($2.30).

Finally, because of Berlin's sudden rise in status to the capital of Germany, **Berlin–Templehof Airport** was resurrected for commercial use, serving mostly domestic flights. Transportation from the airport is via either **bus no. 119,**

Berlin Deals & Discounts

SPECIAL DISCOUNTS   If you're a museum fan, buy the 6€ ($6.90) **Tageskarte**, valid for admission to the Pergamon, Altes Museum, Gemäldegalerie, Alte Nationalgalerie, Neue Nationalgalerie, Egyptian Museum, Berggruen Sammlung, and Museum für Gegenwart at the Hamburger Bahnhof, and all other state-owned museums on the same day. (Note, however, that the Tageskarte is not valid in museums during special exhibitions with increased admission prices.) For longer stays, a 3-day 11€ ($13) **SchauLUST Museen Berlin** museum pass allows entry to all of the approximately 60 museums on 3 consecutive days. For both tickets, children pay half price.

You can save money on both public transport and sightseeing by buying the **Berlin WelcomeCard** for 21€ ($24). It allows unlimited travel throughout Berlin for 3 days and as much as 50% off the prices of selected museums, guided tours, and the performing arts. A bonus for families: Three children under the age of 14 can travel with one paying adult free of charge.

Students can get cheaper admission to most museums by presenting an **International Student Identity Card (ISIC)**. In addition, some theaters and live-music venues offer student reductions. If you've arrived without an ISIC and can show proof of current student status, you can get the card at **STA Travel**, Hardenbergstrasse 9 (*©* **030/310 00 40**), a travel agency in the technical university district not far from Bahnhof Zoologischer Garten. It also offers discount plane fares. The agency is open Monday to Friday 10am to 7pm and Saturday 11am to 3pm.

WORTH A SPLURGE   For an evening of grand entertainment, it's worth forking over the extra euro to see an opera at the **Deutsche Oper Berlin, Staatsoper Unter den Linden,** or **Komische Oper.** If you're lucky enough to get a ticket, it's also worth the money to see the **Berlin Philharmonic.**

If you can't get tickets, console yourself with a cocktail or two high above the city in the **Telecafe of the Fernsehturm.** Although the ride on the elevator adds to the cost, the view is the best in Berlin.

which travels the length of Kurfürstendamm, or **U-Bahn U-6** from the Platz der Luftbrücke station to Friedrichstrasse. In either case, the fare is 2€ ($2.30).

For information on any of Berlin's three airports, call *©* **01805/00 01 86.**

BY TRAIN   If you're arriving by train from western Europe, including Amsterdam, Munich, Frankfurt, and Paris, you'll probably end up at the city center's main train station, **Bahnhof Zoologischer Garten** (aka **Bahnhof Zoo**), not far from Kurfürstendamm with its hotels and nightlife. Both the subway and the bus system connect the train station to the rest of the city. A money exchange counter and EurAide, an English-language info office for train travel and local sightseeing, are in the station. In 2006, a new Central Station (Hauptbahnhof) will open farther east (presently Lehrter Bahnhof).

If you're coming from an eastern European city like Prague or Budapest, you may arrive at **Berlin–Lichtenberg** station, where S-Bahn S-5 or S-7 will take you to Bahnhof Zoo. (Make sure you board the S-Bahn in the correct direction.) *Money-saving tip:* If you arrive at Berlin–Lichtenberg station, your train ticket (or Eurailpass) is valid for immediate onward travel via S-Bahn to Bahnhof Zoo, Savignyplatz, or Charlottenburg, thus saving you the cost of an S-Bahn ticket. It's not valid, however, for transportation on Berlin's U-Bahn or bus systems.

For information on train schedules, call ℂ **0190/50 70 90.**

VISITOR INFORMATION

TOURIST OFFICES If you arrive at Bahnhof Zoo train station, the most convenient stop for information is **EurAide,** on the ground floor in the Reisezentrum (Travel Center). Although the staff's main function is to provide English-speaking visitors with details on train travel, they will also answer questions on local sightseeing. Summer hours are Monday to Friday 8:30am to 12:30pm and 1:30 to 4:30pm; winter hours are Monday to Friday 9am to 12:30pm and 1:30 to 4:30pm (closed Jan).

Berlin's main tourist office, **Berlin Tourismus,** is in the Europa-Center, with its entrance at Budapester Strasse 45, a 4-minute walk from Bahnhof Zoo. Besides stocking maps (.50€/55¢), souvenirs, and brochures, and dispensing sightseeing advice, this office will book a room for you for 3€ ($3.45). It's open Monday to Saturday 10am to 7pm and Sunday 10am to 6pm. Other convenient tourist offices are at **Brandenburger Tor,** at Unter den Linden, and below the **Fernsehturm** (TV tower) on Alexanderplatz; both are open daily 10am to 6pm.

For more information or to book a hotel reservation, call **Berlin Tourismus** at ℂ **030/25 00 25.** For information on Berlin museums and special exhibitions, call the **MD info line** at 030/283 97 444.

English-language publications to look out for include the monthly *ExBerliner,* designed mostly with the expatriate in mind but also containing information on events and nightlife; it costs 2€ ($2.30) and is available at Berlin Tourismus. *Berlin in Your Pocket,* published every 2 months, offers good information on sightseeing, events, and nightlife. But the best publication on Berlin is the monthly *Berlin Programm,* available at the tourist office and at magazine kiosks for 1.60€ ($1.85). Although only in German, it provides an in-depth overview of the opera, concerts, museum exhibitions, and more. Other German publications are the city magazines *tip* (2.60€/$3) and *zitty* (2.40€/$2.75), which come out on alternate weeks with info on fringe theater, film, rock, folk, and all that's happening on the alternative scene.

WEBSITES Details on the city are available on the Internet at **www.berlin-tourist-information.de** and **www.berlin.de**.

CITY LAYOUT

Berlin comprises 12 precincts. The 1990s brought tremendous change, and the city is still being transformed by one of the most extensive and ambitious urban-renewal plans ever undertaken, particularly in former East Berlin and in the vast swath of land once occupied by the Wall and its surrounding no-man's-land. Even Berlin's main train station will find a new home in 2006, when Lehrter Bahnhof completes a transformation that will render it the Hauptbahnhof (Central Station).

Still, one of the most famous streets remains **Kurfürstendamm,** located in former West Berlin and affectionately called the **Ku'damm.** About 4km (2½ miles) long, it starts at the Kaiser–Wilhelm Gedächtniskirche (Memorial Church), a ruin left standing as a reminder of the horrors of war. Near the church is the Bahnhof Zoologischer Garten (currently Berlin's main train station, usually shortened to Bahnhof Zoo); a large park called the Tiergarten (complete with a zoo); and the Europa-Center, a 22-story building with shops, restaurants, bars, and Berlin Tourismus. Along the Ku'damm and its side streets are many of the city's smartest boutiques, as well as the biggest concentration of hotels and pensions.

Nearby **Wilmersdorfer Strasse** is where most of the natives shop. A pedestrian street near a U-Bahn station of the same name and Charlottenburg S-Bahn Station, it boasts a couple of department stores and numerous boutiques and restaurants. Not far away are Charlottenburg Palace and a cluster of fine museums, including the Egyptian Museum, Berggruen Sammlung, and Bröhan Museum. This area around the Ku'damm is part of **Charlottenburg,** western Berlin's most important precinct.

Berlin's other well-known street—and historically much more significant—is **Unter den Linden,** in a precinct called **Berlin-Mitte** (literally, Central Berlin). This was the heart of Old Berlin before World War II, its most fashionable and lively street, and thereafter was part of East Berlin. Today, Mitte has once again become the city center and contains the city's highest concentration of monuments, tourist attractions, and federal government buildings. Although Mitte has undergone dramatic transformation during the past decade, Brandenburg Gate remains the city's most readily recognized landmark, and buildings along the wide tree-lined Unter den Linden Boulevard have been painstakingly restored. Unter den Linden leads past **Friedrichstrasse,** which now rivals the Ku'damm for its smart shops and boutiques; past **Museumsinsel (Museum Island),** which boasts the outstanding Pergamon and other museums; and to the drab modern square called **Alexanderplatz,** once the heart of East Berlin and easily found by its tall TV tower. Nearby is the **Nikolai Quarter,** a reconstructed neighborhood of shops, bars, and restaurants built to resemble Old Berlin. In stark contrast is **Potsdamer Platz,** once Berlin's busiest intersection and reduced to a wasteland during the Cold War; now it's a vibrant center once again, with a glitzy shopping center, a museum dedicated to German film, and headquarters for Sony and Daimler-Benz. Mitte also boasts the city's hottest alternative scene, centered in the old Jewish quarter around **Auguststrasse, Oranienburger-strasse,** and **Sophienstrasse** and filled with art galleries, restaurants, and bars. Nearby **Prenzlauer Berg,** once a working-class district in former East Berlin, has reblossomed into another nightlife hot spot.

Berlin's other important museum district, the **Tiergarten,** is in Mitte near Potsdamer Platz, within easy reach of the city center by subway or bus. **Kreuzberg** has long been Berlin's alternative nightlife scene, though **Friedrichshain** across the Spree River has stolen some of the spotlight. Spread along the city's southwestern edge and accessible by S-Bahn are Berlin's most famous woods, the **Grünewald,** and waterways, the **Havel** and **Wannsee.** In the east, the **Spreewald** is a huge refuge of waterways and woods.

Tips A Note on Ku'damm Addresses

The numbering system of buildings runs on one side of the Ku'damm all the way to the end, then jumps to the other side of the street and runs all the way back. For example, across from Ku'damm 11 is Ku'damm 230. It's a bit complicated, but numbers for each block are posted on street signs.

GETTING AROUND

Berlin has an excellent public transport network, including the **U-Bahn** (underground), the **S-Bahn** (inner-city railway), buses, and trams (in eastern Berlin). All use the same ticket and fare system and are run by the **Public Transport Company Berlin Brandenburg (BVG;** ☎ **030/194 49;** www.bvg.de), which maintains a booth outside Bahnhof Zoo on Hardenbergplatz. Open daily 6am to 10pm, it provides details on how to reach destinations and the various ticket options available and also sells tickets.

BUYING TICKETS   Although Greater Berlin is divided into three fare zones, A, B, and C (zone maps are posted at all U-Bahn and S-Bahn stations), most places of interest to you will require purchase only of the **AB Einzelfahrausweis** single ticket at 2€ ($2.30). With this ticket, you can travel all of the U-Bahn system, most of the S-Bahn network, and buses and trams, including travel to Berlin's three airports and its major attractions. The only exception is Potsdam, for which you must buy a three-zone ABC Einzelfahrausweis for 2.60€ ($3).

If you're traveling only a short distance (six stops by bus or three by subway), you have the option of buying a **Kurzstreckenkarte** for 1.20€ ($1.40).

If you don't want to hassle with individual tickets and plan to travel more than twice on a given day, consider buying a **Tageskarte** (day ticket) for 5.60€ ($6.45), covering zones A and B. If you're going to Potsdam, buy the 6€ ($6.90) Tageskarte valid for all three zones; it's good for local travel within Potsdam as well.

However, if you're going to be in Berlin at least 3 days and plan to do a lot of sightseeing and traveling back and forth, your best bet is the **Berlin Welcome-Card**, available at all tourist offices, major hotels, and transportation ticket offices in major S-Bahn stations. Costing 21€ ($24), it allows one adult and up to three children 13 and under unlimited travel for 72 hours in all three zones (including Potsdam), as well as 25% reductions on guided sightseeing tours, performing arts (including the Deutsche Oper, Komische Oper, and Staatsoper Unter den Linden), and admission to a limited selection of museums and attractions in Berlin and Potsdam over 3 days (major attractions are generally *not* included). The tourist office has brochures listing the participating places; be sure to check whether the discounted museums and attractions include those you're interested in.

Finally, if you're going to be in Berlin for at least a week, an excellent value is the **7-Tage-Karte** (7-day ticket) for 23€ ($27), valid for any 7 consecutive days you want to travel in zones A and B. The 7-day ticket for all three zones is 29€ ($33).

Tickets are available from automatic machines at U-Bahn and S-Bahn stations, ticket windows, bus drivers (except the 7-day ticket), and even some automatic machines at bus stops (most common at bus stops on the Ku'damm). Once you buy a ticket, you must validate it yourself by inserting it into one of the machines at the entrance to S-Bahn and U-Bahn platforms and on buses.

BY U-BAHN & S-BAHN   The U-Bahn (underground) has nine lines with more than 130 stations. Lines run about 4am to midnight or 1am (except for lines U-2, U-5, U-6, U-7, U-8, U-9, and U-15, which run all night on weekends). The S-Bahn (inner-city railway) stretches throughout greater Berlin and is useful for travel between the eastern and western reaches of the city (such as Bahnhof Zoo and Alexanderplatz) and for trips to Potsdam. If you have a valid Eurailpass, you can use it on the S-Bahn but not the U-Bahn.

Berlin U-Bahn & S-Bahn

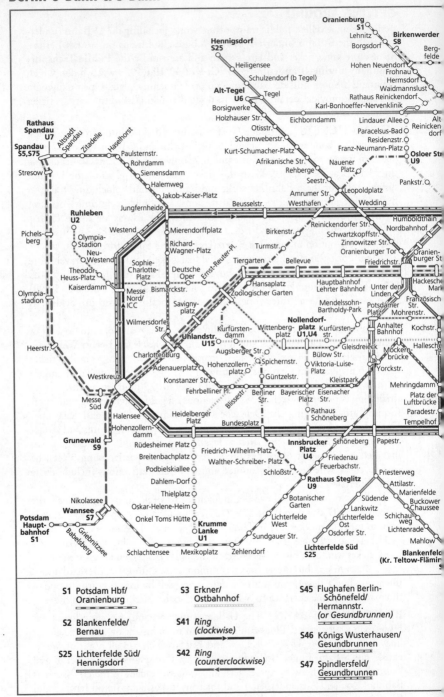

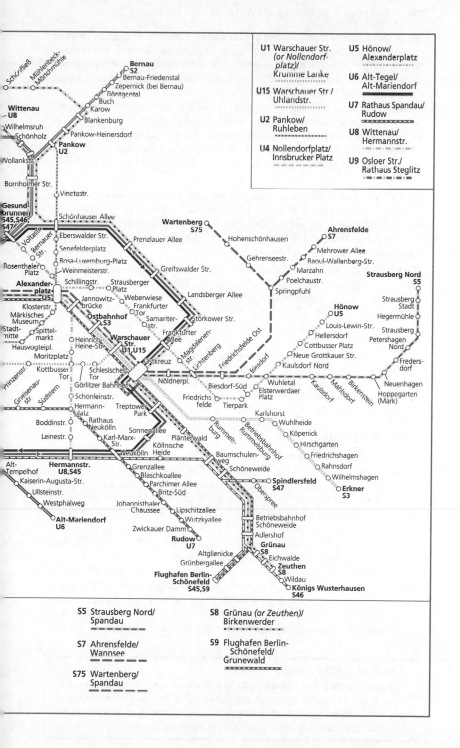

U1 Warschauer Str.
(or Nollendorf-
platz)/
Krumme Lanke

U15 Warschauer Str /
Uhlandstr.

U2 Pankow/
Ruhleben

U4 Nollendorfplatz/
Innsbrucker Platz

U5 Hönow/
Alexanderplatz

U6 Alt-Tegel/
Alt-Mariendorf

U7 Rathaus Spandau/
Rudow

U8 Wittenau/
Hermannstr.

U9 Osloer Str./
Rathaus Steglitz

Schönfließ
Mühlenbeck-Mönchmühle

Bernau
S2
Bernau-Friedenstal
Zepernick (bei Bernau)
Röntgental
Buch
Karow
Blankenburg
Pankow-Heinersdorf

Wittenau
U8
Wilhelmsruh
Schönholz

Pankow
U2

Wollankstr.

Bornholmer Str.

Vinetastr.

Gesund-
brunnen
S45,S46,
S47

Schönhauser Allee

Voltastr.
Bernauer Str.

Eberswalder Str.

Senefelderplatz

Rosenthaler
Platz

Rosa-Luxemburg-Platz
Weinmeisterstr.

Alexander-
platz
U5

Schillingstr.

Jannowitz-
brücke

Klosterstr.

Märkisches
Museum

Stadt-
mitte

Spittel-
markt

Hausvogteipl.

Moritzplatz

Prinzenstr.

Kottbusser
Tor

Greisenau-
str.

Südstern

Hermann-
platz

Boddinstr.

Leinestr.

Alt-
Tempelhof

Hermannstr.
U8,S45

Kaiserin-Augusta-Str.

Ullsteinstr.

Westphalweg

Alt-Mariendorf
U6

Heinrich-
Heine-Str.

Warschauer
Str.
U1,U15

Ostkreuz

Nöldnerpl.

Schlesisches
Tor

Görlitzer Bahnhof

Schönleinstr.

Rathaus
Neukölln

Karl-Marx-
Str.

Neukölln

Grenzallee

Blaschkoallee

Parchimer Allee

Britz-Süd

Johannisthaler
Chaussee

Zwickauer Damm

Rudow
U7

Treptower
Park

Sonnenallee

Köllnische
Heide

Baumschulen-
weg

Schöneweide

Lipschitzallee

Wutzkyallee

Altglienicke

Grünbergallee

Flughafen Berlin-
Schönefeld
S45,S9

Plänterwald

Wartenberg
S75

Hohenschönhausen

Gehrenseestr.

Prenzlauer Allee

Greifswalder Str.

Strausberger
Platz

Weberwiese
Frankfurter
Tor

Samariter-
str.

Frankfurter
Allee

Magdalenenstr.

Lichtenberg

Friedrichsfelde

Friedrichs
felde

Tierpark

Biesdorf-Süd

Elsterwerdaer
Platz

Wuhletal

Karlshorst

Wuhlheide

Köpenick

Hirschgarten

Friedrichshagen

Rahnsdorf

Wilhelmshagen

Erkner
S3

Oberspree

Spindlersfeld
S47

Landsberger Allee

Storkower Str.

Frankfurter-
Allee

Friedrichsfelde Ost

Biesdorf

Kaulsdorf

Mahlsdorf

Birkenstein

Betriebsbahnhof
Rummelsburg

Rummelsburg

Oberspree

Betriebsbahnhof
Schöneweide

Adlershof

Grünau
S8

Eichwalde

Zeuthen
S8

Wildau

Königs Wusterhausen
S46

Ahrensfelde
S7

Mehrower Allee

Raoul-Wallenberg-Str.

Marzahn

Poelchaustr.

Springpfuhl

Hönow
U5

Louis-Lewin-Str.

Hellersdorf

Cottbusser Platz

Neue Grottkauer Str.

Kaulsdorf Nord

Strausberg Nord
S5

Strausberg
Stadt

Hegermühle

Strausberg

Petershagen
Nord

Freders-
dorf

Neuenhagen

Hoppegarten
(Mark)

S5 Strausberg Nord/
Spandau

S7 Ahrensfelde/
Wannsee

S75 Wartenberg/
Spandau

S8 Grünau (or Zeuthen)/
Birkenwerder

S9 Flughafen Berlin-
Schönefeld/
Grunewald

195

BY BUS   Many of Berlin's buses are double-deckers, affording great views of the city. You can buy a single or a day ticket from the bus driver. If you're transferring, simply show the driver your ticket. Double-decker bus no. 100 travels from Bahnhof Zoo through the Tiergarten, past the Reichstag and Brandenburg Gate, and along Unter den Linden with its Museum Island on the way to Alexanderplatz and Prenzlauer Berg, making this an interesting ride between the eastern and western parts of the city. In fact, you might want to ride the bus for an inexpensive sightseeing tour. Apart from the normal day services, more than 50 special buses (Nachtbussen, marked with an N before the route number) run all night. You can pick up the schedule at the BVG office in front of the Bahnhof Zoo.

BY TRAM   East Berlin's most popular form of transportation during the Cold War has been overhauled with new streetcars and improved service. Although tickets bought for buses and the underground are valid on trams, you'll probably find the U-Bahn and S-Bahn more useful. Otherwise, a map showing the tram network is available at BVG.

BY BICYCLE   Riding a bike in Berlin can be a hair-raising experience, but with almost 805km (500 miles) of bicycle paths, parts of the city and parks are pleasant for cycling. **Fahrradstation/Berlin by Bike** rents city and mountain bikes beginning at 15€ ($17) for 1 day or 50€ ($58) for 1 week. Maps and recommended cycling routes are free. Rental bikes are available from several locations, the most convenient of which is probably **Friedrichstrasse Station,** Friedrichstrasse 141–142, open in summer daily 8am to 8pm and in winter Monday to Friday 10am to 7pm and Saturday and Sunday 10am to 4pm. Other Fahrradstation locations are bike shops at Bergmannstrasse 9 in Kreuzberg (U-Bahn: Mehringdamm) and in a complex called Die Hackeschen Höfe at Rosenthaler Strasse 40–41 in Mitte (S-Bahn: Hackescher Markt), open Monday to Friday 10am to 7pm and Saturday 10am to 4pm. For more information, call © **030/28 38 48 48.**

BY TAXI   You shouldn't have to take a taxi, but if you do, there are several companies with the following numbers: © **030/690 22,** 030/26 10 26, or 030/21 01 01. The meter starts at 2.50€ ($2.85), then increases according to a complicated tariff system. However, for short distances (3km or less than 5 min.), a special *kurzstrecke* (short-distance) fare is available for 3€ ($3.45), but you must mention it as soon as you enter the taxi.

BY RENTAL CAR   Several well-known agencies have offices in Berlin. **Avis** has a counter at Tegel Airport (© **030/41 01 31 48**), as well as an office near Bahnhof Zoo at Budapester Strasse 41 (© **030/23 09 37 0**), open Monday to Friday 6:30am to 8pm, Saturday 8am to 2pm, and Sunday 10am to 2pm. **Hertz** has a counter at Tegel Airport (© **030/41 70 46 74**) and at Budapester Strasse 39 (© **030/261 10 53**). The downtown office is open Monday to Friday 9am to 7pm, Saturday 8am to 2pm, and Sunday 9am to 1pm (closed Sun in winter).

Country & City Codes

The **country code** for Germany is **49**. The **city code** for Berlin is **30**; use this code if you're calling from outside Germany. If you're within Germany but not in Berlin, use **030**. If you're calling within Berlin, simply leave off the code and dial only the regular phone number.

Although prices vary, expect to spend about 75€ ($86) for a 1-day rental of a Ford Fiesta or Opel Corsa, including 16% tax and unlimited kilometers. It's cheaper to rent a car over the weekend, when the rate of 99€ ($114) often covers the entire period from noon on Friday to 9am on Monday. It's cheaper to rent from a downtown location than at the airport, but cheapest still is to arrange for the rental before leaving home.

FAST FACTS: Berlin

American Express There are two offices: one at Bayreuther Strasse 37, 10787 Berlin (© 030/214 76 292; U-Bahn: Wittenbergplatz), catty-cornered from KaDeWe department store across Wittenbergplatz; the other in Mitte at Friedrichstrasse 172, 10117 Berlin (© 030/204 55 721), across from Galeries Lafayette. Both are open Monday to Friday 9am to 7pm and Saturday 10am to 1pm. You can cash Amex traveler's checks here without paying a commission (although the rate tends to be lower than at a bank). If you have American Express traveler's checks or an American Express card, you can have your mail sent to these offices free.

Banks Banks are generally open Monday to Friday 9am to 3pm, with slightly longer hours 1 or 2 days a week, depending on the bank. If you need to **exchange money** outside bank hours, your best bet is the **Reise Bank** (© 030/881 71 17), the exchange office just outside Bahnhof Zoo with an entrance on Hardenbergplatz. It's open daily 7:30am to 10pm. For transactions using credit cards, you'll find **ATMs** (*Geldautomat* in German) open 24 hours throughout the city, including banks up and down the Ku'damm and at Bahnhof Zoo. Although transaction fees are high, the exchange rate is better than that offered at banks, making it useful for exchanging large amounts of money.

Business Hours Downtown **businesses** and **shops** open Monday to Friday at about 9 or 10am. While some of the smaller boutiques may close at 6pm, larger stores and department stores remain open to 8pm. On Saturday, shops are generally open 9am to 8pm; stores are closed Sunday, though convenience stores are open at major train stations.

Consulates & Embassies The consulate of the **United States** is in Dahlem at Clayallee 170 (© 030/238 51 74; U-Bahn: Dahlem-Dorf), open Monday to Friday 8:30am to noon. The embassy of **Canada** is at Friedrichstrasse 95 in Berlin-Mitte (© 030/203 12-0; U-Bahn: Friedrichstrasse), open Monday to Friday 9am to noon and 2 to 5pm. The embassy of the **United Kingdom** is at Wilhelmstrasse 70 in Berlin-Mitte (© 030/20 45 70; S-Bahn: Unter den Linden); its consular section is open Monday to Friday 9am to noon and 2 to 4pm. The embassy of **Australia** is at Wallstrasse 76–79 in Berlin-Mitte (© 030/880 08 80; U-Bahn: Märkisches Museum); its consular section is open Monday to Thursday 8:30am to 1pm and 2 to 5pm, and Friday 8:30am to 1pm and 2 to 4:15pm. Since various departments have different hours, call ahead. The embassy of **New Zealand** is at Friedrichstrasse 60 in Berlin-Mitte (© 030/20 62 10; U-Bahn: Friedrichstrasse), open Monday to Friday 9am to 1pm and 2 to 5:30pm (to 4:30pm Fri).

Currency In 2002, Germany adopted the **euro** (€) for its currency. At press time, $1 = .87€, or 1€ = $1.15.

Dentists & Doctors **Berlin Tourismus** in the Europa-Center has a list of English-speaking doctors and dentists. In addition, the **American Hot Line** at © **0177/814 15 10** has a free medical referral service. If you need an emergency doctor in the middle of the night or on the weekend, call © **030/31 00 31**; for life-threatening emergencies, call an ambulance at © **112**. Call an emergency dentist at © **030/890 04-333**.

Emergencies In Berlin, important numbers include © **110** for the **police,** © **112** for the **fire** department or an **ambulance,** and © **030/31 00 31** for **emergency medical service** and to find out which **pharmacies** are open nights.

Holidays Berlin celebrates New Year's Day (Jan 1), Good Friday, Easter Sunday and Monday, Ascension Day, Whitsunday and Monday (variable dates in Apr and May), Labor Day (May 1), German Reunification Day (Oct 3), Day of Prayer and Repentance (3rd Wed in Nov), and Christmas (Dec 25–26).

Internet Access Berlin's largest Internet establishment is the chain **easy-InternetCafe,** Kurfürstendamm 224 (© **030/8870 79 70;** U-Bahn: Uhlandstrasse or Kurfürstendamm), open daily 6:30am to 2am. It has a unique pricing policy, selling tickets from vending machines that fluctuate in value, depending on the time of day and demand (the more the demand, the higher the price; night is generally the cheapest). At any rate, 1€ ($1.15) is the minimum purchase price, and the average rate is about 1.60€ ($1.85) per hour of computer use. In addition to surfing and e-mailing, customers can also download files, print, and burn CDs for an extra charge.

Laundry & Dry Cleaning Ask the staff of your pension or hotel where the most convenient self-service laundry is. You can expect to spend 4€ ($3.55) for a wash cycle with detergent, and a dryer costs .50€ (45¢) per 10 minutes.

Mail Most post offices are open Monday to Friday 8am to 6pm and Saturday 8am to 1pm. For late service, head to the one at Joachimstaler Strasse 7, between Bahnhof Zoo and the Ku'damm, open Monday to Saturday 8am to midnight. Mailboxes in Germany are yellow. Airmail letters to North America cost 1.55€ ($1.80) for the first 20 grams (.7 oz.), while postcards cost 1€ ($1.15). If you want to mail a package (it can't weigh more than 20kg/44 lb. if sent to the U.S.), you can buy boxes complete with tape at post offices; boxes come in several sizes and range from 1.50€ to 2.50€ ($1.70–$2.85).

Police The emergency number for police is © **110**.

Tax Germany's 16% **government tax** is included in the price at restaurants and hotels, including all the locales in this chapter. If you buy more than 25€ ($29) worth of goods from any one store on a given day and are taking your purchases out of the country, you're entitled to partial recovery (up to 12%) of the **value-added tax (VAT),** which is 16% in Germany. Most stores will issue a Global Refund check at the time of purchase. Fill in the reverse side and attach it to the cash receipt. On leaving the *last* E.U. country you visit before heading home, present to Customs the Global Refund check, the receipt from the store, and the articles. Airports in Berlin, Frankfurt, and other large cities will refund your money immediately. If you're leaving Germany by train for a non-E.U. country, ask the Customs official who comes into your train compartment to stamp your check; if traveling by car, stop at the border Customs office. You can then mail your Global Refund check back to the country of purchase in a tax-free envelope provided by the store.

Telephone A **local telephone call** costs .10€ (12¢) for the first 90 seconds; restaurants and shops usually charge more for the use of their public phones, generally .20€ (23¢). To make sure you're not cut off, insert more coins than you think you'll need—unused coins will be returned.

If you're going to make a lot of calls or want to make an international call from a phone booth, you should buy a **telephone card.** For sale at post offices and news kiosks, they come in values of 6€ ($6.90) and 12€ ($14). Simply insert them into the phone slot. Telephone cards are so popular in Germany that it's often difficult finding a phone that accepts coins.

With the deregulation of Germany's telephone industry and Telecom's loss of monopoly over domestic phone service, competition among phone companies has brought other alternatives and lower long-distance rates, especially for private lines. At press time, it costs approximately .45€ (50¢) per minute for a long-distance call to the United States from a phone booth. In contrast, several **prepaid calling cards** are available at cheaper rates, including Median prepaid cards available only at American Express offices in Germany, offering calls from any touch-tone phone (including hotel, pay, and mobile phones) for .07€ (8¢) per minute from Germany to the United States. Unfortunately, Deutsche Telecom, which still controls pay phones, adds a surcharge for each minute spent using a prepaid card, which can vary from .27€ to .33€ (31¢–38¢). A similar card, the CallHome Card, is offered by Reise Bank at Bahnhof Zoo and costs .06€ (7¢) per minute to the United States (plus the surcharge for calls made from pay phones). Both the Median Card and CallHome Card come in values of 6€ ($6.90), 12€ ($14), and 25€ ($29).

For **information** on telephone numbers in Berlin, call 🕾 **11833,** or 11837 for directory assistance in English.

Incidentally, if you come across a number with a dash, the number following the dash is the extension, which you reach directly simply by dialing the entire number.

Tipping Service is already included in hotel and restaurant bills, so you're not obliged to tip. However, it's customary to round up restaurant bills to the nearest euro; if a meal costs more than 5€ ($5.75), most Germans add a 10% tip. For taxi drivers, add a euro. Porters receive 2.50€ ($2.85) for two pieces of baggage.

2 Affordable Places to Stay

Most of Berlin's pensions and hotels are clustered along and around one of its best-known streets, Kurfürstendamm (Ku'damm for short). Even those places farther away aren't very far, usually a 5- or 10-minute subway ride to Zoologischer Garten. A pension is usually a small place with fewer rooms and lower prices than a hotel and often includes breakfast in its rates, but sometimes there's only a fine line between the two. A continental or buffet breakfast is sometimes optional in the lower-priced places.

Value **Getting the Best Deal on Accommodations**

- Try to time your visit to Berlin when there aren't any major trade fairs (called *Messe* and generally held in Mar, May, June, Sept, and Oct), since many hotels and pensions raise their rates during these times.
- Take advantage of winter discounts; always ask whether one is available, especially in January and February. Some accommodations also offer discounts in July and August.
- Book reservations directly with the hotel, saving yourself the 3€ ($3.45) fee charged by the tourist office for the service.
- Save money by taking a room without a private bathroom. In Berlin (unlike in Munich's cheaper accommodations), you rarely have to pay extra for taking a shower in the communal bathroom down the hall.
- When quoted a price for a room, ask whether it's the cheapest room available. Rates are occasionally based on room size or amenities.
- Note that you can find inexpensive lodgings in the heart of town, thus saving on transportation costs.
- Inquire whether breakfast is included in the room rate—if it's buffet style, you can eat as much as you want, perhaps saving on lunch.
- Before dialing, check to see what the surcharge is on local and long-distance phone calls made from the lodging.

Keep in mind that although I've made every effort to be accurate, prices for rooms may increase during the lifetime of this edition. In addition, there are peak times—primarily during major trade fairs *(Messe)* held in March, May, June, September, and October—when many hotels and pensions raise their rates and when it might be difficult to find a room. Be sure to confirm the exact rate when making your reservation. The prices below reflect both low- and peak-season rates.

Note: You'll find most of the lodging choices below plotted on the map on p. 214.

NEAR THE KU'DAMM & BAHNHOF ZOO

Alexandra 🕭🕭   A stone's throw from the Ku'damm in a revitalized neighborhood, this pension, owned by the friendly English-speaking Frau Kuhn, offers spotless, wood-floored rooms with modern or antique furniture, plus shaving/makeup mirrors in the rooms with bathrooms. The stucco-ceilinged breakfast room with antique lighting sets the mood—it's lined with pictures of Old Berlin and has flowers on the tables; guests can order eggs served any style. You'll find reception on the second floor, along with a computer offering Internet access for guest use, but most rooms are on the third floor. Frau Kuhn offers a 10% discount to readers of this book who reserve directly with the pension.

Wielandstrasse 32, 10629 Berlin. ⓒ **030/881 21 07.** Fax 030/885 77 818. www.alexandra-berlin.de. 12 units, 2 with shower only, 9 with bathroom. 39€–49€ ($45–$56) single without bathroom, 50€–72€ ($58–$83) single with shower, 58€–82€ ($67–$94) single with bathroom; 63€–82€ ($72–$94) double with shower, 65€–99€ ($75–$114) double with bathroom. Rates include buffet breakfast. Extra person 25€–35€ ($28–$40). Weekend discounts available. AE, DC, MC, V. S-Bahn: Savignyplatz. U-Bahn: Adenauerplatz. Bus: 109 from Tegel Airport or Bahnhof Zoo to Olivaer Platz. **Amenities:** Laundry service; computer with Internet connection. *In room:* Cable TV, hair dryer, radio.

Arco ✦   On a tree-shaded residential street just minutes from the Ku'damm and KaDeWe, this hotel is an early-1900s renovated building, complete with an outdoor garden serving breakfast in summer. Breakfast is served until 11am. The attractive rooms offer comfortable modern furnishings and spotless, tiled bathrooms; the staff is friendly and accommodating. There's no elevator, but most rooms are on the ground and first floors. Families, however, might be willing to trek to the fourth floor for the large double that connects to a smaller bedroom.

Geisbergstrasse 30, 10777 Berlin. ☏ **030/235 14 80.** Fax 030/21 47 51 78. www.arco-hotel.de. 22 units, 1 with shower only, 21 with bathroom. 57€–75€ ($65–$86) single with bathroom; 75€–80€ ($86–$92) double with shower, 85€–97€ ($98–$112) double with bathroom. Rates include buffet breakfast. Extra person 20€ ($23). AE, DC, MC, V. U-Bahn: Wittenbergplatz, Augsburger Strasse, or Spichernstrasse. *In room:* Satellite TV, hair dryer, safe, radio.

Bogota ✦ *(Finds)*   Just off the Ku'damm, this older hotel with personality is well maintained and has a friendly staff. Built in 1911 as an apartment house and boasting a colorful history captured in old photos (photographer Helmut Newton did his apprenticeship here), the rambling hotel invites exploration—the ground floor reception area is elegantly old-fashioned, and on each floor are lobbies reminiscent of another era. You can spend a quiet evening in the cozy TV room, although now most rooms have TVs with English-language channels. The rooms are unique and vary in size; some have stucco ceilings, others boast balconies. If you shun the monotony of chain hotels, this is the place for you.

Schlüterstrasse 45, 10707 Berlin. ☏ **030/881 5001.** Fax 030/883 58 87. www.bogota.de. 125 units, 12 with shower only, 65 with bathroom. 44€ ($51) single without bathroom, 57€ ($66) single with shower, 72€ ($83) single with bathroom; 69€ ($79) double without bathroom, 77€ ($89) double with shower, 98€ ($113) double with bathroom. Rates include continental breakfast. Extra bed 18€–22€ ($21–$25). Children under 15 stay free in parent's room. Cribs available. AE, DC, MC, V. U-Bahn: Adenauerplatz. Bus: 109 from Tegel Airport or Bahnhof Zoo to Bleibtreustrasse. **Amenities:** TV room with CNN, nonsmoking rooms.

Crystal *(Value)*   A 5-minute walk north of the Ku'damm in the heart of the city, this hotel is housed in an early-1900s building with an updated facade. Yet the interior seems like a relic from the 1950s: outdated, old-fashioned, and comfortable. Owner Dorothee Schwarzrock is friendly, speaks perfect English (in fact, all her employees speak English), and is happy to see American guests. The rooms (with just the basics) are spotless, and cable TVs are available. Though units could use a face-lift, those with bathroom are among the cheapest in the city center.

Kantstrasse 144 (off Savignyplatz), 10623 Berlin. ☏ **030/312 90 47** or 030/312 90 48. Fax 030/312-64-65. 33 units, 7 with shower only, 21 with bathroom. 36€ ($41) single without bathroom, 41€ ($47) single with shower, 41€–62€ ($47–$71) single with bathroom; 47€ ($54) double without bathroom, 57€ ($66) double with shower, 67€–77€ ($77–$89) double with bathroom; 87€–98€ ($100–$113) triple with bathroom. Rates include continental breakfast. Cribs available. AE, MC, V. S-Bahn: Savignyplatz. Bus: 109 from Tegel Airport to Bleibtreustrasse or 149 from Bahnhof Zoo to Savignyplatz. **Amenities:** Small bar with cable TV.

Funk ✦✦   Take the sweeping white-marble staircase up to the first floor of this grand early-1900s building, where you'll find this pension, formerly the home of silent-film star Asta Nielsen, reminiscent of a past era. Manager Michael Pfundt runs the establishment with obvious heart and soul and is happy to impart sightseeing advice. The rooms are large, with authentic Jugendstil (German Art Nouveau) or reproduction Chippendale furnishings and updated modern bathrooms; most have high stucco ceilings. Two units with bathroom even boast balconies overlooking Fasanenstrasse, one of Berlin's most charming residential streets, although those facing the back are quieter. The breakfast room has an old-world drawing-room ambience, an invitation to linger over the extensive buffet. The pension has a great location, just minutes from the Ku'damm and U-Bahn and an 8-minute walk from Bahnhof Zoo.

Fasanenstrasse 69, 10719 Berlin. ℂ **030/882 71 93.** Fax 030/883 33 29. www.hotel-pensionfunk.de. 14 units, 4 with shower only, 8 with bathroom. 35€–45€ ($40–$52) single without bathroom, 59€–72€ ($68–$83) single with shower, 69€–82€ ($79–$94) single with bathroom; 69€–82€ ($79–$94) double without bathroom, 79€–92€ ($91–$106) double with shower, 89€–113€ ($102–$130) double with bathroom. Rates include buffet breakfast. Extra bed 25€ ($29). MC, V. U-Bahn: Uhlandstrasse or Kurfürstendamm. Bus: 109 from Tegel Airport or Bahnhof Zoo to Uhlandstrasse.

Hansablick 🌟🌟 *Finds*   One S-Bahn station north of Bahnhof Zoo or a 15-minute walk, this hotel might not be as conveniently located as those near the Ku'damm, but it has many other advantages that make it highly recommendable. For one thing, the S-Bahn provides convenient transport to East Berlin and Potsdam. Also, it's on a quiet residential street beside the Spree River, lined with willows, and is only a few minutes' walk from the Tiergarten park (and a great weekend flea market). The variously sized rooms, in an early-1900s building without an elevator, are a sophisticated blend of antique and modern, with wood floors, stucco ceilings, high-tech lighting, and modern furniture. The best are those with views of the Spree, the largest (and most expensive) of which even has a balcony. The prices below reflect both room size and the seasons, with the lowest in July, August, January, and February; during other months, Frommer's readers can ask for a 5% discount.

Flotowstrasse 6, 10555 Berlin. ℂ **030/390 48 00.** Fax 030/392 69 37. www.hotel-hansablick.de. 29 units. 70€–90€ ($81–$104) single; 85€–126€ ($98–$145) double. Rates include buffet breakfast. Extra bed 31€ ($28). AE, DC, MC, V. Free parking. S-Bahn: Tiergarten. U-Bahn: U-9 to Hansaplatz. **Amenities:** Small bar; babysitting; laundry service, nonsmoking rooms; theater bookings. *In room:* TV, minibar, hair dryer, safe, radio.

Imperator   With an enviable location just off the Ku'damm, this well-maintained small pension, in business for more than 70 years, is on the second floor of an early-1900s building, reached via an ornate gilded entry and elevator. It offers a variety of mostly large, stylish rooms with tall ceilings and wooden floors and modern or antique furniture. One room even has the luxury of a sunroom (called a winter garden in German). Since all rooms face an inner courtyard, they're quieter than what you'd expect from the busy location. Original artwork decorates the walls. A pleasant breakfast room has the extras of a TV with English channels and a sofa, but you can have breakfast delivered to your room.

Meinekestrasse 5, 10719 Berlin. ℂ **030/881 41 81** or 030/882 51 85. Fax 030/885 19 19. 11 units, 7 with shower only, 2 with bathroom. 40€–45€ ($46–$52) single without bathroom, 50€–55€ ($58–$63) single with shower, 60€–70€ ($69–$81) single with bathroom; 70€–78€ ($81–$90) double without bathroom, 88€–92€ ($101–$106) double with shower, 100€–105€ ($115–$121) double with bathroom. Rates include buffet breakfast. No credit cards. U-Bahn: Uhlandstrasse or Kurfürstendamm. Bus: 109 from Tegel Airport to Uhlandstrasse. **Amenities:** Laundry service. *In room:* No phone.

Knesebeck *Kids*   After acquiring this older pension in 1996, Brigitte Kalinowski has learned some English but makes up for any shortcomings with a gracious personality. With fresh paint and carpeting, most rooms feature tall stucco ceilings and face a quiet inner courtyard. Besides singles and doubles, rooms sleeping three, four, and five are available, including two with a balcony and, on the third floor (no elevator), two double rooms share one bathroom, perfect for families. The breakfast room (with cable TV) is lined with photos of the fall of the Berlin Wall. A washing machine and dryer are available at 4€ ($3.55) per load, including detergent.

Knesebeckstrasse 86, 10623 Berlin. ℂ **030/312 72 55.** Fax 030/313 95 07. www.hotel-ami.de. 12 units, 5 with shower only. 30€–39€ ($35–$45) single without shower, 43€–49€ ($49–$56) single with shower;

56€–61€ ($64–$70) double without shower, 62€–72€ ($71–$83) double with shower. Rates include buffet breakfast. Extra person 26€–30€ ($30–$35). No credit cards. S-Bahn: Savignyplatz. Bus: X9 from Tegel Airport or Bahnhof Zoo to Ernst-Reuter-Platz. **Amenities:** Coin-op laundry. *In room:* No phone.

Nürnberger Eck   Fresh flowers accent the breakfast room and the beautifully decorated hallway with antique lamps in this first-floor pension (no elevator). With its huge doors and high stucco ceilings typical of Old Berlin, it looks like a set for the movie *Cabaret.* The pleasant rooms have comfortable Biedermeier-style furniture and Persian-style carpets, but for a splurge, stay in the most expensive double, romantically decorated with 1920s furniture and chandeliers.

Nürnberger Strasse 24a, 10789 Berlin. © **030/235 17 80.** Fax 030/23 51 78 99. www.nuernberger-eck.de. 8 units, 5 with bathroom. 45€ ($52) single without bathroom, 60€–77€ ($69–$89) single with bathroom; 70€ ($81) double without bathroom, 87€–92€ ($100–$106) double with bathroom. Rates include continental breakfast. MC, V. U-Bahn: Augsburger Strasse. Bus: X9 from Tegel Airport to Bahnhof Zoo. *In room:* Cable TV w/CNN, hair dryer (in units with bathroom).

Peters ⍟ *Kids*   Owned by Annika and Christoph Steiner, a friendly English-speaking Swedish painter and her art-historian German husband, this pension just off tree-shaded Savignyplatz is a 5-minute walk from the Ku'damm and a 10-minute walk from Bahnhof Zoo. It occupies the second floor (no elevator) of an 1890 building, with cheerfully renovated white-walled rooms of various sizes and with modern furniture, including a large, high-ceilinged family room and a great wood-floored room with a kitchen and two balconies. Some rooms sleep up to five or six people. For longer stays, the Steiners rent nearby apartments with kitchens and bathrooms for 53€ to 58€ ($61–$67) for one person and 73€ to 83€ ($84–$95) for two, including breakfast. For independent travelers they also offer six one-room apartments in Berlin-Mitte on Linienstrasse near Hackische Markt; these come with kitchens, bathrooms, balconies, and cable TVs (phones available on request), and cost 50€ ($58) for one, 70€ ($81) for two, 75€ ($86) for three, and 80€ ($92) for four, without breakfast. Even cheaper is the Steiner's **Hotel Pankow** (© **030/4862 600**) on the outskirts of Berlin, where single rooms go for 29€ ($33) without bathroom and 44€ ($51) with bathroom; and doubles go for 39€ ($45) and 59€ ($68) respectively. All come with cable TV and include a breakfast buffet.

Kantstrasse 146 (just east of Savignyplatz), 10623 Berlin. © **030/312 22 78.** Fax 030/312 35 19. penspeters@aol.com. 15 units, 5 with shower only, 7 with bathroom. 36€ ($41) single without shower, 47€ ($54) single with shower, 53€–60€ ($61–$69) single with bathroom; 51€ ($59) double without shower, 63€–68€ ($72–$78) double with shower, 73€–83€ ($84–$95) double with bathroom. Rates include buffet breakfast. Extra person 10€–15€ ($12–$17). Children under 12 stay free in parent's room. AE, DC, MC, V. S-Bahn: Savignyplatz. Bus: 109 from Tegel Airport to Uhlandstrasse or 149 from Bahnhof Zoo to Savignyplatz. **Amenities:** Bicycles; babysitting. *In room:* Cable TV, fridge (in units with bathrooms), no phone.

Viola Nova   About a 5-minute walk from the Ku'damm and a 10-minute walk from Bahnhof Zoo, this updated pension has a cheerful modern breakfast room and a reception area on the ground floor, complete with changing artwork for sale. It offers bright rooms, several of which sleep three to four, with sleek black furniture, modern lighting, and tall stucco ceilings.

Kantstrasse 146 (east of Savignyplatz), 10623 Berlin. © **030/315 72 60.** Fax 030/312 33 14. www. violanova.de. 20 units, 2 with shower only, 10 with bathroom. 40€–45€ ($46–$52) single without bathroom, 50€ ($58) single with shower, 70€ ($81) single with bathroom; 60€–65€ ($69–$75) double without bathroom, 85€ ($98) double with bathroom. Buffet breakfast 6€ ($6.90); included in rates for stays of more than 1 night. Extra bed 15€ ($17). No credit cards. S-Bahn: Savignyplatz. Bus: 109 from Tegel Airport to Uhlandstrasse or 149 from Bahnhof Zoo to Savignyplatz. *In room:* Cable TV (some units).

SOUTH OF THE KU'DAMM

Aletto Jugendhotel *(Value)*   "Luxury on a shoestring" is the motto of this simple budget hotel, opened in 2001 by an experienced group of hoteliers. While describing the bare-boned rooms as luxurious might be a stretch, they are clean and modern and have private bathrooms—a plus for those who don't like traipsing down the hall in the middle of the night. Although it calls itself a "youth hotel," it caters to young and old alike, from backpackers to families, though note that there is no elevator to service its five floors of rooms. Single and double rooms are available, but a majority of rooms sleep three to eight persons. A 30-minute walk south of the Ku'damm, its primary setback is location: While close to subway stations, it requires subway transfers to reach major attractions.

Grunewaldstrasse 33, 10823 Berlin. ℂ 030/21 00 36 80. Fax 030/21 96 66 42. www.aletto.de. 71 units. 35€–55€ ($40–$63) single; 39€–75€ ($45–$86) double; 51€–90€ ($59–$104) triple; 64€–116€ ($74–$133) quad; 14€ ($16) dormitory. Rates include buffet breakfast. No credit cards. U-Bahn: Bayerischer Platz or Eisenacher Strasse. Bus: 146 or 185. **Amenities:** Courtyard cafe (summer only); lounge with cable TV; game room; computers with Internet access. *In room:* Cable TV, radio, no phone.

München *(Finds)*   This third-floor pension is about a 20-minute walk south of the Ku'damm or two stops on the U-Bahn. You can tell immediately that an artist runs it: Original works by Berlin artists adorn the walls, flowers fill the vases, and everything is done with style. Frau Renate Prasse, the charming proprietor, is a sculptor (her work decorates the hall), and her rooms are bright white and spotless, with firm beds. There are two nonsmoking rooms with balconies, as well as an apartment complete with kitchen that goes for 75€ ($86) for two without breakfast.

Güntzelstrasse 62, 10717 Berlin. ℂ 030/857 91 20. Fax 030/857 91 222. www.hotel-pension-muenchen-in-berlin.de. 8 units, 6 with bathroom. 40€ ($46) single without bathroom, 55€–60€ ($63–$69) single with bathroom; 70€–80€ ($81–$92) double with bathroom. Rates include continental breakfast. Extra person 20€ ($23). AE, DC, MC, V. Parking garage 5€ ($5.75). U-Bahn: Güntzelstrasse. *In room:* Cable TV.

NEAR BAHNHOF CHARLOTTENBURG

ART Hotel Charlottenburger Hof *(Value)*   This is one of Berlin's best modern budget hotels, with a friendly young staff. Its white rooms trimmed with primary colors are spread over three floors (no elevator) and come with modern furniture and colored bed sheets; attractive art posters; soundproof windows; and, most amazing of all, a computer in every room with free Internet access. The most expensive doubles boast whirlpool baths. Several rooms are large enough for three or four and have the advantage of two sinks and shower separate from the toilet. For breakfast, you might want to try the adjoining 24-hour Café Voltaire. Although at least a 20-minute hike from the eastern end of the Ku'damm, it offers the convenience of an S-Bahn just a minute's walk away, with easy access to Bahnhof Zoo, Berlin-Mitte, and Potsdam.

Stuttgarter Platz 14, 10627 Berlin. ℂ 030/32 90 70. Fax 030/323 37 23. www.charlottenburger-hof.de. 45 units. 60€–80€ ($69–$92) single; 70€–120€ ($81–$138) double; 92€–145€ ($106–$167) quad. AE, MC, V. S-Bahn: Charlottenburg. Bus: 109 from Tegel Airport or Bahnhof Zoo to Charlottenburg. **Amenities:** 24-hr. cafe; laundry service; coin-op laundry; nonsmoking rooms. *In room:* Satellite/cable TV with more than 50 channels, hair dryer, safe, computer.

IN BERLIN-MITTE

In addition to the accommodations here, **Peters** (p. 203) offers six apartments in Berlin-Mitte.

Am Scheunenviertel   In the heart of Berlin's former Jewish quarter not far from a restored synagogue, this hotel is surrounded by some of Berlin's hippest alternative nightlife venues and avant-garde galleries, and is a 5-minute walk from Museum Island. Upbeat and modern with comfortable rooms, it attracts both business types and well-heeled younger travelers. A young staff cultivates a laid-back atmosphere, evidenced by the fact that breakfast is served until 11am for late-night revelers.

Oranienburger Strasse 38, 10117 Berlin. ℭ 030/282 21 25 or 030/28 30 83 10. Fax 030/282 11 15. 18 units. 70€–85€ ($81–$98) single; 80€–95€ ($92–$109) double. Rates include buffet breakfast. AE, MC, V. S-Bahn: Oranienburger Strasse. U-Bahn: Oranienburger Tor. *In room:* Cable TV.

Artist Riverside Hotel & Spa 🌟🌟 *Finds*   This boutique hotel is my top choice in fast-changing Berlin-Mitte. Although located in a nondescript Communist-era building, it has a great setting beside the Spree River, near Museum Island and the Oranienburger Strasse nightlife. But what sets it apart is its design concept—from the hand-painted Jugendstil detailing in each room to the comfortable cafe with outdoor seating beside the Spree. A spa offers everything from massage and body treatments to saunas and baths. The breakfast buffet is offered until noon. Some rooms boast river views from soundproof windows, including a honeymoon suite with a waterbed, whirlpool, and reproductions of antiques gleaned from a film set. Other suites come with state-of-the-art whirlpools and balconies. But all guest rooms are not created equal: Some have no view, while others have private bathrooms inconveniently across the hall. Still, for individuals who revel in the offbeat, this place is a true find.

Friedrichstrasse 106, 10117 Berlin. ℭ **030/28 49 00.** Fax 03/28 49 04 9. www.greathotel-berlin.com. 40 units. 60€–100€ ($69–$100) single; 80€–140€ ($92–161) double; suites 200€–260€ ($230–$300). Buffet breakfast 11€ ($13). Discounts available for artists. MC, V. S-/U-Bahn: Friedrichstrasse. **Amenities:** Bar; coffee shop; spa; nonsmoking rooms. *In room:* Cable TV, dataport, fridge, hair dryer, safe.

Taunus   The location of this rather unassuming hotel is its best attribute, nestled near Museum Island in a fast-changing, revitalized neighborhood filled with hip bars, restaurants, and shops. Opened in 1996, it offers identical, small rooms sporting tiled bathrooms and soundproof windows that do an adequate job blocking out the many streetcars that clank by daily. A good choice for those wishing to avoid the more touristy area of the Ku'damm.

Monbijouplatz 1, 10178 Berlin. ℭ **030/283 52 54.** Fax 03/283 52 55. 18 units. 70€–100€ ($81–$115) single; 90€–130€ ($104–$150) double. Buffet breakfast 10€ ($12). AE, MC, V. S-Bahn: Hackescher Markt. Bus: 100 or 200. **Amenities:** Nonsmoking rooms. *In room:* Satellite TV.

IN KREUZBERG

Transit 🌟 *Value*   This great place for young travelers opened in 1987 in the inner courtyard of a converted tobacco factory; take the elevator to the fourth floor. The singles are a bit expensive, but the dorms sleeping six are perfect for the truly frugal. All the rooms are painted white and are a bit stark, but they have huge windows, high ceilings, photos of Berlin, and modern furniture. The breakfast room features a buffet (available until noon). Transit has been so successful that it converted another warehouse into a budget hotel, **Hotel Transit Loft,** in Prenzlauer Berg, Greifswalder Strasse 219, 10405 Berlin (ℭ **030/48 49 37 73;** fax 030/44 05 10 74; www.transit-loft.de; bus: 100), with 47 rooms, all with bathroom, going for 59€ ($68) for a single and 69€ ($79) for a double.

Hagelberger Strasse 53–54, 10965 Berlin. ℭ **030/789 04 70.** Fax 030/78 90 47 77. www.hotel-transit.de. 30 units, 21 with shower only or with bathroom, 100 dorm beds. 52€–55€ ($60–$63) single with shower, 59€ ($68) single with bathroom; 60€–65€ ($69–$75) double with shower, 69€ ($79) double with bathroom; 26€ ($30) per person triple and quad rooms; 15€ ($17) per person dormitory room. Rates include buffet breakfast. AE, MC, V. U-Bahn: U-9 from Bahnhof Zoo to Berliner Strasse, then U-7 from Berliner Strasse to

Mehringdamm. Bus: 119 or 219 from Ku'damm to Mehringdamm, or 109 from Tegel Airport to Adenauerplatz and then 119 from Adenauerplatz to Mehringdamm. **Amenities:** 24-hr. bar with cable TV and CNN; rental bikes; coin-operated computer with Internet access. *In room:* No phone.

WORTH A SPLURGE

Tiergarten Berlin 🌾🌾 This intimate hotel with an elevator possesses all the makings of a first-rate hotel: a polite and efficient staff, early-1900s charm and elegance, and light and airy rooms sporting tall stucco ceilings. The bathrooms are modern and spotless. Even the breakfast room with its great buffet is something to write home about. It's the kind of place that appeals to both business and pleasure travelers; it's certainly one of my Berlin favorites. Rates are based on the season and demand; be sure to ask for the best current rate.

Alt-Moabit 89, 10559 Berlin. Ⓒ 030/39 98 96 00. Fax 030/39 98 97 35. www.hotel-tiergarten.de. 60 units. 77€–140€ ($89–$161) single; 125€–155€ ($143–$178) double. Rates include buffet breakfast. Extra person 17€ ($15). Children 11 and under stay free in parent's room. Weekend discounts available. AE, DC, MC, V. U-Bahn: U-9 to Turmstrasse. Bus: JetExpressBus from Tegel Airport to Turmstrasse. **Amenities:** Small bar; laundry service; nonsmoking rooms. *In room:* Cable TV, dataport, minibar, radio.

3 Great Deals on Dining

Berlin has an estimated 6,000 restaurants and bars, a great many of which serve international cuisine, which isn't surprising, considering its large foreign population. Even young Germans are more likely to go out for Greek or Italian than they are for their own heavier cuisine. What's more, ethnic restaurants are often cheaper than their German counterparts.

You'll find many restaurants clustered along and around the Ku'damm. The cheapest of these is the *Imbiss,* a stand-up eatery where everything from sausages to fish sandwiches might be offered. Many of the cheaper restaurants also offer takeout.

Most main dishes served in a German restaurant come with side dishes like potatoes and/or sauerkraut. One of Berlin's best-known specialties is *Eisbein* (pig's knuckle), usually served with sauerkraut and potatoes or puréed peas. *Kasseler Rippenspeer* is smoked pork chops, created by a butcher in Berlin named Kassel. *Bockwurst,* also created in Berlin, is a super-long sausage, and *Boulette* is a type of meatball. Other foods you might encounter on a menu are *Sauerbraten* (marinated beef in sauce), *Leberkäs* (a Bavarian specialty, a type of meatloaf), and *Schnitzel* (breaded veal cutlet). In any case, since most main dishes in a German restaurant include one or two side dishes, that's all you'll need to order. And by all means, try a *Berliner Weisse*—a draft beer with a shot of raspberry, a refreshing summer drink.

In addition to the restaurants below, several nightspots reviewed in "Berlin After Dark," later in this chapter, offer food. In fact, a few of the bars specialize in breakfast for those who stay out all night.

ON OR NEAR THE KU'DAMM

Ashoka *Value* INDIAN Just off Savignyplatz, this hole-in-the-wall eatery gives real bang for the buck—you can eat well for less than 6€ ($6.90). No wonder it's always filled with students and alternative types. A tiny establishment with a few tables, outdoor seating, and an open kitchen, it offers vegetarian dishes ranging from *dal* (lentils) to *subji* (vegetable of the day) as well as meat curries. Particularly recommended is the *Gemüse Benares,* a vegetarian platter with various vegetable curries, spinach, *dal,* yogurt, and rice or Indian bread; or try the Ashoka Platter, which comes with lamb and chicken curries, lentils, and vegetables.

Grolmanstrasse 51 (just north of Savignyplatz). ℂ **030/318 08 154.** Meals 3€–7€ ($3.45–$8.05). No credit cards. Daily noon–midnight. S-Bahn: Savignyplatz.

Avanti *Kids* ITALIAN   I wouldn't be surprised to hear there are more self-service Italian cafeterias than any other ethnic restaurant in Berlin (with the exception of Turkish *Imbisse*). This one with outdoor seating is just off the Ku'damm near the Gedächtniskirche and Wertheim department store. It's clean and modern, with contemporary art on the walls and an ice cream/cocktail/espresso bar. Pizzas and pastas are priced at 8€ ($9.20) and under, and there's a salad bar and daily specials like fish.

Rankestrasse 2. ℂ **030/883 52 40.** Main courses 4€–13€ ($4.60–$15). No credit cards. Daily 11am–2am. U-Bahn: Kurfürstendamm.

Café Hardenberg GERMAN/INTERNATIONAL   In the technical university district, across from the Mensa cafeteria, this cafe is always packed with students and people who work nearby. The portions of the daily specials (ranging from *Schnitzel* to spaghetti) are hearty, there's an English menu, breakfast is served all day, and the place is decorated with museum posters, plants, and ceiling fans. If you want, come just for a cup of coffee. Classical music can be heard until 4pm, when it's replaced by modern hits. In the evening, the atmosphere is more like that of a bar—beer and cocktails are served in addition to dinner. In summer you can sit outside.

Hardenbergstrasse 10. ℂ **030/312 26 44.** Meals 5.50€–11€ ($6.30–$13). No credit cards. Daily 9am–midnight. U-Bahn: Ernst-Reuter-Platz.

Calcutta *Kids* INDIAN   Berlin's first Indian restaurant and open more than 30 years, this small, cheerful establishment with colorful murals and the obligatory Indian background music offers curries, tandoori from a wood-fired clay oven imported from India, vegetarian dishes, and lunch specials priced at 6€ ($6.90) and under. A good place for a relaxed, unhurried meal.

Bleibtreustrasse 17. ℂ **030/883 62 93.** Main courses 8.50€–15€ ($9.75–$17). DC, MC, V. Daily noon–midnight. S-Bahn: Savignyplatz.

Value **Getting the Best Deal on Dining**

- Take advantage of the stand-up food stalls called *Imbisse,* many in the area of the Ku'damm and Wittenbergplatz.
- Ask about the daily special (Tageskarte), which may not be on the menu or might be written only in German. It's often available all day.
- Note that some restaurants offer a fixed-price lunch, making even expensive restaurants affordable for a big noontime meal.
- Eat at the Mensa, a student cafeteria open also to nonstudents, with some of the cheapest meals served in Berlin.
- Be aware that an especially good value in Berlin is department-store cafeterias, like those at KaDeWe and Wertheim.
- Try one of the coffee-shop chains, such as Tschibo or Starbucks, where a café au lait costs 2€ ($2.30) a cup or less.
- Ask whether there's a charge for an extra piece of bread or whether your entree comes with side dishes.

Moments Enjoying Afternoon Coffee & Cake

As the British crave their afternoon tea, the Germans love their afternoon coffee, which naturally requires a slice of cake or torte to accompany it.

The cheapest place for a cup is **Tschibo,** a chain that sells both the beans and the brew. A cup of café au lait costs 2€ ($2.30), which you can drink at one of the stand-up counters. You can find Tschibos at Ku'damm 11 (across the plaza from the Kaiser Wilhelm Memorial Church) and at Wilmersdorfer Strasse 117. The ubiquitous **Starbucks** has also conquered Berlin, with convenient locations next to Wertheim department store at Kurfürstendamm 233 (© **030/88 72 66 24**), and on Pariser Place 4a (© **030/20 61 79 90**), with a view of Brandenburg Gate; both branches have wireless service for customers with laptops.

Another place for afternoon coffee is one of the department-store restaurants (see "Local Budget Bests: Department Stores," below). My favorite place near the Ku'damm, however, is **Café im Literaturhaus,** Fasanenstrasse 23 (© **030/822 54 14**), in a beautiful villa on a tree-lined street next to the Käthe-Kollwitz Museum; in summer you can sit outside surrounded by greenery.

In eastern Berlin, the place to go is the opulent **Operncafe,** Unter den Linden 5 (© **030/20 26 83**). One of Berlin's most celebrated cafes, it's on the ground floor of the Opernpalais, built in 1733, destroyed during World War II, then rebuilt. In summer it has outdoor seating. Try one of the more than 40 tortes, prepared daily.

Einhorn VEGETARIAN/INTERNATIONAL   This simple but pleasant bistro with waitress service and outdoor seating in fine weather, on the opposite end of the square from KaDeWe, specializes in a changing daily menu of vegetarian and international cuisine ranging from fish to Schnitzel to pasta. A business lunch is available weekdays noon to 4pm for 8.80€ ($10). Even cheaper is the adjoining cafeteria with its ready-made vegetarian selections, salads, curries, and pastas ranging from 2.80€ to 5€ ($3.20–$5.75), available 11am to 5pm. There are stand-up counters here where you can eat—but better yet, take your food and sit on one of the benches lining the square.

Wittenbergplatz 5–6. © **030/218 63 47.** Meals 6€–12€ ($6.90–$14). AE, MC, V. Mon–Sat 9am–9:30am. U-Bahn: Wittenbergplatz.

Good Friends CHINESE   This bustling large Cantonese restaurant with sidewalk seating, about a 6-minute walk north of the Ku'damm, includes many Chinese customers among its regular clientele, always a good sign. Service by the Chinese staff is quick, brusque, and matter-of-fact. There are more than 100 items on the English menu, with an additional 20 choices available for weekday lunch to 3pm, priced below 8€ ($9.20).

Kantstrasse 30 (at the corner of Schlüterstrasse). © **030/313 26 59.** Main courses 9€–15€ ($10–$17). AE, MC, V. Daily noon–2am. S-Bahn: Savignyplatz.

Hakuin 𝒦𝒦 VEGETARIAN   This restaurant, entirely nonsmoking and serving vegetarian food with an Asian twist, makes artful use of an unattractive building in a noisy location. With an entry reminiscent of a Japanese temple, it evokes the austerity of a Zen temple with its hushed atmosphere, artwork, and Japanese-style flower arrangements. The menu lists an intriguing selection of kitchen-created meals using fresh organic foods, such as homemade saffron tortellini filled with eggplant, Mediterranean herbs and goat cheese served in basil sauce, or red Thai curry with exotic vegetables in coconut milk. There are also two Japanese meals, nicely presented and delicious but unlike anything served in Japan.

Martin-Luther-Strasse 1. ℂ **030/218 20 27.** Meals 15€–20€ ($17–$23). AE, MC, V. Tues–Sat 5–11:30pm; Sun and holidays noon–11:30pm. U Bahn: Wittenbergplatz. Bus: 119, 219, 129, or 185 to An der Urania.

Karavan TURKISH   Across the plaza from the Kaiser Wilhelm Memorial Church, this tiny takeout is typical of Turkish *Imbisse* where you can sample ethnic food at low prices. I recommend the Turkish pizza, which has a thick soft crust with a thin spread of meat and spices; falafel; or *Spinat-tasche,* a spinach-filled pastry. There are also chicken and vegetarian dishes and fried noodles. Don't worry about a language problem: All the food is visible behind a glass counter, so you can point. There are a few bar stools along a counter, or you can sit on one of the benches in the square and watch the human parade.

Kurfürstendamm 11. ℂ **030/881 50 05.** Main courses 1.60€–3€ ($1.85–$3.45). No credit cards. Daily 9am–midnight. U-Bahn: Kurfürstendamm or Bahnhof Zoologischer Garten.

Marché Mövenpick ⊛ *Finds* INTERNATIONAL   This is one of my favorite places on the Ku'damm for a quick, satisfying meal. A cafeteria, it imitates the neighborhood market, with various stands of fresh dishes—most prepared in front of you. You'll find a salad bar, a vegetable stand, and counters offering meat dishes, soups, pastas, salads, daily specials (most priced at 5.50€ 8€/$6.30–$9.20), desserts, and more. Simply grab a tray and walk around to the various counters. It's a good place to load up on veggies; there are also freshly squeezed fruit and vegetable juices. Look for weekly specials, such as the Sunday brunch for 16€ ($18) available 10am to 2pm, and the all-you-can-eat buffet available nightly from 6pm for 12€ ($14).

Kurfürstendamm 14–15. ℂ **030/882 75 78.** Meals 10€–16€ ($12–$18). AE, MC, V. Mon–Sat 8am–10pm; Sun 10am–10pm. U-Bahn: Kurfürstendamm.

Mensa *Value* GERMAN   There are several places to eat at this student cafeteria, by far the cheapest place to eat near the Ku'damm. The cheapest is up the stairs to the left, offering three or four main dishes such as *Schnitzel* and spaghetti, as well as side dishes, salads, a soup, and dessert. First you have to decide which meal you want and then head to the appropriate counter. Non-students (under the heading *Mitarbeiter* or *Gast*) pay slightly more than students. Less confusing and offering more relaxed dining is the top-floor bistro (take the stairs towards the back to the right). While not an aesthetic place for a meal, it offers a slightly more expansive menu from self-service counters, giving you the chance to point at what you want. Finally, a ground-floor cafeteria (open Mon–Fri 8am–7pm) serves daily specials, side dishes, and salads.

In the Technische Universität, Hardenbergstrasse 34. ℂ **030/31 12 241.** Main courses 2€–3.25€ ($2.30–$3.75). No credit cards. Mon–Fri 11am–2:30pm. U-Bahn: Ernst-Reuter-Platz.

San Marino ⊛ ITALIAN   A 4-minute walk north of the Ku'damm, this restaurant with friendly service is upscale and artsy; in summer you can sit outside with a view of leafy Savignyplatz. Most pizza and pasta dishes are under 8€ ($9.20), but if you feel like splurging, order the much higher-priced steaks and seafood from the English menu. Even better, order one of the four daily fixed-price meals for less than 10€ ($12).

Savignyplatz 12. ℭ 030/313 60 86. Pizzas and pasta 4.80€–9.50€ ($5.50–$11). AE, MC, V. Daily 11am–midnight. S-Bahn: Savignyplatz.

Soup Kultur SOUP   Here's a simple concept: a minuscule *Imbiss* selling eight or nine homemade soups and stews daily, from borscht and leek-and-potato soup to chili, vegetarian choices, and cold soups, depending on the season. There are a few stand-up tables both inside and out, but most customers are people working in the area who order takeout. This shop is so successful that it has opened branches elsewhere, including Kantstrasse 154m on the corner of Fasanenstrasse (ℭ **030/450 868 38**), open Monday to Friday 11:30am to 3pm.

Kurfürstendamm 224 (entrance on Meinekestrasse). ℭ 030/886 29 282. Soups 3.30€–3.80€ ($3.80–$4.35). No credit cards. Mon–Fri noon–7pm; Sat noon–6pm. U-Bahn: Kurfürstendamm or Uhlandstrasse.

IN BERLIN-MITTE

Kartoffel-Laube *(Moments)* GERMAN   The potato in all its glory is the star of this antiques-filled restaurant in the restored Nikolai Quarter, not far from Alexanderplatz. An English menu covers pretty much all the ways Germans love their staple, including fried with onions, ham, or other ingredients; baked with toppings; in casseroles; mashed; and served as fritters, dumplings, salads, side dishes, and soups. In summer, you can sit outside with a view of the Nikolai Church.

Probststrasse 1. ℭ 030/241 56 81. Main courses 5.50€–15€ ($6.30–$17). AE, DC, MC, V. Daily noon–10pm. S-/U-Bahn: Alexanderplatz.

Oren *(☆)* MIDDLE EASTERN/VEGETARIAN   A 5-minute walk north of Museum Island, next to a beautifully restored 100-year-old gold-domed synagogue not far from Mitte's main nightlife scene, this was the former East Berlin's first modern kosher restaurant. Decorated like a 1920s Berlin coffeehouse, with outdoor garden seating and catering to an intellectual crowd, it offers excellent food, with an English menu drawing inspiration from Asia, the Middle East, and international vegetarian cuisine. Perhaps start with the Russian borscht or the falafel with hummus and pita, followed by grilled fish or a daily special. The Orient Express is an assortment of Middle Eastern vegetarian food, like hummus, tahini, falafel, tabbouleh, eggplant salad, and pita.

Oranienburger Strasse 28. ℭ 030/282 82 28. Meals 7€–13€ ($8.05–$15). AE, MC, V. Daily noon–midnight. S-Bahn: Oranienburger Strasse.

Zur Letzten Instanz *(Finds)* GERMAN   Open since 1621, this tiny restaurant claims to be Berlin's oldest *Gaststätte* (neighborhood pub). Its rooms are rustic, with plank floors, wainscoting, and a few antiques. The English menu offers traditional Berlin specialties, including *Boulette,* stewed leg of pork, suckling pig, roast pork with an herb crust, and braised beef, all served with side dishes like dumplings, potatoes, or red cabbage. Be sure to save room for Berlin's famous dessert, *rote Grütze* (cooked fruits with vanilla sauce). Tables are placed outside in summer.

Waisenstrasse 14–16. ℭ 030/242 55 28. Meals 8.90€–13€ ($10–$15). AE, DC, MC, V. Mon–Sat noon–11pm; Sun noon–9pm. U-Bahn: Klosterstrasse.

Zwölf Apostel *(☆)* *(Value)* PIZZA/PASTA   If you're hungry for pizza or pasta after visiting the Pergamon on Museum Island, there's no more popular (or packed) place than this very successful local chain. Catering to everyone from business types to students and occupying colorfully painted vaulted rooms underneath the S-Bahn tracks (you can hear the trains rumble as they pass overhead), it offers very good pastas and pizzas. If you're on a budget, come on a weekday between noon and 4pm, when all pizzas are 6€ ($6.90); with a salad, one pizza is big enough for two to share. There's also a daily business lunch from noon to 4pm for 4.95€ ($5.70). You'll find another Zwölf Apostel at Bleibtreustrasse 49 (© 030/312 14 33; S-Bahn: Savignyplatz), open 24 hours.

Georgenstrasse 2 (underneath the S-Bahn tracks near the Pergamon). © 030/201 02 22. Reservations recommended. Pizzas and pastas 8€–11€ ($9.20–$13). No credit cards. Sun–Thurs noon–midnight; Fri–Sat noon–1am. S-/U-Bahn: Friedrichstrasse.

NEAR TIERGARTEN & POTSDAMER PLATZ

Lindenbräu GERMAN   A good place for a meal or beer after visiting the Gemäldegalerie or other museums in the Tiergarten, this microbrewery is located behind the Filmmuseum Berlin, in the striking Sony Center (look for its Mt. Fuji–like roof, which changes color at night) on Potsdamer Platz. A multilevel modern establishment with a summer beer garden of sorts (it's protected from the elements by the Sony glass roof), it offers its own brewed beer, including very good unfiltered wheat, as well as soups, *Schnitzel*, sausage, Schweinshaxe, fish, *Leberkäse* (meatloaf), Berliner Eisbein, and other Bavarian and Berliner dishes that go well with beer (is there a German dish that doesn't?), all on an English menu.

In the Sony Center, Bellevuestrasse 3–5. © 030/25 75 12 80. Meals 8.50€–15€ ($9.75–$17). AE, MC, V. Daily 11am–11:30pm. S-/U-Bahn: Potsdamer Platz.

NEAR CHARLOTTENBURG PALACE

Luisen-Bräu 🍴 GERMAN   Southeast of Charlottenburg Palace, Luisen-Bräu brews its own beer on the premises (you can see the stainless-steel tanks) and sells German dishes to go with it. An English menu is offered weekdays 11am to 5pm with such items as grilled pork knuckle, sausages, roast pork, meatloaf, ham, and chicken, all with side dishes. After 5pm weekdays and all day on weekends, you have to order food from a counter; choices change daily but may include *Spiessbraten* (skewered meat and vegetables), *kasseler Rippenspeer* (pork chops), *Boulette* (a meatball), *Schweienbraten* (pot-roasted pork), salads, and stews. Dining is at long wooden tables (which fosters conversation with neighbors) or, in summer, outside. Of course, this being a brewery, you can also come just for the beer.

Luisenplatz 1 (at the corner of Spandauer Damm). © 030/341 93 88. Meals 7€–10€ ($8.05–$12). AE, DC, MC, V. Daily 11am–11:30pm. Bus: 109 or 145 to Luisenplatz/Schloss Charlottenburg.

LOCAL BUDGET BESTS: DEPARTMENT STORES

Le Buffet im KaDeWe 🍴🍴 INTERNATIONAL   KaDeWe is short for Kaufhaus des Westens, and on the sixth floor is continental Europe's biggest food department. It's so amazing it might be worth coming to Berlin just to see it— sausages and other meats (more cuts of pork than I could count), cheeses, teas, breads, jams, sweets, vegetables, coffees, spices, wines, salads, live fish, and much more. Interspersed throughout are dining counters specializing in everything from pasta to fish. An even greater selection is available one floor up at a glass-enclosed self-service restaurant reminiscent of a greenhouse, with plants galore. Its selections are sophisticated for a cafeteria—steaks, fish, Chinese food, pasta, an extensive salad bar, an antipasto buffet, Berlin specialties, desserts, and more. A smart-looking bar occupies one end, and there's a large nonsmoking section.

In KaDeWe, Wittenbergplatz. ℂ 030/217 77 39. Meals 8€–15€ ($9.20–$17). AE, DC, MC, V. Mon–Fri 9:30am–7:30pm; Sat 9am–7:30pm. U-Bahn: Wittenbergplatz.

Restaurant Cafe ℱ GERMAN   This is my pick for a quick inexpensive meal with a view. On the top (6th) floor of this department store across from the Kaiser Wilhelm Memorial Church, self-service Le Buffet features counters of salads, vegetables, vegetarian dishes, Asian stir-fries, daily specials of typical German food such as *Schnitzel* and *Eisbein*, juices, and desserts. A glass facade overlooks the rooftops of Berlin. There's a nonsmoking section. This is a great place for a meal, a snack, afternoon cake, or just a coffee break. Set lunches are available weekdays for 4.95€ ($5.70).

In Wertheim, Kurfürstendamm 231. ℂ 030/88 20 61. Meals 4.95€–8€ ($5.70–$9.20). AE, MC, V. Mon–Fri 9:30am–7:30pm; Sat 9am–7:30pm. U-Bahn: Kurfürstendamm.

STREET EATS & PICNICKING

There are a number of *Imbisse* (food stalls) around Wittenbergplatz selling *Würste*, fries, Turkish specialties, and beer. In addition, Einhorn, Karavan, and Soup Kultur (see "On or Near the Ku'damm" in "Great Deals on Dining," earlier in this chapter) sell takeout food at low prices. All **department stores** have large food departments (especially KaDeWe—see above) and counters serving prepared meats, salads, and takeout food. As for a place to consume your picnic, the most convenient green space is the huge **Tiergarten** just northwest of Bahnhof Zoo, packed with families enjoying cookouts on summer weekends. For people-watching, sit on one of the benches or stairs in the shadow of the Kaiser Wilhelm Memorial Church on the Ku'damm.

WORTH A SPLURGE

Desbrosses ℱ FRENCH   The Ritz-Carlton is much too ritzy for our budget, but this classic brasserie—built in 1875 in a French village but dismantled and reassembled here—offers casual dining and standard French fare from a changing menu, which might include *coq au vin, cassoulet* (a bean stew with pork), and steaks. A plat du jour is available daily for 8.50€ to 15€ ($9.75–$17). It's a good choice if you're visiting the many museums in the Tiergarten or the Sony Center, but even though dining here is casual, the rest of the hotel is so upscale it's not the kind of place you want to visit on a bad hair day.

Ritz-Carlton, Potsdamer Platz 3. ℂ 030/33 77 77. Reservations recommended. Meals 12€–17€ ($13–$20). AE, MC, V. Daily 6pm–midnight. S-Bahn: Savignyplatz.

Lutter & Wegner Seit 1811 ℱℱ AUSTRIAN/FRENCH   This wine bar/restaurant dates from 1811, when it opened as a wine cellar in East Berlin. It moved to West Berlin after World War II and still exudes old-world charm, with dark wainscoting, candles on white tablecloths, and changing art exhibits. Lutter & Wegner caters to a professional and artistic crowd, and although the tables are too close together in the tiny restaurant—or perhaps because of it— the atmosphere is convivial. In summer, tables are set up on the sidewalk. In addition to a standard English menu, there's a handwritten daily menu in German with offerings like *Tafelspitz*, salmon in a white wine sauce, and beef filet in Dijon gravy with beans and potato gratin, but the kitchen prides itself in being able to prepare dishes according to individual preference, even if it's not on the menu.

Schlüterstrasse 55. ℂ 030/881 34 40. Reservations recommended. Meals 13€–20€ ($15–$23). AE, MC, V. Daily 6pm–midnight. S-Bahn: Savignyplatz.

4 Seeing the Sights

Berlin has three museum centers: **Charlottenburg,** with its palace and three significant museums, including the Egyptian Museum and a museum devoted to Picasso; **Museumsinsel (Museum Island),** with the world-famous Pergamon Museum and Alte Nationalgalerie; and the **Tiergarten,** center for European art, including the Gemäldegalerie. It makes sense to cover Berlin section by section—saving time and money on transportation.

IN CHARLOTTENBURG

The 6€ ($6.90) Tageskarte bought at either the Ägyptisches Museum or the Sammlung Berggruen entitles entry to both museums, as well as state-owned museums elsewhere in Berlin. Not included are the Bröhan Museum and Schloss Charlottenburg.

Ägyptisches Museum (Egyptian Museum) ★★★   Across from Charlottenburg Palace is this invaluable collection of Egyptian art. Berlin's most famous art object (and probably the world's best-known single piece of Egyptian art) is on the first floor in a dark room reserved just for her: the **bust of Queen Nefertiti.** Created more than 3,300 years ago, the bust amazingly never left the sculptor's studio but rather served as a model for all other portraits of the queen and was left on a shelf when the ancient city was deserted. The bust was discovered in the early 1900s by German archaeologists. In an adjoining room you can see smaller likenesses of Pharaoh Akhenaton (husband of Nefertiti) and the royal family, including Nefertiti's eldest daughter, Princess Meritaton. Look also for

---

Value Getting the Best Deal on Sightseeing

- Take advantage of free admission to all the state museums on the first Sunday of every month, including the Pergamon, Alte Nationalgalerie, Altes Museum, Ägyptisches Museum, Gemäldegalerie, Neue Nationalgalerie, Sammlung Berggruen, and Museum für Gegenwart at Hamburger Bahnhof. But remember, you won't be the only one doing so.
- Note that the 6€ ($6.90) Tageskarte allows entry to all state-owned museums that same day, the 3-day 11€ ($13) SchauLUST Museen Berlin ticket allows entry to all state-owned museums and dozens of others on 3 consecutive days, and the 3-day 21€ ($24) Berlin WelcomeCard offers unlimited transportation around the city and as much as 50% off the admission to a limited number of museums and attractions. (For details on all these, see "Berlin Deals & Discounts," p. 190.) Note, however, that during special exhibitions when admission is higher than 6€ ($6.90), the Tageskarte is not valid for that state-owned museum; rather, a separate ticket must be purchased.
- Take a ride on public bus no. 100, Berlin's best sightseeing deal. It travels from Bahnhof Zoo through Tiergarten and Brandenburger Tor, continuing along Unter den Linden to Alexanderplatz and Prenzlauer Berg.
- Seek out churches for music virtually every day of the week, either for free or for a small fee.

Western Berlin

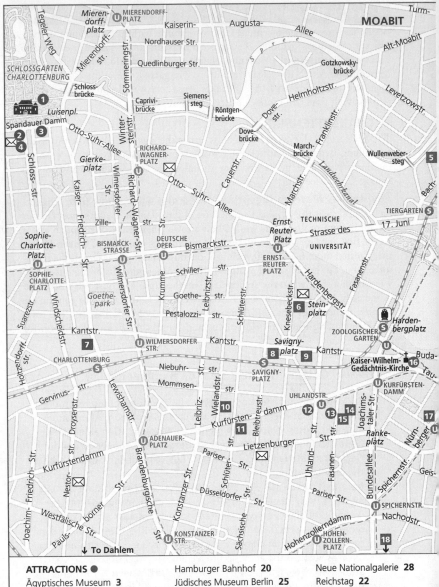

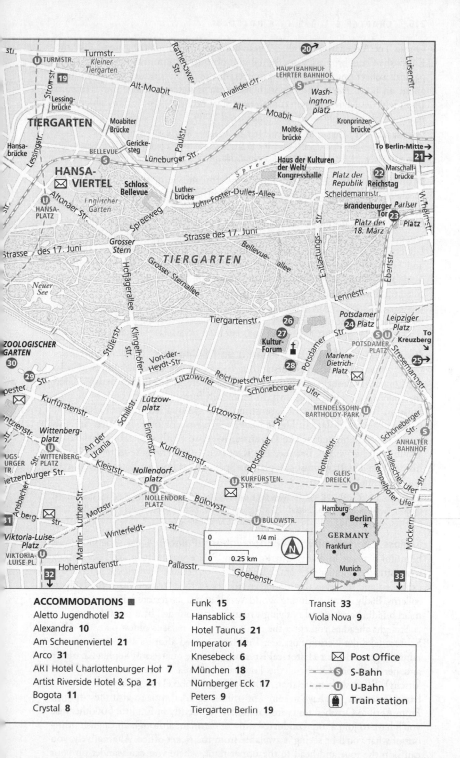

ACCOMMODATIONS ■

Aletto Jugendhotel **32**
Alexandra **10**
Am Scheunenviertel **21**
Arco **31**
ART Hotel Charlottenburger Hof **7**
Artist Riverside Hotel & Spa **21**
Bogota **11**
Crystal **8**

Funk **15**
Hansablick **5**
Hotel Taunus **21**
Imperator **14**
Knesebeck **6**
München **18**
Nürnberger Eck **17**
Peters **9**
Tiergarten Berlin **19**

Transit **33**
Viola Nova **9**

☒ Post Office
Ⓢ S-Bahn
Ⓤ U-Bahn
🛆 Train station

Queen Tiy, Akhenaton's mother. There are many other amazing items, like the Kalabasha Gate, bronzes, vases, burial cult objects, a mummy and sarcophagi, a papyrus collection, and tools used in everyday life. You can tour the museum in about an hour. *Note:* The Egyptian Museum is slated to move into Museum Island's Neues Museum upon completion of its extensive renovation, which after many delays probably won't take place until 2009.

Schlossstrasse 70. ⓒ **030/343 57 311.** www.smpk.de. Admission 6€ ($6.90) adults, 3€ ($3.45) students and children. Tues–Sun 10am–6pm. U-Bahn: U-2 to Sophie-Charlotte-Platz or U-7 to Richard-Wagner-Platz (then a 10-min. walk). Bus: 109 or 145 to Luisenplatz/Schloss Charlottenburg.

Bröhan Museum 🌟🌟 *(Finds)*   This wonderful museum, one of my favorites, specializes in decorative objects of the Art Nouveau (Jugendstil in German) and Art Deco periods (1889–1939), with exquisite vases, figurines, glass, furniture, carpets, silver, paintings of artists belonging to the Berlin Secession, and other works of art arranged in drawing-room fashion, including an outstanding porcelain collection. You'll see glassware by Emile Gallé, furniture by Eugene Gaillard and Hector Guimard, and works by Belgian Art Nouveau artist Henry van de Velde and Vienna Secession artist Josef Hommann. You can easily spend a dream-filled 60 minutes wandering the rooms here.

Schlossstrasse 1a. ⓒ **030/32 69 06 00.** www.broehan-museum.de. Admission 4€ ($4.60) adults, 2€ ($2.30) students and children; more for special exhibits. Tues–Sun 10am–6pm. U-Bahn: U-2 to Sophie-Charlotte-Platz or U-7 to Richard-Wagner-Platz (then a 10-min. walk). Bus: 109 or 145 to Luisenplatz/Schloss Charlottenburg.

Die Sammlung Berggruen: Picasso und Seine Zeit 🌟🌟🌟   Across from the Egyptian Museum, this outstanding collection was previously on display in the London National Gallery but was moved here in 1996 after Berlin offered the collection a home of its own, in renovated former barracks built by August Stüler in 1859. It contains an astonishing 85 works by **Picasso,** from his student years in Madrid to late in life and covering his major periods. There are also works by contemporaries like **Cézanne, Matisse** (with one room devoted to about 12 of his works), **Braque,** and **Klee** (with pieces ranging from 1917 until his death in 1940). A must-see; plan on spending at least an hour here, more if you're mesmerized.

Schlossstrasse 1. ⓒ **030/326 958-15.** www.smpk.de. Admission 6€ ($6.90) adults, 3€ ($3.45) students and children. Tues–Sun 10am–6pm. U-Bahn: U-2 to Sophie-Charlotte-Platz or U-7 to Richard-Wagner-Platz (then a 10-min. walk). Bus: 109 or 145 to Luisenplatz/Schloss Charlottenburg.

Schloss Charlottenburg (Charlottenburg Palace) 🌟🌟🌟   Berlin's most beautiful baroque building, Charlottenburg Palace was built in 1695 for Sophia Charlotte, the popular wife of the future king of Prussia, Frederick I. Later it was expanded and served as the summer residence of the Prussian kings, the Hohenzollerns. Badly damaged during World War II and since restored, it consists of one main building and several outlying structures, surrounded by a beautiful park.

Straight ahead as you enter the main gate is the palace's oldest part, the **Altes Schloss** (aka the Nering-Eosander Building, named after its architects). It contains the ground-floor **Historical Rooms,** once the quarters of Sophia Charlotte and her husband. Of these, the Porcelain Cabinet is the most striking (and kitschy), filled with more than 2,000 pieces of porcelain. Also of note is the baroque chapel. You have to join a 50-minute guided tour to visit these rooms. From April to October, tours are conducted frequently in English, but otherwise you'll have to join a tour conducted only in German, although an English printout of what you'll be seeing is available from the ticket office. Alternatively, you can skip the tour and head to the upper floor, where you can wander on your

A Memorial Update

Taking shape beside Berlin's most famous landmark, the Brandenburg Gate, is a Holocaust memorial dedicated to the six million Jews who perished under the Nazi regime. Designed by American architect Peter Eisenmann, the memorial, scheduled for completion in 2005, will consist of 2,700 concrete slabs of varying heights covering 2 city blocks.

own through rooms containing tapestries; goblets; swords; portraits of Sophie Charlotte, her husband Frederick, and their son (the so-called Soldier King); and other royal possessions, including the Hohenzollern insignia and a stunning silver place setting completed in 1914 but never used by the family because of the outbreak of World War I. If you join the guided tour, a visit to these rooms is included.

To the right of this building is the **Neuer Flügel** (New Wing, also called the Knobelsdorff Flügel), where you can wander through more royal quarters, the state dining hall, and the elaborate Golden Galerie, one of the prettiest rococo ballrooms in Germany. (An audioguide is included in the admission price.) Next head for the **Neuer Pavilion** (known locally as the Schinkel Pavilion) behind the New Wing. This delightful summer house, built in 1825 like an Italian villa and designed by Karl Friedrich Schinkel, Berlin's most important early-19th-century architect, has cozy rooms, each unique and decorated with period arts and crafts. After strolling through the beautiful park (laid out in the French style in 1697 and restored to its baroque form after World War II), visit the **Belvedere,** a former teahouse containing 18th- and 19th-century KPM (Königliche Porzellan-Manufaktur) Berlin porcelain. On the park's west side is the **Mausoleum,** built for Queen Luise in 1810 and also containing the tombs of her son, William I, the first German emperor. If you take the tour and see everything in the park, expect to spend at least 3 hours here.

Spandauer Damm. ② 030/32 09 14 40. www.spsg.de. Individual tickets: Altes Schloss with guided tour of Historical Rooms 8€ ($9.20) adults, 5€ ($5.75) students and children; upper floor of Altes Schloss without guided tour 2€ ($2.30) adults, 1.50€ ($1.75) students and children; Neuer Flügel 5€ ($5.75) adults, 4€ ($4.60) students and children; Neuer Pavilion or Belvedere each 2€ ($2.30) adults, 1.50€ ($1.75) students and children; Mausoleum 1€ ($1.15). Combination ticket to everything except guided tour 7€ ($8.05) adults, 5€ ($5.75) students and children. Altes Schloss (with Historical Rooms) Tues–Fri 9am–5pm, Sat–Sun 10am–5pm (you must enter by 4pm); Neuer Flügel Tues–Fri 10am–6pm, Sat–Sun 11am–6pm; Neuer Pavilion Tues–Sun 10am–5pm; Belvedere summer Tues–Sun 10am–5pm, winter Tues–Fri noon–4pm and Sat–Sun noon–5pm; Mausoleum Tues–Sun 10am–noon and 1–5pm (closed Nov–Mar). U-Bahn: U-2 to Sophie-Charlotte-Platz or U-7 to Richard-Wagner-Platz (then a 10-min. walk). Bus: 109 or 145 to Luisenplatz/Schloss Charlottenburg.

IN BERLIN-MITTE

I suggest you start with a stroll down **Unter den Linden** beginning at the Reichstag and Brandenburg Gate (S-Bahn: Unter den Linden; bus: 100), where you'll pass the **Neue Wache** (dedicated to victims of war and totalitarianism with a statue by Käthe Kollwitz) and the **German Historical Museum** before you reach Museumsinsel with the excellent Pergamon Museum. **Alexanderplatz,** the concrete modern heart of eastern Berlin, is a 5-minute walk farther west on Karl-Liebknecht-Strasse and where you'll find the TV tower with its great views. Nearby is the **Nikolai Quarter,** a reconstructed Old Berlin neighborhood, while **Oranienburger Strasse** and **Prenzlauer Berg** form the heart of Mitte's nightlife. Remember that the 6€ ($6.90) admission to the Pergamon, Alte Nationalgalerie, or Altes Museum entitles you to visit all three museums—and all other state-owned museums—on the same day.

Deutsches Historisches Museum (German Historical Museum) 🐱🐱

Housed in the oldest building on Unter den Linden, the 1695 Zeughaus (Arsenal), the national museum of German history is scheduled to reopen in 2005 with the ambitious goal of chronicling Germany's tumultuous past from the Middle Ages to the present day, utilizing both historic artifacts and audiovisual displays. Clothing, items used in daily life, photographs, furniture, maps, posters, military uniforms, weapons, and more breathe life into the political events, social upheavals, and cultural blossoming that have shaped German history over the past several centuries. The architectural gem of the museum is the inner courtyard with the masks of dying warriors by Andreas Schlüter, now topped by a glass roof. An addition by I. M. Pei houses special exhibitions. You'll spend at least an hour here.

Note: Contact the museum or Berlin Tourismus for a complete update on the museum's opening.

Unter den Linden 2. ℂ 030/20 30 40. www.dhm.de. Admission prices and open hours to be announced. S-/U-Bahn: Friedrichstrasse, Hackescher Markt. Bus: 100 or 200 to Staatsoper.

Pergamon Museum 🐱🐱🐱

Entrance to Berlin's most famous museum is via the bridge on Kupfergraben, behind and to the left of the Altes Museum. It's named after its most prized possession, the **Pergamon Altar,** which together with its frieze is a magnificent masterpiece of Hellenistic art of the 2nd century B.C., and certainly one of the wonders of the ancient world. Essentially a museum of architecture and antiquities, the Pergamon contains the impressive **Roman Market Gate of Milet,** as well as the dazzling **Babylonian Processional Way** leading to the **Gate of Ishtar,** created during Nebuchadnezzar's reign. Greek and Roman sculpture and Islamic art are also on display, including the **facade of Mshatta Palace** from Jordan. If you see only one museum on Museum Island, this should be it. An audioguide in English is included in the admission fee. Expect to spend a minimum of 1 hour here if you stick to the highlights.

Bodestrasse 1–3, on Museum Island. ℂ 030/20 90 50. www.smpk.de. Admission 6€ ($6.90) adults, 3€ ($3.45) students and children. Tues–Sun 10am–6pm (Thurs to 10pm). S-/U-Bahn: Friedrichstrasse, Hackescher Markt. Bus: 100 or 200 to Staatsoper.

Altes Museum

Resembling a Greek temple and designed by Berlin's greatest architect, Karl Friedrich Schinkel, this is Berlin's oldest museum and the first one you see on Museum Island if you approach from Unter den Linden. On its main floor is the **Antikensammlung,** a collection of ancient arts and crafts, primarily Greek and Roman antiquities, including pottery, figurines, statues, busts, glassware, jewelry, Greek helmets, and wood and stone sarcophagi. Outstanding are the **Attic red-figure vases** of the 5th century B.C. and the **treasury** with its silver and exquisite gold jewelry from about 2000 B.C. to late antiquity. To learn more about what you're seeing, be sure to take advantage of the audioguide, included in the admission fee. You'll spend at least 30 minutes here. Special exhibits are held on the upper floor.

On Museum Island. ℂ 030/20 90 5801. www.smpk.de. Admission 6€ ($6.90) adults, 3€ ($3.45) students and children. Tues–Sun 10am–6pm. S-Bahn: Hackescher Markt (the closest), Alexanderplatz, or Friedrichstrasse. Bus: 100 or 200 to Lustgarten.

Alte Nationalgalerie 🐱🐱

Located behind the Altes Museum in an impressive 1876 building, this museum is devoted to 19th-century painting, primarily

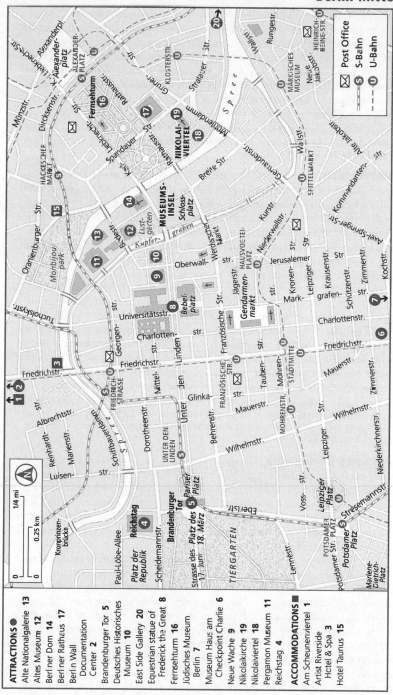

Berlin-Mitte

by artists from Germany but also those from other European countries, including French Impressionists. Of special note is the world's largest collection of works by Berlin artist **Adolph von Menzel.** There are also 19th-century romantic, classical, and Biedermeier paintings, including works by Caspar David Friedrich and Schinkel. Other artists represented include **Waldmüller, Max Liebermann, Lovis Corinth, Max Beckmann, Courbet, Delacroix, Degas, Renoir, Pissarro, Cézanne, van Gogh,** and **Monet.** This gem of a museum can be toured in about an hour.

On Museum Island. (*C*) **030/20 90 50.** www.smpk.de. Admission 6€ ($6.90) adults, 3€ ($3.45) students and children. Tues–Sun 10am–6pm (Thurs to 10pm). S-Bahn: Hackescher Markt (the closest), Alexanderplatz, or Friedrichstrasse. Bus: 100 or 200 to Lustgarten.

Berliner Dom   The most striking structure on Museum Island, this cathedral was built in the early 1900s in Italian Renaissance style to serve as the central church for Prussian Protestants and as the court church and primary burial site of the Hohenzollern imperial family. Severely damaged during World War II, it took decades to restore. Of special note are the gilded **wall altar of the 12 Apostles** by Schinkel; the impressive **Sauer organ** with more than 7,000 pipes; and the ornate **ceremonial coffins** of Frederick I and his wife, Sophie Charlotte, designed by Andreas Schlüter. The basement crypt, the final resting place of Frederick I and Sophie Charlotte, also contains coffins of their children. Worship service is held Sunday and holidays at 10am (English translation via earphones available) and at 6pm, while a musical service in German and English is held Thursday at 6pm. Organ concerts and other performances are given year-round, including Saturday at 6pm—pick up a schedule at the cathedral. Otherwise, because admission is so high (most churches in Germany are free), I think you're better off spending the 30 minutes or so needed to tour this cathedral somewhere else, unless you have a special interest in religious architecture.

In the Lustgarten, on Museum Island. (*C*) **030/20 26 91 36.** www.berliner-dom.de. Admission 5€ ($5.75) adults, 3€ ($3.45) students and seniors, free for children under 14. Mon–Sat 9am–7pm; Sun and holidays noon–7pm (to 6pm in winter). You must enter an hour before closing. S-Bahn: Hackescher Markt or Alexanderplatz. Bus: 100 or 200 to Lustgarten.

Reichstag (Parliament)   Completed in 1894 in neo-Renaissance style to serve as the German house of parliament, the Reichstag had its darkest hour on the night of February 17, 1933, when a mysterious fire broke out that was blamed on the German Communist Party and was used as an excuse by the Nazi government to arrest dissidents and abolish basic democratic rights. Heavily damaged in World War II, it was rebuilt with the exception of a glass cupola that had adorned its center.

The Reichstag again became home of German lawmakers after the fall of the Wall and German reunification in 1990. Following a ceremonial wrapping by artist Christo in 1995, it underwent extensive renovation, including a new glass dome by British architect Sir Norman Foster. Today, you can enter the main (west) entrance for an elevator ride up to the impressive glass dome and its spiraling ramp, with panoramic views from an observation platform and a rooftop restaurant (open daily 9am–4:30pm). A photographic display chronicles the Reichstag's history. Try to arrive early in the morning; until every German has visited, you can expect long lines at the entrance.

Platz der Republik 1. (*C*) **030/22 73 21 52.** Free admission. Daily 8am–midnight (you must enter by 10pm). S-Bahn: Unter den Linden. Bus: 100 or 200 to Reichstag.

Tracing the Wall

The hideous 161km-long (100-mile-long) **Berlin Wall,** built in 1961 to prevent East Germans from fleeing into the sanctity of West Berlin, was reinforced by hundreds of guardhouses, 293 watchtowers, patrol dogs, and a vast swath of no-man's-land. Today the wall is history, but if you're wondering where it once stood, it divided the city into eastern and western sectors at the Brandenburg Gate and stretched roughly north and south from there—its location is now best identified by a string of massive construction sites.

The **Museum Haus am Checkpoint Charlie** and the **AlliiertenMuseum** (p. 222 and p. 226, respectively) are the best places to gain an understanding of what life was like during the Cold War. If you have time, there's also the **Berlin Wall Documentation Center** on Bernauer Strasse (© **030/464 10 30;** www.berliner-mauer-dokumentationszentrum.de; U-Bahn: Bernauer Strasse; S-Bahn: Nordbahnhof). Bernauer Strasse was one of Berlin's most notorious streets during the Cold War, divided its entire length into East and West, with buildings on the East empty and boarded up. Here you'll find a chapel (built on the site of a former church blown up by the Communists in 1985), a Berlin Wall memorial, and a Documentation Center with photographs and other items chronicling in English the historical and political background of the Wall and presenting a personal view of what the Wall meant for Berliners on both sides. The center is open Wednesday to Sunday 10am to 5pm, and admission is free.

A few sections of the Wall have been left standing, most notably on **Niederkirchnerstrasse** (not far from the Museum Haus am Checkpoint Charlie; S-/U-Bahn: Potsdamer Platz), where a 250m (820-ft.) section remains. But the most colorful remainder of the Wall is in former East Berlin on **Mühlenstrasse** (S-Bahn: Ostbahnhof; U-Bahn: Warschauer Strasse). Called the **East Side Gallery,** this kilometer-long section on the banks of the Spree was painted on its east side with more than 100 murals by international artists in 1990. The murals are now a bit faded and chipped, though some artists restored their murals in 2000.

Brandenburger Tor (Brandenburg Gate) During the decades of the Wall, the Brandenburger Tor stood in no-man's-land, marking the boundary of East and West Berlin and becoming the symbol of a divided Germany. After the November 1989 revolution and the fall of the Wall, many Berliners gathered here to rejoice and dance on top of the Wall. The gate was built from 1788 to 1791 by Carl Gotthard Langhans as the grand western entrance onto Unter den Linden. One of the guardhouses serves as a non-denominational **Room of Silence,** a place for reflection; the other is home to a **Berlin tourist office,** open daily 10am to 6pm.

On Unter den Linden. Free admission. Room of Silence summer daily 11am–6pm, winter daily 11am–4pm. S-Bahn: Unter den Linden. Bus: 100 or 200 to Unter den Linden/Brandenburger Tor.

IN KREUZBERG

Jüdisches Museum Berlin (Jewish Museum Berlin) ✶✶✶ *Kids* Opened in 2001 and quickly becoming a top attraction, this addition to the city's roster of impressive museums was designed by Daniel Libeskind, the son of Holocaust refugees. The zinc-clad building's jagged, zigzagging structure (resembling, perhaps, a deconstructed Star of David, and slashed by hundreds of asymmetrical windows) houses collections chronicling 2,000 years of German-Jewish history, from Roman times to the present. Through photographs, artwork, historic artifacts, religious objects, and audiovisual displays, visitors learn about Jewish emigration to Europe 2,000 years ago; the persecution of Jews in medieval times; the integration of Jews in Germany; Jewish life in Berlin; the development of Jewish community and religious life; and Jewish contributions to German culture, politics, economy, and science. Small rooms scattered throughout the museum are designed especially for children, allowing them to enjoy the museum from a different level. Although the Holocaust is addressed, this is far more than a Holocaust museum. Expect to spend up to 2 hours here.

Lindenstrasse 9–14. (© 030/25 99 33-00. www.jmberlin.de. Admission 5€ ($5.75) adults, 2.50€ ($2.85) children, 10€ ($12) families. Mon 10am–10pm; Tues–Sun 10am–8pm. U-Bahn: Hallesches Tor or Kochstrasse. Bus: 129, 240, or 341.

Museum Haus am Checkpoint Charlie 🟊🟊🟊 *Moments*   This is by far the best museum for gaining an understanding of what life was like before, during, and after the fall of the Wall—if you have never been to Berlin before, don't miss it. Near what was once the most frequently used border crossing into East Berlin, Checkpoint Charlie, this collection documents events that took place around the Berlin Wall, including successful and failed attempts to escape East Berlin. With displays in English, the museum aptly illustrates these years in Berlin's history with photographs, items used in escape attempts (such as cars with hidden compartments), videos, artwork, and newspaper clippings. The fall of the wall and the demise of communism in East Germany, Russia, Poland, and Hungary are also documented, and part of the museum is devoted to nonviolent struggles for human rights around the world, including those led by Gandhi, Walesa, and Martin Luther King Jr. Expect to spend a minimum of an hour here, more if you become engrossed in the fascinating displays and newspaper clippings.

Friedrichstrasse 43–45. (© 030/25 37 25 0. www.mauermuseum.de. Admission 7.50€ ($8.60) adults, 4.50€ ($5.15) students and children. Daily 9am–10pm. U-Bahn: Kochstrasse. Bus: 129 to Kochstrasse.

IN THE TIERGARTEN & POTSDAMER PLATZ

Filmmuseum Berlin   This visually rich museum, with explanations in English, chronicles 100 years of the German film industry, with movie clips, photographs, props, and mementos. You'll view movie clips from such classics as Fritz Lang's *Metropolis* or *M* with Peter Lorre; read about silent film stars like Asta Nielsen and Henny Porten; see tricks used in special effects; and learn about the role of cinema during the Nazi regime and the exodus of film personalities to Hollywood. A highlight of the museum is its Marlene Dietrich exhibit, which displays the star's designer gowns and costumes (with clips showing her wearing them), stills, off-screen shots, and personal items such as her makeup case and luggage. The high admission price makes it a must only for film buffs; the museum takes about an hour or so to see.

In the Sony Center, Potsdamer Strasse 2. (© 030/300 90 30. www.filmmuseum-berlin.de. Admission 6€ ($6.90) adults, 4€ ($4.60) college students with school ID, 3€ ($3.45) children, 14€ ($16) families. Tues–Sun 10am–6pm (to 8pm Thurs). S-/U-Bahn: Potsdamer Platz. Bus: 148 or 348.

Gemäldegalerie (Picture Gallery) 🟊🟊🟊   Housed in a modern structure utilizing natural light, Berlin's top art museum offers a comprehensive survey of

European painting from the 13th to the 18th century, presented in chronological order and grouped geographically. Exhibits begin with German paintings of the 13th to the 16th century and include works by **Albrecht Dürer, Lucas Cranach,** and **Holbein the Elder and the Younger.** One of my favorites is Cranach's *Fountain of Youth (Der Jungbrunnen),* which shows old women being led to the fountain, swimming through, and emerging youthful and beautiful. Note that apparently only women need the bath—men regain their youth through relations with younger women! Other highlights are Cranach's *The Last Judgment,* eight paintings by Dürer, and Holbein the Younger's **portrait of merchant Georg Gisze.**

The next sections contain one of the museum's most important collections, Netherlandish paintings of the 15th and 16th centuries, with works by Jan van Eyck, Rogier van der Weyden, and Pieter Bruegel. Look for Bruegel's *100 Proverbs (100 Sprichwörter),* a delight with peasants engaged in proverbial activities—see how many proverbs you can detect, such as "No use crying over spilled milk." The top attractions of the Flemish and Dutch paintings collection are works by **Peter Paul Rubens** and some 20 paintings by **Rembrandt.** Look for Rembrandt's self-portrait and (my favorite) portrait of Hendrickje Stoffels, his common-law wife—the intimacy of their relationship is captured in her face as she gazes at Rembrandt. The famous *Man with the Golden Helmet,* however, is no longer attributed to Rembrandt. Finally, the art lover is treated to works by English, French, and Italian masters, including **Gainsborough, Watteau, Botticelli, Raphael, Tiepolo, Titian, Murillo,** and **Velázquez.**

Of course, this is only a fraction of what the museum offers. You might want to take advantage of free audioguides for the most significant pieces, but even then you'll have to tailor your visit to your interests—the entire tape lasts 8 hours.

Matthäiskirchplatz 4. © 030/266 29 51. www.smpk.de. Admission 6€ ($6.90) adults, 3€ ($3.45) students and children. Tues–Sun 10am–6pm (to 10pm Thurs). S-/U-Bahn: Potsdamer Platz. Bus: 129 from Ku'damm to Potsdamer Brücke.

Hamburger Bahnhof, Museum für Gegenwart (Museum for Contemporary Art) ✸✸

North of the Tiergarten, this 19th-century former train station lends itself perfectly to the massive installations of sculpture, paintings, and other works of contemporary art gracing the spacious halls and upstairs galleries. One room is devoted to works by **Keith Haring** (unless the room is taken over by a special exhibit), while another big hall, dominated by **Andy Warhol**'s huge portrait of Mao Tse-tung, also features works by **Rauschenberg** and **Lichtenstein.** Other artists represented here are **Nam June Paik, Cy Twombly, Anselm Kiefer, Jeff Koons, Sandro Chia, Mondrian,** and **Julian Schnabel,** but again, changing exhibits often change what's on view at any one time. The star is conceptual artist **Joseph Beuys,** with more than 450 drawings from his comprehensive *Secret Block for a Secret Person in Ireland;* a number of his installations; and a film showing him at work. The museum also houses the world's most extensive collection by Bruce Naumann.

Note: During special exhibits, the Tageskarte and SchauLust ticket aren't valid for this museum, nor is the ticket you purchase here valid for any other museum.

Invalidenstrasse 50–51. © **030/397 83 412.** www.smpk.de. Admission 6€ ($6.90) adults, 3€ ($3.45) students and children; more for special exhibits. Tues–Fri 10am–6pm; Sat–Sun 11am–6pm. S-Bahn: Lehrter Bahnhof.

Kunstgewerbe Museum (Museum of Applied Arts) ✸

This museum, next to the Gemäldegalerie in a modern red-brick edifice built for the collection,

Special & Free Events

Berlin festivals revolve around the cultural calendar, beginning with the prestigious **International Film Festival** held in February. The **Lesbian and Gay Street Festival,** one of Europe's largest, takes place in mid-June at Nollendorplatz. Beer lovers rejoice in the **Berlin International Beer Festival,** held in August on Karl-Marx-Allee and featuring almost 200 breweries from more than 70 countries. The **Berlin Jazzfest,** in early November, attracts musicians from Europe and the United States. But Berlin's most popular event for young revelers is the July **Love Parade,** in which several dozen 18-wheeler trucks blasting music and covered with partyers snake their way through the Tiergarten in what is billed as the world's largest gathering for fans of techno music.

If you come any time from the end of November to Christmas Eve, you'll be treated to several colorful **Christmas Markets,** the largest of which is in Spandau with some 280 booths selling homemade arts and crafts. There are also Christmas Markets at Gendarmenmarkt, on Alexanderplatz, and around the Kaiser Wilhelm Memorial Church. New Year's Eve, complete with music and fireworks, is celebrated at Brandenburg Gate.

The best place to turn for information about all events is **Berlin Tourismus** (see "Visitor Information," earlier in this chapter) and its website www.berlin-tourist-information.de.

is devoted to European applied arts from the early Middle Ages to the present, including the Renaissance, baroque, rococo, Jugendstil (German Art Nouveau), and Art Deco periods. Displayed are glassware, porcelain, silver, furniture, jewelry, and clothing. The collection of medieval goldsmiths' works is outstanding, as are the displays of Venetian glass; early Meissen and KPM porcelain; and Jugendstil vases, porcelain, furniture, and objects. The bottom floor has changing exhibits of contemporary crafts and product design, from typewriters to teapots to furniture.

Matthäiskirchplatz. (© 030/266 29 51. www.smpk.de. Admission 3€ ($3.45) adults, 1.50€ ($1.75) students and children. Tues–Fri 10am–6pm; Sat–Sun 11am–6pm. S-/U-Bahn: Potsdamer Platz. Bus: 129 from Ku'damm to Potsdamer Brücke.

Neue Nationalgalerie (New National Gallery) *Overrated* This was one of the first museums to open in the new museum area near the Tiergarten, in 1968. A starkly modern building designed by Mies van der Rohe and set into a vast square surrounded by a sculpture garden, the Nationalgalerie houses art of the 20th century until about 1970. The permanent collection, in the basement, shows German expressionist, realist, abstract, and cubist art, with works by **Munch, Kokoschka, Ernst Ludwig Kirchner, Otto Dix, Picasso, René Magritte, Dalí, Max Beckmann, Max Ernst, Paul Klee, Lyonel Feininger,** and **Frank Stella.** Frequent special exhibitions, however, some of them very good, can severely curtail the permanent exhibit or close it altogether. Check what's showing; if the special exhibition is not to your interest, skip this museum. Otherwise, expect to spend about an hour here.

Potsdamer Strasse 50. (© **030/266 26 51**. www.smpk.de. Admission 6€ ($6.90) adults, 3€ ($3.45) students and children; more for special exhibits. Tues–Fri 10am–6pm (to 10pm Thurs); Sat–Sun 11am–6pm. S-/U-Bahn: Potsdamer Platz. Bus: 129 from Ku'damm to Potsdamer Brücke.

NEAR THE KU'DAMM

Kaiser-Wilhelm Gedächtniskirche (Kaiser Wilhelm Memorial Church)

Completed in 1895 as a memorial to Kaiser Wilhelm I, this church was destroyed by bombs during World War II and left in ruins as a reminder of the horrors of war. Today it contains a small museum with displays and photos related to war and destruction. Beside the ruined church is a new church designed by Prof. Egon Eiermann and finished in 1961; come here for free organ concerts Saturday at 6pm.

Breit-scheidplatz. (© **030/218 50 23**. www.gedaechtniskirche.com. Free admission. Ruined church Mon–Sat 10am–4pm; new church daily 9am–7pm; organ concerts in new church Sat 6pm. U-Bahn: Zoologischer Garten or Kurfürstendamm.

Käthe-Kollwitz Museum *(Finds)*

This small but significant museum shows the powerful drawings, sketches, and sculptures of Käthe Kollwitz (1867–1945), a Berliner who managed to capture human emotions both tender and disturbing in her subjects, mostly the working class. War, poverty, death, hunger, love, grief, and happiness are all deftly rendered with just a few strokes. Who can forget Kollwitz's portrayal of horror on the face of a mother whose child has just been run over or the wonderment expressed by a young mother and her infant gazing into each other's eyes? If you want to know more about her, rent the 2€ ($2.30) audiotape for a 1-hour self-guided tour.

Fasanenstrasse 24 (just off Ku'damm). (© **030/882 52 10**. www.kaethe-kollwitz.de. Admission 5€ ($5.75) adults, 2.50€ ($2.85) students and children. Wed–Mon 11am–6pm. U-Bahn: Uhlandstrasse. Bus: 109, 119, 129, 219, or 249.

The Story of Berlin *(*)*

This multimedia extravaganza ambitiously attempts to portray 8 centuries of the city's history through photos, films, sounds, and colorful displays. Beginning with the founding of Berlin in 1237, it chronicles the plague, the Thirty Years' War, Frederick the Great's reign, military life, the Industrial Revolution and the working poor, the Golden 1920s, World War II, divided Berlin during the Cold War, and the fall of the Wall. Hidden loudspeakers heighten the effects: In a 19th-century tenement courtyard, for example, you hear a dog barking, a baby crying, and other sounds of a densely packed neighborhood, while the sound of breaking glass accompanies a display on Nazis and their treatment of Jews. Lights flash in a media blitz as you enter the display on the fall of the Wall, making you feel like one of the first East Berliners to wonderingly cross to the West. Conclude your tour on the 14th floor with a panoramic view over today's Berlin. Be sure, too, to join the 30-minute tour of the underground bunker built in 1974 at the height of the Cold War to house 3,500 people. Luckily it was never used, since there was only enough food, water, and self-generated power to last 2 weeks. Although the displays are a bit jarring and the historical information is too jumbled to be truly educational, the museum does leave a lasting impression. Allow at least 2 hours.

Ku'damm-Karree, Kurfürstendamm 207–208 (at the corner of Uhlandstrasse). (© **030/88 72 01 00**. www.story-of-berlin.de. Admission 9.30€ ($11) adults, 7.50€ ($8.65) college students, 3.50€ ($4) children, 21€ ($24) families. Daily 10am–8pm (you must enter by 6pm). U-Bahn: Uhlandstrasse. Bus: 109, 110, 119, or 129.

Zoologischer Garten (Berlin Zoo) *(Kids)*

Founded in 1844, the Berlin Zoo is one of Europe's most attractive—and one of my favorites. Just a short walk from the Ku'damm or Bahnhof Zoo, it's home to more than 11,000 animals of almost 2,000 species and is a beautiful oasis in the middle of the city. The aquarium contains more than 10,000 fish (including sharks), reptiles, and amphibians, but since the combination ticket is quite expensive, I recommend seeing only the zoo if you're on a tight budget. Since it's fairly small by today's standards, you can see most of it in a couple of hours—unless you have children.

Budapester Strasse 32 and Hardenbergplatz 8. (© 030/25 40 10. www.zoo-berlin.de. Combination ticket for zoo and aquarium 14€ ($16) adults, 11€ ($13) college students, 7€ ($8.05) children; ticket to zoo only 9€ ($10) adults, 7€ ($8.05) college students, 4.50€ ($5.15) children. Summer daily 9am–6:30pm (to 5pm in winter). S-/U-Bahn: Zoologischer Garten.

IN ZEHLENDORF

AlliiertenMuseum (Allied Museum)   This museum in the heart of the former U.S. military sector documents Berlin's nearly 50 years of Allied occupation (1945–94). Occupying a former base library and cinema, it's easily recognizable by a cargo plane, used during the Berlin Airlift, on its grounds, as well as a guard tower, a section of the Berlin Wall, a building from Checkpoint Charlie, and other symbols of the Cold War. Begin at the cinema, which chronicles the end of World War II and the division of Berlin. The rest of the museum illustrates the changing role of the Western Allies (U.S., British, French), who arrived as an occupying power but gradually became protectors against Stalin and helped shape Germany into a democracy.

Clayallee 135. (© 030/81 81 99-0. www.alliiertenmuseum.de. Free admission. Thurs–Tues 10am–6pm. U-Bahn: Oskar-Helene-Heim. Bus: 115 or 183 to Alliiertenmuseum.

ORGANIZED TOURS

BUS TOURS   Sightseeing tours of Berlin and Potsdam are offered by a number of companies, with buses departing from the Ku'damm area. The oldest and largest is **Severin + Kuhn,** Kurfürstendamm 216 ((© **030/880 41 90;** www.severin-kuehn-berlin.de), open daily 8am to 7pm. Among its many tour options, the best for independent travelers is its 18€ ($21) "Berlin City Circle Tour," which provides commentary but allows you to disembark at more than a dozen stops and reboard the next bus at your convenience (or you can remain on the bus for the entire 2-hr. circuit). Buses run every 15 minutes from 10am to 4pm in summer and every 15 to 30 minutes 10am to 3pm in winter. Stops include the Ku'damm, the KaDeWe department store, Tiergarten museums, Potsdamer Platz, the Jewish Museum, Checkpoint Charlie, Alexanderplatz, Unter den Linden, the Brandenburg Gate, and Charlottenburg Palace. Tickets are valid for 1 day.

BOAT TOURS   May through September, you can climb aboard one of the many pleasure boats plying the Spree River and Havel and Wannsee lakes. One of the largest companies is **Reederei Riedel** ((© **030/691 37 82;** www.reederei-riedel.de), offering 1½-hour trips through Berlin-Mitte with departures from Haus der Kulturen der Welt in the Tiergarten and costing 6.50€ ($7.50) for adults and 3.50€ ($4) for children. **Reederei Bruno Winkler** ((© **030/349 95 95;** www.reedereiwinkler.de) offers 3-hour boat tours through Berlin-Mitte for 14€ ($16), with departures from Schlossbrücke near Charlottenburg Palace at 11am and 3pm daily.

WALKING TOURS   The Original Berlin Walks ((© **030/301 91 94;** www.berlinwalks.com) offers four tours in English, with departures from the Bahnhof Zoo taxi stand. The "Discover Berlin Walk," a 3- to 4-hour general tour taking in the sights of old and new Berlin, departs daily throughout the year at 10am and also at 2:30pm April through October. It costs 12€ ($14) for those 26 and older, and 9€ ($10) for those under 26 (children under 14 are free). Other tours, offered different days of the week April to October and lasting approximately 3 hours, take in the infamous sites of the Third Reich or of Jewish Berlin; the cost of these are 10€ ($12) and 7.50€ ($8.65) respectively. A fourth tour is to a former Nazi concentration camp in Sachsenhausen, lasting approximately 6 hours and costing 15€ ($17) for those 26 and older, and 11€ ($13) for those under 26. There's no need to book in advance; pick up a brochure at the tourist office or EurAide.

5 Shopping

If it exists, you can buy it in Berlin. A look inside **KaDeWe,** established in 1907 and the largest department store on the Continent, made a believer out of me. Start your shopping in KaDeWe, on Wittenbergplatz—with an inventory of 380,000 items and visited by 80,000 shoppers daily, it might be as far as you get.

But that would mean you'd miss the shop-lined **Tauentzienstrasse,** which leads from KaDeWe to the **Ku'damm,** the showcase of Berlin's fashionable boutiques and art galleries. Some of the stores may be a bit pricey, but window-shopping and people-watching are free. Natives head for the pedestrians-only **Wilmersdorfer Strasse,** with its department stores and countless boutiques and restaurants. **Friedrichstrasse,** in Berlin-Mitte, now rivals the Ku'damm with its expensive shops, including the Galeries Lafayette department store and the upscale Quartier 206 shopping mall. **Potsdamer Platz,** once Berlin's busiest intersection and a no-man's-land during the Cold War, is home to the **Arkaden,** an American-style shopping mall with more than 120 stores and restaurants.

Typical souvenirs are stuffed toy bears (the city mascot), Wall fragments, toy Trabants (a former East German car, now virtually extinct), and the Brandenburg Gate pictured on ashtrays and bowls. Most department stores have souvenir sections, as do the tourist offices in the Europa-Center, Brandenburg Gate, and Alexanderplatz. If kitsch doesn't appeal to you, Germany is known for kitchen gadgets and cutlery, linens, those luxuriously fluffy *Federbetten* (feather beds), binoculars and telescopes, cameras, and toys (model trains, tin soldiers, and building blocks). If you like porcelain, brands to look for are Rosenthal, antique Meissen, and Berlin's own Königliche Porzellan-Manufaktur (better known as KPM)—assuming, of course, you have a Swiss bank account.

Berlin's most unique buys are found at the many antiques and flea markets. Some are indoors and are held almost daily; others are open just 1 or 2 days a week. Under the arches of the elevated track, the indoor **Berliner Antik- und Flohmarkt,** on Georgenstrasse between the Friedrichstrasse S-Bahn station and the Pergamon Museum (© **030/208 26 55**), features more than 60 vendors of antiques and curios, including jewelry, porcelain, glassware, dolls, silver, books, lamps, and odds and ends. Prices are relatively high, but you might find a bargain. If you get thirsty, drop by **Die Nolle** (located inside the Antik-und Flohmarkt), a 1920s-style pub/restaurant with outdoor seating. The market is open Wednesday to Monday 11am to 6pm. A minute's walk east of the Tiergarten S-Bahn station is Berlin's best-known and biggest outdoor market, the **Grosser/Berliner Trödelmarkt und Kunstmarkt (Art and Junk Market),** on Strasse des 17 Juni (© **030/26 55 00 96**). A staggering selection of books, CDs, silverware, coins, stamps, china, glass, original artwork, jewelry, clothing, and junk is sold at this market divided into two parts: one with antiques and junk;

the other, across the bridge, with arts and crafts. The market is open Saturday and Sunday 10am to 4pm.

Kreuzberg is home to most of the city's Turkish population, so there you'll find Berlin's most colorful produce market, the **Turkish Market.** Spread along the bank of the Maybachufer Canal, it offers a taste of the exotic, with German and Turkish vendors selling vegetables, fish, sheep's-milk cheese, pita bread, beans, rice, spices, clothing, household goods, bolts of cloth, and odds and ends. The market is open Tuesday and Friday noon to 6:30pm; Friday's markets are livelier, with more vendors. Take the U-Bahn to Kottbusser Tor; from there it's about a 5-minute walk.

Winterfeldplatz, in Schöneberg, is Berlin's largest weekly market of fruits, vegetables, meat, olives, spices, flowers, clothing, and accessories; it's a 5-minute walk south of the Nollendorfplatz U-Bahn station. The biggest market day is Saturday from 8am to 1pm, with a smaller market also on Wednesday. December 1 to Christmas Eve, a **Weihnachtsmarkt** is held in various parts of the city, including the Altstadt of Spandau, Alexanderplatz and Gendarmenmarkt in Berlin-Mitte, and around the Kaiser-Wilhelm Gedächtniskirche on the Ku'damm.

6 Berlin After Dark

Berlin never sleeps. There are no mandatory closing hours for nightclubs, dance clubs, and bars, so you can stay out all night if you want. In fact, a native Berliner once told me, "The reason everyone comes to Berlin is its nightlife"— and he was serious. In any case, no self-respecting reveler dreams of hitting the town before 10pm.

Nightlife in Berlin means everything from far-out bars and dance clubs to world-renowned opera and theater. To find out what's going on in the performing arts, pick up a copy of *ExBerliner* or *Berlin in Your Pocket.* If you read German, a more thorough publication is the monthly *Berlin Programm,* while *tip* and *zitty* are two city magazines covering alternative nightlife and events.

THE PERFORMING ARTS

If you don't mind taking a chance on what's available, the best bargain for last-minute tickets is **Hekticket,** with outlets at Hardenbergstrasse 29d, across from Bahnhof Zoo on Hardenbergplatz on the corner of Deutsche Bank (© **030/230 99 30;** S-/U-Bahn: Bahnhof Zoologischer Garten); and at Karl-Liebknecht-strasse 12, opposite McDonald's near Alexanderplatz (© **030/24 31 24 31;** S-/U-Bahn: Alexanderplatz). Unsold tickets for that evening's performances are available for more than 100 venues, including the Staatsoper Unter den Linden, Komische Oper, classical concerts, pop concerts, and cabaret, most at up to 50% off. The Hardenbergplatz office is open Monday to Saturday 10am to 8pm and Sunday 2 to 6pm, while the Alexanderplatz office is open Monday to Saturday noon to 8pm. If you want to know whether tickets for a performance are available, call first or look on the Internet at **www.hekticket.de.**

If you have your heart set on a specific performance and don't mind paying a commission, you can find a convenient ticket box office at **Centrum,** Meinekestrasse 25 (© **030/882 76 11;** U-Bahn: Kurfürstendamm). **Berlin Tourismus** in the Europa Center also sells tickets, or you can make online bookings at **www.btm.de.** Finally, tickets for theater and opera, often with student and senior discounts, are also available during box office hours and about an hour before the performance starts at the venue itself.

OPERA   The **Deutsche Oper Berlin,** Bismarckstrasse 35, Charlottenburg
((C) **030/341 02 49** for information, or 0700-67 37 23 75 46 for tickets; www.
deutscheoperberlin.de; U-Bahn: Deutsche Oper), is the largest of Berlin's three
opera houses. Works by Mozart, Verdi, and Wagner are perennial favorites, but
it also cultivates forgotten operas and works of the 20th century, staging opera
virtually every evening except when there's ballet. Tickets for most performances
run 17€ to 65€ ($20–$75), with a 25% reduction for children, students, and
seniors available up to 1 week before the performance. On the night of the performance, children and students can buy unsold tickets for 10€ ($12; not avail-
able for all productions). The box office is open Monday to Saturday 11am to
the start of the performance and Sunday 10am to 2pm.

The **Staatsoper Unter den Linden,** Unter den Linden 7, Berlin-Mitte
((C) **030/20 35 44 38** for information, or 030/20 35 45 55 for tickets; www.
staatsoper-berlin.de; U-Bahn: Friedrichstrasse or Französische Strasse; bus: 100
or 200), has long been one of Berlin's famous opera houses, featuring opera, ballet, and concerts under the musical direction of conductor Daniel Barenboim.
Tickets go for 8€ to 80€ ($9.20–$92) for most performances, with a 50%
reduction for students and a 25% reduction for seniors. The box office is open
Monday to Friday 11am to 7pm and Saturday and Sunday 2 to 7pm, and the
hour before performances.

The **Komische Oper (Comic Opera),** Behrenstrasse 55–57, Berlin-Mitte
((C) **030/20 260-666** for information, 030/47 99 74 00 for tickets; www.
komische-oper-berlin.de; S-Bahn: Unter den Linden; U-Bahn: Französische
Strasse; bus: 100), an innovative musical theater company, serves as an alternative
to the grander mainstream productions of the two other opera houses, presenting
a varied program of opera, operetta, symphony concerts, ballet, and even modern
dance. Tickets cost 8€ to 62€ ($9.20–$71) for most performances. The box office
at Unter den Linden 41 is open Monday to Saturday 11am to 7pm and Sunday
1pm to 2 hours before the performance begins. You can also buy tickets for that
evening's performance at the venue itself an hour before the performance begins.

THEATER & CABARET   Popular productions, musicals, and spirited revues
are presented in the attractive early-1900s **Theater des Westens,** Kantstrasse 12
(near the Ku'damm), Charlottenburg ((C) **030/319 03-0;** S-/U-Bahn: Zoologischer Garten). Tickets begin at 16€ to 27€ ($18–$31) depending on the production, with reductions sometimes given Sunday and weekday evenings. The
box office is open Monday to Saturday 11am to 7pm and Sunday 2 to 5pm.

Berlin has a long history of cabaret delivered with political and social satire,
with most performances only in German. One that often features troupes from
the United States, England, and Australia, however, in addition to German
cabaret, with lots of revues, chanson evenings, comedies, and other musical performances, is **Bar Jeder Vernunft,** Schaperstrasse 24 ((C) **030/883 15 82;** www.
bar-jeder-vernunft.de; U-Bahn: Spichernstrasse), housed in a unique Jugendstil
circus tent from the 1920s and offering dinner as well. In summer there's an
outdoor beer garden. Tickets cost 17€ to 26€ ($19–$29), plus a 15% commission on advance tickets; you can save on commission by showing up when
the doors open at 7pm and buying your ticket then if any are still available; or
by coming for the Friday or Saturday 11:30pm show at 14€ ($16). In any case,
it's best to call to ask about the program and availability of tickets. The box office
is open Monday to Saturday noon to 7pm and Sunday 4 to 7pm.

CLASSICAL & CHURCH MUSIC   Performances of the world-renowned
Berliner Philharmonisches Orchester (Berlin Philharmonic Orchestra), founded

in 1882, take place at the **Philharmonie** in the Kulturforum, Herbert-von-Karajan-Strasse 1 ((C) **030/25488-132;** S-/U-Bahn: Potsdamer Platz; bus: 129, 148, 200, 248, or 348). Tickets begin at 14€ ($12), but those for the Berlin Philharmonic usually sell out months in advance. The box office is open Monday to Friday 3 to 6pm and Saturday, Sunday, and holidays 11am to 2pm. The **Konzerthaus Berlin,** on beautiful Gendarmenmarkt in Berlin-Mitte ((C) **030/ 20 30 90**), serves as the venue of the Berlin Symphonic Orchestra (founded in 1952 in the former East Germany) and other musical events, with tickets at 10€ to 15€ ($12–$17), depending on the performance. Its box office is open Monday to Saturday noon to 7pm and Sunday noon to 4pm, as well as 1 hour before performances begin.

One of the least expensive places to hear music is a church. The **Berliner Dom** on Museum Island in Berlin-Mitte features organ, choir, and instrumental classical music concerts most weekends, usually on Saturday at 6pm but also other nights. Prices are generally 5.20€ to 12€ ($6.30–$14), sometimes free. Call (C) **030/ 202 69 136** for more information. The **Kaiser-Wilhelm Gedächtniskirche** on Breitscheidplatz, off the Ku'damm, stages free organ concerts and cantata worship services in its new addition most Saturdays at 6pm, as well as choirs, soloists, and other performances throughout the month. Pick up the brochure listing the month's performances at the church, or call (C) **030/218 50 23.**

LIVE-MUSIC CLUBS

Two popular venues are **A-Trane,** Bleibtreustrasse 1, at the corner of Bleibtreustrasse and Pestalozzistrasse, Charlottenburg ((C) **030/313 25 50;** www. a-trande.de; S-Bahn: Savignyplatz), where musicians perform everything from new and mainstream jazz to bebop and swing; and **Quasimodo,** Kantstrasse 12a, Charlottenburg ((C) **030/312 80 86;** www.quasimodo.de; U-Bahn: Zoologischer Garten), Berlin's oldest jazz club and also a venue for blues, funk, and soul.

PUBS & BARS

AROUND THE KU'DAMM & SAVIGNYPLATZ   Although definitely tourist oriented and a bit too corny for my tastes, **Joe's Wirtshaus zum Löwen,** Hardenbergstrasse 29 ((C) **030/262 10 20**), does a brisk business due to its convenient location (between Bahnhof Zoo and the Kaiser-Wilhelm Gedächtniskirche), huge multilevel beer hall, even larger beer garden, and occasional music. **Zillemarkt,** Bleibtreustrasse 48a ((C) **030/881 70 40;** S-Bahn: Savignyplatz), dates from the early 1900s and is good place for an evening drink as well as breakfast or Saturday and Sunday brunch; with outdoor seating, it's open daily 10am to midnight. **Zwiebelfisch,** Savignyplatz 7–8 ((C) **030/312 73 63;** S-Bahn: Savignyplatz), is a neighborhood bar that's been around for more than 25 years and still enjoys great popularity, especially in the wee hours of the night. **Hard Rock Cafe,** Meinekestrasse 21 ((C) **030/88 46 20;** U-Bahn: Kurfürstendamm), offers occasional live music and karaoke every Tuesday from 10pm, along with the usual burgers and T-shirts. But on a fine summer's day, nothing beats a beer under the trees at **Loretta's Garden** on Lietzenburger Strasse 89 ((C) **030/882 33 54;** U-Bahn: Uhlandstrasse), a huge beer garden open April to September.

IN KREUZBERG & FRIEDRICHSHAIN   Kreuzberg was long the center of Berlin's avant-garde and alternative scene but now shares the spotlight with Berlin-Mitte and with Friedrichshain directly across the Spree River. **Madonna,** Wiener Strasse 22 ((C) **030/611 69 43;** U-Bahn: Görlitzer Bahnhof; bus: 129), is one of Kreuzberg's best-known and longest-running bars. **Morena,** Wiener Strasse 60 (℡ **030/611 47 16;** U-Bahn: Görlitzer Bahnhof; bus: 129), seems to be the watering hole for the hippest avant-garde. It's crowded even during the day, especially in nice weather, when you can sit outside and order breakfast until a late 5pm. In Friedrichshain, **Astro-Bar,** Simon-Dach-Strasse 40 (no phone; S-/U-Bahn: Warschauer Strasse), lures wild partyers with its camp '70s sci-fi decor, old pinball machines, and DJs from Berlin's underground scene spinning electro-pop and retro.

IN BERLIN-MITTE Although the trip to the top is expensive (6.50€/$7.50 adults; 3€/$3.45 children), the **Fernsehturm** on Alexanderplatz is my pick for both the best bird's-eye view of Berlin and a romantic early-evening drink. Its revolving **Telecafe** (℡ **030/242 33 33**), 195m (650 ft.) high, offers a terrific view.

In the heart of the Nikolai Quarter, **Georg Bräu,** Spreeufer 4 (℡ **030/242 42 44;** S-/U-Bahn: Alexanderplatz), is a popular microbrewery that also serves German fare. **Zum Nussbaum,** Am Nussbaum 3 (℡ **030/242 30 95**), is small, cozy, and comfortable, modeled after a bar built in 1507 but destroyed in World War II.

Oranienburger Strasse and its surrounding *Scheunenviertel* in Berlin-Mitte is one of Berlin's hottest alternative nightlife districts. First on the scene was **Tacheles,** Oranienburger Strasse 53–54, which for years sported such an alternative identity that it didn't have a phone or sign outside and didn't seem likely to survive. No wonder: The building was a bombed-out department store, famous for its extreme state of disrepair and taken over in 1990 by squatting artists who transformed it into studio/gallery/living space. On the ground floor is **Zapata** (℡ **030/281 61 09**), a cafe where characters from *Star Wars* would feel right at home; live music is offered most nights beginning at 10 or 11pm. **Kurvenstar,** Kleine Präsidentenstrasse 3 (℡ **030/247 2311-5;** S-Bahn: Hackescher Markt), featuring retro furnishings and a curved bar, is popular for its happy hour (Tues–Sat 7–10pm) and nightly happenings, including live music on Thursday and DJs spinning hip-hop and reggae on Saturday.

GAY & LESBIAN BARS

The neighborhoods of **Prenzlauer Berg, Berlin-Mitte, Nollendorfplatz,** and **Kreuzberg** are the best for their selection of gay bars. Keep an eye out for the free monthly *Out in Berlin,* a city magazine for gays and lesbians in English and German. Further information for gays and lesbians is provided on the city's home page, **www.berlin-tourist-information.de.**

The well-known gay bar **Har Die's Kneipe,** Ansbacher Strasse 29 (℡ **030/ 236 398 42;** U-Bahn: Wittenbergplatz), has been popular for more than 30 years for its laid-back atmosphere and convenient location off Wittenbergplatz. Almost anyone—including women and straight couples—can feel comfortable among the mostly gay older crowd. **Café Berio,** Maasenstrasse 7 (℡ **030/216 19 46;** U-Bahn: Nollendorfplatz), is a popular gay/lesbian cafe and a good starting point for finding out what's going on in Berlin; you can probably find a copy of *Out in Berlin* here.

DANCE CLUBS & DANCE HALLS

Top picks near the Ku'damm include **Big Eden,** Kurfürstendamm 202, Charlottenburg (℡ **030/882 61 20;** U-Bahn: Uhlandstrasse), which attracts young people of every nationality Thursday, Friday, and Saturday nights; and **Far Out,** Kurfürstendamm 156 (℡ **030/320 00 717** or 030/320 00 723; U-Bahn:

Adenauerplatz), which attracts a more sophisticated crowd, especially for its after-work party on Tuesday, when admission is free from 7 to 8pm and 3€ ($3.45) thereafter. Its "Forever Young" Wednesday night draws an older crowd. **Cafe Keese Ball Paradox,** Bismarckstrasse 108, near the Maxim Gorki Theater (© **030/312 91 11;** U-Bahn: Ernst-Reuter-Platz), is a large dance hall popular with the middle-aged and older, but with a difference—here it's always the women who ask the men to dance (except for the hourly Men's Choice, when the green light goes on).

Not far from Oranienburger Strasse, in the direction of Alexanderplatz in Berlin-Mitte, is the beautifully renovated **Die Hackeschen Höfe,** an Art Nouveau complex built around a series of courtyards. In addition to galleries, a cinema, boutiques, and cafes, there's **Oxymoron,** located in the first courtyard, Rosenthaler Strasse 40 (© **030/28 39 18 86;** S-Bahn or tram: Hackescher Markt), with events held several times a month, including Boogie Night Friday starting at 11pm. Top on the list of Berlin's upwardly mobile young professionals is **Adagio,** Marlene-Dietrich-Platz 1 (© **030/259 29 550;** S-/U-Bahn: Potsdamer Platz), a smart-looking club with after-work parties on Wednesday and Thursday, singles night on Friday, and varied events on Saturday. Nearby **Dorian Gray,** Marlene-Dietrich-Platz 4 (© **030/25 93 06 60;** S-/U-Bahn: Potsdamer Platz), is another trendy club, with after-work parties from 7pm every Tuesday; its ThursgayAfterWork event is, you guessed it, on Thursday and aimed primarily at gays and lesbians. Otherwise, it opens at 10pm Friday and Saturday.

7 Side Trips: Potsdam ⭐⭐ & the Spreewald

POTSDAM & SANSSOUCI PALACE

If you take only one excursion outside Berlin, it should be to **Potsdam,** 24km (15 miles) southwest. Potsdam was once Germany's most important baroque town, serving as a garrison and residence of Prussia's kings and royal families from the 17th to the 20th centuries. Its most famous resident was Frederick the Great, who succeeded in uniting Germany under his rule and built himself the delightful rococo palace **Schloss Sanssouci** ("without care"), which he used as a place for quiet meditation away from the rigors of war and government. His palace still stands, surrounded by a 300-hectare (750-acre) estate, Park Sanssouci, with several other magnificent structures, including the Neues Palais.

To reach Potsdam, take **S-Bahn 1** from Berlin (Bahnhof Zoo, Alexanderplatz, Savignyplatz, or many other S-Bahn stations) to Potsdam Hauptbahnhof station. The trip takes about 30 minutes and costs 2.60€ ($3). Or buy a Tageskarte (day ticket) for 6€ ($6.90). With either ticket, from Potsdam Hauptbahnhof station (take the Friedrich-Ebert-Strasse exit) you can then board **bus no. 695** directly for Schloss Sanssouci or Neues Palais. Otherwise, for the most dramatic approach to the palace, take **tram 96** or **98** from Potsdam Hauptbahnhof to Luisenplatz, from which it's a 10-minute walk through Sanssouci Park. Or, if you'd like to see even more of the city, take bus no. 695 only as far as Brandenburger Strasse and walk 30 minutes to Sanssouci, passing through the historic town center along the way.

There's a **Tourist Information** counter in Potsdam Hauptbahnhof (© **0331/270 91 50**), open daily 9am to 8pm, as well as another tourist office in the heart of the old town at Brandenburger Strasse 18 (© **0331/275 58 88;** www.potsdamtourismus.de), open Monday to Friday 10am to 6pm, and Saturday, Sunday, and holidays 10am to 2pm. Otherwise, you can get information on

Schloss Sanssouci and Sanssouci Park from the **Sanssouci Visitor Center,** catty-cornered from Schloss Sanssouci on An der Orangerie across from the windmill (© **0331/96 94 202**). It's open daily: March to October 8:30am to 5pm and November to February 9am to 4pm.

SEEING THE SIGHTS   Potsdam's star attraction is **Schloss Sanssouci** 🏰🏰🏰 Zur Historischen Mühle (© **0331/96 94 202**). Built in the 1740s by Georg von Knobbelsdorff, it served as Frederick the Great's summer residence for almost 40 years. (He died here and is buried on the grounds.) With only a dozen rooms, the one-story palace is exceedingly modest compared to most royal residences, yet its rooms are a delight, filled with paintings, marble, and gold leaf, with playful motifs of grapes, wine, and images of Bacchus. Don't miss the most dramatic view of the palace—from its park side, it sits atop six grassy terraces, cut into the side of a hill like steps in a pyramid, created for Frederick's vineyards. You can visit only on a 40-minute guided tour in German (an English pamphlet is available), departing every 20 minutes and costing 8€ ($9.20) adults and 5€ ($5.75) students/children. Schloss Sanssouci is open Tuesday to Sunday: April to October 9am to 5pm and November to March 9am to 4pm.

At the other end of Sanssouci Park, about a 25-minute walk away, is the estate's largest building, the **Neues Palais** (© **0331/96 94 202**), built 20 years after Schloss Sanssouci as a show of Prussian strength following the devastation of the Seven Years' War. Also serving as a summer residence for the royal Hohenzollerns, it's much more ostentatious than Schloss Sanssouci and in comparison seems grave, solemn, and humorless. Of note is the Grotto Room, its walls and ceiling smothered with shells, mica, minerals, fossils, and semiprecious stones. The Neues Palais is open Saturday to Thursday: April to October 9am to 5pm and November to March 9am to 4pm. November to March, you can see it only on a 1-hour guided tour in German (an English pamphlet is available), but the rest of the year you can tour it on your own. Admission here is 5€ ($5.75) for adults and 4€ ($4.60) students/children.

WHERE TO DINE   The most convenient place for a meal if you're visiting Schloss Sanssouci is the Mövenpick chain's **Zur Historischen Mühle,** across from the palace at An der Orangerie (© **0331/28 14 93;** bus: 695 to Sanssouci). It offers a variety of Continental and traditional German and Swiss meals priced from 9€ to 15€ ($10–$17), as well as a salad bar, a children's menu, and daily specials. In summer there are a shaded outdoor terrace, children's playground, and beer garden with simpler, less expensive fare ranging from sausage to chicken. It's open daily 8am to 11pm and accepts American Express, Diners Club, MasterCard, and Visa.

BOATING THROUGH THE SPREEWALD

The **Spreewald** is one of Middle Europe's most unique landscapes, formed where the Spree River spreads out into countless streams and canals, a labyrinth of waterways through woodlands. For centuries, transportation through the bayou has been via narrow barges and punts, and even today, mail is delivered by boat, firemen arrive by boat, and garbage is collected and transported away by boat. For visitors, the most popular thing to do is take a boat ride through this watery wonderland. **Lübbenau,** in the upper Spreewald, is a convenient starting point for 3-hour boat rides through the region, offered daily in good weather from April to the end of October at 9€ ($10) for adults and half-price for children. Four- and 8-hour rides are also available.

Trains bound for Lübbenau depart every hour or so from Bahnhof Zoo, costing 9.30€ ($11) for the 75-minute trip. Cheaper is the 23€ ($26) Brandenburg Ticket, valid for unlimited travel on any weekday 9am to 3am (you may *not*, however, travel between 4–6pm), for up to five people traveling together. On weekends, up to five people can travel for 30€ ($35) on the Schönes-Wochenende Ticket. Stop by EurAide at Bahnhof Zoo for train schedules and ticket information. From Lübbenau train station, it's about a 20-minute **walk** to the town's boat harbor (walk straight out of the station onto Poststrasse and take a right at Ehm-Welk-Strasse). For more info, contact the **Lübbenau Spreewald information office,** Ehm-Welk-Strasse 15 (© **03542/36 68**), open in summer Monday to Friday 9am to 6pm and Saturday and Sunday 9am to 1pm. In winter it's open Monday to Friday 9am to 4pm. In summer, there's a tourist information kiosk at the small town harbor where boats depart for the Spreewald, open weekends 10am to 4pm. In any case, boats depart regularly from about 9:30am to 3pm, but it's best to arrive by noon. For more information on boat tours, call the **Grosser Spreewaldhafen Lübbenau** at © **03542/22 25.**

7

Bern & the Best of the Berner Oberland

by Darwin Porter & Danforth Prince

Unlike Zurich and Geneva, the federal capital of **Bern,** snuggled in a bend in the Aare River, remains one of the world's greatest landmark centers of the architecture of the Middle Ages. The original wooden city was rebuilt in soft gray stone after a devastating early-15th-century fire and has changed little in more than 500 years. Its streets are lined with wide arcades under whose shade shops prosper and people stroll. Bern's cobblestone streets, painted 16th-century fountains, pitched red roofs, and unified urban plan all led the United Nations to declare it a world landmark in 1983.

However, aside from wandering its medieval streets, taking a float down the Aare, and spending a morning with the world's greatest Paul Klee collection at the art museum, Bern offers little more to detain you. All the better, since Switzerland's greatest sight by far is the alpine landscape less than an hour's train ride south. That's why this chapter gives much space to excursions in the Berner Oberland, the heart of the Swiss Alps. This is a land of flower-strewn meadows and awe-inspiring glaciers, Europe's highest train station and the mighty 4,093m (13,642-ft.) Jungfrau, Interlaken's castle-lined lakes, and more than 483km (300 miles) of hiking trails and some 193km (120 miles) of skiing.

For the frugal traveler, the bad news is that Switzerland remains one of Europe's most expensive countries. You'll have to shell out a little more for anything better than a dorm room and a schnitzel-on-a-stick from a sidewalk stand, but the hotels and restaurants listed will give you a good balance between comfort and economy.

Switzerland has four official **languages:** Italian in the Ticino of the southernmost corner, French in most of the west, Romansch (a vestigial Etrusco-Latin language) in a small zone of the east, but mainly Schwyzerdütsch, a Swiss German dialect even most Germans can't understand. But don't worry: Most of these natural polyglots can help you in English as well.

For more on Bern, see *Frommer's Switzerland.*

Value **Budget Bests**

Bern's most compelling sight is the medieval city itself, and it costs nothing to wander the arcaded shopping streets, admire the 400-year-old fountains, visit the city's mascot bears across the river, and climb to the Rose Gardens for a fantastic cityscape panorama. Also note that the Bern Historical Museum is free (and consequently packed) on Saturday.

Bern Deals & Discounts

SPECIAL DISCOUNTS   The Swiss Museum Passport (30F/$23) is valid for 1 month, but you'd have to visit most of the museums in Bern to make it pay off. If you're interested, you can buy the passport at the tourist office (see "Visitor Information," below) or order it at www.museums.ch/pass.

Students can get some discounts with their international student ID card (even an old university ID will work). For anyone under 26, the budget travel agency **SSR**, Rathausgasse 64 (© **031/302-03-12;** tram/bus: 12), can get you the best travel deals.

WORTH A SPLURGE   So much of Bern's sightseeing is free that there's little to splurge on—which is just as well, because you'll need any extra money for the region's great splurge: a trip up to the skyscraping Jungfraujoch (see "Side Trips: Interlaken & the Berner Oberland," later in this chapter).

1 Essentials

ARRIVING

BY PLANE   The small **Berne-Belp Airport** (© **031/960-2111;** www.alpar.ch), 9km (5½ miles) south of the city, receives flights from several major European cities. There's a shuttle bus from the airport to the city's train station, where you'll find the tourist office; the 20-minute trip costs 14F ($11). A taxi from the airport to the city is around 50F ($38).

Most European and transatlantic passengers fly into **Zurich's Kloten Airport.** From there, an hourly train (50F/$38) makes the 90-minute trip to Bern.

BY TRAIN   Bern's *Hauptbahnhof,* or train station (© **031/328-1212**), is at the west end of the Altstadt (Old Town). Ticketing, track access, and lockers are found in the basement; luggage storage and train and tourist info are on the ground floor. For national rail information, hit the website www.sbb.ch, call © **0900/300-300** (1.20F/90¢ per min.), or use the computers in the SBB train info office (across from the tourist office) to look up and print out your itinerary.

Note: If you leave the train station from the most obvious exit, at the tourist office, you'll be facing south; turn left to head into the Altstadt.

VISITOR INFORMATION

INFORMATION OFFICE   The **Bern Tourist Office** (© **031/328-1212;** www.berne.ch) is in the Hauptbahnhof (train station). June to September, it's open daily 9am to 8:30pm; October to May, it's open Monday to Saturday 9am to 6:30pm and Sunday 10am to 5pm. There's a **smaller information station** inside the building at the Bear Pits (offering a free 20-min. multimedia show on "Bern Past and Present"). June to September, it's open daily 9am to 8:30pm; October and March to May, daily 10am to 4pm; and November to February, Friday to Sunday 10am to 4pm.

WEBSITES   The city's site **(www.berne.ch)** is rather uninformative, but you can make hotel reservations online. You'll find helpful general and ski information on the Berner Oberland at **www.berneroberland.ch**. More Berner Oberland

data, including timetables for the major trains and cable cars, is found at
www.jungfraubahn.ch.

CITY LAYOUT

Bern's layout is easy, but the fact that almost every road changes names each
block (as do the squares those streets cross) adds a bit of confusion. The tourist
office's free map is not really adequate. Pick up a more complete one, including
the outlying areas and a street finder, at the Schweizerischer Bankverein Bank,
Bärenplatz 8.

You'll be spending your time in Bern's pedestrianized **Altstadt (Old Town),**
which is small and easily navigable on foot. Tucked into a sharp U-shaped bend
of the **Aare River,** it's made up of five long arcaded streets, two large squares
(**Bärenplatz/Waisenhausplatz/Bundesplatz** and **Kornhausplatz/Casino-
platz**), and a dozen cross streets. Lots of shop-lined passageways not shown on
most maps cut through buildings from one main drag to another. If you imagine this Aare bend as a U lying on its side, at the western, open end of the U is
the **Hauptbahnhof** (train station).

South of the Altstadt, across the Aare via the **Kirchenfeldbrücke** bridge, are
several museums and the embassy district. North of the Aare are the casino and
a residential neighborhood with a few hotels that are less expensive than those
in the Altstadt.

GETTING AROUND

BY TRAM & BUS   Bern's bus and tram system (© 031/321-8888) is extensive,
but the Altstadt, as mentioned, is small enough to cover on foot. However, you
might want to take bus no. 12 back uphill toward the center and station after you
visit the Bear Pits. Most buses and trams begin and end their routes around the
Hauptbahnhof, many on Bubenbergplatz just to the station's south.

There are two types of **tickets:** the 1.60F ($1.20) version, good for travel for
up to six stops (valid for 45 min.), and the 2.60F ($1.95) version for longer rides
(more than six stops, up to 90 min.). Nothing in this chapter is more than six
stops away, so always buy the cheaper ticket. Purchase your ticket from the
machine at each stop. There's a daily ticket for 9.50F ($7.15), but you'd have to
make an unlikely five trips or more a day to save money.

"Moonliner" **night buses** run Thursday through Saturday at 12:45am, 2am,
and 3:15am, and cost 5F ($3.75); the M3 runs from the Hauptbahnhof through
the Altstadt and returns via the casino.

BY TAXI   If you're restricting your sightseeing to the tiny Altstadt, you'll do
fine on foot. If you want a taxi to your hotel, cabs congregate at the train station, Casinoplatz, and Waisenhausplatz. You can also call © 031/371-1111. The
fare is 6.80F ($5.10), plus a hefty 3.10F ($2.35) per kilometer, or 3.10F ($2.35)
per kilometer between 8am and 6pm and on Sunday and holidays.

BY BICYCLE   The best option is a free loaner from *Berner Zeitung* (see box
titled "A Two-Wheel Deal," below). For mountain bikes, for longer rentals, or in

---

(*Finds* **A Two-Wheel Deal**

Bern's best secret: From May to October, the town's daily paper, *Berner
Zeitung,* Zeughausstrasse 14 (tram/bus: 5, 9, 10, or 12), will lend you a bike
for free. Just bring your passport as ID and leave a 20F ($15) deposit.

Country & City Codes

The country code for Switzerland is **41**. The city code for Bern is **031**; leave off the initial zero when calling from outside Switzerland (so dial 011-41-31, then the number, from the U.S.). If you're calling within Bern, leave off the city code completely and dial the regular phone number.

winter, you'll have to pay at the train station. The bike rental is in the *fly-gepäck* (left-luggage) area (© **900/300-300**). Rentals are 25F to 30F ($19–$23) per day. You can pick up bikes at 250 train stations throughout Switzerland; half-day rentals have to be returned at the same station, but full-day rentals can be returned at any other station for an extra 6F ($4.50).

BY RENTAL CAR   There's no need to rent a car in Bern. However, you might want to explore the countryside or the Alps with your own wheels—and with train prices so high, groups of three or more might enjoy a savings. (Although few alpine resorts besides Grindelwald are accessible by car, you can at least drive to a lift station.) Try **Avis**, Wabernstrasse 41 (© **031/378-1515;** tram/bus: 9); **Hertz**, Casinoplatz (© **031/318-2160;** tram/bus: G, 3, 5, 10, or 19); or **Europcar,** Laupenstrasse 22 (© **031/381-7555;** tram/bus: 11or 12).

Note: You'll save money by arranging your rental before leaving home.

Parking in Bern is never free. Aboveground "blue zones," such as Waisenhausplatz, are metered for 2F ($1.50) per hour—but you can stay only 1 hour Monday to Friday 8am to 7pm and Saturday 8am to 4pm. More convenient are the garages that cost up to 3.50F ($2.65) per hour (depending on time of day) or 28F ($21) per day. Central ones are **Hauptbahnhof** (© **031/311-2252**); **Metro,** under Waisenhausplatz/Bärenplatz (© **031/311-4411**); and **Casino,** under Kochergasse/Kornhausplatz (© **031/311-7776**). Your hotel might sell you a permit to park on the streets, or you can get one at the tourist office.

FAST FACTS: Bern

Banks   Banks are open Monday to Friday 9am to 5pm. ATMs in German are called *Bankomat* and exist at post offices as well as banks.

Business Hours   Most shops are open Monday 2 to 6:30pm; Tuesday, Wednesday, and Friday 8:15am to 6:30pm; Thursday 8:15am to 9pm; and Saturday 8:15am to 4pm.

Currency   The national currency of Switzerland is the **Swiss franc (F),** which is composed of 100 centimes. At press time, the rate of exchange was $1 = 1.35F, or 1F = 75¢.

Doctors & Hospitals   For a list of doctors and dentists, dial © **0900/57-67-47.** For emergency care, go to **Insel Hospital,** Freiburgstrasse (© **031/632-2111;** bus: 11). For an ambulance, dial © **144.**

Embassies   The **U.S. Embassy** is at Jubiläumsstrasse 93 (© **031/357-7011;** www.us-embassy.ch; bus: 19). It's open Monday to Friday from 8:30am to 12:30pm and 1:30 to 5:30pm. The **U.K. Embassy** is at Thunstrasse 50 (© **031/359-7700;** tram/bus: G, 3, or 5). It's open Monday to Friday 8:30am to 12:30pm and 1:30 to 5pm. The **Canadian Embassy** is at Kirchenfeldstrasse 88

((© 031/357-3200; tram/bus: G, 3, or 5). The **Irish Embassy** is at Kirchenfeld-strasse 68 ((© 031/352-1442; tram/bus: 3 or 5).

Emergencies Dial © 117 for the police, © 144 for an ambulance, © 118 to report a fire, and © 140 (not a free call) if your car breaks down.

Holidays Bern's official holidays are January 1 and 2, Good Friday, Easter Sunday and Monday, Ascension, Pentecost and Whit Monday, August 1 (Swiss National Day), and December 25 and 26.

Internet Access Get online at **BTM Medienhaus,** Zeughausgasse 14 ((© 031/327-1188).

Laundry Bern has only one coin-op laundromat, **Jet Wash,** north of the Aare at Dammweg 43 ((© 031/330-2638; tram: 9). It's open Monday to Saturday from 7am to 9pm, Sunday from 9am to 6pm.

Mail Bern's **main post office,** Schanzenpost 1, behind the train station ((© 031/386-6552; tram/bus: 5, 9, 10, 12, 13, 14, 16, or 19), is open Monday to Friday from 7:30am to 9pm, Saturday from 8 to 4pm. There are several branches throughout the Altstadt. For any letter or postcard under 20 grams, rates are 1.30F ($1) airmail anywhere in Europe; 1.80F ($1.35) airmail outside Europe. The slower, ground "economy" rates are 1.10F (85¢) in Europe and 1.40F ($1.05) outside Europe.

Pharmacies **Central-Apotheke Volz & Co.,** Zeitglockenlaub 2, near the Clock Tower ((© 031/311-1094; tram/bus: 9, 10, or 12), employs English-speaking attendants. It's open Monday 9am to 6:30pm, Tuesday to Friday 7:45am to 6:30pm, and Saturday 7:45am to 4pm. To find out which drugstore's turn it is to stay open 24 hours or on Sunday, dial © 031/311-2211.

Police Dial © 117 for the police.

Safety With the exception of the park surrounding Parliament, where heroin addicts often roam after dark, you'll feel comfortable on the streets of Central Bern day or night. But don't let your sense of safety lull you into carelessness; take the usual precautions to protect yourself against crime.

Tax Switzerland's **value-added tax (VAT)** is 7.6%. Foreigners who spend more than 500F ($375) at one store can reclaim it. Ask the store for the forms.

Telephone A local call costs .60F (45¢). Switzerland's phone system is highly advanced—most booths contain digital multilingual phonebooks that dial the number for you after searching it out, and even let you send short e-mails. Few phones still accept coins. You can use your major credit card in most pay phones, or buy a Taxcard (prepaid **phone card**) in denominations of 5F ($3.75), 10F ($7.50), and 20F ($15) at the train station or any newsstand, gas station, or post office. For **direct dialing internationally,** you might want the Value Card version, for 20F ($15) or 50F ($38). Dial © 111 (not free) for directory assistance.

To charge your long-distance call to a **calling card** issued by AT&T, MCI, or Sprint, dial © 800/56-34-12. To **call direct** from Bern abroad, dial 00 followed by the country code (1 for the U.S.), the area code, and the number.

Tipping Bills in Swiss restaurants and other businesses almost always include the service charge, so always ask first. Taxi drivers appreciate an extra 10%; tip porters 2F ($1.50) per bag.

2 Affordable Places to Stay

Bern is small for a national capital, and conventions and international meetings overbook it regularly. Make reservations in advance no matter what the time of year. The folks at the tourist office will **book you a room** for free (call ☎ **031/ 328-1210**), or you can use the big hotel board and free phone just outside the tourist office (at the top of the escalators down to the train tracks).

The dismal news is that, aside from the five-star luxury inns, most hotels in Bern are disconcertingly similar. They almost all have smallish stuccoed rooms with duvets, pancake-flat pillows on the beds, and cramped bathrooms. The only real difference is that pricier properties are closer to the center of town, the units (and, more importantly, bathrooms) are a few microns bigger than the standard offerings, and there might be a minibar.

Note: The lodging choices below are plotted on the map on p. 247.

IN THE ALTSTADT

Glocke Backpackers ⭐ *Value*   You won't find a better price in the heart of town. In late 2000, management gutted the most centrally located hotel in town—around the corner from the Clock Tower—and turned it from a down-at-the-heels inn into a shiny new hotel/hostel aimed at backpackers (hence the new name). Half the units are private rooms; the other half are shared dorms. The cozy private rooms—with wood furnishings and modern bathrooms—occupy the quietest top floors (although the hotel isn't too noisy to begin with). The "dorms" are more like shared rooms, with just two to six beds (bunked) in each, along with lockers and a sink. The more beds in a room, the lower the rates per person. The shared bathrooms are immaculate. Reception hours are 8 to 11am and 3 to 10pm; if you're arriving later, let the staff know, and they'll give you a code so you can get your keycard from the outside box.

Rathausgasse 75, CH-3011 Bern. ☎ **031/311-3771**. Fax 031/311-1008. www.chilisbackpackers.com. 12 units, 3 with bathroom; 48 beds in 12 shared rooms. 60F–75F ($45–$56) single without bathroom; 90F–120F ($68–$90) double without bathroom, 130F–160F ($98–$120) double with bathroom; 29F ($22) bed in shared room. MC, V. Bus: 12. Tram: 3, 5, or 9. **Amenities:** Tour desk; coin-op washer and dryer (from 5.70F/$4.30 per load); Internet access (about 5F/$3.75 for a half-hour); nonsmoking rooms (all). *In room:* No phone.

Goldener Schlüssel ⭐⭐   Now a good budget hotel, this structure dates back 5 centuries when it was a horse stable. It went from there to a checkered career,

---

Value Getting the Best Deal on Accommodations

- Ask at the tourist office about rooms for rent, which tend to be cheaper than hotel rooms.
- Try to bargain down the rates for stays of longer than 3 days.
- Take a room that shares a hall bathroom—it's always cheaper than one with a private bathroom.
- Be aware that, generally, the farther from Bärenplatz you get (north of the Aare or out at the Altstadt's tip), the lower the rates—and Bern is so tiny you needn't fret about getting too "far" from the center.
- Definitely go for the cheapest accommodations first—Bern's hotels vary little in style, and you won't get that much more for your money at the expensive inns.

serving for 2 centuries as a flophouse. For most of the 20th century, it was a brewery before being turned into a hotel in 1980. Jost Troxler runs his hotel and restaurant (p. 244) with care and keeps the prices low for an inn just "99 steps" from the Clock Tower. The modular furnishings show wear but remain sturdy. The bathrooms, however, lack room for even an extra elbow. The back rooms overlook a sweep of medieval rooftops and are the quietest (save for the hourly chimes of the bell tower). Only two rooms open onto the dreary airshaft. The four top-floor accommodations share two toilets and one shower.

Rathausgasse 72 (just off Kornhausplatz), CH-3011 Bern. ℃ **031/311-0216.** Fax 031/311-5688. www. goldener-schluessel.ch. 29 units, 21 with bathroom. 88F ($66) single without bathroom, 115F ($86) single with bathroom; 125F ($94) double without bathroom, 155F ($116) double with bathroom; 225F ($169) triple with bathroom. Rates include continental breakfast. MC, V. Bus: 10 or 12. Tram: 5 or 9. **Amenities:** Restaurant/cafe; concierge; limited room service. *In room:* TV, hair dryer.

Nydeck   The Nydeck's basic but cheap rooms occupy an old building spearheading an acute intersection at the far tip of the Altstadt, a block from the Aare on three sides. You get what you pay for: no elevator and tiny, worn rooms, but at least they're freshly painted and carpeted. The place is removed from the action but ideal if you're a Bears fan—the furry critters live just across the bridge at Bärengraben (Bear Pits). The pleasant little Junkere Bar occupies the ground floor and serves croissants and coffee for less than a continental breakfast would cost if included in the rates.

Gerechtigkeitsgasse 1, CH-3011 Bern. ℃ **031/311-8686.** Fax 031/312-2054. www.hotelnydeck.ch. 13 units. 110F ($83) single; 160F ($120) double. AE, MC, V. Bus: 12. *In room:* TV.

Zum Goldener Adler *(Kids)*   The carpeting is hideous and the modular furnishings worn, but the bathrooms are some of the largest in a city plagued by chronically undersized facilities. If only the same could be said of the rooms themselves. Still, some are quite spacious, including family-perfect no. 15. The back rooms are a smidgen quieter. Downstairs is a good cheap restaurant. This place is nicer than its neighbor the Nydeck (see previous listing), but a bit pricier.

Gerechtigkeitsgasse 38, CH-3011 Bern. ℃ **031/311-1725.** Fax 031/311-3761. www.goldener-adler-bern.ch. 20 units. 130F–150F ($98–$113) single; 160F–180F ($120–$135) double. Rates include breakfast. AE, DC, MC, V. Bus: 12. **Amenities:** Restaurant; laundry service; dry cleaning. *In room:* TV.

NORTH OF THE AARE

Alpenblick *(★)*   This is a large business-oriented hotel in a residential district, but it charges reasonable rates and is a good bet when you can't find a room in the center. The unabashedly international-modern rooms have Paul Klee prints to hint that you're still in Bern. The bathrooms with shower are largish and well kept, and there's a restaurant downstairs if you're not up to the trek into the center.

Kasernenstrasse 29, CH-3013 Bern. ℃ **031/335-6666.** Fax 031/335-6655. www.alpenblick-bern.ch. 48 units. 106F ($80) single; 150F ($113) double; 192F ($144) triple. Rates include buffet breakfast. AE, DC, MC, V. Parking 10F ($7.50) in hotel garage. Tram: 9. **Amenities:** Restaurant. *In room:* TV, dataport, coffeemaker, hair dryer, safe.

Marthahaus *(★★)*   On the whole, the rooms in Bern's only pension are a bit larger than those in the central hotels—and the woman who runs it is a sweetheart. All the bathrooms, private and shared, have been recently overhauled, and with two hall bathrooms per floor, there's rarely a wait. Accommodations with private facilities also come with TVs and phones and have slightly nicer built-in furnishings. The units without bathrooms contain sinks.

Wyttenbachstrasse 22a, CH-3013 Bern. ℃ **031/332-4135.** Fax 031/333-3386. www.marthahaus.ch. 40 units, 6 with bathroom. 65F ($49) single without bathroom, 110F ($83) single with bathroom; 95F ($71) double without bathroom, 125F ($94) double with bathroom; 126F ($95) triple without bathroom, 156F ($117) triple with bathroom. Rates include breakfast. Lower rates for longer stays. MC, V. Parking 10F ($7.50) in 1 of 4 spots. Bus: 20. **Amenities:** Lounge; communal kitchen; laundry/dry-cleaning service; nonsmoking rooms. *In room:* TV.

NEAR THE HAUPTBAHNHOF

Kreuz 𝒢   After undergoing massive renovations early in 2002, the Kreuz is now a government-rated three-star hotel. It's about as central as you can get. Other than being a bit larger than average, the rooms differ little from Bern's standard. The renovated bedrooms are well maintained but still a bit stark and angular, although comfortable nonetheless. Many rooms hide foldaway beds for families; light sleepers should request a room in the back.

Zeughausgasse 39–41, CH-3000 Bern. ℭ **031/329-9595.** Fax 031/329-9596. www.hotelkreuz-bern.ch. 100 units. 139F ($104) single; 200F ($150) double; 230F ($173) triple. Rates include breakfast. AE, DC, MC, V. Tram: 3, 5, or 9. **Amenities:** Restaurant; bar lounge; business center (limited); limited room service; laundry service; nonsmoking rooms. *In room:* TV, hair dryer.

National 𝒢   The prices are low at this imposing 1908 castle-in-the-city because it's outside the center, just south of the station. The place smacks of former grandeur, but there's a tomblike quiet about this hotel, which is too big for its current demand. The elevator doesn't make it up to the fifth floor, where the bathrooms and furnishings are newer and the modern double-glazed windows are more efficient at blocking traffic noise. The accommodations tend to be larger than most in Bern. The hotel's popular South American–themed bar, Shakira, often features live acts.

Hirschengraben 24, CH-3011 Bern. ℭ **031/381-1988.** Fax 031/381-6878. www.nationalbern.ch. 44 units, 30 with bathroom. 60F–70F ($45–$53) single without bathroom; 90F–110F ($68–$83) single with bathroom; 100F ($75) double without bathroom, 135F–150F ($101–$113) double with bathroom; 180F–250F ($135–$188) family room for 3–4 with bathroom. Rates include breakfast. AE, DC, MC, V. 4 free parking spots or 24F ($18) in nearby blue zones. Bus: 11, 13, or 15. Tram: 3 or 5. **Amenities:** Restaurant; bar; babysitting; laundry/dry-cleaning service; 1 room for those w/limited mobility. *In room:* TV (some units).

WORTH A SPLURGE

Bern 𝒢𝒢   Behind an Art Deco facade, this massive hotel is popular with business travelers and discerning guests who appreciate the amenities, the mostly large units and bathrooms, and the dining options. The street-facing rooms are bigger and brighter than those opening onto the small inner courtyard; all are comfortably furnished in modern style. This place is so cutting edge that you can have ISDN wireless modem service in your room if you're staying on the fourth floor (or use the lounge computer for Internet access).

Zeughausgasse 9 (just off Kornhausplatz), CH-3011 Bern. ℭ **031/329-2222.** Fax 031/329-2299. www.hotel bern.ch. 100 units. Mon–Thurs 198F ($149) single, Fri–Sun 165F ($124) single; Mon–Thurs 265F ($199) double, Fri–Sun 239F ($179) double; Mon–Thurs 325F ($244) triple, Fri–Sun 280F ($210) triple. Rates include breakfast. Children under 16 stay free in parent's room (or at 20% discount in separate unit). AE, DC, MC, V. **Amenities:** 2 restaurants; bar; concierge; room service (7am–11:30pm); laundry service/dry cleaning; nonsmoking rooms; rooms for those w/limited mobility. *In room:* TV, dataport, minibar, coffeemaker, hair dryer, safe.

3 Great Deals on Dining

Switzerland's provincial sausage-and-potatoes cuisine has taken on culinary influences from neighboring Germany, France, and Italy, giving Swiss cooking an international flavor.

Cheese is, of course, a holey Swiss ingredient—and there are about 100 varieties besides the sour, riddled Emmenthal we generically refer to as "Swiss cheese." Emmenthal and Gruyère, along with white wine, garlic, and lemon, are

> ### ⸨Value⸩ Getting the Best Deal on Dining
>
> - Note that for smaller appetites—or smaller budgets—most Swiss restaurants offer *halb-portions* (half portions) of many dishes, often at just half the price.
> - Watch what you drink. Swiss wine, while quite good, is notoriously expensive, and restaurants tend to overcharge for all their beverages—averaging 4.50F ($3.40) for a small cola or half-liter bottle of water. Beer is often cheaper, say 3.50F ($2.65), but no potable is reasonably priced. Save your thirst until you can get to a grocery store.
> - Try Bern's street food—it's generally cheap and offers more variety than most restaurants do. Stands hawking Asian, Italian, Middle Eastern, and German foods line the arcaded streets. Have lunch on the run to save both time and money.
> - Skip your usual sit-down dinner, since Bern goes to bed early anyway. Take your restaurant meals at lunch (when you can get the least expensive fixed-price menus) and make a Migros run for picnic dinner supplies to eat in your hotel room.
> - Note that a platter of sausages and *rösti* in a tavern (such as Anker Bern, below) makes for a cheap, filling meal, if not quite the cooking quality you'd find in a proper restaurant.

thrown together in a melting crock and called **fondue,** one of the country's specialties (use the long forks to dip in chunks of bread). The Swiss might also scrape melted cheese over your plate as **raclette,** to be eaten warm with hunks of brown bread, boiled baby potatoes, pickles, and pearl onions.

To go with your cheese, the Swiss offer the omnipresent *rösti* (a sort of hash brown, plain or garnished with any of a number of items such as cheese, bacon, onions, or even a fried egg), lake **fish,** and **sausages.** Another typical Bernese dish is the **Bernerplatte,** a plate of sauerkraut or beans, atop which are piled sausages, ham, pig's feet, bacon, or pork chops. (Can't you just hear the arteries screaming?) *Käseschnitte* is a slab of bread soaked in white wine, smothered in cheese, and baked in the oven, often with ham, a fried egg, or both. Wash it all down with one of Switzerland's seldom-exported but fine white or light red **wines** or a handcrafted local **beer.**

IN THE ALTSTADT

Anker Bern ⸨ℛ⸩ SWISS/ITALIAN   Food at this beer hall is cheap and plentiful, and it's really an outlet for the Anker Brauerei (brewery). This isn't fine dining—the laminated menu with pictures should clue you in to that—but this dark-wood locals' tavern does offer low-cost hearty meals in a convivial atmosphere. It specializes in pizzas (15 types) and *röschti* (nine types, plus a half dozen rotating specials on the "Röschti Festival" menu card), including the *party-roschti,* topped with a skewer of grilled veal, beef, veggies, pork, and chicken, with three sauces to spoon over it all. You can also get cheese fondue for 21F ($16).

Schmiedenplatz 1/Kornhausplatz 16. ℰ 031/311-1113. www.roeschti.ch or www.roestischweiz.ch. Main courses 16F–23F ($12–$17); pizza 11F–18F ($8.25–$14); lunch menus 15F–23F ($11–$17). AE, MC, V. Mon–Thurs 9am–11pm; Fri–Sat 9am–midnight; Sun 9:30am–6pm. Tavern Mon–Sat 7:30am–midnight; Sun 9:30am–6pm. Bus/tram: 5, 9, 10, or 12.

Arlequin ☆ SWISS/ITALIAN   With a bar in back, small tables lined closely against the walls' stone arches, and jazz on the sound system, the wood-beamed Arlequin is a mellow and moderately priced place. Here you can tuck into raclette, *maccaroni casalinga* (macaroni with beef, tomatoes, cheese, and cream), or *pastetli* (puff pastries steaming with veal and mushrooms). A few tables sit under the arcade out front in summer. The service, though, can be seriously slow.

Gerechtigkeitgasse 51. ℭ 031/311-3946. Reservations recommended. Main courses 18F–22F ($14–$17); fixed-price meal 18F–22F ($14–$17). MC, V. Daily 11am–1pm and 6–10pm. Closed Dec 24. Bus: 12.

Goldener Schlüssel ☆☆ SWISS   The broadly arched plank ceiling of this converted 16th-century stable gives you the impression of dining in the keel of an upside-down ship. You can tuck into hearty Swiss regional cooking such as *echtes Bauern Bratwirst erlebnis* (a 200g/7-oz. sausage under an onion sauce with *rösti*) or one of several vegetarian dishes of Indian or Mexican inspiration. Wash it all down with a half-liter of a local brew, Mutzenbügler. There's a budget hotel upstairs (see "Affordable Places to Stay," above).

Rathausgasse 72. ℭ 031/311-0216. www.goldener-schluessel.ch. Reservations recommended. Main courses 19F–35F ($14–$26); fixed-price lunch 18F–22F ($14–$17). AE, MC, V. Sun–Thurs 7am–11:30pm; Fri–Sat 7am–12:30am. Closed Dec 24. Bus: 9, 10, or 12.

Klötzlikeller ☆☆ SWISS   This brick-vaulted room is the best and most authentic of Bern's old-fashioned *keller* (cellar joints). It schedules live music some evenings. Since 1635, it has served big glasses of wine and beer alongside a limited menu of excellent traditional specialties such as *gescnhetzelte kalbsleber* (veal liver with butter and herbs served with *rösti*), sausage with chive-flavored vegetables,

---

Value Quick Bites

Cheap cafes and restaurants line Bern's two main squares, Bärenplatz and Kornhausplatz. They include **Le Mazot** and **Anker Bern** (p. 245 and 243). The arcaded streets of the city are filled with **kiosks** selling *donner kabob* (pita stuffed with spicy lamb and hot sauce), various Asian nibbles, pizzas, pretzel sandwiches, and *Gschnätzltes,* a Bern specialty of fried veal, beef, or pork (order *sur chabis* sauerkraut to go with it). **Metzgerei Adolf Richner,** Aarbergergasse 3 (ℭ **031/311-0211**; tram/bus: 11, 20, or 21), is a butcher who'll hand-carve meat for a **sandwich** or stuff a roll with a hot dog for as little as 4.50F ($3.40), sauerkraut included.

The indoor marketplace **Markthalle,** Bubenbergplatz 11 (tram/bus: 5, 9, 10, 12, or 19), has lots of small **booths** hawking prepared specialty foods to take away or to enjoy at a small table. It's open Monday to Friday 8am to 7pm (to 9pm Thurs) and Saturday 8am to 4pm.

The **supermarkets Migro** (one at the corner of Marktgasse and Zeughausgasse, the other on Bubenbergplatz, adjacent to Markthalle; tram/bus: 5, 9, or 12) and **Coop,** Schlosstrasse 140B (tram/bus: 11, 20, or 21), can provide fresh picnic ingredients, and both have inexpensive **cafeterias** where meals generally weigh in at around 20F ($15). They're open Monday 9am to 6:30pm; Tuesday, Wednesday, and Friday from 8am to 6:30pm; Thursday from 8am to 9pm; and Saturday from 7am to 4pm.

and cheese fondues. In January and February, you can try *Treberwurst*, a sausage cooked in *merc* (an 84-proof aquavit made from the leftovers of the winemaking process). For dessert, try the excellent tart-and-sweet pudding, *Süssmostcrème*.

Gerectigkeitsgasse 62. (C) **031/311-7456.** Main courses 20F–49F ($15–$37). AE, MC, V. Mon–Sat 4pm–midnight. Closed Sun year-round; closed Mon Mar–Sept. Bus: 12.

Le Beaujolais ⭐ FRENCH   You enter through a rustic cafe, but the candlelit-yet-comfortable dining room in back has subtle reminders throughout the decor that, while you may be in Switzerland's capital, you're dining on fine French cuisine. The cooking runs through a range of traditional dishes such as coq au vin and *tripes aux tomates*, as well as monthly specials like *trance de saumon pochée* (sautéed salmon filet in white-wine sauce with vegetables). In winter, the menu includes Swiss specialties such as cheese fondue and raclette.

Aarbergergasse 50 52. (C) **031/311 4886.** Reservations recommended. Fixed-price menus 19Г–40Г ($14–$30). MC, V. Restaurant Mon–Fri 11:30am–2pm and 6–9:30pm. Bus: 5, 9, or 12.

Le Mazot VALAIS/BERNER SWISS   This cozy alpine eatery 10 steps from the Clock Tower is not the best of the Bärenplatz restaurants, but it's an ideal place to sample Swiss specialties on a budget. It offers 15 types of *rösti* and 10 fondues (including one with champagne).

Bärenplatz 5. (C) **031/311-7088.** Main courses 10F–38F ($7.50–$29); fixed-price menus 15F–26F ($11–$20); set lunch platter 13F–16F ($9.40–$12). MC, V. Daily 11am–10:30pm. Bus: 5, 9, or 12.

Menuetto VEGETARIAN   This well-managed restaurant corner in the heart of Bern's oldest section serves inventive vegetarian cuisine that includes such dishes as samurai rice (a fancy permutation of tofu); *nasi goring*, the well-accessorized national rice dish of Indonesia; and a delicious eggplant moussaka. The vegetable broth is superb. Even the wines served here are organic, as is most of the food.

Münstergasse 47 at the Herrengasse. (C) **031/311-1448.** Reservations recommended. Main courses 20F–25F ($15–$19); fixed-price menus 15F–26F ($11–$20). AE, DC, MC, V. Mon–Sat 11:15am–2:15pm and 5:30–10pm. Tram: 9. Bus: 11.

SOUTH OF THE AARE

Kirchenfeld ⭐ *Value* SWISS/INTERNATIONAL   The Kirchenfeld is a good stop during a day at Bern's "other" museums across the river. There's a modern cafe up front—lots of patrons poring over newspapers, and couples conversing—with slightly fancier dining on linen-covered tables in the back. The main courses can verge on expensive but you get a lot for your franc, with heaping portions. The cheap daily menus are a real value. Some of the dishes we've enjoyed here include an entire roast duck with orange sauce, and smoked pork cutlet with mustard sauce and *rösti*. The restaurant also prepares vegetarian variations and traditional Swiss dishes.

Thunstrasse 5 (just over the Kirchenbrücke, take the easy—not the sharp—left fork). (C) **031/351-0278.** Reservations recommended. Main courses 22F–42F ($17–$32). Fixed-price lunches 18F–24F ($13–$18); set 4-course dinner 63F ($47). AE, MC, V. Restaurant Tues–Sat 11:30am–2:30pm and 6–11:30pm. Bistro Tues–Fri 8am–11:30pm; Sat 8am–8pm. Tram: 3 or 5. Bus: 3 or 5.

WORTH A SPLURGE

Della Casa ⭐⭐ SWISS   This creaky local legend is pushing 110 in a building from the 1500s. The friendly staff weaves expertly among the large, crowded tables to bring abundant portions of ravioli and *lamm-médaillons* (tender lamb medallions in rich sauce with rice and green beans) with Swiss efficiency. If you feel like loosening your wallet straps (and your belt), splurge on the local specialty

Bernerplatte, an enormous platter of grilled meats served over beans and kraut—it'll cost 40F ($30) but will probably tide you over for two meals. Most regulars prefer the jovial tavern atmosphere on the ground floor to the fancier, more sedate dining room upstairs.

Schauplatzgasse 16. (C) 031/311-2142. Reservations recommended. Main courses 20F–45F ($15–$34); quick lunch menu 17F–20F ($13–$15); full meal menu 24F ($18). DC, MC, V. Mon–Sat 11:30am–2pm and 6–10pm. Bus: 12 or 16. Tram: 9.

Frohsinn *Finds* FRENCH/SWISS This little restaurant, containing only a dozen tables, stands in the shadow of the Clock Tower. It attracts businesspeople, journalists, and politicians as much for its traditional cuisine as for its cozy atmosphere. The menu might include goose-liver mousse, liver with *rösti,* or filet of rabbit with watercress. Other dishes reflect a southern Italian influence, especially the homemade ravioli. Sabayon with strawberries is a seasonal specialty. You'll relish most of the dishes, all prepared with first-rate ingredients.

Münstergasse 54. (C) 031/311-3768. Reservations required. Main courses 25F–54F ($19–$41). AE, DC, MC, V. Tues–Sat 9am–11:30pm. Closed July 15–Aug 15. Tram: 54.

Ratskeller *Finds* SWISS If you want professional service and excellent meat dishes, this is one of the best splurge deals in town for an understated dinner. The house specialty, *Oberlander rösti,* is cheesy *rösti* layered with bacon and topped with a fried egg. It'll give you the energy to climb an Alp—and enough cholesterol to kill a mountain goat. Those with lighter appetites can go for the chicken Cordon Bleu or one of nine types of steak tartare (made using the finest Swiss cattle), from plain to curried to cooked in cognac. The laid-back brick-vaulted *keller* (cellar) is cheaper and offers four fixed-price meals daily.

Gerechtigkeitsgasse 81. (C) 031/311-1771. Reservations recommended. Main courses 20F–52F ($15–$39); cellar fixed-price lunch menu 20F ($15). AE, DC, MC, V. Daily 12:30–2pm and 6–10pm (cellar open only at lunch). Bus: 12.

4 Seeing the Sights

Bern's greatest sight is itself, a medieval town and shopper's paradise with a uniquely intact urban fabric whose buildings almost all date to the 15th century. Just south of the city is a vista-blessed modest mountain called **Gurtenkulm.** Tram 9 will take you to the funicular station for the ride up to the panoramic top (8.50F/$6.40). It takes 25 minutes each way—buy your ticket at the tourist office.

A STROLL THROUGH THE ALTSTADT

Bern's historic center is comfortably scenic and walkable, with low-key sights such as a dozen statue-topped fountains dating from the 1500s. Since the 16th century, the **Zytgloggeturm (Clock Tower)** *Finds,* on Kramgasse at the corner of Bärenplatz (tram/bus: 3, 5, 9, 12, or 30), has treated Bern to a simple mechanical puppet show 4 minutes before every hour. May to October, there's a 45-minute tour of the clock's inner workings daily at 4:30pm, with another tour at 11:30am July to August; it costs 8F ($6) adults and 4F ($3) children.

Switzerland began as a confederation of three forest cantons in 1291. Today's 23 cantons retain a remarkable degree of autonomy and governmental powers, making this one of the West's least centralized democracies. The federal chambers meet only four times a year for 3-week sessions to debate legislative issues and foreign treaties. If you're curious for a glimpse into such a lean federal machine, you can tour the 1902 **Bundeshaus (Parliament)** *Finds,* Bundesplatz ((C) 031/322-8522; www.parliament.ch; tram/bus: 10 or 19), whose dome was

Bern

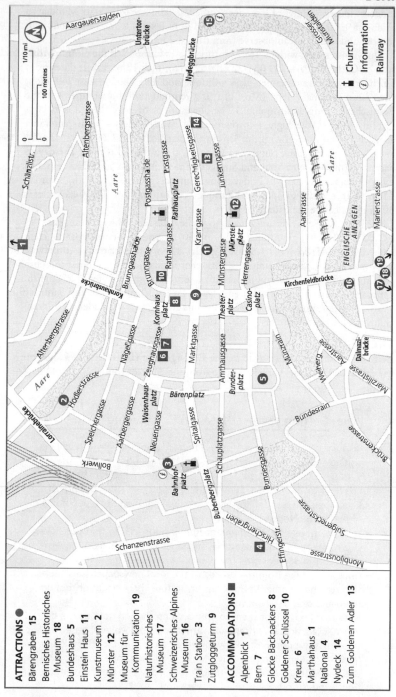

ATTRACTIONS ●

Bärengraben **15**
Bernisches Historisches
  Museum **18**
Bundeshaus **5**
Einstein Haus **11**
Kunstmuseum **2**
Münster **12**
Museum für
  Kommunikation **19**
Naturhistorisches
  Museum **17**
Schweizerisches Alpines
  Museum **16**
Tram Station **3**
Zytgloggeturm **9**

ACCOMMODATIONS ■

Alpenblick **1**
Bern **7**
Glocke Backpackers **8**
Goldener Schlüssel **10**
Kreuz **6**
Matthahaus **1**
National **4**
Nydeck **14**
Zum Goldenen Adler **13**

modeled loosely on that of Florence's cathedral. The free tours start Monday to Friday at 9, 10, and 11am and at 2, 3, and 4pm (except when Parliament is in session, and then you can observe from the galleries).

On Münsterplatz, with its 16th-century Moses fountain, is the Gothic **Münster,** or **Cathedral** 🏆🏆 (✆ **031/312-0462;** tram/bus: 12 or 30). It dates from 1421, with enormous stained-glass windows and an elaborate Last Judgment carved over the main door. (Most of it is a reproduction; the original is in the Bernisches Historisches Museum.) The biggest draw of the cathedral is its 90m (300-ft.) steeple, the highest in Switzerland, which offers a great panorama across Bern and its river with the Alps in the distance (3F/$2.25 adults; 1F/75¢ kids 7–16). From Easter Sunday to October, the cathedral is open Tuesday to Saturday from 10am to 5pm and Sunday from 11:30am to 5pm; November to Easter, hours are Tuesday to Friday from 11am to 1pm and 2 to 4pm, Saturday 11am to 1pm and 2 to 5pm, and Sunday 11:30am to 2pm. The steeple closes 30 minutes before the church.

In 1905, while living at what's now the **Einstein Haus,** Kramgasse 49 (✆ **031/312-0091;** tram/bus: 9, 12, or 30), a young German patent clerk named Albert devised his famous "Special Theory of Relativity" (otherwise known as $E = mc^2$), revolutionizing 20th-century science. The modest museum consists mainly of photos and photocopied letters, most translated into English. February to November, it's open Tuesday to Friday 10am to 5pm and Saturday 10am to 4pm. Admission is 3F ($2.25) adults and 2F ($1.50) students/children; children under 6 enter free.

THE BEAR PITS

Bern's most unusual sight has to be the **Bärengraben (Bear Pits)** 🏆🏆, just on the other side of Nydeggbrücke bridge from the Altstadt (bus: 12). Here you'll

---

⟨Value Getting the Best Deal on Sightseeing

- Be aware that if you're a museum hound, and especially if you'll be visiting museums in other Swiss cities, the monthly Swiss Museum Card gets you into just about every gallery for a mere 30F ($23)—but you have to visit most of Bern's museums before it starts paying off.
- Climb the cathedral bell tower, Switzerland's highest, for a panorama of the city rooftops.
- Tour the stately 1902 Parliament Building for free to find out how one of Europe's oldest countries manages to run a federal government on just $6 per citizen per year.
- Grab a free bike from the offices of the local newspaper (see "Getting Around," earlier in this chapter) to tour the Altstadt or tool up the banks of the Aare River.
- Note that Bern might seem to empty when the sun goes down, but many locals actually disappear into traditional *kellers* (basement taverns) and pubs. Ensconce yourself at a table in the Klöztlikeller (p. 244) or Pery Bar (see "Live-Music & Club Scene," later in this chapter) with a creamy beer or light local wine and watch the notoriously industrious Swiss relax and unwind.

Moments Floating Down the Aare

Unlike most capital cities, Bern has a river so unpolluted the locals actually swim in it regularly. In warm weather (late summer, when the river is slower, is best), join the Bernese for a short hike up the river and then a leisurely float down the Aare to a free public beach just below the Altstadt. (Make sure you get out at the beach, as a dam/waterfall is the river's next stop.) Wear sandals.

---

find up to 12 (usually more like four) very well-fed live examples of Bern's civic symbol roaming around. Bern has had bear pits since at least 1441—formerly on the square still named Bärenplatz, here since 1875. The bears are out daily 9am to 4pm (to 6pm in summer). The keeper sells 3F ($2.25) baggies of fruit to feed them, and these hairy fellows will ham it up to get you to drop them a piece of apple or carrot. Remember, they're strict vegetarians.

To the Bear Pits' left, a long path leads up the hillside to a ridge planted with Bern's fragrant **Rosengarten (Rose Garden),** with scenic views over medieval Bern.

MUSEUMS

Bern's only great museum is the **Kunstmuseum** (p. 250), although the Historical Museum (see below) is worth a visit as well. All except the Kunstmuseum are on or near Helvetiaplatz, just over Kirchenfeld Bridge (tram/bus: 3, 5, 19, or G).

The best of the rest is the **Schweizerisches Alpines Museum (Swiss Alpine Museum)** ⚜, Helvetiaplatz 4 (© **031/351-0434;** www.alpinesmuseum.ch). It explains all you ever wanted to know about the Alps with maps, do-it-yourself slide shows, and a whole passel of scale relief models of Alpine regions, some dating from 1800. Admission is 11F ($8.25) adults, 7.50F ($5.65) students/seniors, 3F ($2.25) children 6 to 16, and free for children under 6; it's open Monday from 2 to 5pm, and Tuesday to Sunday from 10am to 5pm (mid-Oct to May, closed noon–2pm).

Other museums might pique your interest. The **Naturhistoriches Museum (Natural History Museum),** Bernastrasse 15 (© **031/350-7111;** www.nmbe. unibe.ch), is not the best of its kind, but you can pay your respects to Barry (1800–14), the most famous of the old rescue St. Bernards. He saved more than 40 people before retiring to Bern at age 12. The **Museum fur Kommunikation (Museum of Communication),** Helvetiastrasse 16 (© **031/357-5555;** www. mfk.ch), spans everything from stamps to cellphones. Admission at either is 7F ($5.25) adults and 3F ($2.25) students and children 3 to 16. Both are open, roughly, Tuesday to Sunday from 10am to 5pm; the Natural History Museum also opens Monday 2 to 5pm.

Bernisches Historisches Museum (Bern Historical Museum) ⚜   Switzerland's second-largest historical museum occupies a fanciful faux-medieval castle from 1894 and contains a rich collection of artifacts. There's a bit of everything, from Burgundian suits of armor, furnishings, decorative arts, and Flemish tapestries to the original 15th-century carvings from the cathedral's Last Judgment portal and dioramas of everyday life in Bern over the past 3 centuries.

Helvetiaplatz 5. © **031/350-7711.** www.bhm.ch. Admission 13F ($9.75) adults, 8F ($6) students and seniors, free to all Sat. Tues–Sun 10am–5pm (Wed until 10pm). Tram/bus: 3, 5, 19, or G.

Special & Free Events

Bern's not a top festival town, but it does have some fine music fests and seasonal markets. The annual **Easter Egg Market** is kind of cute (except to professional collectors, for whom it's very serious). Much bigger affairs are the May **Geranium Market** and the famed **Onion Market** (4th Mon in Nov), which fills Bern's streets with stalls selling far more than just traditional onions. A **Christmas Market,** starting in late November, does the same with stalls selling toys and lots of hand-carved wood.

The **Jazz Festival** in early May kicks off the musical calendar, followed by Tuesday-evening recitals in the cathedral throughout July and August, and pop and rock concerts on Bern's mini-mountain during the July **Gurten Festival.** All of these are part of the overarching July-to-September Summertime Festival of plays, dance, jazz, and folk music throughout the Altstadt.

Kunstmuseum (Fine Arts Museum) ✶✶✶   This museum preserves the world's largest collection of paintings and drawings by Bern native Paul Klee, offering a unique insight into this early-20th-century master's skill with color and expression. Although it also has a smattering of old masters such as Fra Angelico, Duccio, and Delacroix, the museum's particular strength is late-19th- and early-20th-century art: a few works each by the best Impressionists and surrealists, along with paintings by Kandinsky, Modigliani, Matisse, Picasso, Léger, Pollock, and Rothko.

Hodlerstrasse 12. ✆ **031/311-0944.** www.kunstmuseumbern.ch. Admission 7F ($5.25) adults, 5F ($3.75) students; special exhibitions 8F–14F ($6–$11). Tues 10am–9pm; Wed–Sun 10am–5pm. Tram/bus: 20 or 21 (or 5-min. walk from train station).

ORGANIZED TOURS

The tourist office sponsors a 2-hour **bus tour** of the center and major sights with a multilingual guide, costing 29F ($22) adults and 10F ($7.50) children. It starts at 11am June to September daily; April, May, and October Monday to Saturday; and November to March Saturday only. A 2-hour **walking tour** of the Altstadt costs 14F ($11) and leaves at 11am daily June to September. You can see the city from below on a 90-minute **raft tour** daily at 5pm (45F/$34 adults; 25F/$19 children). This is a genuine rubber raft deal, not a cruise-type riverboat, meaning you help paddle and need to bring a swimsuit. A minimum of five adults is required to run the tour.

5 Shopping

Bern has 6km (3¾ miles) of virtually continuous shopping arcades running down its three parallel main streets, with even more shops crowding the alleys and corridors connecting them. You can buy anything from chocolates to cheesy cuckoo clocks to tapestries to Swiss Army knives. Here are the most popular purchases most budgeters can afford.

Switzerland is home to Nestlé, Lindt, and those triangular Toblerone **chocolates.** You can get the famous factory-made chockies at **Merkur,** Spitalgasse 2

(Tips **Market Watch**

The Tuesday- and Saturday-morning **market stalls** sell handmade knick-knacks on Waisenhausplatz, fruit and produce on the connected Bären-platz, flowers on the southerly Bundesplatz, and meat on Münstergasse. From May to October, the Bärenplatz fruit and flower stalls are open daily to 6pm, later on Thursday. The **Onion Market** fills the city on the fourth Monday in November. The daily December **Christmas Market** is on Mün-sterplatz and Waisenhausplatz.

(© 031/311-0425; tram/bus: 3, 11, or 12). You'll also find handmade sweets from a traditional confectioner—try the truffles, little chocolate spheres with a variety of fillings. **Confisserie Abegglen,** Spitalgasse 36 (© 031/311-2111; tram/bus: 3, 5, 9, or 12), specializes in chocolate truffles, gingerbread, and *caramel mous* (cubes of caramel encased in a soft sugary glaze). **Confisserie Tschirren,** Kram-gasse 73 (© 031/311-1717; tram/bus: 12), offers pastries, chocolates, and a delec-table form of peppermint-infused fudge.

Although the Swiss set their **watches** by the workshops in Geneva, shop-happy Bern has more than its share of outlets—plus every other store in town has a dis-play of Swatches and the ever-popular Swiss Army watches. If you're in the mar-ket for a fine watch, the shop with the most reasonable prices is **Columna,** Spitalgasse 4 (© 031/311-0975; tram/bus: 3, 11, or 12), where Swatches start at 50F ($38) and Tissots at 125F ($94). If you're using this guide mainly to save enough to afford that 3,750F ($2,813) Rolex (that's the cheapest model), put on your best and head to the burnished wood shrine of **Bucherer,** Marktgasse 38 (© 031/328-9090; tram/bus: 3, 5, 9, or 12).

Hullinger Swiss Knife Shop, Aarbergergasse 11 (© 031/311-1992; tram/bus: 11, 20, or 21), carries cutlery in addition to **Swiss Army knives** and Leatherman-type mini-tool sets. The general souvenir shops listed next carry dozens of Victorinox and Wenger knives (the two major brands), but you'll sometimes get the best prices from the locksmith shop **Schlüssel Bern,** Neuen-gasse 5 (© 031/312-1315; tram/bus: 11 or 21). **Stauffacher,** Neuengasse 25 (© 031/311-2411), has a remarkable five floors of books, including a huge selection of new and used books in English on the third floor.

For a little bit of everything Swiss (or at least imagined to be Swiss), from watches and knives to cuckoo clocks, music boxes, and teddy bears, try **Swiss Plaza,** Kramgasse 75 (© 031/311-5616; tram/bus: 12 or 30); or **Edelweiss,** Gerechtigkeitsgasse 21 (tram/bus: 3, 5, 9, or 12). For less touristy (and more genu-ine) but rather more expensive handicrafts—clothing, leather, ceramics, glass, and metalwork—head to **Heimatwerk,** Kramgasse 61 (© 031/311-3000; bus: 12; tram: 3, 5, or 9).

6 Bern After Dark

THE PERFORMING ARTS

The best operas and ballets are at the gorgeous 19th-century **Stadttheater,** Kornhausplatz 14 (© 031/329-5111; tram/bus: 3, 5, 9, 10, 12, or 30). Bern's well-regarded symphony plays in the **Casino music hall,** Herrengasse 25 (© 031/311-4242; www.bernorchester.ch; tram/bus: 3 or 5).

As for traditional Swiss folk music, you can sometimes catch a virtuoso Alphorn player or professional yodeling ensemble at the premier venues above or in a small concert space in the revamped **Kornhaus,** Kornhausplatz 18 (© **031/ 327-7270;** www.kornhaus.org; tram/bus: 3, 5, 9, 10, 12, or 30).

LIVE-MUSIC & CLUB SCENE

The premier lounge for hearing live jazz is **Marian's Jazzroom,** in the Hotel Innere Enge, Engestrasse 54 (© **031/309-6111;** www.bluesline.com; tram/bus: 21). There are live acts Tuesday through Saturday night, plus a Sunday jazz brunch. Bern throws a Jazz Festival in early May.

Much of Bern's nightlife centers on Aarbergerstrasse. **Cafe Aarbergerhof,** Aarbergerstrasse 40 (© **031/311-0870;** tram/bus: 11, 20, or 21), is a spartan but lively cross between a cafe (cheap Swiss dishes and a 15.50F/$12 menu) and a university bar. The stylish **Divino,** Aarbergerstrasse 35 (© **031/311-0200;** tram/bus: 11, 20, or 21), offers the same cafe-bar mix but with a lot more class (and the prices to prove it). Downstairs, its sibling, **Tonis** (© **031/311-0200;** www. tonis.ch), is the hottest city-center disco of the moment.

For a similar but less relentlessly trendy (and cheaper) pairing of bar and disco, head to Gurtengasse 3, where you'll find two interconnected cafes, both of which do a landslide business on weekends. Catering to a crowd in their 30s and over is the **Art Cafe** (© **031/318-2070**), where a medley of pre-recorded jazz and house music keeps the crowd drinking and dancing till late. Right next door, and attracting a 20-something crowd, is **Eclipse** (© **031/318-4700**), a cafe and bar where music focuses on punk and rock. Across the street, at Gurtengasse 3, is **Babalu** (© **031/311-0888**), a small but fun disco that draws a diverse crowd (20s–40s) and charges an entrance fee ranging from 7F to 10F ($5.25–$7.50).

After work, Bern's yuppies loosen their ties under the high postmodern vaults of the revamped **Kornhaus's ground-floor cafe** (see "The Performing Arts," above, for contact information). Drinks aren't the cheapest, but it's a semi-refined schmoozefest, with well-spaced cafe tables and light meals.

If you're looking for a more "Swiss" evening, seek out one of the *keller* taverns like the **Klötzlikeller** (see "Great Deals on Dining," earlier in this chapter). Or head to the **Pery Bar** on the ground floor of Räblus restaurant, Zueghausgasse 3/Kornhausplatz (© **031/311-5908;** tram/bus: 3, 5, 9, 10, 12, or 30). This Swiss pub with excellent wines and drinks strikes just the right balance between an antique atmosphere of carved wood-plank ceilings and a modern meeting place where the DJ plays rock and pop quietly enough that you can converse.

Bar aux Petits Fours, Kramgasse 67 (© **031/312-7374**), is the best gay bar in Bern, attracting a multilingual, attractive, and international group of gay people, mostly men. There's no dance floor and no restaurant on the premises, but what you get is a low-key bar, filled with regular clients, where a newcomer with a bit of effort can usually break the glacial freeze of Swiss reserve. Open daily 6pm to 12:30am.

A CASINO

Grand Casino Kursaal, Kornhausstrasse 3 (© **031/339-5555**), is the only place in town to gamble. Indeed, it's a great spot for novices to learn because serious money rarely changes hands here. It's open daily from noon to 3:30am, and admission is free. Drinks cost 11F to 15F ($8.25–$11). There are three restaurants and two bars, plus a dance hall, which charges a 15F ($11) cover. It's open Friday to Saturday from 9pm to 3:30am and Sunday from 3 to 10pm.

7 Side Trips: Interlaken ⚹ & the Berner Oberland ⚹⚹⚹

The alpine **Berner Oberland** south of Bern encompasses the legendary craggy **Jungfrau,** Queen of the Alps. This most popular area of the Swiss Alps is littered with tiny villages and small resort towns like **Mürren** and **Grindelwald,** either of which puts you halfway between the civilization of Switzerland and the primal wilderness of Europe's grandest mountain range. From the **Jungfraujoch**— at 3,400m (11,333 ft.), Europe's highest rail station—you're treated to one of the world's great panoramas, sweeping across the Alps and encompassing more than half of Switzerland.

The gateway to the Berner Oberland is **Interlaken,** a bustling resort town in the foothills, flanked by a pair of scenic lakes and just an hour's train ride from Bern. Interlaken itself doesn't have too much to entice you, but it makes a good base—and a requisite stop at any rate—for forays into the Alps.

INTERLAKEN & ITS LAKES

Interlaken used to be four separate villages but is now a conglomeration of vaguely alpine-looking modern hotels and a tourist office whose main job is to show you what you can do if you head out of Interlaken in any direction. This vacation base lies at the foothills of the Alps, a few minutes by train from the Lauterbrunnen Valley and the heart of the Berner Oberland. It occupies a brief stretch of the Aare River as it connects two lakes, Thun and Brienz—hence the city's name, "between the lakes."

There are two **trains** an hour from Bern to Interlaken (23F/$17 one-way; 45 min.), some requiring a change in Spiez. Interlaken has two rail stations. Get off at Interlaken Westbahnhof station for the main part of town and the hotels listed in this chapter; disembark at Interlaken Ostbahnhof station to transfer to trains into the Jungfrau region.

The **Tourist Office** is a 7-minute walk from the Westbahnhof, on Harderstrasse just left off Höheweg at the Hotel Metropole (© **033/826-5300;** fax 033/822-5221; www.interlakentourism.ch). It's the central information bureau for the region, with maps and advice on the entire Berner Oberland. It is open Monday to Friday 8am to 6pm and Saturday 9am to noon; in summer, it often stays open until 5pm Saturday and also is open Sunday 5 to 7pm.

SEEING THE SIGHTS   Interlaken makes a good base yet not a thrilling destination. Its marginally interesting **Tourism Museum,** Obere Gasse 26 ((© **033/ 822-9839),** is open May to October, Tuesday to Sunday 2 to 5pm; admission is 5F ($3.75) adults and 3F ($2.25) children. For another low-key thrill, ride the **Harder Klum funicular,** near Ostbahnhof (© **033/828-7216;** www.jungfrau bahn.ch), past a wildlife preserve to the top of the mountain backing Interlaken, and you'll get a vista across forested hills to the Alps beyond Interlaken's lakes (22F/$17 round-trip).

The **Thunersee (Lake Thun)** is the more popular of Interlaken's two lakes ((© **033/251-0000** or 033/654-7266; www.thunersee.ch). A 3-hour boat tour ((© **033/334-5211;** www.bls.ch) runs year-round (eight times per day in summer, once daily in winter) and costs 28F to 40F ($21–$30) adults, 14F to 20F ($11–$15) children. The lake's main town of **Thun** (tourist information at the train station; © **033/222-2340)** lies at the opposite end of the lake from Interlaken. Thun has long since overgrown its island core, perched where the lake flows out to become the Aare River again. On the Aare's right bank lies Thun's **Hauptgasse,** the arcaded and shop-lined main drag. From the 17th-century

---

Value **Get Your Guest Card**

In Interlaken and Berner Oberland resort villages, you'll receive a "guest card" from your hotel that includes significant discounts on everything from the Jungfrau train to adventure outfitters. If you don't get one upon check-in, be sure to ask for it.

---

town hall on Rathausplatz, you can climb a long stairway up to **Schloss Thun** or **Castle Kyburg** (© 033/223-2001), a fortress from the 1100s. It's occasionally open as a museum with military collections, archaeological finds, and a Gobelin tapestry; note that it doesn't always follow these official hours: June to September daily 9am to 6pm; April, May, and October daily 10am to 5pm; winter daily 1 to 4pm. Admission is 6F ($4.50) adults, 2F ($1.50) children. More certain to be open is the **Oberhofen Castle** (© 033/243-1235), on the lake's north shore. Its rooms are set up just as they appeared in various periods from the 16th to the 19th centuries. From mid-May to mid-October, it's open Tuesday to Sunday 11am to 5pm and Monday 2 to 5pm. Admission is 7.50F ($5.65) adults, 3F ($2.25) students and children.

You can also tour **Lake Brienz** (www.brienzersee.ch), out the other end of Interlaken, for 30F ($23). The round-trip takes a little under 3 hours; it stops at the cute lakeside village of Iseltwald and at **Geissbach.** Geissbach has magnificent waterfalls, which you can reach from Iseltwald on foot in under 2 hours, or by funicular (May–Oct only; 4.50F/$2.50) from the boat's final stop, the town of **Brienz,** famous for its wood carving.

Near Brienz, outside the village of **Ballenberg,** is the **Swiss Open-Air Museum** (© 033/951-1123). It consists of 2,000 acres (809 hectares) laid out roughly as a map of Switzerland, with the vernacular architecture of each region and canton re-created using original buildings. Rather than eat at the cafeteria, save your hunger for the freshly made breads, cheeses, and sausages sold at the various working farmhouses and "settlements" that make up the park. This odd but enjoyable establishment is open April 15 to October, daily 10am to 5pm; admission is 16F ($12) adults, 14F ($11) students, and 8F ($6) children. The bus leaves Brienz at 2:26pm, returning from Ballenberg at 4:55pm. (If ferries don't float your boat, you can also take the train from Interlaken to Thun or Brienz.)

WHERE TO STAY   Interlaken's high season is summer, when rates go way up at most hotels. In a pinch, there's a hotel billboard with a phone outside each train station; or the tourist office (© 033/826-5300; www.interlaken tourism.ch) will book you a room for free.

The **Splendid,** Hoheweg 33 (© 033/822-7612; fax 033/822-7679; www. splendid.ch), is a nondescript 35-room modern hotel in the center of town. It offers comfortable accommodations, all with private bathroom, a few amenities, glimpses of the mountains, and a popular corner pub with Internet access. Doubles cost 170F to 210F ($128–$158), depending on the season. Just off the main drag, the 150-room **Chalet-Hotel Oberland** ⋟ (© 033/827-8787; fax 033/827-8770; www.chalet-oberland.ch) offers somewhat nicer, newer, and roomier accommodations for 182F to 222F ($137–$167), depending on the season. Both accept American Express, MasterCard, and Visa; the Chalet-Hotel Oberland also takes Diners Club.

The best deal is the **Swiss Inn Apartments** 🌟🌟, in a residential neighborhood at Général Guisanstrasse 23 (© **033/822-3626;** fax 033/823-2303; www. swiss-inn.com). Reserve early for one of Herr Müller's six huge apartments with kitchenettes, TVs, phones, and mountain views—they cost only 130F to 210F ($98–$158) for two and 220F to 320F ($165–$240) for four (a bit more for each extra person). He also rents five doubles for 100F to 170F ($75–$128), offers a package deal that includes room and rental of a Smart car, and accepts American Express, MasterCard, and Visa. Also check out **Hirschen** (see 261).

WHERE TO DINE   You can fill your daypack for picnics and hikes at the huge **Coop supermarket** center across from the Ostbahnhof, or at **Migros supermarket** on Bahnhofstrasse near Westbahnhof. (Exit the station, and turn left to walk along the tracks toward town; at the intersection at the end of the station parking lot, turn left to cross over the tracks and two narrow branches of the river, and the Migros is on the right.)

Almost every visitor at some point pays a visit to **Schuh,** Höheweg 56 (© **033/822-94-41**), a restaurant/tearoom in the center of town. Housed in a classic alpine building, Schuh's been serving the town's best pastries since 1885, and you can also order reasonably priced set menus here as well. Open Tuesday to Sunday 8am to 11pm; closed October 25 to December 9. American Express, Diners Club, MasterCard, and Visa are accepted.

For relatively cheap, hearty, but surprisingly good food in an unassuming modern tavern atmosphere, head to the **Goldener Anker** 🌟, Marktgasse 57, between the train tracks and the river (© **033/822-1672;** www.anker.ch). Vegetarian or low-fat platters are a special feature here. Open daily 4pm to 12:30am, it accepts American Express, MasterCard, and Visa.

Tips **Preparing for the Alps**

Prepare for the unique climate of the skyscraping Alps before you get on that train to the top of the world. A warm, sunny day in Interlaken might still be sunny atop the Jungfrau, but the wind can drop temperatures deep into negative territory, so bring a heavy jacket. The sun reflects strongly off all that snow, and UV rays are more concentrated, so wear shades and sunscreen. The highest peaks poke into a very thin atmosphere (about 30% less oxygen than at sea level), so it's easy to overexert yourself into dizziness and hyperventilation.

Also check the weather conditions and forecasts before you set off into the mountains. An overcast day can make an excursion to the panoramic terraces of Jungfrau or Schilthorn a moot point, and avalanche warnings might crimp your skiing or hiking plans. Displayed on TVs at train stations, tourist offices, and hotel rooms, and live-linked at www.swisspanorama.com, is a live video feed that switches from the Jungfraujoch to the Schilthorn to Männlichen. The website **www. meteotest.ch** will fax or e-mail you a personalized weather forecast, or you can check in with the local tourist office. Real-time forecasts are available at © **0900/576152** by calling from anywhere in Europe or in Switzerland.

Finds **A Drink with a View**

Even on a budget, you can ride the skyscraping Hotel Metropole's elevator to the 18th floor and the **Top o' Met cafe** 🌟, Höheweg 37 (© **033/828-
6666**). Just 4.50F ($3.40) will buy you a hot cocoa against a backdrop of
Interlaken's best alpine panorama. It's open daily 11am to 11pm, and
accepts American Express, Diners Club, MasterCard, and Visa.

For cheap Italian food and pizzas, try **Pizpaz,** Bahnhofstrasse 1 (© **033/822-
2533**), open Tuesday to Sunday 11am to midnight. For rather better cuisine but
seriously high prices, **Il Bellini** 🌟🌟, in the Hotel Metropole, Höheweg 37
(© **033/828-6666**), is one of the best French/international restaurants in
Switzerland, and a worthy splurge. It's open Tuesday to Saturday 11:30am to
2pm and 6:30 to 10pm. Both restaurants accept American Express, Diners
Club, MasterCard, and Visa.

THE BEST OF THE BERNER OBERLAND

Berner Oberland is dominated by the triple peaks of the **Eiger** (3,908m/13,025
ft.), **Mönch** (4,035m/13,450 ft.), and mighty **Jungfrau** (4,093m/13,642 ft.).
The entire region offers thrilling rides on scenic trains hugging (or punching
through) cliffsides and on ski-lift gondolas dangling high above mountain
passes. Winter and spring bring out the skiers in droves. Spring and summer
seduce hordes of hikers trekking through the high green meadows carpeted with
bright wildflowers, tinkling with cowbells, accented with plunging waterfalls,
and dotted with villages, all set against the backdrop of those glacier-clad Alps.
From late September to mid-December, the resorts become ghost towns as many
hotels close up for the autumn.

Lauterbrunnen Valley runs south from Interlaken, with trains to the
Jungfraujoch branching off to inch up its east cliffside. The resort of **Mürren**
perches on the Lauterbrunnen's west lip toward the valley's end, under the grand
Schilthorn. On the valley floor lie the tiny town and transit stations of **Lauterbrunnen** (where you change from your Interlaken train to one that hauls you
up through the way-station towns of **Wengen** and **Kleine Scheidegg** to the
Jungfraujoch, or another that climbs to **Mürren**). A post-bus ride farther up
the valley, **Stechelberg** is a collection of houses around the cable-car station up
to Mürren and the Schilthorn.

Just over the **Männlichen** massif rising east of this valley is the gentler river-
carved **Grindelwald Valley,** where you'll find the sprawling car-accessible resort
of **Grindelwald.** (You can catch the train or drive from Lauterbrunnen.)

You can get updated info on the entire region at the website
www.jungfraubahn.ch.

GETTING AROUND   The various scenic and private rail lines—plus cog
railways, cable cars, and ski lifts—connecting the peaks and towns can get very
expensive. **Rail passes** such as Swissrail, the Swiss Flexi Pass, and Eurail (or
a regional ski pass; see the box "Alpine Ski Passes & Rentals," below) can get
you on some private rail lines and even lifts free, but on the popular scenic
sections—Lauterbrunnen or Grindelwald to the Jungfraujoch, and Mürren to
the Schilthorn—you get a discount of only 25%. Always ask about **discounts**
for children (if you have some sort of pass, kids under 16 often ride free), seniors,
families, or students. There are special **early-bird morning discount** fares

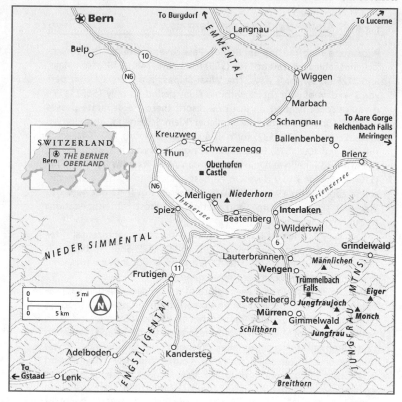

(about 25% off) up to the Jungfraujoch and the Schilthorn. The tourist office in Interlaken has Berner Oberland transportation maps and schedules. Whatever trains or gondolas don't cover, Switzerland's efficient yellow post **buses** do (© **033/828-8828;** www.postauto.ch).

The May-to-October **Berner Oberland Regional Pass** gets you 7 days of travel (3 days free, 4 at 50% off) for 195F ($146), or 15 days of travel (5 days free, 10 at 50% off) for 240F ($180), but again, it grants you a discount only on the Jungfraujoch and Schilthorn rides.

Only Grindelwald is directly accessible by car. For Mürren, you have two options: Drive to Lauterbrunnen and park in the **garage** next to the train station for 10F ($7.50) per day in summer or 12F ($9) in winter, then take the train up to Mürren, or drive to the end of the valley and park in the open lot under the Stechelberg lift (which also gets you up to Mürren) for similar rates.

MÜRREN & THE SCHILTHORN

At 1,634m (5,445 ft.), **Mürren** is the highest town in the Berner Oberland. This little burg of 350 souls feels less like a modern resort than a pleasant Swiss alpine town that just happens to have a cluster of hotels and a dedicated troupe of Swiss and British visitors who return every year. It perches on its ledge atop the west rim of the Lauterbrunnen Valley, a halfway station between the valley floor and the craggy Schilthorn peak with its revolving restaurant and exquisite views across the valley to the even taller Eiger, Mönch, and Jungfrau peaks.

Value   Alpine Ski Passes & Rentals

Prices for a **Jungfrau Top Ski Region Pass** covering trains, lifts, funiculars, and cable cars start at 118F ($89) for 2 days, 248F ($186) for 5 days, and 312F ($234) for 7 days. The **Whal-Skipass** is a flexipass that gets you 3 ski days of your choice within a 7-day period for only 156F ($117). If you're concentrating on just one resort, there are **separate passes** for the Mürren/Schilthorn, Männlichen/Klein Scheidegg, and First ski areas. Each costs 42F ($32) for half a day (after noon), 55F ($41) for a full day, and 100F ($75) for 2 days. **For nonskiers** who just want to ride the lifts and hike in the snow, there's an **Aktiv-Pass** for 138F to 230F ($104–$173) for 3 to 7 days. On all passes, kids 6 to 15 get a 50% discount, those 16 to 19 get 20% off, and seniors over 62 get 10% off. Buy your ski pass at any train station and most cable-car stations throughout the region.

Each town generally has two or three **ski shops,** and **rental** rates tend to be the same everywhere: 38F to 50F ($29–$38) for basic skis (and boots), and 48F to 70F ($36–$53) for test skis or snowboards. Children under 16 often get discounted gear.

If you plan to ski in as many regions of the Bernese Oberland as possible, consider renting your ski equipment from **Intersport,** a sporting goods store that maintains 90 branches throughout Switzerland, with outlets in each of the high-profile resorts of the Oberland, including Lauterbrunne, Mürren, Interlaken, Wengen, and Grindelwald. If you rent equipment from any branch of this outfit, and after a day of using it find that you'd prefer a different make, model, or venue, you can exchange your equipment at any branch of the chain. For more information, contact their main office in Grindelwald (© 033/853-0400), or check out the website at www.intersportrent.ch or www.skiservice-grindelwald.ch.

Trains run every 30 minutes from Interlaken's Ostbahnhof, with a change at Lauterbrunnen (60 min.; 16F/$12). When the funicular/train line from Lauterbrunnen to Mürren is snowed in, take the hourly post bus (15 min.; 9F/$6.75) to Stechelberg and the half-hourly Schilthornbahn cable car (© 033/856-2141; www.schilthorn.ch) up to Mürren (10 min.; 15F/$11).

Mürren's **Tourist Office** is in the Sportszentrum (© 033/856-8686; fax 033/856-8696; www.muerren.ch). Hours are a bit flexible here. In general, the office is open Monday to Friday 9am to 7pm (to 8:30pm on Thurs), Saturday 8am to 7pm, and Sunday 8:30am to 6pm.

SKIING & OTHER ACTIVITIES   Mürren boasts 42km (26 miles) of **ski trails.** The skiing isn't as good as from Grindelwald but is considerably less crowded. The **Ski School,** opposite the Hotel Bellevue (©/fax 033/855-1247), offers private lessons at 110F ($83) for 2 hours and up to four people, or 48F ($36) for a half-day lesson in a class. There are two **ski rental** outfits: the one adjacent to the Sportszentrum (see below), and the **Stäger-Sport** (© 033/855-2355; www.staegersport.ch), which has the wider selection and also rents ice skates (8F/$6 per day).

There's also some decent **hiking** in the area, plus snowshoe trekking in winter. Mürren has a modern **Sportszentrum** sports complex (© 033/856-8686), with an indoor pool, an outdoor skating rink, squash and tennis courts, and free curling lessons Tuesday afternoons to anyone staying in a Mürren hotel, 5F ($2.75) if you're just passing through. At other times, lessons cost from 12F to 22F ($6.60–$12.10).

THE SCHILTHORN   One of the most dramatic excursions is taking the dizzying cable car from Mürren up to the peak of the **Schilthorn** ✮✮✮ (© 033/826-0007; www.schilthorn.ch). The mountain crests at 2,941m (9,804 ft.), and since it's across the Lauterbrunnen Valley from the Big Three peaks, you get a panorama of the Alps' poster children. Half-hourly cable cars from Mürren get you to the top in 20 minutes at a round-trip cost of 92F ($69); discounts are available for various rail- and ski-pass holders. If you're up for a workout, you can hike up in a rather demanding but exhilarating 5 hours. It's a 1,309m (4,363-ft.) climb.

The summit boasts the scenic **Piz Gloria** restaurant (© 033/856-2141), slowly rotating on its dramatic perch with video screens playing a loop of its starring role as SPECTRE headquarters in the James Bond flick *On Her Majesty's Secret Service*. If you can tear your eyes away from the view, sample the hearty Hungarian goulash or sirloin steak. Catch the first car up for a high-altitude breakfast. It accepts American Express, Diners Club, MasterCard, and Visa and is open daily from the first cable car's arrival until the last one's departure (closed Nov 15–Dec 15, 1 week in May, and during blizzards).

WHERE TO STAY & DINE   Although it's quite pricey, one of the top choices is the **Hotel Alpenruh** ✮ (© 033/856-8800; fax 033/856-8888; www.schilthorn.ch), a cozy but well-equipped hotel next to the cable-car station with an excellent restaurant and a private sauna. Doubles run 180F to 360F ($135–$270). It accepts American Express, Diners Club, MasterCard, and Visa; the restaurant closes in November.

If you're after lower prices and panoramic views, head to the cliff-top **Alpina** (© 033/855-1361; fax 033/855-1049; www.muerren.ch/alpina), where the Tauwalder family runs a friendly little hotel and restaurant with great vistas across the Lauterbrunnen Valley. Doubles go for 140F to 200F ($105–$150), depending on the season, with bathrooms but no phones. There's a TV lounge, or you can pay 8F ($6) for a TV in your room. Half-board costs 25F to 30F ($19–$23) extra. Alpina accepts American Express, Diners Club, MasterCard, and Visa.

Try to take at least one meal at the excellent and moderately priced **Eigerstübli** ✮ basement restaurant in the pricey Eiger Hotel (© 033/856-5454), and have breakfast once at the **Piz Gloria** atop the Schilthorn (see above). The cheapest nonhotel eats are at the **Stügerstübli** (© 033/855-1316), a rough-and-ready locals' joint in the town center. It is open daily from noon to midnight and accepts MasterCard and Visa. Nearby is the **Co-op grocery store,** open Monday, Wednesday, and Friday 8am to noon and 1:45 to 6:30pm.

THE JUNGFRAU: ON TOP OF THE WORLD

The most spectacular and rewarding excursion in the region is to **Jungfraujoch** ✮✮✮. At 340m (11,333 ft.)—the highest rail station in Europe—your breath is quickened by the stupendous views and the extremely thin air. An elevator takes you up from the station to the even higher Sphinx Terrace viewpoint to look out over Europe's longest glacier, the 25km (16-mile) **Great Aletsch,** whose melt-off eventually makes its way to the Mediterranean.

The view goes on seemingly forever—on a clear day, you can even see as far as Germany's Black Forest. One of the popular attractions is the *Eispalast* (Ice Palace), a warren of tunnels carved into a living glacier and filled with whimsical ice sculptures, including a family of penguins and a sumo wrestler. There's a mediocre **restaurant** and a **cafeteria** at the top in case you didn't pack lunch.

Trains run every hour from Interlaken's Ostbahnhof (2½ hr.; 168F/$126 round-trip). You change once in Lauterbrunnen (© **033/828-7038**), pause in Wengen, and change again in Kleine Scheidegg (© **033/828-7038**) before making the final run to Jungfraujoch station (© **033/828-7901**). Since 1894, this popular route has run like a machine well oiled with tourist money, so the transfers are smooth. Four of the last 9.5km (6 miles) of track are in tunnels, but the train pauses a few times to let you peer out through windows in the rock at the glaciated surroundings. On your way back down, you can change trains at Kleine Scheidegg to detour west through Grindelwald. For more information, contact the Jungfraubahnen (© **033/828-7901**; www.jungfraubahn.ch).

GRINDELWALD

Cars can reach **Grindelwald** 🚗, so this large, resortlike (and slightly more expensive) village in the eastern alpine foothills gets more crowded than its less accessible neighbors. However, the setting is panoramic: Huge frozen rivers of glaciers spill down the steep sides of its wide valley. And it's an ideal base for both hiking and skiing. Lifts and cable cars reach both the Männlichen ski area on the Grindelwald Valley's west flank and the First ski and hiking area rising to the east; there are 200km (124 miles) of slopes (no joke), 50 lifts, and a vertical drop on some runs of up to 1,980m (6,600 ft.). Grindelwald is also the only area to offer night skiing (Tues, Thurs, and Sat).

Grindelwald is Switzerland's oldest winter ski resort. It was founded in 1888, just 30 years after German and English tourists began coming to the Alps to hike, skate, and marvel at the views—and only 5 years after one visitor had the bright idea to bring along a pair of those weird Norwegian contraptions called skis.

ARRIVING & INFORMATION There are half-hourly **trains** from Interlaken's Ostbahnhof (36 min.; 9.80F/$7.35); be sure you're on the right car, as the train splits in half at Lauterbrunnen. Grindelwald's **Tourist Office** (© **033/854-1212;** fax 033/854-1210; www.grindelwald.ch) is open mid-December to April, Monday to Friday 8am to noon and 1:30 to 6pm, Saturday 8am to noon and 2 to 5pm, Sunday 9am to noon and 3 to 5pm; June to October, Monday to Friday 9am to 7pm, Saturday 8am to 5pm, Sunday 9 to 11am and 3 to 5pm; May and November to mid-December, Monday to Friday 8am to noon and 2 to 8pm, Saturday 8am to noon.

Grindelwald has a branch of the **Swiss Ski School** (© **033/853-5200;** www.grindelwald.ch/skischule), where attending a 3-day course costs 185F ($139). Private lessons go for a whopping 320F ($240) a day, or 80F ($60) an hour. You can **rent ski gear** at Ski-Service near the Grindelwald-Grund station (© **033/853-0400**). The **Sportszentrum** (© **033/854-1230**) offers everything from curling and swimming to a fitness center and an indoor climbing wall.

HIKING The Tourist Office has trail maps covering everything from easy scenic rambles to rock climbing up the sheer eastern face of Mount Eiger.

An hour's hike up to **Milchbach** brings you to the base of the Obere Gletscher glacier, whose milky-white runoff gives the spot its name. If you continue 45 minutes up the side of the glacier, you're treated to the **Blue Ice Grotte.** Glacial ice turns a deep, resonant blue as you get down into it. However, visitors are no longer allowed to go inside the glacier, because the ice is too dangerous. A post bus costing 9.80F ($7.35) will take you from the center of town to a station nearby where you can view the glacier.

One of the region's best picture postcards—the snowcapped Alps rising from behind a flat-glass mini-mountain lake called the **Bachsee**—is a fairly easy hour's uphill hike (only about 70m/232 ft. total elevation) from the first cable-car station above Grindelwald.

WHERE TO STAY & DINE   One of the best and most reasonable places for comfortable rooms and excellent (albeit expensive) Swiss meals is **Hirschen** (© 033/854-8484; fax 033/854-8480; www.hirschen-grindelwald.ch), between the station and the First cable car. Units are stylishly outfitted with oak furnishings and rustic paintings, and some are equipped with four-poster beds. A double costs 150F to 210F ($113–$158), depending on the season. The restaurant accepts American Express, MasterCard, and Visa, and closes only from early November to mid-December.

The year-round **Hotel Grindelwalderhof** (© 033/854-4010; fax 033/854-4019; www.grindelwalderhof.ch) is a 19-room chalet at the heart of town with all the amenities. Opened in 1994, the hotel lies only a 5-minute walk from the railway station. Doubles cost 150F to 260F ($113–$195), depending on the season; American Express, Diners Club, MasterCard, and Visa are accepted. In business since 1994, the pleasant little 16-room **Tschuggen** (© 033/853-1781; fax 033/ 853-2690; tschuggen.grindelwald@bluewin.ch) has double rooms ranging from 150F to 190F ($113–$143) in summer, 230F to 260F ($173–$195) in winter. The cozy, compact, and rather rustic guest rooms contain TV, phone, and mini-bar. They accept American Express, MasterCard, and Visa. On-site and under different management is a reasonably priced Korean restaurant. Most people dine at their hotels or pick up picnic supplies at the **Coop** opposite the Tourist Office or the string of small **shops**—butcher, cheese and wine, and bakery—a block farther on. There are a few cheap restaurants scattered throughout town, including one in the **Sportszentrum** (© 033/853-3277), open daily 7:30am to 11:30pm. It's rather touristy, but the **Restaurant Glacier** (© 033/853-1004) accompanies its moderately priced tasty Swiss cuisine with live folk music Friday nights from January to April. It's open daily noon to 2pm and 6 to 9:30pm (closed Mon in low season) and accepts American Express, Diners Club, MasterCard, and Visa.

8

Brussels & Bruges

by George McDonald

A city with a notable history, **Brussels** is carving out a bright future. Headquarters of the European Union, it both symbolizes the Continent's vision of unity and is a bastion of officialdom, a breeding ground for the regulations that govern and often exasperate the rest of Europe.

Bruxellois have ambivalent feelings about their city's transformation into a power center. At first, the waves of Eurocrats brought a cosmopolitan air to a somewhat provincial city, but as old neighborhoods were leveled to make way for office towers, people wondered whether Brussels was losing its soul. After all, this city doesn't only mean politics and business. It inspired surrealism and Art Nouveau, worships comic strips, prides itself on handmade lace and chocolate, and serves each one of its craft beers in its own unique glass.

Fortunately, not all of Brussels's individuality has been lost. The city's spirit survives in traditional cafes, bars, bistros, and restaurants. Whether elegantly Art Nouveau or eccentrically festooned with posters, curios, and

Value Budget Bests

You can enjoy Brussels's greatest masterpiece, the **Grand-Place,** for free, and can see a great variety of events there—including the daily music-and-light shows on summer evenings—without ever reaching for your wallet. The city's many **markets** are a source of free amusement (unless you want to buy something, of course), as are the **summer music festivals,** the **concerts in the parks,** some **museums,** and the mischievous *Manneken-Pis.* Historic churches such as the **Cathédrale des Sts-Michel-et-Gudule** and **Notre-Dame du Sablon** cost nothing to enter, though you'll pay a modest amount to visit the cathedral crypt.

You don't need to pay the entrance fee to enjoy that towering symbol of Brussels, the **Atomium**—indeed, many visitors are disappointed with the interior. It's more impressive on the outside.

Cafes are a true bargain, for most of them allow you to spend hours lingering over just one moderately priced beer while you enjoy the marvelous decor and the company of the Bruxellois.

Many **Métro stations** contain artworks by leading modern Belgian artists that you can view for free just by entering the Métro station.

Speaking of art, the city prides itself on being a stronghold of **Art Nouveau architecture,** rich in masterpieces of this turn-of-the-19th-century style; with information from the tourist office and a public transportation pass, you can spend a day seeking them out.

Brussels Deals & Discounts

SPECIAL DISCOUNTS   From Friday to Sunday night throughout the year and every day in July and August (unless there's a big convention or Euro-summit in town), many first-class hotels rent their **rooms at discounts** of 30% to 70% to fill vacancies. You can book these discounts through Belgium Tourist Reservations (see "Affordable Places to Stay," later in this chapter), or ask for them at the hotel when you book.

If you plan to visit many attractions that charge admission, consider a **Brussels Card,** available from the Brussels International tourist office in the Grand-Place, from hotels, museums, and offices of the STIB city transit authority, for 30€ ($35). Valid for 3 days, it provides free use of public transportation; free and discounted admission to around 30 of the city's museums and attractions; and discounts at some restaurants and other venues, and on some guided tours.

Select cultural arenas and museums give **senior and student discounts.** See "Seeing the Sights," later in this chapter, for details on museums with reduced admission.

WORTH A SPLURGE   Brussels is known for its fine food and superb selection of beers. So even if funds are limited, try to splurge on at least one truly splendid meal and spend an evening discovering Belgium's amazing brews in one of the many convivial bars and cafes. Some of the most attractive cafes are right on the Grand-Place, but you'll pay around 50% more for the privileged location.

---

knickknacks, such centuries-old establishments provide a warm, convivial ambience that is peculiarly Belgian.

Although international attention is focused on Brussels as "the capital of Europe," in a country the size of Maryland the timeless beauty of Bruges is accessible even to the most hurried visitor. This Flemish city is a showcase of medieval art and architecture. Some of the northern Renaissance's most outstanding paintings hang in its museums and churches.

For more on Brussels and its environs, see *Frommer's Brussels, Bruges, Ghent & Antwerp* and *Frommer's Belgium, Holland & Luxembourg.*

1 Essentials

ARRIVING

BY PLANE   Brussels National Airport (© 0900/70-000 for flight information; www.brusselsairport.be) is 14km (8¾ miles) northeast of the city. In the arrivals hall are currency exchange offices, ATMs, a tourist information office, car-rental desks from the major international rental companies, bars, restaurants, and shops.

A **train** connects the airport with Brussels's three major railway stations (see "By Train," below) every 20 minutes daily, from 5:30am to 11:30pm. A one-way ride is 2.60€ ($3); trip time to Gare Centrale is 25 minutes (other city stops are just minutes away). The **Airport Line bus,** no. 12, departs from the airport one to four times an hour to place Schuman (Métro: Schuman) in the center city, with stops on the way, and costs 3€ ($3.45); **De Lijn bus** BZ connects the airport hourly with Gare du Nord railway station, for the same price. A **taxi** from the airport to the city center is around 30€ ($35); be sure to use only licensed cabs.

BY TRAIN   High-speed **Eurostar** trains from London; **Thalys** from Paris, Amsterdam, and Cologne; and **TGV** from France (not Paris) arrive at **Gare du Midi,** rue de France, south of the city center. Other international trains arrive at Gare du Midi; **Gare Centrale,** Carrefour de l'Europe, downtown, a few blocks from the Grand-Place; and **Gare du Nord,** rue du Progrès, north of the city center. Train information is available from © **02/528-28-28** or on the Web at **www.sncb.be.** All three stations are served by Métro, tram, and bus lines, and have taxi ranks outside.

Warning: Muggers, attracted by rich pickings from international travelers, haunt the environs of Gare du Midi, which are in the middle of a years-long redevelopment. Pickpockets and bag-snatchers work the interior. To avoid this threat, do not travel to or leave the station on foot—take a taxi or public transportation. Inside, keep a close eye on your possessions.

BY BUS   Eurolines (© 02/274-13-50; www.eurolines.com) buses from London, Paris, Amsterdam, and other cities arrive at the bus station adjoining Gare du Nord railway station.

BY CAR   Major expressways to Brussels are E19 from Amsterdam and Paris, and E40 from Bruges and Cologne. Avoid if possible the "hell on wheels" R0 Brussels ring road. Then, do yourself a favor: Leave the car at a parking garage.

VISITOR INFORMATION

TOURIST OFFICE   Brussels International Tourism, Hôtel de Ville, Grand-Place, 1000 Bruxelles (© 02/513-89-40; www.brusselsinternational.be; Métro: Gare Centrale), is on the ground floor of the Town Hall. The office is open April to October, daily from 9am to 6pm; November to December, Monday to Saturday from 9am to 6pm, and Sunday from 10am to 2pm; and January to March, Monday to Saturday from 9am to 6pm.

PRESS   For English-speaking visitors, the most useful publication is the weekly magazine *The Bulletin,* published on Thursdays and filled with local news, articles, shopping, and information on cultural events.

WEBSITES   A good starting point for exploring Brussels and the Wallonia and Flanders regions of Belgium on the Web are the official tourist-office sites **www.brusselsinternational.be, www.visitbelgium.com, www.opt.be,** and **www.toervl.be.** You might also want to check out the independent **www.trabel.com.** A site in English that covers Belgian news, weather, tourism, and more is **www.xpats.com.** A good site to research hotels (where you can compare prices and see pictures of the rooms) is **www.hotels-belgium.com.** For dining-out pointers, go to **www.resto.be.**

CITY LAYOUT

The city center's small, cobbled streets are clustered around the magnificent **Grand-Place.** Two of the most traveled lanes nearby are restaurant-lined **rue des Bouchers** and **Petite rue des Bouchers,** part of an area known as the **Ilôt Sacré.** A block from the Grand-Place is the classical colonnaded **Bourse (Stock Exchange).** A few blocks north, on **place de la Monnaie,** is the Monnaie opera house and ballet theater, named after the coin mint that once stood here. Brussels's busiest shopping street, the pedestrian-only **rue Neuve,** starts from place de la Monnaie and runs north for several blocks.

The Upper Town is spread along an escarpment southeast of the center, where you find the second great square, **place du Grand-Sablon,** the Royal Museums of Fine Arts, and the Royal Palace. If you head southwest and cross the broad **boulevard de Waterloo,** where you find the most exclusive designer stores, you come to **place Louise.** From here, Brussels's most fashionable thoroughfare, **avenue Louise,** runs south all the way to a large wooded park called the **Bois de la Cambre.** Both main streets are flanked by attractive residential side streets.

Between the Palais de Justice and Gare du Midi, the unpretentious working-class **Marolles** area has cozy cafes, drinking-man's bars, and inexpensive restaurants; its denizens even speak their own dialect.

East of this zone, the **Ixelles** district, near the Free University, has many casual, inexpensive restaurants, bars, and cafes. North of Ixelles, the modern European Union district surrounds **place Schuman.**

In this bilingual city, called *Bruxelles* in French and *Brussel* in Dutch, street names and places are in both languages. Grand-Place is *Grote Markt* in Dutch; Gare Centrale is *Centraal Station;* and Théatre Royal de la Monnaie is *Koninklijke Munttheater.* For convenience, only the French names are used in this chapter.

GETTING AROUND

There's no better way to explore the historic core of the town than on foot, especially around the Grand-Place. You'll also enjoy strolling uptown around place du Grand-Sablon. Beyond these areas, you'll want a ride.

BY METRO, TRAM & BUS   Public transportation generally runs from about 6am to midnight. After that, there are infrequent night buses. The **Métro** (subway) network is good for getting to major destinations around and on the edge of town. Métro stations are indicated by signs showing a large white M on a blue background. **Trams** (streetcars) and **buses** are yellow; stop them by extending your arm as they approach. Though not as fast as the Métro, trams are generally faster than buses and are a great way to get around, not least because you can view the cityscape while you ride—lines 92, 93, and 94 cover a bunch of key sights along rue Royale, rue de la Régence, and as far as avenue Louise.

Tickets can be purchased from the driver on trams and buses, from Métro and railway station ticket counters, and (some tickets) from the Brussels International tourist office. A **single ride** (a *direct*) costs 1.40€ ($1.60). You can buy a **1-day pass** for 3.80€ ($3.20), a **five-ride card** for 6.50€ ($7), and a **10-ride card** for 9.80€ ($11). Insert your ticket into the orange machines on buses and trams and at Métro platforms. Your ticket must be inserted each time you enter a new vehicle, but you can transfer free from Métro to tram to bus for up to 1 hour.

Free pocket maps of the public transportation network are available from the tourist office, main Métro stations, and the **S.T.I.B.** public transportation company, Galerie de la Toison d'Or 20 (✆ **02/515-20-00;** www.stib.irisnet.be; Métro: Louise). Maps of the network are posted at all Métro stations and on many bus and tram shelters.

BY TAXI   The meter starts at 2.35€ ($2.70) during the day, 4.35€ ($5) after 10pm; the fare increases by 1.14€ ($1.30) per kilometer inside the city (tariff 1) and 2.28€ ($2.60) per kilometer outside (tariff 2)—make sure the meter is set to the correct tariff. Waiting time is 22€ ($25) an hour. Taxis cannot be hailed on the street, but there are stands at prominent locations around town. Call

Country & City Codes

The **country code** for Belgium is **32**. The **area code** for Brussels is **2**; use this code when you're calling from outside Belgium. If you're within Belgium, use **02**. You need to use this code even if you are calling a city number from within the city limits; in Belgium, you always need to use the area code.

Taxis Bleus (℡ **02/268-00-00**), **Taxis Oranges** (℡ **02/349-43-43**), or **Taxis Verts** (℡ **02/349-49-49**).

BY RENTAL CAR   Going around by car in Brussels is akin to life during the Stone Age: nasty and brutish—though it's rarely short. In some cases (but not always), traffic from the right has the right of way, even if it is coming from a minor road onto a more important one. You can imagine how this plays at multiple-road intersections, particularly since Belgians will relinquish their *priorité* under no known circumstances, cost what it may. If you must drive, all the top international firms rent here: **Avis,** rue de France 2 (℡ **02/527-17-05;** Métro: Gare du Midi); **Budget,** av. Louise 327B (℡ **02/646-51-30;** Métro: Louise); **Europcar,** rue du Page 29 (℡ **02/348-92-12;** tram: 81 or 82); and **Hertz,** bd. Maurice-Lemmonier 8 (℡ **02/717-32-01;** Métro: Anneessens). All of these firms also have desks at the airport. Rates begin at around 45€ ($52) for a small car with unlimited mileage.

   Remember: You get the best deal if you arrange for the rental before leaving home.

BY BIKE   Brussels's hoggish drivers and biased road laws combine to make travel by bike a poor option. If you want to rent a bike anyway, try **Pro Vélo,** rue de Londres 13–15 (℡ **02/502-73-55;** Métro: Porte de Namur). July and August, it's open daily 9am to 6pm; September to June, hours are Monday to Friday 9am to 6pm. Rental is 7.50€ ($9) for a half day, 13€ ($14) for a full day, and 20€ ($23) for a weekend. They also organize bike tours with commentary in English.

BY FOOT   There's no better way to explore the historic core of the town than by walking, especially around Grand-Place. You'll also enjoy strolling uptown around place du Grand-Sablon. Beyond these areas, you'll want to use public transportation. Don't expect cars to stop for you just because you're using a black-and-white "pedestrian crossing." It's only recently that drivers have been obliged legally to stop at these spots, and many of them haven't gotten the message yet.

FAST FACTS: Brussels

American Express   The office at bd. du Souverain 100, 1000 Bruxelles (℡ **02/676-21-11;** Métro: Horrmann-Debroux), is open Monday to Friday 9am to 1pm and 2 to 5pm. Call ahead before visiting, as this is an administrative office only, and is out in the suburbs.

Business Hours   **Banks** are open Monday to Friday 9am to 1pm and 2 to 4:30 or 5pm. Open hours for **offices** are Monday to Friday 9 or 10am to 4 or 5pm. Most **stores** are open Monday to Saturday 9 or 10am to 6 or 7pm; some stay open on Friday to 8 or 9pm.

Currency   Belgium's currency is the **euro** (€). At press time, $1 = .87€, or 1€ = $1.15.

Currency Exchange Banks give the best rates for direct exchange, and currency exchange offices in railway stations come close. Hotels and *bureaux de change* (currency-exchange offices), open regular hours plus evenings and weekends, charge a low commission (or none at all) but give a poor rate. **Thomas Cook**, Grand-Place 4 (© **02/513-28-45**; Métro: Gare Centrale), has fair rates.

There are many ATMs (the best exchange rate of all) around town, identified by BANCONTACT and MISTER CASH signs. A convenient bank with an ATM is **CBC**, Grand-Place 5 (© **02/547-12-11**; Métro: Gare Centrale), open Monday to Friday 9am to 5pm.

Doctors & Dentists For 24-hour emergency medical service, call © **02/479-18-18**; ask for an English-speaking doctor. For emergency dental care, call © **02/426-10-26.**

Drugstores & Pharmacies For both prescription and non-prescription medicines, go to a pharmacy (*pharmacie* in French; *apotheek* in Dutch). Regular pharmacy hours are Monday to Saturday 9am to 6pm (some close earlier on Sat). Try the centrally located **Grande Pharmacie de Brouckère**, Passage du Nord 10–12 (© **02/218-05-07**; Métro: De Brouckère). All pharmacies post locations of nearby all-night and Sunday pharmacies on the door.

Embassies **United States,** bd. du Régent 25–27 (© **02/508-21-11**; Métro: Arts-Loi), open Monday to Friday 9am to noon for visas and 1:30 to 4:30pm for assistance. **Canada,** av. de Tervuren 2 (© **02/741-06-11**; Métro: Mérode), open Monday, Wednesday, and Friday 9am to noon and 2 to 4pm; Tuesday and Thursday 9am to noon. **United Kingdom,** rue Arlon 85 (© **02/287-62-11**; Métro: Maalbeek), open Monday to Friday 9:30am to noon. **Ireland,** rue Wiertz 50 (© **02/235-66-76**; Métro: Schuman), open Monday to Friday 10am to 1pm. **Australia,** rue Guimard 6 (© **02/286-05-00**; Métro: Arts-Loi), open Monday to Friday 9am to 12:30pm and 2 to 4pm. **New Zealand,** Sq. de Meeûs 1 (© **02/512-10-40**; Métro: Trone), open Monday to Friday 9am to 1pm and 2 to 3:30pm.

Emergencies For police assistance, call © **101.** For an ambulance or the fire department, call © **100.**

Holidays January 1 (New Year's Day), Easter Monday, May 1 (Labor Day), Ascension, Pentecost Monday, July 21 (Independence Day), August 15 (Assumption), November 1 (All Saints Day), November 11 (Armistice Day), and December 25 (Christmas). The dates of Easter, Ascension, and Pentecost change each year.

Hospital **Cliniques Universitaires St-Luc,** av. Hippocrate 10 (© **02/764-11-11**; Métro: Alma), has a first-aid department.

Internet Access In the city center, **easyEverything,** place de Brouckère 9–13 (© 02/211-08-20; www.easyeverything.com; Métro: De Brouckère), is open daily from 8am to 11pm; access charges start at 2.50€ ($2.90).

Laundry & Dry Cleaning Laundry chain **Ipsomat** has a branch at rue Blaes 193 (Métro: Louise), open daily 7am to 10pm. Dry-cleaning chain **5 à Sec** has a branch at rue du Marché-aux-Herbes 8 (no phone; Métro: Gare Centrale), open Monday to Friday 9am to 6pm. Both chains have branches around town; check the phone book for the one nearest your hotel.

Mail Most **post offices** are open Monday to Friday 9am to 5pm. The office at Centre Monnaie, place de la Monnaie (② 02/226-21-11; Métro: De Brouckère), is open Monday to Friday 9am to 5pm, Saturday 9:30am to 3pm. The office at Gare du Midi, av. Fonsny 1E/F (② 02/538-33-98; Métro: Gare du Midi), is open 24 hours.

Postage for a postcard or letter to the United States, Canada, Australia, and New Zealand is .85€ ($1); to the United Kingdom and Ireland .45€ (50¢).

Police In an emergency, call ② **101.** In non-urgent situations, go to **Brussels Central Police Station,** rue du Marché-au-Charbon 30 (② **02/279-79-79**), just off the Grand-Place.

Safety Brussels is generally safe, but there's a rise in crime, in particular pickpocketing, theft from cars and of cars, and muggings at Métro stations. Tourists may be targets of pickpockets on the Métro and in tourist areas like the Grand-Place. Don't overestimate the risk, but take sensible precautions, particularly in obvious circumstances such as on crowded Métro trains and when withdrawing cash from an ATM at night.

Taxes There's a **value-added tax (tva** in Belgium) of 6% on hotel bills and 21.5% on restaurant bills and on many purchases. For information on how to recover some of the tax on purchases, see "Shopping," later in this chapter.

Telephone Both **local and long-distance calls** from a pay phone are .25€ (30¢) per minute at peak time (Mon–Fri 8am–7pm) and per 2 minutes at other times. **International calls,** per minute, are: to the United States, Canada, United Kingdom, and Ireland .35€ (40¢); and to Australia and New Zealand 1€ ($1.15). You can use most pay phones in booths all around town with a plastic **Belgacom telecard,** selling for 5€ ($6), 13€ ($15), and 25€ ($29) from post offices, train ticket counters, and newsstands. Some pay phones take coins of .10€, .20€, .50€, and 1€. For information inside Belgium, call ② **1207** or **1307;** for international information, call ② **1405.**

To charge a call to your calling card, dial **AT&T** (② **0800/100-10**); **MCI** (② **0800/100-12**); **Sprint** (② **0800/100-14**); **Canada Direct** (② **0800/100-19**); or **British Telecom** (② **0800/100-24**).

Tipping The prices on most restaurant menus already include a service charge of 16%, so it's unnecessary to tip. If the service is good, however, it's usual to show appreciation with a tip (5%–10%). Service is included in your hotel bill as well. For taxi drivers, you can round up the fare if you like, but you need not add a tip unless you have received an extra service such as help with luggage.

Toilets Be sure to *pay the person* who sits at the entrance to a *toilette.* He or she has a saucer in which you put your money. If you don't, you might have a visitor in the inner sanctum while you're transacting your business. Even if you have paid, in busy places the attendant may have forgotten your face by the time you emerge and will then pursue you out of the toilet and along the street. It's tiresome, but toilet use is usually only about .50€ (60¢).

2 Affordable Places to Stay

If you arrive in Brussels without a reservation, you should stop by **Brussels International Tourism** in the Grand-Place (see "Visitor Information," earlier in this chapter), which makes same-day reservations, if you go in person, for a small fee, which the hotel deducts from its room rate. You can also contact **Belgium Tourist Reservations,** bd. Anspach 111, 1000 Bruxelles (© **02/513-74-84;** www.horeca.be; Métro: Bourse), which reserves hotel rooms throughout Belgium and can often give substantial discounts.

Youth hostels and youth hotels (both open to all ages) naturally have the cheapest deals of all. Brussels has five of them around the city, and all have upgraded their facilities in recent years by adding more single and double rooms and some private bathrooms. For more info on Brussels's hostels, head online to **www.laj.be**.

Note: You'll find the lodging choices below plotted on the map on p. 278.

AROUND THE GRAND-PLACE

La Légende ℛ   The entrance to this popular hotel in an 18th-century building is at the end of a quiet courtyard in the middle of the city's premier restaurant-and-nightlife area. The rooms are immaculately maintained, with bright print bedspreads. The twin-bedded rooms have quite narrow beds; the double beds are a more sleepable size.

Rue du Lombard 35 (a block from Grand-Place), 1000 Bruxelles. © **02/512-82-90.** Fax 02/512-34-93. www. hotellalegende.com. 26 units. 69€–107€ ($79–$123) single; 77€–117€ ($89–$135) double. Rates include continental breakfast. AE, DC, MC, V. Limited street parking. Métro: Gare Centrale. *In room:* TV.

Mozart   Go up a flight from the busy, cheap-eats street level, and guess which famous composer's music wafts through the lobby? Salmon-colored walls, plants, and old paintings create a warm, intimate ambience that's carried over into the guest rooms. Although furnishings are blandly modern, colorful fabrics

---

(*Value*   **Getting the Best Deal on Accommodations**

- Don't be afraid to ask for a discounted rate. Hotel prices drop whenever business travelers aren't around. Weekends, holidays, and July to August are the best times to get discounted rooms.
- Note that there are decent medium-priced hotels in the streets around the Grand-Place and the three main railway stations, and even in the upmarket neighborhood of avenue Louise.
- When choosing a hotel, find out if breakfast is included in the room rate. This isn't always the case, and some hotels charge a disproportionate price for rolls and coffee.
- You pay less for rooms without a private bathroom. Hallway showers and toilets are usually well maintained, and the price reduction is substantial.
- Be aware that if you want to stay at one of the official youth hostels, you can buy an international membership card before leaving home. But you can also pay a nightly surcharge of 2.50€ ($2.90), which after 4 nights makes you a member.

Tips Booking in a B&B

Brussels has two **bed-and-breakfast** organizations: **Bed & Brussels,** rue Kindermans 9, 1050 Bruxelles (ⓒ **02/644-07-37;** www.bnb-brussels.be); and **Windrose,** av. Brugman 11, 1060 Bruxelles (ⓒ **02/534-71-91;** fax 02/534-50-70; nadine@wep-edu.be). Both have a database of several hundred rooms, from the simple to the grand.

---

and exposed beams lend each room a rustic originality. Several are duplexes with a sitting room underneath the loft bedroom. Top-floor rooms have a great view.

Rue du Marché-aux-Fromages 23 (close to the Grand-Place), 1000 Bruxelles. ⓒ **02/502-66-61.** Fax 02/502-77-58. www.hotel-mozart.be. 47 units. 75€ ($86) single; 95€ ($109) double. AE, DC, MC, V. No parking. Métro: Gare Centrale. **Amenities:** Lounge; laundry service. *In room:* TV, fridge.

La Vieille Lanterne ⭐   A tiny place with two rooms on each floor and no elevator, the hotel is diagonally across a narrow street from the *Manneken-Pis.* It can be hard to spot, as you enter through the side door of a trinket store selling hundreds of *Manneken-Pis* replicas. You'll feel right at home in guest rooms with old-style leaded windows, and small bathrooms with marble counters and tiled walls. It's advisable to book well in advance.

Rue des Grands Carmes 29 (facing *Manneken-Pis*), 1000 Bruxelles. ⓒ **02/512-74-94.** Fax 02/512-13-97. 6 units. 65€ ($75) single; 38€–75€ ($56–$86) double. Rates include continental breakfast. AE, DC, MC, V. Limited street parking. Métro: Bourse. *In room:* TV.

AROUND THE BOURSE

George V   This agreeable little hotel is tucked away in a corner of the city center that looks more down-at-the-heels than it really is, and is currently being reborn as a trendy shopping-and-eating area. The George, in an 1859 town house within easy walking distance of the Grand-Place, provides a free shuttle bus to this square and the main museums, and to Gare du Midi. The rooms are plain but clean and have new furnishings.

Rue 't Kint 23 (off place du Jardin-aux-Fleurs), 1000 Bruxelles. ⓒ **02/513-50-93.** Fax 02/513-44-93. www.george5.com. 16 units. 53€–55€ ($60–$63) single; 60€–65€ ($69–$75) double; 75€ ($86) triple; 85€ ($98) quad. Rates include continental breakfast. AE, MC, V. Parking 6.50€ ($7). Métro: Bourse. **Amenities:** Restaurant; bar; 24-hr. room service. *In room:* TV.

THE UPPER TOWN

Albert ⭐ *Value*   This comfortable, reasonably priced place beside the bronze-domed Eglise Ste-Marie (and close to an enclave of the best Turkish restaurants in town), has clean, bright, modern rooms with a dash of design flair and tiled bathrooms (some with showers only). The five studio apartments at the Résidence Albert, next door, include refrigerators. Although the hotel is on the outer edge of the center, trams from a nearby stop take you straight to the Royal Palace, Royal Museums of Fine Arts, and Sablon antiques district.

Rue Royale-Ste-Marie 27–29 (just off place de la Reine), 1030 Bruxelles. ⓒ **02/217-93-91.** Fax 02/219-20-17. www.hotelalbert.com. 19 units. 57€–65€ ($66–$75) single; 70€–75€ ($81–$86) double. Rates include continental breakfast. MC, V. Free parking. Tram: 90, 92, 93, or 94. **Amenities:** Lounge. *In room:* TV, hair dryer.

Sabina   This small hostelry is like a private residence, presided over by hospitable owners. A grandfather clock in the reception area and polished wood along the restaurant walls give it a warm, homey atmosphere. Rooms vary in size, but all are comfortable and simply yet tastefully done in modern style with twin beds.

Rue du Nord 78 (at place des Barricades), 1000 Bruxelles. ℂ 02/218-26-37. Fax 02/219-32-39. www.hotel sabina.be. 24 units. 50€–75€ ($58–$86) single; 50€–90€ ($58–$104) double. Rates include buffet breakfast. AE, DC, MC, V. Limited street parking. Métro: Madou. *In room:* TV, hair dryer.

Tasse d'Argent ⭐   This engaging hotel, in a typical Brussels town house (without elevator), makes you feel like a guest in a friend's home—even though you're in the heart of the administrative quarter, a few blocks from the Belgian Parliament. The rooms are bright and clean and furnished plainly in a modern style. The units have half-size tubs, while a stately grandfather clock presides over the cheerful chintz-trimmed breakfast room.

Rue du Congrès 48 (off place du Congrès), 1000 Bruxelles. ℂ 02/218-83-75. Fax 02/218-83-75. 8 units. 50€ ($58) single; 60€–65€ ($69–$75) double. Rates include continental breakfast. MC, V. Limited street parking. Métro: Madou.

AROUND GARE DU MIDI

Barry   Place Anneessens is a slightly down-at-the-heels square on a busy boulevard running through the center of town. But you're safe and snug in the Barry, in one of the character-filled early-1900s buildings the planners have somehow forgotten to destroy. The rooms are comfortable, representing good value for central Brussels. And when you step out the door, you're right in the heart of the action.

Place Anneessens 25 (off bd. Maurice-Lemmonier), 1000 Bruxelles. ℂ 02/511-27-95. Fax 02/514-14-65. 32 units. 45€ ($52) single; 57€–65€ ($66–$75) double; 87€ ($100) triple; 99€ ($114) quad. Rates include continental breakfast. AE, DC, MC, V. Limited street parking. Métro: Anneessens. **Amenities:** Bar. *In room:* TV.

AROUND AVENUE LOUISE

Berckmans *(Value*   Despite the upscale character of avenue Louise, it's still possible to find inexpensive accommodations in the area. This neat, uncomplicated hotel (without elevator) is tucked in the maze of streets behind place Louise and the exclusive boutiques thereabouts. All of the rooms, which are of reasonable size, have been renewed in recent years, with new furnishings and parquet floors, and bathrooms with showers.

Rue Berckmans 12 (off chaussée de Charleroi), 1060 Bruxelles. ℂ 02/539-15-28. Fax 02/538-09-00. www. hotelberckmans.be. 23 units. 50€–55€ ($58–$63) single; 55€–60€ ($63–$69) double; 70€ ($81) triple. AE, DC, MC, V. Limited street parking. Métro: Hôtel des Monnaies. *In room:* TV.

De Boeck's   In a well-maintained 19th-century town house, this graceful hotel has unusually spacious and quiet rooms. They don't quite measure up to the Victorian elegance of the public spaces but are adequately furnished, with comfortable modern beds and soft carpeting. Some rooms, ideal for families and small groups, can be used as quads or even quints.

Rue Veydt 40 (off chaussée de Charleroi), 1050 Bruxelles. ℂ 02/537-40-33. Fax 02/534-40-37. hotel. deboeck@euronet.be. 38 units. 57€–90€ ($66–$104) single; 62€–100€ ($71–$115) double. Rates include buffet breakfast. AE, DC, MC, V. Limited street parking. Métro: Louise. *In room:* TV, coffeemaker on request, hair dryer.

Les Bluets ⭐   If you're searching for classic European charm or are a fan of American B&Bs, you'll enjoy it here. In a town house from 1864, the effect is more that of a comfortable country residence than a hotel. You feel as though you're staying with friends when you breakfast in the antiques-filled dining room or in the sunroom. A sweeping stairway (no elevator) leads up to the rooms, several of which have 4.25km (14-ft.) ceilings and ornate moldings; all have antiques and knickknacks. This is one of the city's few nonsmoking hotels.

Rue Berckmans 124 (off av. Louise), 1060 Bruxelles. © **02/534-39-83.** Fax 02/543-09-70. www.geocities.com/les_bluets. 10 units. 40€–57€ ($46–$66) single; 53€–81€ ($61–$93) double. Rates include continental breakfast. MC, V. Limited street parking. Métro: Hôtel des Monnaies. *In room:* TV.

Rembrandt 🏠🏠   The high ceilings and oak furniture of the Rembrandt seem a world away from the studied chic of nearby avenue Louise. Although the lobby resembles the cluttered living room of someone's slightly dotty aunt, the guest rooms are relatively spacious (with good-size beds), especially the higher-priced doubles (however, the bathrooms are tiny). The decor is endearingly old-fashioned.

Rue de la Concorde 42 (off av. Louise), 1050 Bruxelles. © **02/512-71-39.** Fax 02/511-71-36. 13 units, some with shower only. 39€ ($45) single with shower only, 58€ ($67) single with bathroom; 60€–80€ ($69–$92) double. Rates include continental breakfast. AE, DC, MC, V. Limited street parking. Métro: Louise. *In room:* TV.

WORTH A SPLURGE

Brussels Welcome Hotel 🏠🏠   The name of this gem of a hotel, overlooking the Fish Market, couldn't be more accurate, thanks to the untiring efforts of its husband and wife proprietors. You can think of it as a country *auberge* (inn) right in the heart of town. Rooms are furnished and styled on individual, unrelated international and travel themes, such as Provence, Tibet, Marrakech (see photo on back cover), Egypt, Africa, Jules Verne, and Laura Ashley, all to a high standard. The fine in-house seafood restaurant La Truite d'Argent closed in 2004, creating space for more rooms, but there's no shortage of good alternatives on the Marché-aux-Poissons. There's a free airport shuttle to and from Brussels National Airport. Book ahead; the Welcome's regular guests are fiercely loyal.

Quai au Bois-à-Brûler 23 (at the Marché-aux-Poissons), 1000 Bruxelles. © **02/219-95-46.** Fax 02/217-18-87. www.hotelwelcome.com. 17 units. 85€ ($98) single; 95€–130€ ($109–$150) double; 150€ ($173) suite. AE, DC, MC, V. Parking 10€ ($12). Métro: Ste-Catherine. **Amenities:** Lounge; Internet desk. *In room:* A/C (some rooms), TV, dataport, minibar, hair dryer, safe.

Comfort Art Hotel Siru 🏠🏠   Set in an area of fancy office towers, this fascinating art-gallery-cum-hotel is not easily forgotten. What sets the Siru apart is that the proprietor persuaded 130 Belgian artists, including some of the country's biggest names, to "decorate" each of the coolly modern, well-equipped rooms and the corridors with a work on the theme of travel. Given the unpredictable nature of reactions to modern art, some clients reserve the same room time after time; others ask to change in the middle of the night.

Place Rogier 1 (opposite Gare du Nord), 1210 Bruxelles. © **800/228-3323** in the U.S. and Canada, or 02/203-35-80. Fax 02/203-33-03. www.comforthotelsiru.com. 101 units. 90€–185€ ($104–$213) single; 90€–210€ ($104–$242) double. Rates include buffet breakfast. AE, DC, MC, V. Parking 15€ ($17). Métro: Rogier. **Amenities:** Restaurant; babysitting; laundry service; same-day dry cleaning; nonsmoking rooms; executive rooms. *In room:* TV w/pay movies, dataport, minibar, hair dryer, safe.

3 Great Deals on Dining

The city's French- and Dutch-speaking residents may have their differences, but they both value a good meal. Indeed, food is a passion in Brussels, and you can always find somewhere to eat well—it's hard to eat badly here—at a reasonable price.

Among the sturdy regional dishes you find on menus around town are *waterzooï,* a creamy casserole of fish or chicken; *stoemp,* a purée of potato and vegetables, accompanied by sausages, bacon, or perhaps a pork chop; *anguilles au vert,*

> **Value   Getting the Best Deal on Dining**
>
> - Take advantage of the *plat du jour* at lunch and one of the set menus at dinner for good food at a bargain rate.
> - Venture into one of the simple Greek places near Gare du Midi, where there's no menu and you go to the kitchen to point out the dishes you want. You can pig out for around 7€ ($8).
> - Remember that many neighborhood bars serve basic meals such as soup, steak with french fries, and spaghetti Bolognese—bland, but better with a dash of Tabasco—at low prices.
> - Fill up on inexpensive and delicious Belgian *frites*, which we mistakenly call french fries (see "Quick Bites," below). You won't be the first tourist who has done Europe by potato express.
> - Be aware that some of the most expensive hotels serve a modestly priced Sunday brunch. At the **Conrad,** av. Louise 71 (*(*© **02/542-42-42;** Métro: Louise), for example, you can raid a lavish buffet for about 20€ ($23).

eels in green herb sauce; *ballekes,* meatballs; and *hochepot,* stew. While most of the city's favorite dishes are based on local products, the famous **mussels**—prepared in countless ingenious variations and served in large tureens—come from Zeeland in neighboring Holland. A selection from Belgium's 300 craft cheeses is a good way to finish off your meal.

Note: If you are a nonsmoker, you're mostly out of luck—get ready to consume a garnish of secondhand smoke with your dinner. Finally, don't fret if the service is slow: Belgians take their time when dining out.

AROUND THE GRAND-PLACE

Armand & KO FRENCH/BELGIAN   This smart Parisian-style bistro serves up dishes of surprising sophistication. Specialties include crispy honeyed duck, spinach-stuffed roast beef, and mussels and game in season. A two-course lunch typically includes soup or green salad and the *plat du jour.* The wine list favors the Bordeaux and Loire Valley regions of France.

Rue des Chapeliers 16 (off the Grand-Place). © 02/514-17-63. Main courses 13€–18€ ($14–$20). AE, DC, MC, V. Daily noon–2:30pm and 7–11pm. Métro: Gare Centrale.

Chez Léon ⭐ *Value* SEAFOOD/TRADITIONAL BELGIAN   Léon has been flexing its mussels since 1893 and now has clones all over Belgium (including one at Bruparck, the city's amusement complex). The big, basic restaurant is the city's most famous purveyor of that marine delicacy, and the mollusks in question are top quality at low prices. If you don't like mussels, there are plenty of other fishy delights—such as *anguilles au vert* (eels in a green sauce), cod, and bouillabaisse.

Rue des Bouchers 18 (2 blocks north of Grand-Place). © 02/511-14-15. www.chezleon.be. Main courses 9.40€–22€ ($11–$25); *menu formule léon* 12€ ($14). AE, DC, MC, V. Daily noon–11pm (Fri–Sat to 11:30pm). Métro: Gare Centrale.

L'Auberge des Chapeliers ⭐⭐ *Value* TRADITIONAL BELGIAN   In a 17th-century building that was once the headquarters of the hatmakers' guild, the Auberge des Chapeliers preserves its historic charm. Behind a beautiful brick facade, the first two floors are graced with timber beams and paneling and connected by a narrow wooden staircase. The food is typical hearty Belgian fare, with an accent on mussels in season and dishes cooked in beer. The prices are modest, considering the location.

Rue des Chapeliers 3 (off of the Grand-Place). ℂ 02/513-73-38. Reservations recommended on weekends. Main courses 8.50€–18€ ($10–$21); fixed-price menus 15€–21€ ($17–$24). AE, DC, MC, V. Mon–Thurs noon–2pm and 6–11pm; Fri noon–2pm and 6pm–midnight; Sat noon–3pm and 6pm–midnight; Sun noon–3pm and 6–11pm. Métro: Gare Centrale.

't Kelderke 🎯🎯 *Finds* TRADITIONAL BELGIAN   The Little Cellar is one of the Grand-Place's most delightful surprises, even if it does have little in the way of frills. It's hidden beneath an ornate guild house, and the entrance isn't easy to spot. But when you descend the steps, you'll find a crowded, lively restaurant in the 17th-century brick-vaulted room at the bottom. As many Bruxellois as tourists throng the long wooden tables. The menu is replete with Belgian favorites such as *stoemp,* served with a pork chop; Flemish beef stew; rabbit in beer; and Zeeland mussels in season, served from an open kitchen.

Grand-Place 15 ℂ 02/513-73-44. Main courses 9.50€–20€ ($11–$22); *plat du jour* 9.75€ ($11). AE, DC, MC, V. Daily noon–2am. Métro: Gare Centrale.

NEAR THE BOURSE

Den Teepot 🎯 VEGETARIAN   Belgium is a country of meat-eaters, and noncarnivores will be amazed to discover there are almost no strictly vegetarian restaurants in Brussels. This is a rare exception, serving imaginative and tasty dishes prepared only with organically grown grains, *pulses* (chickpeas, lentils, beans), and veggies. In fact, you can even enjoy an organic beer or wine with your meal.

Rue des Chartreux 66 (2 blocks west from the Bourse). ℂ 02/511-94-02. Main courses 7.50€–11€ ($9–$12); *plat du jour* 7.50€ ($9). No credit cards. Mon–Sat noon–2pm. Métro: Bourse.

In 't Spinnekopke 🎯🎯 *Finds* TRADITIONAL BELGIAN   The Spider's Web occupies a stagecoach inn from 1762, just far enough off the beaten track downtown to be frequented mainly by those in the know. You dine in a tilting,

---

Tips   **On Your Guard in the Ilôt Sacré**

A few restaurants (not reviewed here) in this colorful restaurant district off the Grand-Place take advantage of tourists. Follow these ground rules to ensure you're not one of them:

- Be wary if inexpensive menu items such as the *plat du jour* (plate of the day), are "sold out."
- Confirm the price of everything you order—especially if the waiter proposes "something special."
- Confirm the price of both the house wine and house aperitif before ordering. Usually the cheapest options, in a few places they are by far the most expensive.
- Confirm both the price and the size of a seafood platter before ordering.
- Don't pay for anything you didn't order or didn't get.

Value **Quick Bites**

You can find plenty of fast-food outlets where you can grab a bite while you're on the run. Naturally, **McDonald's** outposts are everywhere. You might prefer to try **Quick,** the Belgian hamburger chain that's even bigger, locally, than Ronald. Two central locations are rue du Marché-aux-Herbes 103 (② **02/511-47-63**; Métro: Gare Centrale); and rue du Fossé-aux-Loups 5 (② **02/217-65-11**; Métro: De Brouckère).

Then there are all the **Greek, Turkish,** and Israeli places, where you can fill up on moussaka, kabobs, and falafel for as little as 4€ ($4.60). Try **Chez Munir,** rue du Marché-aux-Fromages 17 (② **02/503-33-03**; Métro: Gare Centrale); or **Plaka,** rue du Marché-aux-Fromages 6 (② **02/511-21-27**; Métro: Gare Centrale).

Another seductive invitation is the aroma of **fresh waffles,** sold from street stands all around the city. Generally thicker than American waffles, they cost about 2€ ($2.30) and are smothered in sugar icing.

And don't forget those Belgian *frites* (fries)! These are twice-fried, giving them a delectably crunchy crust and flavorful interior. Brussels is dotted with dozens of fast-food stands serving *frites* in paper cones. Belgians usually eat them with mayonnaise rather than ketchup; though this method might cause apprehension, don't knock it till you've tried it. Prices run from around 1.50€ to 2.50€ ($1.75–$2.90). Toppings, such as peanut or curry sauce, cost extra.

tiled-floor building, at plain tables more likely than not squeezed into a tight space. So traditional is this cafe-restaurant that the menu lists its hardy, recommendable standbys of regional Belgian cuisine in the old Bruxellois dialect. *Stoemp mi sossisse* is hotchpotch with sausage, and *toung ave mei* is sole. The bar stocks a vast selection of traditional beers.

Place du Jardin-aux-Fleurs 1 (off rue Van Artevelde). ② **02/511-86-95**. www.spinnekopke.be. Main courses 11€–20€ ($12–$22); *plat du jour* 8.15€ ($9). AE, DC, MC, V. Restaurant: Mon–Fri noon–3pm and 6–11pm; Sat 6pm–midnight. Métro: Bourse.

NEAR THE FISH MARKET

Le Paon Royal ✦ TRADITIONAL BELGIAN   In a house dating from 1637, this small restaurant has a rustic wood-and-exposed-brick interior and beamed ceiling. You may order just a snack with 1 of the 65 brands of beer from the tiny bar, or try the hearty *plat du jour,* usually a traditional Belgian dish, offered at lunchtime. Specialties include roast suckling pig in a mustard sauce, and filet of cod in a Hoegaarden (white beer) sauce. In fine weather, chairs are usually set out under the trees across the street.

Rue du Vieux Marché-aux-Grains 6. ② **02/513-08-68**. Main courses 9€–15€ ($10–$17); *plat du jour* 15€ ($17). AE, DC, MC, V. Restaurant Tues–Sat noon–9:30pm. Tavern Tues–Sat 8am–10pm. Métro: Ste-Catherine.

IN THE MAROLLES

La Grande Porte ✦ TRADITIONAL BELGIAN   This attractive late-night brasserie is hidden on a side street of the Marolles, the city's old working-class neighborhood. Despite the eclectic decor (paper lanterns, marionettes, antique posters, and rag-rubbed walls), the menu has a reassuringly proletarian flavor.

Discover the substantial worth of dishes such as *ballekes, waterzooï,* and *stoemp,* scaled down and dressed up to match contemporary tastes.

Rue Notre-Seigneur 9 (off rue Haute). ℂ 02/512-89-98. Main courses 9.90€–17€ ($11–$19). MC, V. Mon–Fri noon–3pm and 6pm–2am; Sat 6pm–2am. Bus: 20 or 48.

IN SOUTH BRUSSELS

La Mirabelle 𝒻 TRADITIONAL BELGIAN   Popular with students from the nearby Free University of Brussels for its "democratic" prices, this brasserie/restaurant in Ixelles is equally popular with Bruxellois in general for its convivial atmosphere and consistently good food. Plainly decorated, with wooden tables crowded together, La Mirabelle looks more like a bar than a restaurant and often has a boisterous pub-style atmosphere to match. The steak *frites* (steak with french fries), a Belgian staple, is particularly good. The garden terrace is great for alfresco summer dining.

Chaussée de Boondael 459 (off bd. Général Jacques). ℂ 02/649-51-73. Main courses 9.30€–24€ ($11–$28); *plat du jour* 9.50€ ($11). MC, V. Daily noon–3pm and 6pm–2:45am. Tram: 23 or 90.

Le Mâcon BELGIAN/SWISS   Tasty, uncomplicated Belgian fare, such as mussels *(moules)* and steak with french fries *(steak frites),* is this superior neighborhood cafe-restaurant's stock-in-trade. The extensive menu also has slightly more exotic items—try the *tournedos Rossini* in port sauce. Service is simple, and the cozy, wood-paneled dining area is a style-free zone (smoky, too), but there are a few tables with tablecloths, usually kept for regulars unless you ask for one. A Swiss menu, including fondue, is served every Thursday.

Rue Joseph Stallaert 87 (off av. Winston Churchill). ℂ 02/343-89-37. Main courses 6.50€–20€ ($7–$22); fixed-price menus 9.50€–25€ ($11–$28); Swiss menu 21€ ($24). No credit cards. Daily noon–dawn. Tram: 23 or 90.

Mexican Grill Buffet ⟨Value⟩ ⟨Kids⟩ SEAFOOD/BARBECUE   For the most amazing deal in town, it's worth taking a tram out to this unpretentious restaurant on the old Waterloo road. In the classic tradition of Belgian nuttiness, the Mexican Grill has absolutely no Mexican food. Instead, you can take limitless helpings from a vast buffet stocked with oysters, crab claws, and much more. There's also meat you can barbecue to your personal taste and an unending supply of beer and wine. Kids love the help-yourself ice-cream bar.

Chaussée de Waterloo 782 (at Bois de la Cambre). ℂ 02/375-41-44. All you can eat and drink 25€ ($29) adults, 2.50€ ($2.90) children 7–12, free for children under 7. MC, V. Mon–Sat 6–11:30pm; Sun noon–midnight. Tram: 23 or 90.

PICNICKING

You'll find a large **GB** supermarket, with an extensive cold cut/cheese counter perfect for assembling a picnic lunch, in the basement of the City 2 mall on rue Neuve (Métro: Rogier). It's open Monday to Saturday 9am to 8pm (to 9pm Fri). An equally large and well-stocked **Delhaize** supermarket is at the corner of rue du Marché-aux-Poulets and boulevard Anspach, diagonally across from the Bourse (Métro: Bourse). Both GB and Delhaize have an extensive range of modestly priced good wines.

Or do what many Belgians do and purchase one of the country's numerous brands of beer, many of which are craft beers made by local and regional brewers (though an equal number are produced by the big Interbrew firm whose flagship beer is Stella Artois). If you have a way to get and keep it cool, I recommend the fresh-tasting, cloudy Hoegaarden *blanche* (white) beer, or *witbier* as it's called in the Flanders region where it originates. Or just pick up some ordinary Pilseners, such as Stella, Maes, or Jupiler.

> **Tips A Perfect Brew**
>
> Belgian beer is the perfect accompaniment to your meal. The country is renowned for its 450 brands of beer produced by dozens of breweries. Belgium's chefs use beer in their sauces the way French chefs use wine. Beef, chicken, and fish are often bathed in a savory sauce based on the local Brussels *gueuze, faro,* and *kriek* brews.

You can find ample specialist food stores in the streets around the Grand-Place. The best city center spot for a picnic is the **Parc de Bruxelles**, which extends in front of the Palais Royal (see "Parks," later in this chapter).

WORTH A SPLURGE

Aux Armes de Bruxelles TRADITIONAL BELGIAN   In business since 1921, this large, family-run Art Deco restaurant commands universal respect. It has hosted countless celebrities over the years, from Laurel and Hardy to Danny DeVito to Belgian favorites such as singer Jacques Brel. The service is gracious and rather formal, but the ambience is totally relaxed. The vast menu—a Belgian cuisine primer in itself—includes local specialties like beef stewed in beer, mussels in a variety of guises, a delicious *waterzooï,* and shrimp croquettes, all at quite reasonable prices.

Rue des Bouchers 13 (a block from Grand-Place). ℭ **02/511-55-98.** Lunch menu 13€ ($14); main courses 14€–21€ ($16–$24); dinner menu 28€ ($32). AE, DC, MC, V. Tues–Sun noon–11:15pm. Métro: Gare Centrale.

Taverne du Passage TRADITIONAL BELGIAN   Surrealist painter René Magritte (1898–1967) was a regular at this classic Art Deco brasserie, situated in a glass-roofed arcade. It's easy to imagine him strolling through the door in his bowler hat, sitting at his favorite banquette, and ordering from one of the white-jacketed waiters. The menu hasn't changed much since Magritte's day: Belgian staples such as shrimp croquettes, *waterzooï,* endive with ham, and roast beef carved tableside. The prices are a little steep, but it's worth it for the atmosphere alone. Plus, the food's great—a real Brussels treat.

Galerie de la Reine 30 (in the Galeries Royales St-Hubert). ℭ **02/512-37-32.** Main courses 13€–23€ ($15–$26); *plat du jour* 9.90€ ($11). AE, DC, MC, V. Daily noon–midnight (closed June–July Wed–Thurs). Métro: Gare Centrale.

4 Seeing the Sights

Brussels has such a wonderful variety of things to see. There are more than 75 museums dedicated to just about every special interest under the sun (from cartoons to cars) in addition to impressive public buildings, leafy parks, and interesting squares. History is just around every corner. Fortunately, numerous sidewalk cafes offer respite for weary feet, and there's good public transportation to those attractions beyond walking distance of the compact, heart-shaped city center, which contains many of Brussels's most popular attractions.

THE GRAND-PLACE

Ornamental gables, medieval banners, gilded facades, sunlight flashing off gold-filigreed rooftop sculptures, a general impression of harmony and timelessness—there's a lot to take in all at once when you first enter the **Grand-Place** (Métro: Gare Centrale), the city's historic central square, which has always been the very heart of Brussels. Some call it the world's most beautiful square.

Brussels

Railway
(i) Information
⊠ Post Office
✝ Church

0   1/5 mi
0   0.2 km

Brussels
⊛
BELGIUM

bd. Léopold II
rue Ribaucourt
rue Courtois
rue de l'Avenir
chaussée de Gand
quai des Charbonnages
bd. du Neuvième de Ligne
rue de l'Ecole
rue des Quatre Vents
rue du Comte de Flandres
chaussée de Gand
canal de Charleroi
bd. de Nieuport
Vlaamsesteenweg
r. A. Dansaert
rue Dubois Thorn
quai du Hainaut
rue Barthélemy
rue du Grand Serment
Rempart des Moines
rue N.D. du Sommeil
rue des Fabriques
chaussée de Ninove
rue Heyvaert
rue de Birmingham
bd. de l'Abbatoir
bd. de la Senne
rue Van Artevelde
1
rue d'Anderlecht
rue de Soignies
rue du Dam
2
place **Rouppe**
bd. du Midi
rue Broigniez
bd. Poincaré
bd. Lemonnier
av. de Stalingrad
chaussée de Mons
rue de Vétérinaires
place **Bara**
bd. Jamar
rue des
Zuidlaan
av. de la Porte de Hal
place du Jeu de Balle
Gare du Midi
av. du Fonsny
rue Mérode
rue d'Angleterre
rue Blaes
rue de Deux Gares
⊠
rue de Suède
rue de Claes
rue Fontainas
rue Coenraets
Hallepoort

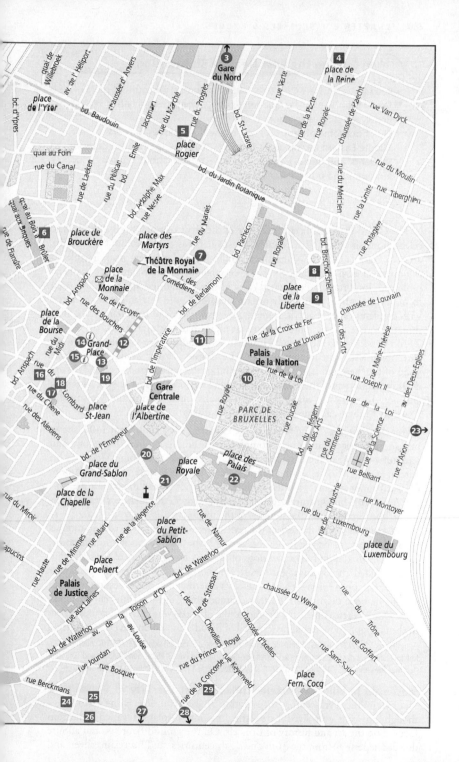

Value   Getting the Best Deal on Sightseeing

- Purchase a **Brussels Card** (see "Brussels Deals & Discounts," p. 263).
- Take advantage of the **free admission** some museums offer on the first Wednesday afternoon of the month.
- Check out some of Brussels's fun **markets**—antiques, flowers, even a Middle Eastern bazaar. See "Outdoor Markets" (p. 286) for details.
- **Students and seniors** should be sure to ask about discounts for museums and other attractions.

The Grand-Place has been the center of the city's commercial life and public celebrations since the 12th century. Most of it was destroyed in 1695 by the army of France's Louis XIV and then rebuilt over the next few years. Thanks to the town's close monitoring, the baroque splendor of these buildings has been preserved. Important guilds owned most of these buildings, and each competed to outdo the others with highly ornate facades of gold leaf and statuary, often with emblems of their guilds. Some now house cafes and restaurants. The illuminated square is even more beautiful at night than during the day.

Top honors go to the Gothic **Hôtel de Ville** and the neo-Gothic **Maison du Roi.** You'll also want to admire no. 9, **Le Cygne,** former headquarters of the guild of butchers and now a tony restaurant of the same name; no. 10, **L'Arbre d'Or,** headquarters of the guild of brewers and location of the Brewing Museum; and nos. 13 to 19, an ensemble of seven mansions known as the **Maison des Ducs de Brabant,** adorned with busts of 19 dukes.

Hôtel de Ville ✹✹   The facade of the dazzling Town Hall, from 1402, shows off Gothic intricacy at its best, complete with dozens of arched windows and sculptures—some of these, such as the drunken monks, a sleeping Moor and his harem, and St. Michael slaying a female devil, display a sense of humor. A 66m (216-ft.) tower sprouts from the middle, yet it's not placed directly in the center. A colorful but untrue legend has it that when the architect realized his "error," he jumped from the summit of the tower.

The building is still the seat of the civic government, and its wedding room is a popular place to tie the knot. You can visit the interior on 40-minute tours, which start in a room full of paintings of the past foreign rulers of Brussels, who have included the Spanish, Austrians, French, and Dutch. In the spectacular Gothic Hall, open for visits when the city's aldermen are not in session, you can see fine baroque decoration. In other chambers are 16th- to 18th-century tapestries. One of these depicts the Spanish duke of Alba, whose cruel features reflect the brutal oppression he and his Council of Blood imposed on the Low Countries.

Grand-Place. ✆ 02/279-43-55. Admission (guided tours only) 3€ ($3.45) adults, 2€ ($2.30) children 5–15, free for children under 5. Guided tours in English Apr–Sept Tues and Wed 3:15pm, Sun 10:45am and 12:15pm; Oct–Mar Tues and Wed 3:15pm. Closed Jan 1, May 1, Nov 1 and 11, Dec 25. Métro: Gare Centrale.

Musée de la Ville de Bruxelles (Museum of the City of Brussels) ✹
Housed in the 19th-century neo-Gothic Maison du Roi (King's House)—though no king ever lived here—the museum displays a varied collection focused on the art and history of Brussels. On the ground floor you can admire detailed tapestries from the 16th and 17th centuries, and porcelain, silver, and

stone statuary. After climbing a beautiful wooden staircase, you can trace the history of Brussels in old maps, prints, photos, and models. Among its most fascinating exhibits are old paintings and scale reconstructions of the historic city center, particularly those showing the riverside ambience along the now-vanished River Senne. On the third floor are more than 650 costumes that have been donated to *Manneken-Pis* (see box below), including an Elvis costume.

Grand-Place. © 02/279-43-50. Admission 3€ ($3.45) adults, 2.50€ ($2.90) seniors and students, 1.50€ ($1.75) travelers with disabilities and children 6–15, free for children under 6. Tues–Fri 10am–5pm; Sat–Sun 11am–5pm. Closed Jan 1, May 1, Nov 1 and 11, and Dec 25. Métro: Gare Centrale.

SOME MEMORABLE MUSEUMS

Centre Belge de la Bande Dessinée (Belgian Comic-Strip Center) 𝓡𝓡

Kids As you'll soon find out, Belgians are crazy for cartoons. The unique "CéBéBéDé," focuses on Belgium's own popular cartoon characters, such as Lucky Luke, Thorgal, and, of course, Tintin, complete with red-and-white-checkered moon rocket, yet it doesn't neglect the likes of Superman, Batman, and the Green Lantern. The building, designed by Art Nouveau architect Victor Horta, is an attraction in itself.

Rue des Sables 20 (off bd. de Berlaimont). © 02/219-19-80. www.brusselsbdtour.com. Admission 6.20€ ($7) adults, 5€ ($6) students and seniors, 2.50€ ($2.90) children under 12. Tues–Sun 10am–6pm. Closed Jan 1, Dec 25. Métro: Gare Centrale.

Musée Horta *Finds* Brussels owes much of its rich Art Nouveau heritage to Victor Horta (1861–1947), a resident architect who led the development of the style. His home and adjoining studio in St-Gilles, restored to their original condition, showcase his use of flowing, sinuous shapes and colors, in both interior decoration and architecture.

Rue Américaine 25 (off chaussée de Charleroi). © 02/543-04-90. www.hortamuseum.be. Admission 4.95€ ($6) adults, 3.70€ ($4.30) seniors and students, 2.50€ ($2.90) children 5–18, free for children under 5. Tues–Sun 2–5:30pm. Closed national holidays. Tram: 81, 82, 91, or 92.

A Cool Little Guy

Two blocks south of the Grand-Place, at the intersection of rue de l'Etuve and rue du Chêne, is the *Manneken-Pis* 𝓡 (Métro: Bourse). A small bronze statue of a urinating child, Brussels's favorite character gleefully does what a little boy's gotta do, generally ogled by a throng of admirers. Children especially enjoy his bravura performance.

No one knows when this child first came into being, but it's clear he dates from quite a few centuries ago—the 8th century, according to one legend. Thieves have made off with the tyke several times in history. One criminal who stole and shattered the statue in 1817 was sentenced to a life of hard labor. The pieces were used to recast another version and that "original" has been removed for safekeeping.

King Louis XV of France began the tradition of presenting colorful costumes to "Little Julian," which he wears on special occasions (during Christmas season he dons a Santa suit, complete with white beard), to make amends for Frenchmen having kidnapped the statue in 1747. The vast wardrobe is housed in the Musée de la Ville de Bruxelles in the Grand-Place (see above).

Special & Free Events

July 21, **National Day,** is marked by various celebrations, including fireworks and a military parade past the Royal Palace; July 21 to August 20 brings the bustling **Brussels Fair** near Gare du Midi; on August 9, the Bruxellois celebrate the 1213 victory of Brussels over Leuven by planting a slightly misnamed **Meiboom (Maytree)** at the intersection of rue des Sables and rue du Marais, as bands and other activities celebrate the event.

It's only natural the magnificent Grand-Place should be the setting for some of Brussels's most memorable free events. April to September, you can watch a free evening **Music and Light Show.** Classical music plays as the historic square's buildings are dramatically highlighted. Or you can stop by at noon, when the tower of the Maison du Roi plays golden **carillon chimes** reminiscent of an earlier European era. On the first Tuesday and Thursday in July, in the Grand-Place, you can watch the **Ommegang,** a parade of noble families dressed in historical costumes. Mid-August in even-numbered years, the **Carpet of Flowers** covers the cobblestones with two million begonias arranged in a kind of tapestry. During **Christmas,** a large tree is erected at the center and a crèche is placed at the lower end, and the square hosts the city's Christmas Market.

Musées Royaux des Beaux-Arts (Royal Museums of Fine Arts) ☆☆☆

In a vast museum of several buildings, this complex combines the **Musée d'Art Ancien** and the **Musée d'Art Moderne** under one roof (connected by a passage). The collection displays mostly Belgian works, from the 14th to the 20th century. Included in the historical collection are **Hans Memling's portraits** from the late 15th century, which are marked by sharp lifelike details; works by **Hieronymus Bosch;** and **Lucas Cranach's** *Adam and Eve.* Be sure to see the works of Pieter Bruegel, including his *Adoration of the Magi* and his unusual *Fall of the Rebel Angels,* with grotesque faces and beasts. But don't fear—many of Bruegel's paintings, such as those depicting Flemish village life, are of a less fiery nature. Later artists represented include **Rubens, Van Dyck, Frans Hals,** and **Rembrandt.**

Next door, in a circular building connected to the main entrance, the modern art section has an emphasis on underground works—if only because the museum's eight floors are all below ground level. The overwhelming collection includes works by van Gogh, Matisse, Dalí, Tanguy, Ernst, Chagall, Miró, and local heroes Magritte, Delvaux, De Braekeleer, and Permeke.

Rue de la Régence 3 (at place Royale). ℂ 02/508-32-11. www.fine-arts-museum.be. Admission 5€ ($6) adults, 3.50€ ($4) students, seniors, and travelers with disabilities, free for children under 12, free for everyone 1st Wed afternoon of the month (except during special exhibits). Tues–Sun 10am–5pm. Closed Jan 1, May 1, Nov 1 and 11, and Dec 25. Métro: Parc.

PARC DU CINQUANTENAIRE

Designed to celebrate the half centenary of Belgium's 1830 independence, the Cinquantenaire Park was a work in progress from the 1870s until well into the 20th century. Extensive gardens have at their heart a triumphal arch topped by a bronze four-horse chariot sculpture, representing *Brabant Raising the National Flag*, flanked by several fine museums.

Autoworld *Kids* Even if you're not a car enthusiast, you'll find this display of 500 historic cars set in the Palais Mondial fascinating. The collection starts with 1899 early motorized tricycles and moves on to a 1911 Model T Ford, a 1924 Renault, a 1938 Cadillac that was the official White House car for FDR and Truman, a 1956 Cadillac used by Eisenhower and later by Kennedy during his June 1963 visit to Berlin, and more.

Parc du Cinquantenaire 11. © 02/736-41-65. www.autoworld.be. Admission 5€ ($6) adults, 3.70€ ($4.30) students, seniors, and travelers with disabilities, 2€ ($2.30) children 6–13, free for children under 6. Apr–Sept Mon–Fri 9:30am–6pm, Sat–Sun 10am–6pm; Oct–Mar daily 10am–5pm. Closed Jan 1, Dec 25. Métro: Mérode.

Musée du Cinquantenaire *⚔* This vast museum shows off an eclectic collection of antiques, decorative arts (tapestries, porcelain, silver, and sculptures), and archaeological finds. Highlights include an Assyrian relief from the 9th century B.C., a Greek vase from the 6th century B.C., a tabletop model of imperial Rome in the 4th century A.D., the 1145 reliquary of Pope Alexander, some exceptional tapestries, and colossal statues from Easter Island.

Parc du Cinquantenaire 10. © 02/741-72-11. www.kmkg-mrah.be. Admission 4€ ($4.60) adults, 2.50€ ($2.90) students and seniors, 1.25€ ($1.45) children 12–18, free for children under 12, free for everyone 1st Wed afternoon of the month (except during special exhibits). Tues–Fri 9:30am–5pm; Sat–Sun and public holidays 10am–5pm. Closed Jan 1, May 1, Nov 1 and 11, Dec 25. Métro: Mérode.

BRUPARCK

Built on the site of the 1958 Brussels World's Fair, this attractions park (Métro: Heysel) is home to the **Atomium** and **Mini-Europe; The Village,** a collection of restaurants and cafes, including a restaurant in a 1930s railway car of the legendary Orient Express; **Océade,** an indoor/outdoor watersports pavilion with water slides, pools, and saunas; a **planetarium;** and **Kinepolis,** a 26-screen movie multiplex.

Atomium *⚔* As the Eiffel Tower is the symbol of Paris, the Atomium is the symbol of Brussels and, as was Paris's landmark, it was built for a world's fair, the 1958 Brussels World's Fair. Closed for renovation through 2004, it's due to reopen early in 2005. Rising 102m (335 ft.) like a giant plaything of the gods that's fallen to earth, the Atomium is an iron atom magnified 165 billion times. Its metal-clad spheres, representing individual atoms, are connected by enclosed escalators and elevators. The topmost atom's restaurant/observation deck provides a sweeping panorama of the metropolitan area.

Bd. du Centenaire, Heysel. © 02/475-47-77. www.atomium.be. Admission 5.50€ ($6.35) adults, 4€ ($4.60) children under 13, free for children under 1.2m (4 ft.). Reduced-rate combination tickets to Atomium and Mini-Europe 15€ ($17) adults, 10€ ($12) seniors, students, and children 12 and under, free for children under 1.2m (4 ft.). Last week Mar to June and Sept daily 9.30am–5pm; July–Aug daily 9.30am–7pm (to 11pm mid-July to mid-Aug); Oct–Dec and New Year holidays 10am–5pm. Métro: Heysel.

Mini-Europe *⚔⚔ Kids* Built at ¹⁄₂₅ the originals' size, Big Ben, the Leaning Tower of Pisa, the Seville bullring, the Channel Tunnel, the Brandenburg Gate, and more, exhibit remarkable detail (Mt. Vesuvius, for example, "erupts"). Although children like Mini-Europe the best, adults certainly find it fun.

Bruparck, Heysel. © 02/478-05-50. www.minieurope.com. Admission 12€ ($13) adults, 8.70€ ($10) children under 13, free for children under 1.2m (4 ft.). Reduced-rate combination tickets to Atomium and Mini-Europe 15€ ($17) adults, 10€ ($12) seniors, students, and children 12 and under, free for children under 1.2m (4 ft.). Apr–June and Sept 9:30am–5pm; July–Aug 9:30am–7pm; mid-July to mid-Aug Fri–Sun 9:30am–11pm; Oct–Dec and 1st week Jan 10am–5pm. Closed rest of Jan–Mar. Métro: Heysel.

A HISTORIC CHURCH

Cathédrale des Sts-Michel-et-Gudule ✴ Victor Hugo considered this magnificent church, dedicated to the city's patron St. Michael and to St. Gudula, to be the "purest flowering of the Gothic style." Begun in 1226, it was officially consecrated as a cathedral only in 1961. The 16th-century Habsburg Emperor Charles V donated the superb stained-glass windows. Apart from these, the spare interior decoration focuses attention on its soaring columns and arches. The bright exterior stonework makes a fine sight. On Sunday at 10am, the Eucharist is celebrated with a Gregorian choir. In July, August, and September, polyphonic Masses are sung by local and international choirs at 10am. August to October, chamber-music and organ concerts are occasionally performed on weekdays at 8pm. In spring and autumn at 12:30pm, Mass is sung accompanied by instrumental soloists and readings by actors (in French).

Parvis Ste-Gudule (off bd. de l'Impératrice 2 blocks west of Gare Centrale). ⓒ **02/217-83-45.** Free admission to cathedral; admission to crypt, treasury, archaeological zone 2.50€ ($2.90). Mon–Fri 8:30am–6pm; Sat–Sun 8am–6pm. Métro: Gare Centrale.

OTHER HISTORIC SQUARES

Considered classier than the Grand-Place (p. 277) by the locals, though busy traffic diminishes your enjoyment of its cafe-terraces, **place du Grand-Sablon** ✴✴ (tram: 92, 93, or 94) is lined with gabled mansions. This is antiques territory, and many of these mansions house antiques stores or private art galleries, with pricey merchandise on display. On Saturday and Sunday (9am–6pm and 9am–2pm, respectively), an excellent antiques market sets up its stalls in front of Notre-Dame du Sablon Church.

Across rue de la Régence, the Grand-Sablon's little cousin, **place du Petit-Sablon** ✴ (tram: 92, 93, or 94), has a small sculptured garden with a fountain and pool at its center. This magical little retreat from the city bustle is surrounded by wrought-iron railings, atop which stand 48 small statues of medieval guildsmen.

At the meeting-point of rue de la Régence and rue Royale, streets on which stand many of the city's premier monuments and attractions, **place Royale** ✴ (tram: 92, 93, or 94) is graced by an equestrian statue of Duke Godefroid de Bouillon, leader of the First Crusade. Also in place Royale is the neoclassical St-Jacques-sur-Coudenberg Church.

PARKS

The most attractive park in town is the **Parc de Bruxelles** ✴✴ (Métro: Parc), extending in front of the Palais Royal. Once the property of the dukes of Brabant, this well-designed park with geometrically divided paths—which form the outline of Masonic symbols—running through it became public in 1776. The many benches make a fine place to stop for a picnic. The park has historic importance, too: The first shots in Belgium's 1830 war of independence were fired here. In 2001, the park was restored as closely as possible to its 18th-century look. The refurbished 1840s bandstand hosts regular summer concerts.

The large public park called the **Bois de la Cambre** ✴ begins at the top of avenue Louise in the southern section of Brussels (tram: 23, 90, 93, or 94) and gets busy on sunny weekends. Its centerpiece is a small lake with an island in its center, which you can reach via an electrically operated pontoon. Some busy roads run through the park, and traffic moves fast on them, so be careful with children at these points.

ORGANIZED TOURS

Brussels City Tours, rue de la Colline 8, off Grand-Place (© 02/513-77-44; www.brussels-city-tours.com; Métro: Gare Centrale), operates a guided 2¾-hour Brussels City Tour by bus for 20€ ($23) adults, 18€ ($21) students and seniors, and 10€ ($11) children. You can book at most hotels, and arrangements can be made for hotel pickup.

June 15 to September 15, **Le Bus Bavard,** rue des Thuyas 12 (© 02/ 673-18-35), gives you a real feel for the city. The 3-hour "chatterbus" tour leaves daily at 10am from the Galeries Royales St-Hubert (Métro: Gare Centrale), a mall next to rue du Marché-aux-Herbes 90, a few steps off the Grand-Place. A walking tour covers the historic center, followed by a bus ride through areas that most visitors never see. The price is 8.75€ ($10). You don't need a reservation for this fascinating experience—just be there by 10am.

5 Shopping

Don't look for many bargains. As a general rule, the upper city around avenue Louise and Porte de Namur is more expensive than the lower city around rue Neuve. You can enjoy a stroll along modern shopping promenades, the busiest of which is pedestrian-only **rue Neuve.** Starting at place de la Monnaie and running north to place Rogier, it is home to boutiques; big department stores like Inno, H&M, and Marks & Spencer; and several malls.

Some of the trendiest boutiques are on **rue Antoine-Dansaert,** across from the Bourse. An interesting street for window-shopping, **rue des Eperonniers,** near the Grand-Place, hosts many small stores selling antiques, toys, old books, and clothing.

For luxury shopping, try stores on avenue Louise and nearby streets, where you'll find names such as **Cartier, Burberry, Vuitton, Benetton,** and **Valentino.** You might not find any bargains, but there's lots to look at.

The **Galeries Royales St-Hubert** (Métro: Gare Centrale) is an airy, glass-topped arcade hosting expensive boutiques, cafes with outdoor terraces, and buskers playing classical music. Opened in 1847, architect Pierre Cluysenaer's Italian neo-Renaissance gallery has a touch of class and is well worth a stroll, even if you have no intention of buying. The elegant gallery is near the Grand-Place, between rue du Marché-aux-Herbes and rue de l'Ecuyer, and split by rue des Bouchers. Opposite is **Galerie Agora,** hip and punky, with lots of chains, leather clothes, and belts.

BEST BUYS

Lace is the overwhelming favorite, followed by crystal, jewelry, antiques, and pewter. Chocolate, beer, and other foods are more economical. And in souvenir stores you find replicas of *Manneken-Pis,* so you can bring the little guy home with you.

In a former guild house, **Maison Antoine,** Grand-Place 26 (© 02/512-48-59; Métro: Gare Centrale), is one of the best places in town to buy lace. The quality is superb, the service is friendly, and the prices are reasonable.

Visit **De Boe,** rue de Flandre 36 (© 02/511-13-73; Métro: Ste-Catherine), a small store near the Marché aux Poissons, for the heavenly aromas of roasted and blended coffee, a superb selection of wines in all price categories, and an array of specialty teas, spices, and epicurean snacks. **Dandoy,** rue au Beurre 31 (© 02/511-03-26; Métro: Bourse), is where cookie and cake fans can try traditional Belgian

Tips   Tax Saver

If you spend over 125€ ($144) in some stores, and you are not a resident of the European Union, you can get a tax refund when you leave the European Union. Stores that display a TAX-FREE SHOPPING sign provide visitors who are not residents in the European Union with the form they need for recovering some of the 21.5% value-added tax (TVA) on purchases. At the airport, show the Customs officials your purchase and receipt and they'll stamp the form. You mail this form back to the Belgian Tax Bureau (the address is on the form) or bring it directly to the Best Change office at the airport, which charges a small commission but gives you an on-the-spot refund.

specialties such as spicy *speculoos* (traditional Belgian cookies made with brown sugar and cinnamon and baked in wooden molds) and *pain à la grecque* (caramelized, sugary, flaky pastries).

If you have a sweet tooth, you'll feel you're in heaven when you see Brussels's famous chocolate stores, filled with sumptuous soft-centered pralines, from around 12€ ($14) per kilogram (2¼ lb.). You find some of the best confections at **Chocolatier Mary,** rue Royale 73 (© 02/217-45-00; Métro: Parc), supplier to the royal court; **Neuhaus,** Galerie de la Reine 25 (© 02/502-59-14; Métro: Gare Centrale); **Wittamer,** place du Grand-Sablon 12 (© 02/512-37-42; tram 92, 93, or 94); and **Léonidas,** bd. Anspach 46 (© 02/218-03-63; Métro: Bourse).

For kids, pick up some Tintin mementos from **Boutique de Tintin,** rue de la Colline 13 (© 02/514-45-50; Métro: Gare Centrale). **Waterstone's,** bd. Adolphe-Max 75 (© 02/219-27-08; Métro: Rogier), has English-language books, newspapers, and magazines.

OUTDOOR MARKETS

The city's favorite *marché-aux-puces* (flea market) is the **Vieux-Marché (Old Market;** Métro: Porte de Hal), on place du Jeu-de-Balle, a large cobblestone square in the Marolles district, open daily 7am to 2pm. You have to sift through lots of junk but can make real finds among the old postcards and vintage clothing. Around the square are cozy cafes and inexpensive restaurants. Marolles denizens even speak their own dialect.

For goods of a higher quality—at decidedly higher prices—check out the **Antiques Market** on place du Grand-Sablon (tram: 92, 93, or 94), open Saturday 9am to 6pm and Sunday 9am to 2pm. You'll also find antiques stores, open throughout the week, on streets in the nearby area.

The Grand-Place (Métro: Gare Centrale) has a **Flower Market,** Tuesday to Sunday from 7am to 2pm. Nearby, at the top end of rue du Marché-aux-Herbes, a weekend **Crafts Market** has lots of fine little specialized jewelry and other items, most of which are inexpensive.

Every Sunday from 7am to 2pm, hundreds of merchants assemble their wares in a **street market** outside Gare du Midi (Métro: Gare du Midi). Because many of the merchants and much of the merchandise are of Arab origin, the scene resembles a *casbah*. You can find many excellent food and household-item bargains. Hold on to your wallet, though, because the market attracts pickpockets.

6 Brussels After Dark

A listing of upcoming events—opera, classical music, dance, theater, live music, film, and other events—is in the *What's On* guide in the weekly English-language magazine *The Bulletin*.

You can order tickets for performing-arts venues from the **Central Booking Office** (℗ **0800/21-221**), open Monday to Friday 9am to 7pm, Saturday 10am to 7pm. The tourist office in the Town Hall on the Grand-Place (see "Visitor Information," earlier in this chapter) can reserve concert/theater tickets for 1€ ($1.15).

THE PERFORMING ARTS

An opera house in the grand style, the **Théâtre Royal de la Monnaie** ⚘⚘, place de la Monnaie (℗ **02/229-12-00**; www.lamonnaie.be; Métro: De Brouckère), is home to the **Opéra Royal de la Monnaie,** which has been called the best in the French-speaking world, and to the **Orchestre Symphonique de la Monnaie.** The resident modern dance company, **Anne Theresa de Keersmaeker's Group Rosas,** is noted for its original moves. The box office is open Tuesday to Saturday 11am to 6pm. Tickets run 8€ to 148€ ($9–$170). Five minutes before a show, they're 8€ ($9) for those under 28.

Bozar, rue Ravenstein 23 (℗ **02/507-82-00**; Métro: Gare Centrale)—formerly the elegantly named Palais des Beaux-Arts until some "bright spark" came up with the idea of trendifying it—is home to the **Belgian National Orchestra.** The box office is open Monday to Saturday 11am to 6pm, with tickets running 10€ to 75€ ($11–$86). The **Cirque Royal,** rue de l'Enseignement 81 (℗ **02/218-20-15**; Métro: Parc), formerly a real circus, now hosts music, opera, and ballet. The box office is open Tuesday to Saturday from 11am to 6pm, with tickets for 8€ to 65€ ($11–$75).

LIVE-MUSIC CLUBS

The jazz café **Marcus Mingus Jazz Spot,** impasse de la Fidelité 10, off rue des Bouchers (℗ **02/502-02-97**; Métro: Gare Centrale), attracts top local performers and an occasional international name. The Art Deco bar **L'Archiduc,** rue Antoine Dansaert 6 (℗ **02/512-06-52**; Métro: Bourse), serves up a sophisticated program of jazz on weekends.

DANCE CLUBS

Top clubs include the always popular **Le Sparrow,** rue Duquesnoy 16 (℗ **02/512-66-22**; Métro: Gare Centrale); **Le Fuse,** rue Blaes 208 (℗ **02/511-97-89**; bus: 20 or 48) for techno; and **Griffin's Night Club,** in the Royal Windsor Hotel, rue Duquesnoy 5 (℗ **02/505-55-55**; Métro: Gare Centrale), fashionable for older hoofers.

Moments Puppet Theater

Traditional Brussels marionette theater is performed at **Théâtre Royal de Toone,** impasse Schuddeveld 6, Petite rue des Bouchers 21 (℗ **02/217-27-23**; Métro: Gare Centrale). In a tiny theater in the old café **Toone VII,** puppet master José Géal presents adaptations of classic tales like *Faust* and *The Three Musketeers.* Some performances are in English, others are in French, Dutch, German, or the local patois, Bruxellois, with plots and characters so familiar that even if you don't understand a word, you'll be able to follow the action. Performances are at 8:30pm Tuesday to Saturday; tickets are 10€ ($11).

GAY & LESBIAN CLUBS

Rue des Riches-Claires and **rue du Marché-au-Charbon** host gay and lesbian bars. **Macho 2,** rue du Marché-au-Charbon 108 (© **02/513-56-67;** Métro: Bourse), a block from rue des Riches-Claires, has a gay men's sauna, pool, steam room, and cafe. **Le Fuse** and **Le Sparrow** (see above) have gay nights. Cover varies.

For more information about clubs and gay life in Brussels, contact **Infor Homo,** av. de Roodebeek 57 (© **02/733-10-24;** Métro: Diamant), open Tuesday to Friday 8am to 6pm. Or stop by the gay and lesbian community center, **Telsquels,** rue du Marché-au-Charbon 81 (© **02/512-45-87;** Métro: Bourse), open Saturday to Thursday 5pm to 2am, Friday 8am to 4am.

CAFES & BARS

It's always satisfying to sit at a sidewalk cafe on the Grand-Place and drink in the beauty of the floodlit golden buildings ringing the square. Drinks on a Grand-Place terrace are more expensive than those in ordinary cafes, but once you've ordered one, you can nurse it for hours—or until the waiter's patience wears out and he grabs the glass from you, empty or not.

The city's oldest cafe, **Le Roy d'Espagne,** Grand-Place 1 (© **02/513-08-07;** Métro: Gare Centrale), accommodates patrons in several areas. In addition to the outdoor tables, you can drink in a room preserving a 17th-century Flemish interior—a masterpiece of wooden architecture with a wooden walkway and wooden beams above and a fireplace covered by a black metal hood. The fourth-floor view of the Grand-Place is spectacular. It's open daily 10am to 1am.

Although its name means "Sudden Death," you'll likely survive **A la Mort Subite,** rue Montagne-aux-Herbes-Potagères 7 (© **02/513-13-18;** Métro: Gare Centrale), a 1911 cafe with stained glass mirrors, old photographs, paintings, and prints, that's a good place to enjoy an afternoon coffee or an evening beer. It's open daily 10am to 1am. A block from the Grand-Place in a 1642 house, **A l'Imaige de Nostre-Dame,** rue du Marché-aux-Herbes 6–8 (© **02/219-42-49;** Métro: Gare Centrale), harbors people of all ages enjoying reasonably priced beer amid wooden ceiling beams, old wooden tables, painted windows, and an antique ceramic fireplace. It's open daily noon to midnight.

Shock reverberated through the city in 1999 when the legendary Art Nouveau tavern **Falstaff,** rue Henri Maus 17–25 (© **02/511-98-77;** Métro: Bourse), went bankrupt. It has reopened, and you can still enjoy a drink in this stunning setting. Across the way, at **Le Cirio,** rue de la Bourse 18 (© **02/512-13-95;** Métro: Bourse), you sip your drink in quiet, refined surroundings that make the exercise seem worthwhile. Many customers look like they've made their pile at the neighboring Stock Exchange and retired here to a state of genteel splendor.

In a 17th-century building, **Le Fleur en Papier Doré,** rue des Alexiens 53, off place de la Chapelle (© **02/511-16-59;** Métro: Bourse), calls itself a temple of surrealism because Magritte used to relax here. Despite its grandmotherly decor, the cafe attracts a wide assortment of arty types. On Friday and Saturday from 9 or 10pm, an accordion player pumps out some tunes, and there are occasional poetry readings upstairs. It's open daily 11am to 11pm.

You can choose from a large selection of beers and wine, coffee, and a few snacks at **De Ultieme Hallucinatie,** rue Royale 316 (© **02/217-06-14;** Métro: Botanique), located in an early-1900s town house on the edge of the center. An expensive Art Nouveau restaurant occupies another room. Downstairs, a futuristic dance club has fluorescent lighting and abstract outer-space art.

7 A Side Trip to Bruges ★★★: Canals & Flemish Charm

From its 13th-century origins as a cloth-manufacturing town to its current incarnation as a tourism mecca, the Flemish city of **Bruges (Brugge)** seems to have changed little. As in a fairy tale, swans glide down winding canals and the stone houses look as if they're made of gingerbread. Even though glass-fronted stores have taken over the ground floors of ancient buildings and swans scatter before tour boats chugging along the canals, Bruges has made the transition from medieval to modern with remarkable grace. The town seems revitalized rather than crushed by the tremendous influx of tourists.

Trains depart every hour from Brussels for Bruges. The trip takes 55 minutes, and the train stops at Ghent. Bruges is well connected to Antwerp, the North Sea resort of Ostend, and the ferry port of Zeebrugge. **Bruges station** (look out for BRUGGE, the town's Dutch name, on the destination boards) is on Station-splein (© **050/38-23-82**), 1.5km (1 mile) from the center, a 20-minute walk or a short bus ride—take any bus labeled CENTRUM and get out at the Markt.

Buses from Brussels, London, Paris, Amsterdam, and other cities, operated by **Eurolines** (© **02/274-13-50;** www.eurolines.com), arrive at the bus station adjoining Bruges railway station.

If you're **driving** from Brussels, take A10/E40. Drop your car at one of the large, prominently signposted underground parking garages around the center—these are expensive for long stays—or at the inexpensive parking lot at the railway station, from where you can take a bus or take the 10- to 15-minute walk into the heart of the city. The network of one-way streets in the center makes driving a trial.

VISITOR INFORMATION **Toerisme Brugge,** Burg 11, 8000 Brugge (© **050/ 44-86-86;** www.brugge.be), in the center of town, is the official dispenser of tourist information. The office, which can make hotel reservations, is open April to September Monday to Friday from 9:30am to 6:30pm, Saturday, Sunday, and holidays from 10am to 12:30pm and 2 to 6:30pm; October to March Monday to Friday from 9:30am to 5pm, and Saturday, Sunday and holidays from 9:30am to 1pm and 2 to 5:30pm.

GETTING AROUND De Lijn city **buses** (© **070/22-02-00**) depart the bus station beside the railway station, and from the big square called 't Zand, west of the Markt. Several bus routes pass through the Markt. **Biking** is a terrific way to get around town. You can rent a bike from the railway station (© **050/ 38-58-71**) for 9€ ($10) a day, plus a deposit. Some hotels and stores rent bikes for 5€ to 9€ ($6–$10) a day.

SEEING THE SIGHTS Walking is the best way to see Bruges, but wear good walking shoes—those cobblestones can be hard going. Narrow streets fan out from two central squares, the **Markt** and the **Burg.** A network of canals threads its way to every section of the small city, and the center is almost encircled by a canal that opens at its southern end to become a swan-filled lake, the **Minnewater**—this translates as Lake of Love, though the name actually comes from the Dutch *Binnen Water,* meaning Inner Harbor—bordered by the Begijnhof and a fine park.

Begin your tour at the **Markt** ★★, where you'll find the 13th- to 16th-century **Hallen (Market Halls)** and its 88m (289 ft.) tower, the **Belfort (Bel-fry)** ★★★ (© **050/87-44-11**). Much of the city's cloth trade and other commerce was conducted in the Hallen in centuries past, and if you have enough energy, you can climb the 366 steps to the Belfry's summit for a panoramic view of the old city—you can pause for a breath at the second-floor Treasury, where the town seal and charters were kept behind multiple wrought-iron grilles. Both are open Tuesday to Sunday 9:30am to 5pm (also Easter and Pentecost Mondays); closed January 1, Ascension Day afternoon, and December 25. Admission is 5€ ($6) adults, 3€ ($3.45) seniors and ages 13 to 26, children under 13 free.

A **sculpture group** in the middle of the Markt depicts two Flemish heroes, butcher Jan Breydel and weaver Pieter de Coninck, who led a bloody 1302 uprising against pro-French merchants and nobles who dominated the city, then went on to an against-all-odds victory over French knights later that same year in the Battle of the Golden Spurs. The large neo-Gothic **Provinciaal Hof,** from 1887 to 1921, houses the government of West Flanders province.

An array of beautiful buildings, which adds up to a trip through the history of Bruges architecture, stands in the **Burg** 𝕬𝕬𝕬, a square just steps away from the Markt. During the 9th century, Count Baldwin "Iron Arm" of Flanders built a castle here at a then tiny riverside settlement that would grow into Bruges.

The beautiful Gothic **Stadhuis,** Burg 12 ((𝐶 **050/44-87-11**), from the late 1300s, is Belgium's oldest town hall. Don't miss the upstairs **Gotische Zaal (Gothic Room)** 𝕬𝕬𝕬, with its ornate, oak-carved vaulted ceiling and murals depicting biblical scenes and highlights of the town's history. The statues in the niches on the Town Hall facade are 1980s replacements for the originals, which had been painted by Jan van Eyck and were destroyed by the French in the 1790s. The Gothic Room is open Tuesday to Sunday 9:30am to 5pm (also Easter and Pentecost Mondays); closed January 1, Ascension Day afternoon, and December 25. Admission is 2.50€ ($3.90) adults, 1.50€ ($1.75) seniors and ages 13 to 26, children under 13 free. The price includes entry to the restored 16th-century Renaissance **Aldermen's Chamber** 𝕬𝕬, in the neighboring, neoclassical **Landhuis van het Brugse Vrije (Palace of the Liberty of Bruges),** Burg 11, which has a superb black marble fireplace decorated with an alabaster frieze. This is surmounted by an oak chimney-piece embellished with sculptures of Emperor Charles V and his illustrious grandparents: Emperor Maximilian of Austria, Duchess Mary of Burgundy, King Ferdinand II of Aragon, and Queen Isabella I of Castile. The open hours are the same as those for the Town Hall's Gothic Room.

Next to the Town Hall is the richly decorated **Heilig-Bloedbasiliek (Basilica of the Holy Blood)** 𝕬𝕬, Burg 10 ((𝐶 **050/33-67-92**). Since 1150, this Romanesque church has been the repository of a fragment of cloth impregnated with what's said to be Christ's holy blood, brought to Bruges after the Second Crusade by the count of Flanders. The relic is in the basilica museum, inside a rock-crystal vial that's kept in a magnificent gold-and-silver reliquary, and is exposed frequently for the faithful to kiss. Every Ascension Day, in the Procession of the Holy Blood, the relic is carried through the streets, accompanied by costumed residents acting out Biblical scenes. The basilica is open April to September daily 9:30am to noon and 2 to 6pm; October to March daily 10am to noon and 2 to 4pm (closed Wed afternoon); closed January 1, November 1, and December 25. Admission to the basilica is free; admission to the museum is 1.50€ ($1.75) adults, .50€ (60¢) children 5 to 18, children under 5 free.

The **Groeninge Museum** 𝕬𝕬𝕬, Dijver 12 ((𝐶 **050/44-87-11**), ranks among Belgium's leading traditional museums of fine arts, with a collection that covers Low Countries painting from the 15th to the 20th centuries. The Flemish Primitives Gallery has 30 works—which seem far from primitive—by such painters as Jan van Eyck (portrait of his wife, Margareta van Eyck), Rogier van der

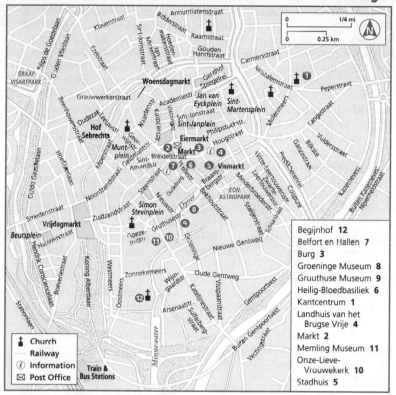

Weyden, Hieronymus Bosch *(The Last Judgment)*, and Hans Memling. Works by Magritte and Delvaux are also on display. The museum is open Tuesday to Sunday 9:30am to 5pm (also Easter and Pentecost Mondays); closed January 1, Ascension Day afternoon, and December 25. Admission (which includes the neighboring Arentshuis) is 8€ ($9) adults, 5€ ($6) seniors and ages 13 to 26, children under 13 free.

In a courtyard next to the Groeninge Museum is the ornate mansion where Flemish nobleman Lodewijk van Gruuthuse lived in the 1400s. Now the **Gruuthuse Museum** ⚑, Dijver 17 (© **050/44-87-11**), it contains thousands of antiques and antiquities, including paintings, sculptures, tapestries, lace, weapons, glassware, and richly carved furniture. The museum is open Tuesday to Sunday 9:30am to 5pm (also Easter and Pentecost Mondays); closed January 1, Ascension Day afternoon, and December 25. Admission (combined ticket with nearby Archaeological Museum) is 6€ ($7) adults, 4€ ($4.60) seniors and ages 13 to 26, children under 13 free.

The former Sint-Janshospitaal (Hospital of St. John), where the earliest wards date from the 13th century, houses the **Memling Museum** ⚑⚑, Mariastraat (© **050/44-87-11**), a magnificent collection of paintings by the German-born artist Hans Memling (ca. 1440–94), who moved to Bruges in 1465. You can view such masterpieces as his triptych altarpiece of St. John the Baptist and St. John the Evangelist, which consists of the paintings *The Mystic Marriage of*

St. Catherine, the *Shrine of St. Ursula,* and the *Virgin with Child and Apple.* A 17th-century apothecary in the cloisters near the hospital entrance is furnished as it was when the building's main function was to care for the sick. The museum is open Tuesday to Sunday 9:30am to 5pm (also Easter and Pentecost Mondays); closed January 1, Ascension Day afternoon, and December 25. Admission is 8€ ($9) adults, 5€ ($6) seniors and ages 13 to 26, under 13 free.

It took 2 centuries (13th–15th c.) to build the magnificent **Onze-Lieve-Vrouwekerk (Church of Our Lady)** 🌟🌟, Onze-Lieve-Vrouwekerkhof-Zuid (© **050/34-53-14**), at Mariastraat. Its soaring spire, 122m (400 ft.) high, is visible from a wide area around Bruges. Among the Church of Our Lady's many art treasures are the marvelous marble *Madonna and Child* 🌟🌟🌟 by Michelangelo (one of his few works outside Italy); the *Crucifixion,* a painting by Anthony Van Dyck; and the impressive side-by-side bronze tomb sculptures of Duke Charles the Bold of Burgundy (d. 1477) and his daughter Mary of Burgundy (d. 1482). The church is open Monday to Friday 9am to 12:30pm and 1:30 to 5pm (also Easter and Pentecost Mondays), Saturday 9am to 12:30pm and 1:30 to 4pm, Sunday 1:30 to 5pm. Admission to the church and the *Madonna and Child* altar is free; admission to the mausoleum of Charles and Mary and the museum is 2.50€ ($2.90) adults, 1.50€ ($1.75) seniors and ages 13 to 26, under 13 free.

One of the most tranquil spots in Bruges is the **Begijnhof** 🌟🌟, Wijngaard-straat (© **050/33-00-11**). Begijns were religious women, similar to nuns, who accepted vows of chastity and obedience, but they did not take vows of poverty. Today, the begijns are no more, but the Begijnhof is occupied by Benedictine nuns who try to keep the begijn traditions alive. Little whitewashed houses surrounding a lawn with trees make a marvelous place of escape. One of the begijns' houses has been set up as a museum. The house is open March and October to November, daily 10:30am to noon and 1:45 to 5pm; April to September, daily 10am to noon and 1:45 to 5:30pm (to 6pm Sun); December to February, Wednesday, Thursday, Saturday, Sunday 2:45 to 4:15pm, and Friday 1:45 to 6pm. Admission is 2€ ($2.30) adults, 1€ ($1.15) children 5 to 18, under 5 free. The Begijnhof itself is permanently open and admission is free.

Bruges lace is famous the world over, and there's no lack of stores to tempt you with the opportunity to take some home. The **Kantcentrum (Lace Center)** 🌟, Peperstraat 3A (© **050/33-00-72**), in the 15th-century Jerusalem Almshouse founded by the Adornes family of Genoese merchants, is where the ancient art of lace-making is passed on to the next generation. You get a firsthand look at

---

⟨*Tips*⟩ Boating the Canals

Open-top **tour boats** 🌟🌟🌟 cruise the canals year-round from five departure points around the center, all marked with an anchor icon on maps available from the tourist office. The boats operate March to November, daily 10am to 6pm; December to February, Saturday, Sunday, and school holidays 10am to 6pm (except if the canals are frozen). A half-hour cruise is 5.20€ ($6) adults, 2.60€ ($3) children 4 to 11 accompanied by an adult, under 4 free. Be sure to wear something warm if the weather is cold or windy.

craftspeople making items for future sale in all the town's lace stores. (Handmade lace is the best, but it's more expensive than machine-made.) The center is open Monday to Saturday 10am to noon and 2 to 6pm (to 5pm Sat). Lace-making demonstrations are in the afternoon. Admission is 2.50€ ($2.90) adults, 2€ ($2.30) seniors and children 7 to 18, under 7 free.

WHERE TO STAY   The recently renovated **Fevery** ⟨★⟩, Collaert Mansionstraat 3 (off Langerei), 8000 Brugge (② **050/33-12-69;** www.hotelfevery.be), on a quiet side street in a quiet part of town just north of the center, has 10 modern and comfortably furnished units (all are nonsmoking). The rates are 60€ to 75€ ($69–$86) single, 60€ to 80€ ($69–$92) double; triples and quads are available. Rates include buffet breakfast. American Express, MasterCard, and Visa are accepted.

Right in the heart of Bruges, the **Lucca** ⟨★⟩, Naaldenstraat 30 (off Sint-Jakobsstraat), 8000 Brugge (② **050/34-20-67;** www.hotellucca.be), has 18 gracious units, 14 with bathroom, in a 14th-century mansion. Rates range from 45€ to 67€ ($52–$77) for a single, 50€ to 82€ ($58–$94) double; triples and quads available. Rates include buffet breakfast. American Express, Diners Club, MasterCard, and Visa are accepted.

One of Bruges's least expensive hotels, **'t Keizershof,** Oostmeers 126 (close to the railway station), 8000 Brugge (② **050/33-87-28;** http://users.belgacom.net/ hotel.keizershof), has seven clean, comfortable units (none with bathroom) in a quiet, peaceful location. The rates are 25€ ($28) single, 36€ ($41) double; triples and quads are available. Rates include continental breakfast. No credit cards are accepted.

WHERE TO DINE   The Markt is lined with cozy traditional restaurants serving decent food, but few bargains.

For real family-style Flemish food, head south of the Markt to the small but popular **Brasserie Erasmus** ⟨★⟩, in the Hotel Erasmus, Wollestraat 35 (② **050/ 33-57-81;** www.hotelerasmus.com). Close to the Markt, it's a fine place to stop after viewing the cathedral and nearby museums. It serves a large variety of Flemish dishes, including a very good *waterzooï* with fish and rabbit in a beer sauce, and has around 150 different brands of beer. Main courses are 15€ to 25€ ($17–$29), and fixed-price menus 20€ to 30€ ($23–$35). MasterCard and Visa are accepted; open Tuesday to Sunday noon to 4pm (also Mon in summer) and 6 to 11pm.

Even nonvegetarians will enjoy the delicious daily lunch at **Lotus,** Wapenmakersstraat 5 (② **050/33-10-78**), off the Burg. For only 7.50€ and 9€ ($9 and $10), you get two menu choices, each with a hearty assortment of imaginatively prepared vegetables, served in a cheerful Scandinavian-style dining room. No credit cards are accepted; open Monday to Saturday 11:45am to 2pm only.

A reliable but slightly more expensive choice is **'t Putje,** 't Zand 31 (② **050/ 33-28-47**), close to the Concertgebouw. This large brasserie/restaurant serves meals centered on expertly grilled meats and seafood enhanced by classic sauces and served with a dollop of potatoes and vegetables. The two-course lunch menu is a bargain at 9€ ($10), and a la carte meals are 14€ to 25€ ($16–$29). You can enjoy light snacks or a drink on the terrace under red-striped awnings. American Express, Diners Club, MasterCard, and Visa are accepted; open daily 8:30am to 1am.

9

Budapest & Lake Balaton

by Joseph S. Lieber & Christina Shea

For much of the 20th century, **Budapest** languished in relative obscurity, off the itinerary and out of the minds of most European travelers. The dramatic political changes of 1989 irreversibly altered the state of the Hungarian capital. Budapest, awakened after its long slumber behind the Iron Curtain, now ranks as one of Europe's hottest travel destinations. One of the great cities of central Europe, Budapest embodies all the elements of the region's peculiar and rich cultural legacy. Poised between East and West, both geographically and culturally, Budapest stands proudly at the center of the region's cultural rebirth.

Budapest came of age in the 19th century. At its start, the towns of Buda and Pest were little more than provincial outposts on the Danube. The dawning of a modern Hungarian identity spawned the city's neoclassical development. The rise of the eclectic style coincided with the great post-1867 boom, creating most of the historic Inner City. Indeed, Budapest, notwithstanding its long and tattered history of Roman, Mongol, and Turkish conquest, is very much a fin-de-siècle city, with a characteristic coffeehouse and music hall culture. The decades after World War I and the fall of the Habsburg monarchy weren't kind to Hungary's charming capital and, until recently, Budapest's glory seemed irretrievably lost. But as the new century dawns over a new Europe, the city is once again attracting visitors from far and wide.

Despite the collapse of the Iron Curtain, however, Budapest has managed to retain an exotic feeling seldom experienced in the "better-known" capital cities of Europe. Take a turn off any main boulevard and you'll quickly find yourself in a quiet residential neighborhood, where the scent of a hearty *gulyás* (goulash) wafts from a kitchen window and cigarette smoke fogs the cavelike entry of the corner pub.

For more on Budapest and its environs, see *Frommer's Budapest & the Best of Hungary.*

1 Essentials

ARRIVING

BY PLANE   Ferihegy II, in the XVIII district in southeastern Pest, handles all civilian flights. (Adjacent Ferihegy I has been turned over to NATO for military use.) There are several main numbers: for arrivals, call © **061/296-5052;** for departures, © **061/296-5883;** and for general info, © **061/296-7155.** Pick up a copy of the free ***LRI Airport Budapest*** magazine, which contains a wealth of valuable phone numbers and transportation-related details, as well as articles on Hungary.

> ### Value Budget Bests
>
> It's hard to know where to begin, so varied are the budget bests in Budapest. Here's a perfect example: This is the place to take in an **opera** or a classical music performance—tickets can be as little as $15—and bring the kids to the **Amusement Park,** where entry is only 300 Ft ($1.35) and rides cost as little as 150 Ft (70¢). This is an amusement park in the great European tradition, in the middle of the city's most popular park. And you don't want to pass on the chance to "take the waters" at one of Budapest's **famed thermal baths**—entry is usually just a few bucks.

The easiest way into the city is probably the **Airport Minibus** (© 1/296-8555; fax 1/296-8993), a public service of the LRI (Budapest Airport Authority). The minibus, which leaves every 10 or 15 minutes throughout the day, takes you directly to any address in the city. From either terminal, it costs 2,100 Ft ($9.45); the price includes luggage transport. The trip takes from 30 minutes to an hour, depending on how many stops are made. The Airport Minibus desk is easily found in the main hall. Minibuses also provide the same efficient service returning to the airport; arrange for your pickup *1 full day in advance.* The minibus will pick up passengers virtually anywhere in the Budapest area.

We strongly *discourage* the use of cabs from the notoriously overpriced **Airport Taxi** fleet (© 061/296-6534). A ride downtown in one of these cabs might cost as much as twice the fare in a recommended fleet. Alas, for reasons no one has been able to explain to us with a straight face, only Airport Taxi fleet cabs are permitted to wait for fares on the airport grounds. This isn't a problem, however—dozens of cabs from the cheaper fleets we recommend wait just off the airport property, ready for radio calls from their dispatchers. Call from the terminal, and a cab will be there for you in a few minutes. See "Getting Around," below, for names and phone numbers. For three or more people traveling together (and maybe even two people), a taxi from a recommended fleet to the city, at approximately 4,500 Ft ($20), will be substantially cheaper than the combined minibus fares. A taxi from the airport to downtown takes about 20 to 30 minutes.

It's also possible (and very cheap) to get to the city by public transportation; the bus-to-Metro-to-town trip takes about 1 hour. Take the red-lettered **bus no. 93** to the last stop, Kőbánya-Kispest. From there, the Blue Metro line runs to the Inner City of Pest. The cost is two transit tickets, 250 Ft ($1.10) altogether; tickets can be bought from the automated vending machine at the bus stop (coins only) or from any newsstand in the airport.

BY TRAIN   Budapest has three major train stations: Keleti pályaudvar (Eastern Station), Nyugati pályaudvar (Western Station), and Déli pályaudvar (Southern Station). The stations' names, curiously, correspond neither to their geographical location in the city nor to the origins or destinations of trains serving them. Each has a Metro station beneath it and an array of accommodations offices, currency-exchange booths, and other services.

Most international trains pull into bustling **Keleti Station** (© 061/314-5010) in Pest's seedy Baross tér. The Red line of the Metro runs below the station; numerous bus, tram, and trolleybus lines serve Baross tér as well. Some

Budapest Deals & Discounts

SPECIAL DISCOUNTS   Although some museums offer **student reductions,** very few discount opportunities are available. This shouldn't worry you, though, because prices are already very low compared to prices elsewhere in Europe. For example, you can eat very well for a fraction of what the same meal would cost in Vienna.

WORTH A SPLURGE   Wine aficionados should drop in at **Le Boutique des Vins,** V. József Attila u. 12, behind the Jaguar dealership (✆ **061/ 317-5919** or 061/266-4397; Metro: Deák tér [all lines]). Here you'll find the city's best selection of native wines, with prices more or less mirroring variations in quality. Splurge on a Villány red. If you appreciate classy handmade women's clothing, visit the **V50 Design Art Studio,** V. Váci u. 50 (✆ **061/337-5320;** Metro: Ferenciek tere [Blue line]). Designer Valeria Fazékas has an eye that's both subtle and elegant.

international trains arrive at **Nyugati Station** (✆ **061/349-0115**). A Blue line Metro station is beneath Nyugati, and numerous tram and bus lines serve busy Nyugati tér. Few international trains arrive at **Déli Station** (✆ **061/375-6293**) in central Buda; the terminus of the Red Metro line is beneath the train station.

The individual train station phone numbers are good daily from 8pm to 6am. During the day, get **in-land train information** over the phone by dialing ✆ **061/461-5400** and **international train information** at ✆ **061/461-5500.** Purchase **tickets** at train station ticket windows or from the MÁV Service Office, VI. Andrássy út 35 (✆ **061/322-8082**), open Monday to Friday 9am to 6pm. You can access a timetable on the Web at **www.elvira.hu**, searchable in English. Other rail information can be found at **www.mav.hu/eng.** *Indul* means "departure" and *Érkezik* means "arrival." The timetables for arrivals are displayed in big white posters, while departures are on yellow posters. The relevant terms in the timetables are *honnan* (from where), *hova* (to where), *vágány* (platform), *munkanap* (weekdays), *hétvége* (weekend), *munkaszüneti nap* (Saturday), *ünnepnap* (holiday), *gyors* (fast train; stops only at major cities, as posted), and *IC* (InterCity; stops only once or twice en route and you must reserve a seat). Ticket terminology is as follows: *jegy* (ticket), *oda* (one-way), *oda-vissza* (round-trip), *helyjegy* (reservation), *első osztály* (1st class), *másodosztály* (2nd class), *nem dohányzó* (nonsmoking), *ma* (today), and *holnap* (tomorrow).

MÁV operates a minibus that will take you from any of the three stations to the airport for 2,100 Ft ($9.45) per person, or between stations for 1,200 Ft ($5.40) per person. To order the minibus, call ✆ **1/353-2722.** Often, however, a taxi fare will be cheaper, especially for groups of two or more travelers.

BY BUS   The **Népliget Bus Station** is the city's newest main bus terminal on the Red Metro line at the Népstadion stop. The Blue line goes to the much smaller **Árpád híd bus station,** which caters to domestic bus service only. The former main bus station at Erzsébet tér was permanently closed in 2002. For domestic and international bus information, call (✆ **1/219-8080**), though you should be aware that it can be rather difficult to get through to the bus stations by phone and to reach an English speaker. Your best bet is to gather your information in person or ask for assistance at the Tourinform office.

BY CAR The border crossings from Austria and Slovakia are generally hassle-free. You may be requested to present your driver's license, vehicle registration, and proof of insurance. (The number plate and symbol indicating country of origin are acceptable proof.) Hungary doesn't require the International Driver's License. Cars entering Hungary are required to have a decal indicating country of registration, a first-aid kit, and an emergency triangle.

BY HYDROFOIL The Hungarian state shipping company **MAHART** operates hydrofoils on the Danube between Vienna and Budapest in spring and summer. It's an extremely popular route, so book your tickets well in advance; contact your local Austrian National Tourist Board. In Vienna, contact MAHART, Handelskai 265 (© **0043/729-2161;** fax 0043/729-2163). The Budapest office of MAHART is at V. Belgrád rakpart (© **061/318-1704** or 061/318-1880). Or visit www.besthotelz.com/hungary/hydrofoil/hydrofoil.htm. Boats and hydrofoils from Vienna arrive at the international boat station next door to the MAHART office on the **Belgrád rakpart,** which is on the Pest side of the Danube, between the Szabadság and Erzsébet bridges. The one-way fare is 830 AS ($69) and round-trip fare is 1,150 AS ($96). (We use the exchange rate of $1 to AS 12 for these purposes.) Children 5 years and under not requiring seats ride free; children between the ages of 6 and 15 are half-price. Eurailpass and ISIC holders also receive a discount, as long as you buy the ticket before boarding.

VISITOR INFORMATION

TOURIST OFFICES For general country information and a variety of pamphlets and maps before you leave, contact the government-sponsored **Hungarian National Tourist Office** (see chapter 2, "Planning an Affordable Trip to Europe").

Since Budapest continues to undergo rapid change, published tourist information is often out of date. The best information source in the city is **Tourinform** (© **1/317-9800** or 1/317-8992; www.hungarytourism.hu), the office of the Hungarian Tourist Board. Centrally located at V. Süt u. 2, just off Deák tér (reached by all three Metro lines) in Pest, the office is open daily from 8am to 8pm. Another Tourinform office is in the bustling entertainment district of Liszt Ferenc tér, open daily from 9am to 7pm (Liszt Ferenc tér is just down the street from Oktogon, reached by the Yellow line of the Metro or by tram no. 4 or 6). **Vista Visitor Center,** V. Paulay Ede u. 7 (© **061/267-8603;** www.vista.hu), also near Deák tér, is another useful source. It's open Monday to Friday 8am to 10pm, Saturday and Sunday 10am to 10pm.

Look for free pamphlets, such as *Visitors Guide, Pesti Est, Programme in Hungary,* and *Budapest Panorama,* at tourist offices and hotels. They contain details on scheduled cultural events. The *Budapest Sun,* an English-language weekly newspaper, also has extensive listings; it's available at most hotels, many newsstands, and online at **www.budapestsun.com**. A similar resource, now available only online, is the former print publication *Budapest Week,* found at www.budapestweek.com.

OTHER WEBSITES The site **www.gotohungary.com** has a wealth of tourist information, as does **www.hungarytourism.hu**. Use the extensive collection of links at **www.hungary.org** as a starting point for learning more about Hungary's history, culture, cuisine, and more.

CITY LAYOUT

The city of Budapest came into being in 1873, the result of a union of three cities: Buda, Pest, and Óbuda. Budapest, like Hungary itself, is defined by the **river Danube (Duna)**, along which many of the city's historic sites lie. Eight bridges connect the two banks, including five in the city center.

On the right bank of the Danube lies **Pest,** the capital's commercial and administrative center. Central Pest is between the Danube and the semicircular **Outer Ring boulevard (Nagykörút)**, stretches of which bear the names of former monarchs: Ferenc, József, Erzsébet, Teréz, and Szent István. The Outer Ring begins at the Pest side of the Petófi Bridge in the south and wraps around the center, ending at the Margit Bridge in the north. Several of Pest's busiest squares are along the Outer Ring, and Pest's major east-west avenues bisect it at these squares. Central Pest is further defined by the **Inner Ring (Kiskörút)**. It starts at Szabadság híd (Freedom Bridge) in the south and is named Vámház körút, Múzeum körút, Károly körút, Bajcsy-Zsilinszky út, and József Attila utca before it ends at the Chain Bridge. Inside this ring is the **Belváros,** the historic Inner City of Pest. **Váci utca** is a popular pedestrian shopping street between the Inner Ring and the Danube. It spills into **Vörösmarty tér,** one of the area's best-known squares. The **Dunakorzó (Danube Promenade),** a popular evening strolling place, runs along the river between the Chain and Erzsébet bridges. The historic Jewish district of Pest is in the **Erzsébetváros,** between the two ring boulevards.

Margaret Island (Margit-sziget) is in the middle of the Danube. Accessible by the Margaret Bridge or Árpád Bridge, it's a popular park without vehicular traffic.

On the left bank of the Danube is **Buda,** as hilly as Pest is flat. **Castle Hill** is widely considered the most beautiful part of Budapest. A number of steep paths, staircases, and small streets go up to Castle Hill, but no major roads do. The easiest access is from Clark Ádám tér (at the head of the Chain Bridge) by funicular, or from Várfok utca (near Moszkva tér) by foot or bus. Castle Hill consists of the royal palace, home to numerous museums, and the **Castle District,** a lovely neighborhood of small winding streets centered on the Gothic Matthias Church. Below Castle Hill, along the Danube, is a long, narrow neighborhood, historically populated by fishermen and other river workers, known as the **Watertown (Víziváros). Central Buda** is a collection of mostly low-lying neighborhoods below Castle Hill. The main square of central Buda is **Moszkva tér,** just north of Castle Hill. Beyond Central Buda, mainly to the east, are the **Buda Hills.**

Óbuda is on the left bank of the Danube, north of Buda. Although the greater part of Óbuda is modern and drab, it contains a beautiful old city center and impressive Roman ruins.

Tips A Note on Addresses

Budapest is divided into 22 districts called *kerűlets* (abbreviated *ker.*). A Roman numeral followed by a period precedes every written address in Budapest, signifying the *kerűlet;* for example, XII. Csörsz utca 9 is in the 12th *kerűlet.* Because many street names repeat in different parts of the city, it's very important to know which *kerűlet* a certain address is in.

GETTING AROUND

Budapest has an extensive, efficient, and inexpensive public transport system. The system's biggest disadvantage is that, except for 17 well-traveled bus and tram routes, all forms of transport shut down around 11:30pm; certain areas of the city, most notably the Buda Hills, are beyond the reach of the limited night service, so you'll have to take a taxi. Be on the alert for pickpockets on public transportation. Keep your money and other valuables inside your clothing in a money belt.

All forms of public transportation in Budapest require the self-validation of pre-purchased tickets *(vonaljegy)*, which cost 125 Ft (55¢) apiece (children under 6 travel free); single tickets can be bought at Metro ticket windows, newspaper kiosks, and the occasional tobacco shop. Automated machines in most Metro stations and at major transportation hubs provide reliable service. For 1,100 Ft ($4.95), you can get a convenient 10-pack *(tizes csomag)*, and for 2,150 Ft ($9.70), a 20-pack *(huszas csomag)*.

The standard ticket is valid on the Metro, but there are several optional single-ride ticket choices, too: a **Metro section ticket** *(metrószakaszjegy)*, at 90 Ft (40¢), is valid for a single Metro trip of three stations or less; a **Metro section transfer ticket** *(metró-szakaszátszállójegy)*, at 140 Ft (65¢), allows transfer from one Metro line to another, but only for a trip totaling five or fewer stops; and a **Metro transfer ticket** *(metróátszállójegy)*, at 205 Ft (90¢), allows transfer from one Metro line to another on the same ticket, without any limit to the number of stations you may travel.

For convenience, we recommend that you purchase a **day pass** or **multiday pass** while in Budapest. Passes are still rather inexpensive and need only be validated once, saving you the hassle of having to validate a ticket every time you board. A pass will probably save you some money, too, as you are likely to be getting on and off public transportation all day. Day passes *(napijegy)* cost 975 Ft ($4.40) and are valid until midnight of the day of purchase. Buy them from Metro ticket windows; the clerk validates the pass at the time of purchase. A **3-day pass** *(turistajegy)* costs 1,950 Ft ($8.75) and a **7-day pass** *(hetijegy)* costs 2,350 Ft ($11); these have the same validation procedure as the day pass.

Dark-blue uniformed inspectors (who reveal a hidden red armband when approaching you—a remnant of the not-too-distant past when they traveled the Metro in plain clothes) frequently check for valid tickets, particularly at the top or bottom of the escalators to Metro platforms. On-the-spot fines of 1,500 Ft ($6.75) are assessed to fare dodgers; pleading ignorance generally doesn't work. Metro tickets are good for 1 hour for any distance along the line you're riding, except for Metro section tickets *(metrószakaszjegy)*, which are valid only for 30 minutes. You may get off and reboard with the same ticket within the valid time period. All public transport operates on rough schedules, posted at bus and tram shelters and in Metro stations. The Budapest Transport Authority (BKV térkép) produces a more detailed transportation map, available at most Metro ticket windows for 250 Ft (90¢).

BY METRO   The Metro is clean and efficient, with trains running every 3 to 5 minutes from about 4:30am to about 11:30pm. The three lines are universally known by color—Yellow, Red, and Blue. Officially they have numbers as well (1, 2, and 3, respectively), but all signs are color-coded. All three lines converge at Deák tér, the only point where any meet. Metro tickets are good for 1 hour for any distance along the line you're riding.

The **Yellow (1) line** is the oldest Metro on the European continent and was fully renovated in 1996. It runs from Vörösmarty tér in the heart of central Pest, out the length of Andrássy út, and past the Városliget (City Park), ending at Mexikói út. Tickets for the Yellow line are self-validated on the train. The **Red (2)** and **Blue (3)** lines are modern Metros. The Red line runs from eastern Pest, through the center, and across the Danube to Déli Station. The Blue line runs from southeastern Pest, through the center, and out to northern Pest. Tickets must be validated at automatic boxes before you descend the escalator. When changing lines at Deák tér, you're required to validate another ticket at the orange validating machines in the hallways between lines.

BY BUS   Many parts of the city, most notably the Buda Hills, are best reached by bus *(busz)*. Most lines are in service from about 4:30am to about 11:30pm, with less frequent weekend service on some. Bus tickets are self-validated on board using the mechanical red box near each door. You can't buy tickets from the driver on Budapest buses (though this is usually possible outside of Budapest). Board the bus by any door. **Black-numbered local buses** constitute the majority of the city's lines. **Red-numbered buses** are express. If an *E* follows the red number on the bus, the bus runs nonstop between terminals (an *É*—with an accent mark—signifies *éjszaka,* meaning "night"). A few buses are labeled by something other than a number; one you'll probably use is the Vár-busz (Palace Bus), a minibus running between Várfok utca, off Buda's Moszkva tér, and the Castle District.

BY TRAM   You'll find Budapest's bright yellow trams *(villamos)* very useful, particularly **nos. 4** and **6,** which travel along the Outer Ring (Nagykörút). Tickets are self-validated on board. As with buses, tickets are valid for one ride, not for the line itself. Trams stop at every station and all doors open, regardless of whether anyone is waiting to get on. The buttons near the tram doors are for emergency stops, not stop requests.

BY HÉV   The HÉV is a suburban railway network connecting Budapest to various points along the outskirts. There are four HÉV lines; only one, the Szentendre line, is of serious interest to visitors. The terminus for the Szentendre HÉV line is Buda's Batthyány tér, also a station of the Red Metro line. To reach Óbuda's Fő tér (Main Square), get off at the Árpád híd (Árpád Bridge) stop. The HÉV runs regularly daily 4am to 11:30pm. For trips within the city limits, you need one transit ticket, available at HÉV ticket windows at the Batthyány tér station or from the conductor on board. The tickets are different from the standard transportation tickets; the conductors punch them. If you have a valid day pass, you don't need to buy a ticket for trips within the city limits.

BY TAXI   We divide Budapest taxis into two categories: **organized fleets** and private taxis. If you follow only one piece of advice in this chapter, it's this: Do business with the former and avoid the latter. Because taxi regulations permit fleets (or private drivers) to establish their own rates (within certain parameters), fares vary greatly between the different fleets and among the private unaffiliated drivers. The best rates are invariably those of the larger fleet companies. We particularly recommended **Fő Taxi** (⟨❄⟩ 1/222-2222). Other reliable fleets include **Volántaxi** (⟨❄⟩ 1/466-6666), **City Taxi** (⟨❄⟩ 1/211-1111), **Tele5** (⟨❄⟩ 1/355-5555), and **6×6** (⟨❄⟩ 1/266-6666). Call one of these companies from your hotel—or ask the clerk to call for you—even if there are other private taxis waiting outside. The same applies to restaurants. You will seldom, if ever, wait more than 5 minutes for a fleet taxi in any but the most remote of neighborhoods.

Budapest Metro

ÓBUDA

PEST

BUDA

Margaret Island

Danube

Blue Line (Line 3)
- Újpest-Központ
- Újpest-Városkapu
- Gyöngyösi u.
- Forgách u.
- Árpád híd
- Dózsa György út
- Lehel tér

Yellow Line (Line 1)
- Mexikói út
- Széchenyi fürdő
- Hősök tere
- Bajza utca
- Kodály körönd
- Vörösmarty utca
- Oktogon
- Opera
- Bajcsy-Zsilinszky út

Nyugati pu.

Moszkva tér
Batthyány tér
Kossuth L. tér
Arany János utca
Déli pu.
Deák tér
Vörösmarty tér
Ferenciek tere

Red Line (Line 2)
- Örs vezér tere
- Népstadion
- Pillangó utca
- Keleti pu.
- Blaha L. tér
- Astoria
- Kálvin tér
- Ferenc körút
- Klinikák
- Nagyvárad tér
- Népliget
- Ecseri út
- Pöttyös u.
- Határ út
- Kőbánya-Kispest

Danube

BY RENTAL CAR We don't recommend using a car for sightseeing in Budapest. Our preferred rental agency is **Fox Auto Rental,** XVI. Vegyesz u. 17–25, 1116 Budapest (*©* **1/382-9000;** fax 1/382-9003), which rents a Fiat Seicento for 29€ ($33) per day and 174€ ($200) per week, insurance and mileage included. You must leave a deposit of 100,000 Ft ($450) on your credit card. Though located far from the city center, Fox will deliver the car to you at your hotel without charge between 8 am to 6pm.

Note: You may save money by arranging for your rental before leaving home.

FAST FACTS: Budapest

American Express Budapest's only American Express office is between Vörösmarty tér and Deák tér in central Pest, at V. Deák Ferenc u. 10, 1052 Budapest (*©* **1/235-4330** or 1/235-4300; fax 1/267-2028). It's open Monday through Friday from 9am to 5:30pm, and Saturday from 9am to 2pm. An American Express cash ATM is located outside, in front of the office. Depending on whether your account allows it, these ATMs dispense either cash (forints only) or traveler's checks (U.S. dollars only). Check with American Express beforehand if you wish to use these ATMs abroad.

For lost traveler's checks, come to the office as soon as you can and they will assist you. If you do not want to wait that long, use a 20 Ft coin to initiate a call to England; the call (*©* **00-800-11128**) is otherwise toll-free. For a lost credit card, make a local call to *©* **1/235-4310** during business hours or to *©* **1/460-5233** after hours. If this is unsuccessful, try calling England at *©* **00-44-181-551-1111** (or dial *©* **00/800-04411** for the U.K. direct operator, and ask to call collect).

Babysitters **Ficuka Baby Hotel,** V. Váci u. 11b, I em. 9 (*©* **1/338-2836** or 1/483-0713 [ask for Livia Nagy]), will send an English-speaking babysitter to your hotel for 850 Ft ($3.80) per hour for one child, or 950 Ft ($4.25) per hour for two children. For four or more children, two babysitters are sent. Babysitters are often university students and are trained in first aid and early childhood learning. Reserve a sitter by phone between 10am and 6pm, Monday through Friday.

Business Hours Most **stores** are open Monday through Friday from 10am to 6pm, and Saturday from 9 or 10am to 1 or 2pm. Some shops close for an hour at lunchtime, and most stores are closed Sunday, except those in the central tourist areas. Some shop owners and restaurateurs also close for 2 weeks in August. On weekdays, food stores open early, at around 6 or 7am, and close at around 6 or 7pm. Certain grocery stores, called "non-stops," are open 24 hours (however, a growing number of shops call themselves "nonstop" even if they close for the night at 10 or 11pm). **Banks** are usually open Monday to Thursday 8am to 3pm and Friday 8am to 1pm.

Currency The basic unit of currency in Hungary is the **forint (Ft).** Coins come in denominations of 1, 2, 5, 10, 20, 50, and 100 Ft. Banknotes come in denominations of 200, 500, 1,000, 5,000, 10,000, and 20,000 Ft. As of this writing, the rate of exchange is $1 = 220 Ft (or 100 Ft = 45¢). At press time, Hungary was poised to become a member of the European Union in 2004; however, the country does not plan to introduce the euro until 2007.

Currency Exchange The best official rates for both cash and traveler's checks are obtained at banks. Exchange booths located throughout the city center, in train stations, and in most luxury hotels almost uniformly offer less favorable rates than banks. This is particularly true of the Inter Change chain, which offers a rate up to 20% less favorable than the going bank rate, depending on the amount you exchange. ATMs are found in front of banks throughout the city or in major shopping malls. You may withdraw forints at the daily exchange rate from your home account through the Cirrus and PLUS networks. Since 2001, with the full convertibility of the Hungarian forint, there are no longer any restrictions regarding re-exchange of forints back into your currency. Consequently, unlike in the past, you need not retain your currency exchange receipts as proof of exchange.

Doctors We recommend the **American Clinic,** in a modern building across from the Mammut shopping center at I. Hattyu u. 14 (© **061/224-9090;** Metro: Moszkva tér [Red line]); it's a newly opened private outpatient clinic with two U.S. board-certified physicians and several English-speaking Hungarian doctors. Check with Vista Visitor Center for discount coupons. For dental work, we recommend **Dr. Susan Linder,** II. Vihorlat u. 23 (© **061/335-5245;** bus: 5, 29), the dentist for the U.S. and British embassies; she did her post-doctoral work at UCSF and speaks flawless English.

Drugstores The Hungarian word is *gyógyszertár* or *patika*. Generally, pharmacies carry only prescription drugs. Hotel "drugstores" are just shops with soap, perfume, aspirin, and other nonprescription items. There are a number of 24-hour pharmacies in the city—every pharmacy posts the address of the nearest one in its window. Your best bet for 24-hour service throughout the year is *Oktogon Patika* on Teréz körút, next to Hotel Béke Radisson (off Oktogon Sq., Yellow Metro line or trams no. 4 or 6).

Embassies The embassy of the **United States** is at V. Szabadság tér 12 (© **061/475-4400;** Metro: Kossuth tér [Red line]). The embassy of **Canada** is at XII. Budakeszi út 32 (© **061/392-3360;** tram: 22 from Moszkva tér). The embassy of the **United Kingdom** is at V. Harmincad u. 6 (© **061/266-2888;** Metro: Deák tér [all lines]). The embassy of **Ireland** is at V. Szabadság tér 7 (© **061/302-9600;** Metro: Kossuth tér [Red line]). The embassy of **Australia** is at XII. Királyhágó tér 8–9 (© **061/457-9777;** Metro: Déli pu. [Red line]). **New Zealand** doesn't have an embassy, but the U.K. embassy handles matters for New Zealand citizens.

Emergencies Dial © **104** for an ambulance, © **105** for the fire department, or © **107** for the police. To report a crime, dial © **1/438-8080** for a 24-hour hot line in English.

Internet Access The best place in town to access the Internet at press time is a 24-hour **Internet Café,** VI. Andrássy út 46 (© **1/331-9102**), providing Internet access (minimum of 15 min. for 200 Ft/90¢), plus other services like CD burning and scanning. We also frequent **Vista Visitor Center,** at V. Paulay Ede u. 7 (© **1/267-8603;** Metro: Deák tér, all three Metro lines), which has about 10 terminals in a small mezzanine area. Access costs 5 Ft (2¢) per minute. It's open Monday through Saturday from 10am to 10pm, and Sunday from 10am to 8pm. Avoid Netvillage, at V. Váci u. 19–21 (in the basement of the recently opened Millennium Center); though conveniently located, it has extremely poor service.

Laundry & Dry Cleaning Self-service launderettes *(patyolat)* are scarce in Budapest. The Mister Minit chain, a locksmith and shoe repair service located in all large shopping centers throughout the Inner City area, now offers laundry service. Many hotels and pensions also provide laundry services. Private room hosts, as well, usually are happy to make a little extra money doing laundry. For 1-hour dry cleaning, try **Ruhatisztító Top Clean,** at the Nyugati Skála Metro department store (across the street from Nyugati train station; no phone); they are open Monday through Friday from 7am to 7pm, and Saturday from 9am to 2pm.

Mail & Post Office Mail can be received by clients at American Express (see "American Express," above); a single Amex traveler's check is sufficient to prove that you're a client. Others can receive mail c/o Poste Restante, Magyar Posta, Petőfi Sándor u. 17–19, 1052 Budapest, Hungary (© **36/1-318-3947** or 487-1100). This confusing office (open Mon–Sat 7am–9pm), not far from Deák tér (all Metro lines), is the city's main post office. Other postal locations are near Keleti and Nyugati Metro stations. The post office near Keleti is at VIII. Baross tér 11/c (© **36/1-322-9013**), and is open Monday to Saturday 7am to 9pm. The post office near Nyugati is at VI. Teréz krt. 51 (© **36/1-312-1480**), and is open Monday to Saturday 7am to 9pm, Sunday 8am to 8pm.

At press time, an airmail postcard costs 150 Ft (65¢); an airmail letter, 230 Ft ($1.05) and up, depending on size of envelope and weight.

Safety By U.S. standards, Budapest is a relatively safe city—muggings and violent attacks are rare. Nevertheless, foreigners are always prime targets. Although they're clearly less of a threat now than a few years ago, teams of professional pickpockets still plague Budapest, operating on crowded trams, Metros, and buses. Be particularly careful on bus no. 26 (Margaret Island), tram nos. 4 and 6, and any other crowded setting. The pickpocket's basic trick is to create a distraction to take your attention away from yourself and your own security. Avoid being victimized by wearing a money belt under your clothes instead of wearing a fanny pack or carrying a wallet or purse. Never keep valuables in the outer pockets of a knapsack.

Taxes Taxes are included in restaurant and hotel rates, and in shop purchases. Refunds of the 10% to 25% **value-added tax (VAT),** which is built into all prices, are available for most consumer goods purchases of more than 50,000 Ft ($225), VAT included (look for stores with the TAX-FREE logo in the window). The refund process, however, is elaborate and confusing. In most shops, the salesperson can provide you with the necessary documents: the store receipt, a separate receipt indicating the VAT amount on your purchase, the VAT reclaim form, and the mailing envelope. The salesperson should also be able to help you fill out the paperwork. Use a separate claim form for each applicable purchase. If you are departing Hungary by plane, you can collect your refund at the **IBUSZ Agency** at Ferihegy Airport; be sure you do so *after* check-in but *before* you pass security control. Otherwise, hold onto the full packet until you leave Hungary, at which point you get your forms certified by Customs. Then, mail in your envelope and wait for your refund. For further information, contact **Global Refund,** XIV. Zászló utca 54, 1143 Budapest (© **1/468-2965;** fax 1/468-2966; www.globalrefund.com).

Telephone The **area code** for Budapest is 1, and all phone numbers in Budapest (except mobile phones) have seven digits. Most other towns in Hungary have a two-digit area code and six-digit telephone numbers. To make a call from one Hungary area code to another, first dial 06; when you hear a tone, dial the area code and number. Numbers that begin with 06-20, 06-30, or 06-70 followed by a seven-digit number are **mobile phone numbers.** Mobile phones are extremely popular and some of the listings in this book are mobile phone numbers. Be aware that all phone calls made to a mobile phone, regardless of location, are charged as long-distance calls. Budapest telephone numbers are constantly changing as the Hungarian telephone company, MATÁV, continues to upgrade its system. Usually, if the number you are dialing has recently changed, you will get a recording first in Hungarian and then in English, indicating the new number. If further information is needed, dial ⓒ **198** for **local directory assistance** and **199** for **international assistance.**

Public **pay phones** charge varying amounts for local calls depending on the time of day that you place your call. It's cheapest to call late in the evenings and on weekends. Public phones operate with 20, 50, and 100 Ft coins or with phone cards (in 50 or 120 units), which can be purchased from post offices, tobacco shops, supermarkets, travel agencies, and any MATÁV customer service office (MATÁV Pont).

Hotels typically add a surcharge to all calls (although some allow unlimited free local calls).

For international calls, there are several options. Our preferred method these days is to make all international calls from abroad through a U.S.-based "callback" service. These services allow you to gain access to a U.S. dial tone from abroad, typically by means of dialing in to a computer in the U.S., which then automatically calls you back with the dial tone. International calls made in this manner are billed at competitive U.S. calling rates, which are still significantly cheaper than Hungarian international rates. These services generally charge an activation fee and a monthly maintenance fee, as well as other fees, so you ought to make a judgment as to whether you are likely to be making enough calls for it to be worthwhile. A company called **Kallback** seems to offer the best package; call ⓒ **800/959-5255** or 800/516-9992; www.kallback.com.

Alternatively, you can use a **phone card** and access the international operator through a public phone, though older phones are less reliable; again, a 20 Ft coin is required to start the call. The phone card will allow you to call the U.S. and Canada for 94 Ft (40¢) per minute, 24 hours a day, 7 days a week. There is a 450 Ft ($2) connecting fee. Purchase either 50-unit (800 Ft/$3.60) or 120-unit (1,800 Ft/$8.10) cards.

Hungarian telephone books list the numbers of all countries that can be directly dialed. MATÁV also publishes a useful English-language pamphlet on international calling that includes country codes. Failing either of these resources, dial **199** for international directory assistance. Direct dial to the **United States** and **Canada** is 00/1; to the **U.K.**, 00/44; to **Australia,** 00/61; and to **Ireland,** 00/353.

You can reach the **AT&T** operator at ⓒ **00/800-01111,** the **MCI** operator at ⓒ **00/800-01411,** and the **Sprint operator** at ⓒ **00/800-01877.**

Other country direct access numbers connect you to operators in the country you're calling, with whom you can arrange your preferred billing. **Australia Direct** is ✆ **00/800-06111**, **Canada Direct** is ✆ **00/800-01211**, **New Zealand Direct** is ✆ **00/800-06411**, and **U.K. Direct** is ✆ **00/800-04411** (BT) or 00/800-04412 (Mercury).

To make **a call to Hungary from abroad,** dial the appropriate numbers to get an international dial tone (011 from the U.S.), then dial 36 (Hungary country code), followed by the appropriate city code (for Budapest, 1), followed by the six- or seven-digit telephone number.

Tipping Business patrons generally tip 10%. Among those who welcome tips are waiters, taxi drivers, hotel employees, barbers, cloakroom attendants, toilet attendants, masseuses, and tour guides.

2 Affordable Places to Stay

One of the happy developments of the post-1989 boom in Budapest has been the proliferation of new pensions and small hotels. The better—and less expensive—choices are usually outside the city center, but all the places we list can easily be reached by public transportation.

Notwithstanding these new places, Budapest retains its reputation as a city without enough guest beds. Indeed, in high season it can be difficult to secure a hotel or pension room or hostel bed, so make reservations and get written confirmation well ahead if possible.

An alternative is a **private room** in someone's apartment. Usually you share the bathroom with the hosts or other guests. Breakfast is not officially included, but the host will often offer a continental spread (bread, butter, jam, coffee or tea) for around 550 Ft to 850 Ft ($2.50–$3.80). You may have limited kitchen privileges (ask in advance). Some landlords will greet you when you arrive, give you a key, and seemingly disappear; others will want to befriend you, change money, show you around, and sometimes even cook for you.

Most rooms are quite adequate, some even memorable, but any number of reasons may cause you to dislike your accommodations: Noisy neighborhoods, tiny bathrooms, and wretched coffee are among the complaints we've heard from the occasional displeased traveler. The great majority of guests, though, are satisfied; certainly, staying in a private room provides a window into everyday Hungarian life that would be missed otherwise (except, perhaps, in some of the family-run pensions).

Prices vary slightly between accommodations agencies but, generally speaking, an average room will cost about 4,500 Ft to 6,000 Ft ($20–$27) for two

Tips A Note on Rates

Accommodations rates in Budapest are among the lowest of any European capital. You'll note that many hotels and pensions list their prices in euros or U.S. dollars (hostel prices are usually listed in forints). This is done as a hedge against forint inflation; everyone accepts payment in forints as well as foreign currencies. We have found that the websites of hotels are frequently inaccurate with respect to rates.

> *Tips* **A Note on Private Rooms**
>
> In Keleti Station, you're likely to be approached by all sorts of people offering you private rooms. Most are honest folks trying to drum up some business personally. Keep in mind that when the middleman (the agency) is eliminated, the prices tend to be slightly better, so you might consider taking a room from one of these people, especially if you arrive late at night when the agencies are closed or long lines drive you to despair. Trust your judgment, but resist people who try to pressure you. Feel free to haggle over prices.

---

people, or 3,800 Ft ($17) for a single, plus a 3% tourism tax (though high-end rooms in fashionable neighborhoods can cost significantly more). Most agencies add a 30% surcharge (to the 1st night only) for stays of less than 4 nights. There's scarcely an address in Budapest that cannot be reached by some form of public transportation, so regard with skepticism anyone who tells you that you must take a taxi. In peak season you may need to shop around a bit for the location you want, but you can always find a room. Arriving at an agency early in the day will afford you the best selection.

The most established agencies are the former state-owned travel agents **Ibusz, Cooptourist,** and **Budapest Tourist.** Although newer, private agencies have proliferated, the older ones tend to have the greatest number of rooms. There are agencies at the airport, all three major train stations, throughout central Pest, and along the main roads into Budapest. The main **Ibusz reservations office** is at Ferenciek tere 10 (€ **1/485-2700;** fax 1/318-2805), reached by the Blue Metro line (open year-round Mon–Fri 8:15am–5pm). All major credit and charge cards are accepted. **Cooptourist,** Nyugati Station (€ **36/1-458-6200**), is open 9am to 4:30pm Monday through Friday and does not accept credit cards. **Budapest Tourist,** Nyugati Station (€ **36/1-318-6552**), is open 9am to 5pm Monday through Friday, and 9am to noon Saturday, and does not accept credit cards. **MÁV Tours,** Keleti Station (€ **36/1-382-9011**), is open 9am to 5pm Monday through Friday and does not accept credit cards.

Note: You'll find the lodging choices below plotted on the map on p. 316.

HOTELS
IN CENTRAL PEST

Hotel MEDOSZ *(Kids)* This hotel's location on sleepy Jókai tér, in the heart of Pest's theater district, is as good as it gets off the river in central Pest: It's just across the street from the bustling Liszt Ferenc tér, Pest's most recent center of night life and a couple of blocks from the Opera House. Although it hasn't been renovated since privatization (it once was a trade-union hotel), it remains a great value given its location, with simple but well-kept rooms. Next door is one of Budapest's special treats for children: a puppet theater *(bábszínház).*

VI. Jókai tér 9, 1061 Budapest. € 1/374-3000. Fax 1/332-4316. www.medoszhotel.hu. 67 units. 47€ ($48) single; 55€ ($63) double. Rates include breakfast. Rates 20% lower in low season. No credit cards. Metered on-street parking difficult in neighborhood; there is an indoor garage in nearby Aradi utca. Metro: Oktogon (Yellow line). **Amenities:** Restaurant; bar; laundry service; solarium. *In room:* TV.

Marco Polo Although this place calls itself a youth hostel, it's really more of a budget hotel. On a recent visit, we noticed that most of the guests were well-dressed

---

Value   Getting the Best Deal on Accommodations

• Take advantage of winter discounts—even major hotel operators grant significant price reductions off season.
• Be aware that rooms in private homes are the cheapest way to go.
• Ask at your hotel if there are rooms without a shower. The staff might assume you want one of the more expensive units with a bathroom.
• If you're willing to stay on the outskirts and spend some time traveling to the city center, you can usually spend less for a room.

---

middle-aged Europeans; this is no backpackers' haunt. Given the central location and tidy rooms, it's a very good deal.

VII. Nyár u. 6, 1072 Budapest. ℂ 1/413-2540. Fax 1/413-6058. www.marcopolohostel.com. 36 doubles, 5 quads, 5 12-bed units (all with shower and toilet). 4,200 Ft ($19) per person in 12-bed unit; 5,500 Ft ($25) per person in quad; 8,000 Ft ($36) per person in double. Rates include breakfast. 10% discount for IYHF members. No credit cards. Parking available for a fee. Metro: Blaha Lujza tér (Red line). **Amenities:** Laundry service; communal kitchen.

Peregrinus ELTE Hotel ⚷   This is the guesthouse of Pest's ELTE University, and its location couldn't be better—in the heart of the Inner City, on a small side street just half a block from the quiet southern end of the popular pedestrians-only Váci utca. Reserve at least a week ahead. The building dates from the early 1900s and was renovated in 1994, when the guesthouse opened. The rooms are simple but comfortable.

V. Szerb u. 3, 1056 Budapest. ℂ 1/266-4911. Fax 1/266-4913. 26 units. 22,000 Ft ($99) double; 18,000 Ft ($81) double in low season. Rates include breakfast. No credit cards. No parking. Metro: Kálvin tér (Blue line). *In room:* A/C in attic rooms, TV, minibar.

IN OUTER PEST

Hotel Délibáb   The ancient Délibáb enjoys a wonderful location across from Heroes' Square and City Park, in an exclusive neighborhood that's home to most of the city's embassies. It's a 30-minute walk or a 5-minute Metro ride to the center of Pest. The well-kept rooms are surprisingly spacious and have nice wood floors; the fixtures are old, but everything works.

VI. Délibáb u. 35, 1062 Budapest. ℂ 1/342-9301 or 1/322-8763. Fax 1/342-8153. www.hoteldelibab.hu. 34 units. 66€ ($76) single; 76€ ($87) double. Rates include breakfast. 20% lower in low season. Major credit cards accepted. Parking in neighborhood difficult; parking in hotel's yard 2,500 Ft ($11) per day. Metro: Hősök tere (Yellow line). **Amenities:** Restaurant; bar; laundry service; nonsmoking rooms. *In room:* TV, fridge (some rooms).

IN CENTRAL BUDA

Charles Apartment House ⚷   Owner Károly Szombati has gradually amassed 70 apartments in a group of apartment buildings in a dull but convenient neighborhood near the large luxury Novotel. All are average Budapest flats with full kitchens, comfortable furnishings, and one to four beds. Hegyalja út is a very busy street, but only two apartments face it; the rest are in the interior or on the side of the building.

I. Hegyalja út 23, 1016 Budapest. ℂ 1/212-9169. Fax 1/202-2984. www.charleshotel.hu. 70 units. 48€–136€ ($55–$156) apt for 1–4. Rates include breakfast. Rates approximately 5% lower in low season. AE, DC, MC, V. Parking 2,000 Ft ($9) per day. Bus: 78 from Keleti pu. to Mészáros utca. **Amenities:** Restaurant; bar; bicycle rental; tour desk; business center; babysitting; laundry service. *In room:* A/C, TV, kitchen, minibar, hair dryer, safe.

IN THE BUDA HILLS

G. G. Panoráma Panzió   G. G. are the initials of Mrs. Gábor Gubacsi, the friendly English-speaking owner of this guesthouse on a steep, quiet street in the elegant Rose Hill (Rózsadomb) section. Several bus lines converge on the neighborhood, making it fairly convenient. All on the top floor, the rooms are small but tastefully furnished; they share a common balcony with a great vista of the hills. There's also a common kitchen and dining area, with full facilities (including a minibar), as well as ample garden space. The Gubacsis take good care of their guests.

II. Fullánk u. 7, 1026 Budapest. ©/fax **1/394-4718** or 1/394-6034. 4 units. $60 double. Breakfast $5 extra. No credit cards. Parking available on street. Bus: 11 from Batthyány tér to Majális utca or 91 from Nyugati pu. **Amenities:** Kitchen; shared phone. *In room:* TV.

Hotel Papillon   The Papillon is a pleasing Mediterranean-style white building on a quiet side street in the area where central Buda begins to give way to the Buda Hills. It's an easy bus ride to the center of the city. An airy feeling pervades the interior and spare pink guest rooms. Seven rooms have terraces. There's a small pool on the premises.

II. Rózsahegy u. 3/b, 1024 Budapest. ©/fax **1/212-4003** or 1/212-4750. www.hotels.hu/papillon. 20 units. 59€ ($68) double. Rates include breakfast. Rates 20%–25% lower in low season. AE, MC, V. Parking: 4 free spaces in secure hotel lot. Bus: 91 from Nyugati pu. to Zivatar utca. **Amenities:** Restaurant; bar; small outdoor pool; car-rental desk; limited room service; babysitting; laundry service. *In room:* TV, fridge.

Vadvirág Panzió 🏵🏵   A 10-minute walk from the bus stop, the Vadvirág is in a gorgeous part of the Buda Hills a few blocks behind the Béla Bartók Memorial House. Sloping gardens and terraces surround it. The guest rooms are all different: on the petite side but tastefully furnished. Half of them have balconies. Room no. 2, a small suite with a balcony, is the best. The cozy restaurant has plenty of outdoor seating.

II. Nagybányai út 18, 1025 Budapest. © **1/275-0200.** Fax 1/394-4292. www.hotels.hu/hotelvadvirag. 15 units. 49€–68€ ($56–$78) double; 75€–80€ ($86–$92) suite. Rates include breakfast. MC, V. Parking available in private garage for 6€ per day or for free on street. Bus: 5 from Március 15 tér or Moszkva tér to Pasaréti tér (the last stop). **Amenities:** Bar; sauna; laundry service. *In room:* TV, minibar, safe.

IN THE CASTLE DISTRICT

Hotel Kulturinnov   This little place is in the heart of Buda's Castle District. This is the guesthouse of the Hungarian Culture Foundation, dedicated to forging ties with ethnic Hungarians in neighboring countries. It's open to the public, but few travelers know about it. The rooms are small and simple; nothing is modern, but everything works and the bathrooms are well maintained. One chagrined traveler reported a nocturnal battle with tiny insects who live inside mattresses, but that has not been our experience. The hotel, in the large building directly across from Matthias Church and the Plague Column, can be hard to find; the entrance is unassuming and practically unmarked. Go through the iron grille door and pass through an exhibition hall, continuing up the grand red-carpeted staircase to the right.

I. Szentháromság tér 6, 1014 Budapest. © **1/355-0122** or 1/375 1651. Fax 1/375 1886. 16 units. 70€ ($81) double. Rates include breakfast. Rates 40% lower in low season. AE, DC, MC, V. No parking available. Bus: "Várbusz" from Moszkva tér or 16 from Deák tér. **Amenities:** 2 restaurants; 2 bars. *In room:* Fridge.

HOSTELS

There is intense competition in Budapest between the leading youth hostel company and various privately run hostels. The leading company is **Travellers' Youth Way Youth Hostels,** also known as **"Mellow Mood Ltd."** (© **1/413-2062;**

www.hostels.hu), which recently swallowed its chief competitor, Universum Youth Hostels. They now run two year-round hostels (Diáksport and Marco Polo) and 11 summer-only hostels.

International trains arriving in Budapest are usually met by young representatives of Travellers' and some of the privately run youth hostels. (Some even board Budapest-bound international trains at the Hungarian border crossing to work the backpacking crowd before the train reaches Budapest.) Your best bet is to book a bed in advance at one of our recommended hostels; if you haven't, you can make phone calls on your arrival and try to secure a hostel bed, or you can try your luck with these hawkers. Since they make a commission on every customer they bring in, they tend to be pushy and say whatever they think you want to hear about their hostel. Shop around and don't let yourself be pressured. Most hostels that solicit at the station also have a van parked outside. The ride to the hostel is usually free, but you may have to wait a while until the van is full.

Travellers' operates a youth hostel placement office at Keleti Station (© **1/343-0748**), off to the side of Track 9 and Track 6 near the international waiting room. This office, open daily 7am to 8pm, can help you book a bed in one of Travellers' hostels or in other hostels.

In July and August, a number of university dormitories and other empty student housing are converted into hostels, many managed by Travellers'. Their locations (as well as their condition) have been known to change from year to year, so we haven't reviewed any of them in this guide. The youth hostels and budget lodgings listed below are all open year-round.

The main office of the **Hungarian Youth Hostel Federation (Magyar Ifjúsági Szállások Szövetsége)** is located on the fourth floor of VII. Almássy tér 6 (near Blaha Lujza tér [Red line Metro]; © **1/395-6530**). They can provide you with a full listing of youth hostels in Hungary, including those in Budapest. You can also pick up an IYHF card (no photo required) for 1,800 Ft ($8.10).

Aquarium Youth Hostel ⚔   This hostel (formerly known as Ananda) is well located just a few minutes by foot from Keleti railway station (where most international trains arrive), on the corner of Alsóerdősor utca and Péterfy Sándor utca. Like most other centrally located, privately run youth hostels in town, Aquarium is sited in a residential building (a classic Pest apartment house), and there is little evidence from the street of its existence within (just a small buzzer that says HOSTEL). This year-round hostel has extremely clean rooms (mixed sexes) and a friendly, engaging staff. Guests are given large lockers in which to store gear. The hostel is frequented in equal parts by tired rail travelers arriving at Keleti station and by meditation-vegetarian types who have been drawn by Mr. Bustos, a magnetic personality somewhat famous among certain circles of locals and European travelers. No curfew.

VII. Alsóerdősor u. 12 (2nd floor). ©/fax **1/322-0502**. 14 beds in 4 units. 2,600 Ft ($12) per person in 4-bed units; 8,000 Ft ($36) for the only double. No credit cards (plans to accept V in 2005). No parking available. Metro: Keleti pu (Red line). **Amenities:** Laundry service; communal kitchen; free Internet access.

WORTH A SPLURGE
Hotel Astra Vendégház ⚔⚔   This little gem opened in the late 1990s in a renovated 300-year-old building on a quiet side street in Buda's lovely Watertown. The rooms are large, with wood floors and classic Hungarian-style furniture; the overall effect is far more homey and pleasant than that of most hotels. Indeed, the hotel is tasteful through and through, and the staff is friendly. Some rooms overlook the inner courtyard, while others face the street.

I. Vám u. 6, 1011 Budapest. ℗ 1/214-1906. Fax 1/214-1907. www.hotelastra.hu. 12 units. All rooms are doubles and cost 90€ ($104) for 1 person and 106€ ($122) for 2. Rates include breakfast. Rates 10% lower in low season. No credit cards. Only meter parking is available on street. Metro: Batthyány tér (Red line). **Amenities:** Restaurant; bar; car rental desk; babysitting (on request). *In room:* A/C, TV, minibar.

Hotel Victoria The Victoria, in Buda's Watertown, occupies a narrow building with only three rooms on each of its nine floors. That makes two-thirds of the units corner rooms, with large double windows providing great views over the Danube to Pest's skyline beyond. Middle rooms, although smaller, also have windows facing the river. Alas, noise from the busy road might disturb your rest. The hotel is just minutes by foot from Batthyány tér and Clark Ádám tér, with dozens of Metro, tram, and bus connections.

I. Bem rakpart 11, 1011 Budapest. ℗ 1/457-8080. Fax 1/457-8088. www.victoria.hu. 27 units. 97€ ($112) single; 102€ ($117) double. Rates include breakfast. Rates 25% lower in low season. AE, DC, MC, V. Parking in garage 9€. Tram: 19 from Batthyány tér to the 1st stop. **Amenities:** Bar; sauna; limited room service; laundry service. *In room:* A/C, TV, dataport, minibar, hair dryer, safe.

3 Great Deals on Dining

Budapest has enjoyed a veritable culinary revolution since 1989, as ethnic restaurants have proliferated; you'll find Chinese, Japanese, Korean, Indian, Middle Eastern, Turkish, Greek, Mexican, and more. Of course, most visitors want Hungarian food. In this city, traditional fare runs the gamut from greasy to gourmet. There are few palates that can't find happiness, and few budgets that'll be much the worse for wear.

Étterem, the most common Hungarian word for restaurant, is used for everything from cafeteria-style eateries to first-class restaurants. A *vendéglő,* or guesthouse, is a smaller, more intimate restaurant, often with a Hungarian folk motif; a *csárda* is a countryside *vendéglő.* An *étkezde* is an informal lunchroom open only in the daytime. *Önkiszolgáló* means self-service cafeteria, typically open only for lunch. Stand-up *büfés* are often found in bus stations and near busy transport hubs. A *cukrászda* or *kávéház* is a classic central European coffeehouse, where lingering has developed into an art form.

At a number of types of places that are primarily for drinking, meals are usually available. A *borozó* is a wine bar; they are often found in cellars (the name may include the word *pince* [cellar] or *barlang* [cave]) and generally feature a house wine. A *söröző* is a beer bar; these places often occupy cellars, too. Sandwiches are usually available in *borozós* and *sörözós.* Finally, a *kocsma* is a sort of roadside tavern on a side street in a residential neighborhood; the Buda Hills are filled with them. Most *kocsmas* serve full dinners, but the kitchens close early.

The customer initiates the paying ritual by summoning the waiter (or any other employee). The waiter usually brings the bill to your table in a little booklet; occasionally you're asked to confirm what you ordered. If you think the bill is wrong, don't be embarrassed to say so; locals commonly do this. After handing over the bill, in most restaurants, the waiter will disappear. The tip (about 10%) should be included in the amount you leave in the booklet. In smaller, less formal lunchroom-type places, waiters will often remain at your table after delivering the bill, waiting patiently for payment. In these face-to-face encounters, state the full amount you're paying (bill plus tip), and the waiter will make change. Never leave a tip on the table. A developing trend among some new restaurants is to dispense with adding a service charge. In these instances, a more robust tip is expected. As many Hungarians and foreigners alike expect that a service charge is already added to the bill, you may find that waiters are not shy about reminding diners of "appropriate" tipping manners.

IN CENTRAL PEST

Bangkok House THAI   Now a veteran eatery in Budapest's ever-evolving gastronomical scene, Bangkok Restaurant features exotic and original Thai cuisine, lovingly prepared with the freshest ingredients, in a lively setting. Folk dance performances on Friday and Saturday evenings accompany the extensive, slightly overwhelming menu. Stick to dishes you already know, or solicit suggestions from the waiter. For a main course, you might try the Mekong catfish soup (a meal in itself) or the grilled shark with wild lemon grass and chili sauce.

V. Só u. 3. ⓒ 1/266-0584. Reservations recommended. Soup 650 Ft–1,950 Ft ($2.95–$8.80); main courses 1,350 Ft–6,500 Ft ($6.10–$29). AE, MC, V. Daily noon–11pm. Metro: Ferenciek tere (Blue line).

Három Dob Vendéglő 🗟🗟 ⟨Value⟩ HUNGARIAN   Formerly known as Kiskacsa Vendéglő ("Little Duck"), this cozy restaurant with rustic furnishings and red-and-white-checked tablecloths has been renovated and renamed "Three Drums" by the current ownership. The place has succeeded in maintaining its local charm, while at the same time taking on a brighter, cheerier atmosphere. This has long been our favorite little eatery in this neighborhood. The food is exceptional for the price range, and the menu incredibly varied. Try the *csirkemell szatmári módra,* chicken breast with dumplings wrapped in bacon and dressed with a creamed carrot sauce. Vegetarians might try *kertész palacsinta,* a crepe stuffed with steamed veggies, served in a cheese sauce.

VII. Dob u. 26 (corner of Kazinczy utca). ⓒ 1/322-6208. Main courses 800 Ft–1,500 Ft ($3.60–$6.75). 10% off for families Sun. Daily noon–midnight. Metro: Astoria (Red line).

Kádár Étkezde 🗟🗟 HUNGARIAN   By 11:45am, Uncle Kádár's, in the heart of the Jewish district, is filled with regulars—from paint-spattered workers to elderly couples. Uncle Kádár, a neighborhood legend, personally greets them as they file in. From the outside, the only sign of the place is a very small red sign saying KÁDÁR ÉTKEZDE. The place is no more than a lunchroom, but it has a great atmosphere: high ceilings, wood-paneled walls with photos (many autographed) of actors and athletes, and old-fashioned seltzer bottles on every table. The food is simple but hearty, and the service friendly. Table sharing is the norm.

VII. Klauzál tér 9. ⓒ 1/321-3622. Soup 300 Ft ($1.35); main courses 500 Ft–750 Ft ($2.25–$3.40). No credit cards. Tues–Sat 11:30am–3:30pm. Metro: Astoria (Red line) or Deák tér (all lines).

Marquis de Salade 🗟🗟 RUSSIAN/MIDDLE EASTERN/ASIAN   Vegetarians will feel right at home here. An Azeri woman owns this recently renovated restaurant on the edge of Pest's theater district. The restaurant employs an eclectic mix of eight cooks from areas around the world (Russia, Bangladesh, Hungary, China, Italy, and the Caucasus Mountains), and turns out an amazing assortment of exceptional dishes. The offerings are sophisticated yet earthy. Try lamb with rice (Azerbaijan) or borscht soup (Russian). A nonsmoking area is available, and tablecloths and other tapestries are for sale.

VI. Hajós u. 43. ⓒ 1/302-4086. Appetizers 900 Ft–3,500 Ft ($4.05–$16); main courses 1,600 Ft–3,000 Ft ($7.20–$14). V. Daily 11am–midnight. Metro: Arany János u. (Blue line).

Vegetariánus Étterem 🗟 VEGETARIAN   This friendly, New Age-y self-serve restaurant offers interesting vegetarian food in a tranquil, smoke-free atmosphere. Choose from 30 different dishes at a set price, including two daily menu options written (in Hungarian and English) on a blackboard, such as stuffed squash with Indian ragout and brown rice; or potato pumpkin casserole with garlic Roquefort sauce, steamed cabbage, and spinach soufflé.

> **Value** **Getting the Best Deal on Dining**
>
> - Take advantage of Budapest's low prices and splurge: Meals here cost a third of what they'd cost in Austria or Germany.
> - Remember that cafeterias are great for simple dining.
> - Try Hungarian wine instead of more expensive imports.
> - Avoid ordering "specials" unless the price is posted or the waiter tells you the price.

V. Vigyázó Ferenc u. 4. ℂ 1/269-1625. Soup 290 Ft ($1.30); main dish 380 Ft ($1.70); small menu meal 1,150 Ft ($5.20); large menu meal 1,450 Ft ($6.50); student menu 520 Ft ($2.35). V, MC. Mon–Sat noon–9pm. Metro: Deák tér (all lines).

IN THE BUDA HILLS

Makkhetes Vendéglő ❀ HUNGARIAN In the lower part of the Buda Hills, Makkhetes is a rustic neighborhood eatery. The crude wood paneling and absence of ornamentation give it a distinctly country atmosphere. The regulars start filing in at 11:30am for lunch; the waiters seem to know everyone. The food is good and the portions are large. We are partial to their *paprikás csirke galuskával* (chicken paprika with dumplings), a spicy and hearty traditional dish.

XII. Némétvölgyi út 56. ℂ 1/355-7330. Soup 370 Ft–690 Ft ($1.65–$3.10); main courses 850 Ft–2,200 Ft ($3.80–$9.90). No credit cards. Daily 11am–10pm. Tram: 59 from Moszkva tér to Kiss János altábornagy utca stop (then walk up hill to the right on Kiss János altábornagy utca).

Szép Ilona HUNGARIAN This cheerful, unassuming restaurant serves a mostly local crowd. There's a good selection of specialties: Try *borjúpaprikás galuskával* (veal paprika) served with *galuska* (a typical central European dumpling). There's a small sidewalk garden for summer dining. The Szép Ilona is in a pleasant neighborhood; after your meal, stroll through the tree-lined streets.

II. Budakeszi út 1–3. ℂ 1/275-1392. Soup 350 Ft–720 Ft ($1.55–$3.25); main courses 600 Ft–3,200 Ft ($2.70–$14). No credit cards. Daily 11:30am–10pm. Bus: 158 from Moszkva tér (departs from Csaba utca, at the top of the stairs, near the stop from which the Várbusz departs for the Castle District).

IN ÓBUDA

Malomtó Étterem ❀❀ HUNGARIAN Across from the Lukács Baths, the Malomtó sits at the base of a hill. There are two well-shaded outdoor terraces, and live guitar music nightly. The menu features a good variety of Hungarian wild game and seafood dishes, in addition to the standards. Main course portions are huge, so you might want to bypass soup and salad. *Bélszín kedvesi módra* (beef and goose liver in creamy mushroom sauce) and *sztrapacska oldalassal* (pork ribs with ewe cheese dumplings) are sumptuous. Service can be slow.

II. Frankel Leó u. 48. ℂ 1/326-2847. Reservations recommended for dinner. Soup 300 Ft–450 Ft ($1.35–$2); main courses 980 Ft–2,800 Ft ($4.40–$13). AE, DC, MC, V. Daily noon–11pm. Tram: 4 or 6 to Margit híd (Buda side), then walk along Frankel Leó utca to the Lukács Baths (Lukács Fürdő).

IN THE CASTLE DISTRICT

Önkiszolgáló ❀ *Value* HUNGARIAN In the Fortuna Courtyard across from the Hilton, this humble self-service cafeteria offers a rare commodity: cheap and hearty meals in the Castle District. Only a small sign bearing the open hours marks the entrance; it's the second door on the left inside the courtyard archway,

Moments Coffeehouse Culture

Imperial Budapest, like Vienna, was famous for its coffeehouse culture. Literary movements and political circles alike were identified in large part by which coffeehouse they met in. You can still go to several classic coffeehouses, all of which offer delicious pastries, coffee, and more in an atmosphere of luxurious splendor. Table sharing is common.

Gerbeaud's, V. Vörösmarty tér 7 (© **061/429-9000;** Metro: Vörösmarty tér [Yellow line]), is probably the city's most famous coffeehouse. Whether you sit inside amid the splendor of the early-1900s furnishings or out on one of Pest's liveliest squares, you'll be sure to enjoy the fine pastries that have made Gerbeaud famous. It's open daily 9am to 9pm.

Across Andrássy út from the Opera House, **Művész Kávéház** ⋈⋈, VI. Andrássy út 29 (© **061/352-1337** or 061/351-3942; Metro: Opera [Yellow line]), boasts a lush interior with marble tabletops, crystal chandeliers, and mirrored walls. Despite its grandeur, Művész retains a casual atmosphere. There are tables on the street, but sit inside for the full effect. It's open daily 9am to 11:45pm.

Central ⋈⋈, V. Károlyi Mihály u. 9 (© **1/266-2110;** Metro: Ferenciek tere [Blue line]), is the latest addition to the Viennese coffeehouse culture in Budapest. It is a perfect replica of the original establishment that originally opened on the premises in 1887, but has long since disappeared. Although high-quality meals are served at the restaurant on the same premises, we consider the place first and foremost a coffee house, with the best flavors of coffee in the Inner City within a very affordable price range of 280 Ft to 950 Ft ($1.25–$4.30). Open Sunday through Thursday 8am to midnight; Friday and Saturday until 1am.

Angelika Cukrászda ⋈, I. Batthyány tér 7, tel **1/201-4847;** Metro: Batthyány tér (Red line), occupies a historic building next to St. Anne's Church in Buda. The sunken rooms of this cavernous cafe provide the perfect retreat on a summer afternoon. The place was recently extended to include a grill restaurant outside and a complex of terraces on three levels. Now you will find a perfect view of the Parliament building and the Chain Bridge. The stained-glass windows and marble floors contrast beautifully with the off-white canvas upholstery and cast-iron furniture. Choose from among a selection of excellent pastries and a good selection of teas (a rarity in this city of coffee drinkers). It's open daily 9am to midnight.

More than 100 years old, **Ruszwurm Cukrászda** ⋈⋈, I. Szentháromság u. 7 (© **061/375-5284;** bus: Várbusz from Moszkva tér or 16 from Deák tér to Castle Hill; funicular: from Clark Ádám tér to Castle Hill), is an utterly charming little place, with tiny tables and chairs and shelves lined with antiques. A particularly tasty pastry is the *dobos torta,* a multilayered cake with a thin caramel top crust. It's open daily 10am to 7pm.

up one flight of stairs. Just follow the stream of locals at lunchtime. Point out your selections, share a table, and bus your own tray.

I. Hess András tér 4 (1st floor in the Fortuna Courtyard). ℂ 1/375-6175. Soup 220 Ft–280 Ft ($1–$1.25); main courses 220 Ft–620 Ft ($1–$2.80). Mon–Fri 11:30am–2:30pm. Bus: Várbusz from Moszkva tér or no. 16 from Deák tér to Castle Hill. Funicular: From Clark Ádám tér to Castle Hill.

IN BUDA'S WATERTOWN

Le Jardin de Paris FRENCH   This wonderful little bistro is in the heart of Watertown, across from the hideous Institut Francais. A cozy cellar space, it's decorated with an eclectic collection of graphic arts. The menu contains nouvelle French specialties, and the wine list features French as well as Hungarian vintages. The presentation is impeccable. A jazz trio entertains diners 7 to 11pm. In summer there's outdoor seating in a new garden area.

I. Fő u. 20. ℂ 1/201-0047. Reservations recommended. Soup 600 Ft–1,200 Ft ($2.70–$5.40); appetizers 800 Ft–1,800 Ft ($3.60–$8.10); main courses 1,200 Ft–4,000 Ft ($5.40–$18). AE, DC, MC, V. Daily noon–midnight. Metro: Batthyány tér (Red line).

WORTH A SPLURGE

Kacsa Vendéglő ⚜ HUNGARIAN   Kacsa (meaning "duck") is located on Fő utca, the main street of Watertown, the Buda neighborhood that lies between Castle Hill and the Danube. Here you'll find an intimate, elegant, and understated dining atmosphere. A string trio is appealing, but the service seems overly attentive and ceremonious. Enticing main courses include roast duck with morello cherries, haunch of venison with grapes, and pike served Russian style. The vegetarian plate is the best we've had. For dessert, sample the assorted strudels, prepared with fruits in season.

Fő u. 75. ℂ 1/201-9992. Reservations recommended. Soup 600 Ft–1,300 Ft ($2.70–$5.85); main courses 2,700 Ft–5,900 Ft ($12–$27). MC, V. Daily noon–3pm and 6pm–1am. Metro: Batthyány tér (Red line).

Kis Buda Gyöngye ⚜⚜ HUNGARIAN   On a quiet side street in a residential Óbuda neighborhood, Kis Buda Gyöngye ("Pearl of Little Buda") is a favorite of Hungarians and visitors. This cheerful place features an interior garden, which sits in the shade of a wonderful old gnarly tree. Inside, an eccentric violinist entertains diners. Consider, if you dare, the goose plate, a rich combination platter including a roast goose leg, goose cracklings, and goose liver.

III. Kenyeres u. 34. ℂ 1/368-6402. Reservations highly recommended. Soup 800 Ft–980 Ft ($3.60–$4.40); main courses 1,900 Ft–3,200 Ft ($8.55–$14). AE, DC, MC, V. Mon–Sat noon–midnight. Closed Sun. Tram: 17 from Margit híd (Buda side).

4 Seeing the Sights

THE TOP ATTRACTIONS
IN PEST

Parliament ⚜   Budapest's great Parliament, an eclectic design mixing the predominant neo-Gothic style with a neo-Renaissance dome, was completed in 1902. Standing proudly on the Danube bank, it has from the outset been one of Budapest's symbols. Before 1989, a democratically elected government convened here only once (just after World War II, before the Communist takeover). Statues of Hungarian kings decorate the main cupola. The interior decor is predominantly neo-Gothic, with ceiling frescoes by Károly Lotz, Hungary's best-known artist of that genre. Note the handmade carpet, purportedly the largest in

Budapest

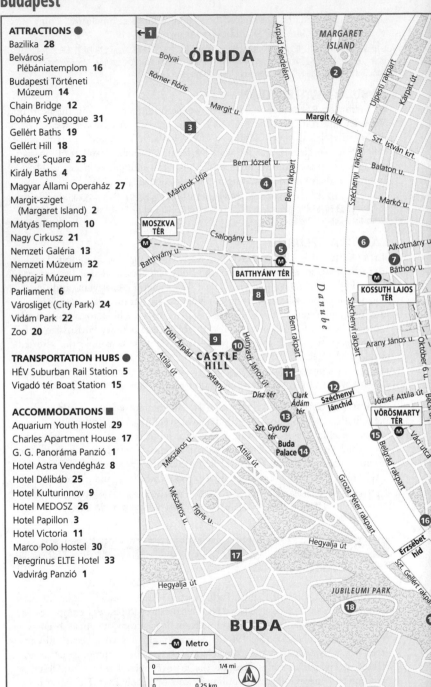

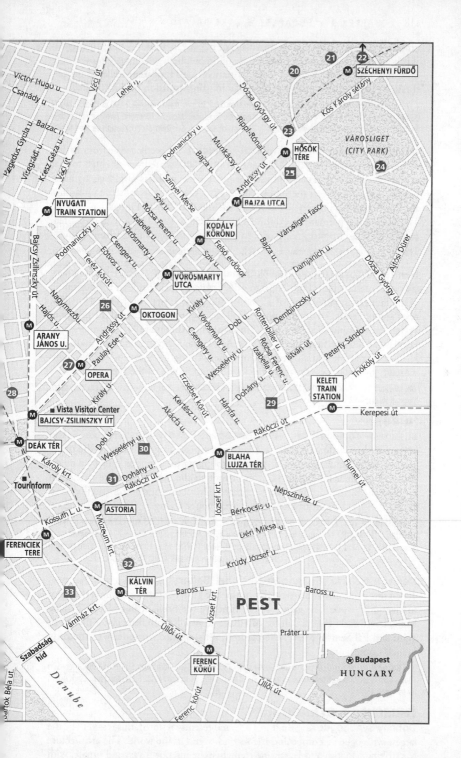

Victor Hugo u.
Csanády u

Hegedűs Gyula u.
Visegrádi u.
Kresz Géza út
Balzac u.
Váci út
Lehel u.
Váci út
Dózsa György út
Rippl-Rónai u.
Podmaniczky u.
Munkácsy u.
Bajza u.
Andrássy út
Kós Károly sétány

20
21
22 SZÉCHENYI FÜRDŐ Ⓜ
23
HŐSÖK TÉRE
25
VÁROSLIGET (CITY PARK)
24

Szinyei Merse
NYUGATI TRAIN STATION Ⓜ
Szív u.
Rózsa Ferenc u.
Izabella u.
Vörösmarty u.
Csengery u.
Eötvös u.
Ⓜ BAJZA UTCA
KODÁLY KÖRÖND Ⓜ
Felső erdősor
Szív u.
Városligeti fasor
Bajza u.
Damjanich u.
Dózsa György út
Aitósi Dürer

Bajcsy Zsilinszky út
Podmaniczky u.
Teréz körút
Nagymező u.
Hajós u.
Andrássy út
26
OKTOGON Ⓜ
Vörösmarty u.
Király u.
Vörösmarty u.
Csengery u.
Dob u.
Wesselényi u.
Rottenbiller u.
Dembinszky u.
Rózsa Ferenc u.
Izabella u.
István út
Péterfy Sándor
Thököly út
VÖRÖSMARTY UTCA Ⓜ

ARANY JÁNOS U. Ⓜ
27 Ⓜ Paulay Ede u.
OPERA Ⓜ
Király u.
Erzsébet körút
Kertész u.
Akácfa u.
Dohány u.
Hársfa u.
29
KELETI TRAIN STATION
Ⓜ
Kerepesi út
28 Ⓜ

■ Vista Visitor Center
BAJCSY-ZSILINSZKY ÚT Ⓜ
DEÁK TÉR Ⓜ
Károly krt.
Dob u.
Wesselényi u.
30
31 Dohány u.
Rákóczi út
BLAHA LUJZA TÉR Ⓜ
Rákóczi út
József krt.
Népszínház u.

■ Tourinform
ASTORIA Ⓜ
Kossuth L. u.
Múzeum krt.
Bérkocsis u.
Déri Miksa u.
Krúdy József u.

FERENCIEK TERE Ⓜ
32
KÁLVIN TÉR Ⓜ
Baross u.
Baross u.
PEST
33
Vámház krt.
Üllői út
József krt.
Práter u.

Szabadság hid
Bartók Béla út
Danube
FERENC KÖRÚT Ⓜ
Üllői út
Ferenc körút

⊛ Budapest
HUNGARY

317

Europe, from the small Hungarian village of Békésszentandrás. The Parliament is also home to the legendary crown jewels of St. Stephen, which were moved here from the National Museum in 2000 as part of the Hungarian millennium celebration. The guided tour is the only way to gain admission to the building.

V. Kossuth tér. ℂ 1/441-4415. Admission (by guided tour only) 30-min. tour in English 1,700 Ft ($7.65), 800 Ft ($3.60) students. Tickets available at gate X; enter at gate XII. Tours given Mon–Fri 10am and 2pm (but not on days on which Parliament is in session, which is usually Tues–Wed), Sat 4pm, Sun 2pm. Metro: Kossuth tér (Red line).

Néprajzi Múzeum (Ethnographical Museum)   Directly across from Parliament, the vast Ethnographical Museum features an ornate interior equal to that of the Opera House. A ceiling fresco of Justitia, the goddess of justice, by artist Károly Lotz, dominates the lobby. Although a third of the museum's holdings are from outside Hungary, concentrate on the items from Hungarian culture. The fascinating permanent exhibit "From Ancient Times to Civilization" features everything from drinking jugs to razor cases to chairs to clothing.

V. Kossuth tér 12. ℂ 1/473-2440. Admission 500 Ft ($2.25). Tues–Sun 10am–6pm. Metro: Kossuth tér (Red line).

Nemzeti Múzeum (Hungarian National Museum) 𝕜𝕜   This enormous neoclassical structure, built from 1837 to 1847, played a major role in the beginning of the Hungarian Revolution of 1848–49. On its wide steps on March 15, 1848, poet Sándor Petőfi and other young radicals are said to have exhorted the people of Pest to revolt against the Habsburgs. The two main exhibits are "The History of the Peoples of Hungary from the Paleolithic Age to the Magyar Conquest" and "The History of the Hungarian People from the Magyar Conquest to 1989." This museum gives you a window into the long, proud history of the Hungarians.

VIII. Múzeum krt. 14. ℂ 1/338-2122. Admission 600 Ft ($2.70). Tues–Sun 10am–6pm (to 5pm in winter). Metro: Kálvin tér (Blue line).

IN BUDA

Budapesti Történeti Múzeum (Budapest History Museum) 𝕜𝕚𝕕𝕤   Also known as the Castle Museum, this is the best place to get a sense of the once-great medieval Buda. It's probably worth splurging for a guided tour by a qualified staff member (6,000 Ft/$27); even though the descriptions are written in English, the history of the palace's repeated destruction and reconstruction is so arcane that it's difficult to understand what you're seeing.

I. In Buda Palace, Wing E, on Castle Hill. ℂ 1/225-7815. Admission 700 Ft ($3.40). Guided tours by qualified staff in English for serious history buffs, at a whopping 6,000 Ft ($27), are available upon advance request. May 15–Sept 15 Wed–Mon 10am–6pm; Sept 16–May 14 Wed–Mon 10am–4pm. Bus: Várbusz from Moszkva tér or no. 16 from Deák tér to Castle Hill. Funicular: From Clark Ádám tér to Castle Hill.

Nemzeti Galéria (Hungarian National Gallery) 𝕜𝕜   Hungary has produced some fine artists, particularly in the late 19th century, and this is the place to view their work. The giants of the time are the brilliant but moody Mihály Munkácsy; László Paál, a painter of village scenes; Károly Ferenczy, a master of light; and Pál Szinyei Merse, the plein-air artist and contemporary of the early French Impressionists.

I. In Buda Palace, Wings B, C, and D, on Castle Hill. ℂ 1/375-5567. Admission 600 Ft ($2.70). Tues–Sun 10am–6pm. Bus: Várbusz from Moszkva tér or no. 16 from Deák tér to Castle Hill. Funicular: From Clark Ádám tér to Castle Hill.

CHURCHES & SYNAGOGUES

Dohány Synagogue 𝕜   Built in 1859 and recently restored, this is said to be the largest synagogue in Europe and the second largest in the world. The architecture has striking Moorish and Byzantine elements; the interior is vast and ornate, with

Value **Getting the Best Deal on Sightseeing**

- Always use the convenient public transport system to maximize your sightseeing time at minimal cost.
- Be aware that the best panoramas of Pest (free, of course) are from the south end of Castle Hill, on the stone-fortified overlooks on the cliff in front of the Budapest History Museum. If you don't have the energy to walk up the hill, you can take the funicular from Clark Ádám tér.
- Remember that a twilight stroll on the Belgrád rakpart embankment in Pest, between the Budapest Marriott Hotel and the Chain Bridge, will give you memorable views against illuminated Castle Hill.

two balconies and the usual presence of an organ in a neologue synagogue. The synagogue has a rich but tragic history. There's a Jewish museum next door.

VII. Dohány u. 2–8. © 1/342-8949. Admission 600 Ft ($2.70). Tues–Thurs 10am–5pm; Fri 10am–2pm; Sun 10am–2pm. Metro: Astoria (Red line) or Deák tér (all lines).

Belvárosi Plébániatemplom (Inner City Parish Church) The Inner City Parish Church, flush against the Erzsébet Bridge in Pest, is one of the city's great architectural monuments. The 12th-century Romanesque church first built on this spot went up inside the remains of the walls of the Roman fortress of Contra-Aquincum. In the early 14th century, a Gothic church was built. This medieval church, with numerous additions and reconstructions reflecting the architectural trends of the time, stands today.

V. Március 15 tér. © 1/318-3108. Free admission. Mon–Sat 6am–7pm; Sun 8am–7pm. Metro: Ferenciek tere (Blue line).

Bazilika (St. Stephen's Church) *Kids* The country's largest church, this basilica took over 50 years to build, and was finally completed in 1906. A full-scale renovation of the church and neighboring square was finished in 2003, and the once-gloomy front of the church now graces a colorful and grand Szent István tér, where tourists sip their coffee in open-air cafes. In the Chapel of the Holy Right (Szent Jobb Kápolna), you can see Hungarian Catholicism's most cherished—and bizarre—holy relic: the preserved right hand of Hungary's first Christian king, Stephen. The ascent to the tower is a great climb for kids, whom it rewards with fabulous views.

V. Szent István tér 33. © 1/317-2859. Free admission to church; admission to treasury 200 Ft (90¢); admission to tower 400 Ft ($1.80). Church daily 7am–7pm, except during services; treasury daily 9am–5pm (10am–4pm in winter); Szent Jobb Chapel Mon–Sat 9am–5pm (10am–4pm in winter) and Sun 1–5pm; tower Apr–Oct 10am–6pm (closed Nov–Mar). Metro: Arany János utca (Blue line) or Bajcsy-Zsilinszky út (Yellow line).

Mátyás Templom (Matthias Church) *Finds* Officially named the Church of Our Lady, this symbol of Buda's Castle District is popularly known as Matthias Church, after the 15th-century king who was married here twice. It dates from the mid–13th century, and, like other old churches in Budapest, it has an interesting history of destruction and reconstruction, always being refashioned in the architectural style of the time. Organ concerts are held every other Friday at 8pm in July and August.

I. Szentháromság tér 2. © 1/355-5657. Admission 400 Ft ($1.80). Daily 9am–6pm. Bus: Várbusz from Moszkva tér or 16 from Deák tér Castle Hill. Funicular: From Clark Ádám tér to Castle Hill.

Special & Free Events

The **Budapest Spring Festival** 🏛🏛 runs for 2 weeks in mid- to late March. Performances of everything from opera to ballet, classical music to drama, take place at all the major halls and theaters. What's more, ticket prices are so low that you can attend virtually every event for the cost of one musical extravaganza in Salzburg. Tickets are available at the Festival Ticket Service, V. 1081 Rákóczi út 65 (© **061/486-3300**).

Except for the 10-day **Summer Opera and Ballet Festival,** which falls in July or August, the wonderful Hungarian State Opera House has no summer performances. Tickets are available at the National Philharmonic Ticket Office (Filharmónia Nemzeti Jegyiroda), relocated to VII. Madách utca 3 (© **1/321-4199**), open Monday through Thursday from 10am to 5:30pm, and Friday from 10am to 5pm; or at the Hungarian State Opera Ticket Office (Magyar Állami Opera Jegyiroda), VI. Andrássy út 20 (entrance inside the courtyard; © **1/353-0170**), open Monday through Friday from 11am to 5pm.

August 20 is **St. Stephen's Day,** Hungary's national day. Cultural events and a dramatic display of fireworks over the Danube celebrate the country's patron saint. On this day, Hungarians also celebrate their constitution and ceremoniously welcome the first bread from the new crop of July wheat. Many festivities are free.

Pepsi Island (Pepsi-sziget), on Óbuda Island in the Danube, is Hungary's very own annual Woodstock. Established in 1994, Pepsi-sziget is a weeklong music festival that draws young people from all over Europe. The event, which usually begins in the second week of August, features foreign and local rock, folk, and jazz groups on dozens of stages playing each day from early afternoon to the wee hours of the morning. Camping is available. Pick up a program schedule at Tourinform.

In mid-August, the Castle District is the site of an annual 3-day **Traditional Handicraft Fair** 🏛🏛, which draws vendors from across Hungary and from Hungarian enclaves in neighboring countries, especially Romania. The wares are generally handmade and of high quality. Admission is free.

ESPECIALLY FOR KIDS

Vidám Park (Amusement Park) 🏛🏛 *Kids*   This is a must if you're traveling with kids, and two rides in particular aren't to be missed. The 100-year-old **Merry-Go-Round** *(Körhinta),* constructed almost entirely of wood, was recently restored to its original grandeur. Riders must actively pump to keep the horses rocking. As authentic Wurlitzer music plays and the carousel spins round and round, it creaks mightily. The **Ferris wheel** *(Óriáskerék)* is also wonderful, although it has little in common with rambunctious modern Ferris wheels. A gangly bright-yellow structure, it rotates at a liltingly slow pace, gently lifting you high for a remarkable view. The Vidám Park also features Europe's longest wooden roller coaster.

XIV. Állatkerti krt. 14–16. © 1/343-0996. Admission 300 Ft ($1.35) adults, free for children under 120cm tall (about 4 ft.); rides 150 Ft–600 Ft (70¢–$2.70). Your best bet is to buy a stack of 20 tickets (plus 2 "free" extra tickets) on entry for 3,000 Ft ($14). Apr–Sept Mon–Fri 10am–7pm, Sat–Sun to 8pm; Oct–Mar Mon–Fri noon–6pm, Sat–Sun 10am–6:30pm. Metro: Széchenyi fürdő (Yellow line).

Nagy Cirkusz (Big Circus) *Kids*   Budapest has a long circus tradition, but most Hungarian stars now opt for more glamorous and financially rewarding careers abroad. Definitely worth seeing, especially if you travel with kids. The box office is open 10am to 7pm.

XIV. Állatkerti krt. 7. (© 1/343-9630. Tickets 900 Ft–1,400 Ft ($4.05–$6.30) adults, 700 Ft–1,200 Ft children ($3.15–$5.40), free for children under 4. Performances Mon–Wed and Fri 3 and 7pm; Thurs 3pm; Sat 10:30am, 3, and 7pm; Sun 3pm. Metro: Hősök tere or Széchenyi fürdő (Yellow line).

PARKS & PANORAMAS

Gellért Hegy (Gellért Hill)   Towering 225m (750 ft.) above the Danube, Gellért Hill offers the city's best panorama. It's named after the Italian bishop who assisted Hungary's first Christian king, Stephen I, in converting the Magyars. Gellért became a martyr when he was rolled in a barrel to his death from the side of the hill on which his enormous statue now stands. On top of Gellért Hill you'll find the Liberation Monument, built in 1947 to commemorate the Red Army's release of Budapest from Nazi occupation. Also atop the hill is the Citadella, built by the Austrians shortly after they crushed the Hungarian War of Independence of 1848–49. Take bus no. 27 from Móricz Zsigmond körtér.

Margaret Island (Margit-sziget) *Kids* has been a public park since 1908. The long, narrow island, connected to both Buda and Pest by the Margaret and Árpád bridges, bars most vehicular traffic. Facilities on the island include the Palatinus Strand open-air baths, which draw on the famous thermal waters under Margaret Island; the Alfréd Hajós Sport Pool; and the Open Air Theater. Sunbathers line the steep embankments along the river, and bicycles are available for rent. Despite all this, Margaret Island is a tranquil place. Take bus no. 26, which runs the length of the island from Nyugati tér, or tram no. 4 or 6, which stop at the entrance to the island midway across the Margaret Bridge. (*Warning:* These are popular lines for pickpockets.)

Finds Where Have All the Statues Gone?

Just over a decade ago, Budapest and Hungary were filled with memorials to Lenin, Marx, Engels, the Red Army, and many other figures of Hungarian and international Communist history. Torn from their pedestals in the aftermath of 1989, they sat for a few years in warehouses until a controversial plan for a **Szoborpark Múzeum (Socialist Statue Park)** was realized. The park's inconvenient location and the relatively small number of statues displayed make it less than it could be. Moreover, the best examples of the genre, from the Stalinist period of the late 1940s and 1950s, were removed before 1989 and have presumably long since been destroyed.

Located in the XXII district (extreme southern Buda) on Balatoni út (© 1/227-7446), the museum park is open daily, from 10am to dusk. Admission is 600 Ft ($2.70). To get there, take the black-lettered bus no. 7 from Ferenciek tere to Kosztolányi Dezső tér. Board a yellow Volán bus (to Érd) at Platform 6 for a 20-minute ride to the park. Or, for a premium, you can take the new and convenient direct bus service from Deák tér for 1,950 Ft ($8.80; admission ticket to the park included). The timetable varies almost monthly, but 11am and 3pm departures remain constant through the year (except Nov–Feb, when the bus does not run at all).

Moments   Enjoying the Thermal Baths

The history of Budapest's baths stretches back to Roman times. Under Turkish occupation, the culture of the baths flourished, and several functioning bathhouses—Király, Rudas, and Rac—are among the architectural relics of that period. In the late 19th and early 20th centuries, Budapest's "golden age," several fabulous bathhouses were built: the extravagant Széchenyi Baths in City Park, the splendid Art Nouveau Gellért Baths, and the neoclassical Lukács Baths. All are still in use.

Because thermal bathing is an activity shaped by ritual, and because bathhouse employees tend to be unfriendly, many foreigners find a trip to the baths confusing at first. The most baffling step may be the ticket window. It lists prices for different facilities and services, often without English translations. You'll want to know *uszoda* (pool), *termál* (thermal pool), *fűrdó* (bath), and *gozfűrdó* (steam bath, massage, and sauna). Towel rental is *törűközó* or *lepedó*. An entry ticket generally entitles you to a free locker in the locker room *(öltözo);* you can usually opt to pay extra for a private cabin *(kabin)*.

Budapest's most spectacular bathhouse, the **Gellért Baths,** is in Buda's Hotel Gellért, XI. Kelenhegyi út 4 (© **061/466-6166;** tram: 47 or 49 from Deák tér to Szent Gellért tér); use the side entrance. The unisex indoor pool is exquisite, with marble columns, majolica tiles, and stone lion heads spouting water. The segregated Turkish-style thermal baths (one to each side of the pool, through badly marked doors) are glorious, although in need of restoration. The outdoor roof pool attracts great attention for 10 minutes every hour on the hour when the artificial wave machine is turned on. Admission to the thermal bath is 2,200 Ft ($9.90) for 4 hours or longer; a 15-minute massage is 2,200 Ft ($9.90). Lockers are free; a cabin can be rented for 500 Ft ($2.25). Admission to all pools and bath is 2,700 Ft ($12) adults, 800 Ft ($3.60) children for 4 hours or longer. Prices and the lengthy list of services are posted in English. The thermal baths are open in summer daily 6am to 7pm; you can also enjoy the bathing facilities at night on Friday and Saturday 8pm to midnight. In winter the baths are open Monday to Friday 6am to 7pm, Saturday and Sunday 6am to 2pm, with the last entrance an hour before closing. The **Király Baths** ☆, I. Fő u. 84 (© **061/202-3688;** Metro: Batthyány tér [Red line]), is one of Budapest's most important architectural monuments to Turkish rule. Here Hungarian culture meets the Eastern culture that influenced it. The baths, from the late 16th century, are housed under an octagonal domed roof. Sunlight filters through stained-glass windows. In addition to the thermal bath, there are saunas and steam baths. After your treatment, wrap yourself in a cotton sheet and lounge with a cup of tea in the relaxation room. Women can use the baths Monday, Wednesday, and Friday from 7am to 5pm. Men are welcome Tuesday, Thursday, and Saturday from 9am to 7pm. The last entrance is an hour before closing. Admission to the baths is 1,000 Ft ($4.50) for 90 minutes only.

City Park (Városliget) is an equally popular place to spend a summer day. Heroes' Square, at the end of Andrássy út, is the logical starting point for a walk. The lake behind the square is used for boating in summer and ice-skating in winter. The park's Zoo Boulevard (Állatkerti körút) is home to the zoo, the circus, and the amusement park. Gundel, Budapest's most famous restaurant, is also here, as are the Széchenyi Baths. The Yellow Metro line stops at Hősök tere (Heroes' Sq.), at the edge of the park, and Széchenyi Fűrdó, in the middle of it.

ORGANIZED TOURS

BUS TOURS   With decades of experience, **Ibusz** (© 061/485-2700; fax 061/ 318-2805; www.ibusz.hu) sets the standard for bus tours in terms of quality and quantity. It offers 11 boat and bus excursions, from basic city tours to special folklore-oriented tours. Tours include a 3-hour Budapest City Tour for 5,500 Ft ($25; children under 12 are free), and a 2-hour Parliament Tour for 7,500 Ft ($34). Ibusz tours operate all year, with an abbreviated schedule off season. Bus tours leave from the Erzsébet tér bus station, near Deák tér (all Metro lines); boat tours leave from the Vigadó tér landing. There's also a free hotel pickup service 30 minutes before departure.

BOAT TOURS   A boat tour is a great way to absorb the scope and scale of the Hungarian capital, and a majority of the city's grand sights can be seen from the river. The Hungarian state company **MAHART** operates daily sightseeing cruises on the Danube. The Budapest office of MAHART is at V. Belgrád rakpart (© 1/318-1704 or 1/489-4013). Boats depart frequently from Vigadó tér (on the Pest waterfront, between the Erzsébet Bridge and the Chain Bridge) on weekends and holidays in the spring and every day in summer.

WALKING TOURS   Of the several companies offering walking tours of historic Budapest, we recommend "The Absolute Walking Tour in Budapest," offered by **Absolute Walking Tours** ✦ (© 06-30/211-8861; www.budapestours. com). From mid-May through September, the daily tours, conducted by knowledgeable and personable guides, start at either pick-up point 1 outside the Evangelical Church in Deák tér (all Metro lines) at 9:30am and 1:30pm, or at pick-up point 2 on the front steps of the Műcsarnok at Hősök tere (Yellow line) at 10am and 2pm. October through mid-December and February through mid-May, tours start daily at 10:30am and 11am only; in January they are offered on weekends only. Tickets are 3,500 Ft ($5.75); children under 12 are free. Show this book (or the company's flyer, on display at many tourist haunts) and you'll get a 500 Ft ($2.25) discount. Buy your ticket from the tour guide at the start of the tour. Tours last anywhere from 3½ to 5 hours, depending on the mood of the group, and take you throughout both central Pest and central Buda. Wear your best walking shoes and leave your heavy backpack at your hotel.

5 Shopping

All year long, shoppers fill the pedestrians-only **Váci utca,** from the stately Vörösmarty tér, the center of Pest, across the roaring Kossuth Lajos utca, all the way to Vámház körút. The **Castle District** in Buda, with many folk-art boutiques and galleries, is another popular area for souvenir hunters. Locals (and budget travelers) might window-shop in these two neighborhoods, but they do their serious shopping elsewhere. One popular street is Pest's **Outer Ring (Nagykörút);** another bustling shopping street is Pest's **Kossuth Lajos utca,** off the Erzsébet Bridge, and its continuation **Rákóczi út,** extending all the way to Keleti Station.

The stores of the state-owned **Folkart Háziipar** should be your main source for Hungary's justly famous folk items. Almost everything is handmade—from tablecloths to miniature dolls, ceramic dishes to sheepskin vests. The main store, **Folkart Centrum,** now relocated in the upper end of the mall at V. Váci u. 58 (© **061/318-5840;** Metro: Deák tér [all lines]), is open daily 10am to 7pm.

See "Taxes" under "Fast Facts," earlier in this chapter, for information about obtaining a VAT refund.

Budapest's largest and best-known **flea market** is the **Ecseri Használtcikk Piac,** XIX. Nagykőrösi út 156 (© **061/280-8840**). Haggling is standard, and merchants accept cash only. The market runs Monday to Friday 8am to 4pm and Saturday 6am to 3pm. Take bus no. 54 from Boráros tér, about a 7-minute ride. The market is on the left side of the street. Open daily 7am to 6pm, **Józsefvárosi Piac,** VIII. Kőbányai út (© **061/459-2100**), is informally known as "Four Tigers" because of the tremendous influx of Chinese vendors. You'll find bargains aplenty. All prices are negotiable. Foreign currency is generally welcomed, but you'll attract far less attention by paying in forints. Dozens of languages are spoken. Take tram no. 28 from Blaha Lujza tér or no. 36 from Baross tér (Keleti Station) and get off at Orczy tér.

6 Budapest After Dark

Budapest is blessed with a rich and varied cultural life. You can still go to the Opera House, one of Europe's finest, for just a few dollars. Almost all of the city's theaters and halls, with the exception of those featuring rock groups on international tours, offer tickets for as little as $5 to $10. The opera, ballet, and theater seasons run September to May or June; most theaters and halls also book performances during the summer festivals. A number of lovely churches and stunning halls offer concerts exclusively in summer. While classical culture has a long and proud tradition in Budapest, jazz, blues, rock, and disco have exploded over the past decade. New clubs and bars have opened everywhere; the parties start late and last until morning.

The most complete schedule of mainstream performing arts is in the free bimonthly *Koncert Kalendárium,* available at the Central Philharmonic Ticket Office in Vörösmarty tér. The *Budapest Sun,* an English-language weekly, has a comprehensive events calendar and lists less-publicized events such as modern dance and folk music performances. *Visitor's Guide,* a free weekly pamphlet, also has pretty good listings. *Programme in Hungary* and *Budapest Panorama,* free monthly tourist booklets, have partial entertainment listings, featuring the editors' pick of highlights.

The **Central Theater Ticket Office (Színházak Központi Jegyiroda),** VI. Andrássy út 18 (© **061/267-1267**), sells tickets to just about everything, from theater and operetta to sports events and rock concerts. The office is open Monday to Friday 10am to 6pm.

THE PERFORMING ARTS

OPERA & CONCERTS   Completed in 1884, the **Magyar Állami Operaház (Hungarian State Opera House),** VI. Andrássy út 22 (© **061/331-2550;** Metro: Opera [Yellow line]), is Budapest's most famous performance hall and an attraction in its own right. Hungarians adore opera, and many seats are sold on a subscription basis; buy your tickets a few days ahead if possible. The box office is open Monday to Friday 11am to 6pm. Guided tours of the Opera House leave daily at 3 and 4pm; the cost is 1,500 Ft ($6.75).

The Great Hall (Nagyterem) of the **Zeneakadémia (Ferenc Liszt Academy of Music)**, VI. Liszt Ferenc tér 8 (© **061/341-4788** or 061/342-0179; Metro: Oktogon [Yellow line]), is Budapest's premier music hall. The academy was built in the Art Nouveau style of the early 20th century, and the acoustics in the Great Hall are said to be the best in the city. Box office hours are 2pm to showtime daily.

The **Budai Vigadó (Buda Concert Hall)**, I. Corvin tér 8 (© **061/317-2754**; Metro: Batthyány tér [Red line]), is the home stage of the Hungarian State Folk Ensemble (Állami Népi Együttes Székháza). The company is the oldest in the country and includes 40 dancers, a 20-member Gypsy orchestra, and a folk orchestra. Under the direction of award-winning choreographer Sándor Timár, it performs folk dances from all regions of historic Hungary. The box office is open daily 10am to 6pm. Performances usually start at 8pm on Tuesday, Thursday, and Sunday.

THEATER   Budapest has an extremely lively theater season September to June. For productions in English, try the **Merlin Theater**, V. Gerlóczy u. 4 (© **061/317-9338** or 061/266-4632; Metro: Astoria [Red line]). For musical productions, check the **Madách Theater**, VII. Erzsébet krt. 29–33 (© **061/478-2041**; tram: 4 or 6 to Wesselényi utca). Also staging musical performances is the **Vigszínház (Merry Theater)**, XIII. Szent István krt. 14 (© **061/340-4650**; Metro: Nyugati pu. [Blue line]), which was recently restored to its original delightfully gaudy neo-baroque splendor.

LIVE-MUSIC CLUBS

The club scene has found fertile ground since 1989's political changes—so much so, in fact, that clubs come in and out of fashion overnight. Check the *Budapest Sun* or *Budapest Week* for up-to-the-minute listings.

Fat Mo's Music Club, V. Nyári Pál u. 11 (© **1/267-3199**; Metro: Kálvin tér [Blue line]), is *the* place and always crowded. Jazz concerts start at 9pm, and the dancing begins around 11pm. Monday nights are the best, when the Hot Jazz Band performs in the style of the 1920s and '30s. Make sure you book a table if you wish to eat here—the food is superb, and the succulent beefsteaks are the best in town. The **Fél 10 Jazz Klub**, VIII. Baross u. 30 (no phone; Metro: Kálvin tér [Blue line]), is a classy multilevel club that features live jazz performances nightly and techno-free dance parties (late night Thurs–Sat). It's open Monday to Friday noon to 4am and Saturday and Sunday 7pm to 4am.

TRAFO, XI. Liliom u. 41 (© **061/215-1600**; www.trafo.hu; tram: 4 or 6 to Üllöi út), is an old electric power station renovated and transformed into a cultural center. It also hosts the hippest disco in town on Tuesday, with deejay Palotai. The party starts at 9pm. **Old Man's**, VIII. Akácfa u. 13 (© **061/322-7645**; Metro: Blaha Luzja tér [Red line]), is the place to take in the best jazz and blues in Hungary. The Pege Quartet plays here, as does Hobo and his blues band. This very hip spot is open daily 3pm to 3am.

BARS

The **Irish Cat Pub**, V. Múzeum krt. 41 (© **061/266-4085**; Metro: Kálvin tér [Blue line]), is an Irish-style pub with Guinness on tap and a whiskey bar. It's a popular meeting place for expats and travelers, serving a full menu. It's open Monday to Saturday 10am to 2 am and Sunday 5pm to 2am. **Morrison's Music Pub**, VI. Révay u. 25 (© **061/269-4060**; Metro: Opera [Yellow line]), is a casual place offering loud live music that's packed by an almost-20-something crowd. It's open Monday to Saturday 8:30pm to 4am.

GAY & LESBIAN BARS

For reliable current information, visit the first Hungarian GLBT website www.pride.hu (not in English).

Angel Bar & Dance Club, VII. Szövetség u. 33 (© **061/351-6490;** Metro: Blaha Lujza tér [Red line]), is a basement place with a bar, restaurant, and huge dance floor. Angel hosts a famous transvestite show at 11:45pm on Friday and Saturday. Sunday is an "open day," welcoming straight folks as well. Hours are Thursday through Sunday 10am to dawn. Cover is 600 Ft ($2.70); free on Thursday. **Mystery Bar,** V. Nagysándor József u. 3 (© **061/312-1436;** Metro: Arany János utca [Blue line]), is a smaller, cozier place, with a larger foreign crowd, perfect for conversation. There's no cover, and it's open daily 4pm to 4am. **Eklektika Café,** V. Semmelweis u. 21 (© **061/266-3054;** Metro: Deák tér [all lines]), is a wonderfully appointed place with 1950s socialist realist furnishings; it features live jazz on Wednesday, Friday, and Sunday. Eklektika hosts a women-only night every second Saturday, starting at 10pm. It's open Monday to Friday noon to midnight and Saturday and Sunday 5pm to dawn.

7 A Side Trip to Lake Balaton ⟨★

Lake Balaton may not be the Mediterranean, but don't tell that to the Hungarians. Somehow over the years they've managed to create their own central European hybrid of a Mediterranean culture along the shores of their shallow milky-white lake. It's Europe's largest, at 80km (50 miles) long and 16km (10 miles) wide at its broadest stretch.

The south shore towns are as flat as Pest; walk 10 minutes from the lake and you're in farm country. The air is still and quiet; in summer, the sun hangs heavily in the sky. Teenagers, students, and young travelers tend to congregate in the hedonistic towns of the south shore, where huge 1970s-style beachside hotels fill to capacity all summer long and music pulsates into the early hours.

On the more graceful north shore, little villages are neatly tucked away in the rolling countryside, where the grapes of the popular Balaton wines ripen in the strong sun. You'll discover the Tihany peninsula, a protected area whose 12 sq. km (4¾ sq. miles) jut into the lake like a knob. Stop for a swim—or the night—in a small town like Szigliget. Moving west along the coast, you can make forays inland to the rolling hills of the Balaton wine country. The city of Keszthely, sitting at the lake's western edge, marks the end of its northern shore.

From Budapest, **trains** to the various towns along the lake depart from Déli Station. The local trains are interminably slow, so try to get on an express.

If you're planning a trip to Lake Balaton for more than a day or 2, consider renting a car. The various towns differ enough from one another that you might want to keep driving until you find the place that's right for you. Wherever you go in the region, you'll find private rooms to be both cheaper and easier to get if you travel a few miles off the lake. Driving directly to the lake from Budapest takes about 1¼ hours. By **car** from Budapest, take the M7 motorway south through Székesfehérvár until you hit the lake. Route 71 circles the lake.

THE TIHANY PENINSULA   The **Tihany** (*Tee*-hine) **peninsula** is a protected area where building is heavily restricted. Consequently, it maintains a rustic charm that's unusual in this region. The peninsula also features a lush protected interior, accessible by a trail from Tihany Village, with several little inland lakes as well as a lookout tower offering views over the Balaton.

> **Value** **Where to Stay Around the Lake**
>
> Anywhere you go on Lake Balaton, you'll see signs advertising rooms for rent in private homes (SZOBA KIADÓ or ZIMMER FREI). Since hotel prices are unusually high in this region, we especially recommend private rooms here. When you take a room without using an agency, prices are generally negotiable. At the height of the season, you shouldn't have to pay more than 6,000 Ft ($27) for a double room within reasonable proximity of the lake.

The rail line circling Lake Balaton doesn't serve the Tihany peninsula. The nearest **rail station** is in Aszófő, about 5km (3 miles) from Tihany Village. A local **bus** runs to Tihany from the nearby town of Balatonfüred. You can also go by **ferry** from Szántód or Balatonföldvár or by **boat** from Balatonfüred. Visitor information is available at **Tourinform,** Kossuth u. 20 (℗/fax **87/448-519**). The office is open May through October only, Monday through Friday from 8:30am to 7pm, and weekends from 8:30am to 12:30pm.

The 18th-century baroque **Abbey Church** ✿ is Tihany Village's main attraction. A resident monk carved the exquisite wooden altar and pulpit in the 18th century. The frescoes are by three of Hungary's better-known 19th-century painters: Károly Lotz, Bertalan Székely, and Lajos Deák-Ébner. Next door is the **Tihany Museum** (℗ **87/448-650**), also in an 18th-century baroque structure. The museum features exhibits on the surrounding region's history and culture. A single fee of 300 Ft ($1.35) covers the church and the museum. They're open daily 9am to 5:30pm.

SZIGLIGET   Halfway between Tihany and Keszthely is the scenic little village of **Szigliget** (*Sig*-lee-get), with thatched-roof houses, lush vineyards, and a lovely Mediterranean quality. **Natur Tourist** (℗ 87/461-197), in the village center, is your best (and only) source of information in Szigliget.

The fantastic ruins of the 13th-century **Szigliget Castle** ✿ stand above the town on **Várhegy (Castle Hill).** In the days of the Turkish invasions, the Hungarian Balaton fleet, protected by the high castle, called Szigliget its home. You can hike up to the ruins for a splendid view of the lake and countryside; look for the path behind the white 18th-century church at the highest spot in the village. A good place to fortify yourself for the hike is the **Vár Vendéglő** (℗ 87/461-990) on the road up to the castle, a casual restaurant with plenty of outdoor seating. It serves traditional Hungarian fare. It's open daily 11am to 11pm. No credit cards are accepted.

The lively **beach** at Szigliget provides a striking contrast to the quiet village. In summer, buses from neighboring towns drop off hordes of beach-goers. The beach area is crowded with fried food and beer stands, ice-cream vendors, a swing set, and a volleyball net. Admission to the beach is 300 Ft ($1.35).

KESZTHELY   At the western edge of Lake Balaton, **Keszthely** (*Kest*-hay), 188km (117 miles) southwest of Budapest, is one the largest towns on the lake. Although it was largely destroyed during the Turkish wars, the town was rebuilt in the 18th century by the Festetics. The aristocratic family made Keszthely their home through World War II.

For visitor information, stop at **Tourinform,** Kossuth u. 28 (©/fax **83/314-144**). It's open daily, Monday through Friday from 9am to 5pm; and on Saturday and Sunday, in high season only, from 9am to 1pm. For private-room bookings, try **Zalatours,** at Kossuth u. 1 (© **83/312-560**); or **Ibusz,** at Kossuth u. 27 (© **83/314-320**), open Monday to Friday 8am to 4pm.

The highlight of a visit to Keszthely is the splendid **Festetics Mansion** *✸*, Szabadsag u. 1 (© **83/312-190**), the baroque 18th-century home (with 19th-c. additions) of the Festetics family. Part of the mansion is now open as a museum, the main attraction of which is the ornate library. The museum also features hunting gear and trophies. The museum is open in summer, daily from 9am to 6pm; in winter, it's open Tuesday through Sunday from 10am to 5pm. Admission for foreigners is 1,700 Ft ($7.65), but it's only 750 Ft ($3.40) for Hungarians. This museum is among the only places in Hungary that maintain this odious Communist-era price discrimination.

The center of Keszthely's summer scene, as in every other place on Lake Balaton, is down by the water on the "strand." Several large hotels dominate Keszthely's **beachfront.** Even if you're not a guest, you can rent **windsurfers, boats,** and other **water-related equipment** from these hotels.

INTO THE HILLS   Northeast of the Danube Bend is Hungary's hilliest region, where you can find its highest peak, 998m (3,327-ft.) **Matra Hill.** Here you can visit the preserved medieval village of **Hollókő,** one of Hungary's most charming spots. This UNESCO World Heritage site is a perfectly preserved but vibrant Palóc village. The rural Palóc people speak an unusual Hungarian dialect and have colorful folk customs and costumes. If you're in Hungary at Easter, by all means consider spending the holiday here: Hollókő's celebration features townspeople in traditional dress and Masses in the town church.

Hollókő sits idyllically in a quiet green valley, surrounded by hiking trails. A recently restored **14th-century castle** is perched on a hilltop over the village. The **Village Museum,** Kossuth Lajos u. 82 (© **32/378-058**), contains exhibits detailing everyday Palóc life from the early 1900s. It's open Tuesday to Sunday 10am to 4pm. Like everything else in town, though, the museum's opening times are flexible. Entry is 100 Ft (45¢).

In Hollókő, traditionally furnished **thatch-roofed peasant houses** are available to rent for a night or longer. You can rent a room in a shared house (with shared facilities) or an entire house. The prices vary depending on the size of the room or house and the number of people in your party, but 8,500 Ft ($38) for a double room is average. Standard private rooms are also available in Hollókő, though credit cards aren't accepted for these. The best information office is the **Foundation of Hollókő,** at Kossuth Lajos út. 68 (© **32/579-010**). In summer it's open weekdays 8am to 8pm, weekends 10am to 6pm; in winter it's open weekdays 8am to 5pm, weekends 10am to 4pm. Additional information is available through **Nograd Tourist** in Salgótarján (© **32/310-660**) or **Tourinform** in Szécsény, at Ady Endre u. 12 (© **32/370-777**); you can also book all accommodations in advance through these agencies.

The most direct way to reach Hollókő is by bus from Budapest's central bus station, Népstadion bus station (© **1/219-8080**), from where the only direct bus to Hollókő departs. It leaves daily at 8:30am, and the trip takes about 2½ hours. The fare is 1,240 Ft ($5.60). Alternatively, you can take a bus from Árpád híd bus station (© **1/320-9229** or 1/317-9886) to Szécsény or Pásztó, where you switch to a local bus to Hollókő, of which there are four daily.

10

Copenhagen & Helsingør

by Darwin Porter & Danforth Prince

Copenhagen, with a quarter of tiny Denmark's population, is an eminently livable capital. Scandinavia's largest city is also one of its most inviting, filled with Danes who are well educated, are English-speaking, and know how to combine urban sophistication with the friendly charm of village life.

Copenhagen (the name means "merchants' harbor") marks the passage between the Baltic and the North seas, sitting on the eastern coast of the island of Sjælland, with Norway to the northwest and Sweden to the east (Denmark once ruled both). It's one of northern Europe's busiest ports, with a vast harbor. The medieval ramparts that came down in the mid–19th century were transformed into breezy lakes, and canals thread through the old city. Slotsholmen, where København was founded in 1167 and where Christiansborg Palace stands today, is actually an island within the island.

No wonder the city's most immediately identifiable symbol is *The Little Mermaid,* or *Den Lille Havfrue.*

Copenhagen's charms sneak up on you gradually and cumulatively. There are plenty of cobblestone streets, squares, and neighborhoods to explore, plus a wide selection of fine museums, royal palaces, parks, and varied nightlife. Tivoli, the great-great-great-granddaddy of amusement parks (it opened in 1843), is an integral part of Copenhagen's urban scene. When the weather is fine, the canalside sidewalks in Nyhavn and along bustling Strøget, a mile-long pedestrian artery, are jammed with cafe tables where Danes and visitors sit, drink, and make merry.

Copenhagen is that rarest of treasures: a big city that hasn't lost its heart.

For more on Copenhagen and its environs, see *Frommer's Denmark* or *Frommer's Scandinavia.*

1 Essentials

ARRIVING

BY PLANE   Copenhagen's **Kastrup Airport** (© 45/3231-3231) is 12km (7¼ miles) from the city center. The Danske Bank in the arrivals hall is open Monday to Friday 6:30am to 10:30pm and Saturday and Sunday 6am to 10pm. In the airport you'll also find a bar/cafe, a small market, duty-free shops, lockers, car-rental counters, and an information desk.

A direct **train,** leaving from the arrivals hall, connects the airport with Central Station (København Hovedbanegården) every 20 minutes from 4:40am (5am on Sat and Sun) to 12:40am; the 12-minute trip costs 23DKK ($3.50) one-way. A **taxi** charges about 140DKK to 170DKK ($22–$27) for the same trip, which takes about 20 minutes.

Value Budget Bests

Copenhagen is an expensive city, but full of bargains. **Tivoli,** the biggest draw, provides one of Copenhagen's cheapest thrills: Adults can get in for 55DKK to 65DKK ($8.60–$10), and kids for half that. You can see Copenhagen's most famous sight, *The Little Mermaid* statue (p. 348), for free. The **Carlsberg Brewery tour** (p. 357), which includes samples of Denmark's best-known beer, is informative, fun, and also free. **Boat tours** (p. 356) of Copenhagen's busy harbor cost 130DKK ($20). And if you're looking for culture, you can attend a world-class **opera** or a **ballet** at the Royal Theater (p. 358) for as little as 30DKK ($4.70).

BY TRAIN   Copenhagen's **Central Station (København Hovedbanegården; ℭ 33-14-17-01**) is relatively easy to negotiate. Shops and self-service eateries are in the center, with more shops, restaurants, banks, ticket windows, and platform entrances around the perimeter; lockers and a baggage checkroom are on the lowest level. Den Danske Bank **currency exchange office,** on the station's platform side, is open daily 8am to 9pm. Commission rates are 20DKK ($3.10) for a cash transaction or per traveler's check, so you'll save money by changing large denominations. May 28 to September 10, holders of InterRail cards and Eurail Youthpasses can shower for 10DKK ($1.55) at the **Interrail Centre,** a popular meeting point for backpackers open daily 6:30 to 10pm; the center is closed in the off season.

The city's **subway (S-tog)** lines converge at Central Station. **Buses** stop outside, where there's also a **taxi** rank.

BY FERRY   Ferries from Malmö and Helsinborg, Sweden, arrive and depart from the ferry terminal at **Havnegade** by Nyhavn. Each of the following ferry companies has its own booking office at the terminal: **Scandlines** (ℭ **33-15-15-15**), **HH Ferries** (ℭ **49-26-01-55**), and **Zonebusserne** (ℭ **49-21-22-01**). Ferries from Norway arrive and depart just north of the Sweden terminal at Kvæsthusbroen; **DFDS,** Sundkrogsgade 11 (ℭ **33-42-30-00;** www.dfdsseaways. com), provides daily ferry service between Copenhagen and Oslo. Both terminals are within easy walking distance of Kongens Nytorv, where you can pick up bus no. 1 or the new Metro, Kongens Nytorv, to Central Station.

VISITOR INFORMATION

TOURIST OFFICES   **Copenhagen Tourist Information** is near Tivoli's main entrance at Bernstorffsgade 1 (ℭ **70-22-24-42;** fax 70-32-24-52; www.visitcopenhagen.dk; S-tog: Central Station). The most useful publication here is the free monthly *Copenhagen This Week* (www.ctw.dk), also available in hotels and other spots around town. The staff can provide details on everything from hostels and hotels to night life, day trips, and longer excursions. You can also buy gifts, postcards, and stamps. Hours are September to October Monday to Saturday 9am to 4pm; November to April Saturday 9am to 2pm.

Use It, on the first floor at Rådhusstræde 13, 2 blocks northwest of Gammel Torv Square off Strøget (ℭ **33-73-06-20;** fax 33-73-06-49; www.useit.dk; bus: 29), offers excellent services and help for young people and budget travelers of all ages. *Playtime,* with details on low-cost restaurants, hotels, and sightseeing, plus a city map, is the most useful of its many free publications. Use It also offers free Internet access, a room-finding service, and a free locker for a day, with a

Copenhagen Deals & Discounts

SPECIAL DISCOUNTS   The **Copenhagen Card** admits you to nearly all museums in the city and environs, offers unlimited use of buses and trains (including trips to Helsingør, Roskilde, Hillerød, and Rungsted-lund), and gives discounts on various sightseeing activities. It's good for 3 days and costs 395DKK ($62) for adults, 225DKK ($35) for children ages 10 to 15. You can buy the card at Central Station's DSB ticket office, the tourist office (see "Visitor Information," below), and many hotels and S-tog stations.

By flashing an **International Student Identification Card (ISIC)**, young people can get discounts at most of the city's museums, at some concert halls, and on planes, trains, and ferries from Denmark. **People over 67** are entitled to half-price tickets at the Royal Theater, reduced admission to many museums, and discounts on ferry trips to Sweden. Check the listings throughout this chapter for more information on student and senior rates.

WORTH A SPLURGE   A trip to the **Louisiana Museum of Modern Art** 𝕸𝕸𝕸 in Humlebæk in North Zealand is memorable; both the museum and its grounds serve as settings for major works of modern art. If you are a fan of Danish author Karen Blixen *(Out of Africa),* you can visit the **Karen Blixen Museum** 𝕸𝕸 in Rungstedlund; it's the family house where she lived and worked after returning from Africa. And you should definitely make a side trip to Roskilde to see the fascinating **Viking Ship Museum** 𝕸𝕸𝕸, the repository of five Viking ships. One of Denmark's top tourist attractions is **Kronborg Castle** 𝕸𝕸 in Helsingør (Elsinore), where Hamlet and his family allegedly played out their days. And castle lovers won't want to miss **Frederiksborg Castle** 𝕸𝕸𝕸 in Hillerød, one of Denmark's greatest historic structures. For more details, see "Side Trips: Helsingør & More," p. 359.

50DKK ($7.80) refundable deposit. June 15 to September 15, it's open daily 9am to 7pm; the rest of the year, hours are Monday to Wednesday 11am to 4pm, Thursday 11am to 6pm, and Friday 11am to 2pm.

WEBSITES   For information on the Net, check out **www.visitdenmark.com**, the Danish Tourist Board's site; or **www.visitcopenhagen.dk**, the Copenhagen Convention and Visitors Bureau's site.

CITY LAYOUT

Nearly everything of interest in Copenhagen occupies a central oval-shaped area bounded to the east by the harbor and to the west by a series of lakes and parks. This entire inner-city area is idyllic for walking and biking.

Life in central Copenhagen revolves around **Strøget** (*Stro*-yet), a vibrant mile-long pedestrian thoroughfare composed of several interconnected streets: Øster-gade, Amagertorv, Vimmelskaftet, Nygade, and Frederiksberggade. Several more pedestrian streets, including **Købmagergade** and **Kompagnistræde,** branch off from Strøget or run parallel to it. Strøget's eastern terminus is **Kongens Nytorv (King's Square),** site of the Royal Theater and the beginning of **Nyhavn**—once

Copenhagen's wild sailors' quarter but now a busy pedestrian area known for its cafes and restaurants. The "New Town" area, with Amalienborg Palace, lies to the north of Nyhavn; this section of Copenhagen was laid out on a grid plan by Christian IV in the 17th century.

Strøget's western terminus opens onto the vast **Rådhuspladsen (Town Hall Square),** presided over by the massive red brick Rådhus (Town Hall). From here, **Vesterbrogade,** a wide busy avenue, runs west past **Tivoli** amusement park and Central Station and into the lovely residential area of **Frederiksberg,** filled with cafes, shops, parks, and B&Bs.

The small island of **Slotsholmen,** a few blocks south of Strøget, is home to Christiansborg Palace, the National Library, and a number of museums. It's where Copenhagen was founded in the 12th century. Across the harbor are the islands of **Amager,** a working-class area; and **Christianshavn,** known as "Little Amsterdam" and home of **Christiania,** an "alternative" free city claimed by squatters in the 1970s.

GETTING AROUND

The compact city center and many pedestrian thoroughfares make walking a breeze. *Playtime,* a free booklet distributed by Use It (see "Visitor Information," above), describes a number of intriguing walking tours. There's virtually no violent street crime in Copenhagen, so you should feel safe at any hour, although the usual precautions are advised.

BY SUBWAY (S-TOG) & BUS   Copenhagen is served by an extensive **bus** and **subway** network. Regular service begins daily at 5am (6am on Sun) and continues until 12:30am. At other times, a limited night-bus service departs from Town Hall Square. Fares are based on a zone system, and most destinations in central Copenhagen cost the minimum 15DKK ($2.35). Buses and subways use the same tickets, and for up to an hour you can transfer between the two.

The subway—called the **S-tog**—works on the honor system. Either pay your fare in the station from which you're departing, or stamp your own strip ticket in the yellow box on the platform. Similarly, when you board a bus, either pay the driver or stamp your ticket in the machine. Beware: Fines for fare dodging are stiff. Bus drivers are helpful and most speak English. If you plan to do a lot of traveling by train or bus, buy a **10-ticket strip (Klippekort)** for 95DKK ($15) or a **24-hour ticket** for 90DKK ($14). You can purchase tickets on buses and at all rail stations. Children under 12 ride for half price; those under 7 ride free. The value-packed **Copenhagen Card** (see "Copenhagen Deals & Discounts," above) allows for unlimited use of public transportation.

Dial © **36-13-14-15** (www.ht.dk) for bus information and © **33-14-17-01** (www.s-tog.dk) for S-tog information.

BY METRO   In 2002, Copenhagen launched its first Metro line, taking passengers from east to west across the city or vice versa. The line is not complete but some phases are operational, including Vanløse Ørestad/Vestamager, linking the heart of Copenhagen and the southeastern branch as far as Lergravsparken. All stations have elevators and escalators. Nørreport is the transfer station to the S-tog system, the commuter rail link to the suburbs. The plan is to run Metro trains every 2 minutes during rush hours and every 15 minutes in the late evening. Fares will be integrated into the existing zonal system (see "By Subway [S-tog] & Bus" above).

BY BICYCLE Scenic, flat Copenhagen is ideal for biking, which is the easiest way to get around the inner city. About half of all Danes ride regularly. May to mid-December, the free bike service **City Bike (Bycyklen)** offers about 1,300 bikes in 125 locked racks around Copenhagen. To release one, insert a 20DKK ($3.10) coin; when you're finished, return the bike to any available rack, and you get your money back. You can use the bikes in the inner city only, you can't lock them with your own lock, and at night you need your own lights.

You can rent a three-speed at **Dan Wheel Rent a Bike,** Colbjørnsensgade 3, across from Weber's Hotel (© **33-21-22-27;** S-tog: Central Station), ranging from 50DKK ($7.80) for a day to 225DKK ($35) for a week, with a 300DKK ($47) refundable deposit. It's open Monday to Friday 9 to 11am and 4 to 5:30pm and Saturday and Sunday 9am to 2pm. You can also rent three-speed, sports, and mountain bikes at **Københavns Cykelbørs,** Gothersgade 157 (© **33-14-07-17;** Metro: Nørreport), open Monday to Friday 8:30am to 5:30pm and Saturday 10am to 1:30pm; and from **Østerport Cykler,** Oslo Plads 9 (© **33-33-85-13;** S-tog: Østerport), open Monday to Friday 8am to 6pm and Saturday 9am to 1pm.

BY TAXI The initial taxi fare for up to four people is 23DKK ($3.60), then about 10DKK ($1.55) per kilometer 4am to 4pm; 11DKK ($1.70) 4pm to 6am; and 13DKK ($2.05) on Saturday and Sunday. You can pay by credit card, with no tip expected. An available cab displays the word FRI. To order a taxi in advance, dial © **70/25-25-25** or 38/77-77-77.

Country & City Codes

The **country code** for Denmark is **45**. The **city code** is an integral part of each telephone number. To reach any phone in Denmark, just dial all eight digits of the number.

BY HARBOR FERRY   The city's "harbor buses" are ferries that sail among several harbor stops (Nordre Toldbod near *The Little Mermaid,* Holmen, Nyhavn, Knippelsbro, and the Royal Library). Tickets cost 50DKK ($7.80) adults, 20DKK ($3.10) children, and are available on board; you can also use these tickets, valid for an hour, on buses and trains. The ferries sail every 30 minutes from early morning to about 7pm.

BY RENTAL CAR   Unless you're planning an extended trip outside Copenhagen, you'll find that keeping a car here is more trouble than it's worth. High parking rates, lots of pedestrian-only streets, and one-way traffic systems help discourage inner-city driving. But if you need a car to leave the city, most major U.S. car-rental firms, including **Hertz** (© 33-17-90-20) and **Avis** (© 33-15-22-99), have offices in Copenhagen and at the airport. Compare big-company prices with those charged by local companies such as **Budget/Pitzner** (© 33-55-70-00) and **Lejtlig (Rent-a-Wreck)** at © 39-29-85-05.

Note: You get the best deal if you arrange the rental before leaving home.

In Denmark, drivers must use their lights at all times, even in daytime, and all occupants of the car, including those in the back seat, must buckle their seat belts.

FAST FACTS: Copenhagen

American Express   American Express is represented throughout Denmark by **Neiman & Schultz,** Nansens (© 33-13-11-81), with a branch in Terminal 3 of the Copenhagen Airport. Fulfilling all the functions of American Express except foreign-exchange services, the main office is open Monday through Thursday from 8:30am to 4:30pm, and Friday from 8:30am to 4pm. The airport office remains open till 8:30pm Monday through Friday. On weekends, and overnight on weekdays, a recorded message, in English, will deliver the phone number of a 24-hour Amex service in Stockholm. This is useful for anyone who has lost a card or traveler's checks. As for foreign exchange, you'll find Neiman & Schultz offices scattered throughout Copenhagen, including a branch that's open 24 hours a day at the railway station.

ATMs   In Denmark, ATMs are also known as "open-air changemakers." You'll find them all over Copenhagen, including inside Central Station (Den Danske Bank).

Babysitters   HH-Babysitting (© 70-20-81-51) charges 40DKK ($6.25) per hour, plus a 40DKK ($6.25) fee. The minimum charge during the day is 3 hours and in the evening 3 hours. Reserve daily 6:30am to 10pm.

Banks   Banks are usually open Monday to Friday 9:30am to 4pm (to 6pm Thurs). Danish banks charge 20DKK ($3.10) per traveler's check for currency exchange, with a minimum 40DKK ($6.25) fee. If you exchange cash, you pay only one fee per transaction. **Forex,** the currency exchange service at the train station, is open daily 8am to 9pm and charges a lower commission than the banks do.

Business Hours **Shops** are usually open Monday to Thursday 9am to 6pm (department stores to 7pm), Friday from 9am to 7 or 8pm, Saturday 9am to 3pm (to 5pm the 1st Sat of the month); shops in the train station stay open later. **Offices** are open Monday to Friday 9 or 10am to 4 or 5pm.

Currency The Danish currency is the **krone (crown),** or **kroner** (designated as **DKK**) in its plural form, made up of 100 øre. Banknotes are issued in 50DKK, 100DKK, 200DKK, 500DKK, and 1,000DKK. Coins come in 25 and 50 øre, and 1DKK, 2DKK, 5DKK, 10DKK, and 20DKK; the 1DKK, 2DKK, and 5DKK coins have a hole in the center.

The rate of exchange used to calculate the dollar values given in this chapter is $1 = about 6.37DKK (or 1DKK = 15¢).

Dentists Emergency care is provided by **Tandlægevagten,** Oslo Plads 14 (© **35-38-02-51;** S-tog: Østerport). The office is open Monday to Friday 8am to 9:30pm and Saturday, Sunday, and holidays 10am to noon. Fees are paid in cash.

Doctors To reach a doctor Monday to Friday 8am to 4pm, dial © **33-93-63-00;** at other times, call © **70-13-00-41.** Doctors' fees are paid in cash.

Embassies Denmark's capital is home to many embassies, including those of the **United States,** Dag Hammerskjölds Allé 24 (© **35-55-31-44;** bus: 1 or 6); **Canada,** Kristen Bernikowsgade 1 (© **33-48-32-00;** bus: 28); the **United Kingdom,** Kastelsvej 36–40 (© **35-44-52-00;** bus: 1 or 6); **Ireland,** Østbanegade 21 (© **35-42-32-33;** S-tog: Østerport); and **Australia,** Strandboulevarden 122 (© **39-29-20-77;** bus: 40).

Emergencies Dial © **112** for **police, fire,** or **ambulance** service. No coins are needed when dialing from a public phone.

Holidays Copenhagen celebrates New Year's Day (Jan 1), Maundy Thursday (Thurs before Easter), Good Friday, Easter Sunday and Monday, Common Prayer Day (late Apr), Ascension Day, Whitsunday and Monday (mid-May), Constitution Day (June 5), Christmas Eve (Dec 24), and Christmas Day (Dec 25). All major businesses, museums, and even some restaurants are closed on these days.

Hospitals Even foreigners staying temporarily in Denmark are entitled to free hospital care in the event of an emergency. **Bispebjerg,** Bispebjerg Bakke 23 (© **35-31-23-73;** bus: 10, 21), is the most centrally located hospital with an emergency ward. For an ambulance, dial © **112.**

Internet Access To check your e-mail or to send messages, go to **Copenhagen Hovebibliotek,** Krystalgade 15 (© **33-73-60-60;** bus: 14 or 16), open Monday through Friday from 10am to 7pm, Saturday from10am to 2pm. Access is free.

Laundry & Dry Cleaning Look for the word *vask* (wash), such as *møntvask* or *vaskeri*. **Quickvask,** Istedgade 45 at Absalomsgade (no phone; S-tog: Central Station), is open daily 7am to 9pm. For dry cleaning, go to **Zens Vask,** Vester Farimagsgade 3 (© **33-12-45-45;** S-tog: Central Station), open daily 8am to 6pm.

Mail **Post offices** are usually open Monday to Saturday 8am to 6pm. Letters and postcards (up to 50g/1.7 oz.) cost 6.25DKK ($1) to North America and Australia and 5.25DKK (80¢) to other countries in Europe. You can receive mail marked *Poste Restante* at the **Main Post Office,** Tietgensgade 39, DK-1570 Copenhagen V (© **33-41-56-00**), open Monday to Friday 11am to 6pm, and Saturday 10am to 1pm. The post office in **Central Station** is open Monday to Friday 8am to 9pm, Saturday 9am to 4pm, and Sunday 10am to 4pm.

Newspapers & Magazines For comprehensive performance listings, pick up a free copy of *What's On in Copenhagen,* available at the tourist office (see "Visitor Information," p. 330). The *Copenhagen Post,* an English-language newspaper available at newsstands on Friday, also has a listing of current city events.

Pharmacy Apotek is the word for "pharmacy," and most are open the same hours as shops. **Steno Apotek,** Vesterbrogade 6C (© **33-14-82-66;** S-tog: Central Station), is a 24-hour pharmacy.

Police In an emergency, dial © **112** from any phone—no coins are needed. For other police matters, call **Police Headquarters,** Polititorvet (© **33-14-14-48**).

Tax Denmark's 25% **value-added tax,** called MOMS (pronounced "mumps" and every bit as painful), is usually included in the prices quoted for hotel rates and on restaurant menus. Many stores offer you the opportunity to reclaim sales tax on purchases over 300DKK ($38).

Telephone Making a **local telephone call** costs a minimum of 5DKK (80¢) for about 2 minutes; a tone sounds when you have to add more coins. On older phones, deposit coins before dialing; although unused coins aren't returned even if you reach a busy signal, they're credited toward another call. On newer phones, wait for the answering party to pick up before inserting money.

There are also phones equipped to take **phone cards.** Plastic phone cards for 30DKK ($4.70), 50DKK ($7.80), and 100DKK ($16) are sold at post offices and newsstands; insert the card in the vertical slit, and time is deducted automatically. *Note:* It costs five times as much—maybe more— to make a local call from a hotel room as it does from a pay phone, which you can usually find in the hotel lobby.

To reach local **directory assistance,** dial © **118.** You can get free **long-distance assistance** by phoning © **80-60-40-55.** To make a **collect call,** dial © **80-60-40-50** and wait for the operator. You can reach a U.S. operator with an **AT&T** calling card by dialing © **800/CALL-ATT.** For **MCI** dial © **800/888-8000.**

Tipping A 15% service charge is included in most restaurant bills. If service has been extraordinary, you might want to round up the bill.

2 Affordable Places to Stay

In the very heart of Copenhagen, it's difficult to find decent and reasonably priced accommodations. During the summer, affordable housing is often booked well in advance (especially during national vacations in early Aug and the jazz festival in late July), so be sure you have reservations. The most

Value Getting the Best Deal on Accommodations

- Try reserving a room in a private home: It costs about half the price of a room in a hotel, and you'll have the chance to get better acquainted with Copenhageners.
- Seek out the hotels immediately southwest of Central Station, along Colbjørnsensgade and Helgolandsgade (off Istedgade). Although many are beyond our budget, some offer excellent values. The area is still a little seedy, with a smattering of porn shops, but it's safe.
- Ask for a room without a private bathroom; you usually get a sink in the room, and the bathroom is just down the hall.

economical way to stay here is by renting a room in a private home, but there are some modestly priced hostels and hotels as well.

The **Accommodation Service (Værelseanvisning),** beside Tivoli's main entrance at Bernstorffsgade 1 (© **70-22-24-42;** fax 70-22-24-52), specializes in booking rooms in private homes, most 10 to 15 minutes by bus or S-tog from the city center, with rates rarely over 190DKK ($30) per person, without breakfast. It also works with some of the best hotels, selling same-day space that would otherwise remain empty. There's a 50DKK ($7.80) fee per room and a deposit required at the time of booking. May to September 14, the desk is open daily 9am to 8pm; September 15 to April, office hours are Monday to Friday 9am to 4:30pm and Saturday 9am to 1:30pm.

Use It (see "Visitor Information," p. 330) can provide a rundown on budget accommodations, and posts last-minute rooming possibilities on its bulletin board. It can also store luggage and hold mail. June 15 to September 15, the office is open daily 9am to 7pm; the rest of the year, hours are Monday to Wednesday 11am to 4pm, Thursday 11am to 6pm, and Friday 11am to 2pm.

Note: You'll find the lodging choices below plotted on the map on p. 350.

PRIVATE HOMES

All the hosts below speak English. There's a strong network among hosts, so if one is booked, he or she can direct you to another. It's important to call ahead to make certain the room is available and to let the hosts know when you'll be arriving. (They have lives, too.) Don't just show up at the door.

IN THE CENTER

Hotel Løven *Value*   Less than a 5-minute walk from the Central Station, this is one of the best budget bets in the heart of the city; it grew from an inn that stood here in 1840. In an old apartment house, the B&B has greatly expanded, offering small and no-frills rooms that, although basic, are decently maintained. Some units are large enough to house three to six guests. Bathrooms with showers have been added to most of the rooms. All guests have use of a kitchen.

Vesterbrogade 30, DK-1620 København. © **21-80-67-20.** Fax 33-79-67-30. www.loeven.com. 50 units, 40 with bathroom. 450DKK ($70) single without bathroom; 550DKK ($86) single with bathroom; 500DKK ($78) double without bathroom; 590DKK ($92) double with bathroom; 245DKK–275DKK ($38–$43) per person in multi-bed room. Extra bed 200DKK–250DKK ($31–$39). AE, DC, MC, V. Bus: 6A. *In room:* TV (on request), no phone.

Margrethe Kaae Christensen 🏖 Ms. Christensen's third-floor apartment in a century-old building is about as close as you can get to living at Amalienborg Palace, 45m (148 ft.) away. The Blue Room has its own sink and a double bed, and the Rose Room its own entrance and two single beds; the two rooms share a bathroom with a tub/shower. Coffee, bread, cheese, and jam are provided for breakfast. Next door is a good budget restaurant, the Amalienborg Special (p. 346).

Amaliegade 26, DK-1256 København. ©/fax **33-13-68-61**. b-b.dk.cph@kaae.com. 2 units, none with bathroom. 400DKK ($62) single; 500DKK ($78) double. Extra bed 150DKK ($23). Rates include breakfast. No credit cards. Bus: 1, 6, or 9. *In room:* TV, coffeemaker, no phone.

Solveig Diderichsen Ms. Diderichsen's seven-room apartment across from Øster Anlæg Park is more than 100 years old, with high ceilings, pine floors, and large rooms. The two comfortable doubles share a big bathroom with a tub/shower and a separate toilet. Breakfast isn't included, but you can store your own food in the guest refrigerator. Nearby are a bakery, a grocery store, and ethnic restaurants; the Botanical Garden is a 5-minute walk away.

Upsalegade 26, DK-2100 København. © **35-43-39-58**. Fax 35-43-22-70. Diderichsen@nypost.dk. 2 units, none with bathroom. 350DKK ($55) single; 400DKK ($62) double. No credit cards. S-tog: Østerport. Bus: 1, 6, or 9. *In room:* TV, coffeemaker, no phone.

Turid Aronsen 🏖 Only a block from Strøget, this apartment is in a 200-year-old building that has been completely modernized. The two large guest rooms are quintessentially Scandinavian, with pine floors and wood trim. They're adjacent to a well-maintained tiled bathroom with a shower. Ms. Aronsen, a former chef, has built up a loyal clientele over the years. Brolægerstræde is around the corner from Use It (see "Visitor Information," p. 330).

Brolægerstræde 13, DK-1211 København. © **33-14-31-46**. 2 units with shared bathroom. 250DKK ($39) single; 350DKK ($55) double. No credit cards. Bus: 6. *In room:* Fridge, coffeemaker, no phone.

IN FREDERIKSBERG

Hanne Løye 🏖 This suburban villa, built in 1928, maintains its original features. The second-floor rooms are filled with period furnishings and exude old-fashioned gentility. Ms. Løye, who's an actress, doesn't offer breakfast or a kitchen, but each room comes with plates, cups, and silverware; bakeries, restaurants, and a supermarket are nearby. The shared bathroom features a sunken tub with shower. There are no singles. The villa is surrounded by old shrubs and trees and an overgrown garden that adds a touch of romance.

Ceresvej 1, DK-1863 Frederiksberg. © **33-24-30-27**. 3 units, none with bathroom. 360DKK ($56) double. Extra bed 180DKK ($28). No credit cards. Bus: 14 or 15. *In room:* Coffeemaker, no phone.

ON AMAGER

Gitte Kongstad 🏖 *Kids* On the island of Amager, across the harbor from central Copenhagen, is this 100-year-old brick house with two cheerful apartments ideal for couples and families. Each apartment (one on the 2nd floor, one on the 3rd) offers a bedroom, a sitting room, a kitchen, and a toilet. There's a well-maintained shower room in the basement. Tea and coffee are provided, as are cooking utensils. This might be the only place in Copenhagen that provides free bikes (you can pedal into town in 10 min.). In warm weather, you can enjoy the compact garden and the barbecue. Two children's playgrounds are across the street.

Badensgade 2, DK-2300 København. © **32-97-71-97**. g.kongstad@post.tele.dk. 3 units. 450DKK ($70) double. Extra person 150DKK ($23). No credit cards. Bus: 2A. Metro: Lergravsvej. *In room:* TV, dataport, kitchen, no phone.

HOTELS
NEAR CENTRAL STATION

Absalon Hotel ★️   Since 1938, the Nedergaard family has been welcoming guests to its hotel, which has grown and expanded over the years in the neighborhood near the rail station. Today the hotel is a combination of a government-rated three-star hotel with private bathrooms, plus a one-star annex without private bathrooms, the two hotels sharing the same entrance and reception. You can stay here in comparative luxury or at budget prices, depending on your accommodations choice. Most bedrooms are medium in size or even somewhat cramped, but all of them are comfortably furnished and well maintained. If you want to stay here luxuriously, opt for one of the large and elegantly furnished top floor rooms in a classical English or else French Louis XIV style.

Helgolandsgade 15, DK-1653. København. (© **33-24-22-11.** Fax 33-24-34-11. www.absalon-hotel.dk. 166 units. Absalon Hotel (with private bathroom) May–Sept 1,235DKK–1,700DKK ($193–$265) double; Oct–Apr 995DKK–1,525DKK ($155–$238) double. Annex (without private bathroom) May–Sept 725DKK ($113) double; Oct–Apr 600DKK ($94) double. Rates include breakfast. AE, DC, MC, V. Closed Dec 19–Jan 2. Bus: 6, 10, 16, 27, or 28. **Amenities:** Breakfast room; lounge; laundry service/dry cleaning; nonsmoking rooms. *In room:* TV, dataport (some rooms), fridge (some rooms), hair dryer (some rooms), safe (some rooms).

Apartment Hotel Valberg   Simple but well kept, this five-story hotel in a charming building from 1903 is about a 10-minute walk from the Central Railroad Station. Renovated in 2003 into apartment-style rooms, each unit now features a kitchenette and bathroom. Breakfast is the only meal served.

Sønder Blvd. 53, DK-1720 København. (© **33-25-25-19.** Fax 33-25-25-83. www.valberg.dk. 15 units. 1,100DKK ($172) double. Extra bed 200DKK ($31). Rates include breakfast. DC, DISC, MC, V. Bus: 10. **Amenities:** Lounge. *In room:* TV, kitchenette, hair dryer.

Hotel Ansgar *(Kids)*   This five-story hotel was built in 1885, but its comfortable, cozy rooms have modern Danish furniture. A dozen large rooms that can accommodate up to six are perfect for families and are available at negotiable rates. All units contain well-kept bathrooms with shower units. You'll often find free parking outside the hotel after 6pm. Guests arriving at Katstrup Airport can take the SAS bus to the Air Terminal at the Central Railroad Station, walk through the station, and be inside the hotel in less than 4 minutes.

Colbjørnsensgade 29, DK-1652 København. (© **33-21-21-96.** Fax 33-21-61-91. www.ansgar-hotel.dk. 81 units. 995DKK–1,200DKK ($155–$187) double. 200DKK ($31) extra bed. Rates include breakfast. AE, DC, MC, V. Bus: 2A, 6, 10, 28, or 41. **Amenities:** Breakfast room; lounge; laundry service/dry cleaning; nonsmoking rooms. *In room:* TV.

Hotel Nebo   Restored in 2003, the Nebo offers very basic small rooms right next to Central Station. Units in front can be noisy. Bathrooms are immaculately maintained and contain shower units. This modest hotel from the 1930s is owned and operated by the Church of Denmark, so it doesn't attract a rowdy crowd, and the staff is helpful. Breakfast is an all-you-can-eat buffet, which you can enjoy in the garden in summer.

Istedgade 6-8, DK-1653 København. (© **33-21-12-17.** Fax 33-23-47-74. www.nebo.dk. 84 units, 48 with bathroom. Apr–Sept 460DKK ($72) single without bathroom, 760DKK ($119) single with bathroom, 690DKK ($108) double without bathroom, 860DKK–1,260DKK ($134–$197) double with bathroom; Oct–Mar 430DKK ($67) single without bathroom, 690DKK ($108) single with bathroom, 560DKK ($87) double without bathroom, 760DKK–1,200DKK ($119–$187) double with bathroom. Extra bed 150DKK ($23). Rates include buffet breakfast. AE, DC, MC, V. S-tog: Central Station. **Amenities:** Breakfast room. *In room:* TV (some units).

Saga Hotel ★️ *(Kids)*   Long a Frommer's favorite, the Saga offers comfortable rooms (several larger ones suitable for families), a good breakfast, and a 5% discount off the rates below for our readers. (Mention Frommer's when booking your room.) All the rooms are unique and nicely furnished. Those with bathrooms have big showers, and some have tub/shower combinations. The friendly reception staff—knowledgeable about Copenhagen and ways to save money—welcomes a congenial group of all ages and nationalities.

Colbjørnsensgade 18–20 (a block from Central Station), DK-1652 København. ℂ **33-24-49-44.** Fax 33-24-60-33. www.sagahotel.dk. 79 units, 29 with bathroom. 380DKK–550DKK ($59–$86) single without bathroom, 475DKK–795DKK ($74–$124) single with bathroom; 480DKK–750DKK ($75–$117) double without bathroom, 600DKK–920DKK ($94–$144) double with bathroom. Extra bed 150DKK–200DKK ($23–$31). Rates include breakfast. AE, DC, MC, V. S-tog: Central Station. **Amenities:** Breakfast room; bar. *In room:* TV.

Selandia Hotel 🏰   This inviting small hotel occupies a corner building just 2 blocks from the train station. The neighborhood isn't particularly scenic, but the hotel from 1928 is immaculately kept and offers well-furnished rooms with soundproof windows. All the rooms have sinks; for those without bathrooms, the facilities are nearby. Deluxe units have full bathrooms and minibars. A buffet breakfast is served. Check out the hotel's website for special deals.

Helgolandsgade 12, DK-1653 København. ℂ **33-31-46-10.** Fax 33-31-46-09. www.hotel-selandia.dk. 87 units, 54 with bathroom. 450DKK–525DKK ($70–$82) single without bathroom, 640DKK–775DKK ($100–$121) single with bathroom; 540DKK–650DKK ($84–$101) double without bathroom, 740DKK–1,150DKK ($115–$179) double with bathroom. Extra bed 200DKK ($31). Children 4–12 half price; children under 4 stay free in parent's room. Rates include breakfast. AE, DC, MC, V. S-tog: Central Station. Bus: 10 or 26. Closed Dec 15–June 5. **Amenities:** Breakfast room; babysitting; laundry service/dry cleaning. *In room:* TV, minibar (some rooms), coffeemaker (some rooms), hair dryer (some rooms), safe, trouser press.

NEAR NØRREPORT STATION

Hotel Jørgensen   This most gay-friendly hotel in a city of gay-friendly hotels is a restored white stucco building, a former textbook publishing house in 1906. It opened on a busy boulevard in central Copenhagen in 1984 and became an instant hit, in no small part because of its helpful staff. Prices are reasonable, and the small to midsize bedrooms are conventional and well organized. Bathrooms, in those units that contain them, are well kept and contain shower/tub combinations. The 11 dormitory rooms each accommodate 6 to 14 guests and are segregated by gender.

Rømersgade 11, DK-København. ℂ **33-13-81-86.** Fax 33-15-51-05. www.hoteljoergensen.dk. 32 units, 11 dormitory units. 575DKK ($90) double without bathroom, 700DKK ($109) double with bathroom. Rates include breakfast. MC, V. Free parking. Bus: 14 or 16. **Amenities:** Breakfast room; lounge. *In room:* TV.

IN VESTERBRO

Hotel Sct. Thomas   This cozy hotel lies in a four-story building a block from Vesterbrogade. Each room is unique: The doubles are spacious (no. 12 especially), while the singles are small but adequate, and many look onto plant-filled courtyards. In the small sitting room, you can avail yourself of a TV, maps, brochures, and free coffee and tea. A pleasant restaurant is next door, and reasonably priced ethnic eateries are nearby.

Frederiksberg Allé 7 (a 15-min. walk from Central Station), DK-1621 København. ℂ **33-21-64-64.** Fax 33-25-64-60. www.hotelsctthomas.dk. 42 units, 8 with shower, 34 with bathroom. 400DKK–525DKK ($62–$82) single with shower, 500DKK–625DKK ($78–$98) single with bathroom; 600DKK–700DKK ($94–$109) double or twin with shower, 745DKK–845DKK ($116–$132) double or twin with bathroom. Extra bed 150DKK ($23). Rates include buffet breakfast. MC, V. Bus: 1, 6, 14, or 26. *In room:* TV, no phone.

IN FREDERIKSBERG

Hotel Cab-Inn Scandinavia 🏰 *Kids*   The Cab-Inn offers well-designed little rooms that resemble ship cabins, with everything built-in. In the doubles and triples, the second and third beds are bunks (with ladders). The compact bathrooms have toilets and showers. It's all very snug, but if you feel claustrophobic, you can head down to the lobby. Toiletries, snacks, and video rentals are available. If the hotel is full, it has an identical property, **Hotel Cab-Inn Copenhagen,** about a block away. Both have rooms designed for travelers in wheelchairs. From either one you can walk to central Copenhagen in 10 minutes.

Vodroffsvej 55, DK-1900 Frederiksberg. (*) 35 36 11 11. Fax 35-36-11-14. www.cab-inn.com. 201 units. 560DKK ($87) single; 730DKK ($114) double or twin; 900DKK ($140) triple; 1,070DKK ($167) family room for 4. Rates include buffet breakfast. AE, DC, MC, V. Parking 60DKK ($9.35). S-tog: Vesterport. Bus: 2A. **Amenities:** Lobby cafe; rooms for those w/limited mobility. *In room:* A/C, TV, coffeemaker.

A GAY B&B

Circuit Q Bed & Breakfast If you're gay or lesbian and want to stay in an inexpensive B&B, this is your best bet. The main apartment is perched high above Copenhagen harbor in a century-old building. The common areas are painted with bold colors and have lots of contemporary artwork. The rooms are much plainer, but everything is done well. Upstairs is a snug dorm area, used mostly during summer, and there's a rooftop terrace. Breakfast is served in your room, or you can cook your own meals in the kitchen. If you'd like more privacy, ask for one of the five small studio apartments (with TVs) in the Nyhavn area.

Christians Brygge 28 (5th floor), DK-1559 København. (*) 33-14-91-07 or 40-50-91-07. www.circuitq.dk. 8 dorm beds, none with bathroom; 14 units, none with bathroom; 5 studios. 165DKK ($26) dorm bed; 480DKK ($75) single; 540DKK ($84) double; 690DKK ($108) triple; 900–1,200DKK ($140–$187) studio. AE, MC, V. S-tog: Central Station. Bus: 48. **Amenities:** Shared kitchen; Finnish sauna; bike rental. *In room:* Fridge, no phone.

A HOSTEL

Copenhagen's hostels are open to visitors of all ages. Sleeping bags aren't permitted; you must supply your own sheet or rent one for about 35DKK ($5.45). In summer, reserve a bed in advance because hostels are popular with all kinds of travelers, including families. Throughout Denmark, a 3-day maximum stay is usual in summer. Holders of **International Youth Hostel Federation (IYHF)** cards receive lower rates; you can buy a card at any hostel for 160DKK ($25).

Bellahøj Vandrerhjem In a residential area northwest of the city center and across from a park, the Bellahøj offers a pleasant lobby lounge, a vending machine, four showers on each floor, and lockers (no kitchen). The hostel is open 24 hours, but the rooms are off limits 10am to 2pm, when they're cleaned. The rooms (a little on the drab and dingy side) contain 4, 6, or 13 beds each.

Herbergvejen 8, DK-2700 Brønshoj. (*) 38-28-97-15. Fax 38-89-02-10. 285 beds in 40 units. 95DKK ($15) per person with IYHF card; 135DKK ($21) without IYHF card. Buffet breakfast 45DKK ($7). MC, V. Closed Jan 2–Feb 3. Bus: 2A. **Amenities:** TV room; table-tennis room; coin-op laundry. *In room:* No phone.

WORTH A SPLURGE

Copenhagen Strand One of the city's most modern hotels, opened in 2000, lies within a pair of former brick-and-timber factories. The savvy architects retained as many of the old-fashioned details as they could. The medium-size rooms are filled with comfortable, contemporary-looking furnishings. The hotel is rated three stars by the Danish government, but frankly, all that it lacks for elevation into four-star status is a full-fledged restaurant.

Havnegade 37, DK-1058 København. (*) 33-48-99-00. Fax 33-48-99-01. www.copenhagenstrand.dk. 174 units. 1,595DKK ($249) double; from 2,795DKK ($436) suite. AE, DC, MC, V. Parking 113DKK ($18). Metro: Kongens Nytorv. **Amenities:** Bar; business center; 24-hr. room service; babysitting; laundry service/dry cleaning; nonsmoking rooms; rooms for those w/limited mobility. *In room:* TV, minibar, hair dryer.

Hotel Cosmopole Operated by a chain that manages several other Danish tourist hotels, the large but unpretentious Hotel Cosmopole comprises two connected 19th-century buildings identified as Cosmopole I and Cosmopole II.

Rooms are simple, efficient, and modern, and include well-kept bathrooms with shower-tub combinations. There's a bar on the premises, and Restaurant City, which serves Danish specialties, is next door.

Colbjørnsensgade 5–11, DK-1652 København. ⓒ **33-21-33-33.** Fax 33-31-33-99. www.choicehotels.dk. 230 units. 1,345DKK ($210) double. Rates include breakfast. Winter discounts available. AE, DC, MC, V. Bus: 6, 10, 16, 28, or 41. **Amenities:** Restaurant; bar; lounge; laundry service/dry cleaning; nonsmoking rooms. *In room:* TV.

Ibsens Hotel 🅐🅐   Ibsens provides an old-fashioned ambience in a 1906 restored building. It's definitely a cut above the Hotel Vestersøhus in terms of style, with antique wooden dressers and decorative cabinets in the rooms and halls. The rooms vary in size. The all-you-can-eat breakfast is served in a congenial dining room. Attached to the hotel is La Rocca restaurant (p. 347). The neighborhood is lively, with markets and shops, and nearby are Ørsteds Park, the Botanical Garden, and Strøget. If the hotel is booked, they'll send you to the **Hotel Kong Arthur,** on the same block (ⓒ **33-11-12-12**), with slightly higher rates.

Vendersgade 23, DK-1363 København. ⓒ **33-13-19-13.** Fax 33-13-19-16. www.ibsenshotel.dk. 118 units. 925DKK–1,025DKK ($144–$160) single; 1,100DKK–1,350DKK ($172–$211) double; 2,100DKK ($328) suite. Rates include breakfast. AE, DC, MC, V. S-tog: Nørreport. **Amenities:** Breakfast room; bar; nonsmoking rooms; rooms for those w/limited mobility. *In room:* TV.

Maritime Hotel   This modern hotel lies on a quiet street. It's near the harbor, a few blocks from Nyhavn, Kongens Nytorv, and Strøget. The airy and well-maintained rooms are good size, and most of the tiled bathrooms (installed in 1996) have showers, but a few contain tubs. On the top floor is a wide terrace overlooking the city and harbor.

Peder Skrams Gade 19, DK-1054 Copenhagen K. ⓒ **33-13-48-82.** Fax 33-15-03-45. www.hotel-maritime.dk. 64 units. 700DKK–1,200DKK ($109–$187) single; 800DKK–1,500DKK ($125–$234) double. Rates include buffet breakfast. AE, DC, MC, V. Bus: 650. **Amenities:** Breakfast room; laundry/dry cleaning; nonsmoking rooms. *In room:* TV, dataport.

3 Great Deals on Dining

If you're staying in a hotel, chances are the rates will include a self-serve **breakfast buffet.** These buffets almost invariably include bread, butter, jam, and boiled eggs, plus an assortment of cheeses, cold cuts, and herring. There's enough protein in these breakfasts to set you up for a good part of the day.

Many restaurants have a very reasonable lunch (sometimes dinner) special: On a sidewalk menu board, *tilbud* and *dagens ret* mean "special of the day." Denmark is known for its open-face sandwiches, *smørrebrød.* The word literally means "bread and butter," but *smørrebrød* is really bread with dozens of toppings—from a single slice of cheese to mounds of sweet shrimp. These sandwiches can be very artfully presented and are eaten with knife and fork. *Smørrebrød* are served in restaurants, but you'll also find sandwich shops where you can get them (more cheaply) for takeout. For lunch, some restaurants serve a typical **Danish buffet,** which begins with fish, then moves on to meat, cheese, fruit, and dessert; a new plate is provided for each course.

For a hot meal, a good choice for dinner (*aftensmad*) that's often offered as a special is *frikadeller* (small fried cakes of minced pork, onions, egg, and spices), served with generous portions of potato salad and pickled vegetables. *Mørbrad,* braised pork loin, is served with a cream sauce. Fresh fish, especially herring (*silde*), is popular and served in dozens of ways.

Danish bakeries are really great if you love freshly baked breads and rolls. *Grov birkes* are tasty nonsweet breakfast rolls. It's a Danish custom to have afternoon

> **Value Getting the Best Deal on Dining**
>
> • Look for low-cost eateries in the very center of Copenhagen (but avoid the tony Kongens Nytorv), and try the bistros in and around Copenhagen University.
> • Take advantage of smorgasbords and other all-you-can-eat restaurants along the Strøget. Although they're not particularly cheap, they can offer good value at lunchtime.
> • Look for ethnic restaurants for lower-cost meals—throughout the city you'll find Middle Eastern, Thai, Indonesian, and Indian restaurants.
> • Try the *tilbud* or *dagens ret*, the daily special, a filling meal offered for lunch and/or dinner at a discount price.
> • Stop for a snack at one of the *pølsevogn* (sausage wagons) parked on the large squares along Strøget—they sell hot grilled sausages costing around 20DKK ($2.50).
> • Search out small, inconspicuous places off the beaten path.

cake and coffee, either at home or at a cafe. Danish pastries *(wienerbrød)*, whichever ones you select, are rich and wonderful. (Napoleon's Hat is exceptional.)

No matter what you eat, however, you might want to follow the Danish custom of drinking a cold Carlsberg or Tuborg beer and an even colder shot of *akvavit*, a 76- to 90-proof potato-based schnapps. (The trade name is Aalborg, after the city in Jutland where it's distilled.) Half a liter of draft beer usually costs about 35DKK ($5.45); a shot of *akvavit* costs about the same.

Tax and tip are included in the price on the menu, and you're not expected to add anything extra. If the service has been great, round up the bill.

NEAR THE TOWN HALL

Feinsmækker LIGHT FARE/SNACKS   Cheese, hummus, roast beef, turkey, chicken, ham, salmon, and tuna are the popular *smørrebrød* fillings at this cozy cafe with half a dozen tables. All the sandwiches are jumbo and served on French bread. There's also fresh-squeezed orange, apple, and carrot juice; carrot cake (in winter); and all kinds of salads. Clients order their sandwiches and salads from a cafeteria-style line, then carry their selections to their tables on trays.

Lars Bjørnsstraede 7. ℂ **33-32-11-32.** Sandwiches 34DKK–38DKK ($5.30–$5.95); salads 44DKK ($6.85). No credit cards. Mon–Sat 10am–4:30pm. Bus: 8.

Husets Cafe ℛ *Value* DANISH/INTERNATIONAL/LIGHT FARE   An adjunct of Use It (see "Visitor Information," p. 330), this cafe serves well-prepared and inexpensive food in a laid-back hip atmosphere. You can choose the all-you-can-eat lunch buffet, a simple one-plate meal (burgers or sandwiches), or just a coffee. The cafe is used for weekly jazz concerts.

Rådhusstræde 13. ℂ **33-15-20-02.** Lunch buffet 45DKK–52DKK ($7–$8.10); sandwiches 25DKK–32DKK ($3.90–$5). MC, V. Daily 11am–midnight (kitchen closes at 2:30pm). S-tog: Central Station.

Kanal Caféen ℛ DANISH   Romantic, authentic, and always crowded with friendly locals, this is the place to go for *smørrebrød*. Even if you have to wait for a table, it's worth it. The waiter will hand you a list of more than 30 choices—everything from herring to roast beef to ham with fried egg—and you mark off what you want. Add a large Carlsberg or some cold Aalborg Jubileum schnapps to make the meal even more memorable. The restaurant is in a mid-1800s building on a canal behind the Parliament Building.

Fredriksholms Kanal 18 (a 2-min. walk from Christiansborg Palace). © **33-11-57-70.** Reservations recommended at lunch. Meals 40DKK–70DKK ($6.25–$11). DC, V. Mon–Sat 11am–7pm. Bus: 6 or 18.

Sabines Cafeteria LIGHT FARE/SNACKS   This undecorated place isn't a cafeteria, but a local cafe with a mixed crowd. Daily specials include smoked salmon, paprika chicken, smoked ham, and more. Copenhageners like to drop in after a movie for coffee and brandy. The food is substantial and adequately prepared without ever going beyond that.

Teglgårdsstræde 4. © **33-14-09-44.** Meals 45DKK–65DKK ($7–$10). No credit cards. Mon–Sat 10am–2am; Sun 2pm–1am. Metro or S-tog: Nørreport. Bus: 14.

OFF STRØGET

Cafe Kreutzberg 🐟 DANISH/LIGHT FARE   This hip cellar cafe/bar with lots of small tables serves generous portions of tasty though hardly exciting cuisine. The menu includes freshly made *smørrebrød*, chili, tapas, and salads with salmon, crab, and chicken. You place your order at the bar and the food is brought to your table. This place is popular with a young crowd and can get smoky. In summer, you can dine on the sidewalk.

Kompagnistræde 14A. © **33-93-48-50.** Main courses 49DKK–95DKK ($7.65–$15). MC, V. Mon–Thurs 10am–midnight; Fri–Sat 10am–2am; Sun noon–7pm. S-tog: Central Station.

Café Sorgenfri *Value* SANDWICHES   Don't come here expecting grand cuisine or even a menu with any particular variety. This place has thrived for 150 years selling beer, schnapps, and a medley of *smørrebrød* that appeal to virtually everyone's sense of workaday thrift. With only about 50 seats, the place is usually very crowded around the lunch hour, with somewhat more space mid-afternoon. Come here for an early dinner. Everything inside reeks of old-time Denmark, from the potted shrubs that adorn the facade to the well-oiled paneling that has witnessed many generations of Copenhageners selecting and enjoying sandwiches. Between two and four of the sandwiches might comprise a reasonable lunch, depending on your appetite. You'll find the cafe in the all-pedestrian shopping zone, in the commercial heart of town.

Brolæggerstræde 8. © **33-11-58-80.** Reservations recommended for groups of 4 or more. Smørrebrød 52FKK–145DKK ($8.10–$23). DC, MC, V. Daily 11am–9pm. Bus: 11 or 12.

Chili AMERICAN   Boisterous, informal, and with an American theme, this is the most recent incarnation of a once-famous 19th-century establishment known to many generations of Danes as Tokanten. Chili serves at least 17 versions of

---

Moments **Dining with the Danes**

For a really memorable dining experience, consider having supper with a Danish family. Anette Waeber is the organizer of **Meet the Danes,** Smallegade 20A (© **33-46-46-46;** www.meetthedanes.dk), a registry that matches visitors with residents. You tell her what your general interests are, and she'll find a compatible Danish family who'll have you over for a meal. The cost is about 225DKK ($28). You can also do this through the tourist office (see "Visitor Information," p. 330).

burgers, available in quarter- and half-pound sizes, whose descriptions read like a map of the world. Choices include Hawaii burgers (with pineapple and curry), English burgers (with bacon and fried eggs), French burgers (with mushrooms in cream sauce), Danish burgers (with fried onions), and all the Texas/chili combo you could want. Also available are sandwiches and grilled steak platters. Service is fast, and the ambience is unpretentious.

Vandkunsten 1. ⓒ **33-91-19-18.** Main courses 59DKK–155DKK ($9.20–$24); burgers and sandwiches 59DKK–100DKK ($9.20–$16). No credit cards. Mon–Sat 11am–midnight; Sun noon–11pm. Bus: 5, 6A, or 16.

Heaven ✿ DANISH/INTERNATIONAL This gay cafe/bar/restaurant on Kompagnistræde, a tony pedestrian street parallel to Strøget, is a celestial spot for everyone. As many straights as gays show up for the good economical lunches served in the first-floor cafe. All kinds of snacks and full meals are available, including omelets, salads, *frikadeller*, fried Camembert, and herring. The lounge area, frequented by a mostly gay clientele, is an elegant candlelit space.

Kompagnistræde 18. ⓒ **33-15-19-00.** Main courses 79DKK ($12). MC, V. Sun–Thurs noon–2am; Fri–Sat noon–5am. S-tog: Central Station.

Københavnercaféen (Copenhagen Cafe) ✿ DANISH This old-fashioned cafe is half a block from Strøget yet seemingly miles from the hustle and bustle outside. The menu comes with an English translation. The cuisine isn't fussy and is typical of what your Danish grandma might prepare. The daily special features herring, fried fish filet, roast pork, and bread; the deluxe version adds roast beef, Danish meatballs, chicken, salad, and cheese. Lunch is served until the kitchen closes (about 5pm), dinner from 5pm on. The cafe is small, so it fills up fast and can get smoky. There's free piano music on Sunday in winter; otherwise, you're free to tickle the ivories whenever the mood strikes.

Badstuestræde 10. ⓒ **33-32-80-81.** Daily special 79DKK ($12) with 5 items, 129DKK ($20) with 7 items; main courses 45DKK–149DKK ($7–$23). AE, DC, MC, V. Daily 11am–midnight (kitchen open 11:30am–10pm). Bus: 6 or 29. Metro: Norreport.

Pasta Basta ITALIAN/INTERNATIONAL Except for its name, Pasta Basta has everything going for it: a tastefully decorated modern interior, large windows overlooking a romantic cobblestone street, and an all-you-can-eat buffet with good food. Most of the food is prepared ahead, which explains the lightning-fast service. House wine is placed on each table in a carafe with marked gradations down the side—you pay for only as much as you drink. The downstairs cafe/bar fills up at night with a young crowd.

Valkendorfsgade 22. ⓒ **33-11-21-31.** Reservations recommended. Main courses 70DKK–165DKK ($11–$26). DC, MC, V. Sun–Thurs 11:30am–3am; Fri–Sat 11:30am–5:30am. Bus: 5.

Riz Raz ✿ *Value* MEDITERRANEAN/VEGETARIAN This popular cafe has low beamed ceilings, one dining niche opening onto the next, and posters and the work of local artists on the walls. The big draw is the buffet: Start with cold dishes like broccoli, string beans, coleslaw, red cabbage, rice, couscous, and eggplant in yogurt. Then move on to hot dishes like kafta, fava beans, zucchini in tomato sauce, potatoes, and carrots. Although Greek, Egyptian, and Moroccan dishes are featured, you can also get pasta. You won't find a more welcoming spot in town, with a staff made up of students, most of whom speak English.

Kompagnistræde 20 (at Knabrostræde). ⓒ **33-15-05-75.** Buffet 59DKK–69DKK ($9.20–$11), half price for children under 12; main courses (including buffet) 99DKK–179DKK ($15–$28). AE, DC, MC, V. Daily 11:30am–midnight (lunch to 4pm, dinner to midnight). Bus: 6A.

IN & NEAR NYHAVN

Amalienborg Special *Æ* (Kids) INTERNATIONAL/PIZZA/PASTA/SNACKS
This no-nonsense, cheap, and cheerful restaurant is near Amalienborg Palace, and palace workers, from secretaries to guardsmen, drop in for a quick lunch or for takeout. The eclectic menu includes a variety of pizzas; Mexican tacos, burritos, and quesadillas; open-face sandwiches; and burgers. Some of these foreign dishes lose a bit of flavor when translated into the Danish kitchen, but it's still reasonably good fare. Steak, fish, and pasta dishes are served with salad and bread. One of the more popular pasta dishes is beef-stuffed tortellini in cream sauce. You can also order a big bag of fries or ice cream in homemade waffle cones. At lunch it's usually packed; after 6pm it's almost deserted.

Amaliengade 26 (a half block south of Amalienborg Sq.). © 33-93-38-39. Pizzas 32DKK–55DKK ($5–$8.60); sandwiches 26DKK–65DKK ($4.05–$10); main courses 50DKK–80DKK ($7.80–$12). No credit cards. Apr–Oct daily 9am–10pm; winter Mon–Fri 8am–9pm, Sun noon–9pm. Bus: 1, 6, 9, or 10.

Cafe Petersborg DANISH   This congenial place close to Churchill Park offers good home cooking, a lively local crowd, and an inviting decor—dark paneling and furniture, exposed beams, and tables trimmed with candles and flowers. Come before or after a visit to the nearby *Little Mermaid*. The English menu lists standard, filling, and good-tasting fare with choices like herring, smoked eel or salmon, ham or mushroom omelet, warm plaice filet with rémoulade, and *frikadeller* (Danish meatballs) with potatoes and cabbage.

Bredgade 76. © 33-12-50-16. Sandwiches 36DKK–69DKK ($5.60–$11); hot meals 45DKK–165DKK ($7–$26). AC, DC, MC, V. Mon–Fri noon–3pm and 5–8:30pm. S-tog: Østerport. Bus: 1, 6, or 15.

Gother's Pizza (Kids) PIZZA/FAST FOOD   There are no tables here, just a few stools around wall counters. Most of the business is fast-food takeout, but if you're in the mood for a pizza, they make good ones (27 kinds are available). They also do salads and quick a la carte meals with chicken, steaks, and fish, but it's best to stick with the pizza.

Gothersgade 7. © 33-12-12-69. Pizzas 35DKK–95DKK ($5.45–$15); lunch specials 30DKK–35DKK ($4.70–$5.45); meals 42DKK–50DKK ($6.55–$7.80). No credit cards. Mon–Sat noon–10pm. Metro: Kongens Nytorv. Bus: 1, 10, or 350.

KFUM Soldaterhjem Cafe (Value) FAST FOOD/DANISH   This place across from Rosenborg Palace is a real find for low prices, and diners come here to fill up on lumberjack portions. You can order sandwiches, burgers, lasagna, salads, and even hot Danish meals. The dining room is casual and plain, with shared tables.

Gothersgade 115 (2nd floor). © 33-15-40-44. Buffet 69DKK ($11). Meals 17DKK–50DKK ($2.65–$7.80). V, MC. Mon–Fri 1–11pm for hot food (snacks to 11pm); Sat–Sun 3–11pm. S-tog: Nørreport.

Restaurant Lai Ho CANTONESE   This 55-seat restaurant 90m (295 ft.) north of Kongens Nytorv is a good choice for Chinese food. The bestsellers are a deliciously prepared sweet corn soup and half a Cantonese duck, complete with trimmings, for 170DKK ($27). Dim sum is available on weekends from noon to 3pm. The interior is pleasant, its mellow walls hung with prints.

Store Kongensgade 18. © 33-93-93-19. Reservations suggested. Main courses 98DKK–150DKK ($15–$23); dim sum dishes 30DKK–55DKK ($4.70–$8.60). AE, DC, MC, V. Daily 5–11pm; Sat–Sun noon–3pm. Metro: Kongens Nytorv. Bus: 1A or 350S.

WORTH A SPLURGE

Bistro DANISH   If you think a fine restaurant in a train station is an oxymoron, you're in for a surprise at the elegant Bistro. To find it from the main area of the train station, you have to walk through the self-serve restaurant called Spisehjårnet. At Bistro, you can choose from several buffets (it's best known for its cold buffet, worth the splurge) or order a la carte. Menu offerings include farmer steak, pork chops, schnitzel, and fish dishes.

In Central Station. ℂ **33-14-12-32.** Buffet 129DKK–175DKK ($20–$27); daily specials 95DKK ($15); main courses (with salad buffet) 109DKK–149DKK ($17–$23). AE, DC, MC, V. Daily 11:30am–9:30pm. S-tog: Central Station.

Els ⭐⭐ NEW DANISH   Els ("elk") is outstanding for its cuisine, location (near Kongens Nytorv), and decor (mid-19th-c. wall paintings of the seasons and the muses). The fixed-price menu changes weekly, ensuring the freshest foods. At dinner, starters often include lime- and garlic-marinated mussels, duck-liver pâté, and caviar. Main courses might be pheasant, tournedos of veal with morel sauce, or filet of sole. Menus change every month. Be sure to try the homemade five-grain bread and the house aperitif, Pousse Rapière (Armagnac with champagne).

Store Strandstræde 3. ℂ **33-14-13-41.** Reservations recommended. Main courses 85DKK–250DKK ($13–$39); fixed-price lunch 158DKK–215DKK ($25–$34). AE, DC, MC, V. Daily noon–3pm and 5:30–10pm. Bus: 1, 6, or 15.

La Rocca ⭐ ITALIAN   This sleek restaurant/cafe is a good choice if you want to dress up and dine in a stylish atmosphere for not a lot of money. Pizzas, as usual, are the least expensive menu items. Featured Italian pasta, fish, and meat dishes run the gamut from *saltimbocca alla romana* to grilled fish. La Rocca serves moderately priced Italian wines as well.

At Ibsens Hotel, Vendersgade 23–25. ℂ **33-14-66-55.** Pizza 80DKK–89DKK ($12–$14); main courses 85DKK–219DKK ($13–$34). AE, DC, MC, V. Daily noon–11pm. S-tog: Nørreport.

L'Education Nationale ⭐ FRENCH   At this authentic bistro, the chef, staff, decor, and food are all *français.* The excellent pâtés and roulettes are made on the premises. The menu reflects every region of France and changes every few months, but it's always interesting and modern. Expect generous servings and casual ambience at this crowded little place, which can get smoky. Check out the big French "breakfast" served 9:30am to 5pm—it includes hearty sandwiches, sausage, and pâté.

Larsbjørnsstræde 12 (near the Town Hall side of Strøget, 2 blocks north of Frederiksberggade). ℂ **33-91-53-60.** Reservations recommended for lunch, required for dinner. Main courses 48DKK–215DKK ($6–$27). MC, V. Mon–Sat noon–10pm; Sun 6pm–midnight. Bus: 6 or 29.

Skindbuksen DANISH   This place is more Danish than the queen. Although located in an expensive neighborhood of tiny establishments, it is not only reasonable in price but is a down-home type of place (that is, down-home Danish style). This atmospheric landmark has long drawn beer drinkers in the neighborhood. Many locals, often old men of the sea, swear by its *lobscouse,* the Danish version of a meat and potato stew that has kept many a mariner from starvation over the years. This dish is so popular it's often sold out at noon. A good variety of smørrebrød is always a luncheon favorite. You can order other dishes here too, including homemade soups, pâtés, fresh shrimp, and a local favorite, tender beef served with a béarnaise sauce. On Sunday afternoons there is live jazz from 4 to 6:30pm.

Lille Kongensgade 4, off Kongens Nytorv. ℂ **33-12-90-37.** Reservations not accepted. Main courses 100DKK–130DKK ($16–$20). AE, DC, MC, V. Daily noon–midnight (kitchen closes at 9:30pm). Bus: 1 or 15.

4 Seeing the Sights

For a city of under two million people, Copenhagen has more than its share of attractions. If you're here on a quick stopover, you'll need to budget your time carefully. Of the three royal palaces, Rosenborg is the most historically interesting. The prehistoric collections in the National Museum are outstanding. Strolling through Nyhavn will give you plenty of photo ops, and a harbor cruise is both fun and informative. Part of the fun of sightseeing in Copenhagen is finding a pleasant cafe, ordering a coffee or a beer, and just watching the world go by.

TIVOLI & THE LITTLE MERMAID

Tivoli *&&& Kids*   When Tivoli opened in 1843, the park was well outside the city center. Today it's Copenhagen's centerpiece, a showcase for Danish culture and music that attracts more than four million visitors annually. Every day brings a full program of open-air concerts, cabaret theater, dancing, pantomime, and other special events. Most are free or moderate in price.

The majority of the performances are staged at night, when the park takes on a magical look. Thousands of lights shimmer through the trees, and every Friday and Saturday fireworks light the sky. Don't overlook an afternoon visit, though, especially from May to the first half of June, when 100,000 brightly colored tulips blossom throughout the park. When you're ready for thrills, hop on the 1914 wooden roller coaster. Its incessant creaking gives you a reason to scream. During the Christmas season, the park hosts a holiday market, a special theatrical production, and ice skating on the lake. **Groften** and **Slukefter** are popular spots for a drink. The former, parts of which are open year-round, serves Danish food, and the latter, beside the main entrance to Tivoli, features jazz and blues year-round.

Open daily, the **Tivoli Billetcenter (Ticket Center),** Vesterbrogade 3, next to the park's main entrance (© 33-15-10-12), sells tickets to concerts and special events in the park and also distributes a free daily schedule.

Vesterbrogade 3. © 33-15-10-01. Admission 55DKK–65DKK ($8.60–$10) adults, 30DKK–35DKK ($4.70–$5.45) children under 14; combination ticket including admission and all rides 190DKK ($30). May to mid-Sept daily 11am–midnight. Partial Christmastime opening from mid-Nov to Christmas Eve (reduced admission). Closed mid-Sept to Apr. Bus: 1 or 16.

Den Lille Havfrue (The Little Mermaid) *& Kids*   This statue of a wistful mermaid is posed on an offshore rock in Copenhagen's harbor. Locals poke fun at the statue's enduring popularity, and more than once this world-famous figure has been the victim of vandals, most recently in 2003. Still, the slightly

---

Value **Getting the Best Deal on Sightseeing**

- Buy the Copenhagen Card, entitling you to museum entries, public transport, and good discounts (see "Copenhagen Deals & Discounts," p. 331).
- Take advantage of the fact that many of Copenhagen's museums offer free admission 1 day a week (usually Wed).
- Check out Copenhagen's most famous monument—*The Little Mermaid*—for free.

over-life-size bronze statue, created in 1913 by Edvard Eriksen and inspired by the Hans Christian Andersen fairy tale, remains the most famous in Copenhagen. Adjacent **Kastellet Park** 🏛🏛, laid out on the remains of Copenhagen's ramparts, is an idyllic area for strolling and picnicking (open daily 7am–5:30pm). Don't miss the nearby **Gefion Fountain** or the **bust of Winston Churchill,** adjacent to St. Alban's Church.

Langelinie on the harbor. S-tog: Østerport. Bus: 1, 6, or 9; during summer a shuttle bus operates between Town Hall Square and the statue.

THE ROYAL PALACES

Amalienborg Slot (Amalienborg Palace) 🏛🏛   The official residence of Denmark's Margrethe II (a cousin of Queen Elizabeth II of England) and her husband, Prince Henrik, is an outstanding example of rococo architecture. Amalienborg is a complex of four mansions dating from 1760 and built around a large square. An equestrian statue of Frederik V is at the center, while the Queen's Guards—bearskin hats and all—stand watch around the perimeter.

In 1994, the palace opened to the public one of its four mansions, **Christian VIII's Palace** 🏛🏛. Within, you can wander through regal private and official rooms of Danish monarchs from 1863 to 1947. Highlights are **Christian IX's study,** a mix of valuables and Victoriana; **Queen Louise's drawing rooms,** more elegant and less cluttered than her husband's study; **Christian X's study,** with mementos from the Faroe Islands, Greenland, and Iceland; and **Frederik VIII's study,** with the original furniture, chandelier, and royal knickknacks. The museum also houses a costume and jewelry gallery.

While you're in the area, stop in to see the ornate **Frederiks Kirke (Frederick's Church),** also known as the "Marble Church," on nearby Bredgade. This baroque Romanesque structure with a landmark dome was intended to be a royal adjunct to Amalienborg when the foundation was laid in 1749. But the cost of the Norwegian marble was so expensive that construction stopped and the church wasn't completed until 1894. It's open daily 10:30am to 4:30pm.

Christian VIII's Palace. 📞 **33-12-21-86.** Admission 45DKK ($7) adults, 25DKK ($3.90) students and seniors, 10DKK ($1.55) children 5–12, free for children under 5. Oct–May Tues–Sun 11am–4pm; June–Aug daily 7am–4pm; Sept daily 11am–4pm. Closed Dec 14–25. Bus: 1, 6, 9, or 10.

Christiansborg Slot (Christiansborg Palace) 🏛   Rebuilt early in the 20th century atop ancient foundations, Christiansborg Palace was home to the royal family until 1794. The ring of water surrounding the tiny island of Slotsholmen once served as a protective moat. Most of the palace's rooms are used as offices by parliamentary and supreme court officials and are off-limits. On guided tours, you can see the **Royal Reception Rooms,** resplendent with Murano chandeliers, Flemish tapestries, and other impressive details; the **Throne Room,** where the queen regularly receives foreign ambassadors; the **Red Room,** named for the red velvet on the walls; the **Long Hall,** still used for state banquets; and the **queen's library,** with 10,000 books. In 2000, a new set of Gobelin tapestries created for the queen's 60th birthday was installed in the **Great Hall.** You can

---

⟨Kids⟩ All the Queen's Men

The noontime **Changing of the Guard** at Amalienborg Slot is as spirited as any, full of pomp and pageantry. It's performed only when the queen is in residence (mainly during colder months).

Copenhagen

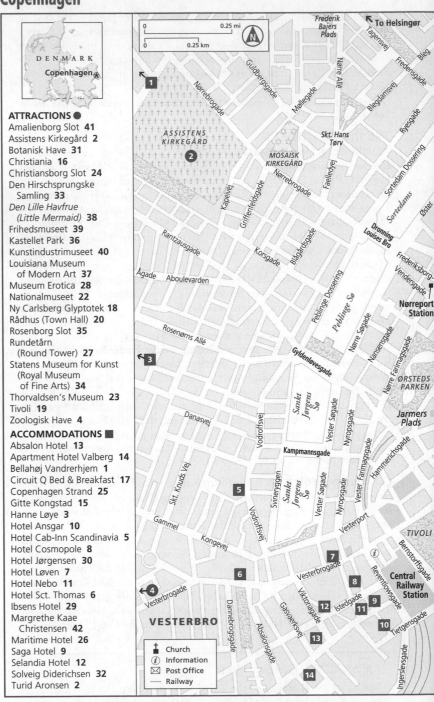

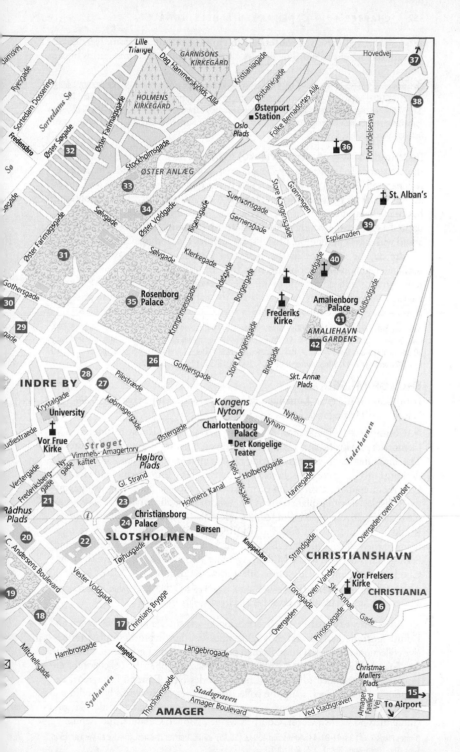

also visit the well-preserved **subterranean ruins** of Bishop Absalon's 1167 castle beneath the present palace. The entrance for them (separate admission) is in the central portal.

Christiansborg Slotsplads. ✆ **33-92-64-92.** Admission to Royal Reception Rooms 50DKK ($7.80) adults, 20DKK ($3.10) children; free admission to parliament; admission to castle ruins 25DKK ($3.90) adults, 10DKK ($1.55) children. Reception rooms guided tours May–Sept daily 11am, 1, and 3pm; Oct–Apr Tues, Thurs, Sun 3pm. Parliament English-language tours daily 11am, 1, and 3pm. Ruins May–Sept daily 10am–4pm. Closed Oct–Apr Mon. Bus: 1, 6, 8, 9, or 42.

Rosenborg Slot (Rosenborg Palace) ✮✮✮   This is the oldest, smallest, and most historically interesting of Copenhagen's three royal palaces. The summer residence of Christian IV (1577–1648), it was built during his reign and served as the official royal residence throughout the late 17th century. Remarkably little has been changed since then; even today the rooms are unheated and lit only by natural light. In the darkly opulent **State Apartments** ✮✮✮, every surface is aswirl with lavish decoration. One display features the clothing Christian IV wore on the day he was shot in the eye—and includes the earrings the intrepid monarch had fashioned for his mistress from the bullet fragments. There's a separate entrance and admission to see the **Crown Jewels,** a collection of gem-encrusted swords, crowns, and necklaces. You can skip the jewels without regret, but do allow yourself time to ramble in the beautifully landscaped gardens.

Øster Voldgade 4a. ✆ **33-15-32-86.** Admission to castle and crown jewels 60DKK ($9.35) adults, 30DKK ($4.70) seniors and students, 10DKK ($1.55) children 5–12. June–Aug daily 10am–5pm; May and Sept daily 10am–4pm; Oct and Dec 27–Dec 30 daily 11am–3pm; Nov 1–Dec 17 and Jan 2–Apr 30 11am–2pm. Closed Feb 7–22 and Apr 8–12. S-tog: Nørreport. Bus: 5, 10, 14, 16, 31, 184, 185, or 350S.

THE TOP MUSEUMS

For details on the great **Louisiana Museum of Contemporary Art** ✮✮✮, see "Side Trips: Helsingør & More," p. 359.

Nationalmuseet (National Museum) ✮✮✮ *Kids*   If you're interested in Denmark's prehistoric and Viking Age past, you don't want to miss this museum. The entire first floor is one fascinating exhibit after another, from 2,000-year-old *lur* horns to Viking-era ships, household utensils, farm implements, and clothing. One room contains a collection of massive rune stones. Everything is imaginatively displayed with explanations in English; to see it all you need at least a couple of hours. If your time is limited, a guide called "10,000 Years in 60 Minutes" is sold at the information desk for 10DKK ($1.55); a free audio guide to highlights of the vast collections is also available here. Less interesting are the second-floor galleries devoted to the Middle Ages and Renaissance. Kids have their own Children's Museum. There's a nice cafe and museum store.

Ny Vestergade 10. ✆ **33-13-44-11.** Admission 50DKK ($7.80) adults, 40DKK ($6.25) students, free for children under 16. Tues–Sun 10am–5pm. Closed Dec 24, 25, and 31. Bus: 1, 5, 6, 8, or 10.

Ny Carlsberg Glyptotek ✮   Specializing in ancient sculpture and French and Danish art from the 19th and early 20th centuries, the Glyptotek displays impressive collections of Greek statues, Roman portrait busts, and Egyptian and Etruscan art. Founded by brewer/arts patron Carl Jacobsen in 1882, the collection of antiquities has continued to grow and now includes Near Eastern, Palmyrene, and Cypriot art. The French sculpture collection features many works by Rodin and Degas. The second-floor modernists are mainly French and include Gauguin (more than 30 works), Corot, Courbet, Manet, Monet, Cézanne, and Renoir.

Dantes Plads 7. ✆ **33-41-81-41.** Admission 40DKK ($6.25) adults, free for children, free for all Wed and Sun. Tues–Sun 10am–4pm. Bus: 1, 2, 5, 6, 8, or 10.

Statens Museum for Kunst (Royal Museum of Fine Arts) 𝒢

The country's largest art museum occupies a monumental building in the Øster Anlæg park. Renovations completed in 1999 added a concert hall and a glassed-in wing for exhibit space. The emphasis of the Danish art collection is on late 18th-century works, but most are overshadowed by outstanding 19th-century landscapes. The foreign art section is heavy on Dutch and Flemish paintings, but other European modernists, like Matisse and Braque, are well represented.

Sølvgade 48–50. © **33-74-84-94.** Admission 30DKK–60DKK ($4.70–$9.35) adults, 25DKK–45DKK ($3.90–$7) students, free for children under 16; higher admission for special exhibitions only. Tues and Thurs–Sun 10am–5pm; Wed 10am–8pm. Bus: 6, 8, 10, 14, 40, 42, 43, 184, or 185.

OTHER MUSEUMS

Den Hirschsprungske Samling (Hirschsprung Collection) 𝒢

Tobacco manufacturer Heinrich Hirschsprung bequeathed his vast collection of 19th-century "Golden Age" Danish art, notably paintings of people and landscapes, to Denmark in 1911. The striking building constructed to house the collection has 16 exhibition areas, a particularly large one devoted to P. S. Krøyer. Works by Anna and Michael Ancher, Viggo Johansen, and Vilhem Hammershoi are prominent. Furniture designed by the artists is exhibited along with the art.

Stockholmsgade 20. © **35-42-03-36.** Admission 35DKK ($5.45) adults, free for children under 16. Wed–Mon 11am–4pm. Bus: 14, 40, 42, 43, 150, or 184.

Frihedsmuseet (Museum of Danish Resistance)

This compact museum is dedicated to the years 1940 to 1945, when Denmark was occupied by Nazi Germany. Exhibits show the development of the Danish resistance movement, including printing of illegal leaflets, sabotage, and rescue of Jewish citizens. It's a moving reminder of Danish humanity during the grim years of World War II. All the texts are translated into English. From May to mid-September, guided tours in English are given on Tuesday, Thursday, and Sunday at 2pm.

Churchillparken. © **33-13-77-14.** Admission 40DKK ($6.25) adults, free for children under 16. May–Sept 15 Tues–Sat 10am–4pm, Sun 10am–5pm; Sept 16–Apr Tues–Sat 11am–3pm, Sun 11am–4pm. Bus: 1 or 6.

Kunstindustrimuseet (Danish Museum of Decorative Art) 𝒢𝒢

Housed in rococo hospital buildings from the mid–18th century, this museum traces Danish design in crafts, furniture, textiles, and decoration back to the Middle Ages. As such, the museum is one of the finest showcases for Danish and Scandinavian crafts and design. You can enjoy it all in about an hour. The museum gift shop has a wonderful assortment of reasonably priced handmade contemporary design gifts.

Bredgade 68. © **33-18-56-56.** Admission 40DKK ($6.25) adults; free for children under 16. Tues–Fri 10am–4pm; Sat–Sun noon–4pm. S-tog: Østerport. Bus: 15, 19, or 29.

Museum Erotica 𝒢

The founding director of this uninhibited museum, Ole Ege, was a well-known Danish nude photographer in the 1960s. Exhibits focus on erotica through the ages, with wall paintings from the 1st century, a Greek vase from the 6th century, Renaissance paintings, and "naughty French postcards" from the Victorian era. Sex toys and chastity belts are part of the show. The last exhibit is a wall of 12 video monitors showing porno films from 1930 to the present. The museum has pin-ups for playgirls as well as playboys.

Købmagergade 24. © **33-12-03-11.** Admission 79DKK ($12) without catalog, 99DKK ($15) with catalog. May–Sept daily 10am–11pm; Oct–Apr Sun–Thurs 11am–8pm, Fri–Sat 10am–10pm. S-tog: Nørreport. Visitors age 16–18 must be accompanied by an adult. No one under 16 admitted.

Special & Free Events

Festivities usually begin at the end of May with the **Copenhagen Carnival**, a raucous Mardi Gras–type party replete with costumes and sambas. **Free park concerts** start in June, including a weekly Saturday rock festival at Femøren, and Sunday concerts in Fælledparken. Free concerts are sometimes held in Nikolaj Church as well. And there's always free entertainment associated with the annual 10-day **Copenhagen Jazz Festival**, starting the first Friday in July. The **Copenhagen Summer Festival**, emphasizing classical music, runs late July to mid-August.

Grabrødre Torv (Gray Friar Square), in the center of Copenhagen, comes alive each summer day with street entertainers, outdoor cafes, and occasional live music.

Now a favorite strolling area, **Nyhavn (New Harbor)**, a historic canal lined with antique buildings, was once a raucous sailors' quarter. Wall-to-wall outdoor cafes serving ice cream and beer attract visitors. Majestic fully rigged ships are moored all along the canal, and you can also see where Hans Christian Andersen lived during different periods of his life—at nos. 18, 20, and 67. Peek into the courtyards at nos. 18 and 20.

Thorvaldsen's Museum ⊛   The personal museum of Bertel Thorvaldsen (1770–1844), Denmark's most celebrated sculptor, features his graceful neoclassical creations as well as other works from his private collection. Among the most striking are his monumental equestrian statues and portrayals of Hercules, Venus, Jason, Mars, Vulcan, Mercury, and Christ and the Apostles. The artist's personal effects, including a gold snuffbox with his monogram in diamonds (a gift from the city of Turin), are on view in the basement. You can see more works by Thorvaldsen in the **Vor Frue Kirke (Copenhagen Cathedral).** The neoclassical church dating from 1829 is at Nørregade 8, next to Copenhagen University; it's open Monday to Friday 9am to 5pm.

Bertel Thorvaldsens Plads 2 (next to Christiansborg Palace). ℭ **33-32-15-32.** Admission 20DKK ($3.10) adults, 10DKK ($1.55) seniors and children under 14, free Wed. Tues–Sun 10am–5pm; guided tours in English July–Aug Sun 3pm. Bus: 1A, 2A, 15, 26, 29, or 650S.

MORE ATTRACTIONS

Christiania   In 1971, organized squatters took over dozens of unused army buildings on the island of Christianshavn, creating the Free Town of Christiania. The public generally supported the group and pressured the government not to take any action. Today some 900 people live in Christiania. The community, with its graffiti, unpaved streets, and generally ramshackle air, looks more like a Third World country than modern Denmark. Hash and marijuana are sold in an open-air market area known as "Pushers' Row" (no hard drugs allowed). But there are some interesting murals, a few wonderfully painted houses, and popular nightspots. Visitors are welcome, but taking photographs along "Pushers' Row" isn't allowed, and elsewhere you should ask permission first. A restaurant called **Spiseloppen** and a jazz club called **Loppen** are housed in the building to your right just inside the main entrance; restrooms and a small gallery are in the same building. There's also a vegetarian restaurant called **Morgenstedet** (no smoking or alcohol).

Christianshavn. Main entrance on Prinsessegade. Free admission. Guided tours sometimes leave from Prinsessegade year-round Sat–Sun, call ✆ **32-57-96-70** for information. Tours require a week's notice; fax requests to 32-57-60-05. Bus: 8.

Rådhus (Town Hall)   Copenhagen's imposing red-brick Town Hall (1905) is one of the city's best-known landmarks because of its clock tower and central location on **Rådhuspladsen,** a vast square right at the beginning of Strøget. The pillar just east of Town Hall (on your left as you face the building) is topped by a bronze statue of two men playing *lurs,* ancient instruments found only in Scandinavia. On the western side of the building is a statue of Hans Christian Andersen. The Town Hall itself is most famous for Jens Olsen's **World Clock,** a gigantic silver-and-gold timepiece on the ground floor—it began ticking in 1955 and is accurate to within half a second. You can get a marvelous **view** 🕊 of the city and harbor from the top of the tower.

Rådhuspladsen. ✆ **33-66-25-82.** Admission to rådhus 30DKK ($4.70); admission to clock 10DKK ($1.55) adults, 5DKK (80¢) children. Guided tour 30DKK ($4.70); tour of Rådhus Mon–Fri 3pm; tour of tower Mon–Sat noon. Bus: 1, 6, or 8.

Rundetårn (Round Tower) 🕊   The best **panoramic view** 🕊🕊 of old Copenhagen is from the top of this observatory built by King Christian IV in 1642. An unusual paved ramp (no steps) spirals around the exterior; at the top is a spiral staircase leading up to a viewing platform.

Købmagergade 52A. ✆ **33-73-03-73.** Admission 20DKK ($3.10) adults, 5DKK (80¢) children. Tower June–Aug Mon–Sat 10am–8pm, Sun noon–8pm; Sept–May Mon–Sat 10am–5pm, Sun noon–5pm. Observatory Oct 15–Mar 20 Tues–Wed 7–10pm. Bus: 5, 14, 16, or 42. Metro: Nørreport.

Zoologisk Have (Copenhagen Zoo) *Kids*   Founded in 1859 and modernized in recent years, this national zoo is home to 2,000 animals, from Nordic species to Asiatic red pandas to giant anteaters from South America. Gorillas and chimpanzees are in the Tropical Zoo, and 25 species of bird occupy the adjacent Tropical Rain Forest. The children's zoo is set up like a farm with cows, llamas, chickens, goats, and other farm animals, as well as a playground, a refreshment stand, and Shetland ponies for riding.

Roskildevej 32. ✆ **72-20-02-80.** Admission 90DKK ($14) adults, 50DKK ($7.80) children. June–Aug daily 9am–6pm; Apr–May and Sept–Oct daily 9am–5pm; Nov–Mar daily 9am–4pm. S-tog: Valby. Bus: 6A, 28, or 39.

PARKS & GARDENS

In addition to the gardens of **Tivoli** (see above), Copenhagen boasts several parks ideal for strolling and picnicking. The city's oldest landscaped park, **Kongens Have (King's Garden),** occupies the grounds around Rosenborg Palace. The charming wooded **Botanisk Have (Botanical Garden),** behind the Royal Museum of Fine Arts, features a rock garden, beds of perennials, and a greenhouse with exotic specimens. May to October, the gates are open daily 8:30am to 6pm (to 4pm the rest of the year).

Kastellet (Park of the Citadel) 🕊🕊, adjacent to the harbor and rocky beach where *The Little Mermaid* sits, is laid out on Copenhagen's ramparts. You can see some brightly colored military barracks and buildings from the 18th century and harborside paths. At its southern end, Kastellet blends into **Churchill Park,** noted for St. Alban's English Church and the monumental Gefion Fountain, depicting the legend of the founding of Denmark. There's also a bulldoggish bust of the park's namesake, Sir Winston Churchill.

Three breezy lakes created from what was once Copenhagen's protective moat cut through the western side of central Copenhagen. Collectively known as "the lakes," they're fringed with strollable greenways and crossed by bridges. **Peblinge,** the most appealing, is a favorite with boaters. Nearby, **Ørsteds Parken,** with its small lake, pleasant paths, and statues, invites meandering. **Assistens Kirkegard,** the parklike cemetery at Nørrebrogade and Kapelvej, is the final resting place of fairy-tale writer Hans Christian Andersen, philosopher Søren Kierkegaard, physicists H. C. Ørsted and Niels Bohr, and tenor sax player Ben Webster. Nearby **Fælledparken** is the scene of exuberant outdoor concerts in summer.

Frederiksberg Park, on the north side of the zoo, is one of the city's largest and prettiest green places and also the backdrop for summer concerts.

ORGANIZED TOURS

GUIDED TOURS   Richard Carpens, of **Richard Carpens Tours** (© 32-84-74-35), conducts an English-language walking tour of a neighborhood within Copenhagen and its environs every day except Sunday, departing at 10:30am and lasting 2 full hours. The cost is 50DKK ($6.25) per person. A minimum of five participants is required. The tours are conducted only between early May and mid-September, and depart from Bernstoffsgade 1.

BUS TOURS   Use It's free *Playtime* booklet takes you through a do-it-yourself tour of all the major sights using city bus no. 6. Those looking for more structure can choose from over a dozen guided bus tours, including the following, offered by **Copenhagen Excursions** (© 32-54-06-06). For orientation, try the 1½-hour **City Tour** (2½ hr. with a visit to a brewery) that covers major scenic highlights like *The Little Mermaid,* Rosenborg Castle, and Amalienborg Palace. On workdays, tours also visit the Carlsberg brewery. Tours depart daily at 1pm from May 30 to September 30 and cost 130DKK ($20) adults and 65DKK ($10) children.

The **City and Harbor Tour,** a 2½-hour trip by launch and bus, departs from Town Hall Square. The boat tours the city's main canals, passing *The Little Mermaid* and the Old Fish Market. It operates from May 30 to September 13. Tours cost 175DKK ($27) adults and 65DKK ($10) children under 12.

Shakespeare buffs will be interested in an afternoon excursion to the castles of North Zealand. The 7-hour English-language tour explores the area north of Copenhagen, including a visit to Kronborg (Hamlet's Castle); a brief trip to Fredensborg, the queen's residence; and a stopover at Frederiksborg Castle and the National Historical Museum. Tours depart from the Town Hall Square May 2 through October 16, Wednesday, Saturday, and Sunday at 9:30am; November to April Wednesday to Sunday 9:30am. The cost is 400DKK ($62) adults, half price for children.

HARBOR & CANAL TOURS   One of the best ways to understand the role of Copenhagen's harbor in its history is to take a boat tour of the city's canals and waterways. An inexpensive guided boat tour is offered between mid-April and mid-September by **Netto-Bådene** (© 32-54-78-00). Tours lasting about 60 minutes each depart at 15-minute intervals every day between 10am and 5pm. Most passengers begin their tour in front of the Holmens Kirke (Church), opposite the Borsen (Stock Exchange), although it's also possible to embark and disembark at Langelinkiekaj (by *The Little Mermaid*) and in the Nyhavn district at Heibnerhgsgade 2–4. The tour costs 20DKK ($3.10) for adults and 10DKK ($1.55) for children under 15.

Roughly equivalent (but pricier) tours, costing 50DKK ($7.80) for adults and 20DKK ($3.10) for children 5 to 14, are conducted by **Canal Tours** (© **33-42-33-20;** www.canal-tours.dk). Tours, each 50 minutes in length, are conducted between April and late October, at 30-minute intervals every day between 10am and 5pm. Points of departure include Gammelstrand, near the main railway station, and Nyhavn, near Kongens Nytorv and the Østerport S-tog station.

BREWERY TOURS The main brewing hall of **Carlsberg Brewery,** Ny Carlsbergsvej 11 (© **33-27-13-14;** bus: 6A), dates from the early 1900s and is dominated by huge copper vats (and a pungent aroma from the hops). It's open Tuesday to Sunday 10am to 4pm. To get to the brewery, take bus no. 6A from Town Hall Square.

5 Shopping

The selection in Copenhagen's stores is wide and varied. The best buys are objects of Danish design made in Denmark—**native silver, porcelain,** and **glassware.** Heavy import duties make non-Danish goods very expensive.

A shopping tour traditionally begins on mile-long pedestrian **Strøget,** the address of many exclusive stores, such as Royal Copenhagen, Bing & Grøndahl, Georg Jensen, Holmegaard, the upscale department store Illum (peek in at the chandeliers and fountain in the atrium), and the home furnishings specialty store Illums Bolighus. A pedestrian street called **Strædet** runs parallel to Strøget and has long been known for its antiques stores but is

> **Value Getting a VAT Refund**
>
> Many stores offer non-Scandinavians the opportunity to recover most of the **value-added tax (VAT)** of 25% on purchases over 300DKK ($47).

gaining a reputation for its galleries, restaurants, and upscale shops. The same is true of **Kompagnistræde.** Perpendicular to Strøget, branching north to the Nørreport S-tog station, is **Købmagergade,** another pedestrian shopping street.

Several other city shopping streets reserved exclusively for walkers are marked in red or green on most maps. Besides the upscale shops, Copenhagen has a good number of secondhand stores and vintage boutiques, especially in and around **Larsbjørnsstræde.** Two favorites are the small shop in **Kvindehuset (Women's House),** Gothersgade 37, and the well-stocked **UFF** at Kultorvet 13 (come here for jeans or Nordic sweaters) or Vesterbrogade 37 at Viktoriagade.

May to October, the lively **Copenhagen Fleamarket,** on Israels Plads (S-tog: Nørreport), is open Saturday 8am to 2pm. It specializes in antiques (vintage Georg Jensen, if you're lucky) and bric-a-brac. On other days, it's a **fruit-and-vegetable market.**

6 Copenhagen After Dark

In Copenhagen, a good night means a late night. On warm weekends, hundreds of rowdy revelers crowd Strøget and Nyhavn until sunrise, and merrymaking isn't just for the young: Jazz clubs, cafes, traditional beer houses, and wine cellars are routinely packed with people of all ages. The city has a more serious cultural side as well, exemplified by excellent theaters, operas, ballets, and a circus.

You can buy tickets for almost all concerts and special events at the centrally located **Tivoli Billetcenter (Ticket Center),** Vesterbrogade 3, next to the park's main entrance (© **33-15-10-12**). It's open Monday to Friday 9am to 5pm.

> ⟨*Value*⟩ **Saving on Tickets**
>
> **Half-price tickets** for some concerts and theater productions are available the day of the performance from the ticket kiosk opposite the Nørreport S-tog station, at Nørrevoldgade and Fiolstræde. It's open Monday to Friday noon to 7pm and Saturday noon to 3pm.

THE PERFORMING ARTS

Copenhagen's cultural scene is dominated by **Det Kongelige Teater (Royal Theater),** at the south end of Kongens Nytorv (© **33-69-69-69;** www.kgl-teater.dk; bus: 1, 6, 9, or 10), staging theater, opera, and ballet under the same roof. Founded in 1748, the theater alternates productions between its two stages. Regular premieres and popular revivals keep the stage lit almost every night of the season (it's dark June and July). Admission is 30DKK to 645DKK ($4.70–$101), half price for seniors 67 and over all times, and for those under 26 (1 week before a show begins). The box office is open Monday through Saturday from 1 to 8pm; phone hours are Monday through Friday 1 to 8pm, Saturday 10am to 8pm, and Sunday 3 hours before a performance (performances are usually at 3pm).

On summer evenings, **outdoor concerts** are held in Fælled Park near the entrance, near Frederik V's Vej; inquire about dates and times at the tourist office.

LIVE-MUSIC CLUBS

Copenhagen's love affair with jazz and blues is one of Europe's most passionate. Danes wholeheartedly embrace jazz as their own, and even though this capital's clubs aren't as plentiful as those in New Orleans or Chicago, they challenge the American variety in both quality and enthusiasm.

A small, rowdy local favorite is **Ca'feen Funke,** Blegdamsvej 2 (© **35-35-17-32;** bus: 3), where live bands perform blues, soul, or funk on Saturday. At the **Copenhagen Jazz House,** Niels Hemmingsensgade 10 (© **33-15-26-00;** bus: 6 or 29), expect to hear Danish jazz 80% of the time and foreign jazz the rest. **Club Absalon,** Frederiksberggade 38 (© **33-16-16-98;** bus: 6 or 29), is a bar/dance hall holding up to 750 on three floors. Jazz is performed in the cellar; the other floors offer live bands and recorded music.

BARS

Named after the contemporary Danish author of westerns and murder mysteries, the convivial **Cafe Dan Turrell,** Store Regnegade 3–5 (© **33-14-10-47;** bus: 6), attracts students and celebrities who converse over burgers, pasta, and cappuccino. Trendy **Cafe Victor,** Ny Østergade 8 (© **33-13-36-13;** bus: 1, 6, or 350), serves crepes, quiches, and omelets. The surroundings are elegant, and most everyone is dressed up; half the patrons come to eat at the restaurant, half to drink. The popular restaurant/bar **Krasnapolsky,** Vestergade 10 (© **33-32-88-00;** bus: 2, 6, 8, or 29), with minimal decor, can be laid-back or loud. It's open Monday to Saturday 10am to midnight.

Both unabashedly upbeat and terminally crowded, the basement bar of **Peder Oxes Vinkælder,** Gråbrødre Torv 11 (© **33-11-11-93;** bus: 6 or 29), is one of the best in the city. **Hviids Vinstue,** Kongens Nytorv 19 (© **33-15-10-64;** bus: 6 or 29), is Copenhagen's most historic wine cellar, open since 1723.

GAY & LESBIAN BARS

A leading nightlife venue, **Oscar Bar & Café,** Radhuspladsen 77 (© **33-12-09-99**), operates a good restaurant serving an international cuisine and also has a cruisy bar. It's an all-around rendezvous point for many of the capital's gay men and women, also attracting a lot of foreign visitors looking for action. The crowd is trendy and hip and the bar is also frequented by straight people for its music and atmosphere. The bar and cafe is open daily from noon to 2am, the restaurant daily from noon to 10pm. **Cosy Bar,** Studiestræde 24 (© **33-12-74-27;** bus: 6 or 29), is a late-night bar for gay men open 11pm to 6am. **Centralhjørnet,** Kattesundet 18 (© **33-11-85-49;** bus: 6 or 29), is the oldest gay bar in Copenhagen (frequented mostly by men). For a more laid-back atmosphere, congenial for both men and women, there's **Café Intime's,** Allegade 25 (no phone; bus: 1 or 14), a piano bar with live music Wednesday to Sunday.

For an update on the scene, call **LBL—National Association for Gays & Lesbians,** at © **33-13-19-48** (www.lbl.dk); or check out **Mermaid Pride Copenhagen** on the Web at www.mermaidpride.dk.

DANCE CLUBS

As in many major cities, dance clubs come and go, and once gone, they're just as quickly forgotten. Take a look at the free *Copenhagen This Week* or ask your hotel for recommendations. Two clubs to consider are **Copenhagen Jazz House** and **Club Absalon** (see "Live-Music Clubs," above).

7 Side Trips: Helsingør & More

There are several easy-to-make side trips from Copenhagen The money-saving **Copenhagen Card** (see "Copenhagen Deals & Discounts," p. 331) is good for the train ride to Helsingør and for train rides and admissions to the Louisiana Museum of Modern Art, the Viking Ship Museum at Roskilde, Frederiksborg Palace at Hillerød, and the Karen Blixen Museum at Rungstedlund.

HELSINGØR (ELSINORE) & HAMLET'S CASTLE

Between the 15th and 19th centuries, **Helsingør** became rich from tolls assessed on passing ships. Today this carefully restored old town, 45km (28 miles) north of Copenhagen at the entrance of Øresund, a narrow strait separating Denmark from Sweden, remains a lively port and tourist mecca.

Helsingør is most famous for its 16th-century **Kronborg Castle** 𝄐𝄐 (© **49-21-30-78;** www.kronborgcastle.com), supposedly the setting for Shakespeare's *Hamlet.* The castle tour features the royal apartments (with paintings and tapestries from the 16th and 17th c.), the banqueting hall, the chapel, and other areas where Hamlet, Gertrude, Claudius, and Ophelia may have lived and met their tragic fates. Admission to the castle is 40DKK ($6.25) adults, 15DKK ($2.35) children 6 to 14. May through September, it's open daily from 10:30am to 5pm; October and April, hours are Tuesday through Sunday from 11am to 4pm; November through March, it's open Tuesday through Sunday from 11am to 3pm (closed Christmas). The castle is 1km (½ mile) from the rail station.

Once you reach Helsingør, 40km (25 miles) north of Copenhagen, you'll be deposited in the center of town and can cover all the major attractions on foot. There are frequent trains from Copenhagen, taking 50 minutes. A one-way ticket is 52DKK ($8.10). Buses leave Copenhagen via the town of Klampenorg for the daily 90-minute trip to Helsingør.

LOUISIANA MUSEUM OF MODERN ART 🏵🏵🏵

One of Europe's top contemporary art museums, the **Louisiana Museum for Moderne Kunst (Louisiana Museum of Modern Art)**, Gammel Strandvej 13, Humlebæk (© **49-19-07-19;** www.louisiana.dk), is in North Zealand, 35km (22 miles) north of Copenhagen, in an area known as the Danish Riviera (about 45 min. by train from Copenhagen's Central Station). This stunning museum houses a permanent collection that includes major works by Warhol, Lichtenstein, Calder, Moore, and Giacometti. In recent years, Hopper, Mapplethorpe, Calder, Monet, and Toulouse-Lautrec have been featured in world-class special exhibits. The museum sits on a spectacular piece of land overlooking Øresund, the strait separating Denmark and Sweden. Sculptures are beautifully situated throughout the landscaped grounds. The museum was founded in 1958 by Knud Jensen, who wanted to showcase his collection of modern art. Jensen had three wives, all named Louise—hence the name Louisiana. Over the years, several new galleries and buildings have been added to the original villalike structure; the Louisiana Children's Wing opened in 1994. In addition to a cinema and concert hall, there's a restaurant/cafe and a museum shop. Admission is 72DKK ($11) adults, 65DKK ($10) students, 20DKK ($3.10) children 4 to 16, and free for children under 4. It's open Thursday through Tuesday from 10am to 5pm, Wednesday from 10am to 10pm; closed December 24, 25, and 31.

The nearest town to Louisiana may be reached by train from Copenhagen (København–Helsingør). Two trains an hour leave from the main station in Copenhagen (trip time: 40 min.). Once you're at Humlebaek, follow signs to the museum, a 15-minute walk.

HILLERØD & FREDERIKSBORG CASTLE 🏵🏵🏵

A not-so-scenic 45-minute train ride to **Hillerød,** 35km (22 miles) north of Copenhagen in Sjælland, brings you to **Frederiksborg Slot (Frederiksborg Castle;** © **48-26-04-39),** often called the "Versailles of northern Europe." The monumental red brick castle, built from 1599 to 1622 in Dutch Renaissance style, served as a residence for Christian IV, king of Denmark and Norway, and for successive monarchs until the 18th century. Earlier buildings from the late 16th century were incorporated into the castle and are connected to it by an S-shaped bridge. Of particular interest are the immense Neptune Fountain in the main courtyard, the elaborate stuccowork ceiling in the Knights Hall, and the richly decorated chapel with an original organ built in 1610 (played on Thurs 3:30–4pm). The interior of the castle serves as the Frederiksborg Museum, displaying historic paintings, furniture, and decorative art. Surrounding the castle are French-inspired landscape gardens laid out in the early 18th century.

The palace is open daily April to October 10am to 5pm, November to March 11am to 3pm. Admission is 60DKK ($9.35) adults, 50DKK ($7.80) students, 15DKK ($2.35) children 6 to 14, free for children under 6.

The **train** takes you to Hillerød, where you then take **bus no. 701** or **702** to the palace (or you can walk). The round-trip train fare is 53DKK ($8.20). If you have a **car,** follow the Ring Route 04 and then Route 16.

ROSKILDE 🏵 & THE VIKING SHIP MUSEUM 🏵🏵🏵

Roskilde, the ancient capital of Denmark, lies at the end of a fiord about 30km (19 miles) west of Copenhagen. There's enough here to keep you busy for a full day, so make your first stop the **Roskilde Turistbureau,** Gullandsstræde 15 off the main pedestrian street (© **46-35-27-00;** www.destination-roskilde.dk), and pick up brochures and a free map. You can also book a hotel room at this office. It's open Monday to Friday 9am to 5pm (to 6pm July–Aug) and Saturday 10am to 1pm (9am–3pm July–Aug).

For centuries Danish kings and queens have been laid to rest in Roskilde's red brick **Domkirke (cathedral)** ℱ, most recently Frederik IX in 1985. The twin-spired edifice, now a UNESCO World Heritage Site, was begun in 1170 and completed some 200 years later. From June to August, free concerts are held in the cathedral every Thursday at 8pm.

Give yourself at least an hour to visit the **Vikingeskibhallen (Viking Ship Museum),** Vindeboder 12 (℃ 46-30-02-00), one of Denmark's most fascinating museums. A pathway from the cathedral leads down through a park to the museum (a 10-min. walk), located on Roskilde Fiord. The museum houses five wooden ships deliberately sunk at the mouth of the harbor around A.D. 1000. The townspeople hoped the sunken ships would act as a barricade against marauding Viking pirates from Norway. A film about the 1962 excavation of the ships is shown throughout the day; ask at the ticket desk when the English version will be playing. Admission to the museum in summer is 60DKK ($9.35) adults and 35DKK ($5.45) children 6 to 15, free for children under 6; in winter it's 45DKK ($7) adults and 28DKK ($4.35) children 6 to 15. May to September, the museum is open daily 9am to 5pm; the rest of the year, it's open daily 10am to 5pm.

Stændertorvet, Roskilde's main square, becomes a fruit, flower, vegetable, and flea market on Wednesday and Saturday mornings. A baroque palace, built on the square in 1733, now houses two museums. The **Palæsamlingerne (Palace Collections;** ℃ 46-35-78-80) is a small but noteworthy collection of 18th- and 19th-century paintings and furniture from local merchant families. It's open May to September daily 11am to 4pm (in winter Sat–Sun noon–4pm) and costs 25DKK ($3.15). The **Museet for Samtidskunst (Museum of Contemporary Art;** ℃ 46-36-88-74) hosts changing exhibits of modern art, including performance art, film, dance, and video. It's open Monday to Friday 11am to 4pm and Saturday and Sunday noon to 5pm; admission is 20DKK ($2.50).

In summer, excursion boats ply the **Roskilde Fiord** and concerts are held throughout the venerable city, as well as in **Byparken** (between the cathedral and the Viking Ship Museum) on Tuesday at 7:30pm. The enormously popular 4-day **Roskilde Festival** (℃ 46-36-66-13; www.roskilde-festival.dk) is held sometime near the end of June every year. This is one of Europe's largest annual open-air events, attracting top-name international performers and drawing more than 60,000 people for some performances. While the emphasis is on rock, there's also folk, blues, and jazz, along with film presentations and theatrical performances. Tickets are sold in Danish post offices beginning May 1.

A half-hour **train** ride (70DKK/$11 round-trip) brings you to Roskilde. From the station you can take **bus no. 233** to town, but it's much easier and more fun to walk everywhere. The main pedestrian-only street begins about a block from the station. If you have a **car,** follow Route 21 going west to Roskilde.

11

Dublin & Environs

by Suzanne Rowan Kelleher

Dublin lies on the shore of a sheltered crescent bay, bisected by the dark waters of the River Liffey. It's a small city, easily traversed on foot, and built on a scale that's comfortable rather than magnificent. The hills and rocky headlands rimming it are lovely in the gentle, unassuming way typical of Ireland's east coast.

"Seedy elegance" may have aptly described much, if not most, of Dublin until quite recently, but no longer. What's amazing is that Dublin has gone from endearingly frumpy to cutting-edge cool so quickly. In 1997, *Fortune* magazine named Dublin the number one European city in which to do business—an accolade fueled, no doubt, by its reputation as the "Silicon Valley" of Europe and strategic Euro-headquarters for computer giants such as Microsoft, Dell, Intel, and Sun Microsystems. Then, in 1998, Dublin became the fifth-most-visited city in Europe—nudging ahead of tourist powerhouses like Rome and Amsterdam. More recently, in 2000, an annual survey of world cities conducted by William M. Mercer Ltd. ranked Dublin among the world's top-10 most livable cities—above New York, Boston, and Washington, D.C.

Needless to say, Dublin is a great place to visit. Over 20 new hotels have sprouted up in the past several years in what seems a nearly hopeless race to keep up with tourist demand. Dublin is the hottest spot on the island.

Still, the transformation has been piecemeal, and a stroll across any of the numerous bridges spanning the Liffey will reveal that the prosperity hasn't been shared equally. The south side of the Liffey has seen the bulk of restoration: Layers of soot have been sandblasted from buildings, expensive shops and restaurants abound, and Continental cafes vie with traditional pubs. In contrast, many of the neighborhoods in North Dublin, known by its postal code, Dublin 1, preserve the language and character that James Joyce recorded, a Dublin of pubs whose pedigree can be measured by the thickness of residue left on their walls by generations of heavy smokers.

Dublin is certainly a city of literary ghosts, and it self-consciously promotes itself as a place of literary pilgrimage. For many, its streets are peopled with the shades of those long dead and those who live only in the pages of Irish novels. Even if your head isn't full of passages from *Ulysses,* you can't walk far without coming across a plaque or statue commemorating some event from Joyce's great celebration of Dublin and its people.

For more on Dublin, see *Frommer's Portable Dublin, Frommer's Ireland, Frommer's Ireland from $80 a Day,* or *Ireland For Dummies.*

Value Budget Bests

The National Museum, National Gallery, National Library, and Natural History Museum all have free admission and are within a block of each other. Other free attractions include the Museum of Modern Art in Kilmainham, and the many fine gardens and parks throughout the city.

Inquire at Dublin Tourism about weekly **lunchtime concerts** offered at the National Concert Hall throughout the year. The cost is reasonable, usually €5 ($5.75). Students and seniors can take advantage of reduced tickets at the Abbey and the Gate, Dublin's premier theatrical venues; standard ticket prices are also low, at €15 to €26 ($17–$30), or below.

Beat the crowds and eat cheap by taking advantage of the **early-bird menus** offered at many of Dublin's restaurants between 5:30 and 7pm.

1 Essentials

ARRIVING

BY PLANE   Dublin International Airport (© 01/814-1111; www.dublin-airport.com) is 11km (7 miles) north of the city center. A Travel Information Desk located in the Arrivals Concourse provides information on public bus and rail services throughout the country.

An excellent airport-to-city bus service called **AirCoach** operates 24 hours a day, making runs at 15-minute intervals. AirCoach runs direct from the airport to Dublin's city center and south side, servicing O'Connell Street, St. Stephen's Green, Fitzwilliam Square, Merrion Square, Ballsbridge, and Donnybrook—that is, all the key hotel and business districts. The one-way fare is €6 ($6.90); you buy your ticket from the driver. While AirCoach is more expensive than the Dublin Bus (see below), it is faster because it makes fewer intermediary stops and it brings you right into the hotel districts. To confirm AirCoach departures and arrivals, call © 01/844-7118 or visit www.aircoach.ie. **Dublin Bus** (© 01/872-0000; www.dublinbus.ie) service runs between the airport and the city center between 6am and 11:30pm. The one-way trip takes about 30 minutes, and the fare is €5 ($5.75). Bus numbers 16a, 33, 41, 41a, 41b, 41c, 46x, 58x, 746, 747, and 748 all serve the city center from Dublin Airport. Consult the Travel Information Desk located in the Arrivals Concourse to figure out which bus will bring you closest to your hotel.

If you need to connect with the Irish bus or rail service, the **Airlink Express Coach** (© 01/873-4222) provides express coach service from the airport into the city's central bus station, **Busaras**, on Store Street, and on to the two main rail stations, **Connolly** and **Heuston**. Service runs daily from 7am until 11pm (Sun 7:30am–8:30pm), with departures every 20 to 30 minutes. One-way fare is €5 ($5.75) for adults and €2 ($2.30) for children under age 12.

Depending on your destination in Dublin, **taxi** fares run between €13 and €19 ($15–$22). Surcharges include €.50 (60¢) for each additional passenger and piece of luggage. Depending on traffic, a cab should take 20 to 45 minutes to get into the city center. A 10% tip is standard. Taxis are lined up at a first-come, first-served taxi stand outside the arrivals terminal.

BY FERRY   Passenger and car ferries from Britain arrive at the **Dublin Ferry-port** (© 01/855-2222), on the eastern end of the North Docks, and at the **Dun**

Dublin Deals & Discounts

SPECIAL DISCOUNTS   You can get **discount passes** for travel on Dublin's extensive network of buses and commuter trains. Here are the most useful passes: the 3-day **Rambler Pass,** which offers unlimited travel on Dublin buses (€9.50/$11); the **1-day "short hop" ticket** (€7.70/ $8.85) valid for unlimited travel on all city bus and rail services; and the **1-day family "short hop" ticket** (€12/$14), which allows two adults and up to four children under 16 unlimited use of all city buses and rail services. Discount passes can be purchased at Dublin Bus, 14 O'Connell St. Upper, any branch of the Dublin Tourism Office (see "Visitor Information," below), most Spar and Centra minimarkets, or online at **www. dublinbus.ie**.

Look for **combination tickets** to closely associated sightseeing attractions. In Dublin, for instance, you can get a combination ticket to the Joyce Tower, the Writer's Museum, and the Shaw Birthplace. (Other combination discounts are noted throughout this chapter.)

FOR STUDENTS   Holders of an International Student Identity Card travel at a 50% discount on trains throughout the Republic with a **Travelsave Stamp,** obtained from the USIT Office, 19 Aston Quay, Dublin 2. The stamp also provides a 15% discount on bus fares outside Dublin, and substantially reduced weekly transit passes in Dublin.

WORTH A SPLURGE   Renting a car for a day or 2 brings the extraordinary beauty of the Wicklow Hills or the grandeur of the ancient monuments at Newgrange and the fabled hill of Tara within easy reach.

Bus Eireann (✆ 01/836-6111) and **Gray Line Tours** (✆ 01/605-7705) offer seasonal sightseeing tours to Glendalough, Wicklow, and Powerscourt Gardens for reasonable rates.

Laoghaire Ferryport. Call **Irish Ferries** (✆ **01/661-0511;** www.irishferries.ie) for bookings and information. There is bus and taxi service from both ports.

BY TRAIN   Irish Rail (✆ **01/836-6222;** www.irishrail.ie) operates daily train service to Dublin from Belfast, Northern Ireland, and all major cities in the Irish Republic, including Cork, Galway, Limerick, Killarney, Sligo, Wexford, and Waterford. Trains from the south, west, and southwest arrive at **Heuston Station,** Kingsbridge, off St. John's Road; from the north and northwest at **Connolly Station,** Amiens Street; and from the southeast at **Pearse Station,** Westland Row, Tara Street.

BY BUS   Bus Eireann (✆ **01/836-6111;** www.buseireann.ie) operates daily express coach and local bus service from all major cities and towns in Ireland into Dublin's central bus station, **Busaras,** Store Street.

BY CAR   If you are arriving by car from other parts of Ireland or on a car ferry from Britain, all main roads lead into the heart of Dublin and are well signposted to An Lar (City Centre). To bypass the city center, the East (toll bridge €1.50/ $1.75) and West Links are signposted, and M50 circuits the city on three sides.

VISITOR INFORMATION

TOURIST OFFICES **Dublin Tourism** operates six walk-in visitor centers in greater Dublin that are open every day except Christmas. The principal center is on Suffolk Street, Dublin 2, open from June to August Monday to Saturday from 9am to 8:30pm, Sunday and bank holidays 10:30am to 2:30pm, and the rest of the year Monday to Saturday 9am to 5:30pm. The Suffolk Street office includes a currency exchange counter, a car-rental counter, an accommodations reservations service, bus and rail information desks, a gift shop, and a cafe. For accommodations reservations throughout Ireland by credit card, contact Dublin Tourism at © **01/605-7700;** www.visitdublin.com.

The five other centers are located as follows: **Dublin Airport,** Arrivals Hall; **Exclusively Irish,** O'Connell Street, Dublin 1; **Baggot Street Bridge,** Baggot Street, Dublin 2; **The Square Towncentre,** Tallaght, Dublin 24; and the new **ferry terminal,** Dun Laoghaire Harbor. (All telephone inquiries should be directed to the number listed above.) All centers are open year-round at least from Monday to Friday 9am to 5:30pm and Saturday 9am to 1pm.

At any of these centers you can pick up the free *Tourism News* or the free *Event Guide* (www.eventguide.ie), a biweekly entertainment guide. *In Dublin,* a biweekly arts-and-entertainment magazine selling for €2.50 ($2.85), is available at most newsstands. For information on Ireland outside of Dublin, call **Bord Fáilte** (© **1850/230330** in Ireland; www.travel.ireland.ie).

WEBSITES The breadth of **www.goireland.com** is almost overwhelming. For information and images of historic sites, parks, gardens, and cultural attractions, try **www.heritageireland.ie.** You'll find the Irish Tourist Board at **www. ireland.travel.ie** and Dublin Tourism at **www.visitdublin.com.**

CITY LAYOUT

Dublin is a relatively small metropolis and easily traversed. The city center—identified in Irish on bus destination signs as AN LAR—is bisected by the River Liffey flowing west to east into Dublin Bay. Canals ring the city center: The Royal Canal forms a skirt through the northern half, and the Grand Canal the southern half. True Dubliners, it is said, live between the two canals.

The focal point of Dublin is the **River Liffey,** with 16 bridges connecting its north and south banks. The most famous of these, O'Connell Bridge, is the only traffic bridge in Europe that is wider than it is long.

On the north side of the river, the main thoroughfare is **O'Connell Street,** a wide, two-way avenue that starts at the riverside quays and runs north to **Parnell Square.** Enhanced by statues, trees, and a modern fountain, the O'Connell Street of earlier days was the glamorous shopping drag of the city. It is still important today, but it's neither as fashionable nor as safe as it used to be. Work is under way, however, to give the north side of the Liffey a mighty makeover and make it once again a focus of attention.

On the south side of the Liffey, pedestrian-only **Grafton Street** is Dublin's main shopping street. The street is the center of Dublin's commercial district, surrounded by a maze of small streets and lanes that boast a terrific variety of shops, restaurants, and hotels. At the south end of Grafton Street is **St. Stephen's Green,** the city's most beloved park and an urban oasis ringed by rows of historic Georgian town houses, fine hotels, and restaurants.

At the north end of Grafton Street, **Nassau Street** rims the south side of **Trinity College.** The street features some fine shops, and leads to **Merrion Square,** another fashionable Georgian park surrounded by historic brick-front town houses. Merrion Square is adjacent to Leinster House, the Irish House of Parliament, the National Gallery, and the National Museum.

Dating from Viking and medieval times, the historic **Old City** includes Dublin Castle, the remnants of the city's original walls, and the city's two main cathedrals, Christ Church and St. Patrick's. In the past few years, Old City has become a hip shopping destination.

Sandwiched between Old City and the Trinity College area, **Temple Bar** took off in the 1990s and was transformed into the city's cultural and entertainment hub. As Dublin's self-proclaimed Left Bank, Temple Bar offers a vibrant array of cafes, unique shops, art galleries, recording studios, theaters, trendy restaurants, and atmospheric pubs. This is largely the stomping ground of young tourists, and it's easy to feel over the hill if you're over 25.

GETTING AROUND

Getting around Dublin is not at all daunting. Public transportation is good and getting better; taxis are plentiful and reasonably priced; and central Dublin is quite walkable. In fact, with its current traffic and parking problems, it's a city where the foot is mightier than the wheel. If you can, don't rent a car while you're in the city.

BY DART   Although Dublin has no subway in the strict sense, there is an electric rapid-transit train, known as the **DART** (Dublin Area Rapid Transit). It travels mostly at ground level or on elevated tracks, linking the city-center stations at **Connolly Station, Tara Street, Pearse Street,** and **Amiens Street** with suburbs and seaside communities as far as Balbriggan to the north and Greystones to the south. Service operates roughly every 10 to 20 minutes Monday to Saturday from 7am to midnight and Sunday from 9:30am to 11pm. The minimum fare is €1 ($1.15). One-day and 10-journey passes, as well as student and family tickets, are available at reduced rates.

For further information, contact **DART,** Pearse Station, Dublin 2 (© **1850/ 366222** in Ireland, or 01/836-6222; www.irishrail.ie).

BY BUS   Dublin Bus operates a fleet of green double-decker buses, single-deck buses, and minibuses (called "imps") throughout the city and its suburbs. Most buses originate on or near O'Connell Street, Abbey Street, and Eden Quay on the north side, and at Aston Quay, College Street, and Fleet Street on the south side. Bus stops are located every 2 or 3 blocks. Destinations and bus numbers are posted above the front windows; buses destined for the city center are marked with the Irish Gaelic words AN LAR. In this chapter, bus information is listed for all places where a bus is a viable transportation option.

Bus service runs daily throughout the city, starting at 6am (10am on Sun), with the last bus at 11:30pm. On Thursday, Friday, and Saturday nights, Nitelink service runs from the city center to the suburbs from midnight to 3am. Buses operate every 10 to 15 minutes for most runs; schedules are posted on revolving notice boards at each bus stop.

Inner-city fares are calculated based on distances traveled. The minimum fare is €.80 (90¢); the maximum fare is €2 ($2.30). The Nitelink fare is a flat €4 ($4.60). Buy your tickets from the driver as you enter the bus; exact change is required, so have your loose change available. Notes of €5 or higher may not be accepted. Discounted 1-day, 3-day, 5-day, and 7-day passes are available. The 1-day bus-only pass costs €5 ($5.75); the 3-day pass costs €9.50 ($11); the 5-day pass goes for €15 ($17); and the 7-day pass costs €18 ($21). For more information, contact **Dublin Bus,** 59 Upper O'Connell St., Dublin 1 ((*C*) **01/87 2-0000;** www.dublinbus.ie).

BY TRAM   The newest addition to Dublin's public transportation network is set to be the sleek light-rail tram known as **LUAS,** due for completion in mid-2004. Traveling at a maximum speed of 70kmph (43 mph) and departing every 5 minutes in peak hours, LUAS aims to appease Dublin's congestion problems and bring the city's transportation into the 21st century. Three lines will link the city center at **Connolly Station** and **St. Stephen's Green** with the suburbs of Tallaght in the southwest and Dundrum and Sandyford to the south. Fares were not yet set as of press time. For further information, contact **LUAS** ((*C*) **01/703-2029;** www.luas.ie).

BY TAXI   Dublin taxis do not cruise the streets looking for fares; instead, they line up at "ranks" (stands). Ranks are located outside all the leading hotels, at bus and train stations, and on prime thoroughfares such as Upper O'Connell Street, College Green, and the north side of St. Stephen's Green near the Shelbourne Hotel. The Dublin taxi market currently suffers from chronic excess demand, with long lines for taxis and little new supply since 1978. More cabs should eventually make the situation better, but for now it can be extremely difficult to catch a cab in the city center—especially on weekend evenings.

You can also phone for a taxi. Some of the companies that operate a 24-hour radio-call service are **Co-Op** ((*C*) **01/676-6666), Shamrock Radio Cabs** ((*C*) **01/ 855-5444),** and **VIP Taxis** ((*C*) **01/478-3333).** If you need a wake-up call, VIP offers that service, along with especially courteous dependability.

Taxi rates are fixed by law and posted in each vehicle. A 2002 survey found the following to be typical travel costs in the city center: A 3.3km (2-mile) journey costs €4.95 ($5.70) by day and €6.85 ($7.90) at night; an 8km (5-mile) journey runs €10 ($12) by day and €12 ($14) at night; and a 16km (10-mile) journey costs €16 ($18) by day and €21 ($24) at night. There's an additional charge for each extra passenger and for each suitcase of €.50 (60¢). And it costs an extra €1.50 ($1.75) for a dispatched pickup. *Be warned:* Some hotel staff members will tack on as much as €4 ($4.60) for calling you a cab, although this practice violates city taxi regulations.

BY RENTAL CAR   Renting a car while you're based in Dublin isn't advisable because of traffic congestion and parking problems, but when exploring the countryside you might want to go by car. If you do rent a car in Dublin, be sure you can park it off the street—car theft and break-ins are all too frequent. Also, remember to keep to the *left-hand side of the road,* and don't drive in bus lanes. The speed limit within the city is 46kmph (29 mph), and seat belts must be worn at all times by driver and passengers.

Most major international **car-rental firms** are represented in Dublin, as are many Irish-based companies. They have desks at the airport, full-service offices downtown, or both. The rates vary greatly according to company, season, type of car, and duration of rental. In high season, the average weekly cost of a car, from subcompact standard to full-size automatic, ranges from €200 to €1,525 ($230–$1,754); you'll be much better off if you've made your car-rental arrangements well in advance from home. (Also see "By Car" under "Getting Around" in chapter 2.).

International firms represented in Dublin include **Avis,** 1 Hanover St. E., Dublin 1 and at Dublin Airport ((*C*) 01/605-7500); **Budget,** in Dublin ((*C*) 01/837-9611), and at Dublin Airport ((*C*) 01/844-5150); **Dan Dooley Rent-a-Car,**

Country & City Codes

The **country code** for Ireland is **353**. The **city code** for Dublin is **1**; use this code when you're calling from outside Ireland. If you're within Ireland but not in Dublin, use **01**. If you're calling within Dublin, simply leave off the code and dial only the seven-digit local phone number.

---

42 Westland Row, Dublin 2 (© 01/677-2723), and at Dublin Airport (© 01/844-5156); **Hertz,** 149 Upper Leeson St., Dublin 4 (© 01/660-2255), and at Dublin Airport (© 01/844-5466); and **Murray's Europcar,** Baggot Street Bridge, Dublin 4 (toll-free © 1850/403803), and at Dublin Airport (© 01/812-0410). **Auto Europe** (© 800/223-5555; fax 207/828-1177; www.autoeurope. com) consistently offers excellent rates and service on overseas rentals and long-term leases. Their agreements are clear, straightforward, and all-inclusive. Better yet, they can beat any bona fide offer from another company; ask for the "Beat Rate Desk." Another well-established firm offering good deals on long-term leases and rentals is **Europe by Car** (© 800/223-1516; www.europebycar.com).

Throughout Dublin, you'll find multibay meters and "pay and display" **disc parking.** In Dublin, a five-pack of discs costs €6.35 ($7.30). Each ticket is good for a maximum of 3 hours. The most reliable and safest places to park are surface parking lots and multistory car parks in central locations such as Kildare Street, Lower Abbey Street, Marlborough Street, and St. Stephen's Green West. Expect to pay €1.90 ($2.20) per hour and €19 ($22) for 24 hours. Night rates run €6.35 to €9 ($7.30–$10) per hour.

FAST FACTS: Dublin

American Express A full-service office is opposite Trinity College at 41 Nassau St., Dublin 2 (© 1890/205511). It's open Monday to Saturday 9am to 5pm. American Express also has a desk at the **Dublin Tourism Office** on Suffolk Street (© 01/605-7709). In an emergency, traveler's checks can be reported lost or stolen by dialing toll-free in Ireland © 1890/706706.

Banks Nearly all banks are open Monday to Friday 10am to 4pm (to 5pm Thurs) and have ATMs that accept Cirrus network cards as well as Master-Card and Visa. Convenient locations include the **Bank of Ireland,** at 28 O'Connell St., Dublin 1, and at 34 College Green, Dublin 2; and the **Allied Irish Bank,** at 64 Grafton St., Dublin 2; 37 O'Connell St., Dublin 1; and 12 St. Stephen's Green, Dublin 2.

Business Hours **Museums** and **sights** are generally open 10am to 5pm Tuesday to Saturday, and 2 to 5pm Sunday. **Shops** are generally open 9am to 6pm Monday to Wednesday and Friday through Sunday, with hours extended on Thursday (stores open later and usually stay open until 7 or 8pm). In the city center, most department stores and many shops are open noon to 6pm Sunday.

Currency & Currency Exchange The Republic of Ireland has adopted the single European currency known as the **euro.** In converting prices into U.S. dollars, we used the rates €1 = $1.15. Currency-exchange services, signposted as BUREAU DE CHANGE, are in all banks and at many branches of the Irish post office system known as **An Post**. Some hotels and travel agencies offer bureau de change services, although the best rate of exchange is usually when you use your bank card at an ATM.

Doctors If you need to see a physician, most hotels and guesthouses will contact a house doctor for you. Otherwise, you can call either the **Eastern Health Board Headquarters,** Dr. Steevens Hospital, Dublin 8 (© **01/679-0700**); or the **Irish Medical Organization,** 10 Fitzwilliam Place, Dublin 2 (© **01/676-7273**), 9:15am to 5:15pm for a referral. The American Embassy (see "Embassies & Consulates," below) can provide a list of doctors in the city and surrounding areas.

Embassies & Consulates The **American** Embassy is at 42 Elgin Rd., Ballsbridge, Dublin 4 (© **01/668-8777**); the **Canadian** Embassy is at 65-68 St. Stephen's Green, Dublin 2 (© **01/678-1988**); the **British** Embassy is at 29 Merrion Rd., Dublin 4 (© **01/205-3700**); and the **Australian** Embassy is at Fitzwilton House, Wilton Terrace, Dublin 2 (© **01/676-1517**).

Emergencies For police, fire, or other emergencies, dial © **999.**

Holidays Dublin holidays are New Year's Day (Jan 1), St. Patrick's Day (Mar 17), Good Friday and Easter Monday, May Day (the 1st Mon in May), summer bank holidays (the 1st Mon in June and Aug), autumn bank holiday (the last Mon in Oct), Christmas Day (Dec 25), and St. Stephen's Day (Dec 26). Many stores stay closed between Christmas and the first Monday after New Year's Day.

Hospitals For emergency care, two of the most modern healthcare facilities are **St. Vincent's Hospital,** Herbert Avenue, Dublin 4 (© **01/269-4533**), on the south side; and **Beaumont Hospital,** Beaumont Road, Dublin 9 (© **01/837-7755**), on the north side.

Internet Access In cyber-savvy Dublin, public access terminals appear in shopping malls, hotels, and hostels throughout the city center. Like all of Dublin's public libraries, the **Central Library,** in the ILAC Centre, off Henry Street, Dublin 1 (© **01/873-4333**), has a bank of PCs with free Internet access. Three centrally located cybercafes are the **Central Cybercafe,** 6 Grafton St., Dublin 2 (© **01/677-8298**); **Planet Cyber Café,** 13 St. Andrews St., Dublin 2 (© **01/670-5182**); and **The Connect Point,** 33 Dorset St. Lower, Dublin 1 (© **01/834-9821**). A half-hour online averages €3.50 ($4).

Laundry & Dry Cleaning Centrally located do-it-yourself choices include **All-American Launderette,** Wicklow Court., Dublin 2 (© **01/677-2779**); **Craft Cleaners,** 12 Upper Baggot St., Dublin 4 (© **01/668-8198**); and **Grafton Cleaners,** 32 S. William St., Dublin 2 (© **01/679-4309**).

Pharmacies Centrally located drugstores, known locally as pharmacies or chemist shops, include **Hamilton Long & Co.,** 5 Lower O'Connell St. (© **01/874-8456**); and **Dame Street Pharmacy,** 16 Dame St., Dublin 2 (© **01/670-4523**). A late-night chemist shop is **Hamilton Long & Co.,** 4 Merrion Rd., Dublin 4 (© **01/668-3287**). It closes at 9pm daily.

Police Dial © **999** in an emergency. Headquarters for the Dublin **Garda Siochana** (police) is in Phoenix Park, Dublin 8 (© **01/666-0000**).

Post Office The **General Post Office (GPO)** is located on O'Connell Street, Dublin 1 (℡ **01/705-7000**). Hours are Monday to Saturday 8am to 8pm, Sunday and holidays 10:30am to 6:30pm. Branch offices, identified by the sign OIFIG AN POST/POST OFFICE, are open Monday to Saturday only, 9am to 6pm.

Tax The Irish sales tax is called VAT (value-added tax) and is usually already included in the price shown on price tags. VAT rates vary—for hotels, restaurants, and car rentals, it is 13.5% and nonrefundable. For souvenirs and gifts, VAT is a whopping 21%, but visitors can get refunds. For full details, see "Frommer's Money-Saving Strategies" in chapter 1.

Telephone The Irish telephone system is known as Eircom. Phone numbers in Ireland are currently in flux and vary in length, as digits are added to accommodate expanded service. Every effort has been made to ensure that the numbers and information in this guide are accurate at the time of writing. If you have difficulty reaching a party, the Irish toll-free number for directory assistance is ℡ **11811**. From the United States, the (toll) number to call is ℡ **00353-91-770220**.

Local calls from a phone booth require pre-paid Callcard. Callcards can be purchased in a range of denominations at phone company offices, post offices, and many retail outlets (such as newsstands). There's a local and international phone center at the General Post Office on O'Connell Street. Be aware that overseas calls from Ireland can be quite costly, whether you use a local phone card or your own calling card. If you think you will want to call home regularly while in Ireland, you may want to open an account with **Swiftcall** (toll-free in Ireland ℡ **1800/929932**; www.swiftcall.com). Its rates represent a considerable savings, not only from Ireland to the United States but vice versa (handy for planning your trip as well as keeping in touch while you're away). **To place a call from your home country to Ireland,** dial the international access code (011 in the U.S., 0011 in Australia, 0170 in New Zealand, 00 in the U.K.), plus the country code (**353** for the Republic, **44** for the North), and finally the number, remembering to omit the initial 0, which is for use only within Ireland (for example, to call the County Kerry number 066/00000 from the U.S., you'd dial 011-353-66/00000).

To place a direct international call from Ireland, dial the international access code **(00)** plus the country code (U.S. and Canada 1, the U.K. 44, Australia 61, New Zealand 64), the area or city code, and the number. For example, to call the U.S. number (212/000-0000), you'd dial (00-1-212/000-0000). The toll-free international access code for **AT&T** is ℡ 1-800/550-000; for **Sprint** it's ℡ 1-800/552-001; and for **MCI** it's ℡ 1-800/551-001. *Note:* To dial direct to Northern Ireland from the Republic, simply replace the 028 prefix with 048.

Tipping Most hotels and guesthouses add a service charge to the bill, usually 12.5% to 15%, although some smaller places add only 10% or nothing at all. Always check. For taxi drivers, hairdressers, and other providers of service, tip 10% to 15%. For restaurants, the policy is usually printed on the menu—either a gratuity of 10% to 15% is automatically added to your bill, or it's left up to you. Always ask if you are in doubt. As a rule, waitstaff at bars do not expect a tip, except when table service is provided.

2 Affordable Places to Stay

It usually pays to book hotels well in advance. Many hotels can be booked through toll-free numbers in the United States, and the quoted prices offered can be appreciably (as much as 40%) lower than those offered at the door. For properties that don't have a U.S. reservation number, the fastest way to reserve is by telephone, fax, or e-mail.

If you arrive in Ireland without a reservation, the staff members at the tourist offices throughout the Republic and Northern Ireland will gladly find you a room using a computerized reservation service known as **Gulliver.** In Ireland, you can call the Gulliver line directly (✆ **00800/668-668-66**). This is a nationwide and cross-border "free-phone" facility for credit card bookings, operated daily 8am to 11pm. Gulliver is also accessible from the United States (✆ **011-800/668-668-66**) and on the Web at **www.gulliver.ie.**

Note: Most of the lodging choices below are plotted on the map on p. 382.

IN THE CITY CENTER—SOUTH OF THE LIFFEY

Fitzwilliam Guesthouse   This guesthouse occupies a meticulously restored 18th-century town house on Fitzwilliam Street, the best-preserved Georgian thoroughfare in Dublin and a convenient location for exploring the city. The entrance parlor has a homey atmosphere, with a carved marble fireplace and antique furnishings. The bright guest rooms have high ceilings; bathrooms are small, but impeccably clean. Tea/coffeemakers are available just outside every room. A full Irish breakfast is served in the vaulted basement dining room.

41 Upper Fitzwilliam St., Dublin 2. ✆ **01/662-5155.** Fax 01/676-7488. 12 units, all with private bathroom. €130 ($150) double. Rates include full breakfast. AE, DC, MC, V. DART to Pearse Station (then a 10-min. walk southeast). Bus: 10. *In room:* TV, hair dryer, iron.

Harding Hotel   Built in 1996 by USIT, Ireland's youth travel organization, the Harding is an unexciting budget hotel with a great location at the foot of Christ Church Cathedral. The units are comfortable and plain; most have a double bed and a couch with a foldout bed. The bathrooms are basic. Units facing west toward Christ Church offer the best views. There's a restaurant on the ground floor, but it doesn't compete with the cheap and cheerful culinary delights of neighboring Temple Bar. So pass on the breakfast and grab something outside.

Copper Alley, Fishamble St., Christ Church, Dublin 2. ✆ **01/679-6500.** Fax 01/679-6504. www.hardinghotel.ie. 53 units, all with private bathroom (shower only). €60 ($69) single; €89–€105 ($102–$121) double or triple. MC, V. Bus: 21A, 50, 50A, 78, 78A, or 78B. **Amenities:** Restaurant. *In room:* TV, tea/coffeemaker, hair dryer.

Jurys Inn Christchurch ⭐ *Value*   A good location in Old City, facing Christ Church cathedral, makes this a solid choice. Totally refurbished in 1998, the rooms are larger than you'd expect and bright, though the decor has the same floral bedspreads and framed watercolors as every other chain hotel you've ever visited. Make your reservations early and request a fifth-floor room facing west for a memorable view of Christ Church. *Tip:* Room nos. 501, 507, and 419 are especially spacious.

Christ Church Place, Dublin 8. ✆ **800/44-UTELL** in the U.S., or 01/454-0000. Fax 01/454-0012. www. jurys.com. 182 units. €112 ($129) double. Service charge included. AE, MC, V. Discounted parking available at adjacent lot. Bus: 21A, 50, 50A, 78, 78A, or 78B. **Amenities:** Restaurant; pub; babysitting; laundry/dry cleaning; nonsmoking rooms. *In room:* A/C, TV, coffeemaker, hair dryer.

Kilronan House ⭐⭐   This extremely comfortable B&B is set on a peaceful, tree-lined road just 5 minutes' walk from St. Stephen's Green. Much of the Georgian character remains, such as the ceiling cornicing, hardwood parquet

Value Getting the Best Deal on Accommodations

- **Book from home.** If your desired hotel has a toll-free number in the United States, get a quote and compare it to what the hotel's front desk offers. Nine times out of ten, the toll-free number's rate will be substantially lower than those offered at the door.
- **Haggle.** Room prices in hotels—especially privately owned hotels in the off season—are often negotiable. Your best bet is to politely ask, "Is that your best rate?" or "Can you do a little bit better?"
- **Use a Consolidator.** Just like with airfares, you can often save money on hotel accommodations if you go through a middleman. On the Web, try www.hotelsireland.net for savings of up to 50% on rack rates for two- to five-star hotels across Ireland.

floors, and fine staircase. The sitting room on the ground floor is particularly intimate, with a fire blazing through the cold months of the year. The rooms are brightly inviting in white and yellow, and those facing the front have commodious bay windows. There's no elevator, so consider requesting a room on a lower floor. The front rooms, facing Adelaide Street, are also preferable to those in back, which face onto office buildings and a parking lot. Breakfast here is especially good, featuring homemade breads.

70 Adelaide Rd., Dublin 2. (℅ 01/475-5266. Fax 01/478-2841. www.dublinn.com/kilronan.htm. 15 units, 13 with private bathroom (shower only). €152 ($175) double. Rates include full breakfast. AE, MC, V. Free private parking. Bus: 14, 15, 19, 20, or 46A. *In room:* TV, tea/coffeemaker, hair dryer.

Kinlay House Hostel   Open year-round and run by USIT, Kinlay House occupies a beautiful redbrick town house in one of Dublin's oldest neighborhoods, steps from Christ Church Cathedral and on the edge of trendy Temple Bar. There's a large self-catering kitchen and dining room on the ground floor and a smaller kitchen on the third floor. Other common spaces include a TV room and a meeting room. The rooms are small but clean. Though there's supposedly a nonsmoking policy, it isn't generally respected by staff or guests. Price ranges given below reflect seasonal fluctuations and midweek versus weekend rates.

2–12 Lord Edward St., Dublin 2. (℅ 01/679-6644. Fax 01/679-7437. www.kinlayhouse.ie. 36 units, 12 with bathroom (shower only); 13 doubles, 6 with bathroom; 23 dorms, 6 with bathroom. €15–€18 ($17–$21) per person dorm; €40–€50 ($46–$58) single; €50–€62 ($58–$71) double without bathroom, €54–€66 ($62–$76) double with bathroom. Rates include continental breakfast. MC, V. Bus: 21A, 50, 50A, 78, 78A, or 78B. **Amenities:** TV room; self-catering kitchen.

Trinity College Accommodation   During the summer months, Trinity College rents student rooms to visitors on a per-night basis, offering a great base from which to explore the city. Trinity is the oldest university in Ireland, occupying a venerable campus within the heart of downtown Dublin. Most rooms are located inside the college walls, either in 19th-century buildings typical of the historic campus or in a group of attractive dorms built in 1990 adjacent to the Beckett Theatre; the rest of the rooms are in Goldsmith Hall, a dormitory built in 1996 next to the Pearse Street DART station. Most rooms have a twin bed, a desk, plenty of built-in cupboards, a closet, and a compact bathroom with shower; rooms with double beds are also available. Other permutations include suites with two (or four) single rooms, a living room, one (or two) shared bathrooms, and minimal kitchen facilities (perfect for families or friends traveling together). The rooms in the Graduate Memorial Building have the most character (high ceilings, views across the green to the Old Library), while the most spacious rooms are in Goldsmith Hall, the newest dorm on campus.

Trinity College, Dublin 2. © **01/608-1177.** Fax 01/671-1267. www.tcd.ie. Units available June 7–Sept 30. 760 units, 360 with bathroom (shower only). €51 ($59) single with shared bathroom, €62 ($71) single with bathroom; €85 ($98) double without bathroom, €109 ($125) double with bathroom. Rates include continental breakfast. MC, V. Discounted rates at nearby parking garage. Bus: 21A, 50, 50A, 78, 78A, or 78B. **Amenities:** Restaurant.

IN THE CITY CENTER—NORTH OF THE LIFFEY

Jurys Inn Custom House ★★ *Value*   Ensconced in the grandiose new financial services district and facing the quays, this Jurys Inn follows the successful formula of affordable comfort without frills. Single rooms have a double bed and a pullout sofa, while double rooms offer both a double and a twin bed. Twenty-two especially spacious rooms, if available, cost nothing extra. Rooms facing the quays also enjoy vistas of the Dublin hills, but those facing the financial district are quieter. Be sure to book well in advance.

Custom House Quay, Dublin 1. © **800/44-UTELL** in the U.S., or 01/607-5000. Fax 01/829-0400. www. jurys.com. 239 units. €89–€99 ($102–$114) single; €103–€112 ($118–$129) double. Rates include service charge. AE, DC, MC, V. Discounted parking available at adjacent lot. DART: Tara Street. Bus: 27A, 27B, or 53A. **Amenities:** Restaurant; bar; laundry/dry cleaning; nonsmoking rooms. *In room:* TV, dataport, tea/coffeemaker, hair dryer, phone.

IN THE SUBURBS—SOUTH OF THE LIFFEY

Ariel House ★★   In the age of the generic, Ariel House remains a bastion of distinction and quality. For Dublin guesthouses, this one sets the standard. Deirdre MacDonald, manager, is a warm and consummate host. Guests are welcome to relax in the Victorian-style drawing room, with its Waterford glass chandeliers, open fireplace, and delicately carved cornices. The guest rooms are individually decorated, with period furniture, fine paintings and watercolors, and crisp Irish linens, as well as an array of modern extras.

50–52 Lansdowne Rd., Ballsbridge, Dublin 4. © **01/668-5512.** Fax 01/668-5845. www.ariel-house.com. 37 units, all with private bathroom. €85–€130 ($98–$150) double. Service charge 10%. MC, V. Private car park. DART to Lansdowne Rd. Station. Bus: 7, 7A, 8, or 45. *In room:* TV, tea/coffeemaker, hair dryer, iron.

Avonlee House ★   Shelagh Moynihan's cozy 19th-century brick town house offers an abundance of simple comforts. The guest rooms are generously proportioned, with refreshingly contemporary furnishings and firm beds; windows are equipped with double-paned glass. The breakfast menu includes smoked salmon and several varieties of omelet in addition to the traditional Irish breakfast. The city center is a 20-minute-walk from the house and there is also a convenient bus stop nearby.

68 Sandford Rd., Ranelagh, Dublin 6. © **01/496-7822.** Fax 01/491-0523. 5 units, all with private bathroom. €57 ($66) single; €102 ($117) double. Rates include full breakfast. MC, V. Closed Christmas to 1st week in Jan. Bus: 11, 11A, 11B, 11C, 44, 44A, 44B, 48A, or 86. *In room:* TV, tea/coffeemaker.

Bewley's Hotel ★   The Bewley's Hotel occupies what was once a 19th-century brick Masonic school building adjacent to the RDS show grounds and next to the British Embassy. A new wing harmonizes well with the old structure, and is indistinguishable in the interior. Public lounges and reception areas are spacious and appointed with mahogany wainscoting, marble paneling, and polished bronze. Rooms, too, are spacious and well furnished—each has a writing desk, an armchair, and either one king-size bed or a double and a twin bed. The studios

---

(Value **More Money-Saving Tips**

- Some Dublin guesthouses offer attractive weekend and 3- or 6-day **package rates** during the low season, with discounts for seniors, so be sure to ask when booking.
- Check with travel agents for package deals including airfare and accommodations—these are usually offered during the off season only. Bus Eireann and Irish Rail (see "Arriving," earlier in this chapter) both offer package holidays with substantial discounts on accommodations, and **Sceptre Tours** regularly offers combined airfare, car rental, and/or accommodations packages at very reasonable rates (© **800/221-0924;** www.sceptretours.com).
- Be aware that if your stay in Dublin is a week or longer, you might save money by booking one of the many apartments available on a **self-catering** basis. Minimum rental is usually 1 week, though some are available for 3-day periods. Inquire about credit card acceptance—many of these operators prefer to work on a cash basis. Check with Dublin Tourism (**www.visitdublin.com**) about available apartments throughout the city.
- Hostels are Ireland's best budget option, and they're as diverse as the people who run them. Many have private rooms at about half the rate you'd pay in the average B&B. Contact **An Óige,** the Irish Youth Hostel Organization (© **01/830-4555;** www.irelandyha.org).

---

have a bedroom with a double bed, plus another room with a foldout couch, a table (seats six), a pullout kitchenette/bar hidden in a cabinet, and an additional bathroom (shower only). The basement restaurant offers very good food at reasonable prices; there's also an informal Bewley's tearoom. The hotel is an excellent value for families and groups; the big downside is its location outside the city center.

Merrion Rd., Ballsbridge, Dublin 4. © **01/668-1111.** Fax: 01/668-1999. www.bewleyshotels.com. 220 units. €99 ($114) double. Rates includes service charge and taxes. AE, DC, MC, V. DART: Sandymount (5 min. walk). Bus: 7, 7A, 7X, 8, or 45. **Amenities:** Restaurant; tearoom. *In room:* TV, dataport, kitchenette, tea/coffeemaker, hair dryer, safe, garment press.

Lansdowne Village   Lansdowne Village is a modest and appealing residential development on the banks of the River Dodder and directly across from Lansdowne Stadium. Within this community, Trident Holiday Homes offers fully equipped two- and three-bedroom rental units, each with an additional pullout double-bed sofa in the living room. They are bright and comfortable, and well maintained, so everything really works. The location is ideal. Not only are you a 5-minute walk from the DART and less than a half-hour's walk from St. Stephen's Green, but the Sandymount Strand, a favorite walking spot for Dubliners, is only 10 minutes away on foot for a pleasant after-dinner stroll. Shops and supermarkets are also nearby, so you can manage here quite well without a car, feeling apart from the city's frenzy and yet not at all cut off.

Newbridge Ave. off Lansdowne Rd., Ballsbridge, Dublin 4. © **01/668-3534.** Fax 01/660-6465. 19 units (2- or 3-bedroom). €700–€960 ($805–$1,104) per week. Shorter periods available at reduced rates Oct–Mar. MC, V. DART: Lansdowne Rd. Station. Bus: 2, 3, 5, 7, 7A, 8, 18, or 45. *In room:* TV, kitchenette, washer/dryer.

Waterloo House 🏵 Waterloo House (actually not one, but two Georgian town houses) is one of the most popular B&Bs in Dublin. Perhaps it's because Evelyn Corcoran and her staff take such good care of you, in a friendly but unobtrusive way. The place is charming in an old-world kind of way, with classical music wafting through the lobby, and an elegant, high-ceilinged drawing room. Guest rooms are comfortable and large (some have two double beds), but it's hard to decide whether the decor, featuring red-patterned carpet and box-pleated bedspreads, is reassuringly traditional or merely dated. The varied breakfast menu is a high point. This is a nonsmoking house.

8–10 Waterloo Rd., Ballsbridge, Dublin 4. ⓒ **01/660-1888.** Fax 01/667-1955. www.waterloohouse.ie. 17 units, all with private bathroom. €78–€175 ($90–$201) double. Rates include full breakfast. MC, V. Free car parking. Closed Christmas week. DART: Lansdowne Rd. Bus: 5, 7, or 8. *In room:* TV, tea/coffeemaker, hair dryer, garment press.

IN THE SUBURBS—NORTH OF THE LIFFEY

Aishling House 🏵 *Kids* A large garden, a location very near the sea, and a warm welcome from hosts Frances and Robert English make Aishling House an exceptionally pleasant base for sightseeing in Dublin. Several Frommer's readers have written to praise this beautifully refurbished Victorian house for the many thoughtful though simple details that distinguish the rooms, including fluffy towels and highly comfortable beds. Three of the rooms are particularly spacious, making them very suitable for families.

19–20 St. Lawrence Rd., Clontarf, Dublin 3. ⓒ **01/833-9097.** Fax 01/833-8400. www.aishlinghouse.com. 9 units, all with private bathroom (shower only). €45 ($52) single; €90 ($104) double. Rates include full breakfast. 50% discount for children staying in parent's room; no charge for children 11 months and under. MC, V. Free parking. Bus: 130. *In room:* TV, hair dryer.

3 Great Deals on Dining

The food scene is changing in Ireland, and while Dublin might not always be at the forefront of this change, it certainly is keeping up. You'll find an increasing number of informal restaurants with small menus and big ambitions, serving food based on the best local ingredients. Plates heaped high with limp vegetables and dubious meats are definitely out—you're more likely to find the capital's culinary imagination at work on an Indian curry, a retake on a great Continental dish, or a succulent spinach cannelloni.

For a taste of Dublin before you leave home, visit **www.ireland.com**, where you can browse archived *Irish Times* restaurant reviews.

IN THE CITY CENTER—SOUTH OF THE LIFFEY

Aya @ Brown Thomas 🏵🏵🏵 JAPANESE The conveyor belt sushi bar has arrived, and Dubliners may never be the same. The good news is that, beyond the trendiness of this buzzing, fashionable annex to Dublin's poshest department store, the food here is damn good. Lunch offers all the classics—tempura, gyoza, and, of course, plenty of sushi—while the dinner menu expands to include yakitori, steaks, and noodle salads. Bypass the table seating (where the a la carte menu is pricier) and head straight for the bar, where afternoon "happy hours" offer small portions of sushi at €2 to €3 ($2.30–$3.45) per plate. (Or come for dinner Sun–Tues for the Sushi55 special: all the sushi you can eat in 55 min., including one complimentary drink, for €24/$28).

49–52 Clarendon St., Dublin 2. ⓒ **01/677-1544.** Reservations recommended for dinner. Lunch €11 ($13); dinner €32 ($37). AE, DC, MC, V. Mon–Sat 10:30am–11pm; Sun noon–10pm. DART: Tara St. Bus: 16A, 19A, 22A, 55, or 83.

Cafe Bell ⚘ *Value* IRISH/SELF-SERVICE   In the cobbled courtyard of early-19th-century St. Teresa's Church, this serene little place is one of a handful of dining options springing up in historic or ecclesiastical surroundings. The menu changes daily but usually includes very good homemade soups, sandwiches, salads, quiches, lasagna, sausage rolls, hot scones, and other baked goods.

St. Teresa's Courtyard, Clarendon St., Dublin 2. ℂ 01/677-7645. All items €3–€6 ($3.45–$6.90). No credit cards. Mon–Sat 9am–5:30pm. Bus: 16, 16A, 19, 19A, 22A, 55, or 83.

Cornucopia Wholefood Restaurant ⚘ *Value* ORGANIC/VEGETARIAN
This little cafe just off Grafton Street is one of the best vegetarian restaurants in the city, and also serves wholesome meals for people on various restricted diets (vegan, nondairy, low sodium, low fat). Soups are particularly good here, as is the baked lasagna made with eggplant.

19 Wicklow St., Dublin 2. ℂ 01/677-7583. Main courses €4–€10 ($4.60–$12). MC, V. Mon–Thurs 8am–7pm; Fri–Sat 8am–10pm. Bus: Any city-center bus.

Dish ⚘⚘ INTERNATIONAL   This is deservedly one of the city's most popular and consistently buzzing restaurants. Chef Gerard Foote uses organic, fresh ingredients and is a master at combining unlikely flavors and coming up with tantalizing results. The griddled scallops with mousseline potatoes and garlic butter are perfect, as is the grilled salmon with avocado, papaya, and tequila-lime dressing. The desserts—including a melt-away vanilla panna cotta and amaretto chocolate cheesecake—are nothing short of sensational.

146 Upper Leeson St., Dublin 4. ℂ 01/664-2135. Reservations recommended. Fixed-price lunch €20 ($23); dinner main courses €16–€26 ($18–$30). AE, DC, MC, V. Daily noon–11:30pm. DART: Tara St. Bus: 21A, 46A, 46B, 51B, 51C, 68, 69, or 86.

Elephant & Castle ⚘⚘ AMERICAN   You'd be forgiven for thinking you could find this kind of food—burgers, chicken wings, omelets—at any old Yankee-style joint, but Noel Alexander elevates casual American fare to an art form, working the stove as if he was brought up in American diners. His chicken wings are scrumptious, his burgers out of this world, his omelets "spot on," as the Irish would say. It's an immensely popular place for breakfast, brunch, lunch, afternoon nibble, dinner, or late dinner.

18 Temple Bar, Dublin 2. ℂ 01/679-3121. Main courses €8–€22 ($9.20–$25). AE, MC, V. Mon–Fri 8am–11:30pm; Sat 10:30am–11:30pm; Sun noon–11:30pm. Bus: 51B, 51C, 68, 69, or 79.

⟨*Value* **Getting the Best Deal on Dining**

- Make lunch your main meal. Most of the city's hippest restaurants offer good-value, set-price lunch menus. It's the best way to eat well for less.
- Make your evening meal an early one, in order to take advantage of early-bird specials offered by many restaurants between 5:30 and 7pm.
- Eat at cafes and pubs; most will feed you well at prices far below those of most restaurants.
- Save by preparing your own meals in the kitchen of your hostel or self-catering apartment.

> **Value Picnic, Anyone?**
>
> The parks of Dublin offer plenty of sylvan settings for a picnic lunch. In particular, try **St. Stephen's Green** at lunchtime (in the summer, there are open-air band concerts), the **Phoenix Park**, and **Merrion Square**. For a good selection of fixings, try any of the following: **Gallic Kitchen**, 49 Francis St., Dublin 8 (✆ **01/454-4912**), has gourmet prepared food to go, from salmon en croûte to pâtés, quiches, sausage rolls, and homemade pies, breads, and cakes; **Magills Delicatessen**, 14 Clarendon St., Dublin 2 (✆ **01/671-3830**), offers Asian and Continental delicacies, meats, cheeses, and salads. For a fine selection of Irish cheeses, luncheon meat, and other delicacies, seek out **Sheridan's Cheesemongers**, 11 S. Anne St., Dublin 2 (✆ **01/679-3143**), perhaps the best of Dublin's cheese emporiums; or the **Big Cheese Company**, 14/15 Trinity St. (✆ **01/671-1399**).

Fitzers Café ✦ INTERNATIONAL   This is one branch of a chain of winning cafes that serve up excellent, up-to-date, and reasonably priced food. Nestled on a street known for its bookshops, this bright, airy, Irish-style bistro has a multiwindowed facade and modern decor. Choices range from chicken breast with hot chile cream sauce or brochette of lamb tandoori with mild curry sauce to gratin of smoked cod. There are also tempting vegetarian dishes made from organic produce. Fitzers has two other Dublin locations: just a few blocks away at the National Gallery, Merrion Square West (✆ **01/661-4496**); and at Temple Bar Square (✆ **01/679-0440**). You'll find the same menu, the same decor theme, and the same good service at each location.

51 Dawson St., Dublin 2. ✆ **01/677-1155**. Dinner main courses €14–€20 ($16–$23). AE, DC, MC, V. Daily 11:30am–11pm. Closed Dec 24–27 and Good Friday. DART: Pearse. Bus: 10, 11A, 11B, 13, or 20B.

The French Paradox ✦✦ *Value* WINE BAR   Just what tony D4 needed: A price-conscious, darling little bistro-cum-*bar de vin* that's endeared itself to everyone in the city. The wine's the thing here, so relax with a bottle of Bordeaux or Côte du Rhone and whatever nibbles you like from the menu. There's a lovely cheese plate named for West Cork cheesemaker Bill Hogan, superb Iberico hams from Spain or, if you're more hungry, the delicious bistro stalwart of confit of duck with vegetables. Whatever you order will be simply delicious and elegantly presented. There are weekday fixed-price specials that change often but always deliver good value.

53 Shelbourne Rd., Dublin 4. ✆ **01/660-4068**. www.thefrenchparadox.com. Reservations recommended. All plates €10–€16 ($12–$18). AE, MC, V. Mon–Sat noon–3pm and 2 evening sittings at 6 and 9pm. DART: Lansdowne Rd. Bus: 5, 6, 7, 8, 18, or 45.

Irish Film Centre Cafe Bar ✦ IRISH/INTERNATIONAL   One of the most popular drinking spots in Temple Bar, the hip Cafe Bar (in the lobby of the city's coolest place to catch a movie) features an excellent, affordable menu that changes daily. Vegetarian and Middle Eastern menus are available for both lunch and dinner. The weekend entertainment usually includes music or comedy.

6 Eustace St., Temple Bar, Dublin 2. ✆ **01/677-8788**. Lunch and dinner €6–€10 ($6.90–$12). MC, V. Mon–Fri 12:30–3pm; Sat–Sun 1–3pm; daily 6–9pm. Bus: 21A, 78A, or 78B.

Juice VEGETARIAN   Juice tempts carnivorous, vegan, and macrobiotic diners alike, using organic produce to create delicious dressings and entrees among its largely conventional but very well prepared offerings. The avocado filet of blue cheese and broccoli wrapped in phyllo is superb, and the spinach and ricotta cheese cannelloni is delicious. Coffees, fresh-squeezed juices, organic wines, and late weekend hours add to the allure of this modern, casual eatery, frequented by mature diners who know their food.

Castle House, 73 S. Great Georges St., Dublin 2. © 01/475-7856. Reservations recommended Fri–Sat. Main courses €12–€15 ($13–$16); early-bird fixed-price dinner (Mon–Fri 5–7pm) €13 ($14). AE, MC, V. Daily 11am–11pm. Bus: 50, 50A, 54, 56, or 77.

Leo Burdock's 🌟 FISH AND CHIPS   Every visitor should go to a Dublin takeout "chipper" at least once, and you might as well do it at the best in town. Established in 1913 across from Christ Church, this quintessential Irish takeout shop remains a cherished Dublin institution, despite a devastating fire in 1998. Rebuilt from the ground up, Burdock's is back. Cabinet ministers, university students, and businesspeople alike can be found in the queue. They're waiting for fish bought fresh that morning and those good Irish potatoes, both cooked in "drippings" (none of that modern cooking oil!). There's no seating, but you can find a nearby bench or stroll down to the park at St. Patrick's Cathedral.

2 Werburgh St., Dublin 8. © 01/454-0306. Main courses €6–€7 ($6.90–$8.05). No credit cards. Mon–Sat noon–midnight; Sun 4pm–midnight. Bus: 21A, 50, 50A, 78, 78A, or 78B.

Mimo Cafe 🌟🌟 *Value* MODERN CONTINENTAL   This chic little cafe in the tony Powerscourt Townhouse shopping minimall is a wonderfully classy and surprisingly budget-minded place to stop for terrific salads, pasta dishes, and inventive sandwiches. Grab one of the leather sofas or armchairs. A piano player is a civilized touch on Thursday and Friday afternoons.

Powerscourt Townhouse, Dublin 2. © 01/674-6712. Main courses €8–€10 ($9.20–$12). MC, V. Daily noon–5:30pm. Bus: Any city-center bus.

One Pico 🌟🌟🌟 MODERN EUROPEAN   About a 5-minute walk from Stephen's Green, on a wee lane off Dawson Street, this is a sophisticated, grown-up, classy place, with excellent service and fantastic food. Try the starter of seared foie gras with pineapple tatin; and the memorable main dishes of scallops with baby beets and lime, confit of duck with fig tatin, or beef with Roquefort ravioli. For dessert, a caramelized lemon tart is the end to a near-perfect meal. This place is a splurge, but worth it.

5–6 Molesworth Place, Schoolhouse Lane, Dublin 2. © 01/676-0300. www.onepico.com. Reservations required. Fixed-price 2-course lunch €22 ($25), 3-course lunch €26 ($30); dinner main courses €20–€27 ($23–$31). AE, DC, MC, V. Mon–Sat 12:30–2pm and 6–10:30pm. DART: Pearse. Bus: 10, 11A, 11B, 13, or 20B.

Queen of Tarts 🌟 TEA SHOP   This tearoom is David to the Goliath of Irish tearooms, Bewley's, but its diminutive physical size packs a solid pie-filled punch. Tarts of ham and spinach or cheddar cheese and chives can be followed up with the flaky sweetness of warm almond cranberry or blackberry pie. The scones here are tender and light, dusted with powdered sugar and accompanied by a little pot of fruit jam. The tarts are delicious. The dining room is small and smoke-free.

4 Corkhill, Dublin 2. © 01/670-7499. Sandwiches and savory tarts €4–€6.50 ($4.60–$7.50); baked goods and cakes €1–€4 ($1.15–$4.60). No credit cards. Mon–Fri 7:30am–7pm; Sat 9am–6pm; Sun 10am–6pm. Bus: Any city-center bus.

The Steps of Rome 🌟 ITALIAN/PIZZA   Word is out that this restaurant, just off the busy shopping thoroughfare of Grafton Street, offers some of the best simple Italian fare in Dublin. Large, succulent pizza slices available for take-out are one way to enjoy the wonders of this authentic Italian kitchen when the dining room is full—the seven tables huddled within this tiny restaurant seem to be perennially occupied.

Chatham Court, off Chatham St., Dublin 2. © 01/670-5630. Main courses €8–€10 ($9.20–$17); pizza slices €3 ($3.45). No credit cards. Mon–Sat 10am–midnight; Sun 1–11pm. DART: Pearse. Bus: Any city-center bus.

Yamamori Noodles ★★ JAPANESE This place has such a pop, casual, and exuberant atmosphere that you may just be startled by how good the food is here. The splendid menu is an encyclopedia of Japanese cuisine, and the prices range from budget to splurge. On a raw, drizzly Dublin day, the chile chicken ramen is a pot of bliss, while the Yamamori yaki soba offers, in a mound of wok-fried noodles, a well-rewarded treasure hunt for prawns, squid, chicken, and roast pork. Vegetarians aren't overlooked. The selective international wine list is well priced and well chosen. The lunch specials are outstanding.

71–72 S. Great George's St., Dublin 2. © 01/475-5001. Reservations only for parties of 4 or more. Main courses €11–€18 ($13–$21). MC, V. Sun–Wed 12:30–11pm; Thurs–Sat 12:30–11:30pm. Bus: 50, 50A, 54, 56, or 77.

THE CITY CENTER—NORTH OF THE LIFFEY

Beshoffs ★ FISH AND CHIPS The Beshoff name is synonymous with fresh fish in Dublin. Ivan Beshoff emigrated here from Odessa, Russia, in 1913 and started a fish business that developed into this top-notch fish-and-chips eatery. Recently renovated in Victorian style, it has an informal atmosphere and a simple self-service menu. Crisp chips are served with a choice of fresh fish, from the original recipe of cod to classier variations using salmon, shark, prawns, and other local sea fare—some days as many as 20 varieties. The potatoes are grown on a 120-hectare (300-acre) farm in Tipperary and freshly cut each day. A second shop is just south of the Liffey at 14 Westmoreland St., Dublin 2 (© 01/677-8026).

6 Upper O'Connell St., Dublin 1. © 01/872-4400. All items €3–€7 ($3.45–$8.05). No credit cards. Mon–Sat 10am–9pm; Sun noon–9pm. DART: Tara St. Bus: Any city-center bus.

Epicurean Food Hall ★★ GOURMET FOOD COURT This wonderful food hall houses a wide variety of artisan produce, delicious local Irish delicacies, and regional specialties. There is limited seating but this place gets uncomfortably jammed during lunchtime midweek, so go midmorning or afternoon.

Middle Abbey St., Dublin 1. No phone. All items €2–€12 ($2.30–$14). No credit cards. Mon–Sat 10am–6pm. Bus: 70 or 80.

Soup Dragon ★★ SOUPS Soup has become the healthy, hip alternative to stodgy sandwiches and fast food, and the Soup Dragon leads the way for cheap and cheerful chow in Dublin. It's a tiny place, with less than a dozen stools alongside a bar, but it's big on drama. Think blue walls, black and red mirrors, orange slices and spice sticks flowing out of giant jugs, and huge flower-filled vases. The menu changes daily, but usually features a few traditional choices (potato and leek, carrot and coriander) as well as the more exotic (curried parsnip and *sag aloo,* a spicy Indian spinach and potato concoction). It's also a good place for dessert. Try the bread-and-butter pudding or the yummy banana bread.

168 Capel St., Dublin 1. © 01/872-3277. All items €3–€8 ($3.45–$9.20). MC, V. Mon–Sat 9:30am–6pm; Sun 1–6pm. Bus: 70 or 80.

The Winding Stair ⭐ HEALTHY EATING   Retreat from the bustle of the north side's busy quays into this darling bookshop's self-service cafe, and indulge in a snack while browsing for secondhand gems. The three floors, chock-full of used books (from novels, plays, and poetry to history, art, music, and sports), are connected by a winding 18th-century staircase. Tall, wide windows provide expansive views of the Ha'penny Bridge and River Liffey. The food is simple and healthy—sandwiches made with additive-free meats or fruits (such as banana and honey), organic salads, homemade soups, and natural juices. Evening events include poetry readings and recitals.

40 Lower Ormond Quay, Dublin 1. ℂ 01/873-3292. All items €2–€8 ($2.30–$9.20). AE, MC, V. Mon–Sat 9:30am–6pm; Sun 1–6pm. Bus: 70 or 80.

4 Seeing the Sights

Dublin's face today mirrors the lines and wrinkles, blemishes and beauty spots left by a long, rich, and colorful history. The past is everywhere for you to explore; it's preserved in stone and parchment, on canvas, and in the heritage of traditional music. But Dublin isn't all about the past: Parts of the city are quickly moving into the future—and moving fast. Be sure to check out the new Dublin at Temple Bar or in one of the city's many hip nightclubs. See "Dublin After Dark," later in this chapter.

DUBLIN'S TOP ATTRACTIONS

The Book of Kells ⭐⭐⭐   The jewel in Ireland's tourism crown is the Book of Kells, a magnificent manuscript of the four Gospels, from around A.D. 800, with elaborate scripting and illumination. This famous treasure and other early Christian manuscripts are on permanent public view at Trinity College, in the Colonnades, an exhibition area on the ground floor of the Old Library. Also housed in the Old Library is the **Dublin Experience,** an excellent multimedia introduction to the history and people of Dublin. The oldest university in Ireland, Trinity was founded in 1592 by Queen Elizabeth I. It occupies a beautiful 16-hectare (40-acre) site just south of the River Liffey, with cobbled squares, gardens, a picturesque quadrangle, and buildings dating from the 17th to the 20th centuries.

College Green, Dublin 2. ℂ 01/608-2320. www.tcd.ie/library/kells.htm. Free admission to college grounds; admission to Library €6 ($6.90) adults, €5 ($5.75) seniors and students, €11 ($13) families, free for children under 12. Combination tickets for the Library and Dublin Experience also available. MC, V. Mon–Sat 9:30am–5pm; Sun noon–4:30pm (opens at 9:30am June–Sept). Bus: 21A, 50, 50A, 78, 78A, or 78B.

Christ Church Cathedral ⭐⭐   Standing on high ground in the oldest part of the city, this cathedral is one of Dublin's finest historic buildings. It dates from 1038, when Sitric, Danish king of Dublin, built the first wooden Christ Church here. In 1171, the original simple foundation was extended into a cruciform and rebuilt in stone by Strongbow. The present structure dates mainly from 1871 to 1878, when a huge restoration took place. Highlights of the interior include magnificent stonework and graceful pointed arches, with delicately chiseled supporting columns. This is the mother church for the diocese of Dublin and Glendalough of the Church of Ireland. The Treasury in the crypt is open to the public, and you can hear bells pealing in the belfry.

Christ Church Place, Dublin 8. ℂ 01/677-8099. cccdub@indigo.ie. Suggested donation €5 ($5.75) adults, €2.50 ($2.90) students and children under 15. Daily 10am–5:30pm. Closed Dec 26. Bus: 21A, 50, 50A, 78, 78A, or 78B.

Dublin Castle 🏛🏛   Built between 1208 and 1220, this complex represents some of the oldest surviving architecture in the city. It was the center of British power in Ireland for more than 7 centuries, until the new Irish government took it over in 1922. Film buffs might recognize the castle's courtyard as a setting in the Neil Jordan film *Michael Collins*. Highlights include the 13th-century Record Tower; the State Apartments, once the residence of English viceroys; and the Chapel Royal, a 19th-century Gothic building with particularly fine plaster decoration and carved-oak gallery fronts and fittings. The newest developments are the Undercroft, an excavated site on the grounds where an early Viking fortress stood, and the Treasury, built between 1712 and 1715 and believed to be the oldest surviving office building in Ireland. Also here are a craft shop, heritage center, and restaurant.

Palace St. (off Dame St.), Dublin 2. © 01/677-7129. dublincastle@eircom.net. Admission €4.25 ($4.90) adults, €3.25 ($3.75) seniors and students, €1.75 ($2) children under 12. 1-hr guided tours every 20–25 min. Mon–Fri 10am–5pm; Sat–Sun and holidays 2–5pm. Bus: 50, 50A, 54, 56A, 77, 77A, or 77B.

Dublinia 🏛   What was Dublin like in medieval times? This historically accurate presentation of the Old City from 1170 to 1540 is re-created through a series of theme exhibits, spectacles, and experiences. Highlights include an illuminated Medieval Maze, complete with visual effects, background sounds, and aromas that lead you on a journey through time from the arrival of the Anglo-Normans in 1170 to the closure of the monasteries in the 1530s. Another segment depicts everyday life in medieval Dublin with a diorama, as well as a prototype of a 13th-century quay along the banks of the Liffey. The medieval Fayre displays the wares of merchants from all over Europe. You can try on a flattering new robe or, if you're feeling vulnerable, stop in at the armorer's and be fitted for chain mail.

St. Michael's Hill, Christ Church, Dublin 8. © 01/679-4611. www.dublinia.ie. Admission €5.75 ($6.60) adults, €4.50 ($5.20) seniors, students, and children, €15 ($17) families. AE, MC, V. Apr–Sept daily 10am–5pm; Oct–Mar Mon–Sat 11am–4pm, Sun 10am–4:30pm. Bus: 50, 78A, or 123.

Dublin Writers Museum 🏛🏛   Housed in a stunning 18th-century Georgian mansion with splendid plasterwork and stained glass, the museum is itself an impressive reminder of the grandeur of the Irish literary tradition. A fine collection of personal manuscripts and mementos that belonged to Yeats, Joyce, Beckett, Behan, Shaw, Wilde, Swift, and Sheridan are among the items that celebrate the written word. One of the museum's rooms is devoted to children's literature.

18–19 Parnell Sq. N., Dublin 1. © 01/475-0854. Admission €6 ($6.90) adults, €5 ($5.75) seniors, students, and children, €17 ($20) families (2 adults and up to 4 children). AE, DC, MC, V. Mon–Sat 10am–5pm (to 6pm June–Aug); Sun and holidays 11am–5pm. DART: Connolly Station. Bus: 11, 13, 16, 16A, 22, or 22A.

Glasnevin Cemetery 🏛🏛   Situated north of the city center, the Irish National Cemetery was founded in 1832 and covers more than 50 hectares (124 acres). Most people buried here were ordinary citizens (especially poignant are the sections dedicated to children who died young), but there are also many famous names on the headstones. They range from former Irish presidents such as Eamon de Valera and Sean T. O'Kelly to other political heroes such as Michael Collins, Daniel O'Connell, Roger Casement, and Charles Stewart Parnell. Literary figures also have their place here, including poet Gerard Manley Hopkins and writers Christy Brown and Brendan Behan. Though open to all, this is primarily a Catholic burial ground, with many Celtic crosses. A heritage map, on sale in the flower shop at the entrance, serves as a guide to who's buried where, or you can take a free 2-hour guided tour.

Dublin

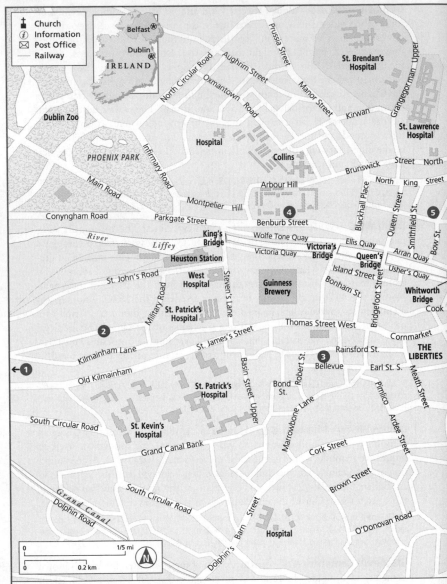

Legend:
- ✝ Church
- ⓘ Information
- ✉ Post Office
- — Railway

IRELAND — Belfast, Dublin

Dublin Zoo
PHOENIX PARK
Main Road
Conyngham Road
Infirmary Road
Parkgate Street
Montpelier Hill
Hospital
Collins
Arbour Hill
Benburb Street ④
Prussia Street
Aughrim Street
Oxmantown Road
North Circular Road
Manor Street
Kirwan
Brunswick
Street North
St. Brendan's Hospital
Grangegorman Upper
St. Lawrence Hospital
North King Street
Blackhall Place
Queen Street
Smithfield St.
Bow St.
⑤

River Liffey
King's Bridge
Heuston Station
St. John's Road
West Hospital
St. Patrick's Hospital
②
Kilmainham Lane
Old Kilmainham
←①
South Circular Road
St. Kevin's Hospital
Grand Canal Bank
Wolfe Tone Quay
Victoria Quay
Victoria's Bridge
Queen's Bridge
Ellis Quay
Arran Quay
Usher's Quay
Island Street
Bonham St.
Bridgefoot Street
Whitworth Bridge
Cook
Guinness Brewery
Thomas Street West
Cornmarket
THE LIBERTIES
St. James's Street
Steven's Lane
Military Road
Basin Street Upper
Bond St.
Marrowbone Lane
Robert St.
Rainsford St.
③ Bellevue
Earl St. S.
Pimlico
Meath Street
Ardee Street
St. Patrick's Hospital
South Circular Road
Cork Street
Brown Street
O'Donovan Road
Grand Canal
Dolphin Road
Dolphin's Barn Street
Hospital

0 — 1/5 mi
0 — 0.2 km
N

ATTRACTIONS ●

The Book of Kells **13**
Christ Church Cathedral **26**
Collins Barracks **4**
Dublin Castle **24**
Dublin Writers Museum **9**
Dublinia **28**

Glasnevin Cemetery **6**
Guinness Storehouse **3**
Hugh Lane Municipal Gallery of Modern Art **8**
Irish Film Centre **23**
Irish Museum of Modern Art **2**
Irish Music Hall of Fame **22**

James Joyce Centre **10**
Kilmainham Gaol Historical Museum **1**
National Botanical Gardens **7**
National Gallery of Ireland **14**
National Museum **15**
Natural History Museum **16**

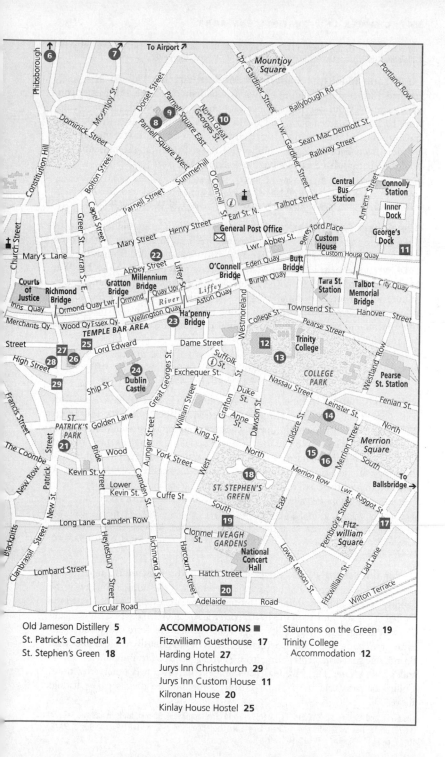

Old Jameson Distillery **5**
St. Patrick's Cathedral **21**
St. Stephen's Green **18**

ACCOMMODATIONS ■
Fitzwilliam Guesthouse **17**
Harding Hotel **27**
Jurys Inn Christchurch **29**
Jurys Inn Custom House **11**
Kilronan House **20**
Kinlay House Hostel **25**

Stauntons on the Green **19**
Trinity College
  Accommodation **12**

Finglas Rd., Dublin 11. © **01/830-1133**. Free admission. Daily 8am–4pm. Free guided tours Wed and Fri 2:30pm from main gate. Map €3.50 ($3.75). Bus: 19, 19A, 40, 40A, 40B, or 40C.

Hugh Lane Municipal Gallery of Modern Art ✿ Housed in a finely restored 18th-century building known as Charlemont House, this gallery contains paintings from the Impressionist and post-Impressionist traditions, sculptures by Rodin, stained glass, and works by modern Irish artists. In 2001, the museum opened the studio of Irish painter Francis Bacon; it was moved piece by piece from Bacon's original studio and reconstructed at the museum. The bookshop is considered the best art bookshop in the city.

Parnell Sq. N., Dublin 1. © **01/874-1903**. Fax 01/872-2182. www.hughlane.ie. Free admission to museum; admission to Francis Bacon studio €7 ($8.05) adults, €3.50 ($4) students. Tues–Thurs 9:30am–6pm; Fri–Sat 9:30am–5pm; Sun 11am–5pm. DART: Connolly or Tara stations. Bus: 3, 10, 11, 13, 16, or 19.

Kilmainham Gaol Historical Museum ✿ This is a key sight for anyone interested in Ireland's struggle for independence from British rule. Within these walls, political prisoners were incarcerated, tortured, and killed from 1796 until 1924, when President Eamon de Valera left as its final prisoner. *Note:* The **War Memorial Gardens** (© **01/677-0236**), along the banks of the Liffey, are a 5-minute walk from Kilmainham Gaol. The gardens, designed by the famous British architect Sir Edwin Lutyens (1869–1944), are fairly well maintained, and continue to present a moving testimony to Ireland's war dead. They are open weekdays 8am to dark, Saturday 10am to dark.

Kilmainham, Dublin 8. © **01/453-5984**. www.heritageireland.ie. 1-hr. guided tour (hours vary) €5 ($5.75) adults, €3.50 ($4.05) seniors, €2 ($2.30) children, €11 ($13) families. Apr–Sept daily 9:30am–4:45pm; Oct–Mar Mon–Fri 9:30am–4pm, Sun 10am–4:45pm. Bus: 51B, 78A, or 79 at O'Connell Bridge.

National Gallery of Ireland ✿✿✿ This museum houses Ireland's national art collection, as well as a superb European collection of art spanning the 14th to the 20th centuries. Every major European school of painting is represented, including fine selections by Italian Renaissance artists (especially Caravaggio's *The Taking of Christ*), French Impressionists, and Dutch 17th-century masters. The highlight of the Irish collection is the room dedicated to the mesmerizing works of Jack B. Yeats, brother of the poet W. B. Yeats. All public areas are wheelchair accessible. The museum has a fine gallery shop and an excellent self-service restaurant.

Merrion Sq. W., Dublin 2. © **01/661-5133**. Fax 01/661-5372. www.nationalgallery.ie. Free admission. Free guided tours (meet in the Shaw Room) Sat 3pm; Sun 2, 3, and 4pm. Mon–Sat 9:30am–5:30pm; Thurs 9:30am–8:30pm; Sun noon–5pm. Closed Good Friday and Dec 24–26. DART: Pearse. Bus: 5, 6, 7, 7A, 8, 10, 44, 47, 47B, 48A, or 62.

National Museum ✿✿✿ Established in 1890, this museum is a reflection of Ireland's heritage from 2000 B.C. to the present. It is the home of many of the country's greatest historical finds, including the Treasury exhibit, which toured the United States and Europe in the 1970s with the Ardagh Chalice, Tara Brooch, and Cross of Cong. Other highlights range from the artifacts from the Wood Quay excavations of the Old Dublin Settlements to "Or," an extensive exhibition of Irish Bronze Age gold ornaments dating from 2200 to 700 B.C. The museum has a shop and a cafe. *Note:* The National Museum encompasses two other attractions, Collins Barracks and the Natural History Museum; see their separate listings above.

Kildare St. and Merrion St., Dublin 2. © **01/677-7444**. Free admission. 90-min. tours (hours vary) €1.50 ($1.70) adults, free for seniors and children. Tues–Sat 10am–5pm; Sun 2–5pm. DART: Pearse. Bus: 7, 7A, 8, 10, 11, or 13.

> ## Value Getting the Best Deal on Sightseeing
>
> - Remember that Dublin's compact size makes it ideal to explore on foot. Heritage Trails and Music Trails are well signposted, and you can follow them with detailed explanatory booklets available from Dublin Tourism (see "Visitor Information," earlier in this chapter).
> - The cobbled squares and tidy cricket lawns of Trinity College (founded in 1592) are a delight to explore, and with the exception of the Old Library and Book of Kells (p. 380), there's no admission charge.
> - Numerous money-saving combination tickets to Dublin attractions are available at Dublin Tourism offices.
> - Take advantage of free admission at the National Museum, National Gallery, National Library, Natural History Museum, and Irish Museum of Modern Art.

Natural History Museum   A division of the National Museum of Ireland, the recently renovated Natural History Museum is considered one of the finest traditional museums in the world. In addition to presenting the zoological history of Ireland, it displays examples of major animal groups from around the world. The Blaschka glass models of marine animals are worth a look.

Merrion St., Dublin 2. © 01/677-7444. www.museum.ie. Free admission. Tues–Sat 10am–5pm; Sun 2–5pm. Bus: 7, 7A, or 8.

St. Patrick's Cathedral ⟨⟩   It is said that St. Patrick baptized converts on this site, and consequently a church has stood here since A.D. 450, making it the oldest Christian site in Dublin. The present cathedral dates from 1190, but because of a fire and 14th-century rebuilding, not much of the original foundation remains. It is mainly early English in style, with a square medieval tower that houses the largest pealing bells in Ireland, and an 18th-century spire. St. Patrick's is closely associated with Jonathan Swift, who was dean from 1713 to 1745 and whose tomb lies in the south aisle. Others memorialized within the cathedral include Turlough O'Carolan, a blind harpist and composer and the last of the great Irish bards; Michael William Balfe, the composer; and Douglas Hyde, the first president of Ireland. St. Patrick's is the national cathedral of the Church of Ireland.

21–50 Patrick's Close, Patrick St., Dublin 8. © 01/475-4817. Fax 01/454-6374. www.stpatrickscathedral.ie. Admission €4 ($4.60) adults, €3 ($3.45) students and seniors, €9 ($10) families. Year-round Mon–Fri 9am–6pm; Nov–Feb Sat 9am–5pm, Sun 9am–3pm. Closed except for services Dec 24–26 and Jan 1. Bus: 65, 65B, 50, 50A, 54, 54A, 56A, or 77.

MORE WORTHY ATTRACTIONS

Guinness Storehouse ⟨⟩   Founded in 1759, the Guinness Brewery is one of the world's largest breweries, producing a distinctive dark stout, famous for its thick, creamy head. Although tours of the brewery itself are no longer allowed, visitors are welcome to explore the adjacent Guinness Hopstore, a converted 19th-century four-story building. It houses the World of Guinness Exhibition, an audiovisual presentation showing how the stout is made; the Cooperage Gallery, displaying one of the finest collections of tools in Europe; the Gilroy Gallery, dedicated to the graphic design work of John Gilroy; and, last but not

> **Tips Finding Your Way**
>
> Wherever you are in Dublin, if you want to reach the city center for shopping, sightseeing, or theater, just hop on any bus marked AN LAR.

least, a bar where visitors can sample a glass of the famous brew. The brewery recently became home to the largest glass of stout in the world, roughly 60m (200 ft.) tall, whose head is in fact an observatory restaurant offering spectacular views of the city.

St. James's Gate, Dublin 8. ℭ 01/408-4800. www.guinness.com. Admission €14 ($16) adults, €12 ($14) seniors, €9 ($10) students, €3 ($3.45) children 6–12, €28 ($32) families. 30-min. guided tours every half-hour. Daily 9:30am–5pm. Bus: 51B, 78A, or 123.

Irish Film Centre ℛ   This art-house film institute is a hip hangout in Dublin's artsy Temple Bar district. The Irish Film Centre houses two cinemas, the Irish Film Archive, a library, a bookshop and cafe, and eight film-related organizations. Free screenings of *Flashback*, a 90-minute history of Irish film since 1896, start at noon Wednesday to Sunday from June to mid-September. Follow with lunch in the cafe for a perfect midday outing.

6 Eustace St., Dublin 2. ℭ 01/679-5744, or 01/679-3477 for cinema box office. Free admission; cinema tickets €6 ($6.90). Centre daily 10am–11pm; cinemas daily 2–11pm; cinema box office daily 1:30–9pm. Bus: 21A, 78A, or 78B.

Irish Museum of Modern Art (IMMA) ℛ   Housed in the splendidly restored 17th-century edifice known as the Royal Hospital, IMMA is a showcase of Irish and international art from the latter half of the 20th century. The buildings and grounds also provide a venue for theatrical and musical events, overlapping the visual and performing arts. The formal gardens, an important early feature of this magnificent structure, have been restored and are open to the public during museum hours.

Military Rd., Kilmainham. ℭ 01/612-9900. www.modernart.ie. Free admission. Tues–Sat 10am–5:30pm; Sun noon–5:30pm. Bus: 79 or 90.

Irish Music Hall of Fame ℛ   The draw here is the exhaustive collection of memorabilia—much of it exclusive—chronicling the history of Irish music, from traditional and folk through pop, rock, and dance. There's loads of great stuff about U2, Van Morrison, Christy Moore, the Chieftains, the Dubliners, Thin Lizzy, Bob Geldof, Enya, the Cranberries, and Sinéad O'Connor, right up to BoyZone, Westlife, and Samantha Mumba.

57 Middle Abbey St., Dublin 1. ℭ 01/878-3345. Free admission. Daily 10am–5:30pm. DART: Connolly. Bus: 25, 26, 34, 37, 38A, 39A, 39B, 66A, or 67A.

James Joyce Centre ℛ   Near Parnell Square and the Dublin Writers Museum, the Joyce center is in a restored 1784 Georgian town house, once the home of Denis J. Maginni, a dancing instructor who appears briefly in *Ulysses*. The Ulysses Portrait Gallery on the second floor has a fascinating collection of photographs and drawings of characters from *Ulysses* who had a life outside the novel. The recently opened Paul Leon Exhibition Room holds the table and writing table used by Joyce in Paris when he was working on *Finnegan's Wake*. Talks and audiovisual presentations are offered daily, as are guided walking tours through the neighborhood streets of "Joyce Country" in Dublin's north inner city.

35 N. Great George's St., Dublin 1. (℃ 01/878-8547. www.jamesjoyce.ie. Admission €4.50 ($5.20) adults,
€3.50 ($4) seniors, students, and children under 10, €13 ($15) families. Separate fees for walking tours and
events. Mon–Sat 9:30am–5pm; Sun 12:30–5pm. Closed Dec 24–26. DART: Connolly. Bus: 3, 10, 11, 11A, 13,
16, 16A, 19, 19A, 22, or 22A.

James Joyce Museum ☆☆   Sitting on the edge of Dublin Bay about 9.7km
(6 miles) south of the city center, this 12m (40-ft.) granite monument is one of
a series of Martello towers built in 1804 to withstand an invasion threatened by
Napoleon. The tower's great claim to fame is that James Joyce lived here in 1904.
He was the guest of Oliver Gogarty, who rented the tower from the Army for an
annual fee of IR£8 (€11/$13). Joyce, in turn, made the tower the setting for the
first chapter of *Ulysses*, and it has been known as Joyce's Tower ever since. Its collection of Joycean memorabilia includes letters, documents, first and rare editions, personal possessions, and photographs.

Sandycove, County Dublin. (℃ 01/280-9265. Admission €6 ($6.90) adults, €5 ($5.75) seniors, students, and
children, €17 ($19) families. Apr–Oct Mon–Sat 10am–1pm and 2–5pm, Sun 2–6pm. Closed Nov–Mar. DART:
Sandycove. Bus: 8.

The Old Jameson Distillery ☆   This museum illustrates the history of Irish
whiskey, known in Irish as *uisce beatha* (the water of life). Housed in a former distillery warehouse in Smithfield Village, a small complex of entertainment venues,
it consists of a short introductory audiovisual presentation, an exhibition area, and
a whiskey-making demonstration. At the end of the tour, visitors can sample
whiskey at an in-house pub, where an array of fixed-price menus (for lunch, tea,

Special & Free Events

For free events, nothing in Dublin beats the free **traditional Irish music**
you can hear every night in pubs all over the city. For details, see "Dublin
After Dark," later in this chapter.

For fans of James Joyce, June 16 is the day to be in Dublin. The city
celebrates **Bloomsday** in memory of Leopold Bloom, whose wanderings
through the city on June 16, 1904, are chronicled in Joyce's *Ulysses*. Contact the James Joyce Centre, 35 N. Great George's St., Dublin 1 (℃ 01/
878-8547; fax 01/878-8488; www.jamesjoyce.ie).

Many Dublin events cater to lovers of classical music. Lunchtime concerts at the **National Concert Hall**, Earlsfort Terrace, Dublin 2 (℃ 01/
475-1572), are offered Tuesdays during June, July, and August, for €5
($5.75). The **AIB Music Festival in Great Irish Houses** is a 10-day festival
of classical music performed by leading Irish and international artists in
some of the Dublin area's great Georgian buildings and mansions. For
more information, call ℃ 01/278-1528 or fax 01/278-1529.

Theater-philes should check out **Eircom Dublin Theatre Festival**, a
unique theatrical celebration that features classic and innovative Irish
drama, plus performances by major overseas theater and dance companies. Call ℃ 01/677-8439 for more details or visit www.eircomtheatre
festival.com.

The biggest sporting events are the **Kerrygold Horse Show** in early
August, the **All-Ireland Hurling and Gaelic Football Finals** in late September, and the **Dublin Marathon** in late October.

or dinner) is available. A new added attraction here at Smithfield Village is **"The Chimney,"** a ride to the top of a 56m (185-ft.) brick chimney built in 1895 and converted to support an observation chamber from which you'll enjoy unparalleled views of the city.

Bow St., Smithfield Village, Dublin 7. ℂ 01/807-2355. Admission €7 ($8.05) adults, €5.75 ($6.60) students and seniors, €3 ($3.45) children, €18 ($21) families. Tours daily 9:30am–6pm (last 30-min. tour at 5pm). Mon–Sat 10am–6pm; Sun 11am–7pm. Bus: 67, 67A, 68, 69, 79, or 90.

PARKS, GARDENS & ZOOS

National Botanic Gardens 𝕽𝕽   Established by the Royal Dublin Society in 1795 on a rolling 20-hectare (50-acre) expanse of land north of the city center, this is Dublin's horticultural showcase. The attractions include more than 20,000 different plants and cultivars, a Great Yew Walk, a bog garden, a water garden, a rose garden, and an herb garden. A variety of Victorian-style glass houses are filled with tropical plants and exotic species. Remember this spot when you suddenly crave refuge from the bustle of the city. All but the rose garden is wheelchair accessible. There's free roadside parking outside the garden gates.

Botanic Rd., Glasnevin, Dublin 9. ℂ 01/837-7596. Free admission; 90-min. guided tour €2 ($2.30). Apr–Oct Mon–Sat 9am–6pm, Sun 11am–6pm; Nov–Mar Mon–Sat 10am–4:30pm, Sun 11am–4:30pm. Bus: 13, 19, or 134.

Phoenix Park 𝕽𝕽 *Kids*   Just 3.2km (2 miles) west of the city center, Phoenix Park, the largest urban park in Europe, is the playground of Dublin. A network of roads and quiet pedestrian walkways traverses its 704 hectares (1,740 acres), which are informally landscaped with ornamental gardens and nature trails. Avenues of trees, including oak, beech, pine, chestnut, and lime, separate broad expanses of grassland. Livestock graze peacefully on pasturelands, deer roam the forested areas, and horses romp on polo fields. The homes of the Irish president and the U.S. ambassador are on the grounds (see below for information on tours). The excellent **Dublin Zoo** (ℂ 01/677-1425; www.dublinzoo.ie) is also found here; in the past few years, the zoo has doubled in size to about 24 hectares (60 acres) and provides a naturally landscaped habitat for more than 235 species of wild animals and tropical birds. Zoo highlights for youngsters include the Children's Pets' Corner and a train ride around the zoo. The Phoenix Park Visitor Centre, adjacent to Ashtown Castle, offers exhibitions and an audiovisual presentation on the park's history. The cafe/restaurant is open 10am to 5pm weekdays, 10am to 6pm weekends. Free car parking is adjacent to the center.

Phoenix Park, Dublin 8. ℂ 01/677-0095. www.heritageireland.ie. Admission to Visitor Centre €2.75 ($2.15) adults, €2 ($2.30) seniors and students, €1.25 ($1.45) children, €9 ($10) families. June–Sept 10am–6pm (call for off-season hours). Bus: 37, 38, or 39.

St. Stephen's Green 𝕽   This park has been preserved as an open space for Dubliners since 1690. A short walk from most city-center locations, this large park is popular for picnics, reading, a quiet stroll, and summertime concerts.

St. Stephen's Green, Dublin 2. No phone. Mon–Sat 8am–dark; Sun 10am–dark. Bus: All city-center buses.

Finds The Secret Garden

While touring St. Stephen's Green, be sure to visit the hidden **Iveagh Gardens** 𝕽, a small garden hidden behind the National Concert Hall. The main entrance is from Clonmel Street, off Harcourt Street; hours are the same as those for the Green.

ORGANIZED TOURS

BUS TOURS   If you want to get a general feel for the city, **Dublin Bus** (© 01/ 873-4222; www.dublinbus.ie) operates a very good, 75-minute hop-on, hop-off **Dublin City Tour** that connects 10 major points of interest, including museums, art galleries, churches, libraries, and historic sites. It departs from the Dublin Bus office at 59 Upper O'Connell St., Dublin 1, and free pickup from many hotels is available for morning tours. Rates are €13 ($15) adults, €6 ($6.90) children under 14, €17 ($20) for a family of four. Daily from 9:30am to 6:30pm. You can buy your ticket from the bus driver or book in advance at the Dublin Bus office or at the ticket desk in the Dublin Tourism Centre on Suffolk Street.

LAND & WATER TOURS   The immensely popular, 2-year-old **Viking Splash Tour** ★★ (© 01/855-3000; www.vikingsplashtours.com) is an especially fun way to see Dublin. Aboard a reconditioned World War II amphibious landing craft, or "duck," this tour starts on land (from Bull Alley St. beside St. Patrick's Cathedral) and eventually splashes into the Grand Canal. Passengers wear horned Viking helmets (a reference to the original settlers of the Dublin area) and are encouraged to issue war cries at appropriate moments. Tours depart roughly every half-hour Monday to Saturday 10am to 5pm and Sunday 11am to 6:30pm and last an hour and 15 minutes. It costs €14 ($16) for adults, €7.95 ($9.15) for children under 12, and €47 ($54) for a family of five. To book with a credit card by phone, call © **086/828-3773.**

WALKING TOURS   Small and compact, Dublin lends itself to walking tours. If you prefer to set off on your own, the **Dublin Tourism Office,** St. Andrew's Church, Suffolk Street, Dublin 2, has been stellar in the development of self-guided walking tours around Dublin; to date, four tourist trails have been mapped out and signposted throughout the city: the Old City Trail for historic sights; the Georgian Trail for landmark buildings, streets, squares, and parks; the Cultural Heritage Trail for top literary sites, museums, galleries, theaters, and churches; and the Rock 'n Stroll Trail, which has a music theme. For each trail, Dublin Tourism has produced a handy booklet that maps out the route and provides commentary about each place along the trail.

A number of firms offer guided tours led by knowledgeable locals. Tour times and charges vary, but most last about 2 hours and cost between €9 and €10 ($10–$12). **Historical Walking Tours of Dublin** (© 01/878-0227; www. historicalinsights.ie) delivers the best introductory walks, with six different 2-hour primers on Dublin's historic landmarks. Guides are history graduates of Trinity College, and participants are encouraged to ask questions.

A very popular evening tour is the **Traditional Music Pub Crawl** (© 01/478-0193), led by two professional musicians who sing as you make your way from one famous pub to another in Temple Bar. The evening is touristy but the music is good. It lasts 2½ hours. Another evening tour is the **Literary Pub Crawl** (© 01/670-5602), a winner of the "Living Dublin Award." The tour follows in the footsteps of Joyce, Behan, Beckett, Shaw, Kavanagh, and other Irish literary greats to local pubs, with actors providing humorous performances and commentary between stops.

The Zosimus Experience (© 01/661-8646; www.zozimus.com) is the latest rage on the walking tour circuit. Its creators call it a "cocktail mix" of ghosts, murderous tales, horror stories, humor, circus, history, street theater, and whatever's left, all within the precincts of medieval Dublin. It's essential to book in advance. The experience lasts approximately 1½ hours.

5 Shopping

The hub of shopping south of the Liffey is **Grafton Street,** crowned by the city's most fashionable department store, Brown Thomas (known simply as BT), and by the city's most exclusive jeweler, Weirs. Sadly, many Irish specialty shops on Grafton Street have been displaced over the years by British chain shops. You'll find better shopping on the smaller streets radiating from Grafton—Duke, Dawson, Nassau, and Wicklow—which have more Irish shops that specialize in books, handcrafts, jewelry, gifts, and clothing. The upscale **Powerscourt Townhouse Centre** and **St. Stephen's Green Centre** shopping malls are examples of Dublin's ongoing gentrification.

A 2-minute walk toward the river brings you to **Temple Bar,** the hub of Dublin's colorful bohemian district and the setting for art and music shops, vintage clothing stores, and a host of other increasingly fine and interesting boutiques, cafes, and restaurants. Dublin's latest "it" shopping district is **Old City,** located just west of Temple Bar and roughly comprising the area between Castle Street and Fishamble Street, with a good mix of hip fashion, modern interior design, crafts, and leisure shops. The center of the action is a cobbled, pedestrian-only street called Cow's Lane, which links Lord Edward Street with Essex Street West.

North of the Liffey, the **O'Connell Street** area is the main inner-city shopping nucleus, along with its nearby offshoots—**Abbey Street** for crafts, **Moore Street** for its open-air market, and, most notably, **Henry Street,** a pedestrian-only strip of chain stores, department stores, and indoor malls such as the **ILAC Centre** and the **Jervis Shopping Centre.**

Generally, Dublin shops are open from 9am to 6pm Monday to Saturday, and Thursday until 9pm. Many of the larger shops also have Sunday hours from noon to 6pm.

All goods and services in Ireland are subject to a 21% tax, known as the **VAT (value-added tax).** All non-European visitors to Ireland are eligible for a **refund** of all VAT tax paid on goods (the tax paid on services is nonrefundable). For details, see chapter 1.

ARTISANAL CRAFTS & GIFTS

Whichcraft, 5 Castlegate, Lord Edward St. (© 01/670-9371), has a large variety of crafts, including wooden bowls, basketry, pottery, jewelry, and batiks. A second Whichcraft is located on Cow's Lane in the burgeoning Old City. For more contemporary Irish design, head to the **Kilkenny Design Centre,** 6–10 Nassau St. (© 01/677-7066), a modern multilevel showplace for original Irish designs and quality products including pottery, glass, candles, woolens, pipes, knitwear, jewelry, books, and prints. Also visit **DESIGNyard,** 12 E. Essex St. (© 01/677-8453); the ground-floor studio of this beautiful emporium showcases exquisite, often affordable works from the very best contemporary Irish jewelry designers. Upstairs in the same building, the Crafts Council Gallery displays and sells Irish-made crafts, including furniture, ceramics, glass, lighting, and textiles. For quality ceramics, the creations of **Louis Mulcahy,** a noted Kerry potter and craftsman, have a Dublin home at 46 Dawson St. (© 01/670-9311).

BOOKSTORES

Established in 1843, **Greene's Bookshop Ltd.,** 16 Clare St. (© 01/676-2554), located near Trinity College, is one of Dublin's treasures for scholarly bibliophiles. It's chock-full of new and secondhand books on every topic from religion to the modern novel.

MARKETS

For a walk into the past with plenty of local color, don't miss the **Moore Street Market**. It's the principal open-air fruit, flower, fish, and vegetable market of the city. It's up and running daily 10am to 4pm—or until the goods run out. **Book Market Temple Bar,** Temple Bar Square, is a weekend book market that makes for excellent browsing—you'll find old and new titles, classics and contemporary novels, science fiction and mysteries, serious biographies, and pulp fiction. It's open Saturday and Sunday, 11am to 4pm. Like Moore Street, **Food Market Temple Bar,** Meeting House Square, is another great pre-picnic shopping spot. Everything here is organic, from fruits and veggies to a delicious selection of homemade cheeses, chutneys, breads, and jams. It's open Saturday and Sunday, 10am to 5pm. The **Mother Red Caps Market,** Back Lane, off High Street (© 01/453-8306), is one of Dublin's best, an enclosed market in the heart of Old Dublin. The stalls offer the usual garage-sale junk mixed in with the occasional hidden treasure, including antiques, used books, coins, silver, handcrafts, leather products, knitwear, music tapes, and furniture. The pickings can be hit or miss, but do make a point of popping by the Ryefield Foods stall (farm-made cheeses, baked goods, marmalades, and jams). Open Friday to Sunday, 10am to 5:30pm.

WOOLENS SHOPS

Blarney Woollen Mills, 21–23 Nassau St. (© 01/671-0068), known for its competitive prices, stocks a wide range of woolen knitwear made at its home base in Blarney, as well as crystal, china, pottery, and souvenirs. **Dublin Woollen Mills,** 41–42 Lower Ormond Quay (© 01/677-5014), is on the north side of the River Liffey next to the Ha'penny Bridge, a leading source of Aran hand-knit sweaters as well as vests, hats, jackets, and tweeds. If you want cashmere, go to **Monaghan's,** 15–17 Grafton Arcade, Grafton Street (© 01/677-0823), which has the best selection of colors, sizes, and styles for both men and women anywhere in Ireland. There's another store at 4–5 Royal Hibernian Way, off Dawson Street (© 01/679-4451).

6 Dublin After Dark

From singing pubs to Broadway-style theater, Dublin offers a wealth of after-dark activities. To find out what's going on, consult *In Dublin* or the *Event Guide,* which offer the most thorough and up-to-date listings. They can be found at any newsstand. The award-winning website of the *Irish Times* (**www.ireland.com**) offers a daily guide to cinema, theater, music, and whatever else you're up for. The **Dublin Events Guide,** at **www.dublinevents.com**, also provides a comprehensive listing of the week's entertainment possibilities. *Time Out* now covers Dublin as well; check their website at **www.timeout.com/Dublin**.

Advance bookings for most large concerts, plays, and so forth can be made through **Ticketmaster Ireland** (© 01/677-9409; www.ticketmaster.ie), with ticket centers in most HMV stores, as well as at the Dublin Tourism Centre, Suffolk Street, Dublin 2.

THE PERFORMING ARTS

For more than 90 years, the **Abbey Theatre,** Lower Abbey St., Dublin 1 (© 01/878-7222; www.abbeytheatre.ie), has been the national theater of Ireland. The box office is open from Monday to Saturday 10:30am to 7pm; performances Monday through Friday begin at 8pm, Saturday at 2:30pm. Tickets are €15 to €26 ($17–$30). In the same building, the **Peacock** (© 01/878-7222) is a

150-seat theater featuring contemporary plays and experimental works, including plays in Gaelic.

The Gate, 1 Cavendish Row, Dublin 1 (© **01/874-4368**), just north of O'Connell Street off Parnell Square, offers a program that includes a blend of modern works and the classics. The Gate is as easily distinguished as the Abbey. The box office is open from Monday to Saturday 10am to 7pm, and shows are held Monday through Saturday at 8pm. Tickets are €21 to €25 ($24–$29).

The **Andrews Lane Theatre,** 9–17 St. Andrews Lane, Dublin 2 (© **01/679-5720**), has a growing reputation for fine theater. It consists of a main theater where contemporary works from home and abroad are presented, and a studio geared for experimental productions. The box office is open from Monday to Saturday 10:30am to 7pm. Tickets are €13 to €20 ($15–$23).

Dublin's main venue for classical music, the **National Concert Hall,** Earlsfort Terrace, Dublin 2 (© **01/475-1572;** www.nch.ie), is home to the National Symphony Orchestra and Concert Orchestra, and host to an array of international orchestras and performing artists. In addition to classical music, there are evenings of Gilbert and Sullivan, opera, jazz, and recitals. The box office is open Monday through Saturday 11am to 7pm and Sunday (when there is a concert) from 7pm on. Tickets are €10 to €32 ($12–$37). Lunchtime concerts are €5 ($5.75).

With a seating capacity of 3,000, **The Point Depot,** East Link Bridge, North Wall Quay (© **01/836-3633**), is one of Dublin's larger indoor theater/concert venues, attracting top Broadway-caliber shows and international stars such as Justin Timberlake and Tom Jones. The box office is open Monday to Saturday 10am to 6pm. Tickets are €13 to €65 ($15–$75).

PUBS

The center of Irish social life, the pub is the place where Dubliners gather for conversation, music, and foaming pints of local brews. Day and night, the pub is for Dubliners an extension of the household, both dining room and parlor. Although pub meals are rarely exciting, they're always filling and offer an inexpensive alternative to the city's restaurants.

Dozens of clubs and pubs all over town feature rock, folk, jazz, and traditional Irish music, usually beginning around 9pm. This includes the so-called "late-night pubs"—pubs with an exemption allowing them to remain open past the usual closing time.

PUBS FOR CONVERSATION

The brass-filled and lantern-lit **Brazen Head,** 20 Lower Bridge St. (© **01/679-5186**), has atmosphere in spades. It's a tad touristy, which isn't surprising when you consider that it's the city's oldest pub—licensed in 1661 and occupying the site of an earlier tavern dating from 1198. On the south bank of the River Liffey, it's at the end of a cobblestone courtyard and was once the meeting place of Irish freedom fighters, such as Robert Emmet and Wolfe Tone.

Converted from an old merchant's warehouse, the **River Club,** in the Ha'penny Theatre, 48 Wellington Quay (© **01/677-2382**), is a wine bar-cum-supper club with soaring ceilings, an enviable position overlooking the river, and contemporary furnishings for an overall feeling of easy-going sophistication. It's a favorite of Ireland's film glitterati for a late drink. Referred to as a "moral pub" by James Joyce in *Ulysses,* **Davy Byrnes,** 21 Duke St., just off Grafton Street (© **01/677-5217**), has drawn poets, writers, and lovers of literature ever since.

Tucked into a busy commercial street, **The Long Hall,** 51 S. Great George's St. (© **01/475-1590**), is one of the city's most photographed pubs, with a beautiful

Victorian decor of filigree-edged mirrors, polished dark woods, and traditional snugs (private alcoves). Adjacent to the back door of the Gaiety Theatre, **Neary's,** 1 Chatham St., Dublin 2 (© **01/677-7371**), is a favorite with stage folk and theatergoers. **Ryan's of Parkgate Street,** 28 Parkgate St. (© **01/677-6097**), located on the north side of the Liffey near Phoenix Park, is a Victorian gem featuring a pressed tin ceiling, beveled mirrors, etched glass, a mahogany bar, and four old-style snugs.

PUBS WITH TRADITIONAL/FOLK MUSIC

Tucked between St. Stephen's Green and Merrion Street, **O'Donoghue's,** 15 Merrion Row, Dublin 2 (© **01/676-2807**), is a smoke-filled kingpin of traditional music pubs. Impromptu music sessions are held almost every night. Situated in the heart of Temple Bar and named for one of Ireland's literary greats, **Oliver St. John Gogarty,** 57-58 Fleet St. (© **01/671-1822**), has an inviting old-world atmosphere, with stacks of dusty books and a horseshoe-shaped bar. Traditional music sessions are held every night from 9 to 11pm, as well as Saturday at 4:30pm, and Sunday from noon to 2pm. **Flannery's Temple Bar,** 47–48 Temple Bar (© **01/497-4766**), in the heart of the trendy Temple Bar district on the corner of Temple Lane, was established in 1840. The decor is an interesting mix of crackling fireplaces, old pictures on the walls, and shelves filled with local memorabilia. There's live Irish music daily. **Chief O'Neill's,** Smithfield Village, Dublin 7 (© **01/817-3838**), is one of the city's best haunts for gimmick-free traditional music, in the hotel of the same name.

GAY & LESBIAN BARS

Check the *Gay Community News, In Dublin,* or *The Event Guide* to find out what's going on in town. The most comprehensive websites for gay organizations, events, issues, and information are **Gay Ireland Online** (www.gay-ireland.com), **Outhouse** (www.outhouse.ie; click on the "Ireland's Pink Pages" link), and **Dublin's Queer Guide** (www.dublinqueer.com). Folks on the help lines **Lesbians Organizing Together** (© **01/872-7770**) and **Gay Switchboard Dublin** (© **01/872-1055**) are also extremely helpful in directing you to activities of particular interest

The city's largest gay bar is **The George,** 89 S. Great George's St., Dublin 2 (© **01/478-2983**), a two-story venue where both the decor and clientele tend toward camp. Check listings magazines for theme nights. **Stonewallz,** Molloy's Bar, High St., Christchurch, Dublin 8 (© **01/872-7770**), is a women-only club open on Saturdays from 8:30pm to 2am. Admission is €5 ($5.75). **Out on the Liffey,** 27 Upper Ormond Quay, Dublin 1 (© **01/872-2480**), is a relaxed, friendly pub catering to a balance of men and women (except Sat, when it's men only). After hours, there's also a late-night venue on the premises called Oscar's, where you can dance (or drink) until you drop.

DANCE & LIVE-MUSIC CLUBS

For club schedules, check *In Dublin* magazine or the *Event Guide.* One of the most popular rock clubs is **Whelan's,** 25 Wexford St., Dublin 2 (© **01/478-0766**). **Annabel's,** Burlington Hotel, Upper Leeson Street, Dublin 4 (© **01/660-5222**), just south of the Lower Leeson Street nightclub strip, boasts a mix of travelers and locals of all ages, and a disco party atmosphere. **Club M,** Blooms Hotel, Anglesea Street, Dublin 2 (© **01/671-5485**), offers Ireland's largest laser lighting system and DJ-driven dance or live music for the over-23 age bracket.

Here are the hippest and hottest clubs (with correspondingly strict door policies): **POD** ("Place of Dance"), 35 Harcourt Street, Dublin 2 (© **01/478-0225**), which is open Wednesday to Saturday from 11pm until at least 2am; **Lillie's Bordello,** Adam Court, off Grafton Street, Dublin 2 (© **01/679-9204**), which is open daily from 11pm to 3am; and **Traffic,** 54 Middle Abbey St., Dublin 1 (© **01/873-4800**), an urban-cool bar and club covering three floors, open Monday to Friday 4pm to 3am, weekends noon to 3am. The quasi-jazz club **Renards,** 23–25 Frederick St. S., Dublin 2 (© **01/677-5876**), offers live music—everything from acid jazz to Latin beats—Sunday to Thursday 11pm to 3am. Though trendy, **Rí-Rá,** 1 Exchequer St., Dublin 2 (© **01/677-4835**), has a friendlier door policy than most of its competition, so this may be the place to try first; it's open daily from 11:30pm until 4am or later.

7 Two Side Trips in the Dublin Countryside

Bus Eireann, in the Busáras Central Bus Station, Store Street (© **01/836-6111;** www.buseireann.ie), offers about 20 half- and full-day excursions from Dublin, including a Glendalough and Wicklow Gap tour, and a Boyne Valley and North Coast tour (including a visit to Newgrange).

GLENDALOUGH 🀫🀫

A large area of County Wicklow, 56km (35 miles) south of Dublin, has been designated a national park and enjoys protection from further development. The core of the park is centered on **Glendalough,** an ancient monastic settlement along the shores of two exquisite mountain lakes. The **Wicklow Mountains National Park Information Center** (© **0404/45325**) at the base of Upper Lake provides details on hiking and touring in the Glendalough Valley and surrounding hills, including maps and route descriptions; it's open May through August daily 10am to 6pm; April and September Saturday and Sunday 10am to 6pm; closed other months. Admission to the park and monastic grounds is free, and both are open year-round. The closest parking is at Upper Lake, where you'll pay €2 ($2.30) per car; to avoid this fee, just walk up from the Glendalough Visitor Center, where the parking is free. If you don't have a car, Gray Line offers a bus tour from Dublin to Glendalough. For information, contact Gray Line Desk, Dublin Tourism Centre, Suffolk Street, Dublin 2 (© **01/605-7705**).

WHERE TO DINE   The best budget dining in the vicinity of Glendalough can be found at the **Avoca Handweavers Tea Shop,** Avoca (© **0402/35105**). They prepare wholesome meals that are often surprisingly imaginative for cafeteria fare, and the shop is open daily all year 9am to 5pm. American Express, MasterCard, and Visa are accepted.

NEWGRANGE 🀫🀫

Just 56km (35 miles) north of Dublin is **Newgrange,** the most prominent of a group of ancient tombs in the Boyne River Valley in County Meath, and one of the archaeological wonders of western Europe. Built as a burial mound more than 5,000 years ago, it sits atop a hill near the Boyne. All visits to Newgrange begin at the **Brú na Bóinne Visitor Centre** (© **041/988-0300**), across the river from Newgrange; admission to the center (including the visit to Newgrange) is €5.50 ($6.35) adults, €4.25 ($4.90) seniors, €2.75 ($3.15) students and children over 6, €14 ($16) family. The center is open daily: November to February 9:30am to 5pm; March, April, and October 9:30am to 5:30pm; May and mid- to late September 9am to 6:30pm; June to mid-September 9am to 7pm. Due to the great numbers of visitors to Newgrange, delays are common and you need to arrive early to guarantee entry.

WHERE TO DINE   On the premises of a fabulously family-friendly working farm, the **Newgrange Farm Coffee Shop,** Slane (© **041/982-4119**), is housed in a converted cow house, and serves comforting favorites including homemade soups, hot scones, and yummy apple tarts. It's open Easter to August daily 10am to 5pm. No credit cards are accepted. The farm has an excellent, hands-on petting zoo that children absolutely adore. Admission is €6 ($6.90) per person, €5 ($5.75) per person in a family.

In Pierce Brosnan's hometown of Navan, County Meath, **Hudson's Bistro,** 30 Railway St., Navan (© **046/29231**), offers such delights as tender Greek lamb kabobs with saffron rice, ratatouille chutney, or the authentic and delicious spicy Thai curry with vegetables. The bistro is open Monday to Saturday 5:30 to 11pm and Sunday 5:30 to 10pm. American Express, MasterCard, and Visa are accepted.

Edinburgh & Environs

by Darwin Porter & Danforth Prince

As it moves deeper into the 21st century, "Auld Reekie" (the Scottish name for **Edinburgh**), has become a bustling, vibrant, and largely self-governing capital. It's still tied to England, of course, but with its own Scottish Parliament—the first in nearly 3 centuries—Edinburghers are taking more control of their own destiny.

Young Edinburgh, in terms of nightlife, art, lifestyle, and other elements, is not quite as cutting edge as London, but it remains among the more sophisticated Europe capitals. The staid reformer and hometown preacher, John Knox, would be shocked by the modern city today.

Most visitors descend at the time of the annual Edinburgh International Festival, but more and more people are arriving year-round to follow in the footsteps of Mary Queen of Scots,

Robert Louis Stevenson, Sir Walter Scott, and Bonnie Prince Charlie, to namedrop just a few.

The city has always extended a friendly welcome to its visitors. Today it is doing so with a resurgence of pride in its identity.

Prepare to walk and to climb hills for the city's legendary panoramic views. Not only views, but also historic sights coupled with a wide diversity of modern culture await you.

Edinburgh has a long and stormy past, of which you'll be reminded every time you gaze up at Edinburgh Castle, one of Europe's most arresting sights. You'll recall it when you follow in the footsteps of Mary Queen of Scots and Lord Darnley through Holyroodhouse. In the Old Town, you'll step from the 21st century back to medieval days when you wander

---

Value **Budget Bests**

Following a series of horrendous delays at the end of the 20th century, rail passengers in droves began deserting the trains in favor of other means of transport to Edinburgh. Many were amazed to discover just how cheap (fares as low as £37/$68 round-trip, most around £70/$130) and convenient it is to fly from London to Edinburgh. The flight takes 55 minutes and, even allowing for travel time to/from the respective airports, is still faster than the train journey, although obviously not as spacious and scenic. The online booking services of **GO** (www.gofly.com), from London's Stansted airport, and **easyJet** (© 0870/600-0000; www.easyjet.com), from London's Luton airport, are simple to use. Booking over the Internet is in both cases the cheapest travel option.

The best values in Edinburgh are the many **free museums** and **galleries**. These include the two Royal Museums, the Scottish National Gallery, and the Museum of Childhood. Other budget bests are **free live music** in pubs and clubs, and great **lunches** in almost any pub.

Edinburgh Deals & Discounts

SPECIAL DISCOUNTS   If you plan to use the public buses, purchase a **Daysaver Ticket** at only £2.50 ($4.65) adults and £1.80 ($3.35) children; it's good for 1 day and allows you to use the LRT buses as often as you wish. An even greater savings is available if you can delay your first journey until 9:30am, after which the Daysaver ticket is just £1.80 ($3.35) adults or children. If you plan to be around for a week, you can get a **City Ridacard** good for unlimited travel at £11 ($20) adults and £7 ($13) children. A Ridacard valid for 2 weeks is £22 ($41) adults and £14 ($26) children; 4 weeks costs £33 ($61) adults and £21 ($39) children.

If you plan on visiting historic properties in and around Edinburgh or elsewhere in Scotland, then buy the **Historic Scotland Explorer Pass,** which allows free admission to around 300 properties and costs £15 ($28) for 3 days, £20 ($37) for 7 days, and £23 ($43) for 10 days. These properties include Edinburgh Castle and Linlithgow Palace, so the pass soon pays for itself. It's available from any of the properties or from the head office of **Historic Scotland,** Longmore House, Salisbury Place, Edinburgh EH9 1SH (© **0131/668-8800;** www.historic-scotland.gov.uk).

WORTH A SPLURGE   In Edinburgh, the budget hotels are quite good, the attractions' admission fees are low, and you won't improve the quality of the food by paying more. The only things you'll have to splurge on are a good bottle of **single-malt whisky** and an occasional **taxi ride.**

through the web of steep alleys (closes) that look down over rooftops or up to soaring spires and castle battlements. It's this uniqueness that has led Edinburgh to be dubbed the "Athens of the north." In striking contrast to the Old Town's twisted closes are the wide streets and spacious squares and crescents of the Georgian New Town.

Although Edinburghers take care to preserve their city's history, they don't ignore their contemporary cultural life. The popular Edinburgh International Festival is held every summer. And during the rest of the year, the theaters, concert halls, live-music clubs, galleries, and museums cater to the Scots' cultural appetite. Every block seems to have its own pub, where you can often hear traditional music while sipping your pint of ale or dram of single-malt whisky. Elegant and expensive shops line Princes Street in the New Town, while antiques shops, boutiques, and unusual import stores fill the Old Town.

For more on Edinburgh and its environs, see *Frommer's Scotland, Scotland For Dummies,* or *Frommer's Scotland's Best-Loved Driving Tours.*

1 Essentials

ARRIVING
BY PLANE   The **Edinburgh Airport** (© **0131/333-1000**) is 13km (8 miles) northwest of the city, and you might want to stop by the **Edinburgh Tourist**

Information Desk (© 0131/473-3800) here before heading on. Double-decker **Airlink buses** regularly make the 25-minute trip into the city at £3.30 ($6.10) one-way or £5 ($9.25) round-trip adults, £2 ($3.70) one-way or £3 ($5.55) round-trip for children. Waverley Bridge, the last stop, is centrally located between the Old Town and the New Town. Airport **taxis** will take you into the city center for £15 to £20 ($28–$37). If you can get one of the standard black taxis to give you a ride, you'll save a little money, but they aren't supposed to pick up fares at the airport.

BY TRAIN   The cheapest available ticket is the **Standard Class Off-Peak Ticket** starting at £25 ($46) round-trip. Flights are subject to availability and you must book in advance. Call © **0044/191-227-5959** or 0345/225-225 from England. You can also book your tickets online at **www.thetrainline.com**. From London, the Intercity 225 service takes 4½ hours to reach **Waverley Station** in downtown Edinburgh. Following the exit signs up the auto ramp, you'll find yourself on Waverley Bridge. Princes Street and the New Town will be to your right and the Old Town to your left.

VISITOR INFORMATION

TOURIST OFFICES   The main **Edinburgh and Scotland Tourist Information Centre,** 3 Princes St. (© 0131/473-3800; bus: all city-center buses), is at the corner of Princes Street and Waverley Bridge, above the underground Waverley Market shopping center. May, June, and September, it's open Monday to Saturday 9am to 7pm and Sunday 10am to 7pm; July and August hours are Monday to Saturday 9am to 8pm and Sunday 10am to 8pm; April and October hours are Monday to Saturday 9am to 6pm and Sunday 10am to 6pm; and November to March hours are Monday to Saturday 9am to 6pm and Sunday 11am to 6pm. There's also an info desk at the airport (see above).

For details on events while you're in town, pick up at the tourist center a free copy of the monthly *Day-by-Day,* listing events, exhibits, theater, and music.

Students who want to find out more about the university scene should head over to the **Edinburgh University Student Centre** on Bristol Square (© 0131/650-2656; bus: 20, 27, or 41), where a large notice board lists events of interest. If you're looking for an apartment for a few months or longer, you'll find ads for roommates there.

WEBSITES   For general information on the Net, check out **www.edinburgh.org**, **www.travelscotland.co.uk**, **www.scotland2000.com**, or **http://aboutscotland.com**. At **www.multimap.com**, you can access detailed street maps of the whole United Kingdom—just key in the location or even just its postal code, and a map of the area with the location circled will appear.

CITY LAYOUT

It's easy to find your way around Edinburgh. The city is divided into the **Old Town** atop the rocky Mound and the **New Town.** They're separated by Princes Street Gardens. Dominating the Edinburgh skyline is **Edinburgh Castle,** standing high on a crag at the western end of the Old Town. At the opposite end of the Old Town and connected to the castle by the **Royal Mile,** a single street bearing four names along its length (Castle Hill, Lawnmarket, High St., and Canongate), is the **Palace of Holyroodhouse,** the Scottish residence of Elizabeth II and many past kings and queens.

Princes Street, New Town's main thoroughfare, is bordered on the north side by department stores and some of Edinburgh's most elegant clothing stores.

Running the length of Princes Street on the south side is **Princes Street Gardens,** a beautiful park filling the valley between the two city sections.

GETTING AROUND

Edinburgh, especially the narrow lanes and closes of the Old Town, is best explored on foot. Almost everything you'll want to see is either along or just a few blocks from the Royal Mile, along Princes Street, or on the nearby streets of the New Town.

BY BUS   Burgundy-and-white **Lothian Region Transport** (✆ **0131/555-6363**) double-deckers run frequently to all parts of the city and its suburbs. Fares vary according to the number of stops you travel, from 60p ($1.10) to £1 ($1.85). You're expected to have the correct fare when boarding—deposit your coins in the slot beside the driver and take your ticket. Be sure to hang onto this ticket in case an inspector asks to see it. From Sunday to Thursday, the buses stop running a little after 11pm, but on Friday and Saturday some buses run all night. The night fare is £2 ($3.70).

You probably won't know how many stops you'll be traveling and thus won't know how much to pay. With plenty of change in hand, ask the driver how much the fare is to your destination. Or you can buy a **Daysaver Ticket** (see "Edinburgh Deals & Discounts," above) from the driver or from LRT Travelshops. (There's one at 2 Cockburn St.) If you're staying for a week, buy a **City Ridacard** (see "Edinburgh Deals & Discounts," above).

BY TAXI   Taxi stands are along Princes Street and at Waverley Station. Fares start at £1.40 ($2.60) and cost 22p (40¢) per mile. From 6pm to 6am, there's an extra charge of 60p ($1.10). You can also call ✆ **0131/228-1211** for a cab.

BY BICYCLE   Because Edinburgh is built on a series of hills and ridges, biking around the city is hard in places but fun. Exploring the surrounding countryside by bike is pleasant. **Edinburgh Cycle Hire and Safaris** (also known as Edinburgh Rent-A-Bike), 29 Blackfriars St. (✆ **0131/556-5560**), offers day rentals from £15 ($28) and weekly rentals from £50 to £70 ($93–$130). It's open daily 9am to 6pm and in summer 9am to 9pm, and requires a credit card for a deposit.

BY RENTAL CAR   For excursions farther afield, you might want to rent a car. In addition to the major international car-rental agencies, all of which have representatives in Edinburgh, you can try **Condor Self Drive,** 45 Lochrin Place (✆ **0131/229-6333;** www.condorselfdrive.co.uk; bus: 10, 11, 15, 16, 17, 23, or 27), offering its smallest cars for about £33 ($61) per day with 200km (124 miles) mileage included per day (unlimited if you rent for more than 4 days). **Capital Car Hire,** 9 Clifton Terrace, Haymarket (✆ **0131/337-5333;** bus: all city-center buses), offers a rate of £22 ($41) per day with unlimited mileage.

Remember: You get the best deal if you arrange the rental before leaving home.

Country & City Codes

The **country code** for the United Kingdom is **44.** The **city code** for Edinburgh is **131;** use this code when you're calling from outside the United Kingdom. If you're within the United Kingdom but not in Edinburgh, use **0131.** If you're calling within Edinburgh, simply leave off the code and dial only the regular phone number.

FAST FACTS: Edinburgh

American Express The office is at 139 Princes St. (© 0131/225-7881; bus: all city-center buses), open Monday to Friday 9am to 5:30pm and Saturday 9am to 4pm.

Banks There are several banks along Princes Street that will change money, offering the best exchange rate and charging a small commission. The **Royal Bank of Scotland**, 142–144 Princes St. (© 0131/226-2555; bus: all city-center buses), is open Monday, Tuesday, Thursday, and Friday 9:15am to 4:45pm, Wednesday 10am to 4:45pm, and Saturday 10am to 2pm.

Business Hours Most **shops** are open Monday to Saturday 10am to 5:30 or 6pm (to 7:30pm Thurs) and Sunday 11am to 5:30pm. Some smaller shops might close for lunch. **Offices** are open Monday to Friday 9am to 5pm.

Consulates The consulate of the **United States** is at 3 Regent Terrace, an extension of Princes Street beyond Nelson's Monument (© 0131/556-8315; bus: 26, 85, or 86); it's open Monday to Friday 1 to 4pm by appointment only. In an emergency, visitors from Canada, Australia, or New Zealand should contact their High Commission in London (see "Fast Facts: London" in chapter 15, "London, Bath & Environs").

Currency The basic unit of currency is the **pound sterling (£)**, which is divided into 100 **pence** (p). The exchange rate at the time we wrote this chapter was £1 ($1.85). Note that although the United Kingdom is part of the E.U., it does not plan to switch to the euro at this time.

Currency Exchange There are currency exchange counters at the Tourist Information Centre in Waverley Market, at Waverley Station, and at many banks on Princes Street and the Royal Mile. The banks charge a lower fee.

Emergencies If you need a doctor or dentist, check the Yellow Pages or ask at your hotel. For **police** assistance or an **ambulance**, dial © 999. There are no 24-hour pharmacies in Edinburgh. **Boots**, 48 Shandwick Place (© 0131/225-6757; bus: all city-center buses), is open Monday to Friday 8am to 9pm and Sunday 10:30am to 4:30pm.

Holidays Edinburgh celebrates New Year's Day (Jan 1), January 2, the first Monday in May, Victoria Day (May 8), Christmas Day (Dec 25), and Boxing Day (Dec 26), plus the spring and autumn bank holidays in mid-April and mid-September, respectively.

Hospital The **Royal Infirmary**, 51 Old Dalkeith Rd. (© 0131/536-1000; bus: 7, 8, 24, 32, 33, 38, 49, or 52), is one of the most convenient hospitals.

Internet Access You can check your e-mail or send messages at **easyEverything**, 58 Rose St., just behind Princes Street; www.easyeverything.com; bus: all Princes St. buses), open 8am to 11pm. Rates are around £1 ($1.85) for an hour, but if you don't use your full time allocation, your ticket (issued before you log on) is valid for 28 days and can be used repeatedly until your hour allocation has expired. There is also free Internet access at any Edinburgh library.

Laundry & Dry Cleaning **Sundial Launderettes**, 62 Portobello High St. (© 0131/667-0825), is open Monday to Friday 8am to 7pm, Saturday 9:30am to 5pm, and Sunday 10:30am to 4pm. For dry cleaning, try **Johnston's**, 23

Frederick St. ((*C* **0131/225-8095**; bus: all city-center buses), open Monday to Friday 8am to 5:30pm and Saturday 8:30am to 4pm.

Mail The **Central Post Office** is at 7 Hope St. (bus: all city-center buses). It's open Monday to Friday 9am to 5:30pm and Saturday 9am to 1pm.

Taxes For details on VAT refunds, see "Shopping," later in this chapter.

Telephone **Public phones** cost 20p (35¢) for the first 3 minutes and accept coins of various denominations. At post offices and newsstands, you can also buy a **phone card** for use in special phones. A 3-minute phone call to the United States costs about £4.80 ($8.90). Alternatively, you can reach an **AT&T** operator, and get U.S. rates for collect or credit card calls by dialing toll free *C* **0800/890 011**; to access **World Phone**, dial *C* **0800/890-222**; and to access **Sprint**, dial *C* **0800/890-877**. To place **collect calls** from Britain to a country besides the United States or Canada, dial *C* **155**, then tell the operator you intend to make a collect call.

Tipping In most restaurants, tax and service charge are included, so it's unnecessary to leave a tip. If a service charge hasn't been included in the bill, the standard tip is 10%. Taxi drivers also expect a 10% tip.

2 Affordable Places to Stay

The cheapest accommodations in Edinburgh, aside from hostels, are home stays. People with an extra bedroom or two in their home will take in paying guests for about £22 ($41) per person per night. Home stays are generally available only in summer but occasionally in other months as well. The **Edinburgh and Scotland Tourist Information Centre** (see "Visitor Information," above) has a list of hundreds of home stays, and its staff will also make reservations for you for £3 ($5.55). You can make phone bookings via **Central Reservations** at *C* **0131/473-3800.**

Note: You'll find the lodging choices below plotted on the map on p. 414.

IN THE CITY CENTER

A-Haven   This semidetached 1862 Victorian house is a 15-minute walk or 5-minute bus ride north of the rail station. Rooms are of various sizes (the biggest are on the 2nd floor). Front rooms open onto views of Arthur's Seat; some rooms in back overlook the Firth of Forth. Manager David Kay extends a Scottish welcome in this family-type place, and is happy to offer sightseeing advice.

180 Ferry Rd., Edinburgh EH6 4NS. *C* 0131/554-6559. Fax 0131/554-5252. www.a-haven.co.uk. 14 units. £30–£50 ($56–$93) per person double. Rates include breakfast. AE, MC, V. Free parking. Bus: 7, 11, or 14. **Amenities:** Restaurant; bar. *In room:* TV, dataport, coffeemaker, hair dryer, iron, trouser press.

Castle Guest House   Don't be confused by the name: This centrally located guesthouse is not actually close to Edinburgh Castle but is located in the New Town less than 2 blocks from Princes Street and about 10 minutes by foot from

---

Tips **A Bed at Festival Time**

If you arrive in Edinburgh during the festival and have no accommodations, contact **Festival Beds**, 38 Moray Place (*C* **0131/225-1101**), which organizes B&B accommodations in private homes.

Value **Getting the Best Deal on Accommodations**

- Be aware that home stays, usually available only in summer, are generally cheaper than hotel rooms—if you don't mind staying in someone else's home, check the tourist office for availability.
- Take advantage of accommodations about a 10- to 15-minute bus ride out of the city center—they tend to be cheaper than those in town.
- Try the guesthouses along Dalkeith Road, near the university residence halls.

Waverley Station. The 200-year-old stone residence offers cozy rooms with good beds and adequate, though not spacious, bathrooms, each with showers. There's no elevator, and to get inside you have to make a steep climb up several flights of stairs, but the place is well maintained and offers a choice of five breakfasts, and the street affords castle views.

38 N. Castle St., Edinburgh EH2 3BN. © 0131/225-1975. Fax 0131/225-1975. 9 units. £35–£45 ($65–$83) single; £70–£90 ($130–$167) double. Rates include full breakfast. Minimum stay 2 nights in July, 3 nights in Aug. No credit cards. Bus: All Princes St. buses. *In room:* TV, coffeemaker, no phone.

Elder York Guest House   It's a steep climb up to this guesthouse (no elevator) occupying the top floors of a 19th-century five-story town house 2 blocks from Waverley Station and right beside the intercity bus terminal. The nonsmoking rooms are small but adequately furnished, with comfortable chairs and good beds. The none-too-spacious bathrooms are well maintained and come with showers. The breakfast room is pleasant but the staff somewhat weary.

38 Elder St., Edinburgh EH1 3DX. © 0131/556-1926. Fax 0131/624-7140. 13 units, 8 singles with bathroom. £35 ($65) single without bathroom; £50–£70 ($93–$130) double with bathroom. Rates include full breakfast. MC, V. Bus: All city-center buses. **Amenities:** Breakfast room; laundry/dry-cleaning service (Mon–Fri). *In room:* TV, coffeemaker, hair dryer, no phone.

Ibis Edinburgh Centre *Value*   This Ibis is part of an international chain, and its rates and location just off the Royal Mile offer excellent value for two people sharing. You're ideally situated for exploring the Old Town, and a short walk over North Bridge brings you to the New Town. The downside is that the rooms have a uniform blandness and the staff is polite but lacking in the warmth that marks Edinburgh's family-run guesthouses. The rooms are medium in size and clean, the fairly low beds are comfortable, and the shower-only bathrooms, though somewhat clinical in design, are adequate. Note that Hunters Square can get noisy from 1 to 3am, when the nearby pubs empty out, so try to get a room at the rear.

6 Hunter Sq., Edinburgh EH1 1QW. © 0131/240-7000. Fax 0131/240-7007. 99 units. £50–£70 ($93–$130) single or double. Breakfast £4.95 ($9.15). AE, DC, MC, V. Bus: All city-center buses. **Amenities:** Breakfast room; bar; laundry service; nonsmoking rooms; rooms for those w/limited mobility. *In room:* TV, dataport, coffeemaker, iron.

Premier Lodge   On a busy street corner below the castle, this 200-year-old town house dominates the block. It's part of a budget chain—it might not brim over with character, but its uniformity means you know exactly what you're getting. That means an ultramodern interior with tidy rooms that range from adequate to extra large, reasonably sized beds, and bathrooms with shower that are spotless. Of course, it's the central location (a cannonball's shot from the castle) that most recommends it, but be warned that Grassmarket can be busy and noisy on weekend nights.

94 Grassmarket, Edinburgh EH1 2JF. © 0131/220-2299. Fax 0870/990-6401. 44 units. £50 ($93) single or double. Continental breakfast £4.25 ($7.85); full Scottish breakfast £6.25 ($12). AE, MC, V. Bus: All city-center buses. **Amenities:** Nonsmoking rooms; rooms for those w/limited mobility. In room: TV, coffeemaker.

Princes Street East Backpackers Hostel This hostel, with 24-hour access, occupies several floors of a small building a block behind Edinburgh's main shopping street. It's a long climb up seemingly endless flights of stairs to reach the congested reception (no elevator), where the staff greets your breathless arrival. The rooms are a little shabby, but if location, value for money, and the chance to meet fellow travelers are what you want, then this is the place. It can accommodate about 250 people in single or double rooms or in dorms sleeping 4 to 12. Sunday dinners are free, and a 7th night is free. (If you have culinary skills, you can get yourself a few nights free here by volunteering to cook this dinner.)

5 W. Register St., Edinburgh EH2 2AA. © 0131/556-6894. www.edinburghbackpackers.com. 110 beds, no units with bathroom. £11 ($20) dorm bed; £30 ($56) double. MC, V. From Waverley Station, turn left onto Princes St., right onto Andrew St., then right onto W. Register St. **Amenities:** TV/video lounge; game room; self-service laundry; 2 self-catering kitchens; luggage storage; Internet access.

Travelodge Edinburgh Another budget chain, the Travelodge offers spacious rooms like any you'll find in similar motels all over the world, with soft "hypnos" mattresses on king-size beds. The beds themselves are quite low, which could pose a problem for those none too agile at getting up. The shower-only bathrooms are tidy and adequately sized if a little claustrophobic. The motel's location a few minutes' walk from the Royal Mile makes it ideal for those seeking central accommodations who don't mind sacrificing character to uniformity.

33 St. Mary's St., Edinburgh EH1 1TA. © 0870/191-1637. www.travelodge.co.uk. 193 units. £50–£70 ($93–$126) double. Continental breakfast £5.25 ($9.70); full Scottish breakfast £8.25 ($15). Special winter discounts sometimes offered. AE, DC, MC, V. Bus: 1 or 6. **Amenities:** Cafe; bar; nonsmoking rooms; rooms for those w/limited mobility. In room: TV, coffeemaker.

SOUTH OF THE CITY CENTER

Arthur's View Guest House James and Elizabeth Woodrow keep this friendly guesthouse that certainly stands out from the numerous "peas in the pod" lining Mayfield Gardens, less than a 10-minute bus ride from the city center. The rooms are attractively furnished and well decorated; they're not overly large but are certainly adequate and have good beds. The shower-only bathrooms tend toward the small, but they're clean and maintained to a high standard.

10 Mayfield Gardens, Edinburgh EH9 2BZ. © 0131/667-3468. 12 units. arthursview@aol.com. £35–£50 ($65–$93) single; £60–£80 ($111–$148) double. Rates include full Scottish breakfast. MC, V. Bus: 3, 7, 8, 29, 31, or 37. In room: TV, coffeemaker, hair dryer.

Gifford House ★★ (Kids) This late-19th-century stone home is run by Mrs. Margaret Dow, who's justifiably proud of her strikingly yet individually decorated large rooms, all renovated in 2000. The hotel is popular with families and parents of students from the nearby university. The beds are good with warm duvets. Unusually for this price bracket, the single room boasts a generous double bed. The bathrooms, above average size, are beautifully decorated, each with shower. The rooms at the back offer views of Arthur's Seat and Salisbury Crags. A variety of dishes is available for breakfast, and special diets are catered to.

103 Dalkeith Rd., Edinburgh EH16 5AJ. ©/fax 0131/667-4688. 7 units. £30–£60 ($56–$111) single; £25–£50 ($46–$93) per person double; £22–£30 ($41–$56) per person triple or quad. Rates include full breakfast. MC, V. Free parking. Bus: 14, 30, or 33. *In room:* TV, coffeemaker, hair dryer, no phone.

Kariba Guest House   This small guesthouse (no elevator) has a warm atmosphere, thanks to owner Agnes Holligan, who's full of information. A lot of time and energy were put into restoring this Victorian home to its former aura, and the plasterwork cornices and ceilings are particularly attractive. The nonsmoking rooms are tastefully furnished in a plain modern fashion, and the beds are good. The bathrooms are clean and well maintained with a choice of tub or shower.

10 Granville Terrace, Edinburgh EH10 4PQ. © 0131/229-3773 or 0131/229-4968. karibaguesthouse@ hotmail.com. 9 units. £20–£40 ($37–$74) single; £40–£70 ($74–$130) double. Rates include full breakfast. AE, MC, V. Bus: 10 or 27. **Amenities:** Laundry service; nonsmoking rooms; 1 room for those w/limited mobility. *In room:* TV, coffeemaker, hair dryer, no phone.

No. 45 Gilmour Road 🎯🎯   This elegant B&B (no elevator) is a hidden gem on a quiet road less than 15 minutes by bus from the city center. You'll be immediately drawn to the polished woodwork of the floors and stairway—the woodwork is an abiding feature of the spacious rooms, all decorated to a high standard, with well-maintained bathrooms with tub or shower. The breakfast room extends into the kitchen so you can keep constant note of how your breakfast is coming along. At the end of a hard day's exploration, you can relax in the front lounge or, during warmer weather, in the garden conservatory.

45 Gilmour Rd., Edinburgh EH16 5NS. © 0131/667-3536. Fax 0131/662-1946. 7 units. £25–£45 ($46–$83) per person single or double. Rates include full breakfast. MC, V. Bus: 3, 7, 8, 30, 31, 36, 63, 69, 80, or 89. *In room:* TV, coffeemaker, hair dryer, no phone.

Pollock Halls   For most of the year, these are nonsmoking dorms for Edinburgh University, but during recess times, the 1,000 singles and doubles, plus the 330 rooms with private bathroom, are available to the public. Many rooms have excellent views of the Salisbury Crags and Arthur's Seat. The entrance gate is beyond the Royal Commonwealth Pool complex; once through the gates, follow the signs to St. Leonard's Hall.

University of Edinburgh, 18 Holyrood Park Rd., Edinburgh EH16 5AY. © 0131/651-2184 or 0800/028-7118. Fax 0131/667-7271. www.edinburghfirst.com. 1,500 units, 400 with bathroom. £27–£46 ($50–$85) single; £69–£75 ($128–$139) double. Rates include full breakfast and showers. No credit cards. Open Mar–Apr and June–Sept. Bus: 14, 21, or 33. **Amenities:** Bars; lounges; TV rooms; self-service laundry.

NORTH OF THE CITY CENTER

Ardenlee Guest House   This comfortable three-floor Victorian town house (no elevator) is run by Alasdair Irving, who offers attractively decorated large rooms with good beds and shower-only bathrooms that are more than adequate in size as well as spotless. Potted plants throughout the house are a nice touch. You have your choice of how you'd like your eggs fixed each morning, and they cater to vegetarians and others on special diets.

9 Eyre Place (off Dundas St.), Edinburgh EH3 5ES. © 0131/556-2838. Fax 0131/557-0937. www.ardenlee. co.uk. 9 units, 7 with bathroom. £39 ($72) single without bathroom; £60–£80 ($111–$148) double with bathroom. Rates include full breakfast. Lower rates apply to low season. DC, MC, V. Bus: 23, 27, or 37. *In room:* TV, coffeemaker, hair dryer, no phone.

Dene Guest House   Five minutes north of Waverley Station by bus is the Dene, operated by Hamish McDougall, who has embarked on upgrading and modernizing this Georgian town house (no elevator) and restoring and enhancing its features. The rooms are simply decorated and cozy. Some of the beds are a little low, although all are comfortable. The shower-only bathrooms, though clean, are on the small side

7 Eyre Place (off Dundas St.), Edinburgh EH3 5ES. ℭ 0131/556-2700. Fax 0131/557-9876. 11 units, 5 with bathroom. £20–£30 ($37–$56) single; £36–£48 ($67–$89) double without bathroom, £44–£60 ($81–$111) double with bathroom. Rates include full breakfast. MC, V. Bus: 23 or 27. *In room:* TV, coffeemaker, hair dryer.

Ravensdown Bed and Breakfast *(Value)*   Away from the city center on a busy main road, this nonsmoking guesthouse (no elevator) run by Mr. and Mrs. Leonard Welch offers above-average rooms that are a good value. Each is large and individually decorated in cheery pastels. The beds have orthopedic mattresses, and all the rooms come with comfortable chairs for relaxing. The shower-only bathrooms are kept to a very high standard. The top-floor triple room has a bathroom on the outside corridor. Try to get one of the south-facing rooms—the view of the Edinburgh skyline is magnificent.

248 Ferry Rd., Edinburgh EH5 3AN. ℭ 0131/552-5438. Fax 0131/552-7559. len@ravensdownfreeserve.co.uk. 7 units. £23–£35 ($43–$65) per person double. Rates include full breakfast. No credit cards. Bus: 17, 23, or 27. *In room:* TV, coffeemaker, no phone.

Terrace Hotel *(Value)*   This landmark Georgian, on a usually pricey elegant street, offers good value. Owner Annie Mann is constantly improving her well-maintained hotel (no elevator). The spacious lounge and breakfast room feature fireplaces, and the sweeping staircase is illuminated by a huge oval skylight. The rooms are spacious, most with 4m (13-ft.) ceilings. The smallest are on the top floor, and the singles in particular are adequate; however, the bathrooms in them are cramped, and reaching the shower can involve maneuvering past the toilet.

37 Royal Terrace, Edinburgh EH7 5AH. ℭ 0131/556-3423. Fax 0131/556-2520. 14 units, 11 with bathroom. £30–£35 ($56–$65) single without bathroom, £40–£50 ($74–$93) single with bathroom; £40–£65 ($74–$120) double without bathroom, £60–£70 ($111–$130) double with bathroom. Rates include full breakfast. Higher prices apply July–Sept, lower rates Jan–Feb. MC, V. Bus: 2, 7, 10, 11, 12, 13, 14, 16, 17, 22, 25, or 87. **Amenities:** All nonsmoking rooms. *In room:* TV, coffeemaker, hair dryer, no phone.

Wayfarer Guest House   This relatively well-located B&B (no elevator) is on a quiet street, and the back rooms overlook an attractive garden. All the units are comfortable, of a reasonable size, and individually decorated, with good beds. The shower-only bathrooms are well kept, although they tend toward the slightly cramped. The ground-floor video library is a nice touch. The breakfast room is dominated by a huge wall mural, painted by a local artist and depicting Ernest Shackleton's last journey, a suitable inspiration as you prepare for your day. The guesthouse is about a 15-minute walk from the city center and especially recommended during the busy summer festival season.

5 Eyre Place, Edinburgh EH3 5ES. ℭ 0131/556-3025. 12 units. £44–£49 ($81–$91) single; £77–£88 ($142–$163) double; £99–£110 ($183–$204) triple. MC, V. Bus: 23 or 27. *In room:* TV, coffeemaker, no phone.

WEST OF THE CITY CENTER

Ashdene House   A two-story brick Edwardian (no elevator), the Ashdene is a B&B on a quiet leafy street about a 15-minute bus ride south of the city center. The house is well kept and renovated annually—a dining room and lounge area are among the latest improvements. The rooms are spacious, airy, and maintained to a high decorative standard. Room no. 3 is very large indeed. The single room has a double bed and during the busy season is available to couples at a bargain rate, but two people might find it cramped. The bathrooms are clean and reasonably sized, each with a shower. Breakfast is served in the garden-facing conservatory.

23 Fountainhall Rd., Edinburgh EH9 2LN. ℂ 0131/667-6026. www.ashdenehouse.com. 5 units. £45 ($83) single; £60–£90 ($111–$167) double; £90–£120 ($167–$222) triple. Rates include full breakfast. Children 16 and under discounted in parent's room. MC, V. Bus: 42. **Amenities:** All nonsmoking rooms. *In room:* TV, coffeemaker, hair dryer.

Beresford Hotel Proprietors Donald and Agnes Mackintosh run the best of the half dozen or so B&Bs on this short block, a stone's throw from the Haymarket BritRail station. Constructed in 1872, the establishment was a private town house until the early 20th century when it became the first hotel in the area, an easy stroll to Princes Street. Every room in this simple but thoroughly adequate home (no elevator) has a good bed, and the standard-size bathrooms are clean, but some of the shower cubicles are a little tiny. A lounge is available for guests.

32 Coates Gardens, Edinburgh EH12 5LE. ℂ 0131/337-0850. Fax 0131/538-7123. www.beresford-edinburgh.com. 12 units. £23–£45 ($43–$83) per person double. Rates include full breakfast. MC, V. Bus: 2, 12, 16, 18, 26, 31, 36, 38, 63, 69, 86, 100, or 284. *In room:* TV, coffeemaker, hair dryer.

Travel Inn *(Kids)* A 10-minute walk from the castle, this branch of Britain's largest budget hotel chain looks almost like a penitentiary. But it offers one of Edinburgh's cheapest rates, so it's often full. You won't find the atmosphere and individuality of older family-run places but will find reasonably sized rooms, uniformly furnished and with good beds. Another **Travel Inn** is at 228 Willowbrae Rd., to the rear of Holyrood Park, Edinburgh EH8 7NG (ℂ **0131/661-3396;** fax 0131/652-2789).

1 Morrison Link, Edinburgh EH3 8DN. ℂ 0870/238-3319. Fax 0131/228-9836. 278 units. £50 ($93) single, double, or family room. Continental breakfast £4.50 ($8.30); full Scottish breakfast £6.50 ($12). AE, MC, V. Bus: 26 or 31. *In room:* TV, coffeemaker.

A GAY & LESBIAN GUESTHOUSE

Mansfield House In Edinburgh's New Town, this friendly guesthouse (no elevator) offers individually decorated rooms of reasonable size, some beds with firm mattresses and some with soft (it's worth stressing your preference at time of booking). There are two extra-large rooms that offer king-size beds. The bathrooms are clean and fairly well proportioned; they come with showers. The hotel is within walking distance of all the gay bars, clubs, and restaurants. It's always busy, so early booking is advised.

57 Dublin St., Edinburgh EH3 6NL. ℂ 0131/556-7980. Fax 0131/466-1315. www.mansfieldguesthouse. com. 9 units, 6 with bathroom. £20–£30 ($37–$56) single without bathroom, £40 ($74) single with bathroom; £50 ($93) double without bathroom, £60 ($111) double with bathroom; £70 ($130) king-size superior room. Rates include continental breakfast. MC, V. Bus: Any bus to George St. *In room:* TV, fridge (some units), coffeemaker, no phone.

WORTH A SPLURGE

Greenside Hotel Royal Terrace is as elegant as its name implies, and at the 1820 Georgian-style Greenside (no elevator) you can experience this at reasonable rates. The rooms vary quite a bit from floor to floor, but all are of adequate size, with fine beds and a reasonable amount of room in the shower-only bathrooms. Ground-floor room no. 5 is extra large and has a larger-than-average bathroom. The neatly landscaped back garden is made for relaxing on summer afternoons, with views over the Firth of Forth.

9 Royal Terrace, Edinburgh EH7 5AB. ℂ 0131/557-0022. www.townhousehotels.co.uk. 15 units. £30–£60 ($56–$111) single; £50–£70 ($93–$130) double. Rates include breakfast. Rates higher at Edinburgh Festival. AE, DC, MC, V. Bus: 4, 15, or 44. **Amenities:** Dining room; bar; access to nearby health club; all nonsmoking rooms; 1 room for those w/limited mobility. *In room:* TV, coffeemaker, hair dryer, iron/ironing board.

Rosslyn Castle *Finds* A 10km (6-mile) drive or a 30-minute bus ride from Edinburgh's center, Rosslyn Castle sits on a rocky crag overlooking a scenic wooded valley. The castle can be yours for a week. For two people it might be expensive. However, it sleeps seven, so for a family or a group of friends, even at the height of summer, that's only around £33 ($61) per person per night. The original castle (now a ruin) dates from 1450, and the wing you rent is from 1622. The rooms are spacious, linen and towels are provided, and you have the romantic luxury of open fires to warm you on cold nights. In the valley, you'll no doubt want to seek out the hidden Wallace's Cave, where Braveheart himself is said to have hidden. The landmark trust has more than 150 similar properties throughout Scotland and the United Kingdom. For details, call the number below or visit **www.landmarktrust.co.uk** on the Web.

Roslin, Midlothian, EH25 9PU. Reservations must be made through Landmark Trust, Shottesbrook, Maidenhead, Berkshire, SL6 3SW. (℃ **0162/882-5925.** 4 units. From £668 ($1,236) per week. MC, V. Bus: 87.

16 Lynedoch Place A short walk from the west end of Princes Street, this 1821 home (no elevator) retains all its original architectural elements. The rooms are attractively furnished with antique armoires and chests, plus good beds. The bathrooms are standard size, tending toward the small, but they're decently maintained. Only one unit comes with a full tub bathroom; the rest come with bathroom with shower. Hosts Andrew and Susie Hamilton make you feel at home, especially when you sample some of Susie's delicious breakfasts. The gardens are a special bonus.

16 Lynedoch Place, Edinburgh EH3 7PY. (℃ **0131/225-5507.** Fax 0131/236-4185. www.16lynedochplace. co.uk. 6 units. £60–£100 ($111–$185) double. Rates include breakfast. MC, V. Bus: 19. **Amenities:** Dining room. *In room:* TV, coffeemaker, hair dryer.

3 Great Deals on Dining

The day when Edinburgh could be considered a backwater of culinary diversity is now long past. The city's restaurants are thriving, and global influences combined with the innovative use of local produce have given Edinburgh a dining scene that's as varied as it is inventive.

IN THE CITY CENTER

Baked Potato Shop VEGETARIAN/STUFFED POTATOES Little bigger than a closet, with seating for only four, the Baked Potato Shop is primarily a takeout place. The potatoes are huge and stuffed with hot and cold vegetarian fillings (such as curry or cauliflower and cheese) or with chili. However, because you're in Scotland, try the vegetarian haggis—it tastes just like the real thing.

Value **Getting the Best Deal on Dining**

- Try to have an early-evening meal—many of the restaurants listed here close at 5:30 or 6pm.
- Take advantage of the department stores along pricey Princes Street—they're surprisingly inexpensive places to eat.
- Eat pub grub or fast food on Sunday—finding a place to eat on Sunday can be a real problem in Edinburgh.

(*Moments* **Tea for Two**

A day spent exploring the Royal Mile can add up to several miles of walking, so if you find your stamina flagging, duck into **Clarinda's Tea Room,** 69 Canongate (✆ **0131/557-1888;** bus: 35), for the very British experience of afternoon tea. (You can have it in the morning, too.) This tiny cubbyhole of a tearoom is only steps from Holyroodhouse and boasts lace tablecloths, bone china, and antique Wedgwood plates on the walls. There are plenty of teas from which to choose, plus a long list of tempting sweets and home-baked scones with jam and cream. Homemade soup, lasagna, baked potatoes with cheese, salads, and similar dishes are also offered. Menu items range from £3 to £4 ($5.55–$7.40). It's open Monday to Saturday 9am to 4:45pm and Sunday 9:30am to 4:45pm.

Another choice is **Ryan's Bar,** 2 Hope St. (✆ **0131/226-6669**), near the northwestern corner of the West Princes Street Gardens. It serves tea daily 10:30am to 10pm (closes Fri–Sat at 1am).

---

56 Cockburn St. ✆ 0131/225-7572. Reservations not accepted. Potatoes £1.05–£3.75 ($1.95–$6.95). No credit cards. Daily 9am–9pm. Bus: 5.

Cafe Hub MODERN SCOTTISH/INTERNATIONAL In the converted church that also houses the Edinburgh Festival office, this cheery large room attracts an artsy/business crowd. Plenty of room is left between tables, and in summer the outdoor terrace is opened to provide extra seating. The varied menu changes regularly and includes simple pasta dishes, the more exotic guinea fowl with a pistachio terrine, grilled Scottish lamb with apricot and red onion, and traditional bubble 'n' squeak (potato and cabbage mashed and fried together with bacon and a poached egg). The service isn't particularly fast.

In the International Festival Centre, Castle Hill, Royal Mile. ✆ 0131/473-2067. Reservations not accepted. Meals £3.50–£9 ($6.50–$75). AE, MC, V. Daily 9:30am–10pm. Bus: All city-center buses.

Chapterhouse Restaurant *Value* SCOTTISH/INTERNATIONAL In a converted church tucked away behind the Museum of Scotland, this spacious restaurant boasts a bold red decor. Although an a la carte menu isn't available, the choices on the fixed-price menu change regularly and offer good value. They might include halibut steaks, Scotch beef braised in red-wine sauce, or broccoli-and-cauliflower flan. The good-tasting portions are more than adequate and well presented.

13 S. College St. ✆ 0131/650-9131. Reservations recommended. 2-course menu £9 ($15). MC, V. Mon noon–2:30pm; Tues–Fri noon–2:30pm and 5–9:30pm. Bus: All city-center buses.

Cornerstone Cafe VEGETARIAN A church crypt is the unlikely location of this quality cafe serving well-priced homemade soups, salads, quiches, baked potatoes, and sandwiches. A quiet oasis in the busiest part of town, the Cornerstone's menu is an alternative to department-store fare, and during warm weather there's outdoor seating that affords excellent views up to the castle.

In St. John's Church, Princes St. at Lothian Rd., West End. ✆ 0131/229-0212. Reservations not accepted. Main courses £3.50–£5 ($6.50–$9.25). No credit cards. Summer Mon–Fri 8:30am–6:30pm, Sat noon–9pm; winter Mon–Sat 9:30am–3:45pm. Bus: All city-center buses.

Duck's at Le Marché Noir ☆ SCOTTISH/FRENCH   The cuisine here is
~~~lish and more tuned to the culinary sophistication of London than at
in Edinburgh. Located in a wood house and dressed in
out, Duck's honors the traditions of Scotland with such
in phyllo pastry on a bed of turnip purée and red wine
ptions include a *boudin* of chicken and foie gras served
d applesauce; seared salmon with leeks, asparagus, zuc-
iger and sesame salad; roasted rack of lamb with thyme
tables; and grilled red snapper with wild rice and lime-
o pickles.

5-1608. Reservations recommended. Set-price 3-course lunch £14 ($26); dinner
8–$39). AE, DC, MC, V. Tues–Fri noon–3pm and 6–10pm; Sun–Mon 6–10pm. Bus:
16 or 23.

Henderson's Salad Table and Wine Bar ☆☆ VEGETARIAN   This Edinburgh institution offers a vast assortment of salads (served by the scoop) and hot
meals available all day in the large basement restaurant. About eight freshly made
hot dishes are posted daily on the blackboard. Batik and stained-glass room parti-
tions, nightly live jazz or similar music, and colorful wall hangings create a relaxing atmosphere. Tempting cakes and pies and a large variety of herbal teas are ideal
for afternoon tea or dessert. About a dozen wines are served by the glass.

94 Hanover St. ✆ 0131/225-2131. Reservations recommended. 2-course fixed-price lunch £7.95 ($15); 2-
course fixed-price dinner £9.35 ($17). AE, MC, V. Mon–Sat 8am–10:45pm; Sun noon–6pm. Bus: All city-cen-
ter buses.

Maxie's Bistro *Value* CONTINENTAL   Maxie's is a popular student lunch
and evening spot, so it's a lively venue and not suited to those seeking an intimate dinner. But for those wanting a varied choice of well-prepared foods at reasonable prices, it's ideal. It's downstairs, making for a cozy cellarlike atmosphere
serving a selection of about 28 wines by the glass. The chalkboard menu changes
daily, but you'll find hearty soups and dishes like cauliflower with cheese; beef
bourguignon; stir-fried beef; prawns; and pheasant, pigeon, and other game in
season—all decently prepared and a good value.

5B Jorenstone Terrace. ✆ 0131/226-7770. Reservations not accepted. Fixed-price lunch £6.95 ($13) for
2 courses, £7.95 ($15) for 3 courses; dinner £5.95–£17 ($11–$31). MC, V. Daily noon–1am. Bus: 27, 28, 35,
41 or 42.

Milne's BRITISH   This cavernous bi-level bar was once Edinburgh's literary
center, attracting both W. H. Auden and Dylan Thomas, who came to meet and
mingle with the city's literati of the 1950s and 1960s. But times have changed,
and you won't find Scottish bards supping here today. However, you will find a
lively atmospheric pub where it's easy to get lost in the labyrinth of rooms. Good
old-fashioned cooking is offered, and to sit in the homelike downstairs dining
room, as the smell of baking crusty pies wafts through the air, is worth the trip.
The gigantic Yorkshire pudding (brimming with mashed potatoes and onion
gravy), accompanied by either hand-carved beef or Theakstone sausage, is more
than sufficient to refuel you after a hard day of sightseeing.

35 Hanover St. ✆ 0131/225-6738. Reservations not accepted. Meals £4.55–£6.45 ($8.40–$12). AE, DC,
MC, V. Mon–Thurs 9am–midnight; Fri–Sat 9am–1am; Sun 12:30pm–midnight. Bus: 19a, 23, 27, 37, 47, 103,
or 203.

The New Bell Restaurant ☆☆ *Value* SCOTTISH/INTERNATIONAL   Iain
Bruce has taken the spacious upstairs room of this large pub (south of the city

center and within walking distance of the Dalkeith Rd., Minto St., and May-field Rd. guesthouses) and created one of Edinburgh's best moderately priced restaurants. The quality and variety of the food coupled with the imaginative use of herbs and spices have made the New Bell popular with locals and visitors alike, and you get splurge quality at budget prices. The pan-fried breast of duck, flavored with balsamic and rosemary, is a winner, but our favorite is marinated slow-roasted salmon flavored with saffron and lemon grass and served with a squid risotto. The wine list is varied and reasonably priced.

233 Causewayside. ℂ **0131/668-2868.** www.thenewbell.com. Reservations recommended. Meals £9.50–£18 ($18–$33). MC, V. Tues–Sun 5:30–10pm. Bus: 42 or 46.

The Queen Street Café SCOTTISH/INTERNATIONAL   A little way past the shop of the National Portrait Gallery, this is an oasis away from the rush of modern Edinburgh. Subdued lighting, a decor of relaxing pastels, exposed red-brick walls hung with portraits of Scottish notables, and a menu combining tra-ditional Scottish baking with the exotic flavors of the east have helped make this a popular lunchtime stop for more than a decade. You can enjoy lentil-and-coconut soup with fresh bread or Malaysian pork-and-potato curry with rice. After 3pm, you can relax with a pot of tea and one or more of the mouthwater-ing cakes and pastries.

National Portrait Gallery, 1 Queen St. ℂ **0131/557-2844.** Reservations not accepted. Meals £4–£5 ($7.40–$15). No credit cards. Mon–Sat 10am–4:30pm; Sun 11am–4:30pm. Bus: 4, 4A, 9, 9A, or 12.

Valvona & Crolla INTERNATIONAL   In 1872, a recent arrival from Italy opened this restaurant, and it's still going strong. The restaurant shares space with a delicatessen and food emporium where exotic coffees, Parma ham, Ital-ian cheeses, and breads, as well as takeaway sandwiches and casseroles, are sold. A satellite room, a few steps down from the main shopping area, contains a cafe and luncheon restaurant where food is very fresh and prices refreshingly low. Here, you can order three kinds of breakfasts (continental, Scottish, or vegetar-ian) for a fixed price of £3.95 ($7.30); platters of pasta, mixed sausages, and cold cuts; and crostini, risottos, and omelets. Don't expect leisurely dining, as the place caters to office workers and shoppers who dash in for midday sustenance, appre-ciating the informality, low prices, and freshness of the food.

19 Elm Row. ℂ **0131/556-6066.** Breakfast £4.95 ($8.90); pizzas, pastas, or platters £3–£10 ($5.55–$17). AE, MC, V. Mon–Fri 8am–6:30pm; Sat 11am–5pm. Bus: 7, 10, 11, 12, or 14.

Whigham's Wine Cellars SCOTTISH/SEAFOOD   This is an appealing spot at the west end of Princes Street. At night, the tables in the cellar alcoves are lit with candles. There's a good selection of wines and fine dishes that range from honey-roasted ham to beef Stroganoff to pasta with garlic and mushrooms in a cream, tomato, and chive sauce. The Thai fishcakes are particularly appeal-ing, as are the fresh Loch Fyne oysters.

13 Hope St., Charlotte Sq. ℂ **0131/225-8674.** Reservations accepted. Meals £5.95–£14 ($11–$26). AE, MC, V. Mon–Wed noon–11pm; Thurs noon–midnight; Fri–Sat noon–1am (Sun too in Aug). Bus: All city-center buses.

LOCAL BUDGET BESTS

PUB GRUB   Pubs along the **Royal Mile** and **Rose Street,** running parallel to Princes Street, offer plenty of local atmosphere and good prices. Pub grub tends to consist of hefty burgers or fish-and-chips, with the older hostelries along the Royal Mile offering haggis, tatties (potatoes), and neeps (turnips) for £4.75 to £5 ($8.80–$9.25).

CAFETERIAS   All the major **department stores** along Princes Street have cafeterias serving economical meals. In addition, many of the smaller stores have small cafes with equally good prices.

Jenner's, 48 Princes St. ((🕽 **0131/225-2442;** bus: all city-center buses), has four restaurants. Menus are posted at the Princes Street doors so you can decide which one appeals to you. The first-floor **Rose Street restaurant** offers breakfast, salads, and hot dishes like beef bourguignon and lemon-and-herb chicken breast. The **Princes Street restaurant** offers a roast of the day and several high teas as well as an afternoon cream tea. The **fifth-floor restaurant** serves breakfast, salads, and hot dishes, while the **Precinct** offers such items as lasagna, haddock and fries, and grilled salmon with lemon-and-dill butter. American Express, Diners Club, and Visa are accepted. It's open Monday, Wednesday, Friday, and Saturday 9am to 5:30pm; Tuesday 9:30am to 6pm; and Thursday 9am to 7:30pm.

PICNICKING

In the basement of **Marks & Spencer,** 64 Princes St. ((🕽 **0131/225-2301;** bus: all city-center buses), stand cooler after cooler of freshly made sandwiches, salads, cakes, cookies, fruits, vegetables, and more. Best of all, the prices are low. American Express, Diners Club, MasterCard, and Visa are accepted. It's open Monday to Wednesday and Friday 7:30am to 7pm, Saturday 8:30am to 6pm, and Sunday 11am to 5pm. Enjoy your picnic fixings in the **Princes Street Gardens,** across the street (see "Parks & Gardens," later in this chapter). If you feel like taking a walk before eating, head up to the top of **Salisbury Crags** or **Arthur's Seat.**

WORTH A SPLURGE

Dubh Prais SCOTTISH   Dubh Prais (Gaelic for "The Black Pot") conjures an image of an old-fashioned Scottish recipe bubbling away in a stewpot above a fireplace. Menu items are time-tested and not at all experimental, but they're flavorful nonetheless. Examples include smoked salmon; ragout of wild mushrooms and Ayrshire bacon served with garlic sauce; saddle of venison with juniper sauce; and salmon with grapefruit-flavored butter sauce.

123B High St., Royal Mile. (🕽 0131/557-5732. Reservations recommended. Lunch main courses £6.50–£9.50 ($12–$18); dinner main courses £13–£17 ($24–$31). AE, MC, V. Tues–Fri noon–2pm; Tues–Sat 6–10:30pm. Bus: 11.

Mussell Inn 🕽 SEAFOOD   This aptly named choice is the brainchild of two Scottish shellfish farmers, and is more functional than fashionable. But it's the freshness of the seafood that matters: You can enjoy mussels and scallops that have been raised without artificial additives at their own farms and then shipped fresh to the restaurant. The kilo pots of mussels, either steamed in their own juices or flavored with the likes of dry cider and horseradish or ginger, lemon grass, and paprika, come with fresh crusty bread. The catch of the day might include rainbow trout or bream served in black butter-caper sauce. King scallops are served four different ways, and are especially enticing when pan-fried with bacon and fresh vegetables with Gruyère cheese.

61–65 Rose St. (🕽 0131/225-5979. Meals £9–£16 ($17–$30). AE, DC, MC, V. Mon–Thurs 11am–3pm and 6–10pm; Fri–Sat noon–10pm; Sun 12:30–10pm. Bus: All Princes St. buses.

Stac Polly 🕽🕽 SCOTTISH   Named for a mountain on Scotland's West Coast, this stone-walled basement restaurant offers a range of classic dishes in unique preparations. The most intriguing starter is the phyllo parcels of haggis with plum sauce, which presents this traditional delicacy in a tangy and different way. The main courses include tender rack of lamb, pan-fried duck breast in red-wine-ginger jus, and saddle of venison topped with herbed black pudding and pickled walnuts. Another branch is at 8–10 Grindlay St. (© **0131/229-5405;** bus: 11, 15, 17, or 24), open Monday to Friday noon to 2pm and 6 to 10pm and Saturday and Sunday 6 to 10pm. It's more spacious than the Dublin Street branch, with a tartan decor that manages to stay just short of kitsch.

29–33 Dublin St. © 0131/556-2231. Main courses £11–£17 ($20–$31). AE, MC, V. Mon–Sat noon–1:45pm and 6–10pm; Sat–Sun 6–10pm. Bus: 19, 20, or 39.

4 Seeing the Sights

THE CASTLE & THE PALACE

Edinburgh Castle 🎔🎔🎔   Perched on a hill overlooking the city, this castle is the most famous building in Edinburgh. Whether it's catching the first rays of the sun, enshrouded in fog, or brightly illuminated at night, Edinburgh Castle is the city's most striking sight. The earliest documented use of this natural redoubt as a fortification dates from the late 11th century, but the oldest remaining building is **St. Margaret's Chapel,** built in the early 12th century. For more than 500 years, Edinburgh Castle was under frequent siege, but the constantly expanding fortifications were never successfully stormed. Among the batteries of cannons that protected the castle, you'll see **Mons Meg,** a 15th-century cannon weighing more than 5 tons. Also within these walls are the **Scottish crown jewels,** the oldest such regalia in the United Kingdom; and the **Stone of Destiny** captured by Edward I and taken to London, where it remained for close to 600 years before being returned to the Scots in 1998. A visit to the castle can take 1 to 4 hours. Don't forget to pick up from the booth opposite the main gate a free audio tour containing 4 hours of detailed info about the castle. (It's on CD so you can shorten the duration by clicking to points of particular interest.)

Castle Hill. © 0131/225-9846. Admission £8.50 ($16) adults, £6.25 ($12) seniors, £2 ($3.70) children. Apr–Oct daily 9:30am–6pm; Nov–Mar daily 9:30am–5pm. Closed Jan 1–2 and Dec 25–26. Bus: 28.

Palace of Holyroodhouse 🎔🎔   Built more than 300 years ago for the kings and queens of Scotland, this palace is still the official residence of the queen when she visits Edinburgh each summer. Holyroodhouse was the home of Mary Queen of Scots, Bonnie Prince Charlie, and Queen Victoria. Uniformed guides will delight in describing to you the grisly death of Queen Mary's personal secretary, David Rizzio, who in 1566 was murdered (56 stab wounds) by associates of her jealous husband, Lord Darnley. Elsewhere in the palace are massive tapestries, ornate plasterwork ceilings, a portrait gallery of the Stuart rulers, the Throne Room, and the State Apartments, still used for entertaining guests. In summer, you can explore the palace on your own (1–2 hr.), but in winter you must be

---

(*Value*)   **Getting the Best Deal on Sightseeing**

- Remember to ask about public transport discount cards.
- Note that the Old Town's narrow lanes (wynds) and closes are fascinating and well worth the effort to explore on foot.
- Combine visits to Edinburgh's free attractions listed below with the climb through Holyrood Park to Arthur's Seat, which at 247m (823 ft.) offers a panoramic view.

Fun Fact **The Face That Launched a Thousand Portraits**

In Holyroodhouse is a portrait gallery of the Stuart rulers in which every one of them has the same face—that of Charles II.

---

escorted by one of the palace guides (around 45 min.), which can mean a long wait if you've just missed a tour—phone ahead to double-check departure times.

Canongate. © 0131/556-1096. Admission £7.50 ($14) adults, £4 ($7.40) seniors, £3.30 ($6.10) children. Apr–Oct daily 9:30am–5:15pm; Nov–Mar daily 9:30am–3:45pm. Closed Nov 24 and 25. Bus: 35 or 64.

THE TOP MUSEUMS & MONUMENTS

Britannia *(Kids)*   It's rumored that some members of the royal family were aghast to hear that the former royal yacht was to be opened to the public, but it's now berthed in Edinburgh's up-and-coming Port of Leith. You'll be struck by just how cramped the admiral's sleeping quarters were—yet compared to the bunks and storage space afforded the 240 ordinary crewmen, they're positively palatial. As you make your way through the royal apartments, you'll note Her Majesty's fondness for chintz. (She and Prince Philip were much involved with the choice of furnishings.) An audioguide helps you explore the five decks, but the commentary is interesting without being revealing. It could gain from being a little more factual about the royal family's time on board or about Gandhi, Churchill, Reagan, Thatcher, Mandela, Yeltsin, Clinton, and others who sailed on the yacht as guests of Her Majesty. Allow an hour for your visit.

Ocean Terminal, Ocean Dr., Leith. © 0131/555-5566. www.royalyachtbritannia.co.uk. Admission £8.95 ($17) adults, £6 ($11) seniors, £4 ($7.40) children 5–15. AE, MC, V. Apr–Aug daily 10am–6pm; Sept–Oct daily 10am–5pm; Nov–Mar Wed–Sun 10am–5pm. Bus: Lothian Regional Transport dedicated bus service from Waverley Bridge £8.50 ($16) adults, £2.50 ($4.60) children round-trip, or bus 10 or 16 from Princes St. (Daysaver ticket covers the trip), then a 5-min. walk.

Dean Gallery *(Finds)*   Across from the Scottish National Gallery of Modern Art, Dean Gallery houses the Modern Art's extensive collections of Dada and Surrealism; all of our favorite artists are here, from Max Ernst to Joan Miró, and, of course, Salvador Dalí. The major exhibits consist in large part of the works of Sir Eduardo Paolozzi, a hip modern Scottish sculptor. Inspired by the mechanization of the 20th century and the culture of the machine, as were many artists before him, Paolozzi created his masterpiece, a mammoth composition of the figure of the robotic *Vulcan* dominating the entrance hall. It looks as if it could break free at any minute and destroy Edinburgh. The collection of prints, drawings, plaster maquettes, molds, and contents of his studio are housed in the gallery.

73 Belford Rd. © 0131/624-6200. Free admission except for special exhibitions (prices vary then). Mon–Sat 10am–5pm; Sun noon–5pm. Bus: 13.

Dynamic Earth *(Kids)*   Standing on the site where James Hutton (1726–97), the founder of modern geology, lived and worked, this futuristic-looking building is set against a backdrop of volcanic rocks and crags. The well-laid-out high-tech exhibits tell the story of the planet, from the big bang to the present and into the future. Simulations of the ice age, earthquakes, and volcanic eruptions, plus journeys beneath the oceans and through the polar regions and tropical rainforests, give you a holistic and at times dizzying view of the planet. The one drawback is that your passage is strictly one-way, so if you miss something or find your curiosity whetted, there's no going back for a second glance. It's also

Edinburgh

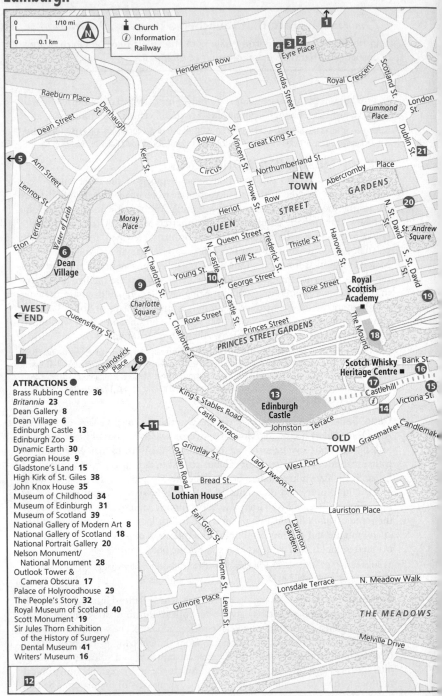

0   1/10 mi
0   0.1 km

N

✝ Church
ⓘ Information
— Railway

1

Henderson Row

4 **3** **2**
Eyre Place

Dundas Street

Royal Crescent

Scotland St.

London St.

Drummond Place

Raeburn Place

Dean Street

Denhaugh St.

Kerr St.

Royal Circus

St. Vincent St.

Great King St.

Northumberland St.

Dublin St.

21

Ann Street

Lennox St.

Water of Leith

Eton Terrace

Moray Place

NEW TOWN

STREET

Abercromby Place

GARDENS

N. St. David St.

20

St. Andrew Square

Heriot Row

Howe St.

QUEEN

6
Dean Village

N. Charlotte St.

N. Castle St.

Queen Street

Hill St.

Thistle St.

Frederick St.

Hanover St.

Rose Street

S. St. David St.

19

WEST END

Queensferry St.

9

Charlotte Square

Young St.

10

Castle St.

George Street

Rose Street

Royal Scottish Academy

7

Shandwick Place

8

S. Charlotte St.

Rose Street

Princes Street

PRINCES STREET GARDENS

The Mound

18

Scotch Whisky Heritage Centre

Bank St.

16

King's Stables Road

13
Edinburgh Castle

Castle Terrace

17
Castlehill

15

14

Victoria St.

ⓘ

Johnston Terrace

OLD TOWN

Grassmarket

Candlemaker

Grindlay St.

Lothian Road

Lady Lawson St.

West Port

Lothian House

Bread St.

Lauriston Place

Earl Grey St.

Home St.

Lauriston Gardens

N. Meadow Walk

Lonsdale Terrace

THE MEADOWS

Gilmore Place

Leven St.

Melville Drive

12

11

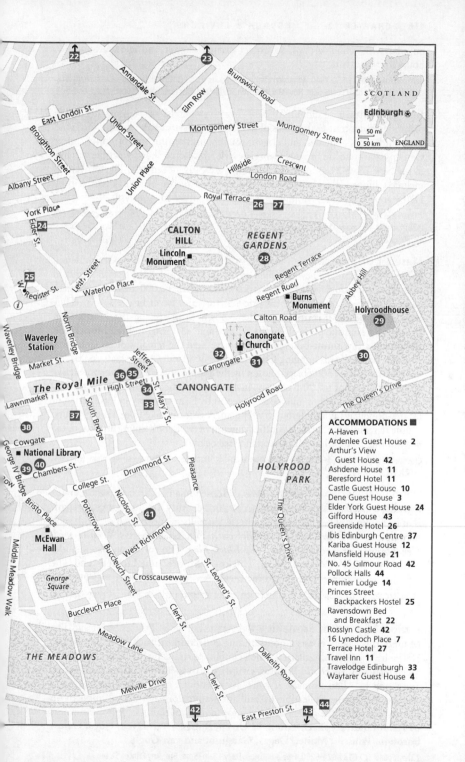

ACCOMMODATIONS ■

A-Haven **1**
Ardenlee Guest House **2**
Arthur's View
  Guest House **42**
Ashdene House **11**
Beresford Hotel **11**
Castle Guest House **10**
Dene Guest House **3**
Elder York Guest House **24**
Gifford House **43**
Greenside Hotel **26**
Ibis Edinburgh Centre **37**
Kariba Guest House **12**
Mansfield House **21**
No. 45 Gilmour Road **42**
Pollock Halls **44**
Premier Lodge **14**
Princes Street
  Backpackers Hostel **25**
Ravensdown Bed
  and Breakfast **22**
Rosslyn Castle **42**
16 Lynedoch Place **7**
Terrace Hotel **27**
Travel Inn **11**
Travelodge Edinburgh **33**
Wayfarer Guest House **4**

popular with school groups, so expect excited chatter and allow around 1½ hours for your visit.

Holyrood Rd. ℭ 0131/550-7800. Admission £8.95 ($17) adults, £5.50 ($10) children and seniors, £6.50 ($12) students. Apr–Oct daily 10am–5pm; Nov–Mar Wed–Sun 10am–5pm (last admission 3:50pm). Bus: 1 or 6.

Georgian House   Edinburgh's New Town is a model of 18th-century urban planning. In contrast to the chaos of the Old Town, symmetry reigns in the grand boulevards, parks, squares, and elegant roughhouses on this side of Princes Street Gardens. Furnished in original Georgian style, this house shows what life was like in the New Town 2 centuries ago, when this area was indeed new. The furnishings include Chippendale, Hepplewhite, and Sheraton pieces, as well as porcelain by Derby and Wedgwood. Around an hour should suffice for your visit.

7 Charlotte Sq. ℭ 0131/226-3318. Admission £5 ($9.25) adults, £3.75 ($6.95) students and children, £14 ($26) families. Mar daily 11am–3pm; Apr–Oct and Nov–Dec 24 daily 11am–3pm. Closed Dec 25–Feb. Bus: 19, 80, or 81.

Museum of Scotland ✸   The six galleries of this state-of-the-art museum, housed in a spectacular new building, are well laid out to tell the story of Scotland from the geological dawn of time to today. More than 12,000 artifacts are imaginatively displayed, many of them priceless treasures never before shown. They include **Lizzie the Lizard,** the earliest-known fossil reptile; the **Hunterston Brooch,** an exquisite piece of jewelry from about A.D. 700; and the **Monymusk Reliquary,** a tiny shrine believed once to have held the remains of St. Columba, who was credited with bringing Christianity to Scotland. On the glass-roofed top floor are more than 300 objects chosen by the people of Scotland as representative of life at the end of the 20th century, including a fragment of the *Declaration of Arbroath* stuffed inside a milk bottle, selected by Sean Connery in recollection of his pre-Bond days as an Edinburgh milkman. A visit can take from 1½ to 3 hours. If time remains, you can also visit the Museum of Scotland's sibling attraction, the neighboring Royal Museum of Scotland (see below).

Chambers St. ℭ 0131/225-7534. Free admission. Mon–Sat 10am–5pm (to 8pm Tues); Sun noon–5pm. Bus: 23, 27, 28, 37, or 45.

National Gallery of Modern Art ✸   Housed in an 1820s neoclassical building, this is Scotland's finest collection of 20th-century art. Its greatest strength is in its holdings of German expressionism, surrealism, and French art, with such masterpieces as **Otto Dix's** *Nude Girl on a Fur,* Giacometti's *Woman with Her Throat Cut,* and **Magritte's** *The Black Flag.* The collection also includes works by **Picasso, Matisse, Miró, Hockney, Moore,** and **Lichtenstein.** The cafe/dining room provides a welcome break. A visit should take 1 to 3 hours.

74 Belford Rd. ℭ 0131/556-8921. Free admission, except for special exhibits. Mon–Sat 10am–6pm; Sun 10am–6pm. Bus: 13.

National Gallery of Scotland ✸✸   At the corner of Princes Street and The Mound, this gallery boasts an outstanding collection for such a small museum. Start with the Scottish galleries, which contain portraits by **Sir Henry Raeburn,** social scenes by **Sir David Wilkies,** evocative seascapes by **William McTaggart,** and works by **Allan Ramsay.** If you're lucky enough to be here in January, you can see the **Turner** collection of brilliant watercolors—displayed annually in that month only. The gallery also has a top-notch collection of European works by **Rembrandt, Raphael, Titian, El Greco, Rubens, Van Dyck, Goya, Gainsborough, Poussin, Monet, Degas, Gauguin,** and **van Gogh.**

2 The Mound. ℭ 0131/624-6200. Free admission. Daily 10am–5pm. Bus: Any Princes St. bus.

National Portrait Gallery ⚡   In a majestic Gothic Revival building, this gallery is an excellent adjunct for those wishing to come to grips with the heroes and heroines, famous or otherwise, of Scottish history. You enter through the foyer, where detailed murals depict great moments from Scotland's past, and pass through galleries containing portraits of the likes of Mary Queen of Scots, Bonnie Prince Charlie, tartan-clad lairds and ladies, and famous 20th- and 21st-century Scots. Allow around 1½ hours for a visit.

1 Queen St. ⓒ 0131/624-6200. Free admission, except for special exhibits. Daily 10am–5pm. Bus: 18, 20, or 41.

Nelson Monument and the National Monument ⚡   A very steep pathway up Calton Hill leads to this telescope-shaped monument, built in 1816 to commemorate Adm. Horatio Lord Nelson, victor at the Battle of Trafalgar. No sooner have you recovered from the ascent than you find yourself confronted with an exhausting climb up 143 spiraling stairs to reach the viewing platform atop this 32m (106-ft.) circular tower. But suddenly the effort has all been worth it, as the vista is spectacular. Edinburgh radiates beneath you, and the beauty of this city becomes apparent, while the views of Arthur's Seat, Holyrood Palace, and the castle are inspiring and unrivaled. Allow 40 minutes for your visit. The "Greek" ruins beside the monument are all that was built of a monument to commemorate Scottish soldiers and sailors who died in the Napoleonic Wars. Lack of funds prevented its completion, and now it's one of the most eye-catching structures in the city, going by the name of Edinburgh's Disgrace.

Calton Hill. ⓒ 0131/556-2716. Admission Nelson Monument £2 ($3.70), joint ticket with Scott Monument £4 ($7.40), free admission to National Monument. Apr–Sept Mon 1–6pm, Tues–Sat 10am–6pm; Oct–Mar Mon–Sat 10am–3pm. Bus: 26, 85, or 86.

Royal Museum of Scotland   A Venetian Renaissance facade hides an unusually bright and airy Victorian interior at this museum of natural history, industry, and decorative arts. Stuffed animals, minerals, steam engines, Egyptian artifacts, and working models of the engines that made the Industrial Revolution possible are on display. Although it's interesting, this is not a "must do" attraction if your time in Edinburgh is limited (you'll spend about 1 hr.), unless there happens to be a special exhibit that appeals. The soaring beauty of the main hall is itself reason enough to visit.

Chambers St. ⓒ 0131/225-7534. Free admission. Mon and Wed–Sat 10am–5pm; Tues 10am–8pm; Sun noon–5pm. Bus: 23, 27, 28, 37, or 45.

Scott Monument   Looking more like a church spire than a monument to a writer, this Gothic structure dominates East Princes Street Gardens. In the center of the spire is a large seated statue of Sir Walter Scott and his dog, Maida. The monument rises to a height of more than 60m (200 ft.), and the climb up 287 steps to reach the observation area at the top is not for the faint-hearted. The view is pleasant, although in all honesty, nowhere near as spectacular as that from the Nelson Monument. You should allow 30 minutes for the ascent and descent.

⟨Tips⟩ A Note on Museum Hours

Be aware that many museums usually closed on Sunday are open on Sunday during the Edinburgh Festival, and some museums open only in summer are open on public holidays, too.

Special & Free Events

You can get details of specific events at many of the festivals below from the official website **www.go-edinburgh.co.uk**.

Hogmany, Box Office and Information, c/o The Hub Festival Centre, Castlehill EH1 1NE (© **0131/473-2001**), is New Year's Eve, celebrated with the ritual kissing of everyone in sight, followed by the time-honored practice of first footing with a lump of coal, a bun, and a drop of the hard stuff. In 1993, the Edinburgh City Council began a 3-day festival that features street theater; lively processions, illuminated by firebrands; and the burning of a long boat. Access to the city center after 8pm on New Year's Eve is by ticket only. If you plan to visit then, contact the box office well before you travel.

January 25 is **Burns' Night,** *the* night when Scots the world over gather to consume the traditional supper of haggis, *neeps* (turnips), and *tatties* (potatoes), accompanied by a wee dram of whisky, while listening to recitals from the works of Scotland's bard, Robert "Rabbie" Burns, whose birthday is being celebrated. You'll find Burns suppers are held all over town.

For 3 weeks in late August and early September, Edinburgh goes on a cultural binge. Dates are subject to change. The city's most famous event, the **Edinburgh International Festival** ⚡, Edinburgh Festival Centre, Castlehill, Edinburgh EH1 1NE (© **0131/473-2000**), encompasses music, dance, opera, performance art, and theater. Tickets are £6 to £40 ($11–$74) per show, but money-saving series tickets are available. Contact the box office by mail, phone, or fax beginning in April. The **Edinburgh Festival Fringe,** 180 High St., Edinburgh EH1 1QS (© **0131/ 226-5257**; www.edfringe.com), is world famous. Among the 13,000-plus performances are found more offbeat and experimental theatrical performances along with musicals, comedy, kids' shows, cabaret, contemporary music, and more. Tickets are £3 to £15 ($5.55–$28), with close to 150 free performances. The **Edinburgh Military Tattoo,** 32 Market St., Edinburgh EH1 1QB (© **0131/225-1188**; fax 0131/225-8627; www. edintattoo.co.uk), is a military musical extravaganza that takes place over 3 weeks in August in front of the castle just before dusk. Tickets cost £9 to £29 ($17–$53).

The **Edinburgh International Jazz and Blues Festival,** 29 St. Stephen's St., Edinburgh EH3 8DD (© **0131/225-2202**; fax 0131/225-3321), features international stars and unknowns at various locales. Tickets are £5 to £25 ($9.25–$46). The **Edinburgh International Film Festival,** 88 Lothian Rd., Edinburgh EH3 9BZ (© **0131/228-4051**), screens world premieres of films along with an eclectic program ($8.25–$13). Dubbed the "Cannes for the literary glitterati," the **Edinburgh Book Festival,** 137 Dundee St., Edinburgh EH11 1BG (© **0131/228-5444**; fax 0131/228-4333), is held in a tented village in Charlotte Square Gardens every August. Thousands of books are displayed, and more than 250 authors participate in a variety of events. Tickets to most events are under £5 ($9.25), and many of the events are free.

E. Princes St. Gardens. ☎ 0131/529-4068. Admission £2.50 ($4.60); joint ticket with Nelson Monument £4 ($7.40). Apr–Sept Mon–Sat 9am–6pm, Sun noon–6pm; Oct–Mar Mon–Sat 9am–3pm, Sun noon–3pm. Bus: 2, 3, 4, 4A, 10, 11, 15, 15A, 16, 43, 44, 80, or 80A.

MORE ATTRACTIONS

Between Edinburgh Castle and the Palace of Holyroodhouse, along the **Royal Mile,** are dozens of interesting shops, old pubs, fascinating little museums, and Edinburgh's oldest cathedral. You'll find many of the sights here down the narrow **closes** leading off the Royal Mile. Regardless of whether they have a specific attraction to offer, all the closes are worth exploring simply for their medieval atmosphere.

Brass Rubbing Centre   This center provides instruction and replicas of medieval church brasses and Neolithic Scottish stone carvings in all sizes for you to make your own rubbings. There are also ready-made rubbings for sale, varying in price. The center is housed in an old church and has a number of rubbings and old brasses on display.

Chalmer's Close, High St. ☎ 0131/556-4364. Free admission; £1.80–£17 ($3.35–$31) for brass rubbing, depending on brass size. Mon–Sat 10am–5pm. Closed Oct–Mar. Bus: 29 or 35.

Edinburgh Zoo *(Kids)*   The zoo covers 32 hectares (80 acres) of parkland and houses nearly 1,500 animals. The main attraction is the **penguin parade,** which takes place daily at 2pm April to September. With more than 100 penguins, this is the world's largest self-supporting captive colony, and they're an unforgettable sight when they go for their afternoon stroll. The latest attraction is the 587m (1,925-ft.) **Darwin Maze,** shaped like a giant turtle and containing 1,600 yew trees. Information boards tell the story of evolution along the way.

134 Corstorphine Rd. ☎ 0131/334-9171. Admission £8 ($15) adults, £5.50 ($10) seniors, £5 ($9.25) children 3–14, free for children under 3. Apr–Sept daily 9am–6pm; Mar and Oct daily 9am–5pm; Nov–Feb daily 9am–4:30pm. Bus: 2, 26, 31, 36, 69, 85, or 86.

Gladstone's Land   This 17th-century merchant's house is furnished and kept in its original style. It's worth a visit on your journey along the Royal Mile, if only to get the impression of the confined living conditions, even for the reasonably well off, before the construction of the New Town. Sadly, this cramped style is the property's biggest drawback, because it doesn't really allow you room to fully appreciate the displays. Allow 30 minutes for your visit.

Finds Seeking Hyde

Near Gladstone's Land is **Brodie's Close,** a stone-floored alleyway. You can wander into the alley for a view of old stone houses that'll make you think you've stepped onto a BBC period set. It was named for the notorious Deacon Brodie—respectable counselor by day, thief by night—who was the inspiration for Robert Louis Stevenson's *The Strange Case of Dr. Jekyll and Mr. Hyde* (though Stevenson set his story instead in foggy London). Across the street is the most famous pub along the Royal Mile: **Deacon Brodie's Tavern,** 435 Lawnmarket (see "Edinburgh After Dark," later in this chapter).

Brodie was hanged in 1788; ironically, it was Brodie himself who had improved the mechanism used for the hangman's scaffolding—for use on others, of course.

477B Lawnmarket. (© 0131/226-5856. Admission £3.50 ($6.50) adults, £2.20 ($4.05) children. Apr–Oct Mon–Sat 10am–5pm, Sun 2–5pm. Bus: 34 or 35.

High Kirk of St. Giles (St. Giles's Cathedral)   This is the spiritual heart of the Church of Scotland. A church has existed on this site since the 9th century, and parts of this one date from 1120. Since then, many alterations have changed the building immensely. Scottish religious reformer John Knox, who established the Protestant religion in Scotland, became the minister here in 1560. The unusual main spire is in the form of a thistle, one of the symbols of Scotland. The **Thistle Chapel of the Ancient and Noble Order of the Thistle** was designed by Sir Robert Lorimer in 1910 and features beautifully crafted stone, wood, and glass. A visit can take 30 to 45 minutes.

High St. (© 0131/225-9442. Free admission. May–Sept Mon–Fri 9am–7pm, Sat 9am–5pm, Sun 1–5pm; Oct–Apr Mon–Sat 9am–5pm, Sun 1–5pm. Bus: 34, 35, 40, or 42.

John Knox House   Although any link between John Knox, the leader of Scotland's Protestant Reformation, and this atmospheric old property, built in 1490, is tenuous, it was the tradition that he lived here from 1561 until his death in 1572 that saved the house from demolition in the mid–19th century. It has been a museum since 1853, with detailed displays telling the story of the Scottish Reformation. There is an audio reenactment of Knox arguing his point with the staunchly Catholic Mary Queen of Scots. Incidentally, this was the home of Royalist social climber James Mossman (the man who made the Scottish Crown displayed at the castle). The idea of contrasting the two men's ideals, including another taped (though purely fictitious) reenactment of a heated exchange between them, works well. The wooden gallery surrounding the upper floors is the last of its kind in the city. Allow 40 minutes.

43–45 High St. (© 0131/556-9579. Admission £2.25 ($4.15) adults, £1.75 ($3.25) seniors, 75p ($1.40) children. MC, V. July Mon–Sat 10am–4:30pm, Sun noon–4pm; Aug Mon–Sat 10:30am–6:30pm, Sun noon–4pm; Sept–June Mon–Sat 10am–4:30pm. Bus: 35.

Museum of Childhood _Kids_   With its displays of antique teddy bears, amazingly detailed dollhouses, riding and pulling toys, board games, and porcelain dolls, this museum is more for adults than for children. Its displays are packed with toys from every conceivable era, and any generation of child will find something to instill nostalgic twinges or even remind them of that anticipated Christmas or birthday present that they never got. There are also some video presentations and an activity area that should keep the kids amused while their parents wipe away the tears of reminiscence. Allow an hour for your visit.

42 High St. (© 0131/529-4142. Free admission. Mon–Sat 10am–5pm. Bus: 35.

Museum of Edinburgh   This tiny museum displays myriad artifacts that tell the story of Edinburgh from the Romans to the 19th century. The method of display, with items crammed together into glass-fronted cases, gives it an old-fashioned feel, but with the help of the guidebook and the attentive guides, you can enjoy a fascinating 40 or so minutes while increasing your understanding of how the city came about. One or two pleasant surprises await you, including the drinking bowl and collar of Greyfriars Bobby.

142 Canongate. (© 0131/529-4143. Free admission. Mon–Sat 10am–5pm (Sun 2–5pm during the festival). Bus: 35.

Outlook Tower and Camera Obscura   A long climb up several flights of stairs awaits those who want to enjoy the view from the Outlook Tower. However, the exhibitions of photography and holography through which you pass on each floor make for an enjoyable ascent. The vista from the top is not as dramatic as that from the top of the Nelson Monument, but it certainly complements it and allows you to gaze down upon Edinburgh from an equally impressive viewpoint. But it's the Camera Obscura that draws visitors to this dizzying height. Installed in 1853 by Edinburgh optician Maria Theresa Short, the device uses a giant lens to project panoramic images onto a white viewing table. The demonstration is given by a guide who takes you on a fascinating journey around the Edinburgh skyline accompanied by a humorous commentary. Allow 45 minutes to an hour for your visit. Note that the Camera Obscura is demonstrated only at specific times, so be sure to ask about the next performance as you purchase your ticket.

Castlehill. (C) 0131/226-3709. Admission £5.95 ($11) adults, £4.75 ($8.80) students, £4.75 ($8.80) seniors, £3.80 ($7) children up to 15. Apr–June and Sept–Oct daily 9:30am–6pm; July–Aug daily 9:30am–7:30pm; Nov Mar daily 10am–5pm. Bus: 23 or 28.

The People's Story   Built in 1591, the Canongate Tolbooth was once the courthouse, prison, and center of municipal affairs for the burgh of Canongate. Now it contains this museum that tells the story of the common folk of Edinburgh from the 18th century to the present. A careful guiding hand has steered the exhibits away from cliché, and thus the sights, sounds, and even smells that help illustrate the story are presented in a thought-provoking way. Allow 30 minutes.

163 Canongate. (C) 0131/529-4057. Free admission. Mon–Sat 10am–5pm (Sun 2–5pm during the festival). Bus: 35.

Sir Jules Thorn Exhibition of the History of Surgery/Dental Museum
Edinburgh's rich medical history and associations make the **Exhibition of the History of Surgery** well worth an hour of your time. On the upper floors of a 19th-century town house in a tucked-away square, you can chart the development of surgery from 1505 to the present. The exhibits, well presented though sometimes macabre, include such gems as a pocketbook made from the skin of the notorious body snatcher William Burke. The **Dental Museum,** its gleaming glass cases full of every conceivable dentistry tool, is certainly not for the squeamish or those experiencing dental problems.

9 Hill Sq. (C) 0131/527-1649. Free admission. Mon–Fri noon–4pm. Bus: 7 or most city-center buses.

Writers' Museum 🐾   Less than 30m (100 ft.) from the George IV Bridge, this museum attracts fans of Scottish literature commemorating as it does Robert Burns, Sir Walter Scott, and Robert Louis Stevenson. Each author has a floor exclusively dedicated to him on which portraits, photographs, personal possessions, and quotes help you get a reasonable understanding of their lives, times, and driving forces. The house was built in 1622 for a prominent merchant and takes its name from Elizabeth, dowager-countess of Stair, who owned it in the early 18th century. From both The Mound and Lawnmarket approaches to the museum, you can follow a series of quotations from various Scottish writers carved into the paving stones and collectively known as Makar's Court. A visit should take 45 minutes to an hour, but you can spend 2 hours if you stop to ponder all the information on display.

Lady Stair's Close, Lawnmarket. (C) 0131/529-4901. Free admission. Mon–Sat 10am–5pm. Bus: 28 or 35.

DEAN VILLAGE 🐾

Beautiful **Dean Village,** in a valley about 30m (100 ft.) below the level of the rest of Edinburgh, is one of the city's most photographed sights. It's a few minutes from the West End, at the end of Bells Brae off Queensferry Street, on the Water of Leith. The settlement dates from the 12th century, and Dean Village's fame grew as a grain-milling center.

You can enjoy a celebrated view by looking downstream under the high arches of Dean Bridge (1830–31), designed by Thomas Telford. The village's old buildings have been restored and converted into apartments and houses. You don't come here for any one particular sight but to enjoy the village as a whole, the way you would New York City's Greenwich Village. You can also walk for miles along the Water of Leith, one of the most tranquil walks in the greater Edinburgh area.

PARKS & GARDENS

Edinburgh is filled with parks and gardens. The largest is **Holyrood Park** *ℜℜ*, which begins behind the Palace of Holyroodhouse (bus: 1 or 6). With rocky crags, a loch, sweeping meadows, and chapel ruins, it's a wee bit of the Scottish countryside in the city. **Arthur's Seat,** at 247m (823 ft.), and the **Salisbury Crags** offer panoramic views over Edinburgh to the Firth of Forth. This is a great place for a picnic.

Princes Street Gardens separate the Old Town from the New Town (bus: any Princes St. bus). Old trees and brilliant green lawns fill the valley between the two city sections. Along the paved footpaths of the gardens are dozens of wooden benches given by Edinburghers in memory of loved ones; they're excellent places to enjoy a picnic lunch or to relax while savoring the views. The gardens are open daily dawn to dusk.

Edinburgh's 28-hectare (70-acre) **Royal Botanic Garden** *ℜ*, Inverleith Row (© 0131/552-7171; bus: 8, 19, 23, 27, or 37), is known for its extensive collection of rhododendrons that flower profusely every spring. With a large arboretum, research facilities, and wild areas providing a sharp contrast to the neatly manicured gardens, this is one of Europe's finest botanical gardens. It's also Britain's second oldest botanical garden, established as a physic garden in 1670 by two physicians. Admission is free. The botanic garden is open daily: April to September 10am to 7pm, October and March 10am to 6pm, and November to February 10am to 4pm.

ORGANIZED TOURS

WALKING TOURS   Free tours are offered by the **Edinburgh Festival Voluntary Guides Association** during the festival. Contact the **Edinburgh Festival Fringe,** 180 High St., EH1 (© 0131/226-5257), for details. **Mercat Tours,** Mercat House, Niddry Street South, EH1 (© 0131/557-6464; www.mercattours. com), has the monopoly on leading tours into the underground Mary Kings Close, a fascinating and spooky nighttime journey. **McEwans Literary Pub Tour,** Suite 2, 97b West Bow, EH1 (© 0131/226-6665; www.scot-lit-tour.co.uk), is a celebration of Edinburgh writers and pubs. **Robins Ghost and History Tour,** 12 Niddry St. S., EH1 (© 0131/557-9933), offers just what the name implies, with the emphasis on the history. **The Witchery Tour,** 84 W. Bow (Victoria St.), EH1 (© 0131/225-6745; www.witcherytours.com), led by highwayman Adam Lyal (deceased), leaves from in front of the Witchery Restaurant and is very much a piece of (at times overacted) street theater. Costs run £4 to £7 ($7.40–$13) and several require reservations, so contact the individual operators for departure details.

BUS TOURS   For a quick introduction to the principal attractions in and around Edinburgh, consider the tours offered April to late October by **Lothian**

Region Transport, 55 Annandale St. (© 0131/555-6363). A curtailed winter program is also offered. You can see most of the major sights by double-decker motor coach, with guided commentary, for £8.50 ($16) adults, £7.50 ($14) seniors/students, and £2.50 ($4.60) children. This ticket is valid all day on any LRT Edinburgh Classic Tour bus, allowing you to get on and off at any of the 15 stops. Buses start from the Waverley Bridge near the Scott Monument daily at 9:30am, departing every 10 minutes in summer and about every 20 minutes in winter; if you remain on the bus without getting off, the trip lasts about 2 hours.

5 Shopping

Princes Street in the New Town is Edinburgh's main shopping area, with several large department stores and dozens of shops selling designer clothes and other equally expensive items. Try the Mill Shop store here for bargains in woolens and knitwear. **George Street,** running parallel to Princes Street, has such luxury stores as Austin Reed. **Victoria Street** and **Grassmarket** in the Old Town both have some unusual shops.

Looking for a knitted memento? Moira-Anne Leask, owner of the **Shetland Connection,** 491 Lawnmarket (© 0131/225-3525; bus: 28), promotes the skills of the Shetland knitter, and her shop is packed with sweaters, hats, and gloves in colorful Fair Isle designs. She also offers hand-knitted mohair, Aran, and Icelandic sweaters. Items range from fine-ply cobweb shawls to chunky ski sweaters handcrafted by skilled knitters in top-quality wool.

If you've ever suspected that you might be Scottish, **Tartan Gift Shops,** 54 High St. (© 0131/558-3187; bus: 35), has a chart indicating the place of origin, in Scotland, of your family name. You'll then be faced with a bewildering array of hunt-and-dress tartans. The high-quality wool is sold by the yard as well as in the form of kilts for both men and women.

Clan Tartan Centre, 70–74 Bangor Rd., Leith (© 0131/553-5161; bus: 7 or 10), is one of the leading tartan specialists in Edinburgh, regardless of which clan you claim as your own. If you want help in identifying a particular tartan, the staff at this shop will assist you. At the same location is the **James Pringle Woollen Mill** (© 0131/553-5161), which produces a large variety of top-quality wool items, including a range of Scottish knitwear—cashmere sweaters, tartan and tweed ties, travel rugs, tweed hats, and tam-o'-shanters. In addition, the mill has the only Clan Tartan Centre in Scotland, where more than 2,500 sets and trade designs are accessible through their research facilities.

The two best department stores in Edinburgh are **Debenham's,** 109–112 Princes St. (© 0131/225-1320; bus: 3 or 31); and **Jenners,** 48 Princes St. (© 0131/225-2442; bus: 3, 26, 31, or 44). Both stock Scottish and international merchandise.

In shops all over Edinburgh you'll see signs saying TAX-FREE SHOPPING. These signs refer to the process by which you as a visitor can recover the **value-added tax (VAT)** that amounts to about 11% of everything you buy. Shops usually require a minimum purchase of £30 to £50 ($56–$93). Once you've filled out the forms, present them to Customs before you leave the country, along with the purchases themselves (pack them in your carry-on luggage). After the forms have been stamped by Customs, mail them back to the store with the envelope provided by the store. Within a few weeks your refund will be mailed to your home address as a check in U.S. dollars or will be credited to your credit card. See chapter 1, "Enjoying Europe on a Budget," for more information.

6 Edinburgh After Dark

Whether your interest is theater, dance, or music (folk, classical, or rock), Edinburgh will entertain you for next to nothing. On any given night you might see a play, stop by a pub for a bit of free traditional music, and then head to a dance club (arrive before 11pm to get in for £3/$5.55 or less)—a jam-packed night out for only £8.50 ($16), not including drinks.

Pick up a free copy of *What's On Scotland* at the Tourist Information Centre at Waverley Market. This pamphlet comes out every 3 months and lists exhibits, theater, music, films, and other information. The best source of listings details is the biweekly *The List,* available at newsstands for £1.80 ($3.30).

THE PERFORMING ARTS

You'll find most of the city's performance venues clustered on or near **Lothian Road** at the west end of Princes Street. Edinburgh, too, has a West End theater district.

THEATER   This is a fine theater town, with good performances at low prices. The culmination of the theater year is the annual summer **Edinburgh International Festival.** Tickets start as low as £6 ($11) at many theaters, and even the most expensive theaters have tickets for under £8 ($15). And it's sometimes possible to catch a free preview. Check *The List* to find the best deals while you're in town.

Festival Theatre, 13–29 Nicolson St. (℃ **0131/662-1112;** bus: most city-center buses), is the glass-fronted showcase for opera, dance, drama, and other entertainment. Guided tours are given, but you need to reserve ahead. Tickets are £5.50 to £45 ($10–$83)—the higher price for opera. The box office is open Monday to Saturday 11am to 6pm (to 8pm on performance nights). The Victorian **King's Theatre,** 2 Leven St. (℃ **0131/529-6000;** bus: most city-center buses), has about 1,300 seats and features a wide variety of performances by repertory companies. Ballet, opera, light opera, pantomime, musicals, and drama all showcase here. Tickets are £5.50 to £23 ($10–$43), and the box office is open Monday to Saturday 10am to 8pm.

Edinburgh's main playhouse, the **Royal Lyceum Theatre,** Grindlay Street off Lothian Road (℃ **0131/248-4848;** bus: most city-center buses), seats 658 and features contemporary and classical dramas and comedies performed by the resident company. Concessionary tickets at a £2 ($3.70) discount are available on a very limited basis. Otherwise, expect to pay £7 to £20 ($13–$37), with student seats £3.10 ($5.75) on Tuesday. The box office is open Monday to Saturday 10am to 7pm (to 6pm on nonperformance nights).

You can catch new experimental productions by English and Scottish playwrights, plus dance and comedy, at the contemporary **Traverse Theatre,** Cambridge Street, off Lothian Road (℃ **0131/228-1404;** bus: most city-center buses). It's one of Britain's best theaters, and its bar and cafe are popular. Tickets cost £4 to £10 ($7.40–$19), and the box office is open Monday 10am to 6pm, Tuesday to Saturday 10am to 8pm, and Sunday 4 to 8pm.

CLASSICAL MUSIC   There are two major halls: **Usher Hall,** on Lothian Road (℃ **0131/228-8616;** bus: most city-center buses), where the Royal Scottish Orchestra performs; and **Queen's Hall,** Clerk Street (℃ **0131/668-2019;** bus: same as above), an 850-seat concert hall that's the home of the Scottish Chamber Orchestra and also features jazz, folk, rock, and dance. Check *What's On Scotland* or *The List* for schedules and programs. Tickets at either hall are £4.50 to £42 ($8.30–$78).

LIVE-MUSIC CLUBS

Fans of folk, rock, and jazz can have a field day in Edinburgh, where most clubs offer free live music every night. At most you might have to pay £3 to £7 ($5.55–$13) on Friday or Saturday for the top local bands. Music usually starts around 11pm. For the greatest concentration of clubs and pubs featuring live music at least 1 night a week, head for **Victoria Street** and **Grassmarket** in the Old Town.

For fine traditional music, try **Bar Alba**, 11–13 Grassmarket (© **0131/229-2665;** bus: most city-center buses), a block west of the end of Victoria Street. On Monday, local musicians get together to play old favorites in a corner of the pub's front room. Admission is free, and it's open Monday to Thursday 9am to midnight, Friday and Sunday 8am to 1am. Located in an old church that has been converted into a commercial building, **Finnegans Wake,** 9A Victoria St. (© **0131/226-3816;** bus: most city-center buses), is one of Edinburgh's most popular spots for Scottish and Irish traditional folk music. Admission is free, and it's open Monday to Thursday 5pm to 1am and Friday to Sunday 1pm to 1am.

Among live-music rock/pop venues is **The Venue,** Calton Road (© **0131/557-3073;** bus: most city-center buses).

PUBS & BARS

There's a pub on nearly every block, and many host live music at least 1 night a week. In all of them, a pint of ale or a shot of Scotch whisky costs £1.75 to £2.25 ($3.25–$4.15). Most pubs also serve lunch noon to 2:30pm. If you want to experience the scene's diversity, stroll along **Rose Street** (parallel to Princes St.), lined with pubs from Milne's at the east end to Scott's at the West.

The ornate Victorian **Guildford Arms,** 1 W. Register St. (© **0131/556-4312;** bus: most city-center buses), is popular with a more upscale older crowd who appreciates the glorious plasterwork ceiling and etched-glass windows. The bar features 12 real ales and is open Monday to Wednesday 11am to 11pm, Thursday to Saturday 11am to midnight, and Sunday 12:30 to 11pm. On the same tiny block is the ever-popular casual **Café Royal,** 17 Register St. (© **0131/556-1884;** bus: most city-center buses), known for its circular bar, stained-glass windows, and unusual painted tiles of famous inventors. Upstairs in the Café Royal Bistro Bar is music spun by a deejay every Friday and other occasional entertainment. It's open Monday to Wednesday 10am to 11pm, Thursday to Saturday 10am to midnight, and Sunday 10am to 11pm.

Whistle Binkies, 4–6 South St. (© **0131/557-5114;** bus: most city-center buses), is a basement dive bar offering live music every night, open 5pm to 3am. A lower level of alcoves offers some privacy away from the main bar area. Elegant it's not, but atmospheric and buzzing it certainly is. The small, dark **Malt Shovel,** 11–15 Cockburn St. (© **0131/225-6843;** bus: most city-center buses), is an Edinburgh legend that has spawned at least two companion pubs in the area. Besides the free live jazz and traditional music on Tuesday, it has one of the best selections of single-malt whiskies in town. It's open Monday to Thursday 11am to midnight, Friday and Saturday 11am to 1am, and Sunday 12:30pm to midnight.

Other notable pubs are the historic **Deacon Brodie's Tavern,** 435 Lawnmarket (© **0131/225-6531;** see "Seeing the Sights," earlier in this chapter); and **Greyfriars Bobby,** 34 Candlemaker Row (© **0131/225-8328**), named after the famous dog, a Skye terrier who kept a 14-year vigil at his master's grave. And for piano entertainment, head for the sophisticated yet comfortable **Fingers Piano Bar,** 61a Frederick St. (© **0131/225-3026**). All three are open daily 11am to 12:30am, and you can take most city-center buses to get there.

GAY & LESBIAN BARS

The heart of the gay community is centered on **Broughton Street** around the Playhouse Theatre. At 36 Broughton St., the **Blue Moon Cafe** (© **0131/556-2788;** bus: 10, 16, or 17) is primarily a dining spot where you can linger over a coffee or enjoy a burger, focaccia sandwich, or salad along with a mixed crowd. Nachos, chili, and other snacks are also offered. It's open Monday to Friday 11am to midnight and Saturday and Sunday 9am to midnight.

Up the street is **C. C. Bloom's,** 23–24 Greenside Place (© **0131/556-9331**), a popular bar with a dance floor downstairs and karaoke 2 nights a week. It's open daily 7pm to 3am. A few doors down is **Planet Out,** 6 Baxter's Place (© **0131/524-0061**), a gay pub where there's no dancing, just quiet conversation depending on the hour. (The later it is, the louder it gets.) It's open Monday to Saturday 4pm to 1am, and Sunday 2pm to 1am. Most gay bars host a weekly lesbian night. The basement **Stand Comedy Club,** 5 York Place (© **0131/558-7272**), stages the monthly **OOT,** a popular gay/lesbian comedy night.

DANCE CLUBS

Dance clubs generally open around 10pm and stay open until 3 or 4am. Beer or hard liquor average £2 ($3.70), and many clubs offer special drink prices on certain nights or early in the evening.

Club Mercado, 36–39 Market St. (© **0131/226-4224;** bus: most city-center buses), is popular with under-25s and features mainstream top-40 dance music. Admission is free Friday to 10:30pm; otherwise it's £3 to £10 ($5.55–$19). It's open Friday to Sunday until 3:30am. **Revolution,** 31 Lothian Rd. (© **0131/229-7670;** bus: most city-center buses), is Edinburgh's largest disco and one of the most popular. Admission is £3 to £6 ($5.55–$11), and it's open Monday and Wednesday to Saturday 10:30pm to 3am.

7 Side Trips: Burghs, Villages & More

Lothian Region Transport, 27 Hanover St. (© **0131/220-2221**), offers more than 20 excursions from Edinburgh. Among the best is the tour to **Loch Ness** and the **Grampian Mountains,** available year-round; it costs £30 ($56) for adults, £23 ($43) children. Along the way toward the home of the fabled Nessie, the Loch Ness monster, the coach travels through beautiful mountains, forests, fields, and farmland.

For a less expensive all-day excursion, try the trip to legendary **Loch Lomond.** In summer, the tour is combined with a visit to the Argyllshire or the Trossachs mountains. In winter, the tour travels through the Argyllshire Mountains. The cost is £16 ($30) adults and £9 ($17) children.

You can also book your Loch Lomond tour at the **Ticket Centre** on Waverley Bridge.

For a completely different and thoroughly enjoyable day out, contact **Walkabout Scotland,** 2 Rossie Place, Edinburgh EH7 5SG (© **0131/661-7168;** www.walkaboutscotland.com), about its day hikes in the mountainous countryside of the Scottish Highlands. The £40 ($74) cost includes a packed lunch, and they can even arrange the proper walking equipment for you.

LINLITHGOW: BIRTHPLACE OF MARY QUEEN OF SCOTS

Mary Queen of Scots was born in the royal burgh (*bur*-ruh) of **Linlithgow,** a county town in West Lothian, 29km (18 miles) west of Edinburgh. Direct **trains** (© **08457/484-950**) depart every 15 minutes, and the journey takes about 20 minutes; avoid traveling on the hour because the journey takes longer and involves a change. The round-trip fare is £5 ($9.25) adults and £2.50 ($4.60) children. **Buses** depart Edinburgh from Waterloo Place (© **0870/8727271**) every 20 minutes and take around an hour; the round-trip fare is £4.15 ($7.70) adults and £2.10 ($3.90) children. If you have a **car,** take A902 to Corstorphine and then A8 to M9, exiting at junction 3 to Linlithgow.

You can still explore the roofless **Linlithgow Palace** ★★ (© **01506/ 842-896**), birthplace of Mary Queen of Scots in 1542, even if it's but a shell of its former self. The queen's suite was in the north quarter but was rebuilt for the homecoming of James VI of Scotland (James I of England) in 1620. The palace burned to the ground in 1746. The Great Hall is on the first floor, and a small display shows some of the more interesting architectural relics. The ruined palace is half a mile from Linlithgow Station (you can walk or take a taxi). Admission is £3 ($5.55) adults, £2.30 ($4.25) seniors, and £1 ($1.85) children. April to September, it's open Monday to Saturday 9:30am to 6:30pm and Sunday 2 to 6pm; October to March, hours are Monday to Saturday 9:30am to 4:30pm and Sunday 2 to 4pm. Allow an hour and a half for your visit.

Just south of the palace stands the medieval *kirk* (church), **St. Michael's Parish Church** (© **01506/842-188**), open daily 9am to 1pm. It has been where many a Scottish monarch has worshiped since its 1242 consecration. Despite being ravaged by the disciples of John Knox and transformed into a stable by Cromwell, it's one of Scotland's best examples of a parish church.

DIRLETON ★★: PRETTIEST VILLAGE IN SCOTLAND

The little town of **Dirleton,** a preservation village 31km (19 miles) east of Edinburgh and 8km (5 miles) west of North Berwick, vies for the title of prettiest village in Scotland. The town plan, drafted in the early 16th century, is essentially unchanged today. It has two greens shaped like triangles, with a pub opposite **Dirleton Castle,** placed at right angles to a group of cottages.

Buses (© **08705/505-950**) leave Edinburgh's St. Andrew's Square station at 10 past and 20 to the hour and take 1 hour. The last bus leaves at 5:10pm. The one-way fare is £2.70 ($5) adults and £1.35 ($2.50) children. If you have a **car,** take A198 from Edinburgh straight to Dirleton.

A rose-tinted 13th-century castle with surrounding gardens, once the seat of the wealthy Anglo-Norman de Vaux family, **Dirleton Castle** (© **01620/850-330**) looks like a fairy-tale fortification, with towers, arched entries, and oak ramp. You can see ruins of the Great Hall and kitchen, as well as what's left of the lord's chamber where the de Vaux family lived. The 16th-century main gate has a hole through which boiling tar or water could be poured to discourage unwanted visitors. The castle's country garden and Bowling Green are still in use. Admission is £3 ($5.55) adults, £2.30 ($4.25) seniors, and £1 ($1.85) children. April to September, it's open daily 9:30am to 6pm; October to March, hours are Monday to Saturday 9:30am to 4pm and Sunday 2 to 4pm. Allow an hour for your exploration of the castle and gardens.

ROSSLYN CHAPEL ★★

The village of **Roslin,** 9.7km (6 miles) south of Edinburgh, is situated in the steeply wooded Esk Valley. Famed for its exquisite carvings, **Rosslyn Chapel,** Roslin, Midlothian (© **0131/440-2159;** www.rosslynchapel.org.uk), stands on the edge of a wooded glen. The chapel itself dates from 1446 and is so rich in ornamental carvings you can spend a good hour appreciating the biblical scenes, mystical carvings, and pagan symbolism adorning its interior. Noteworthy is the reputed face of Robert the Bruce, said to have been carved from his death mask, and the intricate Apprentices Pillar; the carvings on it are so detailed and skillfully executed that the master mason is reputed to have murdered his apprentice in a fit of jealous rage when he saw the finished article! The chapel is open Monday to Saturday 10am to 5pm and Sunday noon to 4:45pm. Admission is £4 ($7.40) adults, £1 ($1.85) children, and £3.50 ($6.45) seniors/students.

Bus 15A or 141 departs regularly from South Bridge in Edinburgh and takes around 25 minutes to reach Roslin. The one-way fare is £1.10 ($2.05) adults and 55p ($1) children, but the Daysaver ticket also includes Roslin. The chapel is about a 5-minute walk from the bus stop. If you're coming by **car,** take A701 south out of Edinburgh to Bilston and then B7003 to Roslin.

Florence & the Best of Tuscany

by Reid Bramblett

Five hundred years ago, **Florence** was the epicenter of European culture and life. It was here, from the 14th through the 16th centuries, that many of the most important developments in Western art, science, literature, and architecture took root and flourished. During the unprecedented years of the Renaissance, Florence was one of the world's wealthiest and most beautiful cities, and much of that Golden Age remains to be seen and experienced today.

Florence is no longer the axis around which the world revolves, but the taste, elegance, and sensibilities that marked the Renaissance are alive and well. The city boasts Europe's richest concentration of artistic wealth, much of which you can see or sense without even entering its world-class museums.

However, not only the sights and the history make Florence special; the nuts and bolts of where you stay and what you eat will make this city special in season and off. Many of the hotels listed below are in imposing palazzi from the time of the Medici and Michelangelo. You might find yourself sleeping beneath a frescoed ceiling or sampling a glass of chianti in the cantina of a palazzo built before Verrazano (who was born, by the way, just outside Florence) even set eyes on New York Harbor. The rustic and delicious Tuscan cuisine is one of Italy's—and the world's—finest, hailing from the heart of the nation's wine- and olive-producing farmland; even the French admit it was Catherine de' Medici's chefs, brought with her from Florence when she was married to

---

Value Budget Bests

With the notable exception of the Uffizi Galleries, the bulk of Florence's **Renaissance heritage** and the works of her greatest artists are free to all, from the statue-studded *piazze* (squares) to the frescoes and paintings decorating the walls of the city's myriad churches, most of which are free.

You're likely to find bargains on almost everything in this shopper's paradise. The famous **San Lorenzo market** stretches for half a dozen blocks, with hundreds of stalls. Leather wallets (around 10€/$12) and jackets (beginning at 80€/$92, if you bargain well) are the best buys, but budget shoppers will be able to find just about anything here at reasonable prices.

You can always save money on food and drink by consuming them **standing up** at one of the city's ubiquitous bars. Prices double—at least— if you sit down. Florence's abundance of **take-away sandwich spots** and *piazze* **with stone benches** make this an easy town in which to indulge in cheap picnic lunches.

Florence Deals & Discounts

SPECIAL DISCOUNTS   Surprisingly, Florence—noble tourist mecca even before the glory days of the Renaissance—has never felt inclined to offer enticing discounts. There's an 11€ ($12) **cumulative ticket** for the museums of the Pitti Palace (see "Seeing the Sights," later in this chapter).

WORTH A SPLURGE   The **major sights**—the Uffizi, Accademia, Palazzo Pitti, Bargello, and so on—are all more than worth the admission fees. What's more, you should definitely spring for the extra buck or two to **reserve your tickets** and entry times to the Uffizi and Accademia; in high season, you could save yourself 3 or more hours of waiting in line. A **walking tour of the city** or **biking tour through the countryside** can be a lovely way to spend the day, and they're not major splurges at 25€ ($29) for the former and 80€ ($70) for the latter; see "Organized Tours," p. 470.

Florence is one of the great culinary centers of Italy. Under "Great Deals on Dining," you'll find a number of restaurants that are particularly worth a splurge. Non-vegetarians should set aside at least one evening to splurge on Tuscany's mighty steak specialty, *bistecca alla Fiorentina*— expensive but absolutely worth it. And while the *vino della casa* (house wine) rarely fails to please, those curious about wine might lay out a few more bucks to tipple some of **Tuscany's famous fine wines**—chianti, Brunello di Montalcino, Vino Nobile di Montepulciano—as well as the so-called **Super Tuscans,** designer wines from top vineyards.

Florence also has an outstanding selection of charming one-of-a-kind **hotels.** If you can afford to spend a little bit more on accommodations, you'll inevitably be treated to an extraordinary and memorable stay—and maybe even a room with a view.

Since the Renaissance, Florence has been known for the impeccable artisanship of its **goldsmiths.** Invest in a family heirloom and take home a little Italian gold—18 karats of beautifully crafted jewelry not easy to come by in the States. A butter-soft **leather jacket** that'll last a few decades wouldn't be bad, either.

Finally, don't miss the *gelato* **(ice cream).** Starting at about 1.65€ ($2) per serving, this creamy delicacy surpasses any ice cream you've ever had and is worth every cent . . . and every yummy calorie.

the king of France, who established what would become French cuisine.

For more on Florence and its environs, see *Frommer's Portable Florence,* *Frommer's Tuscany & Umbria,* *Frommer's Italy from $70 a Day,* *Frommer's Irreverent Guide to Rome & Florence,* *Frommer's Italy,* and *Italy For Dummies.*

1 Essentials

ARRIVING

BY PLANE   Several European airlines now service Florence's expanded **Amerigo Vespucci Airport** (© **055-30-615** switchboard, 055-306-1300 flight updates,

055-306-1700 national flight info, 055-306-1702 international flight info; www.aeroporto.firenze.it), also called **Peretola,** just 5km (3 miles) northwest of town. There are no direct flights to/from the United States, but you can make easy connections through London, Paris, Amsterdam, Frankfurt, and so on. ATAF's regularly scheduled **Vola in Bus** connects the airport with Piazza della Stazione downtown, taking about 30 minutes and costing 4€ ($4.60); buy your ticket onboard. Just as expensive (4€/$4.60) but without the local stops is the half-hourly **SITA bus** to/from downtown's bus station at Via Santa Caterina 15r (© 055-219-383 or 800-373-760; www.sita-on-line.it), behind the train station. Metered **taxis** line up outside the airport's arrival terminal and charge about 13€ ($12) to most hotels in the city center.

The closest major international airport is Pisa's **Galileo Galilei Airport** (© 050-849-111; www.pisa-airport.it), 97km (60 miles) west of Florence. About a dozen **trains** (www.trenitalia.it) per day leave the airport for Florence (80 min.– 2 hr.; 4.95€–5.80€/$5.70–$6.70). Early-morning flights might make train connections from Florence to the airport difficult: The solution is the regular train from Florence into downtown Pisa, with a 10-minute (4€/$4.60) taxi from the Pisa train station to the nearby Pisa Airport. The no. 3 bus (© 800-012-773 in Italy; www.cpt.pisa.it) makes the same hop in twice the time for 1€ ($1.15). July 2003 saw the arrival of **Collective Taxi,** a van service that runs passengers from Pisa's airport to the train station for a flat 2.50€ ($2.90) per person (4€/$4.60 if you want to ride out to the Leaning Tower).

BY TRAIN   Most Florence-bound trains roll into the **Stazione Santa Maria Novella,** Piazza della Stazione (© 055-288-765 or toll-free in Italy 848-888-088; www.trenitalia.it), which you'll often see abbreviated as **S.M.N.** The station is on the northwestern edge of the city's compact historic center, a 10-minute walk from the Duomo and a 15-minute walk from Piazza della Signoria and the Uffizi. The best budget hotels are immediately east of there around Via Faenza and Via Fiume.

With your back to the tracks, you'll find a tiny **tourist info office** with a hotel-booking service office, open daily from 8:30am to 9pm (charging 2.30€–8€/ $2.65–$9), toward the station's left exit next to a 24-hour pharmacy. The **train information office** is near the opposite exit to your right. Walk straight through the central glass doors into the outer hall for tickets at the *biglietteria.* At the head of Track 16 is a 24-hour luggage depot where you can drop your bags (3€/$3.45 per piece for 12 hr.) while you search for a hotel.

Some trains stop at the outlying **Stazione Campo di Marte** or **Stazione Rifredi,** which are worth avoiding. Although there's 24-hour bus service between these satellite stations and S.M.N., departures aren't always frequent and taxi service is erratic and expensive.

BY CAR   Driving to Florence is easy; the problems begin once you arrive. Almost all cars are banned from the historic center—only residents or merchants with special permits are allowed in. You'll likely be stopped at some point by the traffic police, who'll assume from your rental plates that you're a visitor heading to your hotel. Have the name and address of the hotel ready and they'll wave you through. You can drop off baggage there (the hotel will give you a sign for your car advising traffic police you're unloading), but then you must relocate to a parking lot. Ask your hotel which is most convenient: Special rates are available through most of the hotels and their nearest lot.

Standard rates for parking near the center are 1€ to 2€ ($1.15–$2.30) per hour; many lots offer a daily rate of 13€ to 26€ ($15–$30). One option is the 15€ ($17) per day in the vast underground **Parterre lot** at Piazza della Libertà; you must show a hotel receipt to get that tourist rate when you retrieve your car. They'll also loan you a bike for free. Don't park your car overnight on the street; if you're towed and ticketed, it will set you back substantially—and the headaches to retrieve your car are beyond description. For more information on parking in Florence, visit **www.firenzeparcheggi.it**.

VISITOR INFORMATION

TOURIST OFFICES   The city's **largest tourist office** is at Via Cavour 1r (© **055-290-832;** fax 055-276-0383; www.firenzeturismo.it), about 3 blocks north of the Duomo. Outrageously, they now charge for the basic, useful info: .50€ (60¢) for a city map (though there's still a free one that differs only in lacking relatively inane brief descriptions of the museums and sights), 2€ ($2.30) for a little guide to museums, and 1€ ($1.15) each for pamphlets on the bridges and the *piazze* of Florence. The monthly *Informacittà* pamphlet on events, exhibits, and concerts is still free. The tourist office is open Monday to Saturday 8:30am to 6:30pm, Sunday 8:30am to 1:30pm.

At the head of the tracks in Stazione Santa Maria Novella is a **tiny info office** with some maps and a hotel-booking service (see "Affordable Places to Stay," later in this chapter), open Monday to Saturday 9am to 9pm (to 8pm Nov–Mar), but the station's **main tourist office** (© **055-212-245**) is outside at Piazza della Stazione 4. With your back to the tracks, take the left exit, cross onto the concrete median, and turn right; the office is about 30m (100 ft.) ahead. It's usually open Monday to Saturday 8:30am to 7pm (often to 1:30pm in winter), Sunday 8:30am to 1:30pm.

Another office sits on an obscure side street south of Piazza Santa Croce, Borgo Santa Croce 29r (© **055-234-0444**), open Monday to Saturday 9am to 7pm, Sunday 9am to 2pm.

PUBLICATIONS   At the tourist offices, pick up the free monthly *Informacittà*. The bilingual *Concierge Information* (www.florence-concierge.it) magazine, free from the front desks of top hotels, contains a monthly calendar of events and details on attractions. *Firenze Spettacolo* (www.firenzespettacolo.it), an Italian-language monthly sold at most newsstands (1.55€/$1.80), is the most detailed and up-to-date listing of nightlife, arts, and entertainment.

WEBSITES   The official Florence information site, **www.firenzeturismo.it**, contains a wealth of up-to-date information on Florence and its province, including a searchable hotels form allowing you to specify amenities, categories, and the like.

Firenze By Net (www.mega.it/florence), **Firenze.Net** (http://english.firenze. net), and **FlorenceOnLine** (www.fol.it) are all Italy-based websites with English translations and good general information on Florence. The site for **Concierge Information** (www.florence-concierge.it) is an excellent little guide to the current month's events, exhibits, concerts, and theater, as is *Informacittà* (www. informacitta.net), although the English version is still pending for the latter. Other sites worth checking out are **Your Way to Florence** (www.arca.net/florence.htm), **Time Out** (www.timeout.com/florence), and **The Heart of Tuscany** (www. nautilus-mp.com/tuscany).

Tips **The Red & the Black**

Unlike in other Italian cities, there are two systems of street numbering here: black *(nero)* and red *(rosso).* Black numbers are for residential and office buildings and hotels, while red numbers (indicated by an *r* following the number) identify commercial enterprises, such as restaurants and stores. The two numbering systems operate independently of each other—so the doorways on a given street might run 1r, 2r, 3r, 1 (black), 4r, 2 (black).

For years, Florence officials have proclaimed that they're busily renumbering the whole city without the color system—plain 1, 3, 5 on one side, 2, 4, 6 on the other—and will release the new standard soon, but no one is quite sure when. Florentines reluctant for their addresses to change have been holding up the process. This is all compounded by the fact that the color codes occur only in the *centro storico* and other older sections of town; outlying districts didn't bother with the codes and use the international standard system common in the U.S.

CITY LAYOUT

Florence is a compact city best negotiated on foot. No two sights are more than a 20- or 25-minute walk apart, and all the hotels and restaurants in this chapter are in the *centro storico* (historic center).

The city's relatively small and beautiful *centro storico* is loosely bounded by the S.M.N. train station to the northwest, Piazza della SS. Annunziata to the northeast, Piazza Santa Croce to the east, and the Arno River to the south. South of the river is the **Oltrarno** (on the other side of the Arno), considered a "Left Bank" adjunct to the *centro storico,* and home to the Pitti Palace and Florence's lookout-point, Piazzale Michelangiolo. As for the *centro storico:*

Piazza del Duomo, dominated by Florence's magnificent tricolor-marble **cathedral,** bell tower, and baptistery, is the heartbeat of the city. **Borgo San Lorenzo,** a narrow street running north from the baptistery, is best known for the excellent outdoor market at its far end, the **Mercato San Lorenzo,** where everything from marbleized paper-wrapped boxes and frames to leather bags and jackets is for sale. It borders the train station neighborhood, where you'll find a cluster of the city's cheapest hotels.

Via dei Calzaiuoli, Florence's most popular pedestrian thoroughfare and shopping street, runs south from the Duomo, connecting the church with the statue-filled **Piazza della Signoria.** West and parallel to this is **Via Roma,** which becomes **Via Por Santa Maria** on its way to the famed **Ponte Vecchio** bridge, lined with tiny goldsmith's shops, over the Arno. Midway between the two is **Piazza della Repubblica,** a busy caffè-ringed square surrounded by shopping streets. Farther west is **Via de' Tornabuoni,** Florence's boutique-lined Madison Avenue, and its elegant offshoot, **Via della Vigna Nuova.**

From Piazza della Signoria, **Via D. Gondi** leads east, becoming **Borgo dei Greci** on its way to **Piazza Santa Croce** at the center's eastern edge.

GETTING AROUND

Florence—with almost all of its *centro storico* closed to commercial traffic—is one of the most delightful cities in Europe to explore on foot. It's also much, much smaller than other famous capitals; there's rarely a need to take a bus. The best city map is the pocket-size **LAC Firenze** with the yellow-and-blue jacket, available at most newsstands for 2.60€ ($2.30).

BY BUS You'll rarely need to use Florence's efficient **ATAF bus system** (✆ 055-565-0222 or 800-424-500; www.ataf.net), since the city is so wonderfully compact. Many visitors accustomed to big cities like Rome step off their arriving train and onto a city bus out of habit, thinking to reach the center; within 5 minutes they find themselves in the suburbs. The cathedral is a mere 5- to 7-minute walk from the train station.

Bus **tickets** cost 1€ ($1.15), are good for an hour, and must be purchased before you board. A **four-pack** *(biglietto multiplo)* is 3.90€ ($4.50), a **24-hour pass** is 4.50€ ($5), a 2-day pass 7.60€ ($9), a **3-day pass** 9.60€ ($11), and a **7-day pass** 16€ ($18). Tickets are sold at *tabacchi* (tobacconists), bars, and most newsstands. Once on board, validate your ticket in the box near the rear door to avoid a steep fine. If you intend to use the bus system, you should pick up a **bus map** at a tourist office. Since most of the historic center is limited as to traffic, buses make runs on principal streets only, except four tiny electric buses that trundle about the *centro storico.*

BY TAXI You can't hail a cab, but you can find one at **taxi ranks** in or near major *piazze,* or call one to your restaurant or hotel by dialing ✆ **055-4242,** 055-4798, or 055-4390. Taxis charge .80€ (90¢) per kilometer, with a whopping minimum fare of 2.38€ ($2.75) to start the meter (which rises to 4.03€/$4.65 on Sun; 5.16€/$5.95 10pm–6am Sun), plus .57€ (65¢) per bag. Don't forget to include a 10% tip. Taxis are really worth considering only for getting to/from the train station with luggage.

BY BICYCLE OR SCOOTER Despite the relatively traffic-free historic center, biking has not really caught on here, but local authorities are trying to change that with **free bikes** (well, in past years there has been a nominal .50€/60¢ fee). **Firenze Parcheggi,** the public garage authority (✆ **055-500-0453;** www.firenzeparcheggi.it), has set up temporary sites about town (look for stands at the train station, Piazza Strozzi, Via della Nina along the south side of Palazzo Vecchio, and in the large public parking lots) where bikes are furnished free 8am to 7:30pm; you must return the bike to any of the other sites.

If no bikes are left, you'll have to pay for them at a shop like **Alinari,** Via Guelfa 85r (✆ **055-280-500;** www.alinarirental.com), which rents bikes (2.50€/$2.90 per hour; 12€/$14 per day) and mountain bikes (3€/$3.45 per hour; 18€/$21 per day). It also rents 50cc scooters (8€/$9 per hour; 28€/$32 per day) and 125cc mopeds (12€/$14 per hour; 55€/$63 per day). **Florence by Bike,** Via San Zanobi, 120–122r (✆ **055-488-992;** www.florencebybike.it), charges the same as Alinari for bicycles, but mountain bikes start at 3.50€

Country & City Codes

The **country code** for Italy is **39.** Italy no longer uses **city codes.** For folks who have been here before: Florence *used* to have a separate city code of 055, but that's now folded into the number itself (which means for now, all Florentine phone numbers start with a 055, but this could change as they run out of numbers and begin assigning new initial digits). Therefore, unlike in the past, you must dial the whole number—including the initial zero—at all times, whether you are calling from outside or inside Italy or even from within Florence itself.

($4.05) per hour and 18€ ($21) per day, and a 50cc scooter is 23€ ($26) for 5 hours or 30€ ($35) for a day.

BY RENTAL CAR   Don't rent a car for exploring pedestrianized Florence itself, but for day-tripping in the Chianti or exploring Tuscan hill towns, a car is vital. Arrange your rental from home for the best rates. But if you need to do it on the spot, auto-rental agencies in Florence are centered around the Europa Garage on Borgo Ognissanti. **Avis** is at no. 128r (© **055-213-629;** www.avis. com) and **Europcar** nearby at no. 53–55r (© **055-290-438;** www.europcar. com); **Hertz** is at Via Maso Finiguerra 33r (© **055-239-8205;** www.hertz.com). Most rental services have representatives at the Florence and Pisa airports, but you'll probably pay more to pick up a car there and drop it off in town.

FAST FACTS: Florence

American Express   Amex is at Via Dante Alighieri 22r, 50122 Firenze (© **055-50-981**), open Monday to Friday 9am to 5:30pm, Saturday (banking services only) 9am to 12:30pm. All traveler's checks (and not just American Express ones) are changed without a fee. Amex members may receive mail at this office for free. Have the sender address the mail to [your name], Client Mail, American Express, Via Dante Alighieri 22r, 50123 Firenze, Italia/ITALY. Non-members may get the same service for a 1.50€ ($1.75) fee to receive and hold mail. (See "Mail," below, for a better deal.)

Business Hours   In summer, most **businesses** and **shops** are open 9am to 1pm and 3:30 to 7:30pm. Many shops close Monday morning, the majority close on Sunday, and some also close Saturday afternoon. That midday shutdown is a siesta-like naptime called *riposo,* but more and more stores are opting to follow an *orario continuato* (nonstop) schedule. *Alimentari* (small **grocery stores**) are open Monday to Saturday but in low season are closed Wednesday afternoon and in high season are closed Saturday afternoon. Standard **bank** hours are Monday to Friday 8:20am to 1:20pm and 2:45 to 3:45pm. **Restaurants** are required to close at least 1 day per week (their *giorno di riposo*), although the day varies.

Consulates   The consulate of the **United States** is at Lungarno Amerigo Vespucci 38 (© **055-266-951**), near its intersection with Via Palestro; it's open to drop-ins Monday to Friday 9am to 12:30pm. Afternoons from 2 to 4:30pm, the consulate is open by appointment only; call ahead. The consulate of the **United Kingdom** is at Lungarno Corsini 2 (© **055-284-133**), near Via de' Tornabuoni; it's open Monday to Friday 9:30am to 12:30pm and 2:30 to 4:30pm. Citizens of **Australia, New Zealand,** and **Canada** should consult their embassies in Rome (see "Fast Facts: Rome" in chapter 21).

Crime   Pickpocketing is performed deftly and swiftly by Florence's Gypsy *(zingari)* population, despite the efforts of plainclothes police. They show up in small groups at the most touristy spots and jostle or distract you while the kiddies relieve you of your valuables. Gypsy and non-Gypsy incidents alike are known to happen at the crowded markets or on public buses. Use common sense, try to avoid them, and yell *"Polizia!"* if they come too close.

Currency In 2002, Italy adopted the **euro** (€) for its currency. At press time, 1€ = $1.15, or $1 = .87€.

Dentists & Doctors A walk-in clinic ((C) **0330-774-731**) is run by **Dott. (Dr.) Giorgio Scappini** on Tuesday, and his Thursday office hours are brief—5:30 to 6:30pm or by appointment at Via Bonifacio Lupi 32 (just south of the Tourist Medical Service; see "Hospitals," below); Monday, Wednesday, and Friday, go to Via Guasti 2 from 3 to 4pm (north of the Fortezza del Basso). **Dott. (Dr.) Stephen Kerr** keeps a clinic at Via Porta Rossa 1 (toward the south end of Via Calzaiuoli, next to Molteni, the pharmacy; (C) **055-288-055**; www.dr-kerr.com), with weekday morning appointments. Walk-ins are accepted Monday to Friday from 3 to 5pm.

For general dentistry, try **Dott. (Dr.) Camis de Fonseca,** Via Nino Bixio 9, northeast of the city center off Viale dei Mille ((C) **055-587-632**), open Monday to Friday 3 to 7pm; he's also available for emergency weekend calls. The U.S. consulate can provide a list of other English-speaking doctors, dentists, and specialists. See also "Hospitals," below, for medical translator service.

Drugstores You'll find **neon green crosses** above the entrances to most *farmacie* (pharmacies). Three addresses offering English-speaking service and 24-hour schedules are the **Farmacia Communale,** at the head of Track 16 in the train station ((C) **055-216-761**); **Molteni,** Via dei Calzaiuoli 7r, just north of Piazza della Signoria ((C) **055-289-490** or 055-215-472); and **All'Insegno del Moro,** at the Duomo square, Piazza San Giovanni 20r ((C) **055-211-343**).

Emergencies Dial (C) **113** in any **emergency.** You can call (C) **112** for the *carabinieri* (the military-trained and more useful of the two **police** forces). To report a **fire,** dial (C) **115.** For an **ambulance,** dial (C) **118.** For **roadside breakdown** assistance, call (C) **116.**

Holidays See "Fast Facts: Rome" in chapter 21. Florence's patron saint, San Giovanni (John the Baptist), is honored on June 24. Watch for the fireworks and expect many stores to close.

Hospitals The **ambulance number** is (C) **118.** There's a special **Tourist Medical Service,** Via Lorenzo il Magnifico 59, north of the city center between the Fortezza del Basso and Piazza della Libertà ((C) **055-475-411**), open 24 hours; take bus no. 4, 12, 13, 14, 20, 23, 28, or 33 to Viale Lavagnini.

Thanks to socialized medicine, you can walk into most any Italian hospital when ill (but not with an emergency) and get taken care of speedily with no insurance questions asked, no forms to fill out, and no fee charged. They'll just give you a prescription and send you on your way. The most central are the **Arcispedale di Santa Maria Nuova,** a block northeast of the Duomo on Piazza Santa Maria Nuova ((C) **055-27-581**); and the **Misericordia Ambulance Service,** on Piazza del Duomo across from Giotto's bell tower ((C) **055-212-222** for ambulance).

For a **free translator** to help you describe your symptoms, explain the doctor's instructions, and assist you in medical issues in general, call the volunteers at the **Associazione Volontari Ospedalieri (AVO;** (C) **055-234-4567**) Monday, Wednesday, and Friday 4 to 6pm; Tuesday and Thursday 10am to noon.

Internet Access To check or send e-mail, head to the **Internet Train** (www.internettrain.it), with 15 locations, including Via dell'Oriuolo 40r, just blocks from the Duomo (© 055-234-5322), Via Guelfa 54–56, near the train station (© 055-264-5146); and Borgo San Jacopo 30r in the Oltrarno (© 055-265-7935). Access is 4€ ($3.60) per hour, 1€ (90¢) for 10 minutes; they also provide printing, scanning, Webcam, and fax services. Open hours vary but run generally from 11am to 10:30pm or 11pm on weekdays, and noon to 7 or 8pm on weekends. **Thenetgate,** Via Sant'Egidio 14r (© 055-234-4761; www.thenetgate.it), charges 3€ ($3.45) per hour.

Laundry & Dry Cleaning North of the Duomo is one of four modern self-service locations of **Wash & Dry,** Via dei Servi 105r (© 055-580-480 for seven other locations in town; or ask at your hotel). They charge about 7€ ($8) for a wash and dry, and are open daily 8am to 10pm. However, you can get your wash done even more cheaply at a pay-by-weight *lavanderia*—and you don't have to waste a morning sitting there watching it go in circles. The cheapest are around the university (east of San Marco), and one of the best is a nameless joint at **Via Alfani 44r** (© 055-247-9313), where they'll do an entire load for 6€ ($7), have it ready by afternoon, and even deliver it free to your hotel. It's closed Saturday afternoon and Sunday. At other, non-self-service shops, check the price *before* leaving your clothes—some places charge by the item. **Dry cleaning** *(lavasecco)* is much more costly and is available at *lavanderie* throughout the city (ask your hotel for the closest).

Mail You can buy *francobolli* **(stamps)** from any *tabacchi* (tobacconists) or from the central post office. Florence's **main post office** (© **160** for general info, or 055-273-6481) is on Via Pellicceria 3, 50103, Firenze, off the southwest corner of Piazza della Repubblica. You can buy stamps and pick up letters sent *Fermo Posta* (Italian for *Poste Restante*) by showing ID. The post office is open Monday to Saturday 8:15am to 7pm. All packages heavier than 2 kilograms (4½ lb.) must be properly wrapped and brought around to the parcel office at the back of the building (enter at Via dei Sassetti 4, also known as Piazza Davanzati).

To receive mail at the central post office, have it sent to [your name], Fermo Posta Centrale, 50103 Firenze, Italia/ITALY. They'll charge you .26€ (30¢) per letter when you come to pick it up at window 23/24; bring your passport for ID.

Police Dial © 113 for the police or © 112 for the *carabinieri,* a division of the Italian army.

Taxes, Telephone & Tipping See "Fast Facts: Rome" in chapter 21.

2 Affordable Places to Stay

Many budget hotels are concentrated in the area around the train station. You'll find most of the hotels in this convenient and relatively safe, if charmless, area on noisy **Via Nazionale** and its first two side streets, **Via Fiume** and **Via Faenza;** an adjunct is the area surrounding the Mercato San Lorenzo. The area between the Duomo and Piazza della Signoria, particularly along and near **Via dei Calzaiuoli,** is a good though invariably more expensive place to look.

During summer, it's important to arrive early, as many hotels fill up for the night even before all the guests from the previous day have checked out. For

help finding a room, visit the Santa Maria Novella train station for the **Consorzio Informazioni Turistiche Alberghiere (ITA)** office, near Track 9 (© 055-282-893), and the tiny tourist office, near Track 16, both of which will find you a room in your price range (for a small commission). Or go to the official tourist office's website subsection on accommodations at **www.toscanaeturismo.net/dovedormire.** Peak season is mid-March to mid-July, September to early November, and December 23 to January 6. May and September are particularly popular both in the city and in the outlying Tuscan hills.

A **continental breakfast** in an Italian hotel can be one of the great disappointments of budget travel. The usual cost of an unremarkable roll, butter, jam, and coffee is 4€ to 7€ ($4.60–$8); you can get coffee and a *cornetto* (croissant) for about half that standing at any caffè or bar. The hotel breakfast is generally not worth the price, but in many cases is locked into the rates—and can even be a bargain on occasion. Clarify your options on registering, however, not on checkout.

Note: You'll find the lodging choices below plotted on the map on p. 454.

BETWEEN THE DUOMO & THE ARNO

Hotel Alessandra 🄌 *Value*   This old-fashioned *pensione* in a 1507 palazzo just off the river charges little for its simple comfort and kind hospitality. The rooms differ greatly in size and style, and while they won't win any awards from *Architectural Digest,* there are a few antique pieces and parquet floors to add to the charm. There's air-conditioning in 23 of its 27 rooms. The bathrooms are outfitted with fluffy white towels, and the shared bathrooms are ample, clean, and numerous enough that you won't have to wait in line in the morning. They also rent out an apartment in a quiet section of the Oltrarno (across the bridge from the Santa Croce neighborhood) for 775€ ($891) per week for two people; check it out at www.florenceflat.com.

Borgo SS. Apostoli 17 (between Via dei Tornabuoni and Via Por Santa Maria), 50123 Firenze. © 055-283-438. Fax 055-210-619. www.hotelalessandra.com. 27 units, 19 with bathroom. 88€ ($101) single without bathroom; 110€ ($127) single with bathroom; 108€ ($124) double without bathroom; 145€ ($167) double with bathroom; 160€ ($184) double overlooking river; 145€ ($167) triple without bathroom; 191€ ($220) triple with bathroom; 160€ ($184) quad without bathroom, 212€ ($244) quad with bathroom; 160€ ($184) junior suite, 200€ ($230) Baccio suite. Rates include breakfast. Ask about low-season rates. AE, MC, V. Parking in nearby garage 20€ ($23). Bus: A, B, 6, 11, 36, or 37. **Amenities:** Video games (PlayStation on request); concierge; tour desk; limited room service (breakfast); massage; babysitting; laundry service; same-day dry cleaning; nonsmoking rooms (doubles overlooking river and suites). *In room:* A/C (most rooms), TV, hair dryer, safe (most rooms).

Hotel Firenze   A recent renovation has transformed this former student hangout (still partly used as a study-abroad dorm) into a two-star hotel. Its location is divine, tucked away on its own little piazza at the heart of the *centro storico*'s

---

⟨*Tips*⟩ An Elevator Warning

Most of the hotels below are housed in historic palazzi where elevators aren't always common. As one-, two-, and three-star hotels, many exist on just one or two floors in a palazzo, with a lobby rarely at street level—that means it's a one-floor walk up just to get to the front desk and often another story or two to your room. If this is an issue, inquire when booking if there's an elevator, which floor the lobby is on, and which floor your room is on.

> (*Value* Getting the Best Deal on Accommodations
>
> • Try one of the budget hotels in the area east of the train station cen-
>   tered on Via Faenza and Via Fiume.
> • Book early to secure the hotel and price category you want.
> • Get out of paying for breakfast at your hotel and instead enjoy an
>   inexpensive standup breakfast at one of Florence's caffès. Hoteliers
>   are more likely to bend this rule off season. Clarify the breakfast
>   situation when checking in.
> • Ask how many rooms share each hallway bathroom: One or two is
>   minimum traffic, but three or four might mean problems with house-
>   keeping and availability. With a good ratio, the option of a room
>   without a private bathroom should become a real consideration.

pedestrian zone, but it's a bit too institutional to justify the midrange rates. The
rooms are simple, brightly tiled yet bland, but the proprietors are installing air-
conditioning. This is a large operation without any of the warmth or ambience
of a small family-run hotel, and the concierge and management are efficient but
generally uninvolved.

Piazza Donati 4 (on Via del Corso, off Via dei Calzaiuoli), 50122 Firenze. (✆) **055-268-301** or 055-214-203. Fax
055-212-370. 60 units. 67€ ($77) single; 88€ ($101) double; 120€ ($138) triple; 154€ ($177) quad. Continental breakfast 8€ ($9). No credit cards. Bus: A, 14, or 23. **Amenities:** Tour desk. *In room:* TV, hair dryer.

Locanda Orchidea ✮ The elegant English-speaking proprietor, Maria Rosa
Cook, will gladly recount the history of this 13th-century palazzo where Dante's
wife, Gemma Donati, was born (Dante's home and the Casa di Dante aren't far
away). One of its floors houses this old-fashioned *locanda* (inn) whose large,
high-ceilinged rooms are decorated with floral bedspreads and white lace
touches. The furnishings are functional and the beds a little squishy. Room nos.
4 to 7 overlook a tiny junglelike garden rather than the sometimes noisy road.
They have plans to put phones in the rooms, but for now you can use the one
in the common area (where there's also a TV).

Borgo degli Albizi 11 (1st floor, between the Duomo and Santa Croce), 50122 Firenze. (✆)/fax 055-248-0346.
www.hotelorchideaflorence.it. 7 units, none with bathroom, 1 quad with shower. 55€ ($63) single; 75€ ($86)
double; 100€ ($115) triple; 120€ ($138) quad. No credit cards. Bus: A, 14, or 23. **Amenities:** Concierge; tour
desk. *In room:* No phone.

Pensione Maria Luisa de' Medici ✮✮✮ *Kids* *Finds* In the 1950s and '60s,
Angido Sordi was into Italian design, and the rooms of his hotel—each frescoed
with a different Medici portrait by his wife—have lamps, chairs, and tables
you'd normally have to go to New York's Museum of Modern Art to see. In the
1970s and '80s, Sordi got into baroque art, so the halls are hung with canvases
by the likes of Van Dyck, Vignale, and Sustermans. I can't wait to see what he
gets into next. The 1645 palazzo setting goes well with the artistic theme, and
while Dr. Sordi convalesces in a back room, his Welsh partner Evelyn Morris
runs the place, cooking hearty breakfasts served to you in your room. Most
rooms are large enough to accommodate four to five people comfortably. The
firm beds are set on carpeted or tiled floors scattered with thick rugs. There are
four shared bathrooms, so you usually don't have to wait in the morning. One

drawback: You have to walk up three flights. There is a curfew, which varies with the season.

Via del Corso 1 (2nd floor; between Via dei Calzaiuoli and Via del Proconsolo), 50122 Firenze. © 055-280-048. 9 units, 2 with bathroom. 55€ ($63) single without bathroom; 75€ ($86) double without bathroom; 90€ ($104) double with bathroom; 93€ ($107) triple without bathroom, 113€ ($130) triple with bathroom; 118€ ($136) quad without bathroom, 140€ ($161) quad with bathroom. Rates include breakfast. No credit cards. Nearby parking about 24€–28€ ($28–$32). Bus: A, 14, or 23. **Amenities:** Concierge; tour desk. *In room:* Hair dryer, no phone.

NEAR THE TRAIN STATION & THE MERCATO SAN LORENZO

Albergo Azzi/Locanda degli Artisti 🖈 *Value* Musicians Sandro and Valentino, the young owners of this ex-*pensione,* have created a haven for artists, artist *manqués,* and students. It exudes a relaxed Bohemian feel—not all the doors hang straight and not all the bedspreads match, although strides are being made, and they've even discovered some old frescoes in room nos. 3 and 4. In 2003, they overhauled the place to bump up its rating from a "one-star" (bottom end) to a "two-star" (inexpensive/moderate) hotel, adding amenities to the rooms (TVs, phones, A/C, and such), and redoing the reception and public spaces, using recycled and bio-friendly products whenever possible. In June 2004, they added a sauna and Jacuzzi-style shower, plus four large suites with Jacuzzi tubs. You'll love the open terrace with a view where breakfast is served in warm weather, as well as the small library of art books and guidebooks, all of which you can borrow (as long as you return them). The units without full bathroom have at least shower and sink (just no toilet). In the same building, under the same management and with slightly simpler rooms at somewhat lower rates, are the **Anna** (eight units, four with bathroom; © 055-239-8322) and the **Paola** (seven units, four with shower/sink in room and some with frescoes; © 055-213-682). Also in the building, but separately owned, is the **Hotel Merlini** (see below).

Via Faenza 56 (1st floor), 50123 Firenze. ©/fax **055-213-806.** hotelazzi@hotmail.com. 20 units, 13 with bathroom. 25€ ($29) bed in shared room; 35€–48€ ($40–$55) single without bathroom, 50€–65€ ($58–$75) single with bathroom; 45€–65€ ($52–$75) double without bathroom, 65€–95€ ($75–$109) double with bathroom; 90€–150€ ($104–$172) suite with bathroom. Breakfast 5€ ($6). AE, DC, MC, V. Parking in nearby garage 16€ ($18). Bus: A, 4, 7, 10, 11, 12, 25, 31, 32, 33, 36, or 37. **Amenities:** Jacuzzi (shower-style); sauna; concierge; tour desk. *In room:* A/C (on request), TV (on request), hair dryer.

Albergo Mia Cara/Archi Rossi Hostel *Value* The Noto family's old simple hotel had been completely cleared out as this book went to press, and the workmen were busily turning it into a two- or three-star property—rooms complete with private bathroom, air-conditioning, minibars, telephones . . . in short, the works. They expect to have everything finished by mid-2004, and while the particulars are yet to be established, Angela Noto figures they will charge around 100€ to 120€ ($115–$138), including breakfast, for a double room. No matter what the final price, she promises Frommer's readers "a good rate." And by moving the entrance, they finally can make use of the building's elevator.

One thing that hasn't changed much is the family's **Archi Rossi Hostel** (© **055-290-804;** fax 055-230-2601; www.hostelarchirossi.com) downstairs, where units sleep four to six; a unit without bathroom costs 18€ to 20€ ($21–$23) per person, and a unit with bathroom costs 19€ to 22€ ($22–$25) per person depending on how many beds in the room. Private, bathless singles in the hostel go for 29€ ($33), including breakfast; and family rooms sleeping three to five go for 24€ ($27) each room, including breakfast. The hostel does insist on a 2am curfew (up from 1am last year), but no longer closes in the middle of the day. Internet access is free for 30 minutes per customer each day.

Via Faenza 90r, 50123 Firenze. ⓒ **055-216-053.** Fax 055-230-2601. 19 units. Price to be confirmed, but probably 100€–120€ ($115–$138). Breakfast included. Credit cards accepted. 4 parking spots, sometimes free, sometimes up to 8€ ($9). Bus: A, 1, 4, 7, 10, 11, 12, 14, 17, 22, 23, 25, 31, 32, 33, 36, or 37. **Amenities:** Concierge; tour desk; nonsmoking rooms. *In room:* A/C, minibar.

Albergo Serena ⟨★⟩   Run with pride by the Bigazzi family, this unpretentious but dignified place offers pleasant surprises: brand-new nicely tiled bathrooms, patterned stone floor tiles, molded ceilings, and early-1900s stained-glass French doors. The rooms are airy and bright and kept clean as a whistle by the owner's wife. They're awaiting permission to start serving breakfast as well. If this place is full, try the smaller and less expensive **Otello Tourist House** upstairs (ⓒ/fax **055-239-6159**); it has just four simple but lovely units, two with bathroom, and is run by English-speaking Anna and her husband, Otello.

Via Fiume 20 (2nd floor), 50123 Firenze. ⓒ **055-213-643.** Fax 055-280-447. www.albergoserena.it. 8 units. 40€–55€ ($46–$63) single; 55€–80€ ($63–$92) double; 75€ 105€ ($86–$121) triple; 100€–130€ ($115–$150) quad. Breakfast 5€ ($6). AE, MC, V. Parking 18€ ($21). Bus: A, 4, 7, 10, 11, 12, 13, 14, 23, 25, 28, 31, 32, 33, 36, or 37. **Amenities:** Concierge; tour desk; nonsmoking rooms. *In room:* TV, hair dryer (ask at desk), safe (some units).

Hotel Abaco ⟨★★⟩ *(Value)*   Bruno is a bit of a Calabrian dynamo, running his clean, efficient little hotel in a prime location with gusto, and he's one of the more helpful, advice-filled hoteliers in town. The hotel has inherited a few nice touches from its 15th-century palazzo, including high wood ceilings, stone floors (some are parquet), and, in tiny no. 5, a carved *pietra serena* fireplace. Each room is themed after a Renaissance artist, with framed reproductions of the painter's works and a color scheme derived from them. Bruno is slowly replacing the mismatched furnishings with quirky antique-style pieces like gilded frame mirrors and rich half-testers over the beds. The hotel is at a busy intersection, but the double-paned windows help. Internet access is available for guests. Bruno will do a load of laundry for you for 7€ ($8), wash and dry.

Via dei Banchi 1 (halfway between the station and the Duomo, off Via de' Panzani), 50123 Firenze. ⓒ **055-238-1919.** Fax 055-282-289. www.abaco-hotel.it. 7 units, 3 with shower and sink, 3 with full bathroom. 50€ ($58) single without bathroom, 65€ ($75) single with bathroom; 73€ ($84) double without bathroom, 75€ ($86) double with shower only, 90€ ($104) double with bathroom. Breakfast 5€ ($6), free if you pay for room with cash. AE, MC, V (they prefer cash). Valet parking 25€ ($29) in garage. Bus: A, 1, 6, 11, 14, 17, 22, 23, 36, or 37. **Amenities:** Bike rental; concierge; tour desk; car-rental desk; coin-op washer/dryer. *In room:* A/C (5€/$6 per day), TV, dataport, hair dryer.

Hotel Bellettini ⟨★⟩ *(Kids)*   A hotel has existed in this Renaissance palazzo since the 1600s. Gina and Marzia, sisters and third-generation hoteliers, run this gem of terra-cotta tiles, wrought-iron or carved-wood beds, antiques, stained-glass windows, and hand-painted coffered ceilings. Room no. 44 offers a tiny balcony that, blooming with jasmine and geraniums by late spring, makes it second best only to room 45 with its view of the Medici Chapels and the Duomo's dome. The two bedrooms of no. 20 make it perfect for families. Breakfast is an impressive spread. In 2000, they added a lovely six-room annex with frescoes, marble bathrooms, minibars, and coffeemakers; doubles run a bit more at about 160€ ($184).

Via dei Conti 7 (off Via dei Cerretani), 50123 Firenze. ⓒ **055-213-561.** Fax 055-283-551. www.hotelbellettini. com. 28 units. 75€ ($86) single without bathroom; 95€ ($109) single with bathroom; 100€ ($115) double without bathroom, 130€–160€ ($150–$184) double with bathroom; 160€ ($184) triple with bathroom; 200€ ($230) quad with bathroom. Rates include buffet breakfast. AE, DC, MC, V. Nearby parking 18€ ($21). Bus: A, 1, 6, 7, 10, 11, 14, 17, 22, 23, 36, or 37. **Amenities:** Concierge; tour desk; limited room service; laundry service; dry cleaning. *In room:* A/C, TV, minibar (in annex rooms), coffeemaker (in annex rooms), hair dryer (ask at reception), safe.

Hotel Casci 🐕 *Kids* This clean hotel in a 15th-century palazzo is run by the wonderful Lombardi family. The hotel is patronized by a host of regulars who know a good value when they find it. The Lombardis bicker among themselves Italian style, but are amazingly accommodating to guests—their favorite phrase in English is "No problem!" They even offer a free museum ticket to everyone who stays at least 3 nights (and with admissions running nearly $10 for most major museums, that's saying something). The tiny frescoed bar room was, from 1851 to 1855, part of an apartment inhabited by Giacchino Rossini, legendary composer of *The Barber of Seville* and the *William Tell Overture*. The rooms ramble on toward the back forever, overlooking the gardens and Florentine rooftops, and are mouse-quiet except for birdsong. A few large family suites in back sleep four to five. The central location means some rooms (with double-paned windows) over-look busy Via Cavour, so for more quiet ask for a room facing the inner courtyard's magnolia tree. An ample breakfast buffet is served in a frescoed dining room.

Via Cavour 13 (between Via dei Ginori and Via Guelfa), 50129 Firenze. © **055-211-686.** Fax 055-239-6461. www.hotelcasci.com. 25 units. 60€–105€ ($69–$121) single; 90€–145€ ($104–$167) double; 120€–185€ ($138–$213) triple; 150€–225€ ($207–$259) quad. Rates include buffet breakfast. Check website for special offers, especially Nov–Feb. AE, DC, MC, V. Valet parking 23€–25€ ($26–$29), or in nearby garage (no valet) for 15€ ($17). Bus: 1, 6, 11, or 17. **Amenities:** Bar; concierge; tour desk; babysitting; laundry service; dry cleaning; nonsmoking rooms; free Internet access. *In room:* A/C, TV, dataport, fridge, hair dryer, safe.

Hotel Centro 🐕 A block north of the Mercato San Lorenzo, this refurbished hotel occupies a palazzo that was home to Renaissance master painter Raphael in 1505 and 1506. There's precious little he'd recognize in its contemporary reincarnation, with ample-size rooms outfitted in colorful bedspreads and wood veneer furnishings; the bathrooms are tiled in white and brightly lit. New owners Andrea and Sandra Vendali continue to upgrade the place, replacing the furnishing and fabrics with richer versions and laying springy carpet onto the tile floors. Second-floor rooms have air-conditioning (most of the rest get ceiling fans). It's 34 steps to the first-floor reception, but they have an internal elevator after that.

Via Ginori 17 (north of Piazza San Lorenzo), 50123 Firenze. © **055-230-2901.** Fax 055-212-706. www.hotel centro.net. 16 units, 14 with bathroom. 45€–60€ ($52–$69) single without bathroom, 55€–95€ ($63–$109) single with bathroom; 95€–140€ ($109–$161) double with bathroom; 110€–170€ ($127–$196) triple with bathroom. Rates include buffet breakfast. AE, DC, MC, V. Valet parking in nearby garage 20€ ($23). Bus: 1, 6, 7, 10, 11, 14, 17, or 23. **Amenities:** Concierge; tour desk; limited room service (breakfast); babysitting; laundry service; dry cleaning. *In room:* A/C (on request), TV, hair dryer, safe.

Hotel Merlini 🐕 *Value* Run by the Sicilian Gabriella family, this cozy third-floor walkup boasts rooms appointed with wooden carved antique headboards and furnishings (and a few modular pieces to fill in the gaps). It's one of only two hotels in all of Florence with mosquito screens. The optional breakfast is served on a sunny glassed-in terrace decorated in the 1950s with frescoes by talented American art students and overlooking a leafy large courtyard. Room nos. 1, 4 (with a balcony), 6, 7, and 8 all have views of the domes topping the Duomo and the Medici Chapels across the city's terra-cotta roof-scape. A recent renovation tripled the number of private bathrooms and freshened up everything. This is a notch above your average one-star place, the best in a building full of tiny *pensioni*. Curfew at 1am.

Via Faenza 56 (3rd floor), 50123 Firenze. © **055-212-848.** Fax 055-283-939. www.hotelmerlini.it. 10 units, 6 with bathroom. 35€–44€ ($40–$51) single without bathroom; 45€–65€ ($52–$75) double without bathroom, 50€–79€ ($58–$91) double with bathroom; 60€–90€ ($69–$104) triple without bathroom; 80€–100€ ($92–$115) quad without bathroom. Breakfast 6€ ($7). MC, V. Bus: A, 4, 7, 10, 11, 12, 25, 31, 32, 33, 36, or 37. **Amenities:** Concierge; tour desk. *In room:* Hair dryer (ask at desk), no phone.

Hotel Monica 🏵 Gracious polyglot Rhana Cecchini has supervised the face-lift of this two-star hotel, resulting in a bright airy ambience and refinished bathrooms. The prices have increased, but so have the amenities. Highlights are the terrazzo floors, wrought-iron bedsteads, exposed-brick archways, and a wonderful terrace, where breakfast is served the minute the weather turns warm. Most rooms are in the back of the building over the terrace, ensuring a quiet stay and pleasant rooftop views.

Via Faenza 66 (1st floor; at Via Cennini), 50123 Firenze. © **055-283-804** or 055-281-706. Fax 055-283-804. www.hotelmonicafirenze.it. 15 units. 40€–70€ ($46–$81) single; 70€–130€ ($81–$150) double; 30€ ($35) each extra person In room. Rates include buffet breakfast. Frommer's readers can ask for a 5% discount on these prices when booking. AE, DC, MC, V. Bus: A, 1, 4, 7, 10, 11, 12, 22, 23, 25, 31, 32, or 33. **Amenities:** Concierge; tour desk; limited room service (breakfast); laundry service; dry cleaning. *In room:* A/C, TV.

Hotel Nuova Italia 🏵🏵 *Finds* *Kids* A Frommer's fairy tale: With her trusty *Frommer's Europe on $5 a Day* in hand, the fair Eileen left the kingdom of Canada on a journey to faraway Florence. At her hotel, Eileen met Luciano, her baggage boy in shining armor. They fell in love, got married, bought a castle (er, hotel) of their own called the Nuova Italia, and their clients live happily ever after. The staff here really puts itself to task for guests, recommending restaurants, shops, day trips—they gave me tips the tourist office didn't know about. The rooms are two-star standard, medium to small, but the attention to detail makes the Nuova Italia stand out. Every room has a bathroom (with fluffy towels), orthopedic mattress, new furniture custom-designed by Eileen, and triple-paned windows (though some morning rumble from the San Lorenzo market street carts still gets through). It's also one of a handful of hotels in all Tuscany with mosquito screens in the windows. The family's love of art is manifested in framed posters and paintings, and Eileen is a great source about local exhibits. Special rates for Frommer's readers (see below).

Via Faenza 26 (off Via Nazionale), 50123 Firenze. © **055-268-430** or 055-287-508. Fax 055-210-941. www.hotelnuovaitalia.com. 20 units. *For Frommer's readers:* 85€ ($98) single; 125€ ($144) double; 145€ ($167) triple. Rates include continental breakfast. There are frequent discounts, so ask when booking. AE, DC, MC, V. Valet garage parking about 18€–22€ ($21–$25). Bus: A, 1, 4, 7, 10, 11, 12, 25, 31, 32, or 33. **Amenities:** Concierge; tour desk; car-rental desk; babysitting; laundry service; dry cleaning. *In room:* A/C, TV, hair dryer (ask at desk).

Pensione Centrale 🏵🏵 *Kids* The presence of Normandy-born manager Mariethérèse Blot is everywhere in this *pensione* converted from a 14th-century palazzo. Most of the large bright rooms contain matching antique armoires and headboards, and many rooms overlook the Medici Chapels. They've replaced carpeting with synthetic parquet flooring, and have uncovered slightly ruined frescoes on the breakfast room ceiling. Large rooms, including several triples, make this a perfect place for families, but one child under 12 can stay for free in a parent's room. In the off season, the hotel may offer special rates. Plus you get the most ample buffet breakfast in town at this price.

Via dei Conti 3 (2nd floor; off Via Cerretani), 50123 Firenze. © **055-215-761.** Fax 055-215-216. www.pensionecentrale.it. 18 units. 55€–85€ ($63–$98) single; 70€–109€ ($81–$125) double; 88€–136€ ($101–$156) triple; 106€–163 ($122–$187) quad. Rates include buffet breakfast. Ask for discounts in low season. AE, DC, MC, V. Bus: A, 1, 6, 7, 10, 11, 14, 17, 22, 23, 36, or 37. **Amenities:** Concierge; tour desk; limited room service (breakfast); babysitting; laundry service; dry cleaning; nonsmoking rooms; Internet access. *In room:* A/C (in 9, or ask), TV (in 10, or ask), hair dryer (ask at desk).

IN THE OLTRARNO

Albergo La Scaletta 🏵 *Kids* For nearly 30 years, the Barbiere family has run this well-worn old shoe of a place in one of the only remaining palazzi on this block between the Pitti Palace and Ponte Vecchio. The inn's star is the flower-bedecked, sun-kissed terrace offering a 360-degree vista over the Boboli Gardens, the Oltrarno rooftops, and (beyond a sea of antennas) the monumental heart of Florence. Plus there's a shoe-biting turtle they found here when they bought the place. Return visitors book months in advance for the homey rooms that have tiny bathrooms and old tiled floors. Some beds are lumpy to a fault, others fully firm, but street-side accommodations have double-paned windows that really do block the noise, and the worn, dark wood lacquer furniture is pleasantly unassuming. Take all of this with a grain of salt, though: in late 2003, Mrs. Barbiere retired, and her son Manfredo—who for 15€ ($17) will cook you a dinner, if you request it ahead of time at breakfast—is unsure whether he will be able to keep the place running or sell it to a new owner.

Via Guicciardini 13 (2nd floor; near Piazza de Pitti), 50125 Firenze. © 055-283-028 or 055-214-255. Fax 055-289-562. www.lascaletta.com. 13 units, 11 with bathroom. 45€ ($52) single without bathroom, 95€ ($109) single with bathroom; 100€ ($115) double without bathroom, 135€ ($155) double with bathroom; 130€ ($150) triple without bathroom, 155€ ($178) triple with bathroom; 170€ ($196) quad with bathroom. Rates include continental breakfast. Ask about off-season discounts. MC, V. Nearby parking 10€–28€. Bus: C, D, 11, 36, or 37. **Amenities:** Concierge; tour desk; limited room service (breakfast); babysitting; laundry service; dry cleaning. *In room:* A/C (in 8 rooms), TV (in 5, or on request), hair dryer.

Pensione Sorelle Bandini This *pensione* occupies a landmark Renaissance palazzo on one of the city's great squares. You can live like the nobles of yore in appropriately proportioned rooms with 4.5m (15-ft.) ceilings, 3m (10-ft.) windows, and oversize antique furniture. Room no. 9 sleeps five and offers a Duomo view from its bathroom window; room B is a double with a fantastic cityscape out the window. Everything used to seem a bit ramshackle and musty, but a recent renovation has spiffed up the place a bit (though it's still far from luxurious). The highlight is the monumental roofed veranda where Mimmo, the English-speaking manager, oversees breakfast and encourages brown-bag lunches and the chance to relax and drink in the views. Franco Zeffirelli used the *pensione* for some scenes in *Tea with Mussolini*. Quite frankly, their fame as a "typical old-fashioned" *pensione* has gone a bit to their heads—and to the prices, which have slowly crept rather higher than they should be for a budget-class hotel.

Piazza Santo Spirito 9, 50125 Firenze. © **055-215-308**. Fax 055-282-761. pensionebandini@tiscali.it. 13 units, 5 with bathroom. 80€–90€ single ($92–$104) without bathroom, 105€ ($121) single with bathroom; 108€ ($124) double without bathroom, 130€ ($150) double with bathroom. Extra person 35% more. Rates include continental breakfast. No credit cards. Bus: D, 11, 36, or 37. **Amenities:** Concierge; tour desk; car-rental desk; limited room service (breakfast); babysitting. *In room:* No phone.

WORTH A SPLURGE

Hotel Mario's *Finds* In a traditional Old Florence atmosphere, Mario Noce and his enthusiastic staff run a first-rate ship. Your room might have a wrought-iron headboard and massive reproduction antique armoire and look out onto a peaceful garden, or it might feature reproduction Byzantine icons; the amenities include fresh flowers and fruit. The beamed ceilings in the common areas date from the 17th century, although the building became a hotel only in 1872. I'd award Mario's two stars if not for its location—it's a bit far from the Duomo nerve center. Hefty discounts during off-season months (as low as the lowest rates listed below) de-splurge this lovely choice.

Via Faenza 89 (1st floor; near Via Cennini), 50123 Firenze. © **055-216-801**. Fax 055-212-039. www.hotel marios.com. 16 units. 90€–120€ ($104–$138) single; 90€–160€ ($104–$184) double; 100€–180€ ($115–$207) triple. Rates include continental breakfast. AE, DC, MC, V. Valet parking 20€–25€ ($23–$29). Bus: A,

1, 4, 7, 10, 11, 12, 25, 31, 32, 33, 36, or 37. **Amenities:** Concierge; tour desk, limited room service (breakfast); babysitting; laundry service; dry cleaning; nonsmoking rooms. *In room:* A/C, TV, hair dryer, safe.

Hotel Silla ⭐ On a shaded riverside piazza, this 15th-century palazzo's second-floor patio terrace is one of the city's nicest breakfast settings. (In winter, there's a breakfast salon with chandeliers and oil paintings.) The Silla's most recent renovation—mostly new furniture and fresh paint—was in 2001. Many rooms overlook the Arno and, when winter strips the leaves off the front trees, the spire of Santa Croce on the opposite bank. Every room is unique—some with beamed ceilings and parquet floors, others with stylish furnishings. The attention to detail and friendly skilled staff should make this hotel better known; word-of-mouth keeps it regularly full in pricey Florence despite its refreshing low profile.

Via dei Renai 5 (on Piazza Demidoff, east of Ponte delle Grazie), 50125 Firenze. © 055-234 2888. Fax 055-234-1437. www.hotelsilla.it. 35 units. 125€ ($144) single; 170€ ($196) double; 220€ ($253) triple. Rates include buffet breakfast. Ask about off-season discounts. AE, DC, MC, V. Parking in hotel garage 16€ ($18). Often closes late Nov to late Dec. Bus: C, D, 12, 13, or 23. **Amenities:** Concierge; tour desk; limited room service; nonsmoking rooms. *In room:* A/C, TV, minibar, hair dryer, safe.

Hotel Torre Guelfa ⭐⭐ *(Finds)* Giancarlo and Sabina Avuri run one of the most atmospheric hotels in Florence. The first of many reasons to stay here is to drink in the breathtaking 360-degree view from the 13th-century tower, Florence's tallest privately owned tower. Although you're just steps from the Ponte Vecchio, you'll want to put sightseeing on hold and linger in your canopied iron bed. So many people request room no. 15, with a huge private terrace and a view similar to the tower's, they've had to tack 10€ ($12) onto the price. Follow the strains of classical music to the salon, whose vaulted ceilings and lofty proportions hark back to the palazzo's 14th-century origins.

The owners' newest hotel endeavor is the 18th-century **Palazzo Castiglione,** Via del Giglio 8 (© **055-214-886;** fax 055-274-0521; pal.cast@flashnet.it), with four doubles (170€/$196) and two suites (200€/$230). Also ask them about their new Tuscan hideaway, the **Villa Rosa di Boscorotondo,** on a winding road through the woods outside Panzano (© **055-852-577;** fax 055-856-0835; www.resortvillarosa.com), a 35km (22-mile) drive from Florence in the heart of the Chianti, where the 15 doubles are 90€ to 130€ ($104–$150).

Borgo SS. Apostoli 8 (between Via de' Tornabuoni and Via Por Santa Maria), 50123 Firenze. © 055-239-6338. Fax 055-239-8577. www.hoteltorreguelfa.com. 22 units. 90€–110€ ($104–$127) single; 155€–210€ ($178–$242) double; 190€–250€ ($219–$288) triple or junior suite. Rates include continental breakfast. AE, DC, MC, V. Parking in nearby garage 25€ ($29). Bus: B, 6, 11, 36, or 37. **Amenities:** Concierge; tour desk; car-rental desk; courtesy car (for airport); limited room service; babysitting; laundry service; dry cleaning. *In room:* A/C, TV (in all but 6 1st-floor doubles), minibar, hair dryer.

Pensione Burchianti ⭐⭐ *(Finds)* In 2002, rising rents forced the kindly owner of this venerable inn (established in the 19th c.) to move up the block into the *piano nobile* (the floor on which the family resided) of a neighboring 15th-century palazzo. She definitely traded up. Incredible frescoes dating from the 17th century and later decorate every ceiling (save that of one tiny single) and many of the walls. (Actually, virtually all of the walls are so painted but have been whitewashed over; the hotel uncovers these gems as the budget allows.) When I visited, workers were painting the trim, wiping clean the terra-cotta tile floors, and installing inlaid marble bathrooms and period-style furnishings. This promises to become one of the most sought-after little hotels in Florence.

Via del Giglio 8 (off Via Panzani), 50123 Firenze. © 055-212-796. Fax 055-272-9727. www.hotelburchianti. com. 10 units. 70€–120€ ($81–$138) single; 120€–200€ ($138–$230) double; 160€–230€ ($184–$265) junior suite. Rates include continental breakfast. No credit cards. Parking in garage next door about 25€

($29). Bus: A, 1, 4, 6, 7, 10, 11, 12, 14, 17, 22, 23, 25, 32, 33, 36, or 37. **Amenities:** Concierge; tour desk; car-rental desk; limited room service (breakfast); babysitting; laundry service; dry cleaning. *In room:* A/C, TV (on request), minibar (in suite), hair dryer, safe.

3 Great Deals on Dining

Florence is small, so you can turn in any direction and stumble across a good restaurant. There are concentrations of excellent eateries in the neighborhood around (especially west of) Santa Croce, as well as in the Oltrarno across the river. A few good budget options cluster on the piazza just northeast of the Mercato Centrale, north of San Lorenzo in the midst of the outdoor leather market.

Almost all the places below specialize in *cucina povera* or *cucina rustica,* based on the region's rustic and hearty cuisine. Despite its simplicity, Florentine cooking remains one of the most renowned in Italy for its well-balanced flavors and high-caliber ingredients.

Slabs of crusty bread are used for *crostini,* spread with chicken-liver pâté as the favorite Florentine antipasto. Hearty Tuscan peasant soups often take the place of pasta, especially *ribollita* (a stewlike *minestra* of twice-boiled cabbage, beans, and bread) or *pappa al pomodoro* (a similarly thick soup made from tomatoes and drizzled with olive oil).

Look for *pasta fatta in casa* (the homemade pasta of the day) such as the typically Tuscan *pappardelle,* thick flat noodles, usually *al cinghiale* (with a wild boar sauce) or with a simple tomato sauce. Your *contorno* (side dish) of vegetables will likely be the classic *fagioli all'uccelletto* (cannellini beans smothered in a sauce of tomatoes and rosemary or sage); sometimes *fagioli* are served plain, dressed only with extra-virgin olive oil.

Grilled meats are a specialty, the jewel being *bistecca alla Fiorentina,* an inch-thick charcoal-broiled steak on the bone: It's usually the most expensive item on the menu but can easily be shared by two. Florentines also sing the praises of *trippa alla Fiorentina,* but cow's stomach served with onions and tomatoes isn't for everyone.

Although you won't swoon over the unfussy and limited desserts, the puddinglike *tiramisù* made with whipped mascarpone cheese is almost always great, if not actually of Florentine origin. And you can't go wrong with *gelato,* a denser, richer, and more heavenly cousin to ice cream (see the box "Get Thee to a *Gelateria,*" p. 450).

Tuscany's most famous red **wines** are from the designated area known as Chianti between Florence and Siena. You might be pleasantly surprised by the far less expensive *vino della casa* (house wine). Either a full bottle is brought to the table—you'll be charged *al consumo,* according to the amount consumed—or you're served by the quarter or half carafe, as you request.

⌜Tips⌝ Restaurant Hours

Almost all restaurants (and stores and offices for that matter) close *per ferie* (for vacation) at some point in July or August for 2 to 6 weeks, so call ahead during those months. Many restaurants also close at some point over the Christmas and New Year's holidays. A good majority of restaurants serve Sunday lunch but close for Sunday dinner and all day Monday: These meals might need a little advance planning.

Value   Getting the Best Deal on Dining

- Choose a casual eatery where you'll feel comfortable ordering just one course (more easily done at lunch)—although whether a modest pasta dish will satisfy your appetite might be another matter. You won't get the heaping portions commonplace in many American restaurants serving Italian food.
- If the weather is nice, grab a *panino* (sandwich) to go, and choose a different piazza every day for lunch and a lesson on neighborhood life.
- Consider the *menù turistico*, a potential bargain, but first ask about what's included—the selection is often limited and one of the courses is probably a vegetable side dish.
- Try the local *vino della casa* (table wine) instead of a finer bottled wine.
- Round off your dinner with dessert elsewhere: Order an ice cream to go at a neighborhood *gelateria* and stroll the city's side streets.

Italian **meals** consist of three primary courses: the *antipasto* (appetizer), a *primo* (first course, usually a pasta or soup), and a *secondo* (the main course or meat or fish)—to which you must add a separate *contorno* if you want a side of veggies. You're expected to order at least two courses, if not all three.

Note: For details on dining in Italy, see the introduction to "Great Deals on Dining" in chapter 21, "Rome & Environs."

BETWEEN THE DUOMO & THE ARNO

Caffè Caruso *(Kids)* ITALIAN   On a quiet side street between Via Por Santa Maria and the Uffizi, a block from the Ponte Vecchio, this family-run caffè serves a variety of inexpensive hot dishes in what amounts to an expanded bar/*tavola calda* (small cafeteria). It's busy with locals at lunch, but the continuous hours promise less commotion if your appetite is flexible (however, the variety diminishes after the lunch crush). Choose from the display of four or five pastas, a few roasted meats (chicken, pork, roast beef), a dozen pizzas, or lots of vegetable side dishes (making this place great for light eaters and vegetarians). It isn't fancy, but the prices are rock-bottom for this area.

Via Lambertesca 16r (off Via Por Santa Maria). © 055-281-940. *Primi* 4.50€–5.50€ ($5–$6); *secondi* 5€–7€ ($6–$8); pizza and soda 8€ ($7). AE, MC, V. Mon–Sat 8am–6pm. Bus: B.

Caffè Italiano *(★)* ITALIAN   Umberto Montano, the young owner of this handsome caffè, has created an early-1900s ambience in the second-floor dining room and offers a delicious lunch to standing-room-only crowds (come early). The delicate but full-flavored soups, mixed platter of salamis and cheeses, and unusual variety of vegetable *sformati* (terrines) top the list of choices, or you can order one of a dozen oversize salads. Stop by in the afternoon for dessert: Made on the premises by a talented pastry chef, the choices go perfectly with the exclusive blend of African coffees.

Via Condotta 56r (off Via dei Calzaiuoli). © 055-291-082. *Primi* 5.50€ ($6); *secondi* and salads 6€–9€ ($7–$10). No credit cards. Daily 12:30–3pm and 8–10pm. Bar winter daily 7:30am–1am; summer daily to 8pm. Bus: A.

Le Mossacce ⭐ *Value* ITALIAN   Delicious, cheap, abundant, fast home cooking: This tiny *osteria,* filled with lunching businesspeople, farmers in from the hills, locals who've been coming since 1942, and a few knowledgeable tourists, is authentic to the bone. The waiters hate breaking out the printed menu, preferring to rattle off a list of Florentine faves like *ribollita, spaghetti alle vongole, crespelle,* and *lasagne al forno.* Unlike in many cheap joints catering to locals, the *secondi* are pretty good. You could try the *spezzatino* (goulashy beef stew) or a well-cooked, and for once cheap, *bistecca alla Fiorentina,* but I put my money on the excellent *involtini* (thin slices of beef wrapped tightly around a bread stuffing and artichoke hearts, then cooked to juiciness in tomato sauce).

Via del Proconsolo 55r (a block south of the Duomo). ℂ 055-294-361. Reservations suggested for dinner. *Primi* 4.20€–4.70€ ($4.85–$5.40); *secondi* 4.70€–14€ ($5.40–$16). AE, MC, V. Mon–Fri noon–2:30pm and 7–9:30pm. Bus: A, 14, or 23.

Ristorante Casa di Dante (da Pennello) ⭐ ITALIAN   This is one of Florence's oldest restaurants, housed since the late 1400s in a palazzo that once belonged to Renaissance artist Albertinelli (Cellini, Pontormo, and Andrea del Sarto used to dine here). Its claim to fame is the antipasto table, groaning under the day's changing array of two dozen appetizers. Prices vary, but expect to spend 5€ to 8€ ($6–$9) for a good sampling. The best of the *primi* are under the handwritten *lo chef consigla* ("the chef recommends") and *pasta fresa* ("handmade pasta") sections of the menu. They do a perfectly grilled pork chop and, if the antipasti and pasta have done you in, try one of several light omelets for your *secondi.*

Via Dante Alighieri 4r (between Via dei Calzaiuoli and Via del Proconsolo). ℂ **055-294-848**. Reservations suggested. *Primi* 5.50€–8€ ($6–$9); *secondi* 7.50€–13€ ($9–$15); *menù turistico* 20€ ($23) without wine. AE, DC, V. Tues–Sat noon–3pm and 7–10:30pm. Closed Aug. Bus: A, 14, or 23.

NEAR THE TRAIN STATION & THE MERCATO SAN LORENZO

Nerbone ⭐ ITALIAN   Nerbone has been stuffing stall owners and market patrons with excellent Florentine *cucina povera* ("poor people's food") since the Mercato Centrale opened in 1874. You can try *trippa alla Fiorentina, pappa al pomodoro,* or a plate piled with boiled potatoes and a single fat sausage. But the mainstay here is a *panino con bollito,* a boiled beef sandwich that's *bagnato* (dipped in the meat juices). Eat standing with the crowd of old men at the side counter, sipping glasses of wine or beer, or fight for one of the few tables against the wall.

In the Mercato Centrale, entrance on Via dell'Ariento, stand no. 292 (ground floor). ℂ **055-219-949**. All dishes 3.50€–7€ ($4.05–$8). No credit cards. Mon–Sat 7am–3pm. Bus: 1, 4, 6, 7, 10, 11, 12, 17, 25, 31, 32, or 33.

Palle d'Oro ITALIAN   Everyone seems to prefer this trattoria's front bar area, usually packed with the market's vendors and shoppers enjoying a quick lunch of pasta, soup, and vegetable side dishes. The prices aren't much higher for table service in the less-crowded back room, but the front area's advantage is that you don't have to order a full meal and can eat and run. Look for the house specialty pasta, *penne della casa* (with porcini mushrooms, prosciutto, and veal). For a cholesterol boost with a kick, try the homemade *gnocchi alla Gorgonzola.*

⸤*Tips*⸥ Bread & Cover Charge

When figuring your bill, don't forget that lovely Italian invention, *pane e coperto* (bread and cover charge), the 1€ to 10€ ($1.15–$12) you pay simply for the privilege of sitting down to a basket of bread.

Via Sant'Antonio 43–45r (near the Mercato Centrale). ☎ 055-288-383. Reservations suggested for dinner. *Primi* 3.10€–8€ ($3.55–$9.20); *secondi* 5.20€–15€ ($6–$17); fixed-price menu 13€ ($15) without wine. AE, DC, MC, V. Mon–Sat noon–2:30pm and 6:30–9:45pm. Closed Aug. Bus: A, 1, 4, 6, 7, 10, 11, 12, 14, 17, 25, 31, 32, or 33.

Trattoria Zà-Zà 🍴 ITALIAN   This place serves many of the food-market workers from across the way—people who appreciate the importance of using simple, fresh ingredients to make filling dishes. Ask to sit downstairs in the brick barrel vault of the old *cantina* if you want some privacy; if you want company (they make even the small wooden tables communal), sit upstairs, where you can gaze at the dozens of photos of the restaurant's more (but mostly less) famous patrons. The *antipasto caldo alla Zà-Zà* has a bit of everything. If you don't want *ravioli strascicati* (in creamy *ragù*), brace yourself for the *tris di minestre* (three soups: *ribollita, pappa al pomodoro,* and *fagioli con farro*). *Bocconcini di vitella alla casalinga con fagioli all'uccelletto* (veal nuggets with tomato-stewed beans) makes an excellent second course.

Piazza Mercato Centrale 26r. ☎ 055-215-411. www.trattoriazaza.it. Reservations recommended. *Primi* 5.30€–10€ ($6–$12); *secondi* 10€–18€ ($12–$21); *menù turistico* without wine 13€ ($15). AE, DC, MC, V. Mon–Sat noon–3pm and 7–11pm. Closed Aug. Bus: 1, 4, 6, 7, 10, 12, 17, 25, 31, 32, or 33.

AROUND SANTA CROCE

Il Pizzaiolo 🍴🍴 *(Kids)* PIZZERIA/TRATTORIA   Despite their considerable skill in the kitchen, Florentines just can't make a decent pizza. It takes a Neapolitan to do that, so business has been booming ever since Naples-born Carmine opened this pizzeria. Even with a reservation, you'll probably have to wait for a spot at a long, crowded, and noisy marble table. Save the pizza for a main dish; start instead with a Neapolitan first course like *fusilli c'a ricotta* (homemade pasta spirals in creamy tomato-and-ricotta sauce). Of the pizzas, you can't go wrong with a classic *margherita* (mozzarella, tomatoes, and fresh basil); or spice up your evening with a *pizza diavola,* topped with hot salami and olives.

Via de' Macci 113r (at the corner of Via Pietrapiana). ☎ 055-241-171. Reservations required for dinner. Pizza 4.50€–10€ ($5–$12); *primi* 6.50€–13€ ($7–$15); *secondi* 7.50€–13€ ($9–$15). No credit cards. Mon–Sat 12:30–3pm and 7:30pm–midnight. Closed Aug. Bus: B, C, 14, or 23.

Pizzeria I Ghibellini ITALIAN/PIZZERIA   With exposed brick walls and ceilings, curved archways inside, and umbrella-shaded tables on the picturesque piazzetta, I Ghibellini is a good bet year-round. Pizza is the draw, and there's a long list to make your choice difficult: Try the house specialty, pizza *alla Ghibellini* (prosciutto, mascarpone, and pork sausage). The many pastas include *penne alla boccalona,* whose tomato sauce with garlic and a pinch of hot pepper is just spicy enough.

Piazza San Pier Maggiore 8–10r (at the end of Borgo degli Albizi east from Via del Proconsolo). ☎ 055-214-424. Reservations suggested for dinner. Pizza and *primi* 4€–8€ ($4.60–$9); *secondi* 7€–16€ ($8–$18). AE, DC, MC, V. Thurs–Tues noon–4pm and 7pm–12:30am. Bus: A, C, 14, or 23.

Ristorante Acqua al 2 🍴 ITALIAN   Under a barrel-vaulted ceiling and dim sconce lights, diners sit elbow to elbow at tightly packed tables to sample this innovative restaurant's *assaggi* (tastings) courses. Acqua al 2 is proud of its almost cult status, attained through the success of its *assaggio di primi,* which offers you a sampling of five flavorful pastas or *risotti*. If you order the *assaggio* for two, you both just may have room left over for a grilled portobello mushroom "steak," one of the many veal dishes, or something more cross-cultural, like *couscous d'agnello* (lamb). They also offer *assaggi* of salads, cheese, and desserts. Tour companies

---

Moments **Get Thee to a *Gelateria***

Florence is a good spot for *gelato* (ice cream), with a number of great sources around town. The following are not only the best but also have the largest selections and are the most centrally located. Ask for a *cono* (cone) or *coppa* (cup) from 1€ to 6€ ($1.15–$7)—point and ask for as many flavors as can be squeezed in.

Of all the centrally located *gelaterie*, **Festival del Gelato,** Via del Corso 75r, just off Via dei Calzaiuoli (② 055-239-4386), has been the only serious contender to the premier Vivoli (see below), offering about 50 flavors along with pounding pop music and colorful neon. It's open Tuesday to Sunday: summer 8am to 1am and winter 11am to 1am.

Vivoli, Via Isole delle Stinche 7r, a block west of Piazza Santa Croce (② 055-292-334), is still the city's institution. Exactly how renowned is this bright *gelateria?* Taped to the wall is a postcard bearing only the address "Vivoli, Europa," yet it was successfully delivered to this world capital of ice cream. It's open Tuesday to Sunday 9am to 1am (closed Aug and Jan to early Feb).

One of the major advantages of the always crowded **Gelateria delle Carrozze,** Piazza del Pesce 3–5r (② 055-239-6810), is its location at the foot of the Ponte Vecchio—if you're coming off the bridge and about to head straight on to the Duomo, this *gelateria* is immediately off to your right on a small alley that forks off the main street. In summer it's open daily 11am to 1am; in winter, hours are Thursday to Tuesday 11am to 8pm.

---

have started bringing in tourists by the busload on occasion, but the crowd remains a good mix of locals and travelers.

Via della Vigna Vecchia 40r (at Via dell'Acqua). ② **055-284-170.** www.acquaal2.com. Reservations required. *Primi* 7€–8€ ($8–$9); *secondi* 7€–17€ ($8–$20); *assaggio* 8€ ($9) for pasta, 5€ ($6) for dessert. AE, MC, V. Daily 7:30pm–1am. Closed 1 week in Aug. Bus: A, 14, or 23.

Trattoria Cibreo ★★ TUSCAN This is the casual trattoria of celebrated chef-owner Fabio Picchi; its limited menu comes from the same creative kitchen that put on the map his premier and more than twice as expensive *ristorante* next door. The trattoria moved from its back-alley location to the main street in 1999, and this higher visibility has only made the lines longer. Picchi takes his inspiration from traditional Tuscan recipes, and the first thing you'll note is the absence of pasta. After you taste the velvety *passata di peperoni gialli* (yellow bell-pepper soup), you won't care much. The stuffed roast rabbit demands the same admiration. My only complaint: They rush you through your meal in an un-Italian fashion in order to free up tables. Enjoy your after-dinner espresso at the Caffè Cibreo across the way.

Via de' Macci 122r. ② **055-234-1100.** *Primi* 6€ ($7); *secondi* 13€ ($15). AE, DC, MC, V. Tues–Sat 1–2:30pm and 7–11:15pm. Closed July 26–Sept 6. Bus: A, C, or 14.

IN THE OLTRARNO

Bar Ricchi ITALIAN Don't miss this bar when spring arrives and tables appear on one of Florence's best piazzas. Its great, inexpensive lunch menu is available year-round. Four or five pastas are made up on order and, as an alternative to the usual entrees, try one of the super salads. In the evenings, it transforms into a full-fledged seafood restaurant (with a few fish-less dishes on hand for landlubbers).

Piazza Santo Spirito 9r. ① 055-215-864. *Primi* 4.15€ ($4.80) at lunch, 11€–16€ ($13–$18) at dinner; *secondi* 6.20€–7.75€ ($7–$9) at lunch, 5€–13€ ($6–$15) at dinner. AE, V. Mon–Sat noon–2:30pm and 7:30 11pm (bar open to 1am). Bus: D, 6, 11, 36, or 37.

Borgo Antico *(Kids* ITALIAN/PIZZERIA   In the spirit of the Oltrarno's Left Bank atmosphere, the Borgo Antico is a relaxed spot where you can order as little or as much as you want and enjoy it among a mix of visitors and Florentines. The scene inside is always buzzing, but from April to September tables are set out where the million-dollar view of Brunelleschi's church is free. There are a dozen great pizzas and a number of combination super salads. Specialties of the day get equally creative (and expensive!). It's often hectic—if you get the hint they'd like your table, you'd do well not to linger.

Piazza Santo Spirito 6r. ① 055-210-437. Reservations suggested for dinner. Pizza 6€ ($7); *primi* 6€ or 15€ ($7 or $17); *secondi* 10€–22€ ($12–$25). AE, MC, V. Daily 12:45–2:30pm and 7:45pm–midnight. Bus: D, 6, 36, or 37.

Il Cantinone *(Kids* TUSCAN/ENOTECA   With tourists and large groups of locals all seated at long tables under the low arc of a brick ceiling, the convivial noise can sometimes get a bit overwhelming. But the feeling of having walked into a party is part of the charm of this place. The specialty is *crostoni:* slabs of peasant bread with toppings like prosciutto, tomatoes, mozzarella, and sausage—basically, a giant relative of the popular appetizer called *crostini.* The wine list is excellent—due perhaps to this locale's past incarnation as a chianti cellar—and the best way to sample it is through the *degustazione.* You and your companion get an antipasto, two *primi* (usually pasta dishes), and a *secondo,* which might be a tender and tasty wild boar stew. With each course you get a different wine, building from something like a light Orvieto *secco* through a well-chosen chianti to a brawny Brunello for the meat dish.

Via Santo Spirito 6r (off Piazza Santa Trinita). ① 055-218-898 or 055-225-955. *Primi* and *crostoni* 5.50€–8€ ($6–$9); *secondi* 6€–20€ ($7–$23). AE, MC, V. Tues–Sun 12:30–2:30pm and 7:30–10:30pm. Bus: D, 6, 11, 36, or 37.

Trattoria La Casalinga ITALIAN   A recent expansion sadly removed the last wisps of Renaissance aura from La Casalinga, replacing it with a crowded, almost cafeteria-like feeling—but the home cooking of its name is still some of the most genuine in town. The *ribollita* is thick, the *ravioli al sugo di coniglio* (in a rabbit sauce) rich, and the *pasta della nonna* (short, hollow pasta in a sauce of tomatoes, sausage, and onions) excellent. Don't expect anything fancy in the *secondi* department either, just solid favorites like *bollito misto* (a mix of boiled meats with green sauce), *trippa alla Fiorentina,* and *galletto ruspante al forno* (half a young oven-baked chicken). The starving artists and local artisans have been all but driven out by the tourist hordes, but if you want to stuff yourself on huge portions of Oltrarno workman's food, this is the place to come.

Via Michelozzi 9r (between Via Maggio and Piazza Santo Spirito). ① 055-267-9243. *Primi* 3.50€–4€ ($4.05–$4.60); *secondi* 5€–10€ ($6–$12). Mon–Sat noon–2:30pm and 7–10pm. AE, DC, MC, V. Bus: D, 6, 11, 36, or 37.

LUNCH FOR LESS

Lunch is your chance to eat informally, well, and for little, saving your appetite and euros for a special dinner. The traditional cheap lunch will be *panini*—fresh and crusty sandwiches. Most of the bars in the center of town now offer glass cases of point-and-order salads and pastas (about 3€/$3.45) to be eaten standing in the bar area.

Alimentari Orizi SANDWICH BAR At this small *alimentari* (grocery store), Signor Orizi offers a choice of crusty rolls and breads and quality meats and cheeses to be sliced and arranged as you like (now with ketchup, mayonnaise, and mustard). There's a bar and half a dozen stools, but if the sun is shining you can ask for your creation *da portare via* (to take away) and find a piazza bench with a view (Piazza della Repubblica to the east or Piazza Santa Maria Novella to the west). The new coffee machine and fresh pastries make this a good breakfast option.

Via Parione 19r (off Via de' Tornabuoni). ℂ 055-214-067. Sandwiches 2.50€–5€ ($2.90–$6). AE, MC, V. Mon–Fri 8am–3pm and 5–8pm; Sat 8am–8pm. Closed Aug 1–15. Bus: A, B, 6, 11, 36, or 37.

Cantinetta del Verrazzano 🎯 *Value* WINE BAR Owned by the Castello di Verrazzano, one of Chianti's best-known wine-producing estates, this wood-paneled *cantinetta* with a full-service bar/*pasticceria* and seating area helped spawn a revival of stylish wine bars as convenient spots for fast-food breaks. It promises a delicious self-service lunch or snack of focaccia, plain or studded with peas, rosemary, onions, or olives; buy it hot by the slice or as *farcite* (sandwiches filled with prosciutto, arugula, cheese, or tuna). Try a glass of their full-bodied chianti to make this the perfect respite. Platters of Tuscan cold cuts and aged cheeses are also available.

Via dei Tavolini 18–20r (off Via dei Calzaiuoli). ℂ 055-268-590. Focaccia sandwiches 95€–2.85€ ($1.10–$3.25); glass of wine 1.30€–8€ ($1.50–$9). AE, DC, MC, V. Mon–Sat 8am–9pm. Bus: A, 14, or 23.

PICNICKING

There are few supermarkets in Florence. Cold cuts are sold at a *salumeria*, which also sells cheese, although for a wide selection or for yogurt you'll have to find a *latteria*. Vegetables and fruit can be found at a produce stand and store called a *fruttivendolo* or *orto e verdura* and often at a small *alimentari*, the closest thing to a neighborhood grocery store. For bread to put all that between, visit a *forno*, which, along with a *pasticceria*, can supply you with dessert. And for a bottle of wine, search out a shop selling *vino e olio*. **Via dei Neri**, beginning at Via de' Benci near Piazza Santa Croce and stretching over toward Piazza della Signoria, has a handful of small specialty food shops and is a good area for picnic pickings.

For all your picnic needs under one roof, visit the colorful late-19th-century **Mercato Centrale**, a block-long two-story marketplace that's a must-see—and not just for food shoppers. Open Monday to Friday 7am to 2pm, Saturday 7am to 2pm and 4 to 8pm, it's at Via dell'Ariento 12, looming in the midst of the open-air San Lorenzo Market, on the block between Via San Antonino and Via Panicale.

If you're just as happy to have someone else make up your sandwiches, seek out **Forno Sartoni**, Via dei Cerchi 34r, with fresh rolls and breads in front; the crowd in back waits for pizza bubbling from the oven, sold by the slice and weighed by the ounce—the average slice is 1.50€ ($1.70). It also makes up a limited but delicious selection of fresh sandwiches (with prosciutto, mozzarella, and arugula, for example), at about 2€ ($2.30) on freshly baked focaccia. Sartoni is predominantly a baker, so for a greater variety of quality cold cuts, stop by **Alimentari Orizi** (see listing above) and have the combination *panino* of your choice made up as you wait.

The **Boboli Gardens,** on the opposite side of the Arno (see "Parks & Gardens," p. 470) behind the Palazzo Pitti, is without a doubt the best green picnic spot in town. A grand amphitheater behind the palazzo provides historic seating, but it's worth the hike to the top where the grounds join with those of the Fortezza Belvedere for the breathtaking view. If you'd just as soon pull up a park bench in the *centro storico,* a number of the city's most beautiful piazzas have stone benches and open spaces: **Piazza Santa Croce** comes to mind as much for its church's three-toned marble facade as for its proximity to Vivoli's for a post-lunch *gelato.* **Piazza Santa Maria Novella** offers stone benches and the only plots of grass in any of the city's squares. If summer has set in, there are two shady piazzas with benches: **Piazza Massimo d'Azeglio** east of the Accademia near the synagogue; and lovely **Piazza Santo Spirito** in the Oltrarno near the Palazzo Pitti.

WORTH A SPLURGE

Il Latini (★★ (*Value* ITALIAN   Uncle Narcisso Latini opened this cheap locals' eatin' joint in 1950, though it now gets as many tourists as Florentines. Arrive at 7:30pm to get in the crowd massed at the door, for even with a reservation you'll have to wait as they skillfully fit parties together at communal tables. In fact, getting thrown together with strangers and sharing a common meal is part of the fun here. Under hundreds of hanging prosciutto ham hocks, the waiters try their hardest to keep a menu away from you and serve instead a filling, traditional set meal with bottomless wine. This usually kicks off with *ribollita* and *pappa al pomodoro* or *penne strascicate* (in a *ragù* mixed with cream). If everyone agrees on the *arrosto misto,* you can get a table-filling platter heaped high with assorted roast meats. Finish off with a round of *cantucci con vin santo* for everyone.

Via Palchetti 6r (off Via della Vigna Nuova). © 055-210-916. Reservations strongly recommended. *Primi* 6€ ($7); *secondi* 8€–16€ ($9–$18); unofficial fixed-price full meal with limitless wine 30€–35€ ($35–$40). AE, DC, MC, V. Tues–Sun 12:30–2:30pm and 7:30–10:30pm. Closed 15 days in Aug and Dec 24–Jan 6. Bus: A, B, 6, 11, 36, or 37.

Trattoria Antellesi (★★ ITALIAN   This is an attractive spot in a converted Renaissance palazzo. As their restaurant empire expands, the young Florence/ Arizona combination of chef Enrico and manager/sommelier Janice Verrecchia are around less these days, but their skilled staff guarantees a lovely Tuscan dining experience. Never without a smile, they'll talk you through a memorable dinner that should start with their signature antipasto of pecorino cheese and pears. Follow with *crespelle alla Fiorentina* (crepes stuffed with ricotta and spinach and baked) or *spaghetti alla chiantigiana* (pasta with Chianti-marinated beef cooked in tomato sauce). This is the spot to try *bistecca alla Fiorentina*— and one of the excellent moderately priced red wines.

Via Faenza 9r (near the Medici Chapels). © **055-216-990.** Reservations required. *Primi* 6.50€–7.50€ ($7–$9); *secondi* 10€–13€ ($12–$15). AE, DC, MC, V. Mon–Sat noon–2:30pm and 7–10:30pm. Bus: A, 1, 4, 10, 11, 12, 25, 31, 32, 33, 36, or 37.

4 Seeing the Sights

Seeing all of Florence in a short time requires organization, so the first thing you should do is ask at your hotel or stop by a tourist office for an up-to-the-minute listing of museum hours. Establishments (stores, churches, and so on) close for long lunch breaks, and some museums close for the day at 2pm or sooner (remember that the last entrance is at least 30 min. and sometimes as much as 45–60 min. before closing). In addition, many museums are closed on Monday.

Florence

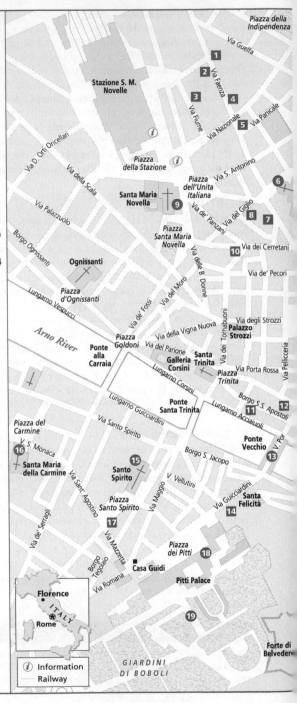

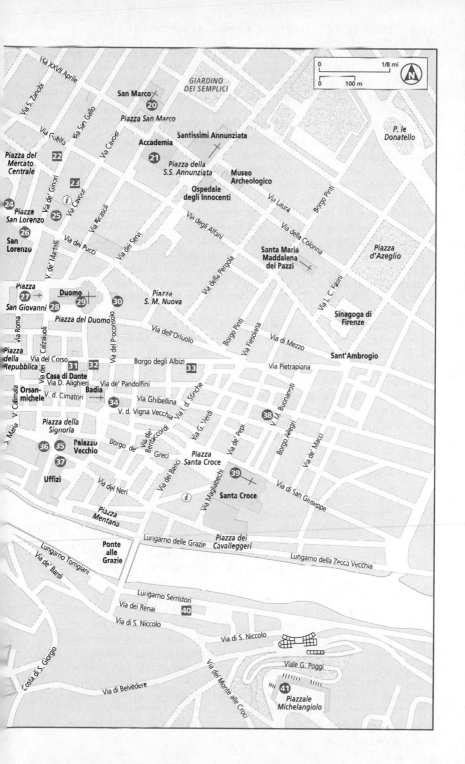

0 1/8 mi
0 100 m

Via XXVII Aprile

Via S. Zanobi

Via San Gallo

Via Guelfa

San Marco
20
Piazza San Marco

GIARDINO
DEI SEMPLICI

P. le
Donatello

Via Cavour

Santissimi Annunziata
Accademia
21
Piazza della
S.S. Annunziata

Museo
Archeologico

Piazza del
Mercato
Centrale
22

Via de' Ginori

23

Via Cavour

Ospedale
degli Innocenti

Via Laura

Borgo Pinti

Via Ricasoli

24
Piazza
San Lorenzo
25

Via degli Alfani

Via della Colonna

San
Lorenzo
26

Via dei Pucci

Via dei Servi

Via della Pergola

Santa Maria
Maddalena
dei Pazzi

Piazza
d'Azeglio

V. de' Martelli

Via L. C. Farini

Piazza
27
San Giovanni
28

Duomo
29
30

Piazza
S. M. Nuova

Sinagoga di
Firenze

Via Roma

Via dei Calzaiuoli

Piazza del Duomo

Via del Proconsolo

Via dell'Oriuolo

Borgo Pinti

Via Fiesolana

Via di Mezzo

Piazza
della
Repubblica

Via del Corso

Borgo degli Albizi
33

Via Pietrapiana

Sant'Ambrogio

V. Calimala

31 **32**
Casa di Dante
Via D. Alighieri
Orsan-
michele
Badia
V. d. Cimatori

Via de' Pandolfini

Via Ghibellina
34
V. d. Vigna Vecchia

Via I. d' Sanche

38
V.M. Buonarroti

S. Maria

Piazza della
Signoria

36 **35**
Palazzo
Vecchio
37

Borgo de'
Greci

Via de'
Bentaccordi

Via G. Verdi

Via de' Pepi

Piazza
Santa Croce

Borgo Allegri

Via de' Macci

Uffizi

Via del Neri

Via de' Benci

Via Magliabechi

39
Santa Croce

Via di San Giuseppe

Piazza
Mentana

Ponte
alle
Grazie

Lungarno delle Grazie

Piazza dei
Cavalleggeri

Lungarno della Zecca Vecchia

Lungarno Torrigiani

Via de' Bardi

Lungarno Serristori
Via dei Renai
40
Via di S. Niccolo

Via di S. Niccolo

Costa di S. Giorgio

Via di Belvedere

Via del Monte alle Croci

Viale G. Poggi

41
Piazzale
Michelangiolo

Over the past few years, summer hours have been extended more and more, and recently this phenomenon has been spreading into the off season as well. Churches and the markets are good alternatives for afternoon touring time, because they usually remain open until 7pm. You won't waste precious hours if you plan in advance and purchase tickets to the top museums ahead of time (see the "Reserving Tickets for the Uffizi & Other Museums" box, p. 459).

Battistero di San Giovanni (Baptistery) ✦✦✦ In front of the Duomo is this octagonal baptistery, dedicated to the city's patron saint, San Giovanni (John the Baptist). The highlight of the Romanesque baptistery, built in the 11th and 12th centuries (most likely on the site of an ancient Roman villa or temple), is Lorenzo Ghiberti's bronze exterior doors called the **Gates of Paradise** ✦✦✦, on the side facing the Duomo (east). The doors were so dubbed by Michelangelo who, upon first seeing them, declared, "These doors are fit to stand at the gates of Paradise." Ten bronze panels depict Old Testament scenes, such as the story of Adam and Eve, in stunning three-dimensional relief. Ghiberti labored over his masterpiece from 1425 to 1452, dying 3 years later. The originals have been removed for restoration and those completed are now permanently displayed in the Museo dell'Opera del Duomo (p. 458); all those exposed here are convincing replicas.

The doors at the north side of the baptistery were Ghiberti's warm-up to the gates and the work that won him, at 23, the original commission. The contest held in 1401 for the design of these doors is considered by some art historians to be the event that launched the Renaissance, since Ghiberti's submission (a bronze panel of *Abraham Sacrificing Isaac* now in the Bargello; p. 462) was chosen based on its dynamism and naturalism—very different from the more static and stylized Gothic panels submitted by other, more well-known sculptor contestants. The doors on the south side, through which you enter, are a good

---

⟨*Value* Getting the Best Deal on Sightseeing

- Save yourself hours of standing in line—call the new agency handling advance-purchase tickets to the Uffizi, the Accademia, and many other museums (see the box "Reserving Tickets for the Uffizi & Other Museums," below).
- Take advantage of the free 40-minute guided tours of the Duomo, led by English-speaking volunteers. They sit at a desk to your right as you enter.
- Florence is the perfect city for walking and simply drinking in the ambience. Its *centro storico* is practically car-free, its maze of streets is lined with imposing Renaissance palazzi and tower residences redolent of the Middle Ages, and its window-shopping opportunities range from the most stylish contemporary boutiques to the goldsmiths of the Ponte Vecchio and the stalls of the San Lorenzo outdoor leather market.
- In summer, check with the tourist office about extended evening hours for museums—these are usually Florence's best-kept secret, so you could avoid the daytime crowds and get the museums nearly to yourself.

example of that older Gothic style, courtesy of Andrea Pisano in 1336. Inside, the **vault** of the baptistery is decorated with magnificent gilded mosaics from the 1200s, dominated by an 8m (26-ft.) figure of Christ—they're the most important Byzantine mosaics in Florence.

Piazza di San Giovanni (adjacent to Piazza del Duomo). ⓒ 055-230-2885. www.operaduomo.firenze.it. Admission 3€ ($3.45), free for children under 6. Mon–Sat noon–7pm; Sun 8:30am–2pm. Last admission 30 min. before closing. Bus: A, 1, 6, 7, 10, 11, 14, 17, 22, 23, 36, or 37.

Campanile di Giotto (Giotto's Bell Tower) ★★
Beginning in 1334, Giotto spent his last 3 years designing the Duomo's Gothic campanile (bell tower), and it's still referred to as Giotto's Tower even though he completed only the first two levels (the next architect had to overhaul the faulty design—Giotto was an astoundingly great painter but a lousy engineer). Clad in the same three colors of marble as the cathedral, it's 6m (20 ft.) shorter than the dome. The bas-reliefs on its slender exterior are copies of works by Andrea Pisano, Francesco Talenti, Luca della Robbia, and Maso di Banco (the originals are in the Museo dell'Opera del Duomo; see below). The view from the top is about equal to that from the Duomo; there are, however, a mere 414 steps here. You'll find fewer crowds on this rooftop, but you won't get the chance to get close to Brunelleschi's architectural masterpiece. Both offer remarkable cityscapes over a beautifully preserved historical center that was never permitted to be built higher than the cathedral's dome.

Piazza del Duomo. ⓒ 055-230-2885. www.operaduomo.firenze.it. Admission 6€ ($7). Daily 8:30am–7:30pm. Last admission 30 min. before closing. Bus: A, 1, 6, 7, 10, 11, 14, 17, 22, 23, 36, or 37.

Duomo (Cathedral of Santa Maria del Fiore) ★★★
The red-tiled **dome** of Florence's magnificent Duomo has dominated the skyline for more than 5 centuries. At the time it was completed in 1434, it was the world's largest unsupported dome, meant to dwarf the structures of ancient Greece and Rome. In Renaissance style, it's a major architectural feat and was the high point of Filippo Brunelleschi's illustrious career. Brunelleschi had to invent many new winch-and-pulley systems to raise his ingenious dome, a brilliant piece of engineering constructed of two shells, both of which thin as they approach each other and the top. You can **climb** ★★★ 463 spiraling steps and clamber up between these two layers to the lantern at the summit for a spectacular panorama (you can enjoy a similar view from the campanile; see below). Entrance to the cupola stairs (there's no elevator) is from outside the church, on the south (bell tower) side.

The cathedral's **exterior** ★ of white-, red-, and green patterned marble (the colors of the Italian flag) is from Tuscan quarries. The modern facade (replacing the original) was added in the late 19th century when Florence briefly became the capital of the united Italy. The tricolor marble mosaic is an interesting contrast to the sienna-colored medieval fortresslike palazzi throughout the city. Although much of the **interior decoration** has been moved to the Museo dell'-Opera del Duomo (p. 458), the cathedral still boasts three stained-glass windows on the entrance wall by Lorenzo Ghiberti (sculptor of the bronze reliefs of the baptistery doors) next to Paolo Uccello's giant clock decorated with portraits of four prophets. In late 1995, an extensive restoration was finally completed on the colorful 16th-century frescoes covering the inside of the cupola and depicting the *Last Judgment*. They were begun by Giorgio Vasari and finished by his less talented student Federico Zuccari. When the restorers began their work, they discovered a surprise: A good portion of the work was executed not in true fresco but in tempera, which is much more delicate.

Beneath the Duomo's floor is the **Scavi della Cripta di Santa Reparata (crypt)**, the ruins of the Romanesque Santa Reparata cathedral, believed to have been founded here in the 5th century. It was continuously enlarged until it was done away with in 1296 to accommodate the present structure. Brunelleschi's tomb, discovered in 1972, is here. The entrance to the excavations is through a stairway near the front of the cathedral, to the right as you enter.

Note: Volunteers offer free tours of the cathedral Monday to Saturday 10am to 12:30pm and 3 to 5pm. Most speak English; if there are many of you and you want to confirm their availability, call © **055-271-0757** (Tues–Fri, mornings only). They can be found sitting at a table along the right (south) wall as you enter the Duomo; they expect no payment, but a nominal donation to the church is always appreciated.

Piazza del Duomo. © **055-230-2885**. www.operaduomo.firenze.it. Free admission to church; admission to Santa Reparata excavations 3€ ($3.45); admission to cupola 6€ ($7), free for children under 6. Church Mon–Wed and Fri 10am–5pm; Thurs 10am–3:30pm; 1st Sat of month 10am–3:30pm, other Sat 10am–4:45pm; Sun 1:30–4:45pm. Free tours of church every 40 min. daily 10:30am–noon and 3–4:20pm. Cupola Mon–Fri 8:30am–7pm; Sat 8:30am–5:40pm (1st Sat of month to 4pm). Last admission to cupola 40 min. before closing. Bus: A, 1, 6, 7, 10, 11, 14, 17, 22, 23, 36, or 37.

Museo dell'Opera del Duomo (Museum of the Duomo) ★★   Opened in 1891, and thoroughly renovated in 1998–2000, this museum behind the cathedral contains much of the art and furnishings that once embellished the Duomo. A bust of Brunelleschi at the entrance is a nod to the architect of the magnificent cupola (some of his original equipment and a death mask are housed upstairs), and over the door hang two glazed della Robbia terra cottas. In the second inner room to your left are sculptures from the old Gothic facade (destroyed in 1587 to make way for today's neo-Gothic facade), including work by the original architect, Arnolfo di Cambio, who was also responsible for the Palazzo Vecchio. Of the various statues, the most noteworthy are Donatello's weathered but noble *St. John* and Nanni di Banco's intriguing *San Luca.*

The museum's most important display is four of the original bronze panels from Ghiberti's **Gates of Paradise door** ★★ for the baptistery (the other six will appear after restoration), housed in the enclosed courtyard. On a landing of the stairs is one of Michelangelo's last *Pietà* sculptures, carved when the master was in his 80s and originally intended for his own tomb until he became so dissatisfied with it he attacked it with a hammer. He later let his students carry it away and finish off a few of the characters—they left the figure of Nicodemus untouched, it's said, because it was a self-portrait of Michelangelo.

The highlights of the center room upstairs are the enchanting twin white marble *cantorie* (choirs) from the 1430s by Donatello and Luca della Robbia. But don't miss the two Donatello statues: *Lo Zuccone (Pumpkin Head)* from Giotto's bell tower, and in a side room his haggard figure of *Mary Magdalene* (a late work in polychrome wood originally in the baptistery) near a priceless 14th- to 15th-century silver-gilt **altarpiece** with scenes from the life of St. John. In the next room are the original bas-reliefs that decorated the first two stories of the exterior of Giotto's campanile, followed by wooden model sand drawings for bits of the cathedral and the various competitions held over the ages to design its facade (not realized until the 19th c.).

Piazza del Duomo 9 (directly behind the dome end of the cathedral). © **055-230-2885**. www.operaduomo. firenze.it. Admission 6€ ($7), free for children under 6. Mon–Sat 9am–7:30pm; Sun 9am–1:40pm. Last admission 40 min. before closing. Bus: A, 1, 6, 7, 10, 11, 14, 17, 22, 23, 36, or 37.

THE TOP MUSEUMS

Galleria degli Uffizi (Uffizi Gallery) ★★★   The Uffizi is one of the world's most important art museums and should be the first stop in Florence for anyone interested in the Renaissance's rich heritage. Six centuries of artistic development are housed in this impressive Renaissance palazzo, built by Giorgio Vasari for Grand Duke Cosimo I de' Medici in 1560 to house the Tuscan Duchy's administrative offices (*uffizi* means "offices"). The collection, whose strong point is Florentine Renaissance art but includes major works by Flemish and Venetian masters, was amassed by the Medici and bequeathed to the people of Florence in 1737 in perpetuity by Anna Maria Ludovica, the last of the Medici line, who stipulated that the unmatched collection of masterworks could never leave Florence.

The gallery consists of 45 rooms where paintings are grouped into schools in chronological order, from the 13th to the 18th century—but as you wander, don't overlook the rich details of the building itself, including frescoed ceilings, inlaid marble floors, and tapestried corridors. The superb collection begins in room no. 2 with Giotto's *Maestà* ★★ (1310), one of the first paintings to make the transition from the Byzantine to the Renaissance style. Look for the differences between Giotto's work and his teacher Cimabue's *Maestà* (1280) nearby. Some of the best-known rooms are dedicated to 15th-century Florentine painting, the eve of the Renaissance. In room no. 7 are major works by Paolo Uccello, Masaccio, and Fra Angelico, and the only works by Piero della Francesca in Florence. As you proceed through room nos. 8 and 9, look for the elegant Madonnas of Filippo Lippi and Pollaiolo's delightful little panels that influenced Botticelli, whose masterworks are next.

For many, the Botticelli rooms (nos. 10–14) are the undisputed highlight. Arguably the most stunning are the recently restored *Primavera (The Allegory of Spring)* ★★, whose three graces form the principal focus; and *The Birth of Venus* ★★. Botticelli's *Adorazione dei Magi (Adoration of the Magi)* is interesting for the portraits of his Medici sponsors incorporated into the scene, as well as a self-portrait of the artist on the far right in yellow.

Other notable works are Leonardo da Vinci's unfinished *Adoration of the Magi* ★ and his famous *Annunciation* ★★★ in room no. 15, Lukas Cranach's *Adam and Eve* in Room no. 20, Michelangelo's circular *Doni Tondo* or *Sacra Famiglia (Holy Family; 1506)* ★★ in room no. 25, Raphael's *Madonna with the Goldfinch* in room no. 26, Titian's *Flora* ★ and *La Venere di Urbino (Venus of Urbino)* ★★ in room no. 28, Caravaggio's *Medusa* and *Baccus* ★★ in room no. 43, two **Rembrandt self-portraits** ★★ in room no. 44, and Canaletto's *Veduta del Palazzo Ducale di Venezia (View of the Ducal Palace in Venice)* in room no. 45.

Tips **Reserving Tickets for the Uffizi & Other Museums**

You can bypass the hours-long ticket line at the **Uffizi Galleries** by reserving a ticket and an entry time in advance. Call **Firenze Musei** at ① **055-294-883** (Mon–Fri 8:30am–7:30pm, Sat to 12:30pm) or visit **www.firenze musei.it**. Entry times can be booked more than a week in advance. You can also reserve for the **Accademia Gallery** (another interminable line, to see *David*), as well as the **Galleria Palatina** in the Pitti Palace, the **Bargello,** and several others. There is a 1.55€ ($1.80) fee—worth every penny—and you can pay by credit card.

The Uffizi

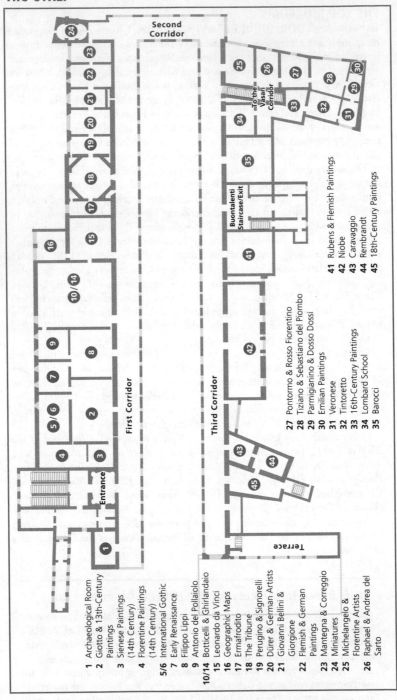

First Corridor

Second Corridor

Third Corridor

Terrace

Entrance

To the Vasari Corridor

Buontalenti Staircase/Exit

1 Archaeological Room
2 Giotto & 13th-Century Paintings
3 Sienese Paintings (14th Century)
4 Florentine Paintings (14th Century)
5/6 International Gothic
7 Early Renaissance
8 Filippo Lippi
9 Antonio del Pollaiolo
10/14 Botticelli & Ghirlandaio
15 Leonardo da Vinci
16 Geographic Maps
17 Ermafrodito
18 The Tribune
19 Perugino & Signorelli
20 Dürer & German Artists
21 Giovanni Bellini & Giorgione
22 Flemish & German Paintings
23 Mantegna & Correggio
24 Miniatures
25 Michelangelo & Florentine Artists
26 Raphael & Andrea del Sarto
27 Pontormo & Rosso Fiorentino
28 Tiziano & Sebastiano del Piombo
29 Parmigianino & Dosso Dossi
30 Emilian Paintings
31 Veronese
32 Tintoretto
33 16th-Century Paintings
34 Lombard School
35 Barocci
41 Rubens & Flemish Paintings
42 Niobe
43 Caravaggio
44 Rembrandt
45 18th-Century Paintings

Tips Seeing *David*

The wait to get in to see *David* can be up to an hour. Try getting to the Accademia before it opens in the morning; or get there an hour or 2 before closing time. Or see the box above, "Reserving Tickets for the Uffizi & Other Museums," to learn how to get advance tickets.

The **Corridoio Vasariano (Vasari Corridor)** is an aboveground "tunnel" running along the rooftops of the Ponte Vecchio buildings and connecting the Uffizi with Duke Cosimo I's residence in the Pitti Palace on the other side of the Arno. The corridor is lined with portraits and self-portraits by a stellar list of international masters, like Bronzino, Rubens, Rembrandt, and Ingres. Tours of the corridor are available Tuesday, Wednesday, and Friday through Saturday. Call © **055-265-4321** for required reservations.

Piazzale degli Uffizi 6 (off Piazza della Signoria). © **055-238-8651**; reserve tickets at © 055-294-883 or www.firenzemusei.it. Gallery info at www.uffizi.firenze.it. Admission 8.50€ ($10). Tues–Sun 8:15am–7pm. Ticket window closes 45 min. before museum. Bus: A, B, or 23.

Galleria dell'Accademia (Accademia Gallery) ★★★

The Accademia is home to Michelangelo's *David* ★★★ (1501–04), his (and perhaps the world's) greatest sculpture. Michelangelo was just 29 and only recently recognized for his promising talents following the creation of the *Pietà* in Rome's St. Peter's Basilica. Sculpted from a 5m (17-ft.) column of white Carrara marble that had been quarried for another sculptor's commission, worked on, then deemed unworkable and left abandoned, *David* looms in stark masculine perfection atop a 2m (6-ft.) marble stand beneath the rotunda of the main room built exclusively for its display in 1873, when it was moved here from Piazza della Signoria (a life size copy stands in its place; a 2nd copy lords it over Piazzale Michelangiolo). Nicknamed *Il Gigante (The Giant),* the statue is protected by a high transparent Plexiglas shield since a 1991 attack damaged its left foot.

The museum houses several other Michelangelos, including four never-finished *Prisoners* or *Slaves* ★★★ struggling to free themselves, commissioned for the tomb of Julius II; Michelangelo believed he could sense their very presence captured within the stone and worked to release their forms. They offer a fascinating insight into how he approached each block of marble that would yield his many masterpieces. The *Palestrina Pietà* here was long attributed to Michelangelo, but most scholars now believe it is the work of his students. The statue of *St. Matthew* ★ (begun in 1504) is, however, by the master. A number of 15th- and 16th-century Florentine artists are here; search out the *Madonna del Mare (Madonna of the Sea)* attributed to Botticelli or his student Filippino Lippi.

In September 2003, just in time for *David's* 500th birthday, Italy's cultural ministry began a controversial cleaning of the statue. Art conservators raged over whether the proposed methods were too abrasive, agreeing only that the process wasn't to hamper visitors' view of the statue. All work was scheduled for completion during press time, so by the time you visit, *David* should be clean once more. You can learn about the restoration by visiting the restoration's Italian-language website, **www.restaurodeldavid.it**.

Via Ricasoli 58–60. © **055-238-8609** or 055-238-8612. www.sbas.firenze.it/accademia. Reserve tickets at © 055-294-883 or www.firenzemusei.it. Admission 6.50€ ($7) adults, 3.25€ ($4) children. Tues–Sun 8:15am–6:50pm. Last admission 30 min. before closing. Bus: C, 1, 6, 7, 11, 17, 20, 25, 31, 32, or 33.

Museo della Casa Buonarroti ("Michelangelo's House" Museum)   This graceful and modest house, which Michelangelo bought late in life for his nephew (but never lived in himself), was turned into a museum by his heirs. Today it houses two of his most important early works: *Madonna alla Scala (Madonna on the Stairs)* and *Battaglia dei Centauri (Battle of the Centaurs)*, both sculpted in his teenage years, when he was still working in bas-relief and before he created the Rome *Pietà*. The museum also houses a sizable collection of his drawings and scale models, particularly the one for the facade of San Lorenzo that was never realized.

Via Ghibellina 70 (5 blocks east of the Bargello). ⓒ 055-241-752. www.casabuonarroti.it. Admission 6.50€ ($7). Wed–Mon 9:30am–2pm. Bus: A, 14, or 23.

Museo di San Marco 🌟🌟   Built in the 13th century, then enlarged and rebuilt by Michelozzo as a Dominican monastery in 1437, this small museum is a monument to the devotional work of the Florentine friar/painter Fra Angelico, one of the early masters of the 15th-century Renaissance. Directly to your right on entering is a room containing the largest collection of his painted panels and altarpieces in Florence. The **Chapter House** nearby is home to Fra Angelico's large and powerful *Crucifixion* 🌟 fresco. On the ground floor, visit the **Refectory,** decorated by Domenico Ghirlandaio (under whom a young Michelangelo apprenticed) with a realistic *Cenacolo (Last Supper)* 🌟, one of the most important of Florence's nine such *Last Suppers* found in ancient refectories (the tourist office has a listing of the others).

At the top of the stairs leading to the **monks' cells** on the second floor is Fra Angelico's masterpiece, the *Annunciation* 🌟🌟. Each of the 44 small dorm cells on this floor are decorated with frescoes from the life of Christ painted by Fra Angelico or one of his assistants under the master's direction from 1439 to 1445 and intended to aid in contemplation and prayer. The frescoes in cell nos. 1, 3, 6, and 9 are the most beautiful. Larger and more luxurious than the others, cell nos. 38 and 39 were designated for the occasional use of Cosimo il Vecchio, originator of the Medici dynasty who financed the enlargement of the monastery, and were frescoed with the aid of Angelico's student Benozzo Gozzoli.

At the end of the corridor is the **cell of Girolamo Savonarola,** which includes a stark portrait of the monastery's former prior by his convert and student, Fra Bartolomeo, as well as his sleeping chamber, his notebook, his rosary, and remnants of the clothes he wore at his execution. Savonarola was a religious fundamentalist who ruled Florence briefly at the head of a mob-rule theocracy, inspiring the people to participate in bonfires of their vanities—the burning of priceless artwork and precious hand-illuminated books. After the pope threatened to excommunicate the entire city for following the mad preacher, Savonarola was hanged and then burned at the stake in Piazza della Signoria for heresy in 1498, depicted here in an anonymous 16th-century painting.

Piazza San Marco 3 (north of the Duomo on Via Cavour). ⓒ 055-238-8608. Admission 4€ ($4.60) adults, 2€ ($2.30) children. Mon–Fri 8:30am–1:50pm; Sat–Sun 8:15am–7pm. Closed 1st, 3rd, and 5th Sun and 2nd and 4th Mon of each month. Bus: 1, 6, 7, 10, 11, 17, 25, 31, 32, or 33.

Museo Nazionale del Bargello (Bargello Museum) 🌟🌟   If the Accademia has whet your appetite for fine Renaissance sculpture, set aside time to see this national museum's outstanding collection—amazingly, the crowds are rarely bad. This daunting 1255 building originated as the seat of the city's *podestà* (chief magistrate) and served as a jail in Renaissance times. In the middle of the majestic courtyard plastered with the coats of arms of the *podestà* is a tank where

Special & Free Events

The **Maggio Musicale (Musical May;** www.maggiofiorentino.com) is Italy's oldest and most important music festival and one of Europe's most prestigious. Events take place at various indoor and outdoor locations, sometimes including the courtyard of the Pitti Palace and the final night's grand concert in Piazza della Signoria. Following in the revered footsteps of creative director Riccardo Muti, Principal Conductor Zubin Mehta often conducts Florence's Maggio Musicale Orchestra. World-class guest conductors and orchestras appear during the festival, which, despite its moniker, runs late April to June (but never later than the 1st few days of July). For schedules and ticket information, inquire at the tourist office.

June to August, the Roman amphitheater in nearby Fiesole comes alive with dance, music, and theater for the **Estate Fiesolana (Summer in Fiesole).** City bus no. 7 travels to Fiesole from the train station and Piazza del Duomo. July sees the annual **Florence Dance Festival** held in the beautiful amphitheater in the Cascine Park. A wide range of dance is performed, varying from classic to modern, with an emphasis on the latter. Again, check with the tourist office for details.

The highlight of June 24, the feast day of Florence's patron saint, **San Giovanni (St. John the Baptist),** is the **Calcio Storico,** a no-holds-barred cross between rugby, soccer, and wrestling with a major dose of ice-hockey attitude, played with a ball and few (if any) rules. Color-coded teams representing Florence's four original parishes/neighborhoods, clad in 16th-century costume, square off against one another in playoff games in dirt-covered Piazza Santa Croce, competing vigorously for that year's bragging rights and final prize: a golden-horned ox. The final *partita* is most worth seeing, often falling on or around June 24 (the feast day of San Giovanni). Fireworks light the sky that night, best viewed from along the north banks of the Arno east of the Ponte Vecchio. See the tourist office for ticket information for seats in the bleachers. No tickets are needed to view the equally dazzling procession in full historical regalia that wends its way through the cobblestone streets and piazzas before each match.

prisoners used to be tortured and executed; some hangings took place out the windows facing Via del Proconsolo for public viewing. Today Il Bargello, named for the 16th-century police chief *(bargello)* who ruled from here, houses three stories of treasures by Florentine Renaissance sculptors and a collection of Mannerist bronzes.

On the ground floor, the first room kicks off with some Michelangelos, including his "other" *David* (also known as *Apollo,* sculpted 30 years after the original), *Brutus,* and *Pitti Tondo,* depicting the Madonna teaching Jesus and St. John the Baptist to read. Take a look at his *Bacchus* ⭐⭐ (1497): It was done at age 22 and was the artist's first major work, effortlessly capturing the Roman god's drunken posture. Among the other important sculptures are Ammanati's *Leda and the Swan;* his student Giambologna's significant *Winged Mercury;* and several of

Donatello's works, including *St. George* ✦, *St. John the Baptist*, and sexually ambiguous *David* ✦✦, the first nude bronze statue to be done by an Italian artist since classical times. In another room are the two **bronze plaques** by Brunelleschi and Donatello's master, Ghiberti, made for the competition in 1401 to decide who would sculpt the baptistery's second set of doors—Ghiberti's won.

Via del Proconsolo 4 (at Via Ghibellina). © 055-238-8606. www.sbas.firenze.it. Reserve tickets at © 055-294-883 or www.firenzemusei.it. Admission 4€ ($4.60). Daily 8:30am–1:50pm. Closed 2nd and 4th Mon and 1st, 3rd, and 5th Sun of each month. Bus: A, 14, or 23.

Palazzo Medici-Riccardi & Cappella dei Magi (Chapel of the Magi) ✦

Built for Cosimo il Vecchio (founder of the Medici dynasty and grandfather of Lorenzo il Magnifico) by Brunelleschi's student Michelozzo, this austere palazzo was the Palazzo Medici from 1460 to 1540 (before Cosimo I moved to the Palazzo Vecchio, and later to the Palazzo Pitti across the Arno) and became the prototype for subsequent noble residences.

Only two rooms are open to the public, but they make your trip worthwhile: A staircase on the right of the courtyard brings you to the tiny **Cappella dei Magi (Chapel of the Magi)** ✦. The jewel-box chapel takes its name from the magnificent frescoes by Benozzo Gozzoli (completed in 1463), who worked several members of the Medici family and a self-portrait into his beautiful depictions of the Wise Men's journey through the Tuscan countryside. Look for Gozzoli's likeness on the far wall as you enter: A young man in the crowd wears a red hat inscribed OPUS BENOTII; he appears beneath the man wearing a light blue hat. The last Magi with the golden locks is a highly idealized version of a young Lorenzo il Magnifico. Upstairs is an elaborate 17th-century baroque gallery commissioned by the subsequent owners, the Riccardi; amid the gilt and stucco are Luca Giordano's frescoes masterfully illustrating the *Apotheosis of the Medici Dynasty.* The palazzo now houses government offices, although parts are frequently used for temporary exhibits.

Via Cavour 3 (north of Piazza del Duomo). © 055-276-0340. Admission 4€ ($4.60). Thurs–Tues 9am–7pm. Number of visitors limited; arrive early or call to book a time to visit. Bus: 1, 6, 7, 10, 11, 14, 17, or 23.

Palazzo Pitti (Pitti Palace) ✦✦✦

This rugged golden palazzo was begun in 1458 for wealthy textile merchant/banker Luca Pitti in his attempt to keep up with the Medici, so it's ironic that it was Medici descendants who bought the palace in 1549 (in what was then a rural area) as the official residence of Florence's rulers when they were still residing in the Palazzo Vecchio. They tripled its size, elaborately embellishing and gracing it with the **Giardini Boboli (Boboli Gardens)** that fan up the hill behind it, once the quarry from which the palazzo's *pietra dura* stone was taken (for more, see "Parks & Gardens," later in this chapter). Today the palace is home to seven museums, the largest collection of galleries in Florence under one roof.

The first-floor **Galleria Palatina** ✦✦ is the star attraction, 26 art-filled rooms home to one of the nation's finest collections of Italian Renaissance and baroque masters after the Uffizi. The art of the 16th century is the forte of the Palatina,

---

⟨*Value* Pitti Cumulative Ticket

An 11€ ($12) **cumulative ticket** will get you into the Galleria Palatina, Giardini Boboli, Galleria d'Arte Moderna, and Museo degli Argenti. Ask if the ticket is still available.

in particular that of Raphael and Titian. Of the outstanding Raphaels displayed, look for the much beloved *Madonna of the Chair* (the best-known of his many interpretations of the Madonna), *Maddalena Doni,* and veiled *La Fornarina (The Baker's Daughter)* ✦—in reality Raphael's Roman mistress—also known as *La Velata.* The museum's treasures include a large collection of works by Andrea del Sarto; Fra Bartolomeo's *San Marco* and his beautiful last work, *Descent from the Cross;* some superb works by Rubens, including *The Four Philosophers* ✦ and *Isabella Clara Eugenia;* canvases by Tintoretto and Veronese; and some stunning Titian portraits, including *Pope Julius II, The Man with the Gray Eyes,* and *The Music Concert.*

The restored **Appartamenti Monumentali** ✦ are gilded and chandeliered, with portraits of the Medicis and tapestries and furnishings from the days of the Medici and later the dukes of Lorraine who inherited the Medici empire. Upstairs, the **Galleria d'Arte Moderna** ✦ houses an interesting array of 19th century Italian Impressionists (called the *macchiaioli* school after its focus on the marks of paint laid on the canvas), said to have inspired the French and early 20th-century art. Visit the **Museo degli Argenti,** on the ground floor, for a look at 16 rooms filled with the priceless private treasures of the Medici (and not just silverware [*argenti*]). Other small museums that seem to open and close without notice are the **Museo della Porecellana** and the **Galleria del Costume.**

Piazza Pitti. **Galleria Palatina:** © 055-238-8614. www.sbas.firenze.it. Reserve tickets at © 055-294-883 or www.firenzemusei.it. Admission 6.50€ ($7) adults, 3.25€ ($4) children; includes admission to Appartamenti Reali and Museo delle Carrozze. Easter–Oct Tues–Sat 8:30am–10pm, Sun 8:30am–8pm; winter Tues–Sat 8:30am–6:50pm, Mon 8:30am–1:50pm. Last admission 45 min. before closing. **Galleria d'Arte Moderna:** © 055-238-8601. Admission 5€ ($6) adults, 2.50€ ($3) children; includes admission to Galleria del Costume. Daily 8:15am–1:50pm. Last admission 30 min. before closing. Closed 1st, 3rd, and 5th Mon and 2nd and 4th Sun of each month. **Galleria del Costume:** © 055-238-8713. Admission 5€ ($6) adults, 2.50€ ($3) children; includes admission to Galleria d'Arte Moderna. Daily 8:15am–1:50pm. Closed 1st, 3rd, and 5th Mon and 2nd and 4th Sun of each month. **Museo degli Argenti/Museo della Porcellana:** © 055-238-8709 or 055-238-8761. Admission 4€ ($4.60) adults, 2€ ($2.30) children; includes admission to both museums and the Giardino Boboli. Nov–Feb daily 8:15am–4:30pm; Mar daily 8:15am–5:30pm; Apr–May and Oct daily 8:15am–6:30pm; June–Sept daily 8:15am–7:30pm. Last admission 30 min. before closing. **Giardino Boboli:** © 055-265-1838. Admission 4€ ($4.60) adults, 2€ ($2.30) children; includes admission to Museo degli Argenti and Museo della Porcellana. Nov–Feb daily 8:15am–4:30pm; Mar daily 8:15am–5:30pm; Apr–May and Oct daily 8:15am–6:30pm; June–Sept daily 8:15am–7:30pm. Last admission 1 hr. before closing. Bus: D, 11, 36, or 37.

Palazzo Vecchio & Loggia dei Lanzi ✦ The elegant **Piazza della Signoria** has been the cultural, political, and social heart of the city since the 14th century. The square is dominated by an imposing rough-hewn fortress, the late-13th-century **Palazzo Vecchio (Old Palace)** ✦, with its severe Gothic style, replete with crenellations and battlements, highlighted by a 92m (308-ft.) campanile that was a supreme feat of engineering in its day. The palazzo served as Florence's city hall for many years (a role it fulfills again today) and then home to Duke Cosimo I de' Medici (that's Giambologna's bronze statue of him on horseback anchoring the middle of the piazza). He lived here for 10 years beginning in 1540, when much of the interior was remodeled in the elegant Renaissance style you see today, before moving to new accommodations in the Palazzo Pitti. You enter through the stunning main courtyard, with intricately carved columns and extraordinarily colorful 16th-century frescos by Vasari; the central focus is the fountain of a *Putto Holding a Dolphin,* a copy of Verrocchio's original (displayed upstairs).

The highlight of the interior is the massive first-floor **Salone dei Cinquecento (Hall of the Five Hundred),** whose rich frescoes by Vasari depict Florence's history; formerly the city's council chambers where the 500-man assembly once gathered, it's still used for government and civic functions. The statue of *The Genius of Victory* is by Michelangelo (1533–34); commissioned for the tomb of Pope Julius II, it was later acquired by the Medici. Upstairs, the richly decorated and frescoed salons, such as the private quarters of Cosimo's wife, Eleanora de Toledo, offer an intriguing glimpse into how the ruling class of Renaissance Florence lived.

A small disk in the ground in front of the piazza's enormous (and controversial) **Fontana dei Nettuno** (*Neptune Fountain;* by Ammanati and Giambologna, 1576) ⚡ marks the spot where religious fundamentalist Savonarola was hanged and then burned at the stake for heresy in 1498—a few years after inciting the original "bonfires of the vanities" while ruling the city during the Medici's temporary exile from Florence (even Botticelli got caught up in the fervor and is said to have tossed in a painting to fuel the flames). Flanking the life-size copy of Michelangelo's *David* (the original is in the Accademia) are copies of Donatello's *Judith and Holofernes* (original in the museum inside) and the *Marzocco* (original in the Bargello), the heraldic lion of Florence. Unfortunately, placed next to *David*'s anatomical perfection (across the stone steps) is Baccio Bandelli's *Heracles* (1534), which comes across looking like the "sack of melons" Cellini described it as.

On the south side of Piazza della Signoria is the 14th-century **Loggia dei Lanzi** ⚡⚡ (also called Loggia della Signoria or, after its designer, Loggia di Orcagna), Florence's captivating outdoor sculpture gallery. Benvenuto Cellini's rare 1545 work *Perseus* ⚡ was returned here in 2000 after a 4-year (and sorely needed) restoration, but in 2001 many of the other statues went under wooden scaffolds for restoration. One that has re-emerged is Giambologna's important *Rape of the Sabine,* a three-dimensional study in Mannerism. Also here, though currently covered, are *Hercules Slaying the Centaur* and *Duke Cosimo de' Medici.* The wallflower statues standing against the back are ancient Roman originals.

During summer evening hours, the following sections, normally closed, are open: the **Loeser Collections,** with paintings by Pietro Lorenzetti and Bronzino and sculptures by Tino di Camaino and Jacopo Sansovino; and, perhaps more fun, the outdoor **Balustrade** running around the roof behind the crenellations—it offers a unique panorama of the city and the piazza below.

Piazza della Signoria. ℂ 055-276-8465. www.museoragazzi.it. Admission 6€ ($7), 4.50€ ($5) age 18–25, 2€ ($2.30) children under 17, 14€ ($16) family ticket for 2 adults and 2 children, 16€ ($18) family ticket for 2 adults and 3 children, 8€ ($9) cumulative ticket for Palazzo Vecchio and Cappella Brancacci. Fri–Wed 9am–7pm; Thurs 9am–2pm. Bus: A, B, or 23.

CHURCHES

Basilica di San Lorenzo & Biblioteca Medicea-Laurenziana ⚡ The **San Lorenzo Basilica,** whose barren unfinished facade looms semi-hidden behind market stalls hawking soccer banners and synthetic-silk scarves, was the Medici's parish church as well as the resting place for most of the clan's early bigwigs, including Cosimo il Vecchio, founder of the family fortune and patron to Donatello (memorialized in front of the high altar with a plaque proclaiming him *pater patriae,* father of his country). Donatello's **two pulpits** ⚡, his final works, are worth a look, as is the **second chapel on the right,** with Rosso Fiorentino's *Marriage of the Virgin.* Designed by Brunelleschi and decorated by Donatello, the **Old Sacristy** ⚡, off the left transept, contains several important works.

The key feature of the main part of the church is the **Biblioteca Medicea-Laurenziana** ★★ (1524), a stunning bit of architecture by Michelangelo housing one of the world's largest and most valuable collections of manuscripts and codices, a few of which are on display. An elaborate Michelangelo stone staircase leads to it from the quiet cloister (off the left aisle), the one real reason to peek in here after a visit to the church next door. San Lorenzo is best known, however, for the **Cappelle Medicee (Medici Chapels)**, but you can't reach them from the church: You enter by going around through the Mercato San Lorenzo to the back of the church (see below).

Piazza San Lorenzo. ✆ **055-216-634**. Admission 2.50€ ($2.90). Church Mon–Sat 10am–5pm. Old Sacristy (usually) Sept–July Mon, Wed, and Fri–Sat 10–11:45am, Tues and Thurs 4–5:45pm. Laurentian Library Mon–Sat 9am–1pm. Bus: 1, 6, 7, 10, 11, 14, 17, or 23.

Basilica di Santa Croce & Cappella Pazzi (Pazzi Chapel) ★★★

Begun in 1294 by Arnolfo di Cambio, the original architect of the Duomo, the cavernous Santa Croce is the world's largest Franciscan church. The humble presence of St. Francis is best felt in the **two chapels** ★★ to the right of the main altar: Entirely covered with faded but important early 14th century frescoes by Giotto, they depict the life of the Assisi-born saint and scenes from the Bible. The Bardi is the more famous of the two, if only as a setting for a scene in the film *A Room with a View;* its deathbed scene of St. Francis is one of the church's most important frescoes. To the left of the main altar is a wooden crucifix by Donatello, whose portrayal of Christ was thought too provincial by early-15th-century standards (Brunelleschi once commented, "Why, Donatello, you've put a peasant on the Cross!").

Santa Croce is the final resting place for many of the most renowned figures of the Renaissance, the Westminster of Florence. More than **270 tombstones** pave the floor of the church, but attention deservedly goes to monumental tombs like that of Michelangelo, designed by Vasari, the first on the right as you enter; the three allegorical figures represent Painting, Architecture, and Sculpture. Dante's empty tomb is right next to him (he was exiled from Florence in 1302 for political reasons, and was buried in Ravenna where he died in 1321; there's also a statue dedicated to the Florentine-born poet on the left side of the steps leading into the church), while Machiavelli rests in the fourth. Galileo and Rossini, among others, were also laid to rest here. Off the right transept and through the sacristy and gift shop is one of Florence's most renowned **leather shops** ★★, where you can watch the artisans at work (great quality; not cheap).

The entrance to the tranquil **Cappella Pazzi** ★ (aka Museo dell'Opera di Santa Croce) is outside the church, to the right of the main doors. Commissioned in 1443 by Andrea de' Pazzi, a key rival of the Medici family, and designed by Filippo Brunelleschi, the chapel is a masterful example of early Renaissance architecture. The 12 glazed terra-cotta roundels of the Apostles are by Luca della Robbia, finished in 1452. Next door, the 13th-century **refectory** today serves as the church's museum, housing many works from the 13th to the 17th centuries, highlighted by one of Cimabue's finest works, the *Crucifixion,* which suffered serious damage in the 1966 flood of the Arno. Completely submerged when floodwaters rose to 1m (3 ft.) in the church and 1.5m (5 ft.) in the museum, it has now been restored and is displayed on an electric cable that will lift it out of reach of future harm.

Piazza Santa Croce. ✆ **055-244-619**. Admission 4€ ($4.60). Mon–Sat 9:30am–5:30pm; Sun 1–5:30pm. Bus: B, C, 12, 13, 14, or 23.

The Ponte Vecchio

Linking the north and south banks of the Arno River at its narrowest point, the **Ponte Vecchio (Old Bridge)** ✸✸ has long been a landmark symbol of the city. It was destroyed and rebuilt many times before the construction of the 1345 bridge you see today, designed by Taddeo Gaddi, and has stood lined with these same goldsmith's shops for centuries. Many of the exclusive gold and jewelry stores are owned by descendants of the 41 artisans set up on the bridge in the 16th century by Cosimo I de' Medici. No longer able to tolerate the smell from the bridge's old butchers and skin tanners on his trips to/from the new Medici residence in the Palazzo Pitti on the other side of the river, Cosimo evicted them and moved in the classier goldsmiths (upping the rent as well).

Florentines tirelessly recount the story of how in 1944 Hitler's retreating troops destroyed all the bridges crossing the Arno (all since reconstructed, often with the original material or at least according to archival designs) with the exception of the Ponte Vecchio. To compensate, they bombed both bridgeheads to block Allied access to it, resulting in the 1950s look of those buildings in the otherwise medieval areas of Via Por Santa Maria and Via Guicciardini.

Basilica di Santa Maria Novella ✸✸✸   Begun in 1246 and completed in 1360 (with a green-and-white marble facade, the top portion of which wasn't added until the 15th c.), this cavernous Gothic church was built to accommodate the masses who had come to hear the Word of God as delivered by the Dominicans. To educate the illiterate, they filled it with cycles of frescoes that are some of the most important in Florence—a claim not to be taken lightly.

In the center of the church hangs the newly restored *Crucifix* (1288–90) ✸✸, one of Giotto's earliest works. In the **Cappella Maggiore (Main Chapel)** ✸, behind the main altar and its bronze crucifix by Giambologna, Domenico Ghirlandaio created a fresco cycle supposedly depicting the *Lives of the Virgin and St. John the Baptist,* when in fact what we see is an illustration of daily life in Renaissance Florence. It's sprinkled with local personalities and snapshot vignettes, and a number of the faces belong to the Tornabuoni family, who commissioned the work. In the **Cappella Filippo Strozzi** ✸, to the right of this, are frescoes by Filippino Lippi (son of Filippo Lippi). To the extreme right is the **Cappella dei Bardi,** covered with 14th-century frescoes; its lunette frescoes of the *Madonna* are believed to be by Cimabue (ca. 1285). To the left of the **Cappella Maggiore** is the **Cappella Gondi** and a 15th-century crucifix by Brunelleschi, his only work in wood. And to the extreme left is the **Cappella Gaddi,** with frescoes by Nardo di Cione (1357); the altarpiece is by Nardo's brother, Orcagna. The chapel awaits the return of Giotto's 13th-century *Crucifix,* now at the restorer. Adjacent is the **sacristy,** worth a peek for the delicate glazed terra-cotta *lavabo* (sink where priests would wash their hands) by Giovanni della Robbia.

In the left aisle near the main entrance is Masaccio's 1428 *Trinity* ✸✸ fresco, the first painting in history to use perfect linear mathematical perspective.

Nearby is Brunelleschi's 15th century **pulpit** from which Galileo was denounced for his heretical theory that the Earth revolved around the sun.

If you're not yet frescoed out, exit the church and turn right to visit the **Museo di Santa Maria Novella,** which comprises the **Chiostro Verde (Green Cloister)** 𝓕 and its **Cappellone degli Spagnoli (Spanish Chapel)** 𝓕, whose captivating series of early Renaissance frescoes (recently restored) by Andrea de Bonaiuto glorify the history of the Dominican church. The chapel got its name from the nostalgic Eleanora de Toledo, wife of Cosimo de' Medici, who permitted her fellow Spaniards to be buried here. The Green Cloister took its name from the prevalent green tinge of Paolo Uccello's 15th-century fresco cycle of *Noah and the Flood* (ironically, themselves heavily damaged in the 1966 Arno flood).

Piazza Santa Maria Novella (just south of train station). ℂ 055-215-918 for church, 055-282-187 for museum. Admission to church 2.50€ ($2.90) adults, 1.50€ ($1.75) age 12–18; admission to museum 1.40€ ($1.60). Church Mon–Thurs and Sat 9:30am–5pm; Fri and Sun 1–5pm. Museum Sat and Mon–Thurs 9am–2pm; Sun 8am–1pm. Bus: A, 1, 4, 6, 7, 9, 10, 11, 12, 14, 17, 13, 25, 36, or 37.

Cappelle Medicee (Medici Chapels) 𝓕𝓕

On entering, you first pass through the massively overwrought marble wonderland of the **Cappella dei Principi (Chapel of the Princes),** added in 1604 but not finished until 1962. Your goal is the far more serene **New Sacristy** 𝓕, which contains the Michelangelo-designed tombs for Lorenzo II de' Medici, duke of Urbino and grandson of Lorenzo il Magnifico (with the sculptor's famous statues of female *Dawn* and male *Dusk*) on the left as you enter. On the opposite wall is the tomb of Giuliano de' Medici, duke of Nemours (with the more famous female *Night* and male *Day*). These two pairs are some of Michelangelo's greatest works (1521–34). Never overlooked by guides is that *Dawn* and *Night* bring to focus the virility with which Michelangelo sculpted females—only marginally less masculine and muscular than males, with breasts tacked on almost as if an afterthought. In the 1980s, a large number of charcoal sketches confirmed to be Michelangelo's were discovered by chance in a **room beneath the sacristy**—it's now open to the public on special request, so inquire at the admission booth.

Piazza Madonna (behind San Lorenzo, where Via Faenza and Via del Giglio meet). ℂ **055-238-8602.** Admission 6€ ($7). Reserve tickets at ℂ 055-294-883 or www.firenzemusei.it. Daily 8:15am–5pm. Closed 1st, 3rd, and 5th Mon and 2nd and 4th Sun of each month. Bus: A, 1, 4, 6, 7, 10, 11, 14, 17, 23, 36, or 37.

Santa Maria del Carmine and Cappella Brancacci 𝓕𝓕

This baroque church dates from the 18th century, when a fire ravaged the 13th-century structure built for the Carmelite nuns; the smoke damage was major, but the fire left the **Brancacci Chapel** miraculously intact. This was a miracle indeed, as the frescoes begun by Masolino in 1425 and continued by his brilliant student Masaccio were a watershed in the history of art—crucial to the development of the Renaissance. The frescoes were painstakingly restored in the 1980s, removing not only the dirt and grime but also the prudish fig leaves across Adam and Eve's privates. Now more clearly evident is the painters' unprecedented expression of emotion as well as their pioneering uses of perspective and chiaroscuro.

Masaccio's *Expulsion of Adam and Eve* (extreme upper-left corner) best illustrates anguish and shame hitherto unknown in painting, while *The Tribute Money* (just to its right) is a study in unprecedented perspective. The bulk of the frescoes depict the *Life of St. Peter* (who appears in a golden-orange mantle). The lower panels were finished by Filippino Lippi (son of the great Filippo Lippi) in 1480, 50 years after the premature death of the Tuscan-born Masaccio at 27; Lippi faithfully imitated the young master's style and technique. Even later masters like

---

Moments   Catching the Sunset from Piazzale Michelangiolo

If you've ever wondered where to go to see the view plastered across those jillions of postcards showing orange-and-pink sunsets over Florence, **Piazzale Michelangiolo** is it. The Technicolor palette of the touched-up postcards might be subdued somewhat by reality, but the breathtaking perspective of the Arno and the trellis of bridges crossing it, Florence's terra-cotta rooftops punctuated by slender bell towers and cupolas, and the hill town of Fiesole beyond is the same and has been for centuries. Caravans of tour buses overwhelm the parking lot—often obliterating the bronze copy of Michelangelo's *David* that gives the *piazzale* (large piazza) its name.

Hop on the no. 13 bus at the Ponte alla Grazie (the 1st bridge east of the Ponte Vecchio) for the 15-minute ride up in time for sunset. If you come a bit earlier, it's an easy walk to nearby **San Miniato al Monte** 🖈, south of the *piazzale* on Via del Monte alle Croci. Dating to the 11th century and the only truly Romanesque structure in town, it's one of Florence's most beloved churches—a favorite site for weddings and Christmas Eve Mass—and at about 4:30pm daily, when the remaining few Benedictine monks sing vespers in Gregorian chant, it's a magical place.

Leonardo da Vinci and Michelangelo came to see what they could learn from this mastery of unprecedented perspective, light, colors, and realism.

Piazza Santa Maria del Carmine (west of Piazza Santo Spirito in the Oltrarno). © 055-238-2195. Free admission to church. Brancacci chapel 4€ ($4.60); cumulative ticket with Palazzo Vecchio 8€ ($9). Mon–Sat 10am–5pm; Sun 1–5pm. Bus: D, 6, 11, 36, or 37.

PARKS & GARDENS

The expansive **Giardini Boboli (Boboli Gardens)** 🖈🖈 (© **055-265-1838**) begin behind the Pitti Palace and fan up to the star-shaped Fortezza Belvedere crowning the hill. Enter the gardens via the rear exit of the Pitti Palace if you're visiting the museum, or via the entrance to the left facing the palace if you're bypassing the museum. The green gardens, particularly beautiful in spring, were laid out in the 16th century by the great landscape artist Tribolo. They're filled with an amphitheater, graveled walks, grottoes, and antique and Renaissance statuary and are the best spot for a **picnic lunch.** The view from the fortress (1590–95) is stunning, but there's not much to see inside unless there's a special exhibit; ask at the tourist office or look for posters around town. The gardens open daily at 8:15am and close at 5:30pm in March, 6:30pm April to May, 7:30pm June to September, and 4:30pm November to February (closed the 1st and last Mon of the month). The last admission is 1 hour before closing. Admission is 4€ ($4.60) adults and 2€ ($2.30) children.

ORGANIZED TOURS

American Express (see "Fast Facts: Florence," earlier in this chapter) teams with venerable **CAF Tours,** Via Roma 4 (© **055-238-2790;** www.caftours.com), to offer two half-day bus tours of town (39€/$45) that include visits to Palazzo Pitti, the Duomo, and Piazzale Michelangiolo. They also offer several half-day walking tours of Florence for 23€ to 33€ ($26–$38); day trips to Pisa, Siena/ San Gimignano, the Chianti, Lucca, or Medici villas for 35€ to 69€ ($40–$79); and farther afield to Venice and Perugia/Assisi for 82€ to 105€ ($94–$121). You can book similar tours through most other travel agencies around town.

Walking Tours of Florence (© **055-264-5033** or 329-613-2730; www. artviva.com) offers 3-hour tours daily at 9:45am for 25€ ($29) adults, 20€ ($23) students under 26, 10€ ($12) kids from 6 to 12, free for kids under 6. Meet at Piazza Santa Stefano 2 (tucked just off Via Por Santa Maria; look for the striped church facade through an archway). They also provide private guides and honor custom requests (but give them a week's notice), and run a morning tour to hilltop Fiesole (49€/$56 includes cheese and wine tastings), as well as a 6-hour jaunt to nearby Siena and San Gimignano (75€/$86). Book all tours in advance.

Call **I Bike Italy** (© **772/388-0783** in the U.S.; www.ihikeitaly.com) to sign up for 1-day rides in the surrounding countryside: Fiesole year-round daily for 80€ ($70), or the Chianti Tuesday to Sunday from April 15 to November for 98€ ($85). They also offer a 2-day trip (Tues–Wed Apr 15–Nov) to Siena for 322€ ($280), which includes a walking tour to Fiesole. A shuttle bus picks you up at 9am at the Ponte delle Grazie and drives you to the outskirts of town, and an enjoyable lunch in a local trattoria is included (though not the return trip to Florence; stay in Siena or catch a public bus or train back). It might stretch your budget, but you should get out of this tourist-trodden stone city for a glimpse of the incomparable Tuscan countryside.

5 Shopping

In terms of good-value shopping, Florence is heaven. Good value usually means high prices, although moderate in comparison to what you might pay back home for similar made-in-Italy products. You'll find something for every taste and price range—whether it's a bargain-price wool sweater at the open-air market or a butter-soft leather jacket that'll blow your budget. Florentine merchants aren't born negotiators and few will encourage or appreciate bartering. A polite suggestion that you're looking for the best price will open (or shut) the door to bargaining. Buy a lot in the off season and pay with cash, and you might get lucky.

THE BEST BUYS

Alta moda fashion in Florence is alive and well on **Via de' Tornabuoni** and its elegant offshoot, **Via della Vigna Nuova,** where some of the high priests of Italian and international design and fashion share space with the occasional bank, which you might have to rob to afford any of their goods. But they make for great window-shopping.

Perpendicular to the top (north) end of Via de' Tornabuoni and of a different caliber entirely is the main drag of **Via dei Cerretani,** which changes into **Via dei Panzani** as it heads from the Duomo west to the train station. Some of the clothing and accessories stores can be rather tasteful, but most of it is mediocre casualwear thrown together with that inborn Florentine flair.

Between the Duomo and the river are the pedestrians-only **Via Roma** (which becomes **Via Por Santa Maria** after passing Piazza della Repubblica and La Rinascente department store before reaching the Ponte Vecchio) and the parallel **Via dei Calzaiuoli;** lined with fashionable jewelry and clothing stores (and the city's 2nd largest department store, Coin), they (and their offshoots) are the main shopping streets. Stores here are less high fashion and resultantly less high-priced than those on Via de' Tornabuoni. A *gelato* stop on your way to/from the Duomo is a guaranteed spirit-lifter. **Via del Corso** and (to a lesser degree) its extension east of Via del Proconsolo, **Borgo degli Albizi**, are also recommended, boasting historic palazzi as well as some approachable boutiques.

Leather is perhaps what Florence is most famous for. For quality and selection, no European city can hold a candle to Florentine quality, but prices in proper stores are higher than you might think. Expect to spend $200 to $300 for a leather jacket with moderate workmanship, detail, and skin quality. However, you can get some quite lovely ones in the **San Lorenzo Market** for as low as $100 if you bargain effectively. (Keep a sharp eye out for glitches in the quality, though. As for those jackets of stiff leather that are astoundingly cheap—if it says *"cavallo,"* it's horse leather.) The area around **Piazza Santa Croce** is the best place to shop for leather. Leather apparel might be beyond your budget, but consider the possibilities of small leather goods, from wallets, belts, and eyeglass cases to fashion accessories, all of which you'll find at the San Lorenzo Market or in myriad *pelletterie* (leather-goods shops) around town.

The Etruscans were known for their **gold** work 28 centuries ago, and the art lives on in Florence, itself known for its gold work since the Renaissance. Jewelry shops of all sizes and levels still abound. Dozens of exclusive gold stores have lined both sides of the pedestrian **Ponte Vecchio** since the days of the Medici. For prices that don't incorporate the high Ponte Vecchio rents, visit the shops lining Via Por Santa Maria or the few scattered along Via de' Tornabuoni. The gold is almost always 18 karat (ask them to point out the teensy obligatory stamp), and the variety of beautifully machine-crafted pieces (handmade is something of generations past) is great—think instant heirlooms. A number of stores specialize in high-quality costume jewelry *(bigiotteria),* where only the price tells you it's not the real thing.

MARKETS

There's nothing in Italy, and perhaps nothing in Europe, to compare with Florence's sprawling open-air **Mercato San Lorenzo** ✸✸✸ north of the Duomo. (To get there, head down the street called Borgo San Lorenzo.) Hundreds of awninged pushcarts crowd along the streets around the San Lorenzo church and the covered early-1900s Mercato Centrale, offering countless varieties of hand-knit and machine-made wool and mohair sweaters, as well as leather jackets, handbags, wallets, and gloves—not to mention the standard array of T-shirts and sweatshirts, wool and silk scarves, Florentine writing paper, and endless other souvenirs. This is one-stop souvenir shopping: Don't think those wooden Pinocchios and soccer T-shirts won't be an instant success back home.

The market stretches for blocks between Piazza San Lorenzo and past the Medici Chapels to Via Nazionale, along Via Canto de' Nelli and Via dell' Ariento, with stalls spilling onto side streets. The days of slashed prices and successful bargaining are getting harder. Convincing a pushcart salesperson (many of whom aren't even Florentine or Italian) to knock 10% off the price is a major accomplishment—and one that might happen only if you're paying in cash. Mid-March to October, the market operates daily 9am to 7pm; November to late March, it's closed Sunday and Monday, and closing hours depend on weather and what kind of day it has been in terms of customer turnout. Many vendors accept credit cards, but there goes the discount. Incidentally, in the heart of the outdoor market hides the **Mercato Centrale** ✸, Florence's covered food market, in a giant 19th-century structure of glass and steel that looks a bit like a railway station.

Much smaller is the outdoor **Mercato del Porcellino,** once known as the Straw Market and today more commonly known as the Mercato Nuovo (New Market), where a couple dozen pushcarts crowd beneath an arcade 2 blocks south of Piazza della Repubblica. Vendors offer mostly handbags, scarves, embroidered linen tablecloths, and miscellaneous souvenirs. The market is named for the bronze boar on the arcade's river (south) side—his snout has been worn smooth by the countless Florentines and visitors who have touched it for good luck. The market is open 9am to 6pm: daily mid-March to November 3, and Tuesday to Saturday the rest of the year.

6 Florence After Dark

The best source for entertainment happenings is the Italian-language monthly *Firenze Spettacolo* (1.55€/$1.80 per issue; or visit www.firenzespettacolo.it), offering comprehensive listings on dance, theater, and music events. The magazine is available at most newsstands. The monthly pamphlet *Informacittà* (in English and Italian) is available from any of the tourist offices, and includes a few coupons.

THE PERFORMING ARTS

One-stop shopping for most of the important venues in town and other major northern Tuscan theaters is the ticket agency **Box Office,** Via Alamanni 39 (© **055-210-804;** www.boxoffice.it), which tacks on a 10% commission. Your hotel can help you place the order by phone, although they have some English-speaking help on staff. In addition to tickets for year-round events of all genres, they handle the summertime Calcio in Costume folkloric festival and the Maggio Musicale (see the box "Special & Free Events," earlier in this chapter).

One of Italy's busiest stages, Florence's contemporary **Teatro Comunale,** Corso Italia 12 (© **055-213-535** or 055-211-158; www.maggiofiorentino.com), offers everything from symphonies to ballet to plays, opera, and concerts. Tickets are 11€ to 85€ ($13–$98), with prices escalating above 100€ ($115) for special or opening-night performances. The Teatro Comunale is the seat of the annual prestigious Maggio Musicale.

The excellent **Teatro Verdi,** Via Ghibellina 99 (© **055-212-320** or 055-239-6242; www.teatroverdifirenze.it), schedules regular dance and classical music events, often with top foreign performers, troupes, and orchestras, and the occasional European pop star. Tickets vary greatly—expect to pay 10€ to 30€ ($12–$35).

BARS, CLUBS & DISCOS

Nightlife isn't Florence's strongest suit, but it has improved considerably over the past few years. It's been in a state of flux lately, with many tried-and-true fixtures of Florence's nightlife scene suddenly closing or radically altering their style, so there's really no telling if these clubs will be around by the time this book hits the shelves! Cover charges (or "minimum consumption" charges) vary anywhere from 10€ to 16€ ($12–$18), depending on the night of the week, the act on stage, and whether you received an invite (usually handed out on the main streets during *passeggiata*).

The big hit of the last few years was **Universale,** Via Pisana 77r (© **055-221-122;** www.universalefirenze.it), housed in a converted 1940s cinema and successfully managing to draw everyone from folks in their early 20s to those pushing 50.

From 8pm it's a popular restaurant in the balcony and a pizzeria on the main floor. Around 11pm a live band takes the main floor stage for an hour or so, after which a DJ comes on board to conduct the disco until 3am.

Of the numerous Irish-style pubs, the **Fiddler's Elbow,** Piazza Santa Maria Novella 7r (© **055-215-056**), is always abuzz.

The professional habitués at upscale **Il Barretto,** Via del Parione 50, off Via de' Tornabuoni (© **055-239-4122**), enjoy the intimate ambience of a small piano bar that now offers a limited traditional Tuscan menu as well.

In the city center near Santa Croce, **Full-Up,** Via della Vigna Vecchia 25r (© **055-293-006**), is a long-enduring disco/piano bar.

Forever known as Yab Yum but reincarnated with a new attitude is **Yab,** Via Sassetti 5r (© **055-215-160**), a dance club for 20-somethings.

Space Electronic, Via Palazzuolo 37 (© **055-293-082**), draws a balanced combination of visitors and Italians—teenagers, students, and an under-30 crowd.

CAFFES

For more conventional caffès, check out the staid and historic bars lining Piazza della Repubblica, particularly **Gilli's** (© **055-213-896**), open Wednesday to Monday; or the early-1900s **Caffè Rivoire** (© **055-214-412**) on Piazza della Signoria, open Tuesday to Sunday.

Piazza Santo Spirito, hiding behind a tangle of back streets just blocks from the Pitti Palace, is the local youths' beloved piazza. Once a haven for drug users, the square has cleaned up its act but still claims enough edginess to be an authentic hangout for the alternative crowd. At the popular **Cabiria Caffè,** Piazza Santo Spirito 4r (© **055-215-732**), there's some seating inside, but the outdoor tables overlook the somber facade of the Santo Spirito church. It's open Monday and Wednesday to Saturday.

The **Caffè degli Artisti/Art Bar,** Via del Moro 4r (© **055-287-661**), also known as Caffè del Moro because of its street location (north of the Ponte alla Carraia), is a longtime favorite that attracts an interesting crowd. It's open Monday to Saturday.

The handsome **Caffè Cibreo,** across the street at Via Andrea del Verrochio 5r (© **055-234-5853**), first became known for its informal and inexpensive lunch and dinner menus, many of whose dishes came from the acclaimed kitchen across the way (dinner 7:30pm–midnight) or from nearby Il Pizzaiolo (see "Great Deals on Dining," earlier in this chapter). But this is also a lovely spot for an attractive older crowd who take their hot chocolate, tea blends, or coffee roasts seriously, or who want to people-watch before or after dining. Open daily.

GAY & LESBIAN BARS

Florence has one of Italy's largest gay communities, with a tradition of gay tolerance that goes back to the early days of the Renaissance and some of the Medicis' homosexual proclivities (Michelangelo didn't specialize in male nudes for nothing). The **Arci-Gay/Arci-Lesbica** office is at Via Manara 12 (© **055-671-298;** fax 055-624-1687; www.gay.it or www.azionegayelesbica.it), offering advice, psychological counseling, HIV testing, and information on the gay community and sponsoring gay-related events. It's open Monday to Saturday 4 to 8pm, with Monday theme nights and Wednesday evenings devoted to lesbians, and Saturday afternoons devoted to the younger set. It also publishes the free gay guide *Il Giglio Fuscia.*

Tabasco, Piazza Santa Cecilia 3, near Piazza della Signoria (© **055-213-000;** www.tabascogay.it), is Florence's (and Italy's) oldest gay dance club. The crowd is mostly men in their 20s and 30s. **Crisco,** Via San Egidio 43r, east of the Duomo (© **055-248-0580;** www.crisco.it), is Florence's leading gay bar. The crowd is international at the **Flamingo Bar** (formerly Santanassa), Via del Pandolfini 26, near Piazza Santa Croce (© **055-243-356).** Thursday to Saturday it's a mixed gay/lesbian party; the rest of the week, it's men only. Cover at these clubs varies but is usually under 10€ ($12), and includes the first drink.

7 Side Trips: Fiesole ⟨★⟨★ & the Tuscan Countryside ⟨★⟨★⟨★

FIESOLE & ITS VIEWS

Ancient **Fiesole** sits on a hill rising above Florence 8km (5 miles) north of town and a half-hour ride on **bus no. 7** leaving from Piazza San Marco. For centuries, families of means have fled the city's summer heat, plagues, and ennui and taken to the cool, cypress-studded environs of Fiesole; consequently, it came to be known for its magnificent hillside villas and million-dollar views. Many of the villas are now associated with some of the 27 American university programs in Florence, such as that of the famous art critic Bernard Berenson, who left his **Villa I Tatti** to Harvard University (today it's a post-doctorate center for studies of the Renaissance topics); or the Rockefellers' **Villa Le Balze,** bequeathed to Georgetown University.

The pre-Roman Etruscans had set up camp here in Faesulae centuries before the Romans established the riverside trading colony and army retirement camp of Fiornetina down below. Their presence is still felt at the important archaeological site called the **Teatro Romano** ★, a vast area of 2,000-year-old Etruscan and Roman ruins (© **055-591-187** or 055-59-477). Its highlight is the 3,000-seat 1st-century B.C. Roman theater used for the June-to-August Estate Fiesolana music, dance, and theater festival. The 6.20€ ($7) admission also gets you into the **Museo Civico (Museo Faesulanum),** whose finds prove the importance of Fiesole over Florence in their nascent days, and into the little **Museo Bardini** to the left of the archaeological site entrance, housing 13th- to 15th-century Florentine paintings. All are open Wednesday to Monday 9:30am to dusk.

The town center surrounds a large square dedicated to sculptor Mino da Fiesole (ca. 1430–84). Fronting the square is the Romanesque **Cattedrale di San Romolo,** from 1000 (although the columns inside are even older, pilfered from neighboring Roman structures) and much altered during the Renaissance. On the right side of the raised presbytery are several important sculptures and tombs carved in the 15th century by Mino da Fiesole. Also on the piazza is the 17th-century **Bishop's Palace** and **Santa Maria Primerana** church.

But Fiesole is all about its lofty **views** over the Arno Valley, and no one leaves without a look at the splendid panorama of Florence and the countryside. For a heart-stopping view (in every sense of the word), you'll have to hike up the very steep pedestrian-only Via di San Francesco west (left) out of the main square— not for the weak of heart. There's a church and museum at the top that follow temperamental hours, but halfway up lies a tiny park **terrace belvedere** ★★ and a view that never ends.

You'll have worked up an appetite by now, but Fiesole's abundant restaurants, bars, and caffès principally work as tourist traps. Sip a Campari or order a *gelato* while waiting for the bus back to reality, but don't plan on eating here.

THE TUSCAN COUNTRYSIDE

The Tuscan heartland is thought by many to be the most beautiful of Italy's 19 regions, its tall hills carpeted with grape vines and olive groves, topped by medieval hill towns, and the ridges between fields picked out by lines of marching cypress trees. Most of its towns are serviced by two bus lines: **SITA,** Via Santa Caterina da Siena 15r ((C) **800-373-760** in Italy or 055-47-821; www.sita-on-line.it), and **LAZZI,** Piazza Stazione 4–6 ((C) **055-363-041;** www.lazzi.it), whose depots are on either side of Florence's train station.

If you want to explore more of this region and its neighbor, say the Chianti district and towns such as Montalcino, Pienza, Perugia, Assisi, Spoleto, and Orvieto, see *Frommer's Tuscany & Umbria.*

SAN GIMIGNANO: THE MEDIEVAL MANHATTAN ✸✸✸

Unique among Italian hill towns, **San Gimignano** "of the Beautiful Towers" retains 14 of its original 72 medieval towers, bristling like stone skyscrapers above the countryside. It's one of Florence's favorite day trips and in high season appears overrun and devoid of magic unless you arrive early or stay late (or overnight). If the crowds dampen your spirits, take to the cool, quiet back streets that promise glimpses of the stunning Tuscan countryside.

Because this town is 55km (34 miles) southwest of Florence and 37km (23 miles) from Siena, plan on a full day and check out the **bus** schedules first (5.90€/ $7 from Florence to San Gimignano, with a change in Poggibonsi; about 5.20€/ $6 from Siena). You can also get a **train** to Poggibonsi and transfer to the bus. By **car,** take the Poggibonsi exit off the Firenze-Siena Autostrada or the SS2; follow the signs to San Gimignano from here, another 12km (7½ miles) away.

The **tourist office,** Piazza del Duomo 1 ((C) **0577-940-008;** fax 0577-940-903; www.sangimignano.com), is open daily, March to October 9am to 1pm and 3 to 7pm, and November to February 9am to 1pm and 2 to 6pm.

SEEING THE SIGHTS   There's only one **admission ticket,** costing 7.50€ ($9) adults, 5.50€ ($6) kids 6 to 18; it covers all the sights and museums in town, including the Collegiata and Torre Grossa (but *not* the privately run Torture Museum).

The heart of town is the ancient **Piazza della Cisterna.** Adjacent is **Piazza del Duomo,** constructed of bricks laid in a herringbone pattern, where you'll find the 12th-century **Collegiata church** ✸✸✸, famous for its wall-to-wall frescoes, including those by Ghirlandaio in the Cappella di Santa Fina. April to October, the church is open Monday to Friday 9:30am to 7:30pm, Saturday 9:30am to 5pm, and Sunday 1 to 5pm; November to March, hours are Monday to Saturday 9:30am to 12:30pm and 3 to 5pm and Sunday 1 to 5pm (closed Jan 27–Feb 28).

Also on the piazza is the **Museo Civico** ✸ ((C) **0577-940-340**), whose *Maestà* by Lippo Mimmi (1317) is the town's masterpiece. The museum is installed in the lower floors of the **Torre Grossa** ✸✸✸, finished in 1311 and the town's highest tower—it's like sitting on top of a flagpole with a view that'll make your heart skip a beat. In summer, they're open daily 9:30am to 7:30pm; November to February, hours are Tuesday to Sunday 9:30am to 1:30pm and 2:30 to 5pm.

WHERE TO STAY   The nicest place in town is **La Cisterna,** Piazza della Cisterna 24, 53037 San Gimignano ((C) **0577-940-328;** fax 0577-942-080; www.hotelcisterna.it), installed in 14th-century tower stumps and used as the setting for films including *Where Angels Fear to Tread* and *Tea with Mussolini.* Many of the doubles, all with TVs and phones, boast views reminding you that, while they're beautiful to view from a distance, Tuscany's hill towns are even more wonderful for the vantage points they offer. Doubles cost 90€ to 95€ ($104– $109) without a view and 105€ to 110€ ($121–$127) with a view. (Add a balcony and it's 115€–120€/$132–$138). Breakfast is included. The hotel is closed January 8 to March 8. Its excellent restaurant, Le Terrazze, crowded at lunch but more romantic at dinner, closes Tuesday and for lunch on Wednesday.

Rooms at the **Bel Soggiorno,** down the block at Via San Giovanni 91, 53037 San Gimignano (© **0577-940-375;** fax 0577-943-149; www.hotelbel soggiorno.it), are a bit more lackluster and modernized (with air-conditioning, TVs, and phones), but it, too, has a fine restaurant and costs 100€ ($115) per double. It closes in January or February for a month. Both La Cisterna and Bel Soggiorno accept American Express, Diners Club, MasterCard, and Visa.

WHERE TO DINE   San Gimignano has plenty of bad pizza joints catering to the tour-bus hordes, but there are a few quality small trattorie where locals actually go. My favorite is **Le Vecchie Mure,** a twisting walk down the first right turn off Via San Giovanni at Via Piandornella 15 (© **0577-940-270;** www.vecchie mura.it), serving hearty peasant cooking in 18th-century brick-vaulted stalls or on a sunny wall-top terrace in summer. It also rents two simple double rooms for 49€ ($56). It's open Wednesday to Monday 5 to 10pm (closed Dec–Feb) and accepts MasterCard and Visa.

If you're willing to splash out a bit more, head to **La Mangiatoia,** near Porta San Matteo at Via Mainardi 5 (© **0577-941-528**), a quirky place with some quite good inventive Tuscan cooking based on ancient Sangimignanese recipes and the chef's whimsy. However, stick to the unusual dishes, as the kitchen doesn't seem to try very hard at the more tried-and-true Italian and Tuscan standards. It's open Wednesday to Monday 12:30 to 2:30pm and 7:30 to 10pm (closed Nov 4– Dec 7) and accepts American Express, Diners Club, MasterCard, and Visa.

MEDIEVAL SIENA 𝒜𝒜𝒜

There's train service to **Siena**, 70km (43 miles) south of Florence in the southern confines of the Chianti area, but buses are more frequent and convenient, because they'll drop you off closer to the center rather than at the remote train station.

For those choosing to forego San Gimignano and head straight for Siena, **SITA buses** leave Florence direct for Siena about every 30 minutes. The bus journey follows a lovely route for the most part, takes about 75 minutes, and costs 6.50€ ($7) each way. Make sure you get on the *rapido* and not the local. You can also take the **train** from Florence in 1½ to 2 hours for 5.40€ ($6), but Siena's station is a 20-minute ride from town on the city bus. By **car,** take the Firenze-Siena Autostrada south from Florence in about 40 minutes (or the much prettier drive down the SS222 through the Chianti countryside in 1–1½ hr.).

The **tourist office** is at Piazza del Campo 56 (© **0577-280-551;** fax 0577/ 281-041; www.siena.turismo.toscana.it). From March 21 to November 11, it's open Monday through Friday from 8:30am to 1pm and 3 to 7pm, and Saturday from 8:30am to 1pm; winter hours are Monday through Saturday from 8:30am to 7:30pm.

SEEING THE SIGHTS   Start at Siena's unique shell-shaped central square, **Piazza del Campo** 𝒜𝒜𝒜, known as **Il Campo.** This piazza is where the famous Palio delle Contrade horse race takes place each year on July 2 and August 16. Here you'll find the **Palazzo Pubblico,** dominated by the 101m (335-ft.) **Torre del Mangia** 𝒜. A sprint up the tower's 505 steps is worth the workout for the unparalleled view of the Tuscan countryside. Admission to the tower is 5€ ($6) with a reservation and 5.50€ ($6) without. Combined admission to the Museo and the Torre del Mangia (see above) is 9€ ($10) with a reservation, 9.50€ ($11) without. The tower opens daily 10am to 7pm (to 4pm Nov–Mar 15). You

---

Siena's Cumulative Tickets

Siena has several **reduced-price cumulative ticket** combinations you can pick up at any of the participating museums or sites. There are also two combined tickets that are valid for 7 days and are seasonally based. From November to March 14, you can get a 13€ ($15), 7-day ticket that includes civic museums—**Museo Civico, Santa Maria della Scala,** and the contemporary art gallery in the **Palazzo delle Papesse** on Via di Città, *plus* the **Museo Dell' Opera Metropolitana, Baptistery,** and **Libreria Piccolomini.** From March 15 to October for 16€ ($18), the same ticket covers all sites listed above plus **S. Bernardino** and **Museo Diocesano.**

Additionally, some attractions sell their own cumulative tickets, like the one for admission to both the **Museo Civico** and **Torre del Mangia**—a savings of 4€ ($4.60) over separate admission tickets. (See the description of the Museo Civico, below.)

---

can reserve a time to climb the tower by calling ℭ **0577-41-169,** faxing 0577-226-265, or e-mailing moira@comune.siena.it.

The palazzo also houses the **Museo Civico** ✿✿✿, repository of the Sienese school of art's most significant works. In the Sala del Mappamondo (Globe Room, named after a long-lost map of the world) are a courtly fresco of a knight riding his horse called *Guidoriccio da Foligno* (1328), and a massive *Maestà* (1315), both by prominent local artist Simone Martini, a student of Duccio. The next room, the Sala di Pace (Hall of Peace), was the meeting place for the medieval Government of Nine and was decorated with the most important piece of secular art to survive from the Middle Ages, local master Ambrogio Lorenzetti's wrap-around fresco on the *Allegory of Good and Bad Government and Their Effects on the Town and Countryside* (1337–39), full of colorful and amusing details on life in 14th-century Siena. A decade later, Siena almost resembled the crumbling city depicted in the "Bad Government" side, when the 1448 Black Death decimated the town, killing over three-quarters of its citizens—including Ambrogio and his equally talented brother Pietro. Admission is 6€ ($7) adults with a reservation, 6.50€ ($7) adults without one; or 3.50€ for students and seniors over 65 with a reservation, 4€ ($4.60) without one. The museum is open daily 10am to 7pm (to 6:30pm Nov–Mar 15). Combined admission to the Museo and the Torre del Mangia (see above) is 9€ ($10) with a reservation, 9.50€ ($11) without.

Nearby on Piazza del Duomo are the stunning **Duomo** ✿✿✿ and its adjacent **Museo dell'Opera Metropolitana** (ℭ 0577-283-048; www.operaduomo.it). Siena's 12th-century black-and-white striped marble Duomo sits atop its highest hill. It's one of Italy's most beautiful and ambitious medieval churches. The entrance will dazzle you: The zebra-striped theme continues, with a priceless 14th- to 16th-century polychrome marble pavement of more than 50 panels only partially on view in the interests of conservation. The octagonal pulpit carved by Nicola Pisano in the 13th century and found in the left transept is one of the many masterpieces. The Duomo is open daily: November to March 15, 10am to 1pm and 2:30 to 5pm; and March 16 to October, 9am to 7:30pm. Admission is 5.50€ ($6), or buy the cumulative ticket (see box).

At an entrance in the Duomo's left aisle is the lavish **Libreria Piccolomini** ✿✿, built in the late 15th century by Cardinal Francesco Piccolomini (the future Pius III—for all of 18 days in office before he died) to house the great illuminated book collection of his uncle, Pope Pius II, the quintessential Renaissance man and humanist. (He commissioned the Sistine Chapel ceiling from Michelangelo.) The elder pontiff's life is the subject of 10 brilliantly colored giant frescoes, together the acknowledged masterpiece of Umbrian artist Pinturicchio (1509); he was assisted by his students, who included a talented young painter named Raphael. The library opens at 10am in winter and 9am in summer, and admission is 1.50€ ($1.75); or buy the cumulative ticket (see box, above).

In 1339, plans were launched to expand the extant cathedral to create Christendom's largest church outside Rome. But the 1348 bubonic plague arrived, money ran dry, and the unfinished structure to the right of the Duomo still stands. Called the Facciatone (Big Facade), it's incorporated into the church's **Museo dell'Opera** 🎨🎨, where masterworks from the Duomo have been brought over the centuries. Upstairs in a room by itself is the celebrated *Maestà* 🎨 (*Madonna Enthroned,* 1311), once the Duomo's altarpiece. One of the most important late medieval paintings, it's a complex work by Duccio di Buoninsegna, a student of Cimabue and native son of Siena. The museum is open daily 9am to 7:30pm (to 1:30pm Nov–Mar 14; to 6pm Oct). Admission is 5.50€ ($6), or buy the cumulative ticket (see box).

The **Pinacoteca Nazionale (Picture Gallery)** 🎨, Via San Pietro 29 (© 0577-281-161), celebrates the greatest Sienese artists (although the true masterpieces of Duccio, Simone Martini, and the Lorenzetti are in the Museo Civico and Museo dell'Opera Metropolitana, both above). The museum does shine, though, with works by 17th-century Mannerist master Beccafumi, including charcoal drawings for his panels in the center of the Duomo floor. It's open Monday 8:30am to 1:30pm, Tuesday to Saturday 8:15am to 7:15pm, and Sunday 8:15am to 1:15pm. Admission is 4€ ($4.60).

After checking out the above, spend your time meandering through the hilly side streets of Siena's large, traffic-free *centro storico.* All roads seem to slide into Il Campo. Instead, head up to the 16th-century **Fortezza Medicea** on Viale Maccari. The fort with a view has been transformed into the **Enoteca Italiana Permanente** 🎨 (© 0577-288-497), an official national repository of wine, a series of cellars installed under the 18th-century brick vaulting of the fortress, and the area's most evocative spot for a wine tasting of Chianti's (and Italy's) best labels. The cost is 2€ to 5€ ($2.30–$6) per glass, and it's open Monday noon to 8pm and Tuesday to Saturday noon to 1am.

WHERE TO STAY   The **Cannon d'Oro,** Via Montanini 28, 53100 Siena (© 0577-44-321; fax 0577-280-868; www.cannondoro.com), is one of Siena's best values, a converted 15th-century palazzo smack on the main drag (the continuation of Via Banchi di Sopra), with plenty of simple rooms—all with phones and some with stylish 19th-century furnishings—for 90€ ($104) double.

For much more charm just off Via Banchi di Sotto, a few steps from Il Campo, the **Piccola Etruria,** Via delle Donzelle 3, 53100 Siena (© 0577-288-088; fax 0577-288-461), is run with pride by the Fattorini family. The 13 doubles run only 75€ ($86), and all rooms have TV and phone. Both lodgings accept American Express, MasterCard, and Visa, and the Piccola Etruria takes Diners Club as well.

WHERE TO DINE   A Tuscan theme prevails at the popular **Antica Trattoria Papei,** Piazza del Mercato 6 (© 0577-280-894), run by three generations of the Papei family. This trattoria has been around a mere 50 years, and its convivial atmosphere, time-tested family specialties (the local specialty is game), and outdoor tables guarantee its future. *Primi* cost 6.20€ ($7) and *secondi* 6.50€ to 10€ ($7–$12). It's open Tuesday to Sunday noon to 3pm and 7 to 10:30pm, and accepts American Express, MasterCard, and Visa.

Tiny **La Torre,** Via Salicotto 7–9 (© 0577-287-548), serves delicious home-made pastas and simple Sienese *secondi* to packed tables under an undulating brick ceiling. It's still a local's joint, despite being just a few feet off the touristy Campo. *Primi* run 6€ to 8€ ($7–$9), second courses 9€ to 10€ ($10–$12). It's open Friday to Wednesday noon to 3pm and 7 to 10pm, and accepts only American Express.

THE WALLED CITY OF LUCCA ✹✹✹

A quintessential Tuscan hill town minus the hill (this picturesque olive-producing corner of Tuscany is uncustomarily flat), **Lucca** has so far mercifully been overlooked by the bus tourism that whizzes by en route to Pisa. That sits just fine with Lucca, a wealthy little city contained within its spectacular Renaissance walls where most residents get around by bike rather than car.

Both **trains** and quasi-hourly **LAZZI buses** from Florence take about 80 minutes and cost about 4.55€ ($5) each way. Pisa is just 22km (14 miles) southwest (76km/48 miles west of Florence) of Lucca and is connected by frequent train and bus service, costing about 2.05€ ($2.35) each way. By **car,** Lucca is 72km (45 miles) west of Florence on the A11 highway. To drive to Pisa from Lucca, take the SS12. **Tourist information** is just inside the city walls at Piazza Santa Maria 35 (© 0583-91-991; fax 0583-469-964; www.lucca.turismo.toscana.it), open daily 9am to 7pm (to 3pm Nov–Mar).

SEEING THE SIGHTS   An unhurried small-town atmosphere prevails within Lucca's protective swath of **walls** ✹✹✹. In summer, **rent bikes** from the tourist office (in winter, go to one of the private outfits on Piazza Santa Maria) for 2.10€ ($2.40) per hour to experience the tree-lined 4km (2½-mile) promenade—also a great jogging path—atop the walls. The 16th-century brick walls were Lucca's third set of ramparts and are Europe's best Renaissance defense walls. This makes Lucca Italy's most perfectly preserved walled city, a mélange of architecture from Roman to medieval to baroque (with neoclassical and Art Deco thrown in). Its straight, level streets follow the grid of ancient Roman roads in a town whose origins go back to the Etruscan days of 600 or 700 B.C. The store-lined **Via Fillungo** is the principal venue for the day's *passeggiata.*

A sophisticated silk and textile trade made this town famous throughout medieval Europe, evident today in the 60-some churches that once numbered far more (many are closed). The two standouts are the Duomo and San Michele in Foro, both exquisite examples of Pisan-Lucchese architecture.

The **Duomo (Cattedrale di San Martino)** ✹✹✹ (© 0583-957-068), Piazza San Martino, was begun in the 11th century and is known for its asymmetrical facade of multiple loggias with carved columns. Competing for historical importance inside is the revered *Volto Santo (Holy Visage of Christ),* said to have been carved by Nicodemus, a contemporary of Christ (art historians attribute it to a much later date). It arrived in Lucca in 782, attracting pilgrims from all over Europe, and was believed to have miraculous powers. One of Lucca's most celebrated monuments is the far more recent **marble tomb of Ilaria del Carretto** ✹✹ by Jacopo della Querica (1408), in the former sacristy on the right (admission 2€/$2.30 adults, 1.50€/$1.75 children 6–12). A beloved figure in local history, Ilaria was the young wife of an affluent lord of Lucca who hired the day's finest sculptor to immortalize her when she died in childbirth 2 years after she wed. The Duomo is open daily 9:30am to 5:45pm (to 6:45pm Sat).

Many people mistake **San Michele in Foro** ★★ (© **0583-48-459**), Piazza San Michele, for the cathedral because its facade is similar but bigger and it resides at the center of town, on the original site of the Roman Forum (hence its name). Begun in 1143, it's dedicated to Archangel Michael, who crowns its exquisite Romanesque facade composed of four tiers of patterned pillars, of which no two are alike. Things are less exuberant inside, where the only works of interest are a painting of Filippino Lippi on the far wall in the right transept and a glazed terra-cotta bas relief by Andrea (or perhaps his uncle, Luca) della Robbia. The church is open daily 7:30am to noon and 3 to 6pm. Admission is free.

All Lucca was a stage for **Giacomo Puccini,** born here in 1858 at Via Poggio 30, just down the block from San Michele in Foro, where both his father and his grandfather were organists and where young Giacomo sang as a choirboy.

WHERE TO STAY   The **Piccolo Hotel Puccini,** a block from San Michele in Foro at Via di Poggio 9, 55100 Lucca (© **0583-55-421;** fax 0583/53-487; www. hotelpuccini.com), is lovely even minus any real competition. The enthusiastic young owners have brightened up the place, giving it the charm so sorely needed. All 14 units have phones and TVs, with doubles at 80€ ($92).

If that's full, the next best bet inside the walls is **Hotel La Luna,** near the ancient Roman amphitheater at Corte Compangi 12, just off Via Fillungo, 55100 Lucca (© **0583-493-634;** fax 0583-490-021; www.hotellaluna.com), a family-run place with fairly pedestrian modern furnishings—save the 17th-century frescoes on the second floor of the hotel's older half—with doubles at 105€ ($121). Both hotels accept American Express, Diners Club, MasterCard, and Visa.

WHERE TO DINE   **Da Giulio,** Via delle Conce 47, north of Piazza San Donato (© **0583-55-948**), is the kind of ultra-Tuscan locale that draws urbane Florentines for a memorable lunch *alla toscana.* Save your appetite for the rustic specialties, from the thick *zuppa di farro,* made with elmer (a barleylike grain), to the roasted or grilled meats. *Primi* run 4.15€ to 5.15€ ($4.75–$6), and *secondi* are 7€ to 25€ ($8–$29). It's open Tuesday to Saturday (and the 3rd Sun of each month) noon to 2:30pm and 7:30 to 10:15pm (closed 10 days in Aug and 10 days around Christmas), and accepts American Express, Diners Club, MasterCard, and Visa.

Da Guido, Via C. Battisti 28, near Piazza Sant'Agostino (© **0583-476-219**), is a no-frills family-run place that in some ways is even more authentic than the polished Giulio's. With the TV locked into the sports channel and amiable Guido running a smooth operation, you can count on *primi* (with a homemade pasta or two usually making an appearance) costing less than 3.80€ ($4.35) and entrees under 5.15€ ($6). It's open Monday to Saturday noon to 2:30pm and 7:30 to 10pm (closed 3–4 weeks in Aug) and accepts American Express, MasterCard, and Visa.

PISA & ITS PERPENDICULARLY CHALLENGED TOWER ★★

The truth about **Pisa** is that unless you're determined to see for yourself whether that certain tower really leans (it does) and to have your photo taken as you pretend to hold it up, you might be disappointed with what's not a quaint little town but a bustling little city—one blessed, however, with a magnificent Campo dei Miracoli (Field of Miracles). This campo's centerpiece, the Leaning Tower, might very well be the most recognized human-built structure anywhere in the Western world.

Half-hourly **trains** from Florence take about an hour and cost 4.95€ ($6). Trains run once or twice an hour from Lucca in 18 to 30 minutes for 2.05€ ($2.35). By **car,** Pisa is 81km (50 miles) west of Florence on the Firenze-Pisa Autostrada. Pisa is also 22km (14 miles) south of Lucca on the SS12.

Although there's a small **tourist office** to the left as you exit the train station, the principal **tourist office** is at Via Cammeo 2 (© **050-560-464;** www.pisa. turismo.toscana.it), just outside the city walls and the Campo dei Miracoli. Hours are Monday to Saturday 9:30am to 7:30pm (to 5:30pm Nov–Apr). Sharing space with it is the **Consorzio Turistico di Pisa** (© **050-830-253;** www.traveleurope.it/ pisa.htm), providing free hotel reservation and information services.

SEEING THE SIGHTS   Medieval Pisa was, together with Genoa, Venice, and Amalfi, one of Italy's (and Europe's) four great maritime powers in the Mediterranean and beyond—until its port silted up. Then it turned much of its revenue and attention to the flourishing of the arts and architecture. Its greatest legacy remains in the spacious green **Campo dei Miracoli.** And in December 2001, the biggest reason—but least budget-friendly—reason for visiting Pisa reopened to the public for the first time since 1990. It took a decade to reverse the lean a total of about 40 centimeters (17 in.) to 4m (13 ft.).

The eight-story white-marble campanile known as the **Leaning Tower of Pisa** 😾😾😾 was begun in 1173 as the free-standing bell tower to the adjacent **Duomo** 😾😾 (begun in 1063), whose **Battistero** 😾😾 (begun in 1153; great Pisano pulpit inside) is the largest of its kind in Italy. It completes the trio of remarkable structures on the emerald-green piazza (itself a rarity for Italy's urban squares). They set the style for Pisa-Romanesque architecture in Italy, with its roots in the great Moorish architecture of Spain's Andalusia. (Pisa had strong trade connections with Spain and Africa.)

Many legends persist about the tower, which, if it were to stand upright, would measure about 54m (180 ft.) tall. (It curves slightly as it goes up, giving it a faint banana shape.) Various manners of ingenious engineering have been employed in the interests of arresting the continuing listing (about 1mm a year), like shoring up its foundation of water-soaked clay. Contrary to hearsay, it wasn't built leaning to prove the inordinate (and assuredly peculiar) talents of the architect; rather, it started to list at some time after the completion of the first three stories when it was discovered, too late, that the foundation wasn't rock solid. Construction was suspended for a century and then resumed, with completion in the late 14th century.

For several decades, a series of complicated and delicate projects has been directed at stabilizing the alluvial subsoil. In 1989, more than a million people climbed the tower, but by 1990 the lean was at about 4.5m (15 ft.) out of plumb and the tower was closed to the public. At 3:25pm on January 7, 1990, with the tower's bells sounding a death knell, the doors were closed indefinitely. In 1992, steel cables were belted around the base to prevent shear forces from ripping apart the masonry. In 1993, even the bells and their dangerous vibrations were silenced, and the same year a series of lead weights was rather unaesthetically stacked on the high side to try to correct the list. In 1997, engineers took a chance on excavating around the base again—this time carefully removing more than 70 tons of soil from the foundation of the high side so the tower could gradually tip back.

In December 2001, righted to its more stable lean of 1838 (when it was a mere 4m/13½ ft. off its center), the tower reopened to the public. Now, however, the number of visitors is strictly controlled via compulsory 35- to 40-minute guided tours—and a massive 17€ ($20) admission charge. Visit **www.opapisa.it/box office** to book tickets. It's wise to book well ahead; when I checked ticket availability in January, tours were sold out a full week in advance. If you show up in Pisa without reservations, you will *not* be able to get into the tower. The tower is open Monday to Friday from 8am to 1:30pm. You are required to show a printed receipt at the ticket office 1 hour prior to your scheduled visit.

WHERE TO DINE   The blocks around the Campo dei Miracoli are filled with sandwich bars and pizza places. One of the best medium-priced restaurants is **Da Bruno,** just outside the walls north of the Campo dei Miracoli at Via Luigi Bianchi 12 (© **050-560-818**), specializing in Pisan cuisine, such as *pasta e ceci* (pasta with chickpeas) and *baccala conporri* (codfish simmered with leeks). Fresh fish makes up a good part of the changing menu but hikes the prices considerably. The restaurant is open Monday noon to 3pm, Wednesday to Sunday noon to 3pm and 7 to 10:30pm; it accepts American Express, Diners Club, MasterCard, and Visa.

14

Lisbon & Environs

by Sascha Segan & Herbert Bailey Livesey

Lisbon is a time machine. In the span of 1 day you may find yourself walking with peacocks on the ramparts of a castle, then sipping espresso at a decades-old cafe, and finally sampling trendy cuisine at a waterfront restaurant. Decaying tile-covered walls rub shoulders with gleaming modern high-rises in this city where the very old and the very new are amicable next-door neighbors.

Once considered a bit of a backwater, Lisbon (pop. 1.9 million) is making great strides to catch up with its fellow capitals in the European Union—especially since it was selected to host Euro 2004, an international soccer event scheduled for press time. The efficient Metro (subway) system has been upgraded and is being extended even further; the impressive Vasco da Gama suspension bridge has been completed; and the airport terminal has been expanded. Much of the 52-hectare (130-acre) Expo '98 site has been converted to permanent use, including a grand aquarium and shopping center. Private interests have converted long strips of empty maritime warehouses into a lively district of nightclubs, bars, cafes, and marinas. Work on the Rossio and adjacent Praça da Figueira is complete, the grand fountains are back in action, the sidewalks are redone, and the sandblasting of the opera house is finished.

The city bears some resemblance to San Francisco: Lisbon sits at the edge of an ocean, is built on seven hills traversed by antique trams, and has a dramatic red-orange suspension bridge spanning its harbor. It has even been subject to devastating earthquakes.

Even though it fronts the Atlantic, Lisbon feels like a Mediterranean city. Pastel-colored houses cling to its steep slopes, and the mosaic sidewalks are composed of black-and-white stones arranged in elaborate patterns. Everywhere you look, palm trees and tropical flora are abundant, and weather patterns can change by the hour.

Value Budget Bests

Inexpensive eating places abound, many self-described as *cervejarias* (beer halls) or *adegas* (taverns). Servings are nearly always ample; half portions *(meia dose)* are often available. In places where you can choose to sit or stand at the counter, standing is usually cheaper.

Because Lisbon's sightseeing centers are compact, in downtown or in outlying Belém you can see most things **on foot** or for the modest price of a **subway** or **tram** ticket.

Many **museums** are free on Sunday morning, and some are free on Wednesday morning. The Centro Cultural in Belém gives free "happy hour" **concerts** three to four times a week.

Lisbon Deals & Discounts

SPECIAL DISCOUNTS   Consider buying a **Lisboa Card,** which provides free admission to dozens of museums and historic buildings and unrestricted access to all forms of public transport. The cards, which can be purchased at the main tourist office, are valid for 24, 48, and 72 hours and cost 13€ ($15), 22€ ($25), and 27€ ($31), respectively. Cards for children are discounted by over 60%. When buying the card, keep in mind the free museum admissions on Sunday and the Monday closings.

WORTH A SPLURGE   An evening at a **fado club** (with dinner and entertainment) might run 40€ ($46) or more per person, but you'll likely want to experience this Portuguese musical form at least once. A dinner reservation guarantees you a seat, but drop in after midnight just for drinks and you'll pay a minimum, typically 10€ to 15€ ($12–$17). The music usually goes on until at least 3am. For recommended fado clubs in Lisbon, see "Lisbon After Dark," later in this chapter.

The Mediterranean that Lisbon evokes isn't an entirely Latin one; the Arabs were here for centuries, and the twisting streets and markets in the Alfama district are reminiscent of Moroccan souks. A grand fortress broods from the crest of the highest hill, and the sunsets turn the ancient buildings dusty shades of pink and rose.

The diversity of the population may come as a surprise; the bloodless 1975 revolution that led to the dissolution of Portugal's remaining African colonies and the return of tens of thousands of overseas citizens made Lisbon one of Europe's most multiethnic, multiracial capitals.

After the devastating 1755 earthquake, which leveled much of the city and killed 40,000 people, Lisbon arose anew under the supervision of the Marquês de Pombal, whose enlightened urban planning continues to serve the city well. The downtown Baixa district is an orderly grid of streets sloping gently up from the harbor to the broad tree-lined Avenida da Liberdade. Sidewalk cafes invite lingering along the way, and throughout the city, parks, gardens, and plazas offer welcome breathing spaces. Most of the damage caused by a fire in 1988 that devastated parts of Baixa and adjoining Chiado has been repaired, and Pombal's vision has been restored.

Portugal remains one of the E.U.'s poorer countries, but it boasted an above-average economic growth rate for much of the last decade before a slowdown in 2001–2003. It was in the first wave of nations to join the monetary union launched in January 1999, which led to its adoption of the euro in 2002. In the wake of that move into Greater Europe, Lisbon's shops have become increasingly chic (and expensive), its restaurants more sophisticated (and expensive), and its nightlife hours longer. Yet while Lisbon dances to a futuristic beat, the culture and vestiges of 19th-century technology are still evident, with 2-hour lunches, creaking trolleys, and narrow streets. Through all of this, its spirit remains open and companionable, sensual and exotic.

For more on Lisbon and its environs, see *Frommer's Portugal.*

1 Essentials

ARRIVING

BY PLANE   During peak travel seasons, the national airline, **TAP** (© 800/221-7370;** www.tap-airportugal.com), may be heavily booked with flights from the U.S.; check fares on other airlines, such as Continental or Northwest/KLM, before making reservations. In addition to TAP, **Portugalia** (© 21/842-5559 in Lisbon; www.pga.pt) operates a shuttle service between Lisbon and Madrid at lower fares than the big lines. **Air Luxor** (© 21/006-2200 in Lisbon; www.airluxor.com) also offers low-fare flights between Lisbon and destinations like London and Paris. Lisbon's **Portela Airport** is only about 13km (8 miles) from the heart of town. Expect to pay 9€ to 15€ ($11–$17) for a **taxi,** depending on traffic and destination. Prepaid taxis (vouchers are available at the Tourist Office counter) are often on the expensive side, but you will avoid being scammed by a less-than-scrupulous driver. The best option, if you don't have too much luggage, is the yellow **Aero-Bus,** which costs 2.30€ ($2.65) for the day; TAP passengers get one trip free. It runs from the airport to the Cais do Sodré rail station every 20 minutes from 7am to 9pm (slightly less often on weekends) and makes 10 intermediate stops, including Praça dos Restauradores and the east side of the Rossio. Look for the Aero-Bus sign at regular bus stops.

BY TRAIN   Rail Europe (© 877/272-RAIL in the U.S., or 800/361-RAIL in Canada; www.raileurope.com) offers a special **Portuguese Railpass,** good for any 4 days in a 15-day period within the country, first class only, for $105. Travelers visiting both Spain and Portugal might want to consider the **Iberic Railpass,** good for any 3 days over 2 months, for $205 in first class. In both cases, children 4 to 11 years pay half the adult fare. The nightly sleeper from Madrid, the Talgo Hotel Train, has several categories, from private cabins with showers to reclining seats in second class for budgeters. From Madrid or Paris, arrivals are at Lisbon's major terminal, the **Estação Santa Apolónia,** by the river near Alfama. There are three stations in addition to Santa Apolónia, which also serves the northern environs: **Rossio** (with trains to Sintra), **Cais do Sodré** (with trains to the Estoril Coast), and **Sul e Sueste** (with trains to the Algarve).

VISITOR INFORMATION

TOURIST OFFICE   The **Tourist Office/Lisboa Welcome Center,** at Palácio Foz, Praça dos Restauradores (© **21/346-3314** or 21/342-5231; Metro: Baixa-Chiado), is the best on-site info source. It's open Monday to Sunday 10am to 6pm. It has few free brochures, but several attendants can answer most questions in English and sell useful publications. A branch office near the airport's arrivals area is open daily 6am to 2am. Attendants there can make hotel reservations at no cost.

For a listing of useful information, addresses, phone numbers, and events, pick up a copy of the bilingual *Follow Me Lisboa* at the tourist office or any major hotel. Additional giveaway guides, usually available at the airport and some hotels, are *Lisboa Tips* and *Your Guide Lisboa.* The best source for up-to-the-minute details on entertainment around town is the Portuguese-language newspaper *Diário de Noticias.*

WEBSITES   For general info on the Net, including weather, history, hotels, dining, and nightlife, check out **www.eunet.pt/lisboa**, **www.portugal.org**, and **www.portugalvirtual.pt**.

CITY LAYOUT

The heart of the city extends some 3.2km (2 miles) from **Praça do Comércio** to **Praça do Marquês de Pombal** (named after the prime minister who rebuilt the city after the 1755 earthquake). Between Praça do Comércio and **Praça Dom Pedro IV** (known as the Rossio, pronounced "Row-*see*-yo") is the **Baixa,** a commercial grid of small shopping streets. If you stand there, facing away from the waterfront, up to the right is **Alfama,** crowned by the Castelo São Jorge (St. George's Castle), and rising to the left is the **Bairro Alto,** a picturesque business and residential district. Connecting the Rossio to Praça do Marquês de Pombal is **Avenida da Liberdade,** Lisbon's version of the Champs-Elysées.

NEIGHBORHOODS Baixa ("Lower Town," pronounced "bye-shah") stretches from the river to the Rossio, once the site of the Inquisition's auto-da-fés. Such streets as Rua do Ouro (Street of Gold) and Rua da Prata (Street of Silver) have diversified their consumer offerings. Rua Augusta and Rua de Santa Justa are pedestrian streets lined with boutiques selling leather goods, real and costume jewelry, handcrafts, and more.

The shopping continues along Rua do Carmo, Rua Garrett, and Largo do Chiado, which link Baixa with the **Bairro Alto** ("Upper Town"). Its steep, claustrophobic streets house many fado clubs and budget eating places, plus increasing numbers of chic restaurants and clubs.

To the east, on the opposite side of Baixa, is **Alfama,** the ancient Arab quarter rising steep and narrow to the walls of Castelo São Jorge. Because it miraculously escaped the 1755 earthquake, its medieval aspect remains intact. Except for the castle, a handful of churches and small museums, and a smattering of shops, restaurants, and fado clubs, this is a colorful but largely residential working-class neighborhood.

To the north of these districts extends the broad **Avenida da Liberdade,** where banks, airline offices, and tour operators rub elbows with souvenir shops, first-run cinemas, and outposts of international fashion houses. Along its lower reaches, a few sidewalk cafes occupy space on the central pedestrian promenade.

Six-and-a-half kilometers (4 miles) from Praça do Comércio is **Belém,** a district that has a separate urban identity. The focal point of Portugal's 16th-century maritime activities, Belém is home to several museums and monuments as well as commemorations of Portugal's colonial glories. Nearby, too, is the eastern end of the impressive suspension bridge, Ponte 25 de Abril, which was completed in the 1960s.

GETTING AROUND

The **tourist pass** (*passe turístico*)—valid for all city buses, trams, subways, the Santa Justa Elevator, and the funiculars—costs 9.95€ ($11) for 4 days and 14€ ($16) for 7. It's sold at the base of the Santa Justa Elevator (see below) daily from 8am to 8pm. To use the pass on the Metro, show it to an agent at a staffed booth and get a special ticket that can be read by the turnstiles.

Most of Lisbon's tourist areas are compact enough to cover on foot, but remember that steep hills can make parts of a sightseeing or shopping trip fairly strenuous. Only the sights in the area of Parque Eduardo VII and the Belém district require public transportation or a car.

BY SUBWAY The Metro (subway) is the top transportation bargain in the city **(www.metrolisboa.pt).** The system has four interconnected lines, with several extensions in the works. Fares are by the ride, not by distance, and include transfers between lines. A *bilhete* (ticket) for a single ride is .65€ (75¢), and a 10-trip *cademeta* is 5.10€ ($5.85). A 7-day unlimited-use version costs 4.80€ ($5.50). Buy tickets from the staffed booth or at the nearby machines, which have instructions in English. Then insert the ticket in the turnstiles and keep it until leaving the destination station; you'll need to insert it into the turnstile again to exit. Handy credit card–size maps are available at the booths. The system operates daily 6:30am to 1am.

BY BUS & TRAM Even more extensive are the bus *(autocarro)* and tram *(eléctrico)* networks, run by Carris (www.carris.pt). A **ticket bought on board** (from the driver on the old trams and buses, or from a machine on the new trams serving Belém) is 1€ ($1.15). Travel two-for-one by buying **prepaid tickets,** bought in pairs from Carris kiosks (1€/$1.15 for the pair). **Multiuse tickets** good for 1 day are 2.35€ ($2.70); for 3 days, 5.65€ ($6.50). Validate a new multitrip ticket by sticking it in the slot of the unlabeled metal box found at the doors of the trams or behind the driver. After that, you only have to show it to the driver. Booths are in most of the major squares (like Rossio and Figueira) and at the base of the Santa Justa Elevator. Route maps are usually available there as well. Buses run daily 6am to midnight and trams 6:30am to midnight.

BY ELEVATOR & FUNICULAR Near the Rossio, the **Elevador de Santa Justa** once linked Rua do Ouro in Baixa with Praça do Carmo I in Bairro Alto. The bridge connection at the top has been closed for some time, and the elevator now goes only to the belvedere and cafe at the top. The round-trip fare is 1€ ($1.15) with the purchase of your prepaid ticket. Hours are Monday to Saturday 7am to 11pm, Sunday 9am to 11pm.

Lisbon's three funiculars are the **Glória,** which dates from 1885 and groans uphill from Praça dos Restauradores to Rua de São Pedro Alcântara; the **Lavra,** from the east side of Avenida da Liberdade to Campo Martires da Pátria; and the **Bica,** from Calçada do Combro to Rua da Boavista. Fares and operating hours are essentially the same as those for the Santa Justa Elevator.

BY TAXI Hail cabs in the street or in ranks in major plazas. If the green roof lights are on, the taxi is occupied. The initial cost is about 1.90€ ($2.20) from 6am to 10pm, and 2.25€ ($2.60) overnight. Fare rules are posted inside the cab; check to make sure the meter is set correctly before your trip begins. Surcharges apply for summoning a taxi by phone and for luggage that has to be carried in the trunk or on the roof (1.50€/$1.75). To call for a cab, try **Radio Taxi** (© 21/ 811-9000 or 21/793-2756).

BY RENTAL CAR Due to maddening traffic, narrow streets, and daredevil drivers, we strongly recommend you use a car only for excursions outside the city. Most international car-rental companies have offices at the airport, but rates

---

⌐Tips Street Smarts

With the closing of the Santa Justa Elevator connection, getting from downtown Baixa to the shops and cafes of the upper Chiado district means a leg-testing climb up very steep Rua do Carmo. To avoid that strenuous workout, go into the Metro station at the west end of Rua Vitoria, take the escalator down to the platform, walk straight across, and take the series of escalators up. You'll arrive on Rua Garrett in front of A Brasileira, Lisbon's oldest cafe, and it won't cost a cent.

Country & City Codes

The **country code** for Portugal is **351**; use this code when calling from outside Portugal. The city code for Lisbon is **21**; use this code when calling from anywhere outside or inside Portugal, even if you're in Lisbon and calling somewhere else in the city.

---

at local firms may be lower. Two in-town firms are **Rupauto,** Beneficiência 99 (© 21/793-3258); and **Viata,** Filipe da Mata 26C (© 21/793-3148). Expect to pay a minimum of around 50€ ($58) per day, plus tax, for the smallest cars with unlimited mileage. Shopping for the best rates is rewarded.

Remember: You get the best deal if you arrange the rental before leaving your home country.

FAST FACTS: Lisbon

Addresses Lisbon addresses consist of a street name, a building number, and the story, denoted by a numeral and the symbol °. "Rua Rosa Araújo 2–5°" means the sixth floor at no. 2 on that street. (As elsewhere in Europe, the ground floor isn't counted as the 1st floor, so 5° means six stories up.)

ATMs ATMs, called *caixas automáticos,* are widely available—look for the sign MULTIBANCO. You can get cash with major credit cards or Cirrus and PLUS network ATM/debit cards. One ATM is in the lobby of the airport terminal, so it's easy to get euros on arrival to cover transportation into the city and tips at the hotel.

Banks Banks are open Monday to Friday 8:30am to 3pm; some offer extended hours, as well as foreign exchange service Monday to Saturday 6 to 11pm. The bank at the airport is always open. You can change money on Saturday and Sunday 8:30am to 8:30pm at the bank at the Santa Apolónia train station.

Business Hours Typically, **shops** are open Monday to Friday 9am to 1pm and 3 to 7pm (some stay open through lunch), Saturday 9am to 1pm. Increasingly, though, shops are open through Saturday afternoon. Shopping malls, especially those with movie theaters, are usually open quite late. **Restaurants** are usually open noon to 2:30pm and 7:30 to 11pm or midnight. Closing times vary substantially, but many restaurants remain shut after Saturday lunch and all day Sunday. **Offices** are generally open Monday to Friday 9am to 1pm and 3 to 5:30pm or 6pm, but this is gradually changing.

Currency In 2002, Portugal adopted the **euro (€)** for its currency. At press time, 1€ = $1.15 and $1=.87€.

Doctors You can find English-speaking doctors at the **British Hospital,** Saraiva de Carvalho 49 (© 21/395-5067). Embassies and hotel concierges can also recommend doctors.

Embassies Lisbon is home to the embassies of many countries, including the **United States,** Avenida das Forças Armadas (© 21/727-3300; Metro: Jardim Zoológico); the **United Kingdom,** São Bernardo 33 (© 21/392-4000); **Canada,** Liberdade 200–3° (© 21/316-4600; Metro: Avenida); and

Australia, Liberdade 200–2° (℘ **21/310-1500;** Metro: Avenida). They're open Monday to Friday, usually 9 or 9:30am to 12:30 or 1pm and 2 or 2:30 to 5 or 5:30pm, but call ahead.

Emergencies Call ℘ **112** for an ambulance, the fire department, or the police. Look in any newspaper or dial ℘ **16** for 24-hour pharmacies. Closed pharmacies post notices indicating the nearest open one.

Holidays Major holidays are New Year's Day (Jan 1), Freedom Day (Apr 25), Worker's Day (May 1), Camões and Portugal Day (June 10), St. Anthony's Day (June 13), Assumption Day (Aug 15), Day of the Republic (Oct 5), All Saints' Day (Nov 1), Independence Day (Dec 1), Feast of the Immaculate Conception (Dec 8), and Christmas (Dec 25). Other public holidays with shifting dates are Good Friday, Shrove Tuesday, and Corpus Christi. When holidays land on Tuesday or Thursday, the intervening Monday or Friday is often declared a day off, making for many 4-day weekends throughout the year. Halloween recently has become an important event, with many workers getting the next day off.

Hospitals See "Doctors," above.

Internet Access You can check your e-mail at **PT Comunicações,** 68 Praça Don Pedro IV (no phone; 1€/$1.15 for 30 min.). You can also try the slightly out-of-the-way **Cyber.bica,** Duques de Bragança 7, in the Chiado district (℘ **21/322-5004;** www.cyberbica.com; Metro: Baixa-Chiado); or ask around for other Internet cafes. If you have a Wi-Fi enabled laptop, free access is available at the open-air plaza by the Oceanarium at the Parc das Nações (Metro: Oriente). More Wi-Fi hotspots are promised very soon.

Laundry Plan ahead. If you request same-day laundry or dry-cleaning service, it will usually cost 50% more than having your clothes returned late the next day. Better still, do it yourself. Two self-service launderettes are **Lava Neve,** Alegria 37 (no phone; Metro: Avenida); and **Lavatax,** Francisco Sanches 65A (℘ **21/812-3392;** Metro: Arroios). *Tinturaria* is the Portuguese word for "dry cleaning."

Mail The **post office** *(correios)* at Praça dos Restauradores 58 (℘ **21/323-8700;** Metro: Restauradores) is open Monday to Friday 8am to 10pm, and Saturday, Sunday, and holidays 9am to 6pm. The airport post office is open 24 hours.

Police Call ℘ **112** for the police.

Tax The **value-added tax (IVA** in Portugal) varies from 8% to 17%. For refund information, see "Shopping" later in this chapter.

Telephone One of the busiest **phone offices** is at the northwest corner of the Rossio, Praça Don Pedro IV 68, diagonally across from the National Theater. Called **PT Comunicações,** it's open daily 8am to 11pm. If you plan to make many calls, consider getting a prepaid phone card. To make international calls, dial "00" and then the country code ("1" for the U.S.), the area code, and the number. Some phones are equipped for credit card calls (Visa and MasterCard) but not phone company cards. If you're calling direct from a hotel, there might be steep surcharges.

To make a **collect call** at more economical U.S. calling-card rates, use **AT&T's USA Direct** by dialing ℘ **05017-1-288** or **MCI's Call USA** by dialing

© **05017-1-234.** Collect calls, or those at U.S. calling-card rates, can be made through an **international operator** by dialing © **098.**

For **long-distance** calls within the country, dial "0" (zero) before the city code and then the number. The dial tone for long-distance calls might be unusual, but make sure there's a tone before you dial and that the tone then stops. Dial steadily, without long pauses; the connection can take up to a minute, during which you might hear some unfamiliar tones. A persistent tone means that the call has failed.

Tipping Although restaurant prices usually include a service charge, it's appropriate to tip an extra 5% to 10%. Taxi drivers get about 10% for long rides and 15% to 20% on short rides. Give .75€ to 1€ (85¢–$1.15) to porters and bellhops for each bag, depending on the weight of the bags and the distance they're carried. It's customary to leave a similar amount for the chambermaid for each night of a hotel stay.

2 Affordable Places to Stay

Budget accommodations abound throughout the city, but the most convenient areas are off Avenida da Liberdade, near Rossio Square, in Baixa, and in the Bairro Alto. The customary admonition that lodgings shouldn't be judged solely by their often grimy or otherwise unpromising exteriors and entry areas applies doubly in Lisbon, although a laudatory byproduct of Expo '98 was the incentive it gave managers of hotels and *pensãos* to undertake needed renovations. Ask to see some rooms before deciding.

Substantial savings can result if you're willing to risk the uncertainty of arriving without reservations. Stop at the tourist info desk in the airport and present your list of preferred lodgings, or simply state the maximum rate you would be willing to pay. The attendant will start making calls, asking the price for available rooms. Except at peak periods, the charge will almost always be substantially lower than published rack rates, sometimes by as much as 50%. Room rates no longer routinely include breakfast, so when they do, that can be considered a bonus.

During high season (Easter until about the end of Oct), most of the cheaper places jack up their prices by as much as 30%. During that period, some can be almost as expensive as the larger hotels. Most room rates include VAT (called IVA in Portugal), but ask to be sure.

Note: You'll find the lodging choices below plotted on the map on p. 505.

OFF AVENIDA DA LIBERDADE

Astória   Half a block off Praça Marquês de Pombal (with its central Metro station and towering monument to the 18th-c. leader), the Astória's small rooms, furnished in light wood, have sculptured ceilings that provide a note of old-world character. Otherwise, the building projects a somewhat worn modernity in need of refreshing. Many of the front-desk employees speak English.

Tips **Rooms on the Web**

For further information about lodging and online booking, try **www. portugal-hotels.com.**

> **_Value_** **Getting the Best Deal on Accommodations**
>
> - Note that *pensãos* and *residências* often offer discounts of at least 10% to guests staying more than a week.
> - Try your hand at **bargaining**—hoteliers won't be offended, especially off season and on weekends. Most three-star hotels have **corporate rates** available for the asking, even if your connection to a firm or corporation is tenuous.
> - Be aware that rooms with shower stalls are nearly always cheaper, often substantially so, than those with full tubs with showerheads. Ask about this when booking.

Braamcamp 10, 1200 Lisboa. ℂ **21/386-1317.** Fax 21/386-0491. 83 units. 43€ ($49) single; 57€ ($65) double. Rates include breakfast. AE, DC, MC, V. Metro: Marquês de Pombal. **Amenities:** Bar; laundry service. *In room:* A/C, TV.

Casal Ribeiro   Immediately adjacent to the Astória (see above), this pension has a promising-looking cream exterior with green trim. The compact, dated rooms off well-lighted halls live up to the low tariffs. Guests can meet in the agreeable lounge by the reception desk. The outgoing staff members speak English.

Braamcamp 10-R/C (west of the Praça Marquês de Pombal), 1200 Lisboa. ℂ **21/386-1544.** Fax 21/386-0067. 30 units. 40€ ($46) single; 50€ ($58) double. Rates include breakfast. DC, MC, V. Metro: Marquês de Pombal. *In room:* TV, radio.

Nacional ✸   If the clamor of downtown Baixa isn't for you, this modern mid-rise in a quieter neighborhood of office and apartment buildings might be the ticket. The pleasant lobby staff is attentive to guests' needs, and many employees speak English. Rooms are crisply furnished and the bathrooms have American-style showers. There's a comfortably furnished lounge with a big-screen TV.

Castilho 34, 1250 Lisboa. ℂ **21/355-4433.** Fax 21/356-1122. www.hotel-nacional.com. 61 units. 68€ ($78) single; 80€ ($92) double. Rates include breakfast. AE, DC, MC, V. Metro: Marquês de Pombal. **Amenities:** Bar; concierge; limited room service; laundry service. *In room:* A/C, TV, minibar (on request), hair dryer, safe.

Roma   One flight up from the narrow street (no elevator), the Roma consists of two floors of rooms, some quite large, with a variety of configurations and furnishings. There are combinations of twins and double beds, with TVs mounted high on the walls and usually a desk or bureau. Front rooms are noisier but have more light. Bar service is available in the old-fashioned lounge at all hours. Housekeeping standards are high, and some members of the genial staff speak English.

Travessa da Glória 22A (1 block west of av. da Liberdade), 1250–118 Lisboa. ℂ **21/346-0557,** -0558, or -0559. Fax 21/346-0557. 48 units. 39€–67€ ($45–$77) single; 48€–80€ ($55–$92) double. Rates include breakfast and taxes. AE, DC, MC, V. Metro: Avenida or Restauradores. **Amenities:** Restaurant; bar; sauna. *In room:* A/C, TV, safe.

IN BAIXA

Duas Nacões   A few strides east of pedestrian rua Augusta, this economical place is a happy surprise, and the management continues to keep the brakes on precipitous price increases. The high-ceilinged doubles are unusually commodious, and those with bathrooms have ample tubs. Breakfast is served in a large dining room with blue and white scenic tile murals. Renovation work is ongoing, so see your room before accepting it. English is spoken.

Victoria 41, 1100 Lisboa. (€) **21/346-0710.** Fax 21/347-0206. www.duasnacoes.com. 66 units, 43 with bathroom. 25€ ($29) single with shower, 39€–50€ ($45–$58) single with bathroom; 37€ ($43) double with shower, 39€–50€ ($45–$58) double with bathroom. Rates include breakfast. AE, DC, MC, V. Metro: Baixa-Chiado. **Amenities:** Bar. *In room:* Safe.

NEAR THE ROSSIO

Florescente   A block east of Praça dos Restauradores, this place offers small, well-kept rooms off narrow tile-lined corridors on four floors (no elevator). The street-level reception area is attractive, and most of the staff members, some multilingual, are welcoming. They'll buzz you in after deciding you pose no danger, although the neighborhood isn't threatening. Some rooms are significantly larger than others. Many coffee shops and budget restaurants are nearby.

Portas de São Antão 99 (opposite the Grand Teatro Politeama), 1100 Lisboa (€) **21/342-6609.** Fax 21/342-7733. www.residencialflorescente.com. 70 units. From 40€ ($46) single; from 50€ ($58) double. AE, MC, V. Metro: Restauradores or Rossio. *In room:* A/C, TV (some units), no phone.

Gerês ⋆   One of the best values in town, the homey Gerês combines clean rooms with a fairly quiet but handy location a little over a block from the Rossio. Its rooms—painted and repainted—occupy two floors; units on the second floor are more desirable. The English-speaking owners have installed video surveillance of the lobby. There's no elevator, but reception is only one floor up. Breakfast is not served.

Calçada do Garcia 6, 1150 Lisboa. (€) **21/881-0497.** www.pensaogeres.web.pt. Fax 21/888-2006. 20 units, 16 with bathroom. 45€–50€ ($52–$58) single; 50€–65€ ($58–$75) double. AE, DC, MC, V. Metro: Rossio. *In room.* TV.

Mundial ⋆⋆   The best business hotel in the Rossio area took a giant step up in appeal with construction that nearly doubled its size. Its new wing looks out on a plaza filled with fountains, shopping, and eateries, while the original structure and its good-size rooms have been repapered, repainted, and outfitted with fresh fabrics. Best of all is its rooftop restaurant, Varanda, affording lovely views of the city and the illuminated castle above. The staff is starting to measure up to its surroundings. Rates have been kept relatively low.

Dom Duarte 4, 1100 Lisboa. (€) **21/884-2000.** Fax 21/884-2110. www.hotel-mundial.pt. 252 units. From 75€ ($86) single; from 83€ ($95) double. Rates include breakfast. AE, DC, DISC, MC, V. Garage parking. Metro: Rossio. Tram: 28. **Amenities:** 2 restaurants; 2 bars; concierge; 24-hr. room service; same-day laundry service/dry cleaning. *In room:* A/C, TV w/pay movies, minibar, hair dryer, safe.

Portugal ⋆ *Finds*   This is a largely unnoticed place, a rejuvenated but appealingly old-fashioned hotel with large guest rooms, high ceilings, and marble bathrooms. It's blissfully quiet despite being barely a block off Praça da Figueira. And it doesn't have the oppressively smoky air found in too many Lisbon hotels. You can meet friends in the offbeat lounge next to the spacious lobby.

João das Regras 4, 1100 Lisboa. (€) **21/887-7581.** Fax 21/886-7343. www.hotelportugal.com. 59 units. 50€ ($58) single; 61€ ($70) double. Rates include breakfast. AE, DC, MC, V. Metro: Rossio. Tram: 12. **Amenities:** Bar. *In room:* A/C, TV.

IN THE BAIRRO ALTO

Casa de São Mamede ⋆   A free-standing former private residence west of the Jardim Botânico, this *pensão* has three floors of rooms (no elevator). They vary substantially in size, but some are quite large, with pine furniture, carpeting, sofas, and glass chandeliers. The mostly amiable staff, tile-lined breakfast salon, and TVs in the rooms enhance the obvious value.

Escola Politécnica 159, 1250 Lisboa. © **21/396-3166.** Fax 21/395-1896. 28 units. 75€ ($86) double; 85€ ($98) triple. Rates include breakfast. Children under 8 stay free in parent's room. No credit cards. Metro: Rato. Tram: 24. *In room:* TV, safe.

NEAR PARQUE EDUARDO VII

Ibis Lisboa-Saldanha   A unit of the monster European chain of economical hotels, this mid-rise is on a busy but not unattractive street 3 blocks from the Saldanha Metro station and under 6.5km (4 miles) from the airport. Warmth isn't a hallmark, but value is. The rooms are small and spare but certainly adequate for those who don't plan to do more than sleep here.

Casal Ribeiro 23, 1100 Lisboa. © **21/319-1690.** Fax 21/319-1699. www.accorhotels.com. 116 units. 59€–72€ ($68–$83) single or double. Rates include taxes. AE, DC, MC, V. Parking in garage 5€ ($5.75). Metro: Saldanha. **Amenities:** Restaurant; bar; nonsmoking rooms. *In room:* A/C, TV.

Miraparque ⭐⭐   This low-key contemporary hotel is worth every cent. Identified by its terra-cotta-hued exterior, it does "look at the park," the one named for Eduardo VII. Management repaints the interior every year or so, and housekeeping standards are high. The rooms are spacious and uncluttered, with desks and an easy chair or two. The buffet breakfast is laid out in the full-service restaurant. The Metro stop is around the corner, and an ornate sports pavilion is across the street. English is spoken.

Sidónio Pais 12, 1050–214 Lisboa. © **21/352-4286.** Fax 21/357-8920. www.miraparque.com. 102 units. 58€–90€ ($67–$103) single; 67€–100€ ($77–$115) double. Rates include breakfast. AE, MC, V. Metro: Parque. **Amenities:** Restaurant; bar; concierge; car-rental desk; limited room service; babysitting; same-day laundry/dry cleaning. *In room:* A/C, TV, minibar, safe.

WORTH A SPLURGE

As Janelas Verdes ⭐⭐⭐   Hopeful travelers eagerly seek charm and affordability, but rarely find that combination in Lisbon lodgings. Here's an exception, at least if you're a couple traveling off season. The innlike 18th-century manse used to be an annex of the better-known York House, down the street, and since its separation, it has doubled its room count. Units in the new wing are spacious but plainer; the original ones are smaller but furnished with attractive antiques. Cable-deprived Yanks in 8-channel Portugal find relief here with numerous TV channels, several of them in English. You aren't likely to regret choosing this alluring retreat.

Rua das Janelas Verdes 47, 1200 Lisboa. © **21/396-8143.** Fax 21/396-8144. www.heritage.pt. 17 units. Low season 165€–198€ ($190–$228) double; high season 195€–245€ ($224–$282) double. Children under 12 stay free in parent's room. AE, DISC, MC, V. Parking 9€ ($10). Bus: 27, 49, or 60. **Amenities:** Honor bar; concierge; 24-hr. room service; babysitting; same-day laundry/dry cleaning; nonsmoking rooms. *In room:* A/C, TV, dataport, minibar, hair dryer, safe.

Dom Rodrigo ⭐⭐   Most of the accommodations here are sizable two-room suites that can house families of three or four. There are two beds in one room and a full marble bathroom. The sitting area contains a convertible sofa and a dining table, and the complete kitchen comes with a stove, a sink, a fridge, and rudimentary utensils. Stated tariffs are nearly always negotiable. The quiet location, 2 blocks uphill from Praça Marquês de Pombal, is desirable. Fluent English is spoken at the front desk. The casual dining room serves light meals.

Rodrigo da Fonseca 44–50, 1200 Lisboa. © **21/386-3800.** Fax 21/386-3000. htdrodrigo@mail.telepoc.pt. 57 units. 106€–124€ ($122–$143) single. Rates include breakfast. AE, DC, MC, V. Garage parking available. Metro: Marquês de Pombal. **Amenities:** Cafe; lobby bar; unheated outdoor pool; limited room service; same-day laundry service/dry cleaning. *In room:* A/C, TV, hair dryer, safe.

Veneza   Opened as a hotel in 1990, the Veneza occupies one of the few remaining 19th-century mansions that once lined Avenida da Liberdade. Inside, a grand staircase leads to the three upper floors. The well-appointed midsize rooms are furnished in a soothing modern style, each with a firm mattress. The staff is extremely pleasant and many speak English.

Av. da Liberdade 189, 1250–141 Lisboa. (€) 21/352-2618. Fax 21/352-6678. www.3khoteis.com. 36 units. 130€–150€ ($150–$173) double. Rates include continental breakfast. AE, DC, MC, V. Parking 11€ ($12). Metro: Avenida. **Amenities:** Bar; car-rental desk; same-day laundry/dry cleaning. *In room:* A/C, TV, minibar, hair dryer, safe.

3 Great Deals on Dining

By far the best areas for budget restaurants are the blocks west of **Rua da Misericórdia** and **Rua de São Pedro Alcântara** in the Bairro Alto, as well as **Rua das Portas de Santo Antão,** east of Praça dos Restauradores. **Rua dos Correiros,** in Baixa, has over a dozen places charging less than 15€ ($17) for a fixed-price three-course meal with wine.

Lisbon's meals are relatively cheap and built around a number of hearty dishes. One is *caldo verde,* a soup with mashed potatoes, shredded kale, and peppery sausage cooked in beef broth. There's the ubiquitous *bacalhau* (cod), available in over 300 recipes. *Frango* (chicken), often spit-roasted and fragrant with generous showers of garlic, is highly popular. *Carne de porco a alentejana* is pork stewed with clams in a sauce spiced with herbs, a classic of the Portuguese kitchen. *Barrigas de freira* ("nuns' tummies") is a popular egg dish, and *cozido a portuguesa* is a flavorful Portuguese version of the New England boiled dinner.

Another common savory dish is **grilled sardines**—large ones, not like those found in cans—with a fresh salad. *Açorda* (a porridge of bread, eggs, and parsley or cilantro, tossed with shrimp or fish, then whipped) is one of those dishes every native had as a child and loves as an adult. Newcomers often find it less adorable. Additional possibilities are *lulas recheadas* (stuffed squid), *leitão* (roast suckling pig), and *ensopada de enguias* (eels stewed with bread).

Be forewarned: Portuguese cooks aren't always fastidious about the removal of bones, shells, or skin. They also have a taste for spicy seasonings, a result of influences from their former colonies in Africa, Asia, and South America. *Piri-piri* is a favorite hot sauce that often shows up, unannounced, in chicken and pork dishes or in a bowl on the table. Use it with caution.

For dessert, try *pudim Molotov,* a cross between a sponge cake and a pudding served with caramel sauce. Any of a dozen types of cheese are also eaten for dessert. A special one is *serra da estrêla,* a creamy smoked sheep's cheese.

As for wine, it's hard to go wrong ordering the unlabeled house version—*vinho da casa.* Slightly more expensive *vinho verde,* a young country white with a slight spritz, goes well with seafood. Increasingly, however, cola, beer, or

---

(*Tips*) Dining Notes

In many *cafetarias,* customers are expected to pre-pay for snacks or beverages to be consumed at the bar. Look for the sign PRÉ-PAGAMENTO. Tell the cashier what you want, pay, and take the receipt to the bar.

Smoking is less pervasive than in years past, but it takes only one puffer to cloud up some of the smaller restaurants, and nonsmoking sections are rare. An option for the allergic is to choose places with outdoor tables.

mineral water is substituted, especially among younger people. Coffee comes in varying forms, the most popular being *bica* (black espresso), *carioca* (espresso with a dash of milk), *garoto* (espresso with more milk), and *galão* (a large glass of coffee with milk). Good Portuguese brandies are **Fim do Seculo** and **Croft.**

Breakfast usually consists of coffee, juice, and a roll or croissant.

NEAR THE PRAÇA DO MARQUÊS DE POMBAL

Grill 20 ✿ PORTUGUESE   Less than 2 blocks west of the top of Avenida da Liberdade, this effervescent restaurant is handy to several of the hotels recommended above. It's airy, bright, and contemporary, making it attractive to the younger professionals who work in the area. There's no need for an *entrada* (appetizer), as the price of each main course includes a visit to the salad bar. This is a grill—every item is meat, mostly beef or pork, in monster slabs or on skewers, all intensely flavorful and cooked precisely to order. The fries are good, as are the aromatic rice side dishes. You should be able to spend under $15, wine and tax included.

Braancamp 62. © **21/385-8888.** Main courses 3.75€–10€ ($4.30–$12). AE, DC, MC, V. Mon–Sat noon–4pm and 7–11pm. Metro: Marquês de Pombal.

IN CHIADO

A Brasileira SANDWICHES/SNACKS   The city's oldest coffee shop, a block from Praça de Camões in the Chiado district, serves aromatic Brazilian espresso for under a dollar. The outside tables are enjoyable for coffee or quick lunches.

⟨Value⟩ Getting the Best Deal on Dining

- Ask about the *ementa turística* (tourist menu), which usually includes an appetizer or soup, a main course, dessert, bread, and a beverage for a price often lower than that of an a la carte main course. Although fewer restaurants offer it than in the past, those that don't always advertise the fact, so you must request it.
- Consider ordering only a main course in places where the *ementa turística* is unappealing or unavailable. They're often served with two starches, typically rice with fried or roasted potatoes, and portions are usually large.
- Be aware that appetizers, many of which involve shellfish, can cost nearly as much as main courses. Soups, on the other hand, are tasty and filling and often cost less than 3€ ($3.45).
- Try *cervejarias*—restaurants where the featured beverage is draft beer. They're large, informal places featuring hearty portions at sensible prices.
- A quick, light meal at a snack bar or *pastelaria* will help you keep to your budget.
- Take advantage of *adegas* and *tascas*—economical, often family-style restaurants with usually decent food at budget prices.
- Be aware that eating and drinking at the bar usually costs less than doing so at a table.
- Enjoy a picnic. Scenic, relaxing spots are plentiful in Lisbon. (See "Fast Food & Picnicking," p. 501.)

> ### *Tips* A Dining Warning
>
> Most restaurants run what amounts to a minor scam: Once you've ordered, a procession of small plates of nibbles arrives unrequested. The items might include olives, cheese, strips of ham, and little aluminum containers of pâté. *Beware:* You'll be charged for anything you consume (and some times even if you don't touch a thing). In addition, there's a *cobierto* (cover charge), usually about 2€ ($2.30) for the bread and butter, whether you eat it or not.

Inside is a fin-de-siècle coffeehouse where conversations swirl, patrons play cards and chess, and the service is offhand at best. Modern paintings occupy the spaces above the large mirrors. There's a dining room downstairs.

Garrett 120–122. ℂ **21/346-9541.** Most items under 3€ ($3.45). No credit cards. Daily 8am–2am. Tram: 28. Metro: Baixa-Chiado.

Bernardí PORTUGUESE   This antiquarian cafe near A Brasileira (see above) is great for a breakfast of coffee and pastries or fresh croissants. A standard version costs about 2€ ($2.30) at the bar or 3.50€ ($4) at a table. Lunch or dinner possibilities include grilled salmon and rice with duck. Keep it in mind for afternoon or late-night hot chocolate or snacks. To imbibe at the bar, prepay the cashier and get a voucher.

Garrett 104–106. ℂ **21/347-3133.** Several items under 10€ ($12). AE, MC, V. Mon–Sat 8am–2am. Metro: Baixa-Chiado. Tram: 28.

Trindade ✷ PORTUGUESE   Open since 1836, this cavernous *cervejaria* occupies the site of the 13th-century Convento dos Frades Tinos. The 1755 earthquake leveled that building, but several rooms with arched ceilings and fine blue-and-white tile murals recall those origins. Its long hours make Trindade desirable when competitors are closed, especially on Sunday and at Saturday lunch. That means the hustling waiters don't have time to smile, let alone engage in happy chat. The kitchen does a better job with seafood than with meat. Beware the pricier items, like spiny lobsters and huge tiger shrimp. Draft beer in foot-high glasses is served as often as wine. The high ceilings of the larger rooms in back help dissipate the clouds of tobacco smoke.

Nova da Trindade 20. ℂ **21/342-3506.** Main courses (other than shellfish) 7€–14€ ($8–$16). AE, DC, MC, V. Daily noon–1am. Tram: 24.

IN THE BAIRRO ALTO

O Barrigas ✷ PORTUGUESE   Unless the dictionary has missed something, the name of this happily hip bistro translates as "The Bellies." That fits, for the woman in charge and very much in evidence is intent on filling that critical organ. Quarters are tight, but diners squeeze in throughout the long evening for unstinting portions of such sturdies as rabbit stew and grilled loin of pork in mustard-cream sauce. Skin-on roasted potatoes sliced so thin they are close to chips accompany meat items. Fans and air-conditioning help dispel smoke. The boss speaks English and will help translate the menu; she brings a complimentary glass of *ginginha*, the traditional liqueur, at the end of the meal.

Travessa da Queimada 31 (near rua da Atalaia). ℂ **21/347-1220.** Main courses 7€–14€ ($8–$16). MC, V. Daily noon–2am. Tram: 24.

Pedro-das-Arábis MOROCCAN   Pete of Arabia? Whatever it means, the owner knows what makes an adventure on the plate. He took over a defunct Spanish restaurant, painted it, hung a few Moroccan ornaments, and began serving food that started packing the place. His kitchen concentrates on several kinds of couscous prepared to order. Appetizers aren't really necessary, because Pedro (who speaks fluent English) brings bowls of spicy olives, ratatouille, cumin-flavored meatballs, and square flat bread. Some prices have increased along with the restaurant's popularity, but the *ementa turística* set meal is still a good deal.

Atalaia 70. © **21/346-8494.** Main courses starting at 8€ ($9.20); *ementa turística* 16€ ($18). AE, MC, V. Daily 7:30pm–2am. Tram: 24.

Stravaganza 𝄐 *Kids* PIZZA/ITALIAN   These bright, clean-lined dining rooms avoid the usual trattoria decorative clichés, and the wood-burning oven produces some of the best pizza in town. The thin-crusted (but not cracker-crisp) pies come in small and large. For the largely under-30 customers it attracts, the kitchen fills orders past midnight, take out or eat in. The friendly manager speaks good English.

Grémio Lusitano 24 (a short walk west of Rua de São Pedro Alcântara). © **21/346-8868.** Main courses 9.50€–17€ ($11–$19). MC, V. Mon–Sat noon–2am. Tram: 24.

ON OR NEAR THE ROSSIO

Bonjardim PORTUGUESE   This self-styled *Rei da Brasa* ("King of the Grill") specializes in spit-roasted chicken. Dining downstairs or at the street tables under umbrellas is much preferable to the loud, smoky room upstairs. Students, merchants, couples, and families come for the unfussy, unadorned food. For about 8€ ($9.20), you get a whole chicken, cooked to tender, juicy perfection; a 10-inch platter of fries is about 2€. Ask for a bowl of *piri-piri* if it's not already on the table, and brush the fiery sauce over the meat (it isn't for wimps). Fish and other meats are available, but chicken's the reason to come here. Across the way is another **Bonjardim (Rei dos Frangos),** at no. 10 (© **21/342-4389**), with the same fare, prices, and hours but a little less elbowroom. It also has outdoor tables in good weather.

Travessa de Santo Antão 8–10. © **21/342-7424.** Main courses 8€–15€ ($9.20–$17). DC, MC, V. Daily noon–11:30pm. Metro: Restauradores.

Pastelaria Suíça PORTUGUESE   Scores of *pastelarias* service the pronounced Portuguese sweet tooth, and many go well beyond tarts and cakes to soups, sandwiches, and even full meals. This always-busy cafe takes up an entire block, with tables on the east side of the Rossio and on the west side of Praça da Figueira; it has been thoroughly refurbished, like the plazas on either side. It covers most bases, with pastry and ice cream counters, tearooms, and bars. Omelets and salads are available, as is a breakfast of juice, croissant, bacon, eggs, and coffee for about 5€ ($5.75).

Praça Dom Pedro IV 105. © **21/321-4090.** Main courses 2€–10€ ($2.30–$12). No credit cards. Daily 7am–10pm. Metro: Rossio.

IN BAIXA

Martinho da Arcada PORTUGUESE   Founded in 1782, this old-timer has plenty of experience in satisfying the needs of its cost-conscious clientele, from breakfast *carioca* to four-course dinners. The bar and cafe at the corner charge significantly lower prices than the restaurant in back and the tables out under the arcade. These include, at about 5€ ($5.75), your choice of roast chicken, duck with rice, or shellfish *açorda*. Even if you opt for soup, main course, wine, and dessert, the tab in the cafe shouldn't be more than 10€ ($12). Figure about double that in the more formal dining room. Attendance at charm academy isn't an employment requirement.

Praça do Comércio 3 (corner of Rua da Prata). © **21/886-6213.** Main courses 10€–15€ ($12–$17); *ementa turística* 13€ ($14). AE, DC, MC, V. Mon–Sat 7am–11pm. Metro: Baixa/Chiado.

O Múni PORTUGUESE   Apart from the fact that it doesn't set tables out on the pedestrian street, there isn't much stylistically to distinguish this *adega* (tavern) from any of the other two dozen or so in central Baixa. Until the food arrives, that is. First up are the trademark deep-fried green beans. Then come roast kid cutlets, the gaminess offset by lashings of onions and garlic, accompanied by potatoes, rice, and lemon wedges. Main courses are divided equally between meats and seafood. Families, couples, and groups of friends occupy the 10 tables; meals proceed at a measured pace.

Correiros 117 (north of Rua da Vitoria). © **21/342-8982.** Main courses 9€–11€ ($10–$13); *ementa turística* 13€ ($15). AE, MC, V. Mon–Fri noon–4pm and 7:30–midnight. Closed Sept. Metro: Baixa/Chiado.

WEST OF THE CENTER

Alcântara Café INTERNATIONAL   You have to see this place: Cast-iron columns and beams hold up the 7.5m (25-ft.) ceiling, and a full-size replica of the Winged Victory looms over the zigzag bar. Fans turn lazily overhead. Half the cavernous space is given to the restaurant, the rest to the drinking trade. The place draws a hip young crowd, and it isn't unusual for patrons to show up for dinner at midnight. They have a wide choice of uncomplicated fare in minimalist presentations, including such items as cold lobster salad, steak tartare, and steamed skate. Friday and Saturday evenings are big, so go another night to be assured of a table. You'll need a taxi coming to and going from this bleak industrial district.

Rua Maria Luisa Holstein 15. © **21/362-1226.** Reservations suggested on weekends. Main courses 14€–16€ ($16–$18). AE, DC, MC, V. Kitchen daily 4pm–1am; bar daily 8pm–3am. Bus: 57, but take a cab.

Sua Excelência PORTUGUESE   Just a block up the hill from the National Art Gallery, the restaurant has an interior resembling a provincial drawing room. Some dishes are uncommon in Portugal, often hailing from outposts of the former empire, including Angolan chicken cooked in palm oil with vegetables. Specialties include spicy prawns *piri-piri*, and *lulas a moda da casa* (squid stewed in white wine, crème fraîche, and cognac). Other possibilities include smoked swordfish and clams cooked at least five ways. One unusual specialty is "little jacks," small fish eaten whole, served with a well-flavored "paste" made from 2-day-old bread.

Rua do Conde 34. © **21/390-3614.** Reservations required. Main courses 13€–16€ ($15–$18). AE, MC, V. Mon–Tues and Thurs–Fri 1–3pm; Thurs–Tues 8–10:30pm. Closed Sept. Bus: 27 or 49. Tram: 25.

ON THE WATERFRONT

Espalha Brasas PORTUGUESE   A few blocks of two-story marine warehouses along the western waterfront—the Ribeirinha—have been converted to restaurants and clubs. This one is among the liveliest. The barbecue in the open kitchen turns out tempting plates like grilled marlin and skewered turbot and shrimp (with salad and baked potato). While you can put together a standard dinner from the menu, this is mainly a grazing place. But even if you order only a side of fried squid, you still get bread, flavored butters, a round of cheese, and four jars of pâtés. The place is much in demand on weekends, so call ahead—the walk-up reservation list can mean a wait of an hour or more. Many of the staff members speak English.

Doca de Santo Amaro, Armazém 12. ℂ **21/396-2059.** Reservations recommended on weekends. Main courses 9€–16€ ($10–$18); *ementa turística* 16€ ($18). AE, MC, V. Mon–Sat 12:30pm–2am. Bus: 12 or 20, but take a cab.

Jardim do Marisco ℱ PORTUGUESE/SEAFOOD   Another product of the ongoing gentrification of the waterfront, this sprawling emporium occupies a shedlike structure several blocks east of the Praça do Comércio. Glass walls afford unobstructed views of river traffic. The first room, on the left, is the *cervejaria*, with a long, curving bar. It serves less expensive meals than the glossy main dining room straight ahead. Before turning into the cafe section, take a moment to walk along the fish display counter bordering the open kitchen. Have the staff call a taxi when you're ready to leave, because they're hard to come by out here.

Doca Jardim do Tabaco, Av. Infante D. Henrique. ℂ **21/882-4242.** www.jardimdomarisco.pt. Main courses 7€–15€ ($8–$17). AE, MC, V. Mon–Sat noon–2am. Bus: 39 or 59.

Porcão ℱ BRAZILIAN   Get ready for this by skipping lunch, because what you have here is a *rodizio*, a carnivore's fantasy realized. If you've yet to experience this Brazilian extravaganza, get to this converted warehouse on the waterfront for the full over-the-top treatment. After you've been seated, cruise the center sushi/cheese/salad bar—over 30 items—then check out the nearby self-serve counter, with enough soup, sausages, rice, and beans to tide you over until the main events. On a signal, waiters march from the kitchen bearing steaming ribs, beef, chicken, lamb, pork, kidneys, and fish. Most are on skewers, and guys wield huge knives with controlled abandon, slicing and pushing all you want onto your plate, cascades of meat that only stop when you cry uncle. (Save room for the trolley of roast suckling pig.) They give you a paper medallion saying "No, thanks" and "Yes, please," but that's just part of the ritual. There's music every night. Take a taxi.

Rua Cintura do Porto de Lisboa, Cais de Santos, Docas. ℂ **21/393-2090.** Reservations suggested. Fixed-price meal 22€ ($24). AE, DC, MC, V. Tues–Sun 12:30–4pm and 7:30–midnight.

IN BELÉM

Rosa dos Mares PORTUGUESE   Stop in for a full meal or just a sandwich. A sample *ementa turística* consists of vegetable soup; a platter-size main course of roast goat (which tastes like rabbit) with rice, potatoes, baked tomato, and puréed spinach; flan or fruit salad; beverage; and coffee. We recommend that you skip dessert and walk a few doors down to the **Antiga Confeitaria de Belém** ℱ (ℂ **21/363-7423**), a landmark bar and tearoom in business since 1837. It serves the beloved *pastéis de Belém,* a cream-filled tart served with a shake of powdered sugar (.75€/85¢ each). Port or a *bica* goes well with one, two, or three.

Belém 110. ℂ **21/364-9275.** Main courses 8€–12€ ($9–$14); *ementa turística* 12€ ($14). MC, V. Mon noon–10pm; Tues–Sun noon–11pm. Closed 2–3 weeks in Feb. Tram: 15.

IN CACILHAS

A brief but popular waterborne excursion takes diners by ferry from the base of Praça do Comércio to the suburb of **Cacilhas,** on the opposite side of the Tejo, where there are plenty of seafood restaurants along the waterfront at the ferry landing, with great views of Lisbon. The trip costs less than 2€ and takes about 10 minutes.

FAST FOOD & PICNICKING

The Portuguese pizza-and-burger chain, **Abracadabra,** is similar to American imports, although service tends to be slower. Three branches are at Centro Comercial Imaviz next to the Sheraton Hotel, on Praça Dom Pedro IV (Rossio), and at Rua Aurea 19 in Baixa. **Ca das Sandes** is a fast-growing chain of soup-and-sandwich shops; two branches are at Calçada do Carmo 9 (1 block off Rossio), and at Rua da Vitoria 57 (near Rua Augusta) in Baixa.

A well-stocked supermarket near the Rossio, **Celeiro,** Dezembro 81 (© 21/342-7495; Metro: Rossio), offers ready-cooked fare like roast chicken at 6€ ($7) per kilo (2.2 lb.). Of the many *charcutarias* downtown, you might make an effort to seek out **Tábuas,** Barros Queiroz 45 (© 21/342-6169; Metro: Rossio), off the northeast corner of the Rossio. It carries prepared salads, wine, bread, fruit, and a large selection of cheese, sausages, and cured hams.

Enjoy your picnic in any of the city's numerous parks. Favorites are the grounds of the **Castelo São Jorge** atop Alfama; the **belvedere of Rua de São Pedro de Alcântara** in the Bairro Alto; and **Parque Eduardo VII,** which has picnic tables.

WORTH A SPLURGE

Conventual ⚜⚜⚜ PORTUGUESE/INTERNATIONAL   On an attractive but secluded plaza northwest of Bairro Alto, this gem hides its considerable light from the tourist hordes. That helps make it a fave of in-the-know executives, the social set, and assorted fashionistas. They dine in a setting that illustrates the ecclesiastical name with such objects as a woodcarving of a bishop, a fragment of a Gothic choir stall, and a relief panel of the Last Supper. But this isn't a spiritual experience unless you are transported by secular victuals (a distinct possibility). Culinary influences from every corner of the former Portuguese empire show up on the parade of plates. Shrimp curry with garnishes of chutney, raisins, and pineapple chunks is typical, as is rich tomato soup poured over a poached egg atop a crouton in the middle of the bowl. At least five people attend you; the diminutive, grandmotherly lady who takes your order is the owner.

Praça das Flores 45. © 21/390-9196. Reservations recommended. Main courses 13€–21€ ($14–$24). AE, DC, MC, V. Mon–Fri 12:30–3pm; Tues–Sat 7:30–11:30pm; Sun 12:30–10pm.

Solar dos Presuntos ⚜⚜ PORTUGUESE   A tank crammed with spiny lobsters stands inside the door next to the service bar. The walls of both ground floor and upstairs dining rooms are filled with photos and caricatures of domestic and international celebs. *Presunto* is a cured Iberian ham similar to Italian prosciutto, and a plate of thin slices arrives as soon as you've ordered. Many of the patrons have been regulars for years, greeted enthusiastically at the door. A specialty is the four lightly fried cod cakes with a side of soupy rice and beans. Most of the year, foreigners are barely in evidence, but some English is spoken by the hurried staff. Find the restaurant at the foot of the funicular east of the Avenida da Liberdad, the Elevador do Lavra.

Portas de Stanto Antão 150. © 21/342-4253. Reservations suggested. Main courses 9.75€–22€ ($11–$26). AE, MC, V. Mon–Sat noon–3pm and 7–11pm.

4 Seeing the Sights

Imperial Portugal established colonies around the world, from Brazil to Angola to Macao. But its explorers and conquerors were less diligently ruthless than some of their rivals in plundering the civilizations they encountered, and so the purloined national patrimony is far less rich than that of such competing powers as England, France, and Spain. The best museums are those showcasing the collected artworks of generous private citizens or groups, such as the Gulbenkian Museum and the Chiado Museum, and those featuring native arts and crafts, including the Museum of Decorative Arts. Otherwise, the sights of greatest interest are architectural in nature, notably the Jeronimos Monastery, or scenic settings, especially St. George's Castle, which is a good place to begin your explorations.

THE CASTLE & THE MONASTERY

Castelo São Jorge (St. George's Castle) 🏰🏰🏰 More than 2,000 years ago, this strategic hill was the site of important Roman and Moorish fortifications, later amplified by the Christian kings. Today it's a place for relaxation in gardens and playgrounds and beside ponds and waterways. Birdsong and avian chatter fill the trees. Free-roaming peacocks shriek and preen, caged roosters crow, and ducks, geese, and mute swans compete for territory. There are keeps and battlements to wander, and many stone benches and tables at which to rest. Take a camera, for there are many photo ops, not just of the city below but also of the play of light over the trees and ancient walls. A moderately expensive restaurant, the **Casa do Leão**, occupies part of a ruined wall, and in front of the entrance is a small **outdoor cafe**. The views are spectacular. It's a steep uphill walk from the nearest bus and tram stops, so you might want to take a taxi all the way to the castle entrance and walk back down.

Alfama district. Free admission. Daily 9am–sunset. Tram: 28. Bus: 37.

Mosteiro dos Jerónimos (Jerónimos Monastery) 🏰🏰 An extravagant expression of gratitude for the discoveries of Vasco da Gama—who's buried here, although some claim otherwise—and other Portuguese navigators, this monastery is unmistakable, gleaming white in the sun. It contains the Gothic-Renaissance **Church of Santa Maria,** famed for its deeply carved stonework. Formerly on the bank of the river, which has since shifted direction, the church evolved from a chapel built by Prince Henry the Navigator to its current soaring majesty, replete with decorative allusions to the sea and the fruits of the empire it spawned. Three Portuguese kings, their sarcophagi decorated with elephants, are also to be found here. Since church admission is free and the entrance fee admits you to only the adjacent cloister, you might want to save the cash for one of the other Belém museums. In the monastery's west wing is the **Museu da Marinha (Maritime Museum);** see below.

Value Getting the Best Deal on Sightseeing

- Remember that many museums are **free on Sunday** morning and some are free Wednesday morning.
- Take advantage of the low-cost **Lisboa Card** (see "Lisbon Deals & Discounts," earlier in this chapter).
- Note that **tram 28** traverses the city's most intriguing neighborhoods, providing a great orientation.
- Be aware that the 1½- to 2-hour **public tram and bus tours** (see "Organized Tours," below) pass most of the important sights at a far lower cost than that charged by private companies.

Praça do Império 10–17, Belém. 🕐 **21/362-0034.** Free admission to church; admission to cloister 3€ ($3.45) adults, 1.50€ ($1.75) seniors and age 15–25, free for children under 15. May–Sept Tues–Sun 10am–6pm; Oct–Apr 10am–5pm. Closed holidays. Tram: 15. Bus: 27, 28, 29, 43, 49, or 51.

THE TOP MUSEUMS

Museu da Fundação Calouste Gulbenkian (Gulbenkian Foundation Museum) 😄😄😄 A magnificent art treasury, this museum houses one of the Continent's largest privately amassed collections of paintings, furniture, ceramics, sculptures, tapestries, and coins. The gift of an Armenian multimillionaire, the made-to-order building contains objects and artworks from 5,000 years of history, with **Egyptian artifacts** from the 3rd millennium B.C., 14th-century **Chinese porcelain,** 17th-century **Japanese prints, Greek gold coins** from 500 B.C., **stone cylinder seals** of Mesopotamia (3000 B.C.), **silk carpets** from Armenia, and paintings by **Rubens, Rembrandt, Gainsborough, Renoir, Turner, Watteau, Monet,** and **Degas.** Keep an eye out for unexpected little displays, such as the room of enchanting **Guardi Venetian cityscapes** and the book-size **Gothic ivory miniatures** of the Passion. If you get hungry, stop at the cafe, as there aren't many options in the immediate neighborhood.

On the opposite side of the extensive garden is the **Museu do Centro de Arte Moderna (Museum of Modern Art),** Rua Dr. Nicolau Bettencourt (🕐 **21/795-0241;** Metro: Praça de Espanha). Centering on contemporary Portuguese artists, it contains works in most mediums, from painting and sculpture to photographs and prints. Musical performances are irregularly scheduled.

Berna 45. ⓒ 21/782-3000. www.gulbenkian.pt. Admission 3€ ($3.45) adults, free for seniors and students, free to all Sun. Tues 4–6pm; Wed–Sun 10am–6pm. Closed holidays. Metro: Praça de Espanha. Tram: 24. Bus: 16, 26, or 30.

Museu da Marinha (Maritime Museum) Contained at the west end of the Mosteiro dos Jerónimos is this large collection of maps, maritime paraphernalia, and finely detailed models of ships old and new, including Egyptian and Greek warships from 3000 B.C. In an annex across the way is an exhibit of life-size royal barges, galleons, and sailing ships. In between is the **Planetário Gulbenkian** (Planetarium), which offers astronomical shows Saturday and Sunday at 5pm. An English version of the show is offered as well. Admission fees are the same as for the Maritime Museum.

Praça do Império, Belém. ⓒ 21/362-0010. Admission 3€ ($3.45) adults, 1€ ($1.15) seniors and children 6–17, free for children under 6. June–Sept Tues–Sun 10am–6pm; Oct–May Tues–Sun 10am–5pm. Closed holidays. Tram: 15 or 17. Bus: 29 or 43.

Museu de Arte Popular Not far from the Torre de Belém (see below), this folkloric museum displays not only traditional Portuguese native art but also costumes, kitchen implements, tools, furniture, leather goods, and ceramics. It's on the wrong (harbor) side of the highway and railroad line. Visitors must walk about 10 minutes west of the Centro Cultural de Belém (see "More Attractions," below) and cross the pedestrian bridge.

Av. Brasília, Belém. ⓒ 21/301-1282. Admission 1.75€ ($2). Tues–Sun 10am–12:30pm and 2–5pm. Closed holidays. Tram: 15. Bus: 27, 28, 29, 43, or 49.

Museu do Chiado This impressive facility houses a permanent collection of post-1850 art and frequent temporary exhibits of painting, sculpture, photography, and mixed-media works. Portuguese artists are featured, and the building itself is at least as interesting.

Serpa Pinto 4. ⓒ 21/343-2148. Admission 3€ ($3.45), free Sun and holidays. Tues 2–6pm; Wed–Sun 10am–6pm. Closed major holidays. Tram: 28. Bus: 58 or 100. Metro: Baixa-Chiado.

Museu-Escola de Artes Decorativas Portuguesas (Museum School of Decorative Arts) In the Azurara Palace, a 17th-century mansion halfway up Alfama hill, this museum displays Portuguese decorative pieces and furniture from the 17th and 18th centuries, most in the Indo-Portuguese style derived from Portugal's Far Eastern colonial experience. On the premises is a school of decorative arts; the work of the foundation includes restoration and reproduction. The artisans are masters of woodcarving, cabinetry, inlay, painting, lacquerwork, and gilding, and they've done restorations for Versailles and Fontainebleau as well as the Rockefellers. Apprentices work at their sides.

Largo das Portas do Sol 2. ⓒ 21/881-4600. www.fress.pt. Admission 5€ ($5.75) adults, 2.50€ ($2.90) seniors, free for children under 12. Tues–Sun 10am–5pm. Closed holidays. Tram: 12 or 28. Bus: 37.

Museu Nacional de Arte Antiga ✷ Take the elevator to the third floor of this former palace built almost 400 years ago and stroll among mostly Portuguese paintings from the early Renaissance to the 18th century. The second floor has ancient ceramics and porcelains from both Europe and Portugal's Asian colonies, supplemented by antique furnishings and textiles. There's a cafe on the ground floor.

Rua das Janelas Verdes. ⓒ 21/391-2800. Admission 3€ ($3.45) adults, 1.50€ ($1.75) seniors and students, free for children under 14. Tues 2–6pm; Wed–Sun 10am–5:50pm. Tram: 15, 18, or 25. Bus: 14, 27, 28, 32, 49, or 60.

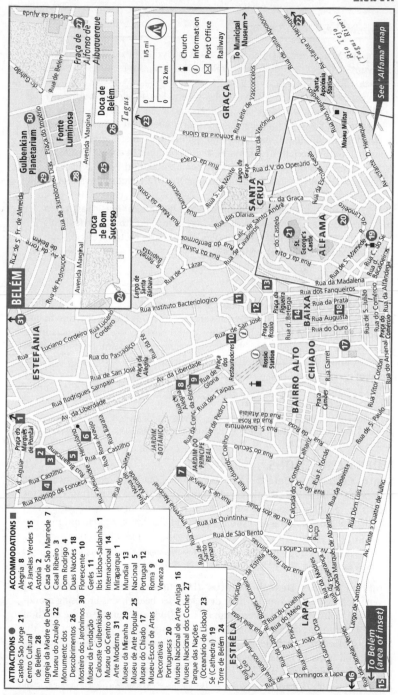

Lisbon

Special & Free Events

In late March, the festival season kicks off with an **outdoor musical event** at the Centro Cultural in Belém. The program includes classical, jazz, rock, and pop performers.

On June 12 and 13, Lisbon celebrates the **Feast Day of St. Anthony** with *marchas* (strolling groups of singers and musicians). On the evening of June 12, costumed revelers parade along Avenida da Liberdade. Festivities include dances, bonfires, and general merriment in the taverns until dawn, especially in Alfama. Festivities on June 24 and 29 in Alfama honor Lisbon's other popular saints—**John, Peter,** and **Paul**—with bonfires and revelry at various sights around the city, including the Castelo São Jorge.

From mid-June to mid-July, Sintra holds its **classical music festival** in various gardens and palaces. It overlaps with the **Estoril jazz festivals** in early July. In the fall, Cascais holds its own **jazz festival.** Check local newspapers or the Web for details.

Museu Nacional dos Coches (Coach Museum) ⋇⋇ The famous collection of hundreds of aristocratic coaches and sedan chairs has returned to its old home, a former royal riding school. Some of the carriages are as long as railroad cars, decorated in mind-bogglingly excessive manner, with lashings of gilt, swags of velvet, and swirls of carving. If ever emblems of wealth were sure to boil the blood of nascent revolutionaries, these would do the trick. The oldest dates from 1581; Elizabeth II of the United Kingdom used the latest, from 1824, during her 1958 state visit.

Praça Afonso de Albuquerque. ⊘ **21/361-0850.** Admission 3€ ($3.45) adults, 1.50€ ($1.75) seniors and age 14–25, free for children under 14, free to all Sun 10am–2pm. Tues–Sun 10am–5:30pm. Closed Mon and holidays. Tram: 15. Bus: 14, 27, 28, 29, 43, 49, or 51.

MORE ATTRACTIONS

Centro Cultural de Belém This vast contemporary structure seems to take inspiration from Moorish palaces, gleaming in the sun like nearby Jerónimos Monastery. Fulfilling its role as a cultural center, it schedules a banquet of activities that include traveling art exhibits, pop and classical concerts, and film festivals. On the premises are several shops and galleries and a cafeteria.

Praça do Império, Belém. ⊘ **21/361-2400.** www.ccb.pt. Free admission to Center; admission for temporary exhibits varies. Daily 11am–8pm. Tram: 15 or 17. Bus: 27, 28, 29, 43, or 49.

Monumento dos Descobrimentos (Monument of the Discoveries)
Several hundred yards from the Torre de Belém (see below), this imposing monument was built in 1960 to commemorate the 500th anniversary of the death of Prince Henry the Navigator, who founded Portugal's first observatory and the Sagres Nautical School. It depicts the prince leading a throng of sailors, captains, priests, and poets to imperial glory. In the pavement is a map chronicling Portuguese discoveries from 1427 to 1541. An elevator runs to the top.

Av. Brasília, Belém. ⊘ **21/303-1950.** Admission 2€ ($2.30). Tues–Sun 9am–5pm (until 6:30pm July–Aug). Tram: 15. Bus: 27, 28, 43, or 49.

Oceanário de Lisboa (Oceanarium) ✦   The imaginatively designed aquarium is the centerpiece of the Parque das Nações. Climb two floors and work your way down. The main element is a large tank as high as the building, meant to represent the open ocean, filled with various sea creatures. Around the perimeter on several levels are both underwater and above-surface exhibits relating to various seas and shores: rocky North Atlantic outcroppings for murres and kittiwakes, a sub-Antarctic island with penguins, a Pacific coastline harboring playful sea otters, and a fragment of Indian Ocean with neon fish below and chattering birds in the palms above. At ground level are smaller tanks with more fragile or exotic specimens—watch for the Australian "sea dragons," which disguise themselves as seaweed.

Parque das Nações, Av. de Berlim. ✆ 21/891-7002. Admission 9€ ($10) adults, 5€ ($5.75) seniors, 4.50€ ($5.20) children 4–12, free for children under 4. Daily 10am–6pm (summer until 7pm). Metro: Oriente.

Parque das Nações   Officials claimed a total attendance of 13 million at Expo '98, but actual results and postmortems were mixed. The exposition area was, in effect, a satellite city on the east bank of the Tejo, northeast of downtown Lisbon. Re-christened the "Park of the Nations," the site contains the Oceanarium as well as the usual futuristic architectural pavilions, some of which have been converted to concert venues and convention centers.

Access is from the Oriente Metro station, through a bi-level shopping mall, the **Centro Vasco da Gama.** Crowded at all hours, the mall is easily the most popular attraction associated with the park. Most of the large park site is modern, windswept, and empty. Getting around requires a lot of walking or use of the shuttle bus. Down the center of the main vehicular promenade, **Alameda dos Oceanos,** a row of fountains erupts at intervals like Old Faithful. You can rent rubber boats and bikes, and there's a cable car to ride. Some of the Expo eating places, none of them memorable, remain open. The best reason to make the trek from downtown is the Oceanarium (reviewed above) and the mall.

Av. de Berlim. ✆ 21/891-9333. Free admission. Sun–Thurs 9:30am 1am; Fri–Sat 9.30am–3am. Metro: Oriente.

Sé (Cathedral)   Built in the 12th century as a fortress-church by Portugal's first Christian king, Afonso Henriques, this is Lisbon's oldest surviving church. Its original Romanesque facade and towers were left largely undamaged by two violent earthquakes, but much of the rest of the exterior and interior has been repeatedly renovated, not always to good effect.

Largo da Sé, Alfama. ✆ 21/886-9145. Free admission. Mon–Sat 10am–5pm. Tram: 12 or 28. Bus: 37.

Torre de Belém (Tower of Belém)   Blending elements of the Gothic and Renaissance in a style known as Manueline, with seafaring motifs and allusions to the purloined fruits of the colonies, this 16th-century watchtower was built as protection against pirates. It now contains a small museum of arms and armor. UNESCO has designated it a World Heritage building. Its upper platform delivers a panoramic view of the Tejo, but because there isn't much else to the interior, you might simply want to appreciate the tower from the outside, without paying admission.

Off Av. Brasília, Belém. ✆ 21/362-0034. Admission 3€ ($3.45) adults, 1.20€ ($1.40) seniors and students, free for children under 15. May–Sept Tues–Sun 10am–6pm; Oct–Apr Tues–Sun 10am–5pm. Tram: 15. Bus: 27, 28, 43, 49, or 51.

PARKS & GARDENS

The most important botanical gardens are the **Jardim Botânico** and **Jardim da Estrêla.** The largest parks are **Parque de Monsanto** and underutilized **Parque**

Eduardo VII, which contains the ornate Sports Pavilion and a small lake with ducks, geese, and a pair of peacocks. The following small parks and terraces offer views of the city: the **Alto de Santa Catarina,** on Rua da Santa Catarina; the **Castelo São Jorge,** at the top of Alfama; the **Luenta dos Quarteis, Moinho dos Mochos, Alto da Serafina,** and **Montes Claros** in the Parque de Monsanto; **Ponte,** at Viaducto Duarte Pacheco; the belvedere of **Santa Luzia** in the Bairro Alto; **Zimborio da Basilica da Estrêla** on Largo da Estrêla; and the park at **Rua de São Pedro de Alcântara.**

ORGANIZED TOURS

BY TRAM   Along its entire route, **tram 28** passes through Lisbon's most picturesque neighborhoods—the Bairro Alto, Alfama, and Graça. With its swoops and sudden swift turns, it is almost as much fun as an amusement park ride.

Since 1901, trams have negotiated the intimate alleys and tight corners of Lisbon's old quarters, and they're still going strong. The city's public transport company, **Carris** (© 21/358-2334; www.carris.pt), offers a 1½-hour tram tour of historic districts and monuments, with guides and interpreters aboard. Departures are from Praça do Comércio four times daily in July and August, twice daily in June. Tickets (sold on board) are 16€ ($18) adults and 8€ ($9.20) children 4 to 10; those under 4 ride free.

BY BUS   Carris (see above) also offers two tours on double-decker buses, allowing you to get on and off at any of the 16 to 18 stops along the Tejo circuit from Baixa to Belém or the Oriente circuit from the center to Parque das Nações. Tickets cost 13€ ($15) adults and 6.50€ ($7.50) children 4 to 10. They're good for a full day (hang onto your ticket), and you can buy them onboard. The buses leave Praça do Comércio hourly from 11am to 4pm in May, June, July, and September, and until 5pm in August. Private companies offering tours in Lisbon (and to such regional destinations as Sintra, Estoril, and Queluz) are **Gray Line** (© 21/352-2594; www.grayline.com), **Cityrama** (© 21/319-1091; www.cityrama.pt), and **Portugal Tours** (© 21/352-2902).

5 Shopping

The **value-added tax** (**IVA** in Portugal) varies according to the item or service sold. In most cases it's 8% to 17%. Visitors from non–European Union countries are entitled to a refund of the tax if purchases in a single duty-free store total at least 59€ ($68), exclusive of IVA. For details on getting your refund, see "Frommer's Money-Saving Strategies" in chapter 1.

Words to remember are *saldos* (sales) and *descontos* (discounts), most often seen after Christmas and in late summer.

The best buys are ceramics, porcelain, pottery, and embroidered and leather goods, but bargains are no longer as common as they once were. To view some of what's available in local pottery and crafts, **Centro de Turismo e Artesanato,**

Tips Market Watch

On Tuesday and Saturday, the **Feira da Ladra** ("Thieves" or Flea Market) runs from 9am to 6pm in Campo de Santa Clara behind the Igreja São Vicente. Take bus no. 12 from the Santa Apolónia Station, or tram 28. You'll find clothing, pottery, glassware, trinkets, electronics, old pieces of tile, and much more.

Castilho 61B (© 21/386-3830), is one of the better shops. The stock is exten sive, and the personable manager speaks fluent English and will arrange for packing and shipping anywhere.

Late-night shoppers might want to seek out the intriguing **Francesinha Handicraft Shop,** Barroca 96, in the Bairro Alto. It's often open past midnight. In Chiado, a few steps from the Largo do Carmo, is **Viúva Lamego,** Calçada do Sacramento 29 (© 21/346-9692), an outlet of the prominent ceramics firm. It displays a great variety of tiles, tureens, vases, bowls, and platters in several tra ditional styles. The store accepts credit cards and ships anywhere.

The smartest shops are on **Ruas Augusta** and **Garrett** in Baixa and in the higher Chiado district. **Rua da Escola Politécnica** is the upper end of a long street with several names (Rua do Alecrim, Rua da Misericórdia, Rua de São Pedro de Alcântara, and Rua Dom Pedro IV). Scattered all along it are many intriguing **antiques** shops.

Although small shops are still the norm, the foreign concept of mega- and mini malls has taken hold in this country of small enterprises. The new **Armazens do Chiado,** a three-level mall with an entrance at Rua do Carmo, opened after the 1988 fire that destroyed much of Chiado. **Colombo,** Avenida Lusiadas, Letras (© 21/716-0250), contains 10 cinemas, 421 stores, 64 restaurants, a 24-lane bowling alley, and a roller coaster. Similar malls are **Imaviz,** next to the Sheraton Hotel, and the **Centro Vasco da Gama,** at the entrance of the Parque das Nações.

The **Livraria Británica,** Luís Fernandes 14 (© 21/342-8472), carries only English-language works, with a British emphasis. While the selection isn't too wide, the **Livraria Europa-América,** Marquês Tomar 1 (© 21/356-3791), stocks books and magazines in several languages, including English.

6 Lisbon After Dark

Lisbon's nightlife has exploded. Only a few years ago, most clubs and discos locked up by 2am. Now, following the lead of their Spanish neighbors, many of them rock until dawn. A few don't bother opening until 6am, thumping on 'til noon! For information on performances and productions, contact the **tourist office** (see "Visitor Information," above) or the **Agência de Bilhetes para Espectáculos Públicos,** a large kiosk on the east side of Praça dos Restauradores (© 21/347- 5823; Metro: Restauradores), open daily 9am to 10pm. The kiosk sells tickets to all cinemas and theaters except the National Theater of São Carlos, and to fre quent concerts by name rock bands stopping in Lisbon on world tours.

The official tourist biweekly guide, *Follow Me Lisboa,* has the latest listings (in English), as does the *Diário de Noticias* (in Portuguese).

THE PERFORMING ARTS

The season for opera, theater, ballet, jazz, and other concerts is October to May, with additional performances throughout the year. The main venues are the **Teatro Nacional de Dona Maria II** (www.teatro-dmaria.pt) in Rossio Square (Metro: Rossio); the **Teatro Nacional de São Carlos** (www.saocarlos.pt), Serpa Pinto 9 (tram: 12); the **Fundação Calouste Gulbenkian** (www.gulbenkian.pt), Berna 45 (tram: 24); the **Teatro Municipal São Luís,** António Maria Cardoso 40 (tram: 28); the **Gran Auditório de la Culturgest,** Rua Arco do Cego (© 21/ 790-5155; Metro: Campo Pequeno); the **Teatro Trindade,** Trinidade 7–A (© 21/ 342-3200; tram: 28); and the **Centro Cultural de Belém** (www.ccb.pt), Praça do Império (© 21/361-2400; tram: 15 or 17).

Tickets might cost as little as 5€ to 25€ ($5.75–$29) and can rise to as high as 75€ ($86). The price varies greatly depending on the artists or companies performing. The Centro Cultural de Belém offers *free* **"happy-hour"** concerts up to four times a week from 7 to 9pm throughout the year. The programs take in everything from fado to pop to jazz.

LIVE-MUSIC CLUBS

Fado is to Lisbon what jazz is to New Orleans and flamenco is to Seville—a native art relying on emotion and spontaneity. While it isn't to everyone's taste, a Lisbon experience isn't complete without it. Fado clubs (*adegas típicas* or *restaurantes típicos*) serve dinner before and during the entertainment, which usually starts about 10pm. You can dine elsewhere and arrive around 11pm to enjoy the show for a lower cover charge. Ask how much it is before entering—it's typically about 13€ to 20€ ($14–$23), which covers admission and a drink or two. There's a fado festival in Lisbon in February.

The well-known fado club **Lisboa à Noite,** Gáveas 69 (© **21/346-8557;** tram: 24), isn't unusually expensive, but the minimum (which covers a couple of highballs, a small carafe of wine, and an appetizer or snack) might rise when the famous owner and diva, Fernanda Maria, is in residence and performing. The interior is more restrained than in other clubs, as are the routine pitches to buy cassettes and souvenirs. It's open Tuesday to Sunday 8:30pm to 3am. There's no cover; the minimum is usually 15€ ($17).

Although **Canto do Camões,** Travessa da Espera 38 (© **21/346-5464;** tram: 24), isn't spared bus tours of tourists, the club has a somehow more authentic—or at least less contrived—air than its many nearby competitors. It's a little less expensive, too, with a minimum of 12€ ($14). Every half-hour or so, a singer takes her place among the patrons, shawl pulled tightly around her and head thrown back, and lets loose. At least one guitarist accompanies her. The food is satisfactory, especially the cod dishes. The club is open Tuesday to Sunday 8pm to 2am, with the last show around 11:30pm.

Patrons often join in the singing at **Parreirinha da Alfama,** Espírito Santo 1 (© **21/886-8209;** bus: 37), one of the less expensive quality fado clubs. Sets are every 20 minutes from 10pm to 3am, and main courses run 5€ to 18€ ($5.75–$21). Go later just for music and drinks. It's open Monday to Saturday 8pm to 2am.

As riveting as fado can be, an evening of it goes a long way. Alternative entertainment is available: Jazz, rock, and Afro-Brazilian pop are popular, and a number of clubs present live groups several nights a week. An entirely new nighttime

---

Moments With or Without Cherries?

All over downtown are open-door, closet-size bars that cater to an informal but revered ritual. Drop in, step up, and raise a finger or say *"ginginha"* (pronounced, very roughly, "zheen-*zheen*-ya"). The man will ask *"Com ou sim?"* meaning "With or without cherries?" He'll pour a shot of ruby-colored liqueur, the nectar that gets its color from the fruit. It can be merely a quick jolt or a chance to linger for a chat.

A classic of the breed is **A Ginjinha,** S. Domingo 8, occupying a cubicle in the end of the building to the right of the National Theater. A pop costs .75€ (85¢). Eat the cherries for an extra punch.

scene has sprung up along the waterfront running west of the city center to the Ponte 25 de Abril, a district known as the **Ribeirinha.**

At **Hot Clube de Portugal,** Praça da Alegria 39 (© 21/346-7369; Metro: Avenida), the sounds of mainstream and fusion jazz fill a traditional subterranean environment that's usually blue with cigarette smoke. It's open Tuesday to Saturday 10pm to 2am, with live performances at 11pm and 12:30am Thursday to Saturday. The cover runs 2.50€ to 8€ ($2.90–$9.20) when there's live music, beginning about 11:30pm.

BARS

A burgeoning crop of night owls is keeping Lisbon bars and clubs open later and later. Many of the popular spots don't even bother to open until 10pm or later.

Across from one of the city's most appealing parks and belvederes, **Harry's Bar,** São Pedro de Alcântara 57 (© 21/346-0760; tram: 28 or Elevador da Glória), is a long-lived cocktail lounge. The **Instituto do Vinho do Porto,** São Pedro de Alcântara 45 (© 21/347-5707; tram: 28 or Elevador da Glória), is a comfortable retreat serving Portugal's trademark tipple. The walls and ceilings of **Pavilhão Chines Bar,** Dom Pedro V 89 (© 21/342-4729; tram: 28), are crammed with an often-kitschy collection of toys, collectibles, and oddities. There are also two billiard tables.

GAY & LESBIAN BARS

Harry's Bar (see above) attracts a mixed straight and gay crowd. Near the Bairro Alto, **Memorial,** Gustavo de Matos Sequeira 42 (© 21/396-8891; Metro: Rato; bus: 6, 27, 49, or 58), is a decent if unremarkable meet-and-greet spot for Lisbon's gay community. The city's largest gay dance club is **Trumps,** Imprensa Nacionale 104B (© 21/397-1059; Metro: Rato; bus: 6, 49, or 58), near the Bairro Alto. It attracts a mixed crowd, but most of its clientele is gay men.

DANCE CLUBS

Lisbon's classier nightspots are permitted to charge an outrageous cover to keep out the riffraff, but well-dressed respectable-looking types are usually admitted free. A moderate admission might be charged if the place is full.

Salsa Latina, Gare Marítima de Alcântara, Docas (© 21/395-0555; bus: 12 or 20), revels in its voluptuous tropical tone. **Lux Frágil,** Avenida Infante D. Henrique (© 21/882-0890; www.luxfragil.com), is popular with the film and fashion crowd, American actor John Malkovich is one of the owners. **Indústria,** Instituto Industrial 6 (© 21/396-4841; tram: 15 or 18; bus: 14, 20, 28, 32, 38, 40, or 43), is located in a converted factory. **Kremlin,** Travessa das Escadinhas da Praia 5 (© 21/397-9103; bus: 14, 20, 22, 28, 32, 38, 40, or 43), is an exemplar of a pounding, frenetic dance club that doesn't open until 2am and is often the last stop on the nocturnal circuit.

7 Side Trips: Palaces & Picturesque Towns

THE ESTORIL COAST

Long favored by aristocratic expatriates, this stretch of Atlantic shore west of the capital still harbors a few representatives of Europe's dwindling nobility. While unrestricted development has taken its toll, the coast remains diverting, if only for day trips or an overnight contrast to the city. Almost 60 trains leave Lisbon's Cais do Sodré station daily 5:30am to 2:30am. Estoril is a 30-minute ride, and Cascais 40 minutes. The round-trip fare to Cascais is 2.50€ ($2.90). By **car** from Lisbon, take either the Coastal Estrada Marginal Road west from Praça do

Comércio or the A-5 Auto-Estrada west from the Praça Marquês de Pombal, following signs.

Estoril is 24km (15 miles) from Lisbon. Its **casino and nightclub** is open daily 3pm to 3am (except Christmas Eve). Dinner starts at 8:30pm; the floor show, which includes topless showgirls, starts at 11pm. International headliners sometimes appear. Figure on spending at least $80 per person for dinner and the show. Bring your passport for entrance.

A few miles farther is **Cascais.** Once a drowsy village, it has followed the familiar progression from fishing port to artists' colony to here-comes-everybody. Working boats still find berths among the pleasure craft, and tamarisk and hibiscus struggle for space between *boîtes* and boutiques. You'll find a pretty beach, umbrella-covered sidewalk cafes, and lively youthful nightlife.

After Cascais, the coast starts to bend north, and you'll need a car to continue. The temper of the sea changes, as the intimidating Atlantic directly rakes the shore. Wave action has bored gaping cavities into the sheer cliffs at **Boca do Inferno,** a popular photo op. Farther along, the land flattens, the vegetation thins, and fine white sand streams in gusts across the road. Eventually, the land lifts again toward the headlands, pocketing the beaches. Breakers belly into milk-green curls before collapsing in an unending thunderous boil. This is prime windsurfing territory, but both surfers and swimmers must be careful of the powerful undertow.

WHERE TO STAY   For an overnight in Cascais, try the unpretentious 105-room **Hotel Baía,** Avenida Marginal, 2754–509 Lisboa (*☎* **21/483-1033;** fax 21/483-1095; www.hotelbaia.com), overlooking the beach and its fishing boats. Its front rooms have small balconies with unobstructed views of the strand and bay, and on the roof is a covered pool. Even in summer, the rates aren't bad (singles from 95€/$109, doubles from 115€/$132, breakfast included), but the rest of the year they drop substantially. Spring for an ocean view. American Express, Diners Club, MasterCard, and Visa are accepted.

WHERE TO DINE   Numerous options abound, but do check out the seafood restaurants on the streets bordering the Cascais fish market. Past the very good but very pricey O Pescador on Rua das Flores, **O Batel,** Travessa das Flores 4 (*☎* **21/483-0215**), faces the market. The *ementa* is a good deal; if you aren't too hungry, consider one of the cheaper main courses, like *arroz de marisco.* The restaurant is open Thursday to Tuesday noon to 3pm and 7 to 10:30pm; it accepts MasterCard and Visa.

SINTRA

Spend an hour in **Sintra,** a place of myth and magic, and you'll likely agree with Lord Byron, who famously called this hill town "a glorious Eden." At every turn of the road is another battlement, spire, or watchtower. About 29km (18 miles) from Lisbon, the town swells regularly with day-trippers from the capital. Botanists thrill to some 90 species of unusual plants thriving in the hills, and romantics revel (as Romantics once reveled) in Sintra's two marvelous palaces.

Three or four **trains** an hour make the run to Sintra from Lisbon's Estação Rossio. The unscenic trip takes 45 minutes and costs 1.25€ ($1.44) one-way. Despite its hilly location, the walk from the station to the center of the town is fairly level and takes only 15 to 20 minutes. A **taxi** costs about 2.50€ ($2.90). The local **tourist office,** Praça da República 23 (*☎* **21/923-1157**), is open daily 9am to 7pm (to 8pm in summer). To **drive** to Sintra, follow the directions above to Cascais, then continue on the N-247 Coastal Road as it turns north and then inland to Sintra.

Huge conical twin chimneys dominate the **main square,** bordered by pastel-colored shops and houses. This is the **Palacio Nacional de Sintra** ✮✮, also known as the Paço Real (© **21/923-0085**). It's open Thursday to Tuesday 10am to 1pm and 2 to 5pm. What survives today dates mainly from the 14th to the 16th centuries, with fragments from a Moorish fortress once on the site. It's largely baroque, with Gothic, Manueline, and Islamic flourishes. Most impressive are the decorative tilework, tapestries, gilded ceilings, and royal kitchen, positioned, logically enough, at the base of those two giant chimneys. Look for the **Sala das Pegas:** The depictions of chattering magpies that cover the ceiling are a king's sour take on the gossiping ladies of the court.

An uphill lane leading to **Seteais** becomes a narrow channel between walls with mottled skins of moss and lichen. Bars of sunlight pierce the canopy of oak and eucalyptus from time to time, and high iron gates permit glimpses of the villas they protect. Byron walked the halls of the **Palácio dos Seteais,** now a luxury hotel. From there, he could see the ocean and, looking farther up, the golden cupolas of the **Palácio da Pena** ✮✮✮ (© **21/924-0861**), perched on a 390m (1,300-ft.) mountaintop. It's an extraordinary piece of romantic architecture from 1839, when it was built as a royal residence. Purists are offended by the palace's agglomeration of styles, not to mention its pink-and-yellow exterior. But Pena has nothing to do with aesthetics and everything to do with fantasy. A fanciful pastiche of Moorish, Gothic, and Manueline conceits, it incorporates a cloister and chapel from the ruins of a 16th-century monastery. It's open Tuesday to Sunday 10am to 1pm and 2 to 5pm (to 6:30pm in summer), with the last entrance 30 minutes before closing.

Admission to both Sintra palaces is 3€ ($3.45) June to September, 2€ ($2.30) October to May.

WHERE TO STAY   If any place in Portugal is worth a splurge, it's Sintra, and here's just the place: the six-room **Quinta das Sequoias** ✮✮, Estrada de Monserrate, 2710 Sintra (© **21/923-0342;** www.quintadasequoias.com). A country manor converted to a guesthouse of exceptional style, it sits on its own 16-hectare (40-acre) forest preserve. Breakfast is served at a long table in a dining room with a massive fireplace. The guest rooms are decorated with considerable flair, including antique furnishings and objects, plus views of Pena Palace from almost every window. They're most affordable in winter but aren't too steep in summer, going for about 145€ ($167) single and 160€ ($184) double, breakfast included. All major credit cards are accepted. The gracious manager is fluent in English. Reserve well in advance. To get there from Sintra, take the Monserrate Road, passing Seteais Palace on the right. After about ½ mile, watch for a private road on the left with a sign, QUINTA DAS SEQUOIAS.

WHERE TO DINE   Across from the National Palace is **Lojo do Vinho,** at the corner of Praça and Rua das Padarias, an unusual wedge-shaped wine shop. It serves light meals of cheese, grilled sausages, crusty bread, and half bottles of the local pressings. The fixed-price menu is a little steep, but smaller snacks and sandwiches cost as little as 1.25€ ($1.45). It's open daily 9am to 9pm in winter and 9am to midnight in summer, and no credit cards are accepted.

For a full meal, walk up from Lojo do Vinho to the tiny family-friendly **Alcobaca,** Rua das Padarias (© **21/923-1651**). The owner speaks English and takes a motherly interest in your well-being. It's open daily noon to 4pm and 7 to 10:30pm and accepts MasterCard and Visa.

15

London, Bath & Environs

by Richard Jones

London is 2,000 years old and swinging like never before. The opening of the Tate Gallery's new building (Tate Modern) on the Thames, opposite St. Paul's, means London can now rival Paris and New York at the cutting edge of art. The city's world-class museums just get better and better, while the smaller, more specialized museums are a joy to discover. The theater scene is unparalleled, the restaurant scene positively blooming, and the shopping scene superb (albeit a bit pricey). Opera, ballet, Brit pop, and Brit film are all thriving, yet traditional London is still alive and kicking, its history and pageantry evident all over the sprawling metropolis.

This rich diversity means London attracts more visitors than any other European city. Many who arrive expecting to see a city of historic buildings are often surprised, and even a little disappointed, by just how modern London is. The past is often not immediately apparent. Yet if you take the time to scratch the surface, you'll find it hidden enticingly away in the "inns of court" around Fleet Street; the "Dickensian" alleyways at the heart of the old city; the squares and peaceful gardens of Bloomsbury around the British Museum; and the pretty streets, mews, and courtyards of villages like Hampstead, Chelsea, and Highgate.

Ken Livingstone, the mayor of London, has instigated several major changes that have impacted the lives and travel habits of Londoners and visitors alike. His congestion charge, whereby cars have to pay a daily rate of £5 ($9.25) for the dubious pleasure of driving into central London, might not be popular with motorists, but it has certainly reduced the amount of traffic on the capital's streets. The pedestrianization of the north side of Trafalgar Square (right in front of the National Gallery) has made a visit to the square and gallery a much more pleasurable experience. Despite these changes, and despite its declining relevance today, Royal London's pomp and pageantry is still more than evident in daily ceremonies like the Changing of the Guard at Buckingham Palace and the Ceremony of the Keys at the Tower of London.

Old and new, London has much to make a visit rich and rewarding. So check out all the top sights, explore the narrow alleys of The City, enjoy lunch in a local pub, attend a free concert in a church, and party the night away in a hot dance club. And be sure to strike up a conversation or two with the locals.

For more on London and its environs, see *Frommer's London, Frommer's London from $90 a Day, Frommer's Irreverent Guide to London, London For Dummies, Frommer's Memorable Walks in London, The Unofficial Guide to London, Suzy Gershman's Born to Shop London, Frommer's England, Frommer's England from $75 a Day,* or *England For Dummies.*

Budget Bests

Not only does London offer many of the world's "bests," but a host of these attractions are either free or cost less than comparable sights elsewhere. Many of London's **museums** are free, as are such attractions as the **Houses of Parliament.** The **Changing of the Guard** at Buckingham Palace is also free, along with the often-acerbic diatribes delivered at **Speakers' Corner** every Sunday in Hyde Park. **Theater tickets** here are still cheaper than those to comparable New York City productions, and **cheap seats** are regularly available at the opera, ballet, and symphony.

1 Essentials

ARRIVING

BY PLANE London is served by three major airports: Heathrow, Gatwick, and Stansted. All have good public transport links to central London. For **rail information,** call © **020/7222-1234** (www.tfl.gov.uk).

Heathrow: The cheapest route from Heathrow is by **Underground** or subway ("the tube"); the 24km (15-mile) journey takes about 45 minutes and costs £3.60 ($6.65) to any downtown station (for discounts, see "Getting Around," below). The service is convenient, as the Underground platforms are directly below the terminals. But Heathrow is big, and even those with light luggage are advised to use one of the free baggage carts for the long walk to the train. Trains operate daily 6am to midnight, departing every 5 minutes at peak times and every 9 minutes at off-peak hours and weekends. A speedier though more expensive link is provided by the **Heathrow Express** (© **0845/600-1515;** www.heathrowexpress.co.uk), taking 15 minutes from the airport to Paddington Station and costing £13 ($24) one-way and £25 ($46) round-trip. Tickets can be purchased on the train itself although this does carry a surcharge of £2 ($3.70) per ticket. Be aware, however, that you will still need to get from Paddington Station to your final destination, so it may not save that much time if, for example, your hotel is in Bloomsbury or Victoria, both of which, unless you indulge in a black cab, can take another 20 to 30 minutes by underground. **Airbus** (© **020/8400-6659**) departs from all Heathrow terminals every 30 minutes and takes a little over an hour and a half into central London, where drop-offs are made at various key locations such as Queensway, Hyde Park, Russell Square, and King's Cross. The cost for adults is £10 ($19) one-way and £15 ($28) round-trip. A more expensive hotel-to-hotel shuttle is operated by **Hotel Link** (© **01293/532-244;** www.hotelink.co.uk); they will meet you and drop you off at your hotel. The cost is £15 ($28) per person each way (or £14/$26 per person each way if booked online) from Heathrow and £22 ($41) per person each way (or £18/$33 per person each way when booked online) from Gatwick.

Gatwick: Convenient nonstop trains (www.gatwickexpress.co.uk) make the 40km (25-mile) trek from Gatwick to Victoria Station in about 30 minutes, at a cost of £11 ($21) one-way or £22 ($40) round-trip. The station is just below the airport, and trains depart daily every 15 minutes 6am to 10pm (hourly, on the hour, at other times). Also see Hotel Link above.

London Deals & Discounts

SPECIAL DISCOUNTS If you enjoy museums and intend to visit as many as you can, you'll be pleased to learn that London's major national museums have now dropped their admission charges to a lower fee or to none at all.

Students in England enjoy discounts on travel, on theater and museum tickets, and at some nightspots. The **International Student Identity Card (ISIC)** is the most readily accepted proof of status. You should buy it before leaving home, but if you've arrived without one and are a good enough talker (or are carrying a registrar-stamped and -signed copy of your current school transcript), you can get one for about £7 ($13) at **S. T. A. Travel,** 40 Bernard St. (℡ **020/7837-9666;** www.statravel.co.uk; tube: Russell Sq.). The office is open Monday to Thursday 9:30am to 6pm, and Saturday 11am to 5pm. There is also a branch at 85 Shaftsbury Ave., W1 (℡ **020/7432-7474;** tube: Piccadilly Circus); it's open Monday to Friday 11am to 7pm (until 8pm Thurs) and 11am to 6pm Saturday. S. T. A. has several other London offices and offers many special travel discounts, including airfares.

In Britain, "senior citizen" usually means a woman of at least 60 or a man of at least 65. Seniors often receive the same discounts as students. Unfortunately for visitors, some discounts are available only to seniors who are also British subjects. More often, however, your passport or other proof of age will also be your passport to cutting costs.

WORTH A SPLURGE London is certainly not one of Europe's budget-friendly cities, and a splurge here can be achieved with minimal effort. But why not do the sights by **black cab?** Sit back and let your driver (who'll be a wealth of local knowledge) get you around the capital. Included should be a trip to the **Tower of London,** the admission to which is pricey but at least you won't lose your head as Anne Boleyn did. Round off your afternoon by spending a few extra pounds (and gaining a few extra pounds) on a wonderful **tea at the Ritz or Brown's.** To cap your splurge day, dine at the trendy **Club Gascon** (if you can get a reservation) and then attend a performance at the newly refurbished **Royal Opera House** in Covent Garden.

Stansted: The **Stansted Skytrain** (℡ **0845/8500-150;** www.Stansted express.com) makes the 40-minute journey from the airport, 48km (30 miles) northeast of London, to Liverpool Street Station for £13 ($24) one-way, £23 ($43) round-trip. Trains depart every half-hour Monday to Friday 5:30am to 11pm, Saturday 6:30am to 11pm, and Sunday 7am to 11pm.

BY TRAIN Trains from Paris arrive at **Waterloo Station** (Eurostar via the Chunnel) and **Victoria Station,** visitors from Amsterdam are deposited at **Liverpool Street Station,** and arrivals from Edinburgh pull into **King's Cross Station.** All four are well connected to the city's extensive bus and Underground network. The stations all contain London Transport Information Centres, luggage lockers, phones, restaurants, and pubs.

VISITOR INFORMATION

TOURIST OFFICES & HOT LINES The **London Tourist Board (LTB)** maintains several **Information Centers.** Its staff distributes city maps, answers questions, and can help you find accommodations for a £5 ($9.25) fee. If you're arriving via Heathrow, visit the LTB in the **arrivals terminal** before making your journey into the city. It's open daily from 9am to 6pm. Those arriving via Gatwick or by train from Paris can visit the well-staffed office in **Victoria Station's forecourt.** Easter to October, it's open daily 9am to 8pm; the rest of the year, hours are Monday to Saturday 9am to 7pm and Sunday 9am to 5pm. Other centers are at the **Liverpool Street Underground Station,** EC2, open Monday to Friday 8am to 6pm and Saturday and Sunday 8:45am to 5:30pm; **Waterloo International Arrivals Hall,** SE1, open daily 8:30am to 10:30pm; and **Southwark Information Centre,** London Bridge, 6 Tooley St., SE1, open Monday to Saturday: March to October, 10am to 6pm, and November to February, 10am to 4pm.

Before leaving home, you can get details on a wide variety of attractions and accommodations on the Internet at the LTB's site: **www.londontouristboard.com**.

Up-to-the-minute info is available from the LTB at ℰ **020/7932-2000.** You will be connected to that bane of modern living, the automated switchboard, but it will at least provide every possible option and phone number you will need. I prefer the online service at **www.londontouristboard.com**, though.

The **Britain Visitor Centre,** 1 Regent St., SW1 (tube: Piccadilly Circus), provides information on all of Britain. It's open Monday to Friday 9am to 6:30pm, Saturday 9am to 5pm, and Sunday 10am to 4pm. Hours are usually slightly reduced in winter.

For information on Scotland, dial ℰ **0845/2255121** (www.visitscotland.com); for Wales, dial ℰ **0870/1211251** (www.visitwales.com); for all of Ireland, dial ℰ **08000/397-000** (www.ireland.travel.ie).

For details on travel by bus, tube, or British Rail, visit a **London Transport Information Centre,** located in the major train stations, or call the **London Regional Transport Travel Information Service** at ℰ **020/7222-1234** (24 hr.).

WEBSITES Designed by the British Tourist Authority expressly for U.S. travelers, **www.usagateway.visitbritain.com** lets you order brochures online, provides trip-planning hints, and even allows e-mail questions for prompt answers. All of Great Britain is covered. For London in particular, visit the official tourist board site **www.londontouristboard.com**. Go to **www.baa.co.uk** for a guide and terminal maps for Heathrow, Gatwick, Stansted, and other lesser airports, including flight arrival times, duty-free shops, airport restaurants, and info on getting from the airports to downtown London. Getting around London can be confusing, so you might want to visit **www.tfl.gov.uk** for up-to-the-minute info on London's transport options. For the latest details on London's theater scene, consult **www.officiallondontheatre.co.uk**. At **www.multimap.com**, you can access detailed street maps of the whole United Kingdom—just key in the location or even just its postal code, and a map of the area with the location circled will appear. For directions to specific places in London, consult **www.streetmap.co.uk**.

CITY LAYOUT

London is often referred to as a "city of villages" that sprang up around the square mile of the original walled Roman city. Most of the walls have long since disappeared, but the political autonomy of **The City of London** still separates it from the surrounding areas. The City has always been London's financial center, and it's crammed with tiny streets and a sense of history befitting its ancient beginnings. The **West End** is the general name of a large, imprecise area west of The City, to Hyde Park. The West End encompasses the Houses of Parliament, Buckingham Palace, and the nation's densest cluster of shops, restaurants, and theaters. You'll get to know this area well.

Beyond the West End, south of Hyde Park, are the fashionable residential areas of **South Kensington** and **Chelsea.** Take a close look at these neighborhoods—you've probably never seen so many beautiful city buildings you'd like to own. Hugging The City's eastern side is one of London's poorest areas. Traditionally, the **East End** was undesirable because both the prevailing winds and the flow of the Thames move from west to east. In the plague-ridden days before sewers, life on the "wrong" side of The City was dangerous indeed. Today the East End is still home to poorer immigrants (mostly from the Indian subcontinent) but is seeing gentrification as well.

The borough of **Southwark,** across the river from The City on the south bank of the Thames, became famous as London's entertainment quarter during Elizabethan times, when theaters and brothels were banned from The City. Today the area is home to the reconstruction of Shakespeare's Globe Theatre and the Tate Gallery's modern art collection. The Millennium Bridge, a pedestrian walkway, now connects Southwark with The City.

Note: In this chapter, street addresses are followed by designations like SW1 and EC1. These are the **postal areas.** The original post office was at St. Martin-le-Grand, in The City, so the postal districts are related to where they lie geographically from there. For example, Victoria is SW1 since it's the first area southwest of St. Martin-le-Grand; Covent Garden is west (west central) and so is WC1 or WC2; and Liverpool Street is east and so is EC1.

GETTING AROUND

Public transportation in London can be difficult to negotiate. It seems as though no two streets run parallel, and even locals regularly consult maps, but in the winding streets of The City and in the tourist area of the West End, there's no better way to go than on foot.

Be warned that cars have the right-of-way over pedestrians; take care even when the light seems to be in your favor.

BY UNDERGROUND & BUS   Commuters constantly complain about it, but visitors find London's public-transport network fast and efficient. **Underground** stations are abundant, and aboveground you can catch one of the famous red double-decker buses. Both the Underground and the buses are operated by **London Transport** (© **020/7222-1234;** www.tfl.gov.uk), which sets fares based on a zone system: You pay for each zone you cross. For most tube trips, you travel in the same zone, and the fare is £1.60 ($3) adults or 60p ($1) children.

To save time at ticket windows or machines, you can buy a **booklet of 10 tickets** for use anywhere in Zone 1, costing £15 ($28) adults or £5 ($9.25) children 5 to 15. A **1-day Travelcard,** costing £4.30 ($8) adults and £2 ($3.70) children 5 to 15, is good for unlimited transport in two zones on the bus and tube after 9:30am Monday to Friday and anytime weekends and public holidays. A **weekly Travelcard** for Zone 1 is £17 ($32) adults and £7 ($13) children 5 to 15, and for Zones 1 and 2 is £20 ($38) and £8.20 ($15), respectively. Children under 5 ride free. You'll need to present a photograph to buy the weekly ticket if you are buying a pass for Zones 3 and above (but you do not need a photo ID for Zones 1 and 2). Photo booths are in tube stations; four passport-size photographs cost about £2.50 ($4.60).

The tube runs every few minutes Monday to Saturday from about 5:30am to midnight (7:30am–11pm Sun). You can buy tickets from the station ticket window or an adjacent coin-operated machine. Many ticket machines now accept credit cards, but be warned that they issue a receipt that is easily mistaken for a ticket before they actually issue the ticket itself. Hold onto your ticket throughout your ride; you'll need it to exit. Pick up a handy tube map, distributed free at station ticket windows. To calculate your journey time, allow 3 minutes for each station passed en route.

London's **red double-deckers** offer a wonderful way to get around as you enjoy the view from the top of the bus. Take a seat, either upstairs or down, and wait for the conductor to collect your fare. On the newer type of bus, pay the driver as you enter and exit through the center doors. The bus fare in central London's Zone 1 is £1 ($1.85) adults or 40p (75¢) children. **One-day bus passes** are available for £2.50 ($4.60) adults or £1 ($1.85) children; **weekly passes** are £9.50 ($18) adults or £4 ($7.40) children for Zones 1, 2, 3, and 4. Note, however, that Travelcards (see above) can be used on both tubes and buses, and will be a better deal for you if you plan on riding both buses and the tube.

Many visitors shy away from buses because their routes can be confusing. Get a free bus map from the tourist office or any Underground ticket office, or ask any conductor about the route and then take advantage of a "top deck" sightseeing adventure. Like the tube, regular bus service also stops after midnight, sometimes making it difficult to get back to your hotel. At night, buses have different routes and different numbers from their daytime counterparts. Service isn't frequent either; if you've just missed your night bus, expect a long wait for the next one or hunt down a minicab (see below). The central London night-bus terminus is Trafalgar Square.

> ## A Map Note
> See the inside back cover of this guide for a map of the London Underground.

BY TAXI For three or four people traveling a short distance, **cabs** can make economic sense. The fare begins at £2 ($3.70), then climbs at a fast clip. There's an extra charge of 40p (75¢) per person, 10p (20¢) per large piece of luggage, and 40p (75¢) on weekends and after midnight. But the thrill of viewing London's famous monuments from the roomy back seat of a taxi is almost enough to get your eye off the meter. If you know in advance you'll be needing a cab, you can try to order one by calling **Computercab** (© **020/7286-0286**), but you'll pay more for it. *Be forewarned:* Booking a cab through this system doesn't guarantee that one will actually turn up at the specified time or, for that matter, at all.

Minicabs are meterless cars driven by entrepreneurs with licenses. Technically, these taxis aren't allowed to cruise for fares but must operate from sidewalk offices—many of which are centered near Leicester Square. A reputable minicab can be more reliable than Computercab and the fare can often be a lot cheaper. Minicabs are also handy at night after the tube stops running and black cabs suddenly become scarce. Always negotiate the fare beforehand. If you're approached by a lone driver on the street, a firm but polite "No, thank you" is called for. Only black cabs are allowed to pick up fares on the streets, and to get into any other vehicle that purports to be a taxi is dangerous.

Country & City Codes

The **country code** for the United Kingdom is **44**. The London **city code** is **20**, and is used when calling from outside the United Kingdom. This code is then followed by an eight-digit number beginning with either 7 or 8. If you're within the United Kingdom but not in London, use **020** followed by the eight-digit number. If you're calling within London, simply leave off the code and dial only the eight-digit number.

BY BICYCLE   Bike lanes are becoming more common here as the cycling lobby grows more vociferous. Cycling can be a quick and convenient way to get around London's increasingly congested roads, but be careful of unyielding motorists. If you want to rent a bike, try **On Your Bike,** 52–54 Tooley St., SE1 (© **020/7378-6669;** tube: London Bridge), open Monday to Friday 8am to 7pm and Saturday 10am to 6pm; Sunday noon to 5pm. Bikes rent for £15 ($28) per day, and you'll have to pay a £200 ($370) deposit. Weekly rental prices are negotiable.

BY RENTAL CAR   Recent security measures have closed many streets in The City, and, since February 2003, a daily congestion charge (see www.tfl.gov.co.uk for up-to-the-minute details) has been in operation from 7am to 6:30pm Monday through Friday, which means that driving in central London incurs a daily charge of £5 ($9.25) per day just for the dubious pleasure of having a car in the capital. It's not smart to keep a car here; however, if you're planning excursions, a rental is worth looking into. To secure the lowest rates, you should reserve and pay for the car before you leave home. The cheapest rates are promised by **www.easyrentacar.com,** which charges around £14 ($26) a day or £85 ($157) a week. However, be aware that only the first 121km (75 miles) per day are free and that thereafter you'll pay 20p (37¢) per 1.5km (1 mile). Also pay extra attention to the condition of the vehicle at the time of rental. Ensure that you have noted with them every scrape on the car's body, however minimal it may seem. **Avis** (© **08700/100287;** www.avis.com) and **Budget** (© **0800/626-063;** https://rent.drivebudget.com) have several branches throughout the city. Gasoline (petrol) costs about £4 ($7.40) per imperial gallon (about $4.65 per U.S. gal.).

FAST FACTS: London

American Express   There are several offices throughout the city, including one at 30–31 Haymarket, SW1 (© 020/7484-9600; tube: Charing Cross), near Trafalgar Square. It's open Monday to Saturday from 9am to 6pm and Sunday from 10am to 5pm.

Babysitters   If your request for a recommendation from a member of your hotel staff is answered by a blank stare, phone **Childminders** at © 020/7935-2049 (www.babysitter.co.uk).

Banks   Most banks are open Monday to Friday 9:30am to 5pm, and some are open Saturday 9:30am to noon. Banks generally offer the best exchange rates, but American Express and Thomas Cook are competitive and don't charge a commission for cashing traveler's checks, no matter what brand. A convenient **Thomas Cook** office is at 1 Woburn Place, Russell Square, WC1 (© 020/7837-5275; tube: Russell Sq.), open Monday to Friday 9am to 5pm (and Sat Apr–Sept only 9am 3pm). Places with the longest hours (sometimes open all night) offer the worst rates. Beware of Chequepoint and other high-commission *bureaux de change*.

Business Hours **Stores** are usually open Monday to Saturday 10am to 6pm and Sunday noon to 6pm. Most also stay open at least an extra hour 1 night during the week. Knightsbridge shops usually remain open until 7pm on Wednesday, while West End stores are traditionally open late on Thursday. Some shops around Covent Garden stay open to 7 or 8pm nightly. Although major stores open on Sunday, many smaller stores still close on Sunday.

Currency The basic unit of currency is the **pound sterling (£)**, divided into 100 **pence (p)**. There are 1p, 2p, 10p, 20p, 50p, £1, and £2 coins; banknotes are issued in £5, £10, £20, and £50. At press time, the rate of exchange (and the rate used in this chapter) was $1 = 55p (or £1 – $1.85).

Note: For now, Britain has opted out of adopting the euro. Several big stores, however, have announced that they will accept euros—though at a price. At the time of this writing, it was suggested that many would build a hidden surcharge into the exchange rate.

Drugstores **Boots** is the largest chain of London drugstores, and you'll find them located all over London (the branches are too numerous to list). They are generally open Monday to Saturday 9am to 10pm and Sunday noon to 5pm.

Embassies & High Commissions The Embassy of the **United States,** 24 Grosvenor Sq., W1 ((C) **020/7499-9000;** tube: Bond St.), is open Monday to Friday 9am to 5pm. The High Commission of **Canada,** Macdonald House, 1 Grosvenor Sq., W1 ((C) **020/7258-6600;** tube: Bond St.), is open Monday to Friday 8 to 11am. The High Commission of **Australia** is in Australia House, The Strand, WC2 ((C) **020/7379-4334;** tube: Charing Cross or Temple), open Monday to Friday 9am to 1pm. The High Commission of **New Zealand** is in New Zealand House, 80 Haymarket, SW1 ((C) **020/ 7930-8422;** tube: Piccadilly Circus), open Monday to Friday 9am to 5pm.

Emergencies **Police, fire,** and **ambulance** services can be reached by dialing (C) **999.** No money is required.

Holidays Most businesses are closed New Year's Day, Good Friday, Easter Monday, the first Monday in May, and December 25 and 26. In addition, many stores close on bank holidays, which are scattered throughout the year. There's no uniform policy for museums, restaurants, and attractions with regard to holidays. To avoid disappointment, always phone before setting out.

Internet Access You can check on your e-mail or send messages at the **easyEverything Internet Shops** (www.easyeverything.com). Branches are open daily 24 hours and located at 9–13 Wilton Rd., SW1 (tube: Victoria); 457–459 The Strand, WC2 (tube: Charing Cross or Embankment); 9–16 Tottenham Court Rd., WC1 (tube: Tottenham Court Rd.); 358 Oxford St., W1 (tube: Bond St.); and 160–166 High St. Kensington, W8 (tube: High St. Kensington). On the boundary between Bayswater and Paddington, try **Internet Café,** 19 Leinster Terrace, W2 ((C) **020/7402-1177;** tube: Bayswater or Paddington), which is open daily 24 hours. For a comprehensive list of Internet cafes across London, go to www.visitlondon.com/directory/eat/ internet_cafes.

Mail Post offices are plentiful and normally open Monday to Friday 9am to 5pm and Saturday 9am to noon. The **Main Post Office,** 24 William IV St., Trafalgar Square, WC2 (✆ **020/7484-9307;** tube: Charing Cross), is open Monday to Saturday 8am to 8pm.

Police In an emergency, dial ✆ **999** from any phone; no money is needed. At other times, dial the operator at ✆ **100** and ask to be connected with the police.

Tax Unlike in the United States, where tax is tacked on at the register, in England, a 17.5% **value-added tax (VAT)** is figured into the price of most items. Foreign visitors can reclaim the VAT for major purchases. See chapter 1, "Enjoying Europe on a Budget," or ask at stores for details.

Telephone There are two kinds of **pay phones.** The first accepts coins and the other operates with a **phone card,** available from newsstands in £1 ($1.85), £2 ($3.70), £4 ($6), £10 ($19), and £20 ($37) denominations. The minimum cost of a **local call** is 20p (37¢) for the first 2 minutes (peak hours). You can deposit up to four coins at a time, but phones don't make change, so unless you're calling long distance, use 10p or 20p coins only. **Phone-card phones** automatically deduct the price of your call from the card; these cards are especially handy if you want to call abroad. Some large hotels and touristy street corners also have phones that accept major credit cards. Lift the handle and follow the instructions on the screen.

To reach the **local operator,** dial ✆ **100.** London **information** ("directory enquiries") can be reached by dialing ✆ **118 118** or **118 500,** and there's a charge of between 20p (37¢) and 40p (74¢). Be aware, however, that the agent will offer to put you straight through to the number. If you do this, you will incur a further charge per minute. It is cheaper to take the number and then dial it yourself.

To make an **international call,** dial ✆ **155** to reach the international operator. To dial direct, dial **00,** then your country code (United States and Canada, 1; Australia, 61; New Zealand, 64), then the local number. You can phone home by dialing a local toll-free number in London and paying with your calling card. To phone Australia, dial ✆ **0800/89-0061;** for New Zealand, ✆ **0800/89-0064;** and for the United States and Canada, ✆ **0800/89-0011** (AT&T), **0800/89-0222** (MCI), or **0800/89-0877** (Sprint).

Tipping Most (but not all) restaurants automatically add a discretionary service charge. The restaurant's policy will be written on the menu. When a service charge isn't included, a 10% to 15% tip is customary. Taxi drivers also expect 10% to 15% of the fare. *Note:* Tipping is rare in pubs.

2 Affordable Places to Stay

Central London accommodations are certainly not cheap and in the height of summer can be difficult to come by. Early booking is highly advisable, and be sure to get written confirmation that you'll have a room and at the price quoted.

The B&B is one of England's greatest traditions. Morning menus differ but usually include cereal, eggs, bacon or sausage, toast, and all the coffee or tea you can drink. The bad news is that, in general, London's budget hotels aren't as nice

> ### ⌒Tips Accommodations Notes
>
> Here are a few things to keep in mind when renting a room in London: Although beds are made up daily, sheets aren't usually changed during a stay of less than a week. If you need new bedding, request it. And remember that even local phone calls made from your room can be deathly expensive; inquire about the rate before dialing.

or as cheap as those on the Continent. The rooms are uniformly small, and wear is often evident. A recent development has been the arrival in central London of budget chains like Travel Inn (p. 530), offering reasonably sized, clean, and comfortable rooms. However, the room price doesn't include breakfast.

You'll also find many affordable rooms provided in family homes. The advantage is affordability; the disadvantage is you'll be 20 or so minutes outside central London. Interested? About a month before you leave, contact **At Home in London,** 70 Black Lion Lane, London W6 9BE (℘ **020/8748-1943;** fax 020/8748-2701; www.athomeinlondon.co.uk); or **London Homestead Services,** Coombe Wood Road, Kingston-upon-Thames, KT2 7JY (℘ **020/7286-5115;** fax 020/7286-5115; www.Lhslondon.com). Prices are £18 to £35 ($33–$65) per person per night in a double with bathroom, including breakfast. Both accept MasterCard and Visa.

Note: You'll find the lodging choices below plotted on the map on p. 540.

IN BAYSWATER & PADDINGTON

Bayswater runs along Hyde Park's northern edge and encompasses Paddington Station. It's a densely packed residential community, populated by a large number of Indians and Pakistanis and jammed with budget hotels. Bayswater's proximity to the park, good restaurants (especially along Queensway and Westbourne Grove), and transport links to the West End make it a desirable place to stay. The Heathrow Express terminates at Paddington Station; the Central and District Underground lines run to Bayswater and Paddington stations. Bus nos. 12, 88, and 289 travel the length of Bayswater Road.

Dean Court Hotel   Big breakfasts, a friendly staff, and a philosophy that's exceptionally kind to the budget traveler are all the hallmarks of this rambling hotel (without elevator) on a quiet Bayswater street. Although wear is evident in many of the rooms, they're of a reasonable size and have high ceilings (the multishares, for example, don't seem cramped). It's a great place to meet up with fellow travelers and it possesses a communal, almost college, atmosphere.

57 Inverness Terrace (1 block from Queensway), London W2. ℘ **020/7229-2961** or 020/7229-9982. Fax 020/7727-1190. www.backpackershostellondon.com. 30 units, none with bathroom; 40 beds in multishare units, none with bathroom. £45 ($83) twin or double; £66 ($122) triple; £15 ($28) per person per night in multishare, £75–£79 ($139–$146) per week. Rates include English breakfast. MC, V. Tube: Bayswater or Queensway. *In room:* No phone.

Dolphin Hotel ⊛ ⟨*Value*⟩   Norfolk Square is a budget hotel–packed horseshoe around a park just steps south of Paddington Station. The Dolphin (without elevator) is one of the best value offerings on the square, and the owners go out of their way to try to add quality to their budget ethos. The tastefully decorated and well-maintained rooms are above average size for budget, the beds have firm mattresses, and the bathrooms are clean as well as reasonably spacious. The shared bathrooms, however, do tend to be on the small side.

34 Norfolk Sq., London W2. © 020/7402-4943. Fax 020/7723-8184. www.dolphinhotel.co.uk. 30 units, 15 with bathroom. £42 ($78) single without bathroom, £52 ($96) single with bathroom; £55 ($102) double without bathroom, £69 ($128) double with bathroom; £69 ($128) triple without bathroom, £79 ($146) triple with bathroom. Rates include continental breakfast. AE, DC, MC, V. Tube: Paddington. **Amenities:** Internet access. *In room:* TV, fridge, coffeemaker.

Hyde Park House   This no-frills budget hotel is on a quiet residential street a short walk from the shops, restaurants, and Underground station on Queensway. The rooms show obvious signs of wear and tear, and although reasonably sized, are very basic with a decor that's not intended to inspire. The beds have firm mattresses. The shared bathrooms have showers only and are tiny. The en suite room is at the very top of the building and involves a long climb up several flights of steep stairs.

48 St. Petersburgh Place, London W2. © 020/7229-1687. 12 units, 1 with bathroom. £30 ($55) single without bathroom; £40 ($74) double without bathroom; £65 ($120) triple with bathroom. Rates include continental breakfast. No credit cards. Tube: Bayswater. **Amenities:** Kitchen. *In room:* TV, fridge, no phone.

Lancaster Hall Hotel   The modern gray facade of this hotel, owned by the German YMCA, is a good indicator of the standards found in the rooms. Elegant and stylish they are not. They're functional rather than fashionable, reasonably spacious, and furnished only with twin beds that aren't overly large. The bathrooms are of adequate size, clean, and well maintained. The hotel has a lively and mixed clientele, and staff that are friendly although a little lacking in enthusiasm. If character and characters are what you seek, then look elsewhere.

35 Craven Terrace, London W2. © 020/7723-9276. Fax 020/7723-9276. www.lancaster-hall-hotel.co.uk. 80 units. £57 ($105) single; £75 ($139) double. Rates include continental breakfast. MC, V. Tube: Lancaster Gate or Paddington. **Amenities:** Bar. *In room:* TV, coffeemaker.

Mitre House Hotel   The high standards maintained at this established family-run hotel are apparent the moment you enter the pleasant reception area, where the staff is exceptionally friendly. The rooms vary in size, ranging from small to well above average, and all are kept to an exceptionally high standard of decoration and furnishing. The beds vary in the firmness of their mattresses. The bathrooms, which are clean and maintained to the high standards evident throughout the hotel, are reasonably spacious.

178–184 Sussex Gardens, London W2. © 020/7723-8040. Fax 020/7402-0990. www.mitrehousehotel.com. 70 units, 50 with bathroom. £70 ($130) single; £80 ($148) double; £90 ($166) triple; £100 ($185) quad; £110 ($204) junior suite, £120 ($222) family suite. Rates include English breakfast. AE, MC, V. Limited parking. Tube: Paddington. **Amenities:** Bar; coffeemaker available 24 hr. at reception. *In room:* TV.

IN VICTORIA

Victoria Station dominates the area, separating pricey Belgravia on its northwest from the more accessible Pimlico to the southeast. If you're shopping around, note that although there are hundreds of hotels here, the majority aren't up to standard. Victoria is known not for its sights, shopping, or entertainment, but for its proximity to busy Victoria Station.

Georgian House Hotel 🄵   This pleasant budget offering (without elevator) is on a busy main road, a few blocks from Victoria Station. The rooms are well maintained and the beds have a mix of mattresses: some soft and others very firm. As with many of the hotels in this area, the bathrooms themselves would win no prizes for generosity, being tiny and offering little room to maneuver between the toilet and shower, but, in general, this is the only drawback here.

Value Getting the Best Deal on Accommodations

- Take advantage of off-season rates. Prices tumble—sometimes by as much as 30%—and often there's room for further negotiation.
- Note that many hotels offer discounts if you stay a week or more.
- Note also that many hotels offer special discounts for Internet bookings. So be sure to check the hotel's website before booking.
- Remember to ask if the hotel has anything cheaper. Never accept a room until you're sure you've secured the lowest price.
- Request to see a room before renting it. Hoteliers are more likely to offer their nicest rooms to travelers who look before they buy.
- If booking in advance, insist on written confirmation of your booking, because there have been instances of travelers arriving to find their booking hasn't been honored.
- Be aware that the London Tourist Board operates a credit card booking line (MasterCard and Visa) at ℭ **020/7932-2020** (fax 014/3823-5099). A £5 ($9.25) fee is charged.

35–39 St. Georges Dr., London SW1. ℭ **020/7834-1438**. Fax 020/7976-6085. www.georgianhousehotel. co.uk. 52 units, 42 with bathroom. £30 ($55) single without bathroom, £50 ($93) single with bathroom; £45 ($83) double without bathroom, £50 ($93) double with bathroom; £68 ($126) triple without bathroom, £72 ($133) triple with bathroom. Rates include full English breakfast. MC, V. Tube: Victoria. *In room:* TV, coffeemaker, hair dryer, safe.

Ivy House and Holly House Hotels A friendly management and attentive staff help make this a reasonable budget choice, located on a quiet side street a short distance from Victoria Station. The rooms, while not overly generous in size, are reasonable and all kept very clean, although some wear is evident. The major drawback is the fact that the bathrooms are tiny and little more than stalls with hardly any room to spare between the hand basins, toilets, and showers. The hotel, however, is a good choice if you're on a strict budget and just seek a place to lay your head at the end of a long day. **Holly House Hotel** next door is run by the same management and offers slightly larger bathrooms.

18–20 Hugh St., London SW1. ℭ **020/7834-5671**. Fax 020/7233-5154. www.hollyhousehotel.co.uk. 9 units, 5 with bathroom. £35 ($65) single without bathroom, £49 ($91) single with bathroom; £49 ($91) double without bathroom, £69 ($128) double with bathroom; £69 ($128) triple without bathroom, £90 ($167) triple with bathroom. Rates include continental breakfast. AE, MC, V. Tube: Victoria. *In room:* TV, fridge, coffeemaker, no phone.

Luna and Simone Hotel This excellent family-run hotel (without elevator) underwent a major refurbishment in 2000 and is now better than ever. The well-decorated rooms are of a reasonable size and are exceptionally well kept. Some rooms even offer small balconies (albeit several overlooking the busy and unattractive Belgrave Rd.). The bathrooms are actually inviting, as opposed to adequate. The beds themselves are comfortable; some have firm mattresses while others have soft mattresses that you can just sink into. Be warned, however, that the hotel is quite a trek from Victoria Station, so you might wish to consider a cab on your first day should you be weighed down with an excess of luggage.

47–49 Belgrave Rd., London SW1. ℭ **020/7834-5897**. Fax 020/7828-2474. www.lunasimonehotel.com. 35 units, 27 with bathroom. £35–£40 ($65–$74) single without bathroom, £50–£60 ($93–$111) single with bathroom; £60–£80 ($111–$148) double with bathroom; £80–£100 ($148–$185) triple with bathroom; £100–£110 ($185–$204) quad with bathroom. Rates include English breakfast. MC, V. Tube: Victoria. *In room:* TV, Internet access, hair dryer.

Melbourne House *Kids* Melbourne House (without elevator), another of the rare breed of recommendable budget hotels on Belgrave Road, is run by friendly John and Manuela. The pleasant fair-size rooms are clean and well maintained and all have firm mattresses on the beds. The bathrooms are above average size for the area and are kept immaculate. The family room consists of two connected rooms (a double with a twin) with a shared bathroom. Because it's located further along Belgrave Road than the Luna and Simone, those with heavy luggage or small children may wish to consider a cab from Victoria to the hotel on the first day.

79 Belgrave Rd., London SW1. © 020/7828-3516. Fax 020/7828-7120. www.melbournehousehotel.co.uk. 16 units, 14 with bathroom. £30–£35 ($56–$65) single without bathroom; £60 ($111) single with bathroom; £85 ($157) double with bathroom; £100 ($185) triple with bathroom; £120 ($222) family room. Rates include English breakfast. No credit cards (except to hold room). Tube: Victoria. *In room:* TV, coffeemaker, hair dryer.

Oxford House Hotel *Finds* This hotel (without elevator) is owned by interior designer Yanus Kader, his wife Terri, and their two sons, and is as homey as you could hope to find in London. Since they live on the premises (the 3rd generation is now in residence), guests have all the advantages of a home stay without the drawbacks. If you want to sit and chat with the family, they'll be more than willing to oblige. If you want to be left to your own devices, then they won't intrude. The rooms are comfortable and pretty, featuring floral motifs, coordinated curtains, and firm mattresses. The shared bathrooms are standard size but kept immaculate. The beautiful dining area, with an open kitchen, is very much the hub of the hotel and a definite home away from home, and there's also a pretty patio area out back for lazing on the rare sunny afternoon.

92–94 Cambridge St. (south of Belgrave Rd. near Gloucester St.), London SW1. © 020/7834-6467. 15 units, none with bathroom. £35–£40 ($65–$74) single; £45–£50 ($83–$93) double; £60–£66 ($111–$122) triple; £80–£84 ($148–$155) quad. Rates include English breakfast. Prices increase by £2 ($3.70) per person if you stay only 1 night. MC, V (add 5% if you pay by credit card). Tube: Victoria.

IN CHELSEA & SOUTH KENSINGTON

The expensive residential areas of Chelsea and South Kensington offer little in the way of accommodations for budgeters. With a few exceptions, the cost of lodging here reflects location rather than quality, since a room in South Kensington is only steps from more than half a dozen top museums and the ritzy boutiques of Knightsbridge.

Oakley Hotel Well-decorated rooms and a fun atmosphere make this economical hotel (without elevator) a welcome oasis in tab-happy Chelsea. The local council of this chic neighborhood forbids a sign, but a knock on the green door will be answered by a friendly Australian. Aside from singles and doubles, the hotel has several multishare rooms at great rates. The bathrooms are tidy but tiny.

73 Oakley St., London SW3. © 020/7352-5599. Fax 020/7727-1190. 13 units, 2 with bathroom. £32 ($59) single without bathroom; £44 ($81) double without bathroom, £56 ($104) double with bathroom; £63 ($117) triple without bathroom, £75 ($139) triple with bathroom; £14 ($26) per person multishare quad. Rates include English breakfast. AE, MC, V. Tube: Sloane Sq.; then take a long walk or the no. 11 or 22 bus down King's Rd. to Oakley St. **Amenities:** Kitchen. *In room:* Hair dryer.

IN EARL'S COURT

Just west of exclusive Chelsea and Knightsbridge, Earl's Court has dozens of hotels; many are hostel types where the quality is often suspect. But the many superbudget accommodations means that cheap restaurants, pubs, and services are also nearby. The Earl's Court tube station is in the middle of Earl's Court Road, which, along with Old Brompton Road to the south, is the area's chief shopping strip. Earl's Court also boasts several gay guesthouses (see "A Gay & Lesbian Hotel," later in this section).

Manor Hotel *(Value)*   Located on a quiet residential street a stone's throw from Earl's Court Underground Station, the Manor Hotel (without elevator) is an exceptional budget find in an area that is awash with hotels that aren't particularly nice. The rooms are above average size for budget accommodations. They're clean and attractively furnished and decorated, while the beds are equipped with firm mattresses. The bathrooms, while not of overly generous proportions, are clean and functional.

23 Nevern Place, London SW5. ℂ 020/7370-6018. Fax 020/7370-6018. 27 units, 11 with bathroom. £30–£55 ($55–$102) single with bathroom; £45 ($83) double without bathroom, £60 ($111) double with bathroom; £58 ($107) triple without bathroom, £80 ($148) triple with bathroom. Rates include continental breakfast. Discount for stays of 1 week or more. MC, V. Tube: Earl's Court. *In room:* TV, coffeemaker, hair dryer.

Mowbray Court Hotel   A few minutes' walk from the Earl's Court Underground station on a reasonably quiet side street, this hotel (without elevator) offers comfortable, reasonably sized rooms with firm mattresses on the beds and bathrooms that are generously sized for the budget category and are certainly well maintained. The decor wouldn't win any prizes, but all the rooms are clean and kept in a good state of repair.

28–32 Penywern Rd., London SW5. ℂ 020/7373-8285. Fax 020/7370-5693. www.mowbraycourthotel. co.uk. 82 units, 75 with bathroom. £45 ($83) single without bathroom, £52 ($96) single with bathroom; £56 ($104) double without bathroom, £67 ($124) double with bathroom; £69 ($128) triple without bathroom, £80 ($148) triple with bathroom; £84 ($155) quad without bathroom, £95 ($176) quad with bathroom. Rates include continental breakfast. AE, DC, MC, V. Tube: Earl's Court. **Amenities:** Internet access; hairdresser; laundry; dry cleaning. *In room:* TV, coffeemaker, safe, trouser press.

IN BLOOMSBURY

Bloomsbury's proximity to the West End in general, and to Soho in particular, has long made it desirable for visitors. The area derives energy from its two most important institutions: the University of London and the British Museum. Gower Street's budget hotels are some of the city's most popular. Most of the B&Bs lining this street are so similar to one another that only their addresses distinguish them. The stairs are steep, the rooms basic, and the prices fairly uniform.

Arran House Hotel *(★)*   The Arran House (without elevator) stands out on the block because of its exceptionally hospitable owner, John Richards, who has ensured that even guests in the front rooms get a quiet night's sleep (he soundproofed the windows). The rooms themselves are above average size for the price range and location, and all the beds have firm mattresses. The bathrooms are a little cramped, but all are clean and well maintained.

77 Gower St., London WC1. ℂ 020/7636-2186. Fax 020/7436-5328. www.london-hotel.co.uk. 28 units, 11 with bathroom. £45 ($83) single without bathroom, £55 ($102) single with bathroom; £55 ($102) double without bathroom, £62 ($115) double with bathroom; £85 ($157) triple without bathroom, £103 ($191) triple with bathroom. Rates include English breakfast. MC, V. Tube: Goodge St. **Amenities:** Kitchen and fridge for guest use; laundry facilities; Internet access. *In room:* TV, coffeemaker.

Garth Hotel   The Japanese-run Garth (without elevator) offers clean though small rooms, although in parts wear is more than evident. Beds have firm mattresses. As with many of the Gower Street properties, street noise can be a problem. You can choose from an English-style breakfast or a traditional Japanese morning meal, including rice, seaweed, and a raw egg.

69 Gower St., London WC1. ℂ 020/7636-5761. Fax 020/7637-4854. www.garthhotel-london.com. 17 units, 11 with shower only, 1 with bathroom. £40 ($74) single without bathroom, £35–£48 ($65–$89) single with

shower; £55 ($102) double without bathroom, £60–£85 ($111–$157) double with shower; £80–£96 ($148–$178) triple with shower. Rates include English or Japanese breakfast. AE, MC, V. Tube: Euston Sq. or Goodge St. *In room:* TV, coffeemaker, no phone.

Hotel Cavendish   This nicely furnished, clean, cozy home (without elevator) is run by Mrs. Edwards. The cheaper doubles are slightly smaller than the more expensive ones, and all the beds have firm mattresses. You have use of a TV lounge and, best of all, there's a shady walled garden for those sunny summer days. The hotel is kept immaculate, including the shared bathrooms.

75 Gower St., London WC1. © 020/7636-9079. Fax 020/7580-3609. www.hotelcavendish.com. 20 units, none with bathroom. £38–£42 ($70–$78) single; £48–£66 ($89–$122) double; £69–£75 ($128–$139) triple; £88–£96 ($169–$178) quad. Rates include English breakfast. AE, DC, MC, V. Tube: Euston Sq. or Goodge St. **Amenities:** TV lounge. *In room:* coffeemaker, no phone.

Jesmond Hotel ⊀   The proprietors, Mr. and Mrs. Beynon, have been to the United States many times and are acutely aware of American expectations. All rooms in the Jesmond (without elevator) are of a reasonable size, with firm mattresses on the beds, and are exceptionally clean. The front rooms have double-glazed windows, minimizing any noise. The bathrooms are a little larger than is the norm for this location and budget, and they, too, are maintained to a high standard and are spotless. The shared bathrooms are slightly larger than the private bathrooms.

63 Gower St., London WC1. © 020/7636-3199. Fax 020/7323-4373. www.jesmondhotel.org.uk. 16 units, 3 with bathroom. £36 ($67) single without bathroom; £46 ($85) single with bathroom; £54 ($100) double without bathroom; £68 ($126) double with bathroom; £70 ($130) triple without bathroom, £80 ($148) triple with bathroom; £80 ($148) quad without bathroom, £90 ($167) quad with bathroom. Rates include English breakfast. MC, V. Tube: Euston Sq. or Goodge St. *In room:* TV, coffeemaker, hair dryer.

LSE Residence High Holborn   This modern block houses the student residences for the London School of Economics (LSE), but the up-to-date flats are available to let throughout the summer vacation. Don't expect opulence, but the location in central London, a few blocks from the British Museum, offers unbeatable value for the price.

178 High Holborn, London WC1. © 020/7379-5589. Fax 020/7379-5640. www.lse.ac.uk. 496 units, 20 with bathroom. £31 ($57) single without bathroom; £49–£58 ($91–$107) double without bathroom; £58–£68 ($107–$126) double with bathroom; £70–£78 ($126–$144) triple with bathroom. Rates include continental breakfast. MC, V. Available July to early Sept. Tube: Holborn.

Ridgemont Hotel ⊀   The Ridgemont is an exceptionally friendly and clean hotel (without elevator) run by warm-hearted Welsh proprietors Royden and Gwen Rees, making it another good choice along the strip. The rooms are cozy, the beds offer firm mattresses, and the bathrooms are certainly adequate if a tad small.

65–67 Gower St., London WC1. © 020/7636-1141. Fax 020/7636-2558. www.ridgemounthotel.co.uk. 34 units, 15 with bathroom. £35 ($65) single without bathroom; £45 ($83) single with bathroom; £50 ($93) double without bathroom; £65 ($120) double with bathroom; £66 ($122) triple without bathroom, £78 ($144) triple with bathroom; £77–£80 ($142–$148) quad without bathroom, £89–£90 ($165–$167) quad with bathroom. Rates include English breakfast. MC, V. Tube: Euston Sq. or Goodge St. **Amenities:** Coffeemaker in lounge. *In room:* TV, hair dryer, no phone.

A GAY & LESBIAN HOTEL

Philbeach Hotel   One of Europe's largest gay hotels, the Philbeach is a Victorian row house (without elevator) on a wide crescent behind the Earl's Court Exhibition Centre. Open to both men and women as well as being transvestite and transgender friendly, it offers a selection of accommodations: from standard budget rooms that, while not huge, are certainly of adequate size, up to larger and more elegant rooms. All the beds have firm mattresses. The bathrooms are just about adequate, but are clean and well maintained, although the showers do tend to be small. The shared bathrooms are clean. Room no. 8A, a double with bathroom, has a balcony overlooking the small back garden.

30–31 Philbeach Gardens, London SW5. © 020/7373-1244. Fax 020/7244-0149. www.philbeachhotel. freeserve.co.uk. 40 units, 16 with bathroom. £55 ($102) single without bathroom, £65 ($120) single with bathroom; £70 ($130) double without bathroom, £90 ($167) double with bathroom; £75 ($139) triple without bathroom, £100 ($185) triple with bathroom. Rates include continental breakfast. AE, DC, MC, V. Tube: Earl's Court (take the Warwick Rd. exit). **Amenities:** Restaurant; bar. *In room:* TV, coffeemaker (some units).

IYHF HOSTELS

The **International Youth Hostel Federation** (**IYHF;** www.yha.org.uk) runs five hostels in central London. (Two are listed below.) To stay at one, you must have a membership card, available for about £9.30 ($17) at any hostel. You can save about £1 ($1.85) per night by supplying your own sheets.

City of London Youth Hostel This top pick, in a wonderfully restored building that was once a school for choirboys, boasts a good number of singles, and most of the multishares have no more than four beds each. The hostel is in the heart of The City on a back street near St. Paul's Cathedral—a location good for sightseeing but poor for dining and nightlife. The hostel's Chorister's restaurant is open until 8pm. Otherwise, most City places close when the bankers go home. Some rooms have TVs.

36 Carter Lane, London EC4. © 020/7236-4965. Fax 020/7236-7681. 197 beds. £19–£21 ($35–$38) per person dorm with 10–15 beds; £20–£23 ($36–$42) per person dorm with 5–8 beds; £21–£24 ($39–$45) per person dorm with 3–4 beds; £23–£26 ($41–$48) per person dorm with 1–2 beds. MC, V. Tube: Blackfriars or St. Paul's. **Amenities:** Restaurant. *In room:* TV (some units).

Holland House Holland House enjoys the most beautiful setting of all London's IYHF hostels, right in the middle of Kensington's Holland Park. The bunk-bedded rooms accommodate 12 people each. You'll find a kitchen, a TV room, a quiet room, and laundry facilities on the premises. Reasonably priced meals are also available.

Holland Walk, Holland Park, London W8 7QU. © 020/7937-0748. Fax 020/7376-0667. 201 beds. £18 ($33) per person under 18; £20 ($37) per person over 18. Rates include English breakfast. MC, V. Tube: High St. Kensington or Holland Park. **Amenities:** Kitchen; TV lounge; self-serve laundry.

WORTH A SPLURGE

Aster House Hotel 🌟 The Aster House (without elevator) is the most beautiful of a number of small B&Bs on this quiet South Kensington street. The pride with which the owners run the place is evident the moment you step onto the interior's plush carpets. All the rooms, with bathrooms featuring amenities usually found in more expensive hotels, are decorated prettily in floral fabrics and have comfortable eclectic furnishings; some beds are even finished off with tent treatments. Take special note of the award-winning rear garden. The breakfast buffet includes the usual eggs and sausages, as well as health-oriented fresh fruits, cold meats, cheeses, yogurt, and muesli. The meal is served in L'Orangerie, the beautiful glass-covered pièce de résistance of this special hotel.

3 Sumner Place, London SW7. © 020/7581-5888. Fax 020/7584-4925. www.asterhouse.com. 14 units. £90–£99 ($167–$183) single; £130–£160 ($241–$296) double. Rates include breakfast. MC, V. Tube: S. Kensington. *In room:* A/C, TV, coffeemaker, hair dryer, safe.

Hampton Court Palace 🌟🌟 Okay, so you can't rent the whole of Henry VIII's magnificent palace (24km/15 miles from central London), but you can become part of its life for 4 to 7 nights. Two self-contained, self-catering locations

⟨*Value* **Local Budget Bests**

The United Kingdom's largest budget hotel chain is **Travel Inn** (ⓒ **01582/ 414-341**; www.travelinn.co.uk), with several branches in London, two of which are centrally located.

The 313-unit **Travel Inn, County Hall,** Belvedere Road, London SE1 (ⓒ **0870/238-3300**; fax 020/7902-1619; tube: Westminster or Waterloo), is across the Thames from Parliament. It offers king-size beds in reasonably spacious rooms, which are comfortable and clean. Family rooms are created by the addition of a sofa bed, but four people sharing the room would find it cramped. It's popular, so book early. Rates are £83 ($154) for a room sleeping up to four. Continental breakfast is £6.50 ($12) and full English breakfast £9.95 ($18). American Express, MasterCard, and Visa are accepted.

Two other branches are **Travel Inn, Euston,** 141 Euston Rd., London NW1 (ⓒ **0870/238-3300**; fax 020/7554-3419; tube: Euston or King's Cross), within walking distance of the British Museum; and **Travel Inn, Tower Bridge,** Tower Bridge Road, London SE1 (ⓒ **0870/238-3300**; tube: London Bridge). Rates are £75 ($139) for a room sleeping up to four. Continental breakfast is £6.50 ($12) and full English breakfast £9.95 ($18). American Express, MasterCard, and Visa are accepted.

Early July to late September (and sometimes during Christmas and Easter), dozens of dorms open their doors to visitors. The rooms are almost all uniformly spartan, and some residence halls offer only singles, but they're inexpensive and centrally located. Try to reserve a space months in advance. The **King's Campus Vacation Bureau** (ⓒ **020/ 7862-8880**; fax 020/7928-5777; www.kcl.ac.uk) handles bookings for several University of London residence halls.

in the palace are available. **Fish Court** is an apartment in the Tudor wing, which was originally home to the "Officers of the Pastry." It's cozy, with two single rooms, a twin, and a double, as well as a kitchen and a living room. It might be expensive for two, but if you're traveling in a group of six in peak season, it's only £51 ($94) per person per night for a week. On a grander scale is the imposing **Georgian House,** built on the palace grounds in 1719 for George, prince of Wales. There you have your own walled garden and magnificent views over the palace roofs from the attic windows. The rooms (two singles, two twins, and one double, plus a kitchen, a sitting room, and a dining room) are airy and spacious, with antique and classic furnishings. If you're traveling with a group of eight, the cost is £47 ($87) per person per night. Needless to say, this is proving to be one of London's most sought-after options, so early booking is advised.

E. Molesey, Surrey. Book through Landmark Trust, Shottesbrooke, Maidenhead, Berks, SL6 3SW. ⓒ 01628/ 825-925. www.landmarktrust.co.uk. Fish Court: Sleeps 6. Price range: 7 nights £1,056 ($1,954) in low season (Jan) to £1,850 ($3,423) in high season (July–Aug). Georgian House: Sleeps 8. Price range: 7 nights £1,176 ($2,176) in low season (Jan) to £2,269 ($4,198) in high season (July–Aug). 4-night stays not available May 27–Sept 1. Train: 30-min. trip from London's Waterloo Station. **Amenities:** TV; dishwasher (in Georgian House).

Harlingford Hotel   The Harlingford (without elevator) is the nicest hotel on Bloomsbury's best-located Georgian crescent. You'll be particularly pleased by the bright ground-floor dining room, where a hearty breakfast is served. The cheery rooms are kept clean and well maintained, but it's worth letting the well-furnished communal lounge entice you away from the TV in your room. All the beds have firm mattresses, and the bathrooms are immaculate and well proportioned. A coffee machine on the landing sits next to a free ice dispenser for chilling your bubbly.

61–63 Cartwright Gardens, London WC1. © 020/7387-1551. Fax 020/7387-4616. www.harlingfordhotel. com. 44 units. £75 ($139) single; £95 ($176) double; £105 ($194) triple; £110 ($204) quad. Rates include English breakfast. AE, DC, MC, V. Tube: Russell Sq., King's Cross. In room: TV, coffeemaker.

Hotel 167 🏵🏵   A favored haunt of ad-men and writers (the *New York Times* and *Paris Match* use it as one of the London bases for their staff), this chic hotel (without elevator) in fashionable "South Ken" offers modern simplicity and rooms that, although a tad small, are individually and brightly decorated as well as imaginatively and colorfully furnished. Art Deco, Japanese, and Victorian are just some of the themes evident in the rooms, all of which have firm mattresses, artwork that's worth looking at, and very clean bathrooms; some even boast antique furnishings. The neighborhood of charming residential streets and serene squares is delightful to explore.

167 Old Brompton Rd., London SW5. © 020/7373-0672 or 020/7373-3221. Fax 020/7373-3360. www.hotel167.com. 19 units. £72 ($133) single; £90–£99 ($167–$183) double. Rates include continental breakfast. AE, DC, MC, V. Tube: S. Kensington or Gloucester Rd. In room: TV, minibar, fridge, coffeemaker.

The Pavilion 🏵   In the early 1990s, a team of fashion industry entrepreneurs took over this Paddington B&B with a blackened Victorian facade of stock bricks and stucco, and radically redecorated the rooms, turning it into an idiosyncratic little hotel (without an elevator). It offers rooms of reasonable size that are exceptionally clean, with firm mattresses on the beds as well as clean, though not overly generously sized, bathrooms. Each room is, to say the least, individually furnished and decorated with a theatrical and often outrageous style. Examples are the kitschy 1970s room ("Honky-Tonk Afro"), the Oriental bordello room ("Enter the Dragon"), and rooms with 19th-century ancestral themes. One Edwardian-style room, a gem of emerald brocade and velvet, is called "Green with Envy."

34–36 Sussex Gardens, London W2. © 020/7262-0905. Fax 020/7262-1324. www.msi.com.mt/pavilion. 27 units. £60–£85 ($111–$157) single; £100 ($185) double; £120 ($222) triple. Rates include continental breakfast. AE, DC, MC, V. Car parking £5 ($9.25) per day. Tube: Edgewater Rd. In room: TV, coffeemaker.

3 Great Deals on Dining

English food has improved immensely in recent years, and even budget fare is now quite palatable, except for the still often overcooked vegetables and the ubiquitous canned peas. There has been a flowering of quality take-aways and quick snack shops, and there is hardly a neighborhood that isn't served by numerous establishments offering decent sandwiches, salads, or even sushi with a drink for under £5 ($9.25). For example, on **Villier's Street,** leading from The Strand to The River, you'll find a variety of nicely priced sandwich bars. On those all too rare, halcyon summer days, what better lunch venue can there be than one of London's many parks and gardens? For indoor dining, London's ethnic restaurants represent the city's best budget values and add spice to the foodscape. Top Indian chefs and good-quality ingredients keep the standards high even in the cheapest of curry houses. Several of London's pubs have risen to the challenge by introducing Thai and Chinese menus. And don't forget the three

---

Fun Fact **What's for Pudding?**

Note that in England appetizers are often called "starters," while desserts of all kinds are referred to as "pudding," "sweets," or "afters." Dinner is often referred to as "supper," and a napkin is called a "serviette." (If you ask for a napkin you might get a strange look—napkins, or nappies, are what the Brits call diapers.)

---

quintessential British experiences: fish and chips, pub grub such as bangers and mash, and afternoon tea with tiny sandwiches (see the "Tea for Two" box, below).

IN & AROUND SOHO, PICCADILLY & TRAFALGAR SQUARE

Cafe in the Crypt ENGLISH   This very atmospheric cafeteria-style restaurant is set in the crypt of the church. Coffee and croissants are available mid-morning; and fresh salads, soups, sandwiches, and hot and cold dishes, both meat and vegetarian, are served at lunch. For example, you might find salmon with lemon-lime and spinach-and-nut roulade. The tables are not large but there is plenty of room between them.

In the Church of St. Martin-in-the-Fields, Trafalgar Sq., WC2. 📞 020/7839-4342. www.stmartin-in-the-fields.org. Rolls and sandwiches £1.75–£2.20 ($3.25–$4.10); main courses £5.95–£6.50 ($11–$12). No credit cards. Mon–Sat 10am–7pm; Sun noon–8pm. Tube: Charing Cross.

Gaby's Deli CONTINENTAL   This small but cozy, fully licensed sandwich bar/cafe offers home-cooked specialties such as stuffed eggplant, cabbage rolls, Hungarian goulash, and lamb curry, which, like most of the main courses, cost around £6.50 ($12), with salad or rice. Everything is made fresh daily according to the chef's mood. The restaurant is known for its sandwiches, especially salt beef, cheapest when you buy it to take out for about £3.50 ($6.50). There's also a broad selection of vegetarian dishes.

30 Charing Cross Rd. (just off Leicester Sq.), WC2. 📞 020/7836-4233. Meals £6.50–£8 ($12–$15). No credit cards. Mon–Sat 9am–midnight; Sun 11am–10pm. Tube: Leicester Sq.

Le Piaf FRENCH   With a comfortable candlelit dining room, pretty good food, and unbeatable prices, this franchised French restaurant has all the hallmarks of permanence. The bistro food includes roast pork with spinach and garlic, as well as chicken in white wine and cream sauce. Vegetables are served on separate side plates, and fresh bread is included with every meal. There are too many other branches to name—check the phone book for the one nearest you.

6 Panton St., SW1. 📞 020/7930-6463. Reservations recommended. Fixed-price lunch £5.95 ($11); pre-theater dinner £8.95 ($17); main courses £6–£11 ($11–$20). AE, MC, V. Daily noon–4pm and 5:30–11pm. Tube: Piccadilly Circus.

New Piccadilly Restaurant ENGLISH/CONTINENTAL   The uninspiring decor and straightforward English cafe menu make this central restaurant a budget mainstay. The long dining room lined with Formica-topped tables is not intended for romance or relaxing, but you can choose from a large number of specialties, like fish and chips, chicken with mushroom sauce, and steak risotto for about £5 ($9.25). For a little less, try one of their pizza or pasta dishes. The place has no liquor license; you're encouraged to bring your own alcohol.

8 Denman St. (just off the bottom of Shaftesbury Ave., a few feet from Piccadilly Circus), W1. 📞 020/7437-8530. Meals £4–£6.75 ($7.50–$13). No credit cards. Daily 11am–9:30pm. Tube: Piccadilly Circus.

New World CHINESE   Reminiscent of Hong Kong's massive catering halls, this giant Cantonese palace seating 700 plus is one of Chinatown's largest restaurants. The immense menu matches the dining rooms in size and reads like a veritable summary of pan-Chinese cookery. The usual poultry, beef, pork, and vegetable stir-fry dishes are represented, and at lunch dim sum is served in the traditional manner, via trolley.

1 Gerrard Place, W1. © 020/7734-0396. Meals £7–£10 ($13–$19); fixed-price meals from £7.20 ($13). AF, DC, MC, V. Mon–Thurs 11am–11:45pm; Fri Sat 11am midnight; Sun 10:45am–10.45pm. Tube: Leicester Sq. or Piccadilly Circus.

Pollo ⚜ ITALIAN   An extremely popular Italian/English restaurant, Pollo offers good food and low, low prices that keep the crowds coming. There must be 150 menu items, with few topping £5 ($9.25). Pastas in myriad shapes and sizes are served with a choice of over a dozen red and white sauces, plus pizzas and a good selection of vegetarian dishes. The list of Italian desserts is impressive, too. The atmosphere is lively, but if you don't like crowds, Pollo isn't for you. Expect to be rushed and jostled.

20 Old Compton St. (near Frith St., a few doors down from the Prince Edward Theatre), W1. © 020/7734-5917. Reservations not accepted. Main courses £4–£7 ($7.50–$21). No credit cards. Mon–Sat 11:30am–11:30pm. Tube: Leicester Sq.

Wong Kei *Value* CHINESE   There are many good, cheap, Chinese restaurants in Soho, most serving Cantonese fare. Wong Kei is one of the area's cheapest, with an extensive menu and very abrupt staff. At least a dozen popular dishes, such as chicken with garlic sauce and beef with vegetables, cost under £5 ($9.25). As is the rule at most Chinese restaurants in London, if you want rice you have to order it separately, for £1.30 ($2.40). Tea is free, and hearty eaters can take advantage of the fixed-price meal of three dishes plus rice for only £7 ($13) per person (two people minimum).

41–43 Wardour St., W1. © 020/7437-3071. Fixed-price menu £7 ($13). No credit cards. Daily noon–11:30pm. Tube: Leicester Sq. or Piccadilly Circus.

IN THE CITY

Al's Cafe ENGLISH   One of London's funkiest cafes is best known for lunch, when it's packed with office types chowing down on half pound bacon cheeseburgers, spicy sausages with grilled onions, and delicious homemade soups like carrot and bean. Most everything comes with thick cut chips, and a long list of salads and sandwiches is also available. Al's gets high marks for service with a

---

Value Getting the Best Deal on Dining

- Seek out the budget restaurants on the side streets around Covent Garden and Soho—the festive atmosphere of these areas makes finding them fun.
- Look for places with a number of taxis parked outside—you can be sure the food is good and the prices are low.
- Remember to take advantage of British standbys like affordable and delicious pub grub and fish and chips.
- Note any restaurants that don't have signs welcoming tourists; they usually care about making you a repeat customer.

⟮Moments⟯ Tea for Two

As much as the tea itself, it's tradition that makes afternoon tea a pleasant and civilized activity. The pot is usually served with a spread of sandwiches and cakes and pastries that more than make a meal. Accordingly, an authentic tea is expensive and usually served in top hotels, where jackets and ties are required for men.

Brown's Hotel, Albemarle and Dover streets, W1 (℃ **020/7493-6020;** tube: Green Park), serves the best fixed-price tea in London, daily 3 to 6pm. For £25 ($46) per person, you can sit in one of three wood-paneled, stained-glass lounges and feel like a millionaire. Tailcoated waiters will make sure you don't leave hungry, as they fill your table with your choice from the variety of teas; tomato, cucumber, and meat sandwiches; scones; and pastries. The **Ritz Hotel,** Piccadilly, W1 (℃ **020/ 7493-8181;** tube: Green Park), is probably the world's most famous spot for afternoon tea, and even at £32 ($59) per person you have to book at least a week in advance. The Ritz is steeped in elegance, and as at Brown's, you have your choice of teas, traditional sandwiches, scones, and yummy pastries. It's served daily 2 to 6pm. And if you're in the mood for tea after visiting Kensington Palace, stop at **The Orangery** (p. 545).

smile and for top ingredients that include Italian focaccia. Good, filling, all-day breakfasts are served, too.

11–13 Exmouth Market, EC1. ℃ 020/7837-4821. Reservations not accepted. Meals £4.50–£6 ($8.50–$11). AE, V. Mon–Fri 7am–11pm; Sat–Sun 10am–8pm. Tube: Angel or Farringdon.

Ferrari's ENGLISH   A popular hangout with London's cab drivers, Ferrari's is famous for its sandwich menu, which includes Norwegian prawn and farmhouse pâté. You can also enjoy a substantial full English breakfast served all day, and the cakes are irresistible.

8 W. Smithfield, EC1. ℃ 020/7236-7545. Meals £2.50–£6 ($4.65–$11). No credit cards. Mon–Fri 5:15am–3pm.Tube: St. Paul's.

Piccolo ENGLISH   This sandwich bar, with fewer than a dozen stools all facing the street, is perfect for a quick bite after visiting St. Paul's Cathedral and offers the widest range of sandwiches you're ever likely to come across. Bacon and turkey, roast chicken, and all the standards are priced below £3 ($5.55). The shop is between St. Paul's Underground station and the Museum of London.

7 Gresham St. (off Martin's Le Grand St.), EC2. No phone. Meals £2–£3 ($3.70–$5.55). No credit cards. Mon–Fri 6am–7:30pm; Sat 6am–4pm. Tube: St. Paul's.

AROUND COVENT GARDEN

Food for Thought VEGETARIAN   This unusual restaurant makes vegetarian food that appeals to all palates and wallets. Delicious dishes, like cauliflower quiche and South Indian curry made with eggplant, carrots, peppers, cauliflower, and spinach, are usually priced around £3.60 ($6.70) and served downstairs in a small pine dining room with a terra-cotta tile floor (no smoking). Evening specials such as cannelloni filled with a julienne of eggplant, sun-dried tomatoes, and mozzarella are only £5 ($9.25). Really tasty soups and salads are also available, plus a good selection of healthful desserts.

31 Neal St. (across from the Covent Garden Underground station), WC2. ℂ 020/7836-9072. Reservations not accepted. Main courses £3.90–£6.50 ($7–$12). No credit cards. Mon–Sat 9:30am–8:30pm; Sun noon–5pm. Tube: Covent Garden.

Neal's Yard Café Society LIGHT FARE   Neal's Yard (an address of a yard of shops located at Seven Dials) boasts several vegetarian and light-fare establishments, all of which are good. However, if you want to sit in reasonably comfortable surroundings, this Mediterranean-style cafe offers clean, though uninspiring, surroundings and a selection of pasta dishes and spicy organic soups that are both warming and filling. You can enjoy large focaccia sandwiches made with mozzarella, spinach, tomato, and avocado, plus a whole range of vegetable and fruit juices. The emphasis is on fresh and healthy, except for the fine ice creams (although they also serve soy ice cream).

13 Neal's Yard, WC2. ℂ **020/7240-1168.** Sandwiches £3.95–£5 ($7.25–$9.25). MC, V. Mon–Sat 9:30am–8pm; Sun 9:30am–7:30pm. Tube: Covent Garden.

Wagamama JAPANESE   This Japanese noodle bar is one of London's hippest and most popular restaurants. There's always a line to get into the minimalist dining room, which is infused with a health-oriented, Zenlike philosophy. The kitchen's offerings are limited to a variety of vegetarian stir-fries and several kinds of steaming noodle soups. Enjoy an ice-cold lager or fresh-squeezed juice while you wait for a table. There's a branch at 10A Lexington St., W1 (ℂ 020/7292-0990; tube: Piccadilly Circus or Oxford Circus); and another right by the Tower of London at 2b Tower Place, EC3 (ℂ 020/7292-0990; tube: Tower Hill). There are more (16 total in London) scattered about town.

4 Streatham St., WC1. ℂ **020/7323-9223.** www.wagamama.com. Reservations not accepted. Meals £8–£10 ($15–$19). AE, DC, MC, V. Mon–Sat noon–11pm; Sun 12:30–10pm. Tube: Tottenham Court Rd.

IN BAYSWATER

Khan's ✹ INDIAN   Khan's is said to have the best Indian food in Bayswater, so it attracts crowds—don't expect a leisurely quiet meal (it'll be rushed and noisy). The menu, which includes all the staples, guarantees that only halal meat is used, conforming to the Muslim dietary code. Curry dishes cost about £4 ($6).

13–15 Westbourne Grove, W2. ℂ **020/7727-5420.** www.khansrestaurant.com. Meals £4.85–£10 ($9–$19). AE, DC, MC, V. Mon–Thurs noon–3pm and 6pm–midnight; Fri–Sun noon–midnight. Tube: Bayswater.

IN BLOOMSBURY

Anwar's INDIAN   Anwar's not only maintains a high standard of quality but is one of the cheapest Indian restaurants in London. Few dishes top £4 ($7.50), and most cost just £3.50 ($6.50). There's a wide choice of meat and vegetable curries and other Indian specialties, including thalis and tandoori chicken for £3 ($5.55). Anwar's is cafeteria style; help yourself and bring your meal to a Formica-covered table. Despite this "canteen" approach, the food is top-notch.

64 Grafton Way, W1. ℂ **020/7387-6664.** Meals £3.30–£5 ($6–$9.25). No credit cards. Daily noon–11pm. Tube: Warren St.

Greenhouse Basement VEGETARIAN   Below the sidewalk, this dining room has an appealing candlelit atmosphere, serving fare that's fresh and healthful. Several salads are offered daily, along with lasagna, mixed vegetable masala, and Eastern/Middle Eastern–inspired dishes.

16 Chenies St., WC1. ℂ 020/7637-8038. Reservations not accepted. Main courses £4.20 ($7.75). No credit cards. Mon–Sat 10am–8:30pm; Sun noon–4pm. Tube: Goodge St.

IN EARLS COURT

The Troubadour ENGLISH   This charming old cafe has been a London fixture since the 1950s and has a long tradition of poetry readings, folk music, and jazz in its basement room; stand-up comedy has recently been added. Bob Dylan, Paul Simon, and even Charlie Watts of the Rolling Stones have all performed here. The ground floor cafe, with its dark wood, candlelit interior, and motley collection of musical instruments and old pots and pans hanging from the ceiling, is vaguely reminiscent of a Parisian bar. The fare, while not overly inspired, is certainly filling and can include spaghetti, garlic prawns, bangers (sausages) and mash, or the justifiably renowned Troubadour omelet, with a choice of fillings, served with salad and either toast or fries. The tables are closely packed so it's not a place for romancing, but you can certainly chill out for a few hours, and even make polite conversation with the occasional latter-day existentialist who has dropped in for a coffee—although the relaxed ambience might convince you that such activity is pointless!

265 Old Brompton Road, SW5. ⓒ 020/7370-1434. Reservations not accepted. Meals £4.95–£9.50 ($9–$18). MC, V. Daily 9am–midnight. Tube: Earl's Court.

IN THE EAST END

Brick Lane Beigel Bakery *(Kids* SANDWICHES   There's always a line for these tiny bagels (here pronounced *bi*-gus), which are made into sandwiches filled with cream cheese, salt beef, chopped herring, or smoked salmon. It's especially busy after midnight, when most other places are shut, and a line of taxi drivers forms curbside by the door. There are two adjacent bagel shops on Brick Lane—this one is the best. Ironically, both are near the corner of Bacon Street.

159 Brick Lane, E1. ⓒ 020/7729-0616. Bagels and cakes 30p–£1.50 (55¢–$2.75). No credit cards. Daily 24 hr. Tube: Aldgate E.

The Spice INDIAN   Brick Lane and the surrounding streets are lined with over 50 curry houses and restaurants. It's where Londoners go to enjoy some of the best Indian food at the keenest prices. The Spice is relatively new to the Lane but already establishing itself as a popular venue. The service is friendly and attentive, and the varied menu includes a range of *birianis* (complete meals in themselves) for around £6 ($11). For those not used to spicy Indian food, I recommend an onion *bhajee* starter at £1.45 ($2.70), followed by chicken *tikka masala* at £5.95 ($11), with *pilau* rice at £1.60 ($3).

8 Brick Lane, E1. ⓒ 020/7375-2709. Meals £4.95–£7.95 ($9–$15). AE, MC, V. Sun–Thurs noon–3pm and 6pm–12:30am; Fri–Sat noon–3pm and 6pm–1am. Tube: Aldgate East.

THE CHAINS

Go to **Pizza Express,** 30 Coptic St., WC1 (ⓒ **020/7636-3232;** www.pizza express.co.uk; tube: Holborn), for terrific pizza that ranges from an ordinary *margherita* (cheese and sauce) to all kinds of imaginative combinations that can include sultanas, olives, capers, pine nuts, and onions. Each of the outlets (located throughout London, though the above-mentioned address is one of the best located) is sleekly decked out with tile and marble, even if it's only faux. Pizza runs £4.25 to £7.15 ($7.85–$13), and American Express, MasterCard, and Visa are accepted. It's open daily noon to midnight.

You will find the upscale sandwich shops of **Prêt à Manger** *(x* all over central London. They operate by a simple philosophy of using the freshest ingredients for their gourmet sandwiches, which can include poached salmon, goat's cheese, chicken and avocado, and tarragon chicken. Although McDonald's took a financial stake in the chain in 2001, they promised faithfully that this would in no

Value Local Budget Bests

FISH & CHIPS   Fast-food restaurants have taken their toll on London, but "chippies" are still to be found. Nowadays, fish and chips are usually offered by Middle Eastern places, too, but the most authentic joints won't have a kabob in sight. Several kinds of fish are used, but when thickly battered and deep-fried, they taste similar; cod is the cheapest. Sitting down will up the price of the meal considerably, so do as most locals do and get it to take away—wrapped in a paper cone, doused with vinegar, and sprinkled with salt. The bill should never top £7 ($13).

Two of the most popular chippies are **Rock & Sole Plaice,** 47 Endell St., at Shorts Gardens, near Covent Garden Market (© 020/7836-3785; tube: Covent Garden), open daily 11:30am to 11pm for takeout; and the **North Sea Fish Bar,** 8 Leigh St., WC1 (© 020/7387-5892; tube: St. Pancras), just southeast of Cartwright Gardens at Sandwich Street in Bloomsbury, open Monday to Saturday noon to 2:30pm and 5:30 to 10:30pm.

PUB GRUB   Pub food can vary from snacks at the bar to a complete restaurant meal, but it's usually cheap, good, and filling. Most pubs offer food, and there are so many pubs that if you don't like what you see in one, you can move on to the next. Most pubs display their dishes so you can select by sight. Popular items are bangers and mash (sausages and mashed potatoes), meat or vegetable pies (including cottage pie, made with ground beef and a whipped potato topping), pasties (meat-filled pastries), and ploughman's lunch (a plate of crusty French bread with several cheeses, salad, and chutney). Wash it all down with a beer (room temperature).

Behind the bar, food and drink are kept apart as vigilantly as an Orthodox rabbi keeps milk from meat. Order and pay for each separately. A good pub lunch will seldom top £7 ($13), and careful ordering can cut that amount.

Many popular pubs are listed under "London After Dark," later in this chapter. These pubs are known especially for their food: **Cittie of Yorke** *, 22 High Holborn, WC1 (© 020/7242-7670; tube: Chancery Lane); **Coal Hole,** 91 The Strand, WC2 (© 020/7836-7503; tube: Temple or Covent Garden); **Australian,** 29 Milner St., Chelsea, SW3 (© 020/589-6027; tube: Sloane Sq.), which has won numerous awards for its excellent food; **Silver Cross,** Whitehall, WC2 (© 020/7930-8350; tube: Westminster or Charing Cross); and **Hung Drawn and Quartered,** 27 Great Tower St., EC3 (© 020/7626-6123; tube: Tower Hill).

way affect the gourmet philosophy of these excellent eateries. There's a small selection of salads and sushi, hot croissants, and a huge assortment of cakes. You line up cafeteria style, then take your meal to matte-black tables. Sandwiches are £1 to £5 ($1.85–$9.25), with no credit cards accepted. All branches are open Monday to Thursday 8am to 10pm, Friday and Saturday 8am to 11pm, and Sunday 10am to 8pm. There are about 50 locations in London.

The Stockpot features contemporary styling and subscribes to a generous budget-minded philosophy. Menus change daily but regularly include two homemade soups; a dozen main courses such as chicken a la king, gammon steak and pineapple, beef Stroganoff, omelets, chili, and fish and chips; and an excellent selection of desserts. Main courses run £3 to £5.50 ($5.55–$10), with no credit cards accepted. Hours usually are Monday to Saturday 11:30am to 11:45pm and Sunday noon to 11pm. Central London locations are 18 Old Compton St., Soho (© **020/7287-1066;** tube: Leicester Sq.); 273 King's Rd., SW3 (© **020/7823-3175;** tube: Sloane Sq.), in Chelsea, a few blocks past the fire station; 6 Basil St., SW3 (© **020/7589-8627;** tube: Knightsbridge), between Harrods and Sloane Street; and 40 Panton St., SW1 (© **020/7839-5142;** tube: Piccadilly Circus), just off Haymarket.

PICNICKING

There are plenty of supermarkets around offering run-of-the-mill staples. Cold cuts and cheeses from the deli counter are usually cheaper than the prewrapped stuff that hangs in the cooler.

For unusual picnic goodies, try the large and fascinating **Loon Fung Supermarket,** 42–44 Gerrard St., W1 (© **020/7437-7332;** tube: Leicester Sq.), in the center of Soho's Chinatown. The most adventurous will try the black-jelly fungus or steamed, congealed chicken's blood. The rest will enjoy dried cuttlefish, a traditional snack that goes well with beer. Loon Fung is open daily 10am to 8:30pm. The last year has seen a mushrooming of major supermarket chains opening neighborhood mini-stores. **Sainsbury, Tesco, Boots,** and **Marks and Spencer** have all opened so called "local" stores across London. They sell a wide range of relatively cheap sandwiches and picnic foods.

For the top picnic spots, see "Parks & Gardens" on p. 552.

WORTH A SPLURGE

Club Gascon ⚔ SOUTHWESTERN FRENCH When Pascal Aussignac sold his St-Tropez restaurant and headed for London, he was taking "the biggest gamble of his life." On the border of newly fashionable Clerkenwell, Club Gascon opened in 1999, and soon booking a table became a major task (a 3-week waiting list isn't uncommon). Marble walls, dark wood floors, subdued lighting, and attentive waiters in crisp white uniforms set the mood. The food, with its emphasis on dishes from the Gascony region, can't be faulted. You have a choice of 12 types of foie gras. The varied selection of main courses changes monthly but is always beautifully presented and delicious. The menu can prove a little overwhelming in its complexity, but the staff is always happy to explain the dishes and make useful suggestions. Pascal insists on only one sitting per night, so the pace is relaxed, and after dinner you might find him wandering from table to table and even pausing for a drink.

57 Smithfield, EC1. © 020/7796-0600. Reservations essential, far in advance. Expect to pay £29–£55 ($54–$102) for a meal. MC, V. Daily noon–2:30pm and 7–10:45pm. Tube: Barbican.

Criterion Brasserie–Marco Pierre White MODERN BRITISH The *enfant terrible* of British cookery, Michelin-starred Marco Pierre White runs his "junior" restaurant here. Before he took over, the Criterion was already a London legend, having been designed by Thomas Verity in the 1870s. This palatial neo-Byzantine mirrored marble hall is now a glamorous backdrop for the master chef's excellent cuisine. The menu is wide ranging, from Paris brasserie food to "nouvelle classical." Perhaps start with squid ink risotto with roast calamari, and follow that with roast skate wing with deep-fried snails, or roast saddle of lamb stuffed with mushrooms and spinach.

224 Piccadilly, W1. © 020/7930-0488. Reservations strongly advised. Main courses £11–£15 ($20–$28); fixed-price lunch £18 ($33) for 2 courses, £20 ($37) for 3 courses. AE, MC, V. Daily noon–2:30pm and 6–11:30pm. Tube: Piccadilly Circus.

Oxo Tower Brasserie ⭐⭐ FRENCH   Even if the food were lousy (it certainly isn't), this stylish Terence Conran dreamchild atop the South Bank's Oxo Tower would rate a star for its breathtaking city views. The Oxo Tower Restaurant is the name it generally goes by, but I recommend the adjacent brasserie, costing about half what you pay to dine on tablecloths on the other side. Plead for a window table (easier if you come early). The starter of chicken liver and mixed-leaf salad with roasted peppers, pancetta, and new potatoes is sublime. The main courses include roast *poussin* (rabbit) with rocket (arugula), French beans, and lemon-and-green-olive butter, as well as seared salmon with spring onion mash and Meaux mustard beurre blanc. The Oxo Tower might be a little hard to find, so hop into a taxi once you get out of the tube station.

Oxo Tower Wharf, Barge House St., SE1. © 020/7803-3888. Reservations essential. Main courses £13–£15 ($23–$27). AE, DC, MC, V. Daily noon–3pm and 5.30–11pm. Tube: Waterloo or Blackfriars.

4 Seeing the Sights

THE TOP ATTRACTIONS

British Library   The British Library is home to one of the world's greatest collections of the written word. Housed in a futuristic, high-tech purpose-built complex, the main collection of over 150 million items is only open to those in possession of the much sought-after Readers Ticket. (Students, researchers, and scholars may apply.) The library's permanent exhibition, however, is open to the general public and is displayed in the **John Ritblat Gallery.** Here you can view over 200 of the library's greatest treasures. On display are world-famous items like the **Lindisfarne Gospels,** the **Gutenberg Bible,** and the **first folio of Shakespeare's plays** (ca. 1623). You can also see one of the few surviving copies of King John's **Magna Carta,** Handel's *Messiah,* and **Beatles manuscripts.** The gallery also contains recordings from the **National Sound Archive,** where visitors can listen to the voices of such historical figures as Florence Nightingale and even James Joyce reading an excerpt from *Ulysses.* Allow 1 to 2 hours for a visit or 1½ hours for the tour.

96 Euston Rd., NW1. © 020/7412-7332 to reserve for tours. www.bl.uk. Free admission. Mon–Fri 9:30am–6pm (8pm on Tues); Sat 9:30am–5pm; Sun 11am–5pm. Tours Mon, Wed, Fri 3pm; Sat 10:30am and 3pm; tours that include a visit to one of the Reading Rooms take place Tues 6:30pm, Sun 11:30am and 3pm. Reading Room tour £7 ($13) adults, £5.50 ($10) seniors and students. Tube: King's Cross or Euston.

British Museum ⭐⭐⭐   Britain's largest and oldest national museum houses an unmatched collection of antiquities, many the spoils of the Empire Where the Sun Never Set. Important finds from Egypt, Greece, Rome, and Cyprus share this warehouse with spectacular collections from Asia and the Middle East. The museum's Great Court is truly dazzling and leads to the absolutely stunning Reading Room that has recently been restored to its original 19th-century splendor. Elsewhere, the **Rosetta Stone** ⭐⭐, at the entrance to the **Egyptian Sculpture Gallery** (room no. 25), is interesting as an artifact, yet even more fascinating because of the way it changed our understanding of hieroglyphics, which had been a mystery for 1,400 years. The **Parthenon Sculptures** ⭐⭐

Inner London

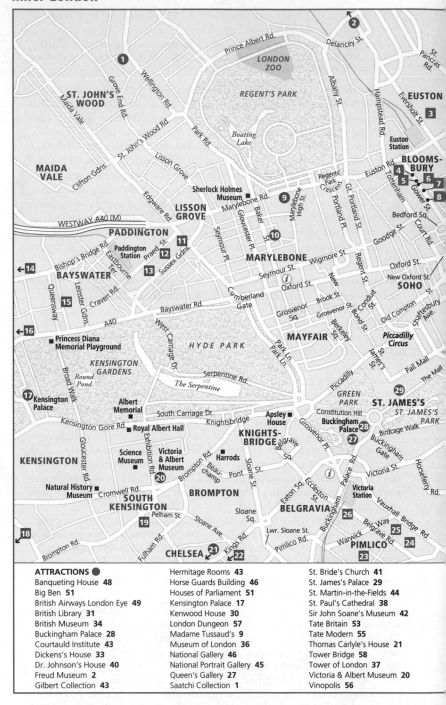

ATTRACTIONS ●

Banqueting House **48**	Hermitage Rooms **43**	St. Bride's Church **41**
Big Ben **51**	Horse Guards Building **46**	St. James's Palace **29**
British Airways London Eye **49**	Houses of Parliament **51**	St. Martin-in-the-Fields **44**
British Library **31**	Kensington Palace **17**	St. Paul's Cathedral **38**
British Museum **34**	Kenwood House **30**	Sir John Soane's Museum **42**
Buckingham Palace **28**	London Dungeon **57**	Tate Britain **53**
Courtauld Institute **43**	Madame Tussaud's **9**	Tate Modern **55**
Dickens's House **33**	Museum of London **36**	Thomas Carlyle's House **21**
Dr. Johnson's House **40**	National Gallery **46**	Tower Bridge **58**
Freud Museum **2**	National Portrait Gallery **45**	Tower of London **37**
Gilbert Collection **43**	Queen's Gallery **27**	Victoria & Albert Museum **20**
	Saatchi Collection **1**	Vinopolis **56**

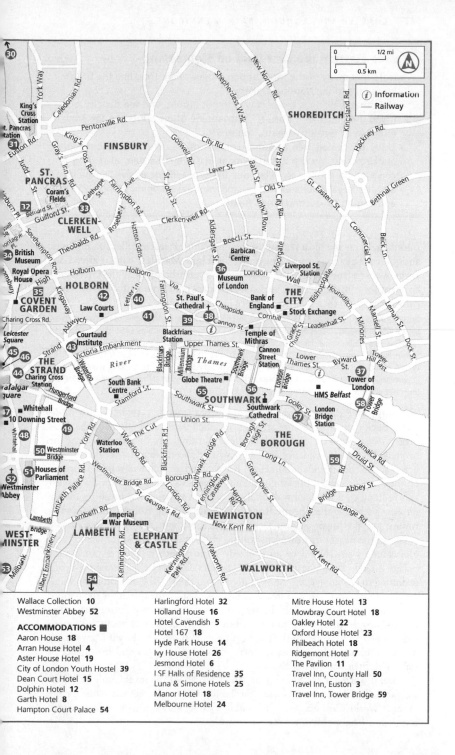

Wallace Collection **10**	
Westminster Abbey **52**	
ACCOMMODATIONS ■	
Aaron House **18**	
Arran House Hotel **4**	
Aster House Hotel **19**	
City of London Youth Hostel **39**	
Dean Court Hotel **15**	
Dolphin Hotel **12**	
Garth Hotel **8**	
Hampton Court Palace **54**	

Harlingford Hotel **32**	
Holland House **16**	
Hotel Cavendish **5**	
Hotel 167 **18**	
Hyde Park House **14**	
Ivy House Hotel **26**	
Jesmond Hotel **6**	
I SF Halls of Residence **35**	
Luna & Simone Hotels **25**	
Manor Hotel **18**	
Melbourne Hotel **24**	

Mitre House Hotel **13**	
Mowbray Court Hotel **18**	
Oakley Hotel **22**	
Oxford House Hotel **23**	
Philbeach Hotel **18**	
Ridgemont Hotel **7**	
The Pavilion **11**	
Travel Inn, County Hall **50**	
Travel Inn, Euston **3**	
Travel Inn, Tower Bridge **59**	

(Value) Getting the Best Deal on Sightseeing

- Note that many of the best London museums are free, like the British Museum and the National Gallery.
- Note that walking is the best way to get around and see the city, but if you use public transport, take advantage of discounts like the Travelcard (see "Getting Around," on p. 518).
- Enjoy the varied free pastimes London offers, like touring outdoor markets, catching the entertainment at Covent Garden, attending a concert in a church, checking out the proceedings at the Old Bailey and the Royal Courts of Justice, and window-shopping along Oxford and Regent streets and King's Road.

(room no. 8) are the most famous of the museum's extensive collection of Greek antiquities. They used to be known as the **Elgin Marbles,** named after Lord Elgin, whose agents removed these treasures from Athens; today the Greek government seeks their return. A visit can take anywhere from half a day to 3 or 4 consecutive days, there's so much to see.

Great Russell St., WC1. ℭ **020/7323-8299**. www.thebritishmuseum.ac.uk. Free admisison to main galleries, but £2 ($3.70) donation requested; special exhibits vary but can be as much as £4.50 ($8.30) adults, £3 ($5.55) seniors, students, and children under 17. Daily 10am–5:30pm (to 8:30pm Thurs–Fri). Museum tours, 90-min. highlight tours of museum's "must-see" objects daily 10:30am, 1, and 3pm (call ℭ 020/7323-8181 to book a tour). Tour £8 ($15) adults, £5 ($9.25) students and children 11–16, free for children under 11. Free "Eyeopener" tours lasting 50–60 min. explore specific galleries, are given by enthusiast volunteer guides, and take place approximately every 30 min. daily 11am–3pm.

Buckingham Palace   As the home of one of the world's few remaining monarchs, Buckingham Palace has strong symbolic interest and is one of the city's biggest draws. Built in 1703 for the duke of Buckingham, the palace became the sovereign's London residence in 1837, when Queen Victoria decided to live here. (When the queen is at home, the Royal Standard is flown from the flagstaff on the building's roof.) Buckingham Palace opens its doors to visitors in August and September, when the royal family is away on vacation. Eighteen rooms are on view, including the **Throne Room,** the **State Dining Room,** three **drawing rooms,** and the **Music Room.** Tickets to see these State Apartments go on sale at 9am at the ticket office on Constitution Hill, on the south side of Green Park. Hours-long waits should be anticipated. Visitors with disabilities can reserve tickets directly from the palace. The **Queen's Gallery** is a permanent space dedicated to changing exhibitions of items from the Royal Collection, the wide-ranging collection of art and treasures held in trust by the queen for the nation. Constructed 40 years ago on the west front of Buckingham Palace out of the bomb-damaged ruins of the former private chapel, the Gallery has recently been redeveloped and is open to the public on a daily basis. The **Royal Mews** is the queen's working stable, displaying ornately gilded carriages and live horses in stalls with their nameplates above.

Note: If you're interested in history and trivia about the royal family of Windsor (actually Saxe-Coburg-Gotha; the family wisely changed its name at the onset of World War I because of the public's strong anti-German feelings), check out their official website, **www.royal.gov.uk.**

Kids **Catch the Change**

The **Changing of the Guard,** outside the palace's front gates, takes place daily just before 11:30am mid-April to July and on alternate days the rest of the year. (It's canceled during bad weather and during major state events, so call © **0906/8663-3440** before setting out.) The Queen's Foot Guards, with their scarlet coats and bearskin hats, march accompanied by barked orders and foot stomping in a half-hour ceremony that replaces the sentries who stand guard in front of the palace.

Okay, it's a touristy cliché, but it's great fun. The Changing of the Guard has become almost *too* popular, and getting a decent view can involve quite a battle with hundreds of fellow visitors all anxious to do likewise. The best way to enjoy the ceremony is to make your way to the traffic lights at the junction of **The Mall** and **Marlborough Road** at 11:05am. At a little after 11:10am, the Regimental Banner, escorted by the Old Guard's commanding officer and a detachment of the guards, will march past you en route for Buckingham Palace. The moment they've passed, cross over **The Mall** and make your way quickly through the gates of St. James's Park opposite, cross the bridge over the lake, turn right, and cut left diagonally across the grass to arrive at the **Wellington Barracks** on **Birdcage Walk.** Position yourself on the corner opposite the main gates, and at 11:25am the New Guard will march past you from their barracks and make their way to Buckingham Palace. Once they've gone by, follow them to the gates of the palace.

The Mall, SW1. © 020/7321-2233 for reservations for visitors with disabilities. www.royal.gov.uk. State Apartments £13 ($23) adults, £11 ($20) seniors, £6.50 ($12) children 5–17; Royal Mews £5.50 ($10) adults, £4.50 ($8.50) seniors, £3 ($5.50) children 5–17. Mar 27–Oct 31 open every day except Fri and Apr 9, May 5, May 29, June 5, June 12, as well as during State Visits. During Buckingham Palace Summer Opening (Aug 2–Sept 26), Royal Mews will be open every day. State Apartments Aug–Sept daily 9:30am–4:30pm; Royal Mews Aug–Sept Mon–Thurs 10:30am–4pm, Oct–July Mon–Thurs noon–3:30pm. Opening times subject to change on short notice. Tube: Victoria, St. James's Park, or Green Park.

Houses of Parliament ☆☆☆   To most people, the Houses of Parliament, with their trademark clock tower, are the ultimate London symbol. Officially known as the New Palace of Westminster, the spectacular 19th-century Gothic Revival building has over 1,000 rooms and 3km (2 miles) of corridors. The clock tower, at the eastern end, houses the world's most famous timepiece: **Big Ben** refers not to the clock tower, as many people assume, but to the largest bell in the chime, a 13½-tonner named for the first commissioner of works. Listen to the familiar chime, which has inspired ostentatious doorbells around the world. At night, a light shines in the tower when Parliament is sitting. You may watch parliamentary debates from the **Stranger's Galleries** of Parliament's two houses.

Rebuilt in 1950 after extensive damage caused by a 1941 German air raid, the **House of Commons** remains small. Only 437 of its 651 members can sit at one time, while the rest crowd around the door and the Speaker's Chair. The ruling party and the opposition sit facing each other, two sword lengths apart. Debates in the **House of Lords** aren't usually as interesting or lively as those in the more

---

⌒ *Tips* In Session?

The Commons sits from mid-October to the end of July, with breaks after Christmas, Easter, and Whitsunday. The Lords is open only when Parliament is in session, but they don't always sit regularly.

---

important Commons, but the line to get in is usually shorter, and a visit here will give you an appreciation for the pageantry of Parliament.

In recent years, 1½-hour guided tours of the **Houses of Parliament** were offered during the summer recess, costing £4 ($7.40) per person. In addition, the magnificent 14th-century **Westminster Hall** was opened to the public. At press time, no decision had been made as to whether this will be repeated in 2005. Visit the website or phone for details.

On the west side of the Houses of Parliament is a pleasant park, **Victoria Tower Gardens.** A little way inside the gardens you'll find a cast of Auguste Rodin's *The Burghers of Calais,* commemorating the heroism of the six burghers upon the surrender of their town to Edward III in 1347.

Parliament Sq., SW1. ⓒ 020/7219-4272. www.parliament.uk. Free admission. House of Commons public admitted Mon–Wed from 2:30pm, Thurs from 11:50am, and Fri (sometimes) from 9:30am. Debates in Westminster Hall Tues 10am–1pm; Wed 9:30am–2pm; Thurs 2:30–5:30pm. House of Lords public admission dependent on debating schedule, so call ⓒ 020/7219-3107. Line up at St. Stephen's Entrance, just past the statue of Oliver Cromwell; debates often run into the night and lines shrink after 6pm. Tube: Westminster.

Kensington Palace   Once the residence of British monarchs, Kensington Palace hasn't been the official home of reigning kings since George II. It was acquired in 1689 by William and Mary as an escape from the damp royal rooms along the Thames. Since the end of the 18th century, the palace has been home to various members of the royal family, and the State Apartments are open for tours. It was here in 1837 that a young Victoria was roused from her sleep with the news that her uncle, William IV, had died and she was now queen of England. You can view a nostalgic collection of Victoriana, including some of her memorabilia. In the apartments of Queen Mary II, wife of William III, is a striking 17th-century writing cabinet inlaid with tortoiseshell. Paintings from the Royal Collection line the walls of the apartments. A rare 1750 lady's court dress and splendid examples of male court dress from the 18th century are on display in rooms adjacent to the State Apartments. Kensington Palace is now the London home of Princess Margaret as well as the duke and duchess of Kent. Of course, it was once the home of Diana, princess of Wales, and her two sons. (William and Harry now live with their father at St. James's Palace.) The palace is probably best known for the millions and millions of flowers that were placed in front of it during the days following Diana's death (and again on the anniversaries of her death). Allow an hour for your visit.

Kensington Gardens are open daily to sunset (they're open even when the palace is closed) for leisurely strolls through the manicured grounds and around the Round Pond. One of the most famous sights here is the **Albert Memorial,** a lasting tribute not only to Victoria's consort but also to the questionable artistic taste of the Victorian era. The monument has now emerged from the scaffolding that hid it for many years and has been restored to its original splendor, complete with gilding. A new addition to the gardens is the **Princess Diana Memorial Playground,** in the northwestern corner.

If you're in the mood for a cuppa (tea) after visiting the palace, in the gardens you'll find **The Orangery**, W8 (© **020/7938-1406**), the brick building about 50 yards north. Queen Anne had this conservatory built in 1704 and used it for royal tea parties. Potted orange trees were (and still are) grown inside amid a collection of urns and statuary. October to March, it's open daily 10am to 5pm (to 6pm Apr–Sept).

The Broad Walk, Kensington Gardens, W8. © 020/7937-9561. www.hrp.org.uk. Admission £11 ($20) adults, £8 ($15) seniors and students, £7 ($13) children. Mar–Oct daily 10am–5pm; Nov–Feb daily 10am–4pm. Tube: Queensway or Bayswater on north side of gardens; High St. Kensington on south side.

National Gallery ✦ The collection is divided chronologically into four wings. The **Sainsbury Wing** houses the gallery's most precious early Renaissance works by Giotto, Masaccio, Raphael, and Piero della Francesca. The **West Wing** carries the story of art forward into the 16th century with works by Correggio, Holbein, Titian, and Bruegel. Rembrandt, Rubens, Ruisdael, and other Spanish and Dutch artists' works are displayed in the **North Wing.** And the **East Wing** focuses on paintings from 1700 to 1920, exhibiting works by Hogarth, Gainsborough, Turner, and Constable as well as Monet and Cézanne. A new state-of-the-art **Micro Gallery** lets you examine any painting in the museum's vast holdings at the touch of a button. There's also a great gift shop. Phone for details on current shows. Allow between 2 and 4 hours for your visit.

Trafalgar Sq. (around the corner from the National Portrait Gallery), WC2. © 020/7747-2885. www.national gallery.org.uk. Free admission to main galleries; admission varies for temporary exhibits. Daily 10am–6pm (to 9pm Wed). Closed Jan 1, Good Friday, and Dec 24–26. Tube: Charing Cross or Leicester Sq.

National Portrait Gallery A walk through this gallery, founded in 1856, takes you back through centuries of British social history. It's home to the only known portrait of William Shakespeare, as well as the best-known painting of the late Diana, princess of Wales. The newest gallery exhibits 20th-century portraiture and photography. A visit can take from as little as an hour up to a half-day.

2 St. Martin's Place (around the corner from the National Gallery), WC2. © 020/7306-0055. www.npg.org.uk. Free admission. Sat–Wed 10am–6pm; Thurs–Fri 10am–9pm. Closed Jan 1, Good Friday, May 1, and Dec 24–26. Tube: Charing Cross or Leicester Sq.

St. Paul's Cathedral ✦ Dedicated to the patron saint of The City of London is architect Sir Christopher Wren's masterpiece. Capped by one of the largest domes in Christendom, the great edifice is one of the few cathedrals ever to be designed by a single architect and completed during his lifetime. Wren is buried in the cathedral's crypt; his epitaph, on the floor below the dome, reads LECTOR, SI MONUMENTUM REQUIRIS, CIRCUMSPICE. (Reader, if you seek his monument, look around you.) You can climb the 259 steps to the **Whispering Gallery,** just below the dome—acoustics here are such that even whispers can be heard on the other side of the dome. Another steep climb to the **Golden Gallery** presents you with an unrivaled view of London. The cathedral has been the setting for many

---

⌒ Fun Fact Try a Whisper

When you climb up to the Whispering Gallery in St. Paul's, try standing on one side of the dome and asking whoever is with you to stand on the other side—you'll be able to hear each other actually speak in whispers across the vast space.

important ceremonies, including the funerals of Admiral Lord Nelson (1806) and Sir Winston Churchill (1965), and the ill-fated wedding of Prince Charles and Lady Diana Spencer (1981). The **Millennium Bridge** can now be reached from St. Paul's (just follow the signs) and provides a pedestrian route over the river Thames to Tate Modern, with some wonderful views en route.

St. Paul's Churchyard, EC4. ℭ 020/7246-8319. www.stpauls.co.uk. Cathedral and crypt £7 ($13) adults, £6 ($11) seniors and students, £3 ($5.50) children under 17. Mon–Sat 8:30am–4pm; Sun services only. 1½-hour guided tours depart 11, 11:30am, 1:30, and 2pm. Tour (in addition to admission) £2.50 ($4.60) adults, £2 ($3.70) seniors and students, £1 ($1.85) children under 17. Tube: St. Paul's.

Tate Britain   When the modern art collection moved to Tate Modern, Tate Britain became a little directionless. But the gallery has now fought back with a major refurbishment and expansion, the results of which are a joy to behold. For a start, it's a lot easier and faster to get to and from the nearby underground stations now, since the opening of a new entrance on Atterbury Street. Once inside, the new and refurbished galleries are driven by the displays, providing the perfect environment in which to view British art from 1500 to the present day. Visitors can appreciate and enjoy in-depth coverage of the works of **Turner, Blake, Hogarth, Gainsborough, Stubbs, Constable,** the **Pre-Raphaelites, Sickert, Hepworth,** and **Moore,** arranged in chronological yet themed order. In short, this classic museum has become much better, far more accessible, and infinitely more interesting.

Millbank, SW1. ℭ 020/7887-8000. www.tate.org.uk. Free admission to permanent collection, donation requested; admission to temporary exhibits varies. Daily 10am–5:50pm. Closed Dec 24–26. Tube: Pimlico.

Tate Modern 🗝🗝   Situated across the Thames from St. Paul's Cathedral, the vast and echoing interior of the former Bankside Power Station, designed by Sir Giles Gilbert Scott in 1947, is now home to the Tate's famous modern art collection and has quickly established itself as one of London's most popular galleries. The use of glass outside and inside makes for bright and airy galleries that provide pleasing and effective surroundings in which to view the works of the 20th century's most influential artists, such as **Picasso, Hockney, Pollock, Dalí, Matisse, Bacon,** and **Warhol.** Dotted around the building are 11 excellent "reading points" where you can browse books and listen to audio commentaries about the artists displayed in the particular galleries. Allow 1 to 3 hours for your visit. The **Millennium Bridge** provides a pedestrian-only walkway from the steps of St. Paul's over the Thames to the new gallery.

Bankside Power Station, Sumner St., SE1. ℭ 020/7401-7271. www.tate.org.uk. Free admission. Sun–Thurs 10am–6pm; Fri–Sat 10am–10pm. Tube: London Bridge or Southwark.

Tower Bridge   Here's a lyrical London landmark you should try not to miss. Inside the towers is an exhibit telling the 100-year story of the bridge, which includes interactive and other displays explaining the way the hydraulic system operates. Unless you're passionate about Victorian engineering, make do with enjoying the splendid panoramic views from the walkways above. A visit takes a little over an hour. The bridge opens about 500 times a year: If you want to see the bridge open, call for information about scheduled openings for the following week.

E1. ℭ 020/7403-3761, or 020/7940-3984 for information about scheduled bridge openings. www.tower bridge.org.uk. Admission £4.50 ($8.30) adults, £3 ($5.50) seniors and children 5–15, free for children under 5. Apr–Oct daily 10am–6:30pm; Nov–Mar daily 9:30am–6pm. Last entry 1¼ hr. before closing. Closed Jan 1, Jan 26, and Dec 24–26. Tube: Tower Hill or London Bridge.

Tips A Tower Ceremony

If you plan ahead, at 9:30pm you can attend the free **Ceremony of the Keys,** during which the Tower is secured for the night and attendees find themselves locked in this imposing fortress. (Don't worry: The Tower has long since ceased to be a prison and you're politely ushered out through a small side door.) You must book tickets at least 6 weeks in advance by writing to Ceremony of the Keys, HM Tower of London, London EC3N 4AB. You should also enclose an International Reply Coupon.

Tower of London Grim, gray, and awe-inspiring, the Tower of London (in fact a collection of towers) has dominated the London landscape and the pages of history since William I (the Conqueror) began its construction in 1078. Over the next 500 years, it evolved into a magnificent royal palace and was home to successive monarchs. It also served as a fortress, a treasury, an armory, and a menagerie. But it's best remembered as a prison, and the names of those who passed through **Traitor's Gate** and were thereafter lost to the world reads like a *Who's Who* of English history. The two young sons of Edward IV are thought to have been murdered here in 1483 (by Richard III?); Henry VIII's second wife, Anne Boleyn, was executed on Tower Green and buried in the church of St. Peter Ad Vicula, as was Lady Jane Grey, the "Nine-Day Queen."

Today, the closest the Tower comes to torture is the suffocating feeling you get on weekends, when it seems as though every tourist in London is there. The Tower is home to the Crown Jewels, displayed in a fortified **Jewel House** built with moving walkways to help the crowds along. The Imperial State Crown, worn by the monarch at major state occasions, is encrusted with more than 2,800 diamonds and is the world's priciest hat. Other valuables are the exquisite Koh-i-noor diamond, in the crown of the Queen Mother; and the Star of Africa, the world's largest cut diamond, set in the cross of the Queen Mother's Orb and Scepter. Make a point to see Henry VIII's anatomically exaggerated armor (you'll know it when you see it) in the **White Tower.**

A visit to the Tower isn't cheap but it's worth every pound. Upon entering, wait by the first gate for the excellent guided free tour.

Tower Hill, EC3. © 0870-756-6060. www.hrp.org.uk or www.tower-of-london.org.uk. Admission £14 ($25) adults, £11 ($20) seniors and students, £9.50 ($18) children 5–15, free for children under 5. Mar–Oct Mon–Sat 9am–5pm, Sun 10am–5pm; Nov–Feb Tues–Sat 9am–4pm, Sun–Mon 10am–4pm. Last tickets sold 1 hr. before closing, but you really need 2½ hr. to see everything. Free guided tours given every half hour from 9:30am. Tube: Tower Hill.

Victoria & Albert Museum In a city of fantastic museums, the V&A is tops, the world's greatest repository of the decorative arts: If it's aesthetic and useful—and has been crafted in the past 15 centuries—you'll find it here. Comprehensive collections from around the world stretch for 11km (7 miles) and include room upon room of porcelain figurines, costume jewelry, hunting tapestries, enamel washing bowls, carved end tables, silver forks and spoons, musical instruments, gilded mirrors, ceramic bowls and plates, ivory letter openers, wax molds, stained-glass lamps, lace doilies—you name it. The famous **Dress Collection** (room no. 40) covers fashion from the 16th century to the present. The stunning **Glass Gallery** (room no. 131) displays 7,000 pieces that vividly illustrate the history of glass. Don't miss the **Raphael Gallery** (room no. 48a), displaying the seven tapestry cartoons by Raphael, and the sumptuous **Silver Galleries** (room nos. 65–69). The breathtaking new **British Galleries** have, in a stroke, transformed what was previously a scattered and noncohesive collection into an inventive and fascinating exhibition that tells the story of British decorative art from the 16th to the 20th centuries. Allow 2 to 3 hours for your visit.

Cromwell Rd., SW7. ℂ 020/7942-2000. www.vam.ac.uk. Admission free. Daily 10am–5:45pm (10pm Wed). Tube: South Kensington.

Westminster Abbey 🏛🏛 The Benedictine abbey, which housed a community of monks as early as A.D. 750, was called Westminster (West Monastery) because of its location west of The City. In 1050, Edward the Confessor enhanced the site and moved his palace next door, making Westminster the primary site of England's church and state. All of England's monarchs have been crowned here since William the Conqueror's coronation on Christmas Day in 1066. Many are buried here too, among a clutter of tombs of statesmen, poets, and benefactors. And as you probably saw on TV, in September 1997, Westminster Abbey was the site of the funeral service for Diana, princess of Wales. Allow 1 to 2 hours for your visit.

When not in use, the **Coronation Chair** (built in 1300) sits behind the High Altar. The abbey's **Henry VII Chapel,** added in 1503, is one of the most beautiful places you may ever see—its exuberant architectural extravagances and exquisite intricate carvings will take your breath away. Comprehensive "Super Tours" condense the abbey's 900-year history into 1½ hours for £3 ($5) per person.

Broad Sanctuary, SW1. ℂ 020/7222-5152. www.westminster-abbey.org. Admission £7.50 ($14) adults, £5 ($9.25) seniors and students, free for children under 11. Abbey Mon–Tues and Thurs–Sat 8am–6pm; Wed 8am–7:45pm (photography permitted only Wed 6–7:45pm). Royal Chapels Mon–Fri 9:20am–3:45pm; Sat 9am–1:45pm. Tube: Westminster or St. James's Park.

MORE ATTRACTIONS

British Airways London Eye 🏛🏛 This extraordinary Ferris wheel is the world's highest observation wheel and towers an amazing 36m (120 ft.) above Big Ben! You are enclosed in a clear capsule that takes you slowly up to a height of 135m (450 ft.), where the views over London, on a clear day at least, are truly spectacular. The only drawback to this high-tech attraction is the lack of air-conditioning in the capsules. Given the fact it's like being in a greenhouse, it can be wilting and uncomfortable on a sunny day, so take plenty of water with you. The ride takes 30 minutes but you should allow around an hour for your visit to include the time spent waiting in line to board.

Jubilee Gardens, SE1. ℂ 0870/500-0600. www.ba-londoneye.com. Admission £12 ($21) adults, £9 ($17) seniors, £5.75 ($11) children under 15. Mar 31–May 25 daily 10am–8pm; May 26–Sept 9 daily 10am–10pm; Sept 10–Sept 30 daily 10am–8pm; Oct 1–Dec 31 daily 10am–7pm. Tube: Westminster or Waterloo.

Courtauld Institute Galleries The glories here are the Impressionist and post-Impressionist works: Manet's *Bar at the Folies Bergère,* Monet's *Banks of the Seine at Argenteuil,* and a number of Cézannes, including *The Card Players.* The collection also includes other remarkable works—a whole gallery of Rubens as well as works by Botticelli, Degas, Renoir, and Bonnard. There's a recently opened Early Renaissance Gallery and a special gallery for exhibiting the Courtauld's collection of old master prints and drawings. Allow 1 to 2 hours for your visit.

In Somerset House, The Strand, WC2. ℂ 020/7848-2526. www.courtauld.ac.uk. Admission £5 ($9.25) adults, £4 ($7.50) seniors and students, free for those under 18, free for all Mon 10am–2pm. Daily 10am–6pm. Tube: Temple, Embankment, or Covent Garden.

> ## *Moments* For Diana Fans
>
> Princess Diana is buried on a picturesque island on the Oval Lake at **Althorp,** the Spencer family estate in Northamptonshire. The grounds are open for a limited time each year between July and August, but you won't have access to the gravesite or island and can view the island only from across the lake. Admission is £11 ($20) adults, £8.50 ($16) seniors, and £5.50 ($10) children. This includes admission to the Diana Museum set up by her brother, Earl Spencer, in the converted stables of the house; it contains an exhibit celebrating Diana's childhood, her royal wedding (including her famous wedding gown), and her charitable works.
>
> Although a limited number of tickets are available at the gate each day, it is advised that you book in advance by calling © **0870/167-9000.** You can also book online and get the most up-to-date information from the website at **www.althorp.com.**
>
> **GETTING THERE   By car:** From London, take the M1 north to junction 16, then the A428, from which Althorp is clearly signposted. **By train:** A regular service connects London Euston with Northampton, from where a special coach service delivers you straight to the house. Details and prices were not available at press time, so call © **08705/125-240** for further information; or visit the Althorp website.
>
> In July 2000, an 11km (7-mile) **walk commemorating the life of Princess Diana** opened. The walk passes through four of London's royal parks: St. James's Park, Green Park, Hyde Park, and Kensington Gardens. Along the way are 70 plaques pointing out sites associated with Diana, including Kensington Palace (her home for 15 years), Buckingham Palace, St. James's Palace (where she once shared an office with Prince Charles), and Spencer House (once her family's mansion and now a museum).

Freud Museum   This was the home of Sigmund Freud, founder of psychoanalysis, who lived, worked, and died in this rather plain house after he and his family left Nazi-occupied Vienna as refugees in 1938. On view are rooms containing original furniture, paintings, photographs, and letters, as well as the personal effects of Freud and his daughter, Anna. Of particular interest is Freud's study and library with his famous couch and large collection of Egyptian, Roman, and Asian antiquities. Exhibits and archive film programs are also on view. Allow an hour for your visit.

20 Maresfield Gardens, Hampstead, NW3. © 020/7435-2002. www.freud.org.uk. Admission £5 ($9.25) adults, £2 ($3.70) students, free for children under 12. Wed–Sun noon–5pm. Tube: Finchley Rd.

Gilbert Collection   This astonishing collection of decorative arts was amassed over a 35-year period by the British-born American entrepreneur, Sir Arthur Gilbert. The galleries positively sparkle with over 800 silver and gold decorative pieces, Italian mosaics, and period furniture. The overall effect, while breathtaking at first, can prove a little too ostentatious. Allow 1 to 2 hours for your visit.

In Somerset House, The Strand, WC2. © 0870/842-2240. www.gilbert.collection.org.uk. Admission £5 ($9.25) adults, £4 ($7.40) seniors, students, and children, free for all Mon 10am–2pm. Mon–Sat 10am–6pm; Sun noon–6pm. Tube: Temple, Embankment, or Covent Garden.

Hermitage Rooms ★★   Somerset House has undergone a major transformation in the past 2 years. Although it's still home to the English IRS, its courtyard has been restructured to hold summer-evening concerts. Fifty-five water jets lead you to what's proving to be one of London's most popular new attractions: the Hermitage Rooms. St. Petersburg's State Hermitage Museum has lent hundreds of its artworks (the 1st time this has been allowed), and a dazzling mix of jewels, metalwork, antiquities, and paintings are displayed. The exhibit changes every 4 months, so it's impossible to suggest highlights. Whatever is on show will be spectacular, and there'll always be a "visiting masterpiece." Allow around 2 hours for your visit.

In Somerset House, The Strand, WC2. ✆ 0870/906-3765. www.hermitagerooms.com. Booking is highly recommended, although a limited number of tickets are on sale at the venue each day. Admission £5 ($9.25), free for children under 16. There is a £1 ($1.85) fee for advance bookings. Daily 10am–6pm. Tube: Embankment or Temple.

Kenwood House ★   Set on 45 hectares (112 acres) of beautiful grounds, about 6.5km (4 miles) from London, this stunning villa is one of the finest examples of the work of master architect Robert Adam. It contains a spectacular library and fine neoclassical furniture and holds the most important private painting collection ever given to the nation. These include Rembrandt's *Self-Portrait* and works by such eminent British artists as Turner, Reynolds, and Gainsborough. You might have seen the house in the film *Notting Hill,* when Hugh Grant visits Julia Roberts on location where she's filming a Henry James novel. Allow a good half-day for your visit.

Hampstead Lane, NW3. ✆ 020/8348-1286. Free admission. Apr–Sept daily 10am–6pm; Oct daily 10am–5pm; Nov–Mar daily 10am–4pm. Closed Jan 1 and Dec 24–25. Tube: Archway, Hampstead, and Golders Green.

London Dungeon   An attraction dedicated to torture and execution might not be everyone's cup of tea, but this infamous museum is extremely popular. It knows its target market and aims straight for the jugular—literally. The exhibits are gruesome and certainly not for the squeamish or those of a nervous disposition. The Jack the Ripper experience is almost sickly in its detail while, elsewhere, there's something tackily compelling about being cast in the role of the condemned and forced to board a barge to float away to meet your fate as you do on the Judgment Day ride. Allow 1½ to 2 hours for your visit.

28–34 Tooley St., SE1. ✆ 020/7403-7221. www.thedungeons.com. Admission £13 ($24) adults, £11 ($21) students and seniors, £9.95 ($19) children 5–15, free for children under 5. Apr–Sept daily 10am–8pm (last admission 7pm); Oct–Mar daily 10:30am–5:30pm (last admission 4:30pm). Tube: London Bridge.

Madame Tussaud's *Overrated*   Eerily lifelike figures have made this century-old waxworks museum world famous. The original moldings of members of the French court, to whom Mme. Tussaud had direct access, are fascinating. But the modern superstars and the Chamber of Horrors, to which this "museum" donates the lion's share of space, are the stuff of tourist traps. Madame Tussaud's is expensive and overrated. If you must go, be there early to beat the crowds; better still, reserve tickets a day in advance, then go straight to the head of the line. Allow a minimum of 2 hours for your visit.

Marylebone Rd., NW1. ✆ 0870/400-3000. (Be warned that when calling off hours you have to suffer a pointless and bland recital that gives you a long-winded sales pitch before any useful information is forthcoming.) www.madame-tussauds.com. Admission £15 ($27) adults, £11 ($21) seniors, £10 ($19) children 5–15, free for children under 5. Mon–Fri 10am–5:30pm; Sat–Sun 9:30am–5:30pm. Closed Dec 25. Tube: Baker St.

Museum of London ★★   This museum provides a perfect introduction to London, enabling you to trace the city's history from its Roman days to the 20th century. Highlights are an audiovisual presentation of the Great Fire as recounted by Samuel Pepys, Elizabethan jewelry, 18th-century prison cells, and the lord mayor's coach. Each era in the city's history is presented in a stimulating and interesting manner, complete with evocative background music. Allow 2 hours for your visit.

150 London Wall, EC2. © 020/7600-3699. www.museumoflondon.org.uk. Free admission. Mon–Sat 10am–5pm; Sun 11:30am–5pm. Tube: St. Paul's or Barbican.

Saatchi Collection ✸✸
Charles Saatchi is as controversial in the art world as he is in the advertising world. Britain's largest private collector of modern art built this personal museum specifically to house his large and brilliant collections, which were reduced by some 100 pieces after a devastating fire in the spring of 2004. Each year the Saatchi holds an exhibit focusing on the freshest talent, making this collector one of the most influential movers on the contemporary art scene.

County Hall, Southbank, SE1. © 020/7928-8195. www.saatchi-gallery.co.uk. Admission £8.50 ($16) adults, £6.50 ($12) seniors and students, free for children under 12. Sun–Thurs 10am–8pm; Fri–Sat 10am–10pm. Tube: Waterloo or Westminster.

Shakespeare's Globe ✸✸
The culmination of years of effort by the late Sam Wanamaker, the New Globe theater now stands on the banks of the Thames as a proud testimony to his memory and to the eventful history of the colorful area where English theater struggled in its formative years. The exhibition is a must for anyone who has even the slightest interest in the history of theater or the life and times of William Shakespeare. The touch screens that guide you through the theater's past and present provide a lively and informative commentary, while the whole experience is superbly informal. The opportunity to record your own rendition from the "bard" is not to be missed! One of the most memorable moments is the opportunity to step into your own booth and listen to the voices of, among too many to list, Ellen Terry, John Barrymore, Laurence Olivier, and Richard Burton recite from Shakespeare. The guides who take you into the theater itself (which is absolutely spectacular, incidentally) are a sheer joy to listen to. Allow 1½ to 2 hours for your visit.

New Globe Walk, Bankside, London SE1. © 020/7902-1500. Fax 020/7902-1515. www.shakespeares-globe.org. Admission £8 ($15) adults, £6.50 ($12) seniors and students, £5.50 ($10) children under 16. May–Sept daily 9am–noon; Oct–Apr daily 10am–5pm. Tube: London Bridge or Southwark.

Sir John Soane's Museum ✸
A fantastic array of archaeological antiquities, architectural drawings, and important works by Hogarth, Turner, and Watteau are housed in the former home of the architect of the first Bank of England. The house is packed with objects, seemingly displayed in a haphazard manner. But enter the small room where Hogarth's *The Rake's Progress* is displayed and ask the guard to show you the room's secret. You'll be convinced there's a method to the madness. Allow an hour for your visit.

13 Lincoln's Inn Fields, WC2. © 020/7405-2107. www.soane.org. Free admission. Tues–Sat 10am–5pm (1st Tues of each month also 6–9pm). Tube: Holborn.

Vinopolis, City of Wine
This "adult theme park" is a multimedia, bacchanalian journey through the world's wine-producing regions. It is a little pricey for the content, with the overall experience similar to a walk through a giant issue of *National Geographic*. However, if you are a wine buff, exhibits are imaginatively laid out and provide an insight into the history of and modern production of wine. Highlights include a virtual-Vespa ride across Chianti country

Special & Free Events

The **Charles I Commemoration,** on the last Sunday in January, is solemnly marked by hundreds of cavaliers marching through central London in 17th-century dress. Prayers are said at the Banqueting House in Whitehall where, on January 30, 1649, Charles I was executed "in the name of freedom and democracy."

The **Chinese New Year** falls in late January or early February (based on the lunar calendar) and is celebrated on the nearest Sunday. Festive crowds line the decorated streets of Soho to watch the famous Lion Dancers.

The **Easter Parade** is London's largest. Brightly colored floats and marching bands circle Battersea Park, kicking off a full day of activities.

The **Chelsea Flower Show** is held in May. This international spectacular features the best of British gardening, with displays of plants and flowers of all seasons. The location, on the beautiful grounds of the Chelsea Royal Hospital, helps make this exposition the rose of garden shows. For tickets, contact the Royal Horticultural Society, Vincent Square, SW1 (© 020/7649-1885; www.rhs.org.uk/chelsea); or check with the British Tourist Authority in your home country (see "Visitor Information," in chapter 2) for the name of the overseas booking agent handling ticket sales.

Trooping the Colour celebrates the queen's official birthday on a Saturday in early June. You can catch all the queen's horses and all the queen's men parading down the Mall from Buckingham Palace.

The end of June signals the start of the **Wimbledon Lawn Tennis Championships,** tennis's most prestigious event. Grounds admission tickets are available at the gate for early rounds of play at about £9

---

or a flight over the vineyards of Australia. Admission includes free tastings of five premium wines, although "taste" is about all you get. The staff, however, is suitably informative and impressively informed. You can spend 3 hours here, although 1 to 1½ hours should suffice.

1 Bank End, Park St., SE1. © 0870/2414040. www.vinopolis.co.uk. Admission £12 ($21) adults, £11 ($20) seniors. Daily 11am–6pm (last admission 3:30pm). Tube: London Bridge or Southwark.

Wallace Collection   It's hard to know which is more impressive here, the art and antiques or the house in which they're displayed. The collection includes masterpieces by **Rembrandt, Rubens, Murillo,** and **Van Dyck,** plus superb examples of 18th-century furniture, Sèvres porcelain, clocks, objets d'art and, quite unexpectedly, an impressive array of European and Asian arms and armor. Allow around 2 hours for a visit.

In Hertford House, Manchester Sq., W1. © 020/7563-9500. www.the-wallace-collection.org.uk. Free admission, donation requested. Mon–Sat 10am–5pm; Sun 2–5pm (from 11am in summer). Tube: Bond St.

PARKS & GARDENS

Hyde Park ⍟ is the park most often associated with London, and it's one of the city's most popular, with its Serpentine Lake and Rotten Row bridle path. As in other Royal Parks, wood-and-canvas deck chairs are scattered about so you can sit in an English garden waiting for the sun. Note, though, that fee collectors will

($17) or £4.50 ($8.30) after 5pm. Advance Center Court and Court 1 seats for later rounds are sold by lottery; some same-day Center Court seats are available the first 9 days of the tournament; same-day Court 1 seats are available throughout the tournament, but lines are long and often form the night before. Apply September to December of the previous year to the All England Lawn Tennis and Croquet Club, P.O. Box 98, Church Road, Wimbledon, SW19 5AE (© 020/8946-2244; www.wimbledon.org).

The **Notting Hill Carnival,** in late August, is one of Europe's largest annual street festivals. This African-Caribbean street fair in the community of Notting Hill attracts over half a million people during its 2 days. Live reggae and soul music combine with great Caribbean food to ensure that a great time is had by all.

You have another chance to see the royals during the **State Opening of Parliament** in late October or early November. Although the ceremony itself isn't open to the public, crowds pack the parade route to see the procession.

Early November is also the season for **Guy Fawkes Day,** commemorating the anniversary of the Gunpowder Plot, an attempt to blow up James I and his parliament. Huge organized bonfires are lit throughout the city, and Guy Fawkes, the plot's most famous conspirator, is burned in effigy.

In early November, the **Lord Mayor's Show** takes to the streets with an elaborate parade celebrating the inauguration of the new chief of The City of London. Colorful floats, military bands, and the lord mayor's 1756 gold coach are all part of the event.

stop by and demand 60p ($1.10) from you for the privilege of using these seats; the benches and grass are free. The park is especially lively on Sunday, when artists hang their wares along the Bayswater Road fence and when the northeast corner, near Marble Arch, becomes the not-to-be-missed Speakers' Corner, where anyone can stand on a soapbox and pontificate on any subject. Although this tradition is often touted as an example of Britain's tolerance of free speech, few people realize this ritual began several hundred years ago when condemned prisoners were allowed some final words before they were hanged on Tyburn gallows, which stood on the same spot. Take the tube to Hyde Park Corner.

A huge irregular circle north of central London, **Regent's Park** ֍ is the city's playground, famous for its zoo, concerts, and open-air theater in summer. A band plays free beside the lake twice daily May to August. Get there by tube to Regent's Park or Baker Street, or Camden Town for the zoo.

St. James's Park ֍֍, opposite Buckingham Palace, is perhaps the most beautiful of London's parks. Swans, geese, and other waterfowl, including a family of pelicans, make their home here (feedings daily at 3pm). A central location, a beautiful lake, and plentiful benches make this park perfect for picnicking. Take the tube to St. James's Park. Adjacent **Green Park** is so named because it lacks flowers (except briefly in spring), offering instead large shade trees under which to picnic on hot summer days.

Literary London

London boasts an extremely long and rich literary tradition. **Geoffrey Chaucer** lived above Aldgate, in the easternmost part of The City until 1386, and playwright **Joe Orton** lived on Noel Road in Islington until his 1967 murder. **Marguerite Radclyffe Hall,** author of the first lesbian novel, *The Well of Loneliness,* lived in Chelsea and is buried in Highgate Cemetery. **Oscar Wilde, Dylan Thomas, Virginia Woolf, Fanny Burney, George Orwell, D. H. Lawrence, George Bernard Shaw, Rudyard Kipling, George Eliot, Dorothy L. Sayers, William Blake**—the list of authors who made London their home goes on and on. Alas, a little blue plaque is usually all that's left to mark the past, but there are some exceptions.

The wonderful Georgian town house where lexicographer Samuel Johnson lived and worked, compiling the world's first English diction-ary, is now a shrine called **Dr. Johnson's House,** 17 Gough Sq., Fleet Street, EC4 (© **020/7353-3745**; tube: Blackfriars, Temple, or Chancery Lane). His original dictionary, on display, includes the definition "Dull: to make dictionaries is dull work." There's not much here in the way of furnishings, but the long upstairs room in which he worked has plenty of ambience. Admission is £4 ($7.40) adults, £3 ($5.55) seniors and students, and £1 ($1.85) children 18 and under. May to September, it's open Monday to Saturday 11am to 5:30pm (to 5pm Oct–Apr).

Thomas Carlyle's House ⟨⟩, 24 Cheyne Row, SW3 (© **020/7352-7087**; tube: Sloane Sq.), is an 18th-century Queen Anne on a beautiful Chelsea back street. The Scottish author/historian/philosopher lived here for 47 years, until his death in 1881. His house remains virtually unaltered, to the extent that some of the rooms are without electric light. In this eerie atmosphere you can imagine yourself sitting in one of the writer's origi-nal Victorian chairs or playing the same piano Chopin himself played. Admission is £3.80 ($7) adults and £1.80 ($3.30) kids under 17. April to October, hours are Wednesday to Sunday 11am to 5pm.

Dickens's House, 48 Doughty St., WC1 (© **020/7405-2127**; www.dickensmuseum.com; tube: Russell Sq.), was home to one of London's most famous novelists for a short but prolific period. It was here that he worked on *The Pickwick Papers, Nicholas Nickleby,* and *Oliver Twist.* His letters, desk and chair, and first editions are on display, along with some memorabilia of his wife, Catherine. Admission is £4 ($7.40) adults, £3 ($5.55) seniors and students, £2 ($3.70) children. It's open Monday to Saturday 10am to 5pm. The book *Walking Dickensian Lon-don* offers a choice of 25 walks around the London that Dickens knew and wrote about.

The **Chelsea Physic Garden,** 66 Royal Hospital Rd., SW3 (© **020/7352-5646;** www.chelseaphysicgarden.co.uk), founded in 1673, is England's second-oldest botanical garden. Set behind high brick walls, it consists of a rare collec-tion of old and exotic plants, shrubs, and trees, including Asian herbs and a 19th-century fruiting olive tree. It was founded by the Society of Apothecaries to teach their apprentices how to identify medicinal plants and has expanded to include rare species from the New World. Admission is £5 ($9.25) adults and £3 ($5.55) students and children. April to October, the garden is open Wednesday noon to 5pm and Sunday 2 to 6pm. Take the tube to Sloane Square or bus no. 11, 19, 22, 211, or 319.

An important research facility, the **Royal Botanic Gardens** 🌺🌺🌺, better known as **Kew Gardens** (© 020/8332-5655; www.rbgkew.org.uk), also happens to be London's most beautiful indoor/outdoor garden. The architectural brilliance of the iron-and-glass greenhouses and Chinese-style pagoda combine with chrysanthemums, rhododendrons, peonies, and one of the world's largest orchid collections to make a visit to Kew unforgettable. The gardens are open daily: April to October 9:30am to 6:30pm, and November to March 9:30am to 4pm. Admission is £8.50 ($16) adults, £6 ($11) seniors and students, 16 and under free. Kew can be reached by tube (Kew Gardens Station) in about 30 minutes. April to October, you can reach the gardens by boat from Westminster Pier, near the Westminster Underground station. The trip upstream takes about 90 minutes, costing adults £6 ($11) one-way or £10 ($19) round-trip, and children 4 to 14 £3 ($5.55) one-way or £5 ($9.25) round-trip; free for children under 4. For information, call © 020/7930-2062.

ORGANIZED TOURS

WALKING TOURS   London's most interesting streets are best explored on foot. If you want to stroll on your own, *Frommer's Memorable Walks in London* details 11 great walks both on and off the beaten path.

If you want to join a tour, several high-quality companies will help you find your way inexpensively. Walks are offered by **The Original London Walks,** P.O. Box 1708, London NW6 (© 020/7624-3978; www.walks.com), which has some experts on its team and constantly updates its program to cover such topics as "Princess Diana's London" and "Jane Austen's London." Be warned that their walks are very popular and can attract around 200 people per walk, which makes hearing the guide a little difficult. Less commercial are the superb walks offered by **Stepping Out** (© 020/8881-2933; www.walklon.ndirect.co.uk), whose series of informative tours, led by qualified historians and blue-badge guides, have a more intimate feel to them since the group sizes rarely number above 20. **Discovery Walks** (© 020/8530-8443; www.discovery-walks.com) offer themes that include "Ghosts," "Jack the Ripper," and "Dickens."

You can also consult the "Around Town" section of *Time Out* for information on other tours. Tours generally cost around £5 ($9.25) and represent one of the best bargains in London.

BUS TOURS   At £15 ($28) and £17 ($32) respectively per person, the panoramic tours offered by **The Original London Sightseeing Tour** (© 020/8877-1722; www.theoriginaltour.com) and **The Big Bus Company** (© 020/7233-9533; www.bigbus.co.uk) are the cheapest. Buses depart frequently from outside the Piccadilly Circus Underground station (Haymarket), Victoria Station (opposite the Palace Theatre), Marble Arch (Speakers' Corner), Baker Street Underground station, St Paul's Cathedral, and Tower of London. You can get on and off the buses to visit any of the attractions you pass. May to mid-September, tours run daily from 9am to as late as 7pm; the rest of the year, tours are given daily 9am to 5pm. For a different type of tour contact **Frog Tours,** County Hall, Westminster Bridge Road, SE1 (© 020/7928-3132; www.frogtours.com; tube: Waterloo or Westminster), whose bright yellow amphibious vehicles take you on a 90-minute journey past West End sights such as Big Ben and Parliament Square before "splashing" into the River Thames for a journey downriver to the London eye. It costs £15 ($28) for adults, £9 ($17) for children.

Do-it-yourselfers should purchase a Travelcard (see "Getting Around," earlier in this chapter) and take the front seat on the upper deck of a public double-decker. Two of the more scenic bus routes are **no. 11,** which passes King's Road, Victoria Station, Westminster Abbey, Whitehall, Horse Guards, Trafalgar Square, the National Gallery, The Strand, the Law Courts, Fleet Street, and St. Paul's Cathedral; and **no. 53,** which passes the Regent's Park Zoo, Oxford Circus, Regent Street, Piccadilly Circus, the National Gallery, Trafalgar Square, Horse Guards, Whitehall, and Westminster Square.

5 Shopping

Even the most jaded capitalists are awed by the sheer quantity of shops in London. The range and variety of goods are so staggering that a quick stop into a store can easily turn into an all-day shopping spree.

January sales are a British tradition, when prices can be reduced by as much as 30%. All the big department stores start their sales just after Christmas, and the smaller shops usually follow suit. Several department stores (chiefly Harrods and Selfridges) compete for all-night lines by offering one or two particularly remarkable specials. Be aware that some goods, shipped in especially for the sales, aren't as high quality as those offered the rest of the year.

The British government encourages visitors to part with their pounds by offering to refund the 17.5% **value-added tax (VAT).** Not all retailers participate in this program, and those that do require a minimum purchase, usually £50 ($93). See "Frommer's Money-Saving Strategies," in chapter 1, for details on getting your VAT refund.

SHOPPING AREAS

The **West End** is the heart of London shopping, and mile-long **Oxford Street** is its main artery. Its sidewalks are terminally congested, with good reason. A solid row of shops stretches as far as the eye can see, so if you have only 1 day to shop, spend it here. At its midsection, Oxford Street is bisected by the more elegant **Regent Street,** lined with boutiques, fine china shops, and jewelers. At **Piccadilly Circus,** Regent Street meets Piccadilly, which, along with **St. James's Street, Jermyn Street,** the **Burlington Arcade,** and **Old** and **New Bond streets,** make up one of the world's swankiest shopping areas. Street fashions galore can be found around **Covent Garden Market** and on **Longacre, Shorts Gardens,** and **Neal Street,** as well as at the famous youth-oriented **Camden Markets.**

The best shops in **Chelsea** are along **King's Road,** a mile-long street straddling the fashion fence between trend and tradition. In the late 1970s and early 1980s, this was the center of punk fashion. Things have quieted down somewhat since, but the chain-store boutiques are still mixed with a healthy dose of the avant-garde.

Kensington is another trendy area for urban designs. The best young fashion flourishes on **Kensington High Street** in general, and in **Hype DF,** 48–52 Kensington High St. (© **020/7938-4343**), in particular.

SOME TOP SHOPS

Department stores are the city's most famous shopping institutions, and a handful stand out as top attractions as well. All of the following accept American Express, Diners Club, MasterCard, and Visa. By many estimates, **Harrods,** 87–135 Brompton Rd., SW1 (© **020/7730-1234;** tube: Knightsbridge), owned by Mohammed al-Fayed, is the world's largest department store, selling everything from pins to pianos. The store claims you can buy anything there—and it might be true. Even if you're not in a shopping mood, the incredible ground-floor food halls are worth a visit. Admire the stained-glass ceiling and the unbelievable fresh-fish fountain in the seafood hall. The store is closed Sunday. **Selfridges,** 400 Oxford St., W1 (© **020/7629-1234;** tube: Marble Arch or Bond St.), seems almost as big and more crowded than its chief rival. Opened in 1909 by Harry Gordon Selfridge, a salesman from Chicago, this store revolutionized retailing with its varied merchandise and dynamic displays.

Liberty, 210–220 Regent St., W1 (© **020/7734-1234;** tube: Oxford Circus), has a worldwide reputation for selling fine textiles in unique surroundings. The pretty old-world store has an incomparable Asian department. If you're British, **Marks & Spencer,** 458 Oxford St., W1 (© **020/7935-7954;** tube: Oxford Circus), is where you buy your quality underwear. M&S is known for well-priced quality family clothes—but don't expect the latest fashion trends. And fans of Edina and Patsy on *Ab Fab* might want to stop by **Harvey Nichols (Harvey Nicks),** 109–125 Knightsbridge, SW1 (© **020/7235-5000;** tube: Knightsbridge), to check out its top-brand designer labels.

Foyle's, 113–119 Charing Cross Rd., WC2 (© **020/7437-5660;** tube: Tottenham Court Rd.), London's leading bookstore, offering books on every subject imaginable, is spread over several massive floors. In addition to stocking London's largest selection of gay and lesbian books, **Gay's the Word Bookshop,** 66 Marchmont St., WC1 (© **020/7278-7654;** www.gaystheword.co.uk; tube: Russell Sq.), holds regular readings and sells calendars, kitsch clothing, jewelry, and associated paraphernalia.

MARKETS

Outdoor markets are where bargain hunters shop for food, clothing, furniture, books, antiques, crafts, and junk. Dozens of markets cater to different communities, and for shopping or browsing, they offer an exciting time. Few stalls officially open before sunrise. Still, flashlight-wielding professionals appear early, snapping up gems before they reach the display table. During wet weather, stalls might close early.

Brixton is the heart of African-Caribbean London, and the **Brixton Market,** Electric Avenue, SW9 (tube: Brixton), is its soul. Electric Avenue (immortalized by Jamaican singer Eddy Grant) is lined mostly with exotic fruit and vegetable stalls. But continue to the end, turn right, and you'll see a good selection of the cheapest secondhand clothes in London. Take a detour off the avenue through the enclosed Granville Arcade for African fabrics, traditional West African teeth-cleaning sticks, reggae records, and newspapers oriented to the African-British community. It's open Monday, Tuesday, Thursday, and Saturday 8am to 6pm, Wednesday 8am to 1pm, and Friday 8am to 7pm.

The **Camden Markets,** along Camden High Street, NW1 (tube: Camden Town), are a trendy collection of stalls in parking lots and empty spaces extending all the way to Chalk Farm Road; they specialize in original fashions by young designers and junk from people of all ages. Cafes and pubs (some offering live music) line the route, making for an enjoyable day. When you've had enough of shopping (and the inevitable crowds), turn north and walk along the peaceful and pretty Regent's Canal. It's open Saturday and Sunday 8am to 6pm.

The market where you're most likely to spot a bargain is the **Bermondsey Market,** also known as the New Caledonian Market, at the corner of Long Lane and Bermondsey Street, SE1 (tube: London Bridge), which sells antiques and bric-a-brac. It's held Friday only, opening at 7am. Although opinions vary about when it closes (anywhere from noon–3pm), it's vital to arrive early. The **Camden Passage Market,** also selling antiques and bric-a-brac, off Upper Street, N1 (© **020/7359-0190;** tube: Angel), is smaller than Portobello (see below) and usually cheaper too. It's open Wednesday 7am to 2pm and Saturday 9am to 5pm. The stores are also open regular hours here, Tuesday to Saturday.

The **Portobello Market,** along Portobello Road, W11 (tube: Notting Hill Gate; you can ask anyone for directions from there), is the granddaddy of them all, famous for its overflow of antiques and bric-a-brac along a road that never seems to end. As at all antiques markets, bargaining is in order. Saturday 8am to 4pm is the best time to go, as the market consists mainly of fruit and vegetable stalls during the week.

6 London After Dark

As the sun sets and a hush descends on the rest of the land, the capital's theaters, clubs, and pubs swing into action. The 24-hour **Ticketmaster** hot line at © **0870/534-4444** (www.ticketmaster.co.uk) makes credit card bookings for theaters, opera, ballet, and pop concerts. Ticketmaster locations include the LTB Information Centre, Victoria Station forecourt (open Mon–Sat 9am–7pm and Sun 9am–5pm); and Harrods department store, Knightsbridge (open Mon–Tues and Thurs–Sat 9am–6pm, Wed 9am–8pm).

Attending a play in London is almost a required experience, one that will most likely deliver great pleasure. More theatrical entertainment is offered here than in any other city, at prices far below New York's. You can check out London's theater scene online at **www.officiallondontheatre.co.uk** or see *Time Out* magazine's listings and comprehensive roundup of the week's events.

THE PERFORMING ARTS

THEATER   The term *West End,* when applied to theater, refers to the commercial theaters around Shaftesbury Avenue and Covent Garden. Currently, there are more than 40 such houses where comedies, musicals, and dramas are regularly staged. Tickets run £10 to £33 ($19–$60), plus a 12.5% booking fee, and are usually most expensive for musicals. But discounts are available. The Society of West End Theatre operates a **discount ticket booth** in Leicester Square where, on the day of the performance, tickets (limit four per person) for many shows are half price, plus a £2 ($3.70) service charge. Credit and debit cards are accepted. The booth is open Monday to Saturday from noon on matinee days (which vary with individual theaters) and from 1 to 6:30pm for evening performances. All West End theaters are closed Sundays.

Blockbuster shows can be sold out months in advance, but if you just *have* to see the most popular show, one of the many high-commission **ticket agencies** can help you. Always check with the box office first for last-minute returns. Free West End theater guides listing the current productions are distributed by tourist offices, hotels, and ticket agencies.

If you have an International Student ID Card (ISIC), you can buy tickets to top shows at drastically reduced prices. Not all theaters participate in this program, however, so call first for availability. Those that participate offer their **student-priced seats** on a standby basis half an hour before the performance.

You can see Shakespeare's plays and other classical and contemporary works at the **Royal National Theatre,** South Bank, SE1 (© **020/7452-3000** for the box office, 020/7452-3400 for info and backstage tours; www.national

Tips **Chamber Music at Lunch**

Lunchtime concerts are regularly scheduled in various churches around London. These concerts, usually by young performers, are all free, but it's customary to leave a small donation. A list of churches offering concerts is available from the London Tourist Board. I've included my favorites here.

St. Bride's Church, Fleet Street, EC4 (tube: Blackfriars), was completed by Christopher Wren in 1703, and its tall tiered spire is said to have become the model for wedding cakes when it was copied by a baker. Concerts begin at 1:15pm and feature professional musicians or top students on Tuesday and Friday, while Wednesday is devoted to organ recitals. You'll want to arrive early to explore the ancient crypt of this handsome church. When Christopher Wren designed **St. James's Church,** 197 Piccadilly, W1 (© 020/7381-0441; tube: Piccadilly Circus), he said it best embodied his idea of what a parish church should be. In addition to regular free recitals Wednesday to Friday at 1:10pm, there are inexpensive evening concerts Thursday to Saturday.

St. Martin-in-the-Fields, Trafalgar Square, WC2 (© 020/7839-8362; www.stmartin-in-the-fields.org; tube: Leicester Sq. or Charing Cross), was once really "in the fields," and its wide tower-topped portico was the model for many colonial churches in America. There are chamber-music recitals Monday, Tuesday, Wednesday, and Friday at 1:05pm, plus concerts by candlelight Thursday to Saturday and many other special performances of oratorios. On Sunday it's worth attending the sublime evensong. Tickets for concerts are £6 to £16 ($11–$30).

theatre.org.uk; tube: Waterloo), and at the new **Globe Theatre,** Bankside, SE1 (© **020/7902-1500;** www.shakespeares-globe.org; tube: London Bridge), an outdoor playhouse built from oak and thatch and based on what little we know of the design for the 1599 theater. There's no heat or light inside and no sound system. The benches seat 1,000; up to 500 "groundlings" can stand, and just as in Shakespeare's day, their commentary on the action is encouraged.

Dozens of **fringe theaters** devoted to "alternative" plays, revivals, contemporary dramas, and even musicals are often more exciting than established West End productions and are certainly lower in price. Expect to pay around £7 to £21 ($13–$39). Among them, the **Almeida Theatre,** Almeida Street, N1 (© **020/7359-4404;** www.almeida.co.uk; tube: Angel), is outstanding; at this small theater you're likely to catch such great talents as Diana Rigg and Ralph Fiennes performing in classics like *Who's Afraid of Virginia Woolf?* and *Ivanov,* or Jonathan Miller directing Shakespeare. Check *Time Out* for current fringe offerings and show times.

OPERA & DANCE Not until the 1946 premiere of Benjamin Britten's *Peter Grimes* did British opera gain serious attention. But since then great composers have lifted British opera onto the world stage. The best thing about dance in London (and true to a lesser extent for opera) is that the major houses offer inexpensive standby seats sold on the day of performance only, and the prices at fringe theaters rarely top £7 ($11). Check *Time Out* for major programs.

The 2,350-seat **London Coliseum,** St. Martin's Lane, WC2 (© **020/7632-8300;** www.eno.org for the box office; tube: Leicester Sq. or Charing Cross), is home to the English National Opera (ENO), an innovative company that continues to thrill enthusiasts and traditionalists. Operas are always sung in English, and many productions have been transported to Germany, France, and the United States. The ENO season runs September to July; visiting companies, often dance groups, perform during summer. The box office is open Monday to Saturday 10am to 8pm, with tickets running £6.50 to £55 ($12–$102).

Home to the Royal Opera and the Royal Ballet, the **Royal Opera House,** Bow Street, Covent Garden, WC2 (© **020/7304-4000;** www.royaloperahouse.org; tube: Covent Garden), is rich in history, having first hosted an opera in 1817. The opera house recently underwent an enormous rebuilding and boasts some of the most advanced computerized set changes in the world. You can explore all this on daily backstage tours Monday to Saturday at 10:30am, 12:30pm, and 2:30pm, costing £7 ($13) adults; £6 ($11) seniors, students, and children under 18. Booking is essential. The box office is open Monday to Saturday 10am to 8pm, and seats cost £15 to £150 ($28–$278). The Royal Opera House Café is open daily from 10:30am to 3:30pm and in summer offers a superb rooftop terrace from which you can enjoy spectacular views over Covent Garden.

A 2-year redevelopment has seen the total rebuilding of the **Sadlers Wells Theatre,** Rosebery Avenue, EC1 (© **020/7863-8000;** www.sadlers-wells.com; tube: Angel), now a state-of-the-art venue with 1,600 seats. Tickets are £7.50 to £40 ($14–$74). The box office is open Monday to Saturday 9am to 8:30pm.

CLASSICAL MUSIC The sprawling, mazelike **Barbican Centre,** Silk Street, EC2 (© **020/7638-8891;** www.barbican.org.uk; tube: Barbican or Moorgate), has an excellent concert hall the London Symphony Orchestra calls home and a theater. Even if you're not attending a performance, pop down before a show for a free concert in the foyer. Concerts and times vary. To find your way from Barbican station, exit the station, go over the traffic lights, and walk through the long tunnel, where you will find the main entrance to the right. The box office is open daily 9am to 8pm, and tickets are £6 to £30 ($11–$56).

The **Royal Albert Hall,** Kensington Gore, SW7 (© **020/7589-8212;** www.royalalberthall.com; tube: S. Kensington), attracts top symphonies (when there's no rock concert or boxing match), despite its infamous echo. The box office is open daily 9am to 9pm. Tickets run £5 to £47 ($9.25–$87), with standing room for as little as £3 ($5.55).

The **Royal Festival Hall and Hayward Gallery,** South Bank, SE1 (© **020/7960-4242;** www.sbc.org.uk; tube: Waterloo or Embankment), contains three well-designed modern concert halls. Concerts are staged nightly and encompass an eclectic range of styles. The Royal Festival Hall is the usual site for major orchestra performances. The smaller Queen Elizabeth Hall is known for its chamber-music concerts and contemporary dance performances, while the intimate Purcell Room usually hosts smaller chamber ensembles and young solo performers. In addition, there are free concerts in the lobby of the Royal Festival Hall Wednesday to Sunday 12:30 to 2pm, and jazz Friday 5:15 to 6:45pm. The box office is open daily 10am to 9pm, with tickets at £5 to £50 ($9.25–$144). The Haywood Gallery (www.hayward-gallery.org.uk), in the same building, holds exhibits of contemporary and historic art.

Perhaps the best auditorium for both intimacy and acoustics, **Wigmore Hall,** 36 Wigmore St., W1 (© **020/7935-2141;** www.wigmore-hall.org.uk; tube: Bond St. or Oxford Circus), presents instrumental and song recitals, chamber music, and early-music and baroque concerts. The Sunday Morning Coffee Concerts, with tickets at £8 or £9 ($15–$17), are great values. Buy the cheapest seats, as it doesn't matter where you sit. The box office is open Monday to Saturday 10am to 8:30pm, with tickets at £6 to £45 ($11–$83).

Britain's clearinghouse and resource center for "serious" music, the **British Music Information Centre,** 10 Stratford Place, W1 (© **020/7499-8567;** www. bmic.co.uk; tube: Bond St.), provides free phone and walk-in information on current and upcoming events. Recitals for as little as £2 or £3 ($3.70 or $5.55) are usually offered weekly, often Tuesday and Thursday at 7:30pm; call for exact times.

LIVE-MUSIC CLUBS

ROCK   Since the 1960s British rock explosion, London hasn't let up on the number of clubs featuring home-grown talent, and the tradition continues with the current demand for Brit pop groups. The West End in general and Soho in particular have a number of intimate places featuring every kind of music. Archaic drinking laws require most late-opening clubs to charge admission, which unfortunately often gets pricey. As usual, check *Time Out* for up-to-the-minute details.

Rock Garden, 6–7 Covent Garden Piazza, WC2 (© **020/7836-4052;** www. rockgarden.co.uk; tube: Covent Garden), is far from fashion conscious. Because this small basement club is near touristy Covent Garden Market, most of the 250 or so revelers are usually foreigners. The quality of music varies, as the club's policy is to give new talent a stage. But Dire Straits, The Police, and many others played here before fame visited them, and triple and quadruple bills ensure a good variety. It's open Monday to Thursday 5pm to 3am, Friday 5pm to 5am, Saturday 4 to 10pm, and Sunday 7:30 to 11:30pm. Admission is free Monday to Friday to 8pm; after 8pm cover is £5 to £8 ($9.25–$15). At 10pm Saturday it becomes Gardens nightclub, for which admission is £12 ($22).

Many of London's best noise polluters are in Camden Town and adjacent Kentish Town, just east of Regent's Park. Smaller, cheaper, and often better than its competitors, the **Bull & Gate,** 389 Kentish Town Rd., NW5 (© **020/7485-5358;** tube: Kentish Town), is the unofficial headquarters of London's pub rock scene. Independent and unknown bands are often presented back-to-back by the half dozen. Music is Monday to Saturday 9 to 11:30pm, with a £3.50 to £5 ($6.50–$9.25) cover. **Camden Palace,** 1A Camden High St., NW1 (© **09062/100 200;** tube: Mornington Crescent or Camden Town), features a variety of music from punk to funk. When the bands stop, records spin and feet keep moving to the beat. It's open Tuesday 10pm to 2am and Friday and Saturday 10pm to 6am, with a cover of £5 to £20 ($9.25–$37).

JAZZ, FUNK & SOUL   You can get information on jazz concerts and events from **Jazz Services** at © **020/7405-0737** (www.jazzservices.org.uk) and from *Time Out.*

In addition to those listed below, the major jazz venues to check out are **Vortex N16,** 139 Stoke Newington Church St. (© **020/7254-6516;** www.vortexjazz. co.uk; BritRail: Stoke Newington); **Pizza Express Jazz Club,** 10 Dean St., W1 (© **020/7439-8722;** tube: Tottenham Court Rd.); and the **606 Club,** 90 Lots Rd., SW10 (© **020/7352-5953;** www.606club.co.uk; tube: Earl's Court or Fulham Broadway).

The austere underground **100 Club,** 100 Oxford St., W1 (© **020/7636-0933;** tube: Tottenham Court Rd.), usually hosts jazz on Wednesday, Friday, and Saturday, with a free jazz session at lunchtime on Friday. The stage is in the center of a smoky basement, looking just the way a jazz club is supposed to look. Sunday is usually given over to rhythm and blues, Monday brings a jitterbug session, while Tuesday and Thursday lean more toward popular sounds. It's open Monday and Wednesday 7:30pm to midnight, Tuesday and Saturday 7:30pm to 1am, Thursday 8pm to 1am, and Friday 8:30pm to 3am. Cover is £5 to £8 ($9.25–$15); a student discount is available. **Ronnie Scotts,** 47 Frith St., W1 (© **020/7439-0747;** www.ronniescotts.co.uk; tube: Leicester Sq.), is the capital's best-known jazz room. Top names from around the world regularly grace this Soho stage, but fans be forewarned: This place is pricey. Call for events and show times. It's open Monday to Saturday 8:30pm to 2am and Sunday 7:30 to 11pm, with a £15 ($28) cover.

PUBS

There's nothing more British than a pub. The public house is exactly that: the British public's place to meet, exchange stories, tell jokes, and drink. Americans tend to think of pubs as evening entertainment, but to the British these institutions are all-day affairs. There's no taboo about spending an afternoon in a pub, and on Sunday afternoon the whole family might go. (Note that children under 14 aren't allowed in pubs at all, and no one under 18 may legally drink alcohol.)

Beer is the main drink sold here; don't even try to order a martini in most places. Sold in imperial half pints and pints (20% larger than U.S. measures), the choice is usually between lager and bitter. Expect to pay £1.75 to £2.50 ($3.25–$4.65) for a pint. Many pubs serve particularly good "real" ales, distinguishable at the bar by hand pumps "pulled" by the barkeep. Real ales are natural "live" beers, allowed to ferment in the cask. Unlike lagers, English ales are served at room temperature and might take some getting used to. For an unusual and tasty alternative to barley pop, try cider, a flavorful fermented apple juice that's so good you'll hardly notice the alcohol—until later.

Generally, there's no table service in pubs, and drinks (and food) are ordered at the bar. Tipping is unusual and should be reserved for exemplary service. Most pubs are open Monday to Saturday 11am to 11pm and Sunday noon to 10:30pm. A few close daily 3 to 7pm.

Carpeted floors, etched glass, and carved-wood bars are the hallmarks of most pubs. But each one looks unique, and each has its particular flavor and crowd. Greater London's 7,000-plus pubs ensure that you'll never have to walk more than a couple of blocks to find one, and part of the enjoyment of pubbing is discovering a special one on your own. Below are a few tried-and-true pubs to help you on your way.

On the south bank of the Thames, offering a stunning vista of St. Paul's and the London skyline opposite, the **Anchor Tavern,** Bank End, Bankside, SE1 (© **020/7407-1577;** tube: Mansion House or London Bridge), was built in 1777 and drips with atmosphere. However, the service can be slow and unenthusiastic, which does let the ambience down slightly. London's only Arts and Crafts pub, the **Blackfriar,** 174 Queen Victoria St., EC4 (© **020/7236-5650;** tube: Blackfriars), is remarkable for its stunning exterior and interior. Marble, beaten copper, brass fittings, and gas lamps adorn both. In the grotto bar, drinkers are watched over by mischievous demons, legs swinging nonchalantly from delicate marble ledges, while copper reliefs of jovial monks enjoy frothing tankards of beer or sing in rustic choirs around the walls.

Chelsea's **Ferret and Firkin,** 114 Lots Rd., SW10 (© **020/7352-6645;** tube: Fulham Broadway or Sloane Sq., then bus no. 11 or 22 down King's Rd.), offers the best pub night out in London. The beer served is brewed in the basement and really packs a punch. But the best thing is the Friday and Saturday night musical entertainment that often turns the place into a raucous sing-along. You don't have to be under 30 to crowd in here, but only the younger revelers will know all the words. Nine other Firkin pubs are just as fun and flavorful, but most are difficult to reach.

The **Lamb & Flag,** 33 Rose St., WC2 (© **020/7497-9504;** tube: Covent Garden or Leicester Sq.), is an old timber-framed pub in a short cul-de-sac off Garrick Street in Covent Garden. It was once nicknamed the "Bucket of Blood" because of the bare-knuckled fistfights held here in the 18th century. Today it's a basic though atmospheric pub, famed for its amazing cheese selection. In the upstairs dining room of the **Sherlock Holmes,** 10 Northumberland St., off Trafalgar Square, WC2 (© **020/7930-2644;** tube: Charing Cross), you'll find a re-creation of Holmes's living room at 221B Baker St., while the head of the hound of the Baskervilles and other relevant "relics" decorate the bar downstairs. The 1667 **Ye Olde Cheshire Cheese,** Wine Office Court, 145 Fleet St., EC4 (© **020/7353-6170;** tube: Blackfriars or St. Paul's), is where Dr. Johnson took his tipple, and it's an attraction in its own right. Ducking through the low doors will transport you back in time, as the cracked black varnish, wooden benches, and narrow courtyard entrance give it authentic period charm. Meals here are delicious and filling but expensive.

It's understandable why **Ye Olde Mitre,** 1 Ely Court, Ely Place off Hatton Garden, EC1 (© **020/7405-4751;** tube: Chancery Lane or Farringdon), is often referred to as London's best-kept secret. This pub is so well tucked down a dingy alley that first-timers often turn back halfway along the passage fearing they've gone the wrong way. The delightful Elizabethan interior has long been a favorite haunt of journalists. Try one of the justifiably famous toasted ham-and-cheese sandwiches. The **Cittie of Yorke,** 22 High Holborn, WC1 (© **020/ 7242-7670;** tube: Chancery Lane), is a vast atmospheric place with reputedly the longest bar in London. It's a favorite gathering place for lawyers and office types, who appreciate the private cubicles. Across the river, galleried 17th-century **The George,** off the Borough High Street in Southwark, SE1 (© **020/ 7407-2056;** tube: London Bridge), is a National Trust Property and advertises itself as London's only surviving coaching inn (the inns that the stage coaches used to stop at), once a haunt of Charles Dickens.

DANCE CLUBS

The hippest Londoners go to "One-Nighters," weekly dance events held at established clubs. The very nature of this scene demands frequent fresh faces, outdating recommendations before ink can dry on a page. *Time Out* is the clubber's bible (on the Internet at **www.timeout.co.uk**). Discount fliers to dance clubs are distributed throughout the West End and can be found most easily at Tower Records on Piccadilly Circus, the Virgin Megastore, and other similar stores. Otherwise, expect to part with some money to get in. Once inside, beware: £5 ($9.25) cocktails aren't uncommon. The lowest prices below are usually for Monday and other weeknights; the highest are for Friday and Saturday. Some places discount prices if you arrive before, say, 10pm. Call ahead and ask if this applies.

Fabric at 77a Charterhouse St., EC1 (© **020/7336-8898;** tube: Barbican or Farringdon), is a relatively new arrival on the club scene but it has established itself as a popular venue. You can expect to hear anything that is on the cutting edge of London's underground music scene; crowds have been known to number 2,500. It's open 9:30pm to 5am on Friday and 10pm to 7am on Saturday. Cover is £12 to £15 ($22–$28). The popular **Hippodrome,** at the corner of Cranbourn Street and Charing Cross Road, near Leicester Square, WC2 (© **020/7437-4311;** tube: Leicester Sq.), is London's big daddy of discos, with a great sound system and lights to match. It's very touristy, very fun, and packed on weekends. It's open Monday to Saturday 9pm to 3am, with a £5 to £12 ($9.25–$22) cover. The **Limelight,** 136 Shaftesbury Ave., WC2 (© **020/7434-0572;** tube: Leicester Sq. or Piccadilly Circus), is the London outpost of a small worldwide chain of churches/dance clubs. The cavernous club features several dance floors and attracts a good-looking crowd. The music is usually mainstream, but phone for special events before heading out. It's open Monday to Friday 10pm to 3am and Saturday 9pm to 3:30am. Cover is £2 to £13 ($3.70–$24).

The best regular weekend raver in England, **Ministry of Sound,** 103 Gaunt St., SE1 (© **020/7378-6528;** tube: Elephant & Castle), has worked hard to keep its underground atmosphere and warehouse style. The vast main floor is frenetic and debauched. No alcohol is served, but for the all-night dancing multitudes, booze isn't the drug of choice. It's open Friday and Saturday 10:30pm to 6:30am, with a £10 to £15 ($19–$28) cover.

And no matter what your sexual orientation, don't forget to check out **Heaven** (see "Gay & Lesbian Clubs," below).

GAY & LESBIAN CLUBS

There's a large gay community here, supported by a plethora of publications, shops, pubs, nightclubs, cafes, and special services. *Capital Gay* is the premier "alternative" paper. Written by and for both men and women, this free weekly features previews, reviews, news, and events listings. The most popular freebies, available in gay pubs, clubs, bars, and cafes, are *Boyz, Pink Paper,* and *QX (Queer Xtra). Gay Times* is a high-quality monthly news-oriented mag available at most newsagents. *Time Out* appears at newsagents on Wednesday. Since the late 1980s, **Soho** has become Gay Central for bars, restaurants, and other businesses. Centered on **Old Compton Street,** or **Gay Street** as it's known, the Soho gay village is trendy, cosmopolitan, and upscale.

The 24-hour **Lesbian and Gay Switchboard** (© **020/7837-7324;** www. llgs.org.uk) offers information, advice, counseling, and a free accommodations agency. If you're looking for books and such, head to **Gay's the Word Bookshop** (p. 557).

A well-established bar with pub hours, **Comptons of Soho,** 53 Old Compton St., W1 (© **020/7479-7961;** tube: Leicester Sq. or Tottenham Court Rd.), is a great pre-club stop, as patrons always know what's going on later and club fliers are available from the barman. You'll find lots of shaved heads and leather bomber jackets. It's open Monday to Saturday 11am to 11pm and Sunday noon to 10:30pm. **Freedom,** 60–66 Wardour St., W1 (© **020/7734-0071;** tube: Piccadilly Circus), is a cafe/restaurant/bar/club attracting a hip artsy crowd. Breakfast and lunch are pretty leisurely, and you can hang out all day if you like, eating the soups, salads, and sandwiches or just nursing a coffee. The scene heats up in the evening and late night. The downstairs bar/club is open Wednesday to Saturday 9:30pm to 3am, with a £5 ($9.25) cover after 10pm.

The place for lipstick lesbians is the **Glass Bar,** West Lodge, Euston Square Gardens, 190 Euston Rd., NW1 (© **020/7387-6184;** www.southopia.com; tube: Euston), where you'll find comfortable couches and candlelight. It's open Monday to Friday from noon to midnight and Saturday from 10pm to 3am, with a £1 ($1.85) cover **The Yard,** 57 Rupert St., W1 (© **020/7437-2652;** tube: Piccadilly Circus), is a pleasant place to while away an afternoon or early evening. There are two bars: The upstairs room is cozy, while the downstairs bar can be cruisy at night. The outdoor courtyard is a welcome summer retreat. The food's pretty good, too. Wednesday night is reserved for stand-up comedy. The Yard is open daily 2pm to 11pm.

Gay or straight, no trip through clubland would be complete without a visit to **Heaven,** Under the Arches, Craven Street, WC2 (© **020/7930-2020;** tube: Embankment or Charing Cross), a colossal danceteria with two dance floors, three bars, and a stage where live bands sometimes perform. The crowd varies, but the sound system is always great. Wednesday is the Fruit Machine, a mixed gay night. Heaven is open Monday, Wednesday, Friday, and Saturday 10pm to 4am, with a £3 to £12 ($5.55–$22) cover. The other "big" scene is the **Fridge,** Town Hall Parade, Brixton Hill, SW2 (© **020/7326-5100;** www.fridge.co.uk; tube: Brixton), which sizzles on Thursday, Friday, and Saturday until 4am. Thursday is currently Breakbeat night. A small cafe/bar is attached. After 11pm, cover is £8 to £12 ($15–$22).

7 Side Trips from London: Bath ✶✶✶ & Windsor Castle ✶✶

Just a few miles from Trafalgar Square, you'll be confronted with an England that's strikingly different from the inner city. The air is cleaner, the people are friendlier, and everything is cheaper.

The **Britain Visitor Centre,** 1 Regent St., W1 (no phone), just south of Piccadilly Circus, offers free leaflets and advice and can book trains, buses, and tours. For train journeys under 81km (50 miles), the cheapest ticket is a Cheap Day Return. Try to avoid day trips on Friday, when fares increase to catch the mass exodus of city dwellers.

You can also purchase rail tickets online at **www.trainline.com**. Be aware that they won't mail tickets overseas, but expect you to pick up your tickets on arrival at the train station. For online bus information, visit **www.nationalexpress.co.uk**.

BATH: A GEORGIAN & VICTORIAN SPA ✶✶✶

In 1702, Queen Anne made the trek from London 185km (115 miles) west to the mineral springs of **Bath,** thereby launching a fad that was to make the city England's most celebrated spa. The most famous personage connected with its popularity was 18th-century dandy Beau Nash. In all the plumage of a bird of paradise, he was carted around in a sedan chair, dispensing (at a price) trinkets to courtiers and aspirant gentlemen.

At least one **train** per hour leaves London's Paddington Station bound for Bath during the day; the trip takes 70 to 90 minutes and costs £41 ($76) round-trip adults and £21 ($38) children. Substantially cheaper is the Super Apex costing £28 ($52), subject to availability; you must reserve it up to a week before you travel and must book your train times both ways. Be warned, however, that the price of rail tickets varies enormously; there being so many offers, you are really better off booking it all online at **www.thetrainline.com**. But if you must book by phone, call © **08457/484-950**. However, be specific about your stations. You'll depart from London-Paddington and your destination is Bath Spa. One **National Express coach** leaves London's Victoria Coach Station every 2 hours during the day for the 2½-hour trip, costing £13 ($24) adults and £6.50 ($12) children, day return; £21 ($39) adult, £11 ($19) children, period return. Call © **08705/808-080** or check online at **www.nationalexpress.co.uk**. By car from London, take the M4 and exit at Junction 18, taking the A46 to Bath.

VISITOR INFORMATION   The **Bath Tourist Information Centre** is at Abbey Chambers, Abbey Church Yard (© **01225/477-101;** www.visitbath.co.uk). May to September, it's open Monday to Saturday 9:30am to 6pm (to 5pm during off season), and Sunday 10am to 4pm.

SEEING THE SIGHTS   Eighteenth-century architects John Wood the Elder and his son provided a proper backdrop for Beau Nash's activities. They designed a city of honey-colored stone from the nearby hills, a feat so substantial and lasting that Bath is England's most harmoniously laid-out city. It attracted a following among leading political and literary figures, such as Dickens, Thackeray, Nelson, Pitt, and (most important) Jane Austen. Canadians may know that General Wolfe lived on Trim Street, and Australians might want to visit the house at 19 Bennett St., where their founding father, Admiral Phillip, lived.

Bath has had two lives. Long before its Georgian and Victorian popularity, it was known to the Romans as Aquae Sulis. The foreign legions founded their baths here (you can visit them today) to ease their rheumatism in the curative mineral springs. Remarkable restoration and planning have ensured that Bath retains its handsome look. It has somewhat of a museum appearance, with the attendant gift shops. Prices—because of the massive tourism—tend to be high, but Bath remains one of the high points of the West Country.

Built on the site of a much larger Norman cathedral, **Bath Abbey,** Orange Grove (© **01225/422-462;** www.bathabbey.org), is a fine example of the late Perpendicular style. When Elizabeth I came to Bath in 1574, she ordered a national fund to be set up to restore the abbey. When you go inside and see its many windows, you'll understand why the abbey is called the "Lantern of the West." Note the superb fan vaulting, with its scalloped effect. Beau Nash was buried in the nave and is honored by a simple monument totally out of keeping with his flamboyant character. Admission to the abbey is free, but a £2 ($3.70) donation is requested. April to October, it's open Monday to Saturday 9am to 6pm; November to March, hours are Monday to Saturday 9am to 4:30pm; year-round, it's also open Sunday 1 to 2:30pm and 4:30 to 5:30pm.

Founded in A.D. 75, the **Roman Baths,** Abbey Church Yard (© **01225/ 477-785;** www.romanbaths.co.uk), were dedicated to the goddess Sulis Minerva. They're among the finest Roman remains in the country and are still fed by Britain's most famous hot-spring water. After centuries of decay, the original baths were rediscovered during Queen Victoria's reign. The site of the Temple of Sulis Minerva has been excavated and is now open to view, and the museum displays many interesting objects from Victorian and recent digs. (Look for the head of Minerva.) You can enjoy coffee, lunch, and tea in the 18th-century **Pump Room,** overlooking the hot springs. There's also a drinking fountain with hot mineral water that tastes horrible but is supposedly beneficial. Admission is £9 ($17) adults, £8 ($15) seniors and students, and £5 ($9.25) children. April to September, the baths are open daily 9am to 6pm (Aug also 8–10pm); October to March, hours are Monday to Saturday 9:30am to 5pm and Sunday 10:30am to 5pm.

Bath's newest attraction, the **Jane Austen Centre,** 40 Gay St. (© **01225/443- 000;** www.janeausten.co.uk), is located in a Georgian town house on an elegant street where Miss Austen once lived. Exhibits and a video convey a sense of what life was like in Bath during the Regency period. The center is open Monday to Saturday 10am to 5:30pm, and Sunday 10:30am to 5:30pm. Admission is £4.45 ($8.25) adults, £3.65 ($6.75) seniors and students, and £2.45 ($4.50) for those under 16.

You'll also want to visit some of Bath's buildings, crescents, and squares. The **North Parade** (where Oliver Goldsmith lived) and the **South Parade** (where

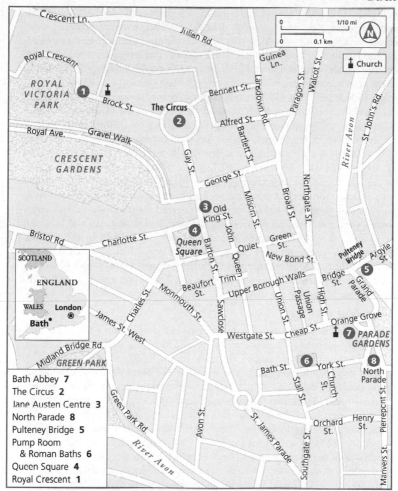

Bath Abbey 7
The Circus 2
Jane Austen Centre 3
North Parade 8
Pulteney Bridge 5
Pump Room
 & Roman Baths 6
Queen Square 4
Royal Crescent 1

English novelist/diarist Frances Burney once resided) represent harmony and are the work of John Wood the Elder. The younger Wood designed the elegant half-moon row of town houses called the **Royal Crescent.** On **Queen Square** (by Wood the Elder), both Jane Austen and Wordsworth once lived. Also of interest is **The Circus,** built in 1754, as well as the shop-lined **Pulteney Bridge,** designed by Robert Adam and often compared to Florence's Ponte Vecchio.

WHERE TO STAY   The elegant Victorian **Number Ninety Three,** 93 Wells Rd., Bath, Avon BA2 3AN (✆ **01225/317-977;** bus: 3, 13, 14, 17, 23, or 33), is a traditional British B&B—small (four rooms with TVs) but immaculate—within walking distance of the city center and the rail and National Bus stations. Its owner is a mine of local information and serves a traditional English breakfast; evening meals are available by prior arrangement. Parking can be difficult in Bath, but the hotel will advise. Rates are £35 to £45 ($65–$83) single, £40 to £65 ($74–$120) double, and £60 to £85 ($111–$157) triple, including breakfast. No credit cards are accepted.

WHERE TO DINE   One of Bath's leading restaurants and wine bars, the **Moon and Sixpence,** 6A Broad St. (© **01225/460-962;** www.moonandsixpence. co.uk), occupies a stone building east of Queen Square, with a conservatory and sheltered patio. The food might not be the equal of that served at more acclaimed choices, but the value is unbeatable. A set lunch is available costing £7.50 ($14). In the upstairs restaurant, full service is offered. Main courses (£11–£14/$20–$26) might include lamb filet with caramelized garlic, or medallions of beef with bacon, red wine, and shallot sauce. Look for the daily specials on the Continental menu. Reservations are recommended. It's open daily noon to 2:30pm and 5:30 to 10:30pm (to 11pm Fri–Sat) and accepts American Express, MasterCard, and Visa.

Bath's best-known French bistro is **Beaujolais,** 5 Chapel Row, Queen Square (© **01225/423-417**). Opened in 1973, it's the oldest restaurant in Bath under its original ownership. Begin with a salad of warm scallops or a rabbit terrine with chutney. You might follow that with an excellent grilled loin of lamb with a julienne of ginger and leeks. One area is reserved for nonsmokers; and vegetarians, people with disabilities (it's well laid out), and parents (special helpings for kids and family-friendly attitude, unlike many places in Bath) will all find comfort here. Reservations are recommended. The two-course lunch is £8.95 ($17) and the two-course dinner £14 ($25); dinner main courses run £11 to £15 ($20–$27). It's open daily noon to 2:30pm and 7 to 11pm, and accepts American Express, MasterCard, and Visa.

WINDSOR CASTLE

Windsor Castle is the largest inhabited castle in the world, on a site that's been a home to monarchs for more than 900 years. On a bend in the Thames about 32km (20 miles) west of London, the castle sits on 1,920 hectares (4,800 acres) of lawn, woodlands, and lakes. You can view the **State Apartments,** formal rooms used for official occasions, furnished with antiques and paintings, including masterpieces by Holbein, Rembrandt, and Van Dyck. The **Gallery** displays a rotating selection of the royal family's collection, including paintings by Dalí, Constable, and Chagall. Queen Mary's Dollhouse is a miniature masterpiece created in 1923 by Sir Edward Lutyens on a 1-to-12 scale; it took 3 years to build. Within the castle precincts, **St. George's Chapel,** dedicated to the Most Noble Order of the Garter, is one of the finest examples of late medieval architecture in the country (and where Prince Edward got married in 1999).

Admission is £12 ($22) adults, £10 ($19) seniors and students, and £6 ($11) kids under 17. Prices are reduced if sections of the castle are closed. The castle is open daily from 10am, closing at 3pm in January and February, at 4pm in March, and at 5pm in April to October. For more information, call © **01753/831118.**

The exclusive **Eton College** is across a cast-iron footbridge in the village of Eton and is usually combined with a visit to the palace. The school's students are famous for attending classes in high collars and tails. If you want a snack, note that Eton High Street has many excellent (but not necessarily budget) restaurants.

Trains to Windsor depart from London's Waterloo Station (© **08457/484-950**) Monday to Saturday every 30 minutes and Sunday every hour. The trip takes approximately 45 minutes. Trains from Paddington Station make the journey to Windsor in 50 minutes but involve changing at Slough Station. The fares from either station are £6.70 ($12) adults and £3.30 ($6) children. You can book your fare online at **www.thetrainline.com.** By **car** from London, take the M4 to Junction 6 and then the A308, which is signposted WINDSOR AND ETON.

16

Madrid & Environs

by Sascha Segan & Herbert Bailey Livesey

Madrid was built to rule. Sprawling over a broad, flat plateau more than 600m (2,000 ft.) above sea level, the city was built practically from scratch beginning in the 16th century. Madrid is neither a port nor an ancient settlement; it was dropped here at the dead center of the Iberian Peninsula to join together Spain's many fractious regions.

It's no wonder, then, that Madrid is Spain's melting pot. That's the city's purpose, and it's succeeded admirably. The most Spanish of Spanish are joined here not only by Basques, Galicians, Catalonians, and Andalusians, but by new immigrants from Africa and South America. Mariachi bands now play in Madrid's subway cars.

Madrid practically quivers with power, ambition, and determination. It was here that Bourbon kings ruled over a grand empire, and from here that Franco sent out his icy decrees to freeze Spain into the 1940s up until 1975.

During the past 25 years, though, Madrid's energy has turned Europe's highest capital into one of its most progressive. In the 1980s, maverick film director Pedro Almodóvar painted a Madrid filled with primary colors, Mambo Taxis, and stiletto heels. Today, it's hard to walk more than a few blocks without running into an exotic restaurant, a gay bar, or a new boutique.

Yet scratch the high-tech surface, and you'll see a core of tradition that runs deep and strong. Tapas, *zarzuela,* flamenco, and the *paseo* continue to be enduring passions among a populace that manages to enjoy the best of both the 21st century and its centuries of history. In that way, Spain's capital is very much a symbol of the new Spanish nation.

For more on Madrid and its environs, see *Frommer's Barcelona, Madrid & Seville; Frommer's Spain;* or *Spain For Dummies.*

1 Essentials

ARRIVING

BY PLANE Madrid's **Barajas Airport** (© **91/305-8343;** www.aena.es/madrid-barajas) is 14km (9 miles) east of the city. The cheapest ride (1.10€/$1.25) into town is on **Metro line 8.** Its disadvantages are that the station is near Terminal 3, a long trek on moving walkways from Terminal 1, where most international flights arrive, and you have to make at least one line change at Nuevos Ministerios, with more walking. The trip is speedy, though: Expect to be downtown about half an hour after you enter the system. For 2.40€ ($2.75), the line 89 **airport bus** runs daily 4:45am to 1:30am (departures every 10–15 min. 6am–10pm, less often at other times) between the airport and Plaza de Colón in the center. A **taxi** costs about 18€ ($21) plus tip and supplemental

Madrid Deals & Discounts

SPECIAL DISCOUNTS Ask about **special promotions** offered by the national airline, **Iberia** (© 800/772-4642; www.iberia.com), usually available November to March. Travelers from the U.K. should consider the discount airline **easyJet** (© 0871/750 0100; www.easyjet.com), which flies to Madrid from Liverpool, Gatwick, and Luton.

If you plan to do a lot of traveling on Madrid's public transit system, purchase a 10-trip **Metrobus ticket,** good for both the bus and Metro (see "Getting Around," under section 1, "Essentials," below). If you plan to tour the country, consider buying the **Spain Rail & Drive Pass,** issued by **Rail Europe** in the United States. It provides 3 days of rail travel and 2 days' use of a rental car within 2 months, a good way to get from Barcelona to Madrid or to make a circle tour of the cities around the capital. For information, call © 877/272-RAIL in the U.S., or 800/361-RAIL in Canada; or log on to **www.raileurope.com**.

Many of Madrid's more luxurious hotels offer weekend or online-only rates that can be far below the usual rack rates, often as low as 70€ to 80€ ($80–$92) per night for a four-star room. Scour the websites for the chain hotels **Sol Melia** (www.solmelia.com; 888/SOL-MELIA in the U.S., 91/567-5901 in Madrid) and **Husa** (www.husa.es; © 90/010-0313) for deals. On Wednesday, Sol Melia posts weekly last-minute deals, which sell out quickly. **Bancotel** (**www.bancotel.com**) uses a voucher system to sell rooms at many upscale Madrid hotels for either 50€ ($58) or 100€ ($115) per night. For details, visit Bancotel's website.

Students should have an **International Student Identity Card (ISIC)** to benefit from discounts on travel, lodging, and admissions. Those who

charges, and the journey takes 30 to 45 minutes, although during rush hours it can take up to an hour.

When **leaving Madrid** from spread-out Barajas, you'll need to know from which of the three terminals your flight departs: **Internacional/T1** (out of the country), **Nacional/T2** (to other destinations in Spain and *many* but not *all* Iberia flights to Germany, Austria, Belgium, Holland, Italy, Luxembourg, and Portugal), or **Puente Aéreo/T3** (the shuttle to Barcelona and some shorter regional flights). You can check in for Iberia, Spanair, Air Europa, and Alitalia flights at the Nuevos Ministerios station and then zip to the airport in 12 minutes on the Metro without your luggage. Taking a cab to Nuevos Ministerios and the Metro from there is a good economical alternative to taking a taxi all the way to Barajas—a savings of about 10€ ($11).

BY TRAIN Trains from France and points in the northeast arrive at **Chamartín** station, far north of central Madrid. The south of Spain is served by Chamartín and the more centrally located **Atocha** station and the northwest by the **Príncipe Pío** (also called Norte) station, just west of the historic part of town. Atocha also handles trains to and from Lisbon. You can reach all these on the Metro (see "Getting Around," below) for easy access to and from anywhere in the city. For information about **RENFE,** the Spanish Railways, including the arrive without an ISIC can get one at the **Instituto de la Juventud,** José Ortega y Gasset 71 (© **91/347-7700;** Metro: Lista), open Monday to Friday 9am to 2pm and 4 to 6pm and Saturday 9am to 2pm (closed Sat July–Aug). The office also issues hostel and student travel cards and provides info on youth discounts. A student travel agency, **TIVE,** Fernando el Católico 88 (© **91/543-0208;** Metro: Moncloa), issues hostel cards and can provide discounts on all forms of public transport to visitors under 26 (under 30 if you're a university student). It's open Monday to Friday 9am to 2pm and Saturday 9am to noon.

Seniors 65 or over can get **half-price train tickets** on all rail travel from the city. Pick up a copy of *Guía del Ocio* (at most newsstands) for details of discounts on events such as concerts staged in Madrid's parks. Most museums tender discounts to seniors (although sometimes only to Spanish or E.U. citizens), and entrance is free at some. When traveling off season and planning to stay in *paradores* in the countryside, seniors are eligible for *Días Dorados* **(Golden Days)** discounts of up to 30%.

WORTH A SPLURGE To really get a feel for the spirit of Spain, spend the money you've saved from a diet of delicious tapas on a **flamenco show,** a *zarzuela* (folkloric light opera), or a lavish production at the gorgeously renovated **Teatro Real.** If you're interested in seeing a **bullfight,** a good seat in the shade *(sombra)* will cost at least $25. You might also want to set aside a few extra euros so you can **rent a car** and explore Madrid's environs, like Aranjuez, El Escorial, and Segovia.

high-speed AVE train between Madrid and Seville, call © **90/224-0202** (daily 7am–11pm). If you don't speak Spanish, however, you might prefer to go to RENFE's ticket office at Alcalá 44 (Metro: Banco de España), which is open Monday through Friday from 9:30am to 8pm. Or buy your tickets online; you can book trips in Spanish or English at **www.renfe.es.**

In the United States, **Rail Europe** sells a variety of **rail passes** valid for use throughout Europe or in one or more specific countries, including Spain (see chapter 1, "Enjoying Europe on a Budget"). For more details, call © **877/272-RAIL** in the U.S. or 800/361-RAIL in Canada; or go to **www.raileurope.com.**

VISITOR INFORMATION

TOURIST OFFICES Barajas Airport has an **Oficina de Información Turística** (© **90/235-3570**), open daily 8am to 8pm. The **regional government's tourism office** in the city is at Duque de Medinaceli 2 (© **90/210-0007;** www.madrid.org; Metro: Banco de España), open Monday to Saturday 9am to 7pm, Sunday and holidays 9am to 3pm. The **Oficina Municipal de Turismo** at Plaza Mayor 3 (© **91/366-5477;** www.munimadrid.es; Metro: Sol) is primarily a distribution center for brochures and maps; not all the attendants are as helpful as you'd like. The office is open Monday to Saturday 9am to 7pm and Sunday and holidays 10am to 3pm.

(Value) Budget Bests

Most restaurants and cafeterias post a changing *menú del día* (available at lunch and sometimes at dinner) that offers soup or salad, a main course, and dessert, plus bread and a glass of wine or other beverage, for 6€ to 15€ ($6.90–$15). Make this your main meal, and in the evening embark on a round of *mesón-* and *taberna*-hopping to sample the tasty and filling snacks called tapas. Or stick to sandwiches or pizzas, which are at least as Spanish as they are American.

For shoppers, the best time to visit Madrid is during the *rebajas* (sales) that take place in January, February, and July. All stores participate, offering discounts that typically increase as those months go on.

July to September in the vicinity of Plaza de España, Puerta del Sol, Plaza Mayor, and the Prado Museum, you'll find **young people** dressed in distinctive blue-and-yellow uniforms whose job is helping visitors. They each speak at least two languages other than Spanish and can offer advice on museums, hotels, restaurants, and special interests.

Even without much Spanish, you should be able to decipher the weekly *Guía del Ocio,* available at newsstands for .90€ ($1.05) or online at www.guiadel ocio.com. It includes the latest on entertainment, concerts, art exhibits, sports, and more. Undubbed movies are designated "V.O.," and most foreign-language films are from the United States or Great Britain. Thursday's edition of the daily newspaper *El País* has a guide to the week's events, as does Friday's edition of *Diario 16.* A monthly giveaway booklet, *en Madrid,* is also useful; it's available at tourist offices and some hotels. And *Shangay,* free at most gay clubs and cafes, lists events and performances of gay and lesbian interest.

WEBSITES   For general info on Spain, check out **www.okspain.org**, the official page of the Tourist Office of Spain; or check the official Madrid city website for tourists at www.munimadrid.es/Principal/ingles/portada.html. For the viewpoints of individual travelers, check www.tripadvisor.com and www.virtual tourist.com/vt/3ff484. The highly personal **www.madridman.com** has a home page that looks frivolous but provides a surprising amount of info, especially on cheap *hostales.* If you're interested in the Prado's treasures, go to **www.mcu.es**.

CITY LAYOUT

Madrid is divided into two distinct parts: old and new. In the old section, whose historic and geographic center is **Puerta del Sol,** the streets randomly curve and wind; in the newer areas to the north and east, the streets are laid out (more or less) in grid patterns. Most of the recommended lodgings in this chapter are around Puerta del Sol. These streets will quickly become familiar: to the north, **Calle de Alcalá, Gran Vía** (with many theaters, cinemas, and stores), and **Plaza de España;** to the south, **Calle Mayor** (off which is **Plaza Mayor**), **Calle de Atocha,** and **Carrera de San Jerónimo.** (By the way, *calle,* "street," is pronounced *cahl*-yeh, while *plaza* is *plah*-thah.)

The streets of new Madrid sprawl endlessly around the strollable old core; sometimes the city seems to stretch halfway to Portugal. **Paseo de la Castellana** is the main north–south thoroughfare bisecting the city. South of Plaza de Colón, it turns into **Paseo de Recoletos,** and after crossing Alcalá it becomes

Paseo del Prado, named for the Prado Museum, which stands on the southeast corner of **Plaza de Canovas del Castillo,** identified by its Neptune fountain. **Moncloa,** the university area, lies in the northwest of the city, and **Calle de Serrano,** with its smart shops, runs through the largely upscale Salamanca district east of Castellana between Plaza de la Independencia and Plaza República de Argentina.

GETTING AROUND

Madrid's subway system is comprehensive and efficient, and the many buses travel in their own lanes on often-congested streets. For **bus** information, call **EMT** at ℂ **91/406-8810,** and for **Metro** info, call ℂ **90/244-4403.** Taxis are plentiful and not too expensive compared to those in London or New York.

BY METRO (SUBWAY)   Consult a map of the Metro system to identify the number of the line on which you want to travel and the name of the station at the end of the line. Metro stations have large maps at their entrances, and pocket-size maps are available at ticket booths. A **single ticket** *(una sencilla)* is 1.10€ ($1.25), and a **10-trip pass** *(metrobús)* a more economical 5.20€ ($6). Ticket machines in the stations accept coins, bills, and credit cards. The subway runs daily 6am to 1:30am; trains are clean and frequent, especially the futuristic-looking lines 8 and 10. For further information, go to **www.metromadrid.es**.

BY BUS   Madrid's bus system, following a series of circuitous routes, can be perplexing. There are both red and yellow buses, the former more numerous and the latter (microbus) more comfortable, with air-conditioning. Route information is available from the **E.M.T. kiosks** in Plaza de Callao, Puerta del Sol, Plaza de Cibeles, and Atocha (open Mon–Fri 8am–8:15pm), or on the Web at www.emtmadrid.es. The booths also sell **single tickets** and the **10-trip pass,** the same used on the Metro. Regular buses run 6am to midnight. A limited night service *(búhos)* runs every half-hour 12:30am to 2am, then every hour to 6am. For obvious reasons, taxis are preferable during that period.

BY TAXI   Metered taxis are white with a diagonal red band on each of their front doors. If they're available, they display a green light on the roof and a sign in the windshield saying LIBRE. The meter starts at 1.45€ ($1.67) and increases by a rate varying from .67€ (80¢) to .95€ ($1.10) per kilometer, with the higher rates applying on weekends and late at night. There's a long list of authorized supplements for trips to/from the bullring, airport, and bus or rail stations; if you're curious, they're all listed at www.radiotelefono-taxi.com/es/tarifas.asp. Taxi drivers are often from other parts of Spain and don't know the city as well as might be expected, so write down the exact address of your destination, preferably with the nearest cross street. To call a taxi, try **Radio Taxi** at ℂ **91/447-3232** or **Radio Telefono Taxi** at ℂ **91/547-8200.**

BY CAR   We strongly recommend you use a car only for out-of-town excursions. City traffic is heavy at nearly all hours and the kamikaze habits of native drivers can be hair-raising. (Spain's accident rate is one of the highest in western

A Traffic Alert

Because traffic is nearly always bad from early morning to late evening, plan to cover distances of under 10 blocks by walking or even by taking the Metro.

Madrid Metro

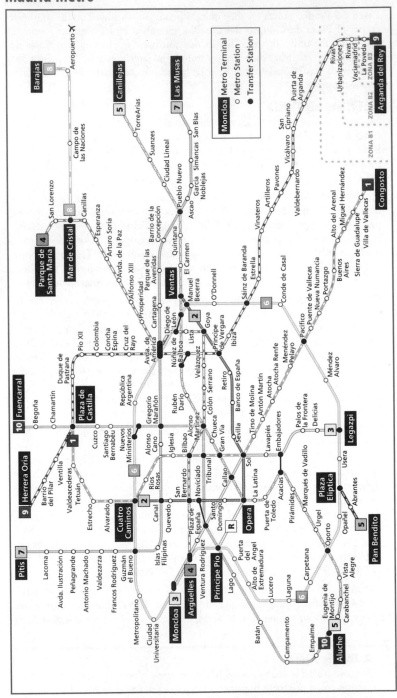

Country & City Codes

The country code for Spain is **34**. The city code for Madrid is **91**. This code has been incorporated into all phone numbers, so all numbers now have nine digits. You must always dial all nine, whether you're outside Spain, within Spain but not in Madrid, or even within Madrid.

Europe.) Street parking spaces are all but nonexistent. If that isn't discouraging enough, renting a car is expensive, though not quite as bad as in some other European countries.

Remember: You get the best deal if you arrange the rental before you leave your home country.

Save money before you leave for Spain by making arrangements with **Auto Europe** (© **800/223-5555;** www.autoeurope.com), which brokers economical rates with established firms abroad, including some of the following ones. But if you want to arrange the rental once you're in Spain, the major in-city firms are **Hertz,** Gran Vía 88 (© **91/542-5805;** www.hertz.com; Metro: Plaza de España); **Avis,** Gran Vía 60 (© **91/548-4204;** www.avis.com; Metro: Gran Vía); **Europcar,** Av. del Partenón 16 (© **91/722-6226;** www.europcar.com; Metro: Campo de las Naciones); and **Atesa,** Paseo de la Castellana 130 (© **91/ 564-5379;** Metro: Serrano). Their offerings change, so shop for the best deal. Many small local firms substantially undercut the rates of the big four, but their services are less comprehensive and cars typically have to be returned to the same stations from which they were rented. Another possibility is the **Spain Rail & Drive Pass,** issued by **Rail Europe** in the United States (see "Madrid Deals & Discounts," p. 570).

Note: You'll need only your state or provincial driver's license to rent a car, but if you're in an accident or stopped on the road by police, a recent regulation stipulates you must produce an **International Drivers Permit.** These are available at AAA offices in the United States for $10 to $15. Take along two passport-size photos; or they can take your picture for another $10. Know, too, that stiff fines are now possible when drivers are caught speaking on a hand-held cellphone while driving.

FAST FACTS: Madrid

American Express The main office is at Plaza de las Cortes 2, 28014 Madrid (© 91/572-0303; Metro: Sevilla), open Monday to Friday 9am to 7:30pm and Saturday 10am to 2pm. They'll replace cards and traveler's checks and hold mail for their customers for up to 1 month free.

Babysitters Babysitters are known as *canguros* in Spanish. Because many *hostales* are family-run, the daughter or son of the house might oblige. Failing that, check under "Servicio Doméstico" in the phone directory for agencies that offer babysitting. Always ask for references.

Business Hours The Spanish **siesta** survives despite pressures from northern Europe and across the Atlantic. Most **offices** operate Monday to Friday 9am to 7pm, taking a long lunch hour from 1:30 or 2pm to 4 or 5pm;

in summer, offices often close at 3pm. **Banks** and **government offices** are open Monday to Friday 9am to 2pm and Saturday 9am to 1pm. Some Puerta del Sol bank offices are open in the afternoon and on weekends in summer. The airport branch of Banco Exterior de España is open 24 hours. **Shops** and **many attractions** open at 10am, close for lunch 1:30 to 5pm, and then reopen until 8pm. (Exceptions are branches of the large department stores El Corte Inglés and FNAC, which stay open through the siesta.) One consequence of these fractured working days is 4 rush hours daily instead of the usual 2.

Consulates The consulate of the **United States** is in the embassy at Calle Serrano 75 ((*©* **91/587-2240** or 91/587-2200 after hours; www.embusa.es/indexbis.html; Metro: Núñez Bilbao), open Monday to Friday 9am to 1pm and 3 to 5:30pm. The consulate of **Canada** is in the embassy at Núñez de Balboa 35 ((*©* **91/423-3250**; Metro: Velázquez), open Monday to Thursday 8:30am to 2pm and 3 to 5:30pm (to 4pm in Aug), Friday 8:30am to 2pm. The consulate of the **United Kingdom** is at Paseo de Recoletos 7/9 ((*©* **91/524-9700**; www.ukinspain.com; Metro: Banco de España), open Monday to Friday roughly 8:30am to 2pm. Hours vary depending on the time of year, so call ahead. The consulate of **Ireland** is at Paseo de la Castellana 46 ((*©* **91/436-4093**; Metro: Serrano), open Monday to Friday 10am to 2pm. The consulate of **Australia** is at Plaza Descubridor Diego de Ordás 3 ((*©* **91/441-6025**; www.embaustralia.es; Metro: Ríos Rosas), open Monday to Thursday 8:30am to 1:30pm and 2:30 to 4:45pm, and Friday 8:30am to 2:15pm. The embassy of **New Zealand** is at Plaza de la Lealtad 2 ((*©* **91/523-0226**; www.nzembassy.com/home.cfm?c=27; Metro: Banco de España), open Monday to Friday 9am to 2pm and 3 to 5:30pm. In July and August, it's open Monday to Friday from 8:30am to 1pm and 1:30 to 4:30pm.

Crime See "Fast Facts: Barcelona" on p. 152.

Currency In 2002, Spain adopted the **euro** (€) for its currency. At press time, 1€ = $1.15, or $1 = .87€.

Currency Exchange Change money or traveler's checks at any **bank** advertising *cambio*. A fixed commission is charged, which makes cashing traveler's checks in small denominations expensive. A number of U.S. banks have representation in Madrid, Citibank being one of the most visible. In an emergency, the Chequepoint offices in such heavily touristed locations as Puerta del Sol are open off-hours and weekends. They don't charge a commission, but their exchange rate is much lower than those prevailing at banks.

ATMs are located throughout the city, especially in tourist and commercial areas. Most machines provide instructions in four to six languages, including English. Some state banks charge excessive fees for this service, so address that before leaving home. As a rule, however, cash obtained through ATMs is dispensed at a more favorable rate, with lower fees than for traveler's checks. If you don't have a four-digit PIN, get one before leaving home. Letters and 6-digit codes don't work in Spain.

Dentists & Doctors For bilingual dental and medical attention, call (*©* **061** or check with the appropriate consulate for its list of approved dentists and doctors.

Emergencies For **street emergencies**, call ℂ **092**. For an ambulance, call ℂ **91/588-4400**. For a **24-hour pharmacy**, phone ℂ **098**. If a pharmacy is closed, it will post a notice giving the address of the nearest open one.

Holidays The majority of Catholic Spain's holidays are religious in origin. Each town celebrates its own saint's day, and in Madrid this is the fiesta of San Isidro, in May, when many businesses close at 2pm all week to enjoy the concerts, plays, art shows, neighborhood fairs, and most important bullfights of the year.

Madrid's holidays are New Year's Day (Jan 1), Three Kings (Jan 6), San José (Mar 19), Maundy Thursday, Good Friday, Easter Sunday, Labor Day (May 1), San Isidro (May 15), Corpus Christi (May or June), Santiago Apóstol (July 25), Feast of the Assumption (Aug 15), Fiesta Hispanidad (Oct 21), All Saints Day (Nov 1), Virgen de la Almudena (Nov 9), Constitution Day (Dec 6), Immaculate Conception (Dec 8), and Christmas Day (Dec 25). August is when Spaniards flee to the beach or mountains, so many of the smaller shops, restaurants, and businesses close for the month.

Hospitals Options are the **Hospital La Paz**, Castellana 261 (ℂ **91/358-2600**; Metro: Begoña), on the north side of town; the **Hospital General Gregorio Marañón**, Dr. Esquerdo 46 (ℂ **91/586-8000**); or the **Hospital 12 de Octubre**, Carretera de Andalucía, Km 5.4 (ℂ **91/390-8000**), on the south side. In the city center, a 24-hour **first-aid clinic** *(casa de socorro)* is at Navas de Tolosa 10 (ℂ **91/521-0025**; Metro: Sol).

Internet Access With more than 100 Internet-connected PCs, **Bbigg**, Alcalà 21 (http://internet.bbigg.com; Metro: Sevilla), lives up to its name. It's open daily from 9am to midnight, and on Friday and Saturday until 2am. Four branches of the ubiquitous global chain **EasyInternetCafé** also dot the city; the biggest is at Montera 10 (www.easyeverything.com; Metro: Sol), open daily 8am to 1am.

Laundry Convenient to many of the *hostales* recommended in these pages is **Lavomatique**, Cervantes 1 (no phone; Metro: Antón Martín), open Monday to Saturday 9am to 8pm. If the machines are full at Lavomatique, try the somewhat more expensive **Ondablu**, just around the corner at Leon 3 (ℂ **91/369-5071**); it's open daily from 9am to 10:30pm.

Mail The main post office, **Correos**, is the grand Palacio de Comunicaciones on Plaza de las Cibeles, 28014 Madrid (ℂ **91/536-0111**; Metro: Banco de España). It's open for stamps Monday to Friday 8am to 9pm and Sunday and holidays 10am to 1pm at Window H. Stamps are also sold at tobacconists' *(estancos)*. An airmail letter or postcard to the United States is .76€ (90¢).

Tax The government sales tax, known as **IVA (value-added tax)**, is currently 7% for most products and services. It's often included in the price.

Telephone The minimum charge for **local telephone calls** is .25€ (30¢). Be aware that many hotels and *hostales* tack on a hefty surcharge for long-distance calls. Most public phones have clear instructions in English, and some high-tech phones provide onscreen instructions in four languages; they accept **phone cards** available for 12€ ($14) at *estancos* (tobacconists), post offices, and the *locutorios telefónicas* (central phone offices) at Gran Vía 30 and Paseo de Recoletos 41 (open Mon–Sat 9am–midnight, Sun and holidays noon–midnight). Another *locutorio* is at the main post office on Plaza de las Cibeles (open Mon–Fri 8am–midnight, Sat–Sun and holidays 8am–10pm).

To make **collect or calling-card calls** at more economical rates, dial © **900/ 99-0011** to access AT&T's USA Direct (to do so from a public phone might require coins or a phone card) or © **900/99-0014** to access MCI's Call USA. When calling from a hotel, check first to make sure there's no service charge or surcharge, or at least to find out how much it is. To make **international calls** to the United States and Canada, dial 00, wait for another tone, and then dial 1, followed by the area code and number.

Tipping The custom is widespread, although the amounts expected are often less than those in other countries. Following is a rough guide: In bars, round out the change and leave at least .10€ (10¢), even after a cup of coffee. In hotels, a service charge is included in the bill, but give the porter 1€ ($1.15); the maid about the same for each night stayed; the doorman .50€ to 1€ (65¢–$1.15) if he goes to some trouble to get a taxi. In restaurants, where a service charge is nearly always incorporated in the total, leave a 5% to 10% tip. Give taxi drivers about 10%, tour guides 10%, and ushers (theater or bullfight) .75€ (85¢).

Water Tap water is entirely safe but doesn't taste very good. Bottled water is widely available, either fizzy *(con gas)* or still *(sin gas)*.

2 Affordable Places to Stay

Most of the lodgings recommended in this section are *hostales*—small, often family-run, limited-service hotels, *not* youth hostels. There are hundreds of *hostales* in Madrid, all graded and loosely overseen by the tourism authorities. The weakened dollar of course makes *hostales* more expensive than they once were, but they're still by far the best deal you'll get in Madrid.

If you're feeling flush enough to spend 70€ ($80) or so per night, remember to check online travel agencies and the websites of major hotel chains Sol Melia (www.solmelia.com) and Husa (www.husa.es) for specials.

Most of the places recommended below are in the old part of the city around Puerta del Sol and Gran Vía or in the neighborhood of the three major art museums that form a Golden Triangle along or near Paseo del Prado. Sometimes two or more *hostales* are in the same building, so if one of the recommended properties is booked, see if there are any on other floors. Standards and sizes vary substantially, so ask to see the guest room and bathroom before accepting. Many *hostales* are in buildings dating from the late 19th or early 20th century, with high ceilings, elaborate moldings, and some ornate or antique furnishings. Don't be put off by entrances, which can be scruffy—they're often in sharp contrast to the scrupulously clean guest rooms.

Spanish hotels and *hostales* typically use twin beds; the queen- and king-size beds routinely found in North American motels are still not common. Taller guests and couples will want to know that a double bed is a *cama matrimonio*.

Air-conditioning isn't universal, and because Madrid summers can be torrid, you might want to take note of the accommodations below that have this facility. Unless otherwise indicated, the rates below don't include breakfast or taxes (IVA in Spain).

Note: You'll find the lodging choices below plotted on the map on p. 596.

NEAR THE PRADO & THYSSEN MUSEUMS

Coruña   They don't come any cleaner or sprightlier than this *hostal* operated with family pride—you might be greeted and shown your room by the teenage daughter. The only drawback is the lack of private bathrooms, but sharing the common bathroom isn't likely to be a problem, except between 8 and 9am. All the freshly painted rooms have bare polished floors and crisp coverlets on the double or twin beds, plus basins. Even the front rooms, facing busy Paseo del Prado, are quiet. The Prado Museum is across the way. No English is spoken.

Paseo del Prado 12 (3rd floor), 28014 Madrid. ℂ **91/429-2543.** 8 units, none with bathroom. 25€ ($29) single; 35€ ($40) double. No credit cards. Metro: Atocha. *In room:* TV, hair dryer.

Gonzalo 🌟 *(Kids)*   The Gonzalo is the best of this building of *hostales* on a quiet street a couple of blocks from the Prado. It has been popular with young travelers for years, but its excellent maintenance (repainting every 3 or 4 years), crisp housekeeping, sturdy furniture, and a family atmosphere make it recommendable to lone travelers and parents with kids, too. Alas, the fans they set up aren't likely to do the trick in summer. English is spoken by the three sons.

Cervantes 34 (3rd floor), 28014 Madrid. ℂ **91/429-2714.** Fax 91/420-2007. 18 units. 40€ ($46) single; 48€ ($55) double. MC, V. Metro: Banco de España. *In room:* TV, no phone.

Mora 🌟 *(Value)*   Long one of Madrid's top budget choices, even with recent rate jumps, the Mora is still an excellent choice. The spacious lobby with chandeliers sets the tone. The narrow but bright halls lead to rooms of varied configuration, but all are sufficiently furnished in muted tones, with carpeting. (Many are too small to contain 2nd thoughts, with mere slivers of bathrooms, so inspect first.) English is spoken by the helpful people at the front desk. The adjacent restaurant, Bango (separate management), attracts a polished crowd for low-cost meals. The Prado is across the street and the Centro de Arte Reina Sofía a short walk away.

Paseo del Prado 32, 28014 Madrid. ℂ **91/420-1569.** Fax 91/420-0564. 62 units. 57€ ($66) single; 75€ ($86) double. AE, DC, MC, V. Metro: Atocha. **Amenities:** Restaurant; bar. *In room:* A/C, TV, safe.

ON OR NEAR THE GRAN VÍA

Anaco   It may not sparkle, but the Anaco is a fine place to stay. The first five floors of this popular hotel have been renovated with witty, alternating red and green color schemes, down to the towels. Double-glazed windows provide blessed silence. The whole second floor is designated nonsmoking. Off the lobby, the busy *cafetería* offers a 7€ ($8.05) *menú del día* and stays open from 7:30am to 2am every day.

Tres Cruces 3 (at Plaza del Carmen), 28013 Madrid. ℂ **91/522-4604.** Fax 91/531-6484. www. anacohotel.com. 40 units. 73€–77€ ($84–$89) single; 92€–97€ ($106–$111) double. AE, DC, MC, V. Metro: Gran Vía. **Amenities:** Restaurant; bar; laundry/dry-cleaning service. *In room:* A/C, TV, hair dryer, safe.

⸤Tips⸥ A *Hostal* Environment

As a rule, Madrid's *hostales* occupy one or two floors of mixed-use buildings, and they're rarely on the ground floor. To gain entrance, it's often necessary to press a button at the doorway and then respond to a shouted *"¿Sí?"* or *"¡Dígame!"* on the intercom. Keep your answer simple—your last name or "Frommer's!" will nearly always get you buzzed in.

(*Value* Getting the Best Deal on Accommodations

- Be aware that some hotels give discounts if you pay in cash instead of with a credit card.
- Note that single rooms are invariably tiny. If you can spend a little extra for more space, ask for a double for individual use—*doble para uso individual.* The price will be more than for a single but less than for the full double.
- Take advantage of the steep weekend discounts offered increasingly by three- and four-star hotels.
- Inquire at the TIVE office at Calle José Ortega y Gasset 71 about which *hostales* offer discounts to people carrying an International Student Identity Card (ISIC).
- Ask if service and taxes are included in the quoted room rate, for they can add as much as 20% to the bill.
- Remember that most places don't include breakfast, so those that do can represent significant savings.

Greco The rooms in this third-floor *hostal* (no elevator) contain quirky blond modern furniture filling relatively large spaces, and those in front have balconies above the quiet street, only a block north of the Gran Vía. The kindly owners have raised their prices only occasionally, in baby steps, over the last decade. A grandmother clock thunks away in the vestibule off the snug TV salon. Little English is spoken.

Infantas 3 (at Hortaleza), 28004 Madrid. © **91/522-4632** or 91/522-4631. Fax 91/523-2361. 18 units. 29€ ($33) single; 45€ ($52) double. MC, V. Metro: Gran Vía. *In room:* TV, safe (most rooms).

Sonsoles Facing a scrubbed-up street with newly planted trees, the gay-friendly Sonsoles' dimly lit entrance gives way to a homey lobby, where a coin-operated Internet computer shares space with the Coke and coffee machines. The rooms are routine and old-fashioned but very clean, with tiny bathrooms. The double-glazed windows muffle street noise. And because they've held prices steady, it's a better value than ever. Just don't expect warmth from the night clerk. By the way, avoid Hostal Odesa, owned by the same people; it's dark, grim, and uninviting.

Fuencarral 18 (2 blocks north of the Gran Vía, 2nd floor), 28004 Madrid. © **91/532-7523** or 91/532-7522. Fax 91/532-7522. www.hostalsonsodesa.com. 27 units. 30€ ($35) single; 43€ ($49) double. Prices negotiable for longer stays. MC, V. Metro: Gran Vía. *In room:* TV, safe.

Triana 🏃 Just south of the Gran Vía, this is a convenient first-floor *hostal* made more appealing by the massive renovations completed a few years ago. Every bathroom on all three floors has been torn out and replaced with fresh fixtures and tiles. Some of the decor, including floral fabrics and lots of white paint and wood, is unusual for Madrid. Interior rooms have ceiling fans. Ask for one of the rooms overlooking the renovated plaza, for they get extra light and are more fetchingly decorated, with small balconies. Some English is spoken.

Salud 13 (on Plaza del Carmen), 28013 Madrid. © **91/532-6812.** Fax 91/522-9729. www.hostaltriana.com. 40 units. 35€ ($40) single; 47€ ($54) double. MC, V. Metro: Gran Vía, Callao, or Sol. *In room:* A/C (exterior rooms), TV.

FROM PUERTA DEL SOL TO PLAZA MAYOR

Aguilar This might be Madrid's biggest hostal. The echoing lobby alone could house the whole of one of its competitors, and its rooms sprawl over the top four floors of a building stretching much of a city block. It has been carved into almost 50 rooms of varying configuration, most with ceilings higher than they are wide, with deeply carved ceiling moldings but minimalist furnishings. More than half have balconies. In some, there are two or three fluted columns with Corinthian capitals. English is spoken.

San Jerónimo 32, 28014 Madrid. ✆ 91/429-5926. Fax 91/429-2661. www.hostalaguilar.com. 46 units. 33€ ($38) single; 45€ ($52) double. MC, V. Metro: Sol or Sevilla. *In room:* A/C, TV.

Europa Hotel locations don't get better than this, in a pedestrian district 1 block north of Puerta del Sol. A massive renovation at the Europa opened up 35 rooms in a wing with marble-floored hallways and pristine wood furnishings; request one of these newer rooms. A pleasant floral smell wafts through most of the older rooms, a result of trying to make an all-smoking hotel palatable to nonsmokers. Some rooms have balconies overlooking an attractive little pedestrian street. You could do worse than take some of your meals in the *cafetería*, with *menús* of 9€ ($10) and 16€ ($18). Fluent English is spoken by some staff, including one American assistant manager.

Carmen 4, 28013 Madrid. ✆ **91/521-2900.** Fax 91/521-4696. www.hoteleuropa.net. 105 units. 59€ ($68) single; 75€ ($86) double. AE, MC, V. Metro: Sol. **Amenities:** Restaurant; bar; concierge; car-rental desk; limited room service; laundry/dry-cleaning service. *In room:* A/C, TV, hair dryer, safe.

Francisco I Under the same ownership as the París, at the other end of Puerta del Sol, this, the preferable property of the two, enjoys an amiable manager and staff. The lobby has wood paneling and marble, and next to the TV lounge is a well-stocked bar. The guest rooms are of sensible size. The sixth-floor dining room shouldn't keep you from going out to eat. Room rates don't rise too often, but bargaining still might be productive off season.

Arenal 15, 28013 Madrid. ✆ **91/548-0204.** Fax 91/542-2899. 58 units. 57€ ($66) single; 79€ ($91) double. Rates include breakfast and taxes. AE, DC, MC, V. Metro: Opera or Sol. **Amenities:** Restaurant; bar; concierge; limited room service; laundry/dry-cleaning service. *In room:* A/C (most rooms), TV, safe.

La Macarena *Value* Known for its reasonable prices and praised by readers for the warmth of its reception, this unpretentious, clean *hostal* has been primped and polished inside and out. One of the *hostal's* assets is its location on a street (admittedly a noisy one) at the bottom of the stairs leading from the southwest corner of the Plaza Mayor. Windows facing the street are double-glazed. No breakfast is served, but there are plenty of cafes nearby. The management runs two other *hostales,* if this one is full.

Cava de San Miguel 8, 28005 Madrid. ✆ **91/365-9221.** Fax 91/364-2757. 25 units. www.hostalsilserranos.com. 53€ ($61) single; 60€ ($69) double. MC, V. Metro: Sol, Opera, or La Latina. **Amenities:** Bar. *In room:* TV, hair dryer.

La Perla Asturiana *Value* This small hostal is sandwiched right between the Puerta del Sol and Plaza Mayor. Stay here for the prices and the location, not for the rooms, which are simply adequate. That said, the staff is courteous, the small rooms are clean, the beds are comfortable, and each unit comes with a shower. There's a small lobby, but you'll probably prefer to hang out in the many tapas bars nearby.

Plaza Santa Cruz 3, 28012 Madrid. ✆ **91/366-4600.** Fax 91/366-4608. www.perlaasturiana.com. 33 units. 33€ ($38) single; 45€ ($52) double. Discounts for online booking and for cash payment. MC, V. Metro: Sol. **Amenities:** Laundry; Internet access. *In room:* TV.

Plaza Mayor 🐞🐞   A crisp hotel in the shell of a 19th-century convent, this is a welcome addition to Madrid's often dreary budget lodgings. Despite the name, the brick-red building wedges into Plaza Santa Cruz, slightly east of Plaza Mayor. A new entrance has been carved out of the ground floor *taberna*. The often oddly shaped rooms are of sufficient size, with double-thick windows sealing off traffic noise; four have double beds. The corner rooms offer light and extra space. English is spoken.

Atocha 2, 28012 Madrid. 📞 **91/360-0606** or 91/360-0828. Fax 91/360-0610. www.h-plazamayor.com. 20 units. 48€ ($55) single; 70€ ($81) double. Rates include breakfast. AE, MC, V. Metro: Sol. **Amenities:** Restaurant; bar. *In room:* A/C, TV, safe.

T.I.J.C.A.L. 🐞🐞   This place was known as the Hostal Montalvo for 30 years, but the current owner imposed this odd label. It's an acronym for "work, equality, justice, culture, friendship, and liberty"—fine values for a hotelier. A sunny, optimistic perspective is visible everywhere, from the exterior to the bathrooms to the room furnishings to the cheerful colors on the walls hung with van Gogh and Gauguin reproductions. If you pay in cash, you get a 10% discount. Considering the prices and the location less than a block from Plaza Mayor, this is a winner.

Zaragoza 6 (east of Plaza Mayor). 📞 **91/365-5910.** Fax 91/364-5260. www.hostaltijcal.com. 31 units. 50€ ($58) single; 60€ ($69) double. MC, V. Metro: Sol. **Amenities:** Car-rental desk; limited room service; laundry service. *In room:* A/C, TV, safe.

T.I.J.C.A.L. 2 🐞🐞   T.I.J.C.A.L. was so nice, they built it twice. The second branch of this *hostal* mini-chain (opened in June 2003) is by far the shiniest in a big building of *hostales*. Rooms vary wildly in size (no. 208 is the biggest) but all are immaculate, with fresh furnishings in pale yellows and oranges. The floors sparkle, and double-glazed windows ensure silence. Four units have bathtubs, 13 have showers. Breakfast and laundry are both unusually cheap, and you get a small discount for paying in cash.

Cruz 26, 28012 Madrid. 📞 **91/360-4628.** Fax 91/521-1477. www.hostaltijcal.com. 17 units. 53€ ($61) single; 63€–69€ ($73–$79) double. MC, V. Metro: Sol. **Amenities:** Limited room service; laundry service. *In room:* A/C, TV, safe.

Victoria III   This is the best of a trio of choices near Puerta del Sol owned and operated by the same conscientious family. The only sign in front is next to the door buzzer. The furnishings are in good condition and the mattresses firm. The room dimensions, however, are often close to claustrophobic, so request one of the larger ones. The reception is pleasant, although English isn't spoken—show this book for a possible discount. If this hostal is full, inquire about availability at the **Victoria I,** Carretas 7, off Puerta del Sol. The reservation phone line handles all three *hostales*, so make sure to specify Victoria III when booking.

San Jerónimo 30 (4th floor), 28014 Madrid. 📞 **91/522-8412.** Fax 91/522-9982. www.hostal-victoria.com. 12 units. 32€ ($37) single; 48€ ($55) double. AE, MC, V. Metro: Sol. **Amenities:** Bar; limited room service. *In room:* A/C, TV, minibar, safe.

AROUND PLAZA SANTA ANA

Inglés   A large ship model in the front window alerts you to this popular hotel. Enter a lobby with deep sofas and armchairs and find that little has changed in recent years, including the room rates and the too-often dour gents at the front desk. Just beyond the TV lounge is the bar/cafeteria where breakfast is served. Many units have sitting areas. Nearby Plaza Santa Ana and Calle de las Huertas jump with tapas and music bars. A parking garage has 25 spaces for guests. Note that only about half the rooms in the hotel are air-conditioned, so ask for an A/C room in summer.

Echegaray 8, 28014 Madrid. ℂ **91/429-6551.** Fax 91/420-2423. 51 units. 70€ ($81) single; 100€ ($115) double. AE, DC, MC, V. Parking 12€ ($14). Metro: Sol. **Amenities:** Restaurant; bar; exercise room; limited room service. *In room:* TV, safe.

Lisboa   Amid one of Madrid's heaviest concentrations of tapas bars, the Lisboa offers rooms spread over four floors; some have double beds with bronze bedsteads. Guests aren't allowed to have visitors in their rooms. The small lounge has a TV and VCR. While there's no restaurant here, the *hostal* is at the top of one of the city's best-known restaurant streets, and there are scores of eating places in all directions. English is spoken, and rates are often negotiable.

Ventura de la Vega 17, 28014 Madrid. ℂ **91/429-4676.** Fax 91/429-9894. www.hostallisboa.com. 22 units. 42€ ($48) single; 51€ ($59) double. Rates include IVA. AE, DC, MC, V. Metro: Antón Martín or Sol. **Amenities:** Limited room service; laundry/dry-cleaning service. *In room:* A/C, TV.

Santander   Little seems to change here, including, for several years, the rates. Even now, with a couple of recent bumps, it's a good deal, aided by the strength of the dollar. The shiny glass-and-brass doorway on Echegaray leads into a foyer with Art Nouveau touches and a carved-wood reception desk. The units are of generally good size, with parquet floors, dressing tables, and wardrobes; some bathrooms have giant tubs. A TV lounge is located next to the bar. Visitors or washing of clothes are not allowed in the rooms.

Echegaray 1 (at the corner of San Jerónimo), 28014 Madrid. ℂ **91/429-9551.** Fax 91/369-1078. 35 units. 64€ ($74) single; 80€ ($92) double. Rates include IVA. MC, V. Metro: Sol. **Amenities:** Cafeteria; bar; laundry service. *In room:* A/C, TV.

NEAR THE PALACE

HH Campomanes 🎯 *Finds*   Up a quiet side street from the opera house is a row of attached houses that has been scooped out and rebuilt to house this spiffy hotel. Contemporary minimalist, it is, stripped to essentials in black, white, and pearl gray, but it's cozy, not chilly. There are two "mini-suites," but they are really just large doubles. Singles aren't too small, and they have full-size beds.

Campomanes 4 (near Arrieta), 28013 Madrid. ℂ **91/548-8548.** Fax 91/559-1288. 30 units. 87€ ($100) single; 99€ ($114) double. Rates include breakfast. AE, MC, V. Metro: Opera. **Amenities:** Bar; laundry/dry-cleaning service. *In room:* A/C, TV, minibar, safe.

Opera 🎯   A couple of blocks from the royal palace and opposite the opera house, this hotel offers first-rate comfort and a warm welcome from the English-speaking staff. Rooms range from medium to surprisingly spacious, some with balconies, and are furnished with twin or double beds with quality mattresses. Bathrooms are excellent, some with whirlpools.

Cuesta de Santo Domingo 2, 28013 Madrid. ℂ **91/541-2800.** Fax 91/541-6923. www.hotelopera.com. 79 units. 90€ ($104) single; 120€ ($138) double. AE, DC, MC, V. Metro: Opera. **Amenities:** Restaurant; bar; limited room service; babysitting; laundry/dry-cleaning service. *In room:* A/C, TV, minibar, hair dryer, safe.

WORTH A SPLURGE

Many top hotels offer deeply discounted weekend rates, allowing you a taste of near-luxury in the middle of an 8-day visit. Also, remember you can often find deeply discounted rates through online travel agency or hotel chain websites.

Best Western Arosa 🎯🎯   Following extensive renovations in 2001, the Arosa has gained four-star status. A doorman watches over the vestibule, where an elevator rises to the reception desk, lobby bar, lounge, and dining room. The broad side of the late-19th-century building occupies a block in the middle of the Gran Vía, but double-paned glass quiets street noise. The rooms vary significantly in size and layout, but with this many rooms, if you're unhappy with yours, a better one is nearly always available. An airport shuttle van runs hourly and costs 6€ ($6.90).

Salud 21, 28013 Madrid. ✆ **91/532-1600.** Fax 91/531-3127. www.bestwestern.com/thisco/bw/ 92043/92043_b.html. 139 units. 90€–110€ ($104–$127) single; 100€–155€ ($115–$179) double. AE, DC, MC, V. Metro: Gran Vía. **Amenities:** Restaurant; bar; limited room service; same-day dry cleaning/laundry. *In room:* A/C, TV, dataport, minibar, hair dryer, safe.

Clarion Hotel Preciados *(Kids)*

A beautiful mingling of old and new has resulted in this gorgeous 2001 hotel in an 1861 building. The original architecture remains, but the rooms are sparkling and breathtakingly well kept, with spacious bathrooms. Light wood furnishings give the rooms a clean, airy feel; hardwood and marble floors recall the hotel's classic past. Wireless Internet access gives it a 21st-century touch. The hotel welcomes families with such extras as beds that can be added to the standard rooms and even a special children's menu in the restaurant. One floor is nonsmoking, and another is for women only. The hotel's Varela restaurant serves innovative Spanish cuisine.

Preciados 37, 28013 Madrid. ✆ **91-454-4400.** Fax 91-454-4401. www.preciadoshotel.com. 73 units. 117€–129€ ($135–$148) double. AE, DC, MC, V. Metro: Santo Domingo or Callao. **Amenities:** Restaurant; bar; room service; babysitting; laundry/dry cleaning. *In room:* A/C, TV, dataport, minibar, hair dryer, iron, safe.

Gaudí

A majestic early-1900s building at the good end of the Gran Vía was gutted to transform it into this near-luxury hotel. That's the pattern for this small Catalan chain. Plaza Mayor and the Prado and Thyssen museums are within walking distance, and retreating at siesta time to these quiet teak-lined quarters is restorative. The weekend rates include an extensive breakfast buffet with hot and cold items, which otherwise costs 13€ ($15) during the week. Rack rates are high, but advance booking can score great deals.

Gran Vía 9, 28013 Madrid. ✆ **91/531-2222.** Fax 91/531-5469. www.hoteles-catalonia.es. 185 units. Rack rates 122€ ($140) single; 198€ ($228) double. Rates can be as low as 80€ ($92) for advance bookings. AE, DC, MC, V. Metro: Gran Vía. **Amenities:** Restaurant; bar; exercise room with sauna/whirlpool; 24-hr. room service; same-day dry cleaning/laundry. *In room:* A/C, TV, dataport, minibar, hair dryer, safe.

La Casa Grande

Despite the small number of rooms (all on the 3rd floor, no elevator), this is a large, gated complex near the airport containing a tavern, a garage, wine *bodegas*, and a 16th-century main building that has served as a royal farmhouse and Jesuit monastery. The rooms are small but sumptuously furnished with antiques, objets d'art, and original paintings. Meals are served in the regal dining room or on the star-lit terrace, where a singer-guitarist entertains nightly in season. Check out the basement gallery's remarkable collection of Russian icons.

28850 Torrejón de Ardoz (19km/12 miles east of Madrid on the Carretera de Barcelona, a few min. from the airport). ✆ **91/675-3900.** Fax 91/675-0691. www.lacasagrande.es. 8 units. 100€ ($115) single; 130€ ($150) double. Rates include breakfast and unlimited use of minibar. AE, MC, V. Closed Aug. **Amenities:** 2 restaurants; 2 bars; sauna; 24-hr. room service; same-day dry cleaning/laundry. *In room:* A/C, TV, fax, minibar, hair dryer, safe.

3 Great Deals on Dining

In Madrid it's always possible to eat well, if not grandly, at relatively low cost. In the old part of the city around Puerta del Sol and Plaza Mayor, the selection of *cafeterías* and *cervecerías* offering decent food is enormous. A little to the east,

> (*Tips* **When Is a *Cafetería* Not a Cafeteria?**
>
> When adapting to Spanish dining hours proves difficult—lunch at 2:30pm and dinner at 10:30pm—look for *cafeterías* and *cervecerías*. A *cafetería* is an inexpensive sit-down restaurant with table service (what Americans call a "cafeteria" is an *autoservicio* or *buffet*). A *cervecería* is usually a cross between a bar and a *cafetería*, with beer on draft as the featured beverage, and food choices ranging from tapas and sandwiches to one-dish *platos combinados* and sometimes full meals.
>
> *Cafeterías* and *cervecerías* stay open longer than regular restaurants, not infrequently 7am to midnight, without a break. They're especially good choices on Sundays, when the relatively few restaurants that choose to stay open are packed in the afternoon, with waits of an hour or more.

in the area bounded by Carrera de San Jerónimo and Calles Huertas, León, Echegaray, and Ventura de la Vega, are dozens of lively tapas bars.

A Spanish **tortilla** is a firm omelet of eggs, potatoes, and onions, generally served at room temperature when eaten as a *tapa*. **Gazpacho** is a cold tomato-based soup made with garlic, vinegar, bread, and olive oil and garnished with chopped onions, green peppers, and egg. **Paella,** a specialty of Valencia, has many variations but is most familiar as rice cooked in saffron with chunks of chicken, fish, and shellfish. *Cocido madrileño* is a boiled dinner served in courses as soup, then vegetables, then meats. A popular first course is *judías,* a simple bean stew. *Perdiz* (partridge) and *codorniz* (quail) appear on menus regularly, along with *cochinillo asado* (roast suckling pig) and *cordero asado* (roast lamb).

An increasing number of foreign restaurants have opened—Moroccan, Cuban, German, Chinese, Greek, Japanese, American . . . you name it. While Spaniards have always been slow to accept other cuisines, partly because their own are so varied and extensive, they are dipping their toes tentatively into this global gastronomic sea. And apart from a few of their tapas, they don't like spicy-hot dishes. That puts a crimp in the efforts of chefs trying for authenticity in Szechuan, Hunan, Tex-Mex, Indian, and Mexican dishes. Of the various foreign cuisines, the one best reproduced is Italian. Pastas and pizzas are nearly as common in Madrid as in Chicago or New York, and most Spanish cooks have learned the meaning of *al dente*. That's why most of the relatively few foreign restaurants below are Italian.

Most Madrid bars and restaurants now serve brewed decaf—ask for *descafinado en máquina*.

NEAR THE PRADO & THYSSEN MUSEUMS

Arrocería Gala (formerly the Champagnería Gala) ⊛ SPANISH Recent price increases are, alas, pushing this well-known restaurant out of the budget category. The front room has blood-orange walls with painted vines coupled with a glassed-over courtyard with real and artificial plants and a Venetian chandelier. *Arroces* (rice dishes) are featured. Italian risottos have joined the paellas and *fideuàs* (a similar dish with thin noodles instead of rice) and come with a choice of 16 components, from cheese and bull's tail to rabbit and fish. Included in the *menú* are do-it-yourself *pa amb tomaquet* (Catalan bread rubbed with garlic and tomato pulp and drizzled with oil), a seasonal salad, wine, aioli and

---

Value   Getting the Best Deal on Dining

- Take advantage of the fixed-price *menú del día* at lunch (and some-times at dinner)—it usually comprises a first course of soup or salad, a main course of meat or fish, bread, and often dessert and wine or another beverage.
- Be aware that unwary choices from the a la carte side of the menu can easily double or triple basic costs when appetizers, wine, desserts, mineral water, and coffee are added.
- Eat tapas instead of ordering full meals, and remember that they're often cheaper if you stand at the bar *(barra)* rather than sit at a table *(mesa).*
- Try the inexpensive *platos combinados* served in *cafeterías, cerve-cerías,* and some bars—they're one-dish meals of meat or fish, rice or fries, and maybe a vegetable and bread and beverage on the side.

---

romesco sauces, dessert, and coffee. Avoid the crowded Sunday afternoons or reserve the day before.

Moratín 22 (west of Paseo del Prado). (C) **91/429-2562.** Main courses 13€–18€ ($15–$21). No credit cards. Daily 1–5pm and 9pm–1:30am. Metro: Atocha.

Bango SPANISH   A paragon of the *cafetería* type of eating place, Bango attracts a surprisingly glossy sort of patron, especially in the evening. It sets out an enticing variety of tapas, as well as freshly squeezed juice at breakfast. Table-cloths are spread for full lunches and dinners, and sandwiches and desserts are available anytime. This is a place to remember on Sunday, when most restau-rants close, or any time when regular Spanish dining hours seem too late.

Paseo del Prado 32 (off the lobby of the Mora hotel, opposite the Botanical Garden). (C) **91/420-0790.** Main courses 6€–12€ ($6.90–$14); *menús del día* 6€ ($6.90) and 9.05€ ($10). MC, V. Daily 7am–midnight. Metro: Atocha.

NORTH OF THE GRAN VIA

Bocaito (R) SPANISH/TAPAS   Many aficionados believe this is Madrid's top tapas bar. Most items are sliced, cooked, and/or assembled to order by the men behind the horseshoe-shaped bar. They aren't doctrinaire—some of the dozen salads contain kiwi fruit. In back are a couple of pleasant dining rooms for sit-down meals. A few dishes do get steep—eggs scrambled with baby eels, a deli-cacy, costs 15€ ($13)—but most main courses are under 9.05€ ($8). For a special treat, take a companion and share the *fritura malaguena* (lightly fried fish and shellfish) at 20€ ($18) for two.

Libertad 4–6 (2 blocks north of the Gran Vía). (C) **91/532-1219.** www.bocaito.com. Main courses 3€–17€ ($2.70–$15). MC, V. Mon–Sat 1–4pm and 8:30pm–midnight. Metro: Chueca or Gran Vía.

Nabucco (R) (Kids) ITALIAN   Uncommonly spacious, with high ceilings, ter-razzo floors, and urns and statuary in niches, Nabucco is a believable echo of a Roman trattoria in the heart of the Chueca nightlife district. The pizzas come with the paper-thin crusts favored in Madrid, and make a great meal for well under $10. On the other hand, those with larger appetites might want to start with *crostini* (slices of bread topped with melted cheese and ham or mushrooms) and go on to the 12€ ($14) osso bucco, a house specialty. Just about everything is available for takeout.

Hortaleza 108 (near Plaza Santa Barbara). ℭ 91/310-0611. Pastas and pizzas 5.50€–8.50€ ($6.30–$9.80); main courses 9.50€–12€ ($11–$14). AE, DC, MC, V. Sun–Thurs 1:30–4:30pm and 8:30pm–12:30am (Fri–Sat to 1am). Metro: Chueca.

Spaghetti & Bollicine ⭐ ITALIAN   In the afternoon, young executives fill this colorful trattoria, and they come back to join models at night, along with neighborhood couples. The pasta menu is inventive and exciting, and the setting is romantic: At night, for example, your server brings a complimentary glass of sparkling *cava* and two small tomato bruschetta and lights the wick of the glass lamp. More than 30 risottos and pastas as well as meal-sized salads are on the menu, so you can forego the more expensive meat courses. Some pastas (*puttanesca,* for example) have a lustier punch than usual. Choose well, and you'll have a fine meal for under 11€ ($13) per person.

Prim 15 (west of Paseo de Recoletos). ℭ 91/521-4514. Main courses 7€–20€ ($8.05–$22). AE, MC, V. Mon–Fri 2–4pm and 9pm–midnight (to 1am Fri); Sat 9pm–1am. Metro: Colón or Banco de España.

Vegaviana ⭐ *Finds* *Kids* VEGETARIAN/ECLECTIC   This little family-run place, where not a word of English is spoken, is way off most tourists' radar and is a true find. Creative vegetarian pizzas, salads, paellas, burritos, and pasta dishes are the stars of the menu; even the hummus is homemade. Meat-eaters can choose from among a half-dozen chicken preparations, such as "Greek" chicken sautéed with yogurt and onions and served with vegetable paella. Many of the mild, home-style dishes would appeal to children.

Pelayo 35 (near Plaza Santa Barbara). ℭ 91/308-0381. www.accua.com/vegaviana. Main courses 5.50€–8.50€ ($6.30–$9.75). MC, V. Tues–Sat 1:30–4pm and 8:30–11:30pm; Sun 1:30–4pm. Metro: Chueca.

AROUND PLAZA SANTA ANA

Artemisa VEGETARIAN   This popular vegetarian restaurant serves mild, pleasant, colorful dishes; a lunch plate may include a bright-orange potato-carrot patty, a vegetable curry, and broccoli smothered in cheese. Desserts are especially good, like the warm chocolate cake, spicy with currants. The walls and floor are of brick, tile, and old stone. This is a nonsmoking place, one of the few in Madrid. Another branch is at Tres Cruces 4 (ℭ 91/521-8721).

Ventura de la Vega 4 (near Carrera de San Jerónimo). ℭ 91/429-5092. Main courses 10€–13€ ($12–$15), *menù del dia* 9€ ($10). MC, V. Mon–Sun 1:30–4pm; Mon–Sat 8:30pm–midnight. Metro: Sol or Sevilla.

Gula Gula ⭐ *Value* INTERNATIONAL   *Buffet libre* doesn't mean it's free, but that it's "all you want to eat." Such buffet restaurants have been sweeping Spain's major cities in recent years; Gula Gula is the pioneer of the system. The menu changes daily, but typical are a couple of soups; several salads of rice, pasta, and greens; meats and poultry with starches; and dessert. The waiter brings beverages and bread. This branch is quieter than the other one at Gran Vía 1 (ℭ **91/ 522-8765;** Metro: Banco de España). But the light lunchtime patronage keeps

---

⸢Tips⸥ Room Service

Some restaurants package meals *para llevar*—to take out—for you to eat back in your hotel room or at a nearby park. Also, the **Tele-Pizza** chain (ℭ **91/212-2122**) delivers on scooters to homes and hotels.

the smoke level down—plus it's a truly good value. Most nights, a hip young crowd fills the room, and transvestite cabaret performances are given.

Infante 5 (between Echegaray and León). (☎ **91/420-2919**. www.gulagula.net. Reservations recommended for dinner. *Menús del día* 9.05€ ($10) at lunch, 12€ ($14) or 17€ ($19) at dinner. AE, DC, MC, V. Tues–Sun 1–5pm and 9pm–3am. Metro: Antón Martín.

La Creazione ✿ ITALIAN On one of Madrid's favorite restaurant streets, this trattoria gratifies several needs. You'll be asked, "Restaurant or pizzeria?" The restaurant has tablecloths, while the tables in the pizzeria are cheerful glass-topped displays of pasta and beans. Both pastas and pizzas are made on the premises and prepared to order. The 25 or so pizza variations are a big star here, with thin, crunchy, airy crusts and improbable mixes of toppings (bacon, oregano, pine nuts, and currants) that are surprisingly quite good. The restaurant menu features sophisticated seafood dishes. Most food is available *para llevar*—for takeout.

Ventura de la Vega 9 (near Carrera de San Jerónimo). (☎ **91/429-0387**. Main courses 13€–16€ ($15–$18); pizzas and pastas 10€–15€ ($12–$17); *menú turístico* 15€ ($17). AE, DC, MC, V. Tues–Sun 1:30–4:30pm; Tues–Sat 9pm–12:30am. Metro: Sol.

La Moderna SPANISH/TAPAS Some of the best tapas around the plaza are served at this upscale tavern—no small feat, given the fierce competition. But look first to the inviting cheese and wine selections. A chalkboard tells of the rotated six or seven pressings available by the glass, which go wonderfully with the many regional cheeses. Each glass comes with a mini-tapa, such as a sardine tail on tomato-rubbed bread. Rations of smoked fish, ham, or sausages cost 6.10€ to 13€ ($7–$15).

Plaza de Santa Ana 12 (near the Hotel Reina Victoria). (☎ **91/420-1582**. Tapas and *raciones* 3€–14€ ($3.45–$16). MC, V. Daily noon–3am. Metro: Sol.

La Trucha SPANISH/TAPAS Trout is the signature dish of this 79-year-old tavern. One version is *trucha a La Trucha*, in the style of the province of Navarre—the whole fish is split open, filled with chopped ham and garlic, then sautéed. Another is the trout filet included in the platter of smoked fish and roe called a *verbena*. Most tapas and larger dishes are cooked to order. This is a favorite stop on the tapas circuit, partly because the men behind the counter make new patrons feel like old friends. There's a larger but similar La Trucha at Manuel Fernández y González 3 (☎ 91/429-5833; Metro: Sol), with the same hours.

Núñez de Arce 6 (near Plaza Santa Ana). (☎ **91/532-0882**. Main courses 15€–30€ ($17–$35). AE, MC, V. Mon–Sat 12:30–4pm and 7:30pm–midnight. Closed July. Metro: Sol.

Tocororo CUBAN Madrid has become a refuge for thousands of Cubans (just like the owner of this well-respected standby). He insists his food is authentic, and it seems to be, with rice and beans, *ceviche* (marinated fish), and *tostones rellenos* (plantains filled with meat and shrimp). The less expensive *platos* are more economical, like the *bandeja sucu-sucu,* black bean soup, white rice, and fried starchy yucca accompanying *ropa vieja* (shredded beef). Photos of old Havana adorn the walls, and Cuban musicians play Friday and Saturday nights. The service has improved but can get distracted when regulars show up. Most of them start with a round of *mojitos;* a gratis shot of fruit liqueur comes with the check.

Prado 3 (at the corner of Echegaray). (☎ **91/369-4000**. Main courses 4.25€–22€ ($4.90–$26); *menú del día* 9.05€ ($10). AE, DC, MC, V. Tues–Sun 1:30–4pm and 8:30pm–midnight (to 2am Fri–Sat). Metro: Sevilla.

Moments   **A True Taste of Spain: Tapas**

Gaining fame around the world, **tapas** are small portions of food served in most Madrid bars. While they often precede lunch or dinner, you can make a complete and tasty meal of tapas alone—a good way to control portions and cost.

Popular tapas are *boquerones* (anchovy-size fish fried or marinated in oil), *croquetas* (fritters of cod or other ingredients), *empanadillas* (pastries filled with tuna or chicken), *setas* (large mushrooms usually fried with garlic), *morcilla* (blood sausage), *pimientos fritos* (fried sweet peppers), *pimientos de Padrón* (grilled jalapeño-size peppers, most of which are mild but a few are little firecrackers), *patatas bravas* (roast potatoes with a piquant sauce), steamed *mejillones* (mussels), *chipirones in su tinta* (baby squid in their ink), stuffed or deep-fried *calamares* (squid), *chorizo* and *salchichón* (sausages), and *queso manchego* (cheese from La Mancha).

Warning: Delectable *jamón de serrano* (air-cured ham) is widely available and should be sampled but is very expensive—a 4-ounce portion can cost 18€ ($20) or more. Equally pricey are the gourmet treats *angulas* (baby eels boiled in oil) and *percebes* (goose barnacles, which look like tiny dragon's feet).

Areas to begin exploration of these delectable Spanish inventions are the streets on and around **Plaza Santa Ana** and **Calle Victoria,** which leads to it, and down **Calle San Miguel,** which borders Plaza Mayor on the west. Trolling through these concentrations of bars, *mesones,* and *tascas* will lead to many delicious discoveries and not a few tales to carry home.

AROUND PUERTA DEL SOL & PLAZA MAYOR

La Finca de Susana *Value* MEDITERRANEAN   A concern for light, healthy eating is far from a priority in most Spanish restaurants. But maybe they'll think again when they see the business this spot is doing. Seated in a space that looks like a former bank, with potted palms and a long bank of windows, you typically have a choice of five vegetable dishes and a similar number of low-calorie options. The manager even declares that the specialty of the house is grilled vegetables. That doesn't mean you'll experience the deprivation caused by spa food or that all diners go the green and leafy route. There's plenty of fish, chicken, and pork on the menu, but prepared with less oil, fat, and salt. All classes of age, profession, and society show up, partly because they'd have to go out of their way to spend more than $14 per person, with wine.

Arlaban 4. (© 91/369-3557. Main courses 5.50€–9€ ($6.30–$10). Lunch menu 6.95€ ($8). MC, V. Daily 1–3:45pm and 8:30–11:45pm. Metro: Sevilla.

Madrid I SPANISH   They've retooled this *cafetería* inside and out from a 1960s lunch counter look to a mock-Renaissance 1660s decor, but nearly all dining bases are still covered. In front is an always-busy tapas bar, with pitchers of *sangría* ready to pour; in back is an equally casual space for *platos combinados* and full meals; upstairs is a slightly more formal dining room. Apart from breakfasts, lunches, and dinners, they offer pizzas, sandwiches, and burgers.

San Jerónimo 16 (east of Puerta del Sol). ℂ **91/523-3556.** *Platos combinados* 9€–14€ ($10–$16); *menús del día* 7.35€ ($8.45) lunch and 12€ ($14) dinner. MC, V. Daily 8am–1am. Metro: Sol.

Museo de Jamón SPANISH/TAPAS   A museum of ham, indeed. This growing chain of bar/butcher shops offers a slew of preparations of Spain's favorite meat, with long rows of ham hocks hanging from the ceiling. Portions range in price from reasonable to stunning—14€ ($16) and higher for 4 ounces at the high end—so the best way to sample this delicacy is in a sandwich, which costs as little as 1.20€ ($1.40). Combo plates are less intimidating, and the *menú especial* includes a first course of ham and melon, followed by scallops or fish for 6.90€ ($7.95). A guitarist plays some nights in the upstairs dining room. Takeout is available from the ground-floor deli counter. Branches of the restaurant are multiplying around town.

Victoria 1/San Jerónimo 6 (a block east of Puerta del Sol). ℂ **91/521-0346.** *Platos combinados* 3€–4.95€ ($3.45–$5.70); *menú del día* 6.90€ ($7.95). MC, V. Daily 9am–midnight. Metro: Sol.

Suite 🎄 *(Finds* INTERNATIONAL   Starting out a couple of years ago as the "Mad Cafe Club," this hip restaurant/bar in the center of Madrid remains a popular haunt for the young and fashionable. There's a garden where patrons languish on hot summer nights and a disco upstairs that cranks it up at midnight. About half the starters are salads, which are good choices, because main courses are comprised almost entirely of the selected flesh, ranging from duck breast with caramelized pears (the least expensive) to lobster in oyster sauce (the most expensive). Preparations are attractive, if minimalist.

Virgin de los Peligros 4 (between Alcalá and Gran Vía). ℂ **91/532-6228.** Reservations recommended. Main courses 11€–16€ ($12–$18); *menú del día* (lunch only) 10€–14€ ($12–$16). AE, DC, MC, V. Mon–Wed 1–4pm and 9:30pm–3am; Thurs–Sat 1–4pm and 9:30pm–4am. Dinner served until 12:30am. Metro: Sevilla, Gran Vía.

Taberna de Cien Vinos SPANISH   Save this serious wine bar for a late light dinner after a big lunch. It serves 14 to 16 wines by the glass; the selections are changed every night and listed on a chalkboard. Although the name declares it a repository of 100 wines, the racks hold considerably more. Simple foods complement the wines, not the other way around. There are usually about 8 *pinchos* (largely skewered meals and fish) and 10 *raciones* of such nibbles as mushroom terrine with foie gras on toast and marinated salmon on bread, but with a repository of over 200 recipes, they are changed constantly. The bar is located just a few blocks southwest of Plaza Mayor. Most diners are of university age or slightly older, but no one is excluded.

Nuncio 17 (off Segovia). ℂ **91/365-4704.** *Pinchos* average 3.25€ ($3.75); *raciones* average 12€ ($14). V. Tues–Sun 1–4pm; Tues–Sat 8–midnight. Metro: Sol.

NEAR THE ROYAL PALACE

Cornucopia 🎄🎄 ECLECTIC   This triumphantly funky, always surprising little joint is crammed into the corner of a 19th-century house opposite the Monasteria de Descalzas Reales. The hostess, an American actress appearing on a Spanish soap opera, co-owns the restaurant with a Frenchman and a Spaniard. The two rooms in ochre and brick, with intricately patterned wood floors and amusing semi-abstract paintings, perfectly suit the international artistic (or at least Bohemian) 30-ish crowd. All that's enough for an entertaining evening, but the food's pretty good, too. A simple salad of roasted red peppers and cheese is warm, mild, and comforting. Later, meatballs arrive covered by a riot of mashed sweet potatoes; a mushroom crepe is stuffed with mushrooms and covered in mushroom sauce.

Flora 1 (west of Plaza Descalzas). (C) **91/547-6465**. www.restaurantecornucopia.com. Reservations recommended for dinner. Main courses 11€–16€ ($12–$18); *menú del día* 10€ ($11). AE, DC, MC, V. Tues–Sat 1:30–4pm and 9pm–midnight. Metro: Sol.

El Buey STEAKHOUSE   When your enthusiasm for exotic seafood starts to pall, head here for a red-meat fix. First courses are standards like thick onion soup and salads that are often meatier than leafy, as with the tuna and pimientos number. Order what everyone does and you are presented with a super-hot earthenware plate, a platter of sliced raw beef filet, and a bowl of fries, steak sauce on the side. You are now to complete your own meal. The half-inch slices, sprinkled with rock salt, take no time to cook on the hot plate, a couple of minutes per side. There is much hilarity from the other patrons, because the food doesn't demand a lot of discussion. Get a table away from the kitchen, if you can, for waiters slam through the doors all evening.

Plaza de la Marina Española 1 (corner of Torija). (C) **91/541-3031**. Reservations essential on weekends. 1 kilo (2.2 lb.) of meat (enough for 4) 37€ ($43); half-kilo 20€ ($23). AE, DC, MC, V. Mon–Sun 1–4:30pm; Mon–Sat 8:30pm–midnight. Metro: España or Santo Domingo.

La Bola REGIONAL SPANISH   Easily spotted by its crimson exterior, La Bola has been on stage since 1870, so you know Hemingway and Ava Gardner were patrons, as attested to by photos above the carved wainscoting. Ask about that history and you get a leaflet. The big menu item is *cocido madrileño,* the traditional Castilian Sunday boiled dinner: Several kinds of meat and vegetables are slow-cooked together for hours; the rich broth is strained off and tiny noodles are dropped in as a first course. That's followed by the vegetables (potatoes, chickpeas, cabbage) and the meats (usually chicken, *chorizo,* beef, pork), mostly cheap cuts with only a couple of bites each. The fish dishes are well suited to smaller appetites.

Bola 5 (2 blocks north of the Teatro Real). (C) **91/547-6930**. Main courses 14€–19€ ($16–$22). No credit cards. Mon–Sun 1:30–4pm; Mon–Sat 9pm–12:30am. Metro: Santo Domingo.

WORTH A SPLURGE

El Olivo Restaurant ⭐ MEDITERRANEAN   French-born chef-owner Jean Pierre Vandelle makes no bones about his enthusiasm for two of his adopted land's most famous products: olive oils and sherry wines. The bar in front is stocked with over 100 versions of the fortified wine, and no matter what you order in the dining room, he wheels over a cart of about three-score olive oils and vinegars and invites you to shake a few drops on what he has cooked for you, which might be marinated and grilled monkfish served with black-olive sauce over a compote of fresh tomatoes, or four preparations of cod (an oft-featured ingredient) arranged on a single platter and served with a spicy pil-pil sauce. Adults will want to dress for the occasion.

General Gallegos 1. (C) **91/359-1535**. Reservations recommended. Main courses 19€–27€ ($21–$30); fixed-price meals 40€–50€ ($46–$58). AE, DC, MC, V. Tues–Sat 1–4pm and 9pm–midnight. Closed Aug 15–31 and 4 days around Easter. Metro: Plaza de Castilla.

La Barraca ⭐⭐ REGIONAL SPANISH   On a narrow side street parallel to the Gran Vía, this place has had since 1935 to take on its folkloric atmosphere of lace curtains, ceramic pitchers, and hanging plates around the (nonworking) fireplace. It excels in *arroces*—the rice dishes of southeastern Spain's Valencia. Most visitors can't get enough of paella but might not be aware it has many variations, from one flavored with squid ink to one substituting thin noodles for rice (*fideuà* *marinera*). If it's your first, you might want to order the paella *mixta*, with bits of chicken, sausage, shrimp, mussels, pork, and squid. Expect some time to pass before you're served, for everything is prepared to order.

Reina 29. ℂ **91/532-7154.** Main courses 12€–20€ ($14–$23). AE, DC, MC, V. Daily 1–4pm and 8:30pm–midnight. Metro: Gran Vía or Banco de España.

La Gamella 🌟🌟 FUSION   For more than 30 years, Illinois-born chef-owner Dick Stephens has taken it upon himself to introduce Madrileños to the creative American cuisine developed over that time. His latest venue is near the Puerta de Alcalá, the interior abloom with vibrant colors, as if Matisse had a hand in the decor. His vegetable and couscous soup is a cheery yet gentle starter, to be followed by such delectables as hake dressed with white truffles and garlic, beef in mustard sauce, or chicken stewed with almonds and saffron. Homesick Yanks may prefer what has been called "the only edible hamburger in Madrid." It's delicious, although it costs a whopping 15€ ($17).

Alfonso XII 4. ℂ **91/532-4509.** www.lagamella.com. Reservations recommended. Main courses 11€–19€ ($12–$22). AE, DC, MC, V. Mon–Fri 1:30–4pm; Mon–Sat 9pm–midnight. Closed 2 weeks around Easter and 2 weeks in Aug. Metro: Retiro.

THE CAFE SCENE

Madrid's cafes hold a special place in the lives of its citizens, serving a function somewhere between tapas bars and restaurants. Food, although always available, is secondary to every Spaniard's favorite occupation—talk. Many of the older cafes, from pre–World War I days and even before, nurture reputations as hotbeds of intellectualism or ideology. Others are favored primarily as meeting places, where a cup of coffee or a beer is the sole price of admission to a table you can hold for hours while writing poetry or postcards, reading a book, or planning your future.

At **Café Comercial,** Glorieta de Bilbao 7 (ℂ **91/521-5655;** Metro: Bilbao), artists and intellectuals have been challenging one another at regular *tertulias* (get-togethers) since the 19th century, reflected in big mirrors beneath the towering ceiling; tables are set outside in good weather. Go for coffee or drinks and the surroundings, not to eat. It's open Monday to Friday 7:30am to 1am, Saturday 8am to 2am, and Sunday 10am to 1am. Hemingway made **Café Gijón,** Paseo de Recoletos 21 (ℂ **91/521-5425;** Metro: Banco de España), famous among Americans, and it's been home to the Spanish tradition of the *tertulia* since 1888. That's a more-or-less formal occasion when friends and colleagues gather for discussions of philosophy, the arts, politics . . . or soccer. Outside in summer or inside in cooler weather, this is a relaxing place to sip a coffee or a beer or read a newspaper. Be prepared for thick cigarette smoke. It's open daily 8am to 2am (to 3am Sat).

With its Belle Epoque interior and nearby neo-Victorian pavilion, **El Espejo,** Paseo de Recoletos 31 (ℂ **91/308-2347;** Metro: Colón), looks as if it has been around as long as nearby Café Gijón. It hasn't, but that doesn't diminish the appeal. The pavilion, on the pedestrian concourse bordering the *paseo,* is a fancy display of glass and wrought iron, with tables inside and out. In summer, a pianist often plays. The cafe is open daily 10:30am to 1am and the pavilion daily 9am to 2am (both close an hour later Fri–Sat). A near-legendary priest originally opened **Café de Oriente,** Plaza de Oriente 2 (ℂ **91/541-1564;** Metro: Opera), to help steer troubled young men and ex-convicts on a better path. It sits at the edge of the plaza, facing the Royal Palace, imposing when illuminated at night. In warm months tables are set outdoors; indoors, much gilt, brass, and velvet are deployed. The dining room in the brick cellar is attractive yet too expensive for these pages; have coffee or a drink instead. An adjacent building has been made over in the same extravagant manner to create **La Botillería,** Plaza de Oriente 4 (© **91/548-4620**), a wine bar with a cellar of over 125 Spanish labels; glasses from a dozen bottles are poured daily. Both places are open daily 8:30am to 1:30am (to 2:30am Fri–Sat).

Madrid's cafe tradition continues to be renewed, as with the handsome bilevel **Café del Español,** Principe 25 (no phone; Metro: Sol), attached to the Teatro Español on Plaza Santa Cruz. The spacious front room with a bar is illuminated by chandeliers that look like eruptions of glassy green mushrooms. The crowd sizes ebb and flow with curtain and dinner times and during departures from discos and dance clubs. Snacks and small *platos combinados* are available. The cafe is open daily 9pm to 2am.

THE CHAINS

Spanish fast-food and casual-dining chains proliferate. **Vips,** Spain's answer to Denny's, has a sleek red-and-black look and waiter service, and an extensive diner menu featuring a wide range of breakfasts. Many branches also have attached convenience store/newsstands. Popular all day long, it's open daily 9am to 3am. Menu items run 3.90€ to 8.45€ ($3.50–$8). Vips branches are at Gran Vía 43 (Metro: Gran Vía), Princesa 5 (Metro: España), Velázquez 136 (Metro: República Argentina), Serrano 41 (Metro: Serrano), Orense 16 and 79 (Metro: Cuzco), Paseo de la Habana 17 (Metro: Colombia), Julián Romea 4 (Metro: Moncloa), and Alberto Aguilera 56 (Metro: San Bernardo); an almost luxurious one is located under the Palace Hotel, facing the Neptune Fountain on Plaza Canovas del Castillo (Metro: Banco de España).

Foster's Hollywood is a popular place to go for your burger or Tex-Mex fix; it's popular with Americans and Spaniards alike. Main courses run 6€ to 17€ ($6.90–$20). The 15 locations include Magallanes 1 (Metro: Quevedo), Apolonio Morales 3 (Metro: Plaza Castilla), and Plaza de Isabel II, behind the Teatro Real (Metro: Opera). Most are open daily 1pm to 1am.

An ever-expanding Barcelona chain, **Pans & Company** (www.pansand company.com) is a little like a Spanish Subway (down to its downscale decor), featuring hot and cold sandwiches on freshly baked baguettes for under 6€ ($6.90). Among the more convenient locations are Princesa 3 (Metro: España), Plaza Callao 3 (Metro: Callao), Goya 5 (Metro: Goya), Gran Vía 30 (Metro: Gran Vía), Serrano 41 (Metro: Serrano), and Orense 8 (Metro: Cuzco). A similar but fancier operation is the chainlet **Bocata y Olé,** at General Martinez Campos 2 (Metro: Iglesia), Goya 45 (Metro: Goya), Fernando VI 2 (Metro: Bilbao), and Glorieta Cuatro Caminos 1 (Metro: Cuatro Caminos). Splashes of pictographic tiles distinguish Bocata y Olé from the simpler Pans, and their sandwiches and salads stay mostly at 3€ to 6€ ($3.45–$6.95).

PICNICKING

To get everything in one place, go to the supermarket at **El Corte Inglés** (see section 5, "Shopping," later in this chapter) or visit the covered **Mercado de San Miguel** on Plaza San Miguel near the northwest corner of Plaza Mayor. Everything at the old market is as fresh as the morning, from sausages and cheeses to dewy produce. Many bake shops and gourmet shops sell salads and sandwiches that are perfect for picnics. Two possibilities are **Rodilla,** on Plaza Callao; and **Ferpal,** at Arenal 7, near Puerta del Sol.

Take your chosen fixings to **El Retiro Park, Parque del Oeste** (northwest of the Royal Palace), or **Casa de Campo.**

4 Seeing the Sights

Capital of Spain since the 16th century, Madrid is the repository of the lion's share of the national patrimony, gathered by monarchs and conquistadors and placed on display in over 50 museums. On view are the surprisingly diminutive sword of the mighty warrior El Cid, sophisticated Iberian sculptures contemporary with the Greeks, the pots and pans of playwright Lope de Vega, the gold and silver of the royal banquet table, the masterworks of Velázquez, and the *Guernica* of Pablo Picasso. Between museums and palaces are the former private hunting grounds of kings, now transformed into vast public parks.

THE TOP MUSEUMS

Monasterio de las Descalzas Reales   In the heart of old Madrid, near Puerta del Sol, this richly endowed royal convent was founded in the mid–16th century in the palace where Juana of Austria, Felipe II's sister, was born. She used it as a retreat and brought the Poor Clare nuns here. For many years, the convent sheltered only royal women, typically the daughters of aristocrats who sequestered the girls until they were old enough for arranged marriages. They didn't live a spartan existence, judging from the wealth of religious artwork that surrounded them, including tapestries, sculptures, and paintings by **Rubens, Bruegel the Elder,** and **Titian.** The main staircase features *trompe l'oeil* paintings and frescoes, and you can view 16 of the 32 lavishly decorated chapels. Compulsory tours for groups of 25 or fewer are conducted in Spanish by guides who hasten visitors from canvas to tapestry to chapel. Try to slow their pace, for there's much to savor.

Plaza de las Descalzas 3. ✆ **91/454-8800.** www.patrimonionacional.es. Admission 5€ ($5.75) adults, 2.50€ ($2.90) seniors, students, and children under 13, free to all Wed. Tues–Thurs and Sat 10:30am–12:45pm and 4–5:45pm; Fri 10:30am–12:45pm; Sun and holidays 11am–1:45pm. Metro: Sol or Callao. Bus: 3, 5, 15, 20, 50, 52, 53, or 150.

Museo Arqueológico Nacional 🏛🏛   Reopened after a couple of years of renovations, this underrated museum is in the same vast building as the National Library (which has a separate entrance on Paseo de Recoletos). It houses antiquities from prehistory to the Middle Ages. Arranged chronologically, the displays are clearly labeled, but only in Spanish. Most of the artifacts

---

⟨*Value* Getting the Best Deal on Sightseeing

- Take advantage of the free admission to most museums on Sunday or Wednesday, or, in several cases after 2:30pm on Saturday.
- Note that over-64 seniors (*jubilados*) are usually accorded half-price admission, as are students. The effective age limit for discounts for young people varies from 12 to 18, while the provision for seniors sometimes applies only to Spanish citizens.
- People-watching from a table at the cafes thrusting into Plaza Mayor can be a treat if you nurse your drinks or snacks. Even if you linger over a soft drink for an hour, no one will suggest you move on.
- Catch the Madrid Vision Bus, which makes a circuit of the major sights and plazas, allowing you to debark and reboard as often as you want for 1 or 2 days.

are related specifically to the development of the Iberian Peninsula, although there are some Egyptian and Greek objects. Most illuminating are the rooms devoted to the Iberian period, before Christ and the waves of sequential conquerors; and those containing relics of the Visigoths, who left relatively little behind, rendering these objects of even greater interest.

A particular treasure is the **Dama de Elche** *(★★*, a resplendent example of 4th century B.C. Iberian sculpture, easily equal to the better-known works produced in Greece at the same time. The Visigothic era (roughly the 5th to the early 8th c. A.D.) is represented by bronzes and funerary offerings from Mérida and some intricate votive crowns and jewelry. Galleries farther on contain several fine Roman mosaic floors, Etruscan pottery, Greek vases, Gothic sculpture and architectural fragments, and Mudéjar woodwork.

Inside the front gate, to the left after you enter, is a reproduction of the **Caves of Altamira.** Because access to the real thing, in northwestern Spain, is sharply restricted, these marginally effective simulations of the 15,000-year-old paintings at least approximate the experience.

Serrano 13 (facing Calle Serrano). © **91/577-7912.** www.man.es. Admission 3€ ($3.45) adults, 1.50€ ($1.75) seniors and students, free for all Sat after 2:30pm. Tues–Sat 9:30am–8:30pm; Sun and holidays 9:30am–2:30pm. Metro: Serrano or Retiro. Bus: 1, 9, 19, 51, 74, or M2.

Museo del Prado *(★★★*   A massive expansion of the Prado, creating two new wings (at press time, scheduled to open in June and Oct 2004), doubles the size of one of the world's most important art museums, giving it enough room to display a good chunk of its 20,000-work collection. Madrid's premier attraction focuses on Spanish painting from the 12th to 19th centuries, as well as Flemish, Italian, and Venetian painters.

Of course, this wouldn't be the Prado if there wasn't a controversy surrounding it: In this case, local residents have been incensed about the destruction of a 15th-century cloister to make way for part of the museum extension.

Whatever the behind-the-scenes problems, this is one of Europe's great treasures. If you have limited time to enjoy this remarkable collection, give priority to the satirical and passionate works of **Goya;** the masterpieces of the unsurpassed technician **Velázquez;** and the sublime, glowing colors of **El Greco,** especially his wrenching *Adoration of the Shepherds.* Velázquez and Goya were court painters, hence the multitude of their paintings here. In the Velázquez rooms, seek out his **portrait of Don Baltasar Carlos,** his depiction of *Los Borrachos (The Drunkards),* and, from the last years of his life, the classic *Las Meninas (★★*. Goya's cartoons are especially popular, although his brutally candid portraits of the royal family and powerful and somber series of **Black Paintings** *(★★* also have their admirers.

Other important canvases are those of the Spaniards **Ribera, Zurbarán,** and **Murillo,** as well as masterpieces by **Hieronymus Bosch** (known to this museum as "El Bosco"), in particular Bosch's nightmarish *Garden of Earthly Delights (★*; still more works are by **Dürer, Titian, Tintoretto, Rubens,** and **Van Dyck.** Too often ignored among these riches are the startling **Gothic diptychs** and

---

Tips **A Plan for the Prado**

A good plan for your visit to the Prado is to focus on two or three specific sections, returning for visits of an hour or so on separate occasions. There's no way you can absorb the whole at one lunge.

Madrid

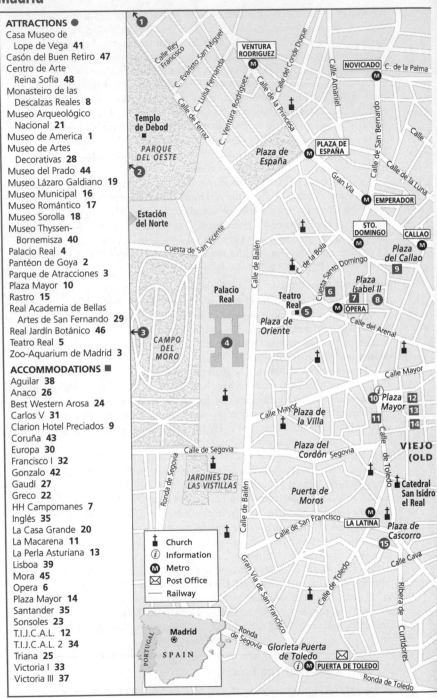

† Church
ⓘ Information
Ⓜ Metro
⊠ Post Office
— Railway

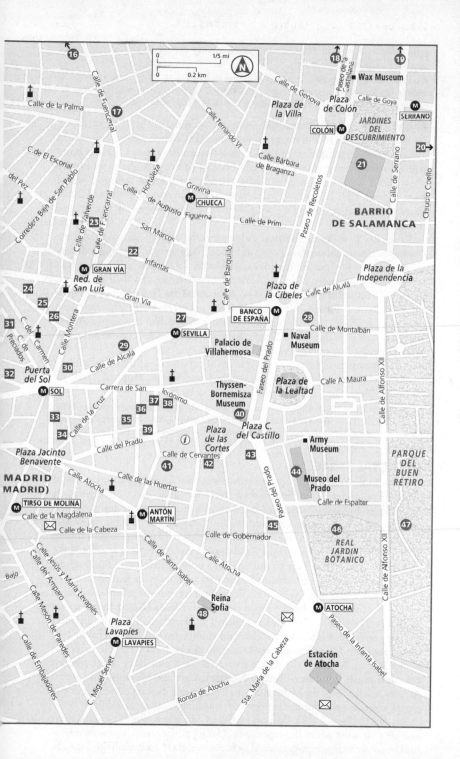

triptychs on the main floor, all in gilded frames carved in the sort of detail accorded facades of cathedrals.

Paseo del Prado. ⓒ 91/330-2800. http://museoprado.mcu.es. Admission 3€ ($3.45) adults, 1.50€ ($1.75) students, free for seniors and children, free for all Sat after 2:30pm and Sun. Tues–Sat 9am–7pm; Sun 9am–2pm. Metro: Atocha or Banco de España. Bus: 1, 2, 9, 10, 14, 19, 27, 34, 37, or 45.

Museo Thyssen-Bornemisza 🎨🎨   On display in the late-18th-century Palacio de Villahermosa and an extension that opened in March 2004 are the works gathered by three generations of the Thyssen-Bornemisza family (*Tees*-ahn Bore-noh-*mees*-uh). The museum's quirky collection of paintings is like an art-history class, with a representation or two of practically every major style and period from the late 13th century to the present. The collection of 19th- and 20th-century paintings is especially strong—certainly the strongest of any Madrid museum.

To see the artworks in historical order, cross the central court and take the central staircase or elevator to the second floor. The gallery numbering indicates the suggested route, proceeding counterclockwise. In the first galleries are Italian primitives of the last centuries before the Renaissance and their successors, including **Tintoretto** and **Bernini.** Also represented are Dutch, Spanish, Flemish, German, and French artists. Of particular note, because they're rarely seen in Spain, are works by 19th-century American artists like landscapist **Albert Bierstadt** and portraitist **John Singer Sargent,** and French Impressionists and Post-Impressionists, such as **Manet, Monet, Renoir,** and **Degas.** They're followed by examples of the modernist schools of cubism, constructivism, surrealism, and abstract expressionism, exemplified by **Picasso, Hopper, Dalí, de Kooning, Mondrian,** and **Cornell.** There is a *cafetería.*

Paseo del Prado 8. ⓒ 91/369-0151. www.museothyssen.org. Admission to permanent collection 4.80€ ($5.50) adults, 3€ ($3.45) seniors and students, free for children under 12; admission to temporary exhibits 3.60€ ($4.15) adults, 2.40€ ($2.75) seniors and students, free for children under 12. Tues–Sun 10am–7pm. Metro: Atocha or Banco de España. Bus: 1, 2, 5, 9, 10, 14, 15, 20, 27, 34, 37, 45, 51, 52, 53, 74, 146, or 150.

THE ROYAL PALACE

Palacio Real 🎨🎨🎨   This opulent palace was built for Felipe V on the site of the medieval Alcázar, a fortified castle that burned in the mid–18th century. It was designed by Giovanni Battista Sacchetti in a mix of baroque and neoclassical styles. Of note are Italian architect Sabatini's majestic staircase, the many dazzling chandeliers, and the superb tapestry collection. There are an astonishing 2,800 rooms, including Gasparini's flamboyantly rococo **drawing room** and the **Throne Room** with its Tiepolo ceiling. (As a point of reference, Buckingham Palace doesn't have even 600 rooms.) About 50 are on view at any one time.

King Juan Carlos and Queen Sofía don't live here, but the palace is still used for state functions. Some lucky visitors get to see the **State Dining Room** set for a banquet. The table, which can seat almost 150, stretches off into the distance, gleaming with silver, gold, and cut glass and illuminated by 15 giant chandeliers. Next door is the **Clock Room,** where over 60 clocks, mostly French, strike the hour together. As well as the palace apartments, the tour takes in the **library, coin and music museums, Royal Pharmacy, Carriage Museum,** and **Royal Armory,** easily one of the highlights with its imposing displays of weaponry and armor, some designed for battle dogs and, touchingly, the royal toddlers.

You can go through the rooms on your own, but take one of the guided tours and get a lot more out of the experience. During peak periods, tours are assembled by common language groups; at slower times, there are multilingual guides.

Special & Free Events

Every year, Madrid launches itself into fiesta after fiesta, with parades, dancing in the streets, fireworks, crafts fairs, bullfights, and concerts. Check the weekly *Guía del Ocio* for full details. Among the highlights:

Around Christmas and New Year's, the city is alive with excitement that culminates in a great gathering beneath Puerta del Sol's big clock on **New Year's Eve**. Take 12 grapes and pop one in your mouth for each strike of the clock at midnight. Those who are up to the challenge will have good luck all year. On January 5, the **Reyes Magos (Three Kings)** arrive (by helicopter nowadays) for an exuberant parade on horseback through the streets.

In March, the **Madrid Theater Festival** attracts a galaxy of international companies. On the Saturday before Lent, hundreds of gaily decorated floats parade down Paseo de la Castellana in a **Carnaval** procession. **Semana Santa (Holy Week)** is celebrated with due solemnity, and processions of the penitents take place all over Madrid, including around Puerta del Sol. Around **Easter** there's a gathering of horses and their riders from Seville, who step through the streets attired in colorful traditional style, beginning and ending their parade at El Retiro Park.

The most important festival celebrates the patron saint of Madrid, **San Isidro,** in mid-May, with a protracted program of activities and the best bullfights of the year. In late June, the gay and lesbian community celebrates with a **Gay Pride Parade** from Puerta de Alcalá to Puerta del Sol. The **Veranos de la Villa** provides summer entertainment for the long, warm evenings, including open-air movies at the Cine del Retiro and flamenco shows in another corner of the park. Fall brings Madrid's acclaimed **jazz festival** and the **Feriarte,** Spain's major antiques fair. The **Fundación Juan March,** Castelló 77 (*©* **91/435-4240**), offers free concerts fall to spring, on Monday and Saturday at noon and Wednesday at 7:30pm, changing the theme monthly.

Religious festivals are celebrated with parades and pageantry, particularly the Procession of the Three Kings on January 5, Carnaval before Lent, and the solemn processions of the penitents during Holy Week.

Plaza de Oriente, Calle de Bailén 2. (*©* **91/454-8800.** www.patrimonionacional.es. Admission 8€ ($9.20) adults, 3.50€ ($4) seniors, students, and children under 12; 1€ ($1.15) extra for guided tours; additional fees for temporary exhibits. Mon–Sat 9:30am–5:30pm; Sun and holidays 9am–3pm. Metro: Opera. Bus: 3, 25, 39, or 148.

MORE MUSEUMS

Casa Museo de Lope de Vega　An extraordinarily prolific 17th-century playwright, Lope de Vega is credited with over 1,800 works. He lived and died in this house on a street ironically named for a contemporary he bitterly resented, Miguel de Cervantes, author of *Don Quijote de La Mancha*. The house, relatively modest considering Vega's substantial popular success, has been carefully reconstructed

---

Tips **Museum Notes**

Always check museum hours before setting out, particularly at the smaller ones, for they're prone to sudden changes and closures. Keep in mind that most museums are closed on Monday, so save that day for the Palacio Real and the Centro de Arte Reine Sofía, which are open. Most museums are also closed January 1, Good Friday, May 1, and December 26, but many, including the Prado, now stay open through the afternoon siesta, when most stores are closed.

---

and declared a national monument. Inside are his study, bedroom, and kitchen; out back is his garden.

Cervantes 11. ℗ **91/429-9216.** www.rae.es. Admission 1.50€ ($1.75) adults, 1€ ($1.15) seniors and students. Tues–Fri 9:30am–2pm; Sat 10am–2pm. Metro: Antón Martín or Sevilla.

Centro de Arte Reina Sofía ⚘ This 19th-century hospital was converted into a museum to serve as a repository of 20th-century art, but its collection remains sparse and unbalanced. The Reina Sofía's direction has been controversial from the outset, with some government members contending it should concentrate on Spanish artists and its directors insisting its mission should focus on currents in international thought. To date, its successes have usually been with temporary exhibits rather than with highlights from its permanent collection. A wing devoted entirely to temporary exhibits was scheduled to open around press time, so check the museum's website for updates.

One triumph was the wresting of Picasso's fabled *Guernica* ⚘⚘⚘ from the Prado, which had held it since its return from New York's Museum of Modern Art after Franco's death. The mural is now the museum's centerpiece, and the once highly restrictive security barriers have been removed. Largely second-rank work by mostly Spanish artists like **Dalí, Miró, Gris,** and **Solana** supplements Picasso's masterwork. For the moment, the center's most interesting element might be the former 18th-century hospital itself, renovated inside and with see-through elevator shafts on the exterior.

Santa Isabel 52 (at the corner of Atocha). ℗ **91/467-5062.** http://museoreinasofia.mcu.es. Admission 3€ ($3.45) adults, 1.50€ ($1.75) students and children under 12, free for all Sat after 2:30, free for seniors and children Sun. Mon–Sat 10am–9pm; Sun 10am–2:30pm. Metro: Atocha.

Museo de América This museum in the University City/Moncloa section received a $15-million renovation and reopened after 13 years. Its expanded galleries are devoted to ethnological and archaeological collections from Spain's former colonies in the Americas and the Philippines. Of note are those rooms dealing with the social organization and daily lives of the various Native American tribes and nations, and the wealth of artifacts related to the observance of their religions. The pre-Columbian jewelry, statuary, and other artifacts are illustrative.

Av. Reyes Católicos 6. ℗ **91/549-2641.** www.geocities.com/museo_de_america. Admission 3€ ($3.45) adults, 1.50€ ($1.75) students and children under 12, free for all Sun. Tues–Sat 10am–3pm; Sun and holidays 10am–2:30pm. Metro: Moncloa.

Museo de Artes Decorativas Crammed with furniture, leatherwork, wall hangings, ceramics, rugs, porcelain, glass, jewelry, toys, dollhouses, clothes, and lace, the museum progresses in chronological order after the introductory ground floor, tracing the development of Spanish interior decoration from the 15th to the 19th centuries. By the fifth floor, the amplitude might become numbing to any but scholars and practitioners, although the immense variety of objects still has the capacity to intrigue.

Montalban 12 (off Plaza de las Cibeles). © **91/532-6499.** mnartesdecorativas.mcu.es. Admission 2.40€ ($2.75) adults, 1.20€ ($1.35) students and children under 12, free for all Sun. Tues–Fri 9:30am–3pm; Sat–Sun and holidays 10am–2pm. Metro: Retiro.

Museo Lázaro Galdiano   Madrid was the beneficiary of financier/author José Lázaro Galdiano's largesse, for when he died, he left the city his 30-room early-1900s mansion and substantial private collection. Every floor attests to his devotion to art. There are paintings from Spain's Golden Age, including works by Spaniards **El Greco, Ribera, Zurbarán, Murillo,** and **Goya.** Among Renaissance Italians represented are **Tiepolo** and **Leonardo da Vinci,** and canvases by Englishmen **Gainsborough** and **Constable** are on view. However, the museum is most admired for its comprehensive array of **enamels, ivories,** and **works in gold and silver,** much of it created during the Middle Ages. A multiyear renovation, scheduled for completion in 2004, will give the collection the space it deserves.

Serrano 122. © **91/561-6084.** www.flg.es/museo/museo.htm Admission 3€ ($3.45) adults, 1.50€ ($1.75) students, free for seniors and children under 12, free for all Sat. Tues–Sun 10am–2pm. Closed holidays and Aug. Metro: Rubén Dario. Bus: 9, 16, 19, 51, or 89.

Museo Municipal   Here Madrid's history is explained through paintings, prints, documents, scale models, carriages, and costumes. In the basement are two large Roman mosaic floors and other artifacts. Easily as interesting is the eye-popping rococo entrance, crowded with cherubim and warriors, designed by Pedro de Ribera to grace what was formerly an 18th-century hospice for the city's poor.
Note: The museum was closed for renovation at press time.

Fuencarral 78. © **91/588-8672.** www.munimadrid.es/museomunicipal. Admission 1.80€ ($2.05) adults, .90€ ($1.05) seniors, students, and children under 18, free for all Wed and Sun. Tues–Fri 9:30am–8pm; Sat–Sun 10am–2pm. Metro: Tribunal.

Museo Romántico (Romantic Museum)   This collection of furniture, paintings, and objets d'art from the Romantic period of the early 19th century was assembled by the philanthropic marquis of La Vega–Inclán. Housed in an 18th-century baroque mansion, it juxtaposes dollhouses and Goyas with antic flair.
Note: The museum was closed for renovations at press time.

San Mateo 13. © **91/448-1045.** museoromantico.mcu.es. Admission 2.40€ ($2.75) adults, 1.20€ ($1.40) students, free for seniors and children under 12, free for all Sun. Tues–Sat 9am–3pm; Sun and holidays 10am–2pm. Closed Aug. Metro: Tribunal. Bus: 3, 37, 40, or 149.

⟨Tips⟩ The Return of the Royal

In late 1997, the 1,750-seat **Teatro Real (Royal Opera House),** Plaza de Oriente s/n (© **91/516-0660;** www.teatro-real.com; Metro: Opera), reopened after almost a decade of false starts and agonizingly slow construction that cost $157 million. It hadn't experienced an operatic performance for more than 70 years, opening and closing irregularly over that time to serve as an orchestral concert hall. Guided tours (4€/$4.60) of the grand hall are available weekdays except Tuesday from 10:30am to 1pm, and Saturday, Sunday, and holidays 11am to 1:30pm.

Museo Sorolla   The museum of painter Joaquín Sorolla has a down-to-earth homeyness after the conspicuous grandeur of many of Madrid's other museums. Sorolla (1863–1923) was born and raised on the coast of Valencia, and his later works, many of them seascapes, were influenced by the French Impressionists. The museum is in the house/studio where he lived and worked the last 11 years of his life—it has been kept (on the ground floor at least) as it was when he died. He was an avid collector, as is evidenced by the large quantity of Spanish ceramics he owned.

General Martínez Campos 37. ℭ 91/310-1584. http://museosorolla.mcu.es. Admission 2.40€ ($2.75) adults, 1.20€ ($1.40) students, free for seniors and children under 12, free for all Sun. Tues–Sat 9:30am–3pm; Sun and holidays 10am–3pm. Metro: Iglesia, Rubén Dario. Bus: 5,

Real Academia de Bellas Artes de San Fernando   This center, in a restored building east of Puerta del Sol, offers a wide variety of works by artists like **El Greco, Zurbarán, Sorolla, Ribera, Murillo, Rubens,** and **Fragonard,** plus one room filled with **Goyas,** produced in the artist's mature years. After a showy display of these heavyweights, the rooms in back contain a diversity of Chinese terra cottas, Egyptian bronzes, and small sculptures.

Alcalá 13. ℭ 91/524-0864. http://rabasf.insde.es. Admission 2.40€ ($2.75) adults, 1.20€ ($1.40) students, free for seniors and children under 18. Tues–Fri 10am–2pm and 5–8pm; Sat–Mon and holidays 10am–2pm. Metro: Sol or Sevilla.

OTHER ATTRACTIONS

Panteón de Goya (Goya's Tomb)   Carlos IV commissioned Francisco de Goya to decorate the ceiling in the chapel dome of this 1797 hermitage. His frescoes, depicting the story of St. Anthony of Padua, are populated with plump cherubs and voluptuous angels who were modeled after members of the Spanish court and Madrid society. Some of the women portrayed were rumored to be prostitutes. Goya is buried here, but somehow his head got lost in transit from Bordeaux, where he was first interred.

San António de la Florida 5. ℭ 91/542-0722. www.munimadrid.es/ermita. Admission 2€ ($2.30) adults, 1€ ($1.15) seniors and children under 18, free for all Wed and Sun. Tues–Fri 10am–2pm and 4–8pm; Sat–Sun 10am–2pm. Metro: Principe Pio. Bus: 41, 46, 75, or C.

Parque de Atracciones (Amusement Park) *Kids*   In the spacious Casa del Campo west of the Royal Palace, this amusement park offers over 40 rides, plus an auditorium staging summer shows (free with admission), restaurants, electronic games, and a cinema. To make a special excursion of the trip, take the **cable car** (*teleférico;* www.teleferico.com) from Paseo del Pintor Rosales, at the western edge of the city, high above the trees of the Casa del Campo. After a ride of a little over 10 minutes, it deposits you within a 10-minute walk of the park. Fares are 2.85€ ($3.30) one-way and 4.10€ ($4.70) round-trip (free for infants).

In Casa de Campo. ℭ 91/463-2900. www.parquedeatracciones.es. Admission to park 5.10€ ($5.85); admission to park and all rides 22€ ($25) adults, 12€ ($14) children under 8; each ride 1.50€ ($1.75). Open hours subject to frequent changes; park open daily noon to past 10pm June to mid-Sept, and at least weekends noon–7pm the rest of the year. Metro: Batan. Bus: 33 or 65.

Zoo-Aquarium de Madrid *Kids*   Madrid's zoo is Spain's best, but it doesn't really compare to such superior facilities as those of San Diego, New York, or Berlin. Most animals are housed in open pens rather than cages, separated from the public by ditches. Over 3,000 mammals, birds, and reptiles are grouped according to their continents of origin. Highlights are the two pandas, **Chang-Chang** and his offspring, **Chu-Lin,** the first panda in Europe to be born in captivity. The **aquarium and dolphin show** (1 and 5pm) also deserve attention, as do the **flights of raptors** staged both morning and afternoon. It's a 15-minute walk from the park's cable-car station (see "Parque de Atracciones," above).

In Casa del Campo. © 91/512-3770. www.zoomadrid.com. Admission 13€ ($15) adults, 10€ ($12) chil-dren 3–7 and seniors, free for infants. Mon–Fri 10:30am–sunset. Metro: Casa de Campo. Bus: 33.

PARKS & GARDENS

The 128-hectare (321-acre) **Parque del Retiro** is what's left of the grounds of a 17th-century palace and grounds built for Felipe IV. Now the tree-lined walk-ways, formal rose garden, Crystal Palace, boating lake, monuments, and grottoes offer a popular retreat for all. *Madrileños* like to see and be seen, and on week-ends entire three- and four-generation families dress up for the *paseo* through the park. Jugglers, tarot readers, musicians, puppeteers, caricaturists, Chinese and Japanese massage therapists, and scantily clad female gymnasts all set up shop along the pathway leading past the lake and the overwrought monument to Alfonso XII that looms over it. The main entrance to the park is on the south side of Plaza de la Independencia. The park is open 24 hours, but avoid it at night.

To the south of the Prado Museum is the **Réal Jardín Botánico,** laid out here in the 18th century, where you can enjoy a wide range of exotic flora. The garden is at its most appealing in spring and summer, of course, but serious gardeners will find plantings of interest even in winter. Admission is 1.50€ ($1.75).

North and west of the Royal Palace, respectively, are the **Jardines de Sabatini** and **Campo del Moro.** Just to the north of them is the **Parque de la Montaña,** which contains the **Templo de Debod,** a 4th-century B.C. Egyptian temple given to Spain in appreciation of its assistance in the building of the Aswan High Dam. Admission is 1.80€ ($2.05), free on Wednesday and Sunday. The temple and the Parque de la Montaña are at the lower end of the larger **Parque del Oeste (West Park),** adjoining **La Rosaleda (The Rose Garden).**

Bordering them on Paseo Pintor Rosales are several open-air bars and the east-ern terminus of the *teleférico* (cable car) that swings out over the Manzanares River and deep into the **Casa del Campo.** This semi-wild preserve, west of the Royal Palace and the city, is an enormous playground for all Madrileños. Here you'll find the zoo-aquarium and the Parque de Atracciones (see reviews above), an exhibition center, a boating lake, a sports center, restaurants, and plenty of space to get away from it all.

ORGANIZED TOURS

The best deals can be found with the two companies whose buses follow set routes allowing you to get off and reboard at more than a dozen museums, plazas, and other major stops. One of them is the distinctive **Madrid Vision Bus** (© **91/767-1743;** www.madridvision.es), whose air-conditioned buses feature multilingual guides who provide info over earphones. Three routes make color-coded, 75-minute loops around themed sets of monuments and buildings; choose Historic Madrid, Modern Madrid, or the length of the Gran Vía. Con-venient places to pick up the bus are at the Puerta de Alcalá and Puerta del Sol. A full-day ticket costs 9.60€ ($11).

Pullmantur, Plaza de Oriente 8 (© **91/541-1807;** www.pullmantur-spain.com; Metro: Opera), is one of Spain's largest tour operators and offers sev-eral guided city tours, including a half-day tour of the Palacio Real and the Prado for 36€ ($41) and a 2-hour nighttime city tour leaving at 8:30pm for 13€ ($14).

Pullmantur also offers full-day excursion tours to Toledo, Avila, and Segovia. Similar out-of-town possibilities are supplied by **Juliá Tours,** Gran Vía 68 (© **91/ 559-9605;** Metro: Gran Vía), and **Trapsatur,** San Bernardo 23 (© **91/542- 6666**). Expect full-day tours to Toledo or to Avila and Segovia to cost around 60€ to 70€ ($69–$81) and half-day tours to run 40€ ($46) or so.

5 Shopping

Madrid's shopping selection is enormous, and the service, particularly in smaller stores, is usually friendly. Everything expected of a modern European capital is at hand, from ultra-modish clothing boutiques to aromatic cigar shops, along the pedestrian walkways **Calle Preciados** and **Calle del Carmen** north of Puerta del Sol (Metro: Sol). Should you desire a splurge or a bit of fantasy-provoking window-shopping, head for the **Salamanca** district, between calles Serrano and Velázquez, Goya, and Juan Bravo (Metro: Serrano), where the tony designer shops compete. The **AZCA area,** between Paseo de la Castellana and Orense, Raimundo Fernández Villaverde, and General Perón, is also worth a visit (Metro: Nuevos Ministerios), especially for its high-fashion mall, **La Moda.** A larger mall known as **Madrid-2** is at La Vaguada (Metro: Barrio del Pilar), with over 350 stores, including an excellent food market.

The major department store chain, **El Corte Inglés,** Preciados 3 (© **91/418- 8800** for information on all branches; Metro: Sol), has just about every category of product, including food markets and bargain basements *(oportunidades)*. All branches have some English-speaking salespeople, as well as those tending the info desks. Other branches are located at Goya 76 (Metro: Goya); Princesa 42 (Metro: España); and Raimundo Fernández Villaverde 79, at the corner of Paseo de la Castellana (Metro: Nuevos Ministerios). Competition for El Corte Inglés has arrived just up the street from the Preciados location in **FNAC,** Preciados 28 (© **91/595-6100;** Metro: Sol), a chain of stores concentrating on photographic and audio equipment, video games, TVs, software, computers, and books. Predictably, El Corte Inglés has opened a mirror-image operation right next door. With a substantial stock of CDs in most musical persuasions, **Madrid Rock,** Gran Vía 25 (© **91/523-2652;** Metro: Gran Vía), also sells tickets to pop concerts. Near Madrid Rock is **La Casa del Libro,** Gran Vía 29 (© **91/521-2113;** Metro: Gran Vía), a large bookstore with a sizable English-language section. **Berkana,** Hortaleza 64 (© **91/522-5599;** Metro: Chueca), Madrid's gay bookstore, is well stocked with Spanish editions of gay books, comic books, magazines, a few gifts, and a spectacularly helpful staff.

For unique craft items, **El Arco de los Cuchilleros Artesiana de Hoy,** Plaza Mayor 9 (basement; © **91/365-2680;** Metro: Sol or Opera), may be a mouthful

---

⌜Tips⌝ Shopping Notes

El Corte Inglés, FNAC, and the larger shopping centers are open straight through from 10am to 9 or 9:30pm; however, almost every place else closes for lunch at 1:30 or 2pm and doesn't reopen until 5pm. In July and August, many stores close on Saturday afternoon, and smaller ones might even close completely for their month's vacation.

January, February, and July are the times for the big sales *(rebajas),* when virtually every store in Madrid offers discounts that increase as the month proceeds.

of a name to remember, but it has an unparalleled array of pottery, leather, textiles, glassware, and jewelry produced by individual artisans throughout Spain. It's open daily 11am to 8pm, even during siesta. Shopping for food in Madrid can be frustrating, as it's illegal to bring most foodstuffs back to North America. So pop into gourmet store **Majorca,** Velázquez 59 (© **91/431-9909;** Metro: Velázquez), to ogle the cheeses, meats, and pâtés, and pick up a few to eat in a local park or back at your hotel.

Bargains are rarely found at the famed **El Rastro flea market,** so forget about plucking an unsigned Goya drawing or a Roman coin from the heaps on display. Still, it's fun to browse. The market takes place in the streets of the triangle formed by the San Isidro church, Puerta de Toledo, and Glorieta de Embajadores. Ribera de Curtidores is its main street and La Latina the nearest metro stop. On Sunday mornings, thousands of Madrileños throng these streets to buy everything from songbirds and sweaters to audiotapes and picture frames. Saturday morning is quieter for browsing through the bordering antiques shops and secondhand stalls. Bargaining is expected. Everyone tells you to be especially protective of your valuables—*believe them.* Pickpockets abound.

6 Madrid After Dark

No city revels in the night as does Madrid. With dinner often ending past midnight, and with clubs and discos staying open until 6am—and even later—the salient question is not what to do, but when to sleep. For details on the former, check the weekly *Guía del Ocio* or the daily entertainment section in *El País,* which publishes a booklet of listings and reviews in its Friday editions. The listings are in Spanish but aren't difficult to decipher. *Shangay,* free at most gay clubs and cafes, lists events and performances of interest to gays and lesbians. On the Web, check **www.in-madrid.com** for current listings; once in town, an English-language printed version is available at selected cafes and tourist offices.

THE PERFORMING ARTS

Madrid's performing arts are enjoying a renaissance, with the high visibility of Spanish tenors Plácido Domingo and José Carreras, and touring organizations such as the National Ballet of Spain and the Compañia Nacional de Danza gathering critical bouquets on five continents.

English-language theatrical productions do stop here from time to time, but more often Broadway, Off-Broadway, and West End productions are presented in Spanish—*My Fair Lady* and *The Vagina Monologues* being recent examples. If you don't understand Spanish you'll hardly be deprived, however, not with the abundant classical and modern dance performances, symphonies and chamber-music recitals, concerts by touring pop and rock stars, opera, and *zarzuela* (a popular native form of operetta with its own dedicated venue).

THEATER, OPERA & *ZARZUELA*   Recent productions at the **Teatro Real,** Plaza de Oriente (© **91/516-0660;** Metro: Opera), reopened in 2000, included productions of *La Traviata, Diary of One Who Disappeared, Tosca,* and *Siegfried,* as well as solo recitals and five ballets.

Among the over 20 theaters showing imported musicals, ballets, *zarzuelas,* and other folkloric singing festivals are the **Teatro Lope de Vega,** Gran Vía 57 (© **90/226-2726;** Metro: Santo Domingo), and **Teatro Alcázar,** Alcalá 20 (© **90/226-2726;** Metro: Sevilla). Classic Spanish plays by authors such as García Lorca and Valle Inclán are the staple at the **Teatro de la Comedia,** Príncipe 14 (© **91/521-5931;** Metro: Sevilla). Run by City Hall, the **Centro Cultural**

Tips   Theater Discounts & Last-Minute Tix

Theater tickets go from 2.40€ to 21€ ($2.75–$24) or more. On certain days (usually Wed or Sun's 1st performance), discounts of up to 50% are available. Most performances are at 10:30pm, but some start at 8 or 9pm. It's best to buy tickets at the theater because agencies charge a considerable markup. If the preferred performance is sold out, you might be able to get tickets at the **Localidades Galicia,** Plaza del Carmen 1 (© **91/531-2732;** www.eol.es/lgalicia; Metro: Sol), to the left of the Madrid Multicine, open Tuesday to Sunday 10am to 1pm and 4:30 to 7:30pm (closed holidays). It also sells bullfight and soccer tickets.

---

de la Villa de Madrid, Jardines del Descubrimiento (© **90/210-1212;** Metro: Colón), a smallish cultural center under Plaza de Colón, puts on plays, recitals, dance events, and concerts of all kinds and is the scene of much activity during the Festival del Otoño (Fall Festival).

Now the venerable **Teatro de la Zarzuela,** Jovellanos 4 (© **91/524-5400;** Metro: Banco de España or Sevilla), can focus on the folkloric musical form for which it's named, since the Teatro Real has reopened. However, it does continue to stage performances of the National Ballet of Spain.

CLASSICAL MUSIC   The National Orchestra of Spain performs in the **Auditorio Nacional de Música (National Auditorium of Music),** Príncipe de Vergara 146 (© **91/337-0139;** www.auditorionacional.mcu.es; Metro: Cruz del Rayo), where 2,000 music lovers can enjoy the best of Spanish and international classical music in a modern setting of wood and marble with excellent acoustics. There's also a smaller concert hall, seating 600. Recitals and chamber-music groups are often presented, frequently for free, at the **Fundación Juan March,** Castelló 77 (© **91/435-4240;** www.march.es; Metro: Núñez Balboa), and at **Círculo de Bellas Artes,** Alcalá 42 (© **91/360-5400;** www.circulobellasartes.com; Metro: Banco de España).

FLAMENCO   The clubs in which flamenco is performed are called *tablaos.* Although not the birthplace of the unique Andalusian meld of music and dance, Madrid does have *tablaos* that are fairly authentic, if expensive. Doors usually open at 9 or 9:30pm, and the show starts at about 10:45pm and ends at 12:30am or even later. To save money, go after dinner, when the still-hefty admission at least includes a drink. The later performances are usually better anyway, after the tour groups leave and the performers are warmed up. These stages feature large troupes with several dancers, two or three guitarists, and one or two singers, all in costume. Among the established *tablaos* are **Torres Bermejas,** Mesonero Romanos 11 (© **91/532-3322;** Metro: Callao); **Corral de la Morería,** Morería 17 (© **91/365-8446;** Metro: Opera); and **Café de Chinitas,** Torija 7 (© **91/559-5135;** Metro: Santo Domingo).

For a flamenco club that doesn't cater primarily to tourists, try **Casa Patas,** Cañizares 10 (© **91/369-0496;** www.casapatas.com; Metro: Antón Martín). In front, it's a restaurant, with a long bar, a high ceiling held up by cast-iron pillars, and three rows of tables with checked tablecloths. A pot-bellied stove at its center provides heat, and photos of matadors and flamenco performers cover the walls. That's not where the shows are, though. Go to the closed door in back. Shortly before showtime, a shuttered window opens, they take your money, and you are allowed to enter. You are seated at tiny tables around the open stage; drink orders are taken. The composition of the performers might vary slightly from the traditional—a flutist as well as guitarists—but the song will be powerful and the dancing fiery and gripping. Shows are held Monday through Thursday at 10:30pm, Friday and Saturday at 9pm and midnight. Call ahead to reserve a table. The cover is 25€ ($29) per person, 30€ ($35) on Friday and Saturday. It's worth the cost and effort, for this is modern flamenco at its best.

With the legendary **La Soleá** now closed, the place to go for *cante hondo* (deep song) is **Monteleón,** Monteleón 46 (© **91/445-6487;** Metro: San Bernardo). Monteleón observes the same format as the older club: one or two guitarists, a few singers, little or no dancing, and audience members occasionally getting caught up in the act. Things get started at 11pm and become really fun around 1am or so. There's no cover, but performers expect tips. La Soleá wasn't especially touristy, and Monteleón is even less so.

JAZZ BARS   Café Central, Plaza del Angel 10 (© **91/369-4143;** www. cafecentralmadrid.com; Metro: Sol or Antón Martín), is *the* place for live jazz and is usually packed with students, tourists, and Madrid's night beauties. Black bench seating, marble topped tables, and glistening brass set the scene. Performances are usually at 10pm and midnight. While jazz is the main course, the cafe also hosts folkies, blues belters, and performers of related music. Calle de las Huertas runs through this plaza, so the cafe can be the start or end of an extended pub-crawl. It's open daily 1:30pm to 2 or 3am, with a cover that usually varies from 10€ to 15€ ($11–$17).

Not far from the Central is **Café Jazz Populart,** Huertas 22 (© **91/429-8407;** www.populart.es; Metro: Antón Martín), a showcase for American blues, Latin salsa, and Caribbean reggae as well as the many shadings of jazz. The large space allows a little elbowroom, and the tone is laid-back at the marble-topped bar or the tables ringing the stage. Admission is often free, but the prices of drinks tend to jump sharply when music is playing. Still, it's cheaper than Central. It's open daily 6pm to 3 or 4am, with shows at 11pm and 12:30am.

BARS & PUBS

AROUND PLAZA DE SANTA ANA   *The* destination for a grand *tapeo,* Plaza de Santa Ana and the streets adjoining it are hip-to-hip with beer pubs and ancient taverns. While sherry *(fino)* is the classic tipple with tapas, red and white wines and beer are more evident, and no one sneers at an order for mineral water or Coca-Cola. Ask for a *copa de tinto, blanco,* or *rosado* (rosé) if you want a small tumbler of the wine, or for a *caña* to get a short glass of about 6 ounces of draft beer.

Half a block west of Plaza de Santa, the tavern **Las Bravas,** Pasaje de Matheu 5 (© **91/521-5141;** Metro: Sol), is supposedly the inventor of *patatas bravas,* the spicily sauced potatoes that are one of the most popular of all tapas. (There are four Las Bravas branches within a 4-block radius, all run by the same crew.) Las Bravas *patatas* feature the official Brava sauce, thin and loaded with paprika, without the mayonnaise component you get everywhere else. Go Friday or Saturday evening for the sideshow barker performances of the auxiliary waiters, who work the crowd shamelessly expediting food service.

As its name suggests, the *tasca* **Cervecería Alemaña,** Plaza de Santa Ana 6 (© **91/429-7033;** Metro: Sol or Antón Martín), was once a popular haunt of German residents; Hemingway liked it, too. It has been in business since 1904, and the bullfighting prints on the wood-paneled walls, the marble-topped tables, and the beamed ceiling provide a vintage atmosphere. Open Sunday to

Thursday 10:30am to 12:30am and Friday and Saturday 10:30am to 2am. **La Fontana de Oro,** Victoria 2 (© **91/531-0420;** Metro: Sol), is a fairly persuasive replica of a Dublin pub, 1 of at least 20 recently opened in Madrid. The music from the corner stage or the DJ, though, is as often Latin or disco as it is Irish. Sunday from 9pm is for dancing to recorded salsa, swing, paso doble, and tango. Guinness Stout is on tap. Open daily 9am to 5am, it's about midway between Puerta del Sol and Plaza de Santa Ana, with plenty of better places to eat all around. No cover. Another example of the breed is the hot **O'Connell St.,** Espoz y Mina 7 (no phone; Metro: Sol), where people line up for an hour to get inside. Bands play Thursday, Friday, and Sunday, and six TVs show soccer, rugby, and NFL football games on Sunday. Happy hour is from 7 to 10pm, with a free shot for every pint of beer.

Pop in for a quick drink to admire the variety of patterned ceramic tiles covering the walls of the five rooms of **Los Gabrieles,** Echegaray 17 (© **91/429-6261;** Metro: Sol or Sevilla), a century-old tavern. Live music, mostly flamenco, is presented Tuesday nights (no cover). It's open daily 1pm to 2:30am (an hour later Fri–Sat). Students and 20-something singles have given the 1890 tavern **Viva Madrid,** Manuel Fernández González 7 (© **91/429-3640;** Metro: Sol or Antón Martín), new life as a trendy meeting place. Both the facade and the interior are resplendent with intricately patterned tiles, and mythical creatures hold up carved ceilings. Light meals and tapas are served in the room behind the bar. It's open daily 1pm to 2am (an hour later Fri–Sat).

ALONG CALLE DE LAS HUERTAS For maxed-out barhopping, Calle de las Huertas, parallel to Calle de Santa María, and the adjoining streets can't be exhausted in a month of Saturdays. It starts a bit east of Plaza Mayor but doesn't shift into high gear until Plaza del Angel, south of Plaza de Santa Ana, when it runs downhill toward Paseo del Prado.

Cervantes lived upstairs over 380 years ago, and **Casa Alberto,** Huertas 18 (© **91/429-9356;** Metro: Sol or Antón Martín), a narrow bar with a rear dining room, has been in business for almost half that time. With a stone bar and an elaborately carved wood ceiling, Alberto is popular with a mixed crowd that drops in for its ambience and tapas Tuesday to Saturday noon to 1am and Sunday noon to 5pm. Full meals are served in back. With rock and Latino music roaring out of every other door, the individualist bar **La Fídula,** Huertas 57 (© **91/429-2947;** Metro: Antón Martín), makes its statement with recitals by performers of classical music, art song, jazz, and poetry Friday and Saturday from about midnight. The room is cozy even without music, and the Irish coffees don't diminish the mood. Performance times, more or less, are Thursday and Sunday at 9 and 11pm and Friday and Saturday at 11:30pm and 1am.

COCKTAIL LOUNGES

Hemingway and his journalist buddies suffered the siege of Madrid during the Civil War at **Chicote,** Gran Vía 12 (© **91/532-6737;** Metro: Gran Vía). Photos on the walls to the left and right of the entrance document the patronage of Coop, Ty, Orson, and Ava. While a superior martini is still available, they've added breakfasts and light meals. At **Cock,** Reina 12 (© **91/532-2826;** Metro: Gran Vía), Madrid's artistic and showbiz elite have been assaulting their livers almost as long on this narrow street parallel to Gran Vía, in this dark, cavernous room. It was given renewed cachet by the presence of internationally known film director Pedro Almodóvar.

If you want to witness a supremely assured professional mixologist in action, head up the same street a few doors. **Del Diego,** Reina 12 (© **91/523-3106;** Metro: Gran Vía), is a stylish contemporary watering hole that attracts exactly the upmarket crowd it seeks, including government ministers and upper-echelon executives. The maestro twirling the swizzle sticks is the eponymous head man, never losing his composure as he shakes and stirs everything from pure martinis to Long Island iced teas and Madrid's drink of the moment, the *mojito* (rum, lime juice, and mint). He put in 32 years at Chicote.

GAY & LESBIAN BARS

The Plaza Chueca area is Spain's hot spot for gays and bohemian straights, with over 60 gay-friendly bars, cafes, and discos. Pick up a map of gay Madrid and a copy of the **Shanguide** pocket-sized nightlife guide at the **Berkana** gay bookstore, Hortaleza 64 (© **91/522-5599**).

A small American-style drinking bar, **Rick's,** Clavel 9 (no phone; Metro: Chueca), brings together gays and straights. **D'Mystic,** Gravina 5 (no phone), and **Wy Not?,** San Bartolomé 6 (no phone), cater more exclusively to gay men. **Truco,** Gravina 10 (© **91/532-8921;** Metro: Chueca), is a hub of Madrid's lesbian community; it's open nightly from 10pm. Ladies are also heavily represented at the **Escape** disco, Gravina 13 (no phone). The waiters fill out their T-shirts and jeans admirably at **XXX Café,** Gran Vía 16 (© **91/532-8415;** Metro: Gran Vía), a gathering place for gay men 3 blocks south of Plaza Chueca, but the erotic undercurrents are subtle enough that straight couples show up, too. Drag shows are featured occasionally.

One of the most popular gay *discotecas* in town, **Refugio,** Doctor Cortezo 1 (© **91/369-4038;** Metro: Tirso de Molina), doesn't get going until midnight, but keeps on until . . . whenever. Cover is only 6.05€ ($6.95) and includes the first drink. **Black & White,** Libertad 34 (© **91/531-1141;** www.discoblack-white. com), is also legendary in the gay scene for offering a little something for everyone (male), with older guys upstairs and buff boys dancing to techno downstairs.

Remember, this is Spain: If you try to go out before 1am, you'll be disappointed. Many clubs and bars don't fill up until 2 or 3am.

DANCE CLUBS

Madrid's most popular dance clubs operate with a selective entrance policy, so dress stylishly and try to look as young, gorgeous, celebrated, and/or rich as possible. Admission, usually including a drink, can exceed 12€ ($14), and even a Coke can cost over 6€ ($6.90). They're usually open nightly until 5am or later, with nothing much happening before 2am. It's easier to get past the unsmiling gents at the door if you arrive before then. Some have a matinee, usually 7 to 9 or 10pm, attended primarily by teenagers. After closing for an hour or two to clear out the youngsters, they reopen to older patrons.

Many years ago, an old Victorian-era theater was transformed into the still-popular disco **Joy Eslava,** Arenal 11 (© **91/366-3733;** www.joy-eslava.com; Metro: Sol or Opera). Laser shows, videos, and energetic performers keep things moving. The best nights are Friday and Saturday, and 20% discount coupons are available around town. It's open daily from 11pm until 5:30am. Cover is 12€ ($14), or 15€ ($17) on Friday and Saturday; it includes the first drink. "Matinees" are Friday and Saturday 7 to 10pm, for ages 14 to 18 only, with no alcohol or tobacco allowed (this may be a good way to occupy teens for a few hours); cover is 7€ ($8).

The most multicultural, multifarious, and multimusical disco in Madrid, **Kapital,** Atocha 125 (© **91/420-2906;** Metro: Atocha), has seven floors, with the main dance floor at street level, a terrace up top, and more bars and dance floors (with different kinds of music) in between. Laser shows, karaoke, a movie room, and what used to be called go-go dancers are added attractions. Throngs of kids show up for the "afternoon" session from 6 to 11pm. Grown-ups arrive after midnight and stay until 6am. The cover is 12€ to 15€ ($14–$17). **Palacio Gaviria,** Arenal 9 (© **91/526-6069;** www.palaciogaviria.com; Metro: Sol), was a vintage mansion near Puerta del Sol that has been converted into a *multispacio* with several salons, each serving up expensive drinks, cabaret, and live or recorded dance music. Tuesday is salsa night, and Thursday features world music. It's open Monday to Thursday 10:30pm to 3am, Friday and Saturday 11pm to 5am, and Sunday 8:30pm to 2am. Cover is 15€ ($17), including the first drink.

Enthusiasm has intensified for things Cuban—food, drink, and music. **La Negra Tomasa,** Cadiz 9, at Espoz y Mina (© **91/523-5830;** Metro: Sol), is a throbbing club serving up all three, made to look like a Santiago cantina, complete with a Che poster. The food is casual but appetizing, chased with daiquiris, piña coladas, *mojitos,* and cigars. Cover on weekends is usually around 6€ ($6.90), including one drink. At **Larios Café,** Silva 4 off Gran Vía (© **91/547-9394;** Metro: Gran Vía), the ceiling towers over glittering masses of glass, metal, and feather sculptures, and constructions you have to see to believe. The garments of the bartenders leave no doubt as to their gender. Almost all their patrons seem immensely impressed with themselves, chic to their fingernails. Dinner goes on in back—for which reservations are essential. Bar action is heavy until very late, with live combos favoring various Latin styles, and there's a disco downstairs that's empty until 3am. No cover, but a drink costs 6.05€ ($7).

After a night of serious clubbing, ritual requires a stop at **La Chocolatería de San Ginés,** Pasadizo de San Ginés 5 (no phone; Metro: Sol), for hot chocolate and *churros* (deep-fried tubes of extruded dough dusted with sugar). It's squeezed up an alley between the Joy Eslava disco and the Iglesia de San Ginés, with a big red neon sign. The line forms before dawn. It's open Tuesday to Thursday 7 to 10pm and 1 to 7am, and Friday and Sunday 7pm to 7am.

7 A Side Trip to Toledo ★★★

Once the capital of Visigothic Spain, **Toledo,** 69km (43 miles) southwest of Madrid, bristles with steeples and towers spread over the pate of an unlikely hill almost completely moated by the River Tajo. Those familiar with the painting of the city by El Greco, who lived most of his creative life here, will be struck by how closely his 16th-century canvas, *View of Toledo,* conforms to the present, in overall impression if not in detail.

Toledo is undeniably a must-see, one of the most photogenic cities on the peninsula, its streets tilting and twisting past buildings sweeping over 15 centuries. Here, too, is history . . . deep, palpable, warming the stones. However, the streets are clogged all year with tour buses and their occupants and crammed with shops hung with Toledo cutlery (samurai and El Cid versions), fake armor, Lladró figurines, and every kind of gaudy souvenir. If possible, stay overnight to get a less feverish picture of the city when it's briefly returned to its citizens. Otherwise, try to leave Madrid early to avoid the worst of the crush.

You can reach Toledo by **train** (six trips daily from Madrid's Atocha Station) or by **bus** (from Madrid's Estación Sur de Autobuses). The one-way trip takes about an hour and 15 minutes by either method. The train fare is 4.90€ ($5.65), while the bus (www.continental-auto.es) costs 3.89€ ($4.50). Taxis are available at the charming neo-Mudéjar train station, but not in great numbers and not always when you want them. We don't recommend driving to Toledo, but if you want to, take Route 401 for 69km (43 miles) south of Madrid. For more information, call the **Toledo Tourist Office,** Puerta de Bisagra (© 925/ 22-0843; www.diputoledo.es/turismo), open Monday through Saturday from 9am to 7pm, and Sunday from 9am to 3pm.

SEEING THE SIGHTS Toledo's most prominent building and the logical first stop is its **Cathedral** ★★, Arco del Palacio 2 ((© 925/22-2241). To get there, walk southwest on Calle Comercio from the triangular Plaza de Zocodover. A glorious example of Spanish Gothic architecture, it was built in large part between the 13th and 15th centuries. Like many Spanish cathedrals, it's nearly enclosed by the town, the surrounding houses snuggling up to and around its base. Surmounted by a 90m (300-ft.) tower, the cathedral boasts five naves and dozens of side chapels. The highlights are the choir and the richly carved altarpiece. In the sacristy are paintings by El Greco, Rubens, and Titian, a collection extraordinary not only for its artistry but also for the fact that it hasn't been spirited away to a museum. The last guided tour is at 12:30pm. Admission is free, but you have to pay 3€ ($3.45) to see the treasury. Summer hours are Monday through Saturday from 10:30am to 1:30pm and 3:30 to 7pm, and Sunday from 10:30am to 1:30pm and 4 to 7pm. Continue past the cathedral in the same general direction you came, and make your next stop the **Iglesia Santo Tomé (Church of St. Thomas),** Plaza Conde (© 925/25-6098). Pass the entrance to the church proper and go around to the glassed entrance on the plaza. Inside is El Greco's famous *The Burial of the Count Orgaz* ★, the only artwork on display but one of his most important. Admission is 1.20€ ($1.40), and summer hours are daily 10am to 7pm (to 6pm the rest of the year).

Return to Calle San Juan de Dios from the church and follow the frequent signs to El Greco's 16th-century house, the **Casa y Museo de El Greco** ★, Samuel Levi 3 (© 925/22-4046). It has long been closed for restoration, but the adjacent museum contains a small collection of the artist's paintings, including a view of the city. Admission is 2.40€ ($2.75). It's open Tuesday to Saturday 10am to 2pm and 4 to 6pm (to 7pm in summer), Sunday 10am to 2pm. A little farther along is the **Synagoga de El Trásito y Museo Sefardi** ★, Samuel Levi ((© 925/22-3665), one of Toledo's two surviving synagogues and one of only three in all of Spain. Beyond the unassuming exterior are some fine examples of Mudéjar craftsmanship (note the *artesonado* ceiling) and a small museum of Jewish relics and archaeological artifacts. Admission is 2.40€ ($2.75). It's open Tuesday to Saturday 10am to 2pm and 4 to 6pm, Sunday 10am to 2pm.

Queen Isabel had a hand in the construction of the 16th-century building housing the **Museo Santa Cruz,** Cervantes 3 (© 925/22-1402), with its impressive Plateresque facade. The paintings within are mostly from the 16th and 17th centuries, with yet another by El Greco. Find the museum immediately east of Plaza de Zocodovar. Admission is free. Hours are Monday to Saturday 10am to 6:30pm; Sunday 10am to 2pm. The **Alcázar,** directly west at Cuesta del Alcázar (© 925/22-1673), is the fortress that occupies the city's highest elevation. It was damaged frequently over its centuries as a fortress and royal residence and was leveled during a siege of the Spanish Civil War. The existing structure is essentially a replica but is built over the old cellars and foundations. Admission is 2€ ($2.30), and hours are daily 9:30am to 2:30pm.

WHERE TO STAY & DINE   It's no surprise that a destination as heavily touristed as Toledo is short on appealing budget hotels. A notable exception is the spic-and-span 12-room **Hostal Nuevo Labrador,** Juan Labrador 10, 45001 Toledo (© **925/22-2620;** fax 925/22-9399), on a quiet lane near the Alcázar. Its virtues include that central location, new facilities and furnishings, and a good restaurant, the **Rincón de Eloy** (© **925/22-9399**), open daily. Rates are 42€ ($48) double, and American Express, MasterCard, and Visa are accepted.

If you want to treat yourself, reserve ahead at the 27-room **El Cardenal** ✿✿, Paseo de Recaredo 24, 45003 Toledo (© **925/22-4900;** fax 925/22-2991; host-cardenal@retemail.es), an 18th-century mansion that also contains the city's top restaurant. Owned by the same people who run the restaurant Botín in Madrid, the dining room is open to all daily, serving traditional Castellano dishes, especially roast lamb and pork. Find the mansion near the Puerta de Bisagra, the only remaining Moorish gate in the city's wall. Room rates are 80€ to 102€ ($92–$118) double, and American Express, Diners Club, MasterCard, and Visa are accepted.

With time and a car, you can cross the Río Tajo to the enormously popular **Parador Conde de Orgaz** ✿✿, Cerro del Emperador, 45002 Toledo (© **925/22-1850;** fax 925/22-1850; www.parador.es), on a promontory opposite the city. From its terrace, the unobstructed view of Toledo recalls El Greco's memorable rendition. Meals in the *parador's* first-class dining room justify a splurge (a three-course meal costs 25€/$29). Alternatively, you can get a sandwich and a beer in the bar. If you want to go all the way and spend the night—120€ ($138) double—you have to reserve *months* in advance. American Express, Diners Club, MasterCard, and Visa are accepted.

17

Munich & Neuschwanstein

by Beth Reiber

Named after the Munichen monks who settled more than 1,200 years ago on the banks of the Isar River, **Munich** is the capital of the state (or Land) of Bavaria and a sprawling city of 1.3 million. Home of industrial giants like BMW and Siemens, it's one of Germany's important cultural capitals, with four symphony orchestras, two opera houses, dozens of world-class museums, more than 50 theaters, and one of Germany's largest universities. The diverse student population and the foreign residents who make up more than 22% of the citizenry ensure an active avant-garde cultural scene and a liberal attitude in an otherwise conservative region.

Munich is striking, largely the product of the exuberant imagination and aspirations of past Bavarian kings and rulers. Royal residences, majestic museums, steepled churches, and ornate monuments celebrate architectural styles from baroque and Gothic to neoclassical and postmodern. Add wide boulevards, spacious parks, thriving nightlife, and at least six breweries, and you have what amounts to one of Germany's most interesting, exciting, and festive cities.

For more on Munich and its environs, see *Frommer's Munich & the Bavarian Alps*, *Frommer's Germany*, or *Frommer's Germany's Best-Loved Driving Tours*.

1 Essentials

ARRIVING

BY PLANE   Germany's own Lufthansa provides the largest number of flights to **Flughafen München Franz Josef Strauss Airport** (© **089/97 52 13 13** for flight information), 40km (25 miles) northeast of the city center in Erding. The easiest way to get into town is from the Flughafen München **S-Bahn station** by boarding S-8 or S-1 for Marienplatz (the city center) or the Hauptbahnhof (main train station). Trains leave every 10 minutes, and the trip to the Hauptbahnhof takes about 40 minutes.

A ticket is 8.40€ ($9.65), but if you have a validated Eurailpass you can ride the S-Bahn free. If you don't have a Eurailpass, you can save with a **Streifenkarte** (strip ticket), allowing 10 short journeys or 5 longer ones for 9.50€ ($11). Note that the trip from the airport is such a long one it takes up eight strips on the ticket. (Fold the ticket to the no. 8 slot and insert it into the machine at the station entrance.) In any case, the trip into town using the Streifenkarte is 7.60€ ($8.75). Alternatively, you can buy a 9€ ($10) **1-day transportation pass** for greater Munich, advisable if you plan on using public transportation at least once more the remainder of the day. Up to five persons can travel with a **1-day Partner Day Ticket** for greater Munich for 16€ ($18). Ticket machines accept credit cards, useful if you haven't yet exchanged money, but if you have any questions about transportation to the city center, stop by the MVV counter in the Zentralbereich (Central Area) of Terminal 1 at the entrance to the S-Bahn escalator; you can also buy tickets here.

Although more expensive, the **Lufthansa City/Airport Bus** departs every 20 minutes from both terminals and the Zentralbereich and costs 9€ ($10) for the 45-minute trip to the Hauptbahnhof. A **taxi** is expensive, costing as much as 52€ ($60) one-way.

BY TRAIN   You'll arrive at the **Hauptbahnhof,** Munich's main train station, in the city center; it serves as a nucleus for the many tram, U-Bahn (underground subway), and S-Bahn (metropolitan railway) lines. In addition to a tourist office (see "Visitor Information," below), beside Track 11 in Room no. 3 is **EurAide,** a special service for English-speaking travelers providing free train and sightseeing info and selling various rail tickets. Summer hours are daily 7:45am to noon and 1 to 6pm; winter hours are Monday to Friday 7:45am to noon and 1 to 4:45pm. It's closed the first 2 weeks in January.

VISITOR INFORMATION
INFORMATION OFFICES   You'll find a branch of Munich's **Tourismus Information** just outside the Hauptbahnhof's main exit at Bahnhofplatz 2. Open Monday to Saturday 9:30am to 6:30pm and Sunday and holidays 10am to 6pm, it distributes city maps for .30€ (35¢) and brochures. For a 10% deposit that goes toward the cost of the room, the staff will find you a hotel room, a valuable service if the places in this book are full. Also at the Hauptbahnhof is **EurAide,** providing train and sightseeing information for English speakers (see above). In the city center is another convenient tourist office in the **Neues Rathaus (New Town Hall)** on Marienplatz, open Monday to Friday 10am to 8pm, Saturday 10am to 4pm. You can book concert tickets here. For more information, call © **089/233 965 00** Monday to Friday 8am to 7pm, Saturday 10am to 6pm.You can also make hotel reservations by calling the **Hotelreservierung Call Center** at © **089/23 39 65 55** during the same hours.

⎛Value⎞ Budget Bests

You can save money by standing up in Munich, whether it's eating or visiting the theater. Eat lunch at an *Imbiss,* a food stall or tiny store selling everything from German sausages and grilled chicken to pizza. Concentrated primarily in the Old Town, most of these places even sell beer to wash it all down. If you'd rather sit for a meal, you can often save money by ordering from the *Tageskarte* (changing daily menu), which includes both the main course and side dishes. Even better, pack a meal and take it to one of Munich's many **beer gardens,** where all you'll have to buy is beer—some even offer free concerts.

Standing up is also the cheapest way to see performances of the **Nationaltheater,** with tickets for students selling for 50% off the usual price. And for getting around, consider buying a **Munich Welcome Card,** which includes unlimited transportation for 1 or 3 days and up to a 50% reduction at several major attractions. But Munich's best sightseeing deal is that several top museums, including the Alte Pinakothek, Neue Pinakothek, and Pinakothek der Moderne, are **free on Sunday** (but also crowded).

Munich Deals & Discounts

SPECIAL DISCOUNTS If you plan on doing a lot of traveling back and forth on Munich's excellent subways, buses, and trams, you can save by buying a **1-day transportation pass** *(Tageskarte)* for 4.50€ ($5.15) or the **Munich Welcome Card** for 6.50€ ($7.50), allowing unlimited 1-day travel on public transportation and up to 50% discounts on admission to museums and sights around Munich. There are also 3-day Welcome Cards. Information is given in more detail in "Getting Around," below.

A student's ticket to lower prices is the **International Student Identity Card (ISIC)**. With it you can realize substantial savings on museum admissions, with 50% or more off the regular price. In addition, the opera and the theater offer student discounts for unsold seats on the night of performance—show up about an hour before the performance to see what's available. A travel agency dealing with student/youth travel, and with reduced-price train or plane tickets, is **Studiosus Urlaubscenter,** Oberanger 6 (© 089/235 05 20; S-/U-Bahn: Marienplatz), open Monday to Friday 9am to 7pm and Saturday 10am to 2pm.

If you're a senior (at least 65), you're entitled to a **50% discount** at most museums in Munich.

WORTH A SPLURGE Although prices can add up, it's worth spending the extra time and money to see Munich's famous museums, particularly the **Alte Pinakothek, Neue Pinakothek, Pinakothek der Moderne, Deutsches Museum,** and **Städtische Galerie im Lenbachhaus,** as well as **Nymphenburg Palace.** To keep costs down, buy a combination ticket whenever possible, or buy the Munich Welcome Card.

If you want to know what's going on in Munich during your stay, pick up a copy of the monthly *Monatsprogramm* at the tourist office. Costing 1.55€ ($1.80), it tells what's being performed and when in the theaters and opera houses and how to get tickets; it also lists concerts (modern and classical), museum hours, and special exhibits. Although much of the info is in German, those who don't understand the language will still find it useful. Keep an eye out also for *in München,* a German-language giveaway with details on popular concerts, nightlife, and events.

A great source in English is *Munich in Your Pocket,* published monthly for 3€ ($3.45) and available at the tourist office. It carries information on nightlife, exhibitions, dining, and other items of interest to visitors. I also like *Munich Found,* an English-language magazine published 10 times a year and available at newsstands for 3€ ($3.45). Besides articles of local interest, including special exhibits and events, it contains a calendar for classical music, opera, ballet, theater, rock concerts, and other nightlife. The only problem is finding a copy because it sells out fast—check the Internationale Presse newsstand at the Hauptbahnhof, across from Track 23.

WEBSITES You can get information in English on the Internet at the Munich Tourist Office's site, **www.munich-tourist.de**. For all things Bavarian, try **www.bavaria.com**.

CITY LAYOUT

The heart of Munich, the **Altstadt (Old Town),** is east of the Hauptbahnhof. Its very center is **Marienplatz,** a cobblestone plaza a 15-minute walk from the train station and connected to the rest of the city by an extensive subway network. Over the centuries, it has served as a market square, a stage for knightly tournaments, and the site of public executions. Today it's no less important, bordered on one side by the impressive Neues Rathaus (New Town Hall), famous for its chimes and mechanized figures appearing daily at 11am and noon (also 5pm in summer). Much of the Old Town is a **pedestrian zone** where you'll find the smartest boutiques, most traditional restaurants, and oldest churches, plus the Viktualienmarkt outdoor market. Most of Munich's museums are within an easy walk or short subway ride from the center.

Schwabing, north of the city center and easily reached by U-Bahn, is home to Munich's university and nightlife. Its Bohemian heyday was in the early 1900s, when it served as a mecca for Germany's most talented young artists and writers, including Kandinsky, Klee, Mann, and Rilke. Today Schwabing is known for its sidewalk cafes, restaurants, and fashionable bars, most on Leopoldstrasse and Occamstrasse. Although brochures like to call Schwabing the Greenwich Village of Munich, most of the people milling about are visitors, including lots of young people from outlying villages in for a night on the town.

As for other areas worth exploring, the **Englischer Garten,** with its wide green expanses and beer gardens, stretches northeast from the city center. Oktoberfest is held at **Theresienwiese,** just south of the Hauptbahnhof, while the **Olympiapark,** home of the 1972 Olympic Games, is on the northern edge of town. **Schloss Nymphenburg,** once the royal family's summer residence, is northwest of town, accessible by streetcar from the train station.

GETTING AROUND

A byproduct of the 1972 Olympics is the extensive downtown **pedestrian zone,** making Munich a perfect city to explore on foot. In fact, many of its museums can be reached on foot from the city center, Marienplatz. All you need is the map issued by the tourist office to set you off in the right direction.

One of the best things about Munich's transportation system is that you can make as many **free transfers** among subways, buses, and trams (streetcars) as you need. A **single journey** to most destinations costs 2.10€ ($2.40). Shorter journeys—trips of at most two stops on the subway or four on the tram or bus—require a ticket called a **Kurzstrecke** at only 1.10€ ($1.25). If in doubt, look at the list of stations allowing a Kurzstrecke indicated on the vending machine.

Just slightly more economical is the **Streifenkarte** (also called a **Mehrfahrtenkarte**), a strip ticket allowing multiple journeys. What I like about this option is that it saves you the hassle of buying individual tickets each time you travel. It costs 9.50€ ($11) and consists of 10 strips worth .95€ ($1.10) each. For short journeys, you use one strip. Most trips in the city, however, require two strips (a total of 1.90€/$2.20 for the ride, slightly less than the 2€/$2.30 for the single ticket above). Simply fold up two segments of the Streifenkarte and insert them into the validating machine.

A simpler solution still is to buy a *Tageskarte* (day ticket), allowing unlimited travel on all modes of transport for 1 day. A 4.50€ ($5.15) Tageskarte is valid for most of Munich's inner city and includes the entire U-Bahn network. If you want to travel to the outskirts, buy the 9€ ($10) card for the metropolitan area (about an 80km/50-mile) radius, including the airport and Dachau). If there are at least

Munich U-Bahn & S-Bahn

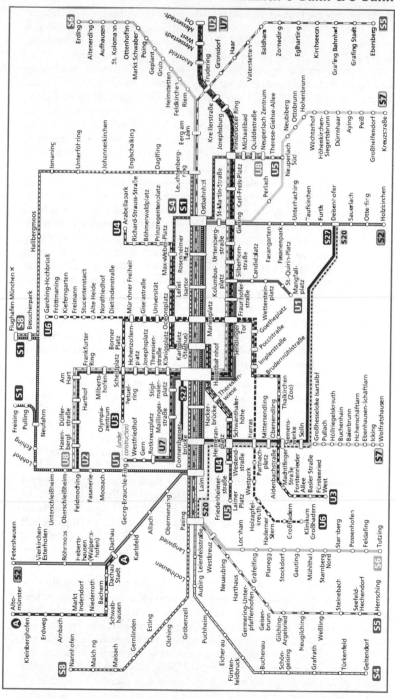

two of you, get the **Partner** *Tageskarte,* which allows five people (two children under 15 count as one person) to travel Munich's inner city for 8€ ($9.20) and the entire metropolitan area for 16€ ($18). **Three-day tickets** are also available, costing 11€ ($13) for one person and 19€ ($21) for up to five people.

If you plan to pack as much sightseeing as you can into 1 day, consider buying the **Munich Welcome Card,** valid for 1 day's unlimited travel in Munich's inner city and costing 6.50€ ($7.50). There's also a 3-day Welcome Card for 16€ ($18) and a 3-day Partner Welcome Card for 23€ ($26), valid for up to five persons (two children up to 14 count as one person). All cards offer a 20% to 50% reduction in admission to the Deutsches Museum, Münchner Stadtmuseum, Nymphenburg Palace, Residenzmuseum, BMW Museum, Städtische Galerie im Lenbachhaus, Hellabrunn Zoo, Bavaria Filmtour, and a handful of other attractions, as well as discounts on guided tours and special offers for several restaurants. For more information or to buy a card, stop by one of the Munich tourist offices.

Otherwise, you can buy the Streifenkarte, *Tageskarte,* and single tickets from the blue vending machines at U-Bahn and S-Bahn stations, as well as from vending machines at some tram stops and in the second car of trams bearing a white-and-green K sign. Bus drivers sell single tickets and the Streifenkarte, while tram drivers sell only single tickets. Strip tickets and day tickets are also sold at tobacco and magazine kiosks displaying the green-and-white K in their window. Three-day tickets are available at ticket windows at major stations and EurAide. After buying your ticket, you must activate it by inserting it into machine slots located on all buses and trams and at entrances to S- and U-Bahn platforms.

For more information about Munich's **public transportation system (MVV),** call © **089/41 42 43 44** or drop by the MVV Kundencenter kiosk inside the Hauptbahnhof or Marienplatz subway station.

BY SUBWAY Munich's wonderful underground network, created in conjunction with the Olympics, is the ultimate in German efficiency. I've seldom waited more than a few minutes for a train. What's more, Munich's subway stations have something I wish every city would adopt—maps of the surrounding streets. You never have to emerge from a station wondering where you are.

Munich's system is divided into the **U-Bahn** (underground subway) and **S-Bahn** (metropolitan railway). Because the S-Bahn is part of the German Federal Railroads, you can use your Eurailpass on these lines. Otherwise, buy a ticket and validate it yourself by inserting it into one of the little machines at the entrance to the track. It's on the honor system, but there are frequent spot checks by undercover controllers—if you're caught without a ticket, you'll pay a stiff fine. Munich's public transport system operates daily about 5am to 1am, with some S-Bahn lines, including one to the airport, operating frequently throughout the night.

BY BUS & TRAM (STREETCAR) Buses and trams go everywhere the subway doesn't. As mentioned above, one ticket allows for many transfers as necessary to reach your destination. In the newer trams, tickets bought from machines aboard the trams are already validated. Otherwise, you must validate tickets yourself by inserting them into the blue machine with the yellow letter *E.* The tourist office map indicates bus and tram routes for the inner city. For night owls, six bus and four tram lines (N17, N19, N20, and N27) run nightly about 1:30 to 5am, designated by an *N* in front of their number. Contact MVV for more information, including a brochure listing the night lines along with their stops and time schedules.

Country & City Codes

The **country code** for Germany is **49.** The **city code** for Munich is **89;** use this code when you're calling from outside Germany. If you're within Germany but not in Munich, use **089.** If you're calling within Munich, simply leave off the code and dial only the regular phone number.

BY TAXI Munich's public transport system is so efficient you should never have to fork over money for a taxi. If you do take a taxi, you'll pay 2.60€ ($3) as soon as you step inside, plus 1.20€ ($1.40) per kilometer for the first 5km (3 miles) and 1.45€ ($1.65) per kilometer after that. If you need to call a taxi, phone ℅ **089/216 10** or **089/194 10.** Taxis ordered by phone add a 1€ ($1.15) surcharge; luggage is an extra .50€ (55¢) per bag.

BY BICYCLE One of the most convenient places to rent bikes is **Radius Touristik,** inside the Hauptbahnhof across from Track 32 (℅ **089/59 61 13**). May to mid-October, it's open daily 10am to 6pm. It charges 14€ ($16) for 1 day's rental of a three-gear bike, and 22€ ($16) for a deluxe 21-speed or mountain bike, plus a 50€ ($58) deposit; 10% discounts are available for students and readers of this book. Weekly rates are also available.

BY RENTAL CAR You'll find counters for all the major rental companies at the Flughafen München Franz Josef Strauss Airport. In addition, there are counters for **Hertz** (℅ **089/550 22 56**), **Avis** (℅ **089/550 22 51**), and **Europcar** (℅ **089/549 02 40**) at the Hauptbahnhof. For other car-rental agencies, check in the phone book under "Autovermeitung."

Although prices vary, expect to spend about 80€ ($92) for a 1-day rental of a two-door VW Polo, Ford Fiesta, or Opel Corsa, including 16% tax and unlimited mileage. It pays to shop around, since car-rental prices vary widely depending on the time of year, the day of the week, and the type of car. It's cheaper to rent a car over the weekend, when the rate of 144€ ($166) often covers the entire period from noon Friday to 9am Monday. It's also cheaper to rent from a downtown location than at the airport.

Remember: You get the best deal if you arrange the rental before leaving your home country.

FAST FACTS: Munich

American Express There's a convenient office in the Old Town just off Karlsplatz at Neuhauserstrasse 47, with an entrance on Herzog-Wilhelm-Strasse (℅ **089/22 80 13 87;** U-Bahn: Marienplatz), open Monday to Friday 9:30am to 6pm and Saturday 10am to 1pm. Another office is at Promenadeplatz 6 (℅ **089/22 80 14 65;** U-Bahn: Karlsplatz/Stachus or Marienplatz), open Monday to Friday 9am to 6pm and Saturday 9:30am to 12:30pm. No fee is charged to cash Amex traveler's checks, though the exchange rate is lower than at banks.

Banks Banks are generally open Monday to Friday 8:30am to 12:30pm and 1:30 to 3:30pm (to 5:30pm Thurs). You can also exchange money at post offices. If you need to exchange money outside bank hours, your best bet is the **Reise Bank currency exchange office** (℅ **089/551 08 13**) at the

Hauptbahnhof's main exit, open daily 7am to 10pm. It has a 24-hour ATM for getting cash from American Express, Diners Club, MasterCard, and Visa.

Business Hours **Department stores** are open Monday to Saturday 9 or 9:30am to 8pm. **Smaller stores** might close at 6pm, while some **neighborhood shops** close for lunch about 12:30 to 2 or 2:30pm.

Consulates Different departments might have different hours, so it's always best to call. The consulate of the **United States,** Königinstrasse 5 (℃ **089/288 80** for general information, 089/288 87 22 for U.S. passport information; bus: 53), is open Monday to Friday 8am to 11am (telephone information available until 5pm). The consulate of the **United Kingdom,** Bürkleinstrasse 10 (℃ **089/21 10 90;** U-Bahn: Lehel), is open Monday to Thursday 8:30 to noon and 1 to 5pm, Friday 8:30am to noon and 1 to 3:30pm. The consulate of **Canada,** Tal Strasse 29 (℃ **089/219 95 70;** S-Bahn: Isartor), is open Monday to Thursday 9am to noon and 2 to 5pm, Friday 9am to noon and 2 to 3:30pm. The consulate of **Ireland,** Denningerstrasse 15 (℃ **089/2080 59 90;** U-Bahn: Richard-Strauss-Strasse), is open Monday to Friday 8am to noon.

Currency In 2002, German adopted the **euro** (€) for its currency. At press time, $1 = .87€, or 1€ = $1.15.

Dentists & Doctors If you need an English-speaking doctor or dentist, contact the American or British consulate. If it's a weekend or evening dental or medical emergency, contact the **Notfallpraxis,** Elisenstrasse 3 (℃ **089/55 17 71;** S-/U-Bahn: Hauptbahnhof; tram: 17, 19, 20, or 21 to Hauptbahnhof), where doctors of various specialties are on hand. It's open Monday, Tuesday, and Thursday 7 to 11pm, Wednesday and Friday 2pm to 11pm, and weekends and holidays 8am to 11pm. For evening and weekend dental emergencies, go to the **Zahnärztliche Klinik,** Lindwurm Strasse 2a (℃ **089/51 60 0;** U-Bahn: Sendlinger Tor), or call an emergency dentist at ℃ **089/723 30 93,** available only weekends and holidays.

Emergencies Important numbers include ℃ **110** for the **police** and ℃ **112** for the **fire** department and **ambulance.** For medical emergencies on weekends or evenings, call the **Notfallpraxis** (see "Dentists & Doctors," above).

Holidays Because of its large Catholic population, Munich has more holidays than much of the rest of the country. While many museums and restaurants remain open, shops and businesses close. Holidays in Bavaria are New Year's Day (Jan 1); Epiphany (Jan 6); Good Friday, Easter Sunday and Monday; Ascension Day, Whitsunday, Whitmonday, and Corpus Christi (all in Apr or May); Labor Day (May 1); Assumption Day (Aug 15); German Reunification Day (Oct 3); All Saints' Day (Nov 1); and Christmas (Dec 25–26). Although it's not an official holiday, note that many museums and shops are also closed for the parade on Faschings Dienstag, the Tuesday before Ash Wednesday.

Hospitals Local hospitals include **Schwabinger Hospital,** Kölner Platz 1 (℃ **089/306 81;** U-Bahn: Scheidplatz); and the **University Clinic,** Ziemssenstrasse 1 (℃ **089/516 00;** U-Bahn: Goetheplatz). If you need to go to a hospital, contact your consulate for advice on which one is best for your ailment. Otherwise, call for an ambulance or the medical emergency service (see "Emergencies," above).

Internet Access Munich's largest Internet-access establishment is **easy-InternetCafe,** located across the main exit of the Hauptbahnhof train station, beside the post office, at Bahnhofplatz 1 (© **089/55 999 696;** S-/U-Bahn: Hauptbahnhof). Open 8am to 1am, it boasts 500 computers with high-speed Internet access. The hourly rate per computer changes depending on the time of day and demand; it typically fluctuates between .80€ and 2.80€ (90¢–$3.20). A monitor at the entrance broadcasts the going rate. In addition to surfing, e-mailing, and chatting, customers can also download files, print, and burn CDs. In the Altstadt, the **Internet Point** is located in the subway station at Marienplatz, near the stairs leading to Viktalienmarkt (© **089/20 70 27 37).** Open 24 hours, it charges 1€ ($1.15) per 30 minutes. In addition, the **Jedermann, Europäischer Hof, Euro Youth Hotel, Helvetia, Hotel Mark,** and **Uhland** hotels offer Internet access for their guests (see "Affordable Places to Stay," below).

Laundry & Dry Cleaning A *reinigung* is a dry cleaner; a *Wäscherei* or *Waschsalon* is a laundry. Most laundries close at 6pm. Ask the staff at your hotel or pension for the location of the closest *Waschsalon;* otherwise, there's the **City SB-Wasch Center** a few minutes' walk south of the main train station at Paul-Heyse-Strasse 21 (© **089/53 13 11;** S-/U-Bahn: Hauptbahnhof). A wash load including detergent costs 4€ ($4.60) for a small load and 8€ ($9.20) for a large one; a dryer costs .70€ (80¢) per 10 minutes. It's open daily 7am to 11pm.

Mail Munich's **main post office** is across from the Hauptbahnhof at Bahnhofplatz 1, 80338 (© **089/599 08 70;** S-/U-Bahn: Hauptbahnhof). If you don't know where you'll be staying, have your mail sent here *Poste Restante.* It's open Monday to Friday 7:30am to 8pm and Saturday 9am to 4pm. You'll find another post office at Residenzstrasse 2, near Marienplatz, open Monday to Friday 8am to 6:30pm and Saturday 9am to 12:30pm.

Mailboxes are yellow. Airmail letters to destinations outside Europe cost 1.55€ ($1.80) for the first 20 grams, while postcards cost 1€ ($1.15). If you want to mail a package back home (it can't weigh more than 20kg/44 lb. if sent to the U.S.), you can buy a box that comes with tape and string at the post office. Boxes come in six sizes and range from 1.50€ to 2.50€ ($1.75–$2.85).

Pharmacies A convenient pharmacy, the **Internationale Ludwigs-Apotheke,** Neuhauser Strasse 11 (© **089/260 30 21),** is open Monday to Saturday 9am to 8pm. It's one of the best places to fill international prescriptions; it can also recommend English-speaking doctors. At the train station is the **Internationale Bahnhof-Apotheke,** Bahnhofplatz 2 (© **089/ 59 41 19).** Pharmacies take turns offering night and weekend services; the names of those offering such services are always posted outside every pharmacy door.

Police The emergency number for the police is © **110.**

Tax Germany's 16% **federal tax** is included in most hotel and restaurant bills, including all the locales in this book. Tax is likewise included in the price of goods, but if you buy more than 25€ ($29) worth of goods from any one store on a given day and are taking your purchases out of the country, you can recover part (up to 11%) of Germany's 16% **value-added tax (VAT).** Many shops will issue a Global Refund Cheque. Fill in the reverse side and, on leaving the last European Union country you visit, present the articles and Refund Cheque to Customs. Airports in Berlin, Frankfurt, Munich, and other large cities have counters that will refund your money immediately.

Telephone Telephone booths in Munich are generally silver and pink. A **local phone call** is .10€ (11¢) for the first 90 seconds; put more coins in to be sure you're not cut off (unused coins will be returned). Phones in some restaurants and shops require .20€ (25¢). Avoid calling from your hotel, since hotels usually add a stiff surcharge.

If you're going to make a lot of phone calls or want to make an **international call** from a phone booth, you'll probably want to buy a **phone card.** For sale at post offices and news kiosks, they come in values of 6€ and 25€ ($6.90 and $29). Simply insert them into the phone slot. Phone cards are so common in Germany that many public phones no longer accept coins. Due to recent deregulation of Germany's phone industry and Telecom's loss of monopoly over domestic service, competition among phone companies has lowered long-distance rates, especially for private lines. At press time, it costs approximately .45€ (50¢) per minute for a long-distance call to the United States from a phone booth. In contrast, several prepaid calling cards are available at cheaper rates, including Median prepaid cards available only at American Express offices in Germany, offering calls from any touch-tone phone (including hotel, pay, and mobile phones) for .07€ (8¢) per minute from Germany to the United States. Unfortunately, Deutsche Telecom, which still controls pay phones, adds a variable surcharge for each minute you use a prepaid card, which can range from .27€ to .33€ (31¢–38¢) per minute. A similar card, the CallHome Card, is offered by Reise Bank at the Hauptbahnhof that costs .06€ (7¢) per minute to the United States (plus the variable surcharge per min. for calls made from pay phones). Both the Median Card and CallHome Card come in values of 6€ ($6.90), 12€ ($14), and 25€ ($29).

Incidentally, if you come across a phone number with a dash, the numbers after the dash are the extension number. Simply dial the entire number as you would any phone number. For directory **information** on local numbers, call ℭ **11833,** or 11837 for directory assistance in English.

Tipping Gratuities are included in hotel and restaurant bills. However, it's customary to round restaurant bills up to the nearest euro; if a meal costs more than 5€ ($5.75), most Germans will give a 10% tip. Don't leave a tip on the table—include it in the amount you give your waiter. For taxi drivers, round up to the nearest euro. Porters charge 2.50€ ($2.85) for two bags.

2 Affordable Places to Stay

Most of Munich's accommodations are clustered around the main train station, the Hauptbahnhof, particularly its south side. While this area might not be the city's most charming, what it lacks in atmosphere it certainly makes up for in convenience. The farther you walk from the station, the quainter and quieter the neighborhoods become.

Although a pension, the German equivalent of a B&B, is generally less expensive than a hotel, there's often only a fine line between the two. In any case, the cheaper the room, the greater the likelihood you'll be sharing a bathroom down the hall. Pensions in Munich often charge a small fee for use of the shower—unless, of course, you have a shower in your room. All rooms in pensions and hotels, however, have their own sink, and most include a continental or buffet breakfast in their rates. Single rooms, alas, are expensive; you can save a lot of money by sharing a room.

Remember that if the accommodations below are full, try the tourist office, whose staff will find a room for you for a 10% deposit of your total room rate. You can also reserve a room in advance through the tourist office by calling © **089/23 39 65 55** or visiting www.muenchen-tourist.de. All prices here include tax and service charge. When indicated, the higher prices are generally those charged April to October, including Oktoberfest, and during major trade fairs *(Messe)*.

Note: You'll find the lodging choices below plotted on the map on p. 636.

PRIVATE HOMES & APARTMENTS

Frau Anita Gross, Thalkirchner Strasse 72 (about a 20-min. walk from Marienplatz), 80337 München (© **089/52 16 81;** bus: 58 from Hauptbahnhof to Kapuziner Strasse), offers two cheerful modern apartments, each with TV, phone, radio, ironing board/iron, and a stocked kitchenette (even coffee, tea, and sugar are provided). The larger apartment has a balcony with table and chairs. Personable Frau Gross, who lives elsewhere but will pick you up at the train station if given notice, speaks perfect English and provides maps and information. The smaller apartment is 60€ ($69) for two, and the larger apartment 76€ ($87) for three or 92€ ($106) for four. No credit cards are accepted.

Frau Audrey Bauchinger, Zeppelinstrasse 37, 81669 München (© **089/48 84 44;** fax 089/48 91 787; Audrey_bauchinger@gmx.de; S-Bahn: Marienplatz, then bus no. 52 to Schweigerstrasse), a former teacher from Virginia, offers six rooms and two apartments on the Isar near the Deutsches Museum. The rooms are clean and quiet and spread on several floors (no elevator). There's one single with a shower (30€/$35); the others are doubles with and without a shower only or with a private bathroom across the hall (54€/$62 without bathroom; 60€–65€/$69–$75 with shower or bathroom). The simple triple is in the Bauchinger apartment and shares the family bathroom (27€/$31 per person). Those looking for greater luxury might like one of the apartments, costing 82€ ($94) for two persons, plus a 26€ ($30) surcharge if they use the attached kitchen. Rates include one shower per night; extra showers are 2.55€ ($2.95). No credit cards are accepted.

Fremdenheim Weigl, Pettenkoferstrasse 32 (just off Georg-Hirth-Platz, about a 10-min. walk south of the Hauptbahnhof), 80336 München (©/fax **089/53 24 53;** dieter.busetti@t-online.de; U-Bahn: Theresienwiese; bus: 58 to

---

Value Getting the Best Deal on Accommodations

- Note that a room without a private shower is usually cheaper than one with—however, you might be charged extra for each shower you take down the hall. If the charge for a shower is high and there are more than two of you, you might save by taking a room with a private shower.
- Be aware that renting a room in a private home can be a bargain, and private apartments with kitchens can help you save on dining bills.
- Ask whether breakfast is included in the room rate—if it's buffet style, you can eat as much as you want and maybe then save on lunch.
- Before placing a call, inquire about the surcharge on local and long-distance phone calls.
- Find out how far the accommodations are from the town center. You might find an inexpensive room on the outskirts, but what you'll end up spending for transportation into the city might negate the savings.
- Avoid coming to Munich during a major trade fair *(Messe)*—rooms can be scarce and many hotels and pensions raise their rates. Munich is most expensive during Oktoberfest.

Georg-Hirth-Platz), consists of three rooms, none with bathroom, on the second floor of a building with an elevator. It's owned/managed by Daniela Busetti, who speaks excellent English and is the granddaughter of the original owner. Although she lives in the same building, her apartment is separate. The cheerful rooms are one single without a sink for 21€ ($24), and two doubles with washbasins for 41€ ($47). No credit cards are accepted.

Note: The listings above prefer guests who stay at least 2 or 3 nights.

HOTELS & PENSIONS

Unless otherwise noted, these accommodations have the same rates year-round.

NEAR THE HAUPTBAHNHOF

Augsburg *Value* One of many hotels and pensions on Schillerstrasse just minutes from the train station, the Augsburg is probably the most economical and the best for its price. Its reception is on the third floor (there's an elevator). Although the rooms are rather small and simple (but carpeted and clean) and the receptionist rather curt, you really can't complain at these prices.

Schillerstrasse 18, 80336 München. ✆ 089/59 76 73. Fax 089/550 38 23. www.pensionaugsburg-muenchen.de. 31 units, 18 with shower only, 3 with bathroom. 25€ ($29) single without bathroom, 31€ ($36) single with shower; 38€–44€ ($44–$51) double without bathroom, 48€–52€ ($55–$60) double with shower, 60€–69€ ($69–$79) double with bathroom; 56€ ($64) triple without bathroom, 66€ ($76) triple with shower, 78€ ($90) triple with bathroom. Rates 4.50€ ($5.15) higher per person during Oktoberfest. Continental breakfast 4.50€ ($5.15); showers 2€ ($2.30). No credit cards. Closed Dec 23–Dec 29. From the main exit of Hauptbahnhof onto Bahnhofplatz, turn right and walk 3 min. *In room:* No phone.

Europäischer Hof ✦ If you're tired of lugging around baggage, you can't get much closer to the train station than this modern hotel with a sleek marble lobby and a courteous staff. Various room types offer various levels of comfort, from bathless rooms with sinks to luxurious doubles with minibars, cable TVs, dataports, and more. Rates are higher in September and during Oktoberfest and major conventions.

Bayerstrasse 31, 80335 München. (℃) **089/55 15 10.** Fax 089/551 51 14 44. www.heh.de. 148 units, 135 with bathroom. 45€–80€ ($51–$91) single without bathroom, 70€–147€ ($80–$168) single with bathroom; 52€–93€ ($60–$107) double without bathroom, 89€–163€ ($102–$187) double with bathroom; 100€–171€ ($115–$197) triple with bathroom. Rates include buffet breakfast and showers. *Frommer's readers:* Discounts available except during major trade fairs and Oktoberfest. AE, DC, MC, V. Parking 9.50€–13€ ($11–$14). Across from Hauptbahnhof's south side. **Amenities:** Restaurant; laundry service; nonsmoking rooms; lobby computer with free Internet access. *In room:* TV.

Euro Youth Hotel ⭐ (Value) Opened in 1998 in a renovated 100-year-old hotel that retains much of its original charm in the high-ceilinged lobby and breakfast room, this well-managed hotel just a few minutes' walk from the train station caters to international travelers of all ages with simple but clean rooms, most of them doubles and triples, and all with sinks. For backpackers, there are dorm rooms with bunks. Note that the price ranges below reflect the seasons, with the highest prices in each category charged during Oktoberfest. This establishment is so successful, it plans to open a second location in 2005 nearby at Schillerstrasse 19, 80336 München (℃) **089/59 90 88 71**), with similar rates.

Senefelderstrasse 5, 80336 München. (℃) **089/59 90 88 11.** Fax 089/59 90 88 77. www.euro-youth-hotel.de. 58 units, 9 with bathroom. 18€–22€ ($20–$25) dorm room; 40€–65€ ($46–$75) single without bathroom; 48€–75€ ($55–$86) double without bathroom, 72€–99€ ($83–$114) double with bathroom; 87€–135€ ($100–$155) triple with bathroom; 19€–30€ ($22–$35) per person triple, quad, and quint rooms without bathroom. Rates include showers; during Oktoberfest, rates include breakfast (except in multi-bed and dorm rooms). Buffet breakfast 4.50€ ($5.15). No credit cards. From main exit of Hauptbahnhof onto Bahnhofplatz, turn right and walk 3 min. **Amenities:** Bar with occasional free live music; coin-op washer and dryer; nonsmoking rooms; public computer with Internet access. *In room:* TV (single and double rooms).

Flora (Kids) A family-owned operation since 1956, the first-floor Flora is now run by the original owner's son, Adolf, and granddaughters Judith and Angy. Great for the price, it features small but clean rooms with wall-to-wall carpeting and high ceilings, though some rooms could stand to lose the cheesy decor. Rooms facing the back are quieter. The apartment with three bedrooms and two bathrooms sleeps seven to nine and is perfect for families. Breakfast is served in a cheerful dining room. The higher prices are charged during Oktoberfest and major trade fairs.

Karlstrasse 49, 80333 München. (℃) **089/59 70 67** or 089/59 41 35. Fax 089/59 41 35. www.hotel-flora.de. 45 units, 25 with bathroom; 1 apt. 45€–65€ ($52–$75) single without bathroom, 55€–75€ ($63–$86) single with bathroom; 60€–85€ ($69–$98) double without bathroom, 75€–110€ ($86–$127) double with bathroom; 70€–95€ ($81–$109) triple without bathroom, 95€–125€ ($109–$144) triple with bathroom; 90€–105€ ($103–$121) quad without bathroom, 110€–130€ ($127–$150) quad with bathroom; 230€ ($265) apt. Rates include buffet breakfast and showers. *Frommer's readers:* 10% discount available. MC, V. From the main exit of Hauptbahnhof onto Bahnhofplatz, turn left and walk north on Dachauer Strasse to Karlstrasse (6-min. walk). *In room:* TV (on request), no phone.

Helvetia ⭐ A good choice on Schillerstrasse just a few minutes' walk from the train station, this pension is under the friendly management of Mr. Kharazi, who is happy to dispense sightseeing advice. He offers clean and fairly large rooms decorated with pine furniture and Persian-style throw rugs. Most of the doubles and triples have two sinks, and several rooms comfortably sleeping up to five even have three sinks. Most rooms face away from the street, ensuring a quiet night's rest, but those facing the front have soundproof windows. A Turkish restaurant (under different management) is on the ground floor. The highest prices are those charged during summer, Oktoberfest, and major conventions.

Schillerstrasse 6, 80336 München. ⓒ **089/59 06 85-0.** Fax 089/59 06 85-70. www.Hotel-Helvetia.de. 46 units, 3 with shower only. 35€–42€ ($40–$48) single without bathroom; 55€–65€ ($63–$75) double without bathroom, 60€–70€ ($69–$81) double with shower; 65€–75€ ($75–$86) triple without bathroom; 85€–100€ ($98–$115) quad without bathroom; 110€–120€ ($127–$138) quint without bathroom. Rates include continental breakfast and showers. AE, MC, V. From main exit of Hauptbahnhof onto Bahnhofplatz, turn right and walk 3 min. **Amenities:** Laundry service (6€/$6.90); lobby computer with free Internet access.

Hotel Mark   Just a 2-minute walk from the station, this older hotel was recently renovated but retains some of its 1950s decor and charm in its lobby and public areas. The rooms, though on the small side, have been updated with modern furniture and facilities, with most facing a quiet courtyard but nonetheless outfitted with soundproof windows. Units with bathrooms have the extras of minibars, radios, and safes. The higher prices are charged during Oktoberfest and trade fairs.

Senefelderstrasse 12, 80336 München. ⓒ **089/55 98 20.** Fax 089/55 98 23 33. www.hotel-mark.de. 95 units, 92 with bathroom. 40€–80€ ($42–$91) single without bathroom, 65€–142€ ($74–$163) single with bathroom; 58€–93€ ($67–$107) double without bathroom, 88€–178€ ($101–$205) double with bathroom. Rates include buffet breakfast and showers. *Frommer's readers:* Discounts available except during major trade fairs and Oktoberfest. AE, MC, V. Parking 9.50€–13€ ($11–$14). From the main exit of Hauptbahnhof onto Bahnhofplatz, turn right. **Amenities:** Bar; nonsmoking rooms; lobby computer with free Internet access. *In room:* Satellite TV.

Ibis München City   What this chain hotel lacks in charm and old-world atmosphere is compensated for by its location (just minutes from the train station) and seamless functionality. All rooms are exactly the same, tiny and with rather awkward configurations, but they're smartly furnished for a budget hotel and are all the same price. In short, this hotel is for those who desire convenience over character, though when you wake up in the morning, there's little to remind you you're in Munich.

Dachauer Strasse 21, 80335 München. ⓒ **089/55 19 30.** Fax 089/55 19 31 02. www.ibishotel.com. 202 units. 69€ ($79) single; 81€ ($93) double. During major trade fairs and Oktoberfest 99€ ($114) single; 111€ ($128) double. Buffet breakfast 9€ ($10) extra. AE, DC, MC, V. Parking 13€ ($15). From the main exit of Hauptbahnhof onto Bahnhofplatz, turn left and walk 5 min. north on Dachauerstrasse. **Amenities:** Small bar; nonsmoking rooms. *In room:* A/C, cable TV, dataport.

Jedermann 𝒦𝒦 *Finds*   The delightful Jedermann has been owned by the English-speaking Jenke family since 1962. Its breakfast room is a pleasant place to start the day with an all-you-can-eat buffet. Nice touches include flowers, antiques, traditional Bavarian furniture, and chocolates left on the pillows; the reception can provide theater, sightseeing, and public transportation tickets. Units with bathroom have such extras as air-conditioning, TV, and phone; a few have interconnecting doors, good for families. The least expensive units, without bathrooms, have sinks but no phone or TV. The higher rates are charged during major trade fairs.

Bayerstrasse 95, 80335 München. ⓒ **089/54 32 40.** Fax 089/54 32 41 11. www.hotel-jedermann.de. 55 units, 1 with shower only, 48 with bathroom. 34€–49€ ($39–$56) single without bathroom, 49€–107€ ($56–$123) single with bathroom; 49€–89€ ($56–$102) double without bathroom, 57€–99€ ($66–$114) double with shower, 67€–157€ ($77–$181) double with bathroom. Extra person 15€–30€ ($17–$35). Rates include buffet breakfast and showers. Crib available. MC, V. Parking 6€ ($6.90). Tram: 18 or 19 to Hermann-Lingg-Strasse. From south exit of Hauptbahnhof, turn right onto Bayerstrasse and walk 8 min. **Amenities:** Small bar; nonsmoking rooms; lobby computer with free Internet access. *In rooms with bathroom:* Satellite TV, dataport, hair dryer, safe, phone, radio.

NEAR THERESIENWIESE

Westfalia ⊕⊕   A century old, this elaborate building is across from the Okto-berfest meadow. (Most rooms overlook it.) The lobby is on the top floor, where you'll be met by English-speaking owner Peter Deiritz and his family. The rooms are bright and cheerful, with Bavarian pine or modern furniture. The pension itself is cozy and comfortable, the breakfast room and corridor featuring 19th-century paintings by Munich artists. The highest prices apply during Oktoberfest.

Mozartstrasse 23, 80336 München. ℂ 089/53 03 77 or 089/53 03 78. Fax 089/543 91 20. www.pension-westfalia.de. 19 units, 12 with bathroom. 40€–55€ ($46–$63) single without bathroom, 55€–65€ ($63–$75) single with bathroom; 55€–78€ ($63–$90) double without bathroom, 75€–98€ ($86–$113) double with bathroom; 69€–88€ ($79–$101) triple without bathroom, 89€–108€ ($102–$124) triple with bathroom. Rates include buffet breakfast. Showers 1.50€ ($1.75). AE, MC, V. U-Bahn: U-3 or U-6 from Marienplatz to Goetheplatz. Bus: 58 from Hauptbahnhof to Goetheplatz. **Amenities:** Nonsmoking rooms. In room: TV.

IN THE OLD TOWN

Am Markt ⊕   Next to Munich's colorful outdoor market, the Viktualien-markt, this hotel has a nostalgic flair. The rooms are a bit plain and small, but the breakfast room and entry are tastefully decorated and display photos of celebrities who have stayed here—and most who haven't. At any rate, the hotel looks more expensive than it is, and you can't beat its location (the best, in my opinion, of all the accommodations in this chapter). It gets many repeat guests, so book early.

Heiliggeistrasse 6, 80331 München. ℂ **089/22 50 14.** Fax 089/22 40 17. hotel-am-markt.muenchen@t-online.de. 31 units, 12 with bathroom. 38€ ($44) single without bathroom, 66€ ($76) single with bath-room; 68€ ($78) double without bathroom, 87€–92€ ($100–$106) double with bathroom; 99€ ($114) triple without bathroom, 123€ ($141) triple with bathroom. Rates include continental breakfast and show-ers. MC, V. Parking 8€ ($9.20). S-Bahn: From Hauptbahnhof, take any S-Bahn to Marienplatz.

Pension Lindner (Value   A stone's throw from the Münchner Stadtmuseum but in a quiet location in a 30 year-plus building, this pension offers simple, clean, and pleasant rooms (three singles and seven doubles) at rates that make it the best bargain in the Old Town. Owner Frau Sinzinger prefers initial inquiries by phone so she can answer questions immediately (mind the time difference) and will reconfirm via fax. You'll usually find her in the pension's ground-floor cafe, where guests are served breakfast. Note that prices are higher during Okto-berfest and trade fairs; call Frau Sinzinger for exact rates.

Dultstrasse 1, 80331 München. ℂ **089/26 34 13.** Fax 089/26 87 60. 10 units, 2 with shower only, 2 with bathroom. 39€ ($45) single without bathroom; 64€ ($74) double without bathroom, 75€ ($86) double with shower, 85€ ($98) double with bathroom. Rates include buffet breakfast and showers. AE, MC, V. S-Bahn: From Hauptbahnhof, take any S-Bahn to Marienplatz. **Amenities:** Coffee shop. In room: TV, no phone.

Pension Stadt München   In the same building as Pension Lindner (see above), this tiny second-floor pension offers simple but clean doubles and twins, with one shared toilet. The owner, who lives elsewhere, is usually here only in the morning, so choose this place if you like being on your own. Rates are more expensive during Oktoberfest and trade fairs (call for exact rates).

Dultstrasse 1, 80331 München. ℂ **089/26 34 17.** Fax 089/26 75 48. 4 units, 3 with shower only. 45€–50€ ($52–$58) single without shower; 65€–70€ ($75–$81) double with shower. Rates include continental break-fast. AE, DC, MC, V. S-Bahn: From Hauptbahnhof, take any S-Bahn to Marienplatz.

IN SCHWABING

Am Kaiserplatz ⊕⊕ (Kids   If you like touches of the Old World, you can't do better than this place for its price and for the friendly service provided by Frau

Jacobi and her son Thomas. On the ground floor of a Jugendstil building almost a century old, this pension features spacious rooms, each in a different style: for example, the English Room, the Farmer's Room, and the Baroque Room. Extravagantly furnished with chandeliers, sitting areas, lace curtains, or washbasins shaped like seashells, they're highly recommended. Some can sleep up to five persons. Breakfast is served in your room.

Kaiserplatz 12, 80803 München. ℂ **089/34 91 90** or 089/39 52 31. 10 units, 7 with shower only. 32€ ($37) single without bathroom, 47€ ($54) single with shower; 48€–53€ ($55–$61) double without bathroom, 55€–57€ ($63–$66) double with shower. Extra person 22€ ($25). 2€ ($2.30) more per person during major trade fairs and Oktoberfest. Rates include continental breakfast and 1 shower per overnight stay. No credit cards. Take any S-Bahn to Marienplatz, changing to U-Bahn U-3 or U-6 for Münchener Freiheit. **Amenities:** Nonsmoking rooms. *In room:* No phone.

BETWEEN THE CITY CENTER & THE ISAR RIVER

Beck *(Kids)*   This astonishingly cheap pension (four floors, no elevator) occupies a century-old building. Frau Beck welcomes families, with four rooms large enough for five. The rooms, with high ceilings, are large and clean, and most have been updated with modern furniture; a few have balconies. Although it's a trek, rooms on the top floor are sunnier. This pension, with a great location near the Deutsches Museum and a 10-minute walk from the city center, is connected to the airport and train station via S-Bahn. Tram 17, which stops outside the front door, travels directly to the Hauptbahnhof and Nymphenburg Palace.

Thierschstrasse 36, 80538 München. ℂ **089/22 07 08** or 089/22 10 92. Fax 089/22 09 25. www.pension-beck.de. 44 units, 8 with bathroom. 33€–36€ ($38–$41) single without bathroom; 48€–52€ ($55–$60) double without bathroom, 69€–75€ ($79–$86) double with bathroom; 22€–23€ ($25–$26) per person triple, quad, or quint without bathroom, 27€–31€ ($31–$36) per person triple, quad, or quint with bathroom. Rates include continental breakfast and showers. Crib available. MC, V. Parking 5.50€ ($6.30). S-Bahn: S-8 or S-1 from airport or any S-Bahn from Hauptbahnhof (toward Ostbahnhof) to Isartorplatz. U-Bahn: Lehel. Tram: 17 from Hauptbahnhof to Mariannenplatz. *In room:* TV.

WORTH A SPLURGE

Occam *(star)*   This 27-year-old family-owned hotel in the heart of Schwabing's nightlife district offers the extra advantage of the expansive Englischer Garten just a short walk away. The rooms, spread on four floors (no elevator), are rather small but have everything you might need and are named after famous artists like Chagall and Klimt in recognition of Schwabing's former status as an artists' community. Kandinsky prints grace corridor walls.

Occamstrasse 7, 80802 München. ℂ **089/33 25 11.** Fax 089/39 05 30. www.hotel-occam.de. 25 units. 70€–100€ ($81–$115) single, 90€–120€ ($104–$138) double; during Oktoberfest and trade fairs 85€–105€ ($98–$121) single, 95€–145€ ($109–$167) double. Rates include buffet breakfast. AE, MC, V. Take any S-Bahn to Marienplatz, changing to U-Bahn U-3 or U-6 for Münchener Freiheit (take the Feilitzschstrasse exit). **Amenities:** Restaurant; nonsmoking rooms. *In room:* Cable TV.

Uhland *(star star) (Kids)*   The facade of this 100-year-old building, in a quiet residential neighborhood just a few minutes' walk from the Oktoberfest field, is striking—ornate neo-Renaissance with flower boxes of geraniums at all the windows. In former days, each floor was its own grand apartment. The building was converted into a hotel more than 50 years ago by the Hauzenberger family and has kept up with the times, offering laptop connections in every room and a small communal living room with a computer. Each room is unique, with some decorated in Bavarian style and others in high-tech modern. Two rooms have waterbeds (both a single and a double with a heated two-mattress bed), a few have balconies, and there's a children's room with bunk beds and a stereo. The higher prices are charged during Oktoberfest and major conventions.

Uhlandstrasse 1 (near the Oktoberfest meadow, about a 10-min. walk from Hauptbahnhof), 80336 München. (*C*) 089/543 35-0. Fax 089/54 33 52 50. www.hotel-uhland.de. 30 units. 68€–130€ ($78–$150) single; 80€–175€ ($92–$201) double. Rates include buffet breakfast. Extra bed 23€–31€ ($26–$36). Crib available. AE, MC, V. Free parking. U-Bahn: U-4 or U-5 to Theresienwiese. Bus: 58 from Hauptbahnhof to Georg-Hirth-Platz. Amenities: Free use of bikes; babysitting; laundry service; nonsmoking rooms; computer with Internet access for small fee. *In room:* TV, dataport, minibar, hair dryer.

3 Great Deals on Dining

Typical Bavarian restaurants are rustic and boisterous, frequently with wooden tables and chairs, beamed ceilings, and half-paneled walls bearing simple hooks on which you can hang your jacket or hat. You sit wherever there's an empty chair (no one will seat you), making it easy to strike up a conversation with others at your table, especially after a few rounds of beer. Since this is Bavaria, which tends toward excess, the meals are hearty and huge. You don't have to spend a fortune for atmosphere or food.

Most of Munich's restaurants are in the city center, around Marienplatz, and in nightlife districts like Schwabing. Since the menu is almost always posted outside, you'll never be in the dark about prices. Many restaurants offer a *Tageskarte* (daily menu) with special complete meals of the day. In fact, most entrees in Munich's German restaurants are complete meals, including a main course and a couple of side dishes (often potatoes and sauerkraut).

With its six breweries, dozens of beer gardens, and the world's largest beer festival, Munich is probably best known for beer, which is almost a complete meal in itself. Bavarians even drink it for breakfast. The freshest is draft beer; *vom Fass. Weissbier* is made from wheat instead of barley and is full of nutritious (that's one way to look at it) sediment. In summer, a refreshing drink is a *Radler,* half beer and half lemon soda. Note that the beer halls under "Munich After Dark," later in this chapter, also serve food. To accompany your beer, you might want to order food. For breakfast, try *Weisswurst* (white sausage), a delicate blend of veal, salt, pepper, lemon, and parsley. Don't eat the skin unless you want to astound those around you—it would be like eating the wrapper around a hamburger. Another popular dish is *Leberkäse* (also *Leberkäs*), which translates as liver cheese but is neither one. It's a kind of German meatloaf of beef and bacon that looks like a thick slab of bologna, often served with a fried egg on top—it's great with a roll, mustard, and sauerkraut or potatoes. Other Bavarian specialties are *Leberknödl* (liver dumplings, often served in a soup or with sauerkraut), *Kalbshaxe* (grilled veal knuckle), *Schweinshaxe* (grilled pork knuckle), *Schweinsbraten* (pot-roasted pork), *Sauerbraten* (marinated beef in a thick sauce), and *Spanferkel* (suckling pig).

NEAR THE HAUPTBAHNHOF

In addition to the choices here, the department store **Hertie am Bahnhof,** catty-corner from the Hauptbahnhof at Bahnhofplatz 7 ((*C*) **089/55 12-0**), has a self-service restaurant on its fourth floor with extensive self-service counters laden with salads, antipasto, veggies, and desserts, along with daily specials in the 4.50€ to 7.50€ ($5–$8.60) range. It's open Monday to Saturday from 10am to 7:30pm and accepts American Express, Diners Club, MasterCard, and Visa.

Value   Getting the Best Deal on Dining

- Try dining at an *Imbiss,* an inexpensive food stall or tiny hole-in-the-wall serving *Wurst,* french fries, beer, and soda. The food is served over the counter and you eat standing up.
- Take advantage of the special menu of the day, the *Tageskarte,* usually a complete meal in itself. It might not be written on the menu and is almost never written in English.
- Note that butcher shops and food sections of department stores offer takeout foods like *Leberkäs,* grilled chicken, and salads.
- For breakfast or an afternoon coffee, go to the coffee-shop chains Tschibo and Eduscho, which sell both the beans and the brew. You can bring your own pastry and drink a cup of coffee standing up for about 2€ ($2.30). Another good bet for afternoon coffee and cake is a department store cafeteria.
- Ask whether there's an extra charge for bread (restaurants in Bavaria charge for each piece of bread consumed) and whether the entree comes with vegetables or side dishes.
- Buy a picnic lunch at a department store, butcher shop, or the Viktualienmarkt and take it to a beer garden.

Dinea GERMAN/VARIED   This self-service cafeteria about a 5-minute walk from the train station in the direction of the Old Town is your best bet for breakfast, lunch, or an early dinner with a panoramic view over the city's rooftops. The fixed-price meals for less than 8€ ($9.20) change daily; the soups and salad bar are cheaper. Desserts are delicious.

In the Kaufhof department store (6th floor), Karlsplatz 21. ⓒ **089/512 51 146.** Meals 5.50€–7.50€ ($6.30–$8.60). AE, DC, MC, V. Mon–Sat 9:30am–7:45pm. S-Bahn: Karlsplatz/Stachus.

Thessaloniki GREEK   In the small Elisenhof shopping center, this reasonably priced restaurant with subdued lighting, murals of Greek landscapes, and the ubiquitous piped-in Greek music offers all the expected specialties from an English-language menu, from gyros and *souvlakia* to *moussaka,* grilled beef, lamb, and seafood, as well as pizza for 6€ ($6.90) or less.

In the Elisenhof (1st floor), Prielmayerstrasse 1 (catty-corner from Hauptbahnhof's main exit). ⓒ **089/59 82 49.** Meals 8€–15€ ($9.20–$17). AE, MC, V. Daily 11am–midnight. S-/U-Bahn: Hauptbahnhof.

Wienerwald (Kids) GERMAN/CHICKEN   The Wienerwald chain is one of the great successes of postwar Germany, with more than a dozen locations in Munich and hundreds more throughout Germany and Austria. Legend has it that the founder came to the Oktoberfest, saw the mass consumption of grilled chicken, and decided to open his own restaurant serving only that at a great price. Half a grilled chicken costs 5.75€ ($6.60). Other menu items are various chicken dishes, schnitzel, soups, salads (including a salad bar), and daily specials available weekdays for less than 5€ ($5.75). A children's menu and a play corner make it family-friendly. Takeout food is available.

Bayerstrasse 35 (across from Hauptbahnhof's south side). ⓒ **089/54 82 97 13.** Meals 6.75€–9.75€ ($7.75–$11). AE, DC, MC, V. Daily 9am–midnight. S-/U-Bahn: Hauptbahnhof.

IN THE OLD TOWN

If you're craving American food like burgers, sandwiches, steaks, fajitas, grilled chicken, and other familiar fare, head to **Hard Rock Cafe,** Platzl 1 (© **089/242 949 0;** S-/U-Bahn: Marienplatz), a startling contrast to Munich's oldest and most famous tourist place, the Hofbräuhaus, across the square. Meals run 8€ to 18€ ($9.20–$20). It's open Sunday to Thursday noon to 1am, Friday and Saturday noon to 2am, and accepts American Express, Diners Club, MasterCard, and Visa.

Bella Italia Am Stachus *Kids* ITALIAN   This popular chain of Italian-staffed restaurants is the best place in town for inexpensive pizza or pasta, including lasagna, tortellini, cannelloni, and spaghetti, all 3.40€ to 6€ ($3.90–$6.90). The daily specials are usually less than 8€ ($9.20). The pizza Bella Italia (with ham, mushrooms, olives, peppers, artichokes, and salami) is especially good. There's indoor seating as well as tables under trees. You'll find another Bella Italia near the Hauptbahnhof at Dachauer Strasse 1 (© **089/55 74 45;** S-/U-Bahn: Hauptbahnhof), open the same hours.

Herzog-Wilhelm-Strasse 8 (just south of Karlsplatz). © 089/59 32 59. Meals 3.40€–8.70€ ($3.90–$10). No credit cards. Daily 11:30am–midnight. S-Bahn: Karlsplatz/Stachus.

Buxs VEGETARIAN   This pleasant self-service restaurant next to the Viktualienmarkt is modern, bright, and spotless, with outdoor seating in summer. It offers more than 40 salads, vegetables, warm dishes, and desserts, which change daily according to what's fresh. About 90% of the ingredients are organically grown. You can select as much or as little of each salad or dish as you want, making it a great place to try a variety of foods—prices are determined by weighing each plate, with each 100 grams at 2€ ($2.30).

Frauenstrasse 9. © 089/29 19 55-0. Meals 9€–12€ ($10–$14). No credit cards. Mon–Fri 11am–6:45pm; Sat 11am–3pm. S-/U-Bahn: Marienplatz.

Donisl *Value* GERMAN   The Donisl is popular with visitors because of its convenient location, typical Bavarian decor, local specialties, English menu, and meals that are all priced at 6.95€ ($8). Try the *Weisswurst, Leberkäse, Schweinsbraten, Schweinshaxe, Wiener schnitzel,* or *Mastente* (duck), each served with a side dish and best washed down with the freshly tapped beer. If all you want is a quick snack, at the entrance is a small *Imbiss* with even lower prices.

Weinstrasse 1 (off Marienplatz). © 089/29 62 64. Meals 6.95€ ($8). AE, DC, MC, V. Daily 9am–11pm. S-/U-Bahn: Marienplatz.

Nürnberger Bratwurst Glöckl am Dom *Finds* GERMAN   You could easily spend 16€ ($18) or more for Bavarian specialties like pork filet and *Schweinshaxe,* but to experience this great place with an English menu, all you have to order is its famous *Rostbratwürstl* (six pork Nürnberger-style sausages with sauerkraut) or one of its other inexpensive sausage plates. This is Bavaria at its finest: a rough wooden floor, wooden tables, hooks for hanging clothing, beer steins and tin plates lining a wall shelf, Bavarian specialties grilled over an open wood fire, and beer served from wooden barrels. Upstairs is the intimate Albrecht Dürer Room, but I prefer the ground floor's liveliness. In summer, there's limited outdoor seating in the shadow of the majestic Frauenkirche church. An evening here could possibly be your most memorable in Munich.

Frauenplatz 9. © 089/29 52 64. Meals 8€–19€ ($9.20–$22). No credit cards. Mon–Sat 10am–10pm; Sun 11am–10pm. S-/U-Bahn: Marienplatz.

Ratskeller ⭐⭐ GERMAN/CONTINENTAL   The Ratskeller is cavernous, with low vaulted, painted ceilings, white tablecloths, and flowers on the tables. This dignified restaurant with an English menu doesn't have a dress code, but shorts aren't appropriate. Besides Bavarian and Franconian specialties such as roast suckling pig, roast pork, Wiener schnitzel, *Wurst*, and *Leberkäs*, it has a few vegetarian dishes, as well as changing specials. This is also a good choice for *Weisswurst* in the morning, an afternoon coffee and dessert, or a glass of Franconian wine in the adjoining wine cellar (open daily from 3pm, with live music nightly).

In Town Hall's cellar, on Marienplatz. ✆ **089/21 99 89-0.** Reservations recommended. Meals 10€–25€ ($12–$29). AE, MC, V. Daily 10am–11pm. S-/U-Bahn: Marienplatz.

Weisses Bräuhaus GERMAN   This boisterous place is famous for its beer (*Bräuhaus* means "brewery"), and the kind to order is wheat beer, either *Weizenbier* or *Weissbier*. With a simple white interior containing a wooden floor and long wooden tables, plus sidewalk seating in summer, this typical Bavarian restaurant has an English-language menu whose cheapest and most famous meal is *Weisswurst* (4€/$4.60 for a pair, available 'til noon). If you're hungry, order the Bavarian Farmer's Feast—roast and smoked pork, pork sausage, liver dumplings, mashed potatoes, and sauerkraut. Other choices are *Leberkäs* ("liver cheese" on the English menu), suckling pig, *Schweinsbraten*, and potato pancakes. It's also a less touristy choice than the Hofbräuhaus.

Tal 7. ✆ **089/290 13 80.** Meals 8.90€–15€ ($10–$17). MC, V. Daily 8:30am–11pm. S-/U-Bahn: Marienplatz.

NEAR THE PINAKOTHEK

The **Mensa Technische Universität**, Arcisstrasse 17 (✆ **089/28 66 39 10**), has a student cafeteria convenient for lunch if you find yourself visiting the area's museums. Even if you're not a student, you can take advantage of cheap meals by going to the *Verwaltung* to the left under the staircase and buying a guest card for 11€ ($13). You can then use the card to purchase a meal ticket from a vending machine. Whatever you don't spend with the guest card is reimbursed when you return the card. Set meals cost 1.15€ to 2.40€ ($1.30–$2.75) for students, and about .40€ (45¢) more for nonstudents. The Mensa is open Monday to Thursday from 11am to 2pm, Friday 11am to 1:45pm. No credit cards are accepted.

Caffè Greco ⭐ GREEK/MEDITERRANEAN/BAVARIAN   Located on the lower level of the Neue Pinakothek with its own outdoor entrance, this casual yet classy restaurant is your best bet for a satisfying meal when visiting the many nearby museums. Gleaming dark woods, photographs hung on white walls, black bentwood chairs, and white tablecloths set the mood for a meal from a limited but varied menu, including a classic Greek salad, various spaghetti dishes, fish of the day, and Bavarian specialties like *Leberkäs*.

Barer Strasse 29 (entrance on Theresienstrasse). ✆ **089/2867 57 50.** Meals 7€–13€ ($8.05–$15). AE, MC, V. Daily 9am–6pm (to 8pm Wed). U-Bahn: U-2 to Theresienstrasse or Königsplatz. Tram: 27 to Pinakothek. Bus: 53 to Schellingstrasse.

IN SCHWABING

Gasthaus Weinbauer ⭐ GERMAN   This longtime neighborhood favorite serves hearty fare in a typical Bavarian setting, with few adornments outside a few antiques. The lunch and dinner menus change daily but might include such main dishes as *Spanferkel, Wiener schnitzel,* or *Wurst.*

Fendstrasse 5. ✆ **089/39 81 55.** Reservations recommended for dinner. Meals 8€–14€ ($9.20–$16). No credit cards. Mon–Fri 11am–midnight; Sat 3pm–midnight. U-Bahn: U-3 or U-6 to Münchener Freiheit.

⟮Moments⟯ Munich's Beer Gardens

The city's beer gardens are as fickle as the weather—if the weather's bad, the beer gardens don't open. By the same token, if suddenly in the middle of February the weather turns gloriously warm, the beer gardens start turning on the taps.

Generally speaking, beer gardens are open on sunny days May to September or October, usually 10 or 11am to 11pm. Ranging from tiny neighborhood gardens accommodating a few hundred to those seating several thousand, they number about 30 in and around Munich, making it the world's beer garden capital. *Note:* Many of the beer gardens are in the middle of huge parks, making them a bit difficult to find. Take note of how you got there; it's even harder to find your way out of the park after you've had a few liters of beer.

These four beer gardens allow you to bring your own food: **Augustiner Keller,** Arnulfstrasse 52 (℡ **089/59 43 93**), about a 10-minute walk northwest of the Hauptbahnhof; **Viktualienmarkt,** in the city center near Marienplatz (℡ **089/29 75 45**), closed Sunday and holidays (see "Picnicking," below); **Chinesischer Turm,** with a lovely location in the Englischer Garten (℡ **089/38 38 73 0**; U-Bahn: U-3 or U-6 to Giselastrasse); and **Hirschgarten,** Hirschgartenstrasse 1 (℡ **089/17 25 91**; S-Bahn: Laim), one of Europe's largest, near Nymphenburg Palace. In the Old Town, the famous **Hofbräuhaus,** Platzl 9 (℡ **089/22 16 76**), also has a beer garden.

Gaststätte Leopold AUSTRIAN/BAVARIAN   This large 100-year-old restaurant with antiques, wainscoting, a hand-painted ceiling, and an atmosphere reminiscent of decades past can be a haven from the Schwabing throngs, although later it can get crowded. In summer, tables and chairs are set outside, where you can watch the passing crowds. It serves Austrian and Bavarian cuisine, such as *Leberkäs* with fried egg and potato salad, *Wiener schnitzel, Schweinshaxe,* and *Tafelspitz,* but oxen dishes are its specialty.

Leopoldstrasse 50. ℡ **089/38 38 680.** Meals 8€–20€ ($9.20–$23). AE, DC, MC, V. Daily 11:30am–11:30pm. U-Bahn: U-3 or U-6 to Giselastrasse.

Mama's Kebap Haus ⟮Value⟯ TURKISH   This small and simple self-service restaurant with a friendly staff in the heart of Schwabing's nightlife district is always crowded with young diners, who stop for an inexpensive meal before or after hitting the nightspots. You can eat the Turkish or Italian pizza by the slice, kabobs, and daily specials at one of the half dozen tables; or get takeout.

Feilitzsch-strasse 7. ℡ **089/39 26 42.** Meals 3.50€–7.50€ ($4–$8.60). No credit cards. Sun–Thurs 10am–1am; Fri–Sat 10am–3am. U-Bahn: U-3 or U-6 to Münchener Freiheit.

PICNICKING

Department stores (like Hertie across from the train station or Kaufhof on Marienplatz) have basement food departments selling fruits and vegetables, cheeses, sausages, breads, drinks, and cakes, as well as ready-made salads, *Leberkäs,* grilled chicken, and more. I especially like Hertie's **Schmankerlgasse,**

an underground passage at Karlsplatz lined with food stalls offering sandwiches, pizza, fish, vegetarian dishes, Chinese food, Greek specialties, pasta, desserts, croissants, fruit juices, cheeses, and vegetables. You can stand and eat here, sit at one of the tables or counters, or take your food with you.

If you want more traditional surroundings, the **Viktualienmarkt** can't be beat. Munich's most famous outdoor market, from the early 1800s, is a colorful affair with permanent little shops and booths, and stalls set up under umbrellas. *Wurst,* bread, cakes, honey, cheese, wine, fruits, vegetables, flowers, and meats are sold, and in the middle of the market there's even a beer garden, where you're welcome to sit at one of the outer tables (only at those without a tablecloth) and eat your purchase. There are also a lot of stand-up fast-food counters offering sausages, sandwiches, and other dishes. The market is open Monday to Friday 8am to 6pm and Saturday 8am to 2pm. Best of all, it's only a couple minutes' walk from Marienplatz in the heart of the Old Town.

And where can you go to eat your goodies? Try along the **Isar River** or somewhere in the huge expanse of the **Englischer Garten.** Better yet, take your food to one of the **beer gardens** (see the box "Munich's Beer Gardens," above), where all you have to buy is one of those famous mugs of foaming beer.

WORTH A SPLURGE

Hundskugel ✸✸ GERMAN   Opened in 1440, this might be Munich's oldest restaurant. Its facade, brightly lit and decorated with flower boxes, hints at what's waiting inside: a tiny dining room with a low-beamed ceiling, little changed over the centuries. It serves Bavarian and German traditional food from an English menu, including suckling pig with dumplings and *kraut* salad; boiled beef cooked in meat stock and sliced; braised beef with gravy; and the *Hundskugel Spezial* (broiled pork tenderloin with potatoes, mushrooms, and vegetables, baked with cheese). Dining here is an experience you won't soon forget.

Hotterstrasse 18. ⓒ **089/26 42 72.** Reservations required. Meals 8.10€–20€ ($9.30–$23); 3-course daily special 10€ ($12) or less. No credit cards. Daily 11am–11pm. S-/U-Bahn: Marienplatz.

Prinz Myshkin ✸✸ VEGETARIAN   This trendy restaurant serves vegetarian dishes in a refined setting with a high vaulted ceiling, artwork, candles, and background music that's likely to be soft jazz. You'll find a variety of changing salads, soups, and appetizers that might include vegetarian quiche, Japanese miso soup, or a wild-rice salad. In addition to pizza, it offers innovative main dishes inspired by the cuisines of Asia, Italy, Greece, and Mexico, which might range from various ravioli to vegetarian sushi to tofu stroganoff. A great alternative to heavier Bavarian food.

Hackenstrasse 2 (off Sendlinger Strasse, a few minutes' walk from Marienplatz). ⓒ **089/26 55 96.** Main courses 9.50€–15€ ($11–$17); fixed-price lunch Mon–Fri 7€ ($8.05); pizza 7€–10€ ($8.05–$12). AE, MC, V. Daily 11:30am–11:30pm. S-/U-Bahn: Marienplatz.

4 Seeing the Sights

THE TOP MUSEUMS & PALACES

Alte Pinakothek ✸✸✸   If you visit only one art museum in Munich, this should be it. Begun as the collection of the Wittelsbach family in the early 1500s, it ranks as one of Europe's most important galleries and contains virtually all European schools of painting from the Middle Ages to the early 19th century, with one of the world's largest collections of Rubens, plus galleries filled with German, Dutch, Flemish, Italian, Spanish, and French masterpieces. Represented are **Dürer, Cranach, Altdorfer, Bruegel the Elder and the Younger, Rembrandt,**

> ### Value   Getting the Best Deal on Sightseeing
>
> - Visit the Alte Pinakothek, Neue Pinakothek, Pinakothek der Moderne, Glyptothek, Antikensammlung, Bayerisches Nationalmuseum, or Münchner Stadtmuseum on Sunday—when admission to the permanent exhibitions is free (but you'll have to brave the crowds).
> - Buy combination tickets wherever possible, such as the combination ticket for the three Pinakothek, cheaper than buying a separate ticket for each.
> - Note that some museums and attractions, such as the Deutsches Museum, the Münchner Stadtmuseum, and the BMW Museum, offer a family ticket that's cheaper than individual tickets for adults and children.
> - If you plan on doing a lot of sightseeing using public transportation, buy the 1- or 3-day Munich Welcome Card, allowing unlimited travel and discounts of up to 50% on selected sights.

Raphael, Titian, Tiepolo, El Greco, Velázquez, Murillo, Poussin, and **Lorrain.** You'll also find galleries of religious allegorical paintings, portraits of peasants and patricians, Romantic landscapes, still lifes, and scenes of war and hunting. They're housed in an imposing structure built by Leo von Klenze from 1826 to 1836 and modeled on Venetian Renaissance palazzi. Plan to spend at least a couple hours here.

Although it's difficult to pick the collection's stars, Dürer is well represented with *Four Apostles, The Baumgartner Altar, Lamentation for the Dead Christ,* and, my favorite, his famous *Self-Portrait (Selbstbildnis im Pelzrock)*. Watch for Titian's *Crowning with Thorns (Die Dornenkrönung)*, Rembrandt's *Birth of Christ* with his remarkable use of light and shadows, and Brueghel's *Land of Cockaigne*. Among the many Rubens are the rather frightening *Last Judgment (Das Grosse Jüngste Gericht)* and *The Damned's Descent into Hell (Der Höllensturz der Verdammten)*, sure to make a convert of the most avowed sinner. In Albrecht Altdorfer's *Battle of Alexander,* which took him 12 years to complete, notice the painstaking detail of the thousands of lances and all the men on horseback. Yet Alexander the Great on his horse is easy to spot amid the chaos, as he pursues Darius fleeing in his chariot. Another favorite is Adriaen Brouwer of the Netherlands, one of the best painters of the peasant genre. The Alte Pinakothek has 17 of his paintings in room no. 11, the largest collection in the world. Brouwer's skill at capturing the life of his subjects as they drink at an inn, play cards, or engage in a brawl is delightful.

Barer Strasse 27 (entrance on Theresienstrasse). ✆ **089/238 05-216**. www.alte-pinakothek.de. Admission 5€ ($5.75) adults, 3.50€ ($4) seniors, students, and children; combination ticket for all 3 Pinakothek 12€ ($14) adults, 7€ ($8.05) seniors, students, and children. Tues 10am–8pm; Wed–Sun 10am–5pm. U-Bahn: U-2 to Theresienstrasse or Königsplatz. Tram: 27 to Pinakothek. Bus: 53 to Schellingstrasse.

Deutsches Museum ✰✰✰ *(Kids)*   I've been to the Deutsches Museum more than any other Munich museum and still haven't seen it all. Munich's most visited museum and the world's largest and oldest technological museum of its kind, it's divided into 53 exhibits, relating to physics, navigation, mining, vehicle engineering, musical instruments, glass technology, writing and printing, photography, textiles, and weights and measures. There's also a planetarium. If

Munich

↑ To Olympiapark

← To Nymphenburg
(see inset)

✝	Church
ⓘ	Information
✉	Post Office
Ⓢ	S-Bahn
Ⓤ	U-Bahn

Zieblandstr.
Schellingstrasse
Theresien- strasse
Hess-Strasse
Augustenstr.
Luisenstrasse
Arcisstrasse
Barerstrasse
Gabelsbergerstrasse
Schleissheimerstrasse
Brienner Strasse
Dachauerstrasse
Augustenstrasse
Karlstrasse
Königs-platz
Meiserstrasse
Karolinen-platz
Max-Joseph-Strasse
Seidlstrasse
Barerstrasse
Marsstrasse
Luisenstrasse
Sophienstrasse
ALTER
BOTANISCHER
GARTEN
Maximilians-platz
Arnulfstrasse
Elisenstrasse
Lenbach-platz
Bahnhof-platz
Prielmayerstrasse
Maxburgstrasse
Hauptbahnhof
Schützenstr.
Bayerstrasse
Karls-platz
Neuhauserstrasse
Senefelderstrasse
Adolf-Kolping-Str.
Herzogspitalstrasse
Schwanthalerstrasse
Hotterstr.
**Deutsches
Theater** ■
Sonnenstr.
Herzog-Wilhelm-Strasse
Josephspitalstr.
Landwehrstrasse
Goethestrasse
Schillerstrasse
Matthildenstrasse
Sendlingerstr.
Pettenkoferstrasse
Sendlingertor-platz
Matthäus-kirche
Beethoven-platz
Nussbaumstrasse
Unterer Anger
Blumen-strasse
Lindwurmstrasse
Müller- strasse
Thalkirchnerstrasse
Jahnstrasse
**ST. STEFAN'S
CEMETERY**

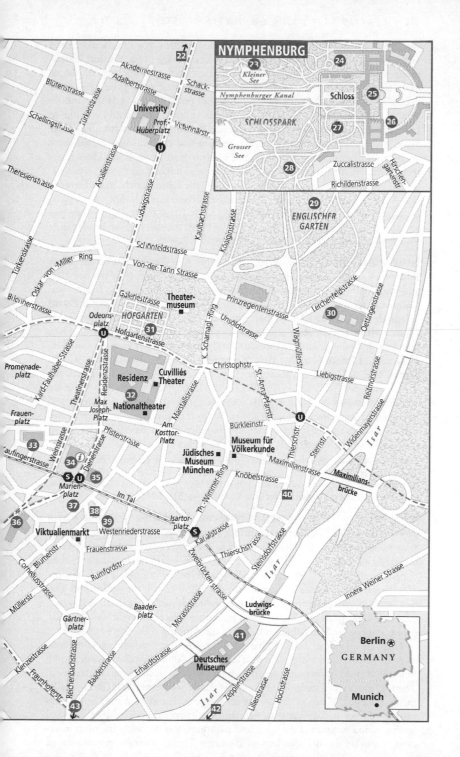

NYMPHENBURG

23 Kleiner See

24

Nymphenburger Kanal

Schloss 25

SCHLOSSPARK

27

26

Grosser See

28

Zuccalistrasse

Richildenstrasse

Akademiestrasse

22

Schack-strasse

Adalbertstrasse

Blütenstrasse

Türkenstrasse

Schellingstrasse

University

Prof.-Huberplatz

Veterinärstr.

U

Arcisstrasse

Ludwigstrasse

Kaulbachstrasse

Königinstrasse

29 ENGLISCHER GARTEN

Theresienstrasse

Schönfeldstrasse

Von-der-Tann Strasse

Lerchenfeldstrasse

Oettingenstrasse

Oskar-von-Miller- Ring

Galeriestrasse

Theater-museum

Prinzregentenstrasse

30

Türkenstrasse

Brennerstrasse

Odeons-platz

U

HOFGARTEN

31

Hofgartenstrasse

K. Scharnagl.-Ring

Unsöldstrasse

Wagmüllerstr.

Promenade-platz

Kard.-Faulhaber-Strasse

Theatinerstrasse

Residenzstrasse

Residenz

Cuvilliés Theater

Christophstr.

St.-Anna-Pfarrstr.

Liebigstrasse

Reitmorstrasse

Isar

Frauen-platz

Max Joseph-Platz

12 Nationaltheater

Marstallstrasse

U

Sternstr.

Widenmayerstrasse

Pfisterstrasse

Am Kosttor-Platz

Bürkleinstr.

33

aufingerstrasse

Weinstrasse

Dienerstrasse

34

i

Jüdisches Museum München

Museum für Völkerkunde

Maximilianstrasse

Thierschstr.

Maximilians-brücke

S

U

35

Knöbelstrasse

36

Marien-platz

37

38

Im Tal

Th.-Wimmer-Ring

40

Isartor-platz

S

39 Westenriederstrasse

Kanalstrasse

Viktualienmarkt

Frauenstrasse

Thierschstrasse

Steinsdorfstraße

Innere Weiner Strasse

Rumfordstr.

Zweibrückenstrasse

Morassistrasse

Isar

Cornelusstrasse

Blumenstr.

Müllerstr.

Gärtner-platz

Baader-platz

Baaderstrasse

Ludwigs-brücke

Berlin ⊛

GERMANY

Kienzestrasse

Reichenbachstrasse

Fraunhoferstr.

41

Erhardtstrasse

Deutsches Museum

Zeppelinstrasse

Lilienstrasse

Hochstrasse

Munich •

43

Isar

42

637

you follow the guideline running through the museum, you'll walk more than 16km (10 miles). You can see a replica of the **Gutenberg press, musical instruments** from electronic drums to a glass harmonica, and an impressive display of **early airplanes** that includes the Wright brothers' first serial plane (a double-decker 1909 Type A). You can descend into the bowels of **coal** and **salt mines**— it takes the better part of an hour just to walk through one. Would you like to ponder the meaning behind the prehistoric drawings of the **Altamira Cave?** What makes the museum fascinating for adults and children alike is that there are buttons to push, gears to crank, and levers to pull (though in today's high-tech world, children used to virtual reality arcades might find the displays a little too tame). There's also a children's section, the **Kinderreich,** geared toward kids 8 and younger. In any case, you could easily spend a half-day here.

Museumsinsel 1 (Ludwigsbrücke). ⊙ **089/217 9 1.** www.deutsches-museum.de. Admission 7.50€ ($8.60) adults, 5€ ($5.75) seniors, 3€ ($3.45) students and children, 15€ ($17) families. Daily 9am–5pm (to 8pm 1st and 3rd Wed of the month). S-Bahn: Isartor. Tram: 18 to Deutsches Museum.

Neue Pinakothek 🏛️🏛️🏛️ Across from the Alte Pinakothek is the Neue Pinakothek, with its comprehensive view of European painting in the late 18th and 19th centuries. It begins with art from around 1800 **(Goya, Turner,** and **Gainsborough)** and works by early romantic landscape painters **Caspar David Friedrich** and **Leo von Klenze,** then continues with works of the Biedermeier era **(Waldmüller**'s romanticized renditions of peasant life are wonderful), German and French Impressionism, symbolism, and Art Nouveau. **Corinth, Courbet, Delacroix, Liebermann, Menzel, Cézanne, Gauguin, Rodin, van Gogh, Degas, Manet, Monet,** and **Renoir** all have canvases here. The building itself is a delight, designed by Alexander von Branca and opened in 1981 to replace the old museum destroyed in World War II. Using the natural lighting of skylights and windows, it's the perfect setting for the paintings it displays, and perimeter ramps make the works accessible by wheelchair or stroller. Follow the rooms chronologically, starting with room no. 1, and expect to spend 1 to 2 hours.

Barer Strasse 29 (entrance on Theresienstrasse). ⊙ **089/238 05-195.** www.neue-pinakothek.de. Admission 5€ ($5.75) adults, 3.50€ ($4) seniors, students, and children; combination ticket for all 3 Pinakothek 12€ ($14) adults, 7€ ($8.05) seniors, students, and children. Wed 10am–8pm; Thurs–Mon 10am–5pm. U-Bahn: U-2 to Theresienstrasse or Königsplatz. Tram: 27 to Pinakothek. Bus: 53 to Schellingstrasse.

Nymphenburg Palace, Marstallmuseum, Amalienburg & the Royal Pavilions 🏛️🏛️🏛️ The former summer residence of the Wittelsbach family who ruled over Bavaria, Nymphenburg is Germany's largest baroque palace. Construction began in 1664 but took more than a century to complete; then the palace stretched 570m (1,870 ft.) long and looked out over a park of some 200 hectares (500 acres). You could spend a whole day in the **sculptured garden** (with its statues, artificial hills, lakes, canals, botanical gardens, and waterfalls) and in the **park pavilions** (each a miniature palace). But first visit the main palace and nearby Marstallmuseum for its outstanding collection of carriages.

There are no guided tours of Nymphenburg—you can either wander on your own in the two open wings or rent a 2.50€ ($2.20) audioguide, worth the 40 minutes of taped information because almost nothing in the rooms is identified. The first room you'll see is the glorious two-story **Steinerner Saal (Stone Hall),** richly decorated in late rococo style with stuccowork and frescoes. The hall was used for parties and concerts; subsequent rooms contain portraits of the royal family, period furniture, tapestries, and paintings. But probably the most interesting room is Ludwig I's **Gallery of Beauties:** The 36 portraits, commissioned by Ludwig, represent the most beautiful women in Munich in his time. Among them are Queen Marie of Bavaria (mother of Ludwig II), Helene Sedlmayr (daughter of a shoemaker, who later married a footman and had 10 children), and Lola Montez (a dancer whose scandalous relations with Ludwig prompted an 1848 revolt by a disgruntled people who forced his abdication). Outside the main palace (to the left as you face the ticket booth) is the **Marstallmuseum,** with a splendid collection of state coaches, carriages, and sleds used for weddings, coronations, and special events. Housed in what used to be the royal stables, the museum culminates in the fantastic fairy-tale carriages of Ludwig II, which are no less extravagant than his castles. On the floor above the Marstallmuseum is the **Museum of Nymphenburg Porcelain,** with a fine collection of delicate figurines, tea services, plates, and bowls from the mid–18th century through the 1920s, including works of Franz Anton Bustelli, considered the most important porcelain sculptor of the 18th century.

Now head for the park, first laid out as a geometrical baroque garden but transformed into an English landscape garden in the early 19th century. To your left is **Amalienburg,** a small pink hunting lodge unlike anything you've ever seen. One of the world's great masterpieces of rococo art, it was built by François de Cuvilliés for Electress Maria Amalia, Charles Albert's wife. Legend has it she used to station herself on a platform on the roof to shoot game that were driven past her. The first couple of rooms in this lodge are simple enough (note the small dog kennels in the 1st room), with drawings in the spirit of the hunt, but then the rooms take off in a flight of fantasy, with an amazing amount of decorative silver covering almost every inch of the walls with vines, grapes, and cherubs. Its **Hall of Mirrors** is as splendid a room as you're likely to find anywhere, far surpassing anything in the main palace. In the park are three pavilions (closed in winter): the **Magdalenenklause,** a meditation retreat for Max Emanuel, complete with artificial cracks in the walls to make it look like a ruin; the **Pagodenburg,** an elegant two-story tea pavilion, with Dutch tiles on the ground floor and Chinese black-and-red lacquered chambers upstairs; and **Badenburg,** Max Emanuel's bathhouse with its Chinese wallpaper and two-story pool faced with Dutch tiles (Europe's 1st heated indoor pool). Afterward, stop for a coffee and cake at the **Schlosscafe** in the Palmenhaus, a greenhouse built in 1820 with outdoor seating. Plan on spending at least 1½ hours to tour the main palace, Marstallmuseum, and Amalienburg.

Schloss Nymphenburg 1. (②) 089/179 08-0. www.schloesser.bayern.de. Combination ticket to everything 10€ ($12) adults, 8€ ($9.20) seniors, students, and children in summer; 8€ ($9.20) and 6€ ($6.90), respectively, in winter; Nymphenburg Palace only 5€ ($5.75) adults, 4€ ($4.60) seniors, students, and children. Apr to mid-Oct daily 9am–6pm (Thurs to 8pm); mid-Oct to Mar daily 10am–4pm. Badenburg, Pagodenburg, and Magdalenenklause closed mid-Oct to Mar. Tram: 17 to Schloss Nymphenburg.

Pinakothek der Moderne 🏵🏵 This spacious, modern museum brings together four major collections under one roof—art, graphics, architecture, and design—making it Germany's largest museum of art from the 20th and 21st centuries. Foremost is the art collection, which features changing exhibitions that might include German expressionists like Ernst Ludwig Kirchner and Max Beckmann (the museum possesses Europe's largest collection of Beckmann's works); surrealists like René Magritte and Dalí; and some of the most important names in modern art, including Picasso, Warhol, Beuys, Rauschenberg, Jasper Johns, and Bruce Nauman. The Architecture Museum displays temporary exhibits on the history of architecture and current developments, while the State Graphic Art Collection stages temporary displays from the beginning of classical modernism to the present. I especially like the New Collection, with its visually pleasing displays of industrial design and applied arts, which can run the gamut from automobiles and computers to teapots and chairs. You can easily spend 2 hours here.

Barer Strasse 40. (€) **089/238 05-360.** www.pinakothek-der-moderne.de. Admission 9€ ($10) adults, 5€ ($5.75) seniors, students, and children; combination ticket for all 3 Pinakothek 12€ ($14) adults, 7€ ($8.05) seniors, students, and children. Tues–Sun 10am–5pm (to 8pm Thurs–Fri). U-Bahn: Odeonsplatz or Theresien-strasse. Tram: 27 to Pinakothek. Bus: 53 to Schellingstrasse.

The Residenz, Residenzmuseum & Schatzkammer ✸✸   While Nymphen-burg Palace was the Wittelsbach summer home, the Residenz was the family's offi-cial town residence for 4 centuries until 1918. The **Residenzmuseum,** a small part of the residence, is open to the public. A mere fraction of the total palace, it's so large that only half the museum's 160 rooms are open to the public in the morn-ing; the other half is open in the afternoon. No matter when you come, you'll see court rooms, apartments, bedchambers, and arcades in everything from Renais-sance and baroque to rococo and neoclassical. The **Antiquarium** is the largest sec-ular Renaissance room north of the Alps; in the **Silver Chamber** is the complete table silver of the House of Wittelsbach—some 3,500 pieces. The **Ancestors Hall** contains the portraits of 121 members of the family—eerie because of the way their eyes seem to follow you as you walk down the hall. Be sure to see the **Emperor's Hall, Rich Chapel, Green Gallery,** and **Rich Rooms** by François de Cuvilliés the Elder, one of the best examples of South German rococo.

In the Residenz is also the **Schatzkammer (Treasure House),** housing an amazing collection of jewelry, gold, silver, insignia, and religious items belong-ing to the Bavarian royalty and collected over 1,000 years, including the royal crown, swords, scepters, goblets, bowls, toiletry objects, serving platters, treas-ures from other countries, and more. The highlight is the 1,586-jewel-studded statue of St. George on his horse. Plan on spending at least 2 hours to tour both the Residenzmuseum and the Schatzkammer, especially if you take advantage of the free audioguide.

Max-Joseph-Platz 3. (€) **089/290 67 1.** www.schloesser.bayern.de. Combination ticket for Residenzmuseum and Schatzkammer 9€ ($10) adults, 8€ ($9.20) seniors and students, free for children under 18; ticket for either Residenzmuseum or Schatzkammer 6€ ($6.90) adults, 5€ ($5.75) seniors and students. Summer daily 9am–6pm; winter daily 10am–4pm. You must enter 30 min. before closing time. S-Bahn: Marienplatz. U-Bahn: U-3, U-4, U-5, or U-6 to Odeonsplatz. Tram: 19 to Nationaltheater.

OTHER MUSEUMS

Antikensammlungen   The Antikensammlungen and the Glyptothek across the square (see below) form one of Germany's largest collections of classical art. The Antikensammlungen houses the state's collection of Greek, Roman, and Etruscan antiquities. The focus is on **Greek amphorae** (two-handled jars with narrow necks used to carry wine or oil), primarily Attic from the 6th and 5th centuries B.C. and beautifully depicting the Greek love of sports, Greek gods, and women performing household duties like spinning. Statues (many of them replicas) and Roman terra-cotta and bronze objects round out the collection. Particularly striking is the **Greek and Etruscan gold jewelry** with its amazing detail and brilliance, including necklaces, bracelets, and earrings—they would look fashionable even today. Alas, the descriptions are only in German. You can tour both the Antikensammlungen and Glyptothek in about an hour or so.

Königsplatz 1. (€) **089/59 98 88 30.** www.antikensammlungen.de. Admission 3€ ($3.45) adults, 2€ ($2.30) sen-iors and students, free for children under 18; combination ticket for Glyptothek and Antikensammlungen 5€ ($5.75) adults, 3€ ($3.45) seniors and students. Tues–Sun 10am–5pm (to 8pm Wed). U-Bahn: U-2 to Königsplatz.

Special & Free Events

Munich's most famous event is the **Oktoberfest**, from mid-September to the first Sunday in October. The celebration began in 1810 to honor Ludwig I's marriage, when the main event was a horse race in a field called the Thereisenwiese. Everyone had so much fun the celebration was held again the following year, and then again and again. Today the Oktoberfest is among the largest fairs in the world.

Every year the festivities get under way with a parade on the first Oktoberfest Sunday, when almost 7,000 participants march through the streets in folk costumes. Most activities, however, are at the Theresienwiese, where huge beer tents sponsored by local breweries dispense both beer and merriment, complete with Bavarian bands and singing. Each tent holds up to 6,000, which gives you some idea of how rowdy things can get. During the 16-day period, an estimated six million visitors guzzle more than a million gallons of beer and eat 700,000 broiled chickens! In addition to the beer tents, there are carnival attractions and amusement rides. Entry to the fairgrounds is free, but rides cost extra.

During the last 2 weeks in April, a smaller **Frühlingsfest (Spring Festival)** is held at Theresienwiese, complete with beer tents and an amusement park; it gives a taste of the Oktoberfest without the crowds and tourists. Young people flock to Olympiapark for the **Tollwood Summer Festival,** an international cultural festival with music, cabaret, and stage performances held mid-June to mid-July; and the **Summer Festival,** a musical feast of rock and jazz the last 2 weeks in August. Munich's other major event is **Fasching (Carnival),** which culminates Shrove Tuesday in a parade through town and a festive atmosphere of food, drink, and dances by market vendors at the Viktualienmarkt. From the end of November until Christmas, an outdoor **Christmas Market** brings color and cheer to the Old Town.

Bayerisches Nationalmuseum ✿ *Value* The Bavarian National Museum emphasizes the historical and cultural development of Bavaria, as well as the rest of Europe, from the Middle Ages to the early 19th century. It complements the Alte Pinakothek, showing what was happening in other genres of art and crafts at the same time that painters were producing their masterpieces. Glass, miniatures, musical instruments, wood and ivory carvings, jewelry, clothing, textiles and tapestries, porcelain, medieval armor and weaponry, furniture, stained-glass windows, sculpture, and religious artifacts and altars are some of the 20,000 items. Outstanding are the **wood sculptures** from the Gothic through rococo periods, especially carvings by **Tilman Riemenschneider** (notice the facial expressions of the 12 Apostles in room no. 16), as well as works by **Erasmus Grasser, Michael Pacher, Johann Baptist Staub,** and **Ignaz Günther.**

One delightful thing about this museum is that the architecture complements the objects. The Late Gothic Church Art Room (room no. 15), for example, is modeled after a church in Augsburg, providing a perfect background for the religious art it displays. My favorite is the basement, partly devoted to folk art, including furniture and complete rooms showing how people lived long ago. Notice the wooden floors and low ceiling (to save heat). The other half of the museum houses an incredible collection of **nativity scenes** *(Krippe)* ⟨★★⟩ from the Alpine region and Italy. Some of the displays are made of paper, but most are amazingly elaborate and lifelike; it's worth visiting the museum for them alone. Otherwise, to do the entire museum justice, plan on devoting at least 2 hours here.

Prinzregentenstrasse 3. ℂ 089/211 24 01. www.bayerisches-nationalmuseum.de. Admission 3€ ($3.45) adults, 2€ ($2.30) seniors and students, free for children under 15; more for special exhibits. Tues–Sun 10am–5pm (to 8pm Thurs). U-Bahn: U-4 or U-5 to Lehel. Tram: 17 to Nationalmuseum.

BMW Museum ⟨★⟩   Anyone interested in cars, motorcycles, and the history of the automobile could easily spend 3 or 4 hours here. Housed in a modern building resembling a giant silver bowl (or is it a wheel?), it features more than two dozen videos (like one describing how the future was imagined by people in the past), slide shows, a cinema, and displays of rare motors and the most important BMW automobiles from the days of the oldies to the age of the robot and beyond. A computer allows you to custom-design your own BMW. Several displays explain in-car navigation systems and how they'll revolutionize personal transport, while others explore alternatives to the combustion engine.

Petuelring 130. ℂ 089/38 22 33 07. Admission 3€ ($3.45) adults, 2€ ($2.30) students, seniors, and children, 6.50€ ($7.50) families. Daily 9am–5pm (you must enter by 4pm). U-Bahn: U-3 to Olympiazentrum.

Glyptothek   The architectural counterpart of the Antikensammlungen (see above), the Glyptothek houses Greek and Roman statues, busts, and grave steles in a setting reminiscent of a Roman bath, and is one of Germany's best examples of neoclassicism. Designed by Leo von Klenze, the building was commissioned to house the personal collection of statues belonging to Crown Prince Ludwig I, whose dream was to transform Munich into another Athens. Indeed, the Glyptothek does resemble a Greek temple. In Room II (to your left as you enter) is the museum's most famous piece, the Greek *Faun Barberini*, a large sleeping satyr from about 220 B.C. In Room IV is the **grave stele of Mnesarete** (daughter of Socrates), depicting a dead mother seated in front of her daughter. Also in the museum are sculptures from the pediments of the **Aphaia Temple in Aegina,** with scenes of the Trojan War. But my favorite is the room overflowing with **Roman busts** of emperors, their families, and other members of nobility.

Königsplatz 3. ℂ 089/28 61 00. www.glyptothek.de. Admission 3€ ($3.45) adults, 2€ ($2.30) seniors and students; combination ticket for Glyptothek and Antikensammlungen 5€ ($5.75) adults, 3€ ($3.45) seniors and students. Tues–Sun 10am–5pm (to 8pm Thurs). U-Bahn: U-2 to Königsplatz.

Münchner Stadtmuseum ⟨★⟩ *(Kids)*   Centrally located in the Old Town and one of my favorite museums, the eclectic Munich City Museum relates the history of the city—but that's not all. The **Puppet Theater Collection** is outstanding, with puppets and theater stages from around the world, as well as fairground art (including the Oktoberfest), while the **Musical Instrument Collection** displays European instruments from the 16th to the 20th centuries and primitive instruments from around the world, including African drums, South American flutes, Indian sitars, and Javanese gamelans. There's also a section devoted to the **history of photography** with original photographs and cameras from 1839 to 1919. The **fashion section** features changing exhibits ranging from historic clothing to the newest of the new. The exhibits on Munich cover the history of the city from the late 15th century to post–World War II, with maps, models, paintings, photographs, and furniture, while a section on National Socialism in Munich from 1918 to 1945 covers the Nazi era with photographs, propaganda posters, and documents (unfortunately only in German). But the most valuable pieces are **Erasmus Grasser's 10 Morris Dancers,** carved in 1480 for display in Munich's old town hall. The morris (or morrice) dance, popular in the 15th century, was a rustic ambulatory dance performed by companies of actors at festivals.

St. Jakobsplatz 1. (C) 089/23 32 23 70. www.stadtmuseum-online.de. Admission 2.50€ ($2.90) adults, 1.50€ ($1.75) seniors, students, and children, 4€ ($4.60) families, free for children under 6; more for special exhibits. Tues–Sun 10am–6pm. S-/U-Bahn: Marienplatz.

Städtische Galerie im Lenbachhaus ★★ The City Gallery is the showcase for Munich's artists from the Gothic period to the present. Its setting couldn't be more perfect: the former Italianate villa of artist Franz von Lenbach, built at the end of the 19th century. Some rooms have been kept as they were then. Although landscape paintings from the 18th and 19th centuries (I particularly like the ones with cityscapes of Munich) and examples of German Jugendstil (Art Nouveau) are part of the collection, the great treasure is the **Blaue Reiter (Blue Rider)** ★★★ group of artists. **Wassily Kandinsky,** one of the great innovators of abstract art, was a key member of this Munich-based group, and Lenbach House has an outstanding collection of works of his early period, from shortly after the turn of the 20th century to the outbreak of World War I. Other Blue Rider artists represented are **Paul Klee, Franz Marc, August Macke,** and **Gabriele Münter.** Expect to spend at least an hour here.

In Lenbach House, Luisenstrasse 33 (off Königsplatz, not far from Glyptothek). (C) 089/233 32 000. www. lenbachhaus.de. Admission 4€–6€ ($4.60–$6.90) adults, 2€–3€ ($2.30–$3.45) seniors, students, and children; more for special exhibits. Tues–Sun 10am–6pm. U-Bahn: U-2 to Königsplatz. Tram: 27 to Karolinenplatz.

ZAM—Zentrum für Aussergewöhnliche Museum (Center for Out-of-the-Ordinary Museums) This is actually six small museums in one, each unique. Where else can you find a museum devoted to the chamber pot? Other collections are devoted to pedal cars (the world's largest collection, according to the *Guinness Book of World Records*), the life of Elisabeth of Austria (much beloved and affectionately called Sisi), guardian angels, perfume bottles, and the Easter rabbit! Each collection has its own room, and you can see the entire complex in about an hour. Explanations are in German only, but there's an English-language pamphlet.

Westenriederstrasse 41. (C) 089/290 41 21. Admission 4€ ($4.60) adults, 3€ ($3.45) students and children 4 and up. Daily 10am–6pm. S-Bahn: Isartor.

OTHER AMUSEMENTS

Bavaria Filmstadt (Kids) A 60-minute guided tour of Germany's Hollywood features movie props from well-known films, including the 51m (170-ft.) metal tube used for the filming of the submarine in *Das Boot,* the spacecraft passage used in *Enemy Mine,* and several characters from Michael Ende's *Neverending Story.* Tours (which begin every 5–10 min. except Nov–Feb, when they're every hour on the hour) are educational as well as entertaining, with insight into how sets are made and how various film tricks are achieved. Alas, they're conducted in German only, although in peak season an English-language tour is given to a large group almost daily (call beforehand to see whether you can join such a group). The Action Show is a stunt show with fist fights, glass and fire stunts, and leaps from dizzying heights, while the Erlebnis Kino features seating that moves in sync with the action of computer-animated thrillers.

Bavariafilmplatz 7. ✆ 089/64 99 20 00. www.filmstadt.de. Guided tour 10€ ($12) adults, 9€ ($10) seniors and students, 7€ ($8.05) children; guided tour, Action Show, and Showscan Kino 17€ ($20) adults, 16€ ($18) seniors and students, 14€ ($16) children. Tours Mar–Oct daily 9am–4pm; Nov–Feb daily 10am–3pm. Erlebnis Kino daily 9am–5pm. Action Show Apr–Oct daily noon, more often in peak season. U-Bahn: U-1 to Wettersteinplatz, then tram 25 to Bavariafilmplatz.

Münchener Tierpark Hellabrunn (Munich Zoo) *(Kids)* Munich's zoo is home to 5,000 animals and includes the Elephant House (built in 1913); Europe's largest walk-through aviary; an aquarium; the Tropical House for gorillas and chimps; and all the usual inhabitants including penguins, rhinos, polar bears, and lions, in environments that mimic native habitats. It also has a petting zoo, playgrounds, camel, and animal shows.

Tierparkstrasse 30. ✆ 089/62 50 80. www.zoo-munich.de. Admission 7€ ($8.05) adults, 5.50€ ($6.35) seniors and students, 4€ ($4.60) children 4–14, free for children under 4. Apr–Sept daily 8am–6pm; Oct–Mar daily 9am–5pm. U-Bahn: U-3 to Thalkirchen.

PARKS & GARDENS

The **Englischer Garten** 🌲 is one of Europe's largest city parks (larger than New York's Central Park). Despite its name, it owes its existence to an American rather than an Englishman. Benjamin Thompson, who fled America during the Revolution because of his British sympathies, was instrumental in the park's creation and landscaping. Stretching 5km (3 miles) along the Isar in the heart of the city, it offers beer gardens, sunbathing (including nude sunbathing, a surprise to quite a few unsuspecting visitors), and recreation.

Much more formal are the 200 hectares (500 acres) of **Nymphenburg Park** (see "The Top Museums & Palaces," in "Seeing the Sights," earlier in this chapter). On the north end of Nymphenburg Park is the **Botanical Garden,** but the most conveniently located garden is the formal **Hofgarten,** off Odeonsplatz and laid out in the Italian Renaissance style.

ORGANIZED TOURS

For guided tours, **Panorama Tours** of the Gray Line (✆ 089/5502 89 95; www.muenchenerstadtrundfahrten.de) offers sightseeing trips of Munich lasting 1 to 2½ hours. The 1-hour trip is adequate for a quick overview, with buses departing from in front of Hertie department store, across from the Hauptbahnhof, several times daily and costing 11€ ($13) adults and 6€ ($6.90) children. Daylong excursions are also offered, including one to Neuschwanstein and Linderhof costing 43€ ($49) adults and 21€ ($24) children; entrance fees are extra.

For a more personal tour, join one of three **Original Munich Walks** (✆ 089/5502 93 74; www.munichwalks.com). The 2-hour walking tours are conducted in English April to October. "Discover Munich," with departures daily at 10am, covers architectural treasures and historic highlights of the Old Town, including Marienplatz, the Frauenkirche, and the Viktualienmarkt, before it ends at the Hofbräuhaus. "Hitler & Third Reich Sites" covers the main sites and buildings of the Nazi era, with departures at 3pm, while the "Jewish Munich Walk" takes in Jewish historic sites daily at 11am. Tours cost 10€ ($12) and depart from inside the Hauptbahnhof at EurAide beside Track 11. If you have more time, you might consider the "Dachau Concentration Camp Memorial Tour" which lasts 5 hours and is offered throughout the year for 18€ ($21), including transportation to Dachau.

If you like cycling, a unique tour in English is offered by **Mike's Bike Tours of Munich.** It passes sights like the Hofbräuhaus and Hofgarten as it follows bike paths along the Isar and through the Englischer Garten and Schwabing, with stops along the way for historic (and often humorous) explanations and picture taking. These leisurely 6.5km (4-mile), 4-hour tours cost 22€ ($25) and depart from beneath the Old Rathaus tower at the east end of Marienplatz daily at 11:30am and 4pm April to Oktoberfest (also at 3:15pm June–July). From March to April 15 and from Oktoberfest to November 10, tours depart at 2pm only. No reservations are required; you can simply show up. There's also a 16km (10-mile), 7-hour tour offered June and July that goes farther afield to the Olympic Park and Nymphenburg Palace and includes two stops at beer gardens. It departs also from the Old Rathaus tower at 10:30am and costs 33€ ($38). Farther afield, an all-day tour offered May through August and during Oktoberfest includes a trip to Neuschwanstein, a bike ride from the castle area to a nearby lake, and a hike through a gorge complete with waterfall. For more information or to reserve the day trip, call (€) **089/255 43 987** or 089/255 43 988. Look for Mike's Bike Tours' helpful pamphlet called *Munich English Information,* available at hotels and the tourist office, or check the website www.mikesbiketours.com.

5 Shopping

As Germany's fashion center, Munich boasts upscale boutiques, department stores, and designer names, primarily in the pedestrian-zoned Old Town. If you're looking for souvenirs (beer mugs, Bavaria's simple blue-and-white pottery, porcelain, and nutcrackers), your best bet in terms of price is the department stores, including **Hertie** (across from the Hauptbahnhof), **Karstadt** (on Karlstor, right off Karlsplatz/Stachus, and at Neuhauser Strasse 44), and **Kaufhof** (Karlsplatz 21–24 and on Marienplatz). For beer mugs, nutcrackers, and cuckoo clocks, try **Max Krug,** Neuhauser Strasse 2 ((€) **089/22 45 01**), in business since 1926. Another good place to hunt for Bavarian and German souvenirs and gifts is along **Orlandostrasse,** about a 5-minute walk from Marienplatz near the Hofbräuhaus. This small pedestrian lane has several shops selling T-shirts, beer steins, dolls in Bavarian costume, pipes, postcards, Christmas tree ornaments, and nutcrackers.

Since the early 1800s, Munich's most famous market is the Old Town **Viktualienmarkt,** where you can buy bread, cheese, honey, cakes, fruit, wine, vegetables, and much more. It's a wonderful place to get picnic supplies. The market is open Monday to Friday 8am to 6pm, and Saturday, its busiest day, 8am to 2pm. There are also many gift/souvenir/craft shops surrounding the market.

From May to October, students set up shop on the east side of Leopoldstrasse, between Münchener Freiheit and Siegestor, to sell their artwork at the **Schwabinger Art Market,** held nightly from 6:30pm. In December, the **Christkindlmarkt (Christmas Market)** on Marienplatz is a colorful hodgepodge of 140 stalls offering everything from Bavarian foods and *Glühwein* (mulled wine) to traditional toys and Christmas decorations. It's open daily from the beginning of December to Christmas Eve. Even better is the **Auer Dult,** a flea market lasting 8 days in April, July, and October. It has been a tradition for more than 600 years, currently held on Mariahilfplatz (take bus no. 52 from Marienplatz). Everything from spices, leather goods, jewelry, and sweaters to antiques, kitchen gadgets, and ceramics is sold, and there are rides and amusements for children.

6 Munich After Dark

Because commercial ticket agencies sell opera and theater tickets at higher prices to make a profit, it makes sense to buy your tickets directly from the theater or opera. To find out where you can buy tickets in advance, get a copy of the monthly *Monatsprogramm* for 1.55€ ($1.80). Both *Munich in Your Pocket* and *Munich Found,* English-language publications selling for 3€ ($3.45), list operas, plays, classical concerts, rock and jazz concerts, movies, and more. Some venues, like the Staatstheater am Gärtnerplatz (see below), offer standing-room tickets you can buy in advance; others allow student discounts.

THE PERFORMING ARTS

THEATER & OPERA   Also known as the Altes Residenztheater, the **Cuvilliés Theater,** Residenzstrasse 1 (© 089/21 85 19 40; S-Bahn: Marienplatz; U-Bahn: Odeonsplatz or Marienplatz), is a small but sumptuous 18th-century work of art and Germany's finest rococo tier-boxed theater. Designed by François de Cuvilliés the Elder and seating 400, it features mainly classical and modern plays and chamber music. The box office, at Max-Joseph-Platz 1, is open Monday to Friday 10am to 6pm and Saturday 10am to 1pm. Tickets begin at 8€ to 14€ ($9.20–$16), depending on the program. You can also tour the famous theater (unless a production or practice is being held): in summer daily 9am to 6pm, and in winter daily 10am to 4pm. The cost is 3€ ($3.45) adults and 2€ ($2.30) students (free for children under 18).

Munich celebrated 350 years of opera in 2004, and the neoclassical-style **Nationaltheater (Bayerische Staatsoper)** on Max-Joseph-Platz (© 089/21 85-1920; S-/U-Bahn: Marienplatz) is Germany's largest opera house. With opera performed in its original language (and some with German subtitles) and under the music direction of Zubin Mehta (and Kent Nagano from 2006), the Nationaltheater's Bavarian State Opera performs mostly Mozart, Wagner, Verdi, and Strauss, though it also stages works from the baroque period. The Nationaltheater also stages ballet. Its box office is open Monday to Friday 10am to 6pm and Saturday 10am to 1pm. Tickets begin at 7€ to 10€ ($8.05–$12) for most opera and 5€ to 8€ ($5.75–$9.20) for ballet. Students can buy standing-room tickets in advance for 50% off the lowest price and can also get unsold seats on the night of the performance for 8€ ($9.20), but only with presentation of a valid ID from your home university (an International Student Identity Card isn't enough).

At the **Residenztheater,** Max-Joseph-Platz 1 (© 089/21 85 19 40; S-/U-Bahn: Marienplatz), the Bayerisches Staatsschauspiel performs classics in German, including Schiller, Goethe, Brecht, Shakespeare, and Pirandello. At 11€ to 36€ ($13–$41), tickets are available in advance at the box office at Max-Joseph-Platz 1, Monday to Friday 10am to 6pm, Saturday 10am to 1pm. And

---

Tips   A Note on Advance Tickets

Tickets you buy in advance for the Bayerische Staatsoper, Staatstheater am Gärtnerplatz, and several other venues are valid for use on Munich's public transport system at least 3 hours before the beginning of the performance until the end of services the same day. When buying your theater ticket, ask whether it's valid on the transport system.

at the **Staatstheater am Gärtnerplatz,** Gärtnerplatz 3 (© **089/21 85 19 60;** U-Bahn: Frauenhoferstrasse; bus: 52 or 56 to Gärtnerplatz), you can see light operas, operettas, ballets, and musicals beautifully performed, usually in German. Tickets begin at 11€ to 18€ ($13–$21) for most productions; standing-room tickets begin at 7€ ($8.05). For students, unsold seats are available for 8€ ($9.20) on the performance night; standing-room tickets are 4.50€ ($5.15).

CLASSICAL MUSIC The **Gasteig,** Rosenheimer Strasse 5 (© **089/480-98-0;** S-Bahn: Rosenheimer Platz; tram: 18 to Gasteig), serves as the stage for major concerts. Its largest concert hall, the Philharmonie, seats 2,400 and features performances of the Munich Philharmonic Orchestra (with Christian Thielemann as chief conductor), the Munich Bach Orchestra and Chorus, the Bavarian Radio Symphony Orchestra (with Mariss Jansons as conductor), and guest orchestras and ensembles. The Kleiner Konzertsaal (Small Concert Hall) features a wide range of musical talent, from flamenco guitar or piano recitals to concerts of Renaissance and baroque music. Smaller venues feature everything from slide presentations and lectures to dance to jazz. Tickets for the Munich Philharmonic Orchestra are 11€ to 52€ ($12–$59).

LIVE-MUSIC CLUBS

The intimate **Schwabinger Podium,** Wagnerstrasse 1, at the corner of Siegesstrasse (© **089/39 94 82;** U-Bahn: U-3 or U-6 to Münchener Freiheit), is a great place in Schwabing to listen to rock, blues, Dixieland jazz, oldies, and other popular music performed nightly. Doors open at 8pm and a cover of 4€ ($4.60) is charged only Friday and Saturday. **Mr. B's,** Herzog-Heinrich-Strasse 38 (© **089/53 49 01;** U-Bahn: Goetheplatz), is one of the smallest places you'll find for jazz, blues, and R&B—only three tables and a bar, with room for about 20 lucky people. Get there when it opens at 8pm for concerts that begin at 9:30pm most Thursdays, Fridays, and Saturdays. Cover is usually 4€ ($4.60), but occasionally 6€ ($6.90) for big names.

Jazzclub Unterfahrt im Einstein, Einsteinstrasse 42 (© **089/448 27 94;** www.unterfahrt.de; U-Bahn: Max-Weber-Platz), is Munich's premier spot for serious jazz, with a varied program from traditional jazz to crossover hip-hop, blues, Brazilian jazz, and other international acts. It opens daily at 8pm, with live music generally from 9pm. The Sunday jam session costs 5€ ($5.75). Otherwise, admission ranges from 12€ to 14€ ($14–$16) for most performances. **Nachtcafe,** Maximiliansplatz 5 (© **089/59 59 00;** U-Bahn: Karlsplatz/Stachus), draws a young professional crowd with its chic setting and outdoor terrace, large selection of drinks and cocktails, and live music nightly ranging from jazz and blues to soul and funk. Drinks are pricey, but there's no cover charge. It's open daily 9pm to 6am, with music performed 11pm to 4am. **Hard Rock Cafe,** opposite the Hofbräuhaus at Platzl 1 (© **089/242 94 90**), stages live music several nights a week starting at 10pm, with the 5€ ($5.75) cover charge including one drink.

BEER HALLS

About 10% cheaper than its sibling Augustiner Restaurant next door, the **Augustiner Bierhalle,** Neuhauser Strasse 27, on the main pedestrian lane in the Old Town (© **089/23 18 32 57;** S-/U-Bahn: Karlsplatz/Stachus or Marienplatz), is much smaller than the Hofbräuhaus, with correspondingly lower prices. It still, however, has typical Bavarian decor, with dark paneled walls, wooden tables, and simple hooks for hats and coats. An English-language menu lists specialties like

Weisswurst, Munich-style *Sauerbraten,* and goulash with potatoes. It's open Monday to Saturday 9am to 11:30pm, Sunday 10am to 11:30pm.

Without a doubt, the **Hofbräuhaus,** Platzl 9 (℃ **089/22 16 76;** S-/U-Bahn: Marienplatz), which celebrated its 415th birthday in 2004, is the world's most famous beer hall. Everyone who has ever been to Munich has probably spent at least one evening here. There are several floors in this huge place, but the main hall is the massive ground-floor Schwemme, with room for 1,300 people. It features your typical Bavarian brass band, waitresses in dirndls, and tables full of friendly Germans who often break into song and link arms as they sway. A beer garden with room for 500 people under spreading chestnut trees is open in fine weather. If you've never been to the Oktoberfest, this place will give you an idea of what it's like. German food is available (there's also a 1st-floor restaurant), including various sausages, *Leberkäs,* boiled pork knuckle with sauerkraut and potatoes, and roast chicken. It's open daily 9am to 11:30pm.

BARS

Once the center of everything Bohemian, **Schwabing** today is more likely to be filled with out-of-towners than with natives. Still, it's definitely worth a stroll through Munich's most famous night district, if you can get through the crowds in summer. The busiest streets are the main **Leopoldstrasse,** scene of a nightly art market in summer, and the smaller side streets, **Feilitzschstrasse** and **Occamstrasse,** near the Münchener Freiheit U-Bahn station. Here are a few places to whet your thirst:

Papa Benz, Occamstrasse 8 (℃ **089/38 88 88 60;** U-Bahn: U-3 or U-6 to Münchener Freiheit), under various names and ownership, has been around for more than 20 years, attracts a slightly older crowd than some of the other bars, and is simply decorated with the usual wooden floor, large bar area, and wooden tables. There's free live music—mostly jazz—some Thursdays and every Sunday from 11:30am to 2pm and 4:30 to 7:30pm. It's open Monday to Thursday 5pm to 1am, Friday 5pm to 3am, Saturday 2pm to 3am, and Sunday 11:30am to 1am. The 111 kinds of beer from 25 countries are the claim to fame of **Haus der 111 Biere,** Franzstrasse 3 (℃ **089/33 12 48;** U-Bahn: U-3 or U-6 to Münchener Freiheit), in operation more than 35 years. It's open Sunday to Thursday 5pm to 1am, Friday and Saturday 5pm to 3am. The two floors are often packed with people from around the world, and it's easy to strike up a conversation. Much newer and trendier than the bars above is **Roxy,** Leopoldstrasse 48 (℃ **089/34 92 92;** U-Bahn: U-3 or U-6 to Giselastrasse), its glass facade overlooking the action on Leopoldstrasse; in summer you can sit at its sidewalk café, great for people-watching. It offers breakfast all day, sandwiches, pasta, and burgers, and is open daily 8am to 3am.

GAY & LESBIAN BARS

Much of Munich's gay and lesbian scene takes place south of the Old Town, particularly on **Müllerstrasse** and **Hans-Sachs-Strasse.**

Nil, Hans-Sachs-Strasse 2 (℃ **089/26 55 45;** U-Bahn: U-1, U-2, U-3, or U-6 to Sendlingertorplatz; tram: 17), is a laid-back gay cafe attracting everyone from students to doctors and serving snacks and light fare; it's open daily 3pm to 3am. Around the corner is **Mylord,** Ickstattstrasse 2a (℃ **089/260 44 98;** U-Bahn: U-1, U-2, U-3, or U-6 to Sendlingertorplatz; tram: 17), opened more than 40 years ago and once a popular lesbian hangout. Today the artsy crowd ranges from mixed to homosexual, transvestite to transsexual, drawn by the living-room atmosphere cultivated by friendly English-speaking proprietress

Marietta. It's open Sunday to Thursday 6pm to 2am and Friday and Saturday 6pm to 3am.

At Munich's premier gay disco, **New York,** Sonnenstrasse 25 (© **089/59 10 56;** U-Bahn: U-1, U-2, U-3, or U-6 to Sendlingertorplatz), the strident rhythms and electronic sounds are accompanied by laser light shows. Club patrons range in age from 20 to 35. Open daily 11pm to 5am, the club has no cover Monday to Thursday; on Friday, Saturday, and Sunday it's 5€ ($5.75), half of which goes toward the first drink. Also check out **Soul City,** Maximiliansplatz 5, with an entrance on Max-Joseph-Strasse (© **089/59 52 72;** U-Bahn: Karlsplatz). It's open Thursday and Saturday from 10pm to 6am, Friday from 11pm to 4am, and attracts a mostly mixed crowd. The 6€ ($6.90) cover on Thursday includes one drink; 2€ ($2.30) of the 5€ ($5.75) cover Friday and Saturday goes toward the first drink.

DANCE CLUBS

Dance clubs in Munich are suffering from elitism. Most have doors with one-way mirrors that can be opened only from the inside—so the doorman can look over potential customers and decide whether they're the right material. In winter, coats must be checked (for a small fee).

One that is not so discriminatory is **Atomic Cafe,** conveniently located in the Old Town at Neuturmstrasse 5 (© **089/228 30 54;** S-/U-Bahn: Marienplatz), a hip dance club featuring both deejays and live bands, including international ones. Featuring hip-hop, funk, garage, punk, and soul, it opens at 10pm Tuesday to Sunday, closing at 3am Sunday to Thursday and 4am Friday and Saturday. Admission usually runs 4€ to 6€ ($4.60–$6.90), though sometimes events and big names cost more.

If you're in your early 20s, head to a former factory turned party city. **Kultfabrik,** located next to Ostbahnhof Station at Grafingerstrasse 6 (© **089/49 00 90 70**), is one of Europe's largest youth entertainment districts, with more than two dozen concert venues, themed bars, and dance clubs featuring everything from heavy metal and hip-hop to Latino (admission to most clubs costs 5€–6€/$5.75–$6.90). Most venues are open only Friday and Saturday, though some are open Wednesday and Thursday as well.

7 Side Trips: Neuschwanstein ⟨⋆⟩⟨⋆⟩⟨⋆⟩, Hohenschwangau ⟨⋆⟩ & Dachau

MAD KING LUDWIG'S NEUSCHWANSTEIN CASTLE & HOHENSCHWANGAU CASTLE

Of the dozens of castles dotting the Bavarian countryside, none is as famous as **Neuschwanstein,** created by the extravagant Bavarian King Ludwig II. No doubt you've seen pictures of this fairy-tale castle, perched on a cliff above the town of Hohenschwangau, but even if you haven't, it'll seem familiar, for this is the castle that served as the model for Walt Disney's castle at Disneyland.

Construction of Ludwig II's most famous castle began in 1869, but only a third of the original plans had been completed at the time of his mysterious death in 1886 (his body, as well as the body of his doctor, was found floating in a lake, but no one has ever proved whether he was murdered or committed suicide). Neuschwanstein, one of several overly ornate castles Ludwig left to the world, is a lesson in extravagance and fantasy, with almost every inch covered in gilt, stucco, wood carvings, and marble mosaics. Swans are used as a motif throughout, and Ludwig's admiration of Richard Wagner is expressed in operatic themes virtually everywhere, including murals illustrating *Tristan and Isolde* in his bedroom, the most opulent room in the palace—it took 14 artisans more than 4 years to produce the elaborate wood carvings.

You can see the castle by joining a 35-minute guided tour, available in English. Incidentally, the guided tour requires climbing 165 stairs and descending 181 stairs; in addition, it takes about 35 minutes to walk up the steep hill from the Hohenschwangau bus stop to Neuschwanstein. An alternative is to hire one of the horse-drawn carriages for 5€ ($5.75) per person or take a shuttle bus for 2.50€ ($2.85), both of which take you two-thirds of the way, but it's still a 10-minute climb to the castle.

Although overshadowed by Neuschwanstein and not quite as fanciful, another worthwhile castle here offers 35-minute tours: **Hohenschwangau Castle,** built in the 1830s by Ludwig II's father, Maximilian II. Young Ludwig spent much of his childhood here, where he was greatly influenced by the castle's many murals depicting the saga of the Swan Knight Lohengrin, immortalized in an opera by Wagner.

For tickets to Neuschwanstein and Hohenschwangau, you must stop by the **Hohenschwangau Ticket-Center,** located in the small town of Hohenschwangau at Alpeestrasse 12 (© **08362/93 08 30;** www.hohenschangau.de); you'll see it after disembarking from the bus. Tours of either Neuschwanstein or Hohenschwangau are 9€ ($10) for adults and 8€ ($9.20) for seniors and students; children under 18 are free. Combination tickets to both cost 17€ ($20) adults, 15€ ($17) seniors and students. Tours are for a specific time (avoid weekends in summer, when the wait for a tour can be as long as 3 hr., or try to be at the ticket office as early as you can after its 8am opening; you can also book online).

Both castles are open daily: April to September 9am to 6pm (last tour) and October to March 10am to 4pm. Neuschwanstein is closed January 1, Shrove Tuesday, and December 24, 25, and 31; Hohenschwangau Castle is closed on December 24.

To reach Neuschwanstein, take the **train** from Munich's Hauptbahnhof to Füssen, a 2-hour trip costing 18€ ($21) one-way. Better yet, if you don't have a Eurailpass, buy a **Bayern Ticket,** allowing travel on local trains throughout Bavaria on a given day. It costs 15€ ($17) for one person or 22€ ($25) for up to five people traveling together, a real savings over one-way tickets to Neuschwanstein. Inquire at **EurAide** at the Hauptbahnhof for more information.

In Füssen, take the **bus** in front of the train station from platform 2 (1.50€/ $1.70) to Hohenschwangau. For more information on the castles or Hohenschwangau, contact the **Hohenschwangau tourist office** (© **08362/81 98 40**), in front of the bus stop and open daily in summer 9am to 6pm and in winter 9:30am to 4pm (closed mid-Nov to mid-Dec). If you have a **car,** take B-17 south from Munich to Füssen, then head east on B-17.

DACHAU

About 19km (12 miles) from Munich is **Dachau,** site of Germany's first concentration camp under the Hitler regime and now a memorial to those who died under the Nazis. Some 200,000 prisoners from 34 countries—primarily political and religious dissidents, Jews, Gypsies, and other undesirables—passed through Dachau's gates between 1933 and 1945, of whom 32,000 lost their lives from disease, starvation, torture, execution, slave labor, and medical experiments.

At the **KZ-Gedenkstätte Dachau (Concentration Camp Memorial)** *★★*, Alte Römerstrasse 75 (© **08131/66 99 70**), a few of the camp's original buildings have been preserved or reconstructed, including a couple of barracks with rows of bunkers, guard towers, a morgue, and a crematorium, in a landscape that's bleak and desolate. But what really makes a visit here a sobering experience is the museum, with photograph after photograph illustrating the horrors of the Holocaust and detailed explanations as to how such atrocities came to pass. Photographs show bodies piled high on top of one another and prisoners so malnourished they can't walk. Be sure to see the museum's 20-minute English documentary, shown at 11:30am, 2pm, and 3:30pm. In addition, free guided tours in English are offered Thursday, Saturday, and Sunday, with a 30-minute tour offered at 12:30pm and a 2½-hour tour at 1:30pm. Audioguides are available for 2.50€ ($2.85), but the museum provides so much information and everything is so well documented, they're not really necessary.

Visiting the Dachau concentration camp, which takes about 3 hours, isn't pleasant, but perhaps it's necessary: A plaque near the museum exit reminds us that those who forget the past are destined to repeat it. Note that the memorial isn't recommended for children under 12.

Admission to the Dachau memorial is free; it's open Tuesday to Sunday 9am to 5pm. To get there, take **S-Bahn S-2** going in the direction of Petershausen to Dachau (about a 20-min. ride). A one-way ticket costs 4.20€ ($4.85), or use four strips on the Streifenkarte; otherwise, buy a *Tageskarte* for the entire metropolitan area for 9€ ($8). In Dachau, transfer to **bus no. 726** to the KZ-Gedenkstätte stop or **bus no. 724** to the K-Z Gedenkstätte-Parkplatz, both a 10-minute ride.

18

Nice & the Côte d'Azur

by Haas Mroue

The name **Côte d'Azur** exerts an almost hypnotic pull on the imagination. The mountains of Provence meet the sea to form one of the world's most dramatic coastlines, studded with harbors and bays, quaint hamlets and perched villages, and luxury villas and beach resorts. Bathed in sun and breezes, this fertile region is carpeted with olive trees, pines, and fragrant flowers.

Painters Paul Signac and Henri Matisse were the first to fall under the spell of the Côte d'Azur (Azure Coast), followed by English aristocrats looking to escape foggy London winters. Pablo Picasso, Marc Chagall, Fernand Léger, and Coco Chanel gravitated to the coast in the first half of the 20th century, transforming fishing villages into flourishing artists' colonies.

The transition from artists' colonies to mega-resorts began with the first Cannes Film Festival in 1946, which added a potent dose of Tinseltown glamour to the region's natural allure. Ten years later, bikini-clad Brigitte Bardot cavorted on a St-Tropez beach in the 1956 film *And God Created Woman* and set off a stampede of visitors in search of sun, sea, and sex. That same year, Grace Kelly married Prince Rainier in Monaco and it seemed that on this rocky coast of fairy-tale beauty, dreams really could come true.

Many people now complain that the area has been ruined by an influx of tourists and rampant overdevelopment. While not exactly a Paradise Lost, it has become a paradise somewhat obscured by horrendous traffic jams, bland apartment blocks, and tacky souvenir shops. Still, this sun-drenched coast offers something for everyone. Whether your passion is browsing art museums, local markets, or chic shops, whether you're a beach stroller or a high roller or simply want to enjoy the dazzling scenery, you'll find your own paradise on the Côte d'Azur.

Nice, among the least expensive of France's resorts, is a good base for exploring the region. At the center of the Côte d'Azur, it's very much a Mediterranean city. Life is lived out on cafe terraces, in parks and gardens, and on the promenade des Anglais curving around the sparkling bay. In Vieux Nice, the medieval part of the city, narrow streets wind through pastel-colored houses and open onto intimate squares.

For more on Nice and the Côte d'Azur, see *Frommer's Provence & the Riviera, Frommer's France, France For Dummies, Frommer's France's Best Bed & Breakfasts & Country Inns,* and *Frommer's France's Best-Loved Driving Tours.*

1 Essentials

ARRIVING

BY PLANE The **Aéroport Nice–Côte d'Azur** (© **08/20-42-33-33;** www.nice.aeroport.fr) at the western edge of town, on the coast only 8km (5 miles) from downtown, ranks just after Paris's airports in terms of activity. Both the airport's

⌈Value⌉ Budget Bests

Most of the **beach** is free in Nice, but it's a beach of pebbles rather than one of comfy sand. Strolling the **promenade des Anglais** along the azure sea is free, and there's no charge for wandering the back streets of **Vieux Nice**.

The fine Mediterranean climate and lush parks make **picnicking** a delight that can cut costs considerably. Try the *pan bagnat,* a small round bread loaf stuffed with *salade niçoise*–type goodies and moistened with olive oil. Look for it in streetside kiosks, *boulangeries* (bakeries), and *charcuteries* (delicatessens). Expect to pay 2.50€ to 6€ ($2.90–$6.90) depending on where you buy it (the vendors closest to the beach are usually the most expensive).

If you'll be visiting a number of museums along the Côte d'Azur, you might want to buy the **Carte Musées Côte d'Azur,** covering most of the main museums—65 in all. A 1-day pass is 8€ ($9.20), a 3-day pass 15€ ($17), and a 7-day pass 25€ ($29). And note there's a **special museum pass *(passe musées)*** for 6€ ($6.90), offering free admission to all Nice museums for a week (within a 15-day period). You can buy these passes at any museum or tourist office or call ⓒ **04/97-03-82-20.** Plus, on the first Sunday of each month, **admission is free** to all museums in Nice.

---

two terminals receive international and domestic flights. Terminal 1 handles airlines such as British Airways, Lufthansa, and Swiss International Air Lines; Terminal 2 handles all Air France domestic and international flights, as well as easyJet flights. The only nonstop from the U.S. arrives into Terminal 2 every morning—a Delta/Air France code-share flight operated by Delta from New York's JFK. Public **bus no. 23** runs between the airport and Nice's central train station Monday to Friday about every 20 minutes, and Saturday and Sunday about every 30 minutes 6am to 10:30pm, charging 1.30€ ($1.50) for the 30-minute trip.

Even more convenient is the airport **Express bus,** running from both terminals along the promenade des Anglais to Nice's bus station (Gare Routière) about every 20 minutes. The 20-minute trip is 3.50€ ($4). For the same price, Express Bus 99 operates direct to Nice's train station (Gare SNCF) between the hours of 7am and 9pm. For information, call ⓒ **04/92-29-88-88.** A **taxi,** by contrast, costs 24€ to 30€ ($28–$35) from the airport into town, depending on your destination and traffic.

BY TRAIN From Paris, you can book a seat on France's state-of-the-art **TGV,** which will get you to Nice in just under 6 hours. There are three daily Paris–Nice TGVs (four to five in summer); otherwise, you may have to change in Marseille or Toulon. The price is about 80€ ($92) one-way, with reductions for students and seniors and for weekend stays. Seat reservations are required and can be made at any travel agency in Paris or any train station, or by contacting the **SNCF** at ⓒ **08/36-35-35-35** or on its website at **www.sncf.fr.**

Nice has two train stations, of which the largest and most convenient is the **Gare Nice-Ville,** avenue Thiers (ⓒ **08/36-35-35-35**), normally called the Gare SNCF (the Société Nationale des Chemins de Fer is France's national rail company). The station has luggage lockers as well as showers and toilets kept moderately clean. The city's helpful tourist office is next to the station (outside

Nice Deals & Discounts

SPECIAL DISCOUNTS   Nice doesn't offer many discounts. However, buying single **bus tickets** (1.30€/$1.50) costs more than buying a group at a kiosk, newsstand, bookstore, or shop. With a **five-trip Suncarte,** the price drops to 1.05€ ($1.20) per trip, and with a **24-trip Suncarte,** it drops to 1€ ($1.15). You can also buy a **Sunpass** *(carte touristique)* allowing unlimited travel for 1, 5, or 7 days costing 4€ ($4.60), 13€ ($15), or 17€ ($19), respectively. The 1-day Sunpass is sold on city buses, but you must buy the 5- or 7-day pass at the Sunbus or tourist offices (see "Visitor Information," below). Both passes allow a free transfer within 59 minutes of stamping the ticket. For more info, ask at the tourist office or anywhere bus tickets are sold; or you can drop in at the **Centre d'Information Sunbus,** 10 av. Félix-Faure, at the corner of rue Gubernatis (© **04/93-13-53-13;** www.sunbus.com), open Monday to Friday 7:15am to 7pm and Saturday 7:15am to 6pm.

Students can save money at some museums by showing the **International Student Identity Card (ISIC).** As with the buses, students with a student ID receive a discount only on month-long transport passes. Apply at the Centre d'Information Sunbus (see above). There are student reductions on local trains. Nice has a major university and a large student population. For information on low-cost youth and student airfares, head for **Usit Voyages,** 10 rue de Belgique (© **04/93-87-34-96);** or the **Centre Régional Information Jeunesse,** 19 rue Gioffrédo (© **04/93-80-93-93).** For details on youth hostels and student accommodations, contact **C.R.O.U.S.,** 18 av. des Fleurs (© **04/92-15-50-50;** www.crous-nice.cnous.fr).

WORTH A SPLURGE   Scrimp on everything else, but budget enough money to **rent a car** for a day or two and enjoy the incomparable scenic drives surrounding Nice. The Grande Corniche running from Nice to Menton offers spectacular views over the coast (but watch those curves—remember Grace Kelly); and on the Route Napoléon twisting north through the Alps to Sisteron (and beyond), you'll pass lakes, lavender fields, and remote mountain villages. Another superb drive is D2210 running through the dramatic Loup Valley gorges on the edge of Vence. Or take the scenic coastal road all the way from Monaco to St-Tropez, passing through lovely little beachside towns.

And while you're traveling along the coast, splurge on a truly **Mediterranean meal:** Order the pricey but wonderful star of Provençal cooking, *bouillabaisse*—a delicate seafood stew made with a variety of fish and shellfish, simmered in white wine and tomato sauce, and served with *rouille* (garlic mayonnaise) and crisp croutons. The perfect accompaniment is a bottle of Cassis (expensive dry white wine from coastal vineyards near Marseille) or some other full-bodied white.

and to the left), and numerous good hotels and restaurants are nearby. Outside the station are also several *bureaux de change,* where you can change money. To go straight to place Masséna in the town center, take **bus no. 15** from the

> (*Value* **Fly for Less**
>
> In 2004, easyJet increased service from Paris (from both Orly and Charles de Gaulle airports) to Nice. Flying on easyJet is frequently cheaper than taking the train; be sure to check www.easyjet.com for the lowest fare for the dates you wish to travel. If you book far enough in advance, the fare can be as low as 15€ ($17) each way, plus tax. Low fares and daily flights are also available to Nice from three London airports: Gatwick, Stansted, and Luton.

station; or turn left and walk to avenue Jean-Médecin and take any bus heading south.

BY BUS   If you arrive by bus, you'll pull into Nice's **Gare Routière** (© **04/93-85-61-81**), between Vieux Nice and place Masséna.

BY CAR   You'll approach on A8, La Provençal, which skirts the city on its northern boundary. Follow the signs for Centre-Ville (downtown) and place Masséna; or follow signs for the promenade des Anglais to get to the waterfront.

VISITOR INFORMATION

TOURIST OFFICE   The **Office de Tourisme** is outside the train station on avenue Thiers (© **04/93-87-07-07;** fax 04/93-16-85-16; www.nice-coteazur. org). It's open daily June to September 7:30am to 8pm, and daily October to May 8am to 7pm. The outlets at the airport (© **04/93-21-44-11**) and in the center of town at 5 promenade des Anglais (© **04/92-14-48-00**) have roughly the same hours.

WEBSITES   The official site of Nice, **www.nice-coteazur.org**, gives general information on the municipality and cultural sites. The best Riviera site is **www.beyond.fr**, which has pages on regional history, wine, gastronomy, and off-the-beaten-track destinations, plus a glossary of French food terms. You can also try **www.crt-riviera.fr**, with a calendar of events and a hotel search. To explore the rest of Provence, head to **www.provence.guideweb.com**.

CITY LAYOUT

Downtown Nice is fairly compact. You'll find almost everything there—hotels, restaurants, the train and bus stations, the beach—easy to reach on foot. City buses are useful for going to some outlying museums, several of which are in the hilly neighborhood of **Cimiez.** Many of the most interesting sights are outside Nice, but you can easily reach them by train or bus.

Imagine downtown Nice as a triangle pointed north. At its apex, the northern point, is the **Gare Nice-Ville** (central train station). Near the station are numerous hotels and restaurants as well as the tourist office. The base of the triangle lies along the waterfront. The eastern point is **Vieux Nice,** the old city, and **Le Château,** a hill on which a castle once stood; the western point is at **Pont Magnan,** to the west of the deluxe Hôtel Négresco and the Musée Masséna.

Near the center of the triangle's base, closer to Vieux Nice than to Pont Magnan, is **place Masséna,** the main square, bordered by the Jardins Albert-1er. Nearby is a pedestrian mall covering several blocks of rue Masséna, rue de France, rue Halévy, and rue Paradis; people come here to stroll, window-shop, and eat at the numerous restaurants.

Avenue Jean-Médecin is the main north–south street, beginning at place Masséna and heading north through the heart of the shopping district, then passing just to the east of the train station. It's the commercial heart of Nice, always busy and lined with shops of all sizes. Along the waterfront, the wide **promenade des Anglais** is the name of the shore road from the center of town westward; the **quai des Etats-Unis** is its name eastward through Vieux Nice to Le Château. This is the most scenic part of the city.

GETTING AROUND

Nice is a good town for walking, with the occasional bus ride thrown in. For your first sightseeing excursion, consider the **Trains Touristiques de Nice,** rubber-tired tourist trolleys traveling a ring route passing Nice's downtown attractions (see "Seeing the Sights," later in this chapter).

BY BUS   For details on Nice's buses, see "Nice Deals & Discounts," above. There's a route map posted at each major bus stop and also a sign indicating the *point de vente le plus proche,* the nearest place where booklets of bus tickets are sold. Free maps of the bus network are handed out at the tourist offices, in hotels, and at the **Sunbus** office at 10 av. Félix-Faure. For more information, log onto www.sunbus.com.

BY TAXI   Taxis are rather expensive and the drivers not overly friendly; the average fare in the city limits is 15€ ($17). If you're traveling in a group of three, the price per person isn't so bad. Call ⓒ **04/93-13-78-78** to order a taxi.

BY TRAIN   Perhaps the best way to move along the Côte d'Azur is by train. Trains run about every hour or two, sometimes much more frequently, depending on the destination. Some of the stations connected by the rail line are (west to east) St-Raphaël–Valescure, Cannes, Juan-les-Pins, Antibes, Biot, Cagnes-sur-Mer, Nice-Ville, Beaulieu-sur-Mer, Eze-sur-Mer, Monaco–Monte Carlo, Menton, and Vintimille (Ventimiglia) on the Italian border.

BY RENTAL CAR   Rentals are expensive and accelerated by a 20.6% value-added tax (called *TVA* in France). The cheapest rates are for standard shifts. If you drive an automatic, it's probably better to make arrangements from your home country because they're substantially more expensive and not always available. Expect to pay about 64€ ($74) per day for a subcompact, including the first 250km (155 miles), tax, and insurance; a compact will run you about 72€ ($83). A week's rental with unlimited kilometers runs about 250€ ($288). If you plan ahead and reserve a car before you arrive in Nice, a rental can be as low as 195€ ($224) per week, including all taxes, insurance, and unlimited mileage. The trick is to book early and ask for the all-inclusive rate; you'll also have to prepay using a credit card. Contact one of the large rental agencies in your home country. Auto fuel costs about $4 per American gallon in France.

In Nice, **Hertz** has an office in each of the two terminals at the airport, in Aérogare 1 (ⓒ **04/93-21-36-72**) and Aérogare 2 (ⓒ **04/93-21-42-72**). **Avis**

ⓕ*Tips* Be a Diesel Driver

It's highly recommended that you ask for a diesel car when you pick up your rental—you can save many euros that way, as a little goes a long way. Diesel cars cannot be confirmed prior to arrival, however.

Country & City Codes

The **country code** for France is **33**. The **city code** for Nice is **4**; use this code when you're calling from outside France. If you're calling Nice from within Nice or from anywhere else in France, use **04**, which is now built into all phone numbers, making them 10 digits long.

---

has three offices: at the train station (℡ **04/93-87-90-11**), at the airport (℡ **04/93-21-42-78**), and downtown off place Masséna at 2 av. des Phocéens (℡ **04/93-80-63-52**). **Europcar** (National, Tilden) has an office at 6 av. de Suéde (℡ **04/92-14-44-50**), 2 short blocks west of place Masséna, and near the train station at 14 av. Thiers (℡ **04/93-16-54-00**). **Thrifty** (known in France as ADA Location de Vehicules) has deeply discounted weekend rates at their airport office inside Terminal 1 (℡ **08/36-68-40-02**).

If you find a place to park in Nice, you'll probably have to pay. Find a parking ticket machine, insert 1.50€ ($1.70) for each 60 minutes you want, push the button to get your ticket, and place the ticket on your dashboard where it will be visible from outside. When your time is up, move the car or buy another ticket. Fines for parking illegally are horribly high. Even parked legally, you might return to find your car trapped by cars bumper-to-bumper with yours. Car break-ins are routine in Nice. Don't leave luggage or valuables anywhere in your car.

BY BICYCLE   The oldest rental agency in Nice is **Arnaud,** 5 rue François-Prémier (℡ **04/93-87-88-55**), near rue Grimaldi between rue Maréchal-Joffre and rue de la Liberté. Daily rental for a regular bike or a mountain bike is 16€ ($18). There's a hefty refundable deposit of 300€ ($345), which you can put on your credit card. The office is open Monday to Saturday 9am to 7pm. Rental motorbikes and mopeds aren't available.

FAST FACTS: Nice

American Express   The office is at 11 promenade des Anglais (℡ **04/93-16-53-53** for exchange, 04/93-16-53-45 for tours), at the corner of rue du Congrés. May to September, hours are Monday to Friday 9am to 7pm and Saturday 9am to noon; October to April, it's open Monday to Friday 9am to noon and 2 to 6pm and Saturday 9am to noon. Cardholders can use the Express Cash machine on the rue du Congrès side of the building. For 24-hour traveler's check refunds, call toll free at ℡ **0800/90-86-00**. *Note:* If you use the exchange office here, you will be charged a whopping 5€ ($5.75) fee. See "Currency Exchange," below, for no-fee exchange shops.

Business Hours   Banks are normally open Monday to Friday 9am to noon and 1 or 1:30 to 4:30pm. Some are open Saturday morning, and some currency exchange booths have long hours (see "Currency Exchange," below). Most museums, shops, and offices open around 9am, close for lunch at noon, and reopen about 2pm, staying open to 7pm in summer or 5 or 6pm in winter. Most shops are open Saturday but closed Sunday and sometimes Monday as well. Post offices are normally open Monday to Friday 8:30am to 7pm and Saturday 8:30am to noon.

Consulates The **U.S. consulate** is at 7 av. Gustave V (© **04/93-88-89-55**). The **Canadian consulate** is at 10 rue Lamartine (© **04/93-92-93-22**). The **U.K. consulate** is at 8 rue Alphonse-Karr (© **04/93-82-32-04**). These consulates don't provide a full range of services but are useful in an emergency. The nearest full-service consulates are in Marseille.

Currency In 2002, France adopted the **euro** (€) for its currency. At press time, $1 = .87€, or 1€ =$1.15.

Currency Exchange When changing money, ask if there's a fee or commission charged—a large one can wipe out the advantage of a good exchange rate. Banks and *bureaux de change* (exchange offices) usually offer better exchange rates than hotels, restaurants, and shops. At the intersection of rue de France and rue Halévy is the **Change Bureau,** 1 rue Halévy, open daily 8am to 7pm; they don't charge a fee here. A block to the west on rue de France at rue Massenet is another exchange office. Check to see which offers more euros for your dollar. As of this writing, neither exacts a commission or fee. ATMs offer the best rate of exchange, and Cirrus and PLUS outlets are plentiful.

Doctors Call **S.O.S. Médecins** at © **08/01-85-01-01,** open 24 hours.

Emergencies The emergency number for the **police** is © **17;** in other cases, call © **04/92-17-20-31,** which specializes in tourist problems. To report a **fire,** dial © **18.** For an **ambulance,** dial © **15.** For **dental emergencies,** call © **04/93-80-77-77.** For a **doctor,** call © **04/93-52-42-42,** open 24 hours. The **Hôpital St-Roch,** 5 rue Pierre-Dévoluy (© **04/92-03-33-75**), has an emergency room open 24 hours. **Pharmacies** at 7 rue Masséna (© **04/93-87-78-94**) and 66 av. Jean-Médecin (© **04/93-62-54-44**) are open 24 hours.

Holidays See "Fast Facts: Paris," in chapter 19.

Internet Access The most convenient and easy-to-find Internet cafe is at 25 promenade des Anglais, close to the Negresco. At Panini Web (© **04/ 93-88-72-75;** web.nice@wanadoo.fr), you can surf the Web or check your e-mail for 2.50€ ($2.90) per 15 minutes. It's open daily from 10am to 11pm in summer and 10am to 8pm in winter.

Laundry Self-service laundries are plentiful outside the central pedestrian zone. Convenient addresses are the **Laverie Automatic,** 29 rue Assalit (© **04/93-80-75-80**); **Laverie du Port,** 22 rue Bonaparte (© **04/93-55-56-44**); and **Laverie Lincoln,** 109 bd. Gambetta (© **04/93-86-66-90**). Most are open daily 7am to 9pm. They charge around 3.50€ ($4) to wash 5 kilograms (11 lb.) of clothing and .50€ (60¢) for 5 minutes of drying up to 7 kilograms (15½ lb.).

Mail Post offices are open Monday to Friday 8:30am to 7pm and Saturday 8:30am to noon. The city's **main post office** is at 23 av. Thiers (© **08/10-82-18-21**), across from the train station. *Poste Restante* is held at the post office on place Wilson, 18 rue de l'Hôtel-des-Postes, 06000 Nice (© **04/93-13-64-10**), 4 blocks east of avenue Jean-Médecin. There's a charge of .50€ (60¢) for each letter retrieved. Airmail letters within western Europe cost .50€ to .65€ (60¢–75¢); to the United States, .90€ ($1); and to Australia, .95€ ($1.10).

Tax France's **TVA (value-added tax)** should already be included in the cost of items you buy, and prices quoted to you should be TTC (*Toutes Taxes Compris,* all taxes included). The rate of tax varies depending on the item or service being purchased. For details about how to get a tax refund on large purchases, see chapter 1, "Enjoying Europe on a Budget."

Telephone See "Fast Facts: Paris," in chapter 19, for more details. Avoid making phone calls from your hotel; many hotels charge at least .50€ (60¢) for a local call. A 1-minute call within western Europe costs about .80€ (92¢), to the United States .90€ ($1), and to Australia .95€ ($1.10). It's always cheaper to call after 8pm or on weekends.

Tipping See "Fast Facts: Paris," in chapter 19.

2 Affordable Places to Stay

Nice's hotels are scattered around town, and the farther they are from the waterfront, the lower the price will generally be. As elsewhere in Europe, each hotel room is different. In the same little hotel you might find rooms you think are wonderful and rooms you can't bear to stay in. Ask to see your room before checking in, and if you don't like it, ask to see another.

In the 19th century, Nice developed as a fashionable winter resort, but since the end of World War II, most of its visitors have come in summer. Prices given here are for the high summer season, when you might be required to pay for breakfast at your hotel. Off season, most hotels lower their prices, so always inquire about possible discounts.

The **Office de Tourisme** at the train station (see "Visitor Information," above) will help you find a room (without a service charge), but in summer there could be quite a wait, so get in line early. The tourism agents won't start calling until 10am because that's when most hotels know whether they'll have vacant rooms. If you can't find exactly the room you want, take one that will do for a night, then spend a little time the next day reserving another for the rest of your stay.

Note: You'll find the lodging choices below plotted on the map on p. 673.

BETWEEN THE TRAIN STATION & AVENUE JEAN-MEDECIN

Hôtel Acanthe   Near Vieux Nice, the promenade des Anglais, and Galeries Lafayette, this large hotel is spread over five floors in an early-1900s building. The rooms, with French windows and high ceilings, are attractively painted in cool pastels; some have narrow balconies. The windows aren't double-glazed, but most rooms are on a quiet side street. If you're a light sleeper, though, ask for a room on an upper floor. There are freshly tiled bathrooms in most rooms.

2 rue Chauvain, 06000 Nice. ⓒ **04/93-62-22-44.** Fax 04/93-62-29-77. www.hotel-acanthe-nice.cote.azur.fr. 50 units, 5 with toilet only, 45 with bathroom. 38€ ($44) single with toilet, 45€ ($52) single with bathroom; 45€ ($52) double with toilet, 56€ ($64) double with bathroom. Continental breakfast 4€ ($4.60). AE, DC, MC, V. Bus: 15. *In room:* TV (rooms with bathroom).

Hôtel Baccarat *(Kids)*   The Baccarat is less than a 5-minute walk from the station. The rooms, spread over five floors, are large and well maintained. The new owner has worked wonders with fabrics, covering the beds and chairs with pretty floral or pastel prints. Six rooms are in a romantic style, with small fabric canopies framing the beds. Several are reserved for nonsmokers, and some hold up to five beds—a good choice for small groups. In the low season, breakfast, which is served in the lounge, is complimentary; otherwise, it's 4€ ($4.60) per person.

39 rue d'Angleterre, 06000 Nice. © **04/93-88-35-73.** Fax 04/93-16-14-25. 33 units. 40€ ($46) single; 44€ ($51) double; 18€ ($21) per bed in 5-bed unit. Breakfast 4€ ($4.60). AE, MC, V. Bus: 1, 2, 4, or 5. *In room:* TV.

Hôtel Carlyna ⍟   The enthusiastic Bouvet family has been whipping this hotel into shape since they bought it in 1998. They've added air-conditioning and double-glazed windows, and outfitted the rooms with firm beds topped by sunny yellow spreads. The large tiled bathrooms contain tubs with hand-held showers and the toilet is in a separate compartment. In 2002, fresh carpets were installed in each room and in 2003 all the mattresses were changed. The hotel is only a few minutes' walk from Vieux Nice and the promenade des Anglais.

8 rue Sacha-Guitry, 06000 Nice. © **04/93-80-77-21.** Fax 04/93-80-08-80. carlyna@int1.com. 24 units. 50€ ($58) single; 58€ ($67) double; 66€ ($76) triple. Continental breakfast 7.50€ ($8.60). Ask about low-season rates. AE, MC, V. Bus: 15. *In room:* A/C, TV.

Hôtel Clair Meublé *(Kids*   The Clair Meublé is 3 blocks from the station and 90m (100 yd.) off avenue Jean-Médecin. Ring a buzzer to enter and go up one flight to the reception (no elevator). Gleaming white-tile floors and blue wallpaper give a sleek modern look to this comfortable hotel. Many of the large sunny rooms have balconies, and the freshly tiled bathrooms are small but perfectly adequate. All the rooms were repainted in 2003. Room no. 5 is ideal for a family, with one large and one small bed and two bunk beds. If you're traveling alone, there are no single rates here but you'll get a discount off the double rate, so be sure to ask.

6 rue d'Italie (at rue d'Angleterre), 06000 Nice. © **04/93-87-87-61.** Fax 04/93-16-85-28. 14 units. 42€ ($48) double; 55€ ($63) triple; 65€ ($75) quad. Extra bed 9.25€ ($12). AE, MC, V. Bus 1, 2, 9, 10,or 23. *In room:* Kitchenette, fridge.

Hôtel du Petit Louvre *(Finds*   English-speaking Mme. Vila and her charming husband run this attractive place and will welcome you enthusiastically. The white-walled rooms are a good size and furnished in a modern style, with freshly tiled bathrooms and shelves or hanging space. Although the hotel is in the commercial center, it's on a quiet side street and the prices are delightfully reasonable. To find it, go to Notre-Dame on avenue Jean-Médecin and look for rue Emma-Tiranty on the east side, a bit south. At breakfast, Monsieur Vila will perform his magic tricks or entertain you with a little bit of humor. The small personal attention you receive in this hotel makes it a very pleasant choice.

10 rue Emma-Tiranty (near Marks & Spencer), 06000 Nice. © **04/93-80-15-54.** Fax 04/93-62-45-08. 34 units, 14 with shower only, 20 with bathroom, none with bathtubs. 33€ ($38) single with shower, 36€ ($41) single with bathroom; 41€ ($47) double with shower, 46€ ($53) double with bathroom. Continental breakfast 5€ ($5.75). MC, V. Closed Nov–Feb. Bus: 15.

⸨*Tips*   A Tax Note

Many hotels don't include the *taxe de séjour* (accommodations tax) in their rates. The tax can range from .50€ to 1€ (60¢–$1.15) per person per day depending on the hotel type and room size. When reserving, ask if this tax is included so you won't be surprised at checkout.

(*Value* **Getting the Best Deal on Accommodations**

- Seek out hotels away from the waterfront—distance from the sea lowers the price.
- Take advantage of low-season discounts.
- Consider staying in a room with a sink or shower only—prices often vary greatly according to how much plumbing a room contains.
- Be sure to make reservations if you plan to visit during high season, as many of Nice's cheaper rooms are booked several months in advance.
- Try to book a room with a kitchenette, which allows you to save money on meals. In addition, these rooms tend to be larger.

Hôtel Durante *Value* The Durante boasts a superb location on a quiet dead-end street. Everything has a touch of elegance, beginning with the unusual *trompe l'oeil* facade, and the staff is cordial. The rooms (renovated in 2003) have French windows opening onto a verdant courtyard as well as plenty of closet space. In fall and winter (except for Christmas and Carnival), a 1-night discount is offered to guests staying for a week.

16 av. Durante, 06000 Nice. © 04/93-88-84-40. Fax 04/93-87-77-76. www.hotel-durante.com. 24 units. 69€ ($79) single; 69€—77€ ($79–$89) double. 4-night minimum for use of kitchenette with 8€ ($9.20) supplement. Buffet breakfast 9€ ($10). AE, MC, V. Free parking. Bus: 1, 2, 4, or 9. *In room:* A/C, TV, kitchenette, fridge, hair dryer, safe.

Hôtel La Résidence This pleasant hotel is set back from the street, a few minutes' walk from the station. The well-maintained large rooms come with newly renovated modern bathrooms. The first-floor rooms were completely renovated in 2000, while the others were redone in the mid-1990s. There's adequate storage space and a toilet on each floor that's used by no more than two rooms. In good weather, breakfast is served on an enclosed terrace.

18 av. Durante. © 04/93-88-89-45. Fax 04/93-88-16-11. www.hotel-laresidence.com. 21 units, 4 with shower only, 17 with bathroom. 45€ ($52) single or double with shower; 48€ ($55) single with bathroom; 58€–72€ ($67–$83) double with bathroom; 76€ ($87) triple with bathroom; 80€ ($92) quad with bathroom. Continental breakfast 6€ ($6.90). AE, DC, MC, V. Free parking. Bus 1, 2, 5, or 23. *In room:* TV.

Hotel L'Oasis *Finds* The Oasis is Nice's best-kept secret. There's a dreamy relaxed feel to the place, set back from the street in an early-1900s Provençal villa surrounded by a lush garden. In this house, Anton Chekhov wrote his infamous play *The Three Sisters,* and Lenin sojourned here for a time in 1911. The staff is friendly, and the rooms are pleasant with clean carpets and bedspreads that reflect the deep blue and yellow colors of Provence. The individual air-conditioning units are quite strong and keep things cool even on the warmest of days; bathrooms are sparkling clean. Breakfast is served in the lovely garden or in the pleasant dining room.

23 rue Gounod, 06000 Nice. © 04/93-88-12-29. Fax 04/93-16-14-40. hotel-oasis-nice.com.fr. 38 units. 65€ ($75) single; 82€ ($94) double; 88€ ($101) double with twin beds; 105€ ($121) triple. Continental breakfast 9€ ($10). AE, DC, MC, V. Parking 6€ ($6.90). *In room:* A/C, TV.

Hôtel Normandie *Value* Two blocks from the station, the five floors of rooms at the Normandie are cheerfully decorated in red, white, and blue. All are in equally good condition, with ample storage space, modern bathrooms, and double-glazed windows; some have balconies. All the mattresses were changed in 2003. It's run by the friendly Beth family (who hail from Normandy, of course) and is popular with tour groups, so book ahead. When you make reservations, identify yourself as a Frommer's reader for a 5% discount.

18 rue Paganini (and 11 rue d'Alsace-Lorraine), 06000 Nice. © **04/93-88-48-83.** Fax 04/93-16-04-33. www.hotel-Normandie.com. 44 units. 59€ ($68) single; 69€ ($79) double; 79€ ($91) triple; 89€ ($102) quad. Buffet breakfast 5.50€ ($6.30). Ask about low-season discounts. AE, DC, MC, V. Bus 1, 2, 4, 5, 12, 17, or 22. *In room:* A/C, TV, dataport, hair dryer, safe.

Hôtel Notre-Dame The very hospitable Yung family manages this hotel 3 blocks from the station, and they work closely with the Clair Meublé (p. 660) and have the same obsession with tip-top maintenance. If one hotel is full, they try to book you into the other. The freshly tiled floors (all redone in 2002) and bathrooms are sparkling white. If you're traveling in a group of four, try to book room no. 3, 9, 16, or 20, each with bunk beds.

22 rue de Russie, Nice 06000. © **04/93-88-70-44.** Fax 04/93-82-20-38. jyung@caramail.com. 17 units. 44€ ($51) single; 54€ ($62) double; 68€ ($78) triple. Extra bed 9.25€ ($11). Continental breakfast 5.50€ ($6.30). AE, MC, V. Bus: 1, 2, 5, 12, 17, or 22.

Sibill's Hotel 🔒 The glistening lobby sets the tone for Sibill's recently renovated (in 2003) and meticulously maintained carpeted rooms, most of which are bathed in cool pastel colors; all are a good size. The double-glazed windows and thick curtains keep out sound and light for a good night's sleep. Some rooms have phone jacks to plug in modems. The train station is a 5-minute walk away, as is the busy shopping district on avenue Jean-Médecin.

25 rue Assalit (at St-Siagre), 06000 Nice. © **04/93-62-03-07.** Fax 04/93-85-37-20. www.sibills-hotel-nice.com. 56 units. 47€ ($54) single; 85€ ($98) double; 93€ ($107) triple; 100€ ($115) quad. Rates include continental breakfast. AE, MC, V. Bus: 15. *In room:* A/C, TV.

NEAR THE SEA

Hôtel Canada *Value* In the midst of Nice's pedestrian zone is the shiny doorway to the Canada, and up 22 marble stairs is the bright lobby, adorned with paintings and mirrors (no elevator). The rooms vary in size, but each has its own touch—a special artwork here, a brass headboard there. Alas, they are showing signs of wear—faded bedspreads, drab curtains, aging carpets. The largest room is no. 5, which adjoins the terrace-garden where breakfast is served in warm weather, but the most desirable rooms are on the third floor and have terraces or balconies with partial sea views. The tiny tiled bathrooms are adequate, the beds firm, and the windows double-glazed. Owner M. Olandj also owns the Hôtel Villa Eden (see below), and you'll receive a warm welcome in both. When making reservations, identify yourself as a Frommer's reader and receive a 10% discount.

8 rue Halévy, 06000 Nice. © **04/93-87-98-94.** Fax 04/93-87-17-12. hotel-canada@caramail.com. 18 units. 30€–75€ ($35–$86) single or double without kitchenette, 60€–75€ ($69–$86) single or double with kitchenette. Extra bed 15€ ($17). Continental breakfast 5.50€ ($6.30). AE, DC, MC, V. Bus: 12. *In room:* A/C, TV.

Hôtel Cronstadt 🔒 *Value* One of Nice's better bargains is on a posh side street, just off the promenade des Anglais, facing the Négresco. The very friendly owners bought the hotel in mid-2002 and try hard to ensure every guest's comfort; they live on the premises and run the place like a cozy B&B. A lush courtyard behind a nondescript residential building leads to the cozy lobby, which in turn leads to the tidy rooms, with lace curtains and flowery bedspreads. They're scattered on three floors (no elevator), including five rooms off the lobby. The upstairs rooms may very well be the quietest accommodations in this price range, in all of Nice. There's a 5€ ($5.75) charge to have breakfast served in your room.

3 rue Cronstadt, 06000 Nice. (©) 04/93-82-00-30. Fax 04/93-16-87-40. www.hotelcronstadt.com. 10 units. 68€ ($78) single; 80€–90€ ($92–$104) double; 107€ ($123) triple. Extra bed 25€ ($29). Rates include continental breakfast. MC, V. Bus: 6, 9, 10, or 22. *In room:* A/C, TV, fridge (ask when reserving).

Hôtel Félix 🎿 *Finds*   The Félix is in a quiet pedestrian zone that's still convenient to the beach and the waterfront's nightlife. The two charming sisters who own/manage the hotel will welcome you in English, French, or Italian and show you to a comfortable room on one of the three floors (no elevator). All rooms had fresh carpeting installed in 2003; bathrooms were also renovated that year and five of the rooms now have sparkling new bathtubs. Most have balconies with flower-filled window boxes. Extras include double-glazed windows, fluffy towels, and firm beds.

41 rue Masséna, 06000 Nice. (©) 04/93-88-67-73. Fax 04/93-16-15-78. 14 units. 50€ ($58) single; 70€ ($81) double; 80€ ($92) triple. Continental breakfast 6€ ($6.90). AE, DC, MC, V. Bus: 2, 5, or 12. *In room:* A/C, TV, hair dryer.

Hôtel Harvey   The Harvey is a good place for families looking for peace and quiet because no outsiders are allowed in the rooms at night. All the rooms in this renovated six-floor hotel have been modernized, and most are relatively large, with good storage space. Many have one double bed and one twin bed, and the fifth-floor rooms boast small balconies with sea views. The bathrooms are attractively tiled, most with tubs with hand-held showers. Avenue de Suède is part of a pedestrian zone; no cars are allowed on the street facing the hotel. Mme. Passeri keeps in personal contact with her guests.

18 av. de Suède (just off promenade des Anglais), 06000 Nice. (©) 04/93-88-73-73. Fax 04/93-82-53-55. hotelharvey@wanadoo.fr. 64 units. 60€–86€ ($69–$99) single or double; 92€ ($106) triple. Continental breakfast 6€ ($6.90). AE, MC, V. Closed Nov–Feb. Bus: 12. *In room:* A/C, TV.

Hôtel Le Lido 🎿🎿 *Finds*   This is, hands down, Nice's best bargain. The Lido opened in 2001 and occupies the second floor of a grand residential building just behind the venerable Hotel Negresco. The location can't be beat, just a block away from the sea. Each of the seven rooms has a new bathroom and contemporary IKEA-style furnishings. In 2004, every room was slowly being renovated to include attractive faux parquet floors and lovely wooden cupboards with electronic safes. The walls are painted a crisp white—a nice contrast to the floral wallpaper found in other discount hotels, and the new air-conditioning system keeps things nice and cool during the hot summer months (very rare in hotels in this price range). No breakfast is served since each unit comes with its own small (but fully equipped) kitchenette. The young manager/owner, Xavier Marinot, offers a discount to Frommer's readers and to those guests staying 5 nights or more, so be sure to ask.

4 rue Commandant Berretta (just behind the Negresco), 06000 Nice. (©)/fax 04/93-88-43-15. X.marinot@ wanadoo.fr. 7 units. Single or double 45€–64€ ($52–$74). AE, MC, V. Bus: 6, 9, 10, or 22. *In room:* A/C, TV, kitchenette, safe.

Hôtel Paradis 🎿   If you'd like to stay in a new, gleaming hotel, you can't go wrong here. On a pedestrian shopping street steps from the beach and the Jardin Albert-1er, this hotel is ideally situated for almost anything you'd want to do. After a complete renovation in 2003, the Paradis is now almost out of our price range, but worth every penny. All the rooms are now soundproof and beautifully furnished with yellow and red heavy fabric; all the mattresses are firm and new. Bathrooms are sparkling, if still a bit small.

1 rue Paradis, 06000 Nice. ℂ **04/93-87-71-23**. Fax 04/93-88-23-16. www.paradishotel.com. 13 units. 60€–90€ ($69–$104) single or double. Continental breakfast 5.50€ ($6.30). Ask about low-season rates. MC, V. Bus: 5. *In room:* TV, minibar.

Hôtel Régence 🖈 Recently renovated, this sleek hotel has been buffed and polished to perfection. The white-tiled bathrooms and white-wicker furniture give the rooms a cheerful look that's enhanced by pretty matching bedspreads and curtains; you'll also find double-glazed windows. The only fault is a shortage of shelf space, but the Régence's location on a pedestrian street near the promenade des Anglais is excellent. Room-service breakfast is available at no extra charge and there's an elevator.

21 rue Masséna, 06000 Nice. ℂ **04/93-87-75-08**. Fax 04/93-82-41-31. www.hotelregence.com. 39 units. 65€–78€ ($75–$90) single or double. Extra bed 16€ ($18). Continental breakfast 6€ ($6.90). AE, DC, MC, V. Bus: 5. *In room:* A/C, TV, dataport.

IN PONT MAGNAN

A 20-minute stroll from avenue Masséna west along promenade des Anglais brings you to Pont Magnan, an upscale residential district with white-and-pastel apartment blocks facing the Mediterranean. It's not near the center of town, but bus transportation is fast and frequent. Take bus no. 24 from the train station; bus no. 3, 10, 12, or 22 from downtown; or bus no. 8 or 11 along promenade des Anglais.

Flots d'Azur *Finds* A good choice for reasonably priced accommodations on the promenade is this three-story villa, which was purchased in 2001 by a friendly younger couple who make sure their multinational guests of all ages are comfortable. The rooms vary widely in size, view, and price, but all have double-glazed windows and new carpets (added in 2002). The basement rooms are larger and quieter but have no view. The priciest rooms are the upper-level seaview units, with large windows; three have small balconies. The bargain 47€ ($54) tiny room with toilet only has a clean shower in the hall. Since it's been a few years since the last renovation, don't expect anything to be too brilliant or new here, but the level of cleanliness is quite high. Breakfast is served on the terrace overlooking the sea, and the oleander bushes help block some of the traffic noise. Although parking is free on the hotel's narrow driveway, space isn't guaranteed; if all the spots are taken, you'll have to pay for parking on the street or in a nearby lot. There is no elevator access.

101 promenade des Anglais, 06000 Nice. ℂ **04/93-86-51-25**. Fax 04/93-97-22-07. www.flotsdazur.com. 20 units, 18 with bathroom, 1 with toilet only. 47€ ($54) single or double with toilet, 65€–105€ ($75–$121) single or double with bathroom. Continental breakfast 6.50€ ($7.50). MC, V. Bus: 3, 9, 10, 12, or 23. *In room:* A/C, TV.

Hôtel Villa Eden *Value* Believe it or not, it's possible to stay in a historic villa on the promenade des Anglais across from the beach and still be within your budget. The homey quarters in high-ceilinged rooms with period furnishings, some with a terrace facing the Mediterranean, are a perfect setting for a pleasant stay. Although all the bathrooms were renovated in late 2003 with new fixtures and sinks, the rooms are aging fast—bedspreads are fading and the carpet is spotted. If you're not going to be spending much time in your room, this is a good choice for its fabulous location. You can breakfast in a small garden with oleander and lemon trees or walk to the beach to swim. The entrance to this

Shangri-La is through a narrow corridor lined with flowers and trees. Identify yourself as a Frommer's reader to receive a 10% discount.

99 bis promenade des Anglais (near sq. Général-Ferrié), 06000 Nice. © **04/93-86-53-70.** Fax 04/93-97-67-97. hotelvillaeden@caramail.com. 14 units. 55€–75€ ($63–$86) single or double. Extra bed 15€ ($17). Continental breakfast 6€ ($6.90). AE, DC, MC, V. Free parking. Bus: 3, 9, 10, 12, or 23. *In room:* A/C, TV.

IN CIMIEZ

Relais International de la Jeunesse Clairvallon   This private hostel is in the northern reaches of Cimiez, one of Nice's finest residential districts. Surrounded by aristocratic villas, the hostel, with pretty grounds, was itself once a villa. Registration is after 5pm, and curfew is 11pm; you don't have to have a hostel card or be a certain age to stay in one of the four- to eight-bed rooms with showers. It's about 5m (3 miles) north of place Masséna, but the bus runs every 10 minutes weekdays and every 15 or 20 minutes weekends. When you get off, turn left onto winding avenue Scuderi, walk about 450m (1,500 ft.) past villas and palm trees, and you'll see the hostel on the right.

26 av. Scuderi, Cimiez, 06100 Nice. © **04/93-81-27-63.** Fax 04/93-53-35-88. 150 beds. 14€ ($16) dorm bed; half-board *(demi-pension)* 24€ ($27); full board *(pension complète)* 29€ ($33). Rates include showers. No credit cards. Bus: 15. **Amenities:** Pool; tennis courts.

A GAY & LESBIAN HOTEL

Hôtel Meyerbeer   This friendly, relaxed hotel is a block from the promenade des Anglais, occupying the first two floors of an older residential building; the lobby is on the second floor (no elevator). David looks after everyone to ensure his or her comfort. The rooms are all a good size, with double-glazed windows and tiled bathrooms with fluffy towels; the twin-bedded rooms are even more spacious and boast well-equipped kitchenettes. The storage space is more than ample, and the wood floors and ceilings create an attractive light look.

15 rue Meyerbeer, 06000 Nice. © **04/93-88-95-65.** Fax 04/93-82-09-25. meyerbeerhotel@aol.com. 20 units. 65€ ($75) single; 72€ ($83) double; 110€ ($127) triple. Breakfast 5.50€ ($6.30). No credit cards. Bus: 12 or 22. *In room:* TV, kitchenette (twin-bedded rooms).

WORTH A SPLURGE

Hi Hotel ★★ *Moments*   The most talked-about hotel in Nice opened in 2003 to much acclaim. A 1930s building, a few blocks off the Promenade, has been totally transformed to house this ultra-modern, quirky, and unique hotel. No two rooms are alike in this space-age Art Deco design. This hotel reeks of pretentious minimalism. Some of the rooms are influenced by what the French designers call "cyber-culture" and come with furniture that looks like computer screens (don't ask, it's hard to explain); others are done totally in white; some have flat-screen TVs. Some bathrooms are separated from the room only by a flimsy designer curtain, so come prepared to be intimate with your roommate. All that said, this place is the most hip and happening of any hotel in Nice. The Happy Bar fills with young local professionals who want to be seen. Even if you're not staying here, it's worth the 6€ ($6.90) splurge for a drink, just to people-watch. You can check your e-mail in the lobby from the public laptops.

3 av. des Fleurs, 06000 Nice. © **04/97-07-26-26.** Fax 04/97-07-26-27. www.hi-hotel.net. 38 units. 155€–200€ ($178 230) double; from 255€ ($293) studio. Rates include buffet breakfast. AE, DC, MC, V. Bus: 3, 12, or 22. **Amenities:** Very hip bar; lounge; small rooftop pool; massage; nonsmoking floors. *In room:* A/C, TV, hair dryer, dataport, safe.

Mercure Marche Aux Fleurs ★ *Finds*   Steps from cours Saleya and the flower market, this hotel is perfectly located right on the Promenade. Most rooms do not overlook the water, however, and are rather small. But they are all sound-proof, clean, and quiet. Every room comes with a small desk, dark blue or gray carpeting, and firm beds. All but four of the bathrooms have tubs and they are all clean and sparkling white. For the ultimate splurge, pay the 55€ ($63) sup-plement to upgrade to a large suite overlooking the sea. The 12€ ($14) break-fast, though pricey, is a lavish buffet. But being this close to Vieux Nice, you might just want to roll out of bed and stroll to the market for your breakfast. Note that this hotel is on two floors and there is no elevator.

91 quai des Etats-Unis, 06000 Nice. © **04/93-83-74-19.** Fax 04/93-13-90-94. www.accor.com. 49 units. 92€–100€ ($106–$115) single; 106€–115€ ($122–$132) double; 161€–170€ ($185–$196) suite. Buffet breakfast 12€ ($14). AE, DC, MC, V. Bus: 1, 2, 4, or 22. **Amenities:** Bar; lounge. *In room:* A/C, TV, hair dryer.

3 Great Deals on Dining

The cuisine along the Côte d'Azur is a refreshing alternative to classical French cooking. Making liberal use of local products like olive oil, garlic, tomatoes, and fresh herbs, the approach to dining is more casual, spontaneous, and often cheaper than that in Paris.

For restaurant dining, the best value is usually a *menu du jour* (fixed-price meal), offering two or three courses, sometimes with wine (look for *vin compris*) at a better price than you'd get by ordering a la carte. An alternative to a multi-course meal is a *plat du jour,* a main-course platter garnished with vegetables and little extras that easily constitutes a filling meal. Service charge and tax are included in prices.

Happily for budget travelers, inexpensive Italian food is popular. You'll find pasta prepared in dozens of imaginative ways, and more pizza shops than there are pebbles on the beach. For lighter fare, you can't do better than *salade niçoise,* usually made with lettuce, tomatoes, onions, anchovies, hard-boiled eggs, olives, and tuna. Hearty and strongly flavored soups are a staple of the local diet. *Soupe au pistou* is a vegetable soup, perked up with garlic and basil pesto (*pistou*). *Soupe au poisson* is a deep red savory soup made from fish, tomatoes, and garlic and served with cheese, croutons, and aioli (Provençal garlic mayon-naise). The most famous Mediterranean soup is **bouillabaisse,** featuring an assortment of local seafood like *rascasse* (rock cod), *congre* (eel), and *dorade* (snapper). Although bouillabaisse can be expensive, try to splurge once on this savory stew.

A particular restaurant may close any day (or part of a day) or week, so be sure to check the hours before heading out to eat. For more dining details, see the

---

⌒Value Street Eats

For a quick bite on the cheap, take to the streets of Nice where vendors offer tasty bake trays of *pissaladière*—onion tarts garnished with anchovies—and sell them for about 2€ ($2.30) a portion. Also look for vendors offering *socca,* a kind of baked pancake made from chickpea flour that's often eaten for breakfast, also costing 2€ ($2.30). For the best *socca* in Nice, visit **Thérèse's** stand in front of 5 cours Saleya. She'll cut the pancake in front of you and sprinkle it with pepper. You could live on healthy and delicious *pan bagnat* (a small, round bread loaf stuffed with *salade niçoise*–type goodies and moistened with olive oil) for the dura-tion of your visit and barely put a dent in your wallet.

> **Value Getting the Best Deal on Dining**
>
> • Take advantage of the street snack stands selling *socca*, pizza, *pissaladière*, and sandwiches.
> • Note that standing at the counter in a cafe rather than sitting at a table with waiter service can save you 30%.
> • Try the *menu du jour* (fixed-price meal), often the most economical and tastiest choice. And there's always the *plat du jour*, cheaper though less filling.
> • Ordering bottled water can increase the cost of your meal by a third. Ask for *une carafe d'eau*—tap water.

introduction to the dining section in chapter 19, "Paris & the Best of the Ile de France."

BETWEEN THE TRAIN STATION & AVENUE JEAN-MEDECIN

Chez Davia *Value* FRENCH   The red-and-white-checkered tablecloths and brisk no-nonsense service place Davia squarely in the French bistro tradition. Staples like cheese soufflé and coq au vin as well as pasta, chicken in curry sauce, and *salade niçoise* are on the menu, and main courses come with a choice of side dishes (vegetables, fried potatoes, salad, or spaghetti). The restaurant is popular with locals, who come for the tasty food and hearty portions at a great price.

11 bis rue Grimaldi. ⓒ **04/93-87-91-39**. Main courses 7€–15€ ($8–$17); 3 course menus 12€ and 17€ ($14 and $20). AE, MC, V. Thurs–Tues noon–2:30pm and 7–10pm. Bus: 1, 2, 15, or 22.

La Nissarda 🌟 NIÇOISE   The charming young M. and Mme. DeTouillons work hard at La Nissarda to maintain Nice's culinary traditions. A 10-minute walk from place Masséna, the space is decorated with unremarkable paintings of Provençal scenes, but it's the food that's the star. The *petits farcis niçois* on the fixed-price menu is a good introduction to the stuffed vegetables that are a Nice specialty, and the *daube à la Provençale* (beef stew) is well prepared. Best of all is the *rouget* (red mullet), marinated in lime and olive oil.

17 rue Gubernatis. ⓒ **04/93-85-26-29**. 3-course menus 16€ and 24€ ($18 and $28). MC, V. Mon–Sat 11:30am–2pm and 6:45–10pm. Bus: 1, 2, 4, 5, 12, 15, 17, or 22.

Le Tire Bouchon SOUTHWESTERN FRENCH   The cuisine of Lyon and southwestern France is rich and flavorful yet delicate and sophisticated; this charming restaurant gives you a taste without breaking your budget. Locals flock to this rustic classic for the *tartiflette savoyarde* (potatoes topped with melted cheese and slow-baked) and the variety of sausages unique to the Lyon region. For a more Provençal meal, the *tarte au saumon fumé au basilic* (pastry filled with smoked salmon and basil) is light and tasty. The *tarte tatin* (warm apple pie) is an excellent choice for dessert. Service is warm and friendly.

19 rue de la Préfecture. ⓒ **04/93-92-63-64**. Main courses 8€–20€ ($9–$23); 3-course menus 17€ and 23€ ($20 and $26). AE, MC, V. Mon–Fri 7–10pm; Sat 7–10:30pm. Bus: 1, 2, 5, or 22.

Restaurant au Soleil FRENCH   Owners Roger and Gaëtane Germain have been serving Frommer's readers at this large, sunny, family eatery for 40 years with pleasure. The *salade niçoise* appetizer on the fixed-price menu includes chunks of tuna, and the breaded veal cutlet is a popular main course. On the higher-priced menu, try the *calamars armoricaine* (squid in tomato sauce). Finish with the fresh chocolate mousse. If you're staying in the neighborhood, drop by for the 6€ ($6.90) full breakfast (served all day).

7 bis rue d'Italie (at rue d'Italie). © **04/93-88-77-74.** *Plat du jour* 6.50€ ($7.50); 3-course menus with wine 12€ and 15€ ($14 and $17). AE, MC, V. Sun–Fri 8am–10pm. Closed Dec–Feb. Bus 3, 4, or 9.

Restaurant le Saetone *(Value* FRENCH/ITALIAN   Le Saetone pleases with a homey decor, friendly service, and good food at unbeatable prices. It offers two three-course *menus du jour,* but the top sellers are the endless pizza varieties, especially the pizza Provençal, topped with tomatoes, herbs of Provence, garlic, olives, and cheese. The *plat du jour* could be anything from ratatouille (sautéed eggplant with green peppers, herbs, and onions) to *lapin sauté* (rabbit sautéed in garlic and white wine). Tables fill up quickly, so get here early.

8 rue d'Alsace-Lorraine (between rue Paganini and rue d'Angleterre). © **04/93-87-17-95.** Pizza 6€–9€ ($7–$10); *plat du jour* 9€ ($10); 3-course menus 11€ and 16€ ($13 and $18). MC, V. Thurs–Tues 11:30am–2pm and 6–10pm.

Voyageur Nissart NIÇOISE   This cozy restaurant is a favorite with retired folks who come for expertly prepared dishes like their grandmothers used to make. The ambience is familial, and you're likely to find grilled sardines, *raviolis niçois* (with a sauce of tomatoes, onions, and olives), *feuilleté aux courgettes* (zucchini tart), *soupe au pistou,* and a superb apple tart. The *lapin à la niçoise* (rabbit stewed with tomatoes, onions, mushrooms, and olives) is especially delicious.

19 rue Alsace-Lorraine. © **04/93-82-19-60.** 3-course menus 11€, 14€, and 17€ ($13, $16, and $20). V. Tues–Sun 11:30am–2pm and 6:30–10pm. Closed Aug. Bus: 1, 2, or 5.

NEAR THE SEA

Bambou Plage FRENCH *(Value*   Below the promenade des Anglais right on the sand, this restaurant is the only affordable choice for beachfront dining. The blue plastic tables and chairs all have pretty umbrellas to keep you shaded. The salad portions are large and the waiters will freshen your bread basket a couple of times if you ask. The menu is simple and consists of sandwiches, salads, and pasta dishes. This is an excellent place to try a delicious *salade niçoise* with a glass of chilled white wine. If you order carefully, you can eat here for less than 12€ ($14) per person while the Mediterranean (literally) laps at your feet.

165 Promenade des Anglais. © **04/93-86-64-15.** Salads and sandwiches 9€–12€ ($10–$14); main courses 14€–21€ ($16–$24). MC, V. Summer daily noon–7pm. Closed mid-Oct to mid-Apr.

La Pizza *(Kids* ITALIAN   Crowded every afternoon and evening, both winter and summer, La Pizza has found the formula: fresh pizzas and fast (though brusque) service at good prices. Salads, omelets, and a *plat du jour,* plus wine and beer, are served as well. You might have a short wait for a table.

34 rue Masséna. © **04/93-87-70-29.** Pizza 7€–9€ ($8–$10); *plat du jour* 10€ ($12); main courses 7€–20€ ($8–$23). AE, MC, V. Daily 11:30am–1am. Bus: 3, 6, 7, or 14.

IN VIEUX NICE

Chez Juliette *(★★* *(Moments* FRENCH   This elegant restaurant, just steps from place Rosetti, is popular with young local professionals. There's a wonderful terrace for summer dining and, indoors, a cozy dining room includes wrought iron tables and thick stone walls. The bargain 17€ ($20) three-course menu includes a fabulous appetizer of marinated peppers and artichokes followed by a delicious chicken baked in a mushroom and cream sauce. For dessert, it's a tough choice between *crème caramel* and luscious homemade sorbet. The service can be slow, but then again, the terrace is perfect for lingering with a glass of wine as you watch the people go by.

1 place Rosetti. ℂ **04/93-92-68-47.** Main courses 12€–19€ ($14–$22); 3-course menu 17€ ($20). MC, V. Wed–Sun 7–11pm. Bus: 1, 2, 4, 5, 12, 15, 17, or 22.

Chez Pipo *Value* NIÇOIS BAKERY   For a very inexpensive and authentic Niçois light meal, this tiny bakery on a side street is always hopping with locals. The focus is the large wood oven where they bake local specialties; there's no cooking and no kitchen, just baking. *Pissaladière* and *socca* (see "Street Eats," p. 666) are served piping-hot out of the oven. For dessert, there's a tasty wheat tart with sugar and lemon. Beer and wine are also served, and you can grab a sidewalk table or a seat at the large communal tables inside.

13 rue Bavastro (behind the large church at the port). ℂ **04/93-55-88-82.** Items 2€–2.50€ ($2.30–$2.90) per portion. No credit cards. Daily 5:30–10pm. Closed Mar. Bus: 1, 2, 9, 10, or 32.

Eclat du Cours *Value* FRENCH   There are many restaurants lining the beautiful cours Saleya, but this tiny pleasant one offers the best bargain. For 15 years, the same chef has been preparing high-quality meals served on the sunny cobblestone terrace or in the (really) tiny bright dining room. The bargain 15€ ($17) menu includes a choice of three appetizers, three main courses, and three desserts. Sample starters include the delicious *soupe de poissons* (fish soup with garlic croutons) or the *moules Provençales* (mussels in a white wine and herb sauce); main courses may include a choice of *escalope de volaille* (breaded chicken filet with mushrooms) or grilled prawns served with rice pilaf. For dessert, there's usually an exquisite tart (pear or apple) and a variety of luscious sorbets to choose from.

11 cours Saleya. ℂ **04/93-85-68-76.** 3-course menu 15€ ($17); main courses 9€–14€. ($10–$16). MC, V. Thurs–Tues 11:30am–2pm; Thurs–Wed 6:30–11pm. Bus: 1, 2, 4, 5, 12, 15, or 22.

Nissa Socca NIÇOISE   Vieux Nice is crammed with casual eateries, but Nissa Socca is the local favorite. This tiny place with beamed ceilings is crowded and noisy as harried waiters rush around trying to satisfy the hungry hordes. The staples of the local cuisine—*socca, beignets, farcis, soupe au pistou*, pizza, and homemade pasta—are all on the menu at easily digestible prices. Get here early for dinner or be prepared for a long wait.

5 rue Ste-Réparate. ℂ **04/93-80-18-35.** Reservations not accepted. *Plat du jour* 9€ ($10); main courses 8€–11€ ($9–$13). No credit cards. Tues–Sat noon–2:30pm; Mon–Sat 7–11pm. Bus: 1, 2, 4, 5, 12, 15, 17, or 22.

Restaurant Acchiardo *⋆* FRENCH   Corncobs and other farm souvenirs decorate the ceiling beams and walls of this tiny place near the St-Jacob church, presaging good eating. The feeling is certainly French provincial, although the smiling staff can get by in English. The seafood is particularly good, including hake; with potatoes, carrots, and celery, this makes a typical big *plat du jour*. Ask for the English menu and don't forget to peek into the catacomb-like wine cellar, built during the reign of Louis XIV.

38 rue Droite (near the corner of rue du Château). ℂ **04/93-85-51-16.** *Plat du jour* 11€ ($13); main courses 10€–17€ ($12–$20). No credit cards. Mon–Sat noon–1:30pm; Mon–Fri 7–9:30pm. Closed Aug. Bus: 1, 2, 4, 5, 12, 15, 17, or 22. Follow signs to the Palais Lascaris, on rue Droite, and walk past the palace and the church.

Samsara *⋆* *Moments* FRENCH   Though the name and decor are part North African, part Southeast Asian, the food here is strictly French and exquisitely prepared. The location, a few steps from the beautiful place Rosetti, can't be beat. There's a small outdoor dining area and a charming dining room overlooking the open kitchen. The place is full of little touches such as the mosaic tables and hand-worked wrought iron chairs. There usually is only one person waiting tables, along with the chef, so you can be sure of very intimate service. The 17€ ($19) fixed-price menu may include an appetizer of warm chèvre served on toast with a green salad, or a smoked salmon terrine; main courses include trout in a basil cream sauce or oven-baked duck served on a bed of extra-fluffy mashed potatoes. You may substitute a cheese course for dessert, and there's a good local wine at 2.50€ ($2.90) a glass. Satisfy your sweet tooth with the variety of home-made pies and ice creams usually available.

2 rue Rosetti. (*C* 04/93-80-70-63. 3-course menu 17€ ($19); main courses 11€–14€ ($13–$16). MC, V. Daily 12:30–11pm. Bus: 1, 2, 4, 5, 12, 17, or 22.

PICNICKING

Buying food in markets is a pleasure in Nice, and there's a wealth of great pic-nic spots. After you stroll through the flower portion of the market at the **cours Saleya** (Tues–Sun 7am–1pm), head to the eastern side to find stands of luscious fruit, pungent cheese, *charcuterie* (smoked sausages), and freshly baked breads. Try *fougasse*—bread stuffed with olives, anchovies, ham, or local cheese. For the best *socca* in Nice, visit **Thérèse** ᏊᏊ in front of 5 cours Saleya. And at **La Poulette,** 12 rue de la Préfecture (*C* 04/93-85-67-96), you'll find the best roasted chicken in Vieux Nice, as well as cheeses and cold meats. For dessert, pick up the best homemade ice cream as well as chocolates and candied chest-nuts from **L'Art Gourmand,** 21 rue du Marche (*C* 04/93-62-51-79).

You can take your feast to the **promenade des Anglais,** grab a chair, and gaze at the sea while eating. You're also only steps from the stairs leading to the park around the hilltop **Château** with magnificent views over the bay.

If you're staying around the train station, you can assemble your picnic from the less touristy **Liberation market** on avenue Malaussena. Open Tuesday to Sunday 7am to 1pm, it also offers numerous stands selling local products.

There's no reason to fast on Monday, when the markets are closed. Head for the **Prisunic department store** on avenue Jean-Médecin between rue Biscarra and avenue Maréchal-Foch. You'll find huge chunks of cheese, *charcuterie,* pâté, and various salads and side dishes at a few euros per 200 grams (7 oz.). Gener-ally the prices are lower than at the markets, but the quality isn't quite as high. When you're done in the grocery section, head for the doors at the corner of avenues Jean-Médecin and Maréchal-Foch, where the bakery is. You can con-sume your picnic on **place Masséna** or in the **Jardins Albert-1er,** or you can head to the **promenade des Anglais** or the **beach.**

WORTH A SPLURGE

Brasserie Flo ᏊᏊ (*Value* FRENCH This is a lovely grand brasserie that, although part of a chain, remains one of the city's most popular restaurants among locals and visitors alike. The open kitchen is visible on a stage behind a thick red curtain, reminiscent of the early 1900s when the restaurant used to be a casino. The food is consistently excellent, the quality is very high, and the serv-ice is extremely gracious for such a large restaurant. The bargain three-course menu may include an appetizer of *tartare de saumon mi-fume* (half-smoked salmon tartar) or a delicate *ravioli aux legumes primavera* (ravioli with spring veg-etables), followed by *magret de canard aux epices, polenta croustillant aux olives* (sliced breast of a fattened duck sautéed with spices and served with crunchy olive polenta), or *gambas geantes* (giant scampi) served with risotto. Dessert includes the delicious bittersweet chocolate meringue or a perfect crème brûlée. All fixed-price menus come with a half-bottle of wine; two diners together who order the same wine get a whole bottle to share.

2–4 rue Sacha Guitry (off Place Massena). (C) **04/93-13-38-38.** Reservations recommended for dinner. 2-course lunch menu and 2-course menu after 10:30pm with wine 21€ ($24); 3-course dinner menu 30€ ($34) with wine; main courses 14€–23€ ($16–$26). AE, DC, MC, V. Daily noon–3pm and 7pm–midnight. Bus: 1, 2, 3, 5, 6, 14, 16, 17, or 25.

Don Camillo 😊😊 (Moments) FRENCH   The talented young chef Stéphane Viano interprets local dishes with flair at this elegant restaurant. Dress up and you won't feel out of place in this intimate and very chic establishment. You'll see Italian influences in the pastas, risotto, and polenta, but the delicate herbs and refined sauces are strictly French. The three-course menu changes daily to take advantage of fresh market ingredients, and the a la carte menu offers a pricey but delicious variety of meat and fish dishes. The regional Château de Berne wines perfectly complement the cuisine.

5 rue des Ponchettes. (C) **04/93-85-67-95.** Reservations suggested. Main courses 16€–24€ ($18–$28); 3-course menu 33€ ($38). AE, MC, V. Tues–Sat noon–2:30pm; Mon–Sat 7–10:30pm. Bus: 1, 2, 3, 5, 6, 14, 16, 17, or 25.

4 Seeing the Sights

A spectacular natural setting is Nice's greatest asset. The promenade des Anglais, running nearly the full length of the Baie des Anges (Bay of Angels), opens the city to sea and sky. Flowers and plants flourish in the mild climate, filling parks and cascading from windowsills. The play of light and color has inspired many fine painters, whose works you can discover in the city's excellent museums.

IN NICE

The wide **promenade des Anglais** 😊😊😊 fronts the bay. Split by islands of palms and flowers, it stretches for about 6.5km (4 miles). Fronting the beach are rows of grand cafes, the Musée Masséna, villas, hotels, and chic boutiques.

Crossing this boulevard in the briefest of bikinis or thongs are some of the world's most attractive golden people. They're heading for the **beach**—"on the rocks," as it's called here. Tough on tender feet, the beach comprises smooth, round pebbles, one of the least attractive (and least publicized) aspects of the cosmopolitan resort. Many bathhouses provide mattresses for about 12€ ($14) a day; arrive after 1pm and take advantage of the half-day rate of around 8€ ($9) per mattress.

Eglise Orthodoxe Russe (Russian Orthodox Church) 😊   Nice was a fashionable resort for Russian aristocrats in the 19th century, and in the early 20th century Tsar Nicholas II and his mother commissioned this church, which was inaugurated in 1912. Its richly decorated interior includes several outstanding

---

(Tips) A Note About Museum Hours

The beaches are open every day, but the museums aren't. Some museums are closed on Monday, others on Tuesday, and many for a month every year, often in rainy November. Check the hours to be sure before heading out. For a complete list of museums and hours, get the free brochure *Les Musées de Nice* at the tourist office.

icons. With six onion domes and vivid colors, the Russian church has become one of Nice's landmarks.

Av. Nicholas-II. ℂ **04/93-96-88-02.** Admission 2.50€ ($2.90). Daily 9am–noon and 2:30–5:30pm (shorter hours in winter).

Le Château 🐾🐾 *Kids*   This hill above Vieux Nice at the eastern end of the quai des Etats-Unis is named for the fortress that once stood here. There are beautiful groves of evergreens and plantings of cacti, with a path to take you around the hilltop. Several viewpoints afford breathtaking vistas of the town and sea. An **elevator** at the end of the quai des Etats-Unis, near the Hôtel Suisse, will transport you uphill for 1€ ($1.15) round-trip; it operates daily 10am to 5:50pm. Also here is the **Tour Bellanda,** an old tower where Berlioz lived for some time; it now houses a small **naval museum** (open Wed–Sun 10am–noon and 2–5pm; admission 2.50€/$2.90). On the northwest side of the hill is the **old cemetery** of Nice, the largest one in France. In addition to magnificent views of the surrounding mountains, the cemetery offers a fascinating display of funeral statuary over the tombs. My favorite is the Gastaud family plot, which shows a hand trying to raise the top of the tomb.

Musée d'Art Moderne et d'Art Contemporain 🐾   Frequently overlooked, the city's modern art museum, between place Masséna and Vieux Nice, offers an interesting collection of avant-garde artists, especially those who've lived or worked in Nice—such as Robert Indiana, Ben, Arman, and Cesar. There's a room dedicated to Yves Klein and his magnificent blue version of the *Winged Victory* that's in the Louvre (see "The Top Museums," in chapter 19). Andy Warhol's acrylic *Dollar Sign* from 1981 is also on display. The collection is large and it might take you over 2 hours to look around; take a break at the ground-floor Café des Artistes, which is popular with local artists for lunch, dinner, and afternoon tea or coffee.

Promenade des Arts. ℂ **04/93-62-61-62.** www.mamac-nice.org. Admission 4€ ($4.60) adults, 2.50€ ($2.90) seniors and children. Tues–Sun 11am–6pm. Bus: 1, 2, 3, 5, 6, 16, or 25.

Musée des Beaux-Arts 🐾🐾   Nice's municipal fine arts museum is housed in a mansion built for Ukrainian Princess Kotschoubey in the 1870s. Here you can see paintings from the 17th and 18th centuries as well as works by Degas, Monet, Sisley, and Bonnard. There's a particularly good collection of works by Jules Chéret, who painted around the same time and in the same manner as Toulouse-Lautrec. Plan on spending at least an hour and a half here.

33 av. des Baumettes. ℂ **04/92-15-28-28.** www.musee-beaux-arts-nice.org. Admission 4€ ($4.60) adults, 2.50€ ($2.90) seniors and children. Tues–Sun 10am–6pm. Closed Jan 1, Easter Sun, May 1, and Dec 25. Bus: 3, 7, 12, 18, 22, or 38.

Musée Masséna 🐾🐾🐾   In a sumptuous villa, the Musée Masséna holds collections of paintings, artifacts, photographs, and other art and memorabilia pertaining to Nice and its region. Primitive paintings, ceramics, jewelry, armor, and memorabilia of Napoléon and Maréchal Masséna fill the grand halls. The front garden is now a little public park with palm trees, shrubs, and benches.

Note: The museum is closed for renovations until mid-2005. Contact the tourist office for the latest details.

When leaving the museum, wander next door to the **Hôtel Négresco,** 37 promenade des Anglais, one of the world's great hotels. Opened in 1913 by Henri Négresco, a native Romanian, the sumptuous guest rooms and grand

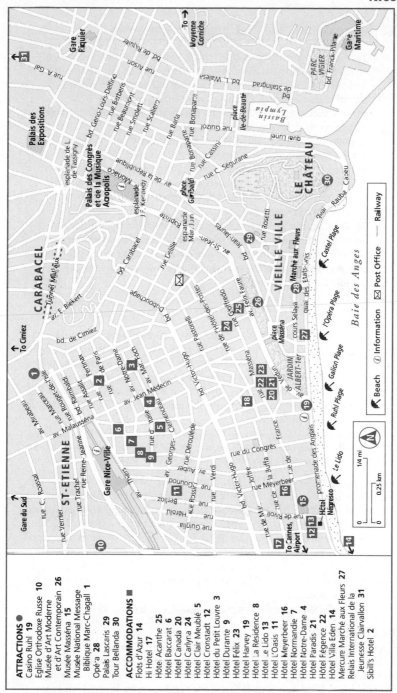

Nice

ATTRACTIONS ●
Casino Ruhl **19**
Eglise Orthodoxe Russe **10**
Musée d'Art Moderne
et d'Art Contemporain **26**
Musée Masséna **15**
Musée National Message
Biblique Marc-Chagall **1**
Opé'a **28**
Palais Lascaris **29**
Tour Bellanda **30**

ACCOMMODATIONS ■
Flots d'Azur **14**
Hi Hotel **17**
Hôte. Acanthe **25**
Hôtel Baccarat **6**
Hôtel Canada **20**
Hôtel Carlyna **24**
Hôtel Clair Meublé **5**
Hôtel Cronstadt **12**
Hôtel du Petit Louvre **3**
Hôtel Durante **9**
Hôtel Félix **23**
Hôtel Harvey **19**
Hôtel La Résidence **8**
Hôte. Le Lido **13**
Hôtel L'Oasis **11**
Hôtel Meyerbeer **16**
Hôtel Normandie **7**
Hôtel Notre-Dame **4**
Hôtel Paradis **21**
Hôtel Fégence **22**
Hôtel Villa Eden **14**
Mercure Marché aux Fleurs **27**
Relais International de la
Jeunesse Clairvallon **31**
Sibili's Hotel **2**

Baie des Anges

↙ Beach ⓘ Information ⊠ Post Office — Railway

(*Value* **Getting the Best Deal on Sightseeing**

- Take advantage of the half of the 3.5km (2-mile) pebbled beach that's free—sunbathe, swim, people-watch, flirt, or just daydream.
- Be aware of the free admission to all Nice museums on the first Sunday of each month—but also be aware of the crowds.
- Buy the special 6€ ($6.90) museum pass *(passe musées)* offering free admission to all Nice museums for a week. And if you'll be visiting a number of museums along the coast, buy the Carte Musées Côte d'Azur (see "Budget Bests," earlier in this chapter).
- Head to Le Château, the only hill facing the sea (at the eastern end of the waterfront), for the best panoramic view of Nice and the beach. You can either walk up 157 easy steps or take an elevator for only 1€ ($1.15) round-trip.
- Stroll along the lovely promenade des Anglais, a pedestrian zone that's as wide as a boulevard. Take a seat in one of the hundred blue wooden chairs (no charge) and just gaze out to sea when you feel like a break. However, beware of the in-line skaters who use the promenade as a racetrack.

---

public spaces of this Belle Epoque palace were converted into a hospital at the beginning of World War I, a year later. By 1918, Négresco was ruined and his hotel left in shambles. The hotel was reborn in 1957, when it was bought by a Belgian company and put in the charge of M. and Mme. Augier, who have worked to restore its former glories. In 1974, it was granted the status of Perpetual National Monument. The deluxe doubles are about $400 per night, so look elsewhere for accommodations.

35 promenade des Anglais, next to the Hôtel Négresco (entrance in the back at 65 rue de France). ℂ 04/93-88-11-34. Admission 4€ ($4.60) adults, 2.50€ ($2.90) seniors and students. Tues–Sun 10am–noon and 2–6pm. Closed for renovations. Bus: 3, 7, 8, 9, 10, 12, 14, or 22.

Palais Lascaris *(Moments*   The Palais Lascaris, deep within the maze of Vieux Nice's winding streets, was the grand home of a prominent Niçois family, the Lascaris-Ventimiglias. This sumptuous palace was built around 1648 and passed through a succession of owners until it was acquired by the city in 1922 and completely restored. The most stunning interior feature is the monumental staircase leading to the second floor. You'll also find Flemish tapestries, 18th-century *trompe l'oeil* ceilings, and a wealth of antique furniture. As you enter, pick up a free sheet (in English) describing the palace in detail; plan to spend at least 45 minutes here.

15 rue Droite, in Vieux Nice. ℂ 04/93-62-05-54. Free admission. Wed–Mon 10am–6pm.

IN CIMIEZ

Founded by the Romans, who called it Cemenelum, **Cimiez,** a hilltop suburb of Nice, was the capital of the Maritime Alps province. All around the **Villa des Arènes** (which contains the Matisse Museum) are the ruins of Cemenelum, including baths and a theater still used for performances. In the 19th century, Queen Victoria and her court made Cimiez their winter home. Even without the museums, Cimiez merits a visit.

Eglise et Monastère de Cimiez/Musée Franciscain (Cimiez Church and Monastery/Franciscan Museum) Not far from the Musée Matisse is this medieval monastery that now houses a museum dedicated to the art and history of the Franciscan order. The church contains a few very fine paintings by the Niçois primitives and a school that flourished here in the 15th and 16th centuries. Writer Roger Martin du Gard and artist Raoul Dufy are buried in the cemetery, and so is Matisse, near an olive grove. Set aside an hour to visit the museum and stroll in the gardens.

Place du Monastère. ℂ 04/93-81-00-04. Free admission. Mon–Sat 10am–noon and 3–6pm. Bus: 15, 17, 20, or 22.

Musée d'Archéologie (Archaeological Museum) Nice's archaeological museum was opened in 1989. Roman Cemenelum was the capital of the province of the Maritime Alps, an important passageway to Gallia and Hispania, and many artifacts found at local excavations are displayed here. There are also Greek and Etruscan pieces. Enter the museum through the archaeological site on avenue Montecroce and set aside an hour for your visit.

160 av. des Arènes de Cimiez. ℂ 04/93-81-59-57. Admission 4€ ($4.60), 2.50€ ($2.90) students. Apr–Sept Tues–Sun 10am–6pm; Oct–Mar Tues–Sun 10am–1pm and 2–5pm. Closed Nov 16–Dec 5. Bus: 15, 17, 20, or 22.

Musée Matisse ★★★ The works of Henri Matisse (1869–1954) are displayed in the 17th-century Villa des Arènes. It's fascinating to view the artist's works—paintings, drawings, sculptures, and studies for the chapel at Vence—in his actual studio. Here you'll find a unique Riviera atmosphere, filled with trees, vistas, and even furniture you might recognize in his paintings. Some fine pieces in the museum's permanent collection include *Nude in an Armchair with a Green Plant* (1937), *Nymph in the Forest* (1935–42), and a chronologically arranged series of paintings from 1890 to 1919. The most famous of these is *Portrait of Madame Matisse* (1905), usually displayed near another portrait of the artist's wife, by Marquet, painted in 1900. You can easily spend half a day taking in this museum's splendors, but plan on spending at least 2 hours. Note that this museum offers free admission the third Sunday of each month (in addition to the usual 1st Sun).

164 av. des Arènes de Cimiez. ℂ 04/93-81-08-08. www.musee-matisse-nice.org. Admission 4€ ($4.60) adults, 2.50€ ($2.90) students. Apr–Sept Wed–Mon 10am–6pm; Oct–Mar Wed–Mon 10am–5pm. Bus: 15, 17, 20, or 22.

Musée National Message Biblique Marc-Chagall (National Biblical Message Marc Chagall Museum) ★ The Chagall family donated 450 of the painter's finer works on biblical subjects to France, his adopted homeland, and they have been put on permanent exhibit in this squat modern building of white stone built at French government expense and set in its own park. It's pleasantly light and airy inside, which is just the right mood for Chagall's lyrical works: three large stained-glass windows in the concert hall, a room of stunning paintings illustrating the Song of Songs, and several rooms of grand-scale canvases portraying Moses and the burning bush, Isaac's sacrifice, and similar themes. This is a small collection and you can see all the paintings in under an hour.

Av. du Docteur-Ménard at bd. de Cimiez. ℂ 04/93-53-87-20. www.musee-chagall.fr. Admission 5.50€ ($6.30) adults, 4€ ($4.60) visitors 18–25 and over 60, free for children under 18; higher admission for special exhibits. July–Sept Wed–Mon 10am–6pm; Oct–June Wed–Mon 10am–5pm. Bus: 15.

Special & Free Events

Nice's big event is **Carnavale,** beginning 2 or 3 weeks before Mardi Gras (Fat Tuesday), just before Ash Wednesday, the beginning of Lent. Depending on the religious calendar, Nice's Carnavale can begin in January or February; most of the action takes place on weekends. Festive decorations fill the city: By day, parades—the *corsi* and *batailles de fleurs* (flower battles)—with marchers and floats pass by reviewing stands in place Masséna; by night, parties and masked balls continue until all hours. On Mardi Gras, the last day of Carnavale, the city puts on a grand fireworks show over the Mediterranean. Many of the events surrounding Carnavale are also free.

Other yearly celebrations are the **Festin des Cougourdons** in April, held at the Jardins des Arènes in Cimiez. This is a popular fête with songs and dances, and you can buy the *cougourdons* (carved and decorated dried gourds). And every Sunday in May at the Jardin des Arènes is the **Fête des Mais,** which celebrates the return of spring with folkloric shows and picnics. On **Bastille Day** (July 14) the city puts on a magnificent fireworks display over the bay; and on the **Fête de la Musique** (June 25), parks, squares, and street corners fill with musicians.

Other events along the Riviera include, of course, the **Festival International du Film** held every May in Cannes, and the International Jazz Festival in Antibes in July. In Nice itself, there's a **Festival de Musique Contemporaine** in January, a **Festival de Musique Sacrée** in June, and both a **Jazz Festival** and a **Festival du Folklore International** in July.

ORGANIZED TOURS

BUS TOURS   Even if you're allergic to bus tours, you might find an organized trip makes it easier to see the sights around Nice. **Santa Azur,** 11 av. Jean-Médecin (© **04/97-03-60-00**), offers a day trip to St-Tropez for 35€ ($40) and a half-day trip to St-Paul-de-Vence for 25€ ($29), among other excursions.

A good introduction to the city is aboard the **Trains Touristiques de Nice,** trolleys that depart from the Albert-1er esplanade across from the Hotel Méridien every 20 minutes, from 10am to 7pm in summer. The trains make a 45-minute tour of the city's high points, including Le Château. The purchase of one ticket at 6€ ($6.90) allows you to reboard anywhere along the route during the day. For information and reservations, call © **04/93-81-58-35.**

BOAT TOURS   The best way to appreciate the coastal scenery around Nice is by boat. May to September, **CIE Trans Côte d'Azur,** quai Lunel (© **04/92-00-42-30**), offers boat trips from Nice to Monaco (20€/$23), to the Iles de Lérins near Cannes (24€/$28), to San Remo, Italy (30€/$35), and to St-Tropez (35€/$40). There are reduced rates for children and students.

5 Shopping

Shopping in Nice runs the gamut from chic designer boutiques to bustling flea and flower markets. The most upscale shopping streets are **rue Paradis** and **avenue de Verdun.** Only a small notch down are the department stores on

avenue Jean-Médecin, which include **Galeries Lafayette** on place Masséna. Don't expect any bargains, however, unless you hit the sales in January and June.

Rue Masséna is lined with moderately priced shops, and the surrounding side streets are where to pick up the usual souvenirs. The best deals in Nice are in shops offering local products. Candied fruit is a specialty, and you'll find the best selection at **Auer** 🌟🌟, 7 rue St-François-de-Paule (© **04/93-85-77-98**), just outside the cours Saleya. The shop dates from 1802 and offers exotic jams and jellies as well. The secret to Provençal cooking is rich, fruity olive oil, and the place to buy it is **Moulin à Huile Alziari** 🌟🌟, 14 rue St-François-de-Paule (© **04/93-85-76-92**), a tiny shop cluttered with attractively labeled bottles and cans of fine olive oil pressed in its own mill *(moulin).* You might also opt for a bottle of flower water containing essence of rose, orange, or witch hazel; a lavender sachet; or a sack of local herbs specially packed for travelers. For more subtle odors, head to **Aux Parfums de Grasse,** 10 rue St-Gaétan (© **04/93-85-60-77**), selling 80 scents in flasks and bottles costing 3.50€ ($4) for a lipstick-size container to 15€ ($17) for 1 liter. The owner will help you combine various brands to create your personal fragrance.

Then there are the markets. The famous, memorable **Marché aux Fleurs (Flower Market)** is held Tuesday to Sunday from 6am to 5:30pm (except Sun afternoon) in Vieux Nice at the cours Saleya. The faded elegance of this 19th-century promenade provides a perfect setting for a market teeming with flowers, fruits, and vegetables. (The food portion closes at 1pm.) When the plant life disappears on Monday, some of the restaurants that cluster along the marketplace close, but a flea market moves in (8am–5pm). Tuesday to Saturday 10am to 6pm, there's another flea market on **place Robilante,** next to the Port.

In the general vicinity of Vieux Nice, on **rue Antoine-Gauthier, rue Catherine-Ségurane,** and **rue Emmanuel-Philibert,** behind Le Château, is the **Marché d'Art des Antiquaires,** featuring antiques Monday to Saturday 10am to noon and 3 to 6:30pm.

Forgot your beach novel? Need a *Newsweek?* Nice has several bookstores that carry books in English. Try **Cat's Whiskers (aka English Books),** 26 rue Lamartine (© **04/93-80-02-66**), a block east of Notre-Dame, just off avenue Jean-Médecin; it's owned and operated by an Englishwoman. And **Maison de la Presse,** 1 place Masséna (© **04/93-87-79-42**), has a variety of international newspapers and magazines and a section devoted to English-language books.

6 Nice After Dark

Nice has an active nightlife, from jazz to opera, from movies to cafe life. Cultural offerings are outlined in *L'Info,* a quarterly giveaway found at the tourist office and at hotels, and in *La Semaine des Spectacles,* which catalogs the week's entertainment for all the towns of the Côte d'Azur.

THE PERFORMING ARTS

OPERA, CONCERTS & BALLET   The **Opéra de Nice,** 4 rue St-François-de-Paule (© **04/93-53-01-14;** www.opera-de-nice.com), has an active winter season. Performances can include anything from the classics done by European masters to Duke Ellington's *Sophisticated Ladies* by New York's Opera Ensemble. The concerts and recitals performed at the Opéra are equally varied. Ballets are often new works or modern interpretations of classical pieces. The box office is open Tuesday to Saturday from 11am to 7pm. Tickets range from 8€ to 50€ ($9–$58).

Nice also sponsors a series of concerts in local churches (Sun at 3pm). For details, contact the **Orchestra d'Harmonie de la Ville de Nice,** 34 bd. Jean-Jaurés (© **04/93-80-08-50**).

THEATER One of the city's main theatrical venues is the **Théâtre de Nice,** promenade des Arts (© **04/93-80-52-60**), which presents a mix of classical and contemporary works and occasional dance and musical programs. Tickets run 8€ to 30€ ($9–$35) and are on sale Tuesday to Saturday 1 to 6pm. The **Théâtre de la Cité,** 3 rue Paganini (©/fax **04/93-16-82-69;** www.art-culture.com/pulsarts), is a cultural center presenting classical and contemporary works. Tickets are 2.50€ to 19€ ($2.90–$22), and the box office is open Tuesday to Saturday 1 to 6pm. All productions are in French, of course.

JAZZ & ROCK CLUBS

One of Nice's prime locations for officially sponsored jazz is **CEDAC de Cimiez,** 49 av. de la Marne (© **04/93-53-85-95**), a cultural center presenting jazz concerts October to June. Tickets run 13€ to 19€ ($14–$21). Contact them for current programs. During July, the Grande Parade de Jazz brings famous musicians to the **Parc et Arènes de Cimiez** (© **04/93-21-22-01**) for outdoor concerts that last long into the night.

BARS

The most active nightlife centers in **Vieux Nice.** As soon as darkness falls, swarms of young Niçois fill the narrow streets, piling into cramped bars and socializing on the cafe terraces. The colorful **cours Saleya** that sells flowers and food by day is transformed into a giant outdoor party at night when one bar after another opens its doors.

By far the most popular hangout in Vieux Nice is **Chez Wayne,** 15 rue de la Préfecture (© **04/93-13-46-99**), drawing a huge crowd of British and American visitors as well as locals. Although the amusingly decorated bar opens at 3pm, the action doesn't really start until 9 or 9:30pm when the band tunes up. You'll be lucky to squeeze in the door, much less elbow your way to the bar. Rock bands play nightly except Monday, when the bar is open but quieter. The cover charge ranges from 5€ to 9€ ($5.75–$10) and includes one drink.

Le Bar des Oiseaux, 5 rue St-Vincent (© **04/93-80-27-33**), is also in Vieux Nice but has a different idea. Open Monday to Saturday 7pm to 2am, it offers a changing program that might include a poetry reading, a philosophy night, or concerts presenting jazz, African music, or Italian songs. There's a 5€ ($5.75) charge for the concerts.

If you'd like to go where the hip and happening local professionals go, head to the new **Happy Bar,** inside the Hi Hotel, 3 av. des Fleurs (© **04/97-07-26-26**). Here, you'll find 30-something Niçois men and women hanging out in the

---

⟨*Tips* A Drink Before Dinner

Remember that in France, most people choose to have alcoholic drinks in a cafe, not a bar. If you're looking to have a pre-dinner drink, then hit one of the cafes lining **cours Saleya.** My favorite is **La Civette du Cours** 𝕽𝕽, 1 cours Saleya (© **04/93-80-80-59**), which is open daily 8am to 2am; drinks are 2.50€ to 6€ ($2.90–$6.90) and you get a little dish of olives with your order. It usually gets quite busy between 6:30 and 9pm. Nice bars below don't get going until after 9 or 9:30pm, even later on weekends.

ultra-fashionable Art Deco basement bar. Drinks are 5€ to 7€ ($5.75–$8) and come with little dishes of olives, radishes, and nuts. In summer, there's a lovely garden area where drinks are served.

GAY & LESBIAN BARS

To find out about happenings on the current gay scene, pick up a free copy of *Exes*, a small gay guide with a foldout map showing the bars and clubs. You can find it at any gay bar or store.

Near the Négresco and promenade des Anglais, **Le Blue Boy,** 9 rue Spinetta (© **04/93-44-68-24**), is the Riviera's oldest gay disco. With two bars and two floors, it's a vital nocturnal stop for passengers of the dozens of all-gay cruises that make regular stops at Nice and such nearby ports as Villefranche. The cover is 10€ ($12) Saturday and 7€ ($8) other days. The trendy hotspot for young gay locals is the new **Pub Six,** 6 rue de la Terrasse (© **04/93 62 66-64**), especially busy on Friday and Saturday after 10pm, when there's usually a live singer and a go-go boy at midnight. They're open daily 6:30pm to 3am, with no cover. Another good address is **Le Klub,** 6 rue Halevy (© **04/60-55-26-61**), where a young and good-looking gay crowd dances to techno Thursday through Sunday from midnight to 4am; the cover is 14€ ($16) and includes a drink.

DANCE CLUBS

Whether in jeans, spangles, or a suit, you'll feel comfortable at **Le Mississippi,** 5 promenade des Anglais (© **04/93-82-06-61**). There's a piano bar downstairs and dancing upstairs with a live band that plays a variety of danceable music. The disco attracts all ages and is open nightly 10pm to 4am. Men pay 14€ ($16) admission every night, but women pay only on weekends.

Two other popular clubs are **Ku de ta,** 29 rue Alphonse-Karr, off rue Masséna (© **04/93-82-37-66**), open Tuesday to Sunday 10pm to 4am, with an admission of 17€ ($20), including two drinks; and **Forum,** 45 promenade des Anglais (© **04/93-96-68-00**), open Thursday to Saturday 11pm to 5am, with an admission of 17€ ($20), including a drink. Nice's newest disco plays world music and attracts a smartly dressed crowd.

7 Side Trips: The Best of the Côte d'Azur

You'll soon find the sights in Nice are only half the story—many great attractions are within an hour's train or bus ride. Trains to points east and west of Nice are cheap and fast. Ask for a train schedule *(fiche horaire)* for St-Raphaël–Vintimille at the station; it lists the hours for trains along the coast from St-Raphaël to the Italian border, via Cannes, Antibes, Nice, and Monaco.

Buses are particularly useful for trips to Vence and St-Paul-de-Vence, sites of the splendid Matisse Chapel and the Fondation Maeght. Buses to both destinations depart from Nice's Gare Routière, the central bus station.

However, if you can afford it, the best way to see the sights of the Azure Coast is via a rental car. You can travel where you want and when you want and can even detour off the beaten path for a scenic drive or two. For details, see "Getting Around," earlier in this chapter.

If you want to explore even more of the towns and sites in this region, check out *Frommer's Provence & the Riviera*.

BEAULIEU-SUR-MER ⊕

The name **Beaulieu-sur-Mer** means "beautiful place by the sea," and it's fitting for the site of one of the most beautiful villas on the Riviera.

> *Tips* **Cheap Coastal Bus Fares**
>
> Several companies run buses along the coast from Nice's Gare Routière, but the cheapest—by about 50%—is **Autocars Broch** (© **04/93-31-10-52**). The fares quoted in this section are for this company, but the catch is that their departures are somewhat less frequent than those of other companies.

The masterpiece **Villa Kérylos** ✶✶✶, rue Gustave-Eiffel (© **04/93-01-01-44;** www.villa-kerylos.com), was created by archaeologist Théodore Reinach and designed by architect Emmanuel Pontremoli in the early 1900s. Fascinated with ancient Greece, Reinach had this amazing classical villa built on a rocky peninsula. His design is purely Hellenic down to its furniture and mosaics, with minimal concessions to the 20th century. But where does neoclassicism end and Art Deco begin? The courtyard, the library, the gardens, and even the baths—everything is lovingly created. Admission is 7€ ($8) adults and 4.30€ ($5) children. It's open daily 10:30am to 6pm.

Take the **train** to Beaulieu from Nice for 1.80€ ($2) one-way, second class, with 15 daily connections. You can also take a **bus** for 1.90€ ($2) round-trip. If you have a **car,** follow the signs for the Basse Corniche (N7) in the direction of Monaco.

ST-JEAN-CAP-FERRAT ✶✶✶

Facing Beaulieu-sur-Mer and the Villa Kérylos across the water is another idyllic spot. The tip of the 15km (9-mile) peninsula of **St-Jean-Cap-Ferrat,** crawling with pine trees, juts out to sea halfway between Nice and Monte Carlo. You could come here just to drive along the main road lined with villas. Behind walls and fences and security systems, these villas belong to the rich and famous from around the world and are empty most of the year. You probably won't be invited to check out any of them, but you can explore one exceptional villa.

The Mediterranean-style **Villa Ephrussi de Rothschild** ✶✶✶, av. Denis-Séméria (© **04/93-01-33-09;** www.villa-ephrussi.com), set in lovely gardens, was once the home of the baronne Ephrussi de Rothschild (sister of baron Edouard de Rothschild), who gave it to the Institut de France in the 1930s. The sumptuous house is filled with her collected treasures: Renaissance tapestries, furniture (including pieces that belonged to Marie Antoinette), porcelain and art objects from Asia, and masterpieces by European painters. Admission to the villa and garden is 8.50€ ($10) adults and 6.50€ ($7.50) for children. The museum is open daily from 10am to 6pm and the gardens Tuesday to Sunday, 9am to noon; both are closed in November.

Take the **train** to Beaulieu-sur-Mer and then the **bus** to St-Jean-Cap-Ferrat, or take the **bus** from Nice's Gare Routière to St-Jean-Cap-Ferrat. The round-trip bus fare is 4.50€ ($5). If you have a **car,** follow the signs for the Basse Corniche (N7) in the direction of Monaco, then turn right at the first intersection, marked ST-JEAN-CAP-FERRAT.

EZE ✶✶✶ & LA TURBIE

The Côte d'Azur is sprinkled with picturesque Mediterranean mountain villages built high on the craggy rocks, well defended by battlements and the occasional tumbledown fort. Pirate raids made these inaccessible spots popular places to live in the Middle Ages. Today they're popular again because of their antique

The Côte d'Azur

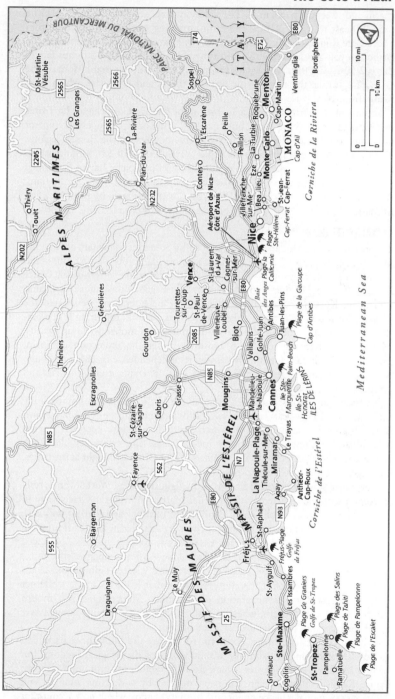

charm and sweeping panoramas. The village of **Eze,** on the Moyenne Corniche (middle coast road), is perhaps the most charming of these. Hop a **bus** from Nice's Gare Routière and get off at Eze to climb its narrow mazelike streets. The farther up you go, the farther back in time you'll travel. Round-trip bus fare to Eze is 2.50€ ($2.90). If you have a **car,** get on E8 heading toward Monaco and exit at La Turbie; the more scenic route is the Grand Corniche, which veers inland from Nice Port.

You might also want to visit **La Turbie** on the Grande Corniche for **La Trofée des Alpes (Trophy of the Alps),** built in 6 B.C. at the order of Augustus, emperor of Rome, to celebrate the defeat of the Alpine peoples by the Roman legions. Nearby is the **Musée de la Trofée des Alpes** (© **04/93-41-10-11**), a minimuseum containing finds from area archaeological digs. It's open daily: July to September 9am to 7pm, October to March 9:30am to 5pm, and April to June 9am to 6pm. Admission is 4€ ($4.60). On weekdays, there are four **buses** a day from Nice and five **buses** a day from Monaco. The one-way fare from Nice is 3.80€ ($4.40).

MONACO ✶✶✶

The principality of **Monaco,** once described by Somerset Maugham as "a sunny place for shady people," is one of Europe's most glamorous destinations—and one of the smallest, at only 148 hectares (370 acres). The current ruler, Prince Rainier III, is part of the Grimaldi dynasty that began with François Grimaldi, a Genoan. Known as La Malizia ("Cunning One"), François penetrated the Monaco fortress in 1297 by disguising himself as a monk, capturing it in a battle memorialized in the Grimaldi coat-of-arms—two monks wielding swords. Monaco passed the succeeding 5 centuries under the protection of Spain, France, and Sardinia before finally gaining its independence in 1861. Although Monaco has its own seat at the United Nations, it retains strong financial and political links to France.

The first casino was set up in 1856 in Monte Carlo, but it only limped along until the arrival a few years later of François Blanc, the director of the Bad Homburg casino. He made sure newspapers around the globe reported on the escapades of dissolute dukes, showy industrialists, and celebrities like Sarah Bernhardt, who reportedly made a suicide attempt after a bad night at the tables. The legend of Monte Carlo was then born.

Nevertheless, Monaco faded from the limelight following World War II, only to come roaring back when Prince Rainier married movie star Grace Kelly in 1956. The princess's Hollywood connection initially appalled conservative Monégasques, but they were soon won over by her charm and dedication to public service. Although the marriage was unhappy, Rainier and Grace produced three children—Caroline, Albert, and Stephanie—whose romantic adventures have been tabloid fodder for decades. Nevertheless, Grace's cultural and charitable projects helped polish the country's somewhat frivolous image while her glamour attracted a new generation of jet-setters. Monégasques still mourn Princess Grace's 1982 death, when an automobile she was driving plunged over a cliff (be careful of the Grand Corniche's hairpin turns!).

With its cobblestone streets, softly tinted houses, and immaculate parks and gardens, Monaco might seem like a subdivision of the Magic Kingdom, but behind its fairy-tale facade lies a hard-nosed scramble for economic viability. Prince Rainier's 50-year reign has been marked by a determination to end Monaco's traditional reliance on income from its casinos, which now account for only 4% of the principality's receipts. Banking, commerce, and tourism provide the bulk of Monaco's revenue, and the prince has encouraged the development of light industry. Real estate is another big money-earner, especially because anyone who can establish a residence in the country is exempt from income taxes. The exemption doesn't apply to French citizens, but Europeans, including Ringo Starr, Claudia Schiffer, Boris Becker, and Plácido Domingo, have found it advantageous to become Monaco residents.

You can reach Monaco by **train** or **bus** from Nice in less than 30 minutes. Round-trip fare for the train is 6.50€ ($7.50) and for the bus 3.50€ ($4). If you have a **car,** get on E8 heading toward Monaco, but the more scenic (although slower) route is taking the Basse Corrniche (N7) along the shore from Nice Port to Monaco. The euro is accepted in Monaco, and you don't need a passport to enter (unless you plan to visit the Casino de Monte Carlo).

Note: Monaco is no longer part of France's telephone system. The new **country code** for Monaco is **377.** The **city code** for all points in Monaco is built into every phone number in the principality. If you're within Monaco, use the complete eight-digit number. If you're calling Monaco from France, dial 00 first, then 377.

THE PRINCIPALITY'S DISTRICTS   Monaco squeezes several districts into its territory. The train station is near **Moneghetti,** site of the Jardin Exotique, prehistoric caves, and an anthropological museum. **Monaco-Ville (The Rock)** is the oldest part of Monaco on a rocky hillside graced by the Palais du Prince, the Oceanographic Museum, lush gardens, narrow streets, and the cathedral where Princess Grace is entombed under a marble slab reading GRATIA. **La Condamine,** the harbor district at the foot of the Rocher, is where most of the Monégasques live, and **Monte Carlo,** famous and infamous, is just uphill from La Condamine. You can walk around virtually all of Monaco in a few hours. Avoid visiting the principality during the **Grand-Prix** (May 19–22, 2005) because many streets are closed to everything but whizzing race cars.

SEEING THE SIGHTS   The **Jardin Exotique** ✿ (© **93/15-29-80**) encloses the world's largest open-air cacti and succulents plantation, over 6,000 species, most of Mexican and African origin, and affords spectacular views over the principality. It's open daily 9am to 6:30pm, with an admission of 7€ ($8) adults and 3.50€ ($4) children/students/seniors. This includes admission to the **Grotte de l'Observatoire,** prehistoric caves of stalactites and stalagmites, and the **Musée d'Anthropologie Préhistorique,** tracing Paleolithic, Neolithic, and Bronze Age societies. You'll be surprised to find that elephants once roamed the Riviera.

From the Jardin Exotique, you can walk or take bus no. 2 to **Monaco-Ville.** The bus deposits you at place de la Visitation, and you can continue straight ahead through the old streets to place du Palais, dominated by the stately **Palais du Prince** ✿✿ (© **93/25-18-31**). The oldest part of the palace, from the 13th century, is the north side. If you get to the old city of Monaco in the morning and if the royal family isn't in residence, you can tour some of the Italianate apartments with their paintings and tapestries, then witness the changing of the guard just before noon. A palace wing is occupied by the **Musée Napoléonien et des Archives du Palais,** an outstanding collection of objects linked to Bonaparte, whose family was related to the princely Grimaldis. The second floor is devoted to exhibits on the history of Monaco. Admission to the palace is 5€ ($5.75), to the museum 3.50€ ($4), and to both 6.50€ ($7.50). From June to September, the palace is open daily 9:30am to 6:30pm. In October, it's open daily 10am to 5pm. December to May, the museum is open Tuesday to Sunday 10:30am to 12:30pm and 2 to 5pm.

When you leave place du Palais, take the road on the right, Col. Bellando de Castro, which leads down to the **Cathédrale de Monaco,** where Princess Grace and other members of the royal family are buried. Built in 1875 from white stone mined in La Turbie, the cathedral is notable for an elaborate altarpiece dedicated to St. Nicolas. It's open daily 9:30am to 7pm. Across the street is an entrance to the **Jardins St-Martin,** a lush collection of exotic tropical plants with splendid views over the Mediterranean. The gardens were created by Prince Albert I, whose statue you can see here gazing at the sea, and they're always open.

The gardens end at the **Musée de l'Océanographie** ✹✹, avenue St-Martin (✆ 93/15-36-00), a fine aquarium founded by naturalist/scientist Prince Albert I. The museum contains his collection of specimens, acquired during 30 years of expeditions aboard his oceanographic boats. For many years, the late explorer Jacques Cousteau directed the museum; the yellow contraption outside is one of Commandant Cousteau's early submersible vessels. Don't miss the magnificent view from the second-floor terrace. Admission is 10€ ($12) adults and 5.50€ ($6.30) children. It's open daily: October and March 9:30am to 7pm; November to February 10am to 6pm; April, May, June, and September 9am to 7pm; and July and August 9am to 8pm.

From Monaco-Ville, you can walk through **La Condamine** to **Monte Carlo** or take bus no. 1 and follow the signs to place du Casino.

The oldest part of the famous **Casino de Monte Carlo** ✹✹✹ was built in 1878 by Charles Garnier, architect of the Paris Opéra. Wander into its posh early-1900s gaming rooms, but don't expect anything as exciting as Mata Hari shooting a Russian spy, which happened here once upon a time. The casino opens at noon and remains receptive, as it were, late into the night (you'll need your passport for entrance). Games played are roulette and blackjack; admission is 8€ ($9), and a minimum token is 3.50€ ($4). Also on place du Casino is the opulent **Hôtel de Paris** ✹✹✹, built in 1864. The doormen can be snooty, but try to take a peek at the lobby that has often served as a movie set. It helps to say that you want to pick up a brochure from reception.

Back down at sea level, follow avenue de Princesse-Grace to the **Musée National** (✆ 93/30-91-26), housed in a villa designed by Charles Garnier. This is a great place to bring the kids because the museum contains one of the world's greatest collections of dolls and mechanical toys. It's open daily: October to Easter 10am to 12:15pm and 2:30 to 6:30pm; and the day after Easter to September 10am to 6pm. Admission is 5€ ($5.75) adults and 3.50€ ($4) children.

Near the museum is Monaco's most popular beach, **Plage de Larvotto** (✆ 93/15-28-76). There's no charge for bathing on this strip of beach, whose sands are frequently replenished with sand hauled in by barge. The beach is open to the public 24 hours a day. If you're looking for a pool, try the stupendous **Stade Nautique Rainier-III** (✆ 93/15-28-75), overlooking the yacht-clogged harbor on quai Albert-1er at La Condamine. This gift from Prince Rainier to his subjects is open daily: July and August 9am to midnight; and March to June and September to November 9am to 6pm. Admission is 3.50€ ($4).

WHERE TO STAY   The best bargain in Monaco (literally 1m/3 ft. from the invisible border—one side of the street is Monaco, the other France), is the **Hôtel Villa Boeri** ✹, 29 bd. Général-Leclerc, 06240 Beausoleil (✆ 04/93-78-38-10; fax 04/93-41-90-95), on a quiet street in a nice residential area and a 5-minute walk from the casino. The 30 bright rooms have been recently renovated, and come with air-conditioning, TVs, and phones; some are tiny but have good-size windows, others are spacious with balconies. Singles are 55€ to 62€ ($63–$71), and doubles 63€ to 95€ ($72–$109); continental breakfast is 5€ ($5.75). MasterCard and Visa are accepted. Nearby is the **Hôtel de France,** 6 rue de la Turbie, MC 98000 Monaco (© **93/30-24-64;** fax 92/16-13-34; hotel.france@ montecarlo.mc), managed by the friendly M. Louis Pauleau. The units are small but neat, with tiny bathrooms like you'd find on a ship, TVs, and phones. Singles are 67€ ($77), doubles are 90€ ($104), and triples are 103€ ($118); continental breakfast is included. MasterCard and Visa are accepted.

WHERE TO DINE   At the **Restaurant and Café de Paris** 🌟🌟, place du Casino (© **92/16-20-20**), you pay for the unique location, in front of the Hôtel de Paris and the casino, but you don't have to eat; sipping coffee or a soda and watching the world pass by is an affordable experience. It's open daily from 9am to 3am; American Express, Diners Club, MasterCard, and Visa are accepted. The **Restaurant le Bistroquet,** Galérie Charles-III (© **93/50-65-03**), is around the downhill corner from the Café de Paris. It doesn't have the same view (from the terrace you get a glimpse of the casino's roof), but the prices are lower. You can get the *plat du jour* or pasta for 10€ ($12). It's open daily noon to 2am (or later). American Express, Diners Club, MasterCard, and Visa are accepted.

Near the Rock in the old part of town, the **Restaurant Le Pinocchio,** 30 rue Comte Félix-Gastaldi (© **93/30-96-20**), is a popular Italian place known for its delicious antipasti, homemade pasta, and veal dishes. The lovely summer terrace makes for excellent people-watching. Main courses are 12€ ($14) for pastas to 17€ ($20) for veal. There's also a prix fixe menu at 24€ ($28). It's open daily 7:30 to 11pm (to midnight June–Sept), and American Express, MasterCard, and Visa are accepted.

On a romantic square just steps from the Rock, **Restaurant Saint-Nicolas** 🌟🌟, 1 place Saint-Nicolas (© **93/30-30-41**), overlooks a fountain and offers excellent prix-fixe menus at 14€ ($16) and 17€ ($20). Feast on endive salad, tender sautéed calamari, pepper-crusted salmon, and excellent homemade desserts. Call ahead for reservations in summer if you want to be seated on the lovely terrace.

MONACO AFTER DARK   Adjoining the lobby in the Loews Monte-Carlo, the **Sun Casino,** 12 av. des Spélugues (© **93/50-65-00**), is a huge room filled with one-armed bandits, blackjack, craps, and American roulette. Additional slot machines are available on the roof starting at 11am—for those who want to gamble with a wider view of the sea. It's open daily 4pm to 4am (to 5am for slot machines). Admission is free. The **Café de Paris,** place du Casino, has a casino (© **92/16-24-29**) offering slot machines from 10am and American roulette, craps, and blackjack from 5pm. It's open late and admission is free.

The **Casino de Monte Carlo** 🌟🌟, place du Casino (© **92/16-20-00**), is the most famous and glamorous in the world. The architect of Paris's Opéra, Charles Garnier, built the oldest part, and it remains an extravagant example of period

---

Monte Carlo Style

If you want to experience how the other half lives, dress up and head to the **Bar Americain (American Bar)** at the swankiest place in town: the Hôtel de Paris, next to the Casino. Order a 7€ ($8) cappuccino or a 6€ ($7) espresso and get a terrific view of the place du Casino for free. For a real taste of the rich-and-famous lifestyle, order a 20€ ($23) Kir Royal (champagne with cassis).

architecture. The Salle des Amériques contains only Las Vegas–style slot machines and opens at 2pm; doors for roulette and *trente-quarante* open at noon. A section for roulette and *chemin-de-fer* (like baccarat) opens at 3pm, and blackjack begins at 9pm (5pm weekends). The gambling continues until very late, with the closing depending on the crowd. To enter the casino, you must carry a passport, be at least 21, and pay an admission fee of 8€ to 16€ ($9–$18) if you want to enter the private rooms. In lieu of a passport, an identity card or driver's license will suffice.

In the **Salle Garnier** of the casino, concerts and operas featuring the Orchestre Philharmonique de Monte Carlo are held regularly. Prices run 16€ to 40€ ($18–$46) for a concert and 28€ to 110€ ($32–$126) for an opera. For information, contact the **Direction du Tourisme et des Congrès,** 2a bd. des Moulin (© 92/16-61-66), open Monday to Saturday 9am to 7pm and Sunday 10am to noon. The casino also contains the **Opéra de Monte-Carlo.** This world-famous house, opened in 1879 by Sarah Bernhardt, presents a winter/spring season that traditionally includes Puccini, Mozart, and Verdi. The famed Ballets Russes de Monte-Carlo, starring Nijinsky and Karsavina, was created here in 1918 by Sergei Diaghilev. The national orchestra and the ballet company of Monaco appear here. Tickets might be hard to come by, but you can make inquiries at the **Atrium du Casino** (© 92/16-22-99), open Tuesday to Sunday 10am to 12:30pm and 2 to 5pm. Standard tickets are 16€ to 90€ ($18–$103).

ST-PAUL-DE-VENCE 🏵🏵 & VENCE

St-Paul-de-Vence is a picture-perfect medieval village perched on a hill with one of the Riviera's finest art collections, the Fondation Maeght, nearby. Vence, a few miles farther, is the site of Henri Matisse's masterful chapel. You can visit the Fondation Maeght and Matisse's chapel with time left over to explore the narrow streets of these towns, but you need to plan carefully because the chapel has limited hours and the Fondation Maeght closes for lunch most of the year.

The town of **St-Paul-de-Vence** is a beautifully preserved example of a fortified hilltop village. In the 1920s, artists Paul Signac, Modigliani, Pierre Bonnard, and Chaim Soutine discovered it, gathering at the restaurant Colombe d'Or, which now contains an impressive art collection. Other artists, writers, and personalities followed, including actor Yves Montand, who made St-Paul his home in later life. At the farthest tip of the village is a cemetery with the tomb of Marc Chagall, another regular visitor. The village contains a number of art galleries (usually closed noon–3pm) and many souvenir shops. The best time to visit is in the late afternoon, when the tour buses leave.

Outside the walled village is the **Fondation Maeght** 🏵🏵🏵, St-Paul-de-Vence (© 04/93-32-81-63; www.fondation-maeght.com), the south of France's best museum. Designed by Spanish architect José Luís Sert, the museum and its park are an organic whole, itself a work of art. Sculpture graces the lawns, placed expertly among the fountains, pools, trees, and shrubs. In the collection is a large number of works by Giacometti, Arp, Braque, Chagall, Bonnard, Kandinsky, Hepworth, Léger, Miró, Calder, Tàpies, and others. Changing exhibits are mounted frequently. There's a library, a bookshop, and a cafeteria. Admission is 7€ ($8) adults and 6€ ($7) children. The museum is open daily: July to September 10am to 7pm, and October to June 10am to 12:30pm and 2:30 to 6pm.

The easiest way to reach St-Paul is by **bus** from Nice's Gare Routière. The trip takes about 40 minutes, and the bus leaves you in front of the entrance to the village before continuing on to Vence. To find the Fondation Maeght, go down the hill in the direction of the bus and turn right at the parking lot to follow the road leading up another hill. One-way bus fare from Nice is 3.50€ ($4). If you have a **car,** take A8 toward Cannes, exit at Cagnes-sur-Mer, and follow the signs to St-Paul and Vence on Route 36.

North of St-Paul, you can visit the sleepy old town of **Vence,** with its Vieille Ville (Old Town). If you're wearing the right kind of shoes, the narrow, steep streets are worth exploring. The cathedral on place Godeau is unremarkable except for some 15th-century choir stalls. But if it's a Tuesday or Thursday (when the chapel is open), most visitors quickly pass through the narrow gates of this once-fortified walled town to where the sun shines more brightly.

It was a golden autumn along the Côte d'Azur in 1946. The great Henri Matisse was 77, and after a turbulent time of introspection he set out to create his masterpiece, the **Chapelle du Rosaire** —in his own words, "the culmination of a whole life dedicated to the search for truth." You might pass right by the chapel of the Dominican nuns of Monteils, on avenue Henri-Matisse just outside Vence (© 04/93-58-03-26), finding it unremarkable—until you spot a 12m (40-ft.) crescent-adorned cross rising from a blue-tile roof.

The light inside picks up the subtle coloring in the simply rendered leaf forms and abstract patterns—sapphire blue, aquamarine, and lemon yellow. In black-and-white ceramics, St. Dominic is depicted in a few lines. The Stations of the Cross are also black-and-white tile, with Matisse's self-styled tormented and passionate figures. The bishop of Nice himself came to bless the chapel in late spring 1951 when the artist's work was completed. Matisse died 3 years later. December 13 to October, the chapel is open Tuesday and Thursday 10 to 11:30am and 2 to 5:30pm; Monday, Wednesday, and Saturday it's open 2 to 5:30pm. Admission is 2.50€ ($2.90); donations are welcome.

ANTIBES & JUAN-LES-PINS

Antibes and Juan-les-Pins compose one municipality at the base of a peninsula, with the exclusive Cap d'Antibes at its tip. Each resort has a different flavor. **Antibes** is a typical Mediterranean town where vines and flowering plants adorn narrow stone streets and the air is redolent with sea and flowers. Founded by Greek settlers in the 4th century B.C., it became a fortified military outpost in the 17th century and a favorite of artists in the 20th. Picasso lived here in 1946 with his wife, Françoise Gilot. **Juan-les-Pins** emerged in the early 20th century as a beach resort of sun, fun, and jazz. Writers like Ernest Hemingway and the fun-loving F. Scott and Zelda Fitzgerald cavorted on the sandy beaches, while jazz musicians Sidney Bechet and Louis Armstrong played. Still renowned for its beaches and the prestigious July jazz festival, Juan-les-Pins is also the center of nightlife along the coast. **Cap d'Antibes** is a highly expensive luxury resort most famous for the Hôtel du Cap, where movie stars reside during the Cannes Film Festival. Nice has its Baie des Anges (Bay of Angels), but Cap d'Antibes has its Baie des Milliardaires (Bay of Multimillionaires), which about sums up its ambience.

Walking the streets of the **old town** is one of the great pleasures of exploring Antibes. Rues de l'Horloge, du Révely, and des Arceaux recall the city's medieval heritage, and the village-within-a-village of **Safronier,** centered on the place of the same name, is replete with intimate squares and tiny cottages half-buried under foliage. A stroll on the **promenade Amiral-de-Grasse** takes you along the city walls and affords magnificent views of the mountainous coast from Cap d'Antibes to Nice.

The 14th-century granite **Château Grimaldi** was built on the ruins of a Roman camp and now houses the **Musée Picasso** (© 04/92-90-54-20).

Picasso came here in 1946 and spent the fall painting and potting. Many of the works you'll see were created in that one season. Inspired by Mediterranean mythology and marine life, Picasso's works from this period include *Ulysses and the Sirens, Fish, Watermelon,* and *Joie de Vivre,* as well as tapestries and 200 ceramics made during his years in nearby Vallauris. The museum also contains works by 20th-century artists Léger, Miró, Ernst, and Calder. Admission is 4.60€ ($5.30) adults, and 2.30€ ($2.60) those 17 to 24 and over 60. It's open Tuesday to Sunday 10am to noon and 2 to 6pm.

The **Musée Archéologique,** on the bastion St-André (© **04/92-90-54-35**), depicts the town's Greek and Roman history through artifacts—there are some very beautiful amphorae—found in the excavations and coastal waters. Admission is 3€ ($3.50) adults and 2€ ($2.30) children/students/under 26; it's open Tuesday to Sunday 10am to noon and 2 to 6pm (closed Nov).

The best **beaches** are in Juan-les-Pins. You can find some free public beaches on boulevard Littoral and boulevard Guillaumont. Otherwise, you'll have to pay 11€ to 14€ ($13–$16) to rent a mattress and a parasol.

Both Antibes and Juan-les-Pins are easy day trips from Nice, accessible by train or bus. There are at least 12 daily **train** connections to Antibes (more in July–Aug). The train station is at the northern end of the old town, and the 24-minute trip costs 3.50€ ($4). There are also **buses** from Nice that leave you at the **Gare Routière** (© **04/93-34-37-60**), near place Général-de-Gaulle in the old town. The train station in Juan-les-Pins is in the center of town. If you have a **car,** take the Basse Corniche (A7) and follow the signs for Antibes and Juan-les-Pins.

WHERE TO STAY   In the center of town, the **Hôtel de l'Etoile,** 2 av. Gambetta, 06600 Antibes (© **04/93-34-26-30;** fax 04/93-34-41-48), offers 30 units with air-conditioning, cable TVs, minibars, double-glazed windows, and phones. The functional good-size doubles are 55€ to 60€ ($63–$69), and the singles are 48€ ($55). Continental breakfast is 5.50€ ($6.30). American Express, Diners Club, MasterCard, and Visa are accepted. This hotel requires payment up front for a 1-night stay. In a former 17th-century coach house with beamed ceilings, **Le Relais du Postillon** ✿✿, 8 rue Championnet, 06600 Antibes (© **04/93-34-20-77;** fax 04/93-34-61-24; www.relaisdupostillon.com), has 15 units with TVs and phones; they're of different sizes and prices, but all have quilted bedspreads, cane chairs, antiques, and hand-stenciled walls. The bathrooms are tiny but adequate. The hotel boasts an excellent restaurant. Singles or doubles are 44€ to 79€ ($51–$91), with a 7€ ($8) buffet breakfast. MasterCard and Visa are accepted.

WHERE TO DINE   There are reasonably priced restaurants in Antibes and Juan-les-Pins, but you might want to make a stop at the **Marché Provençal** ✿✿ on the cours Masséna in Antibes and assemble picnic ingredients. Open daily (except Mon in winter) 6am to 1pm, this canopied market is the best on the coast, presenting a tempting array of Provençal flowers, fruits, vegetables, and fish.

For a taste of the Cote d'Azur's most authentic crepes, **La Crêperie,** 17 rue Dautheville (© **04/93-61-46-15**), in the heart of Juan-les-Pins, offers amazing reasonably priced meals. Try the Popeye crepe (with eggs, spinach, ham, and cheese) or the sweet dessert crepe with crème de marrons (luscious chestnut puree). Crepes run 6.50€ to 10€ ($7.50–$12). It's open daily noon to 11pm; cash only.

For more substantial fare, follow the locals, in Antibes, to the **Taverne du Safranier** ✿✿, 1 place du Safranier (© **04/93-34-80-50**). Nestled in a serene square behind the ramparts, this rustic tavern offers an assortment of delicious Provençal dishes such as mussels *au pistou,* fish soup, grilled fish, pasta, and mesclun salad. You can eat on the terrace under grapevines or in the marine-themed interior. Main courses are 12€ to 16€ ($14–$18). The restaurant is open Tuesday to Sunday noon to 2:30pm and 7 to 10:30pm, and no credit cards are accepted.

Facing the beach in Antibes, the **Restaurant Chez Olive,** 2 bd. du Maréchal-Leclerc (© **04/93-34-42-32**), serves more elaborate Provençal fare at slightly higher prices. On the *menus du jour* for 14€ ($16; lunch only) or 22€ ($25), you might find basil-stuffed mussels, stewed rabbit, or octopus salad. The wine list is good and reasonably priced. The restaurant is open Tuesday to Saturday 11am to midnight and Sunday noon to 2:30pm; American Express, Diners Club, MasterCard, and Visa are accepted.

ANTIBES & JUAN-LES-PINS AFTER DARK   In Antibes, the pedestrian **boulevard d'Aguillon** is lined with bars and cafes that come alive at night. **The Hop Store,** 38 bd. d'Aguillon (© **04/93-34-15-33**), is a friendly Irish-style pub decorated with saddles, scarecrows, and photos of inebriated young Brits. It's open daily 5pm to dawn and often presents live music on weekends. In Juan-les-Pins, **Pam Pam** ☆☆, 137 bd. Wilson (© **04/93-61-11-05**), is a slice of Brazil on the Riviera. During summer, there are Brazilian bands every night, with crowds spilling onto the terrace. The Pam Pam boasts a prime people-watching spot and it's worth paying the steep price for a cocktail on a sidewalk table to watch the endless parade go by. April to October, it's open daily 7pm to dawn. There's no cover, but expect to pay about 12€ to 15€ ($14–$17) for a drink.

Juan-les-Pins has a number of discos. The current favorites are **Voom-Voom,** 1 bd. de la Pinéde (© **04/93-61-18-71**), which attracts a very young crowd, and **Le Bureau,** avenue Georges-Gallice (© **04/93-67-22-74**), which plays techno for 20-somethings. Both places are open nightly in summer and charge a cover of 13€ to 17€ ($15–$20), which includes a drink.

CANNES ☆☆☆

Cannes is a much more glamorous resort than Nice, and the prices reflect that difference, especially during the famous **International Film Festival.** When the festival is on, the town is at its most frenzied, with mobs of paparazzi on the seafront boulevards and mobs of stars and wannabes posing everywhere. It was on the sandy beaches of this chic resort in the 1920s that Coco Chanel soaked up some sun and startled Paris by returning with a tan, a fashion that quickly caught on and became popular worldwide. There are **train** connections about every half-hour from Nice; the 40-minute trip costs 5€ ($5.75). You can also take a bus for about the same price. If you have a car, take A8 toward Cannes, but the more scenic (and slower) route is the Basse Corniche (A7) running along the coast to Cannes.

SEEING THE SIGHTS   Wander down the elegant waterfront **promenade de la Croisette** (aka **La Croisette**) ☆☆, lined with designer boutiques, and have a look at the home of the film festival, the **Palais des Festivals.** The esplanade running along La Croisette is a peaceful oasis of flowers and trees and a great place for a picnic. Above the harbor, the old town of Cannes sits on **Suquet Hill** ☆, where you'll see a 14th-century tower the English dubbed the Lord's Tower.

Nearby is the **Musée de la Castre,** in the Château de la Castre, Le Suquet (© **04/93-38-55-26**), containing fine arts, with a section on ethnography. The latter includes relics and objects from everywhere from the Pacific islands to Southeast Asia, including Peruvian and Mayan pottery. There's also a gallery devoted to relics of ancient Mediterranean civilizations. Five rooms are devoted to 19th-century paintings. The museum is open Wednesday to Monday: April to June 10am to noon and 2 to 6pm, July to September 10am to noon and 3 to 7pm, and October to March 10am to noon and 2 to 5pm. Admission is 3€ ($3.50) adults; children are free.

Another museum of note, the **Musée de la Mer,** Fort Royal (© **04/93-38-55-26**), displays artifacts from Ligurian, Roman, and Arab civilizations, including paintings, mosaics, and ceramics. You can also see the jail where the "Man in the Iron Mask" was incarcerated. Temporary exhibits of photography are also shown. June to September, it's open Wednesday to Monday 10am to noon and 2 to 5pm. Admission is 2€ ($2.30).

Cannes's sandy **beaches** ⋆⋆ extend over 5km (3 miles)—half free (or public) and half owned by hotels charging 14€ to 25€ ($16–$29) for a mattress, towel, and cabin. The choice public beach is **Plage du Midi,** west of the old harborfront, with the best sun in the afternoon. **Plage Gazagnaire,** another good beach, is east of the new port, ideal in the morning.

WHERE TO STAY Cannes has moderately priced hotels, but if you're thinking of coming during the Film Festival (May 11–22, 2005), be aware that prices skyrocket and most hotels are booked a year in advance.

Between the train station and La Croisette, the **Hôtel Splendid** ⋆, 4–6 rue Félix-Faure, 06400 Cannes (© **04/97-06-22-22;** fax 04/93-99-55-02; www.splendid-hotel-cannes.fr), whose facade looks from the waterfront like a sugar wedding cake topped with flags, is the best deal in the splurge category. It offers 62 units, all with air-conditioning, TVs, and phones; 42 have fully equipped kitchenettes. Including continental breakfast, singles start at 119€ ($137) and doubles at 140€ ($161) June to September, but rooms with a view are substantially more expensive. Outside peak season, prices are reduced 20% to 30% (except during the film festival). American Express, Diners Club, MasterCard, and Visa are accepted.

When leaving the Cannes train station, you'll directly face the **Hôtel Atlas,** 5 place de la Gare, 06400 Cannes (© **04/93-39-01-17;** fax 04/93-39-29-57; www.hotel-atlas-cannes.com). The 52 air-conditioned units have TVs, phones, and double-glazed windows—all are modern and attractive. Singles cost 75€ ($86) and doubles begin at 91€ ($105); lower season rates are available October to May, so be sure to ask. The continental breakfast is 10€ ($12). American Express, Diners Club, MasterCard, and Visa are accepted.

The boutique-style **Hôtel America** ⋆⋆, 13 rue St-Honore, 06400 Cannes (© **04/93-06-75-75;** fax 04/93-68-04-58; www.hotel-america.com), is a real find, with a perfect location just a block off the Promenade and close to the main film festival building. Rooms are very modern and attractive and come with spacious marble bathrooms. Singles, in high season, go for 120€ ($138), and doubles are 145€ ($167); be sure to inquire about off-season rates. Continental breakfast is included with all rates.

The best budget find, the **Hôtel National** ⋆, 8 rue du Maréchal-Joffre, 06400 Cannes (© **04/93-39-91-92;** fax 04/92-98-44-06), is halfway between the train station and the beach and owned by an English-French couple, the Potters. There are 17 units on three floors (no elevator), 12 with bathroom. All have phones and TVs; a few have air-conditioning. Singles are 42€ ($48), and doubles run 52€ to 68€ ($60–$78), with continental breakfast at 6€ ($7). The rates are slightly higher in July and August and during the festival. American Express, Diners Club, and MasterCard are accepted.

WHERE TO DINE   Restaurants are expensive in Cannes, but it's easy to supplement restaurant meals with picnics. **Rue Meynadier,** parallel to rue Félix-Faure, has stores selling regional products, and there's a morning food market at **Marché Forville** (Tues–Sun 7am–1pm), where you can pick up fruits, vegetables, and cheese. The **Esplanade G.-Pompidou,** next to the Palais des Festivals, is a tranquil spot to enjoy your goodies.

For excellent dining on a budget, the best address is **Au Bec Fin,** 12 rue du 24-Aout (© **04/93-38-35-86**), steps from the train station. The menu offers a wide selection of bistro dishes with an emphasis on Provençal cuisine. The pastas are made on the premises and include an excellent spaghetti with seafood sauce for 15€ ($17). The hearty *choucroute* is excellent at 16€ ($18), and lamb with curry sauce is another specialty. At lunch there's usually a bargain *plat du jour* at 11€ to 12€ ($13–$14). There's a three-course menu for 18€ ($21); the 21€ ($24) menu often includes a wonderful *bourride* fish filets in a stew spiced with saffron and garlic and served with boiled potatoes. The place attracts a well-heeled crowd of locals who could obviously afford to spend a great deal more on food but prefer to feast here in a convivial ambience. It's open Monday to Saturday 11:30am to 2:30pm and 6:30 to 10pm (except Sat evening), and accepts American Express, MasterCard, and Visa.

A family-run restaurant in Vieux Cannes, **L'Epicerie** ⟨, 4 rue de la Boucherie (© **04/92-98-16-20**), serves expertly prepared, delicious local specialties. The *salade de fruits de mer* ("fruits of the sea") and the *poulet a la provençale* (baked chicken with local herbs) are all good. The three-course *menu du jour* is 18€ ($21); the main dishes range from 8€ to 12€ ($9–$14). The inside room has a cozy atmosphere, but try to sit on the veranda. The restaurant is open Thursday to Tuesday noon to 2:30pm and 7:30 to 10:30pm, and accepts MasterCard and Visa.

The oldest restaurant in Cannes opened in 1860, is still serving delicious meals in a romantic setting, and is surprisingly affordable. Located up the hill in Vieux Cannes, **Auberge Provençale** ⟨⟨, 10 rue Saint-Antoine, Le Suquet (© **04/92-99-27-17**), has a lovely outdoor patio and a charming indoor dining room with exposed stone and antique furnishings. The prix-fixe (24€/$28) menu includes a choice of *soupe de poissons* (traditional fish soup served with garlic mayonnaise and croutons), grilled lamb with basil, and a decadent orange crepe for dessert. Main dishes are 11€ to 16€ ($13–$18). The restaurant is open daily from noon to 2:30pm and 7 to 11pm. American Express, MasterCard, and Visa are accepted.

CANNES AFTER DARK   **Jane's,** in the cellar of the Hôtel Gray d'Albion, 38 rue des Serbes (© **04/92-99-79-79**), is a stylish and appealing nightclub with an undercurrent of coy permissiveness. The crowd is well dressed (the men often wear jackets and ties) and covers a wide gamut of age groups. The cover is 10€ to 17€ ($12–$20), depending on business. A drink is included in the cover, and on Sunday women enter for free. It's open Thursday to Sunday 11pm to 5am. The hottest gay dance club is **Le Disco Sept,** 7 rue Rouguières (© **04/93-39-10-36**). Don't bother coming before midnight. The cover is 10€ to 16€ ($12–$18) and includes one drink.

ST-TROPEZ ⟨⟨⟨

Expensive, flashy, and exclusive, **St-Tropez** is the ultimate beach destination for the rich and famous—a true jet-setter's paradise. Unlike Monaco or Cannes, St-Tropez feels like an island in the middle of the sea, belonging to no country or culture except the culture of decadence and frivolity. This is where topless

Brigitte Bardot frolicked on the beach in the late 1950s and put this once-sleepy fishing village on the celebrity circuit.

St-Tropez has retained its charm because, like an island, it's inaccessible. The nearest airport is in Nice, a 2-hour drive away (the stars arrive by helicopter or private yacht). From Nice, several **trains** per day stop at St-Raphaël (an hour's trip) costing 9€ ($10) one-way. From there, **buses** leave every hour for the 90-minute ride to St-Tropez, costing 8.50€ ($10) each way. There are no buses from Nice to St-Tropez, but a one-way bus fare from Nice to St-Raphaël is 8.30€ ($10). If you have a **car**, take A8 toward Cannes, Fréjus, and St-Raphaël, then take the D25 exit to St-Maxime and follow the signs to St-Tropez.

SEEING THE SIGHTS Despite its inaccessibility, some 100,000 summer visitors per day still find their way to this enchanting village. Most come to stroll around the port, gawking at the multimillion-dollar yachts bobbing in the Mediterranean, or they check out the narrow cobblestone streets inland, all leading to the huge central square, place des Lices, where an open-air market takes place every morning until noon. There is, however, one museum worth visiting.

Facing the port, the 1568 Chapelle de Notre-Dame was converted in 1955 into the **Musée l'Annonciade (Musée de St-Tropez)** 🜨🜨, at place Georges-Grammont (© **04/94-97-04-01**). It's a homage to the many Impressionist and avant-garde artists who flocked to St-Tropez in the first half of the 20th century. Painter Paul Signac was the first to arrive, followed by Pierre Bonnard, Edouard Vuillard, and Henri Matisse. All are well represented in the small collection of paintings on the upper level; the lower level is reserved for temporary exhibits. The museum is open Wednesday to Monday: June to September 10am to noon and 3 to 7pm, and October and December to May 10am to noon and 2 to 6pm. Admission is 5€ ($5.75).

Although St-Tropez is known as the hottest **beach** destination on the Riviera, its beaches are actually 3.2km (2 miles) away in Ramatuelle. Footpaths run from town to the beaches, but catching a bus or renting a bike is much quicker than walking. Inquire at the **Office de Tourisme** on quai Jean-Jaures (© **04/94-97-45-21**); a map of the hiking trails and beaches is available there, as is information on bike rentals. The most famous beach is **La Voile Rouge** 🜨🜨, part of the Plage de Tahiti, Route de Tahiti (© **04/94-18-02**), known to be the main jet-set beach, although its survival is iffy due to a growing environmental outcry at the extreme commercialization of this once serene spot. April to October, the beach and its restaurant are open 10am to 8pm. To save money, come just for a beverage at the bar and forgo paying for a mattress and umbrella. You can stretch your towel out at the numerous public beaches close by.

WHERE TO STAY St-Tropez hotels are notoriously expensive, and finding a bargain can be quite an ordeal in high season. The two hotels below are amazing bargains, but you must book well in advance—for a July trip, call in February. The best bargain in town is the 11-room **Hôtel Le Baron,** 23 rue de l'Aïoli, 83990 St-Tropez (© **04/94-97-06-57**; fax 04/94-97-58-72; hotellebaron@wanadoo.fr), close to the port and place des Lices and popular with a young European crowd. The friendly young owners, Pierre and Christine, stay busy with their ground-floor pub frequented by backpackers and college students. The rooms are small and comfortable (all with TVs and phones), and singles and doubles are 78€ to 110€ ($90–$126). Breakfast is 7€ ($8), and MasterCard and Visa are accepted. Just outside town, a 5-minute walk up a tame hill from the main square, the **Hôtel Lou Troupelen** 🜨🜨, Chemin des Vendanges, 93990 St-Tropez

(© 04/94-97-44-88; fax 04/94-97-41-76; troupelen@aol.com), is a charming country house that has been renovated into 44 comfortable rooms (all with TVs and phones). Many have small balconies opening onto the quiet garden. Singles are 56€ to 64€ ($64–$74), and doubles 76€ to 105€ ($88–$121). American Express, MasterCard, and Visa are accepted.

WHERE TO DINE   Restaurants are expensive in St-Tropez, but you can find many small sandwich and crepe shops for a quick, inexpensive light meal. Avoid the cafes lining the port, as they charge a premium for their prime people-watching outdoor tables. The best bargain, with consistently good food, service, and ambience, is **Chez Maggy** ☆☆, 7 rue Sybille (© 04/94-97-16-12), on a tiny pedestrian-only street in the town center. It's small, lively, and elegant, serving one prix-fixe menu at 24€ ($28) for three courses. The cuisine is a fusion of East and West, and courses might include chicken tandoori, couscous with spicy tuna, salmon steak with sweet-and-sour berry sauce, and excellent lemon meringue pie. It's open daily 7:30 to 11.30pm and accepts MasterCard and Visa.

ST-TROPEZ AFTER DARK   The jet set gathers at **Les Caves du Roy** ☆☆, in the opulent Hôtel Byblos, avenue Paul-Signac (© 04/94-56-68-00), where counts and baronesses sip very expensive cocktails before and after dinner. A fun bar with a mixed/gay/straight crowd is **Chez Nano** ☆, 2 rue Sybille (© 04/94-97-72-69), where locals and visitors alike begin the evening with drinks along with complimentary trays of hors d'oeuvres. **Le Pigeonnier,** 13 rue de la Ponche (© 04/94-97-36-85), is St-Tropez's main nightclub, with good music and a hip, dressed-up crowd. They charge a 10€ ($12) cover Friday and Saturday night. **L'Esquinade,** 2 rue du Four (© 04/94-97-85-45), is the town's main gay dance club, charging a cover of 10€ to 16€ ($12–$18).

19

Paris & the Best of the Ile de France

by Cheryl Pientka

No city is as celebrated as **Paris.** Its landmarks are instantly recognized, it abounds in culture, and its beauty is legendary—bridges connect the city's two banks in graceful arches, the rosy evening light reflecting off buildings unconstrained by right angles. Paris's green spaces, parks, and gardens are numerous and welcome, the antidote to curving and monumental architecture. Turn down one cobblestone street and confront a domed neoclassical structure that wouldn't be out of place in Greece. Make your way down another and discover a stunning view of the Eiffel Tower. You could spend months exploring Paris's treasures without seeing them all.

Paris is modern, despite monuments everywhere attesting to its long history. The city's residents, with their unparalleled knowledge of the fine arts of living, make Paris pulse. Teenagers with cellphones cruise the majestic sweep of the Champs-Elysées, while in-line skaters breeze through centuries-old neighborhoods.

High fashion was born here, and there's no better place to see the world's next fads and fashions than by observing what Parisians wear while simply going about their business.

The food in Paris is unparalleled; nearly every celebrated chef in France has a restaurant here. And though there are more places than ever to have mouthwatering meals in palatial settings, there is also no better place to enjoy the varied flavors of France at down-to-earth, low-priced bistros.

Perhaps the best way to describe Paris is that it's more than a city; it's an encounter. And every visitor will experience the city in a unique way.

For more on Paris and its environs, see *Frommer's Paris, Frommer's Paris from $90 a Day, Frommer's Irreverent Guide to Paris, Paris For Dummies, Frommer's Memorable Walks in Paris, Frommer's France,* or *France For Dummies.*

1 Essentials

ARRIVING

BY PLANE Paris has two airports that handle international traffic: Charles-de-Gaulle and Orly.

AEROPORT CHARLES-DE-GAULLE The larger, busier, and more modern airport, commonly known as CDG and sometimes called **Roissy–Charles-de-Gaulle** (© **01-48-62-12-12** or 08-36-68-15-15; www.adp.fr), is 23km (15 miles) northeast of downtown. Foreign airlines use Terminal 1 (Aérogare 1); Terminal 2 (Aérogare 2) serves Air France, domestic and intra-European airlines, and some foreign airlines, including Air Canada and Delta. Terminal 2 is divided into halls A through F. Because the halls are far apart, it makes sense to know from

(Value Budget Bests

There are many sights to see at low or no cost. It costs nothing to get to the top of department store **La Samaritaine** for unbeatable scenery over the rooftops of Paris. Picnic in one of the city's parks, and admire the museum-quality sculpture for free.

Paris is a great city for **walking**. Stroll on the banks of the Seine close to the **Tour Eiffel**. Watch the sun set from the **Pont des Arts;** the spires of Notre-Dame will be behind you and the river's bridges ahead, silhouetted by the sun. Tour the historic and beautiful iron- and glass-covered **shopping arcades** in the 2e arrondissement. See the sprawling mansions and narrow cobblestone streets of the **Marais,** home to the city's old Jewish quarter and gay population.

Seek out **local watering holes** on side streets instead of tourist traps near popular attractions. If you just want a snack, sit in the cafe side of a brasserie (otherwise you'll be expected to order a full meal), and remember that you'll pay less standing up at the bar.

---

which hall your flight will leave. A third, more remote terminal, known as T9, caters only to charter airlines and all easyJet flights. A free shuttle bus *(navette)* connects the three terminals.

Note: In May 2004, the roof of Charles-de-Gaulle's Terminal 2E collapsed, killing four people. At press time, details of the reorganization of flights was not determined.

There are several ways of getting to and from the airport. The easiest and most comfortable choice is the **Air France buses** (© **01-41-56-89-00;** www.airfrance.com) that run from the two main terminals—and you don't have to fly Air France to use the service. Buy tickets on the bus. **Line 2** runs every 15 minutes from Terminals 1 and 2 to the Porte-Maillot Métro station, next to Paris's huge convention center on the western end of the city, and to place Charles-de-Gaulle–Etoile and the Arc de Triomphe. The 40-minute trip costs 10€ ($12) one-way, 17€ ($20) round-trip. This service is available from 5:45am until 11pm. **Line 4** runs every 30 minutes from Terminals 1 and 2 to Gare Montparnasse, near the Left Bank, and Gare de Lyon, near the Marais. The journey takes about 50 minutes and costs 120€ ($13) one-way or 20€ ($23) round-trip. It runs from 7am to 9pm. **Line 3** operates every 30 minutes and connects Charles-de-Gaulle and Orly from Terminal 1, Porte 34, arrivals level, and Terminal 2 at Porte B2 and Porte C2. The hour-long trip costs 16€ ($18) one-way (round-trips not available). Infants travel free on Air France buses, and there are discounted rates for children under 11. Groups of four passengers or more can receive a 15% discount off the one-way fares.

A less expensive option is the **Roissybus** (© **08-36-68-77-14**), which leaves every 15 minutes for place de l'Opéra; it takes 45 to 50 minutes and costs 8€ ($9.20). It departs from Terminal 1 at Porte 30, arrivals level; Terminal 2 at Porte A10; Porte D12; and Hall F, Port H, arrivals level. Buses run from 5:45am to 11pm.

The **RER Line B suburban train** (www.ratp.fr), which stops near terminals 1 and 2, is also a good bet if you don't have a lot of luggage. A free **shuttle bus** connects all three terminals to the RER train station. From the station, trains depart about every 15 minutes for the half-hour trip into town, stopping at the

Paris Deals & Discounts

SPECIAL DISCOUNTS   If you plan to use public transportation for at least a week, buy the **Carte Orange,** a weekly or monthly pass for all Paris subway or bus lines in zones 1 and 2 (where most major attractions are located). The only catch is that you must supply a passport-size photo of yourself. Bring one from home, or visit a photo booth at one of the many Monoprix stores, major Métro stations, department stores, or train stations. The weekly Carte Orange is on sale Monday through Wednesday morning and is valid through Sunday; the monthly card is only sold the first 2 days of the month. The pass is 13€ ($12) for a week *(coupon hébdomadaire)* valid Monday to Sunday, or 44€ ($40) for a calendar month *(coupon mensuel).*

If you take more than six trains per day, a 5€ ($4.50) 1-day pass, the **Mobilis,** will be your best bet, offering unlimited travel in zones 1 and 2; you'll need a passport-size photo. Otherwise, you can buy a **carnet,** a packet of 10 Métro tickets, for 9.30€ ($8).

If you plan to travel by train, the **Société Nationale des Chemins de Fer (SNCF)** offers a full menu of discounts for children, seniors, and travelers ages 12 to 25. Cards cost from about 43€ to 55€ ($39–$49) and offer discounts from 20% to 50% off regular fares for as long as the card is valid. For more information, ask at any rail ticket office in France; or contact the **SNCF** at ② **08/92-35-35-35** or at its website at www.sncf.fr.

Offering free entrance to 70 monuments and museums in Paris and the Ile de France, **La Carte Musées et Monuments (Museum and Monuments Pass)** is sold at any of the museums honoring it, at any branch of the tourist office, or in Métro and RER stations. A 1-day pass is 13€ ($12), a 3-day pass 26€ ($23), and a 5-day pass 39€ ($35). In addition to the substantial savings, the pass allows you to skip long lines waiting to get into the Louvre.

Anyone 17 and under is **admitted free** to any of France's national museums, including the Louvre, the Musée d'Orsay, and the Musée Picasso. Those 18 to 25 receive a **substantial discount.**

Gare du Nord, Châtelet–Les Halles Métro interchange, and RER stations St-Michel, Luxembourg, Port-Royal, and Denfert-Rochereau, before heading south out of the city. A ticket into town on the RER is 7.60€ ($8.75).

A **taxi** into town from Charles-de-Gaulle takes 40 to 50 minutes and costs about 40€ ($46) from 7am to 7pm, about 40% more at other times. Taxis are required to turn on the meter and charge the price indicated (plus a supplement for baggage—see "Getting Around," later in this chapter). Check the meter before you pay—rip-offs of arriving tourists are not uncommon. If you feel that you have been overcharged, demand a receipt (which drivers are obligated to provide) and contact the **Préfecture of Police** (② **01-55-76-20-00**). Good luck.

AEROPORT D'ORLY   Charter flights and some international airlines fly into **Orly** (② **01-49-75-15-15;** www.adp.fr), 14km (8½ miles) south of the city. The airport has two terminals: French domestic flights land at Orly Ouest, and intra-European and intercontinental flights land at Orly Sud. Shuttle buses connect

Many reductions are offered to holders of a valid **International Student Identity Card (ISIC)**. In Paris, the ISIC office, now called **Council Exchanges,** recently moved to 112 rue Cardinet, 75017 (© 01/58-57-20-50; Métro: Malesherbes). You can gain admission to national museums at half price and get reductions on train, bus, plane, and even cinema and theater tickets. Before leaving home, you can get an ISIC for $22 from the **Council on International Educational Exchange (CIEE),** 205 E. 42nd St., New York, NY 10017 (© 800/2-COUNCIL; www.ciee.org). You can also download the application at www.counciltravel.com/idcards/isic.asp. Flash your ISIC whenever you pay for something—even if no reduction is advertised, you'll be astounded at the discounts granted. If you're not a student but are between 18 and 24, you could be entitled to many of the same reductions. Ask whenever you're going to pay for something—your passport should serve as proof of your age.

For **shopping bargains,** browse at the many shops selling overstock on the **rue St-Placide** in the 6e. You'll also find stylish and inexpensive clothes at Monoprix or Prisunic; there are branches all over the city.

You can buy **half-price theater and other performance tickets** at one of the kiosks by the Madeleine (8e), on the lower level of the Châtelet-Les Halles Métro station, or at the Gare Montparnasse (14e).

WORTH A SPLURGE   It's worth the extra money to experience a meal in one of the city's finest restaurants, where famous chefs make dining an art. For full coverage of the restaurant scene, see *Frommer's Paris.*

Bring some of gourmet Paris back home with you from **Fauchon,** place de la Madeleine, 1e (© 01/47-42-60-11; Métro: Madeleine); or from the city's largest gourmet food store, **La Grande Epicerie,** next to Le Bon Marché department store, 38 rue de Sèvres, 7e (© 01/44-39-81-17; Métro: Sèvres-Babylone). There you'll find some of the best foie gras, pâtés, cheeses, chocolates, truffles, wines, and other fabulous items. Check with the stores to see if there are any restrictions on what you can bring home.

these terminals, and other shuttles connect them to Charles-de-Gaulle every 30 minutes or so.

The cheapest trip into town is on **Jetbus** (© 01-69-01-00-09). It connects Orly with the Métro station Villejuif–Louis Aragon, which is in a southern suburb of Paris; the 15-minute journey costs 5€ ($5.75). The bus leaves every 12 to 15 minutes from Exit G2 in Orly Sud and from Exit C, arrivals level, in Orly Ouest.

Air France coaches (you need not be an Air France passenger) run to the downtown terminal at Invalides every 15 minutes. **Line 1** leaves from Exit D on the arrivals level at Orly Ouest and Exit K at Orly Sud. The trip takes 35 minutes and costs 7.50€ ($8.60) one-way, 13€ ($15) round-trip. You can request that the bus stop at Montparnasse-Duroc (the stop is right in front of the Duroc Métro station). This service operates from 5:45am to 11pm. **Line 3** runs between Orly and Charles-de-Gaulle; see "Aéroport Charles-de-Gaulle," above.

An airport **shuttle bus,** Orly-Rail, leaves every 15 minutes for the RER Pont de Rungis–Aéroport d'Orly station, where you can board a Line C train that stops at several downtown stations, including St-Michel, Invalides, and Gare d'Austerlitz (35 min.). This airport shuttle leaves from Orly Sud Exit F on Platform 1 and from Exit G on the arrivals level at Orly Ouest. It costs 5€ ($5.75).

You can also take the **Orlyval** service at the RER Line B. From Orly Sud it departs from Exit K near the baggage-claim area; from Orly Ouest it departs from Exit W or Exit J on the departures level. You'll connect at the Antony RER station. The trip to Châtelet takes about 30 minutes and costs 8.75€ ($10). You can avoid waiting in line by buying your Orlyval tickets from a machine if you have French coins.

The **Orly Bus** (from Exit J arrivals level at Orly Ouest, and from Exit H Platform 4 at Orly Sud) goes to Denfert-Rochereau and costs 5.50€ ($6.30).

A **taxi** into the city costs about 32€ ($37) and takes 30 to 45 minutes.

AIRPORT SHUTTLES   Cheaper than a taxi for one or two people but more expensive than airport buses and trains is the **Paris Airport Shuttle** (✆ 01-43-90-91-91; www.paris-airport-shuttle.com). An excellent choice for those who over-pack, this service requires advance reservation (reservation@paris-airport-shuttle.com). A minivan will meet you at Orly or Charles-de-Gaulle to take you to your hotel for 18€ ($21) per person for parties of two or more, 24€ ($28) for a single passenger.

The **Blue Shuttle** (✆ 01-30-11-13-00; fax 01-30-11-13-09; www.airport shuttle.fr) offers a similar service, and also requires reservations. It costs 22€ ($25) for one person, 29€ ($33) for two, 44€ ($50) for three, and 59€ ($67) for four.

Both companies have toll-free numbers that you call once you arrive at the airport to confirm your arrival and location of pickup. Be sure to ask for this number when you make your reservations and call as soon as you land, before collecting your luggage, to lessen the amount of time you spend waiting.

BY TRAIN   If you're in Europe, you may want to go to Paris by train, especially if you have a **Eurailpass.** For information, call the national train network, **SNCF** (✆ 01-53-90-20-20) between 6am and 10pm, and ask for someone who speaks English, or go to a travel agent or an information booth at the stations.

Coming from northern Germany or Belgium (and sometimes London), you'll most likely arrive at **Gare du Nord.** Trains from Normandy come into **Gare St-Lazare,** in northwest Paris. Trains from the west (Brittany, Chartres, Versailles, Bordeaux) head to **Gare de Montparnasse;** those from the southwest (the Loire Valley, the Pyrenees, Spain) head to **Gare d'Austerlitz;** those from the south and southeast (the Riviera, Lyon, Italy, Geneva) head to **Gare de Lyon.** From Alsace and eastern France, Luxembourg, southern Germany, and Zurich, the arrival station is **Gare de l'Est.** All stations are next to a Métro station with the same name, and taxis are available at the taxi stand just outside each station. All the above train stations are in the center of Paris.

BY BUS   Buses connect Paris to most major European cities. European Railways operates **Europabus** and **Eurolines.** They do not have American offices, so travelers must make arrangements after arriving in Europe. In **Great Britain,** contact **National Express Eurolines** (✆ 08705/808-080; www.national express.com). In **Paris,** the contact is **Eurolines,** 28 av. du General de Gaulle, 93541 Bagnolet (✆ 08-36-69-52-52); phone access costs .35€ (40¢) per minute. International buses serve **Gare Routière Internationale (International Bus Terminal)** at avenue Charles de Gaulle in the suburb of Bagnolet.

VISITOR INFORMATION

TOURIST OFFICES   The prime source of information is the **Office de Tourisme et des Congrès de Paris,** 127 av. des Champs-Elysées, 8e ((C) 08-92-68-31-12; fax 01-49-52-53-00; www.parisbienvenue.com; Métro: Charles-de-Gaulle–Etoile or George V). It's open daily 9am to 8pm (Sun 11am–7pm Nov–Apr). For a fee, the staff will make a same-day room reservation for you. The charge is 1.50€ ($1.70) for hostels and *foyers* ("homes"), 3€ ($3.45) for one-star hotels, 4€ ($4.60) for two-star hotels, and 6€ ($6.90) for three-star hotels. There are information offices at the airports; the staff will help you make a hotel reservation, but they work only with hotels that charge more than 50€ ($58) a night.

In slow periods, hotels with unsold rooms often sell them at a huge discount through the Office de Tourisme, providing you with a good way to stay in a three-star hotel at a two-star price. The office is very busy in summer, with lines sometimes stretching outside.

The Office de Tourisme has **auxiliary offices** at the Eiffel Tower (May–Sept only, daily 11am–6:40pm) and at the Gare de Lyon (year-round, Mon–Sat 8am–8pm). At the main office you can also reserve concert, theater, or cabaret tickets without an extra fee.

WEBSITES   The Web is a great source of information for your trip to Paris. The sites listed here all have English-language versions, unless otherwise noted. The **Paris Tourist Office's** site, **www.paris-touristoffice.com,** is a good starting point for exploring Paris on the Web, providing up-to-date information on lodging, transportation, events, concerts, exhibits, and fairs. The **Paris Pages, www.paris.org,** has lodging reviews that are organized by area and nearby monuments, plus an events calendar, shop listings, and a map of attractions with details about each. **Bonjour Paris (www.bparis.com;** AOL Keyword: Bonjour) is one of the most comprehensive and fun sites about life in Paris, written from an American expatriate's point of view. Brought to you by the publisher of such magazines as *Living in France, Study in France,* and *What's On in France,* **Paris France Guide (www.parisfranceguide.com)** has lots of useful information about Paris, such as current articles and listings on nightlife, restaurants, events, theater, and music. The online version of the monthly *Paris Voice* (**http://parisvoice.com** or **http://thinkparis.com**) is hip and opinionated for "English-speaking Parisians."

CITY LAYOUT

The river **Seine** divides Paris into the **Right Bank (Rive Droite)** and the **Left Bank (Rive Gauche).** In the middle of the river are two islands, **Ile de la Cité** and **Ile St-Louis,** connected to each other by the **Pont St-Louis.** The heart of

---

Tips Finding an Address

Finding the right neighborhood is usually easy. The last three digits in the postal code indicate the arrondissement; 75005 means the 5e arrondissement ("75" is for Paris), 75019 means the 19e, and so on.

Addresses often include the name of the nearest Métro station. You'll find good neighborhood maps *(plans du quartier)* in the Métro station that will help you locate your street. Addresses on streets that run parallel to the Seine generally follow the direction of the river (east to west). For perpendicular streets, the lowest numbers are closest to the Seine.

Paris and the place from which all distances in France are measured is **Notre-Dame** on Ile de la Cité. Ile St-Louis boasts a beautifully preserved enclave of 17th-century town houses and mansions. Directly north across the river, the sprawling palace of the **Louvre** is the starting point for the city's system of *arrondissements* (**districts**). They're numbered from 1 to 20, progressing in a clockwise spiral from the Louvre's courtyard.

The courtyard of the Louvre is also the tip of the promenade leading west through the **Jardin des Tuileries** up the **Champs-Elysées** to the **Arc de Triomphe** and to the suburb of La Défense, where the **Grand Arche de la Défense** is located. **1er** and the nearby **8e** contain the city's most expensive hotels, restaurants, shops, and cafes. This is where you'll find the designer stores along **avenue Montaigne** and **rue du Faubourg St-Honoré,** the ritzy **place Vendôme,** and the **Palais Royal.** North of the Louvre on the Right Bank is Charles Garnier's ornate 19th-century **Opéra (9e),** surrounded by major department stores such as Galeries Lafayette and Au Printemps; and still farther north is **Montmartre (18e),** topped by **Sacré-Coeur,** the wedding-cake church on the crown of a hill that you can see from all over Paris. East of the Louvre on the Right Bank is the very hip **Marais (3e** and **4e),** home of 17th-century royal mansions, the historic Jewish quarter, and the city's gay neighborhood. East of the Marais is the **Bastille (11e),** site of the new Opéra and lively nightlife. Northeast of the Bastille is the **Père-Lachaise Cemetery (20e)** and the **Ménilmontant** neighborhood, home to the city's North African population, artists, and a burgeoning night scene.

On the Left Bank, the **Latin Quarter (5e)** is home to the **Sorbonne** and the **Panthéon.** The cobblestone streets that once drew medieval scholars are still filled with inexpensive shops and cafes catering to students, although chain stores and fast food are encroaching. The **St-Germain-des-Prés area (6e)** centers on the **St-Germain-des-Prés church** and stretches from the Seine to **boulevard du Montparnasse.** Within its boundaries are the quintessential Parisian park—**Jardin du Luxembourg,** arts and antiques stores along rue Bonaparte and rue de Seine, and the famous literary cafes where Sartre, de Beauvoir, and Hemingway came to write. South of St-Germain-des-Prés is **Montparnasse (14e),** also associated with the literary life of the 1920s and 1930s. East of St-Germain, the **Tour Eiffel, Musée d'Orsay,** and **Hôtel des Invalides** are in the **Faubourg St-Germain (7e),** amid 18th-century mansions that have become embassies, government buildings, or ultra-expensive residences. Beyond the *arrondissements* stretch the vast *banlieue* (**suburbs**) of Greater Paris, where the majority of Parisians live.

GETTING AROUND

BY METRO (SUBWAY) & RER   The first Métro line opened in 1900, and the system is fast, clean, safe for the most part, and easy to navigate. The **RATP** *(Régie Autonome des Transports Parisiens)* operates the Métro and city buses, as well as the *Réseau Express Régional* (RER), which links downtown Paris with its airports and suburbs. The Métro has 16 lines and 380 stations, so there's bound to be one near your destination. It connects with the RER at several stations. Both trains run from 5:30am to around 12:45am. After that, you can wait in line for a taxi (there is a severe shortage), walk, or try the night bus. Both the

A Map Note
See the inside front cover of this guide for a Paris Métro map.

> **Tips A Pickpocket Warning**
>
> Most of the time, the Métro is quite safe. Precautions are in order in the northern parts of the city, in deserted stations, and in long corridors between stations late at night. As a tourist, you are a special mark. You may feel safer riding in the first train car, where the engineer is. Be suspicious if someone pushes up against you or creates a distraction.

Métro and the RER operate on a zone system, at a different fare per zone, but it's unlikely you'll be traveling any farther than zone 2.

A single ticket *(un billet)* costs 1.30€ ($1.50), but if you ask for a booklet *(un carnet),* you'll get 10 loose tickets for 9.60€ ($11), a much better deal. If you're going to be in Paris for more than a week, it might be a better idea to get an unlimited-ride **Carte Orange** (see "Paris Deals & Discounts," earlier in this chapter). At the station, insert your ticket in the turnstile, pass through the entrance, and take your ticket out of the machine. Be sure to keep your ticket until you pass through the exit turnstiles. If you're caught without one at any time before that, you may have to pay a stiff fine. When you ride the RER, it is especially important to keep your ticket because you have to insert it in a turnstile to leave the station.

Many older Métro stations (such as Abesses and Porte Dauphine) are marked by Art Nouveau gateways designed by Hubert Guimard that spell out METRO-POLITAIN; others are marked by big yellow M signs. Once you decide which line you need, make sure you are going in the right direction: Every Métro stop has maps of the system, which are also available at ticket booths. To change train lines, look for the CORRESPONDANCE signs; blue SORTIE signs mark the exits.

On the platform or near the exits is usually a *plan du quartier,* a detailed map of the streets and buildings surrounding each Métro station, with all exits marked. It's a good idea to consult this before you climb the stairs. Or do as Parisians do and carry the pocket-size reference guide *Plan de Paris par Arrondissement.* This book alphabetically lists all streets in Paris from their starting to ending addresses as well as their nearest Métro stations. It carries maps of each arrondissement on which the streets are clearly marked, as well as maps of Métro, RER, and bus routes. The book is available in the travel sections of bookstores such as Barnes & Noble, Borders, W. H. Smith, and travel bookshops. In Paris, it's sold at bookstores and at Monoprix and Prisunic stores.

For more information on public transportation, stop at the **Urbiel/RATP center** on place de la Madeleine, 1er (© **01-40-06-71-45;** www.ratp.fr; Métro: Madeleine); or call © **08-36-68-41-14** for information in English.

BY BUS The bus system is convenient and can be an inexpensive way to sightsee. Each bus shelter has a route map, which you'll want to check carefully. Because of the number of one-way streets, the bus is likely to make different stops depending on its direction. Métro tickets and passes are valid for bus travel, or you can buy your ticket from the conductor. Single tickets are 1.30€ ($1.50). Carnets cannot be bought onboard. Tickets must be punched in the machine and held until the end of the ride. Passes will also get you on the **Balabus** line (© **08-36-68-77-14**), which does a tourist circuit from the Gare de Lyon to the Grande Arche de la Defense; this service only runs on Sundays and holidays from April to September. A one-way trip equals three Métro tickets; pass holders ride free.

BY TAXI   Parisian taxis are fairly expensive, but you should know a few things in case you need one. First, look for the blue taxi sign denoting a taxi stand; although you can hail taxis in the street (look for a taxi with a white light on; an orange light means it's occupied), most drivers will not pick you up if you are near a taxi stand. Check the meter carefully, especially if you are coming from an airport; rip-offs are common. If you feel that you may have been overcharged, demand a receipt (which drivers are obligated to provide) and contact the **Préfecture of Police** (© **01-55-76-20-00**). For one to three people, the drop rate in Paris proper is 2€ ($2.30). The rate per kilometer is .60€ (70¢) from 7am to 7pm; otherwise, it's .95€ ($1.10). The rate per kilometer from the airport is .95€ ($1.10) during the day and 1.15€ ($1.30) at night. You will pay supplements from taxi ramps at train stations and at the Air France shuttle-bus terminals (1€/$1.15) for luggage, and, if the driver agrees to do so, 3€ ($3.45) for transporting a fourth person. It is common practice to tip your driver .50€ to 1€ (60¢–$1.15), except on longer journeys when the fare exceeds 15€ ($17); in these cases, a 5% to 10% tip is appropriate.

BY RENTAL CAR   Streets are narrow, and parking is next to impossible. Nerve, skill, ruthlessness, and a copilot are required if you insist on driving in Paris.

A few tips: Get an excellent street map and ride with another person, because there's no time to think at intersections. You usually must pay to park on the street. Depending on the neighborhood, expect to pay .75€ to 2.50€ (85¢–$2.85) an hour for a maximum of 2 hours. Place coins in the nearest meter, which issues you a ticket to place on your windshield. You can also buy parking cards at the nearest *tabac* for meters that accept only cards. Parking is free on Sundays, holidays, and for the entire month of August.

Drivers and all passengers must wear seat belts. Children under 12 must ride in the back seat. Drivers are supposed to yield to the car on the right, except where signs indicate otherwise, as at traffic circles. Watch for the gendarmes, who lack patience and who consistently countermand the lights. Horn blowing is frowned upon except in emergencies. Flash your headlights instead.

BY BICYCLE   Long accustomed to darting through traffic, bicyclists are gaining new respect and a few amenities. Out of concern for pollution, city planners have been trying to encourage more cycling by setting aside more than 161km (100 miles) of bicycle lanes throughout Paris. The main axes run north-south from the Bassin de La Villette along the Canal St-Martin through the Left Bank, and east-west from Château de Vincennes to the Bois de Boulogne and its miles of bike lanes. For more information and a bike map, pick up the *Plan Vert* from

---

Country, City & Cell Codes

The **country code** for France is **33**. The **city code** for Paris is **1;** use this code if you're calling from outside France. If you're calling Paris from within Paris or from anywhere else in France, use **01**, which is now built into all phone numbers, making them 10 digits long. Cellphones have prefixes of **06;** you should know that calling cellphones in France is more expensive than calling a land line, unless you are calling from another cellphone. Beware of the prefixes **0802, 0803,** and **0836,** which cost .15€ (17¢), .20€ (25¢), and .35€ (40¢) per minute, respectively.

the tourist office; or get the *Mini Paris Vélo* map, on sale at many bookstores around the city for 3,50€ ($4). Some sections along the Seine are closed to cars and open to pedestrians and cyclists Sundays from March to November, 10am to 5pm. It might not make much of a dent in the air quality, but it's a lovely way to spend a Sunday afternoon.

To rent a bicycle, contact **Maison Roue Libre,** 1 Passage Mondetour, 1e (© 08-10-44-15-34; rouelibre@wanadoo.fr), a cycling center run by the RATP at Les Halles. They rent bikes for 12€ ($14) per day, 8€ ($9.20) per half day, or 3€ ($3.45) per hour, and can supply loads of biking info for Paris and the surrounding area. Hours are 9am to 7pm. From April to September, Roue Libre has smaller outlets in several areas around the city, including Place de la Concorde and Bercy, where you may pick up your bike. Contact the main office above for details. ID and a deposit are required for all rentals.

FAST FACTS: Paris

American Express Amex operates a 24-hour phone line (© 01-47-14-50-00) that handles questions about American Express services in greater Paris. Tours, mail drop, money exchange, and wire-transfer services are available at 11 rue Scribe, 9e (© 01-47-14-50-00; Métro: Opéra), and at 38 av. Wagram, 8e (© 01-42-27-58-80; Métro: Ternes). Both are open for banking services Monday to Saturday from 9am to noon and from 2 to 5pm. Foreign exchange and participation in the company's many guided bus tours are offered Monday to Saturday from 9am to 6pm, and Sunday (rue Scribe branch only) from 10am to 4:30pm.

Business Hours The **grands magasins** (department stores) are generally open Monday through Saturday 9:30am to 7pm; some **smaller shops** close for lunch and reopen around 2pm, but this is rarer than it used to be. Many stores stay open until 7pm in summer; others are closed on Monday. Most large **offices** remain open all day, but some close for lunch. **Banks** are normally open weekdays 9am to noon and 1 or 1:30 to 5pm. Many banks also open on Saturday from 9am to noon and 1 to 4pm.

Currency In 2002, France adopted the **euro** (€) for its currency. At press time, $1 = .87€, or 1€ = $1.15.

Currency Exchange Banks and *bureaux de change* (exchange offices) almost always offer better exchange rates than hotels, restaurants, and shops. ATMs offer the best rates; make sure your bank card is on a major network. For good rates and quick service, try the **Comptoir de Change Opéra,** 9 rue Scribe, 9e (© 01-47-42-20-96; Métro: Opéra; RER: Auber). It is open weekdays from 9am to 6pm, Saturday from 9:30am to 4pm. The *bureaux de change* at all train stations (except Gare de Montparnasse) are open daily. **Exchange Corporation France,** 63 av. des Champs-Elysées, 8e (© 01-53-76-40-66; Métro: Franklin-D-Roosevelt), and 140 av. des Champs-Elysées, 8e (© 01-40-75-00-49; Métro: Charles-de-Gaulle–Etoile), keep long hours.

Dentists You can call your consulate and ask the duty officer to recommend a dentist. For dental emergencies, call **SOS Dentaire** (© 01-43-37-51-00), available daily from 9am to midnight.

Doctors Call your consulate and ask the duty officer to recommend a doctor, or call **SOS Médecins** (© 01-47-07-77-77), a reliable 24-hour service. Doctors usually arrive within 1 hour of your call, and most speak at least some English. The cost is 40€ ($46).

Drugstores Pharmacies are marked with a green cross and are often upscale affairs, very expensive; it's cheaper to buy your toiletries elsewhere. After regular hours, ask at your hotel where the nearest 24-hour *pharmacie* is. You'll also find the address posted on the doors or windows of other drugstores in the neighborhood. One all-night drugstore is the **Pharmacie Derhy,** in La Galerie Les Champs, 84 av. des Champs-Elysées, 8e (© 01-45-62-02-41; Métro: George V).

Electricity The French electrical system runs on 220 volts. Adapters are needed to convert the voltage and fit sockets and are cheaper at home than in Paris. Make sure you have an adapter that converts voltage; if you plug a 110 hair dryer into a 220 socket, you can forget about the blow-dried look for the rest of your trip. Many hotels have two-pin (in some cases, three-pin) sockets for electric razors.

Embassies & Consulates If you have a passport, immigration, legal, or other problem, contact your consulate. Call before you go—they often keep strange hours and observe French and home-country holidays. Here's where to find them: **Australia,** 4 rue Jean-Rey, 15e (© 01-40-59-33-00; Métro: Bir-Hakeim); **Canada,** 35 av. Montaigne, 8e (© 01-44-43-29-00; Métro: Franklin-D-Roosevelt or Alma Marceau); **New Zealand,** 7 rue Léonard-de-Vinci, 16e (© 01-45-01-43-43; Métro: Victor-Hugo); **Great Britain,** 16 rue d'Anjou, 8e (© 01-44-51-31-02; Métro: Madeleine); and **United States,** 2 rue St-Florentin, 1er (© 01-43-12-22-22; Métro: Concorde).

Emergencies Call © 17 for the **police.** To report a **fire,** dial © 18. For an **ambulance,** call © 15 for **SAMU** (*Service d'aide médicale d'urgence,* or "emergency services"). For help in English, call **SOS Help** (© 01-47-23-80-80) between 3 and 11pm. The main police station, 1 rue de Lutèce, 4e (© 01-53-71-53-71; Métro: Cité), is open 24 hours a day.

Holidays France has lots of national holidays, most of them tied to the Catholic (the major religion in France) church calendar. On these days, shops, businesses, government offices, and most restaurants are closed: New Year's Day (Jan 1); Easter Monday (late Mar or Apr); Labor Day (May 1); Liberation Day (May 8); Ascension Thursday (May or June, 40 days after Easter); Whit Monday, also called Pentecost Monday (51 days after Easter); Bastille Day (July 14); Assumption Day (Aug 15); All Saints' Day (Nov 1); Armistice Day (Nov 11); and Christmas Day (Dec 25).

In addition, schedules may be disrupted on Shrove Tuesday (the day before Ash Wednesday, in late winter) and Good Friday (late Mar or Apr).

Hospitals Two hospitals with English-speaking staff are the **American Hospital of Paris,** 63 bd. Victor-Hugo, Neuilly-sur-Seine (© 01-46-41-25-25), just west of Paris proper (Métro: Les Sablons or Levallois-Perret); and the **British Hospital of Paris,** 3 rue Barbes Levallois-Perret (© 01-46-39-22-22), just north of Neuilly (Métro: Anatole-France). The American Hospital is quite expensive; French hospitals and doctors' fees are much cheaper. Open Monday to Saturday from 8am to 7pm, **Central Médical**

Europe, 44 rue d'Amsterdam, 9e ((✆ **01-42-81-93-33;** Métro: Liège or St-Lazare), maintains contacts with medical and dental practitioners in all fields. Appointments are recommended. An additional clinic is the **Centre Figuier,** 2 rue du Figuier, 4e ((✆ **01-49-96-62-70;** Métro: St-Paul). Call before visiting.

Internet Access To find cybercafes throughout Paris, go to **www.paris paris.com/fr/multimedia/bodycyber1.html.**

Laundry & Dry Cleaning To find a laundry, ask at your hotel or consult the Yellow Pages under *Laveries.* Take as many .50€, 1€, and 2€ pieces as you can. Washing and drying 6 kilos (13¼ lb.) costs from around 4€ to 7€ ($4.60–$8.05). Dry cleaning is called *nettoyage à sec* or *pressing.*

Liquor Laws Supermarkets, grocery stores, and cafes sell alcoholic beverages. The legal drinking age is 18. Persons under 18 can be served an alcoholic drink if accompanied by a parent or legal guardian.

Mail Large **post offices** are open weekdays 8am to 7pm, Saturday 8am to noon; small post offices may have shorter hours. There are many post offices (PTT) around the city; ask anybody for the nearest one. Airmail letters and postcards to the United States cost .70€ (80¢); western Europe .45€ (50¢); eastern Europe .60€ (70¢); and Australia or New Zealand .85€ (95¢).

The **main post office** is at 52 rue du Louvre, 75001 Paris ((✆ **01-40-28-20-40;** Métro: Louvre-Rivoli). It's open 24 hours for urgent mail, telegrams, and telephone calls. It handles Poste Restante mail—sent to you in care of the post office; be prepared to show your passport and pay .45€ (50¢) for each letter. If you don't want to use Poste Restante, you can receive mail care of **American Express.** Holders of American Express cards or traveler's checks get this service free; others have to pay a fee.

Police Dial (✆ **17** in emergencies; otherwise, call (✆ **01-53-71-53-71.**

Restrooms Public restrooms are plentiful, but you usually have to pay for them. Every cafe has a restroom, but they are supposed to be for customers only. The best plan is to ask to use the telephone; it's usually next to the *toilette.* For .30€ (35¢) you can use the street-side toilets, which are automatically flushed out and cleaned after every use.

Smoking Although restaurants are required to provide nonsmoking sections, you may find yourself next to the kitchen or the restrooms. The best strategy for avoiding smoke is to sit outside.

Telephone All **public phone booths** take only telephone debit cards, called *télécartes,* which can be bought at post offices and at *tabacs.* You insert the card into the phone and make your call; the cost is deducted from the "value" of the card recorded on its chip, or *puce.* The *télécarte* comes in 50- and 120-unit denominations, costing 7.50€ ($8.60) and 15€ ($17), respectively, and can be used only in a phone booth. Ask for a *télécarte France Télécom.*

There is another kind of phone card that is a little more labor intensive but cheaper, especially for international calls. Instead of inserting the card into a public phone, you dial a free number and tap in a code. Tell the cashier at the *tabac* that you would like a *carte téléphonique avec un code,* and which country you want to call (some cards specialize in certain regions). Delta and GTS Omnicom are two good cards for calling North America and Europe.

For placing **international calls from France,** dial 00, then the country code (for the United States and Canada, 1; for Britain, 44; for Ireland, 353; for Australia, 61; for New Zealand, 64), then the area or city code, and then the local number (for example, to call New York, you'd dial 00 + 1 + 212 + 000-0000). For **calling from Paris to anywhere else in France** (called *province*), just dial the number; the area code will always be included in the number you are given. The country is divided into five zones with prefixes beginning 01, 02, 03, 04, and 05; Paris is 01.

If you're **calling France from the United States,** dial the international prefix, 011; then the country code for France, 33; followed by the number but leaving off the initial zero (for example, if you are calling a number in Paris, you would dial 011 + 33 + 1-00-00-00-00).

Avoid making phone calls from your hotel room; many hotels charge at least .50€ (58¢) for local calls, and the markup on international calls can be staggering.

Tipping Service is supposedly included at your hotel, but it is still customary to tip the **bellhop** about 1€ ($1.15) per bag, more in expensive (splurge) hotels. It's not customary to tip housekeepers unless they perform extra work. Tip 2€ to 4€ ($2.30–$4.60) if a **reception staff member** performs extra services.

Although your *addition* (restaurant bill) or *fiche* (cafe check) will bear the words *service compris* (service charge included), it's customary to leave a small tip. Generally, 5% is considered acceptable. Remember, a 15% service charge has supposedly already been paid for.

Taxi drivers appreciate a tip of .30€ to .50€ (35¢–57¢). On longer journeys, when the fare exceeds 15€ ($17), a 5% to 10% tip is appropriate. At the theater and cinema, tip .50€ (60¢) if an usher shows you to your seat. In **public toilets,** the attendant will expect a tip of about .30€ (35¢). Put it in the basket or on the plate at the entrance. **Porters** and **cloakroom attendants** are usually governed by set prices, which are displayed. If not, give a porter 1€ to 1.50€ ($1.15–$1.70) per suitcase, and a cloakroom attendant .50€ to 1€ (60¢–$1.15) per coat.

2 Affordable Places to Stay

Generally, budget French hotels are reliably clean and comfortable. If you're used to the amenities offered for the same money in American motels, however, you might be disappointed. The rooms tend to be smaller, and vary greatly in furnishings. Many older hotels do not have air-conditioning or elevators. Ask to see a room or two before you check in. If you're reserving by phone, and room size is important to you, you would do better to reserve a triple or a suite in a modest hotel than a double in a higher-priced one. Budget triples are generally larger than comparably priced doubles. Also, if you're looking for a double room, note that a double bed is cheaper than two twin beds, but the twin beds are likely to be in a larger room. Though generally quite clean, bathrooms in Parisian hotels can be a bit of an adventure. They usually range in size from tiny to small. Some rooms have only a sink or a shower; most have a toilet with a shower or a tub. If you do get a full (toilet and shower or tub) bathroom, it will always have a sink. The hotels described in this chapter offer private full bathrooms unless specified.

Breakfasts, unless otherwise noted, are continental, meaning croissants, rolls, jam, and a hot beverage. A "buffet breakfast" will usually be an expanded version, including cereal, yogurt, and sometimes cheese or ham. There is rarely an extra charge for having breakfast delivered to your room. If you are anxious to get going and are not a big eater, you will usually spend less at a nearby cafe or bakery.

High season is generally late spring to early summer and early fall; during these periods reserve rooms at least 2 months in advance. The dead of winter and August are lighter months. There are also annual trade shows and events, like the Foire de Paris in late April or the Fête de la Musique in June, when hotels are booked solid. Mid-September to mid-October is one of the busiest times for conventions, and hotel space is scarce. We suggest reserving up to 4 months in advance if you're visiting during these busy periods.

Visiting Paris at any time without a reservation isn't a good idea, especially if you're looking to save money. If you do arrive without a reservation, head early in the day to one of the tourist offices in the airports, at the train stations, or at 127 av. des Champs-Elysées. For a small fee, they'll book a room for you (see "Visitor Information" in "Essentials," earlier in this chapter).

It's important to be flexible about what part of the city you stay in. Paris is relatively small and well connected by public transport. Even on the fringes, you won't be more than half an hour from the center, where hotel rates are highest. The areas around the major train stations, especially the Gare du Nord, Gare de Lyon, and Gare de l'Est, have a large supply of reasonably priced places even if the neighborhoods are a bit bland. Less-frequented residential quarters like the 9e, 11e, 13e, 15e, and 18e also have many small budget hotels.

All rates below include tax.

IN & AROUND THE LATIN QUARTER (5E ARRONDISSEMENT)

The Quartier Latin (Latin Quarter) is the intellectual heart and soul of Paris, home to the Sorbonne, where students once spoke Latin with their teachers. Bookstores abound, and there are schools, churches, Roman ruins, nightclubs, and cheap and boutique clothing stores, as well as the busy boulevards of St-Michel and St-Germain. The rue Mouffetard is home to a wonderful outdoor market, and behind it, atop a hill, is the Panthéon. Room size is often tighter here than in other locations, and rates rise steeply as you approach place St-Michel. Students and tourists keep restaurant prices down, but eateries are mediocre.

Familia Hôtel *(★★ (Finds*   Owner Eric Gaucheron will just about do back flips to please guests at this charming hotel, which has been lovingly maintained and renovated. Window boxes full of flowers, *toile de Jouy* (fabric printed with a scenic design), wallpaper, exposed beams, and stone walls are some of the touches found in the rooms, many of which have balconies with views of the Latin Quarter. From the fifth and sixth floors, you can see Notre-Dame. Some rooms have sepia murals of Parisian scenes, and all the rooms are being fitted with mahogany closet doors. Bathrooms are small but sparkling. The friendly, English-speaking staff can help with directions. Maps and brochures are available at the front desk. If you can't get a room here, try **Hôtel Minerve,** 13 rue des Ecoles (© **01-43-26-26-04**), owned by the same folks.

11 rue des Ecoles, 75005 Paris. © 01-43-54-55-27. Fax 01-43-29-61-77. www.hotel-paris-familia.com. 30 units. 64€–85€ ($74–$98) single; 75€–105€ ($86–$121) double. Breakfast 5.50€ ($6.30). AE, DC, MC, V. Métro: Cardinal Lemoine or Jussieu. **Amenities:** Elevator. *In room:* Satellite TV, minibar, hair dryer.

(Value) Getting the Best Deal on Accommodations

- Plan ahead if you want to find the most attractive room at the best price. During the busiest times—late spring/early summer and early fall—rooms at the best budget hotels are reserved several months in advance and the reservation service at the tourist office might be very busy. The dead of winter and August are slower months.
- Note that a room without a bathroom can be marvelously cheap.
- Try to negotiate the price downward, especially in winter, when there's less demand for budget rooms. You can best do this in the evening.
- Always ask if the hotel offers weekend specials, which typically require you to stay 2 nights. In Paris, you can find this kind of deal September through March at almost all price levels.
- A home swap or short-term apartment rental in Paris is a good option if you don't need the services of a hotel. One company that facilitates home swapping is Trading Homes International (www.HomeExchange.com); for apartment rentals, try www.lodgis.fr.
- Families should consider a hotel offering some units with bathroom and others without—the kids can stay in the simpler room and use their parent's shower.
- Ask for the most recently renovated room; the quality of the rooms can vary widely in a hotel.
- Ask for a corner room; they usually don't cost any more and are often larger and quieter and have more light than standard rooms.
- If you're a light sleeper, ask for a room in the rear and/or make sure the windows are double-glazed. The acoustics in old hotels can be unpredictable; your neighbors' noise might be as annoying as street noise. Bring earplugs.

Hôtel Marignan ✦ (Value) Owners Paul and Linda Keniger are so welcoming, they will let you use the kitchen and the washing machine. You can also bring your own food into the dining area. The lobby is papered with handy tips for travelers, and there's a computer in the basement for guests to use for a small fee. The Kenigers have invested much time and energy in renovating this hotel, keeping much of the building's architectural detailing, such as ceiling moldings and mantle pieces. Mattresses are new and firm, bathrooms expertly tiled—the communal showers and toilets are a pleasure.

13 rue du Sommerard, 75005 Paris. © 01-43-54-63-81. www.hotel-marignan.com. 30 units, 10 with bathroom, 15 with toilet only. 39€–54€ ($45–$62) single; 60€–80€ ($69–$92) double; 85€–110€ ($98–$127) triple; 90€–120€ ($104–$138) quad. Continental breakfast included. No credit cards. Métro: Maubert-Mutualité or St-Michel. **Amenities:** Internet/computer room. *In room:* Hair dryer.

Hôtel St-Jacques ✦ (Finds) This beautifully preserved hotel offers a taste of the Second Empire at reasonable rates. The frescoes in the breakfast room and lounge are recent, but several rooms have restored 18th-century ceiling murals. Most of the ceilings have wedding-cake plasterwork; traditional furniture enhances the romantic effect. The hallways have been painted with *trompe l'oeil* marble and draperies. The guest rooms are spacious and well lit, with fabric-covered walls and ample closet space. Several units have balconies with views of Notre-Dame and the Panthéon. Bathrooms are immaculate and roomy, and some come with glass doors instead of shower curtains. If you don't mind climbing one flight of stairs, the guest rooms on the top floor are less expensive and have great views.

35 rue des Ecoles, 75005 Paris. ☎ **01-44-07-45-45.** Fax 01-43-25-65-50. Hotelsaintjacques@wanadoo.fr. 35 units, 32 with bathroom. 47€–55€ ($54–$63) single without bathroom or with shower only, 72€ ($82) single with bathroom; 81€–107€ ($93–$123) double with bathroom; 126€ ($145) triple with bathroom. Breakfast 7€ ($8.05), in room 8.50€ ($9.75). AE, DC, MC, V. Métro: Maubert-Mutualité. **Amenities:** Elevator. *In room:* Satellite TV, fax (on request), dataport, hair dryer, safe.

Port-Royal Hôtel ☆ (Value) This family-run hotel is a budget traveler's dream. It has the rates of a motel but the perks of a high-class hotel. The lobby is spacious and air-conditioned, halls are freshly painted, and all the guest rooms are in mint condition, decorated with colorful wallpaper and antiques. Many units have nonworking fireplaces, and several bathrooms have been redone and even have towel warmers. There is a breakfast/TV room, and a courtyard for outdoor breakfasts. Communal bathrooms are spotless. The location is away from the center, but for this quality and price it's worth the walk.

8 bd. Port-Royal, 75005 Paris. ☎ 01-43-31-70-06. Fax 01-43-31-33-67. www.portroyalhotel.fr.st. 46 units, 21 with bathroom. 37€–48€ ($43–$55) single with sink, 73€ ($84) single with bathroom; 48€ ($55) double with sink, 73€–87€ ($84–$100) double with bathroom. Shower 2.50€ ($2.90). Breakfast 5€ ($5.75). No credit cards. Métro: Gobelins. **Amenities:** Elevator. *In room:* Towel warmer.

IN & AROUND ST-GERMAIN-DES-PRÉS (6E ARRONDISSEMENT)

Postwar St-Germain was home to intellectuals like Sartre and de Beauvoir, who thought deep thoughts at the Café de Flore. Today you're more likely to find boutiques than philosophers in this pricey neighborhood. It's getting harder to find hotels within our budget here, but it's a great place to hang your hat for the night.

Hôtel des Académies (Value) This no-frills hotel may remind you of a visit to your grandmother's apartment. The small "lobby" on the first floor has a daybed, a bird cage, a clock, and various bits of homey clutter. The rooms are a little worn but clean and exceptionally low-priced for the location—near Montparnasse and a 10-minute walk from the Jardin du Luxembourg. There's no elevator, but rooms on the fourth and fifth floors are cheaper, so the climb pays for itself. The hotel is managed by an elderly couple who insist on quiet after 10pm.

15 rue de la Grande-Chaumière, 75006 Paris. ☎ **01-43-26-66-44.** Fax 01-43-26-03-72. 21 units, 12 with bathroom, 5 with shower only. 41€ ($47) single with sink and toilet, 64€ ($74) single or double with shower only, 68€ ($78) single or double with bathroom. Breakfast 7€ ($8.05). MC, V. Métro: Vavin.

Hôtel du Dragon (Moments) In the heart of St-Germain, this 17th-century hotel has a lot to offer. The sparse and slightly monastic rooms have been renovated with sparkling new bathrooms and contain wood armoires, bed frames, and tables in French country style. There is a patio for summer breakfasts, and a piano in the lounge. Rooms facing the courtyard get plenty of light. There is no elevator, but the top floor has air-conditioning, which could make up for the climb.

36 rue du Dragon, 75006 Paris. ☎ **01-45-48-51-05.** Fax 01-42-22-51-62. www.hoteldudragon.com. 28 units, 27 with bathroom, 1 with shower only. 75€ ($86) single with shower only; 95€ ($109) single or double with bathroom; 108€ ($124) triple with bathroom. Continental breakfast 8€ ($9.20). AE, MC, V. Métro: St-Germain-des-Prés or Sèvres-Babylone. *In room:* A/C (top floor only), satellite TV, dataport, hair dryer.

Hôtel du Globe ☆ (Finds) Loaded with character, this tiny hotel is not what you'd expect to find in such a posh neighborhood. The building dates from the early

17th century, and the decor resembles the 1600s on acid: exposed stone walls and beams, fabric wallpaper in antique patterns, tapestries, bizarre minicanopies over some beds, and orange 1970s bathroom fixtures in the larger rooms. The overall effect is cozy and eclectic, though some might find it just weird. The rooms with tubs are almost twice as large as the rooms with showers, so for the extra expense, you'll get a lot more than just a plumbing improvement. Rooms facing the courtyard are dark. There's no elevator, and the staircase is narrow.

15 rue des Quatre Vents, 75006 Paris. © 01-46-33-62-69. 15 units. 70€ ($81) single with shower; 90€ ($104) double with shower, 105€ ($121) double with bathtub. Breakfast 9€ ($10). MC, V. Métro: St-Sulpice.

Hôtel St-Pierre *Value* If you get a room facing the street in this stylish hotel, you will see what is left of a 13th-century convent—next to the former lodgings of celebrated actress Sarah Bernhardt. Rooms tend to be smallish, but the higher-price doubles are good-sized, and the one with the tub is large, with double sinks in the bathroom. The fabrics, wallpaper, and rugs are in good condition and the bathrooms are new. Closets are ample and windows are double-glazed. The communal toilets on each of the seven floors are immaculate.

4 rue de l'Ecole de Médecine, 75006 Paris. © 01-46-34-78-80. Fax 01-40-51-05-17. Hotel.st-pierre@ wanadoo.fr. 50 units, 45 with bathroom, 5 with shower only. 51€ ($59) single with shower only, 64€ ($74) single with bathroom; 59€ ($68) double with shower only, 74€ ($85) double with bathroom. Breakfast 5€ ($5.75). AE, MC, V. Métro: Odéon. **Amenities:** Elevator. *In room:* Satellite TV, hair dryer.

Regents Hôtel *Finds* This is a charming hotel on a quiet side street. A stone's throw from the Jardin du Luxembourg, it was completely renovated a few years ago and is quite elegant. The decor evokes the south of France, with yellow-and-blue bedspreads and wood-framed mirrors in most rooms; the bathrooms are sparkling. There's a garden overflowing with plants, where breakfast is served in summer, and a cozy indoor lounge where beverages are served. Top-floor rooms have a narrow balcony with delightful views over the rooftops. Don't expect any extra services from the somewhat surly staff, but the wonderful location and quiet atmosphere will help you overlook their shortcomings.

44 rue Madame, 75006 Paris. © 01-45-48-02-81. Fax 01-45-44-85-73. Regents.hotel@wanadoo.fr. 34 units. 80€ ($92) single or double, 98€–110€ ($113–$127) double with balcony. Breakfast 7€ ($8.05). AE, MC, V. Métro: Rennes or St-Sulpice. **Amenities:** Lounge; elevator. *In room:* Satellite TV, hair dryer.

IN & AROUND THE MARAIS (3E, 4E & 11E ARRONDISSEMENTS)

Crisscrossed with narrow, medieval streets and dotted with 17th-century mansions, the Marais is one of the hippest neighborhoods of Paris. Here you can find boutiques and restaurants, a happening gay scene, several museums, and the remnants of the city's Jewish quarter. Hotels book up fast and this is the most challenging area in which to find hotels within our budget. Farther east, the Bastille area offers a wealth of nightspots and a huge modern opera house—an architectural masterpiece or an eyesore, depending on your outlook.

Grand Hôtel Jeanne D'Arc *Finds* Reserve well in advance for this great little hotel near all the major attractions in the area. Housed in an 18th-century building on the place Marché St-Catharine (a lovely square lush with Chinese mulberry trees), the lobby includes a mirror framed in mosaics, and the walls in the breakfast room are hand-painted by local artists. Rooms are colorful and decent-sized and have large bathrooms, but none have views of the square.

3 rue de Jarente, 75004 Paris. © 01-48-87-62-11. Fax 01-48-87-37-31. www.hoteljeannedarc.com. 36 units. 55€–78€ ($63–$90) single; 78€–92€ ($90–$106) double; 108€ ($124) triple; 125€ ($144) quad. Breakfast 5.80€ ($6.70). MC, V. Métro: St-Paul or Bastille. **Amenities:** Elevator. *In room:* Satellite TV, hair dryer, safe.

Hôtel Beaumarchais ✦✦ *Finds*   Situated at the start of ultracool rue Oberkampf, this hotel offers high style for a reasonable price. Rooms are decorated with hyper-modern furniture in bold primary colors, gooseneck lamps, and rugs that could have been designed by Jackson Pollock. Windows have recently been soundproofed, and air-conditioning units have been added in all but three rooms. Bathrooms have recently been overhauled, and their walls are now covered in tile shards and mirror pieces. There's a lovely magnolia tree in the courtyard, where breakfast is served in summer.

3 rue Oberkampf, 75011 Paris. © 01-53-36-86-86. Fax 01-43-38-32-86. www.hotelbeaumarchais.com. 31 units. 69€ ($79) single; 85€–99€ ($98–$114) double. Continental breakfast in breakfast room 7€ ($8.05), in room 9€ ($10). AE, MC, V. Métro: Filles du Calvaire or Oberkampf. **Amenities:** Elevator. *In room:* A/C, satellite TV, hair dryer, safe.

Hôtel de Nevers   Don't mistake this hotel for another in the 7e with the same name. The ebullient Alain Bourdereau, his wife Sophie, and their cats will enthusiastically welcome you to this well-tended hotel. A 1930s vintage wood-paneled elevator brings you to average-size rooms papered with floral prints. The triples on the sixth floor have skylights, sloping ceilings, and views over the rooftops. Double rooms with twin beds are a little bigger, but the beds are quite narrow. Carpets were replaced in 2002 when the rooms were repainted; walls are thin, so if you're a light sleeper, bring earplugs. There is not one TV to be found in this hotel, but there is a computer with free Internet access for guests in the lobby.

53 rue de Malte, 75011 Paris. © 01-47-00-56-18. Fax 01-43-57-77-39. www.hoteldenevers.com. 32 units, 22 with bathroom, 10 with shower only. 32€ ($37) single or double with sink, 42€ ($48) single or double with shower only, 45€–48€ ($52–$55) single or double with bathroom; 60€–74€ ($69–$85) triple with bathroom. Breakfast 4.20€ ($4.85). Shower 4€ ($4.60). MC, V. Métro: République. **Amenities:** Elevator.

Hôtel du Vieux Saule ✦   Smart travelers make tracks for this lovely hotel in the northern Marais that offers not only air-conditioning and Internet access (free for guests in the salon) but a sauna as well. The cheerful, smallish rooms come with satellite TV, trouser press, and small irons with ironing boards. Deluxe rooms on the top floor are large and have slanted ceilings and big bathrooms. You may wish to skip the expensive breakfast and find a cafe tucked away in this neighborhood laced with tiny, narrow streets left over from the medieval era.

6 rue de Picardie, 75003 Paris. © 01-42-72-01-14. Fax 01-40-27-88-21. www.hotelvieuxsaule.com. 31 units. 76€ ($87) single; 91€–121€ ($105–$139) double. Breakfast 9€ ($10). AE, DC, MC, V. Métro: République or Filles du Calvaire. **Amenities:** Free sauna; laundry service; nonsmoking rooms; elevator. *In room:* A/C, satellite TV w/pay movies, hair dryer, iron, safe, trouser press.

Hôtel Sansonnet ✦ *Value*   This cozy hotel, in the southern part of the Marais, is within walking distance of the Centre Pompidou and Les Halles, and just a few paces from the BHV department store and other great shopping on rue de Rivoli. The staircase has a wrought-iron railing, but there is no elevator. The 20 rooms with bathrooms were all painted in warm colors in 2003 and have double-glazed windows and new carpet. The bathrooms are spotless. The management works hard to make sure guests are comfortable.

48 rue de la Verrerie, 75004 Paris. © 01-48-87-96-14. Fax 01-48-87-30-46. www.hotel-sansonnet.com. 25 units, 21 with bathroom, 4 with shower only. 45€ ($52) single with sink, 54€ ($62) single with shower only, 64€–68€ ($74–$78) single with bathroom; 59€ ($68) double with shower only, 74€–78€ ($85–$90) double with bathroom. Breakfast 6.70€ ($7.70). MC, V. Métro: Hôtel de Ville. **Amenities:** Dry cleaning. *In room:* Satellite TV, hair dryer.

Hôtel Sévigné ✦   Just off the rue de Rivoli in the Marais, this comfortable hotel offers a great location and clean, recently spruced-up rooms. There are some great views of the Church of St-Paul for those who don't mind a bit of street noise. Windows are double-glazed and mattresses are firm. Some rooms on the second, third, and fifth floors have narrow balconies.

2 rue Malher, 75004 Paris. ℭ 01-42-72-76-17. Fax 01-42-72-98-28. www.le-sevigne.com. 30 units. 61€ ($70) single; 71€–83€ ($82–$95) double; 98€ ($113) triple. Breakfast 6.40€ ($7.35). MC, V. Métro: St-Paul. **Amenities:** Elevator. *In room:* Satellite TV.

NEAR THE EIFFEL TOWER

The upside: If you stay in this swanky neighborhood, you will be close to the Eiffel Tower and you'll be in a charming residential neighborhood. The downside: You will not be alone. With the Musée d'Orsay and the Invalides in the vicinity, this elegant arrondissement is in constant demand—so book early.

Grand Hôtel Lévêque ⭐ *Value* As you enter, you will pass a collection of framed pages from guidebooks (including this one) hailing the virtues of this venerable establishment. On a colorful market street that is car-free, this large hotel offers good-size rooms, recently renovated with new if not inspired decorations. Air-conditioning was added to every room in 2002; all rooms come with fans, too. The bathrooms are small but in excellent condition and come with shower doors. Staff members are friendly and helpful; if you ask, they may be able to give you a higher-priced room on the fifth floor with a balcony and partial view of the Eiffel Tower. For the price, this is a great deal.

29 rue Cler, 75007 Paris. ℭ 01-47-05-49-15. Fax 01-45-50-49-36. www.hotel-leveque.com. 50 units. 53€ ($61) single; 84€–91€ ($97–$105) double; 114€ ($131) triple. Continental breakfast 7€ ($8.05). AE, MC, V. Métro: Ecole-Militaire or Latour-Maubourg. **Amenities:** Elevator; soda and ice machines. *In room:* A/C, satellite TV, hair dryer, safe (3€/$3.45).

Hôtel Amélie ⭐ *Kids* Hôtel Amélie is as pretty on the outside as its name suggests, with flowerpots brimming at each window. The interior is modest, with small, pleasant rooms. Closets are small, but the bathrooms, renovated in 2002, offer sparkling tiles and good-quality toiletries. Rooms facing the courtyard are brighter than those facing the street. Despite the central location, the atmosphere is peaceful, almost serene. There is no elevator. The Orvilles, the young couple who own the hotel, have kids of their own and are friendly to visitors with little ones.

5 rue Amélie, 75007 Paris. ℭ 01-45-51-74-75. Fax 01-45-56-93-55. www.hotelamelie.fr. 16 units. 82€ ($94) single; 85€–92€ ($98–$106) double; 93€–100€ ($107–$115) twin. Breakfast 7€ ($8.05). AE, DC, MC, V. Métro: Latour-Maubourg. *In room:* Satellite TV, dataport, minibar, hair dryer.

Hôtel de L'Alma ⭐ *Value* This pleasant hotel is on what may be one of the narrowest (and quietest) streets in Paris, a few minutes' walk from the rue Cler market. The hotel is being renovated at the rate of one room per month. Though rather small, rooms are clean and bright with colorful wallpaper and white bathrooms. The new rooms have heavy fabrics with deep burgundy and blue colors, writing desks, new mattresses, and new fixtures in the bathrooms. Top-floor rooms have rooftop views, and no. 64 boasts a view of the Eiffel Tower but usually costs an additional 20€ to 30€ ($23–$35), though it never hurts to ask at check-in for a complimentary upgrade. There is a small garden where breakfast is served in summer, and an Internet cafe a few doors down. Many of the guests are young Americans, affiliated with the American University nearby. When reserving, be sure to identify yourself as a Frommer's reader to qualify for the discount.

32 rue de l'Exposition, 75007 Paris. ℭ 01-47-05-45-70. Fax 01-45-51-84-47. almahotel@minitel.net. 31 units. Special rate for *Frommer's* readers: 72€ ($83) single; 78€ ($90) double. Rates include breakfast. AE, DC, MC, V. Métro: Ecole-Militaire or Alma Marceau. **Amenities:** Elevator. *In room:* Satellite TV, minibar.

Hôtel du Champ de Mars ★★ *(Finds)*   This hotel is a gem tucked around the corner from a market street near the Eiffel Tower. The entire place, from the elegant facade to the cloth-covered chairs in the breakfast room, is as chic as you'd find in a luxury boutique hotel. Flowing curtains, fabric-covered headboards, throw pillows, and high-backed seats make each room charming and comfortable. Bathrooms are in mint condition. Reserve at least 2 months in advance as this hotel is very popular with visiting Americans.

7 rue du Champ de Mars, 75007 Paris. ℰ **01-45-51-52-30.** Fax 01-45-51-64-36. www.hotel-du-champ-de-mars.com. 25 units. 68€–74€ ($78–$85) single; 74€–78€ ($85–$90) double; 94€ ($108) triple. Continental breakfast 6.50€ ($7.50). MC, V. Métro: Ecole-Militaire. RER: Pont de l'Alma. **Amenities:** Elevator. *In room:* Satellite TV, hair dryer.

Hôtel Prince ★   In a stately building near the Eiffel Tower, the Hôtel Prince offers modern, soundproof accommodations with big bathrooms. Lively orange and yellow curtains brighten the rooms, which vary in size but are all comfortable and well kept. If you're too worn out from sightseeing to stagger out the door for meals, the hotel will arrange for a local restaurant to deliver a meal. There's a ground-floor room with facilities for travelers with disabilities.

66 av. Bosquet, 75007 Paris. ℰ **01-47-05-40-90.** Fax 01-47-53-06-62. www.hotel-prince.com. 30 units. 69€ ($79) single; 83€–107€ ($95–$123) double; 115€ ($132) triple. Cold buffet breakfast 7€ ($8.05). AE, DC, MC, V. Métro: Ecole-Militaire. **Amenities:** Elevator. *In room:* Satellite TV, minibar, hair dryer.

IN THE 9E ARRONDISSEMENT
NEAR THE GARE DE L'EST

Although this isn't the most glamorous neighborhood, you'll be near Métro stations with a lot of lines. The area is full of fast-food outlets, cafes, and grocery stores. The Gare de l'Est station becomes rather seedy at night.

Hôtel Little Regina ★★ *(Value)*   Run by the Corbel family since the 1960s, this hotel's warm atmosphere and relatively spacious rooms are a great bargain. The recently renovated rooms are soundproof and have new rugs and furniture, burgundy wallpaper, ample wardrobe space, full-length mirrors, and white-oak desks. The sparkling bathrooms have all been redone. Breakfast can be served in your room, or you can amble downstairs and check out the new breakfast area. The hotel's proximity to the train stations keeps the streets hopping with people until late into the night. Upon arrival, show your Frommer's guide to Mr. Corbel and he'll offer a 20% discount.

89 bd. de Strasbourg, 75009 Paris. ℰ **01-40-37-72-30.** Fax 01-40-36-34-14. www.littleregina.com. 34 units. 57€ ($66) single; 65€ ($75) double. Breakfast 5€ ($5.75). AE, MC, V. Métro: Gare de l'Est. **Amenities:** Elevator. *In room:* TV, hair dryer.

NEAR MONTMARTRE

The Basilica of Sacré Coeur, the Moulin Rouge, and the hectic place de Tertre (which could be renamed "place de Tourisme") are only some of the attractions in this outer arrondissement. The network of streets that wind down the hill from the basilica form an intimate village that seems far removed from the rest of Paris. Dining options are plentiful, if less than outstanding, but you'll be near the newly trendy nightlife on place Pigalle. The Marché aux Puces de la Porte de St-Ouen, the city's most famous flea market, is another landmark a short distance north.

Hôtel Navarin et d'Angleterre *(Value)*   Nestled in a quiet, villagelike neighborhood at the foot of Montmartre, this hotel has been managed by the Maylin family for more than 25 years. The lobby was recently renovated; the guest rooms are in good, if not mint, condition. Rooms with twin beds offer the most space. All units have French windows that let in ample light, but those facing the street are noticeably brighter. Bathrooms are clean, but small. During the warmer months, breakfast is served on a garden patio with an acacia tree. If you book a room facing the garden, you'll be wakened by singing birds.

8 rue de Navarin, 75009 Paris. 🕿 **01-48-78-31-80.** Fax 01-48-74-14-09. Navarin-anglettere@wanadoo.fr. 26 units, 24 with bathroom, 2 with toilet only. 55€ ($63) single with toilet only, 66€ ($76) single with bathroom; 60€ ($69) double with toilet only, 75€ ($86) double with bathroom; 90€ ($104) triple with bathroom. Breakfast 8€ ($9.20). MC, V. Métro: St-Georges or Notre-Dame de Lorettes. **Amenities:** Elevator. *In room:* TV.

NEAR THE GARE ST-LAZARE

Hausmann's famous boulevards radiate out from the neighborhood's center, the ornate Opéra Garnier, and you'll never be far from shopping in this busy middle-class neighborhood. Two of Paris's most visited department stores are here—Galeries Lafayette and Printemps. The Gare St-Lazare train station connects Paris with points west in Normandy, making the neighborhood a good choice for travelers heading to World War II sites.

Hôtel de Parme   This well-managed place is in a quiet neighborhood near the Gare St-Lazare and offers basic, clean accommodations. The English-speaking manager, M. Cornilleau, renovated all the rooms a few years ago, covering the walls with powder-blue wallpaper. The 1970s-style wood furniture and spacious bathrooms are plain but well maintained. Good-size armoires provide storage space, and double-glazed windows keep street noise out. There's one toilet per floor, shared by three rooms, but only one public shower in the hotel. TVs are available in about half the rooms.

61 rue de Clichy, 75009 Paris. 🕿 **01-48-74-40-41.** Fax 01-53-21-91-84. 36 units, 17 with bathroom, 9 with sink only, 10 with shower only. 32€ ($37) single or double with sink only, 40€ ($46) single or double with shower only, 45€–50€ ($52–$58) single or double with bathroom; 60€ ($69) twin or triple with bathroom. Shower 3€ ($3.45). Breakfast 5€ ($5.75). MC, V. Métro: Place Clichy, Trinité, or Liège. **Amenities:** Elevator.

IN & AROUND MONTPARNASSE (14E ARRONDISSEMENT)

The Tour Montparnasse looms over a neighborhood of department stores, crêperies, and literary cafes such as La Coupole. The quarter is also close to havens such as Cimitière de Montparnasse and the Jardin du Luxembourg.

Celtic Hôtel *Value*   In a central Montparnasse location not far from the Square Delambre, the Gare Montparnasse, and the Cimitière de Montparnasse, this hotel is a very good deal. It has cozy features such as (nonworking) fireplaces in many of the surprisingly large rooms. Fifth-floor rooms offer superb views of the Eiffel Tower from narrow balconies. There is no elevator.

15 rue d'Odessa, 75014 Paris. 🕿 **01-43-20-93-53** or 01-43-20-83-91. Fax 01-43-20-66-07. Hotelceltic@ wanadoo.fr. 29 units, 21 with bathroom, 5 with shower only. 43€ ($49) single with sink, 54€ ($62) single or double with shower, 57€ ($66) single or double with bathroom. Shower 3€ ($3.45). Breakfast 3€ ($3.45). MC, V. Métro: Montparnasse or Edgar Quinet. *In room:* Satellite TV.

Hôtel des Bains *Finds*   This quiet hotel is a budget traveler's delight, offering excellent quality and value. A walk from the attractive lobby through the courtyard brings you to a separate building with a winding staircase that leads to three brand-new suites (each on its own floor), with large bathrooms and ample storage space—a boon for families. The elevator in the main building runs to a landing between floors, so you will have to manage some stairs. The rooms were overhauled in 2002 and have either carpeted or frequently waxed wooden floors, desks with reading lights, and bright bedspreads and draperies. Bathrooms are freshly renovated; some showers have smoked-glass doors. Book early.

33 rue Delambre, 75014 Paris. 📞 **01-43-20-85-27.** Fax 01-42-79-82-78. des.bains.hotel@wanadoo.fr. 42 units. 71€ ($82) single or double with 1 bed; 74€ ($85) twin; 91€ ($105) suite for 2, 114€ ($131) suite for 3, 137€ ($158) suite for 4. Buffet breakfast 7€ ($8.05). Métro: Vavin or Edgar-Quinet. **Amenities:** Elevator. *In room:* Satellite TV, hair dryer, safe, trouser press.

YOUTH HOSTELS

Paris has plenty of youth hostels *(auberges de jeunesse)* and *foyers* (literally "homes") to accommodate the hordes of young travelers who descend every summer. Quality differs greatly from place to place, but the superior hostels offer excellent value. Many welcome travelers regardless of age. Hostels in Paris are an especially good deal for solo travelers, since you will meet fellow travelers and since a bed is often less expensive than a single hotel room.

Hostels are starting to take reservations in advance—but there are still some that don't. If you arrive late in the day without a reservation, head to one of the offices of **OTU Voyages,** 119 rue St-Martin in the 4e (Métro: Châtelet); 39 rue George Bernanous in the 5e (Métro: Port Royal); or 2 rue Malus in the 5e (Métro: Place Monge). The phone number for all three is the same: 📞 **01-49-72-57-00.** The staff will help you find lodgings in hostels, budget hotels, or (in summer) University of Paris dorms. They will also negotiate discount rail, bus, and plane tickets; issue student IDs; and provide details about activities of special interest to young people. The offices are open Monday to Friday 10am to 6:30pm, Saturday 10am to 5pm.

The **Office de Tourisme et des Congrès de Paris,** 127 av. des Champs-Elysées, 75008 Paris (📞 **01-49-52-53-35;** Métro: Charles-de-Gaulle–Etoile or George V), will book you a bed in a hostel for a 1€ ($1.15) fee.

Auberge Internationale des Jeunes *(Value* Near place de la Bastille and the nightlife along rue de Charonne, this hostel was renovated in the mid-1990s and offers a higher level of comfort than most Paris hostels. Most rooms contain two to four beds, and about half have bathrooms. Common showers and toilets are on each floor. The hostel is open 24 hours and has an Internet connection (.15€/20¢ per min.).

10 rue Trousseau, 75011 Paris. 📞 **01-47-00-62-00.** Fax 01-47-00-33-16. www.aijparis.com. 50 units, 22 with bathroom. 14€ ($16) per person. Rates include bed sheet and breakfast. MC, V. Métro: Ledru-Rollin.

B.V.J. Louvre Run by the Union des Centres de Rencontres Internationales de France, this hostel is friendly, and its location is excellent. There are 2 to 10 beds in each room, and showers and toilets on each floor. Open 24 hours. UCRIF also runs **B.V.J. Quartier Latin,** 44 rue des Bernardins, 5e (📞 **01-43-29-34-80;** Métro: Maubert-Mutualité), in the Latin Quarter. All rooms have showers, with toilets down the hall. There are some singles, costing 30€ ($35), and double rooms are 27€ ($31) per person; a bed in a room with 10 others is 25€ ($29). Breakfast is included.

20 rue Jean-Jacques-Rousseau, 75001 Paris. 📞 **01-53-00-90-90.** Fax 01-53-00-90-91. 204 beds. 24€ ($28) per person. Rate includes continental breakfast. MC, V. Métro: Palais-Royal–Musée du Louvre.

Youth Hostel le Fauconnier *(Finds* Run by the Maisons Internationales de la Jeunesse et des Etudiants, this hostel is in a historic *hôtel particulier,* or private home, on a quiet street in the Marais, near the Seine. Le Fauconnier has a pleasant courtyard and a beautiful staircase. All the rooms have private showers, and some rooms are singles or doubles—unusual for hostels. Be warned, however, that this hostel is often overrun by groups, so book in advance. Doors close at 1am.

Other MIJE hostels are nearby: **Maubuisson,** 12 rue des Barres, 4e, with 111 beds; and **Fourcy,** 6 rue de Fourcy, 4e, with 190 beds. The rates are identical to Le Fauconnier's. Reservations and information are available at the number listed below.

11 rue du Fauconnier, 75004 Paris. © **01-42-74-23-45.** Fax 01-40-27-81-64. www.mije.com. 135 beds. 24€–26€ ($28–$30) per person in multi-bed room; 30€–36€ ($35–$41) twin; 40€–47€ ($46–$54) single. Rates include continental breakfast. Maximum stay 7 nights. No credit cards. Métro: St-Paul or Pont-Marie.

WORTH A SPLURGE

Grand Hôtel des Balcons 😊 *Value*   Denise and Pierre Corroyer take pride in this gracious hotel, which has modern light-oak furnishings, bright fabrics, and new beds. The stairwells have 19th-century stained-glass windows, and their Art Nouveau design is echoed in the lobby furnishings. All rooms facing the street have small balconies. Although most rooms are small, clever use of space allows for large closets and full-length mirrors. Bathrooms are small but well designed. The higher-priced doubles, triples, and quads are big and luxurious; some have double-sink bathrooms and a separate toilet.

3 Casimir Delavigne, 75006 Paris. © **01-46-34-78-50.** Fax 01-46-34-06-27. www.balcons.com. 50 units. 100€–120€ ($115–$138) single; 100€–150€ ($115–$173) double; 180€ ($201) triple or quad. Buffet breakfast 10€ ($12). AE, DC, MC, V. Métro: Odéon. RER: Luxembourg. **Amenities:** Elevator. *In room:* Satellite TV, dataport, hair dryer.

Hôtel Alison 😊 *Kids*   Surrounded by the rue St-Honoré shopping district and several embassies, this hotel has a sleek, upscale ambience. The large, well-appointed rooms are furnished in a modern style, with black furniture and light walls. The two sets of adjoining rooms on the top floor are great for families.

21 rue de Surène, 75008 Paris. © **01-42-65-54-00.** Fax 01-42-65-08-17. www.hotel-alison.com. 35 units. 78€–110€ ($90–$127) single; 110€–140€ ($127–$161) double. Breakfast 8€ ($9.20). AE, DC, MC, V. Métro: Madeleine or Concorde. **Amenities:** Elevator. *In room:* Satellite TV, dataport, minibar, hair dryer, safe, trouser press.

Hôtel Axial Beaubourg 😊😊   If you like sleek, modern hotels, this is a great choice in a neighborhood known for its more traditional offerings. Its modern, air-conditioned interior is reminiscent of a luxury hotel. Some rooms come with wood-beamed ceilings; all come with dark green drapes and bedspreads and high-thread-count cotton sheets. The bathrooms are sparkling and new, if a bit small. Skip the pricey continental breakfast and amble down to one of several neighborhood cafes just a few steps away.

11 rue du Temple, 75004 Paris. © **01-42-72-72-22.** Fax 01-42-72-03-53. www.axialbeaubourg.com. 39 units. 105€–120€ ($121–$138) single; 140€–175€ ($161–$201) double. Continental breakfast 10€ ($12). AE, DC, MC, V. Métro: Hôtel de Ville. **Amenities:** Laundry/dry cleaning; elevator. *In room:* A/C, satellite TV, dataport, minibar, safe.

Hôtel des Marronniers 😊😊 *Finds*   You might miss the entrance to this delightful hotel—it's in the back of a courtyard on a street lined with antiques stores. Rooms have exposed beams, period furniture, and fabric-covered walls in rich reds or blues. Some bathrooms have ceramic tiling over the tub, and rooms facing the garden have a view of the steeple of St-Germain-des-Prés. The off-street location makes this hotel incredibly peaceful. Book 3 months in advance.

21 rue Jacob, 75006 Paris. © **01-43-25-30-60.** Fax 01-40-46-83-56. www.hotel-marronniers.com. 37 units. 110€–$127) single; 150€–190€ ($173–$219) double; 195€ ($224) triple. Extra bed 38€ ($44). Breakfast 10€ ($12), in room 12€ ($14). MC, V. Métro: St-Germain-des-Prés. **Amenities:** Elevator. *In room:* A/C, TV, hair dryer.

Hôtel du Bois 😊😊 *Finds*   A magnificent location and discreet elegance keep this gem of a place buzzing with returning guests, many of them French. On a side street that juts onto the chic boulevard Victor-Hugo, the Hôtel du Bois has warmly decorated rooms, filled with amenities found in deluxe hotels. Mornings, you could skip breakfast and walk down to one of the city's most renowned patisseries, **Le Nôtre,** 2 blocks away, for croissants. *Note:* To avoid stairs with your luggage, be sure to arrive at the rue du Dôme address.

11 rue du Dôme (at 29 av. Victor-Hugo), 75016 Paris. ℂ **01-45-00-31-96.** Fax 01-45-00-90-05. www.hotel dubois.com. 41 units. 105€ ($121) small single; 129€–135€ ($148–$155) standard double, 165€ ($190) deluxe double. Extra bed 50€ ($58). Breakfast 12€ ($14). AE, MC, V. Métro: Kleber or Victor-Hugo. RER: Etoile. **Amenities:** Elevator. *In room:* Satellite TV, minibar, hair dryer, safe.

Hôtel Mansart 🖈🖈 *(Finds)* This elegant hotel's location may be the best in Paris. Behind the Ritz and steps away from the swanky place de la Vendôme, the Mansart offers old-world luxury at bargain prices. The least expensive doubles are a bargain but are not huge; the more spacious doubles come with two windows, marble-topped dressers, full-length mirrors, and heavy drapes. All bathrooms are new, white, and sparkling.

5 rue des Capucines, 75001 Paris. ℂ **01-42-61-50-28.** Fax 01-49-27-97-44. Hotel.mansart@wanadoo.fr. 57 units. 106€–178€ ($122–$204) double; from 242€ ($278) suite. Breakfast 10€ ($12). AE, MC, V. Métro: Tuileries or Concorde. **Amenities:** Elevator. *In room:* Satellite TV, minibar, hair dryer.

3 Great Deals on Dining

The key to fine dining on a budget is to eat where Parisians eat and to stay away from most restaurants around major tourist attractions. Opt for restaurants in neighborhoods where people live and work, which must keep their prices and quality competitive to satisfy their regular customers. Save your appetite for lunch and enjoy a light meal of café au lait and croissants or a buttered baguette called a *tartine.* Unless the price of your hotel room includes breakfast, go to a cafe and stand at the counter. The experience is inimitably Parisian. You'll rub shoulders with workers downing shots of Calvados with their espresso, and executives perusing the morning *Figaro* before work. The price will also be about 40% to 50% lower at the counter than for sit-down waiter service.

Lunch is an important meal in Paris, and you might want to make it your main meal of the day. The majority of restaurants, bistros, and cafes offer a fixed-price weekday lunch called a **menu du jour** or **formule,** a two- or three-course meal that sometimes includes wine. This can be a terrific bargain, allowing you to eat at otherwise unaffordable restaurants. A few places offer the same menu at dinner, but it will be more expensive, though still cheaper than ordering a la carte.

While lunch is important, dinner is *le plus important,* so if you were galloping through the Louvre all day and grabbed a crepe on the street for lunch, unwind during dinner at a leisurely French pace. Even if you're not feeling flush, you can find a restaurant that offers a wonderful meal at an affordable price, particularly since so many places offer a prix-fixe menu (called *formule* or *menu du*

Moments A Parisian *Pique-nique*

One of the best ways to save money is to picnic. Go to a *fromagerie* for some cheese; to a *boulangerie* for a baguette or two; to a *charcuterie* for some pâté, sausage, or salad; and to a *pâtisserie* for some luscious pastries. Add a friendly bottle of Côtes du Rhone and you'll have the makings of a delightful meal.

> ## *Value* Getting the Best Deal on Dining
>
> - Fill up at lunch when you can get a three-course *menu du jour* or *formule* for a fraction of the price you'd pay at dinner.
> - Stop at sidewalk stands for inexpensive sandwiches and crepes.
> - Crêperies (there are many off the bd. du Montparnasse at the Sq. Delambre) offer great value; you can order meat- or vegetable-filled galettes and dessert crepes in Brittany-inspired surroundings.
> - Order the *plat du jour* for lunch or dinner.
> - Avoid the huge markup on bottled water by ordering *une carafe d'eau*—tap water.
> - Remember that house wine is cheaper than soda.
> - Don't eat breakfast at your hotel. Instead, grab a croissant or *pain au chocolat* from a boulangerie and drink your coffee standing up at a cafe counter for about 1.50€ ($1.70).

jour, as noted above). Another tip: Many ethnic restaurants in Paris are inexpensive and worth trying for some spice in your life. Think couscous!

DINING ESTABLISHMENTS   Bistros, brasseries, and restaurants offer different dining experiences. The typical **bistro** used to be a mom-and-pop operation with a menu of Parisian standbys like *oeuf mayonnaise* (egg salad), *boeuf bourguignon* (cubes of beef in red wine, onions, and mushrooms), and *tarte tatin* (an apple tart). Today many bistros have expanded on the classics while retaining the tradition of hearty, relatively low-priced dishes in a convivial atmosphere. Most **brasseries** are large, cheerful places that open early and close late. Today, all brasseries (except Brasserie Ile St-Louis in the 1er) are part of one chain. While this does not detract from the charm of the legendary eateries, watch out for mundane and repetitive food—it's out there. At brasseries you can usually get a meal at any time of day, and the food is relatively inexpensive. **Restaurants** are where you go to savor French cuisine in all its glory. Classic dishes are expertly interpreted, and new taste sensations are invented. Dining is more formal than in bistros or brasseries, and service is slower. Like bistros, restaurants serve lunch between noon and 2:30pm and dinner between 7:30 and 10pm. Parisians usually dine between 8:30 and 9pm.

IN THE LATIN QUARTER (5E ARRONDISSEMENT)

Le Coupe-Chou *ℛ* FRENCH   If medieval Parisian ambience is what you're looking for, come here, where you'll enjoy sumptuous French bistro cuisine in a series of intimate rooms lit by candles and firelight. Simple puréed vegetable soup or the heartier *Salade Coup-Chou* make an excellent start, followed by a perfect duck breast or succulent leg of lamb.

11 rue de Lanneau, 5e. ⓒ **01-46-33-68-69.** 2-course menu 24€ ($28); 3-course dinner menu 32€ ($37); main courses 14€–21€ ($16–$24). AE, DC, MC, V. Mon-Sat noon–2pm; daily 7pm–1am. Métro: Maubert-Mutualité.

Le Grenier de Notre-Dame *ℛ* *Finds* VEGETARIAN   You may feel like you've just entered a green house, with everything from the tablecloths to the walls to the outdoor patio blanketed in various shades of the verdant color, but it goes with the cuisine you'll find here, which is worth a try. Especially recommended is *cassoulet végétarien*, with white beans, onions, tomatoes, and soy sausage; couscous and cauliflower au gratin are also delicious. And don't forget desserts, such as *tarte de tofu*, for which Le Grenier has a well-deserved reputation. The wine list includes a variety of organic offerings.

18 rue de la Bûcherie, 5e. ℂ 01-43-29-98-29. 3-course menu 13€ ($14); main courses 10€–15€ ($12–$17). MC, V. Sun noon–3pm; Mon–Thurs 12:30–3pm; Fri–Sat noon–2:30pm and 7–11pm; Sun–Thurs 7–10:30pm. Métro: Maubert-Mutualité.

Restaurant Perraudin 🐐 CLASSIC BISTRO   The first reason to come here? If you present your Frommer's guide, you get a free aperitif known as a *communard*, kir made with red bordeaux. The second reason? The service is some of the best in the city, the food is great, and on the walls are pictures of turn-of-the-20th-century Paris when the restaurant opened—*très* cool. The bargain lunch menu offers a choice of three appetizers, two main courses, and cheese or dessert. You might start with tomatoes and mozzarella, then have ham with endives or roast beef, followed by baba au rhum. Classic dishes like duck confit and *gigot d'agneau* with gratin Dauphinois are on the a la carte menu.

157 rue St-Jacques, 5e. ℂ 01-46-33-15-75. 3-course lunch 18€ ($21); 3-course gastronomic menu 26€ ($30); main courses 11€–15€ ($13–$17). No credit cards. Tues–Fri noon–2:15pm; Mon–Sat 7:30–10:15pm. Métro: Luxembourg.

IN ST-GERMAIN-DES-PRÉS (6E & 7E ARRONDISSEMENTS)

Au Pied du Fouet *Value* CLASSIC BISTRO   This minuscule place in one of the most expensive parts of Paris is extremely popular with people who could pay much more. The cooking's homey and appetizing, if never surprising. Start with a salad of hot shredded cabbage with bacon, followed by chicken livers and then by a slice of runny Camembert or maybe an apple tart. Coffee's taken at the bar to make way for the next round of hungry, pennywise diners.

45 rue de Babylone, 7e. ℂ 01-47-05-12-27. Main courses 9€–11€ ($10–$13). No credit cards. Mon–Sat noon–2:30pm; Mon–Fri 7–9:45pm. Closed Aug. Métro: Vaneau.

Bistro Mazarin 🐐 BISTRO   Not far from the St-Germain church, this charming bistro attracts the locals who work in this historic neighborhood. In either of two dining rooms, whose wood paneling has been congenially battered over the years, you can order classics like *petit sale* of pork (salt pork), prepared like a stew; boeuf bourguignon; a midwinter selection of fresh oysters; veal chops sautéed with butter-and-lemon sauce; and a satisfying combination of lentils with charcuterie and herbs. The portions are large, and everything can be washed down with reasonably priced wine. The heaters on the flowery sidewalk provide enough warmth so you can take your meal outdoors in any season.

42 rue Mazarin, 6e. ℂ 01-43-29-99-01. Main courses 10€–16€ ($12–$18). AE, MC, V. Daily noon–3pm and 7:30pm–midnight. Métro: Odéon.

Bouillon Racine *Moments* BELGIAN   This gorgeous Belgian brasserie with its tiled floor and tables, iridescent lime-green walls, and shimmering mirrors is

---

Value Street Eats

You can find a large variety of affordable street food sold everywhere from the Latin Quarter to outside the *grands magasins* on the Right Bank. Tasty grilled sandwiches called *paninis*, crepes, *gaufres* (Belgian waffles with powdered sugar or chocolate sauce), and *frites* are just a few of the items available. All are easy to chow down on if you're on the run.

worth coming to just to admire its breathtaking Belle Epoque style. Fortunately, the food is really good, too, and the selection of beer even better.

3 rue Racine, 6e. ℂ 01-44-32-15-60. 2-course lunch menu 15€ ($17); 3-course menu 25€ ($29); main courses 14€–21€ ($16–$24). AE, MC, V. Daily noon–1am. Métro: Cluny-Sorbonne or Odéon.

La Cigale ⚐ BISTRO   This is a great place to escape the Paris rain with its warm, sunny, yellow walls and heavenly soufflés filled with Camembert, sautéed spinach, poultry, herbs, or vegetables. Other entrées include rump roast and succulent lamb chops. With such great food at very affordable prices, you may find yourself sitting next to a struggling artist or a government minister whose office is nearby. Don't forget dessert, like the sinful chocolate soufflé.

11 bis rue de Chomel, 7e. ℂ 01-45-48-87-87. Reservations recommended. Main courses 9€–18€ ($10–$21). DC, MC, V. Mon–Fri noon–2pm; Mon–Sat 7:30–11pm. Métro: Sèvres-Babylone.

La Fontaine de Mars ⚐ FRENCH   This cozy restaurant is quintessentially Parisian with its red-and-white checkered tablecloths and its windows overlooking pretty Rue Dominique. The food is homey, scrumptious, and filling; no need to order an appetizer. Try the roast duck with garlic potatoes and mushrooms (16€/$18); or the duck and sausage stew with white beans, bacon, and tomato sauce (21€/$24). During the summer you can do your daydreaming on the lovely patio overlooking the fountain.

129 rue St-Dominique, 7e. ℂ 01-47-05-46-44. Reservations required during warmer months. Weekly 2-course lunch menu 15€ ($17); main courses 13€–24€ ($15–$28). V. Daily noon–3pm and 7:30–11pm. Métro: Ecole-Militaire.

Le Polidor ⚐ CLASSIC BISTRO   There is a festive air at this 150-year-old bistro, with people sitting elbow to elbow at picnic-style tables covered with red-and-white checkered tablecloths and walls lined with smoky mirrors with the daily specials written on them. The cooking is earthy and homey, with all desserts and ice creams made on the premises. Begin with spinach salad with nut oil, followed by solid plates of *rognons en madere* (kidneys in Madeira sauce), *blanquette de veau,* boeuf bourguignon, or *ragoût* of pork. Save room for a selection from the array of fresh tartes and pies.

41 rue Monsieur-le-Prince, 6e. ℂ 01-43-26-95-34. 2-course weekday lunch menu 10€ ($12); 3-course dinner menu 18€ ($21); main courses 7€–12€ ($8.05–$14). No credit cards. Mon–Sat noon–2:30pm and 7pm–12:30am; Sun 7–11pm. Métro: Odéon.

NEAR THE CENTRE POMPIDOU (4E ARRONDISSEMENT)

Bistrot de Beaubourg *Value* CLASSIC BISTRO   This cheap bistro, a few steps from the Centre Pompidou, attracts a hip, intellectual crowd. Admire the theater and literature posters on the walls while enjoying the hearty and filling food. Try dishes like chitterling sausage or braised beef with noodles. Wash it down with the good house wine.

25 rue Quincampoix, 4e. ℂ 01-42-77-48-02. Main courses 8€–12€ ($9.20–$14); *plats du jour* from 6€ ($7). MC, V. Daily noon–2am. Métro: Hôtel-de-Ville.

Georges ⚐ INTERNATIONAL/FRENCH   If you're in the mood to immerse yourself in hip, mod Paris with a view to kill, then come to Georges on top of Le Centre Pompidou. The food is a little expensive and the waitresses may look and act like bored models, but who cares when you can sit in one of the Costes brothers' wildly colorful rooms with a 360-degree view of Paris?

Centre Pompidou, 6th floor, rue Rambuteau, 4e. ℂ 01-44-78-47-99. Main courses 11€–23€ ($13–$26). AE, DC, MC, V. Wed–Mon noon–2am. Métro: Rambuteau.

Moments Cafe Society

People-watching is a favorite Parisian pastime, so rest your weary feet while lingering over a cup of coffee or a glass of wine at a sun-splashed sidewalk table. The most popular (and touristy) cafes are in St-Germain-des-Prés, across from the church. Also popular are literary cafes in northern Montparnasse along the boulevard du Montparnasse. All cafes are generally open daily 8am to midnight, although some may close on major holidays.

Café de Flore ★, 172 bd. St-Germain, 6e (© 01/45-48-55-26; Metro: St-Germain-des-Prés); and next-door Les Deux Magots ★, 6 place St-Germain-des-Prés, 6e (© 01/45-88-55-25), are always filled with locals and visitors paying tribute to the literary legends who frequented these cafes (Sartre, Simone de Beauvoir, and Apollinaire among them) and taking in the nightly promenade on the boulevard St-Germain. Before World War II, Montparnasse was a literary and artistic scene, and Ernest Hemingway, Scott Fitzgerald, Anaïs Nin, Pablo Picasso, and scores of others frequented La Coupole, 102 bd. du Montparnasse, 14e (© 01/43-20-14-20). *Hip* is the word for Café Beaubourg ★, 100 rue St-Merri, 4e (© 01/48-87-63-96; Métro: Rambuteau), a funky, Art Deco hotspot next to the Centre Pompidou. La Chaise au Plafond, 10 rue Trésor, 4e (© 01/42-76-03-22), offers an array of tarts and treats on a pedestrian-only side street near the Musée Picasso. With a back room that plays live music several nights a week, Café Charbon 109 rue Oberkampf, 11e (© 01/43-57-55-13; Métro: Parmentier), has become one of the hottest spots in east Paris. You'll be mesmerized by this turn-of-the-20th-century dance hall's Art Nouveau interior. Strictly for locals-in-the-know, Café Lateral, 4 av. Mac-Mahon, 17e (© 01-43-80-20-96; www.cafelateral.com), is hidden a few minutes' walk from the Champs-Elysées.

NEAR LES HALLES (1E ARRONDISSEMENT)

Le Coq-Héron ★ FRENCH   Tucked away down a spiral staircase in a modern, refurbished cellar, Le Coq-Héron serves fabulous food at budget prices. For your main dish, try the three-fish choucroute with a white butter and sauerkraut sauce that melts in your mouth; or try the lovely flan made with carrots and cauliflower. Warm lighting complements the stoned arched ceilings of this cozy, two-room restaurant. This is the perfect place for an intimate dinner, or perhaps something larger—Saturday nights you can rent the whole place for private celebrations.

3 rue Coq-Héron, 1er. © 01-40-26-88-68. 2-course lunch menu with glass of wine and coffee 15€ ($17); main courses 8€–10€ ($9–$12). MC, V. Mon–Fri noon–2:30pm; Fri 7:30–10pm. Métro: Louvre-Rivoli.

ON OR NEAR THE CHAMPS-ELYSÉES (8E ARRONDISSEMENT)

Al Diwan ★ *Finds* LEBANESE   Don't head upstairs to the pricey restaurant; stay on the ground floor in the casual, delicious, and affordable bistro. The Lebanese food here is authentic, fresh, and prepared with care. Start with a *fatoush* salad (tomatoes, romaine, parsley, and green onions tossed in a pomegranate dressing) or pureed lentil soup. Then move on to one of the fantastic main courses such as *sayadiyeh* (flaky whitefish with saffron rice drizzled with a

Taking an Ice-Cream Break

A landmark on Ile St-Louis, **Berthillon**, 31 rue St-Louis-en-l'Ile, 4e (© **01/43-54-31-61**; Métro: Pont Marie), offers a huge selection of delectable ice creams. Try gingerbread, rhubarb, bitter-chocolate mousse, plum, or any exotic fresh fruit in season—more than 50 flavors to choose from and nothing artificial. Open Wednesday to Sunday 10am to 8pm.

lemony tahini dressing) or *kibbe* (balls of ground lamb, mild spices, and bulgur wheat simmered in a yogurt-and-mint sauce).

30 av. George V, 8e. © 01-47-20-18-17. 2-course menu 23€ ($26); main courses 9.50€–22€ ($11–$25). MC, V. Daily noon–3pm and 7–11pm. Métro: Georges V.

Les Muses 🐈 *Value* BRETON/CREPES   Owner Madame Rous will greet you, seat you, and serve you with a smile in this cozy Breton crêpe restaurant. We dine here often to enjoy her hospitality and the wonderful crepes filled with meat, seafood, or vegetables, garnished with portions of salad or crudités followed by a sweet dessert crepe. Wash it all down with a bowl of cider.

45 rue de Berri, 8e. © 01-45-62-43-64. 2-course crepe meal with cider 7.80€ ($9); main-course crepes 1.65€–5.80€ ($1.90–$6.70); dessert crepes 2.30€–5.40€ ($2.65–$6.20). MC, V. Mon–Fri 11:30am–8:30pm. Métro: St-Philippe-du-Roule or George V.

NEAR THE OPERA GARNIER (9E ARRONDISSEMENT)

Chartier 🐈 *Value* FRENCH   Think dark wood, mirrors, brisk waiters, and hazy lighting in this former workers' 1890 canteen that can seat a few hundred rowdy yet well-behaved diners. There is a sense of intrigue here that has been captured in several French films, notably *Borsalino*, with Alain Delon and Jean-Paul Belmondo. There are about 100 items on the menu, including 16 main courses like *poulet rôti* (roasted chicken), a variety of steaks and *frites*, and turkey in cream sauce.

7 rue du Faubourg-Montmartre, 9e. © 01-47-70-86-29. Reservations required for large groups. Main courses 7€–11€ ($8.05–$13). V. Daily 11:30am–3pm and 6–10pm. Métro: Grands Boulevards.

AT OR NEAR THE LOUVRE (1E ARRONDISSEMENT)

Le Petit Machon *Value* FRENCH/LYONNAIS   Sleek and modern, with a wood bar and mirrored ceiling, this restaurant serves good Lyonnais cuisine. Start with the regional specialty *saucisson chaud pommes à l'huile* (warm sausage with potatoes in oil) or salad with Roquefort and walnuts. Follow with *noisette d'agneau* (sliced lamb) in asparagus cream sauce, ham with lentils, or *merlu* (a whitefish similar to hake) in a delicate cream sauce.

158 rue St-Honoré, 1er. © 01-42-60-08-06. 3-course menu 17€ ($19); main courses 11€–13€ ($13–$15). V. Tues–Sun noon–2:30pm and 7–10:30pm. Métro: Palais-Royal–Musée du Louvre.

Universal Restaurant *Value* CAFETERIA/INTERNATIONAL   Next to the inverted pyramid in the Galerie Carrousel du Louvre, this cafeteria offers a rich assortment of ethnic and French specialties at unbeatable prices. At lunch it's a madhouse, as hungry hordes load up their trays at stands that offer Spanish tapas, Chinese lo mein, pasta salad, Mexican burritos, or all-American hamburgers and fries. Other counters display Lebanese food, roast chicken, salads, muffins, ice cream, cheese, and crêpes. The pick-and-choose style allows you to design your own meal—perfect for vegetarians or people on special diets.

99 rue de Rivoli, 1er (enter from rue de Rivoli or the Louvre). © 01-47-03-96-58. Main courses from 4€ ($5); 3 courses a la carte 7€–9€ ($8–$10). V. Daily 11am–10:30pm. Métro: Palais-Royal–Musée du Louvre.

IN OR NEAR THE MARAIS (4E ARRONDISSEMENT)

Bofinger *Moments* ALSATIAN/BRASSERIE Just a few steps from place Bastille, this classic Alsatian brasserie, which opened in 1864, is now one of the best-loved restaurants in the city, with its numerous rooms done in wonderful Belle Epoque decor (dark wood, gleaming brass, bright lights, glass ceiling, and waiters with long white aprons—and solicitous manners). The menu features many Alsatian specialties, such as *choucroute* (sauerkraut with smoked ham), as well as its famed oysters and foie gras. The prices are moderate for Paris, but it doesn't matter—you'd pay a lot more for a sampling of this cuisine. If you feel like something a little smaller and intimate, try Le Petit Bofinger across the street.

5–7 rue de la Bastille, 4e. ✆ 01-42-72-87-82. Weekday lunch menu 21€ ($24); lunch and dinner menu with half bottle of wine 31€ ($35); main courses 13€–28€ ($15–$32). AE, MC, V. Mon–Fri noon–3pm and 6:30pm–1am; Sat–Sun noon–1am. Métro: Bastille.

Jo Goldenberg *Moments* EUROPEAN/DELI A Paris institution, Jo Goldenberg deserves a stop, even if it's only to step into the sumptuous delicatessen in the front, where sausages dangle and baklava beckons. The quintessential Jewish/eastern European restaurant, Jo Goldenberg has a convivial atmosphere. Specialties include *poulet paprika*, goulash, moussaka, and Wiener schnitzel. Deli offerings include pastrami and corned beef—allegedly invented here by Goldenberg senior in the 1920s. Adding to the festive air, Gypsy musicians begin playing around 9pm.

7 rue des Rosiers, 4e. ✆ 01-48-87-20-16. Main courses 11€–14€ ($13–$16). AE, DC, MC, V. Daily 9am–midnight. Métro: St-Paul.

L'As du Fallafel *Value* MIDDLE EASTERN This is one of the neighborhood's most popular falafel bars.

34 rue des Rosiers, 4e. ✆ 01-48-87-63-60. Falafel sandwiches 4€ ($4.60). MC, V. Sun–Thurs noon–midnight; Fri noon–4pm. Métro: St-Paul.

Les Temps des Cerises *Finds* FRENCH This bistro, housed in an 18th-century building, boasts a mosaic tile floor, a pewter bar, and walls covered with artwork. Locals gather to chat over a glass of wine or coffee. It's packed at lunch, but it's a bargain, and service is extremely fast. There's a choice of prix-fixe menus that might tempt you with anything from sardines to eggs with mayonnaise to start, and then with dishes from sausage and red beans to steak with shallot sauce for a main course.

31 rue de la Cerisaie, 4e. ✆ 01-42-72-08-63. Lunch 12€ ($14); main courses 11€–14€ ($13–$16). No credit cards. Mon–Fri 7:45am–8pm (lunch 11:30am–2:30pm). Closed Aug. Métro: Bastille or Sully-Morland.

Trumilou *Value* FRENCH With copper pots lining the walls, red leatherette banquette seats, and a view of the Seine or the arches of Notre-Dame, this is one of the most popular restaurants around Paris's Hôtel de Ville (city hall). The prix-fixe menus always include a grilled fish, or try *manchons de canard à l'ancienne* (old-fashioned duck). Neck of lamb (served medium rare unless you specify otherwise) is tender and juicy, and *canard aux pruneaux* (duck with prunes) is a house specialty.

84 quai de l'Hôtel-de-Ville, 4e. ✆ 01-42-77-63-98. Reservations recommended Sat–Sun. 2-course menu 12€ ($14); 3-course menu 16€ ($18); main courses 12€–18€ ($14–$21). MC, V. Daily noon–3pm and 7–11pm. Métro: Hôtel-de-Ville.

NEAR THE EIFFEL TOWER (15E ARRONDISSEMENT)

Le Café du Commerce *Finds* FRENCH You'll love the ambience here, complete with smoky mirrors, stained-glass windows, and photos of great scribes who supposedly wrote their oeuvres on the premises. The menu includes *escargots en Caquelon* as a main course, and appetizers of beef tartar and duck confit. The wine list is extensive. As in many Paris restaurants, you have to ask for the dessert selection: Profiteroles—puff pastries filled with ice cream and topped with hot chocolate—are a good bet.

51 rue du Commerce, 15e. 🕐 01-45-75-03-27. *Plat du jour* 13€ ($15); main courses 13€–18€ ($15($21). AE, DC, MC, V. Daily noon–11:30pm. Métro: Emile-Zola, Commerce, or La Motte–Picquet.

IN MONTMARTRE

Au Relais–Le Bistrot d'Edouard *(Value* CLASSIC BISTRO Let Chef Edouard Martinez warm you with his extraordinary bistro cuisine, including *salade de gesiers de canard confits* (salad with sautéed gizzards) and an egg mayonnaise specialty. This place has a cozy atmosphere.

48 rue Lamarck, 18e. 🕐 01-46-06-68-32. 3-course weekly lunch menu 13€ ($15); 3-course dinner menu 21€ ($24). Tues–Sat noon–2:30pm and 6:30–10:30pm. MC, V. Métro: Lamarck-Caulaincourt.

Chez Les Fondus ⭐ *(Value* FONDUE Be prepared to wait even if you have reservations for this popular, boisterous, and fun place. Most of the diners are young and intent on having a good time. There are two long wooden tables, and you'll have to jump over the table to get into the inside seats. As soon as you're seated, you'll be served red wine in baby bottles (included in the meal price). Dinner is your choice of fondue *bourguignonne* (meat) or *savoyarde* (cheese), with dried sausage as an appetizer. For dessert, you'll get a whole frozen orange filled with sorbet.

17 rue des Trois-Frères, 18e. 🕐 01-42-55-22-65. Reservations recommended. 3-course menu with wine 15€ ($17). No credit cards. Tues–Sat 7pm–midnight. Métro: Abbesses or Anvers.

Le Moulin de la Galette ⭐ ITALIAN/FRENCH You'll find this glossy restaurant under the Moulin de la Galette windmill, one of the last windmills in Paris and a favorite subject of Renoir. The restaurant was a favorite haunt of French-Egyptian singer Dalida, and fans come to eat fine Italian fare and gaze at her pictures, which grace the walls. The lunch menu (appetizer and main course, or main course and dessert) is a great deal and includes wine. The wide range of offerings includes classic French dishes such as steamed sea bass, and Italian specialties such as a medley of veal tortellini, Spanish ricotta ravioli, and crab ventrilli. There are lovely front and back outdoor terraces.

83 rue Lepic, 18e. 🕐 01-46-06-84-77. 2-course lunch menu with wine 19€ ($22); main courses 15€–29€ ($17–$33). Tues–Sun noon–3pm; Tues–Sat 7:30pm–midnight. MC, V. Métro: Abbesses.

WORTH A SPLURGE

Aux Lyonnais ⭐⭐⭐ FRENCH/LYONNAIS The latest Alain Ducasse creation opened in the fall of 2002 and offers, hands down, the best Lyonnais food in the city. The setting is simple and lovely—a 1890s bistro that has kept its redwood facade and bistro sign. For appetizers, you'll most likely find a pot of homemade foie gras served with cornichons or a dozen tender escargots in a garlicky butter sauce. Move on to the *quenelles* (fish dumplings) baked in a red sauce, or the roasted Cornish hen with mushrooms, tomatoes, and onions. Save room for the St-Marcellin cheese on a shallot-rubbed slice of baguette or the exquisite soufflé with pear liqueur. There are several good wines at under 25€ ($29) a bottle.

32 rue St-Marc, 2e. 🕐 01-42-96-65-04. Reservations required 2 weeks in advance. 3-course menu 32€ ($37); main courses 18€–32€ ($21–$37). AE, DC, MC, V. Tues–Fri noon–2:30pm and 7:30–10:30pm; Sat 7:30–11pm. Métro: Grands Boulevards.

Closerie des Lilas ⭐⭐⭐ FRENCH Literary geniuses Hemingway, James, and Dos Passos hung out under the shady lilac bushes, while Lenin and Trotsky debated politics over chess in this old haunt on the border of St-Germain-des-Prés and Montparnasse that remains one of the city's most historic and romantic sites for a meal. Note that Closerie is split into two different dining areas—a more expensive but dark and romantic restaurant, and a cheaper, brighter brasserie serving more traditional French fare. A meal may start out with a staple such as *oeufs dur* (eggs with mayonnaise), oysters (in season), a moist and tasty *terrine de foie gras canard avec toasts* (terrine of duck liver with toasted bread), or the classic *steak tartare avec frites maison* (marinated raw steak with french fries). Dinners may include a tender *selle d'agneau rotie en croute dorée* (roasted lamb flank in a golden crust), a peppery *filet de boeuf au poivre*, or *homard Breton à votre façon* (Brittany lobster cooked the way you choose). Finish up with coffee and *patisseries du jour* or *crêpes suzette*.

171 bd. du Montparnasse, 6e. (C) **01-40-51-34-50.** Reservations required. Main courses 17€–30€ ($20 $35). AE, DC, MC, V. Daily noon–1am. Métro: Port-Royal.

Spoon, Food, and Wine 🐙🐙 INTERNATIONAL   With its ultramodern white interior, great service, and pretentious crowd, this sleek restaurant feels like it belongs in London or New York. Celebrated chef Alain Ducasse's menu encompasses a variety of international dishes, and the customer chooses (from a list of enticing choices) the condiments, side dishes, and vegetables to complement the main dish. Take, for example, spareribs—try a marmalade of stewed meat, red wine, tomato, and olives alongside a heaping portion of Maxim's potatoes. Spoon also boasts a diverse wine list, with 120 selections from South Africa, Argentina, and New Zealand. For dessert, opt for the oozing, warm chocolate "pizza" over bubble-gum ice cream or, if you can't choose, order the selection of five "mini" desserts (a miniature baba au rhum, slice of cheesecake, chocolate chip cookies, and whatever else the pastry chef has made that day).

14 rue de Marignan, 8e. (C) **01-40-76-34-44.** Reservations recommended 1 month in advance. Main courses 23€–38€ ($26–$44). Mon–Fri 11:45am–2:30pm and 6:30–11:30pm. AE, MC, V. Métro: Franklin-D-Roosevelt.

4 Seeing the Sights
THE TOP MUSEUMS

Centre Georges Pompidou 🐙🐙   The "guts" are on the outside of the Centre National d'Art et de Culture Georges Pompidou, designed by British architect Richard Rogers and Italian architect Renzo Piano in the late 1960s. As with much of Parisian architecture, this building was despised by many at first, but over the years, Parisians have come to love—or at least accept—the very 1970s building, with its "exoskeletal" architecture and bright colors.

The center houses an impressive collection of modern art, a cinema, a library, and spaces for dance and music. Temporary exhibits often include video and computer art. Works from the Musée National d'Art Moderne (the national modern art collection) take up two floors. The Brancusi Atelier features nearly 150 drawings, paintings, and sculptures by sculptor Constantin Brancusi. Be sure to take an escalator to the top floor for a breathtaking view of Paris. Don't miss the nearby Igor Stravinsky fountain, with its fun sculptures by Tinguely and Niki de Saint Phalle that include red lips dripping water and a twirling, grinning skull. Allow about 1½ hours for a visit.

Place Georges-Pompidou, 4e. (C) **01-44-78-12-33.** www.centrepompidou.fr. Admission to museum 5.50€ ($6.30) adults, 3.50€ ($4) visitors 13–26, free for children under 13; admission to special exhibits (museum entry included) 8€ ($9.20) adults, 6.50€ ($7.50) visitors 13–26, free for children under 13. Centre Wed–Mon 11am–10pm. Museum Wed–Mon 11am–9pm. Métro: Rambuteau, Hôtel-de-Ville, or Châtelet–Les Halles.

Paris

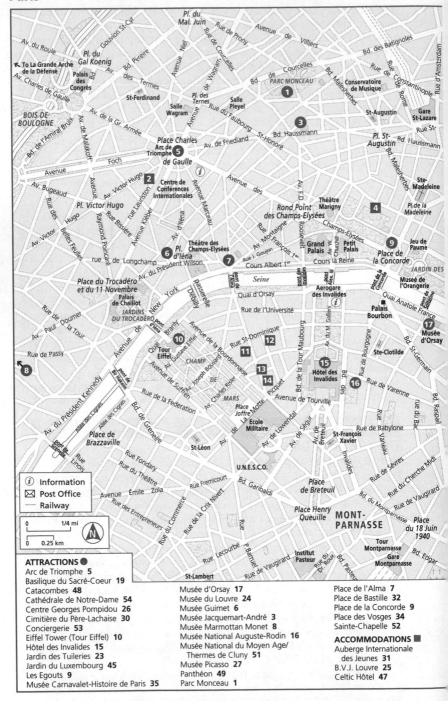

Information
⊠ **Post Office**
· · · · · **Railway**

0 — 1/4 mi
0 — 0.25 km

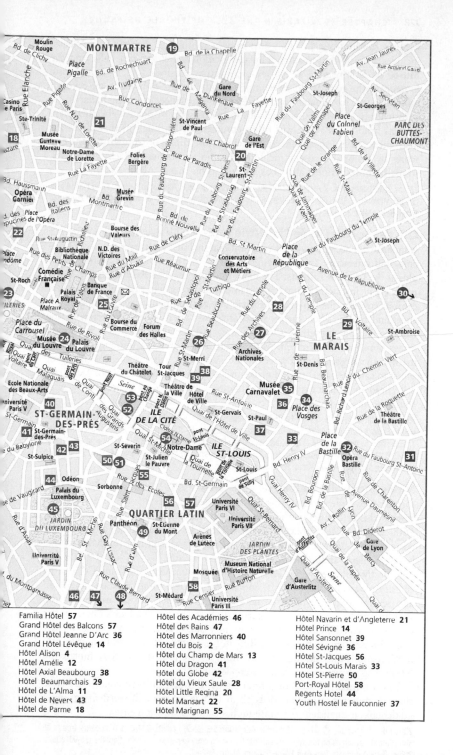

Familia Hôtel **57**
Grand Hôtel des Balcons **57**
Grand Hôtel Jeanne D'Arc **36**
Grand Hôtel Lévêque **14**
Hôtel Alison **4**
Hôtel Amélie **12**
Hôtel Axial Beaubourg **38**
Hôtel Beaumarchais **29**
Hôtel de L'Alma **11**
Hôtel de Nevers **43**
Hôtel de Parme **18**

Hôtel des Académies **46**
Hôtel des Bains **47**
Hôtel des Marronniers **40**
Hôtel du Bois **2**
Hôtel du Champ de Mars **13**
Hôtel du Dragon **41**
Hôtel du Globe **42**
Hôtel du Vieux Saule **28**
Hôtel Little Regina **20**
Hôtel Mansart **22**
Hôtel Marignan **55**

Hôtel Navarin et d'Angleterre **21**
Hôtel Prince **14**
Hôtel Sansonnet **39**
Hôtel Sévigné **36**
Hôtel St-Jacques **56**
Hôtel St-Louis Marais **33**
Hôtel St-Pierre **50**
Port-Royal Hôtel **58**
Regents Hotel **44**
Youth Hostel le Fauconnier **37**

Cité de la Musique ⟨ꭥ⟩ This ultramodern complex in the Parc de la Villette includes a music conservatory, a documentation center, concert halls, and the **Musée de la Musique** ⟨ꭥ⟩. All are architecturally astounding, but the music museum is the gem. Wide, sweeping halls full of light embrace a collection of more than 900 instruments dating from the Renaissance, including Italian lutes, harpsichords, glass flutes, and a 1.8m (6-ft.) bassoon. A portable headset plays extracts from major works and offers commentary (in English) that places the instruments in historical context. Check out the copies of handwritten musical scores by major composers, including Beethoven, Debussy, Bach, and Ravel, whose beautiful script is almost as inspired as his music. Allow 2 hours.

221 av. Jean-Jaurès, 19e. ⟨𝄠⟩ **01-44-84-45-45.** www.cite-musique.fr. Admission 6.10€ ($7) adults, 4.60€ ($5.30) students, 2.30€ ($2.65) children 6–18, free for children under 6. Tues–Sat noon–6pm; Sun 10am–6pm. Métro: Porte de Pantin.

Cité des Sciences et de l'Industrie ⟨ꭥ⟩ *Kids* This mammoth structure is a wonderful science and industry museum that includes a planetarium, a 3-D cinema, and interactive exhibits designed for 3- to 5-year-olds and 5- to 12-year olds at the **Cité des Enfants.** The main museum is called **Explora** and includes models and interactive games that demonstrate scientific principles, as well as exhibits covering the universe, the earth, the environment, space, computer science, and health. There are two *médiathèques* (multimedia centers), one for children and one for adults. Outside, a gigantic metal sphere called the **Géode** shows films on a huge screen. Also outside, kids can climb into an actual submarine, the *Argonaute.* Located in the Parc de la Villette, there is plenty of access to cafes, restaurants, and places to rest tired feet. During school vacations, call ahead to reserve for Cité des Enfants. Depending on your stamina, you could spend a day here.

30 av. Corentin-Cariou, 19e. ⟨𝄠⟩ **01-40-05-80-00,** reservations 01-40-05-12-12. www.cite-sciences.fr. Admission to Explora exhibition 7.50€ ($8.60) adults over 25, 5.50€ ($6.30) visitors 7–25, free for children under 7; admission to Argonaut 3€ ($3.45); admission to planetarium 2.50€ ($2.90); admission to the Géode 8.75€ ($10); admission to Cinaxe theater 5.20€ ($6); admission to Cité des Enfants 5€ ($5.75). Tues–Sat 10am–6pm; Sun 10am–7pm. Métro: Porte-de-la-Villette.

Musée Carnavalet-Histoire de Paris ⟨ꭥꭥꭥ⟩ Also known as the Musée Historique de la Ville de Paris, this museum details the history of the city of Paris from prehistoric times to the present. Two mansions house the museum: the 16th-century Hôtel Carnavalet and the Hôtel Le Peletier de St-Fargeau. Their current look dates to the 17th century, when the architect François Mansart was hired to enlarge and modernize the original structure.

Perfectly preserved period salons, including Louis XV's and Louis XVI's 18th-century blue and yellow rooms, contain ornate furnishings and art. There are also several rooms devoted to the Revolution, which display models of the Bastille, and Marie Antoinette's personal items, including a lock of hair. In the basement, you'll find a collection of prehistoric artifacts, including ancient coins, bronze figures, bowls, and Roman bas-reliefs. The beautiful interior garden, accessible only through the museum, is a sublime spot to contemplate the 3,000 years of history you've just stepped through.

You will need at least 2 or 3 hours to get through this vast collection—note that the museum commentary is all in French, so it's well worth it to buy a guidebook in English at the museum bookshop before you enter.

23 rue de Sévigné, 3e. ⟨𝄠⟩ **01-44-59-58-58.** Admission 5€ ($5.75) adults, 3.50€ ($4) students, free to all Sun 10am–1pm; admission to temporary exhibits (including entry to permanent collection) 6€ ($6.90) adults, 3.80€ ($4.35) students. Tues–Sun 10am–5:40pm. Métro: St-Paul.

Paris's Top Free (or Almost) Attractions

- The **rooftops** of Paris, which can be seen from many vantage points, several for free, like La Samaritaine department store, the Institut du Monde Arabe, and Sacré-Coeur.
- The **neighborhood markets**, such as the Latin Quarter's **rue Mouffetard, rue de Buci** in St-Germain, **rue Lepic** in Montmartre, **rue Montorgueil** near the Bourse, and **rue Daguerre** in Montparnasse.
- The **bird** and **flower markets** on the Ile de la Cité and the **Marché aux Puces** at Porte de Clignancourt (Paris's largest flea market).
- The **churches** of Paris, which have been central to the life of the city. In addition to Notre-Dame and Sacré-Coeur, visit St-Eustache (in the heart of Les Halles), St-Séverin, St-Germain-des-Prés, St-Etienne du Mont, and St-Sulpice for its Delacroix paintings and magnificent organ.
- The **cemeteries** of Paris—especially the famous **Père-Lachaise**. The **Cimetière de Montmartre** and **Cimetière de Montparnasse** also contain the graves of famous writers, artists, and composers.
- **The Louvre on Sunday,** when admission is half price—or, if you're lucky, the first Sunday of the month, when it's free.
- The city's gorgeous gardens and parks. The most famous is the **Jardin des Tuileries**. The **Bois de Boulogne** is the largest, and the **Jardin du Luxembourg** the most beloved. The **Jardins des Plantes,** the oldest public garden in Paris, is a riot of color and variety.
- The **Seine** and its **bridges.** Take a day to stroll along the *quais* (riverbanks)—one of the world's most romantic walks.
- The **antiques stores** and **art galleries** that line rue de Beaune, rue Jacob, rue de Seine, rue Bonaparte, and streets in the St-Germain area.
- The **arcades** winding through the 2e and 9e arrondissements. These 19th-century iron-and-glass–covered passages are ideal for rainy-day shopping.
- The many and various **squares** of Paris: **Place de la Contrescarpe** in the Latin Quarter and the magnificent **place des Vosges** in the Marais are great places to sit and watch life pass by. **Square du Vert-Galant** on the Ile de la Cité is ideal for a picnic by the water

Musée d'Orsay ✿✿✿   In 1986, a renovated train station and the best art of the 19th century were combined to create one of the world's great museums. Thousands of paintings, sculptures, objets d'art, items of furniture, architectural displays, even photographs and movies, illustrate the diversity and richness of the century. They encompass Impressionism, realism, Post-Impressionism, and Art Nouveau. On the ground floor you will find Ingres's *La Source,* Millet's *L'Angelus,* the Barbizon school, Manet's *Olympia,* and other works of early Impressionism. Impressionism continues on the top level, with Renoir's *Le Moulin de la Galette,* Manet's *Déjeuner sur l'Herbe,* Degas's *Racing at Longchamps,* Monet's *Cathedrals,* van Gogh's *Self-Portrait,* and Whistler's *Portrait of the Artist's Mother.* There are also works by Gauguin and the Pont-Aven school, Toulouse-Lautrec, Pissarro, Cézanne, and Seurat. Symbolism, naturalism, and

Art Nouveau are represented on the middle level; the international Art Nouveau exhibit includes wonderful furniture and objets d'art.

62 rue de Lille and 1 rue Bellechasse, 7e. ✆ 01-40-49-48-48. www.musee-orsay.fr. Admission 7€ ($8) adults, 5€ ($5.75) visitors 18–24 and for all on Sun, free for children under 18. Tues–Wed and Fri–Sat 10am–6pm; Thurs 10am–9:45pm; Sun 9am–6pm. June 20–Sept 20 museum opens at 9am. Métro: Solférino. RER: Musée-d'Orsay.

Musée du Louvre 👑👑👑   You could visit the Louvre every day for a month and not see all its 35,000 treasures. To have an enjoyable, nonexhausting experience, you'll need to limit your focus or plan more than one trip.

The Louvre bookstore in the Carrousel de Louvre sells comprehensive guides and maps in English; there are brochures for "visitors in a hurry," and a guide-book, *The Louvre, First Visit.* You can also try the 90-minute tour of the most popular works (*Visite Découverte;* ✆ 01-40-20-52-09), which will give you a quick orientation to the museum's layout. You can set your own pace with the audiotour, which you can rent for 5€ ($5.75) at the entrance to any of the wings. It has an English-language option and is designed to last 4 hours.

If you choose to go it alone, focus on a particular department, collection, or wing. The departments are: Egyptian antiquities; Oriental antiquities; Greek, Etruscan, and Roman antiquities; sculptures; paintings; graphics and the graphic arts; and art objects, spread across three wings: Sully, Denon, and Richelieu.

First-timers usually head to the three most famous works: *Mona Lisa, Winged Victory of Samothrace,* and *Venus de Milo.* Finding your way is easy; signs mark the route, and the flow of other tourists carries you along. In the Denon wing, the *Winged Victory of Samothrace,* dating from the 2nd century B.C., is a master-piece of Hellenic art. Before you climb the staircase topped by this magnificent sculpture, follow the sign that directs you to *Venus de Milo* (in the Sully wing), sculpted in the 1st century B.C. as the quintessence of feminine grace and sen-suality. Don't miss the fragments from the 5th-century-B.C. Parthenon. Also in the Sully wing are the *Seated Scribe,* the crypt of Osiris, the 18th-century rococo paintings of Fragonard and Boucher, and Ingres's *Turkish Bath.* En route from *Winged Victory* to *Mona Lisa,* you will pass David's *Coronation of Napoléon* oppo-site his *Portrait of Madame Récamier.* Stop and admire Ingres's *Grand Odalisque.*

Check out the Italian Renaissance art calmly hanging in the nearby Salle des Sept Cheminées. Here you will find da Vinci's *Virgin with the Infant Jesus and St. Anne* and *The Virgin of the Rocks,* as well as Titian's *Open Air Concert,* Raphael's *La Belle Jardinière,* and Veronese's massive *Marriage at Cana.* Other highlights of the Denon wing include Velasquez's infantas, Ribera's *Club Footed Boy,* Botticelli's frescoes, Michelangelo's *Slaves,* Canova's *Psyche Revived by the Kiss of Cupid,* and works by Murillo, El Greco, and Goya.

The inauguration of the Richelieu wing in 1993 opened several acres of new space, allowing display of some 12,000 works of art in 165 airy, well-lit rooms. Before heading into the galleries, look in at the adjoining cour Marly, the glass-roofed courtyard that houses Coustou's rearing *Marly Horses.* The *Code of Hammurabi* in the Babylonian collection, Rubens's Medici cycle, Rembrandt's self-portraits, Holbein's *Portrait of Erasmus,* and Van Dyck's portrait of Charles I of England are among the works in the Richelieu wing. For a change of pace, see the apartments of Napoleon III (open mornings only), furnished in over-the-top Second Empire style.

In 1997, 9,941 sq. m (107,000 sq. ft.) of exhibition space devoted to Egypt-ian art and antiquities opened in the Sully and Denon wings. The display now totals 7,000 pieces, the largest exhibition of Egyptian antiquities outside Cairo.

> ## *Tips* Maneuvering the Louvre
>
> Long lines outside the Louvre's pyramid entrance are notorious, but here are some tricks for avoiding them:
>
> - Enter through the underground shopping mall Carrousel du Louvre.
> - Enter through the staircases *(Porte des Lions)* next to the Arc du Carrousel.
> - Enter directly from the Palais-Royal–Musée du Louvre Métro station.
> - Buy a *Carte Musées et Monuments* (Museum and Monuments Pass), which allows direct entry through the priority entrance at the Passage Richelieu, 93 rue de Rivoli. The pass costs 15€ ($17) for 1 day, 30€ ($35) for 3 days, and 45€ ($52) for 5 days. The pass is also good for dozens of other museums in Paris.
> - Order tickets via the Internet at www.louvre.fr, or by phone through FNAC (© **08-92-68-36-22,** toll number), and pick them up at any FNAC store (except FNAC photo shops). There is an added service charge of 1€ ($1.15). Or walk into the nearest FNAC and purchase tickets at the *billeterie.* You'll find a branch of FNAC at 71 bd. St-Germain, 5e (© **01-44-41-31-50;** Métro: Cluny). You can also buy tickets at Virgin Megastore, Bon Marché, Printemps, Galeries Lafayette, and BHV.

In 2000, an exhibit featuring 120 pieces from the earliest civilizations in Africa, Asia, Oceania, and the Americas opened on the ground floor. It will be in the Louvre until 2005, when Musée de Quai Branly, to which it belongs, opens.

Rue de Rivoli, 1er. © **01-40-20-51-51** for recorded message, 01-40-20-53-17 for information desk. www.louvre.fr. Admission 7.50€ ($8.60) adults, 5€ ($5.75) after 3pm and Sun, free 1st Sun of month and for children under 18. Mon (certain rooms only 9am–9:45pm) and Wed 9am–9:45pm; Thurs–Sun 9am–6pm. Métro: Palais-Royal–Musée du Louvre.

Musée Guimet ✸✸✸   It was worth the wait. After 5 years of renovations, this superb Asian art museum reopened in 2001, displaying thousands of objects and paintings over five airy floors. At the entrance you will be greeted by a giant seven-headed stone serpent from Cambodia, who leads the way to an enormous room full of peaceful, smiling statues from Southeast Asia. A beautiful portrait of the Khmer monarch Jayavarman VII is just one of the museum's highlights, which include a sublime 11th-century dancing Shiva from southern India, a life-size Chinese ceramic of the Buddhist disciple Luohan, and some spectacular Tibetan mandalas. Be prepared to spend several hours marveling over these and other treasures such as Korean masks, Japanese prints, and Nepalese jewel-encrusted crowns. Don't miss the cupola on the top floor with its magnificent carved lacquer screens from China.

6 place d'Iéna, 16e. © **01-56-52-53-00.** www.museeguimet.fr. Admission 7€ ($8) adults, 5€ ($5.75) visitors 18–25 and for all Sun, free for children under 18. Wed–Mon 10am–6pm. Métro: Iéna.

Musée Jacquemart-André ✸✸   The combination of an outstanding art collection and a splendid 19th-century mansion makes this museum one of the jewels of Paris. The museum is filled with French, Flemish, and Italian paintings, furniture, and Beauvais tapestries. Highlights of the collection include a fresco by Jean Baptiste Tiepolo, Fragonard's *Portrait d'un Vieillard,* Elisabeth Vigée-Lebrun's portrait of *Catherine Skavronskaia,* Rembrandt's portrait of an anxious *Docteur Tholinx,* Van Dyck's *Time Cutting the Wings of Love,* and several rooms filled with paintings of the Italian Renaissance, including Botticelli's *Virgin and Child.* As you wander the ornate rooms, pause in the "winter garden," a tour de force of marble and mirrors that flanks an unusual double staircase. Make sure to take advantage of the fascinating free audio tour; give yourself at least 2 hours to soak up the museum and its atmosphere. The beautiful restaurant on the ground floor makes an excellent lunch stop.

158 bd. Haussmann, 8e. ℭ 01-45-62-11-59. www.musee-jacquemart-andre.com. Admission 8€ ($9.20) adults, 6€ students and children under 18. Daily 10am–6pm. Métro: Miromesnil.

Musée Marmottan Monet ⟨ℛℛ *(Finds*   Located between the Jardin Ranelagh and the edge of the Bois de Boulogne, this jewel celebrates the painter Claude Monet and contains an outstanding collection of his water lily paintings. The museum also displays his more abstract representations of the Japanese Bridge at Giverny, as well as *Impression at Sunrise,* the painting from which the term "Impressionist" derived. Monet's personal collection is also here. It includes works by his contemporaries Pissarro, Manet, Morisot, and Renoir. In addition to these other gems, the stunning Wildenstein collection of late medieval illuminated manuscripts is on display. Give yourself 2 hours for this beautiful museum.

2 rue Louis-Boilly, 16e. ℭ 01-44-96-50-33. www.marmottan.com. Admission 6.50€ ($7.50) adults, 4€ ($4.60) visitors 8–25, free for children under 8. Tues–Sun 10am–5:30pm. Métro: La-Muette.

Musée National Auguste-Rodin ⟨ℛℛℛ   Rodin's extraordinary ability to breathe life into marble and bronze makes this museum a standout in a city full of great art. This wide-ranging collection offers a superlative insight into Rodin's genius and includes all his greatest works, many of which you can see in the garden for only 1€ ($1.15). The most prominent sculpture outdoors is *The Thinker.* The *Gates of Hell* is another standout, a portrayal of Dante's *Inferno.* Intended for the Musée des Arts Décoratifs, these massive bronze doors weren't completed until 7 years after the artist's death. Within the museum is the stunning *The Kiss,*

⟨*Value*   **Getting the Best Deal on Sightseeing**

- If you're age **60 or over,** carry identification proving it and ask for discounts at theaters, museums, attractions, and the Métro.
- Take advantage of the **reduced admission fee at museums,** which usually applies 2 hours before closing and all day Sunday.
- Consider buying the **Carte Musées et Monuments (Museum and Monuments Pass),** but only if you'll be visiting two or three museums a day. The pass costs 15€ ($17) for 1 day, 30€ ($35) for 3 days, and 45€ ($52) for 5 days. Admission to the Louvre is 7.50€ ($8.60), and entrance fees for most other museums are 6€ ($6.90) to 8€ ($9.20) or less; you do the math. The card gives you access to 65 museums and monuments, allowing you to go directly inside without waiting in line—a distinct benefit at the Louvre, for example.
- Also see the box "Paris's Top Free (or Almost) Attractions," earlier in the chapter.

which immortalizes the passion of doomed 13th-century lovers Paolo Malatesta and Francesca da Rimini in a sensuous curve of white marble. Upstairs are two versions of the celebrated and condemned nude of Balzac, his bulky torso rising from a tree trunk. Look also for the few works by Camille Claudel, Rodin's mistress and a brilliant sculptor herself. Give yourself an hour in the gardens and at least an hour in the museum itself. There's a cafe in the garden.

Hôtel Biron, 77 rue de Varenne, 7e. ⓒ **01-44-18-61-10**. www.musee-rodin.fr. Admission 5€ ($5.75) adults, 3€ ($3.45) visitors 18–24 and for all Sun, free for children under 18; garden only 1€ ($1.15). Apr–Sept Tues–Sun 9:30am–5:45pm; Oct–Mar Tues–Sun 9:30am–4:45pm. Garden closes at 6:45pm in summer, last admission at 5:15pm. Métro: Varenne.

Musée National du Moyen Age/Thermes de Cluny ★★   It's difficult not to gawk at the remains of late-2nd- and early-3rd-century baths in one of the Latin Quarter's busiest intersections (the corner of boulevards St-Michel and St-Germain). The baths are part of the Cluny Museum of medieval art and Paris's foremost example of civil architecture from the late Middle Ages.

In the 19th century, the Hôtel de Cluny belonged to a collector of medieval art; upon his death in the 1840s, the government acquired the house and its contents. The exhibits include wood and stone sculpture, brilliant stained glass and metalwork, and rich tapestries. Highlights include jeweled Visigoth crowns, carved ivories from 6th-century Constantinople, and elaborate altarpieces from 16th-century Castille. Don't miss the stunning 15th-century tapestry series of *The Lady and the Unicorn,* an allegory representing the five senses. Allow 2 hours.

6 place Paul-Painlevé, 5e. ⓒ **01-53-73-78-00**. www.musee-moyenage.fr. Admission 5.50€ ($6.30) adults, 4€ ($4.60) visitors 18–25 and for all Sun, free for children under 18. Wed–Mon 9:15am–5:45pm. Métro: Cluny-Sorbonne.

Musée Picasso ★★   Because the works here are exhibited in rotation, you're likely to see something new even if you've visited before. Located in the Hôtel Salé, a 17th-century mansion once owned by a salt tax collector, this is the world's greatest collection of Pablo Picasso's works. After his death in 1973, the artist's heirs arranged to donate this enormous collection in lieu of paying the exorbitant French inheritance taxes. The collection includes more than 200 paintings, almost 160 sculptures, and 88 ceramics, as well as more than 3,000 prints and drawings—but only a fraction are on display at any given time. The museum also displays works of art collected by Picasso, including works by Corot, Cézanne, Braque, Rousseau, Matisse, and Renoir.

Hôtel Salé, 5 rue de Thorigny, 3e. ⓒ **01-42-71-25-21**. Admission 6€ ($6.90) adults, 4€ ($4.60) visitors 18–25 and for all Sun, free for children under 18; free to all 1st Sun each month. Apr–Sept Wed–Mon 9:30am–6pm, Thurs 9:30am–8pm; Oct–Mar Wed–Mon 9:30am–5:30pm, Thurs 9:30am–8pm. Métro: Chemin-Vert, St-Paul, or Filles du Calvaire.

THE TOP CHURCHES

Basilique du Sacré-Coeur ★★   The sensual yet exotic white dome of Sacré-Coeur is almost as familiar as the Arc de Triomphe and the Eiffel Tower; and it, too, is a romantic symbol of Paris. Made famous by Utrillo and other Montmartre artists, Sacré-Coeur is a vaguely Byzantine-Romanesque church built from 1876 to 1919. Construction began after France's defeat in the Franco-Prussian War; Catholics raised money to build this monument to the Sacred Heart of Jesus. There are 237 steps to climb to get up to the dome, but the view is fabulous: almost 50km (30 miles) across the rooftops of Paris on a clear day. You can ease the ascent by taking the elevator up from the Métro and riding the *funiculaire* (which is a sort of tram drawn up and down the side of the hill by cables) to the church. For the staircase-phobic, the panorama from the front of the church is pretty spectacular if you don't mind fending off trinket vendors.

On the other side of Sacré-Coeur is place du Tertre; Vincent van Gogh lived off the place and used it as a scene for one of his paintings. Its charm is long gone and the square is swamped with tourists and quick-sketch artists in the spring and summer. Avoid the hoards and follow any of the small streets winding downhill from the rear of the church to find the quiet side of Montmartre and a glimpse of what Paris looked like before busy Baron Haussmann built his boulevards.

25 rue du Chevalier-de-la-Barre, 18e. ℂ 01-53-41-89-00. Free admission to basilica; admission to dome and crypt 4.60€ ($5.30) adults, 2.45€ ($2.80) students under 25. Basilica daily 6am–11pm; dome and crypt daily 9am–5:45pm. Métro: Abbesses. Take elevator to surface and follow signs to *funiculaire*, which runs to the church (fare: 1 Métro ticket).

Cathédrale de Notre-Dame ✰✰✰   In many ways, Notre-Dame *is* the center of France. Its Gothic loftiness dominates the Seine and the Ile de la Cité, as well as the history of Paris. Napoleon, wishing to emphasize the primacy of the state over the church, crowned himself emperor here, then crowned his wife Joséphine empress. When Paris was liberated during World War II, General de Gaulle rushed to the cathedral after his return, to pray in thanksgiving.

Construction of Notre-Dame started in 1163, but its grounds were sacred long before. Where the cathedral now stands, the Romans built a temple; a Christian basilica and then a Romanesque church succeeded it. As the population grew in the 1100s, Maurice de Sully, bishop of Paris, ordered a brilliant and still unknown architect to build a cathedral. The building was completed in the 14th century.

Parisians, like other urban dwellers in the Middle Ages, learned religious history by looking at the statuary and the stained-glass windows of their cathedral. Built in an age of illiteracy, the cathedral tells the stories of the Bible in its portals, paintings, and stained glass.

Notre-Dame was pillaged during the Revolution: Citizens mistook statues of saints for representations of kings and, in their fervor, took them down. (Some of the statues were found in the 1970s in the Latin Quarter and can be seen in the Musée de Cluny.) Nearly 100 years later, architect Viollet-le-Duc began Notre-Dame's restoration and designed the cathedral's spire, a new feature.

The west front contains 28 statues representing the monarchs of Judea and Israel. The three portals depict, from left to right, the Coronation of the Virgin; the Last Judgment; and the Madonna and Child, surrounded by scenes of Mary's life. The impressive interior, with its slender, graceful columns, holds as many as 6,000 worshipers. The three rose windows—to the west, north, and south—are masterful, their colors a glory to behold on a sunny day.

For a look at the upper parts of the church, the river, and much of Paris, climb the 402 steps to the top of the south tower. (The cleaning of the facade continues through 2004, so expect some views to be obstructed until then.) Lightweights can climb to the first balcony, a mere 255 steps. Allow around 1½ hours including a visit to the tower, but not including the lines.

6 place du Parvis Notre-Dame, Ile de la Cité, 4e. ℂ 01-42-34-56-10. Free admission to cathedral; admission to tower 6€ ($6.90) adults, 4€ ($4.60) students 18–25, free for children under 18. Cathedral Mon–Sat 8am–6:45pm; Sun 8am–7:45pm. Treasury Mon–Sat 9:30am–5:30pm. 6 Masses celebrated on Sun, 4 on weekdays, 1 on Sat. Tower Oct 1–Mar 31 10am–5:30pm; Apr 1–June 30 and Sept 1–30 9am–8pm; July 1–Aug 31 9am–9pm. Free guided visits of the cathedral in English Wed–Thurs noon; Sat 2:30pm. Métro: Cité or St-Michel. RER: St-Michel.

Sainte-Chapelle ✰✰✰   Sainte-Chapelle is an explosion of color. As you enter the lower chapel, you will be surrounded by arches and columns painted in golds, reds, and blues, covered by a starry sky painted on the ceiling. But the real treat awaits when you climb the short, narrow staircase to the upper chapel. The sunlight streaming through its brilliantly hued stained-glass windows is an unforgettable sight. Old and New Testament scenes are illustrated over 612 sq. m (6,588 sq. ft.) of stained glass, to be read from bottom to top and from left to right. The 1,134 scenes trace the Biblical story from the Garden of Eden to the Apocalypse.

St. Louis IX (both king and saint) had the "Holy Chapel" built to house the relics of the crucifixion, including the Crown of Thorns (now in Notre-Dame). The king bought them from the emperor of Constantinople for an astronomical sum—more than twice the cost of the construction of the Sainte-Chapelle itself. The 17th and 18th centuries were not kind to Sainte Chapelle; a fire in 1630 did extensive damage, as did the anticlerical fervor of the French Revolution. Fortunately, plans to raze it were shelved, and renewed interest in the medieval era during the 19th century led to a restoration. Two-thirds of the stained glass is original; the rest is reconstructed. Allow 1 hour to take in this masterpiece.

4 bd. du Palais, Palais de Justice, Ile de la Cité, 4e. (🕐 **01-53-73-78-50**. www.monum.fr (click on "Sainte-Chapelle"). Admission 5.50€ ($6.30) adults, 3.50€ ($4) visitors 18–25, free for children under 18; combined Sainte-Chapelle and Conciergerie ticket 7.65€ ($8.80). Apr–Sept daily 9:30am–6:30pm; Oct–Mar daily 10am–5pm. Closed holidays. Métro: Cité or St-Michel. RER: St-Michel.

TWO PARIS ICONS

Arc de Triomphe ✯✯✯
The world's largest triumphal arch was commissioned by Napoleon in honor of his Grande Armée and its 128 victories. The arch was far from done by the time the imperial army had been swept from the field at Waterloo and wasn't completed until 1836. Although it has come to symbolize the greatness of France and its spirit (or, as Victor Hugo described it, a "stone built on glory"), it has also witnessed some of the country's defeats, as in 1871 and 1940 when German armies marched through the arch and down the Champs-Elysées. Beneath the arch burns an eternal flame honoring France's Unknown Soldier of World War I. On the day of France's liberation from Germany in August 1944, Gen. Charles de Gaulle paid homage here before parading down the Champs-Elysées. Several notable 19th-century sculptures cover the arch, like Rude's *La Marseillaise*, seen on the Champs-Elysées side, and his relief, *Departure of the Volunteers*. To reach the stairs and elevators that climb the arch, take the underpass (via the Métro entrances). From the top, 49m (162 ft.) and 284 steps high, you can see in a straight line the Champs-Elysées, the obelisk in place de la Concorde, and the Louvre. On the other side is a view of the Grande Arche de la Défense, a modern triumphal arch. It's shaped like an open cube and is so large that Notre-Dame could fit beneath it. Set aside at least an hour for your visit here, longer in summer when there's a wait for the elevators.

Place Charles-de-Gaulle, 8e. (🕐 **01-55-37-73-77**. Admission 7€ ($8) adults, 4.50€ ($5.15) visitors 18–25, free for children under 18. Apr–Sept daily 9:30am–11pm; Oct–Mar daily 10am–10:30pm. Closed major holidays. Métro: Charles-de-Gaulle-Etoile.

Eiffel Tower (Tour Eiffel) ✯✯✯ *Kids*
In 1889, Gustave Eiffel beat 699 others in a contest to design what was supposed to be a temporary monument for the 1889 Exposition Universelle (World's Fair), but the Eiffel Tower managed to survive and become the soaring symbol of Paris. Praised by some and damned by others, the tower created as much controversy in its time as I. M. Pei's Louvre pyramid did in the 1980s.

Take the Métro to Trocadéro and walk from the Palais de Chaillot to the Seine to get the full effect of the tower and its surroundings. Besides panoramic views

Special & Free Events

When you arrive, check with the Paris Tourist Office and buy *Pariscope* (a weekly guide with an English-language insert), *Time Out,* or *L'Officiel des Spectacles* for dates, places, and other up-to-date information. Note that telephone access to the **Paris Tourist Office** (© **08-36-68-31-12**) costs .35€ (40¢) per minute.

January
La Grande Parade de Montmartre is a big and noisy New Year's Day parade with bands, majorettes, and elaborate floats. The parade begins at 2pm from Porte St. Martin, 2e (Métro: Strasbourg-St-Denis). During the first weeks of January, the big Parisian stores have their **annual sales**.

February
Foire à la Feraille de Paris. This annual antiques and secondhand fair is held in the Parc Floral de Paris, a garden in the Bois de Vincennes in the 12e arrondissement. For dates, call the **Paris Tourist Office** (see above).

March
The tacky and fun annual **Foire du Trone** carnival has a Ferris wheel, rides and games, hokey souvenirs, and fairground food at the Pelouse de Reuilly in the Bois de Vincennes (20e). Late March to end of May.

April
The **Foire de Paris,** a huge annual fair, signals the start of spring with hundreds of stands selling excellent-priced food and wine, and a variety of clothing and household goods at the Parc des Expositions at the Porte de Versailles. © **01-49-09-61-21.** Late April to early May.

May
During **Les Cinq Jours Extraordinaire (The Five Extraordinary Days),** the antiques shops in the rues du Bac, de Lille, de Beaune, des St-Pères, and de l'Université, and on the quai Voltaire, hold a free open house. © **01-42-61-18-77.** Third week of May.

(especially when the Trocadéro fountains are in full play), you get a free show from the dancers and acrobats in front of the Palais de Chaillot. The spectacle of the tower illuminated against the night sky is unforgettable—but watch out for pickpockets. The tower has elevators in two of its pillars. In summer, the lines for the elevators can be long—up to an hour—so you'll need to factor in 3 hours for this visit. In winter, you can zip up to the top floor in less than 30 minutes. On the top level, historians have re-created the office of engineer Eiffel. The tower has several restaurants and bars.

The vast green esplanade beneath the Eiffel Tower, the **Parc du Champ-de-Mars** 𝔊, extends all the way to the 18th-century Ecole Militaire (Military Academy) at its southeast end. Now a formal lawn, it was once a parade ground for French troops.

Champ-de-Mars, 7e. © **01-44-11-23-45.** www.tour-eiffel.fr. Admission 3.70€ ($4.25) for elevator to 1st level (56m/188 ft.), 7€ ($8) to 2nd level (114m/380 ft.), 10€ ($12) to highest level (318m/1,060 ft.), 3.30€ ($3.80) for stairs to 1st and 2nd levels; discounted admission for children under 12. Sept to mid-June daily 9:30am–11pm; late June to Aug daily 9am–midnight. Fall and winter stairs close at 6:30pm. Métro: Trocadéro, Bir-Hakeim, or Ecole-Militaire. RER: Champ-de-Mars.

June

In late June, a week of expositions and parties climaxes in a massive **Gay Pride Parade,** patterned after those in New York and San Francisco. Call (© **01-43-57-21-47** for the exact date. On the summer solstice (June 21), everyone heads to the streets for the **Fête de la Musique.** Musicians of every caliber perform on nearly every square and street corner.

July

Bastille Day (July 14) commemorates the day a Revolutionary mob stormed the Bastille. Celebrations are held around the city, including a parade down the Champs-Elysées and fireworks near the Eiffel Tower. Also in July is the end of the **Tour de France,** when thousands crowd the Champs-Elysées to witness the finish of this month-long bicycle race.

September

During **Journées Portes Ouvertes,** usually off-limits palaces, churches, and other official buildings throw open their doors to the public for 2 days. Held the weekend closest to Sept. 15; call the Paris Tourist Office (see above).

October

Locals dress in period costumes and the streets come alive with music for the **Fêtes des Vendanges à Montmartre,** the harvest of the wine produced from Montmartre's one remaining vineyard, Clos Montmartre. © **01-46-06-00-32.** First or second Saturday of October.

November

Lancement des Illuminations des Champs-Elysées, the annual lighting of the avenue's Christmas lights, makes for a festive evening that includes jazz concerts. Contact the Tourist Office for exact date and time.

OTHER HISTORIC SITES

Catacombes ⚡ *Kids*   A visit here isn't for the faint of heart: You'll have to descend what seems like an endless narrow staircase, and when you finally arrive way below street level, you'll find dark, dank, eerie tunnels filled with rows of skulls and bones—six million to be exact. There's faint overhead lighting, but bring a flashlight for closer inspection. Wear sneakers or hiking boots to avoid a misstep on the rocky, often slick passageways, and wear a hood to protect yourself from dripping water. The catacombs were the headquarters of the French Resistance during World War II. A visit usually lasts a little over an hour.

1 place Denfert-Rochereau, 14e. © 01-43-22-47-63. Admission 6€ ($6.90) adults, 4€ ($4.60) visitors 8–26, free for children under 8. Sat–Sun 9–11am; Tues–Sun 2–4pm. Métro: Denfert-Rochereau.

Conciergerie ⚡⚡   If you know anything about the French Revolution, you will want to see this infamous edifice. Built in the Middle Ages as a royal palace, it was used as an administrative office of the Crown; torture was frequent at its western tower, the Tour Bonbec. Ravaillac, Henri IV's murderer, was a prisoner here before an angry crowd tore him apart. But the Conciergerie is most famous for its days as a prison during "the Terror" of the French Revolution, when 4,164 "enemies of the people" passed through. More than half headed for the guillotine on place de la Révolution (now place de la Concorde). Besides revolutionary ringleaders Danton and Robespierre, Charlotte Corday and the poet André Chenier were imprisoned here. Marie Antoinette awaited her fate in a tiny, fetid cell.

Marie Antoinette's cell is now a chapel, and the dank cells have been transformed with exhibits and mementos designed to convey a sense of prison life in a brutal era. The Gothic halls built by Philip the Fair in the 14th century are impressive examples of medieval secular architecture. Allow 1½ hours.

Palais de Justice, Ile de la Cité, 1er. © **01-53-73-78-50.** Admission 5.50€ ($6.30) adults, 3.50€ ($4) visitors 18–25, free for children under 18; combined Sainte-Chapelle and Conciergerie ticket 7.60€ ($8.75). Apr–Sept daily 9:30am–6:30pm; Oct–Mar daily 10am–5pm. Métro: Cité, Châtelet–Les Halles, or St-Michel. RER: St-Michel.

Cimetière du Père-Lachaise 🌟🌟 The world's most visited cemetery is more mini-city than somber place of mourning. There are 44 hectares (110 acres) of winding, cobbled streets, park benches, and street signs in addition to tombstones and mausoleums, which are often topped with exquisite marble and stone figures. Many visitors leave flowers or other mementos for their favorites among the famous buried here, who include Balzac, Bizet, Apollinaire, Molière, Colette, Isadora Duncan, Yves Montand, Simone Signoret, Edith Piaf, Oscar Wilde, Chopin, Jim Morrison, Modigliani, Maria Callas, Proust, and Gertrude Stein. A map of the cemetery with famous grave sites marked on it is given free at the entrance, but you can buy a better map from vendors outside the gates. You'll need half a day to leisurely visit this large cemetery. If it's warm, you might want to spend the whole day here and bring a picnic lunch.

16 rue du Repos, 20e. © **01-55-25-82-10.** Free admission. Mar 16–Nov 5 Mon–Fri 8am–6pm, Sat 8:30am–6pm, Sun 9am–6pm; Nov 6–Mar 15 Mon–Fri 8am–5:30pm, Sat 8:30am–5:30pm, Sun 9am–5:30pm. Métro: Père-Lachaise.

Hôtel des Invalides (Napoleon's Tomb) 🌟🌟 Louis XIV, who liked wars and waged many, built this majestic building as a hospital and home for wounded war veterans. To get a sense of the awe that Invalides inspires, access it by crossing the Pont Alexander III Bridge. You'll see the dome of the Eglise du Dôme rising 107m (351 ft.) from the ground, and 16 copper cannons pointed outward in a powerful display. Though the hospital and home for wounded veterans is off-limits, most visitors come for the **Tomb of Napoleon,** a great sarcophagus lying beneath the golden dome of the Invalides. The emperor's body was transferred to this monumental resting place in 1840, almost 2 decades after his death on the remote South Atlantic island of St. Helena, where he was in exile. If you like military lore, you'll want to visit the **Musée de l'Armée,** one of the greatest army museums in the world. It features thousands of weapons from prehistory to World War II. You'll see spearheads and arrowheads, suits of armor, cannons, battle flags, uniforms from all over the world, and all sorts of military paraphernalia. In 2000, the museum unveiled a new series of rooms devoted to World War II, with a focus on General de Gaulle and the Free French—perhaps not the most balanced view, but fascinating nonetheless. Set aside at least 3 hours for a complete visit or just an hour to see the tomb.

Place des Invalides, 7e. © **01-44-42-37-72.** www.invalides.org. Admission 7€ ($8) adults, 5€ ($5.75) students 18–25, free for children under 18. Oct–Mar daily 10am–5pm; Apr–Sept daily 10am–6pm. Tomb of Napoleon open until 7pm June–Sept. Métro: Latour-Maubourg, Invalides, or Varenne.

Les Egouts (Sewers of Paris) 🅚🅲 If you followed Jean Valjean's adventures in *Les Miserables* or have seen movies about World War II French Resistance fighters, a visit to Paris's fascinating sewer system is probably on your list. The tour is popular, so be prepared to wait in line. It starts with a short film about the history of the sewers, followed by a visit to a small museum and finally a short trip through part of this underground city. It was laid out by Belgrand at the same time the *grands boulevards* were built. Streets are clearly labeled, and each branch pipe bears the name of the building to which it's connected. If the mechanical guts of a great city interest you, get in line for an hour's visit on one of the few afternoons when a glimpse is offered. Remember to wear something warm—the temperature is much cooler underground.

Opposite 93 quai d'Orsay/Pont-de-l'Alma, 7e. ✆ 01-53-68-27-82. Admission 5€ ($5.75) adults, 3€ ($3.45) seniors over 60 and students. May–Sept Sat–Wed 11am–5pm; Oct–Apr Sat–Wed 11am–4pm. Closed 3 weeks in Jan. Métro: Alma Marceau. RER: Pont de l'Alma.

Panthéon ✿ This domed neoclassical building near the Sorbonne is the final resting place for many of the nation's greatest men. In the crypt beneath the dome are the tombs of Voltaire, Jean-Jacques Rousseau, Victor Hugo, Louis Braille, Emile Zola, and others. Originally a church commissioned by Louis XV, it was turned into the Panthéon after the Revolution and rededicated as a resting place for France's secular heroes. Most recently, French writer/politician/adventurer André Malraux was honored by a tomb here. A pendulum suspended from the dome re-creates Jean Bernard Foucault's 1851 demonstration proving the rotation of the earth. Plan on spending 2 hours here.

Place du Panthéon, 5e. ✆ 01-44-32-18-00. Admission 7€ ($8) adults, 4€ ($4.60) visitors 18–25, free for children under 18. Apr–Sept daily 9:30am–6:30pm; Oct–Mar daily 10am–6:15pm. Métro: Cardinal-Lemoine. RER: Luxembourg.

HISTORIC SQUARES

The most beautiful square in Paris, the **Place des Vosges** ✿✿✿ sits in the middle of the Marais—a symmetrical block of 36 rose-colored town houses with handsome slate roofs and dormer windows. In the early 17th century, Henri IV transformed this area into the most prestigious neighborhood in France, putting his royal palace here, and the square quickly became the center of courtly parades and festivities. At ground level is a lovely arcaded walkway that's now home to galleries, cafes, antiques dealers, and smart boutiques. Victor Hugo lived at no. 6 for 16 years.

The instantly recognizable names installed on **Place Vendôme** ✿✿✿ (Métro: Opéra) include the Hôtel Ritz and such luxurious stores as Cartier, Van Cleef & Arpels, and Boucheron. Napoleon commissioned the column in the center of this square. The column is modeled on Trajan's column in Rome, to honor those who fought and won the Battle of Austerlitz. During the Paris Commune in 1871, the original column was torn down; it was re-erected before World War I. Napoleon's statue has graced the top of the column at times; there's also been a fleur-de-lis and a statue of Henri IV.

Place de la Concorde ✿✿✿ (Métro: Concorde), at the end of the Champs-Elysées, is a stunning example of artistic, dynamic urban design. During the day, wild traffic whizzes past the formidable administrative buildings toward the Champs-Elysées or Pont de la Concorde. The place takes on a mystical aura when the sun begins to set and the obelisk becomes a piercing silhouette against the sky, its lines mirrored by the Eiffel Tower in the distance. This is one of the centers of Paris. On its perimeter stands the **Hôtel Crillon,** where Benjamin Franklin and Louis XVI signed the Treaty of Friendship and Trade, recognizing the United States of America, in February 1778. Soon thereafter, the octagonal space, designed by

Avant-Garde Architecture in Paris: La Grande Arche de la Défense

This 35-story cube was built for the bicentennial of the French Revolution in 1989. Designed by Danish architect Johan Otto von Spreckelsen as the centerpiece of the La Défense suburb, the view from the top offers a spectacular vista down avenue Charles-de-Gaulle to the Arc de Triomphe, the Champs-Elysées, and the Louvre. On weekend nights in the summer, free jazz concerts are held here. The arch is located at 1 parvis de la Défense (© 01-49-07-27-57). Admission is 7€ ($8) adults, 5.50€ ($6.30) students 15 to 26, 4.50€ ($5.15) children 6 to 14, free for children under 6. Open October to March daily 10am to 7pm; April to September daily 10am to 8pm (Métro: Grande-Arche-de-la-Défense; RER: La Défense–Grande Arche).

Gabriel under Louis XV, became place de la Révolution. The guillotine was installed here, and among the heads severed was that of Louis XVI. From 1793 to 1795, 1,343 people were guillotined—Marie Antoinette, Mme. du Barry, Charlotte Corday, Danton, Robespierre, and Alexandre de Beauharnais among them. After the Reign of Terror, in hopes of peace, the square was renamed place de la Concorde. The **Egyptian obelisk** comes from the temple of Ramses II in Thebes, and is more than 3,000 years old. It was a gift to France from Egypt in 1829.

PARKS & GARDENS

The legendary **Bois de Boulogne** ⊛⊛⊛ (Métro: Les-Sablons, Porte-Maillot, or Porte-Dauphine), in western Paris, was formerly a forest and a royal hunting preserve. Napoleon III donated it to the city, and Baron Haussmann, his town planner, transformed it into a park, using London's Hyde Park as his model. Today the Bois is a vast reserve of more than 880 hectares (2,200 acres). It offers space for jogging, horseback riding, bicycling (rentals are available), and boating on the two lakes. Also here are the famous Longchamp and Auteuil racecourses and the beautiful **Jardin Shakespeare,** a garden containing many of the plants and herbs mentioned in Shakespeare's plays. In addition, you'll find the **Jardin d'Acclimatation** ⊛, a children's amusement park open daily June through August 10am to 7pm and September through May 10am to 6pm. Admission is 2.50€ ($2.90) adults and children 3 and over, free for children under 3. Finally, be sure to visit the **Parc de Bagatelle** ⊛⊛, a delightful collection of thematic gardens. The rose gardens are particularly sublime, and there is also a pond of water lilies—the garden's designer was a friend of Monet. As the sun sets, prostitutes move in (notably along the Porte Dauphine entrance), so the Bois is best enjoyed in daylight.

A study in geometric elegance, the **Jardin des Tuileries** ⊛⊛⊛, located between the Louvre and place de la Concorde, 1er (Métro: Tuileries or Concorde), was laid out in the 1560s to complement Catherine de Medici's Tuileries Palace, which burned down in the 19th century. In 1664, Le Nôtre, creator of French landscaping, redesigned a large section of the garden in the formal, classical style, adding octagonal pools surrounded by statues and terraces. In 1990, the Tuileries got a major overhaul and today it is as stunning as ever. An impressive array of sculpture, both classical and modern, is scattered throughout the gardens, including works by Jean Dubuffet, Alberto Giacometti, David Smith, Max Ernst, Henry Moore, and Henri Laurens.

The 6e arrondissement's **Jardin du Luxembourg** ⊛⊛⊛, commissioned by King Henri IV's queen, Marie de Medici, is one of Paris's most beloved parks. The

French love of order and harmony is expressed in these formal gardens—long gravel walks shaded by trees lead to a central pond and fountain. On the way, flower beds and statues create a calm, inviting space. Parisians flock to the park to read, sunbathe, or people-watch. Sunday-afternoon band concerts draw a crowd in the summer, and the Medici Fountain is a cool, shady spot on a hot day. Children love the park, too, especially for the *parc à jeux* (playground), the toy sailboats in the central pond, and the *théâtre des marionettes* (puppet theater), where the ancient *Guignol* characters live on. Besides pools, fountains, and statues, there are tennis courts and spaces for playing boules. In the southwest corner is an orchard where several hundred species of apple and pear trees blossom each spring. A fenced-in area in the northwest corner houses beehives, and a beekeeping course is taught on weekends in the spring and summer.

The **Palais du Luxembourg,** at the northern edge of the park, was built for Marie de Medici, who was homesick for the Palace Pitti in Florence. Upon the queen's banishment in 1630, the palace passed along to various royals until the Revolution, when it was used as a prison. The *orangerie* here holds the **Musée de Luxembourg** (© 01/42-34-25-95), which presents temporary exhibits several times per year.

The **Bois de Vincennes** *(Métro: Porte-Dorée or Château de Vincennes)* boasts a lake where you can rent boats, a *parc zoologique,* and a petting zoo. There is also a Buddhist center, complete with temple; a castle, the Château de Vincennes; and the **Parc Floral de Paris** *,* which has a butterfly garden, library, and, in the summer, free concerts. Admission is 6€ ($6.90) adults, 4.50€ ($5.15) ages 4 to 16 and seniors (over 60), free for children under 4. The park is open daily 9am to 6pm.

Of Paris's parks and squares, the English-style **Parc Monceau** *(Métro: Monceau)* is the most romantic. A favorite of Proust, it contains some odd features, like a pyramid, ancient columns, and several tombs of unknown origin. The park is in the heart of a well-heeled residential district.

ORGANIZED TOURS

BUS TOURS Paris is the perfect city to explore on your own, but if your time or legs don't permit, consider taking an introductory bus tour. The most prominent company is **Cityrama,** 4 place des Pyramides, 1er (© 01-44-55-61-00; www.cityrama.com; Métro: Palais Royal–Musée du Louvre). The 2-hour orientation with a live guide costs 24€ ($28), free for children under 12 (one free child per paying adult). There are also guided half- and full-day tours for 53€ ($61) and 99€ ($114). Tours to Versailles for 58€ ($67) and to Chartres for 48€ ($55) are a good bargain—they eliminate a lot of hassle. Nighttime illumination tours start at 26€ ($30).

Paris's public transit agency, the RATP, has a sightseeing system called **Paris l'Open Tour** (© 01-43-46-52-06; www.ecityrama.com/opentour). This is a "hop-on, hop-off" setup using open-topped yellow buses that take you from highlight to highlight in the city while you listen to recorded commentary in French and English. Three circuits cover all the sights in central Paris and extensions east to Bercy and north to Montmartre—40 stops in all. You can get on and off the bus as many times as you wish; buses pass the stops about every 20 minutes. The buses run daily throughout the year from around 9:30am to 6:30pm. A 1-day pass costs 23€ ($26), and the 2-day pass is 28€ ($32). You get a 16% discount on a 1-day pass if you have a Paris Visite pass (1- to 3-day pubic transit pass; 9€–20€/$10–$23). Paris l'Open Tour and Paris Visite passes

---

Tips View from the Bus

If you're feeling adventurous and want a bargain tour, the Paris bus system is clean and efficient, and has routes that could come straight from a guidebook. You can get bus maps in most Métro stations; each bus stop will have a map showing the route of the bus that stops there. For more information, contact the city public transit agency, the RATP (© 08-36-68-41-14).

---

are on sale at the Paris Tourist Office and the RATP visitor center at place de la Madeleine.

BOAT TOURS   Among the most popular ways to see Paris is a cruise on the Seine. The **Bateaux-Mouches** (© **01-42-25-96-10**, or 01-42-25-76-10 for reservations; www.bateaux-mouches.fr; Métro: Alma Marceau) sail from the pont de l'Alma on the Right Bank. From March through mid-November, departures are usually on the hour and half-hour; in winter there are 5 to 10 cruises per day, depending on demand. The voyage includes taped commentary in six languages and lasts about an hour. It costs 7€ ($8) for adults, 4€ ($4.60) for children 5 to 13 and seniors (over 65); children under 5 ride free.

Bateaux-Parisiens (© **01-44-11-33-44;** www.bateauxparisiens.com; Métro: Iéna) offers similar tours from the pont d'Iéna on the Left Bank, with the added attraction of an onboard cafeteria and evening departures until 10pm (11pm July–Aug). They cost 9€ ($10) for adults, 4.10€ ($4.70) for children under 13.

Vedettes Pont Neuf (© **01-46-33-98-38;** Métro: Pont Neuf) sails from Square du Vert Galant on the Ile de la Cité, and has smaller boats and live guides. It charges 9€ ($10) for adults, 4€ ($4.60) for children 4 to 12.

Paris Canal (© **01-42-40-96-97;** www.pariscanal.com; Métro: Bastille) offers longer and more unusual tours of Parisian waterways. The 3-hour cruises leave the Musée d'Orsay at 9:30am and end at Parc de la Villette, 19e. The boat passes under the Bastille and enters the Canal St-Martin for a journey along the tree-lined quai Jemmapes. An English-speaking guide is on hand to regale you with local lore as you cruise under bridges and through locks. The boat leaves the Parc de la Villette at 2:30pm for the same voyage in reverse. Reservations are essential. The trip costs 16€ ($18) for adults, 12€ ($13) for seniors over 60, 9€ ($10) for children 4 to 11. Paris Canal also has a 1-day trip that cruises the Seine past Paris and into the countryside and takes a little loop on the Marne; it costs 32€ ($37) not including lunch (no discounts for children). If you are pressed for time and still want to do a canal, **Canauxrama** (© **01-42-39-15-00;** www.canauxrama.com; Métro: Jaurès or Bastille) offers 2-hour tours of both Canal St-Martin and Canal de l'Ourcq. The fare is 13€ ($15) for adults, 11€ ($13) for students and seniors over 60, and 8€ ($9.20) for children 6 to 12; children under 6 ride free. Reservations are required.

BIKE TOURS   Along with renting bicycles, **Maison Roue Libre** (95 bis rue Rambuteau; © **08-10-44-15-34;** Métro: Rambuteau) also runs **bike tours.** Tours cost 16€ ($18) for a 1½-hour tour, 26€ ($30) for a 3-hour tour, and 45€ ($52) for a 1-day tour out of the city to a nearby castle. **Paris a Vélo C'est Sympa** (© **01-48-87-60-01;** Métro: Bastille) offers 3-hour bike tours for 30€ ($35). Reservations are required. They also rent bikes for 13€ ($14) a day, 9.50€ ($11) a half day, or 22€ ($25) from Saturday morning until Sunday evening.

5 Shopping

Paris is truly a shopper's heaven, offering everything from tony haute couture shops to hidden *depot-ventes* (resale shops) selling last year's Yves St-Laurent at bargain prices. Most resale stores are in the stylish 8e, 16e, and 17e arrondissements. For overstock, end-of-series, and *dégriffé* (labels removed) clothes, bargain-hunters head to rue **St-Placide** in the 6e (Métro: Sèvres-Babylone), a street of dreams for frugal shoppers looking for affordable sportswear and men's fashions. **Mouton à Cinq Pattes** (nos. 8, 10, and 48 on rue St-Placide) sells children's, women's, and men's designer clothes. **Rue Paradis** in the 10e (Métro: Poissonière) is filled with wholesale china and porcelain stores such as Paradis Porcelaine at no. 56 and La Tisanière Porcelaine at no. 21. For very off-the-wall end-of-series pieces, visit the **L'Espace Createurs** on the first level of the Forum des Halles, where over 50 young designers (mostly European) sell their (ever so slightly) passé creations at heavy discounts. Shops on **rue d'Alésia** in the 14e (Métro: Alésia) offer last season's Cacharel, Chantal Thomass, Diapositive, Régina Rubens, and Sonia Rykiel, among other midprice lines. Many stores are closed Monday or Monday morning.

France imposes a **value-added tax** (TVA in French) of 20.6% on most goods, but if you're not a European resident you can get a refund. You must spend more than 185€ ($213) in each store and show the clerk your passport. See chapter 1, "Enjoying Europe on a Budget," for details on getting your refund.

FASHION

Réciproque, 89–123 rue de la Pompe, 16e (© **01-47-04-30-28;** Métro: Rue de la Pompe), is the place to go for designer clothes at a bargain, though prices over $1,000 are still all too common. The largest resale store in Paris fills its stores along rue de la Pompe with racks of lightly used clothing for men, women, and children, as well as jewelry, furs, belts, and purses. The sheer number of gently worn Chanel suits is astonishing. Midrange labels are also well represented.

Paris's *grands magasins,* or department stores, offer all kinds of French goods. Two of them, Au Printemps and Galeries Lafayette, offer tourists a 10% discount coupon. If your hotel or travel agent didn't give you one of these coupons (they're sometimes attached to a city map), you can ask for it at the stores' welcome desks—the clerks speak English. With its first two floors recently redone, **Au Printemps,** 64 bd. Haussmann, 9e (© **01-42-82-50-00;** Métro: Havre-Caumartin), is beginning to don a new, sleeker look. The department store's Maison Store is great if you're into home decorating. For the clothes connoisseur, there's a fashion show under the 1920s glass dome at 10:15am on Tuesdays year-round and Fridays March through October. Almost always crowded, the colossal **Galeries Lafayette,** 40 bd. Haussmann, 9e (© **01-42-82-34-56;** Métro: Opéra or Chaussée-d'Antin), is worth checking out for its selection of hip new clothes, which are often very affordable. If you're shopping with *les enfants,* you might want to visit the kiddie entertainment center. The sixth floor self-service cafeteria, Lafayette Café, offers tasty food and has good views of Opéra and the rooftops of Paris.

Near the Marais, **BHV** (Bazar de l'Hôtel de Ville), 52–64 rue de Rivoli, 1er (© **01-42-74-90-00;** Métro: Hôtel de Ville), is a popular department store among Parisians because of its reasonable prices on everything from clothing to luggage. **Au Bon Marché,** 24 rue de Sèvres, 7e (© **01-44-39-80-00;** Métro: Sèvres-Babylone), is the oldest department store in Paris. The clothing here is fabulous! Prices are high, but during the sales you can find tons of deals. Visit the huge basement supermarket, with its many reasonably priced food items; it's the city's largest *épicerie,* and you can find nearly any kind of food.

Located between the Louvre and the Pont Neuf, **La Samaritaine,** 67 rue de Rivoli, 1er (② **01-40-41-20-20;** Métro: Pont Neuf or Châtelet–Les Halles), which is made up of four buildings, feels and looks more quintessentially French than the other department stores. It also has the best view: Look for signs to the *panorama,* a free observation point, to see Paris from up high. The fifth floor of store no. 2 has a fine, inexpensive restaurant.

Clothing is stylish and inexpensive at **Monoprix-Prisunic,** which has various locations around Paris (② **01/55-20-70-00**). These stores are also great for accessories, cosmetics, lingerie, housewares, and groceries.

FOOD

La Maison du Chocolat, 225 rue du Faubourg St-Honoré, 8e (② **01-42-27-39-44;** Métro: Ternes), is the best place in Paris to buy chocolate. **La Grande Epiceriet,** Au Bon Marché, 38 rue de Sèvres, 7e (② **01-44-39-81-00;** Métro: Sèvres-Babylone), is like a food museum, but even better because you can actually buy the goods!

MARKETS

A trip to Paris is not complete without a visit to the vast **Marché aux Puces de la Porte de St-Ouen,** 18e (Métro: Porte-de-Clignancourt). The Clignancourt flea market features thousands of stalls, carts, shops, and vendors selling everything from vintage clothing to antique paintings and furniture. The best times for bargains are at opening and just before closing. Avoid the stalls selling junk on the periphery, and watch out for pickpockets. The market is open Saturday through Monday 9am to 8pm. The market at **Porte de Vanves,** 14e (Métro: Porte de Vanves), is a bit more upscale, but so are its prices. It's open Saturday and Sunday 8:30am to 1pm. The prettiest of all the markets is the **Marché aux Fleurs** (Métro: Cité), the flower market on place Louis-Lépine on the Ile de la Cité. Visit Monday through Saturday to enjoy the flowers, even if you don't buy anything. On Sunday it becomes the **Marché aux Oiseaux,** an equally colorful bird market.

6 Paris After Dark

Paris nightlife is incredibly diverse, with everything from tony bars and tea dances to throbbing clubs to ballet and opera venues to a host of cinemas.

Pariscope (.40€/45¢) is a weekly guide with comprehensive entertainment listings, including a selection of events in its English-language "Time Out Paris" section. The *Paris Free Voice* is an English-language free monthly that spotlights events of interest to English speakers, including readings, plays, and literary evenings at bookstores and libraries. Look for it in English-language bookstores and other Anglophone haunts.

Many concert, theater, and dance tickets are sold through FNAC stores as well as at the box office. There are a dozen or so FNAC outlets; the biggest is 74 av. des Champs-Elysées (Métro: George V). You can also purchase tickets by phone at **FNAC** (② **08-92-68-36-22**).

THE PERFORMING ARTS

CLASSICAL MUSIC More than a dozen churches schedule **organ** recitals and concerts; tickets are free or inexpensive at 9€ to 24€ ($10–$28). Among them are **Notre-Dame** (② **01-42-34-56-10;** Métro: Cité); **St-Eustache,** 1 rue Montmartre, 1er (② **01-42-36-31-05;** Métro: Châtelet); **St-Sulpice,** place

St-Sulpice (© **01-46-33-21-78;** Métro: St-Sulpice), which has the largest organ; **St-Germain-des-Prés,** place St-Germain-des-Prés (© **01-43-25-41-71;** Métro: St-Germain-des-Prés); the **Madeleine,** place de la Madeleine (© **01-44-51-69-00;** Métro: Madeleine); and **St-Louis en l'Ile,** 19 bis rue St-Louis-en-l'Ile (© **01-46-34-11-60;** Métro: Pont-Marie). The Sunday concerts at 6pm at the **American Church,** 65 quai d'Orsay (© **01-40-62-05-00;** Métro: Invalides), are friendly and inviting.

Free concerts occasionally take place in the parks and gardens; check any of the entertainment guides for information. **Maison de la Radio,** 116 av. du President-Kennedy, 16e (© **01-56-40-15-16**), offers free tickets to recordings of some concerts; check out *Pariscope.* Tickets are available an hour before recording starts. **Cité de la Musique,** 221 av. Jean-Jaurès, 19e (© **01-44-84-44-84;** www.cite-musique.fr; Métro: Porte-de-Pantin), offers a concert program that has a universal appeal: chamber music, world music, and new music are all offered here. Tickets are 7€ to 34€ ($8.05–$39). In addition, the **Conservatoire National de Musique** at the Cité de la Musique, 209 av. Jean-Jaurès, 19e (© **01-40-40-46-46**), stages free concerts and ballets by students at the conservatory. The Orchestre de Paris usually plays in the **Salle Pleyel,** 252 rue du Faubourg St-Honoré, 8e (© **01/45-61-53-00;** Métro: Ternes). However, the hall is under renovation until September 2004 so they will be performing a full lineup at the **Theatre Mogador,** 25 rue Mogador, 9e (© **01-56-35-12-00;** Métro: Trinite or Chaussée d'Antin). Tickets are 10€ to 65€ ($12–$75).

OPERA & DANCE   The city's principal opera stage is the **Opéra Bastille,** on place de la Bastille, 12e (© **08-92-89-90-90;** www.opera-de-paris.fr.; Métro: Bastille). Opened to commemorate the 1989 bicentennial of the Revolution, this modernistic performance center was designed by Uruguayan-Canadian architect Carlos Ott and has brought new life to the Bastille neighborhood. Opera tickets are 10€ to 114€ ($12–$131); dance tickets are 8€ to 70€ ($9.20–$81). The gorgeous, newly renovated **Opéra Garnier,** place de l'Opéra, 9e (© **08-92-89-90-90;** www.opera-de-paris.fr; Métro: Opéra), is the home of the Paris Opera Ballet and is mainly dedicated to dance. Dance tickets are 6€ to 70€ ($6.90–$81); opera tickets are 7€ to 114€ ($8.05–$131).

Excellent operas, concerts, recitals, and dance are found at **Châtelet, Théâtre Musical de Paris,** 1 place du Châtelet, 1e (© **01-40-28-28-40;** www.chatelet-theatre.com; Métro: Châtelet). Check out the concert series on Monday, Wednesday, and Friday at 12:45pm for only 9€ ($10). Opera tickets are 12€ to 105€ ($14–$121); ballet tickets are 9€ to 55€ ($10–$63); and concert and recital tickets are 9€ to 55€ ($10–$63).

Théâtre de la Ville, 2 place du Châtelet, 1cr (© **01-42-74-22-77;** www.theatredelaville-paris.com; Métro: Châtelet), is now a major venue for cutting-edge performances, from modern dance to avant-garde theater to an eclectic array of concerts (world music, classical, and French *chanson* are all on the lineup for 2004). Tickets are 15€ to 22€ ($17–$25).

THEATER   Most theatrical performances in Paris are, of course, in French. If Racine in the original is too much for you, don't despair; there are a handful of small **English-language theater companies** in Paris. None have a permanent address, but most advertise their periodic performances in the "Time Out" section of *Pariscope* or in the *Paris Voice.*

The works of Corneille, Racine, Molière, and other classic French playwrights come alive at the 300-year-old refurbished **Comédie-Française,** 2 rue de Richelieu, 1er (© **01-44-58-15-15;** www.comedie-francaise.fr.; Métro: Palais-Royal-Musée-du-Louvre). Nowadays, schedules vary with the addition of modern works and plays translated from other languages. If you aren't fairly fluent in French or aren't familiar with the plays, chances are you will not enjoy the performances. Note that for those under 27, last-minute seats for 10€ ($12) in the upper balcony are sold 1 hour before performances. Most tickets range between 11€ and 30€ ($13–$35).

CABARETS & REVUES

Even before Josephine Baker stunned Paris with her banana costume, Paris's cabarets had a reputation for sensual naughtiness. Though the names Lido, Folies Bergère, Crazy Horse Saloon, and Moulin Rouge conjure up images of Maurice Chevalier and Mistinguett, it's the saucy cancan dancers that still draw in the crowds. However, headlining entertainers have given way to light shows, special effects, canned music, and a bevy of nearly nude women and (sometimes) men. If you must see a Parisian cancan show, you'll pay steeply. The most famous of the cabarets is the **Moulin Rouge,** Place Blanche, 18e (© **01-53-09-82-82;** Métro: Blanche), which has been packing in the crowds since 1889. These days, reputation is what the Moulin Rouge mainly trades on. Its current show, *Féerie,* features a giant aquarium, 100 *artistes,* 60 "Doriss Girls," and lots of feathers. A bar seat and a required two drinks is 63€ ($72); Sunday through Thursday the revue and champagne are 92€ ($106) at 9pm, 82€ ($94) at 11pm; dinner and the show are 130€ ($150) at 7pm, 160€ ($184) at other times. Reserve early.

At **Paradis Latin,** 28 rue Cardinal-Lemoine, 5e (© **01-43-25-28-28;** www. paradis-latin.com; Métro: Cardinal-Lemoine), in a building designed by Gustave Eiffel, the revue called *Paradis d'Amour* is the most typically French of the bunch. The show is less gimmicky than the others around town and relies more on the talents of its singers and dancers. The master of ceremonies banters in French and English and encourages audience participation. Even the waiters get into the act. Performances are Wednesday through Monday at 9:30pm. The revue and a half bottle of champagne are 75€ ($86); the revue and dinner start at 109€ ($125).

JAZZ CLUBS

Parisians have an insatiable craving for American music, especially jazz, and the scene is vibrant as a new generation develops a taste for the sound. Look through the current *Zurban* or *Pariscope* for the artists you admire. You can also check the Paris jazz website: www.jazzvalley.com.

New Morning, 7–9 rue des Petites-Ecuries, 10e (© **01-45-23-51-41;** www. newmorning.com; Métro: Château-d'Eau), is the star of Paris's jazz clubs. The best perform here, from Archie Shepp, Bill Evans, and Elvin Jones to Kevin Coyne and Koko Ateba. Concerts begin at 9pm. Reserve early. Cover is 19€ to 22€ ($21–$25).

Le Baiser Salé, 58 rue des Lombards, 1er (© **01-42-33-37-71;** Métro: Châtelet–Les Halles), is a small club where the jazz sounds are fusion: Jazz funk, Latin jazz, and African jazz are some of the mixes on tap. Cover is 8€ to 13€ ($9.20–$15). Thursdays are free. **Le Duc des Lombards,** 42 rue des Lombards, 1er (© **01-42-33-22-88;** Métro: Châtelet–Les Halles), may be crowded, noisy, and smoky, but this club presents some of the most interesting jazz around. A different band plays every night. Repertoires range from free jazz to hard bop—you won't find traditional jazz here. Cover is 16€ to 19€ ($18–$22).

The interior at **Le Petit Journal Montparnasse,** 13 rue du Commandant Mouchotte, 14e (© **01-43-21-56-70;** Métro: Montparnasse-Bienvenüe), is much more spacious and, in principle, less smoky than other clubs. Current programming includes jazz, blues, boogie, and occasional French songs. The music starts around 10pm and lasts until 1:30am. Cover (including one drink) is 18€ to 22€ ($21–$25). **Le Petit Journal Saint-Michel,** 71 bd. St-Michel, 5e (© **01-43-26-28-59;** Métro: Cluny-Sorbonne), offers a lineup that is at least as prestigious as the one at its sister operation in Montparnasse (see above). You can dine as well as drink here in a warm, relaxed atmosphere. Cover (including one drink) is 18€ to 22€ ($21–$25).

Also see **Caveau de la Hûchette** (p. 749).

BARS

Beautiful people dressed in black come to **La Fabrique,** 53 rue du Faubourg St-Antoine, 11e (© **01-43-07-67-07;** Métro: Bastille), to be seen, drink at the minimalist bar, and eat the Alsatian specialty, *Flammekueche* (large, thin-crusted pizzas topped with cream, herbs, and items of your choice). Deejays arrive around 11pm, as do the crowds.

Stylish but easygoing, the **Lizard Lounge,** 18 rue du Bourg-Tibourg, 4e (© 01/42-72-81-34; Métro: Hôtel-de-Ville), is a pleasant Marais place to hang out with an arty international crowd after dinner. You can also come early in the evening for a reasonably priced light meal from the open kitchen and stay for the deejay spinning dance music in the refurbished basement every night.

Don't look for a sign for this bar owned by Johnny Depp, John Malkovich, and Sean Penn; the entrance to **Man Ray,** 34 rue Marbeuf, 8e (© **01/56-88-36-36;** Métro: F.-D.-Roosevelt), is marked only by a Chinese character and big wrought-iron doors. The upstairs bar area is spacious, and the music leans to jazz in the early evening. Friday nights after 11pm the music takes on a harder edge and the bar hosts a hyper-hip dance party with a pricey 16€ ($18) cover charge.

At **Buddha Bar,** 8 rue Boissy d'Anglas, 8e (© **01-53-05-90-00;** Métro: Concorde), the music is spacey, the atmosphere is electric, and you'll see some of the prettiest people in Paris. For such a trendy spot, the food is mediocre, but food is not the point. The point is to see and be seen and then say you saw it. A trendy young crowd surrounds the U-shaped bar and listens to acid jazz and funk at **Sanz Sans,** Faubourg St-Antoine, 12e (© **01-44-75-78-78;** Métro: Bastille). The *venir accompagner* (men must come accompanied by a woman) policy applies here, as does a hipster dress code.

GAY & LESBIAN CLUBS

They don't call it "Gay Paree" for nothing. The city has one of the world's largest homosexual populations, with many gay clubs, restaurants, organizations, and services.

The Marais is the city's main gay and lesbian neighborhood, and rainbow flags flutter over bars and restaurants dotting its narrow streets. Gay dance clubs come and go so fast that even the magazines devoted to them—*e.m@ale* and *Illico,* both distributed free in the gay bars and bookstores—have a hard time keeping up. For lesbians, the guide *Exes Femmes* publishes a free seasonal listing of bars and clubs. Also look for nightlife listings in **Têtu.**

Le Pulp, 25 bd. Poissonnière, 2e (© **01-40-26-01-93;** Métro: Grands-Boulevards), resembles a 19th-century French music hall, and the music is cutting edge. This is probably the hippest lesbian dance club in Paris, and no one shows up until after midnight. The presence of men is discouraged, although if you're a gay male, you can go to the "separate but equal," side entrance of **Le Scorp** (© 01/40-26-28-30). **Les Scandaleuses,** 8 rue des Ecouffes, 4e (© **01/48-87-39-26;** Métro: St-Paul), is a laid-back lesbian bar attracting a diverse mix of women, with styles running from pink-haired punk to denim and flannel. The place is jammed on weekends when Djette Sex Toy spins house and techno. A few blocks east of avenue de l'Opéra, **La Champmesle,** 4 rue Chabanais, 2e (© **01/42-96-85-20;** Métro: Bourse, Pyramides, Quatre-Septembre, or Opéra), is a comfortable bar for women. Cabaret night on Thursday draws a large crowd.

There's a relaxed and friendly ambience at **Amnesia Café,** 42 rue Vielle-du-Temple, 4e (© **01-42-72-16-94;** Métro Hôtel-de-Ville). The ambience is more friendly than cruisey, and the drinks and food reasonably priced. Restaurant service stops at 5pm when the bar action cranks up. A tiny dance floor in the basement gets hopping at midnight. **Open Café,** 17 rue des Archives, 4e (© **01-42-72-26-18;** Métro: Hotel de Ville), is a great spot to people-watch in the heart of the Marais. This popular gay cafe/bar has lots of outdoor seating and is busy from midafternoon to late at night. The crowd is mostly male and mixed—everything from American travelers nursing beers to young professionals sipping espresso after a day at work to partying Parisians on their way to the dance clubs. Also see Le Queen, under "Dance Clubs," below.

DANCE CLUBS

If you are in search of ultimate cool, some of the hippest bars and dance clubs are in the 8e and the Marais, which is also the focus of gay nightlife. The Bastille proper has lost much of its cachet, but new clubs and bars are appearing farther back near rue de Charonne and rue Keller. In the past few years, rue Oberkampf has exploded with a profusion of bars and restaurants offering a relaxed, "non-scene" scene; the area is still popular.

Most clubs don't open until 11pm, and the music doesn't stop until dawn. The later you go, the better. Check out French magazines *Nova* and *Zurban* and *Pariscope*'s sections *"Paris la Nuit"* (in French) and "Paris Nightlife" (in English) for the latest on hot clubs.

Edith Piaf used to perform at **Le Balajo,** 9 rue de Lappe, 11e (© **01-47-00-07-87;** www.balajo.fr; Métro: Bastille), but now the music is rap, reggae, and salsa combined with the *musette* of yesteryear. The international crowd (ages 18–80) is racially mixed, fun, hip, and wild; the Thursday-night and Sunday-afternoon *bal musette* draw older crowds. It really gets going around 3am. The cover, which includes one drink, is 16€ ($18) on Tuesday, Wednesday, Friday, and Saturday nights. Admission to the *bal musette* on Thursday and Sunday is 8€ ($9.20).

The high-tech **Rex Club,** 5 bd. Poissonnière, 2e (© **01-42-36-10-96;** Métro: Bonne-Nouvelle), has techno on Friday night, and house on Thursday and Saturday nights; Wednesday could be anything. The cover on Wedneday varies; Thursday to Friday cover is 11€ ($24), and Saturday it is 13€ ($15). **Bus Palladium,** 6 rue Fontaine, 9e (© **01/-53-21-07-33;** Métro: Blanche), is the best bet for people who can't stand house and techno. Thursday night is devoted to Motown and the groove sound. On other nights, the emphasis is on mainstream rock. Cover is 16€ ($18).

The doorman will decide whether you'll be allowed in to play with the supermodels, designers, and movie people who frequent **Les Bains,** 7 rue du Bourg-l'Abbe, 3e (© **01-48-87-01-80;** Métro: Etienne Marcel.) Dress as fashionably as you can and show up around 1am. This is one of the best parties in town. Cover (includes one drink) is 20€ ($23).

Not only the busiest gay disco but one of the hottest clubs in town, **Le Queen,** 102 av. des Champs-Elysées, 8e (© **08-92-70-73-30;** www.queen.fr; Métro: George V), attracts the wildest of Paris's night people. The crowd is about two-thirds gay. Women usually get in only with male friends, and Sunday and Monday the crowd is heavily gay. The cover Sunday through Thursday is 10€ ($12); Friday and Saturday (includes one drink) it's 20€ ($23).

If you swing, **Caveau de la Huchette,** 5 rue de la Huchette, 5e (© **01-43-26-65-05;** Métro or RER: St-Michel), is a fabulous place to dance to top-quality jazz bands. The music starts at 9:30pm. Cover Sunday to Thursday is 10€ ($12), Friday and Saturday 12€ ($14).

7 A Side Trip to Versailles ★ & Its Gardens

21km (13 miles) SW of Paris

The Château de Versailles (© **01-39-50-36-22;** www.chateauversailles.fr) is astonishing. The over-the-top magnificence of the vast grounds and gardens and the size and wealth of the castle attest to the excesses of Louis XIV. The "Sun King" reigned for 72 years, beginning in 1643, when he was only 5. He sought to prove his greatness with a château that would be the wonder of Europe. He hired the best: Louis Le Vau and Jules Hardouin-Mansart, France's premier architects; André Le Nôtre, designer of the Tuileries gardens; and Charles Le Brun, head of the Royal Academy of Painting and Sculpture, for the interior. Construction began in 1661.

In 1682, Louis XIV transferred the court to Versailles and, to prevent plots against him, summoned his nobles to live with him. An estimated 3,000 to 10,000 people, including servants, lived at Versailles. When Louis XIV died in 1715, his great-grandson Louis XV succeeded him. The new king continued the pomp and ceremony and made interior renovations until lack of funds forced him to stop. While the aristocrats frivolously played away their lives, often in silly intrigues and games, the peasants on the estates sowed the seeds of the Revolution. Louis XV's son, Louis XVI, and his queen, Marie Antoinette, had simpler tastes and made no major changes. But by then, it was too late. On October 6, 1789, a mob marched on the palace and forced the royal couple to return to Paris, and Versailles ceased to be a royal residence.

The six magnificent **Grands Appartements** are in the Louis XIV style, each named after the allegorical painting on the room's ceiling. The largest is the **Hercules Salon,** with a ceiling depicting the Apotheosis of Hercules. After his death in 1715, the body of Louis XIV lay in state for 8 days in the **Salon of Mercury.** The most famous room at Versailles is the 71m (236-ft.) -long **Hall of Mirrors.** Hardouin-Mansart began work on the hall in 1678, and Le Brun added 17 large windows and corresponding mirrors. Thirty ceiling paintings represent the accomplishments of Louis XIV's government. The German Empire was proclaimed here in 1871. On June 28, 1919, the treaty ending World War I was signed in this room.

Louis XV and Louis XVI and their families lived in the *Petits Appartements.* Louis XV stashed his mistress, Mme. du Barry (and earlier, Mme. de Pompadour), in his second-floor apartment, which can be visited only with a guide. The *appartement* of Mme. de Maintenon, Louis XIV's mistress and later his wife, is also here. Attempts have been made to restore the original decor of the queen's bedchamber, which Marie Antoinette renovated with a huge four-poster bed and silks in a pattern of lilacs and peacock feathers.

Versailles

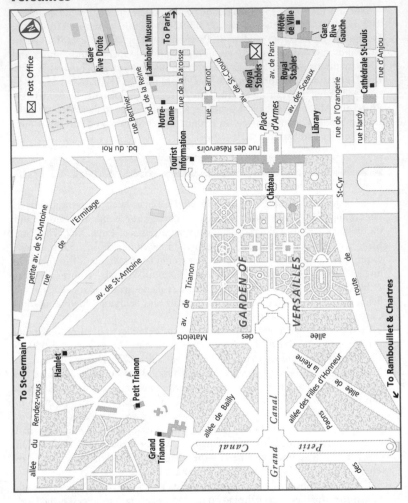

Louis XVI had an impressive library, designed by Ange Jacques Gabriel, but it didn't seem to influence the dim-witted monarch. The library's panels are delicately carved, and the room has been restored and refurnished. The Clock Room contains Passement's astronomical clock, encased in gilded bronze; it took 20 years to make and was completed in 1753. At the age of 7, Mozart played in this room for the court.

At the peak of Versailles's glory, 1,400 fountains splashed (50 remain today) in the **Gardens of Versailles,** where Le Nôtre created a Garden of Eden using ornamental lakes and canals, geometrically designed flower beds, and avenues bordered with statuary.

A long walk across the park leads to the pink-and-white marble **Grand Trianon,** designed in 1687 by Hardouin-Mansart for Louis XIV. It has traditionally housed the country's important guests, although de Gaulle wanted to turn it into his weekend retreat. Napoleon I spent the night, and Nixon slept in the room where Mme. de Pompadour died. The original furnishings are gone; today the Trianon is filled mostly with Empire pieces. Gabriel, who designed place de la Concorde, built the **Petit Trianon** in 1768 for Louis XV. Mme. de Pompadour, who died before it was complete, inspired its construction. Not one to waste a good space, Louis used it for his trysts with Mme. du Barry. It was Marie Antoinette's favorite residence. Many of the current furnishings, including a few in the bedroom, were hers.

Behind the Petit Trianon is the **Hamlet.** Marie Antoinette strolled around these thatched farmhouses, enchanted by the simple tasks of farm life—milking cows, milling grain, and fishing in the lake.

From May 2 to September 30, the palace is open Tuesday to Sunday 9am to 6:30pm; the Grand Trianon and Petit Trianon are open the same days 10am to 6pm. The rest of the year, the palace is open Tuesday to Sunday 9am to 5:30pm; the Grand Trianon and Petit Trianon are open Tuesday to Friday 10am to noon and 2 to 5pm, Saturday and Sunday 10am to 5pm. Admission to the palace is 7.50€ ($8.60) adults; 5.50€ ($6.30) for ages 18 to 24 and seniors (over 60), and for all on Sunday; free for those under 18. Admission to the Grand Trianon and Petit Trianon is 5€ ($5.75) adults, 3€ ($3.45) for ages 18 to 24. Admission to the gardens only is 3€ ($3.45). Admission to the park is free for pedestrians, 4.50€ to 5.50€ ($5.15–$6.30) per car.

To get to the palace, catch RER Line C5 at the Gare d'Austerlitz, St-Michel, Musée d'Orsay, Invalides, Pont de l'Alma, Champs-de-Mars, or Javel stations, and take the train to the Versailles Rive Gauche station. From there, it is a short walk to the château. Holders of a Eurailpass can use it for the trip. The fare is 2.60€ ($2.85) one-way, and the trip takes about half an hour. For the same price, a regular train leaves the Gare Montparnasse for the Versailles Chantier station, and a free shuttle bus runs to the palace. Alternatively, if you plan to buy a Mobilis 1-day travel ticket, ask for a *billet* covering zones 1 to 4 (Versailles falls in zone 4). It'll set you back 8.50€ ($9.75) for the round-trip and unlimited travel in Paris for the day.

Arrive early. Not only is there a lot to see, but more than three million tourists visit Versailles each year—you'll want to get as much of a head start as possible.

20

Prague & Environs

by Hana Mastrini

The Bohemian capital of **Prague** is a city of paradox. For the romantic who still can be a cynic, the aesthete who loves to be a critic, or the deep historian who doubles as a news junkie, beautiful and quirky Prague is the quintessential destination. Here, the past 1,000 years of creative triumphs in art and architecture have collided, often violently, with destructive power, politics, and religious conflicts. While Bohemia has been the fulcrum of wars over the centuries, it has settled into a post–Cold War peace, spiked with a rough transition to a capitalist economy.

While Prague's rich collection of Gothic, baroque, and Renaissance buildings has remained stoically standing through all the strife, the streets and squares fronting the grand halls have often been the stage for tragedy. The well-worn cobblestones have felt the hooves of king's horses, the jackboots of Hitler's armies, the heaving wheels of Soviet tanks, and the shuffling feet of students in passive revolt. Conflicts past and present give Prague an eclectic energy. The atmosphere continually reminds us that monarchs and dictators have tried to possess this city for much of the past millennium.

For more on Prague and environs, see *Frommer's Prague & the Best of the Czech Republic.*

1 Essentials

ARRIVING

BY PLANE   Prague's newly reconstructed **Ruzyně Airport** (© 220-111-111), 7.5km (12 miles) west of the city center, has several bank kiosks for changing money (usually daily 7am–11pm), several car-rental offices (see "Getting Around," below), and a luggage storage office charging 30Kč ($1.05) per item per day. The official Volkswagen sedan airport **taxis** are parked in front of the arrivals hall.

CEDAZ (© 220-114-296; www.aas.cz/cedaz) operates an **airport shuttle bus** to and from náměstí Republiky, Praha 1, every 30 minutes from 6am to 9pm. The shuttle costs 90Kč ($3.20) per person and takes about a half an hour.

Value Budget Bests

In Prague, private rooms are always the best buy—a double might cost 750Kč to 1,500Kč ($27–$54). Compare that to 2,500Kč ($89) or more for a double in a full-service hotel. But for a special affordable getaway, the **Pension Větrník** (© 220-612-404) is hard to beat with its friendly country setting, made-to-order breakfasts, and clay tennis court available when the weather permits.

Prague Deals & Discounts

SPECIAL DISCOUNTS   Prague's public transportation system of subways, buses, and trams is fast, efficient, and affordable. A **1-day pass**, good for unlimited rides, is 70Kč ($2.50), a **3-day pass** 200Kč ($7.15), a **7-day pass** 250Kč ($8.90), a **15-day pass** 280Kč ($10), and a **monthly pass** 420Kč ($15), but a photo is required.

The city's **walks**, affordable **cultural events**, and cheap worldrenowned **Bohemian beer** make it one of Europe's bargains. Many restaurants are in a budget traveler's range, especially **pubs** that provide a hearty meal at a price locals demand.

Prague's **museums** and **galleries** are inexpensive, with admission fees less than 84Kč ($3) and many with student discounts and free days.

Public transportation fares are still incredibly low, and the best draws—**Charles Bridge**, the **Prague Castle gardens and courtyards, Old Town Square**, and the area around them—are free for the walking.

For food, look no further than the local *hospoda* (beer pub). The farther it is from the tourist trail in the city center, and the less English spoken, the cheaper the food will be.

Also note that students get **discount admission** at many sightseeing attractions by showing the internationally recognized **International Student Identity Card (ISIC)**.

WORTH A SPLURGE   Fully experience the baroque elegance of Prague by seeing most any production at the **Estates' Theater (Stavovské divadlo)**. The most sought-after ticket is Mozart's *Don Giovanni*, in its original home for as little as 250Kč ($8.90) or as much as 2,000Kč ($71), depending on whether the box office is sold out and you have to seek tickets through one of the private ticket agencies.

The not-too-inconvenient public transport option is to take the **city bus 119,** which delivers you from just outside the airport baggage claim to the **Dejvická Metro station** (Line A). It costs only 12Kč (40¢), including the Metro ride to the center (either the Můstek or Muzeum Metro stations), with travel time to the center taking about 40 minutes.

BY TRAIN   Of the two central rail stations, **Hlavní nádraží,** Wilsonova třída 80, Praha 1 (© **224-614-071**), is the grander and more popular; however, it's also seedier. The basement holds a 24-hour luggage storage counter charging 15Kč (55¢) per bag up to 15 kilograms (33 lb.) per day (counted from midnight). Although cheaper, the nearby lockers aren't secure and should be avoided. From the main train station, it's a 5-minute stroll to the "top" end of Wenceslas Square or a 15-minute walk to Old Town Square. Metro trains depart from the lower level, and city-center no-transfer tickets, costing 8Kč (30¢), are available at the newsstand near the Metro entrance. Taxis line up outside the station day and night.

Nádraží Holešovice, Partyzánská at Vrbenského, Praha 7 (© **224-615-865**), usually serves trains from Berlin and points north. Although it isn't as centrally located as the main station, its size and position at the end of Metro Line C make it almost as convenient. I advise you to take the Metro from this station, as the taxi drivers waiting here are especially crooked and unpleasant.

BY BUS   The **Central Bus Station Praha–Florenc,** Křižíkova 4–6, Praha 8 (© **12999;** www.jizdnirady.cz), is a few blocks north of the main rail station, and most local and long-distance buses arrive here. Smaller depots are at **Želivského, Smíchovské nádraží,** and **Nádraží Holešovice.**

VISITOR INFORMATION

TOURIST OFFICES   E-Travel.cz has developed a set of websites, including **www.travel.cz,** for general Czech tourist information and accommodations, and **www.apartments.cz,** for booking private apartments online. Any trip planning should start here. E-Travel's office is near the National Theater at Ostrovní 7 (© **224-990-983;** fax 224-990-999). Another agency, especially for those arriving late by train or air, is **AVE Travel Ltd.** (© **224-223-226;** fax 251-556-005; www.avetravel.cz). It has outlets at the airport, open 7am to 10pm; at the main train station, Hlavní nádraží, 6am to 11pm; and at the north train station, nádraží Holešovice, 7am to 8:30pm.

The city's **Cultural and Information Center,** on the ground floor of the Municipal House, Obecní dům), náměstí Republiky 5, Praha 1 (© **222-002-100;** fax 222-002-134; www.obecni-dum.cz/e_index.htm; Metro: Náměstí Republiky), offers advice, tickets, souvenirs, refreshments, and restrooms daily 10am to 6pm.

WEBSITES   The city's own information service, PIS, has regularly updated cultural information in English and acts as a gateway to other tourism websites on **www.pis.cz** or **www.prague-info.cz.** For visa and other consular information, the Foreign Ministry site is **www.czech.cz.** For the latest local news updates and tourism info, try the *Prague Post* at **www.praguepost.cz.** Also, as stated above, **E-Travel.cz** has developed a set of websites, including **www.travel.cz** for general Czech tourist information.

CITY LAYOUT

The river Vltava (more familiar from the German "Moldau") bisects Prague. **Staré Město (Old Town)** and **Nové Město (New Town)** are on the east (right) side of the river, while **Hradčany (Castle District)** and **Malá Strana (Lesser Town)** are on the west (left) bank.

Apart from the castle that hovers over the city, bridges and squares are the most prominent landmarks. The 14th-century **Charles Bridge,** the oldest and most famous of those spanning the Vltava, is at the epicenter and connects Old Town with Lesser Town and the Castle District. Several important streets radiate from Old Town Square, including fashionable **Pařížská** to the northwest,

---

⌐*Tips* Finding an Address

You should know that *ulice* (abbreviated *ul.*) means "street," *třída* means "avenue," *náměstí* (abbreviated *nám.*) is a "square" or "plaza," a *most* is a "bridge," and a *nábřeží* is a "quay." In Czech, none of these is capitalized. In addresses, street numbers follow the street name (like Václavské nám. 25). Each address is followed by a district number, such as Praha 1 (*Praha* means "Prague" in Czech). Praha 1 is the oldest and most historically concentrated district, encompassing Staré Město (Old Town), Hradčany (Castle District), and Malá Strana (Lesser Town). Praha 2 is mostly Nové Město (New Town). The remaining districts are more remote and contain few major attractions.

historic **Celetná** to the east, and **Melantrichova,** connecting to **Wenceslas Square (Václavské náměstí)** to the southeast.

On the west side of Charles Bridge is **Mostecká,** a 3-block-long connection to **Malostranské náměstí,** Malá Strana's main square. Hradčany, the Castle District, is just northwest of the square, while a second hill, **Petřín,** is just southwest.

GETTING AROUND

BY METRO, BUS & TRAM   Prague's public transport network is a vast and usually efficient system of **subways, trams,** and **buses.** You can ride a maximum of four stations on the Metro or 15 minutes on a tram or bus, without transfers, for 8Kč (30¢); kids under 6 are free. This usually suffices for trips in the historic districts. Rides of more than four stops on the Metro and tram, or bus rides longer than 15 minutes with unlimited transfers for up to 1 hour after your ticket is validated, cost 12Kč (40¢). You can buy tickets from coin-operated orange machines in Metro stations or at most newsstands marked TABÁK or TRAFIKA. Hold onto your ticket (which you must validate at the orange or yellow stamp clocks in each tram or bus when you get on board or at the entrance to the Metro) during your ride—you'll need it to prove you've paid if a ticket collector asks.

If you're caught without a valid ticket, you'll have to pay a 400Kč ($14) fine to a plainclothes ticket controller on the spot who must flash an official badge.

A **1-day pass,** good for unlimited rides, is 70Kč ($2.50), a **3-day pass** 200Kč ($7.15), a **7-day pass** 250Kč ($8.90), and a **15-day pass** 280Kč ($10). If you're staying for more than 2 weeks, buy a **monthly pass** for 420Kč ($15). You can buy the day passes at the "DP" windows at any Metro station, but the photo ID monthly pass is available only at the Dopravní podnik (transport department) office on Na bojišti, near the I. P. Pavlova Metro station (© **296-191-111**).

Metro trains operate daily 5am to midnight and run every 3 to 8 minutes. On the three lettered lines (A, B, C), the most convenient central stations are **Můstek,** at the foot of Václavské náměstí (Wenceslas Sq.); **Staroměstská,** for Old Town Square and Charles Bridge; and **Malostranská,** serving Malá Strana and the Castle District.

The 26 **electric tram** (streetcar) lines run practically everywhere, and there's always another tram with the same number traveling back. You never have to hail trams, for they make every stop. The most popular, **no. 22** (the "tourist tram" or "pickpocket express"), has become less crowded with the addition of the **no. 23** tram. Both run past top sights like the National Theater and Prague Castle.

To ride the **bus,** you have to buy the same tickets as for other modes in advance and validate them on boarding. Regular bus and tram service stops at midnight, after which selected routes run reduced schedules, usually only once per hour. If you miss a night connection, expect a long wait for the next one to arrive.

BY FUNICULAR   The cog railway makes the scenic run up and down Petřín Hill every 15 minutes or so from 9:15am to 8:45pm, with a stop at the Nebozízek Restaurant in the middle of the hill overlooking the city. It requires the same 12Kč (40¢) ticket as other public transport. The funicular departs from a small house at the foot of Petřín Hill, just above the middle of Újezd in Malá Strana.

BY TAXI   Avoid taxis in Prague. If you must, however, you can hail one in the streets or in front of train stations, large hotels, and popular attractions, but be forewarned that many drivers simply gouge unsuspecting tourists. The best fare

Prague Metro

you can hope for is 17Kč (60¢) per kilometer, but twice or three times that isn't rare. The rates are usually posted not on the exterior of the car but on the dashboard, making it too late to haggle once you're in and on your way. Negotiate a price and have it written down before getting in. Better yet, go on foot or by public transport. Somewhat reputable companies with English-speaking dispatchers are **AAA Taxi** (© **14014** or **221-102-211**), **ProfiTaxi** (© **14035**), and **SEDOP** (© **271-726-666**).

BY RENTAL CAR Most travelers will find driving in Prague not worth the money or effort. The roads, except for the Prague-Plzeň and Prague-Brno super highways, are frustrating and slow and parking is minimal and expensive. If you want to rent a car to explore the environs, try **Europcar Czech Rent a Car,** at

---

Tips A Taxi Warning

Many of Prague's taxi drivers will try to take advantage of you; obtaining an honestly metered ride from the airport is a challenge. The fare from the airport to Wenceslas Square *should* be no more than about 700Kč to 800Kč ($25–$28). Know where you are going, point it out on the map, and agree on a price before you get in.

Country & City Codes

The **country code** for the Czech Republic is **420**. Since the whole Czech telephone network was digitized in 2002, the **city codes** are connected to the local number in front so each number dialed within the Czech Republic has nine digits. For directory assistance in English and for information on services and rates calling abroad, dial ℂ **1181**. This costs 7Kč (25¢) per minute.

To call Prague direct from the United States, dial 011 (international code), 420 (country code), and the nine-digit local number. From Britain, dial 00 (international code), 420 (country code), and the local number.

Pařížská 28, Praha 1 (ℂ **224-811-290;** Metro: Staroměstská); or at Ruzyně Airport (ℂ **235-364-531;** www.europcar.cz). There's also **Hertz,** Karlovo nám. 28, Praha 2, or Ruzyně Airport, or Hotel Diplomat, Praha 6 (ℂ **220-102-424;** www.hertz.com; Metro: Karlovo náměstí or Dejvická for Hotel Diplomat); and **Budget,** at Ruzyně Airport (ℂ **220-113-253),** and in the Hotel Inter-Continental, náměstí Curieových, Praha 1 (ℂ **224-889-995;** www.budget.cz; Metro: Staroměstská).

Local Czech car-rental companies sometimes offer lower rates than the big international firms. Try **CS Czechocar,** Kongresové centrum (Congress Center at Vyšehrad Metro stop on the C line), Praha 4 (ℂ **261-222-079;** www.czechocar.cz); or Ruzyně Airport, Praha 6 (ℂ **220-113-454**). Also try **SeccoCar,** Přístavní 39, Praha 7 (ℂ **220-800-647;** www.seccocar.cz; Metro: Nádraží Holešovice, then tram 12 or 25).

Remember: You get the best deal if you arrange the rental before leaving home.

FAST FACTS: Prague

American Express For travel arrangements, traveler's checks, currency exchange, and other member services, visit the office at Václavské nám. 56 (Wenceslas Sq.), Praha 1 (ℂ **222-800-237;** fax 222-211-131; Metro: Muzeum), open daily 9am to 7pm. To report lost or stolen cards, call ℂ **222-800-222.**

Babysitters If your hotel can't recommend a sitter, phone **Agentura Domestica,** Lidická 7, Praha 5 (ℂ **257-316-150;** www.domestica.cz; Metro: Anděl), a company providing various domestic services, including babysitting. Make reservations in advance. The fee is 100Kč ($3.55) per hour.

Business Hours Most **banks** are open Monday to Friday from 8am to 5pm. Business **offices** are generally open Monday to Friday from 8am to 6pm. **Pubs** are usually open daily 11am to midnight. Most **restaurants** open for lunch from noon to 3pm and for dinner from 6 to 11pm; only a few stay open later.

Currency The basic unit of currency is the **koruna** (plural, **koruny**) or **crown,** abbreviated **Kč.** Each koruna is divided into 100 haléřů or **hellers.** Always check your change from waiters to make sure they haven't slipped you old "Czechoslovak" bills or other currencies.

The rate of exchange used to calculate the dollar values given in this chapter is $1 = approximately 28Kč (or 1Kč = 3.6¢) and £1 = approximately 45Kč.

Banks generally offer the best exchange rates. Don't hesitate to use a credit or debit card to draw cash for the best rates. **Komerční banka** (© 222-432-111) has three Praha 1 locations with ATMs accepting Visa, MasterCard, and American Express: Na Příkopě 33 (Metro: Můstek), Národní 32 (Metro: Národní třída), and Václavské nám. 42 (Metro: Můstek). The exchange offices of the bank are open Monday to Friday 8am to 5pm, but the ATMs are accessible 24 hours.

Dentists & Doctors If you need a doctor or dentist and your condition isn't life-threatening, you can visit the **Polyclinic at Národní,** Národní 9, Praha 1 (© 222-075-120; Metro: Národní třída). For **emergency medical aid,** call the **Foreigners' Medical Clinic,** Na Homolce Hospital, Roentgenova 2, Praha 5 (© 257-272-146 or 257-272-191 after hours).

Embassies The **U.S. Embassy,** Tržiště 15, Praha 1 (© 257-530-663; Metro: Malostranská), is open Monday to Friday 8am to 4:30pm. The **Canadian Embassy,** Muchova 6, Praha 6 (© 272-101-800; Metro: Hradčanská), is open Monday to Friday 8:30am to 12:30pm and 1:30 to 4:30pm. The **U.K. Embassy,** Thunovská 14, Praha 1 (© 257-402-111; Metro: Malostranská), is open Monday to Friday 8:30am to 12:30pm and 1:30 to 5pm. The **Irish Embassy,** Tržiště 13, Praha 1 (© 257-530-061; Metro: Malostranská), is open Monday to Friday 9:30am to 12:30pm and 2:30 to 4:30pm. You can visit the **Australian Honorary Consul,** Klimentská 10, Praha 1 (© 296-578-350; Metro: Nám. Republiky), Monday to Friday 9am to 1pm and 2 to 5pm. **New Zealand's Honorary Consul** is located at Dykova 19, Praha 10 (© 222-514-672; Metro: Jiřího z Poděbrad); visits by appointment.

Emergencies You can reach Prague's **police** by dialing © 158 from any phone; for **fire** services, call © 150; to call an **ambulance,** dial © 155. All of these are free calls.

Hospitals Particularly welcoming to foreigners is **Nemocnice Na Homolce,** Roentgenova 2, Praha 5 (© 257-272-146 or 257-272-191 after hours; Metro: Anděl, then bus no. 167). The English-speaking doctors there can also make house calls.

Internet Access One of Prague's trendiest places is the **Globe** ⟨★⟩, Pštrossova 6, Praha 1 (© 224-916-264; www.globebookstore.cz), a cafe cum English-language bookstore that provides Internet access. You can surf the Internet for 1.30Kč (5¢) per minute. Open daily from 10am until midnight.

Check your e-mail and surf at the very centrally located new Internet cafe **Inetpoint.cz,** Jungmannova 32, Praha 1 (© 296-245-962). It is open daily from 10am to 10pm and the connection charge is 25 Kč (89¢) per 15 minutes. The **Internet Café u Pavlánských,** near the funicular train at Újezd 31 in Malá Strana, Praha 1, has about a half-dozen PCs in a pleasant setting for 80 Kč ($2.80) per hour, also open daily from 10am to 10pm. Another place for getting on the Internet is **Cyber Cafe-Jáma** at V jámě 7, Praha 1 (© 224-222-383).

Luggage Storage & Lockers The **Ruzyně Airport Luggage Storage Office** never closes and charges 30Kč ($1.05) per item per day. Left-luggage offices are also available at the main train stations, **Hlavní nádraží** and **nádraží Holešovice.** Both charge 15Kč (55¢) per bag (up to 33 lb.) per day (counted from midnight) and are technically open 24 hours, but if your train is departing late at night, check to make sure someone will be around. Luggage lockers are available in all of Prague's train stations, but avoid them since they're not very secure.

Mail Post offices are plentiful and are normally open Monday to Friday from 8am to 6pm. Mailboxes are orange and are usually attached to the sides of buildings. Mail can take up to 10 days to reach its destination. The **Main Post Office (Hlavní pošta),** Jindřišská 14, Praha 1 (© 221-131-111; Metro: Můstek), a few steps from Václavské náměstí, is open 24 hours. You can receive mail here, marked *Poste Restante* and addressed to you, care of this post office.

Pharmacies The most central pharmacy *(lékárna)* is at Václavské nám. 8, Praha 1 (© 224-227-532; Metro: Můstek), open Monday to Friday from 8am to 6pm. The nearest emergency (24-hr.) pharmacy is at Palackého 5, Praha 1 (© 224-946-982; Metro: Můstek). If you're in Praha 2, there's an emergency pharmacy on Belgická 37 (© 222-513-396; Metro: Náměstí Míru).

Police In an emergency, dial © 158. This is a free call.

Restrooms Toilets are in every Metro station and are staffed by cleaning personnel who usually charge 5Kč (20¢) and dispense a few precious sheets of toilet paper. Restaurants and pubs around all the major sights are usually kind to nonpatrons who want to use their facilities. Public toilets are clearly marked with the letters WC.

Safety In Prague's center, you'll feel generally safer than in most Western cities, but you shouldn't walk alone at night around Wenceslas Square—it's one of the main areas for prostitution, as well as a lot of unexplainable loitering. All visitors should be watchful of pickpockets in heavily touristed areas, especially on Charles Bridge, in Old Town Square, and in front of the main train station. Be especially wary in crowded buses, trams, and trains. You shouldn't keep your wallet in a back pocket, and don't flash a lot of cash or jewelry.

Taxes A 22% **value-added tax (VAT)** is built into the price of most goods and services rather than being tacked on at the register. Most restaurants also include VAT in the prices on their menus. If they don't, that fact should be stated somewhere on the menu. (For more information on VAT, see chapter 1, "Enjoying Europe on a Budget.")

Telephone You can get **directory assistance** and information on **services** and **rates,** in English, by dialing © **1181.**

There are two kinds of **pay phones.** The first accepts coins and the other operates only with a phone card, available from post offices and newsstands in denominations from 50Kč to 500Kč ($1.80–$18). The minimum cost of a **local call** is 4Kč (15¢). Coin-op phones, if they work, have displays telling you the minimum price for your call, but they don't make change, so don't load it with more than you have to; you can add more coins as the display nears zero. The more efficient phone card telephones deduct the price of your call from the card. If you're calling home, get a phone card with plenty of points, as calls run about 20Kč (71¢) per minute to the

United States and 15Kč (33p) to the United Kingdom. **Long-distance phone charges** are higher than they are in the United States, and hotels usually add their own surcharge, sometimes as hefty as 100% to 200%, which you might be unaware of until you're presented with the bill. Ask before placing any call from a hotel. Charging to your phone credit card from a public telephone is often the most economical way to call home.

The access number in the Czech Republic for **AT&T's USA Direct** is ⓒ **00 420 00101,** for **MCI's Call USA** ⓒ **00 420 00112,** and for **Sprint Global One** ⓒ **00 420 87187.** Canadians can connect with **Canada Direct** at ⓒ **00 420 00151** and Brits with **BT Direct** at ⓒ **00 420 04401.** From a pay phone in the Czech Republic, your local phone card will be debited only for a local call.

Tipping Rules for tipping in the Czech Republic aren't as strict as they are in the United States. At most restaurants and pubs, locals just round the bill up to the nearest few koruny. When you're presented with good serv-ice at tableclothed places, at least a 10% tip is proper. Washroom and cloakroom attendants usually get a couple of koruny, and porters in air-ports and rail stations usually get 20Kč (71¢) per bag. Taxi drivers expect about 10%, unless they've already ripped you off, which means they often get nothing.

2 Affordable Places to Stay

Prague pensions are much cheaper than hotels, but they're pricey for what you get in Prague's old neighborhoods. Still, those listed below give good value. Do be aware, however, that with the rapid changes in the Czech economy, rates can often vary as the forces of supply and demand battle to find their balance, and exchange rates fluctuate wildly.

Rooms in private homes or apartments offer a budget stay with usually a lit-tle more privacy than hostels provide, but if you don't like feeling as if you're invading somebody else's home and simply want a bed, Prague has several rela-tively clean dorm-type accommodations.

Additionally, full-service hotels have improved recently in the face of heavier international competition: Room rates at top properties often exceed those in many western European hotels of similar or better quality!

If you show up at a hotel and think rooms are going empty, you can always negotiate the price before committing. Use the lack of amenities in specific rooms as a reason for the lower rate or ask if you can get a better rate for stay-ing a few nights.

All kinds of private housing are offered by several local agencies. The leader now is Prague-based **E-Travel.cz,** which offers all types of accommodation at their main site (www.travel.cz), or you can tap their large pictured database of apartments (www.apartments.cz). The office is near the National Theater at Ostrovní 7 (ⓒ **224-990-983;** fax 224-990-999). Another agency, especially for those arriving late by train or air, is **AVE Travel Ltd.** (ⓒ **224-223-226;** fax 251-556-005; www.avetravel.cz). It has outlets at the airport, open 7am to 10pm; at the main train station, Hlavní nádraží, 6am to 11pm; and at the north train station, nádraží Holešovice, 7am to 8:30pm.

Note: You'll find the lodging choices below plotted on the map on p. 772.

NEAR STAROMĚSTSKÉ NÁMĚSTÍ (OLD TOWN SQUARE)

Betlem Club *(Value)* This is one of the most affordable hotels in Old Town, the other being my favorite, the Hotel Cloister Inn (see below). The location is fantastic, too, opposite Bethlehem Chapel. Several restaurants and bars are on or near this quiet square, and Charles Bridge, Wenceslas Square, and Old Town Square are within easy walking distance. The Betlem feels more like a private pension than a central-city hotel, with small rooms that don't encourage extended lounging, but the aura amid the square's cobblestones and old lamps keeps you looking out the window instead of inward. Breakfast is served in a vaulted medieval cellar.

Betlémské nám. 9, Praha 1. ℭ **222-221-575.** Fax 222-220-580. www.betlemclub.cz. 22 units, with tub/shower combination. 3,600Kč ($128) double; 3,900 Kč ($139) suite. Rates include breakfast. No credit cards. Metro: Národní třída. **Amenities:** Babysitting; laundry; safe. *In room:* TV, minibar, hair dryer.

Dům krále Jiřího The "House at King George's" is above two pubs on a narrow side street. The remodeled rooms boast a bit more charm than before but are still pretty bare, although they have high ceilings and attractive dark wooden furniture. Charles Bridge is a few dozen steps and a swing to the left from the pension, but this narrow alley has become more like Bourbon Street than the Royal Route. Ask for a room in back if you want to deaden the pub clamor. Breakfast is served in the remodeled wine cellar.

Liliová 10, Praha 1. ℭ **222-220-925.** Fax 222-221-707. www.hotel.cz/kraljiri. 11 units. 3,300Kč ($117) double; 3,750Kč ($133) suite. Rates include breakfast. AE, MC, V. Metro: Staroměstská. **Amenities:** Safe. *In room:* TV, fridge.

Hotel Cloister Inn *(Value)* Between Old Town Square and the National Theater, this property has been renovated into a good-value mid-range hotel. The original rooms of this unique spot were developed from holding cells used by the Communist secret police (the StB); these cells were converted from a convent. It sounds ominous, but the Cloister Inn rooms are very inviting. Proprietor Jiří Tlaskal has taken over management from the police and the Sisters of Mercy and

---

Value Getting the Best Deal on Accommodations

- Note that in Prague you can find the best value in the center of the city by staying in one of the numerous pensions or hotels near náměstí Míru, just a few blocks above Wenceslas Square.
- Avoid anything that resembles a Western-style full-service hotel— most often they have Europe-standard rates with Warsaw Pact–standard furnishings and service.
- Don't be afraid to rent a room away from the old quarters of town, especially if it's close to a Metro stop. The farther away from the center, the lower the rates will be, and the Metro connections are fast and affordable.
- Always know the latest market exchange rates when budgeting your stay in Prague, and build in some padding for any potential surge. The exact rate at many hotels depends on the daily koruna/euro exchange rate.

Fun Fact **Václav Slept Here**

In the building on Bartolomějská Street known as Pension Unitas/Art Prison Hostel, Václav Havel, ex-president of the Czech Republic, was once a frequent "guest" of the Communist police.

---

refurbished and expanded the place. No Jailhouse Chic here; rooms are thoroughly comfortable with crisp Scandinavian wooden furniture.

Konviktská 14, Praha 1. © 224-211-020. Fax 224-210-800. www.cloister-inn.cz. 73 units, with showers only. 4,200Kč ($150) double. Rates include breakfast. AE, DC, MC, V. Metro: Národní třída. **Amenities:** Concierge; tour and activities desk; safe. *In room:* TV, hair dryer, safe.

Pension Unitas/Art Prison Hostel /Value   With a quirky history (same building complex as Hotel Cloister-Inn; see above) and with an unbeatable location at this price, the Unitas is great value for the money. On a side street between Old Town Square and the National Theater stands this former convent, which was conveniently seized for use as secret police holding cells under the Communists. One of their most frequent guests, before the Unitas was turned into a post-revolution pension, was none other than the pesky dissident and soon-to-be-president Václav Havel. Once the bizarre allure in staying in Havel's former hoosegow wears off, you realize that this is still a pretty artful attempt at providing decent accommodations at a good price. The cells and rooms range from doubles to quads, with comfy mattresses and clean linen provided. A recent rebranding of the complex added some funky wall murals to give it the added subtitle of being an Art Prison Hostel. There is no curfew, and the complimentary breakfast of cold cuts, rolls, and cheese is fresh and plentiful. The joint bathrooms are clean enough to pass. If you feel you are becoming a bit too Bohemian from too many backpacking days on the road, there is a well-equipped laundry room.

Bartolomějská 9, Praha 1. © 224-221-802. Fax 224-217-555. www.unitas.cz. 36 units, with shared bathroom facilities. 1,400Kč ($50) double in pension; 500Kč ($17) per person in room with 2 beds in hostel. Rates include breakfast. AE, MC, V. Metro: Národní třída. **Amenities:** Safe; laundry room; luggage room.

AROUND WENCESLAS SQUARE

Andante ⭐ /Value   The best value choice near Wenceslas Square, the understated Andante is tucked away on a dark side street, about 2 blocks off the top of the square. Despite its less-than-appealing neighborhood, this is the most comfortable property in the $100 to $150 range. It lacks the character of the old Hotel Evropa (see below), but also the neglect. With en suite bathrooms for every room, and with higher-grade Scandinavian furniture, you will gain in comfort what you lose in adventure.

Ve Smečkách 4, Prague 1. © 222-211-616. Fax 222-210-591. www.andante.cz. 32 units, some with shower only, some with tub only. 3,444Kč ($123) double; 4,704Kč ($168) suite. Rates include breakfast. AE, MC, V. Metro: Muzeum. **Amenities:** Restaurant; tours arranged with reception desk; business services; limited room service. *In room:* TV, minibar, hair dryer, iron, safe (available at reception).

Hotel Evropa   Rebuilt in its original style, at the heart of Wenceslas Square, the Evropa has an ornate Art Nouveau facade that recalls more glorious years. Seats on the ground-floor cafe terrace are coveted—for style and people-watching, not food or service. Rooms range from adequate to shabby, with none matching the grandeur of the public areas. The best are the front-facing doubles, half a dozen of which have balconies overlooking Václavské náměstí. Because it is cheaper than most central-city places, I list it here, but the Evropa does not offer the value of the Cloister Inn or the Betlem Club (see above for both).

Václavské nám. 25, Praha 1. ⓒ **224-215-387.** Fax 224-224-544 90 units, 20 with bathroom (tub only). 2,210Kč ($78) double without bathroom, 3,390Kč ($121) double with bathroom; from 3,556Kč ($127) suite. Rates include continental breakfast. AE, MC, V. Metro: Můstek or Muzeum. **Amenities:** Restaurant; cafe; concierge; safe (at reception); luggage room. *In room:* No phone.

Hotel Meran This used to be part of the Hotel Evropa (see above), now known better for its cafe than its spartan accommodations. The Meran is the brighter, narrower building next door, and it is on its own again. Family run, and cozier than the bigger Art Deco landmark that draws so much attention to its gilded facade, the Meran has had a face-lift to make it a fair but not spectacular mid-range choice on Wenceslas Square, in a walkable distance to the main train station. The lobby interior has retained some original Art Nouveau accents, although the room furnishings have few. The front windows overlook the place where hundreds of thousands demonstrated night after night until the Communist government fell in a peaceful coup in 1989.

Václavské nám. 27, Praha 1. ⓒ **222-244-373.** Fax 224-230-411. www.hotelmeran.cz. 20 units with bathroom (tub or shower). 3,950Kč ($141) double. Rates include breakfast. AE, DC, MC, V. Metro: Muzeum or Můstek. **Amenities:** Concierge; exchange. *In room:* TV.

NEAR NÁMĚSTÍ MÍRU

Flathotel Orion 🅰 (Kids) The best family value, the Orion is an apartment hotel. All rooms are one- or two-bedroom flats, sleeping up to six, each with a well-equipped kitchen. They're comfortable but not imaginative, bordered in pale blue with black leather armchairs and dark wooden bed frames. The bathrooms are basic and modern, much like the kitchens. The only extra in the building is a Finnish sauna (200Kč/$7.15 per hour). In this friendly neighborhood, you'll find plenty of restaurants and cafes around náměstí Míru up the street.

Americká 9, Praha 2. ⓒ **222-521-700.** Fax 222-521-701. www.hotel.cz/orion. 26 units, apts with bathroom (tub/shower combination). 2,580Kč ($92) 1-bedroom; 3,320Kč ($118) 2-bedroom. Breakfast 160Kč ($5.70). AE, MC, V. Metro: Náměstí Míru. **Amenities:** Finnish sauna 200Kč ($7.15) per hour; tours and activities arrangements at reception; room service; laundry and dry-cleaning service. *In room:* TV, kitchen, fridge, coffeemaker.

Hotel City The City offers clean characterless rooms, each with one to four beds, typical dark wood-veneer furniture, and Communist-era Day-Glo orange interiors. However, they're large and expandable into triples or quads, with an extra charge for additional people. The best thing about the City is that (like the Orion, above) it's around the corner from the pub Na Zvonařce (p. 765).

Belgická 10, Praha 2. ⓒ **222-521-606.** Fax 222-522-386. www.hotelcity.cz. 19 units, 7 with bathroom (each room sleeps up to 4; tub/shower combination), 12 2-room apts with shared bathrooms. 1,550Kč ($55) double in separate room in apt with shared bathroom, 2,320Kč ($82) double with private bathroom. Rates include breakfast. AE, DC, MC, V. Metro: Náměstí Míru. **Amenities:** Safe (at reception). *In room:* TV (additional 75Kč/$2.70 per night), phone (35Kč/$1.25 per night).

NEAR NÁMĚSTÍ REPUBLIKY

Hotel Axa The Axa added modern bathrooms to the rooms and hiked its prices a few years ago, but this is still one of the most affordable central hotels. The rooms are trying to look updated, but the beds are loudly upholstered particleboard, and the lobby feels like a hospital's. However, you'll find a six-lane 25m (82-ft.) pool here used for local competitions, as well as a fitness center with weight machines, free weights, a sauna, and a solarium. This place might be better cast as a rehabilitation center.

Na Poříčí 40, Praha 1. ℂ **224-816-332.** Fax 224-214-489. 134 units. 3,350Kč ($119) single; 4,150Kč ($148) double. Rates include continental breakfast. AE, DC, MC, V. Metro: Náměstí Republiky or Florenc. **Amenities:** Restaurant; indoor pool; fitness center; tour arrangements at reception desk. *In room:* TV.

OUTSIDE THE CITY CENTER

Pension Větrník ✦ *Finds* A half-hour tram ride from the city center takes you to this secret country hideaway still within the city limits. After getting off the tram, walk behind a bunch of large concrete dorms to find a restored 18th-century white windmill house. Once you buzz at the metal gate (avoid the buzzer for the door to the family residence), Miloš Opatrný will greet you. Lush gardens and a tennis court lead into a quaint guesthouse with a stone staircase, spacious rooms with big beds, open-beam ceilings, and modern amenities. The bathrooms are roomy, with huge stand-up showers. Opatrný, a former foreign service chef, takes pride in whipping up a traditional Czech country dinner and serving it in a small medieval stone cellar with a fire. There's also a patio for drinks. You can't get more romantic than this, especially for the price.

U Větrníku 40, Praha 6. ℂ **220-612-404.** Fax 235-361-406. milos.opatrny@telecom.cz. 6 units, 4 with shower only, 2 with tub/shower combination. 2,000Kč ($71) double. Rates include breakfast. MC. Metro: Line A to Hradčanská station, then tram 1 or 18 to stop Větrník. **Amenities:** Tennis court, lit for night play. *In room:* TV, hair dryer.

HOSTELS

Hostels are most abundant in July and August, when many schools' classrooms are converted into dorms. During the rest of the year, hostel space is thin in Prague, with the two listed below as the most sought-after in the off season. For the latest offerings, contact **AVE Travel Ltd.** (see the beginning of this section, "Affordable Places to Stay," for contact information).

Hostel ESTEC Strahov Across from the giant Strahov Stadium, these converted dormitories, none with private bathroom but open 24 hours, are not much more than a bed and place to throw your things in a pretty clean concrete cell, but the price is right. Dinner is served at the nearby student cafeteria for 100Kč to 150Kč ($3.55–$5.35).

Vaníčkova 5, Praha 1 (on Strahov Hill). ℂ **224-320-202.** Fax 224-323-489. www.czechhostel.cz. 110 units, 20 singles, 75 doubles, 15 triples, all with shared bathrooms and toilets. 300Kč–400Kč ($11–$14) per person. AE, MC, V. From Dejvická Metro station, take bus 143, 149, or 217 to Strahov Stadium.

Traveller's Hostel-Pension Dlouhá ✦ *Value* This is, by far, the best hostel in the city center. The flagship in the local Traveller's group of hostels is open year-round, just a few blocks off Old Town Square and a few floors above the wildest dance club in town, the Roxy. There are a total of 164 beds—which can be arranged into rooms from singles to six-bed rooms—on two floors, all sharing large, well-equipped bathrooms. This hostel attracts a mix of student backpackers and veteran tourists taking advantage of the clean, affordable, modern setting. Traveller's offers other hostels at dormitories throughout town during the high season. Check their website for each season's roster.

Dlouhá 33, Praha 1. ℂ **224-826-662.** Fax 224-826-665. www.travellers.cz. 39 units, expandable from singles to 6-bed rooms. 950Kč ($34) per person single room; 520Kč ($19) 2-bed room; 330Kč ($12) 6-bed room. Rates include breakfast. AE, MC, V. Metro: Nám. Republiky. **Amenities:** Bar; laundry; safe; communal TV; Internet access.

WORTH A SPLURGE

Hotel Neruda ☆☆ Another great writer/philosopher who left his mark on Prague was Jan Neruda. The street that bears his name, Nerudova, is a cozy alley of stores and pubs leading up to the Castle. Between the long row of curiosity shops is a strong contender for the best boutique hotel in Malá Strana—the Hotel Neruda. This recently refurbished 20-room villa has brought a high level of modern elegance while retaining some of the original accents within its 14th-century stone walls. Most of the fixtures—from the fresh new bathrooms to the beds and dining tables—suggest a bold sense of Prague's promising future, but are still enveloped within the hotel's Renaissance past. You will reside just a few hundred paces below the Castle, making this the most convenient for exploring Prague's imperial past.

Nerudova 44, Praha 1. ℂ **257-535-557.** Fax 257-531-492. www.hotelneruda-praha.cz. 20 units. 6,500Kč ($232) double. Rates include breakfast. AE, DC, MC, V. Tram: 22 or 23 to Malostranské nám. **Amenities:** Restaurant/cafe; concierge. *In room:* A/C, TV, VCR, minibar, hair dryer, safe.

Romantik Hotel U raka ☆ *(Finds* Hidden among the stucco houses and cobblestone streets of a pristine medieval neighborhood on the far side of Prague Castle is this most pleasant surprise. In a ravine below the Foreign Ministry gardens, this old-world farmhouse has been lovingly reconstructed and is the quietest getaway in Prague. The rustic rooms have heavy wooden furniture, open-beam ceilings, and exposed brick. The suite has a fireplace and adjoins a private garden, making it a favorite for honeymooners.

Černínská 10, Praha 1. ℂ **220-511-100.** Fax 220-510-511. www.romantikhotels.com/Prag. 6 units, 5 with shower only. 6,200Kč ($221) double; 7,900Kč ($282) suite. Rates include breakfast. AE, MC, V. Tram: 22 or 23. **Amenities:** Laundry service; safe (at reception). *In room:* A/C, TV, minibar, hair dryer.

3 Great Deals on Dining

Czech menus are packed with meat, and the true Czech experience can be summed up in three native words: *vepřo, knedlo, zelo*—pork, dumplings, cabbage. When prepared with care and imagination, Czech food can be hearty and satisfying. Plus, with new restaurants pouring into the city, it's getting easier to eat lighter in Prague.

THE PICK OF THE PUBS

Besides being the center of extracurricular activity, *hospody* are the best places to get a fulfilling, inexpensive meal and a true Czech experience, not to mention the best brews (some call them "liquid bread"). Selections are typically the same: sirloin slices in cream sauce and dumplings *(svíčková na smetaně)*, goulash *(guláš)*, roast beef *(roštěná na roštu)*, or breaded fried *hermelín* cheese *(smažený sýr)*. All can be ordered with fries, rice, potato pancakes *(bramborák)*, or boiled potatoes. Reservations aren't usually accepted, but you might see tables reserved for friends of the waiters or for regulars known as *štamgast*, or just because the waiter doesn't want to serve more tables.

NEAR OLD TOWN SQUARE

Na Zvonařce *(Value* CZECH The best pub choice outside the city center, "The Bellmaker's" in Vinohrady has a huge menu, probably the best all-around pub food in town, and super Pilsner Urquell beer. During summer, it's worth the wait for a table on the patio.

Šafaříkova 1, Praha 2. ℂ **224-251-990.** Main courses 80Kč–150Kč ($2.85–$5.35). V. Daily 11:30am–11pm. Metro: I. P. Pavlova.

Pivnice Radegast ⭐ CZECH   The raucous Radegast dishes up Prague's best pub *guláš* in a single narrow vaulted hall. The namesake Moravian brew seems to never stop flowing from its taps. The Radegast attracts a good mix of visitors and locals and a somewhat younger and upwardly mobile crowd than the other pubs listed. Some western visitors complain about the *guláš* meat being a bit tough at times, and the service being surly. But relative to other local haunts, the Radegast is the best for a gritty Czech pub experience, warts and all.

Templová 2, Praha 1. ⓒ **222-328-237**. Main courses 68Kč–240Kč ($2.40–$8.60). AE, MC, V. Daily 11am–midnight. Metro: Můstek or Náměstí Republiky.

U medvídků ⭐⭐ CZECH   Bright and noisy, the House at the Little Bears serves a better-than-average *vepřo, knedlo,* and *zelo* with two colors of cabbage. The pub on the right after you enter is half as cheap and more alive than the restaurant to the left. It's a hangout mixing locals, German tour groups, and foreign journalists because it serves the original Czech Budweiser beer, the genuine article. In high season, an oompah band plays in the beer wagon in the center of the pub.

Na Perštýně 7, Praha 1. ⓒ **224-211-916**. Main courses 90Kč–250Kč ($3.20–$8.90). AE, MC, V. Daily 11am–11pm. Metro: Národní třída.

NEAR KARLOVO NÁMĚSTÍ
Restaurant U Čížků ⭐ *Value* CZECH   Officially a restaurant and not a pub, this cozy cellar-cum-hunting lodge on Charles Square has the warmth of a 19th-century Bohemian country inn complete with horned trophies. The fare is purely Czech, and the massive portions of game, smoked pork, and other meats are the perfect match for the huge mugs of pilsner.

Karlovo nám. 34, Praha 2. ⓒ **222-232-257**. www.restaurantucizku.cz. Reservations recommended. Main courses 75Kč–175Kč ($2.70–$6.25). AE, MC, V. Daily noon–10pm. Metro: Karlovo náměstí.

THE BEST NON-PUB MEALS
NEAR PRAGUE CASTLE
Saté Indonesian Restaurant INDONESIAN   A lunchtime savior just beyond the foreign ministry (Černínský palác) west of the Castle, the Saté has made quite a business out of its simple Indonesian dishes at simple prices in a casual setting. The unassuming storefront just up from the Swedish Embassy doesn't scream out to you, so look closely. The pork saté comes in a peanut sauce along with a plentiful noodle *mie goreng.*

Pohořelec 152/3, Praha 1. ⓒ **220-514-552**. Main courses 80Kč–200Kč ($2.85–$7.15). No credit cards. Daily 11am–10pm. Tram: 22 or 23.

IN MALÁ STRANA (LESSER TOWN)
Circle Line Brasserie FRENCH/CONTINENTAL   The Cirle Line has a breezy casual ease despite its frequently buttoned-up clientele from the nearby embassies. Starters a rich duck foie gras lightly fried with peaches, and sautéed

---

Tips **A Dining Warning**

Be sure to check restaurant bills and credit card slips carefully, as some shifty waiters will add an extra charge or an extra digit here or there. If you pay with plastic, perhaps write out the total in words on the credit-card slip, as you would on a check.

> ### ⌒Value Getting the Best Deal on Dining
>
> - Stick to Czech and European cuisines; ingredients for other dishes are more rare and expensive. The more the menu varies from pork, cabbage, and dumplings (with the exception of pizza), the higher the price will be. And remember that the farther from the Castle or Old Town you go, generally the cheaper your meal will be.
> - Go for the beer and eat where you drink it. The food won't be stunning but will be filling and usually cheap.
> - Search out fixed-price menus, two-for-one specials, and deals in the local English-language newspapers (see www.praguepost.cz).
> - Watch out for on-table treats like almonds, olives, and appetizers. Some restaurants gouge customers by charging exorbitant amounts for them.

oysters and artichokes. Main courses range from straightforward baked chicken in herbs to poached turbot with slices of Prague ham.

Malostranské nám. 12, Praha 1. ℂ 257-530-021. www.pfd.cz. Main courses 295Kč–995Kč ($11–$36). AE, MC, V. Mon–Fri noon–11pm; Sat–Sun 11am–11pm. Metro: Malostranská.

NEAR VÁCLAVSKÉ NÁMĚSTÍ (WENCESLAS SQUARE)

Café-Restaurant Louvre CZECH/INTERNATIONAL   A big, breezy upstairs hall, the bustling Louvre is great for a coffee, an inexpensive pre-theater meal, or an upscale game of pool. Avoid the always-overcooked pastas and stick to the basic meats and fish. In the billiards parlor in back, you can have drinks and light meals.

Národní třída 20, Praha 1. ℂ 224-930-949. Reservations accepted. Main courses 90Kč–300Kč ($3.20–$11). AE, DC, MC, V. Daily 8am–11:30pm. Metro: Národnítřída.

Jarmark ⋇ CONTINENTAL   This cafeteria-style spot serves a very tasty variety of meats, sides, salads, and, of course, beer. Despite its convenient come-and-shove-it-in system, this is not an all-you-can-eat deal. Everyone gets a ticket upon entering, which will be validated at each pit stop you make among the various rows of steaming hot tables, veggie carts, and drink dispensers. For less than $5, you can sample the heartiest entrees, including roast beef and the traditional Czech roast pork. For just 79Kč ($2.80), you can have the Sote Jarmark, a generous portion of fried potatoes in onions with herbs and spices—nice on a cold, gray afternoon. The seating is spread throughout the bowels of an early-20th-century arcade, which has found a new life, keeping visitors dry and sated.

Vodičkova 30, Dům "U Nováků." ℂ 224-233-733. Reservations not accepted. Main courses 70Kč–150Kč ($2.50–$5.35). No credit cards. Daily 11am–10pm; Mon–Fri breakfast 8am–10am. Metro: Můstek.

NEAR STAROMĚSTSKÉ NÁMĚSTI (OLD TOWN SQUARE)

Klub architektů CZECH/INTERNATIONAL   Tucked into the alcoves of a 12th-century cellar, across the courtyard from Jan Hus's Bethlehem Chapel, this eclectic clubhouse for the city's progressive architects' society is the best nonpub value in Old Town. Choose from baked chicken, pork steaks, pasta, stir-fry chicken, and even vegetarian burritos.

Betlémské nám. 5a, Praha 1. ℂ 224-401-214. Reservations recommended. Main courses 80Kč–130Kč ($2.85–$4.65). AE, MC, V. Daily 11:30am–midnight. Metro: Národní třída.

Kogo ★★ *(Value* ITALIAN This ristorante-pizzeria has become very trendy and popular, because its fresh and well-prepared Italian specialties are served by an above-average waitstaff in a pleasant atmosphere. Beyond the standard and tasty pasta and pizza roster, the roasted veal, *vitello al forno a legna,* should be your choice. For a rare and (for Prague) tasty seafood dish, try the mussels in white wine and garlic *(cozze al vino bianco e aglio).*

Havelská 27, Praha 1. ℂ 224-214-543. www.kogo-prague.cz. Reservations recommended. Main courses 200Kč–400Kč ($7.15–$14). AE, MC, V. Daily 9am–midnight. Metro: Můstek.

Pizzeria Rugantino ★ *(Kids* PIZZA/PASTA Generous iceberg lettuce salads front the best selection of individual pizzas in Prague. Wood-fired stoves and handmade dough create crisp and delicate crusts on which a multitude of cheeses, vegetables, and meats can be placed. The Diabolo with fresh garlic bits and very hot chilies goes nicely with a cool salad and a pull of Krušovice beer. The constant buzz, nonsmoking area, and heavy childproof wooden tables make this a family favorite.

Dušní 4, Praha 1. ℂ 222-318-172. Individual pizzas 100Kč–300Kč ($3.55–$11). No credit cards. Mon–Sat 11am–11pm; Sun 5–11pm. Metro: Staroměstská.

Red Hot & Blues AMERICAN/CAJUN/MEXICAN You won't find a live crawfish or chef Paul Prudhomme lurking about, but the étouffée is excellent and the spicy Cajun shrimp delivers a punch. Tex-Mex regulars, plus burgers and nachos, round out the menu. Sunday brunch is best taken in the small courtyard. The casual French Quarter feel makes this a family-friendly choice. Some evenings you can hear live jazz here from 7 to 10:30pm.

Jakubská 12, Praha 1. ℂ 222-314-639. Main courses 139Kč–499Kč ($4.95–$18). AE, MC, V. Daily 9am–11pm; Sat–Sun brunch 9am–4pm. Metro: Náměstí Republiky.

CAFE SOCIETY
IN STARÉ MĚSTO (OLD TOWN)

Angel Café ★ SANDWICHES/SALADS/LIGHT MEALS The food offerings here are similar in style to Pret a Manger in Britain, but unlike the cash-and-carry Pret, you can sit comfortably and linger over tasty sandwiches on fresh bread. French pastries highlight the breakfast lineup along with properly stiff espresso. Who needs Starbucks?

Opatovická 3, Praha 1. ℂ 224-930-019. Reservations accepted. Main courses 90Kč–310Kč ($3.20–$11). AE, MC, V. Daily 10am–4pm; Tues–Fri 7–10pm. Metro: Národní třída.

Kavárna Obecní dům ★ *(Value* LIGHT FARE Of all the beautifully restored spaces in the Municipal House, the *kavárna* might be the most spectacular. Lofty ceilings, marble accents and tables, an altarlike mantle at the far end, huge windows, and period chandeliers provide the awesome setting for coffees, teas, pastries, and light sandwiches.

In the Municipal House, náměstí Republiky 5, Praha 1. ℂ 222-002-763. Cakes and coffees around 50Kč ($1. 80). AE, MC, V. Daily 7:30am–11pm. Metro: Náměstí Republiky.

Kavárna Slavia *(Finds* LIGHT FARE The Slavia reopened in 1997, saved after half a decade's absence prolonged by a Boston real estate speculator who was sitting on the property. Ex-president Havel, a Slavia regular when it was a dissident hangout, intervened, and after a long legal battle, the Slavia reopened on the Velvet Revolution's eighth anniversary. The restored Art Deco room recalls the place's 100 years as the rendezvous for the city's cultural and intellectual corps.

> ### *Tips* Quick Bites
>
> If you want to take a short break in the main shopping district, **Kogo Minibar,** Na Příkopě 22, Praha 1 (© **221-451-258**), is a breeze. In the newly refurbished shops and cinema center Slovanský Dům, you can get warm or cold sandwiches for 60Kč ($2.15) and delicious salads for 85Kč ($3.05), both served with the same homemade bread from Kogo's home base.
>
> The very Czech-style delicatessen **Kliment-Obchod čerstvých uzenin,** Václavské nám. 39, Praha 1 (© **222-243-236**), offers meat, meat, and more meat on the ground floor of Wenceslas Square's Melantrich Building. The front of the shop is a takeout deli. In the back, it serves goulash, cooked meats, sausages with mustard and a slice of dense bread, and cheap beer. You have to eat standing up, but prices are pure Czech. Expect to pay about 60Kč ($2.15) for a plate of meat and a beer. It's open Monday to Friday from 7am to 7pm and Saturday and Sunday from 9am to 7pm. No credit cards are accepted.
>
> Vegetarians will like **Country Life,** Melantrichova 15, Praha 1 (© **224-213-366**), a health-food store run by the Seventh-Day Adventists; it offers a strictly meatless menu also served to go. You'll find tofu; salads; zesty wheat bread pizzas topped with red pepper, garlic, and onions; and vegetable burgers. Selections are 50Kč to 75Kč ($1.80–$2.65). It's open Monday to Saturday from 11am to 8pm. No credit cards are accepted.

The Slavia still has its relatively affordable menu of light fare served with the riverfront views of Prague Castle and the National Theater.

Národní at Smetanovo nábřeží, Praha 1. © 224-218-493. Coffees and pastries 20Kč–40Kč (70¢–$1.40); salad bar and light menu items 40Kč–120Kč ($1.40–$4.30). AE, MC, V. Daily 8am–midnight. Metro: Národní třída.

WORTH A SPLURGE
IN MALÁ STRANA
Hergetova Cihelna *Kids* INTERNATIONAL/PIZZA   This is the latest addition to the list of Prague's top dining experiences—and it's become a popular spot of social life on the embankment of the river. It's set in an 18th-century former brick factory (*cihelna*), which received extensive reconstruction starting in 2000. Now the interior is divided into a restaurant, cocktail bar, cafe, and music lounge. From the large summer terrace you can experience one of the most exciting and unforgettable views of the river and Charles Bridge. The food is standard and good; I enjoyed their homemade pizza Quattro Stagioni and Czech goulash served with herbed gnocchi.

Cihelná 2b, Praha 1. © 257-535-534. www.cihelna.com. Main courses 195Kč–485Kč ($6.95–$17). AE, MC, V. Daily 9am–2am. Metro: Malostranská.

NEAR NÁMĚSTÍ MÍRU
Osmička *Kids* CONTINENTAL/CZECH   Osmička is an interesting hybrid in Vinohrady, on a side street a few blocks above the National Museum. The "Number 8" is a residential cellar restaurant with local art for sale on the walls and an eclectic menu dominated by Italian standbys, fresh salads, and sandwiches. But this is also still a good ol' Bohemian *hospoda* with *vepřo-knedlo-zelo*

We're Here for the Beer

While most post-Communist Czechs aren't very religious, one thing that elicits a piety unseen in many orthodox countries is *pivo* (beer). The golden nectar has inspired some of the most popular Czech fiction and films, poetry and prayers.

Czechs have brewed beer since the 9th century, but the golden lager *(ležák)* known around the world as Pilsner was born in 1842 in the western Bohemian town of Plzeň (*Pilsen* in German). Before then, beers and ales carried a murky, dull body, but the Pilsner method kept the brew bright and golden. What's unique here, experts say, is the exceptionally light and crisp hops grown in the western Bohemian region of Žatec.

The debate over which Czech beer is best rages on, but here are some top contenders, all readily available in Prague: **Budvar,** the original "budweiser," is a semisweet lager hailing from České Budějovice; **Gambrinus,** smooth and solid, not too bitter, is the best-selling domestic label and comes from the Pilsner breweries; **Pilsner Urquell,** the more familiar, bitter brother of Gambrinus, is packaged mostly for export; **Staropramen,** the flagship label from Prague's home brewery, is a hardy standby and easiest to find; and **Krušovice,** a favorite with American expats bred on light beer, is heavy and somewhat sweet, yet has a spicy aroma that surrounds the back of your gullet.

and other indigenous fare at local prices, served on rustic wood furniture by nicer-than-normal staff.

Balbínova 8, Praha 2. (℃ **222-826-208.** Main courses 60Kč–260Kč ($2.15–$9.30). MC, V. Mon–Thurs 9am–midnight; Fri 9am–2am; Sat noon–midnight; Sun noon–11pm. Metro: I. P. Pavlova or Náměstí Míru.

Radost FX Café VEGETARIAN   Radost is a clubhouse for hip new Bohemians, with plenty of Americans and others lingering, too. The veggie burger is well seasoned and substantial on a grain bun, and the soups are light and full of flavor. Saté vegetable dishes, tofu, and huge Greek salads round out the health-conscious menu. The dining area is a dark rec room in 1960s kitsch.

Bělehradská 120, Praha 2. (℃ **224-254-776.** Reservations not accepted. Main courses 120Kč–250Kč ($4.25–$8.90). MC, V. Daily 10am–5am. Metro: I. P. Pavlova.

4 Seeing the Sights

Prague's intrigue comes from its outdoor sights—architecture and atmosphere—best enjoyed by an aimless wander through the city's heart. If you have the time and energy, try taking a broad view of Prague Castle and the Old Town skyline (best from Charles Bridge) at sunrise, then at sunset. The variations of shadows and silhouettes show you two completely different cities.

Except for busy main streets, Prague is an ideal city for walking. Actually, it's the only way to truly explore it. Many older areas are walking zones, with motor traffic restricted. Wear comfortable, preferably flat, shoes. The crevices in the brick streets have been known to eat stiletto heels.

PRAGUE CASTLE & CHARLES BRIDGE

Dating from the 14th century, **Charles Bridge (Karlův most)** ⊛, Prague's most celebrated structure, links Prague Castle to Staré Město. For most of its 600 years, the 518m (1,700-ft.) span has been a pedestrian promenade, although for centuries walkers had to share the concourse with horse-drawn vehicles and trolleys. Today, the bridge is filled with hordes walking among folksy artists and busking musicians.

The best times to stroll across the bridge are in early morning or around sunset, when the crowds have thinned and the shadows are more mysterious. But you're more than likely to crisscross the bridge several times throughout your stay.

Prague Castle (Pražský Hrad) ⊛ *(Moments* The huge hilltop complex known collectively as **Pražský Hrad (Prague Castle)** encompasses dozens of houses, towers, churches, courtyards, and monuments. A visit to the castle could easily take an entire day or more. Still, you can see the top sights—St. Vitus Cathedral, the Royal Palace, St. George's Basilica, the Powder Tower, plus Golden Lane—in the space of a morning or an afternoon.

St. Vitus Cathedral (Chrám sv. Víta), constructed in A.D. 926 as the court church of the Premyslid princes, was named for a wealthy 4th-century Sicilian martyr and has long been the center of Prague's religious and political life. The key part of its Gothic construction took place in the 14th century under the direction of Mathias of Arras and Peter Parléř of Gmuend. In the 18th and 19th centuries, subsequent baroque and neo-Gothic additions were made. In 1997, Pope John Paul II visited Prague to honor the 1,000th anniversary of the death of 10th-century Slavic evangelist St. Vojtěch. He conferred the saint's name on the cathedral along with St. Vitus's, but officially the Czech state calls it just St. Vitus. Of the massive Gothic cathedral's 21 chapels, the **St. Wenceslas Chapel (Svatováclavská kaple)** ⊛ stands out as one of Prague's few must-see, indoor sights. Located midway toward the high altar on the right, it's encrusted with hundreds of pieces of jasper and amethyst and decorated with paintings from the 14th to the 16th centuries. The chapel sits atop the gravesite of Bohemia's patron saint, St. Wenceslas.

The **Royal Palace (Královský palác),** in the third courtyard of the castle grounds, served as the residence of kings between the 10th and the 17th centuries. Vaulted Vladislav Hall, the interior's centerpiece, was used for coronations and special occasions. It was also here that Václav Havel was inaugurated

---

Value Getting the Best Deal on Sightseeing

- Spend most of your time just wandering on Charles Bridge, in Old Town, and in Malá Strana. Prague's ambience and architecture offer a unique experience for each visitor—and strolling around is free (although it might be tough on your feet and legs).
- For a good orientation to the city, take tram no. 22 or 23 from Prague Castle down through Malá Strana and past the National Theater to Wenceslas Square.
- The best free (and relatively tourist-free) scenic view is from the ramparts atop Vyšehrad citadel at the city's south end. The park within is also perfect for a picnic.

Prague

♟ ----- ♟ Royal Route
⊖ — — ⊖ Metro

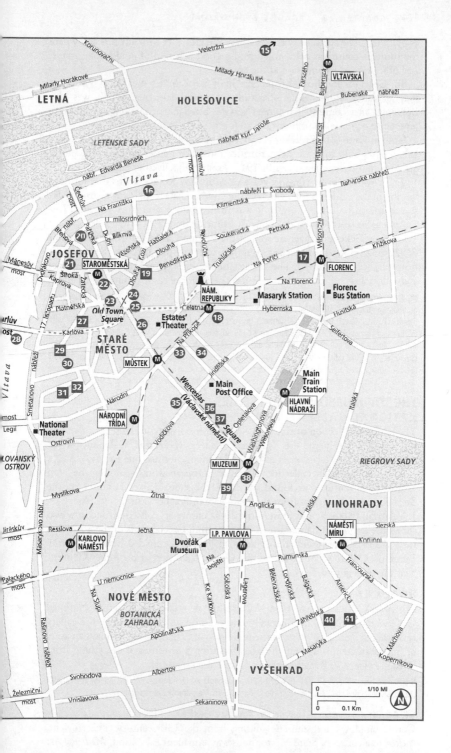

as president. The adjacent Diet was where the king met with advisers and where the supreme court was held. You'll find a good selection of guidebooks, maps, and other related information at the entrance.

St. George's Basilica (Kostel sv. Jiří), adjacent to the Royal Palace, is Prague's oldest Romanesque structure, from the 10th century. It was also Bohemia's first convent. No longer serving a religious function, the building now houses a museum of historic Czech art.

Golden Lane (Zlatá ulička) is a picturesque street of tiny 16th-century servants' houses built into the castle fortifications. The houses now contain shops, galleries, and refreshment bars. In 1917, Franz Kafka lived briefly at no. 22.

The **Powder Tower (Prašná věž aka Mihulka)** forms part of the northern bastion of the castle complex, just off the Golden Lane. Originally a gunpowder storehouse and a cannon tower, it was turned into a laboratory for the 17th-century alchemists serving the court of Emperor Rudolf II.

Getting Tickets: Tickets are sold at the **Prague Castle Information Center** (© **224-373-368**), in the second courtyard after you pass through the main gate from Hradčanské náměstí. The center also arranges tours in various languages and sells tickets for concerts and exhibits held on the castle grounds.

Hradčanské nám., Hradčany, Praha 1. © **224-373-368**. Fax 224-310-896. www.hrad.cz. Free admission to grounds. Combination ticket for tour A to 5 main attractions (St. Vitus Cathedral, Royal Palace, St. George's Basilica, Powder Tower, Golden Lane) without guide 220Kč ($7.85) adults, 110Kč ($3.90) students; with English-speaking guide 300Kč ($11) adults, 190Kč ($6.80) students. Tour B (St. Vitus Cathedral, Royal Palace, Golden Lane) without guide 180Kč ($6.40) adults, 90Kč ($3.20) students; with English-speaking guide 260Kč ($9.30) adults, 170Kč ($6) students. Tour C (only Golden Lane) without guide 40Kč ($1.40); with guide 120Kč ($4.30). Guided tours organized for groups of 5 or more only Tues–Sun 9am–4pm. V. Ticket valid 1 day. Castle daily 9am–5pm (Nov–Mar to 4pm). Metro: Malostranská, then tram 22 or 23, up the hill 2 stops.

THE TOP MUSEUMS & GALLERIES
NATIONAL GALLERY SITES

The national collection of fine art is grouped for display in the series of venues known collectively as the National Gallery **(Národní Galerie), www. ngprague.cz**. This term refers to several locations, not just one gallery.

The most extensive collection of classic European works spanning the 14th to the 18th centuries is found at the Archbishop's Palace complex in the **Šternberský palác** across from the main gate to Prague Castle.

Veletržní Palace houses most of the 20th-century art collection, and now also shows the important national revival works from Czech artists of the 19th century. Much of the rest of the national collection is divided between Kinský Palace on Old Town Square, and the Gothic collection at St. Agnes Convent near the river in Old Town.

HRADČANY
Šternberk Palace (Šternberský palác) ⭐

The jewel in the National Gallery crown (also known casually as the European Art Museum), the gallery at Šternberk Palace, adjacent to the main gate of Prague Castle, displays an array of European art throughout the ages, featuring 5 centuries of everything from Orthodox icons to Renaissance oils from Dutch masters.

Hradčanské nám. 15, Praha 1. © **233-090-570**. www.ngprague.cz. Admission 150Kč ($5.35) adults, 70Kč ($2.50) students and children. Tues–Sun 10am–6pm. Metro: Malostranská or Hradčanská.

St. Agnes Convent (Klášter sv. Anežky České)

This is a complex of early Gothic buildings and churches dating from the 13th century. The convent, tucked in a corner of Staré Město, houses a permanent exhibition, *Medieval Art in Bohemia and Central Europe.* Some famous panel paintings of the Master Theodoric are on display here along with other paintings and sculptures from the 14th to 16th centuries.

U milosrdných 17, Praha 1. © 224-810-628. www.ngprague.cz. Admission 100Kč ($3.65) adults, 50Kč ($1.80) children. Tues–Sun 10am–6pm. Metro: Staroměstská.

St. George's Convent at Prague Castle (Klášter sv. Jiří na Pražském hradě)

Displaying Czech baroque paintings and sculptures from the 17th and 18th centuries, the castle convent is especially packed with works by four key baroque artists: Karel Škréta's portraits and altarpieces; Petr Brandl's and Václav Reiner's painting collections; and the well-known sculptures by Matyas Braun.

Jiřské nám. 33, Praha 1. © 257-320-536. www.ngprague.cz. Admission 100Kč ($3.65) adults, 50Kč ($1.80) students. Tues–Sun 10am–6pm. Metro: Malostranská or Hradčanská.

STARÉ MĚSTO (OLD TOWN)

Kinský Palace (Palác Kinských) *Finds* This reconstructed rococo Palace houses graphic works from the National Gallery collection, including pieces by Georges Braque, André Derain, and other modern masters; Pablo Picasso's 1907 *Self-Portrait* is also here. Good-quality international exhibits have included Max Ernst and Rembrandt retrospectives, as well as shows on functional Arts and Crafts.

Staroměstské náměstí 12, Praha 1. © 224-810-758. www.ngprague.cz. Admission varies for each exhibition. Tues–Sun 10am–6pm. Metro: Staroměstská.

Veletržní Palace (National Gallery) This 1925 constructivist palace, built for trade fairs, was remodeled and reopened in 1995 to hold the bulk of the National Gallery's collection of 19th, 20th, and 21st-century works by Czech and other European artists. Three atrium-lit concourses provide a comfortable setting Czech paintings, sculpture, furniture, and also contemporary multimedia works. Alas, the best cubist works from Braque and Picasso, Rodin bronzes, and many other primarily French pieces have been relegated to the second floor. Other displays are devoted to peculiar works from Czech artists that demonstrate how creativity flowed even under the weight of the Iron Curtain. The first floor features temporary exhibits.

Veletržní at Dukelských hrdinů 47, Praha 7. © 224-301-024. www.ngprague.cz. Admission for 4 floors of Palace 250Kč ($8.90) adults, 120Kč ($4.30) students; admission for 3 floors 200Kč ($7.15) adults, 100Kč ($3.55) students; admission for 2 floors 150Kč ($5.35) adults, 70Kč ($2.50) students; admission for 1 floor 100Kč ($3.55) adults, 50Kč ($1.80) students. Tues–Sun 10am–6pm. Metro: Line C to Vltavská. Tram: 17.

OTHER MUSEUMS

Alfons Mucha Museum (Muzeum Alfonse Muchy) Prague's newest museum celebrates the work of renowned Art Nouveau artist Alphonse Mucha, best known for his theatrical posters created for the dramatic diva of his day, Sarah Bernhardt, and highly patriotic images that turned women into goddesses and warriors. The museum displays some of Mucha's decorative panels, posters, paintings, designs for Czech banknotes, manuscripts, and studio photos. An interesting video provides an overview of his life.

Panská 7, Praha 1. © 221-451-333. www.mucha.cz. Admission 120Kč ($4.30) adults, 60Kč ($2.15) students and children. Daily 10am–6pm. Metro: Můstek.

The Jewish Museum in Prague The Jewish Museum is the organization managing all the Jewish landmarks in Josefov, which forms the northwest quarter of Old Town. The organization provides guided tours as part of the admission price, with an English-speaking guide. The package includes the **Old Jewish Cemetery** and **Ceremonial Hall, Pinkas Synagogue, Klaus Synagogue, Maisel Synagogue,** and **Spanish Synagogue.**

The Maisel Synagogue serves as the exhibition space for the Jewish museum. In 1994, the State Jewish Museum closed; the Torah covers, 100,000 books, and other exhibits once housed there were given to the Jewish community, who then proceeded to return many items to synagogues throughout the country. Most of Prague's ancient Judaica was destroyed by the Nazis. Ironically, those same Germans constructed an "exotic museum of an extinct race," thus salvaging thousands of objects, such as the valued Torah covers, books, and silver now displayed at the synagogue. Also worth seeing, as part of the museum's offerings, is the **Spanish Synagogue** at Vězeňská, 3 blocks down Široká Street from the Old-New Synagogue (see below), with exhibits of more Jewish history in Prague.

Maisel Synagogue, Maiselova 10 (between Široká and Jáchymova 3), Praha 1. ⓒ **222-317-191.** Fax 222-317-181. www.jewishmuseum.cz. Combined admission to all museum parts listed above 300Kč ($11) adults, 200Kč ($7.15) students. Tours Apr–Oct Sun–Fri 9am–6pm (last tour 5pm); Nov–Mar Sun–Fri 9am–4:30pm. Metro: Staroměstská.

Museum Kampa 🎯 This building on Kampa island, called Sovovy Mlýny, served for most of its history as a mill. It holds a picturesque position on the river, but it has been struck by floods, fires, and destructive wars. In September 2003, the Sovovy Mlýny was opened as a museum of modern art by Czech-born American Meda Mládková. She has been collecting works of Czech and central European artists since the 1950s. Here she has fulfilled her dream of presenting her family's extensive collection of abstract works of František Kupka, Otto Gutfreund's cubist sculptures, and Jiří Kolář's graphics, and more than 200 paintings and art pieces from European and American artists.

U Sovov_ch ml_nů 503/2, Praha 1. ⓒ **257-286-147.** www.museumkampa.cz. Admission 120Kč ($4.30) adults, 60Kč ($2.15) students. Daily 10am–6pm. Metro: Malostranská.

National Museum (Národní muzeum) The National Museum, dominating upper Václavské náměstí, looks so much like an important government building it even fooled the Communists, who fired on it during their 1968 invasion. If you look closely you can still see shell marks. The second oldest museum in the Czech lands, this neo-Renaissance-style museum opened in 1893. On the first floor is an exhaustive collection of minerals, rocks, and meteorites from the Czech and Slovak republics. The other floors' exhibits depict the ancient history of the Czech lands through zoological and paleontological displays.

Václavské nám. 68, Praha 1. ⓒ **224-497-111.** www.nm.cz. Admission 80Kč ($2.85) adults, 40Kč ($1.40) students, free for children under 6, free for all 1st Mon of each month. May–Sept daily 10am–6pm; Oct–Apr daily 9am–5pm. Closed 1st Tues each month. Metro: Muzeum.

Old Jewish Cemetery (Starý židovský hřbitov) and Ceremonial Hall (Obřadní síň) From the mid–15th century, the Old Jewish Cemetery is one of Europe's oldest Jewish burial grounds, 1 block from the Old-New Synagogue. Because the local government of the time didn't allow Jews to bury their dead elsewhere, graves were dug deep enough to hold 12 bodies vertically, with each tombstone placed in front of the last. The result is one of the world's most crowded cemeteries: a 1-block area filled with more than 20,000 graves. Among the famous buried here are the celebrated Rabbi Loew (died 1609), who made the legendary golem (a clay "monster" to protect Prague's Jews), and banker Markus Mordechai Maisel (died 1601), then the richest man in Prague and protector of the city's Jewish community during the reign of Rudolf II. The adjoining **Ceremonial Hall**

at the end of the path is worth a look for the heart-wrenching drawings by children held at the Terezín concentration camp during World War II.

U Starého hřbitova; entrance is from Široká 3. © **222-317-191.** Admission to site is part of Jewish Museum package (see above): 300Kč ($11) adults, 200Kč ($7.15) students. Apr–Oct Sun–Fri 9am–6pm; Nov–Mar Sun–Fri 9am–4:30pm. Metro: Staroměstská.

Old-New Synagogue (Staronová synagoga) First called the New Synagogue to distinguish it from an even older one that no longer exists, the Old-New Synagogue, built around 1270, is Europe's oldest Jewish house of worship. Jews have prayed here continuously for more than 700 years, carrying on even after a massive 1389 pogrom in Josefov that killed over 3,000 Jews.

Červená 2. © **222-317-191.** Admission 200Kč ($7.15) adults, 140Kč ($5) students. Sun–Thurs 9am–5pm; Fri 9am–4:30pm. Metro: Staroměstská.

W. A. Mozart Museum (Bertramka) Mozart loved Prague, and when he visited he often stayed with the family who owned this villa, the Dušeks. The villa contains displays that include his written work and harpsichord. Much of the Bertramka villa was destroyed by fire in the 1870s, but Mozart's rooms, where he finished composing *Don Giovanni,* miraculously remained untouched.

Mozartova 169, Praha 5. © **257-318-465.** www.bertramka.cz. Admission 90Kč ($3.20) adults, 50Kč ($1.80) students; concert tickets 350Kč ($13) adults, 230Kč ($8.20) students. Daily 9:30am–6pm (Nov–Mar until 5pm). Tram: 4, 6, 7, 9, 10, 14, or 16 from Anděl Metro station to the Bertramka stop.

MORE ATTRACTIONS

Chrám sv. Mikuláše (Cathedral of St. Nicholas) This church is critically regarded as one of the best examples of the high baroque north of the Alps. K. I. Dienzenhofer's 1711 design was augmented by his son Kryštof's 79m (260-ft.) dome, which dominates the Malá Strana skyline and was completed in 1752. Now concerts of chamber music and choirs are held here regularly throughout the year.

Malostranské nám. 1, Praha 1. © **257-534-215.** Free admission; admission to concerts 390Kč ($14) adults, 290Kč ($10) students. Tues–Sun 10am–5pm (concerts at 5pm). Metro: Malostranská, then tram 22, 23, or 12, 1 stop to Malostranské náměstí.

Estates' Theater (Stavovské divadlo) ⚘ This theater was completed in 1783 by the wealthy Count F. A. Nostitz, and Mozart staged the premier of *Don Giovanni* here in 1787 because he said the conservative patrons in Vienna didn't appreciate him or his passionate and often shocking work. Czech director Miloš Forman returned to his native country to film his Oscar-winning *Amadeus,* capturing Mozart in Prague at the Estates' Theater. The theater doesn't have daily tours, but tickets for performances—and the chance to sit in one of the elegant private boxes—are usually available. Tours are occasionally scheduled; call the city heritage group of the Pražská informační služba (PIS) at © **12444** for information.

Ovocný trh 1, Praha 1. © **224-901-448.** Metro: Můstek.

Strahov Monastery and Library (Strahovský klášter) The second oldest monastery in Prague, Strahov was founded high above Malá Strana in 1143 by Vladislav II. It's still home to Premonstratensian monks, a scholarly order closely related to the Jesuits, and their dormitories and refectory are off-limits. What draws visitors are the monastery's ornate libraries, holding more than 125,000 volumes.

Strahovské nádvoří 1, Praha 1. © **220-516-671.** Admission 60Kč ($2.15) adults, 40Kč ($1.40) students. Daily 9am–noon and 1–5pm. Tram: 22 or 23 from Malostranská Metro station.

Special Events

Mid-May to the first weekend in June, the city hosts the **Prague Spring International Music Festival,** celebrating its 60th year in 2005. If you plan to attend, get tickets as far in advance as possible through the Czech travel agency Čedok, Na Příkopě 18, Praha 1 (toll free ℂ **800-112-112;** www.cedok.cz; Metro: Můstek), open Monday to Friday 9am to 7pm; Saturday 10am to 2pm. Or, for schedules and tickets, contact the Prague Spring International Music Festival, Hellichova 18, 118 00 Praha 1 ((ℂ **257-312-547;** www.festival.cz). Tickets for concerts range from 250Kč to 2,000Kč ($8.90–$71).

In late May, the **Prague International Marathon** (www.pim.cz) has grown to become one of Europe's premier annual running events. It draws a top-flight roster of international champions and tens of thousands of recreational roadsters who navigate the classic marathon or 9km (5½-mile) fun run through Prague's scenic Old Town. The event is regularly scheduled for the third or fourth Sunday in May.

A similar event to its older brother (the Prague Spring Festival), the **Prague Autumn International Music Festival** is expected to be held again for 2 weeks from the last weekend in September. This 1990s addition to Prague's perennial serious music events features more contemporary works and cutting-edge performances. Contact the Festival Office ((ℂ **222-002-127;** www.pragueautumn.cz) for tickets.

National Day, October 28, commemorates the founding of Czechoslovakia as a republic in 1918 (the federation with Slovakia was dissolved at the beginning of 1993). Besides the speeches and military memorials (and the annual clash between police and extremists on Wenceslas Sq.), Prague Castle is opened for a rare tour of the stately baroque salons normally off limits to the public. **Be warned:** While the event is free of charge, a huge line begins forming early in the morning, and many hopefuls are out of luck when the doors close in the late afternoon. There are no human guides, so select one of the many detailed guides in the Castle bookshop the day before and get in line early.

HISTORIC SQUARES

Staroměstské náměstí (Old Town Sq.) is the city's most celebrated square, surrounded by baroque buildings and packed with colorful craftspeople, cafes, and entertainers. In its center stands a **memorial to Jan Hus,** the 15th-century martyr who crusaded against Prague's German-dominated religious and political establishment; it was unveiled in 1915 on the 500th anniversary of Hus's execution. The **Astronomical Clock (orloj)** at Old Town Hall (Staroměstská radnice; Metro: Staroměstská) performs a glockenspiel spectacle daily on the hour from 8am to 8pm. Constructed in 1410, the clock has long been an important symbol of Prague.

Wenceslas Square (Václavské náměstí; Metro: Muzeum or Můstek), and especially its namesake memorial of the Good King Wenceslas (Václav) high atop his horse, has been the focal point of riots, revolutions, and celebrations, such as the raucous spontaneous celebrations in 1918 (for the founding of

Czechoslovakia); the 1968 demonstrations (against the invasion of Soviet tanks); the 1989 "Velvet Revolution;" and February 1998, when Czechs went wild after the national hockey team won Olympic gold in Nagano. Under the steps to the monumental building of the National Museum is a small memorial to Jan Palach, the student who burned himself to death nearby on the square in January 1969 to protest the Soviet-led invasion.

PARKS & GARDENS

Vyšehrad, Soběslavova 1 (© **241-410-348;** tram: 3 from Karlovo náměstí to Výtoň south of New Town), was the first seat of the first Czech kings in the Premyslid dynasty. From this spot, legend has it, Princess Libuše looked out over the Vltava valley toward the present-day Prague Castle and predicted the founding of a great state and capital city. Within the confines of the citadel, lush lawns and gardens are crisscrossed by dozens of paths leading to historic buildings and cemeteries. It's great for quiet picnics.

The **Royal Garden (Královská zahrada)** at Prague Castle, once the site of the sovereigns' vineyards, was founded in 1534. Dotted with lemon trees and surrounded by 16th-, 17th-, and 18th-century buildings, the park is conservatively laid out with abundant shrubbery and fountains. Enter from U Prašného mostu north of the castle complex. On the other side of the castle, the **Garden on the Ramparts (Zahrada na Valech)** overlooks the city. Beyond the beautifully groomed lawns and artful shrubbery is a tranquil view of the castle above and one of the best views of Prague below. Enter the garden from the south side of the castle complex below Hradčanské náměstí. All the gardens are open Tuesday to Sunday from 9am to 5pm (to sundown during winter months).

5 Shopping

Czech authorities make no concerted effort to refund the 22% **value-added tax,** and most stores are shocked if you ask, but some enterprising shops with the TAX FREE FOR TOURISTS sign will provide the required legal paperwork, which then has to be deposited with the Customs officials before you exit the country. Your check will then be mailed to you. For details on getting your VAT refund, see chapter 1.

BEST BUYS

Czech porcelain, glass, and cheap but well-constructed clothing draw hordes of day-trippers from nearby Germany. Craft and specialty shops abound, and you can find good deals in street markets, art studios, and galleries. Shops lining the main route from **Old Town Square to Charles Bridge** are great for browsing. For clothing, porcelain, jewelry, garnets, and glass, stroll around **Wenceslas Square** and **Na Příkopě,** the street connecting Wenceslas Square with náměstí Republiky.

SELECT SHOPS & MARKETS

Bohemian glass, porcelain, jewelry, and other specialty items can be packed and shipped directly from **Celetná Crystal,** Celetná 15, Praha 1 (© **223-243-022;** Metro: Nám. Republiky). At **Cristallino,** Celetná 12, Praha 1 (© **224-225-173;** Metro: Nám. Republiky), you'll find a good selection of stemware and vases in traditional designs at excellent prices.

Havelský trh (Havel's Market), Havelská ulice, Praha 1 (Metro: Můstek), is on a short street running perpendicular to Melantrichova, the main route connecting Staroměstské náměstí with Václavské náměstí. This open-air market (named well before a Havel became president) features private vendors selling seasonal homegrown fruits and vegetables and flowers and cheese. The market is a great place to pick up super-cheap picnic supplies. It's open Monday to Friday from 7am to 6pm.

6 Prague After Dark

Turn to the *Prague Post* (www.praguepost.cz) for listings of cultural events and nightlife around the city; it's available at most newsstands in Old Town and Malá Strana.

Once in Prague, you can buy tickets at theater box offices or from any one of dozens of agencies throughout the city center. Agencies include the **Prague Tourist Center,** Rytířská 12, Praha 1 (© 224-212-209; www.ptc.cz; Metro: Můstek), open daily 9am to 8pm; **Bohemia Ticket International,** Na Příkopě 16, Praha 1 (© 224-215-031; www.ticketsbti.cz; Metro: Můstek), open Monday to Friday 10am to 7pm, Saturday 10am to 5pm, Sunday 10am to 3pm; and **Čedok,** Na Příkopě 18, Praha 1 (© 800-112-112 toll free; www.cedok.cz; Metro: Můstek), open Monday to Friday 9am to 7pm, Saturday 10am to 2pm. Prague's largest computerized ticket service is **Ticketpro,** Salvátorská 10, Praha 1 (© 296-329-999; www.ticketpro.cz). You can buy tickets using Visa, Master-Card, Diners Club, or American Express, or reserve them online.

THE PERFORMING ARTS

Although there's plenty of music year-round, the symphonies and orchestras all come to life during the **Prague Spring Music Festival,** a 3-week series of concerts featuring the country's top performers, as well as noted guest conductors and soloists and visiting symphony orchestras. For more details, see the "Special Events" box on p. 778.

The Czech Philharmonic Orchestra and Prague Symphony Orchestra usually perform at the **Rudolfinum,** náměstí Jana Palacha, Praha 1 (© 227-059-352; Metro: Staroměstská). The Czech Philharmonic is the traditional voice of the country's national pride, often playing works by Dvořák and Smetana; the Prague Symphony often ventures into more eclectic territory. Tickets range from 100Kč to 600Kč ($3.55–$21).

In a city full of spectacularly beautiful theaters, the massive pale-green **Estates' Theater (Stavovské divadlo),** Ovocný trh 1, Praha 1 (© 224-215-001; Metro: Můstek), is one of the most awesome. Built in 1783 and the site of the premiere of Mozart's *Don Giovanni* (conducted by the composer), the theater now hosts many of the classic productions of European opera and drama. Simultaneous English translation, transmitted via headphone, is available for most plays. Tickets cost 200Kč to 1,000Kč ($7.15–$36).

Lavishly constructed in the late Renaissance style of northern Italy, the gold-crowned **Národní divadlo (National Theater),** Národní 2, Praha 1 (© 224-901-448; Metro: Národní třída), overlooking the Vltava River, is one of Prague's most recognizable landmarks. Completed in 1881, the theater was built to nurture the Czech National Revival—a grassroots movement to replace the dominant German culture with that of native Czechs. Today's classic productions are staged in a larger setting than the Estates' Theater, but with about the same ticket prices. The National Theater Ballet performs here, with tickets costing 200Kč to 600Kč ($7.15–$21).

Laterna Magika, Národní 4, Praha 1 (© 224-931-482; Metro: Národní třída), is a performance-art show based in the new wing of the National Theater.

The multimedia show, such as *Odysseus* or *Casanova*, which combines live theater with film and dance, was once considered on the radical edge. They aren't for those easily offended by nudity. Tickets are 400Kč ($14).

ROCK & DANCE CLUBS

The club scene in Prague is limited but lively. Popular spots includes **Lávka,** Novotného lávka 1, Praha 1 (© **222-222-156;** Metro: Staroměstská), where straightforward dance hits attract one of Prague's best-looking young crowds; **Radost FX,** Bělehradská 120, Praha 2 (© **224-254-776;** Metro: I. P. Pavlova), which caters to a mixed gay and model crowd; and **Roxy,** Dlouhá 33, Praha 1 (© **224-826-296;** Metro: Náměstí Republiky), one of the city's most unusual venues, with a subterranean theater and wraparound balcony that overlooks the concrete dance floor.

JAZZ CLUBS

Relatively high prices (100Kč–200Kč/$3.60–$7.15) guarantee the small **AghaRTA Jazz Centrum,** Krakovská 5, Praha 1 (© **222-211-275;** Metro: Muzeum), a predominantly foreign crowd. The **Reduta Jazz Club,** Národní 20, Praha 1 (© **224-933-487;** Metro: Národní třída), is a smoky subterranean room that looks exactly like a jazz cellar should.

GAY & LESBIAN BARS

For details on the gay and lesbian community, call the **SOHO Infocentrum** at © **224-220-327** or check out the listings in *SOHO Revue* and *Amigo* (both in Czech but with helpful maps of bars) and the *Prague Post* (www.praguepost.cz).

Radost FX (see above) is a stylish place to dance. Lesbians should look for **"A" Klub,** Milíčova 32, Praha 3 (no phone; tram no. 9 from the center to the Lipanská stop). **Aqua Club 2000,** Husitská 7, Praha 3 (© **222-540-241;** www.euroshow2000.cz; Metro: Florenc, then bus no. 133 to Husitská), is a multi-activity (such as cabaret) venue that attracts a mixed gay and lesbian crowd. **U Střelce,** Karolíny Světlé 12, Praha 1 (© **224-238-278;** Metro: Národní třída), is a popular nightclub near Charles Bridge that attracts a mixed crowd—gay and straight, local and foreign.

7 A Side Trip to Český Krumlov ★★: Where the Renaissance Lives On

If you have time for only one excursion from Prague, make it **Český Krumlov** ★★, 19km (12 miles) southwest of České Budějovice (see below) and 167km (104 miles) south of Prague. It's a living gallery of elegant Renaissance-era buildings housing cafes, pubs, restaurants, shops, and galleries. In 1992, UNESCO named it a World Heritage Site.

GETTING THERE   The only way to reach Český Krumlov by **train** from Prague is via České Budějovice, a slow ride that deposits you at a station far from the town center. It takes 3½ hours; the fare is 336Kč ($12) first class or 224Kč ($8) second. The nearly 3-hour **bus** ride from Prague usually involves a transfer in České Budějovice. The fare is 150Kč ($5.35), and the bus station in Český Krumlov is a 15-minute walk from the main square. If you choose to **drive,** take Highway 3 leading from the south of České Budějovice and turn onto Highway 159. It takes about 35 minutes to Krumlov, depending on traffic. The roads are clearly marked, with several signs directing traffic to the town. From Prague, it's a 2-hour drive via České Budějovice.

Český Krumlov

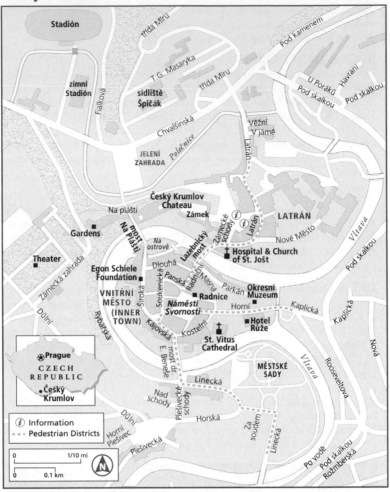

SEEING THE SIGHTS The town is split into the **Inner Town** and **Latrán,** which houses the castle. Begin at the **Okresní muzeum (Regional Museum;** ☏ **380-711-674)** at the top of Horní ulice, containing artifacts and displays relating to Český Krumlov's 1,000-year history. The highlight is a giant model of the town. Admission is 50Kč ($1.80), and it's open daily May through September 10am to 5pm (till 6pm in July and Aug), October through December Tuesday through Friday from 9am to 4pm, and March and April Saturday and Sunday from 1 to 4pm.

Across the street is the **Hotel Růže (Rose),** once a Jesuit student house. Built in the late 16th century, the hotel and the prelature next door show Gothic, Renaissance, and rococo influences. Don't be afraid to walk around and even ask questions at the reception desk. Continue down the street to the impressive Late Gothic **St. Vitus Cathedral.** Be sure to climb the tower for its spectacular view.

Continue down the street to **náměstí Svornosti.** Few buildings show any character, making the main square of such an impressive town a bit disappointing. The **Radnice (Town Hall),** náměstí Svornosti 1, is one of the few exceptions. Its Gothic arcades and Renaissance vault inside are beautiful. From the square, streets fan out in all directions. Take some time just to wander through them. As you cross the bridge and head toward the castle, you'll see immediately to your right the former **hospital and church of St. Jošt.** Founded at the beginning of the 14th century, it has since been turned into apartments.

The second largest castle in Bohemia (after Prague Castle), the **Český Krumlov Château** ⋪ (www.castle.ckrumlov.cz) was built in the 13th century. After a long climb up, the first thing greeting you will be a round 12th century **tower,** with a Renaissance balcony, and then you'll pass over the moat, now occupied by two brown bears. Next is the **Dolní Hrad (Lower Castle)** and then the **Horní Hrad (Upper Castle).**

Tours last 1 hour and depart frequently. The tour costs 140Kč ($5) for adults and 70Kč ($2.50) for students. The castle hours are Tuesday to Sunday: June to August from 9am to noon and 1 to 4pm; April, May, September, and October from 9am to noon and 1 to 5pm. The last entrance is 1 hour before closing. For more information, call ⓒ **380-704-721** or visit www.castle.ckrumlov.cz. Past the main castle building, you can see one of the more stunning views of Český Krumlov from **most Na Plášti,** a walkway that doubles as a belvedere.

WHERE TO DINE   Open daily 11am to 11pm, **Rybářská bašta Jakuba Krčína,** Kájovská 54 (ⓒ **380-712-692**), specializes in freshwater fish, with main courses costing 94Kč to 335Kč ($3.35–$12). Trout, perch, pike, and eel are sautéed, grilled, baked, and fried in a variety of herbs and spices. Venison, rabbit, and other game are also available, along with roast beef and pork cutlet. Reservations are recommended, and American Express, MasterCard, and Visa are accepted.

21

Rome & Environs

by Reid Bramblett

Over the past decade, **Rome** has undergone a touristic renaissance, with new museums and archaeological sites opening and monuments and galleries that had spent decades languishing under scaffolding emerging sparkling clean and with the latest technologies. Visitor information kiosks are now located all over town, the revamped train station/urban mall is among Europe's best, and the city's orchestras, opera, and theaters have come roaring out of the doldrums to inaugurate fabulous new seasons. Sights are staying open longer, monuments and palaces are hosting more exhibits and concerts, and nearly every hotel was renovated in 1999 in preparation for Jubilee Year 2000.

Then, between the last edition and this one, several of the classic old standby hotels that were once famous for supremely basic services but great locations—Abruzzi, Smeraldo, Coronet—started vigorously renovating themselves into fully loaded, three-star status (unfortunately, they've started charging the prices to prove it). Rome has come further in the past few years than it has since 1950.

Modern initiatives aside, Rome is still a place where your attention turns to the past. You come to immerse yourself in the era when the Forum gleamed white with travertine and emperors strode across it, when citizens spent their time at the Circus Maximus's chariot races and the Colosseum's gladiator duels, and when tradesmen and prostitutes hawked their wares at Trajan's Markets.

The Colosseum, the Forum, the Pantheon, the baths, the markets—these monuments of Imperial Rome stand amid a sea of sputtering Fiats and milling tourists. But Rome is the seat of another vast empire, too: Christianity. Since A.D. 312, when Emperor Constantine converted, Christians have shaped the fate of the Western world, covering Rome with grandiose medieval, Renaissance, and baroque churches designed by the likes of Bramante, Michelangelo, Bernini, and Borromini. These hallowed structures were enriched by Byzantine-era mosaics, frescoes, sculptures, and paintings by the finest artists of the Renaissance and baroque: Giotto, Michelangelo, Raphael, and Caravaggio. St. Peter's, with its vast Vatican Museums and the fingers-almost-touching artistic icon of *God Creating Adam* on Michelangelo's Sistine Chapel ceiling, is but the beginning.

For more on Rome and its environs, see *Frommer's Rome, Frommer's Italy from $70 a Day, Frommer's Irreverent Guide to Rome, Frommer's Italy,* and *Italy For Dummies.*

1 Essentials

ARRIVING

BY PLANE   Most international flights land at **Leonardo da Vinci International Airport,** also called **Fiumicino** (✆ **06-6595-3640** or 06-65-951; www.adr.it),

Value Budget Bests

Although the city is full of museums and ancient sites that charge (a generally worthwhile) admission, you'll find plenty of free sites. They range from the Roman Forum itself to dozens of fountain-studded *piazze* (squares), from the perfectly preserved Pantheon to the more than 900 churches (including St. Peter's) filled with Renaissance and baroque masterpieces.

The Vatican Museums are free on the last Sunday of every month. However, because this is common knowledge, dozens of school and tour groups descend in swarms; be prepared to be positively crushed and rushed. Instead, pay full price to go on a (relatively uncrowded) weekday morning to truly enjoy it.

29km (18 miles) west of the city. To get downtown, follow the *treni* signs for half-hourly (6:37am–11:37pm) nonstop trains to the main rail station, Stazione Termini (30 min.; 8.80€/$10). There's also a local train every 15 minutes (30 min. on Sun) to the Tiburtina station (45 min.; 4.70€/$5) from the same tracks. (Get off at Ostiense and walk to the Piramide Metro stop to catch the B line to Termini; 1€/$1.15.)

Many charter and continental flights land at the smaller **Ciampino Airport** (© **06-7934-0297** or 06-794-941), 15km (9 miles) south of the city. The easiest but priciest way downtown is the Terravision Shuttle bus (© **06-7949-4572;** http://shop.terravision.it), which has departures timed to arrivals of major flights, and costs 8€ ($9); it arrives downtown at the Hotel Royal Santina at Via Marsala 22, near Termini. The more common route downtown is to catch a public COTRAL bus (© **800-150-008;** www.cotralspa.it) outside the terminal for 1€ ($1.15); it leaves about twice an hour for the 20-minute trip to Anagnina, the terminus of Metro line A, where you can grab a subway to Stazione Termini (1€/$1.15).

Taxis to/from either airport cost about 40€ ($46), plus around 2€ to 3€ ($2.30–$3.45) for bags.

BY TRAIN There are at least three trains an hour from **Florence** (1½–3½ hr.; 14€–29€/$16–$33), 13 direct trains daily from **Venice** (4½–7 hr.; 30€–45€/$34–$52), hourly runs from **Milan** (4½–9 hr.; 27€–46€/$31–$53), and two to three runs hourly (at least once an hour Sun) from **Naples** (2–2½ hr.; 10€–22€/$12–$25). Although a few long-haul trains stop only at the Tiburtina station in the southern part of the city, Rome's main train station is the recently renovated **Stazione Termini** on Piazza dei Cinquecento (© **06-4730-6599,** or toll-free in Italy 800-888-088; www.trenitalia.com; for station info go to www.romatermini.it).

BY BUS Rome has coach connections with every major Italian city, but it's preferable to travel by train—the price is about the same, and bus trips are longer and less comfortable. However, buses can be handy (but crowded) when the rail system goes on strike (not as common as in the 1980s and '90s, but it still happens a few times a year). For **24-hour info** on all bus lines into and out of Rome, call © **166-845-010** or 800-431-784. Most intercity buses arrive near Stazione Termini or at one of several suburban bus stations, especially Tiburtina (that, and all the others, are at or near a Metro stop).

Rome Deals & Discounts

SPECIAL DISCOUNTS   Rome doesn't offer many official discounts, such as museum passes or travel cards, as do other European capitals. Over the past few years, the tourist office has tested various **discount cards,** but they've never been good for more than reduced admission at some secondary museums and small discounts at a few shops. Check with the tourist office to see if anything's in the works.

There are, however, two cards good on largely **ancient Roman sights. The Museum Card** costs 9€ ($10) and gets you 7 days in which to visit all the branches of the Museo Nazionale Romano (Palazzo Altemps, Palazzo Massimo, Baths of Diocletian, Crypta Balbi); the card is sold at all participating sights save the Crypta Balbi.

With the 20€ ($22) **Roma Archeologia Card,** you get all those sights plus the Colosseum, Palatine Hill, Baths of Caracalla, and, out on the Appian Way, Villa dei Quintili and Mausoleo di Cecilia Metella. You can buy the card at all participating sights except the Palatine and Crypta Balbi.

If you're a **student with an International Student Identity Card (ISIC),** you'll get discounts at many of Rome's museums. Note that, officially, many state- and city-run museums grant reduced admission or free entrance only to citizens of E.U. countries—or, sometimes, citizens of most countries except the U.S. (it's complicated and has to do with a reciprocity treaty the U.S. didn't sign). However, in practice, real people tend to be more generous than the rules dictate, and often ticket offices and museum guards will grant the discount to anyone in the right age bracket (under 18 for freebies; ages 18–25 for reduced admission) without asking your nationality first. In Stazione Termini, you'll find desks for **Wasteels** (© 06-482-5537; www.wasteels.it) and **CTS** (© 06-467-9254; www.cts.it), both open daily 8:30am to 8:30pm to offer discounts to those under 26, mainly for international train travel. Wasteels' main office is at Via Milazzo 8C (© **06-445-6679;** Metro: Termini; bus: any to Termini), and CTS's is at Corso Vittorio Emanuele II 297 (© **06-687-2672;** bus: 40, 46, 62, 64, 571, or 916).

WORTH A SPLURGE   Don't settle for a **hotel** in the dingy streets surrounding the train station just to save a few bucks. Set up housekeeping in the heart of the historic center, where the sights, life, and restaurants of Rome will be but steps from your door.

Don't go to the **Vatican Museums** on the free admission Sunday, when the Sistine Chapel is so overpacked you'll be more miserable from the crushing crowds than moved by the art. Pony up the 12€ ($14) and visit on a calmer morning.

It pays to cough up the extra 2€ ($2.30) to reserve your ticket in advance for the **Galleria Borghese**—often those who tempt fate by showing up ticketless first thing Wednesday morning discover the place is sold out through Saturday.

VISITOR INFORMATION

INFORMATION OFFICES & KIOSKS   The official A.P.T. **tourist office** is at Via Parigi 5 (© **06-3600-4399;** fax 06-481-9316; www.romaturismo.com; Metro: Repubblica), about a 5-minute walk straight out from Stazione Termini and across several *piazze* and traffic circles (it's next door to a corner luxury car dealership). It's open Monday to Saturday 9am to 7pm. The office also runs the official telephone **tourist info line** (© **06-3600-4399)** for events, art and culture, shopping, restaurants, and other useful information.

There's a large new info office **inside the train station** across from Tracks 5/6 (© **06-4890-6300**). It's usually crowded and short on information. However, as it's open daily 8am to 9pm, it can be useful early and late in the day, when the main office is closed. **At Fiumicino airport** is another info desk (© **06-6595-6074**), open daily 8am to 7pm.

Rome has added **info kiosks** dispensing maps and pamphlets at the following locations: **Castel Sant' Angelo** (© 06-6880-9707; bus: 23, 34, 40, 49, 62, 87, 271, 280, 926, 982, or 990); **Largo Goldoni/Via del Corso,** across from the end of Via de' Condotti (© 06-6813-6061; bus: 81, 117, 119, 204, 224, 590, 628, 913, or 926); another one near the Piazza Venezia end of Via del Corso at Via Minghetti, about halfway between the **Pantheon and Trevi Fountain** (© 06-678-2988; bus: 62, 63, 81, 85, 95, 117, 119, 160, 175, 204, 492, 628, 630, or 850); Via dei Foro Imperiali, near the **Roman Forum** (© 06-6992-4307; Metro: Colosseo; bus: 60, 75, 84, 85, 87, 117, 175, 186, 271, 571, 810, or 850); Piazza delle Cinque Lune, off **Piazza Navona** (© 06-6880-9240; bus: 30, 70, 81, 87, 116, 116T, 186, 204, 492, or 628); Piazza Sonnino, in **Trastevere** (© 06-5833-3457; tram: 8; bus: H, 115, 630, or 780); Piazza **San Giovanni in Laterano** (© 06-7720-3535; Metro: San Giovanni; bus: 16, 81, 85, 87, 186, 218, 571, 650, 665, 810, or 850); Via Nazionale in front of the **Palazzo delle Esposizioni** (© 06-4782-4525; bus: H, 40, 60, 64, 70, 71, 116T, 170, or 640); near **Santa Maria Maggiore** church on Via dell'Olmata (© 06-474-0955; bus: 16, 70, 71, 75, 204, 360, 590, 649, or 714); and on Piazza dei Cinquecento in front of **Stazione Termini** (© 06-4782-5194; Metro: Termini; bus: any to Termini). All are open daily 9am to 6pm.

The private firm of **Enjoy Rome,** 2 blocks north of Termini at Via Marghera 8a (© **06-445-1843;** fax 06-445-0734; www.enjoyrome.com), started as a walking-tour outfit but soon became the first stop in Rome for budget travelers, students, and backpackers (for years, this staff wrote the tourist office's "useful info" booklet). In addition to running year-round foot and bike tours of the city, Enjoy Rome's young staff, which hails from English-speaking countries, will provide lots of info on the city and a free room- and apartment-finding service. It's open Monday to Friday 8:30am to 7pm and Saturday 8:30am to 2pm.

WEBSITES   Rome's official sites are **www.romaturismo.com** (click on "Data Bank" for the treasure trove of useful information) and **www.comune.roma.it**. Among the good privately maintained sites, you can check out **www.enjoy rome.com** and **www.roma2000.it** (hasn't been updated since June 2000 but it's chock-full of info); **www.dolcevita.com** is devoted to fashion, cuisine (cookbook goddess Marcella Hazan is on staff), design, and travel. The Vatican maintains its own site at **www.vatican.va**, and **www.christusrex.org** is a religious site that provides a photo tour of the Vatican and its treasures. A great general site covering all of Italy is **www.italytour.com**.

CITY LAYOUT

Rome is strung along an S-shaped bend of the **Tevere (Tiber River)**. The bulk of the *centro storico* (**historic center**) lies east of the Tevere. The north end of the tourist's city is oval **Piazza del Popolo.** From this obelisk-sporting square, three major roads radiate south: **Via del Babuino, Via del Corso,** and **Via di Ripetta.** The middle one, Via del Corso (usually just called the Corso), divides the heart of the city in half.

To the east of the Corso lie the **Spanish Steps** (whence leads Via del Babuino) and the **Trevi Fountain.** Surrounding these monuments are Rome's most stylish shopping streets—including boutique-lined **Via dei Condotti,** running straight from the Spanish Steps to the Corso. Although hotels and restaurants in this area tend to be expensive and touristy, it's a pleasantly pedestrianized zone with some good budget values if you look hard enough. To the west of the Corso spreads the medieval **Tiber Bend** area, home to landmarks like bustling **Piazza Navona,** the ancient **Pantheon,** the market square of **Campo de' Fiori,** countless churches, a few small museums, and the medieval **Jewish Ghetto.** This area is chock-a-block with great restaurants and has some good, inexpensive lodging.

The Corso ends at about Rome's center in **Piazza Venezia.** This major traffic circle and bus juncture is marked by the overbearing, garishly white Vittorio Emanuele II Monument, which you can now climb for free (until sunset) for low-angle city panoramas. Leading west from Piazza Venezia is **Via Plebescito,** which, after passing through the archaeological site–cum–major bus stop **Largo di Torre Argentina/Largo Arenula,** becomes **Corso Vittorio Emanuele II.** This wide street effectively bisects the Tiber Bend as it heads toward the river and the Vatican. (Piazza Navona and the Pantheon lie to the north, Campo de' Fiori and the Jewish Ghetto to the south.)

Back at Piazza Venezia and facing south, go to the right around the Vittorio Emanuele Monument and you'll see a Michelangelo-designed stair ramp leading up behind it to the **Campidoglio (Capitoline Hill),** Rome's seat of government. Around the left side of the monument is **Via dei Fori Imperiali,** a wide boulevard making a beeline from Piazza Venezia to the **Colosseum,** passing the archaeological zone of the **Roman Forum** on the right (slung into the low land between the Capitoline and **Palatine Hills**) and the **Imperial Fori** on the left. South of the Forum and Colosseum rises the shady residential **Aventine Hill,** beyond which is another, smaller hill surrounded by the working-class quarter of **Testaccio,** now a trendy restaurant and nightclub district.

Those are the areas of Rome where you'll spend most of your time. But the first part of the city you'll see lies east of all this, in the grid of 19th-century streets surrounding the main train station, **Termini.** Although many budget hotels surround the station, this area should be your last choice for where to stay—it's generally boring and, though much cleaned up in recent years, still seedy, especially after dark. The streets north of Termini are somewhat cleaner and safer than those south of it. East of Termini is the University district of **San Lorenzo,** home to some fantastic restaurants.

Northwest of Termini (east of the Spanish Steps) is a boulevard zone where many foreign embassies lie, the highlight being the lazy S-curve of the cafe-lined **Via Veneto,** of fashionable 1950s *La Dolce Vita* fame—but thoroughly touristy and overpriced these days. Via Veneto ends at the giant **Villa Borghese park,** studded with museums and expanding northeast of the *centro storico.* (It's also accessible from Piazza del Popolo.)

Across the Tiber are two major neighborhoods. Mussolini razed a medieval district to lay down the wide **Via della Conciliazione** linking the **Ponte Vittorio Emanuele** with **Vatican City** and **St. Peter's.** South of here, past the long parklike **Gianicolo (Janiculum Hill),** lies the once medieval working-class, then trendy, and now touristy district of **Trastevere,** with Rome's highest concentration of bars and restaurants.

GETTING AROUND

All city transport uses the same *biglietto* **(ticket),** which costs 1€ ($1.15) and gives you 75 minutes during which you can transfer as often as you'd like (including one ride on the Metro). Stamp one end of the ticket on the first bus, tram, or Metro turnstile and the other end when you board the final one. Note that there are two types of tickets, both equally valid (they're slowly changing the system), and two little metal boxes on each bus/tram into which you must stick them. The older, narrow tickets you stamp in the boxier, orange ticket stamper; the wider tickets (printed with a bar code) you need to stick into the more streamlined yellow boxes. There are also **daily passes** (4.10€/$4.70), **3-day passes** (11€/$13), and **weekly passes** (16€/$18). You can buy tickets and passes from *tabacchi* (tobacconists), most newsstands, Metro stations, or machines at major bus stops. Hold onto your ticket until you're off the bus or out of the Metro station to avoid paying a huge fine.

BY METROPOLITANA (SUBWAY)   Rome's Metro isn't very extensive— every time workers dig new tunnels, they run across ancient ruins and have to stop so archaeologists can putter about. The city has only two lines (the orange "A" and the blue "B") that etch a rough X on the city map, with Stazione Termini at the intersection. **Line A** runs from Viale Aurelia, past Cipro–Musei Vaticani (the new Vatican Museums stop) and Ottaviano–San Pietro (a dozen blocks from St. Peter's), and makes stops like Flaminia (near Piazza del Popolo), Spagna (Spanish Steps), Termini, and San Giovanni (Rome's cathedral). **Line B** is most useful to shuttle you quickly from Termini to stops like Colosseo (Colosseum), Circo Massimo (Circus Maximus), and Piramide (at the Tiburtina train station, near Testaccio).

BY BUS & TRAM   Rome's bus and tram system is much more extensive than the Metro. Sadly, there is no free official map; buy a *mappa degli autobus* at a newsstand for 6€ ($7) or simply scan the list of stops at your *fermata* (stop) to figure out which lines take you where you need to go. Note that some newer lines are **express** (and labeled as such on the signs) and won't make all the stops.

The most useful bus line is probably the **40,** which makes a beeline from Stazione Termini, past Piazza Venezia (for central Rome) and Largo Argentina (for the historic Tiber Bend area), then across the river to Piazza Pia, right next to Castel Sant'Angelo. This is the new "waiting room" stop for visiting St. Peter's, the place where you pick up shuttle bus no. 62, which just does a loop down the 4 long blocks from Piazza Pia to St. Peter's and back. Of course, as this route is heavily used by tourists, it's also thick with thieves, so be extra careful. Also extremely useful for tourists are nos. **116, 117,** and **119**— all three are teensy electric buses that trundle through the streets of the *centro storico* (historic center). Most buses run daily 5:30am to midnight, with a separate series of **night buses** whose route numbers are prefaced by an *N.* For bus information, call (C) **800-431-784** or go to **www.atac.roma.it** on the Web.

Rome Metropolitana

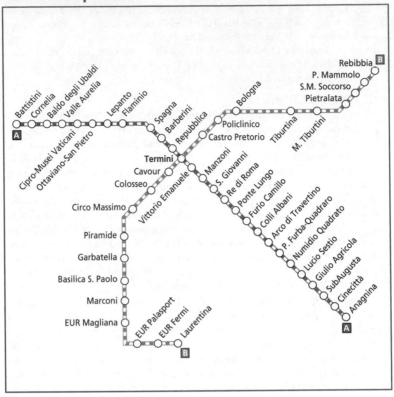

BY TAXI Although you can reach most of Rome's sights easily by bus or foot, trips from the airport or the train station to your hotel might be more comfortable in a taxi. Taxi stands are located at major *piazze* like Piazza Venezia and Largo Argentina, at the Pantheon, and in front of Stazione Termini. You can also **call a taxi** at © **06-3570,** 06-4994, 06-6645, or 06-5551, but the meter begins running when the driver picks up your call. The initial charge is 2.33€ ($2.65), plus .11€ (15¢) per kilometer. There are extra charges for luggage (1.04€/$1.20 per bag) and travel between 10am and 7am (2.58€/$2.95) or on Sunday (1.03€/$1.20).

BY BICYCLE OR SCOOTER Traffic is heavy on the streets of Rome, and bike riding should only be attempted if you're used to biking in city traffic; on Sunday, though, when traffic is relatively light, it's actually pleasant.

There are three places to get a great deal on a rental bike or scooter: **Treno e Scooter,** at Track 1 inside Stazione Termini (© **06-4890-5823;** Metro: Termini; bus: any to Termini)—pick up the bike outside the station on the right; **I Bike Rome,** Via Veneto 156, in section 3 of the underground parking lot (© **06-322-5240;** bus: M, 88, 95, 116, 116T, 204, 490, 491, or 495); and (for scooters only) **Happy Rent,** Via Farini 3 (© **06-481-8185;** www.happyrent.com; Metro: Termini; bus: any to Termini).

Rates are pretty standardized. Regular bikes run about 2€ to 2.60€ ($2.30–$3) per hour or 5.15€ to 7.75€ ($6–$9) per day. A 10-speed runs 3.60€ to 4.15€ ($4.15–$4.75) per hour, 9€ to 10€ ($10–$12) per day.

Country & City Codes

The **country code** for Italy is **39**. Rome's former separate city code of **06** has been folded into each phone number (but this might change as the capital runs out of numbers and begins assigning new initial digits). Therefore, you must dial the whole number—including the initial zero—at all times, whether you're calling from outside or inside Italy or even within Rome itself.

Scooters cost 21€ to 36€ ($24–$41) for 4 hours or 30€ to 70€ ($35–$81) for a day (depending on engine size). *Note:* If you arrive in Rome by train on the same day you rent, bring your canceled rail ticket to Treno e Scooter for a 10% discount on bike or scooter rental for your first day.

BY RENTAL CAR   Don't drive in Rome. Not only are Italian drivers even more manic in the city—and parking is impossible—but the system of one-way roads seems specially designed to keep you from driving anywhere near your intended destination. Much of the historic center is pedestrian-only, but you're allowed to drive to your hotel to drop off luggage. If you plan to rent a car in Italy and are starting your trip in Rome, wait to pick up the car until the day you set out into the countryside; if you're flying home from Rome, drop the rental off the instant you drive into town and spend your days in the capital blissfully car-free.

Your hotel might have a garage or an arrangement with one, or you might be lucky enough to be staying in one of the few scraps of the historic center that haven't yet been designated a *zona blu*—most of the city's parking spaces have been painted with blue stripes, meaning you must pay a **parking meter** (usually a box at the end of the block; you feed it coins and it gives you a slip to leave on the dashboard). The cheapest and biggest **public garage** is **ParkSi** (© **06-322-5934**) under the **Villa Borghese** park in the northeast corner of town. Its entrance is on Viale del Muro Torto, which leads off into the park from the traffic circle at Porta Pinciana, the top of Via Veneto. Rates run 1.15€ ($1.30) per hour (.90€/$1.05 each hour after the 4th) to 14€ ($17) per day.

To rent a car for leaving the city, you'll save lots of money if you arrange the rental before you leave the U.S. (see "Getting Around Without Going Broke: By Car," in chapter 1). The major agencies have offices in Stazione Termini, and many also at the airports.

FAST FACTS: Rome

American Express   The office is to the right of the Spanish Steps at Piazza di Spagna 38, 00187 Roma, Italy (© **06-678-2456** or toll-free within Italy 06-72280-0371; Metro: Spagna). May to September, it's open Monday to Friday 9am to 5:30pm and Saturday 9am to 12:30pm (to 2:30pm May–Oct). To report lost or stolen traveler's checks, call © **800-872-000;** to report lost or stolen Amex cards, call © **800-864-046.**

Business Hours   As in most of Italy, many shops and offices, most churches, and many museums observe a siesta-like midafternoon shutdown called *riposo,* lasting roughly noon or 1pm to 3 or 4pm. It's a good idea to figure out the few sights in town that remain open during *riposo* so you can save them—and a leisurely lunch—to fill this time. However, more and more stores are posting *orario continuato* ("no-stop") signs and staying open through *riposo*. In Rome, most shop hours are Monday 3 or 4pm to 8pm, Tuesday to Saturday 8am to noon or 1pm and 3 or 4pm to 8pm. Food shops are generally also open Monday morning but closed Thursday afternoon.

Currency In 2002, Italy adopted the **euro** (€) for its currency. At press time, $1 = .87€, or 1€ = $1.15.

Doctors & Dentists First aid is available 24 hours a day in the emergency room *(pronto soccorso)* of major hospitals; see "Hospitals" below. Also try the **International Medical Center,** Via Giovanni Amendola 7 (© **488-2371** or 06-488-4051; Metro: Termini; bus: any to Termini). Call the U.S. Embassy at © **06-46-741** for a list of English-speaking doctors and dentists.

Embassies & Consulates The embassy of the **United States** is at Via Vittorio Veneto 121 (© **06-46-741;** www.usembassy.it; bus: 52, 53, 63, 80, 95, 116, 116T, or 119). For passport and consular services, head to the consulate, left of the embassy's main gate, open Monday to Friday 8:30am to 12:30pm. The **Canadian** consulate is on the fifth floor at Via Zara 30 (© **06-445-981;** www.canada.it; tram: 3 or 19; bus: 36, 60, or 140), open Monday to Friday 8:30am to 12:30pm and 1:30 to 4pm. The consulate of the **United Kingdom** is at Via XX Settembre 80 (© **06-4220-0001** or 06-4220-2603; www.britain.it; bus: 16, 36, 60, 61, 62, 84, 90, or 492); summer hours are Monday to Friday 8am to 4pm, and autumn through spring hours are Monday to Friday 9am to 5pm. The consulate of **Australia** is at Corso Trieste 25 (© **06-852-721** or toll-free 800-877-790 for emergencies only; www.australian-embassy.it; tram: 3 or 19; bus: 36, 60, or 140), open Monday to Friday 8:30am to noon and 1:30 to 4:15pm. The **New Zealand** consulate is at Via Zara 28 (© **06-441-7171** or 06-440-2928; nzemb. rom@flashnet.it; tram: 3 or 19; bus: 36, 60, or 140), open Monday to Friday 8:30am to 12:45pm and 1:45 to 5pm.

Emergencies Dial © **113** in any **emergency.** You can call © **112** for the *carabinieri* (the military-trained and more useful of the two **police** forces), © **118** or 06-5510 to summon an **ambulance,** or © **115** for the **fire department.** *Pronto soccorso* means "first aid" and is also the word used for emergency rooms. Call © **116** for **roadside assistance** (not free).

Holidays Many offices and shops, and some sights, are closed in Italy on the following official holidays: January 1, Easter Sunday and Monday, April 25 (Liberation Day), May 1 (Labor Day), August 15 (Assumption of the Virgin), November 1 (All Saints' Day), December 8 (Feast of the Immaculate Conception), December 25, and December 26 (Santo Stefano). Rome also celebrates June 29 as the Feast Day of patron saints Peter and Paul.

Hospitals In an emergency, go the nearest emergency room *(pronto soccorso)* of any hospital *(ospedale).* Convenient ones in the center are **San Giacomo,** Via Canova 29, off Via del Corso 2 blocks from Piazza del Popolo (© **06-3626-6354** or 06-36-261; bus: N25, 81, 117, 119, 204, 224, 590, 628, or 926); **Fatebenefratelli,** Via Cassia 600 on Tiber Island (© **06-3358-2644** or 06-33-581; tram: 8; bus: H, 23, N29, N30, 44, 63, N72, N96, 280, or 780);

and **Ospedale Santo Spirito in Sassia,** Lungotevere in Sassia 1 on the river just south of the Castel Sant'Angelo (© **06-6835-2241** or 06-68-351; bus: 23, N29, N30, 34, 44, N45, 63, 80, 98, N98, 115, 271, 280, 630, or 780). The "H" bus line makes a circular route of all the major hospitals.

Most hospitals will be able to find someone to help you in English, and with Italy's partially socialized medical system, you can often pop into an emergency room and get taken care of speedily without dealing with any forms. English-speaking doctors are always on duty at the private **Rome American Hospital,** Via Emilio Longoni 69, just off the Viale Prenestina (© **06-22-551;** tram: 5 or 14; bus: 516 from just south of Termini, 81 from Piazza del Popolo/Via del Corso/Circus Maximus/behind the Colosseum, or 810 from Piazza Venezia to Largo Preneste, then 112 or 312); and at **Salvator Mundi International Hospital,** Viale delle Mura Gianicolensi 67 (© **06-588-961;** bus: 115 or 870).

A special "H" bus connects Rome's municipal hospitals. It takes the usual 1€ ($1.15) ticket.

Internet Access The best spot to surf the Net is the gargantuan 24-hour **easyInternetcafe,** Via Barberini 2 (no phone; www.easyInternetcafe.com; Metro: Barberini; bus: N25, N45, 52, 53, N55, N60, 61, 62, 63, 80, 95, 116, 116T, 117, 119, 175, 204, 492, 590, or 630), with 350 computers costing 1€ ($1.15) per quarter hour, plus a coffee/snack bar. You can also log on at **Thenetgate** (www.thenetgate.it) with locations in Termini's underground mall (© **06-8740-6008;** Metro: Termini; bus: any to Termini), open daily 6am to midnight, and at Piazza Firenze 25 (© **06-687-9098;** bus: 70, 87, 116, 116T, 186, 204, or 492), open Monday to Saturday 10:30am to 9pm. Access costs 3€ ($3.45) per hour.

You can kill two birds with one stone with the latest Roman traveler's trend: **wired Laundromats.** Most now let you log on for 1€ to 3€ ($1.15–$3.45) per half-hour while your grubby travel togs get clean (see "Laundry," below).

Laundry Self-service *lavanderie* (laundromats) are all over town and generally open every day from 10am to 10pm. Try the **Bolle Blu,** with shops at Via Principe Amedeo 116 (© **06-4470-3098**), and Via Palestro 59 (© **06-446-5804**), both near Termini (Metro: Termini; bus: any to Termini), where they do the wash for you in an hour. For coin-op Laundromats, hit the **Ondablu** chain (www.ondablu.com), with central locations at Via Principe Amedeo 70b (© **06-474-4647**), south of Termini (Metro: Termini; bus: any to Termini), and Via Vespasiano 50 (no phone), near the Vatican (tram: 19; bus: 23, 32, 49, 70, 81, 490, 492, 982, 990, 991, or 999). All charge about 4€ to 7€ ($4.60–$8) per load, and all also now double as cybercafes (see "Internet Access," above).

The bulk of *lavanderie,* though, are full-service, charging ridiculous by-the-piece rates to wash, dry, press, and wrap your T-shirts and undies like Christmas presents. Always ask first if service is *à peso* (by weight, the cheap way) or *al pezzo* (by the piece). However, these full-service joints also usually provide *lavasecco* **(dry cleaning)** service, at prices comparable to those in the States. Your hotel will be able to point out the nearest one.

Mail The Italian mail system is notoriously slow, and friends back home might not receive your postcards for anywhere from 1 to 8 weeks (sometimes longer). The **main post office** is at Piazza San Silvestro 19, 00187 Roma, Italia (off Via del Corso, south of the Spanish Steps; bus: 52, 53, 61, 62, 63, 71, 80, 81, 85, 95, 116, 116T, 117, 119, 160, 175, 204, 492, 590, 628, 630, or 850). It's open Monday to Friday 9am to 6pm, Saturday 9am to 2pm, and Sunday 9am to 6pm. You can pick up stamps at any *tabacchi* (tobacconists).

If you want your letters to get home before you do, use the **Vatican post office**. It costs the same—but you must use Vatican stamps, available only at their post offices—and is much quicker and more reliable. There are three offices: to the left of the basilica steps, just past the information office; behind the right-hand colonnade of Piazza San Pietro (where the alley ends beyond souvenir stands); and in the Vatican Museums.

To receive mail while in Rome (for a modest pickup fee), have it sent to the main post office above, addressed to "Your Name/FERMO POSTA/Roma, Italia/ITALY." Holders of Amex cards can get the same service for free by having mail sent to "Your Name/CLIENT MAIL/American Express/Piazza di Spagna 38/00187 Roma, Italia/ITALY."

Newspapers & Magazines Expat magazines *Wanted in Rome* (.75€/85¢; www.wantedinrome.com) and *Metropolitan* (.80€/90¢) list events along with classified ads and articles on Rome and Italy. If you want to try your hand at Italian, the Thursday edition of the newspaper *La Repubblica* contains the magazine insert **"TrovaRoma"** (www.repubblica.it), with entertainment, event, gallery, and show listings. One other prime resource is the weekly magazine *Roma C'è* (1€/$1.15; www.romace.it), which has a "This Week in Rome" section in English. You'll find all of these at most newsstands. Less complete, but free, is the tourist office's bimonthly events pamphlet *L'Evento*.

Pharmacies Farmacie follow a rotation schedule, posted outside each pharmacy, so several remain open all night and on Sunday and holidays. Pharmacies open 24 hours are at **Piazza Barberini 49** (© **06-487-1195;** Metro: Barberini; bus: N25, N45, 52, 53, N55, N60, 61, 62, 63, 80, 95, 116, 116T, 117, 119, 175, 204, 492, 590, or 630); **Piazza Risorgimento 44** (© **06-3973-8166;** tram: 19; bus: 23, N29, N30, 32, 49, 81, 271, 492, 590, 982, 990, or 991); and **Via Arenula 73** (© **06-6880-3278;** tram: 8; bus: H, N29, 63, N72, N96, 115, 271, 280, 630, or 780). A pharmacy at **Termini** on Piazza del Cinquecento 49–51 (© **06-488-0776;** Metro: Termini; bus: any to Termini) stays open until 10pm.

Police Dial © **113** in emergencies (see also "Emergencies," above).

Safety Random violent crime is extremely rare, but **pickpockets**—especially Gypsy children—target tourists. Thieves favor buses that run between Termini and the major tourist sites (particularly bus no. 64, the "Pickpocket Express"). Watch your wallet especially in Termini, near the Forums and Colosseum, in Piazza del Popolo, and around the Vatican.

Gypsy children roam in packs around tourist areas and infest subway tunnels. They aren't physically dangerous, but whenever they're around, a tourist and his money will soon be parted. They approach looking pitiful, begging and waving scraps of cardboard, occasionally scrawled with a few words in English. This flurry of cardboard is a distraction beneath which their fingers will be busy relieving your pockets of their valuables.

If you see a group of dirty kids dressed in colorful but filthy rags headed your way, give them a wide berth, forcefully yell *"Va via!"* ("Scram!"), or loudly invoke the *polizia*. If they get too close, shove them away violently—don't hold back just because they're kids.

Gypsy mothers usually stick to panhandling but aren't above picking your pocket—one scam is to toss their swaddled baby at you (usually it's a doll in blankets, but sometimes they throw the real thing!), and while you rush to catch it, they or their waiting brood fleece you in the blink of an eye.

Women should be aware there's occasional drive-by purse snatchings by young Vespa-riding thieves. Keep your purse on the wall side of the sidewalk, wear the strap diagonally across your chest, and try to keep from walking along the sidewalk's edge. And if your purse has a flap, keep the clasp side facing your body to deter pickpockets. **Men** should also take precautions: Keep your wallet in your front pocket rather than the rear and your hand on it while riding the bus.

Taxes Italy's national sales tax, IVA (value-added tax) varies with the item or service up to 19% and is always already included in the sticker price of any item (except, oddly, in the most expensive luxury hotels). Non-E.U. citizens who spend more than 155€ ($178) in a single shop are entitled to a refund; see chapter 2 for details.

Telephone Local calls in Italy cost .10€ (12¢). There are two types of public pay phones, those that take both coins and phone cards and those that take only **phone cards** (*carta telefonica* or *scheda telefonica*). You can buy these prepaid phone cards at any *tabacchi* (tobacconists) and most newsstands. Break off the corner before inserting it and don't forget to take the card with you when you leave!

For **operator-assisted international calls** (in English), dial toll-free ✆ **170.** Note, however, that you'll get better rates by calling a home operator for collect calls, as detailed here: To make **calling card calls,** you may have to insert a phone card or .10€ (12¢)—which will be refunded at the end of your call (note that with the new numbers on most phones you don't need to insert that deposit)—and dial the local number for your service: **AT&T** at ✆ **800-172-444, MCI** at ✆ **800-905-825,** or **Sprint** at ✆ **800-172-405.** These numbers—frequent visitors to Italy will notice that all three have recently changed—will raise an American automated operator, and you can also use any one of them to place a **collect call** even if you don't carry that particular phone company's card.

To **dial direct internationally from Italy,** dial ✆ **00,** then the country code, the area code, and the number. Country codes are as follows: the United States and Canada 1; the United Kingdom 44; Ireland 353; Australia 61; New Zealand 64. Make international calls from a public phone if possible because hotels charge ridiculously inflated rates for direct dial, but take along plenty of *schede* to feed the phone.

To call free national **telephone information** (in Italian) in Italy, dial ✆ **12.** International information for Europe is available at ✆ **176** but costs .60€ (70¢) a shot. For international information beyond Europe, dial ✆ **1790** for .50€ (60¢).

Tipping Increasingly in restaurants, a *servizio* (service charge) of 15% is automatically added to your bill, so always ask *"È incluso il servizio?"* ("Is service included?") when you get the check. If not, leave 15%; if yes, it's still customary to leave an extra .50€ (45¢) per person at the table. At a bar, put a .10€ (12¢) piece on the counter with your receipt when you order your espresso or cappuccino; if you're ordering at a table, leave a .20€ coin (22¢) per person. Tip taxi drivers about 10%.

2 Affordable Places to Stay

Even as a budget-conscious traveler, you don't have to settle for the cheap, often squalid accommodations surrounding Stazione Termini. (Although I've recommended several good ones below, the neighborhood leaves something to be desired.) You can still stay well within your budget in a small but comfortable room overlooking the Pantheon, near the Spanish Steps, or hidden in Trastevere.

A few notes on the hotels below. A **price range** reflects seasonal variations. High season (highest rates) runs Easter to October, excluding August, which is often considered part of the low season. If a hotel's season varies significantly from this, I've noted it in the listing. If the price ranges indicate different styles or sizes of accommodations ("standard" versus "superior" double), I've noted that as well. And **parking** rates usually apply to small to midsize cars. If I've given no parking information, the hotel has no special arrangements with a garage, and street parking is metered and/or difficult (when there's ample free street parking, I've noted it). In these cases, your best bet is to use a public garage (see "Getting Around," in "Essentials," earlier in this chapter).

The **tourist offices** (see "Visitor Information" in "Essentials," earlier in this chapter) will help you track down a room but are often loathe to do so when waiting crowds crush behind you during summer. There's also a **hotel reservation desk in Termini** (✆ **06-699-1000**), with branches at the airports, specializing in getting discounts of up to 50% off (especially late in the day in low season when hotels are eager to fill their vacant rooms). You must put down a deposit (they accept most credit cards) that's credited to your room. You may have more luck and certainly get better service at **Enjoy Rome,** a private outfit (see "Visitor Information" in "Essentials," earlier in this chapter). It specializes in finding budget accommodations, even at the last minute. The English-speaking staff will help you for free via phone, in person, or by e-mail.

Note: Most of the lodging choices below are plotted on the map on p. 816.

AROUND ANCIENT ROME

Casa Kolbe *Value* If you love archaeology but don't need too many amenities (just phones and private bathrooms in the units), this monastically quiet converted convent may be perfect. It's as hidden as you can get in the heart of Rome, around the corner from the Forum's "back door" on a side street hugging the Palatine's west flank. Most of the slightly institutional large rooms overlook palm-filled gardens, but those on the second-floor street side enjoy a low panorama of ruins. The furnishings are unmemorably modular, the bathrooms are nice, and the beds could be firmer but aren't bad.

Via San Teodoro 44 (bordering the west side of the Palatine archaeological zone), 00186 Roma. ✆ 06-679-4974. Fax 06-6994-1550. 63 units. 65€ ($75) single; 84€ ($97) double; 105€ ($121) triple. Breakfast

(*Value* **Getting the Best Deal on Accommodations**

- Reserve well in advance to get the best budget room. Rome is predictably popular, and none of the centrally located bargains is a secret; they all fill up quickly, especially in summer.
- Always ask for off-season rates October to Easter or for other special rates for students, seniors, teachers, or professionals—you never know what might work.
- Ask for the cheapest room, as prices often vary according to size, view, amenities, and so on.
- Settle for a room without a private bathroom—it'll invariably be cheaper.
- Be aware that a double bed *(letto matrimoniale)* is still sometimes cheaper than two twin beds *(due letti)* in a double room. (This old loophole, though, is fast disappearing.)
- If possible, opt out of the hotel breakfast; you can get the same *cornetto* (croissant) and cappuccino at the corner bar for a third of the price.

6€ ($7), AE, MC, V. Free parking on street. Bus: H, 30, 44, 63, 81, 95, 160, 170, 204, 271, 628, 630, 715, 716, 780, 781, N44, N72, N91, or N96. **Amenities:** Restaurant; concierge; tour desk; car-rental desk; nonsmoking rooms (all).

AROUND CAMPO DE' FIORI & THE JEWISH GHETTO

Campo de' Fiori ❀ The rooms vary greatly at this central inn—some modern and carpeted, others with brick arches and rustic wood-beam ceilings. Although some aren't much larger than the beds, most of the rooms are sizable. There's no elevator, but room no. 602 is worth the climb for its views across the rooftops and domes—a vista beat only by that of the communal roof terrace. The nightly party noise wafting up from the streets can be annoying, so request a room off the front if you want to sleep more soundly. The bathrooms, shared or private, are very clean. The owners also rent 10 apartments nearby—all with kitchens and some with TVs but no phones—for longer stays and up to seven people (140€/$161 for two with breakfast; discounts available Nov–Mar).

Via del Biscione 6 (just off the northeast corner of Campo de' Fiori), 00186 Roma. ☎ **06-687-4886.** Fax 06-687-6003. www.hotelcampodefiori.com. 27 units, 9 with bathroom. 50€–80€ ($58–$92) single without bathroom, 100€ ($115) single with bathroom; 70€–90€ ($81–$104) double without bathroom, 90€ 110€ ($104–$127) double with shower but no toilet, 110€–140€ ($127–$161) double with bathroom; add 20€ ($23) for triples. MC, V. Parking 21€ ($24) in nearby garage. Bus: 40, 46, 62, 64, 116, 116T, 571, 916, N45, or N98. **Amenities:** Concierge; courtesy car (fee); babysitting. *In room:* Hair dryer (ask at desk).

Sole al Biscione The pillows are rock hard, the cots are sway-backed, and the wall linoleum is peeling in spots, but that's as bad as it gets in Rome's oldest hotel (since 1462). In fact, many rooms are in rather better shape, most aren't minuscule (and you have your choice—bigger room, or better price—as the rates below reflect room size), and the old-fashioned wood furnishings are nicely tooled. Yet even the double-glazed windows on the streetside rooms can't block out the night revelers, so request a room overlooking the garden courtyard. The fourth-floor rooms even get a rooftop view with a few domes and hundreds of TV aerials (and cost a bit extra). This inn is popular—and has actually become something of a good deal, given that prices haven't gone up in 3 years (though the room rate average is still just $1 shy of getting booted into our "Splurge" category)—so book ahead. Although the hotel does have an elevator, you have to climb 33 steps to the first-floor reception before you get to it. In 2003, many bathroomless singles were removed to make room for doubles with private bathrooms, and A/C was added to 16 of the rooms.

Via del Biscione 76 (half a block north of Campo de' Fiori), 00186 Roma. © **06-6880-6873.** Fax 06-689-3787. www.solealbiscione.it. 59 units, 54 with bathroom. 65€ ($75) single without bathroom, 85€ ($98) single with bathroom; 95€ ($109) double without bathroom, 110€–130€ ($126–$150) double with bathroom, 150€ ($172) double with bathroom on top floor with minibar and panoramic view. Ask about discounts in low season. No credit cards. Parking 15€–20€ ($17–$23) in garage. Bus: 30, 40, 46, 62, 64, 80, 116, 116T, 204, 492, 571, 628, 916, N45, N98, or N29. **Amenities:** Concierge; tour desk; laundry service; dry cleaning. *In room:* A/C (16 rooms), TV, minibar (3 rooms).

AROUND PIAZZA NAVONA & THE PANTHEON

Coronet *Finds* Here you can occupy a high-ceilinged room in the 15th-century Palazzo Doria Pamphilj. Simona Teresi and her son preside over baronially sized rooms with tall windows and modest, sometimes worn, yet comfy mismatched furnishings and antiques—though all that may soon change. They're planning a full-bore overhaul of the hotel, installing private bathrooms in each room, replacing the furnishings with modern units, and sticking TVs and minibars and such throughout the hotel (though, even in its current incarnation, a TV is available upon request). The family hopes to do all this in August of 2004, but they admit there's a chance it won't happen until 2005. For now, as we go to press, the beds have orthopedic mattresses (you can request a soft one), and each room without bathroom en suite has its own down the hall. Room nos. 34, 35, and huge 45 boast wood ceilings and sitting corners with sofas. The piazza isn't very noisy, but for absolute quiet ask for a room overlooking the private gardens. Call for reservations, but confirm by fax if possible. The price range reflects a high season of March to May and September to October.

Piazza Grazioli 5, 00186 Roma. © **06-679-2341.** Fax 06-6992-2705. www.hotelcoronet.com. 13 units, 10 with bathroom. 60€–115€ ($69–$132) single without bathroom, 70€–130€ ($80–$150) single with bathroom; 70€–135€ ($80–$155) double without bathroom, 80€–170€ ($92–$196) double with bathroom. Rates include breakfast. AE, MC, V. Free parking on piazza (ask hotel for permit). Bus: 30, 40, 46, 62, 63, 64, 70, 81, 87, 116, 116T, 186, 492, 571, 628, 810, 850, 916, N25, N45, N60, or N99. **Amenities:** Tour desk; courtesy car for arrivals; babysitting; laundry service; nonsmoking rooms; safe at desk. *In room:* TV (free on request), hair dryer.

Marcus *Kids* This is easily one of Rome's best upper-end budget hotels—especially as its prices have actually dropped (no, really) while its competition (most of those hotels mentioned above) has gone the opposite route, renovating everything and jacking up rates. The Marcus remains a smartly updated *pensione* in an 18th-century palazzo with high ceilings and the odd marble fireplace. This place has it where it counts: friendly management by Salvatore and his wife, firm beds, decent bathrooms, Persian rugs on the patterned tile floors (some are carpeted), the occasional classy antique furnishing, walls hung with Roman prints and Art Deco lights, and double-glazed windows. It's welcoming to families, and the larger rooms have futon chairs to sleep a third person.

Via del Clementino 94 (in the renamed final block of Via Fontanella Borghese before Piazza Nicosia, just south of Augustus's Mausoleum), 00186 Roma. © **06-6830-0320.** Fax 06-6830-0312. www.marcushotel.com. 18 units, 17 with bathroom. 65€ ($75) single with or without bathroom; 83€ ($95) standard double with or without bathroom; 95€ ($109) large double (2 with marble fireplace) with bathroom. Each extra person 30% more. Rates include breakfast. AE, MC, V. Parking 16€ ($18) in nearby garage. Bus: 30, 70, 81, 87, 117, 119, 186, 204, 224, 492, 590, 628, 913, 926, N25, N78, or N99. **Amenities:** Concierge; tour desk; car-rental desk;

room service (breakfast); babysitting; laundry service; dry cleaning; nonsmoking rooms. *In room:* A/C, TV, minibar, hair dryer, safe.

Mimosa *(Kids)* This friendly little *pensione* offers a fantastic price for such a central location (but no elevator; you're looking at 52 steps). It's threadbare but very well cared for. The room furnishings are built-in or modular; most accommodations are pretty huge, with multiple beds for families on a budget (a few singles are cramped). The largest and newest rooms (nos. 1, 2, and 3) were redone in 2002 with wrought-iron and brass beds, Oriental rugs, and giant ceiling beams. Otherwise, rooms are plain but efficient; the beds are springy, firm, and spread with attractive comforters; and as of summer 2004, all rooms have A/C—quality touches that separate this caring modest inn from the student dives—and the communal bathrooms are clean. It's rather popular, so book ahead; if they don't respond to your fax within 48 hours, it means they're full.

Via Santa Chiara 61, 00186 Roma. ℭ **06-6880-1753**. Fax 06-683-3557. www.hotelmimosa.net. 11 units, 7 with bathroom. 46€–60€ ($53–$69) single without bathroom, 70€–88€ ($80–$101) single with bathroom; 65€–103€ ($75–$118) double without bathroom, 75€–118€ ($86–$136) double with bathroom. Breakfast 5€ ($6) in low season; included in high season. No credit cards. Few free parking spots on piazza (ask for permit). Tram: 8. Bus: 30, 40, 46, 62, 63, 64, 70, 81, 87, 116, 116T, 186, 204, 492, 571, 628, 630, 810, 916, N78, or N99. **Amenities:** Courtesy car from airport (fee); nonsmoking rooms (all). *In room:* A/C, no phone (pay phone in lobby)

Navona *(★★)* *(Finds)* Cory Natale, the Australian architect who owns the Navona with his parents and sister, seems to be continuously overhauling his charming hotel just off the south end of Piazza Navona—the top floor used to be Percy Bysshe Shelley's apartment. The latest renovation (in 2003) replaced all the modular furnishings with antique reproductions, installed private bathrooms in the last few rooms still lacking them, and added plaster decorations to the ceilings—except in the two rooms where they were surprised to uncover frescoes instead. Despite all this, prices remain (for Rome) fairly modest. The building has no elevator; it's 27 steps up to the front desk and first-floor rooms. If the Navona is full, the Natales might accompany you up to the equally nice six-room **Residence Zanardelli,** which they renovated in a building off the north end of Piazza Navona; doubles there run around 145€ ($167). Or, if you want to set up housekeeping with your own kitchen, they just started renting out two nearby apartments. The larger one runs 180€ ($207); a smaller one installed in a 15th-century chapel, with a spiral staircase up to a wood-ceilinged bedroom, costs 145€ ($167).

Via dei Sedari 8 (off Corso del Rinascimento, between Piazza Navona and the Pantheon), 00186 Roma. ℭ **06-686-4203** or 06-6821-1392. Fax 06-6880-3802. www.hotelnavona.com. 30 units. 90€ ($104) single; 120€ ($138) double with bathroom; 185€ ($213) triple with bathroom. Rates include breakfast. AE, DC, MC, V. Free parking on street (ask hotel for permit). Bus: 30, 40, 46, 62, 63, 64, 70, 81, 87, 116, 116T, 186, 492, 571, 628, 810, 916, N78, or N99. **Amenities:** Concierge; tour desk; nonsmoking rooms (all). *In room:* A/C (on request in all but 5 rooms for 5€/$6), TV, hair dryer.

AROUND THE SPANISH STEPS & PIAZZA DEL POPOLO

Margutta The Margutta isn't for those who need a lot of elbowroom, but it offers a touch of style for an inexpensive central choice on a tranquil side street. The hardworking management—young Enrico Rosati runs the place with the help of his father and uncle—likes to joke around, providing efficient service with a smile in rapid-fire English. The bed frames are beautiful, but the mattresses are lumpy. In 2003—following a brutal summer heat wave—the Margutta installed air-conditioning in all the rooms, along with TVs. Most rooms are immaculate but on the small side of cozy, and some bathrooms are positively minuscule. No. 54

has a small private terrace (and costs 145€–160€/$167–$184); nos. 50 and 52 share a terrace and charge 150€–170€ ($172–$196).

Via Laurina 34 (2 blocks from Piazza del Popolo between Via Babuino and Via del Corso), 00197 Roma. © **06-322-3674.** Fax 06-320-0395. 24 units. 80€–115€ ($92–$132) single; 90€–130€ ($104–$150) double; 140€–155€ ($161–$178) triple; 155€–165€ ($178–$190) quad. Rates include breakfast. AE, DC, MC, V. Metro: Flaminio (not the closest, but the most direct from Termini). Bus: 81, 117, 119, 204, 224, 590, 628, 926, or N25. **Amenities:** Concierge; tour desk; car-rental desk; room service (breakfast); babysitting. *In room:* A/C, TV, hair dryer.

Panda 🟉 *Value* The Panda is just 2 blocks from the Spanish Steps, in the heart of the shopping zone. The owner likes to describe the rooms as "quaintly spartan"—few frills or amenities, but plenty of old-fashioned character and the sort of attractive furnishings found at pricier inns. The first-floor rooms were redone in 1996 with frescoed ceilings, wrought-iron fixtures, and firm beds set on terra-cotta floors; the second-floor rooms were renovated in the same style in 2000 to 2001 (though here the ceilings have stuccoes rather than frescoes). The six rooms downstairs without private bathroom have three to share among them, and the only two upstairs that are bathroomless each has its own bathroom next door in the hall. The lack of an elevator (42 steps to reception) helps keep prices way down for this prime location. They finally added telephones to the rooms in 2002, which, hopefully, will be joined by air-conditioning soon after this book goes to press. (They're shooting for summer 2004; if not, then at least by 2005, when they also plan to install TVs.)

Via del Croce 35, 00187 Rome. © **06-678-0179.** Fax 06-6994-2151. www.hotelpandaparadise.com. 20 units, 12 with bathroom. 42€–48€ ($48–$55) single without bathroom, 62€–65€ ($71–$75) single with bathroom; 65€–68€ ($75–$78) double without bathroom, 93€–98€ ($107–$113) double with bathroom. 10% discount if paying in cash. No breakfast. AE, MC, V. Metro: Spagna. Bus: 81, 116, 116T, 117, 119, 204, 224, 590, 628, 926, or N25. **Amenities:** Concierge; tour desk; car-rental desk.

Parlamento 🟉🟉 *Value* The Parlamento has four-star class at two-star prices with a friendly *pensione*-style reception (but 23 steps up to the elevator; it will soon extend all the way to the ground). The street traffic is so heavy they installed an effective double set of double-glazed windows. The furnishings are antiques or reproductions and the firm beds backed by carved wood or wrought-iron headboards. In 2003, air-conditioning was finally installed in all the rooms, though if you want to turn it on, it'll cost you an extra 12€ ($14) per day. You can enjoy the breakfast room, with its chandelier and trompe-l'oeil mural, or carry your cappuccino to the small roof terrace with a view of San Silvestro's bell tower—the three rooms that open onto this terrace have Jacuzzi tubs and cost a bit extra (they go for 145€–155€/$167–$178).

Via delle Convertite 5 (at the intersection with Via del Corso, near Piazza San Silvestro), 00187 Roma. ©/fax **06-6992-1000.** www.hotelparlamento.it. 23 units. 93€–110€ ($107–$127) single; 103€–130€ ($118–$150) double; 140€–160€ ($161–$184) triple. Rates include breakfast. AE, DC, MC, V. Parking 15€ ($17) in nearby garage. Bus: 52, 53, 61, 62, 63, 71, 80, 85, 95, 116, 116T, 117, 119, 160, 175, 590, 628, 630, N25, N45, N60, or N99. **Amenities:** Concierge; tour desk; car-rental desk; room service (breakfast only). *In room:* A/C, TV, hair dryer, safe.

AROUND VIA VENETO & PIAZZA BARBERINI

Tizi *Value* The Tizi, run by an amicable family and their fluffy cat on two floors in a posh neighborhood south of the Villa Borghese, is favored by young travelers who'd rather have a quiet family atmosphere. It's frill-less but clean and comfy and welcoming—many cheap hotels won't allow you to soak your socks in the sink, but the Tizi actually invites you to use the roof terrace to dry your wash. In the rooms you'll find mostly new modular furnishings with orthopedic mattresses.

The ceilings (especially on the 2nd floor) are high, some with stuccowork, and the private bathrooms are in good working order. The five ground-floor rooms, opened in 2001, have lower ceilings but are stuccoed, and the furnishings and bathrooms are spanking-new. Shared bathrooms are used by two units only. The lower rates are usually applied in the slow periods of November, January, and February.

Via Collina 48 (east of Piazza Sallustio and west of Via Piave), 00187 Roma. ☎ 06-482-0128. Fax 06-474-3266. 24 units, 10 with bathroom. 42€ ($48) single without bathroom; 55€ ($63) double without bathroom, 65€ ($75) double with bathroom. Extra person 30% more (but small children can squeeze in for free). Breakfast 5€ ($6). No credit cards. Parking about 15€ ($17) in nearby garages. Bus: M, 38, 52, 53, 63, 80, 86, 88, 92, 217, 360, 490, 491, 495, 630, 910, or N60. **Amenities:** Nonsmoking rooms. *In room:* No phone.

NEAR STAZIONE TERMINI

Contilia   As the automatic doors part to reveal a stylish marble lobby with Persian rugs and antiques, you might step back to double-check the address. The popular old-fashioned Pensione Tony Contilia of yesteryear has taken over this building's other small hotels and upgraded itself into the best choice in Rome's diciest neighborhood—though the desk staff can be quite surly. The rooms have been redone in modern midscale comfort, with firm beds, stylish built-in units, fabric-covered walls, and Murano-style chandeliers hanging from (occasionally) stuccoed ceilings. The double-glazed windows keep out traffic noise, and the rooms overlooking the cobblestone courtyard are even quieter. Some of the smallish bathrooms come with hydromassage showers. The sunny breakfast room is open-air in summer and sky-lit in winter.

Via Principe Amedeo 79d–81 (2 blocks south of Termini between Via Gioberti and Via Cattaneo), 00185 Roma. ☎ 06-446-6942. Fax 06-446-6904. www.hotelcontilia.com. 41 units. 60€–135€ ($69–$155) single; 75€–165€ ($86–$190) double; 100€–225€ ($115–$259) triple. Rates include breakfast. AE, DC, MC, V. Parking 18€ ($16) in garage. Metro: Termini. Bus: Any to Termini. **Amenities:** Concierge; tour desk; car-rental desk; courtesy car; 24-hr. room service; babysitting; laundry service; dry cleaning; nonsmoking rooms. *In room:* A/C, TV, minibar (on request; only 5 to go around), hair dryer, safe.

Fawlty Towers *Value*   This hotel/hostel is a fave of international students who, like the inn itself, are primarily of the clean-scrubbed variety. It's staffed by friendly young folk from English-speaking countries and has Rome's most comfy hostel-style accommodations. The fifth-floor dorms—really shared rooms sleeping three or four—are as bare as you'd expect but not crowded (no bunk beds, just cots). The sixth-floor simple singles and doubles have functional furnishings; four rooms without full bathrooms do have sinks and showers. The new owners—who are otherwise adamant about keeping the place the same as it always has been—replaced all the mattresses, added TVs to the rooms, and filled the small communal terrace with flowers. Best part: There's no curfew.

Via Magenta 39 (a block north of Termini, between Via Milazzo and Via Marghera), 00185 Roma. ☎ 06-445-0374 or 06-445-4802. Fax 06 4938-2878. www.fawltytowers.org. 16 units, 5 with bathroom. 20€ ($23) bed in dorm without bathroom, 23€ ($26) bed in dorm with bathroom; 45€–52€ ($52–$60) single without bathroom, 48€–59€ ($55–$68) single with shower and sink (no toilet); 60€ 70€ ($69–$81) double without bathroom, 65€–76€ ($75–$87) double with shower and sink (no toilet), 75€–86€ ($86–$99) double with bathroom; 80€–92€ ($92–$106) triple with shower, 90€–98€ ($104–$113) triple without bathroom. No credit cards. Metro: Termini. Bus: any to Termini. **Amenities:** TV lounge with fridge, microwave, and Internet access (free). *In room:* TV, no phone (pay phone in lobby).

Nardizzi Americana 🌟 *Value*   The Nardizzi has always been a steal. Since 2000, Nicola and Fabrizio have transformed their hotel into one of the best two-stars in town but kept the rates way down. The style is inspired by ancient Rome, with a patterned tile decor giving an inlaid-stone look to the public-area floors, and a narrow terrace (open in nice weather, enclosed in winter) where you take breakfast. The rooms now have richly patterned curtains and bedspreads—a few even boast wood-beam ceilings—and new bathrooms. Although the smaller rooms were given built-in dressers, the larger ones got walk-in closets. Several are triples and quads large enough for families. *One drawback:* There's no double-glazing on the old-style windows, so for quiet, avoid rooms on the heavily trafficked Via XX Settembre side. Note that they apply low-season rates June 16 to August as well as in winter.

Via Firenze 38 (just off Via XX Settembre, 2 blocks from Via Nazionale), 00184 Roma. ℂ 06-488-0368. Fax 06-488-0035. www.hotelnardizzi.com. 30 units. 60€–110€ ($69–$127) single; 80€–135€ ($92–$155) double. Rates include breakfast. Frommer's readers get 5% discount (but you must show them the book), if you pay cash. AE, DC, MC, V. Parking around 15€–18€ ($17–$21) in nearby garage. Metro: Repubblica. Bus: H, 36, 40, 60, 61, 62, 64, 70, 71, 84, 116T, 170, 175, 492, 590, 640, 910, N25, N45, N55, N78, or N91. **Amenities:** Concierge; tour desk; courtesy car (more for departures than arrivals); 24-hr. room service; babysitting; laundry service; dry cleaning; nonsmoking rooms; Sony PlayStation and VCR in lounge. *In room:* A/C, TV, dataport, hair dryer, safe.

Papà Germano 🎯🎯 (𝒱𝑎𝑙𝑢𝑒   Gino holds cleanliness in the highest regard and is a terrifically friendly guy who loves to help you settle into Rome. The mattresses are firm to the point of being hard, but everything from the built-in units and box showers (sometimes just showerheads in corners) to the double-glazed windows is either new or kept looking that way—they redo a handful of rooms almost every year. The shared bathrooms are great, and six of the bathroomless rooms can become dorms of two to four beds. Gino has recently installed a few computers so you can use the Internet at 2.60€ ($3) per hour. By the time you arrive, they will be offering breakfast (included in the room rates) as well as in-room air-conditioning (which will cost a bit more, along the lines of 5€/$6 per day). There is no elevator.

Via Calatafimi 14a (4 blocks north of Stazione Termini, on a dead-end street off Via Volturno), 00185 Roma. ℂ 06-486-919. Fax 06-4782-5202. www.hotelpapagermano.com. 17 units, 7 with bathroom. *Rates for Frommer's readers (only if you show this book):* 18€–22€ ($21–$25) bed in shared room (3–4 beds) without bathroom; 35€–40€ ($40–$46) single without bathroom; 45€–65€ ($52–$75) double without bathroom; 60€–80€ ($69–$92) double with bathroom; 55€–75€ ($63–$86) triple without bathroom, 75€–90€ ($86–$104) triple with bathroom. Rates include breakfast. AE, DC, MC, V (although during the slowest winter periods, prices are discounted around 8%–15% if you pay in cash). Parking 13€–18€ ($15–$21) in nearby garage. Metro: Repubblica. Bus: Any to Termini. *In room:* A/C (costs extra to turn on), TV, minifridge (unstocked, only in newest rooms), hair dryer.

IN TRASTEVERE

Carmel (𝒱𝑎𝑙𝑢𝑒   The kosher Carmel lies 2 blocks beyond the daily food market on Piazza San Cosimato, a 6-minute walk from the heart of Trastevere. A 1997 renovation freshened the place up, adding pine headboards and new modular furnishings, fresh floor tiles, and spiffy soft quilts in some rooms. However, the bathrooms could stand to be upgraded in the four rooms that weren't overhauled in 2000 (with new built-in units and fabrics in addition to the bathrooms), and there's no elevator (24 steps). It's on a shady but trafficked residential road, but double-glazed windows help. They always update a few rooms each year.

Via Goffredo Mameli 11 (the continuation of Via E. Morosini off Viale Trastevere), 00153 Roma. ℂ 06-580-9921. Fax 06-581-8853. www.hotelcarmel.it. 11 units. 80€ ($92) single; 90€ ($104) double; 140€ ($161) triple. Rates include breakfast (no breakfast Sun). MC, V. Parking on metered street 1€ ($1.15) per hour 8am–11pm. Tram: 3 or 8. Bus: H, 44, 75, 780, N30, N44, N72, or N96. *In room:* A/C, TV, minifridge (unstocked).

Trastevere 🎯 (𝒱𝑎𝑙𝑢𝑒   What was once the dingiest hotel in Trastevere has renovated itself into one of the classiest. Get here while it's also still one of Rome's best bargains, with cushy new amenities at fantastic prices, a location at the heart of Trastevere's restaurants and nightlife, and a daily market at your doorstep for fresh picnic pickings. (The market's not as noisy as you'd think in the mornings.) The rooms feature fresh tiles and painted stucco, massive modular wood furnishings, and new bathrooms (although with only flat waffle-towels). All except small and dreary nos. 11 and 12 overlook the market square of San Cosimato—colorful but noisy. The apartments next door come with kitchenettes and are lofted onto three levels under a wood-beamed roof.

Via Luciano Manara 24a–25 (just behind Piazza San Cosimato; it's the continuation of Via di Fratte di Trastevere off Viale Trastevere), 00153 Roma. ℭ 06-581-4713. Fax 06-588-1016. hoteltrastevere@tiscalinet.it. 11 units, 3 apts. 77€ ($89) single; 103€ ($118) double; 129€ ($148) triple; 154€ ($177) quad; 103€–181€ ($118–$208) apt, depending on how many guests (up to 5). Rates include breakfast. AE, DC, MC, V. Free parking on street (ask for permit). Tram: 3 or 8. Bus: H, 44, 75, 780, N30, N44, N72, or N96. **Amenities:** Concierge; tour desk; courtesy car (pay); room service (breakfast; also drinks to 11:30pm); babysitting; laundry service; dry cleaning. In room: A/C, TV, hair dryer.

AROUND THE VATICAN

Colors ✦ *Value*   This cheery five-story walk-up *pensione* in upper-middle-class residential Prati is run by the Enjoy Rome folks (see "Visitor Information" in "Essentials," above) who made Fawlty Towers such a success. It's popular with students and the younger set, but mostly of the clean-cut variety—the friendly staff, most of who hail from English-speaking countries, are careful about that. This place has a relaxed air fostered by the fully equipped communal kitchen/lounge (with TV) that opens onto a small terrace, the only place you can smoke. The joint lives up to its name (each sizable room painted in a whimsical cacophony of hues), and while the furnishings are simple and functional, they're new. Two of the rooms without toilet or full bathroom even have showers in the corner, and all rooms have at least sinks. To save a bundle, book one of the five beds in the only shared room. You're near the Vatican and open-air markets, as well as some of the best food shops on Via Cola di Rienzo.

Via Boezio 31, 00192 Roma. ℭ 06-687-4030. Fax 06-686-7947. www.colorshotel.com. 7 units, 1 with bathroom. 22€ ($25) bed in co-ed dorm without bathroom; 75€ ($86) double without bathroom, 85€ ($98) double with shower but no toilet, 90€ ($104) double with bathroom; 95€ ($109) triple with shower but no toilet, 110€ ($126) triple with bathroom. Prices lower in winter. No credit cards. Metered parking in street. Metro: Ottaviano–San Pietro. Bus: 23, 34, 49, 80, 271, 280, 492, 982, 990, N29, N30, N55, or N99. **Amenities:** Concierge; tour desk; coin-op washer/dryer 4€ ($4.60 per load); nonsmoking rooms (all). In room: No phone.

WORTH A SPLURGE

Abruzzi ✦✦   Open your window and the Pantheon is not 30m (100 ft.) away. That's what keeps this hotel special, and keeps it firmly planted in this guidebook, even though in 2003 new owners took what had been an utterly basic comfortable old shoe of a cheap *pensione* with no amenities and turned it into a full-bore, three-star (moderate) hotel. Also, that means *the prices have more than doubled,* which is a downright crying shame. (To tell you the truth, I would have preferred it remain an unadorned budget gem, but that's progress for you.) All the rooms now come with private bathrooms fitted with heated towel racks; they've installed such amenities as telephones, air-conditioning, and TVs; and minibars and cherrywood veneer furnishings now sit on new wood floors. Perhaps more important than all those put together, the new owners have installed double-paned windows—the piazza is a popular hangout until late, so the noise can get annoying, but with this location and that view, who cares? The giant corner rooms, with windows on two sides, are the best in the house. Only a few singles suffer from not getting that stellar view, yet most are large. There's no elevator, and they were not able to carve out space for a breakfast room, so you take the included continental breakfast in one of the nearby cafes on the piazza instead (which is actually nicer than hanging around a hotel for breakfast).

Piazza della Rotonda 69, 00186 Roma. ⓒ **06-679-2021.** Fax 06-6978-8076. www.hotelabruzzi.it. 25 units. 120€–155€ ($138–$178) single; 160€–195€ ($184–$224) double. Rates include breakfast. DC, MC, V. Tram: 8 to Largo di Torre Argentina. Bus: 40, 46, 62, 63, 64, 70, 81, 87, 116, 116T, 186, 492, 571, 628, 630, 780, 810, 850, 916, N25, N78, or N99. **Amenities:** Concierge; tour desk; car rental; babysitting; laundry service; dry cleaning. *In room:* A/C, TV, dataport, minibar, hair dryer, safe.

Alimandi ⚜ The Alimandi is one of the better tour-group hotels, and is 3 blocks from Rome's best daily food market. But its huge selling point is its close proximity to the Vatican Museums. The rooms are standardized, modern, and comfortable, holding few surprises in the built-in wood units and newish bathrooms. The beds sport fresh foam mattresses. The faux medieval bar opens onto a bright lounge, frescoed by the owner's nephew, with a player piano. The pleasant roof terrace sports a touch of Vatican view. They serve breakfast on the roof year-round (open air in summer, enclosed in winter), and offer free Internet access in the lobby. In late 2004 (after this book goes to press), they'll open a 25-room annex nearby—smack-dab in front of the Vatican Museums entrance, in fact. Rooms will be of "superior" three-star quality, but for now, at least, the rates will remain the same as at the main hotel.

Via Tunisi 8 (at Via Veniero and the base of the steps up to Viale Vaticano), 00192 Roma. ⓒ **06-3972-3941.** Fax 06-3972-3943. www.alimandi.org. 35 units. 90€ ($104) single; 150€ ($173) double; 180€ ($207) triple. Rates lower in low season. Rates include breakfast. AE, DC, MC, V. Free parking. Metro: Cipro–Musei Vaticani. Bus: 49, 490, 492, N30, N55, or N99. **Amenities:** Concierge; tour desk; car-rental desk; courtesy car (free for airport); babysitting; laundry service; dry cleaning. *In room:* A/C, TV, small fridge (some rooms), hair dryer, safe.

Astoria Garden ⚜ *Value* The prices (especially at those low-season rates) are fantastic for the comfort and style at this late-19th-century palazzo (without elevator), where the stuccoed ceilings and dark oils of the public areas conjure an old-world atmosphere. Renovations in 2001 gave the rooms reproduction furnishings and soft carpets; about seven even have Jacuzzi tubs (and cost 30€/$34 per day more). The only drawback is that rooms are smallish. The garden rooms (those overlooking it and especially those opening off its back) enjoy the most quiet and the best views. The gravelly garden shaded by palm and orange trees boasts a glassed-in veranda. If you plan to stay several days, tell manager Francesco Cusato that you're traveling with Frommer's, and get a 10% discount. At press time, a room fitted out for guests with disabilities was in the works.

Via V. Bachelet 8, 00185 Roma. ⓒ **06-446-9908.** Fax 06-445-3329. www.hotelastoriagarden.it. 34 units. 62€–129€ ($71–$148) single; 80€–232€ ($92–$267) double; 160€–420€ ($184–$483) junior suite. Rates include breakfast. AE, DC, MC, V. Parking 10€–26€ ($12–$30) in garage (free if staying Sat–Sun nights). Metro: Termini or Castro Pretorio. Bus: Any to Termini. **Amenities:** Restaurant (dinner only); small weight room; concierge; tour desk; airport service (fee); limited room service; nonsmoking rooms. *In room:* A/C, TV, dataport, hair dryer, iron, safe.

Casa di Santa Brigida ⚜⚜ Rome's best (and poshest) convent hotel is run by the friendly sisters of St. Bridget in the building where that Swedish saint died in 1373. It's got a stellar location catty-corner to the Michelangelo-designed Palazzo Farnese on a quiet square just a block from the daily market and nightlife of Campo de' Fiori. The splurge prices are justified by the roomy old-world accommodations with antiques or reproductions on parquet (lower level) or carpeted (upstairs) floors. The bathrooms are a little old but the beds heavenly firm. There's a roof terrace, library, TV lounge, and private church. This retreat is highly requested—often booked months in advance—so reserve as far ahead as possible.

Via Monserato 54 (just off Piazza Farnese). (Postal address Piazza Farnese 96, 00186 Roma.) ⓒ **06-6889-2596.** Fax 06-6889-1573. www.brigidine.org. 24 units. 95€ ($109) single; 170€ ($196) double. Rates include breakfast. DC, MC, V. Bus: 23, 40, 46, 62, 64, 116, 116T, 280, 571, 870, 916, N29, N45, or N98. **Amenities:** Restaurant. *In room:* A/C, hair dryer (on request), iron (on request).

Smeraldo 🏛🏛   For the utmost comfort smack-dab in the heart of Rome (3 blocks from Largo Argentina, 3 from Campo de' Fiori), book the Smeraldo. A complete overhaul and expansion in 2001 gave it the most amenities in its price range—though that range did get jacked up by 15% in 2004 when they finished adding private bathrooms to all rooms and hopped up one classification to become a three-star, or moderate, hotel (which, unfortunately, booted it just over the mark to land it here in the "Splurge" category). Most of the rooms boast fresh mattresses, new bathrooms, and well-chosen built-in furnishings. Everything is extremely quiet, save for some distant traffic rumble on the Via Monte della Farina side. The fourth-floor patio is perfect for shady quiet, and the rooftop terrace (fluttering with hotel sheets) offers sun and a panorama of rooftops. In 2002, they bought the crummy old Hotel Piccolo across the street, renovated it to the standards and comfort level of the Smeraldo, and renamed it **In Parione.** Those 16 rooms cost 10€ ($12) less than at Smeraldo, but breakfast is not included (you can take it at the Smeraldo for 7€/$8).

Vicolo dei Chiodaroli (between Via Chiavari and Via Monte della Farina), 00186 Roma. ⓒ **06-687-5929.** Fax 06-6880-5495. www.smeraldoroma.com. 50 units. 100€ ($115) single; 135€ ($155) double; 165€ ($190) triple. AE, DC, MC, V. Parking 35€ ($40) in nearby garage. Tram: 8. Bus: H, 30, 40, 46, 62, 63, 64, 70, 81, 87, 186, 204, 271, 492, 571, 628, 630, 780, 810, 916, N72, or N96. **Amenities:** Concierge; tour desk; car-rental desk; limited room service. *In room:* A/C, TV, hair dryer.

3 Great Deals on Dining

You could spend a lot on dining in Rome, dropping upward of 50€ ($58) in the many fine *ristorante* and overpriced tourist-oriented *trattorie*, but you don't have to. You'll find plenty of *osterie* and old-fashioned *fiaschetterie* where you can get basic, filling Roman meals for well under 20€ ($23), many places just steps from the touristy sights of the *centro storico.* If you want to wander and find a restaurant on your own, look for the strongest concentration of eateries in Trastevere. And you'll note that trendy "wine bars" (called that even in Italian) have been popping up all over town: places where you can drink remarkable wines by the glass and nibble on cheese platters, salamis, and often inventive small dishes, all pretty cheaply.

Tips Dining Notes

Traditionally, **osterie** are basic tavernlike eateries; **trattorie** are casual family-run places serving simple full meals; and **ristoranti** are fancier places, with waiters in bow ties, printed menus, linen tablecloths, and hefty prices (which usually include a **pane e coperto,** or bread and cover charge, of 1€–10€/$1.15–$12 merely for the privilege of sitting down to a basket of bread). Nowadays, fancy restaurants often go by the name of *trattoria* to cash in on the associated charm factor, trendy spots use *osteria* to show they're of-the-moment hip, and casual inexpensive places sometimes tack on *ristorante* to ennoble themselves. A *tavola calda,* however, is always a glorified bar with a few prepared dishes kept hot under lamps, cafeteria-style.

As for typical Roman cuisine, you start off with an **antipasto (appetizer)**, which in Rome most often means a simple *bruschetta* (a slab of peasant bread grilled, rubbed with garlic, drizzled with olive oil, and sprinkled with salt; *al pomodoro* adds a pile of tomatoes on top). If you see *carciofi* (artichokes), *alla giudea* (flattened and lightly fried) or otherwise, snap up one of Rome's greatest specialties.

Your *primo* (**1st course**) could be a soup—try *stracciatella* (egg and Parmesan in broth)—or a pasta. Available on just about every Roman menu are traditional favorites such as *spaghetti* or *bucatini all'amatriciana* (pasta in a spicy tomato sauce studded with pancetta bacon and dense with onions); *spaghetti alla carbonara* (steaming hot spaghetti mixed with eggs, pancetta bacon, Parmesan, and loads of black pepper—the heat of the pasta cooks the eggs); or *pasta al pomodoro* (pasta in plain tomato sauce). Also try *penne all'arrabbiata* ("hopping mad" pasta quills in spicy tomato sauce), *tagliolini* or *spaghetti cacio e pepe* (pasta simply prepared with black pepper and grated pecorino cheese), the ever-popular poor man's *pasta e fagioli* (pasta with beans), *pasta e ceci* (pasta with chickpeas), or *gnocchi* (potato-based pasta dumplings).

Secondi (**2nd courses**) include traditional local dishes such as the eyebrow-raising but delicious *coda alla vaccinara* (braised oxtail with tomatoes), *pajata* (made of calves' intestines still clotted with mother's milk and often put in tomato sauce on rigatoni), and *trippa* (old-fashioned tripe). Less adventurous main courses are *involtini* (veal layered with prosciutto, cheese, and celery, then rolled and stewed in its own juices with tomatoes), *polpette* (meatballs, served in Italy with sauce as a meat dish, never atop spaghetti), *bocconcini di vitello* (veal nuggets, usually stewed with potatoes and sage), or *pollo arrosto* (roast chicken), usually one of the cheapest entrees and often sided *con patate* (with roast potatoes). *Abbacchio scottaditto* (grilled tender Roman spring lamb chops) are so good, the name avers, you'll "burn your fingers" in your haste to eat them. One of the best Roman *secondi* is *saltimbocca,* literally "jumps-in-the-mouth"—a tender veal cutlet cooked in white wine with sage leaves and a slice of prosciutto draped over it.

The *contorni* on the menu are vegetables and side dishes (*melanzana* is eggplant, *fagioli* are beans, and *patate* are potatoes). Round off your meal with *tiramisù* (a triflelike layer cake of espresso-soaked ladyfingers and sweetened creamy mascarpone cheese dusted with cocoa) or a *tartufo* (an ice-cream ball with a fudge center, dusted with cocoa).

Roman **pizza**—the kind from a cheap sit-down pizzeria, called *pizza al forno*—is large, round, flat, and crispy (unlike its softer Neapolitan cousin). A "plain" tomato sauce, mozzarella, and basil pie is called *pizza margherita.* The adventurous might want to try a *capricciosa,* a "capricious" selection of toppings that often includes anchovies, prosciutto, olives, and an egg cracked onto the hot pizza, where it fries in place. You can also get the Roman version of pizza by the slice, *pizza rustica* (also known as *pizza à taglio*) from hole-in-the-wall joints (see the box "Quick Bites," below).

Although the capital's restaurants are usually blessed with **wine** cellars that draw on the best vineyards throughout Italy, table wine in Rome is usually a light fruity white from the hills south of the city, either a Frascati or the often slightly inferior Castelli Romani.

AROUND ANCIENT ROME

Birreria Peroni 🦌 *Value* ROMAN/GERMAN/BUFFET   Long one of my favorites, this 1906 Italian beer hall is the lunchtime haunt of local businesspeople who pack in for good food at ridiculously low prices (especially at the buffet). The edges of the fan-cooled vaulted ceilings were frescoed in the 1940s with Art Nouveau sporting *putti* drinking beer and espousing homilies like "Beer makes you strong and healthy." Plates run the gamut from *bombolotti all'amatriciana*, *trippa*, and *pollo arrosto con patate* to *arrosto misto alla Peroni* (a huge mix of German Bierhalle eats, like sausage with sauerkraut and goulash with potatoes). The buffet includes goose salami, stuffed olives, beans with tuna, and marinated artichokes. To wash it all down, order a Peroni beer or the "blue ribbon" Nastro Azzurro label—they even offer beer by the 1.5-liter (1.6-qt.) carafe.

Via San Marcello 10 (north of Piazza SS. Apostoli). © 06-679-5310. Dishes 5€–15€ ($6–$17); buffet items 3€–7€ ($3.45–$8). MC, V. Summer Mon–Fri 12:30–11:30pm, Sat 8pm–midnight; winter Mon–Fri 12:30–3:15pm and 7:30pm–midnight, Sat 7pm–midnight. Closed up to 4 weeks in Aug. Bus: H, 40, 60, N60, 62, 63, 64, 70, 81, 85, 95, 117, 119, 160, 170, 175, 204, 492, 628, 630, 850, N25, N45, or N99.

AROUND CAMPO DE' FIORI & THE JEWISH GHETTO

Vegetarians looking for monstrous salads—or if you just want to lay off the heavy Italian for a meal—can find great food at **Insalata Ricca,** Largo dei Chiavari 85 (© **06-6880-3656;** bus: 40, 46, 62, 64, 116, 116T, 571, or 916). See the review of this chain under "Around Piazza Navona & the Pantheon," later in this section.

Da Giggetto 🐨🐨 ROMAN JEWISH This third-generation classic eatery in the old Jewish Quarter rambles back in room after wood-beamed room hung with drying herbs and spices. If you want one of the coveted tables wedged between the Roman temple columns sprouting out of the sidewalk in front, call ahead. Since 1923, neighborhood cronies have rubbed elbows with tourists digging into Roman Jewish specialties like *carciofi alla giudia* (flattened, tender fried artichokes), *fiori di zucchine ripieni* (fried zucchini flowers stuffed with mozzarella and anchovies), and well-prepared Roman dishes such as *bucatini all'amatriciana* and *abbacchio à scottaditto*. It's easy to go overboard, so keep an eye on that mounting bill.

Via del Portico d'Ottavia 21–22. © 06-686-1105. Reservations recommended. *Primi* 7.50€–10€ ($9–$12); *secondi* 9.50€–15€ ($11–$17). AE, MC, V. Tues–Sun 12:30–3pm and 7–11pm. Closed Aug. Tram: 8. Bus: H, 23, 63, 271, 280, 630, 780, N29, N72, or N96.

Da Pancrazio ROMAN/ITALIAN   It doesn't get more atmospheric than this, a restaurant whose basement rooms are set into the restored arcades of Pompeii's 55 B.C. theater. It's like dining in a museum. For a touristy restaurant, the cooking is surprisingly excellent. Among the top dishes are *spaghetti alla carbonara* and delicious *cannelloni alla Pancrazio* (pasta tubes stuffed with meat and cheese). Follow up with *abbacchio al forno con patate* (oven-roasted lamb chops with roasted potatoes) or fresh fish.

Piazza del Biscione 92 (just off the northeast corner of Campo de' Fiori). © **06-686-1246.** Reservations highly recommended. *Primi* 9€–12€ ($10–$14); *secondi* 9€–21€ ($10–$24). AE, DC, MC, V. Thurs–Tues 12:30–2:30pm and 7:30–11pm. Closed 25 days in Aug. Bus: 40, 46, 62, 64, 116, 116T, 571, 916, N29, N45, or N98.

Hosteria Romanesca *★★* ROMAN   If you're looking to buck the tourists packing into the famous but much-declined La Carbonara, but you still want a seat on lively Campo de' Fiori, head to Armando and Enzo's little 110-year-old *osteria*. It's the piazza atmosphere and well-tuned traditional dishes you come for, not the service, which sometimes seems nonexistent. (They work hard, but there are just too many diners for two waiters to handle.) The wine is from the Castelli Romani, and dishes include favorites like excellent *pasta all'a-matriciana*, flawless *abbacchio scottaditto*, and *cervello d'abbacchio* (fried lamb's brains). In colder weather, you can retreat under the wood beams of the tiny interior.

Campo de' Fiori 40. © **06-686-4024.** Reservations recommended. *Primi* 7€–8€ ($8–$9); *secondi* 7€–12€ ($8–$14). No credit cards. Tues–Sun noon–4pm and 7pm–midnight. Closed 20 days in Aug. Bus: 40, 46, 62, 64, 116, 116T, 571, 916, N29, N45, or N98.

L'Angolo Divino WINE BAR/LIGHT MEALS   Massimo Crippa and his brothers have transformed their grandmother's wine shop into a fashionable and lovable wine bar just off Campo de' Fiori. Although old-fashioned in style, with wood ceilings and shelves of *vino,* it's trendy in its culinary offerings—like most wine bars, it offers mixed platters of cheeses, salamis, and smoked fish and *bruschette* with daily dishes like lasagna, *rustica ripiena* (a cousin to vegetable quiche), salads, and delectable vegetable terrines. There's a vast selection of wines by the glass, particularly strong in Italian vintages but with a good number of select foreign labels as well.

Via dei Balestrari 12 (a block southeast of Campo de' Fiori). © **06-686-4413.** Dishes 3€–9.50€ ($3.45–$11). MC, V. Tues–Sun 10am–3pm and 5:30pm–2am. Closed 15 days in Aug. Bus: 40, 46, 62, 64, 116, 116T, 571, 916, N29, N45, or N98.

Sora Margherita *★★* *Finds* ROMAN JEWISH   Margherita Tomassini opened this signless nine-table *osteria* 40 years ago as an outlet for her uncle's Velletri wine. The *vino* still comes from Velletri, and Margherita keeps busy in the kitchen making by hand the fresh *agnolotti* (meat-stuffed ravioli in *ragù*), fettuccine (best sauced *cacio e pepe,* with pecorino and cracked pepper), and gnocchi (on Thurs). She began serving her legendary *polpette* (meatballs) about 20 years ago so her infant son would have something soft to eat—patrons were soon clamoring for them to be included on the menu. Try the heavenly *parmigiana di melanzane*—she loads the eggplant slices with mozzarella and bakes them long and slow in tomato sauce.

Piazza Cinque Scole 30 (west of Via Arenula). © **06-687-4216.** *Primi* 5€–6.50€ ($5.75–$7); *secondi* 7€–11€ ($8–$13). No credit cards. Mon–Fri noon–3pm. Closed Aug 7–Sept 6. Tram: 8. Bus: H, 23, 63, 271, 280, 630, 780, N29, N72, or N96.

AROUND PIAZZA NAVONA & THE PANTHEON

Enoteca Corsi *Kids* ROMAN   It isn't often you find a dirt-cheap old-fashioned *enoteca* that accepts Diners Club. Corsi has kept up with the times—but not the prices—so while the wine shop looks every inch the *vini olii* of 1937, behind it and next door are large fan-cooled rooms with long tables to hold the lunchtime crowds of local workers. Your choices are limited, but every one is excellent in its simplicity. The chalkboard menu changes daily but may include *penne all'arrabbiata, saltimbocca,* and delectable specials like tepid *pasta e patate* soup or *zucchine ripiene* (baked zucchini flowers stuffed with minced meats).

Via del Gesù 87–88 (off Via delle Plebescito). 🕿 **06-679-0821.** *Primi* 5€ ($6); *secondi* 8€ ($9). AE, DC, MC, V. Mon–Sat noon–3:30pm. Closed Aug. Bus: 30, 40, 46, 62, 63, 64, 70, 81, 87, 186, 492, 571, 628, 630, 780, 810, 916, N45, or N98.

Insalata Ricca 2 ITALIAN/SALADS   A need for more vegetarian restaurants and lighter low-fat fare in Rome helped a single little trattoria hawking entree-size salads grow into a small chain of packed restaurants. Most people call ahead for an outdoor table, but on summer days you might prefer the smoke-free air-conditioning inside. The more popular of the oversize salads are the *baires* (lettuce, rughetta, celery, walnuts, apples, Gorgonzola) and *siciliana* (lettuce, rughetta, sun-dried tomatoes, green olives, corn, hard salted ricotta). Also on the menu are dishes like *gnocchi verdi al Gorgonzola* (spinach gnocchi with Gorgonzola sauce) and *pasta integrale* (whole-wheat pasta in tomato-and-basil sauce). The branches near Campo de' Fiori and near the Vatican offer the same basic menu.

Piazza Pasquino 72 (southwest of Piazza Navona). 🕿 **06-6830-7881.** Reservations recommended. *Primi* and salads 5.20€–9€ ($6–$10); *secondi* 6€–13€ ($7–$15). AE, MC, V. Daily 12:30–3:30pm and 6:45pm–12:40am. Bus: 30, 40, 46, 62, 64, 70, 81, 87, 116, 116T, 186, 204, 492, 628, N45, N78, or N99.

Pizzeria Baffetto *Kids Kids* PIZZA   At this pizzeria, the service is fast and furious and the thin-crusted wood-oven pizzas are sublime and bubbling hot. People line up early to squeeze in for a paper-spread table surrounded by photos of the directors, artists, and other international types who've shown up nightly over the past 40 years to slum it with businesspeople, locals, and packs of youngsters. The night's pizzas are chalked on a board, so when the waiter whips past, be ready to order a *piccolo* (small), *media* (medium), or *grande* with the toppings of your choice—"plain" *margherita* is overwhelmingly the most popular.

Via del Governo Vecchio 114 (at the corner of Via Sora). 🕿 **06-686-1617.** Pizza 3.50€–8.50€ ($4–$10). No credit cards. Daily 6:30pm–1am (sometimes closed Sun in winter). Closed Aug 10–30. Bus: 30, 40, 46, 62, 64, 70, 81, 87, 116, 116T, 186, 204, 492, 628, N45, N78, or N99.

AROUND THE SPANISH STEPS & PIAZZA DEL POPOLO

Edy *Kids Finds* ROMAN/SEAFOOD   Edmondo and Luciana run this comfy trattoria near Rome's toniest shopping zone, offering downscale prices—especially on the fish portion of the menu—in an otherwise terminally upscale area. Under an old coffered and painted ceiling or at candlelit tables out on the cobblestones, you can sample their excellent *tagliatelle con ricotta e carciofi* (pasta in ricotta-and-artichoke sauce) or specialty *spaghetti al cartoccio* (pasta and seafood baked in foil). For a *secondo,* try the *abbacchio Romanesco con patate* (spring lamb with potatoes) or *rombo alla griglia con patate* (grilled turbot with potatoes). Don't leave before tasting one of their homemade desserts.

Vicolo del Babuino 4 (off Via del Babuino, 3 blocks from Piazza del Popolo). 🕿 **06-3600-1738.** Reservations highly recommended. *Primi* 8€–12€ ($9–$14); *secondi* 7€–13€ ($8–$15). DC, MC, V. Mon–Sat noon–3:30pm and 7–midnight. Closed 1 week in Aug. Metro: Spagna. Bus: 117, 119, or N25.

Kids Quick Bites

At **Dar Filettaro à Santa Barbara,** just off the southeast corner of Campo de' Fiori at Largo dei Librari 88 (© **06-686-4018;** bus: 40, 46, 62, 64, 116, 116T, 571, or 916), you can join the line of people threading to the back of the bare room to order a filet of *baccalà* (salt cod) fried golden brown *da portar via* (wrapped in paper to eat as you *passeggiata*). It costs precisely 2.85€ ($3.25); they're open Monday to Saturday 5 to 10:40pm.

Lunchtime offers you the perfect opportunity to savor Roman fast food: *pizza rustica,* by the slice (often called *pizza à taglio*), half-wrapped in waxed paper for easy carrying. Rome averages a tiny *pizza rustica* joint every 3 blocks or so. Just pop in, point to the bubbling sheet with your preferred toppings behind the counter, and hand over a couple of euros. For 2€ ($2.30) you'll get a healthy portion of "plain" tomato sauce–basil-and-cheese *pizza margherita. Pizza rossa* (just with sauce) and *pizza con patate* (with cheese and potatoes) cost even less, as does the exquisitely simple *pizza bianca*—plain dough brushed with olive oil and sprinkled with salt and sometimes rosemary.

A *rosticceria* is a *pizza à taglio* with spits of chickens roasting in the window and a few pasta dishes kept warm in long trays. You can also sit down for a quick pasta or prepared meat dish steaming behind the glass counters at a *tavola calda* (literally "hot table") for about half the price of a dish at a trattoria. A Roman bar, although it does indeed serve liquor, is more what we'd call a cafe, a place to grab a cheap *panino* (flat roll stuffed with meat, cheese, or vegetables) or *tramezzino* (large triangular sandwiches on white bread with the crusts cut off—like giant tea sandwiches).

For some luscious gelato or a frothy cappuccino, see *"Gelaterie & Cafes"* in "Rome After Dark," later in this chapter.

Fiaschetteria Beltramme (da Cesaretto) ✿ ROMAN   *Fiaschetteria* refers to the flasks from which wine was once poured, to be accompanied by a simple plate of pasta and roast meat. Little has changed here since 1886—but the menu's a tad longer now and the place has been declared a national monument. Cesare and his hardworking staff keep the lucky 30 or so diners happy in this hole-in-the-wall. At lunch, businesspeople and workers line up to cram themselves at communal tables under whirling fans and framed whatnot on the walls. Dinnertime is just as crowded but features more families and tourists. The *antipasto misto* is good, as is the *rigatoni al cesaretto* (al dente pasta topped with arugula, cherry tomatoes, mozzarella, olive oil, and herbs). The *secondi* are traditionally basic, like *bollito misto* (mix of boiled meats) and *abbacchio scottaditto.*

Via della Croce 39 (4 blocks from the Spanish Steps). No phone. *Primi* 8€ ($9); *secondi* 8€–13€ ($9–$15). No credit cards. Mon–Sat 12:15–2:45pm and 7:15–10:45pm. Metro: Spagna. Bus: 117, 119, or N25.

IN SAN LORENZO

Arancia Blu ✿ INVENTIVE VEGETARIAN ITALIAN   Fabio Bassan and Enrico Bartolucci offer Rome's best vegetarian cuisine. Under soft lighting and wood ceilings, surrounded by wine racks and university intellectuals, the waiters will help you compile a menu to fit any dietary need. The dishes at this trendy spot are inspired by peasant cuisines from across Italy and beyond. The appetizers range from hummus and tabbouleh to zucchini-and-saffron quiche or *insalata verde con mele, Gorgonzola naturale,* and *e aceto balsamico* (salad with apples, Gorgonzola, and balsamic vinegar). The main courses change seasonally and might be lasagna with red onions, mushrooms, zucchini, and ginger; *cous cous con verdure* (vegetable couscous); or ravioli *ripieni di patate e menta* (stuffed with potatoes and mint, served under tomatoes and Sardinian sheep's cheese). They offer 100 wines and inventive desserts like *pere al vino* (pears cooked in wine and juniper, served with orange-honey *semifreddo*).

Via dei Latini 65 (at Via Arunci). ℂ 06-445-4105. Reservations highly recommended. *Primi* and *secondi* 6.70€–12€ ($8–$14). No credit cards. Daily 8pm–midnight; Sun 12:30–3:30pm. Bus: 71.

NEAR STAZIONE TERMINI

Pizzeria Est! Est! Est! ⍟ *(Kids* PIZZA   You can sit outside at the box canyon–like end of the road as part of an old-fashioned Roman street dining scene or opt for the Liberty-style interior of the Ricci family's 103-year-old pizzeria. The starched-shirt service and small pies of Est! Est! Est!—named after a sweet white wine from northern Lazio—have long been popular with the nearby police station and other neighbors as well as visitors. Order an appetizer of *supplì* (gooey fried balls of rice and mozzarella) and *olive ascolane* (green olives stuffed with minced meat, breaded, and fried) before your pizza. The pizza is excellent, with a soft Neapolitan-style crust; try it with *funghi porcini* or *capricciosa* (mushrooms, prosciutto, mozzarella, tomatoes, and a fried egg).

Via Genova 32 (off Via Nazionale). ℂ 06-488-1107. Reservations recommended. Pizza 5.20€–10€ ($6–$12). MC, V. Tues–Sun 7pm–midnight. Closed Aug. Bus: H, 40, 60, 64, 70, 71, 116T, 117, 170, N78, or N91.

IN TESTACCIO

La Torricella ⍟⍟ *(Finds* ROMAN/SEAFOOD   This ultratraditional Testaccio *osteria* is set in the echoing tiled rooms of what appears to be an old dock warehouse, with tall arches, soccer team photos on the walls, and a die-hard crowd of neighborhood families. It ain't fancy but gets stars for its genuineness and huge portions. The menu has only Roman faves like *spaghetti ai frutti di mare* (with seafood), homemade gnocchi (on Thurs), great *rigatoni con pagliata,* tasty *bucatini all'amatriciana, saltimbocca alla romana, abbacchio à scottadito, bistecca di manzo ai pepi verdi* (steak in cream sauce with green peppercorns), and fresh *sogliole* (sole), *spigola* (sea bass), *rombo* (turbot), and other fish.

Via E. Torricelli 2–12 (at Via G. B. Bodoni, just off the Lungotevere a few blocks up from Ponte Testaccio). ℂ 06-574-6311. *Primi* 5€–16€ ($6–$18); *secondi* 7€–20€ ($8–$23). MC, V. Tues–Sun 12:30–3:30pm and 7:30–11:30pm. Closed a few days in Aug. Metro: Piramide. Bus: 95, 170, 719, 781, N29, N30, or N91.

IN TRASTEVERE

Da Augusto ⍟ *(Value* ROMAN   The Silvestri family's modest eatery has found its way into virtually every guidebook as the poster child for Trastevere *osterie.* But the bulk of its patronage remains neighborhood cronies who pack into the pair of rooms and few tables squeezed into the triangular piazza. Perhaps visitors just can't find the place, tucked into a forgotten corner of Trastevere on a tiny square used as a car park. The lucky few sit elbow-to-elbow to dig into standbys like *rigatoni all'amatriciana, fettuccine cacio e pepe, trippa alla romana, involtini,* and succulent *abbacchio.* The place gets rather busy, so don't expect solicitous service, just excellent home cooking.

Piazza de' Renzi 15 (between Vicolo delle Cinque and Via del Moro). ℂ 06-580-3798. *Primi* 3€–5€ ($3.45–$6); *secondi* 4€–7.20€ ($4.60–$8). No credit cards. Mon–Sat noon–3pm; Mon–Fri 7pm–midnight. Tram: 8. Bus: H, 23, 115, 271, 280, 780, N30, N72, or N96.

Il Duca ⭐⭐ ROMAN/PIZZA   The wood-ceilinged interior and Roman murals between the brick arches of this Trastevere standby are as much of an attraction as the excellent cooking and noisy banter—plenty of Roman dialect still mixed in with the tourist tongues. But they really get stars for the outstanding melt-in-your-mouth lasagna, the only version on the planet better than my mother's. (Mom, incidentally, agrees.) Since everyone at the table can't order the same thing, they also offer *spaghetti alla carbonara* and *gnocchi alla Gorgonzola*. For a *secondo*, the *saltimbocca alla romana* is divine, or try the *pollo arrosto con patate* or *abbacchio à scottaditto*. They even have a nonsmoking room.

Vicolo delle Cinque 52–56 (just around the corner from Piazza San Egidio, behind Piazza Santa Maria in Trastevere). ℂ 06-581-7706. Reservations recommended. *Primi* 6€–9€ ($7–$10); *secondi* 7€–15€ ($8–$17); pizza 5.50€–8€ ($6–$9). AE, DC, MC, V. Tues–Sun 7pm–midnight; Sun noon–3pm. Tram: 8. Bus: H, 23, 115, 271, 280, 780, N30, N72, or N96.

La Tana dei Noiantri ROMAN/ITALIAN/PIZZA   This place has a vast menu with seemingly limitless offerings of quite good food, impeccable service by crisply bow-tied waiters, and an enviable location just off Piazza Santa Maria. But everybody really comes for the romance of dining on the cobblestones under the tentlike umbrellas of a pocket-size piazza. The interior is more formal, with wood ceilings and painted coats of arms hanging above baronial fireplaces. Open with the tasty *stracciatella romana* (egg-drop soup with parmigiano reggiano) or the wonderfully spicy *penne all'arrabbiata*. The best among the *secondi* are the *abbacchio arrosto con patate* and *fritto cervello di abbacchio* (fried lamb's brains with zucchini), but the *bistecca di manzo* (beefsteak) is fine as well. There's also a sizable selection of fresh fish and seafood.

Via della Paglia 1–3 (the street leading west out of Piazza Santa Maria in Trastevere). ℂ 06-580-6404. Reservations highly recommended. *Primi* 8.50€–9.50€ ($10–$11); *secondi* 7.50€–16€ ($9–$18); pizza 7.50€–11€ ($9–$12). AE, MC, V. Wed–Mon noon–3pm and 7:30–11:30pm. Closed Jan 8–Feb 2. Tram: 8. Bus: H, 23, 115, 271, 280, 780, N30, N72, or N96.

Pizzeria Ivo ⭐ *Kids* PIZZA/ROMAN   Trastevere's famed pizza parlor is always thronged with locals and visitors, but the hordes haven't led it to compromise taste or prices. The sidewalk tables are hard to come by but the street's fairly trafficked, so I always choose the closely spaced tables inside. The service is swift and brusque in true Trastevere style, and, despite its almost terminal popularity, Ivo remains an excellent place to introduce yourself to genuine Roman wood-oven pizza. My pick is the "plain" *margherita*, but also good are *al prosciutto* and *capricciosa* (at the whim of the chef, but likely to include anchovies, prosciutto, olives, and a fried egg). There are plenty of pastas to choose from as well, but the *secondi* leave enough to be desired to be left alone.

Via San Francesco a Ripa 158 (from Viale Trastevere, take a right onto Via Fratte di Trastevere, then left on Via San Francesco a Ripa). ℂ 06-581-7082. *Primi* 6.20€–7€ ($7–$8); *secondi* 5.20€–13€ ($6–$15); pizza 5€–9€ ($6–$10). AE, DC, MC, V. Wed–Mon 5:30pm–1:30am. Tram: 8. Bus: H, 23, 44, 75, 115, 271, 280, 780, N30, N44, N72, or N96.

AROUND THE VATICAN

The no. 6 branch of **Insalata Ricca,** the popular chain of salad-and-light-meal restaurants (see review under "Around Piazza Navona & the Pantheon," earlier in this chapter), is across from the Vatican walls at Piazza del Risorgimento 5–6 (ℂ **06-3973-0387;** Metro: Ottaviano–San Pietro; bus: 19, 23, 32, 49, 81, 271, 492, 982, 990, N29, or N30).

Il Matriciano ROMAN   This classic and classy *ristorante* has for more than 80 years been beloved by Rome cognoscenti, Prati residents, and film directors for business lunches. At these prices, the portions could be larger and the sauces more ample, but the cooking is impeccable. It would be a sacrilege if you or someone at your table didn't order the namesake *bucatini all'amatriciana* (but they skimp a bit on the meat). Other good *primi* are *fettuccine casarecce* (pasta with tomatoes and basil) and *tagliolini alla gricia.* The pride of their *secondi* is *abbacchio al forno con patate* (lamb with tasty oven-roasted potatoes), but also great are the *ossobuco cremoso con funghi* (osso buco in mushroom-cream sauce) and *filetto di bue* (ox steak).

Via dei Gracchi 55 (at the corner of Via Silla). ✆ **06-321-3040.** Reservations highly recommended. *Primi* 8.50€ ($10); *secondi* 12€–17€ ($14–$20). AE, DC, MC, V. May–Oct Sun–Fri 12:30–3pm and 8–11:30pm; Nov–Apr Thurs–Tues 12:30–3pm and 8–11:30pm. Closed Aug 6–21 and Dec 24–Jan 2. Metro: Ottaviano–San Pietro. Bus: 19, 23, 32, 49, 271, 492, 590, 982, 990, N29, or N30.

PICNICKING

When it comes time to put together that picnic (and I recommend you do so at least once) to enjoy while you sit by the fountain of a piazza, on your day trip, or just back in your hotel room, you can visit a string of little Roman food shops: a *panifici* or *forno* for breads and pastries; a *fruttivendolo* for fresh fruit and veggies; a *latteria* for cheeses; a *vini olii* or *enoteca* for a bottle of wine; and an *alimentari* for packaged goods, salamis, drinks, and a bit of everything else.

For the absolute best and freshest in raw ingredients, nothing beats hitting an outdoor food market (and don't forget your camera). In the *centro storico,* **Campo de' Fiori** has flower stalls at one end but food throughout the rest; in Trastevere, head to rectangular **Piazza San Cosimato;** north of the Vatican there's an indoor market at **Via Cola di Rienzo 53/Piazza dell'Unità,** but I prefer the nearby **Via Andrea Doria** (between Via Santamaura and Via Tunisi, just past Largo Trionfale); the stalls on **Piazza Testaccio** fuel the kitchens of the neighborhood's working-class trattorie, but the hugest Roman market has plans to move from Piazza Vittorio Emanuele to nearby **Via Giovanni Giolitti** (running along the south edge of Termini). Markets are generally open Monday to Saturday 7am to noon or 1pm.

WORTH A SPLURGE

Checchino dal 1887 ✶✶ ULTRA-ROMAN   The Mariani family started this elegant temple of traditional cuisine six generations ago as a blue-collar wine shop patronized by workers from the slaughterhouse across the street, men who received the undesirable "fifth fourth" of the day's butchering (offal, tails, feet, and so on). Checchino has turned these remains into culinary masterpieces of poor man's food, like *rigatoni con patata* and *bucatini alla gracia.* This is the family that nearly 100 years ago managed to make an oxtail appetizing by inventing *coda alla vaccinara* (it's stewed with tomatoes, celery, white wine, bittersweet chocolate, pine nuts, and raisins). They also offer flawless but less adventurous Roman and Italian dishes like the specialty *abbacchio alla cacciatore* (spring lamb browned in olive oil and flavored with anchovies, vinegar, and pepperoncini). You can sample more than two dozen cheeses, lots of homemade desserts, and glasses of wine from among the 500 labels in Rome's most extensive wine cellar.

Via di Monte Testaccio 30 (at the southerly end of Testaccio). ✆ **06-574-6318.** www.checchino-dal-1887.com. Reservations required at dinner, suggested at lunch. *Primi* 9€–12€ ($10–$14); *secondi* 12€–22€ ($14–$25); set-price menus without wine 31€–60€ ($36–$69). AE, DC, MC, V. Tues–Sat 12:30–3pm and 8pm–midnight. Closed Aug and 1 week at Christmas. Metro: Piramide. Bus: 95, 673, 719, N29, N30, or N91.

L'Eau Vive ✶ *Finds* FRENCH/INTERNATIONAL   This is one of Rome's most elegant dining experiences, worth the splurge for its unique food and atmosphere. Fine French cuisine and a daily exotic dish are prepared and served by a lay sisterhood of missionary Christians from five continents who dress in traditional costumes. Nonsmokers can skip the plain stuccoed vaulting downstairs and climb to the *piano nobile* of this 16th-century palazzo, where the high ceilings are gorgeously frescoed. First courses include the specialty *soupe à l'oignon gratinée* (French onion soup) and scrumptious *chèvre chaus aux aumandes* (toasted goat cheese coated with mustard and almond slivers). Main courses include *langouste thermidor* (lobster thermidor) and *magret de canard à l'orange* (duck filet in Grand Marnier sauce with puff-fried potatoes). Most wines are French, with plenty of half-bottles available. At 10pm, the recorded classical music is interrupted so the sisters can sing the "Ave Maria of Lourdes," and some evenings they interpret a short Bible story in ballet. Only then will they bring your *crêpes flambés* (crepes cooked in Grand Marnier sauce). Tip well—the profits go to charity.

Via Monterone 85 (off Piazza Sant'Eustachio). © **06-6880-1095.** Reservations highly recommended. *Primi* 4€–15€ ($4.60–$17); *secondi* 15€–26€ ($17–$30); fixed-price menus with wine 14€–30€ ($16–$35). MC, V. Mon–Sat 12:30–2:30pm and 7:30–10:30pm. Closed Aug. Tram: 8. Bus: H, 40, 46, 62, 63, 64, 70, 81, 87, 116, 116T, 186, 492, 571, 628, 810, 916, N45, or N98.

Sora Lella ⊛ ROMAN/INVENTIVE ITALIAN This classic is best described as refined rustic, with rough-hewn beams, cozy rooms, elegant service, and a great wine list. Aldo Trabalza and his sons honor the memory of Aldo's mother, Sora Lella Fabbrizi—cook, unlikely star of Italian TV back in the 1960s, and archetypal Roman character—by serving traditional favorites, innovative lighter fare, and half-forgotten dishes with centuries of pedigree. The specialty *primo* is *tonnarelli alla cuccagna* (pasta with sausage, eggs, walnuts, cream, and a dozen other ingredients), but the *bombolotti alla ciafruiona* (pasta with tomatoes, artichokes, peas, and tuna) is also great. For a *secondo,* try the rarely found *abbacchio brodettato* (veal pieces sautéed with eggs, lemon, parmigiano reggiano, and parsley) or the *maialino al forno "antica romana"* (sweet-and-sour suckling pig with prunes, raisins, pinoli, almonds, and baby onions). At these prices, the portions could be larger, but the quality is impeccable.

Via Ponte Quattro Capi 16 (on Tiber Island, at the foot of Ponte Fabricio). © **06-686-1601.** Reservations highly recommended. *Primi* 10€–14€ ($12–$16); *secondi* 13€–21€ ($15–$24). AE, DC, MC, V. Mon–Sat 12:45–2:30pm and 8–11pm. Bus: H, 23, 63, 115, 271, 280, 630, 780, N29, N72, or N96.

4 Seeing the Sights

Visiting Rome is like enduring a sightseeing decathlon—its historic and artistic treasures are scattered across a dozen archaeological sites, two dozen galleries, and literally hundreds of churches. You'll never get it all in, so just pace yourself and toss a few coins in the Trevi Fountain to ensure you'll come back to see the rest.

Note: Some of Rome's most popular monuments, archaeological sites, and museums now stay open to 7, 8, or even 11:30pm during summer and offer "Art and Monuments Under the Stars" at least several nights a week. Some even throw in guided tours or a concert. Check events guides from mid-June to September.

Tips A Note on Museum Hours

Many Rome museums close Sunday afternoon and all day Monday. Also, remember that many smaller museums and almost all churches close from around noon or 1pm to 3 or 4pm for *riposo* (siesta).

THE VATICAN & ST. PETER'S

Basilica di San Pietro (St. Peter's Basilica) ✰✰✰   St. Peter's is one of the holiest basilicas in the Catholic faith, the pulpit for a parish priest we call the pope, one of the grandest creations of Rome's Renaissance and baroque eras, and the largest church in Europe. It's absolutely humongous, longer than two football fields and 44m (145 ft.) high inside, but since every part of it is oversize (even the cherubs would dwarf a full-grown man), it doesn't appear nearly that large—until you look 187m (614 ft.) down to the opposite end and see the specks of people walking about. Mocking bronze plaques set in the nave floor mark how short the world's other great cathedrals come up in comparison.

You approach the church through the embracing arms of Bernini's oval colonnade, which encompasses **Piazza San Pietro** ✰✰. Actually, this "oval" is a perfect ellipse described by the twin arms of 284 Doric columns, arranged in four rows and topped with 96 statues of saints. The ellipse creates a neat special effect. Between either of the two fountains and the Egyptian obelisk in the piazza's center is a marble disk in the ground; stand here to see the rows of the colonnade nearest you line up, appearing to be only one column deep. On the left side of Piazza San Pietro is the **Vatican Tourist Office** (© **06-6988-4466** or 06-6988-4866), open Monday to Saturday 8:30am to 7pm with maps, guides, and reservations for Vatican Gardens tours.

The current basilica, which replaced a crumbling 4th-century version, saw many architects—from Bramante in 1506 through Raphael, Peruzzi, Sangallo the Younger, Michelangelo, and Giacomo della Porta—until Carlo Fontana finished it in 1626. Bernini added a baroque flourish to the interior from 1629 through the 1650s. To the right as you enter is the greatest single sight, Michelangelo's **Pietà** ✰✰✰ (1500). The beauty and unearthly grace of sweet-faced Mary and her dead son, Jesus, led some critics of the day to claim the 25-year-old Florentine sculptor could never have carved such a work himself. An indignant Michelangelo returned to the statue and did something he never did before or after: He signed it, chiseling his name unmistakably right across the Virgin's sash. The *Pietà* has been behind protective glass since the 1970s, when a hammer-wielding lunatic attacked it.

Under the fabulous dome is Bernini's twisted-columned **baldacchino** ✰ (1524), a ridiculously fancy 29m (96-ft.) -high altar canopy constructed with bronze taken from the Pantheon. Against the first right pier supporting the dome is Arnolfo di Cambio's late-13th-century bronze *St. Peter,* a holy good-luck talisman whose foot has been worn to a shiny nub by the caresses of the faithful. Alongside the usual embroidered vestments, gilded chalices, and other bejeweled accouterments of the faith in the **Treasury** (entrance just before the left transept) is the enormous bronze slab tomb of Pope Sixtus IV, cast by early Renaissance master Antonio del Pollaiuolo in 1493 and edged with relief panels personifying the scholarly disciplines.

Recessed into that pier with the statue of St. Peter are the steps down to the **Papal Crypt (Vatican Grottoes)** ✰; sometimes they move the entry to another of the central piers. Along with the tomb chapels of lots of dead popes (plus Queen Christina of Sweden), you get to see 15th-century bronze plaques on the *Lives of Sts. Peter and Paul* by Antonio del Pollaiuolo and remaining bits of Constantine's original basilica. See the crypt last, as they usually route you right from this up to the dome, then out onto the piazza, ending your visit.

Rome

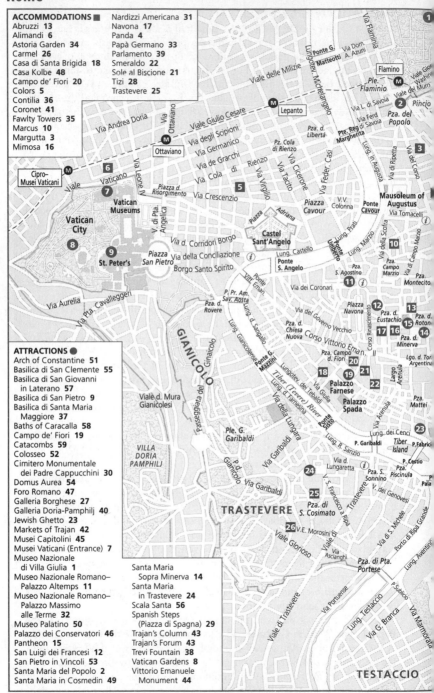

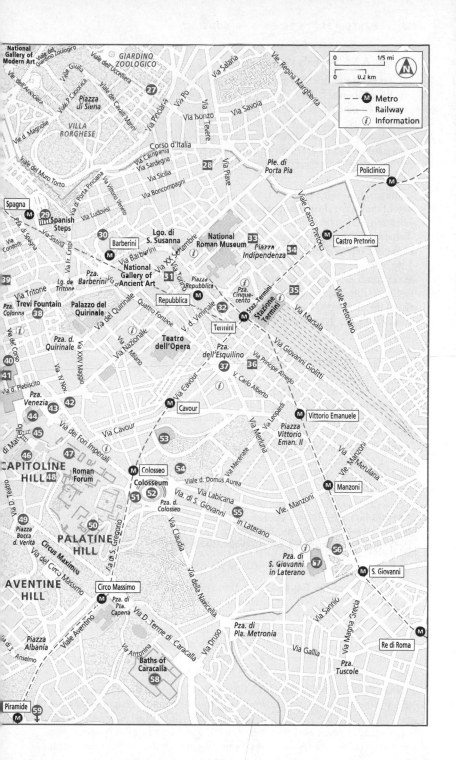

Tips A St. Peter's Warning

St. Peter's has a strict dress code: no shorts, no skirts above the knee, and no bare shoulders. *They will not let you in if you aren't dressed appropriately.* In a pinch, men and women alike can buy a big cheap scarf from a nearby souvenir stand and wrap it around your legs as a long skirt or throw it over your shoulders as a shawl. In summer, some nearby vendors sell paper pants to shorts-wearing tourists (no word on comfort, though).

The last great thing to do at the Vatican is climb (you can ride an elevator for parts of the ascent) **Michelangelo's dome** ⋆⋆, 135m (450 ft.) from the ground at its top and 42m (139 ft.) in diameter—in deference to the Pantheon, Michelangelo made his dome 1.5m (5 ft.) shorter across. Carlo Maderno's dome-top lantern affords you a fantastic and dizzying city panorama.

If the Papal Crypt isn't enough, you can also tour the **subcrypt around St. Peter's tomb** ⋆, with tombs and a necropolis dating from the origins of Christianity. St. Peter was probably martyred in the Circus of Nero, which lies under part of the current St. Peter's, but the actual site of his grave was argued over for centuries. Then 1940s excavations uncovered here what many had thought was just a medieval myth: the Red Wall, behind which St. Peter was fabled to be buried and on which early Christian pilgrims scratched prayers, invocations, thanks, or simply names in Latin. Sure enough, behind this wall they found a small pocket of a tomb in which doctrine now holds the first pope was buried. The only way to visit it is by a 10€ ($12) tour. Apply in advance at the **Ufficio Scavi** (© **06-6988-5318**), through the arch to the left of the stairs up the basilica. Specify your name, the number in your party, your language, and the dates you'd like to visit, and they'll notify you by phone of your admission date and time.

Note: Professors and scholars from Rome's North American College offer free tours of the basilica Monday to Friday at 2:15 and 3pm, Saturday at 10:15am and 2:15pm, and Sunday at 2:30pm. Meet in front of the Vatican info office to the left of St. Peter's main steps.

Piazza San Pietro (there's an information office/bookshop on the south/left side of the basilica steps). © **06-6988-1662** or 06-6988-4466. Free admission to church, sacristy, and crypt; admission to dome 5€ ($6); admission to treasury 4€ ($4.60). Church Apr–Sept daily 7am–7pm; Oct–Mar daily 7am–6pm. Dome Apr–Sept daily 8am–6pm; Oct–Mar daily 8am–5pm. Crypt Apr–Sept daily 7am–6pm; Oct–Mar daily 7am–5pm. Treasury Apr–Sept daily 9am–6:30pm; Oct–Mar daily 9am–5:15pm. Metro: Ottaviano–San Pietro. Tram: 19. Bus: 23, 32, 34, 40, 62, 64, 81, 271, 492, 590, 982, or 990.

Musei Vaticani & Cappella Sistina (Vatican Museums & Sistine Chapel) ⋆⋆⋆

The Vatican harbors one of the world's greatest museum complexes, a series of some 12 collections and apartments whose highlights include Michelangelo's incomparable Sistine Chapel and the Raphael Rooms. It's a good idea to get up extra early and be at the grand new monumental museum entrance (next to the old one) before it opens—30 minutes before in summer—or be prepared to wait behind a dozen busloads of tourists.

PINACOTECA (PICTURE GALLERY) ⋆⋆⋆   One of the top painting galleries in Rome shelters Giotto's *Stefaneschi Triptych* (1320), a Perugino *Madonna and Child with Saints* (1496), Leonardo da Vinci's unfinished *St. Jerome* (1482), Guido Reni's *Crucifixion of St. Peter* (1605), and Caravaggio's *Deposition from the Cross* (1604), alongside works from Simone Martini, Pietro Lorenzetti,

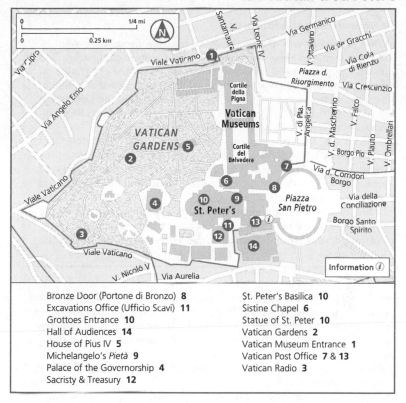

Bronze Door (Portone di Bronzo) **8**
Excavations Office (Ufficio Scavi) **11**
Grottoes Entrance **10**
Hall of Audiences **14**
House of Pius IV **5**
Michelangelo's *Pietà* **9**
Palace of the Governorship **4**
Sacristy & Treasury **12**

St. Peter's Basilica **10**
Sistine Chapel **6**
Statue of St. Peter **10**
Vatican Gardens **2**
Vatican Museum Entrance **1**
Vatican Post Office **7** & **13**
Vatican Radio **3**

Gozzoli, Fra Angelico, Filippo Lippi, Melozzo da Forlí, Pinturicchio, Bellini, Titian, Veronese, and Il Guercino.

But the most famous name here is Raphael, the subject of room VIII, where you'll find his *Coronation of the Virgin* (1503) and *Madonna of Foligno* (1511) surrounded by the Flemish-woven tapestries executed to the master's designs. In the room's center hangs Raphael's greatest masterpiece, the *Transfiguration* ✸✸ (1520). This 4m (14-ft.) -high study in color and light was discovered almost finished in the artist's studio when he died suddenly at 37, and mourners carried it through the streets of Rome during his funeral procession.

STANZE DI RAFFAELLO (RAPHAEL ROOMS) ✸✸✸ Pope Julius II commissioned young Raphael to paint his private chambers in 1508—just a few months after hiring Michelangelo to paint the Sistine Chapel ceiling. As Raphael's fame grew, he turned more of his attention away from this job, and his assistants handled much of the painting in the first and last rooms you visit. But in the Stanza della Segnatura and Stanza d'Eliodoro, the master's brush was busy, and all of these frescoes have been restored. The order in which you visit the rooms is occasionally rearranged.

The first room, the **Stanza dell'Incendio** (1514–17), was painted for Pope Leo X, so the frescoes detail exploits of previous popes named Leo. The best is the Borgo Fire, a conflagration that swept the neighborhood around the Vatican in A.D. 847 and was extinguished only when Pope Leo IV hurled a blessing at it

(Moments Papal Audiences

When schedule allows, the pope holds a public audience every Wednesday at 10am (sometimes as early as 9am in the heat of summer). This means you get to attend a short service performed by the pope, either in the Vatican's large Paolo IV Hall or, when it's really crowded and in summer, out on the piazza itself. You need a ticket for this (see below), but not for the brief Sunday noon blessing the pope tosses out his office window to the people thronging Piazza San Pietro below.

Tickets are free, but you must get them in advance (before Tues would be wise). Monday to Saturday 9am to 1pm, apply in person at the **Prefecture of the Papal Household** (© **06-6988-3114**), located through the bronze door where the curving colonnade to the right of the church begins on Piazza San Pietro. You can also obtain tickets by writing at least 2 weeks before to the Prefettura della Casa Pontifica/Città del Vaticano/00120 ITALIA. Specify your nationality, the number of tickets, and the date you'd like (remember: Wed only). Mid-July to mid-September, his Holiness is at his summer estate, so there are few audiences at the Vatican.

---

from his window. The setting in the fresco, though, is classical, showing Aeneas carrying his jaundiced father, Anchises, and leading his son Ascanius as they escape the fall of Troy. Although Raphael's pupils painted most of this fresco, some experts see the master's hand at work in the surprised woman carrying a jug on her head and possibly in the Aeneas group.

The second room is the best, the **Stanza della Segnatura** 🟊🟊 (1508–11), containing Raphael's famous *School of Athens.* This mythical gathering of philosophers from across the ages is also a catalog of the Renaissance, with many philosophers actually bearing portraits of Raphael's greatest fellow artists, including his mentor, the architect Bramante (on the right as balding Euclid, bent over as he draws on a chalkboard); Leonardo da Vinci (as Plato, the bearded patriarch in the center pointing heavenward); and Raphael himself (looking out from the lower-right corner next to his white-robed buddy Il Sodoma). While painting this masterpiece, Raphael took a sneak peek at what his heretofore rival Michelangelo was painting on the ceiling of the Sistine Chapel down the hall. He was so impressed he returned to the *School of Athens* and added a sulking portrait of Michelangelo (as Heraclitus) sitting on the steps in his stonecutter's boots.

The third room, the **Stanza di Eliodoro** 🟊, was painted from 1510 to 1514. The title fresco, *Heliodorous Expelled from the Temple,* shows the king's lackey trying to carry out orders to steal a Hebrew temple's sacred objects; a heavenly knight appears to help the faithful chase him off while a time-traveling Pope Julius II—a warrior pope whose own battle against enemies of the Church this fresco is metaphorically celebrating—looks on from his litter to the left. At the lower right of *The Miracle of Bolsena* fresco are depicted members of the papal Swiss Guards, a detail that provided some of the historical evidence on which the guards' current retro-Renaissance outfits are based. The fourth room, the **Stanza di Constantino** (1517–24), is the least satisfying and was largely painted after Raphael's death according to his hastily sketched designs, adapted to the prevailing Mannerist style of the day.

APPARTAMENTO DI BORGIA & CAPPELLA DI NICHOLAS V (BORGIA APARTMENT & CHAPEL OF NICHOLAS V) After visiting the Raphael Rooms, you pop out into the Sala dei Chiaroscuro, with a 16th-century wooden ceiling bearing the Medici arms and a little doorway in the corner many people miss. Through this doorway is the Vatican's most gorgeous hidden corner, the closet-size **Chapel of Nicholas V** ✸ (1447–49), colorfully frescoed floor-to-ceiling with early-Renaissance Tuscan genius by that devout little monk of a painter, Fra Angelico. The rooms of the Borgia Apartment downstairs from the Raphael Rooms were occupied by the infamous Spanish Borgia pope, Alexander VI, and are now hung with bland pieces of modern art. But the walls and ceilings retain their rich frescoes, painted by Pinturicchio with wacky early-Renaissance Umbrian fantasy.

CAPPELLA SISTINA (SISTINE CHAPEL) ✸✸✸   The pinnacle of Renaissance painting and the masterpiece of Michelangelo covers the ceiling and altar wall of the Sistine Chapel, the grand hall where the College of Cardinals meets to elect a new pope. Pope Sixtus IV had the Sistine's walls frescoed with scenes from the lives of Moses and Jesus by the greatest early Renaissance masters: Botticelli, Ghirlandaio, Perugino, Pinturicchio, Roselli, and Signorelli. Each of them—fully restored just in time for New Year's 1999—would be a masterpiece in its own right were the group not overshadowed by the famous ceiling.

Pope Julius II had hired Michelangelo to craft a grand tomb for himself, but then pulled the sculptor off the job and asked him instead to decorate the chapel ceiling—which at that time was done in the standard Heavens motif: dark blue with large gold stars. Michelangelo complained that he was a sculptor, not a frescoist, but a papal commission can't be ignored. Luckily for the world, Michelangelo was too much of a perfectionist not to put his all into his work, even at tasks he didn't much care for, and he proposed to Julius that he devise a whole fresco cycle for the ceiling rather than just paint "decorations" as the contract specified. At first Michelangelo worked with assistants, as was the custom, but soon he found he wasn't a good team player and fired them all. And so, grumbling and irritable and working solo, he spent 1508 to 1512 daubing at the ceiling, craning his neck and arching his back, with paint dripping in his eyes and an impatient pope looking over his shoulder.

When the frescoes were unveiled, it was clear they had been worth the wait. Michelangelo had turned the barrel-vaulted ceiling into a veritable blueprint for the further development of Renaissance art, inventing new ways to depict the human body, new designs for arranging scenes and tying a series of them together, and new uses of light, form, and color that would be embraced by generations of painters.

The scenes along the middle of the ceiling are taken from the Book of Genesis and tell the stories of Creation (the 1st six panels) and of Noah (the last three panels, which were actually painted first, with the help of assistants). In thematic order, they are *Separation of Light from Darkness; Creation of the Sun, Moon, and Planets* (scandalous for showing God's behind and the dirty soles of his feet); *Separation of*

⌐Tips A Sistine Chapel Note

To get the best view of the Sistine Chapel's ceiling frescoes, bring along binoculars.

the Waters from the Land; the fingers-almost-touching artistic icon of **Creation of Adam** ⚔️⚔️; *Creation of Eve; Temptation and Expulsion from the Garden* (notice how the idealized Adam and Eve in Paradise become hideous and haggard as they're booted out of Eden); *Sacrifice of Noah; The Flood;* and *Drunkenness of Noah.*

These scenes are bracketed by a painted false architecture to create a sense of deep space (the ceiling is actually nearly flat), festooned with cherubs and *ignudi,* nude male figures reaching and stretching, twisting and turning their bodies to show off their straining muscles and physiques—Michelangelo's favorite theme. Where the slight curve of the ceiling meets the walls, interrupted by pointed lunettes, Michelangelo ringed the ceiling with Old Testament prophets and ancient sibyls (sacred fortune-tellers of the classical age in whose cryptic prophecies medieval and Renaissance theologians liked to believe they found specific foretellings of the coming of Christ). The triangular lunettes contain less impressive frescoes of the ancestors of Christ, and the wider spandrels in each corner depict Old Testament scenes of salvation.

A lengthy and politically charged cleaning from 1980 to 1990 removed centuries of dirt and smoke stains from the frescoes. The techniques used and the amount of grime—and possibly paint—taken off continue to be bones of contention among art historians; some even maintain that later detailing or shading added by Michelangelo were lost during the cleaning.

In 1535, 23 years after he had finished the ceiling, a 60-year-old Michelangelo was called to the Sistine yet again, this time to paint the entire end wall with a **Last Judgment** ⚔️—a masterwork of color, despair, and psychology finished in 1541. The aging master carried on the medieval tradition of representing saints holding the instruments of their martyrdom: St. Catherine carries a section of the spiked wheel with which she was tortured and executed; St. Sebastian clutches some arrows. Look for St. Bartholomew (really a portrait of poet Pietro Aretino) holding his own skin and the knife used to flay it off. Many believe the droopy, almost terminally morose face on the skin is a psychological self-portrait of sorts by Michelangelo, known throughout his life to be a sulky, difficult character (and most likely a severe manic-depressive).

In the lower-right corner is a political practical joke. There's a figure portrayed as Minos, Master of Hell, but it's in reality a portrait of Biagio di Cesena, Master of Ceremonies to the pope and a Vatican bigwig who protested violently against Michelangelo's painting all these shameless nudes (although some of the figures were partially clothed, the majority of the masses were originally naked). As the earlier Tuscan genius Dante had done to his political enemies in his poetic masterpiece *Inferno,* so Michelangelo put Cesena into his own vision of Hell, giving him jackass ears and painting in a serpent eternally biting off his testicles. Furious, Cesena demanded the pope order the artist to paint his face out, to which a bemused Pope Paul III reportedly replied, "I might have released you from Purgatory, but over Hell I have no power."

Twenty-three years and several popes later, the voices of prudery (in the form of Pope Pius IV) got their way and draperies were painted over the objectionable bits of the nudes. These loincloths stayed modestly in place until many were removed during a recent and, yes, controversial cleaning that ended in 1994. Some critics of this restoration claim, among other things, that Michelangelo himself painted some of those cloths after he was done and too many were removed; others wanted all the added draperies stripped from the work. It seems that the compromise, with the majority of figures staying clothed but a few bare bottoms uncovered, pleased nobody.

One thing is for certain: Since the restorations of both the ceiling and the *Last Judgment,* Michelangelo's colors truly pop off the wall in warm yellows, bright oranges, soft flesh tones, and rich greens set against brilliant white or azure. Many still prefer the dramatic, broodingly somber, and muddled tones of the pre-cleaning period. For all the controversy, the revelations provided by the cleanings have forced artists and art historians to reevaluate everything they thought they knew about Michelangelo's color palette, his technique, his painterly skills, and his art.

MUSEO PIO-CLEMENTINO (PIO-CLEMENTINO MUSEUM) ✸✸

This collection of Greek and Roman sculpture is the best of the Vatican's other museums. In the octagonal Belvedere Courtyard you'll find the famed *Laocoön* group, a 1st-century B.C. tangle of a man and his two sons losing a struggle with giant snakes (their fate for warning the Trojans about the Greeks' tricky wooden horse); and the *Apollo Belvedere,* an ancient Roman copy of a 4th-century B.C. Greek original that for centuries continued to define the ideal male body. In the long Room of the Muses is the muscular *Belvedere Torso,* a 1st-century B.C. fragment of a Hercules statue studied by Renaissance artists like Michelangelo to learn how the ancients captured the human physique so well.

OTHER VATICAN COLLECTIONS ✸

The Vatican has many more museums; it would take months to go through them all. Among them are the Museo Gregoriano Egizio (Egyptian Museum) with statues dating back to the 21st century B.C.; the important Museo Gregoriano Etrusco (Etruscan Museum) containing the 4th-century B.C. bronze *Mars of Todi;* and the Museo Pio Cristiano (Pio Christian Museum) of early religious art, including a 3rd-century *Good Shepherd,* the earliest representation of Christ in existence.

You might also want to check out the Collezione d'Arte Religiosa Moderna (Collection of Modern Religious Art), featuring papal robes by Matisse; the outstanding Vatican Library, full of illuminated manuscripts; and the Museo Missionario Ethologico (Ethnological Museum), cataloging 3,000 years of history across all continents. Most of this was missionary booty, although the displays do try to convey the history and meaning behind these non-European religions and the peoples from which they came. The Chinese items are particularly interesting.

GIARDINI VATICANI (VATICAN GARDENS) ✸

The 2-hour foot-and-bus tour of these 16th-century gardens takes you past everything from an 8th-century German graveyard and the 16th-century Mannerist buildings making up the Casina of Pius IV to the Vatican Radio (designed by radio inventor Marconi himself in 1931) and the 1971 Audience Hall courtesy of one of Italy's foremost modern architects, Pier Luigi Nervi. You must book the guided tour—best to book 2 weeks in advance—at the Vatican Tourist Office to the left of St. Peter's entrance (see the St. Peter's entry, above) by calling the number below or by faxing a request to 06-6988-5100. Visits generally run Monday, Tuesday, and Thursday to Saturday at 10am; tickets are 10€ ($12).

Viale Vaticano (on the north side of the Vatican City walls, between where Via Santamaura and the Via Tunisi staircase hit Viale Vaticano; about a 5- to 10-min. walk around the walls from St. Peter's). ☏ 06-6988-4466. www.vatican.va. Admission 12€ ($14) adults, 8€ ($9) students under 26, free to all last Sun of each month (8:45am–1:45pm). Mar–Oct and Dec 20–30 Mon–Fri 8:45am–4:45pm, Sat 8:45am–1:45pm; Nov–Feb Mon–Sat 8:45am–1:45pm. Last admission 75 min. before closing. Closed Jan 1 and 6, Feb 11, Mar 19, Easter Monday, May 1 and 20, June 10 and 29, Aug 14, Nov 1, Dec 8 and 25, and many religious holidays; check website or call ahead. Metro: Cipro–Musei Vaticani. Tram: 19. Bus: no. 49 stops right at the museum entrance; also stopping in the general neighborhood are: 23, 32, 49, 62, 81, 271, 490, 590, 492, 982, or 990.

> ### Value Getting the Best Deal on Sightseeing
>
> - The best value in Rome is undoubtedly wandering the medieval streets of the center, past ancient ruins, Renaissance churches, and baroque palaces. Grab a bus map from a ticket booth outside the train station so you can learn the main routes and use public transport wisely and sparingly.
> - For an inexpensive city overview, the "110 Open" bus—a double-decker with an open top—leaves from Termini at 45-minute intervals daily from 9am to 10:30pm and swings past all Rome's major sights, monuments, and archaeological sites over the next 3 hours. Tickets are 13€ ($15) if purchased from the kiosk opposite the taxi stand on Piazza dei Cinquecento, or 14€ ($16) if purchased onboard.
> - Be aware that the Ancient Rome Cumulative Ticket (see "Rome Deals & Discounts," at the beginning of this chapter) offers free entrance to several of Rome's top archaeological sites and antiquities museums.
> - The Vatican Museums and the Capitoline Museums are free on the last Sunday of each month—but crowds of tourists and local school kids can put a damper on an otherwise brilliant idea. This might save you some cash, but for the real "value," pony up the admission and enjoy these great museums on a relatively calmer weekday morning.
> - Enjoy a free church concert—they're given frequently, especially at holidays.
> - When in Rome, do as the Romans do and set up camp at one of the cafe tables on Piazza Navona or Piazza della Rotonda (Pantheon) for some priceless people-watching, all for the price of a cappuccino or an afternoon Campari.

THE FORUM, THE COLOSSEUM & THE BEST OF ANCIENT ROME

Foro Romano (Roman Forum) ★★★   A gathering of temples and buildings slung between the Palatine and Capitoline hills, the Forum was the cradle of the Roman Republic and epicenter of the ancient world. It takes a healthy imagination to turn dusty chunks of architrave jumbled on the ground, crumbling arches, and a few shakily re-erected columns into the Glory of Ancient Rome, but this archaeological zone is fun to explore nonetheless. You could wander through in an hour or 2, but many people spend 4 or 5 hours and pack a picnic lunch to eat on the Palatine. It gets hot and dusty in August, so visit in the cool morning, wear a brimmed hat, and bring bottled water and sunscreen.

The early Etruscan kings drained this swampy lowland, and under Republican rule it became the heart of the city, a public "forum" of temples, administrative halls, orators' podiums, markets, and law courts. Along with tumbled-down temples and columns set into the bases of medieval churches, you'll see a few bits still in good shape. Turn right at the bottom of the entrance slope to walk west along the old Via Sacra, or "Holy Way" (the Broadway of ancient Rome, down which triumphal military parades and imperial procession marched), toward that arch.

The Forum & Ancient Rome

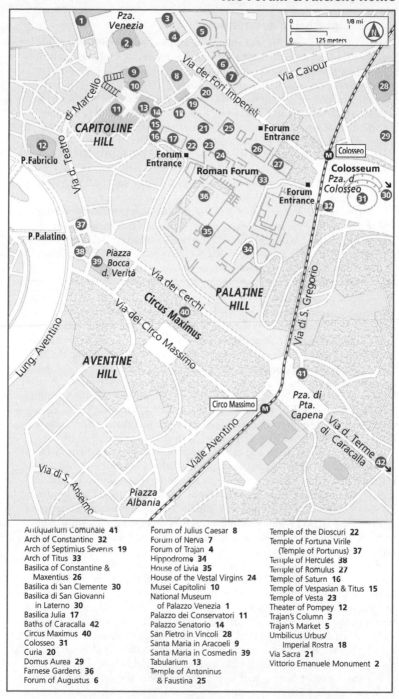

⌒Tips Sightseeing Reservations

Many of Rome's galleries, museums, and sights now offer advance reservations through a single reservations service. **Pierreci** (telephone number varies, see the individual listings throughout the chapter; **www.pierreci.it** for info only, no bookings) charges a 1.50€ ($1.75) fee per ticket, and can be used to make reservations at the following sights: Castel Sant'Angelo, Palazzo Massimo, Palazzo Altemps, Crypta Balbi, Baths of Diocletian, Capitoline Museums, Centrale Montemartini, Domus Aurea, Colosseo, Foro Romano, Palatine and Palatine Museum, Baths of Caracalla, Mausoleo di Cecilia Metella, Villa dei Quintili, Hadrian's Villa at Tivoli, Museo Arceologico, Palestrina.

The reservations office is open Monday to Saturday, 9am to 1:30pm and 2:30 to 5pm.

Reservations aren't necessary at many of Rome's attractions, but during high season or at the more popular sights—such as the Colosseum, or perhaps the Palazzo Massimo (for which you need a timed reservation to visit the frescoes and mosaics)—you might find long lines. At others, however, such as the Domus Aurea, advance reservations are required.

Just before it on your right is the large brick **Curia** ⋐ built by Julius Caesar, the main seat of the Roman Senate (pop inside to see the 3rd-c. marble inlay floor).

The triumphal **Arch of Septimius Severus** ⋐⋐ (A.D. 203) displays time-bitten reliefs of the emperor's victories in what are today Iran and Iraq. During the Middle Ages, Rome became a provincial backwater, and frequent flooding of the nearby river helped rapidly bury most of the Forum. This former center of the Empire became—of all things—a cow pasture. Some bits did still stick out above ground, including the top half of this arch, which was used to shelter a barbershop! It wasn't until the 19th century that people really became interested in excavating these ancient ruins to see what Rome in its glory must once have been like.

Just to the left of the arch, you can make out the remains of a cylindrical lump of rock with some marble steps curving off it. That round stone was the Umbilicus Urbus, considered the center of Rome and of the entire Roman Empire, and the curving steps were of the Imperial Rostra, where great orators and legislators stood to speak and the people gathered to listen. Nearby, the much-photographed trio of fluted columns with Corinthian capitals supporting a bit of architrave form the corner of the Temple of Vespasian and Titus. (Emperors were routinely turned into gods upon dying.)

Head to your left toward the eight Ionic columns marking the front of the Temple of Saturn (rebuilt 42 B.C.), which housed the first treasury of Republican Rome. It was also where they threw one of the Roman year's biggest annual blowout festivals, the December 17 feast of Saturnalia, which, after a bit of tweaking, we now celebrate as Christmas. Now turn left to head back east past the worn steps and stumps of brick pillars outlining the enormous Basilica Julia, built by Julius Caesar. Past it are the three Corinthian columns of the Temple of the Dioscuri, dedicated to the Gemini twins, Castor and Pollux.

Beyond the bit of curving wall that marks the site of the little round Temple of Vesta (rebuilt several times after fires started by the sacred flame housed within), you'll find the partially reconstructed **House of the Vestal Virgins** ⋐ (3rd–4th c. A.D.) against the south side of the grounds. This was home to the consecrated young women who tended the sacred flame in the Temple of Vesta. Vestals were young girls chosen from patrician families to serve a 30-year priesthood. During their tenure, they were among Rome's most venerated citizens, with unique powers like the ability to pardon condemned criminals. The cult was quite serious about the "virgin" part of the job description—if any of Vesta's earthly servants were found to have "misplaced" their virginity, the miscreant Vestal was summarily buried alive. (Her amorous accomplice was merely flogged to death.) The overgrown rectangle of their gardens has lilied goldfish ponds and is lined with heavily worn broken statues of senior Vestals on pedestals (and, at any given time when the guards aren't looking, two to six tourists posing as Vestal Virgins on the empty pedestals).

The path dovetails back to join the Via Sacra at the entrance. Turn right and then left to enter the massive brick remains and coffered ceilings of the 4th-century **Basilica of Constantine and Maxentius** ★. These were Rome's public law courts; their architectural style was adopted by early Christians for their houses of worship (the reason so many ancient churches are called "basilicas").

Return to the path and continue toward the Colosseum, veering right to the second great surviving triumphal arch, the **Arch of Titus** ★★ (A.D. 81), on which one relief depicts the carrying off of treasures from Jerusalem's temple—look close and you'll see a menorah among the booty. The war this arch glorifies ended with the expulsion of Jews from the colonized Judea, signaling the beginning of the Jewish Diaspora throughout Europe. From here you can enter and climb the only part of the Forum archaeological zone that still charges admission, the Palatine Hill (see below).

Via dei Fori Imperiali (across from the end of Via Cavour), or Via delle Foro Romano (just south of the Campidoglio). ✆ 06-699-0110. For reservations ✆ 06-3996-7700 or www.pierreci.it. Free admission (Forum area only; see Palatine Hill listing below). Daily 9am–1 hr. before sunset (generally 7:15pm in summer, 4:30pm in winter). Metro: Colosseo. Bus: 60, 63, 70, 75, 81, 84, 85, 87, 95, 117, 160, 170, 175, 186, 628, 630, 715, 716, 781, 810, or 850.

Palatino (Palatine Hill) & Museo Palatino (Palatine Museum) ★   The

Palatine Hill was where Rome began as a tiny Latin village (supposedly founded by Romulus) in the 8th century B.C. Later it was covered with the patrician and imperial palaces. Today it's an overgrown tree-shaded hilltop of gardens and fragments of ancient villas few visitors bothered to climb even before admission was charged. It can make for a romantic, scenic escape from the crowds, though—a place where you can wander across the grassy floors of ancient palaces and peer down the gated passageways that were once the homes of Rome's rich and famous.

In 1998, the Museo Palatino here finally reopened, displaying a good collection of Roman sculpture from the ongoing digs in the Palatine villas. In summer, they run guided tours in English, Monday to Sunday at noon for 3.10€ ($2.75); call in winter to see if they're still running. If you ask the museum's custodian, he might take you to one of the nearby locked villas and let you in for a peek at surviving frescoes and stuccoes. The entire Palatine is slated for renewed excavations, so be on the lookout for many areas to be roped off at first; but soon, even more than before will open to the public.

From the Palatine's southern flank, you can look out over the long grassy oval that was the Circo Massimo (Circus Maximus), where Ben-Hur types used to race chariots. (It's now used mainly by joggers.)

Main entrance inside the Roman Forum (see listing above); 2nd entrance at Via di San Gregorio 30. ✆ 06-699-0110. For reservations ✆ 06-3996-7700 or www.pierreci.it. Combined admission with Colosseum 8€ ($9), or see "Rome Deals & Discounts" at the start of this chapter. Hours same as Forum (see listing above). Metro: Colosseo. Bus: Same as Forum (see listing above).

Colosseo (Colosseum) ⭐⭐ This wide majestic oval with the broken-tooth profile is the world's most famous sports arena. Started in A.D. 70 on the filled-in site of one of Nero's artificial fish ponds, this grand amphitheater was the "bread and circus" of the Roman Empire, an arena of blood and gore to amuse 50,000 of the masses at a time—the inaugural contest in A.D. 80 lasted 100 days and killed off 5,000 beasts and countless gladiators. If a gladiator was wounded seriously during a match, he'd raise his left arm for mercy. The victor decided his opponent's fate, but when the emperor was around, he made the call, flashing the thumbs-up signal to spare the loser or the thumbs-down signal to finish him off.

Architecturally, the Colosseum is a poster child for classical order: three levels of arcades whose niches were once filled with statues and whose columns became more ornate with each level, following the Greek orders of Doric, Ionic, and Corinthian, respectively. A fourth level, plainer in design, supported an apparatus of pulleys, beams, and canvas that created a retractable roof, winched out by a specially trained troupe of sailors to shade the seats from sun and rain. (Astrodome, eat your heart out!)

The most impressive aspect of the Colosseum is the view of it from afar, where you can admire that unmistakable silhouette, the symbol of Rome itself. The interior is a bit disappointing, although the recent reopening of the upper levels has dramatically improved a visit. The Colosseum fell into disuse as the Empire waned; earthquakes caused considerable damage, and later generations used its stones and marble cladding as a mine of precut building materials. The seats are gone, as is the wooden floor, but one-fifth of it has been restored so you can see how it once appeared. The overall impression, though, is that of a series of nested broken eggshells of crumbling brick, littered with lazing cats and cupping a maze of walls in the center (these walls mark the corridors and holding pens for the animals, equipment, and gladiators).

Standing next to the Colosseum is the Arco di Costantino (Arch of Constantine), one of the largest of Rome's ancient triumphal arches, celebrating Emperor Constantine the Great's A.D. 312 victory over Maxentius at the Milvian Bridge. (Before the battle, Constantine had a vision of the Cross. Because he won by fighting under that symbol, he eventually converted himself, and later the Empire, to Christianity.)

Piazza del Colosseo. ℂ **06-700-4261.** For reservations ℂ 06-3996-7700 or www.pierreci.it. Combined admission with Palatine Hill 8€ ($9), or see "Rome Deals & Discounts" at the start of this chapter. Daily 9am–1 hr. before sunset (generally 7:15pm in summer, 4:30pm in winter). Last admission 1 hr. before closing. Metro: Colosseo. Tram: 3. Bus: 60, 75, 81, 85, 87, 117, 175, 186, 204, 271, 571, 673, 810, or 850.

Domus Aurea (Golden House of Nero) ⭐ Nero's fabulous and fabled Golden House reopened in 1999 after a 15-year restoration. In A.D. 64, Rome was swept by a disastrous fire—although contrary to the gossips of the time, it has never been proved that Nero himself set the fire, much less played his lute while it burned. (Lute? Yes, fiddles weren't invented yet, but the deluded emperor did fancy himself quite the lutist.)

⌒Tips **The Ruins Before & After**

To appreciate the Roman Forum, Colosseum, and other ruins more fully, buy a copy of the small red book *Rome Past and Present* (Vision Publications), sold in bookstores or at stands near the Forum. Its plastic overleafs show you how things looked 2,000 years ago.

The emperor did, however, seize about three-fourths of the burned-out historic core (over 80 hectares/200 acres) to create in just 4 years one of the most sumptuous palaces in history. Subsequent emperors, seeking to distance themselves from their unpopular predecessor, destroyed much of the golden palace by using its vast network of rooms and walls as a foundation for new construction. Trajan installed a baths complex over much of it; Domitian built his own palace atop the Palatine section. Vespasian even filled in the palace's artificial lake to erect his huge Flavian Amphitheater for the people. Some 50 years later, Hadrian raised a temple to Venus and Rome over the palace's vestibule, first removing from it a famed 35m (115-ft.) golden statue of Nero as the Sun King. Hadrian used 24 elephants to drag the statue down to its new home next to the Flavian Amphitheater, and soon that enormous sports complex became nicknamed "The Colosseum" after its gargantuan neighbor. Before long, the fabulous Golden House had become merely underground foundations for the growing city.

Of its original 250 rooms, 30 are now open, decorated with some of the sculptures, mosaics, and frescoes that have survived 2,000 years. Sixteenth-century proto-archaeologists first rediscovered the Golden House—after construction crews in the area started digging up marvelous statues like the Vatican's *Laocoön*—by chopping through the roof and lowering themselves down on ropes. Since the chambers they explored were underground, they called them grottoes, and Renaissance painter Raphael, studying the fanciful and intricate frescoes of curlicues and ivy trails featuring fantastic creatures, christened the decorations "grotesques."

The best bits on view are the Hall of Hector and Andromache, once illustrated with scenes from Homer's *Iliad;* the Hall of Achilles, with a gigantic shell decoration; and the Hall of the Gilded Vault, depicting satyrs raping nymphs, plus Cupid driving a chariot pulled by panthers. The most spectacular sight is the Octagonal Hall, Nero's banquet room, where the menu included casseroles of flamingo tongues and other rare dishes, and the floor is said to have rotated slowly, like a giant lazy Susan, while flower petals rained from the oculus above. When Nero moved in, he shouted, "At last I can start living like a human being!"

Via della Domus Aurea, on the Esquiline Hill. © 06-699-0110. For required advance reservations © 06-3996-7700 or www.pierreci.it. Admission 6.50€ ($7) includes required reservation fee; audio tour 1.55€ ($1.80); guided tour 3.10€ ($2.75). Tues–Sun 9am–7:45pm. Last admission 1 hr. before closing. Metro: Colosseo. Tram: 3. Bus: 60, 75, 81, 85, 87, 117, 175, 186, 204, 271, 571, 673, 810, or 850.

Mercati Traiani (Markets of Trajan) & Foro di Traiano (Trajan's Forum) ⍟

Emperor Trajan built his markets in the 2nd century, but in recent memory they reopened to the public only in 1998. This is the most spectacular section of the Imperial Fori (a series of public forums built by the emperors as the city grew too large for the original Republican-era Roman Forum). You enter a grand bazaar hall lined by former market stalls with marble porticos and barrel-vaulted ceilings. They now contain some sculptural bits and informative placards (in English). You also get to wander the brief but evocative sections of the most intact ancient Roman streets in the city; clamber up to the top terrace for a bird's-eye panorama of the curving market and forums of Trajan and Caesar across the street; and explore the four stories of 150 empty *tabernae* (shops) that made up the world's first multilevel shopping mall.

Don't forget to duck through a tunnel under Via dei Fori Imperiali to Trajan's Forum, sprouting the impressive 29m (98-ft.) **Colonna Traiana (Trajan's Column)** ⍟, today topped by a 16th-century statue of St. Peter. Around the column wraps a 198m (660-ft.) -long cartoon strip of deep relief carvings that use a cast of 2,500 to tell the story of Trajan's victorious A.D. 101 to 106 campaigns to subdue the Dacians (modern-day Romania). It's hard to see the carvings well, but you can get a better glimpse from the street level.

Via IV Novembre 94. (€ **06-679-0048** or 06-6978-0532. www.capitolium.org. Admission 6.20€ ($7). Summer Tues–Sun 9am–6:30pm; winter Mon–Sun 9am–5:30pm. Bus: H, 40, 60, 63, 64, 70, 75, 84, 85, 87, 117, 170, 175, 186, 271, 571, 810, or 850.

Pantheon ✮✮✮   "Simple, erect, severe, austere, sublime." That's Lord Byron groping for the words to capture the magic and power of Rome's best-preserved ancient building, a "pantheon" (temple) to all the gods and an architectural achievement like no other. Emperor Hadrian, an accomplished architect, built it in the early 2nd century, and his engineering skills allowed him to create a mathematically exacting, gravity-defying, and awe-inspiring space.

The bronze entrance doors—1,800-year-old originals—weigh 20 tons each. The interior is circular and the coffered ceiling a perfect half-sphere of a dome with a 16m (18-ft.) oculus (eye) in the center that lets sunlight and rain stream in. The dome is 43m (143 ft.) across and the building 43m (143 ft.) high—in other words, a perfect sphere resting in a cylinder. Such an engineering marvel remained unduplicated until the Renaissance. The roof is made of poured concrete (a Roman invention) composed of light pumice stone, and the weight of it, rather than bearing down, is distributed by brick arches embedded sideways into the fabric of the walls and channeled into a ring of tension around the lip of the oculus. It also helps that the walls are 7.5m (25 ft.) thick.

The decoration is spare but includes the tombs of Italy's short-lived 19th-century monarchical dynasty (three kings total, only two of which are here) and that of the painter Raphael. The Pantheon has survived the ages because it was left alone by the barbarians, who recognized its beauty, and by zealous temple-destroying Christians, who reconsecrated it as a church in 609. Later Christians weren't as charitable. When Pope Urban VIII, a prince of the Barberini family, removed the bronze tiles from the portico and melted them down to make 80 cannons and the baldacchino in St. Peter's, it prompted one local wit to quip, "What even the barbarians wouldn't do, Barberini did."

Piazza della Rotonda. (€ **06-6830-0230**. Free admission. Mon–Sat 8:30am–7:30pm; Sun 9am–6pm. Tram: 8. Bus: 30, 40, 46, 62, 63, 64, 70, 81, 87, 116, 116T, 186, 492, 571, 628, 810, 916, N45, N78, N98, or N99.

MORE TOP MUSEUMS

Galleria Borghese ✮✮✮   Fully reopened in late 1997 after a 14-year restoration, this is one of the world's best small museums, set in a frescoed 1613 villa. The new ticket reservation policy is annoying, but (in summer especially) the museum can be sold out for days, so it's necessary to book well ahead.

Four ground-floor rooms are each devoted to an early masterpiece by the baroque's greatest genius, Gianlorenzo Bernini, including *Aeneas and Anchises* (1613), chipped out at 15 with the help of his father, Pietro; and the *Rape of Persephone* (1621), in which Hades throws back his head in laughter as the grip of his strong hand puckers the fleshy thigh of the young goddess. Also here is *Apollo and Daphne* (1624), in which the 26-year-old sculptor captures the moment the nymph's toes take root and her fingers and hair sprout leaves as her river god father transforms her into a laurel tree to help her escape from a Cupid-struck Apollo hot on her heels.

Bernini's vibrant *David* (1623–24) is a resounding baroque answer to Michelangelo's Renaissance take on the same subject in Florence. The Renaissance *David* is pensive, all about proportion and philosophy. This baroque

---

Tips **A Galleria Borghese Note**

Call ahead at ⓒ **06-328-101** to reserve tickets at least a day beforehand (earlier if possible) to ensure you get the entry time you want. You can arrive without a reservation but it's risky, as limited numbers of entries mean the place is often completely sold out—in summer, sometimes by as much as 2 weeks in advance!

David is a man of action, twisting his body as he's about to let fly the stone from his sling. Bernini modeled the furrowed brow and bitten lip of *David*'s face on his own.

Neoclassical master Canova's sculpted portrait of Napoleon's sister *Pauline Bonaparte* as Venus (1805) reclining on a couch was quite the scandal in its time. When asked whether she wasn't uncomfortable posing half-naked like that, Pauline reportedly responded, "Oh, no—the studio was quite warm." Also on the ground floor is a room with five Caravaggio paintings, including the power-ful *Madonna of the Serpent,* also known as *Madonna dei Palafrenieri* (1605); the *Young Bacchus, Ill* (1653), the earliest surviving Caravaggio and said to be a self-portrait from when the painter had malaria; and the creepy *David with the Head of Goliath* (1610), in which Goliath might be another self-portrait. The second floor contains the rest of the painting collection, starring good works by Andrea del Sarto, Titian, Dürer, Rubens, Antonella Messina, Pinturicchio, and Corregio, plus a masterful 1507 *Deposition* by the young Raphael.

Note: Advance reservations are required. You can visit only during the 2-hour period specified on your regular museum ticket. Audioguides are available for rent for 5€ ($6).

In the northeast corner of Villa Borghese park, off Via Pinciana. ⓒ **06-32-810** or www.ticketeria.it for ticket reservations, 06-841-7645 for main desk. Admission 8.50€ ($10), free for visitors under 18 and over 65. Summer Tues–Sat 9am–10pm, Sun 9am–8pm; winter Tues–Sun 9am–7pm. Metro: Spagna. Bus: M, 52, 53, 63, 86, 88, 92, 95, 116, 116T, 204, 217, 360, 490, 491, 495, 630, or 910.

Galleria Doria-Pamphilj ⭐ The paintings of this collection are displayed more or less as they were in the 19th century—jumbled like a giant jigsaw puzzle on dimly lit walls. Among masterworks by Tintoretto, Correggio, the Carraccis, Bellini, Parmigianino, Jan and Pieter Bruegel the elders, and Rubens, you'll find two stellar paintings by Caravaggio, *Mary Magdalene* and *Rest on the Flight into Egypt,* as well as a copy he made of his *Young St. John the Baptist,* now in the Capitoline Museums. Also here are Titian's *Salome with the Head of St. John the Baptist,* and Bernini's *Bust of Innocent X,* whose sister-in-law started this collection.

Note: The Doria-Pamphilj and Galleria Borghese cooperate to give visitors to both a discount. Show your Borghese ticket at the Doria-Pamphilj within 5 days, and your admission will be reduced to 5.70€ ($7).

Piazza del Collegio Romano 1A (off Via del Corso near Piazza Venezia). ⓒ **06-679-7323.** www.doria pamphilj.it. Advance reservations ⓒ 06-32-810 or www.ticketeria.it. Admission 8€ ($9) adults, 5.70€ ($7) students, seniors over 65, and Villa Borghese ticket holders. Fri–Wed 10am–5pm. Closed Aug 15–31. Bus: 30, 40, 46, 62, 63, 64, 70, 81, 87, 116, 116T, 186, 492, 571, 628, 810, 850, or 916.

Museo Etrusco–Villa Giulia (Etruscan Museum) ⭐ Housed in a 16th-century Mannerist villa, this museum is dedicated to the Etruscans, a Bronze Age people who were Italy's first great culture, controlling what are today the provinces of Tuscany, Umbria, and the north half of Lazio (Rome's province).

The height of their power lasted from the 7th to 5th centuries B.C., when their Tarquin dynasty ruled Rome as her first kings. Etruscan culture is something of a mystery, but they apparently enjoyed a highly developed society as well as equality between the sexes, and appreciated the finer things in life such as banqueting, theater, and art.

The greatest piece here is the touching and remarkably skilled 6th-century B.C. terra-cotta sarcophagus from Cerveteri, whose lid carries full-size likenesses of a husband and wife sitting down to their final, eternal banquet together. Also look for the 4th-century B.C. *Ficoroni Cist,* a bronze marriage coffer richly engraved with tales of the Argonauts, and a large painted terra-cotta statue of Apollo (500 B.C.). The Castellani collection of ancient jewelry spans Minoan civilization through the Hellenistic and Roman eras. But what strikes most visitors are the miles on miles of pots, ranging from pre-Etruscan styles through the Etruscan and Greek eras to the Roman era, many beautifully painted. Seek out the Faliscan Krater, with a scene of Dawn riding her chariot across the sky, and the early 7th-century B.C. Chigi Vase showing hunting scenes and the judgment of Paris.

Piazzale di Villa Giulia 9 (on Viale delle Belle Arti, in the northern reaches of Villa Borghese park). ℂ **06-320-0562.** Reservations ℂ 06-824-529. Admission 4€ ($4.60) adults, 2€ ($2.30) visitors 18–26, free for visitors under 18 and over 65. Tues–Sun 8:30am–7:30pm. Metro: Flaminio. Tram: 2, 3, or 19. Bus: M, 52, 204, or 926.

Museo Nazionale Romano—Terme di Diocleziano (Baths of Diocletian), Aula Ottagona & Santa Maria degli Angeli 🕱

The Baths of Diocletian, built at the turn of the 4th century, have been put to various other uses over the centuries, and today you can visit three main parts. The complex was formerly the sole seat of the National Roman Museum of antiquities, closed for more than a decade until the late 1990s saw the collections split up, with the best pieces going to the nearby Palazzo Massimo alle Terme and the Palazzo Altemps near Piazza Navona (both reviewed separately below). What remains of the Museo in the baths complex itself, reopened in summer 2000, consists of three sections. There's an extensive epigraphy section whose inscriptions aren't particularly interesting (even if exhaustively explained on English placards), although the early Republican terra-cotta statuary is nice. The large exhibit on pre-Latin peoples from the area has informative placards to go along with the usual glass cases filled with Bronze and Iron Age pots and tomb paraphernalia. The huge 79m (264-ft.) -to-a-side Michelangelesque Cloister, supposedly based on a drawing by the master, is lined by headless statues and beat-up sarcophagi. Audioguides are 4€ ($4.60); a guided tour with an archaeologist, offered Saturday and Sunday at noon and 5:30pm, costs 3.50€ ($4).

The museum is mostly installed in modernized rooms of a 16th-century charterhouse. The Great Halls of the baths are open to the public only when filled with temporary exhibits. To catch a glimpse of the ancient structure, duck into the exhibit in the sacristy of **Santa Maria degli Angeli,** a section of the baths converted into a church by Michelangelo. But for the best sense of the baths, drop into the nearby **Aula Ottagona,** a huge and airy brick room unadorned save for a funky modern inner webbing (left from its 1928 gig as a planetarium) and several excellent oversize ancient statues that came from this and other baths complexes around the city.

Various entrances (see additional reviews below). ℂ **06-488-0530.** For reservations ℂ 06-3996-7700, www.pierreci.it, or www.archeorm.arti.beniculturali.it. Admission to museo (entrance at Via E. De Nicola 79, on Piazza dei Cinquecento) 5€ ($6), or see "Rome Deals & Discounts" at the beginning of this chapter; free admission to Aula Ottagona (entrance on Via G. Romita, between Via Cernia and Via Parigi); free admission to Santa Maria degli Angeli (entrance on Piazza della Repubblica). Museo Tues–Sun 9am–7:45pm (last admission 1 hr. before closing). Aula Ottagona Tues–Sat 9am–2pm; Sun 9am–1pm, Santa Maria degli Angeli Mon–Sat 7am–6:30pm; Sun 8am–7:30pm. Metro: Repubblica or Termini. Bus: H, 36, 40, 60, 61, 62, 64, 70, 84, 90, 116, 170, 175, 492, 590, or 910.

Museo Nazionale Romano—Palazzo Altemps 🌟🌟

This is a crown jewel in Rome's touristic renaissance, a prime example of Italy's newfound ability to craft a 21st-century museum that respects both the gorgeous architecture and frescoes of its 16th-century Renaissance space as well as the aesthetic and historic value of the classical sculpture it contains. Rather than stuff statues into every nook and cranny, just a few choice pieces have been placed in each room, allowing you to examine each carefully and read the accompanying placard in English.

Be on the lookout for a 2nd-century A.D. giant *Dionysus with Satyr;* a 1st-century B.C. copy of the (now lost) 5th-century B.C. Athena that once held the place of honor in Athens's Parthenon; a pair of lute-playing Apollos; and a 3rd-century A.D. sarcophagus carved from a single block of marble and depicting in incredible detail the Roman legions fighting off invading Ostrogoth Barbarians. Guided tours (Sat–Sun at 5pm) run 3.50€ ($4). Audioguides are available for rent for 4€ ($4.60).

Piazza Sant'Apollinare 44 (2 blocks north of Piazza Navona). (C) 06-683-3759. For reservations (C) 06-3996-7400, 06-3996-7700, www.pierreci.it, or www.archeorm.arti.beniculturali.it. Admission 5€ ($6) adults, or see "Rome Deals & Discounts" at the beginning of this chapter. Tues–Sun 9am–7:45pm. Last admission 1 hr. before closing. Bus: 30, 70, 81, 87, 116, 116T, 186, 204, 492, or 628.

Museo Nazionale Romano—Palazzo Massimo alle Terme 🌟🌟

Opened in 1998, this museum (paired with the Palazzo Altemps, above) simply blows away anything else you'll find in Rome when it comes to classical statues, frescoes, and mosaics. The 19th century palazzo houses a modernized museum of advanced lighting systems, explanatory placards in English, and a curatorial attention to detail rarely seen on the dusty old Roman museum scene.

Among the imperial portrait busts is a statue of Augustus Caesar wearing his toga pulled over his head like a shawl, a sign he'd assumed the role of a priest (actually, of the head priest, which in Latin is *Pontifex Maximus,* a title the Christian popes would later adopt). Also on the ground floor is a hauntingly beautiful 440 B.C. statue of a wounded Niobid. Among the 2nd-century A.D. masterpieces on the first floor are a discus thrower, a bronze Dionysus fished out of the Tiber, and a well-preserved sarcophagus featuring a tumultuous battle scene between Romans and Germanic barbarians.

On the second floor are Roman frescoes, stuccoes, and mosaics spanning the 1st century B.C. to the 5th century A.D., most never seen by the general public because they were discovered in the 19th century. You can visit only via a 45-minute guided tour at the time specified on your regular museum ticket. The frescoes and stuccoes are mostly countryside scenes, decorative strips, and a few naval battles, all carefully restored and reattached into spaces faithful to the original dimensions of the rooms from which they came. Also up here are halls and rooms lined with incredible mosaic scenes, including the famous *Four Charioteers,* along with rare examples of 4th-century *opus sectile* (marble inlay).

The basement has a section of ancient jewelry and an oversize vault containing Rome's greatest numismatic collection, tracing Italian coinage from ancient Roman Republic monies through the pocket change of Renaissance principalities,

Special & Free Events

At the end of April or the beginning of May, the Spanish Steps are covered with azaleas for the **Festa di Primavera (Feast of Spring)**, while an **International Horse Show** is held in the Villa Borghese's Piazza di Siena. During **Holy Week,** pilgrims flood the city to attend church and glimpse the pope saying Mass at the Colosseum on Good Friday, after which he leads a procession around the ancient amphitheater with pauses for each Station of the Cross. On **Easter Sunday,** the pope speaks a blessing from his balcony in the Vatican overlooking St. Peter's Square.

Rome's **Estate Romana** summer has been drawing concerts, programs, exhibitions, and performers to numerous venues in recent years. Summer is also when the Rome Opera heads outdoors to perform a roster of popular favorites at various evocative venues such as the ancient Baths of Caracalla. The June 23 **Festa di San Giovanni** is celebrated with throngs of people singing and dancing and consuming large amounts of stewed snails and artery-clogging *porchetta* (pork) on Piazza San Giovanni in Laterano. On June 29, the **Festa di Santi Pietro e Paolo** honors the two Big Saints with a street fair on Via Ostiense and Masses at St. Peter's and St. Paul's Outside the Walls.

The Trastevere district celebrates itself during the mid-July **Festa dei Noiantri (Feast of We Others),** immortalized in Fellini's film *Roma.* Rome's most famous old working-class neighborhood sets out long communal tables for a week of feasting with a street fair on Viale Trastevere and outdoor concerts and plays. August 5 is the **Festa della Madonna della Neve** in Santa Maria Maggiore, in which the church's legendary founding is reenacted with a pretty "snowfall" of rose petals over the altar during Mass.

August 15 marks the start of **Ferr'agosto,** when most Romans leave for their 2 weeks at the beach. The city is deserted, public services like buses go on restricted hours, almost every shop not directly catering to tourists shutters up for the duration, and the weather tends to be scorching. Try by any means possible not to be in Rome.

In the first week of September, grape growers from the region come to the Basilica of Maxentius in the Roman Forum to hold a **Sagra dell'Uva (Festival of the Grape),** in the shade of its half-ruined vaults. This harvest festival of half-price grapes is accompanied by costumed musicians and other market stalls.

The pope gives his annual December 25 **Urbi et Orbi** blessing from his Vatican window overlooking St. Peter's, repeating the words in as many languages as the polyglot pontiff can manage. For a more consumerist (but traditional) take on the holiday season, visit the **Christmas fair** on Piazza Navona between mid-December and January 6, where market stalls of handmade crèche figurines and La Befana Christmas Witch dolls still pepper the square between stands hawking mass-market toys.

to the Italian lira, the euro, and a live feed of the Italian stock market. Daily guided tours in English cost 3.10€ ($2.75).

Largo di Villa Peretti 1 (where Piazza dei Cinquecento meets Via Viminale). ℂ 06-4890-3500. Reservations ℂ 06-3996-7700, www.pierreci.it, or www.archeorm.arti.beniculturali.It. Admission 6€ ($7), or see "Rome Deals & Discounts" at the beginning of this chapter. Tues–Sun 9am–7:45pm (might close Sun at 2pm in winter). Metro: Termini or Repubblica. Bus: Any to Termini.

Musei Capitolini (Capitoline Museums) & Capitolino (Capitoline Hill) ★★

The trapezoidal Piazza del Campidoglio at the top of the Capitoline Hill was designed by Michelangelo, who flanked it on three sides by palaces and placed at its center the 2nd-century bronze equestrian statue of Marcus Aurelius, his outstretched hand seeming to bless the city (now replaced by a copy; the original is in the Palazzo Nuovo). The central Palazzo Senatorio houses the mayor's office; the side palaces house two of Rome's top museums, as of 2000 connected by an underground tunnel through the famed Tabularium, the ancient Roman archives under Palazzo Senatorio.

Start with the building on your right, the Palazzo dei Conservatori. The entrance is to the left of a courtyard filled with the oversize marble head, hands, foot, arm, and kneecap of what was once a 12m (40-ft.) statue of Constantine II. The collections have their share of antique statuary—including the 1st-century *Spinario*, a little bronze boy picking a thorn out of his foot, and the Etruscan bronze *She-Wolf*, crafted in the late 6th century B.C. (the suckling toddlers were added in the 16th c.)—but the paintings are the stars. The second-floor gallery houses works by Guercino, Veronese, Titian, Tintoretto, Rubens, Pietro da Cortona, and two by Caravaggio—*the Gypsy Fortune Teller* and the scandalously erotic *St. John the Baptist,* in which the nubile young saint twists to embrace a ram and looks out at us coquettishly. Don't miss the stunning panoramic views from the roof terrace cafe.

Follow that Tabularium tunnel—diverging down the side corridor for a great view across the Roman Forum—to the museum's other half, the Palazzo Nuovo. This section is filled with ancient sculpture like the *Dying Gaul,* busts of ancient philosophers, the *Mosaic of the Doves,* the *Capitoline Venus,* and the original horseback statue of Marcus Aurelius. (The gilded bronze statue had been tossed into the Tiber, and when Christians later fished it out, they mistakenly thought it was Constantine the Great, the first Christian emperor—a misinterpretation that saved it from being hacked to pieces as pagan.)

Note: When a temporary exhibition is on view in Palazzo Caffarelli, the ticket price rises slightly and includes admission to both the show and the museum.

Piazza del Campidoglio 1 (behind Piazza Venezia's Vittorio Emanuele Monument). ℂ 06-6710-2475. For reservations ℂ 06-3996-7700, www.pierreci.it, or www.museicapitolini.org. Admission to museum 6.20€ ($7); admission to exhibition only 4.20€ ($5). Tues–Sun 9am–8pm (in summer may stay open to 9pm; call ahead). Last admission 1 hr. before closing. Metro: Colosseo. Bus: H, 30, 40, 44, 46, 62, 63, 70, 75, 81, 84, 87, 95, 160, 170, 271, 204, 271, 628, 630, 715, 716, 780, 781, 810, or 916.

MORE TOP CHURCHES

Santa Maria in Cosmedin & Bocca della Verità (Mouth of Truth) ★ (Kids

At the western foot of the Palatine Hill sit two small 2nd-century B.C. temples— the square Temple of Portunus and the round Temple of Hercules Victor, the oldest marble structure surviving in Rome—and Santa Maria in Cosmedin, with its early-12th-century bell tower and Cosmatesque floors.

But it's the front porch of this church that draws the crowds (like Audrey Hepburn and Gregory Peck in *Roman Holiday*)—the virtuous eager and prevaricators wary—to stick their hands inside the Mouth of Truth, a 4th-century B.C.

Moments   **A Marvelous View**

Standing on Piazza del Campidoglio, walk around the right side of the Palazzo Senatorio to a terrace overlooking the city's best panorama of the Roman Forum, with the Palatine Hill and the Colosseum as a backdrop (and all floodlit at night).

---

sewer cover carved as a bearded face with a dark slot for a mouth. Medieval legend holds that if you stick your hand in its mouth and tell a lie, it'll clamp down on your fingers. (Apparently, a priest once added some sting to this belief by hiding behind the mouth with a scorpion, dispensing justice as he saw fit.)

Up Via di Teatro Marcello from the piazza out front is the outer wall of what looks like a midget Colosseum with a 16th-century palace grafted atop its curve. This was actually the original model on which the Colosseum was based, **the Teatro di Marcello,** built by Augustus in 11 B.C. and dedicated to his nephew Marcellus.

Piazza Bocca della Verità 18. © **06-678-1419.** Free admission. Church daily 9am–1pm and 3–6pm; portico (containing Mouth of Truth) daily 9am–5pm (in summer, portico gates sometimes open as late as 8pm). Bus: 23, 30, 44, 81, 95, 160, 170, 204, 271, 280, 628, 715, 716, or 781.

San Pietro in Vincoli (St. Peter in Chains) ✦
Besides the chains that supposedly once bound St. Peter in prison (on display under the altar), this 5th-century church is famous for containing one of Michelangelo's masterpieces, which in late 2003 emerged glistening from a multiyear restoration. *The Monument to Pope Julius II,* centered on an imposing statue of Moses, is all that remains of the original grand designs for a project that plagued Michelangelo throughout his life as the pope's whims changed and later his heirs quarreled about the contract. The original plan called for a free-standing tomb adorned with over 40 sculptures—the *Slaves* now in Florence and at the Louvre were originally carved for it—but in the end, all Julius got was this wall monument largely executed by Michelangelo's students.

The muscle-bound Moses was supposed to sit at a corner of the huge tomb, above our heads, and because the master carved it with that perspective in mind, it looks a bit oddly proportioned viewed at ground level. Moses sports satyr's horns—symbolizing the holy rays of light from medieval iconography—and a self-portrait by Michelangelo hides in the flowing beard. Michelangelo might also have wielded the chisel on the more delicate Rachel and Leah figures flanking Moses.

Piazza San Pietro in Vincoli 4 (just off the south side of Via Cavour, sort of hidden up a set of stairs and through a tunnel). © **06-488-2865.** Free admission. Daily 7am–12:30pm and 3:30–6pm. Metro: Cavour. Bus: 75, 84, or 117.

Santa Maria Sopra Minerva ✦
Rome's only Gothic church was built in 1280 over the site of a Temple to Minerva (hence the name "St. Mary over Minerva"). The piazza out front sports a whimsical statute by Bernini (although that attribution has been disputed) of a baby elephant carrying a miniature Egyptian obelisk on its back (1667). The interior was heavily restored in the 19th century, but retains some fine Renaissance art. The last chapel on the right is filled by a sumptuous cycle of frescoes by Filippino Lippi (insert coins to operate the lights). Under the main altar lies the body of the pious medieval activist and

Dominican nun St. Catherine of Siena (1347–80), a skilled theologian/diplomat who was instrumental in returning the papacy from Avignon to Rome.

To the left of the altar steps is Michelangelo's muscular *Risen Christ* (1514–21), leaning nonchalantly on a diminutive cross. (Such a virile and naked Christ wasn't to everyone's taste, and the church later added a sweep of bronze drapery to cover the Lord's loins.) In a corridor to the left of the choir, behind a small fence, is the tomb slab of the early Renaissance master and devout monk Fra Angelico, who died in the attached convent in 1455.

Piazza della Minerva (southeast of the Pantheon). ℂ **06-679-3926.** Free admission. Daily 7am–noon and 4–7pm. Bus: 30, 40, 46, 62, 63, 64, 70, 81, 87, 116, 116T, 186, 492, 571, 628, 810, or 916.

San Luigi dei Francesi ⚛ France's national church in Rome preserves Caravaggio's famous St. Matthew cycle of paintings in the last chapel on the left (insert coins to operate the lights). These huge canvases depict *The Calling of St. Matthew* on the left, the best of the three and amply illustrating Caravaggio's mastery of light and shadow to create mood and drama; *The Martyrdom of St. Matthew* on the right; and *St. Matthew and the Angel* over the altar. Also check out the Domenichino frescoes in the second chapel on the right aisle.

The church of **Sant'Agostino** ⚛ around the corner contains another Caravaggio, an almost Mannerist *Madonna del Loreto*, with dirty-footed pilgrims kneeling before a velvet-robed willowy Virgin carrying a ridiculously oversize Christ child. The third pillar on the right in this church has a Raphael fresco of *Isaiah*. It's open daily 7:45am to noon and 4 to 7:30pm.

Piazza San Luigi dei Francesi 5 (just east of Piazza Navona). ℂ **06-688-271.** Free admission. Fri–Wed 7:30am–12:30pm and 3:30–7pm; also sometimes Thurs mornings. Bus: 30, 70, 81, 87, 116, 116T, 186, 204, 492, or 628.

Santa Maria del Popolo ⚛ The much-restored frescoes in the first right chapel are by the Umbrian early Renaissance master Pinturicchio. For a hidden delight, duck behind the main altar to see the coffered shell-motif apse—one of Bramante's earliest works in Rome. Andrea Sansovino carved the two tombs here in 1505 to 1507, while set higher in the walls are Rome's first stained-glass windows, commissioned in 1509 from French master Guillaume de Marcillat. The vault frescoes are by Pinturicchio. The apse has been filled with scaffolding for the past few years but should reopen by the time you get here.

In the first transept chapel to the left of the altar hang Caravaggio's tensely dramatic *Conversion of St. Paul* and *Crucifixion of St. Peter,* masterpieces of the baroque and among the *chiaroscuro* master's greatest works.

Raphael had barely finished the plans of a memorial chapel for his patron, banking mogul Agostino Chigi, when both died in 1520. Chigi Pope Alexander VII hired other artists to complete the chapel (2nd on the left aisle) to Raphael's designs with a mosaicked minidome. The smoother-bodied statues of Jonah and Elijah were carved by Lorenzetto to match Raphael's sketches, but Bernini stuck to his own active, detailed style to depict Habakkuk with the Angel and Daniel getting his foot licked by a bemused-looking lion. The chapel altarpiece is by Sebastiano del Piombo and the flying skeleton in the floor an addition by Bernini.

Piazza del Popolo 12 (at the Porta del Popolo). ℂ **06-361-0836.** Free admission. Mon–Sat 7am–noon and 4–7pm; Sun 8am–2pm and 4:30–7:30pm. Metro: Flaminio. Tram: 2. Bus: 88, 95, 117, 119, 204, 490, 491, or 495.

Cimitero Monumentale dei Frati Cappuccini (Capuchin Crypt) *(Kids)*
The Capuchins are monks with a creepy but healthy attitude toward their own mortality—and a penchant for making mosaics with the bones of their deceased

brethren. Five chambers in the crypt of this church (entrance halfway up the right exterior stair) were filled between 1528 and 1870 with mosaics made from over 4,000 dearly departed Capuchins. These fantastic displays form morbid patterns and baroque decorative details—from rings of knucklebones and garlands of pelvises to walls made from stacked skulls and scapulae used to create butterflies or hourglasses in an all-too fitting *memento mori* motif.

In Santa Maria Immacolata Concezione church, Via Veneto 27. ℭ **06-487-1185**. www.cappucciniviaveneto.it. Donation of 1€ ($1.15) expected. Fri–Wed 9am–noon and 3–6pm. Metro: Barberini. Bus: 52, 53, 61, 62, 63, 80, 95, 116, 116T, 119, 175, 204, 492, 590, or 630.

Basilica di Santa Maria Maggiore ⨁   Entering this basilica is like stepping back in time, so well is its basic design and decor preserved from the 6th century. It marks the city skyline with Rome's tallest bell tower. The main facade is a baroque mask whose arcades and loggias partially hide the fantastically mosaicked earlier facade from 1294 to 1308 (often you can climb stairs to view these mosaics up close). Some scenes recount the legend that this basilica was founded in the 350s by Pope Liberius, who had a vision of the Madonna telling him to raise a church on the spot and along the outlines that would be marked by a miraculous snowfall the next morning—on August 5. They celebrate the miracle's anniversary every year with a special Mass during which the snowfall is beautifully reenacted using pale rose petals.

The gargantuan interior is some 85m (284 ft.) long, a dark, echoing environment suited to religious pilgrimages. The glowing coffered ceiling is the work of Giuliano da Sangallo, said to be leafed with the very first gold brought back from the Americas by Columbus (a gift from Ferdinand and Isabella to the pope). The floor was inlaid with marble chips in geometric patterns by the Cosmati around 1150, while the mosaics lining the nave and covering the triumphal arch before the altar are glittering testaments to the skills of 5th-century craftsmen (the apse's *Coronation of the Virgin* mosaics were designed by Iacopo Torriti in the 1290s). The most striking later additions are the two magnificent and enormous late Renaissance and baroque chapels flanking the altar to form a transept. (The Sistina Chapel on the left is particularly sumptuous.)

Piazza Santa Maria Maggiore. ℭ **06-483-195** or 06-488-1094. Free admission. Daily 7am–7pm. Tram: 5 or 14. Bus: 16, 70, 71, 75, 84, 105, 204, 360, 590, 649, or 714.

THE CATACOMBS OF THE APPIAN WAY

The Via Appia Antica (Appian Way)—built in 312 B.C.—is now closed to traffic on Sunday, when it fills up with Romans strolling, bicycling, in-line skating, and picnicking.

Mausoleo di Cecilia Metella (Tomb of Cecilia Metella) ⨁⨁   Of the monuments on the Appian Way, the most impressive is the Tomb of Cecilia Metella, within walking distance of the catacombs. The cylindrical tomb honors the wife of one of Julius Caesar's military commanders from the Republican era. Why such an elaborate tomb for such an unimportant person in history? Cecilia Metella happened to be singled out for enduring fame because her tomb has remained and the others have decayed.

Along the Appian Way, patrician Romans built great monuments above the ground and Christians met in the catacombs beneath. You can visit the remains of both. In some dank, dark grottoes (never stray too far from your party or one of the exposed light bulbs), you can still discover the remains of early Christian art. Of those open to the public, the catacombs of St. Callixtus and St. Domitilla are the most rewarding.

Note: Advance reservations are required.

Via Appia Antica 161. © **06-3996-7700** for required reservations. www.plerreci.it. Admission 2€ ($2.30) adults, or see "Rome Deals & Discounts" at the start of this chapter. Admission only with 45-min. guided tours Sun 10am and noon. Bus: 118 from Piramide Metro stop.

Catacombe di San Callisto (Catacombs of St. Callixtus) *(Kids)*

This catacomb has the biggest parking lot and so the largest crowds of tour bus groups—plus the cheesiest, most Disneyesque tour, full of canned commentary and stilted jokes. Some of the tunnels, however, are phenomenal, 21m (70 ft.) high and less than 1.8m (6 ft.) wide, with tomb niches pigeonholed all the way up. These are the largest of all the catacombs—19km (12 miles) of tunnels over 13 hectares (33 acres) and five levels housing the remains of half a million Christians—and were the final resting places of 16 early popes. During the 30- to 40-minute guided tour, you also get to ogle some of the earliest Christian art: frescoes, carvings, and drawings scratched into the rock depicting ancient Christian symbols like the fish, the anchor, and the dove, as well as images relating some of the earliest popular Bible stories.

Via Appia Antica 110–126. © **06-5130-1580** or 06-513-0151. www.catacombe.roma.it. Admission 5€ ($6) adults, 3€ ($3.45) children 6–14. Thurs–Tues 8:30am–noon and 2:30–5pm (to 5:30pm in summer). Closed Feb. Bus: 118 from Piramide Metro stop.

Catacombe di San Domitilla *(Kids)*

This oldest of the catacombs is also the hands-down winner for most enjoyable catacomb experience. The groups are small and most of the guides genuinely entertaining and personable; depending on the mood of the group and your guide, the visit might last 20 minutes or over an hour. You enter through a sunken 4th-century church. There are fewer "sights" than in the other catacombs—although the 2nd-century fresco of the Last Supper is impressive—but some of the guides actually hand you a few bones out of a tomb niche so you can rearticulate an ancient Christian hip. (Incidentally, this is the only catacomb where you'll get to see bones; the rest have emptied their tombs to rebury the remains in ossuaries on the inaccessible lower levels.)

Via delle Sette Chiese 282. © **06-511-0342** or 06-513-3956. www.catacombe.roma.it. Admission 5€ ($6) adults, 3€ ($3.45) children 6–14, free for children under 6. Wed–Mon 8:30am–noon and 2:30–5pm. Closed Jan. Bus: 218 from San Giovanni Metro stop to Largo M. F. Ardeatine, then walk.

PIAZZE, FOUNTAINS & MORE

The most defining aspects of the Roman urban landscape are its *piazze* and bur-bling fountains, fed by a limitless supply of sweet, fresh water—most of it still carried into town from springs in the surrounding hills by 2,000-year-old aqueducts. The city is blessed with hundreds of these open spaces and fanciful baroque waterworks; those described below are but the most famous.

The graceful off-center curves of the **Scalinata di Spagna (Spanish Steps)** ★★★ rising from the hourglass Piazza di Spagna (Metro: Spagna; bus: 116, 116T, 117, 119, 590, or N25) are covered with bright azaleas in spring and teem with visitors, Roman teens, poseurs, and tour groups year-round. The steps were built in the 18th century by the French to lead up to their twin-towered church of Trinità dei Monti. At the foot of the steps lies the beloved Barcaccia ("Ugly Boat") fountain, sculpted by a teenage Bernini and his father, Pietro. Piazza di Spagna has long been the Anglo-American and commercial center of Rome, and flanking the steps are British 19th-century bastions of Babington's Tea Rooms (see "Rome After Dark," later in this chapter) and, at no. 26, the house where Romantic poet John Keats died of tuberculosis at 25. This

Keats-Shelley Memorial House (℡ 06-678-4235; www.keats-shelley-house.org) is now a small museum open Monday to Friday 9am to 1pm and 3 to 6pm, Saturday 11am to 2pm and 3 to 6pm. Admission is 2.60€ ($3). Leading from the bottom of the steps is the überfashionable **Via dei Condotti,** the centerpiece for Rome's toniest fashion boutique shopping scene.

Closed to traffic, studded with fountains, lined with cafes, and filled with tourists, street performers, artists, kids playing soccer, and couples smooching on benches, **Piazza Navona** 🎯🎯🎯 (bus: 30, 40, 46, 62, 63, 64, 70, 80, 81, 87, 116, 116T, 186, 204, 492, 571, 628, 810, 916, N78, or N99) is Rome's archetypal open space. The piazza owes its long, skinny, round-ended shape to the ancient Stadium of Domitian, which lies underneath. (You can see one travertine entrance arch buried under a bank on Piazza di Tor Sanguigna, just outside the piazza.) At Piazza Navona's center soars the **Fontana dei Quattro Fiumi (Fountain of Four Rivers)** 🎯🎯 by Gianlorenzo Bernini (1651), a roiling masterpiece of rearing mer-horses, sea serpents, and muscle-bound figures topped by an obelisk. The giant figures at the four corners represent the world's four great rivers: the Danube (Europe), the bearded Ganges (Asia), the bald Plate (the Americas), and the Nile (Africa, shrouding his head because the source of the Nile was unknown at the time).

Once a meadow *(campo)* filled with flowers *(fiori),* the piazza of **Campo de' Fiori** 🎯 (bus: 30, 40, 46, 62, 64, 70, 81, 87, 116, 116T, 186, 204, 492, 571, 628, 916, N29, N45, or N98) is surrounded by tall medieval buildings in a veritable theater of life. Since 1869, it fills every morning with a colorful collage of sun-beaten canvas awnings shading piles of fruits, vegetables, cheeses, and flowers. The square once did dark duty as an execution site, and the bronze statue of grim Giordano Bruno at the center reminds us that even a great Renaissance philosopher such as he wasn't safe from persecution—he was burned at the stake for heresy on this spot in 1600.

The famous **Fontana di Trevi (Trevi Fountain)** 🎯🎯 (bus: 52, 53, 61, 62, 63, 71, 80, 85, 95, 116, 116T, 119, 160, 175, 204, 492, 590, 628, 630, 850, N25, N45, N60, or N99) is a huge baroque confection of thrashing mer-horses, splashing water, and striding Tritons presided over by a muscular Neptune. It was sculpted in 1762 by Nicolà Salvi to serve as an outlet for the Acqua Vergine aqueduct, built in 19 B.C. and still running (it also supplies the fountains in Piazza Navona and Piazza di Spagna). Tourists and teens throng the cramped little piazza's curving steps from early morning until after midnight. Legend and a host of silly American movies (especially *Three Coins in the Fountain*) hold that if you toss a coin into this fountain, you're guaranteed to return to Rome. Some say you must lob the coin with the right hand backward over the left shoulder. Others insist you must use three coins. Historians point out that the original tradition was to drink the fountain's water, but unless you like chlorine, I'd stick to coins.

The broad lazy **S-**curve of tree-shaded **Via Veneto** (Metro: Barberini; bus: 52, 53, 61, 62, 63, 80, 95, 116, 119, 175, 492, 590, N25, N45, N55, or N60) was laid out in 1866. Lined with extravagant hotels, mansions, and the first grand cafes, it later garnered international fame as the epicenter of the 1950s and 1960s La Dolce Vita ("The Sweet Life"). In this era of "Hollywood on the Tiber," Via Veneto became a hotspot for celebrities, the jet set, and European nobility. This phenomenon—and the street—were immortalized in Fellini's film *La Dolce Vita,* which also introduced a new word into modern vocabulary: *Paparazzo* was the name of the photographer who worked this street getting candid shots of celebrities.

At the base of Via Veneto is **Piazza Barberini,** today a traffic-choked circle of cars around one of Bernini's masterpieces, the travertine **Fontana del Tritone (Triton Fountain)** ☆. This apotheosis of the sea god blowing water through his conch-shell to splash back around his muscular shoulders was built for the princely Barberini family in 1643 and restored in 1998. A few steps up Via Veneto from this piazza sits the small sidewalk **Fontana delle Api (Fountain of the Bees),** crafted by Bernini with a few emblematic bees clinging to a scallop shell. An inscription dedicates the use of the fountain to "the public and their animals."

PARKS & GARDENS

Rome's greatest central green lung is the **Villa Borghese** ☆☆, 90 hectares (226 acres) of gardens, statue- and bust-lined paths, fountains, and artificial lakes; it also contains a biopark zoo, several museums (reviewed above), and the 19th-century Pincio Gardens rising above Piazza del Popolo. You can rent bikes or rent paddle-boats on the small lake with its teensy 19th-century Greek-style temple.

Rising above Trastevere, south of the Vatican, is a long ridge paralleling the Tiber called the **Gianicolo (Janiculum).** Its most attractive feature is simply the sweeping view of Rome across the river, taking in everything from the Pincio Gardens on the left past the domes of the city center beyond the curve of the Colosseum on the right. This panorama is thrilling by day and beautiful by night, when the Gianicolo doubles as Rome's Lover's Lane. Toward its southern end and halfway down the hill (off Via Garibaldi) is the church of San Pietro in Montorio, whose courtyard houses Bramante's *Tempietto,* the epitome of classically inspired Renaissance architecture in miniature. The tiny round Doric temple was built over the spot where, in 1508, it was erroneously believed St. Peter had been crucified.

ORGANIZED TOURS

The tourist office sponsors a variety of **free guided tours** on the weekends (but you might have to pay an admission charge or two if the tour enters museums). Call ② **06-4889-9244** or 06-3600-4399 for more information and the upcoming schedule.

Enjoy Rome, Via Marghera 8a (② **06-445-1843;** www.enjoyrome.com; Metro: Termini; bus: any to Termini), has a young staff from various English-speaking countries who run 3-hour **walking tours** for up to 20 people. Tours of "Ancient Rome" and "Rome at Night" run daily. Tours of the Vatican and the Jewish Ghetto/Trastevere are offered several times a week. They cost 21€ ($24) or 15€ ($17) for those under 26. A more expensive food- and wine-tasting tour—for at least seven people—is 35€ ($40) for those 26 or older and 30€ ($35) for those under 26. Once a week (sometimes twice in summer) they run a walking tour of the catacombs and the Appian Way. They also do 4-hour **bike tours** (bike and helmet included; 10 people) thrice weekly at 20€ ($23) for those under 26, and 25€ ($29) for those 26 and older. Enjoy Rome also does a Pompeii trip (see the end of the chapter).

What kind of **guided bus tour** you get depends on how much you spend. The City-run **"110 Open" bus** (② **06-4695-2252**), a double-decker with an open top, leaves from Termini at 45-minute intervals daily from 9am to 10:30pm for a 3-hour trip past the city's top sights. Tickets are 13€ ($15) if purchased from the kiosk opposite the taxi stand on Piazza dei Cinquecento, or 14€ ($16) if purchased onboard.

Green Line Tours, Via Farini 5A (② **06-482-7017;** www.greenlinetours.com; Metro: Termini; tram: 5 or 14; bus: 16, 70, 71, 75, 105, 204, 360, 590, 649, or

714 to Via Cavour, or any to Termini), gives you an audioguide in the language of your choice for their hop-on/hop-off bus tour costing 18€ ($21) for a 24-hour ticket. They also do eight live-commentary, guided, themed half- and full-day tours from 32€ to 34€ ($36–$39), as does **Vastours,** Via Vittorio Piemonte 32–34 (© **06-481-4309;** www.vastours.it; bus: M, 16, 36, 38, 60, 61, 62, 84, 86, 90, 92, 217, 360, or 492), for 30€ to 42€ ($34–$48).

Ciao Roma (© **06-4897-6161** or 06-4890-7913) runs a hop-on, hop-off trolley tour similar to that of Green Line Tours. For 18€ ($21), or 15€ ($17) after 1pm, you can catch a ride among a dozen of Rome's major attractions.

5 Shopping

You must spend at least 155€ ($178) in a single shop to qualify for a refund on the **value-added tax (VAT),** which on most goods is 19%. Ask the shop for the forms, fill them out, and budget an extra 20 to 30 minutes at the airport of the final European Union country you'll be visiting to process them. Shops that display the TAX-FREE SHOPPING FOR TOURISTS sign will be able to process the forms for you on the spot. See chapter 1, "Enjoying Europe on a Budget," for details on getting the refund.

Rome's best buys are in high fashion, wine, designer housewares, and flea-market bargains. The capital's toniest boutique zone radiates from the Spanish Steps, centered on the matriarch of high fashion streets, **Via dei Condotti.** This zone is bounded by **Via del Corso,** *the* place for Rome's most fashionable see-and-be-seen *passeggiata* (evening stroll).

Via dei Coronari, off the north end of Piazza Navona, has always been the heart of Rome's **antiques district.** Almost every address here is a dealer or restorer, and many of their wares or works-in-progress spill onto the narrow cobbled street. For **art,** the highest concentration of dealers and studios lies along **Via Margutta,** a side street parallel to Via del Babuino.

But while the locals do turn out to *passeggiata* on the Corso and window-shop on Via dei Condotti, the actual shopping in these parts is pretty touristy. To Romans, the city's true shopping nexus is the upper-middle-class residential zone of **Prati,** just northeast of the Vatican, with the economic activity centered on wide **Via Cola di Rienzo.** Here you'll find generally lower prices, more down-to-earth stores, and a much better opportunity to see how the citizens of Rome really live and shop.

A FEW TOP SHOPS

Rome has its share of stock houses selling last year's fashions, irregulars, and overstock at prices of up to 50% to 70% off. The best are **Il Discount dell'Alta Moda,** with branches near the Spanish Steps at Via di Gesù e Maria 16A (© **06-361-3796;** Metro: Spagna; bus: 116, 116T, 117, 119, or 590) and near Stazione Termini at Via Viminale 35 (© **06-482-3917;** Metro: Termini; bus: any to Termini); **Duck Stock** at Via San Marcello 45 (© **06-6692-3620;** Metro: Spagna; bus: 116, 116T, 117, 119, or 590); and tiny **Firmastock,** Via delle Carrozze 18 (© **06-6920-0371;** Metro: Spagna; bus: 116, 116T, 117, 119, or 590). You can avoid all those zeros on the tags at designer footwear boutiques by shopping instead at **Rocco Shoes,** Via Gioberti 22–26 (© **06-446-7299;** Metro: Termini; bus: any to Termini), where you'll find good quality control on minor "Made in Italy" brands. **Il Discount delle Firme,** Via dei Serviti 27, on the teensy road off Largo del Tritone (© **06-482-7790;** Metro: Barberini; bus: 52, 53, 61, 62, 63, 80, 95, 116, 116T, 119, 175, 204, 492, 590, or 630), carries accessories and perfumes from all the top names (and lesser-known Italian designers) at 50% off.

Italians are masters of **industrial design,** making the most utilitarian items into memorable pieces of art like the Pavoni espresso machine or Alessi teapot. The best outlet is the enormous **Spazio Sette,** hidden at Via dei Barberi 7 off Largo di Torre Argentina (© **06-686-9747;** tram: 8; bus: H, 30, 40, 46, 62, 63, 64, 70, 80, 81, 87, 186, 204, 271, 492, 571, 628, 630, 780, 810, or 916). Bargain hunters should head to **Stock Market,** Via dei Banchi Vecchi 51–52 (© **06-686-4238;** bus: 40, 46, 62, 64, 571, or 916), and near Castel Sant'Angelo at Via Tacito 60 (© **06-3600-2343;** bus: 23, 34, 40, 271, 280, or 982), where you'll find mouthwatering prices on last year's models, overstock, and artistic misadventures in design.

For the perfect bottle of **wine,** hit the granddaddy of Rome wine stores, **Trimani,** Via Goito 20 (© **06-446-9661** or toll free in Italy 800-014-625; www.trimani.com; bus: C, H, M, 16, 36, 38, 40, 60, 61, 62, 63, 64, 86, 90, 92, 217, or 360), a family business since 1821 with literally thousands of bottles (and a fantastic, upscale *enoteca* for pricey but excellent lunches). Rome's most peculiar inebriatory experience has to be **Ai Monasteri,** off the east side of Piazza Navona at Corso Rinascimento 72 (© **06-6880-2783;** www.monasteri.it; bus: 30, 70, 81, 87, 116, 116T, 186, 204, 492, or 628). Here are gathered the liqueurs, elixirs, and other alcoholic ingestibles concocted by industrious monks at abbeys and convents across Italy.

The **antiquarian book and print market** on Piazza Borghese (bus: 30, 70, 81, 87, 117, 119, 186, 224, 492, 628, 913, or 926) has good deals on dated art books as well as spiffy Roman prints.

MARKETS

The mother lode of Roman bazaars is **Porta Portese** (tram: 3 or 8; bus: H, 44, 75, or 780), a flea market off Piazza Ippolito Nievo in Trastevere. You'll find everything from antique credenzas to used carburetors, bootleg CDs to birds that squawk "Ciao," all in a carnival atmosphere of haggling and hollering, jostling and junk jockeying, beggars, pickpockets, and shrewd stall owners. It runs every Sunday, dawn to lunchtime. Watch out for those pickpockets.

Snuggled up along a stretch of the Aurelian Wall off Via Sannio are the stalls of the **San Giovanni clothing market** (Metro: San Giovanni; bus: 16, 81, 85, 87, 186, 218, 571, 650, 665, 810, or 850) for inexpensive new and cut-rate used clothing (and cheap army surplus in case you need an extra pack, sleeping bag, or tent). It runs Monday to Friday 10am to 1pm, Saturday 10am to 5pm.

Campo de' Fiori (bus: 40, 46, 62, 64, 116, 116T, 571, or 916), once the site of medieval executions, is today one of Rome's liveliest squares, a cobblestone expanse that starts bustling in the predawn as florists arrange bouquets and produce vendors set up their stalls, and doesn't end till after lunch.

6 Rome After Dark

For all the various events listings magazines and brochures, see "Newspapers & Magazines" in "Fast Facts: Rome," near the beginning of this chapter.

THE PERFORMING ARTS

CLASSICAL MUSIC Always check the events listings for concerts being held in Rome's medieval and baroque churches and, in summer especially, outdoor evening performances in evocative archaeological settings surrounded by ancient columns and ruins.

In 2003, the **Accademia Nazionale di Santa Cecilia** (© **06-808-2058;** www.santacecilia.it), one of Italy's premier musical associations, took up residence in the Auditorium of the stunning Parco della Musica, designed by Renzo Piano in sweeping, bulbous curves, at Viale Pietro de Coubertin 34—just off Corso di Francia behind the Stadio Flaminio on Via Flaminia (© **06-802-411;** www.auditoriumroma.com; bus: M [a special "Musica" bus from Termini runs 5pm until the end of the last show], 53, 217, 231, or 910). Its season runs October to May, with symphonic concerts, chamber music, choral works, and featured soloists from classical violinists to Van Morrison to experimental Japanese drummers.

The **Amici della Musica Sacra** (© **06-6880-5816;** www.amicimusicasacra. com; bus: 62, 63, 81, 85, 95, 116, 116T, 117, 119, 160, 175, 204, 492, 628, 630, 850, N25, N45, N60, or N99) sponsors free choral and other religious music concerts by mostly foreign traveling groups in the theatrical setting of Sant' Ignazio church, between the Corso and the Pantheon. The Teatro dell'Opera (see below) sponsors an October-to-December season of symphonic concerts held in intriguing performance spaces across the city, such as the medieval Santa Maria in Trastevere church or the Teatro Olympico.

OPERA Rome's **Teatro dell'Opera** performs in its newly restored late-19th-century opera house at Piazza B. Gigli 1/Via Torino (© **06-481-7517** or 06-481-601 for information, 06-481-7003 for the box office; www.opera. roma.it; Metro: Repubblica). The season runs January to November, with a special July/August season that changes venues every year—though, after many years of absence, they have once again returned to using the evocative ruins of the Baths of Caracalla as a backdrop to July and August performances.

LIVE-MUSIC CLUBS

Romans go crazy for Latin music (no pun intended), and one of the best clubs is **Caffè Latino,** Via Monte Testaccio 96 (© **06-5728-8556;** Metro: Piramide; bus: 95, 170, 673, 719, 781, N40, N80, or N91). If you have time for only one jazz club, make it **Alexanderplatz,** in Prati at Via Ostia 9 (© **06-3974-2171;** Metro: Cipro–Musei Vaticani, bus: 23, 490, 492, 907, 990, or 991), which has drawn names like Winton Marsalis and Lionel Hampton along with top Italian players. It's usually closed July and August. The Roman home of the blues is in Trastevere at **Big Mamma,** Vicolo San Francesco a Ripa 18 (© **06-581-2551;** tram: 8; bus: H, 23, 115, or 780).

DISCOS & NIGHTCLUBS

Rome's attempt at a major Manhattan- or London-style disco is **Alien,** Via Velletri 13–19 (© **06-841-2212;** www.aliendisco.it; bus: 38, 63, 80, 86, 88, 217, 360, or N60), which opens at 11pm Tuesday through Sunday. More glitzy is perennially packed and popular **Gilda,** Via Mario de Fiori 97 (© **06-678-4838;** www.gildabar.com; bus: 116, 116T, 117, 119, 590, N25, N45, or N60), a disco (opens midnight) with a pizzeria/restaurant (opens 10:30pm) where the beautiful people—and those who want to be near them—congregate in the Spanish Steps area after midnight.

GELATERIE & CAFES

Although Rome isn't quite the ice cream mecca Florence is, its gelato is still heavenly. Any place advertising *produzione propria* (homemade) will have a high-quality, tasty stock, but the parlor in which to enjoy this sweetly sinful snack is the 19th-century **Giolitti,** a few long blocks north of the Pantheon at Via Uffici

---

Tips **See the Cashier First**

At Rome bars, cafes, and *gelaterie*, don't just saunter up to the bar and order two fingers of *vino* or whatever. Go first to the cashier, order what you want, pay for it, and then take the *scontrino* (receipt) to the counter where you can order your cappuccino or your *coppa* (cup) or *cono* (cone) of gelato, putting the receipt down with a .10€ (12¢) piece as a tip.

---

del Vicario 40 (© **06-699-1243;** www.giolitti.it; bus: 116, 116T, N78, or N99). Another Roman institution is **Tre Scalini,** Piazza Navona 28–32 (© **06-6880-1996;** bus: 30, 70, 81, 87, 116, 116T, 186, 204, 492, 628, N78, or N99).

Sant'Eustachio, Piazza Sant'Eustachio 82 (© **06-6880-2048;** www.santeustachioilcaffe.it; bus: 30, 70, 81, 87, 116, 116T, 186, 204, 492, or 628), is a traditional Italian bar serving Rome's best cappuccino since 1938. On Piazza del Popolo, the place to see and be seen—and catch a nightly parade of cruisin' Ferraris and Maseratis—is **Caffè Rosati,** Piazza del Popolo 4–5 (© **06-322-5859;** bus: 117, 119, or 590), which retains its 1922 Art Nouveau decor.

BARS & PUBS

AROUND CAMPO DE' FIORI   On happening Campo de' Fiori, you'll find a full gamut of alcohol-oriented nightspots. The exceedingly popular but rigorously old-fashioned wine bar called simply **Vineria** at no. 15 (© **06-6880-3268;** bus: 40, 46, 62, 64, 116, 116T, 571, 916, N45, or N98) is still holding its own amid the nightly crowds of this newly trendy piazza. A crowded **Taverna del Campo** snack stop with *crostini*, panini, and beer is next door at no. 16 (© **06-687-4402**). The **Drunken Ship** at nos. 20–21 (© **06-6830-0535**) is an American-style bar. Its slightly less obscenely crowded neighbor, **Sloppy Sam's,** is at nos. 9–10 (© **06-6880-2637;** www.sloppysams.com).

NEAR PIAZZA NAVONA & THE PANTHEON   The basement **Black Duke,** Via della Maddalena 29B (© **06-6830-0038;** bus: 30, 40, 62, 64, 70, 81, 87, 116, 116T, 186, 204, 492, 571, 628, 916, N78, or N99), is an Irish pub complete with pub grub. Similar is the **Abbey Theatre Irish Pub,** Via del Governo Vecchio 51–53 (© **06-686-1341;** www.abbey-rome.com). Even more genuine is **St. Andrew's Pub,** Vicolo della Cancelleria 36 (© **06-5820-1405**), so Scottish it's got tartan on the walls. At Corso Vittorio Emanuele II 107 is the ever-popular and crowded **John Bull Pub** (© **06-687-1537**).

The most unique nightspot in the area is **Jonathan's Angels,** Via della Fossa 16 (© **06-689-3426**), a temple to kitsch and one man's artistic vision. The owner was a circus acrobat and restaurateur before opening this funky, dark, casual bar.

NEAR THE SPANISH STEPS & PIAZZA DEL POPOLO   The **Birreria Viennese,** Via della Croce 21 (© **06-679-5569;** Metro: Spagna; bus: 117, 119, or N25), is a Bavarian-tinged *bierhaus*. **L'Enotecantina,** Via della Croce 76b (© **06-679-0896**), is a friendly, relaxed spot, sort of a traditional *enoteca* gone trendy. The **Victoria House Pub,** Via Gesù e Maria 18 (© **06-320-1698**), is a genuine English Victorian-style pub serving good ale and pub grub, with a non-smoking bar at the back and plenty of expat Brits enjoying a pint.

IN TRASTEVERE   **Birreria della Scala,** Piazza della Scala 60 (© **06-580-3763;** tram: 8; bus: H, 23, 115, 271, 280, 780, N30, N72, or N96), is a raucous Italian-style beer hall, with lots of good food, snacks, and desserts. And the **Bar San**

Callisto, Piazza San Callisto 3–4 (© **06-589-5678**), is your run-of-the-mill bar (in the Italian sense of the word), a bit dingier than most, that somehow has become a requisite nightly stop for everyone from trendoids to tourists to Trasteverini.

GAY & LESBIAN CLUBS

The hottest gay club in Rome these days is **L'Alibi,** Via di Monte Testaccio 40–44 (© **06-574-3448;** Metro: Piramide; bus: 23, 60, 95, 271, 280, 716, 719, 769, N29, N30, or N91), with a rotating schedule of DJs and a great summer roof garden. **The Hanger,** Via in Selci 69 (© **06-488-1397;** Metro: Cavour; bus: 75, 84, 204, or N40), is Rome's oldest gay club, frequented by the under-30 crowd and Anglo-American visitors. On men-only Monday they show skin flicks. If you're just looking for a laid-back, low-key gay bar (it welcomes women as well), head to **Garbo,** Vicolo di Santa Margherita 1A (© **06-5832-0782;** tram: 8; bus: H, 23, 115, 271, 280, N30, N72, or N96).

Besides Garbo (see above), lesbians get only a night here or there devoted to women-only at a few clubs across town: **New Joli Coeur,** Via Sirte 5 (© **06-8621-5827;** bus: 38, 80, 86, 88, 93, N6, or N60), on Saturday; and **L'Angelo della Notte,** Via dei Sabelli 101 (© **06-581-6700;** bus: C, 71, 204, 492, or N29), on Friday, with live music.

For more, check out www.gay.it and www.azionegayelesbica.it.

---

7 A Side Trip to Pompeii ⟨ᐟ⟨ᐟ⟨ᐟ

Once a thriving city of 30,000, the Roman colony of **Pompeii** (© **081-861-0744;** www.pompeiisites.org; or for bookings 899-111-178, 081-857-534 outside Italy, or www.arethusa.net) was virtually buried alive in A.D. 79 when nearby Mount Vesuvius erupted, inundating it under 6m (20 ft.) of scalding cinder and volcanic ash (not lava). It was rediscovered in the 16th century, but systematic digs didn't begin until 1860. Today, some two-thirds of the 64-hectare (160-acre) site have been excavated, but work goes on. Much of the remarkable frescoes, mosaics, and statuary you've seen photographed has wound up in Naples's Museo Archeologico Nazionale, but enough has been left *in situ* to make these Europe's most fascinating and best-preserved 2,000-year-old ruins—a veritable ghost town of ancient Rome. Admission is 10€ ($12), and it's open daily: April to October 8:30am to 7:30pm (last entry 6pm), November to March 8:30am to 5pm (last entry 3:30pm).

Daylong trips from Rome to Pompeii (242km/150 miles southeast) are doable, but you've got to catch the 2-hour express train to Naples and then connect to the local Circumvesuviana train (© **081-772-2444;** www.vesuviana.it) to Pompeii—a 4-hour adventure if all goes smoothly. It might be worth the slightly greater expense to take **Enjoy Rome**'s **Pompeii Shuttle** (© **06-445-1843;** www.enjoyrome.com) at 55€ ($63) adults, 45€ ($52) for those under 26, leaving Tuesday and Friday and only if at least 10 people show up; it deposits you at Pompeii's gate and takes you back to Rome after a good day's sightseeing (this is a transportation service; neither site admission nor a tour are included). Or take an organized bus tour: **Vastours** (© **06-481-4309;** www.vastours.it) charges 100€ ($115) for a full-day Pompeii excursion. They will pick you up for free at your hotel around 6:45am (or show up at their Rome terminal at Via Piemonte 32–34 before 7:30am), and will force you to poke around a coral cameo factory outside Naples before lunch (included). You then spend the afternoon at the archaeological site before heading back to Rome via Sorrento and another shopping stop at a wood factory; you get back around 9pm.

22

Salzburg & Innsbruck

by Beth Reiber

Salzburg, surrounded by magnificent Alpine scenery, boasts one of the world's most striking cityscapes—a medieval fortress perched above a perfectly preserved baroque inner city filled with architectural wonders. Like most European cities, it's divided by a river—in this case, the Salzach. The names of the town and river derive from the region's salt mines, which brought Salzburg fame and fortune and are now popular attractions. With only 150,000 inhabitants, Salzburg is also one of Europe's leading cultural centers, especially for classical music. Mozart was born here, and Salzburg boasts one of the grandest music festivals in the world. A short journey by train or car from Munich, it's a very convenient and worthwhile stop for anyone traveling between Germany and Italy or to Vienna. Another must-see is nearby **Innsbruck,** a picturesque village nestled in the Austrian Alps.

For more on Salzburg and its environs, see *Frommer's Austria* or *Frommer's Munich & the Bavarian Alps.*

1 Essentials

ARRIVING

BY PLANE The **Salzburg Airport W. A. Mozart,** Innsbrucker Bundesstrasse 95 (© **0662/85 80-0**), 1.5km (1 mile) southwest of the city, is larger than Innsbruck's airport and much smaller than Munich's. **Bus** no. 2 takes you to Salzburg's main train station for 1.70€ ($1.95); **taxis** charge about 13€ to 15eu] ($15–$17) for the same trip.

BY TRAIN Salzburg is about 1½ to 2 hours from Munich by train and about 3 hours from Vienna. Trains arrive at the **Hauptbahnhof** (main train station), on the right bank of the city center at Südtirolerplatz (© **0662/05 17 17**). Buses depart from Südtirolerplatz to various parts of the city, including the Old City (Altstadt) across the river. It's about a 20-minute walk from the Hauptbahnhof to the heart of the Altstadt.

BY CAR If you come by car, ask at your hotel where the nearest garage is. Street parking (metered) is not only costly but also practically impossible to find, especially in the Altstadt, with its narrow streets and pedestrians-only zones. Note that if you're staying at one of the hotels in the inner city's several pedestrian zones, you can still drive to your hotel for check-in. In the Altstadt, you're required to stop at a ticket booth to get permission to drive to your hotel. In any case, once there, ask the hotel where you should park. You can reach most of Salzburg's sights on foot.

VISITOR INFORMATION

TOURIST OFFICES At the small **tourist kiosk** on Platform 2a of the Hauptbahnhof, Südtirolerplatz (© **0662/889 87-340**), you can buy a city map for .70€ (80¢) or make hotel reservations by paying a deposit of 12% of your first night's payment. In addition, there's a service charge of 2.20€ ($2.55) for two people or 4.40€ ($5.05) for three or more. The office is open daily 9am to 8pm in summer and 9am to 7pm in winter.

A larger **City Tourist Office (Tourismus Salzburg)** is in the heart of the Old City at Mozartplatz 5 (© **0662/889 87-330**). May to September, it's open daily 9am to 7pm; October to April, hours are Monday to Saturday 9am to 6pm. The office also books hotel rooms, sells city maps, stocks brochures, and sells sightseeing, concert, and theater tickets. Be sure to pick up a free copy of *Veranstaltungen,* a monthly brochure listing the concerts in Salzburg's many music halls.

WEBSITES   Further information is available on the Internet at **www. austria-tourism.at/us**, the official site of the Austria National Tourist Office, and at **www.salzburg.info**.

CITY LAYOUT

Most attractions are on the left bank of the **Salzach River,** in the **Altstadt (Old City).** Much of the Altstadt is now a pedestrian zone, including picturesque Getreidegasse with its many shops, Domplatz, and Mozartplatz. The Altstadt is where you'll find such attractions as Mozart's Geburtshaus (Mozart's Birthplace), the Festival House complex, the cathedral, the Catacombs of St. Peter, the Haus der Natur (Museum of Natural History), and Salzburg's landmark, the **Hohensalzburg.** In fact, it's this fortress, towering above the Altstadt on a sheer cliff, that makes Salzburg so beautiful, even from afar. It's lit up at night, making a walk along the Salzach one of the most romantic in Austria.

The **Hauptbahnhof** is on the opposite side of the Salzach, about a 20-minute walk from the Altstadt. This part of the city is newer and contains the Mirabellgarten and a number of nearby hotels and shops, just a short walk across the river from the Altstadt.

Value Budget Bests

Practically everywhere in Salzburg, you'll find open-air food and drink stalls called *Imbisse* or *Würstelbude.* They sell sausages, french fries, soft drinks, and canned beer for much less than restaurants charge. You'll find a convenient *Imbiss* in the center of the Altstadt (Old City) at Alter Markt, selling *Würste* (sausages), fries, and drinks. It's open Friday 5pm to midnight and Saturday, Sunday, and holidays 11am to midnight. On the other side of the Salzach River, at Linzer Gasse and Reitsamer Platz, is another *Imbiss* (with outdoor seating in summer), selling *Würste, Wiener schnitzel,* grilled chicken, *Leberkäse, Gulasch* soup, and drinks. It's open Monday to Friday 9am to midnight, and Saturday, Sunday, and holidays 10am to midnight.

Be sure to visit the **City Tourist Office,** Mozartplatz 5 (© **0662/889 87-330**; bus: 5, 6, 49, 55, or 95 to Mozartsteg), for up-to-date info on such free events as concerts that might take place during your stay. During summer, for example, free brass-band concerts are held in the Mirabellgarten on Wednesday at 8:30pm and Sunday at 10:30am. Free concerts are also given throughout the school year by students at Mozarteum (University of Music and Dramatic Art).

Salzburg Deals & Discounts

SPECIAL DISCOUNTS Discounts on **museum admissions** and reduced **cable car fares** are granted to students and children under 16, provided you can show proof of age (a passport) or an International Student ID Card. These reductions vary from 20% to 50%. Anyone 26 and under can buy heavily reduced **rail and flight tickets** by contacting **STA Travel**, Fanny-v.-Lehnertstrasse 1 (© **0662/45 87 330**; a 3-min. walk from the Hauptbahnhof), open Monday to Friday 9am to 5:30pm.

If you're staying on the outskirts of Salzburg and plan to visit most of the city's attractions, invest in the **Salzburg Card**, which allows unlimited use of the city's public transportation system and includes admission to most of the city's attractions, such as Mozart's Birthplace and Residence, the Hohensalzburg Fortress, the state rooms at the Residenz, Hellbrunn Palace, Haus der Natur, and the Toy Museum. The card, sold at any tourist office and most hotels, is available for 24 hours at 19€ ($22), 48 hours at 26€ ($30), and 72 hours at 32€ ($37), except from mid-June to mid-September, when 2€ ($2.30) are added to the prices above. Children pay half fare.

WORTH A SPLURGE Salzburg is famous for its **music,** presented throughout the year in a number of festivals and concerts, particularly the Salzburg Festival. Tickets aren't always inexpensive and aren't even always available unless you order months in advance. But they're worth the effort and the money, considering that you're in one of the music capitals of the world. For more information, see "Special & Free Events" and "Salzburg After Dark," later in this chapter.

GETTING AROUND

Walking around Salzburg, especially in the Altstadt with its many pedestrian zones, is a pleasure. In fact, because Salzburg is rather compact, you can walk to most of its major attractions. One of the best walks is along the top of Mönchsberg from the Mönchsberg Lift to the fortress, about a 30-minute stroll through woods and past medieval villas, with panoramic views.

BY PUBLIC TRANSPORTATION A quick, comfortable public transport system is provided by 19 **bus lines,** charging 1.70€ ($1.95) per ticket for a single journey, including transfers to your final destination. Children under 16 travel for .90€ ($1.05); children under 6 travel free. If you think you'll be traveling a lot by bus, consider buying a 4€ ($4.60) **24 Stundenkarte,** valid for 24 hours of unlimited travel. If you purchase tickets in advance (not from the bus driver but from tobacco shops or vending machines at the train station), prices are slightly cheaper: 1.40€ ($1.60) for a single journey and 3.20€ ($3.70) for the 24-hour ticket. For more info about the public transportation system, call © **0662/4480-6263.**

Another option is the **Salzburg Card,** which serves as a ticket for unlimited use of the public transport facilities and includes admission to most of the city's attractions (see "Salzburg Deals & Discounts," above).

Country & City Codes

The **country code** for Austria is **43**. The **city code** for Salzburg is **662**; use this code when you're calling from outside Austria. If you're within Austria but not in Salzburg, use **0662**. If you're calling within Salzburg, simply leave off the code and dial only the regular phone number. And if you come across a number with a dash, as in 6580-0, the number after the dash is the extension. Simply dial the entire number.

For information on local telephone numbers in Salzburg, dial ℂ **118877**.

BY TAXI　The average taxi fare from the train station to a hotel or private home within the city limits is 8€ to 14€ ($9.20–$16) and 13€ to 15€ ($15–$17) to the airport. Fares start at 3€ ($3.45); 10pm to 6am and all day Sundays and holidays, fares start at 3.70€ ($4.25). In and around the Altstadt are convenient taxi stands at Hanuschplatz, Residenzplatz, Max-Reinhart-Platz, and the Mönchsberg Lift; on the opposite side of the river are stands at the train station, Makartplatz, and Auerspergstrasse. To phone for a taxi, call ℂ **8111** or 1715.

BY BICYCLE　Biking is becoming more and more popular, as is evident from the more than 160km (99 miles) of bike paths through the city. If you feel like a long ride, try the bike path beside the Salzach River going all the way to Hallein, 15km (9 miles) away. Easter through September, **Top-Bike** (ℂ **6272/ 4656**; www.topbike.at) rents standard, mountain, and city bikes daily from the Hauptbahnhof or the Staatsbrücke bridge at Franz-Josef-Kai, beginning at 13€ ($15) for the whole day.

BY RENTAL CAR　Driving a rental car is much less expensive if you arrange a rental before arriving in Europe rather than if you wait until you arrive in Salzburg to rent one. If you need a car in Salzburg, go to **Hertz,** Ferdinand-Porsche-Strasse 7 (ℂ **0662/87 66 74**), across from the train station, or to its airport office (ℂ **0662/85 20 86**). The downtown office is open Monday to Friday 8am to 6pm and Saturday 8am to 1pm. Also nearby is **Avis,** Ferdinand-Porsche-Strasse 7 (ℂ **0662/87 72 78**), open Monday to Friday 7:30am to 6pm and Saturday 8am to noon; it also has an airport office (ℂ **0662/87 72 78**). Charges for a 1-day rental of a compact car, with unlimited mileage, tax, and insurance, are about 106€ to 118€ ($122–$136). There are always special weekend prices and other promotions, so it pays to shop around.

FAST FACTS: Salzburg

American Express　The office is on Mozartplatz (ℂ **0662/80 80**; bus: 3, 5, 6, 7, 8, 25, or 26 to Mozartsteg), next to the tourist office, open Monday to Friday 9am to 5:30pm. There's no commission charge here to cash American Express traveler's checks.

Babysitters　Students at Salzburg's university earn extra money by babysitting; call ℂ **0662/8044-6000** Monday to Thursday 9am to noon and Friday 9am to 1pm. Or call **ÖVP-Frauen** at ℂ **0662/8698-61**.

Banks　Banks are generally open Monday to Friday 8:30am to 12:30pm and 2 to 4:30pm. If you need to exchange money outside these hours, try the

Wechselstube (Exchange Office) at the Hauptbahnhof (© **0662/87 13 77**), open Monday to Friday 8:30am to 7pm and Saturday 8:30am to 2:30pm. You can get cash from Diners Club, MasterCard, and Visa here, but there's also an ATM on platform 2a (beside the tourist office) where you can get cash from American Express, Diners Club, MasterCard, and Visa 24 hours a day. In the Altstadt, you can exchange money and cash American Express traveler's checks after banking hours at the **Hotel Weisse Taube,** across the square from American Express at Kaigasse 9, open Monday to Friday 7am to 8pm, Saturday noon to 8pm, and Sunday 9am to 8pm.

Business Hours Shops are usually open Monday to Saturday 9am to 6pm. Some shops may close an hour or 2 at noon or Saturday afternoon.

Consulates The consulate general of the **United States** is at Alter Markt 1, 3rd Floor (© **0662/84 87 76;** bus: 3, 5, 6, 7, 8, 25, or 26 to Rathaus), open Monday, Wednesday, and Thursday 9am to noon. The consulate of the **United Kingdom** is at Alter Markt 4 (© **0662/84 81 33**), open Monday to Friday 9:30am to noon. Citizens of **Australia** and **Canada** should contact their respective embassies in Vienna (see "Fast Facts: Vienna," in chapter 26).

Currency In 2002, Austria adopted the **euro** (€) for its currency. At press time, $1 = .87€, or 1€ = $1.15.

Dentists & Doctors If you need a doctor or dentist, head to one of Salzburg's hospitals; the largest is **St.-Johannsspital-Landeskrankenanstalten Salzburg,** Müllner Hauptstrasse 48 (© **0662/4482-0**). Or ask your hotel concierge for the address of the hospital closest to you or inquire at your consulate. If you need an English-speaking doctor on the weekend (7pm Fri to 7am Mon) or on a public holiday, call © **141.**

Emergencies For the **police,** phone © **133;** to report a **fire,** phone © **122;** for an **ambulance,** phone © **144.** For urgent medical assistance on the weekend (7pm Fri to 7am Mon) or a public holiday, or for an English-speaking doctor, contact the **Ärzte-Bereitschaftsdienst,** Dr.-Karl-Renner-Strasse 7 (© **141**).

Holidays Holidays celebrated in Salzburg are New Year's Day (Jan 1), Epiphany (Jan 6), Good Friday (for Protestants), Easter Monday, Labor Day (May 1), Ascension Day, Whitmonday, Corpus Christi, Feast of the Assumption (Aug 15), Austria National Day (Oct 26), All Saint's Day (Nov 1), Feast of the Immaculate Conception (Dec 8), and Christmas (Dec 25–26).

Hospitals Hospitals in Salzburg include St.-Johannsspital-Landeskranke-nanstalten Salzburg, Müllner Hauptstrasse 48 (© **0662/4482-0**), and Unfall-krankenhaus (Accident Hospital), Dr.-Franz-Rehrl-Platz 5 (© **0662/6580-0**).

Internet Access In the Altstadt, the **BIGnet.café** is at Judengasse 5, between Mozartplatz and Rathausplatz (© **0662/84 14 70;** bus: 3, 5, 6, 7, 8, 25, or 26 to Rathaus), open daily 9am to 10pm. It charges 1.50€ ($1.75) for 10 minutes or 3€ ($3.45) for an hour. Near the Hauptbahnhof is **Internetcafe.piterfun,** behind Hotel Europa at Ferdinand-Porsche-Strasse 7 (© **0662/87 84 14;** bus: 1, 2, 3, 5, 6, 23, or 25, to Hauptbahnhof), open daily 11am to 11pm and charging 2€ ($2.30) for 15 minutes and 5€ ($5.75) for an hour.

Laundry There's a self-service laundry east of Mirabellgarten on the right side of the Salzach: **Norge Exquisit,** Paris-Lodron-Strasse 16 (© **0662/87 63**

81; bus: 3, 5, 6, or 25 to Mirabellplatz), open Monday to Friday 7:30am to 6pm and Saturday 8am to noon. It charges 10€ ($12) for 6 kilograms (13 lb.) of clothing washed and dried, including detergent.

Mail The **main post office (Hauptpostamt)** is in the center of the Altstadt at Residenzplatz 9, 5010 Salzburg (© **0662/84 41 21-0;** bus: 3, 5, 6, 7, 8, 25, or 26 to Mozartsteg). It's open Monday to Friday 7am to 7pm and Saturday 8 to 10am. Have your mail sent here *Poste Restante.* There's a **branch post office** beside the train station on Südtirolerplatz (© **0662/88 30 30),** open Monday to Friday 7am to 8:30pm, Saturday 8am to 2pm, and Sunday 1 to 6pm. Postcards to North America cost 1.25€ ($1.45), as do airmail letters weighing up to 20 grams.

Pharmacies A wonderful pharmacy is the 400-year-old **Alte Hofapotheke,** Alter Markt 6 (© **0662/84 36 23;** bus: 3, 5, 6, 7, 8, 25, or 26 to Rathaus), a few blocks from the Mozart house. It's open Monday to Friday 8am to 6pm and Saturday 8am to noon. The names and addresses of pharmacies open on Saturday afternoon, Sunday, and holidays are posted in every pharmacy window.

Tax Government tax and service charge are included in restaurant and hotel bills. If you've purchased goods for more than 75€ ($86) from any one store on a given day, you're entitled to a partial refund of the **value-added tax (VAT)**—see chapter 1, "Enjoying Europe on a Budget."

Telephone Telephone booths are painted either silver with a yellow top or green with a red top and are found on major roads and squares. For **local calls,** you must insert a minimum of .20€ (20¢); .10€, .20€, .50€, 1€, and 2€ coins are accepted. A 1-minute local call costs .12€ (10¢).

Because hotels add a surcharge to calls made from guest rooms, it's a good idea to make your **international calls** from an international pay phone. It costs .38€ (45¢) per minute to call the United States from a post office phone booth. If you're going to make a lot of local calls or want to make international calls from a pay phone, purchase a **telephone card** at any post office, available in values of 3.60€ ($4.15) and 6.90€ ($7.95); then insert the card into the slots of special phones found virtually everywhere.

Alternatively, private companies offer cheaper phone service. One such company is **International Telefon Discount,** a minute's walk from the train station at Kaiserschützenstrasse 8 (© **0662/88 31 94).** Open daily 9am to 11pm, it charges .22€ (25¢) per minute for a call to the United States. It also sells telephone cards for 6€ and 10€ ($6.90 and $12), in which case it costs just .04€ (5¢) per minute for a call to the U.S. You can also make calls from booths at **BIGnet.café** for .21€ (24¢) per minute to the U.S. (see "Internet Access," above).

Tipping A service charge is included in hotel and restaurant bills and taxi fares. It's customary, however, to round up to the nearest 1€ for meals costing less than 10€ ($12); for meals costing more than 10€, add a 10% tip. Likewise, if you're satisfied with the service, tip up to 10% of the bill for taxis and in salons.

2 Affordable Places to Stay

Most of Salzburg's budget accommodations are on the outskirts of town and in neighboring villages, easily reached by bus in less than 30 minutes. The cheapest rooms are often those rented out in private homes; in most cases, you have to share a bathroom down the hall but have a sink in your room. A bit more expensive are bathless doubles in a small pension (often called a *Gasthof* or *Gästehaus*). Not surprisingly, prices are usually higher in more centrally located places. In addition, many of the higher-priced accommodations charge even more during peak season, including Easter, the end of May, July to September, December to New Year's, and during city festivals (see "Special & Free Events," later in this chapter). In January, when tourism is at its lowest, some hotels close completely.

If the places recommended below are full, try the **Salzburg Tourist Offices** at the train station or on Mozartplatz, which will book you a room for a 2.20€ ($2.55) fee if there are two of you, or 4.40€ ($5.05) for three or more, plus a deposit toward your first night's payment. In addition, **Bob's Special Tours** (© **0662/84 95 11;** www.bobstours.com), will book inexpensive accommodations, including rooms in private homes, for no charge.

Note: You'll find the lodging choices below plotted on the map on p. 865.

PRIVATE HOMES

These accommodations are in private homes, which sometimes offer less privacy but are good opportunities for getting to know the Austrians. Note, however, that they all prefer guests who stay longer than 1 night and that you should call in advance to make sure they have an empty room.

⟨Value⟩ Getting the Best Deal on Accommodations

- Book directly with the hotel to avoid the extra charge collected by the tourist office for booking rooms.
- Ask about the winter discounts offered by medium- and upper-range hotels.
- Be aware that some people who rent rooms in private homes will pick you up at the train station, saving you the cost of a taxi or bus ride.
- Note that lower prices are charged for accommodations in surrounding villages than for those in the heart of the city.
- Buy the Salzburg Card to save money if you're staying in the outskirts or in a nearby village.
- Look for accommodations that offer cooking facilities, which will help you save on dining bills.
- Ask whether there's an extra charge for taking a shower and whether breakfast is included in the rates; if it's buffet style, you can eat as much as you want, thereby perhaps saving on lunch.
- Before making a call, find out whether there's a surcharge on local and long-distance calls.

> **Tips   A Word of Warning**
>
> In summer, it has become common practice for some accommodations to employ hustlers at the train station to recruit people fresh off the train. Some of these lodgings are so far out in the countryside you might as well be in Germany. Some recruiters even go so far as to claim they represent accommodations you might have already booked, only in the end to deliver you elsewhere. Stay away!

IN THE CITY

Gästehaus Brigitte Lenglachner *(Kids)*   This small two-story cottage, all nonsmoking, is owned by a traditional Austrian, who wears dirndl costumes and speaks English. Take a look through her guest book—it's chock-full of praise. The rooms, all with sinks and decorated with Austrian knickknacks, are cozy and spotless; some have balconies. Budget travelers can ask for the double with a bunk bed for 28€ ($32). The small apartment with kitchenette and bathroom is good for one or two people, and the large apartment with a bathroom and a balcony with views of the mountains sleeps up to five and is perfect for families. This place is popular, so reserve well in advance. It's about a 15-minute walk from the Hauptbahnhof.

Scheibenweg 8, 5020 Salzburg. ©/fax 0662/43 80 44. mail@trudeshome.com. 8 units, 4 with bathroom, 2 apts. 22€ ($25) single without bathroom; 37€ ($43) double without bathroom, 44€ ($51) double with bathroom; 50€ ($58) triple without bathroom, 61€ ($70) triple with bathroom; apt with kitchenette 37€ ($43) for 1, 56€ ($64) for 2; apt without kitchenette 88€ ($101) for 4, 105€ ($121) for 5. Rates include continental breakfast and showers. 10% more for 1-night stay. No credit cards. Free parking. Walk from the Hauptbahnhof across the Salzach via the Pioniersteg Bridge, turn right, and take the 3rd street left. **Amenities:** Laundry service 8€ ($9.20) per load (only for stays longer than 1 night); nonsmoking rooms. *In room:* Satellite TV, hair dryer, no phone.

Maria Raderbauer   This two-story house (all nonsmoking), about a 20-minute walk from the Hauptbahnhof, is in a quiet neighborhood and has sparkling clean rooms. The triple has a balcony as well as its own bathroom across the hall. Frau Raderbauer, who speaks English, will pick you up at the station.

Schiesstattstrasse 65, 5020 Salzburg. © 0662/43 93 63. Fax 0662/43 93 63 or 0664/577 68 50. 5 units. 25€ ($29) single; 44€ ($51) double; 66€ ($76) triple. Rates include continental breakfast. 2€ ($2.30) extra per person for 1-night stay. No credit cards. Walk from the Hauptbahnhof across the Salzach via the Pioniersteg Bridge. **Amenities:** Sauna (6€/$6.90 per person); nonsmoking rooms. *In room:* No phone.

Trude Poppenberger   Frau Poppenberger offers three comfortable rooms, all opening onto a balcony with tables, chairs, and mountain views. There are two bathrooms. Generous, Austrian-style breakfasts feature homemade cakes. Frau Poppenberger will pick you up at the train station or airport, and she and her husband, both of whom speak English, will happily provide sightseeing info. Both the train station and the Altstadt are within a 20-minute walk.

Wachtelgasse 9, 5020 Salzburg. ©/fax 0662/43 00 94. www.trudeshome.com. 3 units, none with bathroom. For 1-night stays 28€ ($32) single, 42€ ($48) double; for stays of 2 nights or more 25€ ($29) single, 38€ ($44) double. Rates include continental breakfast and showers. No credit cards. Walk from the Hauptbahnhof across the Salzach via the Pioniersteg Bridge. **Amenities:** Laundry service for 8€ ($9.20) per load (only for stays longer than 1 night); nonsmoking rooms. *In room:* No phone.

ON THE OUTSKIRTS

Blobergerhof *(finds)*   This picturesque Salzburg-style farmhouse with flower boxes is managed by a wonderful English-speaking mother and daughter who receive repeated kudos from readers. There are two types of rooms: The more luxurious, with the extras of minibars and dataports, are in a new addition and are reflected by the highest prices in each category below, while the older, less expensive rooms in the farmhouse are nonetheless spacious and modern, decorated in traditional Austrian style. Some rooms have balconies. The owners raise chickens, so you can always be assured of fresh eggs, and there's even a restaurant here serving Austrian cuisine (closed Sun). The owners will pick you up at the station, and if you stay at least 5 nights, a free city tour is included in the price. A true find.

Hammerauerstrasse 4, 5020 Salzburg. © **0662/83 02 27.** Fax 0662/82 70 61. www.blobergerhof.at. 12 units. 36€–51€ ($41–$59) single; 55€–88€ ($63–$101) double. 18€–22€ ($21–$25) extra person. Rates include buffet breakfast. Discounts for stays of 3 nights or more in the off season. MC, V. Free parking. Bus: 1, 3, 5, 6, or 25 from the Hauptbahnhof to Makartplatz, then 16 to Hammerauerstrasse. **Amenities:** Restaurant; free bikes; laundry service; nonsmoking rooms. *In room:* Satellite TV.

Elfriede Kernstock *(Kids* On the western edge of town near the airport, this beautiful bungalow offers more privacy than most homes — the cheerful rooms have their own entry, separate from the family's quarters. One room has hand-painted furniture, while another large room, good for families, has a balcony (overlooking, alas, a trucking company). All rooms have bathrooms. If she's not busy with guests, English-speaking Frau Kernstock will pick you up at the bus stop if you call from the station.

Karolingerstrasse 29, 5020 Salzburg. ©/fax **0662/82 74 69.** www.tiscover.at/hauskernstock. 7 units. 33€ ($38) single; 44€–48€ ($51–$55) double; 66€ ($76) triple; 20€ ($23) per person in apt. Rates include continental breakfast. MC, V. Free parking. Bus: 2 from the Hauptbahnhof to Karolingerstrasse. *In room:* Satellite TV, hair dryer, no phone.

Gästehaus Gassner This modern nonsmoking guesthouse south of the city has well-furnished spacious rooms in two buildings, some with balconies. In summer, you can eat breakfast on the terrace. Sometimes elderly Frau Gassner, who speaks good English, can pick you up at the station. Houseguests also receive a discount on the cable car to Untersberg.

Moosstrasse 126b, 5020 Salzburg. © **0662/82 49 90.** Fax 0662/82 20 75. pension-maria.gassner@ utanet.at. 10 units, 1 with toilet only, 9 with bathroom. 25€ ($29) single with toilet only, 30€–40€ ($35–$46) single with bathroom; 45€–60€ ($52–$69) double; 75€ ($86) triple; 90€ ($104) quad. 10% extra per person for 1-night stay. Rates include buffet breakfast and showers. MC, V. Bus: 1, 3, 5, 6, or 25 from Hauptbahnhof to Makartplatz, then 16 to Sendlweg. **Amenities:** Rental bikes; self-service laundry (1€/$4.60 per wash load); nonsmoking rooms. *In room:* TV, dataport (3 rooms), minibar, hair dryer, no phone (3 rooms).

Haus Ballwein ☆ *(Kids* Located in peaceful surroundings with a view of Untersberg, this converted former home of a *Fiaker,* a carriage driver who kept his horse and carriage in a stable downstairs, now offers newly furnished rooms decorated in rustic country style, some with balconies. Two rooms, connected by a kitchenette, are very good for families.

Moosstrasse 69, 5020 Salzburg. ©/fax **0662/82 40 29.** haus.ballwein@gmx.net. 5 units. 22€–24€ ($25–$28) per person. Rates include continental breakfast. No credit cards. Free parking. Bus: 1, 3, 5, 6, or 25 from the Hauptbahnhof to Makartplatz, then 16 to Gsengerweg. **Amenities:** Nonsmoking rooms. *In room:* No phone.

Mathilde Lindner *(Kids* This nice Alpine cottage is on top of a high hill northeast of Salzburg, with a great view of the mountains and a playground for children. Four rooms have access to a balcony, there's a garden for sunbathing, the breakfast room overlooks the mountain scenery, and there's a small kitchen for guest use. One room, with a double bed and bunk beds, sleeps four and is good for a family or backpackers traveling together. Three rooms are in the house next door, which belongs to Frau Lindner's sister, Christina (the 2nd phone number below), and although none boasts a view, a greenhouselike breakfast room and outdoor terrace do. If they have time, both Frau Lindner and Christina will pick you up from the station; if you're arriving by car, take the Autobahn Nord exit. If you have a Eurailpass, you can ride for free on a local train (the Regionalzug) from the Hauptbahnhof to Maria-Plain.

Panoramaweg 5, 5300 Hallwang. ©/fax **0662/45 66 81** or 0662/45 67 73. www.haus-lindner.at. 8 units, none with bathroom. 15€–17€ ($17–$20) per person. Rates include continental breakfast and showers. No credit cards. Free parking. Train: From the Hauptbahnhof to Maria-Plain. Bus: 1, 3, 5, or 6 from the Hauptbahnhof to Mirabellplatz, then 15 to Werner-von-Siemens-Platz. In room: No phone.

Moser Frau Moser's husband is a hunter, as is evident from the more than 100 sets of antlers decorating the walls of this home. Not far from Frau Lindner's (see above), it also offers a great view of Salzburg, and its two upper-priced doubles have balconies boasting panoramic views. The pleasant breakfast room offers a panoramic view as well, and there's a terrace and garden. Free coffee and tea are available throughout the day; on arrival, you are welcomed by a drink and *Apfelstrüdel* (apple pie). If you phone upon your arrival in town, Frau Moser will give instructions on how best to reach Kasern via a local train and will meet you at the Maria-Plain station or at the local bus stop.

Turnerbühlel 1, 5300 Hallwang. © **0662/45 66 76.** 4 units, none with bathroom. 14€–15€ ($16–$17) per person. Rates include continental breakfast and showers. No credit cards. Train: From the Hauptbahnhof to Maria-Plain. Bus: 1, 3, 5, or 6 from the Hauptbahnhof to Mirabellplatz, then 15 to Werner-von-Siemens-Platz. In room: No phone.

Rosemarie Steiner This modern three-story house south of town offers a communal kitchen, a washing machine, a garden for sunbathing (and a sandbox for children), and adequately furnished clean rooms with bathrooms, three with balconies and views of mountains. The apartments, which sleep up to four, feature a living room, sleeping room, bathroom, and kitchenette. The owner, who speaks English, is happy to give sightseeing advice.

Moosstrasse 156c, 5020 Salzburg. ©/fax 0662/83 00 31. www.haussteiner.com. 4 units, 2 apts. 30€ ($35) single; 50€ ($58) double; 50€ ($58) apt for 2. Extra person 8€ ($9.20). Rates include continental breakfast (except for apt). AE, MC, V. Bus: 1, 3, 5, 6, or 25 from the Hauptbahnhof to Makartplatz, then 16 to Hammerauerstrasse. **Amenities:** Free use of bikes; self-service laundry (4€/$4.60 per wash load); nonsmoking rooms. In room: Satellite TV, fridge (some rooms), teakettle, hair dryer, radio, no phone.

HOTELS & PENSIONS
IN OR NEAR THE ALTSTADT

Bergland ★★ This pleasant, all-nonsmoking pension, owned by the Kuhn family for more than 80 years, is on three floors of a postwar building on a residential street about a 10-minute walk across the river from the Altstadt. What sets it apart is friendly English-speaking Peter Kuhn, who has decorated the pension with his own artwork, oversees breakfast, and is on hand most evenings to converse with guests in the cozy bar/lounge, complete with piano and guitar. There's a small Japanese-style garden where guests can relax in summer. The pension's halls lead to spotless rooms, cheerfully decorated with Scandinavian furniture and a mix of modern design and Austrian antiques.

Rupertgasse 15 (a 12-min. walk south of the Hauptbahnhof), 5020 Salzburg. © **0662/87 23 18-0.** Fax 0662/87 23 18-8. www.berglandhotel.at. 18 units. 58€ ($67) single; 88€ ($101) double; 105€ ($121) triple; 124€ ($143) quad. Rates include buffet breakfast. AE, DC, MC, V. Free parking. **Amenities:** Bar; rental bikes for 6€ ($6.90) per day; nonsmoking rooms; computer with Internet access for small fee; small English-language library. In room: Satellite TV.

Pension Chiemsee ⭐ *Value*   With a great location in the Altstadt, this wonderful tiny pension is owned by Veronika Höllbacher, a Salzburg native who speaks English and gained experience running a restaurant before acquiring the pension. The house itself is 1,000 years old—note how worn the stone stairway is. The reception and small but pleasant breakfast room are up on the first floor, and the guest rooms are on the third (no elevator). The rooms are simple but clean, with natural wood furniture and new bathrooms.

Chiemseegasse 5, 5020 Salzburg. ℂ 0662/84 42 08 or 0664/411 92 97. Fax 0662/84 42 08-70. hotel-chiemsee@aon.at. 6 units. 50€ ($58) single; 82€ ($94) double. Rates include continental breakfast. Winter discounts available. MC, V. Free parking. Bus: 3, 5, 6, 7, 8, 25, or 26 from the Hauptbahnhof to Mozartsteg. *In room:* TV, hair dryer.

Junger Fuchs   This is the inner city's cheapest pension and looks as if it has been here forever. The old stone stairway (no elevator) is narrow and probably medieval; the rooms date from the past century but look no less weary. Although bare, small, and simple, the accommodations are adequate, each with a sink, hooks to hang up your coat, a bed, and a table. Some might smell of cigarette smoke, so ask to see your room first. Basically, this is just a cheap place to sleep in a convenient location, across the river from the Altstadt.

Linzer Gasse 54, 5020 Salzburg. ℂ/fax 0662/87 54 96. 14 units, none with bathroom. 27€–30€ ($31–$35) single; 38€–42€ ($44–$48) double; 48€–50€ ($55–$58) triple. Rates include showers. No credit cards. Bus: 1, 3, 5, 6, or 25 from the Hauptbahnhof to Makartplatz. *In room:* No phone.

Trumer Stube ⭐⭐ *Kids*   This is a personable hotel in the city center, across the river from the Altstadt and within a 5-minute walk of both Mozart's Birthplace and Residence. Ideal for couples and families, it's managed by friendly Silvia Rettenbacher, who speaks English and is happy to give sightseeing tips, make restaurant and guided tour reservations, and do whatever else guests desire. The pension offers cheerful, cozy, and spotless rooms (all nonsmoking), decorated with a feminine touch. The prices below reflect both the low- and high-season rates for each category.

Bergstrasse 6, 5020 Salzburg. ℂ 0662/87 47 76 or 0662/87 51 68. Fax 0662/87 43 26. www.trumer-stube.at. 20 units. 56€–70€ ($64–$81) single; 67€–103€ ($77–$118) double; 81€–125€ ($93–$144) triple; 103€–154€ ($118–$177) quad. Rates include continental breakfast. AE, MC, V. Closed Feb to mid-Mar. Bus: 1, 3, 5, or 6 from the Hauptbahnhof to Mirabellplatz. **Amenities:** Nonsmoking rooms; laptop computer with Internet access guests can use for a small fee. *In room:* Cable TV, no phone.

Wallner *Kids*   On the opposite side of Mönchsberg from the Altstadt, not far from the Augustinerbräu brewery and beer garden, this 45-year-old pension is now managed by the original owner's daughter. It consists of two buildings; the one in back is very quiet. The simple but roomy accommodations, each decorated only with a cross, include a four bed room, with two sleeping quarters, that's good for families. The main drawback: It's not as centrally located as this guide's other in-town selections. Also, there are no single rooms per se, but in the off season lone travelers can stay in double rooms at the "single" prices given below.

Aiglhofstrasse 15, 5020 Salzburg. ℂ 0662/84 50 23. Fax 0662/84 50 23-3. www.pensionwallner.at. 15 units, 13 with bathroom. 26€ ($30) single without bathroom, 43€ ($49) single with bathroom; 42€ ($48) double without bathroom, 62€ ($71) double with bathroom; 78€ ($90) triple with bathroom; 88€ ($101) quad with bathroom. Rates include continental breakfast and showers. No credit cards. Free parking. Bus: 2 or 77 from the Hauptbahnhof to Aiglhof. *In room:* TV.

NEAR THE HAUPTBAHNHOF

Adlerhof *Value*   If you're staying in Salzburg only 1 night and don't want to hassle with buses or taxis, try this simple pension, just a few minutes' walk from the train station (take the main exit and walk straight ahead; its reception is open 24 hr.). Built in 1900 (with an elevator added in 2002), it offers rooms of various sizes, a few large enough for five persons, and some rather old-fashioned in decor, with antlers, wood furniture painted with flowers and other traditional motifs, chandeliers, and landscape paintings (they remind me of the guest room in my Austrian relative's house). A couple rooms even have canopy beds. The price range reflects the seasons.

Elisabethstrasse 25, 5020 Salzburg. (C) **0662/87 52 36.** Fax 0662/87 36 63. www.pension-adlerhof.com. 35 units, 32 with bathroom. 38€–40€ ($44–$46) single without bathroom, 48€–62€ ($55–$71) single with bathroom; 58€–65€ ($67–$75) double without bathroom, 68€–89€ ($78–$102) double with bathroom. Rates include buffet breakfast. *Frommer's readers:* Show this book to receive a 10% discount in off season. No credit cards. *In room:* Satellite TV, radio.

Auerhahn   This well-furnished small hotel is across from a secondary rail track (used only once or twice a day and causing little noise). It has been owned by the same family for more than 30 years (the proprietress speaks fluent English), and has a pleasant and very good restaurant and outdoor terrace, shaded by chestnut trees, serving typical Austrian food popular with locals (closed Sun evenings and Mon). The rooms are upstairs, along corridors that have a hunting lodge feel, with heavy beams and Bauernmöbel (wooden furniture gaily painted Austrian style). Recently renovated, all rooms are modern, with spotless tiled bathrooms and wood furniture. The hotel's only disadvantage is that it's a bit far from the Altstadt, but a bus to the Hauptbahnhof and Altstadt runs every 10 to 15 minutes.

Bahnhofstrasse 15 (a 10-min. walk north of the Hauptbahnhof), 5020 Salzburg. (C) **0662/45 10 52.** Fax 0662/45 10 52-3. www.auerhahn-salzburg.at. 13 units. 43€–46€ ($49–$53) single; 72€–81€ ($83–$93) double; 95€ ($109) triple. Rates include buffet breakfast. AE, DC, MC, V. Free parking. Closed 2 weeks in July. Bus: 3 from the Hauptbahnhof to Werkstättenstrasse. **Amenities:** Restaurant. *In room:* Satellite TV.

Yoho International Youth Hotel *(Value*   With a college dorm atmosphere and a young English-speaking staff, this is the best budget choice in town, centrally located (a 15-min. walk to the Altstadt) and with no age limit. There are two doubles; the rest are triples, quads, and dorms with six to eight beds each. All rooms have sinks, three rooms have showers, and lockers are available. *The Sound of Music* is shown free daily at 10:30am.

Paracelsusstrasse 9, 5020 Salzburg. (C) **0662/87 96 49.** Fax 0662/87 88 10. www.yoho.at. 150 beds. 20€ ($23) per person double without bathroom, 23€ ($26) per person double with bathroom; 18€ ($21) per person triple without bathroom, 21€ ($24) per person triple with bathroom; 17€ ($20) per person quad; 15€ ($17) dorm bed. Rates include 1 free shower daily. Discounts available on 2nd and subsequent nights. AE, DC, MC, V. Walk 10 min. south of the Hauptbahnhof. **Amenities:** Restaurant/bar serving breakfast and dinner (bar stays open to 1am); coin-operated laundry; nonsmoking rooms; Internet corner with computers costing 6€ ($6.90) per hour. *In room:* No phone.

ON THE OUTSKIRTS

Fürstenbrunn *(Finds*   In a quiet wooded location 8km (5 miles) south of Salzburg at the foot of Untersberg mountain, this is a great choice for hikers (in winter when there's snow, you can ski down Untersberg practically to the front door). Owners Manfred and Heidelinde Schnöll, whose family has run the inn for 100 years and are assisted by their two daughters, will pick you up at the train station if they have time. Large immaculate rooms have gaily painted wooden furniture (Bauernmöbel); some rooms have balconies. The restaurant, Gasthof Schnöll, is popular with locals for its terrace and excellent smoked trout. The breakfasts are extensive.

Fürstenbrunnerstrasse 50, 5082 Fürstenbrunn. (C)/fax 06246/73 342. 11 units. 37€ ($43) single; 58€ ($67) double; 66€ ($76) triple; 75€ ($86) quad. Rates include continental breakfast. MC, V. Free parking. Bus: 1, 3,

5, 6, or 25 from the Hauptbahnhof to Makartplatz, then 60 to Fürstenbrunn. **Amenities:** Restaurant. *In room:* TV, hair dryer, no phone.

Helmhof   In Liefering on the northeastern edge of town, this pension with an English-speaking owner might still have rooms when others in the town center are booked up. This attractive country house boasts balconies off most rooms, and flowers on the windowsills. Though the furnishings, carpets, and wallpapers are a few decades from being modern, this is a good choice for a relaxing stay.

Kirchengasse 29, 5020 Salzburg. ⓒ/fax **0662/43 30 79.** helmhof@utanet.at. 16 units, 12 with bathroom. 27€ ($31) single without bathroom, 35€ ($40) single with bathroom; 50€ ($58) double without bathroom, 60€–66€ ($69–$76) double with bathroom. Rates include continental breakfast and showers. No credit cards. Free parking. Bus: 2 from the Hauptbahnhof to Esshaverstrasse, then 4 to Schmiedingerstrasse. **Amenities:** Small outdoor pool. *In room:* Satellite TV (some rooms), no phone (most rooms).

Parkpension Kasern ★★ *(Finds)*   This is a lovely country villa in a park on Salzburg's northern outskirts. Built in 1870 as a private mansion, it's now in its fourth generation of owners and features exquisite artistry throughout. Most rooms are large, with tall ceilings and antique furniture; six tastefully furnished modern rooms were recently added, and there are also a couple two-room suites. Cooking facilities can be arranged for longer stays, and a computer in the entryway with Internet access is available for a small fee. There's also a fine garden with a pond where you can sit in summer. One of my top picks, this is a very relaxing place yet easily connected to the heart of Salzburg by bus.

Wickenburgallee 1, 5028 Salzburg-Kasern. ⓒ **0662/45 00 62.** Fax 0662/45 40 81. www.parkpension.at. 16 units. 43€–50€ ($49–$58) single; 66€–89€ ($76–$102) double. Extra person 25€ ($29). Rates include buffet breakfast. MC, V. Free parking. Bus: 1, 3, 5, or 6 from the Hauptbahnhof to Mirabellplatz, then 15 to Kasern. **Amenities:** Nonsmoking rooms; computer with Internet access for small fee. *In room:* Satellite TV, no phone.

WORTH A SPLURGE

Amadeus ★★   Occupying a 15th-century building and owned by the same family for three generations, this small hotel has a great location in the city center, across the river from the Altstadt. You have your choice of rooms facing either the street or a peaceful cemetery (where Mozart's wife is buried). Recently renovated, the rooms are pleasant with traditional furniture but modern touches, including spotless tiled bathrooms; for families, there are a couple of two-room suites sleeping four to six persons. The buffet breakfast is substantial, offering eggs, cereals, and cold cuts; free coffee and tea are available afternoons in the lobby. The helpful staff can make reservations for concerts, sightseeing tours, and restaurants, but equally popular is the hotel's second-floor terrace overlooking the cemetery, where guests enjoy relaxing in the sun or an evening with drinks. The higher prices in each category are for the peak season, including mid-July to September, weekends in December, New Year's, and Easter.

Linzer Gasse 43–45, 5020 Salzburg. ⓒ **0662/87 14 01.** Fax 0662/87 14 01-7 or 0662/87 61 63-7. www. hotelamadeus.at. 26 units. 72€–82€ ($83–$94) single; 112€–150€ ($129–$173) double; 145€–175€ ($167–$201) triple. Rates include buffet breakfast, afternoon coffee, and showers. Off-season discounts available. AE, DC, MC, V. Bus: 1, 3, 5, 6, or 25 from the Hauptbahnhof to Makartplatz. **Amenities:** Espresso bar; nonsmoking rooms. *In room:* Cable TV, hair dryer, safe.

Elefant ★   This family-run hotel has the best location of all my recommendations—in the Altstadt on a small side street just off Getreidegasse, Salzburg's most famous pedestrian lane. The house itself dates back more than 700 years, but the rooms, which are fairly small, have been modernized with all the creature comforts. The prices reflect the seasons, with peak season running July to mid-October, Christmas, Mozart Week (end of Jan), and Easter.

Sigmund-Haffner-Gasse 4, 5020 Salzburg. © **0662/84 33 97**. Fax 0662/84 01 09-28. www.elefant.at. 31 units. 86€–100€ ($99–$115) single; 130€–190€ ($150–$219) double. Rates include buffet breakfast. AE, DC, MC, V. Bus: 3, 5, 6, 7, 8, 25, or 26 from the Hauptbahnhof to Rathaus. **Amenities:** Restaurant; room service (6–10pm); babysitting; laundry service. *In room:* A/C (some rooms), cable TV, dataport, minibar, hair dryer, safe.

Wolf ⭐ This small hotel in the Altstadt has a good location in a quiet pedestrian zone at the foot of the Hohensalzburg Fortress. The structure itself is a national monument and dates from the 14th century, which is evident in such architectural details as arched ceilings in the breakfast room and 400-year-old plank floors, but otherwise everything is supermodern with all the conveniences, including an elevator. Every room is unique, some with antiques like painted wardrobes, others with modern furniture, but all have nice modern bathrooms. The owner wears dirndl costumes and speaks excellent English. The highest prices are for July to September and the Christmas/New Year's holidays.

Kaigasse 7, 5020 Salzburg. © **0662/84 34 53-0**. Fax 0662/84 24 23-4. www.hotelwolf.com. 15 units. 58€–98€ ($67–$113) single; 80€–158€ ($92–$182) double. Rates include buffet breakfast. AE. Bus: 3, 5, 6, 7, 8, 25, or 26 from the Hauptbahnhof to Mozartsteg. *In room:* Cable TV, hair dryer, safe.

3 Great Deals on Dining

You'll find Salzburg's inexpensive restaurants on both banks of the Salzach, many clustered in and around the Altstadt. Most feature specialties typical of Austria and southern Germany, such as *Leberknödelsuppe* (soup with liver dumplings), *Knoblauchsuppe* (garlic soup), *Bauernschmaus* (a combination dish of pork, ham, sausage, dumplings, and sauerkraut), *Tafelspitz* (boiled beef with vegetables), *Gulasch* (Hungarian stew), *Leberkäse* (German meatloaf), or *Wiener schnitzel* (breaded veal cutlet).

The only real Salzburg dish is *Salzburger Nockerl,* a dessert soufflé made of eggs, flour, butter, and sugar. When served at your table it looks like a blimp, too big for you to possibly eat it all, but as soon as you dig in, the air escapes and it becomes more manageable. Try it at least once while in Salzburg.

IN OR NEAR THE ALTSTADT

Augustiner Bräustübl Kloster Mülln ⭐⭐ AUSTRIAN Founded in 1621 by Augustine monks, this brewery about a 10-minute walk from the Altstadt is a Salzburg institution, a great place for a meal in the huge outdoor beer garden with a children's play area, or upstairs in one of the huge beer halls. Beer is drawn from wooden kegs. You can bring your own food, but there are also counters selling sausages and cold cuts, cheese, pretzels, hamburgers, grilled chicken, soup, salads, boiled pork with horseradish, beef with creamed spinach and potatoes, and more. It's a crowded, noisy place, as a brewery should be; it can also be smoky.

Linderhofstrasse or Augustinergasse 4 (10-min. walk from the Altstadt, north of Mönchsberg). © **0662/43 12 46**. Meals 5€–10€ ($5.75–$12). No credit cards. Mon–Fri 3–10:30pm; Sat–Sun and holidays 2:30–10:30pm. Bus: 10, 16, 18, 24, or 27 from Hanuschplatz (in the Altstadt on the Salzach River) to Landeskrankenhaus.

Gasthaus Wilder Mann ⭐ *Finds* AUSTRIAN This popular simple restaurant has wooden tables, a wood-plank floor, and antlers on the wall. It's the kind of place locals come to drink, eat, and gossip, and you might be the only

---

Value   Getting the Best Deal on Dining

- Try the daily specials, called *Tagesgerichte*, which are usually complete meals offered at discount prices and often not included in the English menu.
- Take advantage of butcher shops and food sections of department stores, which usually offer such takeout food as *Leberkäse* and grilled chicken.
- Eat lunch at a student cafeteria *(Mensa)*, where nonstudents pay slightly higher prices than students for bargain meals.
- Pick up a meal at an inexpensive *Imbiss*, or food stall, selling sausages, snacks, and beer, and eat it in a park or on a bench along the river.
- Ask whether there's an extra charge for each piece of bread consumed and whether your main course comes with vegetables or side dishes.

---

non-Salzburger around. The English menu lists *Gulasch, Wiener schnitzel,* turkey with mushroom sauce, and pork chops, with most meals at less than 9€ ($10). Watch for the reasonable daily specials, written only in German.

Getreidegasse 20/Griesgasse 17 (in a narrow passage between Getreidegasse and Griesgasse). 🕾 0662/84 17 87. Meals 6.50€–14€ ($7.50–$16). No credit cards. Mon–Sat 11am–9pm (last order). Bus: 1, 3, 5, or 16 to Hanuschplatz.

Spaghetti & Co *(Kids* PASTA/PIZZA   Near Mozart's Birthplace in the middle of the Altstadt, this chain of spaghetti parlors with an English menu offers more than a dozen spaghetti dishes, as well as more than 20 kinds of pizza (you can also create your own), soups, and salads. It also has a do-it-yourself salad bar, with a large plate costing 4.90€ ($5.65). A good choice for families.

Getreidegasse 14. 🕾 0662/84 14 00. Pizza and pasta 4.50€–8.50€ ($5.15–$9.75). AE, DC, MC, V. Daily 11am–11:30pm. Bus: 1, 3, 5, or 16 to Hanuschplatz.

Sternbräu ⚜ AUSTRIAN   Opened as a brewery more than 500 years ago, this is one of Salzburg's best moderately priced restaurants, a huge place with various dining halls and two courtyard gardens seating 350, one a restaurant with waitress service and the other a self-service beer garden. The English menu is extensive, including favorites like *Wiener schnitzel* with potatoes, *Tafelspitz,* roasted chicken, pork cutlet, fresh fish, and grilled steak.

Getreidegasse 34–36/Griesgasse 23. 🕾 0662/84 21 40. Meals 7€–15€ ($8.05–$17). AE, DC, MC, V. Daily 10am–11pm. Bus: 1, 3, 5, or 16 to Hanuschplatz.

Stiegl-Keller ⚜ AUSTRIAN   Carved out of the foot of the mountain below the fortress, just a few hundred yards uphill from Residenzplatz, the Stiegl-Keller has been popular since 1820 for its picturesque, shaded beer garden overlooking the Altstadt. It serves hearty Austrian fare such as *Wiener schnitzel, Schweinsbraten* (roast pork), and *Schweinshaxn* (knuckle of roast pork), along with mugs of Stiegl beer and occasional live music.

Festungsgasse 10. 🕾 0662/84 26 81. Meals 7€–13€ ($8.05–$15). AE, DC, MC, V. Daily 11am–11pm. Closed Oct–Apr. Bus: 3, 5, 6, 7, 8, 25, or 26 to Mozartsteg.

Wienerwald Restaurant AUSTRIAN   Part of a chain with branches in Austria, Germany, and Switzerland, this family restaurant specializes in spit-roasted chicken (half a grilled chicken costs 5.95€/$6.85). The Wienerwald is decorated like a Swiss chalet and offers comfortable seating, a salad bar, a nonsmoking section, and an English menu.

Griesgasse 31. © **0662/84 34 70.** Meals 7.50€–11€ ($8.65–$13). AE, DC, MC, V. Daily 11am–11:30pm. Bus: 1, 3, 5, or 16 to Hanuschplatz.

IN OR NEAR THE HAUPTBAHNHOF

Interspar Restaurant *(Value* AUSTRIAN   This self-service restaurant, across from the train station, is up on the first floor of a small shopping complex. It offers two fixed-price meals daily, which can range from *Wiener schnitzel* with a side dish to salmon steak with broccoli and potatoes, as well as a salad bar and other choices in main courses. On weekdays, meals are half price 6 to 7pm. This is a good place for a quick, inexpensive meal while waiting for a train.

Südtirolerplatz 11 (in the Forum Am Bahnhof shopping center). © **0662/45 84 66-851.** Meals 4.90€–7€ ($5.65–$8.05). No credit cards. Mon–Fri 8am–7pm; Sat 8am–5pm. Bus: 1, 3, 5, 6, 23, or 25 to Hauptbahnhof.

Quo Vadis AUSTRIAN   It's rare that I want to eat in a train station, but this station eatery is more inviting than most, with soaring ceilings, marble pillars, white tablecloths, and an attentive staff lending it a civilized air. The English menu lists such perennial favorites as *Wiener schnitzel, Tafelspitz, Gulasch,* and grilled fish, but be sure to ask about the daily specials written in German only and priced under 11€ ($13). Waiting for a train doesn't seem such a chore here.

Rainerstrasse 14. © **0662/87 76 94.** Meals 5.60€–15€ ($6.45–$17). AE, DC, MC, V. Daily 6:30am–10pm. Bus: 1, 3, 5, 6, 23, or 25 to Hauptbahnhof.

Moments **Taking a Break for Coffee & Pastries**

Salzburg is famous for its coffeehouses and pastry shops, where you can linger over pastry and coffee or a glass of wine, read the newspapers (including the *International Herald Tribune*), and watch the passersby. In summer, many cafes have outdoor seating. If you prefer, get some pastries to go and eat them on a park bench or in your hotel.

Café Bazar, Schwarzstrasse 3, on the right side of the Salzach near the Staatsbrücke (© **0662/87 42 78**), features chandeliers and large windows affording stunning views of the river and fortress, and is popular with locals. It also serves snacks and daily specials and is open Monday 10am to 6pm and Tuesday to Saturday 7:30am to 11pm. It accepts no credit cards.

Opened in 1705 and one of Austria's oldest coffeehouses, **Café Tomaselli,** in the heart of the Altstadt at Alter Markt 9 (© **0662/84 44 88**), is still going strong. It's so popular you might have to wait to get a seat. In summer, extra chairs are placed out on the cobblestone square. Have a *Melange* (a large coffee with frothy milk) and dessert or choose from the pastry tray or display case. There's also wine, beer, soft drinks, and snacks, plus ice cream in summer. It's open Monday to Saturday 7am to 9pm and Sunday 8am to 9pm and accepts no credit cards.

StieglBräu Restaurant AUSTRIAN   A 5-minute walk from the train station (under the tracks in the direction of the city center), this restaurant attached to a hotel offers an English menu ranging from fish to *Gulasch* to grilled steak to pork chops, chicken, and sausages, available for lunch and dinner. In addition, there are lunch specials not on the English menu (including a vegetarian lunch) costing 5.70€ to 13€ ($6.55–$14), as well as a salad bar available to 2pm. A snack menu is available 11am to 11pm. Best is the large outdoor garden, a good place for drinking the restaurant's own Stiegl beer in summer (though nearby passing trains can be loud).

Rainerstrasse 14. 𝄞 0662/87 76 94. Meals 9€–15€ ($10–$17). AE, DC, MC, V. Daily 11am–11pm (main menu available daily 11:30am–2pm and 6–9:30pm). Bus: 1, 3, 5, 6, or 25 to Kongresshaus.

A LOCAL BUDGET BEST

Uni-Cafe Toskana, Mensa der Universität *(Value* AUSTRIAN   This student *Mensa*, with a courtyard entrance (from Churfürststrasse, walk straight to the very back courtyard), is in the center of the Altstadt and is by far one of the cheapest places for a meal. It offers two complete meals daily, with slightly higher prices for nonstudents *(Gast)*. Although the fixed-price meals are served only during the hours listed below, the cafe itself is open Monday to Thursday 8:30am to 5pm and Friday 8:30am to 3pm; it serves a few sandwich choices, soup, frankfurters, desserts, and coffee and other drinks. In summer you can sit outside in the courtyard.

Churfürststrasse and Sigmund-Haffner-Gasse (between Alter Markt and Domplatz). 𝄞 0662/8044-69 09. Fixed-price meals 2.70€–3.50€ ($3.10–$4) students, 3.70€–4.50€ ($4.25–$5.15) nonstudents. No credit cards. Mon–Fri 11am–1:30pm. Closed Dec 21–Jan 6. Bus: 1, 3, 5, or 16 to Hanuschplatz.

PICNICKING

There are many *Imbisse* where you can buy sausages and beer. If it's a nice day, you might want to join the other sun worshipers on the benches in the **Mirabellgarten** or along the **Salzach River.** Another good place is at the **Augustiner Bräustübl Kloster Mülln,** a brewery with an outdoor beer garden, described above.

WORTH A SPLURGE

Ährlich ☞ ORGANIC AUSTRIAN/VEGETARIAN   With a rustic yet elegant atmosphere befitting Austria's first licensed organic restaurant, Ährlich uses only organic ingredients (free from chemicals and hormones) in preparing its meat and vegetarian dishes. Even the wine and beers are organic. An English menu lists approximately four meat entrees and four vegetarian choices that change with the seasons but might include vegetable lasagna with bleu cheese; beef steak in red-wine sauce served with broccoli and garnished with bacon and potato gratin; and stuffed chicken in curry sauce.

Wolf-Dietrich-Strasse 7 (just north of Linzer Gasse). 𝄞 0662/87 12 75 39. Reservations recommended. Main courses 11€–17€ ($13–$19). AE, DC, MC, V. Mon–Sat 6–10pm (July–Aug also 11am–2pm). Closed Feb–Mar. Bus: 4 to Hofwirt.

Stiftskeller St. Peter ☞☞ AUSTRIAN   This is probably Salzburg's most popular first-class restaurant. It's under the management of St. Peter's Monastery and was first mentioned in documents from 803, making it Europe's oldest restaurant. There are various dining rooms, each unique but all with a medieval ambience. The changing English menu lists international food as well as local specialties, such as fresh trout, boiled beef with chives, veal *Schnitzel*, and numerous daily specials. Set meals include a vegetarian choice. For wine you might select the Prälatenwein (prelate's wine), the grapes of which are grown in the convent's own vineyards in Wachau. Its traditional desserts are great—try the *Salzburger Nockerl*. For a real splurge, there's the Mozart Dinner Concert (held in the restaurant's elegant Baroque Hall), featuring Mozart music played by period-costumed musicians and a three-course meal based on traditional 17- and 18th-century recipes (see "Dinner Shows," p. 873, for more details).

St. Peter-Bezirk 1 (near St. Peter's Monastery at the foot of the Mönchsberg). (C) **0662/84 12 68-0.** Main courses 14€–24€ ($16–$28); set meals 22€–37€ ($25–$43); Mozart Dinner Concert 45€ ($52). AE, DC, MC, V. Daily 11:30am–2:30pm and 6–10:30pm. Bus: 3, 5, 6, 7, 8, 25, or 26 to Mozartsteg.

4 Seeing the Sights

Because Salzburg is so compact, with most attractions located in the Old City, you can see quite a bit on foot in just a few hours. But be sure to allow for some unstructured wandering, as one of the city's charms is its medieval atmosphere.

MOZART'S BIRTHPLACE & RESIDENCE

Mozart's Geburtshaus (Mozart's Birthplace) ⨁

This is the most heavily visited attraction in Salzburg (in my opinion, however, Mozart's Residence, described below, is more worthwhile if you have time for only one Mozart attraction). Wolfgang Amadeus Mozart was born in this simple third-floor apartment in 1756 and lived in these four rooms with his family until 1773. The museum contains his clavichord, a copy of his pianoforte (he started composing when he was 4), and the violin he played as a boy. Of the several paintings of Amadeus, his sister Nannerl, and his family, only one is known to be a true likeness of the genius—the unfinished one by the pianoforte, done by his brother-in-law. Another is thought to be of the musician when he was 9. In addition to the rooms where the family lived, there are a few adjoining rooms decorated in the style of a typical burgher's house in Mozart's time. You'll also find changing exhibits related to Mozart's works. You can tour the house in a half-hour.

Getreidegasse 9. (C) **0662/84 43 13.** www.mozarteum.at. Admission 5.50€ ($6.35) adults, 4.50€ ($5.15) seniors and students, 2€ ($2.30) visitors 15–18, 1.50€ ($1.75) children 6–14, 13€ ($15) families; combination ticket (Birthplace and Residence) 9€ ($10) adults, 7€ ($8.05) seniors and students, 2.50€–3€ ($2.85–$3.45) children, 20€ ($23) families. July–Aug daily 9am–7pm; Sept–June daily 9am–6pm (you must enter 30 min. before closing). Bus: 3, 5, 6, 7, 8, 25, or 26 to Rathaus.

Mozart-Wohnhaus (Mozart's Residence) ⨁⨁⨁

Mozart's Residence strives to chronicle the musician's life and the influence his family—particularly his father—had on his career, making it more worthwhile than his birthplace for those who know little about the genius's life. A teenage Mozart and his family moved from their small Getreidegasse home to this more spacious elegant residence in 1773; it dates from 1617 and was once used for dancing classes for the aristocracy. Amadeus lived here until 1780, composing symphonies, serenades, piano and violin concertos, and sacred music. His father died here in 1787. Today the home, heavily damaged during World War II and completely rebuilt, contains a museum dedicated to Mozart and his family, period furniture, Mozart's pianoforte, and original music scores. Best, however, are the audio-guides that are automatically activated by the various displays, complete with music, and the movie depicting the child prodigy's life in Salzburg and his tours

Salzburg

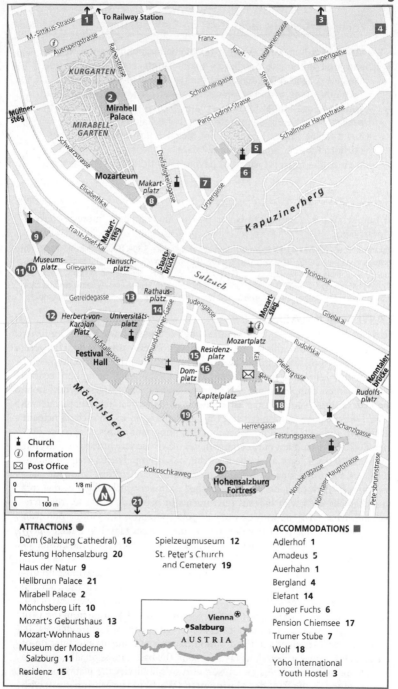

Map Labels

M.-Sittikus-Strasse
To Railway Station
Auerspergstrasse
KURGARTEN
Franz-
Josef-
Stelzhamerstrasse
Rupertgasse
Schrannengasse
Paris-Lodron-Strasse
Strasse
Schallmoser Hauptstrasse
Müllner-steg
Mirabell Palace
MIRABELL-GARTEN
Schwarzstrasse
Mozarteum
Makart-platz
Dreifaltigkeitsgasse
Elisabethkai
Linzergasse
Kapuzinerberg
Franz-Josef-Kai
Makart-steg
Steingasse
Haus der Natur
Museums-platz
Hanusch-platz
Griesgasse
Staats-brücke
Sulzach
Getreidegasse
Rathaus-platz
Judengasse
Mozart-steg
Giselakai
Herbert-von-Karajan Platz
Universitäts-platz
Sigmund-Haffner-Gasse
Rudolfskai
Nonntaler-brücke
Festival Hall
Hofstallgasse
Mozartplatz
Residenz-platz
Pfeifergasse
Rudolfs-platz
Mönchsberg
Dom-platz
Kaigasse
Kapitelplatz
Herrengasse
Festungsgasse
Schanzlgasse
Kokoschkaweg
Hohensalzburg Fortress
Nonnberggasse
Nonntaler Hauptstrasse
Petersbrunnstrasse

Legend

† Church
ⓘ Information
✉ Post Office

0 — 1/8 mi
0 — 100 m
N

ATTRACTIONS ●

Dom (Salzburg Cathedral) **16**
Festung Hohensalzburg **20**
Haus der Natur **9**
Hellbrunn Palace **21**
Mirabell Palace **2**
Mönchsberg Lift **10**
Mozart's Geburtshaus **13**
Mozart-Wohnhaus **8**
Museum der Moderne Salzburg **11**
Residenz **15**
Spielzeugmuseum **12**
St. Peter's Church and Cemetery **19**

Vienna ✱
● Salzburg
AUSTRIA

ACCOMMODATIONS ■

Adlerhof **1**
Amadeus **5**
Auerhahn **1**
Bergland **4**
Elefant **14**
Junger Fuchs **6**
Pension Chiemsee **17**
Trumer Stube **7**
Wolf **18**
Yoho International Youth Hostel **3**

> ### ⟮Value⟯ Getting the Best Deal on Sightseeing
>
> - Buy the **Salzburg Card,** which offers unlimited public transportation and free entry into Salzburg's major sights and museums (see "Salzburg Deals & Discounts," at the beginning of this chapter).
> - Take advantage of the combination ticket for Mozart's Birthplace and Residence—great for Mozart fans. Combination tickets are also available for the Residenz State Rooms and Galerie.
> - Buy a family ticket, if available, at Mozart's Birthplace, the Hohensalzburg Fortress, and Hellbrunn Palace.
> - Walk to the fortress instead of paying for a ticket on the funicular.

of Europe. You can spend the better part of an hour here, more if you're a Mozart fan.

Makartplatz 8. ⟮C⟯ 0662/87 42 27-40. www.mozarteum.at. Admission 5.50€ ($6.35) adults, 4.50€ ($5.15) seniors and students, 2€ ($2.30) visitors 15–18, 1.50€ ($1.75) children 6–14, 13€ ($15) families; combination ticket (Birthplace and Residence) 9€ ($10) adults, 7€ ($8.05) seniors and students, 2.50€–3€ ($2.85–$3.45) children, 20€ ($23) families. July–Aug daily 9am–7pm; Sept–June daily 9am–6pm (you must enter 30 min. before closing). Closed during Mozart Week (end of Jan). Bus: 1, 3, 5, 6, or 25 to Makartplatz.

CASTLES & PALACES

Festung Hohensalzburg (Hohensalzburg Fortress) ⟨★★★⟩ ⟨*Kids*⟩ Dominating the city from a cliff, this impressive medieval fortress/castle was built between the 11th and the 17th centuries as a residence for the prince-archbishops who ruled Salzburg for more than 500 years. It has the honor of being both central Europe's largest completely preserved fortress and Europe's largest fortress from the 11th century. It contains the **State Rooms** of the former archbishops and two related museums, which you can visit on a guided tour in which each participant receives an audioguide that describes the most important rooms. I highly recommend taking the tour, not only because there's otherwise very little to do here, but also because you'll learn a lot about medieval Salzburg. There's even an audioguide geared toward kids, with less history and more anecdotes. The tour takes you through dark corridors and unfurnished chambers, including a dismal torture chamber filled with hideous instruments of pain. You'll also see the archbishops' living quarters, with carvings of gold leaf and a late Gothic porcelain stove from 1501, the most valuable item in the fortress, as well as a huge open-air barrel organ from 1502, once used to signal the daily opening and closing of the city's gates.

Included in the tour is a visit of the **Rainermuseum,** a military museum displaying armor, swords, uniforms, and other related items. You'll also tour the **Burgmuseum (Fortress Museum),** which provides a historic overview of the fortress with displays of weapons used in peasant revolts, furniture from the 14th and 15th centuries, and a macabre collection of medieval torture devices. In addition, you'll see the Sound and Vision Show, a multimedia presentation of the fortress's history. If you don't take the tour, the base admission allows you to wander through the fortress grounds, courtyards, and viewing platforms. Also on the grounds is the **Welt der Marionetten (World of the Marionettes),** with more than 120 marionettes from around the world, including some from Salzburg's own famous marionette theater. There's also a tavern.

The easiest way to reach the fortress is by **funicular** (which includes the admission to fortress grounds, but not the tour). If you want a workout, you might want to approach on foot. A path leading from the Altstadt and winding up the hill, offering changing vistas on the way, makes for a pleasant and slightly strenuous walk. As an alternative, you might want to go up by funicular and descend on foot. If you want to see everything, including time to wander fortress grounds, expect to spend up to 3 hours here.

Mönchsberg 34. (C) 0662/84 24 30-11 for fortress; 0662/84 95 55 for Welt der Marionetten. www.salzburg-burgen.at. Fortress grounds only 3.60€ ($4.15) adults, 2€ ($2.30) children, 8€ ($9.20) families; audio tour including Sound and Vision Show, State Rooms, Burgmuseum, and Rainermuseum 3.60€ ($4.15) adults, 2€ ($2.30) children, 8€ ($9.20) families; Welt der Marionetten 3€ ($3.45) adults, 2€ ($2.30) seniors and students, 1.50€ ($1.75) children. Fortress grounds mid-Mar to mid-June daily 9am–6pm (audio tour 9:30am–5pm); mid-June to mid-Sept daily 9am–7pm (audio tour 9am–5:30pm); mid-Sept to mid-Mar daily 9am–5pm (audio tour 9:30am–4:30pm). Welt der Marionetten July–Aug daily 9:30am–6pm; Apr–June and Sept to mid-Oct daily 10am–5pm. Rainermuseum closed Nov–Apr. Funicular, including entrance to fortress grounds 3.70€ ($4.25) one-way or 8.50€ ($9.75) round-trip adults, 1.90€ ($2.20) and 4.50€ ($5.15), respectively, for children.

Hellbrunn Palace *(Kids)*   Built as a hunting lodge/summer residence for Salzburg's prince-bishops in the early 17th century, this Italian Renaissance–style country villa is an impressive example of the luxury enjoyed by absolute rulers during the Renaissance. The most intriguing features are its water gardens— dozens of trick fountains and water sprays hidden in the large Renaissance gardens, with mysterious grottoes and mythical statues. (You almost invariably get doused, to the delight of children.) You can visit the palace on your own in about 20 minutes with an audioguide. Be sure, too, to take a quick spin through the Volkskundemuseum (Folklore Museum) with its handmade crafts, gaily painted furniture, and household objects. Guided tours of the garden, in English and German, last 30 to 40 minutes and depart every half-hour. During July and August, evening guided tours that take in only the illuminated trick fountains are also given at 7, 8, 9, and 10pm.

Fürstenweg 37 (5km/3 miles south of the city). (C) 0662/82 03 72-0. www.hellbrunn.at. Admission to palace, water garden tour, and Folklore Museum 7.50€ ($8.65) adults, 5.50€ ($6.35) students, 3.50€ ($4) children, 20€ ($22) families; evening garden tours (July–Aug only) 7€ ($8.05) adults, 3.50€ ($4) children. Apr and Oct daily 9am–4:30pm (last tour); May–June and Sept daily 9am–5:30pm (last tour); July–Aug daily 9am–10pm. Closed Nov–Mar. Bus: 55 to Hellbrunn.

Residenz *   The 180-room baroque Residenz, in the heart of the Altstadt, dates from the mid–12th century but was rebuilt extensively in the 16th, 17th, and 18th centuries, offering you a tour through 200 years of classical architecture. It served as the official residence of the archbishops when it was deemed safe for them to move down from the fortress into the city. (After you've toured both places, you won't blame them for preferring the more elegant Residenz.) You can tour 15 **Residenz Prunkräume (State Rooms)** on your own with an audioguide, included in the price, which takes about 40 minutes. You'll see the throne room (the most beautiful, and one of several in which Mozart performed), the bedroom of the archbishop, the library, the audience chamber (the most lavishly decorated, with original furnishings), and other chambers, most with inlaid wooden floors, marble portals, ceiling frescoes relating heroics of Alexander the Great, tapestries, and precious furniture. The **Residenzgalerie** is a 15-room gallery of European art from the 16th to the 19th centuries, with works by Dutch, French, Italian, and Austrian baroque artists, including **Rembrandt, Rubens, Bruegel, Friedrich Loos, Ferdinand Georg Waldmüller,** and

Special & Free Events

Throughout the year, Salzburg hosts annual music festivals. The year kicks off with **Mozart Week** at the end of January, followed by the **Salzburg Easter Festival.**

The city's most famous spectacle is the **Salzburger Festspiele (Salzburg Festival),** which is held from the end of July to the end of August and has a history stretching back 70 years. Tickets are hard to come by and impossible to get once the festival is under way. To find out what's being performed, contact the Salzburg Festival, Postfach 140, 5020 Salzburg (℗ **0662/8045-500;** www.salzburgfestival.at). Among the highlights are Mozart's operas, Hugo von Hofmannsthal's *Everyman,* performances of the Salzburg Marionette Theater, and guest philharmonic orchestras.

Autumn brings the **Salzburg Culture Days,** a 2-week musical event held in October with more opera and concerts given by renowned national orchestras. International jazz stars dazzle with 4 days of concerts and jam sessions at the **Autumn Jazz Festival** in early November. From the end of November until Christmas, a **Christmas Market** is held daily in the square by the Cathedral and Mirabellplatz. Because these festivals are popular, make hotel reservations at least a month or 2 in advance if you want to visit Salzburg during these times, and even more in advance for August.

For free concerts, your best bet is the **Hochschule Mozarteum,** where concerts are given regularly by students. In summer, free brass-band concerts are held in Mirabell Garden on Wednesday at 8:30pm and Sunday at 10:30am.

Hans Makart. Also of special interest are paintings depicting Salzburg through the centuries.

Residenzplatz 1. ℗ **0662/80 42-26 90** for state rooms; 0662/84 04 51 for Residenzgalerie. www.salzburg-burgen.at or www.residenzgalerie.at. Combination ticket (State Rooms and Residenzgalerie) 7.30€ ($8.40) adults, 5.50€ ($6.35) seniors and students, 2.50€ ($2.90) children. State Rooms daily 10am–5pm (closed 2 weeks before Easter and for special events); Residenzgalerie Tues–Sun 10am–5pm. Bus: 3, 5, 6, 7, 8, 25, or 26 to Rathaus.

CHURCHES

Catacombs of St. Peter's Church   This church in the Altstadt, at the foot of Mönchsberg, has a lovely rococo interior and is surrounded by one of the most picturesque cemeteries I've ever seen—definitely worth a walk through. At the entrance to the catacombs (against the cliff) are two of the most important tombs—those of Mozart's sister, Nannerl, and Haydn's brother, Johann Michael Haydn. You can tour the catacombs on your own in less than 30 minutes (an English pamphlet costs .60€/55¢), where you'll see rooms and chapels carved in the face of the cliff, the first dating from A.D. 250 and built by Roman Christians for secret religious ceremonies. *Be forewarned:* There are a lot of stairs to climb.

St. Peter-Bezirk 1. ℗ **0662/84 45 78-0.** Free admission to church and cemetery; admission to catacombs 1€ ($1.15) adults, .60€ (70¢) seniors, students, and children. Cemetery daily 6:30am–6pm. Catacombs May–Sept Tues–Sun 10:30am–5pm; Oct–Apr Wed–Thurs 10:30am–3:30pm, Fri–Sun 10:30am–4pm. Bus: 3, 5, 6, 7, 8, 25, or 26 to Mozartsteg.

Dom (Salzburg Cathedral)   Salzburg Cathedral, in the center of the Altstadt, was first built in the 8th century but destroyed by fire in the 16th. The present Dom, commissioned by Archbishop Wolf-Dietrich and designed by Italian architect Santino Solari, is the finest example of an early baroque building north of the Alps. This is where Mozart was baptized and engaged as a court organist, and it's famed for its three bronze doors and 4,000-pipe organ. Treasures of the Dom, including an 8th-century cross of St. Rupert, are on display in the museum to the right of the front door, but it's worth visiting only if you're interested in religious art.

Domplatz. ℰ **0662/80 47-1860** or 84 41 89. Free admission to Dom (donations appreciated); admission to Dom museum 5€ ($5.75) adults, 3.50€ ($4) seniors, 1.50€ ($1.75) students and children. Dom daily 8am–7pm (to 5pm in winter); Dom museum May–Oct Mon–Sat 10am–5pm, Sun 1–6pm (closed Nov–Apr). Bus: 3, 5, 6, 7, 8, 25, or 26 to Mozartsteg.

MUSEUMS

Haus der Natur (Museum of Natural History) ⭐ *Kids*   On five floors in 80 exhibit rooms, practically everything that lives or grows is brilliantly displayed. Exhibits include model dinosaurs (including one that moves) and other prehistoric animals; the twin roots of a fir tree hundreds of years old; a rock crystal weighing 1,360 pounds; abnormalities like a calf with two heads, a chicken with four legs, and a deer with three legs; a giant model of a DNA molecule; models of the Saturn V rocket; and pieces of moon rock donated by President Nixon in 1973. There's also an aquarium with fresh- and seawater animals, as well as an exhibit on sharks and other ocean inhabitants and the Reptile Zoo with 200 scaly creatures. Without a doubt, this is one of the better natural history museums in Europe, and kids love it. Alas, the descriptions are in German only. With little ones in tow, you can easily spend a couple hours here.

Museumsplatz 5. ℰ **0662/84 26 53-0.** www.hausdernatur.at. Admission 4.50€ ($5.20) adults, 4€ ($4.60) seniors, 2.50€ ($2.90) students and children. Daily 9am–5pm. Bus: 1, 3, 5, or 16 to Hanuschplatz.

Spielzeugmuseum (Toy Museum) *Kids*   Housed in the former Salzburg Municipal Hospital, this delightful museum contains two collections: toys and historic musical instruments. The toy museum displays every conceivable sort of toy—from a hand-carved Noah's Ark to a merry-go-round, from model trains to dolls and dollhouses, cutouts, and cardboard theaters—all from the 16th century to the present. You'll see more adults than children, especially in a section of historic musical instruments. You can see everything in less than an hour.

Bürgerspitalgasse 2. ℰ **0662/62 08 08-300.** www.smca.at. Admission 3.50€ ($4) adults, 2€ ($2.30) seniors, .80€ (90¢) students and children. Daily 9am–5pm. Bus: 1, 4, or 15 to Herbert-von-Karajan-Platz.

Stiegl's Brauwelt (Stiegl's World of Beer)   On the western edge of town near the airport and housed in the former malt house of the Stiegl Brewery (Austria's oldest private brewery), this museum recounts the 500-year history of the brewery, shows the brewing process, and imparts information on the beer-brewing nations. (Did you know, for example, the United States is the largest beer producer in the world?) Displays are in German only, but ask for the English translation at the ticket counter. At the end of your self-guided tour, stop by the pub, where you can choose 2 pints of beer (included in the admission price). The museum itself can be toured in about an hour.

Bräuhausstrasse 9. ℰ **0662/83 87-1492.** www.brauwelt.at. Admission (including 2 pints of beer or a soft drink, a pretzel, and a souvenir) 9€ ($10) adults, 8.30€ ($9.55) seniors and students, 4€ ($4.60) children. Wed–Sun 10am–5pm (you must enter by 4pm). Bus: 1 to Bräuhausstrasse.

PANORAMIC VIEWS

For the best view of Hohensalzburg Fortress towering above Salzburg and the Salzach River, take the **Mönchsberg Lift** from Gstättengasse 13 (© **0662/44 80-62 85**) in the Altstadt to the top of Mönchsberg. It costs 1.60€ ($1.85) one-way and 2.60€ ($3) round-trip adults, .80€ (90¢) one-way and 1.30€ ($1.50) round-trip children. The elevator operates daily 9am to 9pm June to September and 9am to 6pm October to May. At the end of 2004, the lift will also connect the Mönchsberg to the **Museum der Moderne Salzburg** (© **0662/80 42-2541;** www.museumdermoderne.at). The museum will feature changing exhibitions of art and photography from the 20th and 21st centuries (contact the tourist office for current admission prices and open hours).

For added enjoyment, hike the 30 minutes from Mönchsberg Lift to Hohen-salzburg Fortress, passing changing vistas and villas along the way.

Salzburg's tallest mountain at 1,835m (6,115 ft.) above sea level, **Untersberg** is 11km (6¾ miles) south of town. Visiting Untersberg is certainly worth the extra money and might very well be one of the highlights of your stay, especially if this is your only excursion into the Alpine scenery. To get there, take bus no. 25 from the train station or Mozartsteg to St. Leonhard, the last stop, and change to the cable car to ride to the mountaintop. From there, you'll have a glorious view of Salzburg and the Alps. A marked path leads to the peak in about 20 minutes (wear good walking shoes if you plan to hike); if you prefer, you can sit in the restaurant there and enjoy the view. The round-trip fare for the **cable car** (© **06246/724 77**) is 17€ ($20) adults and 8.50€ ($9.80) children. It operates daily July to September 8:30am to 5:30pm, October 8:30am to 5pm, mid-December to February 9am to 4pm. It's closed November to the beginning of December and 2 weeks in April for maintenance.

PARKS & GARDENS

The town's most famous garden, now a public park, is the **Mirabellgarten** on the river's right bank. Designed in the 17th century in baroque style with stat-ues, marble vases designed by Fischer von Erlach, fountains, and ponds, it offers a great view of the Hohensalzburg Fortress. In the middle of the grounds is a palace built by Archbishop Wolf-Dietrich for his mistress (she bore him 14 chil-dren), now used for concerts, weddings, and administrative offices. The park is a popular place for a stroll, and its benches are always occupied by office work-ers and older people catching a few rays. The Orangerie is free, and in spring the garden comes alive with about 17,000 tulips. A small open-air cafeteria sells beverages and snacks. Adjoining the garden is the **Kurgarten,** a tree-lined area with a small hill called Rosenhügel (a good spot for taking snapshots) and an indoor pool and spa center.

ORGANIZED TOURS

In a city as small as Salzburg, it really isn't necessary to spend money on a tour. But if you insist, the tourist office offers hour-long tours of the Altstadt, where you'll learn the history of the Cathedral, St. Peter's Church, Mozart's Birthplace, and other historic locations. Tours cost 8€ ($9.20) and depart daily at 12:15pm from the City Tourist Office on Mozartplatz.

Organized tours are most convenient for visiting out-of-town sights. Readers planning more than a 2-day stay might want to consider an excursion with **Bob's Special Tours** (© **0662/84 95 11;** www.bobstours.com), which has specialized in personable English-language tours for more than 30 years, in buses seating 8 to 20. The "*Sound of Music* Tour" includes a short city tour and takes in most of the major film locations, like Leopoldskron Palace (which served as the von Trapp film home), the Lake district where the opening scene was filmed, and the gazebo at Hellbrunn Palace. The "Bavarian Mountain Tour" includes some *Sound of Music* sights, as well as Berchtesgaden in Germany, Lake Königssee, and the option of visiting Hitler's Eagle's Nest. Both tours last 4 hours and depart daily at 9am and 2pm, with pickup at any guesthouse or hotel. They cost 35€ ($40) for adults (discounts given to seniors, students, children, and families); entrance fees are extra. Other tours take in a visit to salt mines, the ice caves at Eisriesenwelt, King Ludwig's castle at Herrenchiemsee, or Grossglockner (Austria's highest mountain). You can buy tickets at tourist offices and most hotels, but *Frommer's* readers can get a 5€ ($5.75) discount by booking directly at Bob's Special Tours via the Internet or at its office in the Altstadt at Rudolfskai 38, open Monday to Friday 9am to 5pm and Saturday 9am to noon.

Another tour company is **Salzburg Sightseeing Tours,** Mirabellplatz 2 (© **0662/88 16 16;** www.salzburg-sightseeingtours.at), the first company to offer a *Sound of Music* tour (its bus even appeared in the film)—it still offers a 4-hour "The Most Unique *Sound of Music* Tour" in English for 33€ ($38) adults and 17€ ($20) children, with departures daily at 9:30am and 2pm. In addition to a variety of city tours, it offers several countryside excursions. Most interesting is the daily 4-hour trip to the salt mines in Hallein, which includes a visit to an open-air reconstructed Celtic village and an excursion through the mines for 40€ ($46) adults and 33€ ($38) children. For real *Sound of Music* fans, another option is the "Follow Maria's Footsteps Tour," which allows you to join both the "*Sound of Music* Tour" and the "Salt Mine Tour" (the real Maria spent some time in Hallein) at a reduced rate of 62€ ($71) adults and 39€ ($45) children. You can do both tours in 1 day or on separate days. *Note:* Readers who present this book will get a 10% discount on tour prices; students and families receive further reductions on all tours except the "Salt Mine Tour." Prices for all tours include hotel pickup and all admissions.

5 Shopping

Austrian artisanship is of high quality, with correspondingly high prices for Austrian traditional **sweaters, dirndls, leather goods, jewelry,** and other local goods, including **chocolates.** Most shops are concentrated in the Altstadt along **Getreidegasse** and **Alter Markt,** as well as across the river along **Linzer Gasse.**

If you make purchases that total more than 75€ ($67) in one store on any given day, you're entitled to a **partial refund of the 16.67% value-added tax (VAT).** (See chapter 1, "Enjoying Europe on a Budget," for details on how to get a VAT refund.)

Salzburg has two well-known markets. The **Grünmarkt (Green Market)** is held in the Altstadt, in front of the Universitäts church on Universitätsplatz (behind Mozart's Birthplace). It features stalls selling vegetables, fruit, flowers, and souvenirs, as well as a stand-up food stall selling sausages. It takes place Monday to Friday 6am to 7pm and Saturday 6am to 3pm. On the other side of the river, in front of St. Andrew's Church near Mirabellplatz, is the **Schrannenmarkt.** This is where Salzburg's housewives go to shop and socialize, purchasing vegetables, flowers, bread, and even traditional handicraft products. It's held every Thursday (on Wed if Thurs is a public holiday) 6am to 1pm.

6 Salzburg After Dark

As the birthplace of Mozart and site of the Salzburg Festival (see the box "Special & Free Events," above), the city boasts a musical event almost every night of the year. To find out what's going on where, stop by the **City Tourist Office,** Mozartplatz 5 (© **889/87-330**), to pick up a free copy of the monthly *Veranstaltungen.*

The cheapest way to secure theater tickets is to buy them directly at the theater box office. Otherwise, the **Salzburg Ticket Service,** which charges a 20% commission, is at the City Tourist Office on Mozartplatz (© **0662/84 03 10**). Selling tickets for all concerts, it's open Monday to Friday 9am to 6pm and Saturday 9am to noon (mid-July to Aug Mon–Sat 9am–7pm and Sun 10am–6pm).

For the **Salzburg Festival,** you must secure tickets months in advance.

THE PERFORMING ARTS

OPERA, DANCE & MUSIC   The **Festspielhaus,** Hofstallgasse 1 (© **0662/ 80 45-0;** bus: 1, 4 or 15 to Herbert-von-Karajan-Platz or 3, 5, 6, 7, 8, 25, or 26 to Rathaus), is where opera, ballet, and concerts are performed and major events of the Salzburg Festival take place. Performances are in the 1,324-seat Kleines Haus (Small House) or the 2,170-seat Grosses Haus (Large House), and it's best to buy tickets in advance; for the Salzburg Festival, months in advance for major performances. The box office for the Salzburg Festival is at Herbert-von-Karajan-Platz (© **0662/80 45-500**). It's open Monday to Friday 9:30am to 3pm, except from July 1 to the start of the festival, when it's open Monday to Saturday 9:30am to 5pm, and during the festival, when it's open daily 9:30am to 6:30pm. For orchestra concerts, given September to June, you'll find the box office at Kulturvereinigung, Waagplatz 1A (© **0662/84 53 46**), near the tourist office. It's open Monday to Friday 8am to 6pm; performances are usually at 7:30pm. Tickets for orchestra concerts are 23€ to 45€ ($27–$52); during the Salzburg Festival, tickets start at 15€ ($17) for opera, 4€ ($4.60) for concerts and plays.

Orchestra concerts and chamber music are presented in the **Mozarteum,** Schwarzstrasse 26 (© **0662/87 31 54;** bus: 1, 3, 5, 6, or 25 to Makartplatz). The Mozarteum is on the river's right bank, near Mirabellgarten; its box office, open Monday to Thursday 9am to 2pm and Friday 9am to 4pm, is in the Mozart-Wohnhaus, Theatergasse 2. Performances are at 11am and/or 7:30pm, with most tickets at 8€ to 51€ ($9.20–$59).

The **Salzburger Schlosskonzerte (Salzburg Palace Concerts)** take place year-round in the Marble Hall of Mirabell Palace, Mirabellplatz (© **0662/84 85 86;** www.salzburger-schlosskonzerte.at; bus: 1, 3, 5, 6, 51, or 25 to Mirabellplatz). The chamber-music series presents mostly Mozart's music, as well as music by Mozart's contemporaries and others, including works by Haydn, Beethoven, Schubert, and Vivaldi. Concerts, generally at 8 or 8:30pm, are held 3 to 7 nights a week in intimate baroque surroundings, much as they were in Mozart's time. The box office, at Theatergasse 2, is open Monday to Friday 9am to 5:30pm. Tickets are 26€ to 31€ ($30–$36).

Salzburg's landmark, the **Hohensalzburg Fortress,** Mönchsberg 34 (© **0662/ 82 58 58;** www.mozartfestival.at; take the funicular from Festungsgasse), features concerts called the **Salzburger Festungskonzerte** in the medieval Prince's Chamber, performed by the Salzburger Mozart-Ensemble, as well as guest musicians. The box office, at A.-Adlgasser-Weg 22, is open daily 9am to 9pm; performances are given almost daily at 8 or 8:30pm. Tickets are 29€ to 36€ ($33–$41).

THEATER Opera and ballet are performed at the **Salzburger Landestheater,** Schwarzstrasse 22 (© **0662/87 15 12-222;** www.theater.co.at; bus: 1, 3, 5, 6, or 25 to Makartplatz), as well as operettas. During August, the theater takes part in the Salzburg Festival. The Landestheater has a central location on the river's right bank, just south of Mirabellgarten. The box office, on Makartplatz, is open Monday to Friday 10am to 5pm and Saturday 10am to 2pm. Tickets are 15€ to 47€ ($17–$54) for operas and operettas, and 11€ to 36€ ($12–$36) for ballet; students receive discounts on unsold tickets 30 minutes before the performance.

Next door, the **Salzburger Marionettentheater,** Schwarzstrasse 24 (© **0662/ 87 24 06;** www.marionetten.at; bus: 1, 3, 5, 6, or 25 to Makartplatz), was founded in 1913 and tours the world as one of Europe's largest and most famous marionette theaters. Using recordings made by top orchestras and singers, it presents operas and operettas Easter through September, during Christmas, and some dates in January, including *The Magic Flute, Die Fledermaus, The Barber of Seville, The Marriage of Figaro,* and *Don Giovanni.* The box office is open Monday to Saturday 9am to 1pm and 2 hours before the start of each performance, which are usually Monday to Saturday at 7:30pm, with occasional 2 and 4pm matinees. Tickets run 18€ to 35€ ($21–$40).

DINNER SHOWS

For a real splurge, you might consider combining dinner with the music of Mozart. At the **Stiftskeller St. Peter** (see "Great Deals on Dining," above), the **Mozart Dinner Concert** features Mozart music played by period-costumed musicians and a three-course meal based on traditional recipes from the 17th and 18th centuries. Festivities, costing 45€ ($52) per person, begin at 7:15pm three or more times a week (nightly July–Aug). For details, contact the Salzburger Konzertgesellschaft, Pfeifergasse 11 (© **0662/82 86 95-0;** www.mozartdinner concert.com).

In addition, **Candlelight Dinner & Mozart Concert shows** feature dinner beginning between 5:30 and 6:30pm at the Hohensalzburg Fortress or the Restaurant K&K in the Altstadt, followed by concerts 2 hours later at either the Fortress or a State Room of the Residenz (times and places depend on the season). These culinary musical experiences cost 44€ to 48€ ($51–$55) depending on the menu. For details, contact the Salzburger Festungskonzerte box office at A.-Adlgasser-Weg 22 (© **0662/82 58 58**).

Capitalizing on Salzburg's movie fame is **The *Sound of Music* Dinner Show,** held nightly at 7pm May to October at Sternbräu, Griessgasse 23 (© **0662/84 21 40** or 0662/82 66 17). Costing 43€ ($49) per person, it features melodies from the film, tunes from Salzburg operettas, and a documentary video of the von Trapp family.

BARS

The **Augustiner Bräustübl Kloster Mülln,** Augustinergasse 4 (© **0662/43 12 46;** bus: 27 from Mirabellplatz or Hanuschplatz to Augustinergasse), popularly called Augustinerbräu or Müllnerbräu, is one of the cheapest places in town for a brew, with seating in its beer garden or in one of its massive dining halls. There are also counters selling sausages, pretzels, and other foods that go well with beer (see "Great Deals on Dining," above).

One of many bars along Rudolfskai on the banks of the Salzach, the **Altstadtkeller,** Rudolfskai 26 (© **0662/84 96 88;** bus: 3, 5, 6, 7, 8, 25, or 26 to Mozartsteg), occupies a historic cellar vault and features live piano music ranging from swing and blues to Latin American tunes. On Thursday, folk musicians perform typical Austrian and Bavarian songs. There's no cover, and it's open Tuesday to Saturday 7pm to 3am. Nearby at the **Shamrock Irish Pub,** Rudolfskai 12 (© **0662/84 16 10;** bus: 3, 5, 6, 7, 8, 25, or 26 to Rathaus), a young international crowd ranging from students to tourists gathers at Salzburg's hottest bar for Guinness on tap, Salzburg's largest selection of whiskies and alcoholic coffees, and free live music nightly starting around 9pm. It's open Tuesday and Wednesday 3pm to 3am, Thursday 3pm to 4am, Friday and Saturday noon to 4am, and Sunday noon to 2am.

Rockhouse, Schallmooser Hauptstrasse 46 (© **0662/88 49 14;** www. rockhouse.at; bus: 4 to Canavalstrasse), is an alternative music venue that includes a cafe and a tunnel-shaped concert hall featuring local and international bands playing rock, jazz, funk, soul, blues, and techno pop, with concerts three or four times a week. Occupying an 1842 building that formerly served as a wine and ice cellar, this is a welcome addition to the Salzburg music scene. Cover ranges from 6€ to 18€ ($6.90–$21).

A GAY & LESBIAN BAR

2 Stein, beside the Stein Hotel at Giselakai 9 (© **0662/88 02 01;** bus: 1, 2, 5, 6, 51, or 55 to Makartplatz), draws mostly gays but also lesbians and a mixed crowd, especially after other nearby bars close. It's open Sunday to Wednesday 6pm to 4am and Thursday to Saturday 6pm to 5am.

7 A Side Trip to Innsbruck ✦✦

One of the joys of being in **Innsbruck,** capital of the Tyrol province and just 190km (118 miles) southwest of Salzburg, is its mountains—no matter where you are, you can see majestic peaks towering above the rooftops. This Alpine town of 120,000 offers a beautifully preserved medieval Old City (Altstadt) of narrow cobbled streets and Gothic, Renaissance, and baroque buildings, as well as excursions into the stupendously scenic countryside. Little wonder the Winter Olympics were held here in 1964 and 1976—it's a skier's mecca almost year-round, due to the Stubai Glacier 16km (10 miles) south. In summer, it also offers excellent hiking. If you're tired of big cities, come to Innsbruck to unwind.

From Salzburg, it takes about 2 hours to reach Innsbruck by **train.** You'll arrive at Innsbruck's city-center train station, the **Hauptbahnhof,** Südtirolplatz (© **0512/05 17 17** for train info and schedules), a 10-minute walk from the Altstadt.

VISITOR INFORMATION In the Hauptbahnhof, you'll find the **Innsbruck Information Office** (© **0512/58 37 66**) in the main hall, where you can pick up city maps for 1€ ($1.15) and reserve accommodations for a 3€ ($3.45) fee and 15% deposit. It's open daily 9am to 7pm.

In the Altstadt, there's a larger Innsbruck Information Office at Burggraben 3 (© **0512/53 56**), just off Maria-Theresien-Strasse. Computers impart information on destinations and attractions throughout Tyrol, and on-site cameras show skiing conditions. You can also buy bus tickets, exchange money daily (until 5:15pm) at the same rates as at banks, and purchase theater tickets. This office is open daily from 8am to 6pm in winter and from 9am to 6pm in summer. You can visit Innsbruck's home page at **www.innsbruck-tourismus.com.**

GETTING AROUND Most of Innsbruck's major sights are clustered in or around the Altstadt, within easy walking distance of one another. Otherwise, trams and buses provide public transportation around Innsbruck and its

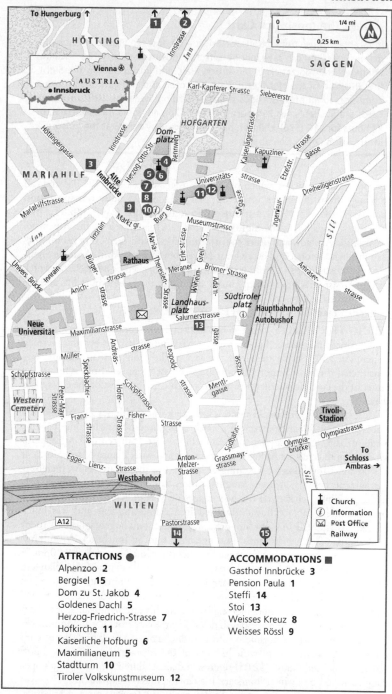

Innsbruck

To Hungerburg ↑

1

2

HÖTTING

Inn

Innstrasse

Vienna ⊛
AUSTRIA
●Innsbruck

Karl-Kapferer Strasse   Siebererstr.

SAGGEN

0   1/4 mi
0   0.25 km

HOFGARTEN

Höttingergasse

Innstrasse

Herzog Otto-Str.

Rennweg

Dom-
platz

Kaiserjägerstrasse

Kapuziner-   Strasse   gasse

Etzelstr.

Dreiheiligenstrasse

MARIAHILF

3

Alte
Innbrücke

4

5

6

Universitäts-   strasse

Engasse

Mariahilfstrasse

7

8

9   10 ⓘ

Burg gr.

11   12

Museumstrasse

Universitätsstrasse... gasse

Sill

Inn

Univers. Brücke

Innrain

Markt gr.

Maria-   Theresien-   Strasse

Erlerstrasse

Greil-   Str.

Burg gr.

Amraser-   strasse

Rathaus

Bürger-   strasse

Meraner

Wilhelm-   Adam-

Brixner Strasse

Anich-   strasse

Neue
Universität

Maximilianstrasse

Andreas-   strasse

Landhaus-
platz
Salurnerstrasse

13

Südtiroler
platz   ⓘ

Hauptbahnhof
Autobushof

Müller-

Speckbacher-

Schöpfstrasse

Leopold-   strasse

Mentl-
gasse

Schöpfstrasse

Peter-Mayr-   Strasse

Hofer-

Franz-

Fisher-   Strasse

Strasse

Strasse

strasse

Western
Cemetery

Tivoli-
Stadion

Egger-   Lienz-   Strasse

Anton-
Melzer-
Strasse

Grassmayr-
strasse

Südbahn-

Olympia-
brücke

Olympiastrasse

To
Schloss
Ambras →

Westbahnhof

Sill

WILTEN

A12

Pastorstrasse

14 ↓

15 ↓

✝ Church
ⓘ Information
✉ Post Office
— Railway

(Value The Innsbruck Card

If you plan to use public transportation a lot and see most of Innsbruck's major sights, you can save money with the **Innsbruck Card,** which includes unlimited transportation in Innsbruck, Hall, and Igls, including the Sightseer Bus; use of the Nordkette, Patscherkofel, and Hungerburg lifts; and admission to all of Innsbruck's sights, including Swarovski Kristallwelten. Cards are available for 24 hours for 21€ ($24), 48 hours for 26€ ($30), or 72 hours for 31€ ($36); children pay half-price. Buy tickets at the Innsbruck Information Office (see above).

---

environs. A **single ticket,** which permits transfers, costs 1.60€ ($1.85) and can be bought from the driver. Other options include a **24-hour transportation pass** for 3.40€ ($3.90) or a **group of four tickets** for 5.10€ ($5.85). Best for visitors, however, is the **Sightseer,** a red bus that travels to the Alpenzoo, Bergisel, the Altstadt, and other tourist attractions, with runs every 30 minutes May through October and every hour November through April. A single Sightseer ticket costs 2.50€ ($2.90), but best is the Day Ticket for 8€ ($9.20), which includes transportation on all city buses and trams, the Hungerburg lift, and the funicular to the Alpenzoo.

To call a **taxi,** dial ✆ 0512/5311 or 0512/1718.

SEEING THE SIGHTS   First mentioned in 12th-century documents, Innsbruck gained international stature under Maximilian I, who became German emperor in 1507, made the town the seat of the Holy Roman Empire, and constructed the most important buildings. Today, these buildings stand at the center of the compact medieval **Altstadt,** which contains most of the city's main attractions.

Most striking is Innsbruck's famous landmark, the **Goldenes Dachl (Golden Roof),** Herzog-Friedrich-Strasse 15, easily recognized by its gleaming balcony made of 2,657 gilded copper tiles. Built in the late 15th century by Emperor Maximilian to celebrate his marriage to his second wife, Bianca Maria Sforza, it was used as a royal box for watching civic events in the square below, including tournaments between armored knights, dances, and theatrics. If you look closely at the building's reliefs, you can see images of Maximilian and his two wives. (His 1st wife, Mary of Burgundy, died in a riding accident and was much grieved; his 2nd wife brought him great wealth and went largely ignored.) Today the building's facade is the most photographed sight in Innsbruck. In summer, Tyrolean Folk Art Evenings are staged in the square on Thursday at 8:30pm.

The best thing to do at the Goldenes Dachl is go inside to the **Maximilianeum** (✆ 0512/58 11 11; www.tiroler-landesmuseum.at), a museum dedicated to Maximilian. Although it's just one room filled with portraits of Maximilian and artifacts of his time, an audioguide explaining the historic significance of the displays and a 20-minute film in English describing the emperor's life and Innsbruck's history make a visit worthwhile. Visitors are also allowed a peek onto the balcony under the Goldenes Dachl with its view of the Altstadt. Admission is 3.60€ ($4.15) adults and 1.80€ ($2.05) seniors/students/children. In summer, it's open daily 10am to 6pm; winter hours are Tuesday to Sunday 10am to 5pm.

Just a stone's throw away is the **Stadtturm (City Tower),** Herzog-Friedrich-Strasse 21 (✆ 0512/56 15 00-3), built in 1450 and at 56m (185 ft.) tall still one of the Altstadt's highest structures. Its viewing platform, reached via 148 stairs, offers magnificent panoramic views of the city and Alps. It's open daily 10am to 5pm (to 8pm in summer) and admission is 2.50€ ($2.90) adults, 2€ ($2.30) seniors/students, and 1€ ($1.15) children.

Innsbruck's most imposing building remains the **Kaiserliche Hofburg (Imperial Court Palace)** 𝕬𝕬, Rennweg 1 (℗ **0512/58 71 86**; www.tirol. com/hofburg-ibk). It's to Innsbruck what Versailles is to Paris—but on a much smaller scale. Built in 1460 and enlarged by Emperor Maximilian in the 1500s as a residence for his second wife, it was reconstructed in the baroque style by Empress Maria Theresa in the mid–18th century. On view are the **Kaiserappartements** used by Maria Theresa and her family whenever they visited, including the royal chapel, dining rooms, and bedrooms, all with original furnishings, tapestries, paintings, and portraits. The most fascinating of the 20-some open rooms is the **Giant's Hall**, lavishly decorated in rococo style with elaborate stucco designs and a painted ceiling. What's most striking about the room, however, are the portraits of Maria Theresa and her 16 children, including her youngest daughter, Antonia, who went on to become that ill-fated queen of France, Marie Antoinette. Admission is 5.45€ ($6.25) adults, 4€ ($4.60) seniors, 3.65€ ($4.15) students, 2.45€ ($2.80) children ages 15 to 18, and 1.10€ ($1.25) children 6 to 14 (free for children under 6). It's open daily 9am to 5pm (you must enter by 4:30pm) and can be toured in 30 minutes.

A minute's walk east of the Kaiserliche Hofburg is the **Hofkirche (Court Church)**, Universitätsstrasse 2 (℗ **0512/58 43 02**; www.hofkirche.at), conceived by Maximilian as his memorial and place of burial. Inside is his elaborate tomb, decorated with reliefs depicting scenes from the emperor's life and surrounded by 28 larger-than-life bronze statues representing his ancestors, relatives, and peers, including his father, two wives, son, and daughter; two of the statues are from designs by German artist Albrecht Dürer. The tomb, however, is empty—Maximilian died before the church was built and was buried in Wiener Neustadt. Several other important figures are interred here, however, including Tyrolean freedom fighter Andreas Hofer and Archduke Ferdinand II. You'll find Ferdinand's final resting place up the stairs in the **Silberne Kapelle (Silver Chapel)**; just outside the chapel's iron gate is the tomb of Ferdinand's wife, Philippine Welser, who, as a mere commoner, wasn't allowed to be buried beside her husband. It's open Monday to Saturday 9am to 5pm, with admission at 3€ ($3.45) adults and 1.50€ ($1.75) children.

For adults, the best deal is to buy a combination ticket for 6.50€ ($7.50) that includes a visit to the **Tiroler Volkskunstmuseum (Tyrolean Folk Art Museum)** 𝕬𝕬𝕬 (℗ **0512/58 43 02**; www.tiroler-volkskunstmuseum.at), housed in a former monastery adjoining the Court Church (and sharing the same entry). My favorite museum in Innsbruck, it's one of Austria's best folk art museums, with a collection of items used by common folk in the Tyrol from the Middle Ages to the 20th century. Included are sleighs; a beautiful collection of painted furniture (Bauernmöbel); ornamental bells for sheep, goats, and cows (you should see the size of some); farming tools and cooking utensils; religious artifacts; traditional clothing; glassware; and a fascinating collection of nativity scenes (Krippe). It also contains more than a dozen reconstructed Tyrolean rooms taken from inns, farmhouses, and patrician homes and furnished in Gothic, Renaissance, and baroque styles. It's open Monday to Saturday 9am to 5pm, Sunday and holidays 9am to noon. If you want to see only the museum and not the Hofkirche, it costs 5€ ($5.75) adults and 1.50€ ($1.75) children.

Although it's not in the Altstadt, very much worth a visit—especially if you have children in tow—is Europe's highest-elevation zoo, the **Alpenzoo (Alpine Zoo)** ⊛, Weiherburggasse 37 (© **0512/29 23 23;** www.alpenzoo.at), boasting great views from its location above the city on the slopes of the Hungerburg. This is the place to see all those animals native to the Alps and Alpine region, like European bison, wolves, lynx, marmots, otters, beavers, vultures, owls, eagles, buzzards, elk, Alpine ibex, rabbits, brown bears, and local fish. There's also a section devoted to domesticated Alpine animals, including cows, goats, and sheep. Admission to the zoo, open daily 9am to 6pm (to 5pm in winter), is 7€ ($8.05) adults, 5€ ($5.75) seniors/students, and 3.50€ ($4) children. To reach the zoo, take tram no. 1 or bus no. 4, D, or E to Talstation, followed by the Hungerburg funicular to Station Alpenzoo. Or take the Sightseer to the Alpenzoo bus stop.

If you're staying overnight, I highly recommend an excursion to nearby **Wattens** to visit the fantastic **Swarovski Kristallwelten (Crystal Worlds)** ⊛⊛⊛, Kristallweltenstrasse 1 (© **05224/51080;** www.swarovski.com/crystalworlds), which you can reach in about 15 minutes by bus from the Innsbruck Busbahnhof (next to the Hauptbahnhof). Buses depart for Wattens every 30 minutes (every 60 min. Sun and holidays); get off at the Kristallwelten stop. Even if you know what Swarovski is—the world's leading producer of full-cut crystal—you won't be prepared for this experiment in fantasy, with theatrical three-dimensional displays that give this attraction a Disney-esque quality and have catapulted it into the status of the region's top tourist draw. Kristallwelten itself is subterranean, hidden from view by a man-made hill but attracting attention with a giant head spouting water. Designed by Viennese multimedia artist Andre Heller, the interior consists of more than a dozen magical cavernlike chambers, with displays relating to crystal. You'll see the world's largest cut crystal (137 lb.); a glass-enclosed wall containing 12 tons of crystal; works by artists ranging from Salvador Dalí to Keith Haring; and costumes, art, and other displays about crystal, including a crystal dome that gives a pretty good idea of what it would be like to be encapsulated inside a crystal. New Age music adds a dreamlike quality. You can see it all in about 40 minutes, not counting the Swarovski shop. Admission is 8€ ($9.20), free for children under 12. Open daily 9am to 6pm.

SKIING & OTHER SPORTS   The Tyrolean Alps surrounding Innsbruck provide a ready-made playground for both summer and winter sports and activities. Most popular, of course, is **skiing,** available October to June. For 1-day skiers, there's the Stubai Package, including ski rental, lift tickets, and transportation

---

⟨*Moments* **A Leap of Faith**

Less than a mile from the center of Innsbruck, easily reached by the Sightseer bus and then funicular (6€/$6.90 adults, 4€/$4.60 children), looms the sleek, futuristic-looking **Bergisel** (© **0512/58 92 59;** www.bergisel.info). Its raison d'être is its famous ski jump, first built in 1925, but the new tower also beckons with an observatory and the Café im Turm offering Continental food, snacks, and desserts. Enclosed by glass on three sides, the cafe boasts panoramic views of Innsbruck, lofty mountain peaks, the ski jump, and, at the bottom of the hill, Innsbruck's largest cemetery. Bergisel is open daily 9am to 5pm.

to/from Stubai Glacier. Offered by the Innsbruck Information Office, it costs 49€ ($56). There are also ski packages covering wider areas for more days. Other winter activities are **cross-country skiing, snowboarding, ice skating,** and **day and evening tobogganing** (rental sleds available; some runs are up to 10km/6 miles long!). Throughout the year, enthusiasts can also partake in rides on a **piloted four-man bobsled.**

In summer, activities include **white-water rafting, hang gliding, mountain biking,** and **hiking.** Particularly good are the **free mountain walks** led by experienced guides, offered daily June to September at 8:45am, including transportation and use of climbing shoes and rucksack. Hikes last about 3 to 5 hours, and no previous experience in mountain hiking is necessary. Another good deal is the **free lantern hikes** offered every Tuesday evening mid-June to mid-September that culminate at an Alpine hut, where you can buy food and drink.

For more details on sports activities, contact the **Innsbruck Information Office,** Burggraben 3 (© **0512/53 56**).

WHERE TO STAY Anyone spending at least a night in one of Innsbruck's pensions or hotels can become a free member of **Club Innsbruck,** which entitles you to free transportation on ski buses, fee reductions to sports facilities, and free guided hikes.

If you can afford it, stay in the Altstadt, just a 10-minute walk from the train station (or tram no. 3 to the 2nd stop, Maria-Theresien-Strasse). One of my top picks is the **Weisses Rössl** 🌟🌟, Kiebachgasse 8, 6020 Innsbruck (© **0512/58 30 57;** fax 0512/58 30 57-5; www.roessl.at). This delightful inn, built in 1410 and recently renovated to enhance its rustic splendor, offers 14 rooms, all with cable TVs, radios, safes, hair dryers, phones, and bathrooms. The inn also boasts a fine traditional restaurant, with an outdoor terrace for summer dining. Rates are 70€ ($81) single and 110€ to 124€ ($126–$143) double, including breakfast buffet. American Express, MasterCard, and Visa are accepted.

Also in the Altstadt is the **Weisses Kreuz** 🌟🌟, Herzog Friedrich-Strasse 31, 6020 Innsbruck (© **0512/59 4 79;** fax 0512/594 79 90; www.weisseskreuz.at), with an enviable location across from the Goldenes Dachl and boasting a 500-year history. Mozart stayed here when he was 13, during a 1769 journey with his father to Italy. Although the inn has been updated with modern conveniences, including an elevator and a smart restaurant serving Continental cuisine, it remains true to its historic atmosphere, offering 40 white-walled rooms furnished with modern or traditional pine furniture, radios, phones, and (in most) cable TVs and bathrooms. Rates reflect both the seasons and various room types: 33€ to 39€ ($38–$45) single without bathroom, 57€ to 61€ ($66–$70) single with bathroom, and 85€ to 110€ ($98–$127) double with bathroom. Rates include a buffet breakfast. American Express, MasterCard, and Visa are accepted.

Although not in the Altstadt, the **Gasthof Innbrücke,** Innstrasse 1, 6020 Innsbruck (© **0512/28 19 34;** fax 0512/27 84 10; www.innsbruck.nethotels. com/innbruecke), is just a 2-minute walk away, on the other side of the Inn River. Managed by the same family for five generations, it occupies three floors (no elevator) of a building whose foundations date from 1425. Of the 27 rooms, about a third have bathrooms and cable TVs. Ask for a room with a view of the river and Altstadt. Facilities include a small bar and a solarium. Including breakfast, rates are 28€ ($32) single without bathroom, 36€ ($41) single with bathroom; 47€ ($54) double without bathroom, and 62€ ($71) double with bathroom. Diners Club, MasterCard, and Visa are accepted. Take Bus D to Innstrasse.

Pension Paula, Weiherburggasse 15, 6020 Innsbruck (© **0512/29 22 62;** fax 0512/29 30 17; www.pensionpaula.at), on a hill near the Alpine Zoo and offering splendid panoramic views of Innsbruck and the surrounding mountainside, is only a 15-minute walk from the Altstadt across the river. Once a farmhouse, with a foundation from the 1600s, this country-style chalet offers 14 rooms, 9 with bathroom and none with phones. Try to get one of the rooms facing the front with a balcony and chairs affording great views of Innsbruck. The owner, a young man named Wolfgang, speaks good English. Including continental breakfast, rates are 27€ ($31) single without bathroom, 34€ ($39) single with bathroom; 46€ ($53) double without bathroom, and 56€ ($64) double with bathroom. No credit cards. Take bus D from the train station to Schmelzergasse, from where it's a 5-minute walk.

Nestled in a mountain village only 5km (3 miles) south of Innsbruck, **Steffi** 🌟🌟, Dorfplatz 2, 6161 Natters (©/fax **0512/54 67 70;** www.pension steffi.at), is a pension beautifully decorated with dried flower arrangements, plants, and antiques. The owners are a charming couple named Brigitte (who wears dirndls in summer) and Edwin Klien-Frech, formerly English teachers. They both speak excellent English, make sure their guests are well cared for, and provide a personal touch that makes staying here a pleasure. The 10 rooms, all with bathrooms, are cozily furnished, and there's a sun terrace and garden with folding chairs, as well as a public lounge with a cable TV. If you give advance notice, they'll pick you up at the train station, a 15-minute ride away, but even the tram ride (tram STB to Natters) straight up the mountain is a hit with guests (to save money, consider buying a weekly pass). You'll love this place. Singles are 26€ ($30), doubles 49€ to 51€ ($56–$59), triples 69€ ($79), and quads 88€ ($101), including continental breakfast. No credit cards are accepted.

A good choice in budget accommodations is **Stoi,** Salurner Strasse 7 (enter from Adamgasse), 6020 Innsbruck (© **0512/58 54 34;** fax 05238/872 82; www.stoi.cjb.net), a 3-minute walk west of the train station. A simple pension (without elevator), it caters primarily to younger travelers, offering 26 clean and perfectly adequate rooms that go for 30€ ($35) single without bathroom, 35€ ($40) single with bathroom; 49€ ($56) double without bathroom, 56€ ($64) double with bathroom. Rooms sleeping three and four are also available. No credit cards are accepted, and no breakfast is served, but a machine dispenses coffee. Because the office closes at 9pm, make sure you check in before then.

WHERE TO DINE   For hearty, reasonably priced Austrian cuisine, head to the **Weisses Rössl,** Kiebachgasse 8 (© **0512/58 30 57**), described above under "Where to Stay." Up on the first floor, this old-fashioned restaurant with a covered outdoor terrace offers an English menu with photographs of *Schnitzel,* beef filet, *Gulasch, Gröstl* (a local stew made of potatoes, beef, and onions), and other meals costing 7€ to 17€ ($8.05–$20). Be sure to top your meal with Apfelstrudel. American Express, MasterCard, and Visa are accepted, and it's open Monday to Friday 11am to 2pm and 5 to 10pm; Saturday 11am to 2pm and 6 to 10pm. It's closed for 2 weeks in April and November.

For a splurge, there's no better place for a taste of Tyrolean history and cuisine than the atmospheric medieval-era **Ottoburg** 🌟, Herzog-Friedrich-Strasse 1 (© **0512/58 43 38**), in the Altstadt between the Goldenes Dachl and the Inn River. First mentioned in 12th-century documents, when it was listed as an apartment house (Maximilian lived here for a year), it was converted to a restaurant 150 years ago. The building is topped by a 1494 Gothic tower and contains four intimate dining rooms with carved wooden ceilings and neo-Gothic decor. In summer, there's outdoor seating on the Altstadt's most famous pedestrian lane. Local and house specialties on the English menu include *Gulasch, Wiener schnitzel,* Ottoburg pork filet, steak with an herb sauce, and Austrian-style gnocchi; meals cost 12€ to 26€ ($14–$30). American Express, Diners Club, MasterCard, and Visa are accepted. It's open Tuesday to Sunday from 11:30am to 2pm and 6:30pm to 10pm; closed 2 weeks in January.

If you're tired of the hearty and somewhat heavy Austrian cuisine, try the mostly vegetarian **Philippine** *⚘*, Templstrasse 2 (© **0512/58 91 57**), a 1-minute walk southwest of Maria-Theresien-Strasse on the corner of Müllerstrasse and Templstrasse. Up on the first floor, it offers a salad buffet and changing a la carte dishes (from an English-language menu) ranging from vegetarian lasagna to Asian-influenced stir-fries and fish. Most dishes cost 7.50€ to 16€ ($8.65–$18). American Express, Diners Club, MasterCard, and Visa are accepted. It's open Monday to Friday 11:30am to 2pm and Monday to Saturday 6 to 10pm. On the ground floor is the restaurant's casual cafe, open the same hours with the same menu.

INNSBRUCK AFTER DARK The **Tiroler Landestheater,** Rennweg 2 (© **0512/52 07 44**), is Innsbruck's most important venue for performances of opera, operetta, and theater. Tickets for opera run 7.50€ to 37€ ($8.65–$43), but standing-room tickets cost only 4€ ($4.60). The box office is open Monday to Saturday 8:30am to 8:30pm, Sunday and holidays 5:30 to 8:30pm.

For an evening of Tyrolean entertainment, including traditional music, yodeling, and folk dancing, see the **Tiroler Alpenbühne** (© **0512/26 32 63**), held in the Gasthaus Sandwirt am Inn, Reichenauerstrasse 151, or in the Messe-Saal at Ing-Etzel Strasse 33. Held daily at 8:40pm April to October, it costs 20€ ($23), which includes a drink. The similar **Tyrolean Party Night** is held Wednesday from about Christmas to mid-April at 8:30pm at Hotel Sailer, at Adamgasse 6–10 (© **0512/53 63**). It costs 32€ ($37), including a snack, drink, and souvenir.

South of the Altstadt is a very popular microbrewery, **Theresien-Bräu,** Maria-Theresien-Strasse 51 (© **0512/58 75 80**). It offers an Austrian menu and is open Monday to Wednesday 11:30am to 1am, Thursday to Saturday 10:30am to 2am, and Sunday 10:30am to midnight. Nearby, at Maria-Theresien-Strasse 9, is **Limerick Bill's Irish Pub** (© **0512/58 20 11**), a popular gathering place for English-speakers featuring Irish tunes; it's open daily 4:30pm to 2am.

In summer there's no finer place to be—judging by the crowds—than the **Hofgarten Cafe** (© **0512/58 88 71**), located in the Hofgarten just north of the Altstadt and offering indoor and outdoor seating and live music. Many natives make it a tradition to stop off for a beer after work—and then perhaps another, and another. In summer, it's open daily 10am to 2am; in winter, hours are Tuesday to Saturday 6pm to 2am.

23

Seville & the Best of Andalusia

by Sascha Segan & Herbert Bailey Livesey

Andalusia is the Spain of myth, where Moorish princes held court and veiled maidens danced *flamenco* under fragrant orange trees. The eight provinces of Spain's southernmost region were held, at least in part, by Muslim rule for 700 years before Ferdinand and Isabella united Spain in 1492. They left a rich heritage of architectural treasures, including Seville's Giralda, Córdoba's Mezquita, and the unforgettable Alhambra in Granada.

Seville, Andalusia's capital, is a city of operatic passion and shimmering romance. Mozart's *Don Juan,* Bizet's *Carmen,* and Rossini's *Figaro* all made their homes in the winding streets of Spain's third-largest city. It's where Christopher Columbus landed and told his queen of a New World beyond the Atlantic. Much of the pleasure of strolling Seville (indeed, all of Andalusia) isn't in visiting specific museums or sites, but rather in kicking back over a *very* long lunch and contemplating the beauty of this beautiful land.

Outside Seville, **Córdoba** still holds the echoes of another era when it was the capital of one of the world's most advanced nations, where Christians, Muslims, and Jews lived in harmony and partook freely of the city's 72 libraries. **Granada** climbs elegantly up a steep hill to a vast palace complex where the Moorish rulers made their last stand against the Christian armies. **Jerez** is home to some of the world's most celebrated sherries.

Andalusia has its problems, of course. One of Europe's most economically struggling regions (on par with parts of Italy), the regional government has been trying to lower the 20% unemployment rate for years. Street crime is an issue in Seville, and some of the locals are less than friendly to tourists (thanks in part to the vast swarm of junior-year-abroad college students encamped in the city). But on a sunny Andalusian day, none of that matters; the city, and the region, glitter like the unique gems they are.

For more on Seville and its environs, see *Frommer's Barcelona, Madrid & Seville; Frommer's Spain;* or *Spain For Dummies.*

1 Essentials

ARRIVING

BY PLANE Discount, advance-purchase airfares between Madrid and Seville are often cheaper than the high-speed AVE train fare. **Iberia** (© **800/772-4642;** www.iberia.com) and **Spanair** (© **888/545-5757;** www.spanair.com) run several flights daily between Madrid and Seville, with flights from North America and most other international cities usually connecting through Madrid's Barajas Airport. There are direct flights to other Iberian cities, though, including Barcelona, Lisbon, Palma de Mallorca, Santiago de Compostela, and the Canary Islands. The **Aeropuerto San Pablo** (© **95-444-9000**) is about 13km (8 miles)

Seville Deals & Discounts

SPECIAL DISCOUNTS If you're staying long enough to take full advantage of it, the 10-ride bus pass called the *bonobús* costs 4.50€ ($5.20) with transfers, saving you at least 50% over the same number of single-ride tickets. You can use the *tarjeta turística* pass as many times as you desire at 3€ ($3.45) for 1 day or 7€ ($8.05) for 3 days. Buy the *tarjeta* from the tourist information booth at Santa Justa railway station or from the TUSSAM bus booth on Plaza Nueva.

Don't drive in Seville itself, but when it comes time to visit its environs, the **Spain Rail & Drive Pass** sold by **Rail Europe** (© 877/272-RAIL in the U.S., 800/361-RAIL in Canada; www.raileurope.com) provides 3 days of rail travel and 2 days' use of a rental car within a 2-month period, making it a good way to get around Andalusia, by train to the larger cities (Granada, Córdoba, Málaga) and by car to the smaller towns (Ronda, the Costa del Sol, and the White Villages). Visitors 65 or over can get **half-price tickets** on rail travel from the city.

An **International Student Identity Card (ISIC)** is often necessary to get discounts on travel, lodging, and admission to museums. Youth hostel cards are issued at **Viajes TIVE,** Jesús de Veracruz 27 (© 95-490-6022).

WORTH A SPLURGE   The **Alfonso XIII,** San Fernando 2 (© 95-422-2850), is one of Spain's most expensive hotels. But you can take in the atmosphere of the mock-Mudéjar 1929 palace for the price of a pre-dinner drink in the courtyard (have dinner elsewhere). Often meals composed of tapas are a good way to keep costs down, but some of these tidbits are rare and pricey, like *angulas* (baby eels boiled in olive oil) and *percebes* (goose barnacles that taste delectably of the ocean).

A sightseeing tour by **horse-drawn carriage** is a fun splurge for children and romantics, and the fare isn't too high when it covers two or more people. Andalusia is the birthplace of the music and dance called **flamenco,** and Seville is the place to experience it. The cover charge for a midnight show is steep, but it at least includes the first drink. Sip slowly and enjoy.

east of downtown on the Seville–Carmona road. A **taxi** (about 15€/$17) is the easiest way into town, but the Route EA **bus** (© 90/221-0317) goes to Puerta de Jerez for only 2.10€ ($2.40), roughly on the hour daily 6:30am to 10:30pm.

BY TRAIN Built for Expo '92, the **Estación Santa Justa,** Avenida Kansas City (© 95-454-0202), now receives all passenger trains. The more desirable of the two long-distance services is the ultra-high-speed **AVE train.** It reduced the travel time between Madrid and Seville, always with a stop in Córdoba and sometimes one or two other cities, from over 7 hours to 2½; there are up to 20 trips each way daily. Each train has three classes (Turista, Preferente, and Club), with one-way fares from 57€ ($66) to 103€ ($118). Two slower daily **ALTARIA** trains take 3½ hours, costing 50€ ($58) in tourist class and 78€ ($90) in first class. Thirty daily trains connect Seville and Córdoba, 50 minutes by AVE (19€/$22) or 80 minutes by the slower **Andalusia Expres** train

(6.95€/$8). Four trains run daily between Granada and Seville (17€/$20), taking 3¼ hours. Frequent buses marked C1 connect the train station to the city center.

For more info and/or to book tickets on the Internet, try **www.raileurope. com** or **www.renfe.es** (the Spanish railway company).

BY BUS   Buses serving Andalusia arrive at and depart from the **bus terminal** at Prado de San Sebastián on Calle José María Osborne (© **95-441-7111**), within walking distance or a short taxi ride east of downtown. Most long-distance lines pick up and discharge passengers at the new **Plaza de Armas terminal** (© **95-490-8040**) at the east end of the Chapina Bridge. Several private companies provide frequent service from Cádiz, Córdoba, Granada, Jerez de la Frontera, Madrid, and other cities in the region. Except for the AVE train, buses are nearly always cheaper and faster for distances under 400km (248 miles). Comforts and conveniences vary from one bus company to another, however, and the trains are more comfortable than any bus. One prominent bus company is **T. Alsina Graells Sur** (© **95-441-8811;** www.continental-auto.es).

BY CAR   Divided highways connect Seville with Jerez, Cádiz, Granada, and Málaga. The two principal routes from Madrid aren't direct; one is via Mérida, the other by way of Ciudad Real and Córdoba. They have four-lane segments for much of the way, though, which are maintained well, and traffic usually isn't heavy. If you arrive by car, I strongly recommend you park it at your hotel or in a garage and not use it again until you're ready to leave or want to drive into the countryside.

VISITOR INFORMATION

TOURIST OFFICE   The **Oficina de Información del Turismo** is at Avenida de la Constitución 21B, a block southwest of the Alcázar (© **95-422-1404**). It has English-speaking attendants and is open Monday to Saturday 9am to 7pm and Sunday and holidays 10am to 2pm. Three helpful giveaway magazines available at hotels and other tourist gathering places are the bimonthly *Tourist* and the monthly *Welcome & Olé!* and *El Giraldillo.*

WEBSITES   Check out **www.okspain.org**, the official page of the Tourist Office of Spain. The site of the city's municipal government, **www.sevilla.org**, features important phone numbers and addresses. Andalusia's regional government supports **www.andalucia.org**. Give a star for quality to **www.sol.com/ Seville**, with its many descriptions of cultural events and fiestas, sights, hotels, and up-to-date weather. Also helpful is **www.sevilla5.com/sevilla**.

CITY LAYOUT

Seville occupies both banks of the **Guadalquivir River.** Most of its attractions and desirable hotels are in the larger eastern portion, dominated by the **cathedral,** Europe's third largest, and its bell tower, the **Giralda.**

Immediately south of the cathedral is the **Alcázar,** a palace built for Pedro the Cruel in the 14th century, and to the east is the pedestrian street maze of the **Barrio de Santa Cruz,** the old Jewish quarter. The 12th-century **Torre de Oro (Tower of Gold)** guards the river, dominating the promenade above the water. These monuments, with the riverside **Plaza de Toros,** form an inverted triangle that's the *centro histórico,* a good place to find lodging, since from there you can reach on foot the city's worthiest *barrios* and architectural relics.

South of the triangle lie the **gardens** of the Alcázar, and a few blocks farther is the **Parque María Luisa,** a refuge shaded by hundreds of trees and containing some remaining structures of a 1929 exposition, notably the **Plaza de España,** with its semicircular canal. The neighborhood north of the triangular old city is **El Arenal.** Along its narrow streets are many shops and cafes. Over toward the river is the **Museo de Bellas Artes,** facing a pleasant square.

On the opposite bank, primarily between the Isabel II and San Telmo bridges, is **Triana.** Long identified as a Gitano (Gypsy) quarter, now it's more notable for its many restaurants and tapas bars, especially those along **Calle Betis,** bordering the river. North of the historic center is the working-class district of **La Macarena,** home to the **Alameda de Hercules** nightlife district.

GETTING AROUND

The best way to explore the city is on foot, and there are plenty of cafes, parks, plazas, and benches on which to rest.

BY TAXI   The principal attractions occupy a fairly compact area, so taxis aren't an unreasonable expense for getting to the more distant points. At night they're almost essential, given the reported level of street crime. Rates are higher at night and on weekends. The meter starts at either .95€ ($1.10) or 1.16€ ($1.35) and increases by .64€ (75¢) or .79€ (90¢) per kilometer. Most rides within the city cost between 3€ and 6€ ($3.45–$6.90). Cabs can be hailed on the street, but at night they're often hard to find. Restaurant staff and hotel *conserjes* will summon taxis for you, or you can call for one at © **95-458-0000** or 95-462-2222.

Sevillano cab drivers have a genetic predisposition to avoid direct routes, stretching rides by at least a few extra blocks. Unless you speak Spanish *and* know Seville's welter of one-way streets, there isn't much you can do to challenge this.

BY BUS & METRO   Due to the many narrow or one-way streets, the orange city buses follow complicated routes. The most useful are the C3 and C4, which run in opposite directions in a ring around the center of the city. A one-ride fare is .90€ ($1.05). If you think you'll find them useful, the 10-ride *bonobús/bonopass* is only 4.50€ ($5) with transfers or 3.80€ ($4.35) without, and the *tarjeta turística* is 3€ ($3.45) for 1 day or 7€ ($6.90) for 3. You can buy them at tobacconists, newsstands, and booths near major stops marked TUSSAM. On the bus, press the orange button on one of the posts to let the driver know you want to get off at the next stop. Find schedules at **www.tussam.es** and pick up maps at the TUSSAM kiosk on Plaza Nueva. Seville's first **Metro** line (www.metrodesevilla.net) will open in 2006, but the east–west line is useless for tourists.

BY CARRIAGE   Horse-drawn carriages muster around the edges of Plaza Virgen de los Reyes, on the east side of the cathedral, at the south end of Plaza de San Francisco, and at the Torre del Oro. They're expensive and undeniably touristy but could serve as a one-time treat just to see the sights. Signs post fares in both English and Spanish. The standard fare is 30€ ($33) for a 1-hour ride. At slow times, you might be able to haggle a discount or get a lower price for a shorter ride, but during the high holidays in April expect fares of up to 50€ ($58).

Country & City Codes

The **country code** for Spain is **34.** The **city code** for Seville **(95)** has now been incorporated into all phone numbers, so you must always dial it, wherever you're calling from.

BY CAR Don't try getting around by driving. Apart from a few wide boulevards, most streets are narrow and many follow confusing one-way patterns. Parking is extremely limited, and even moving cars are a favorite target of criminals. On major streets, men might try to sell you parking spaces they don't own. Ignore them. To rent cars for side trips to Andalusia, there are **Hertz** (© 95-442-6156) and **Avis** (© 95-453-7861) offices at the Santa Justa train station, with branch offices for each at the airport. *Remember:* You get the best deal if you arrange the rental before leaving your home country.

Note: You'll need only your state or provincial driver's license to rent a car, but if you're in an accident or stopped on the road by police, a new regulation stipulates that you must produce an **International Driver's License.** These licenses are available at AAA offices in the United States for $10 or $15. Take along two passport-size photos, or they can take your picture for another $10.

FAST FACTS: Seville

American Express The office is to the left of the entrance of the **Hotel Inglaterra**, Plaza Nueva 7 (© 95-421-1617), open Monday to Friday 9:30am to 1:30pm and 4:30 to 7:30pm; Saturday 10am to 1pm.

Babysitters Called *canguros* in Spanish, babysitters are often available through *conserjes* in the larger hotels. In family-run *hostales,* sons or daughters might oblige.

Business Hours The traditional **siesta period** has greater justification in southern Spain, where the midday sun is fierce 6 months of the year. Most **offices** are open Monday to Friday 9am to 7pm, with a long lunch break from 1:30 or 2pm to 4 or 5pm; in summer, offices often close for the day at 3pm. **Banks** are usually open Monday to Friday 9am to 2pm and Saturday 9am to 1pm. **Shops** and many **attractions** open at 10am, close for siesta from 1:30 or 2pm to 4:30 or 5pm, and then stay open to 8pm.

Consulates The **U.S.** consulate is at Paseo de las Delicias 7 (© 95-423-1885), open Monday to Friday 10am to 1pm and 2 to 4:30pm. The nearest **Canadian** consulates are in Madrid, at Nuñez de Balboa 35 (© 91/423-3250), open Monday to Thursday 8:30am to 4pm and Friday 8:30am to 2pm; and in Malaga, at Plaza de la Malagueta 2 (© 95-222-3346), open Monday to Friday 10am to 1pm. The nearest **British** consulate is also in Malaga, in the south building of the Eurocom complex, at Mauricio Moro Pareto 2 (© 95-235-2300), open Monday to Friday 9am to 2pm. **Ireland's** consulate is at Plaza de Santa Cruz 6 (© 95-421-6361), open Monday to Friday 8am to 3pm. The **Australian** consulate is at Calle Federico Rubio 14 (© 95-422-0971), open Monday to Friday 8am to 3pm.

Crime In a region with nearly 20% unemployment (at press time), Seville suffers a reputation as one of Spain's most crime-ridden cities. Although the chances are strong you'll encounter no unpleasantness, you should follow the usual urban cautions. Cars are particular targets. Leave nothing of value in view. Some experts suggest leaving the glove box open and empty so thieves won't break windows. Keep purses and cameras firmly in hand when riding in the car, for criminals are known to rush out to cars stopped at traffic lights, reach in the window, and snatch whatever comes to hand. Keep the doors locked while driving. For more hints, see "Fast Facts: Barcelona," in chapter 5.

Currency In 2002, Spain adopted the **euro** (€) for its currency. At press time, 1€ = $1.15, or $1 = .87€.

Currency Exchange Change money at banks advertising *cambio*. A set commission is charged, which makes cashing traveler's checks in small denominations expensive. **ATMs** *(cajeros automáticos)* are often a better choice because the rates applied are usually the best available at the time of exchange. Some U.S. banks charge excessive fees for this service, however, so check before leaving. ATMs accept major credit cards or bank cards in the Cirrus and PLUS systems. If a machine rejects your card, don't be alarmed; the next ATM down the street will most likely honor it. If you don't have a four-digit PIN, get one before leaving home.

Dentists & Doctors For bilingual dental or medical attention, ask the hotel *conserje* for referrals, or contact your consulate.

Emergencies For the **police**, dial ℂ 091 (Policia Nacional) or ℂ 092 (Policia Municipal); to report a crime, go to the **station** at Paseo de las Delicias (ℂ 95-461-5450). For **medical emergencies**, dial ℂ 061 or go to the Hospital Universitario Virgen del Rocío, Avenida Manuel Siurot (ℂ 95-501-2000). Also try the Hospital Universitario Virgen Macarena, Avenida Doctor Fedriani (ℂ 95-500-8000).

Holidays For a list of national holidays, see "Fast Facts: Barcelona" in chapter 5.

Internet Access The **Seville Internet Centre,** upstairs at Almirantazgo 2 (ℂ 95-450-0275; www.internetsevilla.com), has 21 terminals available at 3€ ($3.45) per hour. Open Monday to Friday 9am to 10pm, Saturday and Sunday 10 am to 10pm. No food is served.

Laundry To avoid exorbitant hotel fees for laundry, take soiled clothing to the **Lavandería Robledo,** F. Sanchez Bedoya 18 (ℂ 95-421-8123). Cleaning 5 kilos (11 lb.) of wash costs 5.90€ ($6.80). Open Sunday through Friday from 10am to 2 pm and 5 to 8 pm.

Post Office The main post office, **Correos,** is at Avenida de la Constitución 32 (ℂ 95-421-9585), open Monday to Friday 8:30am to 8:30pm and Saturday 9:30am to 2pm.

Telephone The minimum charge for **local telephone calls** is .15€ (15¢). Many hotels and *hostales* tack on a hefty surcharge for long-distance calls. Most public phones have clear instructions in English. Place at least .30€ (35¢) worth of coins in the rack at the top and let them roll in as required (you'll need a slew of .50€/60¢ coins for long-distance calls). Many phones provide onscreen instructions in four languages and accept credit cards as well as the **Tarjeta Telefónica,** a phone card that comes in denominations of 6.05€ ($6.95), 12€ ($14), and 30€ ($35). You can buy it at post offices, *estancos* (tobacconists), and the *Locutorio Público* (phone office) at Sierpes 11, near Calle Rafael Padura. See chapter 5 for more details.

Tipping See "Fast Facts: Barcelona" in chapter 5.

2 Affordable Places to Stay

Virtually all Seville hotels and other lodgings observe three **pricing seasons:** the lowest in January, February, July, and August; the midpriced months of March, June, and September to December; and the high holidays period of April to May, when Semana Santa (Holy Week) and the secular Feria de Abril are celebrated. A doubling of prices from those of the winter months to April's isn't unusual, and some of the lowliest *hostales* even *triple* their rates. (*Hostales* aren't youth hostels, although they are popular with young travelers; they don't provide all the conveniences of conventional hotels but are usually family run and more personal.)

In the listings below, the price ranges are for low to medium months, unless otherwise specified. Reservations for Semana Santa and the Feria need to be made as much as a year in advance. The rest of the year, some hotels have significantly lower weekend rates, but you nearly always must make a specific request for them.

Note: You'll find the lodging choices below plotted on the map on p. 897.

IN THE BARRIO DE SANTA CRUZ

Amadeus ⋆⋆ *Finds*   The former home of a family of music lovers is now a peaceful haven of high culture, run by that same family with warmth, grace, and cheer. Music is everywhere in this hotel, whether at the periodic concerts, on the stereo in the lobby, or in one of the soundproofed practice rooms with pianos. As befits a former private home, rooms vary widely in terms of size and light. All are decorated with antiques and family pieces, and some have Jacuzzis.

Calle Farnesio 6 (1 block east of Calle Mateos Gago), 41004 Seville. (C) **95-450-1443.** Fax 95-450-0019. www.hotelamadeussevilla.com. 14 units. 63€ ($72) single; 76€–88€ ($87–$101) double. MC, V. *In room:* A/C, TV, dataport, minibar, hair dryer, safe.

Arias *Value*   Hidden on a quiet pedestrian lane touching the Alcázar wall, this *hostal* (with a newly installed elevator) has three floors of dimly lit rooms (only a few have windows) that are clean, cool retreats from the summer heat. Some are barely large enough for the bed, but others contain two doubles; nos. 22 and 32 are the largest. The otherwise convivial English-speaking owner insists that rooms be paid for in advance and allows no food or friends in the rooms.

Mariana de Pineda 9 (2 short blocks east of Plaza de la Contratación), 41004 Seville. (C) **95-422-6840.** Fax 95-421-1649. www.hostalarias.com. 14 units. 31€–37€ ($36–$43) single; 41€–47€ ($47–$54) double. AE, DC, MC, V. **Amenities:** Limited room service; laundry service. *In room:* A/C, TV.

Hosteria del Laurel ⋆   Touristy, yes; trashy, absolutely not. Sooner rather than later, every visitor comes upon this atmospheric restaurant in the Barrio's heart, with squat little tables beside the orange trees in the plaza. Most are unaware there's also a spiffy little hotel behind the tavern. The rooms are immaculate, though they vary from tiny to spacious and the marble floors amplify the noise of late-night comings and goings. Tapas in the bar go for 1.35€ to 3.80€

Tips **Rooms on the Web**

A minority of the accommodations recommended here have websites, but several can be found at **www.all-hotels.com**.

> ⌒ **Value**   **Getting the Best Deal on Accommodations**
> _____
>
> - Don't plan to go to Seville in April, when prices are at their highest.
> - Book rooms through the attendant at the hotel reservation booth in the Santa Justa train station; rates are nearly always cheaper than those quoted by reception clerks to walk-in clients.
> - Take advantage of discounts that are often available for stays of a week or more.
> - Don't accept the first rate quoted. Ask if cheaper rooms are available, especially in the off season.
> - Ask if service and taxes are included in the tariff.
> - Stay on a weekend, when some of the larger budget hotels drop their prices 15% to 20%. Ask when reserving ahead.

($1.55–$4.35), and *raciones* (meal-sized serving of tapas) up to 13€ ($15); main dishes in the charming dining room are 7.90€ to 15€ ($9.10–$17).

Plaza de los Venerables 5, 41004 Seville. ℂ **95-422-0295.** Fax 95-421-0450. www.hosteriadellaurel.com. 21 units. 49€–67€ ($56–$77) single; 70€–97€ ($81–$112) double. AE, DC, MC, V. **Amenities:** Restaurant; bar; 24-hr. room service; laundry service. *In room:* A/C, TV, hair dryer.

Hotel Convento La Gloria ⭐⭐   Built in 1363, this was Seville's first post office, then it was converted to a convent, then a pastry factory, before it finally became a hotel in 2003. Some of the rooms are set around a cloister. Walls are covered in beautiful mosaics and studded with random pieces of art from the past 7 centuries. Doubles are sizeable, but feel a little cell-like with nearly barren walls and little light (in many of the rooms); however, you do get nice tile floors and comfortable beds. Request room no. 103, 105, 201, 203, 301, or 302, and you'll be thrilled by the view of the Giralda tower, floodlit at night. Residents get a 50% discount on the set menu at the Don Raimundo restaurant (p. 892) in the same building.

Argote de Molina 26–28, 41004 Seville. ℂ **95-429-3670.** Fax 95-421-8951. 43 units. 76€–88€ ($87–$101) single; 109€–121€ ($125–$139) double. AE, DC, MC, V. **Amenities:** Restaurant; bar; 24-hr. room service; laundry service. *In room:* A/C, TV, hair dryer.

Monreal   The rooms at Monreal vary greatly: No. 315, for example, has a sink rather than a full bathroom, but it also has a big brass double bed and a little balcony with a table and chairs. Others have fetching rooftop views, and some have glimpses of the Giralda. The pretty lobby leads to a ground-floor restaurant in back. No elevator.

Calle Rodrigo Caro 8 (2 short blocks off Mateos Gago), 41004 Seville. ℂ **95-421-4166.** 20 units, 12 with bathroom. 18€ ($14) single without bathroom; 36€ ($32) double without bathroom; 48€ ($43) double with bathroom. AE, MC, V. **Amenities:** Restaurant. *In room:* A/C.

IN EL ARENAL

Maestranza *(Kids)*   This dignified building is at least a century or 2 old—its age is uncertain—but it was thoroughly renovated in 1997. The good-looking lobby, with tile dadoes and marble floors, doesn't oversell the rooms upstairs. Most are freshly painted and airy. The suite can accommodate a family of four.

There's no dining room, but the hotel is on an attractive street with a dozen nearby bars for breakfast and tapas. English is spoken by some of the staff.

Gamazo 12 (between Plaza Nueva and the Plaza de Toros), 41001 Seville. © **95-456-1070** or 95-422-6766. Fax 95-421-4404. www.hotel-maestranza.com. 19 units. 41€–49€ ($47–$56) single; 57€–87€ ($66–$100) double. AE, DC, MC, V. *In room:* A/C, TV, safe.

Simón ⚡ *Kids*   This converted 18th-century mansion, barely half a block from the cathedral, might be the area's top budget hotel. A little more paint here and there would help, but several bathrooms have been renovated, and the walls are often covered all the way to the high ceilings with *azulejos* (ceramic tiles). Good for families or two couples traveling together, several connecting units share bathrooms and sitting rooms. The commodious inner court has lots of cushy chairs for meeting friends. Price increases during the high holidays are kept under 25%.

García de Vinuesa 19 (west of Av. de la Constitución), 41001 Seville. © **95-422-6660**. Fax 95-456-2241. www.hotelsimonsevilla.com. 29 units. 42€–44€ ($49–$51) single; 63€–67€ ($73–$76) double; 90€–95€ ($104–$109) connecting units. AE, DC, MC, V. *In room:* A/C, hair dryer (some rooms), safe.

IN CENTRO

París   Built in 1991 on a quiet, essentially pedestrian street, this little *hostal* (without elevator) is a pretty good deal even when the rates get jacked up during the high holidays. The singles are closet-size and the triples a little snug for any but very close friends or families, but the furnishings are new, including desks, and many rooms have double beds. Most look out into the light-filled center atrium. The owners also have a couple of even humbler *hostales* nearby if this one's full.

San Pedro Mártir 14 (a block south of the Museo de Bellas Artes), 41001 Seville. © **95-422-9861**. Fax 95-421-9645. www.sol.com/hostales-sp. 15 units. 30€–36€ ($35–$41) single; 45€–50€ ($52–$58) double. AE, DC, MC, V. Parking 11€ ($12). **Amenities:** Massage; laundry/dry cleaning. *In room:* A/C, TV, safe.

Puerta de Triana   The windows of some rooms face one of the city's broadest avenues, and a few have small balconies. The decor skews toward the florid, and some mattresses need to be replaced. Most rooms are of decent proportion, though, and they vary considerably in decor and configuration. The *hostal* is within easy walking distance of the Triana *barrio,* the bullring, and the opera house.

Reyes Católicos 5 (2 blocks east of the river), 41001 Seville. © **95-421-5404**. Fax 95-421-5401. www. hotelpuertadetriana.com. 62 units. 40€ ($46) single; 60€ ($69) double. Rates include breakfast. AE, DC, MC, V. *In room:* A/C, TV, hair dryer.

IN LA MACARENA

Baco ⚡⚡   Apart from April and May, when the usual higher rates apply, you can't do better than the Baco at twice the price. Iridescent tiles, polished marble, buffed woods, and glistening brass are generously deployed on all three floors, including in the upscale *charcutería* and accomplished El Bacalao tapas bar/restaurant (open daily) on the ground floor. Breakfast nooks occupy the landings upstairs. The bathrooms have showers that produce more than dribbles.

Plaza Ponce de León 15, 41003 Seville. © **95-456-5050**. Fax 95-456-3654. 25 units. 48€ ($55) single; 71€ ($81) double. AE, DC, MC, V. **Amenities:** Restaurant; bar. *In room:* A/C, TV, minibar, hair dryer.

Plaza Santa Lucia   A sparkling hotel on a quiet street, this unassuming place is a decent and pleasant choice. New modern furnishings are low-key; staff is polite. The hotel is a long walk or short cab ride from the train station, so it's a great choice if you have an early train to catch. (*Parents, be forewarned:* The TVs feature porn channels.)

Santa Lucia 33, 41003 Seville. ℂ **95-427-5442.** Fax 95-428-4426. 28 units. 64€–74€ ($73–$85) single; 82€–92€ ($95–$106) double. Rates include breakfast. Rates lower for 3-night stay AE, DC, MC, V. Free parking. *In room:* A/C, TV, minibar, safe.

WORTH A SPLURGE

Las Casas de la Judería ⋆⋆
About half the units in this row of noble 16th-century residences are suites, typically joining small bedrooms with larger sitting areas. While the exteriors, up a cobblestone lane from a discreet archway, hint at Seville's Moorish past, as do the ochre-and-white interior patios and splashing fountains, the suites bespeak the Victorian era. Room no. 10 is a favorite. Some suites have saunas and whirlpools. Alert but understated attention is provided by the genteel staff, many of whom speak English. Except during the high holidays, you should be able to haggle reductions in the rates below.

Callejón de Dos Hermanas 7 (off Plaza Santa María la Blanca), 41004 Seville. ℂ **95-441-5150.** Fax 95-442-2170. 56 units. 87€–101€ ($100–$129) single; 128€–156€ ($147–$179) double. AE, DC, DISC, MC, V. **Amenities:** Restaurant; bar; room service; laundry/dry cleaning. *In room:* A/C, TV, minibar, hair dryer, safe.

Las Casas de los Mercaderes ⋆⋆
Under the same ownership as Las Casas de la Judería (above) and demonstrating a similar sensibility, this recently converted mansion has a far better location than its older sibling. It's right in the middle of things, with many of the best shops and department stores within 2 or 3 blocks and every major sight within walking distance. The grand lobby leads to an 18th-century inner court with a stained-glass skylight. Guest rooms are larger than average, with carpeting, a small desk, and an easy chair or two.

Calle Alvarez Quintero 9–13 (1 block south of Plaza del Salvador), 41004 Seville. ℂ **95-422-5858.** Fax 95-422-9884. 47 units. 72€–88€ ($83–$101) single; 105€–128€ ($121–$147) double. AE, DC, MC, V. Parking available. **Amenities:** Cafe/bar; room service; laundry/dry cleaning. *In room:* A/C, TV, minibar, hair dryer, safe.

3 Great Deals on Dining

Many restaurants post their menus out front, including at least the a la carte offerings, if not the fixed-price *menú del día* most make available. The latter usually includes soup or an appetizer, a main course, a dessert, and often bread and a beverage. Of course, it will be composed of items from the cheaper end of the card, but they're usually at least satisfactory. By the way, the only sure way to get vegetables with your meal is to order them as a first course. Even then, they're likely to be cooked with bits of ham or pork fat. An *ensalada mixta* (mixed green salad) is a logical flesh-free alternative.

Contrary to what many visitors expect, service is usually swift; you may well be served your entire three-course meal in under 30 minutes. On the other hand, once you sit down, the table is yours. No one will try to move you along, and *Sevillanos* often linger for 2 hours or more. The bill usually isn't presented until you ask for it, which might require repeated efforts.

IN EL ARENAL

Mesón 5 Jotas *Kids* SPANISH   On a blessedly picturesque corner with plenty of outdoor tables, this outpost of ham producer Sanchez Romero Carvajal specializes in top-quality ham. (Cinco Jotas ham isn't cheap, with a *ración* going for 23€/$26. Fortunately, more down-to-earth cuts are served as well.) Tapas are served on upturned barrels in the well-lit bar; the restaurant in the back specializes in meat dishes, mostly porky or pork-enhanced in some way. Potato, egg,

---

Value **Getting the Best Deal on Dining**

- Take advantage of the two- or three-course *menú del día* offered at lunch in many restaurants and at dinner in some.
- Eat and drink at the bar. Many restaurants have two or three prices for the same items, depending on whether you stand, sit indoors, or sit at outside tables.
- Make a meal of a few tapas or a couple of the larger portions, *raciones,* and pay much less than for a conventional meal.
- Keep an eye out for places serving *platos combinados*—usually meat or fish with two vegetables and sometimes bread and a beverage. They're often advertised in the window.
- Have breakfast in a bar rather than in the hotel dining room (unless it's included in the room rate): juice, coffee, and a sweet roll or croissant will cost about half as much, and the coffee will be better.

---

and ham fry-ups go for 9€ to 10€ ($10–$12) and can satisfy that un-Spanish craving for a big breakfast. Try the lentil stew, rich with bits of ham and chorizo and fragrant with sage. Kids, even toddlers, are frequent guests.

Castelar 1 (2 blocks east of the Plaza de Toros). ℂ **95-456-4200**. Main courses 9.30€–19€ ($11–$22); *menú del día* 12€ ($8). AE, DC, MC, V. Daily noon–2:30pm and 8pm–midnight.

IN THE BARRIO DE SANTA CRUZ

Don Raimundo REGIONAL SPANISH In this profusion of mismatched tiles, stained-glass panels, suits of armor, rococo chandeliers, and molded terra cotta, all lit by a hooded fireplace put to work when there's even a hint of chill in the air, the food tends to be a second attraction. It's actually quite satisfactory, some of it allegedly based on recipes developed at the time of the Moors. Game stews and casseroles are tops in the cooler months; the menu switches to lighter fish dishes when they crank up the air-conditioner. At least stop in for a look and a *copa de tinto* (small glass of red wine) in the bar. If you're too full to move after your meal, the restaurant is conveniently attached to the charming Hotel Convento La Gloria (p. 889).

Argote de Molina 26 (at Francos). ℂ **95-422-3355**. Main courses 9.05€–15€ ($8–$13); *menú del día* 24€ ($28). AE, DC, MC, V. Daily noon–3:30pm and 8–11:30pm.

Mesón El Toboso ✿ TAPAS If Modesto (reviewed below) is too crowded or expensive, sit down instead at this incredibly popular tapas shop run by the same owners. Everything's fresh, and shrimp is the most popular dish, though the hot little *jamón serrano*-and-Roquefort sandwiches are also highly addictive. The overworked bartender can never seem to get to people quickly enough.

Cano y Cueto 7. ℂ **95-441-9334**. *Raciones* 5.40€–10€ ($6.20–$12); tapas 1.35€–2.10€ ($1.55–$2.40). AE, DC, MC, V. Thurs–Tues 8am–2am.

Modesto ✿ SPANISH A happy cacophony prevails here, at everyone's favorite *Sevillano* tapas emporium. Although it has a dining room upstairs and lots of tables on the terrace out front, patrons crowd shoulder-to-shoulder into the ground-floor bar. Many items are cooked to order, but because seafood dominates, it arrives quickly. The *fritura modesto* is a tumble of lightly fried onions and peppers topped with shrimp, enough for two or three. A heap of dozens of *coquinas* (tiny clam nubbins smaller than peas) is cooked in sweet oil with slivers of garlic. Modesto is a little fancier than El Toboso, next door (and reviewed above).

Caño y Cueto 5 (at the north end of the Jardines de Murillo). © 95-441-6811. Main courses 7€–22€ ($8.05–$25); *menú de la casa* 17€ ($19). AE, DC, MC, V. Thurs–Tues 8am–2am.

IN CENTRO

El Cairo SPANISH   Despite the name, this busy place is unabashedly Spanish, with ceramic tiles, tables inside and out, a long bar, and a small dining balcony above (where it's quieter and less smoky). The formally dressed waitstaff urgently trucks drinks, tapas, and full meals to their patrons. Drop your napkin on the floor and another is quickly brought, carried between two forks. Pre-meal *fino* (sherry) comes with a plate of olives, caperberries, and pickled garlic cloves. The kitchen does veal and beefsteaks well, but fish (mostly grilled) is the feature; the grilled *dorada* (gilthead bream) is especially good. The main courses come with overcooked potatoes and a green vegetable. More than a few diners settle for one of the several platters piled with various fried seafood, including baby squid, shrimp, and occasional seahorses, skewering tidbits from one another's hoards.

Reyes Católicos 13 (a block east of Paseo de Colón). © 95-421-3089. www.andalunet.com/hosteria-salas/el-cairo/photo02.htm. Main courses 11€–17€ ($12–$20). AE, DC, MC, V. Daily noon–midnight.

Moments   **A True Taste of Spain: Tapas**

Seville pronounces itself the birthplace of that greatest of Spanish culinary inventions, **tapas**. Never mind that the claim is disputed by Madrid. It was here, boosters insist, that a canny tavern keeper first placed a slab of bread over a cup of wine to keep the flies out; here that one of his competitors laid a slice of ham or cheese or a bit of fish on the bread as incentive to drink at *his* place. Inevitable evolution from these modest gastronomic innovations led to *tabernas* and *mesones* all over Spain, their bars lined with dozens of bowls and platters of flavorful fare.

There are hundreds of tapas choices. Some characteristics of Andalusia are *coquinas* (thumbnail-size clams tossed in hot garlic oil), *pescado frito* (lightly breaded fried fish, baby squid, and other sea creatures), *cabrillas* (snails), *pincho moruno* (small marinated and grilled kabobs), *bienmesabe* (fish chunks marinated in lemon juice, floured, and fried), *cabo de toro* (stewed bull's tail), and *almejas a la marinera* (clams in tomato sauce).

These treats often come in three sizes: *tapa* (small), *media ración* (about twice as much), and *ración* (slightly smaller than a main course). This allows budget travelers to control total costs, keeping in mind that certain delicacies almost always cost the world. Beware, on that count, of *angulas* (baby eels), *percebes* (goose barnacles), *langosta* (spiny lobster), and *bogavente* (clawed lobster). Of course, the reason these items are so costly is that they're rare and delicious, so they make a good splurge.

Fun Fact **Savor a Sherry**

One of Spain's most important wine-producing districts, Jerez de la Frontera, is just 89km (55 miles) south of Seville. The area is famous for its sherries, fortified wines with a distinctive taste that comes in several classifications, largely based on sweetness. *Fino,* possessed of an almost dusty dryness, is most often drunk chilled as an aperitif, especially with tapas. *Manzanillas,* softer but still dry, are also popular with appetizers. *Amontillados* and *olorosos* are full-bodied, almost syrupy, and higher in alcoholic content, more likely ordered as *digestifs;* and the sweet **Bristol creams** are best with desserts.

La Dorada ⭐ MEDITERRANEAN   This branch of a national chain lives up to the high standards of its corporate family, especially in the superb quality of the seafood. The small dining room, with an entrance separate from the adjacent bar (where a limited, cheaper menu is available), is a rendition of the captain's lounge of a cruise liner. Boat models, brass engine gauges, and buffed wood trim and floors underscore the theme. The crowd is polished too—mostly prosperous middle-agers and their children. Many of them start with gazpacho, served in an aperitif glass. Main selections are Spanish classics like *lubina* or *dorada al sal* (sea bass or sea bream baked in a hard salt shell), and *arroz caldoso* (soupy rice with lobster chunks). *Pez espada* (swordfish) is one of the less expensive items. Among the many gracious extras is a post-meal icy cordial, often with a sweet of some kind.

Paseo de Colón 3 (south of Reyes Católicos). © **95-422-7828.** Reservations recommended. Main courses 10€–14€ ($12–$16). AE, MC, V. Daily 1–4pm and 9pm–midnight.

Taberna del Alabardero ⭐⭐ NEW SPANISH   The overachievers at the local hotel school bundle together Seville's most imaginative cuisine with one of its most charming small hotels in this restored 18th-century mansion. On the ground floor, a spacious coffee shop and tapas bar lets you kick back with free wireless Internet access. These are tapas with a difference—made to order, not scooped from a tray, and presented with panache. Even with four tapas, wine, and a wedge of cheese or cream tart, you should get out for well under 15€ ($17). In the back, chefs try ambitious new interpretations of Andalusian cuisine. Dinner for one runs about 40€ ($46) all-inclusive, but there's a lunchtime set menu for only 15€ ($17). For the complete experience, and a bit of a splurge, head upstairs to one of the four rooms or three suites, with prices starting at 135€ ($155) for a double.

Zaragoza 20 (west of Plaza Nueva). © **95-456-0637.** Tapas and *raciones* 2.20€–15€ ($2.55–$17). AE, DC, MC, V. Cafetería daily 8am–2am; dining room daily 1–4pm and 9pm–midnight.

IN TRIANA

Kiosco de las Flores SPANISH   This restaurant started in 1930 as a semipermanent stand squeezed up against the stairs to the west end of the Isabel II Bridge. That site is now the entrance to a parking garage, and this favorite *tapeo* stop has moved to the middle of the block, in a new white-brick building bearing no resemblance to the old shed. The tapas were always good, and still are, though prices went up after the move. Fried and grilled fish and shellfish (shrimp, squid, and shark) are featured and can be preceded by bowls of gazpacho.

Calle Betis s/n. ✆ 95-427-4576. www.kioscodelasflores.com. Main courses 9€–20€ ($10–$23). MC, V. Tues–Sun 11am–4pm and 7pm–midnight.

La Albariza SPANISH   Up-ended black barrels serve as stand-up tables in the front bar, buttressing the place's self-description as a *bodega* (a wine bar or cellar), although most customers seem to order beer. The starring edible is *jamón ibérico*, the very best air-cured ham, hand-sliced to order by the man who does little else. Be careful, though, for that undeniable treat can easily cost more than a full meal in the welcoming sit-down salon in the rear. Back there, lamb chops, sole, and meaty shrimp occupy diners' attention.

Calle Betis 6 (near Puente Triana). ✆ 95-433-2016. Main courses 6€–15€ ($7–$17). DC, DISC, MC, V. Tues–Sun noon–5pm and 8pm–midnight.

Los Cuevas ANDALUSIAN   Make a reservation for this hidden gem, because if it's full, there's no waiting allowed; you'll just be booted out the door with a shake of the head. It's worth the effort, though, because this unpretentious neighborhood bar serves up sublime Andalusian regional specialties—creamy chickpea and spinach stew, butter-soft chunks of meat in tomato sauce, feather-light fried zucchini. A slew of salads and sausages also dot the menu, but stick to the "home cooking" section. With two half-portions, a beer, and a cheese tart, it's almost impossible to spend more than 11€ ($13).

Virgen de las Huertas 1 (3 blocks west of the San Telmo bridge). ✆ 95-427-8042. www.servicom.es/loscuevas. Main courses 7€–12€ ($8.05–$14); half-portions available. MC, V. Tues–Sun 1–5pm and 9pm–1am. Closed Aug.

Río Grande SPANISH   Renowned for its unobstructed views of the historic quarter's skyline, this standby at the west end of the San Telmo Bridge has a win-dowed dining room and bar and a sprawling terrace from which to take in views of the Torre del Oro, the Giralda, and sightseeing boats. New management in 2003 promised to shake up a tired menu, and the new entrees focus on creatively sauced seafood, with shrimp, prawns, and lobster playing major roles. Save room for desserts like sweet sherry ice cream with pine nuts. The downside: Prices have risen dramatically with the new ownership.

Calle Betis 70. ✆ 95-427-3956. www.riogrande-sevilla.com. Main courses 9.50€–27€ ($11–$31). AE, DC, MC, V. Dining room daily 1–5pm and 8pm–1am; bar daily 8pm–1am.

San Marco *(Kids* ITALIAN   University students are much in evidence here, but this breezy trattoria also draws seniors and kids in substantial numbers. Billed as a pizzeria, it tosses together many interesting combos, including a great mix of clams, mussels, and shrimp. But there are pastas and familiar Italian meat dishes as well. This is part of a small local chain, with another outlet in the Santa Cruz neighborhood at 6–10 Mesón del Moro (✆ 95-456-4390).

Calle Betis 68 (near Troya). ✆ 95-428-0310. www.san-marco.net. Pastas and pizzas 4.90€–6.80€ ($5.65–$7.80); main courses 6.50€–9.75€ ($7.50–$11). AE, DC, MC, V. Wed–Mon 1:30–4:30pm and 8:30pm–12:30am.

PICNICKING

Gather picnic makings at the **Horno de San Buenaventura,** at the corner of Avenida de la Constitución and Calle García de Vinuesa, opposite the cathedral. Apart from a variety of ready-made sandwiches, it has sumptuous displays of pastries, cold cuts, breads, cheeses, wines, and assorted tapas. Open daily 9am to 7pm. The logical places to take your selections are **Parque María Luisa** near Plaza de España, a 15-minute walk south, or to a bench or the wall along the **Paseo Alcalde Marques del Contadero,** bordering the river.

WORTH A SPLURGE

Casa Robles 🐦🐦 SPANISH   This is as fancy as affordable restaurants get in Seville, with a serious young waitstaff, dining rooms boasting paintings of matadors and genre scenes, and vases of daisies on cream tablecloths (there's also a bar and tables on the street, with heat lamps to extend the season). The kitchen strays somewhat from the traditional, assembling ingredients with a refined eye. A first course of *verduras* (vegetables), for example, combines gently sautéed cauliflowers, carrots, potatoes, and squash, with disks of fresh duck liver imparting an unusual creamy finish. Try the *fritura sevillana* (fried fish) to see how good this Andalusian standard can be. The specials are changed twice a month.

Alvarez Quintero 58 (near the cathedral). 🕿 **95-456-3272.** www.casa-robles.com. Main courses 12€–24€ ($14–$27). AE, DC, MC, V. Daily 1–4:30pm and 8:30pm–1am.

Enrique Becerra SPANISH   Named for the owner who transformed the 19th-century building, this place has a friendly tapas bar in front and dining rooms in back and upstairs; the main room has massive dark beams supported by ancient columns. The greeting of the host and his staff is professional, and they watch out for you throughout the meal. The tables are a decent distance apart from one another, providing some insulation from the large parties of often noisy foreign businesspeople. The waiters stop by with baskets of good breads and then Andalusian dishes of little imagination but considerable expertise, such as *cordero a la miel* (honeyed lamb) or stuffed calamari. You do have to choose carefully to keep the total under 30€ ($35), but you're unlikely to be disappointed.

Gamazo 2 (2 blocks south of Plaza Nueva). 🕿 **95-421-3049.** Main courses 14€–17€ ($16–$19). AE, DC, MC, V. Mon–Sat 1–5pm and 8pm–midnight.

La Albahaca BASQUE/SPANISH   On a corner of an attractive square in the Barrio de Santa Cruz, this elegant little manse dates from 1929 but looks much older. The high ceilings, many antiques and paintings, and extensive use of *azulejos* (ceramic tiles) make it one of the most idyllic dining settings in Seville. In concert with the ministrations of the creative young Basque chef, this makes a most desirable place for a romantic evening. The menu is adjusted seasonally, but look for dishes like vegetables *escabeche* with oysters, or pork loin roasted with pear and vanilla sauce. The service is discreet. At the least, stop for a drink in the intimate snuggery.

Plaza de Santa Cruz 12. 🕿 **95-422-0714.** www.andalunet.com/la-albahaca. Main courses 17€–21€ ($20–$24). AE, DC, MC, V. Mon–Sat 1–4pm and 8pm–midnight.

4 Seeing the Sights

Over the centuries, Seville has been a ripe target of conquerors, from Romans to Visigoths to Moors and on to the drawn-out reconquest of the Spanish kings. The citizens of Seville typically chose to switch sides rather than fight and thus avoided the far greater destruction visited upon more combative cities to the north. A result is a city where evidence of the melding and sharing of cultures abounds—the castle built for the Christian kings by Arab artisans; the massive bell tower that is part Muslim and part Catholic; the ancient quarter that was

Seville

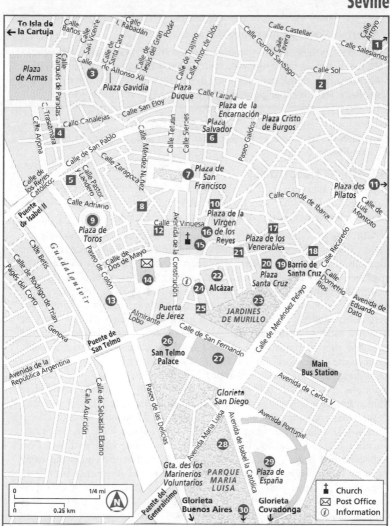

Church †
Post Office ⊠
Information ⓘ

ATTRACTIONS ●

Alcázar **22**
Ayuntamiento **7**
Casa Lonja **24**
Casa-Museo Murillo **19**
Casa de Pilatos **11**
Catedral **15**
Estudio John Fulton **19**
Giralda tower **16**
Hospital de la
  Santa Caridad **14**
Hospital de Venerables
  Sacerdotes **19**
Jardines de Murillo **23**

Museo Arqueológico **30**
Museo de Artes y
  Costumbres Populares **30**
Museo de Bellas Artes **3**
Palacio de San Telmo **26**
Parque María Luisa **28**
Plaza de España **29**
Plaza de Toros/
  La Real Maestranza
  de Caballería **9**
Real Fábrica de Tabacos **27**
Torre del Oro **13**

ACCOMMODATIONS ■

Amadeus **17**
Arias **25**
Baco **2**
Hosteria del Laurel **20**
Hotel Convento La Gloria **10**
Las Casas de la Judería **18**
Las Casas de los Mercaderes **6**
Maestranza **8**
Monreal **21**
París **4**
Plaza Santa Lucia **1**
Puerta de Triana **5**
Simón **12**

Tips A Note on Museum Hours

Almost everything is closed January 1, Good Friday, May 1, and December 25, and hours are highly unpredictable during Holy Week and the Feria de Abril in spring. Check museum hours before setting out, particularly at the smaller ones. They change seasonally and often for no obvious reason.

---

home to both Arabs and Jews; and excavations in and near the city that reveal the long Roman occupation.

THE TOP ATTRACTIONS

In other Spanish cities, most attractions are closed Monday. But in Seville, the cathedral, Giralda, Hospital de los Venerables, and Hospital de la Caridad are all open. Remember that most attractions observe the afternoon siesta.

Alcázar 𝄪𝄪𝄪 This complex is also known by the plural, Reales Alcázares, in a nod to the presence of bits and pieces of an earlier Almohad palace and to the additions of later Christian kings, but most of what's now on view was commissioned by Pedro the Cruel in the 14th century. An admirer of Moorish architecture, he hired Arab craftspeople to design and decorate the place. Arab residents who chose to stay in Spain after their former rulers were vanquished were called Mudéjar, and that name was given to the style they developed for their new masters. Islam didn't allow them to create images of human or animal forms, so they carved intricate stylized floral motifs and intertwined Arabic script in the plasterwork and woodwork of walls and ceilings. You might wonder if the Christian royals knew that much of the scrollwork constituted huzzahs to the glories of Allah. Isabel I received her New World explorers here, and Holy Roman Emperor Carlos V added his own lavish apartments.

You enter the complex through the **Puerta del León** on the south side of Plaza del Triunfo. When lines are long at the counter, look for the nearby machines dispensing tickets. Beyond the entry is a long courtyard with trees and sculptured hedges, and through the arched wall at the end is the larger **Patio de la Montería.** On the right is the **Cuarto del Almirante (Admiral's Apartment),** ordered built by Isabel to house the administrators of the explorations of the New World. Behind it is her own abode in Seville, the **Casa de la Contratación.** The rooms in both are notable for their *artesonado* ceilings and extensive tile murals, but they're closed to the public, in part because they serve as an occasional residence for the present king and queen. Enter the palace proper through the **Puerta Principal** in the Mudéjar facade on the far side. Inside is the **Patio de las Doncellas (Maidens),** appointed with tiles, carved plasterwork, and scalloped arches supported by twined columns. Through the arches to the right is the **Salón de Embajadores (Hall of Ambassadors).** Look up: Its most compelling feature is a domed ceiling of elaborately carved and gilded wood, completed in 1427.

Continuing through the palace, you'll contemplate the harmonious arrangements of slender pillars around reflecting pools. With their sprays of horseshoe arches, they can be interpreted as representations of palms around desert oases, a harkening to the North African origins of the Mudéjar artisans. After a banquet hall and the apartment of Felipe II, the dainty **Patio de las Muñecas (Courtyard of the Dolls)** 𝄪 is another highlight. These were the royal bedrooms, named for the delicate carved heads adorning one of the arches. Descend then to the vaulted subterranean **baths,** surviving from a 12th-century Arab structure. From there, passageways lead to the **Salones de Carlos V,** notable for their 16th-century Flemish tapestries. Adjacent to the apartments are **gardens** where the Holy Roman emperor walked.

Plaza del Triunfo. (℗) 95-450-2323. Admission 5€ ($5.75) adults, free for seniors, students, and children under 13. Apr–Sept Tues–Sat 9:30am–7pm, Sun and holidays 9:30am–5pm; Oct–Mar shorter hours.

Catedral ⚅⚅⚅   The third-largest church in Europe, after St. Paul's in London and St. Peter's in Rome, this Gothic extravaganza was begun in 1401 and took centuries to complete. It replaced a former mosque that had been used as a Catholic church since the Reconquest of Seville in 1248. Expansive though it is and intended to erase the memory of Islam, the builders retained the minaret, which constitutes the lower portion of the adjoining **Giralda bell tower** (see review for Giralda, below), and the adjacent **Patio de los Naranjos (Court of the Orange Trees)** on the north side. Primarily Gothic in design, it does blend in Renaissance elements, a result of the long construction period. Claims that the cathedral contains Columbus's remains are suspect, despite the monumental tomb at the end of the south transept, with four larger-than-life bronze figures shouldering a casket. It's more certain that the grave in the floor by the main door contains his son, Fernando. The cathedral is also the final resting place of Alfonso X, Fernando III, and Pedro the Cruel and his mistress, María de Padilla.

The door in the west facade, on Avenida de la Constitución, is often closed, so go directly to the entrance on the north side, called the **Puerta de San Cristóbal.** (Be flexible, though, for efforts at crowd control cause authorities to change entrances frequently.) The interior is vast, with nearly 40 columns that used to be all but swallowed up in the murk by the ceiling. (New lights have taken away much of the former gloom.) The columns delineate the nave with double aisles to either side and chapels lining the walls. Sunlight illuminates 75 stained-glass windows, a few from the 15th century. At the far end of the north side, the **second chapel** contains two paintings by Seville's most celebrated artist, Murillo. In the **Sala Capitular (Chapter House)** at the east end are several more of his canvases, notably the large *Conception* above the throne. Nearby is the **Sacristía Mayor,** housing the cathedral treasury and its prodigious collection of religious objects and paintings, including two Virgins by Zurbarán. And the adjacent chapel leads to the **Sacristía de los Cálices,** with paintings by Goya and Murillo.

Plaza del Triunfo, Av. de la Constitución. (℗) 95-421-4971. Admission 6€ ($6.90) adults, free for children under 13. Mon–Sat 11am–5pm; Sun 2:30–6pm.

(*Value* **Getting the Best Deal on Sightseeing**

- Bring an ID if you're a university student or a senior (65 and older) for reduced or free admission.
- Take advantage of smaller special-interest museums that are free to all.
- Grab a bench along the esplanade on the east bank of the Guadalquivir for Seville's best sightseeing bargain: the evening *paseo,* after work and before dinner, when *Sevillanos* go out for a stroll.

Giralda 🎯 The 97m (322-ft.) square rosy tower at the northeast corner of the cathedral began in 1198 as the minaret of the mosque that was replaced by the church. It progresses from the austere stonework of the fundamentalist Almohads in control at its inception to the decorative brick latticework and pointed arches of the middle section and culminates in the florid Renaissance-influenced upper floors and bell chamber. Despite the architectural mix, it's surprisingly harmonious visually and serves as the most recognizable symbol of Seville. On the very top is a large weathervane in the shape of an angel, *Faith,* that moves in the wind despite its heft. Determined visitors can climb the 35 ramps (and a few steps at the end) to a **viewing platform** 🎯🎯🎯 at the 69m (230-ft.) level for the best views in the city.

At the foot of the Giralda is a doorway opening onto the **Patio de los Naranjos (Court of the Orange Trees).** Around the corner, on the north side, is an elaborate 16th-century Mudéjar gate and portal, the **Puerta del Perdón.** At last look, both were open Monday to Saturday 11am to 5pm and Sunday 2 to 7pm, but hours are altered frequently.

Plaza Virgen de los Reyes. Admission included in Cathedral ticket; hours same as Cathedral.

Torre del Oro (Tower of Gold) This 12-sided tower at the east end of the San Telmo Bridge long ago lost the sheathing of gold ceramic tiles that might have inspired its name, but it was here to welcome the treasure galleons returning from the New World. Built during the 13th-century Almohad dynasty, it was an important link in their defensive system, connecting with the Alcázar to the east and, by a heavy chain across the Guadalquivir, to a similar tower (no longer extant) on the opposite side. The slender turret atop the main structure was added in the 18th century. Subsequently used as a prison and a gunpowder magazine, it now houses a maritime museum. There are good views from the top.

Paseo de Cristóbal Colón (at Almirante Lobo). 🕐 95-422-2419. Admission 1€ ($1.15); free admission Tues. Tues–Fri 10am–2pm; Sat–Sun 11am–2pm.

MORE ATTRACTIONS

Ayuntamiento (City Hall) The west side of the City Hall, facing Plaza Nueva, presents a graceful uncluttered visage. But go around back to Plaza de San Francisco and you'll discover a diametrically opposite mode of decoration. This side, what's left of it at least, is as florid and overwrought as the other side is austere. Its Plateresque style, in vogue at the time of construction (1534), was so named because its carvings of cherubs, busts, and medallions entwined with vine and floral motifs resembled the intricate silverwork (*plata,* silver) of the period.

Plaza Nueva. 🕐 95-459-0101. Free admission with passport. Guided tours Tues–Thurs 5:30 and 6pm, Sat noon. Closed Aug.

Casa de Pilatos Said to be modeled in part on the house of Pontius Pilate in Jerusalem, this mansion, with its expansive courtyard, is more clearly an example of the blending of Mudéjar, Gothic, and Renaissance styles. Inside are many gleaming *azulejos* and *artesonado* ceilings, as well as the delicately carved stucco associated with Moorish palaces. Among the artworks displayed are Greek and Roman statuary and paintings by mostly second-tier artists, but there are also some works by Goya. Visits to the second floor are by guided tour only.

Plaza Pilatos 1 (slightly west of the intersection of Recaredo and Luis Montoto). 🕐 95-422-5298. Admission to ground floor only 5€ ($5.75); admission to whole house 8€ ($9.20). Daily 9am–7pm; Oct–Feb daily 9am–6pm. Guided tours leave on the half-hour.

Special & Free Events

Two of the most Spanish of folkloric events occur in Seville in early spring. Both are unforgettable. The **Semana Santa** is the Holy Week preceding Easter, with solemn nightly processions led by massive floats bearing polychromed statues of the Virgin Mary, saints, and stages of the Passion of Christ. Called *pasos,* the floats represent 52 neighborhood churches and are maintained by brotherhoods called *las cofradías.* The *pasos* are led and followed by penitents wearing conical hoods, masks, and robes in various hues. (The costumes resemble those of the Ku Klux Klan, but they preceded that racist organization by centuries.)

The Semana Santa is followed 2 or 3 weeks later by the **Feria de Abril,** an annual secular event that had its origins in a long-ago livestock auction but is now a virtually sleepless weeklong party. Its focus is a tent city laid out on dirt streets on a fairground on the Guadalquivir's west side. Behind its giant illuminated gateway are over a thousand canvas *casetas* (little houses) erected by families, labor unions, clubs, and political parties. Nearly all have music, from boom boxes to live orchestras. Many casetas are private, but there are also public casetas that welcome outsiders, as well as a carnival-like section complete with rides, games, and food stands that's open to everyone. The populace dresses in traditional Andalusian costumes of flounced dresses or flat-brimmed hats with bolero jackets and form-fitting pants, and dances the flamenco-like *sevillanas* until dawn. A similar event, combined with a celebration of the grape harvest, takes place in Jerez de la Frontera in early September.

With 2 weeks to get around Andalusia, only a penchant for misfortune will deny you a **fiesta** or two between May and October. A small sampling might include the **Cruces de Mayo** in Córdoba in early May, when patios all over the Judería are ablaze with flowers; the **festival of music and dance** held in various courts and gardens of Granada's Alhambra in late June and early July; and Ronda's principal *feria* in early September, with bullfights performed in the costumes of Goya's time and robust flamenco competitions.

Casa Lonja/Archivo General de Indias (General Archive of the Indies)
Designed by the royal favorite, Juan de Herrera (El Escorial Palace northwest of Madrid was also his commission), this 16th-century financial exchange was later converted to an archive for a priceless collection of maps and documents from Spain's exploration and exploitation of the New World. Included are letters penned by Columbus and Magellan, but they are rarely on display. The exhibits are rotated to minimize damage from exposure to light, so it can't be predicted what might be on view at any given time.

Note: Closed for renovation at press time.

Av. de la Constitución (south of the cathedral). ℰ 95-421-1234. Free admission. Mon–Fri 10am–1pm.

Overrated Itálica: To See or Not to See

A little over 8km (5 miles) northwest of Seville is the town of Santiponce and the remains of the Roman city of Itálica. We mention it only because it appears in virtually all the tourist literature and is a prominent outing for tour companies. Although it's easy to reach by bus from the Empresa Casal company's stop at the Plaza de Armas station, our recommendation is not to bother going, except perhaps as a brief stop on the way to some-where else, like Carmona. The most interesting architectural fragments and artifacts have been moved to Seville's archaeological museum, and nearly all the ancient buildings have been scavenged over the centuries for construction materials. What remains—some mosaic floors, paving stones, and ruins of an amphitheater that once held 25,000—requires a vivid imagination to be appreciated.

Hospital de la Santa Caridad   At the end of the small park running east from the riverbank is the attractive facade of this 17th-century refuge for the poor. Don Miguel de Mañara purportedly was responsible for the building and its charitable activities. The nobleman might have been a model for the semific-tional lothario Don Juan, and this institution is thought to be either his atone-ment for his past debauchery or a monument to the dead wife he deeply loved. One of Mañara's close friends was *Sevillano* artist Murillo—several of the paint-ings in the baroque chapel inside are his. Find it by turning left after entering the red-and-ochre patio.

Temprado 3. (℃ 95-422-3232. Admission 3€ ($3.45). Mon–Sat 9am–1:30pm and 3:30–7:30pm; Sun and holidays 9am–1pm.

Museo Arqueológico   This richly embellished building in María Luisa Park, from the 1929 Exposition, now houses a collection of artifacts from archaeolog-ical sites around Seville province, especially Roman Itálica, but also of Paleolithic, Carthaginian, Greek, and Arab origin. Included are housewares, tools, jewelry, ceramics, and sculptures. One arresting exhibit is a mosaic depicting a generously endowed Hercules in danger of being groped by eager sirens. In all, it's an inter-esting but fairly modest array, but making the trip might be worth it if you also drop by the **Museo de Artes y Costumbres Populares (Museum of Popular Arts and Costumes),** directly opposite the archaeological museum. Admission to this museum is 1.50€ ($1.35), and it's open Tuesday to Sunday 9:30am to 2pm (℃ 95-423-2576).

Plaza de América, Parque María Luisa. (℃ 95-423-2401. Admission 1.50€ ($1.75) adults, free for seniors and students. Tues 3–8pm; Wed–Sat 9am–8pm; Sun 9am–2pm.

Museo de Bellas Artes ★★   Seville's most important art museum is modest by the standards of Barcelona or Madrid, but it definitely deserves a visit. This former 17th-century convent faces a pretty park with a prominent statue of Bartolomé Estéban Murillo, the native son of whom Seville is most proud. Tiles from convents in the Seville region decorate the entrance and the cloister. Works by **Murillo** outnumber those of any other artist, but additional highlights of the collection are canvases by **El Greco, Velázquez,** and **Zurbarán,** whose influence on Murillo is evident. Look for his Virgin and Child called *La Servilleta,* named for the legend that Murillo painted it on a napkin. The 14 galleries contain sculptures and paintings by many worthy artists of the School of Seville, notably **Juan de Valdés Leal,** and range from the Middle Ages to the early 20th century.

Plaza de Museo 9. ⓒ 95-422-0790. Admission 1.50€ ($1.75) Tues 3–8pm; Wed–Sat 9am–8pm; Sun 9am–2pm.

Plaza de Toros & La Real Maestranza de Caballería   The best times to see this historic bullring are during *corridas,* especially those mounted during the Feria de Abril; the season runs late March to early October. The bullring can seat fewer than 13,000 aficionados, so even the cheapest seats most distant from the ring have clear views. But if that spectacle is distasteful to you or merely too expensive, it's still a worthwhile attraction, for both its age and the pleasing visual aspect of its perfect oval surmounted by graceful arches. You can take a 15- to 20-minute tour (in Spanish and English) year-round, though they skip the stables on fight days.

Paseo de Colón 12. ⓒ 95-422-4577. Admission varies for bullfights; admission to tours 4€ ($4.60). Tours daily 9:30am–7pm; 9:30am–3pm on fight days.

Real Fábrica de Tabacos (Royal Tobacco Factory)/Universidad   The prototype of the fiery Carmen of operatic legend worked in this 18th-century *fábrica de tabacos* (tobacco factory). It looks far too grand to have served that function, but in any event it's now part of the city's university. You might have noticed the many young people in the city speaking American English—many of them are studying here in the Junior Year Abroad programs of their home colleges.

San Fernando (between Puerta de Jerez and Menéndez Pelayo). Free admission.

STROLLING AROUND THE BARRIO DE SANTA CRUZ

Before setting out into the Barrio de Santa Cruz, get a copy of the city map from the tourist office near the cathedral, one of the few maps that features actual street names of the city's maze of alleys and narrow lanes. The *barrio* isn't too large, though, so even if you get lost, walk a few short blocks in almost any direction and you'll emerge from the mostly pedestrian-only neighborhood into the rumble of the larger city of cars, trucks, and commerce.

Start in front of the cathedral's main entrance, on **Plaza de la Virgen de los Reyes.** With your back to the church, walk across the square, past the ornate fountain in the middle, and onto Calle Mateos Gogo. Orange trees line the street and its cafes and souvenir shops. After 2 blocks, note the yellow-ochre building with a sign reading MESON DEL MORO. Turn right in front of it. This is the **Barrio de Santa Cruz,** with the winding streets and whitewashed houses that have been characteristic of southern Spain since the 700-year Moorish occupation. It was the Judería, a thriving Jewish community, until the Inquisition began. Palms, bougainvillea, and citrus trees cast cooling shadows over its patios and pocket plazas. Restaurants set tables out beside bubbling fountains, and gated but open doorways invite you to peek in at tiled and planted inner courts.

Bear left at the end of the block, and then turn right onto Calle Santa Teresa. At no. 8 is the **Casa-Museo Murillo** (ⓒ 95-421-7535), one of several small galleries in a city that has only two midsize art museums. It's open Monday to Friday 10am to 1:30pm and 4 to 7pm and charges 1.50€ ($1. 35) admission. Continue along until the street opens onto **Plaza de Santa Cruz.** The small park in the center has a wrought-iron Victorian whimsy incorporating the shapes of saints, winged creatures, and dragons to form a lamp and cross. Note the restaurant **La Albahaca** and the flamenco clubs **Los Gallos** and **El Tamboril,** all of which are recommended in this chapter.

Bear right around the plaza, past Los Gallos, and turn right into Plaza Alfaro. To the left, tall trees mark the edge of the **Jardines de Murillo,** a park with extensive horticultural displays. Lately, it has been dug up and fenced off to facilitate both public and archaeological works. The street next to the gardens is bordered by part of a **fortification** from the 9th century, the early years of the Moorish occupation. Walk down that street. On the right, homeowners often leave their front doors open (behind locked iron gates) so passersby can look into the **patios** and see their *azulejos* and luxuriant potted plants. The second building has a plaque high up on the wall honoring American author Washington Irving, who lived here in 1828 during his brief diplomatic career. Turn right into the narrow Justino de Neve, with its herringbone brick paving. This soon ends in **Plaza de los Venerables.**

To the right is the hotel/restaurant **Hostería del Laurel** (p. 888); straight ahead is the **Hospital de Venerables Sacerdotes** (© **95-456-2696**), now an art gallery with an inner court lined with *azulejos.* It's open daily 10am to 2pm and 4 to 8pm; admission is 3€ ($3.45). Exit the plaza down the alley left of the Hospital and you'll soon reach the smaller **Plaza Doña Elvira.** This square can be a bit bedraggled, in part because it's heavily used as a late-night gathering place of young people who drink, flirt, and play their guitars. Cross diagonally to the opposite corner, past another restaurant, and up the alley called Calle Rodrigo Caro. It makes a sharp left, passing an upscale shop of leather goods and fragrances, then makes another right into the much larger **Plaza de Alianza.** Near the middle of the plaza is a fountain and on the left is the wall of the Alcázar. At the right corner is a shop called the **Estudio John Fulton.** An American drawn to Spain by his dream of becoming a matador, he stayed on after his time in the bullring and pursued a career as a painter, writer, and photographer. He died in 1998. James Michener discussed Fulton at length in his book *Iberia.*

Pass the fountain and turn left down the wide ramp into Calle Joaquín Romero Murube. The Alcázar wall makes that turn too; here you'll see the pointed crenellations typical of Arab fortresses. The street empties into **Plaza del Triunfo.** The cathedral is now on your right, and most of the two plazas connecting the cathedral and the Alcázar have been pedestrianized, with new reassuring lighting for evening strollers. Walk straight ahead and turn left at the next corner. The entrance to the **Alcázar** is up ahead.

PARKS & GARDENS

The western edge of the **Parque María Luisa** runs along the edge of the river south of the **Palacio de San Telmo** and once constituted the bulk of the palace's estate. It served as the principal site for pavilions and other buildings erected for the 1929 Ibero-American Exposition. Several of these structures remain, most notably the neo-Renaissance government house that forms a semicircle around **Plaza de España,** bordered by a half-moon canal and featuring an ornate fountain. Considerable renovations have been necessary to maintain the tile-covered bridges and balustrades. You can rent boats to paddle along the canal. At the south end of the park is **Plaza de America,** bordered by the **Museo de Artes y Costumbres Populares** and the **Museo Arqueológico** (see above).

ORGANIZED TOURS

Sevillatour (© **90/210-1081;** www.citysightseeing-spain.com) caters to English speakers, with both double-decker and single-level trolley buses. The 75-minute tour covers 27 local monuments and takes you around the edges of the entire old city. No reservation is required—just show up at one of their five bus stops; the two most central locations are at the Torre de Oro and the Plaza de España. The fare is 11€ ($13) adults and 5€ ($5.75) children.

Walking tours of the city's historic district are conducted by the guides of **Sevi-Ruta** (© **90/215-8226;** www.sevi-ruta.com). They gather at the statue of San Fernando on the south side of Plaza Nueva, with departures Monday through Friday at 9:30am and 11:30am, and Saturday at 11:30am. You must reserve the 9:30am tour in advance. Tours last approximately 90 minutes. The price is 9€ ($8), and children under 12 are free.

Longer, more informative tours are offered by **Visitours,** Avenida de los Descubrimientos, Isla de la Cartuja (© **95-446-0985;** www.visitours.galeon. com). The comprehensive 3- to 4-hour tours start at 9 or 9:30am and 3 or 3:30pm, with frequent stops and knowledgeable commentary. Prices, however, are steep at 15€ to 37€ ($17–$43). Visitours also has excursions to Granada, Córdoba, Ronda, Jerez de la Frontera, and Cádiz. They're carefully planned, professional in tone and preparation, and expensive. For example, the long day trip to Granada and back was 87€ ($100). For half the price you could buy your own round-trip bus ticket to Granada and get a sightseeing bus ticket there. If you do go to Jerez with Visitours, try to make it on a Thursday, when there's a riding exhibition of the famous Andalusian horses.

Note: All tours are available in English; inquire when booking.

5 Shopping

Start looking along **Calle de las Sierpes,** the pedestrian "Street of the Snakes" running from Plaza Magdalena Campaña to the top of Plaza San Francisco. One block west, the parallel **Calle Tetuan** is similar. They're lined with shops selling clothing, electronics, jewelry, silverware, and leather goods. Bargains are elusive. Items that almost qualify are handmade ceramics (bowls, plates, pitchers, and tureens) decorated with intricate floral traceries, largely blue on white. **Martián,** Calle de las Sierpes 74 (© **95-421-3413**), has a substantial selection. Shopkeepers rarely agree to ship ceramics purchases, but they'll wrap them carefully for carrying by hand—certainly safer than trusting the Spanish postal service.

For more ceramics in a greater variety of styles and shapes, including distinctive Moroccan varieties, cross the river via the Isabel II Bridge to Plaza del Altozano. Turn right on Calle San Jorge, and ahead on the left is **Cerámica Santa Ana** (© **95-433-3304**), with a large stock. For even more selections, turn down narrow **Calle Antillano Campos,** which intersects **Calle Alfareria.** Of the many merchants along Alfareria, watch for **Ceramica R,** no. 45 (© **95-434-4370**), and **Azulejos Santa Isabel,** no. 12 (© **95-434-4608**). Their merchandise runs from simple tiles and dinner plates to elaborate coffee sets and garden fountains. If you'd prefer antique or older-looking ceramics, seek out **Populart,** Pasaje de Vila 4 (© **95-422-9444**), in the Barrio de Santa Cruz.

If Seville suggests lace fans to you, check out **Blasfor,** Calle de las Sierpes 33 (© **95-421-8449**). Past the north end of Sierpes, over to the left, is the local branch of the preeminent national department store, **El Corte Inglés,** Plaza del Duque 10 (© **95-422-1931**).

On Sunday morning in the working-class La Macarena *barrio,* a 5-block, tree-shaded concourse called the **Alameda de Hercules** is the site of a crowded flea market that makes no concession to tourism. Walk among eight-track players, cleavers, hubcaps, Peruvian sweaters, marinated olives, sunglasses, canaries,

videos, comic books, chandeliers, African carvings, lawn jockeys, carved canes—
you name it. If you find something that piques your acquisitive impulse, be prepared to bargain. The two tall columns marking the southern end of the
promenade are Roman, holding aloft statues of Caesar and Hercules.

6 Seville After Dark

A large-format giveaway magazine, *Welcome & Olé!,* is available at many hotels
and at the tourist office. It's in both Spanish and English, with much information
about dining and cultural and popular events in Seville, but it is advertiser-driven
and so not to be considered a sole source. Very similar is the free bimonthly the
Tourist, available in the same places, as is the useful free monthly, *El Giraldillo.*

THE PERFORMING ARTS

Spain's performing artists and organizations draw increasingly enthusiastic attention from audiences and critics worldwide. Two of the fabulously successful
Three Tenors are, after all, Spaniards. Many international performers, including
celebrated rock bands and pop singers as well as ballet companies and symphonies, make Seville a tour stop. Curiously, Seville, the city that inspired a score
of operas by Bizet, Verdi, Mozart, and others, had no proper venue for staging
them until the 1990s. Expo '92 provided the motivation to correct this lack.

Dominating all of Seville's performing-arts venues is the **Teatro de la
Maestranza,** Paseo de Colón 22 (© **95-422-6573;** www.teatromaestranza.
com), 2 blocks south of the Plaza de Toros that bears the same name and a similar circular design. Home to the Real Orquestra Sinfónica de Seville, it seats
1,800 for varied seasons of symphonic and chamber concerts, ballet, opera, and
the Spanish operetta form *zarzuela.*

Until the new opera house opened, the **Teatro Lope de Vega,** Avenida María
Luisa (© **95-459-0867;** www.cultura.sevilla.org/paginas/lope.asp), was the principal performance space. It's still important, hosting traveling companies of
considerable variety, from dramatic productions to jazz to musicals like *West Side
Story.* Curtain time is usually 9pm, but be sure to check ahead. Similar diversity
is provided at the **Teatro Central,** on the Isla de la Cartuja in the Guadalquivir
(© **95-503-7200;** www.teatrocentral.com).

Box offices at all three theaters are open daily 11am to 2pm and 5 to 8pm;
prices vary with the attraction.

FLAMENCO

The profoundly Andalusian art form of **flamenco** degraded into commercialized
pap long ago. Blame it on Franco or on the homogenizing influences of mass
tourism, but flamenco as it's now performed in the land of its birth rarely displays the authentic spontaneity and passion said to have inspired it in the past.
Even in Seville, performances are more often coolly choreographed rather than
improvised and too often descend into the travesty of audience participation.

To gain a hint of what flamenco once must have been, go late, after the tour
groups have left and the performers have worked up a sweat. Watch the older
dancers, often a little thick around the waist but still able to bring fire to their
twirling, twisting, foot-stamping performances, electrified by the kind of stac-
cato hand-clapping you must be born Spanish to master.

For a reliable show, head to the Barrio de Santa Cruz for flamboyant **El
Tamboril,** Plaza de Santa Cruz 15 (© **95-456-1590**). In a room to the right of
the eccentrically decorated bar, guitarists and singers assemble informally most

nights, and patrons get on the floor to perform the *rumba* and *sevillanas*, a dance related to flamenco, as well as improvisations thereon. The bar is open all day, but the dancing doesn't start until midnight. Get there well before then if you want a seat. There's no cover. On the same attractive square is **Los Gallos**, Plaza de Santa Cruz 11 (© 95-421-6981), a *tablao* that's routinely deplored as a tourist trap. That assessment is difficult to dispute, but things get better after midnight, and you're seated close to the action. Shows are at 9 and 11:30pm. The cover (including the 1st drink) is 27€ ($31).

Sol Café Cantante, Sol 5 (© 95-422-5165), in the Macarena neighborhood, says it's a new kind of *flamenco* studio for a new generation. They specialize in young local performers and offer dance lessons (the two, obviously, are linked), but this is truly some of the city's freshest flamenco. Shows are at 9pm Wednesday through Saturday, and admission costs 18€ ($21) for adults and 11€ ($13) for students, including the first drink. A signboard outside lists upcoming performances.

La Carbonería, Leviés 18 (© 95-56-3755), is a curious place, with a vestibule that looks like the entry hall of a grand but decaying farmhouse in the mountains, complete with fireplace to ward off winter chills. Beyond that is a space with tables on a raised platform, then a concrete floor with crude beams for seating beneath a corrugated plastic roof, then a terrace with more tables. Bad abstract paintings adorn (if that is the word) the walls. There is music every night, all year, with at least one guitarist, one singer, and one dancer, all working hard to make themselves heard above the hubbub of 200 or more people; plenty of tourists, plenty of locals. No cover, no minimum.

LIVE-MUSIC CLUBS

Seville isn't yet a routine stop on the tours of superstars like the Stones or Elton John, but the international performers who do drop in often use the open-air **El Auditoro,** on the Isla de la Cartuja (site of Expo '92), or the soccer stadium, **Estadio Ramón Sánchez Pijuan.** Lesser-known bands are usually booked into warehouse spaces in the industrial parks to the north and east of the center city. Keep an eye out for posters and leaflets announcing their appearances.

Jazz remains an enthusiasm, evidenced by the **Festival Internacional de Jazz** held in early November. (Check with the tourist office for details.) More prominent combos and bands appear at the **Teatro Central,** Isla de la Cartuja (© 95-503-7200); or at the **Teatro Lope de Vega,** Avenida María Luisa (© 95-459-0867). Otherwise, watch for the programs of the **Club de Jazz** of the Universidad de Seville. Established jazz clubs that frequently stray into blues and related forms are **Café Lisboa,** Alhóndiga 43; **Café Pavana,** Calle Betis 40; **Blues Box,** Levies 18; and **Blue Moon,** Cavestany. They're usually open Tuesday to Saturday 10am to 4am.

An Irish pub next to a Moorish Spanish cathedral, **Flaherty,** Alemanes 7 (© 95-421-0451), has become so popular it's expanded into the next building. The denizens are usually American exchange students scarfing up plates of nachos, but Porter, Guinness, and Jameson's are poured, and live groups play Irish music on Thursday. With three bars bracketing an open patio, there's plenty of elbow-bending room. There's no cover, and it's open daily noon to 2 or 3am.

TAPAS & COCKTAILS

A *Sevillana* evening inevitably starts with a *tapeo*—the traditional walkabout called a *paseo* combined with stops at several bars for tapas. This segues into drop-ins at *barres de la noche* (bars of the night) emphasizing drinks, mingling, and music. As weekends approach, these are often followed, well after midnight and even 2am, by visits to rock clubs or discos.

Calle Mateos Gago, leading east from the cathedral and into the **Barrio de Santa Cruz,** is lined with pizzerias, *cervecerías,* and bars that get clogged on weekends. Easily the classiest bar on this strip, the **Bodega Belmonte,** Calle Mateos Gago 24 (© **95-421-4014**), boasts a front room surrounded on three sides by rows of bottles from every wine-producing region of the country. Appetizing tapas are available, but they are secondary to the opportunity for an informal tasting of wines, 10 of which you can have by the glass. A dining room has been added. There's no accounting for the popularity of the unremarkable **Bodega Santa Cruz,** Calle Rodrigo Caro 1 (© **95-421-3246**), except that it provides plastic glasses to take beer into the street, where hundreds of young people gather Friday and Saturday. (When you order a drink on those nights, the first question is, "In here or outside?") The favorite snacks are *montaditos,* round toasted rolls with a dozen fillings.

Follow the throngs (for safety, if nothing else) into the heart of the *barrio* and the convivial **Casa Román,** Plaza de los Venerables (© **95-421-6408**). Patrons surge through, snaffling up plates and sandwiches of ham and sausage. Your consumption is chalked directly on the bar. Watch out for the Ibérico ham, a *ración* of which is 15€ ($17). Chauvinistic food historians insist that **El Rinconcillo,** Gerona 40–42 (© **95-422-3183**), was the birthplace of the tapa tradition. That was in 1670, they say, which also makes this one of the country's oldest *tabernas.* The tapas on the short list are only average, but that doesn't stop the hordes who course through its two rooms every day but Wednesday. It's in the lee of the colorful Iglesia de Santa Catalina, which faces Plaza Ponce de León.

The vast plaza of the **Alameda de Hercules** just north of the city center attracts hundreds of college students and a smaller crowd of revelers in their 20s and 30s to chat, drink, flirt, and generally show off. The kids get going around midnight at bars like **Bar la Sirena,** 34 Alameda de Hercules (© **95-438-9414**). A buzzing crowd of 30-somethings packs **La Habanilla,** 63 Alameda de Hercules (© **95-490-2718**); and **Central Café,** 64 Alameda de Hercules (© **95-490-6401**), whose walls are lined with the work of local artists. At the live-music venue at **Fun Club,** 83 Alameda de Hercules (no phone), rock, pop, and hip-hop shows start at 9pm and dancing takes over past midnight. Depending on the band, the crowd's average age may be anywhere from 16 to 25.

GAY BARS

With a large transient population of university students and the inevitable conflict with a socially conservative moral tone, Seville's gay scene is elusive and ephemeral. Bars and clubs open suddenly and close as quickly, sometimes moving a few blocks away and opening again with different names. Start by asking at the gay-friendly bars on the Alameda de Hercules such as **El Bosque Animado,** 5 Arias Montero (© **95-437-6858**), **Central Café,** and **Habanilla.** Just south of the Alameda de Hercules, **Sevilla Monasterio,** Amor de Dios 18 (no phone), is an established club with a mixed gay/straight crowd. Bears and friends should check out **El Hombre et El Oso** (bear), 32 Amor de Dios (no phone). **Triangulo,** Bajos Paseo M. Contadero (no phone), is the one reliably lesbian bar in town, but lesbians are welcome at any of the Alameda de Hercules bars.

7 Side Trips in Andalusia

The Costa del Sol is just the edge of a region staggeringly rich in art, architecture, folklore, and culture. An hour or 2 inland from the resorts of Marbella and Torremolinos are whitewashed villages clinging to steep hillsides and rearing cliffs, and such wonders of the Western world as the Mosque of Córdoba and the fabulous Alhambra of Granada. A comprehensive network of bus routes provides good connections with all but the more remote villages. Trains are less useful, except between Madrid and Málaga and Seville and Córdoba.

Andalusia comprises over 596km (370 miles), about two-thirds of which, from Huelva, west of Seville, to Granada, is served by a new *autopista*, a fast but expensive toll highway. The coastal road from Almeria to Algeciras is free but far slower, passing through dozens of coastal villages and the housing developments called *urbanizaciones*, with traffic at its worst April to September. Secondary roads are far easier to traverse, apart from the likelihood of spending time behind slow-moving trucks.

Seville deserves at least 2 or 3 days, and can serve as a base for day trips to Córdoba, Ronda, and Granada. For more day trips in glorious Andalusia, check out *Frommer's Barcelona, Madrid & Seville.*

CORDOBA ✹✹✹

The road from Seville to **Córdoba** borders the Guadalquivir, once navigable all the way to the ocean but now so shallow and silted that cattle graze on its sandbars. A still-used Roman bridge crosses the river, connecting the uninteresting new city on the south bank to the expansive Moorish quarters on the north.

Córdoba is an intermediate stop on the high-speed AVE train between Madrid and Seville, placing it 1¾ hours from Madrid and 45 minutes from Seville. A taxi ride from the rail station to the Mezquita is about 3€ ($2.70). Once you're there, you can reach all the city's major sights on foot. Buses operated by several companies between Córdoba and Seville make the trip in 2 to 3 hours. The **Tourism Office,** on the Plaza de las Tendillas (© **90/220-1774;** turismo@ayuncordoba.es), is open daily from 10am to 2pm and 5 to 8:30pm.

SEEING THE SIGHTS   Near the north end of the Roman bridge rises the perimeter wall of the **Mezquita** ✹✹✹, one of the most extraordinary sites in Spain, at the corner of Calles de Herrero and de Torrijos (© **95-747-0512**). The Mezquita is a great mosque of immoderate but singularly graceful proportions. When you walk up along the west wall on Torrijos, the building appears pockmarked and battered, with failed intrusions, overlays, and bricked-up doors and windows both Arabic and Spanish. The wonder of it isn't revealed until later. Soon there's a portal in the wall—but for the full effect, continue to the corner, turn right, and enter beneath the Renaissance bell tower **Torre del Alminar,** through the 14th-century Mudéjar **Puerta del Perdón,** and into the **Patio de los Naranjos.** In this traditional arrangement, Muslim worshipers undertook ritual washing at the fountains beneath the orange trees before entering the mosque proper, on the far side of the courtyard.

Recently, the ticket booth has been against the north wall, over to the left after passing through the Puerta del Perdón. Admission is 6.50€ ($7.50) kids 14 and up, 3.25€ ($3.75) kids under 10. Admission to the patio is free. For now, the Mezquita is open from 10am to 7pm daily (to 6pm Oct–Apr).

Walk straight across the patio from the Puerta del Perdón to enter the original section of the mosque. Pause a moment to let your eyes adjust to the gloom. Soon you'll be able to comprehend the vastness of the space and the unique way it has been formed. A flat roof covers nearly 3.2 hectares (8 acres) of floor space. It's supported by what's routinely described as a "forest" of some 850 pillars stretching off into the murk at the distant corners. Those columns support double arches, some of which have scalloped edges and all of which bear alternating bands of white stone and brick. The pillars are made from a variety of materials, including marble, granite, onyx, limestone, and even wood. No two are exactly alike.

Walk straight across from the entrance to the south wall, glancing to the left and right. The stunning magnitude of the building will become even more obvious. Directly ahead is the most dazzling component, commissioned by the second caliph to order an expansion of the mosque: the **Mihrab** ✿, the holiest place, glowing in the shadows. You can no longer enter it, but you can still see the golden, glittery mosaic tiles that encase the triple-domed enclosure known as the *maksourah,* reserved for the supreme ruler. The Mihrab itself is in a niche off this vestibule, its entrance formed by marble columns supporting entwined arches. The whole gleams like jewels on black velvet. Its beauty is enough to make even the faithful excuse the fact that, due to a miscalculation, the Mihrab is oriented to the south rather than to the east and Mecca.

If you turn left (east), a far less felicitous element will make itself glaringly apparent. It's a **cathedral,** the reason for the official designation of this edifice as the **Mezquita-Catedral** and a grotesque tribute to Gothic-baroque excess plunked in the middle of a monument characterized by structural lightness and spare decoration. In the early 16th century, bishops of the Church Triumphant obtained the permission of Carlos V to convert this Muslim house of worship into a cathedral. You might forgive the desecration if the cathedral exemplified *good* baroque style, but this accretion of marble saints, coffered ceilings, rampant cherubim, and curls of stucco, alabaster, and jasper would stand as a visual insult almost anywhere. When Carlos V saw the structure he had authorized, he said, in effect: "What you have made here may be found in many places, but what you have destroyed is to be found nowhere else in the world."

In the bishops' defense, had they not imposed this cathedral and incorporated the rest of the mosque by closing off the once-open sides and building ancillary chapels, the entire Muslim structure might have been razed, as were so many others in the wake of the Christian Reconquest. And the Moors were hardly pure of heart, given that many of those 800-plus pillars were scavenged from Roman temples, Visigothic churches, and various pagan North African and Turkish sites.

Continue past the cathedral into the extension ordered by caliph Alhaken II in the mid–10th century to the small **archaeological museum** displaying relics of the Visigothic church that once stood here. The exit (at press time) is up to the left.

You've just been exposed to manifestations of two of Spain's great religions, so it's appropriate that evocative hints of the third are close at hand. Take the street leading off from the northwest corner of the Mezquita into the quarter known as the **Judería** ✿, the ancient Jewish *barrio.* After a short block of gaudy souvenir shops, turn right on Calle Deanes and a few steps later onto Calle Almanzor Romero. Most of the modest whitewashed homes date from the 18th century but resemble the older Córdoba, and a few pre-date the 1492 expulsion order of Queen Isabel and King Fernando.

Turn left into Plaza Cardenal Salazar and into the connecting Plazuela de Maimónides, passing the **Museo Municipal de Arte Taurino** (© **95-747-2000**),

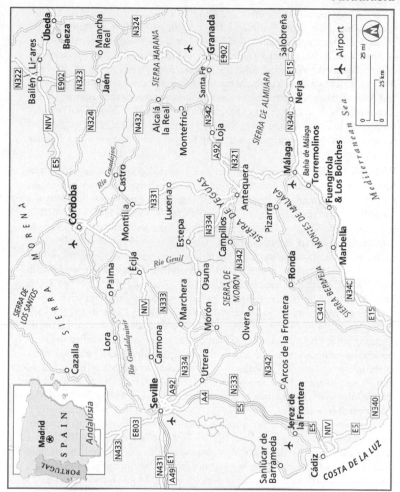

a bullfighting museum that's open May to September Tuesday to Saturday from 10:30am to 2pm and 6 to 8pm, Sunday from 9:30am to 3pm; and October to April Monday to Saturday from 10am to 2pm and 4:30 to 6:30pm, Sunday from 9:30am to 2:30pm. Admission is 3€ ($3.45); free on Tuesday. Around to the right, in the small Plaza Tiberiades, is a **statue of Moses Maimónides.** Given the bitter antipathies among the three creeds in the modern era, it's difficult to imagine the relative tolerance displayed by the ruling Muslims of his time toward the Jews in their midst. But in 12th-century Córdoba, and in his sojourns around the Mediterranean after Islamic sufferance broke down, Maimónides achieved high honor as a physician, theologian, law scholar, and philosopher.

Not far beyond the statue, at Calle Judios 20, is the entrance to **La Sinagoga** (© **95-720-2928**), one of only three intact synagogues remaining in Spain. It dates from the 14th century and has Middle Eastern embellishments in its intricately carved plasterwork; on the walls are Hebrew quotations from the Psalms. The building consists of a small square room, above which is the *ezrat nashim,* the segregated balcony for women and girls. No longer used for worship, La Sinagoga is open Tuesday to Saturday 10am to 2pm and 3:30 to 5:30pm, Sunday 10am to 1:30pm; admission is .30€ (35¢), but is not always collected.

Apart from the Mezquita-Catedral, there are relatively few other monuments of note. You might want to seek out the **Alcázar,** Amador de los Ríos (© **95-742-0151**), 2 blocks southwest of the Mezquita. Its most notable draws are its gardens and Arab baths, supplemented by mosaics from an earlier Roman palace. Admission is 2€ ($2.30), and it's open May through September, Tuesday to Saturday from 10am to 2pm and 6 to 8pm, Sunday 10am to 2pm; October through April it's open Tuesday to Saturday from 9:30am to 3pm and 4:30 to 6:30pm, Sunday from 9:30am to 3pm.

WHERE TO STAY   While you can easily do Córdoba as a day trip from Seville, it's an agreeable city to wander and absorb at leisure, so you might want to stay overnight. Among the most impressive inexpensive hotels is the **González,** Manriquez 3, 14003 Córdoba (© **95-747-9819;** fax 95-748-6187). Especially remarkable are its excellent location in the Judería, a short stroll from the Mezquita, and its ingratiating staff. The 16th-century mansion is pleasantly decorated in Andalusian style, with a dining courtyard. As at most Córdoba hotels, prices are highest during Holy Week and the Feria the last weekend in May. The 27 units have air-conditioning and TV. Doubles cost 52€ to 122€ ($60–$140); the hotel accepts American Express, MasterCard, and Visa.

The new **Mezquita** ♠, Plaza Santa Catalina 1, 14003 Córdoba (© **95-747-5585;** fax 95-747-6219), is very similar to the González, down to the nearly identical rates. That's because it's owned by the same people, and they've incorporated ancient columns and arches and hung genuinely old paintings for a downright grand effect. Opposite the east entrance to the Mezquita, it has 21 fairly large air-conditioned rooms with TV, costing 52€ to 108€ ($60–$124) double, depending on the time of year. American Express, MasterCard, and Visa are accepted here as well.

On the street angling off the northeast corner of the Mezquita, **Los Omeyas,** Encarnación 17, 14003 Córdoba (© **95-749-2267;** fax 95-749-1659), is a crisply maintained hotel, much of it sheathed in marble. Several rooms have double beds, and all can be converted into triples by sliding in an extra bed. Breakfast is served on the attractive patio or in the Moorish-style bar. The 25 rooms have air-conditioning, TVs, and safes, and cost 52€ to 64€ ($60–$74) double. American Express, MasterCard, and Visa are accepted.

WHERE TO DINE   Up an alley opposite the Mezquita's Puerta del Perdón is **El Caballo Rojo** ♠, Cardenal Herrero 28 (© **95-747-5375;** www.elcaballo rojo.com), Córdoba's best-known restaurant. Its menu claims that nine of its entrees are adapted from ancient Sephardic and Moorish cookbooks, but there are adroitly executed Andalusian dishes as well. As soon as you order, the waiter brings a plate of fritters and pours a complimentary *vino.* There are three floors, with plenty of rooms to get away from smokers if you want. Main courses cost around 12€ to 19€ ($14–$22). If the restaurant prices are too steep, step out of the hot sun into the cool bar on the ground floor and order a beer to go with a sandwich or a couple of tapas. American Express, MasterCard, and Visa are accepted. It's open daily 1 to 4:30pm and 8pm to midnight.

Tables are set out in the interior courtyard of **El Churrasco** ♠, Romero 6 (© **95-729-0819;** www.elchurrasco.com), and there's a retractable roof to deflect the summer sun. In winter, the skirts of the tablecloths hide braziers with hot coals, a version of the Arab space heaters of 1,000 years ago. A glass of the sherrylike local wine, Montilla, arrives as soon as you sit down. Try the *salmorejo*, a Córdoba cousin of gazpacho that's a thick paste of cold tomato garnished with bits of ham and egg. Order the pork tenderloin and you get a Bowie-size knife to cut it and two bowls of sauce, one green and garlicky, the other mildly *picante*. Main courses are 10€ to 25€ ($12–$29). Open daily 1 to 4pm and 8pm to midnight; closed in August. MasterCard and Visa are accepted. In business since 1879, the **Taberna Salinas,** Tundidores 3 (© **95-748-0135**), is as atmospheric a tavern as you'll find. Bullfighting memorabilia adorns the walls, and wine casks are installed behind the bar. A list of *raciones* suggests gazpacho, croquettes, and marinated anchovies for 3.60€ to 5.70€ ($3.20–$5). Full meals in the dining room are equally inexpensive (about 8€–12€/$7–$11). Open Monday to Saturday 11:30am to midnight. MasterCard and Visa are accepted.

RONDA 🕊

The road up to **Ronda** from the Costa del Sol used to be an impossibly narrow route, twisting back on itself for a terrifying 48km (30 miles). It was widened and straightened about 10 years ago, though, so it needn't be feared by any but the severely acrophobic (who might want to approach from the less precipitous northern Rtes. 339 and 341).

SEEING THE SIGHTS   Certainly the grandeur of the town's site is undeniable. The flat-topped cliff the city occupies is cleft across its breadth by the narrow Guadalevin gorge, more than 548m (490 ft.) deep, the two sides stitched together by an 18th-century bridge higher than it is long. The southern half of town dates from the Moors, while the bullring built in 1785 in the new section is claimed to be the country's oldest.

Parks and overlooks around the perimeter are the principal diversions, especially the **Alameda del Tajo** and its forever views, but the **Plaza de Toros** on Virgen de la Paz, with a baroque main portal and a neoclassical interior, is intriguing. Said to be the oldest bullring in Spain, it's open daily 10am to 8pm, and admission is 2.10€ ($2.40). On the Moorish side, the 13th-century **Baños Arabes (Arab Baths)** are the sights to see. Alas, they've been closed for years for renovations. Check at the **tourist office** (© **95-218-7119**), open Monday to Friday 10am to 2pm, a block south of the bullring at Plaza de España 9, to find out if they've finally reopened.

If you have a car, an excursion to the **Cuevas de Pileta (Pileta Caves;** www.cuevadelapileta.org) is worthwhile. They're 29km (18 miles) west of Ronda: Take Route 339 toward Jerez de la Frontera for 15km (9 miles), then turn south at the sign for Montejaque along a usually deserted road for 15km (9 miles). There's a climb from the parking lot, and tours, usually 10am to 1pm and 4 to 6pm, are sporadic. Expect to wait for up to an hour, because the caretaker/guide locks the gate whenever he gathers enough people for a tour. For those who've never entered such a place, the black-and-red prehistoric drawings in these cathedral-size caves are startling, especially the etched fish suggesting that a lake or an ocean once lapped at the base of this mountain. The fee for the guided tour is 4.80€ ($5.50).

WHERE TO STAY & DINE   At **Don Miguel,** Plaza de España 4–5 (© **95-287-7722;** fax 95-287-8377; www.dmiguel.com), meals are spiced by the restaurant's position at the rim of the gorge, looking *up* at the bridge. The restaurant is open daily 1 to 4:30pm and 8:30 to 10:30pm. There's no Sunday lunch in July and August, and the restaurant is closed for 2 weeks every January. Some of the 19 bedrooms have views, and all have TVs. Doubles are 66€ ($76). American Express, MasterCard, and Visa are accepted.

For a special treat, the **San Gabriel** 衡, José María Holgado 19 (© **95-219-0392;** fax 95-219-0117; www.hotelsangabriel.com), is an under-publicized charmer of a mansion a block from the old bridge. It dates from the early 18th century, consistent with the old quarter in which it is located. There are 16 air-conditioned bedrooms with TV, with doubles costing 79€ ($91). American Express, MasterCard, and Visa are accepted.

At **Jerez,** Paseo Blas Infante (© **95-287-2098;** www.restaurantejerez.com), you can dine under umbrellas on a terrace next to the Plaza de Toros. Stick to the *platos combinados* rather than full meals and the cost should stay under 10€ ($11). It's open daily 1 to 4:30pm and 8:30 to 11pm. American Express and Visa are accepted.

GRANADA 衡衡衡 & THE ALHAMBRA 衡衡衡

Even visitors intent on nothing more elevating than a sun-blasted, *sangría*-soaked week on the Costa del Sol should make the day trip to **Granada** (127km/79 miles north). The **Alhambra** (www.alhambra-patronato.es), after all, is one of the world's grandest and most elegant monuments, ranking with the Acropolis and the Taj Mahal. Floating above the city like a dream of palaces, its keeps and spires are sharp against the backdrop curtain folds of the **Sierra Nevada,** whose peaks are snowcapped into June. Unlike the Mezquita of Córdoba, the Alhambra (Ahl-*ahm*-bra) isn't a single structure but a regal compound of interlocking gardens, royal residences, pools, citrus groves, waterworks, fortifications, and temples for two of the world's great religions, complete with a supporting cast of hotels and restaurants.

SEEING THE ALHAMBRA   Take the no. 30 bus from the Plaza Nueva downtown (.85€/$1), which drops you off a few steps from the ticket office. The heart of the complex is a series of connected structures and courtyards constituting Iberia's highest achievement of Islamic art. Neglected and abused for centuries after the Christian Reconquest, it became a campground for brigands, smugglers, and other malcontents. American author/diplomat Washington Irving enjoyed a short residence here and wrote *Tales of the Alhambra.* Its popularity inspired the government to undertake restoration after 1828. Much of the palace's interior embellishment was lost, but enough remains to provide a sense of what must have been. This is all the more remarkable because of the delicacy of the plaster ceilings and the breathtaking intricacy of the wall carvings.

With its unchallenged stature as one of Europe's great sights, the Alhambra is inevitably swamped with people, over two million each year. During the high season, from April to October, getting to the ticket office at the stroke of 8:30am doesn't seem to make much difference, not with the first buses of the day arriving at the same time. During late fall or winter, especially if it's raining, you may feel like you have the whole Alhambra to yourself. This amazing place is worth seeing at any time of year, cold or warm, crowded or desolate. Allow at least 2 hours.

The main entrance has been changed, moved to the north end of the complex, and the old ticket office, near the 14th-century Torre de la Justicia, has been closed. The new office has a running notice advising of the next available entrance period. There is also a counter where you can obtain an audioguide, which you can carry through the site, pressing numbered buttons at corresponding points on the map you are provided. It is available in five languages, including English. Rental is 3€ ($3.45) and you must leave your passport, driver's license, or a credit card as security. It's worth it.

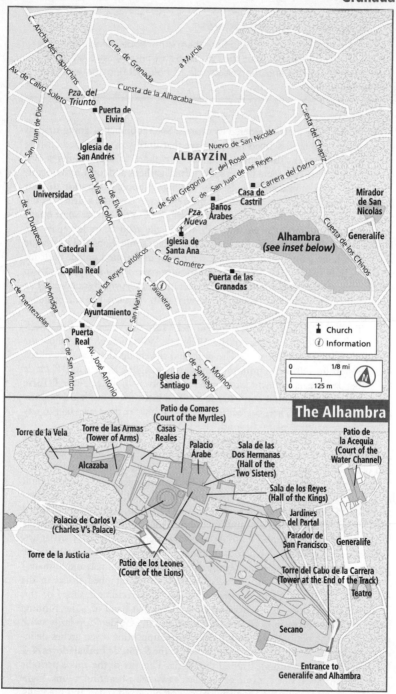

Granada

C. Ancha des Capuchins

Crta. de Granada

a Murcia

Av. de Calvo Soleto

Pza. del Triunto

Cuesta de la Alhacaba

C. San Juan de dios

■ **Puerta de Elvira**

Cuesta del Chapiz

✝ **Iglesia de San Andrés**

ALBAYZÍN

Nuevo de San Nicolás

C. de San Gregoria

C. del Rosal

C. de San Juan de los Reyes

Carrera del Darro

■ **Casa de Castril**

Mirador de San Nicolás

■ **Universidad**

Gran Vía de Colón

C. de Elvira

Pza. Nueva

✝ **Baños Árabes**

Alhambra
(see inset below)

Generalife

C. de la Duquesa

C. de los Reyes Católicos

■ **Catedral** ✝

✝ **Iglesia de Santa Ana**

Cuesta de los Chinos

■ **Capilla Real**

C. de Gomérez

Alhondiga

C. San Matías

C. Pavaneras

ⓘ

■ **Puerta de las Granadas**

C. de Puente-zuelas

■ **Ayuntamiento**

■ **Puerta Real**

C. de San Anton

Av. José Antonio

C. de Santiago

C. Molinos

✝ **Iglesia de Santiago**

■ Church
ⓘ Information

| 0 | 1/8 mi |
| 0 | 125 m |

Ⓝ

The Alhambra

Torre de la Vela

Torre de las Armas (Tower of Arms)

Casas Reales

Patio de Comares (Court of the Myrtles)

Palacio Árabe

Sala de las Dos Hermanas (Hall of the Two Sisters)

Patio de la Acequia (Court of the Water Channel)

Alcazaba

Sala de los Reyes (Hall of the Kings)

Palacio de Carlos V (Charles V's Palace)

Jardines del Partal

Parador de San Francisco

Generalife

Torre de la Justicia

Patio de los Leones (Court of the Lions)

Torre del Cabo de la Carrera (Tower at the End of the Track)

Teatro

Secano

Entrance to Generalife and Alhambra

Tips Dealing with the Crowds

Especially May through September, there's no hope of evading the throngs at the Alhambra, but they do tend to thin at least a bit during the afternoon siesta and the last couple of hours during the extended summer openings.

Entrance is along a path bordered by cypress. Soon it branches, going straight up to the Generalife (described below). Save that until you've finished visiting the Alhambra proper. Turn sharply left onto a short bridge crossing a dry canal and bear left. This route passes some formal gardens and, over to the right, the 16th-century monastery that is now the highly popular **Parador de San Francisco.** Staying here would be a real budget-buster; consider a drink on the patio or lunch in the dining room for a small splurge. On the left are some ongoing archaeological digs. Passing through a gate, the road bears left, past the **Hostal America** (recommended below). Shortly, past some shops and a cafe, the massive building looming ahead on the right is an **unfinished palace** built for Carlos V. Built in ponderous Spanish Renaissance style, it's in sharp contrast to the delicacy of the almost whimsical residences of the emirs you'll soon visit. The circular opening in the roof was to be covered with a dome. The side galleries contain two small museums.

Continue to walk down to the **Puerta del Vino,** the Wine Gate that welcomed visitors to the oldest part of the Alhambra. Walk through and follow the sign reading ALCAZABA (fortress). The walls and towers up ahead are the oldest structures on the hill, some from the 9th century. Angling right across Plaza de los Aljibes past the refreshment kiosk, enter the doorway in the rose-tinted **Torre Quebrada.** This allows you entry to the fortified town that once had a population of over 40,000. There are several places to take in the views of the city below, the agricultural plains beyond, and the mountains behind.

Backtracking to Plaza de los Aljibes, return to the Carlos V palace and turn left in front. Ahead are the **Jardines de Machuca,** a series of patios planted with olive and orange trees around a small pool. Over to the right, stairs lead up into the first of the Arab palaces. Most of the **Casa Real** you're entering was ordered built by princes of the Nasrid dynasty between 1335 and 1410. Courts and chambers are clustered around central patios. Walk through and turn right into a hall called the **Mexuar.** At first it was a council chamber, frequently altered and eventually used as a Christian chapel. From here, follow signs reading CONTINUACION VISITA, through rooms with reliefs of Arabic script and floral motifs carved in the plaster walls. (Islamic law doesn't permit representations of animals and humans.)

This enters the north end of one of the most photographed spaces in the Alhambra, the famed **Patio de Comares** ✦✦. The rectilinear shape of this "Court of the Myrtles" is accentuated by the long, flat band of water running down the center between hedges of sculptured myrtle. Golden carp lazily swish their tails in the pool. At this end, a colonnade supporting seven arches delineates the **Sala de la Barca,** a sort of anteroom to the **Salón de Embajadores** ✦✦ **(Hall of the Ambassadors),** beyond the loggia. This site of the emir's periodic audiences isn't large, but it is one of the place's two most beautiful rooms. Eighteen meters (60 ft.) overhead is a vaulted ceiling of carved cedar, and the walls, covered in intricate script and decorative details, meet dadoes of lustrous ceramic tiles. Portals with scalloped edges frame fragments of ramparts as well as the near and distant hills.

Exiting the hall, walk on the left side of the pool. Near the end is a pair of doors leading to the famous **Patio de los Leones (Court of the Lions)** 🐾🐾. In the center of the court are 12 stylized stone lions in a circle, bearing a large basin on their haunches. Jets of water arc from their mouths. A loggia of 124 marble pillars runs all around the courtyard, and protruding into the court at opposite ends are two pavilions with pyramidal cupolas above small pools. It's conjectured that these pillars and their intricately carved capitals were meant to represent the palm trunks and foliage of ancestral desert oases.

Around the court are several important chambers, including the **Sala de los Abencerrajes,** where a number of assassinations and executions took place; the **Sala de los Reyes (Room of the Kings);** and the **Sala de las Dos Hermanas (Room of the Two Sisters),** named for the two marble slabs set into the floor. Exit through the small doorway with the pointed arch into a corridor with beams above and shuttered windows on the right. This takes you into a room that's obviously not Arabic. It's part of the apartments of Carlos V, adapted to the king's taste about 35 years after his grandparents conquered Granada in 1492. Three centuries later, the apartment was lent to Washington Irving during his brief tenure as an American consular official in 1829.

Taking the staircase down to the **Patio de Lindaraja,** with orange and cypress trees, bear right into the **Baños de Comares.** These royal baths are closed part of the year to reduce wear and tear, but when open they reveal the cool vaulted chambers that may remind you of the sensuous Orientalism depicted by European Romantic painters in the early 19th century. From there, proceed to the **Jardín de Daraxa,** the first of many terraced gardens to the east of the palace. Follow the CONTINUACION VISITA signs past pools, rivulets, and gentle cascades to the **Torre del Cabo de la Carrera (Tower of the End of the Track).** It marks the edge of the palace grounds but not the end of the attractions. Up ahead is the bridge you crossed upon entering the Alhambra.

On the other side, a path leads up to the left toward the grounds of the summer residence of the Moorish kings, the **Generalife** 🐾🐾, pronounced (hay-nay-rahl-*ee*-fay), which means Gardens of Paradise. You'll find no palace up there, just many more luxurious gardens of roses, geraniums, salvias, and oleander. But what draws attention and cameras is the narrow pool running more than 48m (160 ft.) down the center of the **Patio de la Acequia,** with scores of high thin jets of water forming a canopy above the length of the pool.

The crush at the Alhambra has led the authorities to conduct many experiments in crowd control. Micromanagement and calibrations lead to frequent changes, often unannounced, so flexibility is required. A maximum of 8,400 persons is allowed inside each day. Tickets are issued for morning (8:30am–2pm), afternoon (2–6pm), or evening entry. (Mar–Oct: Tues–Sat 10–11:30pm; with entry to Nasrid palaces 10–10:45pm only. Nov–Feb: Fri–Sat 8–9:30pm; with Nasrid entry 8–8:45pm only.) That refers to the Generalife, Alcazaba, and Charles V palace. Your ticket will have an exact time you're allowed to enter the Nasrid palaces, the true stars of the Alhambra. Once inside any area, you can stay as long as you want. Sunday to 3pm is free (and, during summer, packed to the walls). With its many levels, frequent stairs, and relatively long distances to be covered, the Alhambra and Generalife aren't hospitable to visitors with disabilities.

In the winter months, simply asking your hotel *conserje* (concierge) to arrange tickets for the next day is usually sufficient. You may even be able to obtain them walking up to the ticket office cold, although you'll probably have to wander around the Generalife and main court for a while before you can enter the Nasrid palaces. In the heavy months, especially May through September, advance bookings are wise. This can be done through branches of the national bank, BBVA. The booking number is © **91/537-9178.** The tickets can then be collected at a convenient branch. Alternatively, if you plan to be in the country a week or 2 ahead of your projected visit to the Alhambra, you can make arrangements in person at a BBVA branch. You can also book online at **www.alhambratickets.com** and pick up your ticket at the Alhambra ticket office; if you do, remember to print out and bring the confirmation number the site gives you.

For all the fuss, visiting the Alhambra is still a bargain, with an admission fee of 8€ ($9.20) for the whole complex. The information number for the Alhambra is © **95-822-7527.** It's open March through October daily from 8:30am to 8pm, and November through February daily from 8:30am to 6pm. Night visits between March and October to the Nasrid Palaces are Tuesday through Saturday from 10pm to 11:30pm; in winter, Friday and Saturday from 8 to 9:30pm.

SEEING THE CITY If you plan to stay overnight, you'll find a gracious and beautiful city that rewards strolling. The tourism office, at Plaza de Mariana Pineda 10 (© **95-824-7128;** www.granadatur.com or www.granada.org/turismo), provides excellent maps. The major tourist attraction downtown is the **Catedral** ⋒, Plaza de la Lonja, Gran Vía de Colón 5 (© **95-822-2959**). Queen Isabel and King Fernando ordered this splendid Renaissance-baroque cathedral built after their victory over the Moors; the adjoining Flamboyant Gothic **Capilla Real (Royal Chapel)** became their final resting place. Admission to the cathedral is 2.50€ ($2.90), the same for the chapel. Both are open daily 10:45am to 1:30pm and 4 to 7pm (only 4–7pm on Sun).

The city's most picturesque quarter is the **Albayzín** ⋒ (often also spelled Albaicín), a warren of ancient, winding streets climbing the hill opposite the Alhambra north of the Plaza Nueva. Many of the city's most charming hotels and restaurants are here, but it's impossible for non-natives to find anything, which is part of the fun of wandering through the quarter. Car traffic is only allowed 6 hours a day, so walk or take the no. 31 bus (.85€/$1) from the Plaza Nueva deep into the quarter. Many bars and restaurants cluster around the Plaza Larga. You can always get out by walking downhill until you hit the Gran Vía or the river. Take a cab or the no. 31 bus to the **Mirador de San Nicolás** ⋒, near the church of that name. Try to arrive at sunset for the best views of the city, the Alhambra, the Generalife, and the mountains. *Warning:* Street crime, usually of the snatch or grab variety, is a problem in this quarter, so keep tight control of your belongings.

Next to the Albayzin is the heavily touted (but overrated, in our opinion) Gypsy quarter, the **Sacramonte.** The hill it occupies is shot with caves, once inhabited as homes but most now unoccupied after severe flooding in 1962. A remaining few serve as troglodyte nightclubs. That romantic notion evaporates indoors. Strung with colored lights and furnished with stubby little tables and chairs, they function as primitive flamenco *tablaos.* With rare exceptions, the performances of the featured musicians and dancers are execrable. Also, once lured past the door, you'll be pressed to tip the performers and to buy shoddy cassettes, castanets, and vile sherry. Leaflets scattered around the city on *conserje* desks and any available flat surfaces urge you to join various "Granada by Night" tours of the picturesque caves. *Our heartfelt advice:* Don't!

WHERE TO STAY On the grounds of the Alhambra itself, the charmingly quirky **América,** Real de la Alhambra 53, 18009 Granada (© **95-822-7471;** fax 95-822-7470; hamerica@moebius.es), lets you imagine you're Washington Irving. Pass through a sitting room/lobby of off-kilter antiques into the court-yard for copious, homey meals at around 14€ ($13). The snug rooms upstairs are a third the cost of the *parador,* only a few meters away. There are 13 units, with doubles going for 84€ ($75). American Express, MasterCard, and Visa are accepted. Closed November to February.

The location of the **Maciá Plaza,** Plaza Nueva 4, 18010 Granada (© **95-822-7536;** fax 95-822-7533; www.maciahoteles.com), couldn't be better. It's on the square at the base of the main access road to the Alhambra, in the downtown business district and only a few blocks from the cathedral. None of the 44 guest rooms will knock your socks off, but they're at least cheerful and functional, with air-conditioning and TV. Twelve rooms have tiny balconies; avoid the dank ground-floor rooms. Doubles are 66€ ($75). American Express, Diners Club, MasterCard, and Visa are accepted.

Built in 1503, the **Casa del Capitel Nazarí,** Cuesta Accituneros 6 (© **95-821-5260;** www.hotelcasacapitel.com), is the cheapest of a quartet of historic hotels in the Albayzin. Seventeen rooms on three floors cluster around an open-air patio—yes, that means it rains inside sometimes. Units are decorated with tapes-tries and old rugs, with tiny but sparkling bathrooms (showers only, no tubs). Top-floor rooms have gorgeous wood-beam ceilings, and a few have views of the Alhambra. Doubles are 85€ ($98). Visa, MasterCard, and American Express are accepted.

WHERE TO DINE If you just want to chow down on some tapas, the air-conditioned **Chikito,** Plaza del Campillo 9 (© **95-822-3364**), behind El Corte Inglés department store, is a happy choice. While meat dishes are of high qual-ity, the seafood snacks at the bar are the big draw, and a good selection of wines is on hand. There's a dining terrace. Tapas are 3.75€ to 9.95€ ($4.30–$11). MasterCard and Visa are accepted. It's open Thursday to Tuesday 1 to 11pm.

Pilar del Toro ✦, Hospital de Santa Ana 12 (© **95-822-3847**), is in a for-mer home of nobility partially hidden up a flight of stairs near the north end of the Plaza Nueva. Enter an atmospheric bar, then a large inner patio with an array of cushioned wicker chairs arranged around a bubbling fountain; finally, climb the stairs to the dining rooms. Start with the *pimientos de piquillo*—small trian-gular sweet peppers stuffed with a cod brandade—a classic of the Basque kitchen. The veal *solomillo* (tenderloin) is butter-tender, with a mustard and mushroom sauce. Main courses are 9.15€ to 15€ ($11–$17). MasterCard and Visa are accepted. Open daily 1:30 to 4pm and 8:30 to 11pm.

Exciting New Spanish cuisine is served up daily at **Iberos y Patagonicos** ✦✦, Escudo de Carmen 36 (© **95-822-0772**), where at any given time your plate may be adorned with cumin foam, cauliflower mousse, or cheese-and-cinnamon crisp. While dinner entrees are pricey at 11€ to 19€ ($13–$22), the 12€ ($14) lunch menu lets you experience savory creations like "chicken in local beer, with potato foam and garlic vinegar." The cooking is sophisticated, imaginative, and fun. Open Monday through Saturday from 1:30 to 4pm and 8:30 to 11pm. Visa and MasterCard are accepted.

24

Stockholm & Environs

by Darwin Porter & Danforth Prince

Regal **Stockholm** is not only Scandinavia's most classic capital but also one of the world's most beautiful cities. No longer the sadly provincial capital it was for much of the 20th century, it is savvy, sophisticated, and fun to explore, with a well-educated population who speak English as a second language.

It remains a dignified place, filled with grand old buildings, none more imposing than the landmark City Hall, scene of Nobel Prize ceremonies when red carpets come out of mothballs. Stockholm today is a cosmopolitan metropolis, pulsating with life, although it's no Paris or London. As one resident claimed, "We have *lagom*," a Swedish word meaning "just enough" or "just right."

Built on 14 islands between the Baltic and Lake Mälaren, Stockholm boasts a strong maritime flavor. The currents keep Stockholm relatively temperate, which comes as a surprise to many first-time visitors who expect to see polar bears wandering the streets. Hundreds of boats—from giant cargo ships and yachts to local ferries and fishing scows—ply the city's harbor and waterways, many of which are clean enough for swimming and even fishing. It's a royal city, too, with a palace, a cathedral, and a highly democratized monarchy that adds a touch of old-world romance. You'll really feel the romance of Stockholm in Gamla Stan (Old Town), the historic heart of this ancient Hanseatic trading city.

Stockholm is also a well-planned modern metropolis, much of it dating from the 1960s and 1970s. Pedestrians are honored here, so walking is a pleasure. Inner-city streets, for blocks on end, are given over to people on foot. Because it's surrounded by so much water and built on such a human scale, the city never overwhelms its natural surroundings. If you do feel the urge for a bit of solitude, a giant national park called the Djurgården is just minutes away.

With about 1.8 million residents, Stockholm is home to almost a quarter of Sweden's population, who remain on top of every artistic and cultural trend. When it comes to nightlife, Stockholm lets you be as cultured, sophisticated, or wild as you like.

Stockholmers themselves aren't frosty blond Vikings immersed in a Bergmanesque gloom. Once you delve into their city and begin to meet them, you'll find openness, warmth, and hospitality.

For more on Stockholm and its environs, see *Frommer's Sweden* or *Frommer's Scandinavia*.

1 Essentials

ARRIVING

BY PLANE Stockholm's **Arlanda Airport** (© 08/797-60-60) is 45km (28 miles) north of town. Four rainbow-striped **buses** (© 08/600-10-00) leave daily every 10 to 15 minutes 6:40am to 11:45pm for City Terminal, costing

> ## ⟮*Value* Budget Bests
>
> You can get **opera and philharmonic tickets** for little money, and the city's many **theaters** are reasonably priced (see "Stockholm After Dark," p. 946). **Outdoor summer concerts** and other warm-weather events are usually free, as are a host of year-round **special events and activities**. During winter, open-air **ice-skating** in the heart of the city is both exhilarating and inexpensive. At any time, a **stroll along the waterfront** or a **walk through Old Town** are both a look at Stockholm's maritime tradition and an intriguing glimpse into its illustrious past.

89SEK ($12) for everyone except kids under 16, who ride free with a parent; the journey takes 40 minutes. The direct **Arlanda Express train** (✆ 020/22-22-24 within Sweden only; www.arlandaexpress.com) connects the airport with Central Station every 15 minutes daily 4am to 12:05pm, costing 180SEK ($23) adults and 90SEK ($12) seniors/students; those under 8 ride free. **Taxis** are available at the airport, but the ride into town runs about 390SEK to 435SEK ($51–$57). You can change money at several places in the baggage-claim area, before Customs (rates are reasonable; hours are long); beyond Customs, you'll find a post office, a bank, and representatives from most of the major car-rental companies. Pick up a free city map from the 24-hour **information office** at Terminal 5 (✆ 08/797-61-00); the desk also sells telephone cards and bus or train tickets into the city.

BY TRAIN OR BUS Stockholm's train station, **Central Station,** Vasagatan 14 (✆ 020/75-75-75; T-Bana: Centralen), and bus station, **Cityterminalen (City Terminal),** Klarabergsviadukten 72 (✆ 08/440-85-70; T-Bana: Centralen), are across from each other and connected underground by escalators. The tri-level Central Station can be confusing; the more modern bi-level City Terminal is easy to maneuver through and seems more like an international airport. It has an **information desk** to the left of the entrance and a money-exchange window (look for the yellow-and-black FOREX sign). Because neither the bus nor the train station is within easy walking distance of hostels or most budget hotels, you'll probably have to take the subway. You can connect directly to the subway system from the lower level of Central Station. Just follow the signs saying T-BANA or TUNNELBANA.

The ground level of the train station is home to the **tourist office** and the helpful **Hotell Centralen,** where you can book rooms (see "Affordable Places to Stay," p. 927). Look for a sign with a white I on a green background pointing the way.

Train tickets are sold on the ground floor; Tracks 1 to 9 are for trains heading north, and Tracks 10, 17, or 18 for those heading south (13 to 16 are local trains). The ground floor is also home to phones, train information (SJ Information), and the Forex currency exchange, open daily 8am to 9pm (look for the big yellow-and-black sign).

For information about train service within Sweden, call ✆ 0771/75-75-75. For bus information, call ✆ 08/440-85-70 or Swebus at ✆ 20/021-82-18; for airport bus departures, call ✆ 08/600-10-00.

VISITOR INFORMATION
TOURIST OFFICES Your first stop in town should be **Sverige Huset (Sweden House),** Hamnagatan 27 (T-Bana: Kungsträdgården). On the ground

Stockholm Deals & Discounts

SPECIAL DISCOUNTS The **Stockholm Card**—costing adults 220SEK ($29) for 1 day, 380SEK ($49) for 2 days, or 540SEK ($70) for 3 days (children 60SEK/$7.80, 120SEK/$16, and 180SEK/$23, respectively)— buys you unlimited rides on the public transport network, admission to most museums, free guided tours, and a guidebook. You also get boat sightseeing at half price, plus a one-way ticket to Drottningholm Palace. The card, valid for one adult and two children 7 to 17, is sold at the tourist counter at Sweden House and at Hotell Centralen at Central Station (see "Visitor Information" for both, below).

In addition, the city transportation network, SL, sells day passes for subways and buses, available at the SL Center (see "Visitor Information," above). For adults, a 1-day unlimited-use pass for the Stockholm area and the Djurgården ferries is 80SEK ($10), and a 3-day pass 150SEK ($20); for children, they are 45SEK and 90SEK ($5.85 and $12).

Sweden's high taxes on alcohol are sobering. If you want to imbibe without taking out a mortgage, buy duty-free alcohol before you enter the country. Ditto for tobacco. Overseas visitors may import up to 1 quart of alcohol and 200 cigarettes.

A valid **student ID** will get you discounts at some museums and at cultural events, such as the opera and ballet. **Travelers 65 and over** get most of the same discounts as students—and more. Take advantage of the reduced fares on subways and buses. The listings below have even more heartening news for the frugal traveler.

WORTH A SPLURGE Stockholm County encompasses about 24,000 small islands or "islets" that make you believe you're a million miles from anywhere. Most are uninhabited, a few were inhabited hundreds of years ago (and contain meager ruins), while others are jammed every summer with vacationing city dwellers. The Stockholm Information Service (see "Visitor Information," below) will help you plan an excursion as a day trip or an overnight stay. Ferries are usually frequent and cheap, the accommodations (including many small furnished cabins) are more charming and less expensive than those in the city, and camping is always free.

floor is the **Stockholm Tourist Office** (© 08/789-24-90). May to September, it's open Monday to Friday 9am to 7pm and Saturday and Sunday 9am to 3pm; the rest of the year, hours are Monday to Friday 9am to 6pm, Saturday and Sunday 10am to 3pm. Even if you need no other information, get a free copy of *What's On in Stockholm,* with listings for special and free events and a good map. You can buy the Stockholm Card (see "Stockholm Deals & Discounts," above) as well as city tour and archipelago excursion tickets and concert and soccer tickets; there are also two Internet terminals. The staff can reserve a hostel or B&B room for the same day for 60SEK ($7.80).

Hotell Centralen, in the main hall of Central Station (© 08/789-24-56; fax 08/791-86-66; T-Bana: Centralen), makes hotel reservations (see "Affordable

Places to Stay," p. 927) and distributes free maps. It's open Monday to Friday 9am to 6pm, Saturday 9am to 4pm.

SL Center, on the lower level of Sergels Torg in Norrmalm (© 08/686-11-97; T-Bana: Centralen), offers details about local subway and bus transportation and sells a good transport map, as well as tickets for the system. It's open Monday to Friday 7am to 7pm and Saturday and Sunday 10am to 5pm.

WEBSITES   For general information on the Net, check out www.stockholm town.com. For details on the top cities, head to www.cityguide.se.

CITY LAYOUT

Picture the city as the group of islands it is. Bridges and tunnels harmoniously connect them as one. Fortunately, only a handful of the thousands of islands in the archipelago are important for visitors. You'll find a reliable free map at the back of *What's On in Stockholm.*

The heart of modern Stockholm, **Norrmalm** is actually on the mainland, in the northernmost part of the city center. It's where you'll arrive at the train station, shop, and probably find a hotel. **Drottninggatan,** the major pedestrian shopping street, runs approximately north-south and bisects Norrmalm. Along it are the important squares of **Sergels Torg** and **Hötorget,** home to the Åhléns and PUB department stores, respectively. Branching east from Sergels Torg is **Hamngatan,** a short street lined with chain-store outlets, the NK department store (Sweden's largest), Sweden House (home of the Stockholm Tourist Office), and Kungsträdgården (half park/half street, host to many free outdoor events). **Birger Jarlsgatan,** a few blocks east of Kungsträdgården, leads to the Royal Dramatic Theater and the American Express office, and is filled with shops and cafes as far as **Sturegallerian,** the trendy shopping gallery at Stureplan.

Flanking Norrmalm on the east, the upscale **Østermalm** is home to the History Museum, shops, hotels, and restaurants. Due west of Norrmalm, **Kungsholmen** is home to Stockholm's striking City Hall, where the Nobel Prize banquet is held annually.

In Swedish, **Gamla Stan** means "Old Town," and on the city's maps this small island district is always in the center. Gamla Stan is where Stockholm began some 800 years ago, and it's definitely the city's prettiest and most historic part, where the royal palace (Kungliga Slott) and the cathedral (Storkyrka) are located. Eighteenth-century buildings with pastel facades, cobblestone streets, narrow alleys, fashionable restaurants, and interesting shops provide a welcome counterpoint to Norrmalm's big-city landscape. Fast currents on either side of the island once forced sea merchants to portage their goods to vessels waiting on the other side. The paths these porters pounded are now the oldest extant streets in Stockholm and are well worth exploring. Gamla Stan includes **Riddarholmen (Knights' Island),** where the country's law courts are located, and **Helgeandsholmen (Island of the Holy Spirit),** almost entirely covered by the Swedish Parliament buildings.

East of Gamla Stan, across a narrow channel, lies **Skeppsholmen (Ships' Island),** once the home base of the Swedish Royal Navy. Today, this peaceful island is home to two popular youth hostels (one on a ship) and the Museum of Modern Art/Architecture Museum. The quiet streets on the island, as well as the islet connected to it, are ideal for strolling.

South of Gamla Stan lies **Södermalm,** once the "bad" side of town. As the city has gentrified, Södermalm's rents have skyrocketed and chic restaurants, bars, and cutting-edge clubs have moved in. You might stay in one of Södermalm's budget hotels or private rooms, and for a photo op you might want to visit the cliffs overlooking Stockholm Harbor. Farther east still is Stockholm's magnificent **Djurgården (Deer Garden)**, encompassing several of the city's top sights. This shady neck of land with lush oak groves once served as the royal hunting grounds; today it's a protected national park. The *Vasa* Ship Museum, the Skansen outdoor folk museum, and the Gröna Lunds Tivoli amusement park are the area's top draws.

GETTING AROUND

Subways (called Tunnelbana) and buses are operated by the SL transportation network and charge according to a zone system—the price increases the farther you go. The fare for trips within central Stockholm is 20SEK ($2.60), payable at the Tunnelbana and bus entrance.

The **Stockholm Card,** which you can get at Sweden House and Hotell Centralen at Central Station, provides unlimited transportation. You can also buy bus and subway **day passes** at the SL Center (see "Stockholm Deals & Discounts," above). People under 18 and seniors can buy **half-price tickets** for all forms of public transport. For more information, call ℂ **08/600-10-00.**

Walking is the best way to get to know the city. You'll have to explore Gamla Stan on foot, as cars are banned from most streets. Djurgården and Skeppsholmen are other popular haunts for strolling.

BY SUBWAY (TUNNELBANA OR T-BANA)   Stockholm is blessed with a fast and far-reaching subway system called the **T-Bana.** Color-coded maps are on station walls and printed in most tourist publications. Timetables for each train are also posted. Many of the city's 100 subway stations are distinctive for the permanent artwork they display; especially eye-catching are Kungsträdgården, T-Centralen, Rådhuset, Solna, and Slussen.

A **single ticket** costs 20SEK ($2.60) and is good for 1 hour (use it as often as you want), or you can get a **strip of 20 coupons** for 110SEK ($14). A **1-day tourist card** for unlimited use in the Stockholm area is 80SEK ($10) adults and 50SEK ($6.50) seniors and children; a **3-day tourist card** is 150SEK ($20) adults and 90SEK ($12) seniors and children. Unlimited transportation is included in the cost of the Stockholm Card. *Note:* Most subway stops have several well-marked exits; save yourself time by checking your map and choosing the exit closest to your destination.

If you're paying with cash or using a strip ticket, tell the person in the ticket booth where you're going. He or she will ask for your fare or stamp your ticket. If you have a Stockholm Card, just flash it and pass through the stile nearest the ticket booth.

BY BUS   Buses run where the subways don't, comprehensively covering the city. Enter through the front door and pay the driver, show your Stockholm Card, or have your strip ticket stamped. If you plan on taking the bus a lot, buy a transport map from the Tourist Office in Sweden House or at the SL Center (see "Visitor Information," earlier in this chapter). Many buses depart from Norrmalmstorg, catty-corner to Kungsträdgården and 2 blocks from Sweden House.

Country & City Codes

The **country code** for Sweden is **46.** The **city code** for Stockholm is **8;** use this code when you're calling from outside Sweden. If you're within Sweden but not in Stockholm, use **08.** If you're calling within Stockholm, leave off the code and dial the regular phone number.

BY FERRY   Year-round ferries run between Slussen at the southeastern corner of Gamla Stan to Skeppsholmen and Djurgården, providing the best link between these two. In summer, boats depart daily every 20 minutes 9am to midnight (to 10:40pm Sun); winter hours are daily 9am to 6pm. The ride costs 25SEK ($3.25) for adults, half-price for seniors and children 7 to 18, free for children under 7. A Tourist Card is good for transportation on this ferry. Check with the Tourist Office in Sweden House for more details.

BY TAXI   Because Stockholm cabs are expensive, budget travelers may want to use this service only when absolutely necessary. The meter starts at 36SEK ($4.70), and a short ride can easily come to 100SEK ($13), but the tip is included. Avoid Gypsy cabs; always take one with a yellow license plate with the letter T at the end of the number. You can order a cab by calling **Taxi Stockholm** (© 08/15-00-00). **Taxi Kurir** (© 08/30-00-00) has set prices, but always ask if there's an extra charge for a pickup.

BY RENTAL CAR   Unless you're planning an extended trip outside the city, you'll find that keeping a car is more trouble than it's worth. Most major U.S. car-rental firms, including **Hertz** (© 08/797-99-00) and **Avis** (© 08/797-99-70), have counters at the airport and offices in Stockholm. Local companies are often cheaper and are listed under "Biluthyrning" in the phone book. Swedish law requires that motorists drive with their lights on day and night.

Remember: You get the best deal if you arrange the rental before leaving home.

FAST FACTS: Stockholm

American Express   The Stockholm office, Rousenlundsgaten, S-11863 Stockholm (© 08/429-58-00; T-Bana: Østermalmstorg), can exchange money and hold or forward mail and has an ATM on-site. The office is open Monday to Friday 8am to 5pm and Saturday 10am to 3pm.

Banks   Most **banks** are open Monday to Friday 10am to 3pm. Some in central Stockholm stay open to 5:30pm. Exchange rates rarely vary from bank to bank, but commissions do. In general, expect to pay about 35SEK ($4.55) for a traveler's check transaction; you can often exchange up to six checks per transaction, so it's a good idea to change as much money as you think you'll need at one time. There may be no fee to change cash, but the exchange rate is lower. Competitive exchange rates are also offered by many post offices, including the main branch, which keeps long hours (see "Mail," below). The **exchange window (Forex)** at the train station is open daily 8am to 9pm. If you cash American Express traveler's checks at the American Express office, there's no extra charge.

Business Hours   Usually, **shops** are open Monday to Friday 9:30am to 6pm and Saturday 9:30am to 2pm. **Larger stores** might maintain longer hours Monday to Saturday and be open Sunday as well. Most **offices** are open Monday to Friday 9am to 5pm.

Currency   You'll pay your way in Stockholm with Swedish **kronor,** or crowns (singular, krona), abbreviated SEK, which are divided into 100 öre. Coins are minted in 50 öre, as well as 1SEK, 5SEK, and 10SEK. Bills are issued in denominations of 10SEK, 20SEK, 50SEK, 100SEK, 500SEK, and 1,000SEK. At the time of writing, the rate of exchange used to calculate the dollar values given in this chapter is $1 = 7.66SEK (or 1SEK = about 15¢).

Dentists Emergency dental care is available at **Sankt Erik Hospital,** Polhemsgatan 48 (© **08/545-512-20;** T-Bana: Fridhelmsplan). Regular hospital hours for walk-ins are 8am to 8:30pm; an appointment is necessary.

Doctors Normally, emergency medical care is provided by the hospital closest to the area in which you're staying. For information, as well as advice regarding injuries, call the 24-hour **medical care information** line at © **08/32-01-00. City Akuten,** a privately run infirmary, is located at Holländargatan 3 (© **08/412-29-60).** For clinics listed by neighborhood, check the phone directory under "Hälsooch sjukvaørd" (in the blue pages at the beginning of the Företag phone book).

Embassies & Consulates The embassy of the **United States** is at Dagshammarskjölds vög 31 (© **08/783-53-00;** T-Bana: Östermalmstorg). The embassy of **Canada** is at Tegelbacken 4 (© **08/453-30-00;** T-Bana: Centralen). The embassy of the **United Kingdom** is at Skarpögatan 6–8 (© **08/671-30-00;** bus: 69). The embassy of the **Republic of Ireland** is at Östermalmsgatan 97 (© **08/661-80-05;** T-Bana: Östermalmstorg). The embassy of **Australia** is at Sergels Torg 12 (© **08/613-29-00;** T-Bana: Hötorget). The General Consulate of **New Zealand** is at Stureplan 2, S-102 27 (© **08/611-26-25;** T-Bana: Östermalmstorg).

Emergencies For police, fire department, or ambulance service, call **211.**

Holidays Sweden celebrates New Year's Day (Jan 1), Epiphany, Good Friday, Easter and Easter Monday, May Day (May 1), Ascension Day (Thurs of the 6th week after Easter), Whitsunday and Whitmonday (also called Pentecost), Midsummer Day (the Sat closest to June 24), All Saints' Day (the Sat after Oct 30), and Christmas (Dec 24–26).

Internet Access If you want to check on your e-mails or send a message, try **Cafe Nine,** Odengatan 44 (© **08/673-67-97;** info@ninestudios.com; T-Bana: Odenplan), charging .75SEK (10¢) per minute. It's open daily 9am to 1am and Saturday and Sunday 11am to 1am. The coffee shop sells soft drinks, salads, and open sandwiches. Another choice is **Access IT,** on the ground floor of the Kulturhuset at Sergelstorg 31, next to the glass obelisk (© **08/508-314-89;** staff@cafeaccess.se; T-Bana: Centralen), open Tuesday to Friday 10am to 7pm and Saturday and Sunday 11am to 5pm. It charges 20SEK ($2.60) for 30 minutes, including assistance. The **Tourist Office** in Sweden House (see "Visitor Information," p. 921, for address, phone, and hours) charges 15SEK ($1.95) for 10 minutes or 25SEK ($3.25) for 20 minutes to use its Internet terminals.

Laundry & Dry Cleaning The self-service laundry **Tvättomatten,** Västmannagatan 61 (© **08/34-64-80;** T-Bana: Odenplan), is open Monday to Friday 8:30am to 6:30pm and Saturday 9:30am to 3pm.

Mail The **Central Station post office** (T-Bana: Centralen) is open Monday to Friday 7am to 10pm and Saturday and Sunday 10am to 7pm. **Local post offices** are open Monday to Friday 9am to 6pm and Saturday 10am to 7pm. Letters within Europe must be posted with a 5SEK (65¢) stamp and overseas mail with an 8SEK ($1.05) stamp.

Pharmacy For 24-hour service, go to **C. W. Scheele**, Klarabergsgatan 64 (© 08/454-81-00; T-Bana: Centralen).

Police For **emergencies**, dial **211.** For other matters, contact **Polishuset (Police Headquarters)** at Bergsgatan 52 (© 08/401-00-00), open 24 hours.

Tax A 25% **value-added tax (VAT)** is applied to entertainment, restaurants, and food; hotel rooms and other travel-related expenses are taxed 12%. You won't really have to worry about this, as the VAT is already added into the price of most store items, restaurant menus, and hotel costs. Many stores offer non-Scandinavian visitors the opportunity to recover the VAT on purchases over 200SEK ($26). Note that the 200SEK must be spent in one store, on the same day. See "Shopping," p. 945.

Telephone **Local calls** cost 3SEK (40¢) for the first 2 minutes and 2SEK (25¢) more for every couple of minutes after that (depending on distance). There are virtually no coin phones left in Stockholm, so you must buy a phone card (called a **Telekort**), available from any newsstand for 35SEK ($4.55), 60SEK ($7.80), and 100SEK ($13). The easiest way to make **international calls** to North America is via AT&T's USA Direct service. If you have an AT&T Calling Card or call collect, you can reach an American operator at © **800/CALL-ATT.** For **directory listings** for Stockholm or anywhere in Sweden, dial © **118118**; for other parts of Europe, dial © **118119.**

Tipping A 10% service charge is routinely included in hotel and most restaurant bills. If it's been included, no further tipping is necessary. Most Stockholmers add another 10% at restaurants.

2 Affordable Places to Stay

You might have heard about Stockholm's sky-high hotel prices, but less expensive options do exist for those willing to seek them out. Affordable hotels are listed below along with some alternatives. Many Stockholm hotels cut their rates by up to a third during summer and on weekends year-round. And a strong dollar (at least at press time) has made the city more affordable for Americans.

On the ground level of Central Station, **Hotell Centralen** (© **08/789-24-90;** fax 08/791-86-66) can sometimes offer cut-price rooms for same-day occupancy during slow periods. Of course, not all hotels discount rooms, but those that do usually lower their rates as the day wears on. The office is open Monday to Friday 9am to 7pm and Saturday and Sunday 9am to 6pm; October to April it's open Monday to Friday 9am to 6pm and Saturday 9am to 4pm.

Hotelltjänst, Nybrogatan 44, 5th Floor, 11440 Stockholm (© **08/10-44-37;** fax 08/21-37-16; www.hotelltjanst.com), is a small and rather insular family-run organization that maintains dialogues with more than 50 private homes in and around Stockholm, all of which rent rooms to paying overnight clients. There are no service fees, but you'll pay a standardized fee of 400SEK ($52) for a single or 600SEK ($78) for a double, with shared bathroom. Depending on your tastes, you might find the venue a bit fussy and a bit restrictive, but if life as a paying guest in a private home appeals to you, you might want to investigate. The organization also offers discounts, especially in summer, at conventional hotels as well. Management discourages personal visits to this organization's headquarters, preferring communication by phone or fax instead.

(*Value*   **Getting the Best Deal on Accommodations**

- Try renting a room in a private home—it costs less than a hotel room and affords you the opportunity to get to know Swedes in their own environment.
- Take advantage of a room-finding service that can find you cut-price rooms. (See Hotell Centralen and Hotelltjänst, above.)
- Note that hostels are inexpensively priced, well-maintained, clean lodgings for people of all ages.
- If you're booking a hotel room in Stockholm over the weekend or during July and August, a lower rate is almost always in effect.

PRIVATE HOMES

Many of the older apartment buildings in Stockholm are larger than you might have expected, and in many cases, leaseholders, because of absentee children or whatever, find themselves with more rooms than they actually need. Many of these are available for rent to temporary visitors to Sweden at rates that are less expensive than what you will pay in a full-service hotel. In many cases, you might genuinely appreciate your contact with the host family or landlord.

Available apartments drop in and drop out of the rental pool on an erratic basis that's influenced by the personal schedule of the apartment owner or leaseholder.

The best way to tap into the current rental pool is to contact one of two agencies, each of which screens homeowners for their suitability as short-term landlords. Established in 1999 and 2000 by Amira Veronardi and Inger Kjellström, respectively, they are **Bed and Breakfast Agency Sweden,** Mariatorget 8, 11848 Stockholm (© **08/643-80-28;** fax 08/643-80-78; www.bba.nu); and **Bed and Breakfast Service Stockholm,** Sidenvägen 17, 17837 Ekerö (© **08/660-55-65;** fax 08/663-38-22; www.bedbreakfast.a.se).

Both of these agencies require a minimum stay of at least 2 nights and between 25% and 33% of the rental fee in advance. They accept American Express, Diners Club, MasterCard, and Visa as pre-payment deposits. (The balance of your agreed-upon payment must be paid directly to the apartment owner, in cash, at the time of your arrival.) Each of the two agencies maintains a rental pool of between 100 and 150 pre-screened families or individuals.

You'll receive a confirmation in advance of your arrival, and instructions on how to reach your lodgings via public transportation from either the airport, the railway station, or the bus station. Most lodgings are located within Stockholm or its suburbs, and most are contained within homes that have between one and three available bedrooms.

Most of them require that you share bathroom facilities with your hosts, although past experience has shown that this rarely presents any serious inconvenience. Breakfast and use of bed linens and towels are included in the rates, which in the case of both agencies are between 520SEK and 700SEK ($68–$91) for two persons in a double room, and between 360SEK and 700SEK ($47–$91) in a single.

In every case, you'll be given a key to the apartment, allowing you to come and go at your leisure. At both agencies, most arrangements are finalized several weeks in advance, but in some cases, they can be made within about 24 hours, and sometimes less, of your arrival.

HOTELS

Hotell Anno 1647 🐧🐧 This hotel within walking distance of Gamla Stan occupies buildings from the 17th and 18th centuries. Although modernized, rooms retain the warm ambience of a country inn, with hardwood floors and country-style furnishings. Every room is different in size and decoration, some with small sitting areas; the bathrooms have roomy showers. There's no elevator, so if you dislike stairs ask for a ground-floor room; the nonsmoking rooms are on the fourth floor. Beer and wine are sold in the lobby.

Mariagränd 3, 11646 Stockholm. 📞 08/442-16-80. Fax 08/442-16-47. hotell@anno1647.se. 42 units, 13 without bathroom. 595SEK–950SEK ($77–$124) single without bathroom, 995SEK–1,695SEK ($129–$220) single with bathroom; 795SEK–1,025SEK ($103–$133) double without bathroom, 1,395SEK–2,015SEK ($181–$262) double with bathroom. Rates include breakfast. AE, DC, MC, V. T-Bana: Slussen (take the Götgatan exit). **Amenities:** Restaurant; bar; limited room service; nonsmoking rooms. *In room:* TV, dataport, hair dryer.

Hotell Örnsköld *Value* This five-story building is a favorite of actors since it lies across from the Royal Dramatic Theater. Even if you can't act, you're still welcome to this old-fashioned place, built in 1910. The accommodations are spacious and carpeted, and have some antique furniture. The walls and furnishings tend to be on the dark side throughout, but the bathrooms with showers are decent-size. You can walk to the city center in 5 minutes or to Central Station in 10. The hotel isn't fancy, but it's a good, centrally located one with a helpful staff and a lobby that's as comfy as a living room.

Nybrogatan 6, 11434 Stockholm. 📞 08/667-02-85. Fax 08/667-69-91. 27 units. 875SEK–1,175SEK ($114–$153) single; 1,275SEK–1,975SEK ($166–$257) double. Extra bed (up to 4) 200SEK ($26). Rates include continental breakfast delivered to room. AE, MC, V. T-Bana: Östermalmstorg (take the Nybrogatan exit). **Amenities:** Nonsmoking rooms (all). *In room:* TV, minibar, hair dryer.

Kom Hotel 🐧 *Kids* Managed by the Swedish YMCA, the Kom features large rooms with wood floors and tiled bathrooms with heated towel racks and showers. The guest rooms, though not large, have bright modern styling and tasteful Swedish design as befits the hotel's rating as a government-ranked three-star hotel. Some of the units look out on the spire of St. John's Church. The hotel is a favorite with families.

Döbelnsgatan 17, 11140 Stockholm. 📞 08/412-23-00. Fax 08/412-23-10. www.komhotel.se. 99 units. 850SEK–1,320SEK ($111–$172) single; 1,090SEK–1,670SEK ($142–$217) double. Extra bed 250SEK ($33) adult, 180SEK ($23) child. Children under 11 free. Rates include buffet breakfast. AE, DC, MC, V. T-Bana: Rådmansgatan (take the Sveavägen exit). **Amenities:** Breakfast room; gym; sauna; nonsmoking rooms; 1 room for those w/limited mobility. *In room:* TV, dataport, minibar, hair dryer.

Tre Små Rum This hotel's motto is "cheap and clean." The place is modern too, but not unlike a hostel: The rooms are small (and a bit claustrophobic and dark), but the beds are comfortable. Guests share three toilets and three large showers. The rooms book up quickly, so call ahead. Tre Små Rum is in a quiet neighborhood on Södermalm, 3 blocks from the T-Bana and near reasonably priced cafes and a laundry.

Högbergsgatan 81, 11854 Stockholm. 📞 08/641-23-71. Fax 08/642-88-08. www.tresmarum.se. 7 units, none with bathroom. 695SEK ($90) single or double. Extra bed 150SEK ($20). Rates include continental breakfast. AE, MC, V. T-Bana: Mariatorget. **Amenities:** Bike rental 85SEK ($11) per day. *In room:* TV, hair dryer (some rooms), no phone.

HOSTELS

Stockholm has four International Youth Hostel Federation (IYHF) hostels, offering excellently priced, well-maintained lodgings. Two, on Skeppsholmen, provide the best-located lodgings in the city (see the AF *Chapman,* below). All are similarly priced and offer lower rates to IYHF card carriers. If you aren't a member, you have to get a Welcome Card and pay an extra 45SEK ($5.85) per night for up to 6 nights, after which you gain member status. Note that these hostels aren't just for young people.

AF Chapman 🐦🐦   The fully rigged masts of this gallant tall ship are a Stockholm landmark. The vessel sailed under British, Norwegian, and Swedish flags for about half a century before permanently mooring on the island of Skeppsholmen and opening as a hostel in 1949. It's extremely popular, so arrive early to reserve a bed, especially in summer (reception is open 7am–2am). The rooms are closed daily from 11am to 3pm for cleaning. You can buy disposable sheets, rent linen sheets, supply your own, or use a sleeping bag. The lowest rates are for 15-bed dorms, the most expensive for units with only two beds. Toilets and showers (only three for women) are in the corridor. Each room has a locker, but you must supply your own lock. The common area (and the cafe on the deck in summer) is conducive to meeting people of all ages and from all walks of life.

Across the street, on Västra Brobänken, is the STF **Vandrarhem/Hostel Skeppsholmen** (© 08/463-22-66; fax 08/611-71-55), with 293 beds and a TV room. This hostel provides more privacy than the *Chapman* and charges the same rates. Smoking isn't allowed; the curfew is at 2am. The reception desk is on the AF *Chapman.*

Flaggmansvägen 8, Skeppsholmen, 11149 Stockholm. © **08/463-22-66.** Fax 08/611-71-55. www.stfchapman. com. 155SEK–185SEK ($20–$24) person with IYHF card; 200SEK–230SEK ($26–$30) without IYHF card. Paper sheets 30SEK ($3.90); linen sheets 50SEK ($6.50); towels 10SEK ($1.30). Breakfast 55SEK ($7.15). Maximum 5-night stay. AE, V. T-Bana: Kungsträdgården. Bus: 65 (to 6pm).

Hotel/Hostel Gustaf AF Klint 🐦🐦   This floating hotel/hostel rigged with lights is on the riverbank across from Old Town. When the *Klint* served as a radar sounder mapping out the ocean floor, the officers lived in what's now the hotel (four singles, three doubles), while the deckhands occupied what's now the hostel (10 doubles, 17 quads). The hotel is slightly more spacious than the hostel's cramped quarters; all the cabins are equipped with bunk beds. During summer, the ship's deck-top bar and cafe are open, with a panoramic harbor view. Year-round, inexpensive dinners are served in a pub.

Stadsgårdskajen 153, 11645 Stockholm. © **08/640-40-77** or 08/640-40-78. Fax 08/640-64-16. 30 cabins, none with bathroom. Hotel 110SEK ($14) single, 680SEK ($88) double; hostel 160SEK–180SEK ($21–$23) per person. Cotton sheets 50SEK ($6.50); towels 10SEK ($1.30). Breakfast 55SEK ($7.15). MC, V. T-Bana: Slussen (take the Södermalmstorg exit).

WORTH A SPLURGE

Comfort Wellington Hotel 🐦   The staff of this nine-floor hotel is so friendly that guests often linger in the lobby chatting with them. From the comfortable, eclectically furnished rooms you can hear church bells softly chiming the hour. The free sauna is fully equipped with changing room, robes, towels, lotion and shampoo, and shower. There's a nice breakfast room (with filling fare), and they also operate a smart little cafe.

Storgatan 6, 11451 Stockholm. © **08/667-09-10.** Fax 08/667-12-54. www.wellington.se. 60 units. Weekends and June 26–Aug 2 1,045SEK ($136) single, 1,395SEK ($181) double; rest of year 1,845SEK ($240) single, 2,245SEK ($292) double. Rates include buffet breakfast. AE, DC, MC, V. T-Bana: Östermalmstorg (take the Östermalmstorg exit). **Amenities:** Breakfast room; bar; sauna; nonsmoking rooms; 1 room for those w/limited mobility. *In room:* TV, dataport, hair dryer, iron (most rooms), trouser press.

Hotel Aldoria   The Aldoria is a quiet family-oriented hotel. To enter the street door, push button B 0004 and take the elevator to the fifth-floor reception area.

Renovated in 2000, the rooms are of average size and furnished with modern Scandinavian furniture. All come with soundproof windows and well-kept private bathrooms with shower. Friendly owner Wojtek Rybicki is from Poland. All rooms are nonsmoking.

St. Eriksgatan 38, 11234 Stockholm. © **08/693-63-00**. Fax 08/693-63-33. 21 units. 960SEK ($125) single; 1,200SEK ($156) double; 1,500SEK ($195) suite for 3, 1,600SEK ($208) suite for 4. Rates include continental breakfast. Rates 20% less on weekends (2 nights, Fri–Sun) and in summer. AE, DC, MC, V. S-Tog: Fridhelmsplan (take the Eriksgatan exit). **Amenities:** Breakfast room. *In room:* TV, dataport, fridge.

Hotel Rival ★★   Opened in 2003, this completely modernized, stylish hotel is in the heart of Stockholm's most popular restaurant district. Try to book one of the five rooms with balconies overlooking the tree-lined Maria Square. All the units are larger than usual, some with vestibules and sitting alcoves. The bathrooms each contain rich mosaics and are separated from the bedrooms by a glass wall. Much use is made of Swedish yellow stained birch, and beds are covered in Egyptian cotton. Most of the Scandinavian furnishings are by famous designers such as Alvar Aalto.

Mariatorget 3, 17525 Stockholm. © **08/545-789-00**. Fax 08/545-789-24. www.rival.se/undersidor/english1.htm. 74 units. 1,190SEK–1,990SEK ($155–$259) single, 1,340SEK–2,290SEK ($174–$298) double. T-Bana: Mariatorget. **Amenities:** Restaurant; 2 bars; 24-hr. room service; babysitting; laundry service; dry cleaning; nonsmoking rooms; units for those w/limited mobility. *In room:* TV, dataport, minibar, hair dryer, iron/ironing board, safe.

Lady Hamilton Hotel ★★★   On a cobbled street in Gamla Stan (Old Town), just steps from the cathedral and royal palace, this beautifully appointed hotel is one of the most romantic in Stockholm. Fine rustic and nautical-themed antiques are found throughout, and the room fabrics and furnishings have been chosen with care. The roomy bathrooms have tubs as well as showers. An excellent breakfast buffet rounds out the hotel's considerable charms.

Storkyrkobrinken 5, 11128 Stockholm. © **08/506-401-00**. www.lady-hamilton.se. 34 units. 1,090SEK–1,990SEK ($142–$259) single with shower; 1,690SEK–2,390SEK ($220–$311) double with shower, 1,990SEK–2,690SEK ($259–$350) double with shower/tub. Rates include breakfast. AE, DC, MC, V. T-Bana: Gamla Stan. **Amenities:** Bistro; sauna; limited room service; laundry service; dry cleaning; nonsmoking rooms. *In room:* TV, dataport, minibar, hair dryer.

Lille Radmannen Hotel ★★   This charming hotel keeps a low profile, so you won't see a sign from the street. It's in a modern building half a block from Drottninggatan, one of the city's main pedestrian-only shopping streets. Renovated in 2001, the hotel has a small lobby and a large cheerful-looking breakfast room. The rooms have comfortable Scandinavian style furniture and bathrooms with roomy showers and heated towel racks. The buffet breakfast is unusually good. It's a 10-minute walk from the hotel to the city center.

Rådmansgatan 67, 10430 Stockholm. © **08/506-215-00**. Fax 08/506-215-15. www.freyshotels.com. 36 units. 1,295SEK ($168) single, 1,490SEK ($194) double; Fri–Sat year-round and daily June 28–Aug 10 795SEK ($103) single, 990SEK–1,095SEK ($129–$142) double. Extra bed (up to 4) 350SEK ($46). Rates include buffet breakfast. AE, DC, MC, V. T-Bana: Rådmansgatan. Bus: 47 or 69. **Amenities:** Nonsmoking rooms. *In room:* TV, coffeemaker, hair dryer.

3 Great Deals on Dining

For those on a budget, meals can sometimes seem more like a chore than a delight. It's not true, however, that dining out in Stockholm is prohibitively expensive; prices (especially with a strong dollar) are often lower than those found in other northern European capitals. It's easy to find good-value lunch specials (see below), and there are a number of budget cafes and inexpensive bistros and restaurants.

Although price limitations mean you're unlikely to enjoy a full Swedish *smörgåsbord*, you can try other specialties, such as *strömming* (herring), *ärtsoppa* (pea soup), **eel, Swedish meatballs, dill meat fricassee,** and *pytt i panna* (a simple tasty meat-and-potato hash). If you're in Stockholm at Christmastime, when tables are trimmed with traditional colorful holiday cutlery, be sure to sample **ginger cookies** and *glögg,* a potent traditional drink of fortified hot mulled wine with raisins and almonds. Swedish pastry shops are among the best in Europe.

Many restaurants compete for noontime midweek business with **lunch specials** that cost between 60SEK and 90SEK ($7.80–$12); the price generally includes a main course, salad, bread, and a nonalcoholic drink. Lunch is usually served 11am to 3pm. If you don't see a daily special *(dagens rätt)* posted, ask for it. For dinner, look for pasta and pizza houses or vegetarian restaurants. To save even more money, avoid alcohol; state control keeps prices extremely high. A glass of beer costs about 45SEK ($5.85).

In the past it wasn't customary to tip in Swedish restaurants because a service fee is incorporated into the prices. Nowadays, however, many Swedes tip an additional 10% to 15% at dinner, especially if the service has been exceptional.

You'll find that restaurants are generally not smoke-free.

IN NORRMALM & ÖSTERMALM

Bistro Boheme ⊛ CZECH/SWEDISH This busy bistro right on Drottninggatan, one of Stockholm's principal shopping streets, draws its culinary inspiration from Bohemia, an area of the Czech Republic. Best bets are specialties like schnitzel with potato salad or spicy goulash soup. The place fills up at night and on weekends. The tables are set close together, and it can be noisy and smoky.

Drottninggatan 71a. ℭ 08/411-90-41. A la carte meals 85SEK–198SEK ($11–$26). AE, DC, MC, V. Mon–Thurs 11am–midnight; Fri 11am–1am; Sat 1pm–1am; Sun 4–10pm. T-Bana: Hötorget.

Café La Rose SWEDISH/INTERNATIONAL/LIGHT FARE At La Rose you order and pay at the counter and your food is brought to your table when it's ready. The all-purpose cafe serves pastries and coffee but also omelets, well-stuffed sandwiches, filling casseroles, and freshly made salads. The old-fashioned, sometimes smoky interior has small tables and banquettes amid mirrored walls and columns.

Drottninggatan 86. ℭ 08/20-95-45. Meals from 55SEK–70SEK ($7.15–$9.10); set-price lunch 65SEK ($8.45). AE, DC, MC, V. Sun–Fri 11am–3pm and 10am–10pm; Sat 10am–11pm. T-Bana: Hötorget.

Capri ⊛ ITALIAN Although Capri serves meat and fish, it's the extensive and tasty pasta and pizza menu, the courteous service, and well-prepared dishes that attract most diners. Capri's low ceiling makes this popular place feel more intimate. If you come for dinner, look for the nightly special, usually less expensive than the regular menu. Tagliolini with mussels and fettuccine with truffles are two pasta dishes worth trying.

Nybrogatan 15. ℭ 08/662-31-32. Reservations required. Pizza 90SEK ($12); pasta 100SEK–130SEK ($13–$17); fish and meat dishes 170SEK–250SEK ($22–$33). AE, DC, MC, V. Mon–Fri 5pm–midnight; Sat noon–11:30pm; Sun 1–11pm. T-Bana: Östermalmstorg.

Cattelin Restaurant *(Value* SWEDISH This restaurant on a historic street opened in 1897 and continues to serve fish and meat in a boisterous, convivial setting. Don't expect genteel service—the clattering of china can sometimes be almost deafening, but few of the regular patrons seem to mind. First-rate menu

> (*Value* **Getting the Best Deal on Dining**
>
> - Look for low-cost eateries serving filling dinners along Odengatan in the Vasastaden district. For light dining, especially lunch, young Stockholmers frequent the cafes along Skanegatan and Gotgatan in the Södermalm sector.
> - If you're staying in a hotel, the ample buffet breakfast can fuel you for the day. Most hotels lay out a spread that includes cold cuts, cereals, yogurts, orange juice, boiled eggs, bread, cheese, marmalade, fresh fruit, and coffee.
> - Lunch specials are large and considerably less expensive than dinner choices, so order your big meal at midday. You can save even more if you get a sandwich and a soft drink in a sandwich shop.
> - Always ask about a daily special *(dagens rätt)*—it might not always be posted.
> - Try cafes, department-store cafeterias, pasta and pizza houses, and vegetarian restaurants for dinner—they're usually bargains.

choices include various preparations of beef, salmon, trout, veal, and chicken, which frequently make up the daily specials often preferred by lunch patrons. The fixed-price lunch is served only Monday through Friday from 11am to 3pm.

Storkyrkobrinken 9. (*08/20-18-18.* Reservations recommended. Main courses 90SEK–200SEK ($12–$26); *dagens* (daily) menu 62SEK ($8.05). AE, DC, MC, V. Mon–Fri 11am–10pm; Sat noon–3pm. T-Bana: Gamla Stan.

City Lejon *(Value* SWEDISH   In this place bustling with office workers and residents, the lunch special is one of the best values in town. A continuous series of wooden doors covers the restaurant's walls, complemented by wooden tables and stained-glass hanging lamps. The food is filling, and the Wiener schnitzel is particularly good. For the sake of nostalgia, we suggest you order the flank steak, which is famous in Stockholm.

Holländargatan 8 (just off Kungsgatan, a block north of Hötorget). (*08/23-00-80.* Lunch specials 63SEK–95SEK ($8.20–$12); main courses 69SEK–149SEK ($8.95–$19). AE, MC. Mon–Fri 10am–10pm (lunch special Mon–Fri 10:30am–3pm); Sat noon–10pm. T-Bana: Hötorget.

Coffee House LIGHT FARE   This friendly place fills with locals and the low hum of conversation. For breakfast, you can get a ham-and-cheese sandwich with coffee or tea for 20SEK ($2.60). The lunch special (11am to closing) includes a sandwich (it might be pepperoni, shrimp, turkey, or cheese) with juice or coffee. Quiches and large salads are also available.

Odengatan 45 (near Dobelnsgatan). (*08/673-23-43.* Fax 08/673-57-29. Lunch specials 59SEK ($7.65); main courses 59SEK–65SEK ($7.65–$8.45). No credit cards. Mon–Fri 6am–10pm (breakfast 7–10am); Sat–Sun 9am–10pm (breakfast 9–11am). T-Bana: Rådsmansgatan.

Hot WOK Cafe *(Value* ASIAN   The food is good quality, and you won't find a seat (here or at the other eight restaurants) unless you come before noon. It might be noisy, but it's one of the best budget eateries in Stockholm. Twelve small tables face the open kitchen. The most recommended choices are the fried noodles, the chicken surprise with rice, and the yellow prawns.

Kungsgatan 44 (take the escalator down). (*08/20-94-44.* Lunch courses 52SEK–75SEK ($6.75–$9.75); dinner courses after 4pm 72SEK–85SEK ($9.35–$11). AE, DC, MC, V. Daily 11am–10pm. T-Bana: Hötorget.

Leonardo ⓖ ITALIAN   This refurbished Stockholm standard is one of the oldest pizza places in the city. An authentic Italian staff and chef, a good menu, and first-rate food are the real testaments to this trattoria's long success. On a tight budget, you'll have to limit yourself to the homemade pastas and pizzas (topped with mozzarella and fresh tomatoes).

Sveavägen 55. ⓒ 08/30-40-21. Reservations recommended. Pizza and pasta 75SEK–136SEK ($9.75–$18); fish and meat dishes 175SEK–215SEK ($23–$28). AE, DC, MC, V. Mon–Fri 11am–3pm and 5–11pm; Sat 1pm–midnight; Sun 1–10pm. T-Bana: Rådmansgatan. Bus: 52.

Örtagården (Herb Garden) ⓥ𝑎𝑙𝑢𝑒 VEGETARIAN   Lovely Örtagården offers one of the best deals in town with its huge vegetarian *smörgåsbord* and comfortable surroundings. Help yourself to the hot and cold dishes (including soup, salads, fruits, and fresh vegetables), take a seat in the pleasant dining room, and pay when you leave. Desserts cost extra but aren't expensive, and wine is served. Meat dishes are available at lunch only, a platter costing 75SEK ($9.75).

Nybrogatan 31 (2nd floor). ⓒ 08/662-17-28. Reservations recommended at night. All-you-can-eat mini-*smörgåsbord* 120SEK ($16) Mon–Fri 11am–5pm, 120SEK ($16) Mon–Fri after 5pm and all day Sat–Sun. AE, DC, MC, V. Daily 11am–9:30pm. T-Bana: Östermalmstorg.

Restaurang Drottninggatan ⓖ INTERNATIONAL   This is a cool and relaxed place where you can sip a beer, get a good cappuccino, or order an entire meal. Plus, its big windows look out on Drottninggatan, one of the city's busiest pedestrian-only shopping streets. The food is well prepared and the menu changes seasonally. For pasta, you might find tagliolini with scampi, wild mushrooms, saffron, white wine, and cream. Tasty and typical Swedish dishes include barbecued pork filet with chanterelles creamed in port with potato wedges. There's a "little menu" if you prefer to snack.

Drottninggatan 67. ⓒ 08/22-75-22. Pasta 99SEK–149SEK ($13–$19); fish and meat dishes 130SEK–200SEK ($17–$26). AE, DC, MC, V. Mon–Fri 11:30pm–midnight; Sat 3pm–1am; Sun 3pm–midnight. T-Bana: Hötorget.

Teater Baren (Theater Bar) ⓖ SWEDISH   The food and the view, overlooking animated Sergels Torg, make this a great lunch spot. Arrive before noon or after 1pm to avoid the crunch. The freshly prepared and tasty daily special includes a fish, meat, or vegetarian hot dish with bread, salad, soda or light beer, and coffee. For veggies, try the top-notch salad bar.

In the Culture House (Kulturhuset), Sergels Torg 3 (2nd floor). ⓒ 08/145-606. Daily special or salad buffet 66SEK–76SEK ($8.60–$9.90). AE, DC, MC, V. Sat and Mon 11am–6pm; Tues–Fri 10am–7pm; Sun noon–4pm. T-Bana: T-Centralen.

Zoë ⓖ SWEDISH/INTERNATIONAL   Zoë's entire menu changes every 3 months, but lunch always consists of one meat and one fish dish with salad, bread, and coffee. For dinner you might find grilled deer filet with fried Swedish mushrooms. The food—substantial and well prepared—is made with first-rate ingredients. You might be the only non-Swede here, but if you're looking for a relaxing atmosphere off the beaten track, this is the place to go. If you can't decide what to order, let the waiter choose for you. In summer an open-air terrace is a popular gathering place.

Jungfrugatan 6. ⓒ 08/661-27-77. Set-price lunch 75SEK ($9.75); main dinner courses 150SEK–230SEK ($20–$30). Mon–Fri 11am–noon; Mon–Thurs 5–10pm; Fri–Sat 5–11pm. AE, MC, V. T-Bana: Östermalmstorg.

IN GAMLA STAN
Agaton ⓖ ⓚ𝑖𝑑𝑠 PIZZA/PASTA/ITALIAN   Gamla Stan isn't known for its abundance of affordable restaurants, but Agaton is an exception, serving reasonably priced pizzas and pastas. The cost of other dishes in this popular Italian

trattoria will knock the tab up into splurge category. There are nearly two dozen kinds of zesty pizza available, each one large enough for a meal.

Vasterlånggatan 72. ✆ 08/20-72-99. Reservations suggested. Pizzas 89SEK–125SEK ($12–$16); pastas 134SEK–164SEK ($17–$21); meat and fish dishes 247SFK–278SEK ($32–$36). AE, DC, MC, V. Mon–Sat 11:30am–11pm; Sun noon–10pm. T-Bana: Gamla Stan.

ON DJURGÅRDEN

Café Blå Porten LIGHT FARE   There aren't many restaurants on this museum island that don't cater almost exclusively to tourists. The self-service cafe Blue Door (and there is one) is an exception, drawing equal numbers of local students and art enthusiasts visiting the adjacent Liljevalch Art Gallery. Blue Door has an inviting atmosphere and serves homemade soups, freshly made salads, quiche, and decent cold and hot meals, along with wine and beer. In summer, patrons spill into the gallery's courtyard.

Djurgårdsvägen 64. ✆ 08/662-71-62. Main courses 65SEK–118SFK ($8.45–$15). AE, MC, V. Tues–Thurs 11am–9pm; Fri–Sun 11am–7pm. Bus: 47. Ferry: From Slussen or Gamla Stan.

ON SÖDERMALM

Masters Salad Bar LIGHT FARE   Here you'll find two tables, four chairs, and Stockholmers who work or live in this busy part of town. About 90% of the food is for takeout: 35 sandwiches, 20 salads (with five dressings to choose from), and six pasta dishes. The quality and the variety are excellent.

Vasagatan 40 (near Central Station). ✆ 08/10-23-30. Sandwiches 17SEK–50SEK ($2.20–$6.50); salads 45SEK–55SEK ($5.85–$7.15); pasta dishes 45SEK–55SEK ($5.85–$7.15). No credit cards. Mon–Fri 7am–7pm; Sat 9am–4pm. T-Bana: Central Station.

Strömmen SWEDISH   This coffee shop perched above the harbor in a blue building across from the Slussen T-Bana station offers one of the best views in Stockholm. In addition to some of the cheapest dinner dishes in town, Strömmen serves breakfast, so if you're in the mood for an early-morning walk across Gamla Stan to Södermalm, make this your goal for coffee and a roll, sandwich, or pastry. Lunch is nothing special but "a good tuck-in," as an Englishman said, coming with bread, a fresh salad, and beverage.

Södermalmstorg 1. ✆ 08/643-44-70. Meals 98SEK–128SEK ($13–$17); lunch special 65SEK ($8.45). AE, DC, MC, V. Mon–Fri 11am–11pm; Sat noon–midnight; Sun 1–9pm. T-Bana: Slussen (take the Södermalmstorg exit).

FAST FOOD & PICNICKING

At the high-quality fast-food eateries and fresh-food markets around **Hötorget Square,** you can buy picnic supplies, stop for a snack, or have a full meal.

On the south side of the square, enter through the glass doors of **Hötorgshallen** and take the escalator down to a great gourmet market with 35 stands selling high-quality picnic supplies and prepared foreign foods like fresh breads, meats, fish, and cheeses. Head for the coffee bar or sample a falafel for about 40SEK ($5.20). You can get fresh fish lunches and dinners—and sit down—at a popular spot called **Kajsas Fisk,** with daily specials from 65SEK to 90SEK ($8.45–$12). By the escalator, **Piccolino Café** sells sandwiches. Hötorgshallen is open Monday to Friday 10am to 6pm and Saturday 10am to 3pm.

Fruits, vegetables, and a variety of other picnic supplies are available at the **outdoor market** on Hötorget Square itself. It's open Monday to Friday 9am to 6pm and Saturday 9am to 4pm.

Saluhall, on Östermalmstorg at the corner of Nybrogatan and Humel-gaördsgatan, is the fanciest food market of the lot—and Sweden's oldest. Inside the striking brick building, nearly two dozen stalls, a few doubling as casual restaurants, offer high-quality fish, meats, cheeses, fresh produce, and Swedish specialties like *biff Lindström* (beef patties with capers and beets). Figure on spending 75SEK to 125SEK ($9.75–$16). It's open Monday 10am to 6pm, Tuesday to Friday 9am to 6pm, and Saturday 9am to 3pm.

For picnic staples and general foods, try **ICA** and **Konsum,** two of the largest supermarket chains around.

For spots at which to enjoy your picnic, see "Parks & Gardens," p. 944.

WORTH A SPLURGE

Bistro Jarl ✹ SWEDISH/FRENCH   The lunch special at the elegant cafe comes with homemade bread and a rib-sticking main dish that's either meat, fish, or vegetarian. Check the chalkboard menu for the day's offerings. The menu changes every 3 weeks and might feature oysters, whitefish roe on gratinéed potatoes, a delectable roast lamb with truffle purée, grilled salmon (our favorite), or veal liver with onions. There's even a champagne bar; a glass of bubbly goes for 95SEK to 130SEK ($12–$17).

Birger Jarlsgatan 7. ✆ **08/611-76-30.** Lunch specials 110SEK ($14); main courses 165SEK–245SEK ($21–$32). AE, DC, MC, V. Mon–Fri 11:30am–3pm and 5–11pm; Sat 1pm–2am. T-Bana: Östermalmstorg.

Le Bistrot de Wasahof ✹✹ SWEDISH/FRENCH/SEAFOOD   If you're looking for a special night out, give this artful bistro a try. It's basically a fish restaurant with a bit of French kitchen to liven things up. Just south of Odengatan, it's in an area known as Stockholm's "Off Broadway." The crowd is arty, the food good, and the atmosphere convivial. Seafood platters for one or two are specialties; the oysters, imported from France, are always popular and delectable. The menu changes monthly.

Dalagatan 46 (across from Vasa Park). ✆ **08/32-34-40.** Reservations recommended. Dinner 140SEK–243SEK ($18–$32). AE, DC, MC, V. Mon–Sat 5pm–1am. T-Bana: Odenplan.

4 Seeing the Sights

Stockholm combines the old and the new with graceful charm and ingenuity. At the open-air museum of **Skansen,** for instance, centuries-old buildings of every kind from villages and farms all over Sweden have been so skillfully reassembled in natural settings you'll swear you've stepped back in time. The mighty Swedish warship *Vasa,* sunk almost 4 centuries ago on its maiden voyage, now rests, amazingly preserved, in its own specially designed museum. Those are the two most important sights in a city filled with noteworthy attractions. We'd also recommend a visit to the palacelike **City Hall** where the Nobel Prize ceremonies are held. A **boat ride,** out into the harbor or through the maze of canals, is the best introduction to this island city. So is a walk along the cobblestone streets of **Gamla Stan.**

ON DJURGÅRDEN

Several of Stockholm's most intriguing sights are clustered on **Djurgården,** the island east of Gamla Stan and Skeppsholmen. Once the king's private hunting ground, the island today, with its thick oak forests and sweeping harbor views, is protected as a national park. The most enjoyable way to get here in warm weather is by ferry from Slussen (at the southeastern tip of Gamla Stan) or by the streetcar that runs daily during summer and on weekends the rest of the year from the Royal Dramatic Theater in Norrmalmstorg. Bus nos. 44 and 47 stop near the *Vasa* Museum and at the front gate of Skansen, the two top attractions; bus no. 69 loops down to other attractions at the tip of the island.

Value Getting the Best Deal on Sightseeing

- Buy the Stockholm Card for unlimited rides on public transport, admission to most museums, and free guided sightseeing tours (see the "Stockholm Deals & Discounts" box, p. 922).
- Keep in mind that the city's museums are busiest on weekends; many are closed Monday.
- Ask about the discounted admission prices often available for students and seniors.
- Note that getting lost in Gamla Stan's timeless maze of car-free streets is one of Stockholm's greatest pleasures—and it's free.

Vasamuseet (Vasa Museum) ★★★ (Kids) When the wooden warship *Vasa* set sail on its maiden voyage in August 1628, it was the pride of the Swedish fleet. Even before it reached the harbor's mouth, the 64-cannon man-o'-war caught a sudden fierce gust of wind, keeled over, and sank. Forgotten for centuries, it was discovered in 1956. It took 5 years and advanced technology to raise the fragile ship intact, but in 1961 the *Vasa* was reclaimed and placed in a temporary building. In 1988, it was moved into a $35-million climate-controlled museum and became Stockholm's top attraction. You need at least an hour to fully enjoy this remarkable relic. Walkways and balconies allow you to view the "time capsule" ship from every level and angle (take time to examine the carvings on the bow and stern). There are many intriguing exhibits, including the original six sails (the oldest existing sails in the world) and two of the original masts. You can enter a life-size replica of the ship's interior and see how engineers raised the *Vasa* from its watery grave. A 25-minute film about the warship is shown every hour on the hour, and the museum has a good cafe, open August 21 to June 9 daily 11am to 7pm; June 10 to August 20 daily 9:30 to 6:30pm.

Galärvet, Djurgården. (C) **08/51-95-48-00.** www.vasamuseet.se. Admission 70SEK ($9.10) adults, 40SEK ($5.20) students, 10SEK ($1.30) children 7–15, free for children under 7. June 10–Aug 20 daily 9:30am–7pm; Aug 21–June 9 Thurs–Tues 10am–5pm, Wed 10am–8pm. Closed Jan 1, May 1, Dec 23–25, and Dec 31. Ferry: From Slussen at southeastern tip of Gamla Stan. Trolley: 7 (departs daily in summer and weekends year-round from the Royal Dramatic Theater). Bus: 44, 47, or 69.

Skansen ★★★ (Kids) Founded in 1891, this terrific 30-hectare (75-acre) outdoor museum is home to more than 150 buildings from the 16th to the early 20th century. A Swedish version of America's Colonial Williamsburg, it's home to **traditional Nordic log cabins, farm buildings, cottages, schools, summer houses, native stone houses,** and a **12th-century stave church.** Most of the structures were transported from locations all across Sweden. Some cottages (rural dwellings and 18th-c. town houses) maintain their original interiors, including painted wooden walls, fireplaces, spinning wheels, plates, and folk decor. Costumed craftspeople use traditional tools and methods to demonstrate former ways of farming, metalworking, typography, bookbinding, pottery, glassblowing, and other trades. Handcrafted items and baked goods are on sale in the buildings. A map of Skansen (5SEK/65¢), sold at the entrance, comes in handy. Once you start strolling and exploring here, it's easy to spend several hours. A **small zoo** has also been incorporated into the bucolic surroundings. Restaurants (including Tre Byttor, specializing in foods from earlier times) and food stands are scattered

Stockholm

ATTRACTIONS ●

Drottningholm Palace
  & Theater **5**
Hallwylska Museet **18**
Historiska Museet **22**
Katarinahissen **14**
Kungliga Slottet
  (Royal Palace) **9**

Medeltidsmuseet **8**
Millesgården **21**
Moderna Museet/
  Arkitekturmuseet **15**
Nationalmuseet **17**
Nordiska Museet **23**
Skansen **25**
Stadshuset (City Hall) **4**

Storkyrkan
  (Stockholm Cathedral) **10**
Theilska Galleriet **26**
Vasamuseet
  (*Vasa* Museum) **24**
Waldemarsudde **27**

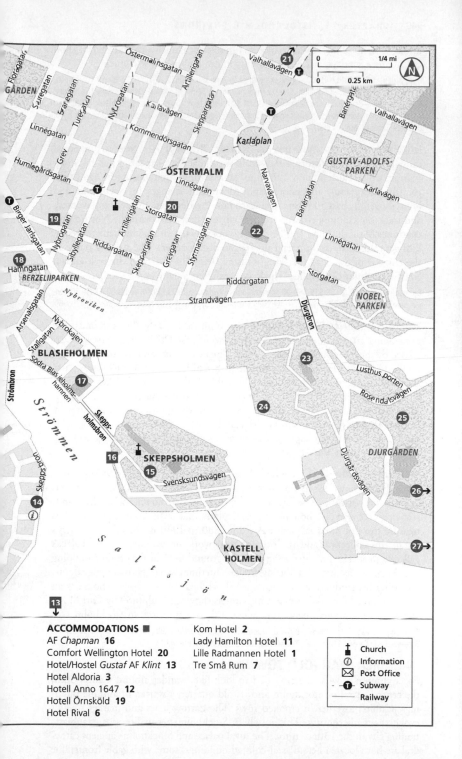

throughout, but if the weather is nice it's fun to pack a lunch and find a picnic spot. On summer Sundays, at 2:30 and 4pm, you can join in the folk dancing.

Djurgården. ℭ 08/442-80-00. www.skansen.se. Admission 30SEK–70SEK ($3.90–$9.10) adults, 20SEK–30SEK ($2.60–$3.90) children, free for children under 7. Museum grounds Oct–Apr daily 10am–4pm; May daily 10am–8pm; June–Aug daily 10am–10pm; Sept daily 10am–5pm. Ferry: From Slussen (southeastern tip of Gamla Stan). Tram: 7 (departing daily in summer and weekends year-round across from the Royal Dramatic Theater). Bus: 44 or 47.

Nordiska Museet (Museum of Nordic History) 𝔎 Sweden's national museum of cultural history is housed in a palatial 19th-century brick building. Exhibits on Swedish fashion, furniture, table settings, dollhouses, the Sami people (from Lapland), and photography document changes in Nordic life and lifestyle over the past 500 years. You learn how Swedes lived, dressed, and worked, and track the culture's evolution to the current day. Start with the **Nordic folk costumes** 𝔎 on the lower level and work your way up. In the children's museum, kids get to dress up and pretend they're Swedish pioneers. The striking statue in the entry is of Sweden's first king, Gustav Wasa (1496–1560), by well-known Swedish sculptor Carl Milles. The large cafe offers a daily lunch special.

Djurgårdsvägen 6–16. ℭ 08/519-560-00. www.nordm.se. Admission 70SEK ($9.10) adults, 50SEK ($6.50) seniors, free for children 18 and under. June–Aug daily 10am–5pm; Sept–May daily 10am–4pm. Bus: 44, 47, or 69.

Thielska Galleriet (Thiel Gallery) 𝔎 Built in the early 1900s to house the burgeoning art collection of banker/art patron Ernst Thiel, the gallery was purchased by the Swedish government when Thiel went bust and was opened to the public in 1924. One room is devoted to Swedish art icon Carl Larsson, and there are minor works by Gauguin, Vuillard, Anders Zorn, Carl Wilhelmson, and Ernst Josephson. Climb to the tower room to see the two dozen Munchs (our favorites) and a fine archipelago view. On the grounds are sculptures by Rodin and the Norwegian Gustav Vigeland.

Sjotullsbacken 6–8. ℭ 08/662-58-84. Admission 50SEK ($6.50) adults, 30SEK ($3.90) students and seniors, free for children under 16. Mon–Sat noon–4pm; Sun 1–4pm. Bus: 69.

Waldemarsudde 𝔎 Once the palace of Prince Eugen (1865–1947), Waldemarsudde is known for its fine architecture, landscaped grounds, sea views, and collection of artworks. The "artist prince," as Eugen is known, was a gifted landscape painter who also bought art, particularly that of his contemporaries. His treasure trove of Swedish paintings from 1880 to 1940 is one of the country's finest; this collection and the prince's own work are exhibited in the palace's gallery annex. The principal rooms on the ground floor of the original building remain largely as they were during Eugen's lifetime, while the two upper floors, including his studio, are used for special exhibits. In an adjacent house is an exhibit on the life of the prince. The gardens showcase sculptures by Carl Milles and Rodin and afford a panoramic view of the sea approach to Stockholm.

Prins Eugen's Väg 6. ℭ 08/545-837-00. Admission 75SEK ($9.75) adults, free for children under 18. Tues–Wed and Fri–Sun 11am–5pm; Thurs 11am–8pm. Closed Nov. Bus: 47.

IN GAMLA STAN (OLD TOWN)

For a glimpse of what the city used to look like, wander around **Gamla Stan,** the central island of Stockholm and its old quarter, a warren of antique buildings jumbled together in crooked rows. The narrow lanes and market squares evoke the 13th century. This is where Stockholm began life as a Hanseatic trading city in the 13th century. The royal palace and Stockholm's ancient cathedral are both located here. Pastel-colored buildings, some with gable fronts, line cobblestone streets illuminated at night by old street lamps. It's mostly car-free, and Stockholmers flock here in droves to shop, stroll, and eat.

Medeltidsmuseet (Museum of Medieval Stockholm) *Kids* Digging for a garage beneath the Parliament Building led to some surprising archaeological finds and the creation of this museum, which shelters part of the 16th-century **city wall,** a cemetery wall from around 1300, and artifacts from 15th-century Stockholm. In some ways, this walk-through environment promises more than it can deliver, but it does manage to convey a sense of what medieval Stockholm was like. A vaulted passage leads from the entrance into the **medieval city,** where you pass through interpretive exhibits on spiritual life in a cloister, domestic life, and commercial life. The **Riddarholm** ship (ca. 1520), excavated in 1930, is displayed, and a spooky **Gallows Hill** reveals the way harsh justice used to be carried out. Near the cemetery wall you can view a **collection of skulls,** some with holes left by a crossbow's arrows. Most texts are in English.

Strömparterren. (C) **08/508-318-08.** Admission 40SEK ($5.20) adults, 20SEK ($2.60) seniors and students 18 and over, 5SEK (65¢) children 7–17, free for children under 7. Sept–June Tues and Thurs–Sun 11am–4pm, Wed 11am–6pm; July–Aug Thurs–Tues 11am–4pm, Wed 11am–6pm. T-Bana: Kungstradgården or Gamla Stan (go down the stairs in the middle of Norrbro, the bridge between Gamla Stan and Norrmalm). Bus: 43 or 62.

Kungliga Slottet (Royal Palace) *☆☆☆* A royal residence has stood on this spot for more than 700 years, and the existing palace, rebuilt between 1697 and 1754, reflects a time when Sweden flourished as one of Europe's major powers. Encompassing 608 rooms, it's used by the Swedish king for ceremonial tasks and state functions. The complex is huge, and although the massive stone facade is rather uninspired, the 18th-century **Royal Apartments** *☆☆☆* are grand, with flamboyantly painted ceilings, crystal chandeliers, tapestries, and other royal riches. (The rooms can close without notice for special occasions.)

You can see the **Royal Treasury (Skattskammeren),** with its collection of Swedish state regalia (sword of state, crowns, orbs, and scepters), in just a few minutes; skip it if your time is limited. Unless you're an avid history buff, you can also skip the **Tre Kronor Museum** in the cellars of the royal palace. It contains remnants of the Tre Kronor (Three Crowns) Castle destroyed by fire in 1697; the three crowns symbolized the kingdoms of Sweden, Norway, and Denmark. Also okay to skip, unless you're a passionate lover of classical antiquities, is **Gustav III's Museum of Antiquities (Gustav III's Antikmuseum).** The museum is Sweden's oldest public art museum but doesn't offer much of interest to the general visitor.

But do save time for the fascinating and well-designed **Royal Armory (Livrustkammaren)** *☆☆,* which has a separate entrance on Slottsbacken to the right of the palace. Here you'll find ceremonial armor for horses and riders, along with royal finery, including coronation robes and wedding costumes worn by the kings and queens of Sweden. There's also a first-rate collection of royal coaches dating back to the 18th century. June to August, the armory is open daily 10am to 5pm; September to May, it's open Tuesday, Wednesday, and Friday to Sunday 11am to 5pm, Thursday 11am to 8pm. And don't forget the colorful and intricate **changing of the guard** spectacle, which includes a guards' parade and a military band (see below for times). Kids love it.

Off Skeppsbron. (C) **08/402-61-30.** www.royalcourt.se. Separate admission for Royal Apts., Treasury, Tre Kronor Museum, or Museum of Antiquities 65SEK ($8.45) adults, 50SEK ($6.50) students, free for children under 7; combination ticket for all 110SEK ($14) adults, 65SEK ($8.45) students. May 15–Aug daily 10am–4pm; Sept–May 14 Tues–Sun 11am–4pm. Changing of the guard June–Aug Mon–Sat at 12:15pm, Sun at 1:15pm; Nov–Mar Wed, Sat noon, Sun 1pm. T-Bana: Gamla Stan.

Special & Free Events

Midsummer Day, celebrated on the Saturday nearest to June 24, is Sweden's answer to Mardi Gras. The entire country goes a little wild, rejoicing in the first day of summer. Stockholm becomes something of a giant party.

From June to August, Norrmalm's Park, **Kungsträdgården,** adjacent to Sweden House, comes alive almost daily with classical music or rock concerts, theater performances, and the like. During winter, an outdoor ice rink provides the best inner-city skating. Summer also means frequent **free and almost-free concerts** in other parts of Stockholm. **Folk dancing** is performed Monday to Saturday evening and Sunday afternoon at the Skansen outdoor museum. The **Parkteatern (Parks Theater)** provides free open-air performances in the city's parks throughout summer.

The exciting weeklong **Stockholm Open tennis championship** is held the last week of October or the first week of November in the Kungliga Tennishallen. The **Nobel Prizes** are awarded on December 10 for excellence in physics, chemistry, medicine, literature, and economics. The prizes are named for the Swedish inventor of dynamite, Alfred Nobel, who first funded them (in part to salve a guilty conscience).

Lucia, the festival of lights, is celebrated on December 13, the shortest day (and longest night) of the year. This is one of the most popular and colorful of all Swedish festivals, designed to "brighten up" an otherwise dark period. The festivities continue on the nearest Sunday, when a Lucia Queen is crowned with candles during a ceremony in Skansen. Concerts are held throughout the city from morning to night.

Finally, few locals miss the **Christmas Markets,** beginning 4 weeks before the holiday. It's held daily in the squares of Gamla Stan, and every Sunday (on a much larger scale) in Skansen. Stalls sell handcrafts, gifts, other seasonal items, and traditional foods like smoked reindeer meat, cloudberry jam, ginger cookies, and hot *glögg.*

Storkyrkan (Stockholm Cathedral) ⊹ Founded in the 13th century, making it the oldest building in Stockholm still used for its original purpose, this church has presided over 700 years of religious ceremonies, including coronations and royal marriages. The spare white-plaster interior with red-brick pillars looks remarkably modern. The cathedral's greatest treasure is a magnificent 15th-century wooden sculpture of St. George and the Dragon, regarded as one of finest medieval sculptures in northern Europe. The 16th-century painting of Stockholm near the front entrance is the earliest representation of the city. Every Saturday at 1pm and Sunday once or twice a month, concerts featuring the church's huge 18th-century organ are given.

Trångsund (next to the Royal Palace). © 08/723-30-00. Suggested donation 10SEK ($1.30) May–Aug; free admission rest of year, free admission to concerts. Daily 9am–4pm (to 8pm in summer). T-Bana: Gamla Stan.

ON KUNGSHOLMEN

Stadshuset (City Hall) ⊹⊹⊹ Stockholm's landmark City Hall is home to the annual Nobel Prize banquet and may be visited only by guided tour. The highlight is undoubtedly the **Golden Hall,** lavishly decorated with nearly 19 million 23k-gold tiles. Dinners honoring Nobel Prize winners were originally held in this room, but swelling guest lists have forced the party to relocate to the even-larger **Blue Hall.** Marble floors, stone columns, and Gothic motifs make City Hall look and feel much older than its 70-plus years. As a piece of architecture, it's a marvel. In summer, you can climb to the top of the distinctive tower for a magnificent view of the city.

Hantverkargatan 1. ℂ 08/508-290-58. Stadshuset 50SEK ($6.50) adults, free for children under 12; tower 20SEK ($2.60) adults, free for children. Tours June–Aug daily 10, 11am, noon, 2, and 3pm; Sept daily 10am, noon, and 2pm; rest of year daily 10am and noon. Tower visits May–Sept daily 10am–4:30pm (closed Oct–Apr). T-Bana: Rådhuset or Centralen.

IN NORRMALM & ÖSTERMALM

Nationalmuseet (National Museum of Fine Arts) 🐾🐾   The collections in this 200-plus-year-old building are well marked in English and nicely displayed. Visitors tend to flock toward the masterpieces by international stars like Rembrandt, Rubens, El Greco, and Renoir. But this is also the place to see the best in Swedish art from the mid-19th to the mid-20th centuries. You'll find these works, by Swedish painters Anders Zorn, Carl Larsson, and Ernst Josephson, on the third floor along with works by Renoir, Degas, Rodin, and Corot. French, Italian, Flemish, and Dutch works from the 16th and 17th century are also exhibited. The second-floor Department of Applied Arts features a remarkable collection of porcelain, glassware, silverwork, and jewelry. On-site are a gift store and a coffee shop.

Sodrä Blasieholmshamnen (at the foot of the bridge to Skeppsholmen). ℂ 08/519-543-00. www.national museum.se. Admission 75SEK ($9.75) adults, 60SEK ($7.80) seniors and students, free for children under 17. Tues and Thurs 11am–8pm; Wed and Fri–Sun 11am–5pm. T-Bana: Kungsträdgården.

Historiska Museet (History Museum) 🐾🐾   If you come for no other reason than to view the opulent treasures in the **Gold Room** 🐾🐾🐾, a visit here is worthwhile. The subterranean spiral gallery contains a stunning collection of gold and silver articles, some from the 5th century. There are coins, jewelry, and a 14th-century gold buckle the size of a small pizza. The **Dune Hoard,** the largest medieval treasure ever found in Scandinavia, consists of 150 items probably buried in A.D. 1361. The other collections in the museum are drawn from archaeological finds dating back to Sweden's earliest hunting cultures and extend up to the Middle Ages. The Viking collection is disappointingly scanty, however.

Narvavägen 13–17. ℂ 08/519-556-00. www.historiska.se. Admission 60SEK ($7.80) adults, 50SEK ($6.50) seniors and students, free for children under 18. Tues–Wed and Fri–Sun 11am–5pm; Thurs 11am–8pm. T-Bana: Karlaplan or Östermalmstorg. Bus: 44, 47, 69, or 76.

Hallwylska Museet (Hallwyl Museum) 🐾   Stockholm's most "personal" museum is a magnificent private palace from the early 1900s filled with 70 years' worth of passionate collecting by Countess Wilhelmina von Hallwyl. It's like entering a time capsule. On display is everything from buttons to Dutch and Swedish paintings, European china and silver, umbrellas, and weapons. The Hallwyls, who lived here from 1898 to 1930, had three daughters, one of whom, Ellen, became a sculptor and studied with Carl Milles. The Hallwyls had a modern bathroom before even the king did. Admission to the house is by 1-hour guided tour only (tours are given on the hour). Arrive early—they fill up quickly.

Hamngatan 4. ℂ 08/519-555-99. Admission 65SEK ($8.45) adults, 30SEK ($3.90) students 7–18, free for children under 7. Visits by guided tour only. Oct–Feb guided tour in English Sun 1pm; Mar–Sept English-language tours daily 1, 2, and 3pm, plus additional tour Wed 6pm. T-Bana: Kungsträdgården.

ON SKEPPSHOLMEN

Moderna Museet (Museum of Modern Art)/Arkitekturmuseet (Museum of Architecture) ★★★ Spanish architect Rafael Moneo designed this impressive museum on the island of Skeppsholmen. After its restoration in early 2004, it is now more user-friendly than before. One part of it is used by the **Architecture Museum,** which hosts changing exhibits. Architecturally, the **Modern Museum** is an almost Zenlike feast of serenity. Its large, uncrowded galleries are filled with major works by seminal artists of the 20th century, including Matisse, Picasso, Duchamp, De Chirico, and Warhol, plus some of the newest contemporary art. Every year the entire collection is rehung, highlighting new themes. There are changing exhibits of Swedish and international contemporary art as well. Late hours Tuesday to Thursday make it ideal for evening sightseeing. If the weather is fine, you might want to linger in the open-air terrace restaurant overlooking the water toward Stockholm.

Skeppsholmen. ℰ **08/519-552-00.** www.modernamuseet.se. Free admission. Tues–Thurs 11am–8pm; Fri–Sun 11am–6pm. Ferry: From Slussen at southeastern tip of Gamla Stan. T-Bana: Kungsträdgården. Bus: 65.

ON SÖDERMALM

Katarinahissen (Katarina Elevator) *Moments* The Katarina Elevator itself isn't the attraction—what you come for is the seven-story view it provides. Located just over the southern bridge from Gamla Stan, the elevator lifts you to a perch high above the port. If you want a cardio workout, take the stairs up the cliff behind the elevator, but don't miss this spectacular view of Stockholm.

Södermalmstorg, Slussen. No phone. Admission 25SEK ($3.25) adults, free for children under 7. Mon–Sat 7:30am–dusk; Sun 10am–dusk. T-Bana: Slussen.

ON LIDINGÖ

Millesgården ★★ One of the greatest Swedish artists, sculptor Carl Milles (1875–1955) lived and worked in the United States from 1931 to 1951, when he returned to Stockholm to design and build a garden on a hill beside his home on Lidingö. Many of the artist's most important works, including the monumental *Hand of God* and exuberant human figures that look airborne on their tall pedestals, are located on the terraces of this outdoor sculpture garden overlooking Stockholm. In Milles's house is his unique collection of medieval and Renaissance art and of art objects from ancient Rome and Greece. The large studio contains Milles's original castings and tools; paintings by Olga Milles are displayed in a smaller studio.

Herserudsvägen 32. ℰ **08/446-75-90.** www.millesgarden.se. Admission 75SEK ($9.75) adults, 60SEK ($7.80) seniors and students, 20SEK ($2.60) children 7–16, free for children under 7. May–Sept daily 10am–5pm; Oct–Apr Tues–Fri noon–4pm, Sat–Sun 11am–5pm. T-Bana: Ropsten (then take a bus to Torsvik; walk about 8 min., following signs to Millesgården; entire trip takes about 40 min.).

PARKS & GARDENS

Parks are among Stockholm's loveliest assets, and many have already been recommended. You might want to bring a picnic to **Skansen,** the open-air folk museum, or to **Waldemarsudde,** Prince Eugen's royal compound, both on the wooded peninsula of **Djurgården.** The grounds of **Millesgården** on the island of Lidingö are also excellent for strolling, and so is the entire island of **Skeppsholmen,** home of the Museum of Modern Art. In Norrmalm, take your lunch to the **Kungsträdgården,** a bustling urban park and the city's summer gathering place.

Tanto Lunden, with tiny cottages and carefully tended gardens near the city center, was created in 1919 so city workers who couldn't afford a country home could still benefit from rural living. The one-room cottages, which are rented from the city for 50 years, look more like dollhouses, with their equally tiny yards filled with birdhouses, shrubs, and flower and vegetable beds. To get here, take bus no. 43 or the T-Bana to Zinkensdamm. Zinkens Väg, where you'll find the Zinkensdamm Hostel and Hotel, dead-ends into Tanto Lunden; climb the wooden steps and enter a world in miniature. There's a delightful house at no. 69.

ORGANIZED TOURS

City Sightseeing (© 08/587-140-30) operates 90-minute and 3-hour bus tours of Stockholm; the tours leave from the Opera House. Mid-October to mid-April, the 90-minute "Panorama" tour departs at 10am and noon (also 11:30am Sat–Sun); mid-April to mid-October, departure times are 10am, noon, and 2pm. The cost is 190SEK ($25) adults and half price children 6 to 11. A 3-hour "Royal Stockholm" tour (300SEK/$39) departs daily at 10am; the "Stockholm in a Nutshell" tour (280SEK/$36) combines 2 hours and 30 minutes of bus sightseeing with an hour-long boat ride around Djurgården and the inner islands of the Stockholm archipelago; departure times are daily at 10am, noon, and 2pm.

Mid-April to mid-December, **Stockholm Sightseeing** (© 08/587-140-20) provides boat tours of the city, departing from Strömkajen, in front of the Grand Hotel. Get tickets at the kiosk topped with yellow flags. The company's "Under the Bridges of Stockholm" tour takes 2 hours and costs 160SEK ($21) adults, half price kids 6 to 15. The hour-long "Royal Canal Tour" is 100SEK ($13). Mid-April to mid-October, boats depart every half-hour 10:30am to 4pm; late October to mid-December, departure times are 10 and 11:30am, and 12:30 and 1:30pm.

Early June to mid-August, **Strömma Sightseeing** (© 08/587-140-00) offers an "Archipelago Boat Tour" with a guide for 190SEK ($25) adults and half price children 6 to 11. The boat leaves from Strandvågen, in front of the Grand Hotel.

5 Shopping

A whopping 25% **goods tax** makes shopping in Sweden expensive, but if the dollar remains strong, you'll be surprised at how far your money can go. You'll find the best deals on items made in Sweden. Swedish design is justly renowned for its beauty, quality, and sophistication; look for crystal, glass, linen, and Scandinavian-design furniture and accessories.

For the best shopping and window-shopping, stroll along the streets of **Gamla Stan** (especially **Västerlånggatan**), filled with boutiques, art and antiques galleries, gift shops, and jewelry stores. Similarly attractive shops and galleries line **Horns-gats-Puckeln** (Hornsgatan-Hunchback, a reference to the shape of the street), on **Södermalm**. **Drottninggatan** is a major pedestrian-only shopping street that passes the train station and Hötorget. Other good browsing streets are **Hamngatan, Birger Jarlsgatan, Biblioteksgatan**, and **Kungsgatan**, all in **Norrmalm**.

NK (Nordiska Kompaniet), Hamngatan 18–20 (© 08/762-90-00; T-Bana: Kungsträdgården), across from Sweden House, is the Harrods of Stockholm. The department store is really an assortment of independent shops built around a four-story atrium, and the quality merchandise is beautifully displayed. There are several cafes. For more reasonable prices, visit the **Åhléns City department store** (pronounced like "Orleans"), a block from Central Station at Klarabergsgatan 50 (© 08/676-60-00; T-Bana: Centralen). This is a good place to buy Swedish-designed crystal, ceramics, and gift items.

Gallerian, at Hamngatan 37 (T-Bana: Kungsträdgården), is a centrally located mall where you can buy luggage and backpacks, toys, cheap postcards, and other items. Its upscale cousin, **Sturegallerian**, is at Stureplan 4 (T-Bana: Östermalmstorg). On Södermalm, near the Medborgarplatsen T-Bana station, is

---

Value Getting a VAT Refund

Many stores offer VAT refunds to visitors spending over 200SEK ($26). When you make your purchase, ask the retailer for a Tax Free Check (valid for 1 month) and leave your purchase sealed until you leave the country. At any border crossing on your way out of Sweden (or at repayment centers in Denmark, Finland, or Norway), show both the check (to which you've added your name, address, and passport number) and the purchase to an official at the tax-free desk. You'll get a cash refund of about 12% to 18% in U.S. dollars (or any of seven other currencies) after the service charge has been deducted. Remember not to pack the purchase in your luggage until after you've received the refund. For more information, call Global Refunds Sweden at ℂ 0410/484-50.

---

a contemporary mall called **Söderhallarna,** where you can combine shopping with dining out and moviegoing.

For Swedish crystal and porcelain, visit **Duka,** Kungsgatan 41, at Sveavägen (ℂ **08/20-60-41;** T-Bana: Hötorget). For authentic Swedish handicrafts, including textiles, metalwork, yarns, baskets, rugs, pottery, and hand-carved items in wood, browse through **Svensk Hemslöjd,** Sveavägen 44 (ℂ **08/23-21-15;** T-Bana: Hötorget), operated by the Swedish Handicraft Society.

6 Stockholm After Dark

The city's concert hall, opera house, and theaters are closed in summer, but three deals are offered in their place. **Free open-air park performances** by the Parkteatern (Parks Theater) begin in June and continue throughout summer; **Sommarnättskonserterna (Summer Night Concerts),** on the main staircase of the National Museum, start in July and run to the end of August; and **folk dancing** at Skansen takes place Monday to Saturday at 7pm. Summer **jazz cruises** are an exhilarating way to experience Stockholm from the water while enjoying upbeat entertainment under the stars. **Churches** often host free concerts.

Always check *What's On in Stockholm* and local newspapers (especially *Dagens Nyheter* Thurs–Sun) for details on upcoming events.

THE PERFORMING ARTS

Filharmonikerna i Konserthuset (Stockholm Concert Hall), Hötorget 8 (ℂ **08/10-21-10;** www.konserthuset.se; T-Bana: Hötorget), is home to the Royal Stockholm Philharmonic Orchestra, and performances are usually August to May on Wednesday, Thursday, and Saturday, while touring companies sometimes light up the stage on other days throughout the year. Carl Milles's sculpture *Orpheus* stands outside the building. The box office is open Monday to Friday 11am to 6pm and Saturday 11am to 3pm. Tickets run 70SEK to 420SEK ($9.10–$55); students/seniors get a 10% discount.

Berwaldhallen (Berwald Concert Hall), Dag Hammarskjöldsväg 3 (ℂ **08/784-18-00;** bus: 69, 56, or 76), an award-winning hexagonal structure built into a granite hillside, is home to the Stockholm Radio Symphony Orchestra and the Swedish Radio Choir. Call or check the entertainment section of local papers for a schedule and times for concerts. The box office is open Monday to Friday noon to 6pm. Tickets run 65SEK to 320SEK ($8.45–$42).

The **English Theater Company (Engelska Teatern)**, Nybrogatan 35 (© **08/660-11-59**; www.englishtheatre.se; T-Bana: Östermalmstorg), stages productions in English at theaters throughout the city. The office is open Monday to Friday 10am to 5pm; tickets are 120SEK to 290SEK ($16–$38). The **Kungliga Dramatiska Teatern (Royal Dramatic Theater)**, on Nybroplan (© **08/667-06-80**; T-Bana: Östermalmstorg), is one of Europe's great playhouses. The plays are performed in Swedish (with the exception of touring companies), but don't let that deter you. During summer, the theater offers a Monday-to-Friday guided tour for 40SEK ($5.20) at 3pm (the rest of the year, at 5:30pm on Sat only). The box office is open Monday noon to 6pm, Tuesday to Sunday noon to 7pm. Tickets run 120SEK to 280SEK ($16–$36) for the large stage or 200SEK ($26) for the small stage; kids under 17 pay half price, and adults 20 to 26 and seniors get a 10% discount on Sunday.

Built in 1898, the **Kungliga Operan (Royal Opera House)**, Gustav Adolfs Torg (© **08/791-43-00**; www.operan.se; T-Bana: Kungsträdgården), houses the Royal Swedish Opera and the Royal Swedish Ballet. Operas are performed in their original languages. The Royal Ballet presents classics as well as contemporary works. The season runs August to June. Call or visit the box office for a current schedule; it's open Monday to Friday noon to 7:30pm (to 6pm when no performance is scheduled), Saturday noon to 3pm (later on performance days). Tickets run 100SEK to 560SEK ($13–$73), with half price for students; there are some "listening seats" (no view, but not standing room) for 35SEK ($4.55); an hour before a performance, all unsold seats are available at a 35% discount.

LIVE-MUSIC CLUBS

A Stockholm tradition since 1968, **Stampen**, Stora Nygatan 5 (© **08/20-57-93** or 08/20-57-94; T-Bana: Gamla Stan), is the city's lively center for jazz, soul, funk, blues, and rock, with two bands performing nightly. It's open Monday to Saturday 8pm to 2am Cover ranges from 100SEK to 120SEK ($13–$16). **Engelen**, Kornhamnstorg 59B (© **08/20-10-92**; T-Bana: Gamla Stan), provides a stage upstairs for local bands nightly and dance discs spin below. The 20-something crowd arrives before 10pm, especially on weekends, when it's packed. It's open daily 4pm to 3am, with cover ranging from none (free before 9pm) to 60SEK to 80SEK ($7.80–$10).

Stockholm's futuristic **Globen (Globe Arena)**, Johanneshov (© **08/600-34-00** for information, or 077/131-00 for the box office; T-Bana: Globen), seats 16,000 and is used for big names like Bruce Springsteen, the Rolling Stones, and Luciano Pavarotti. If you're not a megaconcert fan, you might enjoy taking in a hockey game here. In summer, the box office is open Monday to Friday 10am to 4 or 5pm; winter hours are Monday to Friday 9am to 6pm and Saturday 10am to 3pm. Tickets run 350SEK to 900SEK ($46–$117) for concerts, about 155SEK to 230SEK ($20–$30) for ice hockey.

Small, cozy, and well-known among jazz fans throughout Scandinavia, **Fasching**, Kungsgatan 63 (© **08/534-829-64**; T-Bana: T-Centralen), is one of the most visible of the jazz clubs of Stockholm, with artists appearing from North America, Europe, and around the world. After most live acts there's likely to be dancing to salsa, soul, and perhaps R&B. With many exceptions, varying with performance schedule, the club is usually open nightly. Cover varies from 100SEK to 250SEK ($13–$33).

BARS

Because of the astronomical price of alcohol, most customers nurse their drinks for a long time and understanding waiters don't hurry anyone. For budget-minded visitors, even a trip to the local watering hole is a splurge. With that in mind, here are some favorites:

Black & Brown Inn, Hornsgatan 50B, on Södermalm (© **08/644-82-80;** T-Bana: Mariatorget), is the place to come when you're in the mood to sample many kinds of beer. Scottish and Irish music and classic hits play constantly in this landmark tavern, where fish-and-chips, burgers, and sausage with coleslaw and chips complement the beer. It's open Monday to Wednesday 4pm to midnight, Thursday 4pm to 1am, Friday and Saturday noon to 1am, and Sunday 2 to 11pm. The **Bakfickan (Back Pocket Bar),** Operakällaren, Kungsträdgården (© **08/676-58-00;** T-Bana: Kungsträdgården), is a well-kept secret that's as tiny as its name implies. Patrons sit around the bar (where service is quickest) or at bar stools along the tiled walls. The quietest time is 2 to 5pm. Good food is available all day and includes dishes like salmon or venison with vegetables. It's open Monday to Saturday 11:30am to midnight.

You'll have to fight local artists and journalists for a seat at the bar of Stockholm's oldest pub, **Tennstopet,** Dalagatan 50 (© **08/32-25-18;** T-Bana: Odenplan), with a bright red awning and equally red decor inside. There's a dart room in back. Open Monday to Friday 4pm to 1am, Saturday 1pm to 1am, and Sunday 1pm to 1am (kitchen closes Sun at 9:30pm).

GAY & LESBIAN CLUBS

Gays and lesbians in Sweden have the same legal rights as heterosexuals, including the right to marry. Although there's hardly any visible sign of "gay culture" on the streets, there are a few gay clubs and roving parties. For information on other aspects of gay and lesbian life in Stockholm, pick up the Swedish-English magazine *QX* (www.qx.se) at newsstands, or log onto **www.welcometogay stockholm.com.**

Tuesday seems to be a gay Stockholm institution at **sidetrack,** Wollmar Yxkullsgatan 7 (© **08/641-16-88;** T-Bana: Mariatorget). Small and committed to shunning trendiness, it's open every night from 6pm to 1am.

Many gays and lesbians gather at **Torget,** Mälartorget 13 (© **08/20-55-60;** T-Bana: Gamla Stan), a cozy, Victorian-era cafe and bar in the Old City (Gamla Stan) that's open every afternoon for food and (more importantly) drinks 5pm till around midnight. A gay place with a greater emphasis on food, but with a busy bar area and a particularly helpful staff, is **Babs Kök n bar,** Birger Jarlsgatan 37 (© **08-23-61-01;** T-Bana: Östermalmstorg). It's open Monday to Tuesday 5pm to midnight, Wednesday to Saturday 5pm to 1am, and Sunday 4 to 10pm.

A well-recommended disco that attracts a fun-loving, hard-dancing clientele that's both gay and straight is **Tip-top,** Sveavagen 57 (© **08/32-98-00;** T-Bana: Rädmansgatan). It's open Monday to Saturday from around 7pm till between midnight and 3am, depending on business.

DANCE CLUBS

Most of Stockholm's dance clubs are open for dinner; then there's a lull for a few hours before the night owls arrive around midnight. The nature of this scene requires a constant flow of new places, so ask around and check the listings in newspapers and magazines or on **www.stockholmtown.com** for the latest.

Café Opera, on Kungsträdgården, in the Opera House (© **08/676-58-07;** T-Bana: Kungsträdgården), is the most exclusive place, where even the bouncers are drop-dead gorgeous. While some people choose to eat the expensive dinners, the real socializing starts with the dancing after midnight. To escape the frenzy for a while, turn right instead of left when you enter, pass through the Opera Bar, where artists and journalists gather, and make your way to the congenial Bakficken (see above). It's open daily 5pm to 3am. There's no cover before 11pm, but it's 100SEK ($13) 11pm to 3am.

At **Göta Källare,** Södermalm (© **08/642-08-28;** T-Bana: Medborgarplatsen), well-dressed couples (mostly ages 40–60) who like to dance cheek-to-cheek congregate to enjoy the live bands and large dance floors. Food is served. You must be at least 25. It's open Monday to Saturday 8pm to 3am. The cover is 100SEK ($13) before 9:30pm or 125SEK ($16) after.

7 A Side Trip to Drottningholm Palace ⊛⊛⊛

Drottningholm Slott (Drottningholm Palace; © **08/402-60-00;** www.royalcourt.se) was commissioned in 1662 by Sweden's dowager Queen Hedvig Eleonora. The four-story, 17th-century palace with two-story wings and rococo interior is often referred to as a "little Versailles." It's located just 11km (6¾ miles) from the city center and is makes a great half-day trip from Stockholm. The royal apartments dazzle the eye with painted ceilings framed by gold, crystal chandeliers, opulent furniture, and art from the 17th to the 19th centuries. Landscaped gardens surround the palace, and from time to time you might even spot the down-to-earth royal couple taking a stroll; the palace has been the home of the Swedish royal family since 1981. Admission is 60SEK ($7.80) adults and 30SEK ($3.90) students. It's open daily May to August 10am to 4:30pm and September noon to 3:30pm; October to April, it's open Saturday and Sunday noon to 3:30pm.

Drottningholms Slottsteater (Court Theater) ⊛⊛ (© **08/556-931-00)** is the world's oldest theater preserved in its original state. With original backdrops, props, and stage machinery, it stands exactly as it was on opening night 1766. June to September, 18th-century ballets and operas are performed, authentic down to the costumes. Ask for a schedule at the Stockholm Information Service or check **www.drottningholmslottsteater.dtm.se.** Even if no show is scheduled, visit the theater with a guided tour. Admission is 60SEK ($7.80) adults and 30SEK ($3.90) students; free for ages 16 and under. The theater is open daily: May noon to 4:30pm, June to August 12:30 to 4:30pm, and September 1:30 to 3:30pm.

Kina Slott (Chinese Pavilion) ⊛, near the end of the palace park, was constructed in Stockholm in 1753 as a secret birthday gift from King Adolf Fredrik to his queen. It was floated downriver so it would surprise Lovisa Ulrika when it arrived. Fanciful garden pavilions inspired by Chinese architecture were all the rage among 18th-century European royalty. Extensive renovations have restored this beautiful example to its original appearance. Admission is 60SEK ($7.80) adults and 30SEK ($3.90) seniors/students. It's open Saturday and Sunday: April and October 12:30 to 3:30pm, May to August daily 10am to 4:30pm, and September daily noon to 3:30pm.

There are two ways to reach Drottningholm. The more exciting is by **steamboat,** which takes 50 minutes. The round-trip fare is 110SEK ($14) for adults, 55SEK ($7.15) for children 6 to 11, free for children under 6. The early-1900s steamers leave from Stadshusbron, beside Stockholm's City Hall, daily: June 10 to August 20, 10am to 6pm; April 29 to June 9 and August 21 to September 10, 10am to 3:30pm. Contact **Strömma Kanalbolaget** at © **08/587-140-00** for details. You can also take the **T-Bana** to Brommaplan, then connect to any Mälaro bus for Drottningholm.

25

Venice & Environs

by Reid Bramblett

Yes, the tourist hordes are inescapable. And yes, prices here can be double what they are elsewhere in Italy—but this is **Venice,** *La Serenissima* (the Most Serene), what Lord Byron described as "a fairy city of the heart." For more than a thousand years, people have flocked to this canalled wonder because it's unlike any other city. They come to see the Rio Frescada flowing past houses with centuries-faded facades of muted reds and greens; to travel the truly grand Canal Grande as it winds past stately Gothic and Renaissance palazzi; to experience the unparalleled tranquillity of Campo Santa Margherita, where only the sounds of fruit vendors hawking their produce or shrieking children playing soccer pierce the stillness; and they come to ride the gondolas and *vaporetti* (water buses) that ply its countless canals. Underneath its

unique beauty and weathered decadence, Venice is a living city that seems too exquisite to be genuine, too fragile to survive the never-ending stream of visitors.

Venice was at the crossroads of the Eastern and Western worlds for centuries, resulting in an unrivaled heritage of art, architecture, and culture. It straddled the two worlds, and although traders and merchants no longer pass through as they once did, it nonetheless continues to find itself at a crossroads: an intersection in time between the uncontested period of maritime power that built it and the modern world that keeps it ever-so-gingerly afloat.

For more on Venice and its environs, see *Frommer's Portable Venice, Frommer's Northern Italy, Frommer's Italy, Frommer's Italy from $70 a Day,* or *Italy For Dummies.*

1 Essentials

ARRIVING

BY PLANE   You can fly into Venice from North America via Rome or Milan with **Alitalia** (℃ **800-223-5730;** www.alitalia.it) or a number of other airlines, or by connecting through a major European city with European carriers. No-frills upstart **Ryanair** (℃ **0871-246-0000** in the U.K.; www.ryanair.com) will fly you from London to Venice-Treviso and Venice-Brescia (as well as a number of other Italian cities). Its competitor **easyJet** (www.easyjet.com) flies from London to Milan, Venice, and Bologna. Both usually charge less than £25 ($47) each way for such service.

Flights land at the **Aeroporto Marco Polo,** 7km (4½ miles) north of the city on the mainland (℃ **041-260-9260** for flight info, 041-260-6111 for the switchboard; www.veniceairport.it). There are two bus alternatives. The special **ATVO airport shuttle bus** (℃ **041-520-5530;** www.atvo.it) connects with Piazzale Roma not far from Venice's Santa Lucia train station and the closest

Value Budget Bests

The best free sight in Venice is the **city itself.** The crowds can be taxing in high season, but there's something here you can't buy anywhere else—the quiet. You'll hear conversations going on in dozens of languages but never an agitated automobile horn or a failing car muffler or an annoying Vespa motorbike. Spend an afternoon simply getting lost and loving it in the back alleys of this most serene city.

Venice's many **festivals** and **special events** (see the box "Special & Free Events," later in this chapter) are also budget bests. Most of the revelry is free, and even at the Film Festival and the Biennale you'll find a number of inexpensive screenings and free exhibits.

You can always save money on food and drink by consuming them **standing up** at one of the city's ubiquitous bars or neighborhood *bacari* (wine bars). A 1€ to 3€ ($1.15–$3.45) *panino* (sandwich) and a glass of wine at 1€ ($1.15) make a quick and satisfying lunch. Prices double—at least—if you sit down.

---

point to Venice's attractions accessible by land. Buses leave for/from the airport about every hour, cost 2.60€ ($2.30), and make the trip in about 20 minutes. The less expensive, twice-hourly (once an hour on Sun) **local public ACTV bus** no. 5 (© **041-528-7886**) costs 1.50€ ($1.75) and takes 30 to 45 minutes. Buy tickets for either at the newsstand just inside the terminal from the signposted bus stop. With either bus, you'll have to walk to/from the final stop at Piazzale Roma to the nearby *vaporetto* stop for the final connection to your hotel. It's rare to see porters around who'll help with luggage, so pack light.

A **land taxi** from the airport to the Piazzale Roma to pick up your *vaporetto* will run about 30€ ($34).

The most fashionable and traditional way to arrive in Piazza San Marco is by sea. For 10€ ($12), the **Cooperative San Marco/Alilaguna** (© **041-523-5775;** www.alilaguna.it) operates a large *motoscafo* (**shuttle boat**) service from the airport with two stops at Murano and the Lido before it arrives after about 1 hour in Piazza San Marco. (The *motoscafo* also stops at Arsenale, San Zaccaria, and Zattere.) Call for the daily schedule of a dozen or so trips from about 6am to midnight, which changes with the season and is coordinated with the principal arrival/departure of the major airlines (most hotels have the schedule). If your hotel isn't in the Piazza San Marco area, you'll have to make a connection at the *vaporetto* launches. (Your hotel can help you with the specifics if you've booked before leaving home.)

A **private water taxi** (20–30 min. to/from the airport) is convenient but costly—a legal minimum of 55€ ($63) but usually more around 75€ ($86) for two to four passengers with few bags. However, it's worth considering if you're pressed for time, have an early flight, have a lot of luggage (a Venice no-no), or can split the cost with a friend or two. It may be able to drop you off at the front (or side) door of your hotel or as close as it can maneuver given your hotel's location. (Check with the hotel before arriving.) Your taxi captain should be able to tell you before boarding just how close he can get you. Try **Corsorzio Motoscafi Venezia** (© **041-522-2303;** www.motoscafivenezia.it).

Venice Deals & Discounts

SPECIAL DISCOUNTS   Venice, so delicate it cannot handle the hordes of visitors it receives every year, has been toying with the idea of charging admission to let you get into the city itself. Slightly calmer heads seem to have prevailed, though, and the mayor's office has inaugurated the **Venice Card** (© 899-909-090 in Italy, or 041-271-4747 or 041- outside of Italy; www.venicecard.com). The "blu" version will get you free passage on buses and vaporetti, usage of public toilets, and a reduced daily rate of 6.70€ ($8), along with a reserved spot, at the public ASM parking garage. The "orange" version adds to these services admission to all the sights covered under the expanded version of the Musei di Piazza San Marco cumulative ticket (see below) plus the Ca' Rezzonico; in addition, the card lets you bypass the often long lines. (They're working on arranging reserved, timed entries, the logic being that so many people will have this card, the main sights will be effectively booked-up, thus discouraging visitors who arrive without the card.) They're also encouraging various merchants to jump on the bandwagon in some way.

For adults over 30, the "blu" card costs 14€ ($16) for 1 day, 29€ ($33) for 3 days, or 51€ ($59) for 7 days; for ages 4 to 29, the "blu" card costs 9€ ($10) for 1 day, 22€ ($25) for 3 days, or 49€ ($56) for 7 days. For adults, the "orange" card costs 28€ ($32) for 1 day, 47€ ($54) for 3 days, or 68€ ($78) for 7 days; for ages 4 to 29, the "orange" card costs 18€ ($21) for 1 day, 35€ ($40) for 3 days, or 61€ ($70) for 7 days. You can order it in advance by phone or online, and they'll tell you where to pick it up. Save 1€ to 2€ ($1.15–$2.30) by purchasing your Venice Card (3- or 7-day card only) online or by showing a Trenitalia pass at the ticket office. There are versions that include a ride into town from the airport, but they don't save you any money in the long run, so skip them.

The **Musei di Piazza San Marco** (© 041-520-9070; www.museicivici veneziani.it) joint ticket grants admission to all the piazza's museums— the Palazzo Ducale, Museo Correr, Museo Archeologico Nazionale, and Biblioteca Nazionale Marciana—for 11€ ($13) adults, 5.50€ ($6) students. Add in the Ca' Rezzonico, Museo di Palazzo Mocenigo (Costume Museum), Casa di Goldoni, Museo del Vetro (Glass Museum) on Murano, and Museo del Merletto (Lace Museum) on Burano for a total of 16€ ($18) adults, 10€ ($12) students.

Anyone between 14 and 29 is eligible for the terrific **Rolling Venice pass** (www.commune.venezia.it/rol2), which gives discounts in museums, restaurants, stores, language courses, hotels, and bars across the

BY TRAIN   Trains from **Rome** (4½–7 hr., 30€–45€/$34–$52), **Milan** (2½–3½ hr., 12€–21€/$14–$24), **Florence** (2½–3½ hr., 19€–27€/$22–$31), and all over Europe arrive at the **Stazione Santa Lucia** (© 800/888-088 toll-free from anywhere in Italy; www.trenitalia.it). To get there, all must pass through (but not necessarily stop at) a station marked VENEZIA–MESTRE. Don't be confused: Mestre is a charmless industrial city that's the last stop on the mainland. Occasionally city; just consult the booklet to see where you can use the card. It's valid for a year and costs 3€ ($3.45). July to September, you can stop by the special Rolling Venice office set up in the train station daily 8am to 8pm; in winter, you can get the pass at the Transalpino travel agency just outside the station's front doors and to the right, at the top of the steps, open Monday to Friday 8:30am to 12:30pm and 3 to 7pm, Saturday 8:30am to 12:30pm. Year-round, you can pick one up at the Informagiovani Assessorato alla Gioventù, Corte Contarina 1529, off the Frezzeria west of St. Mark's Square (© 041-274-7650), open Monday to Friday 9:30am to 1pm, Tuesday and Thursday 3 to 5pm.

If you plan to explore a number of the city's secondary churches, many of which charge 2.50 ($2.90) admission, see "For Church Fans," later in the chapter, for information on an 8€ ($9) cumulative ticket.

Some **hotels** offer as much as 30% to 50% discounts in winter (while many just shut down entirely). Look for discounts in the slow months of July and August as well.

Check with a tourist office for **free tours** being offered (erratically and usually during high season) in some of the churches, particularly the Basilica di San Marco and occasionally the Frari.

WORTH A SPLURGE   The cost of living is significantly higher here than in any other city in Italy. Simply visiting Venice is a splurge in and of itself—but a worthy one. To make your euros stretch, book those cheapest rooms in advance and rely less on the serendipity that serves you well in other Italian cities. When it comes to splurges, Venice's offerings are endless. Buying (but then having to carry home—be prepared) **champagne flutes** from Murano means you'll have instant heirlooms as well as a grand way to toast the New Year. Another great souvenir is an elaborate **Carnevale mask**—those from the Commedia dell'Arte are associated with the Venetian Carnevale. And be sure to set aside some euros for a **Venetian dinner of fish or seafood**. It'll be costly but delicious and memorable. If you're in town for **Carnevale** (when the high-season prices mean you'll be splurging no matter what), splash out in a major way at a proper **masked ball** such as the Ballo del Doge (see "The Doge's Ball at Carnevale" box, later in this chapter).

Of course, Venice's top splurge opportunity is a world-famous **gondola ride**. Sure, it might have become a touristy cliché, but it's also a perfect way to experience the essence of the city and see vignettes that are inspiring and inimitably romantic.

trains end in Mestre, in which case you have to catch one of the frequent 10-minute shuttles connecting with Venice; if so, take a moment to look around, as the Mestre station was designed by famed architect Rienzo Piano, who did Paris's Centre Pompidou and the New York Times building currently going up in Manhattan. Still, it's inconvenient, so when booking your ticket, confirm that the final destination is Venezia–Stazione Santa Lucia.

Between the station's large front doors is a small, understaffed **tourist office** (© **041-529-8727** or 041-529-8740), with lines that can be discouraging and a strict "one person allowed in at a time" policy. It's open daily 8am to 7pm (closed Sun in winter). The **train info office,** marked with a lowercase *i,* is also in the station's main hall and staffed daily 8am to 8pm.

On exiting, you'll find the Canal Grande (Grand Canal) in front of you, making a heart-stopping first impression. You'll find the docks for a number of *vaporetto* lines (the city's public ferries or "water buses") to your left and right. Head to the booths to your left, near the bridge, to catch either of the two lines plying the Canal Grande: the **no. 82 express,** which stops only at the station, San Marcula, Rialto Bridge, San Tomà, San Samuele, and Accademia before hitting San Marco (26 min. total); and the misnamed **no. 1 *accellerato,*** which is actually the local, making 14 stops between the station and San Marco (a 31-min. trip). Both leave every 10 minutes or so, but every other no. 82 stops short at Rialto, meaning you'll have to disembark and hop on the next no. 1 or 82 that comes along to continue to San Marco.

Note: The no. 82 goes in two directions from the train station: left down the Canal Grande toward San Marco—which is the (relatively) fast and scenic way—and right, which also gets you to San Marco (at the San Zaccaria stop) but takes twice as long because it goes the relatively boring way around Dorsoduro. Make sure the no. 82 you get on is headed to San Marco.

BY BUS Although rail travel is more convenient and commonplace, Venice is serviced by long-distance buses from all over mainland Italy and some foreign cities. The final destination is Piazzale Roma, where you'll need to pick up *vaporetto* no. 82 or no. 1 (see "By Train," above) to connect you with stops in the heart of Venice and along the Grand Canal.

BY CAR The only wheels you'll see in Venice are those attached to luggage. Venice is a city of canals and narrow alleys. No cars are allowed—even the police and ambulance services use boats. Arriving in Venice by car is problematic and expensive—and downright exasperating if it's high season and the parking facilities are full (they usually are). You can drive across the Ponte della Libertà from Mestre to Venice itself but can go no farther than Piazzale Roma at the Venice end, where many garages eagerly await your money. Do some research before choosing a **garage**—the rates vary widely, from 19€ ($22) per day for an average-size car at the communal **ASM garage** (© **041-272-7211;** www. asmvenezia.it) to 26€ ($30) per day at private outfits like **Garage San Marco** (© **041-523-2213;** www.garagesanmarco.it). If you have reservations at a hotel, check before arriving: Most of them offer coupons for some of the parking facilities with a special daily rate of 10€ ($12) to submit on departure when payment is due. (Ask the hotel which garage you need to park at.)

Vaporetto lines 1 and 82, described under "By Train" above, both stop at Piazzale Roma before continuing down the Canal Grande to the train station and, eventually, Piazza San Marco.

VISITOR INFORMATION

TOURIST OFFICES There's a small office in the train station (above), but the new main office is right when you get off the Vaporetto at the San Marco stop, in a stone pavilion wedged between the small green park on the Grand Canal called the Giardinetti Reali and the famous Harry's Bar. It's called the **Venice Pavilion/Palazzina dei Santi** (© **041-522-5150** or 041-522-6356; www.turismovenezia.it; *vaporetto:* San Marco), and is, frankly, more interested in running its gift shop than in helping tourists. It's open daily, 10am to 6pm. They've kept open the old (but just as indifferent) office under the arcade at the west end of **Piazza San Marco** at no. 71F, on the left of the tunnel-like street leading to Calle dell'Ascensione (© **041-520-8964** or 041-529-8711; fax 041-529-8740; *vaporetto:* San Marco). It's open Monday to Friday 9am to 3:30pm. During peak season, a small info booth with erratic hours operates in the arrivals hall at the Marco Polo Airport.

The tourist office's *LEO Bussola* brochure is useful for museum hours and events, but their map only helps you find *vaporetto* lines and stops. (Buying a street map at a news kiosk is worthwhile; see below.) Even more useful is info-packed monthly *Un Ospite di Venezia* (www.unospitedivenezia.it); most hotels have a handful of copies. Also keep an eye out for the ubiquitous posters around town with **exhibit and concert schedules.** The classical concerts held mostly in churches are touristy but fun, and are advertised by an army of costumed touts handing out leaflets on highly trafficked streets.

WEBSITES The city's **official tourist board site** is **www.turismovenczia.it**; the official site of the city government (also full of good resources) is **www.comune.venezia.it**. A couple of good privately maintained sites are **Meeting Venice** (www.meetingvenice.it), *Un Ospite di Venezia* (www.unospitedi venezia.it), and **Doge of Venice** (www.doge.it).

CITY LAYOUT

Keep in mind as you wander seemingly hopelessly among the *calli* (streets) and *campi* (squares) that the city wasn't built to make sense to those on foot but rather to those plying its canals. No matter how good your map and sense of direction, time after time you'll get lost. Just view it as an opportunity to stumble across Venice's most intriguing corners and vignettes.

Venice lies 4km (2½ miles) from terra firma, connected to the mainland burg of **Mestre** by the Ponte della Libertà, which leads to **Piazzale Roma.** Snaking through the city like an inverted S is the **Canal Grande (Grand Canal),** the wide main artery of aquatic Venice. The "streets filled with water" are 177 narrow *rio* **(canals)** cutting through the interior of the two halves of the city, flowing gently by the doorsteps of centuries-old palazzi. They'd be endlessly frustrating to the landlubber visitors trying to navigate the city on foot if not for the 400 footbridges that cross them, connecting Venice's 118 islands.

Only three **bridges** cross the Grand Canal: the **Ponte degli Scalzi,** just outside the train station; the elegant white marble **Ponte Rialto,** connecting the districts of San Marco and San Polo and by far the most recognizable; and the wooden **Ponte Accademia,** connecting the Campo Santo Stefano area of the San Marco neighborhood with the Accademia museum across the way in Dorsoduro.

Beginning in the 12th century and made official in 1711, the city has been divided into six *sestieri* ("sixths" or **"districts").** **Cannaregio** stretches north and east, from the train station to the Jewish Ghetto and on to the vicinity of the Ca' d'Oro north of the Rialto Bridge. To the east beyond Cannaregio (and skirting the area north and east of Piazza San Marco) is **Castello,** whose tony canalside esplanade, Riva degli Schiavoni, is lined with first-class and deluxe hotels. The central **San Marco** shares this side of the Grand Canal with Castello and Cannaregio, anchored by the magnificent Piazza San Marco and St. Mark's Basilica to the south and the Rialto Bridge to the north; it's the city's commercial, religious, and political heart. On the other side of the Grand Canal, **San Polo** is north of the Rialto Bridge, stretching west to just beyond Campo dei

---

Frari and Campo San Rocco. The residential **Santa Croce** is next, moving north and west, stretching all the way to Piazzale Roma. Finally, the residential **Dorsoduro** is on the opposite side of the Accademia Bridge from San Marco. Most known for the Accademia and Peggy Guggenheim museums, it's the largest *sestiere* and is something of an artists' haven, although escalating rents make it hardly Bohemian these days.

Venice shares its lagoon with several **other islands.** Opposite Piazza San Marco and Dorsoduro is **La Giudecca,** a tranquil working-class place where you'll find a youth hostel and a handful of hotels (including the fabled Cipriani, one of Europe's finest), but mostly residential neighborhoods. The slim 4.5km (7-mile) -long **Lido di Venezia** is the city's sandy beach; separating the lagoon from the sea and permitting car traffic, it's a popular summer destination because of its concentration of seasonal hotels.

Murano, Burano, and Torcello are popular destinations northeast of the city and easily accessible by public transport *vaporetto*. Since the 13th century, **Murano** has exported its glass products worldwide; it's an interesting day trip for those with the time, but you can do just as well in "downtown" Venice's myriad glass stores. Colorful fishing village–style **Burano** was and still is equally famous for its lace, an art now practiced by so few island women that its prices are generally unaffordable. **Torcello** is the most remote and least populated. The 40-minute boat ride is worthwhile for history and art buffs, who will be awestruck by the Byzantine mosaics of the cathedral (some of Europe's finest outside Ravenna's) whose foundation dates to the 7th century, making this the oldest Venetian monument. **San Michele** is the cemetery island where such celebrities as Stravinsky and Diaghilev are buried.

Finally, the industrial city of **Mestre,** on the mainland, is the gateway to Venice and offers no reason to explore it. In a pinch, its host of inexpensive hotels is worth consideration when Venice's hotels are full, but that's about all.

GETTING AROUND

The free map offered by the tourist office and most hotels has good intentions but doesn't even show, much less name or index, all the *calli* (streets) and byways. (As you wander Venice, though, look for the ubiquitous **yellow signs** whose destinations and arrows direct you toward five major landmarks: **Ferrovia** [the train station], **Piazzale Roma,** the **Rialto** [Bridge], [Piazza] **San Marco,** and the **Accademia** [Bridge].) You can buy a more detailed map *(pianta della città)* at a number of bookstores or newsstands. How helpful the more elaborate maps can be is debatable—if you're lost, you're better off asking a Venetian to point you in the right direction.

BY BOAT The various *sestieri* are linked by a comprehensive *vaporetto* **(water bus/ferry)** system of about a dozen lines operated by the **Azienda del Consorzio Trasporti Veneziano (ACTV),** Calle Fuseri 1810, off the Frezzeria in San Marco (© **041-528-7886;** www.actv.it). Transit maps are available at the tourist office and most ACTV stations. It's easier to get around on foot; the *vaporetti* principally serve the Grand Canal (and can be crowded in summer), the outskirts, and the outer islands. The crisscross network of small canals is the province of delivery vessels, gondolas, and private boats.

The **one-way ticket** is a steep 3.50€ ($4.05). A **round-trip ticket** is 6€ ($7) valid until the end of the day, but the **24-hour ticket** at 11€ ($12) is a good buy if you'll be making more than three trips in a day. A **3-day pass** costs 22€ ($25); a **7-day pass** is 32€ ($36). Most lines run every 10 to 15 minutes 7am to midnight, then hourly until morning; most *vaporetto* docks (the only place you can buy tickets) have timetables posted. Note that not all stations sell tickets after dark; if you didn't buy a pass or extra tickets beforehand, you'll have to settle up with the conductor on board (you'll have to find him—he won't come looking for you) for an extra .50€ (60¢) per ticket—or gamble on a 21€ ($24) fine, no excuses accepted.

Just three bridges span the Grand Canal. To fill in the gaps, *traghetti* **skiffs** (oversize gondolas rowed by two standing gondoliers, or *gondolieri*) cross the Grand Canal at eight intermediate points. You'll find a station at the end of any street named Calle del Traghetto on your map and indicated by a yellow sign with the black gondola symbol. The fare is .50€ (60¢), which you hand to the gondolier when boarding. Most Venetians cross standing up. For the experience, try the "S. Sofia" crossing that connects the Ca' d'Oro and the Pescheria fish market, opposite each other on the Grand Canal just north of the Rialto Bridge—the gondoliers expertly dodge water traffic at this point of the canal where it's the busiest and most heart-stopping.

BY WATER TAXI *Taxi acquei* **(water taxis)** charge high prices and aren't for visitors watching their euros. For (unlikely) journeys up to 7 minutes, the rate is 14€ ($16); .25€ (30¢) click off for each 15 seconds thereafter. Each bag over 50 centimeters long costs 1.15€ ($1.35), plus there's a 4.40€ ($5) supplement for

---

Tips Beware the *Acqua Alta*

During the notorious tidal *acqua alta* ("high water") floods, the lagoon backwashes into the city, leaving up to 1.5 or 2km (5 ft. or 6 ft.) of water in the lowest-lying streets. (Piazza San Marco, as the lowest point in the city, goes first.) They can start as early as late September or October, usually taking place November to March. The waters usually recede after just a few hours and are often virtually gone by noon. Walkways are set up around town, but wet feet are a given; a complex system of hydraulic dams being constructed out in the lagoon to cut off these high tides won't be in operation until the end of this decade.

Country & City Codes

The **country code** for Italy is **39**. Italian cities no longer have separate city codes. Venice's used to be 041, but that is now folded into the number itself (which means that for now, all Venetian phone numbers start with a 041, but this might change as Rome runs out of numbers and begins assigning new initial digits). Therefore, unlike in the past, you must dial the whole number—including the initial zero—at all times, whether you are calling from outside or inside Italy or even within Venice itself.

service 10pm to 7am and a 4.65€ ($5.35) surcharge on Sunday and holidays (these last two charges, however, can't be applied simultaneously). If they have to come get you, tack on another 4.15€ ($4.80). Those rates cover up to four people; if any more squeeze in, it's another 1.60€ ($1.85) per extra passenger.

Six water-taxi stations serve key points in the city: the **Ferrovia** (© **041-716-286**), **Piazzale Roma** (© **041-716-922**), the **Rialto Bridge** (© **041-523-0575** or 041-723-112), **Piazza San Marco** (© **041-522-9750**), the **Lido** (© **041-526-0059**), and **Marco Polo Airport** (© **041-541-5084**). **Radio Taxi** (© **041-522-2303** or 041-723-112) will come pick you up any place in the city.

FAST FACTS: Venice

American Express American Express is at San Marco 1471, 30124 Venezia, on Salizzada San Moisè just west of Piazza San Marco (© **041-520-0844**). In summer, the office is open for banking Monday to Saturday 8am to 8pm (for all other services, 9am–5:30pm); in winter, hours are Monday to Friday 9am to 5:30pm, Saturday 9am to 12:30pm (for banking and other services).

Business Hours Standard hours for **shops** are Monday to Saturday 9am to 12:30pm and 3 to 7:30pm. In winter, shops are closed Monday morning, while in summer it's usually Saturday afternoon they're closed. Most **grocers** are closed Wednesday afternoon throughout the year. **Banks** are normally open Monday to Friday 8:30am to 1:30pm and 2:35 to 3:35pm or 3 to 4pm. In Venice and throughout Italy, just about everything is closed **Sunday,** but tourist shops in the San Marco area are permitted to stay open in high season. **Restaurants** are required to close at least 1 day per week *(il giorno di riposo),* but the particular day varies from one trattoria to another. Many are open for Sunday lunch but close for Sunday dinner. Additionally, restaurants that specialize in fish and seafood also typically close Monday, when the fish market is closed. Restaurants close 1 to 2 weeks for holidays *(chiuso per ferie)* sometime in July or August, frequently over Christmas, and sometime in January or February before the Carnevale rush.

Consulates The nearest **U.S. consulate** is in Milan, at Largo Donegani 1 (© **02-290-351**), open Monday to Friday 9am to noon for visas only; from Monday to Friday it's also open for telephone service info 2 to 4pm. The **U.K. consulate** in Venice is at Dorsoduro 1051 (© **041-522-7207**), at the foot of the Accademia Bridge just west of the museum in the Palazzo Querini; it's open Monday to Friday 9am to noon and 2 to 4pm. Like the

United States, **Canada** and **Australia** have consulates in Milan, about 3 hours away by train. Along with **New Zealand,** they all maintain embassies in Rome (see "Fast Facts: Rome," in chapter 21).

Crime Be aware of petty crime like pickpocketing on the crowded *vaporetti,* particularly the tourist routes where passengers are more intent on the passing scenery than on watching their bags. Venice's deserted back streets were once virtually crime-proof; occasional tales of theft are circulating only recently. Generally speaking, Venice is one of Italy's safest cities.

Currency In 2002, Italy adopted the **euro** (€) for its currency. At press time, 1€ = $1.15, or 1$ = .87€.

Dentists & Doctors For a short list, check with the U.S. or U.K. consulate, the American Express office (see above), or your hotel.

Emergencies In Venice and throughout Italy, dial © **113** to reach the **police.** Some Italians recommend that you forgo the police and try the military-trained *carabinieri* (© **112**). For an **ambulance,** phone © **523-0000.** To report a **fire,** dial © **115,** 041-520-0222, or 041-520-0223. For any **tourism-related complaint** (rip-offs, exceedingly shoddy service, etc.), dial the special agency **Venezia No Problem** toll-free (in Italy) at © **800/355-920.**

Holidays See "Fast Facts: Rome," in chapter 21. Venice's patron saint, St. Mark, is honored on April 25.

Internet Access To check e-mail, go to **Venetian Navigator,** Castello 5269 on Calle delle Bande between San Marco and Campo Santa Maria Formosa (© **041-522-6084;** www.venetiannavigator.com; *vaporetto:* San Marco, Zaccaria, Rialto), open daily 10am to 10pm (Nov–Apr 10am–1pm and 2:30–8:30pm) and charging 6€ ($7) per hour. The **Internet Cafe,** San Marco 2976–2958 on Campo San Stefano (© **041-520-8128;** www.nethousecafes.com; *vaporetto:* S. Samuele, Giglio), is open 24 hours and charges a steep 9€ ($10) per hour. **Thenetgate,** San Polo 2925 near Campo San Rocco (© **041-522-9969;** www.thenetgate.it), is open Monday to Saturday 11am to 8pm and Sunday 2 to 8pm. Thenetgate has locations in 29 Italian cities, including Rome and Florence, and they sell a multisession card you can use at any location. All outlets charge about 5.15€ ($4.60) per hour.

Laundry The self-service laundry most convenient to the train station is the **Lavaget** (© **041-715-976**), Cannaregio 1269, to the left as you cross Ponte alle Guglie from Lista di Spagna; the rate is about 9€ ($10) for up to 4.5 kilograms (10 lb.). The laundry place most convenient to San Marco is **Gabriella** (© **041-522-1758**), San Marco 985, on Rio Terrà Colonne (off Calle dei Fabbri), where they wash and dry a load of laundry for you within an hour or 2 for 14€ ($16). They are open Monday to Friday 10am to 12:30pm and 2:30 to 7pm.

Luggage The *deposito bagagli* in the train station (© **041-785-531**) is open daily 6am to midnight. You can store your luggage for 3€ ($3.45) per bag for the first 12 hours, and 2€ ($2.30) per bag for each additional 12-hour period.

Mail Venice's **Posta Centrale** is at San Marco 5554, 30124 Venezia, on the San Marco side of the Rialto Bridge at Rialto Fontego dei Tedeschi (© **041-271-7111** or 041-528-5813; *vaporetto:* Rialto). This office sells stamps at Window 12 Monday to Saturday 8:30am to 6:30pm (for parcels 8:10am–1:30pm). If you're at Piazza San Marco and need postal services, walk through Sottoportego San Geminian, the center portal at the opposite end of the piazza from the basilica on Calle Larga dell'Ascensione. Its usual hours are Monday to Friday 8:30am to 2pm and Saturday 8:30am to 1pm. You can buy *francobolli* (stamps) at any *tabacchi* (tobacconists). The limited mailboxes seen around town are red.

Pharmacies Venice's many drugstores take turns staying open all night. To find out which one is on call in your area, ask at your hotel, check the rotational duty signs posted outside all drugstores, or dial ℂ **041-523-0573**.

Police In an emergency, dial ℂ **112** or 113.

Tax, Telephone & Tipping See "Fast Facts: Rome," in chapter 21.

2 Affordable Places to Stay

Few cities boast as long a high season as Venice, beginning with the Easter period. May, June, and September are the best weatherwise and so the most crowded. July and August are hot—at times unbearably so. (Few of the one- and two-star hotels offer air-conditioning; when they do, it usually costs extra.) Like everything else, hotels are more expensive here than in any other Italian city, with no apparent upgrade in amenities. The least special of those below are clean and functional; at best they're charming and thoroughly enjoyable with the serenade of a passing gondolier thrown in. Some might even provide you with your best stay in Europe.

I strongly suggest you reserve in advance, even off season. If you haven't booked, arrive as early as you can, definitely before noon. The **Hotel Reservations booth** in the train station will book rooms for you, but the lines are long and (understandably) the staff's patience is often thin. For 1€ ($1.15), they'll try to find you a hotel in the price range of your choice; on confirmation from the hotel, they'll accept the deposit from you by credit card and issue you a voucher, and you pay the balance on your arrival at the hotel. There is a similar hotel reservations booth at the airport, but it charges a bit more.

An alternative for reserving the same day as your arrival is the **A.V.A. (Venetian Hoteliers Association),** toll-free from within Italy at ℂ **800/843-006,** or 041-522-2264 (www.veniceinfo.it). Simply state the price range for the room you want to book and they'll confirm a hotel while you wait. There's no fee for the service, and there are offices at the train station, in Piazzale Roma garages, and at the airport. If you're looking to book on the Lido, contact their sister organization, **A.V.A.L.,** toll-free from within Italy ℂ **800/546-788** (www.venicehotels.com), or 041-595-2466 from abroad.

State-imposed ordinances have issued stringent deadlines for the updating of antiquated electrical, plumbing, and sewage systems—costly endeavors. To make up for this, small one- and two-star hotels then raise their rates, often applying for an upgrade in category for which they're now potentially eligible. Even more stuck TVs on the desks and hair dryers in the bathrooms to garner that extra star so they could inflate their rates during the Papal Jubilee in 2000. The good news is that now you'll have accommodations of a better quality; the bad news is that yesteryear's finds are slowly disappearing. The rates below were compiled in 2004. You can expect the usual increase of 4% to 8%, but you

> **Tips   A Note About Rates**
>
> Most hotels usually observe **high- and low-season rates**, but they're gradually adopting a single year-round rate. Even where It's not indicated in the listIngs, be sure to ask when you book or when you arrive at a hotel whether off-season prices are in effect. High season in Venice generally includes the week of Carnevale and the period from mid-March to November 5, with a lull during July and August (when discounts are often offered). Some small hotels close (sometimes without notice) November or December until Carnevale, opening for about 2 weeks around Christmas and New Year's at high-season rates.

might be hit with an increase of as much as 20% if the hotel you pick has been redone recently.

There are a few things most Venice hotels don't offer that you might take for granted: elevators, light, spaciousness, and large bathrooms. Also, canal views aren't half as frequent as our dreams would like them to be. This doesn't mean that a welcoming family-run hotel in an atmospheric neighborhood can't offer a memorable stay. Just don't expect extravagant amenities or Grand Canal vistas (though the latter can be had at the Hotel Galleria, p. 964).

Note: You'll find the lodging choices below plotted on the map on p. 978.

NEAR PIAZZA SAN MARCO

Albergo Ai Do Mori *★★ (Kids (Value* Antonella, the young hands-on owner/manager, creates an efficient yet comfortable ambience, with special care given to Frommer's readers. The more accessible lower-floor rooms (there's no elevator and the hotel begins on the 2nd floor) are slightly larger and offer rooftop views, but the top-floor rooms boast views of San Marco's cupolas and the Torre dell'Orologio, whose two bronze Moors ring the bells every hour. (The large double-paned windows help to ensure quiet.) All guest rooms have firm mattresses and air-conditioning; all but two rooms have a private bathroom. A 2001 renovation revealed the rest of the wood beams on the ceilings; in 2003, the walls were painted in bright colors and comfy new furnishings were added. Room nos. 4 (a small double) and 5 (a triple) share a bathroom and a small hall-way and can be turned into a family suite. Additionally, Antonella has now opened a four-room annex nearby.

San Marco 658 (on Calle Larga San Marco), 30124 Venezia. (☎ **041-520-4817** or 041-528-9293. Fax 041-520-5328. www.hotelaidomori.com. 15 units. 50€–80€ ($58–$92) single; 70€–135€ ($81–$155) double; 180€–220€ ($207–$253) family suite (up to 5 people). Ask about lower off-season rates. MC, V. *Vaporetto:* San Marco (exit Piazza San Marco beneath Torre dell'Orologio; turn right at Max Mara store and hotel is on left, just before McDonald's). **Amenities:** Bar; concierge; nonsmoking rooms. *In room:* A/C, TV, hair dryer, safe.

Albergo al Gambero *★★* Midway on a main strip connecting Piazza San Marco and the Rialto Bridge, one of Venice's former budget hotels underwent a full makeover in 1998. Surrounded by striped damasklike bedspreads and cur-tains, you can slumber in 1 of the 14 canalside rooms (five with bathrooms, including no. 203 with a small balcony). Rooms on the first two floors have higher ceilings, though upstairs rooms are the most freshly renovated (in 2002, when bathrooms were added to all). The entire hotel is nonsmoking. By Venice standards, the budget-level Gambero has all the trappings of a midscale hotel at moderate prices. Guests receive a 10% discount in the lively ground-floor

Value   Getting the Best Deal on Accommodations

- When booking your hotel, confirm whether breakfast is obligatory and, if not, what it costs; you'd spend half as much skipping the hotel charge and noshing at the neighborhood bar instead.
- If you haven't reserved, try to arrive in the city before noon, when it's more likely you'll find a budget room.
- If you're eligible, get a Rolling Venice pass for discounted rates (see "Venice Deals & Discounts," earlier in this chapter); in summer, the Rolling Venice booth at the train station will also help you with reservations for free.
- If Venice's cheap rooms have been snatched up, think about spending the night in Padua if you're on a really tight budget, but incorporate the cost of a round-trip train ticket into your projected savings if you don't have a pass for unlimited train travel. Travel between the cities is about 20 to 40 minutes, and trains run early morning to late at night.
- Remember that July and August, considered peak season elsewhere in parts of Italy, are low season here, but many budget and moderate-price hotels don't offer air-conditioning.
- When arranging for a room in person, always ask if the price quoted is the best available; in slow periods, even during high season, hotels will often entice you with discounted rates rather than have empty rooms, especially if you're standing in front of them.
- If the hotels I've listed are booked, check your luggage at the train station and wander the byways around the station, Lista di Spagna, and the Piazzale Roma area, the realm of budget and moderate-price hotels. Budget hotels closer to St. Mark's are fewer and far between.

Bistrot de Venise (p. 970). The owners acquired an apartment in the adjacent building and intend to knock out the connecting wall and turn this into five more rooms, probably in mid-2005.

San Marco 4687 (on Calle dei Fabbri), 30124 Venezia. © 041-522-4384 or 041-520-1420. Fax 041-520-0431. www.locandaalgambero.com. 27 units, 15 with bathroom. 50€–130€ ($58–$150) single; 70€–190€ ($81–$219) double without view; 90€–190€ ($104–$219) double with view; 110€–240€ ($127–$276) triple with bathroom; 120€–300€ ($138–$345) quad with bathroom. Rates include continental breakfast. MC, V. Vaporetto: Rialto (turn right along canal, cross small footbridge over Rio San Salvador, turn left onto Calle Bembo, which becomes Calle dei Fabbri; hotel is about 5 blocks ahead on left). Amenities: Restaurant (Le Bistrot de Venise); bar (in restaurant); concierge; tour desk; whole hotel nonsmoking. In room: A/C, TV, dataport, minibar, hair dryer, safe.

Al Piave *Kids*   The Puppin family's tasteful hotel is a steal: This level of attention coupled with the sophisticated *buon gusto* in decor and spirit is rare at this price. You'll find orthopedic mattresses under ribbon candy–print or floral spreads, immaculate white lace curtains, stained-glass windows, new bathrooms, and even (in a few rooms) tiny terraces. The family suites—with two bedrooms, minibars, and shared bathrooms—are particularly good deals, as are the small but stylishly rustic apartments with kitchenettes (and washing machines in the two smaller units). A savvy international crowd has discovered this classy spot, so even with renovations that have expanded the hotel's size, you'll need to reserve far in advance.

Castello 4838-40 (on Ruga Giuffa), 30122 Venezia. ✆ 041-528-5174. Fax 041-523-8512. www.hotelalpiave. com. 10 units, 3 apts. Single rates by request (only 1 available); 115€–150€ double ($132–$173); 150€–200€ ($173–$230) triple; 160€–230€ ($184–$265) quad; 160€–230€ ($184–$265) family suite for 3, 200€–280€ ($230–$322) family suite for 4, 220€–300€ ($253–$345) family suite for 5. Rates include continental breakfast. AE, DC, MC, V. Closed Jan 7 to Carnevale. *Vaporetto:* San Zaccaria (walk straight ahead on Calle delle Rasse to small Campo SS. Filippo e Giacomo, take right on Calle San Provolo, and cross over canal to Campo San Provolo; take a left, cross 1st small footbridge, and follow zigzagging street that becomes Ruga Giuffa). **Amenities:** Concierge; tour desk; babysitting. *In room:* A/C, TV, minibar, fridge (family suite), hair dryer, safe.

Foresteria Valdese (Palazzo Cavagnis) ✮ *(Kids* ✓*Value*   Those lucky enough to score a room at this weathered, albeit elegant, 16th-century palazzo will find simple accommodations in a charming *foresteria,* the name given to religious institutions that traditionally provided lodging for pilgrims and guests. Affiliated with Italy's Waldesian and Methodist churches, the large dormitory-style rooms of the palazzo are often filled with visiting church groups, though everyone is warmly welcomed and you'll find an international and inter-religious mix here. Each of the plainly furnished rooms in this once-noble residence opens onto a balcony overlooking a quiet canal. The 18th-century frescoes that grace the high ceilings in some doubles (including corner no. 10) and two of the dorms are by the same artist who decorated the Correr Civic Museum— and these rooms will cost you a few euro extra. The two apartments, complete with kitchen facilities, are the best budget choice in town for traveling families of four or five. (Be aware that guests staying in private rooms or apartments are often required to stay 2 nights; those staying in dormitories can stay just 1.) A sweeping renovation begun in 1995 has *finally* been completed. The reception is open daily from 9am to 1pm and 6 to 8pm. The entire hotel is non-smoking.

Castello 5170 (at the end of Calle Lunga Santa Maria Formosa), 30122 Venezia. ✆ 041-528-6797. Fax 041-241-6238. www.diaconiavaldese.org/venezia. 6 units with bathroom and TV (2–4 beds) often requiring a 2-night stay; 3 dorms (with 8, 11, or 16 beds), none with bathroom; 2 mini-apts (sleeping 4–5; minimum stay often required) with kitchen and bathroom. 20€ ($23) dorm bed (21€/$24 if you stay just 1 night); 56€ ($64) double without bathroom; 74€ ($85) double with bathroom; 102€ ($117) quad with bathroom; 102€ ($117) apt for 4, 115€ ($132) apt for 5. Rates include buffet breakfast, except in apts. DC, MC, V (but pay 3.5% more to use credit cards). Closed 2 weeks in Nov. *Vaporetto:* Rialto. (Head southeast to the Campo Santa Maria Formosa; look for the Bar all'Orologio, just where Calle Lunga Santa Maria Formosa begins. The campo is just about equidistant from Piazza San Marco and the Rialto Bridge.) **Amenities:** Nonsmoking rooms. *In room:* TV (except in dorms), dataport, kitchenette (in apts), no phone.

Hotel Gallini   Though the 1997 fire at La Fenice opera house doused this neighborhood's spark, the Gallini is now back to business as usual. The amiable Ceciliati brothers, Adriano and Gabriele, have been at the helm since 1952 and offer four floors (no elevator) of bright, spacious rooms and big modern bathrooms. (All rooms should have bathrooms by the time you get here.) Ten rooms overlook narrow Rio della Verona, and a few have air-conditioning (for which there may be a small daily fee). Though there's nothing wrong with it in particular, the place is somehow rather charmless. However, it is the largest place I suggest in this area, and moderately priced, so there's a good chance it'll have rooms when the smaller options are full. The housekeeping staff seems to be forever

cleaning. Rich-looking marble floors in green, red, or speckled black alternate with intricate parquet to lend an old-world air.

San Marco 3673 (on Calle della Verona), 30124 Venezia. ☎ 041-520-4515. Fax 041-520-9103. www.hotel gallini.it. 40 units. 75€–103€ ($86–$118) single; 100€–154€ ($115–$177) double; 150€–209€ ($173–$240) triple; 120€–170€ ($138–$196) suite for 2 people, 160€–227€ ($184–$261) suite for 3 people. Rates include continental breakfast. Ask about special discount rates for Frommer's readers (percentage varies depending on how full they are). AE, DC, MC, V. Closed Nov 15–Carnevale. *Vaporetto:* Sant'Angelo (follow zigzagging road south toward Campo Sant'Angelo; exit *campo* at northeast end by taking Calle della Mandola; turn right at the Ottica [optometrist] onto Calle dei Assasini, which becomes Calle della Verona) or Rialto. **Amenities:** Concierge; room service (limited). *In room:* A/C (some rooms), TV (some rooms), minibar (some rooms), hair dryer.

Locanda Fiorita ⭐ *(Value* Everything in the pretty little hotel in a Venetian red palazzo, parts of which date from the 1400s, was renovated in 18th-century Venetian style by the current owners. The wisteria vine partially covering its facade is at its glorious best in May or June, but the Fiorita is excellent year-round, as much for its simply furnished rooms boasting new bathrooms (now with hair dryers) as for its location on a *campiello* off the grand Campo Santo Stefano. Room nos. 1 and 10 have little terraces beneath the wisteria pergola and overlook the *campiello:* They can't be guaranteed on reserving, so ask when you get there. Each of the two bathroomless rooms has private facilities down the hall. Just a few meters away at San Marco 3457A is **Ca' Morosini**, the Fiorita's three-star annex. There you'll find more rooms with views of the *campo* (same phone/fax as Fiorita; www.camorosini.com).

San Marco 3457a (on Campiello Novo), 30124 Venezia. ☎ 041-523-4754. Fax 041-522-8043. www.locanda fiorita.com. 10 units in main house, 8 with bathroom; 6 units in annex. Main house 60€–80€ ($69–$92) single without bathroom; 90€–110€ ($104–$127) double without bathroom, 100€–130€ ($115–$150) double with bathroom. Annex 80€–130€ ($92–$150) single; 80€–140€ ($92–$161) double without bathroom, 140€–180€ ($161–$207) double with bathroom. Extra person 30% more at either. Rates include continental breakfast. Ask about special rates for stays of 3 nights or more during low season. AE, MC, V. *Vaporetto:* S. Angelo (walk to the tall brick building, then turn right around its side; cross a small bridge and turn left down Calle del Pestrin; a bit farther down on your left is a small square 3 stairs above street level; hotel is against the back of it). **Amenities:** Concierge; tour desk; room service; babysitting; nonsmoking rooms. *In room:* A/C, TV, dataport (annex only), minibar (annex only), hair dryer, safe (annex only).

NEAR THE ACCADEMIA (DORSODURO)

Hotel Galleria ⭐⭐ If you've always dreamed of flinging open your hotel window to find the Grand Canal in front of you, choose this 17th-century palazzo. But reserve way in advance—these are the cheapest rooms on the canal and the most charming at these rates, thanks to new owners Luciano Benedetti and Stefano Franceschini. All are done in a modestly sumptuous 17th- and 18th-century style, a rich look that didn't change during a recent, massive overhaul that replaced *everything*—from the floors and bathrooms to the wallpaper and windows—but the old-fashioned air. Although this shouldn't affect prices for 2004, don't be surprised if there are some slight increases in 2005. Still, it's a fantastic deal: Six rooms overlook the canal, while others have partial views that include the Ponte Accademia over an open-air bar/cafe (which can be annoying to anyone hoping to sleep before the bar closes). The bathrooms are small but nicely renovated. Breakfast, with oven-fresh bread, is served in your room.

Dorsoduro 878A (at foot of Accademia Bridge), 30123 Venezia. ☎ 041-523-2489. Fax 041-520-4172. www.hotelgalleria.it. 10 units, 6 with bathroom. 70€ ($81) single without bathroom; 95€–100€ ($109–$115) double without bathroom, 110€–145€ ($127–$167) double with bathroom. Extra bed 30% more. Rates include continental breakfast. AE, DC, MC, V. *Vaporetto:* Accademia (with Accademia Bridge behind you, hotel is just to your left, next to Totem Il Canale gallery). **Amenities:** Concierge; tour desk; room service; babysitting. *In room:* Hair dryer.

Hotel Messner ✦ The Messner and the Pensione alla Salute (below) are the best choices in the Guggenheim area (the choice of those in-the-know looking for a quiet alternative to St. Mark's), at budget-embracing rates. The Messner is a two part hotel: In the *Casa Principale* (Main House) are the handsome beamed-ceiling lobby and public rooms of a 14th-century palazzo and modernized guest rooms with comfortable modular furnishings and Murano chandeliers. (Three overlook the picturesque Rio della Fornace.) The 15th-century *dipendenza* (annex) 18m (60 ft.) away doesn't demonstrate quite as close attention to detail in the decor but is perfectly nice. In summer, you get to take breakfast in a small garden. In 2002, they opened a new annex 27m (90 ft.) away with just six large rooms done in an antique Venetian style.

Dorsoduro 216–217 (on Fondamenta Ca' Balà), 30123 Venezia. ☎ 041-522-7443. Fax 041-522-7266. www.hotelmessner.it. Main House 13 units, annex 20 units. Main House (ask about Frommer's discount in Main House only) 100€–110€ ($115–$127) single; 145€–160€ ($167–$184) double; 165€–180€ ($190–$207) triple; 190€–200€ ($219–$230) quad. Annex 90€ ($104) single; 115€ ($132) double; 145€ ($167) triple; 160€ ($184) quad. Rates include continental breakfast. Ask about discounts such as Aug special: 4 nights for the price of 3. AE, DC, MC, V. Closed Dec 1–27. *Vaporetto:* Salute (follow small canal immediately to right of La Salute; turn right onto 3rd bridge and walk straight until you see white awning just before reaching Rio della Fornace). **Amenities:** Restaurant; bar; concierge; 24-hr. room service; babysitting; nonsmoking rooms. *In room:* A/C (Main House), TV (Main House), dataport (Main House), hair dryer, safe.

Pensione alla Salute (Da Cici) ✦ *Kids* An airy lobby with beamed ceilings and cool marble floors, a small but lovely terrace garden, and a cozy cocktail bar occupy the ground level of this converted 17th-century palazzo on Rio della Fornace. Upstairs, the comfortable guest rooms have high ceilings and huge windows (10 with canal views and 4 facing the garden), many of them large enough to accommodate families of four or even five at an additional charge (ask when booking). Breakfast is served in the garden in warm weather, and the entire hotel is now nonsmoking.

Dorsoduro 222 (on Fondamenta Ca' Balà), 30123 Venezia. ☎ 041-523-5404. Fax 041-522-2271. www.hotel salute.com. 58 units, 12 with shower only, some with bathroom. 80€ ($92) single without bathroom, 115€ ($132) single with bathroom; 100€ ($115) double without bathroom, 140€ ($161) double with bathroom; 140€ ($161) triple without bathroom, 180€ ($207) triple with bathroom. Ask about rooms sleeping 4–5 persons. Rates include continental breakfast. Discounts given Mar, July, and Aug. No credit cards. Often closes in Jan or Feb for upkeep; call ahead. *Vaporetto:* Salute (facing La Salute, turn right and head to 1st small bridge; cross it and walk as straight ahead as possible to next narrow canal, then turn left, before crossing bridge, onto Fondamenta Ca' Balà). **Amenities:** Bar; nonsmoking rooms (whole hotel). *In room:* Hair dryer.

NEAR THE RIALTO BRIDGE

Albergo Guerrato ✦✦ *Value* The Guerrato is as reliable and clean a budget hotel as you're likely to find at these rates. Brothers-in-law Roberto and Piero own this former *pensione* in a 13th-century convent and manage to keep it almost always booked (mostly with Americans). The firm mattresses, good modernish bathrooms, and flea-market finds (hand-carved antique or Art Deco headboards and armoires) show their determination to run a budget hotel in pricey Venice. They don't exaggerate when calling their breakfast, accompanied by classical music, *buonissimo*. The Guerrato is in the Rialto's heart, so think of the 7am noise before you request a room overlooking the marketplace (with a peek down the block to the Grand Canal and Ca d'Oro). In late 2002, Piero and Roberto acquired the building's top floor (great views, no elevator, 70 steps) and installed five nice new double rooms, three with great views. In early 2004, they renovated the entire hotel, adding A/C to all rooms, putting in new floors, and redoing the oldest bathrooms.

Roberto also rents (2-night minimum) two lovely, fully equipped apartments, **Piccolo Guerrato,** between San Marco and the Rialto. The one-bedroom is 120€–130€ ($138–$150) for two or 180€–200€ ($207–$230) for four (though it would be cramped), while the much larger two-bedroom (on three levels) goes for 180€–200€ ($207–$230) for four.

San Polo 240A (on Calle Drio or Dietro la Scimia, near the Rialto Market), 30125 Venezia. ©/fax 041-528-5927. www.pensioneguerrato.it. 20 units, 14 with bathroom. No singles. 95€ ($109) double without bathroom, 125€ ($144) double with bathroom; 120€ ($138) triple without bathroom, 145€ ($167) triple with bathroom; 175€ ($201) quad with bathroom; 185€ ($213) quint with bathroom. Rates include buffet breakfast. Pay in cash, get 5€ ($5.75) per night per room discount. MC, V. Closed Dec 22–26 and Jan 10–31. *Vaporetto:* Rialto (from the north side of the Ponte Rialto, walk straight ahead through the stalls and market vendors; at the corner of Banca di Roma, go 1 more short block and turn right; the hotel is halfway down the narrow street). **Amenities:** Concierge; tour desk; babysitting; nonsmoking rooms. *In room:* A/C, hair dryer.

Hotel Bernardi-Semenzato ☆☆ *(Kids) (Value)* The exterior of this weatherworn palazzo hidden on a side street just off wide Strada Nuova belies its fabulous 1995 renovation. The overhaul exposed hand-hewn ceiling beams, added air-conditioning and antique-styled headboard/spread sets, and modernized and brightly retiled bathrooms. The enthusiastic English-speaking owners, Maria Teresa and Leonardo Pepoli, offer three-star style and amenities, but they're content to offer one-star rates. (Prices get even better off season.) Upstairs rooms enjoy higher ceilings and more light. The *dipendenza* (annex) 3 blocks away offers you the chance to feel as if you've rented an aristocratic apartment, with parquet floors and Murano chandeliers—room no. 5 is in a corner with a beamed ceiling and fireplace, no. 6 (a family-perfect two-room suite) overlooks the confluence of two canals, and no. 2 overlooks the lovely garden of a palazzo next door.

In 2003, the hoteliers opened yet another annex nearby consisting of just four rooms, all done in a Venetian style, including one large family suite (two guest rooms, one of which can sleep four, sharing a common bathroom).

Cannaregio 4363–4366 (on Calle de l'Oca), 30121 Venezia. © 041-522-7257. Fax 041-522-2424. www.hotelbernardi.com. Hotel 18 units, 11 with bathroom; main annex 7 units; new annex 4 units. *For Frommer's readers:* 28€ ($32) single without bathroom, 80€ ($92) single with bathroom; 50€ ($58) double without bathroom, 80€ ($92) double with bathroom; 72€ ($83) triple without bathroom, 88€ ($101) triple with bathroom; 80€ ($92) quad without bathroom, 98€ ($113) quad with bathroom. Rates include continental breakfast. 10% less off season. AE, DC, MC, V. *Vaporetto:* Ca' d'Oro (walk straight ahead to Strada Nova, turn right toward Campo SS. Apostoli, and look for Cannaregio 4309, a stationery/toy store on your left; turn left on Calle Duca, then take 1st right onto Calle de l'Oca). **Amenities:** Concierge; tour desk; room service. *In room:* A/C, TV, dataport, hair dryer, safe.

NEAR THE TRAIN STATION

Adua It ain't too pretty, but it's fairly cheap (in Venice terms, which tells you something right there), conveniently located near the station, clean, and run very well. The Adua family, in the low-end hotel business for more than 30 years, completed a welcome renovation in 1999, giving the largish rooms a unified summery look with contemporary wood furnishings painted pale green. An independent palazzo across the street with six refurbished rooms (without bathroom, TV, or A/C) costs about 20% less.

Cannaregio 233A (on Lista di Spagna), 30121 Venezia. © 041-716-184. Fax 041-244-0162. 13 units, 9 with bathroom. 70€ ($81) single without bathroom, 100€ ($115) single with bathroom; 80€ ($92) double without bathroom, 120€ ($138) double with bathroom; 100€ ($115) triple without bathroom, 180€ ($207) triple with bathroom. Breakfast 6€ ($7). Low-season rates 10%–15% less. MC, V. *Vaporetto:* Ferrovia (exit train station and turn left onto Lista di Spagna). **Amenities:** Concierge; tour desk; room service. *In room:* A/C, TV, dataport, fridge, hair dryer.

Albergo Santa Lucia The flagstone patio/terrace of this contemporary building is bordered by roses, oleander, and ivy—a lovely place to enjoy breakfast, with coffee and tea brought in sterling silver pots. The kindly owner, Emilia Gonzato; her son, Gianangelo; and his wife, Alessandra, oversee everything with pride and it shows: The large rooms are simple but bright and clean, with modular furnishings and a print or pastel to brighten things up.

Cannaregio 358 (on Calle della Misericordia), 30121 Venezia. ✆ 041-715-180. Fax 041-710-610. www. hotelslucia.com. 15 units, 10 with bathroom. 40€ 60€ ($46–$69) single without bathroom, 60€ 80€ ($69–$92) single with bathroom; 50€–85€ ($58–$98) double without bathroom, 70€–110€ ($81–$127) double with bathroom; 100€–140€ ($115–$161) triple with bathroom; 130€–170€ ($150–$196) quad with bathroom. Rates include continental breakfast. AE, MC, V. Generally closed Dec 20–Feb 10. *Vaporetto:* Ferrovia (exit the train station, turn left onto Lista di Spagna, and take the 2nd left onto Calle della Misericordia). **Amenities:** Concierge; tour desk; room service (breakfast). *In room:* Hair dryer (ask at desk).

Hotel Dolomiti For those who prefer to stay near the train station, this is an old-fashioned reliable choice. Because it has so many large, clean, if ordinary rooms spread over four floors (no elevator), your chances of finding a room here are better than at most Venice hotels, which tend to be tiny and fill up fast. It's been in the Basaldella family for generations—the current head manager, Graziella, was even born in a room on the second floor—and they and their efficient polyglot staff supply dining suggestions, umbrellas when necessary, and a big smile after a long day's sightseeing. Rooms without bathrooms always come with sinks.

Cannaregio 73–74 (on Calle Priuli ai Cavalletti), 30121 Venezia. ✆ 041-715-113 or 041-719-983. Fax 041-716-635. www.hoteldolomiti-ve.it. 32 units, 22 with bathroom. 50€–70€ ($58–$81) single without bathroom, 70€–95€ ($81–$109) single with bathroom; 88€ ($101) double without bathroom, 125€ ($144) double with bathroom; 108€ ($124) triple without bathroom, 165€ ($190) triple with bathroom; 130€ ($150) quad without bathroom, 185€ ($213) quad with bathroom. Rates include continental breakfast. Inquire about low-season discounts. MC, V. Closed Nov 15–Jan 31. *Vaporetto:* Ferrovia (exit train station, turn left onto Lista di Spagna, and take 1st left onto Calle Priuli). **Amenities:** Bar; concierge; tour desk. *In room:* A/C (newest rooms), hair dryer (newest rooms).

Hotel San Geremia ★★ *Finds* Mention Frommer's when booking and show this guide when checking in, and you'll get the rates below. If this gem of a two-star hotel had an elevator and was in San Marco, it'd cost twice as much and still be worth it. The tastefully renovated rooms are freshened up almost every year; consider yourself lucky to snag one of the seven overlooking the campo (or, better yet, one of three top-floor rooms with small terraces). The rooms have blond-wood paneling with built-in headboards and closets or whitewashed walls with deep-green or burnished rattan headboards and matching chairs. The small bathrooms offer hair dryers and heated towel racks. Everything is overseen by an English-speaking staff and the owner/manager Claudio, who'll give you helpful tips and free passes to the winter casino.

Cannaregio 290A (on Campo San Geremia), 30121 Venezia. ✆ **041-716-245.** Fax 041-524-2342. www. sangeremia.com (under construction). 20 units. *For Frommer's readers (if you show this book):* 75€–95€ ($86–$109) single; 95€–115€ ($109–$132) double. Rates include continental breakfast. AE, DC, MC, V. *Vaporetto:* Ferrovia (exit the train station, turn left onto Lista di Spagna, and continue to Campo San Geremia). **Amenities:** Concierge; tour desk; room service (breakfast); babysitting. *In room:* TV, hair dryer, safe.

WORTH A SPLURGE

Hotel Campiello ★★ This gem is on a tiny *campiello* just off prestigious Riva degli Schiavoni. The atmosphere is airy and bright, its relaxed hospitality and quality service due to the Bianchini sisters, Monica and Nicoletta. A 1998 renovation transformed much of the rooms' contemporary style into a more traditional decor—most are now done in authentic 18th-century and Art Nouveau antiques—with inlaid *armadios* (armoirelike cabinets) and bas-reliefs on the headboards. The building's original 15th-century marble-mosaic pavement is still evident, a vestige of the days when it was a convent under the patronage of the nearby San Zaccaria; you'll catch a glimpse of it in the lounge area opening onto a pleasant breakfast room. The owners installed an elevator and renovated half the rooms in 2003, and were busily overhauling the other half as we went to press. All of this work has helped them rise one notch up in the local ratings system from a two-star (budget) property to three stars (moderate).

Castello 4647 (on Campiello del Vin), 30122 Venezia. ℭ 041-520-5764. Fax 041-520-5798. www .hcampiello.it. 16 units. 70€–130€ ($81–$150) single; 100€–190€ ($115–$219) double; 120€–220€ ($138–$253) triple; 140€–260€ ($161–$299) quad. Rates include continental breakfast. Ask about discounts in low season. AE, DC, MC, V. *Vaporetto:* S. Zaccaria. **Amenities:** Bar; concierge; 24-hr. room service; babysitting; nonsmoking rooms. *In room:* A/C, TV, dataport, hair dryer, safe.

Hotel Fontana ⭐

Three generations of Stainers have been behind the front desk since 1968 (for centuries prior to that the Fontana was a convent for Austrian nuns), and their warmth seems to pour out the lobby's leaded-glass windows. The four-story hotel offers a *pensione*-like family atmosphere coupled with a crisp, professional operation and rooms with lovely antique furnishings but a decided lack of wattage in the overhead lights. The choice two rooms on the upper floor have private terraces. There's no elevator, but those who brave the climb to the top floors are compensated with views of San Zaccaria's 15th-century facade.

Castello 4701 (on Campo San Provolo), 30122 Venezia. ℭ 041-522-0579. Fax 041-523-1040. www.hotel fontana.it. 16 units. 110€ ($127) single; 170€ ($196) double; 210€ ($242) triple; 240€ ($276) quad. Rates include buffet breakfast. Rates lower in low season, up to 50% off in deepest winter. AE, DC, MC, V. *Vaporetto:* San Zaccaria (from Riva Schiavoni, take any narrow street north to Campiello SS. Filippo e Giacomo; exit this small campo from east side, in direction of Campo San Zaccaria, until reaching Campo San Provolo). **Amenities:** Concierge; tour desk; room service. *In room:* TV, dataport, hair dryer (on request).

Locanda Casa Verardo ⭐

In 2000, Daniela and Francesco took over this one-star *pensione* and transformed it into a fine three-star hotel (and more than doubled its size), while maintaining the feel of a Venetian palazzo romantically faded by time. The wood-paneled lobby is anchored by an ancient stone well. The rooms are done in chipped-stone floors, Murano chandeliers, and eclectic furnishings from imposing armoires and repro 17th century to pseudo Deco and modern functional; three have small terraces. The best accommodations come with stucco wall decorations and scraps of old ceiling frescoes—and tops are the six overlooking a little canal. The airy main hall doubles as a breakfast room. Another renovation in late 2001 installed "deluxe" rooms with A/C, minibars, and cushier furnishings, plus two rooms for travelers with disabilities.

Castello 4765 (at foot of Ponte Storto), 30122 Venezia. ℭ 041-528-6138 or 041-528-6127. Fax 041-523-2765. www.casaverardo.it. 26 units. 60€–120€ ($69–$138) deluxe single; 90€–186€ ($104–$214) classic double, 110€–220 ($127–$253) deluxe double; 130€–275€ ($150–$316) junior suite. 20€–40€ ($23–$46) additional bed. Rates include buffet breakfast. Prices much lower in off season; ask when you book. AE, MC, V. *Vaporetto:* San Zaccaria (walk straight ahead on Calle delle Rasse to Campo SS. Filippo e Giacomo; continue straight through the small *campo* to Calle Chiesa and cross the 1st small bridge, Ponte Storto; hotel is on the left). **Amenities:** Bar; concierge; tour desk; room service (breakfast, drinks); babysitting; nonsmoking rooms. *In room:* A/C, TV, minibar, hair dryer (ask at desk), safe (2 rooms).

Pensione La Calcina ⭐

British author John Ruskin holed up here in 1876 when penning *The Stones of Venice* (you can request his room, no. 2, but good luck getting it), and this hotel on the sunny Zattere in the southern Dorsoduro has remained a quasi-sacred preference of writers, artists, and assorted Bohemians. You can imagine their horror when a recent overhaul was announced—but it was executed so sensitively the third-generation owners refused to add TVs. However, the rates *are* creeping up. Half the unfussy but luminous rooms overlook the Giudecca Canal in the direction of Palladio's 16th-century Redentore. The outdoor floating terrace and the rooftop terrace are glorious places to begin or end any day. The three suites and two apartments were added in 2002.

Dorsoduro 780 (on Zattere al Gesuati), 30123 Venezia. (✆) 041-520-6466. Fax 041-522-7045. www. lacalcina.com. 28 units. 55€–75€ ($63–$86) single without bathroom, 75€–96€ ($86–$110) single with bathroom, 86€–106€ ($99–$122) single with bathroom and canal view; 99€–145€ ($114–$167) double with bathroom, 130€–182€ ($150–$209) double with bathroom and canal view; 187€–239€ ($215–$275) suite or apt. Rates include buffet breakfast. AE, DC, MC, V. *Vaporetto:* Zattere (follow le Zattere east; hotel is on water before 1st bridge). **Amenities:** Restaurant; concierge; 24-hr. room service; laundry service. *In room:* A/C, hair dryer, safe.

3 Great Deals on Dining

You'll see things on Venetian menus you won't see elsewhere, together with local versions of time-tested Italian favorites. Rice grown in the Veneto region makes **risotto** as pervasive as pasta. *Spaghetti alle vongole* or *spaghetti alle verace* (spaghetti served with clams—*vongole verace* are just the local type of clams—preferably ones still in their shells, as otherwise they may be from a can and not fresh) can be wonderful if you choose the restaurant with care; the same holds for *seppie nere con polenta* (stewed cuttlefish in its own black ink over polenta, a thick traditional staple made from corn flour). *Bigoli in salsa* (homemade spaghetti-like pasta in a distinctive but not overpowering anchovy-and-onion sauce) is harder to find but also a regional specialty.

Fresh, delicious *pesce alla griglia* (grilled fish) is readily available (*surgelato* means frozen fish—restaurants are legally obliged to note when the fish or seafood is frozen), but expect to pay handsomely: The price on the menu commonly refers to the *etto* (per 100g)—a fraction of the full cost (have the waiter estimate the cost before you order). Some fish and seafood that are done especially well include *branzino* (a kind of sea bass), *rombo* (turbot or brill), *moeche* (small soft-shelled crab), *granseola* or *granchio* (crab), and *sarde in saor* (sardines in a sauce of onion, vinegar, pine nuts, and raisins). Finally, there's the ubiquitous *frittura mista* (or *fritto misto*), a mix of fried seafood (squid, mussels, clams, and cuttlefish) whose success is in the freshness, quality, and variety of the fish and oil used. More earthly dishes are *risi e bisi* (rice with peas), *pasta e fagioli* (bean-and-pasta soup), and a delicious interpretation of *fegato alla veneziana* (calf's liver with onions), which is heaven when prepared well.

Note: With the exception of the "Budget Bests," where grazing and light dining won't elicit nasty looks, the listings below give prices for a *primo* (1st course) such as pasta, soup, or risotto; and for a *secondo* (main course) of fish or meat. Don't forget to consider nominal charges for *coperto* (bread and cover), *servizio* (tip), *contorno* (a salad or vegetable side dish), and *bevanda* (drink).

Tips A Dining Note

Venetians dine early compared to Romans and those in other points south: You should be seated by 7:30 to 8:30pm. Most kitchens close at 10 or 10:30pm, even though the restaurant might stay open until 11:30pm or midnight. Restaurants usually close for a week or 2 (or more) sometime in January or February before Carnevale and often for 2 to 3 weeks in August.

NEAR PIAZZA SAN MARCO

Da Aciugheta 🏆 *Value* VENETIAN/WINE BAR/PIZZERIA   A long block north of the chic Riva degli Schiavoni hotel lies one of Venice's best wine bars, with an excellent selection of Veneto and Italian wines by the glass, expanded to include an elbow-to-elbow trattoria/pizzeria in back. Its name refers to the toothpick-speared marinated anchovies that join other *cicchetti* lining the popular front bar. The staff is relaxed about those not ordering full multiple-course meals—a pasta and glass of wine or pizza and beer will keep anyone happy. Warm weather moves tables out onto the small piazza.

Castello 4357 (in Campo SS. Filippo e Giacomo east of Piazza San Marco). © 041-522-4292. *Primi* 6€–17€ ($7–$20); *secondi* 6€–17€ ($7–$20). AE, MC, V. Daily 8am–midnight (closed Wed Nov–Mar). *Vaporetto:* San Zaccaria (walk north on Calle delle Rasse to Campo SS. Filippo e Giacomo).

Le Bistrot de Venise 🏆🏆 VENETIAN/FRENCH   This relaxed, popular spot offers outdoor and indoor seating (even a nonsmoking section), young English-speaking waiters, and an eclectic menu. You're made to feel welcome to write postcards over a cappuccino, enjoy a simple lunch like risotto and salad, or dine when most of Venice is shutting down. Linger over an elaborate meal that might include local favorites like *figa' de vedelo a la venexiana* (Venetian calf's liver) and the odd *morete a la caorlotta* (tagliolini made with cocoa, topped by a festival of crustaceans), or dishes from 15th-century Venetian recipes or a classic French cookbook. Peek in the back room (or check the website) to see what's going on in the evening—art exhibits, cabarets, live music, or poetry readings.

San Marco 4687 (on Calle dei Fabbri), below the Albergo al Gambero. © 041-523-6651. www.bistrotdevenise. com. *Primi* 8€–15€ ($9–$17); *secondi* 14€–22€ ($16–$25); classic Venetian tasting menu 35€ ($40); historical Venetian menu 45€ ($52). AE, MC, V. Daily noon–1am. Closed Dec 10–25. *Vaporetto:* Rialto (turn right along canal, cross small footbridge over Rio San Salvador, turn left onto Calle Bembo, which becomes Calle dei Fabbri; Bistrot is about 5 blocks ahead in the direction of St. Mark's Sq.).

Trattoria alla Rivetta 🏆 SEAFOOD/VENETIAN   Lively and frequented by *gondolieri* (always a sign of quality dining for the right price), merchants, and visitors drawn to its bonhomie and bustling popularity, this is one of the safer bets for genuine Venetian cuisine and company in the touristy San Marco area, a 10-minute walk east of the piazza. All sorts of fish—the specialty—decorate the window of this brightly lit place. Another good indicator: There's usually a bit of a wait, even off season.

Castello 4625 (on Salizzada San Provolo). © 041-528-7302. *Primi* 6€–10€ ($7–$12); *secondi* 10€–15€ ($12–$17). AE, MC, V. Tues–Sun noon–2:30pm and 7–10pm. *Vaporetto:* San Zaccaria (with your back to water and facing Hotel Savoia e Jolanda, walk straight ahead to Campo SS. Filippo e Giacomo; trattoria is tucked away next to a bridge off the right side of *campo*).

NEAR THE RIALTO BRIDGE (SAN MARCO SIDE)

Ai Tre Spiedi 🏆🏆 VENETIAN   Venetians bring their visiting friends here to make a *bella figura* (good impression) without breaking the bank, then swear them to secrecy. Rarely will you find as pleasant a setting and appetizing a meal as in this casually elegant small trattoria with some of the most reasonably priced fresh fish dining. Their *spaghetti O.P.A.* (with parsley, pepperoncini, garlic, and olive oil) is excellent, and their *spaghetti al pesto* the best this side of Liguria. Follow it up with the traditional *bisato in umido con polenta* (braised eel). This and Trattoria da Fiore (see below) are the most reasonable choices for an authentic Venetian dinner of fresh fish; careful ordering needn't mean much of a splurge either—though inexplicably, prices have risen dramatically in the past 2 years.

Cannaregio 5906 (on Salizzada San Cazian). ℂ 041-520-8035. Reservations not accepted. *Primi* 4.50€–12€ ($5–$13); *secondi* 9.50€–18€ ($11–$20); *menù turistico* 15€–20€ ($17–$22). AE, MC, V. Tues–Sat noon–3pm; Tues–Sun 7–10pm. Closed July 20–Aug 10. *Vaporetto:* Rialto (on San Marco side of bridge, walk straight ahead to Campo San Bartolomeo and take a left, passing post office, Coin department store, and San Crisostomo; cross 1st bridge after church, turn right at toy store onto Salizzada San Cazian).

Rosticceria San Bartolomeo *(Value)* ITALIAN/TAVOLA CALDA With long hours and a central location, this refurbished old-timer is Venice's most popular *rosticceria* (and for good reason), so the continuous turnover guarantees fresh food. With a dozen pasta dishes and as many fish, seafood, or meat entrees, San Bartolomeo can satisfy any combination of culinary desires. Because the ready-made food is displayed under a glass counter, you don't have to worry about mistranslating—you'll know exactly what you're ordering. There's no *coperto* (cover charge) if you take your meal standing up or seated at the stools in the aroma-filled ground-floor area. For those who prefer to linger, head to the dining hall upstairs —but it costs more and you could do much better than this institutional setting.

San Marco 5424 (on Calle della Bissa). ℂ **041-522-3569**. Pizza and *primi* 3.35€–8€ ($3.85–$9); *secondi* 7€–12€ ($8–$14); *menù turistico* 8€–23€ ($9–$26). Prices are about 20%–30% higher upstairs. AE, MC, V. Daily 9:30am–10pm (until 3:30pm Mon). *Vaporetto:* Rialto (with bridge at your back on San Marco side of canal, walk straight ahead to Campo San Bartolomeo; take underpass slightly to your left marked SOTTO-PORTEGO DELLA BISSA; you'll come across the rosticceria at 1st corner on your right; look for GISLON [its old name] above entrance).

NEAR LA FENICE OPERA HOUSE

Osteria alle Botteghe *(Kids)* PIZZERIA/ITALIAN Easy on the palate, easy on the wallet, and even easy to find (if you've made it to Campo Santo Stefano), this is a great casual choice for pizza, a light snack, or a full meal. You can have stand-up *cicchetti* and fresh sandwiches at the bar or windowside counter, while more serious diners can head to the tables in back to enjoy the dozen pizzas, the pastas, or the *tavola calda,* a glass counter filled with prepared dishes like eggplant parmigiana, lasagna, and fresh-cooked vegetables in season, reheated when you order.

San Marco 3454 (on Calle delle Botteghe, off Campo Santo Stefano). ℂ 041-522-8181. *Primi* 4.15€ ($4.75); *secondi* 7€–8€ ($8–$9); *menù turistico* 8.80€ ($10). DC, MC, V. Mon–Sat 11am–4pm and 7–10pm. *Vaporetto:* Accademia or Sant'Angelo (find your way to Campo Santo Stefano by following the stream of people or by asking; take narrow Calle delle Botteghe at Gelateria Paolin [in northwest corner] across from Santo Stefano).

Trattoria da Fiore *(Finds)* VENETIAN Don't confuse this laid-back trattoria with the expensive Osteria da Fiore. You might not eat better here, but it'll seem that way when your relatively modest bill arrives. Start with the house specialty, the *pennette alla Fiore* for two (with olive oil, garlic, and seven in-season vegetables), and you might be happy to call it a night. Or try the *frittura mista* (over a dozen varieties of fresh fish and seafood). The bouillabaisse-like *zuppa di pesce alla chef* is stocked with mussels, crab, clams, shrimp, and tuna—at only 13€ ($15), it doesn't get any better and is a meal in itself. This is a great place to snack or make a light lunch out of *cicchetti* at the Bar Fiore next door (10:30am–10:30pm).

San Marco 3461 (on Calle delle Botteghe). ℂ 041-523-5310. Reservations suggested. *Primi* 7.80€–16€ ($9–$18); *secondi* 13€–21€ ($15–$24). AE, MC, V. Wed–Mon noon–3pm and 7–10pm. Closed 2 weeks in Jan and 2 weeks in Aug. *Vaporetto:* Accademia (cross bridge to San Marco side and walk straight ahead to Campo Santo Stefano; exit *campo* at northern end, take a left at Bar/Gelateria Paolin onto Calle delle Botteghe).

Value Getting the Best Deal on Dining

- If you qualify for a Rolling Venice pass (see "Venice Deals & Discounts," earlier in this chapter), ask for the discount guide listing dozens of restaurants offering 10% to 30% discounts.
- Remember that standing up at a bar, cafe, or *rosticceria* is less expensive than sitting down—but once you sit, you're rarely rushed.
- Pizza might not be a local specialty, but it's certainly a delicious way to save money (or consider a picnic lunch in one of the piazzas).
- Save your wine consumption for before or after dinner at a characteristic old *bacaro* (wine bar), not at the restaurant.
- Look for the words *servizio incluso* on your menu or at the bottom of your bill—you won't need to leave a 10% to 15% tip if service is already included.
- Check out the breakdown of a *menù turistico* and determine just how hungry you are—you might spend less and be more satisfied with just pasta and a salad a la carte.
- Avoid surprises: Fish is the basis of Venice's traditional cuisine but will hike up your bill substantially. Have the waiter approximate the cost of the entree before you order, as the price typically appears per 100 grams (by the *etto*) on the menu.

Vino Vino 🌟🌟 *Value* WINE BAR/ITALIAN   Vino Vino is an informal wine bar serving well-prepared simple food, but its biggest pull is the impressive selection of local and European wines sold by the bottle or glass (check out the website), with great *cicchetti* to accompany them. The Venetian specialties are written on a chalkboard but also usually displayed at the glass counter. After placing your order, settle down at one of about a dozen wooden tables squeezed into the two storefront-style rooms. Credit the high quality of the food to the fact that Vino Vino shares a kitchen (and an owner) with the eminent and expensive Antico Martini restaurant a few doors down. It's also a great spot for a leisurely self-styled wine tasting (1€–3€/$1.15–$3.45 per glass), with great *cicchetti* bar food. At dinner, the food often runs out around 10:30pm, so don't come too late.

San Marco 2007A (on Ponte delle Veste near La Fenice). ✆ **041-241-7688.** www.vinovino.co.it. *Primi* 5€–9€ ($6–$10); *secondi* 10€–12€ ($12–$14). AE, DC, MC, V. Wed–Mon 10:30am–midnight. *Vaporetto:* San Marco (with your back to basilica, exit Piazza San Marco through arcade on far left side; keep walking straight, pass American Express, cross over canal, and, before street jags left, turn right onto Calle delle Veste).

BETWEEN THE ACCADEMIA & CAMPO SANTA MARGHERITA (DORSODURO)

Taverna San Trovaso 🌟 VENETIAN   Wine bottles line the wood-paneled walls, and low vaulted brick ceilings augment the sense of character in this canalside tavern. The *menù turistico* includes wine, an ample *frittura mista* (assortment of fried seafood), and a dessert. The gnocchi is homemade, the local specialty of calf's liver and onions is great, and the simply grilled fish is the taverna's claim to fame. There's also a variety of pizzas. For a special occasion that'll test your budget but not bankrupt you, consider the four-course menu: It starts with a fresh antipasto of seafood followed by pasta and a fish entree (changing with the day's catch) and includes side dishes, a dessert, and wine. While in the neighborhood, stroll along Rio San Trovaso toward the Giudecca Canal: On your right will be the Squero di San Trovaso, one of the few boatyards that still makes and repairs gondolas.

Dorsoduro 1016 (on Fondamenta Priuli). © 041-520-3703. Reservations recommended. *Pizze* and *primi* 6€–10€ ($7–$12); *secondi* 8€–16€ ($9–$18); *menù turistico* 17€ ($20). AE, DC, MC, V. Tues–Sun noon 2:30pm and 7–9:30pm. *Vaporetto:* Rialto (walk to right around Accademia and take a right onto Calle Gambara; when this street ends at small Rio di San Trovaso, turn left onto Fondamenta Priuli).

Trattoria Ai Cugnai ★★ *(Value* VENETIAN   The storefront of this longtime favorite does little to announce that herein lies some of the neighborhood's best dining. The name refers to the brothers-in-law of the three chefs, all sisters, who serve classic *cucina venexiana,* like the reliably good *spaghetti alle vongole verace* (spaghetti with clams) or *fegato alla veneziana.* The homemade gnocchi and lasagna would meet any Italian grandmother's approval (you won't go wrong with any of the menu's *fatta in casa* choices of daily homemade specialties). Equidistant from the Accademia and the Guggenheim, Ai Cugnai is the perfect place to recharge after an art overload.

Dorsoduro 857 (on Calle Nuova Sant'Agnese). © 041-528-9238. *Primi* 5€–9€ ($6–$10); *secondi* 5€–17€ ($6–$19). AE, MC, V. Tues–Sun 12:30–3pm and 7–10:30pm. *Vaporetto:* Accademia (head east of bridge and Accademia in direction of Guggenheim Collection; on straight street connecting 2 museums, restaurant is on your right).

BUDGET BESTS

Venice offers countless neighborhood bars, cafes, and *bacari* (old-fashioned wine bars) where you can stand or sit with a *panino* (sandwich on a roll), *tramezzino* (triangle-shaped sandwich on sliced white bread), *toast* (grilled ham-and-cheese sandwich), or a tasty variety of the local specialty *cicchetti* (tapaslike finger foods like calamari rings, fried olives, and polenta squares). They'll cost 1€ to 3€ ($1.15–$3.45) if you stand at the bar, as much as double if you take a seat. Bar food is displayed in glass counters and usually sells out by late afternoon, so don't rely on this light grazing for dinner.

You'll find a concentration of popular bars along the Mercerie shopping strip connecting Piazza San Marco with the Rialto Bridge, in Campo San Luca (look for **Bar Torino, Bar Black Jack,** or the primarily pastry **Bar Rosa Salva**) and in Campo Santa Margherita. Avoid the tired-looking pizza you'll find in most bars: Neighborhood pizzerias offer far more savory and fresher renditions for a minimum of 4€ ($4.60), plus your drink and cover charge.

A Le Do Spade ★ WINE BAR/VENETIAN   Since 1415, workers, fishmongers, and shoppers from the nearby Mercato della Pescheria have flocked to this wine bar. There's bonhomie galore amid the locals here for their daily *ombra* (glass of wine)—a large number of excellent Veneto and Friuli wines are available by the glass. A counter is filled with various *cicchetti* (potato croquettes, fried calamari, polenta squares, and cheeses) and a special *picante panino,* whose secret mix of super-hot spices will sear your taste buds. Unlike at most *bacari,* this quintessentially Venetian cantina has added a number of tables and introduced a sit-down menu, while competitor Cantina do Mori (see below) is a better choice for stand-up bar food.

San Polo 860 (on Sottoportego do Spade). © 041-521-0574. www.dospadevenezia.it. *Pizze* 7.30€–9.30€ ($8–$11); *primi* 6€–12€ ($7–$13); *secondi* 7.80€–13€ ($9–$15); *menù fisso* 14€–15€ ($16–$17). AE, MC, V. Mon–Wed and Fri–Sat 9am–3pm and 5–11pm. Closed Jan 7–20. *Vaporetto:* Rialto or San Silvestro (at San Polo side of Rialto Bridge, walk away from bridge and through open-air market until you see covered fish market on your right; take a left and then take 2nd right onto Sottoportego do Spade).

Cantina do Mori *★★* *Finds* WINE BAR/SANDWICHES   Since 1462, this has been the watering hole of choice in the market area; legend even pegs Casanova as a habitué. Here's the best place to try *tramezzini*—you're guaranteed fresh combinations of thinly sliced meats, tuna, cheeses, and vegetables, along with tapaslike *cicchetti*. They're traditionally washed down with an *ombra*. Venetians stop to snack and socialize before and after meals; if you don't mind standing (there are no tables), do as they do. And now with a limited number of *primi* like *melanzane alla parmigiana* (eggplant parmigiana) and *fondi di carciofi saltati* (lightly fried artichoke hearts), my obligatory stop here is more fulfilling than ever.

San Polo 429 (entrances on Calle Galiazza and Calle Do Mori). (C) 041-522-5401. Sandwiches and *cicchetti* bar food 1€–2€ ($1.15–$2.30) per serving. No credit cards. Mon–Sat 8:30am–9:30pm. *Vaporetto:* Rialto (cross Rialto Bridge to San Polo side, walk to end of market stalls, turn left, then turn immediately right, and look for small wooden cantina sign on left).

Da Sandro *★* *Kids* ITALIAN/PIZZERIA   Like most pizzerie/trattorie, Sandro offers a dozen varieties of pizza (his specialty) as well as a full trattoria menu of pastas and entrees. But if you're looking for a cheap (say, 6.20€/$6) pizza-and-beer meal, this is a reliably good spot on the main drag linking the Rialto to Campo San Polo. You won't raise any eyebrows if you order just a pasta or a pizza and pass on the meat or fish. There's communal seating at a few wooden picnic tables placed outdoors, with eight small tables stuffed into the two dining rooms—which, unusually, are on opposite sides of the street.

San Polo 1473 (Campiello dei Meloni). (C) **041-523-4894.** *Primi* and *pizze* 5.50€–16€ ($6–$18); *secondi* 6€–18€ ($7–$21); fixed-price menus 14€–17€ ($16–$20). AE, MC, V. Sat–Thurs 11:30am–11:30pm. *Vaporetto:* San Silvestro (with your back to Grand Canal, walk straight to store-lined Ruga Vecchia San Giovanni and take a left; head toward Campo San Polo until you come on Campiello dei Meloni).

PICNICKING

The enjoyable alternative of a picnic lunch allows you to indulge later with a fine dinner *alla veneziana* while observing the life of the city's few open *piazze* or the aquatic parade on the Grand Canal. Doing your own shopping for food can be an interesting experience because there are few supermarkets as we know them.

Venice's principal **open-air market** is commonly referred to as the **Mercato Rialto.** It has two parts, beginning with the fresh fruit and produce section, whose many stalls, alternating with souvenir vendors, unfold north on the San Polo side of the Rialto Bridge. (Behind these stalls are a few permanent food stores whose delicious cheese, cold cuts, and bread selections alone make the perfect lunch.) At its farthest point is the covered fresh-fish market, located on the Grand Canal opposite the magnificent Ca' d'Oro and still redolent of the ancient days when it was one of the Mediterranean's great fish markets. The fruit and produce vendors are there Monday to Saturday 7am to 1pm, with a number who stay on in the afternoon; the fish merchants take Monday off and work on the other days in the mornings only.

Tuesday to Saturday 8:30am to 1 or 2pm, a number of open-air stalls selling fresh fruit and vegetables set up on spacious **Campo Santa Margherita.** You should have no trouble filling out your picnic spread with the fixings available at the various shops, including an exceptional *panetteria* (**bakery**), **Rizzo Pane,** at no. 2772; a fine *salumeria* (**deli**) at no. 2844; and a good shop for wine, sweets, and other picnic accessories next door. There's even a conventional supermarket, **Merlini,** just off the *campo* in the direction of the quasi-adjacent Campo San Barnaba at no. 3019. This is also the area where you'll find Venice's floating market, operating from a boat moored off Campo San Barnaba at the Ponte dei Pugni. This market is open Monday to Saturday 8am to 1pm and 3:30 to 7:30pm (closed Wed afternoon).

Alas, Venice doesn't have much in the way of green space for a picnic. An enjoyable alternative is to find some of the larger *piazze* or *campi* that have park benches, and in some cases even a tree or two for shade, such as **Campo Santa Margherita** and **Campo San Polo.** For a picnic with a view, scout out the **Punta della Dogana** area near La Salute church for a prime viewing site across the Grand Canal from San Marco and the Palazzo Ducale; pull up a piece of the embankment and watch all the water activity. If you want to copy Katharine Hepburn and Rossano Brazzi as seen in the classic 1950s *Summertime,* take the no. 12 boat out to the near-deserted island of **Torcello** with a hamper full of bread, cheese, and wine. Less time-consuming and perhaps the **best picnic site** in the very heart of Venice is a patch of sun on the marble steps leading down to the water of the Grand Canal, at the foot of the Rialto Bridge on the San Polo side.

WORTH A SPLURGE

Trattoria Alla Madonna *(Overrated* ITALIAN/VENETIAN   Packing them in for more than 50 years, this Venetian institution has a convenient location near the Rialto Bridge, with five large dining rooms and a professional kitchen that prepares a menu of fresh fish and seafood to perfection. With all of this and (by Venetian standards) moderate prices, it's no surprise this place is always jumping, so don't expect the waiter to smile if you linger over dessert. Most of the first courses are served with seafood, like the spaghetti or risotto with *frutti di mare* or the pasta with *sepie* (cuttlefish), blackened by its own natural ink. Most of the day's special fish selections are best simply and deliciously prepared *alla griglia* (grilled).

San Polo 594 (Calle d. Madonna). ✆ 041-522-3824. www.ristoranteallamadonna.com. Reservations not accepted for tables of fewer than 8. *Primi* 9€–11€ ($10–$13); *secondi* 9€–15€ ($10–$17). AE, DC, MC, V. Thurs–Tues noon–3pm and 7–10pm. Closed 2 weeks in Aug and all of Jan. *Vaporetto:* Rialto. From the foot of the Rialto Bridge on the San Polo side of the Grand Canal, turn left and follow the Riva d. Vin along the Grand Canal; Calle d. Madonna (also called Sottoportego d. Madonna) will be the 2nd calle on your right (look for the big yellow sign); the restaurant is on your left.

Trattoria da Remigio *★★* ITALIAN/VENETIAN   Famous for its straightforward renditions of classics, Remigio is the kind of place where you can order simple *gnocchi alla pescatora* (homemade gnocchi in tomato-seafood sauce) and *frittura mista* (a cornucopia of fried seafood that makes a flavorful but light *secondo*) and know they'll be memorable. The restaurant bucks the current Venetian trend by offering excellent food and service at reasonable prices. The English-speaking headwaiter, Pino, will talk you through the day's perfectly prepared fish dishes. You'll even find a dozen meat choices. Remigio's—less abuzz than Alla Madonna (see above)—is well known though not as easy to find, but just ask any local.

Castello 3416 (on Calle Bosello near Scuola San Giorgio dei Greci). ✆ 041-523-0089. Reservations required. *Primi* 3.50€–6€ ($4.05–$7); *secondi* 5€–14€ ($6–$16). AE, DC, MC, V. Wed–Mon 1–3pm; Wed–Sun 7–11pm. *Vaporetto:* San Zaccaria (follow Riva degli Schiavoni east until you come to white Chiesa della Pietà; turn left onto Calle della Pietà, which jags left into Calle Bosello).

4 Seeing the Sights

THE BASILICA & PIAZZA SAN MARCO

Basilica di San Marco 🔑🔑🔑   For centuries, Venice was Europe's principal gateway between the Orient and the West, so the style for the sumptuously Byzantine Basilica di San Marco, replete with five mosquelike bulbed domes, was borrowed from Constantinople (particularly the Hagia Sofia). Legend has it that in 828, two merchants conspired to smuggle the remains of St. Mark the Evangelist from Alexandria by packing them in pickled pork, guaranteeing that Muslim guards would keep their distance. Thus, St. Mark replaced the Greek St. Theodore as Venice's patron saint, and a small chapel was built on this site in his honor. Through the subsequent centuries (much of what you see is from the 11th c.), wealthy Venetian merchants and politicians vied with one another in donating gifts to expand and embellish this cathedral, a symbol of the Venetian Republic's wealth and power. Exotic and mysterious, it's unlike any other Roman Catholic church you'll visit in Europe.

And so it is that the Basilica di San Marco earned its name as the Chiesa d'Oro (Golden Church), its cavernous interior exquisitely gilded with Byzantine mosaics added over 7 centuries (the earliest from the 11th c.), covering every inch of the ceiling and walls. For a close look at many of the most remarkable ceiling mosaics and a better view of the Oriental carpet–like patterns of the inlaid stone pavements, pay the admission to go up to the **Galleria,** or the **Museo Marciano** (entrance in the atrium). This is also the only way to the **Loggia dei Cavalli,** the open balcony running along the basilica's facade above

---

⟨Value⟩ Getting the Best Deal on Sightseeing

- Check with the tourist office about free tours being offered (erratically and usually in high season) in some of the churches, particularly the Basilica di San Marco and Chiesa dei Frari.
- Note that almost all churches offer free admission—but don't show up during lunchtime, when they close for a few hours, reopening at 4 or 5pm.
- To fill the hours when the stores and churches are closed during lunch, head for the museums—but you won't be the only one with this brilliant idea. Recharge your batteries and take that tour of the Grand Canal on the no. 1 *vaporetto* or plan a canalside picnic to watch the water traffic.
- Venice is notorious for changing the hours of its museums and even its churches. At the tourist office, ask for the season's current list of museum and church hours.
- During the peak months, you can enjoy extended museum hours— some places stay open until 7 or even 10pm. Unfortunately, these hours are not released until around Easter of every year.
- Take advantage of the fact that the admission to the Palazzo Ducale includes admission to the Museo Correr and vice versa.
- Plan well: In high season, the museum lines can be long, so leave yourself sufficient time to wait for admission.

Tips **Dress with Respect**

St. Mark's has a strict **dress code:** no shorts, no skirts above the knee, and no bare shoulders. *The guards will not let you in if you are not dressed appropriately.* Women can carry a light shawl to use as a makeshift skirt over shorts or to cover shoulders. You also must remain silent and cannot take photographs.

---

the principal entrance, from which you can enjoy a closer look at the exterior. More important, it lets you mingle with the loggia's copies of the celebrated *Triumphal Quadriga* of gilded bronze horses (from the 2nd or 3rd c. A.D.) brought from Constantinople in 1204 with other booty from the Crusades; together with the Lion of St. Mark (a kind of mascot for the patron saint), they were a symbol of the unrivaled Maritime Republic. The recently restored originals have been moved inside to the otherwise not very interesting museum. A visit to the loggia is a highlight, providing an excellent view of the piazza and what Napoléon called the "most beautiful salon in the world." The Clock Tower is to your right; its multiyear restoration (slated to be finished before you arrive) was timed to coordinate with its 500-year anniversary but ran into overtime. The Campanile di San Marco (bell tower) towers to your left, and beyond are the glistening waters of the Bacino San Marco (St. Mark's Basin). (For more on the clock tower and campanile, see below.)

The church's greatest treasure is the magnificent **Pala d'Oro** ⭐⭐, an enamel-and jewel-encrusted golden altar screen created as early as the 10th century and embellished by master artisans between the 12th and the 14th centuries. This Gothic masterpiece encrusted with close to 2,000 precious gems and 255 enameled panels is behind the main altar whose green marble canopy covers the tomb of St. Mark. Also worth a visit is the **Tesoro (Treasury),** to the altar's far right, with a collection of the Crusaders' plunder from Constantinople. Much of the Venetian fleet's booty has been incorporated into the basilica's interior and exterior in the form of marble, columns, capitals, and statuary. Second to the Pala d'Oro in importance is the 10th-century *Madonna di Nicopeia* ⭐⭐, a bejeweled icon absconded from Constantinople and exhibited in its own chapel to the left of the main altar. She's held as one of present-day Venice's most protective patrons.

Admission to the basilica is free but restricted, and there's often a line in high season—don't leave Venice without visiting its candlelit glittering interior, still redolent of Eastern cultures. In July and August (with much less certainty the rest of the year), church-affiliated volunteers give **free tours** Monday to Saturday, leaving four or five times daily (not all are in English), beginning at 10:30am; groups gather in the atrium, where you'll find posters with schedules. The basilica is open for those wishing to attend **Sunday morning Mass;** all others are strongly discouraged from entering during services (see hours below). There's also a **6:45pm Sunday Mass** during which the mosaics are floodlit. (It's not for "tourists"—if you want to see the spectacle, you have to stay for the full Mass and sit quietly in a pew with the rest of the congregation.)

April through October, you can take a **free guided tour** of the basilica. Tours are offered infrequently. Call ℗ **041-270-2421,** on Tuesday or Thursday mornings only, to reserve a space.

Venice

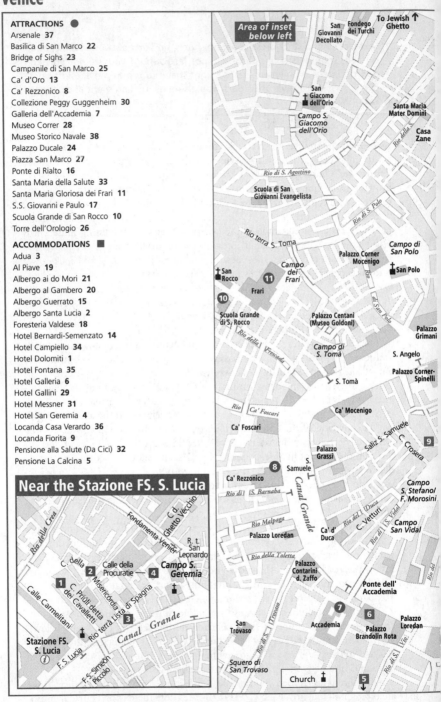

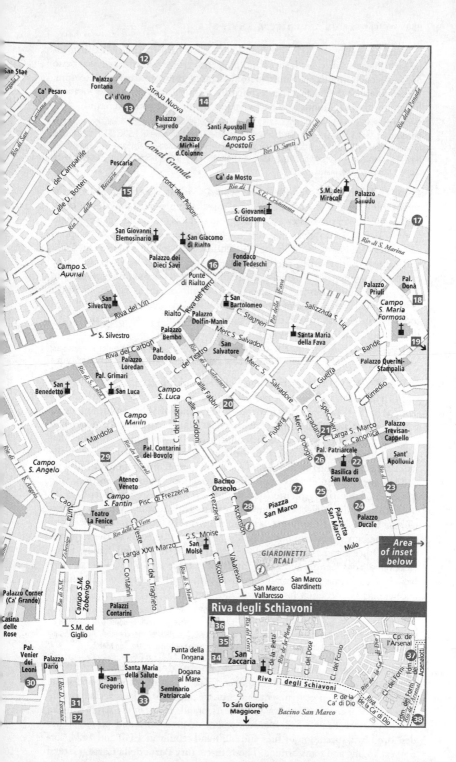

San Stae

Ca' Pesaro

Palazzo
Fontana

Ca' d'Oro

Strada Nuova

Palazzo
Sagredo

Palazzo
Michiel
d.Colonne

Santi Apostoli

Campo SS
Apostoli

Canal Grande

Pescaria

Ca' da Mosto

Rio di

S.G. Crisostomo

S.M. dei
Miracoli

Palazzo
Sanudo

Fond. delle Pegiori

San Giovanni
Elemosinario

San Giacomo
di Rialto

San Giovanni
Crisostomo

Rio di S. Marina

Rio di S. Marina

Campo S.
Aponal

Palazzo dei
Dieci Savi

Fondaco
die Tedeschi

Ponte
di Rialto

San
Silvestro

Riva del Vin

Rialto

San
Bartolomeo

Palazzo
Dolfin-Manin

Palazzo
Priuli

Pal.
Donà

Campo
S. Maria
Formosa

S. Silvestro

Palazzo
Bembo

San
Salvatore

Santa Maria
della Fava

C. Bande

Riva del Carbon

Pal.
Dandolo

Merc. S. Salvador

Palazzo Querini-
Stampalia

Palazzo
Loredan

Pal. Grimani

Mercerie S. Salvatore

C. del Teatro

C. Guerra

Rimedio

San
Benedetto

San Luca

Campo
S. Luca

C. Fiubera

C. Larga S. Marco

Palazzo
Trevisan-
Cappello

Campo
Manin

Calle Fabbri

Merc. Spadaria

C. Canonica

Sant'
Apollonia

C. Mandola

C. dei Fuseri

Pal. Patriarcale

Basilica di
San Marco

Campo
S. Angelo

Pal. Contarini
del Bovolo

Merc. Orologio

Campo
S. Fantin

Bacino
Orseolo

Piazza
San Marco

Piazzetta
San Marco

Palazzo
Ducale

Ateneo
Veneto

Teatro
La Fenice

Frezzeria

C. Ascension

Molo

Area
of inset
below

Palazzo Corner
(Ca' Grande)

C. Larga XXII Marzo

C. Contarini

S.S. Moisè

San
Molsè

GIARDINETTI
REALI

Casina
delle
Rose

C. del Traghetto

S.M. del
Giglio

Campo S.M.
Zobenigo

San Marco
Vallaresso

San Marco
Giardinetti

Pal.
Venier
dei
Leoni

Palazzo
Dario

Santa Maria
della Salute

Punta della
Dogana

Dogana
al Mare

Riva degli Schiavoni

Cp. de
l'Arsenal

San
Zaccaria

San Gregorio

Seminario
Patriarcale

Riva   degli   Schiavoni

P. de la
Ca' di Dio

To San Giorgio
Maggiore

Bacino San Marco

Note: Large bags are no longer allowed inside the basilica, and an "experimental" left luggage office has been set up at Ateneo San Basso in Calle San Basso 315A. It's open Monday to Saturday from 10am to 4pm, Sunday from 2 to 4pm. Please note that the basilica is experimenting with this service, and its location, hours, or other conditions may have changed by the time you visit Venice.

San Marco, Piazza San Marco, 1. ℭ 041-522-5205. Free admission to Basilica; admission to Museo Marciano (St. Mark's Museum, also called La Galleria, includes Loggia dei Cavalli) 1.50€ ($1.75); admission to Tesoro (Treasury) 2€ ($2.30). Basilica, Tesoro, and Pala d'Oro Apr–Oct Mon–Sat 9:45am–5pm, Sun 2–5pm; Nov–Mar Mon–Sat 9:45am–4pm. Museo Marciano summer daily 9:45am–5pm (winter hours may be shorter). *Vaporetto:* San Marco.

Campanile di San Marco (Bell Tower) 🐱🐱

It's an easy elevator ride to the top of this 97m (324-ft.) campanile for a breathtaking view of the cupolas of St. Mark's, the center's red rooftops, church spires, the lagoon, and Venice's neighboring islands. On a clear day you might even see the distant snowcapped Dolomite Mountains. Built in the 9th century, then rebuilt in the 12th, 14th, and 16th centuries (when the pretty marble loggia at its base was added by Jacopo Sansovino), the original cathedral bell tower collapsed unexpectedly in 1902, miraculously hurting no one. It was rebuilt exactly as before, using the same materials, even rescuing one of the five historic bells, which is still used today (each bell was rung for a different purpose, such as war, the death of a doge, religious holidays, and so on).

San Marco, Piazza San Marco. ℭ 041-522-4064. Admission 6€ ($7). Apr–June and Sept–Oct 9am–7:45pm; July–Aug 9am–9pm; Nov–Mar 9:30am–4:15pm (last entrance 1 hr. before closing). *Vaporetto:* San Marco.

Museo Correr

This museum, which you enter through an arcade at the west end of Piazza San Marco, opposite the basilica, is no match for the Accademia (see below) but does include some interesting scenes of Venetian life among its paintings, and a fine collection of artifacts like coins, costumes, the doges' ceremonial robes and hats, and an incredible pair of 15-inch platform shoes that give an interesting feel for aspects of the day-to-day life in *La Serenissima* during its heyday. Bequeathed to the city by the aristocratic Correr family in 1830, it's divided into three sections: the **History Section, Painting Section,** and **Museum of the Risorgimento** (Italy's 19th-c. revolutionary movement).

Of the painting collection from the 13th to 18th century, Vittorio Carpaccio's *Le Cortigiane (The Courtesans),* in room no. 15 on the upper floor, is one of the museum's most famous paintings (are they courtesans or the respected elite?). Other star attractions include paintings by the Bellini family, father Jacopo and sons Gentile and Giovanni. For a glimpse at just how little this city has changed in the past several hundred years, head to room no. 22 and its anonymous 17th-century bird's-eye view of Venice.

San Marco 52, west end of Piazza San Marco. ℭ 041-240-5211. www.museiciviciveneziani.it. Admission 11€ ($13), 5.50€ ($6) students 15–29, 3€ ($3.45) children 6–14, free for children under 6 or for those on San Marco Cumulative Ticket (see "Venice Deals & Discounts," earlier in the chapter). Apr–Oct daily 9am–7pm; Nov–Mar daily 9am–5pm (last entrance 1 hr. before closing). *Vaporetto:* San Marco.

Palazzo Ducale (Doge's Palace) & Ponte dei Sospiri (Bridge of Sighs) 🐱🐱🐱

The Gothic-Renaissance Palazzo Ducale, the pink-and-white marble residence and government center of the doges (or dukes, elected for life) who ruled Venice for more than 1,000 years, stands between the Basilica di San Marco and the Bacino San Marco. Symbol of prosperity and power, it was destroyed by a succession of fires and built and rebuilt in 1340 and 1424, forever expanding and transforming. The 15th-century **Porta della Carta (Gate of**

Paper), the entrance adjacent to the basilica where the doges' proclamations were once posted, opens onto a splendid inner courtyard with a double row of Renaissance arches. Ahead you'll see Sansovino's enormous **Scala dei Giganti (Stairway of the Giants),** scene of the doges' lavish inaugurations and never used by mere mortals; it leads to wood-paneled courts and meeting rooms. The walls and ceilings of these rooms were richly decorated by Venetian masters such as Veronese, Titian, Carpaccio, and Tintoretto to illustrate the history of the puissant Republic while impressing visiting diplomats and emissaries with the prosperity and power it had attained.

If you want to understand something of this magnificent palace, the fascinating history of the 1,000-year-old Maritime Republic, and the intrigue of the government that ruled it, rent an **audioguide** (at entrance: 5.50€/$6) or, even better, book ahead for the fascinating **"Secret Itineraries" tour** of otherwise restricted quarters and hidden passageways, such as the doge's private chambers, the torture chambers where prisoners were interrogated, and the "leads" or prison cells under the roof rafters from which Casanova made his famed escape.

Touring on your own, the first room you'll come to is the spacious **Sala delle Quattro Porte (Hall of the Four Doors),** whose ceiling is by Tintoretto. The next main room, the **Sala del Anti-Collegio** (adjacent to the **Sala del Collegio,** whose ceiling is also by Tintoretto), is where foreign ambassadors waited to be received by this committee of 25 members: It's richly decorated with Tintorettos and Veronese's *Rape of Europa,* considered one of the palazzo's finest. It steals some of the thunder of Tintoretto's *Three Graces* and *Bacchus and Ariadne* (the latter considered one of his best by some critics). A right turn from this room leads into one of the most impressive of the spectacular interior rooms, the richly adorned **Sala del Senato (Senate Chamber),** with Tintoretto's ceiling painting, *The Triumph of Venice.* Here, laws were passed by the Senate, a select group of 200 chosen from the Great Council. The latter was originally an elected body, but from the 13th century onward, it became an aristocratic stronghold that could number as many as 1,700.

After passing again through the Sala delle Quattro Porte, you'll come to the Veronese-decorated **Stanza del Consiglio dei Dieci (Room of the Council of Ten),** which is of particular historical interest: In this room justice was dispensed (and decapitations ordered) by the Republic's dreaded security police. Formed in the 14th century to deal with emergency situations, the Ten were frequently considered more powerful than the Senate and feared by all. Just outside the adjacent chamber, the **Sala della Bussola (Compass Chamber),** notice the **Bocca dei Leoni (lion's mouth),** a slit in the wall into which secret denunciations and accusations of alleged enemies of the state were placed for quick action by the much-feared Council.

The main sight on the next level down—indeed, in the entire palace—is the **Sala del Maggior Consiglio (Great Council Hall)** ★★. This enormous space is made special by Tintoretto's huge *Paradiso* at the far end above the doge's seat. (He was in his 70s when he undertook the project with the help of his son and died 6 years later.) Measuring 7m×68m (23 ft.×75 ft.), it's the world's largest oil painting on canvas; together with Veronese's gorgeous *Il Trionfo di Venezia (The Glorification of Venice)* in the oval panel on the ceiling, it affirms the power that emanated from the Council sessions held here. Tintoretto also did the portraits of the 76 doges encircling the top of this chamber; note that the picture of Doge Faliero, who was convicted of treason and beheaded in 1355, has been blacked out. Venice has never forgiven him. Although elected for life

---

An Insider's Look at the Palazzo Ducale

I cannot recommend the **"Itinerari Segreti" ("Secret Itineraries")** ⭐⭐⭐ guided tours enough. The tours offer an unparalleled look into the world of Venetian politics over the centuries and are the only way to access the otherwise restricted quarters and hidden passageways of this enormous palace. Reserve in advance, by phone if possible—tours are often sold out at least a few days ahead, especially spring through fall—or in person at the ticket desk. Tours are at 10:30am Thursday through Tuesday by reservation only, and cost 13€ ($14) for adults, 7€ ($8) for students, and 4€ ($5) for children 6 to 14.

---

since the 7th century, over time the doge became nothing but a figurehead: The power rested in the Great Council, composed mostly of Venice's nobles and sometimes numbering well over 1,500 members.

Exit the hall via the tiny doorway on the opposite side of Tintoretto's *Paradiso* to find the enclosed **Ponte dei Sospiri (Bridge of Sighs),** connecting the palace with the grim **Palazzo delle Prigioni (Prisons).** The bridge took its current name in the 19th century, when visiting northern European poets envisioned the prisoners' final breath of resignation on viewing the outside world one last time before being locked in their fetid cells awaiting the quick justice of the Terrible Ten. Some of the stone cells still have the original graffiti of past prisoners, many of them locked up interminably for petty crimes.

San Marco, Piazza San Marco. ℂ 041-271-5911. Admission on San Marco Cumulative Ticket (see "Venice Deals & Discounts," earlier in the chapter) or 11€ ($13) adults, 5.50€ ($6) students 15–29, 3€ ($3.45) children 6–14 (includes cumulative ticket, free for children under 5). For "Itinerari Segreti" guided tour in English, see "An Insider's Look at the Palazzo Ducale," above. Apr–Oct daily 9am–7pm; Nov–Mar daily 9am–5pm (ticket office closes 1 hr. earlier). *Vaporetto:* San Marco.

Torre dell'Orologio (Clock Tower)   Alas, the clock tower has been closed for years, despite original plans to reopen it in time for its 500-year anniversary—in 1996. Every year, the tourist office assures me it will open "soon." Hasn't happened yet. As you enter the magnificent Piazza San Marco, it's one of the first things you see, on the north side, next to and towering above the Procuratie Vecchie (the ancient administration buildings for the Republic). The Renaissance tower was built in 1496 and the clock mechanism of that same period still keeps perfect time but has gotten a cleaning by Piaget, the sponsor of its elaborate renovation. The two bronze figures, known as Moors because of the dark color of the bronze, pivot to strike the hour. The base of the tower has always been a favorite *punto di incontro* for Venetians ("meet me at the tower") and is the entrance to the ancient Mercerie (from the word for "merchandise"), the principal souklike retail street of both high-end boutiques and trinket shops that zigzags its way to the Rialto Bridge. Visits to the top will resume on the tower's reopening (when that will be is anybody's guess).

San Marco, Piazza San Marco. ℂ 041-5271-5911. Scheduled to reopen in 2004, but this may change (many other "scheduled" reopening dates have come and gone over the last 7 years). Admission set to be 9€ ($10). Daily 9am–3:30pm. Vaporetto: San Marco.

THE TOP MUSEUMS

Ca' d'Oro (Galleria Giorgio Franchetti) ⭐   The 15th-century Ca' d'Oro is one of the best preserved and most impressive of the hundreds of patrician palazzi lining the Grand Canal. After the Palazzo Ducale, it's the city's finest example of Venetian Gothic architecture. A restoration of its delicate pink-and-white facade (its name, the Golden Palace, refers to the gilt-covered facade that faded long ago) was completed in 1995. Inside, the ornate beamed ceilings and palatial trappings provide an attention-grabbing backdrop for the private collection of former owner Baron Franchetti, who bequeathed his palazzo and artwork to the city during World War I.

The core collection, expanded over the years, now includes sculptures, furniture, 16th-century Flemish tapestries, an impressive collection of bronzes (12th–16th c.), and a gallery whose most important canvases are Andrea Mantegna's *San Sebastiano* and Titian's *Venus at the Mirror,* as well as lesser paintings by **Tintoretto, Carpaccio, Van Dyck, Giorgione,** and **Jan Steen.** For a delightful break, step out onto the palazzo's loggia, overlooking the Grand Canal, for a view up and down the aquatic waterway and across to the Pescheria, a timeless vignette of an unchanged city. Off the loggia is a small but worthy ceramics collection open 10am to noon.

You can book tickets ahead of time by calling ✆ **041-520-0345.** The reservations office is open Monday to Friday from 9am to 6pm and Saturday from 9am to 2pm. There's a 1€ ($1.15) surcharge per ticket to use this service, however, and the museum is generally not so crowded that you need to reserve in advance.

Cannaregio between 3931 and 3932 (on Calle Ca' d'Oro north of Rialto Bridge). ✆ 041-522-2249 for museum information or 041-520-0345 for reservations. www.cadoro.org. Admission 5€ ($6), free for children under 12. Mon 8:15am–2pm; Tues–Sat 8:15am–7:15pm (winter hours may be shorter). Last admission 1 hr. before closing. *Vaporetto:* Ca' d'Oro.

Ca' Rezzonico (Museo del '700 Veneziano; Museum of 18th-Century Venice) 🏛🏛

This museum in a handsome palazzo on the Grand Canal reopened after a complete restoration in late 2001. It offers an intriguing look into what living in a grand Venetian home was like in the final years of the Venetian Republic. Begun by Baldassare Longhena, 17th-century architect of La Salute Church, the Rezzonico home is a sumptuous backdrop for this collection of period paintings (most important, works by Venetian artists Tiepolo and Guardi, and a special room dedicated to the dozens of works by Longhi), furniture, tapestries, and artifacts. This museum is one of the best windows into the sometimes-frivolous life of Venice of 200 years ago, as seen through the tastes and fashions of the wealthy Rezzonico family. The English poet Robert Browning, after the death of his wife Elizabeth Barrett Browning, made this his last home; he died here in 1889.

Dorsoduro (on the Grand Canal on Fondamenta Rezzonico). ✆ 041-241-0100 or 041-520-4036. www.museicivicivenezani.it. Admission 6.50€ ($7) adults, 4.50€ ($5) students 15–29, 2.50€ ($2.90) children 6–14, free for children under 6 or with cumulative ticket (see "Venice Deals & Discounts," earlier in the chapter). Apr–Oct Wed–Mon 10am–6pm; Nov–Mar Wed–Mon 10am–5pm. Last admission 1 hr. before closing. *Vaporetto:* Ca' Rezzonico (walk straight ahead to Campo San Barnabà, turn right at the piazza and go over 1 bridge, then take an immediate right for the museum entrance).

Collezione Peggy Guggenheim 🏛🏛

One of Europe's most comprehensive collections of modern art of the first half of the 20th century, these paintings and sculptures were assembled by the eccentric and eclectic American expatriate Peggy Guggenheim and housed in her Palazzo Venier dei Leoni, which she bought in 1949 and lived in until her 1979 death. Among the major works are Magritte's *Empire of Light,* Picasso's *La Baignade,* Kandinsky's *Landscape with Church (with Red Spot),* Metzinger's *The Racing Cyclist,* and Pollock's *Alchemy.* The museum is also home to several haunting canvases by Max Ernst (whom she married), Giacometti's unique figures, Brancusi's fluid sculptures, and numerous works by Braque, Dalí, Léger, Mondrian, Chagall, and Miró.

A new wing has opened across the inside courtyard, housing an interesting museum shop, temporary exhibit space, and a nice (but pricey) cafe/restaurant.

Check the tourist office for an update on museum hours; it is often open when many others are closed (as on national holidays) and sometimes offers a few hours a week of free admission. Don't be shy about speaking English with the young staff working here on internship; most of them are American. Free English-language tours of the permanent collection are offered on Saturday at 7pm. If you can't make the tour, 5€ ($6) audioguides are available.

Dorsoduro 701 (on Calle San Cristoforo). (℃ 041-240-5411. www.guggenheim-venice.it. Admission 10€ ($9) adults, 5€ ($6) students, free for children under 12 and holders of the Rolling Venice card (see "Venice Deals & Discounts," earlier in the chapter). Wed–Mon 10am–6pm. Vaporetto: Accademia (walk around left side of Accademia, take 1st left, and walk straight ahead following signs—you'll cross a canal, then walk alongside another, until turning left when necessary).

Galleria dell'Accademia ✸✸✸   The glory that was Venice lives on in the Accademia, the treasure house of Venetian painting from the 13th to the 18th centuries, exhibited chronologically in a deconsecrated church and an adjoining *scuola* (confraternity hall). There's no one hallmark masterpiece; this is a comprehensive showcase of works by all the great masters of *La Serenissima:* It includes **Paolo** and **Lorenzo Veneziano** from the 14th century; **Gentile** and **Giovanni Bellini** (and Giovanni's brother-in-law **Andrea Mantegna** from Padua) and **Vittore Carpaccio** from the 15th century; **Giorgione** (whose *Tempest* is one of the gallery's most famous works), **Tintoretto, Veronese,** and **Titian** from the 16th century; and, from the 17th and 18th centuries, Canaletto, Piazzetta, Longhi, and Tiepolo, among others. You'll see in the canvases how little Venice, perhaps least of any European city, has changed. Admission is limited due to fire regulations, and waits in lines, especially in summer, can stretch to 20 or 30 minutes—or more. The new reservations service costs an additional 1€ ($1.15) per ticket, but ought to cut down on your wait.

Dorsoduro, at foot of Accademia Bridge. (℃ 041-522-2247 for museum information or 041-520-0345 for reservations. www.gallerieaccademia.org. Admission 9€ ($10), 5.75€ ($7) children 12–18, free for children under 12 or on cumulative ticket (see "Venice Deals & Discounts," p. 952). Mon 8:15am–2pm; Tues–Sun 8:15am–7:15pm. Last admission 30 min. before closing (winter hours may be shorter). *Vaporetto:* Accademia.

Scuola Grande di San Rocco (Confraternity of St. Roch) ✸✸✸   This museum is a dazzling monument to **Tintoretto**—the largest collection of his

---

Moments   **The Doge's Ball at Carnevale**

Most of the Carnevale balls aren't open to the public, but the candlelit **Doge's Ball (Ballo del Doge)** is a dazzling exception, traditionally held the Saturday before Shrove Tuesday in the 15th-century Palazzo Pisani-Moretta on the Grand Canal. Historic costumes are a must, and you can rent them.

Of course, this ball isn't exactly cheap—in the past, tickets have cost upwards of 260€ ($299) each. If you're interested in finding out more and arranging for a costume rental, contact Antonia Sautter at the Ballo del Doge at (℃ 041-523-3851 (www.ballodeldoge.com).

Did You Know?
Did you know Venice is sinking at a rate of about 6.35cm (2½ in.) per decade?

work anywhere. The series of more than 50 dark and dramatic works took more than 20 years to complete, making this the richest of the many *scuole* (confraternity guilds) that once flourished in Venice. Jacopo Robusti (1518–94), called Tintoretto because his father was a dyer, was a devout, unworldly man who traveled beyond Venice only once. His epic canvases are filled with phantasmagoric light and mystical spirituality.

Begin upstairs in the side chamber called the **Sala dell'Albergo,** where the most notable of the enormous canvases is the moving *La Crocifissione (The Crucifixion).* In the center of the gilt ceiling of the **Great Hall,** also upstairs, is *Il Serpente di Bronzo (The Bronze Snake).* Among the eight paintings downstairs, each depicting a scene from the New Testament, the most noteworthy is *La Strage degli Innocenti (The Slaughter of the Innocents),* so full of dramatic urgency and energy the figures seem almost to tumble out of the frame.

Although dark by nature of the painter's brush, the works were restored in the 1970s. A useful guide to the paintings inside is posted on the wall just before the museum entrance. There are a few Tiepolos among the paintings, as well as a solitary work by Titian. Note that the works on or near the staircase aren't by Tintoretto. The **Accademia di San Rocco** (C 041-962-999; www.musicinvenice. com) sponsors highly recommended chamber orchestra concerts in these evocative environs.

San Polo 3058 (on Campo San Rocco adjacent to Campo dei Frari). C 041-523-4864. www.sanrocco.it (under construction). Admission 5.50€ ($6) adults, 4€ ($4.60) students. Mar 28–Nov 30 daily 9am–5:30pm; Dec–Mar 27 daily 10am–4pm. *Vaporetto:* San Tomà (walk straight ahead on Calle del Traghetto and turn right and immediately left across Campo San Tomà; walk as straight ahead as you can, on Ramo Mandoler, Calle Larga Prima, and Salizzada San Rocco, which leads into *campo* of the same name—look for crimson sign behind Frari Church).

OTHER CHURCHES & SYNAGOGUES

Il Redentore   Antonio Palladio was perhaps the greatest architect of the High Renaissance, his lovely neoclassical "Palladian" style an enormous influence on architects from Christopher Wren (London's St. Paul's Cathedral) to Thomas Jefferson (Virginia's Monticello). One of Palladio's greatest masterpieces is Venice's Il Redentore, commissioned by the city in thanks for being delivered from the great plague of 1575–77, which claimed over a quarter of the population (some 46,000 people). The doge established a tradition of visiting this church by crossing a long pontoon bridge made up of boats from the Dorsoduro's Zattere on the third Sunday of each July, a tradition that survived the demise of the doges and remains one of Venice's most popular festivals.

The interior is done in grand, austere, painstakingly classical Palladian style. The artworks tend to be workshop pieces (from the studios or schools, but not the actual brushes, of Tintoretto and Veronese), but there is a fine *Baptism of Christ* by Veronese himself in the sacristy, which also contains Alvise Vivarini's good *Adoration* and *Angels* alongside works by Jacopo da Bassano and Palma il Giovane, who also did the *Deposition* over the right aisle's third chapel. Recent renovations to the interior have now been completed, and the sacristy is to be next.

Campo del Redentore, La Giudecca. C 041-523-1415. Admission 2€ ($2.30), or 8€ ($9) on cumulative ticket (see "For Church Fans," below). Mon–Sat 10am–5pm; Sun 1–5pm. *Vaporetto:* Redentore.

Special & Free Events

Venice's most special event is the yearly pre-Lenten **Carnevale** ((C) **041-241-0570**; www.carnevale.venezia.it), a theatrical resuscitation of the 18th-century bacchanalia that drew tourists during the final heyday of the Serene Republic. Most of today's Carnevale-related events, masked balls, and costumes evoke that swan-song moment. Many of the concerts around town are free, when baroque to samba to gospel to Dixieland jazz fills the *piazze* and byways; check with the tourist office for a list of events.

The masked balls are often private; those where (exorbitantly priced) tickets are available are sumptuous, with candlelit banquets calling for extravagant costumes you can rent by the day from special shops. If you can score tickets, splurge on the Ballo del Doge (see above). Those not invited to any ball will be just as happy having their faces painted and watching the ongoing street theater from ringside cafes. There's a daily market of Carnevale masks and costumes on Campo Santo Stefano (10am–10pm).

Carnevale builds for 10 days until the big blowout, Shrove Tuesday (Fat Tuesday or Mardi Gras), when fireworks illuminate the Grand Canal, and Piazza San Marco is turned into a giant open-air ballroom for the masses. Book your hotel months ahead, especially for the 2 weekends prior to Shrove Tuesday.

Stupendous fireworks light the night sky during the **Festa del Redentore** ((C) **041-274-7736**), on the third Saturday and Sunday in July. This celebration, marking the July 1576 lifting of a plague that had gripped the city, is centered on the Palladio-designed Chiesa del Redentore (Church of the Redeemer) on the island of Giudecca. A bridge of boats across the Giudecca Canal links the church with the banks of Le Zattere in Dorsoduro, and hundreds of boats of all shapes and sizes fill the Giudecca. It's one big floating *festa* until night descends and an awesome half-hour *spettacolo* of fireworks fills the sky.

Museo Comunità Ebraica and Il Ghetto (Jewish Ghetto) 🏛 Venice's relationship with its Jewish community has fluctuated over time from acceptance to borderline tolerance. In 1516, 700 Jews were forced to move to this then-remote northwestern corner of Venice, to an abandoned site of a 14th-century foundry (*ghetto* is old Venetian dialect for "foundry"). As was commonplace with most of the hundreds of islands making up Venice, the area was surrounded by water. Its two access points were controlled at night and early morning by heavy gates manned by Christian guards (paid for by the Jews), both protecting and segregating its inhabitants. Within a century, the community grew to more than 5,000, representing many languages and cultures. Although the original **Ghetto Nuovo (New Ghetto)** was expanded to include the **Ghetto Vecchio** and later the **Ghetto Nuovissimo (Newest Ghetto),** land was limited and quarters always cramped. A very small, ever-diminishing community of Jewish families continues to live here: Some 2,000 are said to live in all Venice and Mestre.

The **Venice International Film Festival**, in late August and early September, is the most respected celebration of celluloid in Europe after Cannes. Films from all over the world are shown in the Palazzo del Cinema on the Lido as well as at various venues—and occasionally in some of the *campi*. Ticket prices vary, but those for the less sought-after films are usually modest. Check with the tourist office for listings.

Venice hosts the latest in modern and contemporary painting and sculpture from dozens of countries during the prestigious **Biennale d'Arte** (℅ **041-521-8846** or 041-271-9005; www.labiennale.org), one of the world's top international modern-art shows. It fills the pavilions of the public gardens at the east end of Castello from late May to October every odd-numbered year. Many great modern artists have been discovered at this world-famous show.

The **Regata Storica** (℅ **041-274-7735**) that takes place on the Grand Canal on the first Sunday in September is an extravagant seagoing parade in historic costume as well as a genuine regatta. Just about every seaworthy gondola, richly decorated for the occasion and piloted by *gondolieri* in colorful livery, participates in the opening cavalcade. The aquatic parade is followed by three regattas proceeding along the Grand Canal. You can buy grandstand tickets through the tourist office or can come early and pull up a piece of embankment near the Rialto Bridge for the best seats in town.

April 25 is a local holiday, the **feast day of St. Mark,** beloved patron saint of Venice and of the ancient Serene Republic. A special high Mass is celebrated in the Basilica di San Marco, roses are exchanged between loved ones, and a quiet air of *festa* permeates town, where everything pretty much shuts down for the day.

The only way to visit any of the area's five 16th-century synagogues is through a **tour** given in English by the Museo Communità Ebraica (museum admission is included). Your guide will elaborate on the commercial and political climate of those times, the unique skyscraper architecture (overcrowding resulted in many buildings having as many as seven low-ceilinged stories), and the daily lifestyle of the community until the 1797 arrival of Napoléon, who declared the Jews free citizens.

Cannaregio 2902b (on Campo del Ghetto Nuovo). ℅ **041-715-359** or 041-723-007. Museum admission 3€ ($3.45) adults, 2€ ($2.30) children; museum and synagogue tour 8€ ($9) adults, 6.50€ ($7) children. Museum June–Sept Sun–Fri 10am–7pm; Oct–May Sun–Fri 10am–6pm. Early closing Fri possible. Synagogue tours hourly 10:30am–4:30pm. Closed Jewish holidays. *Vaporetto:* Guglie.

Santa Maria della Salute (Church of the Virgin Mary of Good Health) ✸

Referred to as "La Salute," this 17th-century baroque jewel proudly reigns at this commercially and aesthetically important point, almost directly across from Piazza

San Marco, where the Grand Canal empties into the lagoon. The first stone was laid in 1631 after the Senate decided to honor the Virgin Mary of Good Health (La Salute) for delivering Venice from a plague. They accepted the revolutionary plans of a relatively unknown young architect, Baldassare Longhena (he went on to design, among other projects in Venice, the Ca' Rezzonico). He dedicated the next 50 years to overseeing its progress and died a year after its inauguration but 5 years before its completion. The octagonal Salute is recognized as a baroque masterpiece for its exuberant exterior of volutes, scrolls, and more than 125 statues, and for its rather sober interior highlighted by **Luca Giordano altarpieces.** There's a small gallery of important works in the sacristy (enter through a small door to the left of the main altar). A number of ceiling paintings and portraits of the Evangelists and church doctors are all by Titian. On the right wall is Tintoretto's *Marriage at Cana,* one of his best.

Dorsoduro (on Campo della Salute). © 041-522-5558. Free admission to church; admission to sacristy 1.50€ ($1.75). Daily 9am–noon and 3–6pm. *Vaporetto:* Salute.

Santa Maria Gloriosa dei Frari (Church of the Frari) 🦒🦒

Known as i Frari, this immense 13th- and 14th-century Gothic church is around the corner from the Scuola Grande di San Rocco. Built by the Franciscans (*frari* is a dialectal distortion of *frati,* meaning "brothers"), it's something of a memorial to the ancient glories of Venice. Because St. Francis and the order he founded emphasized prayer and poverty, it's not surprising the church is austere inside and out. It does, however, house two **Titian masterpieces** (you might have noticed the scarcity of Titian's works in Venice outside the Accademia and La Salute), the most striking being the *Assumption of the Virgin* 🦒🦒, over the main altar, painted when the artist was only in his late 20s. In his *Virgin of the Pesaro Family* 🦒, in the left nave, Titian's wife posed for the figure of Mary, then died soon afterward in childbirth. The church's other masterwork is Bellini's *Madonna and Child* 🦒🦒, a triptych displayed in the sacristy (take the door on the right as you face the altar); it's one of his finest portraits of Mary. There's also Donatello's *St. John the Baptist,* an almost primitive-looking woodcarving. The **grandiose tombs** of two famous Venetians are also here: Canova (d. 1822), the Italian sculptor who led the revival of classicism; and Titian, who died in 1576 during a deadly plague.

Tips For Church Fans

The **Associazione Chiesa di Venezia** (© 041-275-0462; www.chorusvenezia. org) now curates and maintains most of Venice's important churches. Admission to each church costs 2.50€ ($2.90), and (with a few exceptions) each is open Monday to Saturday 10am to 5pm, Sunday 1 to 5pm. The churches are closed Sundays in July and August. If you plan to visit more than three churches, buy the 8€ ($9) ticket (valid for 1 year), which allows you to visit all the following churches: **Il Redentore** (reviewed above), **Santa Maria del Giglio, Santo Stefano, Santa Maria Formosa, Santa Maria dei Miracoli, San Giovanni Elemosinario, Santa Maria Gloriosa dei Frari** (reviewed above), **San Polo, San Giacomo dell'Orio, San Stae, Sant' Alvise, Madonna dell'Orto, San Pietro di Castello, San Sebastiano,** and **San Marco cathedral's treasury.** The association now offers audioguides at some of the churches for .50€ (60¢).

Moments   Cruising the Canals

A leisurely cruise along the **Canal Grande (Grand Canal)** ★★★ from Piazza San Marco to the Ferrovia—or the reverse—is one of Venice's must-dos. Hop on the **no. 1** *vaporetto* in the late afternoon (it's open in the prow; grab one of the outdoor seats), when the weather-worn colors of the former homes of Venice's merchant elite are warmed by the soft light and reflected in the canal's rippling waters and when the traffic has eased somewhat. Some 200 palazzi, churches, and imposing Republican buildings from the 14th to the 18th centuries (many of the largest now converted into banks, museums, and galleries) line this 3.2km (2-mile) ribbon of water looping through the city like an inverted S, crossed by only three bridges (the Rialto spans it at midpoint). It's the world's grandest Main Street.

As much a symbol of Venice as the winged lion, the **gondola** ★★★ is one of Europe's great traditions, terribly expensive but truly as romantic as it looks (detractors who write it off as too touristy have most likely never tried it). Though it's often quoted in print at differing official rates, expect to pay 62€ ($71) for up to 50 minutes (77€/$89 between 8pm and 8am), with up to six passengers, and 31€ ($36) for another 25 minutes (39€/$45 at night). Aim for late afternoon before sundown when the light does its magic on the canal reflections (and bring a bottle of *prosecco* and glasses). If the price is too high, ask visitors at your hotel or others lingering at the gondola stations if they'd like to share it. Establish the cost, time, and route explanation (any of the back canals are preferable to the trafficked and often choppy Grand Canal) with the gondolier before setting off. They're regulated by the **Ente Gondola** (© **041-528-5075**; www.gondolavenezia.it), so call if you have any questions or complaints.

And what of the serenading gondolier immortalized in film? An ensemble of accordion player and tenor is so expensive it's shared among several gondolas traveling together. A number of travel agents around town book the evening serenades for 30€ ($53) per person. The number of *gondolieri* willing to brave the winter cold and rain are minimal, although some come out of their wintertime hibernation for the Carnevale period.

There are 12 **gondola stations** around Venice, including Piazzale Roma, the train station, the Rialto Bridge, and Piazza San Marco. There's also a number of smaller stations, with gondoliers standing alongside their sleek 11m (36-ft.) black wonders looking for passengers. They all speak enough English to communicate the necessary details.

Free tours in English are sometimes offered by church volunteers during the high-season months; check at the church.

San Polo 3072 (on Campo dei Frari). © 041-275-0462. Admission 2.50€ ($2.90), or 8€ ($9) on cumulative ticket (see "For Church Fans," above). Mon–Sat 9am–6pm, Sun 1–6pm; winter Mon–Sat 10am–5pm, Sun 1–5pm. *Vaporetto:* San Tomà (walk straight ahead on Calle del Traghetto, then turn right and left across Campo San Tomà; walk as straight ahead as you can, on Ramo Mandoler, then Calle Larga Prima, and turn right when you reach beginning of Salizzada San Rocco).

SS. Giovanni e Paolo This massive Gothic church was built by the Dominican order between the 13th and the early 15th centuries. An unofficial Pantheon
where 25 doges are buried (a number of tombs are part of the unfinished facade),
it's also home to a number of artistic treasures. Visit the **Cappella della Rosario**
off the left transept to see the three restored ceiling canvases by Veronese. In the
right aisle is the recently restored and brilliantly colored *Polyptych of St. Vincent
Ferrer* (ca. 1465), attributed to a young Giovanni Bellini. You'll also see the foot
of St. Catherine of Siena encased in glass.

Adjacent to the church is the **Scuola di San Marco,** an old confraternity-like
association now run as a civic hospital, most noteworthy for its beautiful 15th-
century Renaissance facade. Anchoring the large *campo,* a popular crossroads
for this area of Castello, is a **statue of Bartolomeo Colleoni,** a Renaissance *con-
dottiere,* by Florentine master Andrea Verrocchio; it's one of the world's great
equestrian monuments and Verrocchio's best.

Castello 6363 (on Campo Santi Giovanni e Paolo). ⓒ 041-523-7510 or 041-235-5913. Admission 2€
($2.30). Mon–Sat 7:30am–12:30pm and 3:30–5:30pm. *Vaporetto:* Rialto.

ORGANIZED TOURS

Most of the central travel agencies have posters in their windows advertising
half- and full-day walking tours of the city's sights. Most of these tours are piggy-
backed onto those organized by **American Express** (ⓒ **041-520-0844**) and
should cost the same: about 21€ ($24) for a 2-hour tour and 34€ ($39) for a
full day, per person.

Free organized tours of the Basilica di San Marco and some of the other
churches can be erratic, as they're given by volunteers.

Organized 3- to 4-hour visits to **"The Islands of the Venetian Lagoon"**
include brief stops on Murano, famous throughout the world for the products
of its glass factories; tiny Burano, where lace is the claim to fame; and Torcello,
perhaps the most charming of the islands.

5 Shopping

If you have the good fortune of continuing on to Florence or Rome, then shop
in Venice for clothing, leather goods, and accessories with prudence, as most
things are more expensive here. However, if you happen on something that
strikes your fancy, consider it twice on the spot (not back at your hotel), and
then buy it. In this web of alleys, you may never find that shop again.

A mix of low-end trinket stores and middle-market to upscale boutiques lines
the narrow zigzagging **Mercerie** running north between Piazza San Marco and
the Rialto Bridge. More expensive clothing and gift boutiques make for great
window-shopping on **Calle Larga XXII Marzo,** the wide street that begins west
of Piazza San Marco and wends its way to the expansive Campo Santo Stefano
near the Accademia. The narrow **Frezzeria,** also west of the piazza and not far
from Piazza San Marco, offers a grab bag of bars, souvenir shops, and tony clothing stores.

There are few bargains to be had, and there's nothing to compare with
Florence's outdoor San Lorenzo Market; the nonproduce part of the **Rialto
Market** is as good as it gets, where you'll find cheap T-shirts, glow-in-the-dark
plastic gondolas, and tawdry glass trinkets. Venetians, centuries-old merchants,
aren't known for bargaining. You'll stand a better chance when paying in cash or
buying more than one.

Venice is uniquely famous for several local crafts that have been produced here for centuries and are hard to get elsewhere: the **glassware** from the island of Murano, the delicate **lace** from Burano, and the *carta pesca* (papier-mâché) **Carnevale masks** you'll find in endless *botteghe*, where you can watch artisans paint amid their wares.

Now here's the bad news: There's such an overwhelming sea of cheap glass gewgaws it becomes something of a turn-off (shipping and insurance costs make most things unaffordable; the alternative is to hand-carry something so fragile). There are so few women left on Burano willing to spend countless tedious hours keeping alive the art of lacemaking that the few pieces you'll see not produced by machine in Hong Kong are sold at stratospheric prices; ditto on the truly high-quality glass (although trinkets can be cheap and fun). Still, exceptions are to be found in all of the above, and when you find them you'll know. A discerning eye can cut through the dreck to find some lovely mementos.

For details on taxes and getting them back, see "Fast Facts: Rome," in chapter 21.

6 Venice After Dark

Visit one of the tourist info centers for current English-language schedules of the month's special events. The monthly *Ospite di Venezia* is distributed free or online at **www.unospitedivenezia.it**, and is extremely helpful but usually available only in the more expensive hotels. If you're looking for nocturnal action, you're in the wrong town. Your best bet is to sit in the moonlit Piazza San Marco and listen to the caffès' outdoor orchestras, with the illuminated basilica before you—the perfect opera set.

THE PERFORMING ARTS

Several **churches** regularly host classical music concerts (with an emphasis on the baroque) by local and international artists. This was, after all, the home of Vivaldi, and the **Chiesa di Vivaldi** 👁👁 (officially the **Chiesa Santa Maria della Pietà**) is the most popular venue for the music of Vivaldi and his contemporaries.

A number of other churches and confraternities (like **San Stefano, San Stae,** the **Scuola di San Giovanni Evangelista,** and the **Scuola di San Rocco**) also host concerts, but the Vivaldi church, where the red priest was the choral director, offers perhaps the highest-quality ensembles (with tickets slightly more expensive). If you're lucky, they'll be performing *Le Quattro Staggioni (The Four Seasons)*. Tickets are sold at the church's box office (℗ **041-917-257** or 041-522-6405; www.vivaldi.it) on Riva degli Schiavoni, at the front desk of the Metropole Hotel next door, or at many of the hotels around town; they're usually 25€ ($29) adults or 15€ ($17) students. Information and schedules are available from the tourist office; tickets for most concerts should be bought in advance, but the frequency of concerts means they rarely sell out.

After years of construction, the famous **Teatro La Fenice** 👁👁👁 (San Marco 1965, on Campo San Fantin; ℗ **041-786-562** or 786-580; www.teatrola fenice.it) has finally reopened. In January 1996, the city stood still in shock as Venice's principal stage for world-class opera, music, theater, and ballet went up in flames. Carpenters and artisans were on standby to begin working around the clock to re-create the *teatro* (built in 1836) according to archival designs. Inaugural performances in December 2003 included appearances by Riccardo Muti, musical director of La Scala, and Elton John. However, that was just the inaugural. The theater won't actually host a regular schedule until November 2004 at the earliest—though it is expected to open for visitors to tour in summer 2004.

Until then, the Orchestra and Coro della Fenice are performing, as they have since '96, in a substitute venue—a year-round tentlike structure called the **PalaFenice** (© 041-521-0161) in the unlikely area of the Tronchetto parking facilities near Piazzale Roma, convenient to many *vaporetto* lines. To say it ain't the same as La Fenice is something of an understatement. Decent tickets for the PalaFenice start at about 20€ ($23; at 10€/$12 for those "partially obstructed view" seats), and the box office is open Monday to Friday 9am to 6pm.

BARS & BIRRERIE

The **Devil's Forest Pub,** San Marco 5185, on Calle Stagneri (© 041-520-0623; *vaporetto:* San Marco), offers the outsider an authentic chance to take in the convivial atmosphere and find out where Venetians do hang out. It's popular for lunch with the neighborhood merchants and shop owners and ideal for relaxed socializing over beer and a host of games like backgammon, chess, and Trivial Pursuit. A variety of simple pasta dishes and fresh sandwiches runs 3€ to 6€ ($3.45–$7). It's open daily 10am to 1am.

Bácaro Jazz (© 041-285-249; *vaporetto:* Rialto) is a happening cocktail bar (Bellinis are great) with restaurant seating in the back and tasty Venetian cuisine from 7€ ($8). It's across from the Rialto post office at San Marco 5546, just north of Campo San Bartolomeo (the San Marco side of Rialto Bridge). A mix of jazzy music (a bit too loud), rough plank walls, industrial steel tables, and a corrugated aluminum ceiling, it's open Thursday to Tuesday 11am to 2am (happy hour 2–7:30pm).

With a half dozen beers on tap, **ElMoroPub** at Castello 4531 (Calle delle Rasse; © 041-528-2573) is the biggest draw in town. The crowd can be a bit older; post-university types congregate at the bar. TVs sometimes transmit national soccer or tennis matches, and the management welcomes those who linger, but sensitive nonsmokers won't want to.

Good food at reasonable prices would be enough to regularly pack **Paradiso Perduto,** Cannaregio 2540, on Fondamenta della Misericordia (© 041-720-581; *vaporetto:* Ferrovie), but its biggest draw is the live jazz performed on a small stage several nights a week. Popular with Americans and other foreigners living in Venice, this bar was once largely devoid of tourists, primarily because of its hard-to-find location, but lately it looks as if the word is out. The good selection of well-prepared pizzas and pastas goes for under 8€ ($9); arrive early for a table. It's open Thursday to Tuesday 7pm to 1am and sometimes 2am.

CAFFÈS

Nightlife revolves around the city's many bars/caffès on Piazza San Marco, one of the world's most remarkable piazzas. The epicenter of life in Venice, it's also the most expensive and touristed place to linger over a Campari or cappuccino. The nostalgic 18th-century **Caffè Florian** ⟨⟨, San Marco 56A–59A (© 041-520-5641; www.caffeflorian.com), on the south side of the piazza, is the most famous (closed Wed in winter) and most theatrical inside; have a Bellini (*prosecco* and fresh peach nectar) at the back bar and spend half what you'd pay at an indoor table; alfresco seating is even more expensive when the band plays on but is worth every cent for the million-dollar scenario.

On the opposite side of the square, at San Marco 133–134, is the old-world **Caffè Lavena** (© 041-522-4070; closed Tues in winter). At no. 120 is **Caffè**

> ### ⌐Tips Hangin' In a *Campo*
>
> For just plain hanging out in the late afternoon and early evening, popular squares that serve as meeting points include **Campo San Bartolomeo,** at the foot of the Rialto Bridge, and nearby **Campo San Luca;** you'll see Venetians of all ages milling about engaged in animated conversation, particularly from 5pm till dinnertime. In late-night hours, for low prices and a low level of pretension, I'm fond of **Campo Santa Margherita,** a huge open *campo* about halfway between the train station and Ca' Rezzonico. Look for the popular **Green Pub** (no. 3053, closed Thurs), **Bareto Rosso** (no. 2963, closed Sun), and **Bar Salus** (no. 3112). **Campo Santo Stefano** is also worth a visit, namely to sit and sample the goods at the **Bar/Gelateria Paolin** (no. 2962, closed Fri), one of the city's best ice cream sources. Its runner-up, **Gelateria Nico,** is on the Zattere in Dorsoduro 922, south of the Gallerie dell'Accademia. For occasional evenings of live music or cabaret, or for just a relaxed late-night hangout serving a drink and a bite, consider the ever-popular **Le Bistrot de Venise** (p. 970).

Quadri (© **041-528-9299;** www.quadrivenice.com; closed Mon in winter), with a (pricey) romantic restaurant upstairs where two much-requested tables overlook the piazza. At all spots, a cappuccino, tea, or Coca-Cola at a table will set you back about 5€ ($6). But no one will rush you, and if the sun is warm and the orchestras are playing, I can think of no more beautiful public open-air salon in the world. Around the corner (at no. 11) and in front of the pink-and-white marble Palazzo Ducale with the lagoon on your right is the best deal, **Caffè Chioggia** ✦✦✦ (© **041-523-7404** or 041-528-5011; closed Sun). Come here at midnight and watch the Moors strike the hour atop the Clock Tower from your outside table, while the quartet or pianist plays everything from quality jazz to pop until the wee hours (and without taking a break every 6 min.; they also take requests).

THE GAY & LESBIAN SCENE

There are no gay bars in Venice, but you'll find some in nearby Padua, a lovely old city about 35 minutes from Venice by train (see " A Side Trip to Verona, City of Romeo & Juliet," below; and see *Frommer's Gay & Lesbian Europe*). However, Venice does have a local division of a government-affiliated agency, **Arcigay/Arcilesbica,** Via Andrea Costa 38A in Mestre (© **330-777-838;** www.gay.it or www.azionegayelesbica.it). It serves as a home base for the gay community, with info on AIDS services, gay-friendly accommodations, and such. The best hours to call (it's in Mestre, and hard to find) are Monday 7 to 9pm, and Tuesday or Thursday 9 to 11pm.

DANCE CLUBS

Venice is a quiet town at night and offers little in the line of dance clubs. Evenings are best spent lingering over a late dinner, having a pint in a *birrerie,* nursing a glass of *prosecco* in one of Piazza San Marco's tony outdoor cafes, or enjoying popular after-hours places like **Paradiso Perduto** (see Bars & Birrerie,"

above). Dance clubs barely enjoy their 15 minutes of popularity before changing hands or closing; some of those that have survived are open only in summer.

University-age Venetians tend to frequent the Lido or mainland Mestre, but
if you really need that disco fix, you're best off at **Piccolo Mondo,** Dorsoduro
1056, near the Accademia (© **041-520-0371;** *vaporetto:* Accademia). Billed as
a disco/pub (often with live music), it serves sandwiches during lunch to the
tune of America's latest dance music and offers a happy hour in the late afternoon in winter. But the only reason you'd want to come is if you want a disco
night (summer only); the club is frequented mostly by curious foreigners and
the young to not-so-young Venetians who seek them out. It's open daily: 10am
to 4am in summer, 10am to 4pm and 5 to 8pm in winter.

Another club that seems to be surviving is **Casanova** (© **041-275-0199** or
041-534-7479), near the train station on Lista di Spagna 158a. The bar and
restaurant open at 6pm, but at 10pm Thursday to Sunday, the bar becomes a
disco open until 4am. (The restaurant stays open until around midnight.)
Admission is often free (if you arrive before midnight), but sometimes there's a
5€ ($6) or more cover that includes the first drink. Tuesday is "spritz night" (the
Venetian Campari-and-soda, which adds white wine); Wednesday they play
smash hits; Thursday offers rock, pop, and indie favorites; Friday features salsa
and Latino; and Saturday brings house and hip-hop. Casanova doubles as an
Internet cafe; you can go online daily from 9am to 2am.

7 A Side Trip to Verona, City of Romeo & Juliet ⋆⋆⋆

At 113km (70 miles) west of Venice and 52km (32 miles) west of Vicenza, the
Veneto's next most visited city, **Verona,** is on the far side for a day trip except for
the hardy and tireless. You'll most enjoy it if you can spend a night or 2, as there's
much to be taken in other than its major sites. **Trains** run hourly from Venice
and Vicenza. The fare from Venice to Verona is 9.40€ to 12€ ($11–$14).

To get **downtown from the train station,** walk straight out to the bus island
marked MARCIAPIEDE F (parallel to the station) to catch minibus 72 or 73
(1€/$1.15 tickets at the newsstand in the station or the AMT booth on
"Marciapiede A"). Get off on Via Stella at Via Cappello for the center. Alternatively, over half the buses from the station stop at Piazza Brà, so just peruse the
posted route signs.

A central **tourist office** is at the Scavi Scaglieri on Coritle del Tribunali
(© and fax **045-705-0088;** www.tourism.verona.it or www.verona-apt.net).
Summer hours are Monday to Saturday 9am to 8pm, Sunday 10am to 1pm and
4 to 7pm; winter hours are usually shorter, and it's closed Sunday. Another is at
Via degli Alpini 9, adjacent to the Arena off Piazza Brà (© **045-806-8680;** fax
045-801-0682), open Monday to Saturday 9am to 6pm. A small office is at the
train station (© **045-800-0861**), open Tuesday to Saturday 8am to 7:30pm,
Sunday and Monday 10am to 4pm.

Verona reached a cultural and artistic peak during the 13th and 14th centuries under the puissant and often cruel and quirky della Scala (Scalageri)
dynasty that first took up rule in the 1200s. In 1405, it surrendered to mighty
Venice, which remained in charge (hence the presence of St. Mark's winged lion
about town) until the invasion of Napoléon in 1797. This was Verona's heyday,
and the city's locked-in-time atmosphere of magnificent palazzi, towers,
churches, and *piazze* is testimony to its influence and wealth.

Verona

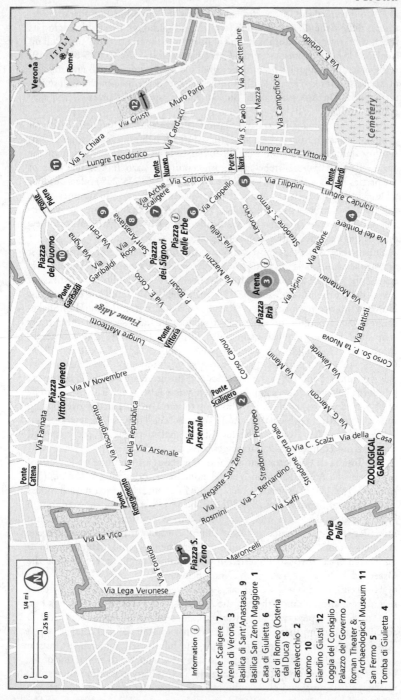

Arche Scaligere **7**
Arena di Verona **3**
Basilica di Sant'Anastasia **9**
Basilica San Zeno Maggiore **1**
Casa di Giulietta **6**
Casi di Romeo (Osteria dal Duca) **8**
Castelvecchio **2**
Duomo **10**
Giardino Giusti **12**
Loggia del Consiglio **7**
Palazzo del Governo **7**
Roman Theater & Archaeological Museum **11**
San Fermo **5**
Tomba di Giulietta **4**

Information ⓘ

ITALY
Verona ● ● Rome

1/4 mi
0.25 km

On the former site of the Roman forum is the city's bustling marketplace, **Piazza delle Erbe** 𝕲, one of Italy's loveliest and (although inevitably edging its way toward tourist-trapdom) still one of its most authentic (closed Sun). Pull up a chair at any of the outdoor cafes—**Caffè Filippini** (no. 26; ℭ **045-800-4549**) is the oldest (although it's been modernized too many times to tell) and still one of the most favored (closed Wed). Another magnet is the hole-in-the-wall stand-up pizzeria, **Da Aldo,** at no. 6. Sicilian Aldo Napoli sells pizza by the slice (closed Wed).

Behind the piazza is **Piazza dei Signori (Piazza Dante),** serene and elegant compared to the bustle of the piazza you've just left behind. Dante, whose 19th-century statue stands in the middle, found exile in Verona as a guest of the Scaligeri family, whose crenellated 13th-century palazzo frames one side of the piazza. The landmark **Antico Caffè Dante** (ℭ **045-595-249**) offers outdoor tables and a chance to sit and take it all in (closed Mon; open in summer to the wee hours). Northeast of the piazza on Via delle Arche Scaligeri are the remark-able **Gothic tombs-on-stilts of the Scaligeri family** 𝕲, which you can view only through the decorative ironwork gates.

But the city is perhaps most famous as the fictional home of history's most famous star-crossed lovers, Romeo and Juliet. There's no doubt Verona's big draw is the **Casa di Giulietta (Juliet's House)** 𝕲, Via Cappello 23, southeast of Piazza delle Erbe (ℭ **045-803-4303**), open Tuesday to Sunday 8am to 7pm. However, no one promises she ever really existed except in the mind of Shake-speare (who, according to some, never set foot in Italy)—even if there really were local feuding families named Del Cappello (Capulet) and Montecchi (Montague). You might not want to pay the 3.10€ ($3.55) adults or 2.10€ ($2.40) students admission to view the spare interior of the 13th-century palazzo (restored in 1996); the ceramics and furniture are authentic of the era but didn't belong to Juliet's family—if there was a Juliet at all. The biggest draw of paying admission is simply the photo-op to stand on the balcony overlooking the courtyard from which the young Veronese allegedly stole a few precious exchanges with her Romeo. The love-struck graffiti plastering the courtyard walls is scrawled in dozens of languages.

The **Tomba di Giulietta (Juliet's Tomb)** is about a 15-minute walk south of here, near the Adige River on Via del Pontiere 5. Admission is 2.60€ ($3) adults, 1.50€ ($1.75) students, but free the first Sunday of each month; hours are Tuesday to Sunday 9am to 6:30pm. The would-be site of the star-crossed lovers' suicide is within the graceful medieval cloisters of the Capuchin monastery of San Francesco al Corso—more evocative than the crowded scene at Juliet's House. The adjacent church is where their secret marriage was said to have taken place. If you're interested in where Romeo might have lived, visit the **Osteria dal Duca** (see "Where to Dine," below).

The well-known opera season takes place every July and August in Verona's magnificent ancient amphitheater, the **Arena** 𝕲𝕲 in Piazza Brà. It's Italy's best known and best preserved after Rome's Colosseum, built about A.D. 100 to accommodate more than 20,000. Admission is 3.10€ ($3.55), and it's open Tuesday to Sunday 9am to 7pm (during the July–Aug summer opera season daily 9am–3:30pm). If you're in town during the season, try to attend one of the live opera performances still put on here. Tickets vary according to seating, weekday versus weekend rates, performance, and cast (*Aïda* is the most sought after, and the most expensive), and are subject to advance booking fees. The cheap seats (unreserved spots on the ancient stone steps) usually cost 22€ ($25) weekdays, 20€ ($22) for Friday or Saturday-night shows. Book via the box office (℧ **045-800-5151;** fax 045-801-3287; www.arena.it) and pick up tickets the day of the performance at Via Dietro Anfiteatro 6b. The cluster of outdoor cafes and trattorias/pizzerias on the western side of the Piazza Brà line a wide marble esplanade called Il Liston; they stay open long after the opera performances end, and some serious après-opera people-watching goes on here.

WHERE TO STAY   The much loved family-run **Locanda Catullo,** Via Catullo 1, 37121 Verona, is just north of the popular Principe V. Mazzini (℧ **045-800-2786**). Doubles without bathroom cost 55€ ($63); those with bathroom 65€ ($75). All rooms are very basic (no phones), but are clean and comfy enough; some have sinks, and some even have small terraces, but it's the well-kept and tasteful ambience that keeps the place full. No credit cards are accepted, and no breakfast is offered (though you can grab a cheap espresso and pastry at the convenient bar downstairs).

Spend a little more and check into the 1996-renovated **Hotel Aurora,** Piazza delle Erbe 2 (℧ **045-594-717** or 045-597-834; fax 045-801-0860), where doubles (with bathroom, A/C, and TV) run 98€ to 130€ ($113–$150). Rates include a nice buffet breakfast. Six rooms overlook the piazza and marketplace, but there's a lovely second-floor terrace for those that don't. American Express, Diners Club, MasterCard, and Visa are accepted.

WHERE TO DINE   A favorite is the welcoming **Osteria del Duca** ⭐⭐, Via Arche Scaligeri 2, east of Piazza dei Signori (℧ **045-594-474**). Legend has it that this colorful 13th-century palazzo was the home of the Mantecchi (Montague) family. There's a daily-changing choice of eight *primi* at 5€ ($6) and 15 *secondi* at 8.50€ ($10), plus an 11€ ($13) fixed-price menu (the English version of which, oddly enough, doesn't include the snail or horsemeat dishes). The unusual *polenta tris* (polenta with Gorgonzola, mushrooms, and salami) and the vegetarian *melanzane con pomodori* (baked eggplant with fresh tomatoes) have long been house specialties. MasterCard and Visa are accepted, and it's open Monday to Saturday 12:30 to 2:30pm and 7 to 10:30pm.

For an unrivaled setting and a great selection of more than 40 varieties, try **Pizzeria Impero,** Piazza dei Signori 8 (℧ **045-803-0160**). A full menu of changing homemade pastas and seafood is available, but you'd never know it from observing the quantity of pizza churned out by the wood-burning stoves. Pizzas range from 6€ to 9€ ($7–$10). You're welcome to linger over a simple but memorable pizza and beer out in one of the world's great piazzas. June to September, it's open daily noon to 2am; the rest of the year, hours are Thursday to Tuesday noon to 3pm and 7pm to midnight. Diners Club, MasterCard, and Visa are accepted.

26

Vienna & Krems

by Beth Reiber

Being in **Vienna** makes me wish I had a time machine so I could go back to the last half of the 18th century, when the city resounded with the music of Haydn and Mozart, and Empress Maria Theresa ruled from Schönbrunn Palace. Or maybe the first decades of the 20th century would be interesting, when Freud was developing his methods of psychoanalysis, Klimt was covering canvases with his Jugendstil figures, and Vienna was whirling to Strauss waltzes.

But I'll settle gladly for Vienna today. Music is still the city's soul, the manifestation of its spirit—from chamber music and opera to jazz and even alternative rock. The Habsburgs, Austria's rulers for 6 centuries, left a rich architectural legacy of magnificent baroque and rococo buildings and palaces, beautifully landscaped gardens, and fabulous art collections from the far corners of their empire.

Vienna, however, isn't resting on past laurels. After the Austro-Hungarian Empire was carved up following World War I, Vienna was a capital without an empire, and when the Iron Curtain descended after World War II, it was suddenly on the edge of western Europe, far from other major capitals. Now, however, Vienna is once again in the center of a unified Europe, and as a springboard for travel to or from Budapest, Prague, and beyond, Vienna has reblossomed into an international city.

For more on Vienna and its environs, see *Frommer's Vienna & the Danube Valley* or *Frommer's Austria*.

1 Essentials

ARRIVING

BY PLANE   The **Vienna International Airport** (℮ 01/7007-0), also known as Schwechat Airport, is 18km (11 miles) southeast of the city center. There's a **tourist information** counter in the arrivals hall, open daily 9am to 7pm. A shuttle bus, the **Vienna Airport Line** (℮ 01/93000-2300; www.oebb.at), departs every 30 minutes for Schwedenplatz in the heart of the city. The trip takes about 20 minutes, and Schwedenplatz is easily connected to the rest of the city via tram, bus, and U-Bahn (subway). Shuttle buses also depart the airport every 30 minutes for the Südbahnhof (a 25-min. trip) and the Westbahnhof (a 40-min. trip), Vienna's two train stations. In any case, the cost of the shuttle to Schwedenplatz or the train stations is 6€ ($6.90) one-way (5€/$5.75 if you have the Vienna Card [see "Vienna Deals & Discounts," p. 1000]).

A cheaper alternative is to take **Schnellbahn (Rapid Transit) 7** from the airport to Wien Mitte, a train/subway station located just east of the Old City. The trip costs 3€ ($3.45) one-way and takes about 25 minutes, with departures every half-hour. But if you're in a hurry, you can take the same trip aboard the

Value Budget Bests

The most wonderful thing you can do for yourself in Vienna is go to a performance at the **Staatsoper (State Opera).** Standing-room tickets start at only 2€ ($2.30), for which you're treated to extravaganzas held on one of Europe's most renowned stages. Even seat tickets aren't prohibitively expensive, starting at 10€ ($12).

The rest of Vienna is affordable, too. All **municipal museums** (including the residences of Mozart, Beethoven, Haydn, and Johann Strauss, and the Historical Museum of the City of Vienna) are free on Friday morning. If you're interested in seeing the famous **Spanish Riding School,** consider going to one of the morning training sessions, when tickets are much cheaper than for actual performances. And if you're willing to stand, you can see the **Vienna Boys' Choir** free. (They perform at Sunday Mass.)

Try to eat at least once at a *Beisl,* a typical blue-collar pub, where you can get hearty home-cooked meals for as little as 11€ ($13). But don't forget Vienna's wonderful **wine cellars,** where you can soak in the atmosphere for the price of a glass of wine, often to the accompaniment of music. And if you want to really save money, eat at a *Würstelstand,* a sidewalk food stand selling various kinds of *Wurst* (sausage) and a roll for less than 3€ ($3.45). They're all around the city and are as much a part of the Viennese scene as the opera house.

City Airport Train (**CAT;** www.cityairporttrain.com), which delivers you to Wien Mitte in 16 minutes for 9€ ($10), with departures every 30 minutes.

Taxis charge about 26€ to 30€ ($30–$35) for the same trip the shuttle buses make. If you make arrangements a day in advance, however, **C & K Airport Service** (© 01/444 44) will deliver you door-to-door to or from the airport for 22€ ($25) per person.

BY TRAIN Vienna has two main train stations, both with currency-exchange counters. Long-distance trains, particularly from Germany, Switzerland, France, Salzburg, and other points west or north, generally arrive at the **Westbahnhof (West Station).** A subway line (U-3) connects the Westbahnhof with Stephansplatz in the center. If you're arriving from the east—from Hungary or Prague—you may arrive at the **Südbahnhof (South Station).** Take tram D from in front of the station if you're heading for the Ring and the city center. Tram 18 travels between the two stations.

It's unlikely you'll arrive at **Franz-Josefs-Bahnhof,** used primarily for local train traffic, but if you do, take tram D for the Ring and the city center. The U-4 Friedensbrücke stop is about a 5-minute walk from the station.

For information on **train schedules,** call © 01/05-1717.

VISITOR INFORMATION

TOURIST OFFICES For a free map, brochures, and details on Vienna (including the current showings and times for the opera, theater, Spanish Riding School, and Vienna Boys' Choir), drop by the main office of **Vienna Tourist Information,** on the corner of Albertinaplatz and Maysedergasse (© 01/24 555; U-Bahn: Stephansplatz), off Kärntner Strasse north of the Staatsoper. It's open daily 9am to 7pm.

Vienna Deals & Discounts

SPECIAL DISCOUNTS If you plan on traveling a lot by public transportation, be sure to buy a **strip ticket**, a **24-hour** or **72-hour ticket**, or even the **Vienna Card**, which for 17€ ($19) allows unlimited transportation on Vienna's subways, buses, and trams for 72 hours. (*E úóñúsÝ* One child under 15 can travel with you for free.) It also gives discounts of 10% to 50% for most of the city's attractions, including Schönbrunn Palace and many museums. You can buy the Vienna Card at major hotels; at Vienna Tourist Information; and at transportation ticket booths at Stephansplatz, Westbahnhof, and other major stations.

Seniors 60 years and older receive discounts to some attractions in Vienna; carry identification to verify your age.

If you're a **student,** you can save 50% or more off the **museum admissions** with an International Student Identity Card (ISIC). If you've arrived in Vienna without an ISIC, you can get one at **STA Travel, Türkenstrasse 6 (© 01/401 48-7608;** U-Bahn: Schottentor), where you can also buy cheap airline and train tickets (for youths under 26). It's open Monday to Friday 9am to 5:30pm.

WORTH A SPLURGE Although it's pricey, you'll find it worth splurging on the longer, 40-room **Grand Tour of Schönbrunn,** Austria's most famous baroque palace. Other attractions worth the high price of admission include the **Kunsthistorisches Museum, Leopold Museum, Hofburg Palace complex,** and **Spanish Riding School's Gala**

A **tourist office** in the arrivals hall at Vienna International Airport is open daily 8:30am to 9pm.

Both Vienna Tourist Information offices will book hotel rooms for a fee of 2.90€ ($3.35). Be sure to pick up the free monthly *Wien-Programm*—it tells what's going on in Vienna's concert halls, theaters, and opera houses. If you're looking for detailed historic information on Vienna's many beautiful buildings, be sure to buy the 3.60€ ($4.15) English-language booklet *Vienna from A to Z.* Its listings are keyed to the unique numbered plaques affixed to the front of every building of historic interest. You'll spot these plaques everywhere: They're heralded by little red-and-white flags in summer.

Although intended more for local citizenry, the **Stadtinformation office,** located in the Rathaus (city hall) with an entrance at Friedrich-Schmidt-Platz (© **01/525 50;** U-Bahn: Rathaus), can answer questions regarding events, theater and concert offerings, museums, and other tourist-related matters; it also stocks brochures and other publications issued by Vienna Tourist Information. It's open Monday to Friday 8am to 6pm.

WEBSITES On the Internet, additional information on Austria in general is available at **www.austria-tourism.at/us**, site of the Austrian National Tourist Office. Information on Vienna is available at **www.info.wien**, site of the Vienna Tourist Board.

CITY LAYOUT

Vienna's **Altstadt (Old City)** is delightfully compact, filled with tiny cobblestone streets leading to majestic squares. In the center is **Stephansplatz,** with Vienna's most familiar landmark, Stephansdom (St. Stephen's Cathedral). From here it's a short walk to the Hofburg (official residence of the Habsburgs) and its many attractions; the Kunsthistorisches Museum (Art History Museum); and the new **MuseumsQuartier Wien,** one of the largest museum complexes in the world and home to the prestigious Leopold Museum and Museum of Modern Art. **Kärntner Strasse,** much of it pedestrian, is the main shopping street, leading from Stephansplatz past the Staatsoper to Karlsplatz.

Circling the Altstadt is the Ring, as Vienna's **Ringstrasse** is commonly called. This impressive circular boulevard, 4km (2½ miles) long and 56m (187 ft.) wide, was built in the mid-1800s along what used to be the city's fortifications (hence its shape as a circle around the Altstadt). Everything inside the Ring is known as the First Bezirk (1st Precinct), denoted by the 1010 postal code in addresses. The rest of Vienna is also divided into precincts.

Trams run along the tree-shaded Ring, which is divided into various sections, including **Opernring** (home of the Staatsoper), **Kärntner-Ring, Burgring** (home of the Hofburg and Kunsthistorisches Museum), and **Schubert Ring. Schönbrunn,** Vienna's top sight, is a few miles southwest of the city center, easily reached by U-Bahn from Karlsplatz. **Mariahilfer Strasse,** lined with department stores, boutiques, and restaurants, is a popular shopping destination for locals; it stretches from the MuseumsQuartier to the Westbahnhof and beyond.

GETTING AROUND

Vienna's transit network consists of five U-Bahn (subway) lines, trams, buses, and several rapid transit and commuter trains. The free map given out by the tourist office shows tram and bus lines, as well as subway stops, although you'll need a magnifying glass to read it. Luckily, most of Vienna's attractions are within walking distance of one another.

For details on Vienna's public transport system, visit the **Informationsdienst der Wiener Verkehrsbetriebe,** in the underground Opernpassage at Karlsplatz, in the U-Bahn station at Stephansplatz, or at the Westbahnhof U-Bahn station. All three are open Monday to Friday 6:30am to 6:30pm, and Saturday, Sunday, and holidays 8:30am to 4pm. The staff can answer questions, such as which bus to take to reach your destination. You can also call ℂ **01/79 09 100.**

A **single ticket** (good for the tram, day and night buses, S-Bahn, or U-Bahn) costs 1.50€ ($1.75) if bought in advance and permits as many transfers as you need to reach your destination as long as you keep moving in the same direction. You can buy advance tickets from machines in U-Bahn stations and at ticket booths or tobacconists. Tickets bought from bus or tram conductors, on the other hand, cost 2€ ($2.30). To save the hassle of buying individual tickets, buy the *Streifenkarte,* a strip ticket with four rides for 6€ ($6.90) or eight rides for 12€ ($13.80). You must buy these tickets in advance from ticket booths at Karlsplatz, Stephansplatz, and other major U-Bahn stations, or from automatic machines at all U-Bahn and train stations (look for the VOR FAHRKARTEN sign).

If you're going to be doing a lot of traveling in 1 day, consider the **Wiener Einkaufskarte (Vienna Shopping Ticket),** valid for as many trips as you wish between 8am and 8pm any day except Sunday and holidays and costing 4€ ($4.60). In addition, there's a **24-hour ticket** for 5€ ($5.75), a **72-hour ticket** for 12€ ($14), and an **8-day pass** for 24€ ($28), which you can use for any 8 days, not necessarily in succession.

For all tickets, you must validate them yourself by inserting them into machines at the entries of S-Bahn and U-Bahn platforms or on buses and trams. Children up to 6 can travel free, while those 7 to 14 travel for half fare, except on Sunday, holidays, and Vienna school holidays, when they travel free.

There are a couple other options worth considering. If you're going to be in Vienna at least 3 days and plan on seeing the major sights, consider buying the **Vienna Card** (see "Vienna Deals & Discounts," p. 1000). Although pricey, the **Vienna Line Hop-On, Hop-Off** is a private bus line that travels three routes to most of the city's major sights, including the State Opera and St. Stephen's Cathedral and outlying sights like the Prater amusement park, KunstHausWien, and Schönbrunn and Belvedere palaces. Guided commentary is provided between each of the 13 stops, and you can get off and on as often as you like. Tickets cost 20€ ($23) for 1 day. For more details, see "Organized Tours," later in this chapter.

BY U-BAHN   The most important U-Bahn line for visitors is U-4, which stops at Schwedenplatz and Karlsplatz before continuing to Kettenbrückengasse (site of Vienna's outdoor market and weekend flea market) and Schönbrunn. U-2 travels around part of the Ring (with plans to extend it east past the Danube in the next few years), while U-1 and U-3 have stations at Stephansplatz (U-3 connects the Westbahnhof with Stephansplatz). U-4, U-2, and U-1 all converge at Karlsplatz.

BY TRAM   Although the U-Bahn and buses have taken over most of the tram routes, trams are still heavily used for traveling around the Ring (trams 1 and 2) and for transportation between the Südbahnhof and the Ring (tram D). Tram 18 travels between the Westbahnhof and the Südbahnhof.

BY BUS   Buses crisscross the entire city. However, only 1A, 2A, and 3A (mostly minibus size) travel inside the Ring, Monday to Saturday. Twenty-one buses operate throughout the night from Schwedenplatz, Oper, or Schottentor to the suburbs (including Grinzing), with departures every half-hour.

BY TAXI   The base price is 2.50€ ($2.90), plus .90€ ($1.05) for each extra kilometer. From 11pm to 6am and all day Sunday and holidays, the base fare is 2.60€ ($3), plus 1€ ($1.15) for each additional kilometer. If you need a taxi, you can call © **31 300,** 40 100, or 60 160 (2€/$2.30 surcharge). Luggage is 1€ ($1.15) extra.

BY BICYCLE   There are more than 650km (403 miles) of marked bike paths in Vienna. Be sure to pick up the brochure *Tips für Radfahrer* at the Vienna Tourist Office. Although written in German only, it contains easy-to-understand maps with suggestions for routes. Keep in mind that you can take bikes along for .80€ (90¢) in specially marked cars of the U-Bahn Monday to Friday 9am to 3pm and 6:30pm to the end of the day, Saturday after 9am, and all day Sunday and holidays.

The most popular places for bike rentals and tours are at the amusement center of Prater and along the banks of the Donaukanal (Danube Canal); several bike-rental agencies at both these spots are open from about April to October. One of the best is **Pedal Power,** Ausstellungsstrasse (© **01/729 72 34;** www. pedalpower.at; U-Bahn: Prater). It goes the extra mile of offering bike delivery and pickup, a free map with suggested routes, and English folders. High-quality

Vienna Metro

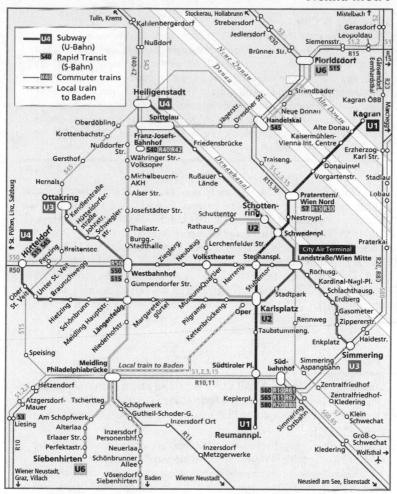

21-gear bikes rent for 32€ ($37) for 24 hours if they're delivered, 27€ ($31) if you pick them up at the shop. Discounts are offered for extra days and families.

BY RENTAL CAR Car-rental agencies include **Avis,** Opernring 3–5 (© 01/587 62 41; U-Bahn: Karlsplatz), and **Hertz,** Kärntner-Ring 17 (© 01/512 86 77; U-Bahn: Stephansplatz). Prices vary, but expect to pay about 106€ to 118€ ($122–$136) for a 1-day rental of a compact car, with unlimited mileage, tax, and insurance. Weekend rates are always lower than weekday rates, promotional bargains are almost always available, and smaller independent companies might offer better deals. **Kalal,** for example, at Rennweg 73 (© 01/715 5925), offers a 1-day rental of a Citroën or Renault with unlimited kilometers and 20% tax starting at 55€ ($63). It pays, therefore, to shop around.

Remember: You get the best deal if you arrange the rental before leaving home.

Country & City Codes

The **country code** for Austria is **43**. The **city code** for Vienna is **1**; use this code when you're calling from outside Austria. If you're within Austria but not in Vienna, use **01**. If you're calling within Vienna, simply leave off the code and dial only the regular phone number. If you come across a phone number with a dash at the end (such as 51553-0), it indicates an extension; treat it as you would any number and simply dial the whole number.

Although every effort has been made to be up-to-date, some phone numbers might no longer be current when you arrive. Call **118 877** for phone numbers in Vienna.

Keep in mind that parking, especially in or near the First Precinct, is practically nonexistent, except in parking garages. Convenient garages in the First Precinct are **Parkgarage Am Hof** (© 01/533 55 71), **Parkgarage Freyung** (© 01/535 04 50), and **Tiefgarage Kärntner Strasse** (© 01/587 17 97). All are open 24 hours and charge about 2.20€ ($2.55) per hour; the U-Bahn stop for all is Stephansplatz. An alternative is to leave your car at the **Park & Ride U-3 Erdberg parking lot,** at the U-3 Erdberg station at the corner of Franzosengraben and Erdbergstrasse (© 01/796 77 17-11); it's open 24 hours and costs only 2.50€ ($2.90) for the entire day. The U-3 subway gets you to the city center in 7 minutes.

FAST FACTS: Vienna

American Express An office at Kärntner Strasse 21–23, 1010 Wien (© 01/ 51 540; U-Bahn: Stephansplatz), is open Monday to Friday 9am to 5:30pm and Saturday 9am to noon. Its cash machine for American Express cards is open 24 hours.

Banks Vienna's main banks within the Ring are open Monday to Friday 8am to 3pm (to 5:30pm Thurs); branches are usually closed for lunch 12:30 to 1:30pm. There are also money exchange counters at the Westbahnhof, open daily 7am to 10pm, and at the Südbahnhof, open daily 6:30am to 9pm, where you can get cash advances as well from Diners Club, Master-Card, and Visa cards. There are ATMs for both MasterCard and Visa at both train stations. You can also exchange money at Intropa, a travel agency located in the tourist office at Albertinaplatz (see "Visitor Information," above) and open the same hours.

Business Hours Shop hours are generally Monday to Friday from 9 or 9:30am to 6:30 or 7pm and Saturday from 9am to 5 or 6pm. Shops outside the city center might close for lunch from noon to 2 or 3pm.

Consulates Be sure to call your consulate in advance before making a special trip, because certain consulate sections might have varying open hours. The hours given here are for passport holders of each respective consulate. If you have questions or problems regarding American passports, contact the consulate of the **United States,** in the Marriott Hotel at Gartenbaupromenade 2 (© 01/313 39; U-Bahn: Stadtpark), open Monday to Friday 8:30am to 5pm. The consular and passport section of the embassy of **Canada,** Laurenzerberg 2 (② **01/531 38-3000;** U-Bahn: Schwedenplatz), is open Monday to Friday 8:30am to 12:30pm and 1:30 to 3:30pm. The consulate of the **United Kingdom,** Jauresgasse 10 (② **01/716 13 5151;** tram: 71 to Unteres Belvedere), is open Monday to Friday 10am to noon and (for British passport holders) 2 to 4pm. The consular and passport section of the embassy of **Australia,** Mattiellistrasse 2 (② **01/506 74;** U-Bahn: Karlsplatz), is open Monday to Friday 9am to 12:30pm and 2 to 4pm.

Currency In 2002, Vienna adopted the **euro** (€) for its currency. At press time, $1 = .87€, or 1€ = $1.15.

Dentists For a list of English-speaking dentists, contact one of the consulates above. If you need dental assistance on a weekend or during the night, call ② **01/512 20 78** for a recorded message listing dentists with weekend or night emergency service.

Doctors The consulates above have lists of English-speaking doctors; or call the **Doctors' Association** at ② **1771** for a referral. If you need an emergency doctor during the night (daily 7pm–7am) or on a weekend, call ② **141.** You can also call **First Care,** inside the Ring at Helferstorferstrasse 2 (② **01/531 16-0;** U-Bahn: Schottentor), a 24-hour doctor service. Call to make an appointment; doctors will also visit your hotel.

Emergencies Dial ② **122** for the **fire** department, ② **133** for the **police,** ② **144** for an **ambulance,** ② **141** for an **emergency doctor** weekends or evenings, and ② **1550** for a recorded message in German to find out which **pharmacy** has night hours. For medical emergencies, see "Dentists" or "Doctors," above, or "Hospitals," below.

Holidays Vienna celebrates New Year's Day (Jan 1), Epiphany (Jan 6), Easter Monday, Labor Day (May 1), Ascension Day, Whitmonday, Corpus Christi, Feast of the Assumption (Aug 15), Austria National Day (Oct 26), All Saints' Day (Nov 1), Feast of the Immaculate Conception (Dec 8), and Christmas (Dec 25–26).

Hospitals The general hospital is the **Neue Allgemeine Krankenhaus,** at Währinger Gürtel 18–20 (② **01/40400-0;** U-Bahn: U-6 to Michelbeuern/ Allgemeine Krankenhaus). Otherwise, free first-aid treatment is available 24 hours at the **Krankenhaus der Barmherzigen Brüder,** Grosse Mohren-Gasse 9 (② **01/21 12 10;** tram: 21). A hospital to serve primarily needy people, it also dispenses medications free of charge.

Internet Access One of the most convenient places for Internet surfing and checking e-mail is the **BIGnet.cafe,** with two locations in the Altstadt: Hoher Markt 8–9 (② **01/533 29 39;** U-Bahn: Stephansplatz), and Kärntner Strasse 61 (② **01/503 98 44;** U-Bahn: Oper). Both are open daily 10am to midnight and charge 1.50€ ($1.75) for 10 minutes and 5.90€ ($6.80) for 1 hour. A third BIGnet.cafe is located just off Mariahilferstrasse at Theobaldgasse 19 (② **01/205 06;** U-Bahn: Volkstheater), open the same hours and charging only 2.60€ ($3) for a minimum of 50 minutes. A drawback is that you must pay in advance for your minutes, and only credit is given for unused time; be conservative in your estimate and then pay more if necessary. Finally, **Speednet-Café,** in the Westbahnhof (② **01/892**

56 66; U-Bahn: Westbahnhof), charges 1.30€ ($1.50) for 10 minutes or 5.80€ ($6.65) for 1 hour; it's open Monday to Saturday 7am to midnight and Sunday 8am to midnight.

Laundry Ask the proprietor of your hotel for directions to the nearest self-service laundry. Otherwise, a convenient coin laundry is the **Münzwäscherei Margaretenstrasse,** Margaretenstrasse 52 (℡ 01/587 04 73; bus: 13A or 59A), open Monday to Friday 7am to 6pm and Saturday 8 to 11am. It costs 10.40€ ($12) to wash and dry 6 kilograms (13½ lb.) of laundry here, including detergent.

Mail Mail boxes are yellow in Austria. Most post offices in Vienna are open Monday to Friday 8am to noon and 2 to 6pm. The post office at Westbahnhof is open daily 7am to 10pm. The main post office, **Hauptpostamt 1010,** open 24 hours daily for long-distance phone calls, telegrams, and stamps, is in the heart of the city inside the Ring at Fleischmarkt 19, Vienna 1010 (℡ 01/51 509; U-Bahn: Schwedenplatz). If you don't know where you'll be staying in Vienna, you can have your mail sent here *Poste Restante.* Postcards sent airmail to North America cost 1.25€ ($1.45), as do airmail letters weighing up to 20 grams.

Tax Government tax and service charge are already included in restaurant and hotel bills. If you've bought goods for more than 75€ ($67) in any one store on a given day, you're entitled to a partial refund of the **value-added tax (VAT).** For details, see "Shopping," later in this chapter.

Telephone It costs .12€ (14¢) to make a 1-minute **local phone call,** but you must insert a minimum of .20€ (23¢) to place the call. Insert several coins—.10€, .20€, .50€, 1€, and 2€ coins are accepted—to prevent being cut off; unused coins will be returned at the end of the call.

Hotels add a surcharge to calls made from their rooms, so you're best off going elsewhere to make **long-distance calls.** At a pay phone, it costs .38€ (45¢) per minute to call the United States. Even cheaper are private companies offering long-distance service. At the **BIGnet.cafe,** for example (see above), you can call the States for .21€ (24¢) per minute. An alternative is to buy a **telephone card,** available at any post office in values of 3.60€ ($4.15) and 6.90€ ($7.95), which you can use in special phones found virtually everywhere (sometimes it's difficult nowadays to find a phone that accepts coins).

Tipping A 15% service charge is included in restaurant bills, but it's customary to round off to the nearest 1€ ($1.15) on bills under 10€ ($12). For more expensive meals, add 10%. The same rule applies to taxi drivers. Porters receive 1.50€ ($1.75) per bag.

2 Affordable Places to Stay

The largest concentration of budget accommodations is near the Westbahnhof, west of the Ring, and in the Altstadt. The most expensive lodgings are those inside the Ring in the old city center. The recommendations below include rooms in private homes, pensions (usually cheaper than hotels and sometimes cheaper than homes), and hotels.

Remember, if the accommodations are full, the **Vienna Tourist Information offices** will book a room for 2.90€ ($3.35), including rooms in private homes. You can also book a room here by phone or Internet (ⓒ **01/24 555;** www.wien. info). The busiest seasons in Vienna are May to mid-June; August and September; and the Christmas, New Year's, and Easter holidays. Reserve well in advance for visits during these times. Note, too, that most hotels have higher rates during these peak times, reflected in the range of prices given for each hotel below.

Note: You'll find the city-center lodging choices below plotted on the map on p. 1020.

PRIVATE HOMES
INSIDE THE RING

Adele Grün On the third floor of an elegant older building, the rooms are comfortable, pleasant, and clean. One has its own tub and two sinks; another can sleep up to four. Frau Grün, in her late 80s, speaks English and is friendly; she requests that people stay a minimum of 2 nights. No breakfast is served, but there are plenty of cafes nearby.

Gonzagagasse 1 (just off Franz-Josefs-Kai), Apt. 19, 1010 Wien. ⓒ **01/533 25 06.** 4 units, none with bathroom. 40€ ($46) single; 80€ ($92) double. Rates include showers. No credit cards. U-Bahn: U-3 from Westbahnhof to Stephansplatz, then U-1 from Stephansplatz to Schwedenplatz. Tram: D from Südbahnhof to Oper, then tram 1 or 2 to Salztorbrücke. *In room:* No phone.

NEAR THE WESTBAHNHOF

Barbara Koller This cheerful private home has its own stairway up to the first floor—look for the iron gate. The rooms wrap around an inner courtyard; they're large and spotless, with sturdy old-fashioned furniture. Although the charges are a bit higher than those at other nearby private homes, keep in mind that all rooms here have bathrooms and that breakfast is included.

Schmalzhofgasse 11 (10-min. walk from train station, near Mariahilfer Strasse), 1060 Wien. ⓒ/fax **01/597 29 35.** 5 units. 23€ ($32) per person. Rates include continental breakfast. No credit cards. U-Bahn: U-3 from Westbahnhof to Zieglergasse (take Webgasse exIt). Tram: 18 from Südbahnhof to Westbahnhof. *In room:* Fridge (some rooms), hair dryer, safe.

Gally Apartments 🛆 *(Kids* Frau Gally and her son, Martin, both of whom speak good English, offer a variety of clean and very nice apartments, all with equipped kitchens (including fridge and coffeemaker). Some are large enough for families with children. Bonuses are the free city map, museum leaflet, and program of events placed in each room, and the Gallys are also happy to answer sightseeing questions.

Arnsteingasse 25 (off Mariahilfer Strasse, 10-min. walk southwest of train station), Apt. 10, 1150 Wien. ⓒ **01/892 90 73.** Fax 01/893 10 28. www.gally.biz. 14 units, 2 with shower only, 12 with bathroom. 30€ ($35) single with shower, 37€ ($43) single with bathroom; 44€ ($51) double with shower, 54€ ($62) double with bathroom; 60€ ($69) triple with shower, 69€–75€ ($79–$86) triple with bathroom. No credit cards. Parking 5€ ($5.75). Tram: 52 or 58 from Westbahnhof to Kranzgasse. *In room:* Satellite TV, kitchenette, hair dryer, radio.

K. & T. Boardinghouse 🛆 *(Finds* On one of Vienna's main shopping streets, not far from the MuseumsQuartier, this third-story walkup has been lovingly restored and decorated by owners Kaled and Tina, who speak excellent English and are happy to give sightseeing tips. Upon your arrival, they'll give you a city map and advice on what to do and how to get there. The baroque-style rooms (each one unique and all nonsmoking) with high ceilings and parquet floors are spacious enough for four persons and are thoughtfully furnished with extras like

> (Value) **Getting the Best Deal on Accommodations**
>
> - Be aware that accommodations outside the Ring are less expensive than those in the Altstadt.
> - Book directly with the hotel, thereby avoiding the 2.90€ ($3.35) booking fee charged by the tourist office.
> - Take a room without a private bathroom, but note that some places charge extra for showers in communal washrooms.
> - Keep in mind that some rates include breakfast and others don't— if you like to start the day with a big meal, the room-only rate might end up costing you more than a rate that includes a shower and breakfast.
> - Note that accommodations offering cooking facilities can help you save money on dining bills.
> - Take advantage of off-season rates offered by some hotels and pensions, generally November to March (excluding the Christmas holidays).
> - Ask whether a surcharge is added to local and long-distance phone calls.

guest slippers and plants; coffee pots and hair dryers are available. The only drawback is a sex shop on the first floor, which is open only during the day.

Mariahilfer Strasse 72 (a 10-min. walk east from the Westbahnhof), 1070 Wien. ☎ 01/523 29 89. Fax 01/522 03 45. www.kaled.at. 4 units, 3 with bathroom. 50€ ($58) single without bathroom, 55€ ($63) single with bathroom; 55€ ($63) double without bathroom, 65€ ($75) double with bathroom; 85€ ($98) triple with bathroom; 105€ ($121) quad with bathroom. Rates include showers. No credit cards. U-Bahn: U-3 from Westbahnhof to Neubaugasse. Bus: 13A from Südbahnhof to Neubaugasse. **Amenities:** Laundry facilities (12€/$14 per load washed and dried, including detergent); computer with free Internet access. *In room:* Cable TV, no phone.

Rooms & Apartments Lauria   People who don't like living in someone's house might prefer staying here, since Frau Lauria lives in a separate apartment in the same building. The atmosphere is laid-back, the rooms are cozy, and guests have access to a fully equipped communal kitchen. The two- and three-room apartments each sleep four to eight. For young travelers counting their pennies, Frau Lauria offers simpler accommodations in the same building (rooms with bunk beds at 36€/$41 for two and 48€/$55 for three). Be sure to call first.

Kaiserstrasse 77, Apt. 8 (15-min. walk north of Westbahnhof), 1070 Wien. ☎ 01/522 25 55. www.lauria-vienna.at. 8 units, 3 with shower only; 2 apts. 36€ ($41) single without bathroom; 36€–46€ ($41–$53) double without bathroom, 62€ ($71) double with shower; 63€ ($72) triple without bathroom, 75€ ($86) triple with shower; 80€ ($92) quad without bathroom, 92€ ($106) quad with shower; 120€ ($138) apt for 4. Rates include showers. MC, V. U-Bahn: U-6 from Westbahnhof to Burggasse/Stadthalle. Tram: 5 from West-bahnhof or Franz-Josefs-Bahnhof to Burggasse. Bus: 13A from Südbahnhof to Kellermann Gasse, then 48A to Kaiserstrasse. *In room:* TV, no phone.

NEAR THE NASCHMARKT & KARLSPLATZ

Hilde Wolf ✦ *Kids*   Elderly English-speaking Frau Wolf offers rooms literally large enough to dance in, with high ceilings and comfortable fin-de-siècle furniture. One room boasts a 120-year-old tiled oven. Frau Wolf, a retired teacher who loves children, welcomes families (she will even babysit), serves a lavish breakfast, and says that readers of this book can ask for second helpings of coffee, bread, butter, and marmalade.

Schleifmühlgasse 7 (few min. walk from Karlsplatz), 1040 Wien. ℂ **01/586 51 03**. 4 units, none with bathroom 33€ ($38) single; 48€ ($55) double; 66€ ($76) triple; 88€ ($101) quad. Rates include continental breakfast and showers. No credit cards. U-Bahn: U-1, U-2, or U-4 to Karlsplatz. Tram: 6 from Westbahnhof to Eichenstrasse, then 62 to Paulanergasse; or D from Südbahnhof or Franz-Josefs-Bahnhof to Oper, then 62 or 65 to Paulanergasse or bus 59A to Schleifmühlgasse. *In room:* No phone.

Renate Halper 🐾 Renate Halper is an outgoing, caring woman who speaks English fluently and offers a nicely furnished two-bedroom apartment with all the comforts, including a well-equipped kitchen, bathroom, and balcony. She prefers that guests stay at least 3 nights. The first telephone number below is her cellphone number.

Straussengasse 5 (less than 12-min. walk from the city center), 1050 Wien. ℂ **0664/180 60 38** or **01/586 31 38**. 1 apt. 35€ ($40) per person. Rates include breakfast. No credit cards. U-Bahn: U-4 to Pilgramgasse; or U-3 from Westbahnhof to Neubaugasse, then bus 13A to Ziegelofen Gasse. Bus: 13A from Südbahnhof to Ziegelofen Gasse. *In room:* Cable TV, no phone.

HOTELS & PENSIONS
INSIDE THE RING

City This small pension, with a great location just a few minutes' walk from Stephansdom, is on the third floor (mezzanine level) of the house where author Franz Grillparzer was born in 1791. The rooms are rather plain and unimaginative but offer all the basic comforts; note that a room with a double bed costs more than a twin room with two single beds. The tiny breakfast room is decorated with Klimt reprints; you can fuel up on the all-you-can-eat breakfast served until a late 11am. (It can also be delivered to your room.)

Bauernmarkt 10 (just west of Stephansplatz), 1010 Wien. ℂ **01/533 95 21**. Fax 01/535 52 16. www.city pension.at. 19 units. 55€–58€ ($63–$67) single; 72€–85€ ($83–$98) double. Extra person 30€ ($35). Rates include buffet breakfast. AE, DC, MC, V. U-Bahn: U-1 or U-3 to Stephansplatz. Tram: D from Südbahnhof to Oper, then bus 3A to Stephansplatz. **Amenities:** Restaurant (in nearby building). *In room:* Satellite TV, minibar, hair dryer, safe, radio.

Dr. Geissler This pension, with a reception area on the eighth floor, has grown over the years, adding more rooms on more floors. The few rooms in the oldest, eighth-floor section have the best views—you can even see the towers of Stephansdom. The rooms are simple and slightly behind the times in decor. The small dining area offers snacks as well as meals that can be ordered in advance.

Postgasse 14 (around the corner from the main post office, 6-min. walk from Stephansplatz), 1010 Wien. ℂ **01/533 28 03**. Fax 01/533 26 35. www.hotelpension.at/dr-geissler. 32 units; 5 with shower only, 24 with bathroom. 32€–48€ ($37–$55) single without bathroom, 39€–68€ ($45–$78) single with shower, 47€–76€ ($54–$87) single with bathroom; 43€–65€ ($49–$75) double without bathroom, 45€–77€ ($52–$89) double with shower, 58€–90€ ($67–$104) double with bathroom. Extra person 20€ ($23). Rates include buffet breakfast and showers. AE, DC, MC, V. U-Bahn: U-1 or U-4 to Schwedenplatz. Tram: 1 or 2 to Schwedenplatz. *In room:* Cable TV, radio.

WEST OF THE RING

Adria Near the university, this first-floor pension with high-ceilinged rooms is simple and somewhat dowdy but clean. It's owned by the English-speaking Mr. Hamde, a Jordanian who now has Austrian citizenship. The buffet breakfast is all-you-can-eat. Mr. Hamde also rents out an apartment near the Südbahnhof and Belvedere; it comes complete with bathroom, kitchen, phone, and cable TV, and costs 36€ to 47€ ($41–$54) for two and 50€ ($58) for three.

Wickenburggasse 23 (northwest of the Ring, 20-min. walk from the city center), 1080 Wien. ℂ **01/402 02 38** or 01/408 39 06. Fax 01/408 39 06-26. reception@hotelpensionadria.com. 14 units, 2 with shower only, 12 with bathroom. 38€–45€ ($44–$52) single with shower, 48€–56€ ($55–$64) single with bathroom; 58€–79€ ($67–$91) double with bathroom; 73€–99€ ($84–$114) triple. Rates include buffet breakfast and showers. MC, V. Tram: D from Südbahnhof to Schottentor or 5 from Westbahnhof or Franz-Josefs-Bahnhof to Lange Gasse. *In room:* Cable TV, fridge, radio.

Astra 🌟 *(Kids)* The rooms in this first-floor pension are clean and quiet with modern furnishings (all but one face away from the street). The manager is the friendly English-speaking Gaby Brekoupil, who goes out of her way to make guests feel welcome. The apartments come with small kitchenettes, making them especially good for families or longer stays.

Alserstrasse 32, 1090 Wien. ℂ **01/402 43 54** or 01/408 22 70. Fax 01/402 46 62-46. www.hotelpension astra.com. 17 units, 2 with shower only, 15 with bathroom; 4 apts. 40€–43€ ($46–$49) single with shower, 58€–60€ ($67–$69) single with bathroom; 58€ ($67) double with shower, 75€–90€ ($86–$103) double with bathroom; 110€ ($127) apt for 3, 130€ ($150) apt for 4. Rates include buffet breakfast. Crib available. Winter discounts available. MC, V. U-Bahn: U-6 from Westbahnhof to Alserstrasse. Tram: 5 from Franz-Josefs-Bahnhof to Spittalgasse/Alserstrasse. Bus: 13A from Südbahnhof to Skodagasse. *In room:* Cable TV, fridge (some rooms).

Kugel *(Value)* The same family has owned this 140-year-old hotel since it opened. A 20-minute walk west of the MuseumsQuartier, it offers a variety of rooms, some small and simple without showers or toilets (referred to by the hotel as "backpacker specials"), and others newly decorated with canopy beds. A few rooms are large enough for four or five people. In July and August, room specials are sometimes offered over the hotel's website.

Siebensterngasse 43/Neubaugasse 46, 1070 Wien. ℂ **01/523 33 55.** Fax 01/523 33 55-5. www.hotel kugel.at. 37 units, 16 with shower only, 21 with bathroom. 33€–35€ ($38–$40) single without bathroom, 43€–46€ ($49–$53) single with shower, 55€–75€ ($63–$86) single with bathroom; 45€–47€ ($52–$54) double without bathroom, 66€–95€ ($76–$109) double with bathroom. Rates include continental breakfast and showers. No credit cards. Closed Jan 7–Feb 10. Tram: 18 from Westbahnhof, then 49 to Neubaugasse; or D from Franz-Josefs-Bahnhof to Westbahnstrasse/Kaiserstrasse, then 49 two stops to Neubaugasse. Bus: 13A from Südbahnhof to Siebensterngasse. **Amenities:** Small bar. *In room:* Satellite TV, minibar (some rooms), radio.

Lindenhof 🌟 This 25-year-old pension is on a quiet road just a few minutes' walk from Mariahilfer Strasse, Vienna's popular shopping street. The new MuseumsQuartier is also nearby. The owner is George Gebrael, an Armenian with Austrian citizenship who's married to a Bulgarian. He speaks seven languages, English among them; his son, Keram, and daughter, Zarek, who attended an international school taught in English, also work here. The long corridor of this second-floor pension (with elevator) is filled with massive plants. The rooms are of various sizes and in various styles: Some are quite spacious and old-fashioned, with super-high ceilings and beautiful wooden floors, and some are smaller, with modern furniture. A few bathroomless rooms even have balconies.

Lindengasse 4, 1070 Wien. ℂ **01/523 04 98.** Fax 01/523 73 62. pensionlindenhof@yahoo.com. 19 units, 6 with bathroom. 29€ ($33) single without bathroom, 36€ ($41) single with bathroom; 49€ ($56) double without bathroom, 65€ ($75) double with bathroom; 73€ ($84) triple without bathroom, 97€ ($116) triple with bathroom; 97€ ($112) quad without bathroom, 129€ ($148) quad with bathroom. Showers 2€ ($2.30). Rates include continental breakfast. No credit cards. U-Bahn: U-3 from Westbahnhof to Neubaugasse (take the Stiftgasse exit). Bus: 13A from Südbahnhof to Kirchengasse. *In room:* No phone.

Wild This pension opened more than 30 years ago with only one bed but now covers several floors and is managed by the original owner's son, English-speaking Peter Wild. Some rooms have been upgraded to equal those in much pricier hotels, with computer outlets, modern tiled bathrooms, and comfortable beds, though simpler rooms are also available. Three apartments with kitchens are available in buildings close by, for 72€ ($83) for two. If you reserve by phone, try to do so between 6am and 10pm European time, or reserve by fax or e-mail.

Lange Gasse 10 (a 10-min. walk from the Ring), 1080 Wien. © 01/406 51 74. Fax 01/402 21 68. www. pension-wild.com. 24 units, 5 with shower only, 14 with bathroom. 37€ ($43) single without bathroom, 45€ ($52) single with shower, 65€ ($75) single with bathroom; 45€ ($52) double without bathroom, 59€ ($68) double with shower, 89€ ($102) double with bathroom. Rates include buffet breakfast. DC, MC, V. U-Bahn: U-3 from Westbahnhof to Volkstheater. Bus: 13A from Südbahnhof to Piaristengasse. *In room:* Cable TV (some rooms), minibar (some rooms).

NEAR THE WESTBAHNHOF

Hostel Ruthensteiner ⭑ This friendly hostel, just a 3-minute walk from the Westbahnhof and run by Erin and Walter Ruthensteiner (Erin is American), is better than most, offering singles, doubles, four- and five-bedded rooms, and dorm rooms, all with sinks, lockers, and bedside reading lamps (and all nonsmoking). You can cook your own food in the kitchen; even better is the outdoor brick patio where you can barbecue, eat, and play chess with oversize figures. There's no age limit or curfew, and youth-hostel cards are not required.

Robert-Hamerling-Gasse 24, 1150 Wien. © 01/893 42 02. Fax 01/893 27 96. www.hostelruthensteiner.com. 24 units, none with bathroom; 30 dorm beds. 24€ ($28) single; 40€ ($46) double; 14€ ($16) per person in multi-bedded room; 13€ ($15) dorm bed (using your own sheets or sleeping bag). Breakfast 2.80€ ($3.20). Sheets 1.50€ ($1.75) extra. Rates include showers. Winter discounts available. AE, MC, V. U-Bahn: U-6 from Franz-Josefs-Bahnhof to the Westbahnhof. Tram: 18 from the Südbahnhof or 5 from Franz-Josefs-Bahnhof to the Westbahnhof. **Amenities:** Laundry facilities; nonsmoking rooms; 2 computers with Internet access. *In room:* No phone.

Wombat's City Hostel *(Value)* This huge, brightly painted facility, just a 5-minute walk from the Westbahnhof, attracts young people in droves with its varied facilities, including rental bikes and in-line skates. In addition to arranging walking tours and day trips, the hotel is also convenient for those wishing to travel onward to Budapest—a bus departs from the hotel for the Hungarian capital every day in summer. In addition to rooms sleeping three to six persons, there are also 19 double rooms, affording more privacy than most hostels. Unusual for these rates, all rooms have bathrooms. The sheer size of this place, however, coupled with its dormitory atmosphere, may prompt travelers seeking quietude to look elsewhere.

Grangasse 6, 1150 Wien. © 01/897 23 36. Fax 01/897 25 77. www.wombats.at. 75 units, all with bathroom. 42€ ($48) double; 16€ ($18) per person in multi-bedded room. Breakfast 3.50€ ($4). No credit cards. U-Bahn: U-6 from Franz-Josefs-Bahnhof to the Westbahnhof. Tram: 18 from the Südbahnhof or 5 from Franz-Josefs-Bahnhof to the Westbahnhof. **Amenities:** Bar; rental bikes and skates; laundry facilities; computers with Internet access. *In room:* No phone.

WORTH A SPLURGE

Aviano ⭑ This centrally located pension, between Stephansplatz and the Staatsoper, is owned by the Pertschy family (see below) and offers elegant rooms decorated in Old Vienna Biedermeier style but with all the modern conveniences. Some rooms even have hot plates, and others feature double-paned windows facing Kärntner Strasse. Babysitting is available (if requested in advance). The reception area is on the fourth floor and serviced by an elevator.

Marco-d'Aviano-Gasse 1 (off Kärntner Strasse), 1010 Wien. © 01/512 83 30. Fax 01/512 83 30-6. www. pertschy.com. 17 units. 72€–90€ ($83–$104) single; 102€–130€ ($117–$150) double. Rates include buffet breakfast. AE, DC, MC, V. U-Bahn: U-3 from Westbahnhof to Stephansplatz. Tram: D from Südbahnhof or Franz-Josefs-Bahnhof to Oper. *In room:* Satellite TV, dataport, minibar, hair dryer, radio, bidet.

Pertschy 🕸🕸 A wonderful splurge inside the Ring not far from the Hofburg and Stephansplatz, the Pertschy occupies the first several floors of a 1723 palace built for a count and now a historic landmark. The ceilings are high and vaulted and the rooms outfitted in updated Biedermeier style, with stucco ceilings, chandeliers, and modern bathrooms. Some rooms have kitchenettes; three rooms even have tile heaters—one is 200 years old. Babysitting is available (if requested in advance). To get from room to room, you walk along an enclosed catwalk on a balcony tracing a courtyard. The Pertschys lived in Canada for 10 years and have run this pension for 40 years—the whole family speaks perfect English.

Habsburgergasse 5 (a few steps off Graben, near Stephansplatz), 1010 Wien. ⓒ 01/534 49-0. Fax 01/534 49-49. www.pertschy.com. 47 units. 67€–110€ ($77–$127) single; 97€–165€ ($112–$190) double. Rates include buffet breakfast. AE, DC, MC, V. U-Bahn: U-1 or U-3 to Stephansplatz. Tram: D from Südbahnhof to Oper, then bus 3A to Habsburgergasse. **Amenities:** Nonsmoking rooms; computer with free Internet access. *In room:* Satellite TV, minibar, radio.

3 Great Deals on Dining

Because many shops and businesses are inside the Ring and along Mariahilfer Strasse west of the Ring, Vienna's best-known restaurants tend to be in these places, too. You don't have to spend a lot of money to eat well, and there's enough variety to keep the palate interested.

Viennese cuisine is the culmination of various ethnic influences, including Bohemian, Hungarian, Croatian, Slovene, German, and Italian. At the top end of the price scale is wild game, followed by various fish, poultry, pork, and beef dishes. Most restaurants serve complete meals, consisting of a main dish and one or several side dishes. Prices listed for each restaurant below, therefore, are usually for complete meals.

For starters, you might try a soup like **Griessnockerlsuppe** (clear soup with semolina dumplings), **Leberknödlsuppe** (soup with liver dumplings), **Rindsuppe** (beef broth), or **Gulaschsuppe** (beef or veal soup, seasoned with paprika). Popular main courses are **Bauernschmaus** (sausages and pork items with sauerkraut and dumplings), **Tafelspitz** (boiled beef with vegetables), **Wiener schnitzel** (breaded veal cutlet), **Schweinebraten** (roast pork), **Spanferkel** (suckling pig), **Backhendl** (fried and breaded chicken), and **Gulasch** (Hungarian goulash). **Nockerl** are little dumplings, usually served with sauce. And then there are desserts: Vienna's **Apfelstrudel** (apple strudel) is probably the best in the world.

Value Dining Notes

The cheapest place for a meal is the **Würstelstand** (sausage stand), which sells various types of drinks and sausages, most at 2.50€ to 3€ ($2.90–$3.45). Convenient stands are those on Seilergasse (off Graben), open Monday to Saturday 8am to 1am and Sunday 9am to 1am; on Kupferschmiedgasse (off Kärntner Strasse), open daily 8am to 9pm; on Albertinerplatz, open daily 8am to 4am; and at the Naschmarkt (see later in this chapter).

For a sit-down lunch, nothing can beat the prices of the **Mensa,** a student cafeteria that serves nonstudents a complete meal for less than $5 (see "A Local Budget Best," later in this chapter). But for atmosphere, don't miss a meal in a **Beisl,** the Austrian word for "pub" or "tavern," many of which serve hearty and inexpensive meals.

(*Value*) **Getting the Best Deal on Dining**

- Take advantage of daily specials (*Tagesmenu*), often posted outside the door of a restaurant, which are complete meals at discount prices. Often available for lunch and dinner, they are rarely listed in English menus, so ask.
- Eat a quick meal at a *Würstelständ*—a food stall selling sausages and beer. For lunch, go to the Mensa, a student cafeteria with very low prices open also to nonstudents.
- Enjoy a few hearty meals in a *Beisl*, a typical Viennese tavern that dishes out home-cooked food at low prices.
- Ask whether there's an extra charge for each piece of bread consumed and whether the main course comes with vegetables or a side dish.
- Note whether there's a per-person table charge (*gedeck*), sometimes levied at more expensive restaurants.

Palatschinken are light sugared pancakes; *Kaiserschmarren* is a diced omelet, served with jam and sprinkled with sugar. A *Sachertorte* is a sinfully rich chocolate cake.

And to top it all off, you'll want coffee, of which there are at least 20 varieties. Introduced 300 years ago by the Turks during their unsuccessful attempt to conquer Vienna, coffee as served in Viennese coffeehouses has become an art form. Among the many kinds are the *kleiner Schwarzer*, a small cup without milk; *kleiner Brauner*, a small cup with cream; *Melange*, a large cup with frothy milk; *Melange mit Schlag*, coffee topped with whipped cream; *Mokka*, strong black Viennese coffee; and *Türkischer*, Turkish coffee boiled in a small copper pot and served in a tiny cup. Coffee is always served with a glass of water.

Note: Unless noted otherwise, the hours given below are exactly the hours the doors remain open. Last orders are generally 1 hour before closing.

INSIDE THE RING

Bizi 🏆 (*Finds*) ITALIAN   This popular self-service restaurant is my top choice for a quick tasty meal inside the Ring. It offers a variety of pizzas and pastas, such as ravioli, gnocchi, tagliatelle, and tortellini, all with a choice of sauces. You can order pizza by the slice (2.40€/$2.75) to take out or to eat at one of the stand-up or sit-down tables. There's also a salad bar, as well as a selection of wines and beer. The decor is upbeat and pleasant, with modern art on the walls, and there's even a nonsmoking section.

Rotenturmstrasse 4 (at the corner of Wollzeile, north of Stephansplatz). (*C*) 01/513 37 05. Pizza and pasta 5€–6.80€ ($5.75–$7.80); meat courses 5.80€–6.80€ ($6.65–$7.80). No credit cards. Daily 10:30am–11:30pm. U-Bahn: Stephansplatz or Schwedenplatz.

GriechenBeisl 🏆 AUSTRIAN   All Viennese know the GriechenBeisl, and many of their ancestors have probably dined here—it dates from the 15th century, built on Roman foundations. Prominent diners have included Beethoven, Schubert, Wagner, Strauss, Brahms, and Twain. Housed in an ancient-looking vine-covered building divided into several small rooms linked by narrow winding passages, the restaurant offers typical Viennese food from its English menu, like *Tafelspitz*, *Wiener schnitzel*, *Gulasch*, stuffed cabbage roulade with bacon and potatoes, pork tenderloin with pepper sauce and potato croquettes, and ragout of venison with burgundy sauce. There's live music from 7:30pm and, in summer, outdoor seating.

Fleischmarkt 11. ⊂ **01/533 19 77.** Meals 14€–19€ ($12–$17). AE, DC, MC, V. Daily 11:30am–11:30pm (last order). U-Bahn: Stephansplatz or Schwedenplatz.

Gulaschmuseum AUSTRIAN   Despite its name, this is not a museum dedicated to that favorite Austrian dish imported from Hungary, but it does offer walls covered with fine art for customers to gaze upon as they dine on more than a dozen variations of *Gulasch*. Probably the world's only restaurant dedicated to Gulasch, it serves traditional Hungarian Gulasch (a spicy meat and paprika dish), as well as Gulasch with unusual ingredients like veal with spinach dumplings; beans with Jamaican pepper sausages; turkey; or fish. A large selection of desserts rounds out the English menu.

Schulerstrasse 20. ⊂ **01/512 10 17.** Reservations recommended for dinner. Main dishes 7.90€–13€ ($9.10–$15). MC, V. Daily 10am–midnight. U-Bahn: Stephansplatz.

Massinger Dombeisl AUSTRIAN   A typical neighborhood *Beisl*, this simple eatery with its wooden floor and plain furniture is behind St. Stephan's Cathedral. Maybe that's why it's a favorite of the Fiaker, the famous Viennese horse-carriage drivers stationed at Stephansplatz. Changing daily specials are posted in German on a chalkboard outside the front door; otherwise, hearty home-cooked meals on the English menu include *Schweinebraten* with *Knödel* (dumplings), *Bratwurst*, *Wiener schnitzel*, and *Fiaker Gulasch*.

Schulerstrasse 4 (at Domgasse). ⊂ **01/512 91 81.** Meals 7€–10€ ($8.05–$12). No credit cards. Mon–Fri 10am–6pm. U-Bahn: Stephansplatz.

Orpheus GREEK   This popular, sophisticated place occupies a 120-year-old building, with an attractive high-ceilinged dining room, candles on every table, modern artwork on the walls, and, in summer, an open facade overlooking sidewalk seating. The emphasis of its English menu is specialties from Crete, especially fish, cooked with homemade extra-virgin olive oil. There's also the usual selection of *gyros*, lamb, *souvlaki*, steaks, calamari, grilled scampi with rice, and fish, plus weekday lunch specials.

Spiegelgasse 10 (parallel to Kärntner Strasse). ⊂ **01/512 38 88.** Meals 8.10€–18€ ($9.30–$21). DC, MC, V. Sun–Thurs noon–11pm; Fri–Sat noon–midnight. U-Bahn: Stephansplatz.

Palmenhaus ⚜ MODERN AUSTRIAN   This stylish, airy restaurant is a good place for a meal on a dreary or rainy day. It occupies the middle section of the Schmetterlinghaus (Butterfly House), an early-1900s Jugendstil greenhouse, set in the midst of the Burggarten park. On fine summer days, you can dine on the outdoor terrace overlooking greenery. It offers a variety of fresh grilled fish and daily specials, as well as what could be described as nouveau Austrian cuisine from an English menu, such as filet of sturgeon in a crust of dark bread with kohlrabi and tomatoes, or sea bass with dried tomatoes, chorizo, and french fries. After your meal, stroll through the Schmetterlinghaus, which boasts 300 butterflies from 40 species in a confined space adjacent to the restaurant. On Friday there's free live music from 9pm.

In the Schmetterlinghaus, Burggarten, Opernring. ⊂ **01/533 10 33.** Main dishes 10€–19€ ($12–$22); lunch special 7.80 ($8.95). AE, DC, MC, V. Daily 11:30am–11:30pm (last order). Closed Nov–Feb Mon–Tues. U-Bahn: Karlsplatz, Stephansplatz, or MuseumsQuartier. Tram: 1, 2, D, or J to Opernring or Burgring.

Moments Coffeehouses Inside the Ring

As Paris has its sidewalk cafes, Vienna has its coffeehouses. All offer newspapers for leisurely perusal, and many also offer live classical music a few times a week. There are literally dozens of ways to order coffee (see the beginning of this section). If all you're looking for is to fuel up with a cheap cup, look for the **Tchibo** chain. There's one at Mariahilfer Strasse 81; U-Bahn: Neubaugasse), where a *Melange* costs 1.80€ ($2.05). It's open Monday to Saturday 8:30am to 6:30pm.

Founded in 1785 by a pastry chef who later served as the pastry supplier to the royal family, **Demel,** Kohlmarkt 14 (© 01/535 17 17-39; U-Bahn: Stephansplatz), is Vienna's most expensive and most famous coffeehouse. Its elegant interior looks like the private parlor of a count, and in summer there's sidewalk seating. A *Melange* is 3.80€ ($4.35), worth the price just for the show of people and waitresses. The tortes and cakes are hard to resist. In apparent recognition of its high prices, Demel even accepts all major credit cards. It's open daily 10am to 7pm.

Equally famous is the 19th-century **Café Sacher,** in the Hotel Sacher Vienna behind the Staatsoper, Philharmonikerstrasse 4 (© 01/514 56-0; U-Bahn: Karlsplatz), where you can indulge in the famous *Sachertorte* (4.50€/$5.20), created in 1832 by 16-year-old Franz Sacher, whose son later founded this hotel. The cafe is open daily 8am to 11:30pm.

Small, dark, and smoky, its walls covered with posters and placards, the **Cafe Hawelka,** Dorotheergasse 6, just off Graben (© 01/512 82 30; U-Bahn: Stephansplatz), attracts students, artists, writers, and other Bohemian types. It's famous for its *Buchtel,* a pastry made fresh daily and available only after 10pm. I prefer this cafe to Demel, and its 2.80€ ($3.20) for a *Melange* is more acceptable. Hawelka is open Monday and Wednesday to Saturday 8am to 2am and Sunday and holidays 4pm to 2am.

On a tiny street connecting Dorotheergasse and Bräunergasse (off Graben), the **Bräunerhof Cafe,** Stallburggasse 2 (© 01/512 38 93; U-Bahn: Stephansplatz), falls between Demel and Hawelka (see both above) as far as style and decoration go. Rather than the dark-paneled walls of many older coffeehouses, this one has a bright and simple interior with gracefully arching lamps by Hoffmann. There are several expensive antiques shops in the area, and a trio entertains customers Saturday, Sunday, and holidays 3 to 6pm. A *Melange* costs 2.90€ ($3.35). It's open Monday to Friday 8am to 9pm, Saturday 8am to 7pm, and Sunday and holidays 10am to 7pm.

Spaghetti & Co. *Kids* PIZZA/PASTA   This conveniently located branch of a chain of spaghetti parlors offers more than a dozen kinds of spaghetti dishes, including one with chili sauce and one with salmon and mushrooms. It also offers a dozen choices of pizzas, as well as salads and a salad bar. It's good for a fast, inexpensive sit-down meal in the heart of the Ring.

Stephansplatz 7 (just north of Stephansdom). ℂ **01/512 14 44**. Pizza and pasta 4.90€–8.20€ ($5.65–$9.45). AE, DC, MC, V. Daily 11am–11:30pm. U-Bahn: Stephansplatz.

Trzesniewski ✦ SANDWICHES   This is one of the most popular cafeterias in all Vienna—and rightly so. It's so small that the mealtime line often snakes through the entire store; try coming at off-peak times. Trzesniewski is a buffet of small open-face finger sandwiches covered with spreads like salami, egg salad, tuna fish, hot peppers, tomatoes, or a couple dozen other selections. Four sandwiches are usually enough for me, along with a *pfiff,* an eighth of a liter of beer. You'll find a convenient branch west of the Ring at Mariahilfer Strasse 95 (ℂ **01/596 42 91;** U-Bahn: Zieglergasse), open Monday to Friday 8:30am to 7pm and Saturday 9am to 5pm.

Dorotheergasse 1 (just off Graben). ℂ **01/512 32 91**. Sandwiches .80€ (90¢). No credit cards. Mon–Fri 8:30am–7:30pm; Sat 9am–5pm. U-Bahn: Stephansplatz.

Wienerwald AUSTRIAN *(Kids*   Wienerwald is a successful chain of grilled-chicken restaurants throughout Austria and Germany, with a dozen locations in Vienna. A half grilled chicken with salad and french fries is 9.65€ ($11). Other dishes on the English-language menu are soups, salads (including a salad bar), *Schnitzel,* and chicken sandwiches, and there's also a children's menu. Other convenient branches are at Freyung 6 (ℂ **01/533 14 20;** U-Bahn: Schottentor/Universität; tram: 1, 2, or D to Schottentor) inside the Ring; and Mariahilfer Strasse 156, west of Westbahnhof (ℂ **01/89 23 306;** U-Bahn: Westbahnhof).

Annagasse 3 (just off Kärntner Strasse). ℂ **01/512 37 66**. Meals 7.40€–11€ ($8.50–$13). AE, DC, MC, V. Daily 11am–11pm. U-Bahn: Stephansplatz or Karlsplatz. Tram: 1, 2, or D to Oper.

Wrenkh ✦ VEGETARIAN   If you're a vegetarian or simply tired of Austria's meat obsession, head to this dark romantic restaurant and treat yourself to innovative dishes influenced by Mediterranean and Asian cuisine. The English-language menu changes often, but past dishes have included tofu salad; zucchini risotto with onions, garlic, herbs, Parmesan, and smoked tofu; or baked potato with mushrooms, chanterelles, apple, and shaved black truffle. For a snack, try the appetizer plate *(Gustoteller),* a celebration of tastes and textures two can share. The wine list is extensive. An adjoining sleek bar, open throughout the day, serves the same menu, plus a great lunch offering a choice of main dish and soup or salad for 7.70€ ($8.85), or with both soup and salad for 9.40€ ($11).

Bauernmarkt 10 (west of Stephansplatz). ℂ **01/533 15 26**. Meals 9.80€–21€ ($11–$24). AE, DC, MC, V. Restaurant daily 11:30am–2:30pm and 6pm–midnight; bar daily 11:30am–midnight. U-Bahn: Stephansplatz.

WEST OF THE RING

Café Leopold ✦ AUSTRIAN/CONTINENTAL   Of the handful of new restaurants in the new MuseumsQuartier, this is probably the most inviting, with a relaxed, cozy atmosphere. From its cubist-style chairs on the outdoor terrace to its beige-colored, low-back chairs grouped around low tables, its camp decor is vaguely reminiscent of a 1950s European cafe but is much more hip. The limited English-language menu lists only a handful of choices like chicken curry with rice, tofu burger, beef *Gulasch,* and *Wiener schnitzel,* so be sure to ask for a translation of the daily special (8.70€/$10), which allows you to choose a soup or salad (like tomato soup or a salad of tofu on basmati rice) as well as a main dish like potato-mushroom strudel with sour cream dip, or lamb with polenta and vegetables. If this place is full, you'll find other restaurants in MuseumsQuartier, including the Italian Il Museo in the Museum of Modern Art and Kantine (serving soups and sandwiches) and Unter'm Hollerbusch (a health-food store also with a deli offering soups and daily specials), both near the main entrance to the quarter. After the museums close, Leopold evolves into a nighttime hangout, with DJs Thursday through Saturday.

Leopold Museum, Museumsplatz 1. ℂ 01/523 67 32. Main courses 6.70€–9.80€ ($7.70–$11). DC, MC, V. Daily 10am–11pm (last order). U-Bahn: MuseumsQuartier.

Cafe Rüdiger Hof ℛ finds AUSTRIAN This is a lovely place for a meal, snack, or drink after visiting the Naschmarkt (outdoor market). Owned by a charming woman who speaks fluent English, it occupies the first floor of an impressive Jugendstil building, built in 1902 by the famous architect and Zionist Oskar Marmorek. With its raised outdoor terrace and garden, it's a popular meeting spot for young people on warm summer nights; it has the distinction of being one of the few outdoor places in Vienna open past midnight. In addition to regular dishes like *Wiener schnitzel,* turkey *schnitzel, Gulasch, Würstl* (sausages), baked sole, and spaghetti on its English-language menu, it offers two daily specials. Breakfast is served until 5pm.

Hamburger Strasse 20 (west of Naschmarkt). ℂ 01/586 31 38. Main dishes 5.10€–7.10€ ($5.85–$8.15); specials 5.70€–6.40€ ($6.55–$7.35). No credit cards. Daily 10am–2am (last order 11pm). Closed Christmas–Jan 7. U-Bahn: Kettenbrückengasse or Pilgramgasse.

Crêperie-Brasserie Spittelberg FRENCH In what used to be Vienna's red-light district but has since become a small enclave of trendy restaurants just a few minutes' walk west of the MuseumsQuartier, this casual yet upscale place with an English-language menu has salads with a great selection of dressings, soups, quiches, pastas, crepes with sweet fillings, and galettes stuffed with ingredients like salami, mozzarella, pepperoni, and oregano or artichoke hearts in a basil-tomato sauce with red pepper and herbed sheep cheese. It's in a modernized old building, with hanging plants and lighting suspended from the super-high ceiling. The glass-enclosed dining areas are pleasant in winter, and in summer there's outdoor seating.

Spittelberggasse 12 (north of Mariahilfer Strasse). ℂ 01/526 15 70. Main dishes 7€–14€ ($8.05–$16). AE, DC, MC, V. Daily 6pm–midnight. U-Bahn: Volkstheater. Tram: 49 from Dr.-Karl-Renner-Ring to Spittelberg.

Gasthaus Witwe Bolte ℛ AUSTRIAN Its facade is fancy baroque, but the interior consists of several simple small rooms, where the emphasis is on home-cooked meals like *Tafelspitz, Schnitzel, Schweinebraten,* lamb, fish, steaks, *Gulasch,* and a few vegetarian selections, all listed on an English menu. There's also a wonderful outdoor dining area. The restaurant is next to the Crêperie-Brasserie Spittelberg (see above) on a narrow lamp-lit cobblestone street just a few minutes' walk west of the MuseumsQuartier. Kaiser Josef II, disguised as an ordinary citizen, is said to have escaped from this building in 1778, when this area was Vienna's red-light district.

Gutenberggasse 13. ℂ 01/523 14 50. Meals 9€–16€ ($10–$18). AE, DC, MC, V. Nov–Apr Mon–Fri 11:30am–3pm and 5:30–10:30pm, Sat–Sun 11:30am–10:30pm; May–Oct daily 11:30am–10:30pm. U-Bahn: Volkstheater. Tram: 49 from Dr.-Karl-Renner-Ring to Spittelberg.

Schnitzelwirt value AUSTRIAN Known also as the Gaststätte Helene Schmidt, this restaurant specializes in variations of the *Schnitzel* and has been one of Vienna's leading budget choices for years. Little wonder—the *Schnitzel* are gigantic, covering the whole plate (you might consider sharing). Choices on the English menu include *Schnitzel* Mexican style, *Wiener schnitzel,* and garlic *Schnitzel.*

Neubaugasse 52 (few blocks north of Mariahilfer Strasse, near the corner of Siebensterngasse). © **01/523 37 71.** Meals 5.20€–8.50€ ($6–$9.80). No credit cards. Mon–Sat 11am–10pm. Closed holidays and mid-July to mid-Aug. U-Bahn: Neubaugasse. Tram: 49 from Dr.-Karl-Renner-Ring to Siebensterngasse. Bus: 13A to Siebensterngasse.

Shalimar INDIAN   This elaborately decorated Indian restaurant with out-door seating in summer offers great tandoori chicken; curry dishes of chicken, pork, lamb, beef, and fish; and a variety of vegetarian dishes. Indian music plays in the background. The fixed-priced meals are good values, especially during lunch, when you can eat for 6€ ($6.90) or less.

Schmalzhofgasse 11 (just south of Mariahilfer Strasse). © **01/596 43 17.** Main courses 7€–14€ ($8.05–$16); fixed-price meals 13€–23€ ($12–$20); *gedeck* (table charge) 1.50€ ($1.75) per person. AE, DC, MC, V. Daily 11:30am–2:30pm and 6–11pm. U-Bahn: Zieglergasse (take Webgasse exit).

Tunnel ⭐ INTERNATIONAL   This informal place is actually a restaurant/bar, with a live-music house in the basement. Catering to Vienna's large student population, it starts the day with huge breakfasts and continues with sand-wiches, salads, vegetarian dishes, pizzas (the larger size is big enough for two), pastas, and Viennese pancakes. The eclectic menu also offers everything from hummus to *moussaka* to grilled lamb. From 11:30am to 2:30pm there are two daily specials (including vegetarian); bread is free with your meal. You can stay as long as you want (it's a good place to write those postcards), and you can come for just a drink.

Florianigasse 39 (behind the Rathaus, about 10-min. walk west of Ring). © **01/405 34 65.** Main courses 3.50€–10€ ($4–$12); daily specials 4€ ($4.60). No credit cards. Daily 9am–1am. U-Bahn: Rathaus. Tram: 5. Bus: 13A.

A LOCAL BUDGET BEST

Mensa *(Value)* AUSTRIAN   Although technically for students, this cafeteria on the first floor of a modern light-green building serves nonstudents for slightly more. It's divided into two parts. The one on the left serves your choice of two fixed-price meals that can range from stews to grilled chicken to spaghetti and includes a drink. On the right is a more extensive cafeteria with slightly higher prices, offering pizza, various main courses, a salad bar, and desserts. Be sure to clear your tray when you're finished.

Technische Universität Wien, Turm B, Wiedner Hauptstrasse 10. © **01/586 65 02** or 01/216 06 68. Fixed-price meals 3.70€–4.40€ ($4.25–$5.05) nonstudents. No credit cards. Mon–Fri 11am–2:30pm. Closed Dec 25–Jan 7. U-Bahn: Karlsplatz.

PICNICKING

The best place for picnic supplies—and one of Vienna's most colorful attractions since its founding in the 1700s—is the **Naschmarkt,** between the Karlsplatz and Kettenbrückengasse U-Bahn stations. Stalls here sell fish, vegetables, fruit, meats, cheeses, spices, Asian foodstuffs, Greek specialties, flowers, and tea. My Viennese friends say this is the best place to shop because of the freshness of the produce and the variety of goods, including exotic items. Among the food stalls are a number of stand-up fast-food counters where you can buy sausages, sand-wiches, pizza, *döner* kabobs, falafel, grilled chicken, sushi, and other ready-made foods. The Naschmarkt is open Monday to Friday 6am to 6:30pm and Saturday 6am to 5pm.

As for picnic settings, Vienna's most accessible parks are the **Stadtpark** and the **Volksgarten,** both on the Ring. In addition, both Schönbrunn and Belvedere palaces have formal gardens. Keep in mind, however, that the Viennese are a bit stodgy and don't look kindly on people who wander off paths and sprawl on the grass. Some parks, in response to Vienna's younger generation, many of whom staged sit-ins in the 1970s to protest the keep-off-the-grass rule, finally opened designated *Liegewiesen* (laying fields). In any case, there are always lots of park benches. Or you can take an excursion to the **Vienna Woods** or the **Danube.**

WORTH A SPLURGE

A number of wine cellars listed under "Vienna After Dark" (later in this chapter) also offer meals. Although you can experience these places for the price of a drink, they're great for a complete meal, which can cost 15€ ($17) and up.

Wiener Rathauskeller 🐟🐟 AUSTRIAN   The Rittersaal (Knights' Hall), in the cellar of Vienna's City Hall, offers elegant a la carte dining in a historical setting. The attractive decor features medieval-style murals on the vaulted ceilings, stained-glass windows, beautiful lamps, and flowers and candles on the tables. The English menu lists traditional Viennese dishes, including Fiaker *Gulasch* with fried egg, sausage, gherkin, and boiled potatoes; prime cuts of ox served in sauce with vegetables and roast potatoes; and in-house specialties like grilled loin of veal or grilled king prawns served on a bed of tomato and leeks with basil butter and curried rice. In the evenings, there's live classical music (with a 1.10€/ $1.25 per-person music charge). Farther down the hall, in the Grinzinger Keller, a fixed-price meal with traditional Viennese entertainment is offered Tuesday to Saturday 7:30 to 11pm from April to October.

Rathausplatz. 🕭 **01/405 12 10.** Reservations recommended for fixed-price meal with traditional entertainment. Main courses 9€–20€ ($10–$23); fixed-price meal 39€ ($45); *gedeck* (table charge) 1.80€ ($2.05). AE, DC, MC, V. Mon–Sat 11:30am–3pm and 6–10pm (last order). U-Bahn: Rathaus. Tram: 1, 2, or D to Burgtheater/Rathausplatz.

4 Seeing the Sights

Remember to buy a copy of *Vienna from A to Z* for an explanation of the city's many historically important buildings. In addition, the *Wien-Programm* lists special exhibits in Vienna's museums and galleries. Both are available at Vienna Tourist Information offices (see "Visitor Information," earlier in this chapter).

SCHÖNBRUNN PALACE

Schönbrunn 🐟🐟🐟 *Finds*   A baroque summer palace with an astounding 1,441 rooms, the lovely Schönbrunn was built between 1696 and 1730 in the midst of a glorious garden. Empress Maria Theresa left the greatest imprint on Schönbrunn. In the course of having 16 children (one of whom was the ill-fated Marie Antoinette) in 20 years, running the country, and fighting a war for her right to sit on the Austrian throne, she found time to decorate and redesign the palace (1744–49), and it remains virtually as she left it. When the French besieged Vienna in the early 19th century, Napoléon was so impressed with Schönbrunn

---

Tips Museum Closings

Most museums are closed on January 1, Good Friday, Easter Sunday, May 1, Whitsunday, Corpus Christi, November 1 and 2, December 24 and 25, and for general elections. Exceptions are the Museum of Fine Arts, Schönbrunn Palace, the Hofburg, and the Imperial Burial Vault, which remain open on Easter Sunday and Whitsunday.

Vienna

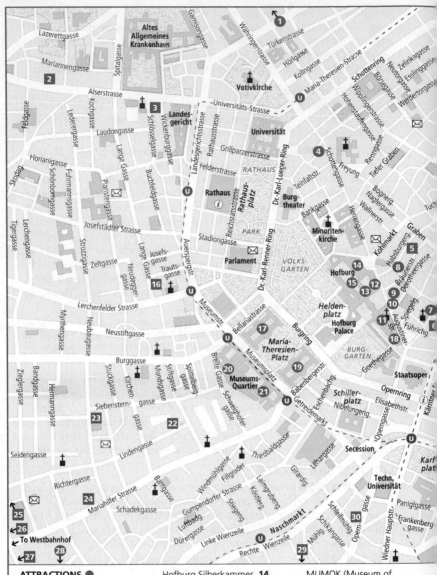

ATTRACTIONS ●

Albertina Museum **18**
Augustinerkirche **11**
Beethoven-Gedenkstätte **4**
Dali im Palais Surreal **10**
Figarohaus **38**
Haydn-Wohnhaus mit
  Brahms-Gedenkraum **28**
Haus der Musik **40**
Hofburg Kaiserappartements **14**

Hofburg Silberkammer **14**
Johann-Strauss-Wohnung **32**
Kapuzinerkirche & Kaisergruft **7**
KunstHausWien **35**
Kunsthistorisches Museum **19**
Leopold Museum **21**
Liechtenstein Museum **1**
Lippizaner Museum **9**
MAK—Österreichisches Museum
  für Angewandte Kunst **36**

MUMOK (Museum of
  Modern Art) **20**
Naturhistorisches Museum **17**
Österreichische Galerie
  Belvedere **42**
Prater **31**
Schatzkammer **15**
Schubert's Birthplace **1**
Sigmund-Freud-Haus **1**
Spanische Reitschule **12**

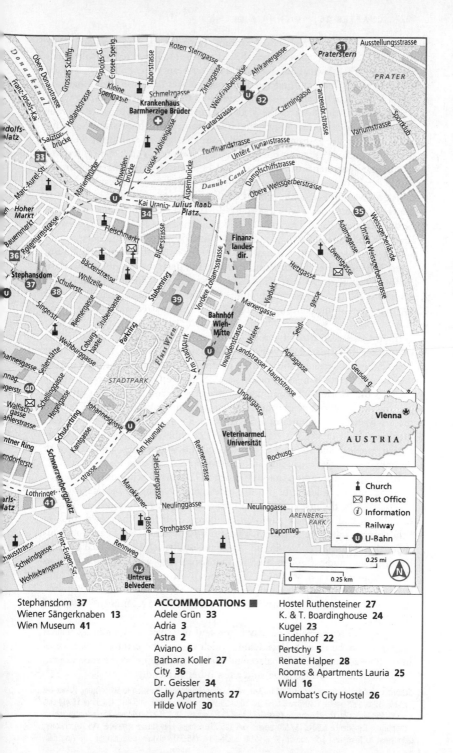

Legend

- ✝ Church
- ✉ Post Office
- ⓘ Information
- —— Railway
- - - ⓤ U-Bahn

Vienna, AUSTRIA

Stephansdom **37**	**ACCOMMODATIONS** ■	Hostel Ruthensteiner **27**
Wiener Sängerknaben **13**	Adele Grün **33**	K. & T. Boardinghouse **24**
Wien Museum **41**	Adria **3**	Kugel **23**
	Astra **2**	Lindenhof **22**
	Aviano **6**	Pertschy **5**
	Barbara Koller **27**	Renate Halper **28**
	City **36**	Rooms & Apartments Lauria **25**
	Dr. Geissler **34**	Wild **16**
	Gally Apartments **27**	Wombat's City Hostel **26**
	Hilde Wolf **30**	

he occupied Maria Theresa's favorite rooms. Franz Josef I, who was born in the palace and reigned for 68 years, was the last emperor to live here. His wife, Elisabeth, popularly known as Sisi, was famed for her beauty (her hair reached to the ground), intelligence, and independent spirit. It was here, too, that Charles I, Austria's last emperor, abdicated and renounced the Imperial Crown.

You can tour the inside of the predominantly white-and-gilt palace on your own, choosing either the 50-minute **Grand Tour** through 40 state rooms for 11€ ($12), or the 35-minute **Imperial Tour** through 22 rooms for 8€ ($7). Both tours include use of an English-language audioguide and allow you to see the **private apartments** of Franz Josef and Elisabeth; **Maria Theresa's nursery** with portraits of her children; the **Hall of Mirrors,** where the 6-year-old Mozart played for Maria Theresa; the exotic **Chinese Cabinets** with inlaid lacquerware; the **Hall of Ceremonies** with a portrait of Maria Theresa; the impressive **Large Gallery,** fashioned after a room in Versailles and used in a 1961 meeting between Kennedy and Khrushchev; and more. The Grand Tour then continues through, among other rooms, the **Chinese Lacquered Room;** the **Napoleon Room,** where Napoléon lived and his only legitimate son died; the delightful **Porcelain Room,** which served as Maria Theresa's study; and the **Millions Room,** decorated with 260 precious parchment miniatures brought from Constantinople and set under glass in the paneling. Because it offers more, I recommend the Grand Tour.

In any case, even the self-guided tours are for a specific time, indicated on your ticket. If there's a long wait (which is possible in summer), you can first explore the 200 hectares (500 acres) of **palace grounds,** one of the most important baroque gardens in the French style. At the top of the hill opposite the palace is the **Gloriette,** a monument to soldiers and also the site of a cafe with glorious views of the Schönbrunn and the spread of Vienna beyond. There's also the lovely **Neptune Fountain;** artificial Roman ruins; a hedge maze; the **Palmenhaus** (built in 1883 as Europe's largest greenhouse and housing Mediterranean, tropical, and subtropical plants); and the **Wagenburg,** a museum with 36 imperial carriages, including an over-the-top carriage used for coronations.

For children, there's the beautifully designed **Tiergarten Schönbrunn,** founded in 1752 and considered the world's oldest zoo. Highlights include its giant pandas, koalas, the first elephant born in Europe using artificial insemination techniques, and a tropical rainforest. Children even have their own tours of Schönbrunn, called the **Schloss Schönbrunn Experience,** which are both educational and fun. After dressing in imperial clothing, children are led by English-speaking guides through original rooms outfitted with hands-on displays that give an insider's view of court life, from why people wore wigs to how folding fans were used to communicate intentions. Tours last 60 to 90 minutes, depending on the children's interest, and reservations are recommended (© 01/811 13-239).

If you plan on spending the day here—and that's very easy to do—consider buying the **Schönbrunn Pass Gold,** which carries the extra convenience of immediate admission to the palace and includes admission to the zoo, Wagenburg, Palmenhaus, hedge maze, and a few other attractions.

Schönbrunner Schlossstrasse. © 01/811 13-0. www.schoenbrunn.at. Admission to Schönbrunn Palace 8€ or 11€ ($7 or $12) adults, 7.40€ or 8.60€ ($8.50 or $9.90) students, 4.30€ or 5.40€ ($4.95 or $5.40) children 6–15; admission to Schönbrunn Pass Gold 36€ ($41) adults, 18€ ($21) children; admission to Schloss Schönbrunn Experience 6.50€ ($7.50) adults, 5€ ($5.75) seniors and students, 4.50€ ($5.20) children; admission to Tiergarten Schönbrunn 12€ ($14) adults, 5€ ($5.75) children. Schönbrunn July–Aug daily

> ### (*Value* Getting the Best Deal on Sightseeing
>
> - Keep in mind that admission to Vienna's municipal museums, including all the composers' homes and the Wien Museum, is free on Friday (excluding holidays) until noon. But remember the crowds!
> - You must enter most museums at least 30 minutes before closing time, but to do main attractions justice, you'll want to allow much more time than that.
> - Buy combination tickets whenever possible.
> - Buy family tickets when available, at museums like the Museum of Military History, Lippizaner Museum, Albertina, Museum of Fine Arts, and Liechtenstein Museum.
> - See the Spanish Riding School without spending a fortune by attending one of the morning training sessions.
> - The Vienna Card (see "Vienna Deals & Discounts," earlier in this chapter) allows unlimited travel in the city for 3 days and offers reduced admission prices to the most important museums and attractions.
> - You can reach Vienna's most important attractions via the Vienna Line Hop-On, Hop-Off, a bus that makes continuous runs through the city with 13 stops along the way and allows you to board/disembark as often as you want.

8:30am–6pm; Apr–June and Sept–Oct daily 8:30am–5pm; Nov–Mar daily 8:30am–4:30pm; closed Jan 1, Nov 1, Dec 25. Schloss Schönbrunn Experience daily 10am 5pm during school holidays; Sat–Sun and holidays when school is in session. Tiergarten Schönbrunn summer daily 9am–6:30pm; winter daily 9am–4:30pm. U-Bahn: Schönbrunn. Tram: 58 to Schloss Schönbrunn.

THE HOFBURG PALACE COMPLEX

The Hofburg was the Imperial Palace of the Habsburgs for more than 6 centuries, during which time changes and additions were made in several architectural styles—Gothic, Renaissance, baroque, rococo, and classical. The entire Hofburg occupies 19 hectares (47 acres); it's a virtual city within a city, with more than 2,600 rooms. Contained in the vast complex are the **Imperial Apartments,** the **Imperial Silver Collection,** the **Treasury,** the **Spanish Riding School,** the **Lippizaner Museum,** and the **Burgkapelle** featuring Sunday Masses with the Vienna Boys' Choir.

Hofburg Kaiserappartements (Imperial Apartments) and Hofburg Silberkammer (Imperial Silver Collection) 🏛🏛🏛   The Imperial Apartments and Silver Collection share the same entrance and are included in the same ticket price. The Imperial Apartments, which served as the winter residence of the Habsburgs, might seem a bit plain if you've already seen the splendor of Schönbrunn, but the Hofburg is so conveniently located it's a shame to pass it up. You can wander at leisure through 22 official and private rooms once belonging to Franz Josef and his wife, Elisabeth, and to Tsar Alexander I of Russia. There are several portraits of a young Elisabeth (including one in Franz Josef's study), who came from the Wittelsbach family of Munich in 1854 to marry Franz Josef at 16. Known as Sisi, she was talented, artistic, and slightly vain—she'd no longer sit for portraits after she turned 30. She was an excellent rider, and in the Hofburg is her own small gymnasium, where she kept in shape (much to the disgust of the court, which thought it improper for a lady). Crown Prince Rudolf, son of Elisabeth and Franz Josef and the only male heir to the throne, committed suicide in a hunting lodge at Mayerling with his young mistress, Baroness Maria Vetsera. Elisabeth was assassinated in 1898 by an anarchist in Geneva. You'll also see the royal dining room laid out with the imperial place settings—notice how the silverware is placed only on the right side and is turned face down, according to Spanish court etiquette, which was the rage at the time. There are five wineglasses for each guest, and each napkin is 1 sq. m ($3\frac{1}{3}$ sq. ft.).

Dating from the 15th century onward, the Imperial Silver Collection of silverware, dinnerware, and tableware provides insight into the imperial household, royal banquets, and court etiquette. It displays items of daily use as well as valuable pieces, everything from cooking molds and pots and pans to table linens, elaborate centerpieces, crystal, silver serving sets, gilded candelabras, silverware, and porcelain table settings.

An English-language audioguide for both the Silver Collection and the Imperial Apartments is available for 3.20€ ($3.70). Expect to spend up to 2 hours touring both.

Michaeler Platz 1 (inside the Ring, 7-min. walk from Stephansplatz; entrance via Kaisertor in Inneren Burghof). ✆ **01/533 75 70.** www.hofburg-wien.at. Admission 7.50€ ($8.65) adults, 5.90€ ($6.80) seniors and students, 3.90€ ($4.50) children. Daily 9am–5pm (to 5:30pm July–Aug). You must enter 30 min. before closing. U-Bahn: Stephansplatz or Herrengasse. Tram: 1, 2, D, or J to Burgring.

Schatzkammer (Treasury) ⚶⚶ The Schatzkammer displays a stunning collection of the secular and ecclesiastical treasures of the Habsburgs. Its priceless imperial regalia and relics of the Holy Roman Empire include royal crowns inlaid with diamonds, rubies, pearls, sapphires, and other gems (like the crown of Charlemagne), as well as swords, imperial crosses, jewelry, altars, christening robes, coronation robes, and other richly embroidered garments. Two prized heirlooms are believed to have mystical and religious significance: the **Agate Bowl,** carved in Constantinople in the 4th century from a single piece of agate and once thought to be the Holy Grail; and the **Ainkhörn,** a huge narwhal tusk, considered a symbol of the unicorn and associated with the Virgin Mary and Christ. The **Holy Lance** was once thought to be the lance used to pierce Christ's side during the crucifixion; next to it is a reliquary containing what's regarded as a piece of the cross. Be sure to pick up the free English-language audioguide, which takes 3 hours if you listen to everything; most visitors stay an hour.

Schweizerhof 1, Hofburg. ✆ **01/533 79 31.** Admission 8€ ($9.20) adults, 6€ ($6.90) seniors and students, free for children under 6. Wed–Mon 10am–6pm. U-Bahn: Stephansplatz or Herrengasse. Tram: 1, 2, D, or J to Burgring.

Spanische Reitschule (Spanish Riding School) ⚶⚶⚶ This prestigious school has roots dating back more than 400 years, when Spanish horses were brought to Austria for breeding; the baroque hall in which they now perform is from the 1730s. The famous graceful Lippizaner horses are a cross of Berber and Arabian stock with Spanish and Italian horses. They're born with dark coats that turn white only between ages 4 and 10.

There are three ways to see the Lippizaners at work. Most impressive are the 80-minute Gala performances. However, tickets for these often sell out (check seat availability at **www.spanische-reitschule.com**), so it's best to purchase them in advance: by writing to the Spanish Riding School, Michaelerplatz 1, 1010 Vienna; by faxing your request to 01/535 01 86; or by e-mailing to tickets@srs.at.

> **Tips See the Lippizaners for Less**
>
> The formal performances of the Lippizaners, with intricate steps and movements, are a sight to see, but cheaper and almost as good are the more frequent morning exercise sessions.

You can also buy tickets for Gala performances through theater ticket and travel agencies such as **American Express,** Kärntner Strasse 21–23 (© **01/515 40 443**), for which you'll pay a 22% commission. In addition to the Gala performances, there is a Final Rehearsal, kind of like a dress rehearsal. Note that tickets for these can be purchased *only* through a ticket or travel agency. Lastly, the least expensive and easiest way to see the horses is at their regular morning exercise sessions with music. Tickets for these are sold on a first-come, first-served basis at the visitor center, Michaelerplatz 1, Tuesday to Saturday from 9am to 5pm, and in the inner courtyard of the Imperial Palace at Josefsplatz, Gate 2, on days of morning exercise from 9am to 12:30pm. Or, purchase a combination ticket at the Lippizaner Museum (see below), which includes both the morning session and entrance to the museum. Stop by the tourist office for a pamphlet with a current schedule.

Note: Children under 3 are not admitted to performances or exercises. No photography or videotaping is permitted.

Josephsplatz, Hofburg. No phone. Fax 01/535 01 86. www.spanische-reitschule.com. Admission to regular Gala performances 40€–145€ ($46–$67) seats, 24€–27€ ($28–$31) standing room; Final Rehearsal 20€ ($23), plus 22% commission; Morning Exercise Sessions 12€ ($13) adults, 8.50€ ($9.80) seniors, 5€ ($5.75) children. Regular Gala performances Mar–June and Sept–Oct most Sun 11am and occasionally Sat 11am or Fri 6pm; Final Rehearsal time and date vary; Morning Exercise Sessions Feb–June, Sept–Oct, and Dec Tues–Sat 10am–noon. U-Bahn: Stephansplatz or Herrengasse.

Lippizaner Museum If you can't get to a performance of the Spanish Riding School or if you're a real horse fan, you might want to visit the Lippizaner Museum in the imperial stables of the Hofburg (off Michaelerplatz). It documents the history of the famous white horses from their origins in the 16th century to the present, with displays of paintings, photographs, uniforms, saddles, and harnesses, but the highlight of the museum is a 40-minute film of the horses, their history, and their performances. Note that combination tickets for Morning Exercise Sessions and the museum are available here.

Reitschulstrasse 2, Stallburg, Hofburg. © 01/533 78 11. www.lippizaner.at. Admission 5€ ($5.75) adults, 3.60€ ($4,15) seniors, students, and children, 10€ ($12) families; combination ticket for Lippizaner Museum and Morning Training Session 15€ ($17) adults, 12€ ($13) seniors, 8€ ($9.20) children. Daily 9am–6pm. U-Bahn: Stephansplatz or Herrengasse.

Wiener Sängerknaben (Vienna Boys' Choir) The Vienna Boys' Choir was founded in 1498 to sing at church services for the Royal Chapel of the Imperial Palace. Joseph Haydn and Franz Schubert sang in the choir, which now consists of four choirs, two of which are usually on world tours. January to June and mid-September to Christmas, you can hear the choir, accompanied by Vienna State Opera orchestra members, every Sunday and some religious holidays at 9:15am Mass in the Burgkapelle of the Hofburg. Reserve seats at least 10 weeks in advance by contacting the Hofmusikkapelle, Hofburg, A-1010 Wien (fax 01/533 99 27-75; hmk@aon.at). Don't enclose money or a check, but rather pay for and pick up your ticket at the Burgkapelle on the Friday preceding

Tips Standing Room for the Vienna Boys' Choir

Standing room for the 9:15am Sunday Mass in the Burgkapelle is free, but there's room for only 20 people on a first-come, first-served basis—get there early if you're interested. Doors open at 8:30am.

the performance 11am to 1pm or 3 to 5pm, as well as Sunday 8:15 to 8:45am. Unsold tickets go on sale at the Burgkapelle on Friday 11am to 1pm and 3 to 5pm for the following Sunday. (It's wise to get there at least 30 min. before tickets go on sale.)

Another opportunity to hear the Vienna Boys' Choir is at performances given occasionally at the **Brahmssaal** of the Musikverein near Karlsplatz, during which mixed programs of motets and madrigals by old masters, waltz music, and folk songs are performed. Tickets, which cost 28€ to 40€ ($32–$46), are available at major hotels and travel agencies or at tickets@musikverein.at.

Burgkapelle, Hofburg (entrance on Schweizerhof). ℂ **01/533 99 27.** No phone. Fax 01/533 99 27-75. www.wsk.at. Admission to Mass 5€–29€ ($5.75–$33) seats, free for standing room. Mass performed mid-Sept to June Sun and some religious holidays 9:15am. U-Bahn: Stephansplatz or Herrengasse.

THE TOP CHURCHES

Stephansdom (St. Stephen's Cathedral) 🎯🎯   In the heart of Old Vienna, Stephansdom is the city's best-known landmark. Built in the 12th century and then enlarged and rebuilt over the next 800 years, it's Vienna's most important Gothic structure and boasts staggering dimensions—106m (352-ft.) long with a nave 38m (128-ft.) high. The highest part is its 135m (450-ft.) -high **south tower,** completed in 1433, with 343 spiral steps. This tower is open to the public (entrance outside the church on its south side) and affords one of the best city views. If you don't like to climb stairs, you can take an elevator (entrance inside the church) to the top of the **north tower,** which was never completed and is only about half as high as the south tower. May to November, organ concerts are given every Wednesday at 8pm; there are also choirs and other concerts throughout the year (pick up a brochure at the cathedral). The **catacombs** contain copper urns bearing the intestines of the Habsburg family. (Their bodies are in the Imperial Burial Vault, reviewed below, while their hearts are in the Augustiner Church.)

Stephansplatz. ℂ **01/515 52-3689.** Free admission to cathedral; admission to south tower 3€ ($3.45) adults, 1€ ($1.15) children; admission to north tower elevator 4€ ($4.60) adults, 1.50€ ($1.75) children; admission to catacombs 4€ ($4.60) adults, 1.50€ ($1.75) children; admission to organ concerts 8€ ($9.20). Cathedral Mon–Sat 6am–10pm, Sun 7am–10pm; south tower daily 9am–5:30pm; north tower summer daily 9am–6pm, winter daily 8:30am–5pm; catacombs Mon–Sat 10–11:30am, Mon–Sun and holidays 1:30–4:30pm; organ concerts May–Nov Wed 8pm. U-Bahn: Stephansplatz.

Kapuzinerkirche and Kaisergruft (Imperial Burial Vault)   The Kapuziner Church contains the Imperial Burial Vault and the coffins of 136 Habsburgs, including 12 emperors and 17 empresses. Some of the coffins are elaborate, made of pewter and adorned with skulls, angels, and other harbingers of death. The biggest belongs to Empress Maria Theresa and her husband and is topped with their reclining statues; it's surrounded by the coffins of their 16 children, many of whom died in infancy. Franz Josef and Elisabeth are also here. The only non-Habsburg to be buried here was the governess to Maria Theresa and her children. Each coffin has two keys, which are kept in separate places.

Only the embalmed bodies are contained inside—the intestines are kept in copper urns in the catacombs of Stephansdom, reviewed above, while the hearts are in the Augustiner Church.

Neuer Markt 1 (inside the Ring, behind the Opera House on tiny Tegetthoffstrasse). (℡ 01/512 68 53-12. www.kapuziner.at. Admission 4€ ($4.60) adults, 3€ ($3.45) seniors and students, 1.50€ ($1.75) children 13 and under. Daily 9:30am–4pm (must enter by 3:40pm). U-Bahn: Stephansplatz.

THE TOP MUSEUMS

In Vienna's bid to become one of Europe's hottest cities for contemporary art, in 2001 it opened the **MuseumsQuartier Wien** just west of the Kunsthistorisches Museum. In addition to the **MUMOK (Museum of Modern Art)** and the

Special & Free Events

If you're coming to Vienna for the opera or theater, avoid July and August—the Staatsoper, Volksoper, Burgtheater, and Akademietheater are all closed then (although the Staatsoper does have an operetta in Aug). In addition, in July and August there are no performances of the Spanish Riding School (nor in Jan or Feb) or the Vienna Boys' Choir. However, Vienna's **Summer of Music** festival features many other events.

It's not surprising that many of Vienna's festivals and events revolve around music. The **Operetta Festival** in early February stages productions at the Volksoper. In February and March there's a **Haydn Festival,** followed by **Osterklang (Sound of Easter Festival),** with performances by famous orchestras the week leading up to Easter. The **Wiener Festwochen (Vienna Festival)** in May and June features primarily new and avant-garde theater productions, with guest companies performing in various languages, including English, as well as jazz and classical concerts and art exhibits. On the last weekend in June, the **Danube Island Festival** is a gigantic open-air party on the banks of the river, complete with rock, pop, and folk music performed on many stages and an evening fireworks display—all free.

In July and August there's something going on almost every night. Vienna's **Klangbogen Wien (Rainbow of Music)** features about 150 concerts and events at the city's most beautiful venues, including weekly operettas, classical concerts, and Viennese waltzes at Schönbrunn. Don't miss the open-air performances of Mozart's operas staged in front of the Roman ruins in Schönbrunn Park. Another popular event is the free **Festival of Music Films,** with evening open-air performances of famous orchestras and conductors shown on a giant screen in front of the Rathaus (City Hall) July through August, and with food stalls offering culinary specialties from around the world.

The annual **Schubert Festival** is in November. December brings the outdoor **Christmas bazaar,** with stalls selling handcrafted items and decorations in front of the Rathaus, on Spittelberg, and on Freyung. Another popular winter event is the **Wiener Eistraum,** which features a large public ice-skating rink in front of the Rathaus, open the end of January to the beginning of March daily 9am to 11pm; after 9pm it becomes an ice-skating disco. Skates are available for rent.

Leopold Museum, described below, other attractions in the complex include the **Architektur Zentrum Wien,** the **Kunsthalle** with temporary exhibits of contemporary art, the **Zoom-Kindermuseum (Zoom Children's Museum),** restaurants, shops, a dance theater, and art studios.

Albertina Museum 🟊🟊 Occupying the southern tip of the Hofburg, this museum is renowned for its graphic arts collection of hand-drawn sketches, drawings, posters, and lithographs dating from the late 15th to 20th centuries. Included in the collection are works by all the great masters—Raphael, Rubens, Rembrandt, Michelangelo, da Vinci, and Dürer, as well as works by Klimt, Schiele, Kokoschka, and other Austrian artists. Exhibitions change every 3 months, drawing on the museum's own collection and international contributions. Several elegant State Rooms are also open for viewing. Expect to spend at least an hour here.

Albertinaplatz 1. ✆ 01/534 83-540. www.albertina.at. Admission 9€ ($10) adults, 7.50€ ($8.65) seniors, 6.50€ ($7.50) students and children, 21€ ($24) families. Daily 10am–6pm (to 9pm Wed). U-Bahn: Karlsplatz or Stephansplatz. Tram: 1, 2, D, or J to Oper.

Heeresgeschichtliches Museum (Museum of Military History) Housed in an elaborate Moorish-Byzantine–style building constructed in the 1850s as part of the Vienna Arsenal, this museum has an admirable collection of Austrian weapons, uniforms, and memorabilia from the Thirty Years' War through World War II. You'll find armor used by knights, Ottoman bows and arrows from the Turkish Wars, an air balloon used by the French for aerial reconnaissance during the Napoleonic wars, sabers, planes, tanks, heavy artillery, and model ships. One room explores 200 years of Austrian naval history (remember, Austria is a landlocked country). Perhaps most interesting are the displays relating to the outbreak of World War I, including the automobile in which Archduke Franz Ferdinand and Archduchess Sophie were riding when they were assassinated in Sarajevo, and even the blood-stained uniform the archduke was wearing. The use of an audioguide in English is included in the price. It takes about an hour to tour the museum.

Arsenal. ✆ 01/79 561-0. www.bmlv.gv.at/hgm. Admission 5.10€ ($5.85) adults, 3.30€ ($3.80) seniors, students, and children, 7.30€ ($7) families, free for children 9 and under. Sat–Thurs 9am–5pm. Tram: D or 18 to Südbahnhof. Bus: 13A to Südbahnhof.

KunstHausWien 🟊🟊 *Finds* This one-of-a-kind museum showcases the life-long works of painter/designer Friedensreich Hundertwasser, famous for his whimsical, fantastical, and dramatically colorful paintings, prints, and architecture. Created from a former Thonet chair factory, the museum, which takes about an hour to tour, houses about 300 of his works, including paintings, prints, tapestries, and architectural models. Temporary shows feature the works of international artists. Typical of Hundertwasser (who died in 2000), the building itself is one of the exhibits, a colorful protest against the mundane gray of modern cities. Be sure to see the **Hundertwasser Haus,** an apartment complex Hundertwasser designed on the corner of Kegelgasse and Löwengasse in the mid-1980s (about a 5-min. walk away). On Kegelgasse is also **Kalke Village,** another Hundertwasser architectural conversion, this time a former stable and gas station turned into a small shopping complex, open daily 9am to 7pm in summer (to 5pm in winter).

Untere Weissgerberstrasse 13. ✆ 01/712 04 91. www.kunsthauswien.com. Admission 8€ ($9.20) adults, 6€ ($6.90) seniors, students, and children, free for children under 10, 50% discount Mon (except holidays); temporary exhibits extra. Daily 10am–7pm. Tram: N or O to Radetzkyplatz.

Kunsthistorisches Museum (Museum of Fine Arts) ★★★

This great museum owes its existence largely to the Habsburgs, who for centuries were patrons and collectors of art. There are several collections, of which the **Egyptian-Oriental Collection** (with sarcophagi, reliefs, statues, and portraits of kings) and the **Picture Gallery** are the most outstanding. Other displays feature coins and medals, as well as sculpture and applied arts from the medieval, Renaissance, and baroque periods. The Picture Gallery, on the first floor, contains paintings by **Rubens, Rembrandt, Dürer, Titian, Giorgione, Tintoretto, Caravaggio,** and **Velázquez.** The high point of the museum is the world's largest collection of **Bruegels,** including the *Turmbau zu Babel (Tower of Babel), Die Jäger im Schnee (The Hunters in the Snow*—you can hardly believe it's not real), the *Kinderspiel* (in which children have taken over an entire town), and *Die Bauernhochzeit (The Peasant Wedding*—notice how the bride is isolated in front of the green cloth, barred by custom from eating or talking). You can easily spend 2 hours here.

Maria-Theresien-Platz. ⓒ 01/525 24-0. www.khm.at. Admission 10€ ($12) adults, 7.50€ ($8.65) seniors, students, and children, 20€ ($23) families, free for children under 7. Tues–Wed and Fri–Sun 10am–6pm; Thurs 10am–9pm. U-Bahn: Volkstheater or MuseumsQuartier. Tram: 1, 2, D, or J to Burgring.

Leopold Museum ★★★

The centerpiece of the MuseumsQuartier, this outstanding collection of Austrian modernist masterpieces covers movements from the late Romantic period to the mid-1900s, including art produced during the Jugendstil, Secessionist, and expressionist periods. Major works by Gustav Klimt, Oskar Kokoschka, Richard Gerstl, Herbert Boeckl, Alfred Kubin, Ferdinand Georg Waldmüller, and Anton Romako are on display, but the absolute highlight of the museum is the world's largest collection of paintings by **Egon Schiele,** who produced 330 oil canvases and more than 2,500 drawings and watercolors before dying at 28; the museum owns some 200 of his works. Also on display are major objects of Austrian arts and crafts such as furniture and glassware from the late 19th and 20th centuries, with works by Otto Wagner, Adolf Loos, Josef Hoffmann, Kolo Moser, and Franz Hagenauer. A must-see; you can easily spend 2 hours here.

Museumsplatz 1. ⓒ 01/525 70-0. www.leopoldmuseum.org. Admission 9€ ($10) adults, 5.50€ ($6.35) seniors, students, and children; combination ticket to Leopold Museum and MUMOK (see below) 16€ ($18) adults, 11€ ($13) seniors, students, and children. Mon and Wed–Fri 10am–9pm; Sat–Sun 10am–7pm. U-Bahn: Volkstheater or MuseumsQuartier.

Liechtenstein Museum ★★

This private collection, housed in an elegant palace built in the late 17th and early 18th centuries by the Prince of Liechtenstein, boasts amazing works of art ranging from Renaissance and baroque portraits to Dutch landscapes, paintings from the Austrian Biedermeier period, and sculpture. Masterpieces by Raphael, Van Dyck, Cranach, Rembrandt, van Ruysdael, Amerling, and Waldmüller are on display in permanent and temporary exhibits, but a highlight of the collection is one of the world's largest holdings of works by Rubens. Decorative arts, including weapons, porcelain, and one of the most beautiful French ceremonial carriages—the rococo Golden Coach—are also on display. You'll spend at least an hour here.

Fürstengasse 1. ⓒ 01/319 57 67-252. www.liechtensteinmuseum.at. Admission 10€ ($12) adults, 8€ ($9.20) seniors, 5€ ($5.70) students and children, 20€ ($23) families. Wed–Mon 9am–8pm. Tram: D to Porzellangasse.

Mak-Österreichisches Museum für Angewandte Kunst (Austrian Museum of Applied Arts) 🕸🕸 Europe's oldest museum of applied arts, this

is a fine collection of Austrian ceramics, furniture, silver, and jewelry, housed in a 19th-century building in Florentine Renaissance style. The exhibits are arranged chronologically, from Romanesque to 20th-century design; English-language leaflets in each room painstakingly describe the exhibits and their historic significance. Highlights include a fascinating collection of Viennese chairs from the 1800s (including Thonet) as well as designs of the Wiener Werkstätte, a remarkable workshop founded in the early 1900s by Josef Hoffmann, Kolo Moser, and Fritz Waerndorfer. The Jugendstil collections are particularly outstanding. There are also exhibits devoted to works from Asia, with lacquerware, porcelain, and Buddha statues. At times, the museum hosts special exhibits of experimental contemporary art from around the world.

Stubenring 5. ⓒ 01/711 36-0. www.mak.at. Admission 7.90€ ($6) adults, 4€ ($4.60) seniors, students, and children, 11€ ($13) families, free admission Sat. Tues 10am–midnight; Wed–Sun 10am–6pm. U-Bahn: Stubentor. Tram: 1 or 2 to Stubentor.

MUMOK (Museum of Modern Art Stiftung Ludwig Wien) 🕸🕸 This

museum in the MuseumsQuartier showcases international 20th-century art, with an emphasis on "classical modern" art from expressionism and cubism to abstraction, pop art, photo realism, and contemporary media art. The museum's biggest contribution to the art world is its preservation of Viennese Actionism, which emerged in the 1960s at the same time as performance art was gaining attention in the United States and shocked audiences with its aggressive attacks on social taboos. Works by Picasso, Kokoschka, Kandinsky, Warhol, Rauschenberg, Roy Lichtenstein, Nam June Paik, Joseph Beuys, Günther Brus, and many others are presented in both permanent and temporary exhibits. Depending on your level of interest, it should take between 1 and 2 hours to wander the five floors here.

Museumsplatz 1. ⓒ 01/525 00. www.mumok.at. Admission 8€ ($9.20) adults, 6.50€ ($7.50) seniors, students, and children; combination ticket to Leopold Museum (see above) and MUMOK 16€ ($18) adults, 11€ ($13) seniors, students, and children. Tues–Wed and Fri–Sun 10am–6pm; Thurs 10am–9pm. U-Bahn: Volkstheater or MuseumsQuartier.

Österreichische Galerie Belvedere (Austrian Gallery) 🕸🕸 The

Belvedere is an airy baroque palace built in the early 1700s as a summer residence for Prince Eugene of Savoy, who protected Austria from Turkish invasion. His reward was to be made minister of war and then prime minister by Emperor Charles VI. He never married, and when he died his estate went to his heiress— frightful Victoria, as the Viennese called her—who promptly sold it. The Imperial Court acquired the buildings and gardens in 1752. It was here that Archduke Franz Ferdinand, heir to the throne, and his wife, Sophie, lived before taking their fateful trip to Sarajevo in 1914.

The Belvedere, which today houses the Austrian Gallery, is actually two palaces separated by a beautiful formal garden. The **Oberes Belvedere** (the one closest to the Südbahnhof) is the more lavish, up on a hill with a sweeping city view. Its **Marble Hall,** used for receptions and the site of the 1955 treaty signaling the withdrawal of Allied troops from Austria, is the palace's most magnificent room. The Oberes Belvedere serves as a gallery for 19th- and 20th-century Austrian and international art, including Viennese art around 1900, the Biedermeier period, and neoclassicism. To make the most of your visit, consider renting the English-language audioguide for 4€ ($3.55). Artists displayed include **Renoir, Monet, Manet, Munch, van Gogh, Pissarro, Max Liebermann,** and

Lovis Corinth, as well as Austrian artists **Hans Makart, Anton Romako, Georg Waldmüller, Oskar Kokoschka** (the leader of Austrian expressionism), **Egon Schiele,** and **Gustav Klimt.** Two rooms are devoted to **Klimt,** the foremost representative of Viennese Jugendstil (Art Nouveau) painting, where you'll see his famous *Der Kuss (The Kiss), Judith* (the frame was made by his brother), and portrait of Fritza Riedler.

A walk through the garden brings you to the **Unteres Belvedere,** home of the **Museum of Austrian Baroque,** with works from the 17th and 18th centuries, including *Napoleon auf dem St. Bernhard* by Jacques Louis David and an amusing series of busts by Franz Xaver Messerschmidt, many with funny grimaces (some of his subjects were sanatorium residents). It's worth a walk through here, however, even if you're not interested in the art, as the palace rooms are finer than the remodeled modern galleries of the Oberes Belvedere. Here, too, in the former Orangerie, is the **Museum of Medieval Art,** which includes Austrian religious sculpture and panel paintings from the end of the 12th to the early 16th centuries. Incidentally, next to the Unteres Belvedere is **SalmBräu,** a microbrewery serving Austrian fare and offering outdoor seating in a small courtyard. Unless you linger over a few beers, you can see Belvedere's galleries in less than 2 hours.

Prinz-Eugen-Strasse 27 (Oberes Belvedere) and Rennweg 6a (Unteres Belvedere). ✆ 01/79 557-0. www.belvedere.at. Admission 7.50€ ($8.65) adults, 5€ ($5.75) seniors and students, 3€ ($3.45) children, free for children under 11. Summer Tues–Sun 10am–6pm. Tram: D to Oberes Belvedere or 71 to Unteres Belvedere.

Sigmund Freud Museum Sigmund Freud, founder of psychoanalysis, lived and worked here (he wrote *The Interpretation of Dreams* and saw patients here) from 1891 to 1938, when he fled the Nazis. This small museum documents his life, with first editions of his works, original waiting-room furniture, personal possessions, and photographs of him, his mother, his wife, and others who influenced his life. A notebook in English identifies everything in the museum, with translations of passages written by Freud. A video shows personal films taken of the Freud family in the 1930s. A visit here takes about 30 minutes.

Berggasse 19. ✆ 01/319 15 96. www.freud-museum.at. Admission 5€ ($5.75) adults, 4€ ($4.60) seniors, 3€ ($3.45) students, 2€ ($2.30) children. Daily 9am–5pm (to 6pm July–Sept). U-Bahn: Schottentor. Tram: D to Schlickgasse.

Wien Museum This museum is devoted to Vienna's 7,000 years of history, from the Neolithic period and the time of the tribal migrations through the Middle Ages to the blossoming of Biedermeier and Jugendstil. You'll see Roman vases; statues and stained-glass windows from Stephansdom; armor used by knights; booty from the Turkish invasions; models of the city; portraits of Maria Theresa, Kaiser Franz Joseph I and his wife Elisabeth; historic photographs; decorative arts by Josef Hoffmann, Kolo Moser, and other artists of the Wiener Werkstätte; and paintings by Klimt, Kokoschka, Waldmüller, and Schiele, among others. One room is the complete interior of poet Franz Grillparzer's Biedermeier-era apartment; another holds the 1903 living room of the architect Loos. You'll spend about 45 minutes here.

Karlsplatz 4. ✆ 01/505 87 47-0. www.wienmuseum.at. Admission 4€ ($4.60) adults, 2€ ($2.30) seniors, students, and children. Tues–Sun 9am–6pm. U-Bahn: Karlsplatz.

AN AMUSEMENT PARK

Prater *(Kids)* Prater is Vienna's amusement park, opened to the general public in 1766 on the former grounds of Emperor Maximilian II's game preserve. Most notable is its giant Ferris wheel, built in 1896 (then rebuilt after its destruction in World War II) and measuring 60m (200 ft.) in diameter; rides take 20 minutes and give a great view of Vienna, especially at night. There are also some 200 booths and both old and new attractions, including the usual shooting ranges, amusement rides ranging from bumper cars and miniature train rides to roller coasters and a bungee ejection-seat, game arcades, restaurants, beer halls, and beer gardens. Compared to today's slick amusement parks, Prater seems endearingly old-fashioned; kids, of course, love it.

Prater Hauptallee. © 01/728 05 16. Free admission to park; charges vary for amusement rides (Ferris wheel and its museum cost 7.50€/$8.65 adults, 3€/$3.45 children). May–Sept daily 9am–midnight; Mar–Apr and Oct daily 10am–10pm. Closed Nov–Feb. U-Bahn: Praterstern.

MEMORIALS TO VIENNA'S MUSICAL GENIUSES

If you're a fan of Mozart, Schubert, Strauss, Haydn, or Beethoven, you've come to the right city. Here you'll find the houses where they lived, the cemetery where most of them are buried, and statues of these musical giants everywhere (especially in the Stadtpark and the Burggarten). Music lovers may also want to walk the **Music Mile "Hall of Fame,"** which stretches from the Theater an der Wien on Linke Wienzeile past the Staatsoper, past the Haus der Musik, and through the Altstadt to Stephansplatz. More than 80 musicians, composers, and conductors are memorialized with imbedded stars along the route, including Mozart, Beethoven, Richard Strauss, Haydn, Schubert, Leonard Bernstein, and Herbert von Karajan

For a one-stop lesson in the origins of sound, the history of the Viennese Philharmonic Orchestra, and the lives of Austria's most famous composers, take in the **Haus der Musik,** Seilerstätte 30 (© **01/516 48-51;** www.hdm.at.), inside the Ring. This hands-on museum explores the world of sound through audiovisual displays; visitors can play futuristic instruments, conduct an orchestra, listen to the gnashing of teeth (and other bodily functions), create a CD (for an extra fee), and listen to an audioguide while wandering through rooms devoted to Haydn, Mozart, Beethoven, Schubert, and other famous composers. Expect to spend about 90 minutes here. Admission is 10€ ($12) for adults, 8.50€ ($9.80) for students and seniors, and 5.50€ ($6.35) for children. It's open daily 10am to 10pm.

In addition, you might like to see the interior of the **Staatsoper,** Opernring 2 (© **01/514 44-2606;** U-Bahn: Karlsplatz). Built from 1861 to 1869 and rebuilt after World War II, it's one of the world's finest opera houses (see "Vienna After Dark," below). Alas, there are no performances during July and August, although other performances (such as concerts) are held here then, and tours of the Staatsoper are conducted throughout the year—check the board outside the entrance on Kärntner Strasse for a schedule of the day's tours, usually twice a day in winter and as many as five times a day in summer, in English and German. Tours, about 40 minutes long, cost 4.50€ ($5.20) adults, 3.50€ ($4) seniors, 2€ ($2.30) students, and 1.50€ ($1.75) children.

You can visit the apartments where the composers lived. Set up as memorials, they're a bit plain and unadorned, of interest only to devoted music fans. With the exception of Figarohaus (see below), all the apartments are open the same hours (Tues–Sun 9am–12:15pm and 1–4:30pm). Admission for each is 2€ ($2.30) for adults and 1€ ($1.15) for students and children; admission is free on Sunday and Friday morning (except holidays).

Ludwig van Beethoven (1770–1827) came to Vienna from Germany when he was 22 and stayed here until his death. From 1804 to 1815 he lived on and off at the **Beethoven-Gedenkstätte,** in the Pasqualati House, Mölker Bastei 8 (℃ **01/ 535 89 05;** U-Bahn: Schottentor; tram: 1, 2, or D to Schottentor). Moody, rebellious, and eventually going deaf, he had habits so irregular (he sometimes played and composed in the middle of the night) that he was constantly being evicted from apartments all over Vienna. One landlord who loved him, however, was Mr. Pasqualati, who kept Beethoven's apartment free—no one else was allowed to live in it, even when the composer wasn't there. Beethoven composed his fourth, fifth, and seventh symphonies here. Adjoining it is the **Adalbert Stifter Memorial,** with paintings and drawings. You can visit other places where Beethoven lived: at **Gedenkstätte Heiligenstädter Testament,** Probusgasse 6 (℃ **01/370 54 08;** tram: 37 to Geweygasse; bus: 38A to Armbrustergasse); and the **Eroica House,** Döblinger Hauptstrasse 92 (℃ **01/369 14 24;** tram: 37 to Pokornygasse).

Inventor of the symphony, Joseph Haydn (1732–1809) bought the tiny **Haydn-Wohnhaus mit Brahms-Gedenkraum,** Haydngasse 19 (℃ **01/596 13 07;** U-Bahn: Zieglergasse), in 1793 and lived here until his death, creating most of his major works here, including *Die Jahreszeiten (The Seasons).* In addition to his letters, manuscripts, and personal mementos are two pianos and his death mask. Earphones allow you to listen to his compositions. There's also a memorial room to Brahms, with a few of his personal items and photos.

Born in Salzburg, Wolfgang Amadeus Mozart (1756–91) moved to Vienna in 1781 but moved around often, occupying more than a dozen apartments. At the **Figarohaus** (📷, Domgasse 5, just off Stephansplatz (℃ **01/513 62 94;** U-Bahn: Stephansplatz), Mozart lived with his wife Constanze and his son from 1784 to 1787. These were his happiest years. Here he wrote *The Marriage of Figaro* and received visits from Haydn and the 16-year-old Beethoven. Set in what used to be a wealthy neighborhood, the Figarohaus was already 200 years old when Mozart lived here. Mozart later lived in poverty and died a pauper. His apartment, open Tuesday to Sunday 9am to 6pm, is on the first floor, which you can reach by walking through a tiny courtyard and up some dark stairs. Headphones with Mozart's music are available for self-guided tours. Admission here is 4€ ($4.60) adults; 2€ ($2.30) seniors, students, and children.

Schubert's Birthplace, Nussdorfer Strasse 54 (℃ **01/317 36 01;** tram: 37 or 38 to Canisiusgasse), is obviously where Franz Schubert was born in 1797, the 12th of 14 children. At that time, as many as 17 families occupied the modest two-story building. A versatile and prolific composer, Schubert is most famous for his songs but also wrote symphonies and chamber music. He died when he was only 31. You can visit the place of his death at Kettenbrückengasse 6 (℃ **01/581 67 30;** U-Bahn: Kettenbrückengasse).

The **Johann-Strauss-Wohnung,** Praterstrasse 54 (℃ **01/214 01 21;** U-Bahn: Nestroyplatz), is where Strauss (1825–99) composed his famous *Blue Danube Waltz,* which is probably better known than the Austrian national anthem. He lived here from 1863 to 1870.

Austria's largest cemetery, the **Zentralfriedhof (Central Cemetery),** Simmeringer Hauptstrasse 234 (℃ **01/760 41;** tram: 71 from Schwarzenbergplatz to Zentralfriedhof), contains the graves of the Strausses (father and sons), Brahms, Schubert, Franz von Suppé, and Beethoven, as well as a commemorative grave for Mozart. To find the Graves of Honor, near the Dr. Karl Lueger

Church where you'll find all the composers buried within a few feet of each other, walk straight ahead from the main entrance (Gate 2) on the large pathway—the graves are to the left just before the path ends at the church. Admission is free. The cemetery is open daily, summer 7am to 7pm and winter 8am to 5pm.

ORGANIZED TOURS

WALKING TOURS   A number of walking tours are conducted in English. **Walks in Vienna** (© 01/774 89 01 or 894 53 63; www.wienguide.at), for example, offers guided walks through medieval Vienna and other parts of the city. It also conducts themed walks that center on Mozart and other famous musicians; the history of Jews in Vienna; the life and times of Sigmund Freud; underground Vienna with its crypts, wine cellars, and excavations; and other topics. Tours (excluding entrance fees) cost 11€ ($13) adults and 6€ ($6.90) children. The brochure *Walks in Vienna* details the various tours, times, and departure points—pick one up at the Vienna Tourist Board. No reservations are necessary for the tours, which last 1½ to 2 hours and are held throughout the year regardless of the weather.

BIKE TOURS   **Pedal Power,** Ausstellungsstrasse 3 (© 01/729 72 34), offers 3-hour bike tours of Vienna May through September at 10am daily, taking cyclists past the Staatsoper, the Hofburg, Stephansdom, and other points of interest. Cost of the tour is 23€ ($26) adults; there are discounts for students and children.

BUS TOURS   A number of companies offer general city tours and specialized tours, which you can book at travel agencies and at top hotels. The oldest tour company is **Vienna Sightseeing Tours,** Stelzhamergasse 4 (© 01/712 46 83-0; www.viennasightseeingtours.com), which offers various tours that include performances of the Spanish Riding School, the Vienna Boys' Choir Sunday Mass performance in the Hofburg chapel, the Vienna Woods and the Mayerling hunting lodge where Crown Prince Rudolph and Baroness Maria Vetsera committed suicide, the wine-growing district of Grinzing, and more. A 3½-hour city tour, which includes a visit through Schönbrunn, costs 33€ ($38) adults and 15€ ($17) children. Departure is from the Staatsoper or major hotels.

For those who prefer to go it alone but would like the convenience of door-to-door transportation with commentary along the way, there's the **Vienna Line Hop-On, Hop-Off** (© 01/712 46 83-0), private buses that travel three routes to most of the city's major sights, including the State Opera and St. Stephen's Cathedral, and outlying sights like the Prater, KunstHausWien, and Schönbrunn and Belvedere palaces. There are 13 stops, with guided commentary provided in between, and you can get off and get back on as often as you like; buses arrive at every stop every hour or 2. Tickets, sold on the bus, cost 20€ ($23) for adults and 7€ ($8.05) for children for 1 day.

Tips **Enjoying Vienna's Outdoor Activities**

Active vacationers should pick up the free *Sports & Nature in Vienna* at the Vienna Tourist Information office. This brochure is packed with information on the where and how of jogging, hiking, swimming, biking, and other outdoor activities in parks and green spaces throughout Vienna.

TRAM TOURS May to September, 1-hour tours of Vienna via a 1929-vintage tramcar are conducted Saturday at 11:30am and 1:30pm and Sunday and holidays at 9:30, 11:30am, and 1:30pm. Departure is from the Otto Wagner Pavilion on Karlsplatz; the cost is 15€ ($17) adults and 5€ ($5.75) children. For details, call ✆ 01/7909-105 or contact the Vienna Tourist Information office (see "Visitor Information" in "Essentials," earlier in this chapter).

BOAT TOURS Boats cruise the Danube during the warmer months, departing from a pier next to the Schwedenbrücke (U-Bahn: Schwedenplatz). One of the most popular is the 1½-hour "Hundertwasser Total Tour" offered by **DDSG Blue Danube** (✆ **01/588 80-0;** www.ddsg-blue-danube.at), departing Reichsbrücke from the end of April to the end of October daily at noon and 4pm on a boat designed by Hundertwasse himself; it includes a trip to KunstHausWien and coffee and cake onboard, and costs 22€ ($25). Other boat trips offered by DDSG include Sunday cruises as far as Krems and Dürnstein (May–Sept), daily cruises between Krems and Melk (Apr–Sept), and evening dinner cruises.

5 Shopping

Vienna is known for the excellent quality of many items, which of course don't come cheap. If money is no object, you might want to shop for petit-point items, hand-painted Augarten porcelain, gold or enamel jewelry, ceramics, and leather goods. Other popular items are suits made of loden (the boiled and rolled wool fabric made into overcoats), hats, and knitted sweaters.

Vienna's most famous **shopping streets** are inside the Ring in the city center, including the pedestrian-only Kärntner Strasse, Graben, Kohlmarkt, and Rotenturmstrasse. Mariahilfer Strasse west of the Ring also has department stores, boutiques, and specialty shops.

If you make a purchase of more than 75€ ($86) at any store on any given day, you're entitled to a partial recovery of the **16.67% value-added tax (VAT).** See chapter 1, "Enjoying Europe on a Budget," for details.

If you're in Vienna on Saturday, head straight for the best-known flea market, held just past the Naschmarkt outdoor market on **Linke Wienzeile** near the Kettenbrücken U-Bahn station. This is the most colorful (and crowded) place to look for curios, antiques, jewelry, ethnic clothing, and junk. Be sure to haggle. It's open Saturday about 8am to dusk (to about 6pm in summer). It's also worth a trip to the adjoining **Naschmarkt,** Vienna's outdoor food-and-produce market, open Monday to Friday 6am to 6:30pm and Saturday 6am to 5pm (see "Great Deals on Dining," earlier in this chapter).

A **market for arts, crafts, and antiques,** held May to August, takes place Saturday 2 to 6pm and Sunday 10am to 8pm along the promenade of the Donaukanal at Franz-Joseph-Kai (near the Schwedenplatz U-Bahn station). May to December, a small **art and antiques market** is held inside the Ring at Am Hof every Friday and Saturday 10am to 7pm, with about 40 vendors. Finally, there's another wonderful market, the **Spittelberg Arts and Crafts Exhibition** (U-Bahn: Volkstheater or MuseumsQuartier; tram: 49 to Spittelberg), held over Easter and in December until Christmas; artists sell arts and crafts up and down historic Spittelberg Street, outside the Ring just west of the MuseumsQuartier.

6 Vienna After Dark

Everything in Vienna is somewhat theatrical, perhaps because of its majestic baroque backdrop. Small wonder that opera and theater reign supreme. It would be a shame if you came all this way without experiencing something that's very dear to the Viennese heart.

To find out what's being played on Vienna's many stages, pick up a copy of *Wien-Programm,* a monthly brochure available free at Vienna Tourist Information. In addition to its details on theatrical productions, concerts, events, and other programs, it lists box offices where you can buy tickets in advance, thereby avoiding the 22% surcharge at travel agencies. If you're a student under 27 with a current valid ID, you can buy tickets at reduced prices for the Staatsoper (Austrian State Opera) and Burgtheater on the night of the performance (a current student card from your university is required; an International Student Identity Card on its own won't be accepted as proof of status). Even if you're not a student, you can see the Staatsoper for as little as 2€ to 3.50€ ($2.30–$4) for standing-room tickets.

THE PERFORMING ARTS

For advance sales of tickets for the Burgtheater, Staatsoper, and several other state theaters, go first to the **Bundestheaterkassen,** Hanushgasse 3 (© **01/514 44-0;** U-Bahn: Karlsplatz), a minute's walk northwest of the Staatsoper. They go on sale a month before the performance. It's open Monday to Friday 8am to 6pm and Saturday, Sunday, and holidays 9am to noon (the 1st Sat of the month 9am–5pm). Tickets for individual theaters are also available at each box office.

You can order tickets for the Staatsoper, Volksoper, or Burgtheater using a credit card by calling © **01/513 15 13** daily 10am to 9pm. You can also order tickets via the Internet at **www.wiener-staatsoper.at** and **www.burgtheater.at**.

OPERA & BALLET   One of the world's leading opera houses and under the musical direction of Seiji Ozawa since 2002, the **Staatsoper,** Opernring 2 (© **01/514 44-2250;** www.wiener-staatsoper.at; U-Bahn: Karlsplatz), stages grand productions throughout the year, except July and August. It's traditional to start each year with Johann Strauss's operetta *Die Fledermaus,* followed by a repertoire of 40 operatic works each season. Opera or ballet, accompanied by the Viennese Philharmonic Orchestra, is presented nightly September to June. (In Aug, an operetta is sometimes performed as well.) A staff of about 1,200, including the stage crew, singers, and production workers, make sure everything runs smoothly. At 488 sq. m (5,300 sq. ft.), the stage area is one of Europe's largest and is even much larger than the spectator floor of the opera house, which holds 2,200 to 1,700 in seats and 500 in the standing-room sections. Tours are given almost daily throughout the year, two to five times a day (see "Seeing the Sights," above).

However, the cheapest way to see the opera house and a performance to boot is to buy 1 of the 500 standing-room tickets available only on the night of the performance. To do so, go to the Staatsoper at least 3 hours before the performance, stand in line, and buy your ticket (tickets go on sale an hour before the performance); once inside, mark your space by tying a scarf to the rail. You can then leave and come back just before the performance. True seats are 10€ to 178€ ($12–$205) for most productions; standing room is 2€ ($2.30) for the Galerie and Balkon (upper balconies) or 3.50€ ($4) for the slightly better Parterrestehplatz (ground floor).

Although not as famous, the **Volksoper,** Währinger Strasse 78 (© **01/514 44-3670;** www.volksoper.at; U-Bahn: Schottentor), also stages operas, operettas, and musicals, with tickets at 4€ to 65€ ($4.60–$75). Student reductions on unsold tickets are available 30 minutes before the performance for 7.50€ ($8.65). Standing-room tickets, available only on the night of performance, cost 1.50€ to 2€ ($1.75–$2.30).

THEATER The **Burgtheater,** Dr.-Karl-Lueger-Ring 2 (*(C)* **01/51444-4140;** www.burgtheater.at; tram: 1, 2, or D to Burgtheater), stages German classics as well as modern plays from new Austrian authors, from Friedrich Schiller's *Wilhelm Tell* to Georg Büchner's *Woyzeck.* Actors consider an engagement here a highlight in their careers. Performances are given most evenings September to June, with seats at 4€ to 44€ ($4.60–$51). Standing room is 1.50€ ($1.75), student prices for unsold tickets are 7€ ($8.05), and last-minute tickets, available an hour before the performance, go for half-price.

The **Theater an der Wien,** Linke Wienzeile 6 (U-Bahn: Karlsplatz), **Ronacher,** Seilerstätte 9 (U-Bahn: Stephansplatz); and the **Raimundtheater,** Wallgasse 18–20 (U-Bahn: Westbahnhof), stage musicals as part of the Vereinigte Bühen (United Theaters). Previous productions have been *Les Misérables, The Phantom of the Opera, Hair, Mozart!, Kiss of the Spider Woman,* and *Dance of the Vampire.* Performances are given daily throughout the year. The box office for all three, a small pavilion called **Wien Ticket,** on Kärntner Strasse beside the Staatsoper (*(C)* **01/58885;** www.wien-ticket.at), is open daily 10am to 7pm. Seats for Theater an der Wien and Raimundtheater start at 10€ ($9), with standing-room tickets (available an hour before the performance) costing 2.50€ ($2.90). Seats for Ronacher start at around 20€ ($23). Half-price tickets for that evening's performance go on sale at Wien Ticket after 2pm.

The English-language **International Theatre,** Porzellangasse 8 (*(C)* **01/319 62 72;** U-Bahn: Rossauer Lände), presents American and British plays, usually offering four productions a year and an annual presentation of Dickens's *A Christmas Carol.* Performances are September to July, Tuesday to Saturday at 7:30pm. The box office is open Monday to Friday 11am to 3pm. Tickets are 22€ ($25); half price for students and seniors. And the **English Theater,** Josefsgasse 12 (*(C)* **01/402 12 60;** www.englishtheater.at; U-Bahn: Rathaus), stages professional productions of both classic and contemporary plays, with performances usually Monday to Saturday at 7:30pm. Tickets are 14€ to 36€ ($16–$41), and its box office is open Monday to Friday 10am to 7:30pm.

CLASSICAL MUSIC Be sure to check *Wien-Programm* for a current listing of concerts. The **Schönbrunner Palace Ensemble** (*(C)* **01/812 500 40**), for example, performs nightly at 8:30pm in the 18th-century Schönbrunn Orangerie, playing works written by Mozart and Strauss; tickets cost 36€ to 50€ ($41–$58). The **Konzerte im Mozarthaus** is a string quartet of musicians dressed in period costumes performing works by Mozart, Haydn, Schubert, and Beethoven; concerts take place in Vienna's oldest concert hall of the Deutsch Ordenshaus, Singerstrasse 7 (*(C)* **01/911 90 77;** www.mozarthaus.at; U-Bahn: Stephansplatz), Thursday, Saturday, and Sunday, and cost 29€ to 35€ ($33–$40). An orchestra playing Johann Strauss waltzes and excerpts from Mozart operas accompany opera singers and ballet dancers at the **Kursalon** in the Stadtpark (*(C)* **01/512 57 90;** www.soundofvienna.at; U-Bahn: Stadtpark) nightly (7:30pm in winter, 8:30pm summer), with tickets starting at 36€ ($41). A great place for **free entertainment** in July and August is in front of the Rathaus, where a giant screen presents performances of famous orchestras and conductors, while stalls offer ethnic food.

LIVE-MUSIC HOUSES

The **Metropol,** Hernalser Hauptstrasse 55 (✆ 01/407 77 407; www.wiener-metropol.at; tram: 43 from Schottentor to Elterleinplatz), has served as a mecca of the Viennese youth scene for more than a decade, with productions ranging from rock, new wave, jazz, and reggae concerts to cabaret and musical retrospectives. It's open Tuesday to Saturday from 8pm, with a 10€ to 36€ ($12–$41) cover. **Planet Music,** Adalbert-Stifter-Strasse 73 (✆ 01/332 46 41; www.planet.tt; tram: 31, 32, or N; bus: 11A or 35A), formerly known as Rockhaus, is one of Vienna's best venues for blues, rock, hip-hop, rap, jazz, new wave, metal, and alternative music, as well as raves and clubbings. International groups provide the main entertainment, while Austrian musicians are usually the warm-up. It's open Tuesday to Sunday; the bar opens at 6pm and concerts begin around 8pm. Cover is 7.50€ to 15€ ($8.65–$17) for local bands and 15€ to 25€ ($17–$29) for international bands.

The basement-level **Tunnel,** Florianigasse 39, behind the Rathaus (✆ 01/405 34 65; www.tunnetl-vienna-live.at; U-Bahn: Rathaus; tram: 5; bus: 13A), attracts a university crowd with its live music 365 nights a year, from blues and rock to folk and jazz. Groups are mainly European, including bands from eastern Europe. Free jazz sessions are featured on Sunday and Monday; otherwise, cover is generally 3€ to 12€ ($3.45–$14). Tunnel's music venue is open daily 8pm to 2am (live music begins around 9pm); an inexpensive ground-floor restaurant/bar is open daily 9am to 2am (see "Great Deals on Dining," earlier in this chapter).

BARS

HISTORIC WINE CELLARS   These two wine cellars, inside the Ring, are among the city's most famous. With a history stretching back several centuries, the **Augustiner Keller,** located below the Albertina Museum at Augustinerstrasse 1 (✆ 01/533 10 26; U-Bahn: Karlsplatz or Stephansplatz), boasts wooden floors, a vaulted brick ceiling, and a long narrow room that once served as a monastery cellar. A *Heuriger* (wine tavern) serving wine from its own vineyards, it offers free traditional *Heurigenmusik* daily starting at 6:30pm. The menu includes grilled chicken, pork cutlet, grilled shank of pork, *Tafelspitz,* and *Apfelstrudel.* Since it can be crowded during mealtimes, you might consider coming for a drink early or late in the evening. The tavern is open daily 11am to midnight. **Zwölf Apostelkeller,** Sonnenfelsgasse 3 (✆ 01/512 67 77; U-Bahn: Stephansplatz), is a huge wine cellar two levels deep. The vaulting of the upper cellar is mainly 15th-century Gothic, while the lower cellar is early baroque. Unlike the Augustiner Keller above, this *Heuriger* offers only a limited menu, so you can come anytime just for drinks. Its Apostel wine is the specialty of the house. The cellar is open daily 4:30pm to midnight.

IN VIENNA'S OLD QUARTER   Most of these bars are in **Rabensteig,** the old Jewish quarter. About a 3-minute walk north of Stephansplatz, the quarter is one of Vienna's most popular nightspots and is popularly referred to as the Bermuda Triangle.

Kaffee Alt Wien, Bäckerstrasse 9 (✆ 01/512 52 22; U-Bahn: Stephansplatz or Schwedenplatz), is a dimly lit cafe/bar in the heart of Old Vienna. It opened in 1936 and is popular with students, artists, and writers. Its tired walls are hidden under a barrage of posters announcing concerts and exhibitions. Come here in the afternoon to read the paper, write letters, and relax; late at night it can get so crowded it's hard to get through the door. The cafe is open daily 10am to 2am.

Roter Engel, Rabensteig 5 (© **01/535 41 05;** U-Bahn: Schwedenplatz), boasts a slightly theatrical modern interior with various levels of seating and artwork on the walls. It opens at 6pm daily, closing at 2am Sunday to Wednesday and 4am Thursday to Saturday; there's occasional live music ranging from piano, folk, blues, and jazz to funk, for which there's a 5€ ($5.75) cover. Across the street is tiny **Casablanca,** Rabensteig 8 (© **01/533 34 63;** U-Bahn: Schwedenplatz), which offers outdoor seating and the usual wine and beer, along with live popular music provided by local bands. It's open daily 6pm to 4am, with live music beginning around 9pm. There's a music charge of 2.40€ ($2.75).

The fact that you can choose from among 50 kinds of beer makes **Krah Krah,** Rabensteig 8 (© **01/533 81 93;** U-Bahn: Schwedenplatz), one of the most popular bars in the area, as does its happy hour Monday to Friday 3:30 to 5:30pm. On Sunday from noon to 3pm, it offers free live music ranging from Dixie and swing to blues and rock. Incidentally, Krah Krah is the sound a raven makes, referring to the street Rabensteig, which means Ravens' Path. It's open Monday to Saturday 11am to 2am and Sunday 11am to 1am. Newer on the Rabensteig scene and catering to a slightly older, professional crowd with its classy decor is **Bermuda Bräu,** Rabensteig 6 (© **01/532 28 65;** U-Bahn: Schwedenplatz). Open daily 11am to 2am; happy hour is Monday to Friday 3:30 to 5:30pm, when beer is half-price. It offers a varied international menu, making this the place to come if you want to dine in the Bermuda Triangle as well as drink.

GAY & LESBIAN BARS

Be sure to pick up the free brochure *Queer Guide* at Vienna Tourist Information, packed with useful information on sightseeing, gay-oriented walking tours, and gay nightlife. Easy to spot with its pink-and-purple exterior, the **Rosa Lila Villa,** Linke Wienzeile 102 (© **01/586 81 50** for lesbians, 585 43 43 for gays; U-Bahn: Pilgramgasse), serves as Vienna's info center for gays and lesbians, dispensing details on cultural activities as well as advice, and holding discussions and encounter groups. The center is open Monday to Friday 5 to 8pm. There's also a cafe here called **Willendorf** (© **01/587 17 89**), open daily 6pm to 2am, operated by gays and lesbians and offering vegetarian food till midnight.

Goldener Spiegel, near the Naschmarkt at Linke Wienzeile 46 with an entrance on Stiegengasse (© **01/586 66 08;** U-Bahn: Kettenbrückengasse), is one of Vienna's most popular gay havens, attracting a lot of foreigners. Attached to the bar is a restaurant serving Viennese food at moderate prices and specializing in *Wiener schnitzel.* It's open daily 7pm to 2am. On the other side of Naschmarkt is the **Alte Lampe,** Heumühlgasse 13 (© **01/587 34 54;** U-Bahn: Kettenbrückengasse), Vienna's oldest gay bar, open since the 1960s, and attracting a mostly mature crowd. It's open Sunday, Wednesday, and Thursday 6pm to 1am, and Friday and Saturday 8pm to 3am. For both these places, you must ring the doorbell for admission. The well-known disco U4 (see below) stages a very popular Heaven Gay Night every Thursday from 11pm.

DANCE CLUBS

U4, Schönbrunner 222 (© **01/815 83 07;** U-Bahn: Meidling Hauptstrasse), is one of Vienna's best-known and most popular discos. In addition to staging themed nights during the week—music of the 1960s and 1970s, Italian pop, and DJ house mix—it has featured a gay night on Thursday for the past 10 years. It's open daily 10pm to 5am and charges a 5€ ($5.75) cover on Sunday and an

8€ ($9.20) cover the rest of the week. **Flex,** on the bank of the Danube Canal near Augartenbrücke (© **01/533 75 25;** U-Bahn: Schottenring), has a long-standing reputation for its grunge party scene. In addition to a super-long bar, it has a club room for DJs and live music once a week that really packs 'em in to the sounds of reggae, techno, rock, heavy bass, and more. Luckily, there's outdoor seating for those who need to cool down. It's open daily 6pm to 4am, with admission starting at 5€ ($5.75) for most events.

Another longtime favorite is **Volksgarten Disco,** located inside the Ring in the Volksgarten (© **01/533 05 18;** U-Bahn: Volkstheater; tram: 1, 2, D, or J to Dr.-Karl-Renner-Ring). It's also been a disco since the 1950s, with an interior that has changed mercifully little since then and includes a terrace and a great dance floor. It really hops Friday and Saturday nights, when it's open from 11am to 5am to the sounds of hip-hop, house, and salsa, with admission ranging from 7€ to 13€ ($8.05–$14). There are also weeknight events with DJs; check www.volksgarten.at for the month's schedule.

7 A Side Trip to the Medieval Village of Krems ★ ★

Krems, 73km (45 miles) northwest of Vienna on the Danube, is a delightful medieval village with a 1,000-year history, making it one of the oldest towns in Austria. Today it encompasses Stein, once a separate village. Krems is a mellow town of courtyards, arched gateways, impossibly narrow cobbled lanes, and partially preserved town walls. It contains more than 700 buildings from the 12th to the 19th centuries, showcasing styles ranging from Romanesque and Gothic to baroque and Renaissance.

In the fertile Wachau region of the Danube valley, Krems stretches narrowly along the river, terraced vineyards rising behind it. This is prime winemaking country, and Krems lives and breathes wine. Just as the Viennese flock to Grinzing and other suburbs to sample new wine in *Heurige,* so the people of the Wachau come here to taste the local vintners' products, which appear in Krems earlier in the year. Krems is famous for two types of wine—classical Grüne Veltliner and Riesling—available at *Heurige* throughout the village.

From Vienna, **trains** depart from the Wien Franz-Josefs-Bahnhof at intervals of 60 minutes or less, arriving in Krems an hour later. In Krems, you can reach most city sights on foot; from the train station, the walk west along the Danube to Stein takes less than 30 minutes. One of your first stops should be the **Austropa Verkehrsbüro Krems,** about a 10-minute walk from the train station at Undstrasse 6 (© **02732/826 76;** www.tiscover.com/krems); head straight out of the station and turn left on Ringstrasse, then right on Reifgasse. April to October, it's open Monday to Friday 8:30am to 6:30pm, Saturday 10am to noon and 1 to 6pm, and Sunday 10am to noon and 1 to 4pm; November to March, hours are Monday to Friday 8:30am to 6pm.

SEEING THE SIGHTS   For an overview of Krems and its history, visit the **Weinstadt Museum,** Körnermarkt 14 (© **02732/801 567;** www.weinstadt museum.at), in the heart of Krems in a restored 13th-century Gothic Dominican monastery. Among its displays is a copy of a 32,000-year-old statuette, Austria's oldest work of art. You'll also find Roman masks, an 18th-century wine press, festive and everyday clothing of the Wachau, and works by Martin Johann Schmidt, who lived in Stein and is recognized as one of Austria's most important baroque painters. Also of interest are the 16th-century cellar tunnels that have been excavated underneath the cloister. Apparently, Krems is riddled with tunnels, used primarily for the storage of wine. The museum is open only March to November, Tuesday to Sunday 10am to 6pm. Admission is 3.60€ ($4.15) adults; 2.50€ ($2.90) seniors, students, and children.

On the way to Stein lies the **Kunst.halle.Krems,** Steiner Landstrasse 8 (© **02732/826 69-14;** www.kunsthalle.at). Occupying a converted 19th-century tobacco factory, it stages a variety of innovative art shows and concerts surprising for a town this size, making it worthwhile to check out what's showing. Admission costs vary; the hours are daily 10am to 6pm. Otherwise, the most interesting part of Krems today is what was once the little village of **Stein,** with narrow streets terraced above the river and flanked by impressive patrician homes. On Kellergasse, you'll find one *Heuriger* after another, as well as a remnant of the old city wall. Be sure, too, to stroll down Krems's main pedestrian lane, **Obere and Untere Landstrasse,** marked by a tower gate. It's popular in summer for its kiosks selling glasses of local wine, which you can sip as you window-shop.

From Krems, it's worth taking a short excursion across the Danube to the region's most striking structure, the **Stift Göttweig (Benedictine Monastery Göttweig;** © **02732/85581-231),** which spreads like a palace atop a hill and commands a breathtaking view of the Wachau. To reach it, one city bus a day departs from the Krems train station at 1:35pm, with a return trip at 4:10pm. Alternatively, you can take a 10-minute train ride from Krems to Furth, followed by a 20-minute walk up a steep incline; a taxi from Krems to the monastery runs about 15€ ($17). The monastery, which lies 50m (164 ft.) above sea level and is home to about 65 monks, was founded in 1083 and rebuilt in its present baroque style in the 18th century. Rivaling the much better-known Melk Monastery in size and splendor, Stift Göttweig contains an ornate abbey church, an original 11th-century medieval chapel, and an imperial wing with one of the most beautiful baroque staircases in Europe. It's open mid-March to mid-November daily from 10am to 6pm. Additionally, guided tours lasting approximately 1 hour are available at 11am and 3pm. Various options are available for sightseeing. To see everything on your own without a guided tour, the cost is 6.50€ ($7.50). Add 2.50€ ($2.90) for the guided tour.

WHERE TO DINE A good choice is **Gozzoburg,** Margaretenstrasse 14 (© **02732/852 47),** in the heart of Krems near Hoher Markt. Very rustic, with a terrace overlooking the town and with exhibits by local artists, it offers Austrian meals for 6€ to 15€ ($5–$13) and is open Wednesday to Monday 11am to 11pm. MasterCard and Visa are accepted.

Index

Not just 4 anoraks

...but 3 duffel coats
59 gorgeous models
5 Tube simulators
4 dead man's handles
3 mucky miners
and 1 brilliant time had by all.

... be *moved*

 **London's Transport
Museum**
Covent Garden Piazza

kids go
FREE

www.ltmuseum.co.uk

Travel Tip: He who finds the best hotel deal has more to spend on facials involving knobbly vegetables.

Hello, the Roaming Gnome here. I've been nabbed from the garden and taken round the world. The people who took me are so terribly clever. They find the best offerings on Travelocity. For very little cha-ching. And that means I get to be pampered and exfoliated till I'm pink as a bunny's doodah.

travelocity®

1-888-TRAVELOCITY / travelocity.com / America Online Keyword: Travel

Travel Tip: Make sure there's customer service for any change of plans — involving friendly natives, for example.

One can plan and plan, but if you don't book with the right people you can't seize le moment and canoodle with the poodle named Pansy. I, for one, am all for fraternizing with the locals. Better yet, if I need to extend my stay and my gnome nappers are willing, it can all be arranged through the 800 number at, oh look, how convenient, the lovely company coat of arms.

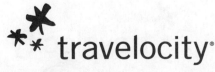

travelocity®

1-888-TRAVELOCITY / travelocity.com / America Online Keyword: Travel